Holt McDougal

Online Learning

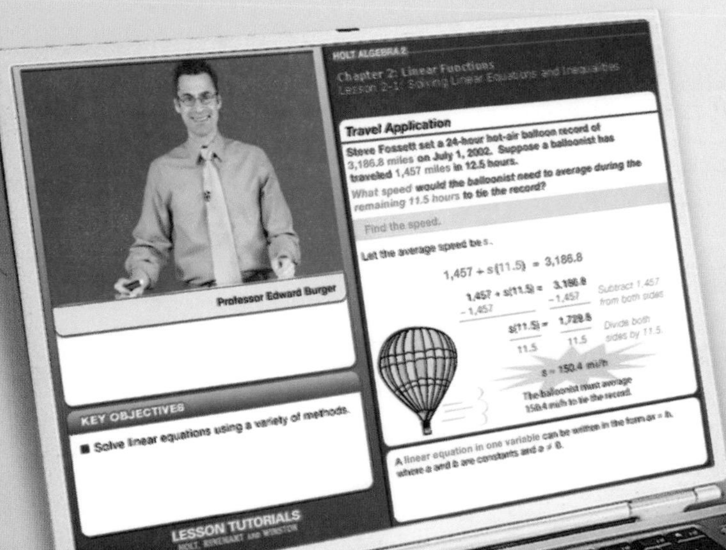

All the help you need, any time you need it.

427 Algebra 2 videos online!

Lesson Tutorial Videos feature entertaining and enlightening videos that illustrate every example in your textbook!

Premier Online Edition
- Complete Student Edition
- Lesson Tutorial Videos for every example
- Interactive practice with feedback

Extra Practice
- Homework Help Online
- Intervention and enrichment exercises
- State test practice

Online Tools
- Graphing calculator
- TechKeys "How-to" tutorials on graphing calculators
- Multilingual glossary

For Parents
- Algebra Refresher
- Parent Resources Online

Log on to **www.go.hrw.com** to access Holt's online resources.

HOLT McDOUGAL

Algebra 2

Edward B. Burger

David J. Chard

Paul A. Kennedy

Steven J. Leinwand

Freddie L. Renfro

Tom W. Roby

Bert K. Waits

HOLT McDOUGAL

HOUGHTON MIFFLIN HARCOURT

Algebra 2

Printed in the U.S.A.

ISBN-13 978-0-030-99576-7

ISBN-10 0-030-99576-0

6 7 8 9 10 0914 20 19 18 17 16 15 14 13 4500419909

Cover photo: © Art by Vladimir Bulatov/Bulatov Abstract Creations/ Photo by Victoria Smith/HMH

AUTHORS

Edward B. Burger, Ph.D., is Professor of Mathematics at Williams College and is the author of numerous articles, books, and videos. He has won several of the most prestigious writing and teaching awards offered by the Mathematical Association of America. Dr. Burger has made numerous television and radio appearances and has given countless mathematical presentations around the world.

Freddie L. Renfro, MA, has 35 years of experience in Texas education as a classroom teacher and director/coordinator of Mathematics PreK-12 for school districts in the Houston area. She has served as a reviewer and TXTEAM trainer for Texas Math Institutes and has presented at numerous math workshops.

David J. Chard, Ph.D., is the Leon Simmons Dean of the School of Education and Human Development at Southern Methodist University. He is a past president of the Divison of Research at the Council for Exceptional Children, a member of the International Academy for Research on Learning Disabilities, and has been the Principal Investigator on numerous research projects for the U.S. Department of Education.

Tom W. Roby, Ph.D., is Associate Professor of Mathematics and Director of the Quantitative Learning Center at the University of Connecticut. He founded and directed the Bay Area-based ACCLAIM professional development program. He also chaired the advisory board of the California Mathematics Project and reviewed content for the California Standards Tests.

Paul A. Kennedy, Ph.D., is a professor and Distinguished University Teaching Scholar in the Department of Mathematics at Colorado State University. Dr. Kennedy is a leader in mathematics education. His research focuses on developing algebraic thinking by using multiple representations and technology. He is the author of numerous publications.

Bert K. Waits, Ph.D., is a Professor Emeritus of Mathematics at The Ohio State University and cofounder of T^3 (Teachers Teaching with Technology), a national professional development program. Dr. Waits is also a former board member of the NCTM and an author of the original NCTM Standards.

Steven J. Leinwand is a Principal Research Analyst at the American Institutes for Research in Washington, D.C. He was previously, for 22 years, the Mathematics Supervisor with the Connecticut Department of Education.

Contributing Authors

Linda Antinone
Fort Worth, TX
Ms. Antinone teaches mathematics at R. L. Paschal High School in Fort Worth, Texas. She has received the Presidential Award for Excellence in Teaching Mathematics and the National Radio Shack Teacher award. She has coauthored several books for Texas Instruments on the use of technology in mathematics.

Carmen Whitman
Pflugerville, TX
Ms. Whitman travels nationally helping districts improve mathematics education. She has been a program coordinator on the mathematics team at the Charles A. Dana Center, and has served as a secondary math specialist for the Austin Independent School District.

Reviewers

Mary Anderson
Mathematics Department Chair
Community High School District 99 South
Downers Grove, IL

Dave Barker
Mathematics Department Chair
Los Alamitos High School
Los Alamitos, CA

MaryLane Blomquist
Mathematics Department Chair
Kewaskum High School
Kewaskum, WI

William L. Bonney
Mathematics Department Chair
Ballard High School
Seattle, WA

Suzanne Castren
Mathematics Teacher
Williamsville South High School
Williamsville, NY

Lala Geraldine Chambers, NBCT
Mathematics Department Chair
Forest Hill High School
Jackson, MS

Joan Chrismer-McNatt
Mathematics Teacher
Clear Creek High School
League City, TX

Roy L. Conwell, Jr.
Mathematics Department Chair
Sam Houston High School
Houston, TX

Patricia Daley
Mathematics Teacher, retired
Fairfield High School
Fairfield, CT

Mohamad Elkhatib
Mathematics Department Chair
Jones High School
Houston Community College Instructor
Houston, TX

Marti Freihofer
Mathematics Department Chair
Scott High School
Taylor Mill, KY

Mary Gesino
Mathematics Department Co-Chair
R. L. Turner High School
Carrollton, TX

Marilyn Gutman
Mathematics Department Chair
Mayfield High School
Las Cruces, NM

Jim Harrington
Supervisor of Mathematics
Omaha Public Schools
Omaha, NE

Marieta W. Harris
Mathematics Specialist
Memphis, TN

Jere Hassberger, PhD
Mathematics Department Chair
Saline High School
Saline, MI

Reviewers

James Patrick Herrington
Mathematics Department Chair
O'Fallon Township High School
O'Fallon, IL

Margie Hill
District Coordinating Teacher for Mathematics, K-12
Blue Valley USD 229
Overland Park, KS

Dr. Douglas Lohnas
Director of Mathematics
Niskayuna Central School District
Niskayuna, NY

Brenda Lynch
Mathematics Department Chair
Montgomery High School
Montgomery, TX

Dr. Charlotte May
Mathematics Teacher
Austin ISD
Austin, TX

Ruth Harbin Miles
K-12 Coordinator of Mathematics
Olathe USD 233
Olathe, TX

Saundra Paschal
Mathematics Department Chair
Lake View High School
San Angelo, TX

Carolyn Randolph
Mathematics Department Chair
Academic Director
Kendrick High School
Columbus, GA

Sarah Ritch
Mathematics Department Chair
Hebron High School
Carrollton, TX

Paul Schwiegerling
Gifted Mathematics Program
SUNY at Buffalo
Buffalo, NY

Katie Smith
Mathematics Department Chair
Berea High School
Greenville, SC

Stephanie Turner
Former Mathematics Teacher
Colleyville Heritage High School
Colleyville, TX

Field Test Participants

Gerri Chambers-McGee
Forest Hill High School
Jackson, MS

Stephanie Cundiff
Mesa Ridge High School
Colorado Springs, CO

Eddie Hancock
Navasota High School
Navasota, TX

Brenda Lynch
Montgomery High School
Montgomery, TX

Lisa Pope
Jacobs High School
Cincinnati, OH

Niki Robinson
Navasota High School
Navasota, TX

Piper Singleton
Pershing High School
Detroit, MI

Dierdre M. Watkins
Dunwoody High School
Dunwoody, GA

Preparing for Standardized Tests

Holt McDougal Algebra 2 provides many opportunities for you to prepare for standardized tests.

Test Prep Exercises

Use the Test Prep Exercises for daily practice of standardized test questions in various formats.

Multiple Choice—choose your answer.

Gridded Response—write your answer in a grid and fill in the corresponding bubbles.

Short Response—write open-ended responses that are scored with a 2-point rubric.

Extended Response—write open-ended responses that are scored with a 3-point rubric.

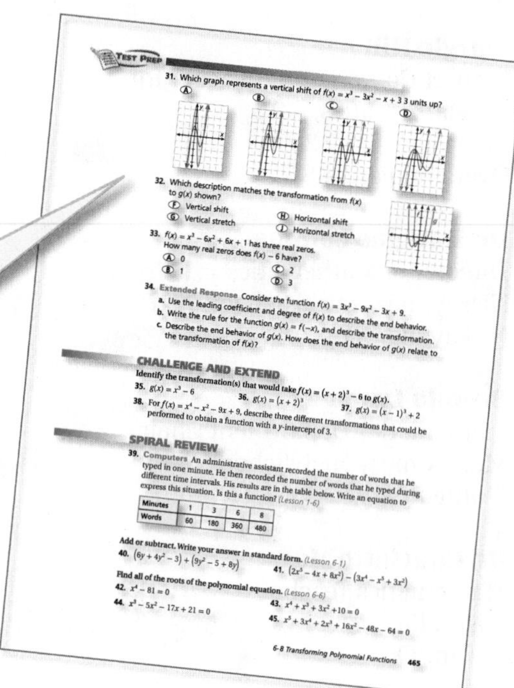

TEST PREP

31. Which graph represents a vertical shift of $f(x) = x^3 - 3x^2 - x + 3$ 3 units up?
Ⓐ Ⓑ Ⓒ Ⓓ

32. Which description matches the transformation from $f(x)$ to $g(x)$ shown?
Ⓕ Vertical shift
Ⓖ Vertical stretch
Ⓗ Horizontal shift
Ⓙ Horizontal stretch

33. $f(x) = x^3 - 6x^2 + 6x + 1$ has three real zeros. How many real zeros does $f(x) - 6$ have?
Ⓐ 0
Ⓑ 1
Ⓒ 2
Ⓓ 3

34. **Extended Response** Consider the function $f(x) = 3x^3 - 9x^2 - 3x + 9$.
a. Use the leading coefficient and degree of $f(x)$ to describe the end behavior.
b. Write the rule for the function $g(x) = f(-x)$, and describe the transformation.
c. Describe the end behavior of $g(x)$. How does the end behavior of $g(x)$ relate to the transformation of $f(x)$?

CHALLENGE AND EXTEND

Identify the transformation(s) that would take $f(x) = (x+2)^3 - 6$ to $g(x)$.

35. $g(x) = x^3 - 6$
36. $g(x) = (x+2)^3$
37. $g(x) = (x-1)^3 + 2$
38. For $f(x) = x^4 - x^2 - 9x + 9$, describe three different transformations that could be performed to obtain a function with a y-intercept of 3.

SPIRAL REVIEW

39. **Computers** An administrative assistant recorded the number of words that he typed in one minute. He then recorded the number of words that he typed during different time intervals. His results are in the table below. Write an equation to express this situation. Is this a function? *(Lesson 1-6)*

Minutes	1	3	6	8
Words	60	180	360	480

Add or subtract. Write your answer in standard form. *(Lesson 6-1)*

40. $(6y + 4y^2 - 3) + (9y^2 - 5 + 8y)$
41. $(2x^5 - 4x + 8x^2) - (3x^4 - x^5 + 3x^2)$

Find all of the roots of the polynomial equation. *(Lesson 6-6)*

42. $x^4 - 81 = 0$
43. $x^4 + x^3 + 3x^2 + 10 = 0$
44. $x^3 - 5x^2 - 17x + 21 = 0$
45. $x^5 + 3x^4 + 2x^3 + 16x^2 - 48x - 64 = 0$

6-8 Transforming Polynomial Functions 465

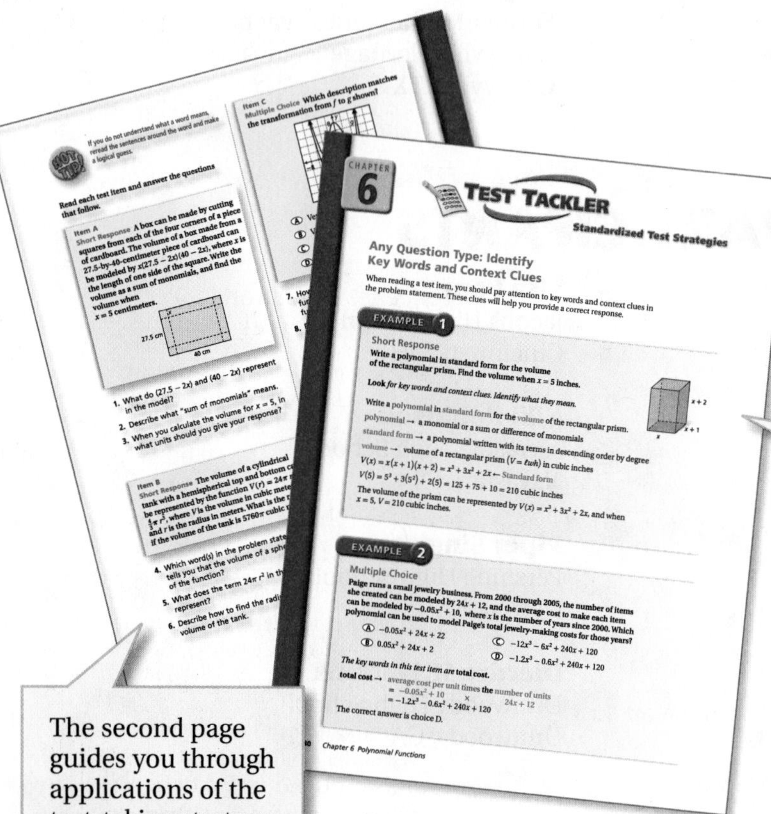

CHAPTER 6

TEST TACKLER

Standardized Test Strategies

Any Question Type: Identify Key Words and Context Clues

When reading a test item, you should pay attention to key words and context clues in the problem statement. These clues will help you provide a correct response.

EXAMPLE 1

Short Response

Write a polynomial in standard form for the volume of the rectangular prism. Find the volume when $x = 5$ inches.

Look for key words and context clues. Identify what they mean.

Write a polynomial in standard form for the volume of the rectangular prism.

polynomial → a monomial or a sum or difference of monomials

standard form → a polynomial written with its terms in descending order by degree

volume → volume of a rectangular prism ($V = \ell wh$) in cubic inches

$V(x) = x(x+1)(x+2) = x^3 + 3x^2 + 2x$ ← Standard form

$V(5) = 5^3 + 3(5^2) + 2(5) = 125 + 75 + 10 = 210$ cubic inches

The volume of the prism can be represented by $V(x) = x^3 + 3x^2 + 2x$, and when $x = 5$, $V = 210$ cubic inches.

EXAMPLE 2

Multiple Choice

Paige runs a small jewelry business. From 2000 through 2005, the number of items she created can be modeled by $24x + 12$, and the average cost to make each item can be modeled by $-0.05x^2 + 10$, where x is the number of years since 2000. Which polynomial can be used to model Paige's total jewelry-making costs for those years?

Ⓐ $-0.05x^2 + 24x + 22$
Ⓑ $0.05x^2 + 24x + 2$
Ⓒ $-12x^3 - 6x^2 + 240x + 120$
Ⓓ $-1.2x^3 - 0.6x^2 + 240x + 120$

The key words in this test item are **total cost.**

total cost → average cost per unit times **the** number of units
$= -0.05x^2 + 10 \times 24x + 12$
$= -1.2x^3 - 0.6x^2 + 240x + 120$

The correct answer is choice D.

Chapter 6 Polynomial Functions

The second page guides you through applications of the test-taking strategy.

Test Tackler

Use the Test Tackler to become familiar with and practice test-taking strategies.

The first page of this feature explains and shows an example of a test-taking strategy.

Standardized Test Prep

Use the Standardized Test Prep to apply test-taking strategies.

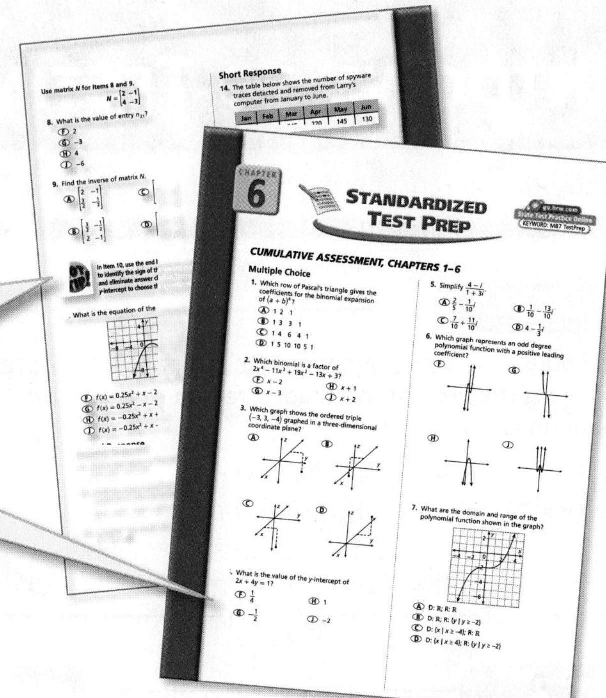

The Hot Tip provides test-taking tips to help you succeed on your tests.

These pages include practice with multiple choice, gridded response, short response, and extended response test items.

Countdown to Testing

Use the Countdown to Testing to practice for your state test every day.

There are 24 pages of practice for your state test. Each page is designed to be used in a week so that all practice will be completed before your state test is given

Each week's page has five practice test items, one for each day of the week.

Test-Taking Tips

- Get plenty of sleep the night before the test. A rested mind thinks more clearly and you won't feel like falling asleep while taking the test.
- Draw a figure when one is not provided with the problem. If a figure is given, write any details from the problem on the figure.
- Read each problem carefully. As you finish each problem, read it again to make sure your answer is reasonable.
- Review the formula sheet that will be supplied with the test. Make sure you know when to use each formula.
- First answer problems that you know how to solve. If you do not know how to solve a problem, skip it and come back to it when you have finished the others.
- Use other test-taking strategies that can be found throughout this book, such as working backward and eliminating answer choices.

Countdown to Testing

Week 1

Day 1

The figure shows a square within a square. Which expression represents the area of the shaded region of the figure in square units?

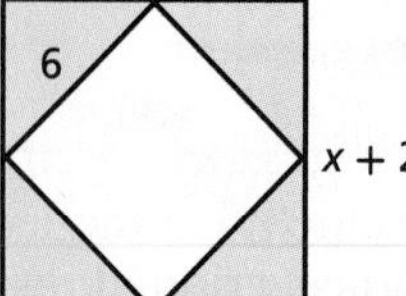

Ⓐ $(x + 2)^2 - 36$
Ⓑ $(x + 2) - 6$
Ⓒ $2(x + 2) - 12$
Ⓓ $(x + 2 - 6)^2$

Day 2

If x is a nonzero real number, which expression is equivalent to $(x + 5) - 8$?

Ⓕ $-8x + 5$
Ⓖ $8 - (x + 5)$
Ⓗ $x + (5 - 8)$
Ⓙ $(x + 8) - 5$

Day 3

If a, b, and c are positive integers, what is the greatest common factor of the expressions $18ab$ and $8abc$?

Ⓐ 18
Ⓑ ab
Ⓒ $2ab$
Ⓓ $72abc$

Day 4

$\triangle ABC$ is a right triangle.

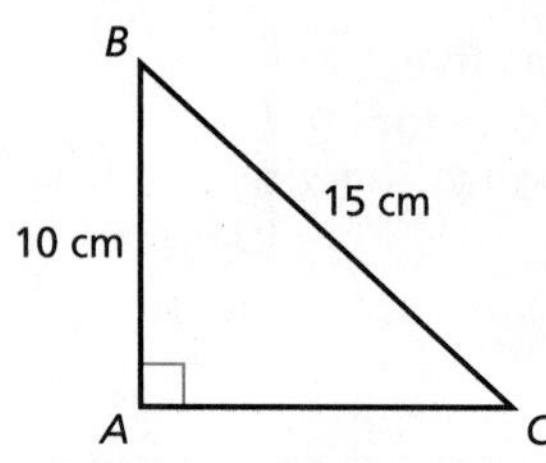

What is the length of $\overline{AC}$?

Ⓕ 5 cm
Ⓖ $5\sqrt{5}$ cm
Ⓗ $5\sqrt{13}$ cm
Ⓙ 25 cm

Day 5

Simplify the expression $5(x^2 + 4x) + 3(x + 6)$.

Ⓐ $12x^2 + 6$
Ⓑ $12x^2 + 18$
Ⓒ $5x^2 + 7x + 6$
Ⓓ $5x^2 + 23x + 18$

Countdown to Testing — WEEK 2

DAY 1

The figure shows a right triangle. Which equation can be solved for the unknown side length c?

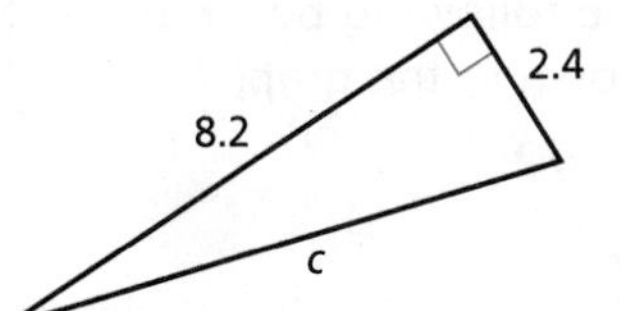

Ⓐ $\sqrt{8.2^2 + 2.4^2} = c$

Ⓑ $\sqrt{(8.2 + 2.4)^2} = c$

Ⓒ $\sqrt{8.2^2 - 2.4^2} = c$

Ⓓ $\sqrt{(8.2 - 2.4)^2} = c$

DAY 2

What is the perimeter in units of a rectangle with a length of $g + 8$ units and a width of $g - 6$ units?

Ⓕ $4g + 2$

Ⓖ $4g + 4$

Ⓗ $g^2 - 16$

Ⓙ $g^2 + 2g - 16$

DAY 3

Which expression is equivalent to $\frac{12x^4y^8}{9xy^4}$?

Ⓐ $\frac{4}{3}xy^2$

Ⓑ $\frac{4}{3}xy^4$

Ⓒ $\frac{4}{3}x^3y^4$

Ⓓ $\frac{4}{3}x^4y^2$

DAY 4

A particular hummingbird averages 60 wing beats per second. At this rate, how many times would the hummingbird beat its wings during an hour of flight?

Ⓕ 2.16×10^3

Ⓖ 2.16×10^4

Ⓗ 2.16×10^5

Ⓙ 2.16×10^6

DAY 5

A marathon is a 26.2-mile race. Kendra's average speed during marathons is 7.2 miles per hour. Which function d represents the distance in miles Kendra has left to run in a marathon t hours after the race begins?

Ⓐ $d(t) = \frac{t}{7.2} - 26.2$

Ⓑ $d(t) = 26.2 - \frac{t}{7.2}$

Ⓒ $d(t) = 7.2t - 26.2$

Ⓓ $d(t) = 26.2 - 7.2t$

DAY 1

Which of the following best represents the domain of the function shown in the graph?

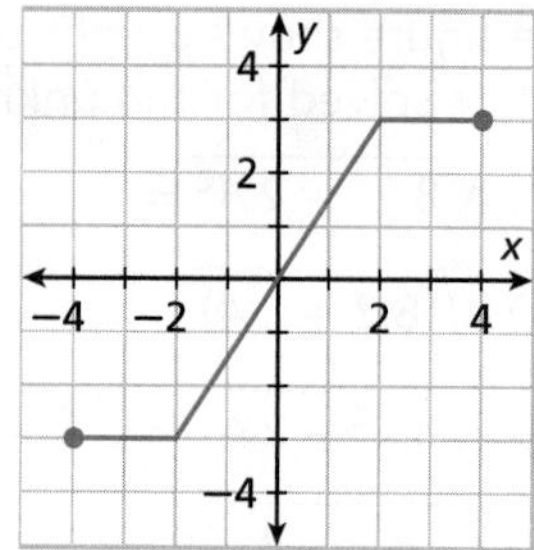

Ⓐ $-2 \le x \le 2$

Ⓑ $-3 \le x \le 3$

Ⓒ $-4 \le x \le 4$

Ⓓ $-5 \le x \le 5$

DAY 2

A diagonal of a rectangle measures 9 meters. The width of the rectangle is 6 meters. What is the length of the rectangle?

Ⓕ $3\sqrt{5}$ m

Ⓖ $9\sqrt{5}$ m

Ⓗ $\sqrt{15}$ m

Ⓙ $\sqrt{117}$ m

DAY 3

If a and b are integers, which expression is equivalent to $6^a \cdot 6^b$?

Ⓐ 6^{a+b}

Ⓑ $6^{a \cdot b}$

Ⓒ 36^{a+b}

Ⓓ $36^{a \cdot b}$

DAY 4

In the diagram, points W, X, Y, and Z are collinear, $WX = YZ$, and $XY = 25$. If WX is a whole number, which is NOT a possible value of WZ?

Ⓕ 27

Ⓖ 30

Ⓗ 35

Ⓙ 37

DAY 5

What is the parent function of the function shown in the graph?

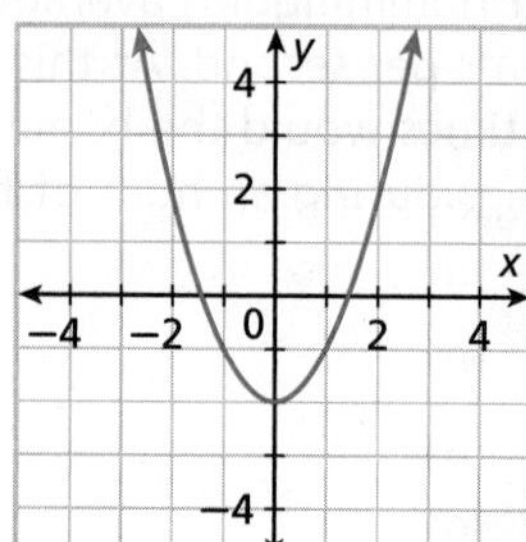

Ⓐ $f(x) = x$

Ⓑ $f(x) = x^2$

Ⓒ $f(x) = x^3$

Ⓓ $f(x) = \sqrt{x}$

Countdown to Testing WEEK 4

DAY 1

Which graph best represents the function $f(x) = \frac{1}{2}x + 2$?

Ⓐ
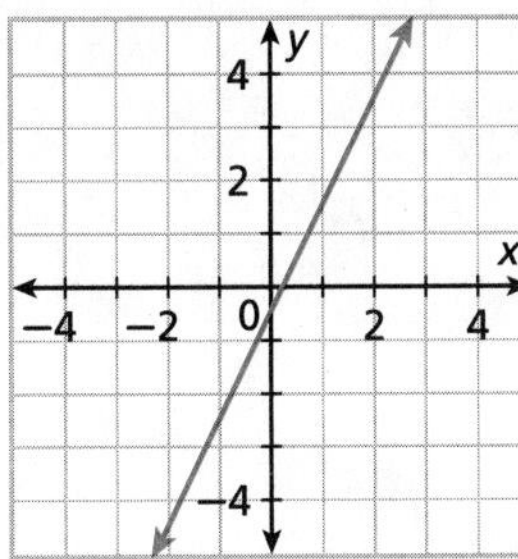

Ⓒ
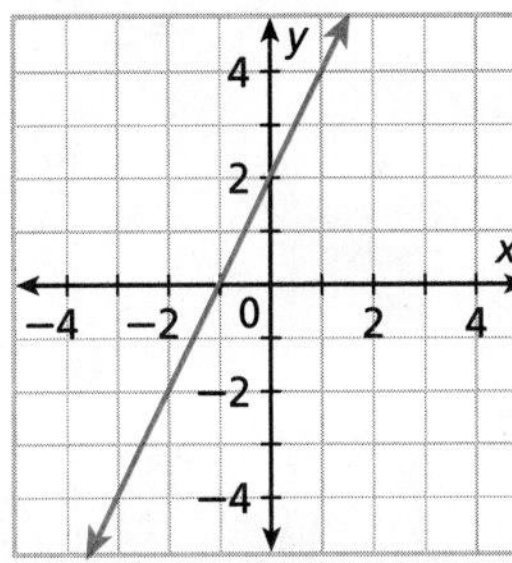

Ⓑ
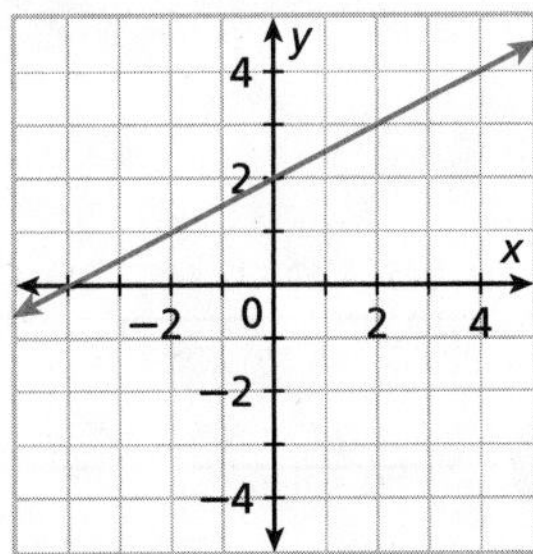

Ⓓ
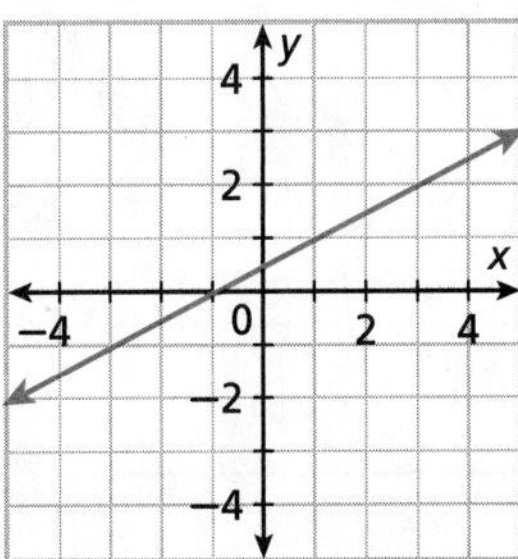

DAY 2

Given that $f(x) = -6x^2 - 12x + 3$, what is $f(-2)$?

Ⓕ -45

Ⓖ 0

Ⓗ 3

Ⓙ 51

DAY 3

What transformation is suggested by the spokes on a stationary bicycle tire?

Ⓐ Rotation

Ⓑ Reflection

Ⓒ Dilation

Ⓓ Translation

DAY 4

Which expression is equivalent to $\left(\frac{6x^2y^4}{x^4y^2}\right)^3$?

Ⓕ $216xy^5$

Ⓖ $216x^2y^{10}$

Ⓗ $216x^{-5}y^5$

Ⓙ $216x^{-6}y^6$

DAY 5

What is the parent function of the graph shown?

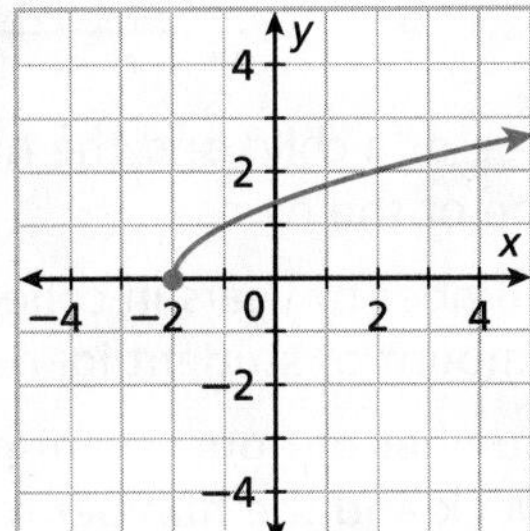

Ⓐ $f(x) = x$

Ⓑ $f(x) = x^2$

Ⓒ $f(x) = x^3$

Ⓓ $f(x) = \sqrt{x}$

Countdown to Testing WEEK 5

DAY 1

Which graph best represents the function $f(x) = x^2$?

Ⓐ
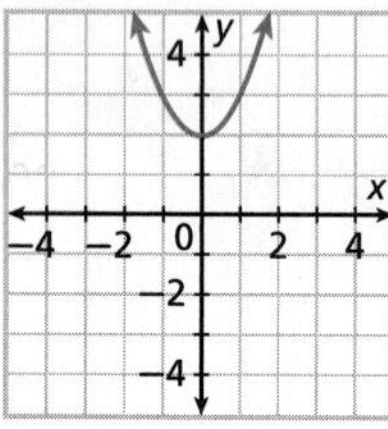

Ⓒ
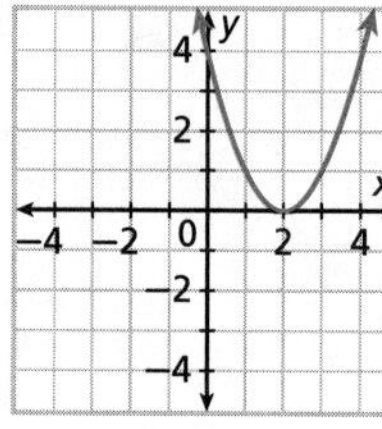

Ⓑ
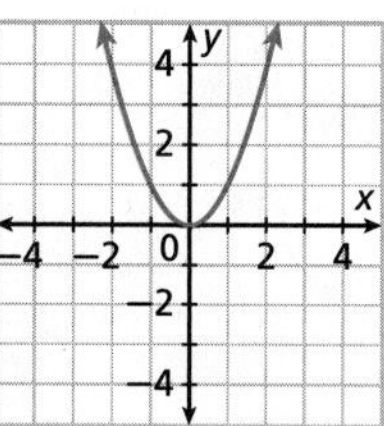

Ⓓ
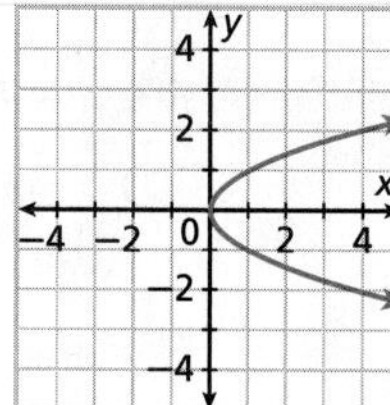

DAY 2

A company determines that 40% of its employees commute for more than 30 minutes each day. If 346 employees commute for more than 30 minutes, how many employees does the company have?

Ⓕ 138
Ⓖ 485
Ⓗ 577
Ⓙ 865

DAY 3

Solve $4z + 16 - 3 = z - 7 + 5z$.

Ⓐ $z = 0$
Ⓑ $z = 2.5$
Ⓒ $z = 10$
Ⓓ $z = 20$

DAY 4

The scatter plot shown is most likely to represent which of the following sets of data?

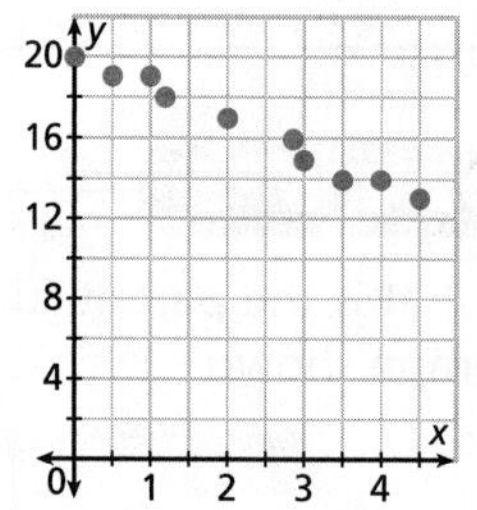

Ⓕ The age of a child and the number of toys he or she owns
Ⓖ The number of years in college and the amount of student loans
Ⓗ The number of hours spent practicing per week and the number of free throws missed per game
Ⓙ The duration of a movie and the cost in millions of dollars to produce it

DAY 5

What transformation of the graph of $f(x) = x$ is the graph of $g(x) = 4x$?

Ⓐ Vertical stretch by a factor of 4
Ⓑ Translation 4 units up
Ⓒ Horizontal stretch by a factor of 4
Ⓓ Translation 4 units right

Countdown to Testing WEEK 6

DAY 1

If $A = \frac{1}{2}bh$, what is the value of A when $b = 10x^3y^2$ and $h = 15x^{-2}y^4$?

Ⓐ $75x^{-1}y^6$ Ⓒ $3xy^8$

Ⓑ $75xy^6$ Ⓓ $150x^5y^2$

DAY 2

Which equation can be used to convert kilometers k to meters m?

Ⓕ $m = 0.001k$ Ⓗ $m = 1000k$

Ⓖ $m = 0.1k$ Ⓙ $m = 10{,}000k$

DAY 3

The graph shows the number of survival kits s a company sells after d days. Which function can best be used to model the data?

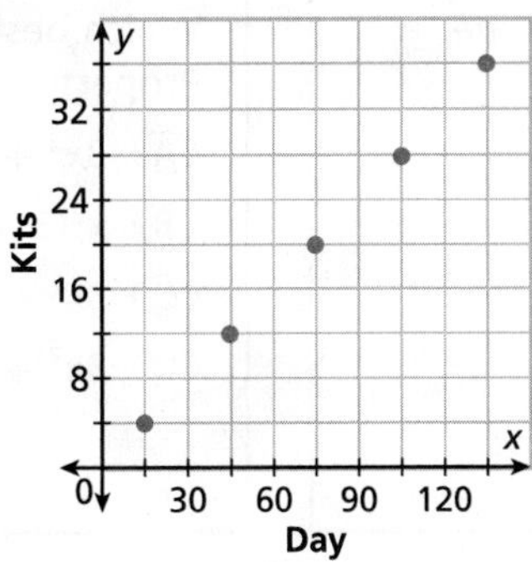

Ⓐ $s = \frac{1}{15}d + 4$ Ⓒ $s = \frac{4}{15}d$

Ⓑ $s = \frac{1}{3}d - 1$ Ⓓ $s = \frac{1}{5}d$

DAY 4

What is the equation of the line shown?

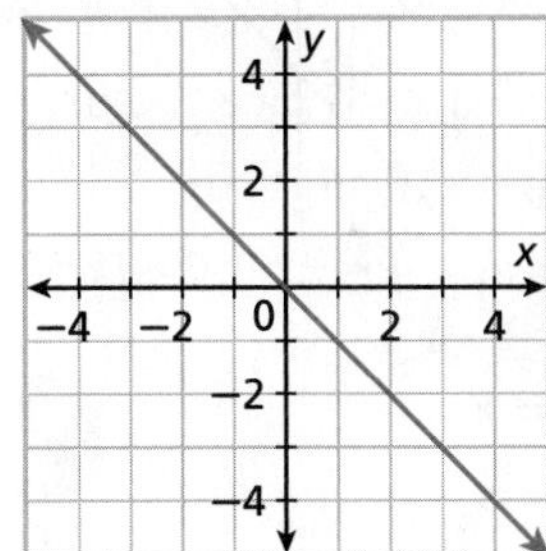

Ⓕ $y = -x$

Ⓖ $y = x$

Ⓗ $y = -2x$

Ⓙ $y = 2x$

DAY 5

The graph represents which system of linear inequalities?

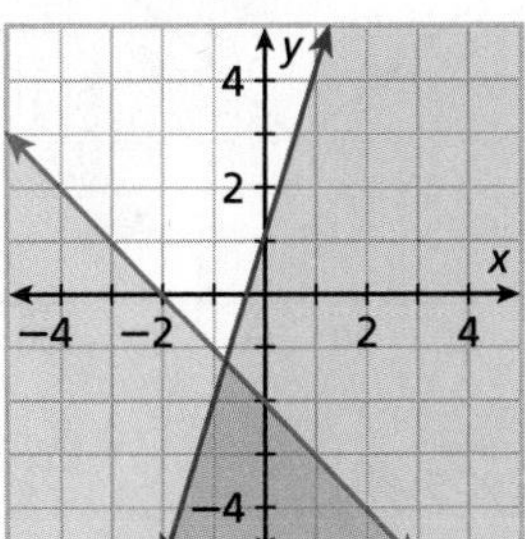

Ⓐ $\begin{cases} y \leq 3x + 1 \\ y \leq -x - 2 \end{cases}$ Ⓒ $\begin{cases} y < 3x + 1 \\ y < -x - 2 \end{cases}$

Ⓑ $\begin{cases} y \leq x + 3 \\ y \leq -2x - 1 \end{cases}$ Ⓓ $\begin{cases} y < x + 3 \\ y < -2x - 1 \end{cases}$

Countdown to Testing — WEEK 7

DAY 1

Which equation fits the data in the table?

x	−3	−1	1	3	5
y	5	3	1	−1	−3

Ⓐ $y = -x + 2$ Ⓑ $y = 2x$ Ⓒ $y = x + 2$ Ⓓ $y = x - 2$

DAY 2

If $a = \frac{1}{2}bh$ and $\frac{1}{2}bh = 25$, which of the following is a true statement?

Ⓕ $bh = 12.5$

Ⓖ $a = 25$

Ⓗ $\frac{1}{2}bh = 25 + a$

Ⓙ $2a = 25$

DAY 3

Which best illustrates the Associative Property?

Ⓐ $3x^2 + 5x^2 - 6 = 3x^2 - 6 + 5x^2$

Ⓑ $x^2(3 + 5) - 6 = (3x^2 + 5x^2) - 6$

Ⓒ $3x^2 + (5x^2 - 6) = (3x^2 + 5x^2) - 6$

Ⓓ $3x^2 + (5x^2 - 6) = (-6 + 3x^2) + 5x^2$

DAY 4

The position of a moving dot on a computer screen over time is given by the graph. What is the domain of this function?

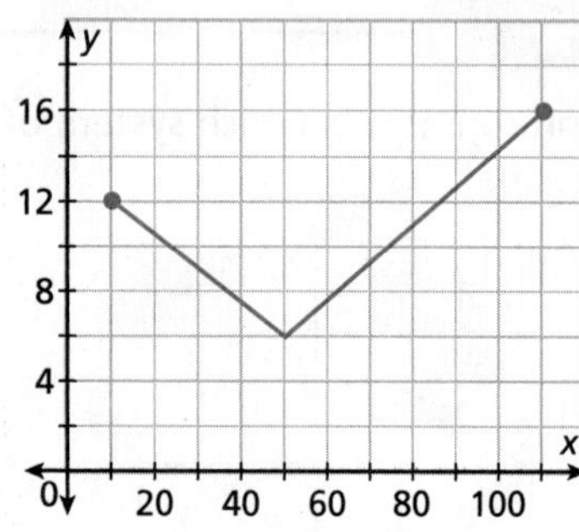

Ⓕ $\{x | 5 \le x \le 40\}$

Ⓖ $\{x | x \ge 10\}$

Ⓗ $\{x | 12 \le x \le 16\}$

Ⓙ $\{x | 10 \le x \le 110\}$

DAY 5

The graph shown represents which linear function?

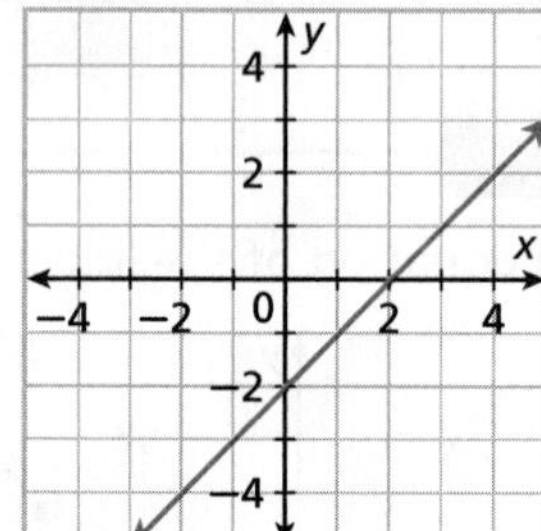

Ⓐ $y = x^2$

Ⓑ $y + 2 = x$

Ⓒ $y - 2 = x$

Ⓓ $2y = \frac{1}{2}x$

Countdown to Testing WEEK 8

DAY 1

What is the domain of the function $y = |x - 1|$?

Ⓐ $\{y | y \geq 0\}$

Ⓑ $\{x | x \geq 0\}$

Ⓒ Positive integers

Ⓓ All real numbers

DAY 2

Identify the property illustrated by the following equation.

$$\frac{2}{3} - \left(\frac{1}{2} - \frac{4}{5}\right) = \frac{2}{3} - \frac{1}{2} + \frac{4}{5}$$

Ⓕ Additive Inverse Property

Ⓖ Commutative Property

Ⓗ Associative Property

Ⓙ Distributive Property

DAY 3

John is a years old and his aunt is b years old. Nine years ago, John's aunt was 3 times as old as he was. Which equation represents the age relationship of these two relatives 9 years ago?

Ⓐ $b = 3a$

Ⓑ $b - 9 = 3a$

Ⓒ $b - 9 = 3(a - 9)$

Ⓓ $b = 3(a - 9)$

DAY 4

Which ordered pair is the solution of the following system?

$$\begin{cases} 3x - 5y = 12 \\ 2x = 4 + 5y \end{cases}$$

Ⓕ $\left(8, 2\frac{2}{5}\right)$

Ⓖ $\left(3\frac{1}{5}, 2\frac{4}{5}\right)$

Ⓗ $\left(16, 7\frac{1}{5}\right)$

Ⓙ $\left(3\frac{2}{5}, \frac{12}{25}\right)$

DAY 5

Teresa has two identical CD binders that are partly filled with CDs.

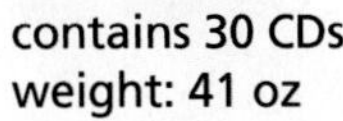

contains 30 CDs
weight: 41 oz

contains 75 CDs
weight: 66.5 oz

How much does each binder weigh when empty, to the nearest ounce?

Ⓐ 1 oz

Ⓑ 2 oz

Ⓒ 24 oz

Ⓓ 26 oz

Countdown to Testing WEEK 9

DAY 1

What is the range of the function $f(x) = -2|x|$?

Ⓐ $y > 0$

Ⓑ $y \leq 0$

Ⓒ $y \leq -2$

Ⓓ All real numbers

DAY 2

What is the solution of the system?

$$\begin{cases} 0.5x + 2.5y = -6.4 \\ 2x - 5y = 19.4 \end{cases}$$

Ⓕ $(10.7, 2.1)$

Ⓖ $(4.\overline{3}, 2.15)$

Ⓗ $(2.2, -3)$

Ⓙ $(0.8, -3.56)$

DAY 3

Cafeteria lunch sales are shown in the table and circle graph. How many vegetarian meals were sold?

Cafeteria Meals Sold	
Hot meal	142
Sandwich	170
Pizza	135
Vegetarian	?
Other	55

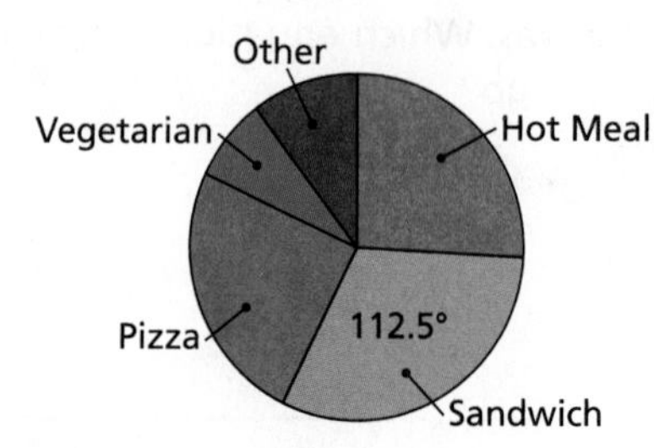

Ⓐ 28 Ⓑ 35 Ⓒ 42 Ⓓ 49

DAY 4

What is the missing number in the following matrix product?

$$\begin{bmatrix} 1 & 3 \\ -1 & 2 \end{bmatrix}\begin{bmatrix} ? & -1 \\ 3 & -2 \end{bmatrix} = \begin{bmatrix} 7 & -7 \\ 8 & -3 \end{bmatrix}$$

Ⓕ −2

Ⓖ 2

Ⓗ 7

Ⓙ Cannot be determined

DAY 5

What is the equation of the line through the origin that is perpendicular to $\overleftrightarrow{AB}$?

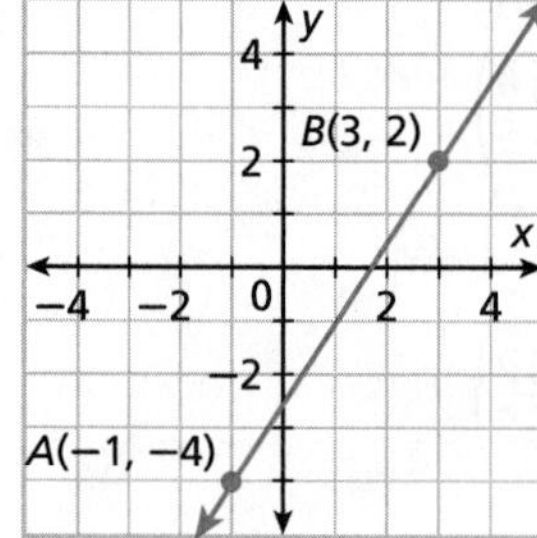

Ⓐ $y = \frac{2}{3}x$

Ⓑ $y = -\frac{2}{3}x$

Ⓒ $y = \frac{3}{2}x$

Ⓓ $y = -\frac{3}{2}x$

DAY 1

Which function is shown in the graph?

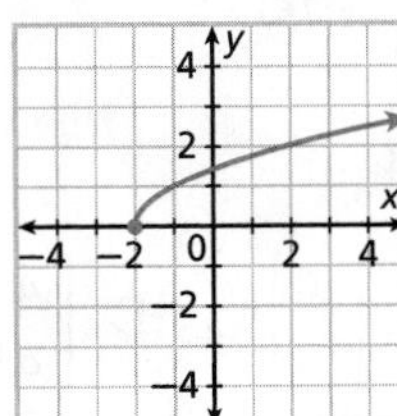

Ⓐ $f(x) = \sqrt{x} + 2$ Ⓒ $f(x) = 2\sqrt{x}$

Ⓑ $f(x) = \sqrt{x + 2}$ Ⓓ $f(x) = \sqrt{x - 2}$

DAY 2

Solve the given system of equations. What is the y-value of the solution?

$$\begin{cases} -6x + 8y = -24 \\ \frac{1}{6}x - 5y = -71 \end{cases}$$

Ⓕ 24

Ⓖ 15

Ⓗ 12

Ⓙ 9

DAY 3

Which is the graph of $f(x) = 3x^2 - 1$?

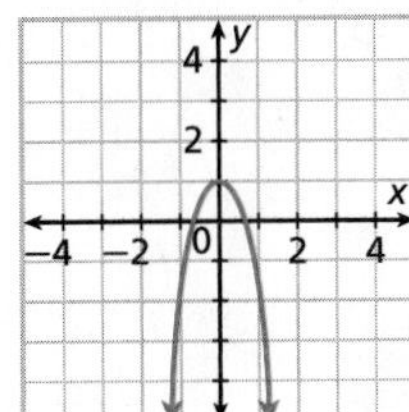

Ⓒ
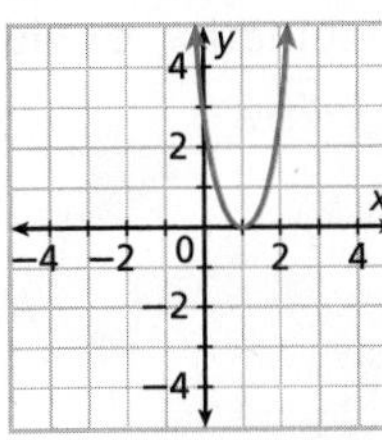

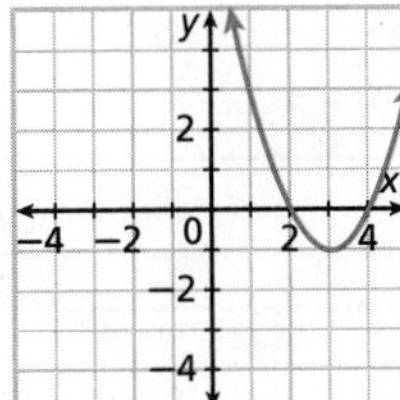

Ⓓ
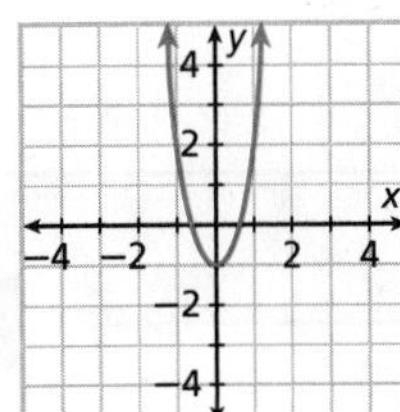

DAY 4

Faith plans to buy no more than 200 doorknobs to sell at her home improvement store. The doorknobs will be made of either brass or wood. Faith wants to buy at most 75 brass doorknobs and at least 110 wood doorknobs. Which of the following purchases meet Faith's requirements?

Ⓕ 5 brass; 150 wood

Ⓖ 20 brass; 90 wood

Ⓗ 40 brass; 175 wood

Ⓙ 80 brass; 112 wood

DAY 5

The equation of a least-squares line is $y \approx 0.15x - 0.21$. Predict the x-value that corresponds to a y-value of 20.

Ⓐ 95.24

Ⓑ 131.93

Ⓒ 134.73

Ⓓ 175.13

Countdown to Testing WEEK 11

DAY 1

What is the range of the function $f(x) = -\frac{1}{4}|x - 2|$?

Ⓐ $y \leq 0$

Ⓑ $y > 0$

Ⓒ $y \leq -2$

Ⓓ $y > 2$

DAY 2

Which matrix product can be used to solve the following system?

$$\begin{cases} 4x = 2y + 6 \\ 8x + 3y = 14 \end{cases}$$

Ⓕ $\begin{bmatrix} 4 & -2 \\ 8 & 3 \end{bmatrix}^{-1} \begin{bmatrix} 6 \\ 14 \end{bmatrix}$

Ⓗ $\begin{bmatrix} 4 & -2 \\ 8 & 3 \end{bmatrix}^{-1} \begin{bmatrix} -6 \\ 14 \end{bmatrix}$

Ⓖ $\begin{bmatrix} 4 & 2 \\ 8 & 3 \end{bmatrix}^{-1} \begin{bmatrix} 6 \\ 14 \end{bmatrix}$

Ⓙ $\begin{bmatrix} 4 & 2 \\ 8 & 3 \end{bmatrix}^{-1} \begin{bmatrix} -6 \\ 14 \end{bmatrix}$

DAY 3

Video games cost \$29.99 each, and DVDs cost \$19.99 each. If Phillipe has at most \$449.99 to spend, which combination of video games and DVDs is NOT a reasonable purchase?

Ⓐ 5 games; 14 DVDs

Ⓑ 10 games; 5 DVDs

Ⓒ 7 games; 13 DVDs

Ⓓ 4 games; 12 DVDs

DAY 4

Which value is equivalent to $30 \div 2 + \sqrt{64} - 4^3(8 - 4)^{-2}$?

Ⓕ -1

Ⓖ 13

Ⓗ 19

Ⓙ 535

DAY 5

The graph shown represents which parent function?

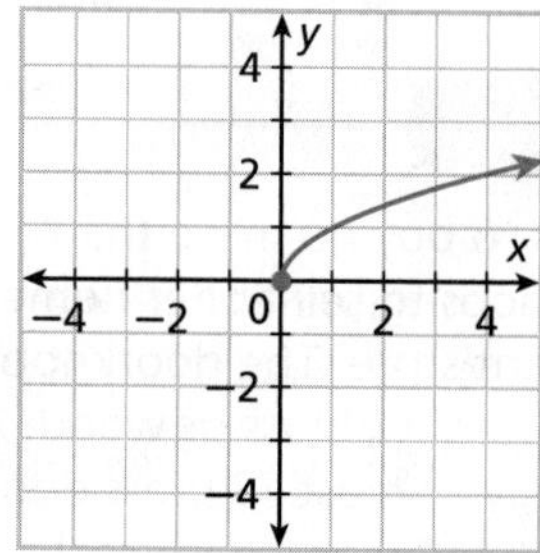

Ⓐ $f(x) = \sqrt{x}$

Ⓑ $f(x) = x^2$

Ⓒ $f(x) = 2$

Ⓓ $f(x) = x^3$

Countdown to Testing WEEK 12

DAY 1

How is the graph of $g(x) = |x| - 4$ transformed from the graph of $f(x) = |x|$?

Ⓐ The graph of f is translated 4 units up.

Ⓑ The graph of f is translated 4 units down.

Ⓒ The graph of f is translated 4 units right.

Ⓓ The graph of f is translated 4 units left.

DAY 2

Given that $f(x)$ is a quadratic function, find the missing value in the table.

x	2	4	6	8
$f(x)$	3	−1	−6	?

Ⓕ 0

Ⓖ −1

Ⓗ −11

Ⓙ −12

DAY 3

The following graph represents which table of data?

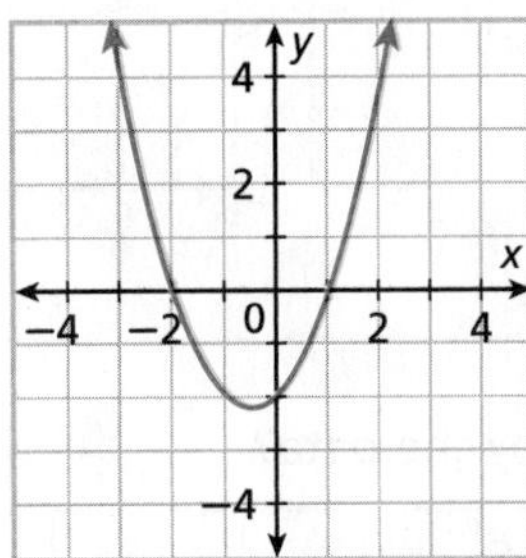

Ⓐ

x	−2	−1	0	1
$f(x)$	2	−2	2	1

Ⓑ

x	0	−2	−2	0
$f(x)$	−2	−1	0	1

Ⓒ

x	−2	−1	0	1
$f(x)$	0	−2	−2	0

Ⓓ

x	−2	−1	0	1
$f(x)$	−1	0	1	2

DAY 4

What is the domain of the function $f(x) = -\frac{1}{2}|x - 4|$?

Ⓕ All real numbers

Ⓖ $x < 0$

Ⓗ $x \geq -2$

Ⓙ $x > 4$

DAY 5

How is the graph of $g(x) = 2(x + 1)^2$ transformed from the graph of $f(x) = x^2$?

Ⓐ The graph of f is translated 2 units left and 1 unit up.

Ⓑ The graph of f is vertically compressed by a factor of $\frac{1}{2}$ and translated 1 unit left.

Ⓒ The graph of f is vertically stretched by a factor of 2 and translated 1 unit up.

Ⓓ The graph of f is vertically stretched by a factor of 2 and translated 1 unit left.

Countdown to Testing WEEK 13

DAY 1

Which of the following best describes the correlation found in the scatter plot?

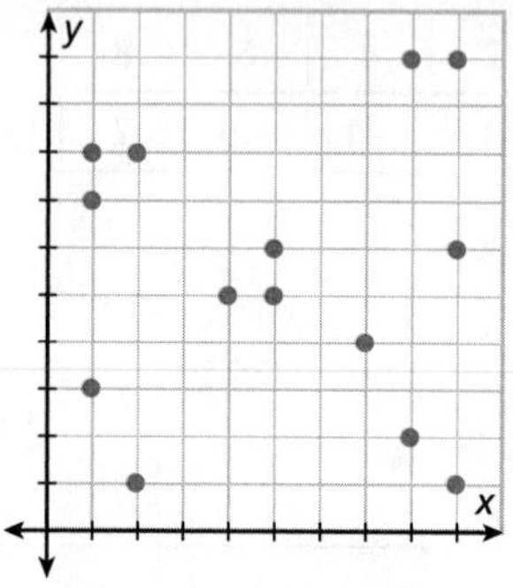

Ⓐ Strong positive correlation

Ⓑ Weak positive correlation

Ⓒ No correlation

Ⓓ Negative correlation

DAY 2

Which of the following best describes how to graph the function $f(x) = (x - 7)^2 + 3$?

Ⓕ Move the parent function to the right 7 units and up 3 units.

Ⓖ Move the parent function to the right 3 units and down 7 units.

Ⓗ Move the parent function to the left 7 units and up 3 units.

Ⓙ Move the parent function to the right 7 units and down 3 units.

DAY 3

Which situation is best represented by the data?

t	0	0.5	1	1.5	2	2.5
$f(t)$	112	108	96	76	48	12

Ⓐ The distance decreases by 4 miles for every 30 seconds traveled.

Ⓑ The height of an object above ground decreases nonlinearly over time.

Ⓒ As the time increases, the speed of a car increases at a constant rate.

Ⓓ As the time increases, the distance traveled decreases at a constant rate.

DAY 4

Which function is equivalent to $f(x) = 30x^2 + 2x - 56$?

Ⓕ $f(x) = (3x - 4)(5x + 14)$

Ⓖ $f(x) = 2(3x + 4)(5x - 7)$

Ⓗ $f(x) = (6x - 4)(5x + 7)$

Ⓙ $f(x) = 2(3x - 4)(5x + 7)$

DAY 5

The height h of a football t seconds after it is kicked is given by $h(t) = -16t^2 + 40t$. What is a reasonable real-world domain for the situation?

Ⓐ all positive real numbers

Ⓑ all real numbers between 0 and 3

Ⓒ all real numbers between 0 and 2.5

Ⓓ all real numbers between 0 and 1.25

Countdown to Testing — WEEK 14

DAY 1

The length x of a rectangle is 6 feet longer than its width. What is a reasonable domain for the function that represents the area of the rectangle?

Ⓐ all real numbers

Ⓑ all positive numbers

Ⓒ $x > 6$

Ⓓ $0 \leq x \leq 6$

DAY 2

Which quadratic equation has nonreal solutions?

Ⓕ $x^2 - 8x + 16 = 0$

Ⓖ $4x^2 - 12x + 9 = 0$

Ⓗ $-x^2 + 4x - 5 = 0$

Ⓙ $x^2 - 3x - 7 = 0$

DAY 3

The function $P = (h - 3)^2 + 174$ models the power, in megawatts, generated between midnight and noon by a power plant, where h represents hours after midnight. How would the graph of the function change if the minimum power generated increased to 250 megawatts?

Ⓐ The vertex would change to (3, 250).

Ⓑ The vertex would change to (250, 174).

Ⓒ The graph of the function would be reflected over the x-axis.

Ⓓ The graph of the function would be horizontally compressed.

DAY 4

To solve the equation $0 = x^2 + 7x - 26$ by completing the square, the first step is to add 26 to both sides of the equation. Which statement best describes the second step?

Ⓕ Add $\frac{9}{4}$ to both sides.

Ⓖ Square the product of 7 and 2.

Ⓗ Take half of 7 and square it.

Ⓙ Rewrite the perfect square trinomial as a binomial squared.

DAY 5

Which quadratic inequality best represents the graph?

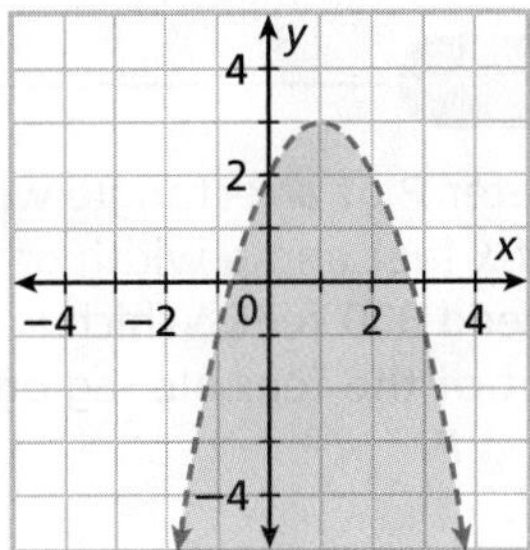

Ⓐ $y < -x^2 + 2x + 2$

Ⓑ $y > x^2 + 2x + 2$

Ⓒ $y \leq -x^2 + 2x + 2$

Ⓓ $y < x^2 - 2x + 2$

Countdown to Testing WEEK 15

DAY 1

The graph represents the solutions of which system of inequalities?

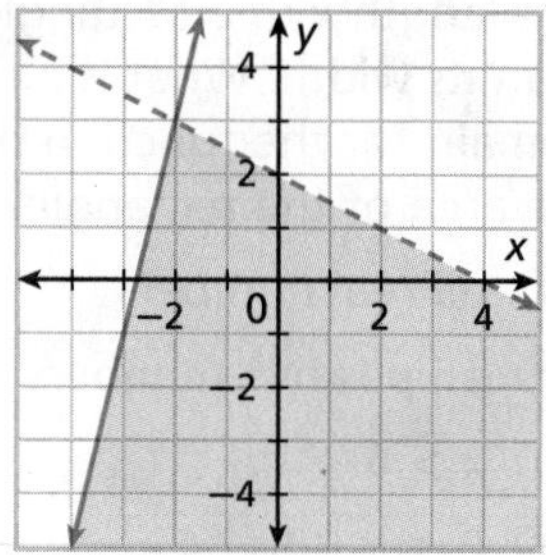

Ⓐ $\begin{cases} y \leq -\frac{1}{2}x + 2 \\ y \leq 4x + 11 \end{cases}$

Ⓑ $\begin{cases} y \leq -\frac{1}{2}x + 2 \\ y \geq 4x + 11 \end{cases}$

Ⓒ $\begin{cases} y > -\frac{1}{2}x + 2 \\ y \leq 4x + 11 \end{cases}$

Ⓓ $\begin{cases} y < -\frac{1}{2}x + 2 \\ y \leq 4x + 11 \end{cases}$

DAY 2

Which best describes $g(x) = \sqrt{2(x - 1)} + 4$ as a transformation of $f(x) = \sqrt{x}$?

Ⓕ g is f horizontally compressed by a factor of $\frac{1}{2}$ and translated left 1 unit and up 4 units.

Ⓖ g is f horizontally stretched by a factor of 2 and translated right 1 unit and up 4 units.

Ⓗ g is f horizontally compressed by a factor of $\frac{1}{2}$ and translated right 1 unit and up 4 units.

Ⓙ g is f horizontally stretched by a factor of 2 and translated left 1 unit and down 4 units.

DAY 3

Which statement is always true of the function $f(x) = \frac{1}{5}x + 6$?

Ⓐ $f(x)$ is less than x.

Ⓑ If x is positive, then $f(x)$ is positive.

Ⓒ If x is negative, then $f(x)$ is negative.

Ⓓ $f(x)$ is greater than x.

DAY 4

The perimeter P of a rectangle with a length of x feet and a width of y feet cannot exceed 300 feet. Which is NOT a constraint of the feasible region representing P?

Ⓕ $x > 0$

Ⓖ $x > 300 - y$

Ⓗ $y > 0$

Ⓙ $x \leq 150 - y$

DAY 5

In which relationship listed are the two quantities independent of one another?

Ⓐ The amount of tax paid for an item and the price of the item

Ⓑ The number of snacks bought from a vending machine and the amount of money in the machine

Ⓒ The number of hours worked at $7.25 per hour and the amount of money earned

Ⓓ The age of a person and the number of telephones in his or her house

Countdown to Testing WEEK 16

DAY 1

What are the solutions of the equation $3x^2 - 6x - 7 = 0$?

Ⓐ $x = \frac{3 \pm 2i\sqrt{3}}{3}$

Ⓑ $x \approx 2.8$ and $x \approx -0.8$

Ⓒ $x \approx 17$ and $x \approx -5$

Ⓓ $x \approx 3.2$ and $x \approx -0.6$

DAY 2

Which function best represents the data in the table?

x	−2	−1	0	1	2	3
$f(x)$	25	13	5	1	1	5

Ⓕ $f(x) = 2x^2 - 6x + 5$

Ⓖ $f(x) = -2x^2 - 6x + 8$

Ⓗ $f(x) = x^2 - 6x + 5$

Ⓙ $f(x) = 2x^2 - 9x + 5$

DAY 3

The graph can be used to determine the solutions to which quadratic equation?

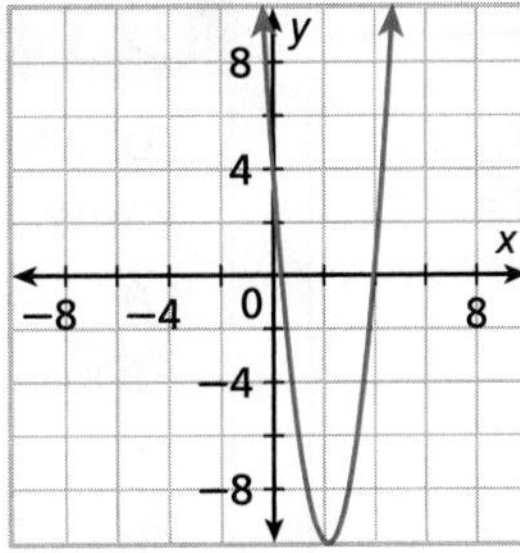

Ⓐ $x^2 - 5x + 4 = 0$

Ⓑ $3x^2 - 7x + 2 = 0$

Ⓒ $3x^2 - 13x + 4 = 0$

Ⓓ $3x^2 - 8x + 4 = 0$

DAY 4

At the beginning of a basketball game, the referee tosses the ball into the air with an initial vertical velocity of 24 feet per second. The ball's initial height is 5 feet above the floor. Which inequality can be used to find the time interval t for which the height of the ball is greater than 10 feet?

Ⓕ $-16t^2 + 24t + 5 < 10$

Ⓖ $-16t^2 + 24t + 5 > 10$

Ⓗ $24t^2 - 16t + 5 > 10$

Ⓙ $24t + 5 > 10$

DAY 5

The function $P = -16(c - 25)^2 + 10{,}000$ models the profit the student council makes from a dance, where c is the cost per ticket in dollars. How does the graph of the function change if the maximum profit is made by selling the tickets for $40?

Ⓐ The graph of the function would be reflected over the y-axis.

Ⓑ The vertex would change to (25, 40).

Ⓒ The vertex would change to(40, 10,000).

Ⓓ The graph of the function would not change.

Countdown to Testing WEEK 17

DAY 1

The school's ticket office sells adult and student tickets to a musical. The auditorium normally holds no more than 2,500 people. There can be no more than 1,200 student tickets and no more than 1,800 adult tickets sold. If *x* represents the number of student tickets sold and *y* represents the number of adult tickets sold, which system of linear inequalities represents the possible combinations of student and adult tickets that can be sold?

Ⓐ $\begin{cases} x + y > 2500 \\ x + y \leq 1200 \\ y \leq 1800 \end{cases}$

Ⓑ $\begin{cases} x + y \geq 2500 \\ x \geq 1200 \\ y \geq 1800 \end{cases}$

Ⓒ $\begin{cases} x + y \leq 1200 \\ x \leq 2500 \\ y \leq 1800 \end{cases}$

Ⓓ $\begin{cases} x + y \leq 2500 \\ x \leq 1200 \\ y \leq 1800 \end{cases}$

DAY 2

In chemistry, pH = $-\log[H^+]$, where $[H^+]$ is the hydrogen ion concentration of a solution in moles per liter. What is $[H^+]$ of a carbonated soda if its pH is 1.5?

Ⓕ $10^{-1.5}$

Ⓖ $10^{1.5}$

Ⓗ $-\log 1.5$

Ⓙ $-\log(-1.5)$

DAY 3

For which of the following functions does *y* vary directly as *x*?

Ⓐ $y = \frac{2}{x}$

Ⓑ $y = -7x$

Ⓒ $10 = xy$

Ⓓ $y = x^0 - 15$

DAY 4

The distance a spring stretches varies directly as the amount of weight hanging from it. A weight of 60 pounds stretches the spring 15 centimeters. How heavy is the weight hanging on the spring when it stretches 12 centimeters?

Ⓕ 3 pounds

Ⓖ 12 pounds

Ⓗ 48 pounds

Ⓙ 52 pounds

DAY 5

The graph represents which parent function?

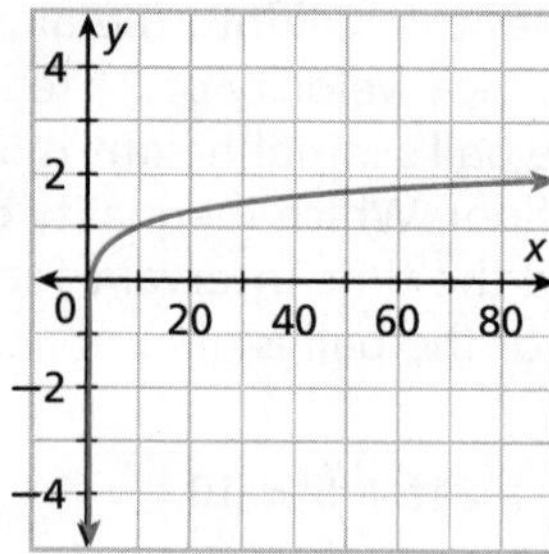

Ⓐ $y = x^2$

Ⓑ $y = x$

Ⓒ $y = \log x$

Ⓓ $y = e^x$

Countdown to Testing WEEK 18

DAY 1

The area of a rectangular parking lot with a length of 1500 feet can be no more than 3,000,000 square feet. Which is the most reasonable domain of the function representing the parking lot's area A in square feet in terms of its width w in feet?

Ⓐ $0 < w \leq 1500$

Ⓑ $0 < w \leq 2000$

Ⓒ $1500 < w \leq 2000$

Ⓓ $1500 < w \leq 3{,}000{,}000$

DAY 2

Which ordered pair is NOT a solution of the exponential inequality shown in the graph?

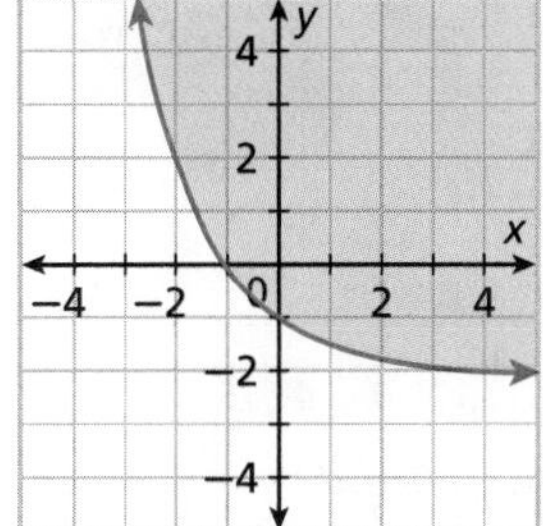

Ⓕ (2, −2)

Ⓖ (5, 1)

Ⓗ (3, 3)

Ⓙ (0, 4)

DAY 3

Determine the y-value of the solution of the system of equations.

$$\begin{cases} y = 4x + 12 \\ y = 2x - 5 \end{cases}$$

Ⓐ −2 Ⓑ −3.5 Ⓒ −8.5 Ⓓ −22

DAY 4

Which function represents the graph of $f(x) = \ln x$ translated 2 units right and 5 units up?

Ⓕ $g(x) = \ln(x + 2) - 5$

Ⓖ $g(x) = \ln(x + 5) - 2$

Ⓗ $g(x) = \ln(x - 2) + 5$

Ⓙ $g(x) = \ln(x - 5) + 2$

DAY 5

Which ordered pair is a solution of the inequality $y > -(x - 3)^2 + 8$?

Ⓐ (5, 0)

Ⓑ (5, 1)

Ⓒ (5, 4)

Ⓓ (5, 6)

Countdown to Testing WEEK 19

DAY 1

The radius of a circle can be determined by dividing the area by π and taking the square root of the result. Which graph best shows the radius as a function of the area?

Ⓐ
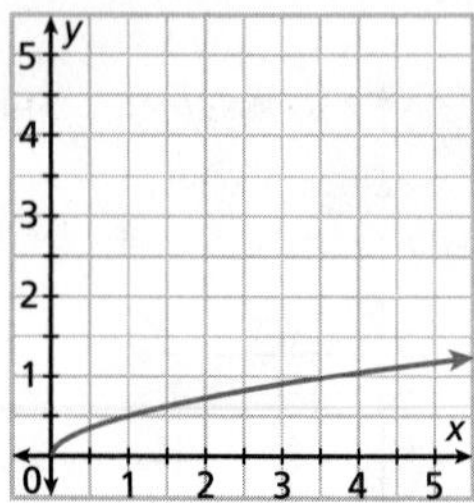

Ⓒ
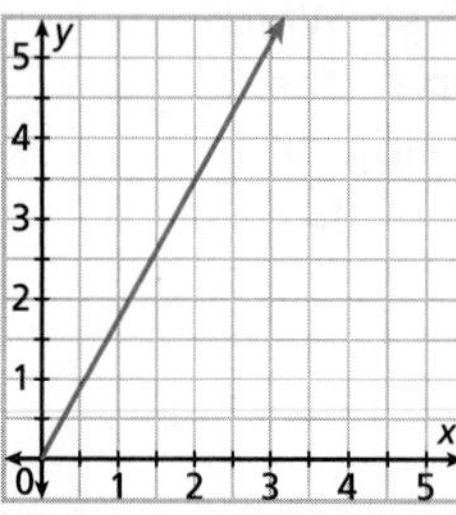

Ⓑ
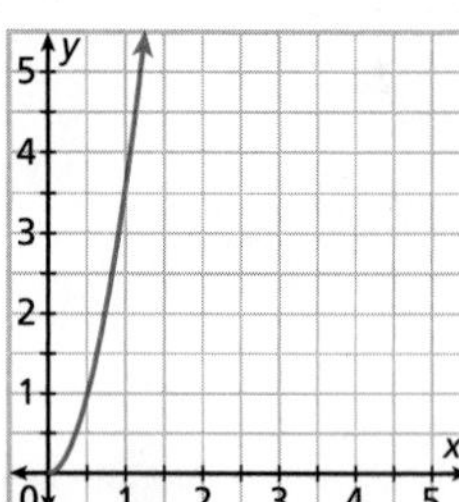

Ⓓ
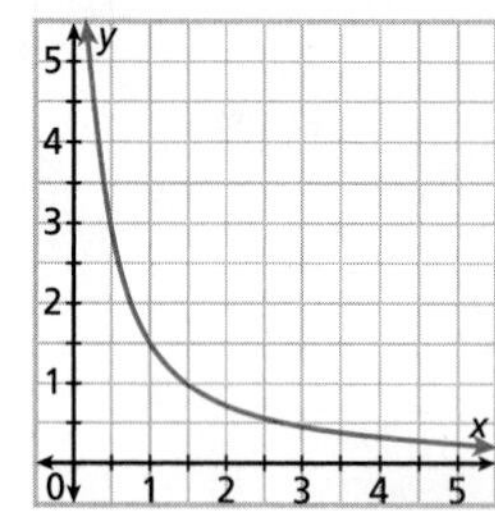

DAY 2

Which of the following relationships would most likely be characterized by a negative correlation?

Ⓕ The number of DVDs purchased and the total cost

Ⓖ The height of a tree and its age

Ⓗ The number of workers on a job and the time it takes to complete the job

Ⓙ The age of a person and his or her hat size

DAY 3

What function best represents the data in the table?

x	f(x)
0	−2
1	−1
4	0
9	1
16	2

Ⓐ $f(x) = x - 2$

Ⓑ $f(x) = (x - 2)^2$

Ⓒ $f(x) = \sqrt{x - 2}$

Ⓓ $f(x) = \sqrt{x} - 2$

DAY 4

How does the graph of $g(x) = \sqrt{-x}$ differ from the graph of $f(x) = \sqrt{x}$?

Ⓕ The graph is reflected across the x-axis.

Ⓖ The graph is reflected across the y-axis.

Ⓗ The graph is rotated 180° about the origin.

Ⓙ The graph is shifted 4 units down.

DAY 5

Where does a hole occur in the graph of $f(x) = \dfrac{(x + 4)(x - 6)}{(x + 2)(x - 6)(x + 3)}$?

Ⓐ $x = 6$

Ⓑ $x = -2$

Ⓒ $x = -3$

Ⓓ $x = -4$

Countdown to Testing WEEK 20

DAY 1

The speed of a sound wave traveling through a thin rod is given by the formula $v = \sqrt{\frac{Y}{p}}$, where v is the speed of the waves in meters per second, Y is 8.0×10^{10} pascals, and p is the density of the rod in kilograms per cubic meter. If you know the value of v, which equation can you use to determine p?

Ⓐ $p = \sqrt{\frac{Y}{v}}$

Ⓑ $p = \frac{Y}{v^2}$

Ⓒ $p = \frac{\sqrt{Y}}{v}$

Ⓓ $p = (Yv)^2$

DAY 2

Martha invested \$12,000 and earned \$840 in interest in one year. She invested some of the money in an account that pays 8% per year and the rest of it in an account that pays 5% per year. Which system can be used to find the amount she invested at each rate?

Ⓕ $\begin{cases} x - y = 12{,}000 \\ 0.08x - 0.05y = 840 \end{cases}$

Ⓖ $\begin{cases} y = 12{,}000 - x \\ 0.08x + 0.05y = 12{,}000 - 840 \end{cases}$

Ⓗ $\begin{cases} xy = 12{,}000 \\ 0.08x - 0.05y = 840 \end{cases}$

Ⓙ $\begin{cases} y = 12{,}000 - x \\ 0.08x + 0.05y = 840 \end{cases}$

DAY 3

Which is the graph of $f(x) = \ln x$?

Ⓐ 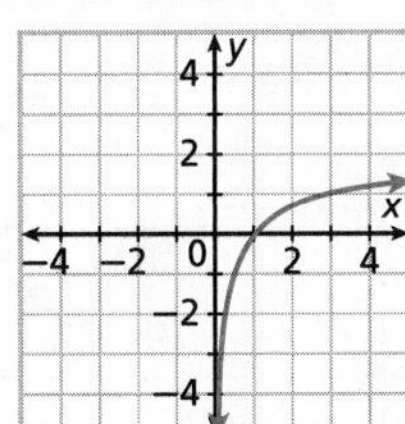

Ⓒ 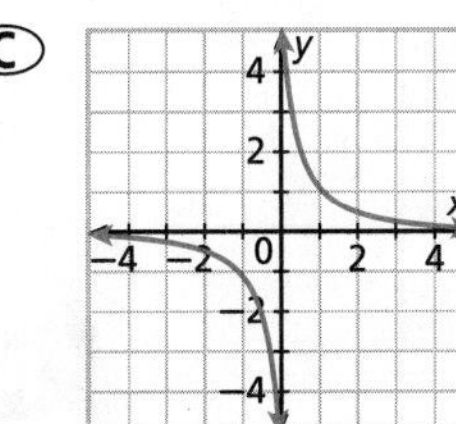

Ⓑ 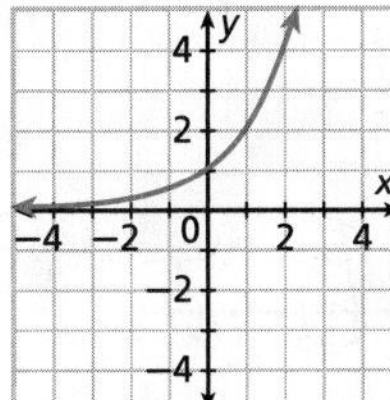

Ⓓ 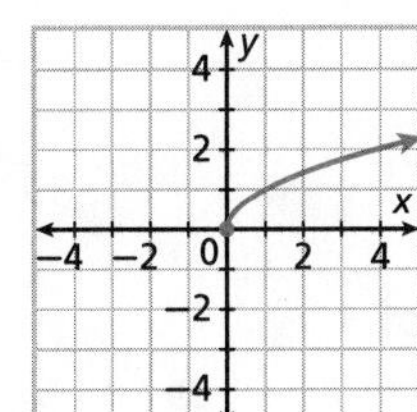

DAY 4

Which function represents a reflection of $f(x) = 2^x$ across the y-axis?

Ⓕ $g(x) = -2^x$

Ⓗ $g(x) = 2^{-x}$

Ⓖ $g(x) = \left(\frac{1}{2}\right)^x$

Ⓙ $g(x) = \left(\frac{1}{x}\right)^2$

DAY 5

Which equation is equivalent to $12^{-x} = 24$?

Ⓐ $\log_{24} 12 = x$

Ⓒ $\log_{12} 24 = -x$

Ⓑ $\log_x 24 = 12$

Ⓓ $\log_{-x} 12 = 24$

Countdown to Testing WEEK 21

DAY 1

The range of a quadratic function is $\{y|y \leq 4\}$. What is the range of the same function after translation 3 units up?

Ⓐ $\{y|y \leq 1\}$
Ⓑ $\{y|y \geq 1\}$
Ⓒ $\{y|y \leq 7\}$
Ⓓ $\{y|y \geq 7\}$

DAY 2

Which function represents a translation of $f(x) = 2^x$ six units right?

Ⓕ $g(x) = 2^x - 6$
Ⓖ $g(x) = 2^{x-6}$
Ⓗ $g(x) = 2^x + 6$
Ⓙ $g(x) = 2^{x+6}$

DAY 3

What is the domain of the function $f(x) = -\sqrt{7 - x}$?

Ⓐ $x \geq -7$
Ⓑ $x \leq -7$
Ⓒ $x \geq 7$
Ⓓ $x \leq 7$

DAY 4

Which transformation was NOT applied to the graph of $f(x) = \sqrt{x}$ to obtain $g(x) = -4\sqrt{6(x + 3)}$?

Ⓕ Vertical translation 3 units up
Ⓖ Reflection across the x-axis
Ⓗ Vertical stretch by a factor of 4
Ⓙ Horizontal compression by a factor of $\frac{1}{6}$.

DAY 5

Which quadratic function is represented by the graph?

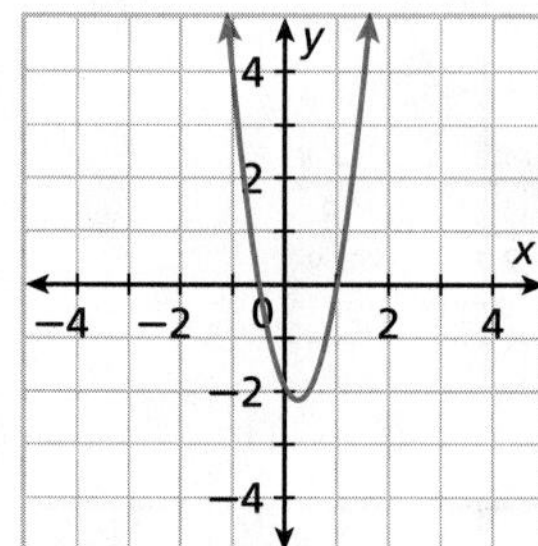

Ⓐ $f(x) = 4x^2 - 2x - 2$
Ⓑ $f(x) = x^2 - 2$
Ⓒ $f(x) = (x + 1)(x - 1)$
Ⓓ $f(x) = (x - 2)^2 - 2$

DAY 1

Francisco wants to make a scatter plot to determine if there is a correlation between duration of a construction highway project and the number of managers assigned to the project. Which table would be best for Francisco to organize his findings?

Ⓐ

Duration of Project			
Manager Names			

Ⓑ

Number of Managers			
Project Number			

Ⓒ

Duration of Project			
Number of Managers			

Ⓓ

Project Number			
Manager Names			

DAY 2

Bobby is on a biking trip that consists of 55 miles on paved roads and 18 miles on unpaved roads. He is able to bike twice as fast on paved roads as on unpaved roads. Which function represents the total time T in hours that Bobby needs to complete the trip in terms of his average speed on unpaved roads x in miles per hour?

Ⓕ $T(x) = \frac{55}{x} + \frac{18}{2x}$

Ⓖ $T(x) = \frac{55}{2x} + \frac{18}{x}$

Ⓗ $T(x) = \frac{55}{x} - \frac{37}{2x}$

Ⓙ $T(x) = \frac{55}{x} - \frac{18}{2x}$

DAY 3

The graph of the inequality $y \geq -(x - 3)^2 + 8$ is shown below. Which of the given points is not in the solution region?

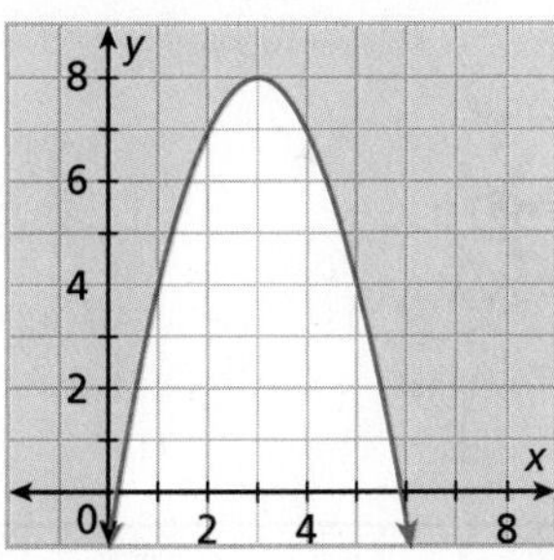

Ⓐ $(-2, -3)$

Ⓑ $(1, 7)$

Ⓒ $(3, 4)$

Ⓓ $(6, 5)$

DAY 4

Solve $\sqrt{x + 14} \leq x - 16$.

Ⓕ $x \geq 16$

Ⓖ $-16 \leq x \leq 22$

Ⓗ $x \leq -22$

Ⓙ $x \geq 22$

DAY 5

What is the relationship between the graph of the function $y = x^2 - 4x$ and the graph of its inverse?

Ⓐ Reflection across the line $y = x$

Ⓑ Translation of 4 units down

Ⓒ 180° rotation about the origin

Ⓓ Vertical stretch by a factor of 4

Countdown to Testing — WEEK 23

DAY 1

What is the domain of $f(x) = \dfrac{3x + 5}{x^2 + 3x - 18}$?

Ⓐ All real numbers

Ⓑ All real numbers except −6

Ⓒ All real numbers except 3

Ⓓ All real numbers except 3 and −6

DAY 2

One leg of a right triangle measures 9 ft and the hypotenuse measures 15 ft. Which equation can you use to find the length of the third side of the triangle?

Ⓕ $b = \sqrt{15^2 - 9^2}$

Ⓖ $b^2 = \sqrt{15^2 - 9^2}$

Ⓗ $b = \sqrt{15^2 + 9^2}$

Ⓙ $b^2 = \sqrt{15^2 + 9^2}$

DAY 3

Which parent function is shown in the graph?

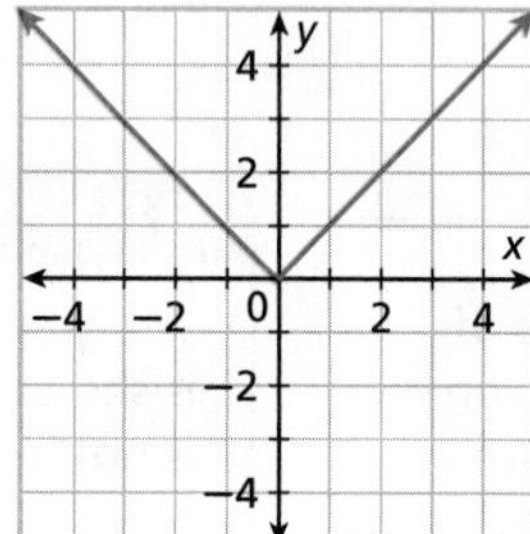

Ⓐ $f(x) = e^x$

Ⓑ $f(x) = \ln x$

Ⓒ $f(x) = \sqrt{x}$

Ⓓ $f(x) = |x|$

DAY 4

Which function does NOT include the values −2, 4, 8, and 12 in the domain?

Ⓕ $f(x) = \sqrt{12x + 24}$

Ⓖ $f(x) = \sqrt{7(x - 4)}$

Ⓗ $f(x) = \sqrt{x^2 + 5x + 6}$

Ⓙ $f(x) = \sqrt{\dfrac{2}{x^2 + 1}}$

DAY 5

A parabola is a conic section formed by the intersection of a plane and a(n) ________.

Ⓐ circle

Ⓑ hyperbola

Ⓒ double cone

Ⓓ ellipse

DAY 1

Which graph can be used to determine the solution of $x^2 = \sqrt{2x}$?

Ⓐ
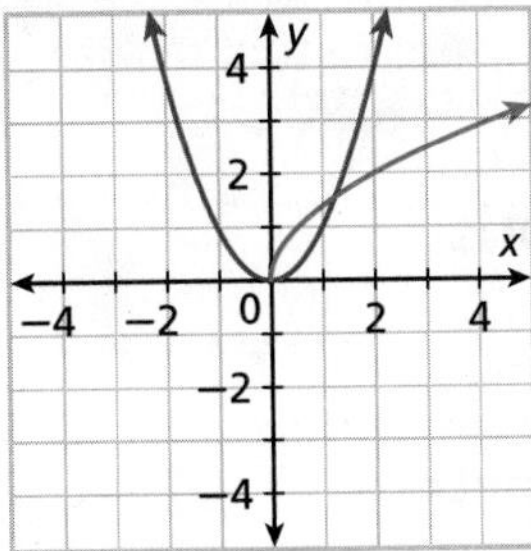

Ⓒ
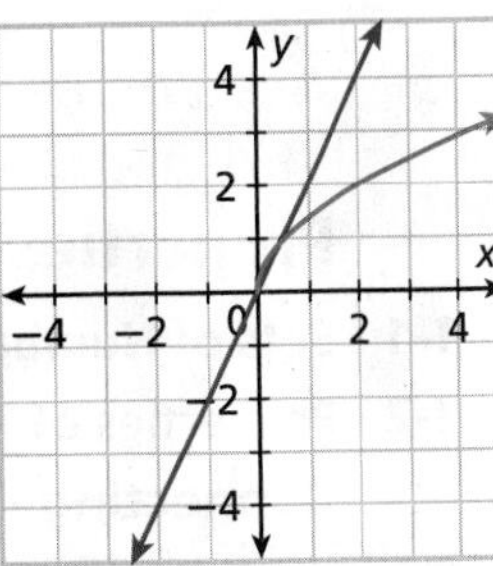

Ⓑ
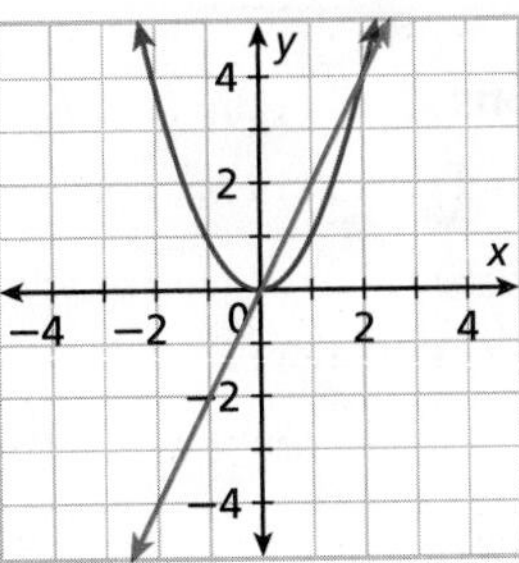

Ⓓ
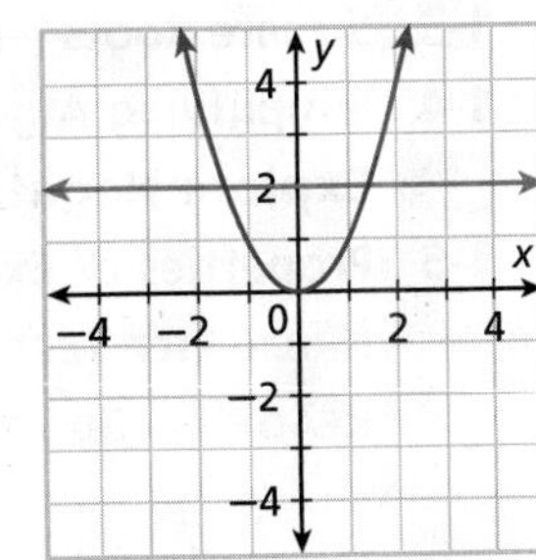

DAY 2

Solve $\frac{x}{x-2} = \frac{3x}{x+2}$.

Ⓕ $x = 2$ or $x = -2$

Ⓖ $x = 0$ or $x = 3$

Ⓗ $x = 0$ or $x = 4$

Ⓙ No real solution

DAY 3

The population of Warren County is 55,000 and is growing at a rate of 3.8% per decade. Which of the following expressions represents the population of Warren County after n decades?

Ⓐ $55{,}000(3.8)^n$

Ⓑ $55{,}000(1.38)^n$

Ⓒ $55{,}000(1.038)^n$

Ⓓ $55{,}000 + (3.8)^n$

DAY 4

What value of x makes the equation $3 = 1 + \log(2x)$ true?

Ⓕ 1

Ⓖ 10

Ⓗ 50

Ⓙ 100

DAY 5

The equation $\frac{x^2}{100} - \frac{y^2}{64} = 1$ represents which conic section?

Ⓐ Circle

Ⓑ Hyperbola

Ⓒ Parabola

Ⓓ Ellipse

Foundations for Functions

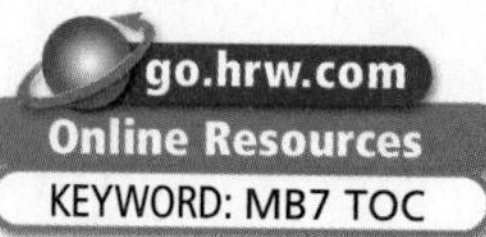

Tools for Success

CHAPTER 2

Linear Functions

go.hrw.com
Online Resources
KEYWORD: MB7 TOC

Table of Contents

Tools for Success

go.hrw.com
Online Resources
KEYWORD: MB7 TOC

Linear Systems

Tools for Success

CHAPTER 4

Matrices

Tools for Success

Quadratic Functions

go.hrw.com
Online Resources
KEYWORD: MB7 TOC

Tools for Success

Polynomial Functions

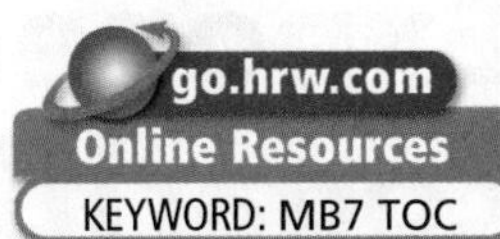

CHAPTER 6

Tools for Success

go.hrw.com
Online Resources
KEYWORD: MB7 TOC

Exponential and Logarithmic Functions

Tools for Success

CHAPTER 8

Rational and Radical Functions

go.hrw.com
Online Resources
KEYWORD: MB7 TOC

Tools for Success

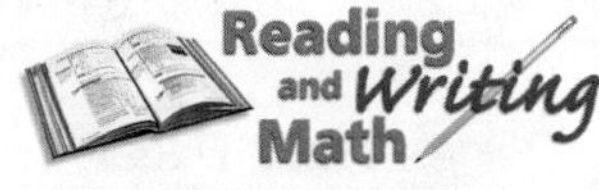

Properties and Attributes of Functions

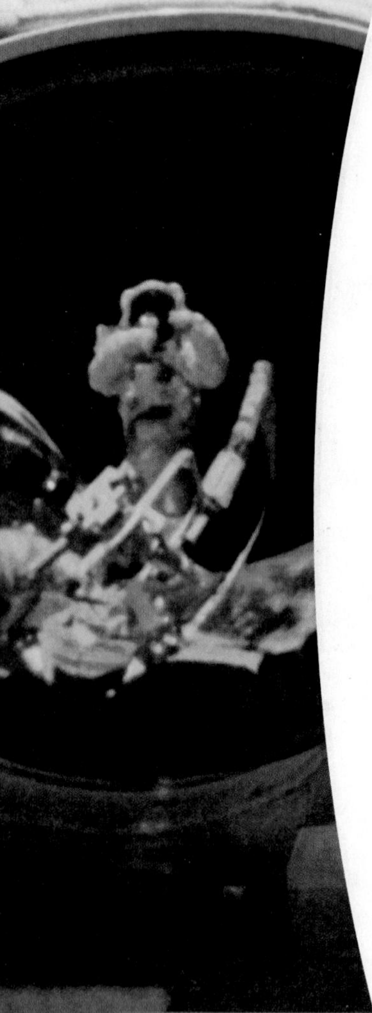

Tools for Success

Conic Sections

Tools for Success

Probability and Statistics

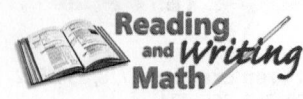

go.hrw.com
Online Resources
KEYWORD: MB7 TOC

Sequences and Series

CHAPTER 12

go.hrw.com
Online Resources
KEYWORD: MB7 TOC

Tools for Success

CHAPTER 13

Trigonometric Functions

go.hrw.com
Online Resources
KEYWORD: MB7 TOC

Tools for Success

CHAPTER 14

Trigonometric Graphs and Identities

go.hrw.com
Online Resources
KEYWORD: MB7 TOC

Tools for Success

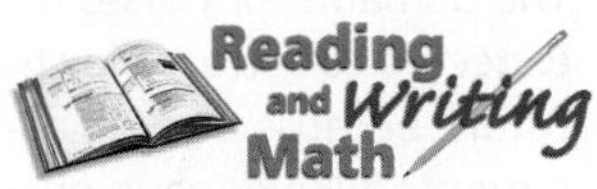

Who Uses Mathematics?

The Career Path features are a set of interviews with young adults who are either preparing for or just beginning in different career fields. These people share what math courses they studied in high school, how math is used in their field, and what options the future holds. Also, many exercises throughout the book highlight the different skills used in various career fields.

Career Path

go.hrw.com
Career Resources Online
KEYWORD: MB7 Career

Career Applications

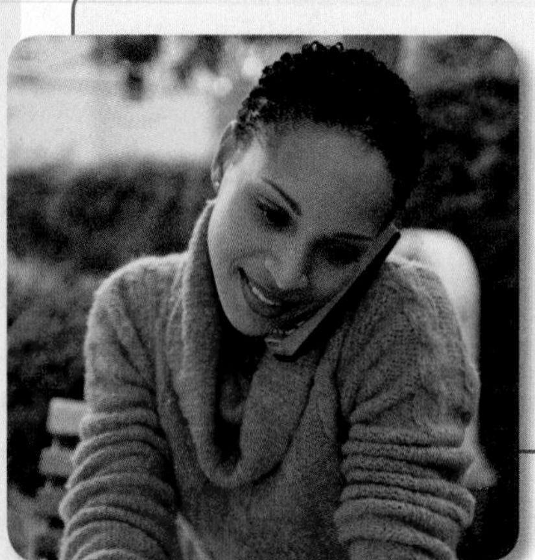

ECONOMIST *p. 277*
Economists help people prepare for the future by analyzing political and business trends and data, and then making predictions. Look on page 277 to learn about the type of training you need for this career path.

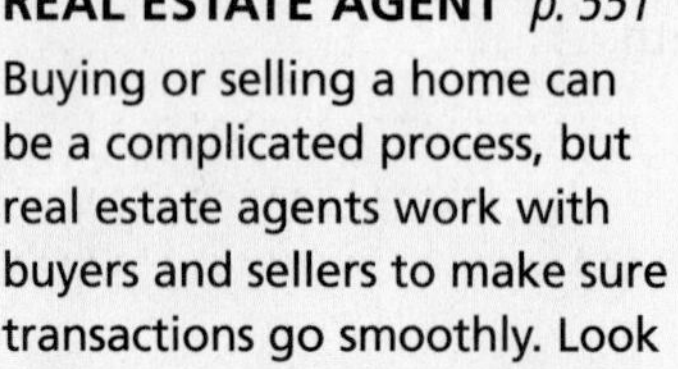

REAL ESTATE AGENT *p. 551*
Buying or selling a home can be a complicated process, but real estate agents work with buyers and sellers to make sure transactions go smoothly. Look at the Career Path on page 551 to see how to become a real estate agent.

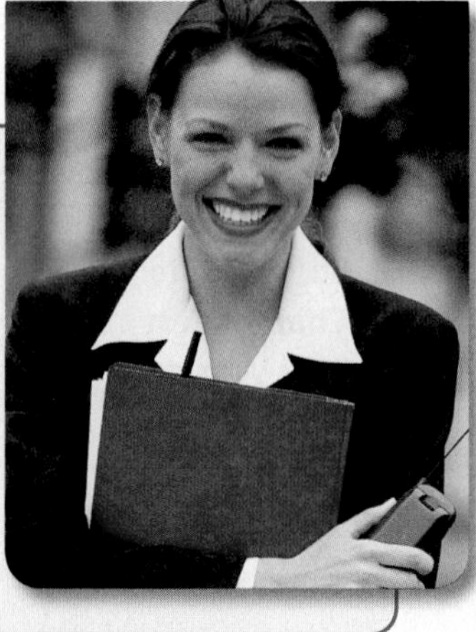

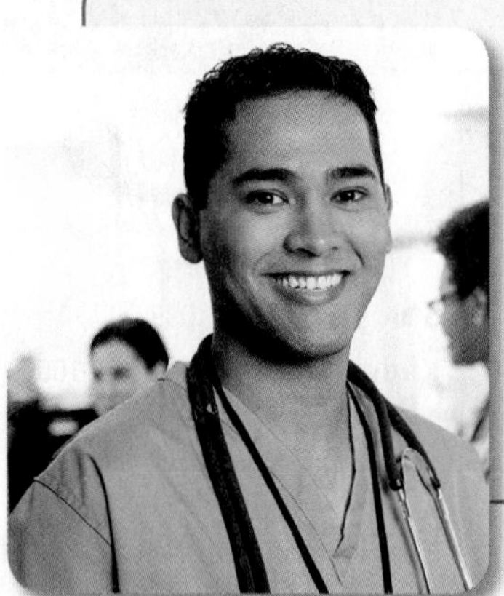

NURSING STUDENT *p. 877*
The demand for nurses is expected to increase in the future because doctors and patients alike depend on their assistance and expertise. The Career Path on page 877 describes what it is like to be a nursing student.

WHY LEARN MATHEMATICS?

Links to interesting topics may accompany real-world applications in the examples or exercises. For a complete list of all applications in *Holt McDougal Algebra 2*, see page IN2 in the Index.

LINK
Architecture

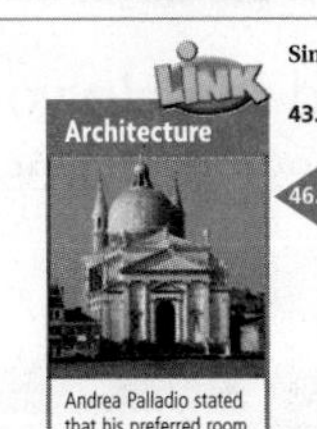

Andrea Palladio stated that his preferred room shapes were squares, circles, and rectangles with precise length-to-width ratios. Some of these shapes can be seen above in Il Redentore church that Palladio designed.

Simplify. Assume that all expressions are defined.

43. $\dfrac{\frac{4}{x+2}}{\frac{x+2}{6}}$ **44.** $\dfrac{\frac{2}{3x-4}}{5x+3}$ **45.** $\dfrac{\frac{1}{2x}+\frac{2}{3x}}{\frac{x-1}{x-3}}$

46. **Architecture** The Renaissance architect Andrea Palladio preferred that the length and width of rectangular rooms be limited to certain ratios. These ratios are listed in the table. Palladio also believed that the height of a room with vaulted ceilings should be the harmonic mean of the length and width.

a. The harmonic mean of two positive numbers a and b is equal to $\dfrac{2}{\frac{1}{a}+\frac{1}{b}}$. Simplify this expression.

b. Complete the table for a rectangular room with a width of 30 feet that meets Palladio's requirements for its length and height. If necessary, round to the nearest tenth.

c. **What if...?** A Palladian room has a length-to-width ratio of 4:3. If the length of this room is doubled, what effect should this change have on the room's width and height, according to Palladio's principles?

Rooms with a Width of 30 ft		
Length-to-Width Ratio	Length (ft)	Height (ft)
2:1	■	■
3:2	■	■
4:3	■	■
5:3	■	■
$\sqrt{2}$:1	■	■

LINKS

Real-World

LINK
Chemistry

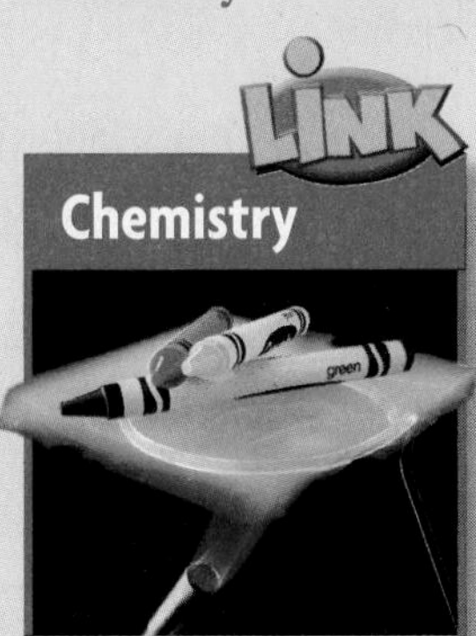

Aerogel has been called the world's lowest density solid. It is 99.8% air and is an excellent heat insulator. As shown above, a layer of aerogel can prevent a flame from melting crayons.

LINK
Geography

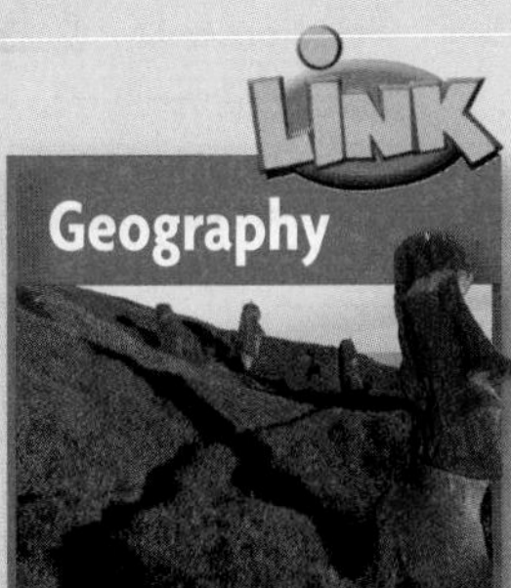

Easter Island, a South Pacific island of Chile, contains more than 600 stone statues. The statues were carved between 1600 and 1730. Most of the heads actually have torsos that have become buried over time.

LINK
Tennis

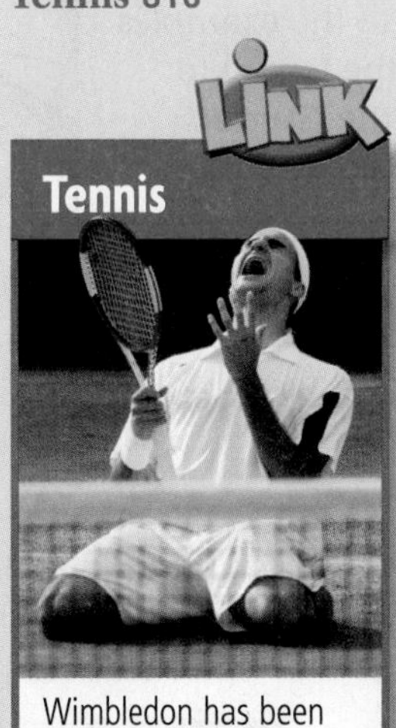

Wimbledon has been played annually since 1877 at the All England Lawn Tennis and Croquet Club.

How to Study Algebra 2

This book has many features designed to help you learn and study effectively. Becoming familiar with these features will prepare you for greater success on your exams.

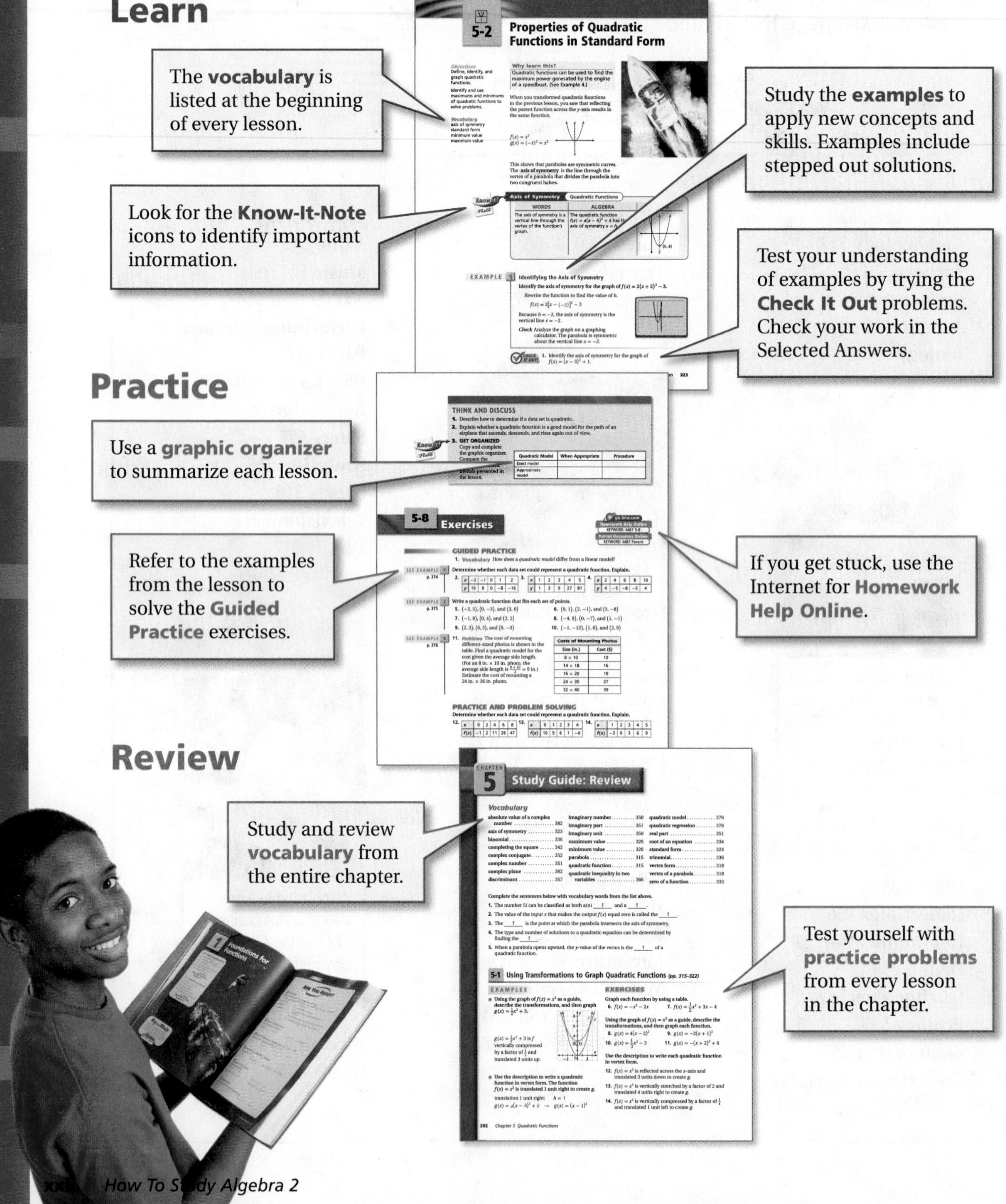

Learn
The vocabulary is listed at the beginning of every lesson.
Look for the Know-It-Note icons to identify important information.
Study the examples to apply new concepts and skills. Examples include stepped out solutions.
Test your understanding of examples by trying the Check It Out problems. Check your work in the Selected Answers.
5-2 Properties of Quadratic Functions in Standard Form
Practice
Use a graphic organizer to summarize each lesson.
Refer to the examples from the lesson to solve the Guided Practice exercises.
If you get stuck, use the Internet for Homework Help Online.
5-8 Exercises
Review
Study and review vocabulary from the entire chapter.
Test yourself with practice problems from every lesson in the chapter.
5 Study Guide: Review

Scavenger Hunt

Use this scavenger hunt to discover a few of the many tools in *Holt McDougal Algebra 2* that you can use to become an independent learner. On a separate sheet of paper, write the answers to each question below. Within each answer, one or more letters will be in a yellow box. After you have answered every question, identify the letters that would be in yellow boxes and rearrange them to finish the quotation at the bottom of the page.

1. What study strategy is discussed on the **Reading and Writing Math** page in Chapter 8?

2. What are you asked to describe in the **Know-it Note** on page 62?

3. What keyword should you enter for **Homework Help** in Lesson 6-2?

   _ _ _ _ _ - _

4. What career is discussed in the **Career Path** on page 277?

5. What is the first vocabulary term listed in the **Study Guide: Review** in Chapter 3?

6. What test-taking strategy is described in the **Test Tackler** in Chapter 5?

7. What type of data display is shown in Item 5 of the **Standardized Test Prep** on page 562?

8. What state is the topic of the **Real-World Connections** on page 176?

Quote!

Do not worry about your difficulties in

_ _ _ _ _ _ _ _ _ _ _.

I can assure you that mine are far greater.

—Albert Einstein, scientist and Nobel Prize winner

CHAPTER 1

Foundations for Functions

- Apply properties and operations of numbers to solve problems.
- Develop symbolic and graphical representations of functions.

Big as a Whale

Humpback whales are among the world's largest animals. You can use expressions and functions to compare the sizes of whales to various objects.

go.hrw.com
Chapter Project Online
KEYWORD: MB7 ChProj

Vocabulary

Match each term on the left with a definition on the right.

1. algebraic expression
2. opposites
3. origin
4. variable

A. the point in the coordinate plane where the *x*-axis and the *y*-axis intersect

B. a value that does not change

C. two numbers that are equal distances from zero on a number line

D. a mathematical phrase that contains one or more variables

E. a symbol that represents a quantity that can change

Fractions and Decimals

Write each fraction as a decimal.

5. $\frac{3}{10}$ **6.** $\frac{3}{5}$ **7.** $-\frac{4}{3}$ **8.** $5\frac{3}{4}$

Graph Numbers on a Number Line

Graph each number on the same number line.

9. 3.5 **10.** -4 **11.** $-\frac{12}{4}$ **12.** $3.\overline{3}$

Compare and Order Real Numbers

Compare using $<$ or $>$.

13. $\frac{5}{6} \blacksquare \frac{2}{3}$ **14.** $3\frac{7}{9} \blacksquare 3\frac{10}{12}$ **15.** $-0.38 \blacksquare -0.3$ **16.** $-\frac{15}{8} \blacksquare -2$

Order of Operations

Simplify each expression.

17. $14 \div 2(-3) + 1$

18. $8^2 - (-12) + 15 \div 3$

19. $-2(25 - 21)^2 + 11$

20. $3\left(\frac{21 - 9}{6} - 1\right) \div 2$

Ordered Pairs

Graph each point on the same coordinate plane.

21. $(0, 2)$ **22.** $(-3, 1)$ **23.** $(2, -1)$ **24.** $(-3, -2)$

CHAPTER 1

Study Guide: Preview

Where You've Been

Previously, you

- used properties of real numbers.
- simplified numeric expressions using the order of operations and exponents.
- used variables, expressions, and equations to represent situations.

In This Chapter

You will study

- using sets of numbers and their properties.
- simplifying algebraic expressions and expressions with exponents.
- using functions and their graphs to represent situations.

Where You're Going

You can use the skills in this chapter

- to quickly calculate tips and discounts in your head.
- to build a foundation for calculus classes.
- to observe patterns and relationships in science and social studies.

Key Vocabulary/Vocabulario

domain	el dominio
element	el elemento
function	la función
parent function	la función elemental
radical symbol	el símbolo de radical
range	el rango
set	el conjunto
subset	el subconjunto
transformation	la transformación

Vocabulary Connections

To become familiar with some of the vocabulary terms in the chapter, consider the following. You may refer to the chapter, the glossary, or a dictionary if you like.

1. The word **subset** begins with the prefix *sub-*. List some other words that begin with *sub-*. What do all of these words have in common?
2. **Element** comes from the Latin word *elementum*, which was used to refer to any one of the four basic substances believed to compose the entire universe (air, water, fire, and earth). What might *element* refer to in a set of numbers?
3. One meaning of the word **function** is "to perform." Give examples of specific machines or tools and the *functions* they perform.
4. What does the word *transform* mean? What do you think a mathematical **transformation** involves?

Study Strategy: Use Your Book for Success

Understanding how your textbook is organized will help you locate and use helpful information.

Pay attention to the **margin notes.** Know-It Note icons point out key information. Helpful Hints, Remember notes, and Caution notes help you understand concepts and avoid common mistakes.

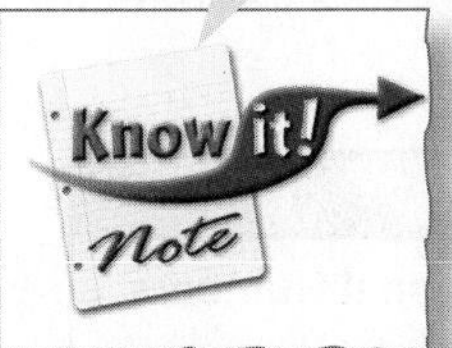

Helpful Hint
A replacement set a set of numbers t can be substitutec

Remember!
Terms that are written without a coefficient have

Caution!
In the expression -5^2, 5 is the base because the nega

The **Glossary** is found in the back of your textbook. Use it as a resource when you need the definition of an unfamiliar word or property.

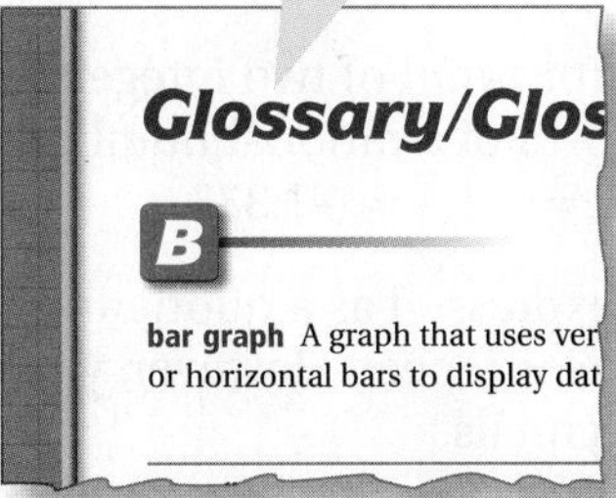

Glossary/Glos
B
bar graph A graph that uses ver
or horizontal bars to display dat

The **Index** is located at the end of your textbook. Use it to locate the page where a particular concept is taught.

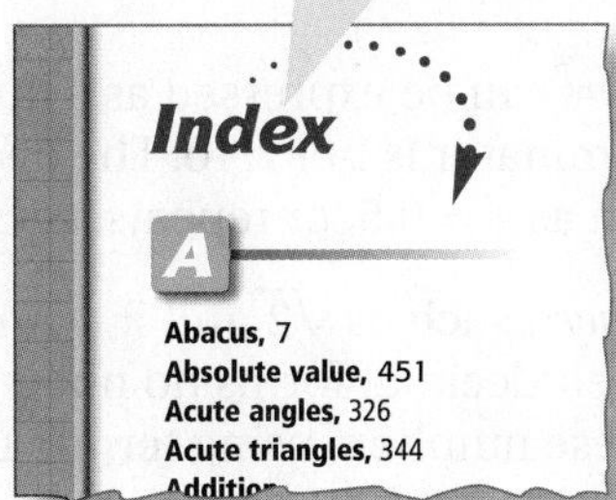

The **Problem Solving Handbook** is found in the back of your textbook. These pages review strategies that can help you solve real-world problems.

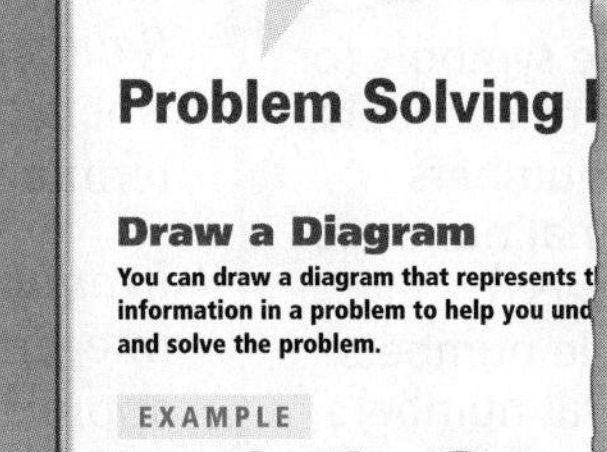

Problem Solving
Draw a Diagram
You can draw a diagram that represents t
information in a problem to help you und
and solve the problem.
EXAMPLE

Try This

Use your textbook for the following problems.

1. Use the index to find the page where each term is defined.

a. range **b.** translation **c.** scientific notation

2. In Lesson 1-4, what fact about coefficients does the **Remember** margin note point out?

3. Use the glossary to find the definition of each term.

a. set **b.** parent function **c.** principal root

1-1 Sets of Numbers

Objective

Classify and order real numbers.

Vocabulary

set
element
subset
empty set
roster notation
finite set
infinite set
interval notation
set-builder notation

Why learn this?

Sets can be used to organize the balls used in the billiard game 8-ball.

A **set** is a collection of items called **elements**. The rules of 8-ball divide the set of billiard balls into three *subsets:* solids (1 through 7), stripes (9 through 15), and the 8 ball. A **subset** is a set whose elements all belong to another set. The **empty set**, denoted ∅, is a set containing no elements. The diagram shows some important subsets of the real numbers.

Real Numbers (ℝ)

Rational Numbers (ℚ): 0.5, $2\frac{7}{9}$, $5.3\overline{12}$

Integers (ℤ): −5, −2

Whole Numbers (𝕎): 0

Natural Numbers (ℕ): 1, 2, 3

Irrational Numbers: $-5\sqrt{3}$, π, $\sqrt{2}$, $\frac{\sqrt{7}}{2}$, e

Reading Math

Note the symbols for the sets of numbers.
ℝ: real numbers
ℚ: rational numbers
ℤ: integers
𝕎: whole numbers
ℕ: natural numbers

Rational numbers can be expressed as a quotient (or *ratio*) of two integers, where the denominator is not zero. The decimal form of a rational number either terminates, such as $\frac{1}{2} = 0.5$, or repeats, such as $-\frac{4}{3} = -1.\overline{3} = -1.333\ldots$.

Irrational numbers, such as $\sqrt{2}$ and π, *cannot* be expressed as a quotient of two integers, and their decimal forms do not terminate or repeat. However, you can approximate these numbers using terminating decimals.

EXAMPLE 1 Ordering and Classifying Real Numbers

Consider the numbers $0.\overline{6}$, $\sqrt{2}$, 0, $-\frac{5}{2}$, and 0.5129.

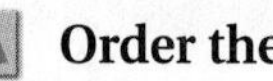

A Order the numbers from least to greatest.

Write each number as a decimal to make it easier to compare them.

$\sqrt{2} \approx 1.414$ — *Use a decimal approximation for $\sqrt{2}$.*

$-\frac{5}{2} = -2.5$ — *Rewrite $-\frac{5}{2}$ in decimal form.*

$-2.5 < 0 < 0.5129 < 0.666\ldots < 1.414$ — *Use < to compare the numbers.*

The numbers in order from least to greatest are $-\frac{5}{2}$, 0, 0.5129, $0.\overline{6}$, and $\sqrt{2}$.

Consider the numbers $0.\overline{6}$, $\sqrt{2}$, 0, $-\frac{5}{2}$, and 0.5129.

B **Classify each number by the subsets of the real numbers to which it belongs. Use a table to classify the numbers.**

Number	Real ($\mathbb{R}$)	Rational ($\mathbb{Q}$)	Integer ($\mathbb{Z}$)	Whole ($\mathbb{W}$)	Natural ($\mathbb{N}$)	Irrational
$-\frac{5}{2}$	✓	✓				
0	✓	✓	✓	✓		
0.5129	✓	✓				
$0.\overline{6}$	✓	✓				
$\sqrt{2}$	✓					✓

Consider the numbers −2, π, −0.321, $\frac{3}{2}$, and $-\sqrt{3}$.

1a. Order the numbers from least to greatest.

1b. Classify each number by the subsets of the real numbers to which it belongs.

There are many ways to represent sets. For instance, you can use words to describe a set. You can also use **roster notation**, in which the elements of a set are listed between braces, { }.

Words	Roster Notation
The set of billiard balls is numbered 1 through 15.	{1, 2, 3, 4, 5, 6, 7, 8, 9, 10, 11, 12, 13, 14, 15}

Helpful Hint

The Density Property states that between any two real numbers there is another real number. So any interval that includes more than one point contains infinitely many points.

A set can be *finite* like the set of billiard ball numbers or *infinite* like the natural numbers {1, 2, 3, 4...}. A **finite set** has a definite, or finite, number of elements. An **infinite set** has an unlimited, or infinite, number of elements.

Many infinite sets, such as the real numbers, cannot be represented in roster notation. There are other methods of representing these sets. For example, the number line represents the set of all real numbers.

The set of real numbers between 3 and 5, which is also an infinite set, can be represented on a number line or by an inequality.

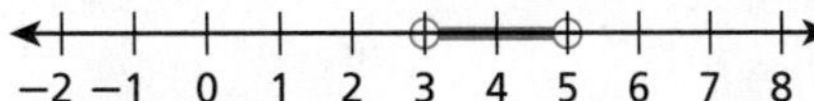

$3 < x < 5$

An interval is the set of all numbers between two endpoints, such as 3 and 5. In **interval notation** the symbols [and] are used to include an endpoint in an interval, and the symbols (and) are used to exclude an endpoint from an interval.

(3, 5) *The set of real numbers between but not including 3 and 5*

An interval that extends forever in the positive direction goes to infinity (∞), and an interval that extends forever in the negative direction goes to negative infinity (−∞).

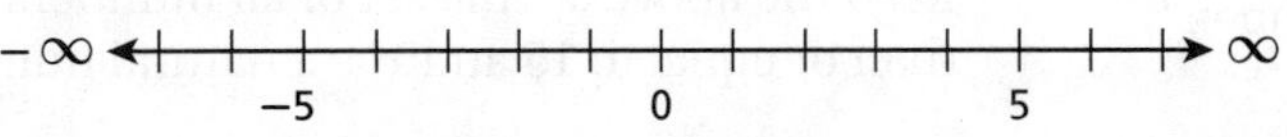

Because ∞ and $-\infty$ are not numbers, they cannot be included in a set of numbers, so parentheses are used to enclose them in an interval. The table shows the relationship among some methods of representing intervals.

Methods of Representing Intervals			
Words	Number Line	Inequality	Interval Notation
Numbers less than 3	−1 0 1 2 3 4 5	$x < 3$	$(-\infty, 3)$
Numbers greater than or equal to −2	−4 −3 −2 −1 0 1 2	$x \geq -2$	$[-2, \infty)$
Numbers between 2 and 4	−1 0 1 2 3 4 5	$2 < x < 4$	$(2, 4)$
Numbers 1 through 3	−2 −1 0 1 2 3 4	$1 \leq x \leq 3$	$[1, 3]$

EXAMPLE 2 Interval Notation

Use interval notation to represent each set of numbers.

A $4 \leq x < 6$

$[4, 6)$ — *4 is included, but 6 is not.*

B

−6 −5 −4 −3 −2 −1 0 1 2 3 4

There are two intervals graphed on the number line.

$[-5, -2]$ — *−5 and −2 are included.*

$(3, \infty)$ — *3 is not included, and the interval continues forever in the positive direction.*

$[-5, -2]$ or $(3, \infty)$ — *The word "or" is used to indicate that a set includes more than one interval.*

Use interval notation to represent each set of numbers.

2a. −4 −3 −2 −1 0 1 2 3 4

2b. $x \leq 2$ or $3 < x \leq 11$

Another way to represent sets is *set-builder notation.* **Set-builder notation** uses the properties of the elements in the set to define the set. Inequalities and the element symbol ($\in$) are often used in set-builder notation. The set of striped-billiard-ball numbers, or $\{9, 10, 11, 12, 13, 14, 15\}$, is represented below in set-builder notation.

Reading Math

The symbol $\in$ means "is an element of." So $x \in \mathbb{N}$ is read "x is an element of the set of natural numbers," or "x is a natural number."

The set of all numbers x such that x has the given properties

Read the above as "the set of all numbers x such that x is greater than 8 and less than or equal to 15 and x is a natural number."

Some representations of the same sets of real numbers are shown.

Methods of Set Notation			
Words	**Roster Notation**	**Interval Notation**	**Set-Builder Notation**
All real numbers except 1	Cannot be written in roster notation	$(-\infty, 1)$ or $(1, \infty)$	$\{x \mid x \neq 1\}$
Positive odd numbers	$\{1, 3, 5, 7, \ldots\}$	Cannot be notated using interval notation	$\{x \mid x = 2n - 1 \text{ and } n \in \mathbb{N}\}$
Numbers within 3 units of 2	Cannot be written in roster notation	$[-1, 5]$	$\{x \mid -1 \leq x \leq 5\}$

EXAMPLE 3 Translating Between Methods of Set Notation

Rewrite each set in the indicated notation.

A $\{x \mid x = 2n \text{ and } n \in \mathbb{N}\}$**; words**

positive even numbers

B **numbers and symbols on a telephone keypad; roster notation**

$\{0, 1, 2, 3, 4, 5, 6, 7, 8, 9, *, \#\}$ *The order of elements is not important.*

C 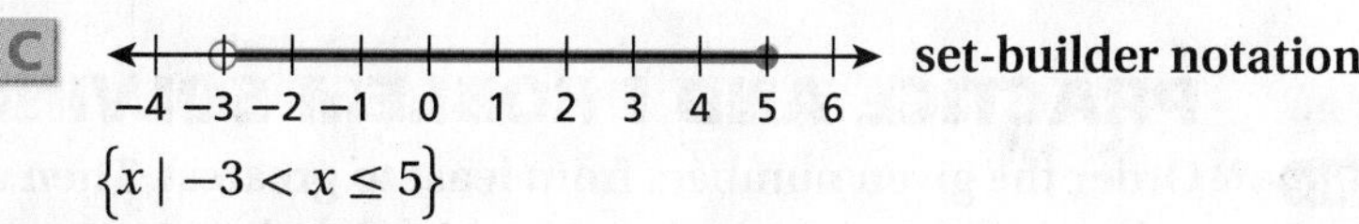

set-builder notation

$\{x \mid -3 < x \leq 5\}$

CHECK IT OUT! **Rewrite each set in the indicated notation.**

3a. $\{2, 4, 6, 8\}$; words

3b. $\{x \mid 2 < x < 8 \text{ and } x \in \mathbb{N}\}$; roster notation

3c. $[99, \infty)$; set-builder notation

THINK AND DISCUSS

1. Compare interval notation with roster notation. Is it possible to have a set that can be represented by both methods?

2. Explain whether it is possible to name a number that belongs to both the set of integers and the set of irrational numbers.

3. GET ORGANIZED Copy and complete the graphic organizer. In each box, show the correct notation for each set.

Set	Roster Notation	Interval Notation	Set-Builder Notation
1, 2, 3, 4, and 5			
$-2 \leq n \leq 2$			
Whole numbers less than 3			

1-1 Exercises

go.hrw.com
Homework Help Online
KEYWORD: MB7 1-1
Parent Resources Online
KEYWORD: MB7 Parent

GUIDED PRACTICE

1. **Vocabulary** Braces, { }, are used in __?__. (*interval notation* or *roster notation*)

SEE EXAMPLE 1 p. 6

Order the given numbers from least to greatest. Then classify each number by the subsets of the real numbers to which it belongs.

2. $3\sqrt{2}, \sqrt{7}, 5.125, 4\frac{3}{5}, 4.\overline{6}$
3. $-\frac{100}{4}, -6.897, \sqrt{4}, \frac{1}{8}, \sqrt{6}$
4. $\sqrt{5}, \frac{\pi}{2}, -\sqrt{3}, 1.\overline{3}, -1\frac{1}{3}$

SEE EXAMPLE 2 p. 8

Use interval notation to represent each set of numbers.

5. $-10 < x \leq 10$
6. 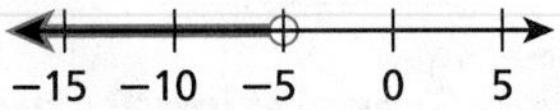

7. $1 \leq x < 20$ or $x > 30$

SEE EXAMPLE 3 p. 9

Rewrite each set in the indicated notation.

8. $\left\{x \mid x = 1 + \frac{1}{2}(n - n) \text{ and } n \in \mathbb{N}\right\}$; words
9. 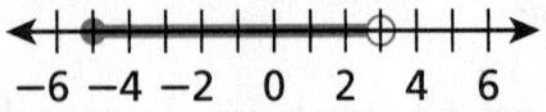

set-builder notation
10. $\{0, 5, 10, 15, 20, \ldots\}$; words
11. integers from −5 to 5; roster notation

PRACTICE AND PROBLEM SOLVING

Independent Practice

For Exercises	See Example
12–14	1
15–17	2
18–21	3

Extra Practice
Skills Practice p. S4
Application Practice p. S32

Order the given numbers from least to greatest. Then classify each number by the subsets of the real numbers to which it belongs.

12. $2.33, 5.\overline{5}, 2\sqrt{5}, -\frac{4}{5}, -0.75$
13. $\frac{1}{2}, -2, -\sqrt{2}, \frac{\sqrt{2}}{3}, -1.\overline{25}$
14. $-\sqrt{9}, 2\pi, -1, 5.\overline{12}, -\frac{7}{2}$

Use interval notation to represent each set of numbers.

15. $x \neq 5$
16. $-15 < x < 0$
17. 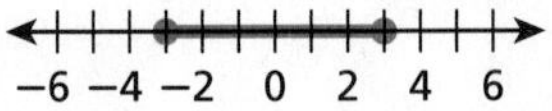

Rewrite each set in the indicated notation.

18. $(-\infty, 3]$ or $(5, 11]$; words
19. positive multiples of 11; roster notation
20. 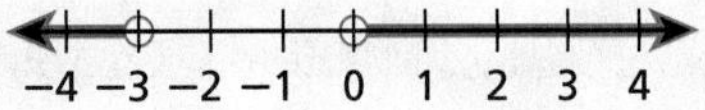

words
21. $\{-9, -7, -5, -3, -1\}$; set-builder notation

Chemistry Use the table for Exercises 22–25.

22. Order the given elements from least to greatest atomic mass.
23. Which subset of the real numbers best describes the atomic masses of these elements? Choose from $\mathbb{R}$, $\mathbb{Q}$, $\mathbb{Z}$, $\mathbb{W}$, and $\mathbb{N}$.
24. Which subset of the real numbers best describes the ionic charges of these elements? Choose from $\mathbb{R}$, $\mathbb{Q}$, $\mathbb{Z}$, $\mathbb{W}$, and $\mathbb{N}$.
25. Explain why interval notation cannot be used to represent the set of atomic masses given.

Elements from the Periodic Table

Element	Atomic Mass (amu)	Ionic Charge
Aluminum	26.982	+3
Calcium	40.078	+2
Chlorine	35.4527	−1
Lithium	6.941	+1
Sulfur	32.066	−2

Complete the table by writing each set in the indicated notations. If a set cannot be written in a given notation, state this in your answer.

	Words	Roster Notation	Interval Notation	Set-Builder Notation
26.	?	$\{-2, -4, -6, -8, \ldots\}$	?	?
27.	?	?	$[-4, 8)$	?
28.	Even numbers between 27 and 39	?	?	?
29.	?	?	?	$\{x \mid 0 < x < 1\}$

Express each set of numbers using interval notation and set-builder notation.

30. 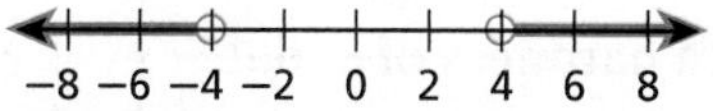

31. 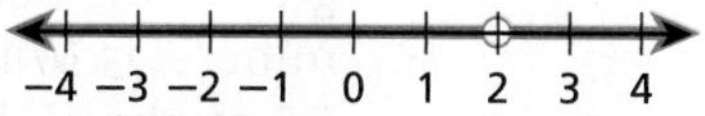

32. $x \leq 2$ or $3 < x < 5$

33. numbers between 1 and 10

34. numbers more than 2 units from 8

35. $x \neq 5$ and $x \leq 10$

Tell whether each statement is true or false. If false, give a counterexample.

36. Every natural number is an integer.

37. Every real number is irrational.

38. Every integer is a whole number.

39. Every integer is NOT irrational.

Sports Use the table of soccer ball sizes for Exercises 40–42.

40. Identify the size of each ball:
soccer ball A: 4.36 in. radius
soccer ball B: 7.54 in. diameter
soccer ball C: 276.2 in^3 volume

Soccer Ball Sizes			
Size	3	4	5
Weight (oz)	11–12	12–13	14–16
Circumference (in.)	23–24	25–26	27–28
Age of Player	Under 8	8–12	Over 12

41. Use set-builder notation to represent the weight range for each soccer ball size.

42. Use interval notation to represent the age range for each soccer ball size.

43. **Critical Thinking** The product of an irrational number and a rational number is an irrational number. Explain why this means that no matter how precisely you measure the diameter of a soccer ball, your calculation for its circumference will NEVER be a rational number.

MULTI-STEP TEST PREP

44. This problem will prepare you for the Multi-Step Test Prep on page 42.

Distances in space are often measured in astronomical units (AU). One AU is defined as the average distance between Earth and the Sun.

a. To which subsets of the real numbers do the numbers in the table belong?

b. Order the bodies from least to greatest average distance from Earth.

c. For a given speed, would it take longer to make a round-trip to Venus or a one-way trip to Mars? Explain.

Average Distances from Earth	
Body	**Distance (AU)**
Mars	$\frac{97}{186}$
Mercury	$\frac{117}{310}$
Moon	0.0026
Venus	0.2774

45. Use interval notation to express the set of numbers NOT represented on the number line.

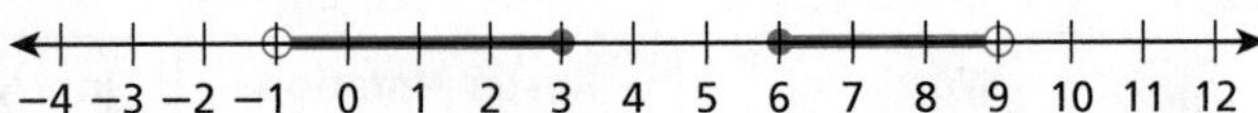

Use a number line to represent each set.

46. $-4 < x \leq 4$ or $x > 5$

47. numbers within 6 units of 5

48. $\{-10, -5, 0, 5, 10\}$

49. $\{x \mid x = \frac{1}{2}n \text{ and } n \in \mathbb{N}\}$

50. numbers more than 5 units from −3

51. $(-\infty, 2)$ or $[-1.75, 1.75]$ or $(2, \infty)$

52. Geology The Mohs scale of hardness gives the increasing order of hardness for minerals. The greater the hardness number, the harder the mineral is. Window glass has a hardness of about 5.5 on the Mohs scale.

a. Use roster notation to represent the set of minerals that are softer than window glass.

b. How many elements does the set of minerals that are harder than window glass have?

c. Explain whether {apatite, diamond, topaz, quartz} is a subset of the set of minerals harder than window glass, the set of minerals softer than window glass, or neither.

Mohs Scale of Hardness	
Talc	1
Gypsum	2
Calcite	3
Fluorite	4
Apatite	5
Orthoclase	6
Quartz	7
Topaz	8
Corundum	9
Diamond	10

Identify which of the real numbers best describes each situation. Choose from $\mathbb{R}$, $\mathbb{Q}$, $\mathbb{Z}$, $\mathbb{W}$, and $\mathbb{N}$.

53. the number of stops a train makes during a trip

54. the cumulative grade point average for a student

55. the squares of the set of integers

56. Critical Thinking Are all square roots irrational numbers? Explain.

57. Careers The graph shows several median salaries by profession.

a. Order the professions by salary from least to greatest.

b. **What if...?** If each salary were increased by \$5000, would the order from part **a** change?

c. **What if...?** If each salary were increased by 15%, would the order from part **a** change?

d. Use roster notation to represent the set of salaries from part **c.**

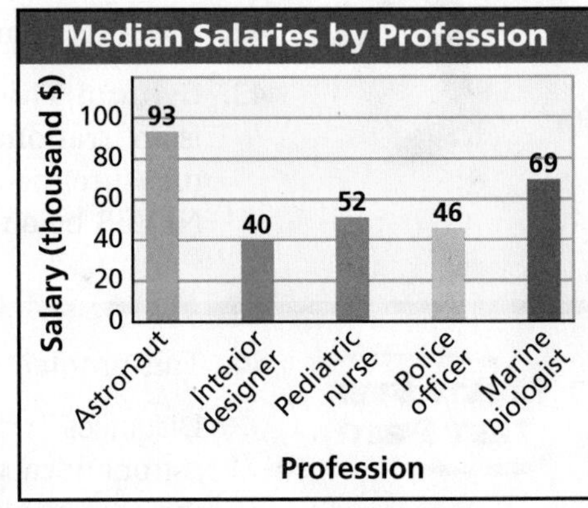

Identify one rational number and one irrational number that belongs to each set. Then explain whether the number 5 is an element of the set.

58. $\{x \mid x = 5c \text{ and } 0 < c \leq 1\}$

59. $-1 < x \leq 1$ or $x > 4$

60. numbers within 4 units of 9

61. $(3, 5)$

62. Write About It People use sets of tools and eat on sets of dishes. How are mathematical sets similar to and different from such everyday sets?

63. Which of the following is NOT equivalent to 4?

Ⓐ $\sqrt{16}$ Ⓑ $3 - (-1)$ Ⓒ $\frac{12}{3}$ Ⓓ $2(-2)$

64. Which list is in order from least to greatest?

Ⓕ $\frac{3}{7}, 0.5, \frac{\sqrt{3}}{2}$ Ⓖ $0.5, \frac{3}{7}, \frac{\sqrt{3}}{2}$ Ⓗ $\frac{3}{7}, \frac{\sqrt{3}}{2}, 0.5$ Ⓙ $\frac{\sqrt{3}}{2}, 0.5, \frac{3}{7}$

65. Which set best describes the numbers graphed on the number line?

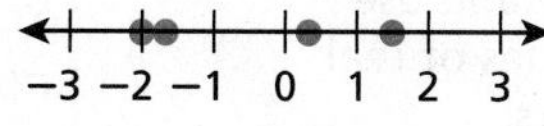

Ⓐ $\{-2, -1.5, 0.5, 1.5\}$

Ⓑ $\{-\sqrt{4}, -\frac{5}{3}, 0.\overline{3}, 1\frac{1}{2}\}$

Ⓒ $\{-\frac{6}{3}, -1.\overline{3}, \frac{3}{4}, \sqrt{2}\}$

Ⓓ $\{-1\frac{1}{3}, 0.\overline{3}, 1.5, 2\}$

66. Which statement can be determined from the diagram?

Ⓕ Every isosceles triangle is equilateral.

Ⓖ Every triangle is either right or isosceles.

Ⓗ No right triangles are isosceles.

Ⓙ No right triangles are equilateral.

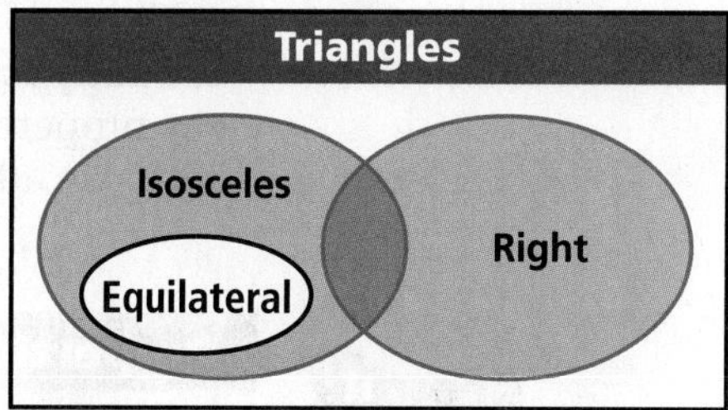

CHALLENGE AND EXTEND

Explain whether each set is finite or infinite. Then identify the subsets of the real numbers to which the set belongs.

67. values in dollars of U.S. coins

68. $\{0.\overline{3}, 0.\overline{6}, 1, 1.\overline{3}, \ldots\}$

69. U.S. Postal Service 5-digit zip codes

70. $\{x \mid x = \frac{c}{4} \text{ and } c \in \mathbb{Z}\}$

71. The symbol π is used to represent the irrational number 3.14159265358.... The fraction $\frac{22}{7}$ and the decimal 3.14 are approximations of π.

a. Find a rational number between 3.14 and π.

b. Find a rational number between $\frac{22}{7}$ and π.

SPIRAL REVIEW

Use the rectangular prism for Exercises 72–74. *(Previous course)*

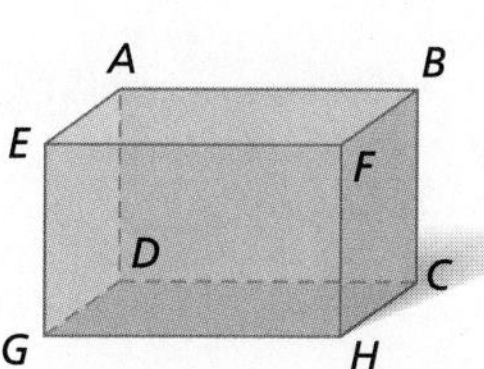

72. Name two edges that intersect to form a right angle.

73. Name two faces that model parallel planes.

74. Name two faces that model perpendicular planes.

75. Debra went shopping with three bills in her wallet. She returned home from shopping with less than $1.00 in her wallet. She made purchases of $21.49, $11.59, and $12.95, all with 6.5% sales tax. What bills did Debra have in her wallet when she went shopping? *(Previous course)*

76. The Wildcat pep squad is enlarging the Wildcats' team logo to create a square banner. The ratio of the side length of the logo shown to the side length of the banner is 1:120. What is the area of the banner in square centimeters? *(Previous course)*

1-2

Properties of Real Numbers

"The tax and tip I understand, but what's this charge for shipping and handling?"

Andrew Toos/CartoonResource.com

Objective
Identify and use properties of real numbers.

Why learn this?
You can use properties of real numbers to quickly calculate tips in your head. (See Example 3.)

The four basic math operations are addition, subtraction, multiplication, and division. Because subtraction is addition of the opposite and division is multiplication by the reciprocal, the properties of real numbers focus on addition and multiplication.

Know it! Note

Properties of Real Numbers — **Identities and Inverses**

For all real numbers *n*,

WORDS	NUMBERS	ALGEBRA
Additive Identity Property The sum of a number and 0, the additive identity, is the original number.	$3 + 0 = 3$	$n + 0 = 0 + n = n$
Multiplicative Identity Property The product of a number and 1, the multiplicative identity, is the original number.	$\frac{2}{3} \cdot 1 = \frac{2}{3}$	$n \cdot 1 = 1 \cdot n = n$
Additive Inverse Property The sum of a number and its opposite, or additive inverse, is 0.	$5 + (-5) = 0$	$n + (-n) = 0$
Multiplicative Inverse Property The product of a nonzero number and its reciprocal, or multiplicative inverse, is 1.	$8 \cdot \frac{1}{8} = 1$	$n \cdot \frac{1}{n} = 1\ (n \neq 0)$

Recall from previous courses that the opposite of any number a is $-a$ and the reciprocal of any nonzero number a is $\frac{1}{a}$.

EXAMPLE 1 **Finding Inverses**

Find the additive and multiplicative inverse of each number.

 -9

additive inverse: 9 — *The opposite of -9 is $-(-9) = 9$.*

Check $-9 + 9 = 0$ ✔ — *The Additive Inverse Property holds.*

multiplicative inverse: $\frac{1}{-9}$ — *The reciprocal of -9 is $\frac{1}{-9}$.*

Check $-9 \cdot \left(\frac{1}{-9}\right) = 1$ ✔ — *The Multiplicative Inverse Property holds.*

Find the additive and multiplicative inverse of each number.

B $\frac{4}{5}$

additive inverse: $-\frac{4}{5}$ — *The opposite of $\frac{4}{5}$ is $-\frac{4}{5}$.*

multiplicative inverse: $\frac{5}{4}$ — *The reciprocal of $\frac{4}{5}$ is $\frac{5}{4}$.*

Find the additive and multiplicative inverse of each number.

1a. 500 **1b.** -0.01

Properties of Real Numbers — **Addition and Multiplication**

For all real numbers *a* and *b*,

WORDS	NUMBERS	ALGEBRA
Closure Property The sum or product of any two real numbers is a real number.	$2 + 3 = 5$ $2(3) = 6$	$a + b \in \mathbb{R}$ $ab \in \mathbb{R}$
Commutative Property You can add or multiply real numbers in any order without changing the result.	$7 + 11 = 11 + 7$ $7(11) = 11(7)$	$a + b = b + a$ $ab = ba$
Associative Property The sum or product of three or more real numbers is the same regardless of the way the numbers are grouped.	$(5 + 3) + 7 = 5 + (3 + 7)$ $(5 \cdot 3)7 = 5(3 \cdot 7)$	$(a + b) + c = a + (b + c)$ $(ab)c = a(bc)$
Distributive Property When you multiply a sum by a number, the result is the same whether you add and then multiply or whether you multiply each term by the number and then add the products.	$5(2 + 8) = 5(2) + 5(8)$ $(2 + 8)5 = (2)5 + (8)5$	$a(b + c) = ab + ac$ $(b + c)a = ba + ca$

Reading Math

Based on the Closure Property, the real numbers are said to be *closed* under addition and *closed* under multiplication.

EXAMPLE 2 Identifying Properties of Real Numbers

Identify the property demonstrated by each equation.

A $(3\sqrt{3} + 5)2 = (3\sqrt{3})2 + (5)2$ — *The 2 has been distributed to each term.*

Distributive Property

B $(3 + 6) + (-6) = 3 + [6 + (-6)]$ — *The numbers have been regrouped.*

Associative Property of Addition

Identify the property demonstrated by each equation.

2a. $9\sqrt{2} = (\sqrt{2})9$ **2b.** $9(12\pi) = (9 \cdot 12)\pi$

The properties described in this lesson are sometimes called *field properties.* You can apply field properties of real numbers to simplify numeric expressions and solve problems mentally.

EXAMPLE 3 Consumer Economics Application

Use mental math to find a 15% tip for the bill shown.

Think: $15\% = 10\% + 5\%$

$(10\% + 5\%)24.80$

$10\%(24.80) + 5\%(24.80)$ — *Distributive Property*

Think: Find 10% of \$24.80

$10\%(24.80) = 2.480 = 2.48$ — *Move the decimal point left 1 place.*

Think: $5\% = \frac{1}{2}(10\%)$

$\frac{1}{2}(2.48) = 1.24$ — *5% is half of 10% so find half of 2.48.*

$2.48 + 1.24 = 3.72$ — *Add 10% of 24.80 to 5% of 24.80.*

A 15% tip for a meal that totaled \$24.80 is \$3.72.

3. Use mental math to find a 20% discount on a \$15.60 shirt.

EXAMPLE 4 Classifying Statements as Sometimes, Always, or Never True

Classify each statement as sometimes, always, or never true. Give examples or properties to support your answer.

A $c + d = c$ **when** $d = 2$

never true

counterexample: $1 + 2 \neq 1$

By the Additive Identity Property, $c + 0 = c$, so $c + d = c$ is only true when $d = 0$, not when $d = 2$.

B $a - c = c - a$

sometimes true

true example: $5 - 5 = 5 - 5$

false example: $5 - 2 \neq 2 - 5$

True and false examples exist. The statement is true when $a = c$ and false when $a \neq c$.

Classify each statement as sometimes, always, or never true. Give examples or properties to support your answer.

4a. $a + (-a) = b + (-b)$ **4b.** $a - (b + c) = (a - b) + (a - c)$

THINK AND DISCUSS

1. Explain whether the Commutative Property applies to subtraction and division.

2. Tell why zero has no multiplicative inverse.

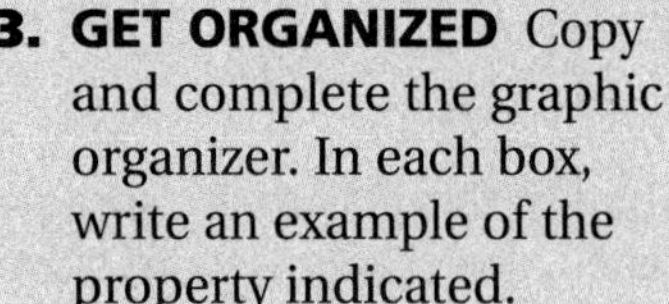

3. GET ORGANIZED Copy and complete the graphic organizer. In each box, write an example of the property indicated.

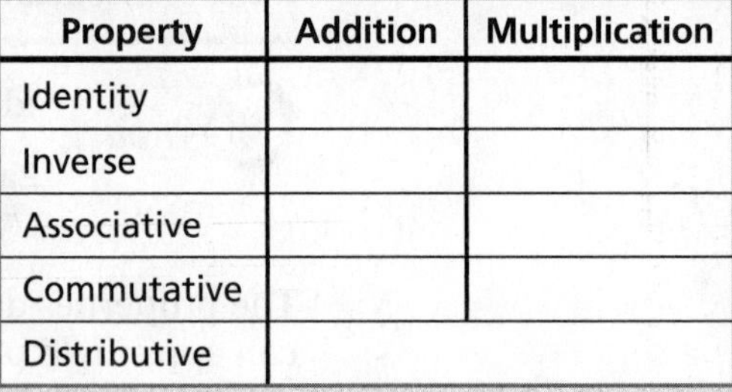

Property	Addition	Multiplication
Identity		
Inverse		
Associative		
Commutative		
Distributive		

1-2 Exercises

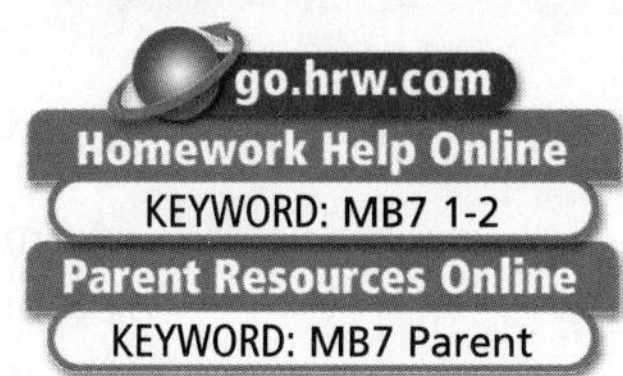

GUIDED PRACTICE

SEE EXAMPLE 1 p. 14

Find the additive and multiplicative inverse of each number.

1. -36 **2.** -0.05 **3.** $2\sqrt{2}$

4. $\frac{2}{5}$ **5.** $-\frac{1}{500}$ **6.** 0.25

SEE EXAMPLE 2 p. 15

Identify the property demonstrated by each equation.

7. $3(2\sqrt{5}) = (3 \cdot 2)\sqrt{5}$ **8.** $x + 7y = 7y + x$ **9.** $\frac{1}{3}(28)(9) = \frac{1}{3}(9)(28)$

SEE EXAMPLE 3 p. 16

Use mental math to find each value.

10. cost of 3 items at $2.55 each **11.** a $33\frac{1}{3}$% discount on a $21.99 item

SEE EXAMPLE 4 p. 16

Classify each statement as sometimes, always, or never true. Give examples or properties to support your answer.

12. $20a + 20b = 5(4a + 4b)$ **13.** $a \div b = b \div a$ **14.** $a + (bc) = (a + b)(a + c)$

PRACTICE AND PROBLEM SOLVING

Independent Practice

For Exercises	See Example
15–20	1
21–23	2
24–25	3
26–27	4

Extra Practice

Skills Practice p. S4
Application Practice p. S32

Find the additive and multiplicative inverse of each number.

15. -2.5 **16.** 0.75 **17.** 2π

18. $-\frac{2}{3}$ **19.** $\frac{1}{20}$ **20.** 6231

Identify the property demonstrated by each equation.

21. $z(x - y) = zx - zy$ **22.** $4abc = 4acb$ **23.** $(a + 0) + b = a + b$

Use mental math to find each value.

24. 9% sales tax on a $150 purchase **25.** cost of 5 items at $1.96 each

Classify each statement as sometimes, always, or never true. Give examples or properties to support your answer.

26. $a - (b - c) = a - b + c$ **27.** $ab\left(\frac{1}{ab}\right) = 0$ for $a \neq 0$ and $b \neq 0$

Shopping **Use the advertisement for Exercises 28–31. Write an expression to represent each total cost and then simplify it.**

28. cost of 2 pencil sets and 3 paintbrush sets

29. cost of 4 acrylic paints minus a refund for 2 pencil sets

30. cost of 4 paintbrush sets at a 15% discount

31. cost of 3 sketch books at a 10% discount and 5 acrylic paints at a 25% discount

Estimation Use the map for Exercises 32–34.

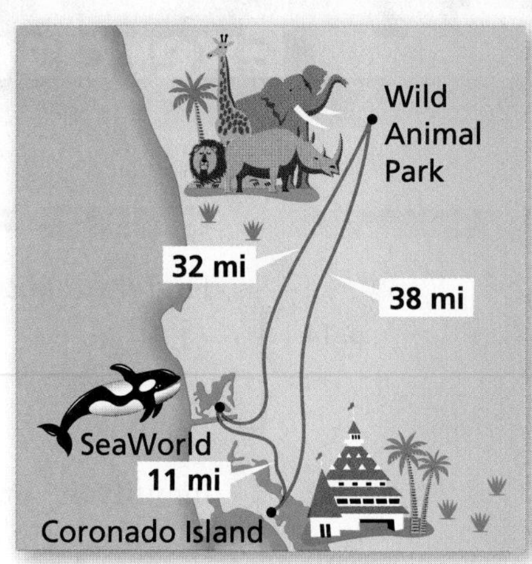

A San Diego tour van starts at Coronado Island, stops at SeaWorld, then at the Wild Animal Park, and then returns to Coronado Island.

32. Estimate how long it would take the van to make one loop at an average speed of 40 mi/h.

33. **Multi-Step** The tour van gets 8 mi/gal, and the gas tank holds 24 gal. Estimate the number of loops the tour van can make on one tank.

34. **What if...?** The van adds another stop that increases the length of its loop by 20%. Estimate the number of loops the van could make in one 10 h day if it averaged 40 mi/h.

LINK

Math History

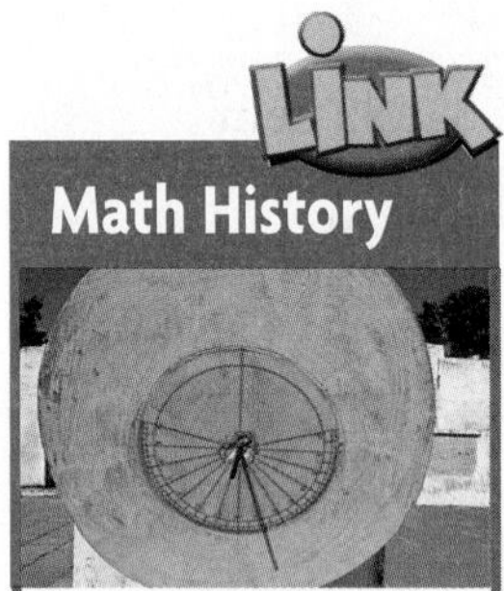

Brahmagupta, an Indian mathematician (598–668), was one of the first to use zero as a number. He was also head of the ancient astronomical observatory at Ujjain, India. The photo shows a sundial from the observatory at Ujjain.

Complete each statement, and state the property illustrated.

35. $(10 + \blacksquare) + 23 = 10 + (5 + 23)$ **36.** $12 + \frac{11}{15}x = \blacksquare + 12$ **37.** $j + \blacksquare = j$

38. $5 \cdot 4 + 5 \cdot 3 = \blacksquare \cdot (4 + 3)$ **39.** $\frac{4}{5} \cdot \blacksquare = 1$ **40.** $ab = b\blacksquare$

41. **Consumer Economics** A store is offering a 25% discount on every item purchased. To find the total discount on a purchase, Gary found the sum of the prices and then multiplied the sum by $\frac{1}{4}$. Maria found the total discount by multiplying each price by $\frac{1}{4}$ and then adding the discounts. Do both methods give the same result? Use properties of real numbers to explain why or why not.

42. **Travel** The base price for an airplane ticket from Austin to Houston is $185. The final price includes an additional $16 for airport fees and a $12 fuel surcharge. José purchased a ticket online for 40% off the base price. Explain how to use mental math to find José's final price to the nearest dollar.

43. **Critical Thinking** Use the terms *additive inverse* and *additive identity* to define the set of integers and the set of rational numbers in terms of the set of natural numbers. For example, the set of whole numbers is made up of the set of natural numbers and the additive identity.

Identify which properties make each statement true for all real values of *c*.

44. $-c + (c + 4) = 4$ **45.** $(10c) \cdot 1 = 10c$

46. $3(2 + c) = (c + 2)3$ **47.** $4c + 5 = 4(c + 2) - 3$

48. $\frac{1}{2}(1 - 5c) = \frac{-5c + 1}{2}$ **49.** $8 - 16c = 8(1 - 2c)$

50. This problem will prepare you for the Multi-Step Test Prep on page 42.

Astronauts use a 24-hour clock to tell time. The 24-hour cycle is an example of *modular arithmetic,* arithmetic performed on a circle. The circle shows mod 24. You can perform arithmetic by moving around the circle. For example, $22 + 8 = 6$ in mod 24, because if you move 8 units clockwise from 22, you end up at 6.

a. What is $18 + 13$ in mod 24?

b. Is addition commutative in mod 24? Give an example to support your answer.

c. Is addition associative in mod 24? Give an example to support your answer.

51. Business A television repair store was offering a 5% discount on parts and a 5% discount on labor. An employee placed a sign in the store window that read "Receive 10% off of your total costs." Use properties of real numbers to explain whether the sign was correct.

52. Write About It Explain the difference between the reciprocal of a number and the opposite of a number. Be sure to discuss the relationship between the signs of the numbers.

TEST PREP

53. Which equation illustrates the Associative Property of Multiplication?

Ⓐ $12(8 \cdot 9) = 12(9 \cdot 8)$

Ⓑ $12 + (8 + 9) = 12 + (9 + 8)$

Ⓒ $12 + (9 + 8) = (12 + 9) + 8$

Ⓓ $12(9 \cdot 8) = (12 \cdot 9)8$

54. Let a and b be real numbers such that $a \neq b$. Which statement is sometimes true?

Ⓕ $a\left(\frac{1}{b}\right) = 1$

Ⓖ $a - b = 0$

Ⓗ $a(1) = b$

Ⓙ $a = 4 + b$

55. Let c and d represent real numbers such that $c \neq 0$ and $d \neq 0$. Which expression represents the multiplicative inverse of $\frac{2c}{d}$?

Ⓐ $-\frac{2c}{d}$

Ⓑ $-\frac{2d}{c}$

Ⓒ $\frac{d}{2c}$

Ⓓ $\frac{c}{2d}$

56. Short Response Show two different methods of simplifying $4(1 + 3)$. Justify each step by using the order of operations or properties of real numbers.

CHALLENGE AND EXTEND

57. A positive real number n is 4 times its multiplicative inverse. What is the value of n?

58. Consider the four pairs of algebraic expressions below.

$a + b$ and $b + a$ $\quad$ $a - b$ and $b - a$ $\quad$ $a \cdot b$ and $b \cdot a$ $\quad$ $a \div b$ and $b \div a$

a. For $a = 3$ and $b = 5$, perform each pair of calculations. Identify which pairs result in a natural number for both calculations.

b. If a and b are natural numbers, which pairs of algebraic expressions always represent natural numbers?

c. Under which operations is the set of natural numbers closed?

d. Under which operations is the set of integers closed?

SPIRAL REVIEW

59. Mr. Connelly planted a 12 ft × 8 ft garden last summer. He wants to increase the size to 16 ft × 10 ft this summer. Find the percent increase in the area of his garden to the nearest tenth. *(Previous course)*

Use the following numbers for Exercises 60–62: 0.89, $\sqrt{9}$, −2, $-\frac{1}{3}$, π, −0.125, $3.\overline{09}$, 0, and $-4\sqrt{2}$. Identify each of the following. *(Lesson 1-1)*

60. greatest value $\quad$ **61.** least value $\quad$ **62.** irrational numbers

Write the inequality $-10 < x \leq 0$ using the indicated method. If the method is not possible, write "cannot be notated." *(Lesson 1-1)*

63. interval notation $\quad$ **64.** set-builder notation $\quad$ **65.** roster notation

The Pythagorean Theorem

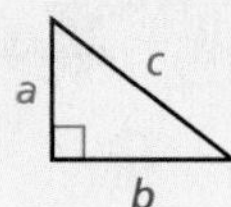

The three sides of a right triangle are related. If you know two of the side lengths, you can find the third.

In a right triangle, the side opposite the right angle is the longest side and is called the hypotenuse. The other two sides are called the legs

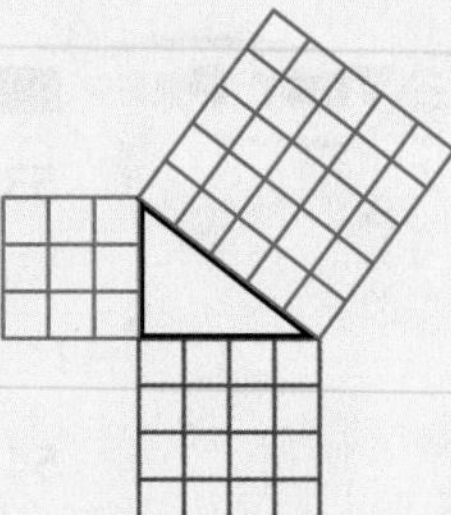

The Pythagorean Theorem
If a triangle is a right triangle with legs of length a and b and hypotenuse of length c, then $a^2 + b^2 = c^2$.

Example

Find the unknown side length in the right triangle.

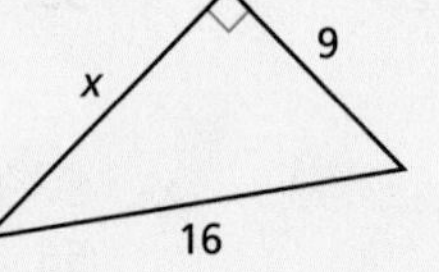

Step 1 The unknown side length is marked with an x. Use the Pythagorean Theorem to write an equation relating the side lengths. Remember that the hypotenuse c is the side opposite the right angle.

$a^2 + b^2 = c^2$

$x^2 + 9^2 = 16^2$ *Use 9 for either side a or side b.*

Step 2 Square the given side lengths and solve for x. Use a calculator to approximate the square root.

$x^2 + 81 = 256$

$x^2 + 81 - 81 = 256 - 81$ *Subtract 81 from both sides.*

$x^2 = 175$

$\sqrt{x^2} = \sqrt{175}$ *Take the square root of both sides.*

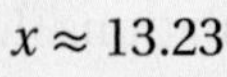

$x \approx 13.23$

Try This

Find the unknown side length in each right triangle. Round your answer to the nearest hundredth.

1.

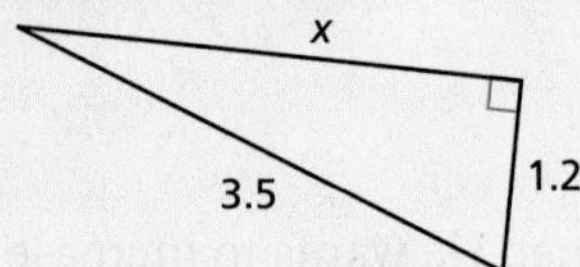

2.

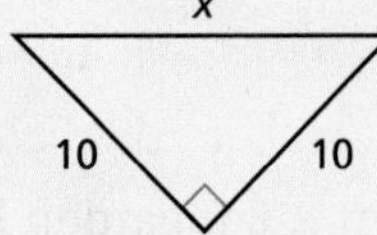

3.

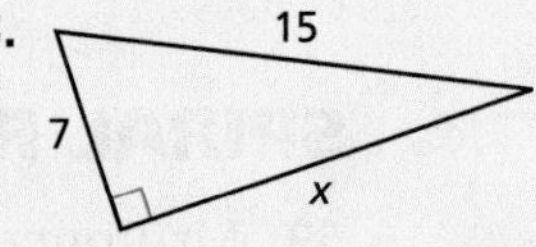

4. The set $\{3, 4, 5\}$ is an example of a Pythagorean triple, three natural numbers that satisfy the Pythagorean Theorem. Show that $\{20, 21, 29\}$ is a Pythagorean triple.

5. The converse of the Pythagorean Theorem states that if the three sides of a triangle satisfy the Pythagorean Theorem, then the triangle is a right triangle. Is a triangle with sides of 36 ft, 77 ft, and 85 ft a right triangle? Explain.

6. Find the diagonal of a square with 10 cm sides. (*Hint:* See Problem 2.)

7. $\triangle PQR$ is isosceles with altitude $\overline{QS}$. Find the length of the altitude if the side lengths of the triangle are 20, 20, and 8.

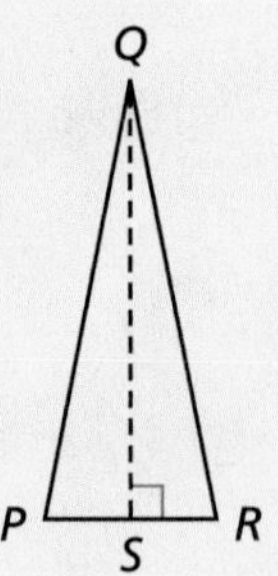

1-3 Square Roots

Objectives

Estimate square roots.

Simplify, add, subtract, multiply, and divide square roots.

Vocabulary

radical symbol
radicand
principal root
rationalize the denominator
like radical terms

Who uses this?

Mosaic artists can use square roots to calculate dimensions based on certain areas.

The largest mosaic in the world is located on the exterior walls of the central library of the Universidad Nacional Autónoma de México in Mexico City. It covers an area of 4000 square meters. If it were laid out as a square, you could use square roots to find its dimensions. (See Exercise 42.)

The side length of a square is the square root of its area. This relationship is shown by a **radical symbol** $(\sqrt{\ })$. The number or expression under the radical symbol is called the **radicand**. The radical symbol indicates only the positive square root of a number, called the **principal root**. To indicate both the positive and negative square roots of a number, use the plus or minus sign $(\pm)$.

$$\sqrt{25} = 5 \qquad -\sqrt{25} = -5 \qquad \pm\sqrt{25} = \pm 5 = 5 \text{ or } -5$$

Numbers such as 25 that have integer square roots are called *perfect squares.* Square roots of integers that are not perfect squares are irrational numbers. You can estimate the value of these square roots by comparing them with perfect squares. For example, $\sqrt{5}$ lies between $\sqrt{4}$ and $\sqrt{9}$, so it lies between 2 and 3.

EXAMPLE 1 **Estimating Square Roots**

Estimate $\sqrt{34}$ to the nearest tenth.

$\sqrt{25} < \sqrt{34} < \sqrt{36}$ *Find the two perfect squares that 34 lies between.*

$5 < \sqrt{34} < 6$ *Find the two integers that $\sqrt{34}$ lies between.*

Because 34 is closer to 36 than to 25, $\sqrt{34}$ is closer to 6 than to 5.

Try 5.8: $5.8^2 = 33.64$ *Too low, try 5.9.*

$5.9^2 = 34.81$ *Too high*

Because 34 is closer to 33.64 than to 34.81, $\sqrt{34}$ is closer to 5.8 than to 5.9.

$\sqrt{34} \approx 5.8$

Check On a calculator $\sqrt{34} \approx 5.830951895 \approx 5.8$ rounded to the nearest tenth. ✔

1. Estimate $-\sqrt{55}$ to the nearest tenth.

Square roots have special properties that help you simplify, multiply, and divide them.

Properties of Square Roots

For $a \geq 0$ and $b > 0$,

WORDS	NUMBERS	ALGEBRA
Product Property of Square Roots The square root of a product is equal to the product of the square roots of the factors.	$\sqrt{12} = \sqrt{4 \cdot 3}$ $= \sqrt{4} \cdot \sqrt{3} = 2\sqrt{3}$ $\sqrt{8} \cdot \sqrt{2} = \sqrt{8 \cdot 2}$ $= \sqrt{16} = 4$	$\sqrt{ab} = \sqrt{a} \cdot \sqrt{b}$ $\sqrt{a} \cdot \sqrt{b} = \sqrt{ab}$
Quotient Property of Square Roots The square root of a quotient is equal to the quotient of the square roots of the dividend and the divisor.	$\sqrt{\frac{25}{16}} = \frac{\sqrt{25}}{\sqrt{16}} = \frac{5}{4}$ $\frac{\sqrt{18}}{\sqrt{2}} = \sqrt{\frac{18}{2}} = \sqrt{9} = 3$	$\sqrt{\frac{a}{b}} = \frac{\sqrt{a}}{\sqrt{b}}$ $\frac{\sqrt{a}}{\sqrt{b}} = \sqrt{\frac{a}{b}}$

Notice that these properties can be used to combine quantities under the radical symbol or separate them for the purpose of simplifying square-root expressions. A square-root expression is in simplest form when the radicand has no perfect-square factors (except 1) and there are no radicals in the denominator.

EXAMPLE 2 Simplifying Square-Root Expressions

Simplify each expression.

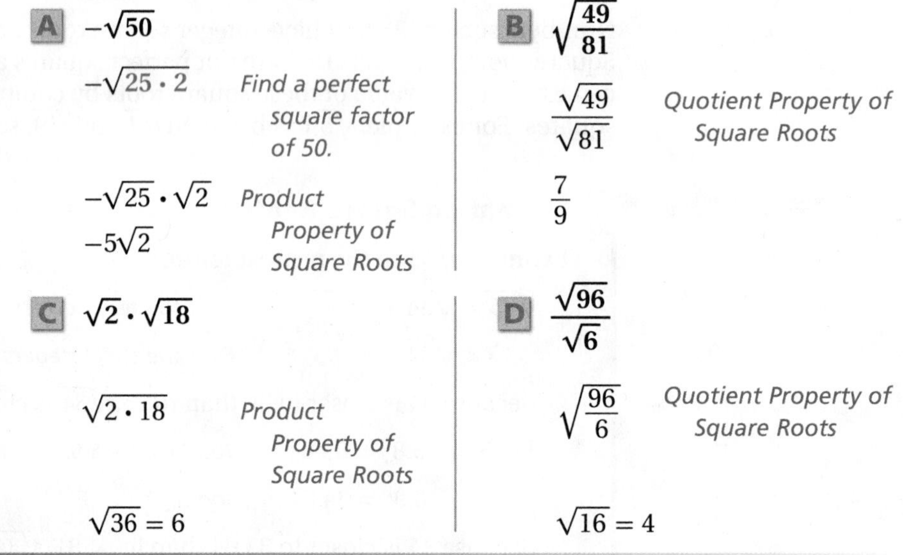

A $-\sqrt{50}$

$-\sqrt{25 \cdot 2}$ *Find a perfect square factor of 50.*

$-\sqrt{25} \cdot \sqrt{2}$ *Product Property of Square Roots*

$-5\sqrt{2}$

B $\sqrt{\frac{49}{81}}$

$\frac{\sqrt{49}}{\sqrt{81}}$ *Quotient Property of Square Roots*

$\frac{7}{9}$

C $\sqrt{2} \cdot \sqrt{18}$

$\sqrt{2 \cdot 18}$ *Product Property of Square Roots*

$\sqrt{36} = 6$

D $\frac{\sqrt{96}}{\sqrt{6}}$

$\sqrt{\frac{96}{6}}$ *Quotient Property of Square Roots*

$\sqrt{16} = 4$

Simplify each expression.

2a. $\sqrt{48}$ **2b.** $\sqrt{\frac{36}{16}}$ **2c.** $\sqrt{5} \cdot \sqrt{20}$ **2d.** $\frac{\sqrt{147}}{\sqrt{3}}$

If a fraction has a denominator that is a square root, you can simplify it by **rationalizing the denominator**. To do this, multiply both the numerator and denominator by a number that produces a perfect square under the radical sign in the denominator.

EXAMPLE 3 Rationalizing the Denominator

Simplify by rationalizing each denominator.

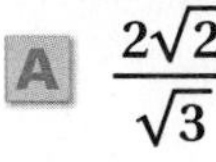

A $\dfrac{2\sqrt{2}}{\sqrt{3}}$

$\dfrac{2\sqrt{2}}{\sqrt{3}} \cdot \dfrac{\sqrt{3}}{\sqrt{3}}$ *Multiply by a form of 1.*

$\dfrac{2\sqrt{2 \cdot 3}}{3}$ *$\sqrt{3} \cdot \sqrt{3} = 3$*

$\dfrac{2\sqrt{6}}{3}$

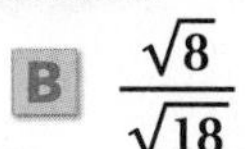

B $\dfrac{\sqrt{8}}{\sqrt{18}}$

$\dfrac{\sqrt{8}}{\sqrt{18}} \cdot \dfrac{\sqrt{2}}{\sqrt{2}}$ *Multiply by a form of 1.*

$\dfrac{\sqrt{8 \cdot 2}}{6}$ *$\sqrt{18} \cdot \sqrt{2} = 6$*

$\dfrac{\sqrt{16}}{6} = \dfrac{4}{6} = \dfrac{2}{3}$ *$\sqrt{16} = 4$*

Simplify by rationalizing each denominator.

3a. $\dfrac{3\sqrt{5}}{\sqrt{7}}$ **3b.** $\dfrac{5}{\sqrt{10}}$

Square roots that have the same radicand are called **like radical terms**.

Like Radicals	$\sqrt{2}$ and $3\sqrt{2}$	$-6\sqrt{15}$ and $7\sqrt{15}$	$\sqrt{ab^2}$ and $4\sqrt{ab^2}$
Unlike Radicals	$2\sqrt{5}$ and $\sqrt{2}$	$\sqrt{x}$ and $\sqrt{3x}$	$\sqrt{xy^2}$ and $\sqrt{x^2y}$

To add or subtract square roots, first simplify each radical term and then combine like radical terms by adding or subtracting their coefficients.

EXAMPLE 4 Adding and Subtracting Square Roots

Add or subtract.

A $5\sqrt{2} + 3\sqrt{2}$

$(5 + 3)\sqrt{2}$

$8\sqrt{2}$

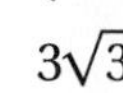

B $5\sqrt{3} - \sqrt{12}$

$5\sqrt{3} - \sqrt{4 \cdot 3}$ *Simplify radical terms.*

$5\sqrt{3} - 2\sqrt{3}$

$(5 - 2)\sqrt{3}$ *Combine like radical terms.*

$3\sqrt{3}$

Add or subtract.

4a. $3\sqrt{5} + 10\sqrt{5}$ **4b.** $\sqrt{80} - 5\sqrt{5}$

THINK AND DISCUSS

1. Compare $3\sqrt{50}$ with $5\sqrt{18}$.
2. Give two different ways to simplify $\sqrt{16} \cdot \sqrt{4}$.
3. **GET ORGANIZED** Copy and complete the graphic organizer. Write examples of each operation with square roots.

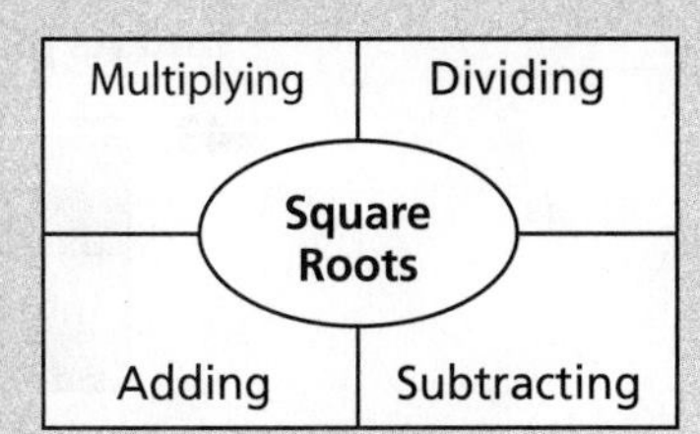

1-3 Exercises

go.hrw.com
Homework Help Online
KEYWORD: MB7 1-3
Parent Resources Online
KEYWORD: MB7 Parent

GUIDED PRACTICE

1. **Vocabulary** The number under the square root symbol is the __?__. (*radicand* or *radical*)

SEE EXAMPLE 1 p. 21

Estimate to the nearest tenth.

2. $\sqrt{75}$ 3. $\sqrt{20}$ 4. $-\sqrt{93}$ 5. $\sqrt{13}$

SEE EXAMPLE 2 p. 22

Simplify each expression.

6. $-\sqrt{300}$ 7. $\sqrt{24} \cdot \sqrt{6}$ 8. $\dfrac{\sqrt{72}}{\sqrt{2}}$ 9. $\sqrt{80}$

SEE EXAMPLE 3 p. 23

Simplify by rationalizing each denominator.

10. $\dfrac{1}{\sqrt{2}}$ 11. $\dfrac{5\sqrt{6}}{-\sqrt{3}}$ 12. $\dfrac{\sqrt{50}}{\sqrt{12}}$ 13. $\dfrac{\sqrt{3}}{-\sqrt{21}}$

SEE EXAMPLE 4 p. 23

Add or subtract.

14. $6\sqrt{7} + 7\sqrt{7}$ 15. $5\sqrt{32} - 15\sqrt{2}$ 16. $4\sqrt{5} + \sqrt{245}$ 17. $-\sqrt{50} + 6\sqrt{2}$

PRACTICE AND PROBLEM SOLVING

Independent Practice

For Exercises	See Example
18–21	1
22–29	2
30–33	3
34–37	4

Extra Practice
Skills Practice p. S4
Application Practice p. S32

Estimate to the nearest tenth.

18. $\sqrt{60}$ 19. $-\sqrt{15}$ 20. $\sqrt{47}$ 21. $\sqrt{99}$

Simplify each expression.

22. $\sqrt{162}$ 23. $-\sqrt{\dfrac{1}{121}}$ 24. $\sqrt{\dfrac{50}{9}}$ 25. $-2\sqrt{10} \cdot \sqrt{8}$

26. $\dfrac{\sqrt{288}}{\sqrt{8}}$ 27. $\sqrt{85} \cdot \sqrt{5}$ 28. $\dfrac{2\sqrt{126}}{\sqrt{14}}$ 29. $-\sqrt{189}$

Simplify by rationalizing each denominator.

30. $\dfrac{2}{\sqrt{3}}$ 31. $\dfrac{3\sqrt{27}}{2\sqrt{6}}$ 32. $-\dfrac{18}{\sqrt{6}}$ 33. $\dfrac{\sqrt{11}}{5\sqrt{132}}$

Add or subtract.

34. $4\sqrt{3} - 9\sqrt{3}$ 35. $\sqrt{112} + \sqrt{63}$ 36. $\sqrt{8} - 15\sqrt{2}$ 37. $\sqrt{12} + 7\sqrt{27}$

38. $\sqrt{45} + \sqrt{20}$ 39. $5\sqrt{28} - 2\sqrt{7}$ 40. $2\sqrt{48} + 2\sqrt{12}$ 41. $\sqrt{150} - 8\sqrt{6}$

42. **Art** The largest mosaic in the world is on the walls of the central library of the Universidad Nacional Autónoma de México in Mexico City. The mosaic depicts scenes from the nation's history and covers an area of 4000 m^2. If the entire mosaic were on one square wall, what would its dimensions be?

Geometry **Each figure below is made from squares. Given the area of each figure, find its perimeter to the nearest tenth.**

43.

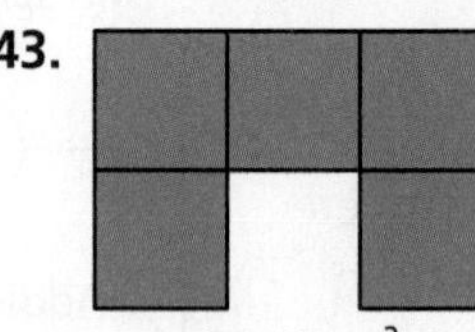

$A = 40$ cm^2

44.

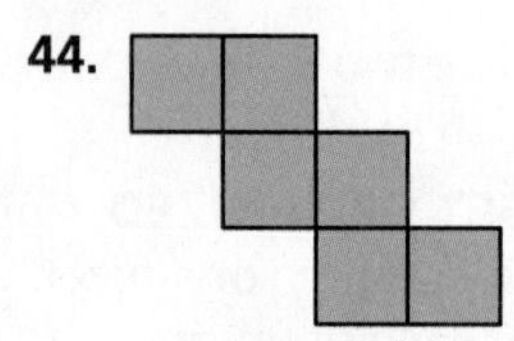

$A = 90$ ft^2

45.

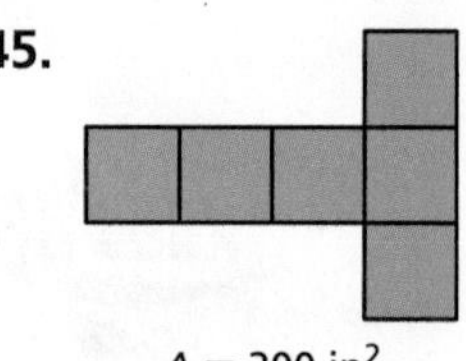

$A = 300$ in^2

46. **Sports** A baseball diamond is a square with an area of 8100 square feet. The length of the diagonal of any square is equal to $\sqrt{2}$ times its side length. Find the distance from home plate to second base (the length of the diagonal) to the nearest hundredth of a foot.

47. **Estimation** A painter's canvas will cover 600 square inches. Estimate the dimensions of a square wall mural that is the size of 4 complete canvases. Explain your thinking.

Simplify each expression. Assume that all variables are positive.

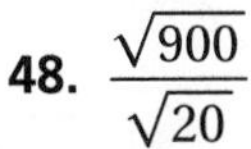

48. $\frac{\sqrt{900}}{\sqrt{20}}$

49. $3\sqrt{50} \cdot 3\sqrt{8}$

50. $-3\sqrt{x} + \sqrt{9x}$

51. $2\sqrt{5} - 5\sqrt{2}$

52. $\sqrt{25x} - 6\sqrt{x}$

53. $\frac{3\sqrt{7} + 1}{\sqrt{5}}$

54. $\frac{4\sqrt{10} - \sqrt{90}}{\sqrt{2}}$

55. $\frac{4\sqrt{32}}{\sqrt{5}}$

56. $\sqrt{75x} + \sqrt{45x}$

LINK Geography

Savannah, Georgia, was the first American city to include squares and wards.

Source: www.pps.org/gps

57. **Geography** The original design for the city of Savannah, Georgia, was based on a gridlike system of wards. At one time the city included a total of 24 wards. Each ward was approximately square, and together the wards covered a total area of about 8,640,000 square feet. Find the approximate dimensions of a ward.

Measurement **Use the table for Exercises 58–61. Find the side length, to the nearest tenth of a foot, of a square with the given area.**

58. 10 acres

59. 2 mi^2

60. 5 hectares

61. 6.2 km^2

Unit of Area	Square Feet
Acre	43,560
Hectare	107,600
Square kilometer	10,760,000
Square mile	27,880,000

Determine whether each statement is sometimes, always, or never true for positive integers *a* and *b*. Give examples to support your conclusion.

62. $\sqrt{a} + \sqrt{b} = \sqrt{ab}$

63. $\frac{\sqrt{ab}}{\sqrt{a}} = \sqrt{b}$

64. $a\sqrt{b} + a\sqrt{b} = 2ab$

65. **Critical Thinking** Given that $\sqrt{2+2} = 2$, does $\sqrt{a+a} = a$? Explain.

66. **Write About It** Find the value of $\sqrt{2}$ on your calculator. Square this value by entering the number and pressing x^2 and ENTER. Is the result 2? Explain why or why not.

MULTI-STEP TEST PREP

67. This problem will prepare you for the Multi-Step Test Prep on page 42.

Gravity on the Moon is much weaker than on Earth. The expression $\sqrt{\frac{h}{0.82}}$ can be used to approximate the time in seconds it takes for an object to reach the surface of the Moon when dropped from an initial height of h meters.

a. How long would it take for an object dropped from a height of 50 meters to land on the Moon?

b. The expression $\sqrt{\frac{h}{4.89}}$ can be used to model the time it takes for an object to reach Earth's surface from a height of h meters. How long would it take for an object dropped from a height of 50 meters to land on Earth?

TEST PREP

68. Which expression is NOT equivalent to the others?

Ⓐ $\sqrt{20}$ Ⓑ $\sqrt{8} \cdot \sqrt{5}$ Ⓒ $2\sqrt{10}$ Ⓓ $\dfrac{5\sqrt{8}}{\sqrt{5}}$

69. What is the approximate perimeter of a square with an area of 30 square meters?

Ⓕ 5.5 m Ⓖ 11 m Ⓗ 22 m Ⓙ 30 m

70. Which list is in order from least to greatest?

Ⓐ $\sqrt{\frac{9}{4}}, \sqrt{4}, 2\sqrt{2}, 2.5$ Ⓒ $0, \sqrt{\frac{1}{4}}, \frac{1}{4}, \sqrt{1}$

Ⓑ $\sqrt{25}, 5.1, 2\sqrt{5}, 6$ Ⓓ $\frac{1}{\sqrt{2}}, 1, \sqrt{2}, 2$

71. Gridded Response By the Pythagorean Theorem, the length d of a diagonal of a rectangle is given by $d = \sqrt{\ell^2 + w^2}$. Find the length in feet of diagonal $\overline{AC}$ to the nearest tenth.

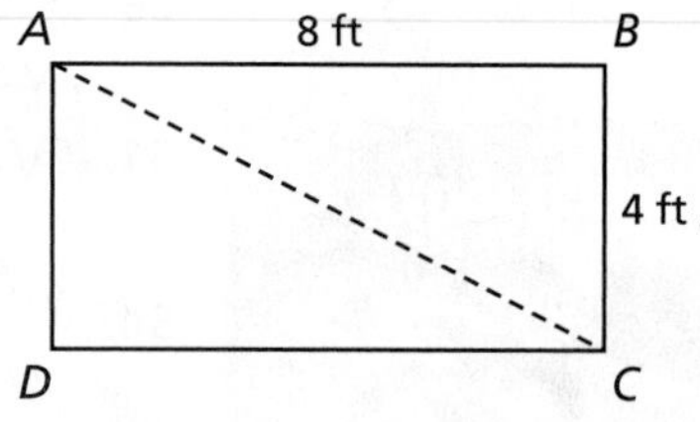

CHALLENGE AND EXTEND

72. Evaluate $\dfrac{a\sqrt{b} - 3a\sqrt{5ab}}{3\sqrt{b}}$ for $a = 5$ and $b = 6$.

73. Geometry The Pythagorean Theorem relates the side lengths a and b of a right triangle to the length of its hypotenuse c, with the formula $a^2 + b^2 = c^2$.

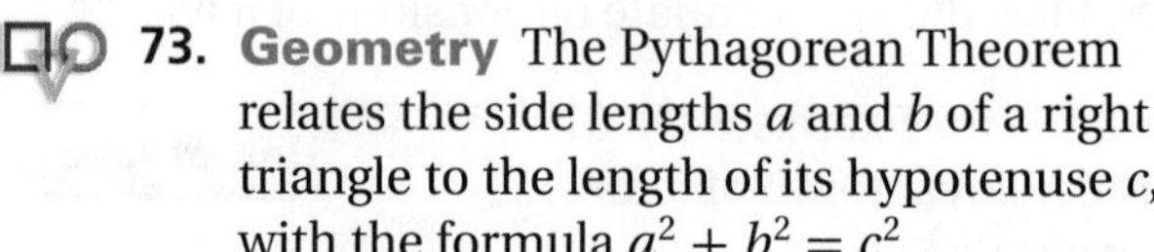

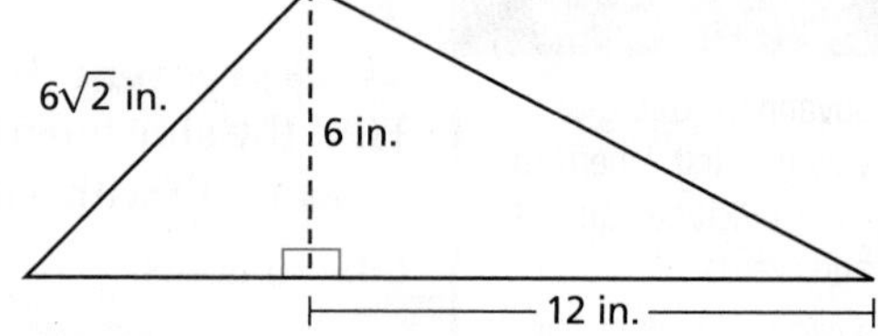

a. Use the Pythagorean Theorem to determine the unknown dimensions of the triangle.

b. Find the area of the triangle.

c. Find the perimeter of the triangle.

74. Simplify $\dfrac{\sqrt{x^3y^5}}{x^2\sqrt{48y^3}}$. Assume all variables are positive.

SPIRAL REVIEW

Identify the three-dimensional figure from the net shown. *(Previous course)*

75.

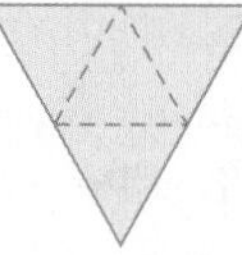

76.

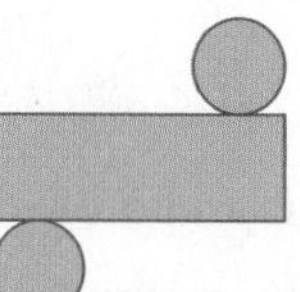

77.

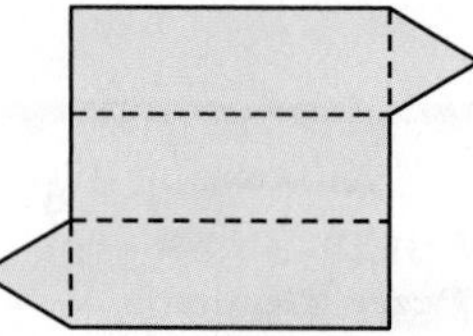

Write an inequality for each set of numbers. *(Lesson 1-1)*

78. $(-7, 1]$ **79.** $(1.5, 8)$ **80.** $[2, 12]$ **81.** $\left(\frac{3}{4}, \frac{5}{2}\right)$

Identify the property demonstrated by each equation. *(Lesson 1-2)*

82. $(a \cdot 1)b = ab$ **83.** $(x + y) + z = z + (x + y)$

84. $8p(q) = 8(pq)$ **85.** $st + 3s = s(t + 3)$

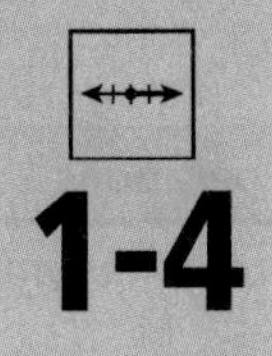

1-4 Simplifying Algebraic Expressions

Objective
Simplify and evaluate algebraic expressions.

Why learn this?

You can model the total points scored in a basketball game by using an algebraic expression.

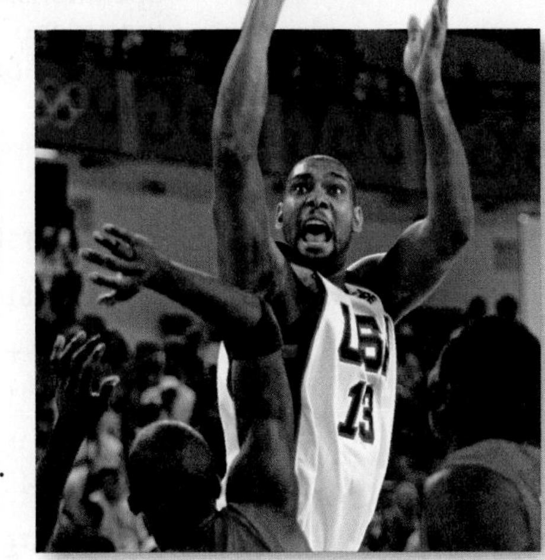

There are three different ways in which a basketball player can score points during a game. There are 1-point free throws, 2-point field goals, and 3-point field goals. An algebraic expression can represent the total points scored during a game.

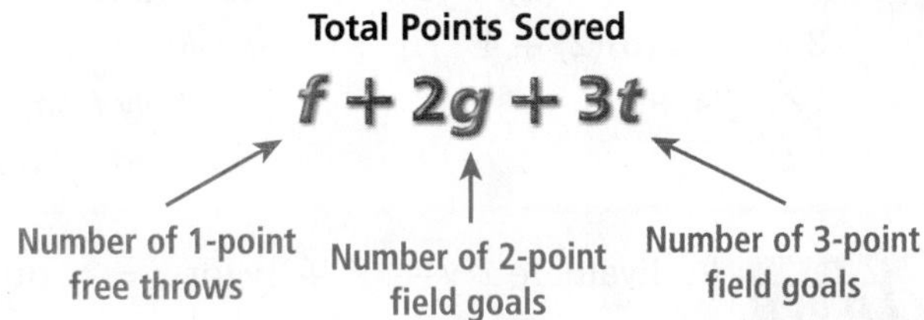

To translate a real-world situation into an algebraic expression, you must first determine the action being described. Then choose the operation that is indicated by the type of action and the context clues.

Action	Operation	Possible Context Clues
Combine	Add	How many total?
Combine equal groups	Multiply	How many altogether?
Separate	Subtract	How many more? How many remaining?
Separate into equal groups	Divide	How many in each group?

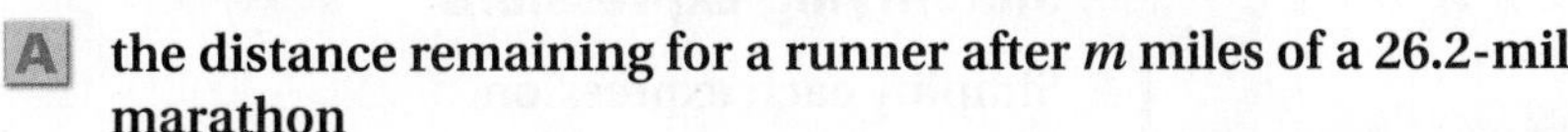

EXAMPLE 1 Translating Words into Algebraic Expressions

Write an algebraic expression to represent each situation.

A **the distance remaining for a runner after m miles of a 26.2-mile marathon**

$26.2 - m$ *Subtract m from 26.2.*

B **the number of hours it takes to fly 1800 miles at an average rate of n miles per hour**

$\frac{1800}{n}$ *Divide 1800 by n.*

Write an algebraic expression to represent each situation.

1a. Lucy's age y years after her 18th birthday

1b. The number of seconds in h hours

To evaluate an algebraic expression, substitute a number for each variable and simplify by using the order of operations. One way to remember the order of operations is by using the mnemonic PEMDAS.

Order of Operations
1. **P**arentheses and grouping symbols
2. **E**xponents
3. **M**ultiply and **D**ivide from left to right.
4. **A**dd and **S**ubtract from left to right.

EXAMPLE 2 Evaluating Algebraic Expressions

Evaluate each expression for the given values of the variables.

A $x + 3xy - 2y$ **for** $x = 4$ **and** $y = 7$

$(4) + 3(4)(7) - 2(7)$ *Substitute 4 for x and 7 for y.*

$4 + 84 - 14$ *Multiply from left to right.*

74 *Add and subtract from left to right.*

B $b^2z - 2bz + z^2$ **for** $b = 6$ **and** $z = 2$

$(6)^2(2) - 2(6)(2) + (2)^2$ *Substitute 6 for b and 2 for z.*

$36(2) - 2(6)(2) + 4$ *Evaluate exponential expressions.*

$72 - 24 + 4$ *Multiply from left to right.*

52 *Add and subtract from left to right.*

2. Evaluate $x^2y - xy^2 + 3y$ for $x = 2$ and $y = 5$.

Recall that the terms of an algebraic expression are separated by addition or subtraction symbols. *Like terms* have the same variables raised to the same exponents. Constant terms are like terms that always have the same value.

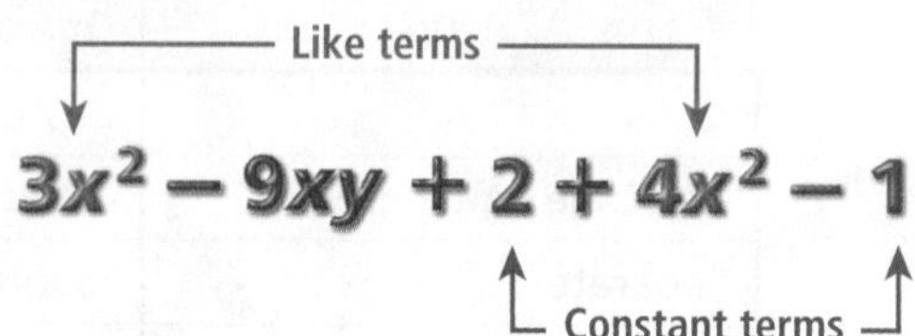

To simplify an algebraic expression, combine like terms by adding or subtracting their coefficients. Algebraic expressions are equivalent if they contain exactly the same terms when simplified.

EXAMPLE 3 Simplifying Expressions

Remember!

Terms that are written without a coefficient have an understood coefficient of 1.

$x^2 = 1x^2$

Simplify each expression.

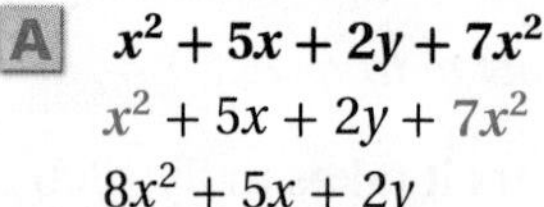

A $x^2 + 5x + 2y + 7x^2$

$x^2 + 5x + 2y + 7x^2$ *Identify like terms.*

$8x^2 + 5x + 2y$ *Combine like terms.* $1x^2 + 7x^2 = 8x^2$

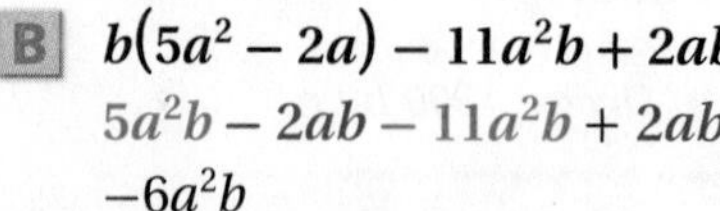

B $b(5a^2 - 2a) - 11a^2b + 2ab$

$5a^2b - 2ab - 11a^2b + 2ab$ *Distribute, and identify like terms.*

$-6a^2b$ *Combine like terms.* $-2ab + 2ab = 0$

3. Simplify the expression $-3(2x - xy + 3y) - 11xy$.

Student to Student

Checking Simplified Expressions

Nadia Torres
Madison High School

To check that I simplified an expression correctly, I substitute the same numbers into both expressions. If I get the same value for each expression, my answer is probably correct.

Original Expression		***Simplified Expression***
$3x + 5y - 2x$		$x + 5y$
$3(2) + 5(3) - 2(2)$	*Use $x = 2$ and $y = 3$.*	$2 + 5(3)$
$6 + 15 - 4$	*Multiply.*	$2 + 15$
17	*They are equal.*	17

EXAMPLE 4 ***Transportation Application***

Holly's hybrid car gets 45 miles per gallon on the highway and 25 miles per gallon in the city.

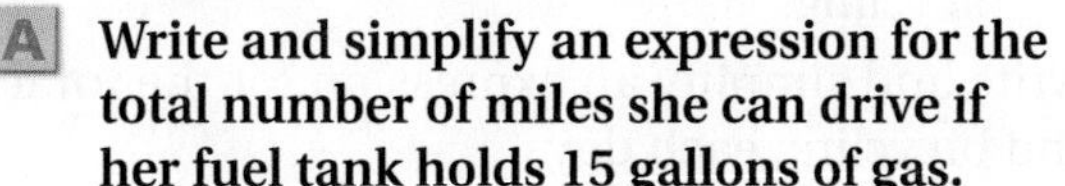

A **Write and simplify an expression for the total number of miles she can drive if her fuel tank holds 15 gallons of gas.**

Let h be the number of gallons used on the highway. Then $15 - h$ is the remaining number of gallons used in the city.

$$45h + 25(15 - h) = 45h + 375 - 25h \quad \textit{Distribute 25.}$$
$$= 20h + 375 \quad \textit{Combine like terms.}$$

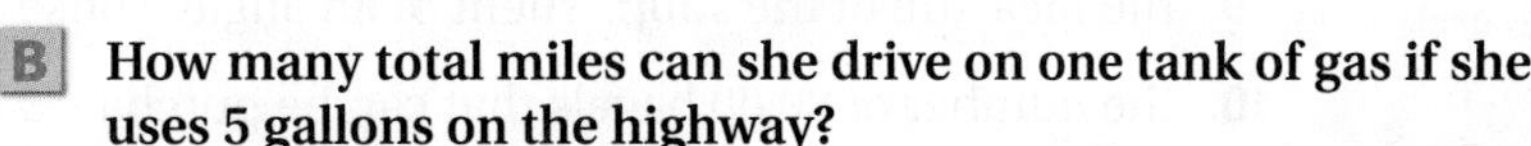

B **How many total miles can she drive on one tank of gas if she uses 5 gallons on the highway?**

Evaluate $20h + 375$ for $h = 5$.

$20(5) + 375 = 475$

Holly can travel 475 miles if she uses 5 gallons on the highway.

CHECK IT OUT!

4. A travel agent is selling 100 discount packages. He makes \$50 for each Hawaii package and \$80 for each Cancún package.

a. Write an expression to represent the total the agent will make selling a combination of the two packages.

b. How much will he make if he sells 28 Hawaii packages?

THINK AND DISCUSS

1. Tell how many addition or subtraction symbols an expression with five terms will have. Explain.

2. Explain how adding like terms involves the Distributive Property.

3. GET ORGANIZED Copy and complete the graphic organizer. In each box, write key words that may indicate each operation.

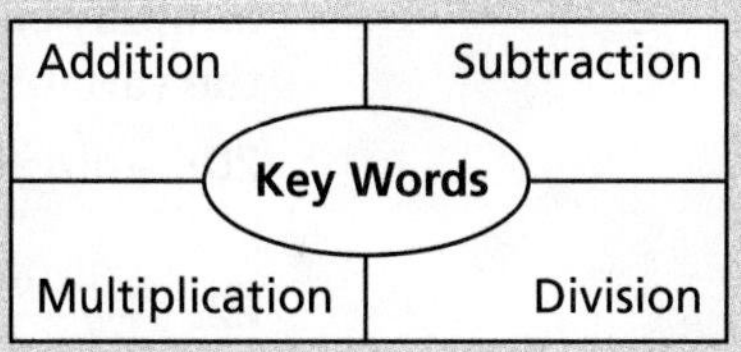

1-4 Exercises

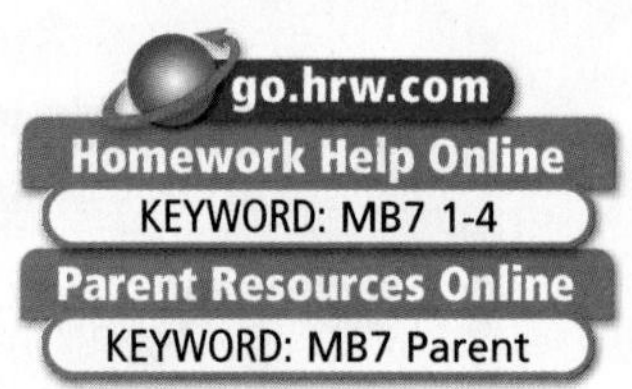

GUIDED PRACTICE

SEE EXAMPLE 1 p. 27

Write an algebraic expression to represent each situation.

1. the cost of c containers of yogurt at \$0.79 each
2. the area of a rectangle with length ℓ meters and width 8 meters

SEE EXAMPLE 2 p. 28

Evaluate each expression for the given values of the variables.

3. $a^2 + b^2 - 2ab$ for $a = 5$ and $b = 8$
4. $\dfrac{3xy}{x^2 - 9y + 2}$ for $x = 2$ and $y = 4$

SEE EXAMPLE 3 p. 28

Simplify each expression.

5. $-8a + 9 - 5a + a$
6. $-2(2x + y) - 7x + 2y$
7. $1 + (ab - 5a)5 - b^2$

SEE EXAMPLE 4 p. 29

8. **Athletics** Regan runs and bicycles every day for a total of 60 minutes. Her body uses 9 Calories per minute during running and 7 Calories per minute during bicycling.
   a. Write and simplify an expression for the total Calories Regan uses running and bicycling each day.
   b. How many Calories does she use on a day when she runs for 20 minutes?

PRACTICE AND PROBLEM SOLVING

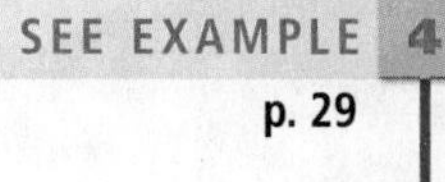

Independent Practice

For Exercises	See Example
9–10	1
11–14	2
15–18	3
19	4

Extra Practice

Skills Practice p. S4
Application Practice p. S32

Write an algebraic expression to represent each situation.

9. the measure of the supplement of an angle whose measure is $x°$
10. the number of \$0.60 bagels that can be purchased with d dollars

Evaluate each expression for the given values of the variables.

11. $6c - 3c^2 + d^3$ for $c = 5$ and $d = 3$
12. $y^2 - 2xy^2 - x$ for $x = 2$ and $y = 3$
13. $3a^2b - ab^3 + 5$ for $a = 5$ and $b = 2$
14. $\dfrac{2s - t^2}{st^2}$ for $s = 5$ and $t = 3$

Simplify each expression.

15. $-x - 3y + 4x - 9y + 2$
16. $-4(-a + 3b) - 3(a - 5b)$
17. $5 - (3m + 2n)$
18. $x(4 + y) - 2x(y + 7)$
19. **Home Economics** Enrique is baking muffins and bread. He wants to bake a total of 10 batches. Each batch of muffins bakes for 30 minutes, and each batch of bread bakes for 50 minutes. Let m represent the number of batches of muffins.
    a. Write an expression for the total time required to bake a combination of muffins and bread if each batch is baked separately.
    b. If Enrique makes 2 batches of muffins, how long will it take to bake all 10 batches?

Simplify each expression. Then evaluate the expression for the given values of the variables.

20. $-a(a^2 + 2a - 1)$ for $a = 2$
21. $(2g - 1)^2 - 2g + g^2$ for $g = 3$
22. $\dfrac{u^2 - v^2}{uv}$ for $u = 4$ and $v = 2$
23. $\dfrac{a^2 - 2(b^2 - a)}{2 + a}$ for $a = 3$ and $b = 5$

Copy and complete each table. Identify which expressions are equivalent for the given values of x.

24.

x	$(x+3)^2$	x^2+9	x^2+6x+9
1	■	■	■
2	■	■	■
3	■	■	■
4	■	■	■

25.

x	$(x-4)^2$	x^2+16	$x^2-8x+16$
1	■	■	■
2	■	■	■
3	■	■	■
4	■	■	■

Super Bowl

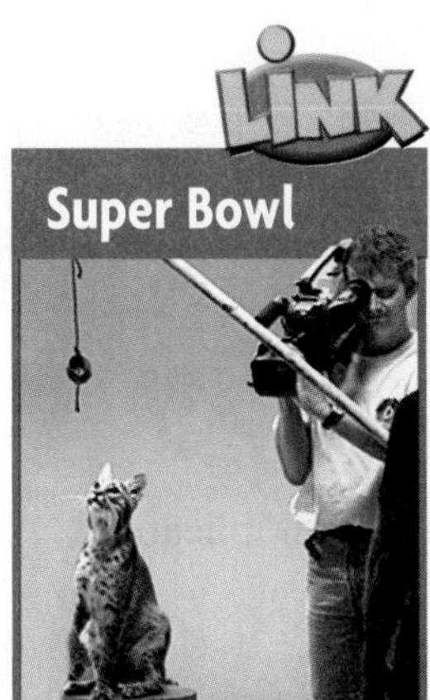

The average cost of producing a 30-second television commercial was more than $370,000 in 2003.

Source: Mediapost.com

26. Super Bowl The cost for a 1-minute commercial during the first Super Bowl was $85,000. The cost per 30-second commercial during Super Bowl XXXVIII was $2,300,000.

a. Write expressions to represent the cost of an m-minute commercial during the first Super Bowl and during Super Bowl XXXVIII.

b. If a commercial cost $170,000 during the first Super Bowl, how much would it have cost during Super Bowl XXXVIII? How do the costs compare?

c. About 60 million viewers watched the first Super Bowl, and about 800 million watched Super Bowl XXXVIII. Write expressions to represent how much an m-minute commercial cost per 1000 viewers during each Super Bowl.

d. What was the cost per 1000 viewers of a 2-minute commercial during each Super Bowl? How do the costs compare?

Geometry **Write and simplify an expression for the perimeter of each figure.**

27.

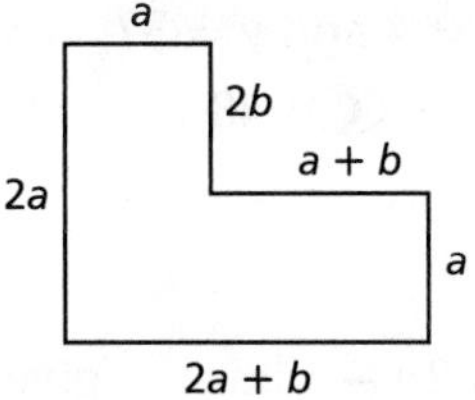

28.

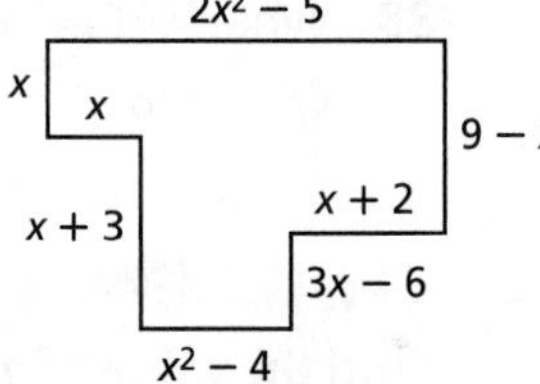

29. Travel The Dane family is going on a 15-day vacation to travel and visit relatives. They budget $100 per day when visiting relatives and $275 per day when traveling.

a. Write an expression for the total budgeted cost of the vacation if they visit relatives for d days.

b. What is the budgeted cost if they stay with relatives for 5 days?

c. How does this cost change for each additional day they stay with relatives?

30. This problem will prepare you for the Multi-Step Test Prep on page 42.

While Neil Armstrong and Buzz Aldrin walked on the Moon, the *Apollo 11* command module completed 1 orbit every 119 minutes.

a. Write an expression for the time in minutes needed to complete n orbits.

b. Modify your expression from part **a** so that it represents the time in hours needed to complete n orbits.

c. The *Apollo 11* module made 30 orbits. For how many hours did it orbit the Moon?

d. Estimate the number of orbits the *Apollo 11* module would make in 1 week if it continued at the same rate.

For each equation find the value of y when $x = -3, -2, 0, 2,$ and 3.

31. $y = -2x^2 + 5x - 7$ **32.** $y = -\dfrac{3x + 9}{x^2 - 1}$ **33.** $y = x^3 - 11x + 1$

34. **ERROR ANALYSIS** The expression below was simplified two different ways. Which is incorrect? Explain the error.

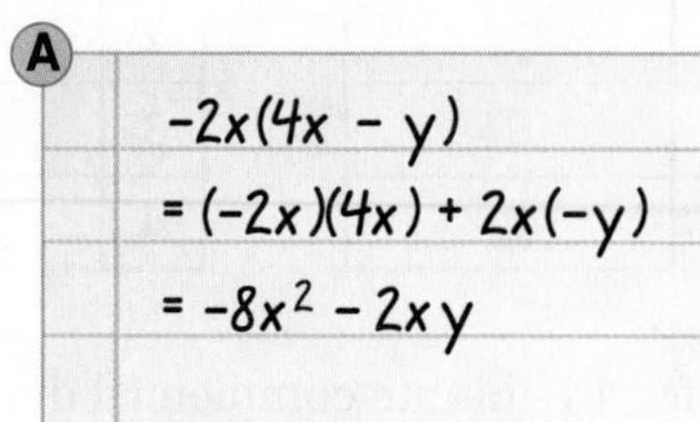

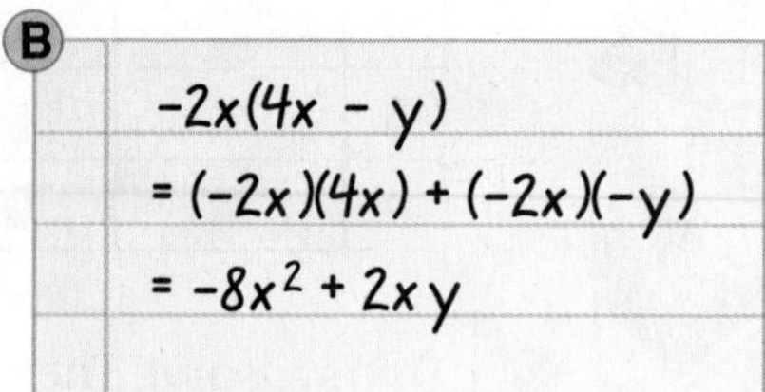

35. **Write About It** What property of real numbers relates addition and multiplication, and how does it relate them?

TEST PREP

36. Which expression is NOT equivalent to the others?

Ⓐ $-2x(1 - 3x)$ Ⓑ $2(3x - 1)x$ Ⓒ $(3x - 1)2x$ Ⓓ $6x^2 + 2x$

37. Which expression is greatest when $s = 10$?

Ⓕ Number of inches in s feet
Ⓗ Number of days in s weeks
Ⓖ Number of minutes in s hours
Ⓙ Number of inches in s yards

38. What is the value of $3x(y - 1)^2$ when $x = 4$ and $y = 3$?

Ⓐ 576 Ⓑ 81 Ⓒ 48 Ⓓ 24

CHALLENGE AND EXTEND

Find the value of a for which the expression $2a - 5$ has the given value.

39. 11 **40.** -5 **41.** 39 **42.** 225

43. Consider the expression $\dfrac{3(x + 2)^2}{(x - 1)(x - 3)}$.

a. Evaluate the expression for $x = 0, 1, 2, 3, 4,$ and 5.

b. Identify the values of x for which the expression cannot be evaluated.

c. Use your results from part **b** to identify the set of reasonable values for x.

SPIRAL REVIEW

Name the three-dimensional figure that has the given shapes as its faces. *(Previous course)*

44. three rectangles and two triangles **45.** one square and four triangles

Classify each number by the subsets of the real numbers to which it belongs. *(Lesson 1-1)*

46. 0 **47.** $\dfrac{5}{16}$ **48.** -6.5 **49.** $3\sqrt{2}$

Simplify each expression. *(Lesson 1-3)*

50. $\sqrt{\dfrac{52}{25}}$ **51.** $\sqrt{24} + \sqrt{6}$ **52.** $\dfrac{4\sqrt{27}}{18}$ **53.** $\sqrt{28} \cdot \sqrt{7}$

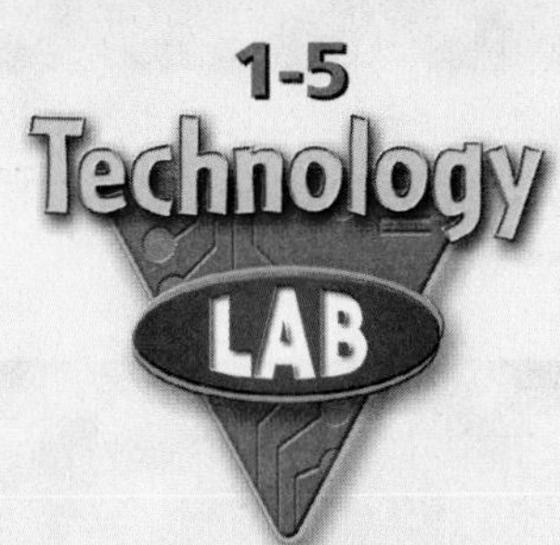

Explore Negative Exponents

You can use the caret key [^] to evaluate powers with a graphing calculator by entering (base) [^] (exponent).

Use with Lesson 1-5

Activity

Use a table to evaluate 10^x and 10^{-x} for $x = 0, 1, 2, 3, 4$, and 5.

1. Press [Y=] and enter **10** [^] **X** for **Y1** and **10** [^] [(−)] **X** for **Y2**. Note that the calculator key for a negative sign [(−)] is different from the calculator key for subtraction [−].

2. Press [2nd] [WINDOW] (TBLSET) to select the **TABLE SETUP** menu. Set the starting value, **TblStart**, to 0 and the step value, **ΔTbl**, to 1 so that the difference between each x-value in the table will be 1.

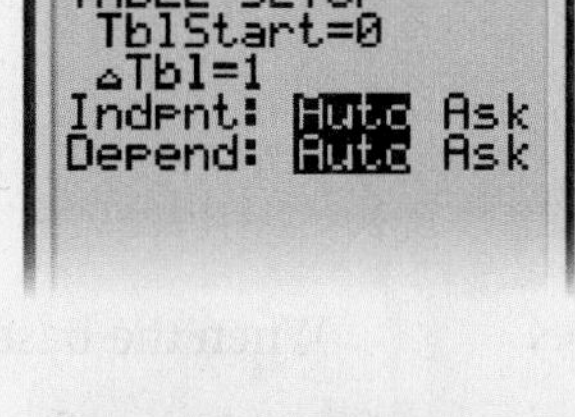

3. Press [2nd] [GRAPH] (TABLE) to view the table of values for 10^x and 10^{-x}.

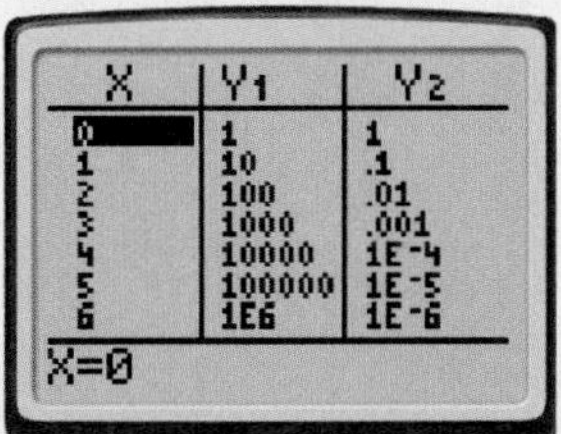

X	Y1	Y2
0	1	1
1	10	.1
2	100	.01
3	1000	.001
4	10000	1E-4
5	100000	1E-5
6	1E6	1E-6

X=0

Try This

Use a table to evaluate each pair of expressions for the given x-values.

1. 2^x and 2^{-x} for $x = -2, -1, 0, 1$, and 2
2. 3^x and 3^{-x} for $x = -4, -3, -2, -1$, and 0
3. 4^x and 4^{-x} for $x = -2, -1, 0, 1$, and 2
4. 5^x and 5^{-x} for $x = -4, -2, 0, 2$, and 4
5. Use a table to compute 2^{-x} and $\frac{1}{2^x}$ for $x = 0, 1, 2, 3, 4$, and 5. Explain what you notice.
6. **Make a Conjecture** Use the tables you created for Problems 1–5 to calculate the product of **Y1** and **Y2** for each value of x. Then make a conjecture about the product of a^x and a^{-x} for any nonzero value of a.
7. **Make a Conjecture** For what values of x is $2^{-x} > 2^x$?

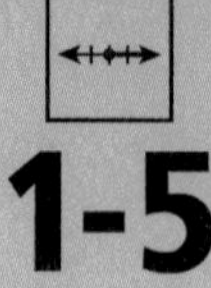

1-5 Properties of Exponents

Objectives
Simplify expressions involving exponents.

Use scientific notation.

Vocabulary
scientific notation

Who uses this?
Astronomers use exponents when working with large distances such as that between Earth and the Eagle Nebula. (See Example 5.)

In an expression of the form a^n, a is the base, n is the exponent, and the quantity a^n is called a power. The exponent indicates the number of times that the base is used as a factor.

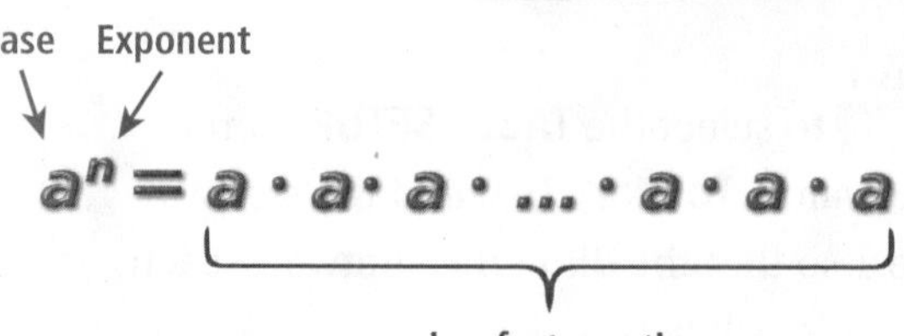

Reading Math

A *power* includes a base and an exponent.
The expression 2^3 is a power of 2.
It is read "2 to the third power" or "2 cubed."

When the base includes more than one symbol, it is written in parentheses.

Exponential Form	Base	Expanded Form
$-2x^3$	x	$-2(x \cdot x \cdot x)$
$-(2x)^3$	$2x$	$-(2x)(2x)(2x)$
$(-2x)^3$	$-2x$	$(-2x)(-2x)(-2x)$

EXAMPLE 1 Writing Exponential Expressions in Expanded Form

Write each expression in expanded form.

A $(4y)^3$

$(4y)^3$ *The base is 4y, and the exponent is 3.*

$(4y)(4y)(4y)$ *4y is a factor 3 times.*

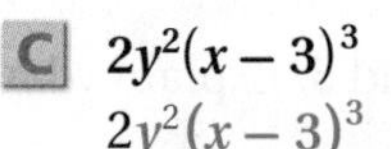

B $-a^2$

$-a^2$ *The base is a, and the exponent is 2.*

$-(a \cdot a) = -a \cdot a$ *a is a factor 2 times.*

C $2y^2(x-3)^3$

$2y^2(x-3)^3$ *There are two bases: y and x − 3.*

$2(y)(y)(x-3)(x-3)(x-3)$ *y is a factor 2 times, and x − 3 is a factor 3 times.*

CHECK IT OUT! **Write each expression in expanded form.**

1a. $(2a)^5$ **1b.** $3b^4$ **1c.** $-(2x-1)^3y^2$

Zero and Negative Exponents

For all nonzero real numbers *a* and *b* and integers *n*,

WORDS	NUMBERS	ALGEBRA
Zero Exponent Property A nonzero quantity raised to the zero power is equal to 1.	$100^0 = 1$	$a^0 = 1$
Negative Exponent Property A nonzero base raised to a negative exponent is equal to the reciprocal of the base raised to the opposite, positive exponent.	$7^{-2} = \left(\frac{1}{7}\right)^2 = \frac{1}{7^2}$ $\left(\frac{3}{2}\right)^{-4} = \left(\frac{2}{3}\right)^4$	$a^{-n} = \left(\frac{1}{a}\right)^n = \frac{1}{a^n}$ $\left(\frac{a}{b}\right)^{-n} = \left(\frac{b}{a}\right)^n$

EXAMPLE 2 Simplifying Expressions with Negative Exponents

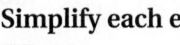

Caution!

Do not confuse a negative exponent with a negative expression.
$a^{-n} \neq -a^n \neq \frac{1}{-a^n}$

Simplify each expression.

 2^{-3}

$\frac{1}{2^3}$ *The reciprocal of 2 is $\frac{1}{2}$.*

$\frac{1}{2 \cdot 2 \cdot 2} = \frac{1}{8}$

 $-\left(\frac{3}{4}\right)^{-4}$

$-\left(\frac{4}{3}\right)^4$ *The reciprocal of $\frac{3}{4}$ is $\frac{4}{3}$.*

$-\frac{4}{3} \cdot \frac{4}{3} \cdot \frac{4}{3} \cdot \frac{4}{3} = -\frac{256}{81}$, or $-3\frac{13}{81}$

Simplify each expression.

2a. $\left(\frac{1}{3}\right)^{-2}$ **2b.** $(-5)^{-5}$

You can use the properties of exponents to simplify powers.

Properties of Exponents

For all nonzero real numbers *a* and *b* and integers *m* and *n*,

WORDS	NUMBERS	ALGEBRA
Product of Powers Property To multiply powers with the same base, add the exponents.	$4^3 \cdot 4^2 = 4^{3+2} = 4^5$	$a^m \cdot a^n = a^{m+n}$
Quotient of Powers Property To divide powers with the same base, subtract the exponents.	$\frac{3^7}{3^2} = 3^{7-2} = 3^5$	$\frac{a^m}{a^n} = a^{m-n}$
Power of a Power Property To raise one power to another, multiply the exponents.	$(4^3)^2 = 4^{3 \cdot 2} = 4^6$	$(a^m)^n = a^{m \cdot n}$
Power of a Product Property To find the power of a product, apply the exponent to each factor.	$(3 \cdot 4)^2 = 3^2 \cdot 4^2$	$(ab)^m = a^m b^m$
Power of a Quotient Property To find the power of a quotient, apply the exponent to the numerator and denominator.	$\left(\frac{3}{5}\right)^2 = \frac{3^2}{5^2}$	$\left(\frac{a}{b}\right)^m = \frac{a^m}{b^m}$

An algebraic expression is *simplified* when it contains no negative exponents, no grouping symbols, and no like terms.

EXAMPLE 3 Using Properties of Exponents to Simplify Expressions

Simplify each expression. Assume all variables are nonzero.

A $2x^3(-5x)$

$2 \cdot (-5) \cdot x^3 \cdot x^1$

$-10x^{3+1}$ *Product of Powers*

$-10x^4$ *Simplify.*

B $\left(\dfrac{ab^4}{b^7}\right)^2$

$(ab^{4-7})^2 = (ab^{-3})^2$ *Quotient of Powers*

$a^2(b^{-3})^2$ *Power of a Product*

$a^2b^{(-3)(2)}$ *Power of a Power*

$a^2b^{-6} = \dfrac{a^2}{b^6}$ *Negative Exponent Property*

Simplify each expression. Assume all variables are nonzero.

3a. $(5x^6)^3$ **3b.** $(-2a^3b)^{-3}$

Remember!

When you multiply by a power of 10, move the decimal to the right if the exponent is positive. Move the decimal to the left if the exponent is negative.

Scientific notation is a method of writing numbers by using powers of 10. In scientific notation, a number takes the form $m \times 10^n$, where $1 \leq m < 10$ and n is an integer.

Scientific Notation	Move the decimal	Standard Notation
1.275×10^7	Right 7 places	12,750,000
3.5×10^{-7}	Left 7 places	0.00000035

You can use the properties of exponents to calculate with numbers expressed in scientific notation.

EXAMPLE 4 Simplifying Expressions Involving Scientific Notation

Simplify each expression. Write the answer in scientific notation.

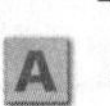

A $\dfrac{9.1 \times 10^{-3}}{1.3 \times 10^8}$

$\left(\dfrac{9.1}{1.3}\right) \times \left(\dfrac{10^{-3}}{10^8}\right)$ $\dfrac{a \cdot b}{c \cdot d} = \dfrac{a}{c} \cdot \dfrac{b}{d}$

7.0×10^{-11} *Divide 9.1 by 1.3 and subtract exponents: $-3 - 8 = -11$.*

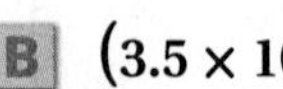

B $(3.5 \times 10^8)(5.2 \times 10^5)$

$(3.5)(5.2) \times (10^8)(10^5)$

18.2×10^{13} *Multiply 3.5 and 5.2 and add exponents: $8 + 5 = 13$.*

1.82×10^{14} *Because $18.2 > 10$, move the decimal point left 1 place and add 1 to the exponent.*

Simplify each expression. Write the answer in scientific notation.

4a. $\dfrac{2.325 \times 10^6}{9.3 \times 10^9}$ **4b.** $(4 \times 10^{-6})(3.1 \times 10^{-4})$

EXAMPLE 5 **Problem-Solving Application**

PROBLEM SOLVING

Light travels through space at a speed of about 3×10^5 kilometers per second. How many minutes does it take light to travel from the Sun to Jupiter?

Distances from the Sun	
Object	**Approximate Average Distance from Sun (m)**
Mercury	5.8×10^{10}
Venus	1.1×10^{11}
Earth	1.5×10^{11}
Mars	2.3×10^{11}
Jupiter	7.8×10^{11}
Saturn	1.4×10^{12}
Uranus	2.9×10^{12}
Neptune	4.5×10^{12}
Pluto	5.9×10^{12}

1 Understand the Problem

The **answer** will be the time it takes for light to travel from the Sun to Jupiter.

List the important information:

- The speed of light in space is 3×10^5 kilometers per second.
- The distance from the Sun to Jupiter is 7.8×10^{11} meters.

2 Make a Plan

Use the relationship: rate, or speed, equals distance divided by time.

$$\text{speed} = \frac{\text{distance}}{\text{time}}, \text{ so time} = \frac{\text{distance}}{\text{speed}}$$

3 Solve

First, convert the speed of light from $\frac{\text{kilometers}}{\text{second}}$ to $\frac{\text{meters}}{\text{minute}}$.

$$3 \times 10^5 \frac{\cancel{\text{km}}}{\cancel{\text{s}}}\left(\frac{10^3 \text{ m}}{1 \cancel{\text{km}}}\right)\left(\frac{60 \cancel{\text{s}}}{1 \text{ min}}\right)$$

There are 1000, or 10^3, meters in every kilometer and 60 seconds in every minute.

$$(3 \cdot 60) \times (10^5 \cdot 10^3) \frac{\text{m}}{\text{min}}$$

$$180 \times 10^8 \frac{\text{m}}{\text{min}} = 1.8 \times 10^{10} \frac{\text{m}}{\text{min}}$$

Use the relationship between time, distance, and speed to find the number of minutes it takes light to travel from the Sun to Jupiter.

$$\text{time} = \frac{\text{distance}}{\text{speed}} = \frac{7.8 \times 10^{11} \text{ m}}{1.8 \times 10^{10} \frac{\text{m}}{\text{min}}}$$

$$\frac{m}{\left(\frac{m}{min}\right)} = \cancel{m}\left(\frac{min}{\cancel{m}}\right) = min$$

$$= 4.\overline{3} \times 10 \text{ min} \approx 43.33 \text{ min}$$

It takes light approximately 43.33 minutes to travel from the Sun to Jupiter.

4 Look Back

Light traveling at 3×10^5 km/s for $43.33(60) \approx 2600$ seconds travels a distance of $780{,}000{,}000 = 7.8 \times 10^8$ km, or 7.8×10^{11}m. The answer is reasonable.

5. How many minutes does it take light to travel from the Sun to Earth?

THINK AND DISCUSS

1. Tell which properties of exponents apply only to expressions with the same base.
2. List the steps for writing a number in scientific notation.

3. **GET ORGANIZED** Copy and complete the graphic organizer by providing a numerical and algebraic example of each property.

Property	Numerical Example	Algebraic Example
Product of Powers		
Quotient of Powers		
Power of a Power		
Power of a Product		
Power of a Quotient		

1-5 Exercises

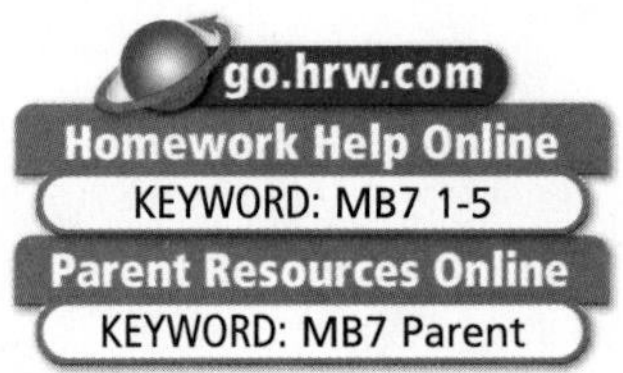

GUIDED PRACTICE

1. **Vocabulary** Describe the requirements for a number to be expressed in *scientific notation.*

SEE EXAMPLE 1 p. 34

Write each expression in expanded form.

2. $4(a - b)^2$ 3. $(12xy)^4$ 4. $-s^3(-2t)^5$ 5. $\left(-\frac{1}{2}d\right)^3$

SEE EXAMPLE 2 p. 35

Simplify each expression.

6. $\left(-\frac{3}{5}\right)^{-2}$ 7. 5^0 8. $\left(\frac{2}{3}\right)^{-3}$ 9. 10^{-1}

SEE EXAMPLE 3 p. 36

Simplify each expression. Assume all variables are nonzero.

10. $(-3a^2b^3)^2$ 11. $c^3d^2(c^{-2}d^4)$ 12. $\frac{5uv^6}{u^2v^2}$ 13. $10\left(\frac{y^5}{x^2}\right)^2$

14. $-2s^{-3}t(7s^{-8}t^5)$ 15. $-4m(mn^2)^3$ 16. $\frac{(4b)^2}{2b}$ 17. $\frac{x^{-1}y^{-2}}{x^3y^{-5}}$

SEE EXAMPLE 4 p. 36

Simplify each expression. Write the answer in scientific notation.

18. $(2.2 \times 10^5)(4.5 \times 10^{11})$ 19. $\frac{7.8 \times 10^8}{2.6 \times 10^{-3}}$ 20. $\frac{16 \times 10^{-3}}{4.0 \times 10^4}$

SEE EXAMPLE 5 p. 37

21. **Technology** Nanotechnology is a branch of engineering that works with devices that are smaller than 100 nanometers. The width of one string on the playable nanoguitar created by scientists at Cornell University in 2003 is 2.0×10^{-7} meters. If the width of a human hair is about 80 microns, how many nanoguitar strings would have the same width as a human hair? (*Hint:* 1 micron = 10^{-6} meters)

PRACTICE AND PROBLEM SOLVING

Independent Practice

For Exercises	See Example
22–25	1
26–29	2
30–33	3
34–36	4
37	5

Extra Practice

Skills Practice p. S4

Application Practice p. S32

Write each expression in expanded form.

22. $(m + 2n)^3$ **23.** $5x^3$ **24.** $(-9fg)^3h^4$ **25.** $2a(-b^2 - a)^2$

Simplify each expression.

26. $(-4)^{-2}$ **27.** $\left(-\frac{3}{4}\right)^{-1}$ **28.** $\left(-\frac{5}{2}\right)^{-3}$ **29.** -6^0

Simplify each expression. Assume all variables are nonzero.

30. $\frac{-100s^3t^{-5}}{25s^{-2}t^6}$ **31.** $(-x^4y^2)^5$ **32.** $(16u^4v^6)^{-2}$ **33.** $8a^2b^5(-2a^3b^2)$

Simplify each expression. Write the answer in scientific notation.

34. $(3.2 \times 10^6)(1.7 \times 10^{-4})$ **35.** $\frac{5.1 \times 10^4}{3.4 \times 10^{-5}}$ **36.** $(6.8 \times 10^3)(9.5 \times 10^5)$

37. Computer Science A computer with a 5.4 GHz microprocessor can make 5.4×10^9 calculations in one second. If a total of 5.02×10^{11} calculations are required to convert a given MP3 file to audio, how many minutes will the computer take to convert the file? Round your answer to the nearest hundredth.

LINK

Biology

King cobras are native to Asia. They may grow more than 12 feet in length and feed primarily on other snakes.

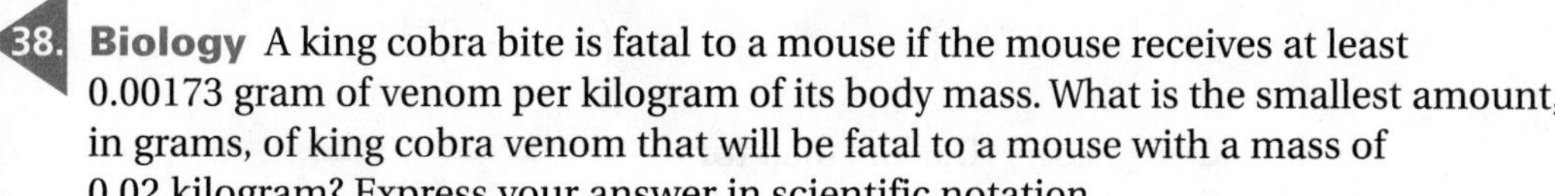

38. Biology A king cobra bite is fatal to a mouse if the mouse receives at least 0.00173 gram of venom per kilogram of its body mass. What is the smallest amount, in grams, of king cobra venom that will be fatal to a mouse with a mass of 0.02 kilogram? Express your answer in scientific notation.

Order each list from least to greatest by first rewriting each number with a base of 2.

39. $8^2, 4^1, 2^5, 16^{-2}$ **40.** $2^{-1}, -4^3, 4^2, 8^{-2}$ **41.** $-8^2, 4^0, 16^1, 2^{-2}$

42. Multi-Step There are approximately 1.3×10^{15} gallons of water in Lake Michigan. If a faucet is leaking at a rate of 1.5 ounces per minute, how many years would it take for the amount of water that has leaked to be equivalent to the volume of Lake Michigan? (*Hint:* 1 gallon = 128 ounces)

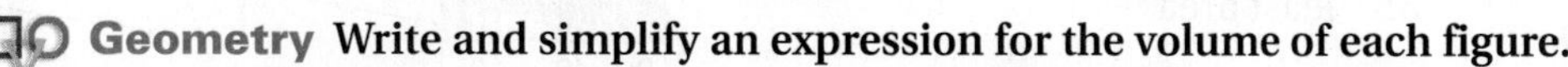

Geometry **Write and simplify an expression for the volume of each figure.**

43.

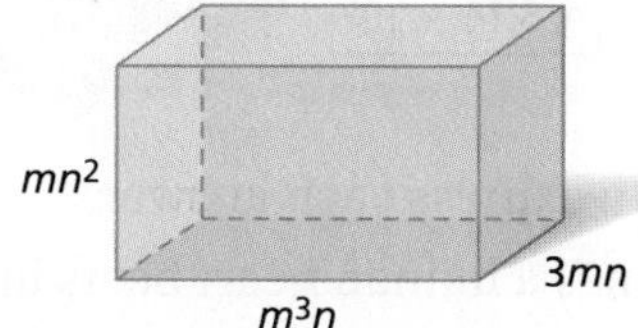

44.

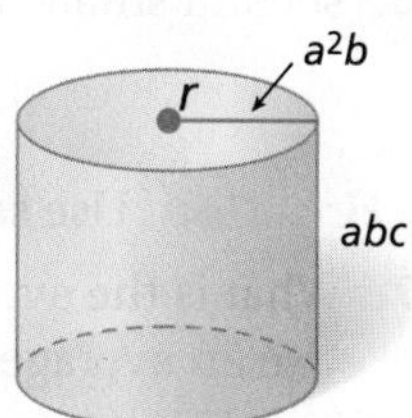

Simplify each expression. Assume all variables are nonzero.

45. $\frac{27x^3y}{18x^2y^4}$ **46.** $\left(\frac{3a^3b}{2a^{-1}b^2}\right)^2$ **47.** $12a^0b^5(-2a^3b^2)$

48. $\frac{72a^2b^3}{-24a^2b^5}$ **49.** $\left(\frac{5mn}{-3m^2}\right)^{-2}$ **50.** $6x^5y^3(-3x^2y^{-1})$

Measurement **Calculate each of the following.**

51. number of square inches in a square yard

52. number of square centimeters in a square meter

53. number of cubic inches in a cubic foot

54. number of cubic meters in a cubic kilometer

55. This problem will prepare you for the Multi-Step Test Prep on page 42.

The *Apollo 11* took approximately 102 hours and 45 minutes to get to the Moon, which is located about 384,500 km from Earth.

a. What was the average speed of the *Apollo 11* to the nearest kilometer per hour?

b. In theory, spaceships of the future might be able to travel at the speed of light, 3×10^5 km/s. How many times as fast is this than the average speed of the *Apollo 11*?

c. How long would it take future space travelers traveling at the speed of light to get to the Moon?

Simplify each expression. Assume all variables are nonzero.

56. $-9a^2b^6(-7ab^{-4})$

57. $\dfrac{14x^{-2}y^3}{-8x^{-5}y^5}$

58. $-\left(\dfrac{20x^6}{2x^2}\right)^3$

59. $\left(10x^{-2}y^0z^{-3}\right)^2$

60. $(-3a^2b^{-1})^{-3}$

61. $(8m^4n^{-2})(-3m^{-2}n)^0$

Geography **Use the map for Exercises 62–66. Identify which country fits the description, and then find its population density, or population per square mile, to the nearest tenth.**

62. greatest population

63. median area

64. median population

65. least area

66. second smallest population

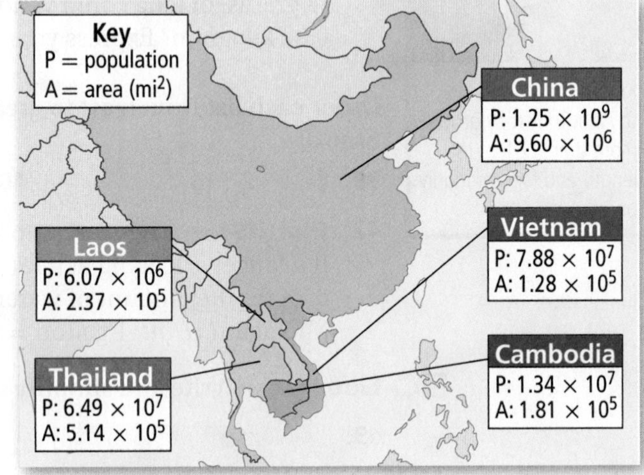

Estimation **Use scientific notation to express each answer.**

67. What is the average number of times a human heart beats in an average lifetime? Use an average rate of 1.2 heartbeats per second and an average lifespan of 75 years.

68. What is the average number of breaths a person takes in a lifetime? Use an average rate of 16 breaths per minute and an average lifespan of 75 years.

69. What is the average number of hairs on a human head? Use an average of 254 hairs per square centimeter and an average scalp size of 500 square centimeters.

Identify the property of exponents illustrated in each equation.

70. $(x^5)^3 = x^{15}$

71. $(m^2n^5)^4 = m^8n^{20}$

72. $\dfrac{3a^3}{a^{-2}} = 3a^5$

73. $\left(\dfrac{st^5}{s^3}\right)^4 = \dfrac{s^4t^{20}}{s^{12}}$

74. **Language** Statements such as "The population of the country is 3.8 million" are commonly used to describe large numbers. Express this value in scientific notation and explain the relationship between the mathematical representation of the number and the words used to describe it.

75. **Critical Thinking** Use the Quotient of Powers Property to show why 0^0 is undefined.

Graphing Calculator The key sequence 2nd EE , on a calculator is used for scientific notation. To enter the number 2.8×10^5 into your calculator, you would enter 2.8 2nd EE , 5. The calculator screen will display 2.8E5. Use your calculator to find the value of each expression.

76. $(3.7 \times 10^{-3})(8.1 \times 10^{-5})$ **77.** $\dfrac{2.08 \times 10^{-8}}{3.2 \times 10^{6}}$ **78.** $(4.75 \times 10^{2})(4.2 \times 10^{-7})$

79. $\dfrac{8.4 \times 10^{9}}{2.4 \times 10^{-5}}$ **80.** $\dfrac{17.068 \times 10^{-4}}{6.8 \times 10^{3}}$ **81.** $(1.83 \times 10^{13})(6.2 \times 10^{10})$

82. Write About It How can you tell which of two numbers written in scientific notation is greater? Use examples to explain your answer.

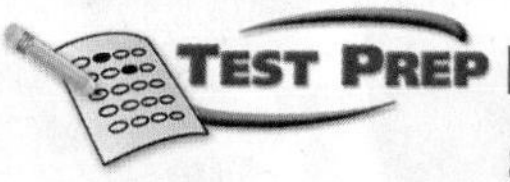

TEST PREP

83. Which number is greatest?

(A) 0.000025 (B) 2.5×10^{-6} (C) 2.5×10^{-4} (D) 2.5×10^{-5}

84. Which number is expressed correctly in scientific notation?

(F) 11×10^5 (G) 58.5×10^4 (H) 0.245×10^{-7} (J) 7.25×10^0

85. Which expression is equivalent to $(-5)(-5)(-5)(-5)(-5)(-5)$?

(A) 5^{-6} (B) $(-5)^{-6}$ (C) $(-5)^6$ (D) -5^6

86. If a and c are nonzero, which expression is equivalent to $\dfrac{a^4b^{-3}}{a^2c^0}$?

(F) $\dfrac{a^2}{b^3c}$ (G) $\dfrac{a^2c}{b^3}$ (H) $\dfrac{a^{-2}}{b^{-3}c}$ (J) $\dfrac{a^2}{b^3}$

CHALLENGE AND EXTEND

Simplify each expression. Write your answer in scientific notation.

87. $\left(\dfrac{7.82 \times 10^6}{5.48 \times 10^8}\right)^2$ **88.** $\left[(6.18 \times 10^7)(2.05 \times 10^8)\right]^2$

89. Give examples of numbers that are greater than 1 when raised to the exponent −2. Make a generalization about the types of numbers that are greater than 1 when raised to a negative exponent.

90. Notice that $2^4 = 4^2$. For whole numbers a and b such that $a < b$, give three examples of values of a and b such that $a^b > b^a$ and three examples such that $a^b < b^a$.

SPIRAL REVIEW

91. When two people play the game rock, paper, scissors, each person's hand simultaneously shows the player's choice of rock, paper, or scissors. What is the probability that both players will make the same choice? *(Previous course)*

Complete each statement. *(Lesson 1-2)*

92. $\dfrac{1}{3} \cdot ■ = 1$ **93.** $4(-3 + ■) = -12 + 32$ **94.** $0 = \sqrt{7} + ■$

Evaluate each expression for the given values of the variables. *(Lesson 1-4)*

95. $\dfrac{2mn}{n^2 - 2n + 5m}$ for $n = -1$ and $m = 3$

96. $2x(9y - x^2)$ for $x = -3$ and $y = 10$

CHAPTER 1

MULTI-STEP TEST PREP

SECTION 1A

Properties and Operations

Man on the Moon On July 20, 1969, the U.S. *Apollo 11* lunar module landed on the Moon. A few hours later, Neil Armstrong was the first human to set foot on the Moon's surface. The *Apollo 11* mission led to many scientific discoveries about Earth's nearest neighbor.

	Earth	Moon
Mean Diameter (km)	12,742	3476
Volume (km^3)	1.08321×10^{12}	2.199×10^{10}
Mass (kg)	5.9736×10^{24}	7.349×10^{22}
Mean Density (kg/m^3)	5515	3342
Surface Gravity (m/s^2)	9.78	1.64
Escape Velocity (km/s)	11.2	2.38

1. *Apollo 11* was launched at 9:32 A.M. eastern daylight time (EDT) on July 16, 1969. The mission lasted 195 h 18 min. What was the date and time when the mission ended?
2. The gravity on the Moon is about $\frac{1}{6}$ of Earth's gravity. Based on the data in the table, is the actual surface gravity on the Moon less than or greater than $\frac{1}{6}$ of Earth's surface gravity? Explain.
3. Classify the numbers in the indicated row of the table by the sets of the real numbers to which they belong.

   a. mean diameter **b.** surface gravity **c.** escape velocity
4. The expression $\sqrt{\frac{h}{0.82}}$ can be used to approximate the time in seconds it takes for an object to reach the surface of the Moon when dropped from a height of h meters. The *Apollo 11* lunar module was about 7.2 meters tall. Suppose Neil Armstrong jumped from the top of the lunar module. How long would it have taken him to land on the surface of the Moon?
5. The expression $\sqrt{\frac{h}{4.89}}$ can be used to model the time it takes to reach Earth's surface from a height of h meters. To the nearest tenth of a second, how much longer would it take for an object to fall from a height of 125 m to the surface on the Moon than it would take on Earth?
6. Approximately how many Moons would it take to equal the volume of Earth?

READY TO GO ON?

Quiz for Lessons 1-1 Through 1-5

1-1 Sets of Numbers

Order the given numbers from least to greatest. Then classify each number by the subsets of the real numbers to which it belongs.

1. $2.5, -3\frac{1}{3}, \sqrt{5}, -\frac{4}{5}, 0.\overline{75}$
2. $\sqrt{3}, -\frac{\pi}{2}, \frac{5}{6}, -1.\overline{15}, -2$

Rewrite each set in the indicated notation.

3. $\{x \mid -4 \le x < 2\}$; interval notation
4. 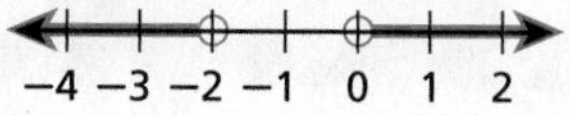

set-builder notation

1-2 Properties of Real Numbers

Identify the property demonstrated by each equation.

5. $3(2a + b) = 3(2a) + 3b$
6. $21 + 0 = 21$
7. $(2\pi)r = 2(\pi r)$
8. Use mental math to find the amount of a 12% shipping fee for an item that costs \$250. Explain your steps.

1-3 Square Roots

9. A rental company rents portable dance floors in three different sizes: 75 square feet, 125 square feet, and 150 square feet. Estimate the dimensions of each square dance floor to the nearest tenth of a foot. Then identify which of the three sizes is the largest dance floor that would fit in a room 11 feet wide and 13 feet long.

Simplify each expression.

10. $-\sqrt{72}$
11. $5\sqrt{12} + 9\sqrt{3}$
12. $\frac{-4\sqrt{10}}{\sqrt{2}}$
13. $\sqrt{32} \cdot \sqrt{6}$

1-4 Simplifying Algebraic Expressions

Evaluate each expression for the given values of the variables.

14. $\frac{a^2}{3} + \frac{ab}{4}$ for $a = 3$ and $b = -4$
15. $\frac{d^2}{2cd}$ for $c = -1$ and $d = 2$

Simplify each expression.

16. $2x^2 - 3y + 5x^2 - x^2$
17. $3(x + 2y) - 5x + y$

1-5 Properties of Exponents

Simplify each expression. Assume all variables are nonzero.

18. $(x^{11}y^{-2})^4$
19. $\frac{-3s^3t^2}{s^{-2}t^8}$
20. $4(a^2b^6)^{-3}$
21. $\left(\frac{m^4}{-5m^{-2}n^3}\right)^2$
22. The atomic mass of an element from the periodic table is the mass, in grams, of one *mole*, or 6.02×10^{23} atoms. Suppose a sample of oxygen contains 4.515×10^{26} atoms. How many moles of oxygen atoms are in the sample?

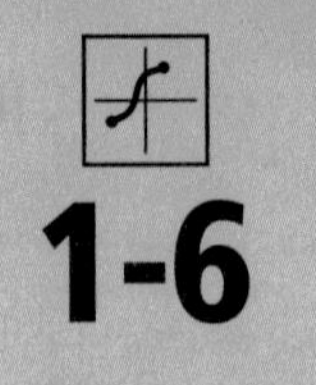

1-6 Relations and Functions

Objectives
Identify the domain and range of relations and functions.

Determine whether a relation is a function.

Vocabulary
relation
domain
range
function

Why learn this?
The relationship between the numbers and the letters on the keys of a cell phone can be described using relations.

When you create a text message on a cell phone, you enter letters by pressing the numbered keys that they appear on. For instance, you would press the 2 key to enter an *A*, *B*, or *C*. This relationship can be represented by a mapping diagram or a set of ordered pairs.

Mapping Diagram

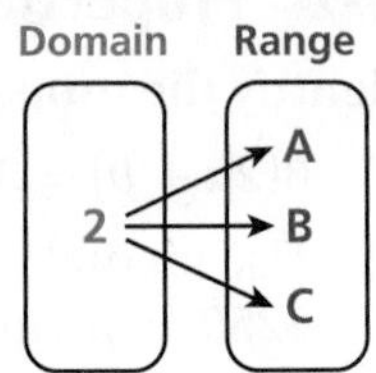

Set of Ordered Pairs

{(2, A), (2, B), (2, C)}

$(x, y) \rightarrow$ (input, output) $\rightarrow$ (domain, range)

A **relation** is a pairing of input values with output values. It can be shown as a set of ordered pairs (x, y), where x is an input and y is an output.

The set of input values for a relation is called the **domain**, and the set of output values is called the **range**.

EXAMPLE 1 Identifying Domain and Range

Give the domain and range for the relation shown.

First-Class Stamp Rates						
Year	1900	1920	1940	1960	1980	2000
Rate (¢)	2	2	3	4	15	33

List the set of ordered pairs:

$\{(1900, 2), (1920, 2), (1940, 3), (1960, 4), (1980, 15), (2000, 33)\}$

Domain: $\{1900, 1920, 1940, 1960, 1980, 2000\}$ *The set of x-coordinates*

Range: $\{2, 3, 4, 15, 33\}$ *The set of y-coordinates*

Helpful Hint

Notice that the rate 2¢ appears twice in the table but is listed only once in the set of range values. When the domain or range of a relation is listed, each value is listed only once.

1. Give the domain and range for the relation shown in the graph.

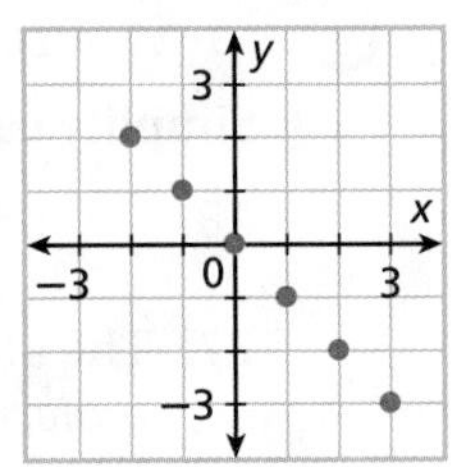

Suppose you are told that a person entered a word into a text message using the numbers 6, 2, 8, and 4 on a cell phone. It would be difficult to determine the word without seeing it because each number can be used to enter three different letters.

Number $\{$**Number, Letter**$\}$

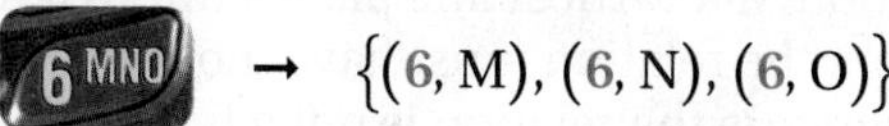

6 MNO → $\{(6, M), (6, N), (6, O)\}$

2 ABC → $\{(2, A), (2, B), (2, C)\}$

8 TUV → $\{(8, T), (8, U), (8, V)\}$

4 GHI → $\{(4, G), (4, H), (4, I)\}$

The numbers 6, 2, 8, and 4 each appear as the first coordinate of three different ordered pairs.

However, if you are told to enter the word *MATH* into a text message, you can easily determine that you must use the numbers 6, 2, 8, and 4, because each letter appears on only one numbered key.

$\{(M, 6), (A, 2), (T, 8), (H, 4)\}$

The first coordinate is different in each ordered pair.

A relation in which the first coordinate is never repeated is called a *function.* In a **function**, there is only one output for each input, so each element of the domain is mapped to exactly one element in the range.

Although a single input in a function cannot be mapped to more than one output, two or more different inputs can be mapped to the same output.

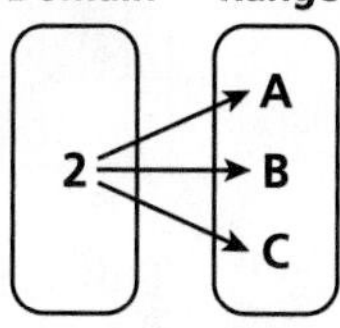

Not a function: The relationship from number to letter is *not* a function because the domain value 2 is mapped to the range values A, B, and C.

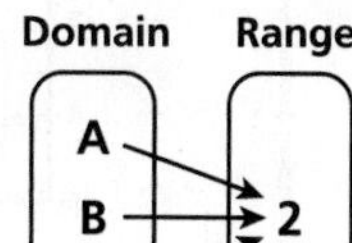

Function: The relationship from letter to number is a function because each letter in the domain is mapped to only one number in the range.

EXAMPLE 2 Determining Whether a Relation Is a Function

Determine whether each relation is a function.

A

Instant Rice Cooking Times				
Servings	2	4	6	8
Cooking Time (min)	5	8	10	11

There is only one cooking time for each number of servings. The relation from number of servings to cooking time is a function.

B **from last name to Social Security number**

A last name, such as Smith, from the domain would be associated with many different Social Security numbers. The relation from last name to Social Security number is not a function.

Determine whether each relation is a function.

2a.

Shoe Prices			
Size	7	8	9
Price ($)	35	35	35

2b. from the number of items in a grocery cart to the total cost of the items in the cart

Every point on a vertical line has the same x-coordinate, so a vertical line cannot represent a function. If a vertical line passes through more than one point on the graph of a relation, the relation must have more than one point with the same x-coordinate. Therefore the relation is not a function.

Know it! Note

Vertical-Line Test

WORDS	EXAMPLES	
If any vertical line passes through more than one point on the graph of a relation, the relation is not a function.	Function	Not a Function

EXAMPLE 3 Using the Vertical-Line Test

Use the vertical-line test to determine whether each relation is a function. If not, identify two points a vertical line would pass through.

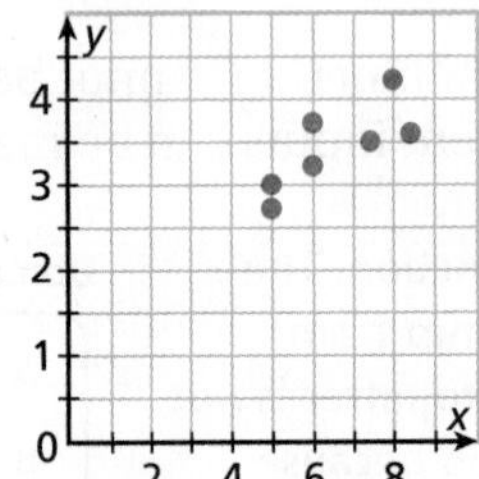

This is *not* a function. A vertical line at $x = 6$ would pass through $(6, 3.25)$ and $(6, 3.75)$.

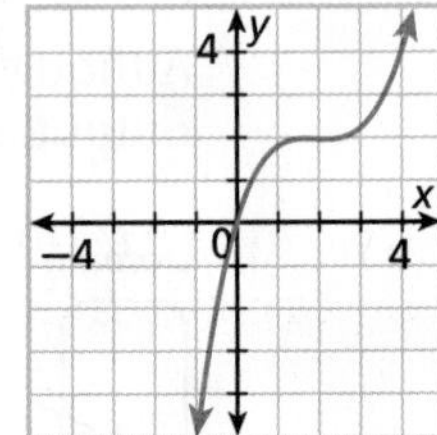

This *is* a function. Any vertical line would pass through only one point on the graph.

Use the vertical-line test to determine whether each relation is a function. If not, identify two points a vertical line would pass through.

3a.

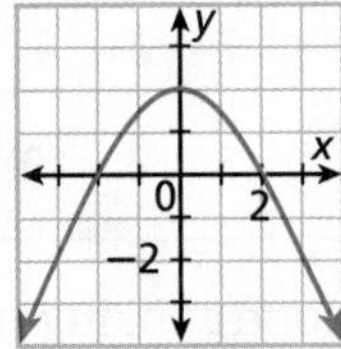

3b.

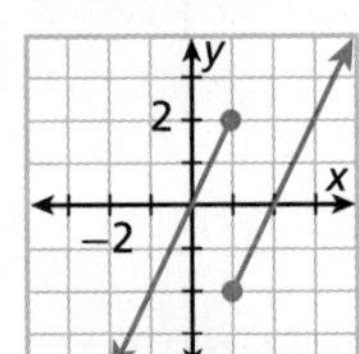

THINK AND DISCUSS

1. Name four different ways to represent a relation or function.
2. Explain why the vertical-line test works.
3. **GET ORGANIZED** Copy and complete the graphic organizer. In each box, give an example of a table, a graph, and a set of ordered pairs.

Know it! Note

Relation

Function

1-6 Exercises

go.hrw.com
Homework Help Online
KEYWORD: MB7 1-6
Parent Resources Online
KEYWORD: MB7 Parent

GUIDED PRACTICE

1. **Vocabulary** The set of output values of a function is its __?__. (*domain* or *range*)

SEE EXAMPLE 1
p. 44

Give the domain and range for each relation.

2. 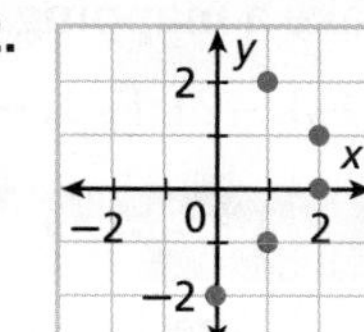

3.

Average Movie Ticket Price	
Year	**Price**
2000	\$5.39
2001	\$5.65
2002	\$5.80
2003	\$6.03

SEE EXAMPLE 2
p. 45

Determine whether each relation is a function.

4.

Math Test Scores				
Name	Jan	Helen	Luke	Soren
Score	90	84	88	84

5. from car models to car colors

SEE EXAMPLE 3
p. 46

Use the vertical-line test to determine whether each relation is a function. If not, identify two points a vertical line would pass through.

6. 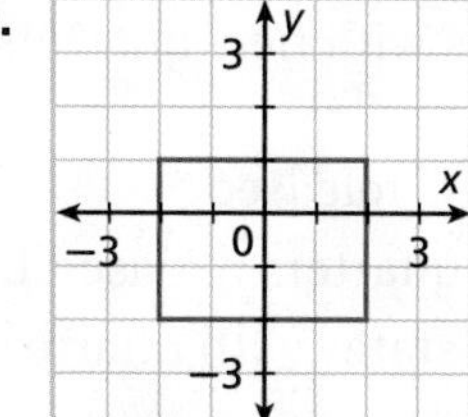

7. 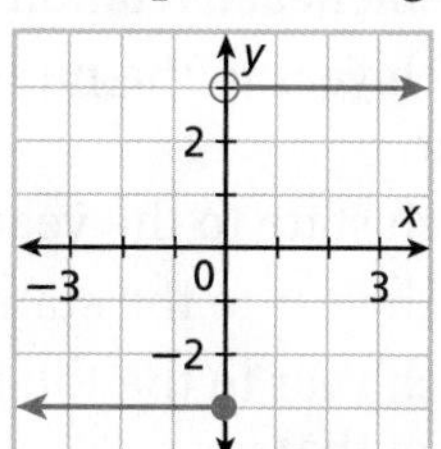

8. 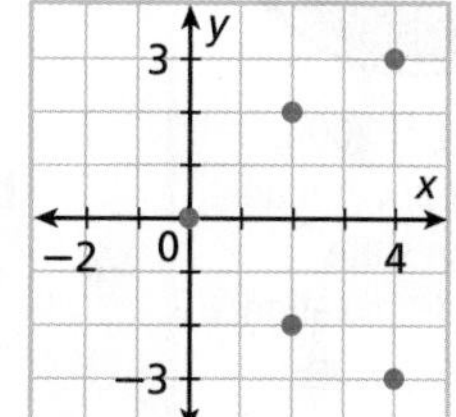

PRACTICE AND PROBLEM SOLVING

Independent Practice	
For Exercises	See Example
9–10	1
11–12	2
13–15	3

Extra Practice
Skills Practice p. S5
Application Practice p. S32

Give the domain and range for each relation.

9. 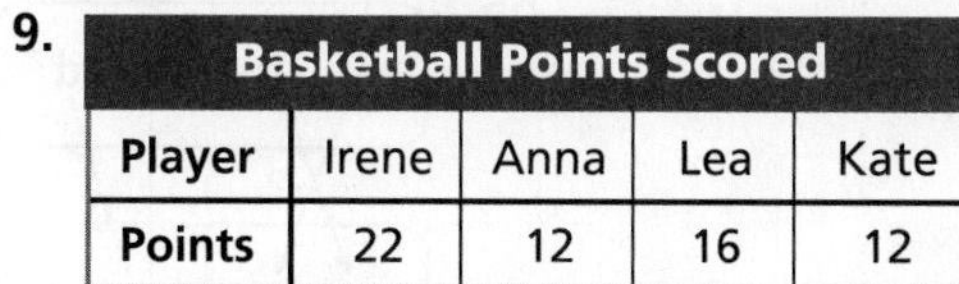

Basketball Points Scored				
Player	Irene	Anna	Lea	Kate
Points	22	12	16	12

10. 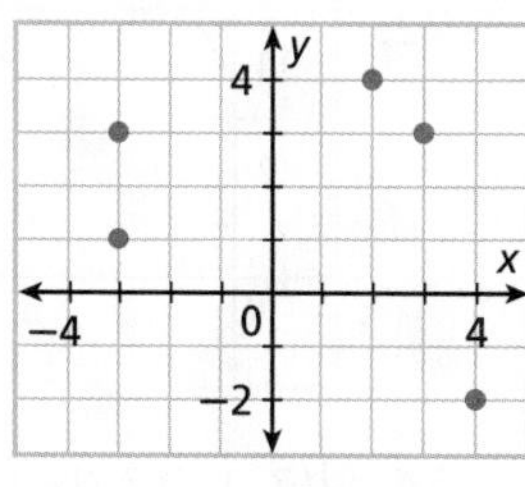

Determine whether each relation is a function.

11.

Women's Glove Sizes			
Size	S	M	L
Maximum Hand Length (in.)	6.5	7.5	8.5

12. 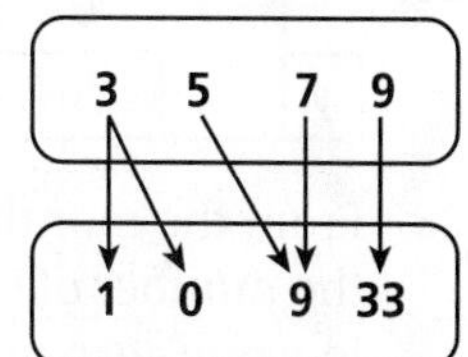

Use the vertical-line test to determine whether each relation is a function. If not, identify two points a vertical line would pass through.

13.

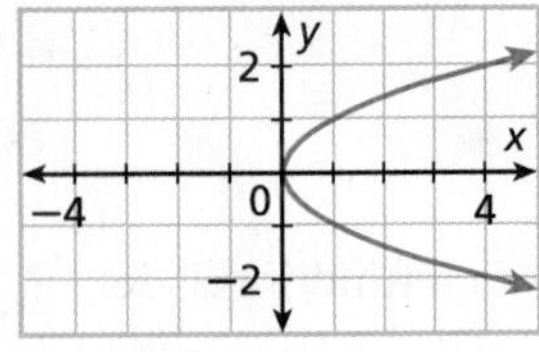

14.

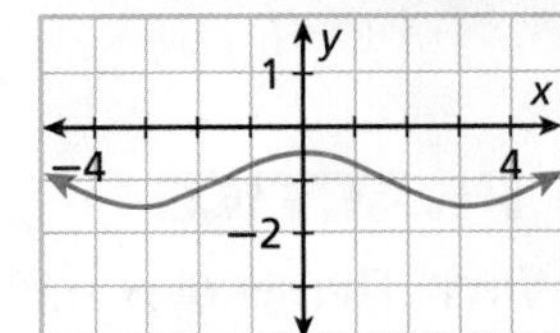

15.

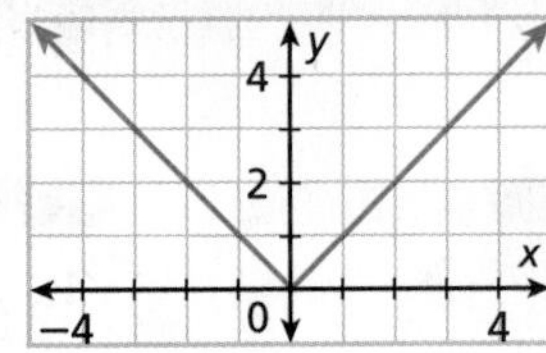

Give the domain and range of each relation and make a mapping diagram.

16. $\{(-5, 0), (0, -5), (5, 0), (0, 5)\}$

17. $\{(-2, -2), (-1, -2), (0, 0), (1, 2), (2, 2)\}$

18.

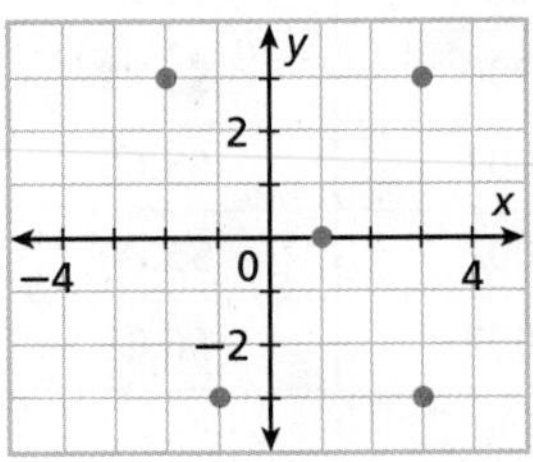

19.

Average Egg Weights	
Size	**Weight (oz)**
Jumbo	2.5
Extra large	2.25
Large	2
Medium	1.75

Money

By the end of 2004, there were more than 17.6 billion state quarters in circulation.
Source: www.usmint.gov

20. from each unique letter in the word *seven* to the number that represents the position of that letter in the alphabet

21. **Money** In 1999 the U.S. Mint began releasing quarters to commemorate each of the 50 states. The release schedule specified that each year for a total of 10 years, new quarters commemorating 5 different states would be released. Explain whether each relation is a function.

a. from each year to the number of states with new quarters released in that year

b. from each state to the year its quarter is released

c. from each year to the states with new quarters released in that year

d. from each year to the total number of states with quarters released by the end of that year

e. from the number of new quarters released each year to the year

Give the domain and range of each relation. Then explain whether the relation is a function.

22.

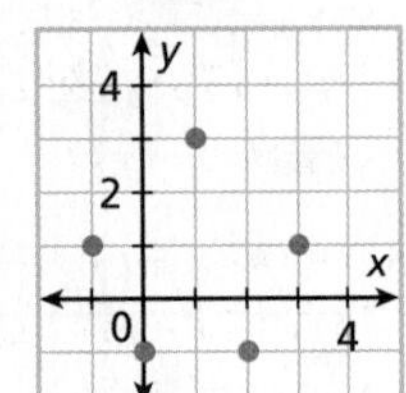

23.

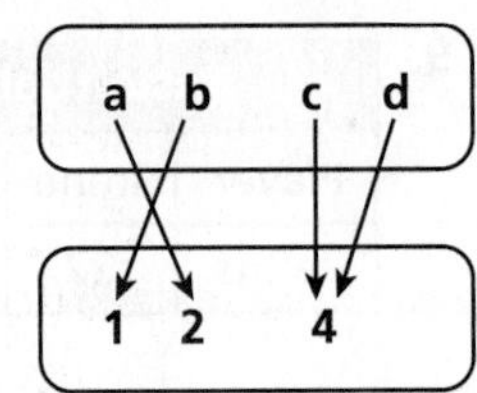

24. $\{(7, 1), (7, 2), (7, 3), (7, 4), (7, 6)\}$

25. $\{(9, 3), (7, 3), (5, 3), (3, 3), (1, 3)\}$

26.

x	3	0	0	−1	−3
y	−4	−3	−1	−2	0

27.

x	7	6	5	4	3
y	−1	2	−1	2	3

28. From the months of the year to the number of days in that month in a non-leap year

29. From day of the week to the number of hours in that day

MULTI-STEP TEST PREP

30. This problem will prepare you for the Multi-Step Test Prep on page 74.

a. The relation $(0, 20)$, $(-20, 0)$, $(0, -20)$, and $(20, 0)$ can be plotted to produce the vertices of a shape very common in Native American art. What shape is this?

b. Does this relation represent a function? Why or why not?

c. What is the domain of this relation?

d. What is the range of this relation?

Explain whether the relation from A to B is a function, the relation from B to A is a function, or both are functions.

	A	B
31.	Date of birth	Person
32.	Thumbprint	Person
33.	Area code	State
34.	Amount of sales tax	Purchase total
35.	Sales tax percentage	Purchase total
36.	Jersey number	NFL football player
37.	Jersey number	current Cleveland Browns player

38. **/// ERROR ANALYSIS ///** Identify which statement is incorrect. Explain the error.

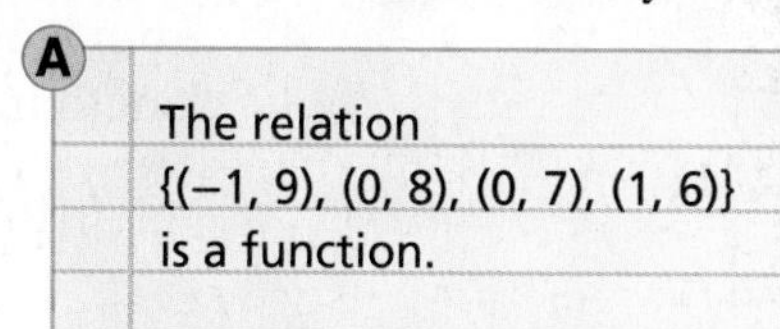
A
The relation
$\{(-1, 9), (0, 8), (0, 7), (1, 6)\}$
is a function.

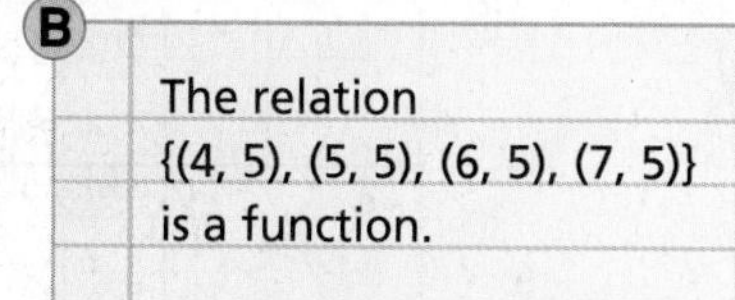
B
The relation
$\{(4, 5), (5, 5), (6, 5), (7, 5)\}$
is a function.

Carpentry **Use the table for Exercises 39–41.**

Common Wire Nail Data

Size	Length (in.)	Gauge	Number (per lb)
2d	1	15	876
3d	$1\frac{1}{4}$	14	568
4d	$1\frac{1}{2}$	$12\frac{1}{2}$	316
5d	$1\frac{3}{4}$	$12\frac{1}{2}$	271
6d	2	$11\frac{1}{2}$	181

39. If you know the gauge of a nail, can you determine its size? What does this indicate about the relation from gauge to size?

40. Identify the pattern in the nail lengths as size increases. Does the pattern indicate that the relation from length to size is a function?

41. Consider the relation from nail size to the number of nails per pound.

a. Does the relation represent a function?

b. Explain the relationship between a nail's size and its average weight.

c. Confirm your answer to part **b** by finding the average weight for each nail size. (*Hint:* 1 pound = 16 ounces)

42. **Critical Thinking** If you switch the domain and range of any function, will the resulting relation always be a function? Explain by using examples.

43. **Write About It** Explain how you would determine whether each of the following represents a function: a set of ordered pairs, a mapping diagram, and a graph.

44. Which relation is NOT a function?

Ⓐ $\{(0, 1), (1, 0), (2, 0), (3, 1)\}$

Ⓑ $\{(-1, 5), (-2, 4), (-2, 3), (-3, 2)\}$

Ⓒ $\{(1, 1), (2, 2), (3, 3), (4, 4)\}$

Ⓓ $\left\{\left(2, \frac{1}{2}\right), \left(4, \frac{1}{4}\right), \left(8, \frac{1}{8}\right), \left(16, \frac{1}{16}\right)\right\}$

45. Which set represents the domain of $\{(99, -2), (99, -3), (96, -4), (96, -5)\}$?

Ⓕ $\{96, 99\}$

Ⓖ All negative integers

Ⓗ $\{-2, -3, -4, -5\}$

Ⓙ $\{-2, -3, -4, -5, 96, 99\}$

46. Which is an element of the range of the graphed function?

Ⓐ −2

Ⓑ 0

Ⓒ 1

Ⓓ 4

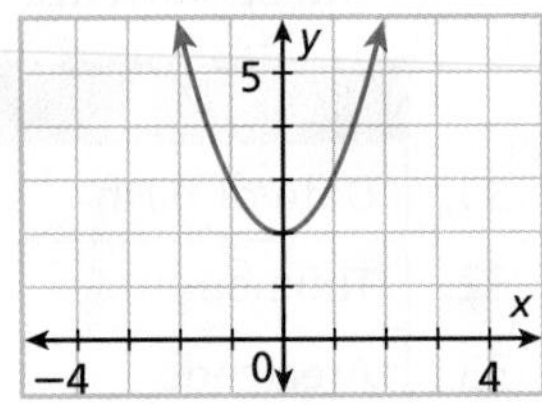

CHALLENGE AND EXTEND

47. Find the conditions for a and b that make $\{(a, b), (-a, b), (2a, b), (a^2, b)\}$ a function.

A *one-to-one function* is a function in which each output corresponds to only one input. Explain whether each function is one to one.

48.

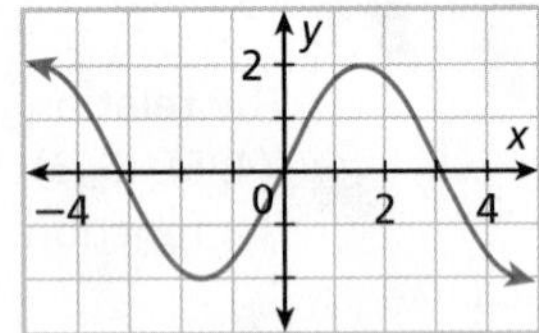

49. from length in inches to length in feet

50. Find the conditions for a and b that make $\left\{(2, b), (3, ab), \left(4, \frac{ab}{2}\right)\right\}$ a one-to-one function.

SPIRAL REVIEW

Use the diagram of the basketball court for Exercises 51–53. *(Previous course)*

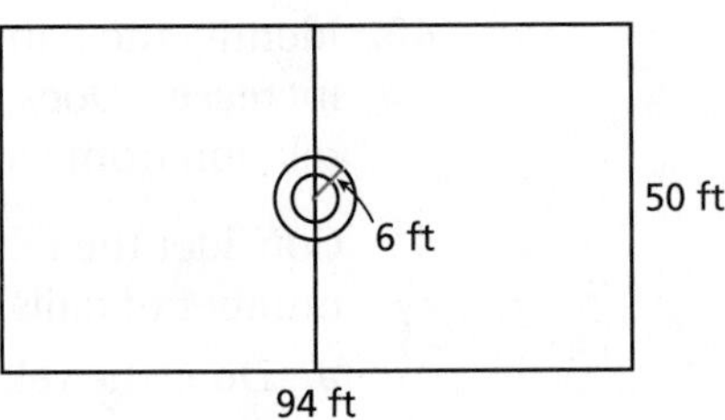

51. What is the perimeter of the basketball court?

52. What is the area of the basketball court?

53. To the nearest tenth, what is the area of the outermost circle at center court?

Estimate to the nearest tenth. *(Lesson 1-3)*

54. $\sqrt{42}$

55. $\sqrt{22}$

56. $-\sqrt{8}$

57. $\sqrt{90}$

Simplify each expression. Assume all variables are nonzero. *(Lesson 1-5)*

58. $(-3y^4)^3$

59. $\frac{(10w^2)^2}{5w^5}$

60. $(4c^6d^2)^2$

61. $\left(\frac{x^3}{z}\right)^7$

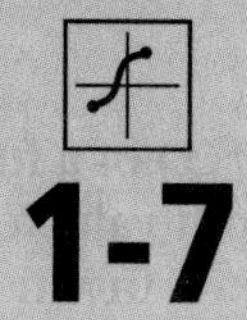

1-7 Function Notation

Objectives

Write functions using function notation.

Evaluate and graph functions.

Vocabulary

function notation
dependent variable
independent variable

Why learn this?

Function notation can be used to indicate the distance traveled by a Japanese bullet train. (See Example 3.)

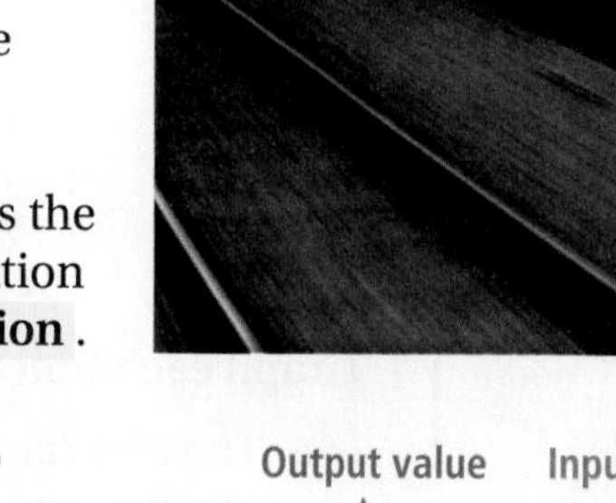

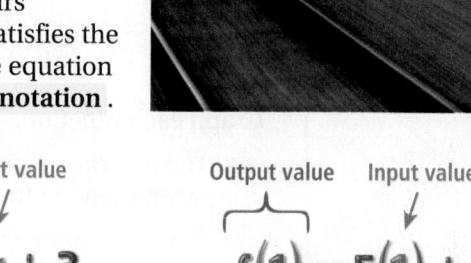

Some sets of ordered pairs can be described by using an equation. When the set of ordered pairs described by an equation satisfies the definition of a function, the equation can be written in **function notation**.

Output value: $f(x)$; Input value: x

$$f(x) = 5x + 3$$

f of *x* equals 5 times *x* plus 3.

Output value: $f(1)$; Input value: 1

$$f(1) = 5(1) + 3$$

f of 1 equals 5 times 1 plus 3.

The function described by $f(x) = 5x + 3$ is the same as the function described by $y = 5x + 3$. And both of these functions are the same as the set of ordered pairs $(x, 5x + 3)$.

$$y = 5x + 3 \rightarrow (x, y) \rightarrow (x, 5x + 3)$$
$$f(x) = 5x + 3 \rightarrow (x, f(x)) \rightarrow (x, 5x + 3)$$

Notice that $y = f(x)$ for each x.

The graph of a function is a picture of the function's ordered pairs.

Caution!

$f(x)$ is *not* "*f* times *x*" or "*f* multiplied by *x*." $f(x)$ means "the value of *f* at *x*." So $f(1)$ represents the value of *f* at $x = 1$.

EXAMPLE 1 Evaluating Functions

For each function, evaluate $f(0)$, $f\left(\frac{1}{2}\right)$, and $f(-2)$.

A $f(x) = 7 - 2x$

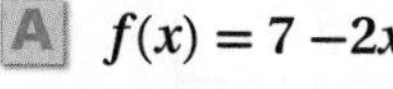

Substitute each value for *x* and evaluate.

$f(0) = 7 - 2(0) = 7$

$f\left(\frac{1}{2}\right) = 7 - 2\left(\frac{1}{2}\right) = 6$

$f(-2) = 7 - 2(-2) = 11$

B

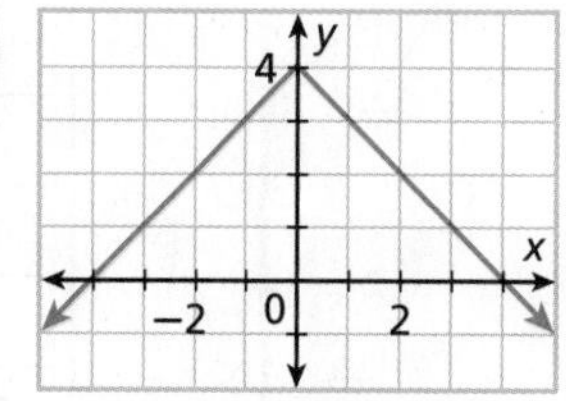

Use the graph to find the corresponding *y*-value for each *x*-value.

$f(0) = 4 \quad f\left(\frac{1}{2}\right) = 3\frac{1}{2} \quad f(-2) = 2$

For each function, evaluate $f(0)$, $f\left(\frac{1}{2}\right)$, and $f(-2)$.

1a. $f(x) = x^2 - 4x$

1b. $f(x) = -2x + 1$

In the notation $f(x)$, f is the *name* of the function. The output $f(x)$ of a function is called the **dependent variable** because it *depends* on the input value of the function. The input x is called the **independent variable**. When a function is graphed, the independent variable is graphed on the horizontal axis and the dependent variable is graphed on the vertical axis.

$d(t) = 65t$

Dependent variable — Independent variable

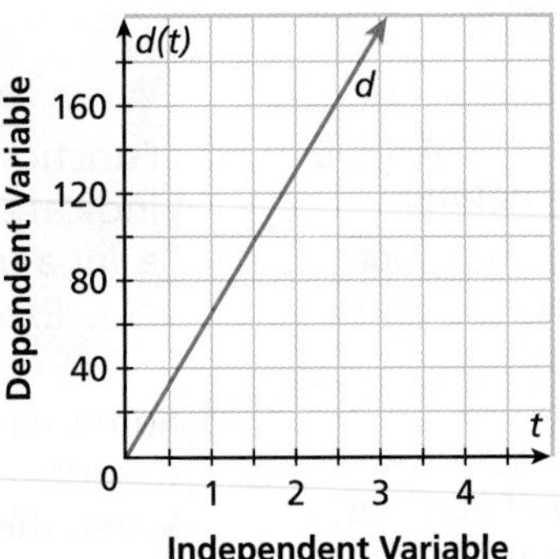

EXAMPLE 2 Graphing Functions

Graph each function.

A **The diagram shows the maximum recommended heart rate for women by age.**

Graph the points.

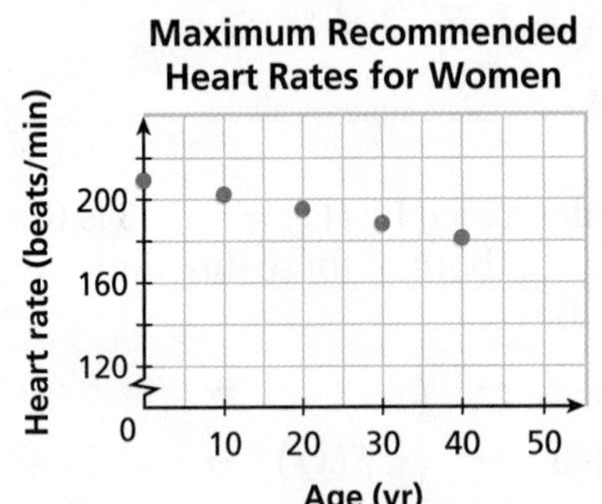

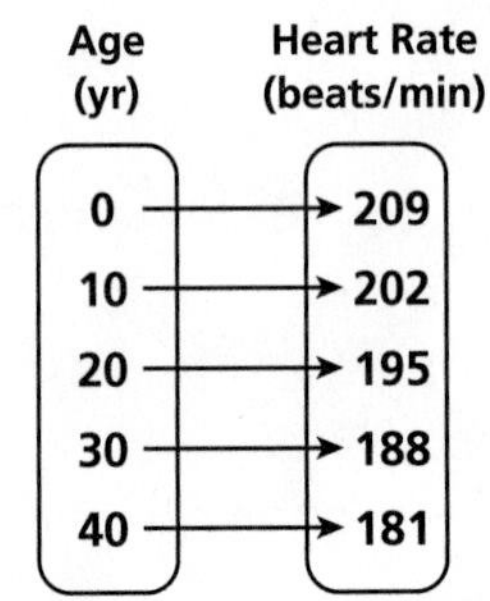

Do not connect the points, because the values between the given points have not been defined.

Reading Math

A function whose graph is made up of unconnected points is called a *discrete* function.

B **The maximum recommended heart rate h for men is a function of age a and can be calculated with $h(a) = 214 - 0.8a$.**

Make a table.

a	$214 - 0.8a$	$h(a)$
0	$214 - 0.8(0)$	214
20	$214 - 0.8(20)$	198
40	$214 - 0.8(40)$	182
60	$214 - 0.8(60)$	166
80	$214 - 0.8(80)$	150

Connect the points with a line because the function is defined for $0 \le a \le 100$.

Graph the points.

Graph each function.

2a.

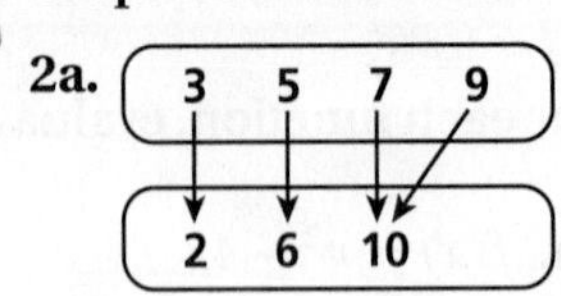

2b. $f(x) = 2x + 1$

The algebraic expression used to define a function is called the function rule. The function described by $f(x) = 5x + 3$ is defined by the function rule $5x + 3$. To write a function rule, first identify the independent and dependent variables.

EXAMPLE 3 *Transportation Application*

The Japanese bullet train that travels from Tokyo to Kyoto averages about 156 km/h. The distance from Tokyo to Kyoto is 380 km.

a. Write a function to represent the distance remaining on the trip after a certain amount of time.

Time traveled is the independent variable, and distance remaining is the dependent variable.

Let t be the time in hours and let d be the distance in kilometers remaining on the trip.

Write a word equation to represent the problem situation. Then replace the words with expressions.

distance remaining	=	total distance	−	distance traveled
$d(t)$	=	380	−	$156t$

b. What is the value of the function for an input of 1.5, and what does it represent?

$d(1.5) = 380 - 156(1.5)$ *Substitute 1.5 for t and simplify.*

$d(1.5) = 146$

The value of the function for an input of 1.5 is 146. This means that there are 146 kilometers remaining in the trip after 1.5 hours.

A local photo shop will develop and print the photos from a disposable camera for $0.27 per print.

3a. Write a function to represent the cost of photo processing.

3b. What is the value of the function for an input of 24, and what does it represent?

THINK AND DISCUSS

1. Identify a reasonable domain for the function in Example 3. Explain your answer.

2. Explain three things you can determine about a function from the notation $g(t)$.

3. GET ORGANIZED Copy and complete the graphic organizer. In each blank, fill in the missing portion of the label.

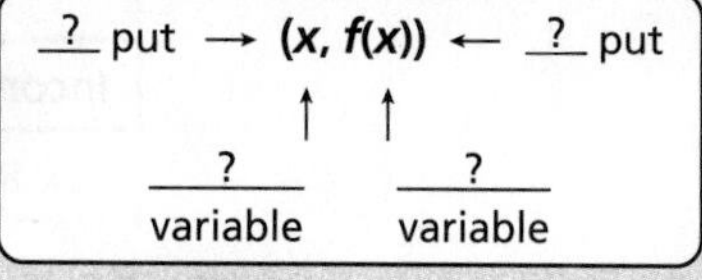

1-7 Exercises

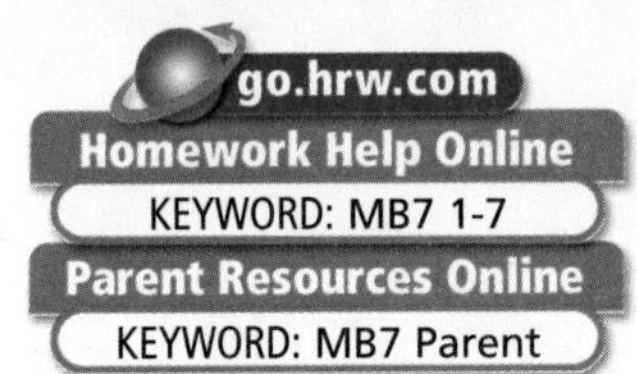

go.hrw.com
Homework Help Online
KEYWORD: MB7 1-7
Parent Resources Online
KEYWORD: MB7 Parent

GUIDED PRACTICE

1. **Vocabulary** In function notation, the variable x is generally used to represent the __?__ variable. (*dependent* or *independent*)

SEE EXAMPLE 1
p. 51

For each function, evaluate $f(0)$, $f(1.5)$, and $f(-4)$.

2. $f(x) = 3x - 4$
3. $f(x) = x^2 + 9$
4. $f(x) = 3x^2 - x + 2$

5.

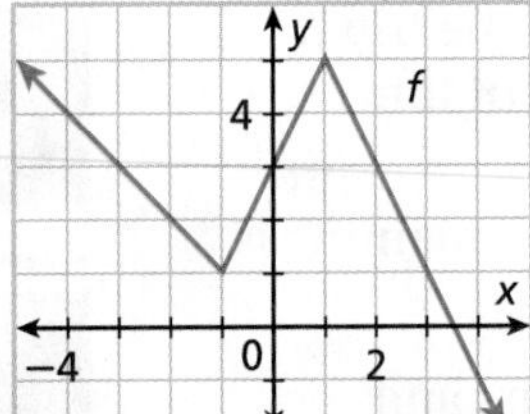

6.

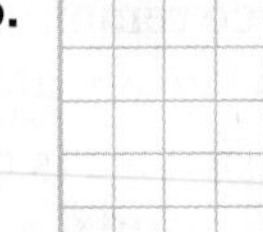

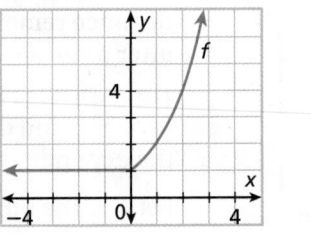

7.

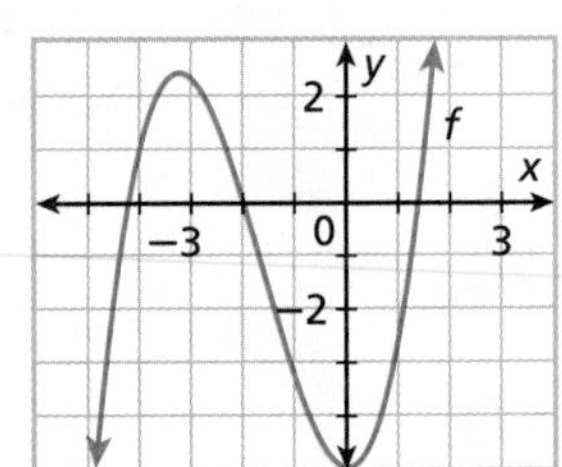

SEE EXAMPLE 2
p. 52

Graph each function.

8.

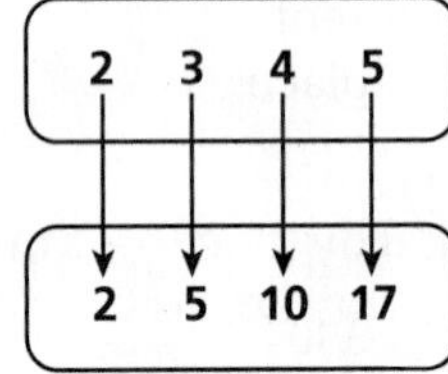

9. $g(x) = -3x + 12$

10.

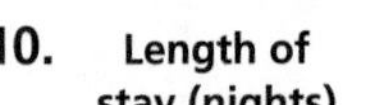

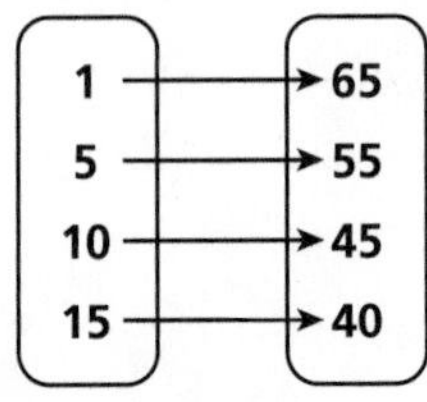

SEE EXAMPLE 3
p. 53

11. **Business** A furniture company misprinted a sales ad for a living room set but honors the advertised price. For each customer who purchases the living room set, the company suffers a loss of \$125. Write a function to represent the company's total loss. What is the value of the function for an input of 50, and what does it represent?

PRACTICE AND PROBLEM SOLVING

Independent Practice

For Exercises	See Example
12–17	1
18–20	2
21	3

Extra Practice

Skills Practice p. S5
Application Practice p. S32

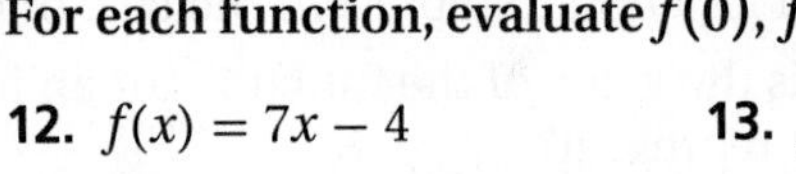

For each function, evaluate $f(0)$, $f\left(\frac{3}{2}\right)$, and $f(-1)$.

12. $f(x) = 7x - 4$
13. $f(x) = -x^2 + x$
14. $f(x) = -2x^2 + 1$

15.

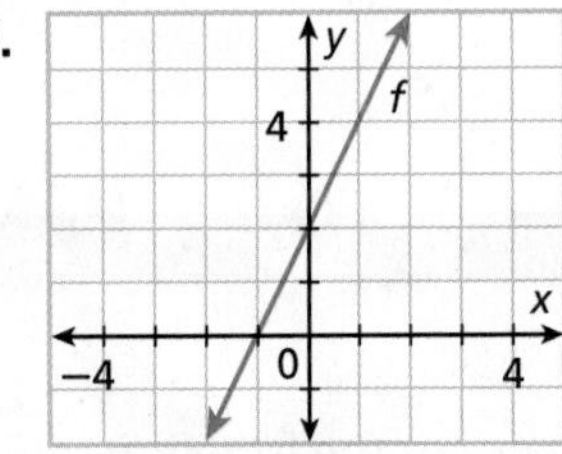

16.

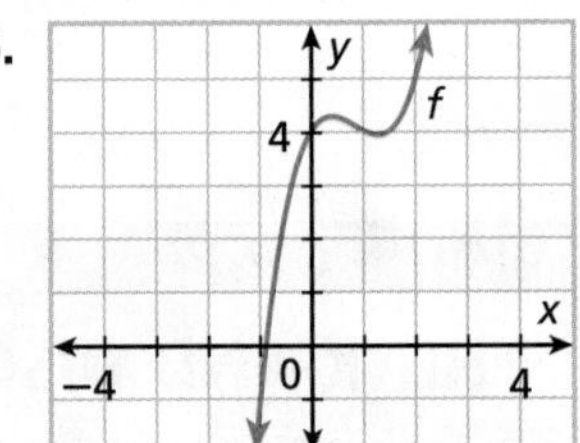

17.

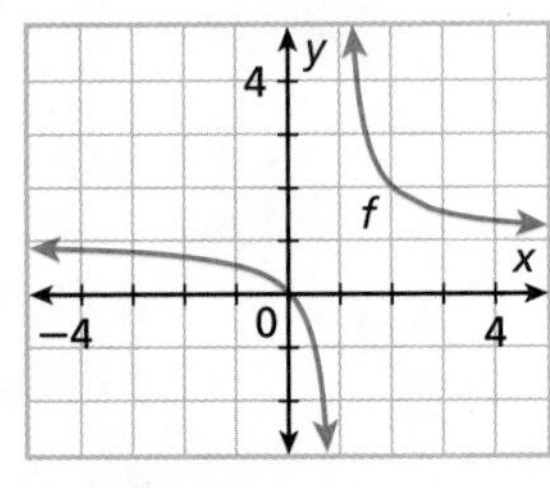

Graph each function.

18.

2003 Federal Income Tax Rates					
Income ($)	25,000	50,000	75,000	100,000	150,000
Tax Rate (%)	15	25	28	28	33

19. $f(x) = \sqrt{x}$ for $x \geq 0$

20. $f(x) = \frac{1}{2}x + 1$ for $-6 < x < 6$

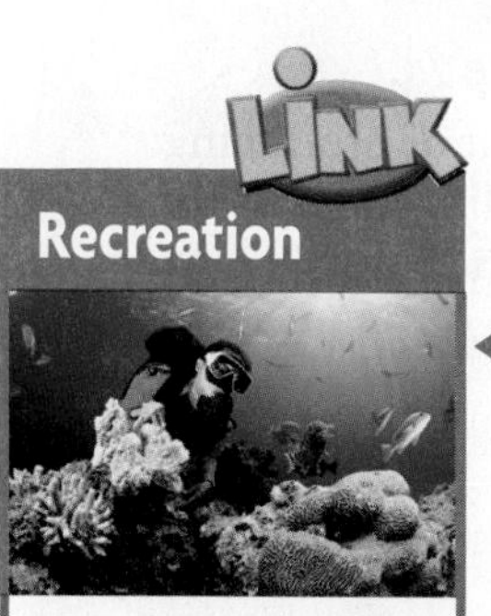

At a depth of 33 feet, a scuba diver is exposed to approximately twice the pressure he or she would experience at the surface.

21. **Safety** In a certain county, the fines for speeding in a school zone are \$160 plus an additional \$4 for every mile per hour over the speed limit. Write a function to represent the speeding fines. What is the value of the function for an input of 8, and what does it represent?

22. **Recreation** In order to scuba dive safely, divers must be aware that the water pressure in the ocean is a function of depth. The water pressure increases by 0.445 pounds per square inch (psi) for each foot of depth. The pressure at the surface is 14.7 psi. Write a function to represent water pressure. What is the value of the function for an input of 50, and what does it represent?

A set of input values is sometimes referred to as the *replacement set* for the independent variable. Evaluate each function for the given replacement set.

23. $f(x) = 3x - 6; \left\{-3.5, -1, \frac{1}{4}, 2, 11\right\}$

24. $f(x) = x(1 - 2x); \left\{-8, \frac{2}{3}, 1, 9, 4\right\}$

25. $f(x) = \frac{2x - 1}{3}; \left\{-4, 0, \frac{1}{2}, 5\right\}$

26. $f(x) = (x - 1)^2 + 4; \left\{-6, -\frac{3}{2}, 1, 4\right\}$

27.

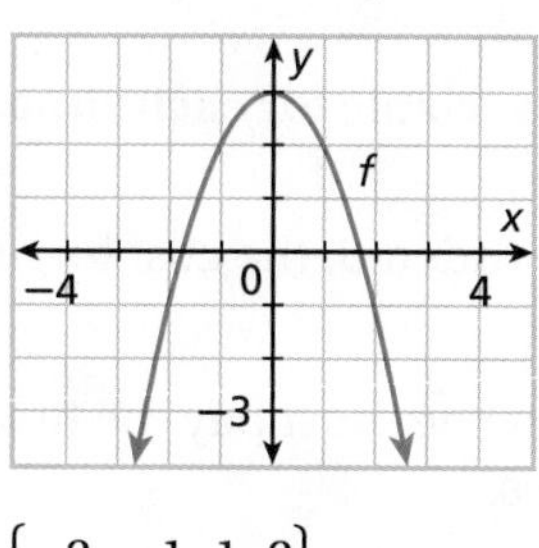

$\{-2, -1, 1, 2\}$

28.

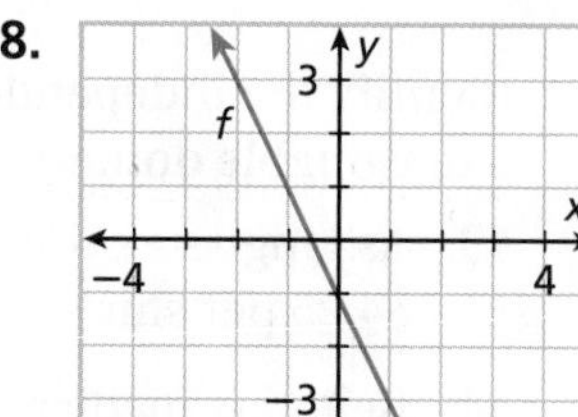

$\left\{-\frac{3}{2}, -1, 0, \frac{1}{2}\right\}$

Explain what a reasonable domain and range would be for each situation. Then explain why the situation represents a function.

29. the number of boxes of kitchen tile that must be purchased to cover a floor with an area of A square feet

30. the number of horseshoes needed to shoe h horses

31. the vertical position of a diver in relation to the surface of the pool t seconds after diving from a 10-meter platform into a 16-foot-deep pool (*Hint:* 1 meter ≈ 3.28 feet)

32. the temperature in degrees Fahrenheit at an Antarctic research station h hours after 12:00 A.M.

Banking **The graph at right shows the functions that represent two different savings plans. Use the graph for Exercises 33–37.**

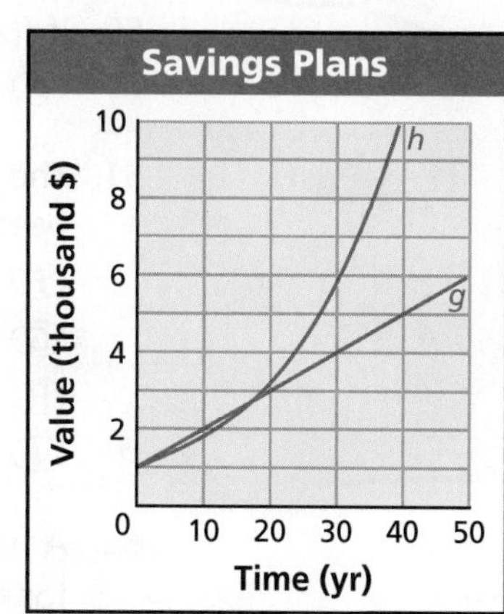

33. If t represents time in years, for what value of t will h have a value of \$7500? What does this value of t represent?

34. Use function notation to represent the value of each savings plan at 25 years. Estimate these values.

35. For what value of t is $g(t)$ approximately equal to $\frac{1}{2}h(t)$? Explain what this value of t represents.

36. Approximately how many years will it take for each savings plan to double from its original value?

37. What is the value of $h(40) - g(40)$, and what is its real-world meaning?

38. This problem will prepare you for the Multi-Step Test Prep on page 74.
   a. The function $c(p) = 175 + 3.5p$ can be used to define the cost of producing up to 200 ceramic pots. If the materials are \$175 and the additional cost to produce each pot is \$3.50, how much will it cost to produce 125 pots?
   b. How many pots can be produced if the budget is limited to \$450?
   c. What would the graph of this function look like?

Critical Thinking For Exercises 39–41, explain why $-5 < x < 5$ is not a reasonable domain for each function.

39. $f(x) = \dfrac{1}{x-3}$

40. $g(x) = \sqrt{x-1}$

41. $f(x)$ is the distance traveled in x hours at a rate of 55 mi/h.

42. If $f(2) = 8$ and $f(3) = 11$, name two points that lie on the graph of f.

Identify the independent and dependent variable for each situation. Then state a reasonable domain.

43. As long as a minimum of 15 shirts are ordered, the cost for an order of T-shirts is \$4.25 per shirt.

44. Belinda's medical insurance states that she must pay the first \$500 for a hospital stay plus 15% of the remaining charges.

Write a function to represent each situation. Graph your function.

45. The price for a tank of gasoline is \$2.37 per gallon.

46. Raul earns \$7.50 per hour for baby-sitting.

47. The sale price is 20% off of the original price.

48. Leona's weekly salary is \$250 plus 5% of her total sales for the week.

49. **Write About It** Explain what is meant by reasonable domain and range. Give examples.

50. If $f(x) = 5 - 3x$ and $g(x) = 12x + 2$, which statement is NOT true?
   Ⓐ $f(0) > g(0)$ Ⓑ $g(5) > f(5)$ Ⓒ $f(1) > g(1)$ Ⓓ $f(-1) > g(-1)$

51. The function $h(t) = 20t - 5t^2$ gives the height of an object t seconds after it has been thrown into the air. Which statement is true?
   Ⓕ The height at 4 seconds is the same as the height at 2 seconds.
   Ⓖ The height at 2 seconds is less than the height at 3 seconds.
   Ⓗ The height at 3 seconds is the same as the height at 1 second.
   Ⓙ The height at 4 seconds is greater than the height at 1 second.

52. A function is described by the equation $f(x) = -3x^2 + 12$. If the replacement set for the independent variable is $\{1, 3, 4, 9, 10\}$, which is an element of the corresponding set for the dependent variable?
   Ⓐ 1 Ⓑ 3 Ⓒ 4 Ⓓ 9

53. **Gridded Response** Given $f(x) = 3(x - 2)^2 + 4$, find $f(-1)$.

CHALLENGE AND EXTEND

Determine each value for the given function. Simplify your answer.

54. $f(2c)$ for $f(x) = \sqrt{x^3}$

55. $g\left(-\dfrac{h}{4}\right)$ for $g(x) = \dfrac{6x + h}{2x}$, where $h \neq 0$

56. $h(t^2 + 3t)$ for $h(x) = 4x + 7t$

57. $r(t^4)$ for $r(x) = \sqrt{x^2 + \left(\dfrac{2}{x}\right)^2}$

58. **Geometry** The area of a triangle is $\frac{1}{2}$ the product of its base length b and its height h.

a. If $b = 4$, explain whether the equation for the area of a triangle represents a function.

b. Explain whether the equation that represents the area of a triangle is a function for the domain $\{(b, h) \mid b > 0 \text{ and } h > 0\}$.

SPIRAL REVIEW

Simplify each expression. Assume all variables are nonzero. *(Lesson 1-4)*

59. $4(x + 2) - x(y - 8)$

60. $(2a)^2 + 6a^2$

61. $\dfrac{3c - 10 + 2c}{5c}$

62. $s(s + 7) - 4s$

Name the conditions for b that would make each set of ordered pairs a function. *(Lesson 1-6)*

63. $\{(1, 2), (6, 0), (0, 1), (-8, b)\}$

64. $\{(b, 2), (0, 3), (5, 4), (-3, 5)\}$

Determine whether each relation is a function. *(Lesson 1-6)*

65. $\left\{(-1, -5), (-2, 0.5), (-4, 5), \left(-5, \frac{1}{2}\right)\right\}$

66. $\{(-1, 3), (-1, 4), (-1, 5), (-1, 6)\}$

Career Path

go.hrw.com
Career Resources Online
KEYWORD: MB7 Career

Adam Leung
Radio announcer

Q: What math classes did you take in high school?

A: I took Algebra 1, Geometry, and Algebra 2.

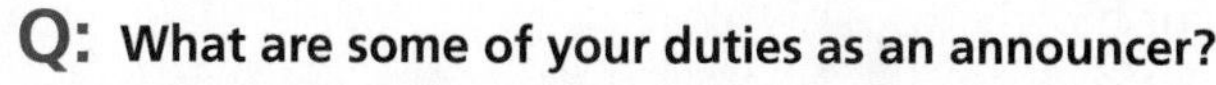

Q: What are some of your duties as an announcer?

A: During the day, I read the traffic reports and the news in addition to playing music. On weekends, I have more freedom to play music and take calls from listeners.

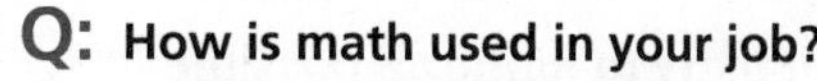

Q: How is math used in your job?

A: I've got to be sure all the scheduled music, ads, news, and traffic reports are covered in my shift. I use math to calculate how much time I need. I also use math to help create contests.

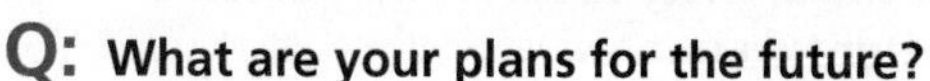

Q: What are your plans for the future?

A: I'll probably continue to work as an announcer for a while. After that, I'd like to become a station manager or a radio engineer. Engineers are responsible for making sure all the equipment at the station works properly.

Use with Lesson 1-8

Chess Translations

You can use the game of chess to explore transformations.

A chessboard consists of 64 squares arranged into 8 rows (numbered 1 through 8) and 8 columns (lettered *a* through *h*). Each square is named by its column letter and row number. For instance, the square in the lower left corner is **a1**.

Chessboard Notation

Selected Rules of Movement	
Bishop	Diagonally any number of squares
King	One square in any direction
Knight	L-shape: two squares horizontally or vertically and then one square perpendicularly
Rook	Horizontally or vertically any number of squares

You move each chess piece by applying the rules of movement. Pieces of the same color cannot move onto a space occupied by another piece, and the knight is the only piece that can jump over other pieces.

Activity

Use the chessboard at right to name all possible locations of the bishop on f7 after one move.

The bishop can move diagonally any number of spaces, but it cannot move into or through any other pieces.

The bishop at f7 can move to any of the marked spaces: e6, e8, g6, g8, or h5.

Try This

Use the chessboard from the activity to name all possible locations of each piece after one move.

1. the king on b1
2. the rook on d7
3. the knight on a6

Use the chessboard from the activity to name all possible locations of each piece after two moves.

4. the king on b1
5. the rook on d7
6. the knight on a6
7. **Critical Thinking** In the last move of a chess game a knight is moved to d5. What are the possible squares that it came from?
8. **Make a Conjecture** Explain the connection between the position labeling in chess and points in the coordinate plane.

1-8 Exploring Transformations

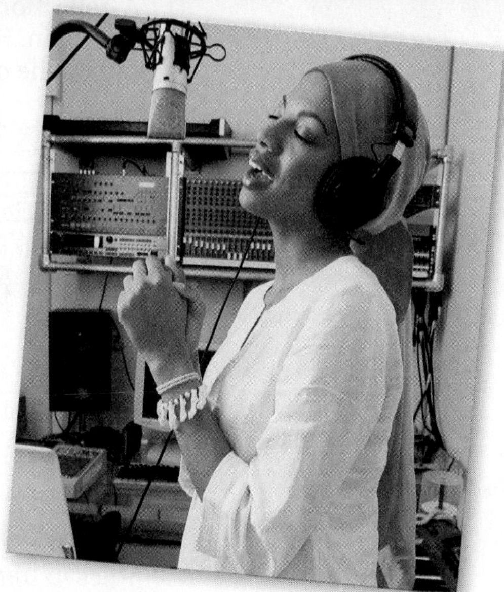

Objectives
Apply transformations to points and sets of points.
Interpret transformations of real-world data.

Vocabulary
transformation
translation
reflection
stretch
compression

Why learn this?
Changes in recording studio fees can be modeled by transformations. (See Example 4.)

A **transformation** is a change in the position, size, or shape of a figure. A **translation**, or slide, is a transformation that moves each point in a figure the same distance in the same direction.

EXAMPLE 1 Translating Points

Perform the given translation on the point $(2, -1)$. Give the coordinates of the translated point.

 **4 units left**

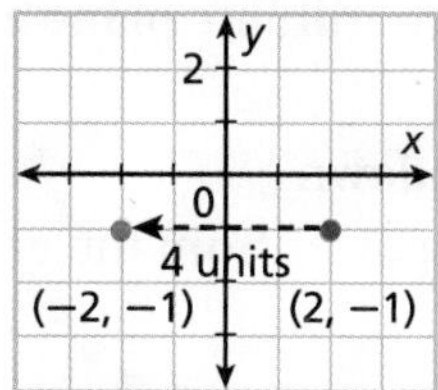

Translating $(2, -1)$ 4 units left results in the point $(-2, -1)$.

 **2 units right and 3 units up**

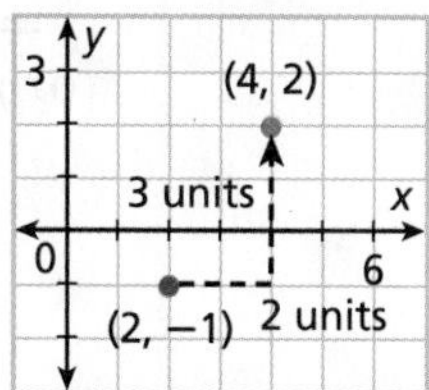

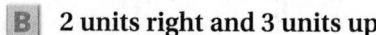

Translating $(2, -1)$ 2 units right and 3 units up results in the point $(4, 2)$.

Perform the given translation on the point $(-1, 3)$. Give the coordinates of the translated point.

1a. 4 units right

1b. 1 unit left and 2 units down

Notice that when you translate left or right, the x-coordinate changes, and when you translate up or down, the y-coordinate changes.

Translations

Horizontal Translation	Vertical Translation
Each point shifts *right* or *left* by a number of units.	Each point shifts *up* or *down* by a number of units.
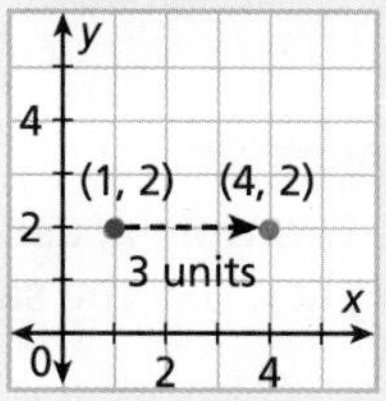 [graph: points (1, 2) and (4, 2), 3 units] The x-coordinate changes. $(1, 2) \rightarrow (1 + 3, 2)$ $(x, y) \rightarrow (x + h, y)$	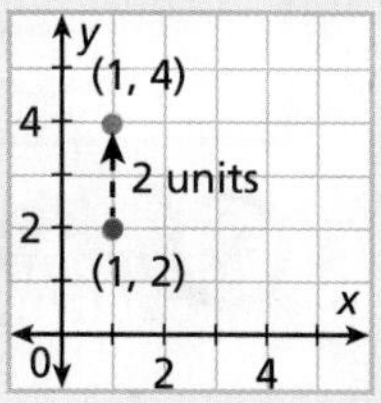 [graph: points (1, 2) and (1, 4), 2 units] The y-coordinate changes. $(1, 2) \rightarrow (1, 2 + 2)$ $(x, y) \rightarrow (x, y + k)$
left if $h < 0$ right if $h > 0$	down if $k < 0$ up if $k > 0$

A **reflection** is a transformation that flips a figure across a line called the line of reflection. Each reflected point is the same distance from the line of reflection, but on the opposite side of the line.

Know it! Note

Reflections	
Reflection Across y-axis	**Reflection Across x-axis**
Each point flips across the y-axis.	Each point flips across the x-axis.
(−1, 2) (1, 2) 1 unit 1 unit x y −2 0 2 The x-coordinate changes. $(1, 2) \rightarrow (-1, 2)$ $(x, y) \rightarrow (-x, y)$	y 2 (1, 2) 2 units x 0 2 units −2 (1, −2) The y-coordinate changes. $(1, 2) \rightarrow (1, -2)$ $(x, y) \rightarrow (x, -y)$

You can transform a function by transforming its ordered pairs. When a function is translated or reflected, the original graph and the graph of the transformation are *congruent* because the size and shape of the graphs are the same.

EXAMPLE 2 Translating and Reflecting Functions

Use a table to perform each transformation of $y = f(x)$. Use the same coordinate plane as the original function.

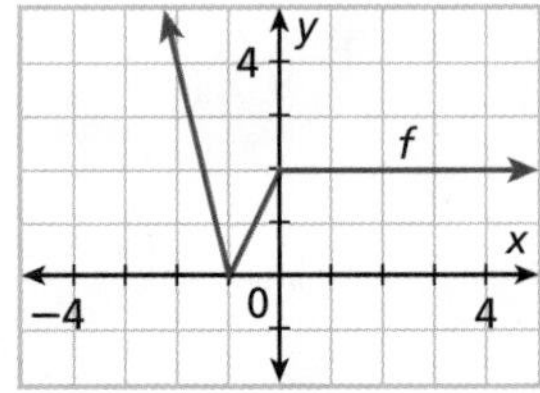

A translation 2 units down

Identify important points from the graph and make a table.

x	y	y − 2
−2	4	4 − 2 = 2
−1	0	0 − 2 = −2
0	2	2 − 2 = 0
2	2	2 − 2 = 0

The entire graph shifts 2 units down. Subtract 2 from each y-coordinate.

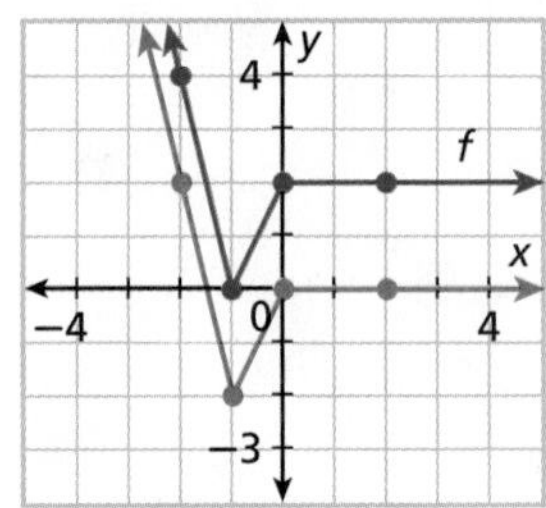

Helpful Hint

Transform *x* by adding a table column on the left side; transform *y* by adding a column on the right side.

B reflection across *y*-axis

Identify important points from the graph and make a table.

−x	x	y
−1(−2) = 2	−2	4
−1(−1) = 1	−1	0
−1(0) = 0	0	2
−1(2) = −2	2	2

Multiply each x-coordinate by −1. The entire graph flips across the y-axis.

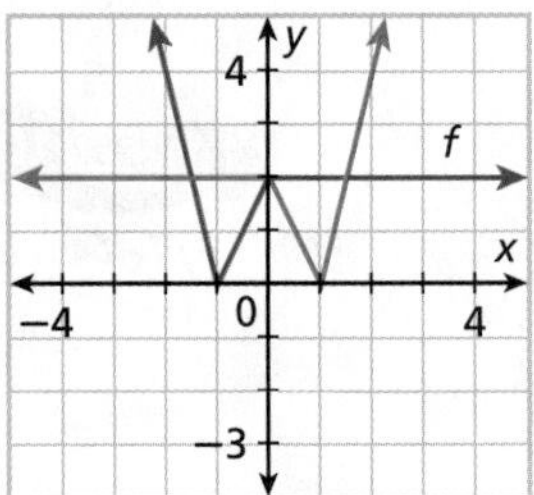

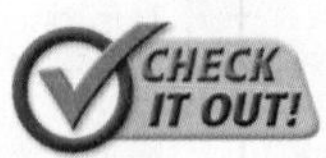

For the function from Example 2, use a table to perform each transformation of $y = f(x)$. Use the same coordinate plane as the original function.

2a. translation 3 units right **2b.** reflection across *x*-axis

Imagine grasping two points on the graph of a function that lie on opposite sides of the y-axis. If you pull the points away from the y-axis, you would create a horizontal **stretch** of the graph. If you push the points towards the y-axis, you would create a horizontal **compression**.

Stretches and compressions are not congruent to the original graph.

Stretches and Compressions		
	Horizontal	**Vertical**
Stretch	Each point is *pulled away* from the y-axis. The x-coordinate changes. $(4, 0) \rightarrow (2(4), 0)$ $(x, y) \rightarrow (bx, y)$ $\lvert b \rvert > 1$	Each point is *pulled away* from the x-axis. The y-coordinate changes. $(0, 4) \rightarrow (0, 2(4))$ $(x, y) \rightarrow (x, ay)$ $\lvert a \rvert > 1$
Compression	Each point is *pushed toward* the y-axis. The x-coordinate changes. $(4, 0) \rightarrow \left(\frac{1}{2}(4), 0\right)$ $(x, y) \rightarrow (bx, y)$ $0 < \lvert b \rvert < 1$	Each point is *pushed toward* the x-axis. The y-coordinate changes. $(0, 4) \rightarrow \left(0, \frac{1}{2}(4)\right)$ $(x, y) \rightarrow (x, ay)$ $0 < \lvert a \rvert < 1$

EXAMPLE 3 Stretching and Compressing Functions

Use a table to perform a horizontal compression of $y = f(x)$ by a factor of $\frac{1}{2}$. Use the same coordinate plane as the original function.

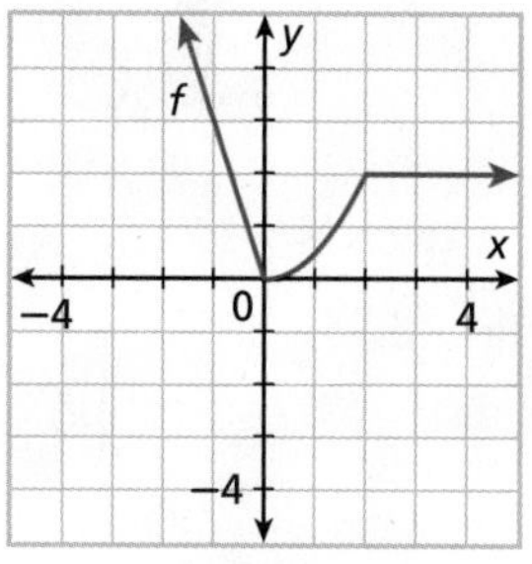

Identify important points from the graph and make a table.

$\frac{1}{2}x$	x	y
$\frac{1}{2}(-1) = -\frac{1}{2}$	−1	3
$\frac{1}{2}(0) = 0$	0	0
$\frac{1}{2}(2) = 1$	2	2
$\frac{1}{2}(4) = 2$	4	2

Multiply each x-coordinate by $\frac{1}{2}$.

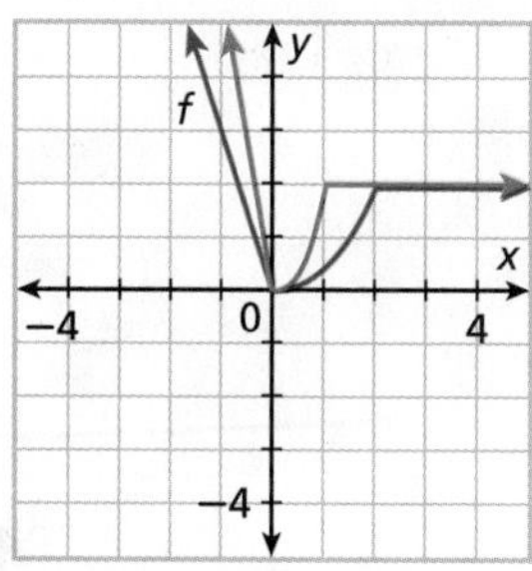

3. For the function from Example 3, use a table to perform a vertical stretch of $y = f(x)$ by a factor of 2. Graph the transformed function on the same coordinate plane as the original function.

EXAMPLE 4 Business Application

Recording studio fees are usually based on an hourly rate, but the rate can be modified due to various options. The graph shows a basic hourly studio rate. Sketch a graph to represent each situation below and identify the transformation of the original graph that it represents.

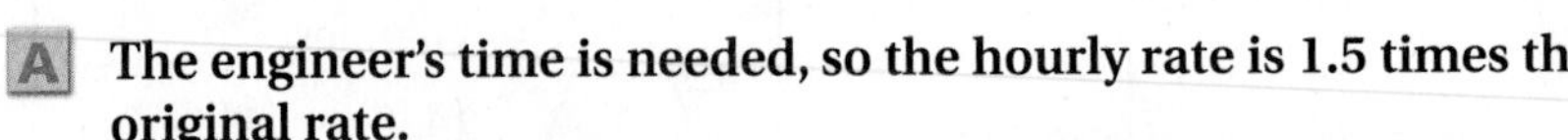

A The engineer's time is needed, so the hourly rate is 1.5 times the original rate.

If the fees are 1.5 times the basic hourly rate, the value of each y-coordinate would be multiplied by 1.5. This represents a vertical stretch by a factor of 1.5.

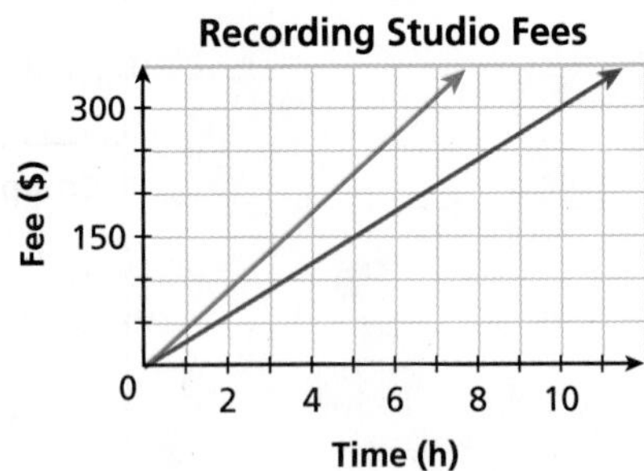

B A $20 setup fee is added to the basic hourly rate.

If the prices are $20 more than the original estimate, the value of each y-coordinate would increase by 20. This represents a vertical translation up 20 units.

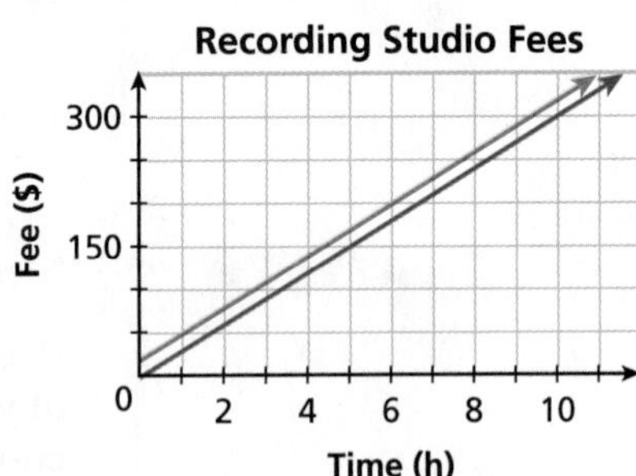

4. **What if...?** Suppose that a discounted rate is $\frac{3}{4}$ of the original rate. Sketch a graph to represent the situation and identify the transformation of the original graph that it represents.

THINK AND DISCUSS

1. Describe two ways to transform $(4, 2)$ to $(2, 2)$.
2. Compare a vertical stretch with a horizontal compression.

3. **GET ORGANIZED** Copy and complete the graphic organizer. In each box, describe the transformations indicated by the given rule.

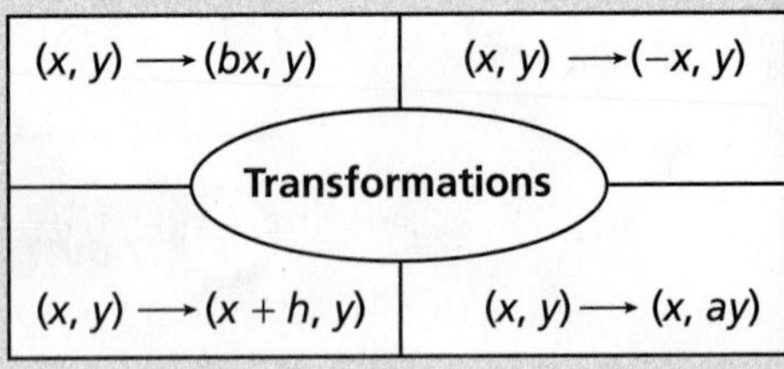

1-8 Exercises

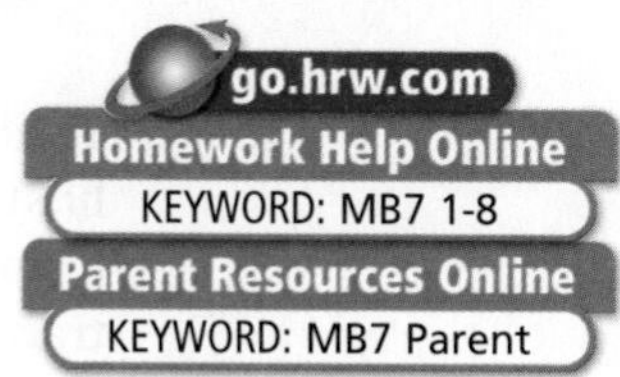

GUIDED PRACTICE

1. **Vocabulary** A transformation that pushes a graph toward the x-axis is a __?__. (*reflection* or *compression*)

SEE EXAMPLE 1 p. 59

Perform the given translation on the point $(4, 2)$ and give the coordinates of the translated point.

2. 5 units left
3. 3 units down
4. 1 unit right, 6 units up

SEE EXAMPLE 2 p. 60

Use a table to perform each transformation of $y = f(x)$. Use the same coordinate plane as the original function.

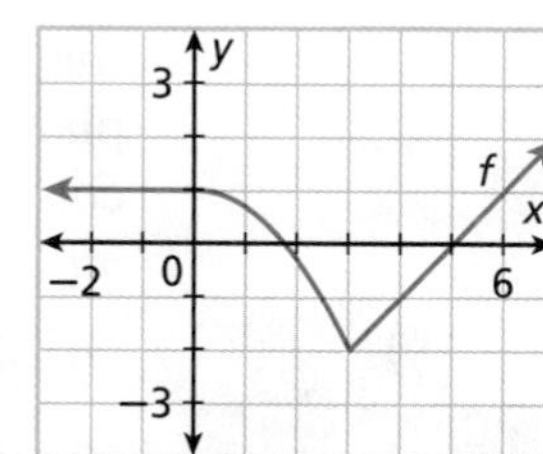

5. translation 2 units up
6. reflection across the y-axis
7. reflection across the x-axis

SEE EXAMPLE 3 p. 61

Use a table to perform each transformation of $y = f(x)$. Use the same coordinate plane as the original function.

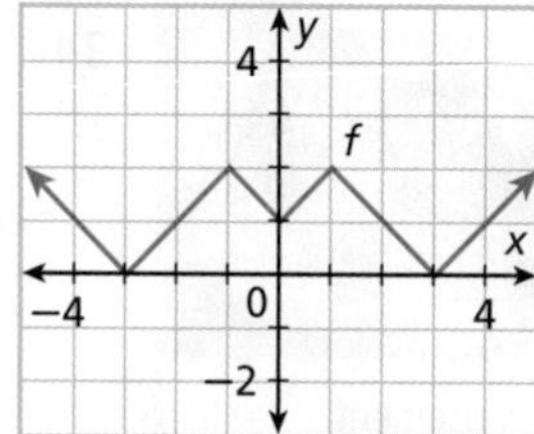

8. horizontal stretch by a factor of 3
9. vertical stretch by a factor of 3
10. vertical compression by a factor of $\frac{1}{3}$

SEE EXAMPLE 4 p. 62

Recreation **The graph shows the price for admission by age at a local zoo. Sketch a graph to represent each situation and identify the transformation of the original graph that it represents.**

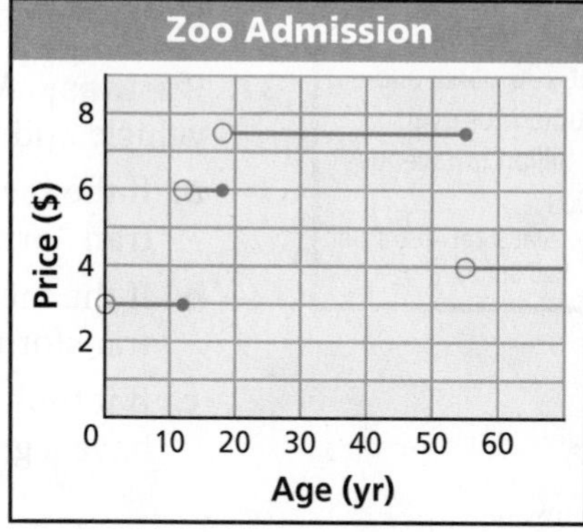

11. Admission is half price on Wednesdays.
12. To raise funds for endangered species, the zoo charges $1.50 extra per ticket.
13. The maximum age for each ticket price is increased by 5 years.

PRACTICE AND PROBLEM SOLVING

Independent Practice

For Exercises	See Example
14–16	1
17–20	2
21–24	3
25–27	4

Extra Practice

Skills Practice p. S5
Application Practice p. S32

Perform the given translation on $(3, 1)$. Give the coordinates of the translated point.

14. 2 units right
15. 4 units up
16. 5 units left, 4 units down

Use a table to perform each transformation of $y = f(x)$. Use the same coordinate plane as the original function.

17. translation 2 units down
18. reflection across the x-axis
19. translation 3 units right
20. reflection across the y-axis
21. vertical compression by a factor of $\frac{2}{3}$
22. horizontal compression by a factor of $\frac{1}{2}$
23. horizontal stretch by a factor of $\frac{3}{2}$
24. vertical stretch by a factor of 2

Technology **The graph shows the cost of Web page hosting depending on the Web space used. Sketch a graph to represent each situation and identify the transformation of the original graph that it represents.**

25. The prices are reduced by \$5.

26. The prices are discounted by 25%.

27. A special is offered for double the amount of Web space for the same price.

Web Page Hosting

Price (\$): 0, 20, 40, 60, 80

Web space (MB): 25, 50, 75, 100

Estimation **The table gives the coordinates for the vertices of a triangle. Estimate the area of each transformed triangle by graphing it and counting the number of squares it covers on the coordinate plane. How does the area of each transformed triangle compare with the area of the original triangle?**

x	y
−2	2
2	−4
4	−2

28. reflection across the y-axis

29. 5 units left, 3 units up

30. horizontal stretch by a factor of 2

31. horizontal compression by a factor of $\frac{2}{3}$

32. vertical compression by a factor of $\frac{2}{3}$

33. reflection across the x-axis

34. 1 unit left, 6 units down

35. vertical stretch by a factor of 3

LINK

Entertainment

The amusement park industry in the United States includes about 700 parks and accounted for over \$8.5 billion in revenues in 2001.

Source: Statistical Abstract of the United States

36. **Entertainment** The revenue from an amusement park ride is given by the admission price of \$3 times the number of riders. As part of a promotion, the first 10 riders ride for free.

    a. What kind of transformation describes the change in the revenue based on the promotion?

    b. Write a function rule for this transformation.

37. **Business** An automotive mechanic charges \$50 to diagnose the problem in a vehicle and \$65 per hour for labor to fix it.

    a. If the mechanic increases his diagnostic fee to \$60, what kind of transformation is this to the graph of the total repair bill?

    b. If the mechanic increases his labor rate to \$75 per hour, what kind of transformation is this to the graph of the total repair bill?

    c. If it took 3 hours to repair your car, which of the two rate increases would have a greater effect on your total bill?

MULTI-STEP TEST PREP

38. This problem will prepare you for the Multi-Step Test Prep on page 74.

    The student council wants to buy vases for the flowers for the school prom. A florist charges a \$20 delivery fee plus \$1.25 per vase. A home-decorating store charges a \$10 delivery fee plus \$1.25 per vase.

    a. The function $f(x) = 20 + 1.25x$ models the cost of ordering x vases from the florist, and the function $g(x) = 10 + 1.25x$ models the cost of ordering x vases from the home-decorating store. What do the graphs of these functions look like?

    b. How are the graphs related to each other?

    c. How could you modify these functions so that their graphs are identical?

    d. If the florist decided to waive the \$20 delivery fee as long as the number of vases ordered was more than 150, how would the graph of f change? How would it compare with the graph of the other function?

Transportation **Use the graph and the following information for Exercises 39–43.**

Roberta left her house at 10:00 A.M. and drove to the library. She was at the library studying until 11:30 A.M. Then she drove to the grocery store. At 12:15 P.M. Roberta left the grocery store and drove home. The graph shows Roberta's position with respect to time.

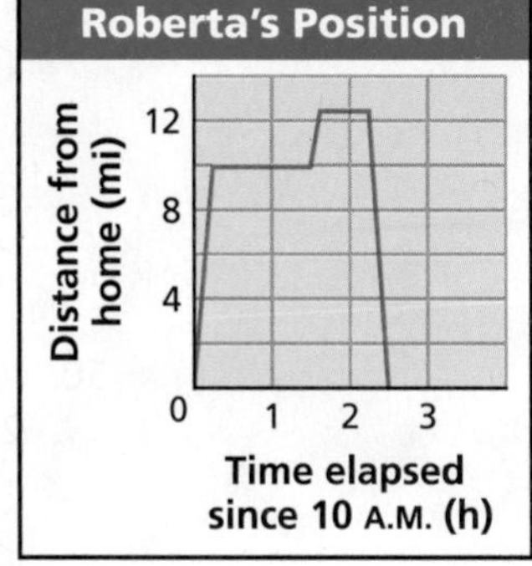

Sketch a graph to reflect each change to the original story. Assume the time Roberta spends inside each building remains the same.

39. Roberta drove at half the speed from her house to the library.

40. The grocery store she went to is twice as far from the library.

41. The grocery store is 2.5 miles closer to the house than the library is.

Change the original story about Roberta to match each graph.

42.

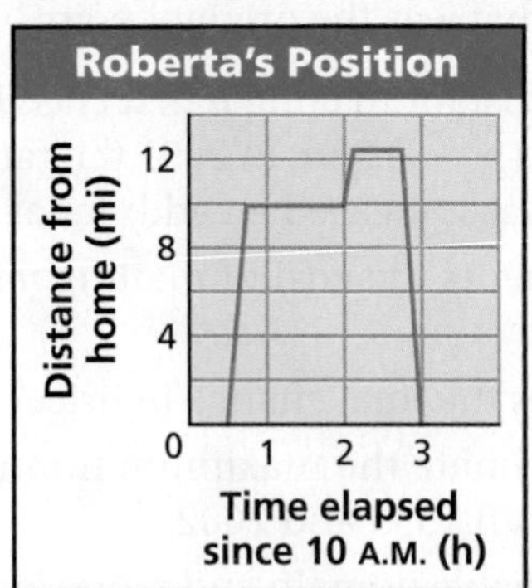

43.

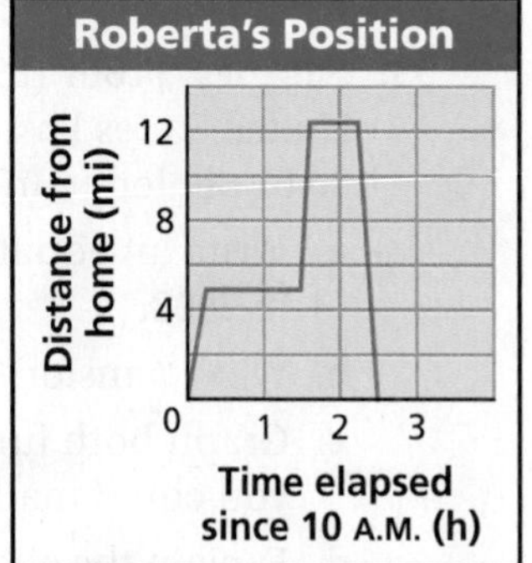

44. **Critical Thinking** Suppose two transformations are performed on a single point: a translation and a reflection. Does the order in which the transformations are performed make a difference? Does the type of translation or reflection matter? Explain your reasoning.

45. **Write About It** Describe how transformations might make graphing easier.

46. The function $c(p) = 0.99p$ represents the cost in dollars of p pounds of peaches. If the cost per pound increases by 10%, how will the graph of the function change?

Ⓐ Translation 0.1 unit up
Ⓑ Translation 0.1 unit right
Ⓒ Horizontal stretch by a factor of 1.1
Ⓓ Vertical stretch by a factor of 1.1

47. Which transformation would change the point $(5, 3)$ into $(-5, 3)$?

Ⓕ Reflection across the x-axis
Ⓖ Translation 5 units down
Ⓗ Reflection across the y-axis
Ⓙ Translation 5 units left

48. The graph of the function f is a line that intersects the y-axis at the point $(0, 3)$ and the x-axis at the point $(3, 0)$. Which transformation of f does NOT intersect the y-axis at the point $(0, 6)$?

Ⓐ Translation 3 units up
Ⓑ Translation 3 units right
Ⓒ Vertical stretch by a factor of 2
Ⓓ Horizontal compression by a factor of $\frac{1}{2}$

49. Which transformation is displayed in the graph?

Ⓕ Reflection across the x-axis

Ⓖ Translation 5 units down

Ⓗ Reflection across the y-axis

Ⓙ Translation 5 units left

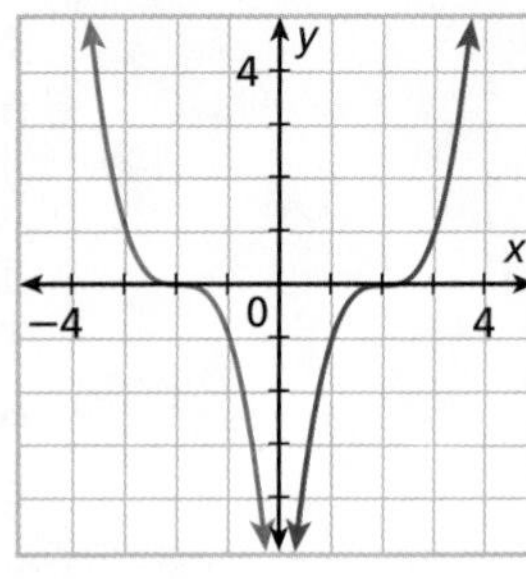

50. Which represents a translation 4 units right and 2 units down?

Ⓐ From (4, 2) to (0, 0)

Ⓑ From (4, −2) to (0, 0)

Ⓒ From (−4, −2) to (0, 0)

Ⓓ From (−4, 2) to (0, 0)

51. **Short Response** Graph the points (−1, 3) and (−1, −3). Describe two different transformations that would transform (−1, 3) to (−1, −3).

CHALLENGE AND EXTEND

52. Suppose the rule $(x, y) \rightarrow (2x, y - 3)$ is used to translate a point. If the coordinates of the translated point are (22, 7), what was the original point?

53. **History** From 1999 to 2001 the cost for mailing n first class letters through the United States Postal Service was $c(n) = 0.33n$. In 2001 the rate was increased by \$0.01 per letter. In 2002 the rate was increased an additional \$0.03 per letter.

  a. Write an equation that represents the cost of mailing n first class letters in 2002.

  b. What transformation describes the total change in price?

  c. Graph both functions and estimate the maximum number of first class letters you could mail for \$5.00 in both 1999 and 2002.

  d. Explain the effect of the reasonable domain and range for these functions on your answer for part **c**.

54. Name a point that when reflected across the x-axis has the same coordinates as if it were reflected across the y-axis. How many points are there that satisfy this condition?

SPIRAL REVIEW

55. **Sports** Katrina's mean bowling score for three games was 144. If the score of her first game was 172 and the score of her second game was 150, what was the score of her third game? *(Previous course)*

Use the vertical-line test to determine whether each relation is a function. *(Lesson 1-6)*

56.

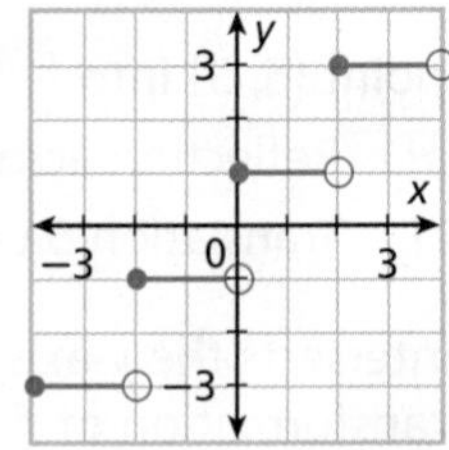

57.

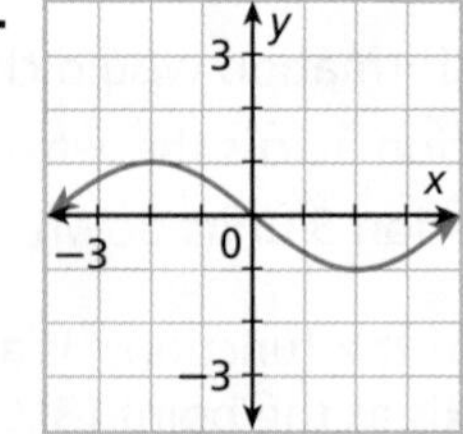

58.

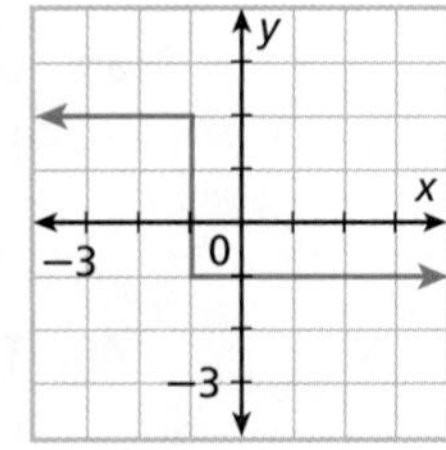

For each function evaluate $f(1)$, $f(-3)$, and $f\left(\frac{1}{4}\right)$. *(Lesson 1-7)*

59. $f(x) = \dfrac{4x - 5}{2}$

60. $f(x) = 2x^3$

61. $f(x) = (1 - x^2)^2$

1-9 Introduction to Parent Functions

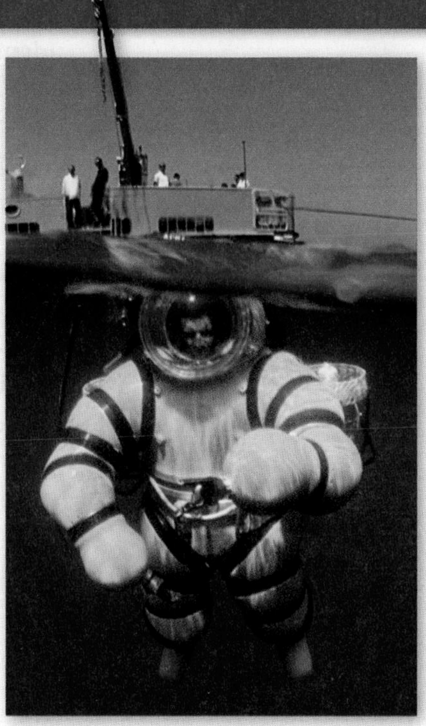

Objectives
Identify parent functions from graphs and equations.

Use parent functions to model real-world data and make estimates for unknown values.

Vocabulary
parent function

Who uses this?
Oceanographers use transformations of parent functions to approximate data sets such as wave height versus wind speed. (See Example 3.)

Similar to the way that numbers are classified into sets based on common characteristics, functions can be classified into *families of functions*. The **parent function** is the simplest function with the defining characteristics of the family. Functions in the same family are transformations of their parent function.

Parent Functions					
Family	Constant	Linear	Quadratic	Cubic	Square root
Rule	$f(x) = c$	$f(x) = x$	$f(x) = x^2$	$f(x) = x^3$	$f(x) = \sqrt{x}$
Graph					
Domain	$\mathbb{R}$	$\mathbb{R}$	$\mathbb{R}$	$\mathbb{R}$	$x \geq 0$
Range	$y = c$	$\mathbb{R}$	$y \geq 0$	$\mathbb{R}$	$y \geq 0$
Intersects *y*-axis	$(0, c)$	$(0, 0)$	$(0, 0)$	$(0, 0)$	$(0, 0)$

EXAMPLE 1 Identifying Transformations of Parent Functions

Identify the parent function for *g* from its function rule. Then graph *g* on your calculator and describe what transformation of the parent function it represents.

A $g(x) = x + 5$

$g(x) = x + 5$ is linear. *x has a power of 1.*

The linear parent function $f(x) = x$ intersects the y-axis at the point $(0, 0)$.

Graph $\mathbf{Y_1 = X + 5}$ on a graphing calculator. The function $g(x) = x + 5$ intersects the y-axis at the point $(0, 5)$.

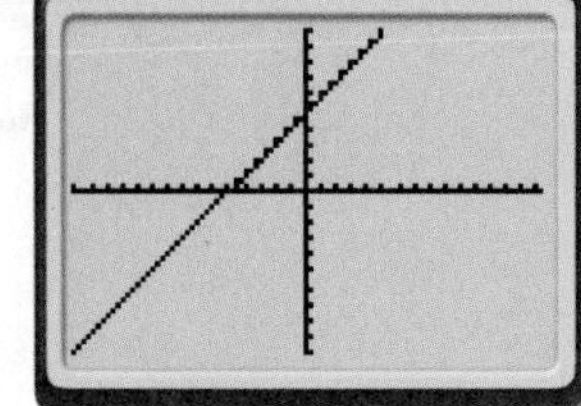

So $g(x) = x + 5$ represents a vertical translation of the linear parent function 5 units up.

Helpful Hint

To make graphs appear accurate on a graphing calculator, use the standard square window. Press  ZOOM, choose **6:ZStandard**, press ZOOM again, and choose **5:ZSquare**.

Identify the parent function for g from its function rule. Then graph g on your calculator and describe what transformation of the parent function it represents.

B $g(x) = (x - 3)^2$

$g(x) = (x - 3)^2$ is quadratic. *$x - 3$ has a power of 2.*

The quadratic parent function $f(x) = x^2$ intersects the x-axis at the point $(0, 0)$.

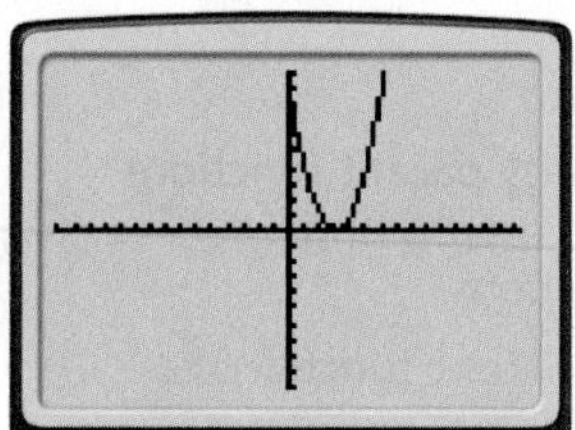

Graph $Y_1 = (X - 3)^2$ on a graphing calculator. The function $g(x) = (x - 3)^2$ intersects the x-axis at the point $(3, 0)$.

So $g(x) = (x - 3)^2$ represents a horizontal translation of the quadratic parent function 3 units right.

Identify the parent function for g from its function rule. Then graph g on your calculator and describe what transformation of the parent function it represents.

1a. $g(x) = x^3 + 2$ **1b.** $g(x) = (-x)^2$

It is often necessary to work with a set of data points like the ones represented by the table at right.

x	−4	−2	0	2	4
y	8	2	0	2	8

With only the information in the table, it is impossible to know the exact behavior of the data between and beyond the given points. However, a working knowledge of the parent functions can allow you to sketch a curve to approximate those values not found in the table.

EXAMPLE 2 Identifying Parent Functions to Model Data Sets

Graph the data from the table. Describe the parent function and the transformation that best approximates the data set.

x	−4	−2	0	2	4
y	8	2	0	2	8

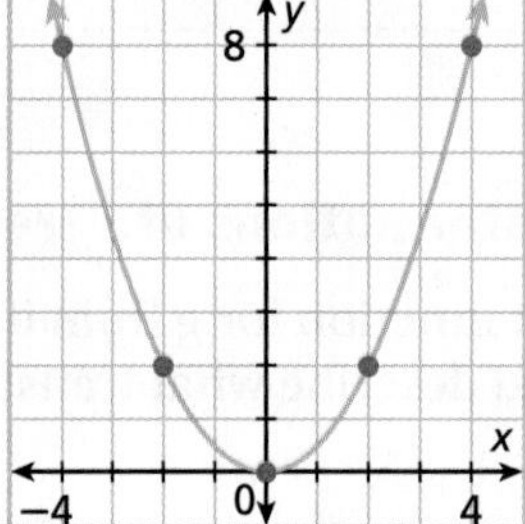

The graph of the data points resembles the shape of the quadratic parent function $f(x) = x^2$.

The quadratic parent function passes through the points $(2, 4)$ and $(4, 16)$. The data set contains the points

$(2, 2) = \left(2, \frac{1}{2}(4)\right)$ and $(4, 8) = \left(2, \frac{1}{2}(16)\right)$.

The data set seems to represent a vertical compression of the quadratic parent function by a factor of $\frac{1}{2}$.

2. Graph the data from the table. Describe the parent function and the transformation that best approximates the data set.

x	−4	−2	0	2	4
y	−12	−6	0	6	12

Consider the two data points $(0, 0)$ and $(1, 1)$. If you plot them on a coordinate plane you might very well think that they are part of a linear function. In fact they belong to each of the parent functions below.

Linear	Quadratic	Cubic	Square Root
$f(x) = x$	$f(x) = x^2$	$f(x) = x^3$	$f(x) = \sqrt{x}$

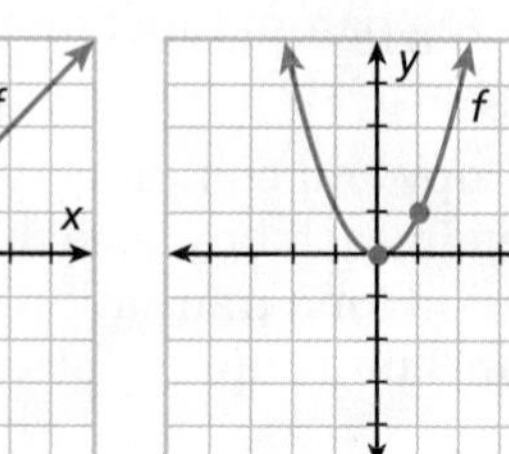
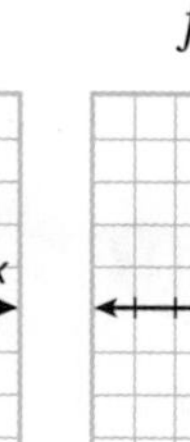

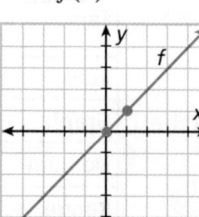

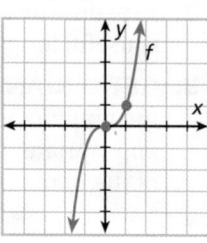

Helpful Hint

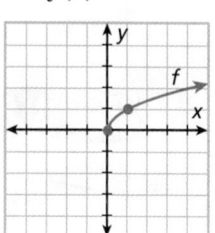

A greater number of data points increases your chances of correctly identifying the parent function that best describes the data.

Remember that any parent function you use to approximate a set of data should never be considered exact. However, these function approximations are often useful for estimating unknown values.

EXAMPLE 3 *Oceanography Application*

An oceanographer wants to determine a model that can be used to estimate wind speed based upon wave height. Graph the relationship from wave height to wind speed and identify which parent function best describes it. Then use the graph to estimate the wave height when the wind speed is 10 knots.

Ocean Waves	
Wave Height (ft)	**Wind Speed (knots)**
2	8.8
4	12.4
6	15.2
8	17.5
10	19.6

Step 1 Graph the relation.

Graph the points given in the table. Draw a smooth curve through them to help you see the shape.

Step 2 Identify the parent function.

The graph of the data set resembles the shape of the square-root parent function $f(x) = \sqrt{x}$.

Step 3 Estimate the wave height when the wind speed is 10 knots.

The curve indicates that a wind speed of 10 knots would create a wave that is approximately 2.5 feet high.

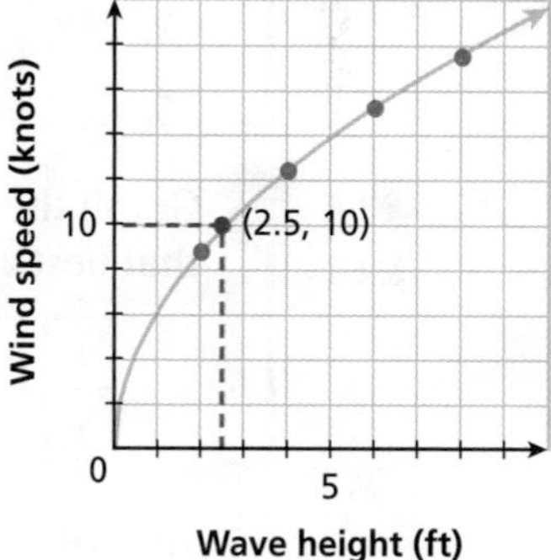

3. The cost of playing an online video game depends on the number of months for which the online service is used. Graph the relationship from number of months to cost, and identify which parent function best describes the data. Then use the graph to estimate the cost for 5 months of online service.

Cost of Online Video Game					
Time (mo)	1	3	6	9	12
Cost ($)	40	56	80	104	128

THINK AND DISCUSS

1. Explain how to determine the parent function for a given equation.
2. Explain why recognizing parent functions is useful for graphing.

3. **GET ORGANIZED** Copy and complete the graphic organizer. In each box, give the appropriate information for a translation of the parent function 3 units up.

Transformed Parent Functions			
Family	Linear	Quadratic	Square root
Rule			
Graph			
Domain			
Range			
Intersects *y*-axis			

1-9 Exercises

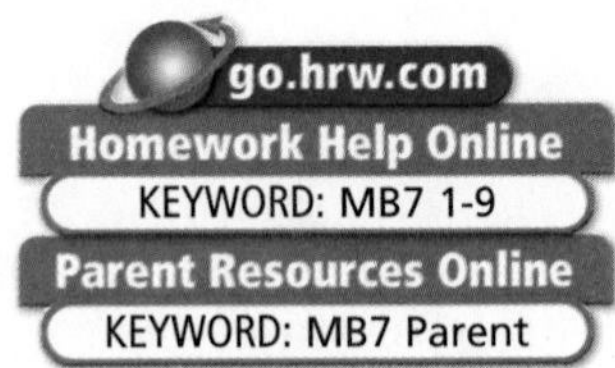

GUIDED PRACTICE

1. **Vocabulary** Explain how transformations, families of functions, and *parent functions* are related.

SEE EXAMPLE 1 p. 67

Identify the parent function for *g* from its function rule. Then graph *g* on your calculator and describe what transformation of the parent function it represents.

2. $g(x) = (x - 1)^3$
3. $g(x) = (x + 1)^2$
4. $g(x) = -x$
5. $g(x) = \sqrt{x + 3}$
6. $g(x) = x^2 + 4$
7. $g(x) = x - \sqrt{2}$

SEE EXAMPLE 2 p. 68

Graph the data from the table. Describe the parent function and the transformation that best approximates the data set.

8.

x	−3	−1	0	1	3
y	−15	−5	0	5	15

9.

x	−3	−1	0	1	3
y	−1	$-\frac{1}{27}$	0	$\frac{1}{27}$	1

SEE EXAMPLE 3 p. 69

10. **Physics** The time it takes a pendulum to make one complete swing back and forth depends on its string length.
    a. Graph the relationship from string length to time.
    b. Identify which parent function best describes the data.
    c. Use your graph to estimate the string length of a pendulum that takes 4.5 seconds to make one complete swing.
    d. Use your graph to estimate the time it takes to make a complete swing for a string of length 14 meters.

Pendulum Swing	
String Length (m)	**Time (s)**
2	2.8
4	4.0
6	4.9
8	5.7
10	6.3

PRACTICE AND PROBLEM SOLVING

Independent Practice	
For Exercises	See Example
11–13	1
14–15	2
16	3

Extra Practice

Skills Practice p. S5

Application Practice p. S32

Identify the parent function for g from its function rule. Then graph g on your calculator and describe what transformation of the parent function it represents.

11. $g(x) = x^2 - 1$ **12.** $g(x) = \sqrt{x - 2}$ **13.** $g(x) = x^3 + 3$

Graph the data from the table. Describe the parent function and the transformation that best approximates the data set.

14.

x	-3	-1	0	1	3
y	3	$\frac{1}{3}$	0	$\frac{1}{3}$	3

15.

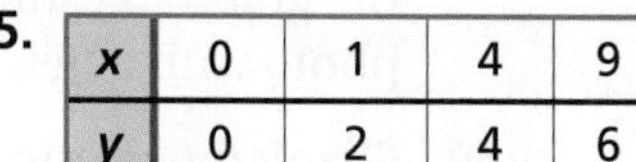

x	0	1	4	9	16
y	0	2	4	6	8

16. Geometry The number of segments required to connect a given number of points is shown in the table.

a. Graph the relationship from the number of points to the number of segments.

b. Identify which parent function best describes the data.

c. Use your graph to estimate the number of points if there are 45 segments.

d. Use your graph to estimate the number of segments if there are 7 points.

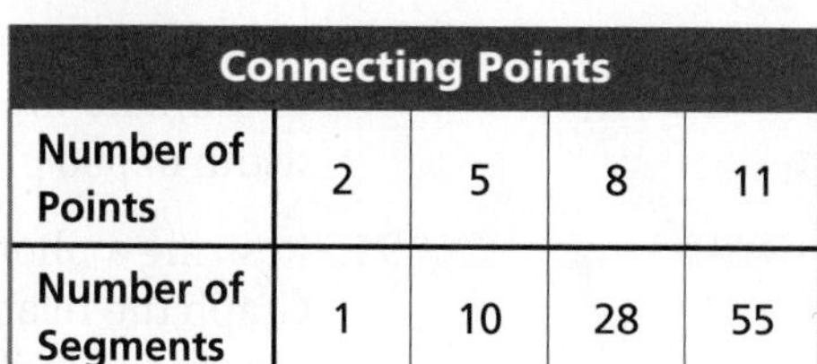

Connecting Points				
Number of Points	2	5	8	11
Number of Segments	1	10	28	55

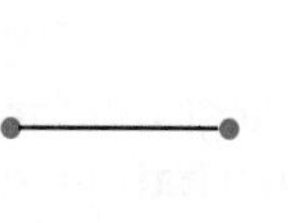

2 points
1 segment

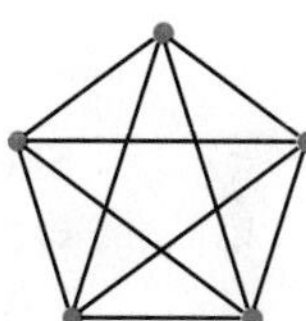

5 points
10 segments

Graphing Calculator **Graph each function with a graphing calculator. Identify the domain and range of the function, and describe the transformation from its parent function.**

17. $g(x) = 3\sqrt{x}$ **18.** $g(x) = \frac{2}{3}x$ **19.** $g(x) = -\sqrt{x}$

20. $g(x) = -(x - 2)^2$ **21.** $g(x) = -x^2 + 1$ **22.** $g(x) = -\frac{1}{2}x^3$

23. Sports Based on the information in the table, what is the total cost of 15 tickets to the hockey game? Explain how you determined your answer.

Hockey Tickets				
Number of Tickets	1	5	8	12
Total Cost ($)	13	65	104	156

Graph each function. Identify the parent function that best describes the set of points, and describe the transformation from the parent function.

24. $\{(-2, 8), (-1, 1), (0, 0), (1, -1), (2, -8)\}$ **25.** $\{(5, 4), (7, 0), (9, 4), (10, 9), (11, 16)\}$

26. $\{(0, 0), (-1, 1), (-4, 2), (-9, 3), (-16, 4)\}$ **27.** $\{(-4, 3), (-2, 1), (0, -1), (2, -3), (4, -5)\}$

28. This problem will prepare you for the Multi-Step Test Prep on page 74.

a. One function used in the Multi-Step Test Prep in Lesson 1-8 was $f(x) = 20 + 1.25x$. What is its parent function?

b. The graph for a given function has a U shape. What could be the parent function?

c. Plot the data set $\{(0, 0), (1, 2), (4, 4), (9, 6), (16, 8), (25, 10)\}$. Which parent function best models the data set?

Photography When resizing a digital photo, it is often important to preserve its *aspect ratio*, the ratio of its width to its height. Use the table for Exercises 29–31.

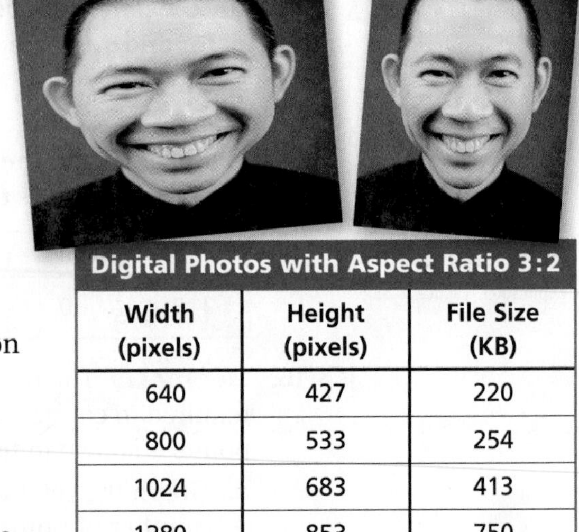

Digital Photos with Aspect Ratio 3:2

Width (pixels)	Height (pixels)	File Size (KB)
640	427	220
800	533	254
1024	683	413
1280	853	750

29. Graph the relationship from width to height and identify which parent function best describes the data. Use the graph to estimate the width of a photo with a height of 1000 pixels.

30. Graph the relationship from height to width and identify which parent function best describes the data. Use the graph to estimate the height of a photo with a width of 500 pixels.

31. Resizing a photo changes the file size. Graph the relationship from width to file size and identify which parent function best describes the data. Use the graph to estimate the width of a photo with a file size of 1000 KB.

Sketch a graph for each situation and identify the related parent function. Then explain what the reasonable domain and range for the function is and compare it with the domain and range of the parent function.

32. distance traveled after h hours at a speed of 55 mi/h

33. volume of a cube with side length ℓ

34. area of a room with width w and a length of 15 feet

35. cost to wash n loads of laundry at $1.00 per load

36. cost of an item with original price p after a 15% discount

37. side length of a square with area A

LINK

Chemistry

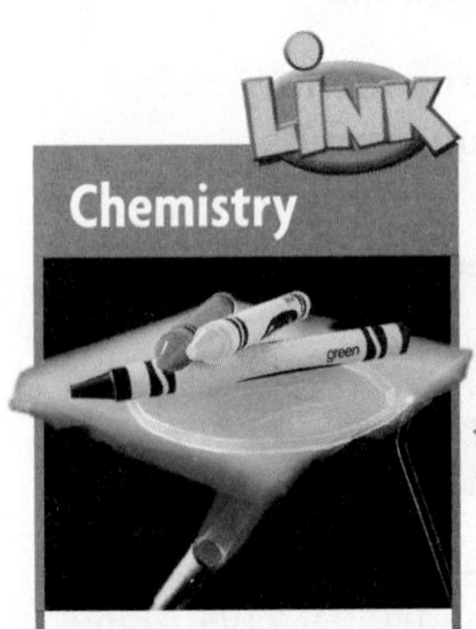

Aerogel has been called the world's lowest density solid. It is 99.8% air and is an excellent heat insulator. As shown above, a layer of aerogel can prevent a flame from melting crayons.

38. **Chemistry** The table shows properties of aerogel. Graph the relationship from mass to volume, and then estimate the volume of 1 gram of aerogel.

Aerogel Properties

Mass (mg)	30	90	300	450
Volume (cm³)	10	30	100	150

39. **What if...?** Use the set of points $\{(-1, -1), (0, 0), (1, 1)\}$ to answer each question.

a. What parent function best describes the set of points?

b. If the points $(-2, 8)$ and $(2, 8)$ were added, what parent function would best describe the set?

c. If the point $(1, 1)$ were replaced with $(1, -1)$, what parent function would best describe the set?

d. If the point $(-1, -1)$ were replaced with $(4, 2)$, what parent function would best describe the set?

e. **Multi-Step** If the x-coordinate of each point were doubled and 3 were added to each y-coordinate, what parent function would best describe the set? What transformation of the parent function would the set represent?

40. **Critical Thinking** Explain any relationship you have noticed between the quadratic parent function and a function rule that represents a horizontal translation, a vertical translation, or a reflection across the x-axis.

41. Write About It Order the parent functions covered in this lesson from least to greatest by the rate at which $f(x)$ increases as x increases for $x > 1$. Explain your answer.

TEST PREP

42. Which situation could be represented by the graph?

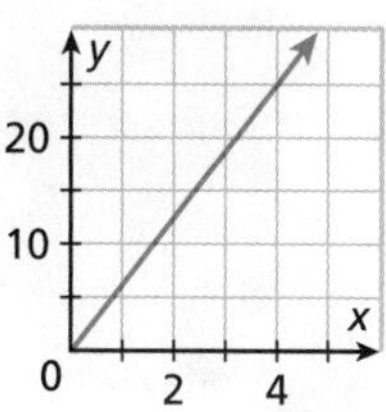

(A) The area of a circle based on its radius
(B) The volume of a sphere based on its radius
(C) The surface area of a sphere based on its radius
(D) The circumference of a circle based on its radius

43. Which graph best represents the function $f(x) = 2x^2 - 2$?

(F) 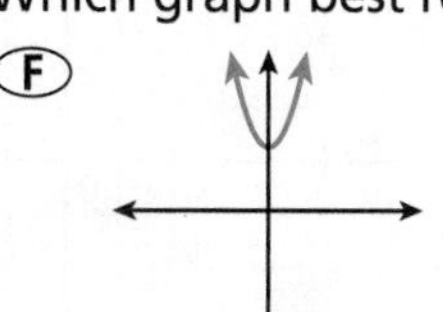 (G) 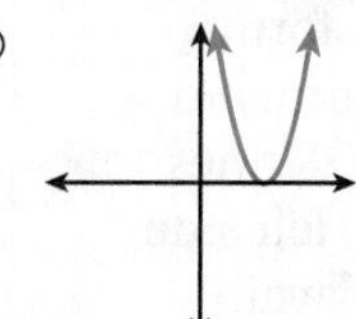 (H) 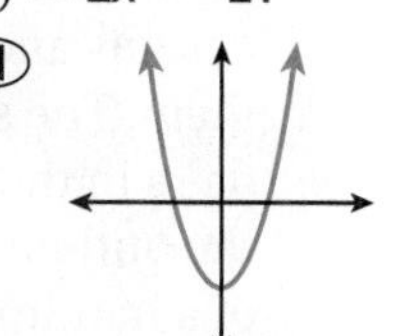 (J) 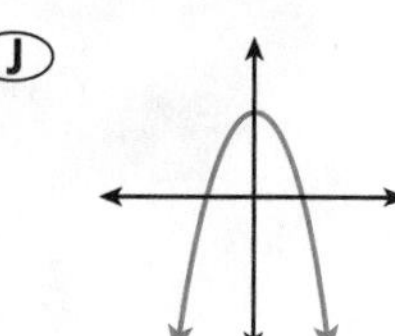

44. Which equation describes a relationship in which every nonzero real number x corresponds to a negative real number y?

(A) $y = -x^3$ (B) $y = -x^2$ (C) $y = (-x)^2$ (D) $y = -x$

45. For which function is -1 NOT an element of the range?

(F) $y = -1$ (G) $y = (-x)^2$ (H) $y = -x$ (J) $y = x^3$

46. What type of function can be used to determine the side length of a square if the independent variable is the square's area?

(A) Cubic (B) Linear (C) Quadratic (D) Square root

CHALLENGE AND EXTEND

Identify the parent function for each function.

47. $g(x) = 3(x - 1)^2 - 6$ **48.** $h(x) = \left(4x^3\right)^0 + 2$ **49.** $g(x) = 5(3x - 2) - 11x$

50. Another parent function is an exponential function of the form $f(x) = a^x$.

a. Graph $f(x) = 2^x$.
b. Find the domain and range of the function.
c. Identify the point where the function crosses the y-axis.
d. Predict where $f(x) = 3^x$ crosses the y-axis and explain your answer.

SPIRAL REVIEW

Simplify each expression. Write each answer in scientific notation. *(Lesson 1-5)*

51. $(1.5 \times 10^{-4})(5.0 \times 10^{13})$ **52.** $(8.1 \times 10^3)^2$ **53.** $\dfrac{1.9 \times 10^{-6}}{9.5 \times 10^{18}}$

Evaluate each function for the given set of input values. *(Lesson 1-7)*

54. $f(x) = \frac{1}{2}x + 3; \left\{-3, 0, \frac{1}{3}, 6\right\}$ **55.** $f(x) = x(x + 2); \left\{-5, -\frac{2}{3}, 1.6, 4\right\}$

Perform each transformation on the point $(3, -5)$. Give the coordinates of the translated point. *(Lesson 1-8)*

56. left 2 , up 6 **57.** right 1, down 5 **58.** reflected across the y-axis

CHAPTER 1

MULTI-STEP TEST PREP

SECTION 1B

Introduction to Functions

Native American Art Much of Native American art, in particular Navajo and Cherokee, displays symmetrical designs.

To reproduce these designs, artists can determine the points that make up the designs and transform them. The set of ordered pairs in the table defines the outline of the left side of a handmade Navajo vase. The graph shows the plotted points.

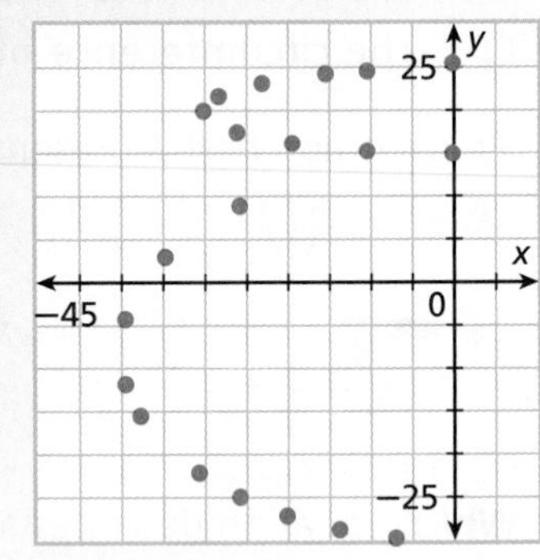

Vase Outline	
x	y
0	25.5
−10.3	24.6
−15.3	24.3
−23.0	23.2
−28.2	21.7
−30.0	20.0
−26.0	17.5
−19.3	16.2
−10.3	15.3
0	15.0
−25.7	8.9
−34.6	3.0
−39.4	−4.2
−39.4	−11.8
−37.6	−15.5
−30.6	−22.1
−25.7	−24.9
−20.0	−27.1
−13.7	−28.7
−6.9	−29.7

1. What is the domain of this relation?
2. What is the range of this relation?
3. Is this relation also a function? Explain why or why not.
4. If the coordinates were plotted such that the vase appears to be on its side (that is, the x- and y-coordinates switched places), would the relation be a function? Explain why or why not.
5. If the vase appears to be on its side, which parent function would best represent the bottom of the vase?
6. What transformation would create the right side of the upright vase?
7. What kind of transformation could be done on the relation in the table to make the vase shorter?
8. What kind of transformation could be done on the relation in the table to make the vase narrower?

READY TO GO ON?

Quiz for Lessons 1-6 Through 1-9

1-6 Relations and Functions

Give the domain and range for each relation. Then tell whether the relation is a function.

1. 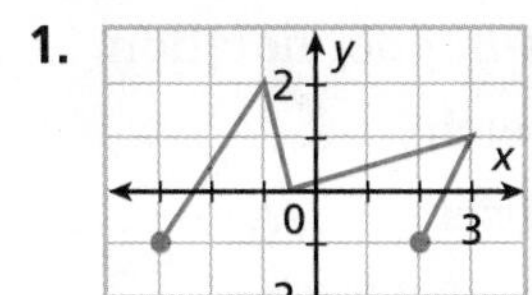

2.

x	0	2	4	6	2
y	5	8	10	20	12

3. 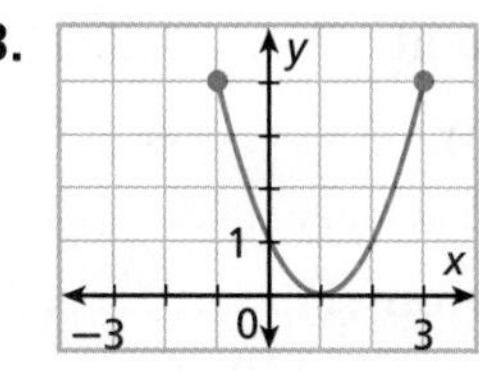

1-7 Function Notation

For each function, evaluate $f(0)$, $f(1)$, and $f(-2)$.

4. $f(x) = 12 - 3x$

5. $f(x) = 3x^3 + 1$

6. $f(x) = 4 - x^2$

7. In a certain city, taxi fares are regulated at \$1.75 per ride plus \$0.25 for each $\frac{1}{4}$ mile.
   a. Write a function to represent the taxi fare per mile.
   b. Graph your function.
   c. What is the value of the function for an input of 5.5, and what does it represent?

1-8 Exploring Transformations

The graph shows some credit card fees for cash advances. Sketch a graph to represent each situation and identify the transformation of the original graph that it represents.

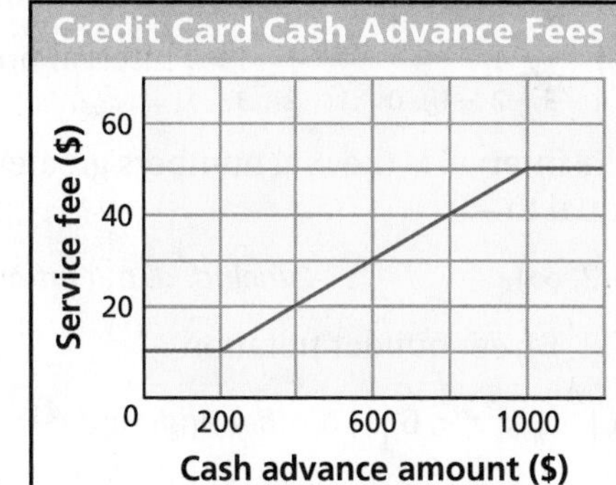

8. Each fee is increased by \$15.

9. Each fee is decreased by 40%.

1-9 Introduction to Parent Functions

Identify the parent function for g from its equation. Then graph g on your calculator and describe what transformation of the parent function it represents.

10. $g(x) = -x^2$

11. $g(x) = \sqrt{x - 3}$

12. $g(x) = 1.5x$

13. The table lists the maximum load of a three-strand nylon rope based on its diameter. Graph the relationship from diameter to maximum load and identify which parent function best describes the data. Then use your graph to estimate the diameter of a three-strand nylon rope that has a maximum load of 7920 kilograms.

Nylon Rope Maximum Load					
Diameter (mm)	8	10	12	14	16
Maximum Load (kg)	1920	2720	3750	5100	6640

CHAPTER 1

Study Guide: Review

Vocabulary

Complete the sentence below with vocabulary words from the list above.

1. For a function, the ___?___ is the set of input values, and the ___?___ is the set of output values.

1-1 Sets of Numbers *(pp. 6–13)*

EXAMPLES

Rewrite each set in the indicated notation.

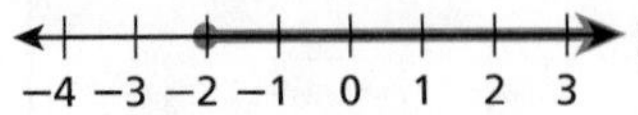

- [number line from −4 to 3, closed point at −2, arrow to the right]; interval notation

  The interval is the real numbers greater than or equal to −2.

  $[-2, \infty)$ *−2 included, but infinity is not.*

- $(-1, 6)$; set builder notation

  $\{x \mid -1 < x < 6\}$ *Neither endpoint is included.*

EXERCISES

Rewrite each set in the indicated notation.

2. $[-5, \infty)$; set-builder notation
3. 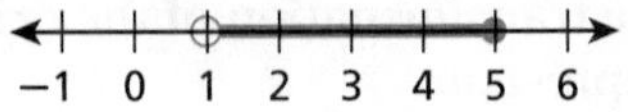 [number line from −1 to 6, open point at 1, closed point at 5] interval notation
4. $\{x \mid x > 3 \text{ and } x \in \mathbb{N}\}$; roster notation
5. $(-\infty, -2)$ or $(5, \infty)$; set-builder notation
6. $\{x \mid -4 < x \le 5 \text{ and } x \in \mathbb{Z}\}$; words
7. $5.5 \le x \le 5.6$; interval notation

1-2 Properties of Real Numbers *(pp. 14–19)*

EXAMPLE

- **Identify the property demonstrated by the equation $3(8x) = (3 \cdot 8)x$.**

  In the equation, the factors have been regrouped. The property of multiplication that allows regrouping is the Associative Property.

EXERCISES

Identify the property demonstrated by each equation.

8. $2x\sqrt{3} = \sqrt{3} \cdot (2x)$
9. $9.9x - 2x = (9.9 - 2)x$

Find the additive and multiplicative inverse of each number.

10. 0.55
11. $-\frac{7}{8}$
12. $1.\overline{2}$

1-3 Square Roots *(pp. 21–26)*

EXAMPLE

- **Simplify the expression $\frac{3\sqrt{2}}{\sqrt{6}}$.**

$\frac{3\sqrt{2}}{\sqrt{6}} \cdot \frac{\sqrt{6}}{\sqrt{6}}$ *Rationalize the denominator.*

$\frac{3\sqrt{12}}{6}$ *Product Property of Square Roots*

$\frac{3\sqrt{4 \cdot 3}}{6}$ *Product Property of Square Roots*

$\frac{6\sqrt{3}}{6} = \sqrt{3}$

EXERCISES

Estimate to the nearest tenth.

13. $\sqrt{12}$ **14.** $\sqrt{55}$

15. $\sqrt{74}$ **16.** $\sqrt{29}$

Simplify each expression.

17. $\sqrt{32}$ **18.** $\frac{\sqrt{64}}{\sqrt{4}}$

19. $2\sqrt{2} - \sqrt{72}$ **20.** $\sqrt{3} \cdot \sqrt{21}$

21. $\frac{7}{\sqrt{2}}$ **22.** $\frac{2\sqrt{20}}{5\sqrt{8}}$

1-4 Simplifying Algebraic Expressions *(pp. 27–32)*

EXAMPLES

- **Evaluate $6c - 3c^2 + d^3$ for $c = -1$ and $d = 3$.**

$6(-1) - 3(-1)^2 + (3)^3$ *Substitute −1 for c and 3 for d.*

$-6 - 3(1) + 27 = 18$

- **Simplify the expression $3m + (m - 5n)2$.**

$3m + (2m - 10n)$ *Distribute the 2.*

$3m + 2m - 10n$ *Identify like terms.*

$5m - 10n$ *Combine like terms.*

EXERCISES

Evaluate each expression for the given values of the variables.

23. $x^2y - xy^2$ for $x = 6$ and $y = -2$

24. $-\frac{x^2}{2} + 5xy - 9y$ for $x = 4$ and $y = 2$

25. $\frac{n^2 + mn - 1}{4m^2n}$ for $m = 2$ and $n = -1$

Simplify each expression.

26. $-x - 2y + 9x - y + 3x$ **27.** $7 - (5a - b) + 11$

28. $-4(2x + 3y) + 5x$ **29.** $c(a^2 - b) + 3bc$

1-5 Properties of Exponents *(pp. 34–41)*

EXAMPLE

- **Simplify the expression $\frac{6m^4n^{-3}}{18m^3n}$. Assume all variables are nonzero.**

$\frac{6}{18}(m^{4-3}n^{-3-1})$ *Quotient of Powers Property*

$\frac{1}{3}(mn^{-4})$ *Simplify.*

$\frac{m}{3n^4}$ *Negative Exponent Property*

EXERCISES

Simplify each expression. Assume all variables are nonzero.

30. $(-2x^5y^{-3})^3$ **31.** $\frac{-24x^4y^{-6}}{14x^{-3}y^3}$

32. $\left(\frac{r^2s}{s^3}\right)^2$ **33.** $4mn(m^5n^{-5})$

Simplify each expression. Write each answer in scientific notation.

34. $\frac{7.7 \times 10^5}{1.1 \times 10^{-2}}$ **35.** $(4.5 \times 10^{-2})(1.2 \times 10^3)$

1-6 Relations and Functions *(pp. 44–50)*

EXAMPLE

■ **Give the domain and range for the relation. Then determine whether the relation is a function.**

Arcade Game Costs				
Games	1	2	3	4
Cost ($)	0.50	1.00	1.50	2.00

Domain: $\{1, 2, 3, 4\}$ *Independent variable*

Range: $\{0.50, 1.00, 1.50, 2.00\}$ *Dependent variable*

Each number of games has only one cost associated with it.

The relation from number of games to cost is a function.

EXERCISES

Give the domain and range for each relation. Then determine whether the relation is a function.

36. 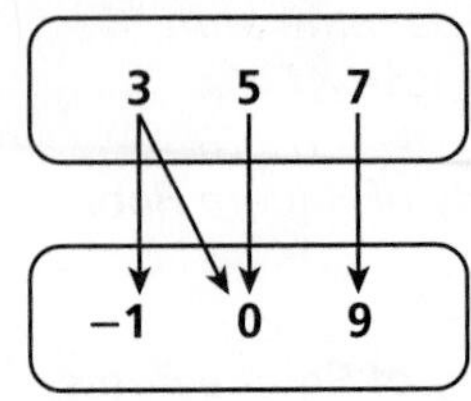

37. 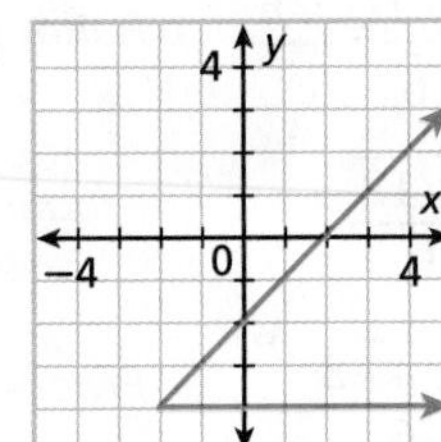

38. $\{(3, 4), (4, 3), (0, 3), (-2, 4)\}$

39.

x	5	10	15	20	25
y	−5	−4	−3	−2	−1

40. from the first three letters of the alphabet to the U.S. states that begin with that letter

1-7 Function Notation *(pp. 51–57)*

EXAMPLE

■ **A cell phone company charges $40 per month for the first 500 minutes plus $0.75 for each additional minute used. Write a function to represent the total monthly cost based on the number of minutes used. What is the value of the function for an input of 30, and what does it represent?**

Let c be the total monthly cost and m be the number of additional minutes used.

cost	=	monthly fee	+	rate	·	additional minutes
$c(m)$	=	40	+	0.75	·	m

$c(30) = 40 + 0.75(30)$

$= 40 + 22.5$

$= 62.5$

The value of $c(m)$ for an input of 30 is $c(30) = 62.5$. This means that the monthly cost when 30 additional minutes are used is $62.50.

EXERCISES

For each function, find $f(2)$, $f\left(\frac{1}{2}\right)$, and $f(-2)$.

41. $f(x) = -x^2 + 2$

42. $f(x) = -5x - 6$

43. 

44. 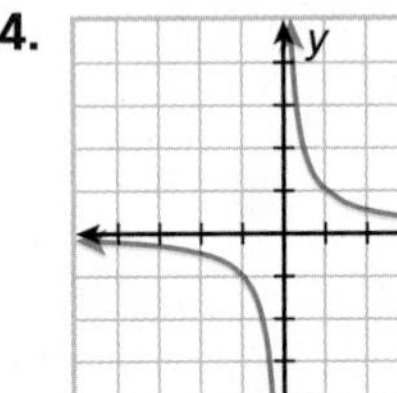

Graph each function.

45. 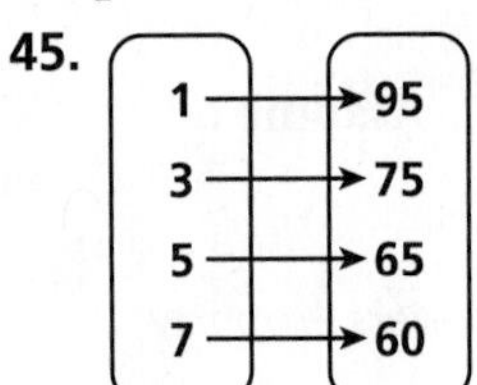

46. $f(x) = 10 - 2x$

47. **Geometry** The surface area of a cube is 6 times the square of its side length. Write a function to represent the surface area of a cube. What is the value of the function for an input of 10 centimeters, and what does it represent?

1-8 Exploring Transformations *(pp. 59–66)*

EXAMPLE

- **The graph shows household alarm monitoring fees. Sketch a graph to represent a $\frac{1}{5}$ fee reduction on long-term contracts. Then identify the transformation of the original graph that the new graph represents.**

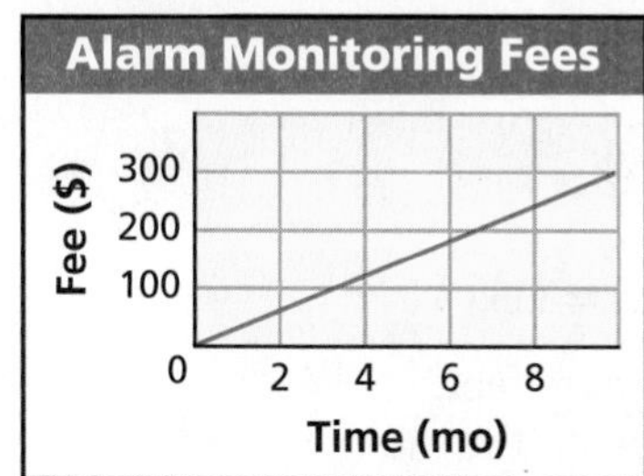

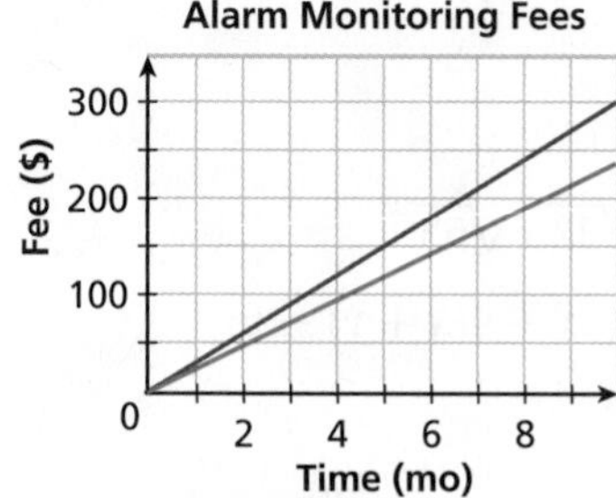

Each price is $\frac{4}{5}$ of the original price. This represents a vertical compression of the graph by a factor of $\frac{4}{5}$.

EXERCISES

Perform the given transformation to the point $(5, -1)$. Give the coordinates of the new point.

48. 5 units left, 4 units down

49. reflection across the x-axis

The graph shows parking garage fees. Sketch a graph to represent each situation and identify the transformation of the original graph that it represents.

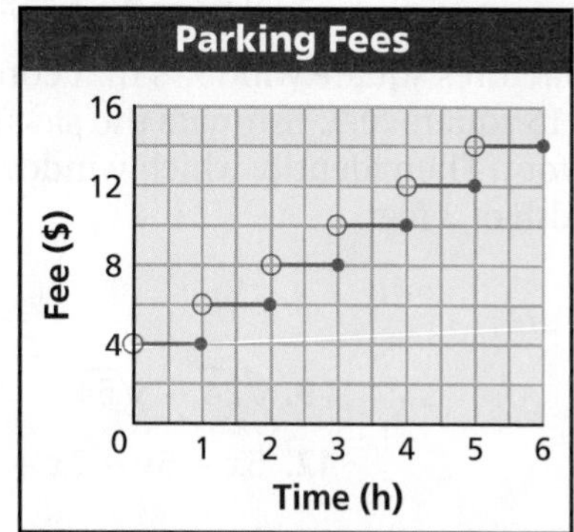

50. The fees are half price on weekends.

51. The fees are increased by 10%.

52. All fees are increased by $1.00.

1-9 Introduction to Parent Functions *(pp. 67–73)*

EXAMPLE

- **Identify the parent function for $g(x) = \sqrt{x-4}$ from its equation. Then graph g on your calculator and describe what transformation of the parent function it represents.**

$g(x) = \sqrt{x-4}$ is a square-root function.

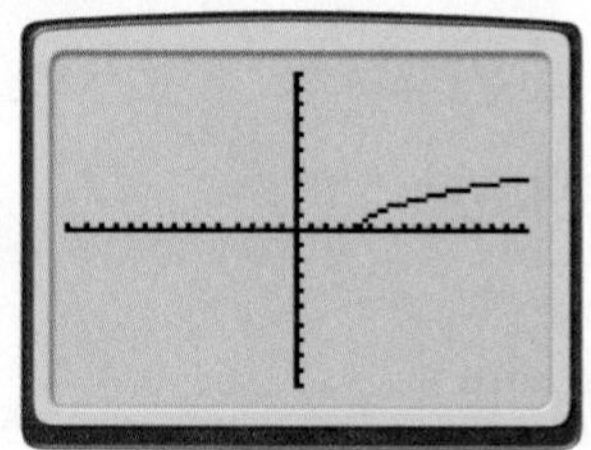

The graph of the square-root parent function intersects the x-axis at the point $(0, 0)$.

The graph of the function $g(x) = \sqrt{x-4}$ intersects the x-axis at the point $(4, 0)$.

So $g(x) = \sqrt{x-4}$ represents a translation of the square-root parent function 4 units right.

EXERCISES

Identify the parent function for g from its equation. Then graph g on your calculator and describe what transformation of the parent function it represents.

53. $g(x) = x^2 - 1$

54. $g(x) = -\sqrt{x}$

55. Graph the data from the table. Describe the parent function that would best approximate the data set. Then use the graph to estimate the tire pressure for a 95-pound rider.

Bicycle Road-Tire Pressures

Weight of Rider (lb)	110	140	170	200	230
Pressure (psi)	95	105	115	125	135

CHAPTER 1 CHAPTER TEST

1. Order $1.\overline{5}$, -2, 0.95, $-\sqrt{3}$, and 1 from least to greatest. Then classify each number by the subsets of the real numbers to which it belongs.

Rewrite each set in the indicated notation.

2. 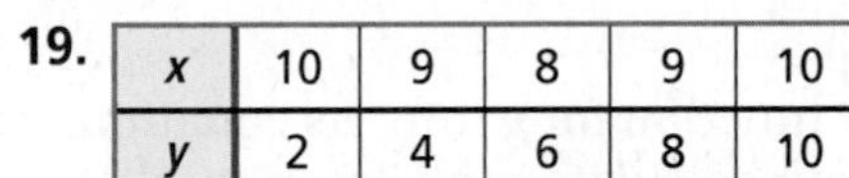 interval notation

3. $(-\infty, 12]$; set-builder notation

Identify the property demonstrated by each equation.

4. $x + y = y + x$

5. $9 \cdot 2 + 9 \cdot 7 = 9 \cdot (2 + 7)$

6. $x = (1)x$

7. A company manufactures square windows that come in three sizes: 6 square feet, 8 square feet, and 15 square feet. Estimate the side length of each window to the nearest tenth of a foot. Then identify which window is the largest one that could fit in a wall with a width of 3 feet.

Simplify each expression.

8. $-2\sqrt{3} + \sqrt{75}$

9. $\sqrt{24} - \sqrt{54}$

10. $\sqrt{22} \cdot \sqrt{55}$

11. $2(x + 1) + 9x$

12. $5x - 5y - 7x + y$

13. $12x + 4(x + y) - 6y$

Simplify each expression. Assume all variables are nonzero.

14. $8a^2b^5(-2a^3b^2)$

15. $\dfrac{28u^{-2}v^3}{4u^2v^2}$

16. $(5x^4y^{-3})^{-2}$

17. $\left(\dfrac{3x^2y}{xy^2}\right)^{-1}$

18. German shepherds are often used as police dogs because they have 2.25×10^8 smell receptors in their nose. Humans average only 5×10^6 smell receptors in their nose. How many times as great is the number of smell receptors in a German shepherd's nose as that in a human's nose?

Give the domain and range for each relation. Then tell whether each relation is a function.

19.

x	10	9	8	9	10
y	2	4	6	8	10

20. 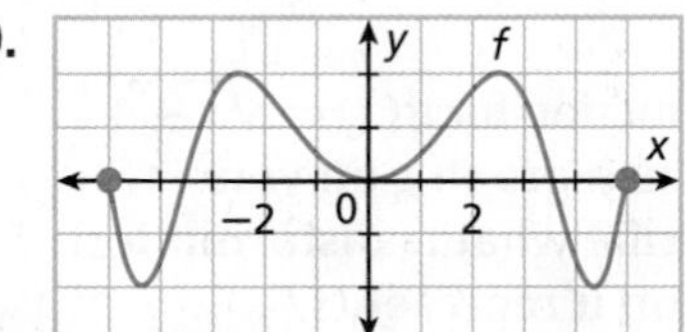

For each function, evaluate $f(-2)$, $f\left(\frac{1}{2}\right)$, and $f(0)$.

21. $f(x) = -4x$

22. $f(x) = -3x^2 + x$

23. $f(x) = \sqrt{x + 3}$

24. The table shows how the distance from the top of a building to the horizon depends on the building's height. Graph the relationship from building height to horizon distance, and identify which parent function best describes the data. Then use your graph to estimate the distance to the horizon from the top of a building with a height of 80 m.

Horizon Distances					
Height of Building (m)	5	10	20	40	100
Distance to Horizon (km)	8.0	11.3	15.9	22.5	35.6

COLLEGE ENTRANCE EXAM PRACTICE

FOCUS ON SAT

The SAT* measures the math and verbal reasoning skills needed for academic success. Your SAT scores show you how you compare with other students taking the test and can be used by colleges to determine admission and to award merit-based financial aid.

On SAT multiple-choice questions, you receive one point for each correct answer, but you lose a fraction of a point for each incorrect response. Guess only when you can eliminate at least one of the answer choices.

You may want to time yourself as you take this practice test. It should take you about 6 minutes to complete.

1. Which element is in the range of the function $\{(-9, -2), (2, 4), (3, -7), (8, 1), (10, 0), (5, 6)\}$?

(A) -9

(B) -1

(C) 2

(D) 3

(E) 6

2. What is the value of $7z^2 + 4 \cdot 3w$ when $w = 8$ and $z = -3$?

(A) 1608

(B) 537

(C) 412

(D) 159

(E) -4068

3. Which of the following is NOT equivalent to $\frac{(mn^3)^4}{m^2n}$?

(A) m^2n^{11}

(B) $\frac{m^4n^{12}}{m^2n}$

(C) $m^{-1}n^{11}$

(D) $(mn^3)^4m^{-2}n^{-1}$

(E) $m^2\frac{(n^3)^4}{n}$

4. If $2 \le x \le 6$, which of the following has the greatest value?

(A) $\sqrt{x}$

(B) $\sqrt{x+1}$

(C) $\sqrt{x+2}$

(D) $\sqrt{x-1}$

(E) $\sqrt{x-2}$

5. Which function is graphed below?

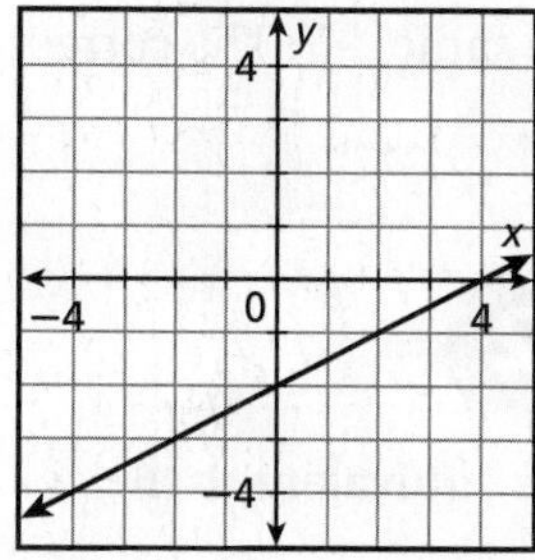

(A) $y = \frac{1}{2}x - 2$

(B) $y = 2x - 2$

(C) $y = \frac{1}{2}(x - 2)$

(D) $y = 2(x - 2)$

(E) $y = \frac{1}{2}x + 2$

*SAT is a registered trademark of the College Board, which was not involved in the production of, and does not endorse, this product.

CHAPTER 1

TEST TACKLER

Standardized Test Strategies

Multiple Choice: Use Multiple Methods

Many mathematical problems can be solved by more than one method. After solving a multiple-choice test item, you can use another method to check your answer. If your answers are not the same, you may have made a typical error for that type of question—likely mistakes are generally answer choices!

EXAMPLE 1

Evaluate the expression $\frac{1}{2}(nm - m^2 + n)$ for $n = 10$ and $m = -2$.

Ⓐ 13 Ⓑ -3 Ⓒ -7 Ⓓ -59

Select a method to evaluate.

$\frac{1}{2}(nm - m^2 + n)$

$\frac{1}{2}[10(-2) - (-2)^2 + 10]$ *Substitute.*

$\frac{1}{2}(-20 - 4 + 10)$ *Simplify.*

$\frac{1}{2}(-14) = -7$

Use an alternative method to check.

$\frac{1}{2}(nm - m^2 + n)$

$\frac{1}{2}nm - \frac{1}{2}m^2 + \frac{1}{2}n$ *Distribute.*

$\frac{1}{2}(10)(-2) - \frac{1}{2}(-2)^2 + \frac{1}{2}(10)$ *Substitute.*

$-10 - 2 + 5 = -7$

The answers are the same, -7. The correct choice is C.

EXAMPLE 2

Which expression is equivalent to $(6^3)^4$?

Ⓕ 6^{12} Ⓖ 6^7 Ⓗ 18^4 Ⓙ 72

Select a method. Suppose you add the exponents.

$(6^3)^4 = 6^{(3+4)}$

$= 6^7$ *6^7 is choice G.*

Check using an alternative method.

$(6^3)^4 = 6^3 \cdot 6^3 \cdot 6^3 \cdot 6^3$ *Rewrite in expanded form.*

$= 6^{(3+3+3+3)}$ *Product of Powers Property*

$= 6^{12}$ *6^{12} is choice F.*

Notice that the answers are different! Both answers are given as choices, so a common error was made in one of the methods. Look closely at the first method; the Power of a Power Property was incorrectly used. The exponents should have been *multiplied, not added.* The correct choice is F.

When a multiple-choice test item is created, incorrect answer choices known as *distracters* are created by solving the problem and intentionally making typical mistakes. Even if your answer choice is given, it is not a guarantee that it is the correct answer. Check your work!

Read each test item and answer the questions that follow.

Item A

A pet store has a dog pen discounted 20%. If the original cost of the dog pen is $82.80, what is the amount of the discount?

Ⓐ $1.66 Ⓒ $16.56

Ⓑ $8.28 Ⓓ $66.24

1. Explain how to use mental math to solve this problem.
2. Describe another method you can use to solve this problem. Then explain how you can use this method to check your answer.

Item B

The area of the rectangle is $\sqrt{8} \cdot \sqrt{24}$. This product simplifies to which of the following expressions?

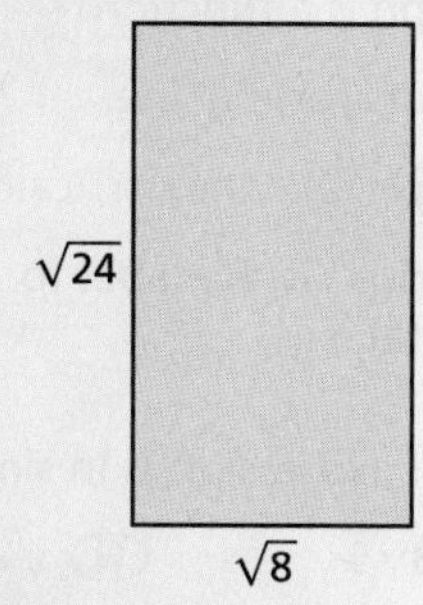

Ⓕ $8\sqrt{3}$ Ⓗ $2\sqrt{8}$

Ⓖ $4\sqrt{8}$ Ⓙ $2\sqrt{12}$

3. Explain two different ways you can simplify the product.
4. Explain how you can use these two methods to check whether your answer is correct.

Item C

The volume of the cube can be simplified to which of the following expressions?

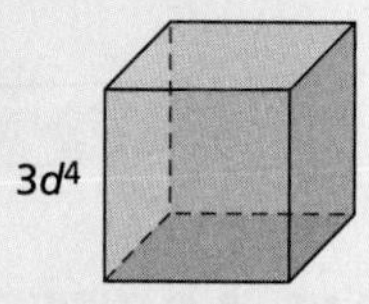

Ⓐ $27d^{12}$ Ⓒ $9d^{12}$

Ⓑ $27d^{7}$ Ⓓ $9d^{7}$

5. Describe the method you would use to solve this problem.
6. Explain an alternative method you can use to solve this problem. Then explain how you can use this method to check your answer.
7. Choices B, C, and D are distracters. What common errors were made to generate these expressions?

Item D

Consider the function $f(x) = 6x - 12$. What is $f(-3)$?

Ⓕ −216 Ⓗ −18

Ⓖ −30 Ⓙ −6

8. Explain how you would evaluate this function.
9. How could you use graphing to check your answer?

Item E

The expression $-8(-9 + 12 - 6)$ simplifies to which value?

Ⓐ −216 Ⓒ 11

Ⓑ −72 Ⓓ 24

10. Describe two different methods you can use to simplify the expression.
11. If your answers to each method are not the same, explain what you would do next.

STANDARDIZED TEST PREP

go.hrw.com
State Test Practice Online
KEYWORD: MB7 TestPrep

CUMULATIVE ASSESSMENT, CHAPTER 1

Multiple Choice

1. Which function translates $f(x) = x^2$ left 7 units?

- (A) $g(x) = x^2 - 7$
- (B) $g(x) = x^2 + 7$
- (C) $g(x) = (x + 7)^2$
- (D) $g(x) = (x - 7)^2$

2. For which function does $f(-8) = -6$?

- (F) $f(x) = 2x^2 - 6$
- (G) $f(x) = 10x - 6$
- (H) $f(x) = x^2 - 10$
- (J) $f(x) = 2x + 10$

3. The circumference of Jena's hula hoop is 32π in. Which subset of the real numbers best describes 32π?

- (A) Natural numbers
- (B) Irrational numbers
- (C) Whole numbers
- (D) Rational numbers

4. The following procedure was used to design a logo. The letter *A* was positioned upright in the first quadrant of a coordinate plane and then reflected across the *x*-axis. Then both figures were reflected across the *y*-axis. Which is the correct logo?

- (F)
- (H)
- (G)
- (J)

5. Which expression simplifies to $x^2 - 3x$?

- (A) $2(x^2 + x) - 3x^2 + 5x$
- (B) $2(x^2 - x) + 3x^2 - 5x$
- (C) $-2(x^2 + x) - 3x^2 + 5x$
- (D) $-2(x^2 - x) + 3x^2 - 5x$

6. The quotient of 7.84×10^{-3} and which divisor is 5.6×10^{-4}?

- (F) 1.4×10^{1}
- (H) 1.4×10^{-7}
- (G) 2.24×10^{-7}
- (J) 2.24×10^{1}

7. If milk price is the dependent variable and number of ounces is the independent variable, which statement is true for the graph of the data in the table?

Milk Prices

Package Size	Number of Ounces	Milk Price
1 pint	16	\$0.90
1 quart	32	\$1.29
1 half gallon	64	\$1.95
2 quarts	64	\$2.58
1 gallon	128	\$3.90

- (A) The graph is a function.
- (B) The points form a line.
- (C) The graph fails the vertical-line test.
- (D) "Milk price" is the label for the horizontal axis.

8. Which radical expression is in simplest form?

- (F) $\sqrt{45} + 3\sqrt{5}$
- (H) $\sqrt{2} \cdot \sqrt{10}$
- (G) $4\sqrt{30}$
- (J) $\frac{\sqrt{27}}{9}$

9. Simplify $-\left(5x^2y^{-1}z^{-3}\right)^2$.

- (A) $-\frac{5x^4}{y^2z^6}$
- (B) $25x^4y^{-2}z^{-6}$
- (C) $-25x^4y^{-2}z^{-6}$
- (D) $-\frac{25x^4}{y^2z^6}$

10. Which does not represent the set shown on this number line?

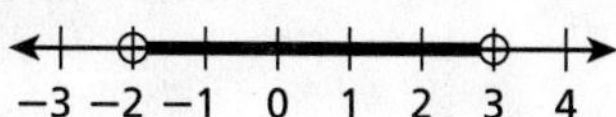

(F) All real numbers between −2 and 3

(G) $-2 < x < 3$

(H) $(-2, 3)$

(J) All real numbers −2 through 3, inclusive

11. The lengths of the legs of a right triangle are 2 and $4\sqrt{3}$. What is the perimeter of the triangle?

(A) $\sqrt{52}$

(B) $6\sqrt{3} + 2\sqrt{13}$

(C) $2 + 4\sqrt{3} + 2\sqrt{13}$

(D) $9\sqrt{39}$

Use mental math to calculate 10% of an amount by moving the decimal point left one place. Then you can use that amount to find 5% by taking half of the amount or find 20% by doubling the amount.

12. Which expression can be used to determine 7.5% of a $210 purchase?

(F) $0.1(210) - \frac{1}{2}(0.1)(210)$

(G) $\frac{1}{2}(0.1)(210) + \frac{1}{4}(0.1)(210)$

(H) $0.1(210) + \frac{1}{4}(0.1)(210)$

(J) $\frac{1}{2}(0.1)(210) - \frac{1}{4}(0.1)(210)$

Gridded Response

13. Craig is mowing lawns and trimming hedges as a community service project. It takes 35 minutes to mow one lawn and 45 minutes to trim the hedges on a property. He plans to work for 4 hours on Saturday. If he mows 3 lawns, how many hedges can he trim?

14. For what missing quantity would price NOT be a function of quantity?

Quantity	Price
12	$132
15	$150
■	$132

15. Evaluate $\frac{5x^4y^{-4}z}{25x^2y^{-7}z^2}$ for $x = 5$, $y = -1$, and $z = -5$.

Short Response

16. A city worker is dividing a community garden into square plots.

a. One plot will have an area of 30 square meters. Find an approximate value for the side length of the plot without using a calculator or a square-root table. Explain each step and show your work. Give your answer to the nearest hundredth of a meter.

b. How can you use the fact that $\sqrt{2} \approx 1.41$ to approximate the side length of a plot with an area of 50 square meters?

17. Shown in the table are some of the world's largest cities, ranked according to population statistics.

Selected Cities		
City	**Country**	**Population**
Houston, TX	United States	1.953×10^6
Seoul	South Korea	1.023×10^7
Hong Kong	China	6.843×10^6
Chicago, IL	United States	2.896×10^6
Cairo	Egypt	6.800×10^6
Istanbul	Turkey	8.260×10^6

Source: **Citymayors.com**

a. Order the cities from greatest population to least population.

b. Two other U.S. cities are in a list of the largest 100 cities in the world. Los Angeles, California, has a population of 3,694,000. New York, New York, has a population of about 8 million. Where would these cities rank if they were included in the table?

Extended Response

18. Change machines charge a fee of $0.089 for every dollar of change turned into cash. The fee is taken from the cash amount returned to the user.

a. Write a function that represents the amount returned in cash.

b. Sketch and label the function graph.

c. Identify the parent function for this function.

d. What amount is returned from $21.91 of change converted to cash?

CHAPTER

2 Linear Functions

Chapter Focus

- Apply linear relationships to solve real-world problems.
- Develop linear models to make predictions.

Sky High

You can use linear functions to compare data sets based on the tallest buildings in the world, including the Taipei 101 tower.

go.hrw.com
Chapter Project Online
KEYWORD: MB7 ChProj

ARE YOU READY?

Vocabulary

Match each term on the left with a definition on the right.

1. absolute value
2. function
3. transformation
4. scatter plot

A. a relation in which each first coordinate is paired with exactly one second coordinate
B. a change in the position, size, or shape of a figure
C. the distance from a number to zero on the number line
D. a symbol used to represent a quantity that can change
E. a graph on a coordinate plane with points plotted to represent relationships between data sets

Connect Words and Algebra

Write an equation for each phrase.

5. The sum of a number and 4 times another number is 25.
6. The difference of 3 times a number and 20 is greater than 10.
7. A number divided by 12 is less than 15 divided by the same number.

Solve One-Step Equations

Solve each equation for *x*.

8. $-8 + x = -20$
9. $-12 = -3x$
10. $x - 19 = -12$
11. $0.75 = \frac{x}{5}$

Percent Problems

Solve each percent problem.

12. Fifteen is 30% of what number?
13. What number is 40% of 140?
14. What percent of 140 is 105?
15. What number is 150% of 90?

Convert Units of Measure

Convert the units of measure.

16. 12 quarts to gallons
17. 15 feet to yards
18. 1.5 hours to minutes
19. 3.5 gallons to quarts
20. 17 yards to feet
21. 200 minutes to hours
22. 107 centimeters to meters
23. 2.5 kilometers to meters
24. 50 milliliters to liters

Absolute Value

Find the absolute value of each expression.

25. $|16 - 22|$
26. $|32 - 20|$
27. $|8 - 17 + 9|$
28. $|-0.75 + 0.625|$

CHAPTER 2

Study Guide: Preview

Where You've Been

Previously, you

- used the properties of real numbers and properties of exponents.
- studied relations and functions.
- graphed parent functions.
- explored transformations.

In This Chapter

You will study

- using properties of equality to write and solve linear equations.
- writing and graphing linear functions.
- solving problems involving transformations of the linear parent function.
- transformations of the absolute-value parent function.

Where You're Going

You can use the skills learned in this chapter

- to model data and make predictions in sports, travel, and financial affairs.
- in fields such as health, chemistry, physics, and economics.
- in your future math classes, including Calculus and Statistics.

Key Vocabulary/Vocabulario

absolute-value function	función de valor absoluto
correlation	correlacíon
identity	identidad
indirect measurement	medición indirecta
line of best fit	línea de mejor ajuste
linear function	función lineal
proportion	proporción
rate	tasa
regression	regresión
scale factor	factor de escala
slope	pendiente
y-intercept	intersección con el eje y

Vocabulary Connections

To become familiar with some of the vocabulary terms in the chapter, consider the following. You may refer to the chapter, the glossary, or a dictionary if you like.

1. What does the word *identical* mean? When do you think an equation might be called an **identity**?
2. How is the word **rate** related to the word **ratio**?
3. What does it mean to *intercept* a message? Why would the value at the crossing location for a line and an axis be called an **intercept**?
4. The word *regress* means "to go back." How can you use the definition of *regress* to understand **regression** in mathematics?

Reading Strategy: Read a Lesson for Understanding

As you read a lesson, read with a purpose. Lessons are centered on one or two specific objectives given at the top of the first page. Reading with the objectives in mind will help guide you through the lesson. You can use some of the following tips to help you follow the math as you read.

Reading Tips

Objective
Identify and use properties of real numbers.

Identify the **objectives** of the lesson. Then skim through the lesson to get a sense of where the objectives are covered.

"What is an inverse?"

"What is an integer?"

As you read through the lesson, list any questions, problems, or trouble spots you may have.

EXAMPLE:
Find the additive and multiplicative inverse of –9.

Additive inverse: 9 *The opposite of –9 is $-(-9) = 9$*

Check $-9 + 9 = 0$ ✓ *The Additive Inverse Property holds.*

Multiplicative inverse: $\frac{1}{-9}$ *The reciprocal of –9 is $\frac{1}{-9}$.*

Check $-9\left(\frac{1}{-9}\right) = 1$ ✓ *The Multiplicative Inverse Property holds.*

Work through each example, as the examples help demonstrate the objectives.

Practice your skills in the Check It Out sections to verify your understanding of the lesson.

Try This

Use Lesson 1-4 in your textbook to answer each question.

1. What is the objective of the lesson?
2. What new terms are defined in the lesson?
3. Fraction bars, square root symbols, and absolute value symbols are all forms of what type of symbol?
4. What skill is being practiced in the first Check It Out problem in the lesson?

2-1 Solving Linear Equations and Inequalities

Objectives
Solve linear equations using a variety of methods.

Solve linear inequalities.

Vocabulary
equation
solution set of an equation
linear equation in one variable
identity
contradiction
inequality

Who uses this?
A hot-air balloonist can use linear equations to calculate the average speed needed to set a world record. (See Example 1.)

An **equation** is a mathematical statement that two expressions are equivalent. The **solution set of an equation** is the value or values of the variable that make the equation true. A **linear equation in one variable** can be written in the form $ax = b$, where a and b are constants and $a \neq 0$.

Linear Equations in One Variable	Nonlinear Equations
$4x = 8$	$3\sqrt{x} + 1 = 32$
$3x - \frac{2}{3}x = -9$	$\frac{2}{x^2} = 41$
$2x - 5 = 0.1x + 2$	$3 - 2^x = -5$

Notice that the variable in a linear equation is not under a radical sign and is not raised to a power other than 1. The variable is also not an exponent and is not in a denominator.

Solving a linear equation requires isolating the variable on one side of the equation by using the properties of equality.

Properties of Equality

For all real numbers *a*, *b* and *c*,

WORDS	NUMBERS	ALGEBRA
Addition If you add the same quantity to both sides of an equation, the equation will still be true.	$3 = 3$ $3 + 2 = 3 + 2$	$a = b$ $a + c = b + c$
Subtraction If you subtract the same quantity from both sides of an equation, the equation will still be true.	$3 = 3$ $3 - 2 = 3 - 2$	$a = b$ $a - c = b - c$
Multiplication If you multiply both sides of an equation by the same quantity, the equation will still be true.	$3 = 3$ $3(2) = 3(2)$	$a = b$ $ac = bc$
Division If you divide both sides of an equation by the same nonzero quantity, the equation will still be true.	$3 = 3$ $\frac{3}{2} = \frac{3}{2}$	$a = b$ If $c \neq 0$, $\frac{a}{c} = \frac{b}{c}$

To isolate the variable, perform the inverse, or opposite, of every operation in the equation on both sides of the equation. Do inverse operations in the reverse order of the order of operations.

EXAMPLE 1 Travel Application

Steve Fossett set a 24-hour hot-air balloon record of 3186.8 miles on July 1, 2002. Suppose a balloonist has traveled 1239 miles in 10.5 hours. What speed would the balloonist need to average during the remaining 13.5 hours to tie the record?

Let v represent the speed in miles per hour the balloonist will need to average.

Model

distance already traveled	plus	average speed	times	time remaining hours	=	total distance
1239	+	v	·	13.5	=	3186.8

Solve

$$\begin{aligned} 1239 + 13.5v &= 3186.8 \\ -1239 \quad & \quad -1239 \end{aligned}$$ *Subtract 1239 from both sides.*

$$\frac{13.5v}{13.5} = \frac{1947.8}{13.5}$$ *Divide both sides by 13.5.*

$$v \approx 144.3$$

The balloonist must average about 144.3 mi/h for the remaining 13.5 hours.

1. Stacked cups are to be placed in a pantry. One cup is 3.25 in. high and each additional cup raises the stack 0.25 in. How many cups fit between two shelves 14 in. apart?

EXAMPLE 2 Solving Equations with the Distributive Property

Solve $5(y-7)=25$.

Method 1

The quantity $(y-7)$ is multiplied by 5, so divide by 5 first.

$$\frac{5(y-7)}{5} = \frac{25}{5}$$ *Divide both sides by 5.*

$$y - 7 = 5$$

$$+7 \quad +7$$ *Add 7 to both sides.*

$$y = 12$$

Method 2

Distribute before solving.

$$5y - 35 = 25$$ *Distribute 5.*

$$+35 \quad +35$$ *Add 35 to both sides.*

$$5y = 60$$

$$\frac{5y}{5} = \frac{60}{5}$$ *Divide both sides by 5.*

$$y = 12$$

Check

$5(y-7)$	25
$5(12-7)$	25
$5(5)$	25
25	25 ✓

Solve.

2a. $3(2-3p)=42$

2b. $-3(5-4r)=-9$

If there are variables on both sides of the equation, (1) simplify each side. (2) Collect all variable terms on one side and all constant terms on the other side. (3) Isolate the variable as you did in the previous problems.

EXAMPLE 3 Solving Equations with Variables on Both Sides

Solve $6y + 21 + 7 = 4y - 20 + 5y$.

$6y + 28 = 9y - 20$ *Simplify each side by combining like terms.*

$-6y \qquad -6y$ *Collect variables on the right side.*

$28 = 3y - 20$ *Subtract.*

$+20 \qquad +20$ *Collect constants on the left side.*

$\frac{48}{3} = \frac{3y}{3}$ *Isolate the variable.*

$16 = y$

Check Substitute 16 for y on both sides of the the original equation. You can use a calculator to make sure they are equal.

```
6(16)+21+7
             124
4(16)-20+5(16)
             124
```

3. Solve $3(w + 7) - 5w = w + 12$

You have solved equations that have a single solution. Equations may also have infinitely many solutions or no solution.

An equation that is true for all values of the variable, such as $x = x$, is an **identity**. An equation that has no solution, such as $3 = 5$, is a **contradiction** because there are no values that make it true.

EXAMPLE 4 Identifying Identities and Contradictions

Solve.

A $3x + 4x + 5 = 7x + 5$

$7x + 5 = 7x + 5$ *Simplify.*

$-7x \qquad -7x$

$5 = 5$ ✔ *Identity*

The solution set is all real numbers, or $\mathbb{R}$.

B $8(y + 7) = 6y - 8 + 2y$

$8y + 56 = 8y - 8$ *Simplify.*

$-8y \qquad -8y$

$56 = -8$ ✘ *Contradiction*

The equation has no solution. The solution set is the *empty set,* which is represented by the symbol $\varnothing$.

Solve.

4a. $5(x - 6) = 3x - 18 + 2x$ **4b.** $3(2 - 3x) = -7x - 2(x - 3)$

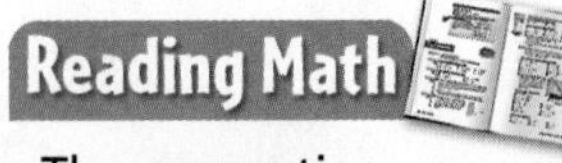

The properties of equality and inequality are also called the axioms of equality and inequality.

An **inequality** is a statement that compares two expressions by using the symbols $<$, $>$, $\leq$, $\geq$, or $\neq$. The graph of an inequality is the solution set, the set of all points on the number line that satisfy the inequality.

The properties of equality are true for inequalities, with one important difference. If you multiply or divide both sides by a negative number, you must *reverse* the inequality symbol.

Inequalities — Multiplying or Dividing by a Negative Number

For all real numbers *a*, *b*, and *c*,

WORDS	NUMBERS	ALGEBRA
If you multiply both sides of an inequality by the same negative quantity and reverse the inequality symbol, the inequality will still be true.	$4 < 6$ $4(-2) > 6(-2)$ $-8 > -12$	$a < b$ If $c < 0$, $ac > bc$
If you divide both sides of an inequality by the same negative quantity and reverse the inequality symbol, the inequality will still be true.	$4 < 6$ $\frac{4}{-2} > \frac{6}{-2}$ $-2 > -3$	$a < b$ If $c < 0$, $\frac{a}{c} > \frac{b}{c}$

These properties also apply to inequalities expressed with $>$, $\geq$, and $\leq$.

EXAMPLE 5 Solving Inequalities

Solve and graph $9x + 4 < 12x - 11$.

$$9x + 4 < 12x - 11$$
$$\underline{-12x} \quad \underline{-12x} \qquad \textit{Subtract 12x from both sides.}$$
$$-3x + 4 < -11$$
$$\underline{-4} \quad \underline{-4} \qquad \textit{Subtract 4 from both sides.}$$
$$-3x < -15$$
$$\frac{-3x}{-3} > \frac{-15}{-3} \qquad \textit{Divide both sides by –3 and reverse the inequality.}$$
$$x > 5$$

Helpful Hint

To check an inequality, test
- the value being compared with *x* (5 in Example 5),
- a value less than that, and
- a value greater than that.

Check Test values in the original inequality:

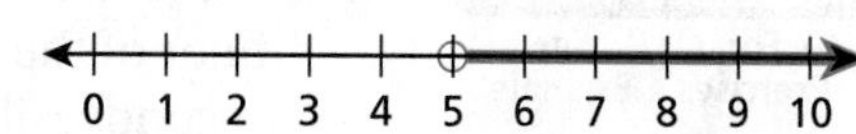

Test $x = 0$.	Test $x = 5$.	Test $x = 7$.
$9(0) + 4 \overset{?}{<} 12(0) - 11$	$9(5) + 4 \overset{?}{<} 12(5) - 11$	$9(7) + 4 \overset{?}{<} 12(7) - 11$
$4 < -11$ ✗	$49 < 49$ ✗	$67 < 73$ ✓
So 0 is not a solution.	So 5 is not a solution.	So 7 is a solution.

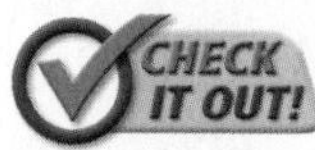

5. Solve and graph $x + 8 \geq 4x + 17$.

THINK AND DISCUSS

1. Give an example of an equation containing $3x$ that has no solution and another containing $3x$ with all real numbers as solutions.

2. Explain why you must reverse the inequality symbol in an expression when you multiply by a negative number. Use the inequality $-3 < 3$ as an example.

3. GET ORGANIZED Copy and complete the graphic organizer. Note the similarities and differences in the properties and methods you use.

Similarities — **Solving Equations and Inequalities** — Differences

2-1 Exercises

go.hrw.com
Homework Help Online
KEYWORD: MB7 2-1
Parent Resources Online
KEYWORD: MB7 Parent

GUIDED PRACTICE

1. **Vocabulary** The statement $4 = 4$ is a(n) __?__. (*identity* or *contradiction*)

SEE EXAMPLE 1 p. 91

2. **Consumer Economics** Shanti has just joined a DVD rental club. She pays a monthly membership fee of \$4.95, and each DVD rental is \$1.95. If Shanti's budget for DVD rentals in a month is \$42, how many DVDs can Shanti rent in her first month if she doesn't want to go over her budget?

SEE EXAMPLE 2 p. 91

Solve.

3. $8(x - 5) = 72$
4. $1.5(x - 4) = 9.6$
5. $-27 = 3(x - 3)$

SEE EXAMPLE 3 p. 92

6. $5 - 4c = c + 20$
7. $24 + 7x = -4x - 9$
8. $3(x - 5) = 5x + 9$
9. $x = -2(x - 3)$
10. $(t - 3)7 = 6t + 21$
11. $-0.5(r - 2) = -r - 2$

SEE EXAMPLE 4 p. 92

12. $-4t + 1 = 3t + 1 - 7t$
13. $2(3x + 1) = 3(2x + 1)$
14. $2(3n + 3) - 9 = 6n$
15. $2h + 4 - 5h = -3h + 4$
16. $4(2 - 6m) = 6(2 - 4m)$
17. $0.5(-8p + 1) = -4p + 1$

SEE EXAMPLE 5 p. 93

Solve and graph.

18. $5x - 12 > 8$
19. $62 - 18x < 20$
20. $23 + 3x \leq 15 - x$

PRACTICE AND PROBLEM SOLVING

Independent Practice

For Exercises	See Example
21	1
22–26	2
27–31	3
32–36	4
37–39	5

Extra Practice

Skills Practice p. S6
Application Practice p. S33

21. **Aerospace** A pen floating in the weightlessness of space is 30 inches above the floor of the space capsule and is rising at 1.5 inches per second. In how many seconds will it reach the 6-foot-high ceiling?

Solve.

22. $-30 = 6(x - 3)$
23. $5(x - 8) - (x + 6) = 18$
24. $2(x + 4) - 5(x - 3) = 32$
25. $\frac{1}{3}(2x - 7) = 4$
26. $3x - 8(3 - x) = 53$
27. $6n - 7 = 2n + 17$
28. $3n - 40 = \frac{1}{2}n + 35$
29. $5(x - 4) - 1 = -7x + 3$
30. $12x + 20 = 6(x + 4)$
31. $8t + 11 - 6t = 5t + 35$
32. $2x + 4(x + 1) = 6\left(x + \frac{2}{3}\right)$
33. $8 = -8x + 4(4 + 2x)$
34. $-4(2n - 5) = -8n - 20$
35. $9(3 - 2x) = -6(3x - 5)$
36. $4x - 2(3 + 2x) = -6$

Solve and graph.

37. $-3x + 8 \leq 14$
38. $3(x - 1) > 7(x + 3)$
39. $5(x - 2) \geq 4(2x + 6) + 2$

40. **Business** Pat is paid a salary of \$500 a month plus a commission of 15% of the value of the jewelry she sells. Find the value of the jewelry Pat must sell in a month to earn at least \$2000.

41. **Economics** In 1902, 44 loaves of bread cost the same amount as 1 loaf of bread in 2006. A loaf of bread in 2006 cost \$1.72 more than in 1902. Find the cost of a loaf of bread in 1902. Explain how you can use estimation to check your answer.

42. **Football** In 2004, three wide receivers for the Indianapolis Colts caught a total of 37 touchdown passes. Reggie Wayne caught 2 more than Brandon Stokely, and Marvin Harrison caught 3 more than Reggie Wayne. How many touchdown passes did each receiver catch?

43. **Technology** A digital answering machine has a total capacity of 32 min for the personal announcement and incoming messages. Incoming messages are limited to 3 min each, and the announcement is 30 s long.

a. Find the possible number of 3 min messages the machine can record.

b. The average length of an incoming message is 1.5 min. How many messages of average length can the machine record?

c. **What If...?** A friend has left 2 maximum length messages on your machine. In addition you have 5 minutes worth of saved messages. How many more average length messages can your machine record?

Geometry Find the measure of each angle in the triangles below. (*Hint:* The sum of angle measures in a triangle is 180°.)

44. Triangle ABC with angles $x°$ at A, $2x°$ at B, $(x - 20)°$ at C.

45. Right triangle DEF with angles $3.5x°$ at D, $x°$ at E, right angle at F.

46. Triangle GHJ with angles $\frac{1}{10}x°$ at G, $x°$ at H, $(x - 135)°$ at J.

LINK Literature

Shakespeare's plays have been made into more than 500 movies and television shows.

Source: IMDB.com

47. **Literature** William Shakespeare wrote 37 plays, including tragedies, comedies, and histories. He wrote the same number of tragedies and histories, but the number of comedies he wrote is 3 less than twice the number of tragedies. How many of each type of play did Shakespeare write?

48. **Chemistry** As an experiment, a student filled a water glass with 5 in. of water. The chart shows the height of the water after each day.

a. How much water evaporates each day?

b. When will the height of the water drop below 2.5 in.?

c. If the pattern continued, what would the height of the water be after 30 days? Is this reasonable in the context of the problem?

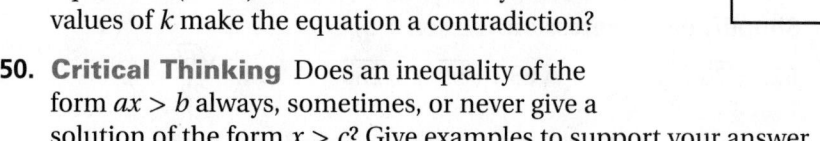

Evaporation of Water

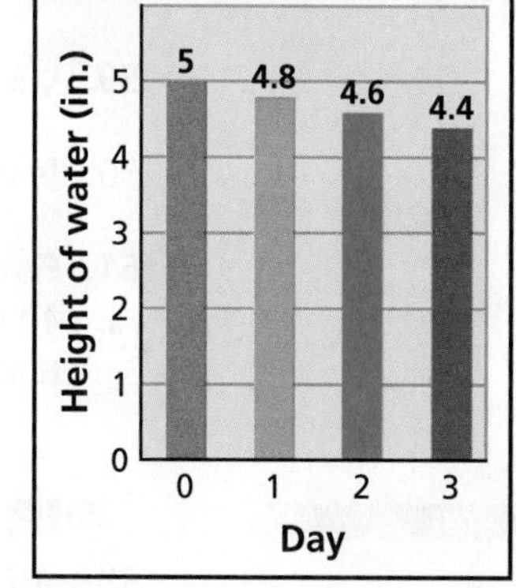

49. **Critical Thinking** What values of k make the equation $2(x - k) = 2x + 20$ an identity? What values of k make the equation a contradiction?

50. **Critical Thinking** Does an inequality of the form $ax > b$ always, sometimes, or never give a solution of the form $x > c$? Give examples to support your answer.

51. **Write About It** How do you recognize when an equation has no real solution or an infinite number of solutions?

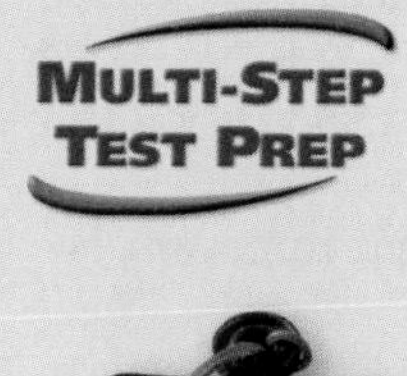

52. This problem will prepare you for the Multi-Step Test Prep on page 132. There are 360° of longitude at the equator.

a. The length of a nautical mile initially represented $\frac{1}{60}$ degree of longitude at the equator, and is very close to that measurement today. How many nautical miles is the circumference of the earth at the equator?

b. The circumference of the earth at the equator is 24,901.55 common or *statute* miles. Is the length of a nautical mile longer or shorter than a statute mile? Explain.

53. If $5 + 3x = 17$, then which equation is true?

Ⓐ $x = \frac{5 - 17}{3}$ Ⓑ $x = \frac{17 - 3}{5}$ Ⓒ $x = \frac{17 - 5}{3}$ Ⓓ $x = \frac{3 - 17}{5}$

54. Which expression does NOT simplify to a? (for $a \neq 0$, for $b \neq 0$)

Ⓕ $(a \div b) \cdot b$ Ⓖ $(a - b) + a + b$ Ⓗ $(a \cdot b) \div b$ Ⓙ $(a + b) - b$

55. Bob has 3 times as much money as Amy has, and Sam has \$5 more than Bob has. Bob, Amy, and Sam have a total of \$75. Which equation can be used to find out how much money Amy has?

Ⓐ $x + 3x + (x - 5) = 75$ Ⓒ $x + 3x + (3x - 5) = 75$

Ⓑ $x + 3x + (x + 5) = 75$ Ⓓ $x + 3x + (3x + 5) = 75$

56. If the perimeter of the rectangle can be at most 100 feet, which inequality can be used to find the width?

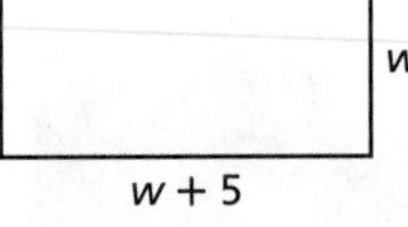

Ⓕ $w + (w + 5) \leq 100$ Ⓗ $w + (w + 5) \geq 100$

Ⓖ $2w + 2(w + 5) \leq 100$ Ⓙ $2w + 2(w + 5) \geq 100$

57. **Gridded Response** If $12 = 15 - 2x$, find the value of $8x$.

CHALLENGE AND EXTEND

Solve.

58. $2x\sqrt{3} + 10 = x\sqrt{3} + 16$

59. $\sqrt{5}(x + 1) > \sqrt{45}(2x + 3)$

60. Is the statement $4(x - 2) \neq 2(-4 + 2x)$ an identity or a contradiction? Explain.

61. **Estimation** There are 90 people in line at a theme park ride. Every 5 minutes, 40 people get on the ride and 63 join the line. Estimate how long it would take for 600 people to be in line. About how long will the 600th person have to wait?

SPIRAL REVIEW

Simplify each expression. *(Lesson 1-3)*

62. $\sqrt{75}$ 63. $\sqrt{90} + \sqrt{250}$ 64. $\frac{\sqrt{68}}{22}$ 65. $\frac{5\sqrt{12}}{\sqrt{5}}$

Determine whether each relation is a function. *(Lesson 1-6)*

66.  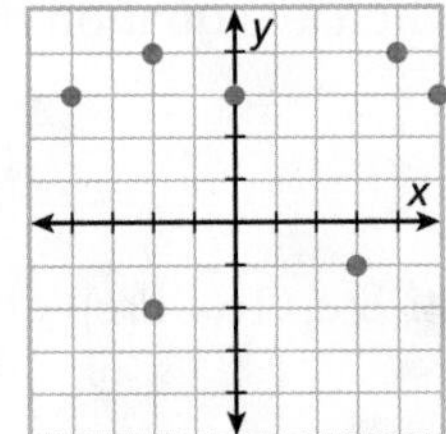

67. 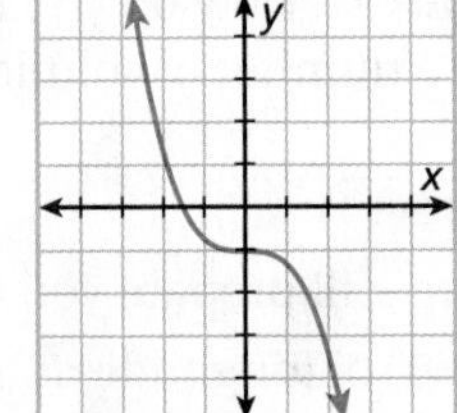

68. 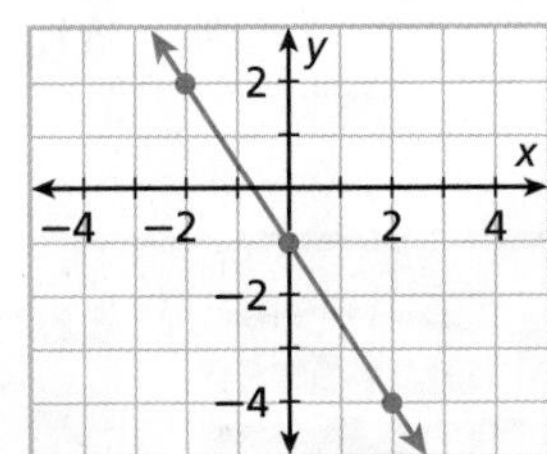

69. **Economics** The table shows the federal minimum wage at four-year intervals. Is minimum wage a function of year? Explain. *(Lesson 1-6)*

Federal Minimum Wage					
Year	1988	1992	1996	2000	2004
Minimum Wage	\$3.35	\$4.25	\$4.75	\$5.15	\$5.15

2-2 Proportional Reasoning

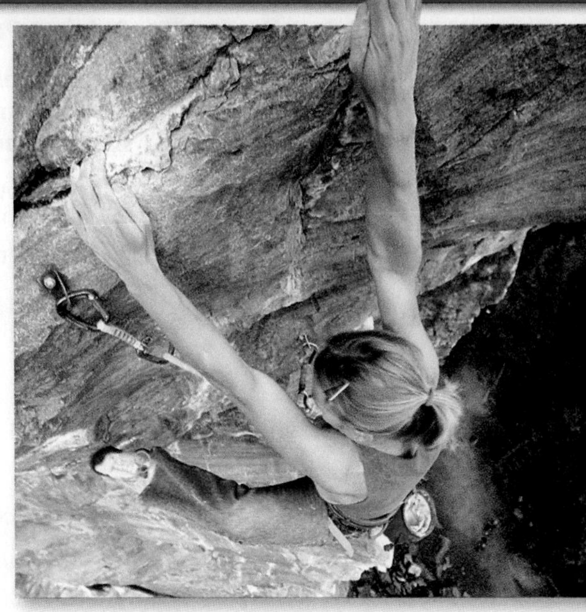

Objective
Apply proportional relationships to rates, similarity, and scale.

Vocabulary
ratio
proportion
rate
similar
indirect measurement

Who uses this?
Rock climbers can use proportions to indirectly measure the height of cliffs. (See Example 5.)

Recall that a **ratio** is a comparison of two numbers by division and a **proportion** is an equation stating that two ratios are equal. In a proportion, the cross products are equal.

Cross Products Property

WORDS	NUMBERS	ALGEBRA
The cross products of a proportion are equal.	$\frac{3}{5} = \frac{9}{15}$ $3(15) = 5(9)$ $45 = 45$	For real numbers *a*, *b*, *c*, and *d*, where $b \neq 0$ and $d \neq 0$: If $\frac{a}{b} = \frac{c}{d}$, then $ad = bc$.

If a proportion contains a variable, you can cross multiply to solve for the variable. When you set the cross products equal, you create a linear equation that you can solve by using the skills that you learned in Lesson 2-1.

EXAMPLE 1 Solving Proportions

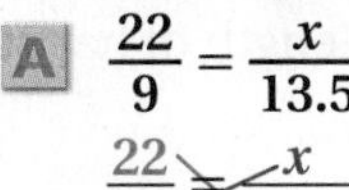

Reading Math
In $a \div b = c \div d$, *b* and *c* are the *means,* and *a* and *d* are the *extremes.* In a proportion, the product of the means is equal to the product of the extremes.

Solve each proportion.

A $\frac{22}{9} = \frac{x}{13.5}$

$\frac{22}{9} \times \frac{x}{13.5}$

$297 = 9x$ *Set cross products equal.*

$\frac{297}{9} = \frac{9x}{9}$ *Divide both sides.*

$33 = x$

B $\frac{512}{16} = \frac{64}{w}$

$\frac{512}{16} \times \frac{64}{w}$

$512w = 1024$

$\frac{512w}{512} = \frac{1024}{512}$

$w = 2$

Solve each proportion.

1a. $\frac{y}{12} = \frac{77}{84}$ **1b.** $\frac{15}{x} = \frac{2.5}{7}$

Because percents can be expressed as ratios, you can use the proportion $\frac{\text{percent}}{100} = \frac{\text{part}}{\text{whole}}$ to solve percent problems.

EXAMPLE 2 Solving Percent Problems

A college brochure states that 11.5% of the students attending the college are majoring in engineering. If 2400 students are attending the college, how many are majoring in engineering?

You know the percent and the total number of students, so you are trying to find the part of the whole (the number of students who are majoring in engineering).

> **Remember!**
>
> Percent is a ratio that means *per hundred.* For example:
>
> $30\% = 0.30 = \frac{30}{100}$

Method 1 Use a proportion.

$$\frac{\text{percent}}{100} = \frac{\text{part}}{\text{whole}}$$

$$\frac{11.5}{100} = \frac{x}{2400}$$

$11.5(2400) = 100x$ *Cross multiply.*

$\frac{27600}{100} = x$ *Solve for x.*

$x = 276$

Method 2 Use a percent equation

$11.5\% = 0.115$ *Divide the percent by 100.*

Percent (as decimal) • whole = part

$0.115 \cdot 2400 = x$

$276 = x$

So 276 students at the college are majoring in engineering.

2. At Clay High School, 434 students, or 35% of the students, play a sport. How many students does Clay High School have?

A **rate** is a ratio that involves two different units. You are familiar with many rates, such as miles per hour (mi/h), words per minute (wpm), or dollars per gallon of gasoline. Rates can be helpful in solving many problems.

EXAMPLE 3 *Fitness Application*

A pedometer measures how far a jogger has run. To set her pedometer, Rita must know her stride length. Rita counts 328 strides as she runs once around a 400 m track. A meter is about 39.37 in. How long is her stride in inches?

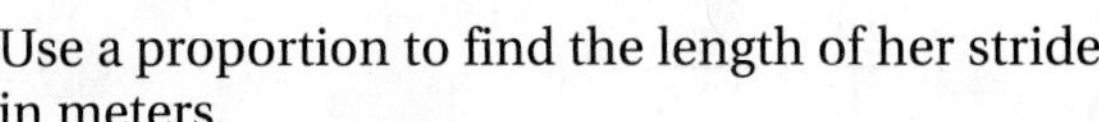

Use a proportion to find the length of her stride in meters.

$\frac{400 \text{ m}}{328 \text{ strides}} = \frac{x \text{ m}}{1 \text{ stride}}$ *Write both ratios in the form $\frac{\text{meters}}{\text{strides}}$.*

$400 = 328x$ *Find the cross products.*

$x \approx 1.22 \text{ m}$

Convert the stride length to inches.

$\frac{1.22 \not{\text{m}}}{1 \text{ stride length}} \cdot \frac{39.37 \text{ in.}}{1 \not{\text{m}}} \approx \frac{48 \text{ in.}}{1 \text{ stride length}}$ *$\frac{39.37 \text{ in.}}{1 \text{ m}}$ is the conversion factor.*

Rita's stride length is approximately 48 inches.

3. Luis ran the same 400 m track in 297 strides. Find his stride length in inches.

Similar figures have the same shape but not necessarily the same size. Two figures are **similar** if their corresponding angles are congruent and corresponding sides are proportional.

EXAMPLE 4 Scaling Geometric Figures in the Coordinate Plane

Geometry

$\triangle ABC$ has vertices $A(0, 0)$, $B(8, 4)$, and $C(8, 0)$. $\triangle ADE$ is similar to $\triangle ABC$ with a vertex at $E(2, 0)$. Graph $\triangle ABC$ and $\triangle ADE$ on the same grid.

Step 1 Graph $\triangle ABC$. Then draw $\overline{AE}$.

Step 2 To find the height of $\triangle ADE$, use a proportion.

$$\frac{\text{width of } \triangle ADE}{\text{width of } \triangle ABC} = \frac{\text{height of } \triangle ADE}{\text{height of } \triangle ABC}$$

$$\frac{2}{8} = \frac{x}{4}$$

$$8x = 8, \text{ so } x = 1$$

Step 3 To graph $\triangle ADE$, first find the coordinates of D.

The height is 1 unit, and the width is 2 units, so the coordinates of D are $(2, 1)$.

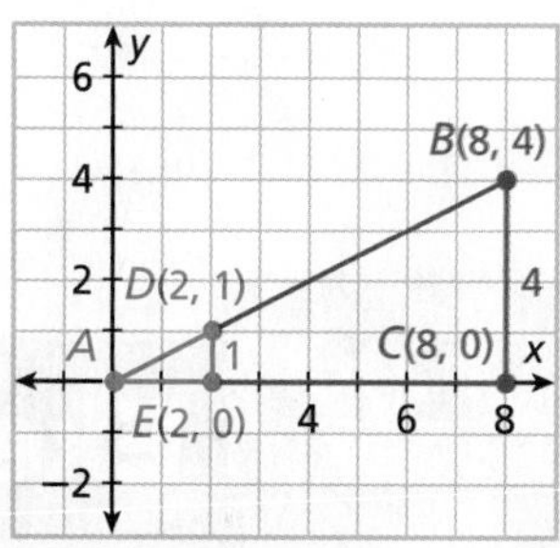

> **Reading Math**
>
> The ratio of the corresponding side lengths of similar figures is often called the *scale factor*.

4. $\triangle DEF$ has vertices $D(0, 0)$, $E(-6, 0)$, and $F(0, -4)$. $\triangle DGH$ is similar to $\triangle DEF$ with a vertex at $G(-3, 0)$. Graph $\triangle DEF$ and $\triangle DGH$ on the same grid.

Indirect measurement uses known lengths, similar figures, and proportions to measure objects that cannot easily be measured.

EXAMPLE 5 *Recreation Application*

A rock climber wants to know the height of a cliff. The climber measures the shadow of her friend, who is 5 feet tall and standing beside the cliff, and measures the shadow of the cliff. If the friend's shadow is 4 feet long and the cliff's shadow is 60 feet long, how tall is the cliff?

Sketch the situation. The triangles formed by using the shadows are similar, so the rock climber can use a proportion to find h the height of the cliff.

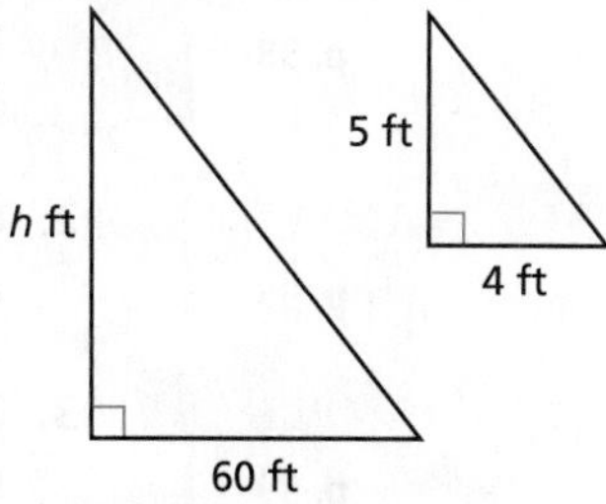

$\frac{4}{5} = \frac{60}{h}$ $\quad$ $\frac{\textit{shadow of friend}}{\textit{height of friend}} = \frac{\textit{shadow of cliff}}{\textit{height of cliff}}$

$4h = 300$

$h = 75$

The cliff is 75 feet high.

5. A 6-foot-tall climber casts a 20-foot-long shadow at the same time that a tree casts a 90-foot-long shadow. How tall is the tree?

THINK AND DISCUSS

1. Use algebra to explain why equal cross products imply that two ratios are equal.
2. How is it possible to find a length or distance without physically measuring it?
3. **GET ORGANIZED** Copy and complete the graphic organizer. In each box, write examples of each item that relate to the concept of proportion.

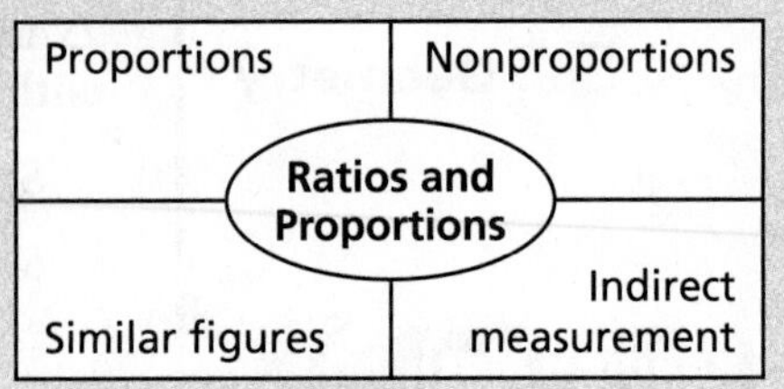

2-2 Exercises

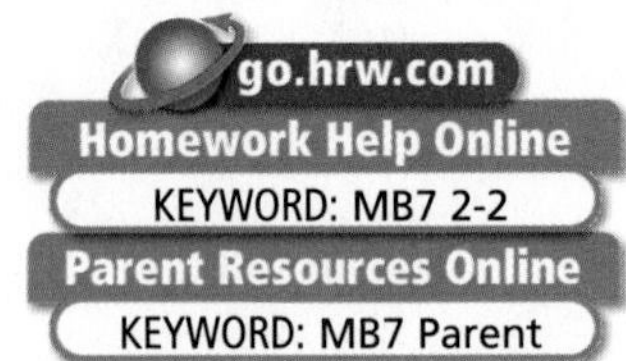

GUIDED PRACTICE

1. **Vocabulary** *Miles per hour* is a(n) __?__. (*rate, ratio,* or *indirect measurement*)

SEE EXAMPLE 1 p. 97

Solve each proportion.

2. $\frac{6.4}{x} = \frac{2}{3}$
3. $\frac{2}{13} = \frac{n}{52}$
4. $\frac{4}{14} = \frac{24}{x}$
5. $\frac{\frac{1}{3}}{3} = \frac{6}{t}$
6. $\frac{8}{x} = \frac{5}{12}$
7. $\frac{4}{9} = \frac{x}{45}$
8. $\frac{-2}{5} = \frac{18}{x}$
9. $\frac{x}{-15} = \frac{63}{45}$

SEE EXAMPLE 2 p. 98

10. **School** A college brochure claims that 24% of the students attending the college are majoring in business. If there are 420 students at the college who are majoring in business, how many students are attending the college?

SEE EXAMPLE 3 p. 98

11. **Travel** Jesse drove from Los Angeles to Las Vegas, a distance of 463 km. He used 12 gal of gas on the trip. Find the gas mileage in miles per gallon of Jesse's car. (*Hint*: 1 km ≈ 0.62 mi)

SEE EXAMPLE 4 p. 98

12. **Geometry** $\triangle ABC$ has vertices $A(0, 0)$, $B(0, 8)$, and $C(-6, 8)$. $\triangle ADE$ is similar to $\triangle ABC$ with a vertex at $D(0, 4)$. Graph $\triangle ABC$ and $\triangle ADE$ on the same grid.

SEE EXAMPLE 5 p. 99

13. **Surveying** A surveyor uses similar triangles to measure the distance across a canyon. What is the distance across the canyon, according to the diagram?

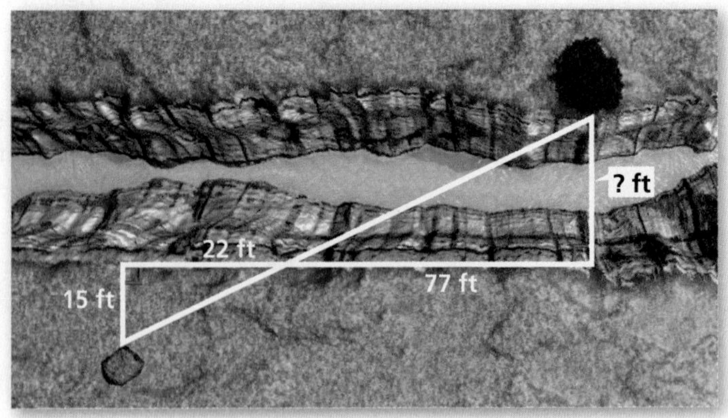

PRACTICE AND PROBLEM SOLVING

Independent Practice

For Exercises	See Example
14–17	1
18	2
19	3
20	4
21	5

Extra Practice

Skills Practice p. S6
Application Practice p. S33

Solve each proportion.

14. $\frac{55}{200} = \frac{143}{n}$ **15.** $\frac{1.24}{3} = \frac{y}{15}$ **16.** $\frac{22}{11} = \frac{7}{x}$ **17.** $\frac{0.1}{x} = \frac{1.1}{110}$

18. Business A quality control inspector has found that 3.2% of the garments produced at Standard Garments contain a defect. If Standard Garments produces 4117 garments in one day, how many of those garments are expected to have a defect?

19. Communication Latanya made a 17-minute phone call from her hotel in France and was charged 17 euro. At the time, \$1 was worth 0.82 euro. Find the cost per minute of the call in dollars.

20. Geometry $\triangle ABC$ has vertices $A(0, 0)$, $B(6, 0)$, and $C(6, -4.5)$. $\triangle ADE$ is similar to $\triangle ABC$ with a vertex at $D(8, 0)$. Graph $\triangle ABC$ and $\triangle ADE$ on the same grid.

21. Measurement A basketball rim 10 ft high casts a shadow 15 ft long. At the same time, a nearby building casts a shadow that is 54 ft long. How tall is the building?

Solve.

22. $\frac{4}{9} = \frac{r+3}{45}$ **23.** $\frac{2.8}{1.5} = \frac{t}{0.09}$ **24.** $\frac{9+m}{5} = \frac{15}{4}$ **25.** $\frac{2}{u-5} = \frac{6}{9}$

26. $\frac{12}{27} = \frac{3r}{3}$ **27.** $\frac{-11}{0.11h} = \frac{10}{3}$ **28.** $\frac{25}{75} = \frac{80}{5x}$ **29.** $\frac{0}{17} = \frac{0.5x}{170}$

30. Food A sample of students was asked what type of restaurant they visit most often. Their answers are shown in the circle graph. If 126 students chose Chinese restaurants, how many students were polled?

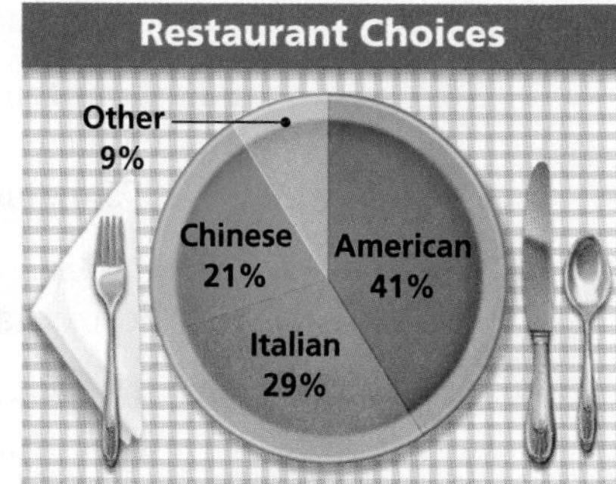

31. Critical Thinking If $a \neq 0$, $b \neq 0$, $c \neq 0$, $d \neq 0$, and $\frac{a}{b} = \frac{c}{d}$, explain why $\frac{d}{c} = \frac{b}{a}$ is also true.

32. What if...? Suppose you double the lengths of the sides of a rectangle.

a. What is the relationship between the perimeter of the new rectangle and the perimeter of the original rectangle?

b. What is the relationship between the area of the image and the area of the preimage?

33. Critical Thinking In a film, the 555-feet-tall Washington Monument casts a 100-feet-long shadow, whereas the main character in the film casts a 4 feet-long shadow nearby. Why is this considered a film "goof"?

34. Estimation The distance from La Paz to Cabo San Lucas on Mexico's Baja Peninsula is 92 miles, or 148 kilometers.

a. The red bar representing the scale of the map represents approximately how many miles?

b. About how many kilometers is El Pescadero from Los Barilles?

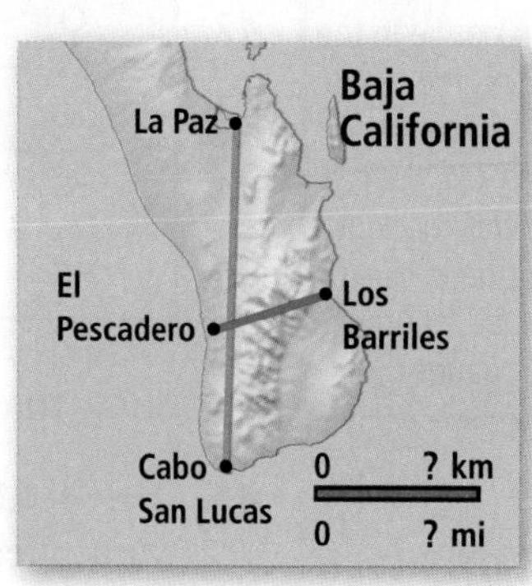

35. This problem will prepare you for the Multi-Step Test Prep on page 132.

Nautical speed was once measured by throwing a rope into the water from the ship. The rope had knots every 47 ft 3 in., and its wedge-shaped end would "grab" the water. The speed was the number of rope knots that went into the water while a 28 s hourglass ran down.

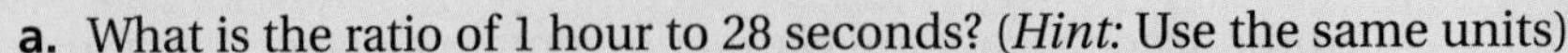

a. What is the ratio of 1 hour to 28 seconds? (*Hint:* Use the same units).

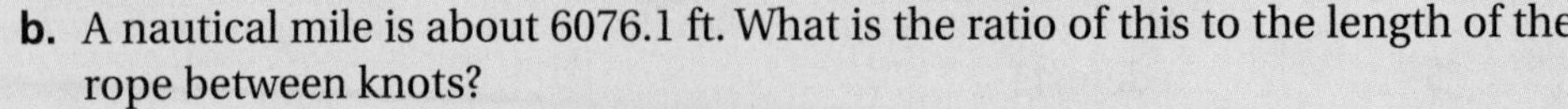

b. A nautical mile is about 6076.1 ft. What is the ratio of this to the length of the rope between knots?

c. What proportion might have been set up to determine the correct length of rope between knots?

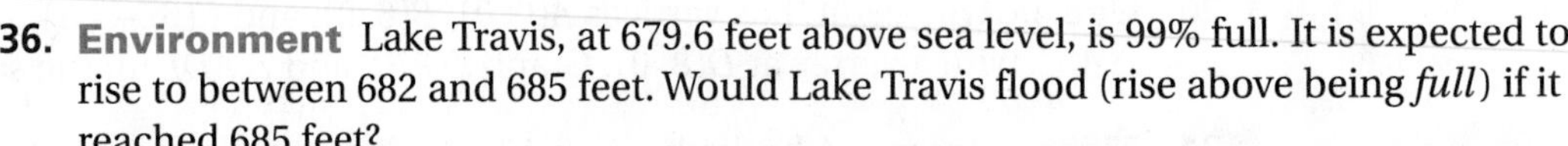

36. Environment Lake Travis, at 679.6 feet above sea level, is 99% full. It is expected to rise to between 682 and 685 feet. Would Lake Travis flood (rise above being *full*) if it reached 685 feet?

37. Chemistry There are about 1,400,000 drops in 25 gallons of a liquid. What percent of a gallon is a single drop?

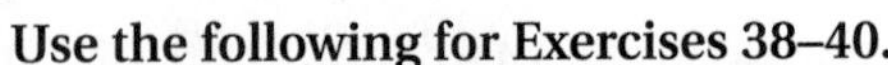

Use the following for Exercises 38–40.

Grade is a measure of the steepness of surfaces, such as roads and ramps. Grade is expressed as a percent based on the ratio $\frac{\text{vertical rise}}{\text{horizontal run}}$. For example, a ramp that is 5 feet long and rises 1 foot has a grade of $\frac{1}{5}$, or 20%.

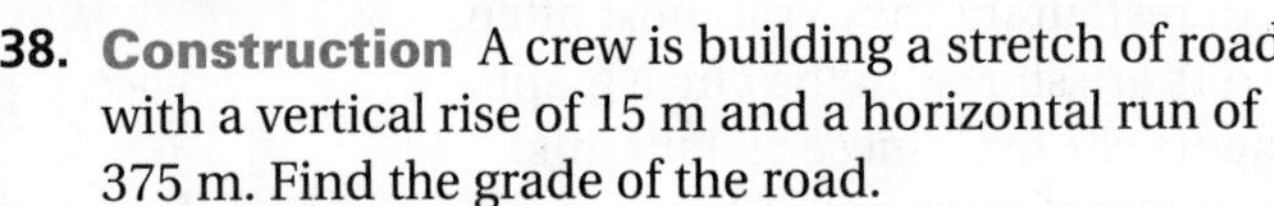

38. Construction A crew is building a stretch of road with a vertical rise of 15 m and a horizontal run of 375 m. Find the grade of the road.

39. Fitness A treadmill has a 9% grade. If the treadmill has a horizontal run of 5 feet, what is the treadmill's vertical rise in inches?

40. Accessibility The Americans with Disabilities Act set the maximum grade for wheelchair-accessible ramps at $8\frac{1}{3}$%. What is the minimum horizontal run in feet required for a ramp designed to rise 30 inches?

41. Geometry In the diagram shown, $\triangle ABC$ is similar to $\triangle DEF$. Find the lengths of sides $\overline{AB}$ and $\overline{EF}$.

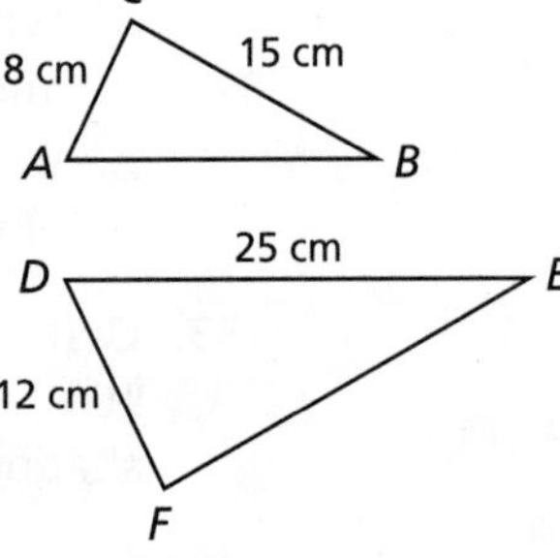

LINK

Hobbies

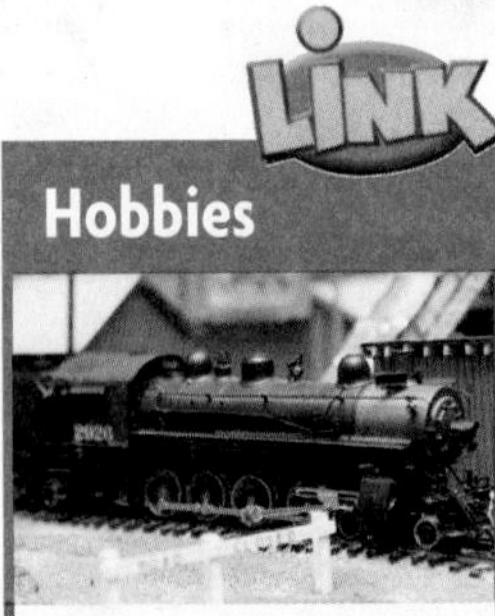

HO is the most popular model train gauge in the United States. The name may have originally meant "Half-O," because it was thought to be about half the size of an O gauge, another model train gauge.

Hobbies **Use the information about model trains to complete the table.**

	Railroad Gauge	Scale Length (in.)	Actual Length (ft)
42.	O	96	■
43.	■	36	261
44.	S	■	80
45.	HO	20	■

Model Trains

Railroad Gauge	HO	O	S
Model Scale	$\frac{1}{87}$	$\frac{1}{48}$	$\frac{1}{64}$

46. Show that if $b \neq 0$, $d \neq 0$, and $\frac{a}{b} = \frac{c}{d}$, then $\frac{a+b}{b} = \frac{c+d}{d}$.

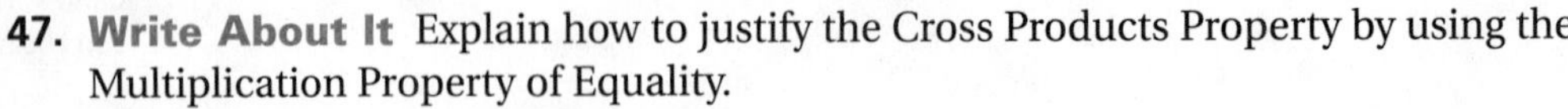

47. Write About It Explain how to justify the Cross Products Property by using the Multiplication Property of Equality.

48. **Chemistry** The energy output from a chemical reaction depends on the amount of chemicals used. The table shows this relationship. What is a reasonable amount of energy from the reaction of 40 moles of the chemical?

Energy Output of a Chemical Reaction				
Amount of Chemical (moles)	5	8	12	15
Energy Output (joules)	29.89	48.01	71.96	90.12

Ⓐ 120 joules Ⓑ 160 joules Ⓒ 240 joules Ⓓ 300 joules

49. **Technology** A 38 MB file is downloading from the Internet at a constant rate. After 1 min, 18% of the file has downloaded. About how much more time should the download take?

Ⓕ 5.6 min Ⓖ 4.6 min Ⓗ 6.75 min Ⓙ 2.1 min

50. A blueprint uses a scale of $\frac{1}{4}$ inch equals 1 foot. A wall on the drawing measures $4\frac{1}{2}$ inches long. How long will the wall be in the actual building?

Ⓐ $\frac{11}{8}$ feet Ⓑ 9 feet Ⓒ 16 feet Ⓓ 18 feet

51. **Geometry** In a circle graph, how many degrees does 1% represent?

Ⓕ 1° Ⓖ 3.6° Ⓗ 6° Ⓙ 10°

CHALLENGE AND EXTEND

Solve.

52. $\frac{-2}{x+5} = \frac{8}{x-3}$ 53. $\frac{h+4}{9} = \frac{h-3}{4}$ 54. $\frac{n-2}{4} = \frac{3n+3}{18}$ 55. $\frac{z}{12.8} = \frac{5}{z}$

56. **Construction** A concrete mix has the ratio 1 part cement, 2 parts water, and 3 parts sand. How much water can be used if 78 kg of sand and 21 kg of cement are available? How much concrete can be made?

57. **Critical Thinking** The graph intends to show the increase in the number of dogs registered. Do the icons accurately represent the data? Justify your answer.

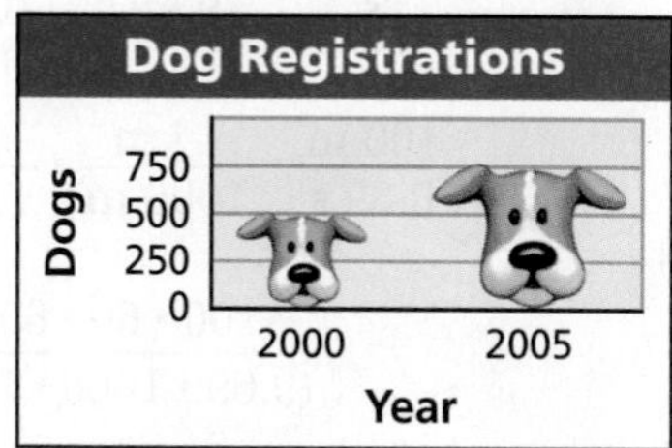

SPIRAL REVIEW

Convert each measure using the given units. *(Previous course)*

58. $\frac{1}{5}$ h = ■ min 59. 108 in. = ■ yd 60. 4.5 lb = ■ oz

61. 3.5 m = ■ cm 62. 12 mm = ■ cm 63. 25 mL = ■ L

Name the three-dimensional figure that each real-world object models. *(Previous course)*

64. tennis ball 65. megaphone 66. pad of paper 67. unsharpened pencil

Identify the parent function for *h* from its function rule. Describe what transformation of the parent function it represents. *(Lesson 1-9)*

68. $h(x) = x^2 - 10$ 69. $h(x) = 3x + 4$ 70. $h(x) = 2x^3$ 71. $h(x) = -\sqrt{x+1}$

Dimensional Analysis

Dimensional analysis involves examining the dimensions (such as mass, length, and time) used in a problem. You can use dimensional analysis to check calculations involving unit conversions and formulas.

The table shows some equivalent measures in the customary and metric systems. Equivalent measures can be used to write conversion factors. A *conversion factor* is a ratio that compares the same quantity in different units.

	Customary	Metric	Customary and Metric
Length	1 ft = 12 in. 1 mi = 5280 ft	1 m = 100 cm 1 km = 1000 m	1 in. = 2.54 cm 1 mi ≈ 1.61 km
Mass/Weight	1 lb = 16 oz 1 ton = 2000 lb	1 g = 1000 mg 1 kg = 1000 g	1 oz ≈ 28.35 g 1 lb ≈ 0.454 kg
Capacity	1 c = 8 fl oz 1 gal = 4 qt	1 L = 1000 mL	1 fl oz ≈ 29.57 mL 1 gal ≈ 3.785 L

In the 2008 Summer Olympics, Usain Bolt ran 100 meters in 9.69 seconds. What was his average speed in miles per hour?

$$\frac{100\text{ m}}{9.69\text{ s}}$$

Use the given information to write a rate that compares distance to time.

$$\frac{100\text{ m}}{9.69\text{ s}} \cdot \frac{1\text{ km}}{1000\text{ m}} \cdot \frac{1\text{ mi}}{1.61\text{ km}}$$

Multiply by conversion factors to convert meters to miles.

$$\frac{100\text{ m}}{9.69\text{ s}} \cdot \frac{1\text{ km}}{1000\text{ m}} \cdot \frac{1\text{ mi}}{1.61\text{ km}} \cdot \frac{60\text{ s}}{1\text{ min}} \cdot \frac{60\text{ min}}{1\text{ h}}$$

Multiply by conversion factors to convert seconds to hours.

$$\frac{(100 \cdot 60 \cdot 60)\text{ mi}}{(9.69 \cdot 1000 \cdot 1.61)\text{ h}} \approx 23.1\text{ mi/h}$$

Simplify. Use dimensional analysis to check that the units cancel correctly.

Bolt's average speed was about 23.1 miles per hour.

Convert each measure. Round to the nearest tenth if necessary.

1. $3\frac{1}{2}$ lb to ounces **2.** 280 m to kilometers **3.** 2 L to fluid ounces

4. 60 mi/h to ft/s **5.** 15 g/mL to kg/L **6.** 9.5 km/L to mi/gal

7. Vincent drives his SUV an average of 20 miles per day. The SUV produces an average of 1.25 pounds of carbon dioxide per mile driven. How many tons of carbon dioxide will the SUV produce per year? Round your answer to the nearest tenth.

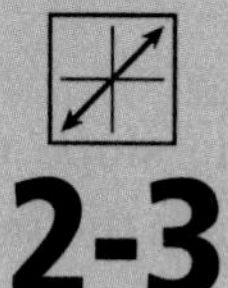

2-3 Graphing Linear Functions

Objectives

Determine whether a function is linear.

Graph a linear function given two points, a table, an equation, or a point and a slope.

Vocabulary

linear function
slope
y-intercept
x-intercept
slope-intercept form

Who uses this?

Meteorologists can use linear functions to predict when a hurricane will reach land.

Meteorologists begin tracking a hurricane's distance from land when it is 350 miles off the coast of Florida and moving steadily inland.

The meteorologists are interested in the rate at which the hurricane is approaching land.

Reading Math

The differences in the y-values for equally-spaced x-values are called *first differences.*

(Time: +1, +1, +1, +1)

Time (h)	0	1	2	3	4
Distance from Land (mi)	350	325	300	275	250

(Distance: −25, −25, −25, −25)

This rate can be expressed as $\frac{\text{change in distance}}{\text{change in time}} = \frac{-25 \text{ miles}}{1 \text{ hour}}$. Notice that the rate of change is constant. The hurricane moves 25 miles closer each hour.

Functions with a constant rate of change are called *linear functions.* A **linear function** can be written in the form $f(x) = mx + b$, where x is the independent variable and m and b are constants. The graph of a linear function is a straight line made up of the set of all points that satisfy $y = f(x)$.

EXAMPLE 1 Recognizing Linear Functions

Determine whether each data set could represent a linear function.

A

(x: +2, +2, +2)

x	0	2	4	6
$f(x)$	−1	2	5	8

(f(x): +3, +3, +3)

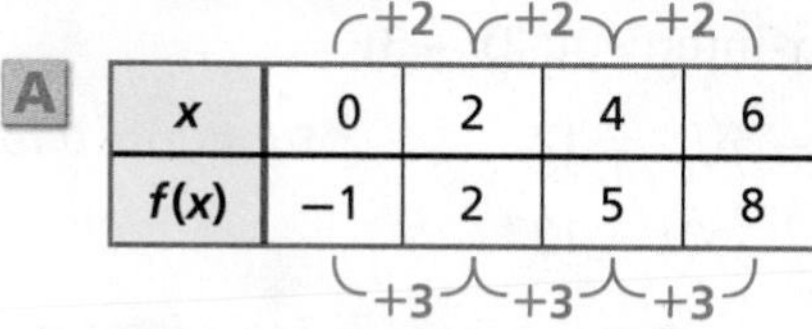

The rate of change, $\frac{\text{change in } f(x)}{\text{change in } x}$, is constant $\frac{3}{2}$. So the data set is linear.

B

(x: +3, +3, +3)

x	−1	2	5	8
$f(x)$	0	1	3	6

(f(x): +1, +2, +3)

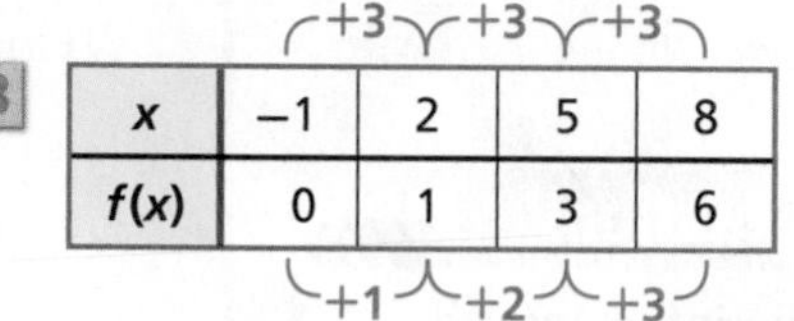

The rate of change, $\frac{\text{change in } f(x)}{\text{change in } x}$, is not constant. $\frac{1}{3} \neq \frac{2}{3} \neq \frac{3}{3}$. The data set is not linear.

CHECK IT OUT! **Determine whether each data set could represent a linear function.**

1a.

x	4	11	18	25
$f(x)$	−6	−15	−24	−33

1b.

x	10	8	6	4
$f(x)$	7	5	1	−7

The constant rate of change for a linear function is its *slope*. The **slope** of a linear function is the ratio $\frac{\text{change in } f(x)}{\text{change in } x}$, or $\frac{\text{rise}}{\text{run}}$. The slope of a line is the same between any two points on the line. You can graph lines by using the slope and a point.

EXAMPLE 2 Graphing Lines Using Slope and a Point

Graph each line.

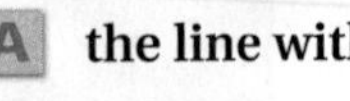

A the line with slope $\frac{2}{3}$ that passes through $(1, 1)$

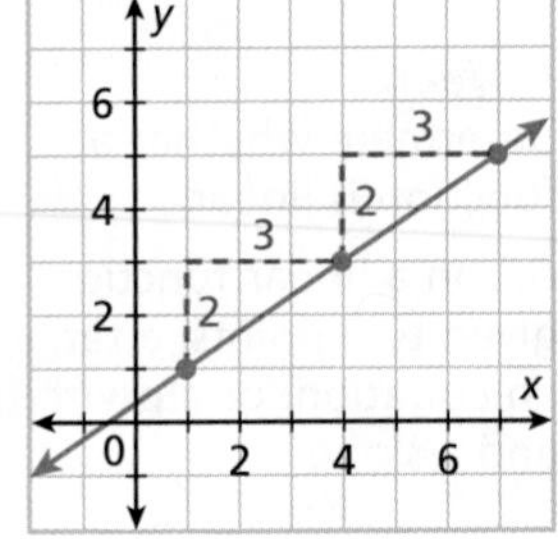

Plot the point $(1, 1)$. The slope indicates a rise of 2 and a run of 3. Move up 2 and right 3 to find another point. Repeat. Then draw a line through the points.

B the line with slope $-\frac{1}{3}$ that passes through $(-2, 3)$

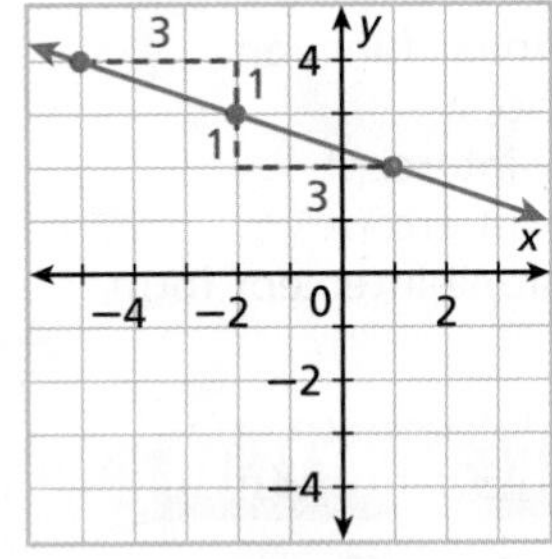

Plot the point $(-2, 3)$. The negative slope can be viewed as $\frac{-1}{3}$ or $\frac{1}{-3}$.

You can move down 1 unit and right 3 units, or move up 1 unit and left 3 units. Notice that all three points are on the same line.

CHECK IT OUT! 2. Graph the line with slope $\frac{4}{3}$ that passes through $(3, 1)$.

Recall from geometry that two points determine a line. Often the easiest points to find are the points where a line crosses the axes. The **y-intercept** is the *y*-coordinate of a point where the line crosses the *y*-axis. The **x-intercept** is the *x*-coordinate of a point where the line crosses the *x*-axis.

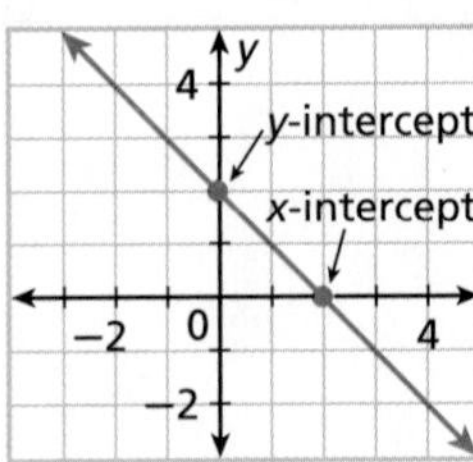

EXAMPLE 3 Graphing Lines Using the Intercepts

Find the intercepts of $2x - 3y = 12$, and graph the line.

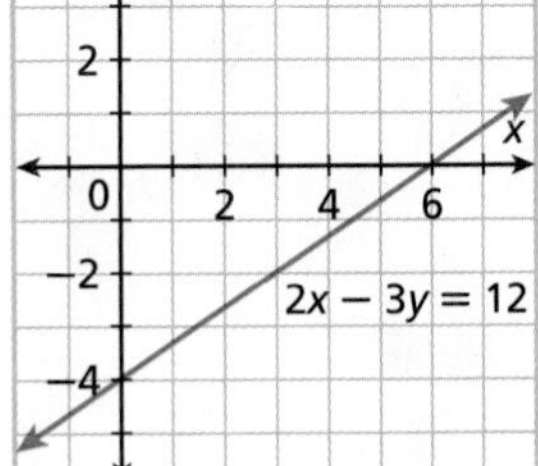

Caution!

The intercept is a single value, not an ordered pair or a point.

Find the *x*-intercept: $2x - 3y = 12$

$2x - 3(0) = 12$ *Substitute 0 for y.*

$2x = 12$

$x = 6$ *The x-intercept is 6.*

Find the *y*-intercept: $2x - 3y = 12$

$2(0) - 3y = 12$ *Substitute 0 for x.*

$-3y = 12$

$y = -4$ *The y-intercept is –4.*

Draw the line through $(6, 0)$ and $(0, -4)$.

CHECK IT OUT! 3. Find the intercepts of $6x - 2y = -24$, and graph the line.

Linear functions can also be expressed as linear equations of the form $y = mx + b$. When a linear function is written in the form $y = mx + b$, the function is said to be in **slope-intercept form** because m is the slope of the graph and b is the y-intercept. Notice that slope-intercept form is the equation solved for y.

EXAMPLE 

Graphing Functions in Slope-Intercept Form

Write each function in slope-intercept form. Then graph the function.

A $3x + y = 5$

Solve for y first.

$$3x + y = 5$$
$$\underline{-3x \qquad -3x} \qquad \textit{Add } -3x \textit{ to both sides.}$$
$$y = -3x + 5$$

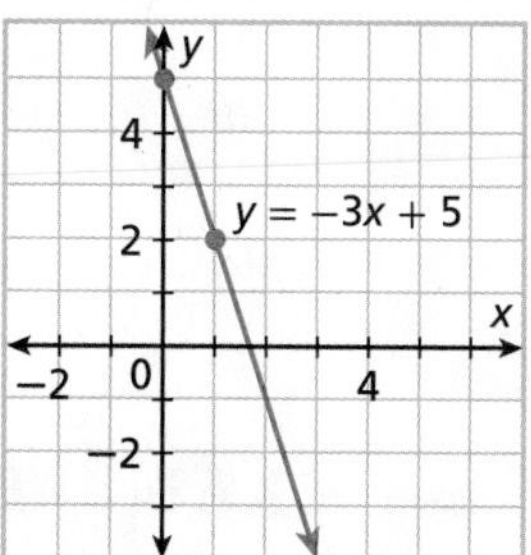

The line has y-intercept 5 and slope -3, which is $\frac{-3}{1}$. Plot the point $(0, 5)$. Then move down 3 and right 1 to find other points.

Helpful Hint

Most graphing calculators require equations to be solved for y, so slope-intercept form is the easiest to enter.

You can also use a graphing calculator to graph. Choose the standard square window to make your graph look like it would on a regular grid. Press ZOOM, choose **6:ZStandard**, press ZOOM again, and then choose **5:ZSquare**.

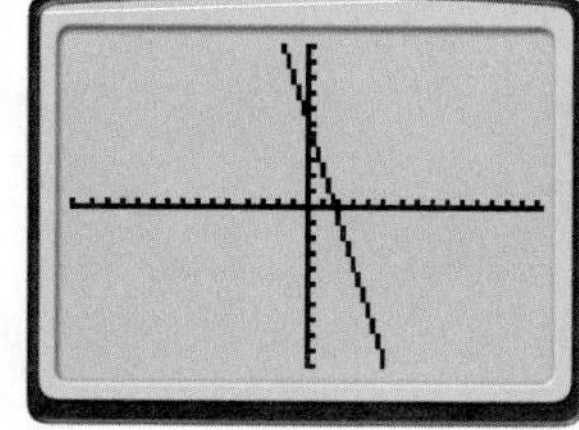

B $\frac{3}{2}y = x - 3$

Solve for y first.

$$\frac{2}{3}\left(\frac{3}{2}y\right) = \frac{2}{3}(x - 3) \qquad \textit{Multiply both sides by } \frac{2}{3}.$$
$$y = \frac{2}{3}(x) - \frac{2}{3}(3) \qquad \textit{Distribute.}$$
$$y = \frac{2}{3}x - 2$$

The graph of the line has y-intercept -2 and slope $\frac{2}{3}$. Plot the point $(0, -2)$. Then move up 2 and right 3 to find other points.

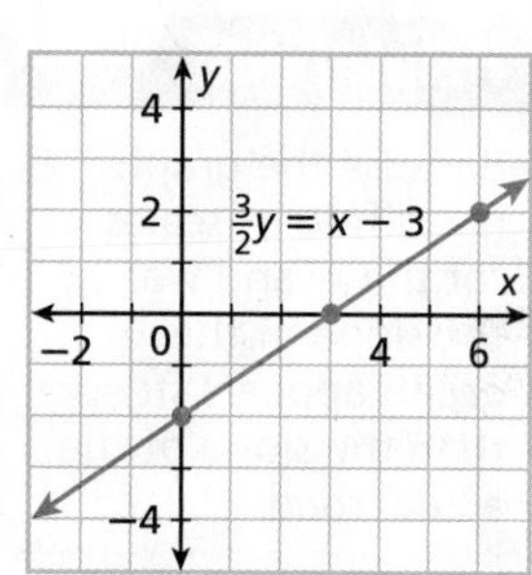

Write each equation in slope-intercept form. Then graph the function.

4a. $2x - y = 9$ **4b.** $5x = 15y + 30$

An equation with only one variable can be represented by either a vertical or a horizontal line.

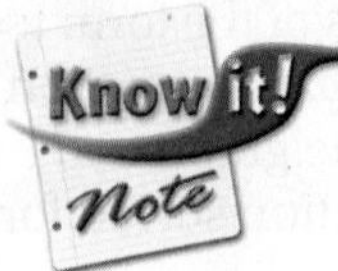

Vertical and Horizontal Lines	
Vertical Lines	**Horizontal Lines**
The line $x = a$ is a vertical line at a.	The line $y = b$ is a horizontal line at b.
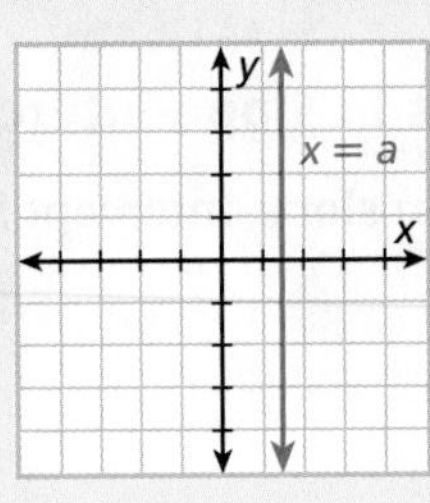	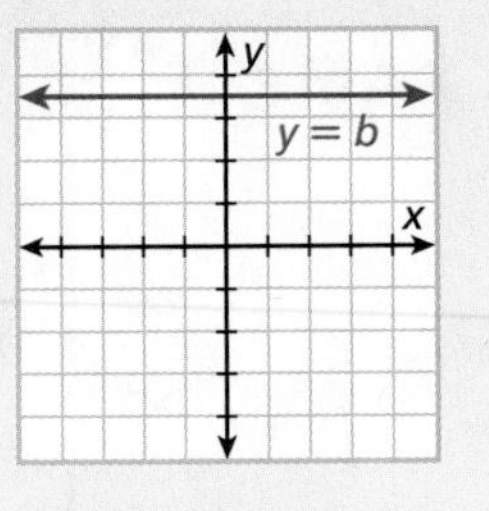

The slope of a vertical line is undefined. The slope of a horizontal line is 0.

EXAMPLE 5 Graphing Vertical and Horizontal Lines

Determine if each line is vertical or horizontal. Then graph.

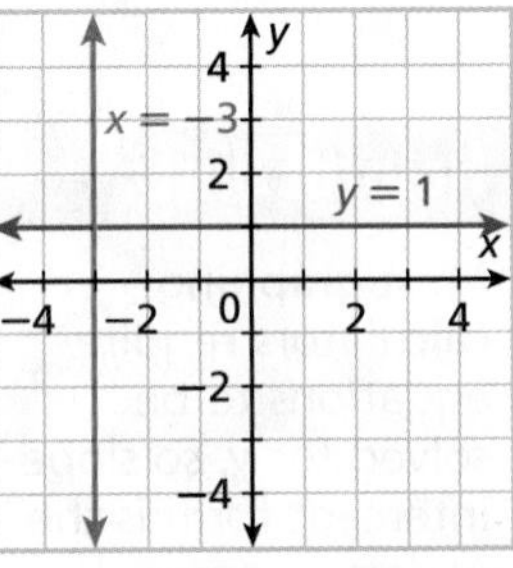

 **A** $x = -3$

This is a vertical line located at the x-value -3. (Note that it is not a function.)

 **B** $y = 1$

This is a horizontal line located at the y-value 1.

CHECK IT OUT! **Determine if each line is vertical or horizontal. Then graph.**

5a. $y = -5$ **5b.** $x = 0.5$

EXAMPLE 6 *Travel Application*

Suppose a road rises from 2500 ft above sea level to 7000 ft in 10 mi. Find the average slope of the road. Graph the elevation against distance.

Helpful Hint

Because the graph has different scales for the x- and y-axis, the slope of the graph appears steeper than the slope of the actual road.

Step 1 Find the slope.

The rise is $7000 - 2500$, or 4500 ft.
The run is 10 mi.

Convert miles to feet:

$10 \text{ mi} = 10(5280) = 52{,}800 \text{ ft}.$

The slope is $\frac{4500}{52{,}800} \approx 0.085$.

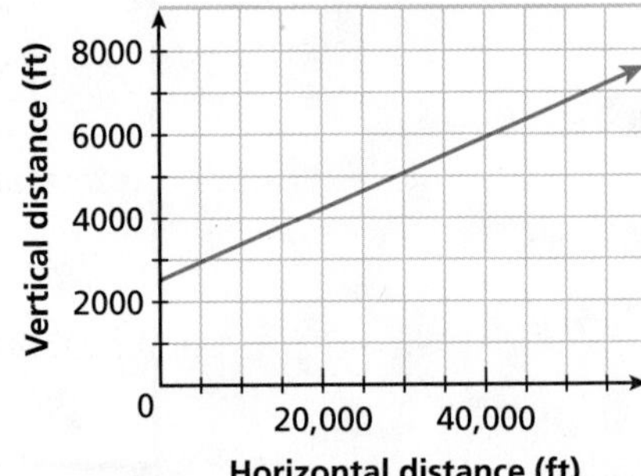

Step 2 Graph the line.

The y-intercept is the original altitude, 2500 ft. Use $(0, 2500)$ and $(52{,}800, 7000)$ as two points on the line. Select a scale for each axis that will fit the data, and graph the function.

CHECK IT OUT! **6.** A truck driver is at mile marker 624 on Interstate 10. After 3 hours, the driver reaches mile marker 432. Find his average speed. Graph his location on I-10 in terms of mile markers.

THINK AND DISCUSS

1. Explain two different ways to graph the equation $4x = 2y - 12$.
2. Can a line have more than one slope? Explain.
3. What are the slope and y-intercept for the line that models the hurricane data at the beginning of this lesson? Explain.

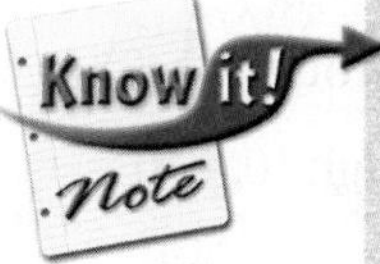

4. **GET ORGANIZED** Copy and complete the graphic organizer for linear functions.

Definition	Characteristics
Linear Function	
Examples	Nonexamples

2-3 Exercises

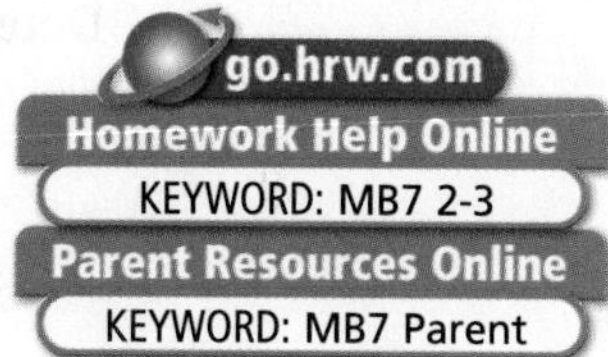

GUIDED PRACTICE

Apply the vocabulary from this lesson to answer each question.

1. **Vocabulary** How does the *y-intercept* differ from the *x-intercept*?
2. **Vocabulary** The rate of change of a linear function is its __?__. (*intercept* or *slope*)

SEE EXAMPLE 1 p. 105

Determine whether each data set could represent a linear function.

3.

x	2	5	8	11
f(x)	9	17	25	33

4.

x	3	9	15	21
f(x)	1	4	10	19

SEE EXAMPLE 2 p. 106

Graph each line.

5. slope $\frac{5}{2}$; passes through $(0, 2)$
6. slope 2; passes through $(4, -5)$
7. slope $-\frac{4}{3}$; passes through $(-2, -1)$
8. slope $-\frac{2}{5}$; passes through $(3, 0)$

SEE EXAMPLE 3 p. 106

Find the intercepts of each line, and graph the line.

9. $5x + 6y = 30$
10. $2x - 3y = 24$
11. $5x - 2y = -30$
12. $-4x + 5y = 10$

SEE EXAMPLE 4 p. 107

Write each function in slope-intercept form. Then graph the function.

13. $5x + y = 4$
14. $-y = -8x$
15. $3y = 15 - 6x$
16. $2x - 5y = -6$

SEE EXAMPLE 5 p. 108

Determine if each line is vertical or horizontal. Then graph the line.

17. $x = 7$
18. $y = \frac{5}{4}$
19. $x = 0$
20. $y = -4$

SEE EXAMPLE 6 p. 108

21. **Business** Art's cash register contained \$150 when he opened the store. After 8 hours, the register contained \$738. Find the average sales per hour, and graph the hourly amount of cash in the register.

PRACTICE AND PROBLEM SOLVING

Independent Practice

For Exercises	See Example
22–23	1
24–27	2
28–31	3
32–35	4
36–39	5
40	6

Extra Practice

Skills Practice p. S6
Application Practice p. S33

Determine whether each data set could represent a linear function.

22.

x	2	3	4	5
$f(x)$	0	1	2	1

23.

x	−3	−1	1	3
$f(x)$	1	1.5	2	2.5

Graph each line.

24. slope 2; passes through $(-3, 0)$

25. slope −2.5; passes through $(1, 6)$

26. slope $-\frac{1}{4}$; passes through $(-1, -2)$

27. slope $\frac{1}{2}$; passes through $(0, -8)$

Find the intercepts of each line, and graph the line.

28. $x + y = -3$

29. $2x - y = 8$

30. $5x - 2y = 10$

31. $-3x + 2y = 6$

Write each function in slope-intercept form. Then graph the function.

32. $2x + y = 6$

33. $-y = -3x + 2$

34. $3y = -6 + x$

35. $8x - 6y = -12$

Determine if each line is vertical or horizontal. Then graph the line.

36. $x = -1$

37. $y = 0$

38. $x = 3.7$

39. $y = -\frac{4}{5}$

40. **Architecture** The fastest elevator in the world is in the Taipei 101 tower in Taiwan. Descending from the observation deck, the elevator travels between the two heights shown in about 7 seconds.

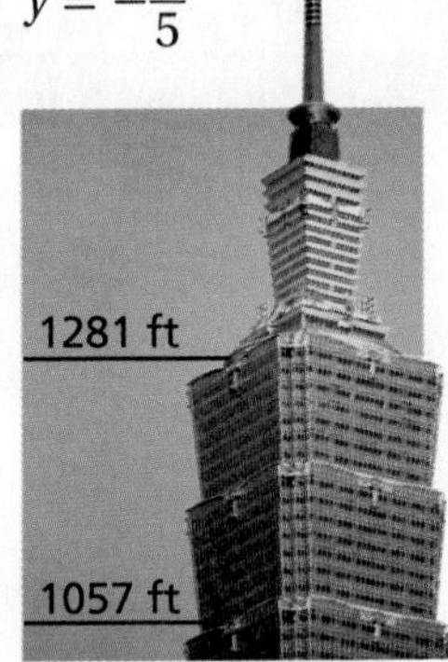

a. Find the average speed of the elevator, and graph the height against the time.

b. Use your graph to estimate when the elevator will reach ground level.

Graph each function.

41. $y = -\frac{1}{3}x + 2$

42. $x + y = 8$

43. $y = \frac{4}{7}x - 6$

44. $2y = 3x - 1$

45. $y = 4 - \frac{1}{8}x$

46. $0.2x + 0.6y = 1.8$

47. The beverage prices for a diner are shown.

a. Are the beverage prices a linear function of the number of ounces?

b. How much should a 32 oz drink cost?

c. What is the y-intercept? What does it represent?

d. **What if...?** Suppose the prices are all decreased by \$0.20. How do your answers to parts **a**, **b**, and **c** change? What answers remain the same?

Tell whether each statement is sometimes, always, or never true.

48. If the slope of a linear function is 0, then the line is parallel to the y-axis.

49. If the y-intercept and the x-intercept of a linear function are equal, then the slope is 1.

50. If the y-intercept of a linear function is positive and the slope is negative, then the x-intercept is positive.

51. This problem will prepare you for the Multi-Step Test Prep on page 132.

The deepest point in the world's oceans, in the Marianas Trench, is 35,840 ft deep. A nautical mile is about 6,076.1 ft.

a. A league is 3 nautical miles. How many leagues deep is the Marianas Trench?

b. Graph the relationship between leagues and feet, using feet as the independent variable. Show a point representing the Marianas Trench on your graph.

c. What does the slope of the line represent?

d. The novel *20,000 Leagues Under the Sea* was written by Jules Verne in 1870. How many feet are in 20,000 leagues? Using this answer, find out how many times the depth of the Marianas Trench 20,000 leagues is.

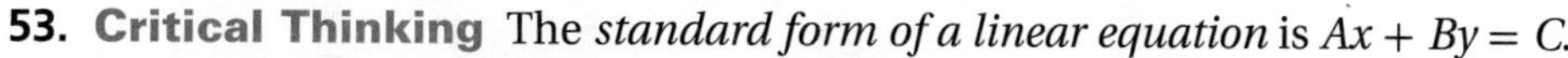

52. **Critical Thinking** If the y-intercept of a linear function is 0, what is the x-intercept? How do you know?

Meteorology

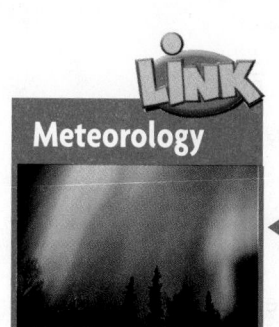

Swedish astronomer Anders Celsius (1701–1744), for whom the Celsius temperature scale is named, published numerous observations of the aurora borealis.

53. **Critical Thinking** The *standard form of a linear equation* is $Ax + By = C$.

a. Find the slope and the y-intercept of a line with this equation.

b. Use your answer to part **a** to quickly find the slope and the y-intercept for the line $12x - 4y = 18$.

54. **Meteorology** The table shows temperatures in both degrees Fahrenheit and degrees Celsius.

Temperature Equivalents						
Temperature (°C)	−5	0	5	10	15	20
Temperature (°F)	23	32	41	50	59	68

a. Explain why this data set is linear.

b. Use Celsius temperature as the independent variable. Find the slope and the y-intercept of the line that passes through the points.

c. Graph these data. Use your graph to estimate the Celsius equivalent of 55°F.

55. **School** The revenue in dollars from a school play is given by the expression $5x + 2y$, where x is the number of adult tickets sold and y is the number of student tickets sold.

a. How much does each type of ticket cost if the revenue is $220?

b. Find the x- and y-intercepts. What do the intercepts represent?

c. **What if...?** Suppose that after the equation is modified and graphed, the y-intercept decreases and the x-intercept remains the same. What could this indicate in the context of the problem?

56. Determine whether the data in the table are linear. Explain.

Time (s)	5	18	20	26	40
Distance (ft)	19.5	32.5	37.5	72	107

57. **Write About It** Explain how to find the slope of a line from a table of data.

58. **Building** A roof is 12 feet high at its edge and rises to a height of 20 feet at a point 10 feet horizontally from the edge. What is the slope of the roof?

59. At what point does the x-intercept of the line $5x - 4y = 40$ occur?

Ⓐ (5, 0) Ⓑ (0, −10) Ⓒ (0, −4) Ⓓ (8, 0)

60. The graph shown could be which of these functions?

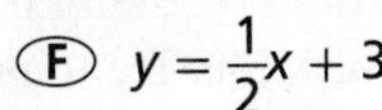

Ⓕ $y = \frac{1}{2}x + 3$

Ⓖ $y = 2x + 3$

Ⓗ $y = -\frac{1}{2}x + 3$

Ⓙ $y = -2x + 3$

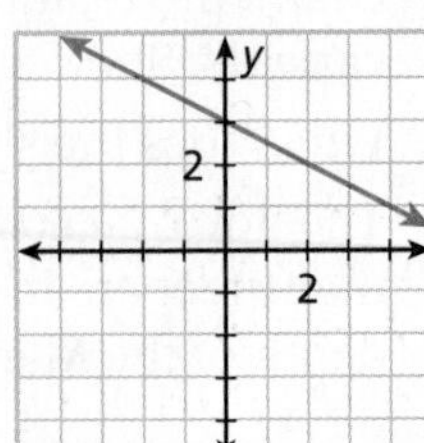

61. If the slope of the line $y = 7 - 3x$ were changed to 5, what would the new equation be?

Ⓐ $y = 7 - 5x$ Ⓑ $y = 7 + 5x$ Ⓒ $y = 5 - 3x$ Ⓓ $y = -5 - 3x$

62. What is the slope of the line $5(y - 4) = -8x$?

Ⓕ $-\frac{5}{8}$ Ⓖ $\frac{5}{4}$ Ⓗ $-\frac{8}{5}$ Ⓙ $\frac{4}{5}$

63. **Gridded Response** If the rise and run are reversed for the linear equation $y = 8x + 4$, what is the slope of the new line?

CHALLENGE AND EXTEND

64. Find the slope and the y-intercept of the line $y = -4$. Does the line have an x-intercept? Explain.

65. The *double-intercept form* of a linear equation is $\frac{x}{a} + \frac{y}{b} = 1$.
    a. Find the slope, the y-intercept, and the x-intercept of the line $\frac{x}{4} - \frac{y}{9} = 1$.
    b. Using your answer to part **a**, explain the meaning of the values a and b in the double-intercept form of a line.
    c. Write the equation of the line $5x + 2y = 30$ in double-intercept form.

66. What happens when you try to find the slope and y-intercept for the equation $3(y + 2) + 6x = 3(4 + 2x + y)$?

SPIRAL REVIEW

Multiply and simplify. *(Previous course)*

67. $\frac{3}{4}\left(\frac{2}{3}\right)$ 68. $\frac{4}{6}\left(\frac{8}{3}\right)$ 69. $-\frac{9}{12}\left(\frac{9}{8}\right)$

Use the set of test scores for Exercises 70–72. Find each measure.
{68, 72, 98, 80, 92, 76, 85, 90, 72, 86} *(Previous course)*

70. mode 71. mean 72. median

For each function, evaluate $f(0)$ and $f(-3)$. *(Lesson 1-7)*

73. $f(x) = \frac{1}{3}x + 7$ 74. $f(x) = -4x^2 - 1$ 75. $f(x) = \frac{x^3}{3}$

Solve. *(Lesson 2-1)*

76. $7(x + 9) = 8(x - 3)$ 77. $\frac{3}{4}(x + 12) + \frac{1}{2}(x + 6) = -18$

78. $7n + 4(n - 1) = 3(n + 4)$ 79. $9t - 3(t - 5) = 51$

Explore Graphs and Windows

When using a graphing calculator to explore graphs, it is important to understand how the WINDOW settings affect the *visual* behavior of the graph. The standard window is usually not the best window and does not usually show the more accurate graph.

Activity 1

Graph $y = 19 - x$ in a window that shows both x- and y-intercepts.

1. Enter $19 - x$ in **Y1**, and press ZOOM **6:ZStandard** to obtain the standard window, $[-10, 10]$ by $[-10, 10]$. You see only a small piece of the graph.

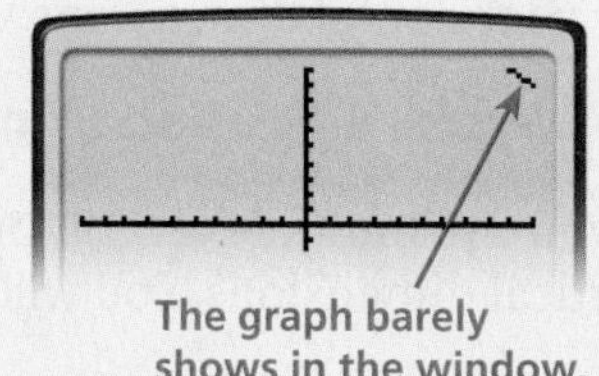

The graph barely shows in the window.

2. Press WINDOW and change the window settings as shown and graph again. By increasing the window dimensions, you can now see both intercepts, but the line looks flatter than the same line graphed on grid paper.

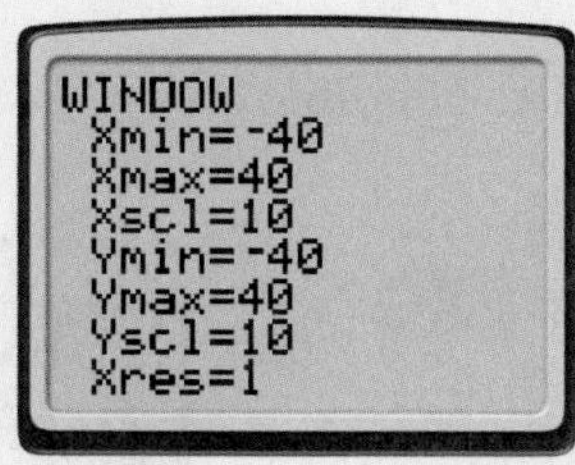

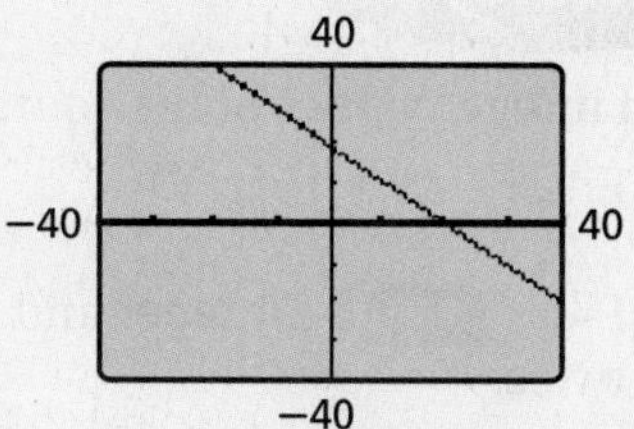

The graphing calculator screen is about 1.5 times as wide (95 pixels) as it is high (63 pixels), so it distorts graphs when the horizontal and vertical dimensions are the same. To correct for this, use a square viewing window.

3. Press ZOOM **5:ZSquare**. **Xmin** and **Xmax** will change to show an accurate graph that displays both intercepts. Notice the change in the window settings.

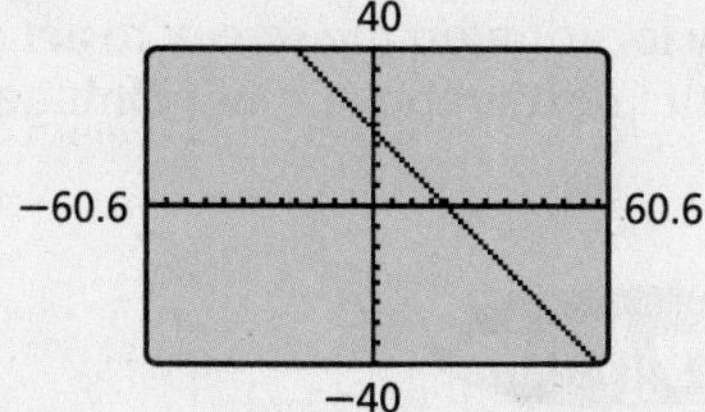

Try This

Graph each function in a window that shows both the x- and y-intercepts.

1. $y = 2x - 25$ **2.** $y = -3x - 50$ **3.** $y = 20 + 0.8x$

4. When you enter and graph a function and only a piece of the graph is visible in the lower left, what adjustments can you make to see the key features of the graph?

5. How can you see the graph of $y = 0.01x$?

6. **What if...?** Suppose that you wanted to make $y = 0.5x$ look very steep or $y = 10x$ look flat in the calculator window. How would you change the window settings?

When you use the TRACE function, x-values are often long decimals. A *friendly* window allows you to trace along simpler x-values. There are several built-in ZOOM windows that give friendly trace values, such as **ZInteger**, and **ZDecimal**.

Activity 2

Find decimal values of the coordinates of points on $y = 2x - 1$.

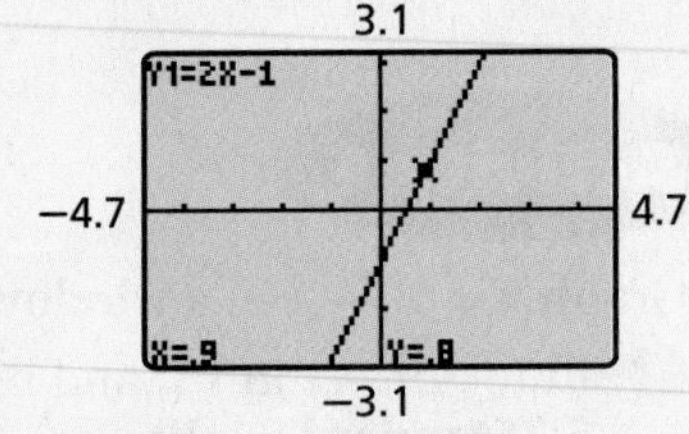

1. Enter $2x - 1$ in **Y1**. Press ZOOM **4:ZDecimal**.

2. TRACE right or left to find the decimal values.

Note the following in the decimal window:

Horizontal dimensions: **Xmax** − **Xmin** = 4.7 − (−4.7) = 9.4 and

Vertical dimensions: **Ymax** − **Ymin** = 3.1 − (−3.1) = 6.2

If you use multiples of 9.4 for the horizontal dimensions and multiples of 6.2 for the vertical dimensions, you will always have simple x-values and an undistorted graph.

Activity 3

Find integer values of the coordinates of points on $y = -4x + 15$.

1. Enter $-4x + 15$ in **Y1**.

2. Press ZOOM **8:ZInteger** and press ENTER twice.

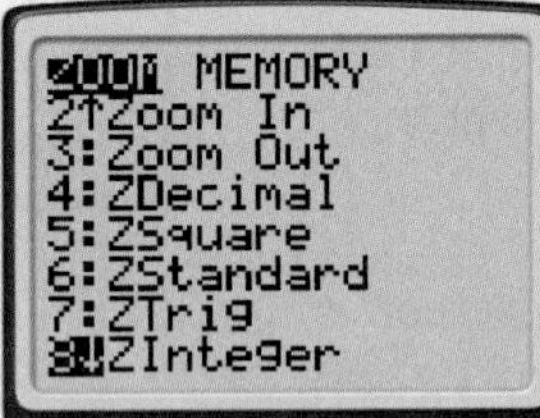

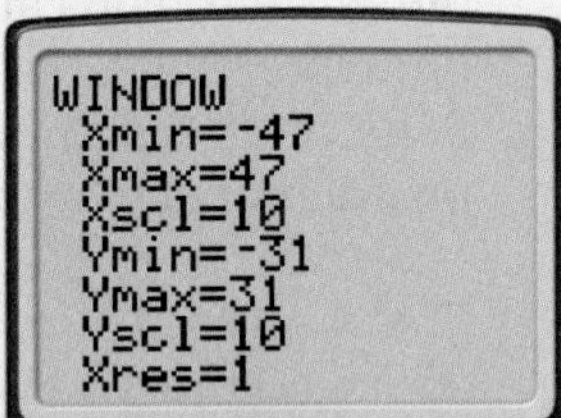

The window changes so that the x-values are integers and tracing to the right increases x-values by 1. The window is also square since **Xmax** − **Xmin** = 94 and **Ymax** − **Ymin** = 62.

3. TRACE to find the integer values.

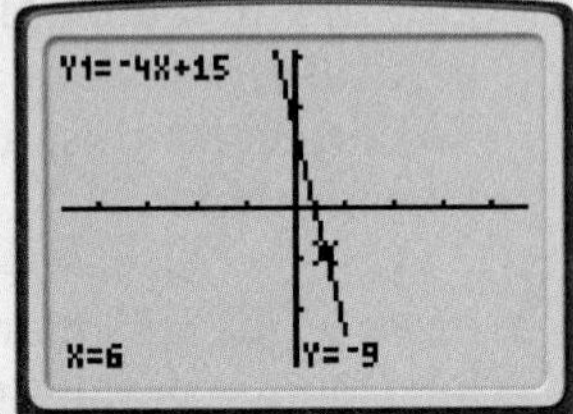

After graphing the function, you can move to any location on the screen to act as the center of the next graph and use **ZInteger** again.

Try This

7. If you ZOOM out on the point (0.9, 0.8) shown in the graph in Activity 3, the window changes to [−8.5, 10.3] by [−5.4, 7]. Find **Xmax** − **Xmin** and **Ymax** − **Ymin**. Use TRACE and the arrow keys to view the coordinates of points on the line. Why is the window friendly?

8. Explain how to graph $y = 3x - 50$ so that the line "looks like" a line with a slope of 3 and allows you to trace to friendly x-values.

9. Graph $y = x + 0.5$ in the standard window.

   a. How can you make the slope of the graph appear to be 1?

   b. Which ZOOM window would create a space between the y-intercept and the origin while keeping an accurate representation of the slope?

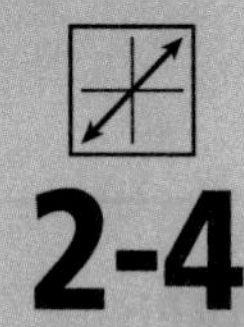

2-4 Writing Linear Functions

Objectives
Use slope-intercept form and point-slope form to write linear functions.

Write linear functions to solve problems.

Vocabulary
Point-slope form

Why learn this?
When you play Monopoly, it's easy to calculate the rent of most properties by looking at the selling price. (See Example 4.)

Recall from Lesson 2-3 that the slope-intercept form of a linear equation is $y = mx + b$, where m is the slope of the line and b is its y-intercept.

In Lesson 2-3, you graphed lines when you were given the slope and y-intercept. In this lesson you will write linear functions when you are given graphs of lines or problems that can be modeled with a linear function.

EXAMPLE 1 Writing the Slope-Intercept Form of the Equation of a Line

Write the equation of the graphed line in slope-intercept form.

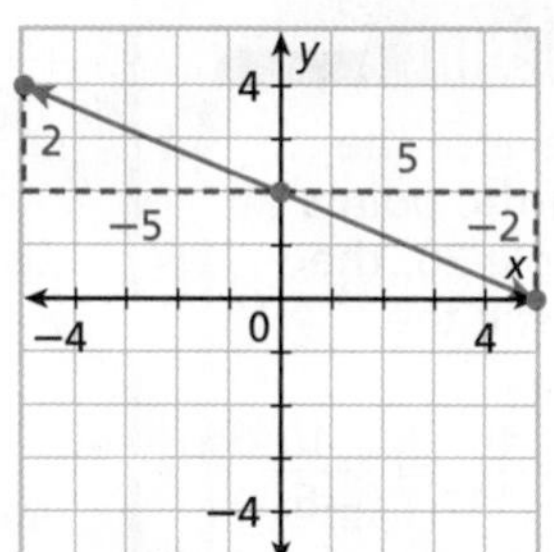

Step 1 Identify the y-intercept.
The y-intercept b is 2.

Step 2 Find the slope.

Choose any two convenient points on the line, such as $(0, 2)$ and $(5, 0)$. Count from $(0, 2)$ to $(5, 0)$ to find the rise and the run. The rise is –2 units and the run is 5 units.

Slope is $\frac{\text{rise}}{\text{run}} = \frac{-2}{5} = -\frac{2}{5}$.

Step 3 Write the equation in slope-intercept form.

$y = mx + b$

$y = -\frac{2}{5}x + 2$ *$m = -\frac{2}{5}$ and $b = 2$*

The equation of the line is $y = -\frac{2}{5}x + 2$.

Remember!
To express a line as a linear function, replace y with $f(x)$.

$y = -\frac{2}{5}x + 2$

$f(x) = -\frac{2}{5}x + 2$

1. Write the equation of the graphed line in slope-intercept form.

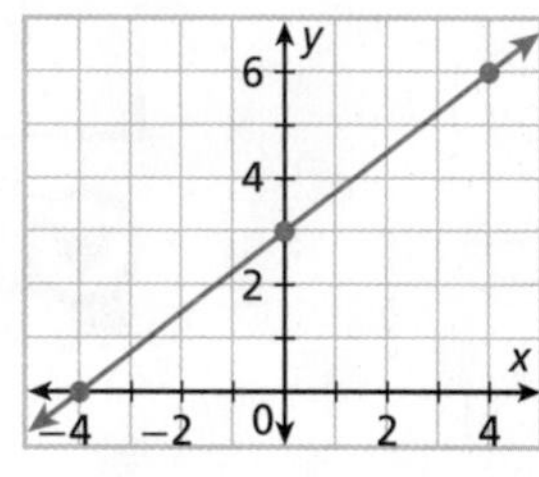

Notice that for two points on a line, the rise is the difference in the y-coordinates, and the run is the difference in the x-coordinates. Using this information, we can define the slope of a line by using a formula.

Slope Formula

WORDS	ALGEBRA	GRAPH
Given two points on a line, the slope is the ratio of the difference in the *y*-values to the difference in the corresponding *x*-values, or rise over run.	The slope of the line containing (x_1, y_1) and (x_2, y_2) is $m = \frac{y_2 - y_1}{x_2 - x_1}$.	(x_2, y_2) rise $= y_2 - y_1$ (x_1, y_1) run $= x_2 - x_1$

EXAMPLE 2 **Finding the Slope of a Line Given Two or More Points**

Find the slope of each line.

A **the line through (3, –2) and (–1, 2)**

Let be (x_1, y_1) be $(3, -2)$ and (x_2, y_2) be $(-1, 2)$.

$$m = \frac{y_2 - y_1}{x_2 - x_1} = \frac{2 - (-2)}{-1 - 3} = \frac{4}{-4} = -1$$ *Use the slope formula.*

The slope of the line is –1.

Helpful Hint

If you reverse the order of the points in Example 2B, the slope is still the same.

$$m = \frac{6 - 16}{5 - 11} = \frac{-10}{-6} = \frac{5}{3}$$

B

x	2	5	8	11
y	1	6	11	16

Let (x_1, y_1) be $(5, 6)$, and (x_2, y_2) be $(11, 16)$. *Choose any two points.*

$$m = \frac{y_2 - y_1}{x_2 - x_1} = \frac{16 - 6}{11 - 5} = \frac{10}{6} = \frac{5}{3}$$ *Use the slope formula.*

The slope of the line is $\frac{5}{3}$.

C **The line shown.**

Either point may be chosen as (x_1, y_1).

Let (x_1, y_1) be $(2, -1)$ and (x_2, y_2) be $(2, 3)$.

$$m = \frac{y_2 - y_1}{x_2 - x_1} = \frac{3 - (-1)}{2 - 2} = \frac{4}{0}$$

Because division by zero is undefined, the slope of the line is undefined.

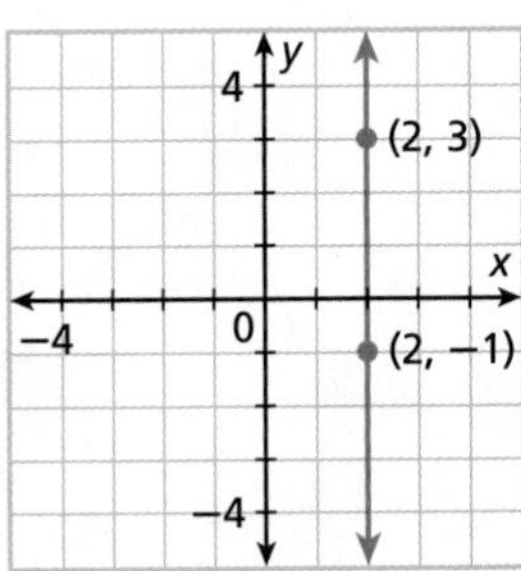

Find the slope of each line.

2a.

x	–6	–4	–2
y	–3	–1	1

2b. the line through (2, –5) and (–3, –5)

Because the slope of a line is constant, it is possible to use any point on a line and the slope of the line to write an equation of the line in **point-slope form**.

Point-Slope Form

The equation of a line with a slope of m and the point (x_1, y_1) is

$$y - y_1 = m(x - x_1).$$

EXAMPLE 3 Writing Equations of Lines

In slope-intercept form, write the equation of the line that contains the points in the table.

x	−3	−1	1	3
y	1.5	1	0.5	0

First, find the slope. Let (x_1, y_1) be $(-1, 1)$ and (x_2, y_2) be $(3, 0)$.

$$m = \frac{y_2 - y_1}{x_2 - x_1} = \frac{0 - 1}{3 - (-1)} = \frac{-1}{3 + 1} = -\frac{1}{4}$$

Next, choose a point and use either form of the equation of a line.

Method A Point-Slope Form

Using $(3, 0)$:

$y - y_1 = m(x - x_1)$

$y - (0) = -\frac{1}{4}(x - 3)$ *Substitute.*

$y = -\frac{1}{4}(x - 3)$ *Simplify.*

Rewrite in slope-intercept form.

$y = -\frac{1}{4}(x - 3)$

$y = -\frac{1}{4}x + \frac{3}{4}$ *Distribute.*

Method B Slope-Intercept Form

Using $(3, 0)$, solve for b.

$y = mx + b$

$0 = \left(-\frac{1}{4}\right)3 + b$ *Substitute.*

$0 = -\frac{3}{4} + b$ *Simplify.*

$b = \frac{3}{4}$ *Solve for b.*

Rewrite the equation using m and b.

$y = -\frac{1}{4}x + \frac{3}{4}$ *$y = mx + b$*

The equation of the line is $y = -\frac{1}{4}x + \frac{3}{4}$.

Write the equation of each line in slope-intercept form.

3a. with slope –5 through $(1, 3)$

3b. through $(-2, -3)$ and $(2, 5)$

Student to Student

Slope and Point-Slope Form

Jennifer Chang
Jefferson High School

I learned the point-slope form by relating it to the formula for slope. The formula for slope and point-slope form are basically the same equation in different forms.

Begin with the slope formula:	$m = \frac{y_2 - y_1}{x_2 - x_1}$
Substitute (x, y) for (x_2, y_2):	$m = \frac{y - y_1}{x - x_1}$
Multiply both sides by $(x - x_1)$:	$m(x - x_1) = y - y_1$
Reverse the equation:	$y - y_1 = m(x - x_1)$

EXAMPLE 4 *Entertainment Application*

In the game of Monopoly, a player who lands on a property that is owned by another player must pay rent to the owner of the property. For most color properties, the rent can be modeled by a linear function of the selling price.

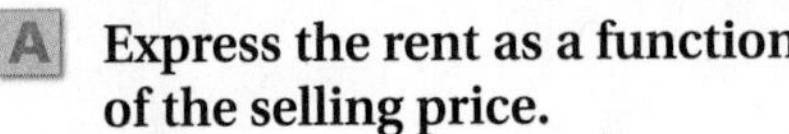

A **Express the rent as a function of the selling price.**

Let x = selling price and y = rent.

Find the slope by choosing two points. Let (x_1, y_1) be $(60, 2)$ and (x_2, y_2) be $(100, 6)$.

$$m = \frac{y_2 - y_1}{x_2 - x_1} = \frac{6 - 2}{100 - 60} = \frac{4}{40} = \frac{1}{10}$$

Monopoly Prices and Rents

Property Name	Selling Price ($)	Rent ($)
Mediterranean Ave.	60	2
Vermont Ave.	100	6
Tennessee Ave.	180	14
Marvin Gardens	280	24
Pennsylvania Ave.	320	28

To find the equation for the rent function, use point-slope form.

$y - y_1 = m(x - x_1)$

$y - 2 = \frac{1}{10}(x - 60)$ *Use the data for Mediterranean Ave.*

$y = \frac{1}{10}x - 4$ *Simplify.*

B **Graph the relationship between the selling price and the rent. How much is the rent for Illinois Ave., which has a selling price of $240?**

Graph the function using a scale that fits the data.

To find the rent for Illinois Avenue, use the graph or substitute its selling price of $240 into the function.

$y = \frac{1}{10}(240) - 4$ *Substitute.*

$y = 24 - 4$

$y = 20$

The rent for Illinois Avenue is $20.

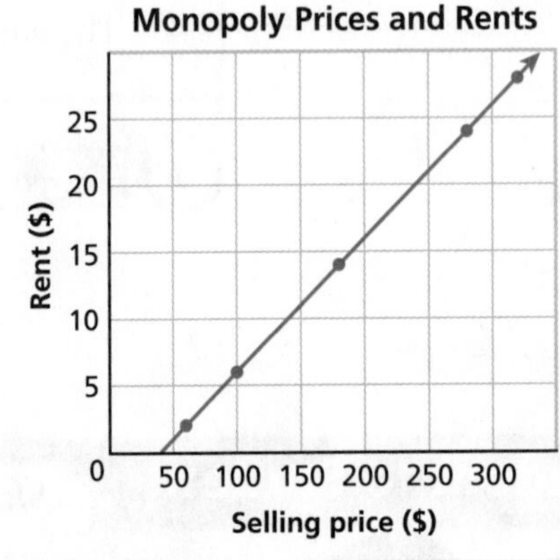

4a. Express the cost as a linear function of the number of items.

4b. Graph the relationship between the number of items and the cost. Find the cost of 18 items.

Items	Cost ($)
4	14.00
7	21.50
18	■

By comparing slopes, you can determine if lines are parallel or perpendicular. You can also write equations of lines that meet certain criteria.

Parallel and Perpendicular Lines

WORDS	GRAPH	ALGEBRA
Parallel Lines If both slopes are defined, the slopes of parallel lines are equal. The slopes of parallel vertical lines are undefined.	$y = 2x + 1$ $y = 2x - 3$	$y_1 = 2x + 1$, so $m_1 = 2$ $y_2 = 2x - 3$ so $m_2 = 2$ $m_1 = m_2$ $2 = 2$
Perpendicular Lines If both slopes are defined, the slopes of perpendicular lines are opposite reciprocals. Their product is −1. A vertical line and a horizontal line are perpendicular.	$y = -\frac{3}{2}x + 4$ $y = \frac{2}{3}x - 3$	$y_1 = -\frac{3}{2}x + 4$, so $m_1 = -\frac{3}{2}$ $y_2 = \frac{2}{3}x - 3$, so $m_2 = \frac{2}{3}$ $(m_1)(m_2) = -1$ $\left(-\frac{3}{2}\right)\left(\frac{2}{3}\right) = -1$

Remember!
A vertical line has an undefined slope.

EXAMPLE 5 Writing Equations of Parallel and Perpendicular Lines

Write the equation of each line in slope-intercept form.

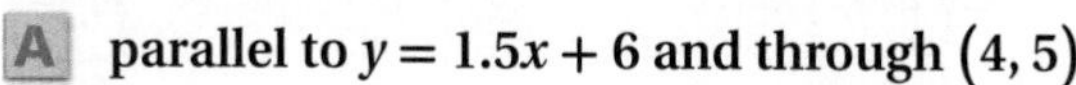

A **parallel to $y = 1.5x + 6$ and through $(4, 5)$**

$m = 1.5$ *Parallel lines have equal slopes.*

$y - 5 = 1.5(x - 4)$ *Use $y - y_1 = m(x - x_1)$ with $(x_1, y_1) = (4, 5)$.*

$y - 5 = 1.5x - 6$ *Distributive property.*

$y = 1.5x - 1$ *Simplify.*

B **perpendicular to $y = -\frac{3}{4}x + 2$ and through $(6, -4)$**

The slope of the given line is $-\frac{3}{4}$, so the slope of the perpendicular line is the opposite reciprocal, $\frac{4}{3}$.

$y + 4 = \frac{4}{3}(x - 6)$ *Use $y - y_1 = m(x - x_1)$. $y + 4$ is equivalent to $y - (-4)$.*

$y + 4 = \frac{4}{3}x - 8$ *Distributive property.*

$y = \frac{4}{3}x - 12$ *Simplify.*

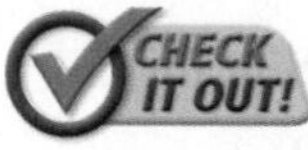

Write the equation of each line in slope-intercept form.

5a. parallel to $y = 5x - 3$ and through $(1, 4)$

5b. perpendicular to $y = \frac{5}{6}x - 7$ and through $(0, -2)$

THINK AND DISCUSS

1. Explain why the slope of a vertical line such as $x = 2$ is undefined.
2. Describe the information that you need in order to write the equation of a line.

3. **GET ORGANIZED** Copy and complete the graphic organizer. In each box, write any appropriate formulas and examples of equations.

Slope-intercept form	Point-slope form
Lines	
Parallel	Perpendicular

2-4 Exercises

go.hrw.com
Homework Help Online
KEYWORD: MB7 2-4
Parent Resources Online
KEYWORD: MB7 Parent

GUIDED PRACTICE

SEE EXAMPLE 1 p. 114

Write the equation of each line in slope-intercept form.

1. a line with slope 2 and intercept 1
2. a line with slope $-\frac{1}{7}$ and y-intercept -2

3. 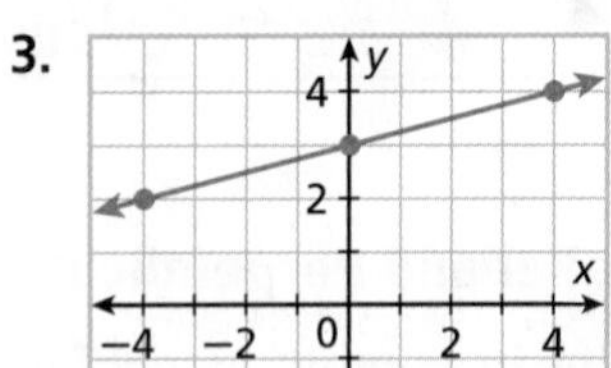

4.  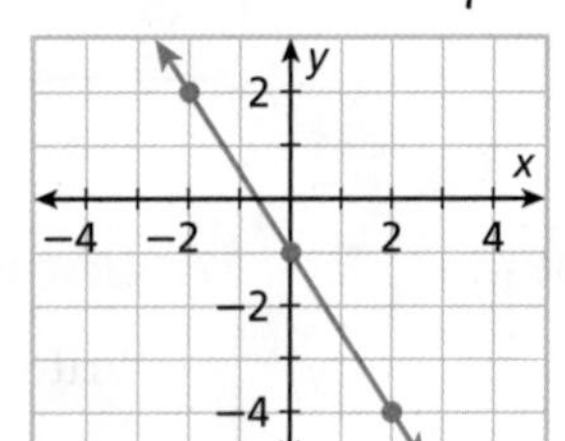

SEE EXAMPLE 2 p. 115

Find the slope of each line.

5.

x	2	7	12	17
y	3	10	17	24

6. a line through $(12, 3)$ and $(3, -4)$

SEE EXAMPLE 3 p. 116

Write the equation of each line in slope-intercept form.

7. a line with slope $-\frac{4}{3}$ passing through $(4, -8)$

8.

x	−2	2	6	10
y	−10	−7	−4	−1

SEE EXAMPLE 4 p. 117

9. **Physics** The boiling point of water can be modeled as a linear function of altitude. The boiling point of water at sea level is 212°F, and the boiling point of water at 1100 ft above sea level is 210°F.
   a. Express the boiling point as a function of altitude.
   b. Graph the relationship between boiling point and altitude.
   c. Find the boiling point of water at an altitude of 11,000 ft.

SEE EXAMPLE 5 p. 118

Write the equation of each line in slope-intercept form.

10. parallel to $y = 3x + 4$ passing through $(0, 9)$
11. perpendicular to $y = \frac{5}{9}x + 4$ passing through $(0, -4)$

PRACTICE AND PROBLEM SOLVING

Independent Practice

For Exercises	See Example
12–14	1
15–16	2
17–18	3
19	4
20–21	5

Extra Practice

Skills Practice: S6
Application Practice: S33

Write the equation of each line in slope-intercept form.

12.

13. 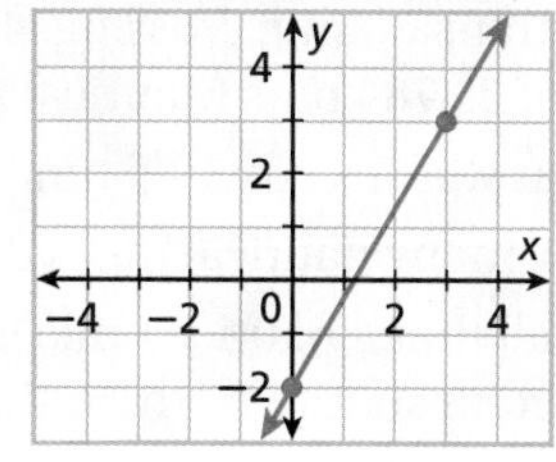

14. 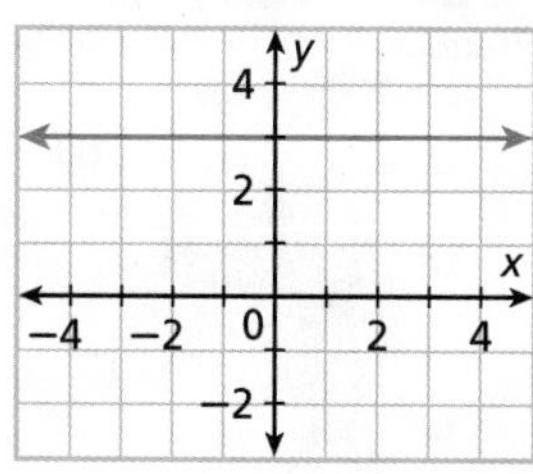

Find the slope of each line.

15.

x	0	1	2	3
y	$-\frac{1}{3}$	$\frac{1}{3}$	1	$\frac{5}{3}$

16. line $\overleftrightarrow{AB}$ through $A(-1, 3)$ and $B(1, -4)$

Write the equation of each line in slope-intercept form.

17. passing through $(3, 11)$ with slope $\frac{7}{3}$

18.

x	10	15	20	25
y	−2	−7	−12	−17

19. **Biology** The table shows the number of times a firefly flashes per minute at various temperatures.

a. Express the flashing rate $f(T)$ as a function of temperature T.

b. Graph the relationship between temperature and the number of flashes per minute.

c. At what temperature would a firefly flash 25 times per minute?

d. How many times per minute would a firefly flash at 35°F. Is this reasonable?

Firefly Flashing Rate

Temperature (°F)	Flashes per Minute
84	16
93	20
66	8

Math History (LINK)

It is unknown why the letter *m* is used to represent slope. Some have claimed that French mathematician René Descartes used it to represent the French word *monter* (to climb). However, this theory has proven to be false.

Write the equation of each line in slope-intercept form.

20. parallel to $y = -\frac{1}{5}x - 7$ and through $(2, 3)$

21. perpendicular to $y = 3x$ and through $(0, 3)$

22. **Clothing** Men's shoe sizes are a linear function of foot length.

a. Write an equation for a man's shoe size as a function of foot length. What men's size shoe is needed for a foot that measures 9.5 in.?

b. Women's shoe sizes are marked $1\frac{1}{2}$ sizes larger than men's sizes for the same foot length. What size shoe is needed for a women's foot that measures 8.5 in.?

Men's Shoe Sizes

Foot Length (in.)	Shoe Size
10	$7\frac{1}{2}$
11	$11\frac{1}{2}$

Determine if each pair of lines is parallel, perpendicular, or neither.

23. $y = \frac{1}{4}x + 9$
$y = 4x - 9$

24. $y = 5 - \frac{1}{8}x$
$y = 8x + 2$

25. $-3x + 4y = 15$
$9x - 12y = 24$

Write each linear function.

26. $f(x)$, where $f(3) = 3$ and $f(-1) = 4$

27. $f(x)$, where $f(-2) = -5$ and $f(1) = 1$

28. This problem will prepare you for the Multi-Step Test Prep on page 132.

Steve Fossett, the balloonist in Lesson 2-1, holds the world sailing record for the fastest transatlantic crossing: 4 days, 17 hours, 28 minutes, 6 seconds, at an average speed of 25.78 knots (nautical mi/h).

a. What was his crossing time, in hours, as a decimal value to the nearest tenth?

b. How many nautical miles did he travel, to the nearest tenth?

c. Recall that a nautical mile is about 1.15 statute miles. What was Fossett's average speed in statute mi/h, to the nearest tenth?

For Exercises 29–37, write the equation of the line with the given properties.

29. a slope of 4 passing through $(1, 7)$

30. a slope of $-\frac{1}{2}$ passing through $(7, -3)$

31. passing through $(-5, 7)$ and $(3, -4)$

32. passing through $(-3, 3)$ and $(1, -1)$

33.

x	4	7.5	8
y	44	117.5	128

34.

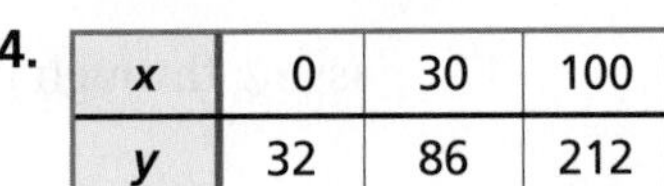

x	0	30	100
y	32	86	212

35.

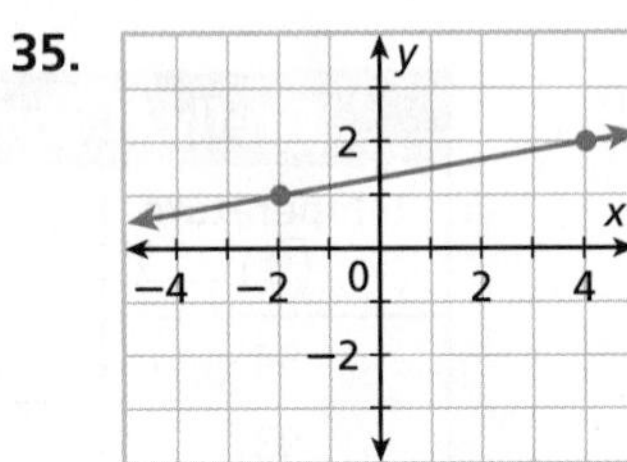

36.

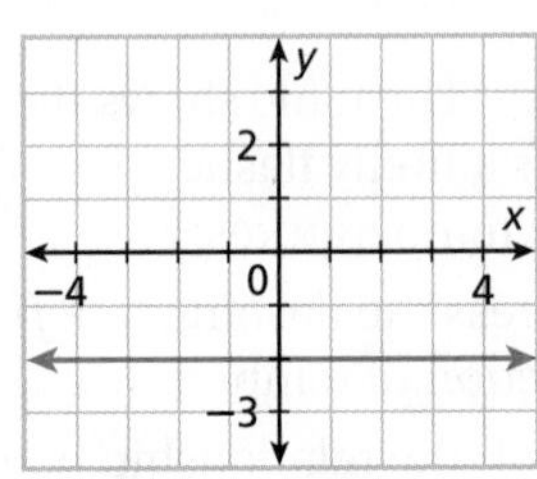

37.

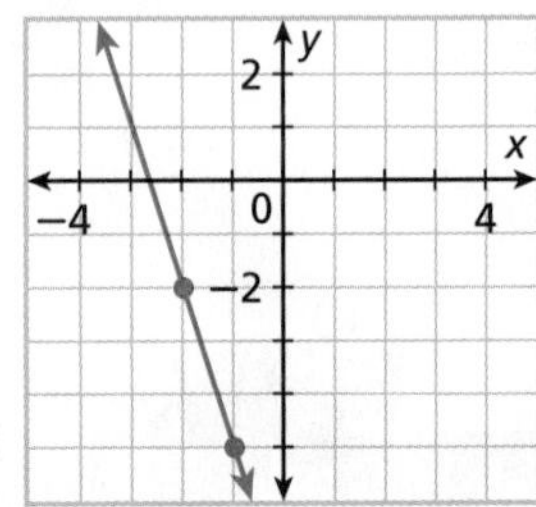

38. **Critical Thinking** Which of the Monopoly properties in the table does not conform to the rent function, $y = \frac{1}{10}x - 4$? Explain.

Monopoly Prices and Rents

Property Name	Selling Price ($)	Rent ($)
Connecticut Ave.	120	8
Kentucky Ave.	220	18
Park Place	350	35

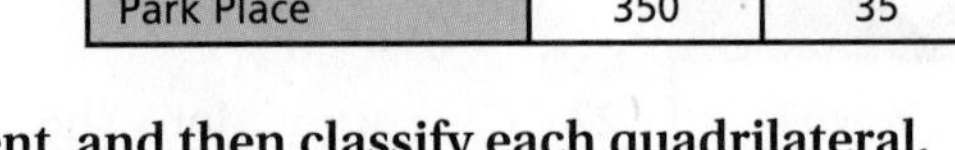

Geometry **Find the slope of each segment, and then classify each quadrilateral.**

39.

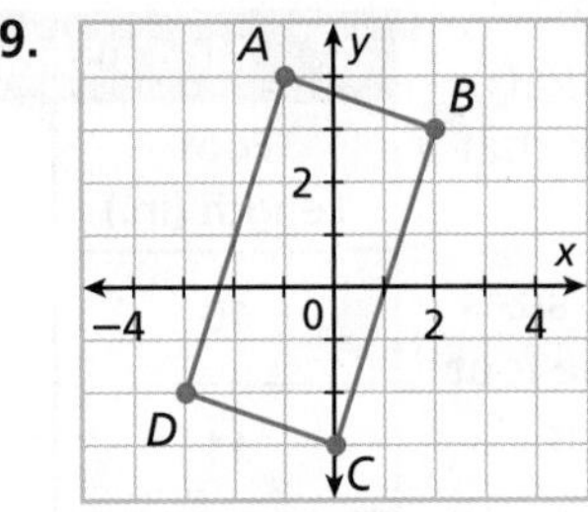

40.

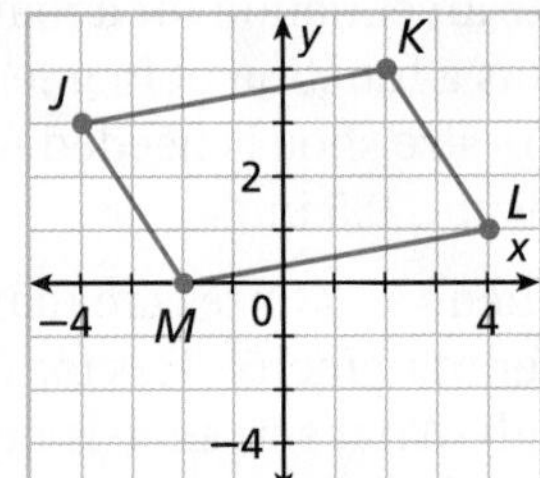

41.

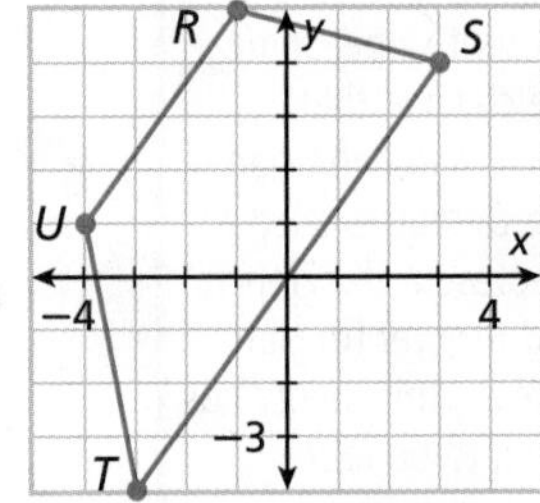

42. **ERROR ANALYSIS** Two attempts to find the slope of the line containing $(5, 8)$ and $(12, 7)$ are shown. Identify which calculation is incorrect. Explain the error.

A

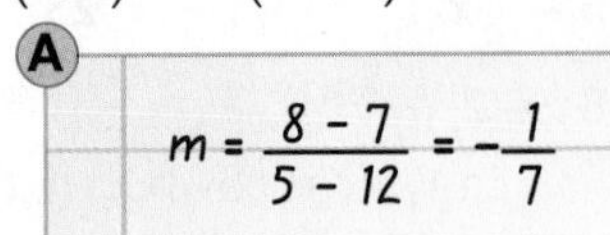

$$m = \frac{8 - 7}{5 - 12} = -\frac{1}{7}$$

B

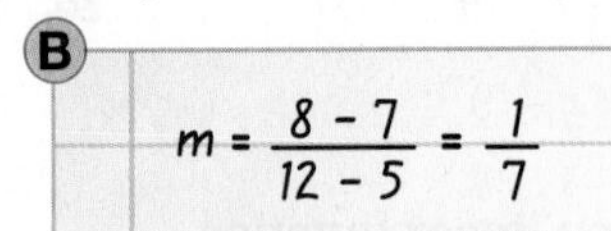

$$m = \frac{8 - 7}{12 - 5} = \frac{1}{7}$$

43. **Write About It** Explain how to write the equation of a line from its graph.

44. A carpenter determines the cost of a job by using the formula $C = 25 + 25h$, where h is the number of hours he works. He has decided to increase the amount he charges per hour to \$30. Which formula will he use now?

Ⓐ $C = 30 + 25h$ Ⓑ $C = 30 + 30h$ Ⓒ $C = 25 + 30h$ Ⓓ $C = 25h + 30$

45. Which graph best shows a line perpendicular to $y = 3x - 2$?

Ⓕ

Ⓖ
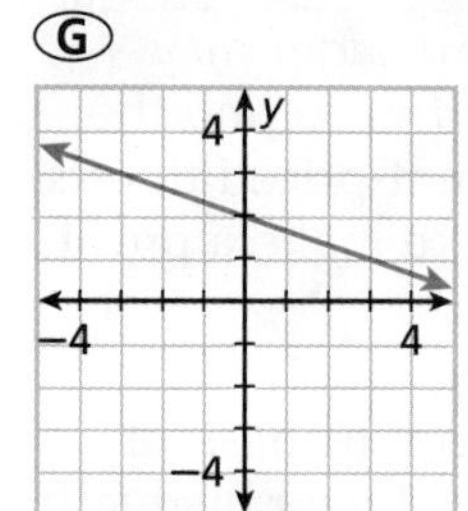

Ⓗ
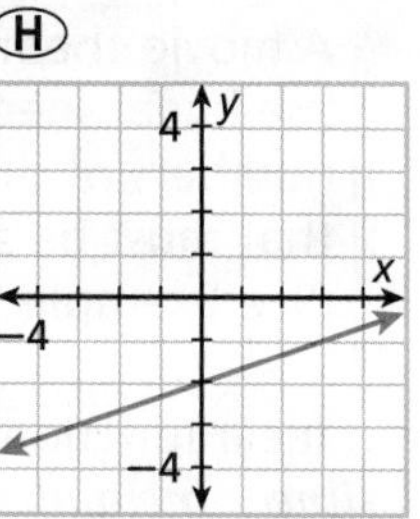

Ⓙ
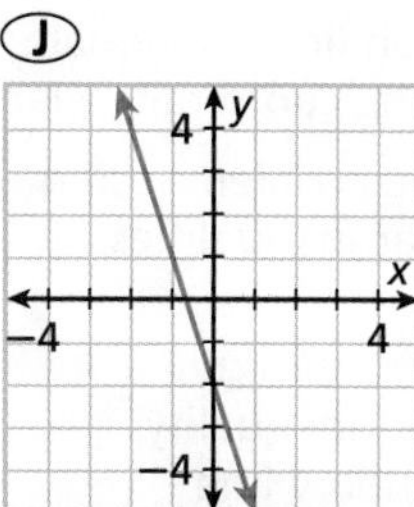

46. An equation can be used to relate the cost c of carpeting a room to the area a of the room in square feet. Which equation accurately reflects the data in the table?

Ⓐ $c = 2a - 125$ Ⓒ $c = a + 275$

Ⓑ $c = 1.5a + 75$ Ⓓ $c = 2a - 1500$

Carpeting Costs

Area (ft²)	Cost (\$)
400	675
550	900
900	1425

CHALLENGE AND EXTEND

47. Show that $y = \frac{2}{5}x + \frac{1}{4}$ and $y - \frac{25}{4} = \frac{2}{5}(x - 15)$ represent the same line.

48. Find the value of k so that the line containing $(4, -3k)$ and $(2k, 5)$ has a slope of $m = \frac{5}{2}$.

49. Are the points $(2, 6)$, $(5, 10)$, and $(9, 15)$ on the same line? Explain.

50. The slope-intercept form of a linear equation can be derived from the point-slope form. Illustrate this statement by substituting the point $(0, b)$ for (x_1, y_1) into the point-slope equation and solving for y.

51. **Aeronautics** A rule that airline pilots use to estimate outside temperature in degrees Fahrenheit at an altitude of h thousand feet is to double h, subtract 15, and multiply the result by –1. State a rule for the altitude in feet based upon the outside temperature. At what altitude is outside temperature about –51°F?

SPIRAL REVIEW

Use interval notation to represent each set of numbers. *(Lesson 1-1)*

52. $-4 \le x \le 8$ or $x > 12$

53. 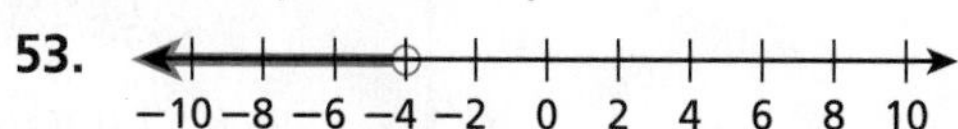

Determine whether the ordered pair is a solution of both $2x + y = 5$ and $\frac{3}{4}x < -5y$. *(Lesson 2-1)*

54. $(0, 0)$ 55. $(-1, 6)$ 56. $(2, 1)$ 57. $(3, -1)$

58. **Entertainment** A scaled replica of the Eiffel Tower at Kings Island Amusement Park is 331 ft 6 in. tall. The Eiffel Tower in Paris is 994 ft 6 in. tall. What percent of the height of the Eiffel Tower is the replica's height? *(Lesson 2-2)*

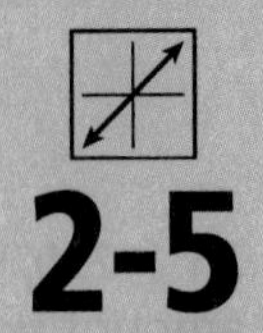

2-5 Linear Inequalities in Two Variables

Objectives

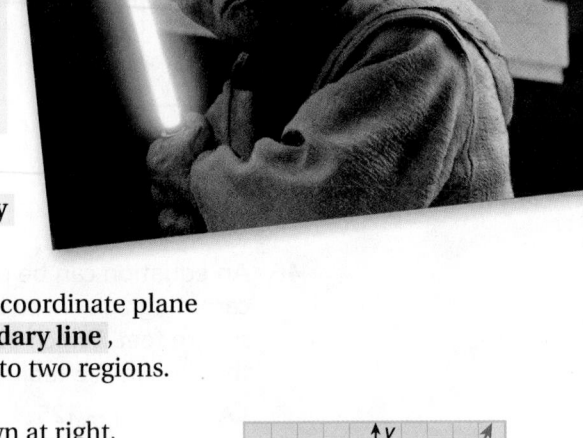

Graph linear inequalities on the coordinate plane.

Solve problems using linear inequalities.

Vocabulary

linear inequality

boundary line

Who uses this?

A movie theater manager may use linear inequalities to find the numbers of different-priced tickets that must be sold to make a profit. (See Example 3.)

Linear functions form the basis of *linear inequalities*. A **linear inequality** in two variables relates two variables using an inequality symbol, such as $y > 2x - 4$. Its graph is a region of the coordinate plane bounded by a line. The line is a **boundary line**, which divides the coordinate plane into two regions.

For example, the line $y = 2x - 4$, shown at right, divides the coordinate plane into two parts: one where $y > 2x - 4$ and one where $y < 2x - 4$. In the coordinate plane higher points have larger y values, so the region where $y > 2x - 4$ is above the boundary line where $y = 2x - 4$.

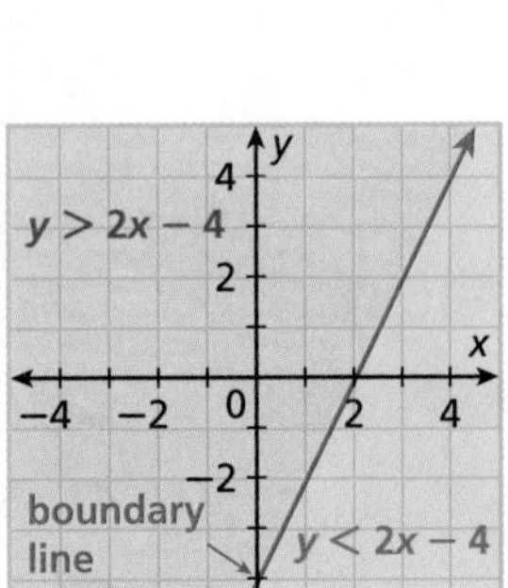

To graph $y \geq 2x - 4$, make the boundary line solid, and shade the region above the line. To graph $y > 2x - 4$, make the boundary line dashed because y-values equal to $2x - 4$ are not included.

Helpful Hint

Think of the underlines in the symbols $\leq$ and $\geq$ as representing solid lines on the graph.

EXAMPLE 1 **Graphing Linear Inequalities**

Graph each inequality.

A $y < \frac{1}{2}x + 1$

The boundary line is $y = \frac{1}{2}x + 1$, which has a y-intercept of 1 and a slope of $\frac{1}{2}$.

Draw the boundary line dashed because it is not part of the solution. Then shade the region below the boundary line to show $y < \frac{1}{2}x + 1$.

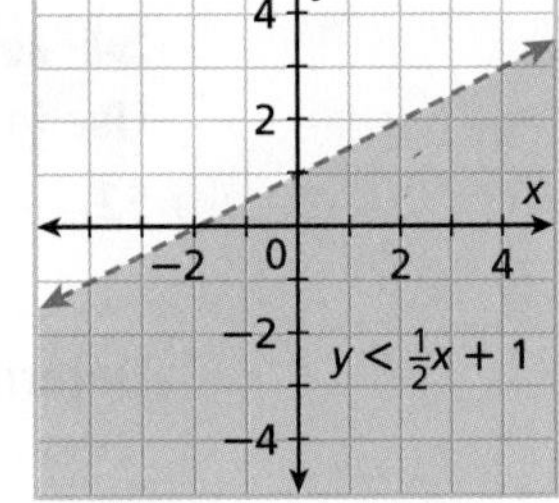

Check Choose a point in the solution region, such as (0, 0) and test it in the inequality.

$$y < \frac{1}{2}x + 1$$

$$0 \overset{?}{<} \frac{1}{2}(0) + 1$$

$$0 \overset{?}{<} 1 \checkmark$$

The test point satisfies the inequality, so the solution region appears to be correct.

Graph each inequality.

B $y \geq 2$

Recall that $y = 2$ is a horizontal line.

Step 1 Draw a solid line for $y = 2$ because the boundary line is part of the graph.

Step 2 Shade the region above the boundary line to show where $y > 2$.

Check The point $(0, 4)$ is a solution because $4 \geq 2$. Note that any point on or above $y = 2$ is a solution, regardless of the value of x.

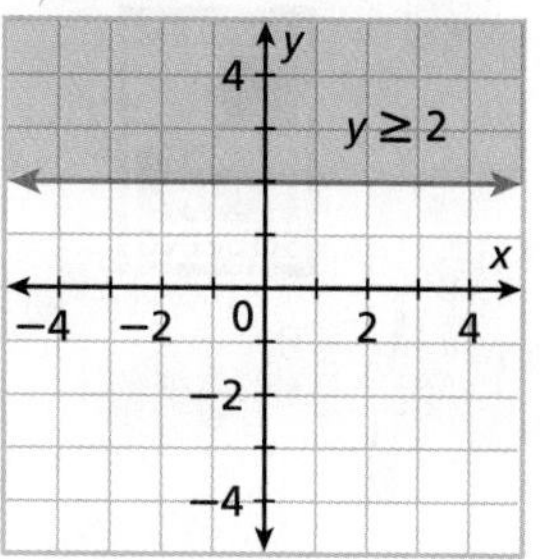

Graph each inequality.

1a. $y \geq 3x - 2$ **1b.** $y < -3$

If the equation of the boundary line is not in slope-intercept form, you can choose a test point that is not on the line to determine which region to shade. If the point satisfies the inequality, then shade the region containing that point. Otherwise, shade the other region.

EXAMPLE 2 Graphing Linear Inequalities Using Intercepts

Graph $2x + 3y \geq 6$ using intercepts.

Step 1 Find the intercepts.

Substitute $x = 0$ and then $y = 0$ into $2x + 3y = 6$ to find the intercepts of the boundary line.

***y*-intercept**	***x*-intercept**
$2x + 3y = 6$	$2x + 3y = 6$
$2(0) + 3y = 6$	$2x + 3(0) = 6$
$3y = 6$	$2x = 6$
$y = 2$	$x = 3$

Step 2 Draw the boundary line.

The line goes through $(0, 2)$ and $(3, 0)$. Draw a solid line for the boundary because it is part of the graph.

Step 3 Find the correct region to shade.

Substitute $(0, 0)$ into the inequality. Because $0 + 0 \geq 6$ is false, shade the region that does *not* contain $(0, 0)$.

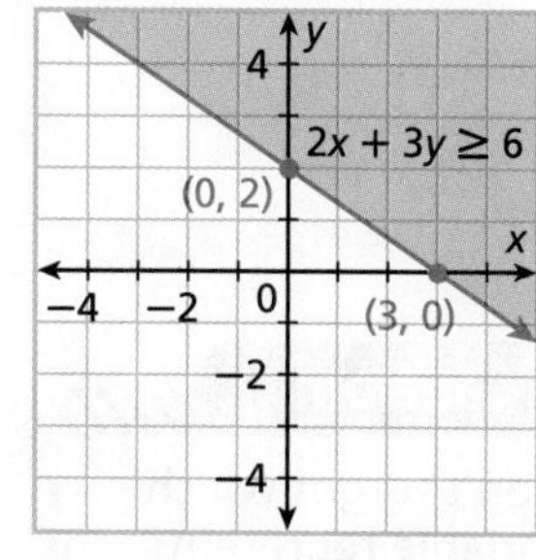

Helpful Hint

The point $(0, 0)$ is the easiest point to test if it is not on the boundary line.

2. Graph $3x - 4y > 12$ using intercepts.

Many applications of inequalities in two variables use only nonnegative values for the variables. Graph only the part of the plane that includes realistic solutions.

EXAMPLE 3 Problem-Solving Application

A local theater charges \$7.50 for adult tickets and \$5.00 for discount tickets. The theater needs to make at least \$240 to cover the rent of the building. How many of each type of ticket must be sold to make a profit? If 20 discount tickets are sold, how many adult tickets must be sold?

1 Understand the Problem

The **answer** will be in two parts: (1) an inequality graph showing the number of each type of ticket that must be sold to make a profit (2) the number of adult tickets that must be sold to make at least \$240 if 20 discount tickets are sold.

List the important information:

- The theater sells tickets for \$7.50 and \$5.00.
- The theater needs to make at least \$240.

2 Make a Plan

Let x represent the number of adult tickets and y represent the number of discount tickets that must be sold. Write an inequality to represent the situation.

Adult price	times	number of adult tickets	plus	discount price	times	number of discount tickets	is at least	total.
7.50	$\cdot$	x	$+$	5.00	$\cdot$	y	$\geq$	240

An inequality that models the problem is $7.5x + 5y \geq 240$.

3 Solve

Find the intercepts of the boundary line.

$7.5(0) + 5y = 240$ $\qquad$ $7.5x + 5(0) = 240$

$y = 48$ $\qquad$ $x = 32$

Graph the boundary line through $(0, 48)$ and $(32, 0)$ as a solid line. Shade the region above the line that is in the first quadrant, as ticket sales cannot be negative.

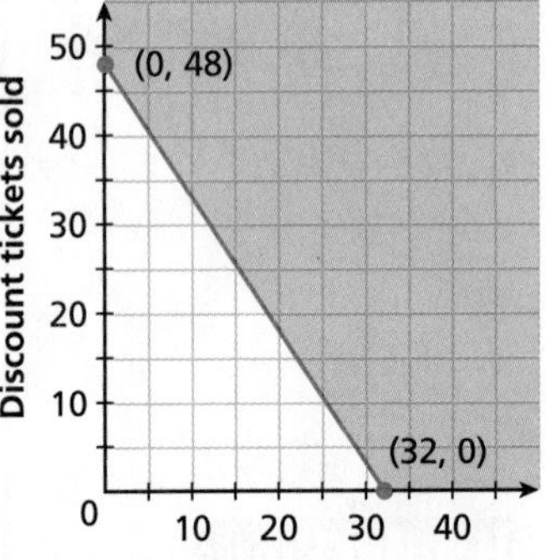

Caution!

Don't forget which variable represents which quantity.

If 20 discount tickets are sold,

$7.5x + 5(20) \geq 240$ *Substitute 20 for y in $7.5x + 5y \geq 240$.*

$7.5x + 100 \geq 240$ *Multiply 5 by 20.*

$7.5x \geq 140$, so $x \geq 18.\overline{6}$ *A whole number of tickets must be sold.*

At least 19 adult tickets must be sold.

4 Look Back

$19(\$7.50) + 20(\$5.00) = \$242.50$, so the answer is reasonable.

3. A café gives away prizes. A large prize costs the café \$125, and the small prize costs \$40. The café will not spend more than \$1500. How many of each prize can be awarded? How many small prizes can be awarded if 4 large prizes are given away?

You can graph a linear inequality that is solved for y with a graphing calculator.

Press **Y=** and use the left arrow key to move to the left side.

Each time you press **ENTER** you will see one of the graph styles shown here. You are already familiar with the line style.

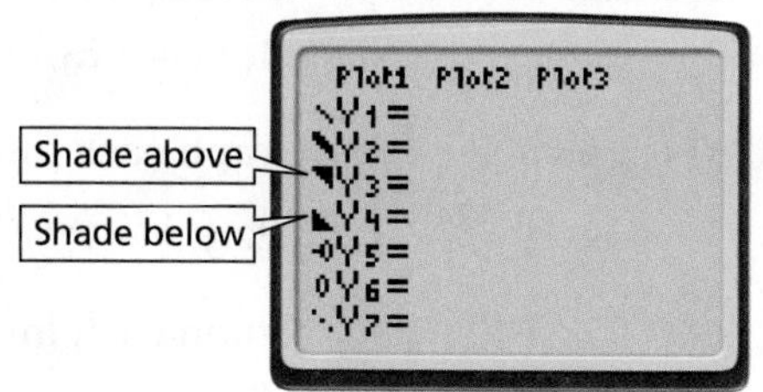

EXAMPLE 4 Solving and Graphing Linear Inequalities

Solve $\frac{2}{3}(2x - y) < 2$ for y. Graph the solution.

$\frac{3}{2} \cdot \frac{2}{3}(2x - y) < \frac{3}{2} \cdot 2$ *Multiply both sides by $\frac{3}{2}$.*

$2x - y < 3$

$-y < -2x + 3$ *Subtract 2x from both sides.*

$y > 2x - 3$ *Multiply by −1, and reverse the inequality symbol.*

Use the calculator option to shade above the line $y = 2x - 3$.

Note that the graph is shown in the standard square window (**ZOOM** **6:ZStandard** followed by **ZOOM** **5:ZSquare**).

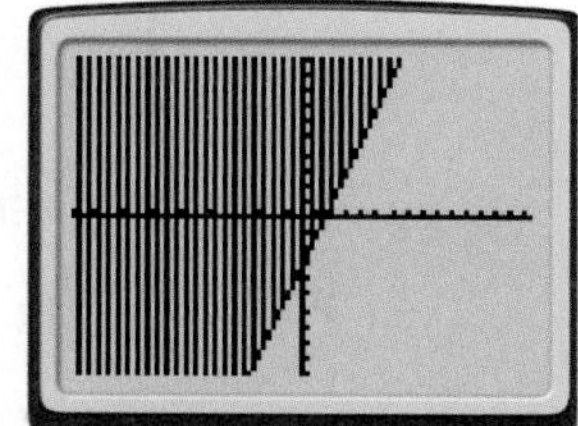

Remember!

When multiplying or dividing an inequality by a negative number, reverse the inequality symbol.

4. Solve $2(3x - 4y) > 24$ for y. Graph the solution.

THINK AND DISCUSS

1. Compare the open and closed circles in graphs of inequalities with the dashed and solid lines in graphs of linear inequalities.
2. Describe what the graph of $x \geq 4$ would look like on a coordinate plane.
3. Explain whether you can use $(0, 0)$ to determine which side of the graph of $3x + 5y \leq 0$ to shade.
4. **GET ORGANIZED** Copy and complete the graphic organizer. For each graph description, give examples of corresponding inequalities solved for y and inequalities in other forms.

Dashed Line, Shaded Above	Dashed Line, Shaded Below	Solid Line, Shaded Above	Solid Line, Shaded Below

2-5 Exercises

go.hrw.com
Homework Help Online
KEYWORD: MB7 2-5
Parent Resources Online
KEYWORD: MB7 Parent

GUIDED PRACTICE

1. **Vocabulary** Explain how the graph of $y = 3x - 4$ can be a *boundary line.*

SEE EXAMPLE 1 p. 124

Graph each inequality.

2. $y > -4$
3. $y \leq 2$
4. $y \geq x - 3$
5. $y < -\frac{1}{3}x + 2$

SEE EXAMPLE 2 p. 125

Graph each inequality using intercepts.

6. $3x + 2y > 12$
7. $5x - 2y \leq 20$
8. $-4x + 5y < -20$

SEE EXAMPLE 3 p. 126

9. **Consumer** Charisse is buying two different types of cereals from the bulk bins at the store. Granola costs \$2.29 per pound, and muesli costs \$3.75 per pound. She has \$7.00. Use x as the amount of granola and y as the amount of muesli.
   a. Write and graph an inequality for the amounts of each cereal she can buy.
   b. How many pounds of granola can she buy if she buys 1.5 pounds of muesli?

10. **School** The senior class sells hamburgers and hot dogs at a football game and makes a profit of \$1.75 on each hamburger and \$1.25 on each hot dog. The class would like a profit of at least \$280. Let x represent the number of hamburgers and y represent the number of hot dogs sold.
    a. Write and graph an inequality for the profit the senior class wants to make.
    b. If the senior class sells 100 hot dogs and 50 hamburgers, will the class make its goal?

SEE EXAMPLE 4 p. 127

Solve each inequality for y. Graph the solution.

11. $\frac{1}{2}(6x - 2y) \geq 4$
12. $-\frac{3}{5}x + y \geq 2$
13. $3(3x - y) > -12$

PRACTICE AND PROBLEM SOLVING

Independent Practice

For Exercises	See Example
14–16	1
17–18	2
19–21	3
22–24	4

Extra Practice
Skills Practice p. S6
Application Practice p. S33

Graph each inequality.

14. $y \geq 6$
15. $y < x + 4$
16. $y > -\frac{2}{5}x - 3$

Graph each inequality using intercepts.

17. $4x + 2y \geq 8$
18. $3x - 6y < 12$

19. **Marketing** Quarter page ads in the local papers cost \$200 per day, and one minute ads on the local radio stations cost \$500. Sheena's Lawn Care has an advertising budget of \$10,000. Let x be the number of quarter page ads in newspapers and y be the number of one minute radio ads. Write and graph an inequality for the advertising that Sheena's Lawn Care can afford.

20. **Astronomy** The rockets of a Mars probe require oxygen to lift off from the surface and return to Earth. Suppose the probe can produce 0.78 L of oxygen for every kg of water and 0.32 L of oxygen for every kg of carbon dioxide. At least 56 L of oxygen are needed. Let x represent the kg of water available and y represent the kg of carbon dioxide.
    a. Write and graph an inequality for the liters of oxygen that will be sufficient for liftoff.
    b. If the probe collects 36 kg of water and 88 kg of carbon dioxide, will it be enough for liftoff?

21. Recreation Amber has a $200 gift card for boat rentals. She rents kayaks at $8 and canoes at $12 per hour. Let x be the number of hours of kayak rentals and y be the number of hours of canoe rentals.

a. Write and graph an inequality for the possible number of hours of each that she can rent.

b. If Amber rents kayaks for 10 hours, how many hours can she rent canoes for?

Solve each inequality for *y*. Graph the solution.

22. $-4y < 4(3x - 5)$

23. $-3(-10x + 2y) \geq 24$

24. $-\frac{1}{3}x + \frac{1}{5}y \leq -1$

Graph each inequality.

25. $-4y > 10x - 20$

26. $y - 5 \geq 4(x - 2)$

27. $6x + 3y < 0$

28. $y + \frac{3}{4} \leq \frac{5}{2}\left(x - \frac{1}{2}\right)$

29. $\frac{9 - 3y}{2} \geq 6x$

30. $x \leq 4$

31. $4x - 5y < 7x - 3y$

32. $2x - 5y \leq -4x + 15$

33. $x > -2$

34. School Tickets to the math club dance cost $5 if bought in advance and $6 at the door. The math club needs to make a total of at least $600 from ticket sales for the dance.

a. Let x be the number of tickets sold in advance and y be the number of tickets sold at the door. Write and graph an inequality for the total amount in ticket sales that the math club needs.

b. If the math club sells 30 tickets in advance, how many tickets must be sold at the door for the math club to reach its goal?

35. Fund-raising The junior class is selling pizza and beverages at a basketball game. The class makes a profit of $1.25 on each slice of pizza and $0.50 on each beverage. Let x be the number of pizza slices and y be the number of beverages.

a. Write and graph an inequality that shows the number of pizza slices and number of beverages the class must sell to make a profit of at least $150.

b. If the junior class sells 75 slices of pizza and 150 beverages, will the class make its goal?

36. Critical Thinking Tickets to an event cost $5 for adults and $2 for students. Total ticket sales were more than $300. Jane and Erin graphed the situation as an inequality. Jane let x be the number of adult tickets sold, and Erin let x be the number of student tickets sold. How did their graphs differ? Which graph, if either, was incorrect?

37. This problem will prepare you for the Multi-Step Test Prep on page 132.

A ship starting 500 nautical miles from port can travel at a speed of 27 knots or less.

a. How long does the trip to port take?

b. Graph the ship's distance over the trip. What do the points above the boundary line represent?

c. **What if...?** Suppose the minimum speed at any point during the trip is 10 knots. How far from port is the ship after 12 hours?

Write an inequality for each graph.

38. 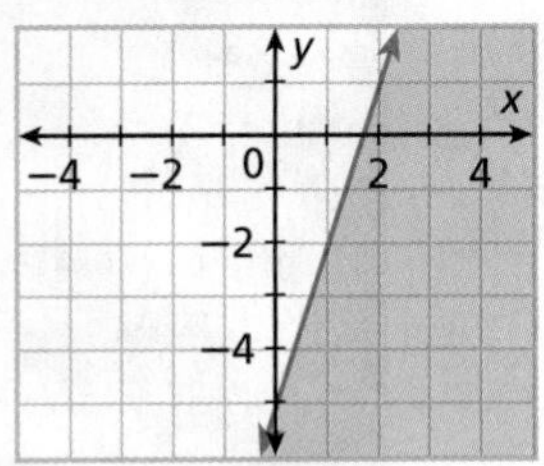

39. 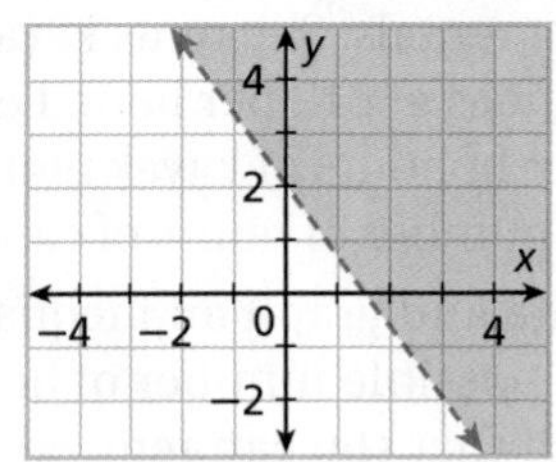

40. 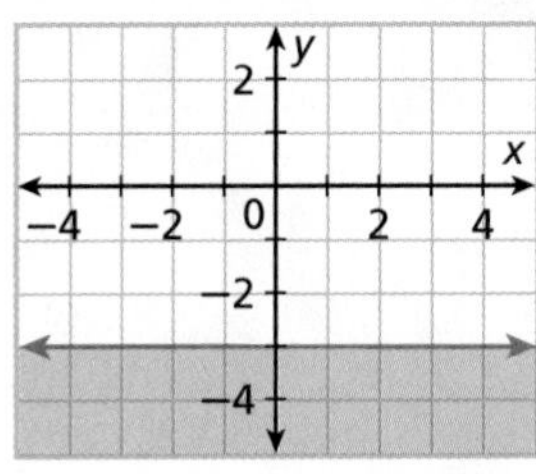

41. **Critical Thinking** Compare the graphs of $30y < 90 + x$ and $30y + x < 90$. How are they alike? How are they different?

42. **Home Economics** Omar uses almonds and raisins in a high-fiber recipe. Almonds have 3.3 g of fiber per ounce and raisins have 2.7 grams of fiber per ounce. He wants at least 5 grams of fiber from these ingredients in a recipe.

   a. Let x be the number of ounces of almonds and y be the number of ounces of raisins. Write and graph an inequality for the amount of fiber from almonds and raisins that Omar wants in the recipe.
   b. If Omar uses 0.5 ounce of almonds, how many ounces of raisins can he use?
   c. **What if...?** Suppose Omar uses 2 ounces of almonds. What happens to the value of y in the inequality? What does this mean in the context of the problem?

43. A banquet room is to be filled with round tables and rectangular tables. The round tables have 8 chairs each, and the rectangular tables have 6 chairs each. Let x be the number of round tables and y be the number of rectangular tables.
   a. Write and graph an inequality for the number of each type of table needed to have at least 220 chairs.
   b. Due to fire regulations, there can be no more than 300 chairs. Write and graph an inequality to reflect this.
   c. Compare your graphs. How do they differ?

TEST PREP

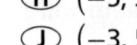

44. Which inequality best represents the set of points graphed here?

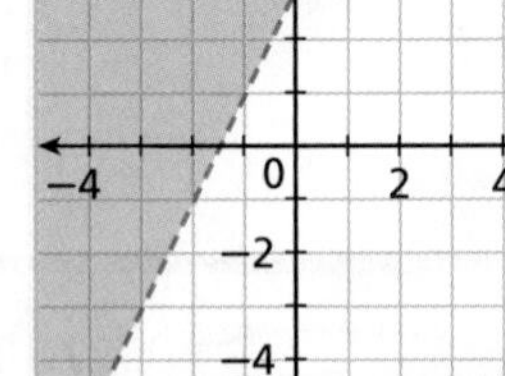

   Ⓐ $y < 2x + 3$
   Ⓑ $4x - 2y < -6$
   Ⓒ $y \geq 2x + 3$
   Ⓓ $4x + 2y > 6$

45. Which point is NOT a solution of $5x - 3y < 30$?
   Ⓕ (0, 0)
   Ⓖ (3, −5)
   Ⓗ (−5, 3)
   Ⓙ (−3, 5)

46. Which inequality is equivalent to $7x - 3y \geq 4$?
   Ⓐ $y \leq \frac{7}{3}x - \frac{4}{3}$
   Ⓑ $y \leq -\frac{7}{3}x + \frac{4}{3}$
   Ⓒ $y \geq -\frac{7}{3}x - \frac{4}{3}$
   Ⓓ $y \geq \frac{7}{3}x + \frac{4}{3}$

47. What points represent the intercepts of the boundary line of the graph of $y \leq 3x - 9$?

Ⓕ (0, 9) and (3, 0)
Ⓖ (0, 3) and (−9, 0)
Ⓗ (0, 9) and (−3, 0)
Ⓙ (0, −9) and (3, 0)

48. Each dime adds 8 minutes to the time on a parking meter, and each quarter adds 20 minutes. The maximum time is 3 hours. The previous driver left 37 minutes of time. Adding which coins would NOT result in getting the maximum time?

Ⓐ 3 dimes and 6 quarters
Ⓑ 13 dimes and 2 quarters
Ⓒ 8 dimes and 4 quarters
Ⓓ 5 dimes and 5 quarters

49. **Short Response** Describe a problem situation using inequalities in which it would make sense to have negative *x*- or *y*-values.

CHALLENGE AND EXTEND

Graph each inequality.

50. $4(4x - 3y) < 5(2 + 3x) - 10y$

51. $\dfrac{4 + 3y - 2x}{6} \geq \dfrac{3x - 2 - 3y}{-4}$

52. **What if...?** Suppose when you graph a $y >$ inequality on a graphing calculator, you find that the entire screen is shaded. What does this indicate about the inequality? What might you do to show the graph of the inequality more accurately?

53. The graph of $y = 500(x - 1)$ is shown in the **ZDecimal** window.

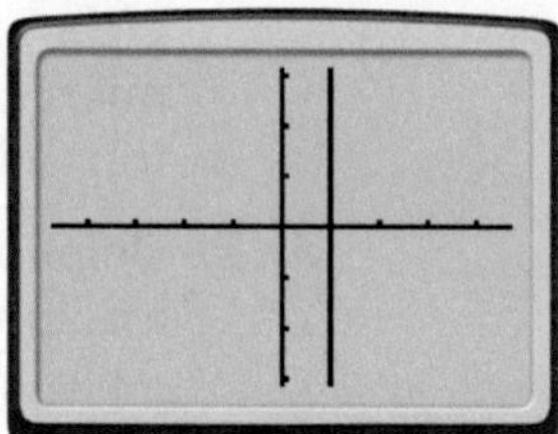

a. Is the line really vertical? Explain.

b. For the graph of $y \leq 500(x - 1)$, which side of the line should be shaded? Justify your answer.

SPIRAL REVIEW

Use the vertical line test to determine whether each graph represents a function. *(Lesson 1-6)*

54.

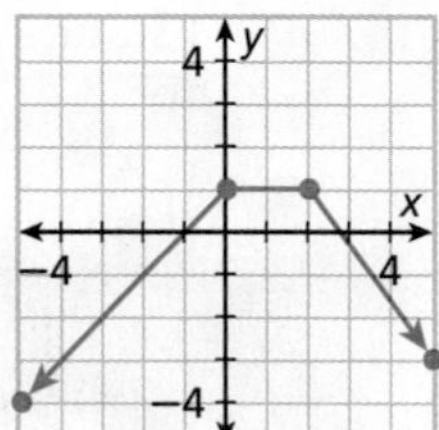

55.

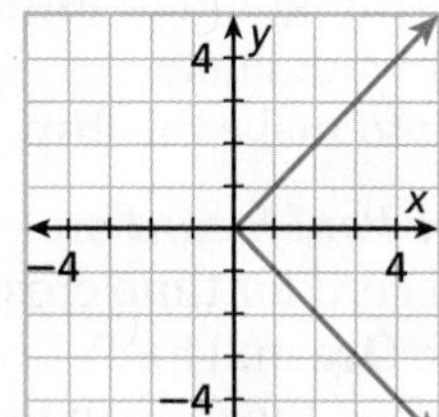

56.

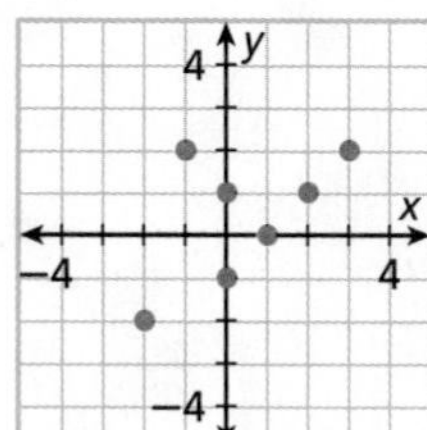

Give the coordinates of the translated point when the original point is (−4, 3). *(Lesson 1-8)*

57. horizontal translation of −1

58. reflection across the *y*-axis

59. vertical translation of 3

60. $(x + 7, y - 5)$

Write an equation of each line in slope-intercept form. Each line passes through the point (1, −7). *(Lesson 2-4)*

61. passing through (1, 3)

62. parallel to $y = \frac{1}{2}x - 5$

63. with a slope of 0.25

64. perpendicular to $3x - y = -4$

CHAPTER 2

MULTI-STEP TEST PREP

SECTION 2A

Linear Equations and Inequalities

Sailing Away Crossing the Atlantic Ocean in a sailboat is a prestigious feat that many sailors attempt. Some of the speed records for the west-to-east trip from New York to England are shown in the table.

Transatlantic Sailing Records (New York to England)

Yacht	Year	Country	Average Speed (knots)
Atlantic	1905	USA	10.02
Royale II	1986	France	15.47
Jet Services V	1990	France	18.62
PlayStation	2001	USA	25.78

1. The length of the course that each yacht sailed, from the Ambrose Light Tower in New York to Lizard Point in England, is 3364 statute miles. How much longer did the *Atlantic* take to complete the trip than the *PlayStation*?

2. Dolphins can swim about 20 statute miles per hour. If a dolphin were racing against each of the yachts in the table, in which place would the dolphin finish?

3. Graph the distance in nautical miles that the *PlayStation* could cover over a period from 0 to 48 hours. The sailing distance from New York to Florida is 947 nautical miles. Use your graph to estimate how long it would take the *PlayStation* to make this trip.

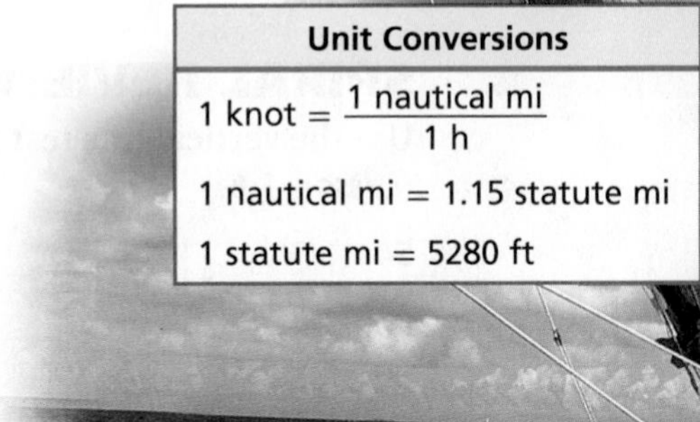

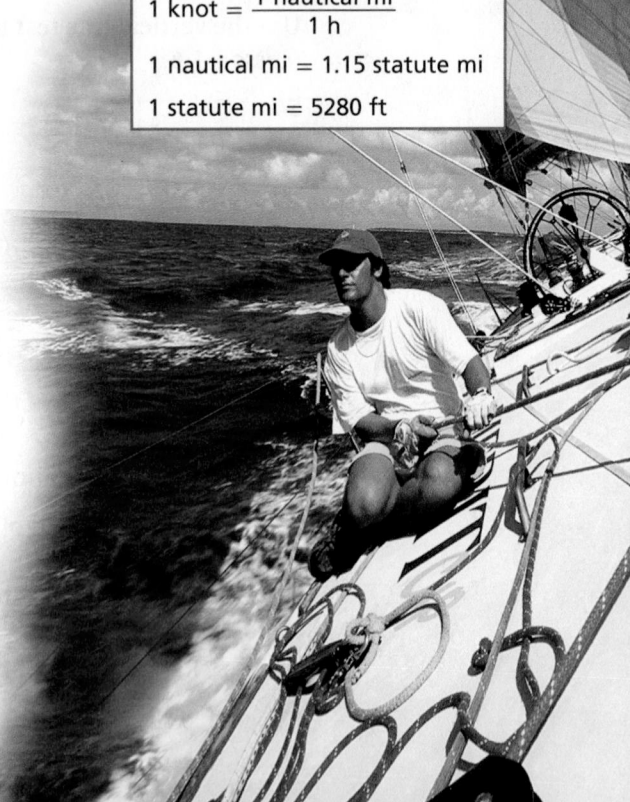

Unit Conversions

$1 \text{ knot} = \frac{1 \text{ nautical mi}}{1 \text{ h}}$

1 nautical mi = 1.15 statute mi

1 statute mi = 5280 ft

4. In 1980, the *Paul Ricard* broke the *Atlantic's* record for time crossing the Atlantic Ocean. The *Paul Ricard* finished the crossing in 10 days, 5 hours, and 14 minutes. Write a linear equation that describes the distance in nautical miles that the *Paul Ricard* covered as a function of time in hours.

5. Write and graph an inequality to show the possible distance d in statute miles that the *Atlantic* could cover in t hours. Is the point $(7.5, 85)$ a solution to the inequality? Explain the meaning of this point in the context of the problem.

READY TO GO ON?

Quiz for Lessons 2-1 Through 2-5

2-1 Solving Linear Equations and Inequalities

Solve.

1. $15 + 8x = 3x$
2. $\frac{3}{2}(5x + 7) = 16$
3. $12 - 15x = 25 - 5x$
4. $3(x + 5) - 8(x - 3) = 20$

Solve and graph.

5. $45 \geq -25 + 10x$
6. $12 - 4x < 24$
7. $4(9 - 2x) \leq 3(4x + 2)$
8. $5x - 4(2x + 6) \geq 15$
9. Marie has \$55 in her bank account, and she would like to buy a video game system that costs \$395. Marie saves \$6 for each hour she works. How many hours must Marie work to have enough money to buy the video game system?

2-2 Proportional Reasoning

Solve each proportion.

10. $\frac{x}{12} = \frac{8}{3}$
11. $\frac{3}{5} = \frac{4x}{9}$
12. $\frac{5}{-x} = \frac{2.5}{8}$
13. $\frac{5}{9} = \frac{4}{2x - 3}$
14. A building casts a 24-foot shadow at the same time that a 6-foot-tall person casts an 8-foot shadow. How tall is the building?

2-3 Graphing Linear Functions

Find the intercepts and graph each line.

15. $2x + 3y = 18$
16. $5x - 3y = -15$
17. $\frac{1}{2}x + 2y = 6$
18. $-x - y = \frac{7}{2}$

Write each function in slope-intercept form. Then graph the function.

19. $y - 3x = 1$
20. $4x + 2y = 8$
21. $3x - 10 - 5y = 0$
22. $5 - x = \frac{y}{3}$

2-4 Writing Linear Functions

Write an equation in slope-intercept form for each line.

23. through $(3, 12)$ and $(6, 27)$
24. slope $\frac{3}{4}$ and through $(4, -6)$
25. parallel to $y = \frac{3}{2}x - 6$ and through $(-6, 2)$
26. perpendicular to $5x + 2y = 8$ and through $(5, 3)$

2-5 Linear Inequalities in Two Variables

Solve for y in each inequality. Then graph.

27. $y - 1 \leq 5$
28. $2x + 5y > 10$
29. $3x - 4y > 5x + 12$
30. $3(2x - 1) + y > 6x - 4$
31. Dorothy has \$30 to spend on holiday cards. Large cards cost \$2.50 each, and small cards cost \$1.50 each. Write and graph an inequality for the number of cards Dorothy can purchase.

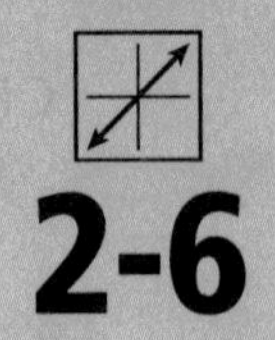

2-6 Transforming Linear Functions

Objectives

Transform linear functions.

Solve problems involving linear transformations.

Why learn this?

Transformations allow you to visualize and compare many different functions at once.

In Lesson 1-8, you learned to transform functions by transforming each point. Transformations can also be expressed by using function notation.

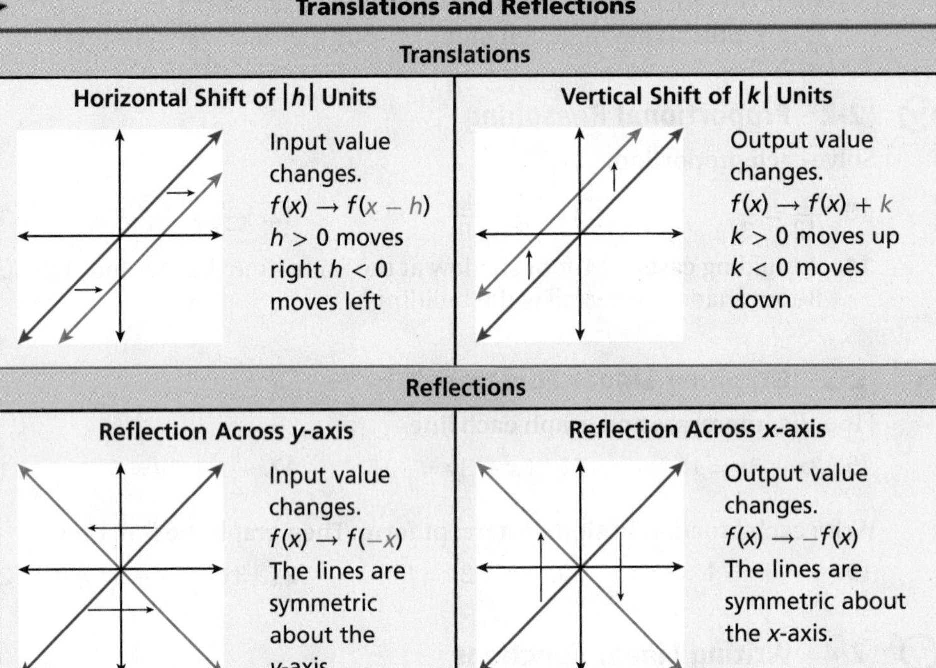

Translations and Reflections

Translations	
Horizontal Shift of $\lvert h \rvert$ Units	**Vertical Shift of $\lvert k \rvert$ Units**
Input value changes. $f(x) \to f(x-h)$ $h > 0$ moves right $h < 0$ moves left	Output value changes. $f(x) \to f(x) + k$ $k > 0$ moves up $k < 0$ moves down
Reflections	
Reflection Across y-axis	**Reflection Across x-axis**
Input value changes. $f(x) \to f(-x)$ The lines are symmetric about the y-axis.	Output value changes. $f(x) \to -f(x)$ The lines are symmetric about the x-axis.

Helpful Hint

To remember the difference between vertical and horizontal translations, think: "Add to y, go high." "Add to x, go left."

EXAMPLE 1 **Translating and Reflecting Linear Functions**

Let $g(x)$ be the indicated transformation of $f(x)$. Write the rule for $g(x)$.

A **$f(x) = 2x + 3$; vertical translation 4 units up**

Translating $f(x)$ 4 units up adds 4 to each output value.

$g(x) = f(x) + 4$ *Add 4 to $f(x)$.*

$g(x) = (2x + 3) + 4$ *Substitute $2x + 3$ for $f(x)$.*

$g(x) = 2x + 7$ *Simplify.*

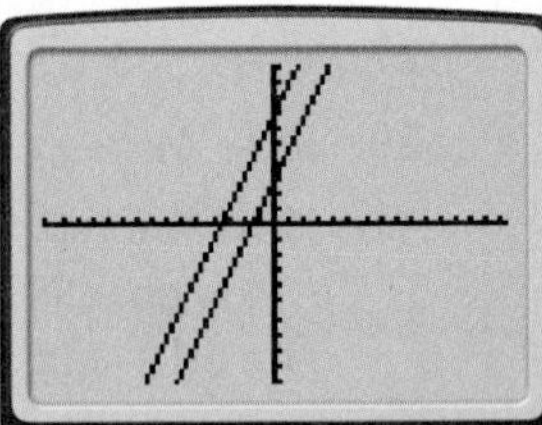

Check Graph $f(x)$ and $g(x)$ on a graphing calculator. The slopes are the same, but the y-intercept has moved 4 units up from 3 to 7. ✔

Let $g(x)$ be the indicated transformation of $f(x)$. Write the rule for $g(x)$.

B **linear function defined in the table; reflection across y-axis**

x	$f(x)$
−1	0
0	2
1	4

Step 1 Write the rule for $f(x)$ in slope-intercept form.

The y-intercept is 2. *The table contains (0, 2).*

Find the slope:

$m = \dfrac{2-0}{0-(-1)} = \dfrac{2}{1} = 2$ *Use (−1, 0) and (0, 2).*

$y = mx + b$ *Slope-intercept form*

$y = 2x + 2$ *Substitute 2 for m and 2 for b.*

$f(x) = 2x + 2$ *Replace y with f(x).*

Step 2 Write the rule for $g(x)$. Reflecting $f(x)$ across the y-axis replaces each x with $-x$.

$g(x) = 2(-x) + 2$ *$g(x) = f(-x)$*

$g(x) = -2x + 2$

Check Graph $f(x)$ and $g(x)$ on a graphing calculator. The graphs are symmetric about the y-axis. ✔

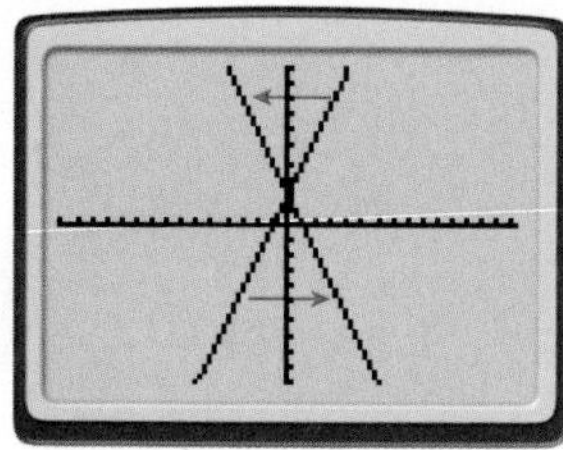

Let $g(x)$ be the indicated transformation of $f(x)$. Write the rule for $g(x)$.

1a. $f(x) = 3x + 1$; translation 2 units right

1b. linear function defined in the table; a reflection across the x-axis

x	−1	0	1
y	1	2	3

Stretches and compressions change the slope of a linear function. If the line becomes steeper, the function has been stretched vertically or compressed horizontally. If the line becomes flatter, the function has been compressed vertically or stretched horizontally.

Stretches and Compressions	
Horizontal	**Vertical**
Horizontal Stretch/Compression by a Factor of b	**Vertical Stretch/Compression by a Factor of a**
Input value changes. $f(x) \rightarrow f\left(\frac{1}{b}x\right)$	Output value changes. $f(x) \rightarrow a \cdot f(x)$
$b > 1$ stretches away from the y-axis. $0 < \lvert b \rvert < 1$ compresses toward the y-axis.	$a > 1$ stretches away from the x-axis. $0 < \lvert a \rvert < 1$ compresses toward the x-axis.

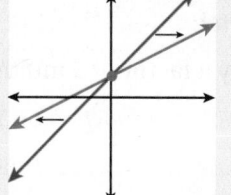

EXAMPLE 2 Stretching and Compressing Linear Functions

Let $g(x)$ be a horizontal compression of $f(x) = 2x - 1$ by a factor of $\frac{1}{3}$. Write the rule for $g(x)$, and graph the function.

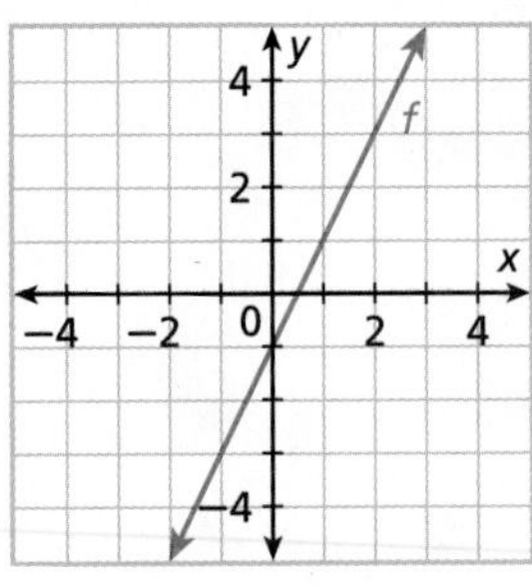

Horizontally compressing $f(x)$ by a factor of $\frac{1}{3}$ replaces each x with $\frac{1}{b}x$ where $b = \frac{1}{3}$.

$g(x) = 2\left(\frac{1}{b}\right)x - 1$ *For horizontal compression, use $\frac{1}{b}$.*

$= 2\left(\frac{1}{\frac{1}{3}}\right)x - 1$ *Substitute $\frac{1}{3}$ for b.*

$= 2(3x) - 1$ *Replace x with 3x.*

$g(x) = 6x - 1$ *Simplify.*

Check Graph both functions on the same coordinate plane. The graph of $g(x)$ is steeper than $f(x)$, which indicates that $g(x)$ has been horizontally compressed from $f(x)$, or pushed toward the y-axis.

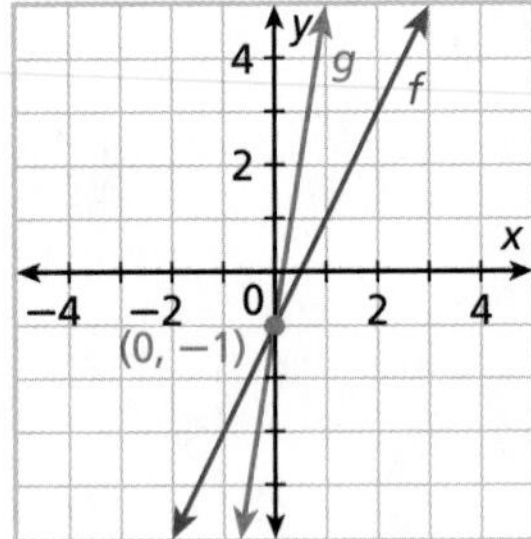

Helpful Hint

These don't change!
- y-intercepts in a horizontal stretch or compression
- x-intercepts in a vertical stretch or compression

2. Let $g(x)$ be a vertical compression of $f(x) = 3x + 2$ by a factor of $\frac{1}{4}$. Write the rule for $g(x)$.

Some linear functions involve more than one transformation. Combine transformations by applying individual transformations one at a time in the order in which they are given.

For multiple transformations, create a temporary function—such as $h(x)$ in Example 3 below—to represent the first transformation, and then transform it to find the combined transformation.

EXAMPLE 3 Combining Transformations of Linear Functions

Let $g(x)$ be a vertical shift of $f(x) = x$ down 2 units followed by a vertical stretch by a factor of 5. Write the rule for $g(x)$.

Step 1 First perform the translation.

Translating $f(x) = x$ down 2 units subtracts 2 from the function. You can use $h(x)$ to represent the translated function.

$h(x) = f(x) - 2$ *Subtract 2 from the function.*

$h(x) = x - 2$ *Substitute x for f(x).*

Step 2 Then perform the stretch.

Stretching $h(x)$ vertically by a factor of 5 multiplies the function by 5.

$g(x) = 5 \cdot h(x)$ *Multiply the function by 5.*

$g(x) = 5(x - 2)$ *Because $h(x) = x - 2$, substitute $x - 2$ for $h(x)$.*

$g(x) = 5x - 10$ *Simplify.*

3. Let $g(x)$ be a vertical compression of $f(x) = x$ by a factor of $\frac{1}{2}$ followed by a horizontal shift 8 units left. Write the rule for $g(x)$.

EXAMPLE 4 *Fund-raising Application*

The Dance Club is selling beaded purses as a fund-raiser. The function $R(n) = 12.5n$ represents the club's revenue in dollars where n is the number of purses sold.

a. The club paid \$75 for the materials needed to make the purses. Write a new function $P(n)$ for the club's profit.

The initial costs must be subtracted from the revenue.

$R(n) = 12.5n$ *Original function*

$P(n) = 12.5n - 75$ *Subtract the expenses.*

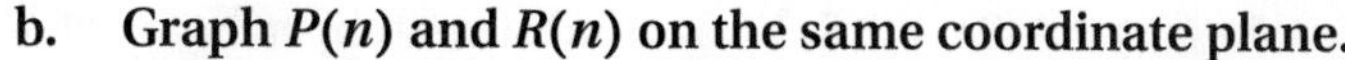

b. Graph $P(n)$ and $R(n)$ on the same coordinate plane.

Graph both functions. The lines have the same slope but different y-intercepts.

Note that the profit can be negative but the number of purses sold cannot be less than 0.

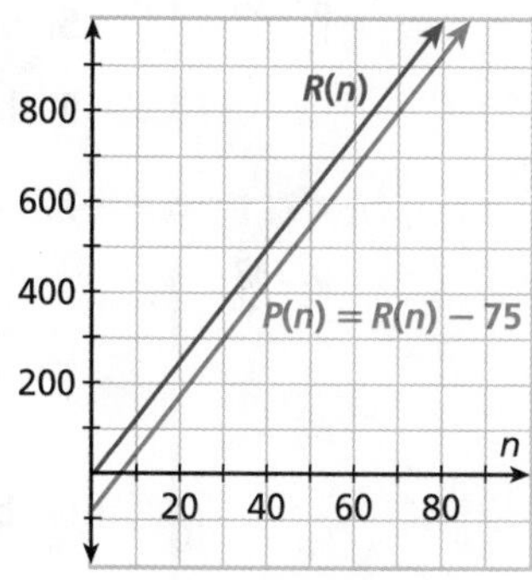

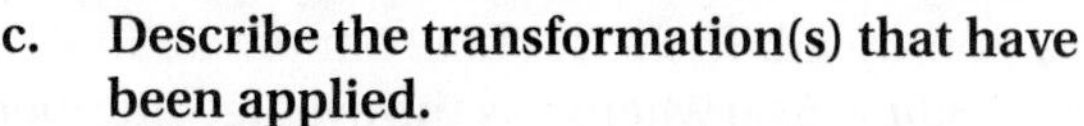

c. Describe the transformation(s) that have been applied.

The graphs indicate that $P(n)$ is a translation of $R(n)$. Because 75 was subtracted, $P(n) = R(n) - 75$. This indicates a vertical shift 75 units down.

4. **What if...?** The club members decided to double the price of each purse.
   - **a.** Write a new profit function $S(n)$ for the club.
   - **b.** Graph $S(n)$ and $P(n)$ on the same coordinate plane.
   - **c.** Describe the transformation(s) that have been applied.

THINK AND DISCUSS

1. Identify the horizontal translation that would have the same effect on the graph of $f(x) = x$ as a vertical translation of 6 units.
2. Give an example of two different transformations of $f(x) = 2x$ that would result in $g(x) = 2x - 6$.
3. Describe the transformation that would cause all of the function values to double.
4. **GET ORGANIZED** Copy and complete the graphic organizer. In each box, give an example of the indicated transformation of the parent function $f(x) = x$. Include an equation and a graph.

Know it! Note

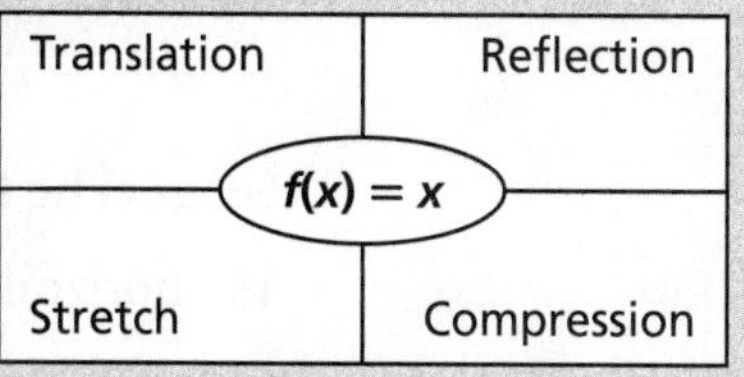

2-6 Exercises

GUIDED PRACTICE

SEE EXAMPLE 1 p. 134

Let $g(x)$ be the indicated transformation of $f(x)$. Write the rule for $g(x)$.

1. linear function defined by the table; vertical translation 1.5 units up

x	−2	−1	0
$f(x)$	3.5	2	0.5

SEE EXAMPLE 2 p. 136

2. $f(x) = -x + 5$; horizontal translation 2 units left
3. $f(x) = \frac{1}{3}x - 2$; vertical stretch by a factor of 3
4. $f(x) = -2x + 0.5$; horizontal stretch by a factor of $\frac{4}{3}$.

SEE EXAMPLE 3 p. 136

Let $g(x)$ be the indicated combined transformation of $f(x) = x$. Write the rule for $g(x)$.

5. vertical compression by a factor of $\frac{2}{3}$ followed by a vertical shift 6 units down
6. horizontal shift right 4 units followed by a horizontal stretch by a factor of $\frac{3}{2}$

SEE EXAMPLE 4 p. 137

7. **Advertising** An electronics company is changing its Internet ad from a banner ad to a pop-up ad. The cost of the banner ad in dollars is represented by $C(n) = 0.30n + 5.00$ where n is the average number of hits per hour. The cost of the pop-up ad will double the cost per hit.
   a. Write a new cost function $D(n)$ for the ads.
   b. Graph $C(n)$ and $D(n)$ on the same coordinate plane.
   c. Describe the transformation(s) that have been applied.

PRACTICE AND PROBLEM SOLVING

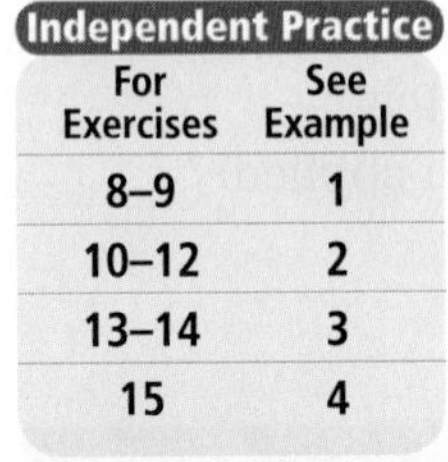

For Exercises	See Example
8–9	1
10–12	2
13–14	3
15	4

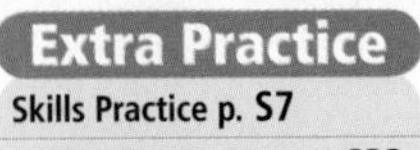

Independent Practice

Extra Practice
Skills Practice p. S7
Application Practice p. S33

Let $g(x)$ be the indicated transformation of $f(x)$. Write the rule for $g(x)$.

8. 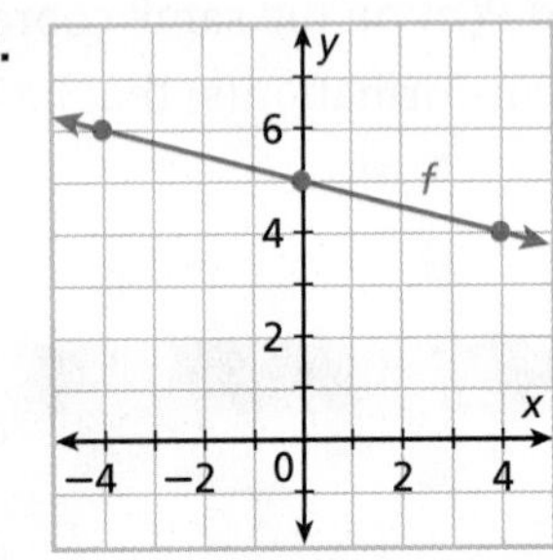

Reflection across the x-axis

9. 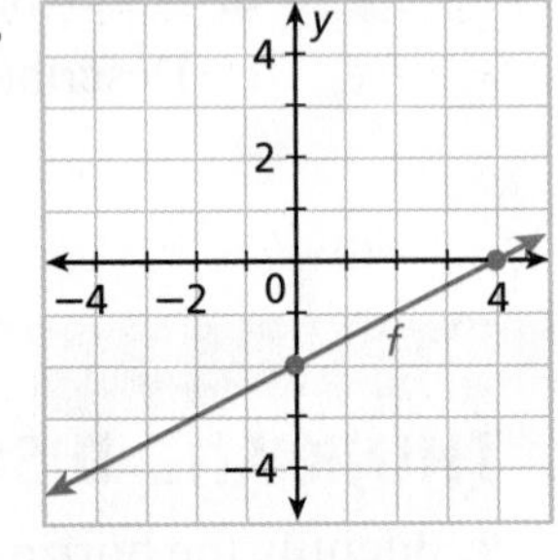

Vertical translation 2 units down

10. 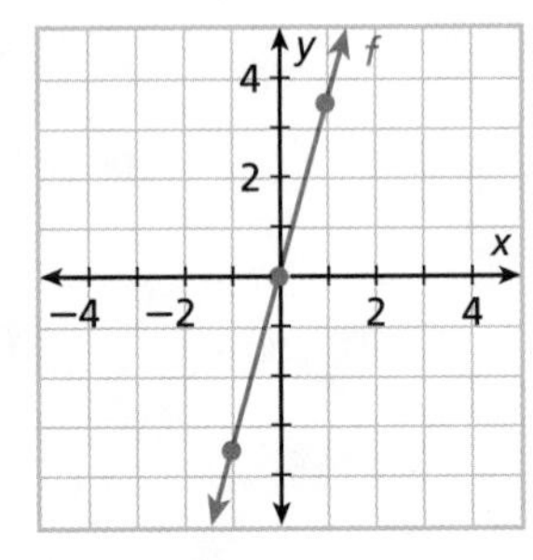

Horizontal compression by a factor of 0.5

11. linear function defined by the table; vertical stretch by a factor of 1.2 units

x	1	5	9
$f(x)$	0	−2	−4

12. $f(x) = -3x + 7$; vertical compression by a factor of $\frac{3}{4}$

Let $g(x)$ be the indicated combined transformation of $f(x) = x$. Write the rule for $g(x)$.

13. horizontal stretch by a factor of 2.75 followed by a horizontal shift 1 unit left
14. vertical shift 6 units down followed by a vertical compression by a factor of $\frac{2}{3}$

15. **Consumer Economics** In 1997, Southwestern Bell increased the price for local pay-phone calls. Before then, the price of a call could be determined by $f(x) = 0.15x + 0.25$, where x was the number of minutes after the *first* minute. The company increased the cost of the first minute by 10 cents.

 a. Write a new price function $g(x)$ for a phone call.

 b. Graph $f(x)$ and $g(x)$ on the same coordinate plane.

 c. Describe the transformation(s) that have been applied.

Write the rule for the transformed function $g(x)$ and graph.

16. 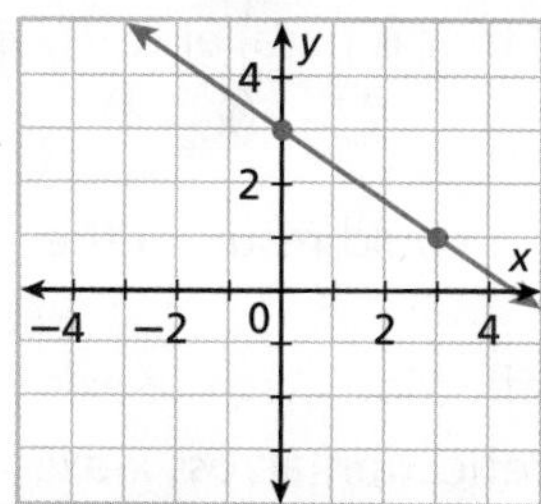

Reflection across the y-axis

17. 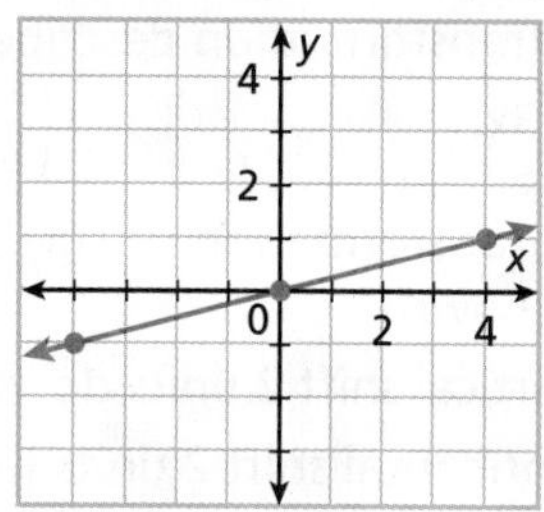

Vertical stretch by a factor of 8

18. 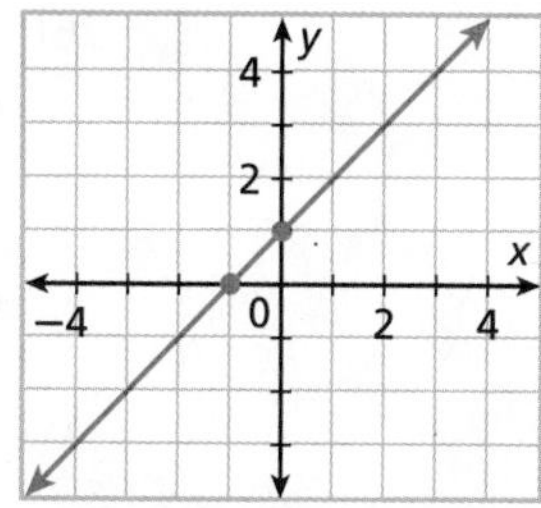

Horizontal stretch by a factor of 3

History **Historic tolls for traveling on the Cumberland Road in Pennsylvania are shown on the sign. Toll was paid every 15 miles.**

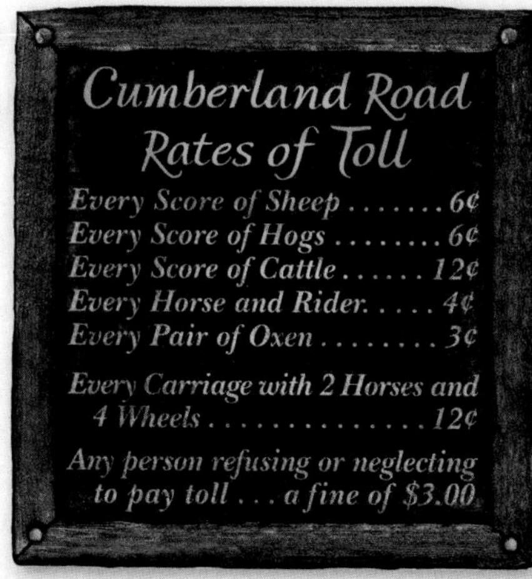

Cumberland Road
Rates of Toll
Every Score of Sheep .... 6¢
Every Score of Hogs .... 6¢
Every Score of Cattle ...... 12¢
Every Horse and Rider ..... 4¢
Every Pair of Oxen .... 3¢
Every Carriage with 2 Horses and 4 Wheels .... 12¢
Any person refusing or neglecting to pay toll . . . a fine of $3.00

19. Write a function to represent the cost for 1 horse and rider to travel n miles with a score of sheep. What transformation describes the change in cost if the sheep were replaced by cattle?

20. Write a function to represent the cost for a carriage with 2 horses and 4 wheels to travel n miles. Name two different transformations that would represent a 6¢ increase in the toll rate.

21. **Critical Thinking** Consider the linear function $f(x) = x$.

 a. Shift $f(x)$ 2 units up and then reflect it over the x-axis.

 b. Perform the same transformations on $f(x)$ again but in reverse order.

 c. Make a conjecture about the order in which transformations are performed.

22. **Write About It** Which transformations affect the slope of a linear function, and which transformations affect the y-intercept? Support your answers.

MULTI-STEP TEST PREP

23. This problem will prepare you for the Multi-Step Test Prep on page 164. Use the data set $\{1, 5, 10, 17, 23, 23, 38, 60\}$.

 a. Find the mean, median, mode, and range.

 b. How does adding 7 to each number affect the mean, median, mode, and range?

 c. How does multiplying each number by 4 affect the mean, median, mode, and range?

 d. How does multiplying each number by 2 and then adding 5 affect the mean, median, mode, and range?

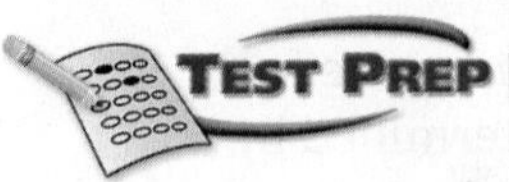

24. The cost function C of rent at an apartment complex increased \$50 last year and another \$60 this year. Which function accurately reflects these changes?

   (A) $60(C + 50)$ (B) $60(50C)$ (C) $(C + 50) + 60$ (D) $50C + 60$

25. Given $f(x) = 28.5x + 45.6$, which function decreases the y-intercept by 20.3?

   (F) $g(x) = 8.2x + 45.6$ (H) $g(x) = 28.5x + 25.3$

   (G) $g(x) = 8.2x + 66.1$ (J) $g(x) = 28.5x + 66.1$

26. Which transformation describes a line that is parallel to $f(x)$?

   (A) $f(3x)$ (B) $f\left(\frac{x}{2}\right)$ (C) $f(x - 4)$ (D) $f(-2x)$

27. Which transformation of $f(x) = \frac{1}{2}x - 1$ could result in the graph shown?

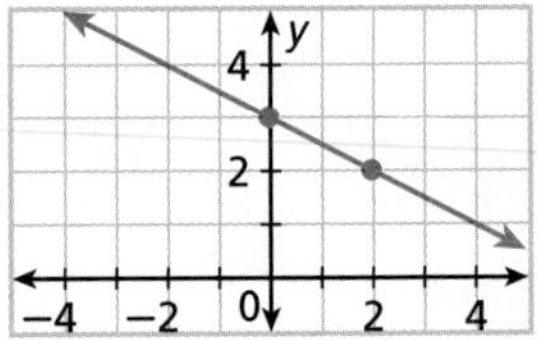

   (F) vertical shift 2 units down and reflection across x-axis

   (G) horizontal shift 2 units left and reflection across x-axis

   (H) vertical shift 2 units up and reflection across x-axis

   (J) horizontal shift 2 units right and reflection across x-axis

CHALLENGE AND EXTEND

28. Give two different combinations of transformations that would transform $f(x) = 3x + 4$ into $g(x) = 15x - 10$.

29. Give an example of two transformations of $f(x) = x$ that can be performed in any order and result in the same transformed function.

30. **Education** The graph shows the tuition at a university based on the number of credit hours taken. The rate per credit hour varies according to the number of hours taken: less than 12 hours, 12 to 18 hours, and greater than 18 hours.

   a. Write the linear function that represents each segment of the graph.

   b. Write the linear functions that would reflect a 12% increase in all tuition costs.

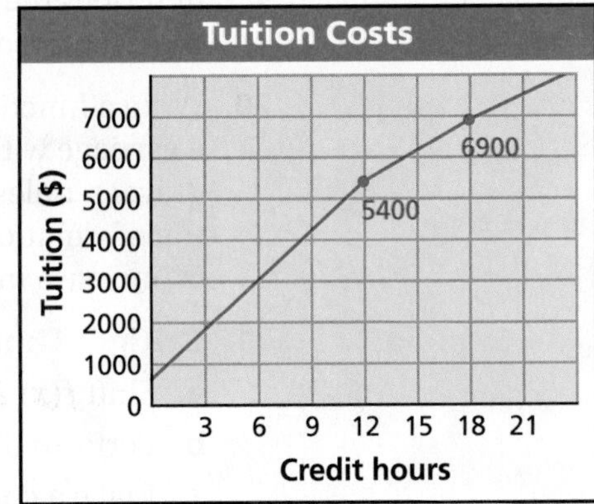

SPIRAL REVIEW

Write each expression in expanded form. *(Lesson 1-5)*

31. $\left(\frac{3}{5}d^2\right)^3$ 32. 2^{-3} 33. $-(2n)^4$ 34. $-a^5(6a)^{-1}$

Determine if each line is vertical, horizontal, or neither, and graph the line. *(Lesson 2-3)*

35. $y = -6$ 36. $x = \frac{3}{7}$

37. $y = -x$ 38. $5.1 = y$

39. **Money** Express Henry's bonus as a function of the ads that Henry sells. How many ad spots must Henry sell to earn \$520 as a bonus? *(Lesson 2-4)*

Henry's Bonus	
Ads Sold	**Bonus ($)**
12	65
16	195
21	357.50

Statistical Graphs

Statistical data may be displayed in bar graphs or circle graphs. Use a bar graph to compare numerical amounts. Use a circle graph to compare parts of a whole.

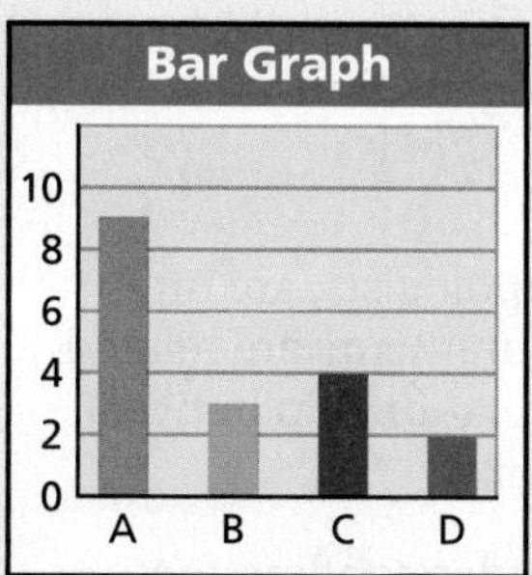

A bar graph compares numerical amounts.

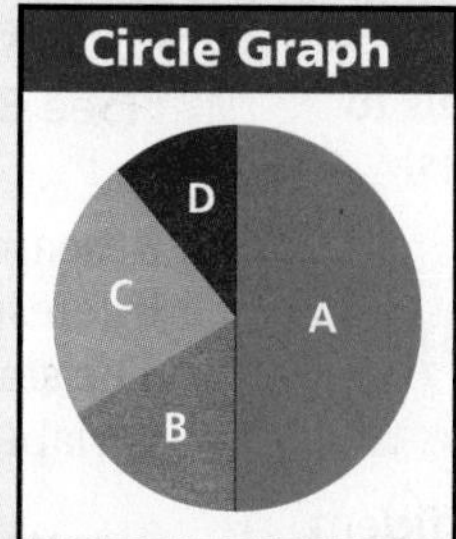

A circle graph compares parts of a whole.

The bar graph shows the numbers of pets owned by a group of students in a pet owners club.

Example

Use the bar graph. Find the central angle measure for the named category in a related circle graph, to the nearest degree.

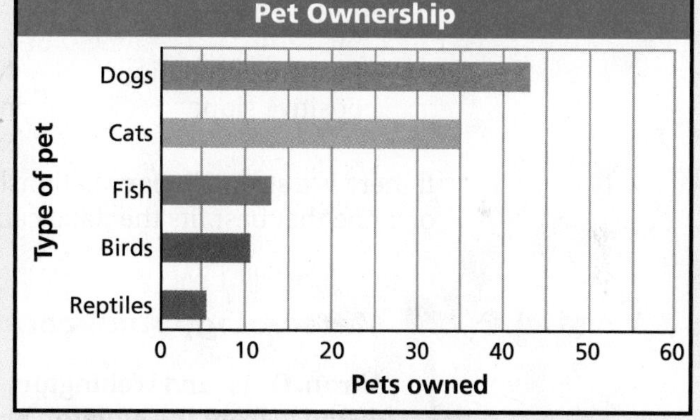

Category: birds

1. Compute the total number of pets.
   Add the number of dogs, cats, fish, birds, and reptiles.
   $43 + 35 + 13 + 11 + 6 = 108$

2. Find the number of pets in the category.
   11 birds

3. A circle consists of 360°. Write and solve a proportion.
   $$\text{Part} \rightarrow \frac{11}{108} = \frac{n}{360} \leftarrow \text{Circle part}$$
   $$\text{Whole} \rightarrow \qquad \leftarrow \text{Circle whole}$$

4. Solve for the measure of the central angle.
   $11 \cdot 360 = 108n$
   $37° \approx n$

Try This

Find the central angle measure for each category, to the nearest degree.

1. fish
2. reptiles
3. dogs
4. cats
5. fish, birds, and reptiles combined
6. What categories combined give a central angle of approximately 207°?

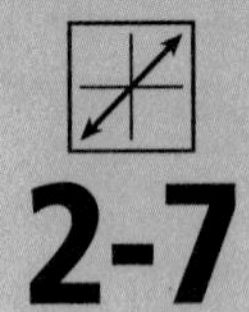

2-7 Curve Fitting with Linear Models

Objectives

Fit scatter plot data using linear models with and without technology.

Use linear models to make predictions.

Vocabulary

regression
correlation
line of best fit
correlation coefficient

Who uses this?

Anthropologists can use linear models to estimate the heights of ancient people from bones that the anthropologists find. (See Example 2.)

Researchers, such as anthropologists, are often interested in how two measurements are related. The statistical study of the relationship between variables is called **regression**.

A *scatter plot* is helpful in understanding the form, direction, and strength of the relationship between two variables. **Correlation** is the strength and direction of the linear relationship between the two variables.

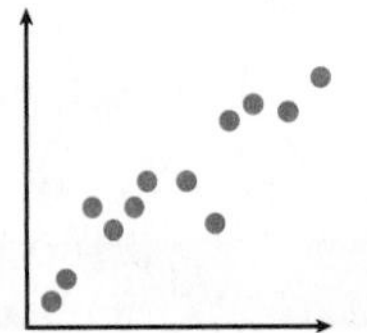

Positive correlation, positive slope

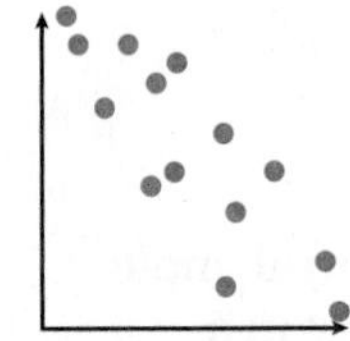

Negative correlation, negative slope

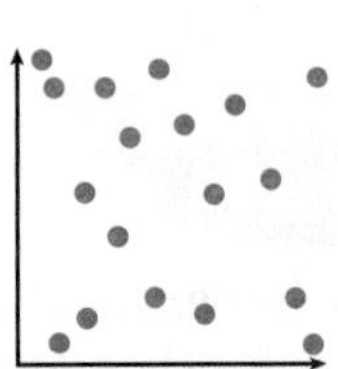

Relatively no correlation

If there is a strong linear relationship between two variables, a **line of best fit**, or a line that best fits the data, can be used to make predictions.

EXAMPLE 1 ***Meteorology Application***

Akron, Ohio, and Wellington, New Zealand, are about the same distance from the equator. Make a scatter plot for the temperature data, identify the correlation, and then sketch a line of best fit and find its equation.

Average High Temperatures (°F)

	Jan	Feb	Mar	Apr	May	Jun	Jul	Aug	Sep	Oct	Nov	Dec
Akron	33	37	48	59	70	78	82	80	73	61	49	38
Wellington	67	67	65	61	56	53	51	52	55	57	60	64

Step 1 Plot the data points.

Step 2 Identify the correlation.

Notice that the data set is negatively correlated—as the temperature rises in Akron, it falls in Wellington.

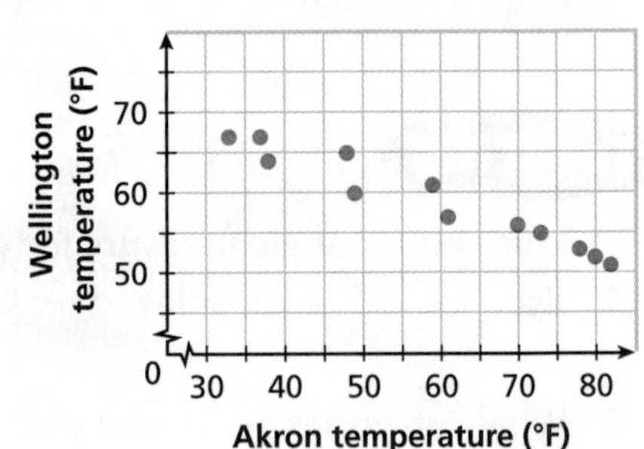

Reading Math

In a set of *bivariate* data, there are two variables for each observation. A set of data displayed in a scatter plot represents bivariate data.

Step 3 Sketch a line of best fit.

Draw a line that splits the data evenly above and below.

Step 4 Identify two points on the line.

For this data, you might select $(30, 70)$ and $(80, 52)$.

Step 5 Find the slope of the line that models the data.

$$m = \frac{70 - 52}{30 - 80} = \frac{18}{-50} = -0.36$$

Use the point-slope form.

$y - y_1 = m(x - x_1)$ *Point-slope form*

$y - 70 = -0.36(x - 30)$ *Substitute.*

$y = -0.36x + 80.8$ *Simplify.*

An equation that models the data is $y = -0.36x + 80.8$.

1. Basketball Make a scatter plot for this set of data. Identify the correlation, sketch a line of best fit, and find its equation.

Points Scored in Ten Games										
Minutes Played	28	35	8	20	39	23	19	27	15	30
Points Scored	16	13	2	12	31	10	9	15	4	19

The **correlation coefficient** r is a measure of how well the data set is fit by a model.

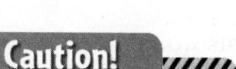

Properties of the Correlation Coefficient r

r is a value in the range $-1 \le r \le 1$.

If $r = 1$, the data set forms a straight line with a positive slope.

If $r = 0$, the data set has no correlation.

If $r = -1$, the data set forms a straight line with a negative slope.

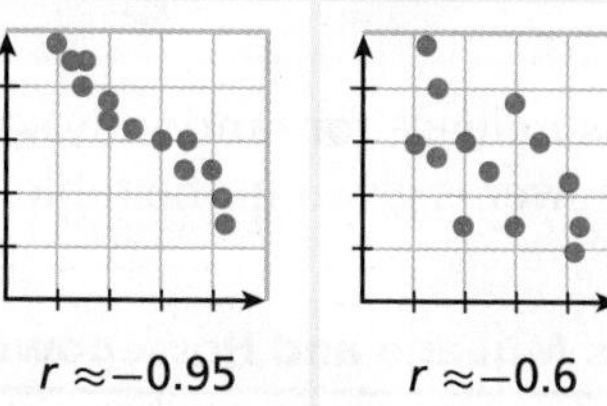

$r \approx -0.95$ $r \approx -0.6$

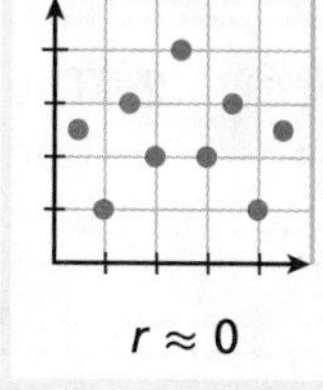

$r \approx 0$

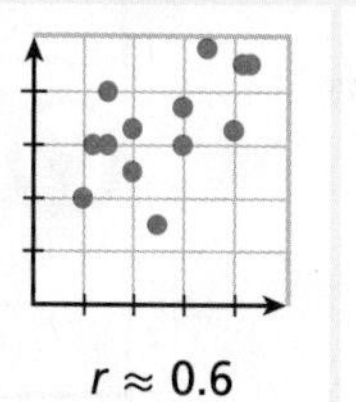

$r \approx 0.6$

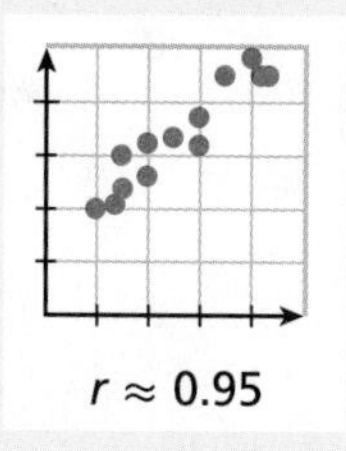

$r \approx 0.95$

Caution!

Don't confuse slope with the *value* of r. Whether a line has a slope of 10 or a slope of $\frac{1}{10}$, it can have an r-value of 1. The r-value and the slope have the same sign.

You can use a graphing calculator to perform a linear regression and find the correlation coefficient r. To display the correlation coefficient, you may have to turn on the diagnostic mode. To do this, press 2nd 0 (CATALOG), and choose the **DiagnosticOn** mode.

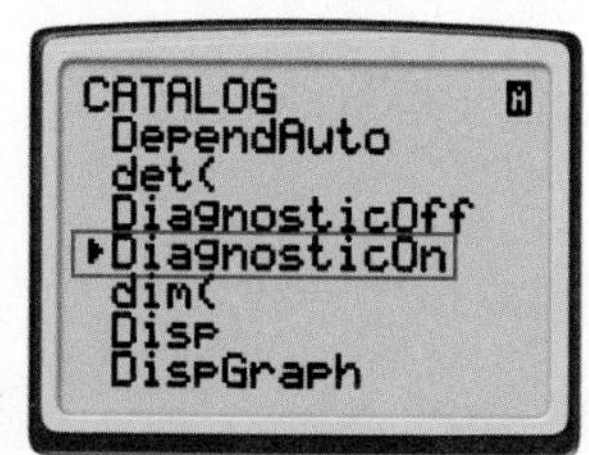

EXAMPLE 2 Anthropology Application

Anthropologists use known relationships between the height and length of a woman's humerus bone, the bone between the elbow and the shoulder, to estimate a woman's height. Some samples are shown in the table.

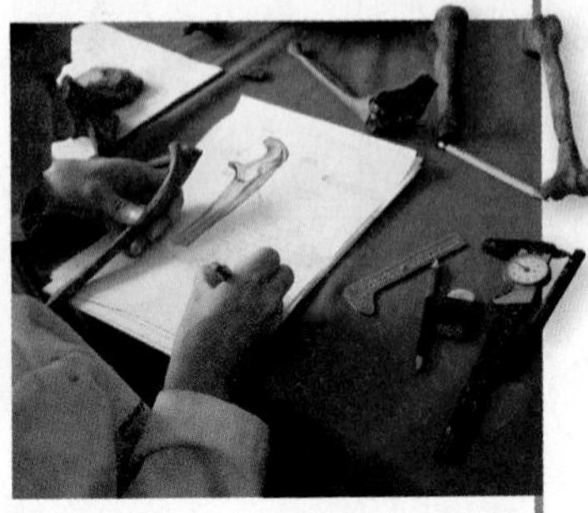

Bone Length and Height in Women								
Humerus Length (cm)	35	27	30	33	25	39	27	31
Height (cm)	167	146	154	165	140	180	149	155

a. Make a scatter plot of the data with humerus length as the independent variable.

The scatter plot is shown at right.

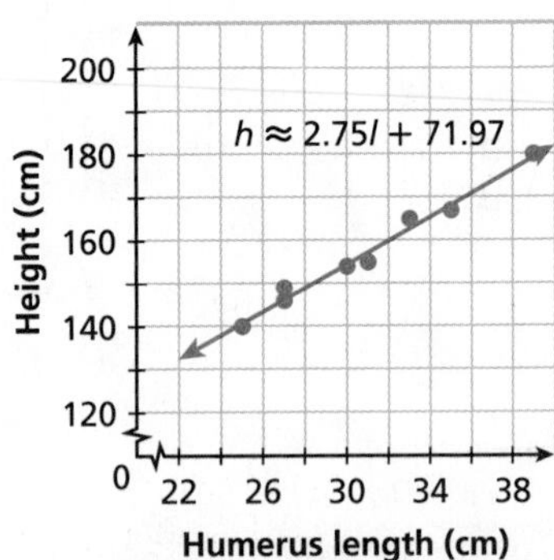

b. Find the correlation coefficient r and the line of best fit. Interpret the slope of the line of best fit in the context of the problem.

Enter the data into lists **L1** and **L2** on a graphing calculator. Use the linear regression feature by pressing STAT, choosing **CALC**, and selecting **4:LinReg**. The equation of the line of best fit is $h \approx 2.75\ell + 71.97$.

The slope is about 2.75, so for each 1 cm increase in humerus length, the predicted increase in a woman's height is 2.75 cm.

The correlation coefficient is $r \approx 0.991$, which indicates a strong positive correlation.

Helpful Hint

To enter data into lists on a graphing calculator, press STAT and select **1:Edit**. Enter the x-values in the **L1** column and the y-values in the **L2** column.

c. A humerus 32 cm long was found. Predict the woman's height.

The equation of the line of best fit is $h \approx 2.75\ell + 71.97$. Use the equation to predict the woman's height. For a 32-cm-long humerus,

$h \approx 2.75(32) + 71.97$ *Substitute 32 for ℓ.*

$h \approx 159.97$

The height of a woman with a 32-cm-long humerus would be about 160 cm.

2. The gas mileage for randomly selected cars based upon engine horsepower is given in the table.

Gas Mileage and Horsepower of Cars										
Horsepower	175	255	140	165	115	120	190	180	110	125
Mileage (mi/gal)	22	13	25	18	32	28	15	21	35	30

a. Make a scatter plot of the data with horsepower as the independent variable.

b. Find the correlation coefficient r and the line of best fit. Interpret the slope of the line in the context of the problem.

c. Predict the gas mileage for a 210-horsepower engine.

EXAMPLE 3 Nutrition Application

Find the following information for this data set on the number of grams of fat and the number of calories in sandwiches served at Dave's Deli.

Dave's Deli Sandwiches Nutritional Information								
Fat (g)	5	9	12	15	12	10	21	14
Calories	360	455	460	420	530	375	580	390

Reading Math

A line of best fit may also be referred to as a *trend line*.

a. Make a scatter plot of the data with fat as the independent variable.
The scatter plot is shown below.

b. Find the correlation coefficient and the equation of the line of best fit. Draw the line of best fit on your scatter plot.
The correlation coefficient is $r = 0.682$.
The equation of the line of best fit is
$y \approx 11.1x + 309.8$.

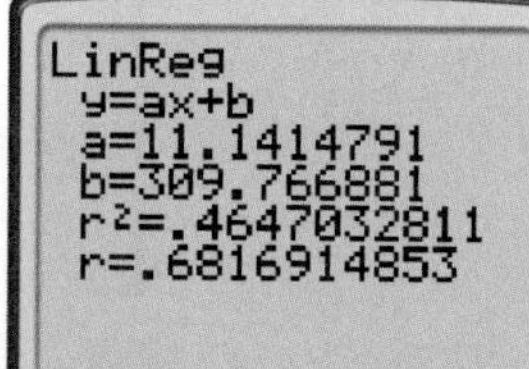

c. Predict the amount of fat in a sandwich with 500 Calories. How accurate do you think your prediction is?

$500 \approx 11.1x + 309.8$ *Calories is the dependent variable.*

$190.2 \approx 11.1x$

$17.1 \approx x$

The line predicts 17.1 grams of fat, but the scatter plot and the value of r show that fat content by itself is *not* a good predictor of the number of calories in a sandwich at Dave's.

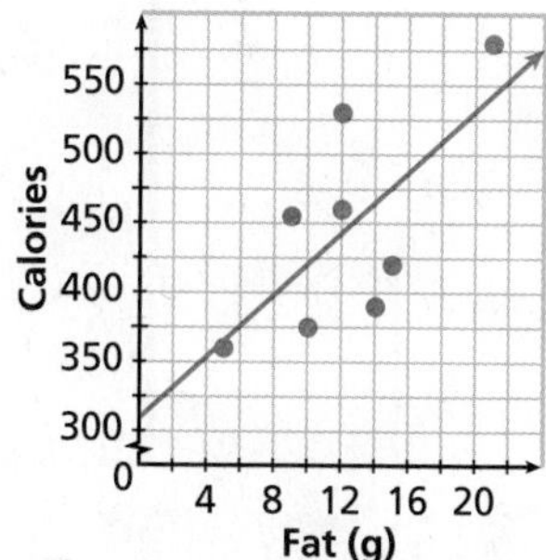

3. What If...? Use the equation of the line of best fit to predict the number of grams of fat in a sandwich with 420 Calories. How close is your answer to the value given in the table?

THINK AND DISCUSS

1. Explain whether the r-value is positive or negative if the line of best fit for data from two variables is $y = 3.2x - 12.5$.

2. Tell which correlation coefficient, $r = 0.65$ or $r = -0.75$, indicates a stronger linear relationship between two variables. Justify your answer.

3. GET ORGANIZED Copy and complete the graphic organizer. Make a scatter plot for each type of correlation and estimate the r-value.

Correlation	Scatter Plot	Estimated r-value
Strong positive		
Weak positive		
No correlation		
Weak negative		
Strong negative		

2-7 Exercises

go.hrw.com
Homework Help Online
KEYWORD: MB7 2-7
Parent Resources Online
KEYWORD: MB7 Parent

GUIDED PRACTICE

1. **Vocabulary** Explain what the following *correlation coefficients* tell you about two sets of data.
   a. $r = 0.4$ b. $r = -0.96$ c. $r = -0.02$

SEE EXAMPLE 1 p. 142

2. **Driving** Make a scatter plot for this data set using gallons as the independent variable. Identify the correlation, sketch a line of best fit, and find its equation.

Distance Traveled							
Gallons	11.2	9.8	10.6	10.1	12.3	8.7	10.1
Distance (mi)	338	296	332	324	368	263	305

SEE EXAMPLE 2 p. 144

3. **Home Economics** Use the data relating the average temperature in a month to the heating bill at Claire's house that month.

Claire's Heating Bills							
Mean Temperature (°F)	38	42	44	36	42	49	38
Heating Bill ($)	93	79	75	83	74	67	86

   a. Make a scatter plot using mean temperature as the independent variable.
   b. Find the correlation coefficient and the equation of the line of best fit. Draw the line of best fit on your scatter plot.
   c. Predict the heating bill for a month in which the average temperature is 40° F. How accurate do you think your prediction is?

SEE EXAMPLE 3 p. 145

4. **School** Here are the number of teachers and the number of students at a randomly selected sample of high schools in a city.

Teachers and Students at Selected Schools								
Teachers	92	52	114	49	110	62	76	84
Students	1050	653	753	381	1312	813	496	910

   a. Make a scatter plot of the data using teachers as the independent variable.
   b. Find the correlation coefficient and the equation of the line of best fit. Draw the line of best fit on your scatter plot.
   c. Predict the number of teachers in a high school that has 600 students. How accurate do you think your prediction is?

PRACTICE AND PROBLEM SOLVING

5. **Chemistry** Make a scatter plot for this data set using the atomic number as the independent variable. Identify the correlation, sketch a line of best fit, and find its equation.

Selected Chemical Elements														
Atomic Number	89	13	95	51	18	33	85	56	97	4	83	107	5	35
Atomic Mass	227	27	243	122	40	75	210	137	247	9	209	264	11	80

Independent Practice	
For Exercises	See Example
5	1
6	2
7	3

Extra Practice

Skills Practice p. S7
Application Practice p. S33

6. **Biology** Hummingbird wing beat rates are much higher than those in other birds. Estimates for various species are given in the table.

Hummingbird Wing Beats							
Mass (g)	3.1	2.0	3.2	4.0	3.7	1.9	4.5
Wing Beats (per *s*)	60	85	50	45	55	90	40

   a. Make a scatter plot of the data using mass as the independent variable.
   b. Find the correlation coefficient and the equation of the line of best fit. Draw the line of best fit on your scatter plot.
   c. Predict the wing beats rate for a Giant Hummingbird with a mass of 19 g. How accurate do you think your prediction is?

7. **Ticket Pricing** The manager of a band has kept track of the price of tickets and the attendance at the band's recent concerts.

Concert Attendance by Ticket Price									
Price ($)	6	5	8.5	8	10	5.50	7	7.5	8
Attendance	213	256	155	194	160	267	258	210	235

   a. Make a scatter plot of the data using price as the independent variable.
   b. Find the correlation coefficient and the equation of the line of best fit. Draw the line of best fit on your scatter plot.
   c. Predict the attendance at a concert where the price of tickets is $9. How accurate do you think your prediction is?

8. Make a scatter plot for this data set. Estimate to find the equation of the line of best fit.

x	2	8	15	21	24	30	33	37
y	71	63	64	194	160	267	258	210

Estimation Estimate the value of *r* for each scatter plot.

9.
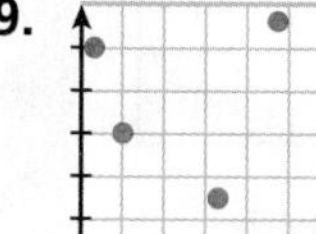
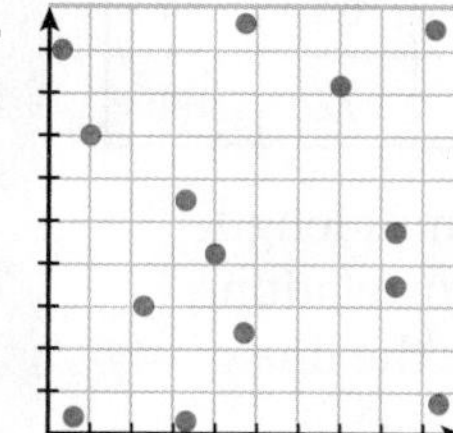

10.
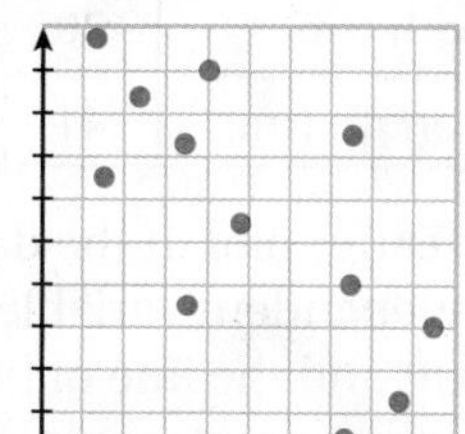

11.
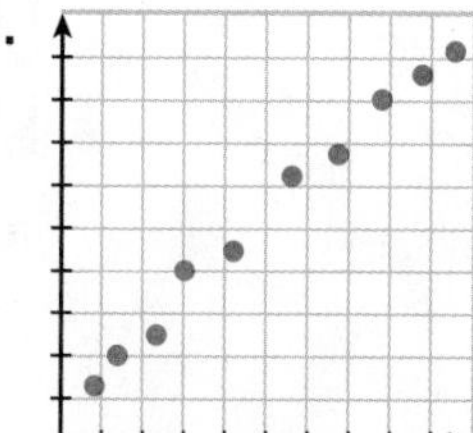

12. **Aviation** Make a scatter plot for the lengths and wingspans of planes in the American Airlines fleet. Sketch a line of best fit with length as the independent variable, and find its equation.

	737	Super 80	757	767	A300	777
Wingspan	113 ft	108 ft	124 ft	147 ft	156 ft	200 ft
Length	130 ft	148 ft	155 ft	178 ft	180 ft	209 ft

13. This problem will prepare you for the Multi-Step Test Prep on page 164.

The table gives the scores of the first 10 entries in a livestock show competition.

Competition Results			
Place	Score	Place	Score
1	95	6	90
2	93	7	89
3	92	8	87
4	91	9	86
5	90	10	85

a. What equation could you use to estimate the score from the place? Graph the equation.

b. Suppose each score is increased by 5. How would this affect the equation and graph of the line?

14. **Athletics** Use the data set relating the number of steps per second to speed for a group of top female runners at different speeds.

Steps Taken by Distance Runners							
Speed (ft/s)	15.86	16.88	17.5	18.62	19.97	21.06	22.11
Steps per second	3.05	3.12	3.17	3.25	3.36	3.46	3.55

Make a scatter plot of the data using speed as the independent variable. Find the correlation coefficient and the line of best fit, and draw it on your scatter plot. Use your equation to predict the number of steps per second taken by a runner going 18 feet per second. How accurate is your prediction? Explain.

15. **Paleontology** The table below shows the lengths of the femur, a leg bone, and the humerus, an arm bone, for five fossil specimens of the archaeopteryx, an extinct animal that had feathers and characteristics of a reptile.

Archaeopteryx Bone Lengths					
Femur Length (cm)	38	56	59	64	74
Humerus Length (cm)	41	63	70	72	84

a. Make a scatter plot of the data using femur length as the independent variable. Find the correlation coefficient and the line of best fit. Draw the line of best fit on your scatter plot.

b. What does the slope of your line mean for the archaeopteryx?

c. Use your equation to predict the length of the femur of an archaeopteryx whose humerus is 50 cm long. How accurate do you think your prediction is?

16. **Critical Thinking** Does a strong linear relationship between two variables mean that one causes the other (for example, if higher daily bee stings correspond to higher ice cream sales)? Explain.

17. **Data Collection** Use a graphing calculator and a motion detector. Stand in a doorway and measure the distance to a person as the person walks from the opposite side of the room toward the motion detector. Is a linear model a good model for distance versus time? Explain.

18. **Write About It** Describe the process of finding a line of best fit.

TEST PREP

19. The equation of the line of best fit for a set of data is $y = 1.05x - 1.3$. Which of the following could be the correlation coefficient for the set of data?

Ⓐ $r = -1.3$ Ⓑ $r = -0.7$ Ⓒ $r = 0.8$ Ⓓ $r = 1.05$

20. Which of the following best describes the correlation shown?

Ⓕ Strong positive Ⓗ Strong negative

Ⓖ Weak positive Ⓙ Weak negative

21. Which of the following relationships would likely have a negative correlation coefficient for an automobile?

Ⓐ Age and total miles Ⓒ Length and width

Ⓑ Age and resale value Ⓓ Highway mileage and city mileage

CHALLENGE AND EXTEND

Are the data linear? Are the data related? Explain.

22.

x	2	7	13	15	22
y	4	4	4	4	4

23.

x	35	45	55	65	75
y	30	34	36	34	30

24. The following data sets were developed by statistician Frank Anscombe. Make a scatter plot of each set of data, and find r and a line of best fit. Why is it important to plot the data before using a linear model to make predictions?

x	10	8	13	9	11	14	6	4	12	7	5
y	9.14	8.14	8.74	8.77	9.29	8.1	6.13	3.1	9.13	7.26	4.74

x	10	8	13	9	11	14	6	4	12	7	5
y	7.46	6.77	12.74	7.11	7.81	8.84	6.08	5.39	8.15	6.42	5.73

SPIRAL REVIEW

Simplify each expression. *(Lesson 1-4)*

25. $3(x^2 - 2) + 4xy - 10x^2y + 5x^2$

26. $-a^4 + 3ab + (2a^2)^2$

27. $-3g^2 + 3(g - 4) - 2(g - g^2)$

28. $n(4t^2 - t) - 10nt^2 + nt$

Solve and graph. *(Lesson 2-1)*

29. $3x < x - 12$

30. $44 + 6x > -5x$

31. $-2(q - 4) + 3q \leq 1 + q$

Write the equation for each function graphed. Describe $g(x)$ as a transformation of $f(x)$. *(Lesson 2-6)*

32.

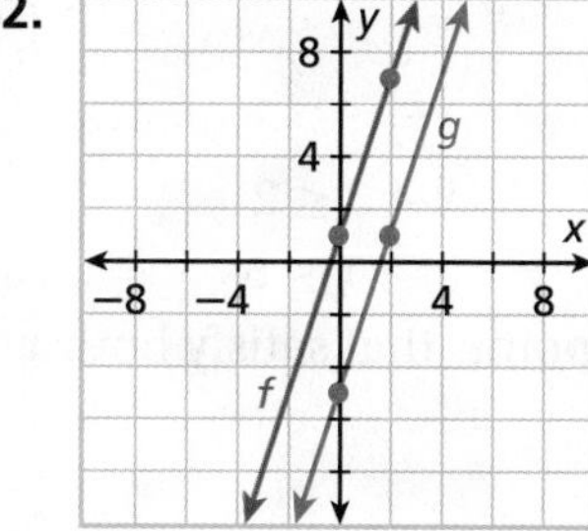

33.

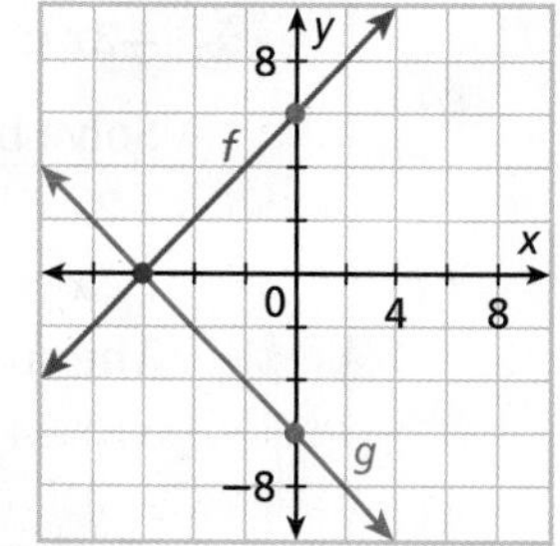

2-8 Solving Absolute-Value Equations and Inequalities

Objectives

Solve compound inequalities.

Write and solve absolute-value equations and inequalities.

Vocabulary

disjunction
conjunction
absolute value

Who uses this?

Absolute value can be used to represent the acceptable ranges for the dimensions of baseball bats classified by length or weight. (See Exercise 43.)

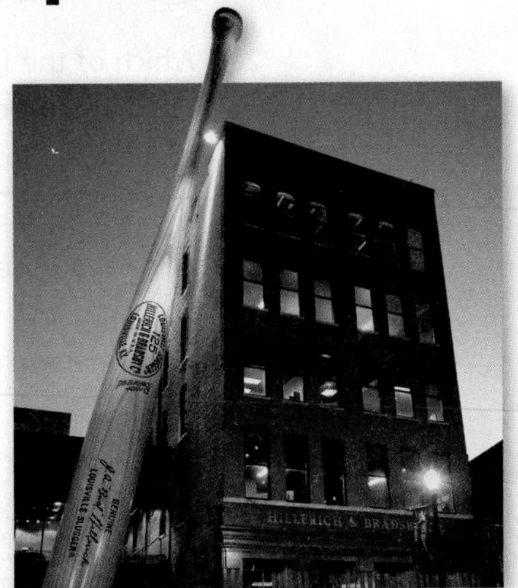

A compound statement is made up of more than one equation or inequality.

A **disjunction** is a compound statement that uses the word *or.*

−8 −6 −4 −2 0 2 4 6 8

Disjunction: $x \leq -3$ OR $x > 2$ Set builder notation: $\{x|x \leq -3 \cup x > 2\}$

A disjunction is true if and only if at least one of its parts is true.

A **conjunction** is a compound statement that uses the word *and.*

−8 −6 −4 −2 0 2 4 6 8

Conjunction: $x \geq -3$ AND $x < 2$ Set builder notation: $\{x|x \geq -3 \cap x < 2\}$
A conjunction is true if and only if all of its parts are true. Conjunctions can be written as a single statement as shown.

$$x \geq -3 \text{ and } x < 2 \rightarrow -3 \leq x < 2$$

Reading Math

Dis- means "apart." Disjunctions have two separate pieces. *Con-* means "together." Conjunctions represent one piece.

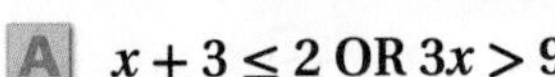

EXAMPLE 1 **Solving Compound Inequalities**

Solve each compound inequality. Then graph the solution set.

A $x + 3 \leq 2$ OR $3x > 9$

Solve both inequalities for x.

$x + 3 \leq 2$	*or*	$3x > 9$
$x \leq -1$		$x > 3$

The solution set is all points that satisfy $\{x|x \leq -1 \text{ or } x > 3\}$.

−8 −6 −4 −2 0 2 4 6 8 $(-\infty, -1] \cup (3, \infty)$

B $-2x < 8$ AND $x - 3 \leq 2$

Solve both inequalities for x.

$-2x < 8$	*and*	$x - 3 \leq 2$
$x > -4$		$x \leq 5$

The solution set is the set of points that satisfy both $x > -4$ and $x \leq 5$, $\{x|-4 < x \leq 5\}$

−8 −6 −4 −2 0 2 4 6 8 $(-4, 5]$

Solve each compound inequality. Then graph the solution set.

 **$x + 3 > 7$ OR $3x \geq 18$**

Solve both inequalities for x.

$x + 3 > 7$ *or* $3x \geq 18$

$x > 4$ $\quad$ $x \geq 6$

Because every point that satisfies $x \geq 6$ also satisfies $x > 4$, the solution set is $\{x \mid x > 4\}$.

$(4, \infty)$

Solve each compound inequality. Then graph the solution set.

1a. $x - 2 < 1$ or $5x \geq 30$

1b. $2x \geq -6$ and $-x > -4$

1c. $x - 5 < 12$ or $6x \leq 12$

1d. $-3x < -12$ and $x + 4 \leq 12$

Recall that the **absolute value** of a number x, written $|x|$, is the distance from x to zero on the number line. Because absolute value represents distance without regard to direction, the absolute value of any real number is nonnegative.

Know it! Note

Absolute Value

WORDS	NUMBERS	ALGEBRA
The absolute value of a real number x, $\|x\|$, is equal to its distance from zero on a number line.	$\|5\| = 5$ $\|-5\| = 5$	$\|x\| = \begin{cases} x \text{ if } x \geq 0 \\ -x \text{ if } x < 0 \end{cases}$

Absolute-value equations and inequalities can be represented by compound statements. Consider the equation $|x| = 3$.

Helpful Hint

Think: Greator inequalities involving $>$ or $\geq$ symbols are disjunctions.
Think: Less thand inequalities involving $<$ or $\leq$ symbols are conjunctions.

The solutions of $|x| = 3$ are the two points that are 3 units from zero. The solution is a disjunction: $x = -3$ or $x = 3$.

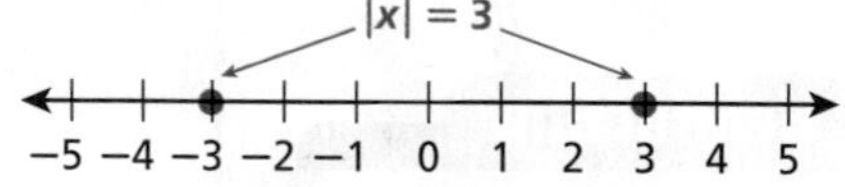

The solutions of $|x| < 3$ are the points that are less than 3 units from zero. The solution is a conjunction: $-3 < x < 3$.

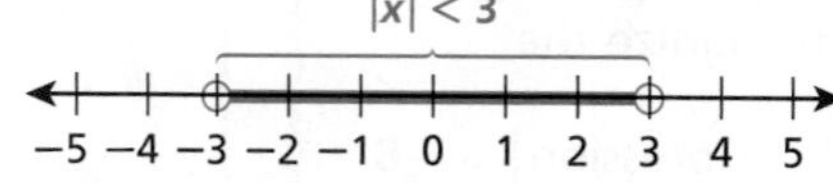

The solutions of $|x| > 3$ are the points that are more than 3 units from zero. The solution is a disjunction: $x < -3$ or $x > 3$.

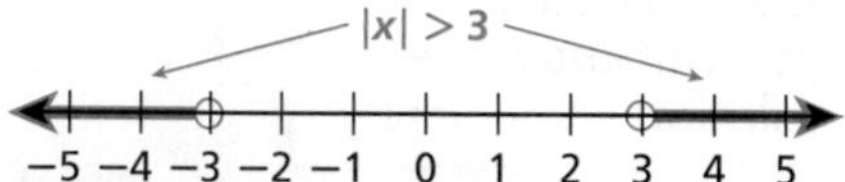

Absolute-Value Equations and Inequalities

For all real numbers x and all positive real numbers a:

$\|x\| = a$	$\|x\| < a$	$\|x\| > a$
$x = -a$ OR $x = a$	$x > -a$ AND $x < a$ $-a < x < a$	$x < -a$ OR $x > a$

Note: The symbol $\leq$ can replace $<$, and the rules still apply. The symbol $\geq$ can replace $>$, and the rules still apply.

EXAMPLE 2 Solving Absolute-Value Equations

Solve each equation.

A $|x-7|=5$ — *This can be read as "the distance from x to 7 is 5."*

$x-7=5$ or $x-7=-5$ — *Rewrite the absolute value as a disjunction.*

$x=12$ or $x=2$ — *Add 7 to both sides of each equation.*

B $|3x|+5=14$

$|3x|=9$ — *Isolate the absolute-value expression.*

$3x=9$ or $3x=-9$ — *Rewrite the absolute value as a disjunction.*

$x=3$ or $x=-3$ — *Divide both sides of each equation by 3.*

Solve each equation.

2a. $|x+9|=13$ **2b.** $|6x|-8=22$

You can solve absolute-value inequalities using the same methods that are used to solve an absolute-value equation.

Solving an Absolute-value Inequality
1. Isolate the absolute-value expression, if necessary.
2. Rewrite the absolute-value expression as a compound inequality.
3. Solve each part of the compound inequality for x.

EXAMPLE 3 Solving Absolute-Value Inequalities with Disjunctions

Solve each inequality. Then graph the solution set.

A $|2x+1|>5$

$2x+1>5$ or $2x+1<-5$ — *Rewrite the absolute value as a disjunction.*

$2x>4$ or $2x<-6$ — *Subtract 1 from both sides of each inequality.*

$x>2$ or $x<-3$ — *Divide both sides of each inequality by 2.*

$\{x \mid x>2 \cup x<-3\}$

−8 −6 −4 −2 0 2 4 6 8 $(-\infty, -3) \cup (2, \infty)$

To check, you can test a point in each of the three regions.

$|2(-4)+1|>5$ $|-7|>5$ ✔ $|2(0)+1|>5$ $|1|>5$ ✘ $|2(5)+1|>5$ $|11|>5$ ✔

> **Helpful Hint**
>
> In Example 3B, if you recognize that
>
> $|\text{expression}| > -8$
>
> is always true, you will know the solution immediately.

B $|4x|+16>8$

$|4x|>-8$ — *Isolate the absolute-value expression.*

$4x>-8$ or $4x<8$ — *Rewrite the absolute value as a disjunction.*

$x>-2$ or $x<2$ — *Divide both sides of each inequality by 4.*

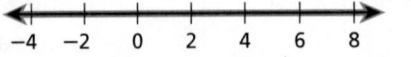

−4 −2 0 2 4 6 8 $(-\infty, \infty)$

The solution set is *all real numbers*, $\mathbb{R}$.

Solve each inequality. Then graph the solution set.

3a. $|4x-8|>12$ **3b.** $|3x|+36>12$

EXAMPLE 4 Solving Absolute-Value Inequalities with Conjunctions

Solve each inequality. Then graph the solution set.

A $\dfrac{|3x-9|}{2} \le 12$

$|3x-9| \le 24$ — *Multiply both sides by 2.*

$3x - 9 \le 24$ and $3x - 9 \ge -24$ — *Rewrite the absolute value as a conjunction.*

$3x \le 33$ and $3x \ge -15$ — *Add 9 to both sides of each inequality.*

$x \le 11$ and $x \ge -5$ — *Divide both sides of each inequality by 3.*

The solution set is $\{x \mid -5 \le x \le 11\}$.

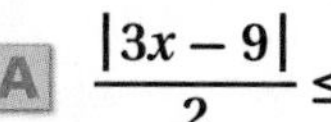

Helpful Hint

In Example 4B, if you recognize that

$|\text{expression}| \le -2$

is never true, you will know the solution immediately.

B $-4|x+3| \ge 8$

$|x+3| \le -2$ — *Divide both sides by −4, and reverse the inequality symbol.*

$x + 3 \le -2$ and $x + 3 \ge 2$ — *Rewrite the absolute value as a conjunction.*

$x \le -5$ and $x \ge -1$ — *Subtract 3 from both sides of each inequality.*

Because no real number satisfies both $x \le -5$ and $x \ge -1$, there is *no solution.* The solution set is ∅.

Solve each inequality. Then graph the solution set.

4a. $\dfrac{|x-5|}{2} \le 4$ **4b.** $-2|x+5| > 10$

THINK AND DISCUSS

1. Explain why the solution set to $|7x| > -1$ is all real numbers.
2. Explain why there is no solution to $|x+3| \le -2$. Give another example of an absolute-value equation that has no solution.
3. Write an absolute-value inequality to model "the distance between x and 5 is greater than 10."

4. **GET ORGANIZED** Copy and complete the graphic organizer. Use the flowchart to explain the decisions and steps needed to solve an absolute-value equation or inequality.

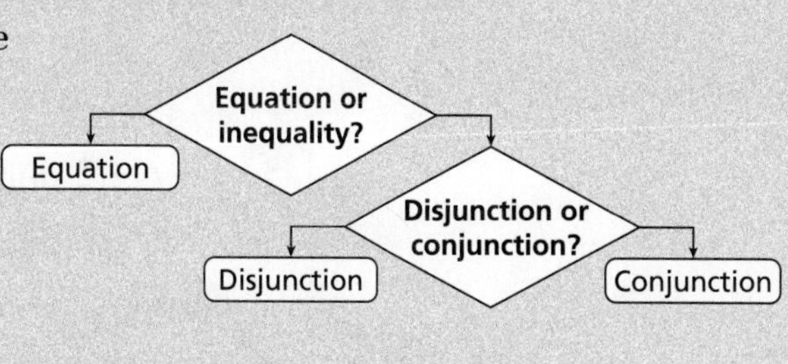

2-8 Exercises

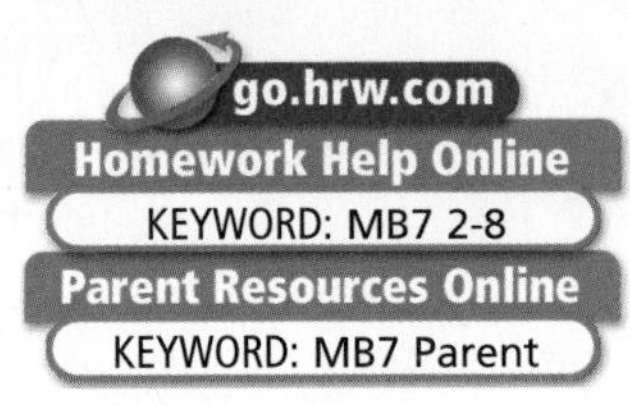

GUIDED PRACTICE

1. **Vocabulary** A graph of an inequality on a number line with two parts is a ___?___. (*conjunction, disjunction*)

SEE EXAMPLE 1 p. 150

Solve each compound inequality. Then graph the solution set.

2. $x - 7 > -3$ OR $5x \leq -15$
3. $3x \leq 18$ AND $x + 4 > 2$
4. $x - 2 > -5$ OR $5x \geq 25$

SEE EXAMPLE 2 p. 152

Solve each equation.

5. $|x + 5| = 2$
6. $|2x| - 6 = 4$
7. $|-x| + 4 = 7$

SEE EXAMPLE 3 p. 152

Solve each inequality. Then graph the solution set.

8. $|2x - 3| \geq 5$
9. $2|x - 3| > 8$
10. $|3x| + 8 > 5$

SEE EXAMPLE 4 p. 153

11. $\dfrac{|4x + 8|}{3} < 8$
12. $|9 - 3x| \leq 6$
13. $-5|x - 3| \geq 15$

PRACTICE AND PROBLEM SOLVING

Independent Practice

For Exercises	See Example
14–15	1
16–19	2
20–23	3
24–27	4

Extra Practice
Skills Practice p. S7
Application Practice p. S33

Solve each compound inequality. Then graph the solution set.

14. $2x - 3 \geq 7$ OR $x + 5 < 2$
15. $3x + 6 \leq 21$ AND $4x - 2 \geq -6$

Solve each equation.

16. $|-3x| = 9$
17. $|x + 7| = 2$
18. $|3x - 9| = 6$
19. $5|2x| - 6 = 24$

Solve each inequality. Then graph the solution set.

20. $|-2x| < 2$
21. $|x + 5| \geq 2$
22. $|8x| + 56 \geq 40$
23. $|7x + 14| \geq 35$
24. $|-0.5x| > 1$
25. $6|2x + 5| > 66$
26. $-8|x + 4| > 48$
27. $\dfrac{|8x + 4|}{6} < 10$

Write a compound inequality for each graph.

28. −8 −6 −4 −2 0 2 4 6 8
29. −8 −6 −4 −2 0 2 4 6 8
30. −8 −6 −4 −2 0 2 4 6 8
31. −8 −6 −4 −2 0 2 4 6 8

Solve and graph.

32. $5x - 9 > 11$ AND $7x + 12 \leq 61$
33. $7x + 4 \leq 3x - 12$ OR $\dfrac{9x - 15}{5} > 6$
34. $4(3 - 2x) < -20$ AND $\dfrac{3}{2}x - 4 < 5$
35. $5x + 12 > 2x - 3$ OR $3 - 5x < -17$

36. **///ERROR ANALYSIS///** Find and explain the error in one solution below.

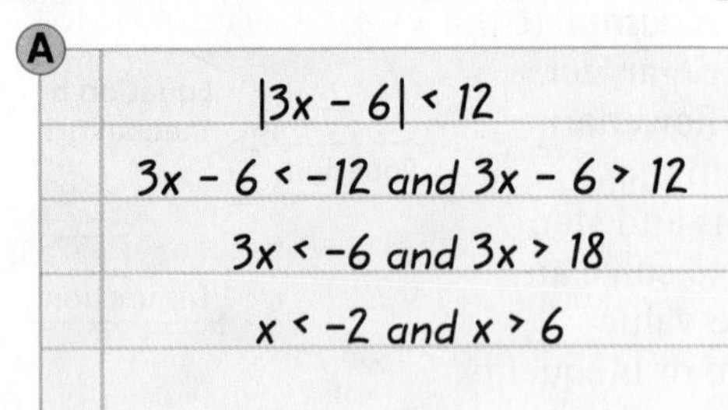

A
|3x - 6| < 12
3x - 6 < -12 and 3x - 6 > 12
3x < -6 and 3x > 18
x < -2 and x > 6

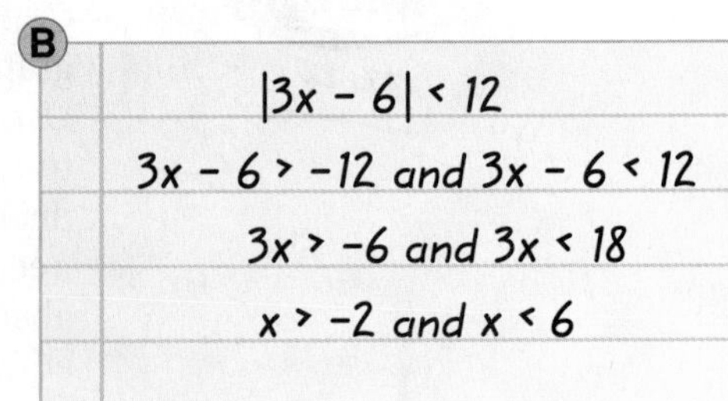

B
|3x - 6| < 12
3x - 6 > -12 and 3x - 6 < 12
3x > -6 and 3x < 18
x > -2 and x < 6

Solve and graph.

37. $|5x - 8| = 27$ **38.** $8|3x - 10| - 12 = 20$ **39.** $|4(2x - 5)| \geq 4$

40. $\left|\frac{2x + 1}{5}\right| < 3$ **41.** $\frac{|4x + 5|}{3} + 9 > 15$ **42.** $|5 - 6x| - 10 \leq 8$

43. Estimation The table shows a sample of baseball bats considered to be within and outside the 32.5-inch-length class by the National Collegiate Athletics Association (NCAA). Write a possible absolute-value inequality to represent the bat lengths considered within the 32.5 inch class of bats.

Bat Lengths (in.)	
32.5-Inch Class	Outside 32.5-Inch Class
32.60	32.18
32.48	32.90
32.36	32.77
32.74	32.24

44. Psychology The IQ scores for the middle 50% of the population can be written as $\left|\frac{x - 100}{15}\right| \leq \frac{2}{3}$, where x is a person's IQ. Write and solve a compound inequality to find an interval for the IQ scores for the middle 50% of the population.

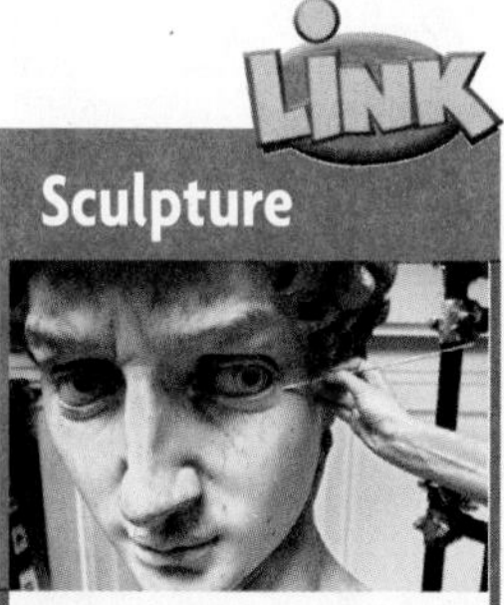

Michelangelo's *David* was sculpted from a single block of Carrara marble. It is nearly 18 feet tall and weighs well over 9 tons.

45. Geology Twenty cubic feet of marble can weigh 3400 pounds, plus or minus 100 pounds. Write and solve an absolute-value inequality for the possible weights of a cubic foot of marble.

46. Business A grocery scale is accurate to within 1 ounce. Write the error in the price when weighing an item that costs \$9 per pound as an absolute value expression.

47. Critical Thinking Is $c|a + b| = |ca + cb|$ always, sometimes, or never true? Justify your answer.

48. Manufacturing The acceptable tolerance of a machine part is 1 foot $\pm \frac{3}{64}$ in. Write the tolerance as an absolute-value equation in feet.

The solutions of an absolute-value equation are given. What is the equation?

49. $x = 2 \pm 3$ **50.** $x = -\frac{5}{2} \pm \frac{9}{2}$ **51.** $x = b \pm 2a$

52. Astronomy During 2007, Earth will travel around the Sun along a path that is not a perfect circle. Earth will be closest to the Sun on January 20, at a distance of 91.4 million miles, and farthest on July 7, at a distance of 94.5 million miles. Write and solve an absolute-value inequality for the distance between Earth and the Sun throughout the year.

53. Write About It When is $|x| = |-x|$? When is $|x| = -|x|$? Explain.

MULTI-STEP TEST PREP

54. This problem will help prepare you for the Multi-Step Test Prep on page 164.

For a livestock competition, the weight classes for goats are shown in this table.

Goat Weight Classes	
Class	Weight Range (lb)
Light	40–50
Medium	50–60
Heavy	60–73

a. What is the center of each weight class?

b. How would you express each weight class as an absolute-value expression?

c. Is there exactly one class for any goat in the weight range shown in the table? Explain.

d. What if...? Suppose just the upper range of the heavy class were increased by 1 lb. How would the absolute-value expression change to reflect the increase?

55. Which statement is equivalent to $|x - y|$?

Ⓐ $|x + y|$ Ⓑ $|y - x|$ Ⓒ $x + y$ Ⓓ $y - x$

56. Which of the following is NOT a solution of $|x - 8| \leq 12$?

Ⓕ $x = 20$ Ⓖ $x = 3$ Ⓗ $x = -2$ Ⓙ $x = -10$

57. How many solutions does $-5|3x + 5| - 6 = 4$ have?

Ⓐ An infinite number Ⓑ 2 Ⓒ 1 Ⓓ 0

58. A thermometer measures 5 body temperatures accurately to within ±0.15°F. Which of the following is an expression for the actual temperature t of a person if this thermometer measures the person's temperature as 98.5°F?

Ⓕ $|t - 98.5| \leq 0.15$ Ⓗ $|t - 98.5| \geq 0.15$

Ⓖ $|t + 98.5| \leq 0.15$ Ⓙ $|t + 98.5| \geq 0.15$

CHALLENGE AND EXTEND

59. Solve $|3x - 8| = 5x$.

60. Solve $|5x + 2| + 3x \leq 8$.

61. If x is an integer, which statement is equivalent to $|x - 3| < 16$? Explain.

a. $|x - 3| \leq 16$ **b.** $|x - 3| \leq 15$ **c.** $|x - 3| \leq 17$ **d.** $|x - 2| \leq 16$

62. Are the solution sets of $|x + a| = b$ and $|x| + a = b$ the same? Explain.

63. Consider the equation $(a + b) + c = a + (b + c)$.

a. What property of real numbers does this demonstrate?

b. Is $|a + b| + c = a + |b + c|$ a true statement? Support your answer.

c. What can you conclude about this property with respect to absolute value?

64. **Technology** A binary search repeatedly divides records of a sorted file in half until the correct record is found. For example, to find data in record 6 of an 8-record file, the binary search will examine records 1–8, then it would narrow the search to records 5–8, then 5–6, then locate the data in record 6. Write absolute-value statements for the records searched in the first three search intervals.

SPIRAL REVIEW

65. **Travel** Pamela filled her 15 gal gas tank before a trip. She added 13 gal after driving 385 mi and 14 gal after another 412 mi. Estimate the number of mi/gal her car got on this trip. *(Previous course)*

Determine the value of n. Identify the property demonstrated. *(Lesson 1-2)*

66. $7 \cdot n = 1$

67. $24 + 16 = (n + 4)4$

68. $(2 + 3) + n = 0$

Geometry Find the measure of each angle in the quadrilaterals below. (Hint: The sum of the angle measures in a quadrilateral is 360°.) *(Lesson 2-1)*

69.

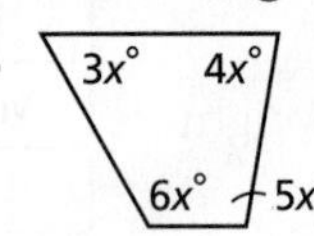

70.

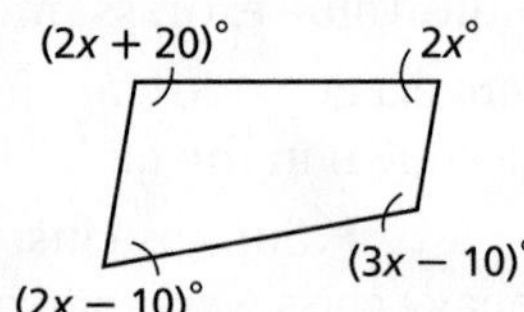

71.

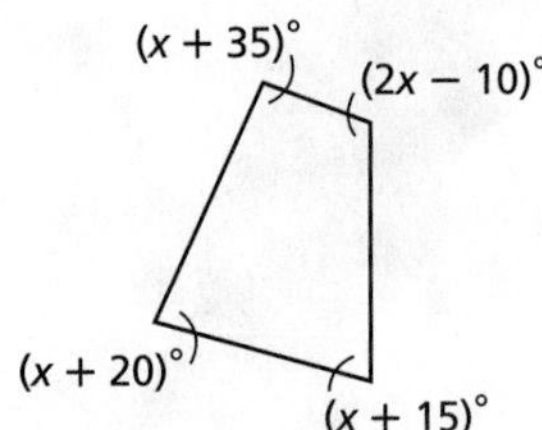

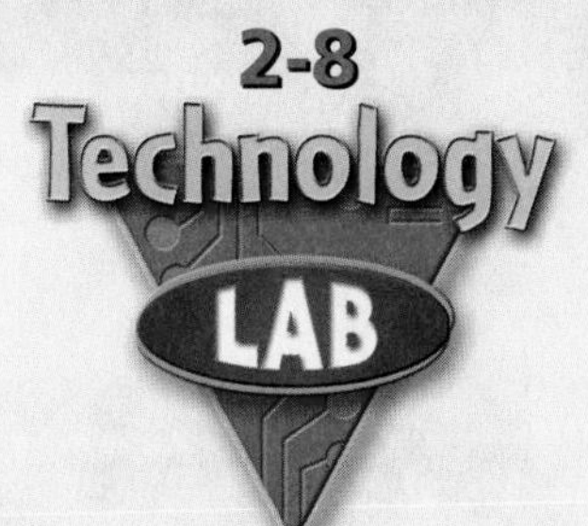

Solve Absolute-Value Equations and Inequalities

A graphing calculator is helpful for visualizing solutions of absolute-value equations and inequalities.

Activity

1 Use a graph to solve $2|x-3|=4$. Check your answer.

Enter the left side of the equation as **Y1** and the right side as **Y2**. To enter the absolute value expression, press MATH, select the **NUM** menu, and choose **1:abs(**.

Graph in a friendly window. The x-values of the points where **Y1** = **Y2** are the solutions of the equation. To find each intersection of **Y1** and **Y2**, press CALC TRACE and select **5:intersect.**

Move the cursor to **Y1**; press ENTER. Repeat for **Y2**. Then move the cursor close to an intersection. Press ENTER to display the coordinates.

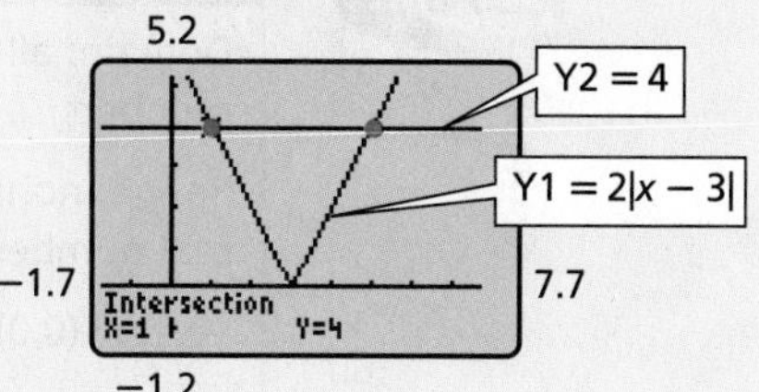

The graphs intersect at (1, 4) and (5, 4), so the solution set of $2|x-3|=4$ is $\{1, 5\}$.

Check

$2\|x-3\|=4$	
$2\|1-3\|$	4
4	4 ✓

$2\|x-3\|=4$	
$2\|5-3\|$	4
4	4 ✓

2 Use a graph to solve $|3x-15|\le 6$.

Enter the left side as **Y1** and the right side as **Y2**.

Graph in a friendly window. The x-values of the points where **Y1** ≤ **Y2** are the solutions of the inequality. Use the intersect feature to find the intersection points.

The graphs intersect at (3, 6) and (7, 6), and **Y1** ≤ **Y2** for $3 \le x \le 7$. The solution set of $|3x-15| \le 6$ is $\{x|3 \le x \le 7\}$ or $[3, 7]$.

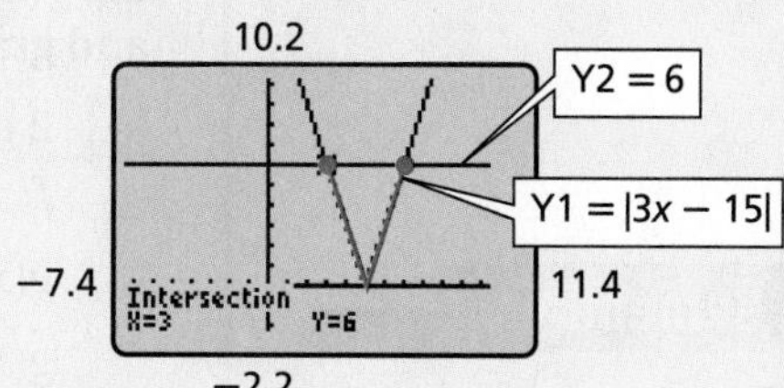

Try This

Use a graph to solve each equation or inequality. Check your answer.

1. $3|x-1|=6$
2. $5|x+3|=0$
3. $|-x|-5=2$
4. $|2x|-10\le 4$
5. $|x|-5\ge -2$
6. $|x+3|<3$
7. Use a graphing calculator to graph the left side of the equation $2|x+1|=-4$ as **Y1** and the right side of the equation as **Y2**.
   a. How many times does **Y1** intersect **Y2**?
   b. **Make a Conjecture** What does your answer to part **a** tell you about the solution set of the equation $2|x+1|=-4$?

2-9 Absolute-Value Functions

Objective
Graph and transform absolute-value functions.

Vocabulary
absolute-value function

Who uses this?
Park rangers can use absolute value to monitor the movement of an animal as it passes a specific location. (See Exercise 30.)

An **absolute-value function** is a function whose rule contains an absolute-value expression. The graph of the parent absolute-value function $f(x) = |x|$ has a V shape with a minimum point or vertex at $(0, 0)$.

The Absolute-Value Parent Function $f(x) = |x|$

Domain: all real numbers

Range: nonnegative real numbers

Vertex: (0,0)

x	$y = \|x\|$
−10	10
−5	5
0	0
5	5
10	10

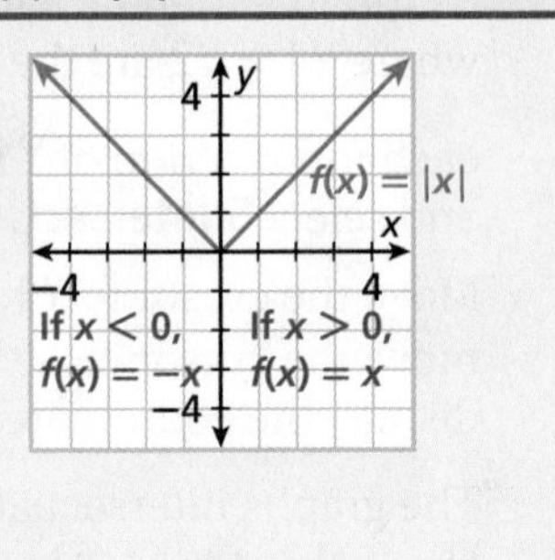

The absolute-value parent function is composed of two linear pieces, one with a slope of −1 and one with a slope of 1. In Lesson 2-6, you transformed linear functions. You can also transform absolute-value functions.

EXAMPLE 1 Translating Absolute-Value Functions

Let $g(x)$ be the indicated transformation of $f(x) = |x|$. Write the rule for $g(x)$ and graph the function.

A 2 units up

$f(x) = x$

$g(x) = f(x) + k$

$g(x) = x + 2$ *Substitute.*

The graph of $g(x) = |x| + 2$ is the graph of $f(x) = |x|$ after a vertical shift of 2 units up. The vertex of $g(x)$ is $(0, 2)$.

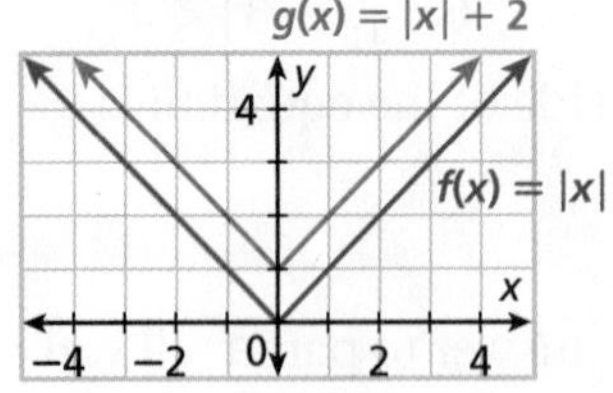

B 3 units left

$f(x) = |x|$

$g(x) = f(x - h)$

$g(x) = |x - (-3)| = |x + 3|$ *Substitute.*

The graph of $g(x) = |x + 3|$ is the graph of $f(x) = |x|$ after a horizontal shift of 3 units left. The vertex of $g(x)$ is $(-3, 0)$.

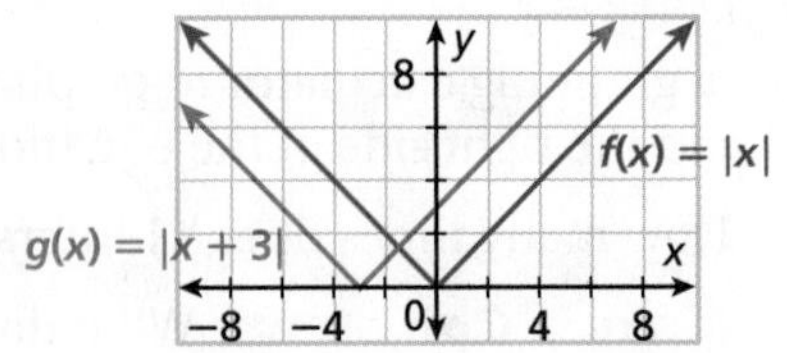

Remember!
The general forms for translations are
Vertical:
$g(x) = f(x) + k$

Horizontal:
$g(x) = f(x - h)$

Let $g(x)$ be the indicated transformation of $f(x) = |x|$. Write the rule for $g(x)$ and graph the function.

1a. 4 units down **1b.** 2 units right

Because the entire graph moves when shifted, the shift from $f(x) = |x|$ determines the vertex of an absolute-value graph.

Vertex of an Absolute-Value Function

The graph of $g(x) = |x - h| + k$ is the image of $f(x) = |x|$ after a horizontal shift of h units and a vertical shift of k units so that the vertex is at (h, k).

EXAMPLE 2 Translations of an Absolute-Value Function

Translate $f(x) = |x|$ so that the vertex is at $(-5, 3)$. Then graph.

$g(x) = |x - h| + k$

$g(x) = |x - (-5)| + 3$ *Substitute.*

$g(x) = |x + 5| + 3$

The graph of $g(x) = |x + 5| + 3$ is the graph of $f(x) = |x|$ after a vertical shift up 3 units and a horizontal shift left 5 units.

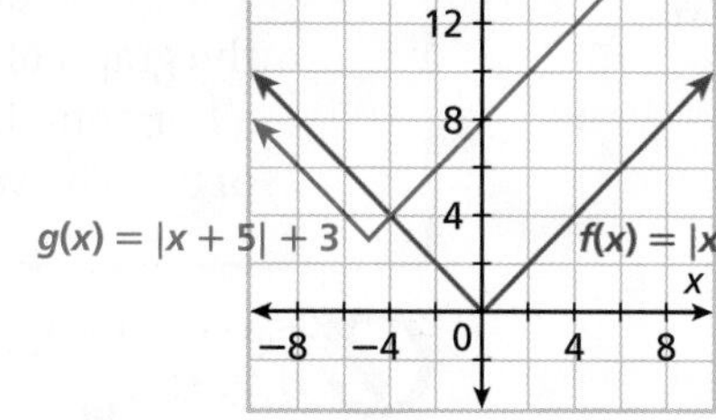

The graph confirms that the vertex is $(-5, 3)$

2. Translate $f(x) = |x|$ so that the vertex is at $(4, -2)$. Then graph.

Absolute-value functions can also be stretched, compressed, and reflected.

EXAMPLE 3 Transforming Absolute-Value Functions

Remember!

Reflection across x-axis:
$g(x) = -f(x)$

Reflection across y-axis:
$g(x) = f(-x)$

Perform each transformation. Then graph.

A **Reflect the graph of $f(x) = |x + 2| + 1$ across the x-axis.**

$g(x) = -f(x)$ *Take the opposite of the entire function.*

$g(x) = -(|x + 2| + 1)$ *Distribute the negative sign.*

The vertex of the graph of $g(x) = -|x + 2| - 1$ is $(-2, -1)$. The graph is reflected across the x-axis.

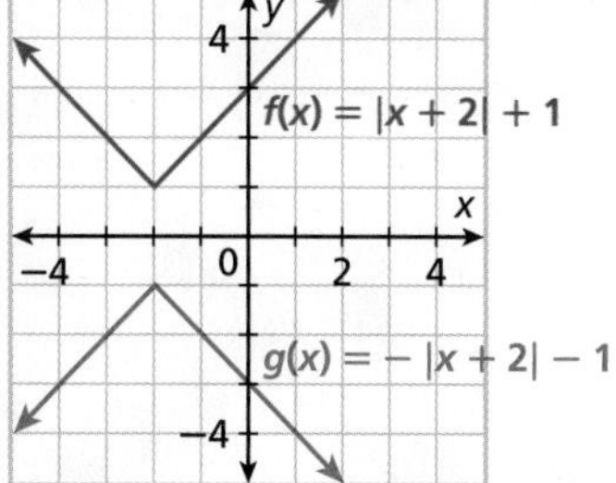

Perform each transformation. Then graph.

B **Stretch the graph of $f(x) = |x| - 2$ vertically by a factor of 3.**

$g(x) = af(x)$

$g(x) = 3(|x| - 2)$ *Multiply the entire function by 3.*

$g(x) = 3|x| - 6$

The graph of $g(x) = 3|x| - 6$ is the graph of $f(x) = |x| - 2$ after a vertical stretch by a factor of 3. The vertex of g is at $(0, -6)$.

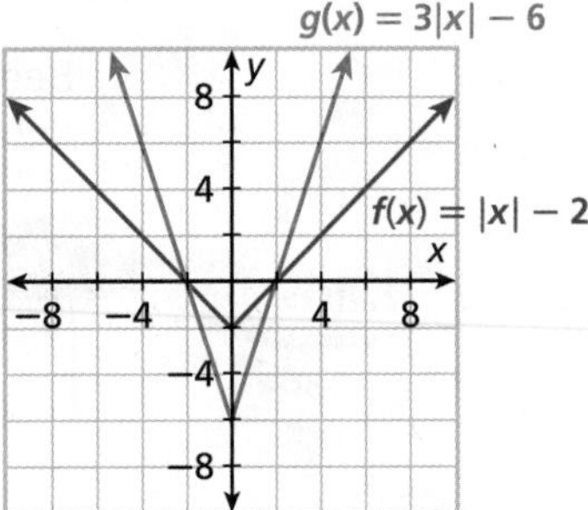

Remember!

Vertical stretch and compression:
$g(x) = af(x)$

Horizontal stretch and compression:
$g(x) = f\left(\frac{1}{b}x\right)$

C **Compress the graph of $f(x) = |x - 1| - 3$ horizontally by a factor of 0.5.**

$g(x) = f\left(\frac{1}{b}x\right)$

$g(x) = \left|\frac{1}{0.5}x - 1\right| - 3$ *Substitute 0.5 for b.*

$g(x) = |2x - 1| - 3$ *Simplify.*

The graph of $g(x) = |2x - 1| - 3$ is the graph of $f(x) = |x - 1| - 3$ after a horizontal compression by a factor of 0.5. The vertex of g is $\left(\frac{1}{2}, -3\right)$.

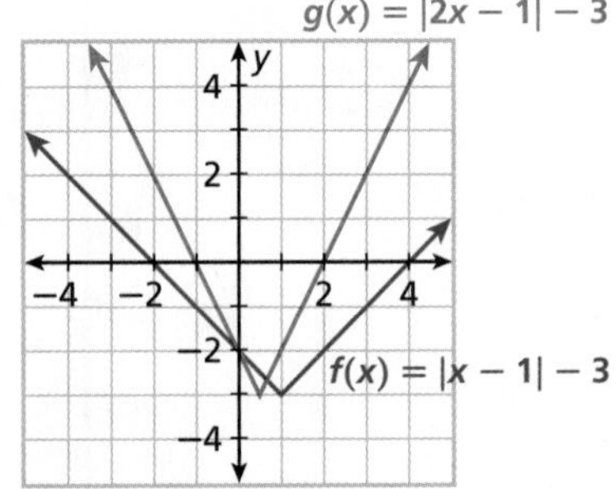

Perform each transformation. Then graph.

3a. Reflect the graph of $f(x) = -|x - 4| + 3$ across the y-axis.

3b. Compress the graph of $f(x) = |x| + 1$ vertically by a factor of $\frac{1}{2}$.

3c. Stretch the graph of $f(x) = |4x| - 3$ horizontally by a factor of 2.

THINK AND DISCUSS

1. Explain why the vertex of $f(x) = |x|$ stays the same when the graph is stretched but not when the graph is shifted.

2. Tell what the graph of $y = |-x|$ looks like.

3. GET ORGANIZED Copy and complete the graphic organizer. Fill in the table with examples of absolute-value transformations.

Transformation	Absolute-Value Function	Transformed Function	Graph
Vertical translation			
Horizontal translation			
(h, k) translation			
Stretch			
Compression			
Reflection			

2-9 Exercises

go.hrw.com
Homework Help Online
KEYWORD: MB7 2-9
Parent Resources Online
KEYWORD: MB7 Parent

GUIDED PRACTICE

1. **Vocabulary** Explain the reason for the shape of the graph of an *absolute-value function.*

SEE EXAMPLE 1 p. 158

Let $g(x)$ be the indicated transformation of $f(x) = |x|$. Write the rule for $g(x)$ and graph the function.

2. 5 units down
3. 4 units left

SEE EXAMPLE 2 p. 159

Translate $f(x) = |x|$ so that the vertex is at the given point. Then graph.

4. $(-4, -5)$
5. $(1, 6)$

SEE EXAMPLE 3 p. 159

Perform each transformation. Then graph.

6. Reflect the graph of $f(x) = |2x + 3| - 4$ across the y-axis.
7. Stretch $f(x) = |x + 3|$ vertically by a factor of 2.
8. Compress $f(x) = |x + 3|$ horizontally by a factor of $\frac{2}{3}$.

PRACTICE AND PROBLEM SOLVING

Independent Practice

For Exercises	See Example
9–11	1
12–14	2
15–17	3

Extra Practice

Skills Practice p. S7
Application Practice p. S33

Let $g(x)$ be the indicated transformation of $f(x) = |x|$. Write the rule for $g(x)$ and graph the function.

9. 2 units right
10. 1 unit down
11. 4 units left

Translate $f(x) = |x|$ so that the vertex is at the given point. Then graph.

12. $(8, 0.5)$
13. $(1.5, 4.5)$
14. $(-2.5, 3)$

Perform each transformation. Then graph.

15. Reflect $f(x) = |x - 5| + 2$ across the x-axis.
16. Compress $f(x) = |2x| - 3$ vertically by a factor of $\frac{1}{4}$.
17. Stretch $f(x) = |2x| - 3$ horizontally by a factor of $\frac{3}{2}$.
18. **Football** Yard lines of a football field have the relationship shown in the table below (0 yard lines are the goal lines).

Football Field Yard Lines

Distance from One End Zone (yd)	0	10	20	30	40	50	60	70	80	90	100
Marked Yard Line	0	10	20	30	40	50	40	30	20	10	0

a. Write an absolute-value function to find the marked yard line for a given distance from the end zone. (*Hint:* Graph the ordered pairs to find the transformation from $f(x) = |x|$.)

b. What yard line is 195 feet from the end zone?

c. **What if...?** Suppose the absolute-value function is based on the distance from the end zone *in feet.* How would this relationship affect the function?

State the transformation from the graph of $f(x) = |x|$. Then graph the transformed function and state its domain and range.

19. $g(x) = |x| - 6$ **20.** $g(x) = |x - 6|$ **21.** $g(x) = 2|x - 1|$

Find the vertex of the graph of each function.

22. $g(x) = |x - 12| + 8$ **23.** $g(x) = |x + 5| + 9$ **24.** $g(x) = 6 + |x - 7|$

25. Write About It How do the slopes of the two parts of an absolute-value function compare? Justify your answer and give examples.

26. Critical Thinking Name two different transformations that move the vertex of $f(x) = |x|$ 4 units up.

Find an absolute-value function for each graph.

27.

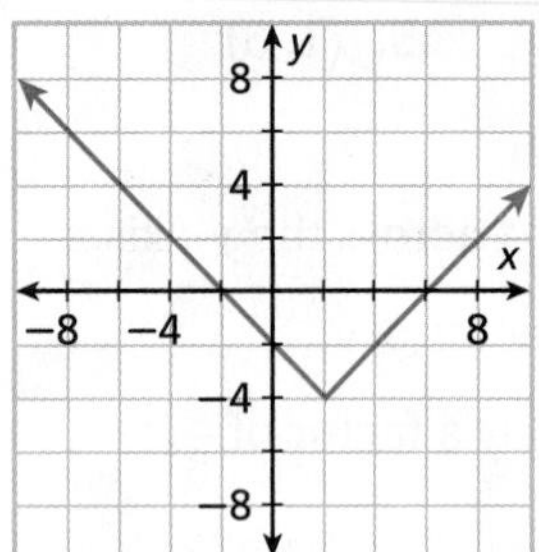

28.

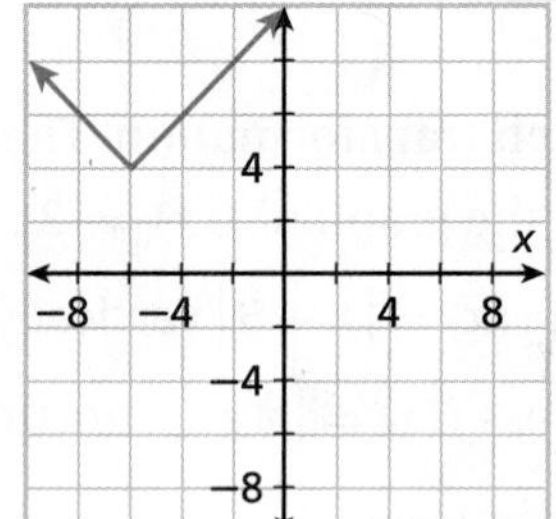

29.

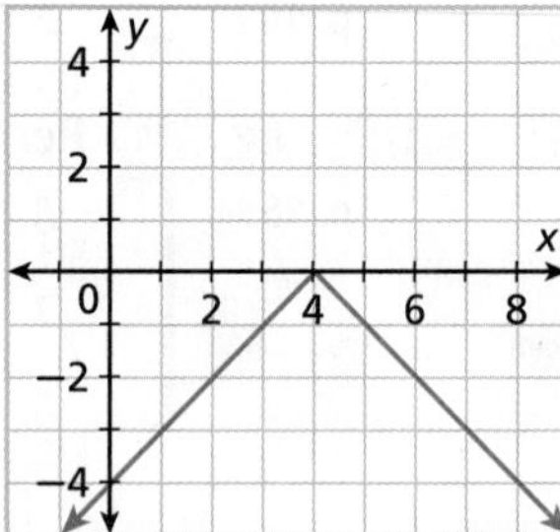

30. Zoology Park rangers track a panther by using a radio transmitter. The panther's distance from the ranger station can be modeled by the function $d = \left|760 - \frac{4}{3}t\right| + 10$, where d is distance in meters and t is the time in seconds since the rangers started timing.

a. How fast is the panther walking along the path?

b. Find the vertex of the function. How long will it take the panther to reach its closest point to the ranger station?

c. How long will the panther be within 200 meters of the ranger station?

d. How far from the ranger station will the panther be after 15 minutes?

31. Critical Thinking Compare vertical stretch to horizontal compression. How are they different? How are they the same?

MULTI-STEP TEST PREP

32. This problem will prepare you for the Multi-Step Test Prep on page 164.

In a livestock competition, hogs in the heavy weight class can be no more than 10 pounds above or below a weight of 240 pounds.

a. Write a function f that gives the absolute value of the difference between the weight w of a hog in pounds and 240 pounds.

b. Graph the function.

c. What is the reasonable domain of the function for hogs in the heavy weight class?

d. What is the reasonable range?

TEST PREP

33. Which function best describes the graph shown?

Ⓐ $y = |x - 2|$ Ⓒ $y = -|x| - 2$

Ⓑ $y = |-x| + 2$ Ⓓ $y = -|x + 2|$

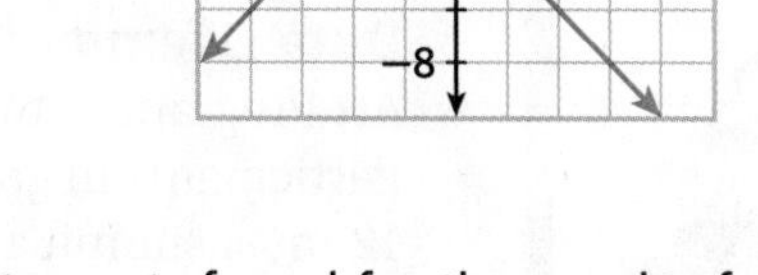

34. The graph of which function is the same as the graph of $f(x) = |x|$?

Ⓕ $g(x) = \left|\frac{1}{x}\right|$ Ⓗ $g(x) = |-x|$

Ⓖ $g(x) = -\left|\frac{1}{x}\right|$ Ⓙ $g(x) = -|x|$

35. At which of the following points are the x-intercepts found for the graph of $f(x) = |3x| - 9$?

Ⓐ $(9, 0)$ and $(-9, 0)$ Ⓒ $(0, 9)$ and $(0, -9)$

Ⓑ $(3, 0)$ and $(-3, 0)$ Ⓓ $(0, 3)$ and $(0, -3)$

36. For which function does y correspond to a nonnegative real number?

Ⓕ $y = |x| - 3$ Ⓖ $y = |x - 3|$ Ⓗ $y = -|3 - x|$ Ⓙ $y + 3 = |x + 3|$

37. If $g(x)$ is the reflection of $f(x) = |x + 1| - 2$ across the y-axis, at which of the following points does the graph of $g(x)$ cross the x-axis?

Ⓐ $(-3, 0)$ and $(-1, 0)$ Ⓒ $(-3, 0)$ and $(1, 0)$

Ⓑ $(3, 0)$ and $(-1, 0)$ Ⓓ $(3, 0)$ and $(1, 0)$

CHALLENGE AND EXTEND

38. Graph $y < |x + 2|$.

39. Graph $|y| \le 4$ on a coordinate plane.

40. **Geometry** Graph the triangle that is above the x-axis below the graph of $f(x) = -|2x| + 8$. Find the area.

41. Write an absolute-value equation for $f(x) = \begin{cases} 2x + 6 \text{ if } x \ge -3 \\ -2x - 6 \text{ if } x < -3 \end{cases}$. Then graph.

42. Graph $x = |y|$. Is the graph a function? Explain.

SPIRAL REVIEW

Perform the indicated operation. Write each answer in scientific notation. *(Lesson 1-5)*

43. $(1.5 \times 10^{-4})(5.0 \times 10^{13})$

44. $(9.8 \times 10^{7})(8.9 \times 10^{-7})$

45. $(8.1 \times 10^{3})^2$

46. $\dfrac{6.2 \times 10^7}{3.1 \times 10^{-4}}$

47. $\dfrac{1.9 \times 10^{-6}}{9.5 \times 10^{18}}$

48. $\dfrac{2 \times 10^{-3}}{5 \times 10^{-3}}$

Perform the given transformation on the point $(3, -5)$, and give the coordinates of the translated point. *(Lesson 1-8)*

49. 2 units left, 6 units up

50. 10 units down

51. 3 units right

52. reflected across the x-axis

53. 1 unit right, 5 units down

54. reflected across the y-axis

Solve. *(Lesson 2-1)*

55. $-2x + 3(1 - x) = -\dfrac{10x}{2}$

56. $0.75(-4x - 12) = -3(3 + x)$

CHAPTER 2

SECTION 2B

MULTI-STEP TEST PREP

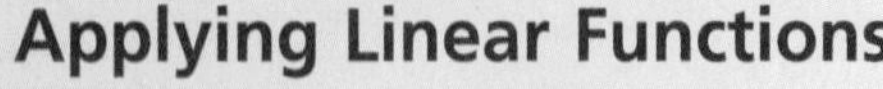

Applying Linear Functions

Data Dilemma The Livestock Show and Rodeo School Art Program is an annual competition for students. Participants in grades ranging from kindergarten through 12 must submit an original art project based on Western culture, history, or heritage. Projects are judged by the show's School Art Committee. Each school district selects the top 20 students to compete in this annual citywide competition. The scores for the top entries in the East District are shown in the table.

The Art Committee guidelines state that the top score awarded in district competitions should be 100. The East District judges have decided to add 5 points to each score in order to comply with the competition guidelines.

Competition Results	
Entry	**Score**
1	95
2	93
3	92
4	91
5	90
6	90
7	89
8	87
9	86
10	85
11	84
12	83
13	82
14	81
15	80
16	79
17	77
18	74
19	71
20	65

1. Create a table to show the new scores. Compare the mean and median of the original scores with those of the modified scores.
2. Graph the original scores using the entry number as the x-coordinate and the score as the y-coordinate. Describe the parent function to which this graph belongs.
3. Predict how the graph of the modified scores will compare with the graph of the original scores. Graph the modified scores on the same graph as the original scores to check your prediction.
4. If $y = f(x)$ represents the function rule for the original scores, determine a function rule for the modified scores. Explain.
5. One judge suggested that the original scores should be multiplied by a factor that would make the highest score 100 points. What factor should be used?
6. Make a table showing the new scores. Compare the mean and median of the original scores with those of these new scores.
7. Graph the newest set of scores on the same graph as the original scores, and describe the transformation.
8. Which method do you think the judges should use to adjust the scores? Explain your answer.

READY TO GO ON?

CHAPTER 2

SECTION 2B

Quiz for Lessons 2-6 Through 2-9

2-6 Transforming Linear Functions

Let $g(x)$ be the indicated transformation(s) of $f(x)$. Write the rule for $g(x)$.

1. $f(x) = x$; horizontal translation 5 units right
2. $f(x) = 2x$; vertical stretch by a factor of 5
3. $f(x) = x + 6$; vertical compression by a factor of $\frac{1}{3}$ followed by a horizontal translation left 4 units
4. $f(x) = 3x - 5$; vertical translation 6 units up followed by a horizontal stretch by a factor of $\frac{3}{2}$

2-7 Curve Fitting with Linear Models

5. Lea keeps track of the number of hours she works in a week and her income for the week. Here are the results from a randomly selected sample of weeks.

Hours	8	23	18	30	12	28
Income ($)	152	465	315	530	240	525

   a. Draw a scatter plot of the data using hours as the independent variable.
   b. Use your graphing calculator to find the correlation coefficient and the equation of the line of best fit for the data. What does the slope of the line of best fit mean for Lea?
   c. Use your equation to predict how much Lea would make in a 40-hour week.

2-8 Solving Absolute-Value Equations and Inequalities

Solve each equation.

6. $|9 - 2x| = 15$
7. $2|x| - 12 = 16$
8. $\frac{|3x - 4|}{-5} = 6$
9. $|2x - 5| = x + 3$

Solve each inequality. Then graph the solution.

10. $|5x + 15| > 20$
11. $\left|\frac{x - 2}{4}\right| \leq 5$
12. $-3|5x - 8| - 5 \geq 6$
13. $|12 - 4x| - 4 > 20$

2-9 Absolute-Value Functions

Translate $f(x) = |x|$ so that the vertex is at the given point. Then graph.

14. $(0, -4)$
15. $(2, 7)$
16. $(-2, 0)$
17. A food order at a restaurant is paid for with a $10 bill.
   a. What function represents the difference between the cost of the food and the change returned? Assume that this difference is nonnegative.
   b. Graph the function.

CHAPTER 2

Study Guide: Review

Vocabulary

Complete the sentences below with vocabulary words from the list above.

1. If there are no values that make an equation true, then the equation is a(n) ___?___ .

2. The equation $y - 5 = 2(x - 1)$ is in ___?___ .

3. ___?___ is the strength and direction of the linear relationship between two variables.

2-1 Solving Linear Equations and Inequalities *(pp. 90–96)*

EXAMPLES

Solve.

■ $5(x + 4) = 3x - 2$

$5x + 20 = 3x - 2$ *Use the Distributive Property.*

$2x + 20 = -2$ *Subtract 3x from both sides.*

$2x = -22$ *Subtract 20 from both sides.*

$x = -11$ *Divide both sides by 2.*

■ $\frac{15 - 3x}{2} < 12$

$15 - 3x < 24$ *Multiply both sides by 2.*

$-3x < 9$ *Subtract 15 from both sides.*

$x > -3$ *Divide both sides by –3x, and reverse the inequality.*

EXERCISES

Solve.

4. $35 = 7(2x - 8)$

5. $3x + 12 - 9x = 12 - 6x$

6. $4(3x + 5) = 12 - 2x$

7. $3x - 5(x + 3) = 16 - 4x$

8. $\frac{5}{2}\left(3x - \frac{3}{2}\right) - \frac{3}{4} = \frac{2}{3}x + 4$

9. Magnets cost \$10 plus \$1.25 each to produce. You sell them for \$1.75. How many magnets were sold if you made a profit of \$60?

10. $24 \geq 6x - 18$

11. $8x + 12 < 5x - 20$

12. $\frac{13 - 5x}{8} \geq -4$

Write an equation or inequality, and solve.

13. Ali's health club membership costs \$19.95 per month. Ali pays \$2.75 each time he works out. If Ali wants to spend less than \$50 per month at the health club, how often can he visit?

2-2 Proportional Reasoning *(pp. 97–103)*

EXAMPLE

Solve the proposition.

■ $\frac{x+2}{12} = \frac{15}{20}$

$20(x+2) = (12)(15)$ *Set cross products equal.*

$20x + 40 = 180$

$20x = 140$

$x = 7$

EXERCISES

Solve each proportion.

14. $\frac{12}{x} = \frac{4}{11}$

15. $\frac{-9}{4} = \frac{3x}{20}$

16. $\frac{x-3}{4} = -\frac{5}{3}$

17. $\frac{4}{5-2x} = \frac{3}{3x-1}$

18. If a flagpole that is 20 feet tall casts a 6 foot shadow, how long a shadow would a building that is 15 feet tall cast at the same time of day?

2-3 Graphing Linear Functions *(pp. 105–112)*

EXAMPLES

Find the intercepts. Then graph.

■ $2x - 3y = 12$

$2x = 12$ *Set y equal to 0 to find the x-intercept.*

$x = 6$

$-3y = 12$ *Set x equal to 0 to find the y-intercept.*

$y = -4$

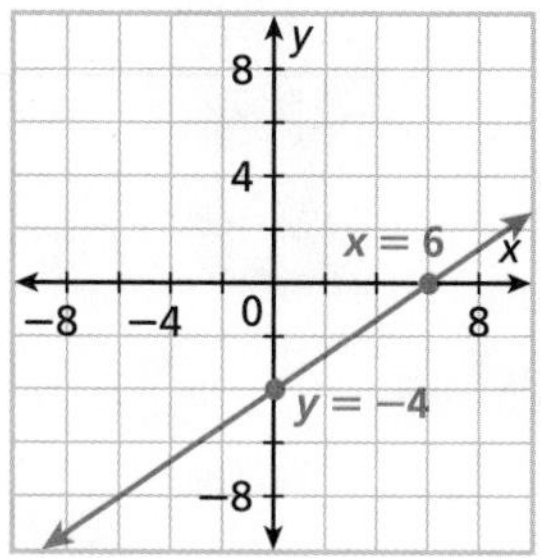

Write each function in slope-intercept form. Then graph.

■ $4x + 3y = 24$

$3y = -4x + 24$ *Isolate the y-term.*

$y = -\frac{4}{3}x + 8$ *Divide both sides by 3.*

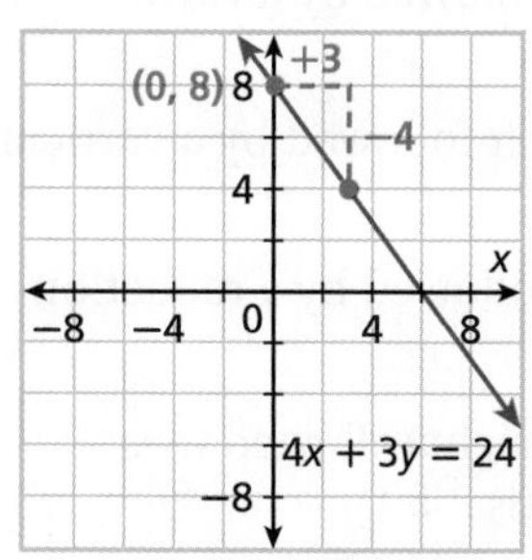

EXERCISES

Determine whether the data set could represent a linear function.

19.

x	1	4	7	10
f(x)	3	−2	−7	−12

Find the intercepts. Then graph.

20. $2x + 5y = 10$

21. $-6x + 9y = -18$

22. $8x = 12y - 18$

23. $y = 6 - 4x$

Write each function in slope-intercept form. Then graph.

24. $6x + 3y = 15$

25. $5x - 3y = -9$

26. $9x = 12 - 6y$

27. $\frac{8}{9}x + \frac{4}{3}y = 12$

Determine whether each line is vertical or horizontal. Then graph.

28. $-3 = x$

29. $y = \frac{5}{2}$

30. A rock climber is descending down a 500-ft-tall cliff. After 8 min, the rock climber has descended to a height of 280 ft. Find the height as a linear function of the time, and graph the function.

2-4 Writing Linear Functions *(pp. 115–123)*

EXAMPLE

- Write the equation of the line through $(3, 4)$ and $(5, 10)$ in slope-intercept form.

  Find the slope $m = \frac{10-4}{5-3} = 3$

  Write an equation:

Method 1	Method 2	
$y - y_1 = m(x - x_1)$	$y = mx + b$	
$y - 4 = 3(x - 3)$	$y = 3x + b$	
$y - 4 = 3x - 9$	$4 = 3(3) + b$	
$y = 3x - 9 + 4$	$-5 = b$	*−5 is the*
$y = 3x - 5$	$y = 3x - 5$	*y-intercept*

EXERCISES

Write the equation of each line in slope-intercept form.

31. passing through $(4, 6)$ with slope $\frac{1}{2}$

32. passing through $(2, 6)$ and $(3, 9)$

33. through $(4, -2)$ and parallel to $y = \frac{3}{2}x + 9$

34. through $(-3, 4)$ and perpendicular to $y = \frac{3}{2}x + 9$

2-5 Linear Inequalities in Two Variables *(pp. 124–131)*

EXAMPLE

Solve for *y*. Graph the solution.

- $3x - 5y \le 10$

  $-5y \le -3x + 10$

  $y \ge \frac{3}{5}x - 2$

  Use a solid boundary line and shade the region above the boundary.

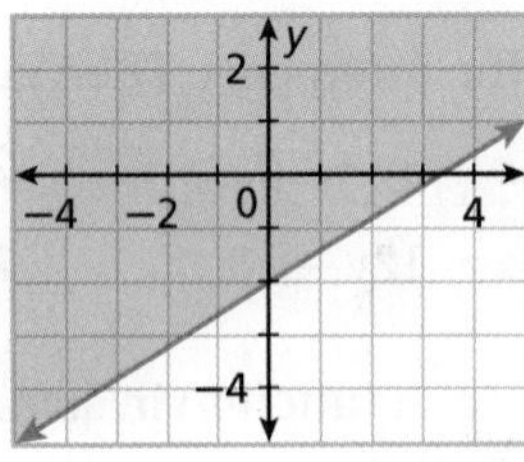

EXERCISES

Solve for *y*. Graph the solution.

35. $y > -3$

36. $y \le x + 3$

37. $2x + 4y > -12$

38. $6x - 2y > 8$

39. Write an inequality for the graph.

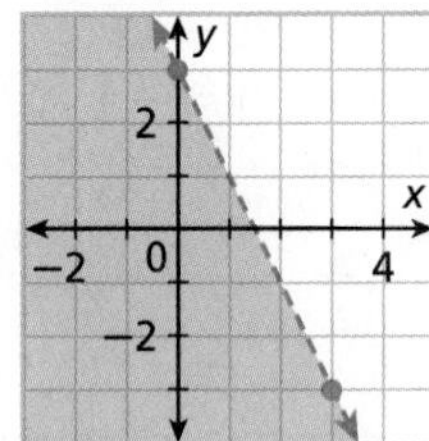

40. A gallery offers a limited-access ticket for \$12 and a standard ticket for \$21. More than \$2520 in tickets were sold. Write and graph an inequality for the numbers of each type of ticket sold.

2-6 Transforming Linear Functions *(pp. 134–140)*

EXAMPLE

Let $g(x)$ be the indicated transformation of $f(x) = x$. Write the rule for $g(x)$.

- horizontal shift 5 units left followed by a horizontal stretch by a factor of 3

  Translating $f(x)$ 5 units left replaces each x with $(x + 5)$.

  Let $h(x) = f(x + 5)$

  Replace each x with $\left(\frac{x}{3}\right)$.

  $g(x) = h\left(\frac{x}{3}\right) = \frac{x}{3} + 5$

EXERCISES

Let $g(x)$ be the indicated transformation of $f(x) = x$. Write the rule for $g(x)$.

41. horizontal shift 8 units right

42. vertical shift 5 units up followed by a vertical stretch by a factor of 3

43. horizontal shift 3 units left followed by a vertical shift down 7 units

44. vertical shift 5 units up followed by a reflection across the x-axis

45. horizontal shift 12 units right followed by a reflection across the y-axis

2-7 Curve Fitting with Linear Models *(pp.142–149)*

EXAMPLE

- **Make a scatter plot of the data. Find the correlation coefficient *r* and the equation of the line of best fit.**

x	2	5	9	13	16
y	8	10	24	16	29

The scatter plot is shown at right

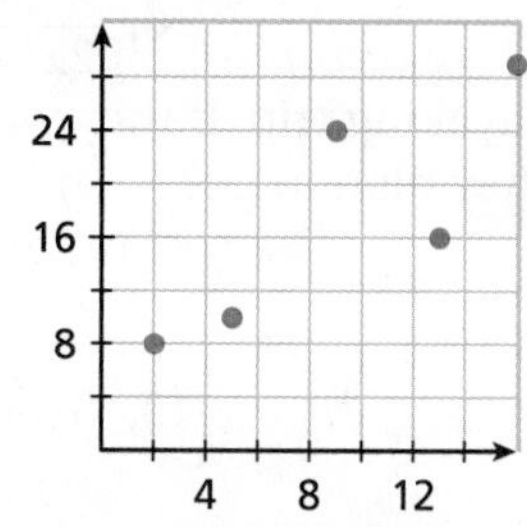

Use **LinReg** on your graphing calculator.

$r \approx 0.834$. The equation of the line of best fit is $y \approx 1.32x + 5.56$.

EXERCISES

46. Find the following for this set of data on median income and median home price.

a. Make a scatter plot of the data using median income as the independent variable.

b. Find the correlation coefficient *r* and the line of best fit for these data.

Median Income (thousands)	Median Home Price (thousands)
69.5	130.2
46.3	94.5
56.7	115.5
65.2	106.4
54.7	98.6
59.6	115.5

2-8 Solving Absolute-Value Equations and Inequalities *(pp.150–156)*

EXAMPLE

Solve the inequality. Then graph the solution set.

- $|2x + 8| - 10 \leq 2$

$|2x + 8| \leq 12$

$2x + 8 \leq 12$ and $2x + 8 \geq -12$ *Conjunction*

$2x \leq 4$ and $2x \geq -20$

$x \leq 2$ and $x \geq -10$

The solution set is $\{x \mid -10 \leq x \leq 2\}$

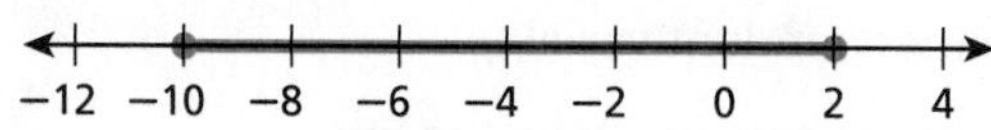

EXERCISES

Solve.

47. $|x - 8| = 20$

48. $\left|\frac{x - 6}{5}\right| = 12$

49. $4|3x - 8| + 16 = 2$

Solve each inequality. Then graph the solution.

50. $3x + 6 > 15$ or $5x + 13 < -12$

51. $2(3x + 6) \leq 32 + 2x$ AND $5x + 15 \geq 2x + 9$

52. $|4x - 8| < 4$

53. $|5x + 10| \geq 30$

2-9 Absolute Value Functions *(pp.158–163)*

EXAMPLE

- Reflect the graph of $f(x) = |x + 3| - 2$ across the x-axis, and graph the function.

$g(x) = -(|x + 3| - 2)$ *$g(x) = -f(x)$*

$g(x) = -|x + 3| + 2$

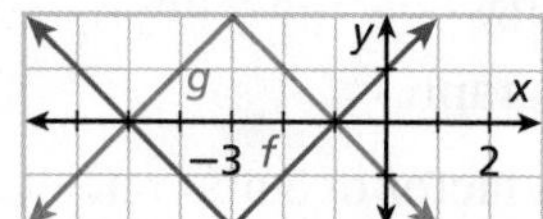

EXERCISES

Translate $f(x) = |x|$ so the vertex is at the given point.

54. $(-5, 7)$

55. $(6, -9)$

Perform each transformation. Then graph.

56. $f(x) = |x - 4| + 1$ reflected across the y-axis

57. $f(x) = |3x + 1|$ compressed vertically by $\frac{1}{3}$

58. $f(x) = |x - 3| + 5$ reflected across the x-axis

CHAPTER 2

Chapter Test

Solve.

1. $5(3x - 4) - 12 = 73$
2. $2x + 12 - 8x = 9 - x - 5x$
3. $4(3 - 3x) - 8x = 15 - 2(5x + 8)$
4. $\frac{-5}{4} = \frac{12}{x}$
5. $\frac{3x - 9}{15} = \frac{18}{12}$
6. $\frac{2}{2x - 5} = \frac{3}{x + 1}$
7. Tim and Kim took 4.6 hours to complete a 25.3 mile kayaking trip. If they want to paddle for 3 hours on their next trip, how far should they plan to go?

Graph.

8. $y = \frac{5}{3}x - 4$
9. $6x + 8y = 24$
10. $6x + 2y < 10$

Write the equation of each line in slope-intercept form.

11. passing through $(9, 12)$ and $(7, 2)$
12. parallel to $9x - 5y = 8$ and through $(-10, 2)$
13. perpendicular to $y = -\frac{2}{7}x + 3$ and through $(6, 4)$
14. The Spanish Club is selling T-shirts and hats and would like to raise at least \$2400. It sells T-shirts for \$15 and hats for \$8. Write and graph an inequality representing the number of T-shirts and hats the club must sell to meet its goal.

Let $g(x)$ be the indicated transformation(s) of $f(x) = x$. Write the rule for $g(x)$.

15. vertical stretch by a factor of 4
16. horizontal translation 6 units right
17. horizontal compression by a factor of $\frac{1}{6}$ followed by a vertical shift 4 units down
18. A consumer group is studying how hospitals are staffed. Here are the results from eight randomly selected hospitals in a state.

Full-Time Hospital Employees								
Hospital Beds	23	29	35	42	46	54	64	76
Full-Time Employees	69	95	118	126	123	178	156	176

   a. Make a scatter plot of the data with hospital beds as the independent variable.

   b. Find the correlation coefficient and the equation of the line of best fit. Draw the line of best fit on your scatter plot.

   c. Predict the number of beds in a hospital with 80 full-time employees.

19. Solve $|12 + 4x| - 6 = 26$.

Solve and graph.

20. $16 \leq \frac{24 - 8x}{5}$
21. $|3x - 9| > 12$
22. $3|12 - 4x| + 4 \leq 28$
23. A pollster predicts the actual percent p of a population that favors a political candidate by using a sample percent s plus or minus 3%. Write an absolute-value inequality for p.
24. Translate $f(x) = |x|$ so that its vertex is at $(4, -2)$. Then graph.
25. Find $g(x)$ if $f(x) = |2x| - 3$ is stretched horizontally by a factor of 3 and reflected across the x-axis.

FOCUS ON ACT

The ACT measures college-preparedness by testing skills in English, mathematics, reading, and science. The Mathematics Test is a 60-minute test with 60 multiple-choice questions. There is no penalty for incorrect answers.

All questions on the ACT Mathematics Test can be answered without using a calculator, but you are allowed to use one. If you bring a calculator to the test center, make sure it is one of the types of calculators approved for the test, as many types are prohibited.

You may want to time yourself as you take this practice test. It should take you about 5 minutes to complete.

1. In a school choir, the ratio of boys to girls is 3:5. If there are a total of 24 singers in the choir, how many girls are in the choir?

(A) 6

(B) 9

(C) 14

(D) 15

(E) 40

2. If $12 - 3(x + 2) = x + 8$, then what is the value of x?

(A) $-\frac{5}{2}$

(B) $-\frac{1}{2}$

(C) $\frac{1}{2}$

(D) $\frac{3}{2}$

(E) $\frac{5}{2}$

3. What are the values of x where $2|x + 4| < 6$?

(A) $x < -1$ and $x < -7$

(B) $x > -1$ or $x < -7$

(C) $x < -1$ or $x > -7$

(D) $x > -1$ and $x < -7$

(E) $x < -1$ and $x > -7$

4. Line ℓ passes through $(1, -3)$ and is perpendicular to $y = \frac{1}{5}x - 7$. What is the equation of line ℓ?

(A) $y = -5x + 2$

(B) $y = -5x - 2$

(C) $y = \frac{1}{5}x - \frac{14}{5}$

(D) $y = -\frac{1}{5}x - \frac{14}{5}$

(E) $y = 5x + 2$

5. Which of the following inequalities is equivalent to $-3y - 5x \le 15$?

(A) $y \ge \frac{5}{3}x + 5$

(B) $y \le -\frac{5}{3}x - 5$

(C) $y \ge -\frac{5}{3}x - 5$

(D) $y \ge \frac{5}{3}x - 5$

(E) $y \le -\frac{5}{3}x + 5$

6. In a state park, any trout caught that weighs less than 10 oz or greater than 30 oz must be returned to the water. Which of the following represents the weights of trout that may be kept?

(A) $|x - 20| \le 10$

(B) $|x - 10| \le 10$

(C) $|x - 10| \ge 20$

(D) $|x - 30| \ge 10$

(E) $|x - 20| \le 30$

CHAPTER 2

TEST TACKLER

Standardized Test Strategies

Gridded Response: Write Gridded Responses

To answer a gridded-response test item, you must write your answer correctly in the top of the provided grid and fill in the bubbles accurately, or the item will be marked as incorrect. Answers may be gridded using several correct formats.

The answer to a gridded-response item is always a *whole number,* a *fraction,* or a *decimal.* Non-numerical signs and symbols, such as units of measure, the percent sign, the degree sign, the negative sign, variables, and commas, cannot be gridded.

EXAMPLE 1

Gridded Response: Solve the equation. $25 - 3(5x - 4) = 32$

1	/	3		

0	.	3	3	3

$$25 - 3(5x - 4) = 32$$
$$25 - 15x + 12 = 32$$
$$-15x = -5$$
$$x = \frac{5}{15} = \frac{1}{3}$$

Grid $\frac{1}{3}$ or its rounded decimal equivalent 0.333 or .3333:

Write your answer in the boxes at the top of the grid. Put only a digit, the fraction bar, or the decimal point in each box.

Put the first digit of your answer in the box on the left OR put the last digit of your answer in the box on the right. Do not leave a blank box in the middle of an answer.

Shade the bubble of each digit or symbol in its corresponding column.

EXAMPLE 2

Gridded Response: Find the slope of the line that passes through $(-2, -5)$ and $(8, 10)$.

3	/	2		

$$m = \frac{y_2 - y_1}{x_2 - x_1} = \frac{10-(-5)}{8-(-2)} = \frac{15}{10} = 1\frac{1}{2}$$

The slope of the line is $1\frac{1}{2}$, but a mixed number must be converted to either a decimal or an improper fraction before the answer can be written on the grid.

Grid the answer 1.5 or $\frac{3}{2}$ following the instructions in Example 1.

Read each statement, and then answer the questions that follow.

Sample A

A student solved a proportion for x and got $\frac{4}{5}$ as a result. He then gridded his answer as shown.

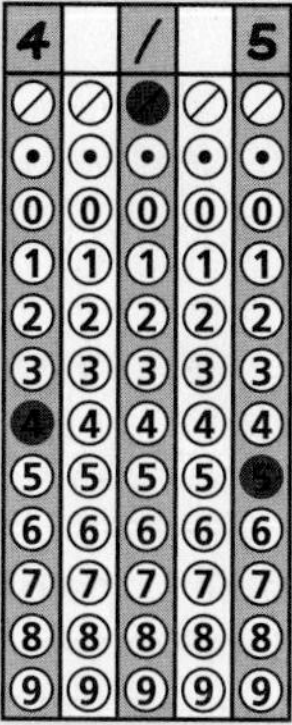

1. Is it possible to grid fractional answers? Explain.
2. If the student solved the proportion correctly, why was the answer marked as incorrect?
3. Describe one way to correctly grid the response $\frac{4}{5}$.

Sample B

What is the x-intercept of the linear function $6x + 9y = 18$?
Wyatt found that the x-intercept point occurs at $(3, 0)$, and then he filled out the grid.

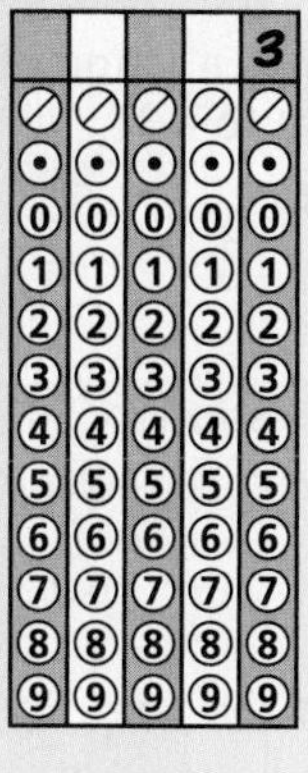

4. Will Wyatt's answer be marked as correct? Explain.
5. Anita got the same answer as Wyatt, but her answer was marked as correct. She did not place the 3 in the last column. Describe Anita's grid.

When filling out a grid, be sure to completely fill in the bubbles, and be careful not to rip the paper.

Sample C

For a gridded-response test item, Jill had to determine the slope of a linear function. She correctly determined the slope to be $2\frac{1}{2}$ and then gridded her answer as shown.

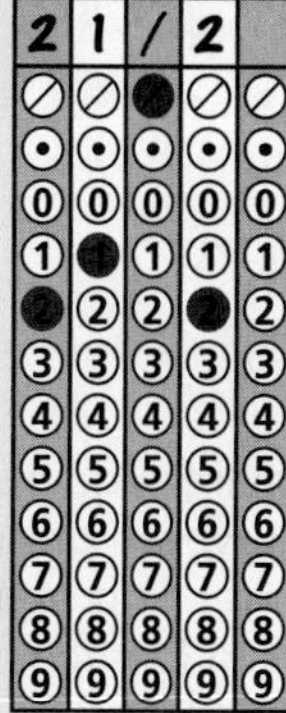

6. Read the number in the answer box grid. What number is recorded in the grid?
7. Why does gridding a mixed number result in an incorrect response?
8. Write a decimal equivalent for $2\frac{1}{2}$, and then write $2\frac{1}{2}$ as an improper fraction. Explain how to correctly grid these values.

Sample D

Daniel is taking an exam where he has to determine the y-intercept of the function shown below.

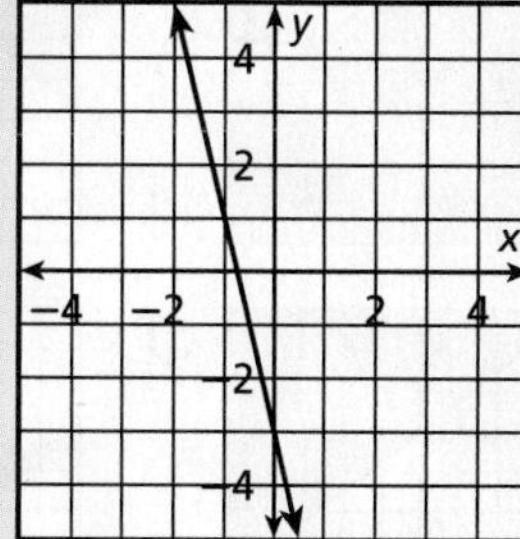

9. Is the y-intercept a positive or negative value?
10. Explain why the answer to this test item cannot be recorded on an answer grid.

CHAPTER 2

STANDARDIZED TEST PREP

go.hrw.com
State Test Practice Online
KEYWORD: MB7 TestPrep

CUMULATIVE ASSESSMENT, CHAPTERS 1–2

Multiple Choice

1. For which function is $g(-3) > g(5)$?

Ⓐ $g(x) = 5x - 9$

Ⓑ $g(x) = x^2 - 12$

Ⓒ $g(x) = (x + 5)^2$

Ⓓ $g(x) = (x - 9)^2$

2. A television commercial claims that 4 out of every 5 dentists surveyed preferred Freshen toothpaste to the leading brand. If 120 dentists in the survey preferred Freshen, how many dentists participated in the survey?

Ⓕ 30 Ⓗ 150

Ⓖ 96 Ⓙ 180

3. Which is an equation of a line with a slope of -3 that passes through $(-2, 7)$?

Ⓐ $y = -3x - 1$

Ⓑ $y = -3x + 1$

Ⓒ $y = -3x + 13$

Ⓓ $y = -\frac{1}{3}x + 1$

4. Which of the following shows the graph of $y + \frac{3}{4}x \geq 2$?

Ⓕ

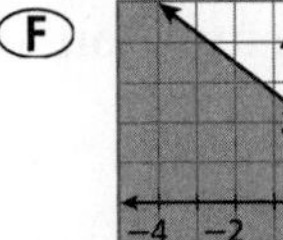

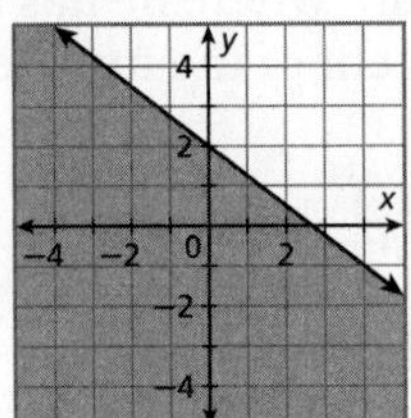

Ⓗ

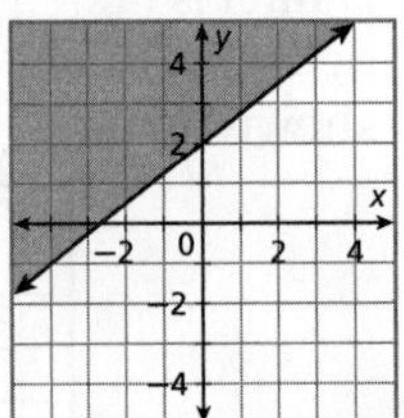

Ⓖ

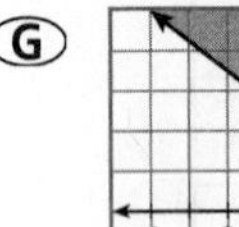

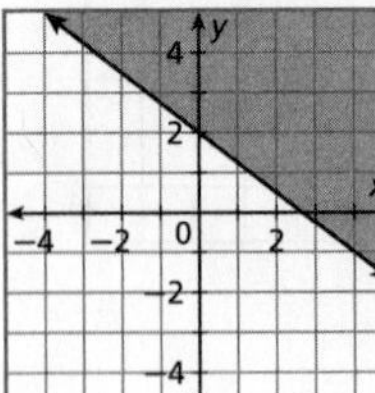

Ⓙ

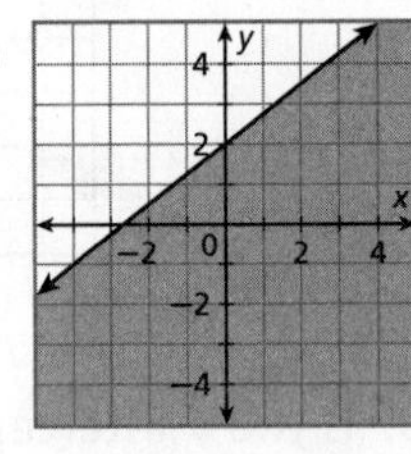

5. In which of the following number sets does -3 NOT belong?

Ⓐ Integers Ⓒ Real numbers

Ⓑ Rational numbers Ⓓ Whole numbers

6. What is a reasonable slope of the line of best fit of the salary data for teachers in a New York school district, as shown in the table below?

Salaries of Teachers	
Years of Experience	**Salary**
0	\$33,407
2	\$34,273
5	\$37,882
8	\$40,185
10	\$42,977
12	\$45,864
15	\$53,811

Ⓕ 450 Ⓗ 1275

Ⓖ 750 Ⓙ 2650

7. Which function has a range of all real numbers less than or equal to -3?

Ⓐ $y = -|x - 3|$ Ⓒ $y = -|x| - 3$

Ⓑ $y = |x| - 3$ Ⓓ $y = |x - 3|$

8. Simplify the expression $4\sqrt{50} + 3\sqrt{72}$.

Ⓕ $4\sqrt{7}$ Ⓗ $12\sqrt{5}$

Ⓖ $7\sqrt{112}$ Ⓙ $38\sqrt{2}$

9. Find the slope of the line $-3y = 6x + 12$.

Ⓐ -4 Ⓒ $-\frac{1}{2}$

Ⓑ -2 Ⓓ $-\frac{1}{4}$

When a word problem contains information about dimensions used to solve a problem, you might find it useful to draw a diagram. The diagram should be clearly labeled and sketched close to scale.

10. A lamppost casts a shadow that is 24 feet long. Tad, who is 6 feet tall, is standing directly next to the lamppost. His shadow is 15 feet long. About how tall is the lamppost?

Ⓕ 10 feet

Ⓖ 15 feet

Ⓗ 33 feet

Ⓙ 60 feet

11. What is the effect on the graph of $y = 2x + 2$ when it is changed to $y = 2x - 2$?

Ⓐ The slope of the line becomes steeper.

Ⓑ The line slants down and right instead of up and right.

Ⓒ The y-intercept is translated 4 units down.

Ⓓ The line is reflected across the y-axis.

12. The cost of renting a moving van is \$39.95 plus \$0.40 per mile. Which equation best represents the relationship between cost c and the number of miles driven m?

Ⓕ $c = 39.95 + 0.40$

Ⓖ $c = 39.95m + 0.40$

Ⓗ $c = 39.95 + 0.40m$

Ⓙ $c = 39.95m + 0.40m$

Gridded Response

13. The baseball statistic "total bases" is calculated by adding the number of singles, twice the number of doubles, three times the number of triples, and four times the number of home runs. In 2001, a player collected 411 total bases, including 49 singles, 32 doubles and 2 triples. How many home runs did the player hit that year?

14. The function $g(x)$ is the reflection across the y-axis of $f(x) = -\frac{2}{3}x - 5$. What is the slope, to the nearest hundredth, of $g(x)$?

15. Evaluate $h^2 - hk + 2k^3 - 2$ for $h = 4$ and $k = -1$.

16. Write the product of $(1.2 \times 10^{-8})(6.8 \times 10^{10})$ in standard form.

17. What is the y-intercept of $3x + 4y = 24$?

Short Response

18. Consider the inequality $|5x + 6| \geq 11$.

a. Solve the inequality.

b. Graph your solution on a number line.

19. The city would like to construct a community amphitheater in the park. The stage of the amphitheater should be 25 feet across and 12 feet deep. The production group that uses the facility has anticipated that at least 5 feet of space should be a sufficient amount for each row. The area allotted for placement of the amphitheater's stage and seating is 2000 ft^2.

a. Write an equation that can be used to determine the maximum number of rows that can be constructed.

b. Determine the maximum number of rows that can be constructed.

c. Suppose the city would like to construct a fence at least 200 feet away from the stage and all of the seats. Find the perimeter of fencing needed.

Extended Response

20. A container is filled with water at a constant rate. The water level over time is shown in the graph.

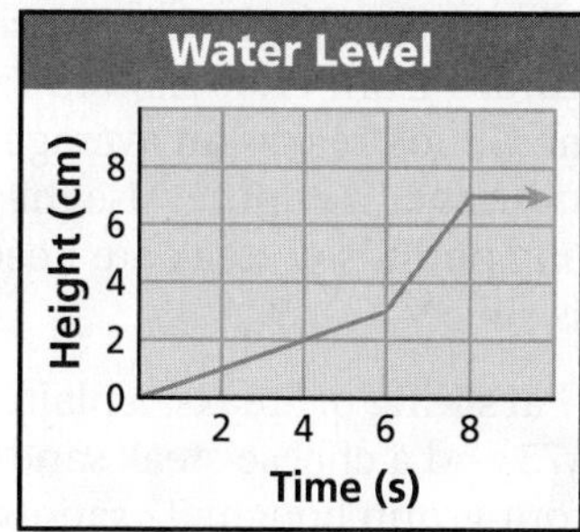

a. What does the flat portion of the graph represent?

b. Sketch a possible shape for the container.

c. Suppose the container is filled twice as fast. Sketch a graph to represent the situation, and identify the transformation of the original graph that it represents.

d. Suppose the container initially contains 2 cm of water. Would the new graph be a vertical translation of the original graph? Justify your answer.

The Philly Cheese Steak Sandwich

Philadelphia's best-known sandwich was created in 1930 when a hot dog vendor tossed some steak and onions onto the grill and then served them on a hot dog bun. Cheese was soon added to the recipe, and the Philly cheese steak sandwich has been a local specialty ever since.

Choose one or more strategies to solve each problem.

1. At Geno's Steaks, the busiest shift of the week is on Saturday from 11:00 A.M. to 7:00 P.M. During that time Geno's makes an average of 1.5 cheese steak sandwiches a minute. Use the recipe below. How many pounds of steak are needed to get through this shift?
2. At Pat's King of Steaks, a plain steak sandwich costs \$5.75 and a cheese steak sandwich costs \$6.00. A tour group bought 32 sandwiches for a total of \$189.00. How many of each type did they buy?
3. In 1930, the first steak sandwich sold for 2 cents. In 2004, a cheese steak sandwich cost \$6. Assuming that cost is a linear function of time, predict the cost of a cheese steak sandwich in 2011.
4. You can expect to find a line at many cheese steak stands, but service is quick. Once an order is placed, the sandwich is made and served in 1 minute and 15 seconds. Suppose it takes 18 seconds for each person in line to place an order. What is the maximum number of people who can be in line ahead of you if you want to have your sandwich in less than 10 minutes from the time you get in line?

Philly Cheese Steak Recipe

5 oz steak
2 1/2 oz. American cheese
Fried onions
9 1/2 in. roll

Thinly slice steak and fry on grill. Just before it's done, cover with cheese and cook until melted. Serve on roll, topped with onions.

The Amazing Maize Maze

Cherry-Crest Farm, located in the heart of Pennsylvania Dutch Country, welcomes visitors by telling them to get lost—in an enormous cornfield maze! The design of the maze changes from year to year, but it always includes bridges and tunnels. There are also clues to discover along the way.

Choose one or more strategies to solve each problem.

1. Corn is usually planted at 30,000 plants per acre. The Amazing Maize Maze measures 360 feet by 660 feet. Assuming that 60% of that area is covered with corn plants, about how many plants form the maze? $\left(\textit{Hint: } 1 \text{ acre} = 43{,}560 \text{ ft}^2\right)$

2. Admission to Cherry-Crest Farm is \$11 for adults and \$9 for children. One group of visitors paid \$213 for admission, and there were more adults than children in the group. How many of each were in the group?

For 3, use the table.

3. Getting through the maze depends on two things: the speed at which you walk and your luck in choosing the right path. The table shows the average walking speeds of eight visitors and the time it took them to exit the maze. Predict the time it would take you to exit the maze if you walked at an average speed of 3.5 mi/h.

Average Walking Speed (mi/h)	2.5	3.0	4.0	3.1	2.8	3.9	4.0	2.7
Time to Exit Maze (min)	72	61	45	58	66	50	51	69

4. For most visitors, the time in minutes that it takes to exit the maze satisfies the inequality $|t - 60| \leq 15$.

   However, people who have already been through the maze usually improve their time by about 7 minutes. What are the minimum and maximum times it takes to exit the maze for repeat visitors?

CHAPTER 3

Linear Systems

Chapter Focus

- Generalize relationships between two or more variables by using systems.
- Develop proficiency in solving systems of equations and inequalities.

Whooping It Up!

You can use linear systems to plan a fund-raiser in which calendars featuring endangered whooping cranes are sold.

go.hrw.com

Chapter Project Online

KEYWORD: MB7 ChProj

Vocabulary

Match each term on the left with a definition on the right.

1. equation
2. inequality
3. solution set
4. slope

A. an equation whose solutions form a line on a coordinate plane
B. steepness of a line given as a ratio of rise over run
C. a mathematical statement using >, <, ≥, or ≤
D. a mathematical statement that says two expressions are equal
E. the set of values that make a statement true

Least Common Multiple

Find the least common multiple, or LCM, for each pair of numbers.

5. 3, 18
6. 28, 8
7. 8, 36
8. 15, 27

Slopes of Parallel and Perpendicular Lines

State whether the linear equations in each pair are parallel, perpendicular, or neither.

9. $\begin{cases} y = 5x - 4 \\ y = -\frac{1}{5}x - 4 \end{cases}$
10. $\begin{cases} 5x - 10y = 3 \\ y = \frac{1}{2}x - 6 \end{cases}$
11. $\begin{cases} x - y = 3 \\ x + y = -4 \end{cases}$
12. $\begin{cases} 2x - 3y = -4 \\ 3y - x = 5 \end{cases}$

Evaluate Expressions

Evaluate each expression for the given values of the variables.

13. $1.5x + 3y$ for $x = 8, y = 14$
14. $5x - \frac{3}{4}y$ for $x = 6, y = -4$
15. $4x - \sqrt{2}y$ for $x = 0.25, y = \sqrt{2}$
16. $-\frac{75x}{3y}$ for $x = 1, y = \frac{1}{3}$

Solve Multi-Step Equations

Solve each equation.

17. $8x + 19 = -5$
18. $5x + 4 = 25 - 2x$
19. $9x - (x + 12) = -13$
20. $-3(4x - 5) - 1 = 20$

Solve Equations with Fractions

Solve each equation.

21. $\frac{1}{4}x + \frac{2}{3}x = 8$
22. $\frac{2}{5}x + \frac{1}{6} = -4$
23. $x + \frac{1}{2} = -\frac{1}{5}$
24. $-\frac{1}{2} = 3x - \frac{1}{3}x$

CHAPTER 3

Study Guide: Preview

Where You've Been

Previously, you

- graphed linear equations.
- graphed linear inequalities.
- solved linear equations.
- studied three-dimensional figures such as cubes and prisms.

In This Chapter

You will study

- graphing systems of linear equations.
- graphing systems of linear inequalities.
- solving systems of linear equations.
- the three-dimensional coordinate system.

Where You're Going

You can use the skills in this chapter

- to solve more complicated systems of equations.
- to understand linear systems in other classes, such as Chemistry, Physics, and Economics.
- outside of school to organize fund-raisers, plan a trip, or spend money wisely.

Key Vocabulary/Vocabulario

constraint	restricción
elimination	eliminación
feasible region	región factible
linear programming	programación lineal
linear system	sistema lineal
substitution	sustitución
system of equations	sistema de ecuaciones
system of linear inequalities	sistema de desigualdades lineales
three-dimensional coordinate system	sistema de coordenadas tridimensional

Vocabulary Connections

To become familiar with some of the vocabulary terms in the chapter, consider the following. You may refer to the chapter, the glossary, or a dictionary if you like.

1. What does the word **eliminate** mean? What might the *elimination* method refer to when solving mathematical equations?
2. **Constraint** refers to a restriction or limitation. What might a mathematical *constraint* refer to?
3. The word **feasible** means “capable of being done or used.” Give examples of sentences that use the word *feasible*. Then discuss what a *feasible region* might refer to.
4. What can you say about a **three-dimensional coordinate system** from its name? If x and y are used for the first two, which letter would be a logical choice for the third coordinate?

Writing Strategy: Keep a Math Journal

Keeping a math journal will help you improve your writing and reasoning skills. By expressing yourself in a journal, you can make sense of confusing or frustrating math situations.

You can use your journal to reflect on what you learned in class, write out any troubles you are having, summarize important concepts and vocabulary, or express your thoughts about a particular topic. Most importantly, though, a math journal helps you see your progress as you continue through Algebra 2.

Journal Entry: Read the entry a student made in his journal.

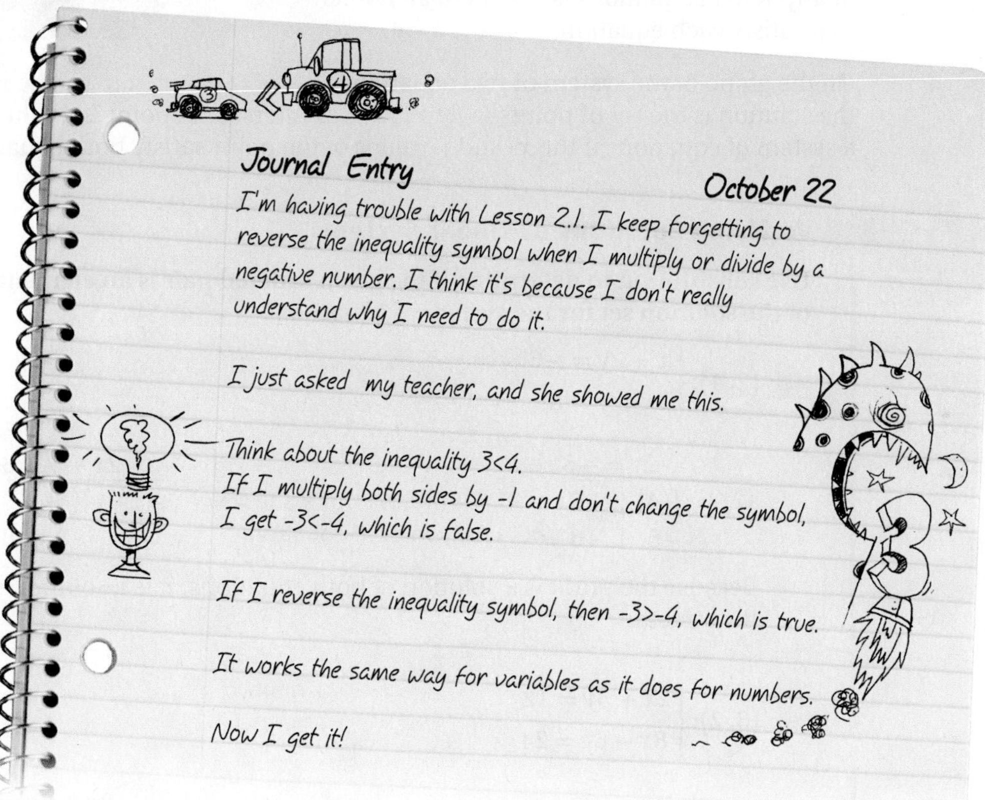

Journal Entry

October 22

I'm having trouble with Lesson 2.1. I keep forgetting to reverse the inequality symbol when I multiply or divide by a negative number. I think it's because I don't really understand why I need to do it.

I just asked my teacher, and she showed me this.

Think about the inequality $3<4$.
If I multiply both sides by -1 and don't change the symbol, I get $-3<-4$, which is false.

If I reverse the inequality symbol, then $-3>-4$, which is true.

It works the same way for variables as it does for numbers.

Now I get it!

Try This

Begin a math journal. Use these ideas to begin your journal entry each day for this week. Be sure to date and number each page.

- What I already know about this lesson is . . .
- What I am unsure about in this lesson is . . .
- The skills I need in order to finish this lesson are . . .
- What trouble spots did I find? How did I handle these difficulties?
- What I enjoyed/did not enjoy about this lesson was . . .

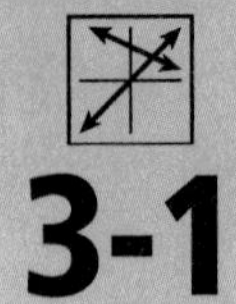

3-1 Using Graphs and Tables to Solve Linear Systems

Objectives

Solve systems of equations by using graphs and tables.

Classify systems of equations, and determine the number of solutions.

Vocabulary

system of equations
linear system
consistent system
inconsistent system
independent system
dependent system

Who uses this?

Winter sports enthusiasts can use systems of equations to compare the costs of renting snowboards. (See Example 4.)

A **system of equations** is a set of two or more equations containing two or more variables. A **linear system** is a system of equations containing only linear equations.

Recall that a line is an infinite set of points that are solutions to a linear equation. The solution of a system of equations is the set of all points that satisfy each equation.

On the graph of the system of two equations, the solution is the set of points where the lines intersect. A point is a solution to a system of equations if the x- and y-values of the point satisfy both equations.

EXAMPLE 1 Verifying Solutions of Linear Systems

Use substitution to determine if the given ordered pair is an element of the solution set for the system of equations.

A $(2, 4); \begin{cases} x - 2y = -6 \\ 2x + y = 8 \end{cases}$

$x - 2y = -6$	
$(2) - 2(4)$	-6
-6	-6 ✔

Substitute 2 for x and 4 for y in each equation.

$2x + y = 8$	
$2(2) + (4)$	8
8	8 ✔

Because the point is a solution of both equations, it is a solution of the system.

B $(3, 2); \begin{cases} 2x + 3y = 12 \\ 8x - 6y = 24 \end{cases}$

$2x + 3y = 12$	
$2(3) + 3(2)$	12
12	12 ✔

Substitute 3 for x and 2 for y in each equation.

$8x - 6y = 24$	
$8(3) + 6(2)$	24
36	24 ✘

Because the point is not a solution of both equations, it is not a solution of the system.

Use substitution to determine if the given ordered pair is an element of the solution set for the system of equations.

1a. $(4, 3); \begin{cases} x + 2y = 10 \\ 3x - y = 9 \end{cases}$

1b. $(5, 3); \begin{cases} 6x - 7y = 1 \\ 3x + 7y = 5 \end{cases}$

Recall that you can use graphs or tables to find some of the solutions to a linear equation. You can do the same to find solutions to linear systems.

EXAMPLE 2 Solving Linear Systems by Using Graphs and Tables

Use a graph and a table to solve each system. Check your answer.

$$\begin{cases} x + y = 4 \\ 2y + 4 = x \end{cases}$$

Solve each equation for y. $\begin{cases} y = -x + 4 \\ y = \frac{1}{2}x - 2 \end{cases}$

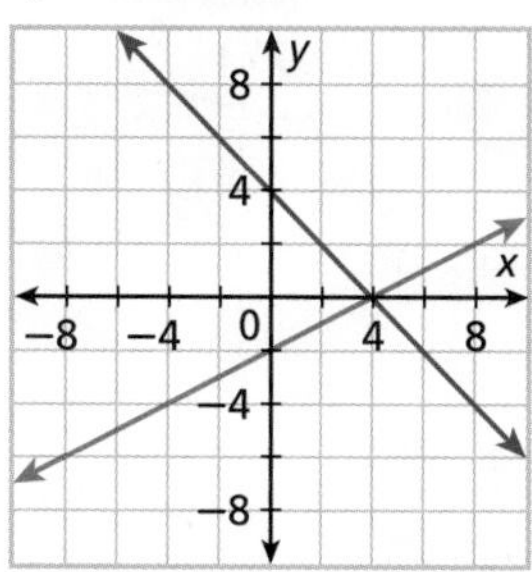

On the graph, the lines appear to intersect at the ordered pair $(4, 0)$.

Make a table of values for each equation. Notice that when $x = 4$, the y-value for both equations is 0.

$y = -x + 4$

x	y
1	3
2	2
3	1
4	0

$y = \frac{1}{2}x - 2$

x	y
1	$-\frac{3}{2}$
2	-1
3	$-\frac{1}{2}$
4	0

The solution to the system is $(4, 0)$.

$$\begin{cases} 3x - y = -2 \\ x - y = -4 \end{cases}$$

Solve each equation for y. $\begin{cases} y = 3x + 2 \\ y = x + 4 \end{cases}$

Helpful Hint

To enter the equations into your calculator, let $\mathbf{Y_1}$ represent $y = 3x + 2$ and let $\mathbf{Y_2}$ represent $y = x + 4$.

Use your graphing calculator to graph the equations and make a table of values. The lines appear to intersect at $(1, 5)$. This is confirmed by the table of values.
The solution to the system is $(1, 5)$.

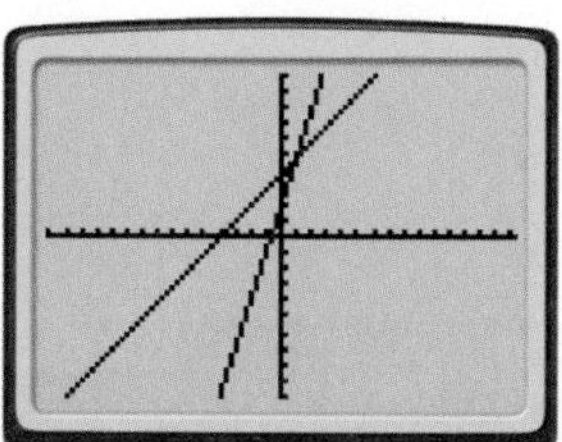

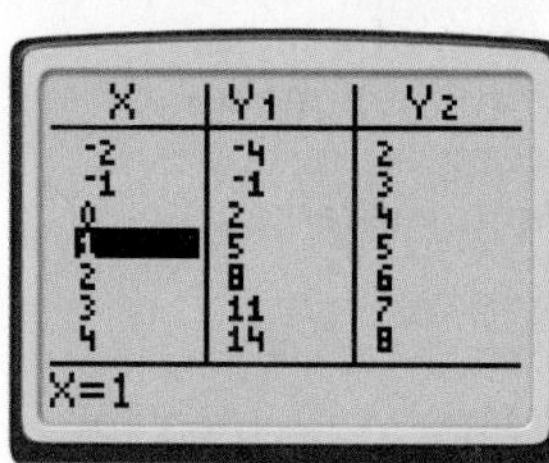

Check Substitute $(1, 5)$ in the original equations to verify the solution.

$$\begin{array}{r|l} 3x - y = & -2 \\ \hline 3(1) - (5) & -2 \\ -2 & -2 \checkmark \end{array} \qquad \begin{array}{r|l} x - y = & -4 \\ \hline (1) - (5) & -4 \\ -4 & -4 \checkmark \end{array}$$

Use a graph and a table to solve each system. Check your answer.

2a. $\begin{cases} 2y + 6 = x \\ 4x = 3 + y \end{cases}$ **2b.** $\begin{cases} x + y = 8 \\ 2x - y = 4 \end{cases}$ **2c.** $\begin{cases} y - x = 5 \\ 3x + y = 1 \end{cases}$

The systems of equations in Example 2 have exactly one solution. However, linear systems may also have infinitely many or no solutions. A **consistent system** is a set of equations or inequalities that has at least one solution, and an **inconsistent system** will have no solutions.

You can classify linear systems by comparing the slopes and y-intercepts of the equations. An **independent system** has equations with different slopes. A **dependent system** has equations with equal slopes and equal y-intercepts.

Classifying Linear Systems

EXACTLY ONE SOLUTION	INFINITELY MANY SOLUTIONS	NO SOLUTION
Consistent, independent The graphs are intersecting lines with different slopes.	Consistent, dependent The graphs are coinciding lines; they have the same slope and same y-intercept.	Inconsistent The graphs are parallel lines; they have the same slope but different y-intercepts.

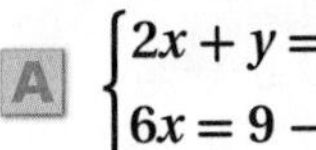

EXAMPLE 3 Classifying Linear Systems

Classify each system and determine the number of solutions.

A $\begin{cases} 2x + y = 3 \\ 6x = 9 - 3y \end{cases}$

Solve each equation for y. $\begin{cases} y = -2x + 3 \\ y = -2x + 3 \end{cases}$

The equations have the same slope and y-intercept and are graphed as the same line.

The system is dependent with infinitely many solutions.

B $\begin{cases} 3x + y = 3 \\ 2 + y = -3x \end{cases}$

Solve each equation for y. $\begin{cases} y = -3x + 3 \\ y = -3x - 2 \end{cases}$

The equations have the same slope but different y-intercepts and are graphed as parallel lines.

The system is inconsistent and has no solution.

Check A graph shows parallel lines.

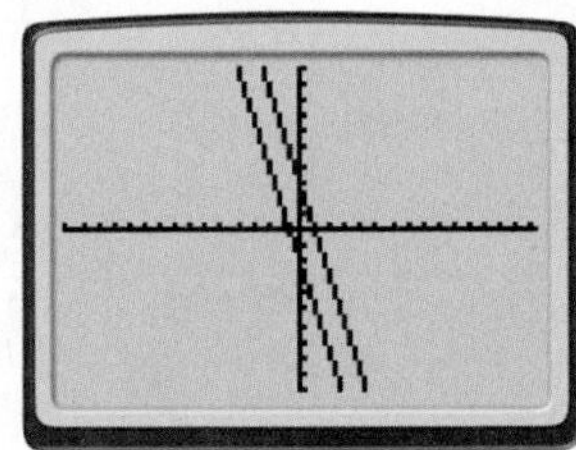

Remember!

The slope-intercept form of a linear equation makes comparing slopes and y-intercepts easy.

$y = mx + b$

Slope (m), y-intercept (b)

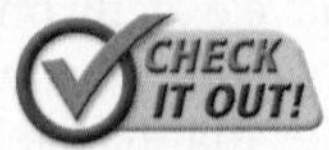

Classify each system and determine the number of solutions.

3a. $\begin{cases} 7x - y = -11 \\ 3y = 21x + 33 \end{cases}$ **3b.** $\begin{cases} x + 4 = y \\ 5y = 5x + 35 \end{cases}$

EXAMPLE 4 Winter Sports Application

Big Dog Snowboard Co. charges \$15 for equipment rental plus \$35 per hour for snowboarding lessons. Half-Pipe Snowboards, Inc. charges \$40 for equipment rental plus \$25 per hour for lessons. For what number of hours is the cost of equipment and lessons the same for each company?

Step 1 Write an equation for the cost of equipment rental and lessons at each company.

Let x represent the number of hours and y represent the total cost in dollars.

Big Dog Snowboard Co.: $y = 35x + 15$

Half-Pipe Snowboards, Inc.: $y = 25x + 40$

Because the slopes are different, the system is independent and has exactly one solution.

Step 2 Solve the system by using a table of values.

Use increments of $\frac{1}{2}$ to represent 30 min.

When $x = 2\frac{1}{2}$, the y-values are both 102.5. The cost of equipment rental and a $2\frac{1}{2}$-hour snowboard lesson is \$102.50 at either company. So the cost is the same at each company for $2\frac{1}{2}$ hours.

$y = 35x + 15$

x	y
1	50
$1\frac{1}{2}$	67.5
2	85
$2\frac{1}{2}$	102.5
3	120

$y = 25x + 40$

x	y
1	65
$1\frac{1}{2}$	77.5
2	90
$2\frac{1}{2}$	102.5
3	115

4. Ravi is comparing the costs of long distance calling cards. To use card A, it costs \$0.50 to connect and then \$0.05 per minute. To use card B, it costs \$0.20 to connect and then \$0.08 per minute. For what number of minutes does it cost the same amount to use each card for a single call?

THINK AND DISCUSS

1. Explain how to find the number of solutions of a system of equations using only a graph.
2. Explain why a system of equations whose graphs are distinct parallel lines has no solution.
3. **GET ORGANIZED** Copy and complete the graphic organizer. In each box, give information about or examples of each solution type.

Know it! Note

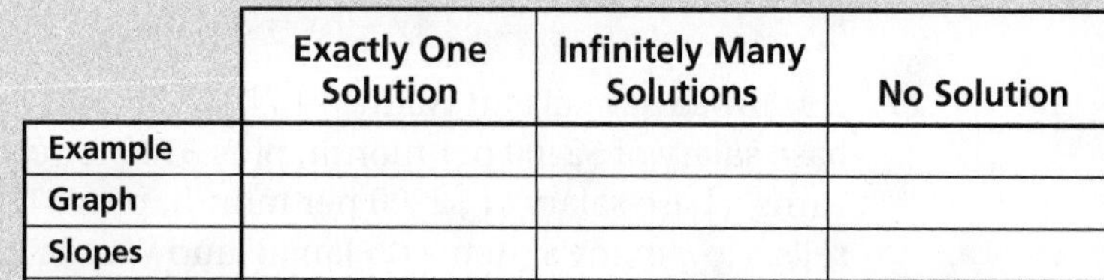

	Exactly One Solution	Infinitely Many Solutions	No Solution
Example			
Graph			
Slopes			
y-intercepts			

3-1 Exercises

go.hrw.com
Homework Help Online
KEYWORD: MB7 3-1
Parent Resources Online
KEYWORD: MB7 Parent

GUIDED PRACTICE

1. **Vocabulary** A system of equations with no solution is __?__. (*consistent* or *inconsistent*)

SEE EXAMPLE 1 p. 182

Use substitution to determine if the given ordered pair is an element of the solution set for the system of equations.

2. $(3, 3)$ $\begin{cases} 2x - y = 3 \\ y + x = 6 \end{cases}$

3. $(1, -3)$ $\begin{cases} y - 4x = -7 \\ 5x + y = -6 \end{cases}$

4. $(-2, 2)$ $\begin{cases} 5y - 5x = 10 \\ 3x + 10 = 2y \end{cases}$

5. $(-1, 4)$ $\begin{cases} y = 3 - x \\ 6x + 2y = 2 \end{cases}$

SEE EXAMPLE 2 p. 183

Use a graph and a table to solve each system. Check your answer.

6. $\begin{cases} y + x = 5 \\ 3x - 5y = -1 \end{cases}$

7. $\begin{cases} 3y + 6x = 3 \\ x - y = -7 \end{cases}$

8. $\begin{cases} y - x = 0 \\ 8x + 4y = -24 \end{cases}$

9. $\begin{cases} x - y = -1 \\ 4x - 2y = 2 \end{cases}$

SEE EXAMPLE 3 p. 184

Classify each system and determine the number of solutions.

10. $\begin{cases} 7x + y = 13 \\ 28x + 4y = -12 \end{cases}$

11. $\begin{cases} 2x - 3y = -15 \\ 3y - 2x = 15 \end{cases}$

12. $\begin{cases} 8y - 24x = 64 \\ 9y + 45x = 72 \end{cases}$

13. $\begin{cases} 2x + 2y = -10 \\ 4x + 4y = -16 \end{cases}$

SEE EXAMPLE 4 p. 185

14. **Aquariums** Marco is draining his two aquariums. The tanks are the same size. One tank has 7 in. of water in it. It is being drained at a rate of 1 in./min. The other tank has 5 in. of water in it. It is being drained at a rate of 0.5 in./min. After how many minutes will the tanks contain the same amount of water?

PRACTICE AND PROBLEM SOLVING

Independent Practice

For Exercises	See Example
15–18	1
19–22	2
23–26	3
27	4

Extra Practice
Skills Practice p. S8
Application Practice p. S34

Use substitution to determine if the given ordered pair is an element of the solution set for the system of equations.

15. $(-2, 2)$ $\begin{cases} x + y = 0 \\ 7y - 14x = 42 \end{cases}$

16. $(-3, -5)$ $\begin{cases} 2y - 6x = 8 \\ 4y = 8x + 4 \end{cases}$

17. $(3, 2)$ $\begin{cases} y = 2 \\ y + 8 = 6x \end{cases}$

18. $(6, 1)$ $\begin{cases} y = 8x + 2 \\ x - 3y = 3 \end{cases}$

Use a graph and a table to solve each system. Check your answer.

19. $\begin{cases} 2 + y = x \\ x + y = 4 \end{cases}$

20. $\begin{cases} 4y - 2x = 4 \\ 10x - 5y = 10 \end{cases}$

21. $\begin{cases} 12x + 4y = -4 \\ 2x - y = 6 \end{cases}$

22. $\begin{cases} y = 10 - x \\ 3x - 3y = 0 \end{cases}$

Classify each system and determine the number of solutions.

23. $\begin{cases} 24x - 27y = 42 \\ -9y + 8x = 14 \end{cases}$

24. $\begin{cases} \frac{3}{2}x + 9 = y \\ 4y - 6x = 36 \end{cases}$

25. $\begin{cases} 7y + 42x = 56 \\ 25x - 5y = 100 \end{cases}$

26. $\begin{cases} 3y = 2x \\ -4x + 6y = 3 \end{cases}$

27. **Business** Jamail and Wanda sell home theater systems. Jamail earns a base salary of \$2400 per month, plus \$100 for each system he sells. Wanda earns a base salary of \$2200 per month, plus \$120 for each system she sells. How many systems do Jamail and Wanda have to sell before they earn the same amount of money?

Determine if the given ordered pair is a solution of the system of equations. If it is not, give the correct solution.

28. $(4, 2)$
$$\begin{cases} y - x = 2 \\ 2x + y = 8 \end{cases}$$

29. $(-1, 2)$
$$\begin{cases} 3x + y = -1 \\ 8x + 6 = -y \end{cases}$$

30. $(7, 2)$
$$\begin{cases} x + y = 9 \\ 4y + 4 = x \end{cases}$$

31. $(0, 6)$
$$\begin{cases} 3x + 4y = -9 \\ y = 2x + 6 \end{cases}$$

32. Bicycling Roberto is competing in a bicycle race. He has traveled 12 mi and is maintaining a steady speed of 15 mi/h. Alexandra is competing in the same race but got a flat tire. She has traveled 8 mi and is maintaining a steady speed of 18 mi/h.

a. Write and graph a system of equations that could be used to model the situation.

b. How long will it take Alexandra to catch Roberto?

c. How many miles into the race will they be when they meet?

LINK — Aviation

When in the air, pilots must follow certain flight-path restrictions to avoid collisions. The direction the airplane travels determines its required altitude. For example, airplanes traveling west fly at even-numbered thousands of feet.

33. Aviation Lynn is piloting a plane at an altitude of 10,000 feet. She begins to descend at a rate of 200 feet per minute. Miguel is flying a different plane at an altitude of 5000 feet. At the same time that Lynn begins to descend, Miguel begins to climb at a rate of 50 feet per minute.

a. Write and graph a system of equations that could be used to model the situation.

b. In how many minutes will the planes be at the same altitude?

c. What will that altitude be?

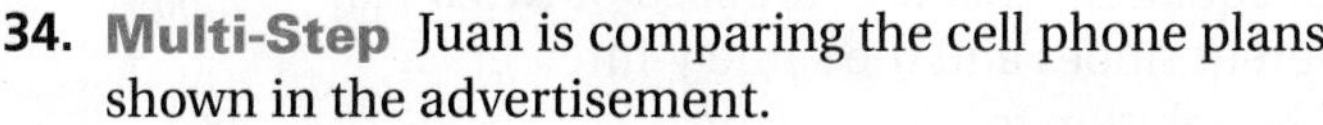

34. Multi-Step Juan is comparing the cell phone plans shown in the advertisement.

a. Write and graph a system of equations that could be used to model the situation.

b. For what number of minutes of use do the plans cost the same?

c. If Juan expects to use the phone for about 2 hours a month, which plan should he choose? Explain.

Write equations for each system graphed below. Then classify the system and find the solution set.

35.

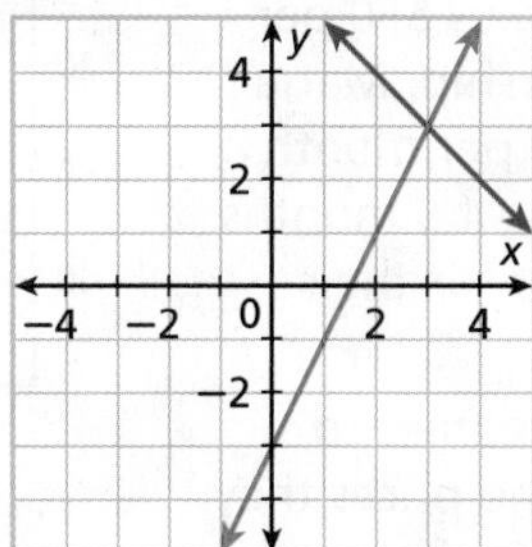

36.

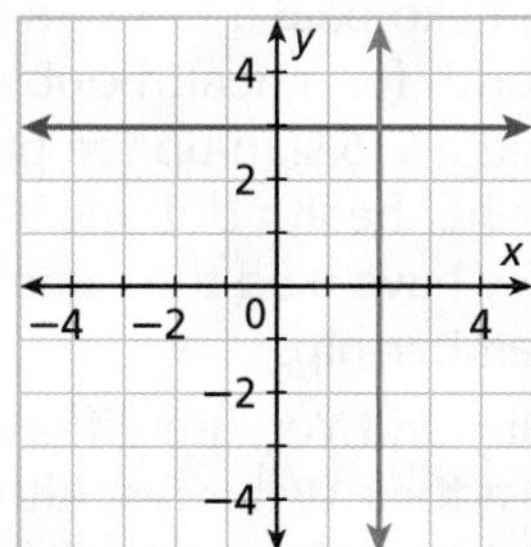

37.

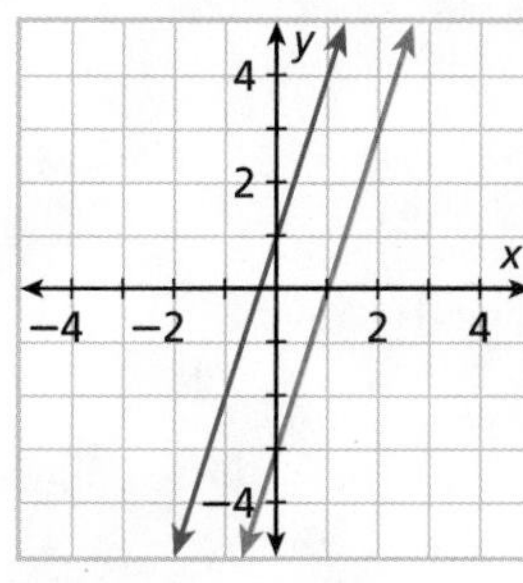

Graphing Calculator **The graphing calculator can find points of intersection. Use the intersect feature of a graphing calculator by pressing 2nd TRACE (CALC), then select 5: Intersect to find the solution to each system of equations. Round each solution to the nearest thousandth.**

38. $\begin{cases} y = -7x + 11 \\ y = 5x - 13 \end{cases}$

39. $\begin{cases} y = 4x + 5 \\ y = 12x + 7 \end{cases}$

40. $\begin{cases} 43 + y = 27x \\ 18x - y = -15 \end{cases}$

41. $\begin{cases} 32x = 121 + y \\ 45x + y = 97 \end{cases}$

MULTI-STEP TEST PREP

42. This problem will prepare you for the Multi-Step Test Prep on page 212.

The fuel tank of a compact truck holds 17 gallons. On a full tank, the truck can travel about 408 miles in the city or 476 miles on the highway. The fuel tank of a compact car holds 14 gallons. On a full tank, the car can travel about 364 miles in the city or 490 miles on the highway.

a. Compare the fuel use of the car and the truck in miles per gallon.

b. How many hours of highway driving are required for each to empty its tank? Assume an average speed of 60 miles per hour.

c. If the car travels at a constant 60 miles per hour on the highway, at what speed must the truck travel if it is to empty its tank at the same time as the car?

43. Critical Thinking One equation in a linear system is $x + 2y = 4$. What is an equation that would cause the system to have an infinite number of solutions? no solutions? one solution?

44. Estimation Use a graph to estimate the solution of the following system.

$$\begin{cases} y = 1.25x - 4 \\ y = -1.4x + 5 \end{cases}$$

45. Critical Thinking How would you classify a system of equations that is composed of two lines with different slopes and the same y-intercepts? What is the solution to the system?

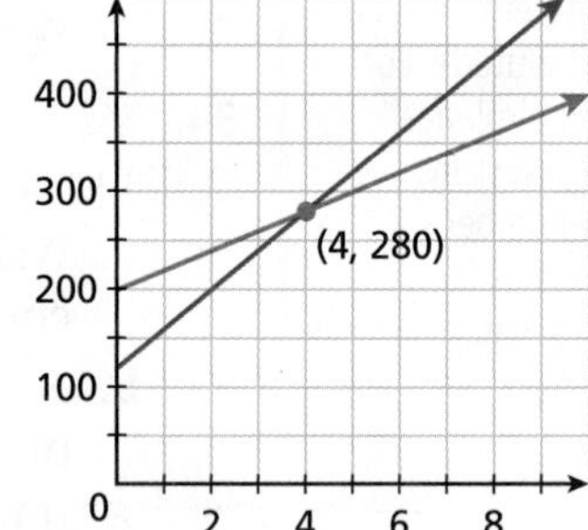

46. Write About It Describe a situation involving two hot-air balloons that could be modeled by the graph shown.

TEST PREP

47. Which of the situations below best matches the graph of the system of equations shown?

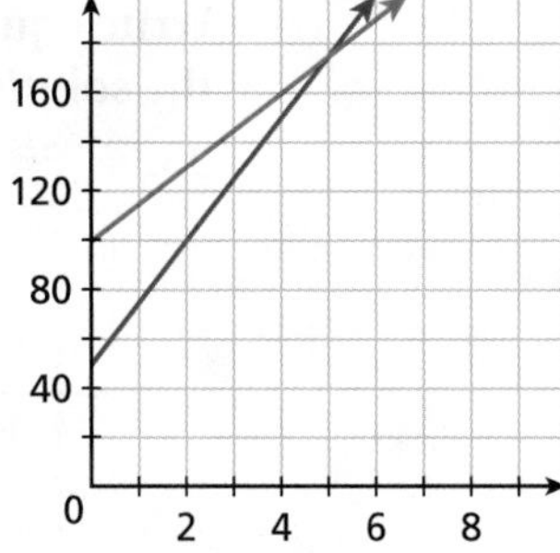

Ⓐ Kameko paid a \$25 sign-up fee plus \$50 per month for a health club membership. Maria paid a \$15 sign-up fee plus \$100 per month for her health club membership. At 5 months, they have paid the same amount for their memberships.

Ⓑ Ruby and Yuri use different companies to host their Web sites. Although the prices they pay are different, if each has 5 gigabytes of traffic per month, Ruby and Yuri pay the same amount, \$200.

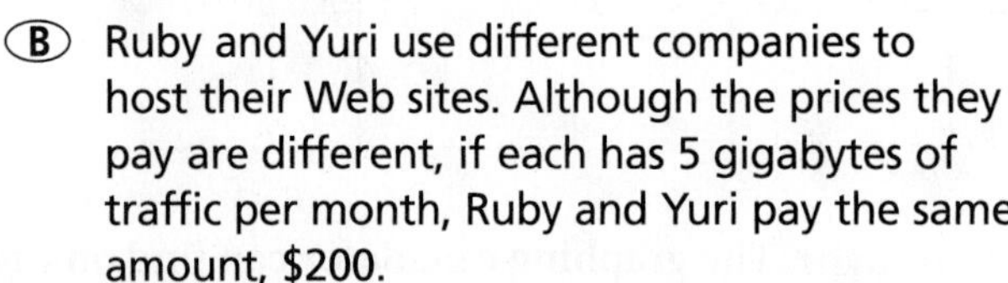

Ⓒ James and Renee paid \$100 plus \$15 per day to rent a small sailboat. They kept the boat for 5 days and paid \$175.

Ⓓ Esteban and Ted belong to different country clubs, and they pay different monthly dues and different amounts to play golf. However, they've found that if they play 5 rounds of golf in a month, they each pay the same amount, \$175, in dues and golf fees.

48. Which system of equations is accurately represented on the graph?

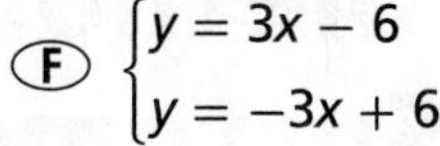

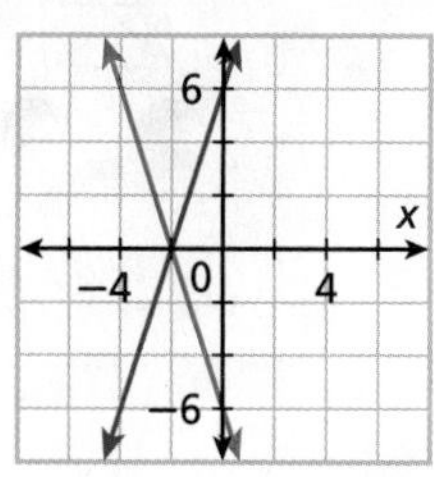

Ⓕ $\begin{cases} y = 3x - 6 \\ y = -3x + 6 \end{cases}$ Ⓗ $\begin{cases} y = 6x - 3 \\ y = -6x + 3 \end{cases}$

Ⓖ $\begin{cases} y = 3x + 6 \\ y = -3x - 6 \end{cases}$ Ⓙ $\begin{cases} y = 6x + 3 \\ y = 6x - 3 \end{cases}$

49. Adam's truck has 5 gal of fuel left in the tank and uses 0.1 gal/mi. Zoe's truck has 6 gal of fuel left in the tank and uses 0.15 gal/mi. Which of the following graphs best represents the system of equations that can be used to find the distance driven at which the trucks will have the same amount of fuel?

Ⓐ

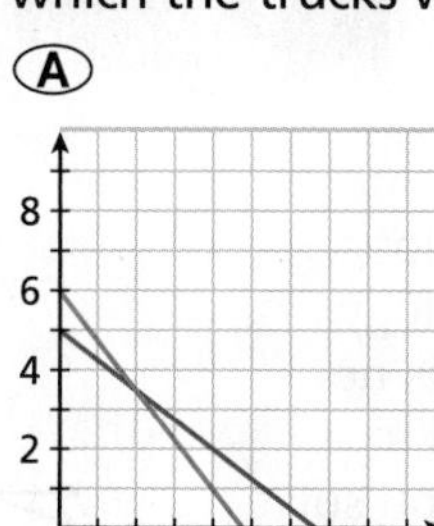

Ⓑ

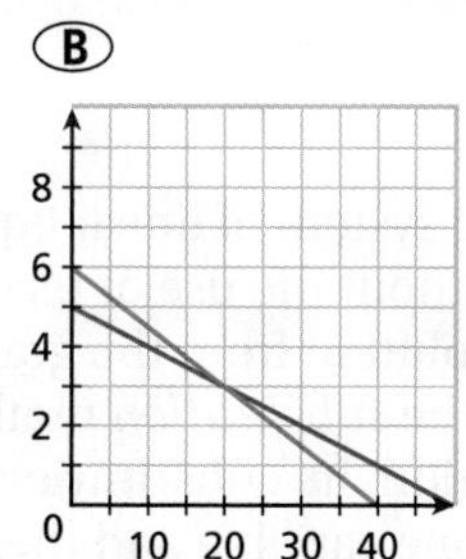

Ⓒ

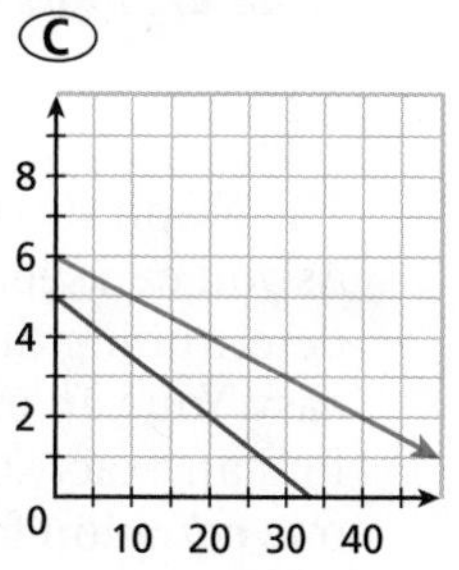

Ⓓ

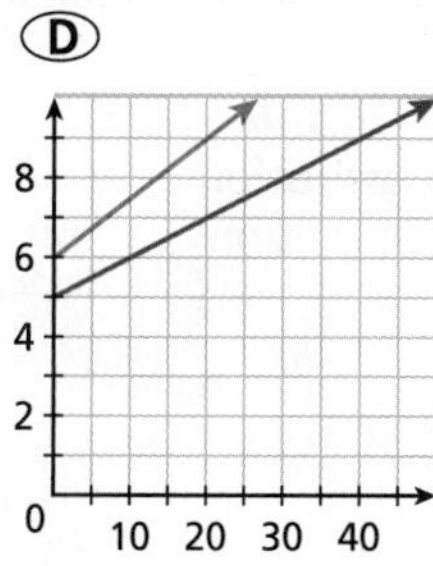

50. **Gridded Response** What is 3 times the y-coordinate of the solution to the following system? $\begin{cases} -x + y = 8 \\ y = 4x \end{cases}$

CHALLENGE AND EXTEND

Solve each system. Round your answer to the nearest thousandth.

51. $\begin{cases} y = 55x + 100 \\ y = 20x + 600 \end{cases}$ 52. $\begin{cases} 20x + 5y = 135 \\ y = -50x + 32 \end{cases}$ 53. $\begin{cases} 9x + 18y = 126 \\ 14y = -7x + 98 \end{cases}$ 54. $\begin{cases} 0.25x - y = 2.25 \\ y = 0.75x + 3.75 \end{cases}$

55. **Business** An economist is studying a system of linear equations representing cost functions for two different products over time. She finds that the solution to the system is $(-6, -200)$. What does the solution tell her about the cost functions?

56. **Multi-Step** Brad is a farmer. He feeds his hogs 12 pounds of feed per day and has 70 pounds of feed in his barn. Cliff is also a farmer. He feeds his hogs 15 pounds of feed per day and has 100 pounds of feed in his barn.

  a. In how many days will Brad and Cliff have the same amount of feed left? Use a system of equations to find your answer.

  b. Does your answer to part **a** make sense?

  c. How would your answer change if both Brad and Cliff receive a shipment of 100 pounds of feed on day 4?

SPIRAL REVIEW

Simplify by rationalizing each denominator. *(Lesson 1-3)*

57. $\dfrac{4}{\sqrt{12}}$ 58. $\dfrac{1}{2\sqrt{5}}$ 59. $\dfrac{\sqrt{6}}{\sqrt{12}}$ 60. $\dfrac{7\sqrt{14}}{\sqrt{5}}$

Solve each equation and check your answer. *(Lesson 2-1)*

61. $\frac{5}{2}x - 1 = \frac{1}{2} + 3x$ 62. $6(7n + 2) = (34 + 11n)3$

63. **Manufacturing** On one assembly line, 45 pounds of cheese are sliced and packaged every two hours. How many hours are needed for 900 pounds of cheese to be sliced and packaged on that assembly line? *(Lesson 2-2)*

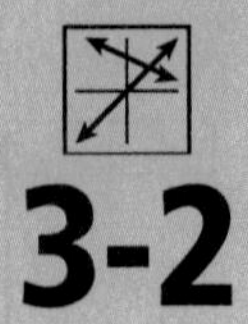

3-2 Using Algebraic Methods to Solve Linear Systems

Objectives
Solve systems of equations by substitution.
Solve systems of equations by elimination.

Vocabulary
substitution
elimination

Who uses this?
Zookeepers use algebraic methods to solve systems of linear equations that model mixtures of animal foods. (See Example 4.)

The graph shows a system of linear equations. As you can see, without the use of technology, determining the solution from the graph is not easy. You can use the *substitution* method to find an exact solution. In **substitution**, you solve one equation for one variable and then substitute this expression into the other equation.

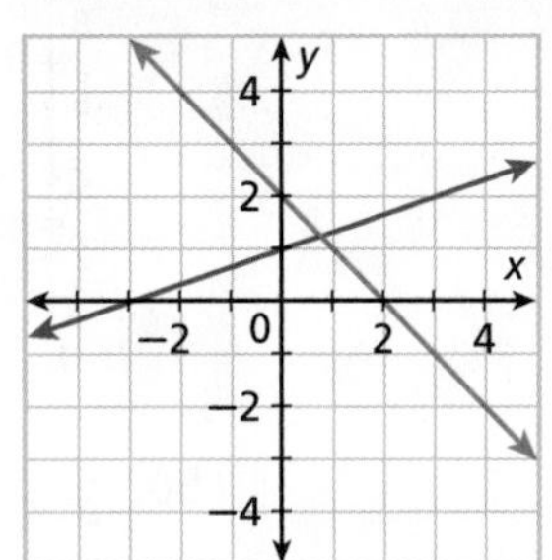

EXAMPLE 1 Solving Linear Systems by Substitution

Use substitution to solve each system of equations.

A $\begin{cases} y = x + 2 \\ x + y = 8 \end{cases}$

Step 1 Solve one equation for one variable.
The first equation is already solved for y: $y = x + 2$.

Step 2 Substitute the expression into the other equation.

$x + y = 8$
$x + (x + 2) = 8$ *Substitute $(x + 2)$ for y in the other equation.*
$2x + 2 = 8$ *Combine like terms.*
$2x = 6$
$x = 3$

Step 3 Substitute the x-value into one of the original equations to solve for y.

$y = x + 2$
$y = (3) + 2$ *Substitute $x = 3$.*
$y = 5$

The solution is the ordered pair $(3, 5)$.

Check A graph or table supports your answer.

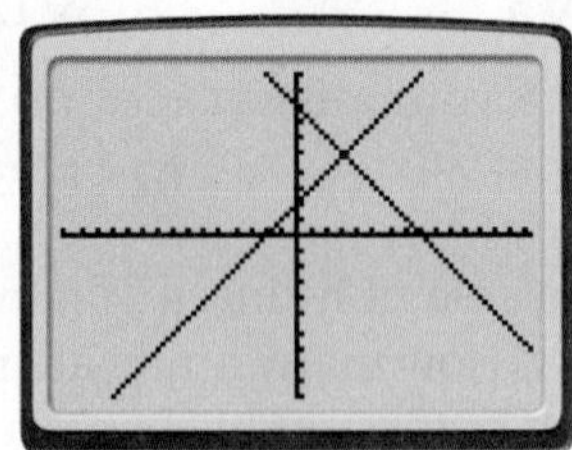

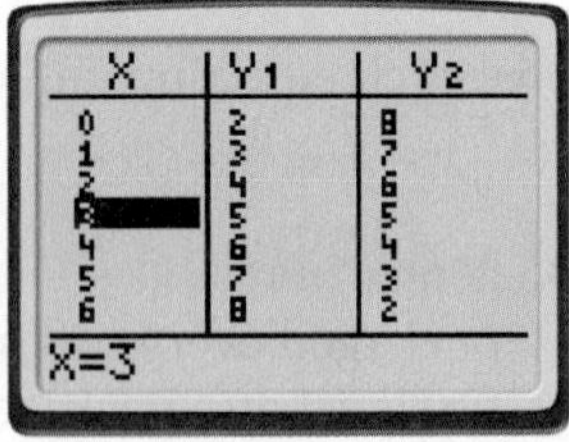

Caution!
The solution to an independent system of equations is an ordered pair. Do not stop working when you have found only one value.

Use substitution to solve each system of equations.

B $\begin{cases} 2x + y = 6 \\ y - 8x = 1 \end{cases}$

Method 1 Isolate y.		**Method 2** Isolate x.
$2x + y = 6$	*First equation*	$2x + y = 6$
$y = 6 - 2x$	*Isolate one variable.*	$x = \frac{6 - y}{2} = 3 - \frac{y}{2}$
$y - 8x = 1$	*Second equation*	$y - 8x = 1$
$(6 - 2x) - 8x = 1$	*Substitute the expression into the second equation.*	$y - 8\left(3 - \frac{y}{2}\right) = 1$
$6 - 10x = 1$	*Combine like terms.*	$y - 24 + 4y = 1$
$-10x = -5$		$5y = 25$
$x = \frac{1}{2}$	*First part of the solution*	$y = 5$

Substitute the value into one of the original equations to solve for the other variable.

$y - 8\left(\frac{1}{2}\right) = 1$	*Substitute the value to solve for the other variable.*	$2x + (5) = 6$
$y - 4 = 1$		$2x = 1$
$y = 5$	*Second part of the solution*	$x = \frac{1}{2}$

By either method, the solution is $\left(\frac{1}{2}, 5\right)$.

Use substitution to solve each system of equations.

1a. $\begin{cases} y = 2x - 1 \\ 3x + 2y = 26 \end{cases}$ **1b.** $\begin{cases} 5x + 6y = -9 \\ 2x - 2 = -y \end{cases}$

You can also solve systems of equations with the *elimination* method. With **elimination**, you get rid of one of the variables by adding or subtracting equations. You may have to multiply one or both equations by a number to create variable terms that can be eliminated.

EXAMPLE 2 Solving Linear Systems by Elimination

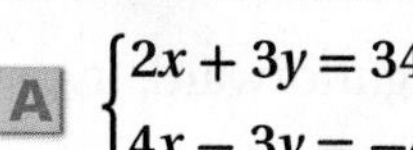

The elimination method is sometimes called the *addition method* or *linear combination*.

Use elimination to solve each system of equations.

A $\begin{cases} 2x + 3y = 34 \\ 4x - 3y = -4 \end{cases}$

Step 1 Find the value of one variable.

$$\begin{array}{r} 2x + 3y = 34 \\ +\ 4x - 3y = -4 \\ \hline 6x \qquad = 30 \\ x = 5 \end{array}$$

The y-terms have opposite coefficients.

Add the equations to eliminate y.

First part of the solution

Step 2 Substitute the x-value into one of the original equations to solve for y.

$2(5) + 3y = 34$

$3y = 24$

$y = 8$ *Second part of the solution*

The solution to the system is $(5, 8)$.

Use elimination to solve each system of equations.

B $\begin{cases} 2x + 4y = -10 \\ 3x + 3y = -3 \end{cases}$

Step 1 To eliminate x, multiply both sides of the first equation by 3 and both sides of the second equation by -2.

$$\begin{aligned} 3(2x + 4y) &= 3(-10) \\ -2(3x + 3y) &= -2(-3) \end{aligned} \quad \rightarrow \quad \begin{aligned} 6x + 12y &= -30 \\ \underline{-6x - 6y} &= \underline{\ \ 6} \\ 6y &= -24 \end{aligned} \qquad \textit{Add the equations.}$$

$$y = -4 \qquad \textit{First part of the solution}$$

Step 2 Substitute the y-value into one of the original equations to solve for x.

$$\begin{aligned} 3x + 3(-4) &= -3 \\ 3x - 12 &= -3 \\ 3x &= 9 \\ x &= 3 \end{aligned} \qquad \textit{Second part of the solution}$$

The solution to the system is $(3, -4)$.

Check Substitute 3 for x and -4 for y in each equation.

$2x + 4y = -10$	
$2(3) + 4(-4)$	-10
-10	-10 ✓

$3x + 3y = -3$	
$3(3) + 3(-4)$	-3
-3	-3 ✓

Use elimination to solve each system of equations.

2a. $\begin{cases} 4x + 7y = -25 \\ -12x - 7y = 19 \end{cases}$

2b. $\begin{cases} 5x - 3y = 42 \\ 8x + 5y = 28 \end{cases}$

In Lesson 3-1, you learned that systems may have infinitely many or no solutions. When you try to solve these systems algebraically, the result will be an identity or a contradiction.

EXAMPLE 3 Classifying Systems with Infinitely Many or No Solutions

Remember!

An *identity,* such as $0 = 0$, is always true and indicates infinitely many solutions.
A *contradiction,* such as $1 = 3$, is never true and indicates no solution.

Classify the system and determine the number of solutions.

$\begin{cases} \mathbf{2x + y = 8} \\ \mathbf{6x + 3y = -15} \end{cases}$

Because isolating y is straightforward, use substitution.

$$\begin{aligned} 2x + y &= 8 \\ y &= 8 - 2x && \textit{Solve the first equation for y.} \\ 6x + 3(8 - 2x) &= -15 && \textit{Substitute } 8 - 2x \textit{ for y in the second equation.} \\ 6x + 24 - 6x &= -15 && \textit{Distribute.} \\ 24 &= -15 \ \times && \textit{Simplify.} \end{aligned}$$

Because 24 is never equal to -15, the equation is a contradiction. Therefore, the system is inconsistent and has no solution.

Classify the system and determine the number of solutions.

3a. $\begin{cases} 56x + 8y = -32 \\ 7x + y = -4 \end{cases}$

3b. $\begin{cases} 6x + 3y = -12 \\ 2x + y = -6 \end{cases}$

EXAMPLE 4 *Zoology Application*

A zookeeper needs to mix feed for the prairie dogs so that the feed has the right amount of protein. Feed A has 12% protein. Feed B has 5% protein. How many pounds of each does he need to mix to get 100 lb of feed that is 8% protein?

Let a represent the amount of feed A in the mixture.

Let b represent the amount of feed B in the mixture.

Write one equation based on the amount of feed:

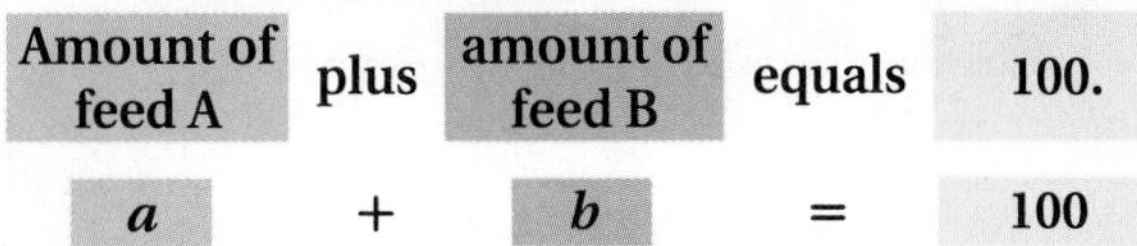

Amount of feed A	plus	amount of feed B	equals	100.
a	$+$	b	$=$	100

Write another equation based on the amount of protein:

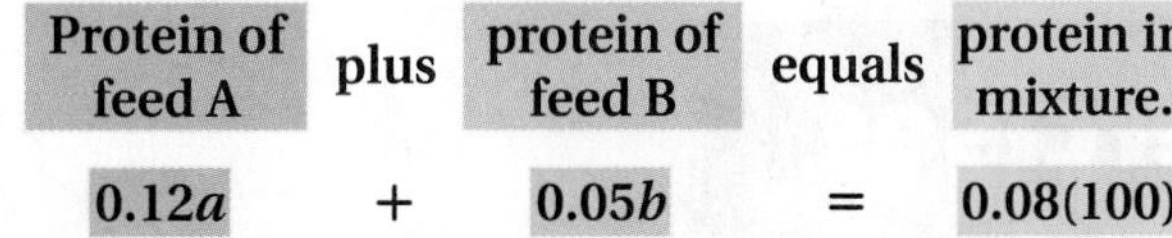

Protein of feed A	plus	protein of feed B	equals	protein in mixture.
$0.12a$	$+$	$0.05b$	$=$	$0.08(100)$

Solve the system. $\begin{cases} a + b = 100 \\ 0.12a + 0.05b = 8 \end{cases}$

$a + b = 100$	*First equation*
$b = 100 - a$	*Solve the first equation for b.*
$0.12a + 0.05(100 - a) = 8$	*Substitute (100 − a) for b.*
$0.12a + 5 - 0.05a = 8$	*Distribute.*
$0.07a = 3$	*Simplify.*
$a \approx 42.9$	*Round to the nearest tenth.*

Substitute a into one of the original equations to solve for b.

$(42.9) + b \approx 100$	*Substitute the value of a into one equation.*
$b \approx 57.1$	*Solve for b.*

The mixture will contain about 42.9 lb of feed A and 57.1 lb of feed B.

4. A coffee blend contains Sumatra beans, which cost \$5/lb, and Kona beans, which cost \$13/lb. If the blend costs \$10/lb, how much of each type of coffee is in 50 lb of the blend?

Student to Student *Solving Systems*

Victor Cisneros
Reagan High School

Choosing a method to solve a system of linear equations can be confusing. Here is how I decide which method to use:

Graphing and tables— *when I'm interested in a rough solution or other values around the solution*

Substitution— *when it's simple to solve one of the equations for one variable (for example, solving 3x + y = 7 for y)*

Elimination— *when variables have opposite coefficients, like 5x and −5x, or when I can easily multiply the equations to get opposite coefficients*

THINK AND DISCUSS

1. Explain which method you would use to solve the system $\begin{cases} 3x + y = 8 \\ 7x - y = 5 \end{cases}$.

2. **GET ORGANIZED** Copy and complete the graphic organizer. In each box, show an example of the given method of solving a linear system.

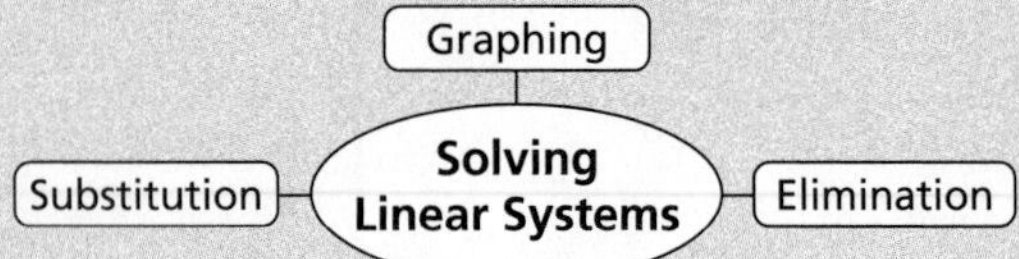

3-2 Exercises

GUIDED PRACTICE

1. **Vocabulary** The __?__ method solves a system of linear equations by adding or subtracting equations. (*substitution* or *elimination*)

SEE EXAMPLE 1 p. 190

Use substitution to solve each system of equations.

2. $\begin{cases} x + y = 17 \\ y = x + 7 \end{cases}$
3. $\begin{cases} y = x - 19 \\ 2x - y = 27 \end{cases}$
4. $\begin{cases} 2x - y = 2 \\ 3x - 2y = 11 \end{cases}$
5. $\begin{cases} y = 3x + 5 \\ x = -3y - 5 \end{cases}$

SEE EXAMPLE 2 p. 191

Use elimination to solve each system of equations.

6. $\begin{cases} 2x + y = 12 \\ -5x - y = -33 \end{cases}$
7. $\begin{cases} 2x - 5y = -5 \\ -2x + 8y = -58 \end{cases}$
8. $\begin{cases} 2x + 6y = -8 \\ 5x - 3y = 88 \end{cases}$
9. $\begin{cases} \frac{1}{2}x + y = 4 \\ -2x - 2y = -6 \end{cases}$

SEE EXAMPLE 3 p. 192

Classify each system and determine the number of solutions.

10. $\begin{cases} 5x - y = -3 \\ 15x - 3y = -9 \end{cases}$
11. $\begin{cases} x - 2y = -8 \\ 4x = 8y - 56 \end{cases}$
12. $\begin{cases} 8x + 12y = 60 \\ 2x + 3y = -24 \end{cases}$
13. $\begin{cases} x - \frac{1}{3}y = -2 \\ 6x - 2y = -12 \end{cases}$

SEE EXAMPLE 4 p. 193

14. **Alternative Fuels** Denise owns a car that runs on a mixture of gasoline and ethanol. She can buy fuels that have 85% ethanol or 25% ethanol. How much of each type of fuel should she buy if she wants to fill her 20 gal tank with a mixture of fuel that contains 50% ethanol?

PRACTICE AND PROBLEM SOLVING

Use substitution to solve each system of equations.

15. $\begin{cases} -4y = x \\ 2x + 6y = -3 \end{cases}$
16. $\begin{cases} 12x + y = 21 \\ 18x - 3y = -36 \end{cases}$
17. $\begin{cases} y = 4x \\ 32x + 21y = 29 \end{cases}$
18. $\begin{cases} y + 1 = x \\ -2x + 3y = 2 \end{cases}$

Use elimination to solve each system of equations.

19. $\begin{cases} 4x - 9y = 26 \\ 4x - 5y = 2 \end{cases}$
20. $\begin{cases} 6x - 3y = -6 \\ -5x + 7y = 41 \end{cases}$
21. $\begin{cases} 12x - 3y = -15 \\ 8x + 8y = -58 \end{cases}$
22. $\begin{cases} 3x + y = 7 \\ -3x + 2y = 11 \end{cases}$

Independent Practice	
For Exercises	See Example
15–18	1
19–22	2
23–26	3
27	4

Extra Practice

Skills Practice p. S8
Application Practice p. S34

Classify each system and determine the number of solutions.

23. $\begin{cases} 4y - x = -24 \\ 3x = 12y + 72 \end{cases}$ **24.** $\begin{cases} 10x - 2y = 22 \\ 5y - 25x = 65 \end{cases}$ **25.** $\begin{cases} 4y - 3x = 32 \\ 8y - 6x = 64 \end{cases}$ **26.** $\begin{cases} -x + \frac{3}{4}y = 4 \\ 8x - 6y = -8 \end{cases}$

27. Business An office is printing 1200 copies of a document using two printers. During the process, printer A gets a paper jam and prints only half as many copies as printer B. Write and solve a system of equations to determine the number of copies each printer will produce.

Use substitution or elimination to solve each system of equations.

28. $\begin{cases} y + 3x = -21 \\ x = 3y + 3 \end{cases}$ **29.** $\begin{cases} y = -2x + 14 \\ 1.5x - 3.5y = 2 \end{cases}$ **30.** $\begin{cases} \frac{4}{5}y - 3x = \frac{1}{5} \\ y - x = 8 \end{cases}$ **31.** $\begin{cases} x + 5y = 5 \\ \frac{1}{5}x + 2y = -2 \end{cases}$

32. Exercise Ahmit gets exercise on the weekend by working around the house. On Saturday, he worked for 3 hours mowing the lawn and raking leaves. He burned 885 Calories.

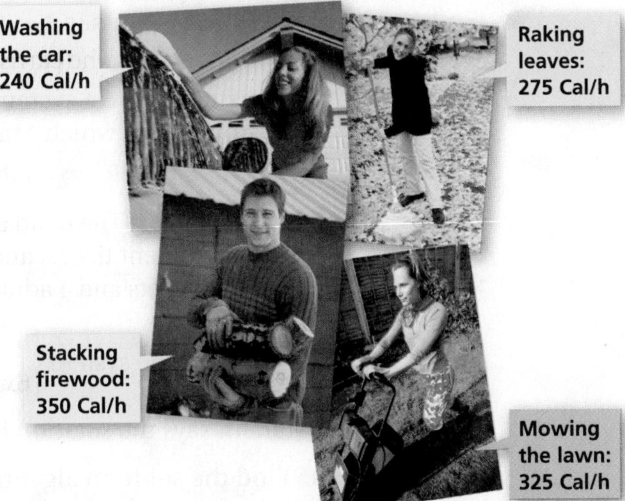

a. Write a system of equations that can be used to describe the amount of time Ahmit worked and the number of Calories he burned by mowing and raking.

b. Determine how much time Ahmit spent on mowing and on raking.

33. Vanessa has collected \$2.10 in dimes and nickels.

a. **Critical Thinking** In how many different ways might Vanessa have combined dimes and nickels to total \$2.10?

b. **Critical Thinking** How does the total number of coins change as the number of dimes decreases? Explain.

c. If Vanessa has exactly 30 coins, how many of each type of coin does she have?

34. ///ERROR ANALYSIS/// Two students attempted to solve the system of equations $\begin{cases} 2x + 4y = 38 \\ 2x - 2y = -4 \end{cases}$ and found different answers. Which solution is incorrect? Explain the error.

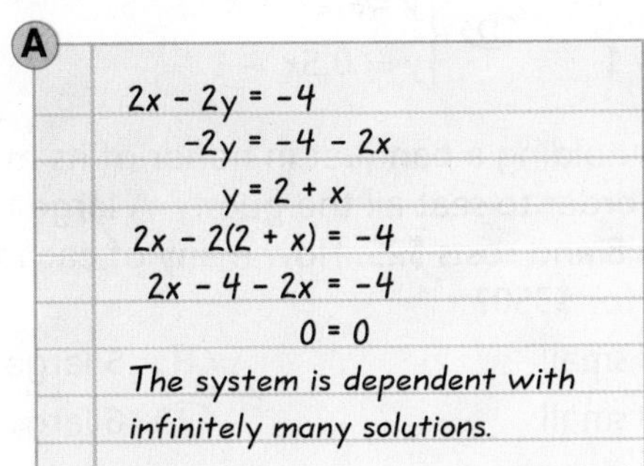
A

$2x - 2y = -4$
$-2y = -4 - 2x$
$y = 2 + x$
$2x - 2(2 + x) = -4$
$2x - 4 - 2x = -4$
$0 = 0$
The system is dependent with infinitely many solutions.

B

$2x - 2y = -4$
$-2y = -4 - 2x$
$y = 2 + x$
$2x + 4(2 + x) = 38$
$2x + 8 + 4x = 38$ $y = 2 + x$
$6x = 30$ $y = 2 + 5$
$x = 5$ $y = 7$
The solution is (5, 7).

35. This problem will prepare you for the Multi-Step Test Prep on page 212.

A car race is made up of 500 laps around a 0.533-mile track.

a. How many miles long is the race?

b. The course record for one lap is 14.94 seconds. Write an equation that could be used to model the distance in miles traveled by the record-setting car if it continues at the same pace.

c. If a second car travels at 125 miles per hour, use your answer to part **b** to determine the distance between the two cars when the lead car finishes the race.

36. Multi-Step Malcolm and Owen work for a bottled water distributor. Malcolm makes \$300 per week plus \$45 for each new customer who signs a contract. Owen has more sales experience, so he earns \$325 per week plus \$60 for each new customer.

a. Write and solve a system of equations to determine the number of new customers for which Malcolm and Owen will have the same income.

b. Critical Thinking Is the solution reasonable? Explain.

37. Entertainment The band and the orchestra are attending a concert. The band bought 16 student tickets and 3 adult tickets for \$110.50. The orchestra bought 12 student tickets and 4 adult tickets for \$96. Find the cost of each type of ticket.

38. The graph of the system $\begin{cases} 3x - 6y = -13 \\ 6x + 3y = 24 \end{cases}$ is shown.

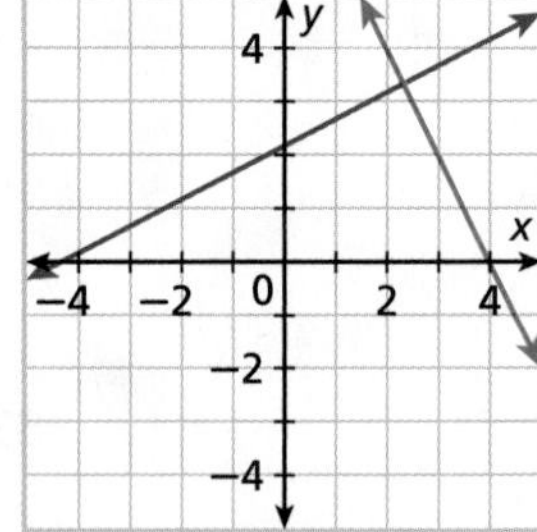

A student says the solution is $\left(2\frac{1}{2}, 3\frac{1}{2}\right)$.

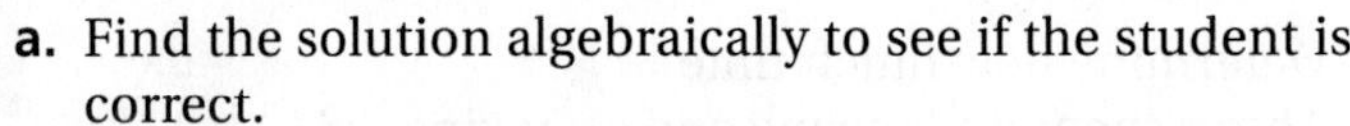

a. Find the solution algebraically to see if the student is correct.

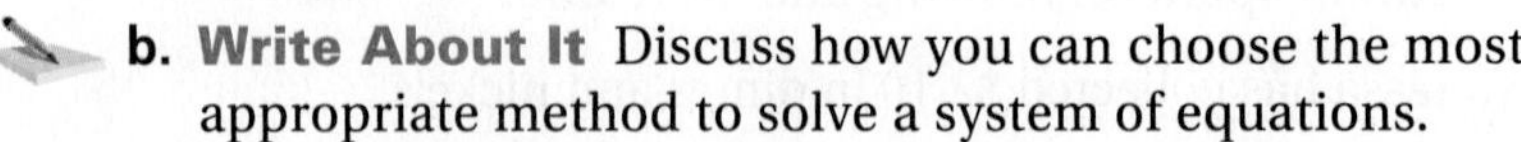

b. Write About It Discuss how you can choose the most appropriate method to solve a system of equations.

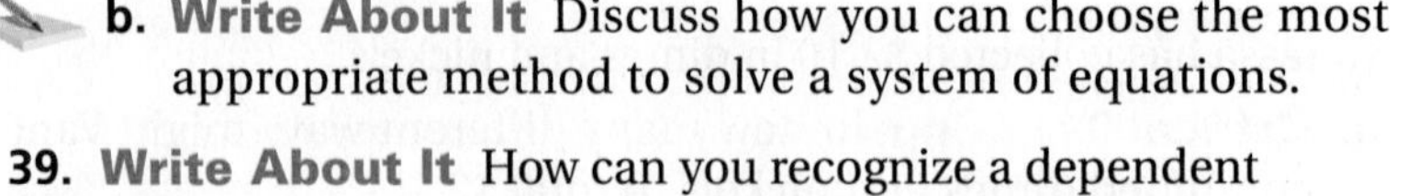

39. Write About It How can you recognize a dependent system of equations by analyzing the equations?

TEST PREP

40. Which of the following systems of equations represents the graph at right?

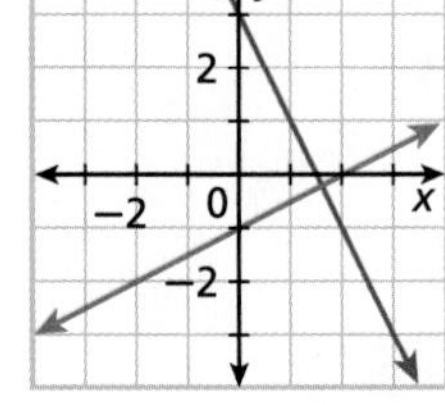

Ⓐ $\begin{cases} y = 2x + 3 \\ y = 0.5x - 1 \end{cases}$

Ⓑ $\begin{cases} y = 2x + 3 \\ y = -0.5x - 1 \end{cases}$

Ⓒ $\begin{cases} y = -2x + 3 \\ y = -0.5x - 1 \end{cases}$

Ⓓ $\begin{cases} y = -2x + 3 \\ y = 0.5x - 1 \end{cases}$

41. An organization is holding a banquet in honor of its member of the year. Tables must be rented in order to seat all the guests. A large table seats 12 and costs \$50. A small table seats 8 and costs \$25. How many of each type of table must be rented to seat 100 guests for \$350?

Ⓕ 8 large and 3 small

Ⓖ 3 large and 8 small

Ⓗ 5 large and 5 small

Ⓙ 6 large and 2 small

42. Solve the system. $\begin{cases} x + y = 7 \\ x - y = -3 \end{cases}$

Ⓐ (2, 5) Ⓑ (5, 2) Ⓒ (−2, 5) Ⓓ (−5, 2)

43. **Short Response** What is the solution to the system of equations $\begin{cases} x - 4y = 6 \\ y = -4x + 7 \end{cases}$? Classify the system.

44. Two cyclists are competing in a 10 mi time trial. The older cyclist, who rides at a speed of 22 mi/h, is given a 1 mi head start. The younger cyclist rides at a speed of 25 mi/h. Let x represent time in hours and let y represent distance in miles. Which of the following systems of equations represents the situation?

Ⓕ $\begin{cases} y = 25 \\ y = 22 + 1 \end{cases}$ Ⓖ $\begin{cases} y = 25x + 1 \\ y = 22x \end{cases}$ Ⓗ $\begin{cases} y = 25x \\ y = 22x + 1 \end{cases}$ Ⓙ $\begin{cases} y = 25x \\ y = 22 + x \end{cases}$

CHALLENGE AND EXTEND

45. One equation in a linear system is $x + 2y = 4$. Write another equation so that the system has the unique solution $(-2, 3)$.

46. The following system has a solution. Find the solution and explain your method. How do you know you are correct?

$$\begin{cases} y - x = 4 \\ y - 1 = -2x \\ y + x - 2 = 0 \end{cases}$$

47. **Economics** A software company is considering the release of a new product. The research department has modeled the current market with a set of equations in terms of price p and quantity q.

Supply: $p = 5 + 2q$ **Demand:** $q = 100 - 4p$

a. The equilibrium price and quantity occur when supply meets demand. Find the equilibrium price and quantity for the current market.

b. **What if...?** After the release of the new product, the supply function changes to $p = 3 + 0.5q$. How will the equilibrium price and quantity change?

SPIRAL REVIEW

Simplify each expression. Then evaluate the expression for the given value of the variable. *(Lesson 1-4)*

48. $-b^2(2b + 4) + b^5,\ b = -1$

49. $3c^2 + 1 + (5c)^2,\ c = 3$

50. $\dfrac{20 - 2x^2}{x},\ x = -2$

51. $y^{-3}\left(\dfrac{2y}{9}\right),\ y = -3$

Write the equation of the line in slope-intercept form that includes the points in the table. *(Lesson 2-4)*

52.

x	2	6	10	14	20	26
f(x)	2	4	6	8	11	14

53.

x	1	2	3	4	5	6
f(x)	−2	−3.5	−5	−6.5	−8	−9.5

Graph each inequality. *(Lesson 2-5)*

54. $y > -5$

55. $3x - y \leq 2(x - 2)$

56. $5x + 4y > 18$

Properties of Polygons

A *polygon* is a closed plane figure formed by three or more line segments. Polygons are classified by the properties of their sides and angles.

Polygons can be named by the number of sides they have.

Two angles with the same measure or segments with the same length are *congruent*. If all the sides and angles of a polygon are congruent, the polygon is *regular*. The first four regular polygons are shown.

Number of Sides	3	4	5	6
Name	Triangle	Quadrilateral	Pentagon	Hexagon
	△	◇	⬠	⬡

Here are some other ways of classifying polygons.

Classifying Triangles	
By Angles	
Acute	Three acute angles (greater than 0° and less than 90°)
Obtuse	One obtuse angle (greater than 90° and less than 180°)
Right	One right angle (90°)
By Sides	
Scalene	No congruent sides
Isosceles	At least two congruent sides
Equilateral	Three congruent sides

Classifying Quadrilaterals	
Types of Quadrilaterals	
Parallelogram	Two pairs of opposite parallel and congruent sides
Trapezoid	Exactly one pair of opposite parallel sides
Types of Parallelograms	
Rectangle	Four right angles
Square	Four congruent sides, 4 right angles
Rhombus	Four congruent sides

Example

Identify each polygon.

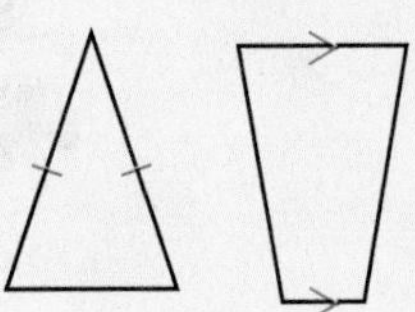

Start by counting the number of sides. Then look at the types of angles and pairs of parallel sides. Compare angles to the corner of a square: acute angles measure less than 90°; obtuse angles measure greater than 90°.

a. Two sides of the triangle are congruent, so it is isosceles.

b. This quadrilateral has one pair of parallel sides. It is a trapezoid.

Try This

Identify each polygon.

1. 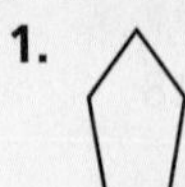

2. 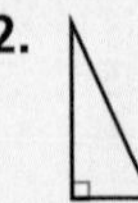

3. 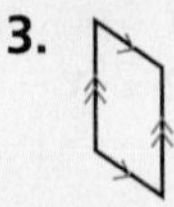

4. 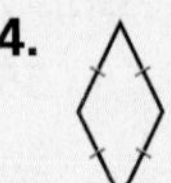

5. 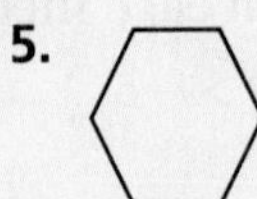

6. 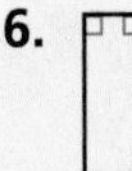

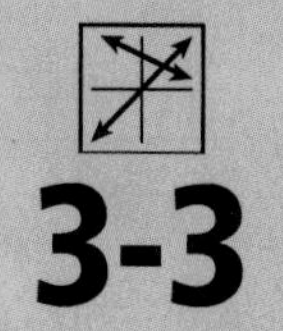

3-3 Solving Systems of Linear Inequalities

Objective
Solve systems of linear inequalities.

Vocabulary
system of linear inequalities

Who uses this?
Explorers can use systems of inequalities to determine the rates at which they must travel to avoid bad weather. (See Example 2.)

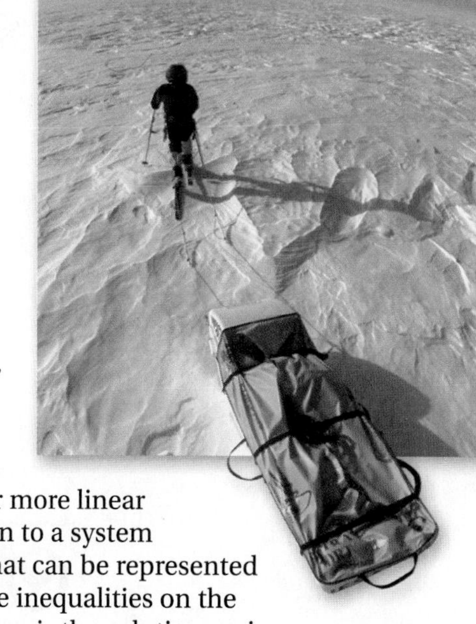

When a problem uses phrases like "greater than" or "no more than," you can model the situation using a system of linear inequalities.

A **system of linear inequalities** is a set of two or more linear inequalities with the same variables. The solution to a system of inequalities is often an infinite set of points that can be represented graphically by shading. When you graph multiple inequalities on the same graph, the region where the shadings overlap is the solution region.

EXAMPLE 1 Graphing Systems of Inequalities

Graph each system of inequalities.

A $\begin{cases} y \le -2x + 4 \\ y > x - 3 \end{cases}$

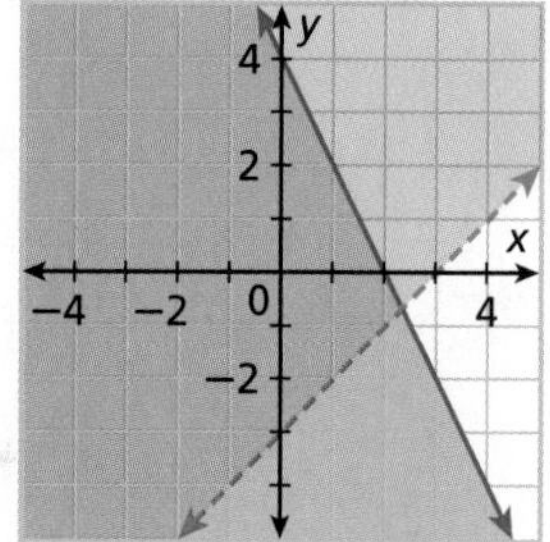

For $y \le -2x + 4$, graph the solid boundary line $y = -2x + 4$, and shade below it. For $y > x - 3$, graph the dashed boundary line $y = x - 3$, and shade above it.

The overlapping region is the solution region.

Helpful Hint
If you are unsure which direction to shade, use the origin as a test point.

Check Test a point from each region on the graph.

Region	Point	$y \le -2x + 4$	$y > x - 3$
Left	(0, 0)	$0 \overset{?}{\le} -2(0) + 4$ $0 \overset{?}{\le} 4$ ✔	$0 \overset{?}{>} 0 - 3$ $0 \overset{?}{>} -3$ ✔
Right	(4, 0)	$0 \overset{?}{\le} -2(4) + 4$ $0 \overset{?}{\le} -4$ ✘	$0 \overset{?}{>} 4 - 3$ $0 \overset{?}{>} 1$ ✘
Top	(2, 2)	$2 \overset{?}{\le} -2(2) + 4$ $2 \overset{?}{\le} 0$ ✘	$2 \overset{?}{>} 2 - 3$ $2 \overset{?}{>} -1$ ✔
Bottom	(2, −2)	$-2 \overset{?}{\le} -2(2) + 4$ $-2 \overset{?}{\le} 0$ ✔	$-2 \overset{?}{>} 2 - 3$ $-2 \overset{?}{>} -1$ ✘

Only the point from the overlapping (left) region satisfies both inequalities.

Graph each system of inequalities.

B $\begin{cases} y \geq \frac{3}{2}x + 2 \\ x < 3 \end{cases}$

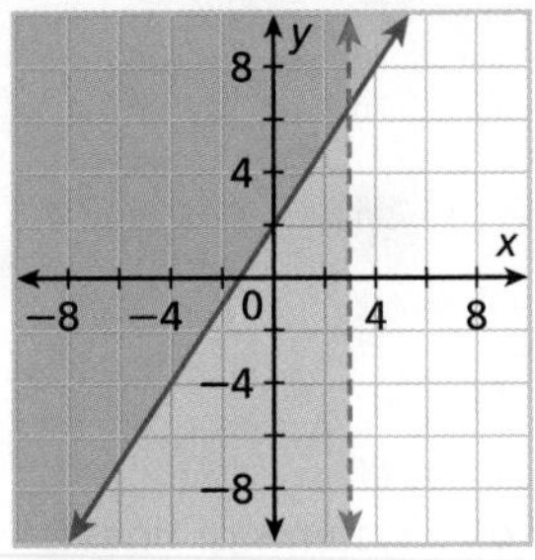

For $y \geq \frac{3}{2}x + 2$, graph the solid boundary line $y = \frac{3}{2}x + 2$, and shade above it. For $x < 3$, graph the dashed boundary line $x = 3$, and shade to the left. The overlapping region is the solution region.

Check Choose a point in the solution region, such as $(-4, 0)$, and test it in both inequalities.

$y \geq \frac{3}{2}x + 2$ | $x < 3$

$0 \geq \frac{3}{2}(-4) + 2$ | $-4 < 3$ ✔

$0 \geq -4$ ✔

The test point satisfies both inequalities, and suggests that the solution region is correct.

Graph each system of inequalities.

1a. $\begin{cases} x - 3y < 6 \\ 2x + y > 1.5 \end{cases}$

1b. $\begin{cases} y \leq 4 \\ 2x + y < 1 \end{cases}$

EXAMPLE 2 *Expedition Application*

A polar expedition is 240 miles away from base camp, and a snowstorm is predicted to reach the area in 48 hours. The expedition will travel as far as possible by boat and then walk the remaining distance to camp before the storm hits. The explorers can navigate the boat through the ice at a rate of 12 miles per hour or walk with the equipment at a rate of 3 miles per hour. Write and graph a system of inequalities that can be used to determine how long the explorers may travel by foot or by boat to reach base camp before the storm.

Let x represent the number of hours traveled on foot, and let y represent the number of hours traveled by boat.

The total number of hours can be modeled by the inequality $x + y \leq 48$. The number of miles covered by the explorers can be modeled by $3x + 12y \geq 240$.

The system of inequalities is $\begin{cases} x + y \leq 48 \\ 3x + 12y \geq 240 \end{cases}$.

Graph the solid boundary line $x + y = 48$, and shade below it. Graph the solid boundary line $3x + 12y = 240$, and shade above it. The overlapping region is the solution region.

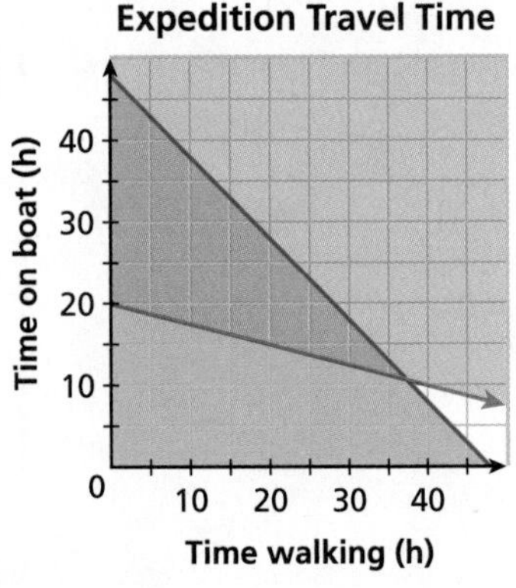

Check Test the point $(15, 25)$ in both inequalities. This point represents traveling 15 hours by foot and 25 hours by boat.

$x + y \leq 48$ | $3x + 12y \geq 240$

$(15) + (25) \leq 48$ | $3(15) + 12(25) \geq 240$

$40 \leq 48$ ✔ | $345 \geq 240$ ✔

2. Leyla is selling hot dogs and spicy sausages at the fair. She has only 40 buns, so she can sell no more than a total of 40 hot dogs and spicy sausages. Each hot dog sells for $2, and each sausage sells for $2.50. Leyla needs at least $90 in sales to meet her goal. Write and graph a system of inequalities that models this situation.

Systems of inequalities may contain more than two inequalities.

EXAMPLE 3 Geometry Application

Geometry

Graph the system of inequalities, and classify the figure created by the solution region.

$$\begin{cases} y \leq 5 \\ y \geq 2 \\ y \leq 3x + 1 \\ y \geq 3x - 4 \end{cases}$$

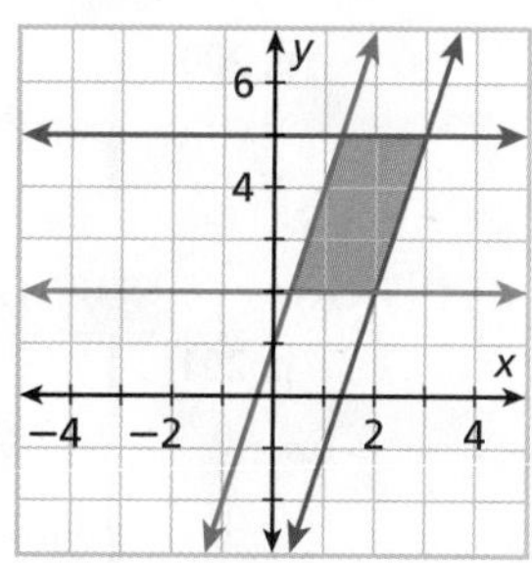

Graph the solid boundary lines $y = 5$ and $y = 3x + 1$, and shade below them. Graph the solid boundary lines $y = 2$ and $y = 3x - 4$, and shade above them. The overlapping region is the solution region.

The solution region is a four-sided figure, or quadrilateral. Notice that the boundary lines $y = 5$ and $y = 2$ are parallel, horizontal lines. The boundary lines $y = 3x + 1$ and $y = 3x - 4$ have the same slope and are also parallel. A quadrilateral with two sets of parallel sides is a parallelogram. The solution region is a parallelogram.

Remember!

Parallel lines have the same slope.

Graph the system of inequalities, and classify the figure created by the solution region.

3a. $\begin{cases} x \leq 6 \\ y \leq \frac{1}{2}x + 1 \\ y \geq -2x + 4 \end{cases}$

3b. $\begin{cases} y \leq 4 \\ y \geq -1 \\ y \leq -x + 8 \\ y \leq 2x + 2 \end{cases}$

THINK AND DISCUSS

1. Explain how you know which region of the graph of a system of linear inequalities contains the solutions.
2. Find the minimum number of inequalities necessary for a triangular solution region and for a square solution region. Give examples that support your answer.
3. **GET ORGANIZED** Copy and complete the graphic organizer. For each region, write the system of inequalities whose solution it represents.

Know it! Note

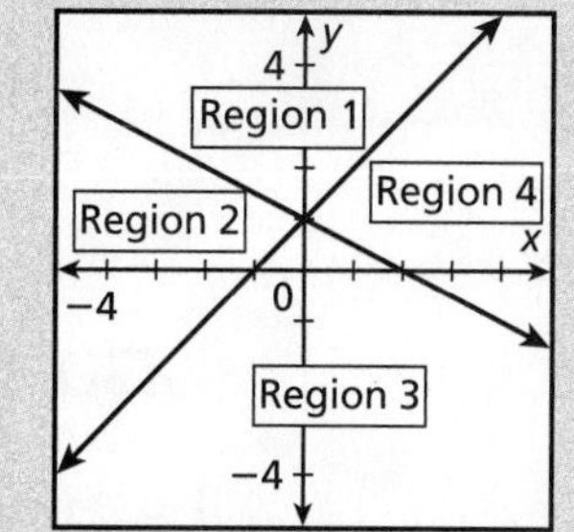

3-3 Exercises

go.hrw.com
Homework Help Online
KEYWORD: MB7 3-3
Parent Resources Online
KEYWORD: MB7 Parent

GUIDED PRACTICE

1. **Vocabulary** Compare a *system of linear inequalities* with a system of linear equations.

SEE EXAMPLE 1 p. 199

Graph each system of inequalities.

2. $\begin{cases} y \geq 4x - 4 \\ y \geq 3x - 3 \end{cases}$
3. $\begin{cases} x + y > 5 \\ x - y < -3 \end{cases}$
4. $\begin{cases} 7x < y - 16 \\ y \leq -5x - 2 \end{cases}$
5. $\begin{cases} 2x + 2y \leq 4 \\ 3x - y > 1 \end{cases}$

SEE EXAMPLE 2 p. 200

6. **Fund-raising** A charity is selling T-shirts in order to raise money. The cost of a T-shirt is \$15 for adults and \$10 for students. The charity needs to raise at least \$3000 and has only 250 T-shirts. Write and graph a system of inequalities that can be used to determine the number of adult and student T-shirts the charity must sell.

SEE EXAMPLE 3 p. 201

Graph the system of inequalities and classify the figure created by the solution region.

7. $\begin{cases} x \geq 9 \\ y \geq -18 \\ x \leq 13 \\ y \leq -4 \end{cases}$
8. $\begin{cases} y \leq 7 \\ 2x - y \leq 3 \\ x + 2y \geq -6 \end{cases}$
9. $\begin{cases} x \leq -1 \\ y \leq 3x + 2 \\ y \geq -3x - 10 \end{cases}$
10. $\begin{cases} y \geq x \\ y \leq x + 6 \\ x \leq 6 \\ x \geq -2 \end{cases}$

PRACTICE AND PROBLEM SOLVING

Independent Practice

For Exercises	See Example
11–14	1
15	2
16–19	3

Extra Practice

Skills Practice p. S8
Application Practice p. S34

Graph each system of inequalities.

11. $\begin{cases} 5x - y > 0 \\ y < x \end{cases}$
12. $\begin{cases} 3y \geq 2x - 3 \\ y \geq 3x + 8 \end{cases}$
13. $\begin{cases} x + y > 5 \\ -2x + y \leq 2 \end{cases}$
14. $\begin{cases} y > 4 \\ x + 4y \geq 8 \end{cases}$

15. **Music** A musician is releasing a new CD. The record company will manufacture the basic CD plus a special promotional version to distribute to radio stations. No more than 10,000 CDs will be made, and the number of promotional CDs will be at most 20% of the number of basic CDs. Write and graph a system of inequalities that describes the possible number of each type of CD.

Graph the system of inequalities and classify the figure created by the solution region.

16. $\begin{cases} x \geq 0 \\ -\frac{1}{3}x + y \geq -4 \\ \frac{1}{3}x + y \leq -1 \end{cases}$
17. $\begin{cases} y \leq 2.5 \\ y \geq -0.5 \\ y \leq -x + 8 \\ y \leq 2x + 4 \end{cases}$
18. $\begin{cases} y \leq x + 6 \\ y \geq x + 1 \\ y \leq -x + 6 \\ y \geq -x - 1 \end{cases}$
19. $\begin{cases} y \leq x \\ y \leq -x + 2 \\ y \geq 0 \end{cases}$

20. **Sports** In 2003, LaDainian Tomlinson led the National Football League in yards from scrimmage, a combination of rushing yards and receiving yards. He had a total of 2370 yards from scrimmage, including 1645 rushing yards. The runner-up, Jamal Lewis, had fewer yards from scrimmage but more rushing yards. Write and graph a system of inequalities that models the possible rushing and receiving yardage for Jamal Lewis.

Geometry Write a system of linear inequalities whose solution region forms the given shape.

21. a rectangle
22. a square
23. a right triangle
24. a trapezoid

25. This problem will prepare you for the Multi-Step Test Prep on page 212.

Most race cars are subject to various size and weight restrictions, depending on their classification. Champ cars must weigh a minimum of 1565 pounds without the driver. Formula One cars must weigh at least 1322.77 pounds with the driver.

a. Write a system of linear inequalities that could be used to compare the possible weights of Champ cars and Formula One cars without drivers.
b. Identify a reasonable domain and range for the system.
c. Graph the system.

26. **Multi-Step** Frostbite is a dangerous condition where skin freezes because of exposure to cold temperatures and wind. People can develop frostbite in 10 to 30 minutes under conditions modeled by the system $\begin{cases} w \geq 2.4t + 23 \\ w \leq 1.4t + 43 \end{cases}$, where t represents temperature (°F) and w represents wind speed (mi/h).

a. Identify a reasonable domain and range for the system.
b. Graph the solution region for the system of inequalities.
c. If the temperature is 15°F and the wind speed is 55 mi/h, can a person develop frostbite in 10 to 30 minutes? Explain.

27. **Income Tax** Brian and Maria are married and file their taxes jointly. Currently, they have a combined income within the 25% tax bracket, and Maria earns at least $2000 more per year than Brian. Use the data in the table to write and graph a system of inequalities that models their possible incomes.

2003 Tax Rate Schedule (Married Filing Jointly)

Income	Tax Rate
$14,000 to $56,800	15%
$56,801 to $114,650	25%
$114,651 to $174,700	28%

Graph the solution region for the system of inequalities shown. Then identify three points in the solution region.

28. $\begin{cases} -5y < 2x \\ 5y \geq 2x - 20 \end{cases}$

29. $\begin{cases} y + 7 > 0 \\ y < 2x + 5 \\ y < -3x + 4 \end{cases}$

30. $\begin{cases} y \geq -8 \\ x + 2y < 4 \\ x > -6 \end{cases}$

31. $\begin{cases} \frac{1}{2}x + 3y \leq 2 \\ x - y > 3 \end{cases}$

32. **Critical Thinking** If the boundary lines in a system of inequalities are parallel, what are the possible solution regions?

33. **Write About It** Is it possible for a system of two inequalities to have no solution? Explain.

34. Which of the following systems of inequalities describes the graph shown?

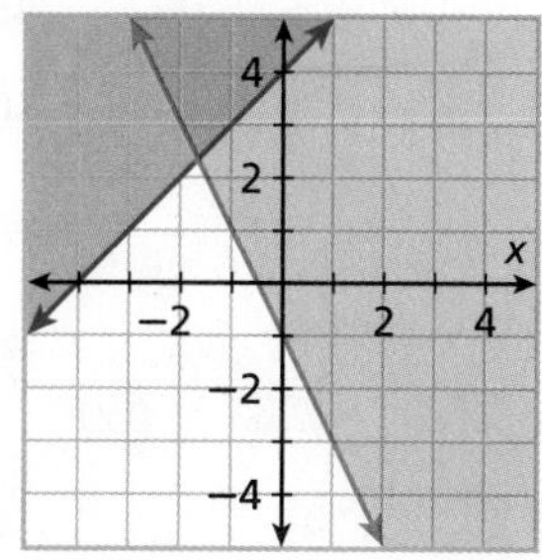

Ⓐ $\begin{cases} y > x + 4 \\ y < -2x - 1 \end{cases}$

Ⓒ $\begin{cases} y \leq x + 4 \\ y \geq -2x - 1 \end{cases}$

Ⓑ $\begin{cases} y > x + 4 \\ y > -2x - 1 \end{cases}$

Ⓓ $\begin{cases} y \geq x + 4 \\ y \geq -2x - 1 \end{cases}$

35. A manufacturing company produces gizmos. It costs at least $300 plus $1.25 per gizmo to produce the items. Each gizmo sells for $2.50 at most. Which of the following systems of inequalities, where *c* is the cost and *n* is the number of gizmos produced or sold, has a solution region that can be used to represent the company's possible profit?

(F) $\begin{cases} c \leq 2.5n \\ c \leq 300 + 1.25n \end{cases}$

(H) $\begin{cases} c \geq 2.5n \\ c \leq 300 + 1.25n \end{cases}$

(G) $\begin{cases} c \leq 2.5n \\ c \geq 300 + 1.25n \end{cases}$

(J) $\begin{cases} c \geq 2.5n \\ c \geq 300 + 1.25n \end{cases}$

36. Which of the tables below contains possible solutions to the following system of inequalities? $\begin{cases} 3x - 12y > 8 \\ x + 5y > -5 \end{cases}$

(A)

x	y
1	−2
2	0
3	0
4	−2

(B)

x	y
1	−2
2	1
3	1
4	−2

(C)

x	y
1	−1
2	−1
3	0
4	0

(D)

x	y
1	−2
2	−2
3	−1
4	−1

CHALLENGE AND EXTEND

37. Write a system of linear inequalities whose solution region is a pentagon.

38. In the following system of inequalities, is there a value of *m* that will cause the system to have no solution? If so, find the value. If not, explain. $\begin{cases} y > -3x + 2 \\ y < mx - 3 \end{cases}$

39. Kira is investing $30,000 divided between two separate simple interest accounts. One pays 5% and has very low risk, and the other pays 7% and has slightly higher risk. What is the least she can invest in the riskier account and still earn at least $1900 after one year?

SPIRAL REVIEW

Find the additive and multiplicative inverse for each number. *(Lesson 1-2)*

40. 7
41. $-\frac{3}{4}$
42. 2.48
43. −1

Write the equation of each line. *(Lesson 2-4)*

44. through $(2, -7)$ and $(1, 1)$
45. with slope 0 through $(3, -3)$
46. through $(1, -1)$ and $(0, 0)$
47. with slope $-\frac{1}{3}$ through $(9, 6)$
48. perpendicular to $y = 4x - 1$ and through $(-2, 4.5)$
49. parallel to $y = -x - 7$ and through $(3, 2)$

50. The youth baseball league charted the number of players and coaches in each age bracket. Find the correlation coefficient to the nearest thousandth and the equation of the line of best fit. *(Lesson 2-7)*

Players	32	18	55	37	50	86
Coaches	3	2	6	5	6	10

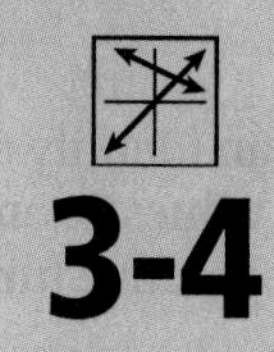

3-4 Linear Programming

Objective
Solve linear programming problems.

Vocabulary
linear programming
constraint
feasible region
objective function

Who uses this?
Landscape architects can use linear programming to determine which plants to plant on a green roof.

Green roofs are roofs covered with plants instead of traditional materials like concrete or shingles to help lower heat and improve air quality.

The plants landscape architects choose might depend on the price, the amount of water they require, and the amount of carbon dioxide they absorb.

Linear programming is a method of finding a maximum or minimum value of a function that satisfies a given set of conditions called *constraints*. A **constraint** is one of the inequalities in a linear programming problem. The solution to the set of constraints can be graphed as a **feasible region**.

EXAMPLE 1 Graphing a Feasible Region

Gillian is planning a green roof that will cover up to 600 square feet. She will use two types of plants: blue lagoon sedum and raspberry red sedum. Each blue lagoon sedum will cover 1.2 square feet. Each raspberry red sedum will cover 2 square feet. Each plant costs \$2.50, and Gillian must spend less than \$1000. Write the constraints, and graph the feasible region.

Let $b =$ the number of blue lagoon sedums, and
$r =$ the number of raspberry red sedums.

Write the constraints:

$$\begin{cases} b \geq 0 \\ r \geq 0 \\ 1.2b + 2r \leq 600 \\ 2.50b + 2.50r \leq 1000 \end{cases}$$

The number of plants cannot be negative.
The combined area is less than or equal to 600 ft².
The combined cost is less than or equal to \$1000.

Graph the feasible region. The feasible region is a quadrilateral with vertices at $(0, 0)$, $(400, 0)$, $(250, 150)$, and $(0, 300)$.

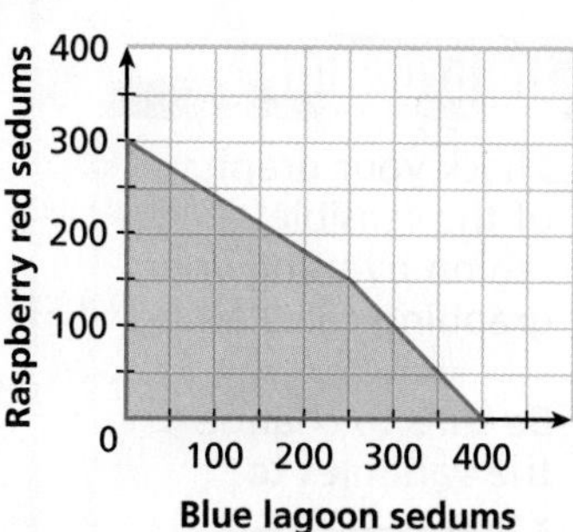

Check A point in the feasible region, such as $(100, 100)$, satisfies all of the constraints. ✔

1. Graph the feasible region for the following constraints.

$$\begin{cases} x \geq 0 \\ y \geq 1.5 \\ 2.5x + 5y \leq 20 \\ 3x + 2y \leq 12 \end{cases}$$

In most linear programming problems, you want to do more than identify the feasible region. Often you want to find the best combination of values in order to minimize or maximize a certain function. This function is the **objective function**.

The objective function may have a minimum, a maximum, neither, or both depending on the feasible region.

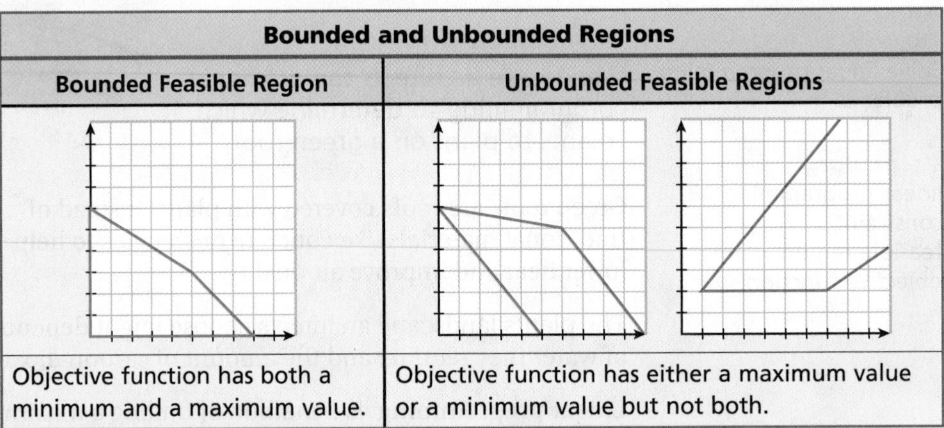

Bounded and Unbounded Regions	
Bounded Feasible Region	**Unbounded Feasible Regions**
Objective function has both a minimum and a maximum value.	Objective function has either a maximum value or a minimum value but not both.

More advanced mathematics can prove that the maximum or minimum value of the objective function will always occur at a vertex of the feasible region.

The Vertex Principle of Linear Programming

If an objective function has a maximum or minimum value, it must occur at one or more of the vertices of the feasible region.

EXAMPLE 2 **Solving Linear Programming Problems**

One of Gillian's priorities for the green roof is to help control air pollution. To do this, she wants to maximize the amount of carbon dioxide the plants on the roof absorb. Use the carbon dioxide absorption rates and the data from Example 1 to find the number of each plant Gillian should plant.

Blue Lagoon Sedum
1.4 lb of CO_2 per year

Raspberry Red Sedum
2.1 lb of CO_2 per year

Helpful Hint

Check your graph of the feasible region by using your graphing calculator.

Be sure to change the variables to *x* and *y*.

Step 1 Let $C =$ the number of pounds of carbon dioxide absorbed.

Write the objective function:
$C = 1.4b + 2.1r$

Step 2 Recall the constraints and the graph from Example 1.

$$\begin{cases} b \geq 0 \\ r \geq 0 \\ 1.2b + 2r \leq 600 \\ 2.50b + 2.50r \leq 1000 \end{cases}$$

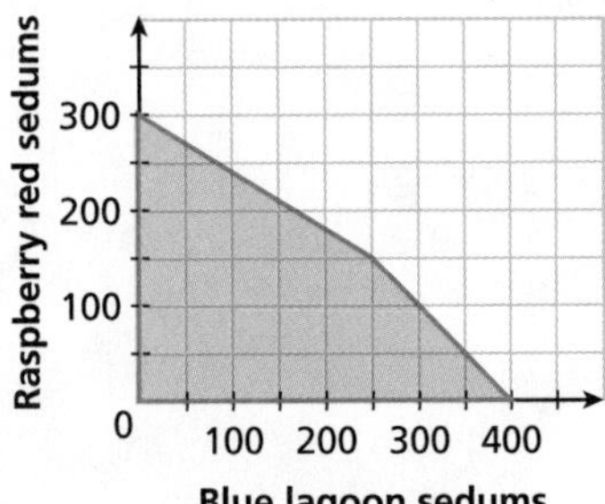

Step 3 Evaluate the objective function at the vertices of the feasible region.

(b, r)	1.4b + 2.1r	C(lb)
(0, 0)	1.4(0) + 2.1(0)	0
(0, 300)	1.4(0) + 2.1(300)	630
(250, 150)	1.4(250) + 2.1(150)	665
(400, 0)	1.4(400) + 2.1(0)	560

The maximum value occurs at the vertex (250, 150).

Gillian should plant 250 blue lagoon sedums and 150 raspberry red sedums to maximize the amount of carbon dioxide absorbed.

2. Maximize the objective function $P = 25x + 30y$ under the following constraints. $\begin{cases} x \geq 0 \\ y \geq 1.5 \\ 2.5x + 5y \leq 20 \\ 3x + 2y \leq 12 \end{cases}$

EXAMPLE 3 *Problem-Solving Application*

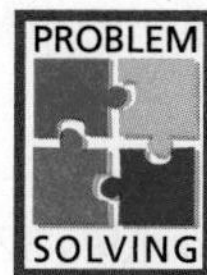

Brad is an organizer of the Bolder Boulder 10K race and must hire workers for one day to prepare the race packets. Skilled workers cost \$60 a day, and students cost \$40 a day. Brad can spend no more than \$1440. He needs at least 1 skilled worker for every 3 students, but only 16 skilled workers are available. Skilled workers can prepare 25 packets per hour, and students can prepare 18 packets per hour. Find the number of each type of worker that Brad should hire to maximize the number of packets produced.

1 Understand the Problem

The **answer** will have two parts—the number of skilled workers and the number of students that will be hired.

List the important information:

- Skilled workers cost \$60 per day. Students cost \$40 per day.
- Brad can spend no more than \$1440.
- Skilled workers can prepare 25 packets per hour. Students can prepare 18 packets per hour.
- Brad needs at least 1 skilled worker for every 3 students.
- Only 16 skilled workers are available.

2 Make a Plan

Let x = the number of students and y = the number of skilled workers. Write the constraints and objective function based on the important information.

$$\begin{cases} x \geq 0 \\ y \geq 0 \\ 40x + 60y \leq 1440 \\ y \geq \frac{1}{3}x \\ y \leq 16 \end{cases}$$

The number of workers cannot be negative.

Cost of labor must be no more than \$1440.

At least 1 skilled worker for every 3 students

Only 16 experienced workers are available.

Let P represent the number of packets prepared each hour. The objective function is $P = 18x + 25y$.

Solve

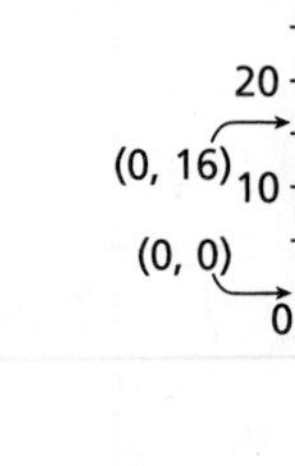

Graph the feasible region, and identify the vertices. Evaluate the objective function at each vertex.

$$P(0, 0) = 18(0) + 25(0) = 0$$
$$P(0, 16) = 18(0) + 25(16) = 400$$
$$P(12, 16) = 18(12) + 25(16) = 616$$
$$P(24, 8) = 18(24) + 25(8) = 632$$

The objective function is maximized at $(24, 8)$, so Brad should hire 24 students and 8 skilled workers.

Look Back

Check the values $(24, 8)$ in the constraints.

$x \geq 0$	$y \geq 0$	$y \leq 16$
$24 \geq 0$ ✔	$8 \geq 0$ ✔	$8 \leq 16$ ✔
	$y \geq \frac{1}{3}x$	$40x + 60y \leq 1440$
	$8 \geq \frac{1}{3}(24)$	$40(24) + 60(8) \leq 1440$
	$8 \geq 8$ ✔	$1440 \leq 1440$ ✔

3. A book store manager is purchasing new bookcases. The store needs 320 feet of shelf space. Bookcase A provides 32 ft of shelf space and costs \$200. Bookcase B provides 16 ft of shelf space and costs \$125. Because of space restrictions, the store has room for at most 8 of bookcase A and 12 of bookcase B. How many of each type of bookcase should the manager purchase to minimize the cost?

THINK AND DISCUSS

1. Explain why linear programming problems often have $x \geq 0$ and $y \geq 0$ as constraints.

2. Explain why an objective function based on the constraints $\begin{cases} x + y > 0 \\ y \leq 4 \end{cases}$ will have a maximum or a minimum, but not both.

3. How can you tell whether a piece of information relates to the constraints or to the objective function?

4. GET ORGANIZED Copy and complete the graphic organizer. In each box, write an example of the given characteristic, using data from Examples 1 and 2.

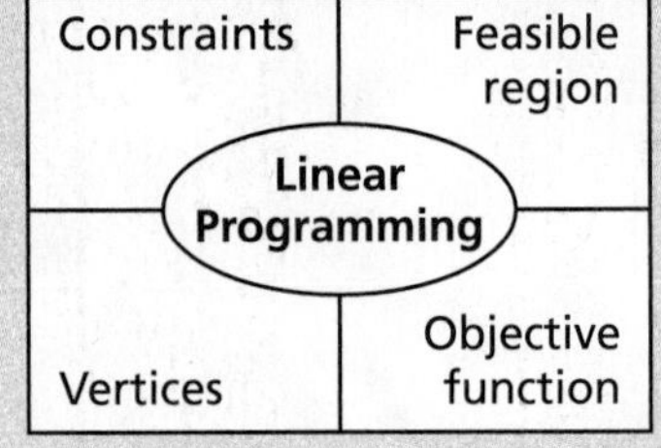

3-4 Exercises

go.hrw.com
Homework Help Online
KEYWORD: MB7 3-4
Parent Resources Online
KEYWORD: MB7 Parent

GUIDED PRACTICE

1. **Vocabulary** The inequalities in a linear programming problem are called ___?___. (*constraints* or *objective functions*)

SEE EXAMPLE 1 p. 205

Graph each feasible region.

2. $\begin{cases} x \geq 0 \\ y \geq 0 \\ y \leq 3x + 3 \\ y \leq -x + 7 \end{cases}$

3. $\begin{cases} x \geq 0 \\ y \geq -1 \\ y \leq x + 1 \\ y \leq -\frac{1}{4}x + 6 \end{cases}$

4. $\begin{cases} x \geq -2 \\ y \leq 1 \\ y \geq 0.5x - 2 \\ y \leq -2x + 3 \end{cases}$

SEE EXAMPLE 2 p. 206

Maximize or minimize each objective function.

5. Maximize $P = 10x + 16y$ for the constraints from Exercise 2.
6. Minimize $P = 3x + 5y$ for the constraints from Exercise 3.
7. Maximize $P = 2.4x + 1.5y$ for the constraints from Exercise 4.

SEE EXAMPLE 3 p. 207

8. **Dentistry** Dr. Lee's dentist practice is open for 7 hours each day. His receptionist schedules appointments, allowing $\frac{1}{2}$ hour for a cleaning and 1 hour to fill a cavity. He charges \$40 for a cleaning and \$95 for a filling. Dr. Lee cannot do more than 4 fillings per day. Find the number of each type of appointment that maximizes Dr. Lee's income for the day.

PRACTICE AND PROBLEM SOLVING

Independent Practice

For Exercises	See Example
9–11	1
12–14	2
15	3

Extra Practice
Skills Practice p. S9
Application Practice p. S34

Graph each feasible region.

9. $\begin{cases} x \geq 0 \\ y \geq 0 \\ y \geq 4x - 4 \\ y \leq x + 5 \end{cases}$

10. $\begin{cases} x \leq 0 \\ y \geq 0 \\ y \leq 9 \\ y \geq -2x - 7 \end{cases}$

11. $\begin{cases} x \geq 0 \\ x \leq 5 \\ y \geq \frac{1}{5}x - 3 \\ y \leq -x + 4 \end{cases}$

Maximize or minimize each objective function.

12. Maximize $P = -21x + 11y$ for the constraints from Exercise 9.
13. Minimize $P = -2x - 4y$ for the constraints from Exercise 10.
14. Maximize $P = x + 3y$ for the constraints from Exercise 11.
15. **Advertising** A concert tour plans to advertise upcoming tour dates. The advertising budget is \$60,000, and the tour manager will focus on prime-time television and radio commercials. She would like to have between 30 and 60 radio commercials. Use the table to find the number of prime-time television and radio commercials that will maximize the on-air time of the advertisements but will stay within the budget.

Type	Time(s)	Cost (\$)
Radio	20	400
Television (prime time)	30	1500
Television (late night)	30	1200
Newspaper	■	300

16. This problem will prepare you for the Multi-Step Test Prep on page 212.

Tickets to a car race cost \$25 for the upper deck and \$45 for the lower deck. The track may admit no more than 160,000 spectators by order of the fire marshal.

a. If the lower deck can seat no more than 60,000 fans and the upper deck can seat no more than 120,000 fans, how many of each ticket type should be sold to maximize profit?

b. How do the system and solution change if race officials expect to make an additional \$60 per person in the upper deck and \$30 per person in the lower deck from the sale of food and merchandise?

17. **Manufacturing** A camping supply company produces backpacks in two models, journey and trek. The journey model requires 4 hours of labor, and the company makes a profit of \$40. The trek model requires 6 hours of labor, and the company makes a profit of \$80. The distributor will accept no more than 4 trek models and 15 journey models per week. What is the minimum number of hours of labor that are required for the company to make a profit of at least \$400 per week?

Geometry Given the graph of the feasible region, identify the figure and write the inequalities that represent the constraints.

18. 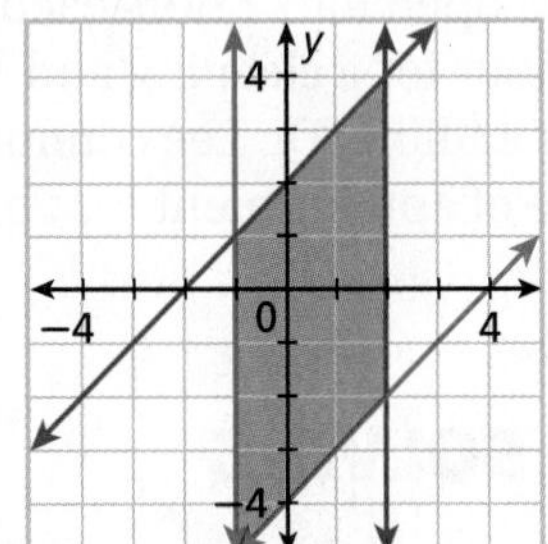

19. 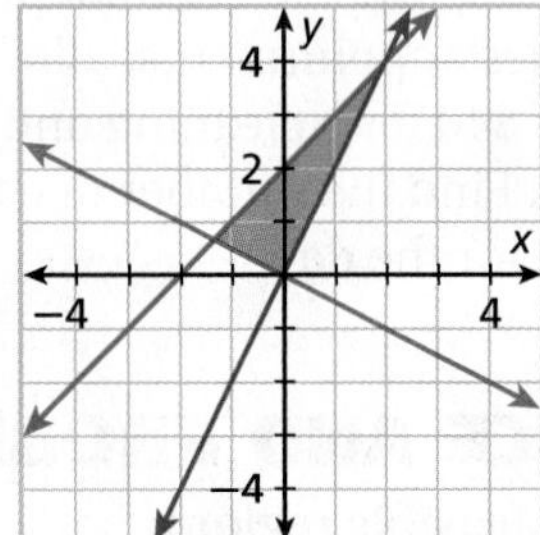

20. 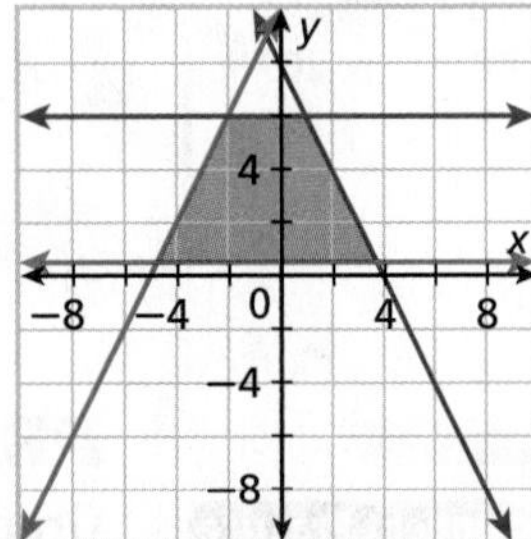

Math History

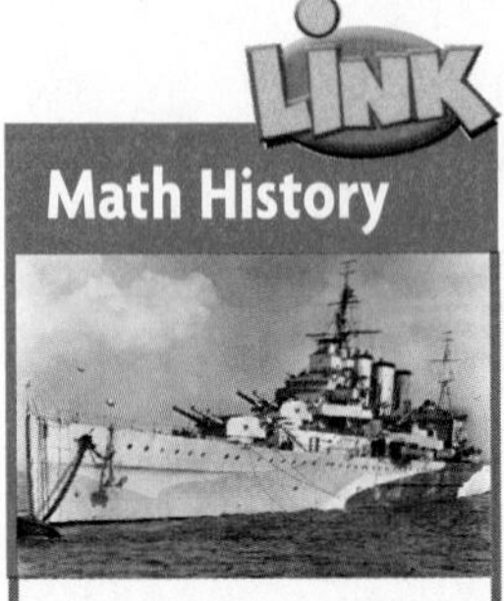

Linear programming was developed during World War II. Also known as Operations Research (OR), the process played an important part in World War II by helping the military effectively allocate its resources.

21. **Highway Traffic** To prevent traffic jams, a city funds a courtesy patrol to aid stranded drivers on local roads. The patrol can repair a flat tire, provide the motorist with 2 gallons of gas, or call a tow truck for more serious problems. It takes 15 minutes to help a driver who is out of gas and 45 minutes to help a driver with a flat tire. The courtesy patrol driver carries 28 gallons of gas. What is the maximum number of stops for flat tires or empty gas tanks that the courtesy patrol can make in an 8-hour shift?

22. **Critical Thinking** Is it possible for a linear programming problem to have no solution? Give an example to support your answer.

23. **Nutrition** A health food store is creating smoothies with soy protein and vitamin supplements. A Soy Joy smoothie costs \$2.75 and uses 2 ounces of soy and 1 ounce of vitamin supplement. A Vitamin Boost smoothie costs \$3.25 and uses 3 ounces of vitamin supplement and 1 ounce of soy protein. The store has 100 ounces each of vitamin supplement and soy protein in stock. How many of each type of smoothie should the store make in order to maximize revenue?

24. **Critical Thinking** Give an example of a problem situation where the feasible region might include negative values.

25. **Write About It** Describe how to recognize when you have found the maximum or minimum value of an objective function for a given set of constraints.

26. **Write About It** Describe how to find the coordinates of the vertices of the feasible region.

TEST PREP

27. Which point gives the minimum value of $P = -x + y$ in the feasible region shown at right?

Ⓐ P Ⓒ R

Ⓑ Q Ⓓ S

28. A feasible region has vertices $(0, 0)$, $(-1, 2)$, and $(-2, 6)$. Which of the following objective functions has a minimum value less than zero over this region?

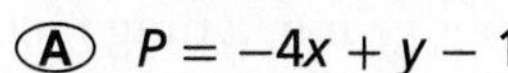

Ⓐ $P = -4x + y - 1$ Ⓒ $P = 12x + 7y$

Ⓑ $P = -x + 3y + 2$ Ⓓ $P = -5x - y$

29. A real estate developer plans to divide a 300,000-square-foot piece of land into commercial and residential properties. Each residential property requires 2500 square feet, and each commercial property requires 30,000 square feet. The developer makes a profit of \$1000 for each residential site and \$20,000 for each commercial site but is limited to no more than six commercial sites because of zoning ordinances. Which of the following gives the objective function for the maximum profit of the developer?

Ⓕ $P = 2500x + 30{,}000y$ Ⓗ $P = 2500x + 1000y$

Ⓖ $P = 1000x + 20{,}000y$ Ⓙ $P = 300{,}000 - x - 6y$

CHALLENGE AND EXTEND

30. **Medicine** A pharmaceutical company is testing a new antibiotic on two sample strains of bacteria. To properly assess the effectiveness of the antibiotic, more than 700 viable bacteria samples must be tested, at least 400 of which must be type B. The company would like to minimize the amount of money spent on bacteria.

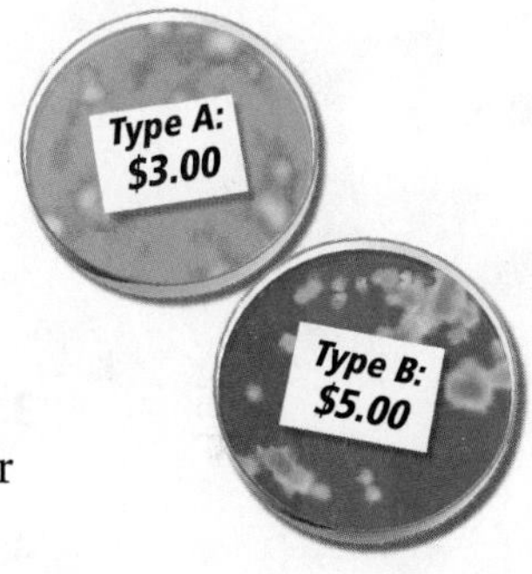

a. Graph the feasible region.

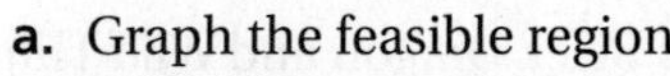

b. What do the points $(350, 400)$ and $(400, 350)$ represent for this problem situation?

c. Do the points satisfy the constraints? Why or why not?

SPIRAL REVIEW

For each function, evaluate $f(7)$ and $f\left(-\frac{1}{2}\right)$. *(Lesson 1-7)*

31. $f(x) = \dfrac{1}{2x - 3}$

32. $f(x) = 0.5x$

33. $f(x) = \dfrac{x^2 - 1}{x - 1}$

Translate $f(x) = |x|$ so that the vertex is at the given point. Then graph. *(Lesson 2-9)*

34. $(6, -3)$

35. $\left(\frac{1}{3}, \frac{4}{3}\right)$

36. $(-2.5, 0.75)$

Geometry **Graph the system of inequalities and classify the figure created by the solution region.** *(Lesson 3-3)*

37. $\begin{cases} y \le 6 \\ y - 2x \ge 0 \\ x \ge 0 \end{cases}$

38. $\begin{cases} y \ge 0 \\ y \le 2 \\ y \le x \\ x + y \le 6 \end{cases}$

CHAPTER 3

SECTION 3A

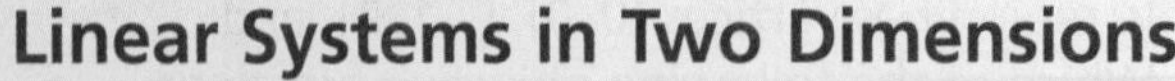

Linear Systems in Two Dimensions

What a Drag! Drag racers measure fuel efficiency differently than most drivers. Instead of using miles per gallon, a drag racing team is more likely to consider gallons per second or gallons per mile to gauge a dragster's fuel consumption and performance. Suppose a drag-racing team is trying to choose a car from four possible entrants. The results of a $\frac{1}{4}$-mile test run are shown in the table.

Dragsters' Results

Dragster	Top Speed (mi/h)	Fuel Used (gal)	Time (s)
Black Dragon	288	14.2	6.1
Lucky Lady	302	15.8	5.9
Red Rocket	274	13.7	6.4
Wild Thing	318	16.5	5.4

1. Using gallons per second as a measure, which car was the most fuel efficient? Which car was the least fuel efficient?
2. Black Dragon and Red Rocket each have 18-gallon fuel tanks, and Wild Thing and Lucky Lady have 20-gallon fuel tanks. Write and graph a system of four linear equations that could be used to model the fuel remaining in these cars after *t* seconds.
3. After how many seconds would Black Dragon and Wild Thing have the same amount of fuel left in their tanks?
4. After how many seconds would Red Rocket and Lucky Lady have the same amount of fuel left in their tanks?
5. Suppose that Black Dragon is located at the team garage and Lucky Lady is located 1000 miles away. Use the maximum speeds of the cars to write and graph a system of linear inequalities that can be used to determine when and where the cars would meet if they travel directly toward one another.
6. Is the point $(1.5, 500)$ a possible solution to the system of linear inequalities? Explain.

READY TO GO ON?

Quiz for Lesson 3-1 Through 3-4

3-1 Solving Linear Systems by Using Graphs and Tables

Solve each system by using a graph and a table. Check your answer.

1. $\begin{cases} 2x + y = -5 \\ x + 2y = 2 \end{cases}$
2. $\begin{cases} x + y = -1 \\ x - 2y = -4 \end{cases}$
3. $\begin{cases} x = y - 2 \\ 3x - y = 2 \end{cases}$

Classify each system and determine the number of solutions.

4. $\begin{cases} 8x - 12y = 48 \\ 3y = 2x - 4 \end{cases}$
5. $\begin{cases} 5x - 6y = 14 \\ x + 3y = 15 \end{cases}$
6. $\begin{cases} x = 2y - 10 \\ y = 5 + \frac{1}{2}x \end{cases}$

3-2 Solving Linear Systems by Using Algebraic Methods

Use substitution or elimination to solve each system of equations.

7. $\begin{cases} y = x + 3 \\ 2x + 4y = 24 \end{cases}$
8. $\begin{cases} x = 5 \\ 2x + 3y = 19 \end{cases}$
9. $\begin{cases} x - y = 5 \\ 3x - 2y = 14 \end{cases}$
10. $\begin{cases} x + 2y = 15 \\ x - 2y = -9 \end{cases}$
11. $\begin{cases} 5x - 4y = 0 \\ 8x - 4y = 12 \end{cases}$
12. $\begin{cases} 4x + 2y = 12 \\ 2x + 6y = -4 \end{cases}$

3-3 Solving Systems of Linear Inequalities

Graph each system of inequalities.

13. $\begin{cases} y - x < 3 \\ y + x < 3 \end{cases}$
14. $\begin{cases} y + x \leq 0 \\ y \leq 4 - x \end{cases}$
15. $\begin{cases} y \geq 2x + 3 \\ y > -x \end{cases}$

16. **Travel** Karen traveled almost 350 mi in under 7 h of highway driving. She stopped for a brief rest that was not included in her driving time. Karen averaged 60 mi/h for the first part of her trip and 50 mi/h for the second part of the trip. Write and graph a system of inequalities that can be used to determine how many hours Karen spent driving in each part of her trip.

3-4 Linear Programming

Graph each feasible region, and maximize or minimize the objective function $P = 4x + 5y$.

17. minimize; $\begin{cases} x \geq 0 \\ y \geq 0 \\ y \leq x - 1 \\ y \leq -\frac{1}{2}x + 4 \end{cases}$
18. maximize; $\begin{cases} x \leq 2 \\ y \geq 0 \\ y \leq 2x + 4 \\ y \leq -3x + 9 \end{cases}$

19. **Finance** A beauty salon schedules appointments for haircuts for 30 minutes and for special services, such as tinting or curling, for 1 hour. Each haircut costs $20, and special services cost $45. The beauty salon wants to schedule no more than 4 special services each day per beautician. Find the number of each type of appointment that produces the maximum income per beautician in a workday of 8 hours at most.

3-5 Linear Equations in Three Dimensions

Objective
Graph points and linear equations in three dimensions.

Vocabulary
three-dimensional coordinate system
ordered triple
z-axis

Why learn this?

You can participate in Geocaching, an outdoor treasure-hunting game, by using three-dimensional coordinates to pinpoint locations on Earth.

A Global Positioning System (GPS) gives locations using the three coordinates of latitude, longitude, and elevation. You can represent any location in three-dimensional space using a **three-dimensional coordinate system**, sometimes called *coordinate space.*

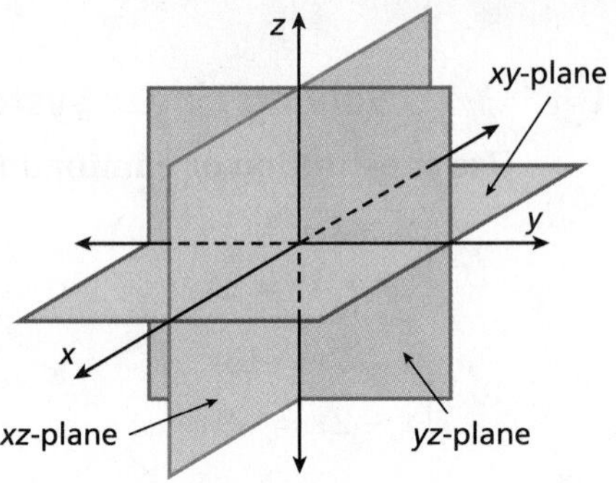

Each point in coordinate space can be represented by an **ordered triple** of the form (x, y, z). The system is similar to the coordinate plane but has an additional coordinate based on the **z-axis**. Notice that the axes form three planes that intersect at the origin.

EXAMPLE 1 Graphing Points in Three Dimensions

Graph each point in three-dimensional space.

A $A(2, 3, -2)$

From the origin, move 2 units forward along the x-axis, 3 units right, and 2 units down.

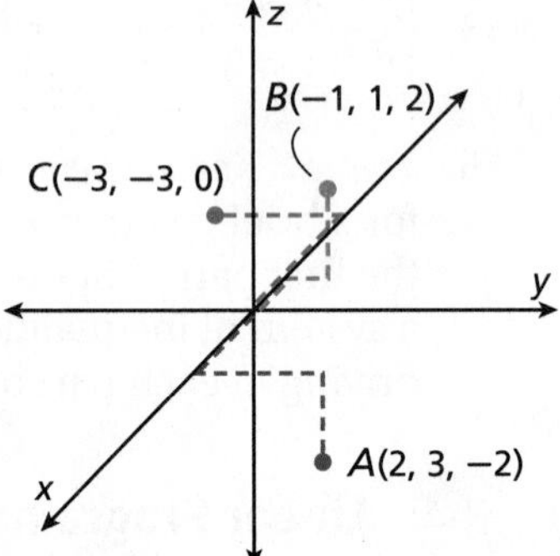

B $B(-1, 1, 2)$

From the origin, move 1 unit back along the x-axis, 1 unit right, and 2 units up.

C $C(-3, -3, 0)$

From the origin, move 3 units back along the x-axis and 3 units left. Notice that this point lies in the xy-plane because the z-coordinate is 0.

Graph each point in three-dimensional space.

1a. $D(1, 3, -1)$ **1b.** $E(1, -3, 1)$ **1c.** $F(0, 0, 3)$

Recall that the graph of a linear equation in two dimensions is a straight line. In three-dimensional space, the graph of a linear equation is a plane. Because a plane is defined by three points, you can graph linear equations in three dimensions by finding the three intercepts.

EXAMPLE 2 Graphing Linear Equations in Three Dimensions

Helpful Hint

To find an intercept in coordinate space, set the other two coordinates equal to 0.

Graph the linear equation $3x + 4y + 2z = 12$ in three-dimensional space.

Step 1 Find the intercepts:

x-intercept: $3x + 4(0) + 6(0) = 12$

$x = 4$

y-intercept: $3(0) + 4y + 2(0) = 12$

$y = 3$

z-intercept: $3(0) + 4(0) + 2z = 12$

$z = 6$

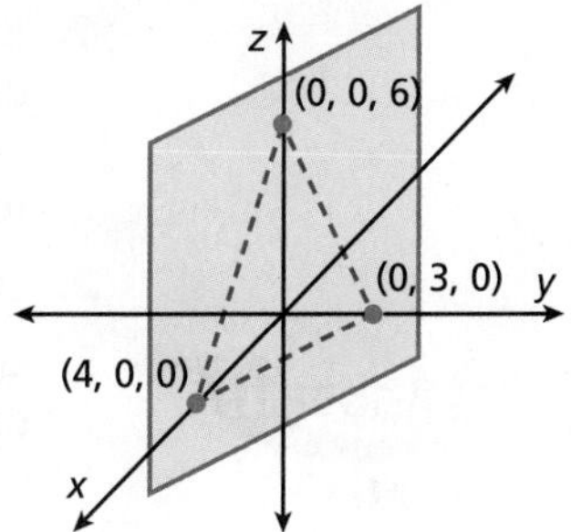

Step 2 Plot the points $(4, 0, 0)$, $(0, 3, 0)$, and $(0, 0, 6)$. Sketch a plane through the three points.

2. Graph the linear equation $x - 4y + 2z = 4$ in three-dimensional space.

EXAMPLE 3 *Technology Application*

A computer game uses a role-playing scenario in which players build civilizations. Each player begins with 100 gold coins to buy resources. The players then compete for the survival of their civilizations. Each unit of food costs 2 gold coins, wood costs 4 gold coins, and stone costs 5 gold coins.

Write a linear equation in three variables to represent this situation.

Let f = units of food, w = units of wood, and s = units of stone.

Write an equation:

cost of food	+	cost of wood	+	cost of stone	+	100 gold pieces
$2f$	+	$4w$	+	$5s$	+	100

B **Use the table to find the number of units of stone each player can buy.**

Bonnie: $2(20) + 3(10) + 5s = 100$

$s = 6$

Chad: $2(15) + 3(15) + 5s = 100$

$s = 5$

Frederico: $2(40) + 3(5) + 5s = 100$

$s = 1$

LaToya: $2(25) + 3(10) + 5s = 100$

$s = 4$

Player	Units of Food	Units of Wood	Units of Stone
Bonnie	20	10	■
Chad	15	15	■
Frederico	40	5	■
LaToya	25	10	■

Bonnie can purchase 6 units of stone, Chad can purchase 5 units, Frederico can purchase 1 unit, and LaToya can purchase 4 units.

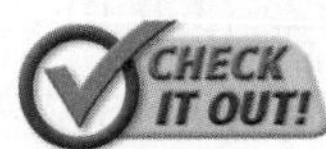

Steve purchased \$61.50 worth of supplies for a hiking trip. The supplies included flashlights for \$3.50 each, compasses for \$1.50 each, and water bottles for \$0.75 each.

3a. Write a linear equation in three variables to represent this situation.

3b. Steve purchased 6 flashlights and 24 water bottles. How many compasses did he purchase?

THINK AND DISCUSS

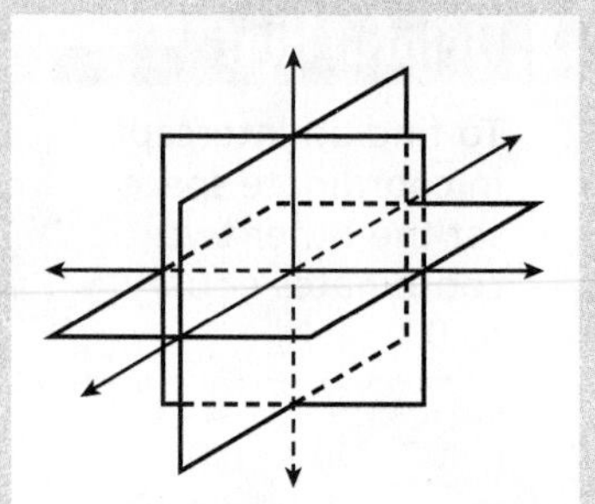

1. Estimate your current coordinates in three-dimensional space using the front left bottom corner of your classroom as the origin. Let 1 foot represent 1 unit.
2. Describe a plane that has only two intercepts

3. **GET ORGANIZED** Copy and complete the graphic organizer. Label each axis, plane, and line shown.

3-5 Exercises

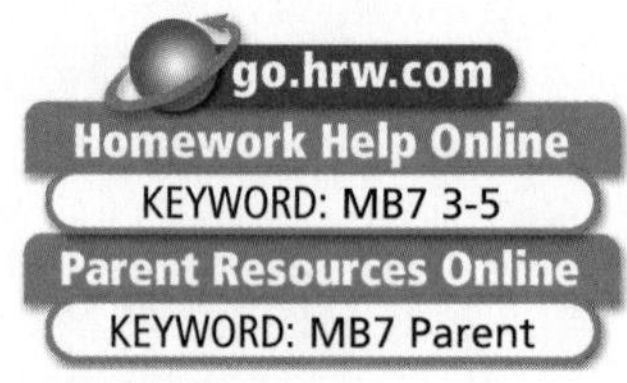

GUIDED PRACTICE

1. **Vocabulary** Explain the difference between the two- and three-dimensional coordinate systems.

SEE EXAMPLE 1 p. 214

Graph each point in three-dimensional space.

2. $(-3, -2, 1)$ 3. $(0, 2, 2)$ 4. $(1, 4, 5)$ 5. $(-1, 2, 4)$

SEE EXAMPLE 2 p. 215

Graph each linear equation in three-dimensional space.

6. $x + y + z = 3$ 7. $5x - 2y - 4z = 10$ 8. $1.5x + 3y - 2z = -6$

SEE EXAMPLE 3 p. 215

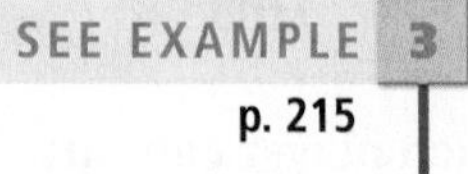

9. **Multi-Step** Whitney's delivery truck has a weight limit of 1.5 tons. She delivers refrigerators that weigh 225 lb, dishwashers that weigh 150 lb, and ovens that weigh 300 lb. (*Hint:* 1 ton = 2000 lb)

Appliance SUPERSTORE

Refrigerators	8	■	4	10
Dishwashers	6	1	■	5
Ovens	■	5	4	■

   a. Write a linear equation in three variables to represent this situation.
   b. Complete the table for the possible numbers of appliances the truck can hold.
   c. **Estimation** Estimate the maximum number of appliances the truck can hold.

PRACTICE AND PROBLEM SOLVING

Independent Practice

For Exercises	See Example
10–17	1
18–23	2
24	3

Graph each point in three-dimensional space.

10. $(2, -4, 3)$ 11. $(-1, 1, 4)$ 12. $(3, 0, 0)$ 13. $(1, -2, 0)$

14. $(-3, -3, -3)$ 15. $(5, 0, 2)$ 16. $(0, -3, 2)$ 17. $(-4, -1, 1)$

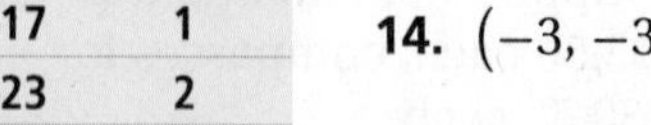

Graph each linear equation in three-dimensional space.

Extra Practice
Skills Practice p. S9
Application Practice p. S34

18. $x + y - z = -1$ 19. $2x - y + 2z = 4$ 20. $2x + \frac{1}{2}y + z = -2$

21. $5x + y - z = -5$ 22. $8x + 6y + 4z = 24$ 23. $3x - 3y + 2.5z = 7.5$

24. **Aquariums** Gordon has \$80 to purchase a combination of cinnamon clownfish, anemones, and hermit crabs for his aquarium. Clownfish cost \$10 each, anemones cost \$15 each, and hermit crabs cost \$2.50 each.

a. Write a linear equation in three variables to represent this situation.

b. Complete the table for the possible numbers of sea creatures Gordon may purchase.

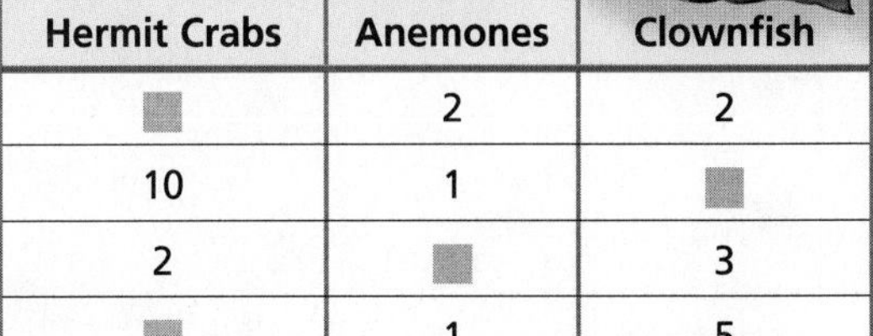

Hermit Crabs	Anemones	Clownfish
	2	2
10	1	
2		3
	1	5

25. **Sports** Basketball players can score in three different ways: one-point free throws, two-point field goals, or three-point field goals. Cindy Brown of Long Beach State holds the Division 1 NCAA women's record for the most points in a single game, 60, including 20 free throws. Identify five possible combinations of two-point field goals and three-pointers that she may have had in the game.

 **Geometry** **Identify the unlabeled vertices of each cube.**

26.

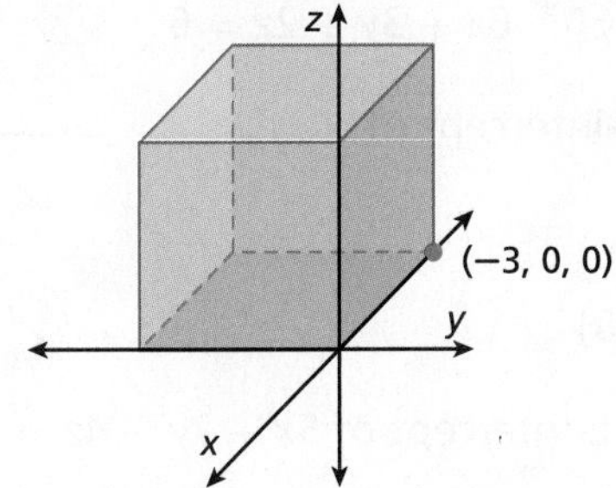

27.

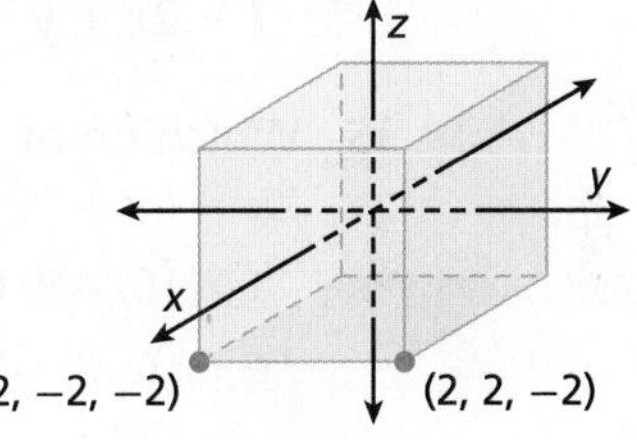

28. **Architecture** An architect is planning the flooring for a 2000 ft^2 home. There will be three types of flooring: hardwood, tile, and carpet. The architect has budgeted \$8000 for the floors and has decided to buy 400 ft^2 of tile. Is it possible for the rest of the flooring to be half wood and half carpet? Explain.

Flooring Sale!

Laminate: \$1.50/ft^2

Carpet: \$2/ft^2

Ceramic Tile: \$4/ft^2

Hardwood Flooring: \$6/ft^2

29. **Critical Thinking** Does moving forward and backward along a line represent two dimensions? Explain.

30. **Write About It** A friend calls you on the phone and asks you how to draw a three-dimensional coordinate system. What would you tell your friend?

31. This problem will prepare you for the Multi-Step Test Prep on page 228.

Engineers use three-dimensional coordinates to design construction projects. An overhead light is anchored at the point (7, 12, 10) in a design where the floor of a building is represented by the *xy*-plane and increments on the plane are in feet.

a. Lights are spaced 4 feet apart in each direction. What are the coordinates of the anchors for two other lights?

b. The light fixture will hang 1.5 feet below the anchor in the ceiling. What are the coordinates of the fixture?

c. What would the new coordinates of the light be if the engineers want to raise the ceiling 4 feet?

32. **ERROR ANALYSIS** Below are two methods of finding the x-intercept of $-5x + 3z = 15$. Which is incorrect? Explain the error.

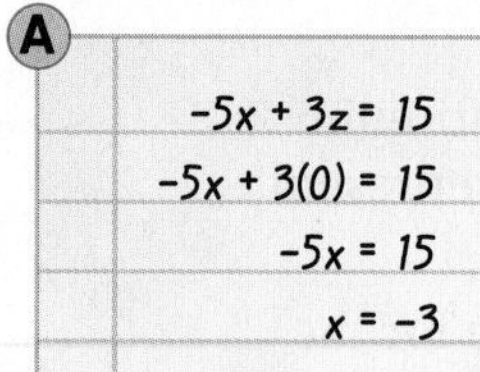

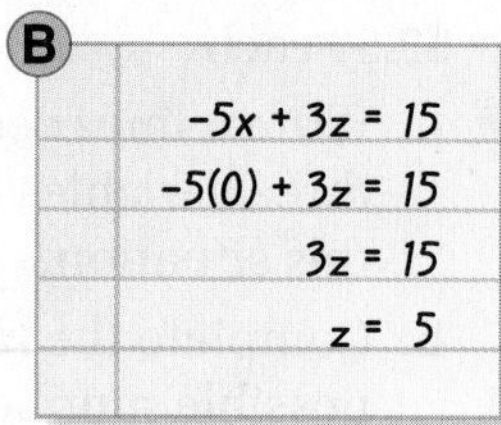

33. Which point is 5 units away from (1, 1, 4)?

Ⓐ (−4, 1, 4)　Ⓑ (1, −4, 9)　Ⓒ (2, 3, 6)　Ⓓ (6, 6, 9)

34. The graph of which equation is shown?

Ⓐ $x + 2y + 3z = 6$　Ⓒ $3x + 6y + 2z = 6$

Ⓑ $2x + y + 3z = 6$　Ⓓ $6x + 3y + 2z = 6$

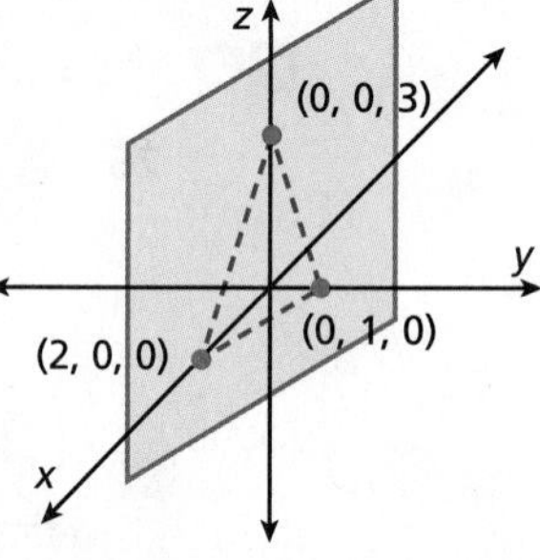

35. Which point is located at the y-intercept of $2x - 4y + 3z = -12$?

Ⓕ (0, −3, 0)　Ⓗ (0, 3, 0)

Ⓖ (0, 0, −3)　Ⓙ (3, 0, 0)

36. **Gridded Response** Find the z-intercept of $5x - 2y - 4z = -3$.

CHALLENGE AND EXTEND

When a linear equation involves only two variables, its graph in three-dimensional space is a plane parallel to one of the axes. Graph each linear equation in three-dimensional space.

37. $x + y = 2$　38. $y - 2z = 4$　39. $x + z = 3$　40. $\frac{1}{2}x + \frac{1}{4}y = 1$

Write a linear equation in three dimensions with the indicated intercepts.

41. x-intercept = 4; y-intercept = 2; z-intercept = −1

42. x-intercept = 25; y-intercept = 50; z-intercept = 10

SPIRAL REVIEW

Name the three-dimensional solid with the given number of edges and vertices. *(Previous course)*

43. 5 vertices, 8 edges　44. 6 vertices, 9 edges　45. 0 vertices, 0 edges

46. **Fund-raising** The Wheels for Charity cycling club rode 1920 miles from Maryland to Montana to raise money for homeless shelters. Each day, the cyclists traveled about 120 miles. How many days of cycling did the trip take? *(Lesson 2-2)*

Use substitution or elimination to solve each system of equations. *(Lesson 3-2)*

47. $\begin{cases} 5y = x \\ \frac{2}{5}x + 7y = 18 \end{cases}$　48. $\begin{cases} 6x - y = 5 \\ 4y - 3x = 1 \end{cases}$　49. $\begin{cases} x + 3y = 6 \\ 2x - 3y = 9 \end{cases}$

Views of Solid Figures

Here are four different ways to represent the same three-dimensional object.

Oblique Grid

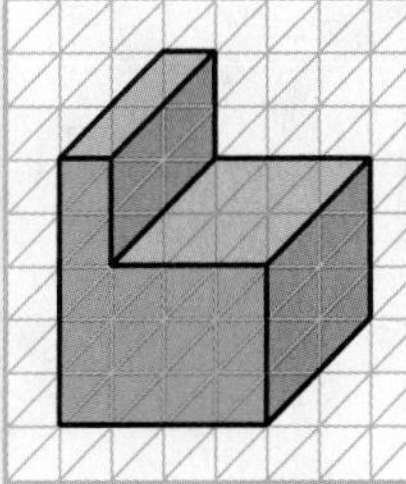

3-D Axes

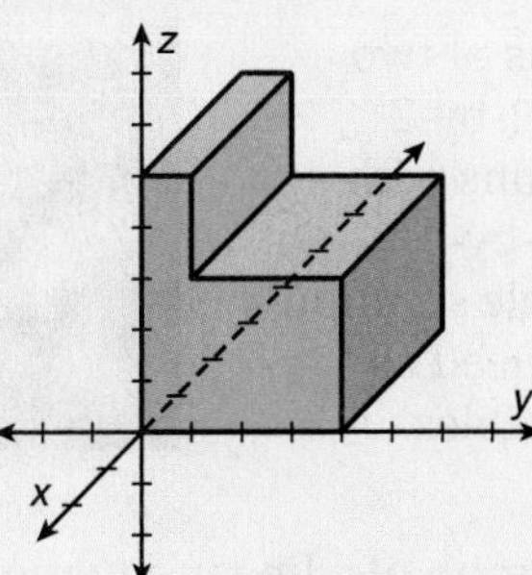

Isometric Grid

Orthographic Views

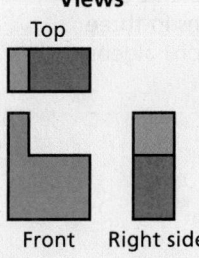

Top

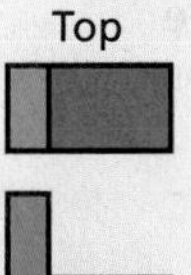

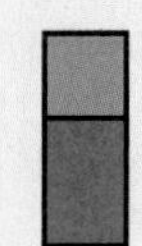

Front   Right side

Example

Use graph paper. Show what this figure looks like from the back.

1. Draw the front of the figure. The answer is shown in figure 1.
2. The back view is the mirror image of the front view. Flip the front view to get the back view. The answer is shown in figure 2.

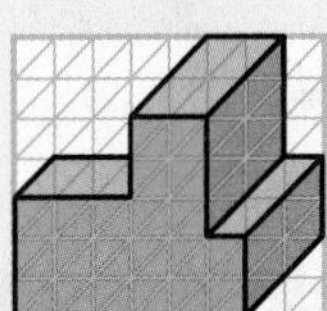

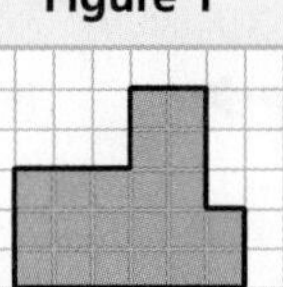

Figure 1

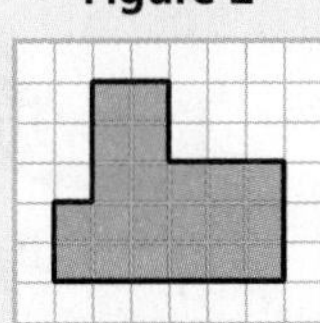

Figure 2

Try This

Use figures 3–6 for Problems 1–5.

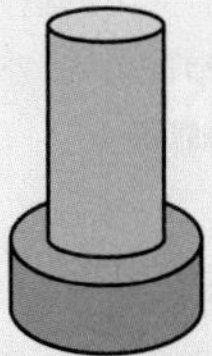

Figure 3

Figure 4

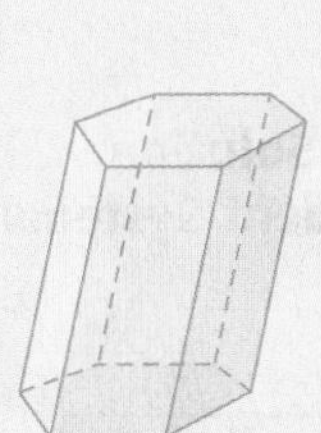

Figure 5

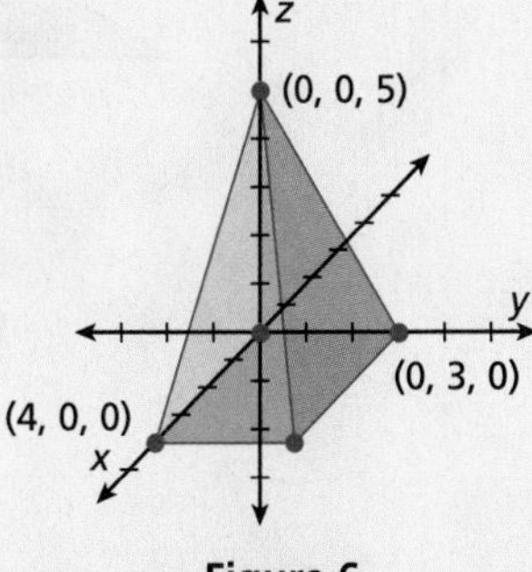

Figure 6

1. Figure 3 is made from two cylinders, one centered on top of the other. Draw front, top, and right-side views of figure 3.
2. In figure 4, the blue cube represents 1 cubic unit. How many of the blue cubes are needed to build the figure?
3. Draw front, top, and right-side views of figure 4.
4. Figure 5 shows an oblique prism. The lateral faces do not make right angles with the bases. Describe the bases and lateral faces of this prism.
5. In figure 6, three of the vertices are labeled. What are the coordinates of the other two vertices? What is the name of this solid figure?

3-6 Solving Linear Systems in Three Variables

Objectives

Represent solutions to systems of equations in three dimensions graphically.

Solve systems of equations in three dimensions algebraically.

Why learn this?

You can use systems of equations in three variables to find out the scoring systems for sports awards. (See Example 2.)

You have learned to solve systems of two equations with two variables, or 2-by-2 systems. Systems of three equations with three variables are often called 3-by-3 systems. In general, to find a single solution to *any* system of equations, you need as many equations as you have variables.

Recall from Lesson 3-5 that the graph of a linear equation in three variables is a plane. When you graph a system of three linear equations in three dimensions, the result is three planes that may or may not intersect. The solution to the system is the set of points where all three planes intersect. These systems may have one, infinitely many, or no solution.

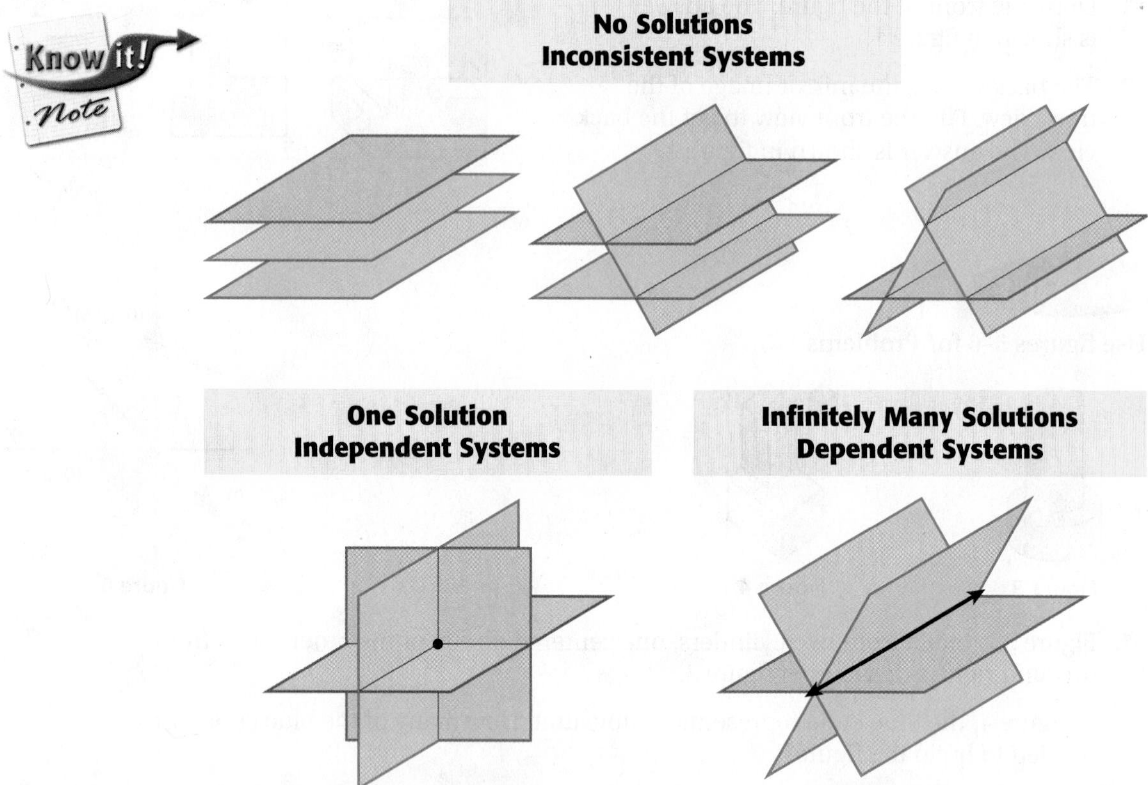

Identifying the exact solution from a graph of a 3-by-3 system can be very difficult. However, you can use the methods of elimination and substitution to reduce a 3-by-3 system to a 2-by-2 system and then use the methods that you learned in Lesson 3-2.

EXAMPLE 1 Solving a Linear System in Three Variables

Use elimination to solve the following system of equations.

$$\begin{cases} x + 2y - 3z = -2 & ❶ \\ 2x - 2y + z = 7 & ❷ \\ x + y + 2z = -4 & ❸ \end{cases}$$

Step 1 Eliminate one variable.

In this system, y is a reasonable choice to eliminate first because the coefficients of y are opposites in the equations ❶ and ❷.

$$\begin{array}{rl} ❶ & x + 2y - 3z = -2 \\ ❷ & \underline{2x - 2y + z = 7} \\ & 3x - 2z = 5 \; ❹ \end{array}$$

Add equations ❶ and ❷.

Use equations ❶ and ❸ to create a second equation in x and z.

$$\begin{array}{lll} ❶ & x + 2y - 3z = -2 & x + 2y - 3z = -2 \\ ❸ & \underline{-2(x + y + 2z = -4)} \rightarrow & \underline{-2x - 2y - 4z = 8} \\ & & -x - 7z = 6 \; ❺ \end{array}$$

Multiply equation ❸ by −2, and add to equation ❶.

You now have a 2-by-2 system. $\begin{cases} 3x - 2z = 5 & ❹ \\ -x - 7z = 6 & ❺ \end{cases}$

Step 2 Eliminate another variable. Then solve for the remaining variable.

You can eliminate x by using methods from Lesson 3-2.

$$\begin{array}{lll} ❹ & 3x - 2z = 5 & 3x - 2z = 5 \\ ❺ & \underline{3(-x - 7z = 6)} \rightarrow & \underline{-3x - 21z = 18} \\ & & -23z = 23 \\ & & z = -1 \end{array}$$

Multiply equation ❺ by 3, and add to equation ❹.

Solve for z.

Step 3 Use one of the equations in your 2-by-2 system to solve for x.

❺ $-x - 7z = 6$

$-x - 7(-1) = 6$ *Substitute −1 for z.*

$x = 1$ *Solve for x.*

Step 4 Substitute for x and z in one of the original equations to solve for y.

❸ $x + y + 2z = -4$

$(1) + y + 2(-1) = -4$ *Substitute 1 for x and −1 for z.*

$y = -3$ *Solve for y.*

The solution is $(1, -3, -1)$.

1. Use elimination to solve the following system of equations.

$$\begin{cases} -x + y + 2z = 7 \\ 2x + 3y + z = 1 \\ -3x - 4y + z = 4 \end{cases}$$

You can also use substitution to solve a 3-by-3 system. Again, the first step is to reduce the 3-by-3 system to a 2-by-2 system.

EXAMPLE 2 Sports Application

In 2001, Randy Johnson of the Arizona Diamondbacks won Major League Baseball's Cy Young Award as the best pitcher in the National League. The winner is the pitcher who receives the most points, and a different number of points are given for each first-, second-, and third-place vote. The table shows the votes for the top three finishers. Find the number of points awarded for each vote.

Player	1st Place	2nd Place	3rd Place	Total Points
Randy Johnson	30	2	0	156
Curt Schilling	2	29	1	98
Matt Morris	0	1	28	31

Step 1 Let x represent the number of points for a first-place vote, y for a second-place vote, and z for a third-place vote.

Write a system of equations to represent the data in the table.

$$\begin{cases} 30x + 2y = 156 & ❶ \\ 2x + 29y + z = 98 & ❷ \\ y + 28z = 31 & ❸ \end{cases}$$

Randy Johnson's votes
Curt Schilling's votes
Matt Morris's votes

Some variables are "missing" in the equations; however, the same solution methods apply. Substitution is a good choice because solving for y is straightforward.

Step 2 Solve for y in equation ❶.

❶ $30x + 2y = 156$

$y = -15x + 78$ *Solve for y.*

Step 3 Substitute for y in equations ❷ and ❸.

$$\begin{cases} 2x + 29(-15x + 78) + z = 98 & ❷ \\ (-15x + 78) + 28z = 31 & ❸ \end{cases}$$ *Substitute −15x + 78 for y.*

$$\begin{cases} -433x + z = -2164 & ❹ \\ -15x + 28z = -47 & ❺ \end{cases}$$ *Simplify to find a 2-by-2 system.*

Step 4 Solve equation ❹ for z.

❹ $-433x + z = -2164$

$z = 433x - 2164$ *Solve for z.*

Step 5 Substitute for z in equation ❺.

❺ $-15x + 28(433x - 2164) = -47$ *Substitute 433x − 2164 for z.*

$12{,}109x = 60{,}545$

$x = 5$ *Solve for x.*

Step 6 Substitute for x to solve for z and then for y.

❹ $z = 433x - 2164$
$z = 433(5) - 2164$
$z = 1$

❸ $y + 28z = 31$
$y + 28(1) = 31$
$y = 3$

The solution to the system is $(5, 3, 1)$. So, a first-place vote is worth 5 points, a second-place vote is worth 3 points, and a third-place vote is worth 1 point.

2. Jada's chili won first prize at the winter fair. The table shows the results of the voting.

How many points are first-, second-, and third-place votes worth?

Winter Fair Chili Cook-off				
Name	1st Place	2nd Place	3rd Place	Total Points
Jada	3	1	4	15
Maria	2	4	0	14
Al	2	2	3	13

The systems in Examples 1 and 2 have unique solutions. However, 3-by-3 systems may have no solution or an infinite number of solutions.

EXAMPLE 3 Classifying Systems with Infinitely Many Solutions or No Solution

Classify the system as consistent or inconsistent, and determine the number of solutions.

$$\begin{cases} 4x - 2y + 4z = 8 & ❶ \\ -3x + y - z = -4 & ❷ \\ -2x + 2y - 6z = 4 & ❸ \end{cases}$$

The elimination method is convenient because the numbers you need to multiply the equations by are small. First, eliminate y.

$$\begin{array}{lrl} ❶ & 4x - 2y + 4z = 8 & \\ ❸ & \underline{-2x + 2y - 6z = 4} & \\ & 2x \quad\quad - 2z = 12 & ❹ \end{array}$$

Add equations ❶ and ❸.

$$\begin{array}{rcl} 4x - 2y + 4z = 8 & & 4x - 2y + 4z = 8 \\ \underline{2(-3x + y - z = -4)} & \rightarrow & \underline{-6x + 2y - 2z = -8} \\ & & -2x \quad\quad + 2z = 0 \quad ❺ \end{array}$$

Multiply equation ❷ by 2, and add to equation ❶.

You now have a 2-by-2 system: $\begin{cases} 2x - 2z = 12 & ❹ \\ -2x + 2z = 0 & ❺ \end{cases}$

Eliminate x.

$$\begin{array}{lr} ❹ & 2x - 2z = 12 \\ ❺ & \underline{-2x + 2z = 12} \\ & 0 = 12 \ ✗ \end{array}$$

Add equations ❹ and ❺.

Because 0 is never equal to 12, the equation is a contradiction. Therefore, the system is inconsistent and has no solution.

Remember!

Consistent means that the system of equations has at least one solution.

Classify the system, and determine the number of solutions.

3a. $\begin{cases} 3x - y + 2z = 4 \\ 2x - y + 3z = 7 \\ -9x + 3y - 6z = -12 \end{cases}$

3b. $\begin{cases} 2x - y + 3z = 6 \\ 2x - 4y + 6z = 10 \\ y - z = -2 \end{cases}$

THINK AND DISCUSS

1. Look at the inconsistent and dependent systems shown on page 220. Describe one other arrangement of three planes that results in an inconsistent system. Describe one other arrangement that results in a dependent system.

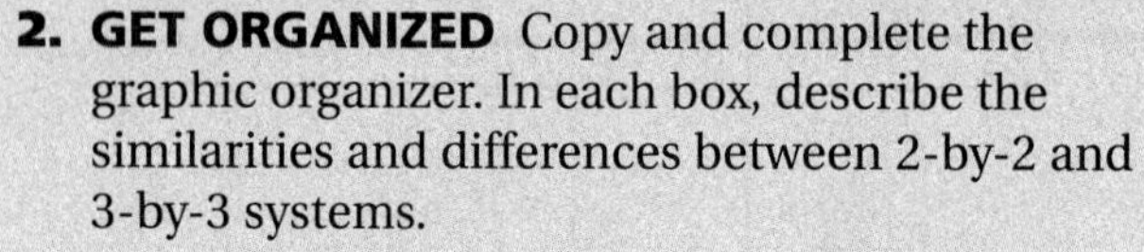

2. **GET ORGANIZED** Copy and complete the graphic organizer. In each box, describe the similarities and differences between 2-by-2 and 3-by-3 systems.

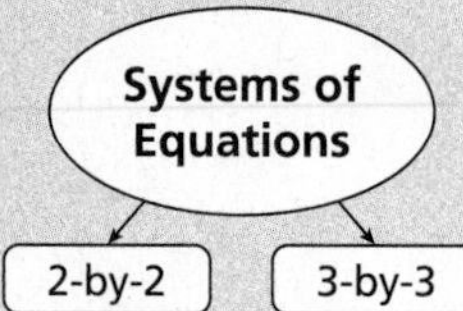

3-6 Exercises

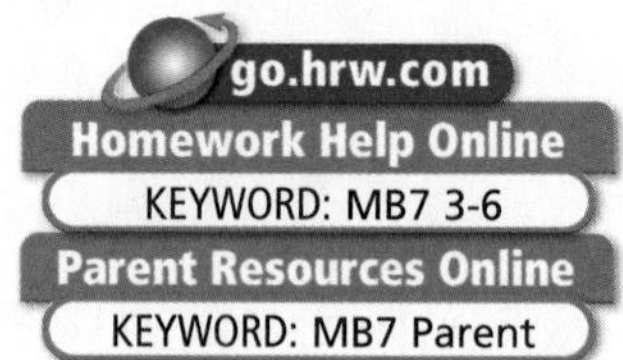

GUIDED PRACTICE

SEE EXAMPLE 1 p. 221

Use elimination to solve each system of equations.

1. $\begin{cases} -2x + y + 3z = 20 \\ -3x + 2y + z = 21 \\ 3x - 2y + 3z = -9 \end{cases}$

2. $\begin{cases} x + 2y + 3z = 9 \\ x + 3y + 2z = 5 \\ x + 4y - z = -5 \end{cases}$

3. $\begin{cases} x + 2y + z = 8 \\ 2x + y - z = 4 \\ x + y + 3z = 7 \end{cases}$

SEE EXAMPLE 2 p. 222

4. **Business** Mabel's Mini-Golf has different prices for seniors, adults, and children. The table shows the total revenue for three hours on a particular night. How much does each type of ticket cost?

Mabel's Mini-Golf Prices				
Time	Senior	Adult	Child	Revenue
6:00 P.M.–7:00 P.M.	5	10	12	\$310
7:00 P.M.–8:00 P.M.	5	5	4	\$155
8:00 P.M.–9:00 P.M.	4	2	3	\$92

SEE EXAMPLE 3 p. 223

Classify each system as consistent or inconsistent, and determine the number of solutions.

5. $\begin{cases} 2x + 4y - 2z = 4 \\ -x - 2y + z = 4 \\ 3x + 6y - 3z = 10 \end{cases}$

6. $\begin{cases} 2x + 4y - 5z = -10 \\ -x - 2y + 8z = 16 \\ -2x + 4y + 2z = 4 \end{cases}$

7. $\begin{cases} -2x + 3y + z = 15 \\ x + 3y - z = -1 \\ -5x - 6y + 4z = -16 \end{cases}$

PRACTICE AND PROBLEM SOLVING

Use elimination to solve each system of equations.

8. $\begin{cases} 2x - y - 3z = 1 \\ 4x + 3y + 2z = -4 \\ -3x + 2y + 5z = -3 \end{cases}$

9. $\begin{cases} 5x - 6y + 2z = 21 \\ 2x + 3y - 3z = -9 \\ -3x + 9y - 4z = -24 \end{cases}$

10. $\begin{cases} 4x + 7y - z = 42 \\ -2x + 2y + 3z = -26 \\ 2x - 3y + 5z = 10 \end{cases}$

Independent Practice	
For Exercises	See Example
8–10	1
11	2
12–14	3

Extra Practice

Skills Practice p. S9

Application Practice p. S34

11. Entertainment On the *Star Quality* show, judges score contestants in three categories: Talent, Presentation, and Star Quality. Each category is worth a percent of the final score. Based on the scores in the table below, what percent of the final score is each category worth?

Star Quality Scores				
Contestant	Talent	Presentation	Star Quality	Final Score
Wanda Wynn	8	9	10	9.2
Amiya Starr	9	7	8	8.1
Kenny Singh	6	10	8	7.8

Classify each system as consistent or inconsistent, and determine the number of solutions.

12. $\begin{cases} 4x - 3y + z = -9 \\ -3x + 2y - z = 6 \\ -x + 3y + 2z = 9 \end{cases}$

13. $\begin{cases} 3x + 3y + 3z = 4 \\ 2x - y - 5z = 2 \\ 5x + 2y - 2z = 8 \end{cases}$

14. $\begin{cases} -x + y + z = 8 \\ 2x - 2y - 2z = -16 \\ 2x - y + 4z = -6 \end{cases}$

15. Geometry In triangle ABC, the measure of angle A is twice the sum of the measures of angles B and C. The measure of angle B is three times the measure of angle C. What are the measures of the angles?

16. Sports Louie Dampier was the leading scorer in the history of the American Basketball Association (ABA). His 13,726 points were scored on three-point baskets, two-point baskets, and one-point free throws. In his ABA career, Dampier made 2144 more two-point baskets than free throws and 1558 more free throws than three-point baskets. How many three-point baskets, two-point baskets, and free throws did Dampier make?

17. Critical Thinking The following system of equations has three variables and two equations. $\begin{cases} x + 2y + 4z = 4 \\ 2x + 3y + z = 12 \end{cases}$

a. Describe what happens when you attempt to solve this system.

b. Explain why a system of equations must have at least as many equations as there are variables to have a single solution.

18. Write About It The graphs of two equations in a 3-by-3 system intersect in a line. What types of solutions could the system have? Explain.

19. This problem will prepare you for the Multi-Step Test Prep on page 228.

The roof lines of a building can be described by the system of equations

$\begin{cases} x + y + z = 53 \\ 3x - 2y + z = 69 \\ -x + 2y - z = -59 \end{cases}$, where the floor is represented by the xy-plane and measurements are in feet.

a. Find the point of intersection of the roof lines.

b. A support column will be placed under the intersection point. How tall must the column be to reach from the floor to the intersection point?

c. What are the coordinates of the center of the base of the column?

TEST PREP

20. Which point is the solution to this system of equations? $\begin{cases} 2x + y + 3z = -1 \\ 4x + 2y + 3z = 1 \\ x - y + 4z = -6 \end{cases}$

Ⓐ (2, −2, −1) Ⓑ (0, 2, −1) Ⓒ (2, 1, −1) Ⓓ (3, −2, 2)

21. Ann, Betty, and Charlotte are sisters. Ann is twice as old as Betty, and Betty is 12 years younger than Charlotte. In 5 years, Charlotte will be twice as old as Betty. What are the sisters' ages?

Ⓕ Ann is 6, Betty is 3, and Charlotte is 15.

Ⓗ Ann is 5, Betty is 10, and Charlotte is 22.

Ⓖ Ann is 34, Betty is 17, and Charlotte is 29.

Ⓙ Ann is 14, Betty is 7, and Charlotte is 19.

22. **Short Response** What is the value of the *x*-coordinate of the solution to the following system of equations? $\begin{cases} x + 4y = 6 \\ 2x + 3z = 12 \\ 4y + z = 10 \end{cases}$

CHALLENGE AND EXTEND

23. Use any method to solve the following 4-by-4 system. $\begin{cases} w + 2x + 2y + z = -2 \\ w + 3x - 2y - z = -6 \\ -2w - x + 3y + 3z = 6 \\ w + 4x + y - 2z = -14 \end{cases}$

24. **Economics** Three investors each put \$1000 into their retirement accounts. They had three funds to choose from—fund A, fund B, and fund C. Each investor divided the money differently, as shown in the table below. The table also shows the gain for each investor for the year. Find the yield in percents for each fund.

Investor	Fund A	Fund B	Fund C	Gain
M. Nguyen	\$300	\$300	\$400	\$56
A. O'Sullivan	\$600	\$200	\$200	\$76
T. Lane	\$100	\$300	\$600	\$30

SPIRAL REVIEW

Perform the given translation of the point $(-3, 2)$, and give the coordinates of the translated point. *(Lesson 1-8)*

25. 6 units right and 1 unit up

26. 4 units left and 2 units down

27. **Construction** The blueprint for a house showed the kitchen as 11 cm by 8 cm. If the blueprint is drawn to a 1 cm:0.65 m scale, what are the dimensions of the kitchen in the house? *(Lesson 2-2)*

Write each equation in slope-intercept form, and then graph. *(Lesson 2-3)*

28. $4x - 3y = -6$

29. $3y - 2x = -12$

30. $2x + 5y = 15$

Explore Parametric Equations

A set of *parametric equations* is a system of two equations with the same independent variable, usually t. The independent variable t is called the *parameter*.

Use with Lesson 3-6

go.hrw.com
Lab Resources Online
KEYWORD: MB7 Lab3

Activity

Follow the steps to graph the following parametric equations. $\begin{cases} x = 2t \\ y = 5t \end{cases}$

Press MODE, and change the graphing mode to **PAR** (for parametric). Press Y=. Enter $2t$ for the first equation (X_{1T}) and $5t$ for the second equation (Y_{1T}). To enter the variable t, use the X,T,θ,n key. Graph the equations.

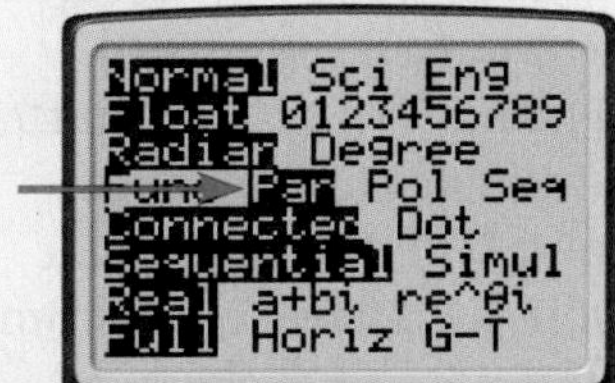

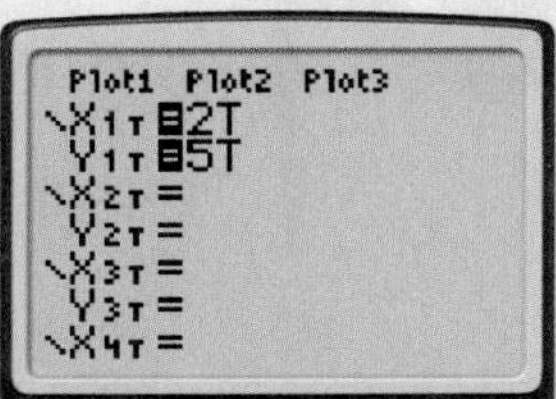

You can use the TRACE key to view values of both equations and t. You can change the look of the graph and the values by adjusting the WINDOW settings.

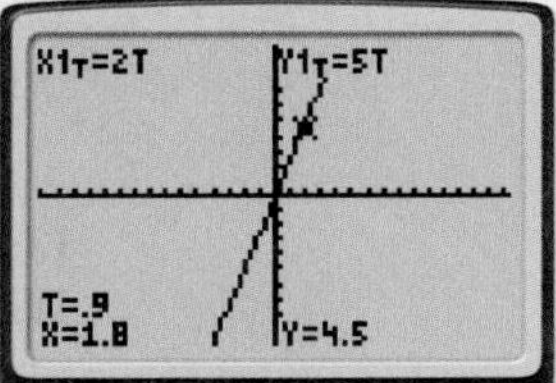

Try This

1. Consider $\begin{cases} x = 2t \\ y = \frac{1}{2}t \end{cases}$.
   a. Graph the relation and estimate the slope of the line created by the graph. Use the following window settings: **Tmin = −10**, **Tmax = 10**, and **Tstep = 0.1**, and use the square viewing window.
   b. **Critical Thinking** How does the slope of the line relate to the slope of the two parametric equations?
2. An airplane is traveling at a constant horizontal speed of 500 ft/s and is ascending at a constant rate of 50 ft/s. A model of the path of the airplane is given parametrically by $\begin{cases} x = 500t \\ y = 50t \end{cases}$ for t s.
   a. Graph the path of the airplane for $t = 20$ to $t = 180$ s and identify the location of the plane after 50 s.
   b. When will the plane reach an altitude of 5000 ft? (*Hint:* You may have to adjust your viewing window.)
3. **Critical Thinking** Create a graph of the line $y = x$ by using parametric equations.
4. **Extension** Consider $\begin{cases} x = t^2 \\ y = t \end{cases}$.
   a. Graph the relation. Use the following window settings: **Tmin = −10**, **Tmax = 10**, and **Tstep = 0.1**, and use the square viewing window.
   b. Describe the relation and write the formula in terms of x and y only. Is the relation a function?

CHAPTER 3

MULTI-STEP TEST PREP

SECTION 3B

Linear Equations in Three Dimensions

Building Bridges A bridge is to be constructed between two buildings. The cross sections of the bridge are 12 steel rectangles 16 feet wide by 11 feet high. The bridge will be represented by a three-dimensional model.

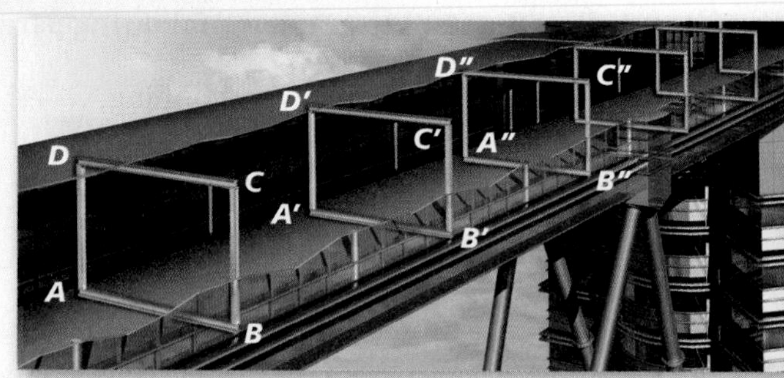

1. The coordinates of the vertices defining the first cross section are $A(0, 0, 0)$, $B(0, 16, 0)$, $C(0, 16, 11)$, and $D(0, 0, 11)$. What are the coordinates of the points A', B', C', and D' if the rectangular cross sections are 30 feet away from each other?

2. What are the coordinates of the points A'', B'', C'', and D''?

3. A supervisor changes the sketch so that point A has coordinates $(150, 0, -16)$. What are the new coordinates for points B, C, and D? What are the new coordinates for points A', B' C', and D'? What about A'', B'', C'', and D''?

4. The steel cross sections will be rigged with sliding metal fire doors that will close in case of emergency. What is the area covered by one of these doors?

5. Due to some budget restrictions, the bridge has to be reduced to a width of 14 feet and a height of 9 feet. What will be the coordinates of points A, B, and D if point C is defined as the origin $(0, 0, 0)$?

Quiz for Lessons 3-5 Through 3-6

3-5 Linear Equations in Three Dimensions

Graph each point in three-dimensional space.

1. $(-3, 2, 1)$ 2. $(2, -3, -2)$ 3. $(3, 1, -3)$

Graph each linear equation in three-dimensional space.

4. $2x - 2y + 4z = 8$ 5. $2x + y - 2z = -4$ 6. $x + 5y + 3z = 15$

Finance **Use the following information and the table for Problems 7 and 8.** A dental office charges \$50 for teeth cleanings, \$100 for performing a one-surface filling, and \$75 for an initial visit with X rays. The dental office's total income was exactly \$3500 for each of the days shown in the table.

Day	Cleaning	Filling	Initial Visit
Monday	20	22	■
Tuesday	■	18	6
Wednesday	16	■	4
Thursday	25	21	■

7. Write a linear equation in three variables to represent this situation.
8. Complete the table for the possible numbers of appointments each day.

3-6 Solving Linear Systems in Three Variables

Use elimination to solve each system of equations.

9. $\begin{cases} x + y + z = 0 \\ 2x + y - 2z = -8 \\ -x + 4z = 10 \end{cases}$ 10. $\begin{cases} x + 2y + z = 7 \\ x - 2y - 4z = 0 \\ 2x - y + 4z = -3 \end{cases}$ 11. $\begin{cases} 2x + 2y + z = 10 \\ x - 2y + 3z = 13 \\ x - y + 3z = 12 \end{cases}$

Business **Use the following information and the table for Problems 12 and 13.** JoJo's Pretzel Stand has three different types of pretzels, indicated by type A, type B, and type C. The table shows the total revenue for three hours on a particular afternoon.

Time	Type A	Type B	Type C	Revenue
2:00 P.M.–3:00 P.M.	6	8	14	\$65
3:00 P.M.–4:00 P.M.	10	10	15	\$80
4:00 P.M.–5:00 P.M.	12	6	9	\$60

12. Write a system in three variables to represent the data in the table.
13. How much does each type of pretzel cost?

Classify each system as consistent or inconsistent, and determine the number of solutions.

14. $\begin{cases} 2x - 2y + 3z = -2 \\ 4y + 6z = 1 \\ 4x - 4y + 6z = 5 \end{cases}$ 15. $\begin{cases} 4x - y + z = 5 \\ 3x + y + 2z = 5 \\ 2x - 5z = -8 \end{cases}$ 16. $\begin{cases} 2x + y - 3z = 4 \\ x - 3y + z = -8 \\ -x + 3y - z = 8 \end{cases}$

EXTENSION Parametric Equations

Objectives
Graph parametric equations, and use them to model real-world applications.

Write the function represented by a pair of parametric equations.

Vocabulary
parameter
parametric equations

As an airplane ascends after takeoff, its altitude increases at a rate of 45 ft/s while its distance on the ground from the airport increases at 210 ft/s.

Both of these rates can be expressed in terms of time. When two variables, such as x and y, are expressed in terms of a third variable, such as t, the third variable is called a **parameter**. The equations that define this relationship are **parametric equations**.

EXAMPLE 1 Writing and Graphing Parametric Equations

As an airplane ascends after takeoff, its altitude increases at a rate of 45 ft/s while its distance on the ground from the airport increases at 210 ft/s.

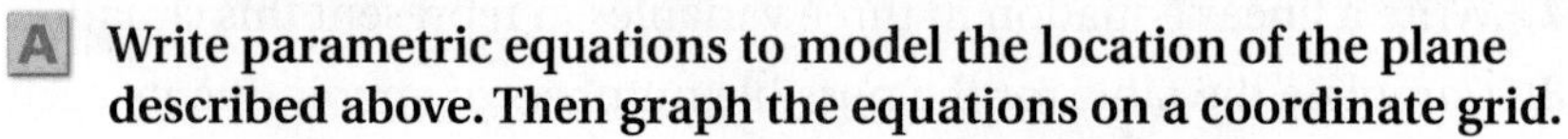

A **Write parametric equations to model the location of the plane described above. Then graph the equations on a coordinate grid.**

Using the horizontal and vertical speeds given above, write equations for the ground distance x and altitude y in terms of t.

$$\begin{cases} x = 210t \\ y = 45t \end{cases}$$ *Use the distance formula $d = rt$*

Make a table to help you draw the graph. Use different t-values to find x- and y-values. The x and y rows give the points to plot.

t	0	2	4	6	8
x	0	420	840	1260	1680
y	0	90	180	270	360

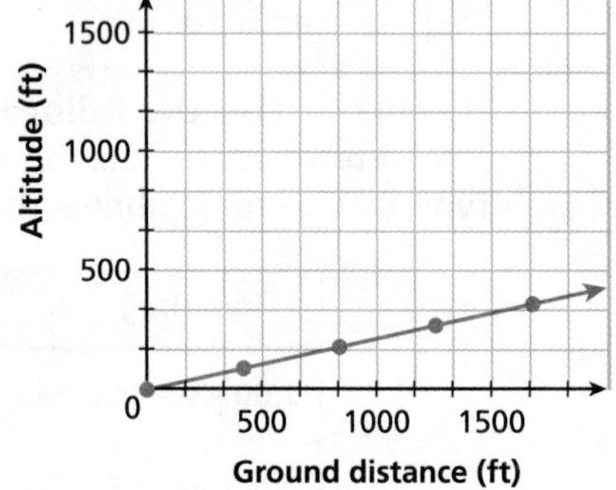

Plot and connect $(0, 0)$, $(420, 90)$, $(840, 180)$, $(1260, 270)$, and $(1680, 360)$.
The graph is shown at right.

B **Find the location of the airplane 15 seconds after takeoff.**

$x = 210t = 210(15) = 3150$ *Substitute $t = 15$*
$y = 45t = 45(15) = 675$

At $t = 15$, the airplane has a ground distance of 3150 feet from the airport and an altitude of 675 feet.

CHECK IT OUT! **A helicopter takes off with a horizontal speed of 5 ft/s and a vertical speed of 20 ft/s**

1a. Write equations for and draw a graph of the motion of the helicopter.

1b. Describe the location of the helicopter at $t = 10$ seconds.

You can use parametric equations to write a function that relates the two variables by using the substitution method.

EXAMPLE 2 Writing Functions Based on Parametric Equations

Use the data from Example 1 to write an equation for the airplane's altitude y in terms of ground distance x.

Solve one of the two parametric equations for t. Then substitute to get one equation whose variables are x and y.

$x = 210t$, so $\frac{x}{210} = t$ — *Solve for t in the first equation.*

$y = 45t$ — *Second equation*

$y = 45\left(\frac{x}{210}\right) = \frac{3}{14}x$ — *Substitute and simplify.*

$y = \frac{3}{14}x$

The equation for the airplane's altitude in terms of ground distance is $y = \frac{3}{14}x$.

Recall that the helicopter in Check It Out Problem 1 takes off with a horizontal speed of 5 ft/s and a vertical speed of 20 ft/s.

2. Write an equation for the helicopter's motion in terms of only x and y.

EXTENSION Exercises

Draw a graph to represent each set of parametric equations.

1. $\begin{cases} x = 4t \\ y = 2t \end{cases}$ **2.** $\begin{cases} x = t - 2 \\ y = 4t \end{cases}$ **3.** $\begin{cases} x = \frac{t}{4} \\ y = -3t \end{cases}$ **4.** $\begin{cases} x = 20t \\ y = 10t + 10 \end{cases}$

Write one equation for each set of parametric equations in terms of only x and y.

5. $\begin{cases} x = 3t \\ y = 2t \end{cases}$ **6.** $\begin{cases} x = 2t + 4 \\ y = 5t \end{cases}$ **7.** $\begin{cases} x = \frac{3}{5}t \\ y = 6t \end{cases}$ **8.** $\begin{cases} x = 7.5t \\ y = 20t + 2 \end{cases}$

9. Oceanography Suppose a research submarine descends from the surface with a horizontal speed of 1.8 m/s and a vertical speed of 0.9 m/s.

a. Write equations for and draw a graph of the motion of the submarine.

b. Find the depth of the submarine after 50 s.

c. Find the submarine's depth after 1 day. Does this answer make sense? Explain.

10. Hiking From her starting point, a hiker walks along a straight path. Her north-south speed is 3 mi/h (to the north), and her east-west speed is 0.4 mi/h (to the east). Let x represent how far east of her starting point the hiker is, and let y represent how far north she is. Write an equation for her motion in terms of only x and y. Find the location of the hiker when $x = 2$.

CHAPTER 3

Study Guide: Review

Vocabulary

Complete the sentences below with vocabulary words from the list above.

1. A consistent and ___?___ system has infinitely many solutions.
2. ___?___ involves adding or subtracting equations to get rid of one of the variables in a system.
3. In a linear programming problem, the solution to the ___?___ can be graphed as a(n) ___?___.
4. Each point in a(n) ___?___ can be represented by a(n) ___?___.
5. A(n) ___?___ system is a set of equations or inequalities that has at least one solution.

3-1 Using Graphs and Tables to Solve Linear Systems *(pp. 182–189)*

EXAMPLES

■ Solve $\begin{cases} x + y = 3 \\ 3x - 6y = -9 \end{cases}$ by using a graph and a table.

Solve each equation for *y*.

$$\begin{cases} y = -x + 3 \\ y = \frac{1}{2}x + \frac{3}{2} \end{cases}$$

Make a table of values.

$y = -x + 3$

x	y
0	3
1	2
4	1

$y = \frac{1}{2}x + \frac{3}{2}$

x	y
0	1.5
1	2
4	2.5

Graph the lines.

The solution is (1, 2).

EXERCISES

Solve each system by using a graph and a table.

6. $\begin{cases} y = 2x \\ 3x - y = 5 \end{cases}$

7. $\begin{cases} x + y = 6 \\ x - y = 2 \end{cases}$

8. $\begin{cases} x - 6y = 2 \\ 2x - 5y = -3 \end{cases}$

9. $\begin{cases} x - 3y = 6 \\ 3x - y = 2 \end{cases}$

Classify each system and determine the number of solutions.

10. $\begin{cases} y = x - 7 \\ x + 9y = 16 \end{cases}$

11. $\begin{cases} \frac{1}{2}x + 2y = 3 \\ x + 4y = 6 \end{cases}$

12. $\begin{cases} 5x - 10y = 8 \\ x - 2y = 4 \end{cases}$

13. $\begin{cases} 4x - 3y = 21 \\ 2x - 2y = 10 \end{cases}$

14. **Security** A locksmith charges $25 to make a house call and $15 for each lock that is re-keyed. Another locksmith charges $10 to make a house call and $20 for each lock that is re-keyed. For how many locks will the total costs be the same?

3-2 Using Algebraic Methods to Solve Linear Systems *(pp. 190–197)*

EXAMPLES

■ **Use substitution to solve** $\begin{cases} y = x + 6 \\ 4x - 5y = -18 \end{cases}$.

$4x - 5(x + 6) = -18$ *Substitute for y.*
$4x - 5x - 30 = -18 \rightarrow x = -12$

Substitute the x-value into either equation.

$y = x + 6 \rightarrow y = (-12) + 6 \rightarrow y = -6$

The solution to the system is $(-12, -6)$.

■ **Use elimination to solve** $\begin{cases} 7x - 2y = 2 \\ 3x + 4y = 30 \end{cases}$.

Multiply the first equation by 2 to eliminate y.

$\begin{cases} 7x - 2y = 2 \\ 3x + 4y = 30 \end{cases} \rightarrow \begin{matrix} 2(7x - 2y = 2) \\ 3x + 4y = 30 \end{matrix} \rightarrow \begin{matrix} 14x - 4y = 4 \\ 3x + 4y = 30 \end{matrix}$

Add the equations. $17x = 34$
First part of the solution $x = 2$

Substitute the x-value into either equation.

$3x + 4y = 30 \rightarrow 3(2) + 4y = 30$

$\rightarrow y = 6$ *Second part of the solution*

The solution to the system is $(2, 6)$.

EXERCISES

Use substitution to solve each system of equations.

15. $\begin{cases} y = 3x \\ 2x - 3y = -7 \end{cases}$ **16.** $\begin{cases} y = x - 1 \\ 4x - y = 19 \end{cases}$

17. $\begin{cases} 4x - y = 0 \\ 6x - 3y = 12 \end{cases}$ **18.** $\begin{cases} 5x = -10y \\ 8x - 4y = 40 \end{cases}$

Use elimination to solve each system of equations.

19. $\begin{cases} 4x + 5y = 41 \\ 7x + 5y = 53 \end{cases}$ **20.** $\begin{cases} -4x - y = -16 \\ -4x - 5y = -32 \end{cases}$

21. $\begin{cases} 2x - y = 8 \\ x + 2y = 9 \end{cases}$ **22.** $\begin{cases} 9x - 5y = 13 \\ 4x - 6y = 2 \end{cases}$

23. Mixtures A popular mixture of potpourri includes pine needles and lavender. If pine needles cost \$1.50 per ounce and lavender costs \$4.00 per ounce, how much of each ingredient should be mixed to make 80 oz of the potpourri that is worth \$200?

3-3 Solving Systems of Linear Inequalities *(pp. 199–204)*

EXAMPLE

■ **The combined annual sales for a company's two divisions was almost \$12 million. One of the divisions accounted for at least 75% of the total sales. Write and graph a system of inequalities that can be used to determine the possible combinations of sales for both divisions of the company.**

Let x be one division, and let y be the other division with 75% of the sales.

Write the system of inequalities.

$\begin{cases} x + y < 12 \\ y \geq 0.75(x + y) \end{cases} \rightarrow \begin{cases} x + y < 12 \\ y \geq 3x \end{cases}$ *dashed line* / *solid line*

Graph the boundary lines, and shade accordingly. Notice also that $x > 0$ and $y > 0$.

The overlapping region is the solution for the system.

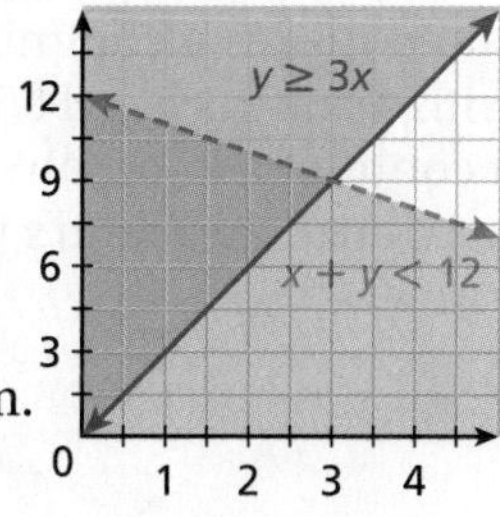

EXERCISES

Graph each system of inequalities.

24. $\begin{cases} y + 1 > 4x \\ y \leq x + 1 \end{cases}$ **25.** $\begin{cases} y - 3x < 3 \\ 3y \geq x + 3 \end{cases}$

Graph the system of inequalities and classify the figure created by the solution region.

26. $\begin{cases} y \leq -x + 2 \\ x > -1 \\ y > -1 \end{cases}$ **27.** $\begin{cases} y \geq 2x \\ y < 4 \\ y > 2 \\ y \leq \frac{1}{2}x + 4 \end{cases}$

28. Business A coffee shop wants to make a maximum of 120 lb of a coffee mixture that costs less than \$10/lb. The shop will mix coffee that is sold at \$8/lb with coffee sold at \$11.50/lb. Write and graph a system of inequalities that shows the possible mixtures of the two coffee types.

3-4 Linear Programming *(pp. 205–211)*

EXAMPLE

■ **A café sells cold sandwiches and hot entrées. The range of items sold is shown in the table. The café has never sold more than a total of 125 sandwiches and entrées in one day. If the café makes a profit of \$0.75 on each sandwich and \$1 on each hot entrée, how many of each item would maximize the café profit?**

Menu Item	Minimum Sold	Maximum Sold
Cold sandwiches	60	80
Hot entrées	40	60

Let x be the number of cold sandwiches, and let y be the number of hot entrées.

Write the constraints.

$$\begin{cases} 60 \le x \le 80 & \textit{Number of sandwiches} \\ 40 \le y \le 60 & \textit{Number of hot entrées} \\ x + y < 125 & \textit{Number of items sold} \end{cases}$$

Graph the feasible region and identify vertices.

The feasible region has five vertices at (60, 40), (60, 60), (65, 60), (80, 45), and (80, 40).

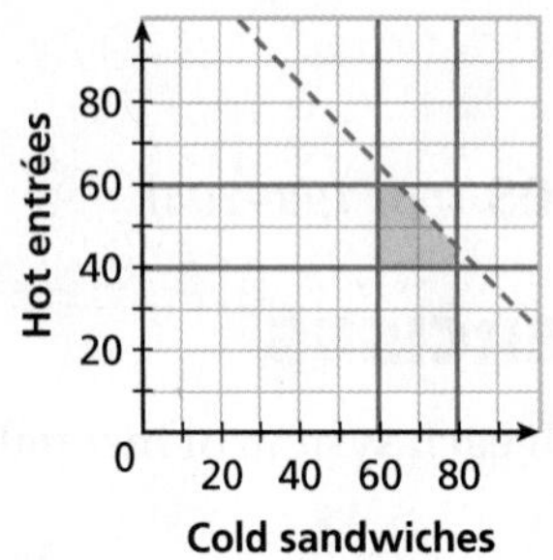

Write the objective function.

The objective function is $P = 0.75x + y$.
$P(0, 0) = 18(0) + 25(0) = 0$

Evaluate the objective function at each vertex.

$P(60, 40) = 0.75(60) + 40 = 85$
$P(60, 60) = 0.75(60) + 60 = 105$
$P(65, 60) = 0.75(65) + 60 = 108.75$
$P(80, 45) = 0.75(80) + 45 = 105$
$P(80, 40) = 0.75(80) + 40 = 100$

The objective function is maximized at (65, 60). The maximum profit of \$108.75 is obtained when 65 cold sandwiches and 60 hot entrées are sold.

EXERCISES

Graph each feasible region.

29. $\begin{cases} x \ge 0 \\ y \ge 0 \\ y \le 3x + 1 \\ y \le -\frac{3}{4}x + 6 \end{cases}$

30. $\begin{cases} x < 3 \\ y \ge 0 \\ y < 2x + 1 \\ y \le -x + 4 \end{cases}$

31. $\begin{cases} x > 0 \\ y < 0 \\ y > \frac{1}{2}x - 6 \end{cases}$

32. $\begin{cases} x \le 2 \\ y \ge -1 \\ x \ge -1 \\ y \le -x + 3 \end{cases}$

Maximize or minimize each objective function.

33. Maximize $P = 6x + 10y$ for the constraints from Exercise 29.

34. Minimize $P = 14x + 9y$ for the constraints from Exercise 30.

Manufacturing A shoe insole company produces two models of insoles: an extra thick insole for sports shoes and a thinner insole for dress shoes. The thick insole requires 6 min of manufacturing time and generates a profit of \$8. The thin insole requires 4 min of manufacturing time and generates a profit of \$9. The manufacturing line runs at most 12 h a day, or 720 min. Because of demand, the company manufactures at least twice as many thick insoles as thin insoles.

35. Write the constraints, and graph the feasible region.

36. Write the objective function for the company's profit.

37. What is the maximum profit that can be generated in one day?

38. **Sales** Each day, a cell phone stand sells between 10 and 25 cell phones with new service contracts, and between 5 and 10 cell phones without contracts. The stand never sells more than 30 new cell phones per day. The cell phone stand makes a commission of \$35 for each phone with a contract and \$5 for each phone without a contract. How many of each option would maximize the stand's profit?

3-5 Linear Equations in Three Dimensions *(pp. 214–218)*

EXAMPLES

- **Graph (2, −1, 3) in three-dimensional space.**

From the origin, move 2 units forward along the x-axis, 1 unit left, and 3 units up.

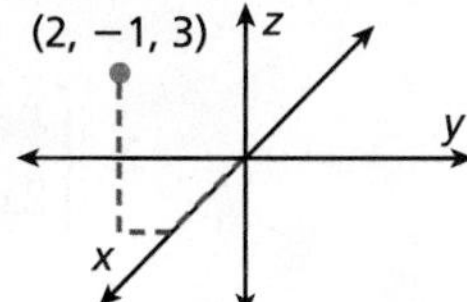

- **Graph the linear equation $3x + 6y - z = -6$ in three-dimensional space.**

Find the intercepts.

x-intercept: $3x = -6 \rightarrow x = -2$

y-intercept: $6y = -6 \rightarrow y = -1$

z-intercept: $-z = -6 \rightarrow z = 6$

Plot the points (−2, 0, 0), (0, −1, 0), and (0, 0, 6). Sketch a plane through the three points.

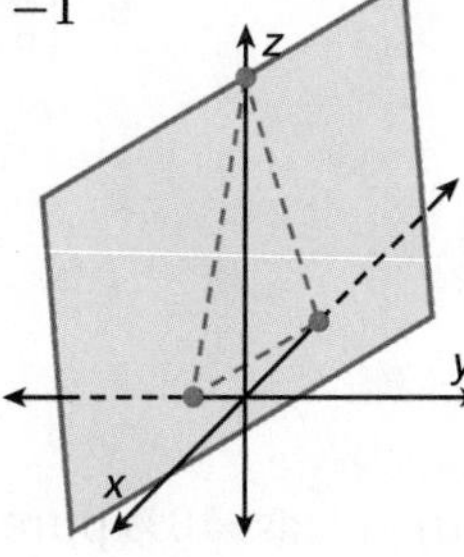

EXERCISES

Graph each point in three-dimensional space.

39. (−1, 0, 3) **40.** (2, −2, 1)

41. (0, −1, 1) **42.** (3, 1, 0)

Graph each linear equation in three-dimensional space.

43. $x - 3y + 2z = 6$ **44.** $2x - 4y - 2z = 4$

45. $-x + y - 5z = 5$ **46.** $3x + 2y + z = -6$

47. Consumer Economics Lee has $35 to purchase a combination of drinks, pizza, and ice cream for a party. Each drink costs $2, each pizza costs $9, and each quart of ice cream costs $4. Write a linear equation in three variables to represent this situation.

3-6 Solving Linear Systems in Three Variables *(pp. 220–226)*

EXAMPLES

- **Use elimination to solve** $\begin{cases} 3x + 2y - z = -1 \\ x + 3y - z = -10 \\ 2x - y - 3z = -3 \end{cases}$.

First, eliminate z to obtain a 2-by-2 system.

$$\begin{array}{r} 3x + 2y - z = -1 \\ \underline{x + 3y - z = -10} \\ 2x - y \qquad = 9 \end{array} \qquad \begin{array}{r} 3(x + 3y - z = -10) \\ \underline{2x - y - 3z = -3} \\ x + 10y \qquad = -27 \end{array}$$

The resulting 2-by-2 system is $\begin{cases} 2x - y = 9 \\ x + 10y = -27 \end{cases}$.

Eliminate x.

$$\begin{array}{r} 2x - \quad y = 9 \\ \underline{-2(x + 10y = -27)} \\ -21y = 63 \rightarrow y = -3 \end{array}$$

Substitute to solve for x and then z.

$2x - y = 9 \rightarrow 2x - (-3) = 9 \rightarrow x = 3$

$3x + 2y - z = -1 \rightarrow 3(3) + 2(-3) - z = -1 \rightarrow z = 4$

The solution to the system is (3, −3, 4).

EXERCISES

Use elimination to solve each system of equations.

48. $\begin{cases} x + 3y + 2z = 13 \\ 2x + 2y - z = 3 \\ x - 2y + 3z = 6 \end{cases}$

49. $\begin{cases} x + y + z = 2 \\ 3x + 2y - z = -1 \\ 3x - y = 4 \end{cases}$

Classify each system as consistent or inconsistent, and determine the number of solutions.

50. $\begin{cases} x + y + z = -2 \\ -x + 2y - 5z = 4 \\ 3x + 3y + 3z = 5 \end{cases}$

51. $\begin{cases} -x - y + 2z = -3 \\ 4x + 4y - 8z = 12 \\ 2x + y - 3z = -2 \end{cases}$

CHAPTER 3

CHAPTER TEST

Solve each system by using a graph and a table.

1. $\begin{cases} x - y = -4 \\ 3x - 6y = -12 \end{cases}$ **2.** $\begin{cases} y = x - 1 \\ x + 4y = 6 \end{cases}$ **3.** $\begin{cases} x - y = 3 \\ 2x + 3y = 6 \end{cases}$

Classify each system and determine the number of solutions.

4. $\begin{cases} 6y = 9x \\ 8x + 4y = 20 \end{cases}$ **5.** $\begin{cases} 12x + 3y = -9 \\ -y - 4x = 3 \end{cases}$ **6.** $\begin{cases} 3x - 9y = 21 \\ 6 = x - 3y \end{cases}$

Use substitution or elimination to solve each system of equations.

7. $\begin{cases} y = x - 2 \\ x + 5y = 20 \end{cases}$ **8.** $\begin{cases} 5x - y = 33 \\ 7x + y = 51 \end{cases}$ **9.** $\begin{cases} x + y = 5 \\ 2x + 5y = 16 \end{cases}$

Graph each system of inequalities.

10. $\begin{cases} 2y - 4x \geq 4 \\ y - x \geq 1 \end{cases}$ **11.** $\begin{cases} x + y \geq 3 \\ y - 4 \leq 0 \end{cases}$

12. Chemistry A chemist wants to mix a new solution with at least 18% pure salt. The chemist has two solutions with 9% pure salt and 24% pure salt and wants to make at most 250 mL of the new solution. Write and graph a system of inequalities that can be used to find the amounts of each salt solution needed.

13. Minimize the objective function $P = 5x + 9y$ under the following constraints. $\begin{cases} x \geq 0 \\ y \geq 0 \\ y \leq 2x + 1 \\ y \leq -3x + 6 \end{cases}$

Graph each point in three-dimensional space.

14. $(2, -1, 3)$ **15.** $(0, -1, 3)$ **16.** $(-2, 1, -1)$

Business **Use the following information and the table for Problems 17 and 18.**
A plumber charges \$50 for repairing a leaking faucet, \$150 for installing a sink, and \$200 for an emergency situation. The plumber's total income was exactly \$1000 for each day shown in the table.

Day	Repair Faucet	Install Sink	Emergency
Monday	2	2	
Tuesday		3	2
Wednesday	1		4
Thursday	4	4	

17. Write a linear equation in three variables to represent this situation.

18. Complete the table for the possible numbers of tasks each day.

Solve each system of equations using elimination, or state that the system is inconsistent or dependent.

19. $\begin{cases} x - y + z = -2 \\ 4x - y + 2z = -3 \\ 2x - 3y + 2z = -7 \end{cases}$ **20.** $\begin{cases} 3x - y - z = -1 \\ x + y + 2z = 8 \\ 6x - 2y - 2z = 5 \end{cases}$

CHAPTER 3

FOCUS ON SAT MATHEMATICS SUBJECT TESTS

In addition to the SAT, the SAT Mathematics Subject Tests are required by some colleges for admission. Colleges that don't require the SAT Mathematics Subject Tests may still use the scores to learn about your academic background and possibly place you in the appropriate college math class.

Take the SAT Mathematics Subject Tests while the subject matter is fresh in your mind. You are not expected to be familiar with all the content covered on the tests, but you should have completed at least three years of college-prep math.

You may want to time yourself as you take this practice test. It should take you about 6 minutes to complete.

1. Which of the following systems of equations is represented by the graph?

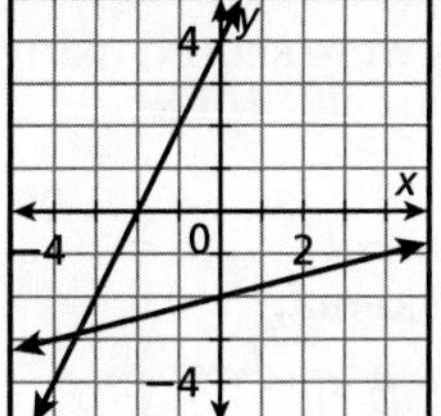

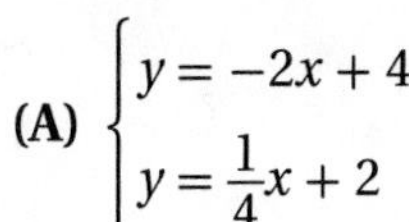

(A) $\begin{cases} y = -2x + 4 \\ y = \frac{1}{4}x + 2 \end{cases}$

(B) $\begin{cases} y = 2x - 4 \\ y = -\frac{1}{4}x - 2 \end{cases}$

(C) $\begin{cases} y = 2x + 4 \\ y = \frac{1}{4}x - 2 \end{cases}$

(D) $\begin{cases} y = \frac{1}{2}x + 4 \\ y = 4x - 2 \end{cases}$

(E) $\begin{cases} y = \frac{1}{2}x - 4 \\ y = 4x + 2 \end{cases}$

2. If $x - 2y = 1$ and $2x - y = -4$, then $x + y = ?$

(A) -9

(B) -7

(C) -5

(D) -3

(E) -1

3. In a fruit salad, there are two more bananas than apples and eight times as many cherries as apples. If a total of 22 pieces of fruit are used, how many of each type are in the salad?

(A) 2 apples, 4 bananas, 18 cherries

(B) 2 apples, 4 bananas, 16 cherries

(C) 2 apples, 0 bananas, 20 cherries

(D) 4 apples, 2 bananas, 12 cherries

(E) 4 apples, 8 bananas, 32 cherries

4. Which of the following inequalities is NOT graphed in the figure?

(A) $y > -3x + 2$

(B) $2y \leq x - 6$

(C) $0.5x \geq y + 3$

(D) $3x + y \geq 2$

(E) $6x + 2y > 4$

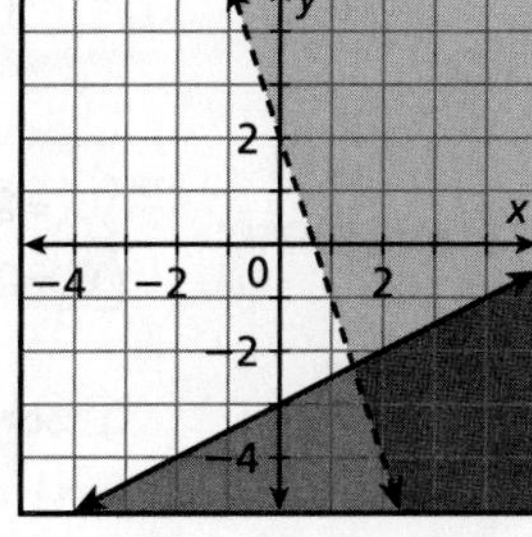

5. If $r = 3s + 1$ and $t = s - 4$, then what is r in terms of t?

(A) $3t + 13$

(B) $t + 4$

(C) -2.5

(D) $3t + 5$

(E) $3t + 1$

CHAPTER 3

TEST TACKLER

Standardized Test Strategies

Short Response: Write Short Responses

Short-response test items are designed to measure understanding and reasoning skills. Typically, you must show how you solved the problem and explain your answer. Short-response questions are scored using a scoring rubric.

EXAMPLE 1

Short Response Kathie earns \$20 per day plus \$0.15 for each newspaper she delivers. Kevin earns \$25 per day plus \$0.10 for each newspaper he delivers. After how many deliveries do they each earn the same amount of money for that day? Write and solve a system of linear equations that models this situation.

Here are examples of how three different responses were scored using the scoring rubric shown.

2-point response:

Let x= the number of newspapers delivered.
Let y= the total amount of money earned.

$\begin{cases} y = 20 + 0.15x \\ y = 25 + 0.10x \end{cases}$ Set up a system of equations.

$20 + 0.15x = 25 + 0.10x$ Use substitution to solve.
$0.05x = 5$
$x = 100$

Check:
$\begin{cases} y = 20 + 0.15x = 20 + 0.15(100) = 35 \\ y = 25 + 0.10x = 25 + 0.10(100) = 35 \end{cases}$ ✓

Kathie and Kevin will make the same amount of money, \$35, if they both deliver exactly 100 newspapers on any given day.

1-point response:

$\begin{cases} y = 20 + 0.15x \\ y = 25 + 0.10x \end{cases}$ Set up a system of equations.

I solved the system using my graphing Calculator and determined that x = 100 newspapers.

Notice that the variables are not defined, and there is no sketch of the graph. Although the answer is correct, no explanation is provided.

0-point response:

Kathie and Kevin will never make the same amount of money on the same day.

Notice that the student provided an incorrect response without showing any work or explanation.

Scoring Rubric

2 points: The student writes and correctly solves a system of equations, showing all work. The student defines the variables, answers the question in a complete sentence, and provides an explanation.

1 point: The student writes and correctly solves a system of equations but does not show all work, does not define the variables, or does not provide an explanation.

1 point: The student writes and solves a system of equations but gives an incorrect answer. The student shows all work and provides an explanation for the answer.

0 points: The student gives no response or provides a solution without showing any work or explanation.

Never leave a short response test item blank. Showing your work and providing a reasonable explanation will result in at least partial credit.

Read each test item, and answer the questions that follow using this scoring rubric.

Scoring Rubric

- **2 points:** The student demonstrates a thorough understanding of the concept, correctly answers the question, and provides a complete explanation.
- **1 point:** The student shows all work and provides an explanation but answers the question incorrectly.
- **1 point:** The student correctly answers the question but does not show all work or does not provide an explanation.
- **0 points:** The student gives a response showing no work or explanation or gives no response.

Item A

Write a real-world situation that can be modeled by this system of equations.

$$\begin{cases} 12x + 15y = 69 \\ 40x + 30y = 170 \end{cases}$$

Solve for x, and make sure that its value makes sense to your situation.

Let x equal the cost of one bag of soil, and let y equal the cost of one potted plant. A landscaper purchased 12 bags of soil and 15 potted plants for $69. He returned to the same store later that week and purchased 40 bags of soil and 30 potted plants for $170. Each bag of soil cost $2, and each potted plant cost $3.

1. How would you score the student's response? Explain.
2. Rewrite the response so that it receives full credit.

Item B

Describe the graph of an independent linear system. Give an example of this type of system, and list the number of solutions it has.

The graph of an independent system is hard to describe because the graph of each equation is independent of the other, and therefore has many solutions.

3. Score the response, and provide your reasoning for the score.
4. Give a response that would receive full credit.

Item C

Explain how to use the intercepts to graph this linear equation in three dimensions. Then graph the equation.

$4x + 3y + 4z = 24$

By finding the x-, y-, and z-intercepts of the linear equation, you can plot three solutions. The plane defined by these points represents the solution set.

x-intercept: $4x + 3(0) + 4(0) = 24$; $x = 6$
y-intercept: $4(0) + 3y + 4(0) = 24$; $y = 8$
z-intercept: $4(0) + 3(0) + 4z = 24$; $z = 6$

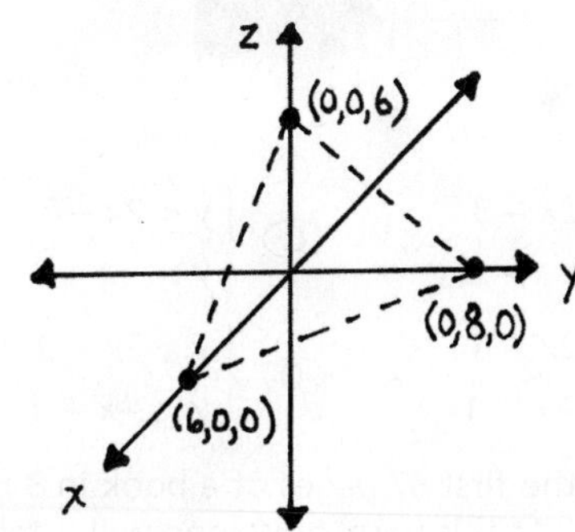

5. Should this response receive full credit? Explain your reasoning.

CHAPTER 3

STANDARDIZED TEST PREP

go.hrw.com
State Test Practice Online
KEYWORD: MB7 TestPrep

CUMULATIVE ASSESSMENT, CHAPTERS 1–3

Multiple Choice

1. What are the intercepts of the linear equation $2x + y - 5z = 20$?

Ⓐ $x = 0, y = 0, z = 0$

Ⓑ $x = 2, y = 1, z = -5$

Ⓒ $x = 10, y = 20, z = -4$

Ⓓ $x = 10, y = 20, z = 4$

2. Sam attends college 440 miles from home. He figures he can make the trip home in about 8 hours driving an average highway speed of 60 miles per hour. Which function represents how many miles Sam is from home after he has been driving for *x* hours at 60 miles per hour?

Ⓕ $f(x) = 440 - 60x$

Ⓖ $f(x) = 440 + 60x$

Ⓗ $f(x) = 440 - 8x$

Ⓙ $f(x) = 60x$

3. Which system of inequalities corresponds to the graph?

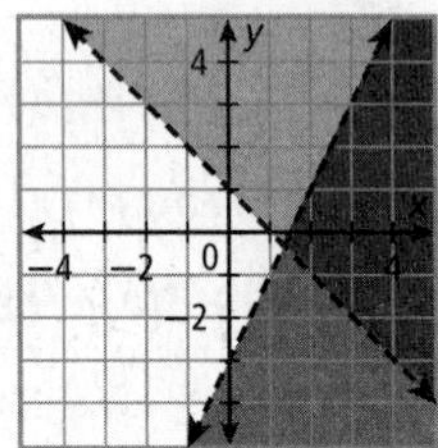

Ⓐ $\begin{cases} y \le 2x - 3 \\ y \ge -x + 1 \end{cases}$

Ⓑ $\begin{cases} y \le 2x - 3 \\ y > -x + 1 \end{cases}$

Ⓒ $\begin{cases} y < 2x - 3 \\ y > -x + 1 \end{cases}$

Ⓓ $\begin{cases} y \ge 2x - 3 \\ y < -x + 1 \end{cases}$

4. Kylie read the first 87 pages of a book in 3 hours 40 minutes. At this pace, how long will it take her to finish the book if it has a total of 214 pages?

Ⓕ 1 hour 25 minutes

Ⓕ 5 hours 5 minutes

Ⓗ 9 hours 1 minute

Ⓙ 12 hours 41 minutes

5. What is the equation of a line with a slope of $-\frac{2}{5}$ passing through (1, 4)?

Ⓐ $y = -\frac{2}{5}x + 4\frac{2}{5}$

Ⓑ $y = -\frac{2}{5}x + 2\frac{3}{5}$

Ⓒ $y = -\frac{1}{4}x - \frac{1}{10}$

Ⓓ $y = \frac{2}{5}x + 3\frac{3}{5}$

6. Which system of equations is an independent system?

Ⓕ $\begin{cases} 2y + 3x = -8 \\ 9x = -24 - 6y \end{cases}$

Ⓖ $\begin{cases} y = -x + 4 \\ 3y + 3x = -21 \end{cases}$

Ⓗ $\begin{cases} 2y + 7x = 24 \\ 5y - 6 = -4x \end{cases}$

Ⓙ $\begin{cases} 2y = 3x - 6 \\ 8y - 12x = 80 \end{cases}$

7. Which relation is a function?

Ⓐ $\{(1, 4), (4, 1), (1, 0), (0, 4)\}$

Ⓑ

x	3	5	8	8	12
y	5	6	7	8	9

Ⓒ

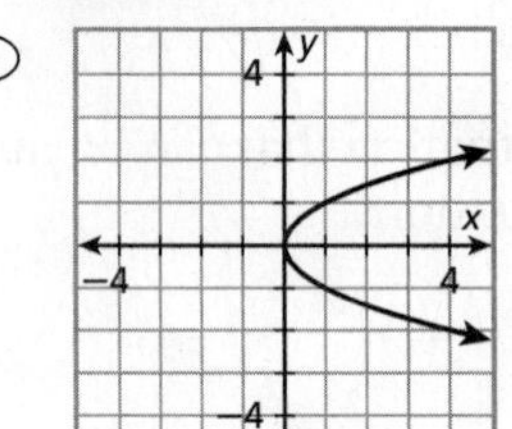

Ⓓ

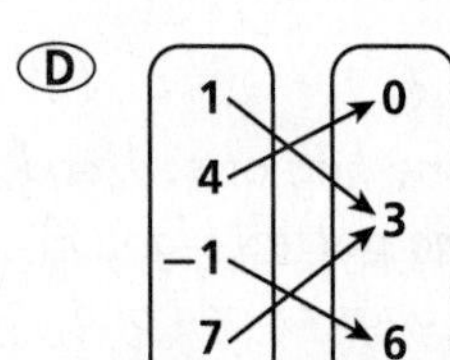

8. A feasible region has vertices (0, 0), (−2, 6), (3, −1), (−1, 1), and (−5, −5). What is the maximum value of the objective function $P = 4x - y$ over this region?

Ⓕ 0

Ⓖ 7

Ⓗ 13

Ⓙ 25

9. Mark has two bowls of cookie dough. One has 30% raisins, and the other has 5% raisins. How much of each dough should he mix to get 18 ounces of cookie dough that has 15% raisins?

Ⓐ 14.4 ounces of the dough with 30% raisins and 3.6 ounces of the dough with 5% raisins

Ⓑ 5.4 ounces of the dough with 30% raisins and 0.9 ounces of the dough with 5% raisins

Ⓒ 8.8 ounces of the dough with 30% raisins and 9.2 ounces of the dough with 5% raisins

Ⓓ 7.2 ounces of the dough with 30% raisins and 10.8 ounces of the dough with 5% raisins

In Exercise 10, to solve for the final exam percent, it is not necessary to find the percent for homework or quizzes first.

10. A final grade is based on a student's performance on homework, quizzes, and the final exam. All homework, quizzes, and the final exam are worth 100 points. Each category is worth a different percentage of the final grade. Given the scores of three students in the table below, what percent of the final grade is the final exam worth?

	Homework	Quizzes	Final Exam	Final Grade
Andy	100	82	73	82
Mia	66	94	88	82
Nick	82	46	98	88

Ⓕ 50%　　Ⓗ 75%

Ⓖ 60%　　Ⓙ 86%

Gridded Response

11. Find the lowest positive whole number that is a solution of $\frac{|438 - 3x|}{3} > 816$.

12. Peter eats 8 wings and 3 pieces of pizza and consumes a total of 975 Calories. K.J. eats 6 wings and 4 pieces of pizza and consumes a total of 950 Calories. How many Calories are in one piece of pizza?

Short Response

13. One group of people going to the zoo bought 5 child tickets and 4 adult tickets for a total of $68. Another group bought 17 child tickets and 12 adult tickets for a total of $216.

a. Write a system of equations that models this problem.

b. Solve the system using a graph.

c. Solve the system using another method. Explain why the method you used may be better than using the graphing method. What is the price of each kind of ticket?

14. Point *A* has coordinates (3, 4). Point *B* is a reflection of point *A* across the *x*-axis.

a. Give the coordinates of point *B*.

b. Point *C* is a translation of point *B* 3 units left and 2 units down. Give the coordinates of point *C*.

15. The function $g(x)$ is a vertical translation of $f(x) = 4x - 3$ down 5 units.

a. Write the rule for $g(x)$.

b. The function $h(x)$ is a reflection of $g(x)$ across the *x*-axis. Write the rule for $h(x)$.

Extended Response

16. A curtain manufacturer has 820 lots of cotton fiber and 1250 lots of synthetic fiber. A discount curtain uses 18 lots of cotton fiber and 32 lots of synthetic fiber. A premium curtain uses 36 lots of cotton fiber and 28 lots of synthetic fiber.

a. Write the constraints.

b. Graph the feasible region. Give the vertices of the polygon that defines the feasible region.

c. The manufacturer makes a profit of $170 on each discount curtain sold and a profit of $190 on each premium curtain sold. Write the objective function.

d. How many of each kind of curtain should be manufactured to maximize profit?

CHAPTER

4 Matrices

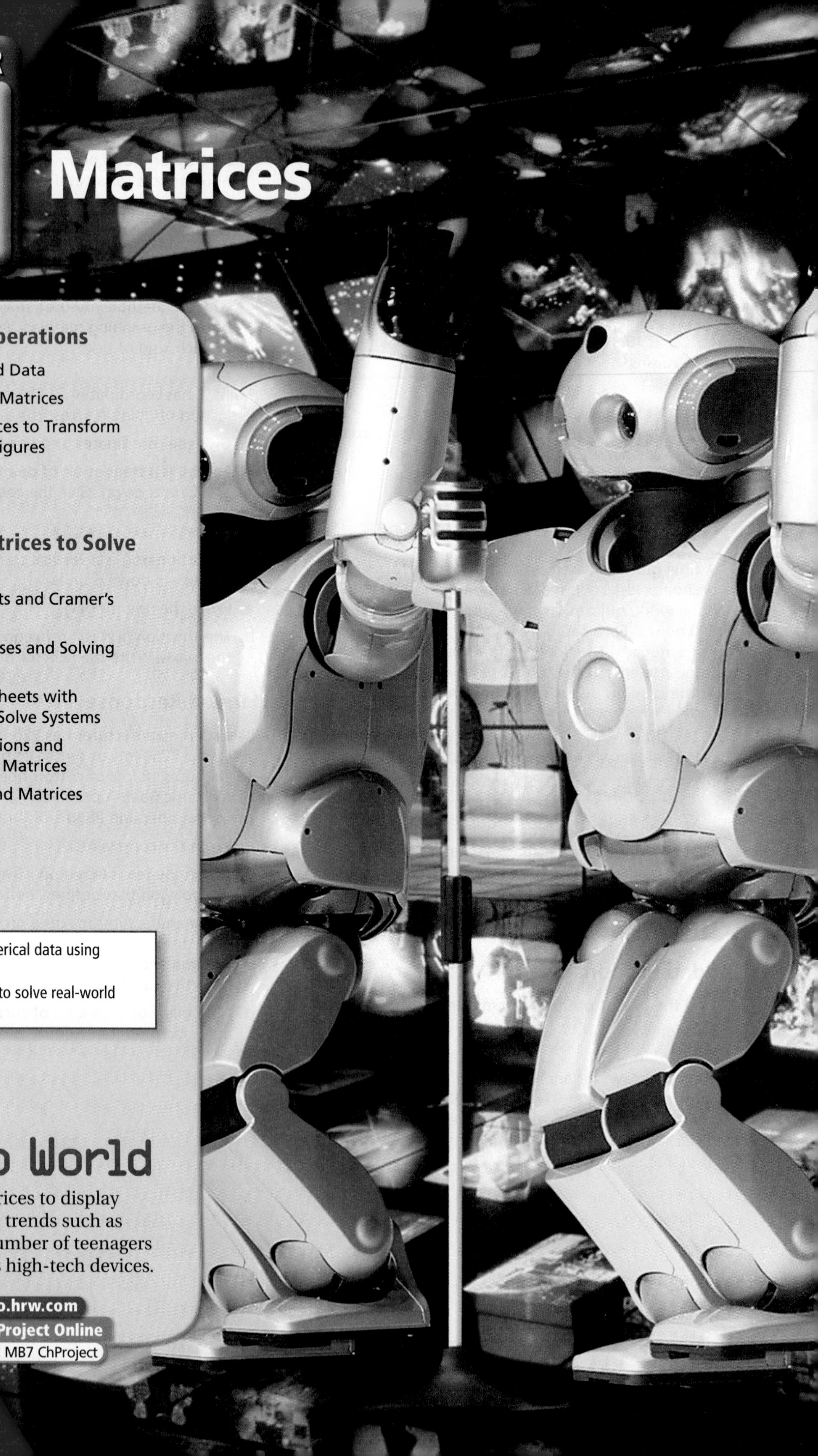

Chapter Focus

- Represent numerical data using matrices.
- Apply matrices to solve real-world problems.

Techno World

You can use matrices to display data and analyze trends such as the increasing number of teenagers who own various high-tech devices.

go.hrw.com
Chapter Project Online
KEYWORD: MB7 ChProject

ARE YOU READY?

Vocabulary

Match each term on the left with a definition on the right.

1. radius
2. dependent system
3. inconsistent system
4. transformation

A. an operation that can be performed in either order, as in $a + b = b + a$ and $ab = ba$
B. the distance from the center of a circle to the circle
C. A system of equations or inequalities that has no solution
D. A change in the position, size, or shape of a figure or graph
E. A system of equations that has infinitely many solutions

Add and Subtract Integers

Simplify each expression.

5. $2 + 7 + (-10)$
6. $-8 + 14 + (-3)$
7. $-2 + (-3) + (-5)$
8. $-9 + 15 - 7 + 1$
9. $20 - (-5) + (-3) - 2$
10. $9 + 8 - 7 + 5 - (-3) + 2$

Multiply and Divide Integers

Multiply or divide.

11. $-18 \div 9$
12. $-6(-1)$
13. $16(-2)$
14. $-15 \div (-3)$

Order of Operations

Simplify each expression.

15. $2(0.5) + 2(0.6)$
16. $0(6.7) + 1(0.3) - 5(2) - 3(8)$
17. $3(2 + 7 + 0) - 5(3 + 6 + 4)$
18. $4(3 - 6 + 2) - 5(2 + 0 - 1)$

Identify Similar Figures

19. Identify which figures are similar.

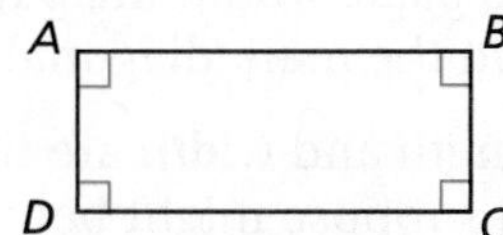

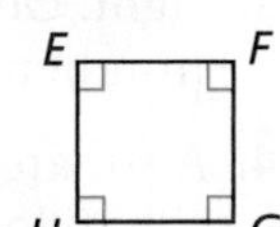

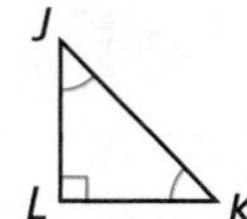

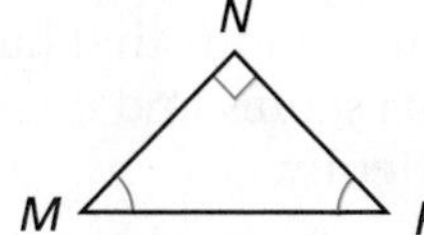

Find Missing Measures in Similar Figures

20. $\triangle ABC$ is similar to $\triangle DEF$. $m\angle FDE = 35°$. What other angle has a measure of 35°?
21. $\triangle FGH$ is similar to $\triangle JKL$. $JL = 12$, $GH = 12$, and $FH = 8$. Find KL.

CHAPTER 4

Study Guide: Preview

Where You've Been

Previously, you

- organized data into tables.
- performed operations with real numbers.
- solved systems of linear equations.

In This Chapter

You will study

- organizing data into matrices.
- operating with matrices.
- solving systems of equations several ways by using matrices.

Where You're Going

You can use the skills in this chapter

- as you study other fields of mathematics, such as geometry, statistics, and business math.
- in competitions that have various scores and degrees of difficulty.
- outside of school to set up and manipulate data as you analyze the possible effects of changes.

Key Vocabulary/Vocabulario

address	dirección
dimensions	dimensiónes
entry	entrada
main diagonal	diagonal principal
matrix	matriz
row operation	operación por filas
scalar	escalar
square matrix	matriz cuadrada

Vocabulary Connections

To become familiar with some of the vocabulary terms in the chapter, consider the following. You may refer to the chapter, the glossary, or a dictionary if you like.

1. The **address** for a number in a matrix tells you the row and column of that number. To locate a specific house in a neighborhood, what two pieces of information do you need in the address?
2. The **dimensions** of a matrix tell how many rows and how many columns the matrix has. What do the dimensions of a 3 in. by 5 in. index card tell you?
3. The **main diagonal** of a matrix goes from the upper left corner to the lower right. On this page, would the page number be on the main diagonal?
4. A square's length and width are the same. What do you suppose might be true of a **square matrix**?
5. A **scalar** scales the numbers in a matrix by using multiplication. What number used as a scalar would double a group of numbers?

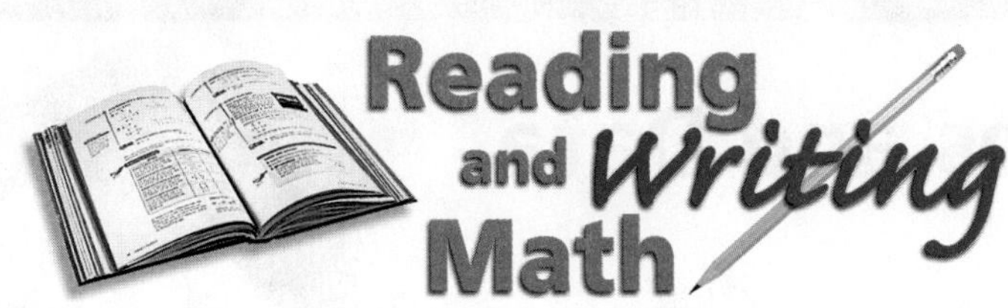

Reading Strategy: Read and Interpret Math Symbols

Interpreting math symbols is a necessary skill that you need in order to comprehend new material. As you study each lesson in this textbook, read aloud the expressions involving symbols and notations. This practice will help you become proficient at translating symbols into words.

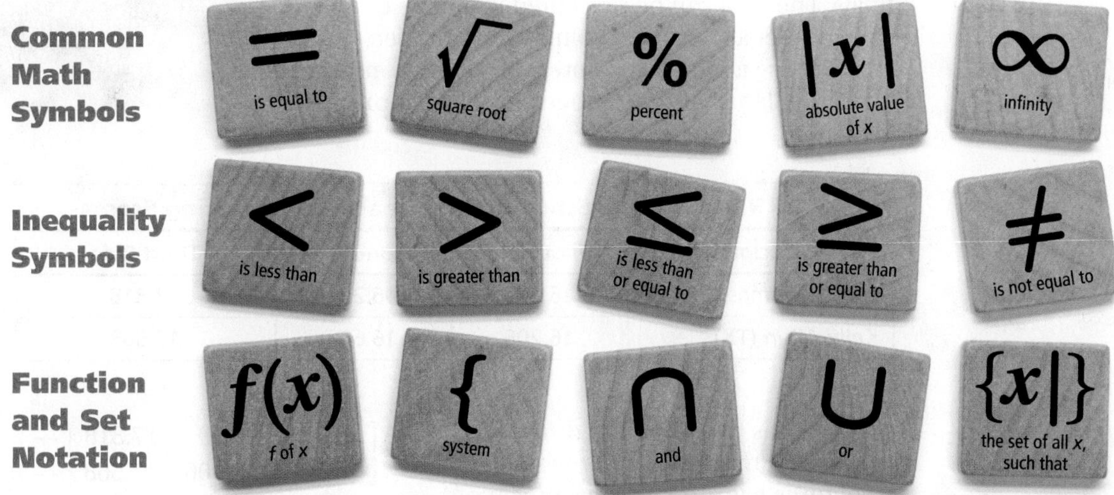

In Algebra, symbols are used to communicate information. As you study each lesson, read aloud expressions involving symbols and expressions. This can help you translate symbols into words.

Expressions	Words
$f(x) = \sqrt{16x} - 4$	*f* of *x* is equal to the square root of 16 times *x*, minus 4.
$\frac{\lvert x - 15\rvert}{6} \leq 12$	The absolute value of the quantity *x* minus 15, divided by 6, is less than or equal to 12.
$\{x \mid x \leq -19 \cup x > 8\}$	The set of all numbers *x* such that *x* is less than or equal to negative 19 OR *x* is greater than 8
$\begin{cases} y \leq -4x + 8 \\ y > x - 6 \end{cases}$	The system of inequalities containing "*y* is less than or equal to negative 4*x* plus 8" and "*y* is greater than *x* minus 6"

Try This

Translate these mathematical expressions into words.

1. $\{x \mid x \geq -7 \cup x \leq -1\}$
2. $f(y) = \lvert 15y \rvert + \frac{y}{2}$
3. $\begin{cases} y = 2x + 3 \\ y = x \end{cases}$
4. $[-5, \infty)$

Rewrite the statement as an algebraic expression.

5. The set of all numbers *x* such that *x* is between negative 8 and 10.

4-1 Matrices and Data

Objectives

Use matrices to display mathematical and real-world data.

Find sums, differences, and scalar products of matrices.

Vocabulary

matrix
dimensions
entry
address
scalar

Who uses this?

Rodeo scorekeepers may use matrices to determine scores of participants for events such as barrel racing.

The table shows the top scores for girls in barrel racing at the 2004 National High School Rodeo finals. The data can be presented in a table or a spreadsheet as rows and columns of numbers. You can also use a *matrix* to show table data. A **matrix** is a rectangular array of numbers enclosed in brackets.

2004 National High School Rodeo Finals—Barrel Racing Scores

Participant	First Ride	Second Ride	Third Ride
Sierra Thomas (UT)	16.781	16.29	17.318
Kelly Allen (TX)	16.206	16.606	17.668

Matrix A has two rows and three columns. A matrix with m rows and n columns has **dimensions** $m \times n$, read "m by n," and is called an $m \times n$ matrix. A has dimensions 2×3. Each value in a matrix is called an **entry** of the matrix.

$$A = \begin{bmatrix} 16.781 & 16.29 & 17.318 \\ 16.206 & 16.606 & 17.668 \end{bmatrix} \begin{matrix} \leftarrow \text{Row 1} \\ \leftarrow \text{Row 2} \end{matrix}$$

Column 1 Column 2 Column 3

The **address** of an entry is its location in a matrix, expressed by using the lowercase matrix letter with the row and column number as subscripts. The score 16.206 is located in row 2 column 1, so a_{21} is 16.206.

$$A = \begin{bmatrix} 16.781 & 16.29 & 17.318 \\ 16.206 & 16.606 & 17.668 \end{bmatrix}$$

a_{21}

EXAMPLE 1 **Displaying Data in Matrix Form**

Use the packaging data for the costs of the packages given.

Cost of 4-Inch Cubic Box ($)

	Plastic	Paper
Total Cost	0.48	0.72
Cost per in^2	0.005	0.0075
Cost per in^3	0.0075	0.01125

a. Display the data in matrix form.

$$C = \begin{bmatrix} 0.48 & 0.72 \\ 0.005 & 0.0075 \\ 0.0075 & 0.01125 \end{bmatrix}$$

b. What are the dimensions of C?

C has three rows and two columns, so it is a 3×2 matrix.

c. What is the entry at c_{12}? What does it represent?

The entry at c_{12}, in row 1 column 2, is 0.72. It is the total cost of a 4 in. paper box.

d. What is the address of the entry 0.005?

The entry 0.005 is at c_{21}.

Use matrix M to answer the questions below.

$$M = \begin{bmatrix} 2 & 1 & 5 & 0 \\ 1 & 5 & 0 & 9 \\ 2 & 11 & 4 & 12 \end{bmatrix}$$

1a. What are the dimensions of M?

1b. What is the entry at m_{32}?

1c. The entry 0 appears at what two addresses?

Corresponding entries in two or more matrices are entries with the same address, such as a_{32} and b_{32} in matrices A and B.

Adding and Subtracting Matrices

WORDS	NUMBERS	ALGEBRA
To add or subtract two matrices, add or subtract the corresponding entries.	$\begin{bmatrix} 1 & 2 \end{bmatrix} + \begin{bmatrix} 5 & 10 \end{bmatrix} = \begin{bmatrix} 6 & 12 \end{bmatrix}$	$\begin{bmatrix} a_{11} & a_{12} \end{bmatrix} + \begin{bmatrix} b_{11} & b_{12} \end{bmatrix} = \begin{bmatrix} a_{11} + b_{11} & a_{12} + b_{12} \end{bmatrix}$

You can add or subtract two matrices only if they have the same dimensions.

✔ Same Dimensions

$$\begin{bmatrix} 1 & 2 \\ 6 & 7 \end{bmatrix} + \begin{bmatrix} 2 & 1 \\ 7 & 6 \end{bmatrix} \qquad \begin{bmatrix} 5 \\ 6 \\ 7 \end{bmatrix} + \begin{bmatrix} 2 \\ 8 \\ 1 \end{bmatrix}$$

✘ Different Dimensions

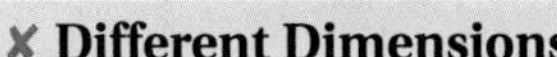

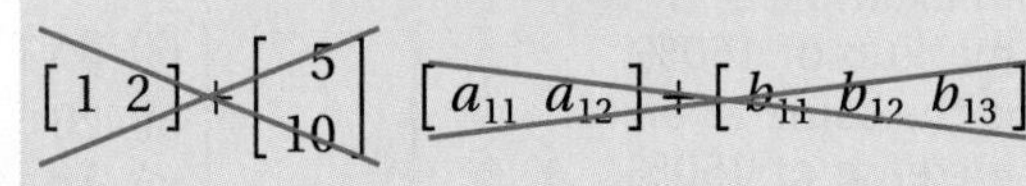

$$\begin{bmatrix} 1 & 2 \end{bmatrix} + \begin{bmatrix} 5 \\ 10 \end{bmatrix} \qquad \begin{bmatrix} a_{11} & a_{12} \end{bmatrix} + \begin{bmatrix} b_{11} & b_{12} & b_{13} \end{bmatrix}$$

EXAMPLE 2 Finding Matrix Sums and Differences

$$A = \begin{bmatrix} 4 & -2 \\ -3 & 10 \\ 2 & 6 \end{bmatrix} \quad B = \begin{bmatrix} 4 & -1 & -5 \\ 3 & 2 & 8 \end{bmatrix} \quad C = \begin{bmatrix} 3 & 2 \\ 0 & -9 \\ -5 & 14 \end{bmatrix} \quad D = \begin{bmatrix} 0 & 1 & -3 \\ 3 & 0 & 10 \end{bmatrix}$$

Add or subtract, if possible.

A $A + C$

Add each corresponding entry.

$$A + C = \begin{bmatrix} 4 & -2 \\ -3 & 10 \\ 2 & 6 \end{bmatrix} + \begin{bmatrix} 3 & 2 \\ 0 & -9 \\ -5 & 14 \end{bmatrix} = \begin{bmatrix} 4+3 & -2+2 \\ -3+0 & 10+(-9) \\ 2+(-5) & 6+14 \end{bmatrix} = \begin{bmatrix} 7 & 0 \\ -3 & 1 \\ -3 & 20 \end{bmatrix}$$

B $C - A$

Subtract each corresponding entry.

$$C - A = \begin{bmatrix} 3 & 2 \\ 0 & -9 \\ -5 & 14 \end{bmatrix} - \begin{bmatrix} 4 & -2 \\ -3 & 10 \\ 2 & 6 \end{bmatrix} = \begin{bmatrix} 3-4 & 2-(-2) \\ 0-(-3) & -9-10 \\ -5-2 & 14-6 \end{bmatrix} = \begin{bmatrix} -1 & 4 \\ 3 & -19 \\ -7 & 8 \end{bmatrix}$$

C $C + B$

C is a 3×2 matrix, and B is a 2×3 matrix. Because C and B do not have the same dimensions, they cannot be added.

CHECK IT OUT! **Add or subtract, if possible.**

2a. $B + D$ **2b.** $B - A$ **2c.** $D - B$

You know that multiplication is repeated addition. The same is true for matrices.

For example, let $E = \begin{bmatrix} 2 & 0 \\ 1 & 5 \end{bmatrix}$.

$$E + E = \begin{bmatrix} 2 & 0 \\ 1 & 5 \end{bmatrix} + \begin{bmatrix} 2 & 0 \\ 1 & 5 \end{bmatrix} = \begin{bmatrix} 2+2 & 0+0 \\ 1+1 & 5+5 \end{bmatrix} = \begin{bmatrix} 2(2) & 2(0) \\ 2(1) & 2(5) \end{bmatrix} = \begin{bmatrix} 4 & 0 \\ 2 & 10 \end{bmatrix}$$

$E + E$ can be written as $2E$. You can multiply a matrix by a number, called a **scalar**. To find the product of a scalar and a matrix, or the *scalar product*, multiply each entry by the scalar.

$$2\begin{bmatrix} 2 & 0 \\ 1 & 5 \end{bmatrix} = \begin{bmatrix} 2(2) & 2(0) \\ 2(1) & 2(5) \end{bmatrix}$$

EXAMPLE 3 *Business Application*

A ticket service marks up prices on tickets to rodeos and other events by 150%. Use a scalar product to find the marked-up prices.

Rodeo Ticket Prices		
Days	**Plaza**	**Balcony**
1–2	\$60	\$35
3–8	\$50	\$28
9–10	\$80	\$45

You can multiply by 1.5 and add to the original numbers.

$$\begin{bmatrix} 60 & 35 \\ 50 & 28 \\ 80 & 45 \end{bmatrix} + 1.5\begin{bmatrix} 60 & 35 \\ 50 & 28 \\ 80 & 45 \end{bmatrix}$$

$$= \begin{bmatrix} 60 & 35 \\ 50 & 28 \\ 80 & 45 \end{bmatrix} + \begin{bmatrix} 90 & 52.5 \\ 75 & 42 \\ 120 & 67.5 \end{bmatrix} = \begin{bmatrix} 150 & 87.5 \\ 125 & 70 \\ 200 & 112.5 \end{bmatrix}$$

The marked-up prices are shown below.

Ticket Service Prices		
Days	**Plaza**	**Balcony**
1–2	\$150	\$87.50
3–8	\$125	\$70.00
9–10	\$200	\$112.50

Helpful Hint

In Example 3, a markup of 150% is the same as an increase of 150%.

CHECK IT OUT! **3.** Use a scalar product to find the prices if a 20% discount is applied to the ticket service prices.

EXAMPLE 4 **Simplifying Matrix Expressions**

$$A = \begin{bmatrix} 4 & -2 \\ -3 & 10 \end{bmatrix} \quad B = \begin{bmatrix} 4 & -1 & -5 \\ 3 & 2 & 8 \end{bmatrix} \quad C = \begin{bmatrix} 3 & 2 \\ 0 & -9 \end{bmatrix} \quad D = \begin{bmatrix} -6 & 3 & 8 \end{bmatrix}$$

A **Evaluate $2A - 3B$, if possible.**

$$2\begin{bmatrix} 4 & -2 \\ -3 & 10 \end{bmatrix} - 3\begin{bmatrix} 4 & -1 & -5 \\ 3 & 2 & 8 \end{bmatrix}$$

A and B do not have the same dimensions; they cannot be subtracted after the scalar products are found.

Helpful Hint

A matrix bracket is a grouping symbol. So in an expression like $C - 2A$, you distribute -2 to all of the entries in A before adding, just as you do with numbers.

B **Evaluate $C - 2A$, if possible.**

$$= \begin{bmatrix} 3 & 2 \\ 0 & -9 \end{bmatrix} - 2\begin{bmatrix} 4 & -2 \\ -3 & 10 \end{bmatrix}$$

$$= \begin{bmatrix} 3 & 2 \\ 0 & -9 \end{bmatrix} + \begin{bmatrix} -2(4) & -2(-2) \\ -2(-3) & -2(10) \end{bmatrix}$$ *Multiply each entry by −2.*

$$= \begin{bmatrix} 3 & 2 \\ 0 & -9 \end{bmatrix} + \begin{bmatrix} -8 & 4 \\ 6 & -20 \end{bmatrix} = \begin{bmatrix} -5 & 6 \\ 6 & -29 \end{bmatrix}$$

Evaluate, if possible.

4a. $3B + 2C$ **4b.** $2A - 3C$ **4c.** $D + 0.5D$

Some properties of equality also apply to matrices.

Know it! Note

Properties of Equality for Matrices

WORDS	NUMBERS	ALGEBRA
Commutative Property Matrix addition is commutative.	$\begin{bmatrix} 7 & 2 \\ 3 & 4 \end{bmatrix} + \begin{bmatrix} 1 & 2 \\ 4 & 1 \end{bmatrix} = \begin{bmatrix} 1 & 2 \\ 4 & 1 \end{bmatrix} + \begin{bmatrix} 7 & 2 \\ 3 & 4 \end{bmatrix}$	$A + B = B + A$
Associative Property Matrix addition is associative.	$\left(\begin{bmatrix} 2 \\ 3 \end{bmatrix} + \begin{bmatrix} 0 \\ 1 \end{bmatrix}\right) + \begin{bmatrix} 5 \\ 4 \end{bmatrix} = \begin{bmatrix} 2 \\ 3 \end{bmatrix} + \left(\begin{bmatrix} 0 \\ 1 \end{bmatrix} + \begin{bmatrix} 5 \\ 4 \end{bmatrix}\right)$	$A + B + C = (A + B) + C = A + (B + C)$
Additive Identity The *zero matrix* is the *additive identity matrix O*.	$\begin{bmatrix} 7 & 2 \\ 3 & 4 \end{bmatrix} + \begin{bmatrix} 0 & 0 \\ 0 & 0 \end{bmatrix} = \begin{bmatrix} 7 & 2 \\ 3 & 4 \end{bmatrix}$	$A + O = A$
Additive Inverse The *additive inverse* of matrix A contains the opposite of each entry in matrix A.	$\begin{bmatrix} 5 & -2 \\ -6 & 9 \end{bmatrix} + \begin{bmatrix} -5 & 2 \\ 6 & -9 \end{bmatrix} = \begin{bmatrix} 0 & 0 \\ 0 & 0 \end{bmatrix}$	If $A + B = O$, then A and B are additive inverses.

THINK AND DISCUSS

1. Find the possible dimensions of a matrix that contains eight entries.

2. Describe a matrix operation that reverses the signs of every entry.

3. GET ORGANIZED Copy and complete the graphic organizer. Give examples for matrices and real numbers.

Property or Operation	Real Numbers	Matrices
Addition		
Subtraction		
Multiplication by a number		

4-1 Exercises

go.hrw.com
Homework Help Online
KEYWORD: MB7 4-1
Parent Resources Online
KEYWORD: MB7 Parent

GUIDED PRACTICE

1. **Vocabulary** The value at a particular place in a matrix is an __?__ . (*address* or *entry*)

SEE EXAMPLE 1 p. 246

2. Kade, Bo, and Tanner record their ticket-selling activities for a fund-raising carnival.

Carnival Ticket Prices			
Student	Single Tickets	Ticket Packages	Total Collected
Kade	39	15	$114
Bo	103	8	$143
Tanner	13	25	$138

a. Display the data in the form of a matrix T.
b. What are the dimensions of T?
c. What is the entry at t_{13}? What does it represent?
d. What is the address of the entry 143?

SEE EXAMPLE 2 p. 247

Use the following matrices for Exercises 3–6. Add or subtract, if possible.

$$A = \begin{bmatrix} 1.5 & 3.8 & 3 \\ -1.2 & 2.4 & 0 \end{bmatrix} \quad B = \begin{bmatrix} 0 & 4 & 1 \\ 0 & -2 & 1 \end{bmatrix} \quad C = \begin{bmatrix} -1 & 1.1 & 6 \\ 4 & 0 & 1 \\ 1 & 2.3 & 1 \end{bmatrix}$$

3. $A + B$ 4. $B - C$ 5. $B - A$ 6. $B + A$

SEE EXAMPLE 3 p. 248

7. **Consumer** The table shows prices for three types of clothing. Use a scalar product to find the price with 8.25% sales tax on each item.

Cost of Athletic Clothing ($)			
	Plain	Team Logo	Individualized
T-shirt	9.00	13.00	14.00
Shorts	6.00	9.50	11.00
Jogging Pants	15.00	21.00	23.00

SEE EXAMPLE 4 p. 248

Use the following matrices for Exercises 8–11. Evaluate, if possible.

$$A = \begin{bmatrix} 1 & 3 & 3 \\ -1 & 2 & 0 \end{bmatrix} \quad B = \begin{bmatrix} 0 & 4 & 1 \\ 0 & -2 & 1 \end{bmatrix} \quad C = \begin{bmatrix} -1 & 1 & 6 \\ 4 & 0 & 1 \\ 1 & 2 & 1 \end{bmatrix}$$

8. $3B$ 9. $\frac{1}{2}C$ 10. $A - 2B$ 11. $2C - A$

PRACTICE AND PROBLEM SOLVING

12. Use the data to answer the questions.
a. Display the data as a matrix, P.
b. What are the dimensions of P?
c. What is the entry at p_{32}? What does it represent?
d. What is the address of the entry 385.98?

Travel Options			
	Airfare	Hotel	Car Rental
Deluxe	425.50	398.00	65.99
Business	385.98	245.50	45.90
Economy	275.12	103.25	29.50

Independent Practice	
For Exercises	See Example
12	1
13–16	2
17	3
18–21	4

Extra Practice

Skills Practice p. S10
Application Practice p. S35

Use the following matrices for Exercises 13–16. Add or subtract, if possible.

$$D = \begin{bmatrix} 5.1 & 2.5 \\ -2 & 0 \\ 0 & 1.5 \end{bmatrix} \quad E = \begin{bmatrix} 3.2 & -1 \\ -1.5 & 2.4 \end{bmatrix} \quad F = \begin{bmatrix} -4.2 & -1 \\ 2.2 & 0 \end{bmatrix}$$

13. $F - E$ **14.** $D + E$ **15.** $D + F$ **16.** $E + F$

17. College The following table shows estimated college costs in 2004.

Estimated College Costs (per Year) in 2004			
	Private School	In-State Public School	Out-of-State Public School
Cost ($)	27,677	12,841	19,188

Costs are expected to increase 5% per year. Use a scalar product to find the estimated costs for each type of college in 2005.

Use the following matrices for Exercises 18–21. Evaluate, if possible.

$$G = \begin{bmatrix} 5 & 2 \\ -2 & 0 \\ 0 & 1 \end{bmatrix} \quad H = \begin{bmatrix} 0 & -1 \\ -1 & 2 \\ 0 & 2 \end{bmatrix} \quad J = \begin{bmatrix} 4 \\ 1 \\ -2 \end{bmatrix} \quad K = \begin{bmatrix} 2 & 3 \\ 3 & -1 \\ 5 & 0 \end{bmatrix}$$

18. $2G$ **19.** $\frac{1}{2}(H + J)$ **20.** $2K - G$ **21.** $J - 0.3G$

22. Estimation Trey recorded his total expenses for February and March in a spreadsheet and graphed the results. Write 3×1 matrices to represent his expenses in February and March, and show the matrix sum for his total expenses.

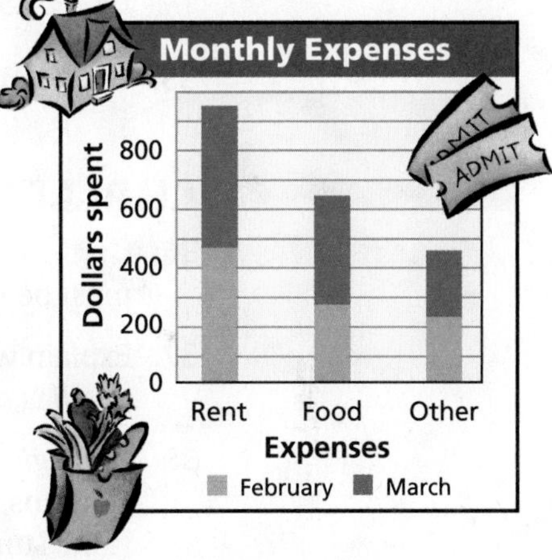

23. Geometry The matrix $R = \begin{bmatrix} 2 & 2.5 \\ 3 & 3.5 \end{bmatrix}$ shows the radii of four circles.

a. Write the matrix operation that gives the related circumferences.

b. Is there an addition or scalar-multiplication matrix operation that could show the related areas of the circles? Explain.

Critical Thinking **Tell whether each statement is sometimes, always, or never true.**

24. If matrices A and B have an equal number of entries, then $A + B$ is defined.

25. If matrices A and B have a different number of entries, then $A + B$ is defined.

26. If matrices A and B each have four rows and three columns, then $A + B$ is defined.

27. If $A + B$ is defined, then $A - B$ is defined.

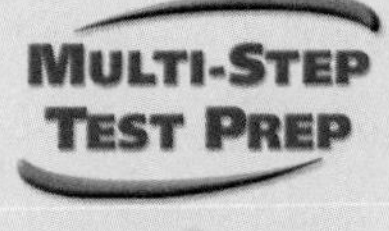

28. This problem will prepare you for the Multi-Step Test Prep on page 268.

a. Place the vertices of the triangle in a matrix so that the x-coordinates are in row 1 and the y-coordinates are in row 2.

b. Use a matrix operation to add 3 to each x-coordinate and 1 to each y-coordinate.

c. Draw a new triangle using the new coordinates. Describe the new triangle.

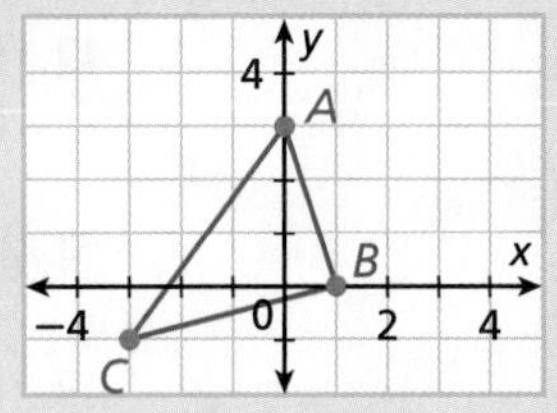

29. Solve for a, b, and c in the matrix equation. $\begin{bmatrix} 3 & a \\ -2 & -8 \end{bmatrix} + \begin{bmatrix} 11 & -4 \\ b & 12 \end{bmatrix} = \begin{bmatrix} 14 & -10 \\ 9 & c \end{bmatrix}$

30. **ERROR ANALYSIS** Explain the error. $\begin{bmatrix} 2 & 8 \\ 4 & 7 \end{bmatrix} + \begin{bmatrix} 6 & 3 & 0 \\ 4 & 1 & 9 \end{bmatrix} = \begin{bmatrix} 8 & 11 & 0 \\ 8 & 8 & 9 \end{bmatrix}$

31. **Write About It** Is subtraction of matrices commutative? Give an example to support your answer.

TEST PREP

32. $P = \begin{bmatrix} 1 & 0.1 & 2 \\ 1.5 & 2.1 & 0 \end{bmatrix}$ $Q = \begin{bmatrix} 2 & 0.4 & 6 \\ 6 & 6.4 & 0 \end{bmatrix}$. Which expression results in $\begin{bmatrix} 1 & 0 & 1 \\ 0 & 1 & 0 \end{bmatrix}$?

Ⓐ $2Q - \frac{1}{2}P$ Ⓑ $Q - 2P$ Ⓒ $P - 2Q$ Ⓓ $2P - \frac{1}{2}Q$

33. For an $m \times n$ matrix E, which statement is always true?

Ⓕ It has $m \cdot n$ entries.
Ⓗ It has $m + n$ entries.
Ⓖ It has an entry e_{nm}.
Ⓙ It has m columns and n rows.

34. Solve for w: $8\begin{bmatrix} 12 & 8 \\ 2 & 7 \end{bmatrix} = w\begin{bmatrix} 48 & 32 \\ 8 & 28 \end{bmatrix}$.

Ⓐ 0.25 Ⓑ 0.5 Ⓒ 2 Ⓓ 4

35. **Gridded Response** Solve for x: $\begin{bmatrix} 2 & -2 \end{bmatrix} - 2\begin{bmatrix} 5 & -x \end{bmatrix} = \begin{bmatrix} -8 & -1 \end{bmatrix}$.

CHALLENGE AND EXTEND

36. **Critical Thinking** If the number of entries in a matrix is a prime number, what must be true about the dimensions of the matrix? Explain.

37. Explain why, for any two $m \times n$ matrices A and B, $A - B$ is equivlent to $A + (-B)$.

38. In *magic squares* like those shown, the rows, columns, and diagonals all have the same sum. Is the sum of the two magic squares also a magic square? Explain.

39. $3\begin{bmatrix} 2 & -1 \\ 0 & -4 \end{bmatrix} - 2B = \begin{bmatrix} 1 & 5 \\ -2 & 2 \end{bmatrix}$. Find B.

SPIRAL REVIEW

Write an algebraic expression to represent each situation. *(Lesson 1-4)*

40. the perimeter of a triangle with side lengths that are consecutive even integers

41. the total number of raffle tickets sold if 20 people each sold n tickets

42. **Money** Nyla has 36 nickels and dimes. She has twice as many dimes as nickels. How much money does Nyla have? *(Lesson 2-1)*

Determine if the given point is a solution of the system of equations. *(Lesson 3-1)*

43. $(2, -2)\begin{cases} x - y = 4 \\ 5x + 6y = 2 \end{cases}$

44. $(4.5, 2)\begin{cases} y = 2 \\ 2x - 4y = 1 \end{cases}$

4-2 Multiplying Matrices

Objectives
Understand the properties of matrices with respect to multiplication.

Multiply two matrices.

Vocabulary
matrix product
square matrix
main diagonal
multiplicative identity matrix

Who uses this?
Skateboard shop owners can use matrices to find the value of their inventory. (See Example 3.)

In Lesson 4-1, you multiplied matrices by a number called a *scalar*. You can also multiply matrices together. The product of two or more matrices is the **matrix product**. The following rules apply when multiplying matrices.

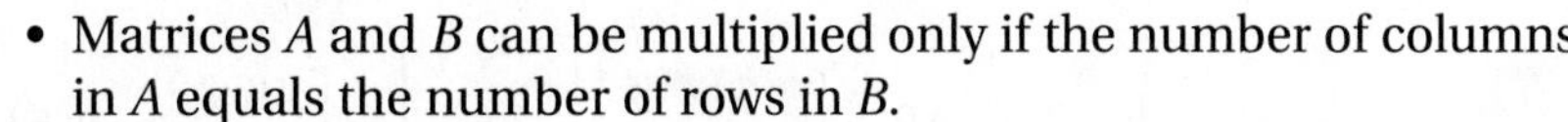

- Matrices A and B can be multiplied only if the number of columns in A equals the number of rows in B.
- The product of an $m \times n$ and an $n \times p$ matrix is an $m \times p$ matrix.

Helpful Hint

The CAR key:
Columns (of A)
As
Rows (of B)
or matrix product AB won't even start

$$A = \begin{bmatrix} 3 & 5 & 7 \\ 4 & 1 & 2 \end{bmatrix} \quad B = \begin{bmatrix} 2 & 3 & 3 & 8 \\ 9 & 5 & 2 & 0 \\ 0 & 1 & 6 & 7 \end{bmatrix}$$

A B AB
$2 \times 3 \quad 3 \times 4 = 2 \times 4$ matrix
columns = rows

$$C = \begin{bmatrix} 3 & 5 \\ 4 & 1 \\ 5 & 8 \end{bmatrix} \quad D = \begin{bmatrix} 2 & 3 & 3 & 8 & 4 \\ 9 & 5 & 2 & 0 & 6 \\ 0 & 1 & 6 & 7 & 2 \end{bmatrix}$$

C D
$3 \times 2 \quad 3 \times 5$
columns $\neq$ rows

✗ CD is not defined $(2 \neq 3)$

An $m \times n$ matrix A can be identified by using the notation $A_{m \times n}$.

EXAMPLE 1 Identifying Matrix Products

Tell whether each product is defined. If so, give its dimensions.

A $P_{2 \times 5}$ **and** $Q_{5 \times 3}$; PQ

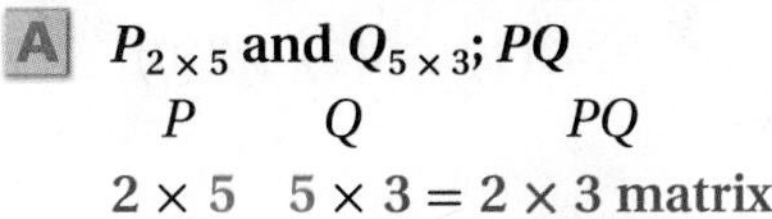

P Q PQ
$2 \times 5 \quad 5 \times 3 = 2 \times 3$ matrix

The inner dimensions are equal $(5 = 5)$, so the matrix product is defined. The dimensions of the product are the outer numbers, 2×3.

B $R_{4 \times 3}$ **and** $S_{4 \times 5}$; RS

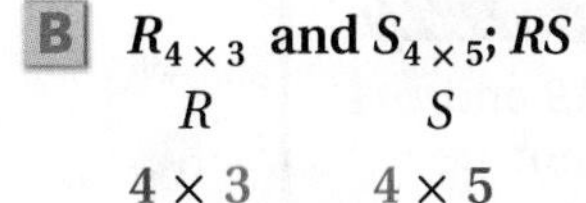

R S
$4 \times 3 \quad 4 \times 5$

The inner dimensions are not equal $(3 \neq 4)$, so the matrix product is not defined. ✗

Use the matrices in Example 1. Tell whether each product is defined. If so, give its dimensions.

1a. QP **1b.** SR **1c.** SQ

Just as you look across the columns of A and down the rows of B to see if a product AB exists, you do the same to find the entries in a matrix product.

Multiplying Matrices

WORDS	NUMBERS	ALGEBRA
In a matrix product $P = AB$, each element p_{ij} is the sum of the products of consecutive entries in row i in matrix A and column j in matrix B.	$P = \begin{bmatrix} 1 & 2 \\ 3 & 4 \end{bmatrix}\begin{bmatrix} 5 & 6 \\ 7 & 8 \end{bmatrix} = \begin{bmatrix} 1 \cdot 5 + 2 \cdot 7 & 1 \cdot 6 + 2 \cdot 8 \\ 3 \cdot 5 + 4 \cdot 7 & 3 \cdot 6 + 4 \cdot 8 \end{bmatrix}$	$P = \begin{bmatrix} a_1 & a_2 \\ b_1 & b_2 \end{bmatrix}\begin{bmatrix} c_1 & c_2 \\ d_1 & d_2 \end{bmatrix} = \begin{bmatrix} a_1c_1 + a_2d_1 & a_1c_2 + a_2d_2 \\ b_1c_1 + b_2d_1 & b_1c_2 + b_2d_2 \end{bmatrix}$

EXAMPLE 2 Finding the Matrix Product

Find each product, if possible. $A = \begin{bmatrix} 0 & 4 & 9 \\ -3 & 3 & 2 \end{bmatrix}$ $B = \begin{bmatrix} 5 & 1 \\ -2 & 7 \\ 6 & 0 \end{bmatrix}$ $C = \begin{bmatrix} 11 & -1 \\ 12 & 10 \end{bmatrix}$

A AB

Check the dimensions. A is 2×3, B is 3×2. AB is defined and is 2×2.

Multiply row 1 of A and column 1 of B as shown. Place the result in ab_{11}.

$$AB = \begin{bmatrix} 0 & 4 & 9 \\ -3 & 3 & 2 \end{bmatrix}\begin{bmatrix} 5 & 1 \\ -2 & 7 \\ 6 & 0 \end{bmatrix} = \begin{bmatrix} 46 & ? \\ ? & ? \end{bmatrix} \leftarrow 0(5) + 4(-2) + 9(6)$$

Multiply row 1 of A and column 2 of B. Place the result in ab_{12}.

$$\begin{bmatrix} 0 & 4 & 9 \\ -3 & 3 & 2 \end{bmatrix}\begin{bmatrix} 5 & 1 \\ -2 & 7 \\ 6 & 0 \end{bmatrix} = \begin{bmatrix} 46 & 28 \\ ? & ? \end{bmatrix} \leftarrow 0(1) + 4(7) + 9(0)$$

Multiply row 2 of A and column 1 of B. Place the result in ab_{21}.

$$\begin{bmatrix} 0 & 4 & 9 \\ -3 & 3 & 2 \end{bmatrix}\begin{bmatrix} 5 & 1 \\ -2 & 7 \\ 6 & 0 \end{bmatrix} = \begin{bmatrix} 46 & 28 \\ -9 & ? \end{bmatrix} \leftarrow -3(5) + 3(-2) + 2(6)$$

Multiply row 2 of A and column 2 of B. Place the result in ab_{22}.

$$\begin{bmatrix} 0 & 4 & 9 \\ -3 & 3 & 2 \end{bmatrix}\begin{bmatrix} 5 & 1 \\ -2 & 7 \\ 6 & 0 \end{bmatrix} = \begin{bmatrix} 46 & 28 \\ -9 & 18 \end{bmatrix} \quad AB = \begin{bmatrix} 46 & 28 \\ -9 & 18 \end{bmatrix}$$

$$-3(1) + 3(7) + 2(0)$$

Caution!

Notice that AB and BA are different products.

The Commutative Property does not hold for multiplication of matrices!

B BA

Check the dimensions. B is 3×2, and A is 2×3, so the product is defined and is 3×3.

$$BA = \begin{bmatrix} 5(0) + 1(-3) & 5(4) + 1(3) & 5(9) + 1(2) \\ -2(0) + 7(-3) & -2(4) + 7(3) & -2(9) + 7(2) \\ 6(0) + 0(-3) & 6(4) + 0(3) & 6(9) + 0(2) \end{bmatrix} = \begin{bmatrix} -3 & 23 & 47 \\ -21 & 13 & -4 \\ 0 & 24 & 54 \end{bmatrix}$$

C AC

Check the dimensions: $2 \times 3 \quad 2 \times 2$. The product is not defined. The matrices cannot be multiplied in this order.

Find the product, if possible.

2a. BC **2b.** CA

Businesses can use matrix multiplication to find total revenues, costs, and profits.

EXAMPLE 3 Inventory Application

A skateboard kit comes in two styles. Two stores have inventories as shown in the first table. Find the total cost of the skateboards for each store.

Skateboard Kit Inventory

	Complete	Super Complete
Store 1	14	10
Store 2	7	8

Skateboard Kit Profits

	Revenue ($)	Store Cost ($)	Profit ($)
Complete	89	44	45
Super Complete	119	58	61

Use a product matrix to find the revenue, cost, and profit for each store.

$$\begin{bmatrix} 14 & 10 \\ 7 & 8 \end{bmatrix}\begin{bmatrix} 89 & 44 & 45 \\ 119 & 58 & 61 \end{bmatrix} =$$

$$\begin{bmatrix} 14(89) + 10(119) & 14(44) + 10(58) & 14(45) + 10(61) \\ 7(89) + 8(119) & 7(44) + 8(58) & 7(45) + 8(61) \end{bmatrix}$$

$$\begin{matrix} \textit{Revenue} & \textit{Cost} & \textit{Profit} \end{matrix}$$

$$= \begin{bmatrix} 2436 & 1196 & 1240 \\ 1575 & 772 & 803 \end{bmatrix} \begin{matrix} \textit{Store 1} \\ \textit{Store 2} \end{matrix}$$

The total cost for skateboards for store 1 is \$1196 and for store 2 is \$772.

3. Change store 2's inventory to 6 complete and 9 super complete. Update the product matrix, and find the profit for store 2.

A **square matrix** is any matrix that has the same number of rows as columns; it is an $n \times n$ matrix. The **main diagonal** of a square matrix is the diagonal from the upper left corner to the lower right corner.

The **multiplicative identity matrix** is any square matrix, named with the letter I, that has all of the entries along the main diagonal equal to 1 and all of the other entries equal to 0.

$$I_{2 \times 2} = \begin{bmatrix} 1 & 0 \\ 0 & 1 \end{bmatrix} \qquad I_{3 \times 3} = \begin{bmatrix} 1 & 0 & 0 \\ 0 & 1 & 0 \\ 0 & 0 & 1 \end{bmatrix}$$

Matrix I is the multiplicative identity when A is any square matrix and $AI = IA = A$.

For $A = \begin{bmatrix} 5 & 7 \\ -1 & 4 \end{bmatrix}$, $I = \begin{bmatrix} 1 & 0 \\ 0 & 1 \end{bmatrix}$ and

$$AI = \begin{bmatrix} 5 & 7 \\ -1 & 4 \end{bmatrix}\begin{bmatrix} 1 & 0 \\ 0 & 1 \end{bmatrix} = \begin{bmatrix} 5(1) + 7(0) & 5(0) + 7(1) \\ -1(1) + 4(0) & -1(0) + 4(1) \end{bmatrix} = \begin{bmatrix} 5 & 7 \\ -1 & 4 \end{bmatrix} = A$$

$$IA = \begin{bmatrix} 1 & 0 \\ 0 & 1 \end{bmatrix}\begin{bmatrix} 5 & 7 \\ -1 & 4 \end{bmatrix} = \begin{bmatrix} 1(5) + 0(-1) & 1(7) + 0(4) \\ 0(5) + 1(-1) & 0(7) + 1(4) \end{bmatrix} = \begin{bmatrix} 5 & 7 \\ -1 & 4 \end{bmatrix} = A$$

Because square matrices can be multiplied by themselves any number of times, you can find powers of square matrices.

EXAMPLE 4 Finding Powers of Square Matrices

$$A=\begin{bmatrix}7&3\\-2&0\end{bmatrix}\quad B=\begin{bmatrix}2&4&1\\5&0&-2\\1&-1&3\end{bmatrix}\quad C=\begin{bmatrix}1&0&1\\2&0&-2\end{bmatrix}\quad I=\begin{bmatrix}1&0\\0&1\end{bmatrix}$$

Evaluate, if possible.

A A^2

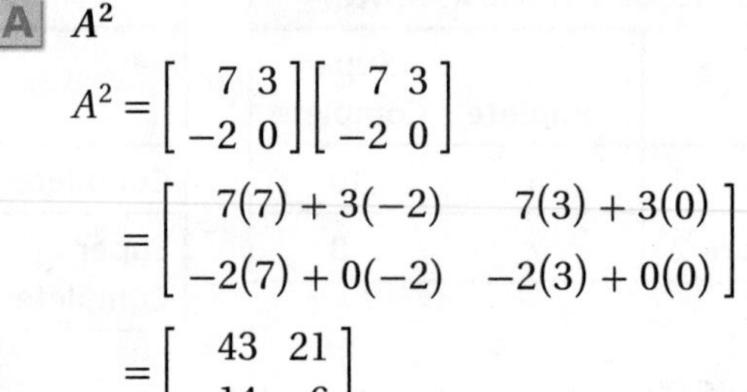

$$A^2=\begin{bmatrix}7&3\\-2&0\end{bmatrix}\begin{bmatrix}7&3\\-2&0\end{bmatrix}$$

$$=\begin{bmatrix}7(7)+3(-2)&7(3)+3(0)\\-2(7)+0(-2)&-2(3)+0(0)\end{bmatrix}$$

$$=\begin{bmatrix}43&21\\-14&-6\end{bmatrix}$$

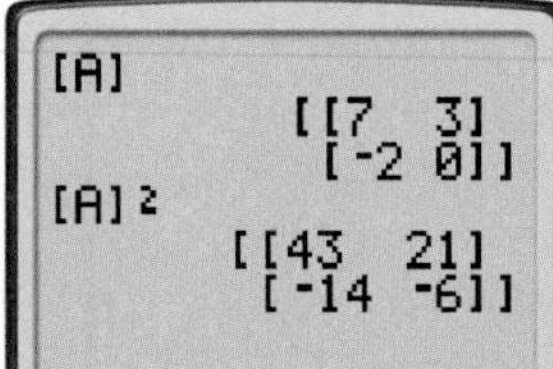

Check Use a calculator.

B B^2

For large matrices, use a graphing calculator.

[B]
[[2 4 1]
[5 0 -2]
[1 -1 3]]

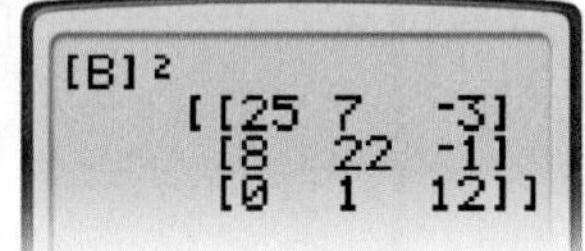

Evaluate, if possible.

4a. C^2 **4b.** A^3 **4c.** B^3 **4d.** I^4

THINK AND DISCUSS

1. Describe what happens when you try to find the first element of *AB* if both *A* and *B* have dimensions 2 × 3.
2. Tell whether matrix multiplication is commutative.
3. *A* is a 4 × 2 matrix. Can you find A^2? Why or why not?

4. **GET ORGANIZED** Copy and complete the graphic organizer. In the decision diamond, enter a question to determine whether *AB* is defined. Then give the general procedure for finding *AB*, if it is defined.

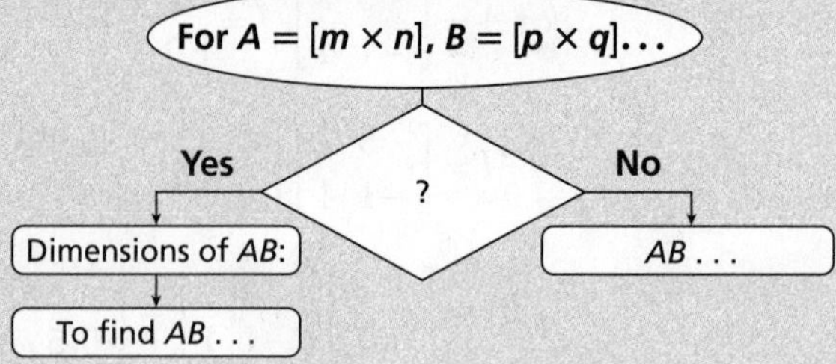

4-2 Exercises

go.hrw.com
Homework Help Online
KEYWORD: MB7 4-2
Parent Resources Online
KEYWORD: MB7 Parent

GUIDED PRACTICE

1. **Vocabulary** A 2 × 2 matrix with every entry equal to 1 is a __?__. (*square matrix* or *multiplicative identity matrix*)

SEE EXAMPLE 1 p. 253

Tell whether each product is defined. If so, give its dimensions.

2. $A_{4\times5}$ and $B_{5\times3}$; AB
3. $A_{4\times5}$ and $B_{5\times3}$; BA
4. $C_{9\times5}$ and $D_{5\times9}$; CD
5. $C_{9\times5}$ and $D_{5\times9}$; DC
6. $E_{6\times2}$ and $F_{2\times6}$; EF
7. $E_{6\times2}$ and $F_{2\times6}$; FE

SEE EXAMPLE 2 p. 254

Use the following matrices for Exercises 8–13. Find each product, if possible.

$$A=\begin{bmatrix}0&7&3\\-2&3&0\end{bmatrix}\quad B=\begin{bmatrix}4&2\\1&-3\end{bmatrix}\quad C=\begin{bmatrix}-3&1\\5&-2\\0&1\end{bmatrix}\quad D=\begin{bmatrix}3&-1&7&10\\1&-1&3&5\end{bmatrix}\quad I=\begin{bmatrix}1&0\\0&1\end{bmatrix}$$

8. BA
9. CA
10. CB
11. DC
12. BI
13. IB

SEE EXAMPLE 3 p. 255

14. **Recycling** Students collected recyclables for fund-raising over a three-week period. Use matrix multiplication to find the total amount of money collected for each type of item.

Recyclables Collected (lb)			
Item	Week 1	Week 2	Week 3
Glass	29	25	16
Cans	8	11	6
Newspaper	163	127	206
Office paper	53	107	84

Price Per Pound ($)				
Week	Glass	Cans	News-paper	Office Paper
1	0.02	0.70	0.02	1.06
2	0.02	0.55	0.01	1.00
3	0.01	0.42	0.02	1.03

SEE EXAMPLE 4 p. 256

Use the following matrices for Exercises 15–18. Evaluate, if possible.

$$A=\begin{bmatrix}-1&-2\\1&0\end{bmatrix}\quad B=\begin{bmatrix}3&4&2\\-1&0&0\\3&0&1\end{bmatrix}\quad C=\begin{bmatrix}3&1\\0&-2\\1&1\end{bmatrix}$$

15. A^2
16. A^3
17. C^2
18. B^2

PRACTICE AND PROBLEM SOLVING

Independent Practice	
For Exercises	See Example
19–24	1
25–29	2
30	3
31–40	4

Extra Practice
Skills Practice p. S10
Application Practice p. S35

Tell whether each product is defined. If so, give its dimensions.

19. $A_{2\times1}$ and $B_{2\times3}$; AB
20. $A_{2\times1}$ and $B_{2\times3}$; BA
21. $C_{3\times5}$ and $D_{5\times1}$; CD
22. $C_{3\times5}$ and $D_{5\times1}$; DC
23. $E_{7\times7}$ and $F_{6\times7}$; EF
24. $E_{7\times7}$ and $F_{6\times7}$; FE

Use the following matrices for Exercises 25–29. Find each product, if possible.

$$A=\begin{bmatrix}4\\-1\\2\end{bmatrix}\quad B=\begin{bmatrix}-3&0\\7&-2\\0&1\end{bmatrix}\quad C=\begin{bmatrix}-2&3&-4\\1&-1&1\\4&1&3\end{bmatrix}\quad I=\begin{bmatrix}1&0&0\\0&1&0\\0&0&1\end{bmatrix}$$

25. AB
26. CA
27. CB
28. IC
29. CI

30. Inventory A pet stroller comes in two sizes. Two stores have inventories as shown in the first table. Find the total cost of the pet strollers for each store.

Pet Stroller Inventory

	Standard	Large
Store 1	11	7
Store 2	8	6

Pet Stroller Profits

	Revenue ($)	Store Cost ($)	Profit ($)
Standard	130	75	55
Large	190	110	80

Use the following matrices for Exercises 31–40. Simplify, if possible.

$$Q=\begin{bmatrix}4 & 13 & -9\end{bmatrix}\quad S=\begin{bmatrix}1 & 2\\ -1 & 0\end{bmatrix}\quad T=\begin{bmatrix}2 & 1 & 0\\ 2 & 0 & 1\\ 1 & 2 & 1\end{bmatrix}\quad A=\begin{bmatrix}0 & -1\\ -1 & 4\\ 2 & 3\end{bmatrix}\quad B=\begin{bmatrix}2 & 1 & 3\\ 0 & 3 & 5\end{bmatrix}\quad C=\begin{bmatrix}-1 & 1\\ 1 & -1\end{bmatrix}$$

31. S^2 **32.** B^2 **33.** T^2 **34.** S^3 **35.** Q^3

36. AB **37.** BA **38.** $2BA - C$ **39.** $3CB + 2B$ **40.** $(BA)^2$

Diving

Chinese diver Guo Jingjing won two gold medals at the 2004 Summer Olympic Games in Athens, Greece.

41. Diving In a diving competition, the point total for each dive is multiplied by an assigned degree of difficulty to determine the diver's score.

Points for Each Dive

Diver	Dive 1	Dive 2	Dive 3
Ted	23.0	18.5	19.5
Chloe	24.0	28.5	25.0
Biko	19.0	22.0	21.5
Hana	27.0	26.5	28.0

Degree of Difficulty Multiplier

Dive	Ted	Chloe	Biko	Hana
1	1.2	1.6	2.0	1.8
2	2.3	2.0	2.8	2.5
3	2.7	2.6	3.2	3.1

a. Organize the tables as matrices, and multiply.
b. Use the product matrix to find the scores for each of the four divers.
c. Explain why only the numbers on the main diagonal of the product matrix are meaningful in the context of the problem.

Critical Thinking For Exercises 42–45, tell whether each statement is always, sometimes, or never true for matrices *A* and *B*. Explain your answer.

42. If A is 2×3 and B has three rows, then AB is defined.

43. If A is 2×3 and B has three columns, then AB is defined.

44. If AB is defined, then BA is defined.

45. If both AB and BA are defined, both are square matrices.

MULTI-STEP TEST PREP

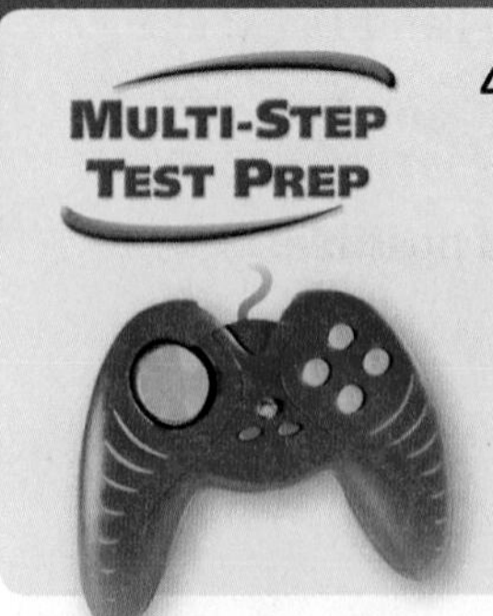

46. This problem will prepare you for the Multi-Step Test Prep on page 268.

a. Place the vertices of the triangle in a matrix so that the x-coordinates are in row 1 and the y-coordinates are in row 2.

b. Use the matrix $\begin{bmatrix}2 & 0\\ 0 & 2\end{bmatrix}$ to multiply each x- and y-coordinate by 2.

c. Draw a new triangle using the new coordinates. Describe the new triangle.

47. Solve for x: $\begin{bmatrix} 4 & 3 \\ 5 & 6 \end{bmatrix}\begin{bmatrix} 6 & \frac{x}{2} \\ -1 & -1 \end{bmatrix} = \begin{bmatrix} 21 & -19 \\ 24 & -26 \end{bmatrix}$

48. **Write About It** Explain why $\begin{bmatrix} 1 & 0 \\ 0 & 1 \end{bmatrix}\begin{bmatrix} a & b \\ c & d \end{bmatrix} = \begin{bmatrix} a & b \\ c & d \end{bmatrix}$.

49. **Fiber Arts** The first table shows points awarded by the judges at the New England Sheep & Wool Fair for each competition. The second table shows the multiplier used for the degree of difficulty of each piece. Find the total score for each contestant.

Points Awarded			
Contestant	Wall Hanging	Clothing	Rug
Madison	16.5	18.0	17.5
Devyn	12.5	14.0	17.0
Ali	16.0	19.5	18.0

Degree of Difficulty Multiplier			
Category	Madison	Devyn	Ali
Wall Hanging	2	3	2
Clothing	3	3	1
Rug	2	2	1

50. **Sales** Old and new commission rates for shoe sales are given.
 a. Find the product matrix. How much did each person make under each rate?
 b. Which salesperson benefited the most from the change in rates? Explain.

Total Sales ($)			
Salesperson	Men's	Women's	Children's
Leigh	5200	4200	2300
Khalid	8100	8400	3100
Ari	2700	7400	630

Commission Rates		
Shoe	Old Rate	New Rate
Men's	9%	9.5%
Women's	9%	10%
Children's	13%	12%

51. **Puzzle** Contestants in a reality TV show need to get to a location given by entries in the following matrix product:

$$P = \begin{bmatrix} 5 & 1 \\ -11 & 2 \end{bmatrix}\begin{bmatrix} 5 & -2 \\ 9 & -3 \end{bmatrix}$$

latitude: p_{21} (north if positive, south if negative)

longitude: p_{12} (east if positive, west if negative)

What is the location that the contestants must make their way to?

52. **Football** Find the total number of points scored by each team.

Team	Touchdowns	Extra Points	Field Goals
Redcliffe	11	9	4
Mayson	15	12	6
Rye Harbor	6	5	9

Type of Score	Points
Touchdown	6
Extra point	1
Field goal	3

53. **Critical Thinking** Write A as a scalar product where each entry is a whole number.

$$A = \begin{bmatrix} \frac{1}{2} & \frac{1}{3} \\ \frac{3}{4} & \frac{5}{6} \end{bmatrix}$$

TEST PREP

54. B is a 5×12 matrix. For AB to be defined, what characteristic must A have?

Ⓐ 5 columns Ⓑ 12 columns Ⓒ 5 rows Ⓓ 12 rows

55. Which result is NOT equal to the other three?

Ⓕ $2\begin{bmatrix} a & b \\ c & d \end{bmatrix}$ Ⓖ $\begin{bmatrix} 2 & 2 \\ 2 & 2 \end{bmatrix}\begin{bmatrix} a & b \\ c & d \end{bmatrix}$ Ⓗ $\begin{bmatrix} a & b \\ c & d \end{bmatrix} + \begin{bmatrix} a & b \\ c & d \end{bmatrix}$ Ⓙ $\begin{bmatrix} a & b \\ c & d \end{bmatrix}\begin{bmatrix} 2 & 0 \\ 0 & 2 \end{bmatrix}$

56. For the matrix product $P = \begin{bmatrix} 7 & -1 \\ 4 & 2 \end{bmatrix}\begin{bmatrix} -2 & 5 \\ 3 & 8 \end{bmatrix}$, which expression gives the value of p_{22}?

Ⓐ $4(-2) + 2(3)$ Ⓑ $7(5) + (-1)8$ Ⓒ $4(5) + 2(8)$ Ⓓ $(-1)3 + 2(8)$

57. Short Response For $A = \begin{bmatrix} 3 & 4 \\ -4 & 5 \end{bmatrix}$ and $B = \begin{bmatrix} 3 & -6 \\ 6 & 8 \end{bmatrix}$, tell whether AB, BA, or neither equals $\begin{bmatrix} 33 & -18 \\ -14 & 64 \end{bmatrix}$.

CHALLENGE AND EXTEND

58. Is matrix multiplication associative? That is, does $ABC = (AB)C = A(BC)$ if the products are defined? Give an example to support your answer.

59. To write the *transpose* A^T of a matrix A for $A = \begin{bmatrix} 2 & 0 & 1 \\ 3 & 1 & 4 \end{bmatrix}$, $A^T = \begin{bmatrix} 2 & 3 \\ 0 & 1 \\ 1 & 4 \end{bmatrix}$, reverse its rows and columns.

a. Can a matrix always be multiplied by its transpose? Explain.

b. Find $P = AA^T$ for $\begin{bmatrix} a & b \\ c & d \end{bmatrix}$. Which entries of the product are equal?

60. On a calculator, enter matrix $A = \begin{bmatrix} 1 & 1 \\ 1 & 0 \end{bmatrix}$. Multiply A by itself, and record the value of the entry in row 2 column 2 of the product matrix. Continue to multiply by A and record the entry in this location. What is the relationship between successive recorded values?

SPIRAL REVIEW

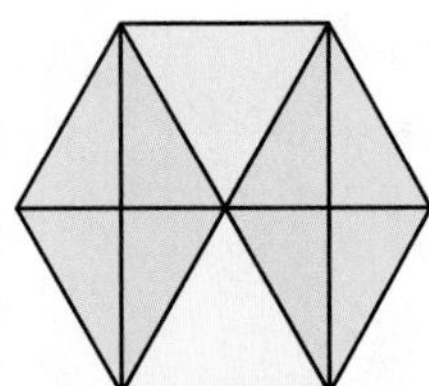

Graphic Design The outer shape of this design is a regular hexagon. The green triangle is an equilateral triangle. *(Previous course)*

61. How many pairs of vertical angles are in the design?

62. How many triangles are congruent to the green triangle?

63. How many line segments are congruent to one side of the hexagon?

Graph each point in three-dimensional space. *(Lesson 3-5)*

64. $(0, 4, -5)$ **65.** $(2, 2, 6)$ **66.** $(-3, -3, 3)$ **67.** $(1, -1, -1)$

Evaluate, if possible. *(Lesson 4-1)*

$$S = \begin{bmatrix} 2 & 4 \\ -1 & 0 \end{bmatrix} \quad T = \begin{bmatrix} 0.5 & 0.83 \\ 5 & 0 \end{bmatrix} \quad V = \begin{bmatrix} 2 & 3 & 0 \\ -4 & 1 & -1 \end{bmatrix}$$

68. $S + T$ **69.** $V - T$ **70.** $4T$

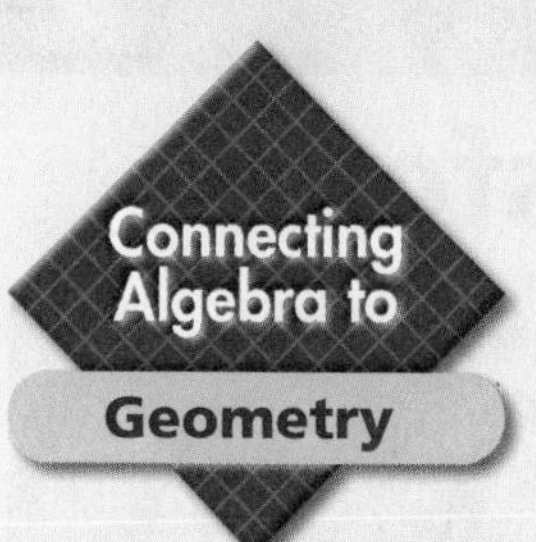

Transformations

A *transformation* describes a way of moving or resizing a geometric figure. *Rigid transformations*, or *isometries*, do not change the size and shape of figures. However, not all transformations are rigid.

Transformations are described by distances, angle measures, and lines of reflection, depending on the type of transformation. The properties of a transformation tell you what attributes of the figure remain unchanged.

	Translation	Reflection	Rotation	Dilation
What You Need to Describe It	Horizontal and vertical distance	Line of reflection	Center angle of rotation	Center scale factor
What Does Not Change	Size and shape, area, orientation	Size and shape, area	Size and shape, area, orientation	Orientation

Example

Reflect $\triangle DEF$ across the line $y = x$.

Step 1 Draw a line through D perpendicular to the line of reflection. Mark point D' as the image of point D. Point D and point D' must be the same distance from the line of reflection.

Step 2 Repeat Step 1 for points E and F. Connect the points to make $\triangle D'E'F'$.

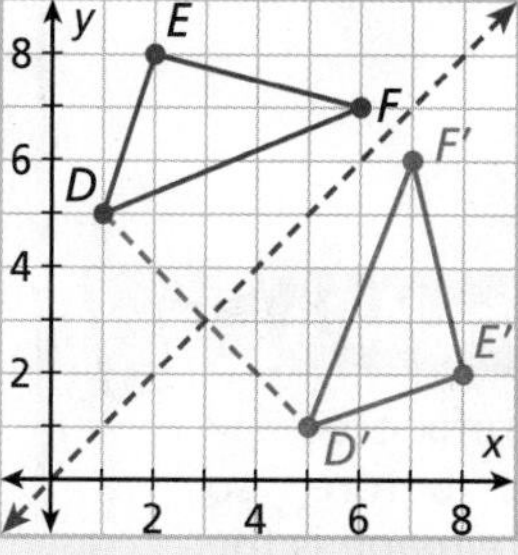

Try This

Use graph paper to show each transformation.

1. Plot rectangle $PQRS$ with vertices $P(3, 1)$, $Q(3, -2)$, $R(-2, -2)$, and $S(-2, 1)$. Rotate the rectangle 90° clockwise. Use vertex P as the center of rotation.
2. Plot $\triangle ABC$ with vertices $A(1, 4)$, $B(6, 4)$, and $C(4, 6)$. Enlarge the triangle using the origin as the center of dilation with a scale factor of 1.5.
3. The identity transformation I maps each point of the plane onto itself. Describe consecutive reflections that are equivalent to the identity transformation.
4. Draw the horizontal line $y = 4$. Use $\triangle DEF$ from the example. Translate the triangle 3 units to the right, and then reflect it across the line. Repeat twice. This is an example of a *glide reflection*, the product of a reflection in a line and a translation along the same line.

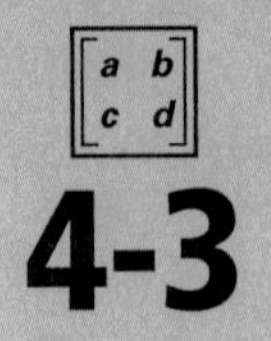

4-3 Using Matrices to Transform Geometric Figures

Objective
Use matrices to transform a plane figure.

Vocabulary
translation matrix
reflection matrix
rotation matrix

Who uses this?
Artists, such as M. C. Escher, may use repeated transformed patterns to create their work. (See Exercise 16.)

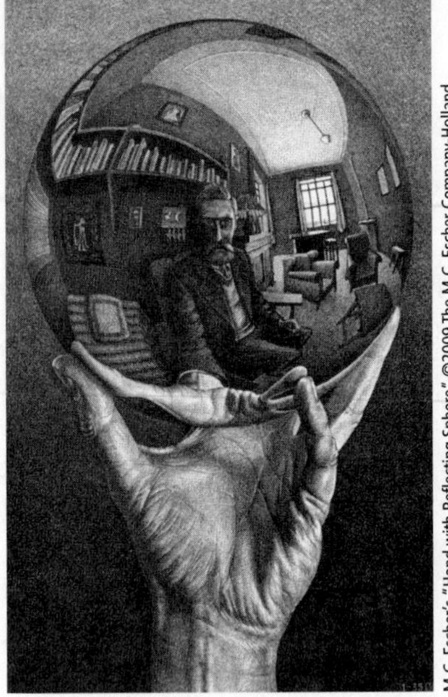

You can describe the position, shape, and size of a polygon on a coordinate plane by naming the ordered pairs that define its vertices.

The coordinates of $\triangle ABC$ below are $A(-2, -1)$, $B(0, 3)$, and $C(1, -2)$.

You can also define $\triangle ABC$ by a matrix:

$$P = \begin{bmatrix} -2 & 0 & 1 \\ -1 & 3 & -2 \end{bmatrix} \begin{matrix} \leftarrow x\text{-coordinates} \\ \leftarrow y\text{-coordinates} \end{matrix}$$

A **translation matrix** is a matrix used to translate coordinates on the coordinate plane. The matrix sum of a *preimage* and a translation matrix gives the coordinates of the translated *image*.

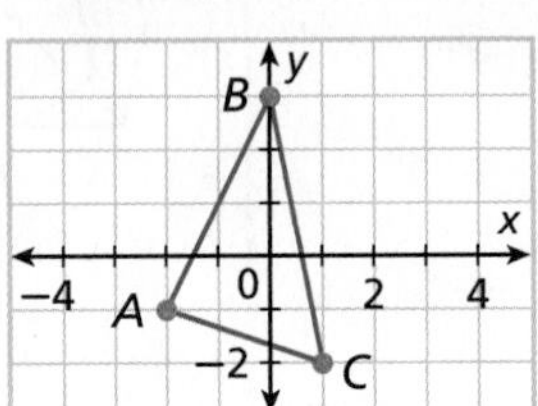

EXAMPLE 1 **Using Matrices to Translate a Figure**

Translate $\triangle ABC$ with coordinates $A(-2, -1)$, $B(0, 3)$, and $C(1, -2)$ 2 units right and 3 units down. Find the coordinates of the vertices of the image, and graph.

The translation matrix will have 2 in all entries in row 1 and −3 in all entries in row 2.

$$\begin{bmatrix} 2 & 2 & 2 \\ -3 & -3 & -3 \end{bmatrix} \begin{matrix} \leftarrow x\text{-translation} \\ \leftarrow y\text{-translation} \end{matrix}$$

Coordinate matrix + *Translation matrix*

$$\begin{bmatrix} -2 & 0 & 1 \\ -1 & 3 & -2 \end{bmatrix} + \begin{bmatrix} 2 & 2 & 2 \\ -3 & -3 & -3 \end{bmatrix} = \begin{bmatrix} -2+2 & 0+2 & 1+2 \\ -1-3 & 3-3 & -2-3 \end{bmatrix}$$

$$= \begin{bmatrix} 0 & 2 & 3 \\ -4 & 0 & -5 \end{bmatrix}$$

$A'B'C'$, the image of $\triangle ABC$, has coordinates $A'(0, -4)$, $B'(2, 0)$, and $C'(3, -5)$.

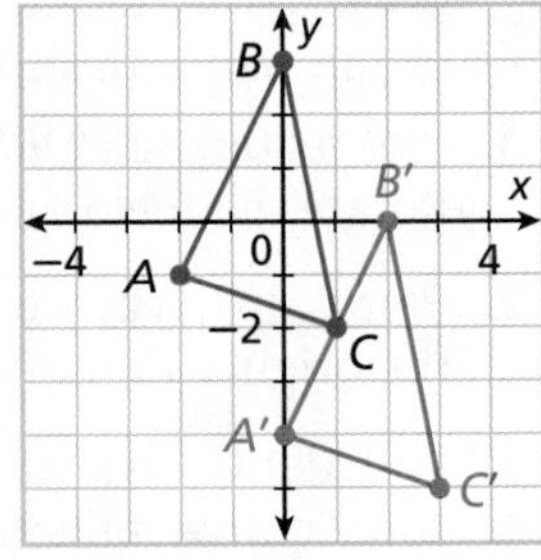

Reading Math

The prefix *pre-* means "before," so the *preimage* is the original figure before any transformations are applied. The *image* is the resulting figure after a transformation.

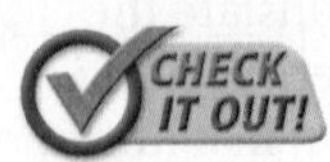

1. Translate $\triangle GHJ$ with coordinates $G(2, 4)$, $H(3, 1)$, and $J(1, -1)$ 3 units right and 1 unit down. Find the coordinates of the vertices of the image and graph.

A *dilation* is a transformation that scales—enlarges or reduces—the preimage, resulting in similar figures. Remember that for similar figures, the shape is the same but the size may be different. Angles are congruent, and side lengths are proportional.

When the *center of dilation* is the origin, multiplying the coordinate matrix by a scalar gives the coordinates of the dilated image. In this lesson, all dilations assume that the origin is the center of dilation.

EXAMPLE 2 Using Matrices to Dilate a Figure

Reduce triangle $\triangle ABC$ with coordinates $A(-4, 0)$, $B(2, 4)$, and $C(4, -2)$ by a factor of $\frac{1}{2}$. Find the coordinates of the vertices of the image, and graph.

Multiply each coordinate by $\frac{1}{2}$ by multiplying each entry by $\frac{1}{2}$.

$$\frac{1}{2}\begin{bmatrix} -4 & 2 & 4 \\ 0 & 4 & -2 \end{bmatrix} = \begin{bmatrix} \frac{1}{2}(-4) & \frac{1}{2}(2) & \frac{1}{2}(4) \\ \frac{1}{2}(0) & \frac{1}{2}(4) & \frac{1}{2}(-2) \end{bmatrix} = \begin{bmatrix} -2 & 1 & 2 \\ 0 & 2 & -1 \end{bmatrix} \begin{matrix} \leftarrow x\text{-coordinates} \\ \leftarrow y\text{-coordinates} \end{matrix}$$

$A'B'C'$, the image of $\triangle ABC$, has coordinates $A'(-2, 0)$, $B'(1, 2)$, and $C'(2, -1)$.

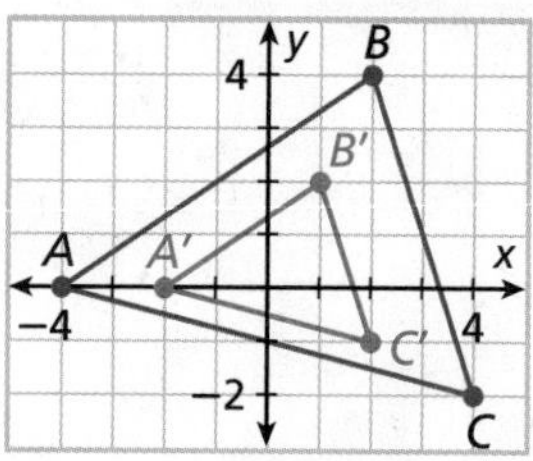

2. Enlarge $\triangle DEF$ with coordinates $D(2, 3)$, $E(5, 1)$, and $F(-2, -7)$ a factor of $\frac{4}{3}$. Find the coordinates of the vertices of the image, and graph.

A **reflection matrix** is a matrix that creates a mirror image by reflecting each vertex over a specified line of symmetry. To reflect a figure across the y-axis, multiply $\begin{bmatrix} -1 & 0 \\ 0 & 1 \end{bmatrix}$ by the coordinate matrix. This reverses the x-coordinates and keeps the y-coordinates unchanged.

EXAMPLE 3 Using Matrices to Reflect a Figure

Reflect $\triangle JKL$ with coordinates $J(3, 4)$, $K(4, 2)$, and $L(1, -2)$ across the y-axis. Find the coordinates of the vertices of the image, and graph.

$$\begin{bmatrix} -1 & 0 \\ 0 & 1 \end{bmatrix}\begin{bmatrix} 3 & 4 & 1 \\ 4 & 2 & -2 \end{bmatrix} = \begin{bmatrix} -3 & -4 & -1 \\ 4 & 2 & -2 \end{bmatrix}$$

Each x-coordinate is multiplied by -1.

Each y-coordinate is multiplied by 1.

The coordinates of the vertices of the image are $J'(-3, 4)$, $K'(-4, 2)$, and $L'(-1, -2)$.

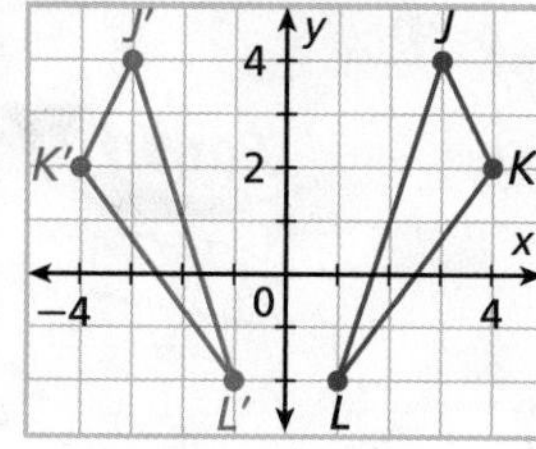

Caution!

Matrix multiplication is not commutative. So be sure to keep the transformation matrix on the left!

3. To reflect a figure across the x-axis, multiply by $\begin{bmatrix} 1 & 0 \\ 0 & -1 \end{bmatrix}$.

Reflect $\triangle JKL$ across the x-axis. Find the coordinates of the vertices of the image and graph.

A **rotation matrix** is a matrix used to rotate a figure. Example 4 gives several types of rotation matrices.

EXAMPLE 4 Using Matrices to Rotate a Figure

Use each matrix to rotate polygon *JKLM* with coordinates $J(0, 0)$, $K(4, 2)$, $L(2, -5)$, and $M(-1, -3)$ about the origin. Graph and describe the image.

A $\begin{bmatrix} 0 & -1 \\ 1 & 0 \end{bmatrix}$

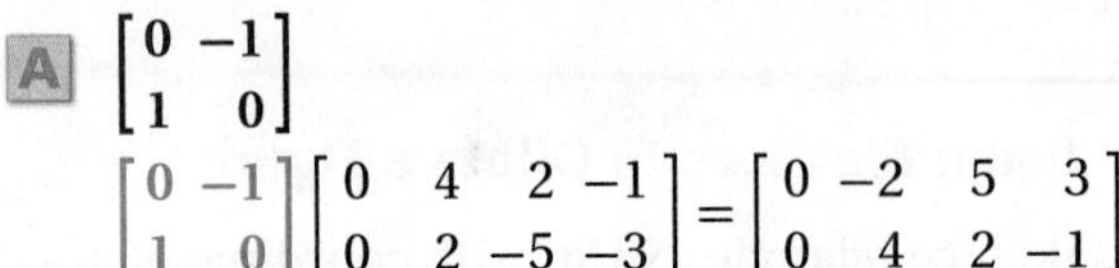

$$\begin{bmatrix} 0 & -1 \\ 1 & 0 \end{bmatrix}\begin{bmatrix} 0 & 4 & 2 & -1 \\ 0 & 2 & -5 & -3 \end{bmatrix} = \begin{bmatrix} 0 & -2 & 5 & 3 \\ 0 & 4 & 2 & -1 \end{bmatrix}$$

The image is rotated 90° counterclockwise.

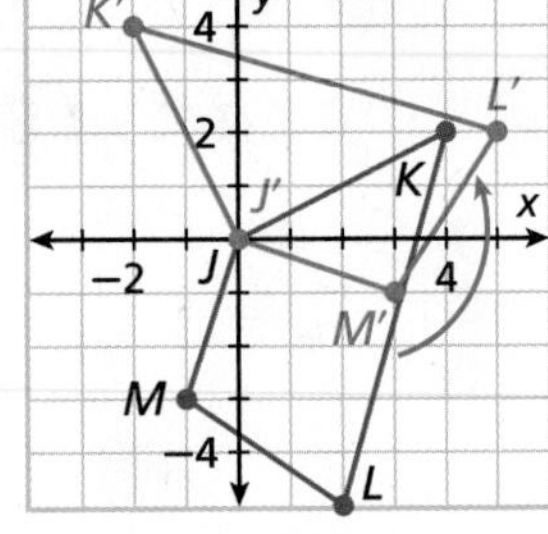

Helpful Hint

Multiplying a coordinate by −1 results in the opposite of the coordinate.

B $\begin{bmatrix} 0 & 1 \\ -1 & 0 \end{bmatrix}$

$$\begin{bmatrix} 0 & 1 \\ -1 & 0 \end{bmatrix}\begin{bmatrix} 0 & 4 & 2 & -1 \\ 0 & 2 & -5 & -3 \end{bmatrix} = \begin{bmatrix} 0 & 2 & -5 & -3 \\ 0 & -4 & -2 & 1 \end{bmatrix}$$

The image is rotated 90° clockwise.

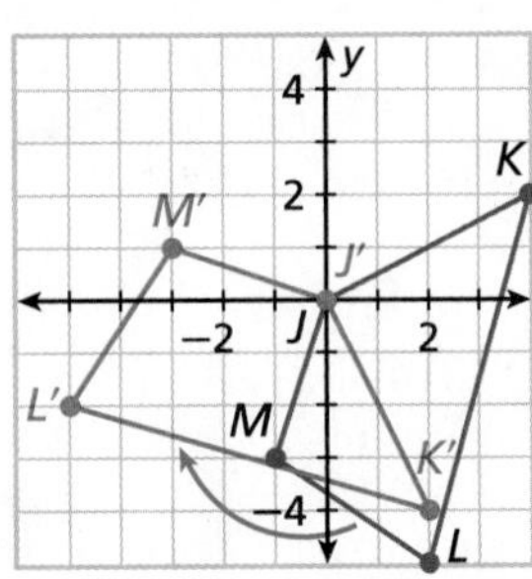

CHECK IT OUT! **4.** Use $\begin{bmatrix} -1 & 0 \\ 0 & -1 \end{bmatrix}$. Rotate $\triangle ABC$ with coordinates $A(0, 0)$, $B(4, 0)$, and $C(0, -3)$ about the origin. Graph and describe the image.

THINK AND DISCUSS

1. Describe the transformation resulting from multiplying a coordinate matrix by $\begin{bmatrix} 1 & 0 \\ 0 & 1 \end{bmatrix}$.

2. Describe what happens to an *x*-coordinate in a matrix when multiplied by this row of a transformation matrix.

a. $\begin{bmatrix} 1 & 0 \end{bmatrix}$ **b.** $\begin{bmatrix} 0 & 1 \end{bmatrix}$ **c.** $\begin{bmatrix} 0.5 & 0 \end{bmatrix}$ **d.** $\begin{bmatrix} 1 & 1 \end{bmatrix}$

3. GET ORGANIZED Copy and complete the graphic organizer. *Q* is a triangle represented by its 2 × 3 coordinate matrix. Complete the summary by filling in a matrix expression.

Transformation	Matrix Operation
Translate *Q* vertically	
Translate *Q* horizontally	
Enlarge or reduce *Q*.	
Reflect *Q* across the *x*-axis or *y*-axis	
Rotate *Q* 90° clockwise or counterclockwise.	

4-3 Exercises

go.hrw.com
Homework Help Online
KEYWORD: MB7 4-3
Parent Resources Online
KEYWORD: MB7 Parent

GUIDED PRACTICE

1. **Vocabulary** A __?__ creates a mirror image of a set of points. (*reflection matrix* or *translation matrix*)

SEE EXAMPLE 1 p. 262

Translate the polygon with coordinates $P(-2, 4)$, $Q(3, 1)$, $R(1, -4)$, and $S(-2, -2)$ as indicated. Find the coordinates of the vertices of the image, and graph.

2. 2 units left and 1 unit up
3. 1 unit right and 0 units down

SEE EXAMPLE 2 p. 263

Use a matrix to reduce or enlarge the polygon with coordinates $P(-2, 4)$, $Q(3, 1)$, $R(1, -4)$, and $S(-2, -2)$ by the given factor. Find the coordinates of the vertices of the image, and graph.

4. Reduce polygon *PQRS* by a factor of 0.5.
5. Enlarge polygon *PQRS* by a factor of 2.

SEE EXAMPLE 3 p. 263

Reflect the figure with coordinates $A(-2, 3)$, $B(0, 4)$, $C(2, 3)$, $D(2, 1)$, and $E(-1, -1)$ across the given line. Find the coordinates of the vertices of the image, and graph.

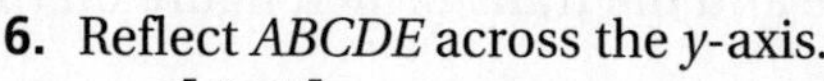

6. Reflect *ABCDE* across the *y*-axis.
7. Use $\begin{bmatrix} 0 & 1 \\ 1 & 0 \end{bmatrix}$ to reflect *ABCDE* across the line $y = x$.

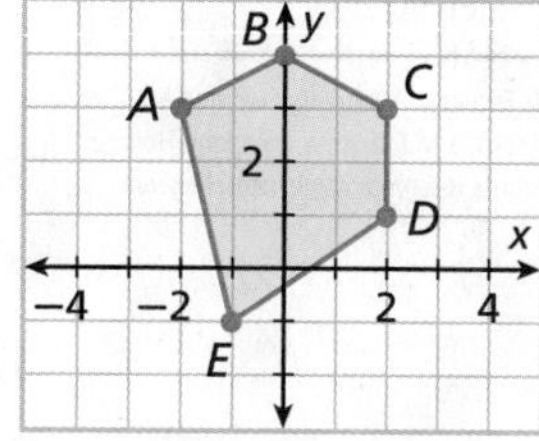

SEE EXAMPLE 4 p. 264

Use each matrix to rotate the figure with coordinates $L(1, 3)$, $M(4, 2)$, $N(1, 1)$, and $O(1, -1)$ about the origin. Graph and describe the image.

8. $\begin{bmatrix} 0 & 1 \\ -1 & 0 \end{bmatrix}$
9. $\begin{bmatrix} -1 & 0 \\ 0 & -1 \end{bmatrix}$

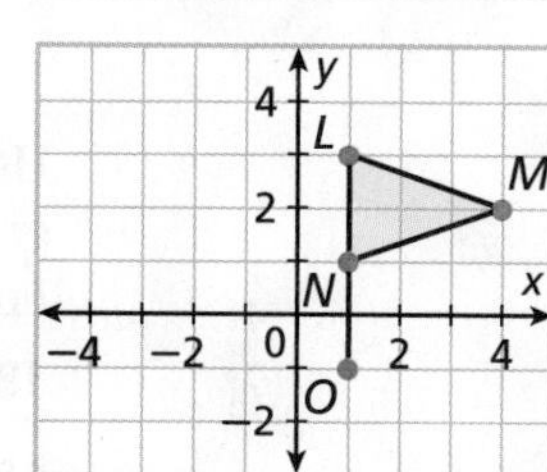

PRACTICE AND PROBLEM SOLVING

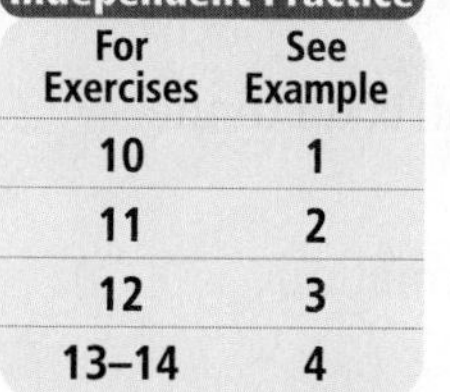

Independent Practice

For Exercises	See Example
10	1
11	2
12	3
13–14	4

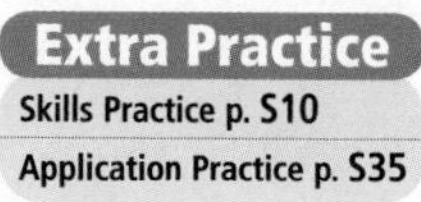

Extra Practice
Skills Practice p. S10
Application Practice p. S35

10. Translate the polygon with coordinates $D(0, 4)$, $E(-3, -1)$, $F(1, -5)$, and $G(1, 0)$ 3 units right and 3 units up. Find the coordinates of the vertices of the image, and graph.

11. Dilate the polygon with coordinates $W(1, 2)$, $X(-2, 3)$, $Y(-3, 4)$, and $Z(-4, 1)$ by a factor of $\frac{3}{2}$. Find the coordinates of the vertices of the image, and graph.

12. Reflect the figure with coordinates $A(-2, 3)$, $B(0, 4)$, $C(2, 3)$, $D(2, 1)$, and $E(-1, -1)$ across the *x*-axis. Graph and describe the image.

Use each matrix to rotate the figure *PQRST* with coordinates $P(-3, 2)$, $Q(0, 0)$, $R(-4, 1)$, $S(-4, 4)$, and $T(-1, 4)$. Graph and describe the image.

13. $\begin{bmatrix} 0 & -1 \\ 1 & 0 \end{bmatrix}$
14. $\begin{bmatrix} 0 & 1 \\ -1 & 0 \end{bmatrix}$

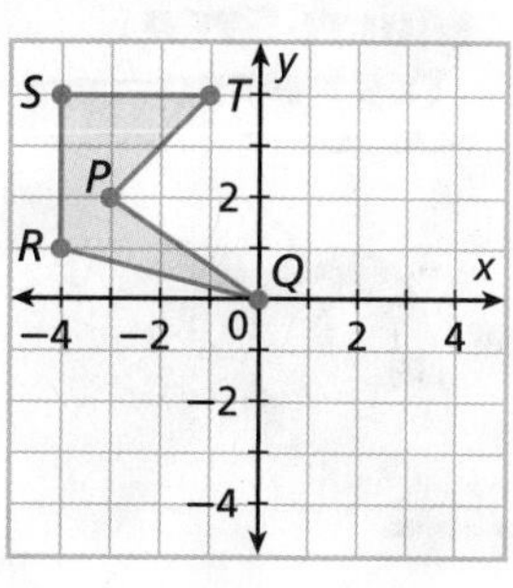

15. **Design** Skye creates a design based on a starfish as a background for her school ecology club Web page. On a coordinate plane, the ends of the arms of the first image are $S(0, 4)$, $T(4, 1)$, $R(2.5, -4)$, $F(-2.5, -4)$, and $H(-4, 1)$.

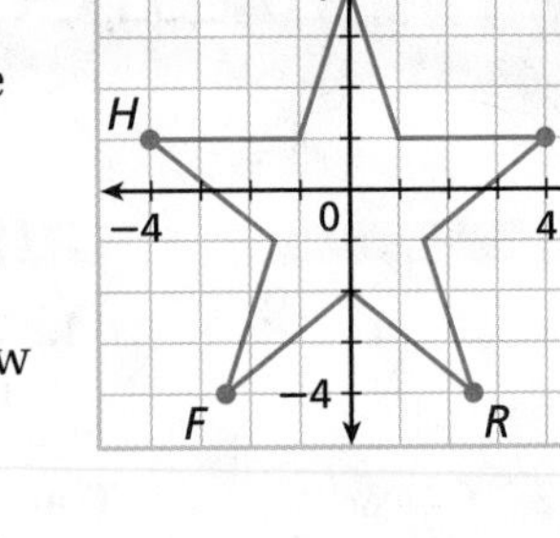

a. Use the matrix $\begin{bmatrix} 0.81 & -0.59 \\ 0.59 & 0.81 \end{bmatrix}$ to rotate the star through $\frac{1}{10}$ of a circle. Round the coordinates of the new image to the nearest half-unit.

b. Does the star rotate clockwise or counterclockwise? Explain.

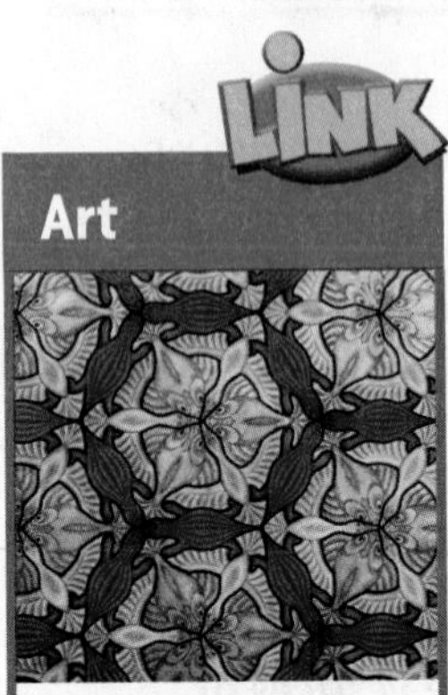

Art

Artist M. C. Escher (1898–1972) transformed symmetric geometric shapes into birds, reptiles, and other figures.

16. **Art** To make a *tessellation,* which is a picture made entirely of repeated transformations of figures without gaps or overlaps, an artist creates the initial figure and transforms it repeatedly.

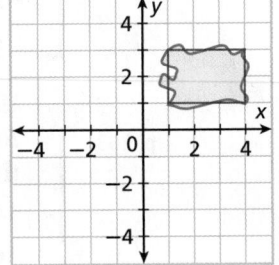

a. The artist first rotates the figure 180°. Write a rotation matrix for this transformation.

b. Find the vertices of the figure after the rotation matrix is applied.

c. Next, the artist translates the figure 4 units up and 2 units right. Write a translation matrix for this transformation.

d. Find the vertices of the figure after this second transformation is applied.

e. Sketch the original figure and the transformed figure on the same coordinate grid.

17. **Critical Thinking** $T = \begin{bmatrix} 0 & 1 \\ -1 & 0 \end{bmatrix}$. Explain what happens if you multiply T by the coordinate matrix of a figure and then multiply T by the result.

Use a matrix to perform each transformation on the graph representing the constellation the Big Dipper. Find the coordinates of the image.

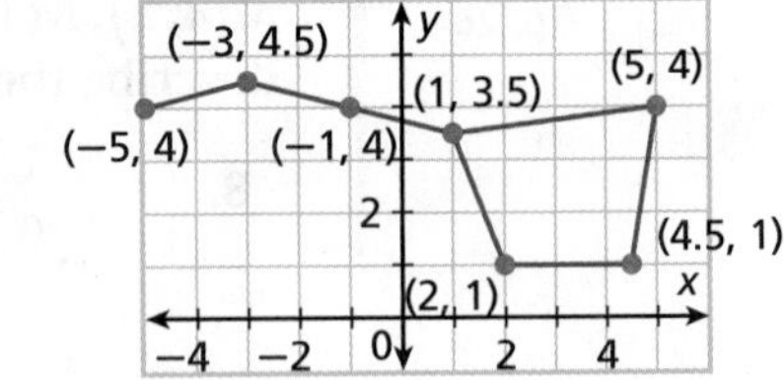

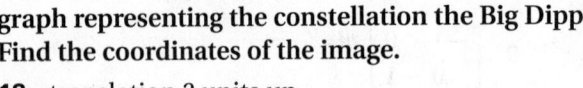

18. translation 2 units up

19. translation 1 unit down and 3 units left

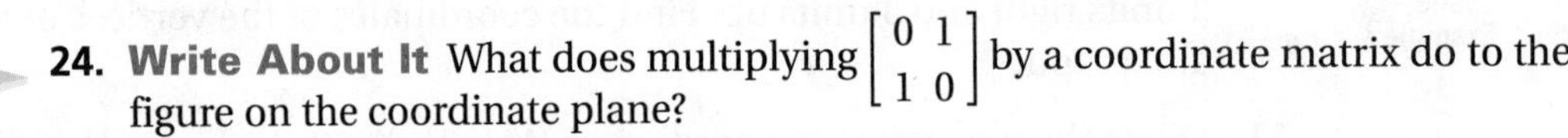

20. enlargement by a factor of 2

21. reflection across the x-axis

22. rotation 90° clockwise

23. rotation 90° counterclockwise

24. **Write About It** What does multiplying $\begin{bmatrix} 0 & 1 \\ 1 & 0 \end{bmatrix}$ by a coordinate matrix do to the figure on the coordinate plane?

25. What transformation matrix represents $g(x) = -f(x)$? What transformation represents $g(x) = f(-x)$?

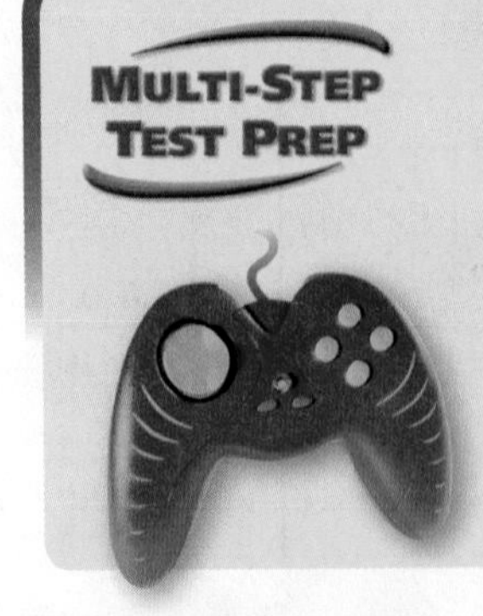

MULTI-STEP TEST PREP

26. This problem will prepare you for the Multi-Step Test Prep on page 268.

a. Place the vertices of the triangle in a coordinate matrix.

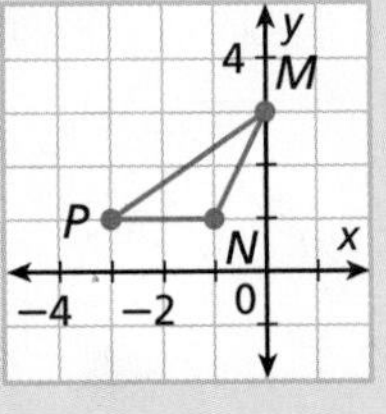

b. Multiply the matrix $\begin{bmatrix} -1 & 0 \\ 0 & -1 \end{bmatrix}$ by the coordinate matrix.

c. Draw a new triangle using the new coordinates. Describe the image.

d. Repeat parts **b** and **c** using the new triangle as the preimage. Describe the final triangle.

27. To create a quilt pattern, Morgan dilates a figure, rotates it 90° clockwise, and reflects it across the y-axis. Which sequence results in the image?

Ⓐ scalar multiplication; matrix addition; matrix multiplication

Ⓑ scalar multiplication; matrix multiplication; matrix multiplication

Ⓒ matrix addition; matrix multiplication; matrix addition

Ⓓ matrix multiplication; matrix addition; scalar multiplication

28. What effect does multiplying $\begin{bmatrix} 0 & 2 \\ -2 & 0 \end{bmatrix}$ by the coordinates of a figure have?

Ⓕ The figure is enlarged and rotated 90° clockwise.

Ⓖ The figure is reduced and rotated 90° counterclockwise.

Ⓗ The figure is reduced and reflected across the x-axis.

Ⓙ The figure is enlarged and reflected across the y-axis.

29. Which matrix can be used to rotate a figure 180° about the origin?

Ⓐ $\begin{bmatrix} 0 & -1 \\ -1 & 0 \end{bmatrix}$ Ⓑ $\begin{bmatrix} 1 & -1 \\ -1 & 1 \end{bmatrix}$ Ⓒ $\begin{bmatrix} -1 & 0 \\ 0 & -1 \end{bmatrix}$ Ⓓ $\begin{bmatrix} -1 & 1 \\ 1 & -1 \end{bmatrix}$

CHALLENGE AND EXTEND

30. What matrix could you use to reflect a figure across the line $y = -x$?

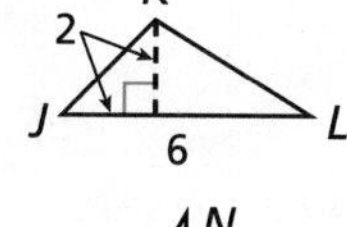

31. Position $\triangle JKL$ on a coordinate plane, and assign coordinates to the vertices.

   a. How can you transform $\triangle JKL$ to create a symmetrical compass with four points N, E, S, and W?

   b. Use matrices to transform $\triangle JKL$, and give the coordinates of the four points N, E, S, and W.

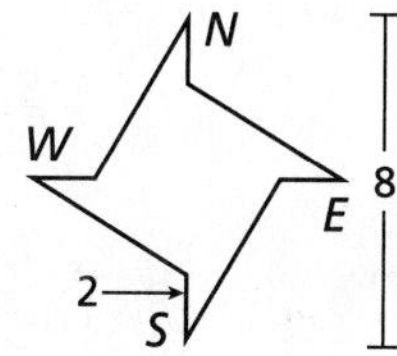

32. Transform a figure using $\begin{bmatrix} -\frac{2}{3} & 0 \\ 0 & \frac{3}{2} \end{bmatrix}$. Describe the transformation. What would happen if this transformation were performed repeatedly?

SPIRAL REVIEW

33. Determine whether the data set could represent a linear function. *(Lesson 2-3)*

Tickets	2	5	8	11
Cost ($)	35.00	87.50	140.00	192.50

Determine if the given point is a solution of the system of inequalities. *(Lesson 3-3)*

34. $(2, -4); \begin{cases} y > 2x - 8 \\ y \le \frac{1}{4}x + 2 \end{cases}$

35. $(0, 5); \begin{cases} y > 0 \\ y \ge 2x - 11 \\ 5x + y < 5.5 \end{cases}$

Evaluate, if possible. *(Lesson 4-2)*

36. $\begin{bmatrix} 5 & -5 \\ 2 & 1 \end{bmatrix}\begin{bmatrix} 10 & 1 \\ -2 & 0 \end{bmatrix}$

37. $\begin{bmatrix} 3 & 1 & -1 \\ 0 & 2 & 1 \end{bmatrix}\begin{bmatrix} 1 & 1 \\ -2 & 1 \end{bmatrix}$

38. $\begin{bmatrix} 3 & 1 & -1 \end{bmatrix}\begin{bmatrix} 4 \\ 5 \\ 6 \end{bmatrix}$

CHAPTER 4

MULTI-STEP TEST PREP

SECTION 4A

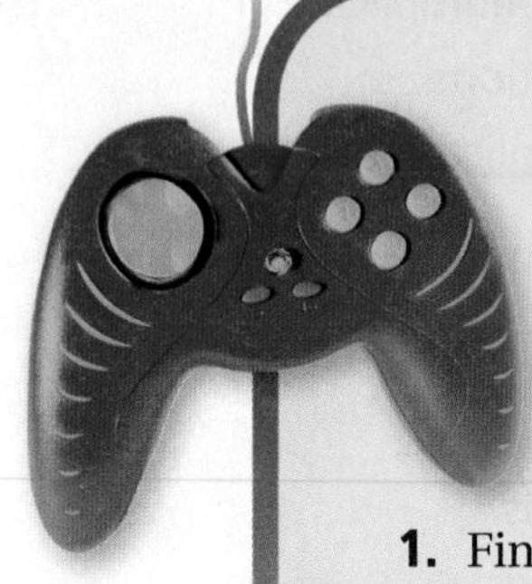

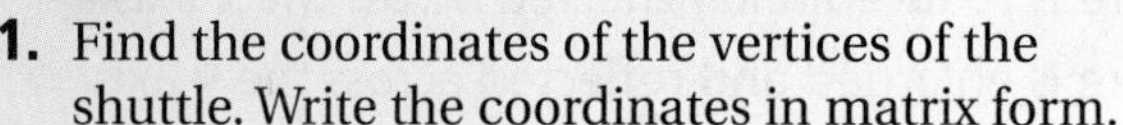

Games Away

You are making a video game using the space shuttle figure shown on the grid. By applying different transformations to the shuttle, you can simulate different moves.

1. Find the coordinates of the vertices of the shuttle. Write the coordinates in matrix form.
2. The *hyperjump* button causes the shuttle to immediately rise 4 units. What transformation represents the shuttle after hyperjump? Write the transformation matrix, and show the matrix operation.
3. What transformation will make the shuttle reverse direction? Write the transformation matrix, and show the matrix operation.
4. What transformation will make the shuttle fly upside down? Write the transformation matrix, and show the matrix operation.
5. What matrix will rotate the shuttle 180° about the origin? Show the matrix operation.
6. Suppose you reflect the shuttle over one axis and then the other. Compare the result to the rotation in Problem 5.
7. If the shuttle is hit by an asteroid, it is reduced by a factor of $\frac{1}{2}$. What matrix operation will show the reduction? What is the ratio of the area of the preimage to that of the image?

READY TO GO ON?

CHAPTER 4

SECTION 4A

Quiz for Lessons 4-1 Through 4-3

4-1 Matrices and Data

Use the table for Problems 1–4.

1. Display the data in the form of a matrix M.

2. What are the dimensions of M?

3. What is the value of the matrix entry with the address m_{32}? What does it represent?

4. What is the address of the entry that has the value 90?

Olympic Medal Specifications

	Gold	Silver	Bronze
Weight (lb)	1.25	1.25	1
% copper	7.5	7.5	90
Hours of handicrafting	19.65	18.30	18.45

Use the matrices below for Problems 5–8. Evaluate, if possible.

$$A = \begin{bmatrix} 3 & 4 \\ 1 & -2 \\ 0 & -1 \end{bmatrix} \quad B = \begin{bmatrix} 4 & 0 \\ 0 & 4 \end{bmatrix} \quad C = \begin{bmatrix} 1 & -1 \\ 3 & 2 \\ 5 & -1 \end{bmatrix} \quad D = \begin{bmatrix} 5 & 1 & -1 \\ -1.5 & 2 & -2 \end{bmatrix}$$

5. $A + C$ **6.** $2B$ **7.** $C - D$ **8.** $C - 3A$

4-2 Multiplying Matrices

Use the matrices named below for Problems 9–12. Tell whether each product is defined. If so, give its dimensions.

$P_{5\times2}$, $Q_{2\times5}$, $R_{1\times5}$, and $S_{5\times2}$

9. PQ **10.** QR **11.** RS **12.** SP

Use the matrices below for Problems 13–16. Evaluate, if possible.

$$E = \begin{bmatrix} 1 & -2 & -1 \\ 5 & 3 & 0 \\ -1 & -1 & 2 \end{bmatrix} \quad F = \begin{bmatrix} 0.5 & 0.75 & -1 \end{bmatrix} \quad G = \begin{bmatrix} 1 & 2 \\ 2 & -1 \end{bmatrix} \quad H = \begin{bmatrix} -1 & 4 \\ 2 & 0 \\ 0 & -1 \end{bmatrix}$$

13. EF **14.** FH **15.** HG **16.** G^2

4-3 Using Matrices to Transform Geometric Figures

For Problems 17–20, use polygon $WXYZ$ with coordinates $W(0, 0)$, $X(1, 4)$, $Y(3, 5)$, and $Z(4, 2)$. Give the coordinates of the image and graph.

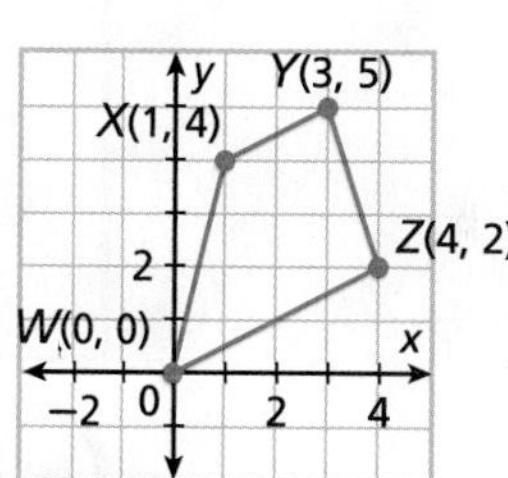

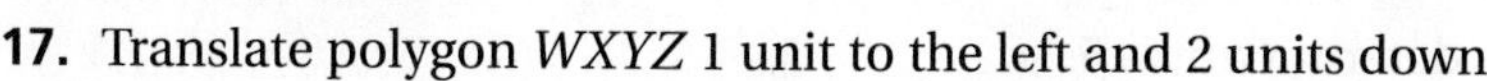

17. Translate polygon $WXYZ$ 1 unit to the left and 2 units down.

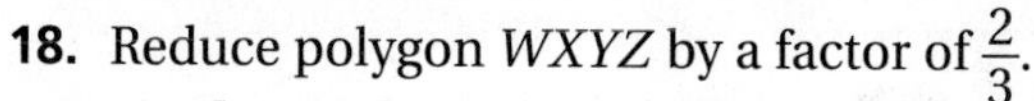

18. Reduce polygon $WXYZ$ by a factor of $\frac{2}{3}$.

19. Use $\begin{bmatrix} 1 & 0 \\ 0 & -1 \end{bmatrix}$ to transform polygon $WXYZ$. Describe the image.

20. Use $\begin{bmatrix} 0 & 1 \\ -1 & 0 \end{bmatrix}$ to transform polygon $WXYZ$. Describe the image.

21. How does multiplying by $\begin{bmatrix} 0 & 2 \\ 2 & 0 \end{bmatrix}$ transform polygon $WXYZ$?

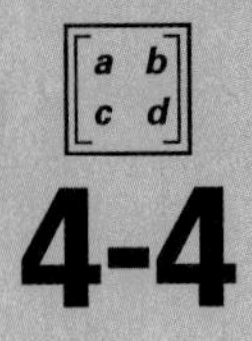

4-4 Determinants and Cramer's Rule

Objectives
Find the determinants of 2 × 2 and 3 × 3 matrices.

Use Cramer's rule to solve systems of linear equations.

Vocabulary
determinant
coefficient matrix
Cramer's rule

Who uses this?

Sports nutritionists planning menus need to solve systems of equations for Calories and grams of protein, fat, and carbohydrates. (See Example 4.)

Every square matrix (n by n) has an associated value called its *determinant,* shown by straight vertical brackets, such as $\begin{vmatrix} 1 & 2 \\ 3 & 4 \end{vmatrix}$. The determinant is a useful measure, as you will see later in this lesson.

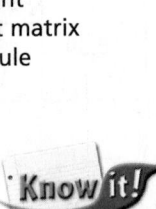

Determinant of a 2 × 2 Matrix

WORDS	NUMBERS	ALGEBRA
The **determinant** of a 2 by 2 matrix is the difference of the products of the diagonals	$\det \begin{bmatrix} 1 & 2 \\ 3 & 4 \end{bmatrix} = \begin{vmatrix} 1 & 2 \\ 3 & 4 \end{vmatrix} = (1)(4) - (3)(2) = -2$	$\det \begin{bmatrix} a & b \\ c & d \end{bmatrix} = \begin{vmatrix} a & b \\ c & d \end{vmatrix} = ad - cb$

EXAMPLE 1 Finding the Determinant of a 2 × 2 Matrix

Find the determinant of each matrix.

A $\begin{bmatrix} 6 & 5 \\ 8 & 3 \end{bmatrix}$

$\begin{vmatrix} 6 & 5 \\ 8 & 3 \end{vmatrix} = 6(3) - 8(5)$ *Find the difference of the cross products.*

$= 18 - 40 = -22$

The determinant is −22.

Reading Math

The determinant of matrix *A* may be denoted as det *A* or $|A|$. Don't confuse the $|A|$ notation with absolute value notation.

B $\begin{bmatrix} \frac{1}{3} & \frac{2}{3} \\ -6 & 3 \end{bmatrix}$

$\begin{vmatrix} \frac{1}{3} & \frac{2}{3} \\ -6 & 3 \end{vmatrix} = \frac{1}{3}(3) - (-6)\left(\frac{2}{3}\right) = 1 + 4 = 5$

The determinant is 5.

Find the determinant of each matrix.

1a. $\begin{bmatrix} 0.2 & 30 \\ -0.3 & 5 \end{bmatrix}$ **1b.** $\begin{bmatrix} \frac{1}{3} & 3 \\ \frac{5}{6} & \frac{3}{4} \end{bmatrix}$ **1c.** $\begin{bmatrix} \frac{1}{2} & \frac{1}{8} \\ 4 & 2\pi \end{bmatrix}$

You can use the determinant of a matrix to help you solve a system of equations. For two equations with two variables written in $ax + by = c$ form, you can construct a matrix of the coefficients of the variables.

For the system $\begin{cases} a_1x + b_1y = c_1 \\ a_2x + b_2y = c_2 \end{cases}$, the coefficient matrix is $\begin{bmatrix} a_1 & b_1 \\ a_2 & b_2 \end{bmatrix}$.

The **coefficient matrix** for a system of linear equations in standard form is the matrix formed by the coefficients for the variables in the equations.

The determinant D of the coefficient matrix is $\begin{vmatrix} a_1 & b_1 \\ a_2 & b_2 \end{vmatrix}$.

Cramer's Rule for Two Equations

$\begin{cases} a_1x + b_1y = c_1 \\ a_2x + b_2y = c_2 \end{cases}$ has solutions $x = \dfrac{\begin{vmatrix} c_1 & b_1 \\ c_2 & b_2 \end{vmatrix}}{D}$, $y = \dfrac{\begin{vmatrix} a_1 & c_1 \\ a_2 & c_2 \end{vmatrix}}{D}$, where $D = \begin{vmatrix} a_1 & b_1 \\ a_2 & b_2 \end{vmatrix}$.

You can use Cramer's rule to tell whether the system represented by the matrix has one solution, no solution, or infinitely many solutions.

Solutions of Systems		
If $D \neq 0$, the system is consistent and has one unique solution.	If $D = 0$ and *at least one* numerator determinant is 0, the system is dependent and has infinitely many solutions.	If $D = 0$ and *neither* numerator determinant is 0, the system is inconsistent and has no solution.
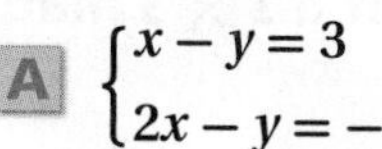		

EXAMPLE 2 Using Cramer's Rule for Two Equations

Use Cramer's rule to solve each system of equations.

A $\begin{cases} x - y = 3 \\ 2x - y = -1 \end{cases}$

Step 1 Find D, the determinant of the coefficient matrix. $\begin{bmatrix} 1 & -1 \\ 2 & -1 \end{bmatrix}$

$D = \begin{vmatrix} 1 & -1 \\ 2 & -1 \end{vmatrix} = 1(-1) - 2(-1) = 1$ *$D \neq 0$, so the system is consistent.*

Step 2 Solve for each variable by replacing the coefficients of that variable with the constants as shown below.

$$x = \frac{\begin{vmatrix} c_1 & b_1 \\ c_2 & b_2 \end{vmatrix}}{D} = \frac{\begin{vmatrix} 3 & -1 \\ -1 & -1 \end{vmatrix}}{1} = -4$$

$$y = \frac{\begin{vmatrix} a_1 & c_1 \\ a_1 & c_2 \end{vmatrix}}{D} = \frac{\begin{vmatrix} 1 & 3 \\ 2 & -1 \end{vmatrix}}{1} = -7$$

The solution is $(-4, -7)$.

Use Cramer's rule to solve each system of equations.

B $\begin{cases} y - 2 = 3x \\ 3x - y = 7 \end{cases}$

Step 1 Write the equations in standard form. $\begin{cases} 3x - y = -2 \\ 3x - y = 7 \end{cases}$

Step 2 Find the determinant of the coefficient matrix.

$$D = \begin{vmatrix} 3 & -1 \\ 3 & -1 \end{vmatrix} = -3 - (-3) = 0$$

$D = 0$, so the system is either inconsistent or dependent. Check the numerators for x and y to see if either is 0.

$$x = \frac{\begin{vmatrix} c_1 & b_1 \\ c_2 & b_2 \end{vmatrix} \rightarrow \begin{vmatrix} -2 & -1 \\ 7 & -1 \end{vmatrix} = 9}{0} \qquad y = \frac{\begin{vmatrix} a_1 & c_1 \\ a_2 & c_2 \end{vmatrix} \rightarrow \begin{vmatrix} 3 & -2 \\ 3 & 7 \end{vmatrix} = 27}{0}$$

Neither numerator is 0. The system is inconsistent with no solutions.

2. Use Cramer's rule to solve. $\begin{cases} 6x - 2y = 14 \\ 3x = y + 7 \end{cases}$

To apply Cramer's rule to 3 × 3 systems, you need to find the determinant of a 3 × 3 matrix. One method is shown below.

Rewrite the first two columns at the right side of the determinant.

Add the sum of the products of the red diagonals. Then **subtract** the sum of the blue diagonals.

$$\det \begin{bmatrix} a_1 & b_1 & c_1 \\ a_2 & b_2 & c_2 \\ a_3 & b_3 & c_3 \end{bmatrix} = \begin{vmatrix} a_1 & b_1 & c_1 \\ a_2 & b_2 & c_2 \\ a_3 & b_3 & c_3 \end{vmatrix} \begin{matrix} a_1 & b_1 \\ a_2 & b_2 \\ a_3 & b_3 \end{matrix} \quad a_1b_2c_3 + b_1c_2a_3 + c_1a_2b_3 - (a_3b_2c_1 + b_3c_2a_1 + c_3a_2b_1)$$

EXAMPLE 3 Finding the Determinant of a 3 × 3 Matrix

Find the determinant of A.

$$A = \begin{bmatrix} 4 & -2 & 0 \\ -3 & 10 & 1 \\ 2 & 6 & -1 \end{bmatrix} \quad \det A = \begin{vmatrix} 4 & -2 & 0 \\ -3 & 10 & 1 \\ 2 & 6 & -1 \end{vmatrix}, \text{ so write } \begin{vmatrix} 4 & -2 & 0 \\ -3 & 10 & 1 \\ 2 & 6 & -1 \end{vmatrix} \begin{matrix} 4 & -2 \\ -3 & 10 \\ 2 & 6 \end{matrix}$$

Helpful Hint

Lightly draw the diagonals to help you locate the six products needed to find the determinant.

Step 1 Multiply each "down" diagonal and add.
$4(10)(-1) + (-2)(1)(2) + 0(-3)(6) = -44$

$$\begin{vmatrix} 4 & -2 & 0 \\ -3 & 10 & 1 \\ 2 & 6 & -1 \end{vmatrix} \begin{matrix} 4 & -2 \\ -3 & 10 \\ 2 & 6 \end{matrix}$$

Step 2 Multiply each "up" diagonal and add.
$(2)(10)(0) + (6)(1)(4) + (-1)(-3)(-2) = 18$

Step 3 Find the difference of the sums.
$-44 - 18 = -62.$

The determinant is -62.

Check Use a calculator.

3. Find the determinant of $\begin{bmatrix} 2 & -3 & 4 \\ 5 & 1 & -2 \\ 10 & 3 & -1 \end{bmatrix}$.

Cramer's rule can be expanded to cover 3×3 systems.

Know it! Note

Cramer's Rule for Three Equations

The system $\begin{cases} a_1x + b_1y + c_1z = d_1 \\ a_2x + b_2y + c_2z = d_2 \\ a_3x + b_3y + c_3z = d_3 \end{cases}$ has solutions given by

$$x = \frac{\begin{vmatrix} d_1 & b_1 & c_1 \\ d_2 & b_2 & c_2 \\ d_3 & b_3 & c_3 \end{vmatrix}}{D},\ y = \frac{\begin{vmatrix} a_1 & d_1 & c_1 \\ a_2 & d_2 & c_2 \\ a_3 & d_3 & c_3 \end{vmatrix}}{D},\ z = \frac{\begin{vmatrix} a_1 & b_1 & d_1 \\ a_2 & b_2 & d_2 \\ a_3 & b_3 & d_3 \end{vmatrix}}{D} \text{ where } D = \begin{vmatrix} a_1 & b_1 & c_1 \\ a_2 & b_2 & c_2 \\ a_3 & b_3 & c_3 \end{vmatrix} \text{ and } D \neq 0.$$

If $D \neq 0$, then the system has a unique solution.

If $D = 0$ and no numerator is 0, then the system is inconsistent. If $D = 0$ and at least one numerator is 0, then the system may be inconsistent or dependent.

EXAMPLE 4 Nutrition Application

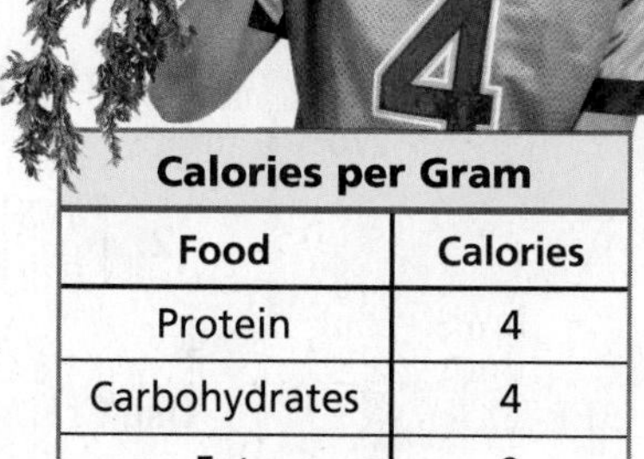

A nutritionist planning a diet for a football player wants him to consume 3600 Calories and 750 grams of food daily. Calories from protein and from fat will be 60% of the total Calories. How many grams of protein, carbohydrates, and fat will this diet include?

Calories per Gram	
Food	Calories
Protein	4
Carbohydrates	4
Fat	9

The diet will include p grams of protein, c grams of carbohydrates, and f grams of fat.

$4p + 4c + 9f = 3600$ *Equation for total Calories*

$p + c + f = 750$ *Total grams of food*

$4p + 0c + 9f = 2160$ *Calories from protein and fat, 60%(3600) = 2160*

Use a calculator.

$$D = \begin{vmatrix} 4 & 4 & 9 \\ 1 & 1 & 1 \\ 4 & 0 & 9 \end{vmatrix} = -20 \quad p = \frac{\begin{vmatrix} 3600 & 4 & 9 \\ 750 & 1 & 1 \\ 2160 & 0 & 9 \end{vmatrix}}{D} \quad c = \frac{\begin{vmatrix} 4 & 3600 & 9 \\ 1 & 750 & 1 \\ 4 & 2160 & 9 \end{vmatrix}}{D} \quad f = \frac{\begin{vmatrix} 4 & 4 & 3600 \\ 1 & 1 & 750 \\ 4 & 0 & 2160 \end{vmatrix}}{D}$$

$$p = \frac{-5400}{-20} \quad c = \frac{-7200}{-20} \quad f = \frac{-2400}{-20}$$

$$p = 270 \quad c = 360 \quad f = 120$$

The diet includes 270 grams protein, 360 grams carbohydrates, and 120 grams fat.

Caution!

When an equation is missing one variable, be sure to write the missing term with a coefficient of zero.

$4p + 0c + 9f = 2160$

4. **What if...?** A diet requires 3200 calories, 700 grams of food, and 70% of the Calories from carbohydrates and fat. How many grams of protein, carbohydrates, and fat does the diet include?

THINK AND DISCUSS

1. Describe a matrix S that has no determinant.
2. Explain how you know what the three determinants will be when you apply Cramer's rule to a two-equation system in which one equation is a multiple of the other.

3. **GET ORGANIZED** Copy and complete the graphic organizer. In each box, write the appropriate formula.

	2 × 2 Matrix	3 × 3 Matrix
Determinant		
Cramer's Rule		

4-4 Exercises

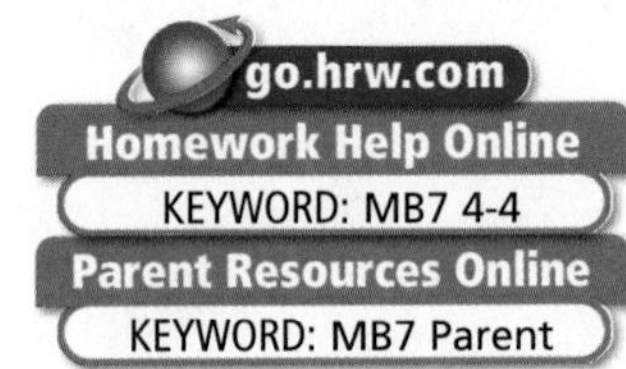

GUIDED PRACTICE

1. **Vocabulary** Explain the meaning of a 0 entry in a *coefficient matrix.*

SEE EXAMPLE 1 p. 270

Find the determinant of each matrix.

2. $\begin{bmatrix} 7 & 5 \\ 9 & 2 \end{bmatrix}$ 3. $\begin{bmatrix} 1.5 & 0.25 \\ 6 & 2.5 \end{bmatrix}$ 4. $\begin{bmatrix} \frac{1}{2} & \frac{2}{3} \\ \frac{3}{4} & -4 \end{bmatrix}$ 5. $\begin{bmatrix} -3 & 40 \\ -5 & 66\frac{2}{3} \end{bmatrix}$

SEE EXAMPLE 2 p. 271

Use Cramer's rule to solve each system of equations.

6. $\begin{cases} 6x = 2 - y \\ 3x + 1 = 2y \end{cases}$ 7. $\begin{cases} 4x + y + 6 = 0 \\ 8x + 2y = 9 \end{cases}$ 8. $\begin{cases} 5x - 2y = 3 \\ 2.5x - y = 1.5 \end{cases}$ 9. $\begin{cases} 2y = 2 - x \\ -3x + 6y = -9 \end{cases}$

SEE EXAMPLE 3 p. 272

Find the determinant of each matrix.

10. $P = \begin{bmatrix} 1 & 2 & -1 \\ 4 & 0 & 1 \\ 1 & -2 & 3 \end{bmatrix}$ 11. $S = \begin{bmatrix} 0 & -5 & -1 \\ 4 & 1 & 6 \\ 2 & 0.5 & 3 \end{bmatrix}$ 12. $E = \begin{bmatrix} 1 & -1 & 1 \\ -1 & 1 & -1 \\ 1 & -1 & 1 \end{bmatrix}$

SEE EXAMPLE 4 p. 273

13. **Consumer** Naomi buys 2 pounds of trail mix, 1.5 pounds of mixed nuts, and 3 pounds of dried fruit for a total of \$28.42. Briana buys 4.5 pounds of mixed nuts and 2 pounds of dried fruit for a total of \$39.39. The price per pound of trail mix plus the price per pound of dried fruit is the same as the price per pound of mixed nuts. What is the price per pound of each product?

PRACTICE AND PROBLEM SOLVING

Find the determinant of each matrix.

14. $\begin{bmatrix} 3 & -0.4 \\ 5 & 0.3 \end{bmatrix}$ 15. $\begin{bmatrix} -1 & 0 \\ 0 & 1 \end{bmatrix}$ 16. $\begin{bmatrix} -\frac{2}{5} & 8 \\ -\frac{1}{2} & 10 \end{bmatrix}$ 17. $\begin{bmatrix} r & -1 \\ -2r^2 & \pi r \end{bmatrix}$

Independent Practice	
For Exercises	See Example
14–17	1
18–21	2
22–24	3
25	4

Extra Practice

Skills Practice p. S11

Application Practice p. S35

Use Cramer's rule to solve each system of equations.

18. $\begin{cases} 0.5x + 6y = 2 \\ 0.25x + 3y = 0.5 \end{cases}$ **19.** $\begin{cases} x + 2y = 3.5 \\ 3x - y = 2.7 \end{cases}$ **20.** $\begin{cases} 2x + y = 3 \\ x + \frac{y}{2} = 2 \end{cases}$ **21.** $\begin{cases} 3y - x = 7 \\ 2x + 3y = -7 \end{cases}$

Find the determinant of each matrix.

22. $A = \begin{bmatrix} 2.5 & 1.5 & 0 \\ 3.2 & 1 & -4 \\ 6.4 & -5 & 2.1 \end{bmatrix}$ **23.** $L = \begin{bmatrix} -2.4 & 1 & 0 \\ 3 & 0 & 0.5 \\ 0 & 3.5 & 1 \end{bmatrix}$ **24.** $W = \begin{bmatrix} 1 & 0 & 2 \\ 0 & -5 & 0 \\ 3 & 0 & 4 \end{bmatrix}$

25. Fitness Cameron records the hours he exercises and the total Calories he burns each day. How many Calories are burned per hour for each of the three activities? Use Cramer's rule to solve.

Cameron's Activity Log

	Bicycling	Racquetball	Swimming	Calories Burned
Monday	1.5 h	1 h	0.75 h	1620
Wednesday	0.75 h	■	1 h	915
Friday	1 h	1.5 h	■	1230

Geography LINK

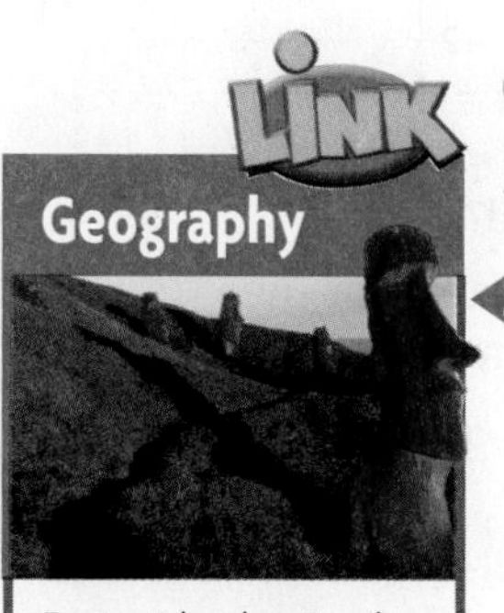

Easter Island, a South Pacific island of Chile, contains more than 600 stone statues. The statues were carved between 1600 and 1730. Most of the heads actually have torsos that have become buried over time.

Geometry The area of a triangle with vertices (x_1, y_1), (x_2, y_2), and (x_3, y_3) is equal to the absolute value of A. Use this information for Exercises 26 and 27.

$$A = \frac{1}{2}\begin{vmatrix} x_1 & x_2 & x_3 \\ y_1 & y_2 & y_3 \\ 1 & 1 & 1 \end{vmatrix}$$

26. Geography Find the area of Easter Island.

27. Find the area of $\triangle FGH$.

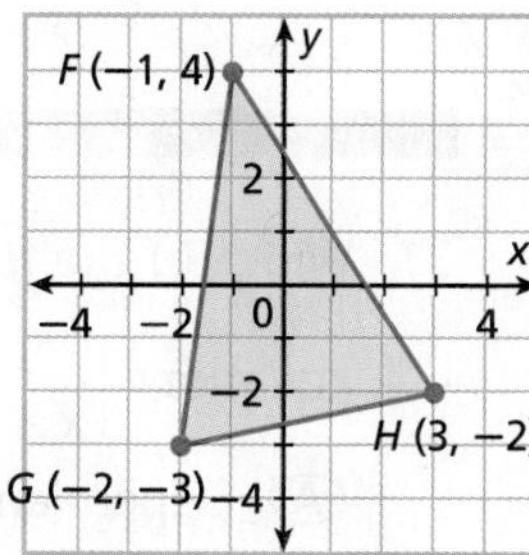

28. Critical Thinking For the system of equations $2x + y = 6$ and $cy = 3 - x$, for what value of c is the determinant zero? Explain your reasoning.

29. Internet John's site asks readers to rate his articles with 1, 2, or 3 points. There were 38 votes, twice as many 3's as 1's, and the point total was 85. How many people gave each rating?

Find the determinant of each matrix.

30. $A = \begin{bmatrix} x & x-1 \\ x+1 & x \end{bmatrix}$ **31.** $B = \begin{bmatrix} x-2 & x+2 \\ x+2 & x+6 \end{bmatrix}$ **32.** $C = \begin{bmatrix} 6x^2 & -6x + 2x^2 \\ 3x & x-3 \end{bmatrix}$

33. Currency The United States Code specifies that dimes weigh 2.268 grams each and nickels weigh 5 grams each. The approximate weight of 425 dimes and nickels is 1483 grams.

a. How many of each coin are there?

b. What is the total value of the coins?

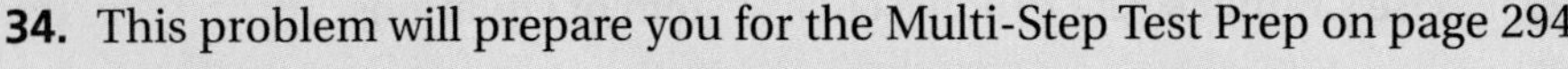

MULTI-STEP TEST PREP

34. This problem will prepare you for the Multi-Step Test Prep on page 294.

At an amusement park, 6 Wild rides and 3 Mild rides require 48 tickets, while 2 Wild rides and 10 Mild rides require 52 tickets. Let x be the number of tickets for a Wild ride and y be the number of tickets for a Mild ride.

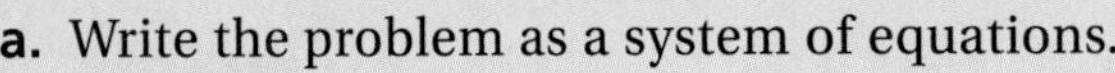

a. Write the problem as a system of equations.

b. Write the coefficient matrix, and find its determinant.

c. How many solutions are there?

d. Use Cramer's rule to find x and y. ⟶ $x = \dfrac{\begin{vmatrix} c_1 & b_1 \\ c_2 & b_2 \end{vmatrix}}{D}$ and $y = \dfrac{\begin{vmatrix} a_1 & c_1 \\ a_2 & c_2 \end{vmatrix}}{D}$

e. How many tickets are required for each ride?

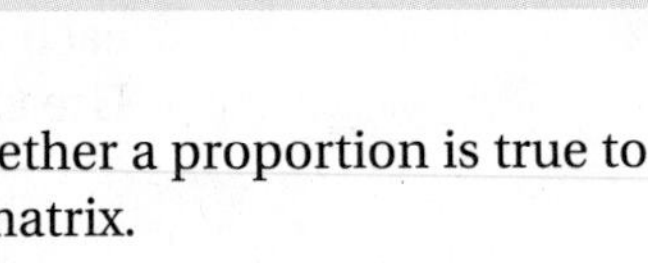

35. Write About It Compare the process of deciding whether a proportion is true to the process of determining whether $D = 0$ for a 2×2 matrix.

36. Multi-Step The points $(5, 0)$ and $(1, 3)$ determine a parallelogram with respect to the origin as shown.

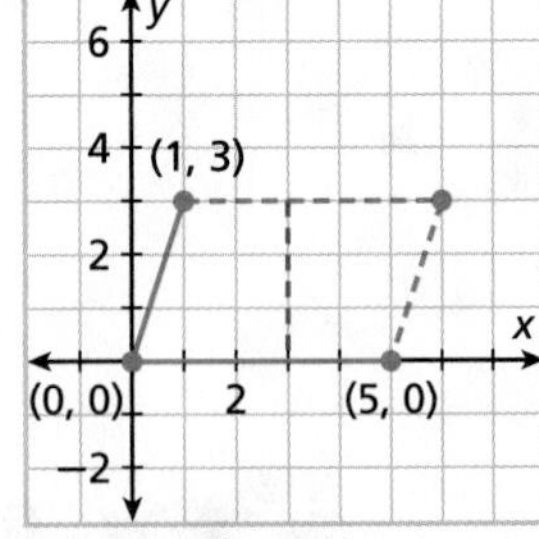

a. Find the area of the parallelogram.

b. Enter the two points in order into $\begin{vmatrix} x_1 & x_2 \\ y_1 & y_2 \end{vmatrix}$, and evaluate. How does this value relate to the area of the parallelogram?

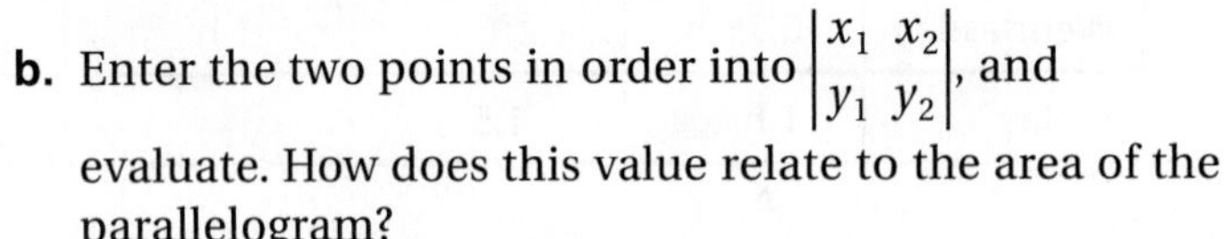

c. Change the width and height of the parallelogram, and find the area and the determinant. Does the relationship between the area and the determinant still hold?

d. Reverse the points in part **b** so that (x_1, y_1) is $(1, 3)$. Do the same for the parallelogram in part **c.** How does the order affect the determinant?

TEST PREP

37. Which of the following statements describes the system of equations $\begin{cases} 3x = y - 1 \\ x + 2y = 16 \end{cases}$?

Ⓐ Dependent; many solutions

Ⓑ Inconsistent; no solution

Ⓒ Inconsistent; many solutions

Ⓓ Consistent; one solution

38. Which matrix has a determinant of 1?

Ⓕ $\begin{bmatrix} 3 & 11 \\ 1 & 4 \end{bmatrix}$ Ⓖ $\begin{bmatrix} 3 & -11 \\ 1 & 4 \end{bmatrix}$ Ⓗ $\begin{bmatrix} -3 & 11 \\ 1 & 4 \end{bmatrix}$ Ⓙ $\begin{bmatrix} 3 & 11 \\ -1 & 4 \end{bmatrix}$

39. Gridded Response The determinant of $\begin{bmatrix} 4 & -5 \\ 1 & 2x \end{bmatrix}$ is 25. Find x.

CHALLENGE AND EXTEND

40. Suppose a 3×3 matrix has a row or column of zeros. Explain the effect on the determinant.

41. Write $x^2 + y^2$ as a determinant.

42. If $x = \dfrac{\begin{vmatrix} 1 & 2 \\ 3 & 4 \end{vmatrix}}{5}$ and $y = \dfrac{\begin{vmatrix} 7 & a \\ b & c \end{vmatrix}}{5}$, find the values of a, b, and c.

43. **Civics** A ballot measure received the vote percentages shown in the table. There were a total of 4826 votes. How many of the votes came from Southside?

Ballot Measure Voting		
District	**In Favor**	**Opposed**
Northside	47%	53%
Southside	85%	15%
Total	49%	51%

SPIRAL REVIEW

44. **Consumer Economics** Trish has \$125 and a coupon for \$10 off her total at the Toasty Coats Outlet. She finds a coat that is marked 25% off. Write an inequality for the maximum amount that the coat can be priced before the markdown so Trish can afford to buy it. *(Lesson 2-1)*

Use substitution to solve each system of equations. *(Lesson 3-2)*

45. $\begin{cases} x = \frac{1}{3}y \\ 6x - 6y = 16 \end{cases}$

46. $\begin{cases} x + y = -5 \\ 2x - y = -7 \end{cases}$

47. $\begin{cases} 2x = y \\ 4x + y = -2 \end{cases}$

Use a matrix to transform the polygon with coordinates $D(1, 1)$, $E(4, -2)$, $F(-2, -3)$, and $G(-1, -1)$. *(Lesson 4-3)*

48. Translate 5 units right and 3 units up.

49. Reflect *DEFG* across the *x*-axis.

50. Translate *DEFG* 1 unit left and 2 units down.

51. Dilate *DEFG* by a factor of 3.

Career Path

go.hrw.com
Career Resources Online
KEYWORD: MB7 Career

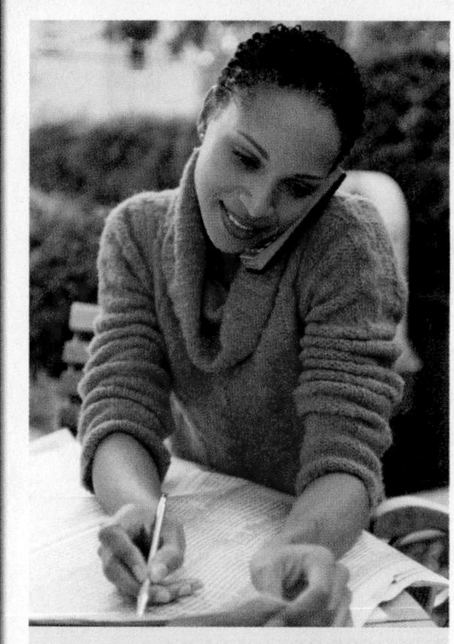

Karen Michaels
Economist

Q: What math classes did you take in high school?

A: I took Algebra 1 and 2, Geometry, and Precalculus.

Q: What math classes did you take in college?

A: Math and economics are closely related, so I took several math classes—Statistics, Calculus, Mathematical Economics.

Q: Any topics you found particularly interesting?

A: Game theory. You wouldn't think it applies, but it has a lot of applications in math, economics, and political science. It's about how people make decisions that affect other people.

Q: How do you use math as an economist?

A: I've conducted research projects on energy costs, interest rates, inflation, and employment levels. I collect, analyze, and summarize data and forecast economic trends.

4-5 Matrix Inverses and Solving Systems

Objectives
Determine whether a matrix has an inverse.

Solve systems of equations using inverse matrices.

Vocabulary
multiplicative inverse matrix
matrix equation
variable matrix
constant matrix

Who uses this?

Cryptographers, who create and crack codes, may use matrices to protect the privacy of messages. (See Example 4.)

You can encode a message using a matrix. The receiver can use an inverse process to decode your message.

A matrix can have an inverse only if it is a square matrix. But not all square matrices have inverses. If the product of the square matrix A and the square matrix A^{-1} is the identity matrix I, then $AA^{-1} = A^{-1}A = I$, and A^{-1} is the **multiplicative inverse matrix** of A, or just the *inverse* of A.

EXAMPLE 1 **Determining Whether Two Matrices Are Inverses**

Determine whether the two given matrices are inverses.

Remember!

The identity matrix I has 1's on the main diagonal and 0's everywhere else.

$$\begin{bmatrix} 1 & 0 & 0 \\ 0 & 1 & 0 \\ 0 & 0 & 1 \end{bmatrix}$$

A $\begin{bmatrix} 2 & 0 & 1 \\ 4 & 1 & 2 \\ 2 & 0 & 4 \end{bmatrix}$ and $\begin{bmatrix} \frac{2}{3} & 0 & -\frac{1}{6} \\ -2 & 1 & 0 \\ -\frac{1}{3} & 0 & \frac{1}{3} \end{bmatrix}$

```
[A]*[B]
        [[1 0 0]
         [0 1 0]
         [0 0 1]]
```

```
[B]*[A]
        [[1 0 0]
         [0 1 0]
         [0 0 1]]
```

The product is the identity matrix I, so the matrices are inverses.

B $\begin{bmatrix} 2 & 3 \\ 7 & 10 \end{bmatrix}$ and $\begin{bmatrix} -10 & 6 \\ 7 & -4 \end{bmatrix}$

```
[A]*[B]
        [[1 0]
         [0 2]]
[B]*[A]
    [[22  30 ]
     [-14 -19]]
```

Neither product is I, so the matrices are not inverses.

1. Determine whether the given matrices are inverses.

$\begin{bmatrix} -1 & 0 & 2 \\ 4 & 1 & -1 \\ 2 & 0 & 1 \end{bmatrix}$ and $\begin{bmatrix} -0.2 & 0 & 0.4 \\ 1.2 & 1 & -1.4 \\ 0.4 & 0 & 0.2 \end{bmatrix}$

Inverse of a 2 × 2 Matrix

The inverse of a 2 × 2 matrix $A = \begin{bmatrix} a & b \\ c & d \end{bmatrix}$ is $A^{-1} = \frac{1}{\det A}\begin{bmatrix} d & -b \\ -c & a \end{bmatrix}$.

If the determinant is 0, $\frac{1}{\det A}$ is undefined. So a matrix with a determinant of 0 has no inverse. It is called a *singular* matrix.

EXAMPLE 2 Finding the Inverse of a 2 × 2 Matrix

Find the inverse of the matrix, if it is defined.

A $A = \begin{bmatrix} -2 & 2 \\ 3 & -4 \end{bmatrix}$

First, check that the determinant is nonzero. The determinant is $(-2)(-4) - 3(2) = 8 - 6 = 2$, so the matrix has an inverse.

For $\begin{bmatrix} a & b \\ c & d \end{bmatrix}$, the inverse is $\frac{1}{\det A}\begin{bmatrix} d & -b \\ -c & a \end{bmatrix}$.

So the inverse of $A = \begin{bmatrix} -2 & 2 \\ 3 & -4 \end{bmatrix}$ is $A^{-1} = \frac{1}{2}\begin{bmatrix} -4 & -2 \\ -3 & -2 \end{bmatrix} = \begin{bmatrix} -2 & -1 \\ -\frac{3}{2} & -1 \end{bmatrix}$.

Use a calculator to check, as in Example 1.

B $B = \begin{bmatrix} \frac{1}{2} & 2 \\ 3 & 12 \end{bmatrix}$

The determinant is $\frac{1}{2}(12) - 3(2) = 0$, so B has no inverse.

Helpful Hint

To find $\begin{bmatrix} d & -b \\ -c & a \end{bmatrix}$ from $A = \begin{bmatrix} a & b \\ c & d \end{bmatrix}$, think "switch ops" for the cross products. *Switch a* and *d*. Take the *opposites* of *b* and *c*.

2. Find the inverse of $\begin{bmatrix} 3 & 2 \\ 3 & -2 \end{bmatrix}$, if it is defined.

You can use the inverse of a matrix to solve a system of equations. This process is similar to solving an equation such as $5x = 20$ by multiplying each side by $\frac{1}{5}$, the multiplicative inverse of 5.

To solve systems of equations with the inverse, you first write the **matrix equation** $AX = B$, where A is the coefficient matrix, X is the **variable matrix**, and B is the **constant matrix**.

The matrix equation representing $\begin{cases} x + y = 8 \\ 2x + y = 1 \end{cases}$ is shown.

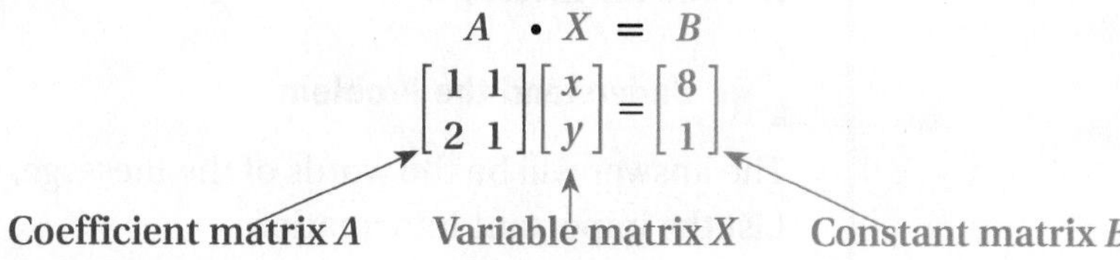

$$\begin{bmatrix} 1 & 1 \\ 2 & 1 \end{bmatrix}\begin{bmatrix} x \\ y \end{bmatrix} = \begin{bmatrix} 8 \\ 1 \end{bmatrix}$$

To solve $AX = B$, multiply both sides by the inverse A^{-1}.

$A^{-1}AX = A^{-1}B$

$IX = A^{-1}B$ *The product of A^{-1} and A is I.*

$X = A^{-1}B$

EXAMPLE 3 Solving Systems Using Inverse Matrices

Write the matrix equation for the system, and solve.

$$\begin{cases} x + y = 8 \\ 2x + y = 1 \end{cases}$$

Step 1 Set up the matrix equation.

$$\begin{array}{ccc} A & X & = & B \end{array}$$

$$\begin{bmatrix} 1 & 1 \\ 2 & 1 \end{bmatrix} \begin{bmatrix} x \\ y \end{bmatrix} = \begin{bmatrix} 8 \\ 1 \end{bmatrix}$$

Write: coefficient matrix • variable matrix = constant matrix.

> **Caution!**
>
> Matrix multiplication is not commutative, so it is important to multiply by the inverse *in the same order* on both sides of the equation. A^{-1} comes *first* on each side.

Step 2 Find the determinant.

The determinant of A is $1 - 2 = -1$.

Step 3 Find A^{-1}.

$$A = \begin{bmatrix} 1 & 1 \\ 2 & 1 \end{bmatrix}, \text{ so } A^{-1} = \frac{1}{-1} \begin{bmatrix} 1 & -1 \\ -2 & 1 \end{bmatrix} = \begin{bmatrix} -1 & 1 \\ 2 & -1 \end{bmatrix}$$

$$\begin{array}{ccc} X & = & A^{-1} \quad B \end{array}$$

$$\begin{bmatrix} x \\ y \end{bmatrix} = \begin{bmatrix} -1 & 1 \\ 2 & -1 \end{bmatrix} \begin{bmatrix} 8 \\ 1 \end{bmatrix}$$

Multiply.

$$= \begin{bmatrix} -7 \\ 15 \end{bmatrix}$$

The solution is $(-7, 15)$.

3. Write the matrix equation for $\begin{cases} x + y = 4 \\ 2x + 3y = 9 \end{cases}$ and solve.

EXAMPLE 4 *Problem-Solving Application: Cryptography*

You receive a coded instant message from Lupe.

Both you and Lupe use the same encoding matrix $E = \begin{bmatrix} 6 & 5 \\ 7 & 6 \end{bmatrix}$.

Upon decoding the message, you will get a matrix where letters are represented by numbers (*A* is 1, *B* is 2, ... *Z* is 26, and 0 is a space). Decode the message.

1 Understand the Problem

The **answer** will be the words of the message, uncoded.

List the important information:

- The encoding matrix is E.
- Lupe used M as the message matrix, with letters written as the integers 0 to 26, and then used EM to create the two-row code matrix C.

$$C = \begin{bmatrix} 240 & 48 & 70 & 5 & 173 & 6 & 245 & 183 & 159 \\ 284 & 56 & 83 & 6 & 205 & 7 & 290 & 216 & 189 \end{bmatrix}$$

Make a Plan

Because $EM = C$, you can use $M = E^{-1}C$ to decode the message into numbers and then convert the numbers to letters.

- Multiply E^{-1} by C to get M, the message written as numbers.
- Use the letter equivalents for the numbers in order to write the message as words so that you can read it.

Solve

Use a calculator to find E^{-1}.

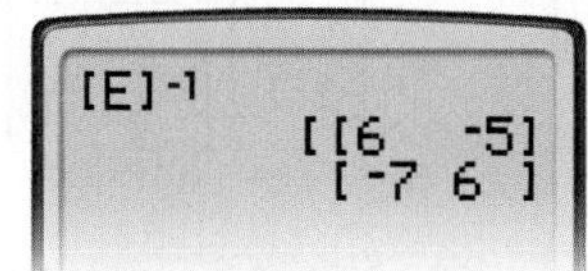

$$E^{-1} = \begin{bmatrix} 6 & -5 \\ -7 & 6 \end{bmatrix}$$

Multiply E^{-1} by C.

20 = T, and so on

$$M = E^{-1}C = \begin{bmatrix} 20 & 8 & 5 & 0 & 13 & 1 & 20 & 18 & 9 \\ 24 & 0 & 8 & 1 & 19 & 0 & 25 & 15 & 21 \end{bmatrix}$$

T H E _ M A T R I
X _ H A S _ Y O U

The message in words is "The matrix has you."

Look Back

You can verify by multiplying E by M to see that the decoding was correct. If the math had been done incorrectly, getting a different message that made sense would have been very unlikely.

4. Use the encoding matrix $E = \begin{bmatrix} 3 & 1 \\ 5 & 2 \end{bmatrix}$ to decode this message.

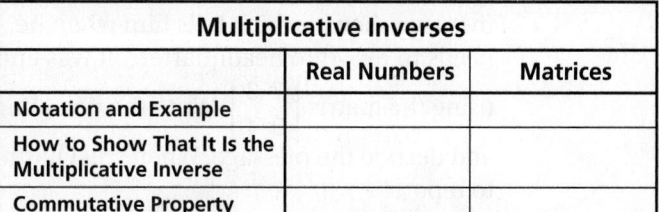

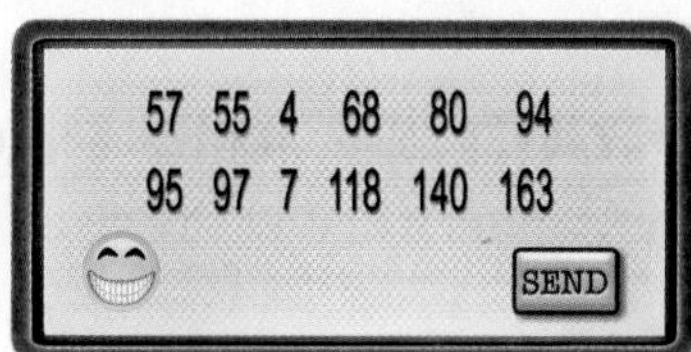

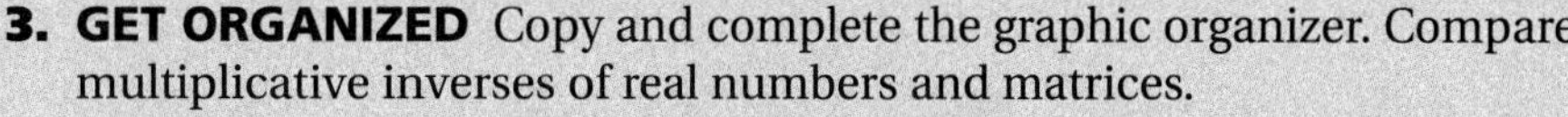

THINK AND DISCUSS

1. Explain what the existence of the inverse of matrix S, S^{-1}, tells you about matrix S.
2. Describe the inverse of an identity matrix.

3. **GET ORGANIZED** Copy and complete the graphic organizer. Compare multiplicative inverses of real numbers and matrices.

Multiplicative Inverses		
	Real Numbers	**Matrices**
Notation and Example		
How to Show That It Is the Multiplicative Inverse		
Commutative Property		

4-5 Exercises

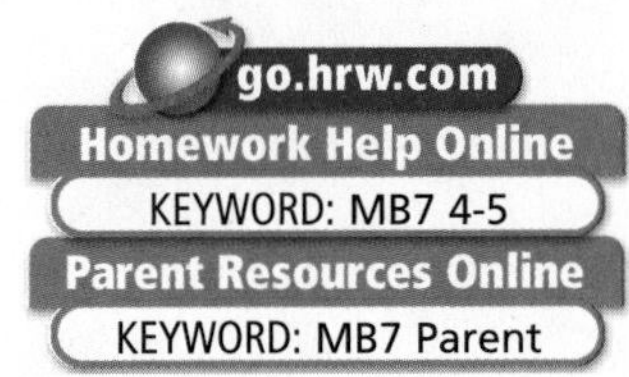

GUIDED PRACTICE

1. **Vocabulary** Describe how to create a *matrix equation* from a system of equations.

SEE EXAMPLE 1 p. 278

Determine whether the given matrices are inverses.

2. $\begin{bmatrix} 8 & 4 \\ 2 & 1 \end{bmatrix}\begin{bmatrix} -\frac{1}{8} & \frac{3}{2} \\ \frac{1}{2} & -1 \end{bmatrix}$

3. $\begin{bmatrix} 1 & 0.4 & 1 \\ 1.2 & 0 & 0.8 \\ -1.6 & 0.2 & -1 \end{bmatrix}\begin{bmatrix} 3 & 12.5 & 2 \\ -1.6 & 2 & -1 \\ 5 & 1 & -10 \end{bmatrix}$

4. $\begin{bmatrix} 1 & 1 \\ 0 & 1 \end{bmatrix}\begin{bmatrix} 1 & -1 \\ 0 & 1 \end{bmatrix}$

SEE EXAMPLE 2 p. 279

Find the inverse of the matrix, if it is defined.

5. $\begin{bmatrix} \frac{1}{2} & 0 \\ -\frac{1}{6} & \frac{1}{3} \end{bmatrix}$

6. $\begin{bmatrix} 1 & 7 \\ 2 & 6 \end{bmatrix}$

7. $\begin{bmatrix} \frac{1}{3} & 2 \\ \frac{3}{2} & 9 \end{bmatrix}$

8. $\begin{bmatrix} -1 & -1 \\ -1 & -1 \end{bmatrix}$

9. $\begin{bmatrix} 8 & 7 \\ 9 & 8 \end{bmatrix}$

SEE EXAMPLE 3 p. 280

Write the matrix equation for the system, and solve.

10. $\begin{cases} 3x - y = 5 \\ y = 2x - 4 \end{cases}$

11. $\begin{cases} 5x + 9y = 1 \\ 2 - 4x - 7y = 4 \end{cases}$

12. $\begin{cases} 2x + 4y = 3 \\ 2x + 3y = 1 \end{cases}$

SEE EXAMPLE 4 p. 280

13. **Cryptography** Rayanne receives the message shown, giving Sara's current location somewhere in Asia. The message was encoded using $\begin{bmatrix} 3 & 4 \\ 5 & 7 \end{bmatrix}$. Write the decoding matrix, and decode the message.

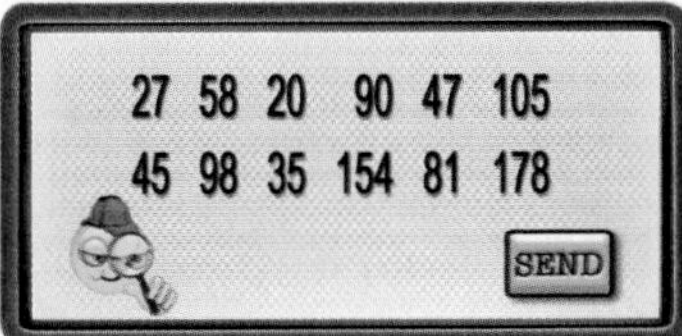

PRACTICE AND PROBLEM SOLVING

Independent Practice

For Exercises	See Example
14–16	1
17–21	2
22–24	3
25	4

Extra Practice
Skills Practice p. S11
Application Practice p. S35

Determine whether the given matrices are inverses.

14. $\begin{bmatrix} 0 & 1 \\ 1 & 1 \end{bmatrix}\begin{bmatrix} 0 & 1 \\ 1 & -1 \end{bmatrix}$

15. $\begin{bmatrix} -1 & \frac{1}{2} \\ \frac{1}{4} & -2 \end{bmatrix}\begin{bmatrix} -\frac{16}{15} & -\frac{4}{15} \\ -\frac{2}{15} & -\frac{8}{15} \end{bmatrix}$

16. $\begin{bmatrix} 1 & 5 & -1 \\ 1 & 0 & -1 \\ 1 & 0 & 0 \end{bmatrix}\begin{bmatrix} 0 & 0 & 1 \\ 0.2 & -0.2 & 0 \\ 0 & -1 & 1 \end{bmatrix}$

Find the inverse of the matrix, if it is defined.

17. $\begin{bmatrix} -0.25 & -0.5 \\ -1.5 & -2 \end{bmatrix}$

18. $\begin{bmatrix} 7 & 14 \\ 3 & 6 \end{bmatrix}$

19. $\begin{bmatrix} 2 & 3 \\ 5 & 8 \end{bmatrix}$

20. $\begin{bmatrix} 5 & 4 \\ 4 & 3 \end{bmatrix}$

21. $\begin{bmatrix} -2 & -3 \\ 7 & 11 \end{bmatrix}$

Write the matrix equation for the system, and solve.

22. $\begin{cases} x - y = 5 \\ 2y - x = 6 \end{cases}$

23. $\begin{cases} x + 2y = 6 \\ 2x + y = 9 \end{cases}$

24. $\begin{cases} 4x + 7y = 10 \\ 3x + 5y = 9 \end{cases}$

25. **Cryptography** Quinn receives the coded message shown, which tells him when he needs to report to headquarters. It was encoded using the matrix $\begin{bmatrix} 7 & 3 \\ 9 & 4 \end{bmatrix}$. Write the decoding matrix, and decode the message. When will Quinn need to report?

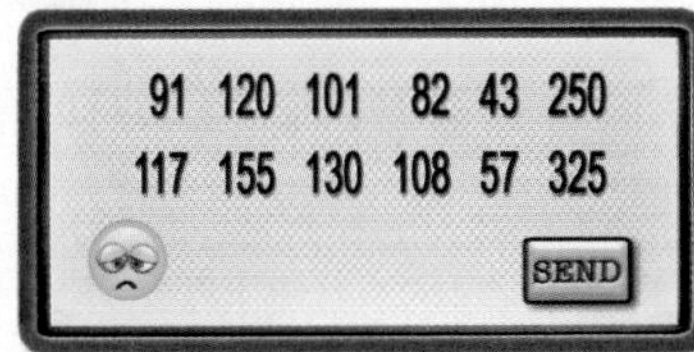

26. **Packaging** Cara compares three fruit and nut gift packs. Write the matrix equation and solve to find the cost per pound of pears, pecans, and nectarines.

27. **Multi-Step** On an outdoor trip, the organizers take seven inflatable boats, 6-person boats and 2-person boats, for 34 people. The system of equations that represents this situation is $\begin{cases} 6x + 2y = 34 \\ x + y = 7 \end{cases}$, where x represents the number of 6-person boats and y the number of 2-person boats.
    a. Write the coefficient matrix.
    b. Write the appropriate matrix equation.
    c. Find the inverse of the coefficient matrix.
    d. Solve the matrix equation to find how many of each size boat the group takes.

28. **Critical Thinking** How are the inverse matrix and identity matrix related?

29. E is an encoding matrix for message M that gives a coded message C. What are the dimension restrictions on E, M, and C?

30. **///ERROR ANALYSIS///** Which inverse is incorrect for $\begin{bmatrix} 2 & 3 \\ 4 & 5 \end{bmatrix}$? Explain the error.

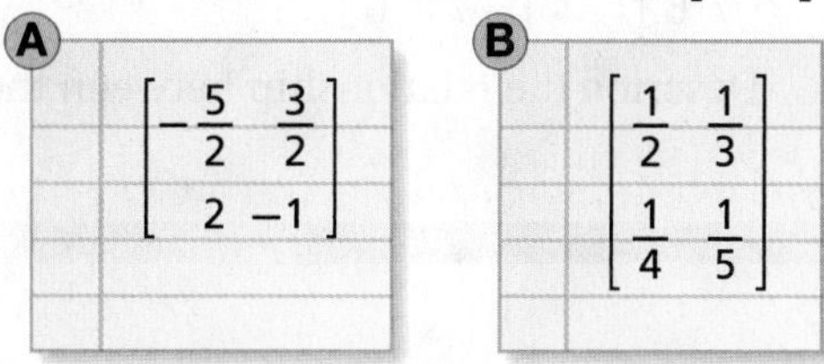

A
$\begin{bmatrix} -\frac{5}{2} & \frac{3}{2} \\ 2 & -1 \end{bmatrix}$
B
$\begin{bmatrix} \frac{1}{2} & \frac{1}{3} \\ \frac{1}{4} & \frac{1}{5} \end{bmatrix}$

31. **Entertainment** A game show host says that he has $5000 in $50 bills and $100 bills and he will give you the $5000 if you can tell him how many of each type of bill he has. He gives you a hint that he has 73 bills. Use an inverse matrix to find how many of each he has.

32. **Water** A fountain operating 24 hours a day can be set at three different speeds, low, medium, and high. Find the number of kL/h the fountain uses at each speed.

	Time on Low (h)	Time on Med (m)	Time on High (h)	Kiloliters Used
Monday	15	7	2	199
Tuesday	16	4	4	208
Wednesday	12	8	4	236

33. **What if...?** Suppose the entries of $\begin{bmatrix} 3 & 5 \\ 2 & 4 \end{bmatrix}$ are doubled.
    a. What happens to the entries of the inverse matrix?
    b. Suppose the entries of a square matrix are multiplied by n. Make a conjecture about the entries of the inverse matrix.

34. This problem will prepare you for the Multi-Step Test Prep on page 294.

At a carnival, 2 meals and 7 rides require 24 tickets, while 4 meals and 13 rides require 46 tickets. Let x be the number of tickets for a meal and y be the number of tickets for a ride.

a. Write the problem as a system of equations.
b. Is the determinant $D = 0$? How many solutions are there?
c. Write the coefficient matrix, and find its inverse.
d. Use $X = A^{-1}B$ to find x and y.
e. How many tickets are required for each item?

35. a. Critical Thinking Prove that the inverse of matrix $\begin{bmatrix} a & b \\ c & d \end{bmatrix}$ is $\frac{1}{ad - bc}\begin{bmatrix} d & -b \\ -c & a \end{bmatrix}$.

b. If the determinant of matrix $\begin{bmatrix} a & b \\ c & d \end{bmatrix}$ is 1, what is its inverse?

c. If a, b, c, and d are integers, why does the inverse contain only integers?

36. Complete the matrix $\begin{bmatrix} 2 & ? \\ 4 & 3 \end{bmatrix}$ so that it has no inverse.

37. Suppose A is the 1-entry matrix $\begin{bmatrix} a \end{bmatrix}$. What is its inverse?

38. Chemistry A laboratory has one solution of 15% hydrochloric acid (HCl) and one solution of 40% HCL. A mixture requires 50 liters of 35% HCL. How many liters of each must be used?

39. Write About It Find the product of
$\begin{bmatrix} 6 & 5 \\ 7 & 6 \end{bmatrix}$ and $\begin{bmatrix} 6 & -5 \\ -7 & 6 \end{bmatrix}$.

Describe the relationship between these matrices.

40. Which is the correct matrix equation for the system $\begin{cases} 3x + 2y = 8 \\ x = y + 1 \end{cases}$?

Ⓐ $\begin{bmatrix} 3 & 2 \\ 1 & -1 \end{bmatrix}\begin{bmatrix} 8 \\ 1 \end{bmatrix} = \begin{bmatrix} x \\ y \end{bmatrix}$

Ⓑ $\begin{bmatrix} 3 & 2 \\ 1 & -1 \end{bmatrix}\begin{bmatrix} x \\ y \end{bmatrix} = \begin{bmatrix} 8 \\ 1 \end{bmatrix}$

Ⓒ $\begin{bmatrix} 3 & 2 \\ 1 & 1 \end{bmatrix}\begin{bmatrix} 8 \\ 1 \end{bmatrix} = \begin{bmatrix} x \\ y \end{bmatrix}$

Ⓓ $\begin{bmatrix} 3 & 2 \\ 1 & 1 \end{bmatrix}\begin{bmatrix} x \\ y \end{bmatrix} = \begin{bmatrix} 8 \\ 1 \end{bmatrix}$

41. Which statement is a true statement about matrix $G = \begin{bmatrix} 2 & -3 \\ 6 & -9 \end{bmatrix}$?

Ⓕ G has an inverse because the determinant is NOT 0.
Ⓖ G has an inverse because the determinant is 0.
Ⓗ G has no inverse because the determinant is 0.
Ⓙ G has no inverse because the determinant is NOT 0.

42. B is the inverse of $\begin{bmatrix} -1 & 6 \\ 4 & 3 \end{bmatrix}$. What is entry b_{11}?

Ⓐ 1 Ⓑ $-\frac{1}{9}$ Ⓒ 3 Ⓓ $-\frac{1}{27}$

43. In matrix $A = \begin{bmatrix} a & b \\ c & d \end{bmatrix}$, $a > 0$, $b < 0$, $c < 0$, $d > 0$, and $\det A \neq 0$. Which of the following is true?

Ⓕ A^{-1} has no negative entries.
Ⓖ A^{-1} has one negative entry.
Ⓗ A^{-1} has two negative entries.
Ⓙ A^{-1} has three negative entries.

44. **Extended Response** An art gallery gives away small prints valued at $25 for donations of $500, and larger prints valued at $50 for donations of $1000 and above. The gallery raises $24,000 and gives away 35 prints. Find the number of each size print that the gallery gives away.

CHALLENGE AND EXTEND

45. **Hobbies** A fantasy league rating system rates NBA point guards by assigning a rating multiplier to each of the following categories: points per game, assists per game, turnovers per game, and steals per game. What multiplier is assigned to each category?

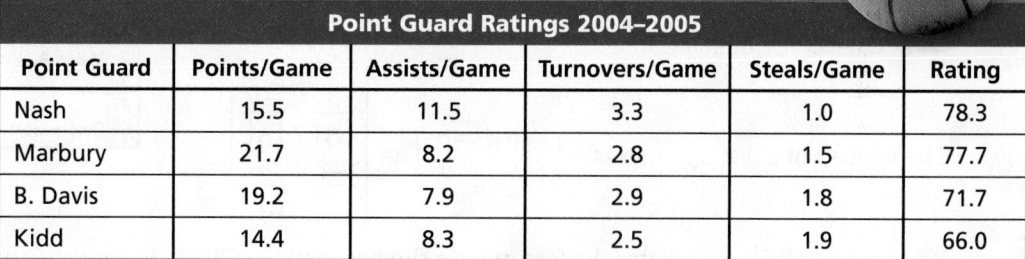

Point Guard Ratings 2004–2005					
Point Guard	Points/Game	Assists/Game	Turnovers/Game	Steals/Game	Rating
Nash	15.5	11.5	3.3	1.0	78.3
Marbury	21.7	8.2	2.8	1.5	77.7
B. Davis	19.2	7.9	2.9	1.8	71.7
Kidd	14.4	8.3	2.5	1.9	66.0

46. For what values of e, f, g, and h will matrix $\begin{bmatrix} e & f \\ g & h \end{bmatrix}$ be its own inverse?

47. Quinn uses a 3×3 decoding matrix on the message shown, where each entry on the main diagonal and above it is 1 and each entry below the main diagonal is 0.

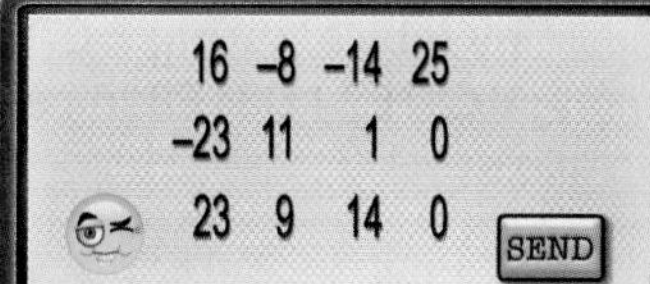

a. What message did he receive?
b. What encoding matrix does he use?
c. He sends the reply "I will try" by using the corresponding encoding matrix. What coded message does he send?

SPIRAL REVIEW

Solve. *(Lesson 2-2)*

48. $\frac{12}{30} = \frac{2x}{10}$

49. $\frac{100}{7} = \frac{0.5}{0.2x}$

50. 125% of $x = 117$

Use elimination to solve each system of equations. *(Lesson 3-6)*

51. $\begin{cases} x + y - z = 2 \\ 2x + 3y - 6z = 5 \\ -4x - 5y + 0.25z = -9 \end{cases}$

52. $\begin{cases} y - x - 3z = 4 \\ 2x + y - 4z = -3 \\ 0.25x + 8z + 3 = 2y \end{cases}$

Find the determinant of each matrix. *(Lesson 4-4)*

53. $\begin{bmatrix} 5 & -6 \\ 1 & 0.5 \end{bmatrix}$

54. $\begin{bmatrix} \frac{1}{6} & 3 \\ 1 & 12 \end{bmatrix}$

55. $\begin{bmatrix} -4 & 1 & 6 \\ 1 & 2 & 1 \\ 3 & -1 & 0 \end{bmatrix}$

56. $\begin{bmatrix} \frac{4}{9} & 8 \\ \frac{3}{2} & -81 \end{bmatrix}$

Use Spreadsheets with Matrices to Solve Systems

You can use matrix inversion on a spreadsheet to solve systems of equations.

Activity

Solve the system $\begin{cases} 7x + 2y = -8 \\ -3x + y = 9 \end{cases}$.

You can find determinants and inverses and solve $X = A^{-1}B$ by using a spreadsheet. To find A^{-1}, first find the determinant of A by using the spreadsheet (subtracting cross products).

Enter the four coefficients of the constant matrix into cells B2, C2, B3, and C3. Calculate its determinant by entering **=B2*C3–B3*C2** in cell C5.

C5 | fx =B2*C3-B3*C2

	A	B	C	D
1				
2	Matrix A	7	2	
3		-3	1	
4				
5	Determinant A		13	

The inverse of a 2 × 2 matrix is $\frac{1}{|A|}\begin{bmatrix} d & -b \\ -c & a \end{bmatrix}$, or $\begin{bmatrix} \frac{d}{|A|} & \frac{-b}{|A|} \\ \frac{-c}{|A|} & \frac{a}{|A|} \end{bmatrix}$.

Begin with cell C7, and enter the formula for the first entry **=C3/C5**. Enter the formulas for the other three entries, D7: **=–C2/C5**, C8: **=–B3/C5**, D8: **=B2/C5**.

The solution is the 2 × 1 matrix $A^{-1}B$. Enter the constant matrix in cells E7 and E8. Multiply A^{-1} by B by entering **=C7*E7+D7*E8** in cell D10 and **=C8*E7+D8*E8** in cell D11.

fx =C7*E7+D7*E8

	A	B	C	D	E
6					Matrix B
7	Inverse A or A^{-1}		0.076923	-0.15385	-8
8			0.230769	0.538462	9
9					
10		Solution A^{-1}B		-2	
11					

The solution is $x = -2$ and $y = 3$. You now have a solving "machine" for any 2 × 2 system. See what happens when you change one or more entries in A or in the constant matrix.

D11 | fx =C8*E7+D8*E8

	A	B	C	D	E
6					Matrix B
7	Inverse A or A^{-1}		0.076923	-0.15385	-8
8			0.230769	0.538462	9
9					
10		Solution A^{-1}B		-2	
11				3	

Try This

1. Change the constants to –5 and 9, and solve the system by using a spreadsheet.
2. How can you check your answers by using the spreadsheet?
3. **Critical Thinking** Solve a system you know to be inconsistent by using the spreadsheet. Solve a system you know to be dependent. How can you tell from the spreadsheet whether a system is inconsistent or dependent?

4-6

Row Operations and Augmented Matrices

Objective
Use elementary row operations to solve systems of equations.

Vocabulary
augmented matrix
row operation
row reduction
reduced row-echelon form

Who uses this?
Workers at an animal shelter can use augmented matrices to analyze the contents of shipments. (See Example 3.)

In previous lessons, you saw how Cramer's rule and inverses can be used to solve systems of equations. Solving large systems requires a different method using an *augmented matrix*. An **augmented matrix** consists of the coefficients and constant terms of a system of linear equations.

$$\begin{cases} 7x + 3y = 4 \\ 2x - 3y = 10 \end{cases} \qquad \left[\begin{array}{cc|c} 7 & 3 & 4 \\ 2 & -3 & 10 \end{array}\right]$$

A vertical line separates the coefficients from the constants.

EXAMPLE 1 Representing Systems as Matrices

Write the augmented matrix for the system of equations.

A $\begin{cases} -3y = x + 12 \\ -2y = 7 \end{cases}$

Step 1 Write each equation in $ax + by = c$ form.

$$-x - 3y = 12$$
$$0x - 2y = 7$$

Step 2 Write the augmented matrix, with coefficients and constants.

$$\left[\begin{array}{cc|c} -1 & -3 & 12 \\ 0 & -2 & 7 \end{array}\right]$$

B $\begin{cases} x - y = 5 \\ z - x = 7 \\ y = z + 6 \end{cases}$

Step 1 Write each equation in $Ax + By + Cz = D$ form.

$$x - y + 0z = 5$$
$$-x + 0y + z = 7$$
$$0x + y - z = 6$$

Step 2 Write the augmented matrix, with coefficients and constants.

$$\left[\begin{array}{ccc|c} 1 & -1 & 0 & 5 \\ -1 & 0 & 1 & 7 \\ 0 & 1 & -1 & 6 \end{array}\right]$$

Write the augmented matrix.

1a. $\begin{cases} -x = y \\ 2 - y = x \end{cases}$

1b. $\begin{cases} -5x - 12 = 4y \\ z = 3 - x \\ 10 = 3z + 4y \end{cases}$

You can use the augmented matrix of a system to solve the system. First you will do a **row operation** to change the form of the matrix. These row operations create a matrix equivalent to the original matrix. So the new matrix represents a system equivalent to the original system.

For each matrix, the following row operations produce a matrix of an equivalent system.

Elementary Row Operations	
• Switch any two rows.	$\left[\begin{array}{cc:c} 1 & 2 & 3 \\ 4 & 5 & 6 \end{array}\right] \to \left[\begin{array}{cc:c} 4 & 5 & 6 \\ 1 & 2 & 3 \end{array}\right]$
• Multiply a row by a nonzero constant.	$\left[\begin{array}{cc:c} 1 & 2 & 3 \\ 4 & 5 & 6 \end{array}\right] \to \left[\begin{array}{cc:c} 2 & 4 & 6 \\ 4 & 5 & 6 \end{array}\right]$
• Replace a row with the sum or difference of that row and another row. $\left[\begin{array}{cc:c} 1 & 2 & 3 \\ 4 & 5 & 6 \end{array}\right] \to \left[\begin{array}{cc:c} 1 & 2 & 3 \\ 1+4 & 2+5 & 3+6 \end{array}\right]$	
• Combine these operations.	

Row reduction is the process of performing elementary row operations on an augmented matrix to solve a system. The goal is to get the coefficients to reduce to the identity matrix on the left side.

This is called **reduced row-echelon form**. $\left[\begin{array}{cc:c} 1 & 0 & 5 \\ 0 & 1 & 2 \end{array}\right] \begin{array}{l} \to 1x = 5 \\ \to 1y = 2 \end{array}$

EXAMPLE 2 Solving Systems with an Augmented Matrix

Write the augmented matrix, and solve.

A $\begin{cases} 6x + y = 9 \\ 3x + 2y = 0 \end{cases}$

Step 1 Write the augmented matrix. $\left[\begin{array}{cc:c} 6 & 1 & 9 \\ 3 & 2 & 0 \end{array}\right]$

Step 2 Multiply row 2 by 2.

$$\left[\begin{array}{cc:c} 6 & 1 & 9 \\ 3 & 2 & 0 \end{array}\right] \quad 2❷ \to \left[\begin{array}{cc:c} 6 & 1 & 9 \\ 6 & 4 & 0 \end{array}\right]$$

Step 3 Subtract row 1 from row 2. Write the result in row 2.

$$❷ - ❶ \to \left[\begin{array}{cc:c} 6 & 1 & 9 \\ 0 & 3 & -9 \end{array}\right]$$

Although row 2 is now $3y = -9$, an equation easily solved for y, row operations can be used to solve for both variables.

Step 4 Multiply row 1 by 3.

$$3❶ \to \left[\begin{array}{cc:c} 18 & 3 & 27 \\ 0 & 3 & -9 \end{array}\right]$$

Step 5 Subtract row 2 from row 1. Write the result in row 1.

$$❶ - ❷ \to \left[\begin{array}{cc:c} 18 & 0 & 36 \\ 0 & 3 & -9 \end{array}\right]$$

Remember!

2 ❷ is read as "2 times row 2."
❷ − ❶ is read as "row 2 minus row 1."

Step 6 Divide row 1 by 18 and row 2 by 3.

$$\begin{array}{l} ❶ \div 18 \rightarrow \\ ❷ \div 3 \rightarrow \end{array} \left[\begin{array}{cc:c} 1 & 0 & 2 \\ 0 & 1 & -3 \end{array}\right] \begin{array}{l} \rightarrow 1x = 2 \\ \rightarrow 1y = -3 \end{array}$$

The solution is $x = 2$, $y = -3$. Check the result in the original equations.

Write the augmented matrix and solve.

B $\begin{cases} x + y = 5 \\ 3x + 3y = 7 \end{cases}$

$\left[\begin{array}{cc:c} 1 & 1 & 5 \\ 3 & 3 & 7 \end{array}\right]$ *Write the augmented matrix.*

$3❶ \rightarrow \left[\begin{array}{cc:c} 3 & 3 & 15 \\ 3 & 3 & 7 \end{array}\right]$ $❷ - ❶ \rightarrow \left[\begin{array}{cc:c} 1 & 1 & 5 \\ 0 & 0 & -8 \end{array}\right]$

The second row means $0 + 0 = -8$, which is always false.
The system is inconsistent.

C $\begin{cases} -4y = 1 - 6x \\ 3x = 2y + \frac{1}{2} \end{cases}$

Write each equation in standard form.

$\begin{cases} 6x - 4y = 1 \\ 3x - 2y = \frac{1}{2} \end{cases}$

$\left[\begin{array}{cc:c} 6 & -4 & 1 \\ 3 & -2 & \frac{1}{2} \end{array}\right]$ *Write the augmented matrix.*

$2❷ - ❶ \rightarrow \left[\begin{array}{cc:c} 6 & -4 & 1 \\ 0 & 0 & 0 \end{array}\right]$

The second row means $0 + 0 = 0$, which is always true.
The system is dependent.

Write the augmented matrix, and solve.

2a. $\begin{cases} 4x + 4y = 32 \\ x + 3y = 16 \end{cases}$ **2b.** $\begin{cases} 3y = 15 - 9x \\ -6x = 2y + 10 \end{cases}$

On many calculators, you can add a column to a matrix to create the augmented matrix and can use the row reduction feature. So, the matrices in the Check It Out problem are entered as 2×3 matrices.

Student to Student

Solving Systems of Equations

Marcus Barrett
Memorial High School

I'm glad I learned all of the different methods for solving systems, but if I have a graphing calculator available, I prefer $A^{-1}B$. At first I thought, "Why'd they wait so long to give us this?"

Without a graphing calculator or a spreadsheet, I'd use elimination for most cases.

Another thing I might do—I might use a spreadsheet on my computer, find determinants, and use Cramer's rule. Cramer's rule is good when you just want the value of one variable.

Now, if I had to solve a 20 by 20 system...

EXAMPLE 3 Charity Application

An animal shelter receives a shipment of items worth a total of \$1890. Large bags of dog food are \$8 each, pet blankets are \$5 each, and dog toys are \$4 each. There are 5 bags of dog food for each dog toy and twice as many blankets as dog toys. How many of each item are in the shipment? Solve by using row reduction on a calculator.

Use the facts to write three equations.

$5b + 8d + 4t = 1890$ *b = blankets*

$d - 5t = 0$ *d = bags of dog food*

$b - 2t = 0$ *t = toys*

```
[A]
 [[5 8 4  1890]
  [0 1 -5 0   ]
  [1 0 -2 0   ]]
```

Enter the 3×4 augmented matrix as A.

Press 2nd x^{-1} (MATRX), select **MATH**, and move down the list to **B:rref(** to find the reduced row-echelon form of the augmented matrix.

```
rref([A]
   [[1 0 0 70 ]
    [0 1 0 175]
    [0 0 1 35 ]]
```

There are 70 blankets, 175 bags of dog food, and 35 toys.

3a. Solve by using row reduction on a calculator.
$$\begin{cases} 3x - y + 5z = -1 \\ x + 2z = 1 \\ x + 3y - z = 25 \end{cases}$$

3b. A new freezer costs \$500 plus \$0.20 a day to operate. An old freezer costs \$20 plus \$0.50 a day to operate. After how many days is the cost of operating each freezer equal? Solve by using row reduction on a calculator.

THINK AND DISCUSS

1. Explain what the rows $\begin{bmatrix} 0 & 1 & 0 & \vdots & 3 \end{bmatrix}$ and $\begin{bmatrix} 0 & 0 & 0 & \vdots & 3 \end{bmatrix}$ tell you about a system of equations when you solve a system of three equations by using augmented matrices and reduced row-echelon form.
2. Tell how you know when an augmented matrix is in reduced row-echelon form.

3. **GET ORGANIZED** Copy and complete the graphic organizer. Fill in the augmented matrix for a three-equation system. Then write an example of the given operation in each box. Tell whether the operation produces an equivalent system.

	System of Equations	Augmented Matrix
Interchange rows or equations.		
Replace a row or equation with a multiple.		
Replace a row or equation with a sum or difference.		
Combine the above.		

4-6 Exercises

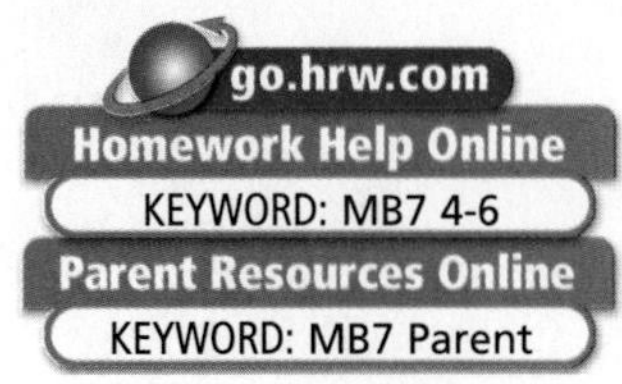

GUIDED PRACTICE

1. **Vocabulary** In an *augmented matrix*, where do you place the coefficients of the variables from the related system of equations?

SEE EXAMPLE 1 p. 287

Write the augmented matrix for each system of equations.

2. $\begin{cases} y - 3 = 2x \\ 3x = -y \end{cases}$
3. $\begin{cases} x + y + z = 10 \\ 2x + z = 12 \\ z - y = 3 \end{cases}$
4. $\begin{cases} 2x - 9 = y \\ 2z = 3y + 7 \\ z = 6 - x \end{cases}$
5. $\begin{cases} y + 2 = 3x \\ \frac{1}{4}y = z - 1 \\ z - 8 = \frac{x}{2} \end{cases}$

SEE EXAMPLE 2 p. 288

Write the augmented matrix, and use row reduction to solve.

6. $\begin{cases} 2y = x + 1 \\ 3x - 2 = y \end{cases}$
7. $\begin{cases} 8y = x + 7 \\ 3y + \frac{x}{2} = 0 \end{cases}$
8. $\begin{cases} x = 2y + 3 \\ y = \frac{1}{2}(x - 3) \end{cases}$
9. $\begin{cases} y = 4 + x \\ 4y - 3 = 4x \end{cases}$

SEE EXAMPLE 3 p. 290

10. **School** During a game, high school students sell snacks. They sell cold sandwiches for \$2.50, hot dogs for \$1.50, and hamburgers for \$2. By the end of the day, the students have collected \$1060.50 and sold 562 items. Casey estimates that the students sold twice as many hot dogs as cold sandwiches. If his estimate is correct, how many of each item did they sell? Solve by using row reduction on a calculator.

PRACTICE AND PROBLEM SOLVING

Independent Practice

For Exercises	See Example
11–13	1
14–16	2
17	3

Extra Practice

Skills Practice p. S11
Application Practice p. S35

Write the augmented matrix for each system of equations.

11. $\begin{cases} \frac{1}{2}(x + 3y) = z \\ y = 2x + 4 \\ x + y + z = 3 \end{cases}$
12. $\begin{cases} 2y + z = 5 \\ y = 2z \end{cases}$
13. $\begin{cases} 0.1x + 0.2y + 0.15z = 1.0 \\ x + y = z \\ 2y = 1.3x \end{cases}$

Write the augmented matrix, and use row reduction to solve.

14. $\begin{cases} y + 2z = 9 \\ 2y + 4z = 13 \end{cases}$
15. $\begin{cases} 5x = y + 2 \\ y - x = 4 \end{cases}$
16. $\begin{cases} x + y = 4 \\ 3x = 9 - 2y \end{cases}$

17. **Math History** The Hundred Fowl problem asks, "A rooster is worth 5 coins, a hen 3 coins, and 3 chicks 1 coin. With 100 coins, we buy 100 of them. How many roosters, hens, and chicks are there?" There are seven times as many chicks as roosters. Write a set of equations and an augmented matrix for this problem. Solve by using row reduction on a calculator.

18. **Geometry** Write an augmented matrix to find the point of intersection of the two lines given by the equations $5y + 4x = 25$ and $y = 3x - 14$. Solve by using row reduction.

Write a system of equations for each augmented matrix.

19. $\left[\begin{array}{cc|c} 2 & 5 & -4 \\ 0 & 1 & -2 \end{array}\right]$
20. $\left[\begin{array}{ccc|c} 1 & 0 & -1 & 0 \\ 0 & 1 & -1 & -2 \\ -1 & 9 & 1 & -9 \end{array}\right]$
21. $\left[\begin{array}{ccc|c} 0 & -1 & 0 & 3 \\ -7 & 0 & 2 & 0 \\ 0 & 0 & -10 & 4 \end{array}\right]$

Write the augmented matrix, and use row reduction to solve.

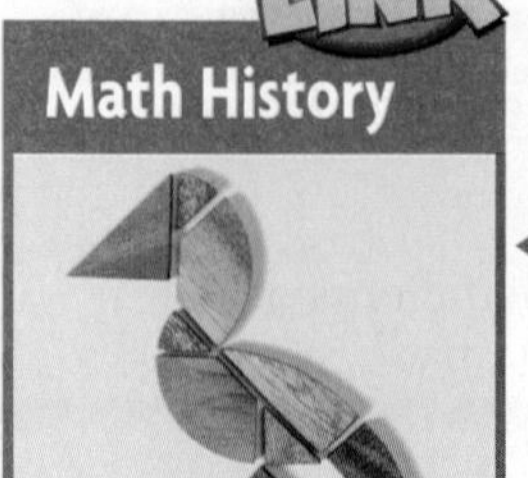

22. $\begin{cases} 2x + 5y = 8 \\ y - x = 10 \end{cases}$

23. $\begin{cases} 3x - y = -9 \\ 7y - 4x = 12 \end{cases}$

24. $\begin{cases} 3y = x + 5 \\ 9y - 3x = 15 \end{cases}$

25. $\begin{cases} 2x + 5y = z \\ 3y + 7 = x \\ x + 7z = 25 \end{cases}$

The ancient Chinese were fascinated with mathematical puzzles, such as tangrams, which were used to form many shapes.

26. **Math History** Around the second century B.C.E., a Chinese mathematician posed a problem. He set up a table to show different combinations—A, B, C—of bundles of three types of corn—1, 2, 3—and found the number of measures of corn in each bundle. Use an augmented matrix to solve this problem.

Chinese Math Puzzle			
	A	B	C
Type-1 Bundles	3	2	1
Type-2 Bundles	2	3	2
Type-3 Bundles	1	1	3
Total Measures of Corn	39	34	26

27. **Multi-Step** Voting data for the 2003 Heisman Trophy is given in the table.
   a. Write a system of equations to represent the data.
   b. Solve by using an augmented matrix. Show it in reduced row-echelon form. Find the number of points that each vote is worth.

2003 Heisman Trophy Votes				
Player	First Place	Second Place	Third Place	Points
Jason White	319	204	116	1481
Larry Fitzgerald	253	233	128	1353
Eli Manning	95	132	161	710

28. **Write About It** Explain the difference between a coefficient matrix and an augmented matrix.

Solve the system by using row reduction on a calculator.

29. $\begin{cases} 3x = 5 - 4z \\ x + y + z = 5 \\ y = 2z \end{cases}$

30. $\begin{cases} x + y = z \\ 5y - 2z = 4 \\ 5y - 2x = 8 \end{cases}$

31. $\begin{cases} 2x + y - z = 5 \\ z = -2x - y \\ y = x \end{cases}$

32. **Critical Thinking** How can you identify a dependent or inconsistent system by looking at an augmented matrix in reduced row-echelon form?

MULTI-STEP TEST PREP

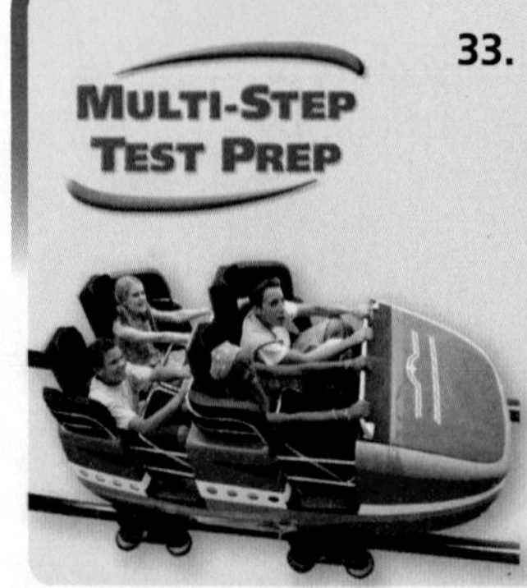

33. This problem will prepare you for the Multi-Step Test Prep on page 294.

At a carnival, 3 meals and 8 rides require 64 tickets, while 4 meals and 11 rides require 87 tickets. Let x be the number of tickets for a meal and y be the number of tickets for a ride.
   a. Write the problem as a system of equations.
   b. Write the augmented matrix.
   c. Use row reduction to solve.
   d. How many tickets are required for each item?

34. **Photography** The yearbook photographer sells sets of photos in three sizes. The price of each set includes a base price and the price for each size of print. The base price is twice the price of a large print. Find the base price and the price for each size of print.

TEST PREP

35. Which operation cannot be used to solve a system of equations by using an augmented matrix and row reduction?

Ⓐ Multiply any two rows together.
Ⓑ Subtract one row from another.
Ⓒ Switch any two rows.
Ⓓ Multiply a row by a constant.

36. Which row-reduced matrix indicates a dependent system of equations?

Ⓕ $\left[\begin{array}{cc|c} 1 & 0 & 1 \\ 0 & 1 & 1 \end{array}\right]$
Ⓖ $\left[\begin{array}{cc|c} 4 & 5 & 7 \\ 0 & 0 & \frac{2}{3} \end{array}\right]$
Ⓗ $\left[\begin{array}{cc|c} 4 & 5 & 7 \\ 0 & 0 & \frac{0}{5} \end{array}\right]$
Ⓙ $\left[\begin{array}{cc|c} 1 & 0 & 0 \\ 0 & 1 & 0 \end{array}\right]$

37. Which is the solution to the system represented by $\left[\begin{array}{cc|c} 2 & 0 & 5 \\ 0 & 3 & -3 \end{array}\right]$?

Ⓐ (5, −3)
Ⓑ (2.5, −3)
Ⓒ (2.5, −1)
Ⓓ (5, −1)

CHALLENGE AND EXTEND

38. Write an augmented matrix in which transposing two rows would be the best first step. Justify your reasoning.

39. The system represented by $\left[\begin{array}{cc|c} 1 & -2 & 5 \\ 3 & 1 & 8 \\ -2 & 4 & -10 \end{array}\right]$ has a solution. Explain why.

SPIRAL REVIEW

Describe each transformation of $f(x) = x^3$. *(Lesson 1-9)*

40. $f(x) = x^3 - 5$
41. $f(x) = \frac{3}{8}x^3$
42. $f(x) = (x + 3)^3$

43. Maximize $P = 3x + 2y$ given the constraints $x \geq 0$, $y \geq 0$, $x \leq y$ and $-2x + 3 \geq y$, and identify the point where P is maximized. *(Lesson 3-4)*

Write the matrix equation for the system, and solve. *(Lesson 4-5)*

44. $\begin{cases} 5y = x + 12 \\ 2y = 2x + 8 \end{cases}$

45. $\begin{cases} 3x - y = 0 \\ x + 2y = 7 \end{cases}$

MULTI-STEP TEST PREP

The Mild and Wild Amusement Park

Three friends, Travis, Kaitlyn, and Karsyn, spent the day at Mild and Wild Amusement Park, which features rides classified as Mild, Wild, or Super Wild. The park had two ticket packages as shown in the table.

Mild and Wild Amusement Park Ticket Packages		
Package	**Admission Fee**	**Ride Tickets**
Pick-ur-Tix	$5	Your choice at regular price
Mombo Combo	$5	8 of each type of ride at a 20% discount

The three friends chose the Pick-ur-Tix package. By the end of the day, Travis had ridden on 4 Mild rides, 8 Wild rides, and 8 Super Wild rides for a total ticket cost of $26. Kaitlyn had ridden on 8 Mild rides, 7 Wild rides, and 5 Super Wild rides for a total ticket cost of $24.25. Karsyn had ridden on 7 Mild rides, 6 Wild rides, and 4 Super Wild rides for a total ticket cost of $20.50.

1. Determine the ticket price for each type of ride. Solve an algebraic system for this situation by using matrices and a calculator or spreadsheet.
2. Determine the amount each person would spend if he or she had chosen the Mombo Combo. Explain which method of payment would have been bestfor each person.
3. Suppose that the amusement park had a fourth type of ride, called Colossal Wild. In addition to the other rides, Travis rode 12 Colossal Wild rides and spent $30. Kaitlyn rode 3 Colossal Wild rides and spent $30.25. Karsyn rode 1 Colossal Wild ride and spent $22.50. Would you be able to write and solve a matrix equation for this new situation? Explain.

Highlight or underline each part of the test item. Verify that your response addresses each part of the problem before you move on.

Read each test item, and answer the questions that follow.

Item A

Extended Response Explain what row operations were performed to create the new matrix.

$$\left[\begin{array}{cc|c} 4 & 3 & 1 \\ 3 & -2 & 5 \end{array}\right] \Rightarrow \left[\begin{array}{cc|c} -17 & 0 & -17 \\ 7 & 1 & 6 \end{array}\right]$$

1. Tyler wrote this response:

First, add row 1 to row 2 to get a new row 2. This makes a new matrix, $\begin{bmatrix} 4 & 3 & 1 \\ 7 & 1 & 6 \end{bmatrix}$. Then multiply the new row 2 by -3 and add it to row 1. This makes the resulting matrix, $\begin{bmatrix} -17 & 0 & -17 \\ 7 & 1 & 6 \end{bmatrix}$.

Item B

Extended Response Write the matrix that represents the vertices of figure *ABCD*. Then, determine and explain what matrix and which operations you would use to create figure *EFGH*.

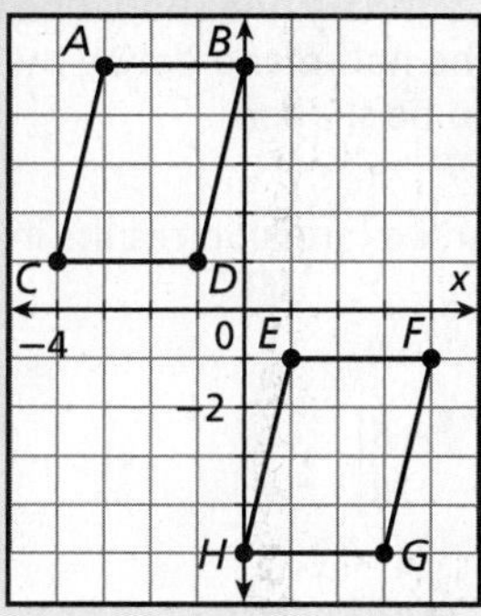

2. Make a list of what needs to be included in a response to this test item so that it receives full credit.

3. Sarah wrote this response:

The matrix for figure ABCD is $\begin{bmatrix} -3 & 0 & -1 & -4 \\ 5 & 5 & 1 & 1 \end{bmatrix}$, where the columns represent points A, B, C, and D and the rows represent the x- and y-coordinates.

Score Sarah's response, and provide your reasoning for the score.

4. Give a response that would receive full credit.

Item C

Extended Response Create a matrix that does not have an inverse. Explain your reasoning.

5. Should the following response receive full credit? Explain your reasoning.

The matrix $\begin{bmatrix} 4 & 3 \\ 12 & 9 \end{bmatrix}$ does not have an inverse because its determinant equals zero.

$\begin{vmatrix} 4 & 3 \\ 12 & 9 \end{vmatrix} = (4 \cdot 9) - (12 \cdot 3) = 36 - 36 = 0$

Item D

Extended Response Consider the system of equations $\begin{cases} x - 4y = 1.5 \\ 2x + y = 8.2 \end{cases}$. Describe which method—row operations, inverse matrices, or Cramer's rule—you would use to solve the system. Explain your reasoning.

6. Score the following response, and explain your score.

$D = \begin{vmatrix} 1 & -4 \\ 2 & 1 \end{vmatrix} = 1 - (-8) = 9$

$x = \dfrac{\begin{vmatrix} 1.5 & -4 \\ 8.2 & 1 \end{vmatrix}}{9} = \dfrac{1.5 - (-32.8)}{9} = \dfrac{34.3}{9} \approx 3.81$

$y = \dfrac{\begin{vmatrix} 1 & 1.5 \\ 2 & 8.2 \end{vmatrix}}{9} = \dfrac{8.2 - 3}{9} = \dfrac{5.2}{9} \approx 0.58$

7. How would you rewrite this response so that it receives full credit?

CHAPTER 4

STANDARDIZED TEST PREP

go.hrw.com
State Test Practice Online
KEYWORD: MB7 TestPrep

CUMULATIVE ASSESSMENT, CHAPTERS 1–4

Multiple Choice

1. Jack is two less than four times Macy's age. Kirstin is six more than half of Jack's age. If x is Macy's age and y is Jack's age, which expression represents Kirstin's age?

   (A) $\frac{1}{2}x + 6$
   (B) $2x + 5$
   (C) $4x + \frac{1}{2}y + 4$
   (D) $\frac{1}{2}(4x + 2) - 6$

2. The matrix below is the augmented matrix for a system of equations. What is the solution of the system of equations?

   $$\left[\begin{array}{cc|c} 6 & 8 & 5 \\ 12 & 4 & 16 \end{array}\right]$$

   (F) $\left(-\frac{3}{2}, \frac{1}{2}\right)$
   (G) $\left(-\frac{1}{2}, \frac{3}{2}\right)$
   (H) $\left(\frac{2}{3}, -2\right)$
   (J) $\left(\frac{3}{2}, -\frac{1}{2}\right)$

3. **PUTTER'S MINIATURE GOLF**
   1 putt—HOLE-IN-ONE!
   2 putts—BIRDIE
   3 putts—PAR
   4 putts—BOGEY

   Grace played 18 holes of miniature golf. On each hole, she made a birdie, a par, or a bogey. She made four more pars than birdies and bogeys combined. Her total score was 55. How many birdies did Grace get?

   (A) 3
   (B) 4
   (C) 7
   (D) 11

4. When stopping a car, a driver takes about 1.5 seconds to react before beginning to brake. A car traveling at 30 miles per hour moves 66 feet before the driver's foot touches the brake pedal. A car traveling at 45 miles per hour moves 99 feet, and a car traveling at 55 miles per hour moves 121 feet. Which set consists of only domain values for the given data?

   (F) $\{1.5\}$
   (G) $\{30, 66\}$
   (H) $\{30, 45\}$
   (J) $\{66, 99, 121\}$

5. The graph below shows the graph of an equation that is the boundary line of an inequality. The ordered pairs (21, 83) and (16, 62) are NOT solutions of the inequality. Which of these is true of the graph of the inequality?

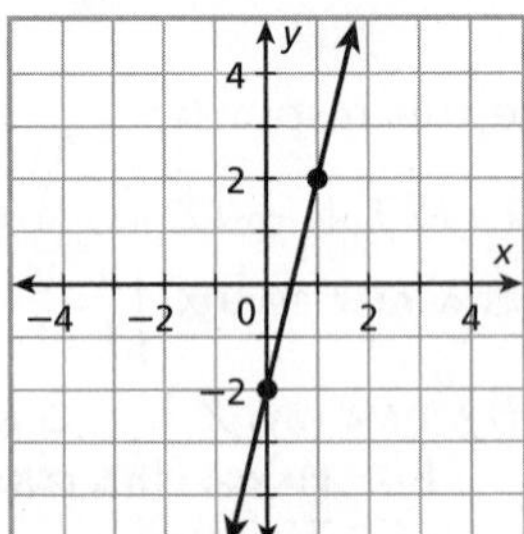

   (A) The boundary line should be dashed, and the half-plane above the line should be shaded.
   (B) The boundary line should be solid, and the half-plane above the line should be shaded.
   (C) The boundary line should be dashed, and the half-plane below the line should be shaded.
   (D) The boundary line should be solid, and the half-plane below the line should be shaded.

6. Which matrix expression results in the matrix $\begin{bmatrix} 2 & -4 \\ 11 & 14 \end{bmatrix}$?

   (F) $\frac{1}{2}\begin{bmatrix} 4 & -8 \\ 22 & 28 \end{bmatrix}$
   (G) $2\begin{bmatrix} 0 & -6 \\ 9 & 12 \end{bmatrix}$
   (H) $\begin{bmatrix} 2 & -4 \\ 11 & 14 \end{bmatrix} + \begin{bmatrix} 1 & 0 \\ 0 & 1 \end{bmatrix}$
   (J) $\begin{bmatrix} -6 & 17 \\ 8 & 10 \end{bmatrix} + \begin{bmatrix} 8 & -13 \\ -3 & 4 \end{bmatrix}$

7. On March 27, 2004, NASA's hypersonic research aircraft X-43A reached a speed of Mach 7. Traveling at seven times the speed of sound, an aircraft moves 16 miles every 12 seconds. Which of these functions represents the number of miles an aircraft traveling at Mach 7 can go in s seconds?

Ⓐ $f(s) = 16x + 12s$

Ⓑ $f(s) = \frac{3}{4}s$

Ⓒ $f(s) = 16s$

Ⓓ $f(s) = 1\frac{1}{3}s$

In order for the correlation coefficient to be displayed when you calculate the linear regression, your calculator should be set to DiagnosticOn.

8. After a conference, Brent was asked to rate each of the five workshops he attended on a scale from 1 to 10. The table below shows the length and Brent's rating of each workshop.

Minutes	53	93	48	120	32
Rating	7	4	5	9	8

What is the correlation coefficient, rounded to the nearest hundredth, for the relationship between the length and Brent's rating of each workshop?

Ⓕ 0.01 Ⓗ 0.88

Ⓖ 0.12 Ⓙ 6.13

Gridded Response

9. Examine the graphs of $f(x) = -|x|$ and $g(x) = f(x - h)$. What is the value of h?

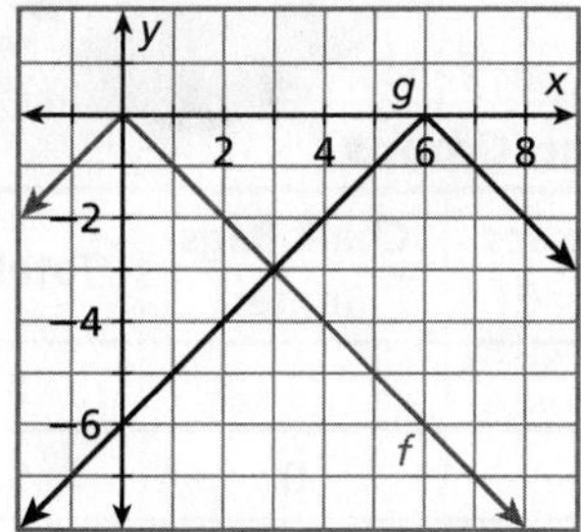

10. Find the determinant of the matrix $\begin{bmatrix} \frac{2}{5} & -1 \\ 0.4 & 10 \end{bmatrix}$.

Short Response

11. a. Name the system of inequalities.

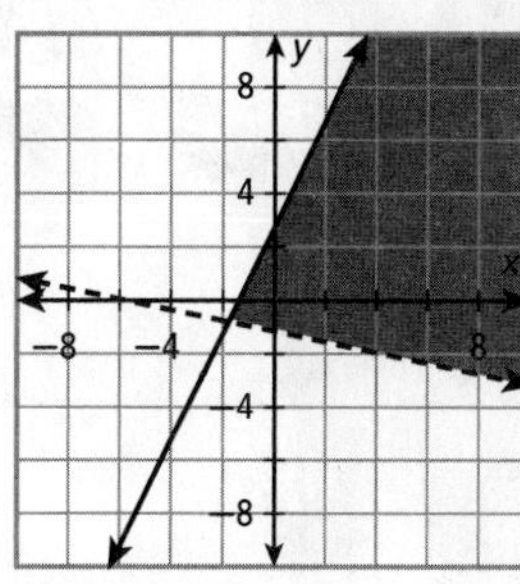

b. Name the system of inequalities.

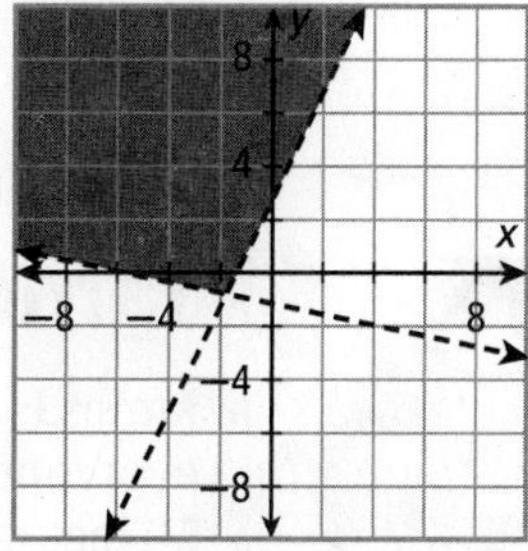

c. Describe how the system in part **a** differs from the system in part **b**.

12. Use a matrix and $\triangle ABC$ with coordinates $(-1, 0)$, $(4, 3)$, and $(2, -1)$ for the transformations.

a. Translate $\triangle ABC$ 1 unit to the right and 4 units up. Give the coordinates of $\triangle A'B'C'$.

b. Reflect $\triangle A'B'C'$ across the y-axis. Give the coordinates of $\triangle A''B''C''$.

Extended Response

13. Use the linear function $2x - 3y = -15$.

a. Explain how to rewrite the equation in slope-intercept form.

b. Describe why the slope-intercept form is usually the best way to write an equation before you graph it.

c. Write a step-by-step explanation on how to graph the equation.

Real-World CONNECTIONS

James Island County Park

James Island County Park in Charleston, South Carolina has something for everyone, but the park may be best known for its climbing wall. Standing 50 feet tall, the structure can accommodate up to 16 climbers at a time, making the park an ideal destination for families and groups of friends.

Choose one or more strategies to solve each problem.

1. County residents pay \$8 to use the climbing wall and nonresidents pay \$10. A group of 11 friends pays a total of \$96 to climb on the wall. How many county residents are in the group?
2. The table shows how many pairs of shoes, harnesses, and chalk bags were rented at the park by three different groups of climbers. The table also shows the total cost of the rentals for each group. What is the cost of renting each item?

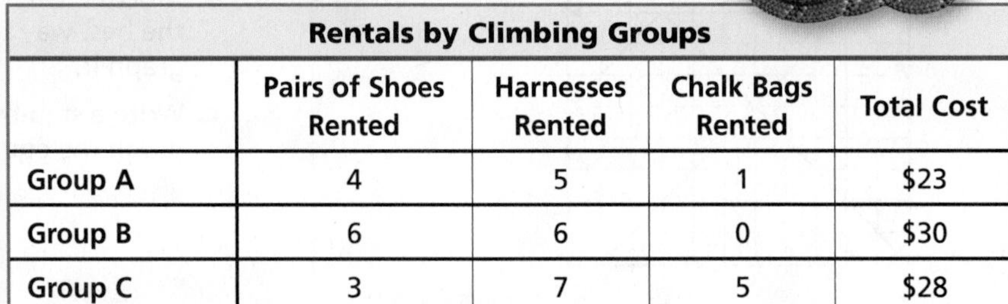

Rentals by Climbing Groups

	Pairs of Shoes Rented	Harnesses Rented	Chalk Bags Rented	Total Cost
Group A	4	5	1	\$23
Group B	6	6	0	\$30
Group C	3	7	5	\$28

3. A climber climbs up the lower part of the wall at a rate of 1.2 ft/min. The upper part of the wall is more difficult, and she climbs at 0.8 ft/min. She reaches the top of the wall in 51.5 min. How long did it take her to climb the lower part of the wall? At what height on the wall did her rate change?

Angel Oak

Many people believe Angel Oak is the oldest living thing in the United States east of the Rockies. This sprawling live oak has stood on John's Island for 1400 years. As is typical of the oldest oaks, its massive limbs touch the ground before curving upward, creating a majestic canopy that covers more than 17,000 square feet.

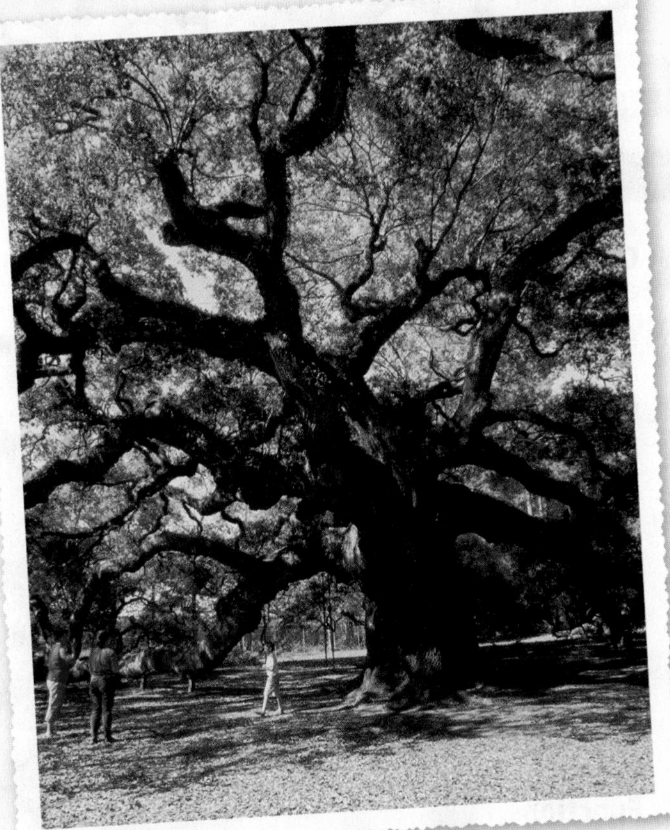

Choose one or more strategies to solve each problem.

1. Tree enthusiasts use a point system to compare trees. They assign a number of points for each inch of circumference, foot of height, and foot of crown spread. The table shows the measurements and point totals for some of South Carolina's champion trees. How many points are assigned to one unit of each measurement?

Champion Trees of South Carolina

	Circumference (in.)	Height (ft)	Crown Spread (ft)	Total Points
Angel Oak	306	65	144	407
Green Ash Tree	181	143	96	348
Redwood Tree	168	105	44	284

2. An oak tree produces acorns at two different rates. Until it reaches maturity, it produces an average of 900 acorns a year. Once it reaches full maturity, it produces an average of 2200 acorns a year. Angel Oak has produced about 2.9 million acorns in its lifetime. At what age did it reach maturity?

3. A botanist is studying the growth rates of live oaks. He wants to know the rates at which the height and circumference increase. He knows that the height typically increases 16 times as fast as the circumference. He measures a 10-year-old live oak and finds that

$$\text{height} + \text{circumference} = 255 \text{ in.}$$

Find the growth rates, in inches per year, for the height and circumference.

Real-World Connections

CHAPTER

5 Quadratic Functions

Chapter Focus

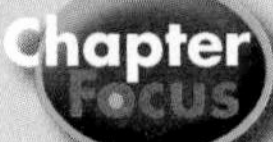

- Make connections among representations of quadratic functions.
- Use various methods to solve quadratic equations and apply them to real-world problems.

Planetary Pass

How far could you throw a football if you were on Mars or Saturn? You can find the answer by using quadratic functions.

go.hrw.com
Chapter Project Online
KEYWORD: MB7 ChProj

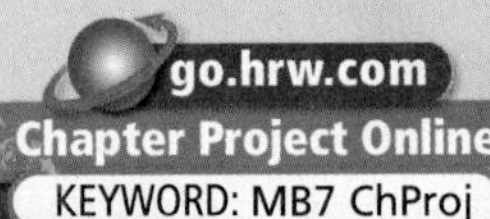

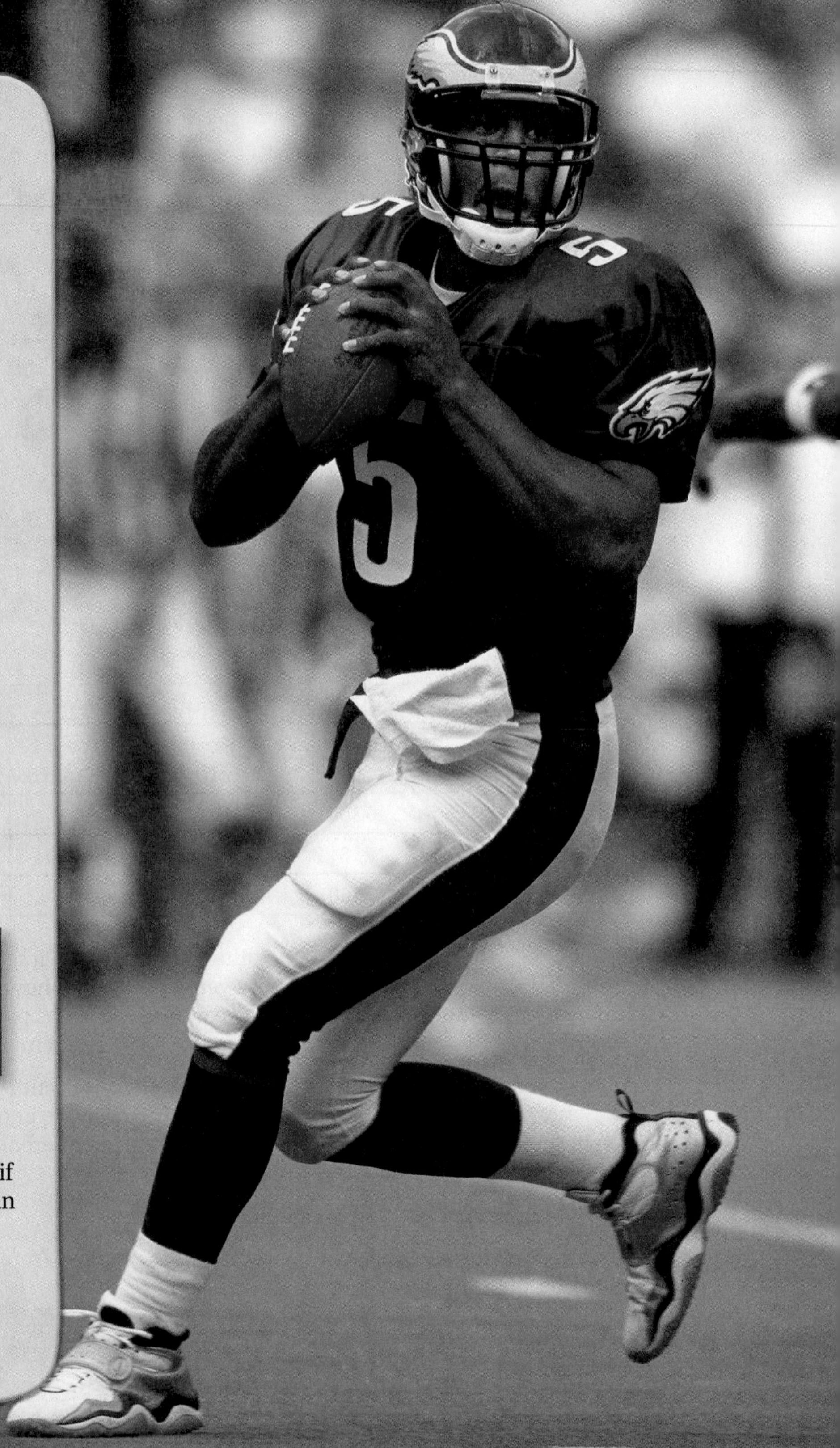

ARE YOU READY?

Vocabulary

Match each term on the left with a definition on the right.

1. linear equation
2. solution set
3. transformation
4. x-intercept

A. a change in a function rule and its graph
B. the x-coordinate of the point where a graph crosses the x-axis
C. the group of values that make an equation or inequality true
D. a letter or symbol that represents a number
E. an equation whose graph is a line

Squares and Square Roots

Simplify each expression.

5. 3.2^2
6. $\left(\frac{2}{5}\right)^2$
7. $\sqrt{121}$
8. $\sqrt{\frac{1}{16}}$

Simplify Radical Expressions

Simplify each expression.

9. $\sqrt{72}$
10. $2\left(\sqrt{144} - 4\right)$
11. $\sqrt{33} \cdot \sqrt{75}$
12. $\frac{\sqrt{54}}{\sqrt{3}}$

Multiply Binomials

Multiply.

13. $(x - 2)(x - 6)$
14. $(x + 9)(x - 9)$
15. $(x + 2)(x + 7)$
16. $(2x - 3)(5x + 1)$

Solve Multi-Step Equations

Solve each equation.

17. $2x + 10 = -32$
18. $2x - (1 - x) = 2$
19. $\frac{2}{3}(x - 1) = 11$
20. $2(x + 5) - 5x = 1$

Graph Linear Functions

Graph each function.

21. $y = -x$
22. $y = 2x - 1$
23. $y = -3x + 6$
24. $y = \frac{1}{3}x + 2$

CHAPTER 5

Study Guide: Preview

Where You've Been

Previously, you

- graphed and transformed linear functions.
- solved linear equations and inequalities.
- fit data using linear models.
- used and performed operations with real numbers.

In This Chapter

You will study

- graphing and transforming quadratic functions.
- solving quadratic equations and inequalities.
- fitting data to quadratic models.
- using and performing operations with imaginary and other complex numbers.

Where You're Going

You can use the skills in this chapter

- in advanced math classes, including Precalculus.
- in other classes, such as Chemistry, Physics, and Economics.
- outside of school to identify patterns and model data.

Key Vocabulary/Vocabulario

absolute value of a complex number	valor absoluto de un número complejo
complex conjugate	conjugado complejo
complex number	número complejo
imaginary number	número imaginario
maximum value	valor máximo
minimum value	valor mínimo
parabola	parábola
quadratic function	función cuadrática
vertex form	forma en vértice
zero of a function	cero de una función

Thinking About Vocabulary

To become familiar with some of the vocabulary terms in the chapter, consider the following. You may refer to the chapter, the glossary, or a dictionary if you like.

1. **Quadratic** is from the Latin *quadrum,* which means "square." A quadratic function always contains a *square* of the variable, such as x^2. What is a quadrilateral, and how does it relate to a square? What are some other words that use the root *quad-*, and what do they mean?
2. The word **conjugate** can mean "joined together, especially in pairs." Name some mathematical relationships that involve pairs.
3. What might the terms **maximum value** or **minimum value** of a function refer to?
4. The word *vertex* can mean "highest point." What might the **vertex form** of a quadratic function indicate about the function's graph?

Study Strategy: Use Multiple Representations

The explanation and example problems used to introduce new math concepts often include various representations of information. Different representations of the same idea help you fully understand the material. As you study, take note of the tables, lists, graphs, diagrams, symbols, and/or words used to clarify a concept.

From Lesson 3-2

EXAMPLE 1 **Solving Linear Systems by Substitution**

Use substitution to solve each system of equations.

A $\begin{cases} y = x + 2 \\ x + y = 8 \end{cases}$

Symbols

Step 1 Solve one equation for one variable.
The first equation is already solved for y: $y = x + 2$.

Step 2 Substitute the expression into the other equation.

$x + y = 8$

$x + (x + 2) = 8$ *Substitute $(x + 2)$ for y in the other equation.*

$2x + 2 = 8$ *Combine like terms.*

$2x = 6$

$x = 3$

Step 3 Substitute the x-value into one of the original equations to solve for y.

$y = x + 2$

$y = (3) + 2$ *Substitute $x = 3$.*

$y = 5$

The solution is the ordered pair $(3, 5)$.

Caution! The solution to an independent system of equations is an ordered pair. Do not stop working when you have found only one value.

Check A graph or table supports your answer.

Graph

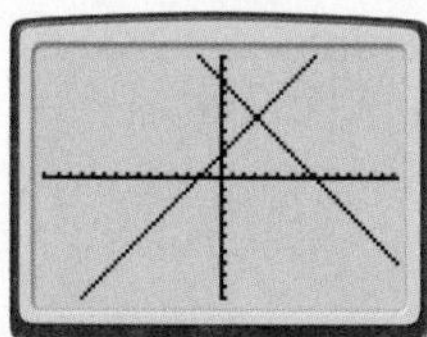

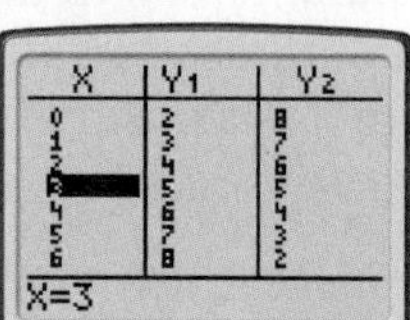

Table

Try This

Describe two representations you could use to solve each problem.

1. A triangle with coordinates $A(3, 5)$, $B(2, 2)$, and $C(3, -2)$ is translated 3 units left and 2 units up. Give the coordinates of the image.

2. A bottle of juice from a vending machine costs $1.50. Hiroshi buys a bottle by inserting 8 coins in quarters and dimes. If Hiroshi receives 5 cents in change, how many quarters did he use? how many dimes?

3. What is the slope of the line that passes through the point $(6, 9)$ and has a y-intercept of 3?

Explore Parameter Changes

You can use a graphing calculator to explore how changes in the parameters of a quadratic function affect its graph. Recall from Lesson 1-9 that the quadratic parent function is $f(x) = x^2$ and that its graph is a parabola.

Activity

Describe what happens when you change the value of k in the quadratic function $g(x) = x^2 + k$.

1. Choose three values for k. Use 0, −5 (a negative value), and 4 (a positive value). Press **Y=**, and enter **X²** for **Y1**, **X² − 5** for **Y2**, and **X² + 4** for **Y3**.

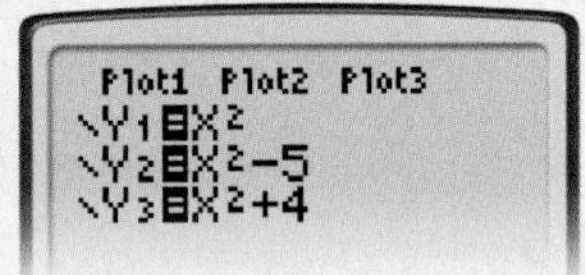

2. Change the style of the graphs of **Y1** and **Y2** so that you can tell which graph represents which function. To do this, move the cursor to the graph style indicator next to **Y1**. Press **ENTER** to cycle through the options. For **Y1**, which represents the parent function, choose the thick line.

3. Next, change the line style for **Y2** to the dotted line.
4. Graph the functions in the square window by pressing **ZOOM** and choosing **5 : ZSquare**.

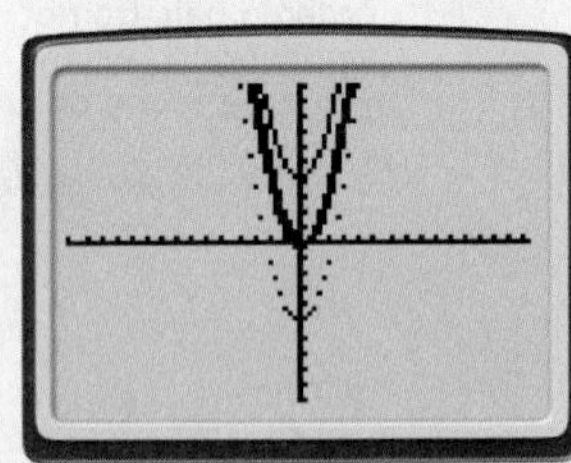

Notice that the graphs are identical except that the graph of **Y2** is shifted 5 units down and the graph of **Y3** has been shifted 4 units up from the graph of **Y1**.

You can conclude that the parameter k in the function $g(x) = x^2 + k$ has the effect of translating the parent function $f(x) = x^2$ k units up if k is positive and $|k|$ units down if k is negative.

Try This

Use your graphing calculator to compare the graph of each function to the graph of $f(x) = x^2$. Describe how the graphs differ.

1. $g(x) = (x - 4)^2$
2. $g(x) = (x + 3)^2$
3. $g(x) = -x^2$
4. **Make a Conjecture** Use your graphing calculator to determine what happens when you change the value of h in the quadratic function $g(x) = (x - h)^2$. Check both positive and negative values of h.
5. **Make a Conjecture** Use your graphing calculator to determine what happens when you change the value of a in the quadratic function $g(x) = ax^2$. Check values of a that are greater than 1 and values of a that are between 0 and 1.

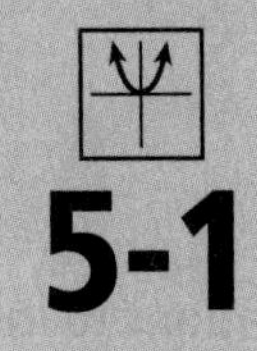

5-1 Using Transformations to Graph Quadratic Functions

Objectives
Transform quadratic functions.

Describe the effects of changes in the coefficients of $y = a(x - h)^2 + k$.

Vocabulary
quadratic function
parabola
vertex of a parabola
vertex form

Why learn this?
You can use transformations of quadratic functions to analyze changes in braking distance. (See Example 5.)

In Chapters 2 and 3, you studied linear functions of the form $f(x) = mx + b$. A **quadratic function** is a function that can be written in the form $f(x) = a(x - h)^2 + k \ (a \neq 0)$. In a quadratic function, the variable is always squared. The table shows the linear and quadratic parent functions.

Linear and Quadratic Parent Functions

ALGEBRA	NUMBERS						GRAPH
Linear Parent Function $f(x) = x$	x	−2	−1	0	1	2	
	$f(x) = x$	−2	−1	0	1	2	
Quadratic Parent Function $f(x) = x^2$	x	−2	−1	0	1	2	
	$f(x) = x^2$	4	1	0	1	4	

Notice that the graph of the parent function $f(x) = x^2$ is a U-shaped curve called a **parabola**. As with other functions, you can graph a quadratic function by plotting points with coordinates that make the equation true.

EXAMPLE 1 Graphing Quadratic Functions Using a Table

Graph $f(x) = x^2 - 6x + 8$ by using a table.

Make a table. Plot enough ordered pairs to see both sides of the curve.

x	$f(x) = x^2 - 6x + 8$	$(x, f(x))$
1	$f(1) = 1^2 - 6(1) + 8 = 3$	(1, 3)
2	$f(2) = 2^2 - 6(2) + 8 = 0$	(2, 0)
3	$f(3) = 3^2 - 6(3) + 8 = -1$	(3, −1)
4	$f(4) = 4^2 - 6(4) + 8 = 0$	(4, 0)
5	$f(5) = 5^2 - 6(5) + 8 = 3$	(5, 3)

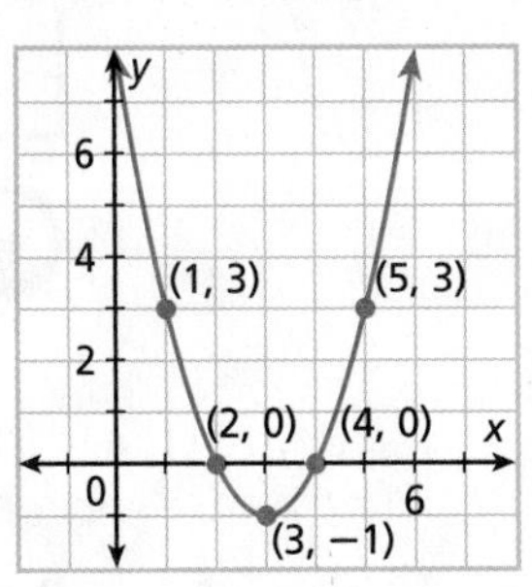

1. Graph $g(x) = -x^2 + 6x - 8$ by using a table.

You can also graph quadratic functions by applying transformations to the parent function $f(x) = x^2$. Transforming quadratic functions is similar to transforming linear functions (Lesson 2-6).

Translations of Quadratic Functions	
Horizontal Translations	**Vertical Translations**
Horizontal Shift of $\|h\|$ Units	**Vertical Shift of $\|k\|$ Units**
$f(x) = x^2$ $f(x - h) = (x - h)^2$ Moves left for $h < 0$ Moves right for $h > 0$	$f(x) = x^2$ $f(x) + k = x^2 + k$ Moves down for $k < 0$ Moves up for $k > 0$

EXAMPLE 2 **Translating Quadratic Functions**

Using the graph of $f(x) = x^2$ as a guide, describe the transformations, and then graph each function.

A $g(x) = (x + 3)^2 + 1$

Identify h and k.

$$g(x) = \left(x - (-3)\right)^2 + 1$$

($h = -3$, $k = 1$)

Because $h = -3$, the graph is translated 3 units left.
Because $k = 1$, the graph is translated 1 unit up.
Therefore, g is f translated 3 units left and 1 unit up.

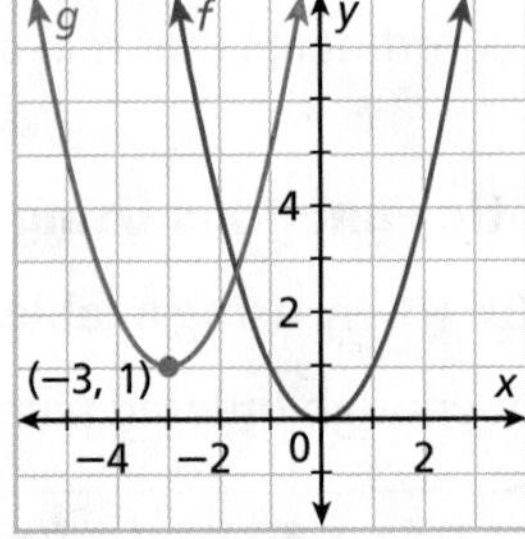

B $g(x) = (x - 2)^2 - 1$

Identify h and k.

$$g(x) = (x - 2)^2 + (-1)$$

($h = 2$, $k = -1$)

Because $h = 2$, the graph is translated 2 units right.
Because $k = -1$, the graph is translated 1 unit down.
Therefore, g is f translated 2 units right and 1 unit down.

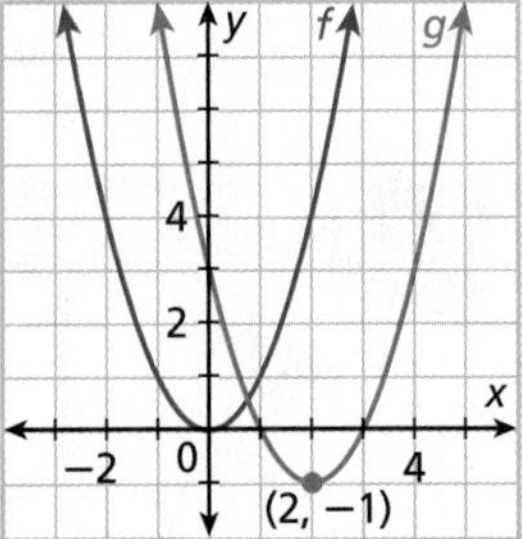

Using the graph of $f(x) = x^2$ as a guide, describe the transformations, and then graph each function.

2a. $g(x) = x^2 - 5$

2b. $g(x) = (x + 3)^2 - 2$

Recall that functions can also be reflected, stretched, or compressed.

Reflections, Stretches, and Compressions of Quadratic Functions	
Reflections	
Reflection Across *y*-axis	**Reflection Across *x*-axis**
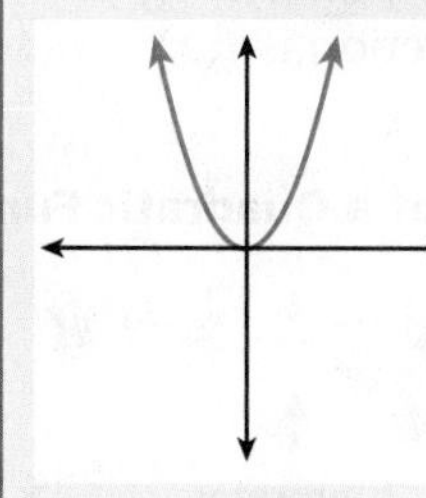 Input values change. $f(x) = x^2$ $f(-x) = (-x)^2 = x^2$ The function $f(x) = x^2$ is its own reflection across the *y*-axis.	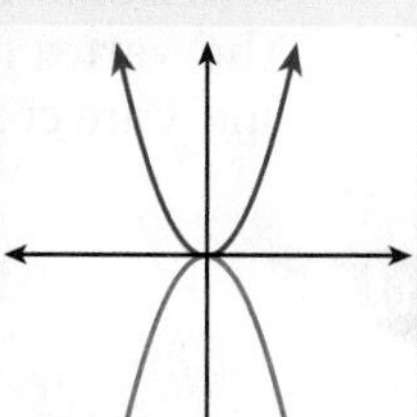 Output values change. $f(x) = x^2$ $-f(x) = -(x^2) = -x^2$ The function is flipped across the *x*-axis.
Stretches and Compressions	
Horizontal Stretch/Compression by a Factor of $\lvert b \rvert$	**Vertical Stretch/Compression by a Factor of $\lvert a \rvert$**
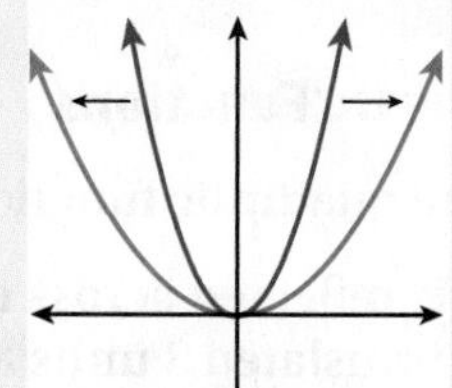 Input values change. $f(x) = x^2$ $f\left(\frac{1}{b}x\right) = \left(\frac{1}{b}x\right)^2$	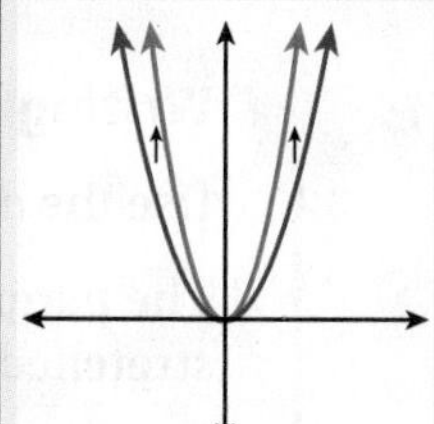 Output values change. $f(x) = x^2$ $a \cdot f(x) = ax^2$
$\lvert b \rvert > 1$ stretches away from the *y*-axis. $0 < \lvert b \rvert < 1$ compresses toward the *y*-axis.	$\lvert a \rvert > 1$ stretches away from the *x*-axis. $0 < \lvert a \rvert < 1$ compresses toward the *x*-axis.

EXAMPLE 

3 Reflecting, Stretching, and Compressing Quadratic Functions

Using the graph of $f(x) = x^2$ as a guide, describe the transformations, and then graph each function.

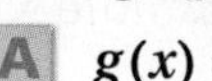

A $g(x) = -4x^2$

Because a is negative, g is a reflection of f across the x-axis. Because $|a| = 4$, g is a vertical stretch of f by a factor of 4.

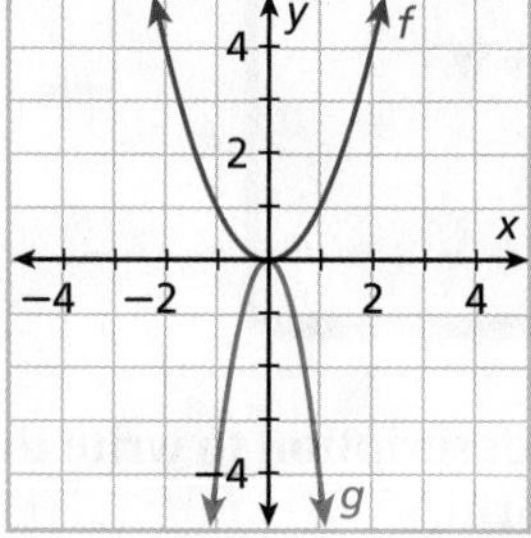

B $g(x) = \left(\frac{1}{2}x\right)^2$

Because $b = 2$, g is a horizontal stretch of f by a factor of 2.

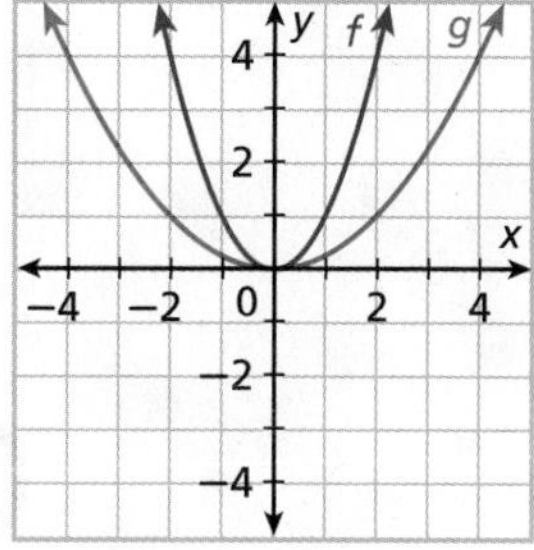

Using the graph of $f(x) = x^2$ as a guide, describe the transformations, and then graph each function.

3a. $g(x) = (2x)^2$

3b. $g(x) = -\frac{1}{2}x^2$

If a parabola opens upward, it has a lowest point. If a parabola opens downward, it has a highest point. This lowest or highest point is the **vertex of a parabola** .

The parent function $f(x) = x^2$ has its vertex at the origin. You can identify the vertex of other quadratic functions by analyzing the function in *vertex form.* The **vertex form** of a quadratic function is $f(x) = a(x - h)^2 + k$, where a, h, and k are constants.

Know it! Note

Vertex Form of a Quadratic Function

$$f(x) = a(x - h)^2 + k$$

a indicates a reflection across the *x*-axis and/or a vertical stretch or compression.

h indicates a horizontal translation.

k indicates a vertical translation.

Because the vertex is translated h horizontal units and k vertical units from the origin, the vertex of the parabola is at (h, k).

EXAMPLE 4 Writing Transformed Quadratic Functions

Use the description to write the quadratic function in vertex form.

The parent function $f(x) = x^2$ is reflected across the *x*-axis, vertically stretched by a factor of 6, and translated 3 units left to create *g*.

Step 1 Identify how each transformation affects the constants in vertex form.

reflection across *x*-axis:	a is negative	$a = -6$
vertical stretch by 6:	$\lvert a \rvert = 6$	
translation left 3 units:	$h = -3$	

Helpful Hint

When the quadratic parent function $f(x) = x^2$ is written in vertex form, $y = a(x - h)^2 + k$, $a = 1$, $h = 0$, and $k = 0$.

Step 2 Write the transformed function.

$g(x) = a(x - h)^2 + k$ *Vertex form of a quadratic function*

$= -6(x - (-3))^2 + 0$ *Substitute –6 for a, –3 for h, and 0 for k.*

$= -6(x + 3)^2$ *Simplify.*

Check Graph both functions on a graphing calculator. Enter *f* as **Y1** and *g* as **Y2**. The graph indicates the identified transformations.

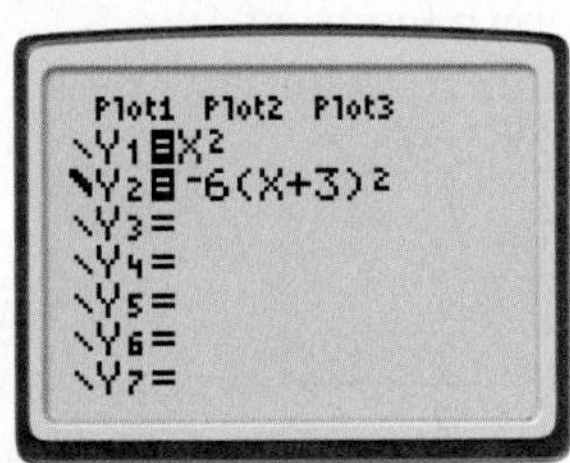

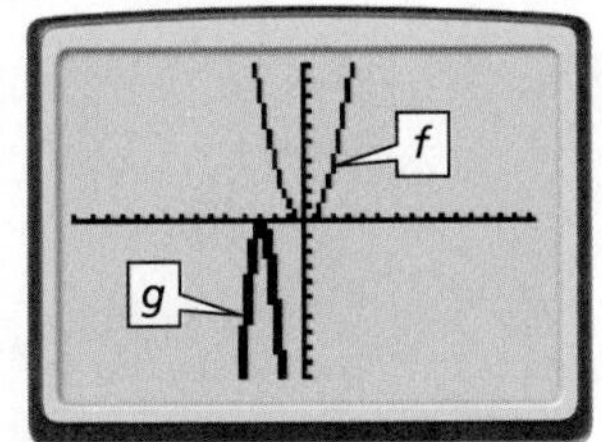

Use the description to write the quadratic function in vertex form.

4a. The parent function $f(x) = x^2$ is vertically compressed by a factor of $\frac{1}{3}$ and translated 2 units right and 4 units down to create *g*.

4b. The parent function $f(x) = x^2$ is reflected across the *x*-axis and translated 5 units left and 1 unit up to create *g*.

EXAMPLE 5 Automotive Application

The minimum braking distance d in feet for a vehicle on dry concrete is approximated by the function $d(v) = 0.045v^2$, where v is the vehicle's speed in miles per hour. If the vehicle's tires are in poor condition, the braking-distance function is $d_p(v) = 0.068v^2$. What kind of transformation describes this change, and what does the transformation mean?

Examine both functions in vertex form.

$$d(v) = 0.045(v - 0)^2 + 0 \qquad d_p(v) = 0.068(v - 0)^2 + 0$$

The value of a has increased from 0.045 to 0.068. The increase indicates a vertical stretch.

Find the stretch factor by comparing the new a-value to the old a-value:

$$\frac{a \text{ from } d_p(v)}{a \text{ from } d(v)} = \frac{0.068}{0.045} \approx 1.5$$

The function d_p represents a vertical stretch of d by a factor of approximately 1.5. Because the value of each function approximates braking distance, a vehicle with tires in poor condition takes about 1.5 times as many feet to stop as a vehicle with good tires does.

Check Graph both functions on a graphing calculator. The graph of d_p appears to be vertically stretched compared with the graph of d.

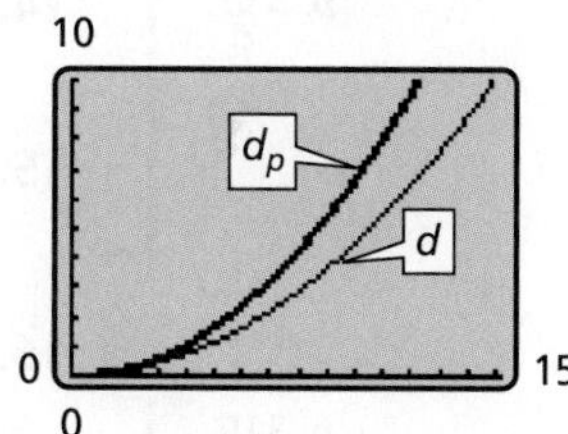

Use the information above to answer the following.

5. The minimum braking distance d_n in feet for a vehicle with new tires at optimal inflation is $d_n(v) = 0.039v^2$, where v is the vehicle's speed in miles per hour. What kind of transformation describes this change from $d(v) = 0.045v^2$, and what does this transformation mean?

THINK AND DISCUSS

1. Explain how the values of a, h, and k in the vertex form of a quadratic function affect the function's graph.
2. Explain how to determine which of two quadratic functions expressed in vertex form has a narrower graph.

3. **GET ORGANIZED** Copy and complete the graphic organizer. In each row, write an equation that represents the indicated transformation of the quadratic parent function, and show its graph.

Transformation	Equation	Graph
Vertical translation		
Horizontal translation		
Reflection		
Vertical stretch		
Vertical compression		

5-1 Exercises

go.hrw.com
Homework Help Online
KEYWORD: MB7 5-1
Parent Resources Online
KEYWORD: MB7 Parent

GUIDED PRACTICE

1. **Vocabulary** The highest or lowest point on the graph of a quadratic function is the ___?___. (*vertex* or *parabola*)

SEE EXAMPLE 1 p. 315

Graph each function by using a table.

2. $f(x) = -2x^2 - 4$
3. $g(x) = -x^2 + 3x - 2$
4. $h(x) = x^2 + 2x$

SEE EXAMPLE 2 p. 316

Using the graph of $f(x) = x^2$ as a guide, describe the transformations, and then graph each function.

5. $d(x) = (x - 4)^2$
6. $g(x) = (x - 3)^2 + 2$
7. $h(x) = (x + 1)^2 - 3$

SEE EXAMPLE 3 p. 317

8. $g(x) = 3x^2$
9. $h(x) = \left(\frac{1}{8}x\right)^2$
10. $p(x) = 0.25x^2$
11. $h(x) = -(5x)^2$
12. $g(x) = 4.2x^2$
13. $d(x) = -\frac{2}{3}x^2$

SEE EXAMPLE 4 p. 318

Use the description to write each quadratic function in vertex form.

14. The parent function $f(x) = x^2$ is vertically stretched by a factor of 2 and translated 3 units left to create g.
15. The parent function $f(x) = x^2$ is reflected across the x-axis and translated 6 units down to create h.

SEE EXAMPLE 5 p. 319

16. **Physics** The safe working load L in pounds for a natural rope can be estimated by $L(r) = 5920r^2$, where r is the radius of the rope in inches. For an old rope, the function $L_o(r) = 4150r^2$ is used to estimate its safe working load. What kind of transformation describes this change, and what does this transformation mean?

PRACTICE AND PROBLEM SOLVING

Independent Practice

For Exercises	See Example
17–19	1
20–25	2
26–28	3
29–30	4
31	5

Extra Practice

Skills Practice p. S12
Application Practice p. S36

Graph each function by using a table.

17. $f(x) = -x^2 + 4$
18. $g(x) = x^2 - 2x + 1$
19. $h(x) = 2x^2 + 4x - 1$

Using the graph of $f(x) = x^2$ as a guide, describe the transformations, and then graph each function.

20. $g(x) = x^2 - 2$
21. $h(x) = (x + 5)^2$
22. $j(x) = (x - 1)^2$
23. $g(x) = (x + 4)^2 - 3$
24. $h(x) = (x + 2)^2 + 2$
25. $j(x) = (x - 4)^2 - 9$
26. $g(x) = \frac{4}{7}x^2$
27. $h(x) = -20x^2$
28. $j(x) = \left(\frac{1}{3}x\right)^2$

Use the description to write each quadratic function in vertex form.

29. The parent function $f(x) = x^2$ is reflected across the x-axis, vertically compressed by a factor of $\frac{1}{2}$, and translated 1 unit right to create g.
30. The parent function $f(x) = x^2$ is vertically stretched by a factor of 2.5 and translated 2 units left and 1 unit up to create h.
31. **Consumer Economics** The average gas mileage m in miles per gallon for a compact car is modeled by $m(s) = -0.015(s - 47)^2 + 33$, where s is the car's speed in miles per hour. The average gas mileage for an SUV is modeled by $m_u(s) = -0.015(s - 47)^2 + 15$. What kind of transformation describes this change, and what does this transformation mean?

32. **Pets** Keille is building a rectangular pen for a pet rabbit. She can buy wire fencing in a roll of 40 ft or a roll of 80 ft. The graph shows the area of pens she can build with each type of roll.

a. Describe the function for an 80 ft roll of fencing as a transformation of the function for a 40 ft roll of fencing.

b. Is the largest pen Keille can build with an 80 ft roll of fencing twice as large as the largest pen she can build with a 40 ft roll of fencing? Explain.

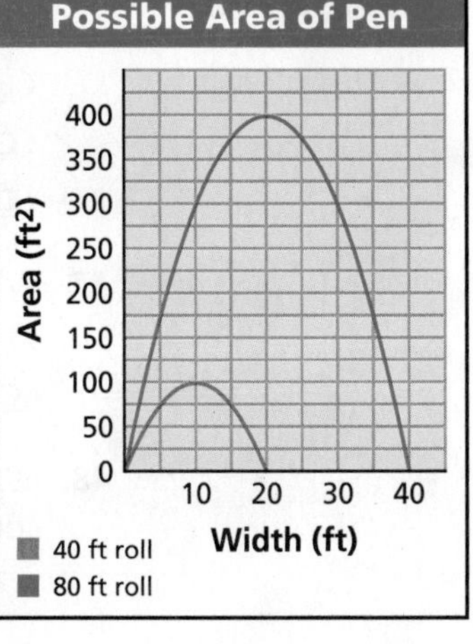

Using $f(x) = x^2$ as a guide, describe the transformations for each function.

33. $p(x) = -(x - 4)^2$

34. $g(x) = 8(x + 2)^2$

35. $h(x) = 4x^2 - 2$

36. $p(x) = \frac{1}{4}x^2 + 2$

37. $g(x) = (3x)^2 + 1$

38. $h(x) = -\left(\frac{1}{3}x\right)^2$

Match each graph with one of the following functions.

A. $a(x) = 4(x + 8)^2 - 3$

B. $b(x) = -2(x - 8)^2 + 3$

C. $c(x) = -\frac{1}{2}(x + 3)^2 + 8$

39.

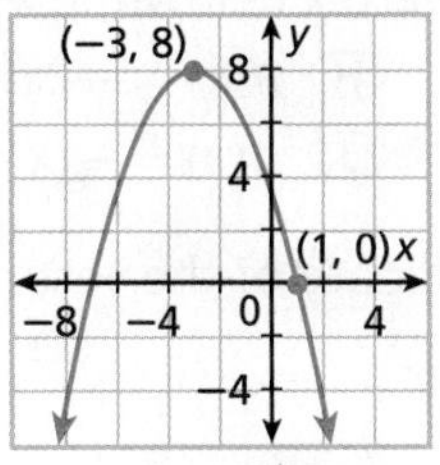

40.

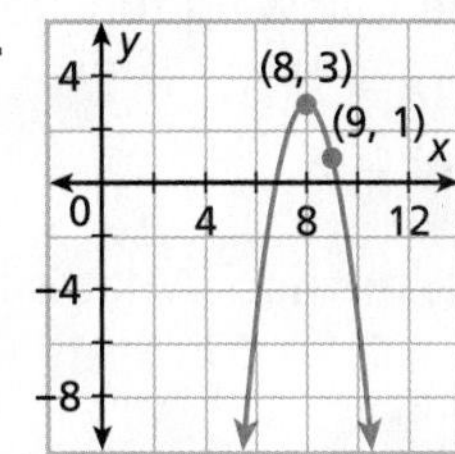

41.

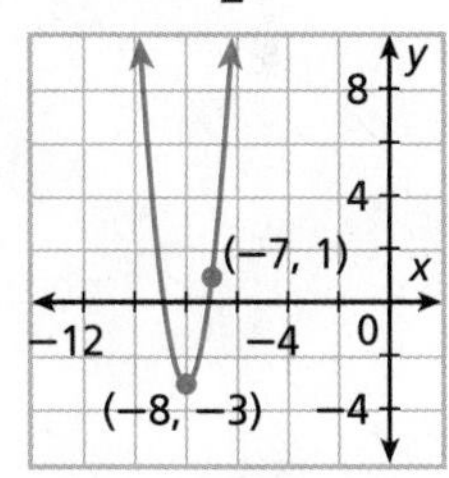

42. **Geometry** The area A of the circle in the figure can be represented by $A(r) = \pi r^2$, where r is the radius.

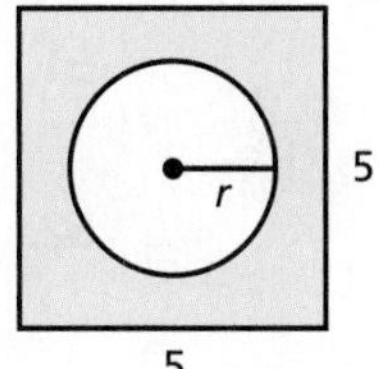

a. Write a function B in terms of r that represents the area of the shaded portion of the figure.

b. Describe B as a transformation of A.

c. What are the reasonable domain and range for each function? Explain.

43. **Critical Thinking** What type of graph would a function of the form $f(x) = a(x - h)^2 + k$ have if $a = 0$? What type of function would it be?

44. **Write About It** Describe the graph of $f(x) = 999{,}999(x + 5)^2 + 5$ without graphing it.

45. This problem will prepare you for the Multi-Step Test Prep on page 364.

The height h in feet of a baseball on Earth after t seconds can be modeled by the function $h(t) = -16(t - 1.5)^2 + 36$, where -16 is a constant in ft/s² due to Earth's gravity.

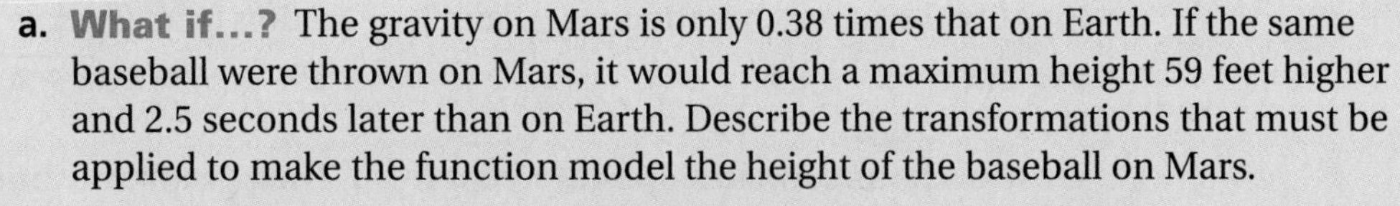

a. **What if...?** The gravity on Mars is only 0.38 times that on Earth. If the same baseball were thrown on Mars, it would reach a maximum height 59 feet higher and 2.5 seconds later than on Earth. Describe the transformations that must be applied to make the function model the height of the baseball on Mars.

b. Write a height function for the baseball thrown on Mars.

Use the graph for Exercises 46 and 47.

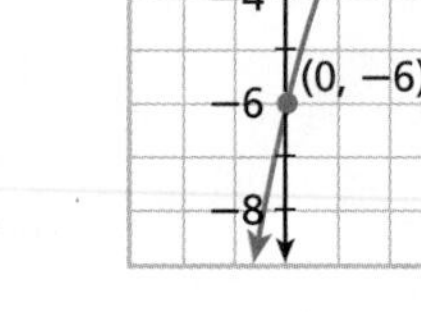

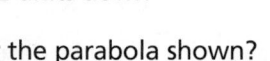

46. Which best describes how the graph of the function $y = -x^2$ was transformed to produce the graph shown?
   (A) Translation 2 units right and 2 units up
   (B) Translation 2 units right and 2 units down
   (C) Translation 2 units left and 2 units up
   (D) Translation 2 units left and 2 units down

47. Which gives the function rule for the parabola shown?
   (F) $f(x) = (x + 2)^2 - 2$
   (G) $f(x) = -(x + 2)^2 - 2$
   (H) $f(x) = (x - 2)^2 - 2$
   (J) $f(x) = -(x - 2)^2 - 2$

48. Which shows the functions below in order from widest to narrowest of their corresponding graphs?

   $m(x) = \frac{1}{6}x^2$ $\quad n(x) = 4x^2$ $\quad p(x) = 6x^2$ $\quad q(x) = -\frac{1}{2}x^2$

   (A) m, n, p, q
   (B) q, m, n, p
   (C) m, q, n, p
   (D) q, p, n, m

49. Which of the following functions has its vertex below the *x*-axis?
   (F) $f(x) = (x - 7)^2$
   (G) $f(x) = x^2 - 8$
   (H) $f(x) = -2x^2$
   (J) $f(x) = -(x + 3)^2$

50. **Gridded Response** What is the *y*-coordinate of the vertex of the graph of $f(x) = -3(x - 1)^2 + 5$?

CHALLENGE AND EXTEND

51. Identify the transformations of the graph of $f(x) = -3(x + 3)^2 - 3$ that would cause the graph's image to have a vertex at $(3, 3)$. Then write the transformed function.

52. Consider the functions $f(x) = (2x)^2 - 2$ and $g(x) = 4x^2 - 2$.
   a. Describe each function as a transformation of the quadratic parent function.
   b. Graph both functions on the coordinate plane.
   c. Make a conjecture about the relationship between the two functions.
   d. Write the rule for a horizontal compression of the parent function that would give the same graph as $f(x) = 9x^2$.

SPIRAL REVIEW

53. **Packaging** Peanuts are packaged in cylindrical containers. A small container is 7 in. tall and has a radius of 2 in. A large container is 5.5 in. tall and has a radius twice that of the small container. The price of the large container is three times the price of the small container. Is this price justified? Explain. *(Previous course)*

Identify the parent function for *g* from its function rule. *(Lesson 1-9)*

54. $g(x) = 4x + \sqrt{3}$

55. $g(x) = 3\sqrt{x + 4}$

Write each function in slope-intercept form. Then graph the function. *(Lesson 2-3)*

56. $2y + 5x = 14$

57. $x - \frac{1}{2}y + 4 = -1$

5-2 Properties of Quadratic Functions in Standard Form

Objectives
Define, identify, and graph quadratic functions.

Identify and use maximums and minimums of quadratic functions to solve problems.

Vocabulary
axis of symmetry
standard form
minimum value
maximum value

Why learn this?
Quadratic functions can be used to find the maximum power generated by the engine of a speedboat. (See Example 4.)

When you transformed quadratic functions in the previous lesson, you saw that reflecting the parent function across the y-axis results in the same function.

$f(x) = x^2$
$g(x) = (-x)^2 = x^2$

This shows that parabolas are symmetric curves. The **axis of symmetry** is the line through the vertex of a parabola that divides the parabola into two congruent halves.

Know it! Note — **Axis of Symmetry** — Quadratic Functions

WORDS	ALGEBRA	GRAPH
The axis of symmetry is a vertical line through the vertex of the function's graph.	The quadratic function $f(x) = a(x - h)^2 + k$ has the axis of symmetry $x = h$.	(h, k)

EXAMPLE 1 **Identifying the Axis of Symmetry**

Identify the axis of symmetry for the graph of $f(x) = 2(x + 2)^2 - 3$.

Rewrite the function to find the value of h.

$f(x) = 2[x - (-2)]^2 - 3$

Because $h = -2$, the axis of symmetry is the vertical line $x = -2$.

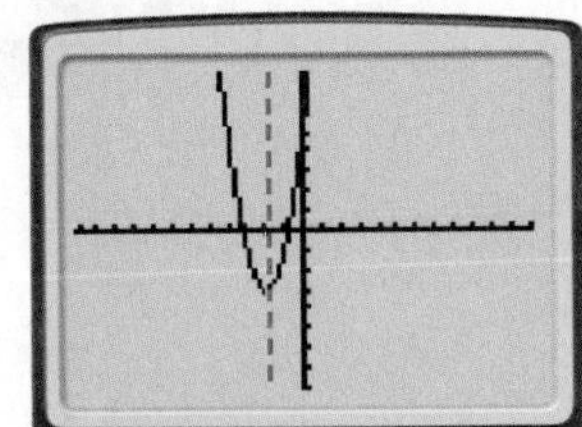

Check Analyze the graph on a graphing calculator. The parabola is symmetric about the vertical line $x = -2$.

1. Identify the axis of symmetry for the graph of $f(x) = (x - 3)^2 + 1$.

Another useful form of writing quadratic functions is the *standard form*. The **standard form** of a quadratic function is $f(x) = ax^2 + bx + c$, where $a \neq 0$.

The coefficients a, b, and c can show properties of the graph of the function. You can determine these properties by expanding the vertex form.

$f(x) = a(x - h)^2 + k$

$f(x) = a(x^2 - 2xh + h^2) + k$ *Multiply to expand $(x - h)^2$.*

$f(x) = a(x^2) - a(2hx) + a(h^2) + k$ *Distribute a.*

$f(x) = ax^2 + (-2ah)x + (ah^2 + k)$ *Simplify and group like terms.*

$a = a$ $\quad -2ah = b \quad ah^2 + k = c$

$$f(x) = ax^2 + bx + c$$

$a = a$ — a in standard form is the same as in vertex form. It indicates whether a reflection and/or vertical stretch or compression has been applied.

$b = -2ah$ — Solving for h gives $h = \frac{b}{-2a} = -\frac{b}{2a}$. Therefore, the axis of symmetry, $x = h$, for a quadratic function in standard form is $x = -\frac{b}{2a}$.

$c = ah^2 + k$ — Notice that the value of c is the same value given by the vertex form of f when $x = 0$: $f(0) = a(0 - h)^2 + k = ah^2 + k$. So c is the y-intercept.

These properties can be generalized to help you graph quadratic functions.

Know it! Note

Properties of a Parabola

For $f(x) = ax^2 + bx + c$, where a, b, and c are real numbers and $a \neq 0$, the parabola has these properties:

The parabola **opens** upward if $a > 0$ and downward if $a < 0$.

The **axis of symmetry** is the vertical line $x = -\frac{b}{2a}$.

The **vertex** is the point $\left(-\frac{b}{2a}, f\left(-\frac{b}{2a}\right)\right)$.

The **y-intercept** is c.

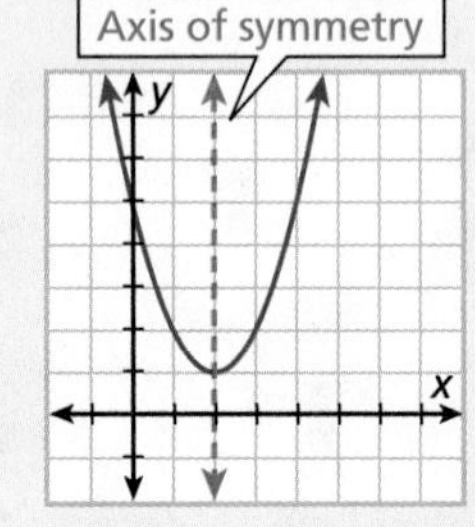

EXAMPLE 2 Graphing Quadratic Functions in Standard Form

A **Consider the function $f(x) = x^2 - 4x + 6$.**

a. Determine whether the graph opens upward or downward.

Because a is positive, the parabola opens upward.

b. Find the axis of symmetry.

The axis of symmetry is given by $x = -\frac{b}{2a}$.

$x = -\frac{(-4)}{2(1)} = 2$ *Substitute −4 for b and 1 for a.*

The axis of symmetry is the line $x = 2$.

c. Find the vertex.

The vertex lies on the axis of symmetry, so the x-coordinate is 2. The y-coordinate is the value of the function at this x-value, or $f(2)$.

$$f(2) = (2)^2 - 4(2) + 6 = 2$$

The vertex is $(2, 2)$.

d. Find the y-intercept.

Because $c = 6$, the y-intercept is 6.

e. Graph the function.

Graph by sketching the axis of symmetry and then plotting the vertex and the intercept point, $(0, 6)$. Use the axis of symmetry to find another point on the parabola. Notice that $(0, 6)$ is 2 units left of the axis of symmetry. The point on the parabola symmetrical to $(0, 6)$ is 2 units right of the axis at $(4, 6)$.

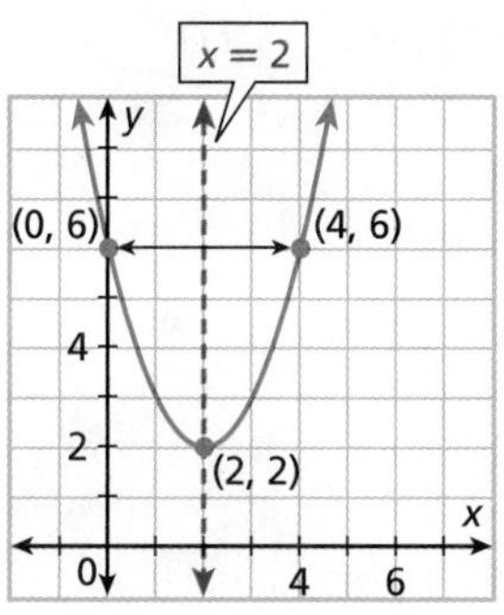

B **Consider the function $f(x) = -4x^2 - 12x - 3$.**

a. Determine whether the graph opens upward or downward.

Because a is negative, the parabola opens downward.

Helpful Hint

When a is positive, the parabola is happy (∪). When a is negative, the parabola is sad (∩).

b. Find the axis of symmetry.

The axis of symmetry is given by $x = -\frac{b}{2a}$.

$$x = -\frac{(-12)}{2(-4)} = -\frac{3}{2} \quad \textit{Substitute } -12 \textit{ for b and } -4 \textit{ for a.}$$

The axis of symmetry is the line $x = -\frac{3}{2}$, or $x = -1.5$.

c. Find the vertex.

The vertex lies on the axis of symmetry, so the x-coordinate is -1.5. The y-coordinate is the value of the function at this x-value, or $f(-1.5)$.

$$f(-1.5) = -4(-1.5)^2 - 12(-1.5) - 3 = 6$$

The vertex is $(-1.5, 6)$.

d. Find the y-intercept.

Because $c = -3$, the y-intercept is -3.

e. Graph the function.

Graph by sketching the axis of symmetry and then plotting the vertex and the intercept point, $(0, -3)$. Use the axis of symmetry to find another point on the parabola. Notice that $(0, -3)$ is 1.5 units right of the axis of symmetry. The point on the parabola symmetrical to $(0, -3)$ is 1.5 units left of the axis at $(-3, -3)$.

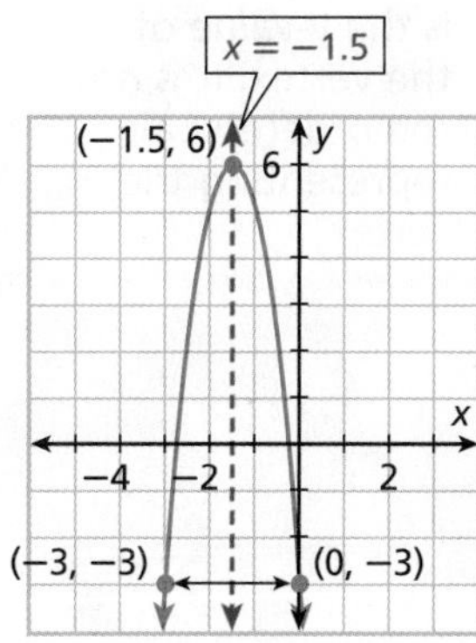

CHECK IT OUT! **For each function, (a) determine whether the graph opens upward or downward, (b) find the axis of symmetry, (c) find the vertex, (d) find the y-intercept, and (e) graph the function.**

2a. $f(x) = -2x^2 - 4x$ **2b.** $g(x) = x^2 + 3x - 1$

Substituting any real value of x into a quadratic equation results in a real number. Therefore, the domain of any quadratic function is all real numbers, $\mathbb{R}$. The range of a quadratic function depends on its vertex and the direction that the parabola opens.

Minimum and Maximum Values

OPENS UPWARD	OPENS DOWNWARD
When a parabola opens upward, the y-value of the vertex is the **minimum value**.	When a parabola opens downward, the y-value of the vertex is the **maximum value**.
D: $\{x \mid x \in \mathbb{R}\}$ R: $\{y \mid y \geq k\}$ (h, k)	D: $\{x \mid x \in \mathbb{R}\}$ R: $\{y \mid y \leq k\}$ 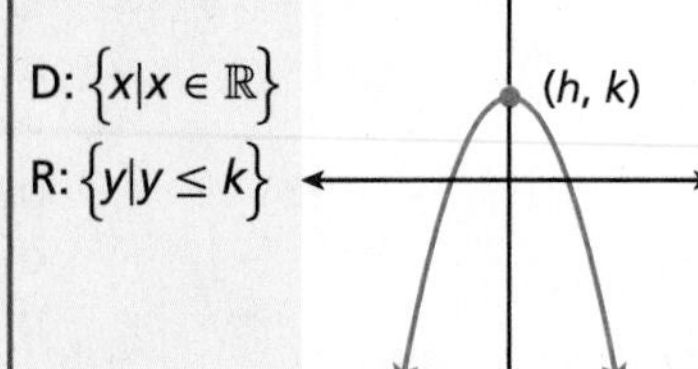
The domain is all real numbers, $\mathbb{R}$. The range is all values greater than or equal to the minimum.	The domain is all real numbers, $\mathbb{R}$. The range is all values less than or equal to the maximum.

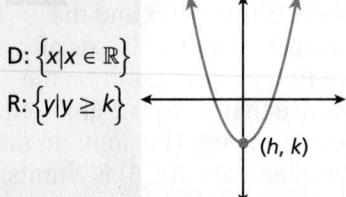

EXAMPLE 3 Finding Minimum or Maximum Values

Find the minimum or maximum value of $f(x) = 2x^2 - 2x + 5$. Then state the domain and range of the function.

Step 1 Determine whether the function has a minimum or maximum value. Because a is positive, the graph opens upward and has a minimum value.

Step 2 Find the x-value of the vertex.

$$x = -\frac{b}{2a} = -\frac{(-2)}{2(2)} = \frac{2}{4} = \frac{1}{2}$$ *Substitute −2 for b and 2 for a.*

Step 3 Then find the y-value of the vertex, $f\left(-\frac{b}{2a}\right)$.

$$f\left(\frac{1}{2}\right) = 2\left(\frac{1}{2}\right)^2 - 2\left(\frac{1}{2}\right) + 5 = 4\frac{1}{2}$$

The minimum value is $4\frac{1}{2}$, or 4.5. The domain is all real numbers, $\mathbb{R}$. The range is all real numbers greater than or equal to 4.5, or $\{y \mid y \geq 4.5\}$.

Check Graph $f(x) = 2x^2 - 2x + 5$ on a graphing calculator. The graph and table support the answer.

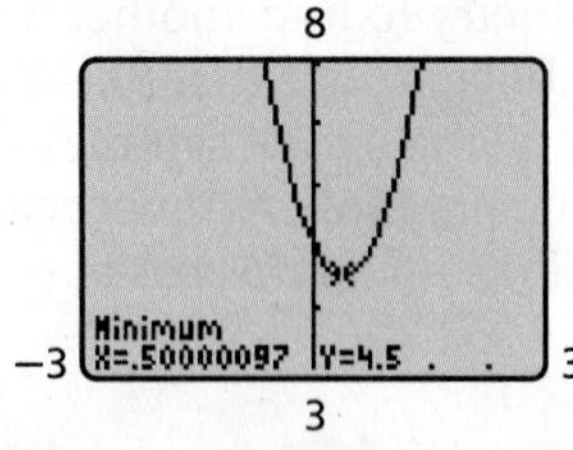

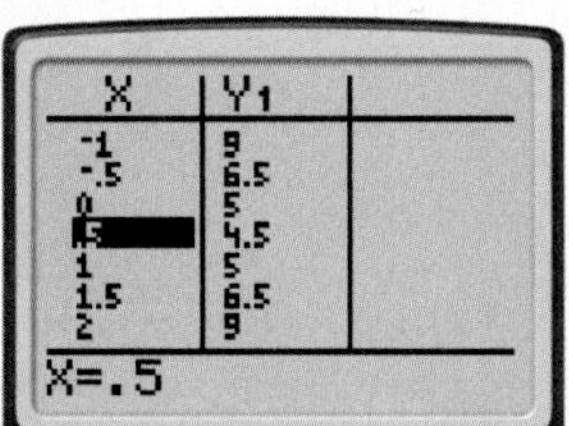

Caution!

The minimum (or maximum) value is the *y-value* of the vertex. It is *not* the ordered pair representing the vertex.

Find the minimum or maximum value of each function. Then state the domain and range of the function.

3a. $f(x) = x^2 - 6x + 3$ **3b.** $g(x) = -2x^2 - 4$

EXAMPLE 4 Transportation Application

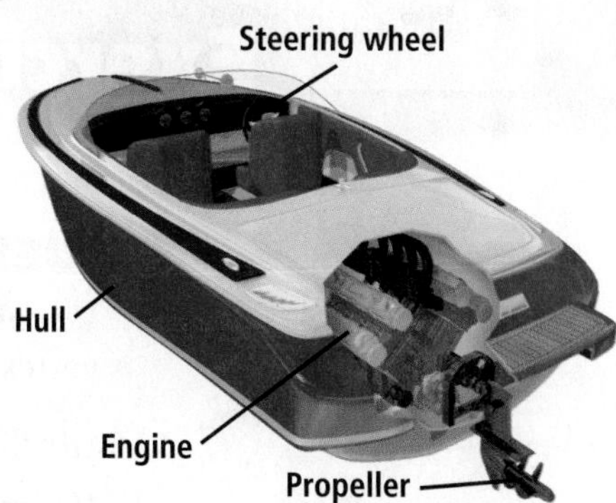

The power p in horsepower (hp) generated by a high-performance speedboat engine operating at r revolutions per minute (rpm) can be modeled by the function $p(r) = -0.0000147r^2 + 0.18r - 251$. What is the maximum power of this engine to the nearest horsepower? At how many revolutions per minute must the engine be operating to achieve this power?

The maximum value will be at the vertex $(r, p(r))$.

Step 1 Find the r-value of the vertex using $a = -0.0000147$ and $b = 0.18$.

$$r = -\frac{b}{2a} = -\frac{0.18}{2(-0.0000147)} \approx 6122$$

Step 2 Substitute this r-value into p to find the corresponding maximum, $p(r)$.

$$p(r) = -0.0000147r^2 + 0.18r - 251$$

$$p(6122) = -0.0000147(6122)^2 + 0.18(6122) - 251$$ *Substitute 6122 for r.*

$$p(6122) \approx 300$$ *Use a calculator.*

The maximum power is about 300 hp at 6122 rpm.

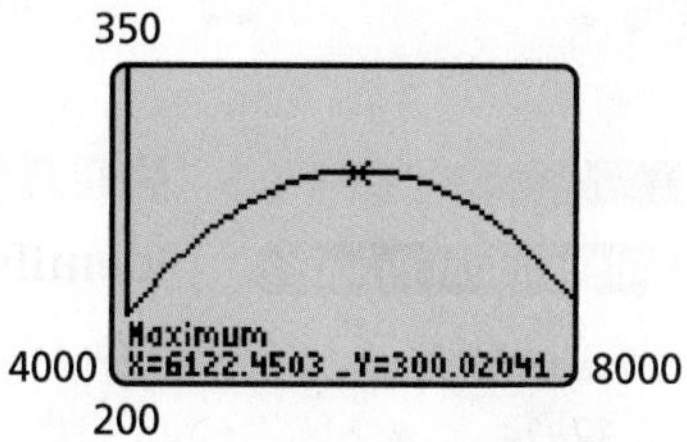

Check Graph the function on a graphing calculator. Use the **maximum** feature under the **CALCULATE** menu to approximate the maximum. The graph supports your answer.

4. The highway mileage m in miles per gallon for a compact car is approximated by $m(s) = -0.025s^2 + 2.45s - 30$, where s is the speed in miles per hour. What is the maximum mileage for this compact car to the nearest tenth of a mile per gallon? What speed results in this mileage?

THINK AND DISCUSS

1. Explain whether a quadratic function can have both a maximum value and a minimum value.

2. Explain why the value of $f(x) = x^2 + 2x - 1$ increases as the value of x decreases from -1 to -10.

3. **GET ORGANIZED** Copy and complete the graphic organizer. In each box, write the criteria or equation to find each property of the parabola for $f(x) = ax^2 + bx + c$.

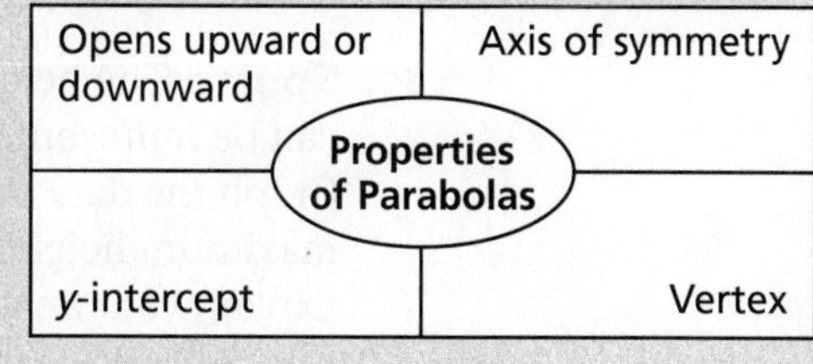

5-2 Exercises

go.hrw.com
Homework Help Online
KEYWORD: MB7 5-2
Parent Resources Online
KEYWORD: MB7 Parent

GUIDED PRACTICE

1. **Vocabulary** If the graph of a quadratic function opens upward, the y-value of the vertex is a __?__ value. (*maximum* or *minimum*)

SEE EXAMPLE 1 p. 323

Identify the axis of symmetry for the graph of each function.

2. $f(x) = -2(x-2)^2 - 4$ 3. $g(x) = 3x^2 + 4$ 4. $h(x) = (x+5)^2$

SEE EXAMPLE 2 p. 324

For each function, (a) determine whether the graph opens upward or downward, (b) find the axis of symmetry, (c) find the vertex, (d) find the y-intercept, and (e) graph the function.

5. $f(x) = -x^2 - 2x - 8$ 6. $g(x) = x^2 - 3x + 2$ 7. $h(x) = 4x - x^2 - 1$

SEE EXAMPLE 3 p. 326

Find the minimum or maximum value of each function. Then state the domain and range of the function.

8. $f(x) = x^2 - 1$ 9. $g(x) = -x^2 + 3x - 2$ 10. $h(x) = -16x^2 + 32x + 4$

SEE EXAMPLE 4 p. 327

11. **Sports** The path of a soccer ball is modeled by the function $h(x) = -0.005x^2 + 0.25x$, where h is the height in meters and x is the horizontal distance that the ball travels in meters. What is the maximum height that the ball reaches?

PRACTICE AND PROBLEM SOLVING

Independent Practice

For Exercises	See Example
12–14	1
15–23	2
24–29	3
30	4

Extra Practice
Skills Practice p. S12
Application Practice p. S36

Identify the axis of symmetry for the graph of each function.

12. $f(x) = -x^2 + 4$ 13. $g(x) = (x-1)^2$ 14. $h(x) = 2(x+1)^2 - 3$

For each function, (a) determine whether the graph opens upward or downward, (b) find the axis of symmetry, (c) find the vertex, (d) find the y-intercept, and (e) graph the function.

15. $f(x) = x^2 + x - 2$ 16. $g(x) = -3x^2 + 6x$ 17. $h(x) = 0.5x^2 - 2x - 4$
18. $f(x) = -2x^2 + 8x + 5$ 19. $g(x) = 3x^2 + 2x - 8$ 20. $h(x) = 2x - 1 + x^2$
21. $f(x) = -(2 + x^2)$ 22. $g(x) = 0.5x^2 + 3x - 5$ 23. $h(x) = \frac{1}{4}x^2 + x + 2$

Find the minimum or maximum value of each function. Then state the domain and range of the function.

24. $f(x) = -2x^2 + 7x - 3$ 25. $g(x) = 6x - x^2$ 26. $h(x) = x^2 - 4x + 3$
27. $f(x) = -\frac{1}{2}x^2 - 4$ 28. $g(x) = -x^2 - 6x + 1$ 29. $h(x) = x^2 + 8x + 16$

30. **Weather** The daily high temperature in Death Valley, California, in 2003 can be modeled by $T(d) = -0.0018d^2 + 0.657d + 50.95$, where T is temperature in degrees Fahrenheit and d is the day of the year. What was the maximum temperature in 2003 to the nearest degree?

31. **Sports** The height of a golf ball over time can be represented by a quadratic function. Graph the data in the table. What is the maximum height that the ball will reach? Explain your answer in terms of the axis of symmetry and vertex of the graph.

Golf Ball Height

Time (s)	0	0.5	1	2	3
Height (ft)	0	28	48	64	48

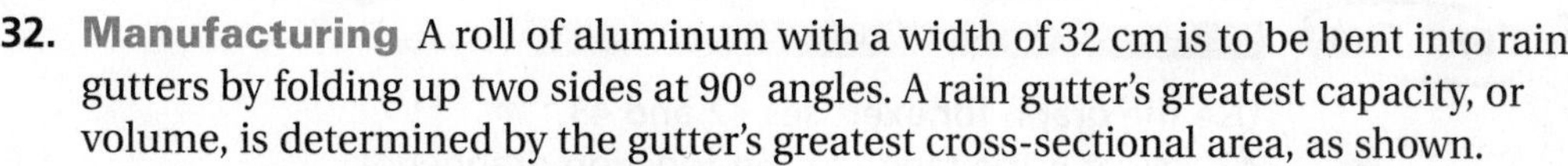

32. Manufacturing A roll of aluminum with a width of 32 cm is to be bent into rain gutters by folding up two sides at 90° angles. A rain gutter's greatest capacity, or volume, is determined by the gutter's greatest cross-sectional area, as shown.

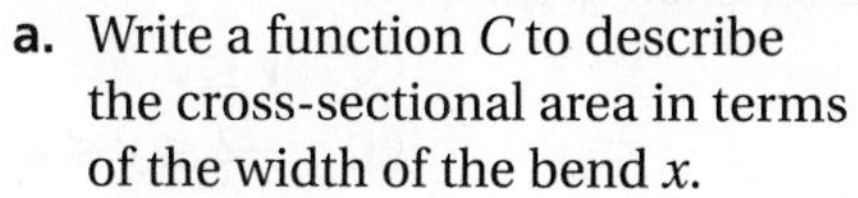

a. Write a function C to describe the cross-sectional area in terms of the width of the bend x.

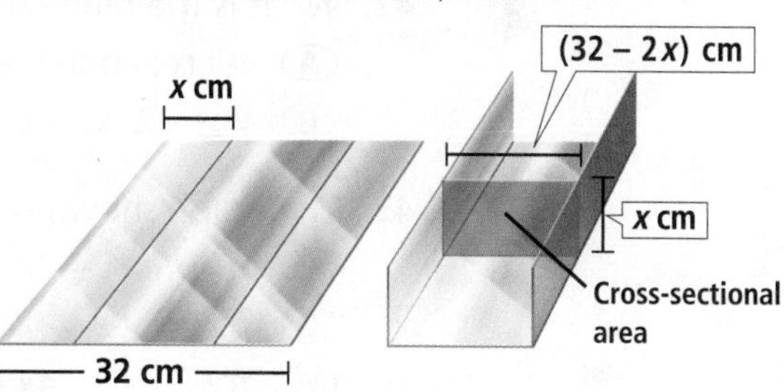

b. Make a table, and graph the function.

c. Identify the meaningful domain and range of the function.

d. Find the value of x that maximizes the cross-sectional area.

LINK Biology

Spittlebugs are insects that feed on the sap of plants. Young spittlebug larvae use sap to produce a layer of bubbles around themselves. The bubbles help to keep the larvae from drying out and may protect them from predators.

33. Biology The spittlebug is the world's highest jumping animal relative to its body length of about 6 mm. The height h of a spittlebug's jump in millimeters can be modeled by the function $h(t) = -4000t^2 + 3000t$, where t is the time in seconds.

a. What is the maximum height that the spittlebug will reach?

b. What is the ratio of a spittlebug's maximum jumping height to its body length? In the best human jumpers, this ratio is about 1.38. Compare the ratio for spittlebugs with the ratio for the best human jumpers.

c. **What if...?** Suppose humans had the same ratio of maximum jumping height to body length as spittlebugs. How high would a person with a height of 1.8 m be able to jump?

34. Gardening The function $A(x) = x(10 - x)$ describes the area A of a rectangular flower garden, where x is its width in yards. What is the maximum area of the garden?

Graphing Calculator Once you have graphed a function, the graphing calculator can automatically find the minimum or maximum value. From the **CALC** menu, choose the **minimum** or **maximum** feature.

Use a graphing calculator to find the approximate minimum or maximum value of each function.

35. $f(x) = 5.23x^2 - 4.84x - 1.91$

36. $g(x) = -12.8x^2 + 8.73x + 11.69$

37. $h(x) = \frac{1}{12}x^2 - \frac{4}{5}x + \frac{2}{3}$

38. $j(x) = -\frac{5}{3}x^2 + \frac{9}{10}x + \frac{21}{4}$

39. Critical Thinking Suppose you are given a parabola with two points that have the same y-value, such as $(-7, 11)$ and $(3, 11)$. Explain how to find the equation for the axis of symmetry of this parabola, and then determine this equation.

40. Write About It Can a maximum value for a quadratic function be negative? Can a minimum value for a quadratic function be positive? Explain by using examples.

MULTI-STEP TEST PREP

41. This problem will prepare you for the Multi-Step Test Prep on page 364.

A baseball is thrown with a vertical velocity of 50 ft/s from an initial height of 6 ft. The height h in feet of the baseball can be modeled by $h(t) = -16t^2 + 50t + 6$, where t is the time in seconds since the ball was thrown.

a. Approximately how many seconds does it take the ball to reach its maximum height?

b. What is the maximum height that the ball reaches?

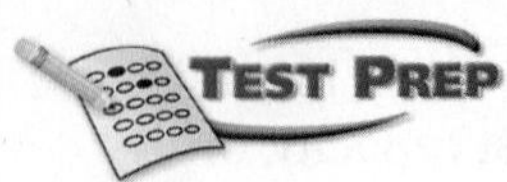

TEST PREP

Use the graph for exercises 42 and 43.

42. What is the range of the function graphed?

Ⓐ All real numbers Ⓒ $y \leq 2$

Ⓑ $y \geq -2$ Ⓓ $-2 \leq y \leq 2$

43. The graph shown represents which quadratic function?

Ⓕ $f(x) = x^2 + 2x - 2$

Ⓖ $f(x) = -x^2 + 4x - 2$

Ⓗ $f(x) = x^2 - 4x - 2$

Ⓙ $f(x) = -x^2 - 2x + 2$

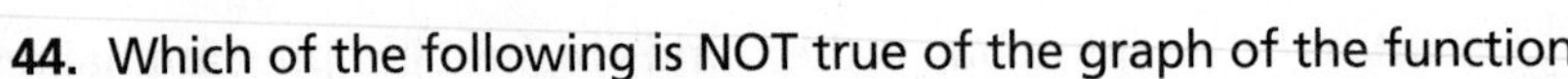

44. Which of the following is NOT true of the graph of the function $f(x) = -x^2 - 6x + 5$?

Ⓐ Its vertex is at $(-3, 14)$. Ⓒ Its maximum value is 14.

Ⓑ Its axis of symmetry is $x = 14$. Ⓓ Its y-intercept is 5.

45. Which equation represents the axis of symmetry for $f(x) = 2x^2 - 4x + 5$?

Ⓕ $x = -4$ Ⓖ $x = 1$ Ⓗ $x = 2$ Ⓙ $x = 5$

46. Short Response Explain how to find the maximum value or minimum value of a quadratic function such as $f(x) = -x^2 - 8x + 4$.

CHALLENGE AND EXTEND

47. Write the equations in standard form for two quadratic functions that have the same vertex but open in different directions.

48. The graph of a quadratic function passes through the point $(-5, 8)$, and its axis of symmetry is $x = 3$.

a. What are the coordinates of another point on the graph of the function? Explain how you determined your answer.

b. Can you determine whether the graph of the function opens upward or downward? Explain.

49. Critical Thinking What conclusions can you make about the axis of symmetry and the vertex of a quadratic function of the form $f(x) = ax^2 + c$?

50. Critical Thinking Given the quadratic function f and the fact that $f(-1) = f(2)$, how can you find the axis of symmetry of this function?

SPIRAL REVIEW

Simplify each expression. *(Lesson 1-3)*

51. $\sqrt{40} \cdot \sqrt{180}$ **52.** $2\sqrt{8} \cdot 4\sqrt{3}$ **53.** $\sqrt{54} \div \sqrt{30}$ **54.** $\sqrt{304}$

For each function, evaluate $f(0)$, $f\left(\frac{1}{2}\right)$, and $f(-2)$. *(Lesson 1-7)*

55. $f(x) = (x - 3)^2 + 1$ **56.** $g(x) = 2\left(x - \frac{1}{2}\right)^2$

57. $f(x) = -4(x + 5)$ **58.** $g(x) = x^3 - 4x + 8$

Write the equation of each line with the given properties. *(Lesson 2-4)*

59. a slope of 3 passing through $(1, -4)$ **60.** passing through $(-3, 5)$ and $(-1, -7)$

61. a slope of -2 passing through $(3, 5)$ **62.** passing through $(4, 6)$ and $(-2, 1)$

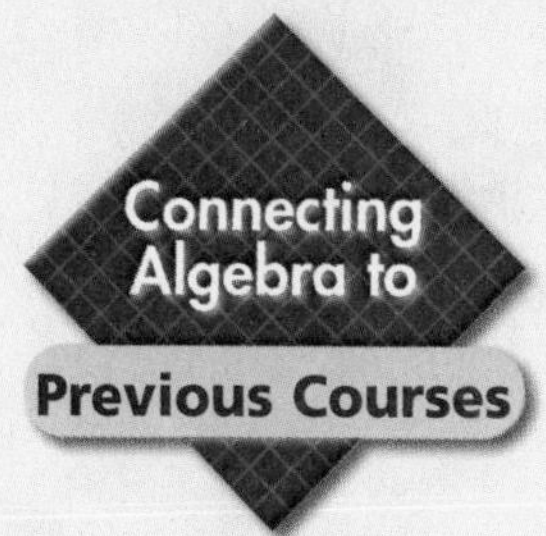

Factoring Quadratic Expressions

Review the methods of factoring quadratic expressions in the examples below. Recall that the standard form of a quadratic expression is $ax^2 + bx + c$.

Examples

Factor each expression.

1 $x^2 - 3x - 10$

Because $a = 1$, use a table to find the factors of -10 that have a sum of -3. These factors are 2 and -5.

Factors of -10	Sum
-2 and 5	3 ✗
-1 and 10	9 ✗
1 and -10	-9 ✗
2 and -5	-3 ✓

Rewrite the expression as a product of binomial factors with 2 and -5 as constants.

$$x^2 - 3x - 10 = (x + 2)(x - 5)$$

Check your answer by multiplying.

$$(x + 2)(x - 5) = x^2 - 5x + 2x - 10$$
$$= x^2 - 3x - 10 \checkmark$$

2 $6x^2 - 15x$

Find the greatest common factor (GCF) of the terms.

$$6x^2 = 2 \cdot 3 \cdot x \cdot x$$
$$15x = 3 \cdot 5 \cdot x$$ *The GCF is 3x.*

Factor $3x$ from both terms.

$$6x^2 - 15x = 3x(2x - 5)$$

Check your answer by multiplying.

$$3x(2x - 5) = 3x(2x) - 3x(5)$$
$$= 6x^2 - 15x \checkmark$$

3 $-x^2 + 3x + 4$

Because a is negative, factor out -1.

$$-x^2 + 3x + 4 = -1(x^2 - 3x - 4)$$

Use the method from Example 1 to factor the expression in parentheses.

$$-(x^2 - 3x - 4) = -(x + 1)(x - 4)$$

Check your answer by multiplying.

$$-(x + 1)(x - 4) = -(x^2 - 3x - 4)$$
$$= -x^2 + 3x + 4 \checkmark$$

Try This

Factor each expression.

1. $4x^2 + 10x$
2. $16x - 2x^2$
3. $x^2 - 6x + 8$
4. $x^2 + 4x + 3$
5. $x^2 - 8x + 15$
6. $x^2 + 10x - 24$
7. $x^2 - x - 56$
8. $x^2 - 6x + 9$
9. $x^2 + 48x - 100$
10. $-x^2 + 12x - 32$
11. $-x^2 + x + 20$
12. $-x^2 - 14x - 13$
13. $4x^2 + 6x$
14. $x^2 + 14x + 24$
15. $x^2 - 16$
16. $2x^2 - x - 3$
17. $3x^2 + 16x + 5$
18. $2x^2 - 9x + 7$

5-3 Technology LAB

Explore Graphs and Factors

You can use graphs and linear factors to find the x-intercepts of a parabola.

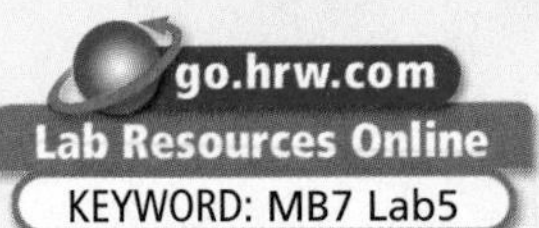

Activity

Graph the lines $y = x + 4$ and $y = x - 2$.

1. Press **Y=**, and enter **X + 4** for **Y1** and **X − 2** for **Y2**. Graph the functions in the square window by pressing **ZOOM** and choosing **5 : ZSquare**.
2. Identify the x-intercept of each line. The x-intercepts are -4 and 2.
3. Find the x-value halfway between the two x-intercepts. This x-value is the average of the x-intercepts: $\frac{-4+2}{2} = -1$.

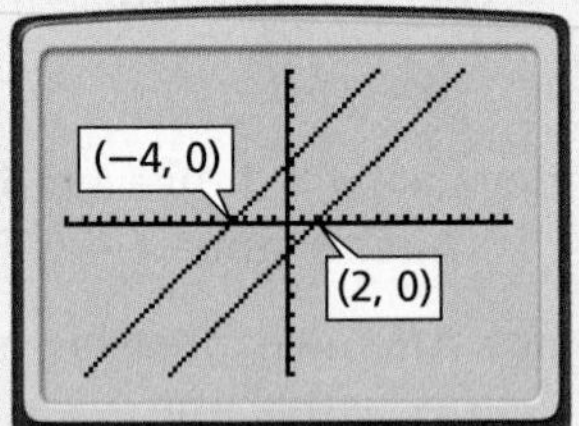

Graph the quadratic function $y = (x + 4)(x - 2)$, which is the product of the two linear factors graphed above.

4. Press **Y=** and enter **(X + 4)(X − 2)** for **Y3**. Press **GRAPH**.
5. Identify the x-intercepts of the parabola. The x-intercepts are -4 and 2. Notice that they are the same as those of the two linear factors.
6. Examine the parabola at $x = -1$ (the x-value that is halfway between the x-intercepts). The axis of symmetry and the vertex of the parabola occur at this x-value.

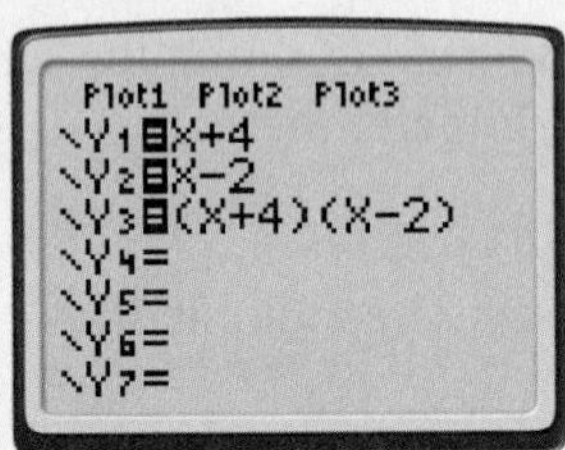

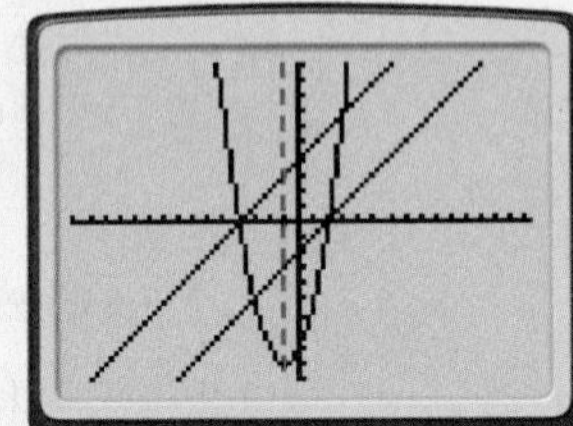

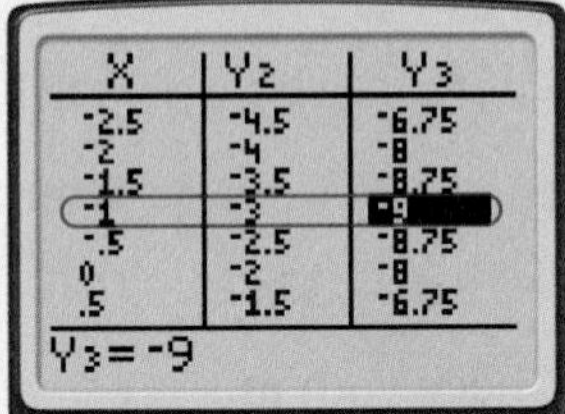

X	Y2	Y3
-2.5	-4.5	-6.75
-2	-4	-8
-1.5	-3.5	-8.75
-1	-3	-9
-.5	-2.5	-8.75
0	-2	-8
.5	-1.5	-6.75

Y3=-9

Try This

Graph each quadratic function and each of its linear factors. Then identify the x-intercepts and the axis of symmetry of each parabola.

1. $y = (x - 2)(x - 6)$
2. $y = (x + 3)(x - 1)$
3. $y = (x - 5)(x + 2)$
4. $y = (x + 4)(x - 4)$
5. $y = (x - 5)(x - 5)$
6. $y = (2x - 1)(2x + 3)$
7. **Critical Thinking** Use a graph to determine whether the quadratic function $y = 2x^2 + 5x - 12$ is the product of the linear factors $2x - 3$ and $x + 4$.
8. **Make a Conjecture** Make a conjecture about the linear factors, x-intercepts, and axis of symmetry of a quadratic function.

5-3 Solving Quadratic Equations by Graphing and Factoring

Objectives

Solve quadratic equations by graphing or factoring.

Determine a quadratic function from its roots.

Vocabulary

zero of a function
root of an equation
binomial
trinomial

Why learn this?

You can use quadratic functions to model the height of a football, baseball, or soccer ball. (See Example 3.)

When a soccer ball is kicked into the air, how long will the ball take to hit the ground? The height h in feet of the ball after t seconds can be modeled by the quadratic function $h(t) = -16t^2 + 32t$. In this situation, the value of the function represents the height of the soccer ball. When the ball hits the ground, the value of the function is zero.

A **zero of a function** is a value of the input x that makes the output $f(x)$ equal zero. The zeros of a function are the x-intercepts.

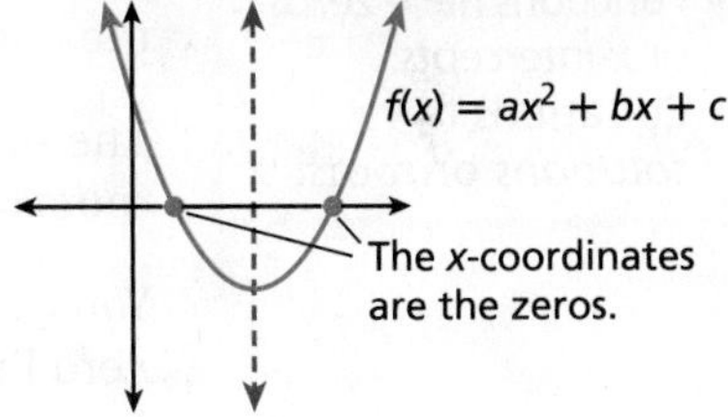

Unlike linear functions, which have no more than one zero, quadratic functions can have two zeros, as shown at right. These zeros are always symmetric about the axis of symmetry.

EXAMPLE 1 **Finding Zeros by Using a Graph or Table**

Find the zeros of $f(x) = x^2 + 2x - 3$ by using a graph and table.

Method 1 Graph the function $f(x) = x^2 + 2x - 3$.

The graph opens upward because $a > 0$. The y-intercept is -3 because $c = -3$.

Find the vertex: $x = -\frac{b}{2a} = -\frac{2}{2(1)} = -1$ *The x-coordinate of the vertex is $-\frac{b}{2a}$.*

Find $f(-1)$: $f(x) = x^2 + 2x - 3$

$f(-1) = (-1)^2 + 2(-1) - 3$ *Substitute -1 for x.*

$f(-1) = -4$

The vertex is $(-1, -4)$.

Helpful Hint

Recall that for the graph of a quadratic function, *any* pair of points with the same y-value are symmetric about the axis of symmetry.

Plot the vertex and the y-intercept. Use symmetry and a table of values to find additional points.

x	-3	-2	-1	0	1
$f(x)$	0	-3	-4	-3	0

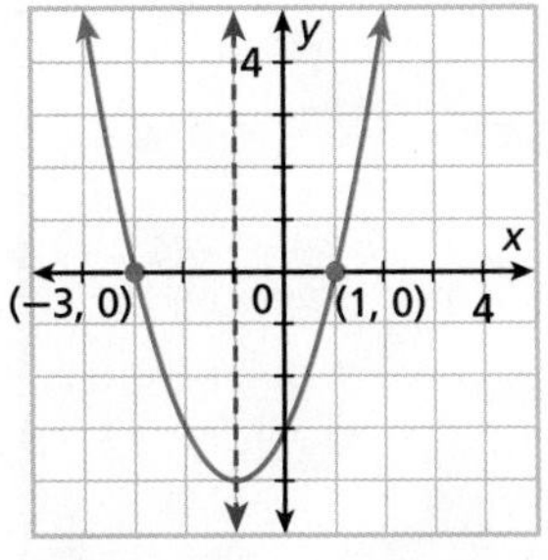

The table and the graph indicate that the zeros are -3 and 1.

Find the zeros of $f(x) = x^2 + 2x - 3$ by using a graph and table.

Method 2 Use a calculator.

Enter $y = x^2 + 2x - 3$ into a graphing calculator.

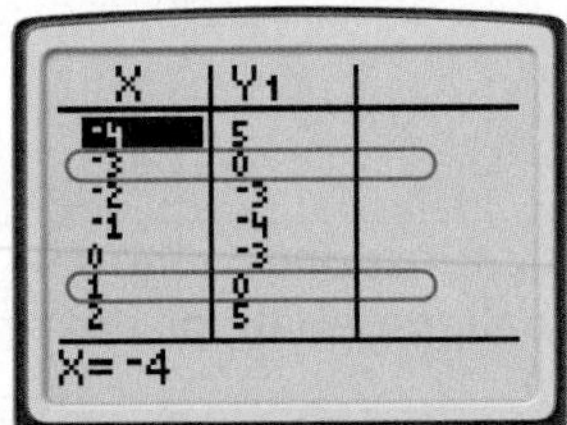
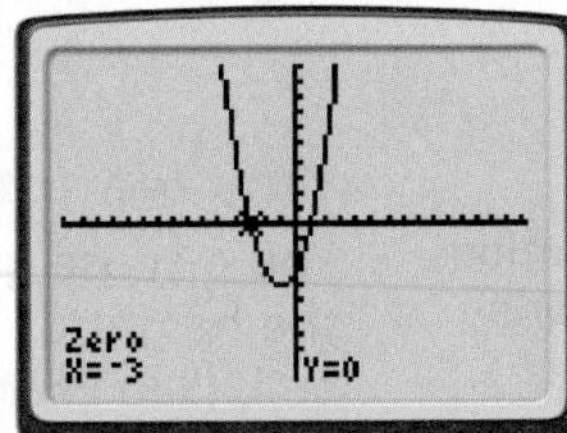

Both the table and the graph show that $y = 0$ at $x = -3$ and $x = 1$. These are the zeros of the function.

1. Find the zeros of $g(x) = -x^2 - 2x + 3$ by using a graph and a table.

Reading Math

- Functions have *zeros* or *x-intercepts*.
- Equations have *solutions* or *roots*.

You can also find zeros by using algebra. For example, to find the zeros of $f(x) = x^2 + 2x - 3$, you can set the function equal to zero. The solutions to the related equation $x^2 + 2x - 3 = 0$ represent the zeros of the function.

The solutions to a quadratic equation of the form $ax^2 + bx + c = 0$ are *roots*. The **roots of an equation** are the values of the variable that make the equation true.

You can find the roots of some quadratic equations by factoring and applying the Zero Product Property.

Know it! Note

Zero Product Property

For all real numbers *a* and *b*,

WORDS	NUMBERS	ALGEBRA
If the product of two quantities equals zero, at least one of the quantities equals zero.	$3(0) = 0$ $0(4) = 0$	If $ab = 0$, then $a = 0$ or $b = 0$.

EXAMPLE 2 **Finding Zeros by Factoring**

Find the zeros of each function by factoring.

A $f(x) = x^2 - 8x + 12$

$x^2 - 8x + 12 = 0$ *Set the function equal to 0.*

$(x - 2)(x - 6) = 0$ *Factor: Find factors of 12 that add to −8.*

$x - 2 = 0$ or $x - 6 = 0$ *Apply the Zero Product Property.*

$x = 2$ or $x = 6$ *Solve each equation.*

Check

$x^2 - 8x + 12 = 0$	
$(2)^2 - 8(2) + 12$	0
$4 - 16 + 12$	0
0	0 ✓

$x^2 - 8x + 12 = 0$	
$(6)^2 - 8(6) + 12$	0
$36 - 48 + 12$	0
0	0 ✓

Substitute each value into the original equation.

Find the zeros of each function by factoring.

B $g(x) = 3x^2 + 12x$

$3x^2 + 12x = 0$ *Set the function equal to 0.*

$3x(x + 4) = 0$ *Factor: The GCF is 3x.*

$3x = 0$ or $x + 4 = 0$ *Apply the Zero Product Property.*

$x = 0$ or $x = -4$ *Solve each equation.*

Check Check algebraically and by graphing.

$$\begin{array}{r|l} 3x^2 + 12x & = 0 \\ \hline 3(0)^2 + 12(0) & 0 \\ 0 + 0 & 0 \checkmark \end{array} \qquad \begin{array}{r|l} 3x^2 + 12x & = 0 \\ \hline 3(-4)^2 + 12(-4) & 0 \\ 48 - 48 & 0 \checkmark \end{array}$$

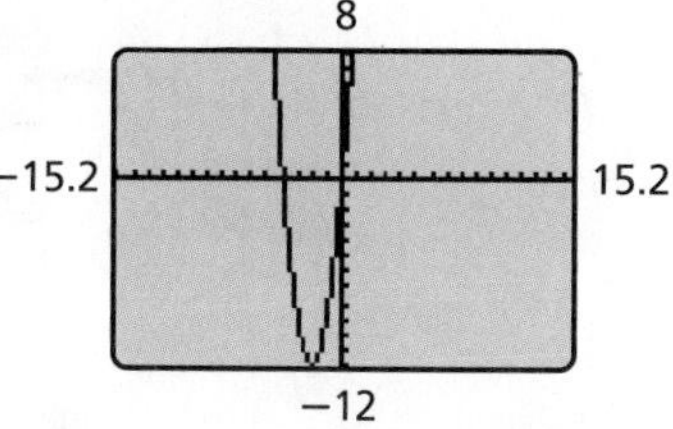

Find the zeros of each function by factoring.

2a. $f(x) = x^2 - 5x - 6$ **2b.** $g(x) = x^2 - 8x$

Any object that is thrown or launched into the air, such as a baseball, basketball, or soccer ball, is a *projectile*. The general function that approximates the height h in feet of a projectile on Earth after t seconds is given below.

$$h(t) = -16t^2 + v_0 t + h_0$$

Constant due to Earth's gravity in ft/s^2 (points to -16)

Initial vertical velocity in ft/s (at $t = 0$) (points to v_0)

Initial height in ft (at $t = 0$) (points to h_0)

Note that this model has limitations because it does not account for air resistance, wind, and other real-world factors.

EXAMPLE 3 *Sports Application*

A soccer ball is kicked from ground level with an initial vertical velocity of 32 ft/s. After how many seconds will the ball hit the ground?

$h(t) = -16t^2 + v_0 t + h_0$ *Write the general projectile function.*

$h(t) = -16t^2 + 32t + 0$ *Substitute 32 for v_0 and 0 for h_0.*

The ball will hit the ground when its height is zero.

$-16t^2 + 32t = 0$ *Set $h(t)$ equal to 0.*

$-16t(t - 2) = 0$ *Factor: The GCF is $-16t$.*

$-16t = 0$ or $(t - 2) = 0$ *Apply the Zero Product Property.*

$t = 0$ or $t = 2$ *Solve each equation.*

The ball will hit the ground in 2 seconds. Notice that the height is also zero when $t = 0$, the instant that the ball is kicked.

Check The graph of the function $h(t) = -16t^2 + 32t$ shows its zeros at 0 and 2.

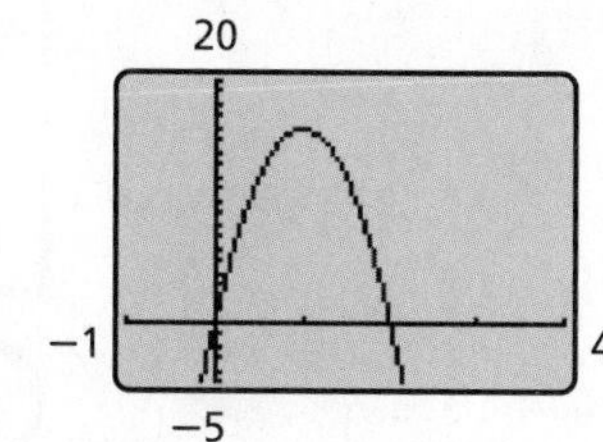

3. A football is kicked from ground level with an initial vertical velocity of 48 ft/s. How long is the ball in the air?

Quadratic expressions can have one, two, or three terms, such as $-16t^2$, $-16t^2 + 25t$, or $-16t^2 + 25t + 6$. Quadratic expressions with two terms are **binomials**. Quadratic expressions with three terms are **trinomials**. Some quadratic expressions with perfect squares have special factoring rules.

Special Products and Factors

Difference of Two Squares	Perfect-Square Trinomial
$a^2 - b^2 = (a + b)(a - b)$	$a^2 - 2ab + b^2 = (a - b)^2$ $a^2 + 2ab + b^2 = (a + b)^2$

EXAMPLE 4 Finding Roots by Using Special Factors

Find the roots of each equation by factoring.

A $9x^2 = 1$

$9x^2 - 1 = 0$ *Rewrite in standard form.*

$(3x)^2 - (1)^2 = 0$ *Write the left side as $a^2 - b^2$.*

$(3x + 1)(3x - 1) = 0$ *Factor the difference of squares.*

$3x + 1 = 0$ or $3x - 1 = 0$ *Apply the Zero Product Property.*

$x = -\frac{1}{3}$ or $x = \frac{1}{3}$ *Solve each equation.*

Check Graph each side of the equation on a graphing calculator. Let **Y1** equal $9x^2$, and let **Y2** equal 1. The graphs appear to intersect at $x = -\frac{1}{3}$ and at $x = \frac{1}{3}$.

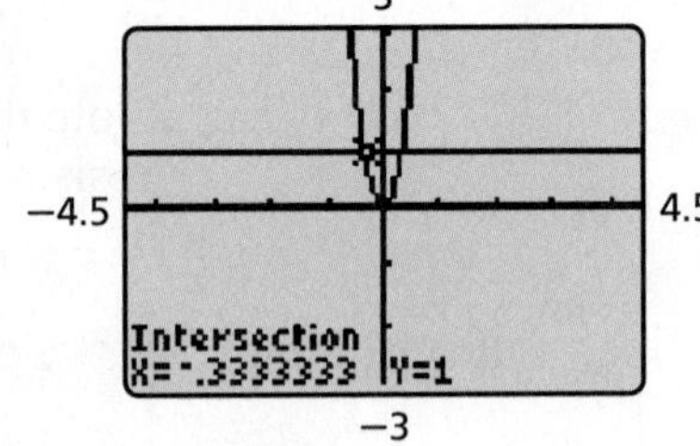

B $40x = 8x^2 + 50$

$8x^2 - 40x + 50 = 0$ *Rewrite in standard form.*

$2(4x^2 - 20x + 25) = 0$ *Factor. The GCF is 2.*

$4x^2 - 20x + 25 = 0$ *Divide both sides by 2.*

$(2x)^2 - 2(2x)(5) + (5)^2 = 0$ *Write the left side as $a^2 - 2ab + b^2$.*

$(2x - 5)^2 = 0$ *Factor the perfect-square trinomial: $(a - b)^2$.*

$2x - 5 = 0$ or $2x - 5 = 0$ *Apply the Zero Product Property.*

$x = \frac{5}{2}$ or $x = \frac{5}{2}$ *Solve each equation.*

Check Substitute the root $\frac{5}{2}$ into the original equation.

$40x$	$= 8x^2 + 50$
$40\left(\frac{5}{2}\right)$	$8\left(\frac{5}{2}\right)^2 + 50$
100	100 ✓

Helpful Hint

A quadratic equation can have two roots that are equal, such as $x = \frac{5}{2}$ and $x = \frac{5}{2}$. Two equal roots are sometimes called a double root.

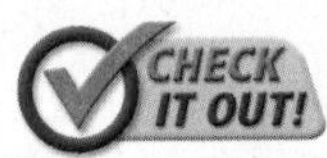

Find the roots of each equation by factoring.

4a. $x^2 - 4x = -4$

4b. $25x^2 = 9$

If you know the zeros of a function, you can work backward to write a rule for the function.

EXAMPLE 5 Using Zeros to Write Function Rules

Write a quadratic function in standard form with zeros 2 and −1.

$x = 2$ or $x = -1$	*Write the zeros as solutions for two equations.*
$x - 2 = 0$ or $x + 1 = 0$	*Rewrite each equation so that it equals 0.*
$(x - 2)(x + 1) = 0$	*Apply the converse of the Zero Product Property to write a product that equals 0.*
$x^2 - x - 2 = 0$	*Multiply the binomials.*
$f(x) = x^2 - x - 2$	*Replace 0 with f(x).*

Check Graph the function $f(x) = x^2 - x - 2$ on a calculator. The graph shows the original zeros of 2 and −1.

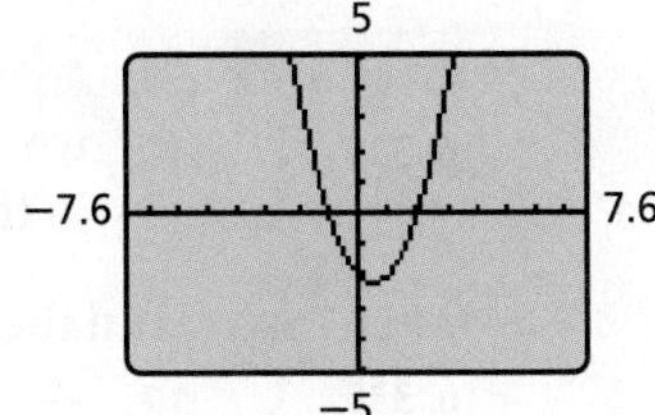

5. Write a quadratic function in standard form with zeros 5 and −5.

Note that there are many quadratic functions with the same zeros. For example, the functions $f(x) = x^2 - x - 2$, $g(x) = -x^2 + x + 2$, and $h(x) = 2x^2 - 2x - 4$ all have zeros at 2 and −1.

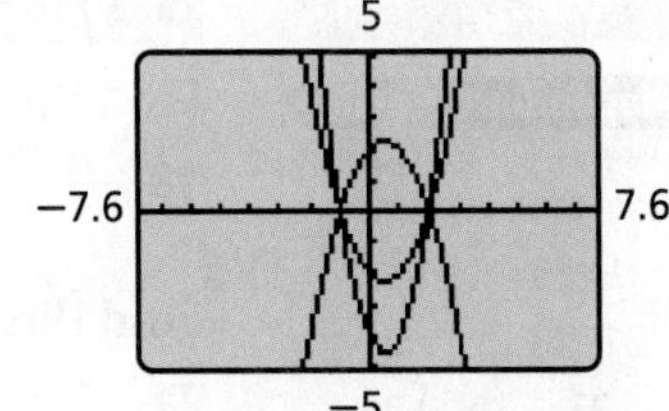

THINK AND DISCUSS

1. Describe the zeros of a function whose terms form a perfect square trinomial.

2. Compare the x- and y-intercepts of a quadratic function with those of a linear function.

3. A quadratic equation has no real solutions. Describe the graph of the related quadratic function.

4. GET ORGANIZED Copy and complete the graphic organizer. In each box, give information about special products and factors.

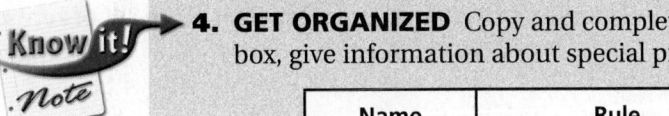

Name	Rule	Example	Graph
Difference of Two Squares			
Perfect-Square Trinomial			

5-3 Exercises

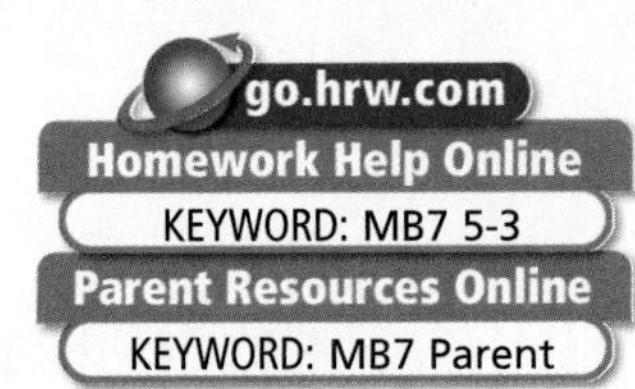

GUIDED PRACTICE

1. **Vocabulary** The solutions of the equation $3x^2 + 2x + 5 = 0$ are its __?__ . (*roots* or *zeros*)

SEE EXAMPLE 1 p. 333

Find the zeros of each function by using a graph and table.

2. $f(x) = x^2 + 4x - 5$
3. $g(x) = -x^2 + 6x - 8$
4. $f(x) = x^2 - 1$

SEE EXAMPLE 2 p. 334

Find the zeros of each function by factoring.

5. $f(x) = x^2 - 7x + 6$
6. $g(x) = 2x^2 - 5x + 2$
7. $h(x) = x^2 + 4x$
8. $f(x) = x^2 + 9x + 20$
9. $g(x) = x^2 - 6x - 16$
10. $h(x) = 3x^2 + 13x + 4$

SEE EXAMPLE 3 p. 335

11. **Archery** The height h of an arrow in feet is modeled by $h(t) = -16t^2 + 63t + 4$, where t is the time in seconds since the arrow was shot. How long is the arrow in the air?

SEE EXAMPLE 4 p. 336

Find the roots of each equation by factoring.

12. $x^2 - 6x = -9$
13. $5x^2 + 20 = 20x$
14. $x^2 = 49$

SEE EXAMPLE 5 p. 337

Write a quadratic function in standard form for each given set of zeros.

15. 3 and 4
16. -4 and -4
17. 3 and 0

PRACTICE AND PROBLEM SOLVING

Independent Practice

For Exercises	See Example
18–20	1
21–26	2
27	3
28–33	4
34–36	5

Extra Practice

Skills Practice p. S12
Application Practice p. S36

Find the zeros of each function by using a graph and table.

18. $f(x) = -x^2 + 4x - 3$
19. $g(x) = x^2 + x - 6$
20. $f(x) = x^2 - 9$

Find the zeros of each function by factoring.

21. $f(x) = x^2 + 11x + 24$
22. $g(x) = 2x^2 + x - 10$
23. $h(x) = -x^2 + 9x$
24. $f(x) = x^2 - 15x + 54$
25. $g(x) = x^2 + 7x - 8$
26. $h(x) = 2x^2 - 12x + 18$
27. **Biology** A bald eagle snatches a fish from a lake and flies to an altitude of 256 ft. The fish manages to squirm free and falls back down into the lake. Its height h in feet can be modeled by $h(t) = 256 - 16t^2$, where t is the time in seconds. How many seconds will the fish fall before hitting the water?

Find the roots of each equation by factoring.

28. $x^2 + 8x = -16$
29. $4x^2 = 81$
30. $9x^2 + 12x + 4 = 0$
31. $36x^2 - 9 = 0$
32. $x^2 - 10x + 25 = 0$
33. $49x^2 = 28x - 4$

Write a quadratic function in standard form for each given set of zeros.

34. 5 and -1
35. 6 and 2
36. 3 and 3

Find the zeros of each function.

37. $f(x) = 6x - x^2$
38. $g(x) = x^2 - 25$
39. $h(x) = x^2 - 12x + 36$
40. $f(x) = 3x^2 - 12$
41. $g(x) = x^2 - 22x + 121$
42. $h(x) = 30 + x - x^2$
43. $f(x) = x^2 - 11x + 30$
44. $g(x) = x^2 - 8x - 20$
45. $h(x) = 2x^2 + 18x + 28$

46. **Movies** A stuntwoman jumps from a building 73 ft high and lands on an air bag that is 9 ft tall. Her height above ground h in feet can be modeled by $h(t) = 73 - 16t^2$, where t is the time in seconds.

a. **Multi-Step** How many seconds will the stuntwoman fall before touching the air bag? (*Hint:* Find the time t when the stuntwoman's height above ground is 9 ft.)

b. **What if...?** Suppose the stuntwoman jumps from a building that is half as tall. Will she be in the air for half as long? Explain.

LINK

Entertainment

The Guinness world record for the greatest number of people juggling at one time was set in 1998 by 1508 people, each of whom juggled at least 3 objects for 10 seconds.

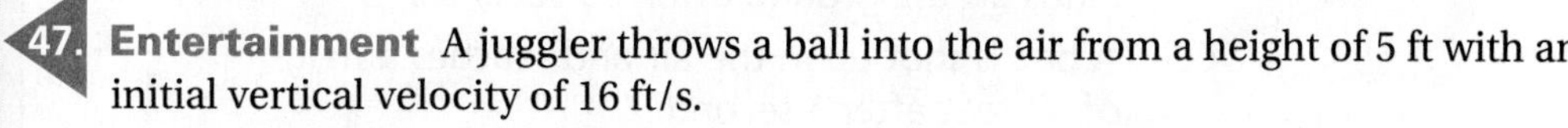

47. **Entertainment** A juggler throws a ball into the air from a height of 5 ft with an initial vertical velocity of 16 ft/s.

a. Write a function that can be used to model the height h of the ball in feet t seconds after the ball is thrown.

b. How long does the juggler have to catch the ball before it hits the ground?

Find the roots of each equation.

48. $x^2 - 2x + 1 = 0$
49. $x^2 + 6x = -5$
50. $25x^2 + 40x = -16$
51. $9x^2 + 6x = -1$
52. $5x^2 = 45$
53. $x^2 - 6 = x$

For each function, (a) find its vertex, (b) find its y-intercept, (c) find its zeros, and (d) graph it.

54. $f(x) = x^2 + 2x - 8$
55. $g(x) = x^2 - 16$
56. $h(x) = x^2 - x - 12$
57. $f(x) = -2x^2 + 4x$
58. $g(x) = x^2 - 5x - 6$
59. $h(x) = 3x^2 + x - 4$

60. **Geometry** The hypotenuse of a right triangle is 2 cm longer than one leg and 4 cm longer than the other leg.

a. Let x represent the length of the hypotenuse. Use the Pythagorean Theorem to write an equation that can be solved for x.

b. Find the solutions of the equation from part **a.**

c. Are both solutions reasonable in the context of the problem situation? Explain.

Geometry **Find the dimensions of each rectangle.**

61. $A = 80$ ft^2; width x; length $x + 16$

62. $A = 210$ cm^2; width x; length $x + 1$

63. $A = 50$ m^2; width $x - 3$; length $x + 2$

64. **Critical Thinking** Will a function whose rule can be factored as a binomial squared ever have two different zeros? Explain.

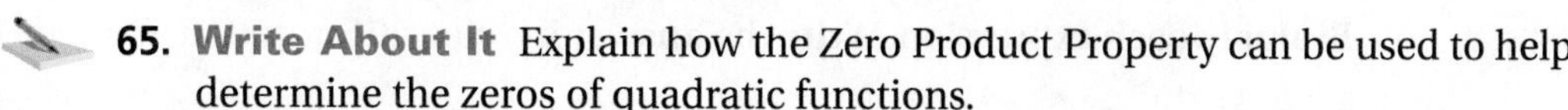

65. **Write About It** Explain how the Zero Product Property can be used to help determine the zeros of quadratic functions.

MULTI-STEP TEST PREP

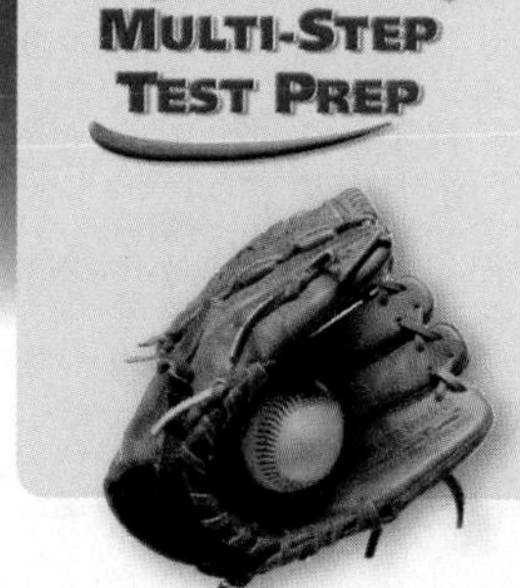

66. This problem will prepare you for the Multi-Step Test Prep on page 364.

A baseball player hits a ball toward the outfield. The height h of the ball in feet is modeled by $h(t) = -16t^2 + 22t + 3$, where t is the time in seconds. In addition, the function $d(t) = 85t$ models the horizontal distance d traveled by the ball.

a. If no one catches the ball, how long will it stay in the air?

b. What is the horizontal distance that the ball travels before it hits the ground?

TEST PREP

67. Use the graph provided to choose the best description of what the graph represents.

Ⓐ A ball is dropped from a height of 42 feet and lands on the ground after 3 seconds.

Ⓑ A ball is dropped from a height of 42 feet and lands on the ground after 1.5 seconds.

Ⓒ A ball is shot up in the air and reaches a height of 42 feet after 1 second.

Ⓓ A ball is shot up in the air, reaches a height of 42 feet, and lands on the ground after 1.5 seconds.

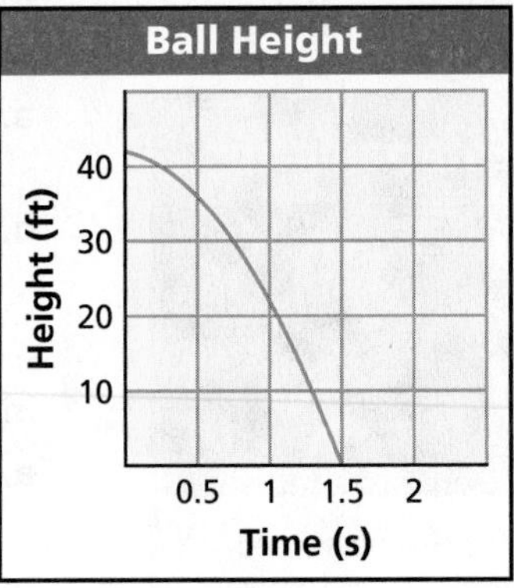

68. Which function has -7 as its only zero?

Ⓕ $f(x) = x(x - 7)$

Ⓖ $h(x) = (x - 7)^2$

Ⓗ $g(x) = (x + 1)(x + 7)$

Ⓙ $j(x) = (x + 7)^2$

69. Which expression is a perfect square trinomial?

Ⓐ $25y^2 - 16$

Ⓑ $25y^2 - 20y + 16$

Ⓒ $25y^2 - 40y + 16$

Ⓓ $25y^2 - 10y + 16$

70. Gridded Response Find the positive root of $x^2 + 4x - 21 = 0$.

CHALLENGE AND EXTEND

Find the roots of each equation by factoring.

71. $3(x^2 - x) = x^2$

72. $x^2 = \frac{1}{3}x$

73. $x^2 - \frac{3}{4}x + \frac{1}{8} = 0$

74. $x^2 + x + 0.21 = 0$

75. Another special factoring case involves perfect cubes. The sum of two cubes can be factored by using the formula $a^3 + b^3 = (a + b)(a^2 - ab + b^2)$.

a. Verify the formula by multiplying the right side of the equation.

b. Factor the expression $8x^3 + 27$.

c. Use multiplication and guess and check to find the factors of $a^3 - b^3$.

d. Factor the expression $x^3 - 1$.

SPIRAL REVIEW

Evaluate each expression. Write the answer in scientific notation. *(Lesson 1-5)*

76. $(1.4 \times 10^8)(6.1 \times 10^{-3})$

77. $(2.7 \times 10^{10})(3.2 \times 10^2)$

78. $\dfrac{(3.5 \times 10^6)}{(1.4 \times 10^{-4})}$

79. $\dfrac{(3.12 \times 10^{-6})}{(4.8 \times 10^3)}$

Solve each proportion. *(Lesson 2-2)*

80. $\frac{12}{7.5} = \frac{n}{5}$

81. $\frac{1.2}{4.8} = \frac{w}{8.8}$

82. $\frac{6.8}{4.5} = \frac{r}{90}$

Using the graph of $f(x) = x^2$ as a guide, describe the transformations, and then graph each function. *(Lesson 5-1)*

83. $h(x) = 0.5x^2$

84. $d(x) = x^2 + 2$

85. $g(x) = (x + 1)^2$

5-4 Completing the Square

Objectives

Solve quadratic equations by completing the square.

Write quadratic equations in vertex form.

Vocabulary

completing the square

Why learn this?

You can solve quadratic equations to find how long water takes to fall from the top to the bottom of a waterfall. (See Exercise 39.)

Many quadratic equations contain expressions that cannot be easily factored. For equations containing these types of expressions, you can use square roots to find roots.

Know it! Note

Square-Root Property

WORDS	NUMBERS	ALGEBRA
To solve a quadratic equation, you can take the square root of both sides. Be sure to consider the positive and negative square roots.	$x^2 = 15$ $\lvert x\rvert = \sqrt{15}$ $x = \pm\sqrt{15}$	If $x^2 = a$ and a is a nonnegative real number, then $x = \pm\sqrt{a}$.

EXAMPLE 

Solving Equations by Using the Square Root Property

Solve each equation.

A $3x^2 - 4 = 68$

$3x^2 = 72$ *Add 4 to both sides.*

$x^2 = 24$ *Divide both sides by 3 to isolate the squared term.*

$x = \pm\sqrt{24}$ *Take the square root of both sides.*

$x = \pm 2\sqrt{6}$ *Simplify.*

Check Use a graphing calculator.

```
3*(2√(6))²-4
            68
3*(-2√(6))²-4
            68
```

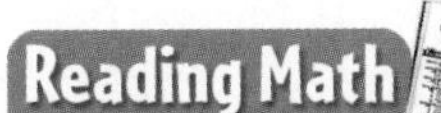

Read $\pm\sqrt{a}$ as "plus or minus square root of *a*."

B $x^2 - 10x + 25 = 27$

$(x - 5)^2 = 27$ *Factor the perfect square trinomial.*

$x - 5 = \pm\sqrt{27}$ *Take the square root of both sides.*

$x = 5 \pm \sqrt{27}$ *Add 5 to both sides.*

$x = 5 \pm 3\sqrt{3}$ *Simplify.*

Check Use a graphing calculator.

```
(5+3√(3))²-10(5+
3√(3))+25
              27
(5-3√(3))²-10(5-
3√(3))+25
              27
```

Solve each equation.

1a. $4x^2 - 20 = 5$

1b. $x^2 + 8x + 16 = 49$

The methods in the previous examples can be used only for expressions that are perfect squares. However, you can use algebra to rewrite any quadratic expression as a perfect square.

You can use algebra tiles to model a perfect square trinomial as a perfect square. The area of the square at right is $x^2 + 2x + 1$. Because each side of the square measures $x + 1$ units, the area is also $(x + 1)(x + 1)$, or $(x + 1)^2$. This shows that $(x + 1)^2 = x^2 + 2x + 1$.

If a quadratic expression of the form $x^2 + bx$ *cannot* model a square, you can add a term to form a perfect square trinomial. This is called **completing the square**.

Completing the Square

WORDS	NUMBERS	ALGEBRA
To complete the square of $x^2 + bx$, add $\left(\frac{b}{2}\right)^2$.	$x^2 + 6x + \blacksquare$ $x^2 + 6x + \left(\frac{6}{2}\right)^2$ $x^2 + 6x + 9$ $(x + 3)^2$	$x^2 + bx + \blacksquare$ $x^2 + bx + \left(\frac{b}{2}\right)^2$ $\left(x + \frac{b}{2}\right)^2$

The model shows completing the square for $x^2 + 6x$ by adding 9 unit tiles. The resulting perfect square trinomial is $x^2 + 6x + 9$. Note that completing the square does not produce an equivalent expression.

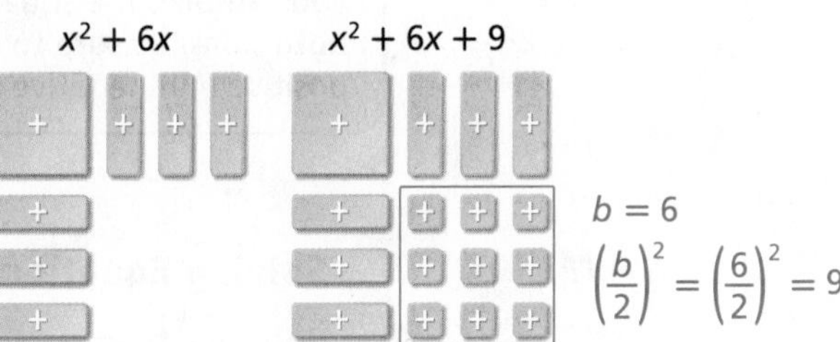

EXAMPLE 2 Completing the Square

Complete the square for each expression. Write the resulting expression as a binomial squared.

A $x^2 - 2x + \blacksquare$

$\left(\frac{-2}{2}\right)^2 = (-1)^2 = 1$ *Find* $\left(\frac{b}{2}\right)^2$.

$x^2 - 2x + 1$ *Add.*

$(x - 1)^2$ *Factor.*

Check Find the square of the binomial.

$(x - 1)^2 = (x - 1)(x - 1)$

$= x^2 - 2x + 1$

B $x^2 + 5x + \blacksquare$

$\left(\frac{5}{2}\right)^2 = \frac{25}{4}$ *Find* $\left(\frac{b}{2}\right)^2$.

$x^2 + 5x + \frac{25}{4}$ *Add.*

$\left(x + \frac{5}{2}\right)^2$ *Factor.*

Check Find the square of the binomial.

$\left(x + \frac{5}{2}\right)^2 = \left(x + \frac{5}{2}\right)\left(x + \frac{5}{2}\right)$

$= x^2 + 5x + \frac{25}{4}$

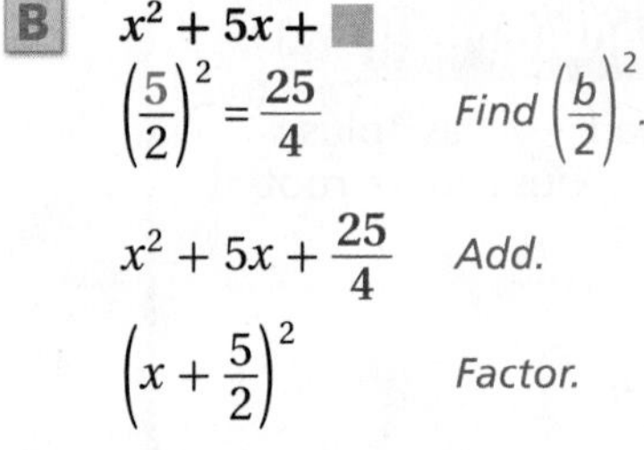

Complete the square for each expression. Write the resulting expression as a binomial squared.

2a. $x^2 + 4x + \blacksquare$ **2b.** $x^2 - 4x + \blacksquare$ **2c.** $x^2 + 3x + \blacksquare$

You can complete the square to solve quadratic equations.

Solving Quadratic Equations $ax^2 + bx + c = 0$ by Completing the Square

1. Collect variable terms on one side of the equation and constants on the other.
2. As needed, divide both sides by a to make the coefficient of the x^2-term 1.
3. Complete the square by adding $\left(\frac{b}{2}\right)^2$ to both sides of the equation.
4. Factor the variable expression as a perfect square.
5. Take the square root of both sides of the equation.
6. Solve for the values of the variable.

EXAMPLE 3 Solving a Quadratic Equation by Completing the Square

Solve each equation by completing the square.

A $x^2 = 27 - 6x$

$x^2 + 6x = 27$	*Collect variable terms on one side.*
$x^2 + 6x + \blacksquare = 27 + \blacksquare$	*Set up to complete the square.*
$x^2 + 6x + \left(\frac{6}{2}\right)^2 = 27 + \left(\frac{6}{2}\right)^2$	*Add $\left(\frac{b}{2}\right)^2$ to both sides.*
$x^2 + 6x + 9 = 27 + 9$	*Simplify.*
$(x+3)^2 = 36$	*Factor.*
$x + 3 = \pm\sqrt{36}$	*Take the square root of both sides.*
$x + 3 = \pm 6$	*Simplify.*
$x + 3 = 6$ or $x + 3 = -6$	*Solve for x.*
$x = 3$ or $x = -9$	

Caution!

To keep the equation balanced, you must add $\left(\frac{b}{2}\right)^2$ to both sides of the equation.

B $2x^2 + 8x = 12$

$x^2 + 4x = 6$	*Divide both sides by 2.*
$x^2 + 4x + \blacksquare = 6 + \blacksquare$	*Set up to complete the square.*
$x^2 + 4x + \left(\frac{4}{2}\right)^2 = 6 + \left(\frac{4}{2}\right)^2$	*Add $\left(\frac{b}{2}\right)^2$ to both sides.*
$x^2 + 4x + 4 = 6 + 4$	*Simplify.*
$(x+2)^2 = 10$	*Factor.*
$x + 2 = \pm\sqrt{10}$	*Take the square root of both sides.*
$x = -2 \pm \sqrt{10}$	*Solve for x.*

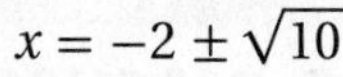

Solve each equation by completing the square.

3a. $x^2 - 2 = 9x$ **3b.** $3x^2 - 24x = 27$

Recall the vertex form of a quadratic function from Lesson 5-1: $f(x) = a(x - h)^2 + k$, where the vertex is (h, k).

You can complete the square to rewrite any quadratic function in vertex form.

EXAMPLE 4 Writing a Quadratic Function in Vertex Form

Helpful Hint

In Example 3, the equation was balanced by adding $\left(\frac{b}{2}\right)^2$ to *both* sides. Here, the equation is balanced by adding and subtracting $\left(\frac{b}{2}\right)^2$ on *one* side.

Write each function in vertex form, and identify its vertex.

A $f(x) = x^2 + 10x - 13$

$$f(x) = \left(x^2 + 10x + \blacksquare\right) - 13 - \blacksquare$$ *Set up to complete the square.*

$$f(x) = \left[x^2 + 10x + \left(\frac{10}{2}\right)^2\right] - 13 - \left(\frac{10}{2}\right)^2$$ *Add and subtract $\left(\frac{b}{2}\right)^2$.*

$$f(x) = (x+5)^2 - 38$$ *Simplify and factor.*

Because $h = -5$ and $k = -38$, the vertex is $(-5, -38)$.

Check Use the axis of symmetry formula to confirm the vertex.

$$x = -\frac{b}{2a} = -\frac{10}{2(1)} = -5 \qquad y = f(-5) = (-5)^2 + 10(-5) - 13 = -38 \checkmark$$

B $g(x) = 2x^2 - 8x + 3$

$$g(x) = 2\left(x^2 - 4x\right) + 3$$ *Factor so the coefficient of x^2 is 1.*

$$g(x) = 2\left(x^2 - 4x + \blacksquare\right) + 3 - \blacksquare$$ *Set up to complete the square.*

$$g(x) = 2\left(x^2 - 4x + \left(\frac{-4}{2}\right)^2\right) + 3 - 2\left(\frac{-4}{2}\right)^2$$ *Add $\left(\frac{b}{2}\right)^2$. Because $\left(\frac{b}{2}\right)^2$ is multiplied by 2, you must subtract $2\left(\frac{b}{2}\right)^2$.*

$$g(x) = 2\left(x^2 - 4x + 4\right) - 5$$ *Simplify.*

$$g(x) = 2(x-2)^2 - 5$$ *Factor.*

Because $h = 2$ and $k = -5$, the vertex is $(2, -5)$.

Check A graph of the function on a graphing calculator supports your answer.

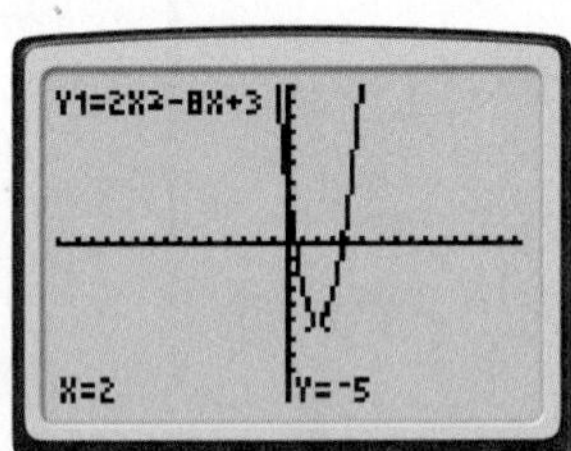

Write each function in vertex form, and identify its vertex.

4a. $f(x) = x^2 + 24x + 145$ **4b.** $g(x) = 5x^2 - 50x + 128$

THINK AND DISCUSS

1. Explain two ways to solve $x^2 = 25$.
2. Describe how to change a quadratic function from standard form to vertex form by completing the square.

3. **GET ORGANIZED** Copy and complete the graphic organizer. Compare and contrast two methods of solving quadratic equations.

Using Square-Root Property vs. Completing the Square

Similarities	Differences

5-4 Exercises

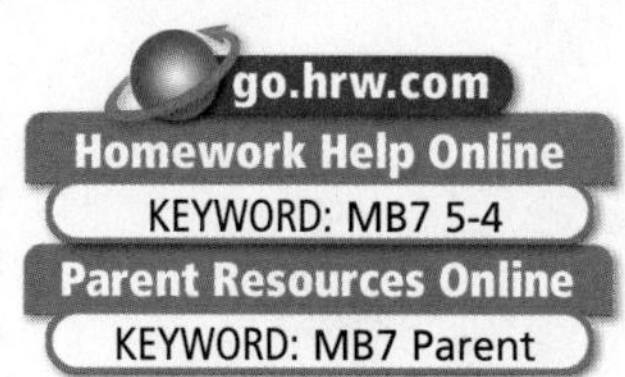

GUIDED PRACTICE

1. **Vocabulary** What must you add to the expression $x^2 + bx$ to *complete the square*?

SEE EXAMPLE 1 p. 341

Solve each equation.

2. $(x - 2)^2 = 16$
3. $x^2 - 10x + 25 = 16$
4. $x^2 - 2x + 1 = 3$

SEE EXAMPLE 2 p. 342

Complete the square for each expression. Write the resulting expression as a binomial squared.

5. $x^2 + 14x + \blacksquare$
6. $x^2 - 12x + \blacksquare$
7. $x^2 - 9x + \blacksquare$

SEE EXAMPLE 3 p. 343

Solve each equation by completing the square.

8. $x^2 - 6x = -4$
9. $x^2 + 8 = 6x$
10. $2x^2 - 20x = 8$
11. $x^2 = 24 - 4x$
12. $10x + x^2 = 42$
13. $2x^2 + 8x - 15 = 0$

SEE EXAMPLE 4 p. 344

Write each function in vertex form, and identify its vertex.

14. $f(x) = x^2 + 6x - 3$
15. $g(x) = x^2 - 10x + 11$
16. $h(x) = 3x^2 - 24x + 53$
17. $f(x) = x^2 + 8x - 10$
18. $g(x) = x^2 - 3x + 16$
19. $h(x) = 3x^2 - 12x - 4$

PRACTICE AND PROBLEM SOLVING

Independent Practice

For Exercises	See Example
20–22	1
23–25	2
26–31	3
32–37	4

Extra Practice

Skills Practice p. S12

Application Practice p. S36

Solve each equation.

20. $(x + 2)^2 = 36$
21. $x^2 - 6x + 9 = 100$
22. $(x - 3)^2 = 5$

Complete the square for each expression. Write the resulting expression as a binomial squared.

23. $x^2 - 18x + \blacksquare$
24. $x^2 + 10x + \blacksquare$
25. $x^2 - \frac{1}{2}x + \blacksquare$

Solve each equation by completing the square.

26. $x^2 + 2x = 7$
27. $x^2 - 4x = -1$
28. $2x^2 - 8x = 22$
29. $8x = x^2 + 12$
30. $x^2 + 3x - 5 = 0$
31. $3x^2 + 6x = 1$

Write each function in vertex form, and identify its vertex.

32. $f(x) = x^2 - 4x + 13$
33. $g(x) = x^2 + 14x + 71$
34. $h(x) = 9x^2 + 18x - 3$
35. $f(x) = x^2 + 4x - 7$
36. $g(x) = x^2 - 16x + 2$
37. $h(x) = 2x^2 + 6x + 25$

38. **Engineering** The height h above the roadway of the main cable of the Golden Gate Bridge can be modeled by the function $h(x) = \frac{1}{9000}x^2 - \frac{7}{15}x + 500$, where x is the distance in feet from the left tower.

a. Complete the square, and write the function in vertex form.
b. What is the vertex, and what does it represent?
c. **Multi-Step** The left and right towers have the same height. What is the distance in feet between them?

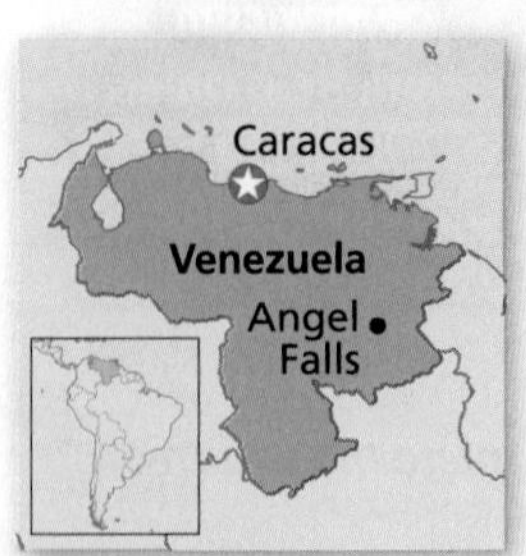

39. **Waterfalls** Angel Falls in Venezuela is the tallest waterfall in the world. Water falls uninterrupted for 2421 feet before entering the river below. The height h above the river in feet of water going over the edge of the waterfall is modeled by $h(t) = -16t^2 + 2421$, where t is the time in seconds after the initial fall.

   a. Estimate the time it takes for the water to reach the river.

   b. **Multi-Step** Ribbon Falls in California has a height of 1612 ft. Approximately how much longer does it take water to reach the bottom when going over Angel Falls than when going over Ribbon Falls?

40. **Sports** A basketball is shot with an initial vertical velocity of 24 ft/s from 6 ft above the ground. The ball's height h in feet is modeled by $h(t) = -16t^2 + 24t + 6$, where t is the time in seconds after the ball is shot. What is the maximum height of the ball, and when does the ball reach this height?

Solve each equation using square roots.

41. $x^2 - 1 = 2$
42. $25x^2 = 0$
43. $8x^2 - 200 = 0$
44. $-3x^2 + 6 = -1$
45. $(x + 13)^2 = 7$
46. $\left(x + \frac{1}{4}\right)^2 - \frac{9}{16} = 0$
47. $\left(x + \frac{3}{2}\right)^2 = \frac{25}{2}$
48. $x^2 + 14x + 49 = 64$
49. $9x^2 + 18x + 9 = 5$

50. **ERROR ANALYSIS** Two attempts to write $f(x) = 2x^2 - 8x$ in vertex form are shown. Which is incorrect? Explain the error.

A

$f(x) = 2x^2 - 8x$
$f(x) = 2(x^2 - 4x)$
$f(x) = 2(x^2 - 4x + 4) - 4$
$f(x) = 2(x - 2)^2 - 4$

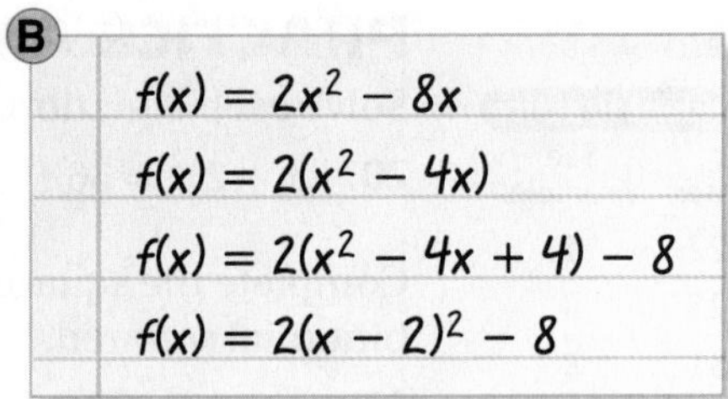

Solve each equation by completing the square.

51. $x^2 + 8x = -15$
52. $x^2 + 22x = -21$
53. $3x^2 + 4x = 1$
54. $2x^2 = 5x + 12$
55. $x^2 - 7x - 2 = 0$
56. $x^2 = 4x + 11$
57. $x^2 + 6x + 4 = 0$
58. $5x^2 + 10x - 7 = 0$
59. $x^2 - 8x = 24$

LINK

Sports

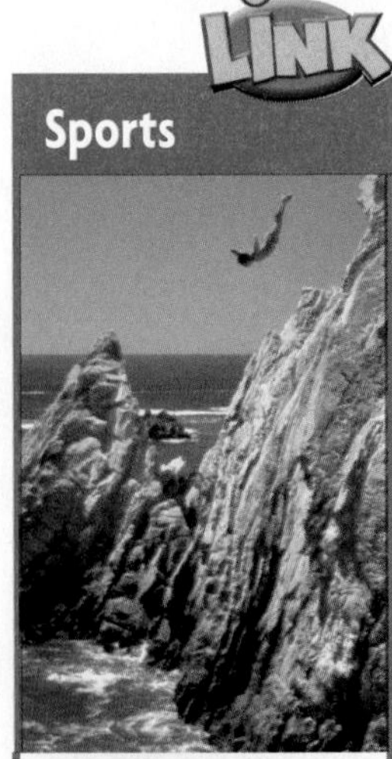

Acapulco, Mexico, is famous for its cliff-diving shows. Divers perform complicated acrobatic dives from heights of up to 80 feet.

60. **Sports** A diver's height h in meters above the water is approximated by $h(t) = h_0 - 5t^2$, where h_0 is the initial height in meters, -5 is a constant based on the acceleration due to gravity in m/s^2, and t is the time in seconds that the diver falls through the air.

   a. Find the total time that the diver falls through the air for each type of dive in the table.

   b. How high is a dive that keeps the diver in the air twice as long as a 5-meter dive?

   c. The speed of a diver entering the water can be approximated by $s = 18t$, where s is the speed in kilometers per hour and t is the time in seconds. Using your results from part **a**, find the speed of the diver entering the water for each dive height.

   d. How many times as high is a dive that results in a speed that is twice as fast?

Dive Heights

Type	Height (m)
Platform	5
Platform	10
Cliff	20
Cliff	30

MULTI-STEP TEST PREP

61. This problem will prepare you for the Multi-Step Test Prep on page 364.

The height h in feet of a baseball hit from home plate can be modeled by the function $h(t) = -16t^2 + 32t + 5.5$, where t is the time in seconds since the ball was hit. The ball is descending when it passes 7.5 ft over the head of a 6 ft player standing on the ground.

a. To the nearest tenth of a second, how long after the ball is hit does it pass over the player's head?

b. The horizontal distance between the player and home plate is 120 ft. Use your answer from part **a** to determine the horizontal speed of the ball to the nearest foot per second.

62. Estimation A bag of grass seed will cover 525 square feet. Twenty bags of seed are used to cover an area shaped like a square. Estimate the side length of the square. Check your answer with a calculator.

63. Critical Thinking The functions f and g are defined by $f(x) = x^2 + 2x - 2$ and $g(x) = (x + 1)^2 - 3$. Use algebra to prove that f and g represent the same function.

64. Sports A player bumps a volleyball with an initial vertical velocity of 20 ft/s.

a. Write a function h in standard form for the ball's height in feet in terms of the time t in seconds after the ball is hit.

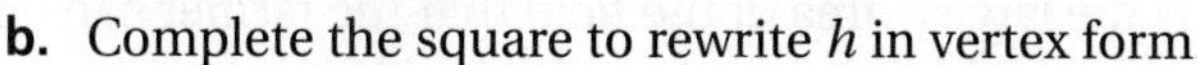

b. Complete the square to rewrite h in vertex form.

c. What is the maximum height of the ball?

d. What if...? Suppose the volleyball were hit under the same conditions, but with an initial velocity of 32 ft/s. How much higher would the ball go?

Graphing Calculator Use a graphing calculator to approximate the roots of each equation to the nearest thousandth.

65. $x^2 - 15 = 40$

66. $x^2 = 2.85$

67. $1.4x^2 = 24.6$

68. $(x + 0.6)^2 = 7.4$

69. $\frac{x^2}{7} = \frac{1}{3}$

70. $\left(x + \frac{1}{4}\right)^2 = \frac{5}{6}$

71. Critical Thinking Why do equations of the form $x^2 = k$ have no real solution when $k < 0$?

72. Write About It Compare the methods of factoring and completing the square for solving quadratic equations.

TEST PREP

73. Which gives the solution to $3x^2 = 33$?

Ⓐ $\pm\sqrt{3}$

Ⓑ $\pm\sqrt{11}$

Ⓒ 11

Ⓓ 121

74. Which equation represents the graph at right?

Ⓕ $y = (x - 2)^2 + 1$

Ⓖ $y = (x - 2)^2 - 1$

Ⓗ $y = (x + 2)^2 + 1$

Ⓙ $y = (x + 2)^2 - 1$

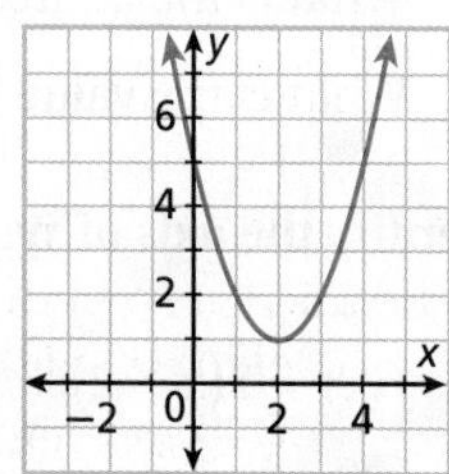

75. Which gives the vertex of the graph of $y = 3(x - 1)^2 - 22$?

Ⓐ $(1, -22)$ Ⓑ $(-1, -22)$ Ⓒ $(3, -22)$ Ⓓ $(-3, -22)$

76. Which number should be added to $x^2 + 14x$ to make a perfect square trinomial?

Ⓕ 7 Ⓖ 14 Ⓗ 49 Ⓙ 196

77. **Gridded Response** What is the positive root of the equation $2x^2 - x = 10$?

78. **Extended Response** Solve the quadratic equation $x^2 - 6x = 16$ by completing the square. Explain each step of the solution process, and check your answer.

CHALLENGE AND EXTEND

Find the value of b in each perfect square trinomial.

79. $x^2 - bx + 144$

80. $4x^2 - bx + 16$

81. $3x^2 + bx + 27$

82. $ax^2 + bx + c$

Find the zeros of each function.

83. $f(x) = x^2 - 4x\sqrt{5} + 19$

84. $f(x) = x^2 + 6x\sqrt{3} + 23$

85. **Farming** To create a temporary grazing area, a farmer is using 1800 feet of electric fencing to enclose a rectangular field and then to subdivide the field into two plots. The fence that divides the field into two plots is parallel to the field's shorter sides.

a. What is the largest area of the field that the farmer can enclose?

b. What are the dimensions of the field with the largest area?

c. **What if...?** What would be the largest area of a square field that the farmer could enclose and divide into two plots?

Plot 1

Plot 2

SPIRAL REVIEW

Express each set of numbers using set-builder notation. *(Lesson 1-1)*

86. $(72, \infty)$

87. numbers within 10 units of 4

88. positive multiples of 4

89. 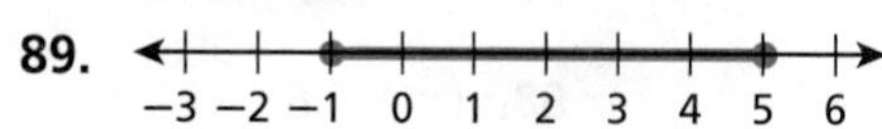

Use the table for Exercises 90–93. *(Lesson 4-1)*

Monthly Budget	Food	Housing	Auto
Aboline family	\$352	\$895	\$426
Hernandez family	\$675	\$1368	\$642
Walker family	\$185	\$615	\$295

90. Display the data in the form of a matrix B.

91. What are the dimensions of the matrix?

92. What is the address of the entry that has the value 185?

93. What is the value of the matrix entry with the address b_{22}? What does it represent?

Identify the axis of symmetry and the vertex of the graph of each function. *(Lesson 5-2)*

94. $f(x) = 3(x - 2)^2$

95. $g(x) = \frac{2}{5}x^2 - 1$

96. $h(x) = 6x^2 + 2.5$

Areas of Composite Figures

Quadratic equations can be used to solve problems involving the areas of composite figures. Write an equation that represents the information given in the problem. Then solve the equation.

Example

The diagram shows a rectangular garden surrounded by a walkway. The garden measures 10 m by 34 m. The total area of the garden and walkway is 640 m². What is the width x of the walkway?

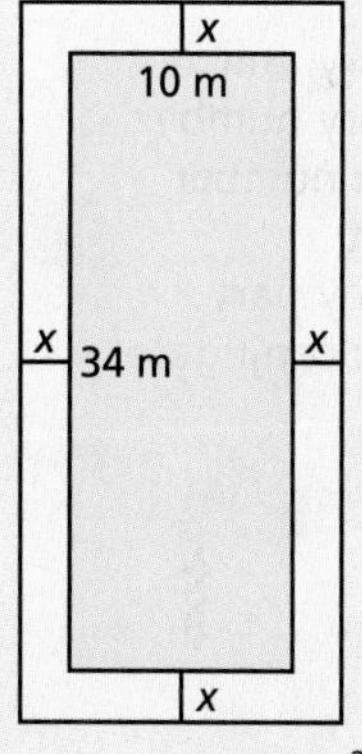

Total area = 640 m²

The total area is equal to the total length multiplied by the total width. The total length is $2x + 34$ m, and the total width is $2x + 10$ m.

$A = \ell \times w$	*Write the formula for total area.*
$640 = (2x + 34)(2x + 10)$	*Substitute.*
$640 = 4x^2 + 88x + 340$	*Multiply the binomials.*
$0 = 4x^2 + 88x - 300$	*Subtract 640 from both sides.*
$0 = x^2 + 22x - 75$	*Divide both sides by 4.*
$0 = (x - 3)(x + 25)$	*Factor.*
$x - 3 = 0$ or $x + 25 = 0$	*Use the Zero Product Property.*
$x = 3$ or $x = -25$	*Solve for x.*

The width cannot be negative. Therefore, the width of the walkway is 3 m.

Try This

Write an equation that represents each problem. Then solve.

1. Use figure 1 below. A ring of grass with an area of 314 yd² surrounds a circular flower bed. Find the width x of the ring of grass.
2. Use figure 2 below. Sid cuts four congruent squares from the corners of a 30-in.-by-50-in. rectangular piece of cardboard so that it can be folded to make a box. Find the side length s of the squares, given that the area of the bottom of the box is 200 in².
3. Use figure 3 below. Harriet has 80 m of fencing materials to enclose three sides of a rectangular garden. She will use the side of her garage as a border for the fourth side. Find the width x of the garden if its area is to be 700 m².

Figure 1

x
10 yd

Grass area = 314 yd²

Figure 2

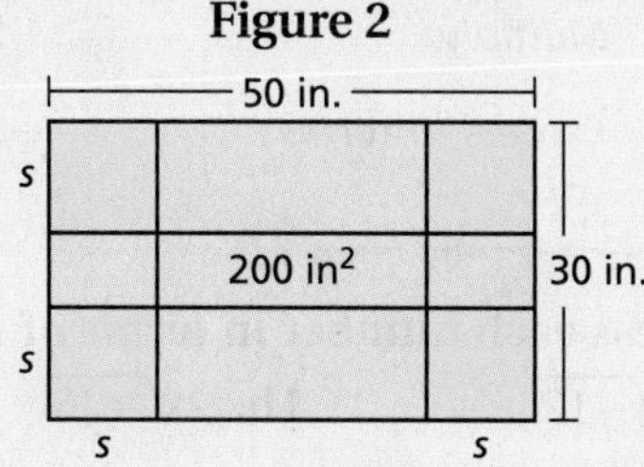

Figure 3

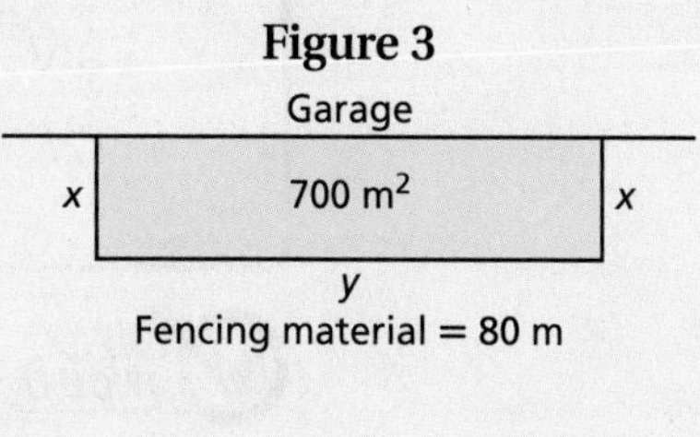

Fencing material = 80 m

5-5 Complex Numbers and Roots

Objectives
Define and use imaginary and complex numbers.

Solve quadratic equations with complex roots.

Vocabulary
imaginary unit
imaginary number
complex number
real part
imaginary part
complex conjugate

Why learn this?

Complex numbers can be used to describe the zeros of quadratic functions that have no real zeros. (See Example 4.)

Andrew Toos/CartoonResource.com

You can see in the graph of $f(x) = x^2 + 1$ below that f has no real zeros. If you solve the corresponding equation $0 = x^2 + 1$, you find that $x = \pm\sqrt{-1}$, which has no *real* solutions.

However, you can find solutions if you define the square root of negative numbers, which is why *imaginary numbers* were invented. The **imaginary unit** i is defined as $\sqrt{-1}$. You can use the imaginary unit to write the square root of any negative number.

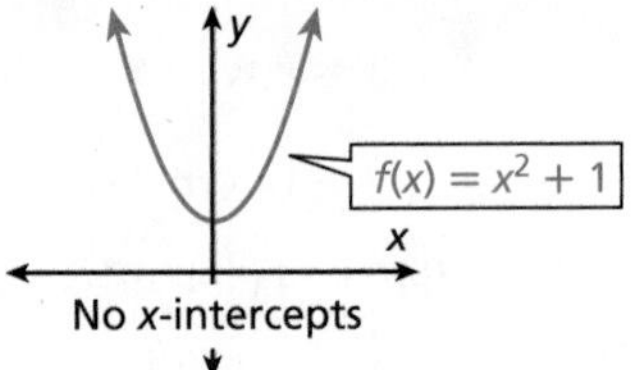

Know it! Note — **Imaginary Numbers**

WORDS	NUMBERS	ALGEBRA
An **imaginary number** is the square root of a negative number.	$\sqrt{-1} = i$	If b is a positive real number,
Imaginary numbers can be written in the form bi, where b is a real number and i is the imaginary unit.	$\sqrt{-2} = \sqrt{-1}\sqrt{2} = i\sqrt{2}$ $\sqrt{-4} = \sqrt{-1}\sqrt{4} = 2i$	then $\sqrt{-b} = i\sqrt{b}$ and $\sqrt{-b^2} = bi$.
The square of an imaginary number is the original negative number.	$\left(\sqrt{-1}\right)^2 = i^2 = -1$	$\left(\sqrt{-b}\right)^2 = -b$

EXAMPLE 1 Simplifying Square Roots of Negative Numbers

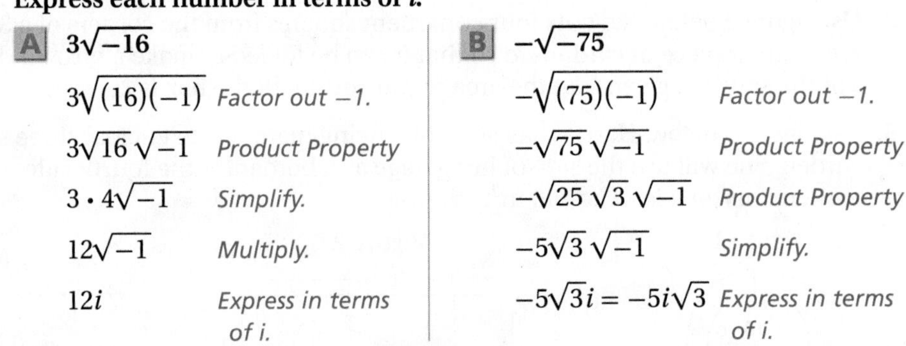

Express each number in terms of *i*.

A $3\sqrt{-16}$

$3\sqrt{(16)(-1)}$	*Factor out −1.*
$3\sqrt{16}\sqrt{-1}$	*Product Property*
$3 \cdot 4\sqrt{-1}$	*Simplify.*
$12\sqrt{-1}$	*Multiply.*
$12i$	*Express in terms of i.*

B $-\sqrt{-75}$

$-\sqrt{(75)(-1)}$	*Factor out −1.*
$-\sqrt{75}\sqrt{-1}$	*Product Property*
$-\sqrt{25}\sqrt{3}\sqrt{-1}$	*Product Property*
$-5\sqrt{3}\sqrt{-1}$	*Simplify.*
$-5\sqrt{3}i = -5i\sqrt{3}$	*Express in terms of i.*

Express each number in terms of *i*.

1a. $\sqrt{-12}$ **1b.** $2\sqrt{-36}$ **1c.** $-\frac{1}{3}\sqrt{-63}$

EXAMPLE 2 Solving a Quadratic Equation with Imaginary Solutions

Solve each equation.

A $x^2 = -81$

$x = \pm\sqrt{-81}$ *Take square roots.*

$x = \pm 9i$ *Express in terms of i.*

Check

$x^2 = -81$	
$(9i)^2$	-81
$81i^2$	-81
$81(-1)$	-81 ✔

$x^2 = -81$	
$(-9i)^2$	-81
$81i^2$	-81
$81(-1)$	-81 ✔

B $3x^2 + 75 = 0$

$3x^2 = -75$ *Add −75 to both sides.*

$x^2 = -25$ *Divide both sides by 3.*

$x = \pm\sqrt{-25}$ *Take square roots.*

$x = \pm 5i$ *Express in terms of i.*

Check

$3x^2 + 75 = 0$	
$3(\pm 5i)^2 + 75$	0
$3(25)i^2 + 75$	0
$75(-1) + 75$	0 ✔

Solve each equation.

2a. $x^2 = -36$ **2b.** $x^2 + 48 = 0$ **2c.** $9x^2 + 25 = 0$

A **complex number** is a number that can be written in the form $a + bi$, where a and b are real numbers and $i = \sqrt{-1}$. The set of real numbers is a subset of the set of complex numbers $\mathbb{C}$.

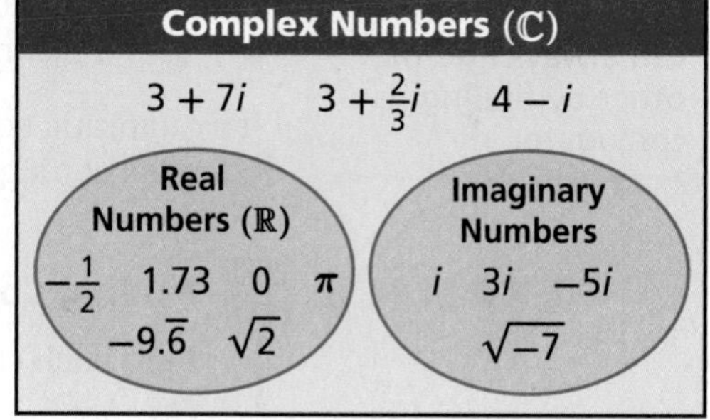

Every complex number has a **real part** a and an **imaginary part** b.

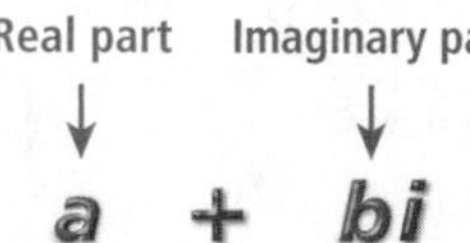

Real numbers are complex numbers where $b = 0$. Imaginary numbers are complex numbers where $a = 0$ and $b \neq 0$. These are sometimes called *pure imaginary numbers.*

Two complex numbers are equal if and only if their real parts are equal and their imaginary parts are equal.

EXAMPLE 3 Equating Two Complex Numbers

Find the values of x and y that make the equation $3x - 5i = 6 - (10y)i$ true.

Real parts

$$3x - 5i = 6 - (10y)i$$

Imaginary parts

$3x = 6$ *Equate the real parts.* $-5 = -(10y)$ *Equate the imaginary parts.*

$x = 2$ *Solve for x.* $\frac{1}{2} = y$ *Solve for y.*

Find the values of x and y that make each equation true.

3a. $2x - 6i = -8 + (20y)i$ **3b.** $-8 + (6y)i = 5x - i\sqrt{6}$

EXAMPLE 4 Finding Complex Zeros of Quadratic Functions

Find the zeros of each function.

A $f(x) = x^2 - 2x + 5$

$x^2 - 2x + 5 = 0$	*Set equal to 0.*
$x^2 - 2x + \blacksquare = -5 + \blacksquare$	*Rewrite.*
$x^2 - 2x + 1 = -5 + 1$	*Add $\left(\frac{b}{2}\right)^2$.*
$(x - 1)^2 = -4$	*Factor.*
$x - 1 = \pm\sqrt{-4}$	*Take square roots.*
$x = 1 \pm 2i$	*Simplify.*

B $g(x) = x^2 + 10x + 35$

$$x^2 + 10x + 35 = 0$$
$$x^2 + 10x + \blacksquare = -35 + \blacksquare$$
$$x^2 + 10x + 25 = -35 + 25$$
$$(x + 5)^2 = -10$$
$$x + 5 = \pm\sqrt{-10}$$
$$x = -5 \pm i\sqrt{10}$$

Find the zeros of each function.

4a. $f(x) = x^2 + 4x + 13$ **4b.** $g(x) = x^2 - 8x + 18$

Helpful Hint

When given one complex root, you can always find the other by finding its conjugate.

The solutions $-5 + i\sqrt{10}$ and $-5 - i\sqrt{10}$ in Example 4B are related. These solutions are a *complex conjugate* pair. Their real parts are equal and their imaginary parts are opposites. The **complex conjugate** of any complex number $a + bi$ is the complex number $a - bi$.

If a quadratic equation with real coefficients has nonreal roots, those roots are complex conjugates.

EXAMPLE 5 Finding Complex Conjugates

Find each complex conjugate.

A $2i - 15$

$-15 + 2i$	*Write as a + bi.*
$-15 - 2i$	*Find a − bi.*

B $-4i$

$0 + (-4)i$	*Write as a + bi.*
$0 - (-4)i$	*Find a − bi.*
$4i$	*Simplify.*

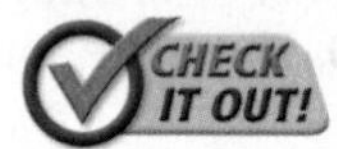

Find each complex conjugate.

5a. $9 - i$ **5b.** $i + \sqrt{3}$ **5c.** $-8i$

THINK AND DISCUSS

1. Given that one solution of a quadratic equation is $3 + i$, explain how to determine the other solution.

2. Describe a number of the form $a + bi$ in which $a \neq 0$ and $b = 0$. Then describe a number in which $a = 0$ and $b \neq 0$. Are both numbers complex? Explain.

3. GET ORGANIZED Copy and complete the graphic organizer. In each box or oval, give a definition and examples of each type of number.

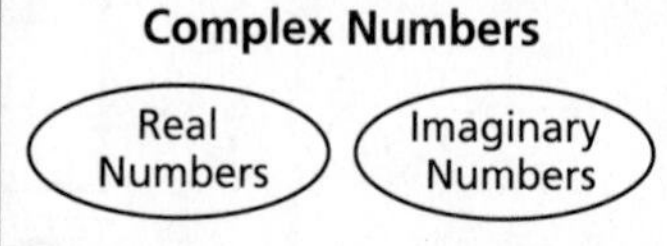

5-5 Exercises

go.hrw.com
Homework Help Online
KEYWORD: MB7 5-5
Parent Resources Online
KEYWORD: MB7 Parent

GUIDED PRACTICE

1. **Vocabulary** The number 7 is the __?__ part of the complex number $\sqrt{5} + 7i$. (*real* or *imaginary*)

SEE EXAMPLE 1 p. 350

Express each number in terms of i.

2. $5\sqrt{-100}$
3. $\frac{1}{2}\sqrt{-16}$
4. $-\sqrt{-32}$
5. $\sqrt{-144}$

SEE EXAMPLE 2 p. 351

Solve each equation.

6. $x^2 = -9$
7. $2x^2 + 72 = 0$
8. $4x^2 = -16$
9. $x^2 + 121 = 0$

SEE EXAMPLE 3 p. 351

Find the values of x and y that make each equation true.

10. $-2x + 6i = (-24y)i - 14$
11. $-4 + (y)i = -12x - i + 8$

SEE EXAMPLE 4 p. 352

Find the zeros of each function.

12. $f(x) = x^2 - 12x + 45$
13. $g(x) = x^2 + 6x + 34$

SEE EXAMPLE 5 p. 352

Find each complex conjugate.

14. $-9i$
15. $\sqrt{5} + 5i$
16. $8i - 3$
17. $6 + i\sqrt{2}$

PRACTICE AND PROBLEM SOLVING

Independent Practice

For Exercises	See Example
18–21	1
22–25	2
26–27	3
28–31	4
32–35	5

Extra Practice

Skills Practice p. S13
Application Practice p. S36

Express each number in terms of i.

18. $8\sqrt{-4}$
19. $-\frac{1}{3}\sqrt{-90}$
20. $6\sqrt{-12}$
21. $\sqrt{-50}$

Solve each equation.

22. $x^2 + 49 = 0$
23. $5x^2 = -80$
24. $3x^2 + 27 = 0$
25. $\frac{1}{2}x^2 = -32$

Find the values of x and y that make each equation true.

26. $9x + (y)i - 5 = -12i + 4$
27. $5(x - 1) + (3y)i = -15i - 20$

Find the zeros of each function.

28. $f(x) = x^2 + 2x + 3$
29. $g(x) = 4x^2 - 3x + 1$
30. $f(x) = x^2 + 4x + 8$
31. $g(x) = 3x^2 - 6x + 10$

Find each complex conjugate.

32. i
33. $-\frac{\sqrt{3}}{2} - 2i$
34. $-2.5i + 1$
35. $\frac{i}{10} - 1$

36. **What if...?** A carnival game asks participants to strike a spring with a hammer. The spring shoots a puck upward toward a bell. If the puck strikes the bell, the participant wins a prize. Suppose that a participant strikes the spring and shoots the puck according to the model $d(t) = 16t^2 - 32t + 18$, where d is the distance in feet between the puck and the bell and t is the time in seconds since the puck was struck. Is it possible for the participant to win a prize? Explain your answer.

18 ft

Given each solution to a quadratic equation, find the other solution.

37. $1 + 14i$ **38.** $\frac{5}{7}i$ **39.** $4i - 2\sqrt{5}$

40. $-12 - i$ **41.** $9 - i\sqrt{2}$ **42.** $-\frac{17i}{3}$

Find the values of c and d that make each equation true.

43. $2ci + 1 = -d + 6 - ci$ **44.** $c + 3ci = 4 + di$ **45.** $c^2 + 4i = d + di$

Solve each equation.

46. $8x^2 = -8$ **47.** $\frac{1}{3}x^2 = -27$ **48.** $2x^2 + 12.5 = 0$

49. $\frac{1}{2}x^2 + 72 = 0$ **50.** $x^2 = -30$ **51.** $2x^2 + 16 = 0$

52. $x^2 - 4x + 8 = 0$ **53.** $x^2 + 10x + 29 = 0$ **54.** $x^2 - 12x + 44 = 0$

55. $x^2 + 2x = -5$ **56.** $x^2 + 18 = -6x$ **57.** $-149 = x^2 - 24x$

LINK

Math History

The Granger Collection, New York

The Swiss mathematician Leonhard Euler (1707–1783) was the first to use the notation i to represent $\sqrt{-1}$. He also introduced the notation $f(x)$ to represent the value of a function f at x.

Tell whether each statement is always, sometimes, or never true. If sometimes true, give examples to support your answer.

58. A real number is an imaginary number.

59. An imaginary number is a complex number.

60. A rational number is a complex number.

61. A complex number is an imaginary number.

62. An integer is a complex number.

63. Quadratic equations have no real solutions.

64. Quadratic equations have roots that are real and complex.

65. Roots of quadratic equations are conjugate pairs.

Find the zeros of each function.

66. $f(x) = x^2 - 10x + 26$ **67.** $g(x) = x^2 + 2x + 17$ **68.** $h(x) = x^2 - 10x + 50$

69. $f(x) = x^2 + 16x + 73$ **70.** $g(x) = x^2 - 10x + 37$ **71.** $h(x) = x^2 - 16x + 68$

72. Critical Thinking Can you determine the zeros of $f(x) = x^2 + 64$ by using a graph? Explain why or why not.

73. Critical Thinking What is the complex conjugate of a real number?

74. Write About It Explain the procedures you can use to solve for nonreal complex roots.

MULTI-STEP TEST PREP

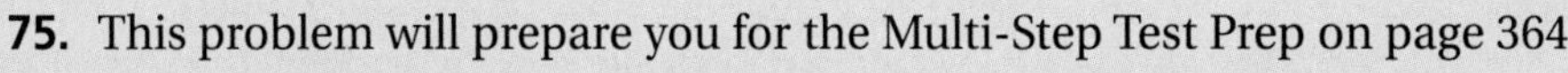

75. This problem will prepare you for the Multi-Step Test Prep on page 364.

A player throws a ball straight up toward the roof of an indoor baseball stadium. The height h in feet of the ball after t seconds can be modeled by the function $h(t) = -16t^2 + 112t$.

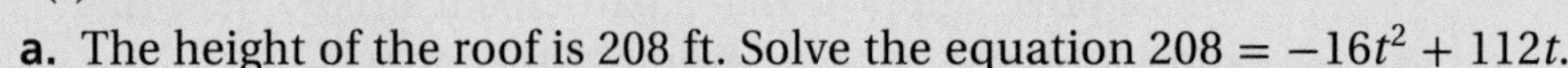

a. The height of the roof is 208 ft. Solve the equation $208 = -16t^2 + 112t$.

b. Based on your answer to part **a**, does the ball hit the roof? Explain your answer.

c. Based on the function model, what is the maximum height that the ball will reach?

76. What is the complex conjugate of $-2 + i$?

Ⓐ $2 + i$ Ⓑ $2 - i$ Ⓒ $i - 2$ Ⓓ $-2 - i$

77. Express $\sqrt{-225}$ in terms of i.

Ⓕ $15i$ Ⓖ $-15i$ Ⓗ $i\sqrt{15}$ Ⓙ $-i\sqrt{15}$

78. Find the zeros of $f(x) = x^2 - 2x + 17$.

Ⓐ $1 \pm 4i$ Ⓑ $4 \pm i$ Ⓒ $-1 \pm 4i$ Ⓓ $-4 \pm i$

79. What value of c makes the equation $3 - 4i - 5 = (9 + ci) - 11$ true?

Ⓕ -2 Ⓖ -4 Ⓗ 2 Ⓙ 4

80. Which of the following equations has roots of $-6i$ and $6i$?

Ⓐ $-\frac{1}{6}x^2 = 6$ Ⓒ $\frac{1}{4}x^2 = 9$

Ⓑ $x^2 - 30 = 6$ Ⓓ $20 - x^2 = -16$

81. **Short Response** Explain the types of solutions that equations of the form $x^2 = a$ have when $a < 0$ and when $a > 0$.

CHALLENGE AND EXTEND

82. Find the complex number $a + bi$ such that $5a + 3b = 1$ and $-5b = 7 + 4a$.

83. Can a quadratic equation have only one real number root? only one imaginary root? only one complex root? Explain.

84. Given the general form of a quadratic equation $x^2 + bx + c = 0$, determine the effect of each condition on the solutions.

a. $b = 0$ **b.** $c \leq 0$ **c.** $c > 0$

d. What is needed for the solutions to have imaginary parts?

SPIRAL REVIEW

Use the following matrices for Exercises 85–88. Evaluate, if possible. *(Lesson 4-2)*

$$S = \begin{bmatrix} 1 & -5 \\ -2 & 0 \end{bmatrix} \quad T = \begin{bmatrix} -4 & 1 & -2 \\ 0 & -3 & 1 \\ 2 & -2 & 2 \end{bmatrix} \quad V = \begin{bmatrix} 10 & 1 \\ 0 & -1 \\ -5 & 5 \end{bmatrix}$$

85. T^2 **86.** TV **87.** ST **88.** S^2

For each function, (a) determine whether the graph opens upward or downward, (b) find the axis of symmetry, (c) find the vertex, (d) find the y-intercept, and (e) graph the function. *(Lesson 5-2)*

89. $f(x) = \frac{1}{5}x^2 + x - 10$ **90.** $f(x) = -x^2 + 3$

91. $f(x) = 2x^2 + 4x - 3$ **92.** $f(x) = -\frac{1}{2}x^2 + 3x + 1$

Find the roots of each equation by factoring. *(Lesson 5-3)*

93. $x^2 + 5x = 14$ **94.** $6x^2 = -x + 2$

95. $4x^2 + 9 = 15x$ **96.** $4x^2 = 1$

97. $x^2 + 11x = -24$ **98.** $x^2 = -7x$

5-6 The Quadratic Formula

Objectives

Solve quadratic equations using the Quadratic Formula.

Classify roots using the discriminant.

Vocabulary

discriminant

Who uses this?

Firefighting pilots can use the Quadratic Formula to estimate when to release water on a fire. (See Example 4.)

You have learned several methods for solving quadratic equations: graphing, making tables, factoring, using square roots, and completing the square. Another method is to use the *Quadratic Formula,* which allows you to solve a quadratic equation in standard form.

By completing the square on the standard form of a quadratic equation, you can determine the Quadratic Formula.

Numbers		Algebra
$3x^2 + 5x + 1 = 0$		$ax^2 + bx + c = 0 \ (a \neq 0)$
$x^2 + \frac{5}{3}x + \frac{1}{3} = 0$	*Divide by a.*	$x^2 + \frac{b}{a}x + \frac{c}{a} = 0$
$x^2 + \frac{5}{3}x = -\frac{1}{3}$	*Subtract $\frac{c}{a}$.*	$x^2 + \frac{b}{a}x = -\frac{c}{a}$
$x^2 + \frac{5}{3}x + \left(\frac{5}{2(3)}\right)^2 = -\frac{1}{3} + \left(\frac{5}{2(3)}\right)^2$	*Complete the square.*	$x^2 + \frac{b}{a}x + \left(\frac{b}{2a}\right)^2 = -\frac{c}{a} + \left(\frac{b}{2a}\right)^2$
$\left(x + \frac{5}{6}\right)^2 = \frac{25}{36} - \frac{1}{3}$	*Factor.*	$\left(x + \frac{b}{2a}\right)^2 = \frac{b^2}{4a^2} - \frac{c}{a}$
$x + \frac{5}{6} = \pm\sqrt{\frac{13}{36}}$	*Take square roots.*	$x + \frac{b}{2a} = \pm\sqrt{\frac{b^2 - 4ac}{4a^2}}$
$x = -\frac{5}{6} \pm \frac{\sqrt{13}}{6}$	*Subtract $\frac{b}{2a}$.*	$x = -\frac{b}{2a} \pm \frac{\sqrt{b^2 - 4ac}}{2a}$
$x = \frac{-5 \pm \sqrt{13}}{6}$	*Simplify.*	$x = \frac{-b \pm \sqrt{b^2 - 4ac}}{2a}$

Remember!

To subtract fractions, you need a common denominator.

$$\frac{b^2}{4a^2} - \frac{c}{a}$$

$$\frac{b^2}{4a^2} - \frac{c}{a}\left(\frac{4a}{4a}\right)$$

$$\frac{b^2 - 4ac}{4a^2}$$

The symmetry of a quadratic function is evident in the next to last step, $x = -\frac{b}{2a} \pm \frac{\sqrt{b^2 - 4ac}}{2a}$. These two zeros are the same distance, $\frac{\sqrt{b^2 - 4ac}}{2a}$, away from the axis of symmetry, $x = -\frac{b}{2a}$, with one zero on either side of the vertex.

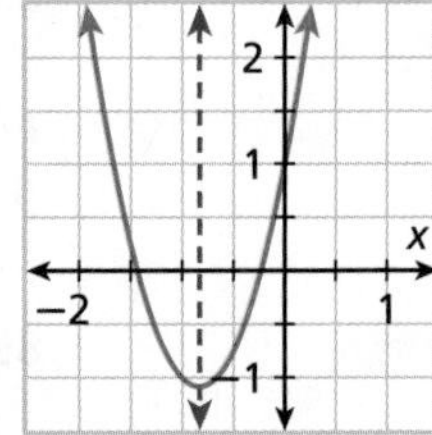

The Quadratic Formula

If $ax^2 + bx + c = 0 \ (a \neq 0)$, then the solutions, or roots, are

$$x = \frac{-b \pm \sqrt{b^2 - 4ac}}{2a}.$$

You can use the Quadratic Formula to solve any quadratic equation that is written in standard form, including equations with real solutions or complex solutions.

EXAMPLE 1 Quadratic Functions with Real Zeros

Find the zeros of $f(x) = x^2 + 10x + 2$ by using the Quadratic Formula.

$x^2 + 10x + 2 = 0$ *Set f(x) = 0.*

$x = \dfrac{-b \pm \sqrt{b^2 - 4ac}}{2a}$ *Write the Quadratic Formula.*

$x = \dfrac{-10 \pm \sqrt{(10)^2 - 4(1)(2)}}{2(1)}$ *Substitute 1 for a, 10 for b, and 2 for c.*

$x = \dfrac{-10 \pm \sqrt{100 - 8}}{2} = \dfrac{-10 \pm \sqrt{92}}{2}$ *Simplify.*

$x = \dfrac{-10 \pm 2\sqrt{23}}{2} = -5 \pm \sqrt{23}$ *Write in simplest form.*

Check Solve by completing the square.

$$x^2 + 10x + 2 = 0$$
$$x^2 + 10x = -2$$
$$x^2 + 10x + 25 = -2 + 25$$
$$(x + 5)^2 = 23$$
$$x = -5 \pm \sqrt{23} \checkmark$$

Find the zeros of each function by using the Quadratic Formula.

1a. $f(x) = x^2 + 3x - 7$ **1b.** $g(x) = x^2 - 8x + 10$

EXAMPLE 2 Quadratic Functions with Complex Zeros

Find the zeros of $f(x) = 2x^2 - x + 2$ by using the Quadratic Formula.

$2x^2 - x + 2 = 0$ *Set f(x) = 0.*

$x = \dfrac{-b \pm \sqrt{b^2 - 4ac}}{2a}$ *Write the Quadratic Formula.*

$x = \dfrac{-(-1) \pm \sqrt{(-1)^2 - 4(2)(2)}}{2(2)}$ *Substitute 2 for a, −1 for b, and 2 for c.*

$x = \dfrac{1 \pm \sqrt{1 - 16}}{4} = \dfrac{1 \pm \sqrt{-15}}{4}$ *Simplify.*

$x = \dfrac{1 \pm i\sqrt{15}}{4} = \dfrac{1}{4} \pm \dfrac{\sqrt{15}}{4}i$ *Write in terms of i.*

2. Find the zeros of $g(x) = 3x^2 - x + 8$ by using the Quadratic Formula.

The **discriminant** is part of the Quadratic Formula that you can use to determine the number of real roots of a quadratic equation.

$$x = \frac{-b \pm \sqrt{b^2 - 4ac}}{2a} \leftarrow \textbf{Discriminant}$$

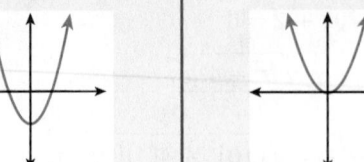

Discriminant

The discriminant of the quadratic equation $ax^2 + bx + c = 0$ $(a \neq 0)$ is $b^2 - 4ac$.

$b^2 - 4ac > 0$	$b^2 - 4ac = 0$	$b^2 - 4ac < 0$
two distinct real solutions	one distinct real solution	two distinct nonreal complex solutions
	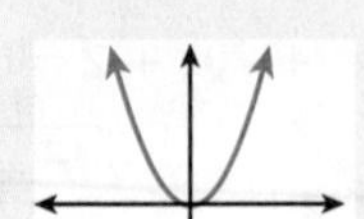	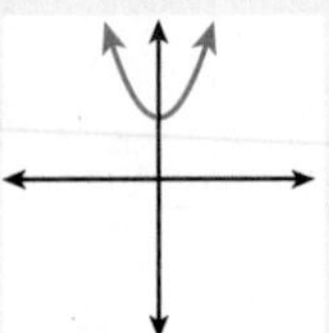

EXAMPLE 3 Analyzing Quadratic Equations by Using the Discriminant

Caution!

Make sure the equation is in standard form before you evaluate the discriminant, $b^2 - 4ac$.

Find the type and number of solutions for each equation.

A $x^2 - 6x = -7$

$x^2 - 6x + 7 = 0$

$b^2 - 4ac$

$(-6)^2 - 4(1)(7)$

$36 - 28 = 8$

$b^2 - 4ac > 0$; the equation has two distinct real solutions.

B $x^2 - 6x = -9$

$x^2 - 6x + 9 = 0$

$b^2 - 4ac$

$(-6)^2 - 4(1)(9)$

$36 - 36 = 0$

$b^2 - 4ac = 0$; the equation has one distinct real solution.

C $x^2 - 6x = -11$

$x^2 - 6x + 11 = 0$

$b^2 - 4ac$

$(-6)^2 - 4(1)(11)$

$36 - 44 = -8$

$b^2 - 4ac < 0$; the equation has two distinct nonreal complex solutions.

Find the type and number of solutions for each equation.

3a. $x^2 - 4x = -4$ **3b.** $x^2 - 4x = -8$ **3c.** $x^2 - 4x = 2$

The graph shows the related functions for Example 3. Notice that the number of real solutions for the equation can be changed by changing the value of the constant c.

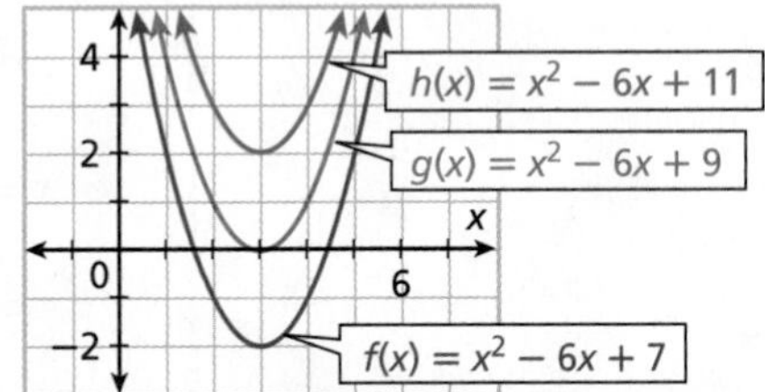

Student to Student

Double-Checking Roots

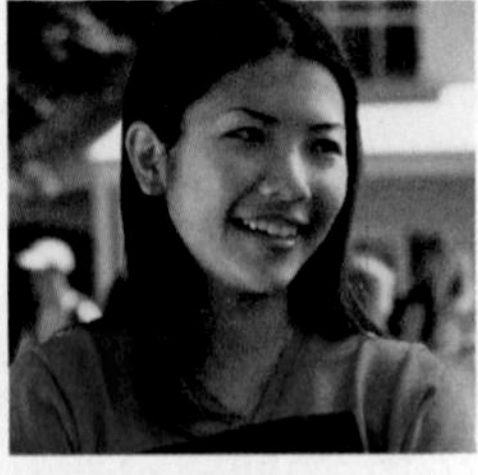

Terry Cannon,
Carver High School

If I get integer roots when I use the Quadratic Formula, I know that I can quickly factor to check the roots. Look at my work for the equation $x^2 - 7x + 10 = 0$.

Quadratic Formula:

$$x = \frac{-(-7) \pm \sqrt{(-7)^2 - 4(1)(10)}}{2(1)}$$

$$= \frac{7 \pm \sqrt{9}}{2} = \frac{10}{2} \text{ or } \frac{4}{2} = 5 \text{ or } 2$$

Factoring:

$x^2 - 7x + 10 = 0$

$(x - 5)(x - 2) = 0$

$x = 5$ or $x = 2$

EXAMPLE 4 Aviation Application

The pilot of a helicopter plans to release a bucket of water on a forest fire. The height y in feet of the water t seconds after its release is modeled by $y = -16t^2 - 2t + 500$. The horizontal distance x in feet between the water and its point of release is modeled by $x = 91t$. At what horizontal distance from the fire should the pilot start releasing the water in order to hit the target?

Step 1 Use the first equation to determine how long it will take the water to hit the ground. Set the height of the water equal to 0 feet, and use the quadratic formula to solve for t.

$$y = -16t^2 - 2t + 500$$

$$0 = -16t^2 - 2t + 500 \qquad \textit{Set y equal to 0.}$$

$$t = \frac{-b \pm \sqrt{b^2 - 4ac}}{2a} \qquad \textit{Use the Quadratic Formula.}$$

$$t = \frac{-(-2) \pm \sqrt{(-2)^2 - 4(-16)(500)}}{2(-16)} \qquad \textit{Substitute for a, b, and c.}$$

$$t = \frac{2 \pm \sqrt{32{,}004}}{-32} \qquad \textit{Simplify.}$$

$$t \approx -5.65 \text{ or } t \approx 5.53$$

The time cannot be negative, so the water lands on the target about 5.5 seconds after it is released.

Caution!

Once you have found the value of t, you have solved only part of the problem. You will use this value to find the answer you are looking for.

Step 2 Find the horizontal distance that the water will have traveled in this time.

$$x = 91t$$

$$x = 91(5.5) \qquad \textit{Substitute 5.5 for t.}$$

$$x = 500.5 \qquad \textit{Simplify.}$$

The water will have traveled a horizontal distance of about 500 feet. Therefore, the pilot should start releasing the water when the horizontal distance between the helicopter and the fire is 500 feet.

Check Use substitution to check that the water hits the ground after about 5.53 seconds.

$$y = -16t^2 - 2t + 500$$

$$y = -16(5.53)^2 - 2(5.53) + 500$$

$$y \approx -0.3544 \checkmark \qquad \textit{The height is approximately equal to 0 when } t = 5.53.$$

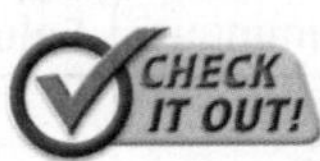

Use the information given above to answer the following.

4. The pilot's altitude decreases, which changes the function describing the water's height to $y = -16t^2 - 2t + 400$. To the nearest foot, at what horizontal distance from the target should the pilot begin releasing the water?

Summary of Solving Quadratic Equations		
Method	**When to Use**	**Examples**
Graphing	Only approximate solutions or the number of real solutions is needed.	$2x^2 + 5x - 14 = 0$ $x \approx -4.2$ or $x \approx 1.7$
Factoring	$c = 0$ or the expression is easily factorable.	$x^2 + 4x + 3 = 0$ $(x + 3)(x + 1) = 0$ $x = -3$ or $x = -1$
Square roots	The variable side of the equation is a perfect square.	$(x - 5)^2 = 24$ $\sqrt{(x-5)^2} = \pm\sqrt{24}$ $x - 5 = \pm 2\sqrt{6}$ $x = 5 \pm 2\sqrt{6}$
Completing the square	$a = 1$ and b is an even number.	$x^2 + 6x = 10$ $x^2 + 6x + \blacksquare = 10 + \blacksquare$ $x^2 + 6x + \left(\frac{6}{2}\right)^2 = 10 + \left(\frac{6}{2}\right)^2$ $(x + 3)^2 = 19$ $x = -3 \pm \sqrt{19}$
Quadratic Formula	Numbers are large or complicated, and the expression does not factor easily.	$5x^2 - 7x - 8 = 0$ $x = \frac{-(-7) \pm \sqrt{(-7)^2 - 4(5)(-8)}}{2(5)}$ $x = \frac{7 \pm \sqrt{209}}{10}$

Helpful Hint

No matter which method you use to solve a quadratic equation, you should get the same answer.

THINK AND DISCUSS

1. Describe how the graphs of quadratic functions illustrate the type and number of zeros.

2. Describe the values of c for which the equation $x^2 + 8x + c = 0$ will have zero, one, or two distinct solutions.

3. GET ORGANIZED Copy and complete the graphic organizer. Describe the possible solution methods for each value of the discriminant.

Value of Discriminant	Type of Solutions	Possible Solution Methods
Negative		
Zero		
Positive		

5-6 Exercises

go.hrw.com
Homework Help Online
KEYWORD: MB7 5-6
Parent Resources Online
KEYWORD: MB7 Parent

GUIDED PRACTICE

1. **Vocabulary** What information does the value of the *discriminant* give about a quadratic equation?

SEE EXAMPLE 1 p. 357

Find the zeros of each function by using the Quadratic Formula.

2. $f(x) = x^2 + 7x + 10$
3. $g(x) = 3x^2 - 4x - 1$
4. $h(x) = 3x^2 - 5x$
5. $g(x) = -x^2 - 5x + 6$
6. $h(x) = 4x^2 - 5x - 6$
7. $f(x) = 2x^2 - 19$

SEE EXAMPLE 2 p. 357

8. $f(x) = 2x^2 - 2x + 3$
9. $r(x) = x^2 + 6x + 12$
10. $h(x) = 3x^2 + 4x + 3$
11. $p(x) = x^2 + 4x + 10$
12. $g(x) = -5x^2 + 7x - 3$
13. $f(x) = 10x^2 + 7x + 4$

SEE EXAMPLE 3 p. 358

Find the type and number of solutions for each equation.

14. $4x^2 + 1 = 4x$
15. $x^2 + 2x = 10$
16. $2x - x^2 = 4$

SEE EXAMPLE 4 p. 359

17. **Geometry** One leg of a right triangle is 6 in. longer than the other leg. The hypotenuse of the triangle is 25 in. What is the length of each leg to the nearest inch?

PRACTICE AND PROBLEM SOLVING

Independent Practice

For Exercises	See Example
18–23	1
24–29	2
30–35	3
36	4

Extra Practice

Skills Practice p. S13
Application Practice p. S36

Find the zeros of each function by using the Quadratic Formula.

18. $f(x) = 3x^2 - 10x + 3$
19. $g(x) = x^2 + 6x$
20. $h(x) = x(x - 3) - 4$
21. $g(x) = -x^2 - 2x + 9$
22. $p(x) = 2x^2 - 7x - 8$
23. $f(x) = 7x^2 - 3$
24. $r(x) = x^2 + x + 1$
25. $h(x) = -x^2 - x - 1$
26. $f(x) = 2x^2 + 8$
27. $f(x) = 2x^2 + 7x - 13$
28. $g(x) = x^2 - x - 5$
29. $h(x) = -3x^2 + 4x - 4$

Find the type and number of solutions for each equation.

30. $2x^2 + 5 = 2x$
31. $2x^2 - 3x = 8$
32. $2x^2 - 16x = -32$
33. $4x^2 - 28x = -49$
34. $3x^2 - 8x + 8 = 0$
35. $3.2x^2 - 8.5x + 1.3 = 0$

36. **Safety** If a tightrope walker falls, he will land on a safety net. His height h in feet after a fall can be modeled by $h(t) = 60 - 16t^2$, where t is the time in seconds. How many seconds will the tightrope walker fall before landing on the safety net?

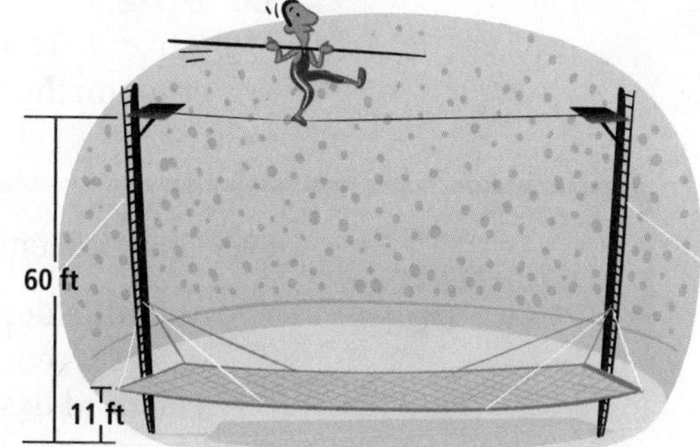

37. **Physics** A bicyclist is riding at a speed of 20 mi/h when she starts down a long hill. The distance d she travels in feet can be modeled by the function $d(t) = 5t^2 + 20t$, where t is the time in seconds.
    a. The hill is 585 ft long. To the nearest second, how long will it take her to reach the bottom?
    b. **What if...?** Suppose the hill were only half as long. To the nearest second, how long would it take the bicyclist to reach the bottom?

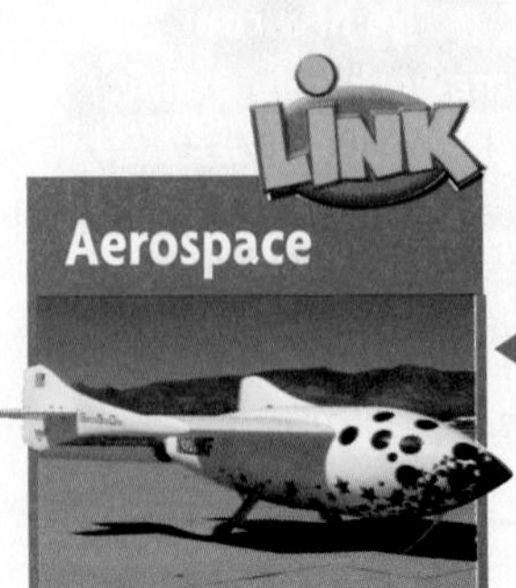

Aerospace

SpaceShipOne was the winner of the Ansari X Prize competition. The X Prize was awarded to the first nongovernmental spacecraft to reach an altitude of at least 100 km twice within a 2 week period.

Find the zeros of each function. Then graph the function.

38. $f(x) = 3x^2 - 4x - 2$
39. $g(x) = 2x^2 - 2x - 1$
40. $h(x) = 2x^2 + 6x + 5$
41. $p(x) = 2x^2 + 3x - 1$
42. $h(x) = 3x^2 - 5x - 4$
43. $r(x) = x^2 - x + 22$

44. **Aerospace** In 2004, the highest spaceplane flight was made by Brian Binnie in *SpaceShipOne*. A flight with this altitude can be modeled by the function $h(t) = -0.17t^2 + 187t + 61{,}000$, where h is the altitude in meters and t is flight time in seconds.
    a. Approximately how long did the flight last?
    b. What was the highest altitude to the nearest thousand meters?
    c. The table shows the altitudes of layers of Earth's atmosphere. According to the model, which of these layers did *SpaceShipOne* enter, and at what time(s) did the spaceplane enter them?

Earth's Atmosphere

Layer	Altitude (in km)
Troposphere	0 to 10
Stratosphere	10 to 50
Mesosphere	50 to 85
Thermosphere	85 to 600

Solve each equation by any method.

45. $x^2 - 3x = 10$
46. $x^2 - 16 = 0$
47. $4x^2 + 4x = 15$
48. $x^2 + 2x - 2 = 0$
49. $x^2 - 4x - 21 = 0$
50. $4x^2 - 4x - 1 = 0$
51. $6x^2 = 150$
52. $x^2 = 7$
53. $x^2 - 16x + 64 = 0$

54. **Critical Thinking** If you are solving a real-world problem involving a quadratic equation, and the discriminant is negative, what can you conclude?

55. **Multi-Step** The outer dimensions of a picture frame are 25 inches by 20 inches. If the area inside the picture frame is 266 square inches, what is the width w of the frame?

Critical Thinking Find the values of c that make each equation have one real solution.

56. $x^2 + 8x + c = 0$
57. $x^2 + 12x = c$
58. $x^2 + 2cx + 49 = 0$

59. **Write About It** What method would you use to solve the equation $-14x^2 + 6x = 2.7$? Why would this method be easier to use than the other methods?

MULTI-STEP TEST PREP

60. This problem will prepare you for the Multi-Step Test Prep on page 364.

    An outfielder throws a baseball to the player on third base. The height h of the ball in feet is modeled by the function $h(t) = -16t^2 + 19t + 5$, where t is time in seconds. The third baseman catches the ball when it is 4 ft above the ground.

    a. To the nearest tenth of a second, how long was the ball in the air before it was caught?
    b. A player on the opposing team starts running from second base to third base 1.2 s before the outfielder throws the ball. The distance between the bases is 90 ft, and the runner's average speed is 27 ft/s. Will the runner reach third base before the ball does? Explain.

61. Which best describes the graph of a quadratic function with a discriminant of -3?

Ⓐ Parabola with two x-intercepts
Ⓑ Parabola with no x-intercepts
Ⓒ Parabola that opens upward
Ⓓ Parabola that opens downward

62. What is the discriminant of the equation $2x^2 - 8x = 14$?

Ⓕ 48 Ⓗ 176
Ⓖ -48 Ⓙ -176

63. Which function has zeros of $3 \pm i$?

Ⓐ $f(x) = x^2 + 6x + 10$ Ⓒ $g(x) = x^2 - 6x + 10$
Ⓑ $f(x) = x^2 + 6x - 10$ Ⓓ $h(x) = x^2 - 6x - 10$

64. Which best describes the discriminant of the function whose graph is shown?

Ⓕ Positive Ⓗ Negative
Ⓖ Zero Ⓙ Undefined

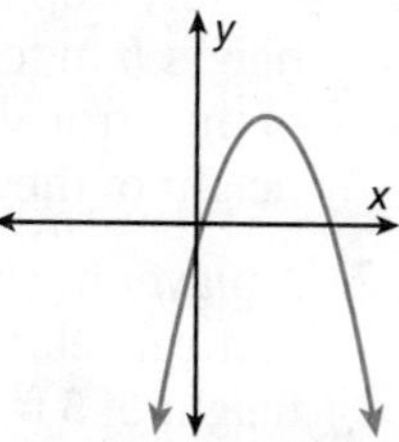

CHALLENGE AND EXTEND

65. **Geometry** The perimeter of a right triangle is 40 cm, and its hypotenuse measures 17 cm. Find the length of each leg.

66. **Geometry** The perimeter of a rectangle is 88 cm.
   a. Find the least possible value of the length of the diagonal. Round to the nearest tenth of a centimeter.
   b. What are the dimensions of the rectangle with this diagonal?

Write a quadratic equation whose solutions belong to the indicated sets.

67. integers 68. irrational real numbers 69. complex numbers

70. A quadratic equation has the form $ax^2 + bx + c = 0\ (a \neq 0)$.
   a. What is the sum of the roots of the equation? the product of the roots?
   b. Determine the standard form of a quadratic equation whose roots have a sum of 2 and a product of -15.

71. Describe the solutions to a quadratic equation for which $a = b = c$.

SPIRAL REVIEW

72. **Biology** The length of a human hair is a linear function of time. Juan's hair grows 2.1 cm in 60 days. Express the growth in centimeters of Juan's hair as a function of the number of days since his last haircut. *(Lesson 2-4)*

Write the augmented matrix, and use row reduction to solve. *(Lesson 4-6)*

73. $\begin{cases} 3y = 2x + 7 \\ x - 6y = 1 \end{cases}$ 74. $\begin{cases} 2x = -3y + 12 \\ x + y = 14 \end{cases}$ 75. $\begin{cases} 4x + 5y = -1 \\ 9 + 7y = 2x \end{cases}$

Solve each equation by completing the square. *(Lesson 5-4)*

76. $x^2 - 5x = 1$ 77. $2x^2 = 16x - 4$ 78. $3x = 5x^2 - 12$

CHAPTER 5

MULTI-STEP TEST PREP

SECTION 5A

Quadratic Functions and Complex Numbers

Ballpark Figures When a baseball is thrown or hit into the air, its height h in feet after t seconds can be modeled by $h(t) = -16t^2 + v_y t + h_0$, where v_y is the initial vertical velocity of the ball in feet per second and h_0 is the ball's initial height. The horizontal distance d in feet that the ball travels in t seconds can be modeled by $d(t) = v_x t$, where v_x is the ball's initial horizontal velocity in feet per second.

1. A short stop makes an error by dropping the ball. As the ball drops, its height h in feet is modeled by $h(t) = -16t^2 + 3$. A slow-motion replay of the error shows the play at half speed. What function describes the height of the ball in the replay?
2. A player hits a foul ball with an initial vertical velocity of 70 ft/s and an initial height of 5 ft. To the nearest foot, what is the maximum height reached by the ball?
3. A pitch will be a strike if its height is between 2.5 ft and 5 ft when it crosses home plate. The pitcher throws the ball from a height of 6 ft with an initial vertical velocity of 5 ft/s and a horizontal velocity of 116 ft/s. Could this pitch be a strike? Explain.
4. The next pitch crosses home plate 1 ft too high to be a strike. The pitch is thrown from a height of 6 ft with an initial vertical velocity of 8 ft/s. What is the initial horizontal velocity of this pitch?
5. A player throws the ball home from a height of 5.5 ft with an initial vertical velocity of 28 ft/s. The ball is caught at home plate at a height of 5 ft. Three seconds before the ball is thrown, a runner on third base starts toward home plate at an average speed of 25 ft/s. Does the runner reach home plate before the ball does? Explain.

Quiz for Lessons 5-1 Through 5-6

5-1 Using Transformations to Graph Quadratic Functions

Using the graph of $f(x) = x^2$ as a guide, describe the transformations, and then graph each function.

1. $g(x) = (x + 2)^2 - 4$
2. $g(x) = -4(x - 1)^2$
3. $g(x) = \frac{1}{2}x^2 + 1$

Use the description to write each quadratic function in vertex form.

4. $f(x) = x^2$ is vertically stretched by a factor of 9 and translated 2 units left to create g.
5. $f(x) = x^2$ is reflected across the x-axis and translated 4 units up to create g.

5-2 Properties of Quadratic Functions in Standard Form

For each function, (a) determine whether the graph opens upward or downward, (b) find the axis of symmetry, (c) find the vertex, (d) find the y-intercept, and (e) graph the function.

6. $f(x)= x^2 - 4x + 3$
7. $g(x) = -x^2 + 2x - 1$
8. $h(x) = x^2 - 6x$
9. A football kick is modeled by the function $h(x) = -0.0075x^2 + 0.5x + 5$, where h is the height of the ball in feet and x is the horizontal distance in feet that the ball travels. Find the maximum height of the ball to the nearest foot.

5-3 Solving Quadratic Equations by Graphing and Factoring

Find the roots of each equation by factoring.

10. $x^2 - 100 = 0$
11. $x^2 + 5x = 24$
12. $4x^2 + 8x = 0$

5-4 Completing the Square

Solve each equation by completing the square.

13. $x^2 - 6x = 40$
14. $x^2 + 18x = 15$
15. $x^2 + 14x = 8$

Write each function in vertex form, and identify its vertex.

16. $f(x) = x^2 + 24x + 138$
17. $g(x) = x^2 - 12x + 39$
18. $h(x) = 5x^2 - 20x + 9$

5-5 Complex Numbers and Roots

Solve each equation.

19. $3x^2 = -48$
20. $x^2 - 20x = -125$
21. $x^2 - 8x + 30 = 0$

5-6 The Quadratic Formula

Find the zeros of each function by using the Quadratic Formula.

22. $f(x) = (x + 6)^2 + 2$
23. $g(x) = x^2 + 7x + 15$
24. $h(x) = 2x^2 - 5x + 3$
25. A bicyclist is riding at a speed of 18 mi/h when she starts down a long hill. The distance d she travels in feet can be modeled by $d(t) = 4t^2 + 18t$, where t is the time in seconds. How long will it take her to reach the bottom of a 400-foot-long hill?

5-7 Solving Quadratic Inequalities

Objectives
Solve quadratic inequalities by using tables and graphs.

Solve quadratic inequalities by using algebra.

Vocabulary
quadratic inequality in two variables

Who uses this?

Tour companies and other businesses use quadratic inequalities to make predictions of profits. (See Example 4.)

Many business profits can be modeled by quadratic functions. To ensure that the profit is above a certain level, financial planners may need to graph and solve *quadratic inequalities.*

A **quadratic inequality in two variables** can be written in one of the following forms, where a, b, and c are real numbers and $a \neq 0$. Its solution set is a set of ordered pairs (x, y).

$$y < ax^2 + bx + c \qquad y > ax^2 + bx + c$$
$$y \leq ax^2 + bx + c \qquad y \geq ax^2 + bx + c$$

In Lesson 2-5, you solved linear inequalities in two variables by graphing. You can use a similar procedure to graph quadratic inequalities.

Graphing Quadratic Inequalities

To graph a quadratic inequality	
1. Graph the parabola that defines the boundary.	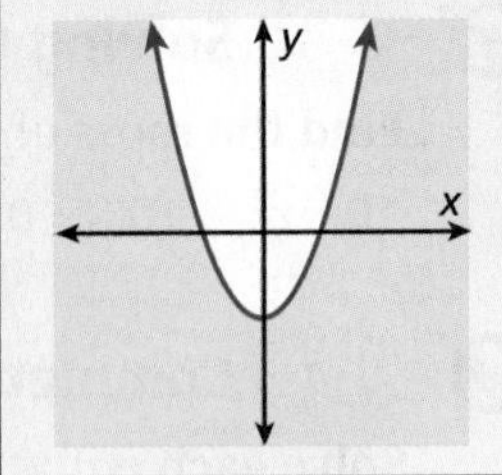
2. Use a solid parabola for $y \leq$ and $y \geq$ and a dashed parabola for $y <$ and $y >$.	
3. Shade above the parabola for $y >$ or $\geq$ and below the parabola for $y \leq$ or $<$.	

EXAMPLE 1 **Graphing Quadratic Inequalities in Two Variables**

Graph $y < -2x^2 - 4x + 6$.

Step 1 Graph the boundary of the related parabola $y = -2x^2 - 4x + 6$ with a dashed curve.

Its y-intercept is 6, its vertex is $(-1, 8)$, and its x-intercepts are -3 and 1.

Step 2 Shade below the parabola because the solution consists of y-values less than those on the parabola for corresponding x-values.

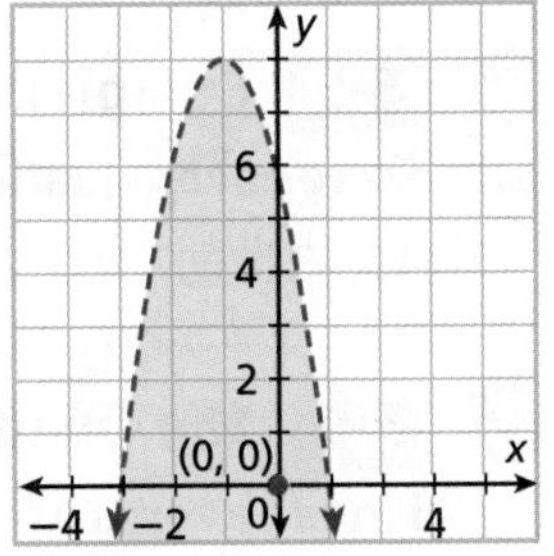

Check Use a test point to verify the solution region.

$$y < -2x^2 - 4x + 6$$
$$0 < -2(0)^2 - 4(0) + 6 \qquad \textit{Try } (0, 0).$$
$$0 < 6 \checkmark$$

CHECK IT OUT! **Graph each inequality.**

1a. $y \geq 2x^2 - 5x - 2$ **1b.** $y < -3x^2 - 6x - 7$

Quadratic inequalities in one variable, such as $ax^2 + bx + c > 0\ (a \neq 0)$, have solutions in one variable that are graphed on a number line.

EXAMPLE 2 Solving Quadratic Inequalities by Using Tables and Graphs

Solve each inequality by using tables or graphs.

A $x^2 - 6x + 8 \leq 3$

Use a graphing calculator to graph each side of the inequality. Set **Y1** equal to $x^2 - 6x + 8$ and **Y2** equal to 3. Identify the values of x for which **Y1** $\leq$ **Y2**.

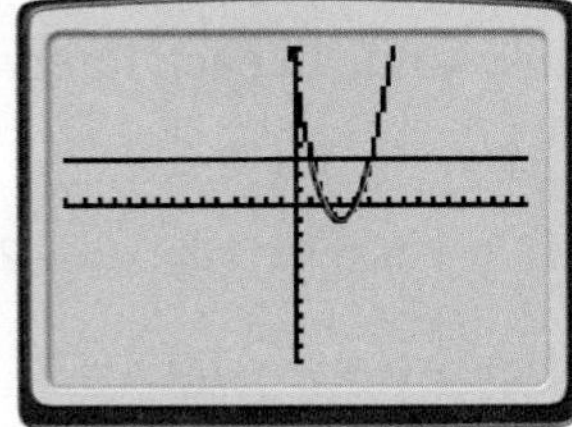

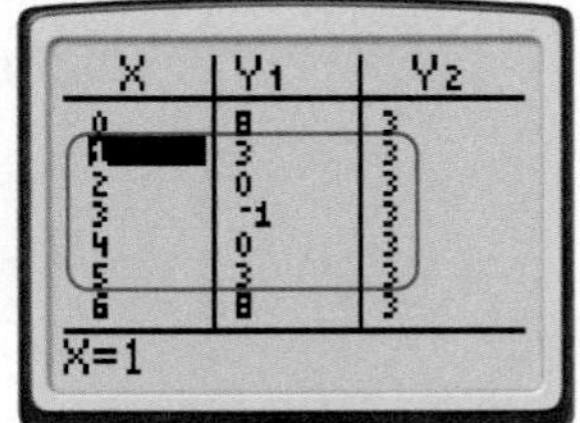

The parabola is at or below the line when x is between 1 and 5 inclusive. So, the solution set is $1 \leq x \leq 5$, or $[1, 5]$. The table supports your answer.

The number line shows the solution set.

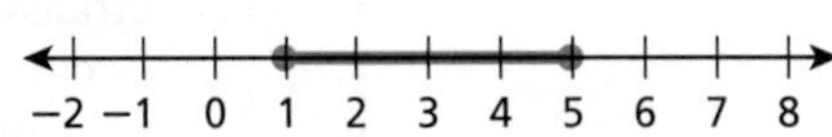

B $x^2 - 6x + 8 > 3$

Use a graphing calculator to graph each side of the inequality. Set **Y1** equal to $x^2 - 6x + 8$ and **Y2** equal to 3. Identify the values of x for which **Y1** $>$ **Y2**.

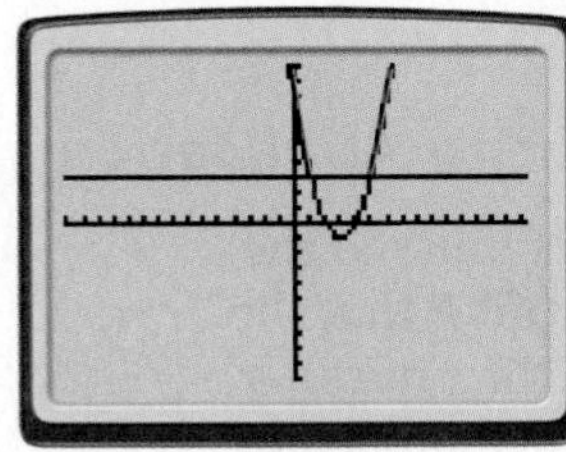

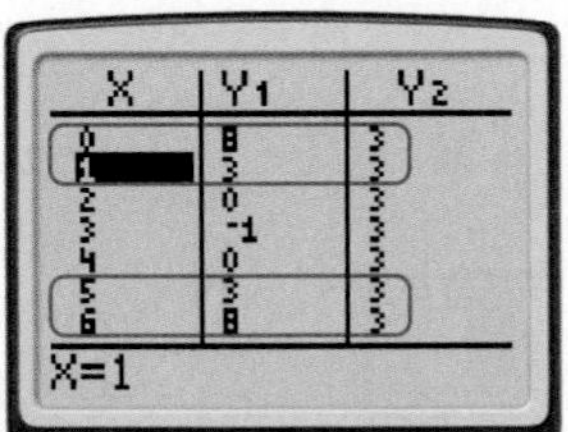

The parabola is above the line $y = 3$ when x is less than 1 or greater than 5. So the solution set is $x < 1$ or $x > 5$, or $(-\infty, 1) \cup (5, \infty)$.

The number line shows the solution set.

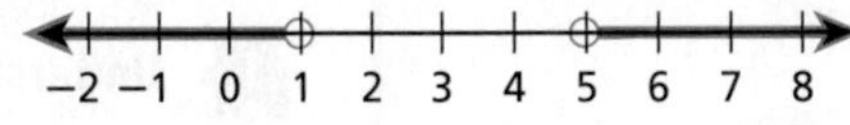

For **and** statements, *both* of the conditions must be true. For **or** statements, *at least one* of the conditions must be true.

CHECK IT OUT! **Solve each inequality by using tables or graphs.**

2a. $x^2 - x + 5 < 7$ **2b.** $2x^2 - 5x + 1 \geq 1$

The number lines showing the solution sets in Example 2 are divided into three distinct regions by the points 1 and 5. These points are called *critical values*. By finding the critical values, you can solve quadratic inequalities algebraically.

EXAMPLE 3 Solving Quadratic Inequalities by Using Algebra

Solve the inequality $x^2 - 4x + 1 > 6$ by using algebra.

Step 1 Write the related equation.

$$x^2 - 4x + 1 = 6$$

Step 2 Solve the equation for x to find the critical values.

$x^2 - 4x - 5 = 0$ *Write in standard form.*

$(x - 5)(x + 1) = 0$ *Factor.*

$x - 5 = 0$ or $x + 1 = 0$ *Zero Product Property*

$x = 5$ or $x = -1$ *Solve for x.*

The critical values are 5 and −1. The critical values divide the number line into three intervals: $x < -1$, $-1 < x < 5$, and $x > 5$.

Step 3 Test an x-value in each interval.

$$x^2 - 4x + 1 > 6$$

$(-2)^2 - 4(-2) + 1 > 6$ ✔ *Try x = −2.*

$(0)^2 - 4(0) + 1 > 6$ ✘ *Try x = 0.*

$(6)^2 - 4(6) + 1 > 6$ ✔ *Try x = 6.*

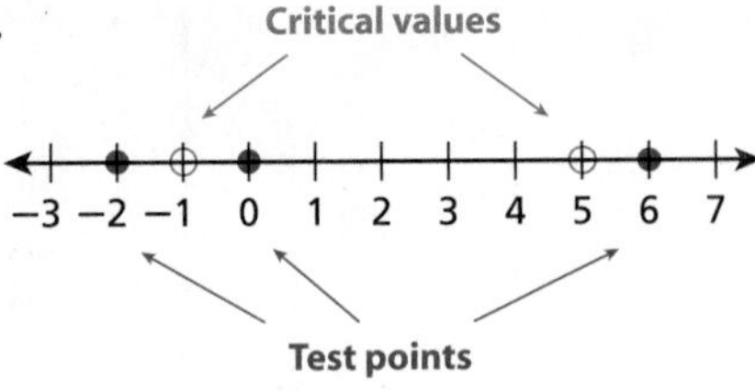

Shade the solution regions on the number line. Use open circles for the critical values because the inequality does not contain *or equal to.*

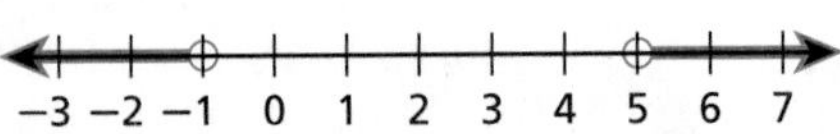

The solution is $x < -1$ or $x > 5$, or $(-\infty, -1) \cup (5, \infty)$.

Solve each inequality by using algebra.

3a. $x^2 - 6x + 10 \geq 2$ **3b.** $-2x^2 + 3x + 7 < 2$

EXAMPLE 4 *Problem-Solving Application*

PROBLEM SOLVING

A business offers tours to the Amazon. The profit P that the company earns for x number of tourists can be modeled by $P(x) = -25x^2 + 1000x - 3000$. How many people are needed for a profit of at least \$5000?

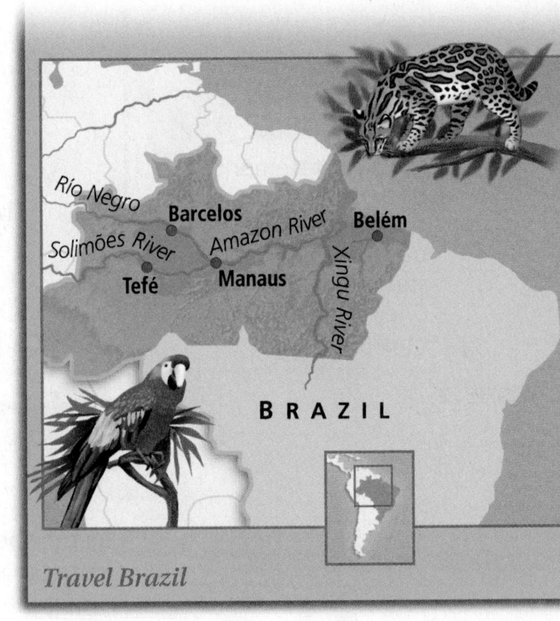

1 Understand the Problem

The **answer** will be the number of people required for a profit that is greater than or equal to \$5000.

List the important information:

- The profit must be at least \$5000.
- The function for the profit is $P(x) = -25x^2 + 1000x - 3000$.

2 Make a Plan

Write an inequality showing profit greater than or equal to \$5000. Then solve the inequality by using algebra.

3 Solve

Write the inequality.

$$-25x^2 + 1000x - 3000 \geq 5000$$

Find the critical values by solving the related equation.

$$-25x^2 + 1000x - 3000 = 5000 \quad \textit{Write as an equation.}$$

$$-25x^2 + 1000x - 8000 = 0 \quad \textit{Write in standard form.}$$

$$-25(x^2 - 40x + 320) = 0 \quad \textit{Factor out } -25 \textit{ to simplify.}$$

$$x = \frac{-b \pm \sqrt{b^2 - 4ac}}{2a} = \frac{-(-40) \pm \sqrt{(-40)^2 - 4(1)(320)}}{2(1)} \quad \textit{Use the Quadratic Formula.}$$

$$= \frac{40 \pm \sqrt{320}}{2} \quad \textit{Simplify.}$$

$$x \approx 28.94 \text{ or } x \approx 11.06$$

Test an x-value in each of the three regions formed by the critical x-values.

$$-25(10)^2 + 1000(10) - 3000 \overset{?}{\geq} 5000 \quad \textit{Try } x = 10.$$

$$4500 \geq 5000 \; ✗$$

$$-25(20)^2 + 1000(20) - 3000 \overset{?}{\geq} 5000 \quad \textit{Try } x = 20.$$

$$7000 \geq 5000 \; ✓$$

$$-25(30)^2 + 1000(30) - 3000 \overset{?}{\geq} 5000 \quad \textit{Try } x = 30.$$

$$4500 \geq 5000 \; ✗$$

Remember!

A compound inequality such as $12 \leq x \leq 28$ can be written as $\{x \mid x \geq 12 \cup x \leq 28\}$, or $x \geq 12$ and $x \leq 28$. (See Lesson 2-8.)

Write the solution as an inequality. The solution is approximately $11.06 \leq x \leq 28.94$. Because you cannot have a fraction of a person, round each critical value to the appropriate whole number.

$$12 \leq x \leq 28$$

For a profit of at least \$5000, from 12 to 28 people are needed.

4 Look Back

Enter $y = -25x^2 + 1000x - 3000$ into a graphing calculator, and create a table of values. The table shows that integer values of x between 12 and 28 inclusive result in y-values greater than or equal to 5000.

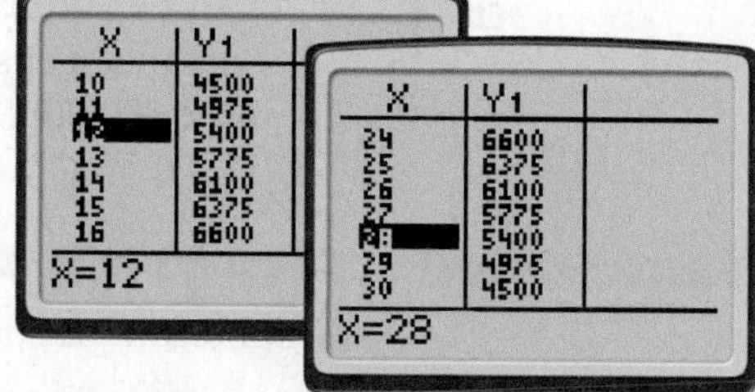

4. The business also offers educational tours to Patagonia, a region of South America that includes parts of Chile and Argentina. The profit P for x number of persons is $P(x) = -25x^2 + 1250x - 5000$. The trip will be rescheduled if the profit is less than \$7500. How many people must have signed up if the trip is rescheduled?

THINK AND DISCUSS

1. Compare graphing a quadratic inequality with graphing a linear inequality.
2. Explain how to determine if the intersection point(s) is/are included in the solution set when you solve a quadratic inequality by graphing.

3. **GET ORGANIZED** Copy and complete the graphic organizer. Compare the solutions of quadratic equations and inequalities.

	Equation (=)	"Less Than" Inequality (< or ≤)	"Greater Than" Inequality (> or ≥)
Example			
Graph			
Solution Set			

5-7 Exercises

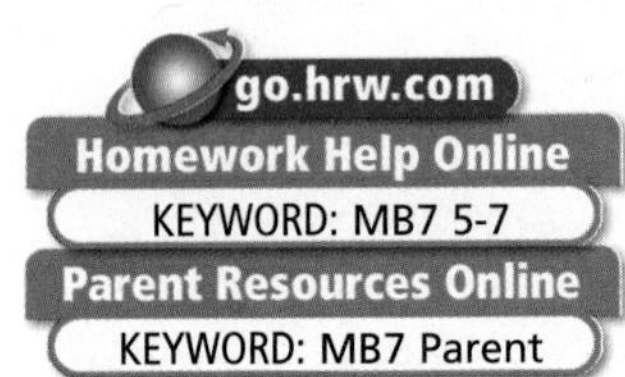

GUIDED PRACTICE

1. **Vocabulary** Give an example of a *quadratic inequality in two variables.*

SEE EXAMPLE 1 p. 366

Graph each inequality.

2. $y > -(x+1)^2 + 5$
3. $y \le 2x^2 - 4x - 1$
4. $y \le -3x^2 + x + 3$

SEE EXAMPLE 2 p. 367

Solve each inequality by using tables or graphs.

5. $x^2 - 5x + 3 \le 3$
6. $3x^2 - 3x - 1 > -1$
7. $2x^2 - 9x + 5 \le -4$

SEE EXAMPLE 3 p. 368

Solve each inequality by using algebra.

8. $x^2 + 10x + 1 \ge 12$
9. $x^2 + 13x + 45 < 5$
10. $-2x^2 + 3x + 12 > 10$

SEE EXAMPLE 4 p. 368

11. **Business** A consultant advises the owners of a beauty salon that their profit p each month can be modeled by $p(x) = -50x^2 + 3500x - 2500$, where x is the average cost that a customer is charged. What range of costs will bring in a profit of at least $50,000?

PRACTICE AND PROBLEM SOLVING

Graph each inequality.

12. $y < x^2 + 2x - 5$
13. $y > -\frac{1}{2}x^2 + 3$
14. $y \le 2(x-1)^2 - 3$
15. $y \ge x^2 + 6$
16. $y < (x+1)(x+4)$
17. $y \le x^2 - 2x + 6$

Solve each inequality by using tables or graphs.

18. $x^2 - x + 5 < 11$
19. $2x^2 + 3x + 6 \ge 5$
20. $x^2 - 5x + 12 > 6$
21. $x^2 - 2x - 8 > 0$
22. $x^2 + 7x + 6 \le 6$
23. $x^2 - 12x + 32 < 12$

Independent Practice

For Exercises	See Example
12–17	1
18–23	2
24–26	3
27	4

Extra Practice

Skills Practice p. S13
Application Practice p. S36

Solve each inequality by using algebra.

24. $x^2 - 11x + 13 \le 25$ **25.** $-2x^2 + 3x + 4 \ge -1$ **26.** $x^2 - 5x - 4 < -9$

27. Sports A football thrown by a quarterback follows a path given by $h(x) = -0.0095x^2 + x + 7$, where h is the height of the ball in feet and x is the horizontal distance the ball has traveled in feet. If any height less than 10 feet can be caught or knocked down, at what distances from the quarterback can the ball be knocked down?

Graph each quadratic inequality.

28. $y \le 2x^2 + 4x - 3$ **29.** $y < 3x^2 - 12x - 4$ **30.** $y \ge -3x^2 + 4x$

31. $y > -2(x + 3)^2 + 1$ **32.** $y > -x^2 - 2x - 1$ **33.** $y \le \frac{1}{3}x^2 + 2x - 1$

34. Circus The human cannonball is an act where a performer is launched through the air. The height of the performer can be modeled by $h(x) = -0.007x^2 + x + 20$, where h is the height in feet and x is the horizontal distance traveled in feet. The circus act is considering a flight path directly over the main tent.

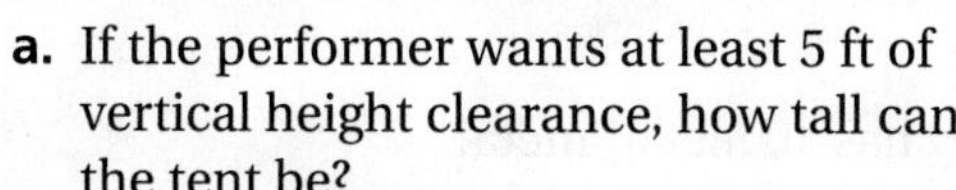

a. If the performer wants at least 5 ft of vertical height clearance, how tall can the tent be?

b. How far from the central pole should the "cannon" be placed?

Solve each inequality by using any method.

35. $x^2 - 5x - 24 \le 0$ **36.** $x^2 - 14 \ge 2$ **37.** $-2x^2 - x + 8 > 6$

38. $x^2 - 4x - 5 \le -9$ **39.** $3x^2 + 6x + 11 < 10$ **40.** $4x^2 - 9 > 0$

41. $3x^2 + 5x + 13 \le 16$ **42.** $-2x^2 + 3x + 17 \ge 11$ **43.** $5x^2 - 2x - 1 \ge 0$

44. $(x - 2)(x + 11) \ge 2$ **45.** $x^2 + 27 > 12x$ **46.** $-2x^2 + 3x + 6 > 0$

47. Multi-Step A medical office has a rectangular parking lot that measures 120 ft by 200 ft. The owner wants to expand the size of the parking lot by adding an equal distance to two sides as shown. If zoning restrictions limit the total size of the parking lot to 35,000 ft^2, what range of distances can be added?

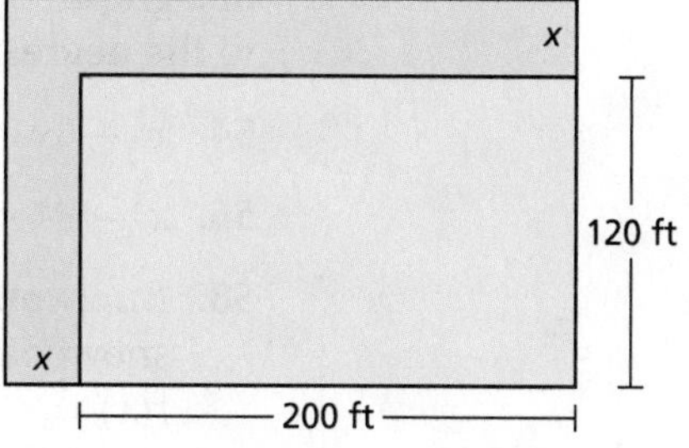

Match each graph with one of the following inequalities.

A. $y < x^2 + 2x - 3$ **B.** $y > -x^2 - 2x + 3$ **C.** $y < x^2 - 2x + 3$

48.

49.

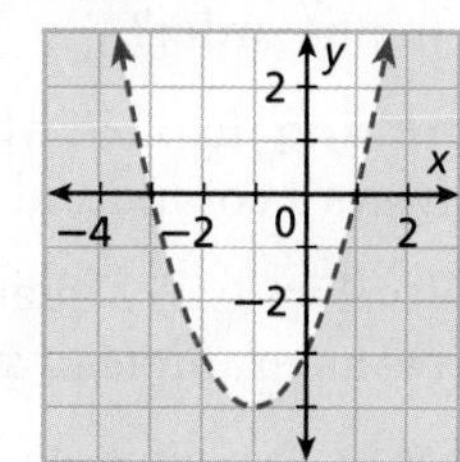

50.

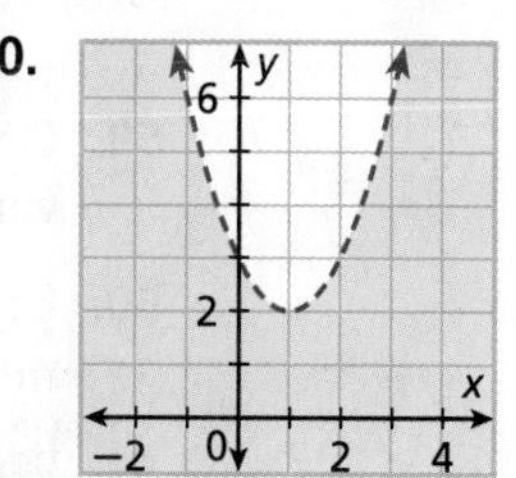

51. This problem will prepare you for the Multi-Step Test Prep on page 390. A small square tile is placed on top of a larger square tile as shown. This creates four congruent triangular regions.

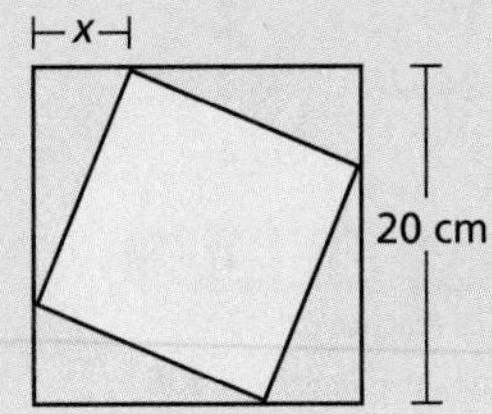

a. Write a function for the area A of one of the triangular regions in terms of x.

b. For what values of x, to the nearest tenth, is the area of each triangular region at least 30 cm^2?

c. For what values of x, to the nearest tenth, is the area of each triangular region less than 40 cm^2?

52. **Music** A manager estimates a band's profit p for a concert by using the function $p(t) = -200t^2 + 2500t - c$, where t is the price per ticket and c is the band's operating cost. The table shows the band's operating cost at three different concert locations. What range of ticket prices should the band charge at each location in order to make a profit of at least \$1000 at each concert?

Band's Costs	
Location	**Operating Cost**
Freemont Park	\$900
Saltillo Plaza	\$1500
Riverside Walk	\$2500

53. **Gardening** Lindsey has 40 feet of metal fencing material to fence three sides of a rectangular garden. A tall wooden fence serves as her fourth side.

a. Write a function for the area of the garden A in terms of x, the width in feet.

b. What measures for the width will give an area of at least 150 square feet?

c. What measures for the width will give an area of at least 200 square feet?

Graphing Calculator Use the intersect feature of a graphing calculator to solve each inequality to the nearest tenth.

54. $x^2 + 6x - 13 > 4$

55. $x^2 - 15x + 20 \leq 7$

56. $x^2 - 24 < 28$

57. $2x^2 + 3x + 5 \geq 8$

58. **Business** A wholesaler sells snowboards to sporting-good stores. The price per snowboard varies based on the number purchased in each order. The function $r(x) = -x^2 + 125x$ models the wholesaler's revenue r in dollars for an order of x snowboards.

a. To the nearest dollar, what is the maximum revenue per order?

b. How many snowboards must the wholesaler sell to make at least \$1500 in revenue in one order?

59. **Critical Thinking** Explain whether the solution to a quadratic inequality in one variable is always a compound inequality.

60. **Critical Thinking** Can a quadratic inequality have a solution set that is all real numbers? Give an example to support your answer.

61. **Write About It** Explain how the solutions of $x^2 - 3x - 4 \leq 6$ differ from the solutions of $x^2 - 3x - 4 = 6$.

TEST PREP

62. Which is the solution set of $x^2 - 9 < 0$?

Ⓐ $-3 < x < 3$
Ⓑ $-9 < x < 9$
Ⓒ $x < -3$ or $x > 3$
Ⓓ $x < -9$ or $x > 9$

63. Which is the graph of the solution to $x^2 - 7x + 10 \geq 0$?

Ⓕ 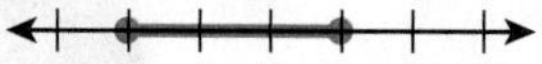

Ⓗ 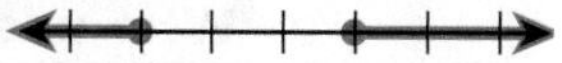

Ⓖ 

Ⓙ 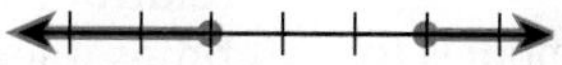

64. Which is the solution set of $x^2 - 7x \leq 0$?

Ⓐ $0 < x < 7$
Ⓑ $0 \leq x \leq 7$
Ⓒ $x < 0$ or $x > 7$
Ⓓ $x \leq 0$ or $x \geq 7$

65. **Short Response** Demonstrate the process for solving $x^2 + 4x + 4 > 1$ algebraically. Justify each step in the solution process.

CHALLENGE AND EXTEND

Graph each system of inequalities.

66. $\begin{cases} y \leq x^2 \\ y \geq -x^2 + 5 \end{cases}$

67. $\begin{cases} y \geq x^2 - 3 \\ y \leq -x^2 - 2x + 9 \end{cases}$

68. $\begin{cases} y \geq 2x^2 - 12x + 20 \\ y \geq \frac{1}{3}x^2 - 2x + 8 \end{cases}$

Geometry The area inside a parabola bounded from above or below by a horizontal line segment is $\frac{2}{3}bh$, where b is the length of the line segment and h is the vertical distance from the vertex of the parabola to the line segment. Find the area bounded by the graphs of each pair of inequalities.

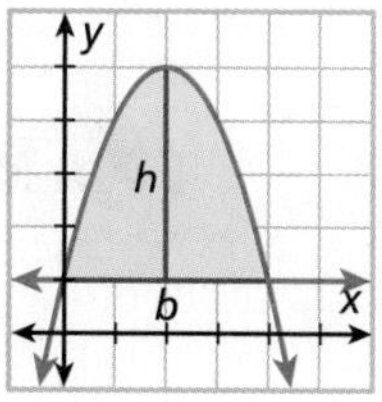

69. $y > x^2 + 5x - 6$; $y < 8$

70. $y < -2x^2 + 3x + 9$; $y > -5$

SPIRAL REVIEW

71. **Community** Once a month, four teams of teens (lawn team, shopping team, cleaning team, and laundry team) spend a day assisting elderly residents of their neighborhood. Lynnette started the assignment chart for June but was interrupted. Complete the chart. Each home has only one team helping during each shift. *(Previous course)*

Shifts	Reed Home	Brown Home	Sondi Home	Clem Home
7:00 A.M.–9:30 A.M.	Lawn	Cleaning	?	?
10:00 A.M.–12:30 P.M.	?	Shopping	?	Lawn
1:00 P.M.–3:30 P.M.	?	?	Laundry	?
4:00 P.M.–6:30 P.M.	Cleaning	?	?	?

Graph each inequality by using intercepts. *(Lesson 2-5)*

72. $4x - 3y > 15$

73. $6x - y \leq 8$

74. $8x + 5y < 40$

Find the values of c that make each equation true. *(Lesson 5-5)*

75. $4 - 2c + 7i = 7i - 14$

76. $4c + 2 - 3i + 2(i - 5) = 4(2i - 6) - 9i$

5-8 Curve Fitting with Quadratic Models

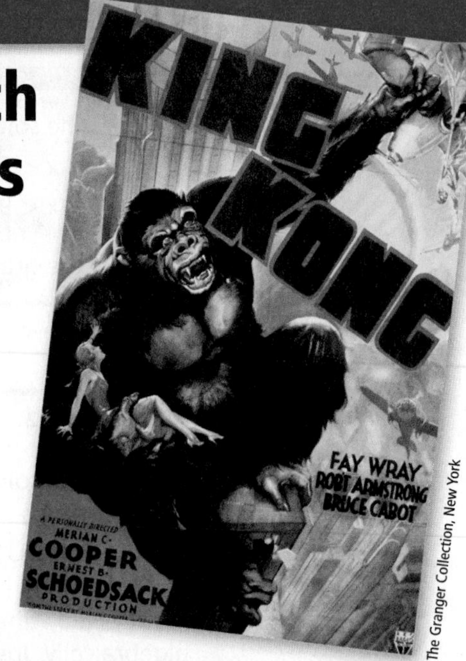

The Granger Collection, New York

Objectives
Use quadratic functions to model data.

Use quadratic models to analyze and predict.

Vocabulary
quadratic model
quadratic regression

Who uses this?
Film preservationists use quadratic relationships to estimate film run times. (See Example 3.)

Recall that you can use differences to analyze patterns in data. For a set of ordered pairs with equally spaced x-values, a quadratic function has constant nonzero second differences, as shown below.

Equally spaced x-values

x	−3	−2	−1	0	1	2	3
$f(x) = x^2$	9	4	1	0	1	4	9

1st differences −5 −3 −1 1 3 5
2nd differences 2 2 2 2 2

Constant 2nd differences

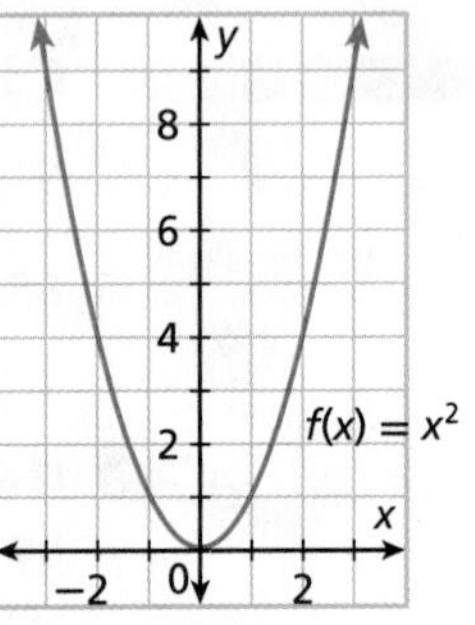

EXAMPLE 1 Identifying Quadratic Data

Determine whether each data set could represent a quadratic function. Explain.

x	0	2	4	6	8
y	12	10	9	9	10

Find the first and second differences.

Equally spaced x-values

x	0	2	4	6	8
y	12	10	9	9	10

1st −2 −1 0 1
2nd 1 1 1

Quadratic function; second differences are constant for equally spaced x-values.

x	−2	−1	0	1	2
y	1	2	4	8	16

Find the first and second differences.

Equally spaced x-values

x	−2	−1	0	1	2
y	1	2	4	8	16

1st 1 2 4 8
2nd 1 2 4

Not a quadratic function; second differences are not constant for equally spaced x-values.

Determine whether each data set could represent a quadratic function. Explain.

1a.

x	3	4	5	6	7
y	11	21	35	53	75

1b.

x	10	9	8	7	6
y	6	8	10	12	14

Just as two points define a linear function, three noncollinear points define a quadratic function. You can find the three coefficients, a, b, and c, of $f(x) = ax^2 + bx + c$ by using a system of three equations, one for each point. The points do not need to have equally spaced x-values.

EXAMPLE 2 Writing a Quadratic Function from Data

Write a quadratic function that fits the points $(0, 5)$, $(2, 1)$, and $(3, 2)$.

> **Reading Math**
>
> *Collinear* points lie on the same line. *Noncollinear* points *do not* all lie on the same line.

Use each point to write a system of equations to find a, b, and c in $f(x) = ax^2 + bx + c$.

(x, y)	$f(x) = ax^2 + bx + c$	System in a, b, c
$(0, 5)$	$5 = a(0)^2 + b(0) + c$	$c = 5$ ❶
$(2, 1)$	$1 = a(2)^2 + b(2) + c$	$4a + 2b + c = 1$ ❷
$(3, 2)$	$2 = a(3)^2 + b(3) + c$	$9a + 3b + c = 2$ ❸

Substitute $c = 5$ from equation ❶ into both equation ❷ and equation ❸.

❷ $4a + 2b + c = 1$
$4a + 2b + 5 = 1$
$4a + 2b = -4$ ❹

❸ $9a + 3b + c = 2$
$9a + 3b + 5 = 2$
$9a + 3b = -3$ ❺

Solve equation ❹ and equation ❺ for a and b using elimination.

❹ $3(4a + 2b) = 3(-4) \rightarrow 12a + 6b = -12$ *Multiply by 3.*
❺ $-2(9a + 3b) = -2(-3) \rightarrow -18a - 6b = 6$ *Multiply by −2.*
$-6a = -6$ *Add the equations.*
$a = 1$

Substitute 1 for a into equation ❹ or equation ❺ to find b.

❹ $4a + 2b = -4 \rightarrow 4(1) + 2b = -4$
$2b = -8$
$b = -4$

Write the function using $a = 1$, $b = -4$, and $c = 5$.

$$f(x) = ax^2 + bx + c \rightarrow f(x) = 1x^2 - 4x + 5, \text{ or } f(x) = x^2 - 4x + 5$$

Check Substitute or create a table to verify that $(0, 5)$, $(2, 1)$, and $(3, 2)$ satisfy the function rule.

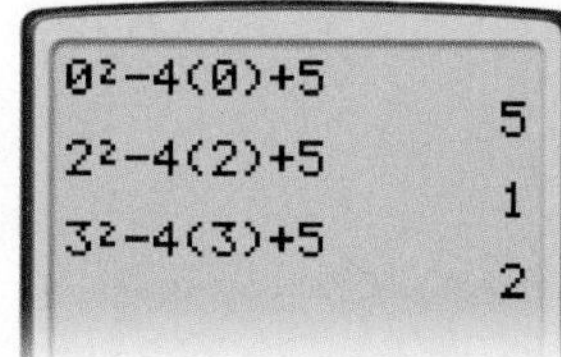

2. Write a quadratic function that fits the points $(0, -3)$, $(1, 0)$, and $(2, 1)$.

You may use any method that you studied in Chapters 3 or 4 to solve the system of three equations in three variables. For example, you can use a matrix equation as shown.

$$\begin{cases} c = 5 \\ 4a + 2b + c = 1 \\ 9a + 3b + c = 2 \end{cases} \rightarrow \begin{bmatrix} 0 & 0 & 1 \\ 4 & 2 & 1 \\ 9 & 3 & 1 \end{bmatrix} \begin{bmatrix} a \\ b \\ c \end{bmatrix} = \begin{bmatrix} 5 \\ 1 \\ 2 \end{bmatrix} \rightarrow \begin{bmatrix} a \\ b \\ c \end{bmatrix} = \begin{bmatrix} 1 \\ -4 \\ 5 \end{bmatrix}$$

[A]⁻¹[B]
[[1]
[-4]
[5]]

A **quadratic model** is a quadratic function that represents a real data set. Models are useful for making estimates.

In Chapter 2, you used a graphing calculator to perform a *linear regression* and make predictions. You can apply a similar statistical method to make a quadratic model for a given data set using **quadratic regression.**

EXAMPLE 3 *Film Application*

The table shows approximate run times for 16 mm films, given the diameter of the film on the reel. Find a quadratic model for the run time given the diameter. Use the model to estimate the run time for a reel of film with a diameter of 15 in.

Film Run Times (16 mm)

Diameter (in.)	Reel Length (ft)	Run Time (min)
5	200	5.55
7	400	11.12
9.25	600	16.67
10.5	800	22.22
12.25	1200	33.33
13.75	1600	44.45

Helpful Hint

The coefficient of determination R^2 shows how well a quadratic model fits the data. The closer R^2 is to 1, the better the fit. In this model, $R^2 \approx 0.996$, which is very close to 1, so the quadratic model is a good fit.

Step 1 Enter the data into two lists in a graphing calculator.

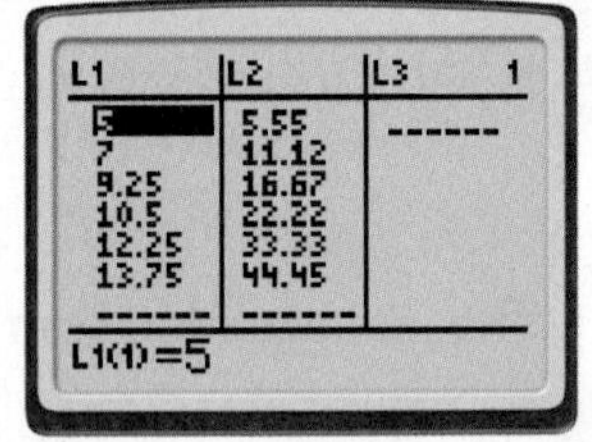

Step 2 Use the quadratic regression feature.

Step 3 Graph the data and function model to verify that the model fits the data.

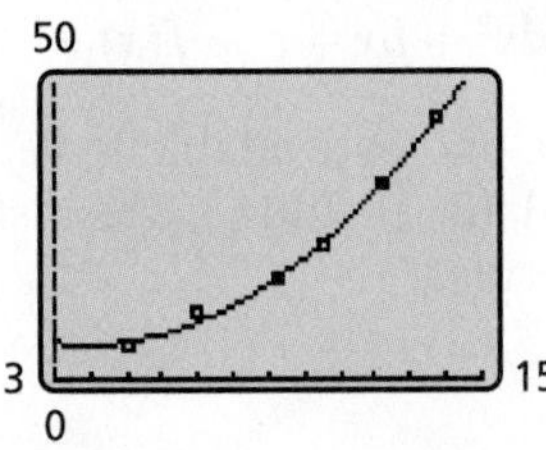

Step 4 Use the table feature to find the function value at $x = 15$.

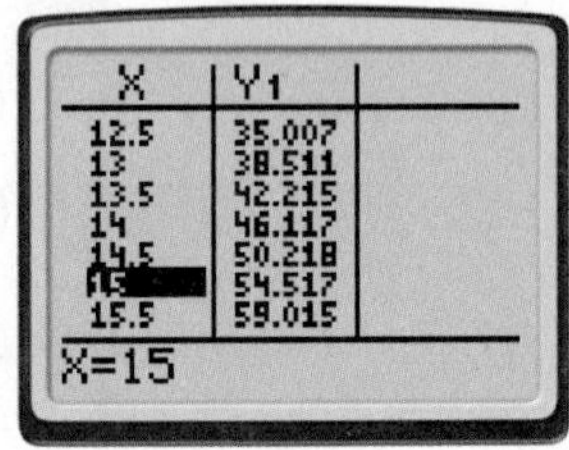

A quadratic model is $T(d) \approx 0.397d^2 - 3.12d + 11.94$, where T is the run time in minutes and d is the film diameter in inches.

For a 15 in. diameter, the model predicts a run time of about 54.5 min, or 54 min 30 s.

Use the information given above to answer the following.

3. Find a quadratic model for the reel length given the diameter of the film. Use the model to estimate the reel length for an 8-inch-diameter film.

THINK AND DISCUSS

1. Describe how to determine if a data set is quadratic.
2. Explain whether a quadratic function is a good model for the path of an airplane that ascends, descends, and rises again out of view.

3. **GET ORGANIZED** Copy and complete the graphic organizer. Compare the different quadratic models presented in the lesson.

Quadratic Model	When Appropriate	Procedure
Exact model		
Approximate model		

5-8 Exercises

GUIDED PRACTICE

1. **Vocabulary** How does a *quadratic model* differ from a linear model?

SEE EXAMPLE 1 p. 374

Determine whether each data set could represent a quadratic function. Explain.

2.

x	−2	−1	0	1	2
y	16	8	0	−8	−16

3.

x	1	2	3	4	5
y	1	3	9	27	81

4.

x	2	4	6	8	10
y	4	−5	−8	−5	4

SEE EXAMPLE 2 p. 375

Write a quadratic function that fits each set of points.

5. $(-2, 5)$, $(0, -3)$, and $(3, 0)$
6. $(0, 1)$, $(2, -1)$, and $(3, -8)$
7. $(-1, 8)$, $(0, 4)$, and $(2, 2)$
8. $(-4, 9)$, $(0, -7)$, and $(1, -1)$
9. $(2, 3)$, $(6, 3)$, and $(8, -3)$
10. $(-1, -12)$, $(1, 0)$, and $(2, 9)$

SEE EXAMPLE 3 p. 376

11. **Hobbies** The cost of mounting different-sized photos is shown in the table. Find a quadratic model for the cost given the average side length. (For an 8 in. × 10 in. photo, the average side length is $\frac{8 + 10}{2} = 9$ in.) Estimate the cost of mounting a 24 in. × 36 in. photo.

Costs of Mounting Photos

Size (in.)	Cost ($)
8 × 10	10
14 × 18	16
16 × 20	19
24 × 30	27
32 × 40	39

PRACTICE AND PROBLEM SOLVING

Determine whether each data set could represent a quadratic function. Explain.

12.

x	0	2	4	6	8
f(x)	−1	2	11	26	47

13.

x	0	1	2	3	4
f(x)	10	9	6	1	−6

14.

x	1	2	3	4	5
f(x)	−3	0	3	6	9

Independent Practice	
For Exercises	See Example
12–14	1
15–18	2
19	3

Extra Practice

Skills Practice p. S13
Application Practice p. S36

Write a quadratic function that fits each set of points.

15. $(-2, 5), (-1, 0)$, and $(1, -2)$

16. $(1, 2), (2, -1)$, and $(5, 2)$

17. $(-4, 12), (-2, 0)$, and $(2, -12)$

18. $(-1, 2.6), (1, 4.2)$, and $(2, 14)$

19. **Gardening** The table shows the amount spent on water gardening in the United States between 1999 and 2003. Find a quadratic model for the annual amount in millions of dollars spent on water gardening based on number of years since 1999. Estimate the amount that people in the United States will spend on water gardening in 2015.

Water Gardening

Year	Amount Spent (million $)
1999	806
2000	943
2001	1205
2002	1441
2003	1565

Write a function rule for each situation, and identify each relationship as linear, quadratic, or neither.

20. the circumference C of a bicycle wheel, given its radius r

21. the area of a triangle A with a constant height, given its base length b

22. the population of bacteria P in a petri dish doubling every hour t

23. the area of carpet A needed for square rooms of length s

24. **Physics** In the past, different mathematical descriptions of falling objects were proposed.

a. Which rule shows the greatest increase in the distance fallen per second and thus the greatest rate of increase in speed?

b. Identify each rule as linear, quadratic, or neither.

c. Describe the differences in da Vinci's rule, and compare it with the differences in Galileo's.

d. The most accurate rule is sometimes described as the odd-number law. Which rule shows an odd-number pattern of first differences and correctly describes the distance for falling objects?

Relative Distance Fallen (units)

Time Interval (s)	Aristotle's Rule	da Vinci's Rule	Galileo's Rule
0	0	0	0
1	1	1	1
2	2	3	4
3	3	6	9
4	4	10	16

Find the missing value for each quadratic function.

25.

x	−1	0	1	2	3
$f(x)$	0	1	0	■	−8

26.

x	−3	−2	−1	0	1
$f(x)$	12	2	■	0	8

27.

x	−2	0	2	4	6
$f(x)$	−2	■	2	7	14

MULTI-STEP TEST PREP

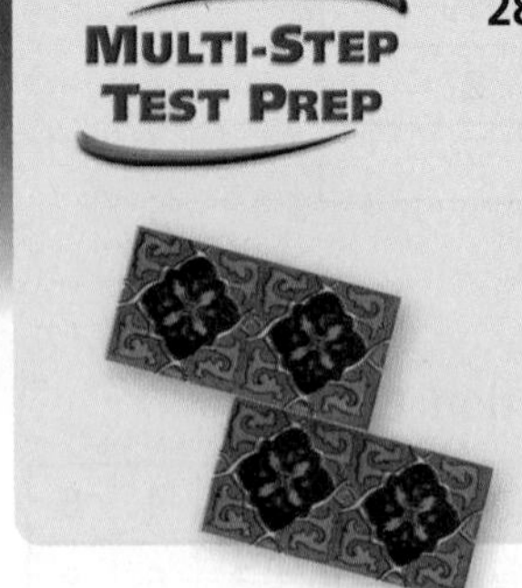

28. This problem will prepare you for the Multi-Step Test Prep on page 390. A home-improvement store sells several sizes of rectangular tiles, as shown in the table.

a. Find a quadratic model for the area of a tile based on its length.

b. The store begins selling a new size of tile with a length of 9 in. Based on your model, estimate the area of a tile of this size.

Length (in.)	Area (in^2)
4	28
6	54
8	88
10	130

29. **Food** The pizza prices for DeAngelo's pizza parlor are shown at right.

a. Find a quadratic model for the price of a pizza based upon the size (diameter).

b. Use the quadratic model to find the price of a pizza with an 18 in. diameter.

c. Graph the quadratic function. Does the function have a minimum or maximum point? What does this point represent?

d. **What if...?** According to the model, how much should a 30 in. pizza cost? How much should an 8 in. pizza cost?

e. Is the quadratic function a good model for the price of DeAngelo's pizza? Explain your reasoning.

Determine whether each data set could represent a quadratic function. If so, find a quadratic function rule.

30.

x	0	1	2	3	4
y	−1	0	−1	−4	−9

31.

x	1	2	3	4	5
y	10	20	40	60	80

32.

x	2	4	6	8	10
y	−1	0	1	3	5

33.

x	−2	−1	0	1	2
y	16	3	0	7	24

34.

x	0	1	2	3	4
y	9	5	3	1	0

35.

x	−2	−1	0	1	2
y	0	3	9	27	81

36. **Winter Sports** The diagram shows the motion of a skier following a jump. Find a quadratic model of the skier's height h in meters based on time t in seconds. Estimate the skier's height after 2 s.

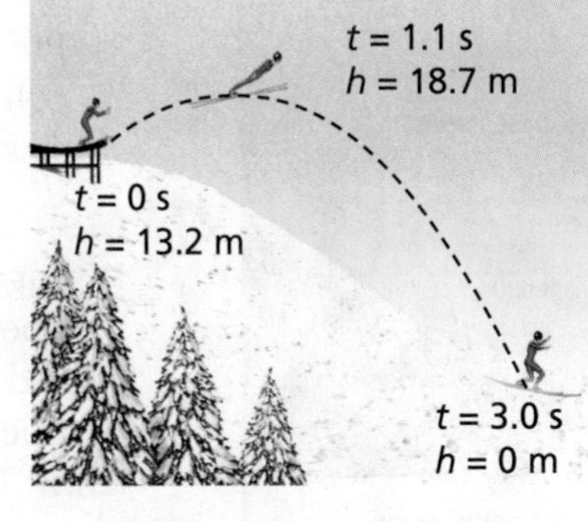

37. **Data Collection** Use a graphing calculator and a motion detector to measure the height of a basketball over time. Drop the ball from a height of 1 m, and let it bounce several times. Position the motion detector 0.5 m above the release point of the ball.

a. What is the greatest height the ball reaches during its first bounce?

b. Find an appropriate model for the height of the ball as a function of time during its first bounce.

38. **Safety** The light produced by high-pressure sodium vapor streetlamps for different energy usages is shown in the table.

High-Pressure Sodium Vapor Streetlamps

Energy Use (watts)	35	50	70	100	150
Light Output (lumens)	2250	4000	5800	9500	16,000

a. Find a quadratic model for the light output with respect to energy use.

b. Find a linear model for the light output with respect to energy use.

c. Apply each model to estimate the light output in lumens of a 200-watt bulb.

d. Which model gives the better estimate? Explain.

39. **Sports** The table lists the average distance that a normal shot travels for different golf clubs.

Average Distance for Normal Shot								
Club Iron (no.)	2	3	4	5	6	7	8	9
Loft Angle	16°	20°	24°	28°	32°	36°	40°	44°
Distance (yd)	186	176	166	155	143	132	122	112

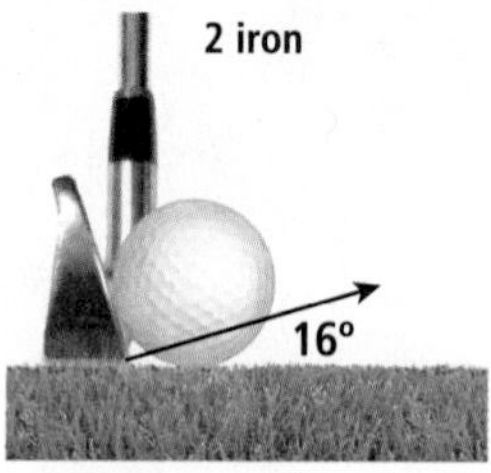

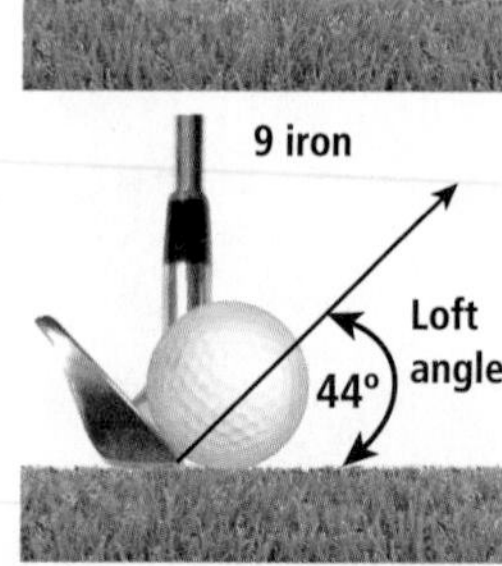

a. Select three data values (club number, distance), and use a system of equations to find a quadratic model. Check your model by using a quadratic regression.

b. Is there a quadratic relationship between club number and average distance of a normal shot? Explain.

c. Is the relationship between club number and loft angle quadratic or linear? Find a model of this relationship.

40. **Multi-Step** Use the table of alloy-steel chain data.

a. Do each of the last two columns appear to be quadratic functions with respect to the nominal chain size? Explain.

b. Verify your response in part a by finding each of the quadratic regression equations. Do the models fit the data well? Explain.

c. Predict the values for the last two columns for a chain with a nominal size of $\frac{5}{8}$ in.

Alloy-Steel Chain Specifications		
Nominal Size (in.)	**Maximum Length 100 Links (in.)**	**Maximum Weight 100 Links (lb)**
$\frac{1}{4}$	98	84
$\frac{1}{2}$	156	288
$\frac{3}{4}$	208	655
1	277	1170
$1\frac{1}{4}$	371	1765

LINK

Math History

Pythagoras made numerous contributions to mathematics, including the Pythagorean Theorem, which bears his name.

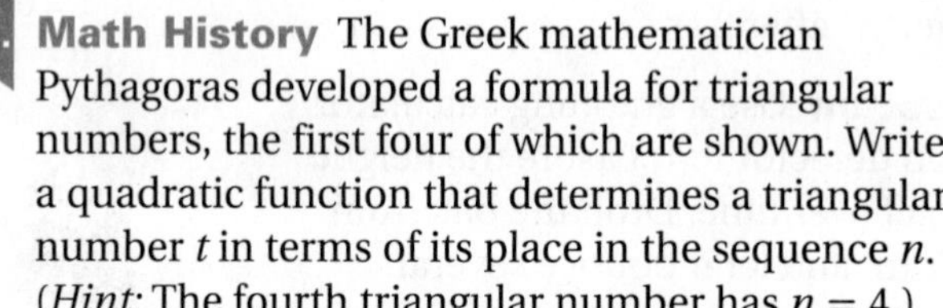

41. **Math History** The Greek mathematician Pythagoras developed a formula for triangular numbers, the first four of which are shown. Write a quadratic function that determines a triangular number t in terms of its place in the sequence n. (*Hint:* The fourth triangular number has $n = 4$.)

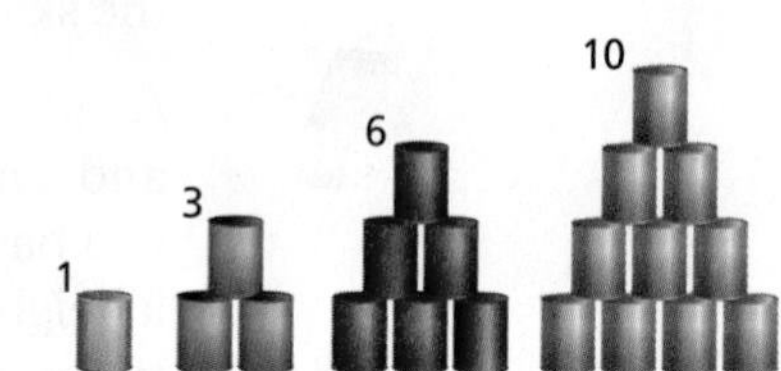

42. **Critical Thinking** Two points define a unique line. How many points define a unique parabola, and what restriction applies to the points?

43. **Critical Thinking** Consider the following data set.

x	10	8	13	9	11	14	6	4	12	7	5
y	9.14	8.14	8.74	8.77	9.29	8.1	6.13	3.1	9.13	7.26	4.74

a. Create a scatter plot of the data.

b. Perform a linear regression on the data.

c. Perform a quadratic regression on the data.

d. Which model best describes the data set? Explain your answer.

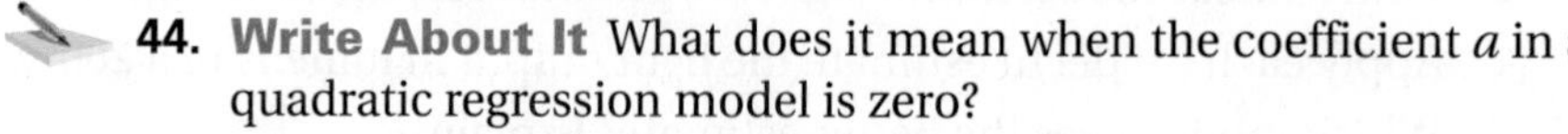

44. **Write About It** What does it mean when the coefficient a in a quadratic regression model is zero?

45. Which of the following would best be modeled by a quadratic function?

Ⓐ Relationship between circumference and diameter

Ⓑ Relationship between area of a square and side length

Ⓒ Relationship between diagonal of a square and side length

Ⓓ Relationship between volume of a cube and side length

46. If (7, 11) and (3, 11) are two points on a parabola, what is the *x*-value of the vertex of this parabola?

Ⓕ 3 Ⓖ 5 Ⓗ 7 Ⓙ 11

47. If *y* is a quadratic function of *x*, which value completes the table?

x	−2	0	2	4	6
y	−8	0	12	28	■

Ⓐ 12 Ⓑ 20 Ⓒ 44 Ⓓ 48

48. The graph of a quadratic function having the form $f(x) = ax^2 + bx + c$ passes through the points (0, −8), (3, 10), and (6, 34). What is the value of the function when $x = -3$?

Ⓕ −32 Ⓖ −26 Ⓗ −20 Ⓙ 10

49. **Extended Response** Write a quadratic function in standard form that fits the data points (0, −5), (1, −3), and (2, 3). Use a system of equations, and show all of your work.

CHALLENGE AND EXTEND

50. Three points defining a quadratic function are (1, 2), (4, 6), and (7, *w*).
   a. If $w = 9$, what is the quadratic function? Does it have a maximum value or a minimum value? What is the vertex?
   b. If $w = 11$, what is the quadratic function? Does it have a maximum value or a minimum value? What is the vertex?
   c. If $w = 10$, what function best fits the points?

51. Explain how you can determine from three points whether the parabola that fits the points opens upward or downward.

SPIRAL REVIEW

Determine whether each data set could represent a linear function. *(Lesson 2-3)*

52.

x	−2	1	4
f(*x*)	−5	7	1

53.

x	−8	−6	0
f(*x*)	−1	0	3

Find the inverse of the matrix, if it is defined. *(Lesson 4-5)*

54. $\begin{bmatrix} \frac{1}{3} & 0 \\ -4 & 1 \end{bmatrix}$ 55. $\begin{bmatrix} 2 & -2 \\ 1 & -1 \end{bmatrix}$ 56. $\begin{bmatrix} -2 & 0 & 1 \\ 0 & 0 & 1 \\ 4 & 2 & 2 \end{bmatrix}$ 57. $\begin{bmatrix} 3 & -4 \\ 0 & -\frac{1}{2} \end{bmatrix}$

Find the zeros of each function by using the Quadratic Formula. *(Lesson 5-6)*

58. $f(x) = 2x^2 - 4x + 1$ 59. $f(x) = x^2 + 9$ 60. $f(x) = -3x^2 + 10x + 12$

5-9 Operations with Complex Numbers

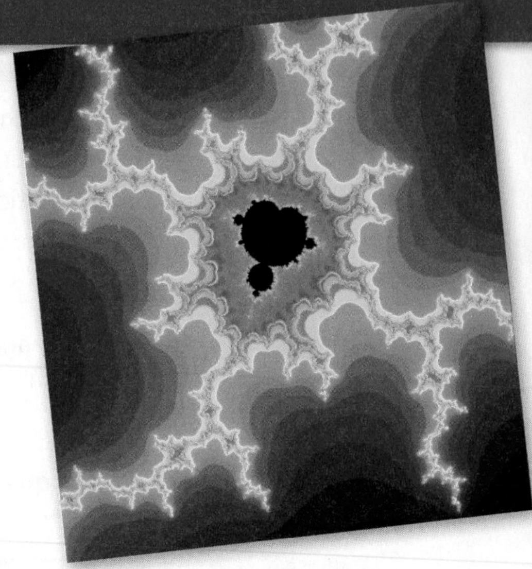

Objective
Perform operations with complex numbers.

Vocabulary
complex plane
absolute value of a complex number

Why learn this?
Complex numbers can be used in formulas to create patterns called fractals. (See Exercise 84.)

Just as you can represent real numbers graphically as points on a number line, you can represent complex numbers in a special coordinate plane.

The **complex plane** is a set of coordinate axes in which the horizontal axis represents real numbers and the vertical axis represents imaginary numbers.

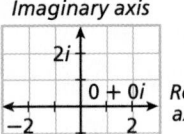

Imaginary axis
$2i$, $0 + 0i$, -2, 2, $-2i$
Real axis

EXAMPLE 1 Graphing Complex Numbers

Helpful Hint
The real axis corresponds to the x-axis, and the imaginary axis corresponds to the y-axis. Think of $a + bi$ as $x + yi$.

Graph each complex number.

A $-3 + 0i$

B $-3i$

C $4 + 3i$

D $-2 + 4i$

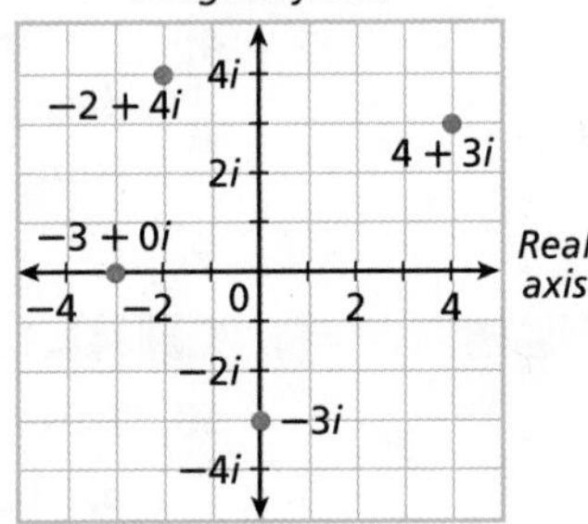

Graph each complex number.

1a. $3 + 0i$ **1b.** $2i$ **1c.** $-2 - i$ **1d.** $3 + 2i$

Recall that the absolute value of a real number is its distance from 0 on the real axis, which is also a number line. Similarly, the absolute value of an imaginary number is its distance from 0 along the imaginary axis.

Know it! Note

Absolute Value of a Complex Number

WORDS	ALGEBRA	EXAMPLE
The **absolute value of a complex number** $a + bi$ is the distance from the origin to the point (a, b) in the complex plane, and is denoted $\lvert a + bi \rvert$.	$\lvert a + bi \rvert = \sqrt{a^2 + b^2}$	*Imaginary axis*; $4i$; $3 + 4i$; $\lvert 3 + 4i \rvert$; 4; 3; 0; 2; 4; *Real axis* $\lvert 3 + 4i \rvert = \sqrt{3^2 + 4^2}$ $= \sqrt{9 + 16}$ $= 5$

EXAMPLE 2 Determining the Absolute Value of Complex Numbers

Find each absolute value.

A $|-9 + i|$

$|-9 + 1i|$

$\sqrt{(-9)^2 + 1^2}$

$\sqrt{81 + 1}$

$\sqrt{82}$

B $|6|$

$|6 + 0i|$

$\sqrt{6^2 + 0^2}$

$\sqrt{36}$

6

C $|-4i|$

$|0 + (-4)i|$

$\sqrt{0^2 + (-4)^2}$

$\sqrt{16}$

4

Find each absolute value.

2a. $|1 - 2i|$ **2b.** $\left|-\frac{1}{2}\right|$ **2c.** $|23i|$

Adding and subtracting complex numbers is similar to adding and subtracting variable expressions with like terms. Simply combine the real parts, and combine the imaginary parts.

The set of complex numbers has all the properties of the set of real numbers. So you can use the Commutative, Associative, and Distributive Properties to simplify complex number expressions.

EXAMPLE 3 Adding and Subtracting Complex Numbers

Add or subtract. Write the result in the form $a + bi$.

A $(-2 + 4i) + (3 - 11i)$

$(-2 + 3) + (4i - 11i)$ *Associative and Commutative Properties*

$1 - 7i$ *Add real parts and imaginary parts.*

B $(4 - i) - (5 + 8i)$

$(4 - i) - 5 - 8i$ *Distributive Property*

$(4 - 5) + (-i - 8i)$ *Associative and Commutative Properties*

$-1 - 9i$ *Add real parts and imaginary parts.*

C $(6 - 2i) + (-6 + 2i)$

$(6 - 6) + (-2i + 2i)$ *Associative and Commutative Properties*

$0 + 0i$ *Add real parts and imaginary parts.*

0

D $(10 + 3i) - (10 - 4i)$

$(10 + 3i) - 10 - (-4i)$ *Distributive Property*

$(10 - 10) + (3i + 4i)$ *Associative and Commutative Properties*

$0 + 7i$ *Add real parts and imaginary parts.*

$7i$

Helpful Hint

Complex numbers also have additive inverses. The additive inverse of $a + bi$ is $-(a + bi)$, or $-a - bi$.

Add or subtract. Write the result in the form $a + bi$.

3a. $(-3 + 5i) + (-6i)$ **3b.** $2i - (3 + 5i)$ **3c.** $(4 + 3i) + (4 - 3i)$

You can also add complex numbers by using coordinate geometry.

EXAMPLE 4 Adding Complex Numbers on the Complex Plane

Find $(4 + 3i) + (-2 + i)$ by graphing on the complex plane.

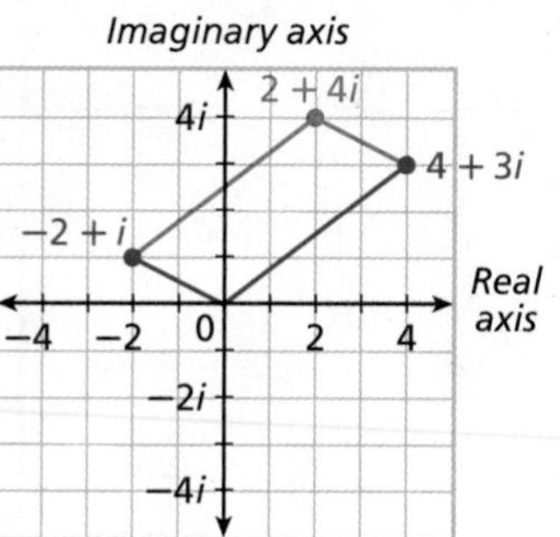

Step 1 Graph $4 + 3i$ and $-2 + i$ on the complex plane. Connect each of these numbers to the origin with a line segment.

Step 2 Draw a parallelogram that has these two line segments as sides. The vertex that is opposite the origin represents the sum of the two complex numbers, $2 + 4i$. Therefore, $(4 + 3i) + (-2 + i) = 2 + 4i$.

Check Add by combining the real parts and combining the imaginary parts.

$$(4 + 3i) + (-2 + i) = [4 + (-2)] + (3i + i) = 2 + 4i$$

Find each sum by graphing on the complex plane.

4a. $(3 + 4i) + (1 - 3i)$ **4b.** $(-4 - i) + (2 - 2i)$

You can multiply complex numbers by using the Distributive Property and treating the imaginary parts as like terms. Simplify by using the fact $i^2 = -1$.

EXAMPLE 5 Multiplying Complex Numbers

Multiply. Write the result in the form $a + bi$.

A $2i(3 - 5i)$

$6i - 10i^2$ *Distribute.*

$6i - 10(-1)$ *Use $i^2 = -1$.*

$10 + 6i$ *Write in a + bi form.*

B $(5 - 6i)(4 - 3i)$

$20 - 15i - 24i + 18i^2$ *Multiply.*

$20 - 39i + 18(-1)$ *Use $i^2 = -1$.*

$2 - 39i$

C $(7 + 2i)(7 - 2i)$

$49 - 14i + 14i - 4i^2$ *Multiply.*

$49 - 4(-1)$ *Use $i^2 = -1$.*

53

D $(6i)(6i)$

$36i^2$

$36(-1)$ *Use $i^2 = -1$.*

-36

Multiply. Write the result in the form $a + bi$.

5a. $2i(3 - 5i)$ **5b.** $(4 - 4i)(6 - i)$ **5c.** $(3 + 2i)(3 - 2i)$

Helpful Hint

Notice the repeating pattern in each row of the table. The pattern allows you to express any power of *i* as one of four possible values: *i*, −1, −*i*, or 1.

The imaginary unit *i* can be raised to higher powers as shown below.

Powers of *i*		
$i^1 = i$	$i^5 = i^4 \cdot i = 1 \cdot i = i$	$i^9 = i$
$i^2 = -1$	$i^6 = i^4 \cdot i^2 = 1 \cdot (-1) = -1$	$i^{10} = -1$
$i^3 = i^2 \cdot i = -1 \cdot i = -i$	$i^7 = i^4 \cdot i^3 = 1 \cdot (-i) = -i$	$i^{11} = -i$
$i^4 = i^2 \cdot i^2 = -1 \cdot (-1) = 1$	$i^8 = i^4 \cdot i^4 = 1 \cdot 1 = 1$	$i^{12} = 1$

EXAMPLE 6 Evaluating Powers of i

A **Simplify $-3i^{12}$.**

$-3i^{12} = -3(i^2)^6$ *Rewrite i^{12} as a power of i^2.*

$= -3(-1)^6 = -3(1) = -3$ *Simplify.*

B **Simplify i^{25}.**

$i^{25} = i \cdot i^{24}$ *Rewrite as a product of i and an even power of i.*

$= i \cdot (i^2)^{12}$ *Rewrite i^{24} as a power of i^2.*

$= i \cdot (-1)^{12} = i \cdot 1 = i$ *Simplify.*

6a. Simplify $\frac{1}{2}i^7$. **6b.** Simplify i^{42}.

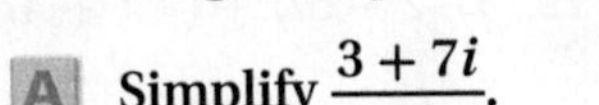

The complex conjugate of a complex number *a* + *bi* is *a* − *bi*. (Lesson 5-5)

Recall that expressions in simplest form cannot have square roots in the denominator (Lesson 1-3). Because the imaginary unit represents a square root, you must rationalize any denominator that contains an imaginary unit. To do this, multiply the numerator and denominator by the complex conjugate of the denominator.

EXAMPLE 7 Dividing Complex Numbers

A **Simplify $\frac{3+7i}{8i}$.**

$\frac{3+7i}{8i}\left(\frac{-8i}{-8i}\right)$ *Multiply by the conjugate.*

$\frac{-24i-56i^2}{-64i^2}$ *Distribute.*

$\frac{-24i+56}{64}$ *Use $i^2 = -1$.*

$\frac{-3i+7}{8} = \frac{7}{8} - \frac{3}{8}i$ *Simplify.*

B **Simplify $\frac{5+i}{2-4i}$.**

$\frac{5+i}{2-4i}\left(\frac{2+4i}{2+4i}\right)$

$\frac{10+20i+2i+4i^2}{4+8i-8i-16i^2}$

$\frac{10+22i-4}{4+16}$

$\frac{6+22i}{20} = \frac{3}{10} + \frac{11}{10}i$

7a. Simplify $\frac{3+8i}{-i}$. **7b.** Simplify $\frac{3-i}{2-i}$.

THINK AND DISCUSS

1. Explain when a complex number $a + bi$ and its conjugate are equal.
2. Find the product $(a + bi)(c + di)$, and identify which terms in the product are real and which are imaginary.

3. **GET ORGANIZED** Copy and complete the graphic organizer. In each box, give an example.

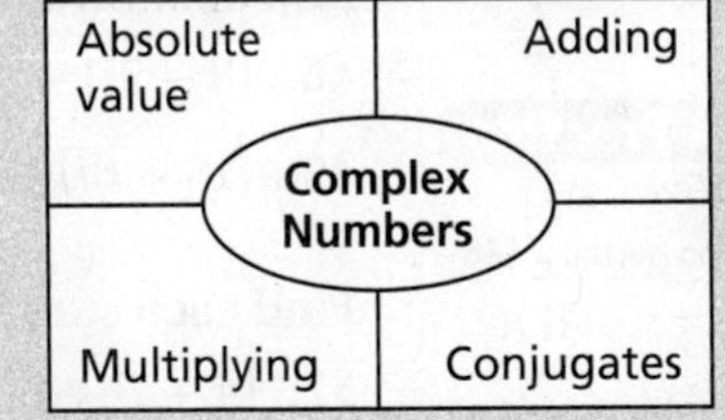

5-9 Exercises

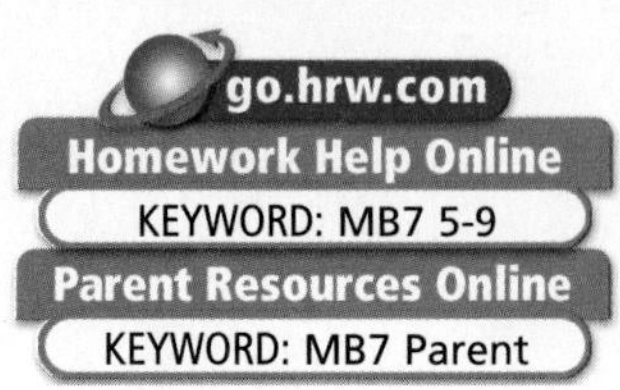

GUIDED PRACTICE

1. **Vocabulary** In the complex number plane, the horizontal axis represents __?__ numbers, and the vertical axis represents __?__ numbers. (*real, irrational,* or *imaginary*)

SEE EXAMPLE 1 p. 382

Graph each complex number.

2. 4 3. $-i$ 4. $3 + 2i$ 5. $-2 - 3i$

SEE EXAMPLE 2 p. 383

Find each absolute value.

6. $|4 - 5i|$ 7. $|-33.3|$ 8. $|-9i|$
9. $|5 + 12i|$ 10. $|-1 + i|$ 11. $|15i|$

SEE EXAMPLE 3 p. 383

Add or subtract. Write the result in the form $a + bi$.

12. $(2 + 5i) + (-2 + 5i)$ 13. $(-1 - 8i) + (4 + 3i)$ 14. $(1 - 3i) - (7 + i)$
15. $(4 - 8i) + (-13 + 23i)$ 16. $(6 + 17i) - (18 - 9i)$ 17. $(-30 + i) - (-2 + 20i)$

SEE EXAMPLE 4 p. 384

Find each sum by graphing on the complex plane.

18. $(3 + 4i) + (-2 - 4i)$ 19. $(-2 - 5i) + (-1 + 4i)$ 20. $(-4 - 4i) + (4 + 2i)$

SEE EXAMPLE 5 p. 384

Multiply. Write the result in the form $a + bi$.

21. $(1 - 2i)(1 + 2i)$ 22. $3i(5 + 2i)$ 23. $(9 + i)(4 - i)$
24. $(6 + 8i)(5 - 4i)$ 25. $(3 + i)^2$ 26. $(-4 - 5i)(2 + 10i)$

SEE EXAMPLE 6 p. 385

Simplify.

27. $-i^9$ 28. $2i^{15}$ 29. i^{30}

SEE EXAMPLE 7 p. 385

30. $\frac{5 - 4i}{i}$ 31. $\frac{11 - 5i}{2 - 4i}$ 32. $\frac{8 + 2i}{5 + i}$
33. $\frac{17}{4 + i}$ 34. $\frac{45 - 3i}{7 - 8i}$ 35. $\frac{-3 - 12i}{6i}$

PRACTICE AND PROBLEM SOLVING

Independent Practice

For Exercises	See Example
36–39	1
40–45	2
46–51	3
52–54	4
55–60	5
61–63	6
64–69	7

Extra Practice
Skills Practice p. S13
Application Practice p. S36

Graph each complex number.

36. -3 37. $-2.5i$ 38. $1 + i$ 39. $4 - 3i$

Find each absolute value.

40. $|2 + 3i|$ 41. $|-18|$ 42. $\left|\frac{4}{5}i\right|$
43. $|6 - 8i|$ 44. $|-0.5i|$ 45. $|10 - 4i|$

Add or subtract. Write the result in the form $a + bi$.

46. $(8 - 9i) - (-2 - i)$ 47. $4i - (11 - 3i)$ 48. $(4 - 2i) + (-9 - 5i)$
49. $(13 + 6i) + (15 + 35i)$ 50. $(3 - i) - (-3 + i)$ 51. $-16 + (12 + 9i)$

Find each sum by graphing on the complex plane.

52. $(4 + i) + (-3i)$ 53. $(5 + 4i) + (-1 + 2i)$ 54. $(-3 - 3i) + (4 - 3i)$

Multiply. Write the result in the form $a + bi$.

55. $-12i(-1 + 4i)$ **56.** $(3 - 5i)(2 + 9i)$ **57.** $(7 + 2i)(7 - 2i)$

58. $(5 + 6i)^2$ **59.** $(7 - 5i)(-3 + 9i)$ **60.** $-4(8 + 12i)$

Simplify.

61. i^{27} **62.** $-i^{11}$ **63.** $5i^{10}$

64. $\frac{2 - 3i}{i}$ **65.** $\frac{5 - 2i}{3 + i}$ **66.** $\frac{3}{-1 - 5i}$

67. $\frac{19 + 9i}{5 + i}$ **68.** $\frac{8 + 4i}{7 + i}$ **69.** $\frac{6 + 3i}{2 - 2i}$

Write the complex number represented by each point on the graph.

70. A

71. B

72. C

73. D

74. E

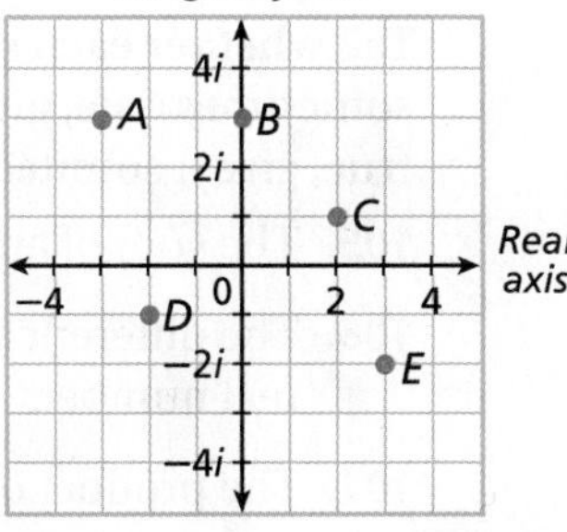

Find the absolute value of each complex number.

75. $3 - i$ **76.** $7i$ **77.** $-2 - 6i$

78. $-1 - 8i$ **79.** 0 **80.** $5 + 4i$

81. $\frac{3}{2} - \frac{1}{2}i$ **82.** $5 - i\sqrt{3}$ **83.** $2\sqrt{2} - i\sqrt{3}$

LINK

Fractals

Fractals are self-similar, which means that smaller parts of a fractal are similar to the fractal as a whole. Many objects in nature, such as the veins of leaves and snow crystals, also exhibit self-similarity. As a result, scientists can use fractals to model these objects.

84. Fractals Fractals are patterns produced using complex numbers and the repetition of a mathematical formula. Substitute the first number into the formula. Then take the result, put it back into the formula, and so on. Each complex number produced by the formula can be used to assign a color to a pixel on a computer screen. The result is an image such as the one at right. Many common fractals are based on the Julia Set, whose formula is $Z_{n+1} = (Z_n)^2 + c$, where c is a constant.

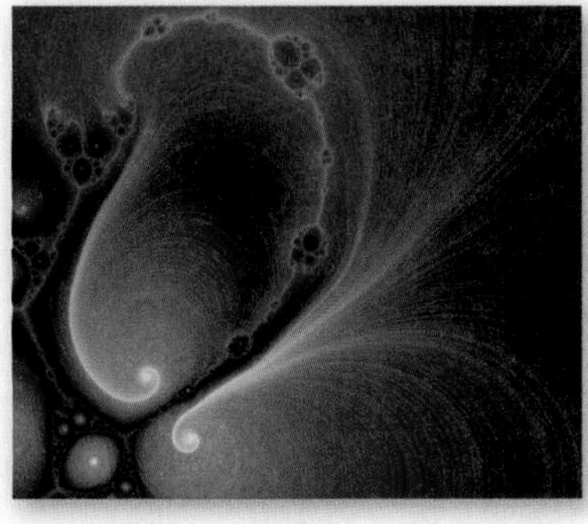

a. Find Z_2 using $Z_2 = (Z_1)^2 + 0.25$. Let $Z_1 = 0.5 + 0.6i$.

b. Find Z_3 using $Z_3 = (Z_2)^2 + 0.25$. Use Z_2 that you obtained in part **a.**

c. Find Z_4 using $Z_4 = (Z_3)^2 + 0.25$. Use Z_3 that you obtained in part **b.**

Simplify. Write the result in the form $a + bi$.

85. $(3.5 + 5.2i) + (6 - 2.3i)$ **86.** $6i - (4 + 5i)$ **87.** $(-2.3 + i) - (7.4 - 0.3i)$

88. $(-8 - 11i) + (-1 + i)$ **89.** $i(4 + i)$ **90.** $(6 - 5i)^2$

91. $(-2 - 3i)^2$ **92.** $(5 + 7i)(5 - 7i)$ **93.** $(2 - i)(2 + i)(2 - i)$

94. $3 - i^{11}$ **95.** $i^{52} - i^{48}$ **96.** $i^{35} - i^{24} + i^{18}$

97. $\frac{12 + i}{i}$ **98.** $\frac{18 - 3i}{i}$ **99.** $\frac{4 + 2i}{6 + i}$

100. $\frac{1 + i}{-2 + 4i}$ **101.** $\frac{4}{2 - 3i}$ **102.** $\frac{6}{\sqrt{2} - i}$

Multi-Step ***Impedance*** **is a measure of the opposition of a circuit to an electric current. Electrical engineers find it convenient to model impedance Z with complex numbers. In a parallel AC circuit with two impedances Z_1 and Z_2, the *equivalent* or total impedance in ohms can be determined by using the formula $Z_{eq} = \frac{Z_1 Z_2}{Z_1 + Z_2}$.**

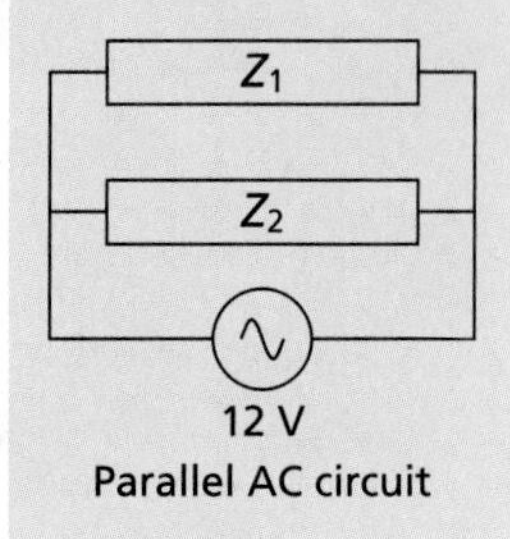

Parallel AC circuit

103. Find the equivalent impedance Z_{eq} for $Z_1 = 3 + 2i$ and $Z_2 = 1 - 2i$ arranged in a parallel AC circuit.

104. Find the equivalent impedance Z_{eq} for $Z_1 = 2 + 2i$ and $Z_2 = 4 - i$ arranged in a parallel AC circuit.

Tell whether each statement is sometimes, always, or never true. If the statement is sometimes true, give an example and a counterexample. If the statement is never true, give a counterexample.

105. The sum of any complex number $a + bi$ and its conjugate is a real number.

106. The difference between any complex number $a + bi$ $(b \neq 0)$ and its conjugate is a real number.

107. The product of any complex number $a + bi$ $(a \neq 0)$ and its conjugate is a positive real number.

108. The product of any two imaginary numbers bi $(b \neq 0)$ and di $(d \neq 0)$ is a positive real number.

109. **/// ERROR ANALYSIS ///** Two attempts to simplify $\frac{3}{2 + i}$ are shown. Which is incorrect? Explain the error.

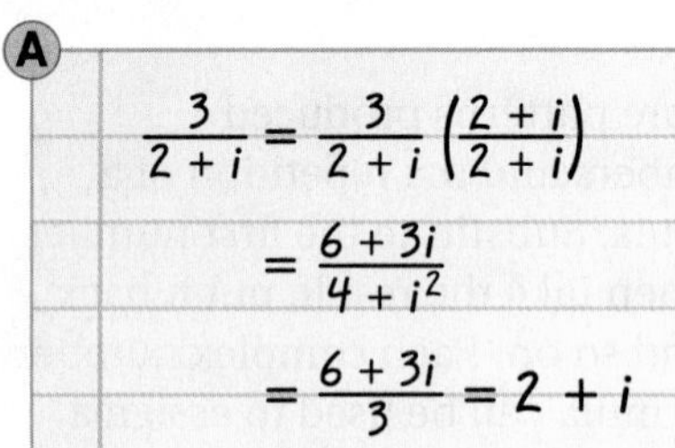

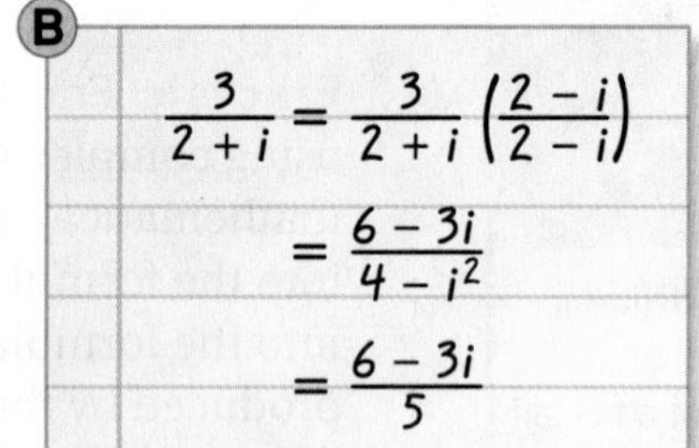

110. Critical Thinking Why are the absolute value of a complex number and the absolute value of its conjugate equal? Use a graph to justify your answer.

111. Write About It Discuss how the difference of two squares, $a^2 - b^2 = (a + b)(a - b)$, relates to the product of a complex number and its conjugate.

MULTI-STEP TEST PREP

112. This problem will prepare you for the Multi-Step Test Prep on page 390.

You have seen how to graph sums of complex numbers on the complex plane.

a. Find three pairs of complex numbers whose sum is $4 + 4i$.

b. Graph each of the sums on the same complex plane.

c. Describe the results of your graph.

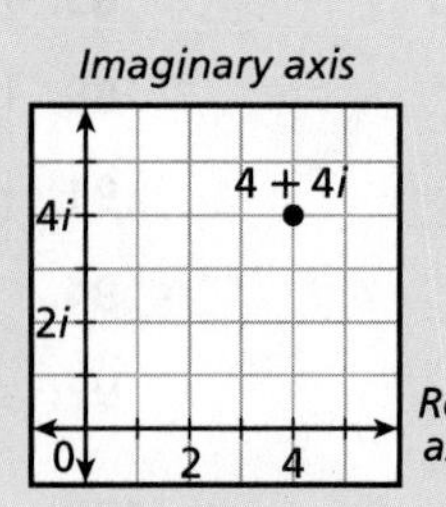

Use the graph for Exercises 113–114.

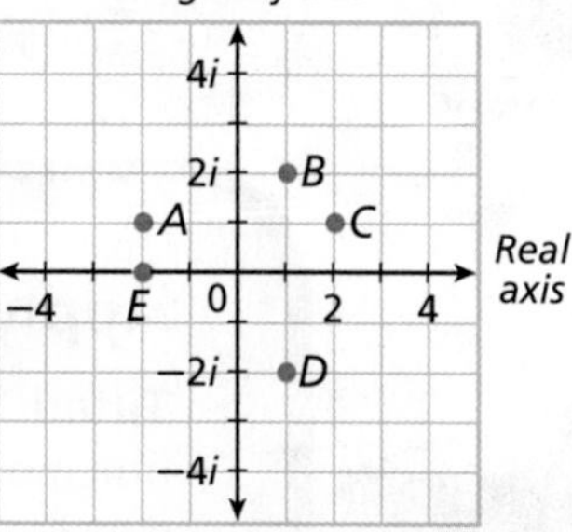

113. Which point on the graph represents $1 - 2i$?

Ⓐ A Ⓒ C

Ⓑ B Ⓓ D

114. What is the value of the complex number represented in the graph by E?

Ⓕ -2 Ⓗ $-2i$

Ⓖ 2 Ⓙ $2i$

115. Which expression is equivalent to $(2 - 5i) - (2 + 5i)$?

Ⓐ $10i$ Ⓑ $4 + 10i$ Ⓒ $-10i$ Ⓓ $4 - 10i$

116. Which expression is equivalent to $(-5 + 3i)^2$?

Ⓕ $16 - 15i$ Ⓖ $16 - 30i$ Ⓗ $34 - 15i$ Ⓙ $34 - 30i$

CHALLENGE AND EXTEND

117. Consider the powers of i.

a. Complete the table, and look for a pattern.

$i^1 = ■$	$i^0 = ■$	$i^{-1} = ■$	$i^{-2} = ■$	$i^{-3} = ■$	$i^{-4} = ■$	$i^{-5} = ■$

b. Explain the pattern that you observed for i raised to negative powers. What are the only possible values of i raised to a negative integer power?

c. Simplify i^{-12}, i^{-37}, and i^{-90}.

Find the general form of the result for each complex operation.

118. $(a + bi)(c + di)$

119. $\dfrac{a + bi}{c + di}$

SPIRAL REVIEW

120. Money The table shows the amount that James spent for lunches each week over an eight-week period. Make a scatter plot of the data. Sketch a line of best fit, and find its equation. *(Lesson 2-7)*

Lunches Purchased	5	7	3	5	6	2	4	5
Weekly Cost ($)	10	13	8	9	8	5	10	11

Solve each inequality by using algebra. *(Lesson 5-7)*

121. $0 \geq 3x^2 - 6x$

122. $10 < x^2 - 4x - 11$

123. $-6 \geq 2x^2 + 7x - 21$

124. $3 - x^2 < 7 - 5x$

Determine whether each data set could represent a quadratic function. Explain. *(Lesson 5-8)*

125.

x	-2	-1	0	1
y	5	-1	-3	-1

126.

x	0	2	4	6
y	18	10	2	-6

CHAPTER 5

SECTION 5B

Applying Quadratic Functions

Tilted Tiles Mitch and Jacob are making mosaics in an art class. To make one mosaic, Mitch first divides a wall into a grid made up of squares with a side length of 20 cm. Then Jacob glues a tile on each square, making sure that each corner of the tile touches a side of the grid square.

They measure the side length of each tile as well as the distance x from the upper right corner of the grid square to a corner of the tile. They find that for each tile there are two possible values of x, as shown.

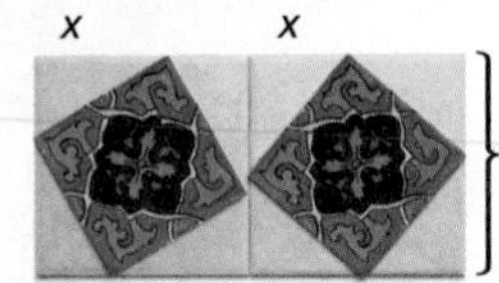

1. Complete the table by finding the area of each tile and the ratio y of the area of each tile to the area of the grid square.
2. Make a scatterplot of the ordered pairs (x, y). Find and graph a quadratic model for the data. Is the model a reasonable representation of the data? Explain.
3. Describe the domain for the problem situation. Explain why the domain of the problem situation is different from the domain of the model.
4. Use your model to determine the value of y when $x = 3.8$. Explain the meaning of your answer in the context of the problem.
5. For what values of x does a tile cover at least 75% of the grid square? Round to the nearest tenth.

Side Length of Tile (cm)	x (cm)	Area of Tile (cm^2)	y
15	6.4		
15	13.6		
15.5	5.5		
15.5	14.5		
16	4.7		
16	15.3		
17	3.3		
17	16.7		
18	2.1		
18	17.9		
19	1.1		
19	18.9		
20	0		

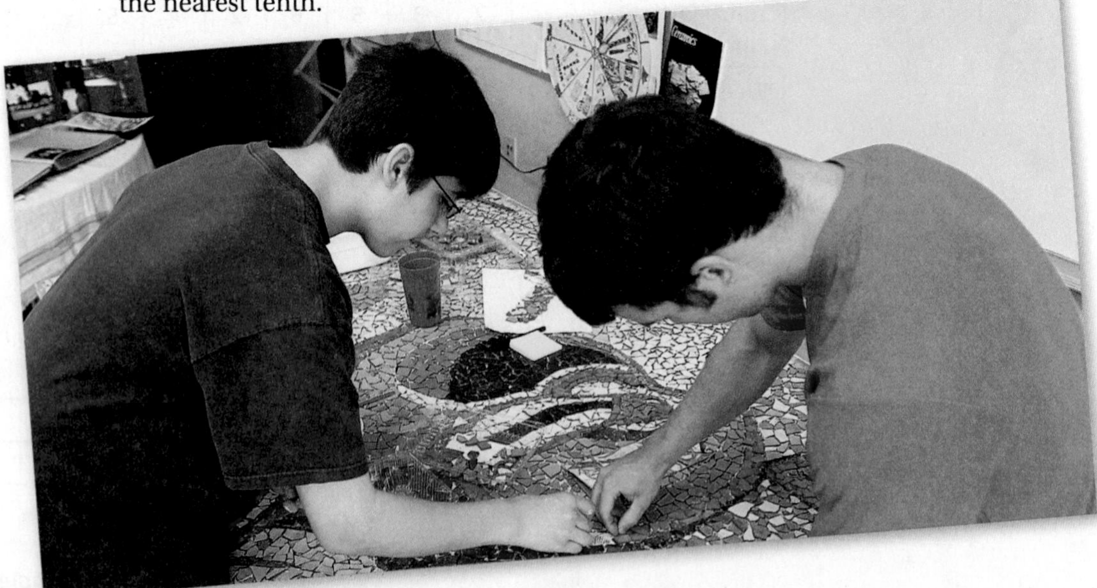

READY TO GO ON?

Quiz for Lessons 5-7 Through 5-9

5-7 Solving Quadratic Inequalities

Graph each inequality.

1. $y > -x^2 + 6x$
2. $y \leq -x^2 - x + 2$

Solve each inequality by using tables or graphs.

3. $x^2 - 4x + 1 > 6$
4. $2x^2 + 2x - 10 \leq 2$

Solve each inequality by using algebra.

5. $x^2 + 4x - 7 \geq 5$
6. $x^2 - 8x < 0$
7. The function $p(r) = -1000r^2 + 6400r - 4400$ models the monthly profit p of a small DVD-rental store, where r is the rental price of a DVD. For what range of rental prices does the store earn a monthly profit of at least $5000?

5-8 Curve Fitting with Quadratic Models

Determine whether each data set could represent a quadratic function. Explain.

8.

x	5	6	7	8	9
y	13	11	7	1	−7

9.

x	−4	−2	0	2	4
y	10	8	4	8	10

Write a quadratic function that fits each set of points.

10. (0, 4), (2, 0), and (3, 1)
11. (1, 3), (2, 5), and (4, 3)

For Exercises 12–14, use the table of maximum load allowances for various heights of spruce columns.

Maximum Load Allowance No. 1 Common Spruce	
Height of Column (ft)	**Maximum Load (lb)**
4	7280
5	7100
6	6650
7	5960

12. Find a quadratic regression equation to model the maximum load given the height.
13. Use your model to predict the maximum load allowed for a 6.5 ft spruce column.
14. Use your model to predict the maximum load allowed for an 8 ft spruce column.

5-9 Operations with Complex Numbers

Find each absolute value.

15. $|-6i|$
16. $|3 + 4i|$
17. $|2 - i|$

Perform each indicated operation, and write the result in the form $a + bi$.

18. $(3 - 5i) - (6 - i)$
19. $(-6 + 4i) + (7 - 2i)$
20. $3i(4 + i)$
21. $(3 + i)(5 - i)$
22. $(1 - 4i)(1 + 4i)$
23. $3i^{15}$
24. $\dfrac{2 - 7i}{-i}$
25. $\dfrac{3 - i}{4 - 2i}$

CHAPTER 5

Study Guide: Review

Vocabulary

Complete the sentences below with vocabulary words from the list above.

1. The number $5i$ can be classified as both a(n) __?__ and a __?__.
2. The value of the input x that makes the output $f(x)$ equal zero is called the __?__.
3. The __?__ is the point at which the parabola intersects the axis of symmetry.
4. The type and number of solutions to a quadratic equation can be determined by finding the __?__.
5. When a parabola opens upward, the y-value of the vertex is the __?__ of a quadratic function.

5-1 Using Transformations to Graph Quadratic Functions *(pp. 315–322)*

EXAMPLES

■ **Using the graph of $f(x) = x^2$ as a guide, describe the transformations, and then graph $g(x) = \frac{1}{2}x^2 + 3$.**

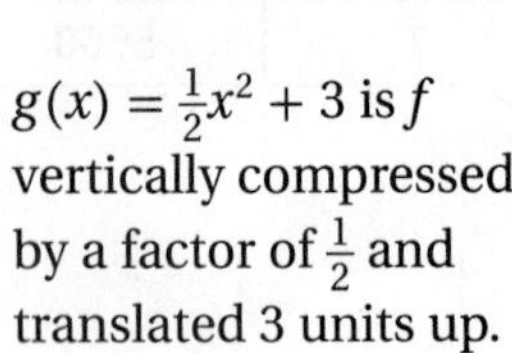

$g(x) = \frac{1}{2}x^2 + 3$ is f vertically compressed by a factor of $\frac{1}{2}$ and translated 3 units up.

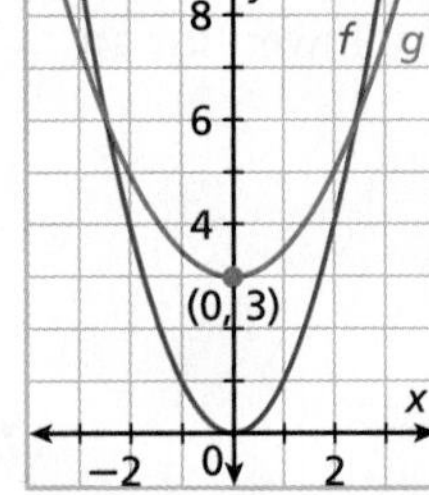

■ **Use the description to write a quadratic function in vertex form. The function $f(x) = x^2$ is translated 1 unit right to create g.**

translation 1 unit right: $h = 1$

$g(x) = a(x - h)^2 + k \rightarrow g(x) = (x - 1)^2$

EXERCISES

Graph each function by using a table.

6. $f(x) = -x^2 - 2x$
7. $f(x) = \frac{1}{2}x^2 + 3x - 4$

Using the graph of $f(x) = x^2$ as a guide, describe the transformations, and then graph each function.

8. $g(x) = 4(x - 2)^2$
9. $g(x) = -2(x + 1)^2$
10. $g(x) = \frac{1}{3}x^2 - 3$
11. $g(x) = -(x + 2)^2 + 6$

Use the description to write each quadratic function in vertex form.

12. $f(x) = x^2$ is reflected across the x-axis and translated 3 units down to create g.
13. $f(x) = x^2$ is vertically stretched by a factor of 2 and translated 4 units right to create g.
14. $f(x) = x^2$ is vertically compressed by a factor of $\frac{1}{4}$ and translated 1 unit left to create g.

5-2 Properties of Quadratic Functions in Standard Form *(pp. 323–330)*

EXAMPLE

- **For $f(x) = -x^2 + 2x + 3$, (a) determine whether the graph opens upward or downward, (b) find the axis of symmetry, (c) find the vertex, (d) find the y-intercept, and (e) graph the function.**

a. Because $a < 0$, the parabola opens downward.

b. axis of symmetry:

$$x = -\frac{b}{2a} = -\frac{2}{2(-1)} = 1$$

c. $f(1) = -1^2 + 2(1) + 3 = 4$

The vertex is $(1, 4)$.

d. Because $c = 3$, the y-intercept is 3.

e.

EXERCISES

For each function, (a) determine whether the graph opens upward or downward, (b) find the axis of symmetry, (c) find the vertex, (d) find the y-intercept, and (e) graph the function.

15. $f(x) = x^2 - 4x + 3$ **16.** $g(x) = x^2 + 2x + 3$

17. $h(x) = x^2 - 3x$ **18.** $j(x) = \frac{1}{2}x^2 - 2x + 4$

Find the minimum or maximum value of each function.

19. $f(x) = x^2 + 2x + 6$ **20.** $g(x) = 6x - 2x^2$

21. $f(x) = x^2 - 5x + 1$ **22.** $g(x) = -2x^2 - 8x + 10$

23. $f(x) = -x^2 - 4x + 8$ **24.** $g(x) = 3x^2 + 7$

5-3 Solving Quadratic Equations by Graphing and Factoring *(pp. 333–340)*

EXAMPLES

- **Find the roots of $x^2 + x = 30$ by factoring.**

$x^2 + x - 30 = 0$ *Rewrite in standard form.*

$(x - 5)(x + 6) = 0$ *Factor.*

$x - 5 = 0$ or $x + 6 = 0$ *Zero Product Property.*

$x = 5$ or $x = -6$ *Solve each equation.*

- **Write a quadratic function with zeros 8 and −8.**

$x = 8$ or $x = -8$ *Write zeros as solutions.*

$x - 8 = 0$ or $x + 8 = 0$ *Set equations equal to 0.*

$(x - 8)(x + 8) = 0$ *Converse Zero Product Property*

$f(x) = x^2 - 64$ *Replace 0 with $f(x)$.*

EXERCISES

Find the roots of each equation by factoring.

25. $x^2 - 7x - 8 = 0$ **26.** $x^2 - 5x + 6 = 0$

27. $x^2 = 144$ **28.** $x^2 - 21x = 0$

29. $4x^2 - 16x + 16 = 0$ **30.** $2x^2 + 8x + 6 = 0$

31. $x^2 + 14x = 32$ **32.** $9x^2 + 6x + 1 = 0$

Write a quadratic function in standard form for each given set of zeros.

33. 2 and −3 **34.** 1 and −1

35. 4 and 5 **36.** −2 and −3

37. −5 and −5 **38.** 9 and 0

5-4 Completing the Square *(pp. 342–349)*

EXAMPLE

- **Solve $x^2 - 8x = 12$ by completing the square.**

$x^2 - 8x + \blacksquare = 12 + \blacksquare$ *Set up equation.*

$x^2 - 8x + 16 = 12 + 16$ *Add $\left(\frac{b}{2}\right)^2$.*

$(x - 4)^2 = 28$ *Factor.*

$x - 4 = \pm\sqrt{28}$ *Take square roots.*

$x = 4 \pm 2\sqrt{7}$ *Solve for x.*

EXERCISES

Solve each equation by completing the square.

39. $x^2 - 16x + 48 = 0$ **40.** $x^2 + 20x + 84 = 0$

41. $x^2 - 6x = 16$ **42.** $x^2 - 14x = 13$

Write each function in vertex form, and identify its vertex.

43. $f(x) = x^2 - 4x + 9$ **44.** $g(x) = x^2 + 2x - 7$

5-5 Complex Numbers and Roots *(pp. 350–355)*

EXAMPLE

- **Solve $x^2 - 22x + 133 = 0$.**

$x^2 - 22x + \blacksquare = -133 + \blacksquare$ *Rewrite.*

$x^2 - 22x + 121 = -133 + 121$ *Add $\left(\frac{b}{2}\right)^2$.*

$(x - 11)^2 = -12$ *Factor.*

$x - 11 = \pm\sqrt{-12}$ *Take square roots.*

$x = 11 \pm 2i\sqrt{3}$ *Solve.*

EXERCISES

Solve each equation.

45. $x^2 = -81$

46. $6x^2 + 150 = 0$

47. $x^2 + 6x + 10 = 0$

48. $x^2 + 12x + 45 = 0$

49. $x^2 - 14x + 75 = 0$

50. $x^2 - 22x + 133 = 0$

Find each complex conjugate.

51. $5i - 4$

52. $3 + i\sqrt{5}$

5-6 The Quadratic Formula *(pp. 356–363)*

EXAMPLES

- **Find the zeros of $f(x) = 3x^2 - 5x + 3$ by using the Quadratic Formula.**

$x = \dfrac{-b \pm \sqrt{b^2 - 4ac}}{2a}$ *Quadratic Formula*

$x = \dfrac{-(-5) \pm \sqrt{(-5)^2 - 4(3)(3)}}{2(3)}$ *Substitute.*

$= \dfrac{5 \pm \sqrt{-11}}{6} = \dfrac{5}{6} \pm i\dfrac{\sqrt{11}}{6}$ *Simplify.*

- **Find the type and number of solutions for $x^2 + 9x + 20 = 0$.**

$b^2 - 4ac = 9^2 - 4(1)(20)$

$= 81 - 80 = 1$

There are two distinct real roots because the discriminant is positive.

EXERCISES

Find the zeros of each function by using the Quadratic Formula.

53. $f(x) = x^2 - 3x - 8$

54. $h(x) = (x - 5)^2 + 12$

55. $f(x) = 2x^2 - 10x + 18$

56. $g(x) = x^2 + 3x + 3$

57. $h(x) = x^2 - 5x + 10$

Find the type and number of solutions for each equation.

58. $2x^2 - 16x + 32 = 0$

59. $x^2 - 6x = -5$

60. $x^2 + 3x + 8 = 0$

61. $x^2 - 246x = -144$

62. $x^2 + 5x = -12$

63. $3x^2 - 5x + 3 = 0$

5-7 Solving Quadratic Inequalities *(pp. 366–373)*

EXAMPLE

- **Solve $x^2 - 4x - 9 \geq 3$ by using algebra.**

Write and solve the related equation.

$x^2 - 4x - 12 = 0$ *Write in standard form.*

$(x + 2)(x - 6) = 0$ *Factor.*

$x = -2$ or $x = 6$ *Solve.*

The critical values are -2 and 6. These values divide the number line into three intervals: $x \leq -2$, $-2 \leq x \leq 6$, and $x \geq 6$.

Testing an x-value in each interval gives the solution of $x \leq -2$ or $x \geq 6$.

EXERCISES

Graph each inequality.

64. $y > x^2 + 3x + 4$

65. $y \leq 2x^2 - x - 5$

Solve each inequality by using tables or graphs.

66. $x^2 + 2x - 4 \geq -1$

67. $-x^2 - 5x > 4$

Solve each inequality by using algebra.

68. $-x^2 + 6x < 5$

69. $3x^2 - 25 \leq 2$

70. $x^2 - 3 < 0$

71. $3x^2 + 4x - 3 \leq 1$

5-8 Curve Fitting with Quadratic Models *(pp. 374–381)*

EXAMPLE

- **Find a quadratic model for the wattage of fluorescent bulbs F given the comparable incandescent bulb wattage I. Use the model to estimate the wattage of a fluorescent bulb that produces the same amount of light as a 120-watt incandescent bulb.**

Wattage Comparison					
Incandescent (watts)	40	60	75	90	100
Fluorescent (watts)	11	15	20	23	28

Enter the data into two lists in a graphing calculator. Use the quadratic regression feature.

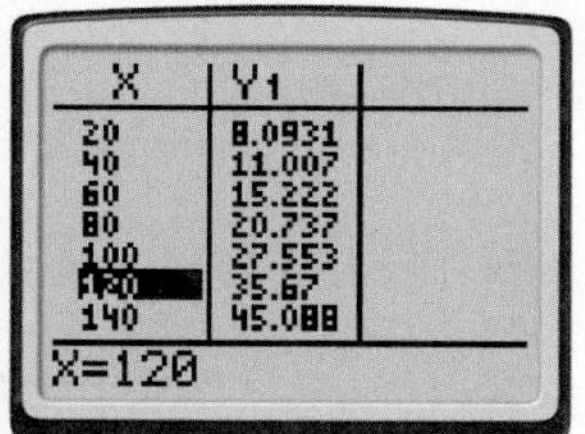

The model is $F(I) \approx 0.0016I^2 + 0.0481I + 6.48$. A 36-watt fluorescent bulb produces about the same amount of light as a 120-watt incandescent bulb.

EXERCISES

Write a quadratic function that fits each set of points.

72. $(-1, 8)$, $(0, 6)$, and $(1, 2)$

73. $(0, 0)$, $(1, -1)$, and $(2, -6)$

Construction **For Exercises 74–77, use the table of copper wire gauges.**

Common U.S. Copper Wire Gauges		
Gauge	Diameter (in.)	Resistance per 1000 ft (ohms)
24	0.0201	25.67
22	0.0254	16.14
20	0.0320	10.15
18	0.0403	6.385

74. Find a quadratic regression equation to model the diameter given the wire gauge.

75. Use your model to predict the diameter for a 12-gauge copper wire.

76. Find a quadratic regression equation to model the resistance given the wire gauge.

77. Use your model to predict the resistance for a 26-gauge copper wire.

5-9 Operations with Complex Numbers *(pp. 382–389)*

EXAMPLES

Perform each indicated operation, and write the result in the form $a + bi$.

- $|-2 + 4i|$

$\sqrt{(-2)^2 + 4^2} = \sqrt{4 + 16} = \sqrt{20} = 2\sqrt{5}$

- $(3 + 2i)(4 - 5i)$

$12 - 15i + 8i - 10i^2$

$12 - 7i - 10(-1) = 22 - 7i$

- $\dfrac{-5 + 3i}{1 - 2i}$

$$\frac{-5 + 3i}{1 - 2i}\left(\frac{1 + 2i}{1 + 2i}\right) = \frac{-5 - 7i + 6i^2}{1 - 4i^2}$$

$$= \frac{-11 - 7i}{1 + 4} = -\frac{11}{5} - \frac{7}{5}i$$

EXERCISES

Perform each indicated operation, and write the result in the form $a + bi$.

78. $|-3i|$

79. $|4 - 2i|$

80. $|12 - 16i|$

81. $|7i|$

82. $(1 + 5i) + (6 - i)$

83. $(9 + 4i) - (3 + 2i)$

84. $(5 - i) - (11 - i)$

85. $-5i(3 - 4i)$

86. $(5 - 2i)(6 + 8i)$

87. $(3 + 2i)(3 - 2i)$

88. $(4 + i)(1 - 5i)$

89. $(-7 + 4i)(3 + 9i)$

90. i^{32}

91. $-5i^{21}$

92. $\dfrac{2 + 9i}{-2i}$

93. $\dfrac{5 + 2i}{3 - 4i}$

94. $\dfrac{8 - 4i}{1 + i}$

95. $\dfrac{-12 + 26i}{2 + 4i}$

CHAPTER 5

CHAPTER TEST

Using the graph of $f(x) = x^2$ as a guide, describe the transformations, and then graph each function.

1. $g(x) = (x + 1)^2 - 2$

2. $h(x) = -\frac{1}{2}x^2 + 2$

3. Use the following description to write a quadratic function in vertex form: $f(x) = x^2$ is vertically compressed by a factor of $\frac{1}{2}$ and translated 6 units right to create g.

For each function, (a) determine whether the graph opens upward or downward, (b) find the axis of symmetry, (c) find the vertex, (d) find the y-intercept, and (e) graph the function.

4. $f(x) = -x^2 + 4x + 1$

5. $g(x) = x^2 - 2x + 3$

6. The area A of a rectangle with a perimeter of 32 cm is modeled by the function $A(x) = -x^2 + 16x$, where x is the width of the rectangle in centimeters. What is the maximum area of the rectangle?

Find the roots of each equation by using factoring.

7. $x^2 - 2x + 1 = 0$

8. $x^2 + 10x = -21$

Solve each equation.

9. $x^2 + 4x = 12$

10. $x^2 - 12x = 25$

11. $x^2 + 25 = 0$

12. $x^2 + 12x = -40$

Write each function in vertex form, and identify its vertex.

13. $f(x) = x^2 - 4x + 9$

14. $g(x) = x^2 - 18x + 92$

Find the zeros of each function by using the Quadratic Formula.

15. $f(x) = (x - 1)^2 + 7$

16. $g(x) = 2x^2 - x + 5$

17. The height h in feet of a person on a waterslide is modeled by the function $h(t) = -0.025t^2 - 0.5t + 50$, where t is the time in seconds. At the bottom of the slide, the person lands in a swimming pool. To the nearest tenth of a second, how long does the ride last?

18. Graph the inequality $y < x^2 - 3x - 4$.

Solve each inequality.

19. $-x^2 + 3x + 5 \geq 7$

20. $x^2 - 4x + 1 > 1$

For Exercises 21 and 22, use the table showing the average cost of LCD televisions at one store.

Costs of LCD Televisions				
Size (in.)	15	17	23	30
Cost ($)	550	700	1500	2500

21. Find a quadratic model for the cost of a television given its size.

22. Use the model to estimate the cost of a 42 in. LCD television.

Perform the indicated operation, and write the result in the form $a + bi$.

23. $(12 - i) - (5 + 2i)$

24. $(6 - 2i)(2 - 2i)$

25. $-2i^{18}$

26. $\frac{1 - 8i}{4i}$

FOCUS ON SAT MATHEMATICS SUBJECT TESTS

The SAT Mathematics Subject Tests assess knowledge from course work rather than ability to learn. The Level 1 test is meant to be taken by students who have completed two years of algebra and one year of geometry, and it tests more elementary topics than the Level 2 test.

You will need to use a calculator for some of the problems on the SAT Mathematics Subject Tests. Before test day, make sure that you are familiar with the features of the calculator that you will be using.

You may want to time yourself as you take this practice test. It should take you about 8 minutes to complete.

1. For what value of c will $3x^2 - 2x + c = 0$ have exactly one distinct real root?

(A) $-\frac{2}{3}$

(B) $-\frac{1}{3}$

(C) 0

(D) $\frac{1}{3}$

(E) $\frac{2}{3}$

2. If m and n are real numbers, $i^2 = -1$, and $(m - n) - 4i = 7 + ni$, what is the value of m?

(A) -4

(B) -3

(C) 1

(D) 3

(E) 4

3. If $x^2 - 5x + 6 = (x - h)^2 + k$, what is the value of k?

(A) $-\frac{25}{4}$

(B) $-\frac{5}{2}$

(C) $-\frac{1}{4}$

(D) 0

(E) 6

4. What is the solution set of $y^2 - 2y \leq 3y + 14$?

(A) $y \geq -2$

(B) $y \leq 7$

(C) $y \leq -2$ or $y \geq 7$

(D) $-7 \leq y \leq 2$

(E) $-2 \leq y \leq 7$

5. Which of the following is a factor of $(a - 1)^2 - b^2$?

(A) $a + b - 1$

(B) $a - b$

(C) $a - 1$

(D) $a - b + 1$

(E) $1 - b$

6. If $z = 5 - 4i$ and $i^2 = -1$, what is $|z|$?

(A) 1

(B) 3

(C) 9

(D) $\sqrt{41}$

(E) $\sqrt{42}$

CHAPTER 5

TEST TACKLER

Standardized Test Strategies

Multiple Choice: Work Backward

When taking a multiple-choice test, you can sometimes work backward to determine which answer is correct. Because this method can be time consuming, it is best used only when you cannot solve a problem in any other way.

EXAMPLE 1

Which expression is equivalent to $2x^2 - 3x - 14$?

Ⓐ $(2x + 7)(x + 2)$　　Ⓒ $(2x - 7)(x + 2)$

Ⓑ $(2x - 7)(x - 2)$　　Ⓓ $(2x + 7)(x - 2)$

If you have trouble factoring the quadratic expression given in the question, you can multiply the binomials in the answer choices to find the product that is the same as $2x^2 - 3x - 14$.

Try Choice A: $(2x + 7)(x + 2) = 2x^2 + 11x + 14$

Try Choice B: $(2x - 7)(x - 2) = 2x^2 - 11x + 14$

Try Choice C: $(2x - 7)(x + 2) = \mathbf{2x^2 - 3x - 14}$

Choice C is the answer.
Note: *Trying choice D can help you check your work.*

EXAMPLE 2

What is the solution set of $x^2 - 36 < 0$?

Ⓕ $x < -6$ or $x > 6$　　Ⓗ $-36 < x < 36$

Ⓖ $-6 < x < 6$　　Ⓙ $x < -36$ or $x > 36$

If you have trouble determining the solution set, substitute values of x into the inequality. Based on whether the values make the inequality true or false, you may be able to eliminate one or more of the answer choices.

Substitute 0 for x: $x^2 - 36 < 0 \rightarrow (0)^2 - 36 \overset{?}{<} 0 \rightarrow -36 < 0$ ✔

When $x = 0$, the inequality is true. Therefore, the solution set must include $x = 0$. Because choices F and J do not include $x = 0$, they can be eliminated.

Substitute 10 for x: $x^2 - 36 < 0 \rightarrow (10)^2 - 36 \overset{?}{<} 0 \rightarrow 64 \overset{?}{<} 0$ ✘

When $x = 10$, the inequality is false. Therefore, the solution set does not include $x = 10$. Because choice H includes $x = 10$, it can be eliminated.

The only remaining choice is choice G. Therefore, choice G must be correct.

You can also work backward to check whether the answer you found by another method is correct or reasonable.

Read each test item, and answer the questions that follow.

Item A
What are the zeros of the function $g(x) = 6x^2 - 8x - 4$, rounded to the nearest hundredth?

(A) -10.32 and 2.32 (C) 1.72 and -0.39

(B) -1.72 and 0.39 (D) 10.32 and -2.32

1. Rachel cannot remember how to determine the zeros of a quadratic function, so she plans to pick one of the answer choices at random. What could Rachel do to make a more educated guess?
2. Describe how to find the correct answer by working backward.

Item B
A portable television has a screen with a diagonal of 4 inches. The length of the screen is 1 inch greater than its width. What are the dimensions of the screen to the nearest hundredth?

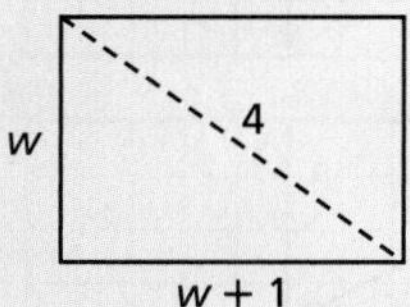

(F) 1.28 inches by 2.28 inches

(G) 1.28 inches by 3.28 inches

(H) 2.28 inches by 2.28 inches

(J) 2.28 inches by 3.28 inches

3. Can any of the answer choices be eliminated immediately? If so, which choices and why?
4. Describe how you can determine the correct answer by using the Pythagorean Theorem and working backward.

Item C
Which of the following is a solution of $(x + 4)^2 = 25$?

(A) $x = -9$ (C) $x = 0$

(B) $x = -1$ (D) $x = 9$

5. Explain how to use substitution to determine the correct answer.
6. Check whether choice A is correct by working backward. Explain your findings. What should you do next?

Item D
The height h of a golf ball in feet t seconds after it is hit into the air is modeled by $h(t) = -16t^2 + 64t$. How long is the ball in the air?

(F) 2 seconds (H) 12 seconds

(G) 4 seconds (J) 16 seconds

7. The measurements given in the answer choices represent possible values of which variable in the function?
8. Describe how you can work backward to determine that choice F is not correct.

Item E
The base of a triangle is 4 in. longer than twice its height. If the triangle has an area of 24 in^2, what is its height?

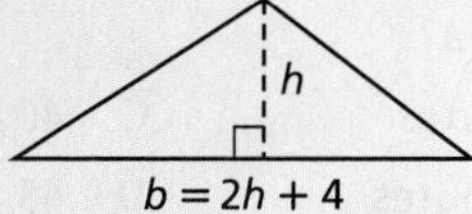

(A) 2 in. (C) 6 in.

(B) 4 in. (D) 8 in.

9. What equation do you need to solve to find the value of h?
10. Try choice A by working backward. Explain your findings. What should you do next?

CHAPTER 5

STANDARDIZED TEST PREP

go.hrw.com
State Test Practice Online
KEYWORD: MB7 TestPrep

CUMULATIVE ASSESSMENT, CHAPTERS 1–5

Multiple Choice

1. $M = \begin{bmatrix} 6 & -2 \\ 3 & 7 \end{bmatrix}$ $N = \begin{bmatrix} -1 & 8 & 2 \\ 0 & 1 & 6 \end{bmatrix}$

   What is the matrix product $2MN$?

   (A) $\begin{bmatrix} -24 & 184 & 0 \\ -12 & 124 & 192 \end{bmatrix}$

   (B) $\begin{bmatrix} -12 & 92 & 0 \\ -6 & 62 & 96 \end{bmatrix}$

   (C) $\begin{bmatrix} -24 & -12 \\ 184 & 124 \\ 0 & 192 \end{bmatrix}$

   (D) $\begin{bmatrix} -12 & -6 \\ 92 & 62 \\ 0 & 96 \end{bmatrix}$

2. Which of these functions does NOT have zeros at −1 and 4?

   (F) $f(x) = x^2 - 3x - 4$

   (G) $f(x) = 2x^2 + 6x - 8$

   (H) $f(x) = -x^2 + 3x + 4$

   (J) $f(x) = 2x^2 - 6x - 8$

3. Dawn and Julia are running on a jogging trail. Dawn starts running 5 minutes after Julia does. If Julia runs at an average speed of 8 ft/s and Dawn runs at an average speed of 9 ft/s, how many minutes after Dawn starts running will she catch up with Julia?

   (A) 5 minutes
   (B) 27 minutes
   (C) 40 minutes
   (D) 45 minutes

4. Which equation has intercepts at (20, 0, 0), (0, 40, 0), and (0, 0, 5)?

   (F) $20x + 40y + 5z = 0$

   (G) $20x + 40y + 5z = 1$

   (H) $4x + 8y + z = 5$

   (J) $2x + y + 8z = 40$

5. Which graph represents the function $f(x) = -\frac{1}{2}(x - 3) - 4$?

   (A)
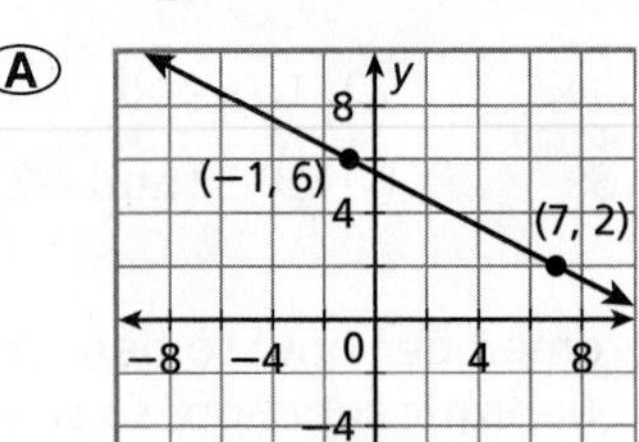

   (B)
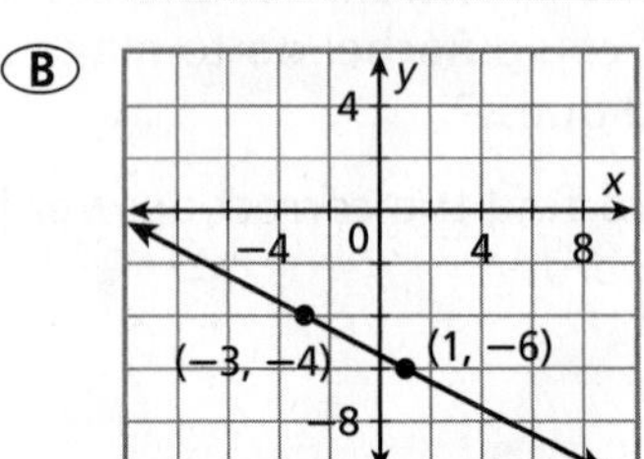

   (C)
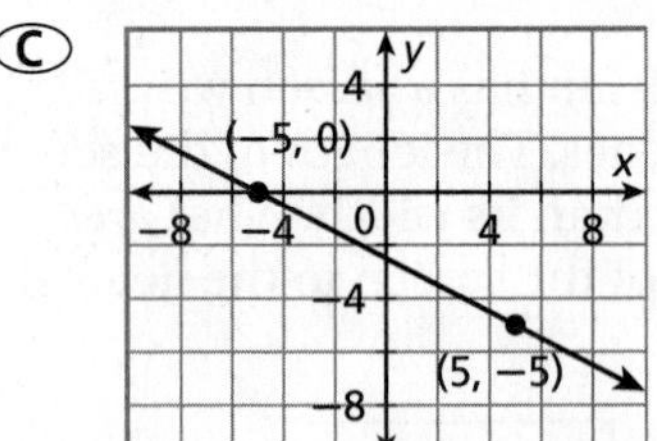

   (D)
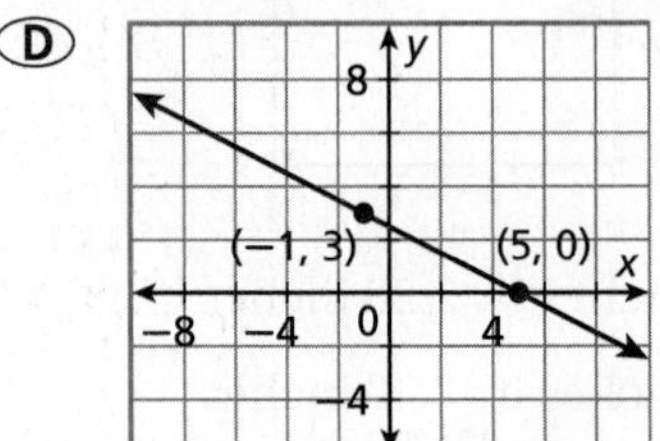

6. What is the equation of the function graphed below?

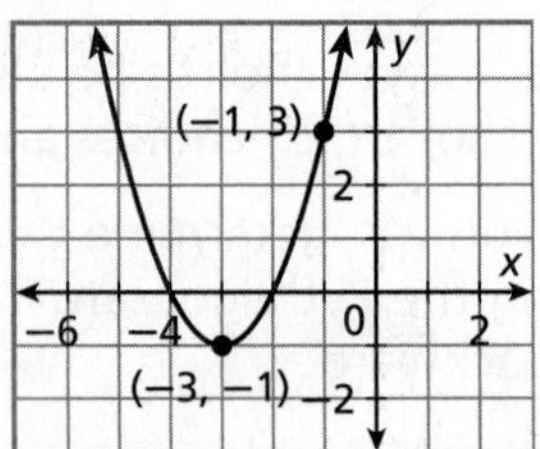

   (F) $y = (x - 3)^2 - 1$
   (G) $y = (x + 3)^2 - 1$
   (H) $y = (x - 1)^2 - 3$
   (J) $y = (x + 1)^2 - 3$

7. If the relationship between x and y is quadratic, which value of y completes the table?

x	−3	−1	1	3	5
y	21	7	■	27	61

(A) 3
(B) 7
(C) 9
(D) 17

8. Which is equivalent to the expression $\frac{5(6-8i)}{2-i}$?

(F) $-20 + 10i$
(G) $15 - 8i$
(H) $15 - 40i$
(J) $20 - 10i$

9. What is the inverse of the following matrix?

$$\begin{bmatrix} -2 & -4 \\ 4 & 2 \end{bmatrix}$$

(A) $\begin{bmatrix} -\frac{1}{6} & -\frac{1}{3} \\ \frac{1}{3} & \frac{1}{6} \end{bmatrix}$

(B) $\begin{bmatrix} -\frac{1}{2} & -\frac{1}{4} \\ \frac{1}{4} & \frac{1}{2} \end{bmatrix}$

(C) $\begin{bmatrix} \frac{1}{6} & \frac{1}{3} \\ -\frac{1}{3} & -\frac{1}{6} \end{bmatrix}$

(D) $\begin{bmatrix} 2 & 4 \\ -4 & -2 \end{bmatrix}$

In nearly all standardized tests, you cannot enter a negative value as the answer to a gridded-response question. If you get a negative value as an answer to one of these questions, you have probably made a mistake in your calculations.

Gridded Response

10. What value of x makes the equation $x^2 + 64 = 16x$ true?

11. The table shows the fees that are charged at an airport parking lot for various lengths of time. What is the slope of the linear function that models the parking fee f in dollars for h number of hours?

Time (h)	1	3	5	7
Parking Fee ($)	3.35	5.05	6.75	8.45

12. What is the x-value of the vertex of $f(x) = 2x^2 - 15x + 5$?

13. What is the value of c given that the following system is dependent?

$$\begin{cases} 2y - x + 10 = 0 \\ 3x - 6y - c = 16 \end{cases}$$

Short Response

14. $\begin{cases} -4x + 8y - 2z = 8 \\ 4x - 4y + 2z = -5 \\ x + 4y - 2z = 15 \end{cases}$

a. Write the augmented matrix that could be used to solve the system of equations given above.

b. Find the solution of the system, and explain how you determined your answer.

15. The graph below shows a feasible region for a set of constraints.

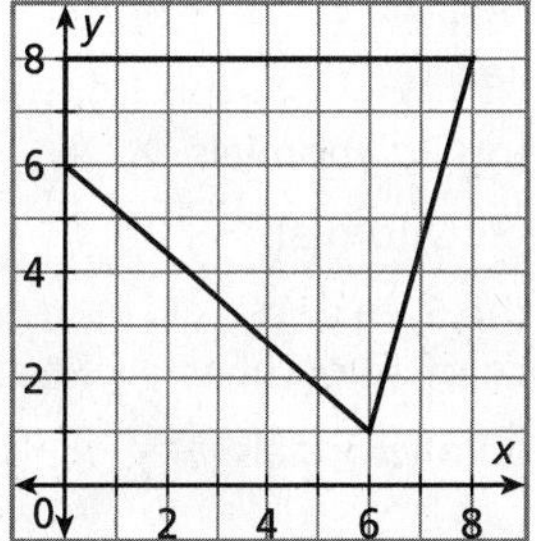

a. Write the constraints for the feasible region.

b. Maximize the objective function $P = 3x - 4y$ under these constraints.

16. Consider the function $f(x) = x^2 - 2x - 48$.

a. Determine the roots of the function. Show your work.

b. The function f is translated to produce the function g. The vertex of g is the point $(3, 30)$. Write the function rule for g in vertex form, and explain how you determined your answer.

Extended Response

17. A small alteration store charges $15.00 per hour plus a $12.50 consulting fee for alterations. A competing store charges $20.00 per hour but does not charge a consulting fee.

a. For each store, write a linear function c that can be used to find the total cost of an alteration that takes h hours.

b. For which values of h is the small alteration store less expensive than the competing store? Explain how you determined your answer.

c. The small store wants to adjust its pricing so that it is less expensive than the competing store for any alteration job that takes an hour or more. By how much should the small store lower its consulting fee in order to make this adjustment?

CHAPTER

6 Polynomial Functions

Chapter Focus

- Solve problems with polynomials.
- Identify characteristics of polynomial functions.

FILL IT UP!

You can use polynomials to predict the shape of containers.

ARE YOU READY?

Vocabulary

Match each term on the left with a definition on the right.

1. coefficient
2. like terms
3. root of an equation
4. x-intercept
5. maximum of a function

A. the y-value of the highest point on the graph of the function
B. the horizontal number line that divides the coordinate plane
C. the numerical factor in a term
D. a value of the variable that makes the equation true
E. terms that contain the same variables raised to the same powers
F. the x-coordinate of a point where a graph intersects the x-axis

Evaluate Powers

Evaluate each expression.

6. 6^4
7. -5^4
8. $(-1)^5$
9. $\left(-\frac{2}{3}\right)^2$

Evaluate Expressions

Evaluate each expression for the given value of the variable.

10. $x^4 - 5x^2 - 6x - 8$ for $x = 3$
11. $2x^3 - 3x^2 - 29x - 30$ for $x = -2$
12. $2x^3 - x^2 - 8x + 4$ for $x = \frac{1}{2}$
13. $3x^4 + 5x^3 + 6x^2 + 4x - 1$ for $x = -1$

Multiply and Divide Monomials

Multiply or divide.

14. $2x^3y \cdot 4x^2$
15. $-5a^2b \cdot ab^4$
16. $\frac{-7t^4}{3t^2}$
17. $\frac{3p^3q^2r}{12pr^4}$

Surface Area

Find the surface area of each solid.

18. cube with side length 4 cm
19. rectangular prism with height 3 ft, width 1.5 ft, and length 8 ft

Volume

Find the volume of each solid.

20. rectangular prism with height 1 in., width 6 in., and length $\frac{2}{3}$ in.
21. rectangular prism with height 5 cm and a square base with side length 2 cm

CHAPTER 6

Study Guide: Preview

Where You've Been

Previously, you

- used transformations to graph quadratic functions.
- solved quadratic equations.
- used the Zero Product Property to find the zeros of quadratic functions.
- modeled data with quadratic models.

In This Chapter

You will study

- using transformations to graph polynomial functions.
- solving polynomial equations.
- the zeros of polynomial functions.
- modeling data with polynomial models.

Where You're Going

You can use the skills in this chapter

- to solve problems in future math classes, including College Algebra and Trigonometry.
- to solve real-life problems in physics and graphic arts.
- to predict the value of stocks.
- to maximize or minimize volume and area.

Key Vocabulary/Vocabulario

end behavior	comportamiento extremo
leading coefficient	coeficiente principal
local maximum	máximo local
local minimum	mínimo local
monomial	monomio
multiplicity	multiplicidad
polynomial	polinomio
polynomial function	función polinomial
synthetic division	división sintética
turning point	punto de inflexión

Vocabulary Connections

To become familiar with some of the vocabulary terms in the chapter, consider the following. You may refer to the chapter, the glossary, or a dictionary if you like.

1. In what position would you find the *leading* runner in a race? In what position do you suppose you would find the **leading coefficient** in a polynomial?
2. A **local minimum** of a function is a value less than any other value in the region around it. Which of the vocabulary terms do you think describes the value of a function that is greater than any other value in the region around it?
3. The word **monomial** begins with the root *mono-*. List some other words that begin with *mono-*. What do all of these words have in common?
4. The everyday meaning of **turning point** is "a point at which a change takes place." What might happen at a *turning point* on the graph of a polynomial function?

Study Strategy: Remember Theorems and Formulas

In math, there are many formulas, properties, theorems, and rules that you must commit to memory. To help you remember an important rule, write it on an index card. Include a diagram or an example, and add notes about the important details. Study your index cards on a regular basis.

From Lesson 5-6

The Quadratic Formula

If $ax^2 + bx + c = 0$ $(a \neq 0)$, then the solutions, or roots, are

$$x = \frac{-b \pm \sqrt{b^2 - 4ac}}{2a}.$$

Sample Index Card

Quadratic Formula

If $ax^2 + bx + c = 0$ $(a \neq 0)$, then the roots are

$$x = \frac{-b \pm \sqrt{b^2 - 4ac}}{2a}.$$

- *This can be used to solve any quadratic equation.*
- *Before using the formula, make sure the equation is written in standard form.*
- $f(x) = x^2 + 2x - 24 \rightarrow x = \frac{-(2) \pm \sqrt{(2)^2 - 4(1)(-24)}}{2(1)}$

Try This

1. Create index cards for the discriminant formulas shown in the table below.
2. Explain why you need to understand the principles and concepts of the quadratic formula prior to memorizing the discriminant properties.
3. Describe a plan to help you memorize the quadratic formula and the discriminant formulas.

Discriminant

The discriminant of the quadratic equation $ax^2 + bx + c = 0$ $(a \neq 0)$ is $b^2 - 4ac$.

If $b^2 - 4ac > 0$, the equation has two distinct real solutions.	If $b^2 - 4ac = 0$, the equation has one distinct real solution.	If $b^2 - 4ac < 0$, the equation has two distinct nonreal complex solutions.
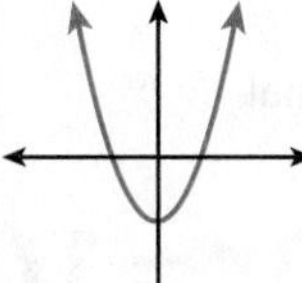	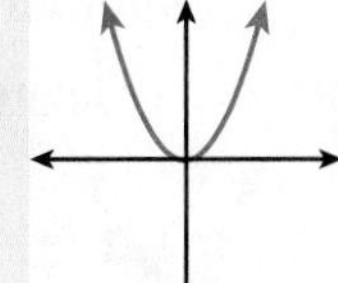	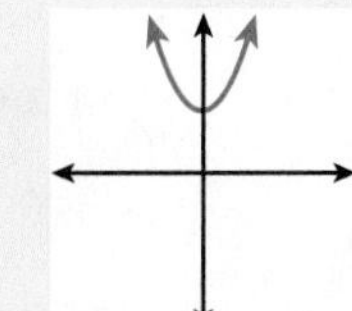

6-1 Polynomials

Objectives
Identify, evaluate, add, and subtract polynomials.

Classify and graph polynomials.

Vocabulary
monomial
polynomial
degree of a monomial
degree of a polynomial
leading coefficient
binomial
trinomial
polynomial function

Who uses this?
Doctors can use polynomials to model blood flow. (See Example 4.)

A **monomial** is a number or a product of numbers and variables with whole number exponents. A **polynomial** is a monomial or a sum or difference of monomials. Each monomial in a polynomial is a term. Because a monomial has only one term, it is the simplest type of polynomial.

Polynomials have no variables in denominators or exponents, no roots or absolute values of variables, and all variables have whole number exponents.

Polynomials:	$3x^4$	$2z^{12} + 9z^3$	$\frac{1}{2}a^7$	$0.15x^{101}$	$3t^2 - t^3$
Not polynomials:	3^x	$\lvert 2b^3 - 6b \rvert$	$\frac{8}{5y^2}$	$\frac{1}{2}\sqrt{x}$	$m^{0.75} - m$

The **degree of a monomial** is the sum of the exponents of the variables.

EXAMPLE 1 Identifying the Degree of a Monomial

Identify the degree of each monomial.

 x^4

x^4 *Identify the exponent.*

The degree is 4.

 12

$12 = 12x^0$ *Identify the exponent.*

The degree is 0.

 $4a^2b$

$4a^2b^1$ *Add the exponents.*

The degree is 3.

 x^3y^4z

$x^3y^4z^1$ *Add the exponents.*

The degree is 8.

Identify the degree of each monomial.

1a. x^3 **1b.** 7 **1c.** $5x^3y^2$ **1d.** a^6bc^2

The **degree of a polynomial** is given by the term with the greatest degree. A polynomial with one variable is in standard form when its terms are written in descending order by degree. So, in standard form, the degree of the first term indicates the degree of the polynomial, and the **leading coefficient** is the coefficient of the first term.

Standard Form

Leading coefficient — Degree of polynomial

$$5x^3 + 8x^2 + 3x - 17$$

Degree of term: 3 2 1 0

A polynomial can be classified by its number of terms. A polynomial with two terms is called a **binomial**, and a polynomial with three terms is called a **trinomial**. A polynomial can also be classified by its degree.

Classifying Polynomials by Degree

Name	Degree	Example
Constant	0	-9
Linear	1	$x - 4$
Quadratic	2	$x^2 + 3x - 1$
Cubic	3	$x^3 + 2x^2 + x + 1$
Quartic	4	$2x^4 + x^3 + 3x^2 + 4x - 1$
Quintic	5	$7x^5 + x^4 - x^3 + 3x^2 + 2x - 1$

EXAMPLE 2 Classifying Polynomials

Rewrite each polynomial in standard form. Then identify the leading coefficient, degree, and number of terms. Name the polynomial.

A $2x + 4x^3 - 1$

Write terms in descending order by degree.

$4x^3 + 2x - 1$

Leading coefficient: 4

Degree: 3

Terms: 3

Name: cubic trinomial

B $7x^3 - 11x + x^5 - 2$

Write terms in descending order by degree.

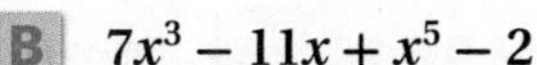

$1x^5 + 7x^3 - 11x - 2$

Leading coefficient: 1

Degree: 5

Terms: 4

Name: quintic polynomial with four terms

Rewrite each polynomial in standard form. Then identify the leading coefficient, degree, and number of terms. Name the polynomial.

2a. $4x - 2x^2 + 2$

2b. $-18x^2 + x^3 - 5 + 2x$

To add or subtract polynomials, combine like terms. You can add or subtract horizontally or vertically.

EXAMPLE 3 Adding and Subtracting Polynomials

Add or subtract. Write your answer in standard form.

A $(3x^2 + 7 + x) + (14x^3 + 2 + x^2 - x)$

Add vertically.

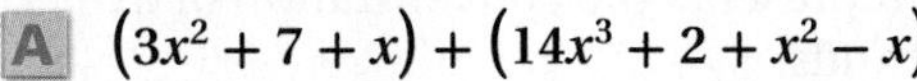

$(3x^2 + 7 + x) + (14x^3 + 2 + x^2 - x)$

$3x^2 + x + 7$	*Write in standard form.*
$+\ 14x^3 + x^2 - x + 2$	*Align like terms.*
$14x^3 + 4x^2 + 0x + 9$	*Add.*
$14x^3 + 4x^2 + 9$	*Combine like terms.*

Add or subtract. Write your answer in standard form.

B $(1 - x^2) - (3x^2 + 2x - 5)$

> **Remember!**
> To subtract a polynomial, distribute the negative to all terms.

Add the opposite horizontally.

$(1 - x^2) - (3x^2 + 2x - 5)$

$(-x^2 + 1) + (-3x^2 - 2x + 5)$ *Write in standard form.*

$(-x^2 - 3x^2) + (-2x) + (1 + 5)$ *Group like terms.*

$-4x^2 - 2x + 6$ *Add.*

Add or subtract. Write your answer in standard form.

3a. $(-36x^2 + 6x - 11) + (6x^2 + 16x^3 - 5)$

3b. $(5x^3 + 12 + 6x^2) - (15x^2 + 3x - 2)$

A **polynomial function** is a function whose rule is a polynomial. In this course, you will study only polynomial functions with one variable.

EXAMPLE 4 *Medical Application*

Cardiac output is the amount of blood pumped through the heart. The output is measured by a technique called dye dilution. A doctor injects dye into a vein near the heart and measures the amount of dye in the arteries over time.

The cardiac output of a particular patient can be approximated by the function $f(t) = 0.0056t^3 - 0.22t^2 + 2.33t$, where t represents time (in seconds after injection, $0 \le t \le 23$) and $f(t)$ represents the concentration of dye (in milligrams per liter).

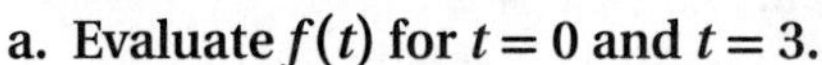

a. Evaluate $f(t)$ for $t = 0$ and $t = 3$.

$f(0) = 0.0056(0)^3 - 0.22(0)^2 + 2.33(0) = 0$

$f(3) = 0.0056(3)^3 - 0.22(3)^2 + 2.33(3) = 5.1612$

b. Describe what the values of the function from part a represent.

$f(0)$ represents the concentration of dye, 0 mg/L, in the artery at the start of the dye dilution process.

$f(3)$ represents the concentration of dye, 5.1612 mg/L, in the artery after 3 seconds.

4. For a different patient, the dye dilution can be modeled by the function $f(t) = 0.000468x^4 - 0.016x^3 + 0.095x^2 + 0.806x$. Evaluate $f(t)$ for $t = 4$ and $t = 17$, and describe what the values of the function represent.

Graphing polynomial functions can be a challenge. Throughout this chapter, you will learn skills for analyzing, describing, and graphing higher-degree polynomials. Until then, the graphing calculator will be a useful tool.

EXAMPLE 5 Graphing Higher-Degree Polynomials on a Calculator

Caution!

Depending on your viewing window, a calculator may not show all of the important features of a graph. Watch out for hidden behavior.

Graph each polynomial function on a calculator. Describe the graph, and identify the number of real zeros.

A $f(x) = x^3 - x$

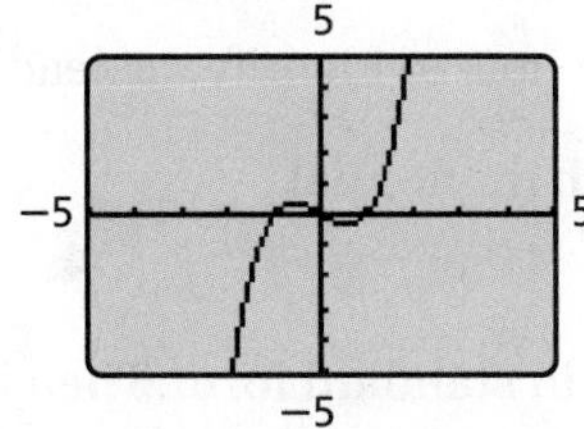

From left to right, the graph increases, decreases slightly, and then increases again. It crosses the x-axis three times, so there appear to be three real zeros.

B $f(x) = 3x^3 + 2x + 1$

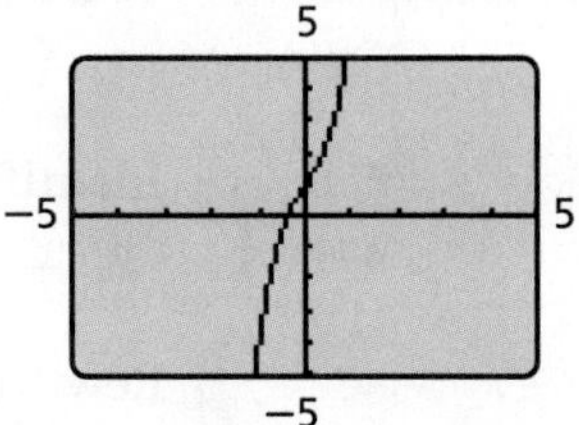

From left to right, the graph increases. It crosses the x-axis once, so there appears to be one real zero.

C $h(x) = x^4 - 8x^2 + 1$

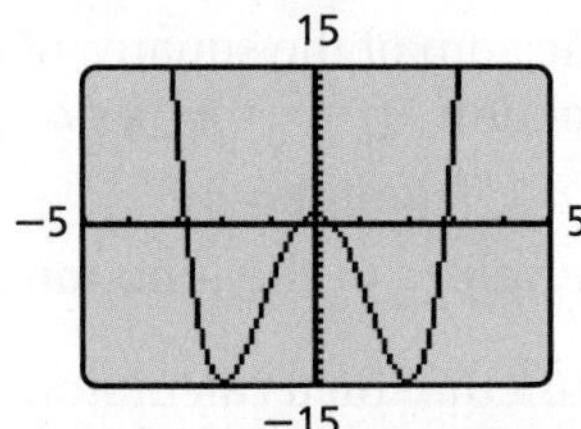

From left to right, the graph alternately decreases and increases, changing direction three times. It crosses the x-axis four times, so there appear to be four real zeros.

D $k(x) = x^4 + x^3 - x^2 + 2x - 3$

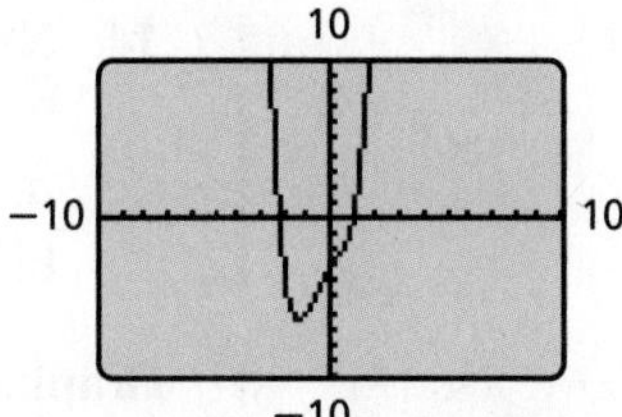

From left to right, the graph decreases and then increases. It crosses the x-axis twice, so there appear to be two real zeros.

Graph each polynomial on a calculator. Describe the graph, and identify the number of real zeros.

5a. $f(x) = 6x^3 + x^2 - 5x + 1$ **5b.** $f(x) = 3x^2 - 2x + 2$

5c. $g(x) = x^4 - 3$ **5d.** $h(x) = 4x^4 - 16x^2 + 5$

THINK AND DISCUSS

1. Can a polynomial have a leading coefficient of $\sqrt{3}$? Explain.
2. What is the degree of the sum of a quartic polynomial and a cubic polynomial? Explain.
3. Is the sum of two trinomial polynomials always a trinomial? Explain.
4. **GET ORGANIZED** Copy and complete the graphic organizer.

Know it! Note

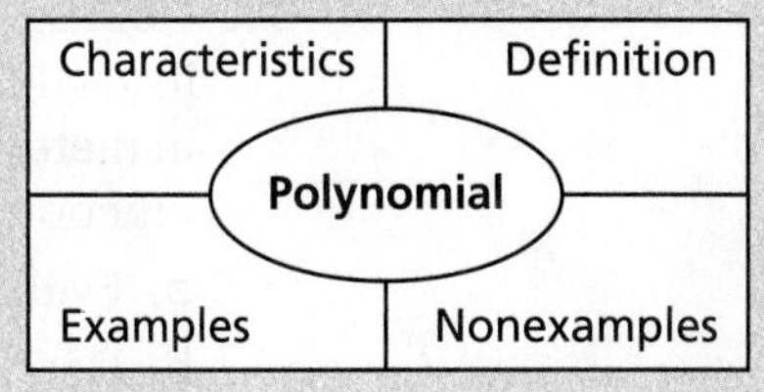

6-1 Exercises

go.hrw.com
Homework Help Online
KEYWORD: MB7 6-1
Parent Resources Online
KEYWORD: MB7 Parent

GUIDED PRACTICE

1. **Vocabulary** Explain how to identify the leading coefficient of a polynomial.

SEE EXAMPLE 1 p. 406

Identify the degree of each monomial.

2. $-7x$
3. $4x^2y^3$
4. 13
5. m^3n^2p

SEE EXAMPLE 2 p. 407

Rewrite each polynomial in standard form. Then identify the leading coefficient, degree, and number of terms. Name the polynomial.

6. $4x + 2x^2 - 7 + x^3$
7. $3x^2 + 5x - 4$
8. $5x^2 - 4x^3$
9. $4x^4 + 8x^2 + 1 - 3x$

SEE EXAMPLE 3 p. 407

Add or subtract. Write your answer in standard form.

10. $(15x^2 - 3x + 11) + (2x^3 - x^2 + 6x + 1)$
11. $(12x - 1 + 2x^2) + (x^2 + 4)$
12. $(3x^2 - 5x) - (-4 + x^2 + x)$
13. $(x^2 - 3x + 7) - (6x^2 + 4x + 12)$

SEE EXAMPLE 4 p. 408

14. **Number Theory** The sum of the squares of the first n natural numbers is given by the polynomial function $F(n) = \frac{1}{3}n^3 + \frac{1}{2}n^2 + \frac{1}{6}n$.
    a. Evaluate $F(n)$ for $n = 5$ and $n = 10$.
    b. Describe what the values of the function from part **a** represent.

SEE EXAMPLE 5 p. 409

Graph each polynomial function on a calculator. Describe the graph, and identify the number of real zeros.

15. $f(x) = 4x^3 + 2x + 1$
16. $g(x) = \frac{1}{4}x^4 - 3x^2$
17. $h(x) = -3x^3 - 6$
18. $p(x) = -4x^4 + 6x^3 - 3x^2$

PRACTICE AND PROBLEM SOLVING

Independent Practice

For Exercises	See Example
19–22	1
23–26	2
27–30	3
31	4
32–35	5

Extra Practice

Skills Practice p. S14
Application Practice p. S37

Identify the degree of each monomial.

19. x^8
20. $6x^3y$
21. 8
22. $a^4b^6c^3$

Rewrite each polynomial in standard form. Then identify the leading coefficient, degree, and number of terms. Name the polynomial.

23. $3x^3 + 2x^4 - 7x + x^2$
24. $6x - 4x^4 + 5^7$
25. $2x^3 + 10x - 9$
26. $3x^2 + 2x^6 - 4x^4 - 1$

Add or subtract. Write your answer in standard form.

27. $(x^2 - 3x + 4) + (x^3 + 3x - 4)$
28. $(x^2 - 3x + 4) - (3x + x^3 - 4)$
29. $(5y^3 - 2y^2 - 1) - (y^2 - 2y - 3)$
30. $(2y^2 - 5y + 3) + (y^2 - 2y - 5)$
31. **Recreation** The distance d, in centimeters, that a diving board bends below its resting position when you stand at its end is dependent on your distance x, in meters, from the stabilized point. This relationship can be modeled by the function $d(x) = -4x^3 + x^2$.
    a. Evaluate $d(x)$ for $x = 1$ and $x = 2$.
    b. Describe what the values of the function from part **a** represent.

Graph each polynomial function on a calculator. Describe the graph, and identify the number of real zeros.

32. $f(x) = -2x^2 + x - 1$

33. $g(x) = x^3 + 1$

34. $h(x) = x^4 - 6x^2 + 10$

35. $p(x) = -x^5 + x - 1$

Complete the table.

	Polynomial	Standard Form	Leading Coefficient	Degree
36.	$8x + 3x^2 - 5$	■	■	■
37.	$3x^2 + x^4 - 2$	■	■	■
38.	$x^3 - x^4 + x - 1$	■	■	■
39.	$64 + x^2$	■	■	■

40. Critical Thinking Write a quartic trinomial with a leading coefficient of 2.

Geometry **Find a polynomial expression in terms of *x* for the surface area of each figure.**

41.

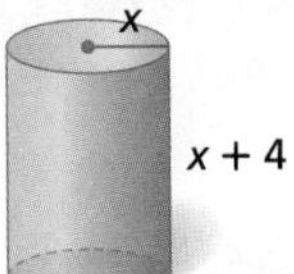

42.

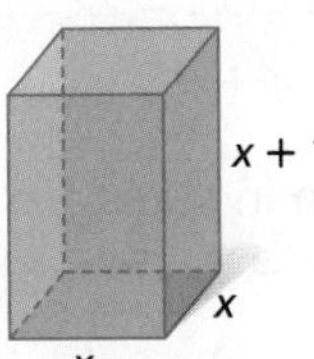

43.

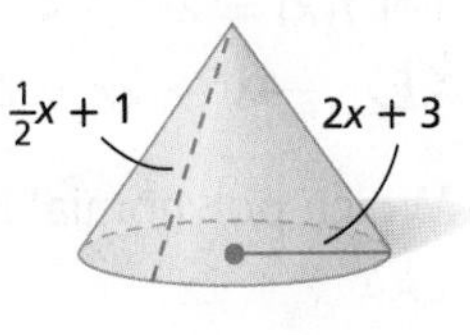

44.

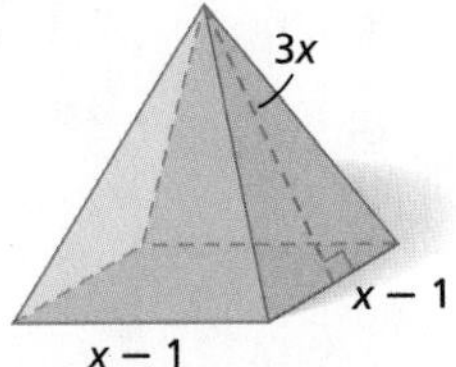

45. Business The manager of a gift-basket business will ship the baskets anywhere in the country. The cost to mail a basket based on its weight x, in pounds, is given by $C(x) = 0.03x^3 - 0.75x^2 + 4.5x + 7$.

a. What is the cost of shipping a 7-pound gift basket?

b. What is the cost of shipping a 19-pound gift basket?

46. Estimation Estimate the value of $P(x) = -2.03x^3 + \pi x^2 - x + 5.8$ for $P(-2.78)$.

Tell whether each statement is sometimes, always, or never true. If it is sometimes true, give examples to support your answer.

47. A quadratic polynomial is a trinomial.

48. The degree of a polynomial in standard form is equal to the degree of the first term.

49. The leading coefficient of a polynomial is the greatest coefficient of any term.

MULTI-STEP TEST PREP

50. This problem will prepare you for the Multi-Step Test Prep on page 436.

The total number of lights in a triangular lighting rig is related to the triangular numbers, as shown at right. The nth triangular number is given by $T(n) = \frac{1}{2}n^2 + \frac{1}{2}n$.

a. Write a polynomial function that represents the $(n + 1)$th triangular number, $T(n + 1)$.

b. The difference between two consecutive triangular numbers is $T(n + 1) - T(n)$. Subtract these two polynomial functions, and state a conclusion about the difference between consecutive triangular numbers.

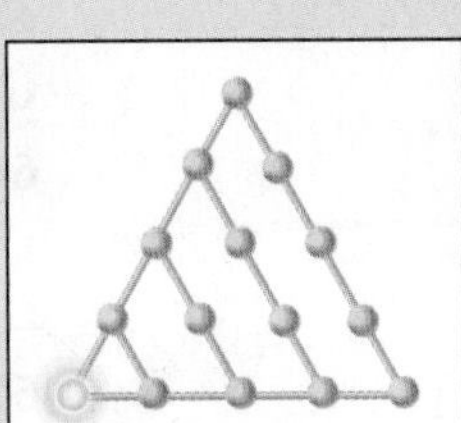

Triangular numbers: 1, 3, 6, 10, 15, . . .

51. **Graphing Calculator** The functions below are polynomials in factored form. Graph each function. Identify the x-intercepts. What can you say about the x-intercepts and the linear binomial factors in the functions?

  a. $f(x) = (x + 3)(x - 1)(x - 4)$

  b. $g(x) = (x + 1)(x + 2)(x - 3)(x - 1)$

  c. $h(x) = x(x + 1)(x - 2)$

  d. $k(x) = (x + 2)(x - 3)$

  e. $j(x) = x\left(x + \frac{1}{2}\right)\left(x - \frac{1}{2}\right)$

Write About It Recall the properties of real numbers from Lesson 1-2.

52. Is the addition of polynomial functions commutative? Explain.

53. Is the addition of polynomial functions associative? Explain.

TEST PREP

54. What is the degree of the monomial $5xy^4z$?

  Ⓐ 6 Ⓑ 1 Ⓒ 4 Ⓓ 5

55. For $f(x) = 2x^2 + 4x - 6$ and $g(x) = 2x^2 + 2x + 8$, find $f(x) - g(x)$.

  Ⓕ $-4x^2 - 2x + 2$ Ⓖ $2x + 2$ Ⓗ $4x^2 + 6x + 2$ Ⓙ $2x - 14$

56. Which polynomial is written in standard form?

  Ⓐ $7 + 2x^4 - x^6$ Ⓑ $3x^3 - x^5$ Ⓒ x^4 Ⓓ $x^2 + 3 - 2x$

57. What is the degree of the polynomial function $h(x) = 7x^3 - x^6 + x$?

  Ⓕ 10 Ⓖ 3 Ⓗ −1 Ⓙ 6

58. **Short Response** Evaluate $P(x) = \frac{1}{2}x^3 - x^2 + 8$ for $x = -2$.

CHALLENGE AND EXTEND

$P(x)$ and $R(x)$ are polynomials. $P(x)$ is a trinomial. Give examples of $P(x)$ and $R(x)$ that meet the given conditions.

59. $P(x) - R(x)$ is a binomial.

60. $P(x) - R(x)$ is a trinomial.

61. $P(x) - R(x)$ is a polynomial with four terms.

62. $P(x) - R(x)$ is a quartic.

63. $P(x) - R(x)$ is a quintic.

SPIRAL REVIEW

Graph each line. *(Lesson 2-3)*

64. slope $\frac{3}{4}$, point $(0, -1)$

65. slope -2, point $(3, 0)$

66. slope 1, point $(1, 2)$

Determine if each line is vertical or horizontal. Then graph the line. *(Lesson 2-3)*

67. $x = 4$

68. $y = -2$

69. $y = \frac{3}{4}$

Using $f(x) = x^2$ as a guide, graph each function and describe the transformations. *(Lesson 5-1)*

70. $g(x) = (x - 5)^2 + 6$

71. $g(x) = (x + 3)^2 + 2$

72. $h(x) = \frac{1}{5}x^2 + 2$

Pascal's Triangle

Each number in Pascal's triangle is the sum of the two numbers diagonally above it. All of the outside numbers are 1.

Many interesting number patterns can be found in Pascal's triangle, such as Fibonnacci's sequence and powers of 2.

Pascal's Triangle is useful for many different mathematical situations, such as expanding binomials and probability.

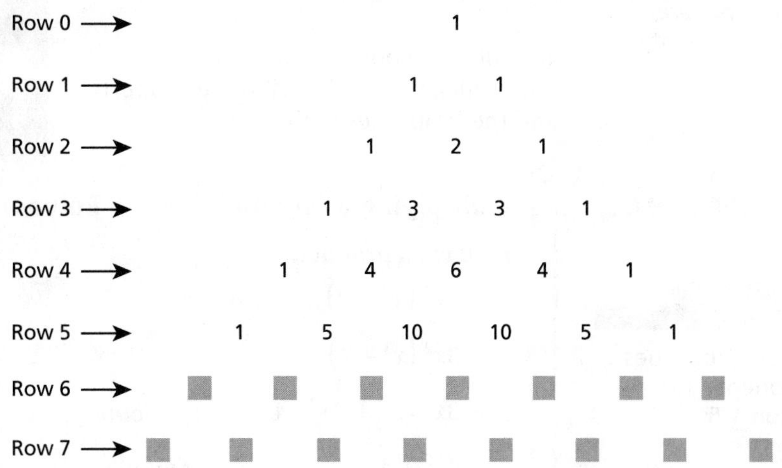

Activity

Find rows 6 and 7 of Pascal's triangle.

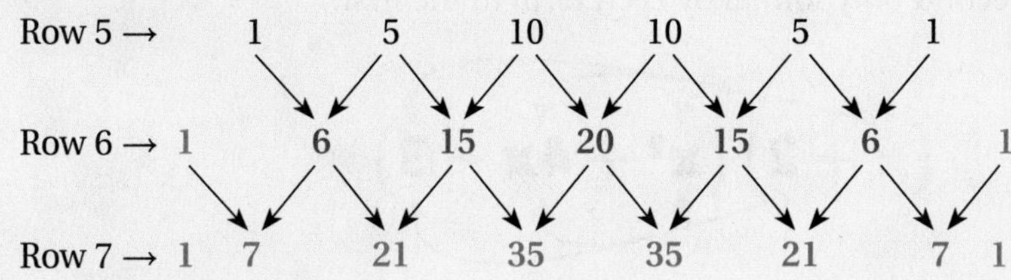

All of the outside numbers are 1. Fill in values by adding the numbers in row 5 that are diagonally above the new values.

Repeat the process for row 7.

Try This

1. Find rows 8, 9, and 10 of Pascal's triangle.
2. **Make a Conjecture** What can you say about the relationship between the row number and the number of terms in a row?
3. **Make a Conjecture** What can you say about the relationship between the row number and the second term in each row?
4. **Make a Conjecture** Expand $(x + 1)(x + 1)$ *and* $(x + 1)(x + 1)(x + 1)$, and use your answers to make a conjecture about the relationship between Pascal's triangle and the multiplication of binomials.
5. Test your conjecture from Problem 4 by expanding $(x + 1)(x + 1)(x + 1)(x + 1)$ with multiplication and by using Pascal's triangle.

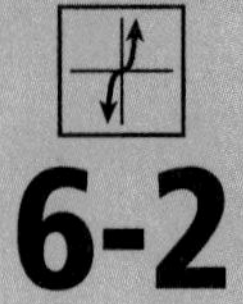

6-2 Multiplying Polynomials

Objectives
Multiply polynomials.

Use binomial expansion to expand binomial expressions that are raised to positive integer powers.

Who uses this?
Business managers can multiply polynomials when modeling total manufacturing costs. (See Example 3.)

To multiply a polynomial by a monomial, use the Distributive Property and the Properties of Exponents.

EXAMPLE 1 Multiplying a Monomial and a Polynomial

Remember!
To review Properties of Exponents, refer to Lesson 1-5.

Find each product.

 $3x^2(x^3+4)$

$3x^2(x^3+4)$

$3x^2 \cdot x^3 + 3x^2 \cdot 4$ *Distribute.*

$3x^5 + 12x^2$ *Multiply.*

 $ab(a^3+3ab^2-b^3)$

$ab(a^3+3ab^2-b^3)$

$ab(a^3)+ab(3ab^2)+ab(-b^3)$

$a^4b+3a^2b^3-ab^4$

Find each product.

1a. $3cd^2(4c^2d-6cd+14cd^2)$ **1b.** $x^2y(6y^3+y^2-28y+30)$

To multiply any two polynomials, use the Distributive Property and multiply each term in the second polynomial by each term in the first.

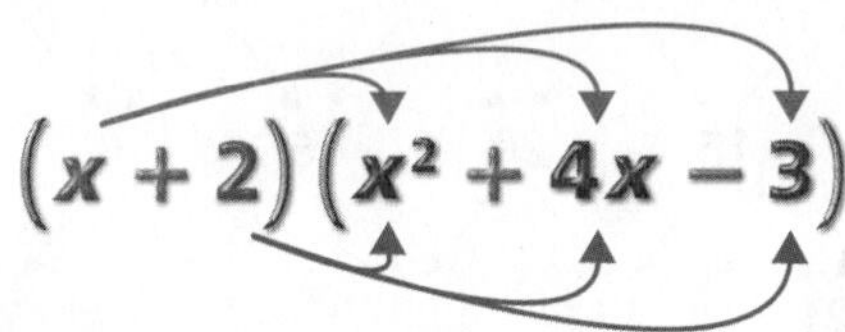

Keep in mind that if one polynomial has m terms and the other has n terms, then the product has mn terms before it is simplified.

EXAMPLE 2 Multiplying Polynomials

Find each product.

 $(x-2)(1+3x-x^2)$

Method 1 Multiply horizontally.

$(x-2)(-x^2+3x+1)$ *Write polynomials in standard form.*

$x(-x^2)+x(3x)+x(1)-2(-x^2)-2(3x)-2(1)$ *Distribute x and then −2.*

$-x^3+3x^2+x+2x^2-6x-2$ *Multiply. Add exponents.*

$-x^3+5x^2-5x-2$ *Combine like terms.*

Method 2 Multiply vertically.

$-x^2 + 3x + 1$	*Write each polynomial in standard form.*
$x - 2$	
$2x^2 - 6x - 2$	*Multiply $(-x^2 + 3x + 1)$ by -2.*
$-x^3 + 3x^2 + x$	*Multiply $(-x^2 + 3x + 1)$ by x, and align like terms.*
$-x^3 + 5x^2 - 5x - 2$	*Combine like terms.*

Find each product.

B $(x^2 + 3x - 5)(x^2 - x + 1)$

Multiply each term of one polynomial by each term of the other. Use a table to organize the products.

	x^2	$-x$	$+1$
x^2	x^4	$-x^3$	$+x^2$
$+3x$	$+3x^3$	$-3x^2$	$+3x$
-5	$-5x^2$	$+5x$	-5

The top left corner is the first term in the product. Combine terms along diagonals to get the middle terms. The bottom right corner is the last term in the product.

$$x^4 + (3x^3 - x^3) + (-5x^2 - 3x^2 + x^2) + (5x + 3x) + (-5)$$

$$x^4 + 2x^3 - 7x^2 + 8x - 5$$

Helpful Hint

When using a table to multiply, the polynomials must be in standard form. Use a zero for any missing terms.

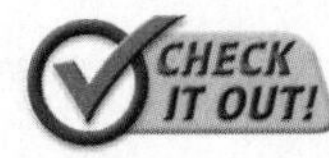

Find each product.

2a. $(3b - 2c)(3b^2 - bc - 2c^2)$ **2b.** $(x^2 - 4x + 1)(x^2 + 5x - 2)$

EXAMPLE 3 *Business Application*

Mr. Silva manages a manufacturing plant. From 1990 through 2005, the number of units produced (in thousands) can be modeled by $N(x) = 0.02x^2 + 0.2x + 3$. The average cost per unit (in dollars) can be modeled by $C(x) = -0.002x^2 - 0.1x + 2$, where x is the number of years since 1990. Write a polynomial $T(x)$ that can be used to model Mr. Silva's total manufacturing costs.

Total cost is the product of the number of units and the cost per unit.

$T(x) = N(x) \cdot C(x)$.

Multiply the two polynomials.

$$\begin{array}{r} 0.02x^2 + 0.2x + 3 \\ \times\ -0.002x^2 - 0.1x + 2 \\ \hline 0.04x^2 + 0.4x + 6 \\ -0.002x^3 - 0.02x^2 - 0.3x \\ -0.00004x^4 - 0.0004x^3 - 0.006x^2 \\ \hline -0.00004x^4 - 0.0024x^3 + 0.014x^2 + 0.1x + 6 \end{array}$$

Mr. Silva's total manufacturing costs, in thousands of dollars, can be modeled by $T(x) = -0.00004x^4 - 0.0024x^3 + 0.014x^2 + 0.1x + 6$.

3. What if...? Suppose that in 2005 the cost of raw materials increases and the new average cost per unit is modeled by $C(x) = -0.004x^2 - 0.1x + 3$. Write a polynomial $T(x)$ that can be used to model the total costs.

You can also raise polynomials to powers.

EXAMPLE 4 Expanding a Power of a Binomial

Find the product.

$(x + y)^3$

$(x + y)(x + y)(x + y)$ — *Write in expanded form.*

$(x + y)(x^2 + 2xy + y^2)$ — *Multiply the last two binomial factors.*

$x(x^2) + x(2xy) + x(y^2) + y(x^2) + y(2xy) + y(y^2)$ — *Distribute x and then y.*

$x^3 + 2x^2y + xy^2 + x^2y + 2xy^2 + y^3$ — *Multiply.*

$x^3 + 3x^2y + 3xy^2 + y^3$ — *Combine like terms.*

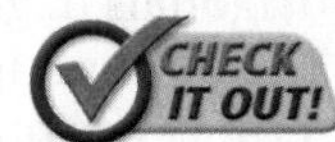

Find each product.

4a. $(x + 4)^4$ **4b.** $(2x - 1)^3$

Notice the coefficients of the variables in the final product of $(x + y)^3$. These coefficients are the numbers from the third row of Pascal's triangle.

	Binomial Expansion	Pascal's Triangle (Coefficients)
$(a + b)^0 =$	1	1
$(a + b)^1 =$	$a + b$	1 1
$(a + b)^2 =$	$a^2 + 2ab + b^2$	1 2 1
$(a + b)^3 =$	$a^3 + 3a^2b + 3ab^2 + b^3$	1 3 3 1
$(a + b)^4 =$	$a^4 + 4a^3b + 6a^2b^2 + 4ab^3 + b^4$	1 4 6 4 1
$(a + b)^5 =$	$a^5 + 5a^4b + 10a^3b^2 + 10a^2b^3 + 5ab^4 + b^5$	1 5 10 10 5 1

Each row of Pascal's triangle gives the coefficients of the corresponding binomial expansion. The pattern in the table can be extended to apply to the expansion of any binomial of the form $(a + b)^n$, where n is a whole number.

Binomial Expansion

For a binomial expansion of the form $(a + b)^n$, the following statements are true.

1. There are $n + 1$ terms.
2. The coefficients are the numbers from the nth row of Pascal's triangle.
3. The exponent of a is n in the first term, and the exponent decreases by 1 in each successive term.
4. The exponent of b is 0 in the first term, and the exponent increases by 1 in each successive term.
5. The sum of the exponents in any term is n.

This information is formalized by the *Binomial Theorem,* which you will study further in Chapter 11.

Student to Student

Expanding Binomials

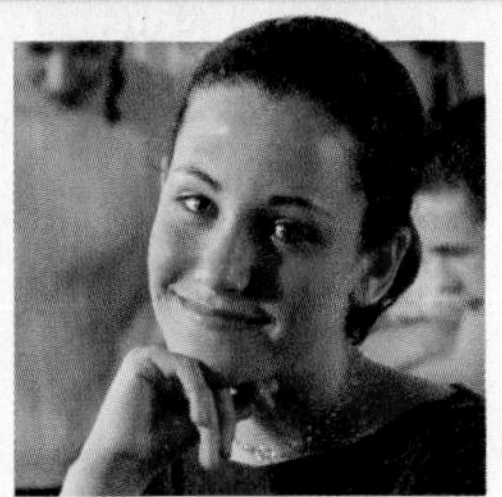

Caitlin Humphrey
Hillcrest High School

I like to use a chart to expand binomials. I will use the binomial $(x + 2)^4$ as an example.

I write the coefficients from Pascal's triangle in the top row. I write the decreasing powers in the second row.

Then I shift one column to the right and write the increasing powers in the third row.

1	4	6	4	1
x^4	x^3	x^2	x	
	2	4	8	16

Finally, I multiply vertically to get $x^4 + 8x^3 + 24x^2 + 32x + 16$.

EXAMPLE 5 **Using Pascal's Triangle to Expand Binomial Expressions**

Expand each expression.

A $(y - 3)^4$

1 4 6 4 1   *Identify the coefficients for n = 4, or row 4.*

$$\left[1y^4(-3)^0\right] + \left[4y^3(-3)^1\right] + \left[6y^2(-3)^2\right] + \left[4y^1(-3)^3\right] + \left[1y^0(-3)^4\right]$$

$y^4 - 12y^3 + 54y^2 - 108y + 81$

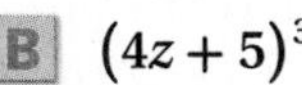

B $(4z + 5)^3$

1 3 3 1   *Identify the coefficients for n = 3, or row 3.*

$$\left[1(4z)^3 5^0\right] + \left[3(4z)^2 5^1\right] + \left[3(4z)^1 5^2\right] + \left[1(4z)^0 5^3\right]$$

$64z^3 + 240z^2 + 300z + 125$

CHECK IT OUT! **Expand each expression.**

5a. $(x + 2)^3$ **5b.** $(x - 4)^5$ **5c.** $(3x + 1)^4$

THINK AND DISCUSS

1. The product of $(3x^4 - 2x^2 - 1)$ and a polynomial $P(x)$ results in a polynomial of degree 9. What is the degree of $P(x)$? Explain.

2. After $(2x + 8)^7$ is expanded, what is the degree of the result, and how many terms does the result have? Explain.

3. GET ORGANIZED Copy and complete the graphic organizer. In each box, write an example and find the product.

Multiplying Polynomials
- Binomial × trinomial (horizontal method)
- Binomial × trinomial (vertical method)
- Monomial × trinomial
- Trinomial × trinomial
- Expand a binomial

6-2 Exercises

go.hrw.com
Homework Help Online
KEYWORD: MB7 6-2
Parent Resources Online
KEYWORD: MB7 Parent

GUIDED PRACTICE

Find each product.

SEE EXAMPLE 1 p. 414

1. $-4c^2d^3(5cd^2 + 3c^2d)$
2. $3x^2(2y + 5x)$
3. $xy(5x^2 + 8x - 7)$
4. $2xy(3x^2 - xy + 7)$

SEE EXAMPLE 2 p. 414

5. $(x - y)(x^2 + 2xy - y^2)$
6. $(3x - 2)(2x^2 + 3x - 1)$
7. $(x^3 + 3x^2 + 1)(3x^2 + 6x - 2)$
8. $(x^2 + 9x + 7)(3x^2 + 9x + 5)$

SEE EXAMPLE 3 p. 415

9. **Business** A businessman models the number of items (in thousands) that his company sold from 1998 through 2004 as $N(x) = -0.1x^3 + x^2 - 3x + 4$ and the average price per item (in dollars) as $P(x) = 0.2x + 5$, where x represents the number of years since 1998. Write a polynomial $R(x)$ that can be used to model the total revenue for this company.

SEE EXAMPLE 4 p. 416

Find each product.

10. $(x + 2)^3$
11. $(x + y)^4$
12. $(x + 1)^4$
13. $(x - 3y)^3$

SEE EXAMPLE 5 p. 417

Expand each expression.

14. $(x - 2)^4$
15. $(2x + y)^4$
16. $(x + 2y)^3$
17. $(2x - y)^5$

PRACTICE AND PROBLEM SOLVING

Independent Practice

For Exercises	See Example
18–21	1
22–25	2
26	3
27–30	4
31–34	5

Extra Practice

Skills Practice p. S14
Application Practice p. S37

Find each product.

18. $7x^3(2x + 3)$
19. $3x^2(2x^2 + 9x - 6)$
20. $xy^2(x^2 + 3xy + 9)$
21. $2r^2(6r^3 + 14r^2 - 30r + 14)$
22. $(x - y)(x^2 - xy + y^2)$
23. $(2x + 5y)(3x^2 - 4xy + 2y^2)$
24. $(x^3 + x^2 + 1)(x^2 - x - 5)$
25. $(4x^2 + 3x + 2)(3x^2 + 2x - 1)$
26. **Measurement** A bottom for a box can be made by cutting congruent squares from each of the four corners of a piece of cardboard. The volume of a box made from an 8.5-by-11-inch piece of cardboard would be represented by $V(x) = x(11 - 2x)(8.5 - 2x)$, where x is the side length of one square.

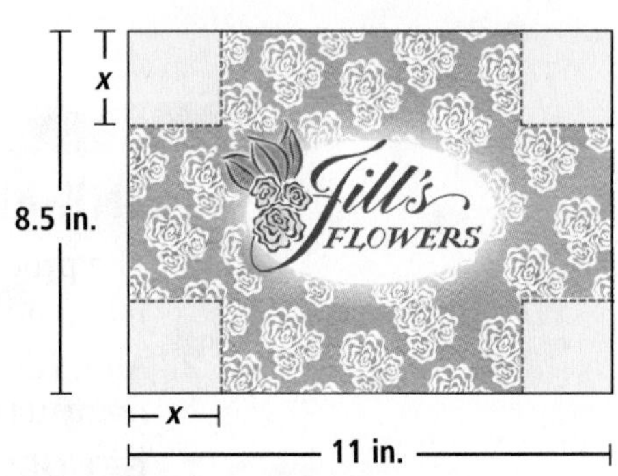

    a. Express the volume as a sum of monomials.
    b. Find the volume when $x = 1$ inch.

Find each product.

27. $(2x - 2)^3$
28. $\left(x + \frac{1}{3}\right)^4$
29. $(x - y)^4$
30. $(4 + y)^3$

Expand each expression.

31. $(x - 3y)^4$
32. $(x - 2)^5$
33. $(x + y)^5$
34. $(2x - 3y)^4$

Graphing Calculator **Compare each pair of expressions with your graphing calculator. Use the table feature to make a conjecture about whether the expressions are equivalent.**

35. $(x-6)^3;\ x^3-18x^2+108x-216$

36. $(11x+10)(11x+1);\ 121x^2+121x+10$

37. $(3x^2+2x)(3x+2);\ 9x^3+12x^2+4$

38. $(2x+1)^4;\ 16x^4+32x^3+24x^2+8x+1$

39. **Business** Ms. Liao runs a small dress company. From 1995 through 2005, the number of dresses she made can be modeled by $N(x)=0.3x^2-1.6x+14$ and the average cost to make each dress can be modeled by $C(x)=-0.001x^2-0.06x+8.3$, where x is the number of years since 1995. Write a polynomial that can be used to model Ms. Liao's total dressmaking costs, $T(x)$, for those years.

LINK

Math History

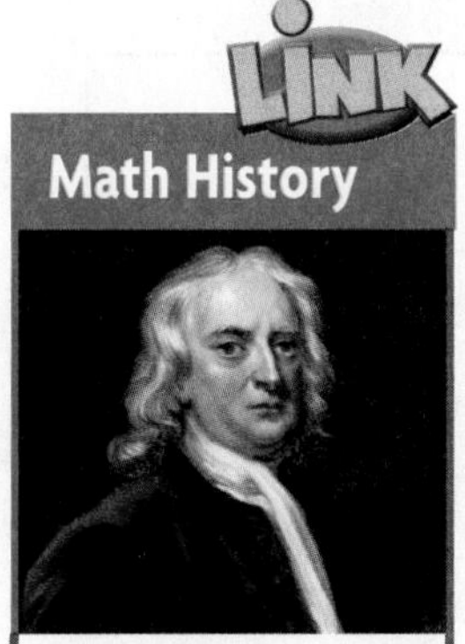

The Binomial Theorem was discovered by Sir Isaac Newton in 1665 or 1666. At this time, Trinity College, in Cambridge, England, was closed because of the plague, and Newton, working in solitude, was able to focus solely on his mathematical studies.

Multiply.

40. $-6x^3(15y^4-7xy^3+2)$

41. $(p-2q)^3$

42. $(x^2-2yz-y^2)(y^2+x)$

43. $(x^4+xy^3)(x^2+y^3)$

44. $(3-3y)^4$

45. $(5x^3+x^2-9x)(y+2)$

46. $(3+x-2x^2)(x-1)$

47. $3(x-2)^4$

48. $(x-6)(x^4-2x^3+x^2+1)$

49. $(30+x^3+x^2)(x-15-x^2)$

50. $\left(\frac{1}{2}+z\right)^4$

51. $(2x-3)(x^5-4x^3+7)$

52. Generate the coefficients that would be used to expand $(a+b)^7$ by using binomial expansion.

53. **Physics** An object t seconds after it is thrown in the air has a velocity that can be described by $v(t)=-9.8t+24$ (in meters/second) and a height $h(t)=-4.9t^2+24t+60$ (in meters). The object has mass $m=2$ kilograms. The kinetic energy of the object is given by $K=\frac{1}{2}mv^2$, and the potential energy is given by $U=9.8mh$. Can you find a polynomial expression for the total kinetic and potential energy $K+U$ as a function of time, t? Explain.

54. **///ERROR ANALYSIS///** Two students used binomial expansion to expand $(a+b)^2$. Which answer is incorrect? Identify the error.

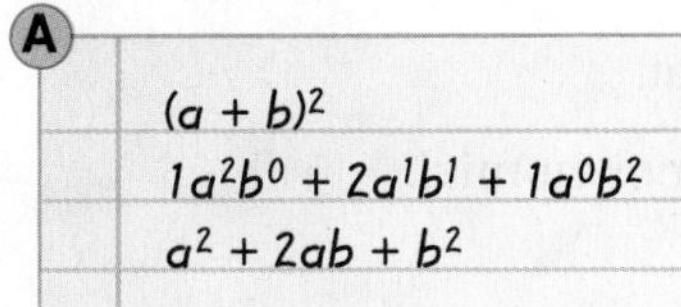

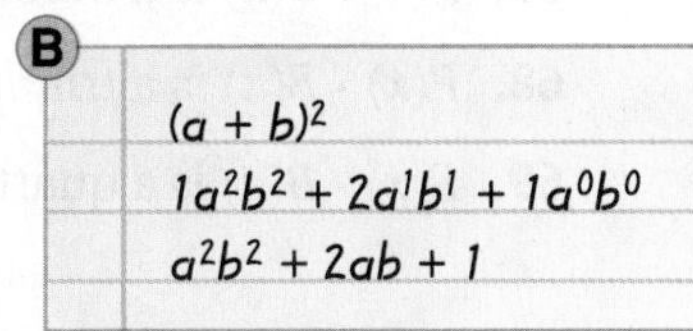

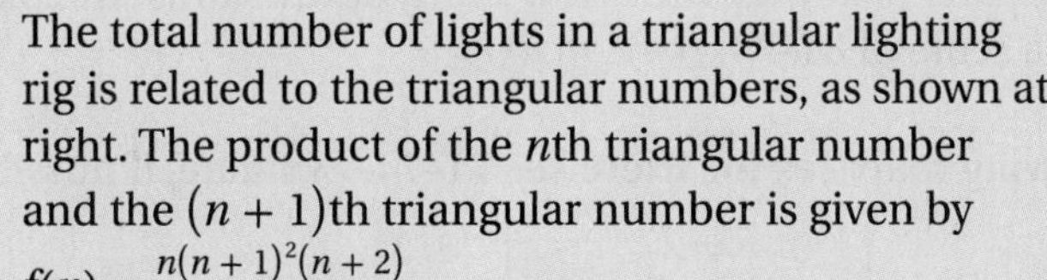

55. This problem will prepare you for the Multi-Step Test Prep on page 436.

The total number of lights in a triangular lighting rig is related to the triangular numbers, as shown at right. The product of the nth triangular number and the $(n+1)$th triangular number is given by $f(n)=\frac{n(n+1)^2(n+2)}{4}$.

a. Write $f(n)$ as a polynomial function.

b. Find the product of the twelfth and thirteenth triangular numbers.

c. Evaluate $f(n)$ for $n=20$ and describe what this value represents.

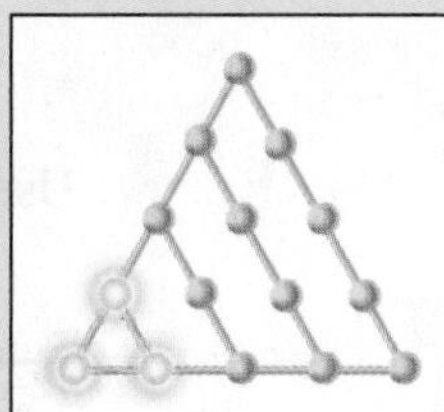

Triangular numbers: 1, 3, 6, 10, 15, . . .

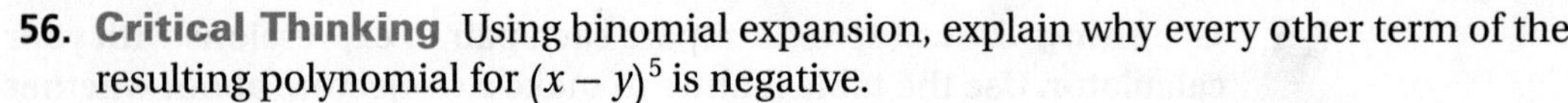

56. **Critical Thinking** Using binomial expansion, explain why every other term of the resulting polynomial for $(x - y)^5$ is negative.

57. **Write About It** Explain how to expand a binomial raised to a power by using Pascal's Triangle.

TEST PREP

58. Multiply $(y - 3)(y^2 - 6y - 9)$.
    Ⓐ $y^3 + 18y - 9$
    Ⓑ $y^3 - 3y^2 + 3y + 27$
    Ⓒ $y^3 + 9y^2 + 27y + 27$
    Ⓓ $y^3 - 9y^2 + 9y + 27$

59. The rectangle shown is enlarged such that each side is multiplied by the value of the width, $2x$. Which expression represents the perimeter of the enlarged rectangle?

    Ⓕ $4x + 2y$
    Ⓖ $6x + 4xy$
    Ⓗ $8x^2 + 2y$
    Ⓙ $8x^2 + 4xy$

60. What is the third term of the binomial expansion of $(x - 4)^6$?
    Ⓐ $240x^4$ Ⓑ $15x^4$ Ⓒ $160x^3$ Ⓓ $8x^3$

61. Find the product $a^2b(2a^3b - 5ab^4)$.
    Ⓕ $-3a^4b^{-2}$ Ⓖ $2a^6b - 5a^2b^4$ Ⓗ $2a^5b^2 - 5a^3b^5$ Ⓙ $2a^5b^2 - 5ab^4$

62. **Short Response** Expand $(4 - x)^4$ by using binomial expansion.

CHALLENGE AND EXTEND

Find the product.

63. $(x - 1)^{10}$ 64. $(14 + y)^5$ 65. $(m - n)^3(m + n)^3$ 66. $(ab + 2c)^4$

Suppose $P(x) = x + 3$. Find a binomial $B(x)$ that satisfies the given condition.

67. $P(x) \cdot B(x)$ is a binomial.

68. $P(x) \cdot B(x)$ is a trinomial.

69. $P(x) \cdot B(x)$ is a quartic polynomial.

SPIRAL REVIEW

70. **Athletics** A basketball coach makes his players run five sprints for every point they lost by in a game. Write a function to represent the number of sprints the team has to run after losing a game. How many sprints must the players run if they lose a game by a score of 84–73? *(Lesson 1-7)*

Use the following matrices for Exercises 71–74. Evaluate, if possible. *(Lesson 4-2)*

$$A = \begin{bmatrix} -2 & 1 \\ 4 & 3 \end{bmatrix} \quad B = \begin{bmatrix} 0 & 4 & 2 \\ 2 & -1 & 1 \\ -2 & 1 & 3 \end{bmatrix} \quad C = \begin{bmatrix} 6 & 3 \\ -1 & 5 \\ 0 & 7 \end{bmatrix}$$

71. A^2 72. CA 73. B^2 74. BC

Rewrite each polynomial in standard form. Then identify the leading coefficient, degree, and number of terms. Name the polynomial. *(Lesson 6-1)*

75. $3x + 5x^2 + 4x^4 - 6x^3$ 76. $10x^2 + 5x^3 - x$ 77. $9 - 4x^2 + 3x^5 - 2x$

Connecting Algebra to Geometry

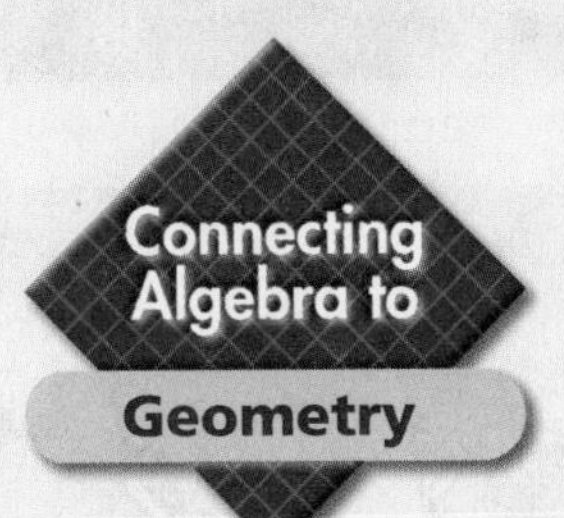

Nets

For a prism, volume equals the area of the base times the height. For a pyramid, volume equals $\frac{1}{3}$ the area of the base times the height. To find the surface area of a solid, add the areas of all of the faces.

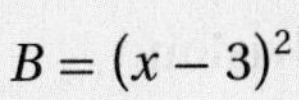

Activity

Find the volume and surface area of the square pyramid shown by this net.

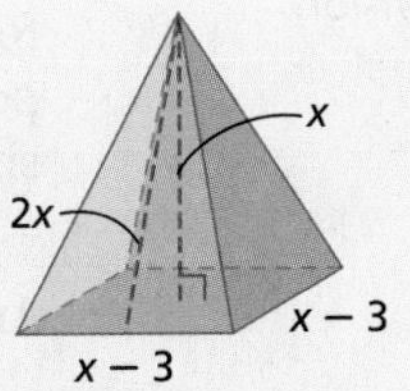

For the volume, multiply the area of the square base by the height and then multiply by $\frac{1}{3}$.

$B = (x - 3)^2$ *Find the area of the square base.*

$V = \frac{1}{3}(x - 3)^2 x$ *The height of the pyramid is x.*

$V = \frac{x^3}{3} - 2x^2 + 3x$ *Multiply the polynomials, and simplify.*

For the surface area, add the area of the square base to the area of the four triangular faces.

$B = (x - 3)^2$ *Find the area of the square base.*

$A = \frac{1}{2}(x - 3) \cdot 2x$ *Find the area of 1 triangular face.*

$L = 4A = 4 \cdot \frac{1}{2}(x - 3) \cdot 2x$ *Find the area of 4 triangular faces.*

$SA = (x - 3)^2 + 4 \cdot \frac{1}{2}(x - 3) \cdot 2x$ *Add the area of the base to the area of the four triangular faces.*

$SA = (x^2 - 6x + 9) + (4x^2 - 12x)$ *Multiply.*

$SA = 5x^2 - 18x + 9$ *Add.*

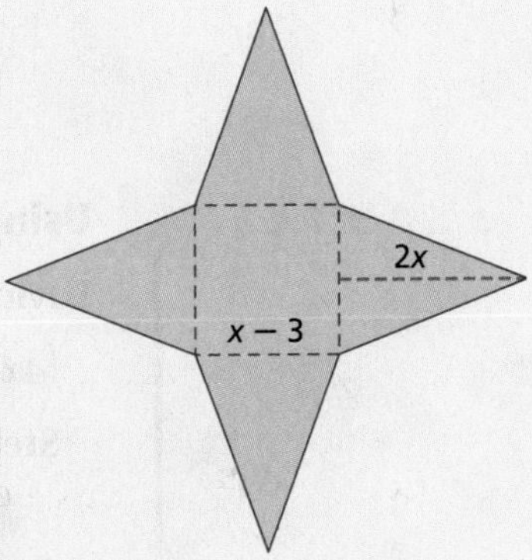

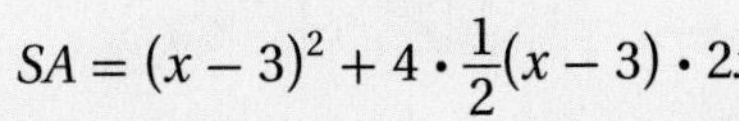

Try This

Find the volume and surface area of the solid shown by each net.

1.

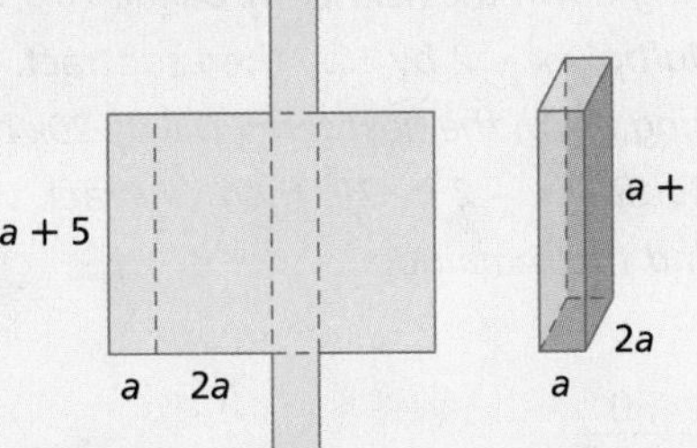

2.

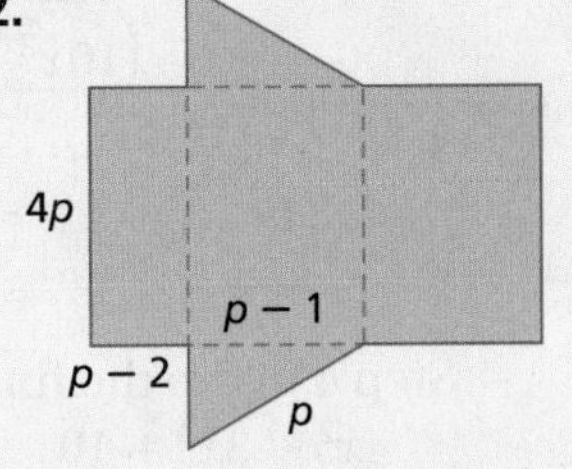

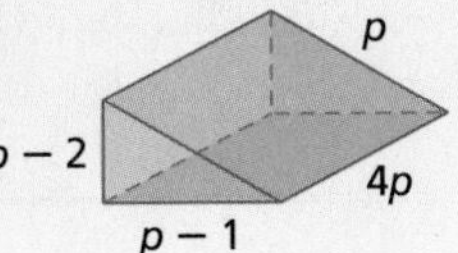

3. The volume of a rectangular prism is $6c^3 - 22c^2 - 8c$. Find the length and width of this prism if the height is $2c$.

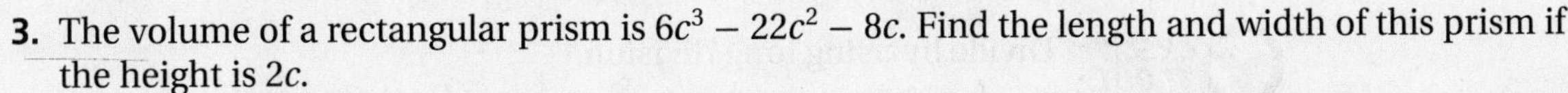

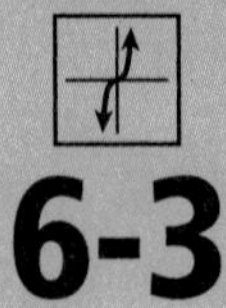

6-3 Dividing Polynomials

"Okay, Copper—what's the charge? Assault and Battery? I have contacts, you know"

© Cartoon Stock

Objective
Use long division and synthetic division to divide polynomials.

Vocabulary
synthetic division

Who uses this?
Electricians can divide polynomials in order to find the voltage in an electrical system. (See Example 4.)

Polynomial long division is a method for dividing a polynomial by another polynomial of a lower degree. It is very similar to dividing numbers.

Arithmetic Long Division

Divisor 12; Quotient 23; Dividend 277

$$\begin{array}{r} 23 \\ 12\overline{)277} \\ \underline{24} \\ 37 \\ \underline{36} \\ 1 \end{array}$$

1 ← Remainder

Polynomial Long Division

Divisor $x + 2$; Quotient $2x + 3$; Dividend $2x^2 + 7x + 7$

$$\begin{array}{r} 2x + 3 \\ x + 2\overline{)2x^2 + 7x + 7} \\ \underline{2x^2 + 4x} \\ 3x + 7 \\ \underline{3x + 6} \\ 1 \end{array}$$

1 ← Remainder

EXAMPLE 1 **Using Long Division to Divide Polynomials**

Divide by using long division.

$(4x^2 + 3x^3 + 10) \div (x - 2)$

Step 1 Write the dividend in standard form, including terms with a coefficient of 0.

$3x^3 + 4x^2 + 0x + 10$

Step 2 Write division in the same way as you would when dividing numbers.

$x - 2\overline{)3x^3 + 4x^2 + 0x + 10}$

Step 3 Divide.

$$\begin{array}{r} 3x^2 + 10x + 20 \\ x - 2\overline{)3x^3 + 4x^2 + 0x + 10} \\ \underline{-(3x^3 - 6x^2)} \\ 10x^2 + 0x \\ \underline{-(10x^2 - 20x)} \\ 20x + 10 \\ \underline{-(20x - 40)} \\ 50 \end{array}$$

Notice that x times $3x^2$ is $3x^3$. Write $3x^2$ above $3x^3$.
Multiply $x - 2$ by $3x^2$. Then subtract.
Bring down the next term. Divide $10x^2$ by x.
Multiply $x - 2$ by 10x, then subtract.
Bring down the next term. Divide 20x by x.
Multiply $x - 2$ by 20, then subtract.
Find the remainder.

Step 4 Write the final answer.

$$\frac{4x^2 + 3x^3 + 10}{x - 2} = 3x^2 + 10x + 20 + \frac{50}{x - 2}$$

Divide by using long division.

1a. $(15x^2 + 8x - 12) \div (3x + 1)$ **1b.** $(x^2 + 5x - 28) \div (x - 3)$

Synthetic division is a shorthand method of dividing a polynomial by a linear binomial by using only the coefficients. For synthetic division to work, the polynomial must be written in standard form, using 0 as a coefficient for any missing terms, and the divisor must be in the form $(x - a)$.

Synthetic Division Method

Divide $(2x^2 + 7x + 9) \div (x + 2)$ by using synthetic division.

WORDS	NUMBERS
Step 1 Write the coefficients of the dividend, 2, 7, and 9. In the upper left corner, write the value of a for the divisor $(x - a)$. So $a = -2$. Copy the first coefficient in the dividend below the horizontal bar.	$\begin{array}{r\|rrr} -2 & 2 & 7 & 9 \\ & \downarrow & & \\ \hline & 2 & & \end{array}$
Step 2 Multiply the first coefficient by the divisor, and write the product under the next coefficient. Add the numbers in the new column.	$\begin{array}{r\|rrr} -2 & 2 & 7 & 9 \\ & & -4 & \\ \hline & 2 & 3 & \end{array}$
Repeat Step 2 until additions have been completed in all columns. Draw a box around the last sum.	$\begin{array}{r\|rrr} -2 & 2 & 7 & 9 \\ & & -4 & -6 \\ \hline & 2 & 3 & \boxed{3} \end{array}$
Step 3 The quotient is represented by the numbers below the horizontal bar. The boxed number is the remainder. The others are the coefficients of the polynomial quotient, in order of decreasing degree.	$= 2x + 3 + \frac{3}{x+2}$

EXAMPLE 2 Using Synthetic Division to Divide by a Linear Binomial

Divide by using synthetic division.

A $(4x^2 - 12x + 9) \div \left(x + \frac{1}{2}\right)$

Step 1 Find a. Then write the coefficients and a in the synthetic division format.

$a = -\frac{1}{2}$ *For $\left(x + \frac{1}{2}\right)$, $a = -\frac{1}{2}$.*

$$\begin{array}{r|rrr} -\frac{1}{2} & 4 & -12 & 9 \\ \hline & & & \boxed{} \end{array}$$

Write the coefficients of $4x^2 - 12x + 9$.

Caution!

Be careful to use the correct a value when doing synthetic division. If the divisor is $(x - a)$, use a. If the divisor is $(x + a)$, use $-a$.

Step 2 Bring down the first coefficient. Then multiply and add for each column.

$$\begin{array}{r|rrr} -\frac{1}{2} & 4 & -12 & 9 \\ & & -2 & 7 \\ \hline & 4 & -14 & \boxed{16} \end{array}$$

Draw a box around the remainder, 16.

Step 3 Write the quotient.

$4x - 14 + \frac{16}{x + \frac{1}{2}}$ *Write the remainder over the divisor.*

Check Multiply $\left(x + \frac{1}{2}\right)\left(4x - 14 + \frac{16}{x + \frac{1}{2}}\right)$.

$$4x\left(x + \frac{1}{2}\right) - 14\left(x + \frac{1}{2}\right) + \frac{16}{x + \frac{1}{2}}\left(x + \frac{1}{2}\right) = 4x^2 - 12x + 9 \checkmark$$

Divide by using synthetic division.

B $(x^4 - 2x^3 + 3x + 1) \div (x - 3)$

Step 1 Find a.

$a = 3$ *For $(x - 3)$, $a = 3$.*

Step 2 Write the coefficients and a in the synthetic division format.

$$\begin{array}{r|rrrrr} 3 & 1 & -2 & 0 & 3 & 1 \\ & & & & & \\ \hline & & & & & \end{array}$$

Use 0 for the coefficient of x^2.

Step 3 Bring down the first coefficient. Then multiply and add for each column.

$$\begin{array}{r|rrrrr} 3 & 1 & -2 & 0 & 3 & 1 \\ & & 3 & 3 & 9 & 36 \\ \hline & 1 & 1 & 3 & 12 & \boxed{37} \end{array}$$

Draw a box around the remainder, 37.

Step 4 Write the quotient.

$x^3 + x^2 + 3x + 12 + \frac{37}{x-3}$ *Write the remainder over the divisor.*

Divide by using synthetic division.

2a. $(6x^2 - 5x - 6) \div (x + 3)$ **2b.** $(x^2 - 3x - 18) \div (x - 6)$

You can use synthetic division to evaluate polynomials. This process is called synthetic substitution. The process of synthetic substitution is exactly the same as the process of synthetic division, but the final answer is interpreted differently, as described by the Remainder Theorem.

Remainder Theorem

THEOREM	EXAMPLE
If the polynomial function $P(x)$ is divided by $x - a$, then the remainder r is $P(a)$.	Divide $x^3 - 4x^2 + 5x + 1$ by $x - 3$. $\begin{array}{r\|rrrr} 3 & 1 & -4 & 5 & 1 \\ & & 3 & -3 & 6 \\ \hline & 1 & -1 & 2 & \boxed{7} \end{array}$ $P(3) = 7$

EXAMPLE 3 Using Synthetic Substitution

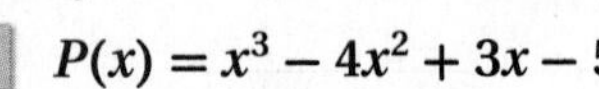

Use synthetic substitution to evaluate the polynomial for the given value.

A $P(x) = x^3 - 4x^2 + 3x - 5$ for $x = 4$

$$\begin{array}{r|rrrr} 4 & 1 & -4 & 3 & -5 \\ & & 4 & 0 & 12 \\ \hline & 1 & 0 & 3 & \boxed{7} \end{array}$$

Write the coefficients of the dividend. Use $a = 4$.

$P(4) = 7$

Check Substitute 4 for x in $P(x) = x^3 - 4x^2 + 3x - 5$.

$P(4) = 4^3 - 4(4)^2 + 3(4) - 5$

$P(4) = 64 - 64 + 12 - 5$

$P(4) = 7$ ✔

Use synthetic substitution to evaluate the polynomial for the given value.

B $P(x) = 4x^4 + 2x^3 + 3x + 5$ for $x = -\frac{1}{2}$

$$\begin{array}{r|rrrrr} -\frac{1}{2} & 4 & 2 & 0 & 3 & 5 \\ & & -2 & 0 & 0 & -\frac{3}{2} \\ \hline & 4 & 0 & 0 & 3 & 3\frac{1}{2} \end{array}$$

Write the coefficients of the dividend. Use 0 for the coefficient of x^2 and $a = -\frac{1}{2}$.

$P\left(-\frac{1}{2}\right) = 3\frac{1}{2}$

Use synthetic substitution to evaluate the polynomial for the given value.

3a. $P(x) = x^3 + 3x^2 + 4$ for $x = -3$

3b. $P(x) = 5x^2 + 9x + 3$ for $x = \frac{1}{5}$

EXAMPLE 4 *Physics Application*

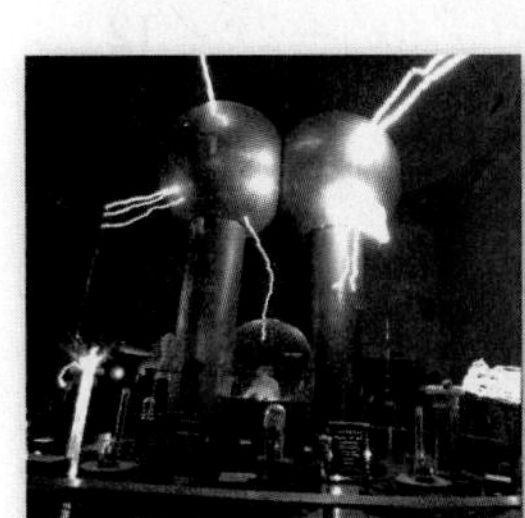

A Van de Graaff generator is a machine that produces very high voltages by using small, safe levels of electric current. One machine has a current that can be modeled by $I(t) = t + 2$, where $t > 0$ represents time in seconds. The power of the system can be modeled by $P(t) = 0.5t^3 + 6t^2 + 10t$. Write an expression that represents the voltage of the system.

The voltage V is related to current I and power P by the equation $V = \frac{P}{I}$.

$V(t) = \frac{0.5t^3 + 6t^2 + 10t}{t + 2}$ *Substitute.*

$$\begin{array}{r|rrrr} -2 & 0.5 & 6 & 10 & 0 \\ & & -1 & -10 & 0 \\ \hline & 0.5 & 5 & 0 & 0 \end{array}$$

Use synthetic division.

The voltage can be represented by $V(t) = 0.5t^2 + 5t$.

4. Write an expression for the length of a rectangle with width $y - 9$ and area $y^2 - 14y + 45$.

THINK AND DISCUSS

1. Can you use synthetic division to divide a polynomial by $x^2 + 3$? Explain.

2. Explain how to quickly find $P(6)$ for the function $P(x) = 2x^3 - 11x^2 - 5x + 2$ without using a calculator. Find $P(6)$.

3. GET ORGANIZED Copy and complete the graphic organizer.

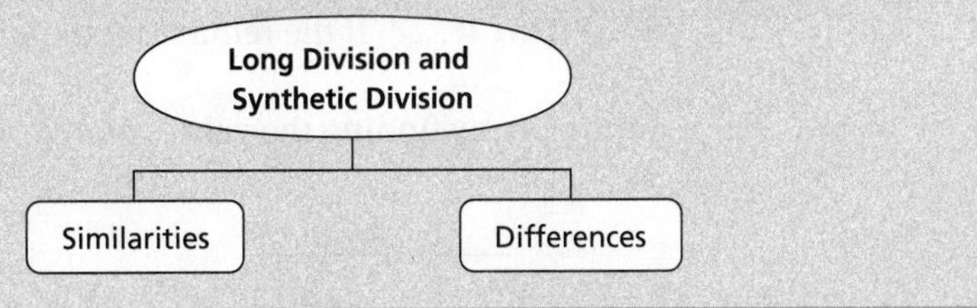

6-3 Exercises

go.hrw.com
Homework Help Online
KEYWORD: MB7 6-3
Parent Resources Online
KEYWORD: MB7 Parent

GUIDED PRACTICE

1. **Vocabulary** Describe *synthetic division* in your own words.

SEE EXAMPLE 1 p. 422

Divide by using long division.

2. $(20x^2 - 13x + 2) \div (4x - 1)$
3. $(x^2 + x - 1) \div (x - 1)$
4. $(x^2 - 2x + 3) \div (x + 5)$

SEE EXAMPLE 2 p. 423

Divide by using synthetic division.

5. $(7x^2 - 23x + 6) \div (x - 3)$
6. $(x^4 - 5x + 10) \div (x + 3)$
7. $(x^2 + x - 42) \div (x + 7)$

SEE EXAMPLE 3 p. 424

Use synthetic substitution to evaluate the polynomial for the given value.

8. $P(x) = 2x^3 - 9x^2 + 27$ for $x = 2$
9. $P(x) = x^2 - x - 30$ for $x = -8$
10. $P(x) = 3x^3 + 5x^2 + 4x + 2$ for $x = \frac{1}{3}$
11. $P(x) = 3x^5 + 4x^2 + x + 6$ for $x = -1$

SEE EXAMPLE 4 p. 425

12. **Geometry** Find an expression for the width of a rectangle whose length is represented by $x - 2$ and whose area is represented by $2x^3 - 8x^2 + 2x + 12$.

PRACTICE AND PROBLEM SOLVING

Independent Practice

For Exercises	See Example
13–18	1
19–24	2
25–28	3
29	4

Extra Practice
Skills Practice p. S14
Application Practice p. S37

Divide by using long division.

13. $(2x^2 + 10x + 8) \div (2x + 2)$
14. $(9x^2 - 18x) \div (3x)$
15. $(x^3 + 2x^2 - x - 2) \div (x + 2)$
16. $(x^4 - 3x^3 - 7x - 14) \div (x - 4)$
17. $(x^6 - 4x^5 - 7x^3) \div (2x^3)$
18. $(6x^2 - 7x - 5) \div (3x - 5)$

Divide by using synthetic division.

19. $(x^2 + 5x + 6) \div (x + 1)$
20. $(x^4 + 6x^3 + 6x^2) \div (x + 5)$
21. $(x^2 + 9x + 6) \div (x + 8)$
22. $(2x^2 + 3x - 20) \div (x - 2)$
23. $(2x^2 + 13x - 8) \div \left(x - \frac{1}{2}\right)$
24. $(4x^2 + 5x + 1) \div (x + 1)$

Use synthetic substitution to evaluate the polynomial for the given value.

25. $P(x) = 2x^2 - 5x - 3$ for $x = 4$
26. $P(x) = 4x^3 - 5x^2 + 3$ for $x = -1$
27. $P(x) = 3x^3 - 5x^2 - x + 2$ for $x = -\frac{1}{3}$
28. $P(x) = 25x^2 - 16$ for $x = \frac{4}{5}$
29. **Physics** An experimental electrical system has a voltage that can be modeled by $V(t) = 0.5t^3 + 4.5t^2 + 4t$, where t represents time in seconds. The resistance in the system also varies and can be modeled by $R(t) = t + 1$. The current I is related to voltage and resistance by the equation $I = \frac{V}{R}$. Write an expression that represents the current in the system.
30. **What if...?** If the remainder of polynomial division is 0, what does it mean?

Complete by finding the values of *a*, *b*, and *c*.

31.
$$\begin{array}{r|rrrrr} 2 & 3 & -4 & 0 & 7 & -1 \\ & & 6 & 4 & b & 30 \\ \hline & 3 & a & 4 & 15 & c \end{array}$$

32.
$$\begin{array}{r|rrr} -2 & 1 & 5 & 6 \\ & & a & c \\ \hline & 1 & b & 0 \end{array}$$

33.
$$\begin{array}{r|rrrr} 3 & a & -2 & 3 & c \\ & & b & 21 & 72 \\ \hline & 3 & 7 & 24 & 68 \end{array}$$

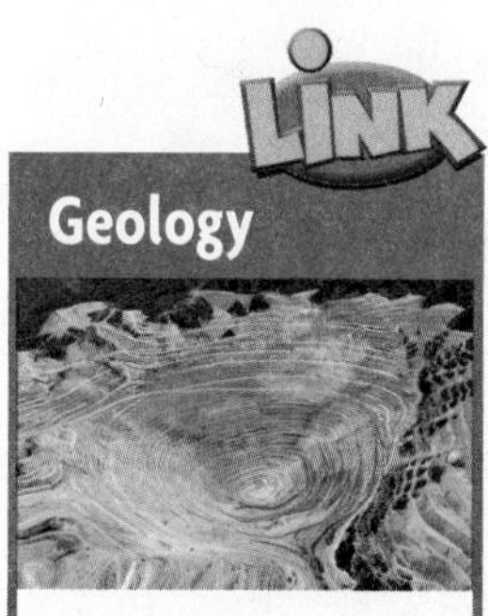

Bingham Canyon copper mine in Utah is the largest copper mine in the world in terms of both total metal production and size. Nicknamed "the richest hole on Earth," the mine has produced more than 14.5 million tons of copper.

Fill in each box to illustrate the Remainder Theorem for $P(x) = x^2 + 3x - 7$ and divisor $x - 2$.

34. Divide $P(x)$ by $(x - 2)$: $\quad \dfrac{P(x)}{x-2} = \square$

35. Multiply both sides by $\square$: $\quad P(x) = (x + 5)(x - 2) + 3$

36. Evaluate $P(2)$: $\quad P(2) = \square$

37. Geology Geologists have taken a collection of samples of a substance from a proposed mining site and must identify the substance. Each sample is roughly cylindrical, and the volume of each sample as a function of cylinder height (in centimeters) is $V(h) = \frac{1}{4}\pi h^3$. The mass (in grams) of each sample in terms of height can be modeled by $M(h) = \frac{1}{4}h^3 - h^2 + 5h$. Write an expression that represents the density of the samples. (*Hint:* $D = \frac{M}{V}$)

38. Geometry The volume of a hexagonal pyramid is modeled by the function $V(x) = \frac{1}{3}x^3 + \frac{4}{3}x^2 + \frac{2}{3}x - \frac{1}{3}$. Use polynomial division to find an expression for the area of the base. (*Hint:* For a pyramid, $V = \frac{1}{3}Bh$.)

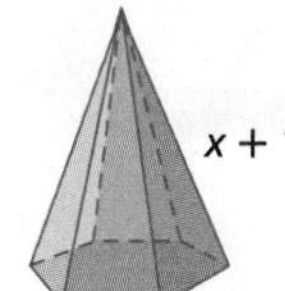

Divide.

39. $\left(y^4 + 9y^2 + 20\right) \div \left(y^2 + 4\right)$

40. $\left(2x^2 - 5x + 2\right) \div \left(x - \frac{1}{2}\right)$

41. $\left(3x^3 - 11x^2 - 56x - 48\right) \div (3x + 4)$

42. $\left(60 - 16y^2 + y^4\right) \div \left(10 - y^2\right)$

43. $\left(t^3 - 7t^2 + 12t\right) \div \left(t^2 - 3t\right)$

44. $\left(y^2 - 18y + 14\right) \div (y - 1)$

45. $\left(x^4 - 3x^3 - 28x^2 + 59x + 6\right) \div (x - 6)$

46. $\left(2d^2 + 10d + 8\right) \div (2d + 2)$

47. $\left(x^4 - 7x^3 + 9x^2 - 22x + 25\right) \div (x - 6)$

48. $\left(6x^3 - 14x^2 + 10x - 4\right) \div (x - 1)$

49. ERROR ANALYSIS Two students used synthetic division to divide $x^3 - 2x - 8$ by $x - 2$. Determine which solution is correct. Find the error in the other solution.

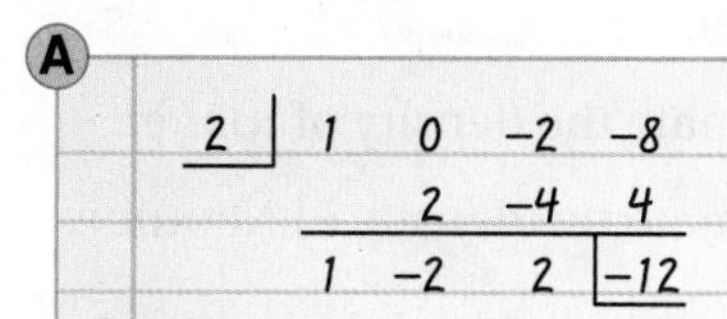

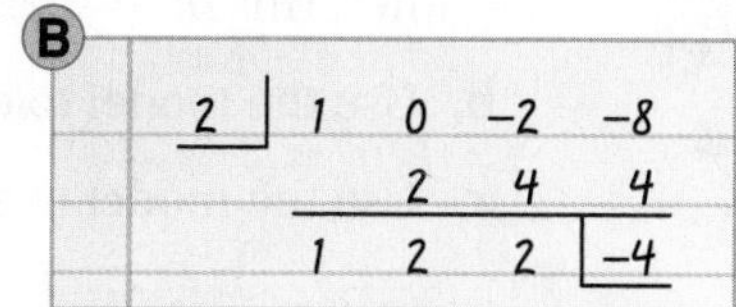

50. Critical Thinking Is $x + 3$ a factor of $3x^3 + 5x^2 + 2x - 12$? Explain.

51. Write About It What conditions must be met in order to use synthetic division?

MULTI-STEP TEST PREP

52. This problem will prepare you for the Multi-Step Test Prep on page 436.

The total number of lights in a triangular lighting rig is related to the triangular numbers, as shown at right. The sum of the first n triangular numbers is given by the polynomial function $g(n) = \frac{1}{6}n^3 + \frac{1}{2}n^2 + \frac{1}{3}n$.

a. Find the sum of the first five triangular numbers in the figure at right, and verify that the formula works when $n = 5$.

b. Use synthetic substitution to find the sum of the first 24 triangular numbers.

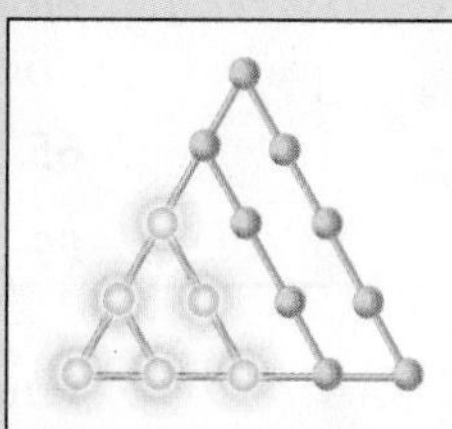

Triangular numbers: 1, 3, 6, 10, 15, . . .

53. What is the remainder when $2x^2 + 6x + 3$ is divided by $x + 3$?

Ⓐ 39 Ⓑ 3 Ⓒ 1 Ⓓ 0

54. Which expression is equivalent to $\frac{6a^2b + 9b^2}{3a^2}$?

Ⓕ $6b + \frac{9b^2}{a^2}$ Ⓖ $\frac{3a^2}{6a^2b + 9b^2}$ Ⓗ $2b + \frac{3b^2}{a^2}$ Ⓙ $\frac{2a^2b + 3b^2}{3a^2}$

55. Which expression is equivalent to $(x^2 + 3x - 28) \div (x - 4)$?

Ⓐ $x + 7 + \frac{3}{x - 4}$ Ⓑ $x - 7$ Ⓒ $28 + \frac{4}{x - 7}$ Ⓓ $x + 7$

56. **Gridded Response** Use synthetic substitution to evaluate $f(x) = 3x^4 - 6x^2 + 12$ for $x = -2$.

CHALLENGE AND EXTEND

Evaluate $P(x) = 4x^9 + 7x^7 - 6x^6 - 5x^4 - x^2 + 3x - 2$ for the given value of x.

57. $x = -4$ 58. $x = -1$ 59. $x = 1$ 60. $x = 3$

61. If -3 is a zero of $P(x) = 2x^3 + 3x^2 - kx - 27$, find the value of k.

62. Divide $(5a^2b - 3ab^2 - 2b^3)$ by $(ab - b^2)$

63. **Astronomy** The volumes of several planets in cubic kilometers can be modeled by $V(d) = \frac{1}{6}\pi d^3$, where d is the diameter of the planet in kilometers. The mass of each planet in kilograms in terms of diameter d can be modeled by $M(d) = (3.96 \times 10^{12})d^3 - (6.50 \times 10^{17})d^2 + (2.56 \times 10^{22})d - 5.56 \times 10^{25}$.

a. The density of a planet in kilograms per cubic kilometer can be found by dividing the planet's mass by its volume. Use polynomial division to find a model for the density of a planet in terms of its diameter.

b. Use the model to estimate the density of Jupiter.

c. Use the model to estimate the density of Neptune.

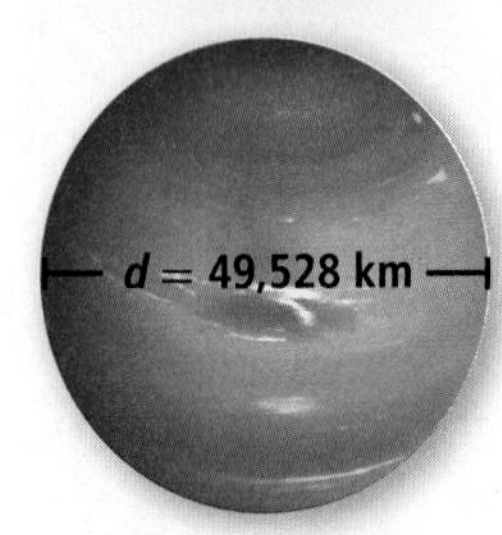

SPIRAL REVIEW

64. A class conducted a survey on eye color. The class found that 70% of students have brown eyes. If 448 students have brown eyes, how many students took the survey? *(Lesson 2-2)*

Find the maximum or minimum value of each function. Then state the domain and range of the function. *(Lesson 5-2)*

65. $f(x) = -4x^2 + 2x + 1$ 66. $g(x) = \frac{1}{2}x^2 - 5x + 6$

67. $f(x) = \frac{1}{3}x^2 - 4x + 10$ 68. $g(x) = -\frac{1}{4}x^2 - 2x + 6$

Find each product. *(Lesson 6-2)*

69. $4x^2y(3xy^2 + 6x + 5y^3)$ 70. $5y^2(3xy + 4x^2y^2 - 8x^3y)$

71. $(2x - 2y)(2x^2 - 2xy + 2y^2)$ 72. $2(y - 2)^4$

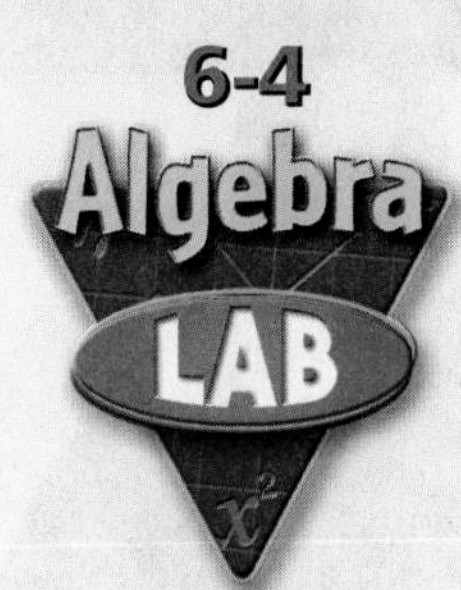

Explore the Sum and Difference of Two Cubes

You can use a diagram of a cube with a corner removed to discover how to factor the difference of two cubes. You can use a similar diagram to discover how to factor the sum of two cubes.

Activity

The figure shown is a large cube with a small cube removed from one corner.

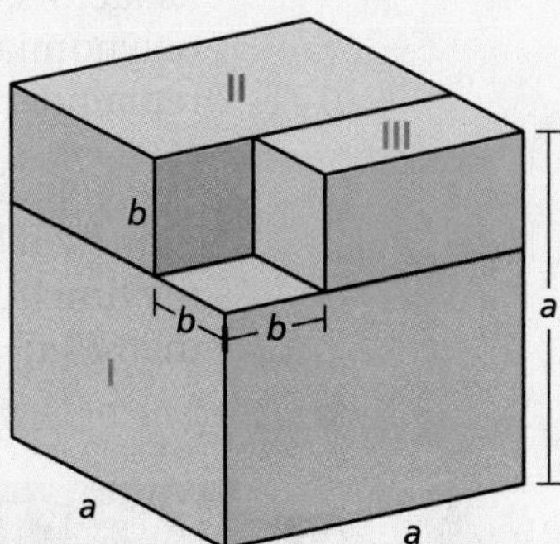

1 Explain why the volume of the figure is $a^3 - b^3$. How is this related to the volumes of the rectangular prisms labeled I, II, and III?

The volume of the complete cube is a^3, and the volume of the cube removed from the corner is b^3. The volume of the figure with the corner removed is $a^3 - b^3$ and can be expressed as the sum of the volumes of the rectangular prisms I, II, and III: $a^3 - b^3 = V_{\text{I}} + V_{\text{II}} + V_{\text{III}}$.

2 Use the diagram to write an algebraic expression for the volume of each rectangular prism.

$V_{\text{I}} = a^2(a - b)$ $\qquad V_{\text{II}} = ab(a - b)$ $\qquad V_{\text{III}} = b^2(a - b)$

3 Write the equation for $a^3 - b^3$ by using the expressions for the rectangular prisms labeled I, II, and III from Problem 2. Factor to get the factored form of $a^3 - b^3$.

$$a^3 - b^3 = V_{\text{I}} + V_{\text{II}} + V_{\text{III}}$$

$$a^3 - b^3 = a^2(a - b) + ab(a - b) + b^2(a - b)$$

$$a^3 - b^3 = (a - b)(a^2 + ab + b^2)$$

Try This

The figure shown is a large cube with a small cube added to one corner.

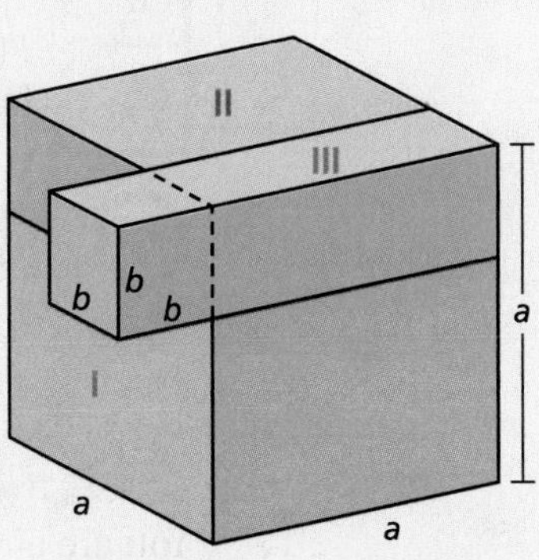

1. Explain why the volume of the figure is $a^3 + b^3$. How is this related to the volumes of the rectangular prisms labeled I, II, and III?
2. Use the diagram to write an algebraic expression for the volume of each rectangular prism.
3. Write the equation for $a^3 + b^3$ by using the expressions for the rectangular prisms labeled I, II, and III from Problem 2. Factor to get the factored form of $a^3 + b^3$. (*Hint:* Factor the expressions for I and II before adding the expression for III.)

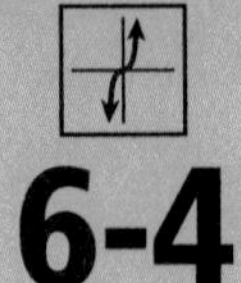

6-4 Factoring Polynomials

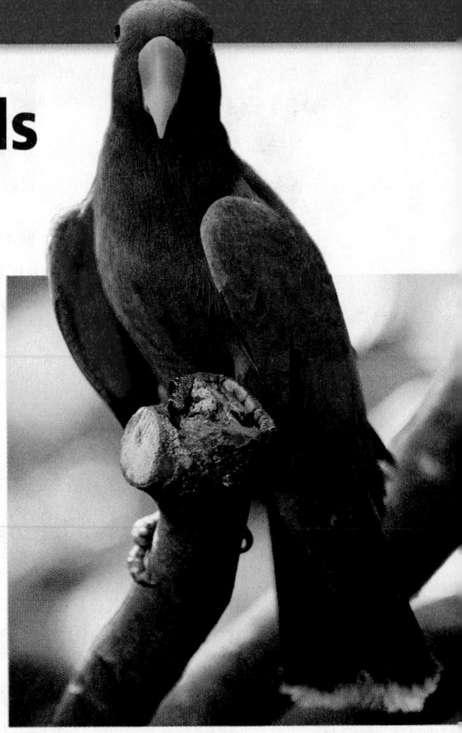

Objectives

Use the Factor Theorem to determine factors of a polynomial.

Factor the sum and difference of two cubes.

Who uses this?

Ecologists may use factoring polynomials to determine when species might become extinct. (See Example 4.)

Recall that if a number is divided by any of its factors, the remainder is 0. Likewise, if a polynomial is divided by any of its factors, the remainder is 0.

The Remainder Theorem states that if a polynomial is divided by $(x - a)$, the remainder is the value of the function at a. So, if $(x - a)$ is a factor of $P(x)$, then $P(a) = 0$.

Factor Theorem

THEOREM	EXAMPLE
For any polynomial $P(x)$, $(x - a)$ is a factor of $P(x)$ if and only if $P(a) = 0$.	Because $P(1) = 1^2 - 1 = 0$, $(x - 1)$ is a factor of $P(x) = x^2 - 1$.

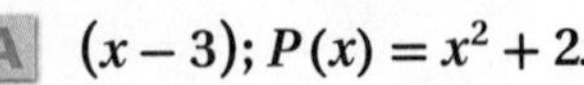

EXAMPLE 1 Determining Whether a Linear Binomial is a Factor

Determine whether the given binomial is a factor of the polynomial $P(x)$.

A $(x - 3);\ P(x) = x^2 + 2x - 3$

Find $P(3)$ by synthetic substitution.

$$\begin{array}{r|rrr} 3 & 1 & 2 & -3 \\ & & 3 & 15 \\ \hline & 1 & 5 & \boxed{12} \end{array}$$

$P(3) = 12$

$P(3) \neq 0$, so $(x - 3)$ is not a factor of $P(x) = x^2 + 2x - 3$.

B $(x + 4);\ P(x) = 2x^4 + 8x^3 + 2x + 8$

Find $P(-4)$ by synthetic substitution.

$$\begin{array}{r|rrrrr} -4 & 2 & 8 & 0 & 2 & 8 \\ & & -8 & 0 & 0 & -8 \\ \hline & 2 & 0 & 0 & 2 & \boxed{0} \end{array}$$

$P(-4) = 0$, so $(x + 4)$ is a factor of $P(x) = 2x^4 + 8x^3 + 2x + 8$.

Determine whether the given binomial is a factor of the polynomial $P(x)$.

1a. $(x + 2);\ P(x) = 4x^2 - 2x + 5$

1b. $(3x - 6);\ P(x) = 3x^4 - 6x^3 + 6x^2 + 3x - 30$

You are already familiar with methods for factoring quadratic expressions. You can factor polynomials of higher degrees using many of the same methods you learned in Lesson 5-3.

EXAMPLE 2 Factoring by Grouping

Factor $x^3 + 3x^2 - 4x - 12$.

$(x^3 + 3x^2) + (-4x - 12)$	*Group terms.*
$x^2(x + 3) - 4(x + 3)$	*Factor common monomials from each group.*
$(x + 3)(x^2 - 4)$	*Factor out the common binomial $(x + 3)$.*
$(x + 3)(x + 2)(x - 2)$	*Factor the difference of squares.*

Check Use the table feature of your calculator to compare the original expression and the factored form.

X	Y1	Y2
-3	0	0
-2	0	0
-1	-6	-6
0	-12	-12
1	-12	-12
2	0	0
3	30	30

The table shows that the original function and the factored form have the same function values. ✔

Factor each expression.

2a. $x^3 - 2x^2 - 9x + 18$ **2b.** $2x^3 + x^2 + 8x + 4$

Just as there is a special rule for factoring the difference of two squares, there are special rules for factoring the sum or difference of two cubes.

Factoring the Sum and the Difference of Two Cubes

METHOD	ALGEBRA
Sum of two cubes	$a^3 + b^3 = (a + b)(a^2 - ab + b^2)$
Difference of two cubes	$a^3 - b^3 = (a - b)(a^2 + ab + b^2)$

EXAMPLE 3 Factoring the Sum or Difference of Two Cubes

Factor each expression.

Remember!

GCF stands for "greatest common factor." Always factor out the GCF before using other methods.

A $5x^4 + 40x$

$5x(x^3 + 8)$	*Factor out the GCF, 5x.*
$5x(x^3 + 2^3)$	*Rewrite as the sum of cubes.*
$5x(x + 2)(x^2 - x \cdot 2 + 2^2)$	*Use the rule $a^3 + b^3 = (a + b)(a^2 - ab + b^2)$.*
$5x(x + 2)(x^2 - 2x + 4)$	

B $8y^3 - 27$

$(2y)^3 - 3^3$	*Rewrite as the difference of cubes.*
$(2y - 3)[(2y)^2 + 2y \cdot 3 + 3^2]$	*Use the rule $a^3 - b^3 = (a - b)(a^2 + ab + b^2)$.*
$(2y - 3)(4y^2 + 6y + 9)$	

Factor each expression.

3a. $8 + z^6$ **3b.** $2x^5 - 16x^2$

You can also use a graph to help you factor a polynomial. Recall that the real zeros of a function appear as x-intercepts on its graph. By the Factor Theorem, if you can determine the zeros of a polynomial function from its graph, you can determine the corresponding factors of the polynomial.

EXAMPLE 4 *Ecology Application*

The population of an endangered species of bird in the years since 1990 can be modeled by the function $P(x) = -x^3 + 32x^2 - 224x + 768$. Identify the year that the bird will become extinct if the model is accurate and no protective measures are taken. Use the graph to factor $P(x)$.

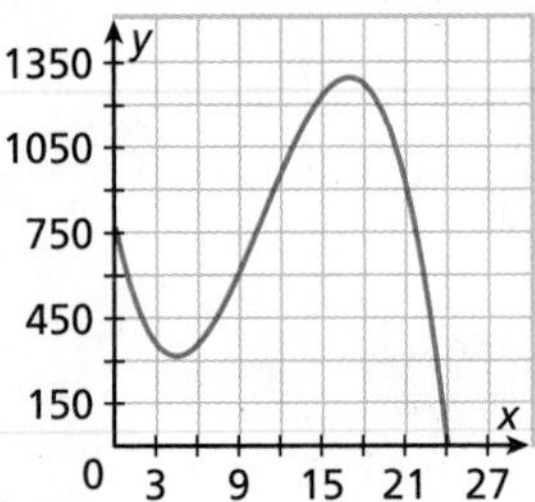

Because $P(x)$ represents the population, the real zero of $P(x)$ represents a population of zero, meaning extinction. $P(x)$ has only one real zero at $x = 24$, which corresponds to the year 2014.

If the model is accurate, the bird will become extinct in 2014.

The corresponding factor is $(x - 24)$.

$$\begin{array}{r|rrrr} 24 & -1 & 32 & -224 & 768 \\ & & -24 & 192 & -768 \\ \hline & -1 & 8 & -32 & \boxed{0} \end{array}$$

Use synthetic division to factor the polynomial.

$P(x) = (x - 24)(-x^2 + 8x - 32)$ *Write P(x) as a product.*

$P(x) = -(x - 24)(x^2 - 8x + 32)$ *Factor out −1 from the quadratic.*

4. The volume of a rectangular prism is modeled by the function $V(x) = x^3 - 8x^2 + 19x - 12$, which is graphed at right. Identify the values of x for which $V(x) = 0$, and use the graph to factor $V(x)$.

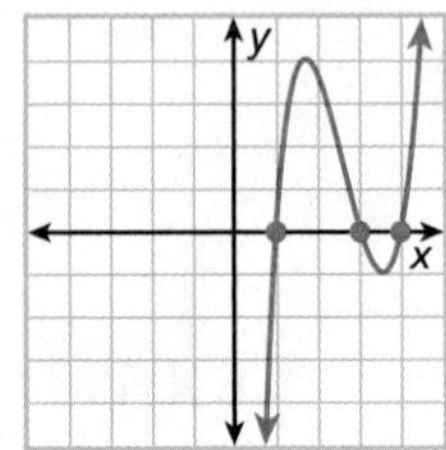

THINK AND DISCUSS

1. Explain how to use the Factor Theorem to determine whether a linear binomial is a factor of a polynomial.

2. Explain how you know when to use the sum or difference of cubes to factor a binomial.

3. GET ORGANIZED Copy and complete the graphic organizer. For each method, give an example of a polynomial and its factored form.

Method	Polynomial	Factored Form
Difference of Two Squares		
Difference of Two Cubes		
Sum of Two Cubes		

6-4 Exercises

go.hrw.com
Homework Help Online
KEYWORD: MB7 6-4
Parent Resources Online
KEYWORD: MB7 Parent

GUIDED PRACTICE

SEE EXAMPLE 1 p. 430

Determine whether the given binomial is a factor of the polynomial $P(x)$.

1. $(x + 1)$; $P(x) = 2x^4 + 2x^3 - x^2 - 5x - 4$

2. $(x - 2)$; $P(x) = 5x^3 + x^2 - 7$

3. $(2x - 4)$; $P(x) = 2x^5 - 4x^4 + 2x^2 - 2x - 4$

SEE EXAMPLE 2 p. 431

Factor each expression.

4. $x^3 + x^2 - x - 1$ **5.** $x^3 + 5x^2 - 4x - 20$ **6.** $8x^3 + 4x^2 - 2x - 1$

7. $2x^3 - 2x^2 - 8x + 8$ **8.** $2x^3 - 3x^2 - 2x + 3$ **9.** $12x^2 + 3x - 24x - 6$

SEE EXAMPLE 3 p. 431

10. $8 - m^6$ **11.** $2t^7 + 54t^4$ **12.** $x^3 + 64$

13. $27 + x^3$ **14.** $4t^5 - 32t^2$ **15.** $y^3 - 125$

SEE EXAMPLE 4 p. 432

16. The volume of a cargo container is modeled by the function $V(x) = x^3 - 39x - 70$. Identify the values of x for which $V(x) = 0$, and use the graph to factor $V(x)$.

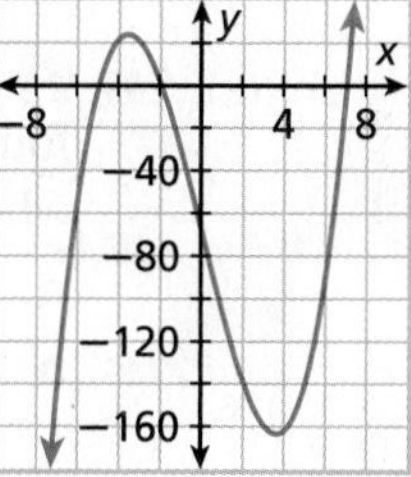

PRACTICE AND PROBLEM SOLVING

Independent Practice	
For Exercises	See Example
17–19	1
20–25	2
26–31	3
32	4

Extra Practice
Skills Practice p. S14
Application Practice p. S37

Determine whether the given binomial is a factor of the polynomial $P(x)$.

17. $(x - 3)$; $P(x) = 4x^6 - 12x^5 + 2x^3 - 6x^2 - 5x + 10$

18. $(x - 8)$; $P(x) = x^5 - 8x^4 + 8x - 64$

19. $(3x + 12)$; $P(x) = 3x^4 + 12x^3 + 6x + 24$

Factor each expression.

20. $8y^3 - 4y^2 - 50y + 25$ **21.** $4b^3 + 3b^2 - 16b - 12$ **22.** $3p^3 - 21p^2 - p + 7$

23. $3x^3 + x^2 - 27x - 9$ **24.** $8z^2 - 4z + 10z - 5$ **25.** $5x^3 - x^2 - 20x + 4$

26. $125 + z^3$ **27.** $s^6 - 1$ **28.** $24n^2 + 3n^5$

29. $6x^4 - 162x$ **30.** $40 - 5t^3$ **31.** $y^5 + 27y^2$

32. Recreation The volume of a bowling ball can be modeled by the function $V(x) = 168 - 28x - 28x^2$, where x represents the radius of the finger holes in inches. Identify the values of x for which $V(x) = 0$,and use the graph to factor $V(x)$.

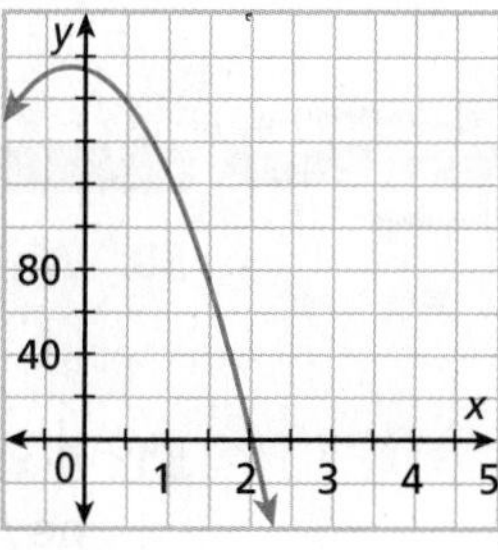

Factor completely.

33. $x^6 - 14x^4 + 49x^2$ **34.** $2x^3 + x^2 - 72x - 36$ **35.** $4x^3 + x^2 - 16x - 4$

36. $9x^9 - 16x^7 + 9x^6 - 16x^4$ **37.** $8x^7 - 4x^5 - 18x^3 + 9x$ **38.** $x^{13} - 15x^9 - 16x^5$

39. Critical Thinking The polynomial $ax^3 + bx^2 + cx + d$ is factored as $3(x - 2)(x + 3)(x - 4)$. What are the values of a and d? Explain.

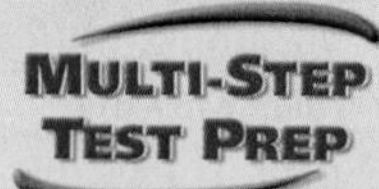

40. This problem will prepare you for the Multi-Step Test Prep on page 436.

The total number of lights in a triangular lighting rig is related to the triangular numbers, as shown at right. The sum of the first n triangular numbers is given by the polynomial function $g(n) = \frac{1}{6}n^3 + \frac{1}{2}n^2 + \frac{1}{3}n$.

a. Find the sum of the first seven triangular numbers.

b. Explain why $n - 7$ must be a factor of $n^3 + 3n^2 + 2n - 504$.

c. Factor $n^3 + 3n^2 + 2n - 504$.

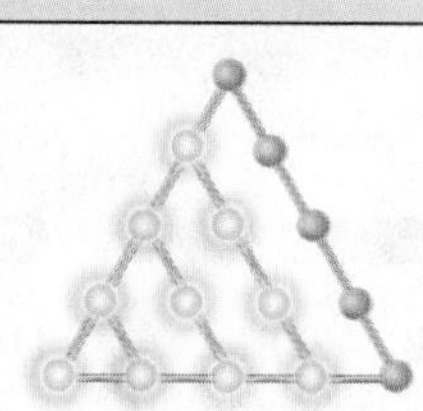

Triangular numbers: 1, 3, 6, 10, 15, . . .

Use the Factor Theorem to verify that each linear binomial is a factor of the given polynomial. Then use synthetic division to write the polynomial as a product.

41. $(x - 2)$; $P(x) = x^4 - 2x^3 + 5x^2 - 9x - 2$.

42. $(x - 1)$; $P(x) = 4x^6 - 4x^5 - 2x^4 + 3x^3 - x^2 - 7x + 7$.

43. $(x + 2)$; $P(x) = 2x^5 + 4x^4 - 6x^2 - 9x + 6$.

44. $(x - 4)$; $P(x) = 2x^4 - 9x^3 + 7x^2 - 14x + 8$.

45. Business The profit of a small business (in thousands of dollars) since it was founded can be modeled by the polynomial $f(t) = -t^4 + 44t^3 - 612t^2 + 2592t$, where t represents the number of years since 1980.

a. Factor $f(t)$ completely.

b. What was the company's profit in 1985?

c. Find and interpret $f(15)$.

d. What can you say about the company's long-term prospects?

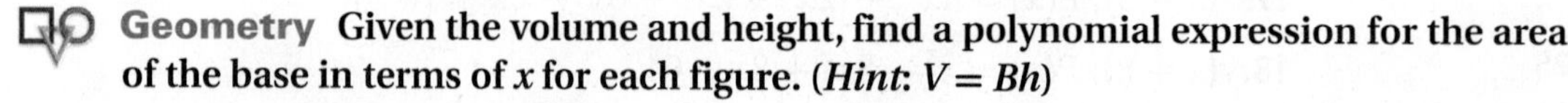

Geometry Given the volume and height, find a polynomial expression for the area of the base in terms of x for each figure. (*Hint*: $V = Bh$)

46. $V(x) = 2x^3 - 17x^2 + 27x + 18$ **47.** $V(x) = x^4 - 16$ **48.** $V(x) = 3x^6 + 3x^3$

$h = x - 6$

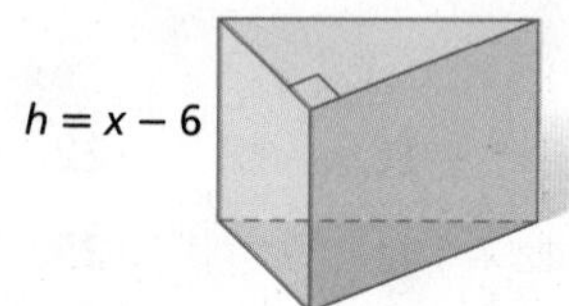

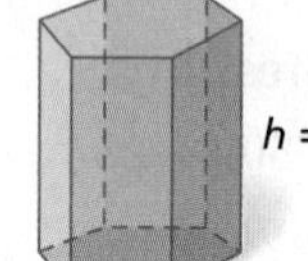

$h = x + 2$

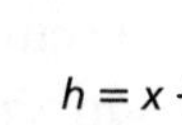

$h = x + 1$

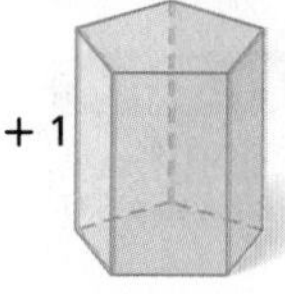

49. Write About It Describe how synthetic division can be used to factor a polynomial.

50. Which is a factor of $x^3 + 2x^2 - 9x + 30$?

(A) $x + 2$ (B) $x - 3$ (C) $x + 5$ (D) $x - 6$

51. $P(x)$ is a polynomial, and $P(4) = P(-2) = P(-1) = 0$. Which of the following could be $P(x)$?

(F) $x^3 + 7x^2 + 14x + 8$

(G) $-x^2 + 2x + 8$

(H) $x^2 + 3x + 2$

(J) $x^3 - x^2 - 10x - 8$

52. Short Response Factor $4p^5 - 16p^3 - 20p$ completely.

CHALLENGE AND EXTEND

53. Factor $(x - 3)^3 + 8$ as the sum of two cubes. Then simplify each factor.

54. Factor $(2a + b)^3 - b^3$ as the difference of two cubes. Then simplify each factor.

55. Divide $(x^2 - 1)$, $(x^3 - 1)$, and $(x^4 - 1)$ by $(x - 1)$ using synthetic division. Use the pattern you observe to find a formula for $(x^n - 1)$ divided by $(x - 1)$.

The polynomial $au^2 + bu + c$ is in quadratic form when u is any function of x. Identify u, and factor each expression, simplifying the factors if possible.

56. $x + 3\sqrt{x} + 2$

57. $(3x - 8)^2 + 6(3x - 8) + 9$

58. $2x^{\frac{1}{2}} - 2x^{\frac{1}{4}} - 12$

59. $\frac{1}{2}\left(x - \frac{1}{3}\right)^2 + \frac{5}{2}\left(x - \frac{1}{3}\right) - 42$

SPIRAL REVIEW

60. **Finance** Amy invests \$100 total in the stock of three companies. She buys 20 shares of Big-Mart stock, 15 shares of Total Telephone, and 25 shares of Zoom Motors. Write a linear equation in three variables to represent this situation. *(Lesson 3-5)*

Simplify. Write the result in the form $a + bi$. *(Lesson 5-9)*

61. $(2 + 4i)(2 - 4i)$

62. $4i(6 + 9i)$

63. $\frac{3 + 4i}{5 + i}$

64. $\frac{8 - 2i}{i}$

Use synthetic substitution to evaluate the polynomial for the given value. *(Lesson 6-3)*

65. $P(x) = 3x^2 - 2x - 1$ for $x = 5$

66. $P(x) = x^3 - 4x^2 + x - 2$ *for* $x = -2$

67. $P(x) = 8x^2 - 5x + 7$ for $x = -1$

68. $P(x) = 6x^2 - 3x - 8$ for $x = 3$

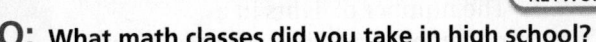

Career Path

go.hrw.com
Career Resources Online
KEYWORD: MB7 Career

Katherine Shields
Nuclear propulsion officer candidate

Q: What math classes did you take in high school?

A: I took Algebra 1 and 2, Geometry, Trigonometry, and Precalculus.

Q: What math classes are you taking now?

A: I've taken two calculus classes. Right now, I'm taking Physics and an engineering class, both of which use a lot of math.

Q: How do you use math in the navy?

A: Nuclear propulsion officers operate aircraft carriers and nuclear-propelled submarines. It's amazing how much math is behind the theory and mechanics of nuclear propulsion.

Q: What are your future plans?

A: There are many options available after my nuclear officer training. While serving as an officer, I'd like to go to graduate school for an advanced degree in nuclear engineering.

CHAPTER 6

MULTI-STEP TEST PREP

SECTION 6A

Operations with Polynomials

In the Spotlight A lighting rig is a large bank of lights that is used to create lighting effects at concerts and sporting events. A company makes rigs with lights arranged in polygonal patterns. The number of lights in a rig depends on the shape of the rig and the number of rows of lights. For example, a triangular rig may have 1, 3, 6, 10, or 15 lights, depending on the number of rows. The figures show the number of lights in a variety of rigs.

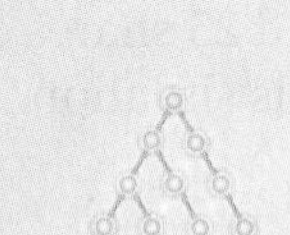

Triangular rig
Number of lights:
1, 3, 6, 10, 15, . . .

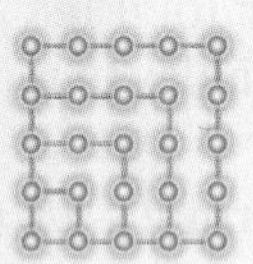

Square rig
Number of lights:
1, 4, 9, 16, 25, . . .

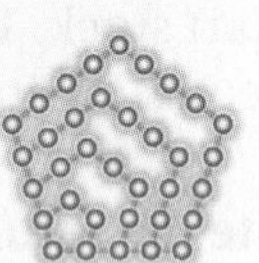

Pentagonal rig
Number of lights
1, 5, 12, 22, 35, . .

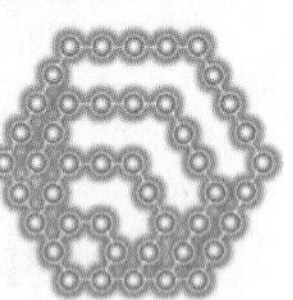

Hexagonal rig
Number of lights:
1, 6, 15, 28, 45, . .

1. The number of lights in a triangular rig with n rows is given by $T(n) = \frac{1}{2}n^2 + \frac{1}{2}n$. Find the number of lights in triangular rigs with 1 to 10 rows.
2. The number of lights in a square rig with n rows is given by $S(n) = n^2$. Find the number of lights in square rigs with 1 to 10 rows.
3. The number of lights in a pentagonal rig with n rows is given by $P(n) = \frac{3}{2}n^2 - \frac{1}{2}n$. Find the number of lights in pentagonal rigs with 1 to 10 rows.
4. Write a polynomial function, $H(n)$, that gives the number of lights in a hexagonal rig with n rows. (*Hint:* Look for a pattern in the coefficients of the polynomial functions in parts **a–c**.)
5. Find $T(n) + P(n)$. What do you notice about this sum?
6. Find $H(n) \div S(n)$. What can you say about the ratio of the number of lights in a hexagonal rig with n rows to the number of lights in a square rig with n rows as n gets larger and larger?

READY TO GO ON?

CHAPTER 6

SECTION 6A

Quiz for Lesson 6-1 Through 6-4

6-1 Polynomials

Rewrite each polynomial in standard form. Then identify the leading coefficient, degree, and number of terms. Name the polynomial.

1. $4x^2 + 3x^5 - 5$
2. $7 + 13x$
3. $1 + 5x^3 + x^2 - 3x$
4. $8x + 2x^4 - 5x^3$

Add or subtract. Write your answer in standard form.

5. $(3x^2 + 1) + (4x^2 + 3)$
6. $(9x^3 - 6x^2) - (2x^3 + x^2 + 2)$
7. $(11x^2 + x^3 + 7) + (5x^3 + 4x^2 - 2x)$
8. $(x^5 - 4x^4 + 1) - (-7x^4 + 11)$
9. The cost of manufacturing x units of a product can be modeled by $C(x) = x^3 - 15x + 15$. Evaluate $C(x)$ for $x = 100$, and describe what the value represents.

Graph each polynomial function on a calculator. Describe the graph, and identify the number of real zeros.

10. $f(x) = -\frac{1}{4}x^5 - x^2$
11. $h(x) = \frac{1}{5}x^3 + x^2 - 2$
12. $f(x) = -2x^6 - 1$

6-2 Multiplying Polynomials

Find each product.

13. $2y(4x^2 + 7xy)$
14. $(a + b)(3ab + b^2)$
15. $\left(2x + \frac{1}{3}\right)^2$
16. $(2x - 3)(x^3 - x^2 + 3x + 5)$

Expand each expression.

17. $(x - 3)^4$
18. $(x + 2y)^3$
19. $(4x - 1)^4$
20. Find a polynomial expression in terms of x for the volume of the rectangular prism shown.

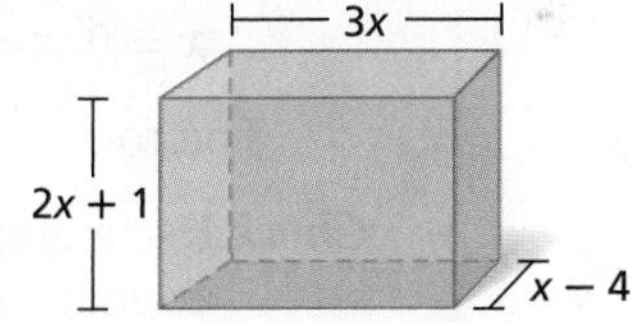

6-3 Dividing Polynomials

Divide.

21. $(6y^2 + 13y - 8) \div (2y - 1)$
22. $(3x^3 + 11x^2 + 11x + 15) \div (x + 3)$

Use synthetic substitution to evaluate the polynomial for the given value.

23. $P(x) = x^3 + 2x^2 - 5x + 6$ for $x = -1$
24. $P(x) = x^4 + x^2 + x - 6$ for $x = 2$

6-4 Factoring Polynomials

Factor each expression.

25. $3t^3 - 21t^2 - 12t$
26. $16y^2 - 49$
27. $y^3 + 7y^2 + 2y + 14$
28. $a^6 + 125$
29. The volume of a box is modeled by the function $V(x) = x^3 + 2x^2 - 11x - 12$. Identify the values of x for which the volume is 0 and use the graph to factor $V(x)$.

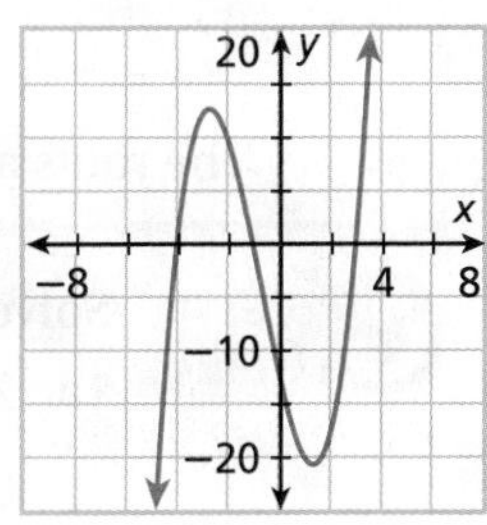

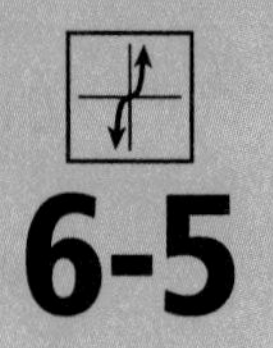

6-5 Finding Real Roots of Polynomial Equations

Objectives
Identify the multiplicity of roots.

Use the Rational Root Theorem and the Irrational Root Theorem to solve polynomial equations.

Vocabulary
multiplicity

Who uses this?
Package designers can use roots of polynomial equations to set production specifications. (See Example 3.)

In Lesson 6-4, you used several methods for factoring polynomials. As with some quadratic equations, factoring a polynomial equation is one way to find its real roots.

Recall the Zero Product Property from Lesson 5-3. You can find the *roots*, or *solutions*, of the polynomial equation $P(x) = 0$ by setting each factor equal to 0 and solving for x.

EXAMPLE 1 Using Factoring to Solve Polynomial Equations

Solve each polynomial equation by factoring.

A $3x^5 + 18x^4 + 27x^3 = 0$

$3x^3(x^2 + 6x + 9) = 0$ *Factor out the GCF, $3x^3$.*

$3x^3(x + 3)(x + 3) = 0$ *Factor the quadratic.*

$3x^3 = 0,\ x + 3 = 0, \text{ or } x + 3 = 0$ *Set each factor equal to 0.*

$x = 0,\ x = -3, \text{ or } x = -3$ *Solve for x.*

The roots are 0 and −3.

Check Use a graph. The roots appear to be located at $x = 0$ and $x = -3$. ✓

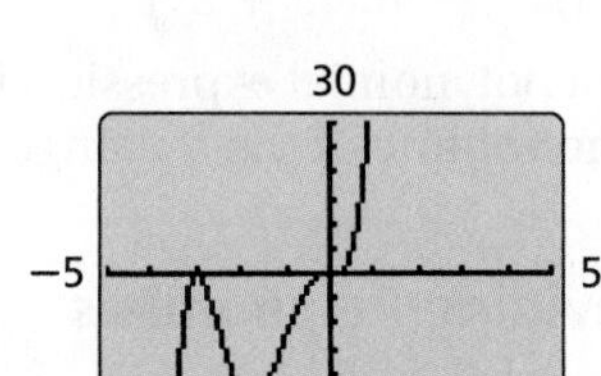

B $x^4 - 13x^2 = -36$

$x^4 - 13x^2 + 36 = 0$ *Set the equation equal to 0.*

$(x^2 - 4)(x^2 - 9) = 0$ *Factor the trinomial in quadratic form.*

$(x + 2)(x - 2)(x + 3)(x - 3) = 0$ *Factor the difference of two squares.*

$x + 2 = 0,\ x - 2 = 0,\ x + 3 = 0, \text{ or } x - 3 = 0$

$x = -2,\ x = 2,\ x = -3, \text{ or } x = 3$

The roots are −2, 2, −3, and 3.

Solve each polynomial equation by factoring.

1a. $2x^6 - 10x^5 - 12x^4 = 0$ **1b.** $x^3 - 2x^2 - 25x = -50$

Sometimes a polynomial equation has a factor that appears more than once. This creates a *multiple root*. In Example 1A, $3x^5 + 18x^4 + 27x^3 = 0$ has two multiple roots, 0 and −3. For example, the root 0 is a factor three times because $3x^3 = 0$.

The **multiplicity** of root r is the number of times that $x - r$ is a factor of $P(x)$. When a real root has even multiplicity, the graph of $y = P(x)$ touches the x-axis but does not cross it. When a real root has odd multiplicity greater than 1, the graph "bends" as it crosses the x-axis.

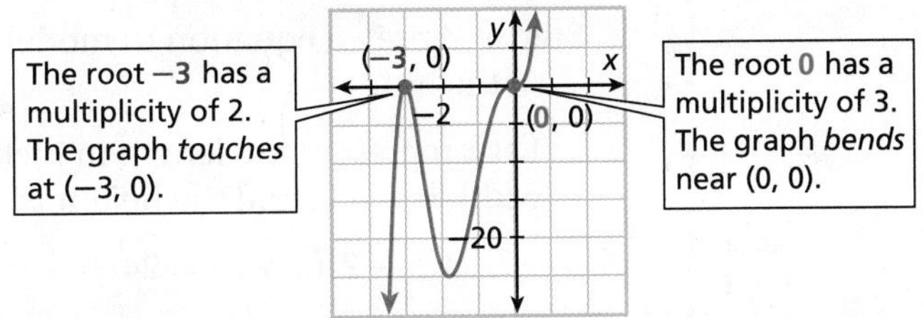

You cannot always determine the multiplicity of a root from a graph. It is easiest to determine multiplicity when the polynomial is in factored form.

EXAMPLE 2 Identifying Multiplicity

Identify the roots of each equation. State the multiplicity of each root.

A $x^3 - 9x^2 + 27x - 27 = 0$

$x^3 - 9x^2 + 27x - 27 = (x - 3)(x - 3)(x - 3)$

$x - 3$ is a factor **three times**.

The root 3 has a **multiplicity of 3**.

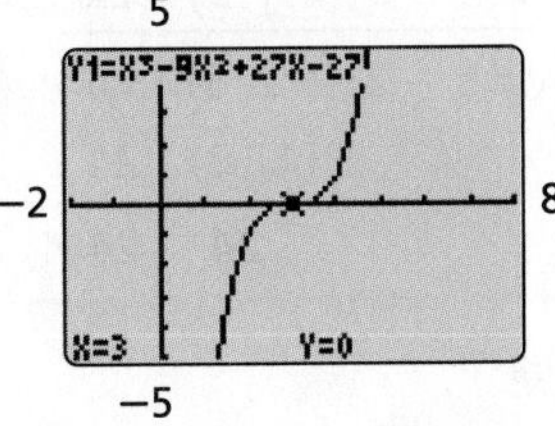

Check Use a graph. A calculator graph shows a bend near (3, 0). ✓

B $-2x^3 - 12x^2 + 30x + 200 = 0$

$-2x^3 - 12x^2 + 30x + 200 = -2(x - 4)(x + 5)(x + 5)$

$x - 4$ is a factor once, and $x + 5$ is a factor twice.

The root 4 has a multiplicity of 1.

The root −5 has a multiplicity of 2.

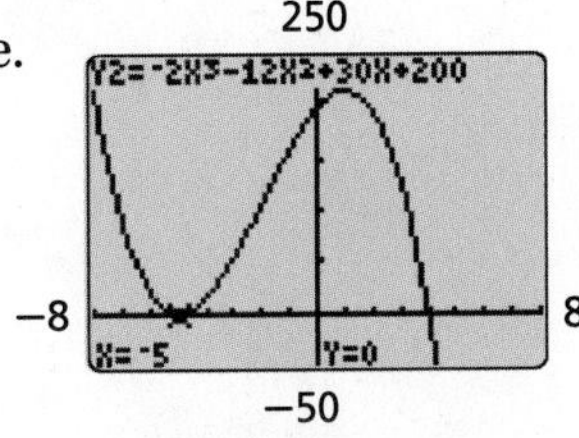

Check Use a graph. The graph crosses at (4, 0) and touches at (−5, 0). ✓

Identify the roots of each equation. State the multiplicity of each root.

2a. $x^4 - 8x^3 + 24x^2 - 32x + 16 = 0$

2b. $2x^6 - 22x^5 + 48x^4 + 72x^3 = 0$

Not all polynomials are factorable, but the Rational Root Theorem can help you find all possible rational roots of a polynomial equation.

Rational Root Theorem

If the polynomial $P(x)$ has integer coefficients, then every rational root of the polynomial equation $P(x) = 0$ can be written in the form $\frac{p}{q}$, where p is a factor of the constant term of $P(x)$ and q is a factor of the leading coefficient of $P(x)$.

EXAMPLE 3 Marketing Application

A popcorn producer is designing a new box for the popcorn. The marketing department has designed a box with the width 2 inches less than the length and with the height 5 inches greater than the length. The volume of each box must be 24 cubic inches. What is the length of the box?

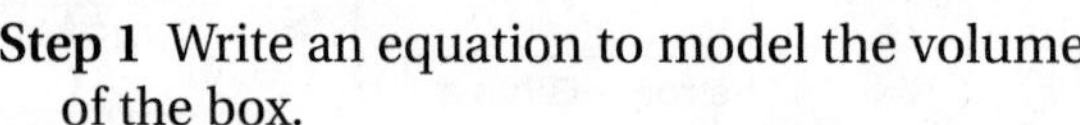

Step 1 Write an equation to model the volume of the box.

Let x represent the length in inches. Then the width is $x - 2$, and the height is $x + 5$.

$x(x-2)(x+5) = 24$	*$V = \ell wh$.*
$x^3 + 3x^2 - 10x = 24$	*Multiply the left side.*
$x^3 + 3x^2 - 10x - 24 = 0$	*Set the equation equal to 0.*

Step 2 Use the Rational Root Theorem to identify all possible rational roots.

Factors of -24: $\pm1, \pm2, \pm3, \pm4, \pm6, \pm8, \pm12, \pm24$

Step 3 Test the possible roots to find one that is actually a root. The length must be positive, so try only positive rational roots.

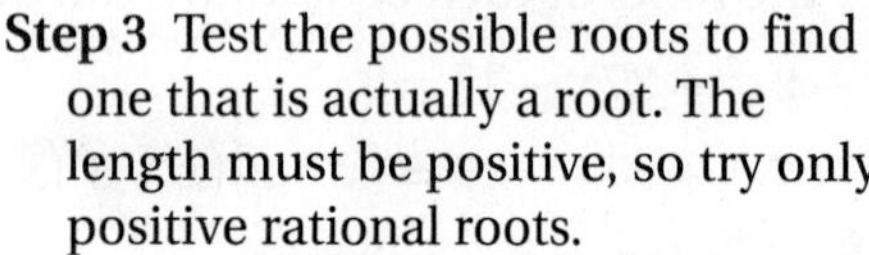

Use a synthetic substitution table to organize your work. The first row represents the coefficients of the polynomial. The first column represents the divisors and the last column represents the remainders. Test divisors to identify at least one root.

$\frac{p}{q}$	1	3	−10	−24
1	1	4	−6	−30
2	1	5	0	−24
3	1	6	8	0
4	1	7	18	48

Helpful Hint

In Example 3, substitute 3 for x to check your (answer).

$x(x-2)(x+5) = 24$

$3(3-2)(3+5)$	24
$3(1)(8)$	24
24	24 ✓

Step 4 Factor the polynomial. The synthetic substitution of 3 results in a remainder of 0, so 3 is a root and the polynomial in factored form is $(x-3)(x^2+6x+8)$.

$(x-3)(x^2+6x+8) = 0$	*Set the equation equal to 0.*
$(x-3)(x+2)(x+4) = 0$	*Factor $x^2 + 6x + 8$.*
$x = 3, x = -2, \text{ or } x = -4$	*Set each factor equal to 0, and solve.*

The length must be positive, so the length should be 3 inches.

Check Substitute 3 for x in the formula for volume.

$$x(x-2)(x+5) = 24$$
$$3(3-2)(3+5) = 24$$
$$24 = 24 \checkmark$$

CHECK IT OUT!

3. A shipping crate must hold 12 cubic feet. The width should be 1 foot less than the length, and the height should be 4 feet greater than the length. What should the length of the crate be?

Polynomial equations may also have irrational roots.

Irrational Root Theorem

If the polynomial $P(x)$ has rational coefficients and $a + b\sqrt{c}$ is a root of the polynomial equation $P(x) = 0$, where a and b are rational and $\sqrt{c}$ is irrational, then $a - b\sqrt{c}$ is also a root of $P(x) = 0$.

The Irrational Root Theorem says that irrational roots of the form $a + b\sqrt{c}$ come in conjugate pairs. For example, if you know that $1 + \sqrt{2}$ is a root of $x^3 - x^2 - 3x - 1 = 0$, then you know that $1 - \sqrt{2}$ is also a root.

Recall that the real numbers are made up of the rational and the irrational numbers. You can use the Rational Root Theorem and the Irrational Root Theorem together to find *all* of the real roots of $P(x) = 0$.

EXAMPLE 4 Identifying All of the Real Roots of a Polynomial Equation

Identify all of the real roots of $4x^4 - 21x^3 + 18x^2 + 19x - 6 = 0$.

Step 1 Use the Rational Root Theorem to identify possible rational roots.

$$\frac{\pm 1, \pm 2, \pm 3, \pm 6}{\pm 1, \pm 2, \pm 4} = \pm 1, \pm 2, \pm 3, \pm 6, \pm \frac{1}{2}, \pm \frac{3}{2}, \pm \frac{1}{4}, \pm \frac{3}{4}$$

$p = -6$ and $q = 4$

Step 2 Graph $y = 4x^4 - 21x^3 + 18x^2 + 19x - 6$ to find the x-intercepts.

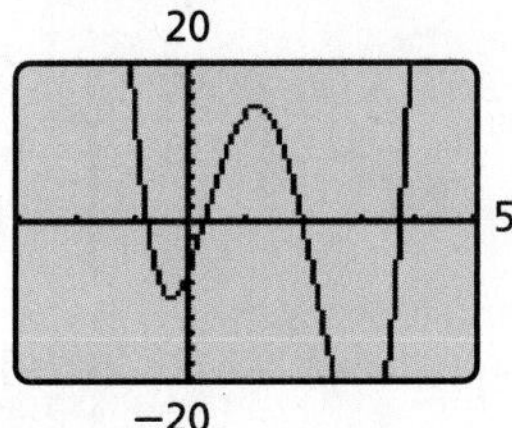

The x-intercepts are located at or near −0.75, 0.27, 2, and 3.73. The x-intercepts 0.27 and 3.73 do not correspond to any of the possible rational roots.

Helpful Hint

In Example 4, the x-intercepts 0.27 and 3.73 correspond to the irrational roots $2 - \sqrt{3}$ and $2 + \sqrt{3}$.

Step 3 Test the possible rational roots 2 and $-\frac{3}{4}$.

$$\begin{array}{r|rrrrr} 2 & 4 & -21 & 18 & 19 & -6 \\ & & 8 & -26 & -16 & 6 \\ \hline & 4 & -13 & -8 & 3 & 0 \end{array}$$

Test 2. The remainder is 0, so $(x - 2)$ is a factor.

The polynomial factors into $(x - 2)(4x^3 - 13x^2 - 8x + 3)$.

$$\begin{array}{r|rrrr} -\frac{3}{4} & 4 & -13 & -8 & 3 \\ & & -3 & 12 & -3 \\ \hline & 4 & -16 & 4 & 0 \end{array}$$

Test $-\frac{3}{4}$ in the cubic polynomial. The remainder is 0, so $\left(x + \frac{3}{4}\right)$ is a factor.

The polynomial factors into $(x - 2)\left(x + \frac{3}{4}\right)(4x^2 - 16x + 4)$.

Step 4 Solve $4x^2 - 16x + 4 = 0$ to find the remaining roots.

$4(x^2 - 4x + 1) = 0$ *Factor out the GCF of 4.*

$x = \dfrac{4 \pm \sqrt{16 - 4}}{2} = 2 \pm \sqrt{3}$ *Use the quadratic formula to identify the irrational roots.*

The fully factored equation is $4(x - 2)\left(x + \frac{3}{4}\right)\left[x - (2 + \sqrt{3})\right]\left[x - (2 - \sqrt{3})\right] = 0$.

The roots are 2, $-\frac{3}{4}$, $2 + \sqrt{3}$, and $2 - \sqrt{3}$.

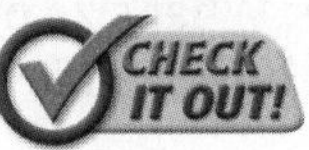

4. Identify all of the real roots of $2x^3 - 3x^2 - 10x - 4 = 0$.

THINK AND DISCUSS

1. Explain how to recognize the multiplicity of a root of a polynomial in factored form.
2. **GET ORGANIZED** Copy and complete the graphic organizer. Give roots that satisfy each theorem and write a polynomial equation that has those roots.

Theorem	Roots	Polynomial
Rational Root Theorem		
Irrational Root Theorem		

6-5 Exercises

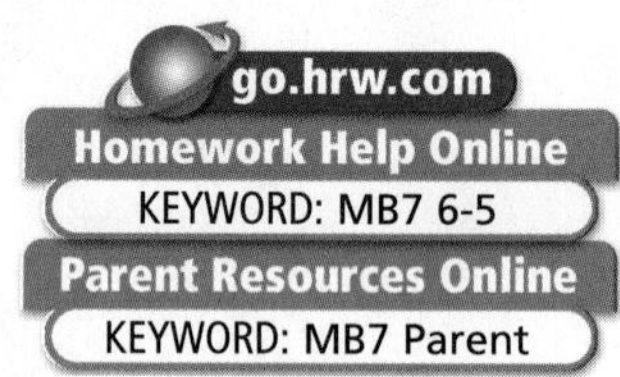

GUIDED PRACTICE

1. **Vocabulary** Explain how *multiplicity* is related to the word *multiple*.

SEE EXAMPLE 1 p. 438

Solve each polynomial equation by factoring.

2. $2x^4 + 16x^3 + 32x^2 = 0$
3. $x^4 - 37x^2 + 36 = 0$
4. $4x^7 - 28x^6 = -48x^5$
5. $3x^4 + 11x^3 = 4x^2$
6. $2x^3 - 12x^2 = 32x - 192$
7. $x^4 + 100 = 29x^2$

SEE EXAMPLE 2 p. 439

Identify the roots of each equation. State the multiplicity of each root.

8. $2x^5 + 12x^4 + 16x^3 - 12x^2 - 18x = 0$
9. $x^6 - 12x^4 + 48x^2 - 64 = 0$

SEE EXAMPLE 3 p. 440

10. **Storage** A cedar chest has a length that is 3 feet longer than its width and a height that is 1 foot longer than its width. The volume of the chest is 30 cubic feet. What is the width?

SEE EXAMPLE 4 p. 440

Identify all of the real roots of each equation.

11. $x^3 + 6x^2 - 5x - 30 = 0$
12. $3x^3 - 18x^2 - 9x + 132 = 0$
13. $2x^3 - 42x + 40 = 0$
14. $x^4 - 9x^2 + 20 = 0$

PRACTICE AND PROBLEM SOLVING

Independent Practice

For Exercises	See Example
15–20	1
21–22	2
23	3
24–26	4

Extra Practice

Skills Practice p. S14
Application Practice p. S37

Solve each polynomial equation by factoring.

15. $x^3 + 3x^2 - 9x = 27$
16. $4x^5 - 8x^3 + 4x = 0$
17. $10x^3 - 640x = 0$
18. $x^4 - 12x^2 = -36$
19. $2x^3 - 5x^2 - 4x + 10 = 0$
20. $4x^3 + 7x^2 - 5x = 6$

Identify the roots of each equation. State the multiplicity of each root.

21. $8x^5 - 192x^4 + 1536x^3 - 4096x^2 = 0$
22. $x^4 + 2x^3 - 11x^2 - 12x + 36 = 0$

23. **Measurement** An open box is to be made from a square piece of material with a side length of 10 inches by cutting equal squares from the corners and turning up the sides. What size of square would you cut out if the volume of the box must be 48 cubic inches?

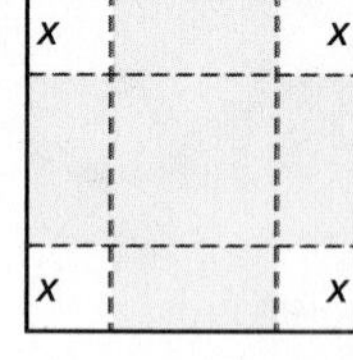

Identify all of the real roots of each equation.

24. $x^4 - 3x^2 - 4 = 0$ **25.** $3x^3 + 4x^2 - 6x - 8 = 0$ **26.** $x^4 - 2x^3 - 2x^2 = 0$

27. Graphing Calculator Consider the polynomial function $f(x) = x^4 + 3x^3 - 3x^2 - 12x - 4$.

a. Use the Rational Root Theorem to list the possible rational roots of this equation.

b. Graph the polynomial on a graphing calculator. Which possible rational roots are zeros of $f(x)$?

c. According to the graph, how many other real zeros does the function have?

d. Approximate these zeros to the nearest hundredth by using the zero feature.

28. Multi-Step A manufacturing company must design a box in the shape of a cube.

a. Let the side length of the box in inches equal x. Write a polynomial equation to represent the volume V of the box in cubic inches.

b. The box must have a volume of 125 cubic inches. Identify all possible rational roots of the resulting equation.

c. Identify the real roots of the equation, and state the multiplicity of each root.

d. What is the side length of the box?

e. Assuming no overlap of the sides, how many square inches of cardboard are needed to make each box?

Identify all of the real roots of each equation.

29. $x^3 - 7x^2 + 14x - 6 = 0$ **30.** $\frac{5}{3}x^3 + \frac{8}{3}x^2 - \frac{4}{3}x = 0$

31. $x^4 - x^3 - 31x^2 + 25x + 150 = 0$ **32.** $3x^4 + 19x^2 + 27x + 6 = 23x^3$

33. $x^5 - 4x^4 - 2x^3 + 4x^2 + x = 0$ **34.** $x^3 + 9 - 6x^2 = -4(11x - 2x^2)$

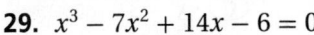

Entertainment

The SheiKra roller coaster at Busch Gardens in Tampa is Florida's tallest roller coaster and includes a 138 ft dive into an underground tunnel.

35. Entertainment The paths of some roller coasters may be modeled by a polynomial function, where t is the time, in tens of seconds, after the ride has started and $h(t)$ is the height, in feet. Some roller coasters go underground as well as above the ground. In factored form, the beginning part of one roller-coaster ride can be modeled by the function $h(t) = \frac{1}{4}(t - 2)(t - 4)(t - 7)(t - 9)$.

a. What is the starting height of this roller coaster?

b. Graph this function on your graphing calculator, and describe the path of the roller coaster for the first 100 seconds.

c. Write an equation of a polynomial function that can be used to model a portion of a roller-coaster ride when the coaster starts 45 feet above the ground, enters an underground tunnel after 30 seconds, and then emerges from underground 20 seconds later.

36. This problem will prepare you for the Multi-Step Test Prep on page 472.

A type of cheese is packaged in a cardboard box shaped like a pyramid. As shown in the figure, the height is 2 cm greater than the length of the base.

$x + 2$, x, x

a. Write a polynomial function for the volume of the box.

b. The volume of the box must be 147 cm³. Write a polynomial equation with integer coefficients that you can solve in order to find the length of the base.

c. What are the dimensions of the box?

37. **Critical Thinking** Suppose you are looking at a graph to identify which possible rational roots correspond to zeros. You see an x-intercept near 4. You have 4 as a possible rational root, but $P(4) \neq 0$. What can you say about the zero that you located on the graph?

38. **Write About It** Graph the functions $f(x) = (x - 2)^2(x + 2)^3$, $g(x) = (x - 2)^2$, and $h(x) = (x + 2)^3$ on your graphing calculator. How does the behavior of f compare to the behavior of g near $x = 2$? How does the behavior of f compare to the behavior of h near $x = -2$? Explain.

39. **Write About It** How does the graph of $5x^4 - 20x^3$ behave near $(0, 0)$? How can you determine the behavior by factoring the expression?

40. Find the solutions to the equation $8x^3 - 2x^2 - 43x + 30 = 0$.

(A) 2 and $\frac{-7 \pm \sqrt{42}}{8}$
(B) 2, $-\frac{5}{2}$, and $\frac{3}{4}$
(C) 2, 15, and 1
(D) 1, 2, and -3

41. How many real zeros does the polynomial $f(x) = 4x^2 - 3x + 2x^4 - 5x^3 - 7$ have?

(F) 2 (G) 3 (H) 4 (J) 5

42. Which of the following is NOT a factor of $g(x) = 6x^3 + 13x^2 - 4$?

(A) $x + 2$ (B) $2x - 1$ (C) $x - 3$ (D) $3x + 2$

43. Use the graph shown at right to identify the multiplicity of the roots of $f(x) = 0$.

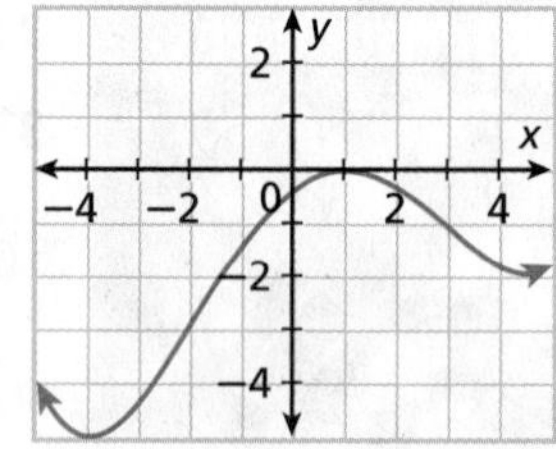

(F) Root 2 with a multiplicity of 1
(G) Root 2 with a multiplicity of 2
(H) Root 1 with a multiplicity of 2
(J) Root 1 with a multiplicity of 3

CHALLENGE AND EXTEND

44. Give a polynomial function that has the zeros 0, 1, and $3 - \sqrt{5}$.

Identify the value of k that makes the x-value a solution to the cubic equation.

45. $x^3 + 3x^2 - x + k = 0; x = 2$

46. $kx^3 - 2x^2 + x - 6 = 0; x = -3$

47. $6x^3 - 23x^2 - kx + 8 = 0; x = 4$

SPIRAL REVIEW

48. **Physics** A water balloon is dropped from the top of an 85-foot-tall building. The height of the water balloon in feet after t seconds is modeled by $h(t) = 85 - 16t^2$. What is the height of the water balloon after 2 seconds? *(Lesson 5-3)*

Solve each inequality by using algebra. *(Lesson 5-7)*

49. $x^2 + x + 5 > 11$

50. $x^2 - 10x + 2 \leq -23$

51. $x^2 < 1$

Factor each expression. *(Lesson 6-4)*

52. $x^3 + 3x^2 - 4x - 12$

53. $8x^3 + 4x^2 - 8x - 4$

54. $x^3 + 27$

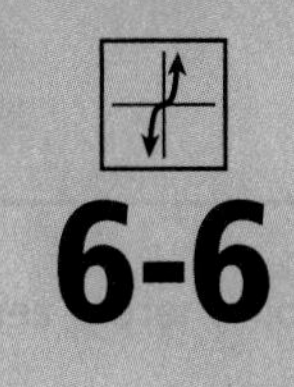

6-6 Fundamental Theorem of Algebra

Objectives

Use the Fundamental Theorem of Algebra and its corollary to write a polynomial equation of least degree with given roots.

Identify all of the roots of a polynomial equation.

Who uses this?

Aerospace engineers may find roots of polynomial equations to determine dimensions of rockets. (See Example 4.)

You have learned several important properties about real roots of polynomial equations.

The following statements are equivalent:
A real number r is a root of the polynomial equation $P(x) = 0$.
$P(r) = 0$
r is an x-intercept of the graph of $P(x)$.
$x - r$ is a factor of $P(x)$.
When you divide the rule for $P(x)$ by $x - r$, the remainder is 0.
r is a zero of $P(x)$.

You can use this information to write a polynomial function when given its zeros.

EXAMPLE 1 **Writing Polynomial Functions Given Zeros**

Write the simplest polynomial function with zeros $-3, \frac{1}{2}$, and 1.

$$P(x) = (x+3)\left(x - \frac{1}{2}\right)(x-1)$$ *If r is a zero of P(x), then x − r is a factor of P(x).*

$$P(x) = \left(x^2 + \frac{5}{2}x - \frac{3}{2}\right)(x-1)$$ *Multiply the first two binomials.*

$$P(x) = x^3 + \frac{3}{2}x^2 - 4x + \frac{3}{2}$$ *Multiply the trinomial by the binomial.*

$$P(x) = x^3 + \frac{3}{2}x^2 - 4x + \frac{3}{2}$$

Write the simplest polynomial function with the given zeros.

1a. $-2, 2, 4$

1b. $0, \frac{2}{3}, 3$

Notice that the degree of the function in Example 1 is the same as the number of zeros. This is true for all polynomial functions. However, all of the zeros are not necessarily real zeros. Polynomial functions, like quadratic functions, may have complex zeros that are not real numbers.

The Fundamental Theorem of Algebra

Every polynomial function of degree $n \geq 1$ has at least one zero, where a zero may be a complex number.

Corollary: Every polynomial function of degree $n \geq 1$ has exactly n zeros, including multiplicities.

Using this theorem, you can write any polynomial function in factored form.

To find all roots of a polynomial equation, you can use a combination of the Rational Root Theorem, the Irrational Root Theorem, and methods for finding complex roots, such as the quadratic formula.

EXAMPLE 2 Finding All Roots of a Polynomial Equation

Solve $x^4 + x^3 + 2x^2 + 4x - 8 = 0$ by finding all roots.

The polynomial is of degree 4, so there are exactly four roots for the equation.

Step 1 Use the Rational Root Theorem to identify possible rational roots.

$$\frac{\pm 1, \pm 2, \pm 4, \pm 8}{\pm 1} = \pm 1, \pm 2, \pm 4, \pm 8$$

$p = -8$ and $q = 1$

Step 2 Graph $y = x^4 + x^3 + 2x^2 + 4x - 8$ to find the real roots.

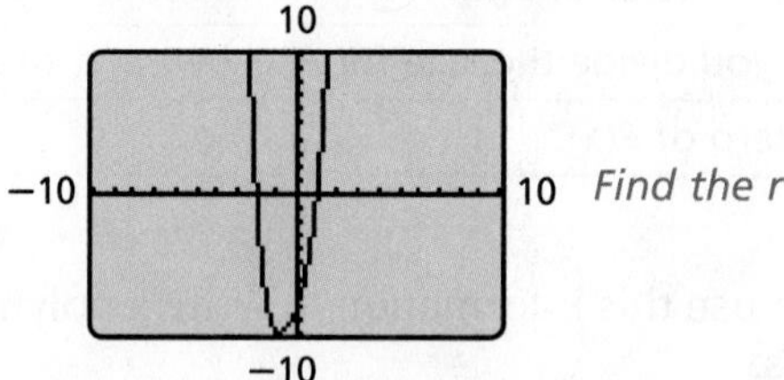

Find the real roots at or near −2 and 1.

Step 3 Test the possible real roots.

$$\begin{array}{r|rrrrr} 1 & 1 & 1 & 2 & 4 & -8 \\ & & 1 & 2 & 4 & 8 \\ \hline & 1 & 2 & 4 & 8 & \boxed{0} \end{array}$$

Test 1. The remainder is 0, so $(x - 1)$ is a factor.

The polynomial factors into $(x - 1)(x^3 + 2x^2 + 4x + 8) = 0$.

$$\begin{array}{r|rrrr} -2 & 1 & 2 & 4 & 8 \\ & & -2 & 0 & -8 \\ \hline & 1 & 0 & 4 & \boxed{0} \end{array}$$

Test −2 in the cubic polynomial. The remainder is 0, so $(x + 2)$ is a factor.

The polynomial factors into $(x - 1)(x + 2)(x^2 + 4) = 0$.

Step 4 Solve $x^2 + 4 = 0$ to find the remaining roots.

$$x^2 + 4 = 0$$
$$x^2 = -4$$
$$x = \pm 2i$$

The fully factored form of the equation is $(x - 1)(x + 2)(x + 2i)(x - 2i) = 0$.

The solutions are 1, -2, $2i$, and $-2i$.

2. Solve $x^4 + 4x^3 - x^2 + 16x - 20 = 0$ by finding all roots.

The real numbers are a subset of the complex numbers, so a real number a can be thought of as the complex number $a + 0i$. But here the term *complex root* will only refer to a root of the form $a + bi$, where $b \neq 0$. Complex roots, like irrational roots, come in conjugate pairs. Recall from Chapter 5 that the complex conjugate of $a + bi$ is $a - bi$.

Complex Conjugate Root Theorem

If $\mathbf{a + bi}$ is a root of a polynomial equation with real-number coefficients, then $\mathbf{a - bi}$ is also a root.

EXAMPLE 3 **Writing a Polynomial Function with Complex Zeros**

Write the simplest polynomial function with zeros $1 + i$, $\sqrt{2}$, and -3.

Step 1 Identify all roots.

By the Irrational Root Theorem and the Complex Conjugate Root Theorem, the irrational roots and complex roots come in conjugate pairs. There are five roots: $1 + i$, $1 - i$, $\sqrt{2}$, $-\sqrt{2}$, and -3. The polynomial must have degree 5.

Step 2 Write the equation in factored form.

$$P(x) = [x - (1 + i)][x - (1 - i)](x - \sqrt{2})[x - (-\sqrt{2})][x - (-3)]$$

Step 3 Multiply.

$$P(x) = (x^2 - 2x + 2)(x^2 - 2)(x + 3)$$
$$= (x^4 - 2x^3 + 4x - 4)(x + 3)$$
$$P(x) = x^5 + x^4 - 6x^3 + 4x^2 + 8x - 12$$

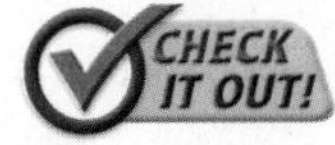

3. Write the simplest polynomial function with zeros $2i$, $1 + \sqrt{2}$, and 3.

EXAMPLE 4 ***Problem-Solving Application***

An engineering class is designing model rockets for a competition. The body of the rocket must be cylindrical with a cone-shaped top. The cylinder part must be 60 cm tall, and the height of the cone must be twice the radius. The volume of the payload region must be 558π cm³ in order to hold the cargo. Find the radius of the rocket.

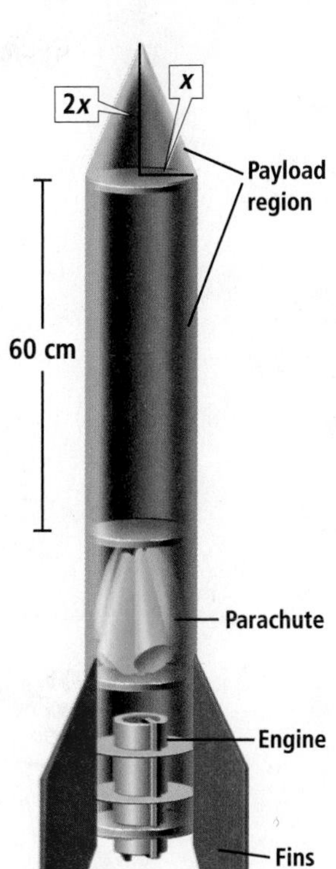

1 Understand the Problem

The cylinder and the cone have the same radius, x. The answer will be the value of x.

List the important information:

- The cylinder is 60 cm tall.
- The height of the cone part is twice the radius, $2x$.
- The volume of the payload region is 558π cm³.

2 Make a Plan

Write an equation to represent the volume of the body of the rocket.

$V = V_{\text{cone}} + V_{\text{cylinder}}$

$V(x) = \frac{2}{3}\pi x^3 + 60\pi x^2$ *$V_{cone} = \frac{1}{3}\pi x^2 h$ and $V_{cylinder} = \pi x^2 h$*

Set the volume equal to 558π.

$\frac{2}{3}\pi x^3 + 60\pi x^2 = 558\pi$

3 Solve

$\frac{2}{3}\pi x^3 + 60\pi x^2 - 558\pi = 0$ *Write in standard form.*

$\frac{2}{3}x^3 + 60x^2 - 558 = 0$ *Divide both sides by π.*

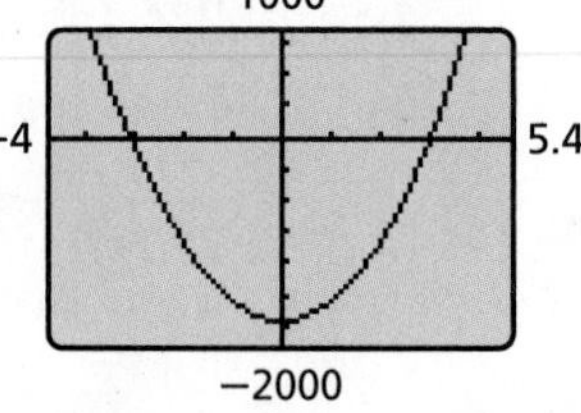

The graph indicates a possible positive root of 3. Use synthetic division to verify that 3 is a root, and write the equation as $(x - 3)\left(\frac{2}{3}x^2 + 62x + 186\right) = 0$. By the quadratic formula, you can find that −3.1 and −89.9 are approximate roots of $\frac{2}{3}x^2 + 62x + 186 = 0$. The radius must be a positive number, so the radius of the rocket is 3 cm.

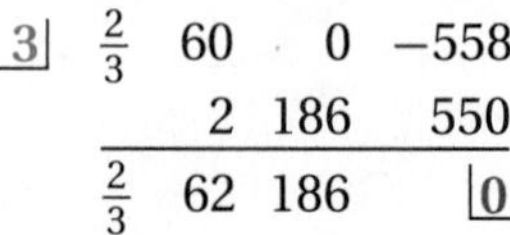

3	$\frac{2}{3}$	60	0	−558
		2	186	550
	$\frac{2}{3}$	62	186	0

4 Look Back

Substitute 3 cm into the original equation for the volume of the rocket.

$V(3) = \frac{2}{3}\pi(3)^3 + 60\pi(3)^2$

$V(3) = 558\pi$ ✔

4. A grain silo is in the shape of a cylinder with a hemisphere top. The cylinder is 20 feet tall. The volume of the silo is 2106π cubic feet. Find the radius of the silo.

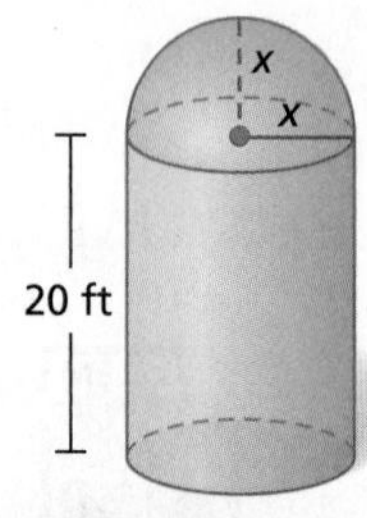

THINK AND DISCUSS

1. Explain why a polynomial equation with real coefficients and root $1 - i$ must be of degree two or greater.

2. If $P(x)$ is the product of a linear polynomial and a cubic polynomial, how many roots does $P(x) = 0$ have? Explain.

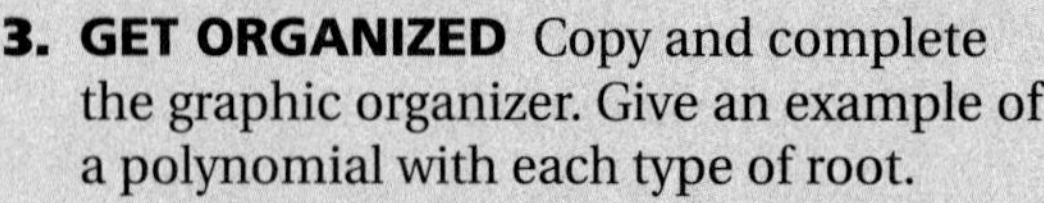

3. GET ORGANIZED Copy and complete the graphic organizer. Give an example of a polynomial with each type of root.

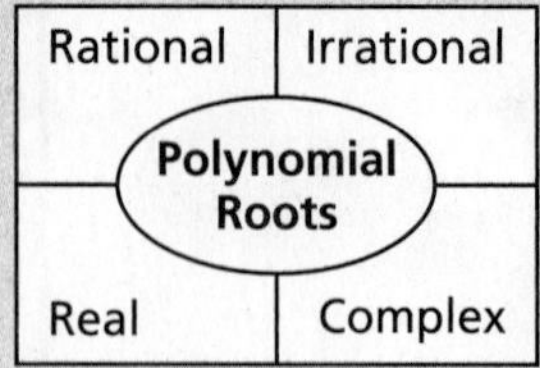

6-6 Exercises

go.hrw.com
Homework Help Online
KEYWORD: MB7 6-6
Parent Resources Online
KEYWORD: MB7 Parent

GUIDED PRACTICE

SEE EXAMPLE 1 p. 445

Write the simplest polynomial function with the given zeros.

1. $\frac{1}{3}, 1, 2$
2. $-2, 2, 3$
3. $-2, \frac{1}{2}, 2$

SEE EXAMPLE 2 p. 446

Solve each equation by finding all roots.

4. $x^4 - 81 = 0$
5. $3x^3 - 10x^2 + 10x - 4 = 0$
6. $x^3 - 3x^2 + 4x - 12 = 0$

SEE EXAMPLE 3 p. 447

Write the simplest polynomial function with the given zeros.

7. $1 - i$ and 2
8. $1 + \sqrt{5}$ and 3
9. $2i, \sqrt{2}$, and 2

SEE EXAMPLE 4 p. 447

10. **Farming** A grain silo is shaped like a cylinder with a cone-shaped top. The cylinder is 30 feet tall. The volume of the silo is 1152π cubic feet. Find the radius of the silo.

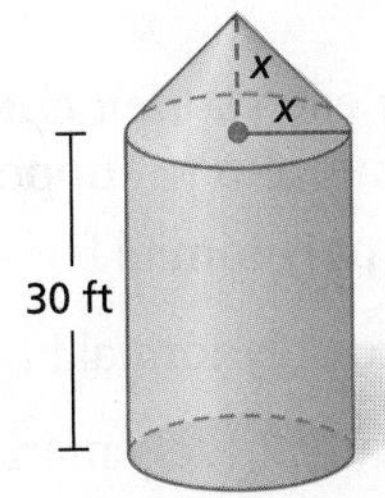

PRACTICE AND PROBLEM SOLVING

Independent Practice	
For Exercises	See Example
11–13	1
14–19	2
20–22	3
23	4

Extra Practice
Skills Practice p. S15
Application Practice p. S37

Write the simplest polynomial function with the given zeros.

11. $-1, -1, 2$
12. $2, 1, \frac{2}{3}$
13. $-4, -1, 2$

Solve each equation by finding all roots.

14. $x^4 - 16 = 0$
15. $x^3 - 7x^2 + 15x - 9 = 0$
16. $x^4 + 5x^2 - 36 = 0$
17. $2x^3 - 3x^2 + 8x - 12 = 0$
18. $x^4 - 5x^3 + 3x^2 + x = 0$
19. $x^4 - 4x^2 + 3 = 0$

Write the simplest polynomial function with the given zeros.

20. $2 - i, \sqrt{3}$, and 2
21. $2\sqrt{2}, \sqrt{5}$, and -3
22. $-2i$ and $1 + i$
23. **Storage** A storage bin is shaped like a cylinder with a hemisphere-shaped top. The cylinder is 45 inches tall. The volume of the bin is 4131π cubic inches. Find the radius of the bin.

Solve each equation by finding all roots.

24. $x^4 - 3x^3 + 5x^2 - 27x - 36 = 0$
25. $x^4 + 4x^3 - 3x^2 - 14x - 8 = 0$
26. $x^3 + 3x^2 + 3x + 1 = 0$
27. $x^4 + 4x^3 + 6x^2 + 4x + 1 = 0$
28. $6x^3 + 11x^2 - 3x - 2 = 0$
29. $x^3 - 2x^2 - 2x - 3 = 0$
30. $x^3 - 6x^2 + 11x - 6 = 0$
31. $x^4 - 13x^3 + 55x^2 - 91x = 0$
32. $x^4 + x^2 - 12 = 0$
33. $x^4 + 14x^2 + 45 = 0$
34. $x^3 + 13x - 85 = 31$
35. $x^3 - 4x^2 + x + 14 = 8$
36. **Geometry** The volume of the rectangular prism is 105 cubic units. Find the dimensions of the prism.

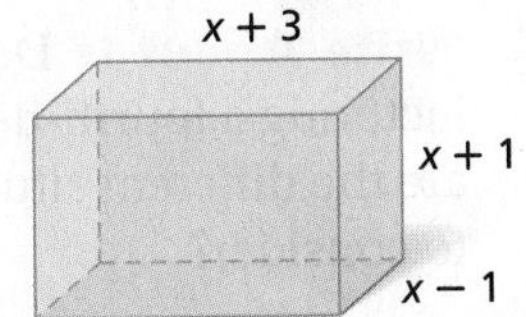

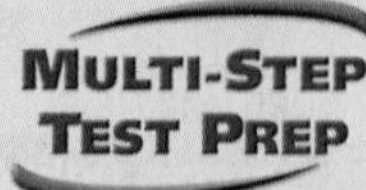

37. This problem will prepare you for the Multi-Step Test Prep on page 472.

The volume of a pyramid-shaped tent with a square base can be represented by the function $V(x) = \frac{1}{3}x^3 - 2x^2$, where x is the length of the base in meters.

a. The volume of the tent is 81 m^3. Write a polynomial equation with integer coefficients that you can solve in order to find the length of the base.

b. Find the length of the base.

c. What can you say about the other roots of the polynomial equation? Why?

Write the simplest polynomial function with the given zeros.

38. $0, \sqrt{5}$, and 2

39. $4i$, 2, and -2

40. 1, -1 (multiplicity of 3), and $3i$

41. 1, 1, and 2

42. $1 - \sqrt{2}$, and $2i$

43. 3 (multiplicity of 2), and $3i$

Tell whether each statement is sometimes, always, or never true. If it is sometimes true, give examples to support your answer.

44. A cubic polynomial has no real zeros.

45. A quartic polynomial has an odd number of real zeros.

46. There are infinitely many polynomials with zeros a, b, and c.

47. The multiplicity of a root is equal to the degree of the polynomial.

Use your graphing calculator to approximate the solutions of each equation by finding all roots. Round your answer to the nearest thousandth.

48. $3x^4 - x = 6x^2 + \sqrt{2}$

49. $2\sqrt{3}x^4 - x^2 = 0$

50. $-6x^3 = -5\sqrt{3}x + \sqrt{2}$

51. $\sqrt{7}x^3 - 11x^2 + 8 = 0$

LINK

Forestry

The sequoias in Sequoia National Park in California are among the largest trees in the world. Many are as tall as a 26-story building and wider than some city streets.

52. **Forestry** The volume of a giant sequoia can be modeled by $V(h) = 0.485h^3 - 362h^2 + 89889h - 7379874$, where h represents the height of a tree in feet and $220 \leq h \leq 280$.

a. Find the height of a tree with volume 39,186 cubic feet.

b. The Lincoln tree in the Giant Forest in Sequoia National Park has a volume of 44,471 cubic feet. What are its possible heights?

c. The actual height of the Lincoln tree is 255.8 feet. What is the difference between the true volume of the tree and the volume given by the model?

53. The volume of a cylindrical propane tank with a hemispherical top and bottom can be represented by the function $V(r) = 33\pi r^2 + \frac{4}{3}\pi r^3$, where V is the volume in cubic inches and r is the radius in inches. What is the radius if the volume of the tank is 1476π cubic inches?

54. **Critical Thinking** What is the least degree of a polynomial equation that has $3i$ as a root with a multiplicity of 3? Explain.

55. **Estimation** Use the graph to estimate the roots of $y = 3x^3 - 2x^2 - 15x + 10$. Then find the exact roots. (*Hint:* Factor by grouping.)

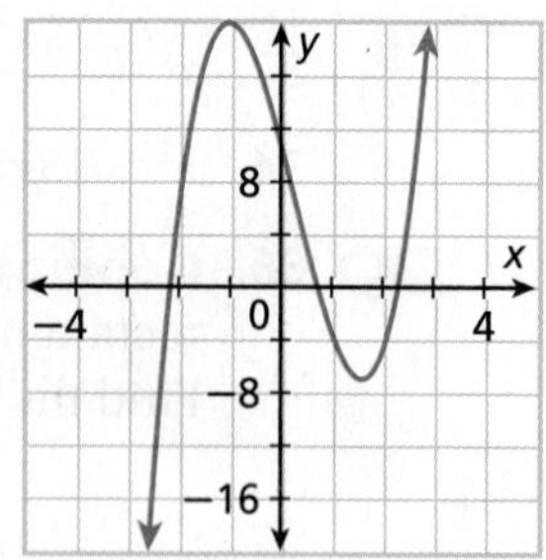

56. **Write About It** Describe your method for factoring a fourth-degree polynomial. What are the different situations that you need to consider?

57. What is the multiplicity of the root -1 in the equation $y = x^4 - 2x^3 - 3x^2 + 4x + 4$?

Ⓐ 1 Ⓑ 2 Ⓒ 3 Ⓓ 4

58. What is the conjugate of $-6 - 5i$?

Ⓕ $-6 - 5i$ Ⓖ $-6 + 5i$ Ⓗ $6 - 5i$ Ⓙ $6 + 5i$

59. Which polynomial function has zeros 0, i, and $-i$?

Ⓐ $P(x) = x^3 + 2x^2 + 1$ Ⓒ $P(x) = x^3 + 2x^2 + x$

Ⓑ $P(x) = x^3 + x^2$ Ⓓ $P(x) = x^3 + x$

60. A polynomial has zeros $3 - \sqrt{2}$, 4, and $6i$. What is the minimum degree of the polynomial?

Ⓕ 3 Ⓖ 4 Ⓗ 5 Ⓙ 6

61. Which polynomial function has zeros $1 + \sqrt{3}$ and $1 - \sqrt{3}$?

Ⓐ $f(x) = x^2 + 8$ Ⓒ $f(x) = x^2 - x + \sqrt{3}$

Ⓑ $f(x) = x^2 - 3x + 9$ Ⓓ $f(x) = x^2 - 2x - 2$

62. **Short Response** Solve the equation $2x^3 - 6x^2 + 8x - 24 = 0$ by finding all roots.

CHALLENGE AND EXTEND

63. Use synthetic substitution to evaluate $f(x) = x^3 - 3x^2 + 9x - 27$ for $x = 3i$ and $x = -\sqrt{3}$. Is either $x = 3i$ or $x = -\sqrt{3}$ a zero of f?

64. $2i$ is a zero of $P(x) = x^3 - 2ix^2 - 4x + 8i$. Find the other zeros of P.

65. One zero of $Q(x) = x^3 - \sqrt{2}x^2 + 9x - 9\sqrt{2}$ is $\sqrt{2}$. Find the other zeros of Q.

66. **Critical Thinking** Based on your answers to Exercises 64 and 65, what can you say about a polynomial function with nonreal or irrational coefficients?

67. Factor the sum $a^2 + b^2$.

68. Factor the sum $a^4 + b^4$.

69. Factor the sum $a^6 + b^6$.

70. **Critical Thinking** Does your answer to Exercise 67 help you answer Exercises 68 or 69? Explain.

71. **Critical Thinking** Give an example of a fourth-degree polynomial equation that has no real zeros. What are the roots of your example?

SPIRAL REVIEW

State the transformation that maps the graph of $f(x) = |x|$ onto the graph of each function. Then graph each function. *(Lesson 2-9)*

72. $f(x) = |x + 5| - 7$

73. $f(x) = -|x - 2| + 3$

Find the vertex of the graph of each function. *(Lesson 2-9)*

74. $g(x) = |x + 3| - 4$

75. $f(x) = |x - 9| - 3$

Solve each equation by factoring. *(Lesson 6-5)*

76. $4x^4 + 32x^3 + 64x^2 = 0$

77. $x^3 - 43x^2 + 42x = 0$

78. $3x^5 + 18x^4 - 81x^3 = 0$

79. $2x^3 + 12x^2 = 32x$

Use with Lesson 6-7

Explore Power Functions

A power function can be written in the form $f(x) = ax^n$, where a and n are real numbers and $a \neq 0$. When n is a positive integer, a power function is also a polynomial function.

End behavior is a description of the values of a function as x approaches positive infinity ($x \to +\infty$) or negative infinity ($x \to -\infty$).

Activity

Describe the end behavior of $f(x) = \frac{1}{5}x^4$, and give the function's domain and range.

1 Enter the function as **Y1**, and graph it in a friendly window.

2 Examine the end behavior. As x increases for positive values of x, the values of f appear to increase. As x decreases for negative values of x, the values of f also appear to increase.

3 Find the domain and range. Substituting any real value of x into the function results in a real number, so the domain is $\mathbb{R}$.

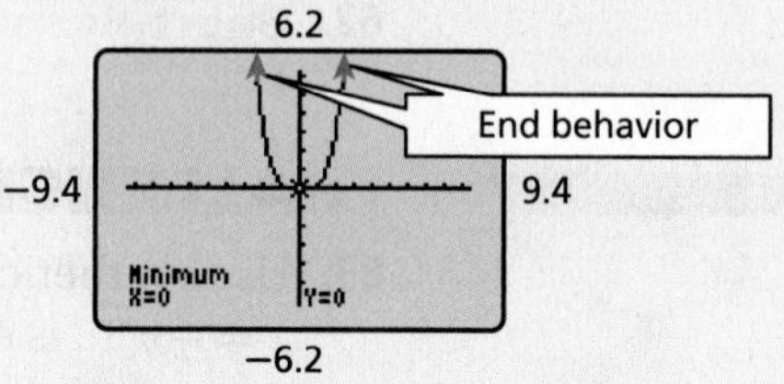

The function has a minimum value, so the minimum determines the range. To find the minimum, press 2nd CALC TRACE and select **3:minimum.**

Move the cursor to the left of the point containing the minimum; press ENTER. Repeat on the right. Then move the cursor close to the point containing the minimum. Press ENTER to display its coordinates.

The minimum is 0, so the range is $\{y \mid y \geq 0\}$ or $[0, \infty)$.

Try This

Describe the end behavior of each function, and give the function's domain and range.

1. $f(x) = \frac{1}{2}x^3$
2. $f(x) = -5x^2$
3. $f(x) = -2x^3$
4. $f(x) = \frac{1}{10}x^3$
5. $f(x) = x^5$
6. $f(x) = -3x^4$
7. **Make a Conjecture** Make a conjecture about the domain and range of polynomial power functions that meet each given condition. Graph as many functions as needed in order to make the conjecture.
   a. n is odd.
   b. a is positive, and n is even.
   c. a is negative, and n is even.
8. **Make a Conjecture** Make a conjecture about the end behavior of polynomial power functions that meet each given condition. Graph as many functions as needed in order to make the conjecture.
   a. a is positive, and n is odd.
   b. a is negative, and n is odd.
   c. a is positive, and n is even.
   d. a is negative, and n is even.

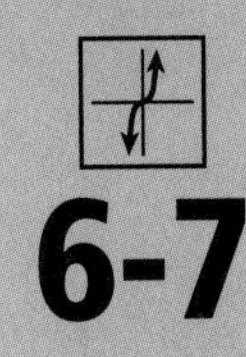

6-7 Investigating Graphs of Polynomial Functions

Objectives

Use properties of end behavior to analyze, describe, and graph polynomial functions.

Identify and use maxima and minima of polynomial functions to solve problems.

Vocabulary

end behawvior
turning point
local maximum
local minimum

Who uses this?

Welders can use graphs of polynomial functions to optimize the use of construction materials. (See Example 5.)

Polynomial functions are classified by their degree. The graphs of polynomial functions are classified by the degree of the polynomial. Each graph, based on the degree, has a distinctive shape and characteristics.

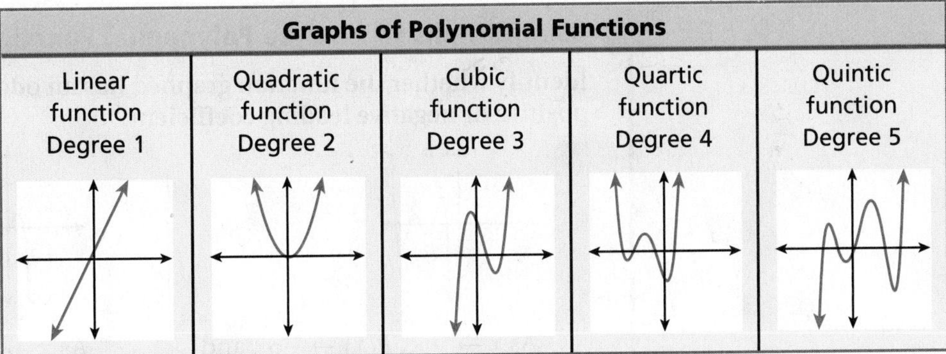

Graphs of Polynomial Functions

Linear function Degree 1	Quadratic function Degree 2	Cubic function Degree 3	Quartic function Degree 4	Quintic function Degree 5

End behavior is a description of the values of the function as x approaches positive infinity ($x \to +\infty$) or negative infinity ($x \to -\infty$). The degree and leading coefficient of a polynomial function determine its end behavior. It is helpful when you are graphing a polynomial function to know about the end behavior of the function.

Polynomial End Behavior

$P(x)$ has...	Odd Degree	Even Degree
Leading coefficient $a > 0$	As $x \to +\infty$, $P(x) \to +\infty$ As $x \to -\infty$, $P(x) \to -\infty$ Domain: $\mathbb{R}$ Range: $\mathbb{R}$	As $x \to -\infty$, $P(x) \to +\infty$ As $x \to +\infty$, $P(x) \to +\infty$ Domain: $\mathbb{R}$ Range: all values $\geq$ minimum
Leading coefficient $a < 0$	As $x \to -\infty$, $P(x) \to +\infty$ As $x \to +\infty$, $P(x) \to -\infty$ Domain: $\mathbb{R}$ Range: $\mathbb{R}$	As $x \to -\infty$, $P(x) \to -\infty$ As $x \to +\infty$, $P(x) \to -\infty$ Domain: $\mathbb{R}$ Range: all values $\leq$ maximum

EXAMPLE 1 Determining End Behavior of Polynomial Functions

Identify the leading coefficient, degree, and end behavior.

Helpful Hint

Both the leading coefficient and the degree of the polynomial are contained in the term of greatest degree. When determining end behavior, you can ignore all other terms.

A $P(x) = -4x^3 - 3x^2 + 5x + 6$

The leading coefficient is -4, which is negative.

The degree is 3, which is odd.

As $x \to -\infty$, $P(x) \to +\infty$, and as $x \to +\infty$, $P(x) \to -\infty$.

B $R(x) = x^6 - 7x^5 + x^3 - 2$

The leading coefficient is 1, which is positive.

The degree is 6, which is even.

As $x \to -\infty$, $P(x) \to +\infty$, and as $x \to +\infty$, $P(x) \to +\infty$.

Identify the leading coefficient, degree, and end behavior.

1a. $P(x) = 2x^5 + 3x^2 - 4x - 1$

1b. $S(x) = -3x^2 + x + 1$

EXAMPLE 2 Using Graphs to Analyze Polynomial Functions

Identify whether the function graphed has an odd or even degree and a positive or negative leading coefficient.

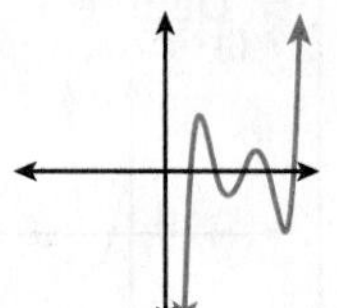

As $x \to -\infty$, $P(x) \to -\infty$, and as $x \to +\infty$, $P(x) \to +\infty$.

$P(x)$ is of odd degree with a positive leading coefficient.

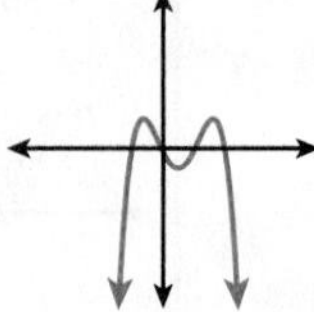

As $x \to -\infty$, $P(x) \to -\infty$, and as $x \to +\infty$, $P(x) \to -\infty$.

$P(x)$ is of even degree with a negative leading coefficient.

Identify whether the function graphed has an odd or even degree and a positive or negative leading coefficient.

2a.

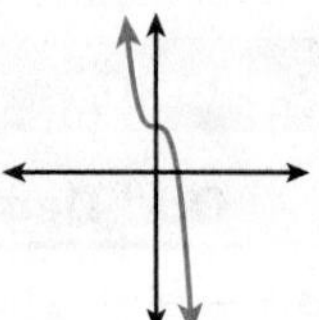

2b.

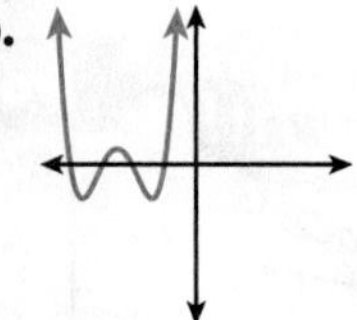

Now that you have studied factoring, solving polynomial equations, and end behavior, you can graph a polynomial function.

Steps for Graphing a Polynomial Function
1. Find the real zeros and *y*-intercept of the function.
2. Plot the *x*- and *y*-intercepts.
3. Make a table for several *x*-values that lie between the real zeros.
4. Plot the points from your table.
5. Determine the end behavior of the graph.
6. Sketch the graph.

EXAMPLE 3 Graphing Polynomial Functions

Graph the function.

$f(x) = x^3 + 3x^2 - 6x - 8$

Step 1 Identify the possible rational roots by using the Rational Root Theorem.

$\pm 1, \pm 2, \pm 4, \pm 8$ *$p = -8$ and $q = 1$*

Step 2 Test possible rational zeros until a zero is identified.

Test $x = 1$.

1	1	3	−6	−8
		1	4	−2
	1	4	−2	−10

Test $x = -1$.

−1	1	3	−6	−8
		−1	−2	8
	1	2	−8	0

$x = -1$ is a zero, and $f(x) = (x + 1)(x^2 + 2x - 8)$.

Step 3 Factor: $f(x) = (x + 1)(x - 2)(x + 4)$.

The zeros are −1, 2, and −4.

Step 4 Plot other points as guidelines.

$f(0) = -8$, so the y-intercept is −8.

Plot points between the zeros. Choose $x = -3$ and $x = 1$ for simple calculations.

$f(-3) = 10$ and $f(1) = -10$

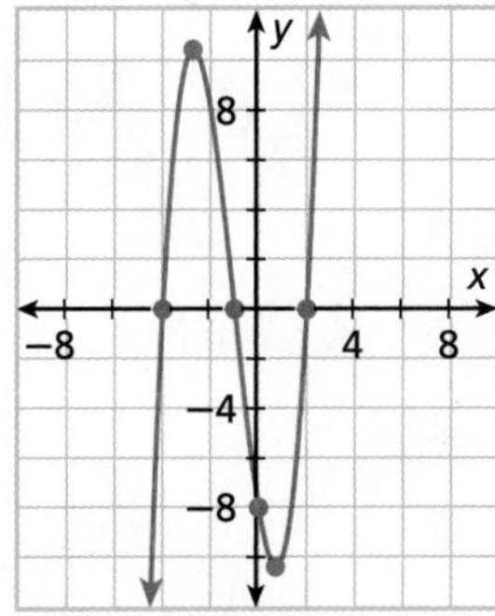

Step 5 Identify end behavior.

The degree is odd and the leading coefficient is positive so as $x \to -\infty$, $P(x) \to -\infty$, and as $x \to +\infty$, $P(x) \to +\infty$.

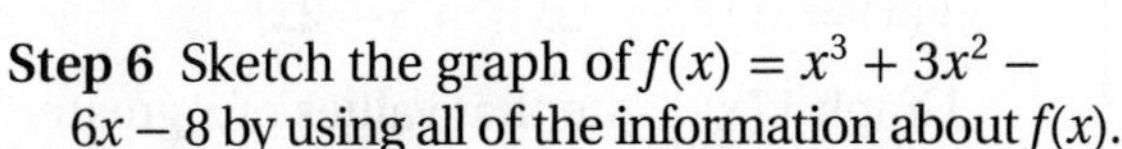

Step 6 Sketch the graph of $f(x) = x^3 + 3x^2 - 6x - 8$ by using all of the information about $f(x)$.

Graph each function.

3a. $f(x) = x^3 - 2x^2 - 5x + 6$ **3b.** $f(x) = -2x^2 - x + 6$

A **turning point** is where a graph changes from increasing to decreasing or from decreasing to increasing. A turning point corresponds to a *local maximum* or *minimum*.

Local Maxima and Minima

For a function $f(x)$, $f(a)$ is a **local maximum** if there is an interval around a such that $f(x) < f(a)$ for every x-value in the interval except a.

For a function $f(x)$, $f(a)$ is a **local minimum** if there is an interval around a such that $f(x) > f(a)$ for every x-value in the interval except a.

A polynomial function of degree n has at most $n - 1$ turning points and at most n x-intercepts. If the function has n distinct real roots, then it has exactly $n - 1$ turning points and exactly n x-intercepts. You can use a graphing calculator to graph and estimate maximum and minimum values.

EXAMPLE 4 Determine Maxima and Minima with a Calculator

Graph $g(x) = 2x^3 - 12x + 6$ on a calculator, and estimate the local maxima and minima.

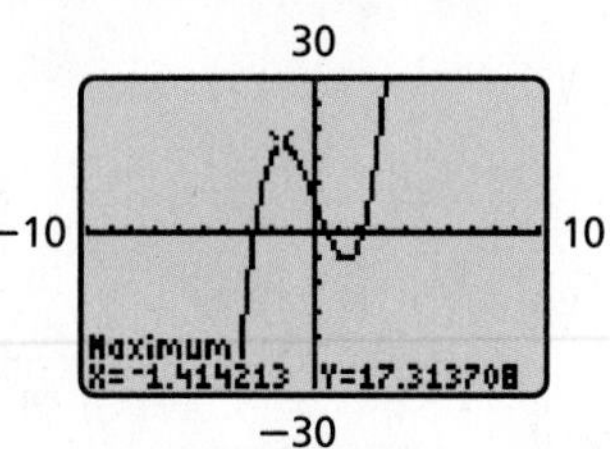

Step 1 Graph.

The graph appears to have one local maximum and one local minimum.

Reading Math

Maxima is the plural form of *maximum*. *Minima* is the plural form of *minimum*.

Step 2 Find the maximum.

Press 2nd TRACE (CALC) to access the **CALC** menu. Choose **4:maximum**.

The local maximum is approximately 17.3137.

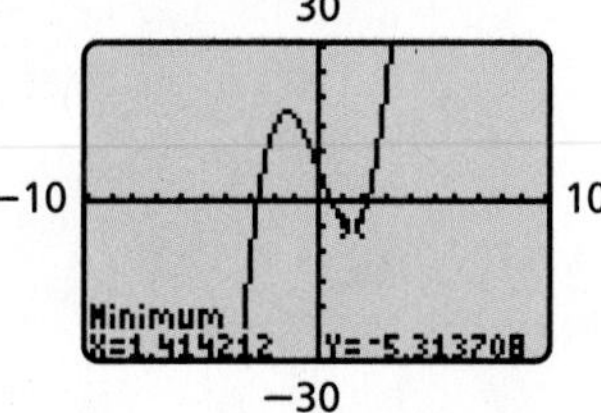

Step 3 Find the minimum.

Press 2nd TRACE (CALC) to access the **CALC** menu. Choose **3:mininum**.

The local minimum is approximately −5.3137.

CHECK IT OUT! **Graph each function on a calculator, and estimate the local maxima and minima.**

4a. $g(x) = x^3 - 2x - 3$ **4b.** $h(x) = x^4 + 4x^2 - 6$

EXAMPLE 5 *Industrial Application*

A welder plans to construct an open box from an 18.5 ft by 24.5 ft sheet of metal by cutting squares from the corners and folding up the sides. Find the maximum volume of the box and the corresponding dimensions.

Find a formula to represent volume.

$V(x) = x(18.5 - 2x)(24.5 - 2x)$ $V = \ell wh$

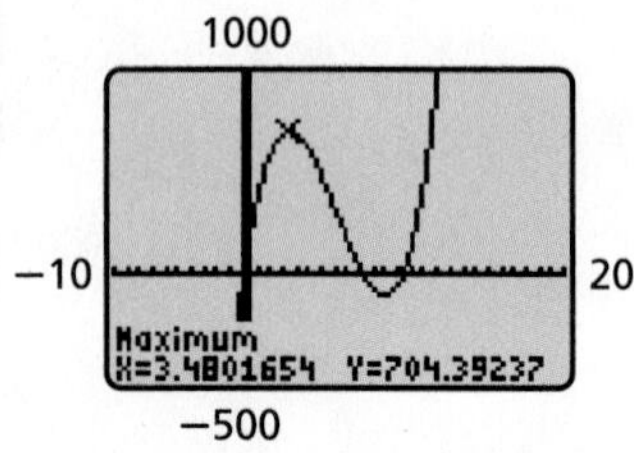

Graph $V(x)$. Note that values of x greater than 9.25 or less than 0 do not make sense for this problem.

The graph has a local maximum of about 704.4 when $x \approx 3.48$. So, the largest open box will have a volume of 704.4 ft^3.

CHECK IT OUT! **5.** What is the maximum volume of a box made from a 16 ft by 20 ft sheet of metal?

THINK AND DISCUSS

1. Explain why a polynomial function that has exactly n distinct real roots must have $n - 1$ turning points.

2. GET ORGANIZED Copy and complete the graphic organizer. In each box, sketch a graph that fits the description.

Leading Coefficient	Odd Degree	Even Degree
Positive		
Negative		

6-7 Exercises

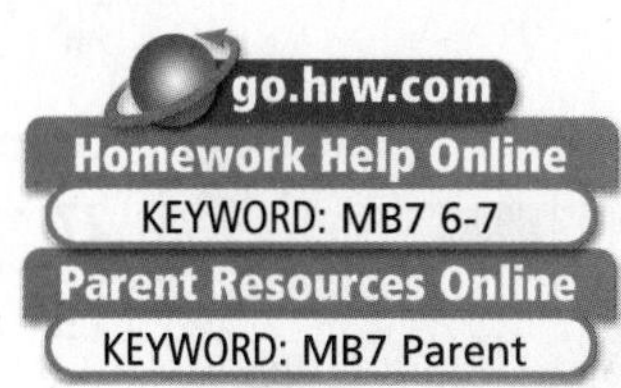

GUIDED PRACTICE

1. **Vocabulary** Explain why a *turning point* is appropriately named.

SEE EXAMPLE 1 p. 454

Identify the leading coefficient, degree, and end behavior.

2. $P(x) = -4x^4 - 3x^3 + x^2 + 4$
3. $Q(x) = -2x^7 + 6x^5 + 2x^3$
4. $R(x) = x^5 - 4x^2 + 3x - 1$
5. $S(x) = 3x^2 + 6x - 10$

SEE EXAMPLE 2 p. 454

Identify whether the function graphed has an odd or even degree and a positive or negative leading coefficient.

6. 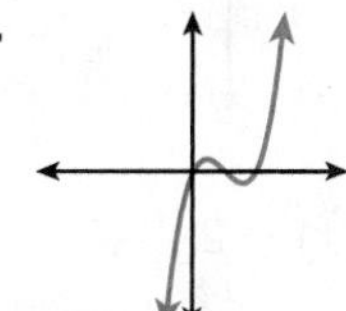
7. 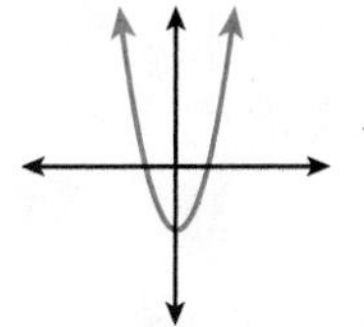
8. 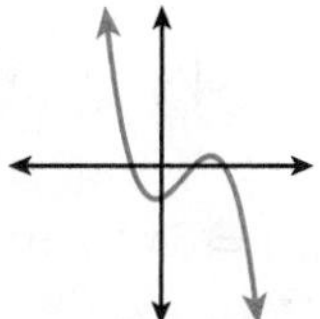
9. 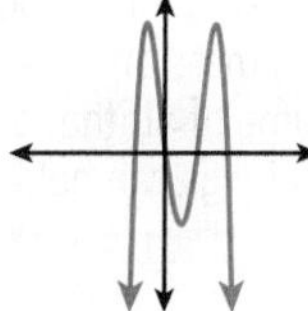

SEE EXAMPLE 3 p. 455

Graph each function.

10. $f(x) = x^2 - 5x - 50$
11. $f(x) = -x^3 + \frac{3}{2}x^2 + 25x + 12$

SEE EXAMPLE 4 p. 456

Graph each function on a calculator, and estimate the local maxima and minima.

12. $f(x) = x^4 - 4x^3 + 3x + 5$
13. $f(x) = 2x^3 - 3x^2 - 6x - 5$

SEE EXAMPLE 5 p. 456

14. **Landscape Design** Vera has 60 ft of fencing and wants to enclose a patio, using an existing wall for one side as shown. The area of the patio can be modeled by $A(x) = 60x - 3x^2$, where x is in feet. Find the maximum area of the patio.

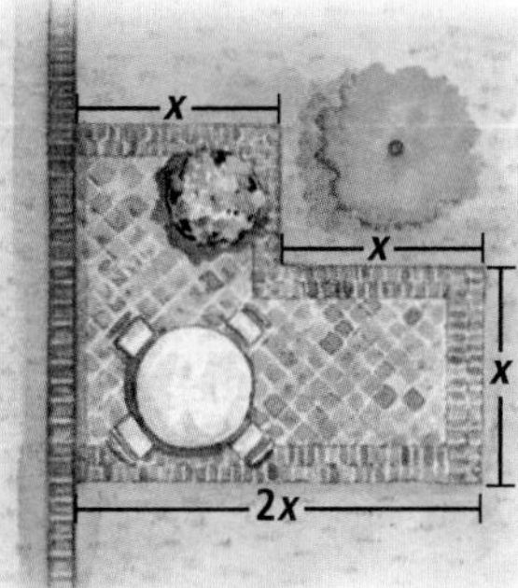

PRACTICE AND PROBLEM SOLVING

Independent Practice

For Exercises	See Example
15–18	1
19–22	2
23–26	3
27–30	4
31	5

Skills Practice p. S15
Application Practice p. S37

Identify the leading coefficient, degree, and end behavior.

15. $P(x) = 2x^3 + 3x^2 - 4x$
16. $Q(x) = -3x^4 - 8x^2$
17. $R(x) = -x^5 + 5x^4 + 1$
18. $S(x) = 5.5x^8 + 7.5x^4$

Identify whether the function graphed has an odd or even degree and a positive or negative leading coefficient.

19. 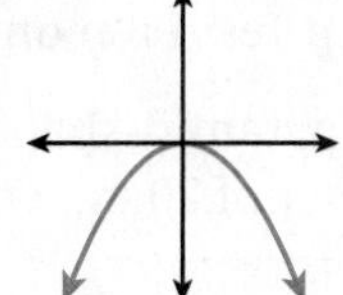
20. 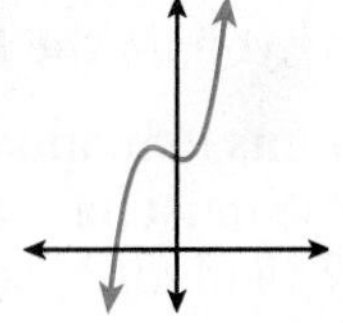
21. 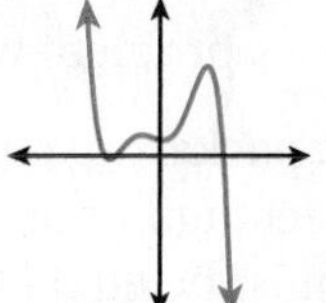
22. 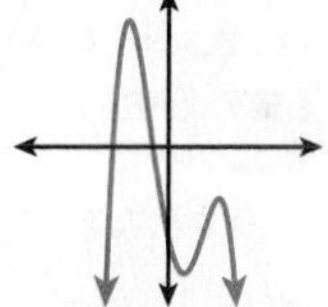

Graph each function.

23. $f(x) = x^3 - \frac{7}{3}x^2 - \frac{43}{3}x + 5$
24. $f(x) = 25x^2 - 4$
25. $f(x) = x^4 + x^3 - 28x^2 + 20x + 48$
26. $f(x) = x^3 + \frac{13}{2}x^2 + 11x + 4$

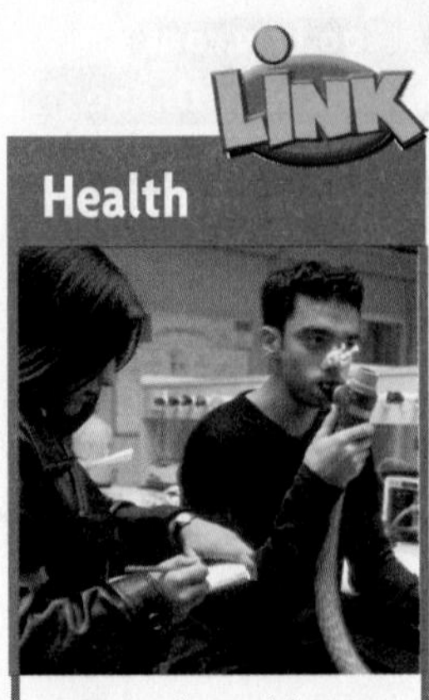

Health

A person's total lung capacity depends on many factors. Typically, age, weight, gender, and physical fitness affect the volume of air that a person's lungs can hold.

Graph each function on a calculator, and estimate the local maxima and minima.

27. $f(x) = 9x^6 + 20$

28. $f(x) = x^3 - 4x^2 + x + 1$

29. $f(x) = -x^2 + 6x - 10$

30. $f(x) = -5x^2 + 7$

31. Health The volume of air (in liters) in the human lung during one normal breath can be modeled by the function $V(t) = -1.7t^2 + 1.7t + 3$, for $0 \le t \le 1$. What is the maximum volume of air in the lungs during a normal breath, and at what time does it occur?

Use the degree and end behavior to match each polynomial function to its graph.

A. **B.**

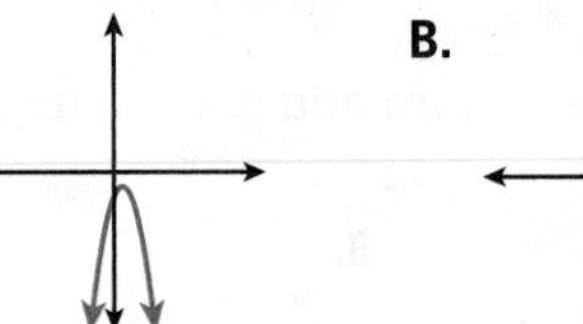

C.

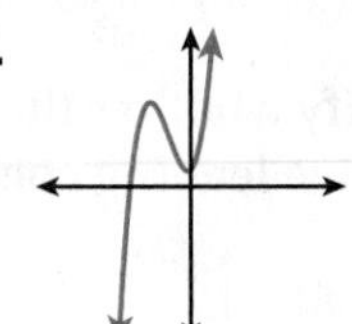

D.

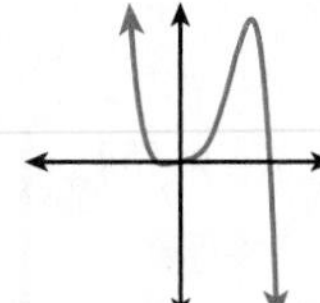

32. $f(x) = 5x^3 + 9x^2 + 1$

33. $f(x) = 2x^6 + 3x^4 + 5x^2$

34. $f(x) = 3x^4 - x^5 + x$

35. $f(x) = -4x^2 + 3x - 1$

Describe the end behavior of each function by completing the statements $f(x) \to$ _______ as $x \to -\infty$, and $f(x) \to$ _______ as $x \to +\infty$.

36. $f(x) = 2x^5 - x^2 + 75$

37. $f(x) = 10x^4 + 9x^2$

38. $f(x) = -5x^3 + x - 8$

39. $f(x) = 1000x^4 - 0.0002x^8$

40. $f(x) = x^{13} - x^7 + 12x$

41. $f(x) = -331x^{44} + 98$

42. Retail Hiromi sells 12 T-shirts each week at a price of \$13.00. Past sales have shown that for every \$0.25 decrease in price, 4 more T-shirts are sold. Knowing that revenue is a product of price and quantity, Hiromi models his revenue by $R(x) = (13 - 0.25x)(12 + 4x)$, where x represents the number of times there is a reduction in price.

a. Graph the function on a graphing calculator.

b. What is the maximum revenue Hiromi can generate each week?

c. How many \$0.25 reductions will maximize Hiromi's revenue? What would be the price per T-shirt, given the price is $13 - 0.25x$?

43. Critical Thinking Why are the leading coefficient and degree of the first term of the polynomial the only characteristics that determine end behavior?

44. Which of the following has a range that is different from the others? Explain.

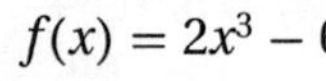

$f(x) = 2x^3 - 6$ $\qquad g(x) = x^4 + x - 7$ $\qquad h(x) = 3x^5 + x^2$

MULTI-STEP TEST PREP

45. This problem will prepare you for the Multi-Step Test Prep on page 472.

A packaging company wants to manufacture a pyramid-shaped gift box with a rectangular base. The base must have a perimeter of 20 in., and the height of the box must be equal to the length of the base.

a. Write a polynomial function, $V(x)$, for the volume of the box, where x is the length of the base.

b. Find the maximum volume of the box.

c. What dimensions result in a box with the maximum volume?

46. **Critical Thinking** Is there always an x-intercept between two turning points? Explain.

47. **Write About It** Describe the steps for graphing a polynomial by hand.

48. How many turning points will a quartic function with four real zeros have?

Ⓐ 1 Ⓑ 2 Ⓒ 3 Ⓓ 4

49. Which function could describe the graph?

Ⓕ $f(x) = -2x^5 + x - 4$

Ⓗ $f(x) = 3x^3 - 9x$

Ⓖ $f(x) = -x^3 + 5x^2 + 4x + 3$

Ⓙ $f(x) = \frac{1}{4}x^2 + \frac{1}{2}x + 1$

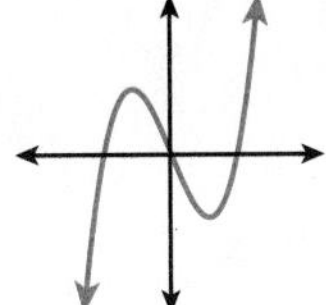

50. **Extended Response** Consider the polynomial function $f(x) = 2x^4 + 12x^3 + 24x^2 + 16x$.
   a. Find all solutions to the equation $f(x) = 0$.
   b. Describe the end behavior of $f(x)$. Explain your reasoning.
   c. Sketch a graph of $f(x)$ by using your answers to part **a** and part **b**.

CHALLENGE AND EXTEND

Graph each function without using a graphing calculator.

51. $3x^6 - 57x^4 + 6x^3 + 144x^2 - 96x$

52. $-2x^5 - 14x^4 - 30x^3 - 18x^2$

Examine the behavior of the cubic polynomials $f(x) = x^3$ and $g(x) = x^3 - 6x^2 + 4x - 20$ for the given values of x by using a spreadsheet or graphing calculator.

53. Complete the table.

x	f(x)	g(x)	$\frac{f(x)}{g(x)}$
5	■	■	■
10	■	■	■
50	■	■	■
100	■	■	■
500	■	■	■
1000	■	■	■
5000	■	■	■

54. Use your answer to Exercise 50 to complete this statement.

As $x \to +\infty$, $\frac{f(x)}{g(x)} \to$ ______.

55. Explain what the statement in Exercise 54 implies about the end behavior of $f(x)$ and $g(x)$.

SPIRAL REVIEW

Use substitution to determine if the given point is a solution to the system of equations. *(Lesson 3-1)*

56. $(2, -2)\begin{cases} 2x + y = 2 \\ 6x - 2y = 16 \end{cases}$

57. $(3, -1)\begin{cases} x + 3y = 0 \\ 8x + 4y = 21 \end{cases}$

58. $(5, -5)\begin{cases} x + y = 5 \\ x - y = 10 \end{cases}$

59. **Sports** A tennis ball is served with an initial velocity of 64 ft/s^2 from 6 ft above the ground. The tennis ball's height in feet is modeled by $h(t) = -16t^2 + 64t + 6$, where t is the time in seconds after the tennis ball is hit. Write the function in vertex form and identify the vertex. *(Lesson 5-4)*

Divide by using long division. *(Lesson 6-3)*

60. $x + 3\overline{)x^2 + 4x + 10}$

61. $x + 1\overline{)10x^2 + 8x + 6}$

62. $x + 8\overline{)x^2 + x - 64}$

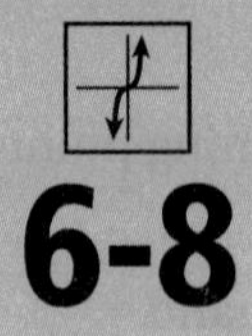

6-8 Transforming Polynomial Functions

Objective
Transform polynomial functions.

Why learn this?
Transformations can be used in business to model sales. (See Example 5.)

You can perform the same transformations on polynomial functions that you performed on quadratic and linear functions.

Transformations of $f(x)$

Transformation	$f(x)$ Notation	Examples	
Vertical translation	$f(x) + k$	$g(x) = x^3 + 3$	3 units up
		$g(x) = x^3 - 4$	4 units down
Horizontal translation	$f(x - h)$	$g(x) = (x - 2)^3$	2 units right
		$g(x) = (x + 1)^3$	1 unit left
Vertical stretch/compression	$af(x)$	$g(x) = 6x^3$	stretch by 6
		$g(x) = \frac{1}{2}x^3$	compression by $\frac{1}{2}$
Horizontal stretch/compression	$f\left(\frac{1}{b}x\right)$	$g(x) = \left(\frac{1}{5}x\right)^3$	stretch by 5
		$g(x) = (3x)^3$	compression by $\frac{1}{3}$
Reflection	$-f(x)$	$g(x) = -x^3$	across x-axis
	$f(-x)$	$g(x) = (-x)^3$	across y-axis

EXAMPLE 1 **Translating a Polynomial Function**

For $f(x) = x^3 + 4$, write the rule for each function and sketch its graph.

A $g(x) = f(x) + 3$

$g(x) = (x^3 + 4) + 3$

$g(x) = x^3 + 7$

To graph $g(x) = f(x) + 3$, translate the graph of $f(x)$ 3 units up.

This is a vertical translation.

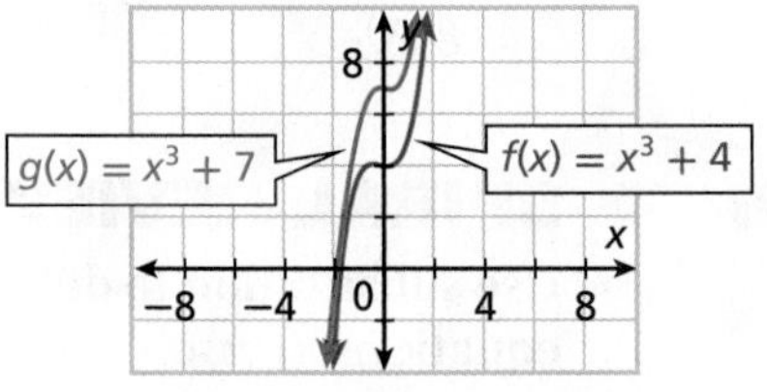

Helpful Hint
You can use a calculator to check your graph.

B $g(x) = f(x - 5)$

$g(x) = (x - 5)^3 + 4$

$g(x) = (x - 5)^3 + 4$

To graph $g(x) = f(x - 5)$, translate the graph of $f(x)$ 5 units right.

This is a horizontal translation.

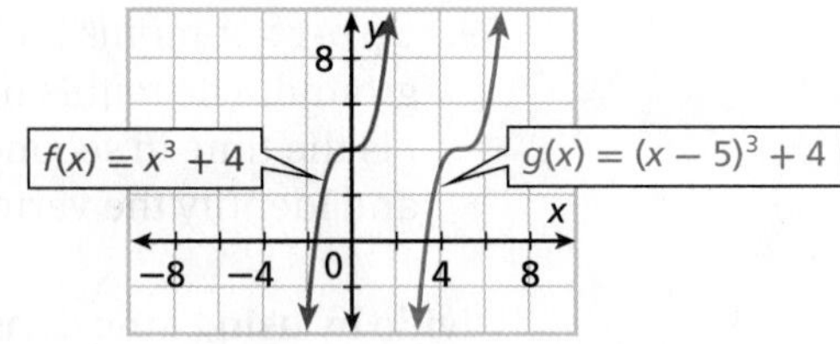

For $f(x) = x^3 + 4$, write the rule for each function and sketch its graph.

1a. $g(x) = f(x) - 5$

1b. $g(x) = f(x + 2)$

EXAMPLE 2 Reflecting Polynomial Functions

Let $f(x) = x^3 - 7x^2 + 6x - 5$. Write a function g that performs each transformation.

A **Reflect $f(x)$ across the x-axis.**

$g(x) = -f(x)$

$g(x) = -\left(x^3 - 7x^2 + 6x - 5\right)$

$g(x) = -x^3 + 7x^2 - 6x + 5$

Check Graph both functions. The graph appears to be a reflection. ✔

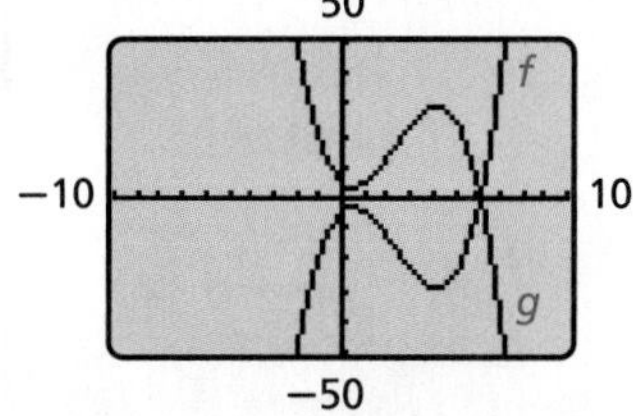

B **Reflect $f(x)$ across the y-axis.**

$g(x) = f(-x)$

$g(x) = (-x)^3 - 7(-x)^2 + 6(-x) - 5$

$g(x) = -x^3 - 7x^2 - 6x - 5$

Check Graph both functions. The graph appears to be a reflection. ✔

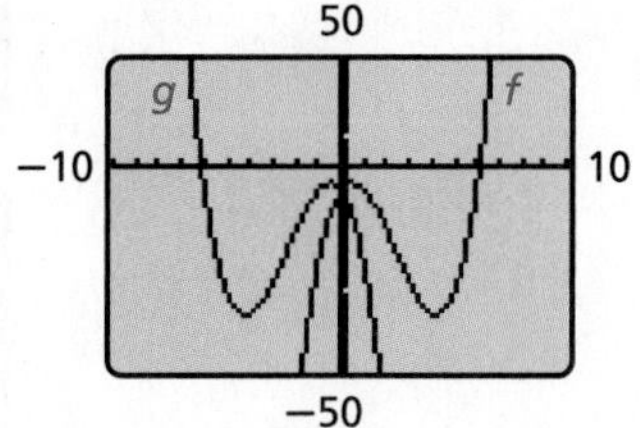

Let $f(x) = x^3 - 2x^2 - x + 2$. Write a function $g(x)$ that performs each transformation.

2a. Reflect $f(x)$ across the x-axis.

2b. Reflect $f(x)$ across the y-axis.

EXAMPLE 3 Compressing and Stretching Polynomial Functions

Let $f(x) = x^4 - 4x^2 + 2$. Graph f and g on the same coordinate plane. Describe g as a transformation of f.

A $g(x) = 2f(x)$

$g(x) = 2\left(x^4 - 4x^2 + 2\right)$

$g(x) = 2x^4 - 8x^2 + 4$

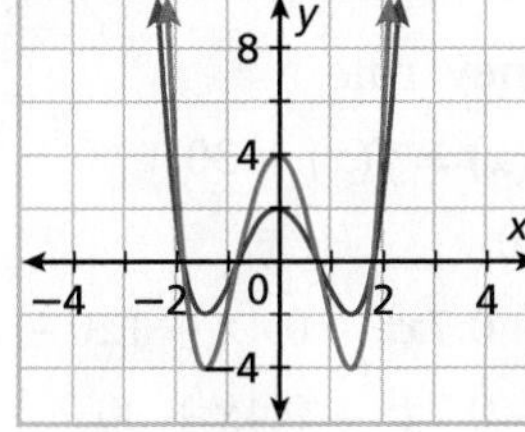

$g(x)$ is a vertical stretch of $f(x)$.

B $g(x) = f(3x)$

$g(x) = (3x)^4 - 4(3x)^2 + 2$

$g(x) = 81x^4 - 36x^2 + 2$

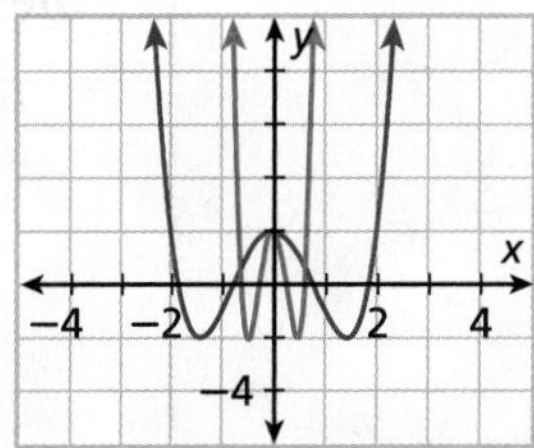

$g(x)$ is a horizontal compression of $f(x)$.

Let $f(x) = 16x^4 - 24x^2 + 4$. Graph f and g on the same coordinate plane. Describe g as a transformation of f.

3a. $g(x) = \frac{1}{4}f(x)$

3b. $g(x) = f\left(\frac{1}{2}x\right)$

EXAMPLE 4 Combining Transformations

Write a function that transforms $f(x) = 3x^3 + 6$ in each of the following ways. Support your solution by using a graphing calculator.

A **Stretch vertically by a factor of 2, and shift 3 units left.**

A vertical stretch is represented by $af(x)$, and a horizontal shift is represented by $f(x - h)$. Combining the two transformations gives $g(x) = af(x - h)$.

Substitute 2 for a and 3 for h.

$g(x) = 2f(x + 3)$

$g(x) = 2\left(3(x + 3)^3 + 6\right)$

$g(x) = 6(x + 3)^3 + 12$

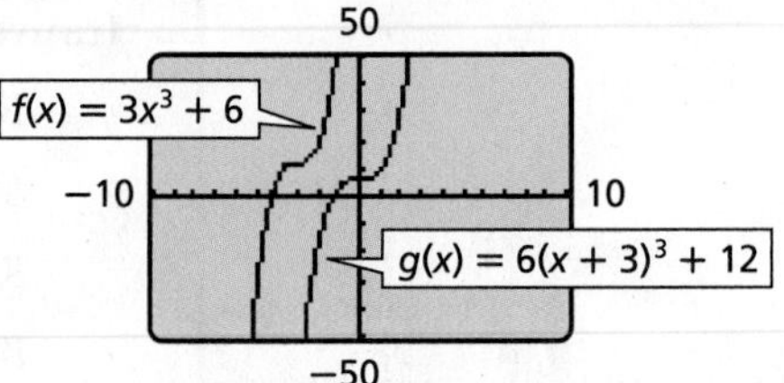

B **Reflect across the x-axis and shift 3 units up.**

A reflection across the x-axis is represented by $-f(x)$, and a vertical shift is represented by $f(x) + k$. Combining the two transformations gives $h(x) = -f(x) + k$.

Substitute 3 for k.

$h(x) = -f(x) + 3$

$h(x) = -\left(3x^3 + 6\right) + 3$

$h(x) = -3x^3 - 3$

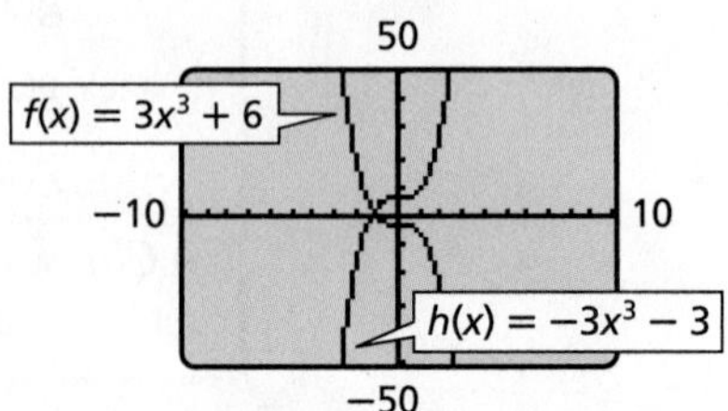

Write a function that transforms $f(x) = 8x^3 - 2$ in each of the following ways. Support your solution by using a graphing calculator.

4a. Compress vertically by a factor of $\frac{1}{2}$, and move the x-intercept 3 units right.

4b. Reflect across the x-axis, and move the x-intercept 4 units left.

EXAMPLE 5 *Bicycle Sales*

The number of bicycles sold per month by a business can be modeled by $f(x) = 0.01x^3 + 0.7x^2 + 0.4x + 120$, where x represents the number of months since January. Let $g(x) = f(x) - 30$. Find the rule for g, and explain the meaning of the transformation in terms of monthly bicycle sales.

Step 1 Write the new rule.

The new rule is $g(x) = f(x) - 30$.

$g(x) = f(x) - 30$

$g(x) = 0.01x^3 + 0.7x^2 + 0.4x + 120 - 30$

$g(x) = 0.01x^3 + 0.7x^2 + 0.4x + 90$

Step 2 Interpret the transformation.

The transformation represents a vertical shift 30 units down, which corresponds to a decrease in sales of 30 units per month.

5. Let $g(x) = f(x - 5)$. Find the rule for g, and explain the meaning of the transformation in terms of monthly bicycle sales.

THINK AND DISCUSS

1. How does shifting $f(x) = x^4 - 4$ up 5 units affect the number of real zeros? What if $f(x)$ is shifted 5 units down?
2. Does a horizontal shift affect the number of real zeros of a function? Explain.

3. **GET ORGANIZED** Copy and complete the graphic organizer.

Transformation	Vertical shift	Horizontal shift	Vertical stretch	Horizontal compression
Example				

6-8 Exercises

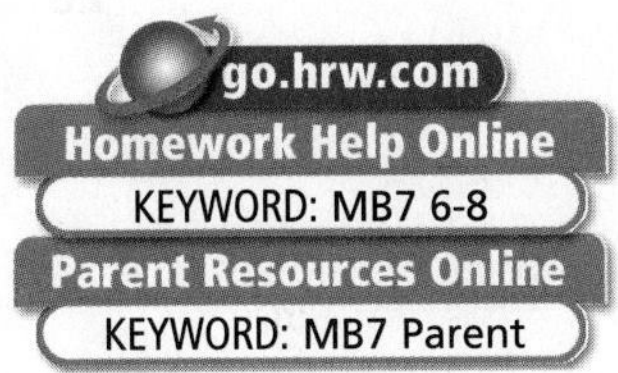

GUIDED PRACTICE

SEE EXAMPLE 1 p. 460

For $f(x) = x^4 - 8$, write the rule for each function, and sketch its graph.

1. $g(x) = f(x) + 4$ 2. $h(x) = f(x - 2)$ 3. $j(x) = f(3x)$ 4. $k(x) = f(x) - \frac{1}{2}$

SEE EXAMPLE 2 p. 461

Let $f(x) = -x^3 + 3x^2 - 2x + 1$. Write a function g that performs each transformation.

5. Reflect $f(x)$ across the y-axis. 6. Reflect $f(x)$ across the x-axis.

SEE EXAMPLE 3 p. 461

Let $f(x) = x^3 - 4x^2 + 2$. Graph f and g on the same coordinate plane. Describe g as a transformation of f.

7. $g(x) = f\left(\frac{1}{2}x\right)$ 8. $g(x) = 3f(x)$ 9. $g(x) = f(2x) + 4$

SEE EXAMPLE 4 p. 462

Write a function that transforms $f(x) = 4x^3 + 2$ in each of the following ways. Support your solution by using a graphing calculator.

10. Compress vertically by a factor of $\frac{1}{2}$, and move the y-intercept 2 units down.
11. Reflect across the y-axis, and compress horizontally by a factor of $\frac{1}{2}$.
12. Move 2 units right, move 3 units down, and reflect across the x-axis.

SEE EXAMPLE 5 p. 462

13. **Manufacturing** The cost to manufacture x units of a product can be modeled by the function $C(x) = 2x^3 - 3x + 30$, where the cost is in thousands of dollars. Describe the transformation $2C(x)$ by writing the new rule and explaining the change in the context of the problem.

PRACTICE AND PROBLEM SOLVING

For $f(x) = x^3 - 4$, write the rule for each function and sketch its graph.

14. $g(x) = f(x) - 3$ 15. $h(x) = f(x - 3)$ 16. $j(x) = f(x) + 5$

Let $f(x) = x^3 - 2x^2 + 5x - 3$. Write a function g that performs each transformation.

17. Reflect $f(x)$ across the x-axis. 18. Reflect $f(x)$ across the y-axis.

Independent Practice	
For Exercises	See Example
14–16	1
17–18	2
19–21	3
22–24	4
25	5

Extra Practice

Skills Practice: S15

Application Practice: S37

Let $f(x) = 2x^4 - 8x^2 - 2$. Graph f and g on the same coordinate plane. Describe g as a transformation of f.

19. $g(x) = 2f(x)$ **20.** $g(x) = \frac{1}{2}f(x)$ **21.** $g(x) = f\left(\frac{1}{2}x\right)$

Write a function that transforms $f(x) = x^4 - 6$ in each of the following ways. Support your solution by using a graphing calculator.

22. Reflect across the x-axis, and move the x-intercept 3 units left.

23. Compress vertically by a factor of $\frac{1}{3}$, and move 1 unit up.

24. Stretch horizontally by a factor of 2, move 4 units down, and reflect across the y-axis.

25. Geometry The volume of a rectangular prism can be modeled by the function $V(x) = x^3 + 3x^2 + x + 8$, where V is the volume in cubic meters and x represents length in meters. Describe the transformation $V\left(\frac{2}{3}x\right)$ by writing the new rule and explaining the change in the context of the problem.

26. ///ERROR ANALYSIS/// Students were asked to write a function g that translates f 3 units to the right. Which answer is incorrect? Identify and explain the error.

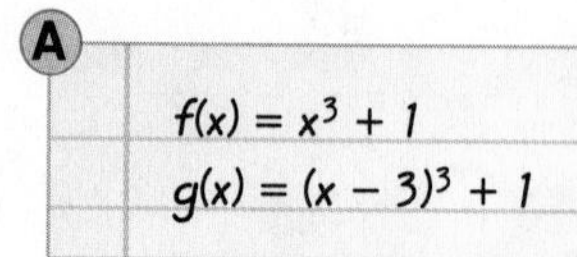

A

$f(x) = x^3 + 1$

$g(x) = (x - 3)^3 + 1$

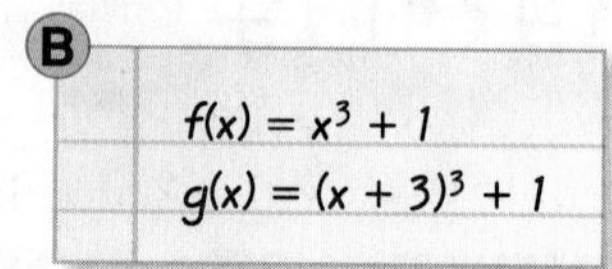

B

$f(x) = x^3 + 1$

$g(x) = (x + 3)^3 + 1$

27. Fish Some flying fish travel in the air up to a quarter of a mile by using a lift force F to overcome their weight W while in the air. The lift force is modeled by $F(v) = 0.24v^2$, where $v \geq 0$ is the initial air speed in meters per second.

a. Graph $F(v) = 0.24v^2$. For $W = 1$, find the values of v such that $F > W$.

b. A flying fish swimming with a current leaps out of the water with a speed that is 5 units greater than normal. Write a function $G(v)$ for the lift force. What transformation does this represent?

c. Find the values of v for which $G > W$.

d. $H(v) = 20v^2$ represents the underwater lift force. What transformation of $F(v)$ does this represent?

28. Critical Thinking In the function $f(x) = (x + 5)^4 + k$, for which values of k does the function have two real solutions? no real solutions? Explain.

29. Write About It Explain in your own words what happens to the graph of a function when you reflect it across the x-axis.

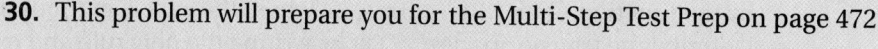

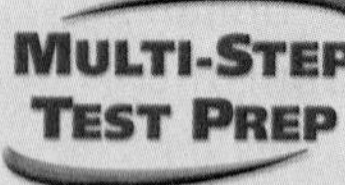

30. This problem will prepare you for the Multi-Step Test Prep on page 472.

The volume of a pyramid with a square base is modeled by the function $V(x) = \frac{1}{3}x^3 + x^2$, where x is the length of the base in inches.

a. Write a new function, $W(x)$, that gives the volume of the pyramid in cubic inches when the length of the base is expressed in feet.

b. Write $W(x)$ in terms of $V(x)$.

c. Graph W and V on the same coordinate plane. How is the graph of W related to the graph of V?

d. How would your answer to part **c** be different if the length of the base were expressed in centimeters?

31. Which graph represents a vertical shift of $f(x) = x^3 - 3x^2 - x + 3$ up 3 units?

Ⓐ
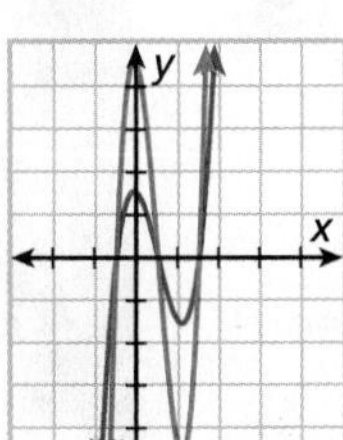

Ⓑ
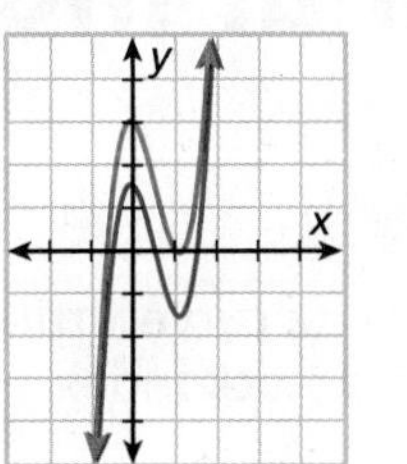

Ⓒ
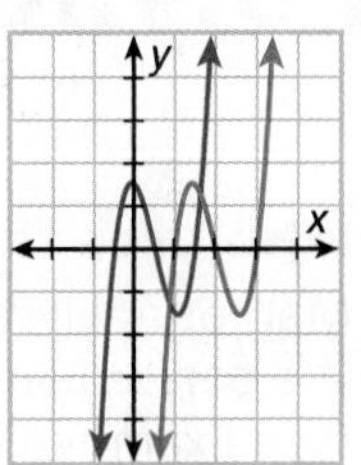

Ⓓ
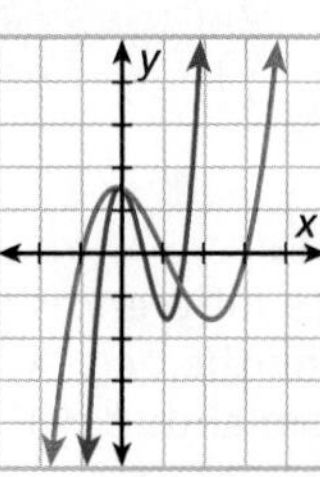

32. Which description matches the transformation from $f(x)$ to $g(x)$ shown?

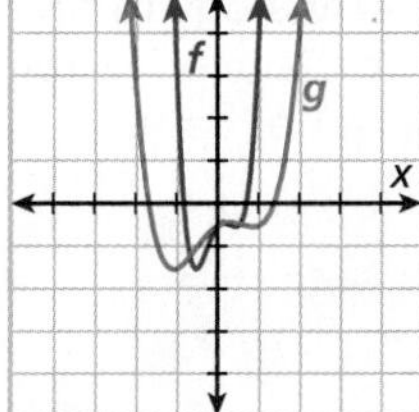

Ⓕ Vertical shift　　Ⓗ Horizontal shift

Ⓖ Vertical stretch　　Ⓙ Horizontal stretch

33. $f(x) = x^3 - 6x^2 + 6x + 1$ has three real zeros. How many real zeros does $f(x) - 6$ have?

Ⓐ 0　　Ⓒ 2

Ⓑ 1　　Ⓓ 3

34. **Extended Response** Consider the function $f(x) = 3x^3 - 9x^2 - 3x + 9$.

a. Use the leading coefficient and degree of $f(x)$ to describe the end behavior.

b. Write the rule for the function $g(x) = f(-x)$, and describe the transformation.

c. Describe the end behavior of $g(x)$. How does the end behavior of $g(x)$ relate to the transformation of $f(x)$?

CHALLENGE AND EXTEND

Identify the transformation(s) that would take $f(x) = (x + 2)^3 - 6$ to $g(x)$.

35. $g(x) = x^3 - 6$　　36. $g(x) = (x + 2)^3$　　37. $g(x) = (x - 1)^3 + 2$

38. For $f(x) = x^4 - x^2 - 9x + 9$, describe three different transformations that could be performed to obtain a function with a y-intercept of 3.

SPIRAL REVIEW

39. **Computers** An administrative assistant recorded the number of words that he typed in one minute. He then recorded the number of words that he typed during different time intervals. His results are in the table below. Write an equation to express this situation. Is this a function? *(Lesson 1-6)*

Minutes	1	3	6	8
Words	60	180	360	480

Add or subtract. Write your answer in standard form. *(Lesson 6-1)*

40. $(6y + 4y^2 - 3) + (9y^2 - 5 + 8y)$　　41. $(2x^5 - 4x + 8x^2) - (3x^4 - x^5 + 3x^2)$

Find all of the roots of the polynomial equation. *(Lesson 6-6)*

42. $x^4 - 81 = 0$　　43. $x^4 + x^3 + 3x^2 + 5x - 10 = 0$

44. $x^3 - 5x^2 - 17x + 21 = 0$　　45. $x^5 + 3x^4 + 2x^3 + 16x^2 - 48x - 64 = 0$

6-9 Curve Fitting with Polynomial Models

Objectives

Use finite differences to determine the degree of a polynomial that will fit a given set of data.

Use technology to find polynomial models for a given set of data.

Who uses this?

Market analysts can use curve fitting to predict the performance of a stock index. (See Example 3.)

The table shows the closing value of a stock index on the first day of trading for various years.

Year	1994	1995	1996	1997	2000	2001	2003	2004
Price ($)	774	751	1053	1293	4186	2474	1347	2011

To create a mathematical model for the data, you will need to determine what type of function is most appropriate. In Lesson 5-8, you learned that a set of data that has constant second differences can be modeled by a quadratic function. Finite differences can be used to identify the degree of any polynomial data.

Finite Differences of Polynomials

Function Type	Degree	Constant Finite Differences
Linear	1	First
Quadratic	2	Second
Cubic	3	Third
Quartic	4	Fourth
Quintic	5	Fifth

EXAMPLE 1 Using Finite Differences to Determine Degree

Use finite differences to determine the degree of the polynomial that best describes the data.

Remember!

To find the differences in the y-values, subtract each y-value from the y-value that follows it. For the first differences,
$-4 - (-10) = 6$
$-1.4 - (-4) = 2.6$
$0 - (-1.4) = 1.4$
and so on.

x	−2	−1	0	1	2	3
y	−10	−4	−1.4	0	2.4	8

The x-values increase by a constant 1. Find the differences of the y-values.

y	−10	−4	−1.4	0	2.4	8

First differences: 6   2.6   1.4   2.4   5.6   Not constant
Second differences: −3.4   −1.2   1   3.2   Not constant
Third differences: 2.2   2.2   2.2   Constant

The third differences are constant. A cubic polynomial best describes the data.

Use finite differences to determine the degree of the polynomial that best describes the data.

x	−6	−4	−2	0	2	4
y	−30	15	30	34	41	60

The x-values increase by a constant, 2. Find the differences of the y-values.

First differences: 45 15 4 7 19 Not constant
Second differences: −30 −11 3 12 Not constant
Third differences: 19 14 9 Not Constant
Fourth differences: −5 −5 Constant

The fourth differences are constant. A quartic polynomial best describes the data.

1. Use finite differences to determine the degree of the polynomial that best describes the data.

x	12	15	18	21	24	27
y	3	23	29	29	31	43

Once you have determined the degree of the polynomial that best describes the data, you can use your calculator to create the function.

EXAMPLE 2 Using Finite Differences to Write a Function

The table below shows the population of a city from 1950 to 2000. Write a polynomial function for the data.

Year	1950	1960	1970	1980	1990	2000
Population (thousands)	2853	4011	5065	6720	9704	14,759

Helpful Hint

Keep the scale of the original data in mind. In Example 2, the population ranges from 2853 to 14,759. The gap between 705 and 728 is small in comparison.

Step 1 Find the finite differences of the y-values.

Let x represent the number of years since 1950. The years increase by a constant amount of 10. The populations are the y-values.

First differences: 1158 1054 1655 2984 5055
Second differences: −104 601 1329 2071
Third differences: 705 728 742 Close

Step 2 Determine the degree of the polynomial.

Because the third differences are relatively close, a cubic function should be a good model.

Step 3 Use the cubic regression feature on your calculator.

$f(x) \approx 0.12x^3 - 4.21x^2 + 146.37x + 2851.64$

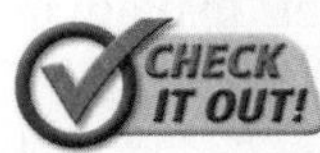

2. The table below shows the gas consumption of a compact car driven a constant distance at various speeds. Write a polynomial function for the data.

Speed	25	30	35	40	45	50	55	60
Gas (gal)	23.8	25	25.2	25	25.4	27	30.6	37

Often, real-world data can be too irregular for you to use finite differences or find a polynomial function that fits perfectly. In these situations, you can use the regression feature of your graphing calculator. Remember that the closer the R^2-value is to 1, the better the function fits the data.

EXAMPLE 3 *Finance Application*

The table shows the opening value of a stock index on the first day of trading in various years. Use a polynomial model to estimate the value on the first day of trading in 2002.

Year	Price ($)	Year	Price ($)
1994	774	2000	4186
1995	751	2001	2474
1996	1053	2003	1347
1997	1293	2004	2011

Step 1 Choose the degree of the polynomial model.

Let x represent the number of years since 1994. Make a scatter plot of the data.

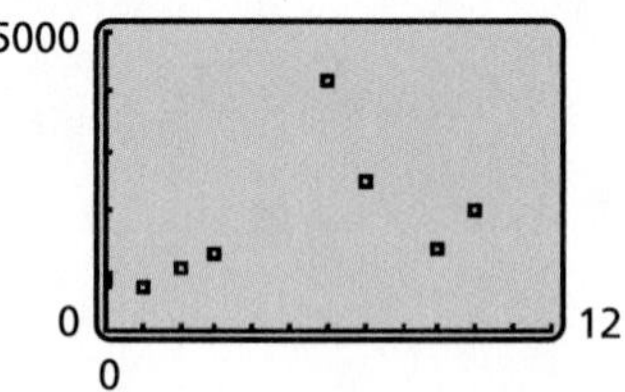

The function appears to be cubic or quartic. Use the regression feature to check the R^2-values.

cubic: $R^2 \approx 0.6279$ quartic: $R^2 \approx 0.8432$

The quartic function is a more appropriate choice.

Step 2 Write the polynomial model.

The data can be modeled by
$f(x) = 9.27x^4 - 191.56x^3 + 1168.22x^2 - 1702.58x + 999.60$

Step 3 Find the value of the model corresponding to 2002.

2002 is 8 years after 1994. Substitute 8 for x in the quartic model.

$f(x) = 9.27(8)^4 - 191.56(8)^3 + 1168.22(8)^2 - 1702.58(8) + 999.60 =$ 2036.24

Based on the model, the opening value was about $2036.24 in 2002.

3. Use a polynomial model to estimate the value of the index in 1999.

Year	1994	1995	1996	2000	2003	2004
Price ($)	3754	3835	5117	11,497	8342	10,454

THINK AND DISCUSS

1. Suppose that finite differences are used to determine that a quartic polynomial best describes a particular data set. What is the minimum number of data pairs in the data set? Explain.

2. GET ORGANIZED Copy and complete the graphic organizer. For each type of function, indicate the degree and the constant differences and give an example of a data set.

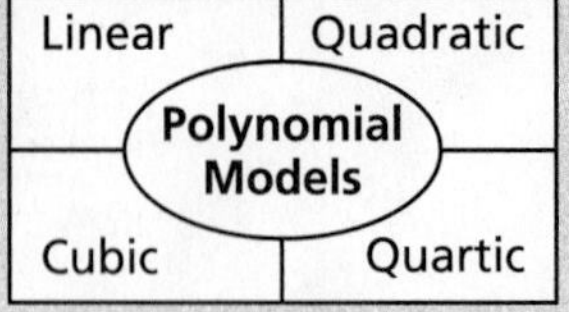

6-9 Exercises

go.hrw.com
Homework Help Online
KEYWORD: MB7 6-9
Parent Resources Online
KEYWORD: MB7 Parent

GUIDED PRACTICE

SEE EXAMPLE 1 p. 466

Use finite differences to determine the degree of the polynomial that best describes the data.

1.

x	y
−2	22
−1	16
0	10
1	4
2	−2
3	−8

2.

x	y
−2	0
−1	−5
0	−3
1	5
2	18
3	35

3.

x	y
−2	23
−1	−2
0	1
1	2
2	−5
3	−2

SEE EXAMPLE 2 p. 467

4. **Business** The table below shows the number of square feet of retail space available for rent in various years. Write a polynomial function for the data.

Year	1957	1967	1977	1987	1997	2007
Retail Space (billion ft^2)	2.8	6.7	14.7	27.3	44.9	67.9

SEE EXAMPLE 3 p. 468

5. **Health** The table below shows the number of infected patients at various stages of a flu outbreak. Use a polynomial model to estimate the number of infected patients after 120 hours.

Time (h)	12	24	48	96	144	240
Patients	21	301	679	973	562	320

PRACTICE AND PROBLEM SOLVING

Independent Practice

For Exercises	See Example
6–8	1
9	2
10–11	3

Extra Practice

Skills Practice p. S15

Application Practice p. S37

Use finite differences to determine the degree of the polynomial that best describes the data.

6.

x	y
−5	−20
−4	−19
−3	−9
−2	5.5
−1	20
0	30

7.

x	y
−2	−2
−1	−6
0	0
1	10
2	20
3	28

8.

x	y
−2	−3
−1	1
0	4.3
1	6.9
2	8.8
3	10

9. **Hobbies** The table below shows the number of Chess Club members in various years. Write a polynomial function for the data.

Year	2002	2003	2004	2005	2006	2007
Members	23	23	23	25	29	35

10. **Tourism** The table below shows the number of Canadian visitors to the United States. Use a polynomial model to predict the number of visitors in 2005.

Year	1996	1998	2000	2001	2002	2003
Visitors (millions)	15.3	13.4	14.6	13.5	13.0	12.7

11. **Education** The table shows the total high school graduates in the United States. Use a polynomial model to estimate the total graduates in 1999.

Year	1989	1991	1995	1996	1998	2000
Graduates (thousands)	59,336	61,272	56,450	56,559	58,174	58,086

12. **Weather** The figure shows the latitude, longitude, and average January minimum temperature of various locations.

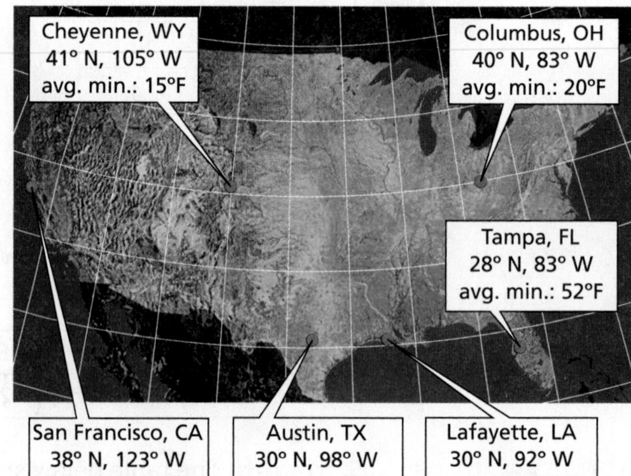

a. Which pair of variables has a closer polynomial relationship: latitude and temperature or longitude and temperature? Give numerical data to support your answer.

b. Is the relationship between latitude and temperature a function? Explain.

c. Is a polynomial model relating longitude and temperature a function? Explain.

13. **Multi-Step** The table shows the total December clothing sales in the United States in billions of dollars.

Year	1997	1998	1999	2001	2002	2003
Sales (billions of $)	12.1	12.7	13.5	14.1	14.6	15.3

a. Write a cubic polynomial to model the data. What is the R^2-value?

b. Write a quartic polynomial to model the data. What is the R^2-value?

c. Is the difference in R^2-values significant?

d. What do the R^2-values say about your answers to part **a** and part **b**?

MULTI-STEP TEST PREP

14. This problem will prepare you for the Multi-Step Test Prep on page 472. You can make a pyramid by stacking balls in triangular layers. For example, three balls can be arranged as a triangle with a fourth ball on top of the other three.

Number of Balls on One Side of the Bottom Layer	1	2	3	4	5
Total Number of Balls in the Pyramid	1	4	10	20	35

a. Use finite differences to determine the degree of the polynomial that best describes the data.

b. Write a polynomial function for the data.

c. How many balls are in a pyramid that has 12 balls on one side of the bottom layer?

15. **Critical Thinking** The fourth differences of a given data set are 0.01, 0, 0, and −0.01. Is a cubic polynomial appropriate to model the data? Explain.

16. **Write About It** Describe the process you would use to determine the appropriate type of polynomial for a given data set.

17. What type of polynomial best models the data below?
$\{(0, 1), (1, 21), (2, 27), (3, 27), (4, 29), (5, 41)\}$
Ⓐ Linear Ⓑ Quadratic Ⓒ Cubic Ⓓ Quartic

18. Which cubic function represents the graph?
Ⓕ $f(x) = -(x + 2)(x - 1)(x - 3)$
Ⓖ $f(x) = (x + 2)(x - 1)(x - 3)$
Ⓗ $f(x) = -(x - 2)(x + 1)(x + 3)$
Ⓙ $f(x) = (x - 2)(x + 1)(x + 3)$

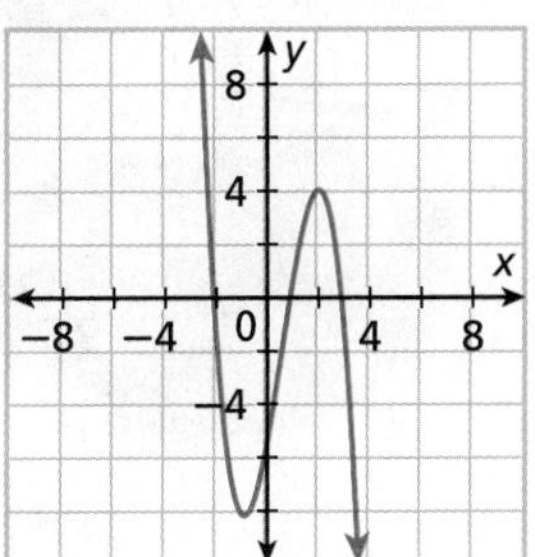

19. **Short Response** Give a cubic polynomial that can be used to model the data below.
$\{(0, 4), (-1, 8), (1, 0), (-2, 6), (2, 2)\}$

CHALLENGE AND EXTEND

The *average slope* of the graph of $f(x)$ between $x = a$ and $x = b$ is the slope of the line through $(a, f(a))$ and $(b, f(b))$. Use the table at right to complete Exercises 20–22.

x	$f(x)$
−3	−5.5
−2	−1
−1	1.5
0	2
1	0.5
2	−3

20. What is the average slope between $x = -2$ and $x = 2$?

21. How can you use first differences to find the average slope between each pair of points given in the table?

22. What happens to the average slope of the graph as the chosen points get closer to the maximum point?

23. Use finite differences to create a data set that could be modeled by a quartic polynomial.

SPIRAL REVIEW

Simplify each expression. *(Lesson 1-4)*

24. $-b^2(2b^2 + 5b - 3)$ 25. $a + 3a - 5a^2(6a - a)$ 26. $\dfrac{u^2 - v + 3v}{v(v^2 - u)}$

27. **Multi-Step** The chart below shows the number of copies sold (in thousands) of a new music CD for 5 weeks. Graph the data. Describe the parent function and the transformation that best approximates the data set. *(Lesson 1-9)*

Week	1	2	3	4	5
Copies Sold (thousands)	2	3	10	29	66

Identify the leading coefficient, degree, and end behavior. *(Lesson 6-7)*

28. $f(x) = x^4 - x^2 + 3x - 1$ 29. $f(x) = 4x^5 - x^3 + 10$ 30. $f(x) = -3x^6 + 5x$

CHAPTER 6

SECTION 6B

Applying Polynomial Functions

Pyramid Pile-Up You can build a pyramid by stacking blocks in layers. The blocks in each layer are arranged in a square, and the layers grow successively larger as shown below.

1. The figure shows the relationship between the number of layers and the total number of blocks in the pyramid. Make a table that shows the relationship for the first five layers.

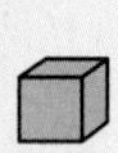
1 layer
1 block

2 layers
5 blocks

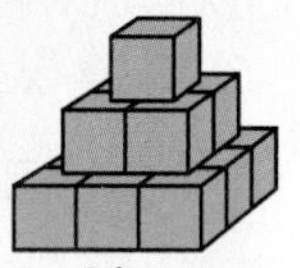
3 layers
14 blocks

2. Use finite differences to determine the degree of the polynomial that best describes the data.
3. Write a polynomial function for the data.
4. The Great Pyramid in Giza, Egypt, has 201 layers. Use your function to estimate the number of blocks in the pyramid.
5. A pyramid contains a total of 285 blocks. How many layers are in the pyramid?
6. Is it possible to build a pyramid that uses exactly 811 blocks? Why or why not? Give an explanation in terms of the solutions to a polynomial equation.
7. A pyramid is known to contain at least 10,000 blocks. What is the minimum number of layers in the pyramid?

READY TO GO ON?

CHAPTER 6

SECTION 6B

Quiz for Lessons 6-5 Through 6-9

6-5 Finding Real Roots of Polynomial Equations

1. The yearly profit of a company in thousands of dollars can be modeled by $P(t) = t^4 - 10t^2 + 9$, where t is the number of years since 2000. Factor to find the years in which the profit was 0.

Identify the roots of each equation. State the multiplicity of each root.

2. $x^3 + 6x^2 + 12x + 8 = 0$
3. $2x^3 + 8x^2 - 32x - 128 = 0$
4. $x^4 - 6x^3 + 9x^2 = 0$

6-6 Fundamental Theorem of Algebra

Write the simplest polynomial function with the given roots.

5. 1, 1, 2
6. $i, -1, 0$
7. Solve $x^4 - 2x^3 + 6x^2 - 18x - 27 = 0$ by finding all roots.

6-7 Investigating Graphs of Polynomial Functions

Graph each function.

8. $f(x) = x^4 - 13x^2 + 36$
9. $f(x) = x^3 - 4x^2 - 15x + 18$

Identify whether the function graphed has an odd or even degree and a positive or negative leading coefficient.

10.

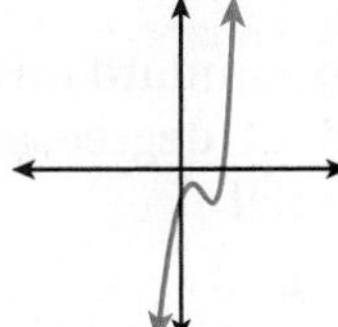

11.

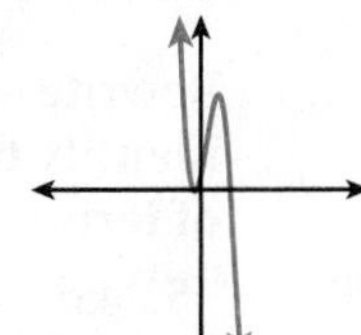

12.

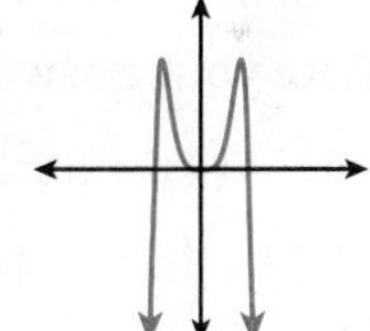

6-8 Transforming Polynomial Functions

Let $f(x) = x^4 - 3x^2 + 6$. Write a function $g(x)$ that performs each transformation.

13. Reflect $f(x)$ across the x-axis.
14. Reflect $f(x)$ across the y-axis.

Let $f(x) = 8x^4 - 12x^2 + 2$. Graph $f(x)$ and $g(x)$ on the same coordinate plane. Describe $g(x)$ as a transformation of $f(x)$.

15. $g(x) = 3f(x)$
16. $g(x) = f\left(\frac{1}{2}x\right)$
17. $g(x) = f(x - 4)$

6-9 Curve Fitting with Polynomial Models

18. The table shows the population of a bacteria colony over time. Write a polynomial function for the data.

Time (*h*)	1	2	3	4	5
Bacteria	44	112	252	515	949

CHAPTER

6 Study Guide: Review

Vocabulary

degree of a monomial 406
degree of a polynomial 406
end behavior 453
leading coefficient 406
local maximum 455
local minimum 455
monomial 406
multiplicity 439
polynomial 406
polynomial function 408
synthetic division 423
turning point 455

Complete the sentences below with vocabulary words from the list above.

1. A(n) ___?___ is a number or product of numbers and variables with whole number exponents.
2. A method of dividing a polynomial by a linear binomial of the form $x - a$ by using only the coefficients is ___?___.
3. The number of times $x - r$ is a factor of $P(x)$ is the ___?___ of r.
4. The ___?___ of a function is a description of the function values as x approaches positive infinity or negative infinity.

6-1 Polynomials *(pp. 406–412)*

EXAMPLES

■ **Subtract. Write your answer in standard form.**

$(6x - 2x^2 + 1) - (4x - 5x^2)$

$(-2x^2 + 6x + 1) + (5x^2 - 4x)$ *Add the opposite.*

$(-2x^2 + 5x^2) + (6x - 4x) + 1$ *Combine like terms.*

$3x^2 + 2x + 1$

■ **Graph $f(x) = -x^3 + 4x + 1$ on a calculator. Describe the graph, and identify the number of real zeros.**

From left to right, the function decreases, increases, and then decreases again. It crosses the x-axis three times. There appear to be three real zeros.

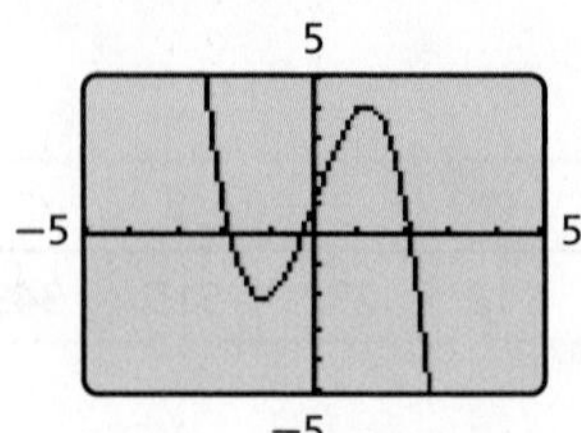

EXERCISES

Rewrite each polynomial in standard form. Then identify the leading coefficient, degree, and number of terms. Name the polynomial.

5. $4x^2 - 3x^3 + 6x + 7$
6. $5x^3 - x^5 + 8x + 2x^4$
7. $1 - 11x + 9x^2$
8. $-6x^2 + x^4$

Add or subtract. Write your answer in standard form.

9. $(8x^3 - 4x^2 - 3x + 1) - (1 - 5x^2 + x)$
10. $(6x^2 + 7x - 2) + (1 - 5x^3 + 3x)$
11. $(5x - 2x^2) - (4x^2 + 6x - 9)$
12. $(x^4 - x^2 + 4) + (x^2 - x^3 - 5x^4 - 7)$

Graph each polynomial function on a calculator. Describe the graph, and identify the number of real zeros.

13. $f(x) = -x^4 + 4x^2 + 1$
14. $f(x) = x^3 + 2x^2 + 1$
15. $f(x) = x^4 - 5x^2 + 2$
16. $f(x) = x^3 - 3x^2 + 2$

6-2 Multiplying Polynomials (pp. 414–420)

EXAMPLE

■ **Find the product.**

$(x-3)(5-x-2x^2)$

Multiply horizontally.

$(x-3)(-2x^2-x+5)$ *Write in standard form.*

$x(-2x^2)+x(-x)+x(5)-3(-2x^2)-3(-x)-3(5)$

$-2x^3-x^2+5x+6x^2+3x-15$ *Multiply.*

$-2x^3+5x^2+8x-15$ *Combine like terms.*

EXERCISES

Find each product.

17. $5x^2(3x-2)$ **18.** $-3t(2t^2-6t+1)$

19. $ab^2(a^2-a+ab)$ **20.** $(x-2)(x^2-2x-3)$

21. $(2x+5)(x^3-x^2+1)$ **22.** $(x-3)^3$

23. $(x+4)(x^4-3x^2+x)$ **24.** $(2x+1)^4$

25. A cylinder has a height of x^2-x-3 and a radius of $2x$ as shown. Express the volume of the cylinder as a sum of monomials.

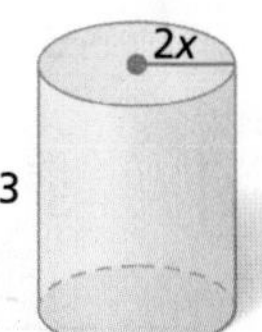

6-3 Dividing Polynomials (pp. 422–428)

EXAMPLE

■ **Divide by using synthetic division.**

$(x^3-3x^2+8)\div(x+2)$

$a=-2$

x^3-3x^2+0x+8 *Write in standard form.*

−2	1	−3	0	8
		−2	10	−20
	1	−5	10	−12

Write the coefficients of the terms.

$$\frac{x^3-3x^2+8}{x+2}=x^2-5x+10+\frac{-12}{x+2}$$

EXERCISES

Divide by using long division.

26. $(x^3-5x^2+2x-7)\div(x+2)$

27. $(8x^4+6x^2-2x+4)\div(2x-1)$

Divide by using synthetic division.

28. $(x^3-4x^2+3x+2)\div(x-3)$

29. $(x^3+2x-1)\div(x-2)$

30. A spool of ribbon has a length of x^3+x^2 inches. Write an expression that represents the number of strips of ribbon with a length of $x-1$ inches that can be cut from one spool.

6-4 Factoring Polynomials (pp. 430–435)

EXAMPLES

Determine whether each binomial is a factor of the polynomial $P(x)=2x^2+x-10$.

■ $(x+5)$

−5	2	1	−10
		−10	45
	2	−9	35

$x+5$ is not a factor of $P(x)$.

■ $(x-2)$

2	2	1	−10
		4	10
	2	5	0

$x-2$ is a factor of $P(x)$.

EXERCISES

Determine whether the given binomial is a factor of the polynomial $P(x)$.

31. $(x+3)$; $P(x)=x^3+2x^2-5$

32. $(x-1)$; $P(x)=4x^4-5x^2+3x-2$

33. $(x-2)$; $P(x)=2x^3-3x^2+x-6$

Factor each expression.

34. $x^3-x^2-16x+16$ **35.** $4x^3-8x^2-x+2$

36. $3x^3+81$ **37.** $16x^3-2$

6-5 Finding Real Roots of Polynomial Equations *(pp. 438–444)*

EXAMPLE

- **Identify all of the real roots of $x^4 - 4x^3 + 4x^2 - 1 = 0$.**

By the Rational Root Theorem, possible roots are ± 1.

$$\begin{array}{r|rrrrr} 1 & 1 & -4 & 4 & 0 & -1 \\ & & 1 & -3 & 1 & 1 \\ \hline & 1 & -3 & 1 & 1 & \boxed{0} \end{array} \quad \textit{Try 1.}$$

$$\begin{array}{r|rrrr} 1 & 1 & -3 & 1 & 1 \\ & & 1 & -2 & -1 \\ \hline & 1 & -2 & -1 & \boxed{0} \end{array} \quad \textit{Try 1 again.}$$

Factor $x^2 - 2x - 1$ by using the quadratic formula.

$$x = \frac{-(-2) \pm \sqrt{(-2)^2 - 4(1)(-1)}}{2(1)} = 1 \pm \sqrt{2}$$

The roots are 1 with a multiplicity of 2, and $1 \pm \sqrt{2}$.

EXERCISES

Identify all of the real roots of each equation.

38. $x^3 - 5x^2 + 8x - 4 = 0$
39. $x^3 + 6x^2 + 9x + 2 = 0$
40. $x^3 + 3x^2 + 3x + 1 = 0$
41. $x^4 - 12x^2 + 27 = 0$
42. $x^3 + x^2 - 2x - 2 = 0$
43. $x^3 - 5x^2 + 4 = 0$
44. A rectangular prism has length that is twice its width and height that is 4 meters longer than its width. The volume of the rectangular prism is 48 cubic meters. What is the width of the rectangular prism?

6-6 Fundamental Theorem of Algebra *(pp. 445–451)*

EXAMPLES

- **Write the simplest polynomial function with roots −2, −1, and 4.**

$P(x) = 0$ — *If r is a root of P(x), then x − r is a factor of P(x).*

$a(x + 2)(x + 1)(x - 4) = 0$

$a(x^3 - x^2 - 10x - 8) = 0$ — *Multiply. For the simplest equation, let a = 1.*

$x^3 - x^2 - 10x - 8 = 0$

- **Solve $x^3 + 2x^2 + x + 2 = 0$ by finding all roots.**

The graphing calculator shows −2 as a root. Use synthetic division to write the equation as $(x + 2)(x^2 + 1) = 0$. Solve $x^2 + 1 = 0$ to find the remaining roots. The solutions are −2, i, and $-i$.

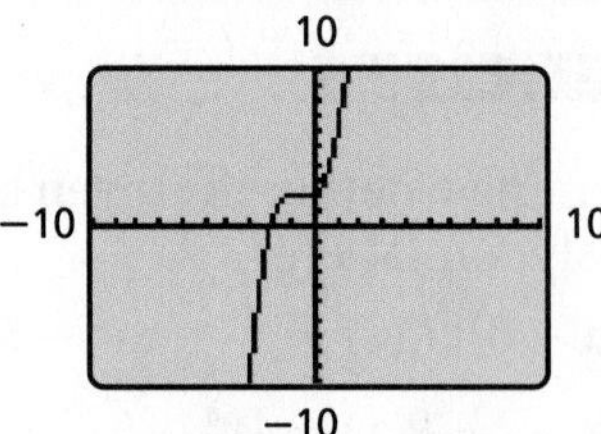

EXERCISES

Write the simplest polynomial function with the given roots.

45. −3, 2, 4
46. $-\frac{1}{2}$, −2, 3
47. $-\sqrt{2}$, −1
48. −3, i
49. $\sqrt{2}, \sqrt{3}$
50. $1 + \sqrt{3}$, $2i$

Solve the equation by finding all roots.

51. $x^3 - x^2 + 4x - 4 = 0$
52. $x^4 - x^2 - 2 = 0$
53. $x^4 - \frac{63}{4}x^2 - 4 = 0$
54. $x^3 + 3x^2 - 5x - 15 = 0$

6-7 Investigating Graphs of Polynomial Functions *(pp. 453–459)*

EXAMPLE

- **Graph the function $f(x) = x^3 + 2x^2 - 5x - 6$.**

  Leading coefficient: 1; Degree: 3;
  End behavior: $x \to -\infty, f(x) \to -\infty$
  $x \to +\infty, f(x) \to +\infty$

  The zeros are $-3, -1, 2$. *Factor to find the zeros.*

  $f(0) = -6; f(-2) = 4; f(1) = -8$ *Evaluate f(x) at values between the roots. Plot these points.*

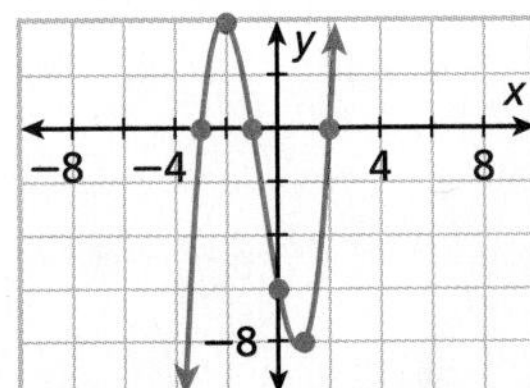

EXERCISES

Identify the leading coefficient, degree, and end behavior.

55. $-2x^3 + 5x^2 + 3$

56. $x^4 + 2x^3 - 3x + 1$

57. $-3x^6 + 9x^3 - 2x - 9$

58. $7x^5 + x^4 - 2x^2 + 5$

Graph each function.

59. $f(x) = x^3 - x^2 - 5x + 6$

60. $f(x) = x^4 - 10x^2 + 9$

61. $f(x) = -x^3 + 5x^2 + x - 5$

6-8 Transforming Polynomial Functions *(pp. 460–465)*

EXAMPLE

- **Write a function that transforms $f(x) = x^3 + 5$ by reflecting it across the x-axis and shifting it 2 units right. Support your solution by using a graphing calculator.**

  $g(x) = -f(x - 2)$

  $g(x) = -(x - 2)^3 - 5$

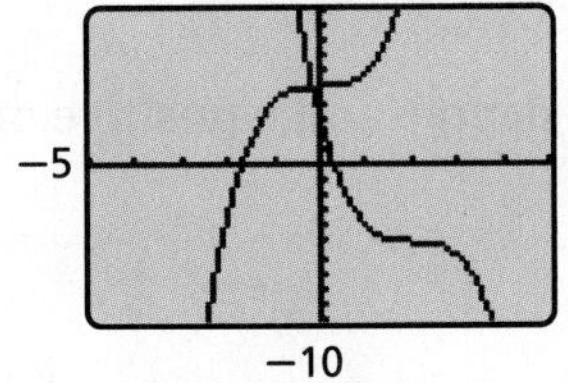

EXERCISES

Write a function that transforms $f(x) = x^4 - 6x^2 - 4$ in each of the following ways. Support your solution by using a graphing calculator.

62. Stretch vertically by a factor of 2, and move 9 units up.

63. Move 2 units down, and reflect across the x-axis.

64. Move 3 units right, and reflect across the y-axis.

6-9 Curve Fitting with Polynomial Models *(pp. 466–471)*

EXAMPLE

- **The table shows the profit for a company in thousands of dollars for the years shown. Write a polynomial function for the data.**

Year	1999	2000	2001	2002	2003
Profits	\$286	\$401	\$507	\$671	\$960

First differences: 115 106 164 289
Second differences: −9 58 125
Third differences: 67 67 *Constant*
A cubic polynomial best describes the data. Use the cubic regression feature on your graphing calculator.

$f(x) = 11.17x^3 - 38x^2 + 141.3x + 286$

EXERCISES

65. The chart shows the attendance for a new movie theater over five days. Write a polynomial function for the data.

Day	1	2	3	4	5
Attendance	248	298	318	388	428

66. The chart shows the population of a city for five years. Write a polynomial function for the data.

Year	1	2	3	4	5
Population (thousands)	1891	2674	3376	4480	6469

CHAPTER 6

CHAPTER TEST

Add or subtract. Write your answer in standard form.

1. $(3x^2 - x + 1) + (x)$
2. $(6x^3 - 3x + 2) - (7x^3 + 3x + 7)$
3. $(y^2 + 3y^2 + 2) + (y^4 + y^3 - y^2 + 5)$
4. $(4x^4 + x^2) - (x^3 - x^2 - 1)$
5. The cost of producing x units of a product can be modeled by $C(x) = \frac{1}{10}x^3 - x^2 + 25$. Evaluate $C(x)$ for $x = 15$, and describe what the value represents.

Find each product.

6. $xy(2x^4y + x^2y^2 - 3xy^3)$
7. $(t + 3)(2t^2 - t + 3)$
8. $(x + 5)^3$
9. $(2y + 3)^4$

Divide.

10. $(5x^2 - 6x - 8) \div (x - 2)$
11. $(2x^3 - 7x^2 + 9x - 4) \div (2x - 1)$
12. Use synthetic substitution to evaluate $x^4 + 3x^3 - x^2 + 2x - 6$ for $x = 3$.

Factor each expression.

13. $-2x^2 - 6x + 56$
14. $m^5 + m^4 - 625m - 625$
15. $4x^3 - 32$
16. Identify the roots of the equation $2x^4 - 9x^3 + 7x^2 + 2x - 2 = 0$. State the multiplicity of each root.
17. Write the simplest polynomial function with roots of 1, 4, and -5.

Identify whether the function graphed has an odd or even degree and a positive or negative leading coefficient.

18.

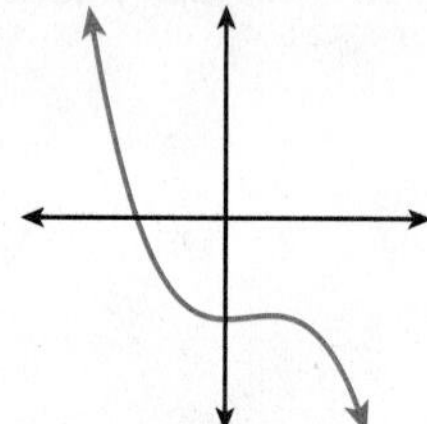

19.

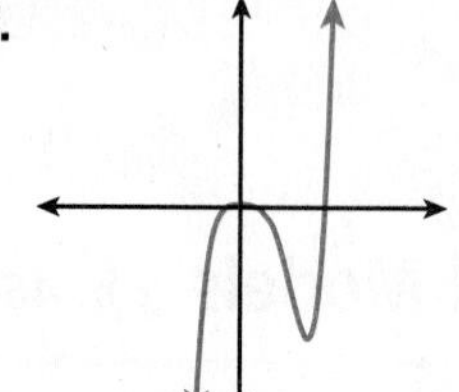

20.

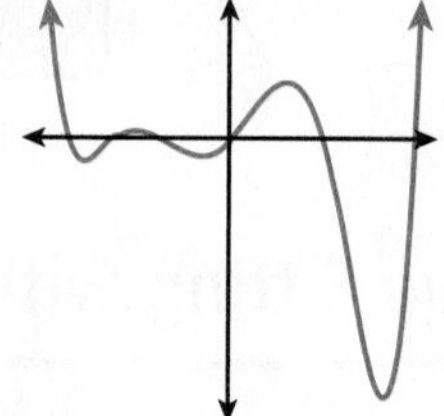

Let $f(x) = 12x^3 + 4$. Graph $f(x)$ and $g(x)$ on the same coordinate plane. Describe $g(x)$ as a transformation of $f(x)$.

21. $g(x) = f(-x)$
22. $g(x) = \frac{1}{2}f(x)$
23. $g(x) = -f(x) + 3$
24. The table shows the number of bracelets Carly can make over time. Write a polynomial function for the data.

Time (h)	1	2	3	4	5	6
Bracelets	3	5	11	21	35	53

25. The table shows the number of sandwiches sold each day at a deli over 5 days. Write a polynomial function for the data.

Day	1	2	3	4	5
Sandwiches	57	72	101	89	66

College Entrance Exam Practice

FOCUS ON SAT MATHEMATICS SUBJECT TESTS

SAT Mathematics Subject Test results include scaled scores and percentiles. Your scaled score is a number from 200 to 800, calculated by using a formula that varies. The percentile indicates the percentage of people who took the same test and scored lower than you did.

You may want to time yourself as you take this practice test. It should take you about 7 minutes to complete.

The questions are written so that you should not need to do any lengthy calculations. If you find yourself getting involved in a long calculation, think again about all of the information in the problem to see if you might have missed something helpful.

1. If $x^4 - 7x^3 - 24x^2 + 112x + 128$ has a rational root a. Which could NOT be the value of a?

(A) 0

(B) 16

(C) 24

(D) 32

(E) 64

2. If there is a remainder of 3 when you divide $p(x) = x^3 + 4x^2 - hx + 30$ by $x - 3$, what is the value of h?

(A) -90

(B) 4

(C) 12

(D) 27

(E) 30

3. The graph of $q(x) = ax^4 + bx^3 + cx^2 + dx + f$ is shown below. Which of the following is true?

(A) $q(x)$ has an odd degree.

(B) $q(x) = (x + 3)h(x)$ for some polynomial $h(x)$.

(C) $f > 0$

(D) $q(0)$ is a local minimum.

(E) $q(x) \to \infty$ as $x \to \infty$

4. Which of the following is the expanded form of $(3x + 2)^3$?

(A) $9x + 6$

(B) $27x^3 + 8$

(C) $27x^3 + 90x + 8$

(D) $27x^3 + 60x^2 + 30x + 8$

(E) $27x^3 + 54x^2 + 36x + 8$

5. If $f(x)$ is a polynomial, which of the following transformations may affect the number of zeros of $f(x)$?

(A) Reflecting $f(x)$ across the y-axis

(B) Reflecting $f(x)$ across the x-axis

(C) Translating $f(x)$ 2 units to the right

(D) Translating $f(x)$ 6 units down

(E) Vertically stretching by a factor of 2

6. Which of the following is a possible root of the polynomial $16x^4 + 80x^3 - 191x^2 + 8x + 15$?

(A) $\frac{1}{12}$

(B) $\frac{1}{5}$

(C) $\frac{3}{8}$

(D) $\frac{3}{5}$

(E) $\frac{8}{3}$

TEST TACKLER

Standardized Test Strategies

Any Question Type: Identify Key Words and Context Clues

When reading a test item, you should pay attention to key words and context clues in the problem statement. These clues will help you provide a correct response.

EXAMPLE 1

Short Response

Write a polynomial in standard form for the volume of the rectangular prism. Find the volume when $x = 5$ inches.

Look *for key words and context clues. Identify what they mean.*

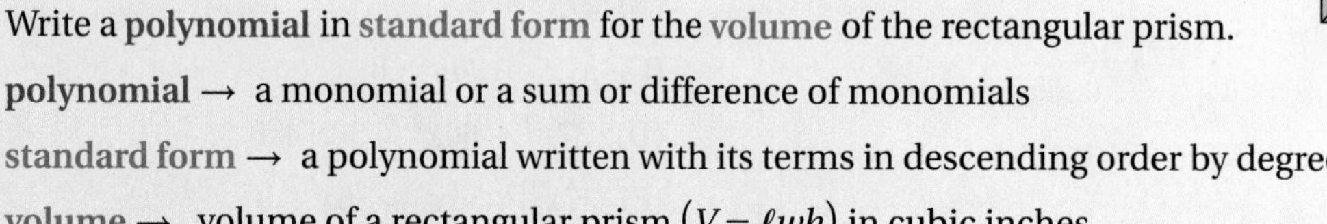

Write a **polynomial** in **standard form** for the **volume** of the rectangular prism.

polynomial → a monomial or a sum or difference of monomials

standard form → a polynomial written with its terms in descending order by degree

volume → volume of a rectangular prism ($V = \ell wh$) in cubic inches

$V(x) = x(x+1)(x+2) = x^3 + 3x^2 + 2x \leftarrow$ **Standard form**

$V(5) = 5^3 + 3(5^2) + 2(5) = 125 + 75 + 10 = 210$ cubic inches

The volume of the prism can be represented by $V(x) = x^3 + 3x^2 + 2x$, and when $x = 5$, $V = 210$ cubic inches.

EXAMPLE 2

Multiple Choice

Paige runs a small jewelry business. From 2000 through 2005, the number of items she created can be modeled by $24x + 12$, and the average cost to make each item can be modeled by $-0.05x^2 + 10$, where x is the number of years since 2000. Which polynomial can be used to model Paige's total jewelry-making costs for those years?

(A) $-0.05x^2 + 24x + 22$

(B) $0.05x^2 + 24x + 2$

(C) $-12x^3 - 6x^2 + 240x + 120$

(D) $-1.2x^3 - 0.6x^2 + 240x + 120$

The key words in this test item are **total cost.**

total cost → average cost per unit times the number of units

$= -0.05x^2 + 10 \quad \times \quad 24x + 12$

$= -1.2x^3 - 0.6x^2 + 240x + 120$

The correct answer is choice D.

If you do not understand what a word means, reread the sentences around the word and make a logical guess.

Read each test item and answer the questions that follow.

Item A

Short Response A box can be made by cutting squares from each of the four corners of a piece of cardboard. The volume of a box made from a 27.5-by-40-centimeter piece of cardboard can be modeled by $x(27.5 - 2x)(40 - 2x)$, where x is the length of one side of the square. Write the volume as a sum of monomials, and find the volume when $x = 5$ centimeters.

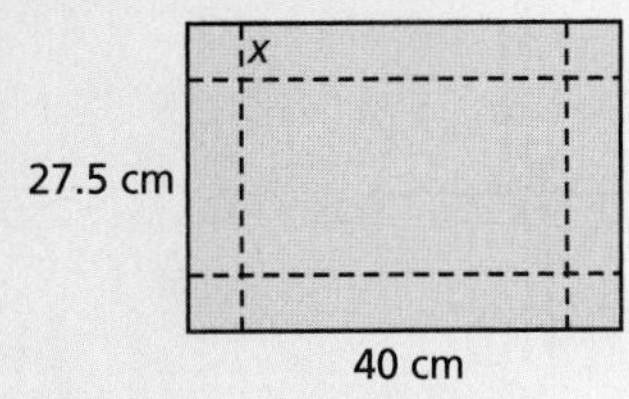

1. What do $(27.5 - 2x)$ and $(40 - 2x)$ represent in the model?
2. Describe what "sum of monomials" means.
3. When you calculate the volume for $x = 5$, in what units should you give your response?

Item B

Short Response The volume of a cylindrical tank with a hemispherical top and bottom can be represented by the function $V(r) = 24\pi r^2 + \frac{4}{3}\pi r^3$, where V is the volume in cubic meters and r is the radius in meters. What is the radius if the volume of the tank is 5760π cubic meters?

4. Which word(s) in the problem statement tells you that the volume of a sphere is part of the function?
5. What does the term $24\pi r^2$ in the function represent?
6. Describe how to find the radius given the volume of the tank.

Item C

Multiple Choice Which description matches the transformation from f to g shown?

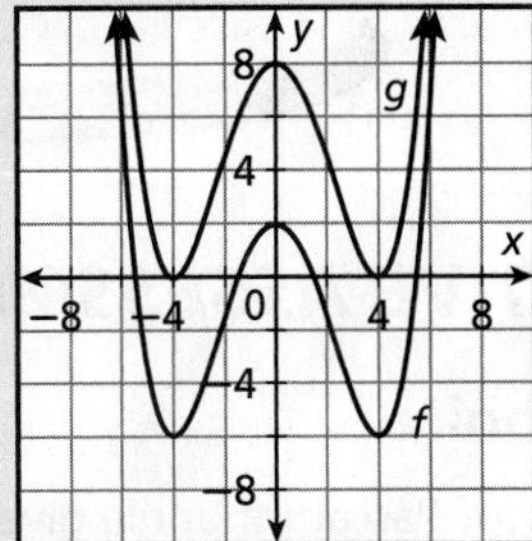

Ⓐ Vertical shift of 3 units

Ⓑ Vertical stretch by a factor of 3

Ⓒ Horizontal shift of 3 units

Ⓓ Horizontal stretch by a factor of 3

7. How do you know which is the original function and which is the image of the function?
8. Because the graphs are shown with an x- and y-scale of 1, how can you use the grid to identify a shift of 3 units?

Item D

Gridded Response A rectangular storage compartment has a length equal to its width and a height that is 5 feet greater than its width. The volume of the compartment is 72 cubic feet. What is the width?

9. Make a list of the key words given in the problem statement, and link each word to its mathematical meaning.
10. Write expressions representing the length and height of the compartment in terms of width.
11. Write an expression for the volume of the compartment.

CHAPTER 6

STANDARDIZED TEST PREP

go.hrw.com
State Test Practice Online
KEYWORD: MB7 TestPrep

CUMULATIVE ASSESSMENT, CHAPTERS 1–6

Multiple Choice

1. Which row of Pascal's triangle gives the coefficients for the binomial expansion of $(a + b)^4$?

(A) 1 2 1

(B) 1 3 3 1

(C) 1 4 6 4 1

(D) 1 5 10 10 5 1

2. Which binomial is a factor of $2x^4 - 11x^3 + 19x^2 - 13x + 3$?

(F) $x - 2$ (H) $x + 1$

(G) $x - 3$ (J) $x + 2$

3. Which graph shows the ordered triple $(-3, 3, -4)$ graphed in a three-dimensional coordinate plane?

(A)

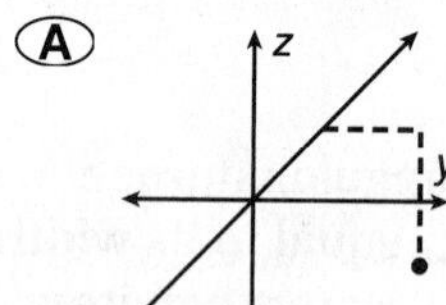

(B)

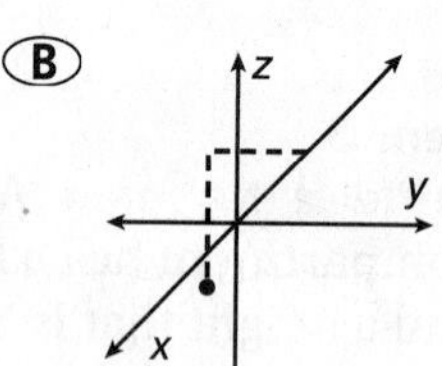

(C)

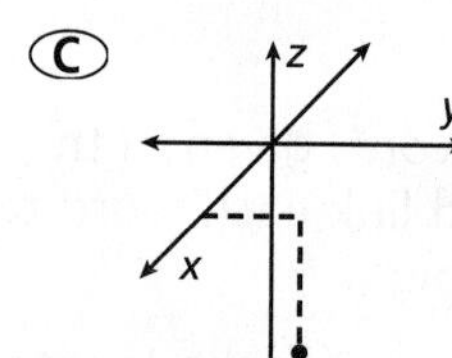

(D)

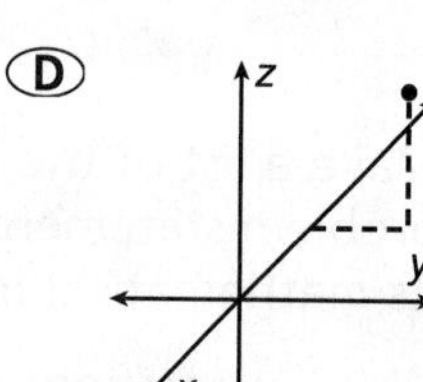

4. What is the value of the y-intercept of $2x + 4y = 1$?

(F) $\frac{1}{4}$ (H) 1

(G) $-\frac{1}{2}$ (J) -2

5. Simplify $\frac{4 - i}{1 + 3i}$.

(A) $\frac{2}{5} - \frac{1}{10}i$ (B) $\frac{1}{10} - \frac{13}{10}i$

(C) $\frac{7}{10} + \frac{11}{10}i$ (D) $4 - \frac{1}{3}i$

6. Which graph represents an odd degree polynomial function with a positive leading coefficient?

(F)

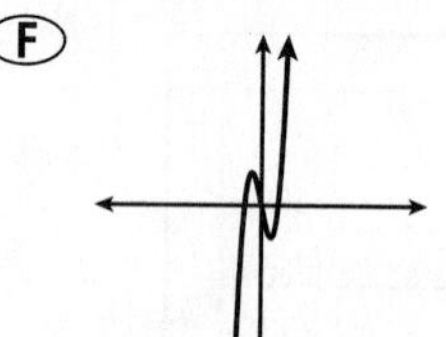

(G)

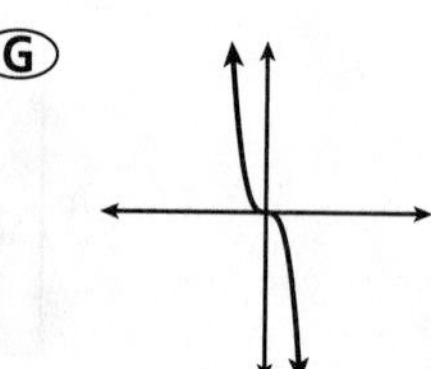

(H)

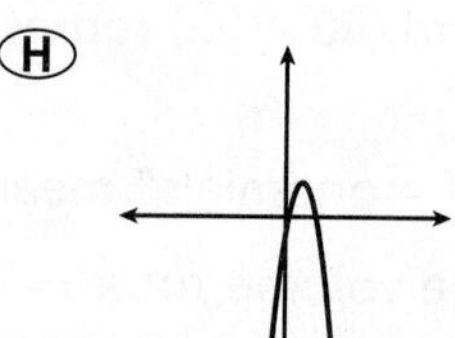

(J)

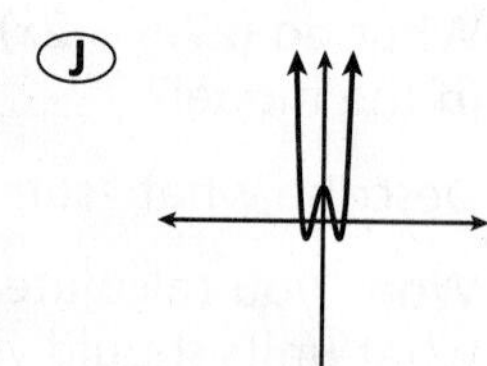

7. What are the domain and range of the polynomial function shown in the graph?

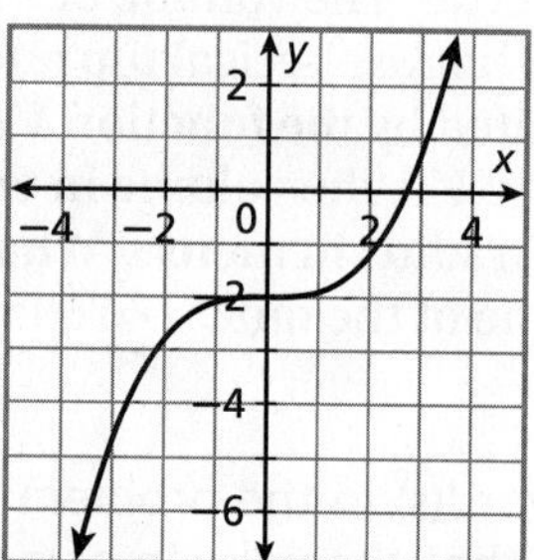

(A) D: $\mathbb{R}$; R: $\mathbb{R}$

(B) D: $\mathbb{R}$; R: $\{y \mid y \geq -2\}$

(C) D: $\{x \mid x \geq -4\}$; R: $\mathbb{R}$

(D) D: $\{x \mid x \geq 4\}$; R: $\{y \mid y \geq -2\}$

Use matrix N for Items 8 and 9.

$$N = \begin{bmatrix} 2 & -1 \\ 4 & -3 \end{bmatrix}$$

8. What is the value of entry n_{21}?

(F) 2

(G) −3

(H) 4

(J) −6

9. Find the inverse of matrix N.

(A) $\begin{bmatrix} 2 & -1 \\ \frac{3}{2} & -\frac{1}{2} \end{bmatrix}$

(C) $\begin{bmatrix} \frac{3}{2} & -2 \\ 2 & -1 \end{bmatrix}$

(B) $\begin{bmatrix} \frac{3}{2} & -\frac{1}{2} \\ 2 & -1 \end{bmatrix}$

(D) $\begin{bmatrix} 2 & -1 \\ \frac{3}{2} & -2 \end{bmatrix}$

In Item 10, use the end behavior of the graph to identify the sign of the leading coefficent and eliminate answer choices. Then use the *y*-intercept to choose the correct response.

10. What is the equation of the parabola shown?

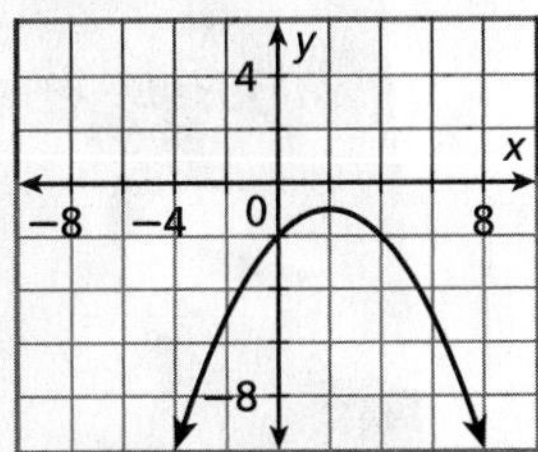

(F) $f(x) = 0.25x^2 + x - 2$

(G) $f(x) = 0.25x^2 - x - 2$

(H) $f(x) = -0.25x^2 + x + 2$

(J) $f(x) = -0.25x^2 + x - 2$

Gridded Response

11. What is the degree of the polynomial $7x^4 + 3x^2 - x^6 + 4$?

12. Divide by using long division. Identify the numerator of the remainder.

$$(2x^5 + 6x^4 - 10x^3 - 2x^2 + 54x + 14) \div (x - 4)$$

13. Complete the square for the expression $x^2 - 3x + ■$.

Short Response

14. The table below shows the number of spyware traces detected and removed from Larry's computer from January to June.

Jan	Feb	Mar	Apr	May	Jun
120	395	545	220	145	130

a. Write a cubic function for the data.

b. Using your answer to part **a**, about how many traces can Larry expect to find in July?

15. Consider $5x^3 + 5x^2 - 40x - 60 = 0$.

a. Identify the roots of the equation.

b. State the multiplicity of each root. Explain what the multiplicity means in terms of the graph.

16. Write the simplest polynomial function with zeros −1, 3, and 4.

17. Use synthetic substitution to evaluate $f(x) = x^3 + 5x^2 - 4x - 20$ for $x = -2$ and $x = 3$.

Extended Response

18. The functions g and h are the result of transformations of the function f.

a. $f(x) = x^3 - 5x^2 + 8x - 1$ is reflected across the x-axis to produce $g(x)$. Write the equation for $g(x)$.

b. Use a graphing calculator to graph f and g. Explain how the graph supports your answer to part **a**.

c. $f(x) = 4(x + 1)^3 + 4$ is translated 1 unit to the right and 3 units down to produce $h(x)$. Write the equation for $h(x)$.

d. Use a graphing calculator to graph f and h. Explain how the graph supports your answer to part **c**.

Real-World CONNECTIONS

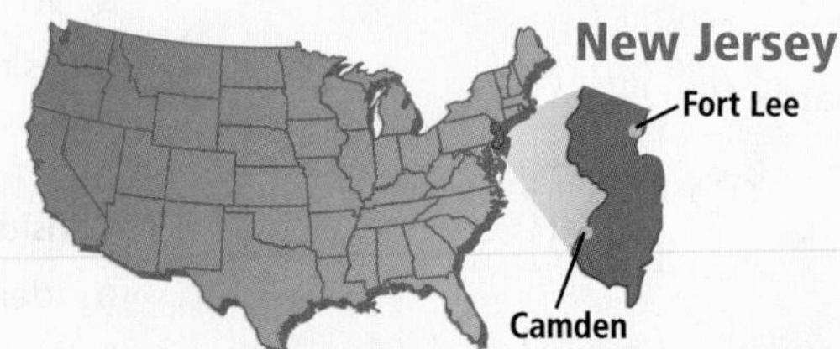

The Camden Waterfront

Located along the Delaware River, the Camden Waterfront offers a variety of attractions, including the Camden Riversharks minor league baseball team and the former home of poet Walt Whitman. The waterfront's most popular destination is the interactive Adventure Aquarium, which features two huge tanks: a 760,000-gallon open tank and a two-story, 550,000-gallon shark tank.

Choose one or more strategies to solve each problem. For 1 and 2, use the table.

Adventure Aquarium		
Tank	**Volume (gal)**	**Volume (m³)**
Open Ocean	760,000	2877
Shark Realm	550,000	2082

1. The volume of a cylindrical tank can be modeled by the function $V(h) = \pi(h^3 + 6h^2 + 9h)$, where h is the tank's height in meters. Use this model to find the height of the Open Ocean tank.
2. The Shark Realm tank has a viewing tunnel along its length. The volume of the tank can be modeled by $V(\ell) = \ell(\ell - 3.2)(\ell + 6.8)$, where ℓ is the tank's length in meters. What is the length of the viewing tunnel?
3. The children's garden at the Camden Waterfront includes a 1200-square-foot room where visitors can walk among hundreds of flying butterflies. During one month of the year, the population of butterflies is modeled by $P(x) = 0.026x^3 - 1.3x^2 + 15.3x + 200$, where x is the number of days since the beginning of the month. What is the maximum population of butterflies during the month?

The George Washington Bridge

When the George Washington Bridge opened to traffic in 1931, it was the world's longest suspension bridge. Since then, it has been eclipsed by longer spans, but it remains one of the world's busiest bridges. On a typical day, more than 300,000 vehicles use the bridge to cross the Hudson River between Upper Manhattan and Fort Lee, New Jersey.

Choose one or more strategies to solve each problem.

1. The height in feet of the main cable above the roadway can be modeled by the equation $h = \frac{2}{15625}(x - 1750)^2$, where x is the distance in feet from the west tower. Find the height of the west tower.
2. The cable touches the roadway at the midpoint between the two towers. What is the length of the span between the towers?
3. The distance d traveled by a vehicle moving at an initial velocity of v_0 mi/h with a constant acceleration of a mi/h^2 is given by $d = \frac{1}{2}at^2 + v_0t$, where t is the time in hours. Given that the George Washington Bridge is 0.9 mi long, how long does it take a motorist to cross the bridge if she enters the bridge at 50 mi/h and accelerates at 10 mi/h^2?

For 4, use the table.

4. The table shows the average hourly volume of eastbound traffic into Manhattan. Use a quadratic model to predict the hourly volume of traffic during the rush-hour peak from 6:00 A.M. to 7:00 A.M.

George Washington Bridge, Eastbound

Hour	Average Vehicular Volume
3:00 A.M. to 4:00 A.M.	1274
4:00 A.M. to 5:00 A.M.	2035
5:00 A.M. to 6:00 A.M.	5581

Real-World Connections

CHAPTER 7

Exponential and Logarithmic Functions

Chapter Focus

- Communicate the relationship between exponential and logarithmic functions.
- Solve problems using exponential and logarithmic functions.

MEET "*e*" IN ST. LOUIS

The Gateway Arch is the tallest national monument. Its shape is a *catenary*. You will examine features of catenaries in the Chapter 7 project.

go.hrw.com
Chapter Project Online
KEYWORD: MB7 ChProj

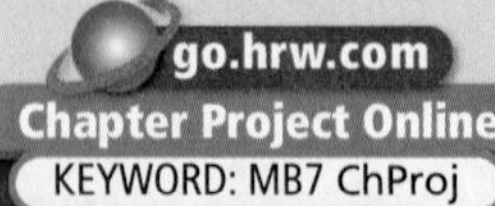

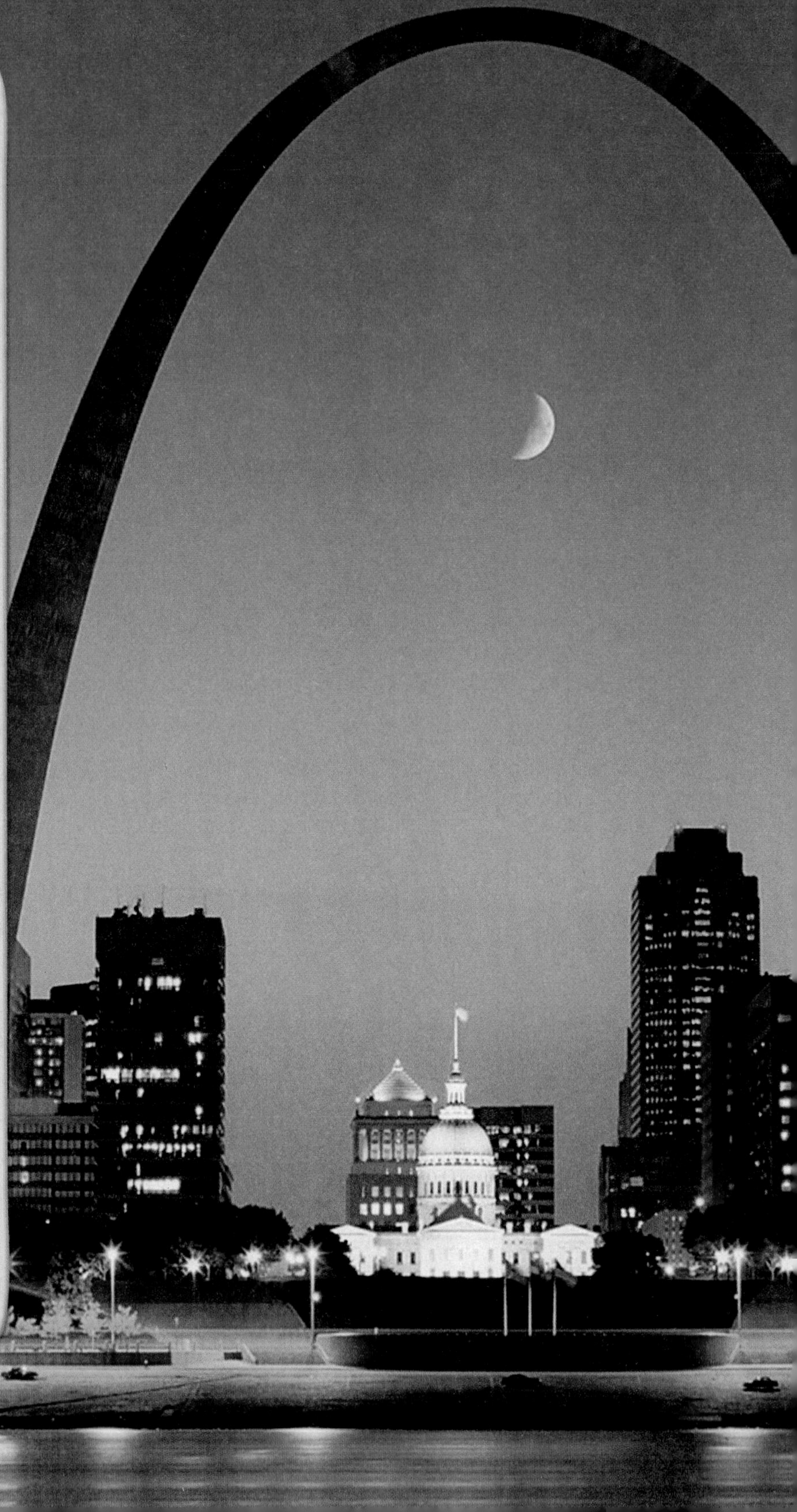

ARE YOU READY?

Vocabulary

Match each term on the left with a definition on the right.

1. exponent
2. function
3. relation
4. variable

A. a symbol used to represent one or more numbers
B. the set of counting numbers and their opposites
C. a relation with at most one y-value for each x-value
D. the number of times the base of a power is used as a factor
E. a set of ordered pairs

Properties of Exponents

Simplify each expression. Assume all variables are positive.

5. $x^2(x^3)(x)$
6. $3y^{-1}(5x^2y^2)$
7. $\dfrac{a^8}{a^2}$
8. $y^{15} \div y^{10}$
9. $\dfrac{x^2y^5}{xy^6}$
10. $\left(\dfrac{x}{3}\right)^{-3}$
11. $(3x)^2(4x^3)$
12. $\dfrac{a^{-2}b^3}{a^4b^{-1}}$

Simple Interest

Use the simple interest formula, $I = Prt$, where I is the interest, P is the initial amount (the principal), and r is the interest rate for Problems 13–15.

13. Find the simple interest on an investment of \$3000 at 3% for 2 years.
14. A savings account of \$2000 earned \$90 simple interest in 3 years. Find the interest rate.
15. Jeri got a loan at 6% simple interest for 3 years. She paid back a total of \$5310. How much was the loan?

Solve for a Variable

Solve each equation for x.

16. $3x - y = 4$
17. $y = -7x + 3$
18. $\dfrac{x}{2} = 3y - 4$
19. $y = \dfrac{3}{4}x - \dfrac{1}{2}$

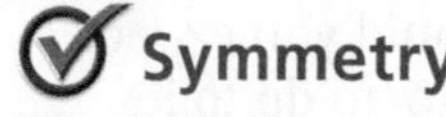

Symmetry

20. Copy the graph, and use the line of symmetry to complete the figure.

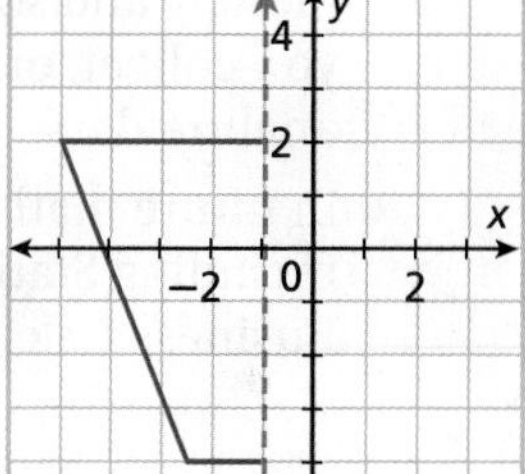

Scientific Notation

Write in scientific notation.

21. 7,000,000,000
22. 0.0000000093
23. 16.75

Write in standard notation.

24. 9.4×10^{-6}
25. 4.7×10^{5}
26. 7.8×10^{4}

CHAPTER 7

Study Guide: Preview

Where You've Been

Previously, you

- used the properties of exponents to simplify expressions.
- performed inverse operations.
- solved problems involving linear, quadratic, and polynomial functions.

In This Chapter

You will study

- exponential functions.
- logarithms, the inverse of exponents, and logarithmic functions.
- solving problems involving exponents and logarithms.

Where You're Going

You can use the skills in this chapter

- to solve problems involving compound interest.
- in scientific fields such as biology and sociology where you collect, organize, and analyze data.
- in future math classes, including Statistics and Business Calculus.

Key Vocabulary/Vocabulario

asymptote	asíntota
base	base
common logarithm	logaritmo común
exponential equation	ecuación exponencial
inverse function	función inversa
logarithmic equation	ecuación logarítmica
logarithmic function	función logarítmica
natural logarithm	logaritmo natural

Vocabulary Connections

To become familiar with some of the vocabulary terms in the chapter, consider the following. You may refer to the chapter, the glossary, or a dictionary if you like.

1. You can think of the **base** as carrying its exponent. Which number in $10^3 = 1000$ is the base?
2. A logarithm is an exponent. The base for common logarithms is 10. What would you think would be the **common logarithm** of 1000?
3. Where would you expect to find the variable x in an **exponential equation**?
4. Multiplication and division are *inverse functions.* What would you expect an **inverse function** to do to its corresponding function?
5. The base of a **natural logarithm** is the number e. What are other constant values that are often named by a letter or symbol?
6. The Greek word *asymptōtos* means "not meeting." How do you think a line on a graph called an **asymptote** would relate to a curve on a graph?

Writing Strategy: Use Your Own Words

When studying a difficult mathematical concept, rewrite the concept using your own words so that you can better comprehend the material. You may also find it helpful to provide your own example.

The **degree of a polynomial** is given by the term with the greatest degree. A polynomial with one variable is in standard form when its terms are written in descending order by degree. So, in standard form, the degree of the first term indicates the degree of the polynomial, and the **leading coefficient** is the coefficient of the first term.

REWRITE the above paragraph with short phrases and sentences to clarify important concepts about polynomials.

Polynomials:

1. The term with the highest degree gives the degree of the polynomial.
2. Standard form—terms are in decreasing order of degree.
3. In standard form, the degree of the first term is the degree of the polynomial.
4. The coefficient of the first term is called the leading coefficient.

INCLUDE an example to connect the words and the mathematics.

Example:
Standard form: $2x^4 - 5x^3 + 3x^2 - 9x + 10$

Leading coefficient: 2
Degree of polynomial: 4

Read the following paragraph from Lesson 6-5, and rewrite it using your own words.

The Irrational Root Theorem states that irrational roots come in conjugate pairs. For example, if you know that $1 + \sqrt{2}$ is a root of $x^3 - x^2 - 3x - 1 = 0$, then you know that $1 - \sqrt{2}$ is also a root.

Recall that the real numbers are made up of the rational and the irrational numbers. You can use the Rational Root Theorem and the Irrational Root Theorem together to find *all* of the real roots of $P(x) = 0$.

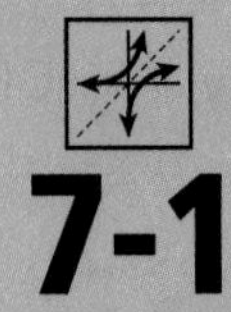

7-1 Exponential Functions, Growth, and Decay

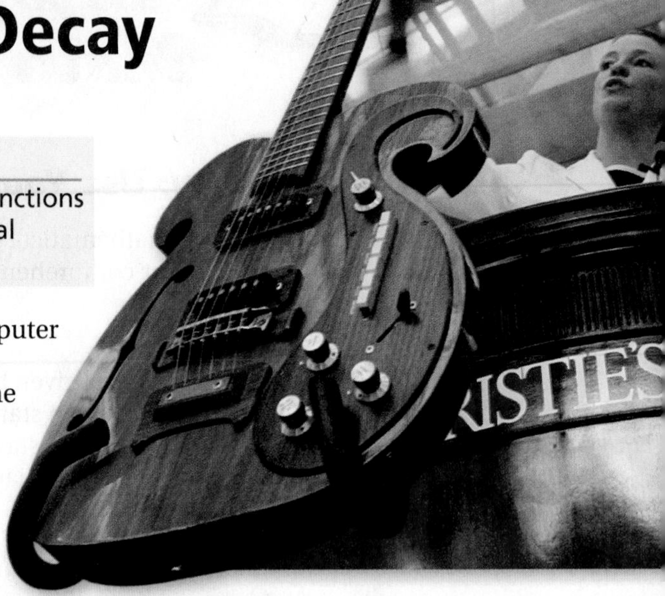

Objective
Write and evaluate exponential expressions to model growth and decay situations.

Vocabulary
exponential function
base
asymptote
exponential growth
exponential decay

Who uses this?
Collectors can use exponential functions to model the value of rare musical instruments. (See Example 2.)

Moore's law, a rule used in the computer industry, states that the number of transistors per integrated circuit (the processing power) doubles every year. Beginning in the early days of integrated circuits, the growth in capacity may be approximated by this table.

Transistors per Integrated Chip

Year	1965	1966	1967	1968	1969	1970	1971
Transistors	60	120	240	480	960	1920	3840

×2 ×2 ×2 ×2 ×2 ×2

Remember!
In the function $y = b^x$, y is a function of x because the value of y *depends* on the value of x.

Growth that doubles every year can be modeled by using a function with a variable as an exponent. This function is known as an *exponential function*. The parent **exponential function** is $f(x) = b^x$, where the **base** b is a constant and the exponent x is the independent variable.

Base Exponent

$$f(x) = b^x, \text{ where } b > 0, b \neq 1$$

The graph of the parent function $f(x) = 2^x$ is shown. The domain is all real numbers and the range is $\{y \mid y > 0\}$.

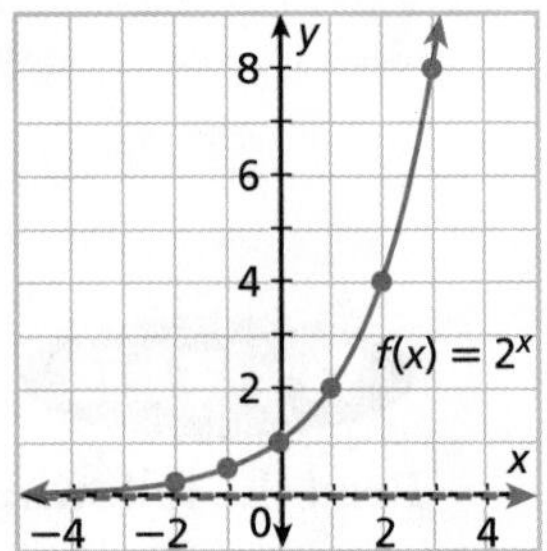

x	−2	−1	0	1	2	3
$f(x) = 2^x$	$\frac{1}{4}$	$\frac{1}{2}$	1	2	4	8

Notice that as the x-values decrease, the graph of the function gets closer and closer to the x-axis. The function never reaches the x-axis because the value of 2^x cannot be zero. In this case, the x-axis is an *asymptote*. An **asymptote** is a line that a graphed function approaches as the value of x gets very large or very small.

A function of the form $f(x) = ab^x$, with $a > 0$ and $b > 1$, is an **exponential growth** function, which increases as x increases. When $0 < b < 1$, the function is called an **exponential decay** function, which decreases as x increases.

EXAMPLE 1 Graphing Exponential Functions

Tell whether the function shows growth or decay. Then graph.

A $f(x) = 1.5^x$

Step 1 Find the value of the base.

$f(x) = 1.5^x$ *The base, 1.5, is greater than 1. This is an exponential growth function.*

Step 2 Graph the function by using a table of values.

x	−2	−1	0	1	2	3	4
$f(x)$	0.4	0.7	1	1.5	2.3	3.4	5.1

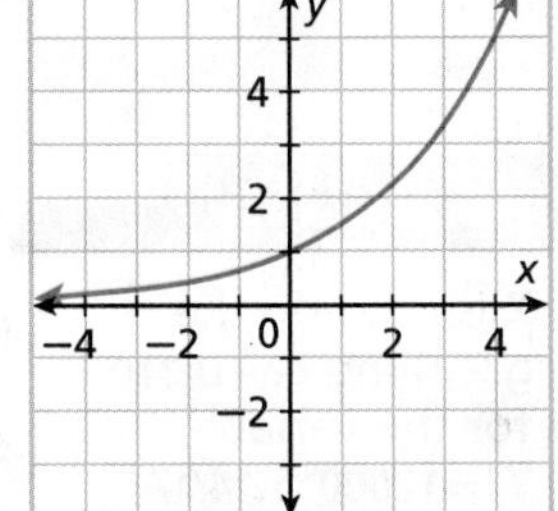

B $g(x) = 30(0.8^x)$

Step 1 Find the value of the base.

$g(x) = 30(0.8^x)$ *The base, 0.8, is less than 1. This is an exponential decay function.*

Step 2 Graph the function by using a graphing calculator.

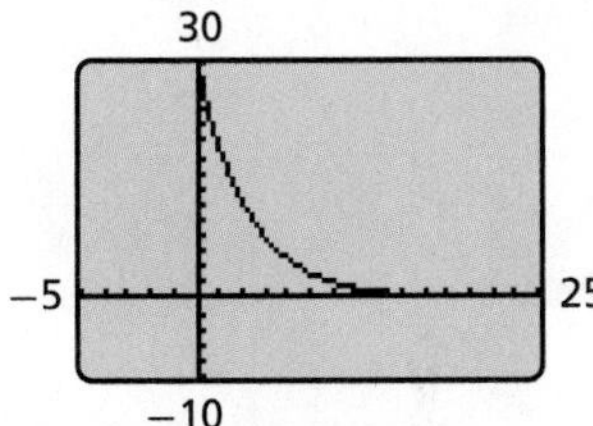

Remember!

Negative exponents indicate a reciprocal. For example:

$x^{-2} = \frac{1}{x^2}$

CHECK IT OUT! **1.** Tell whether the function $p(x) = 5(1.2^x)$ shows growth or decay. Then graph.

You can model growth or decay by a constant percent increase or decrease with the following formula:

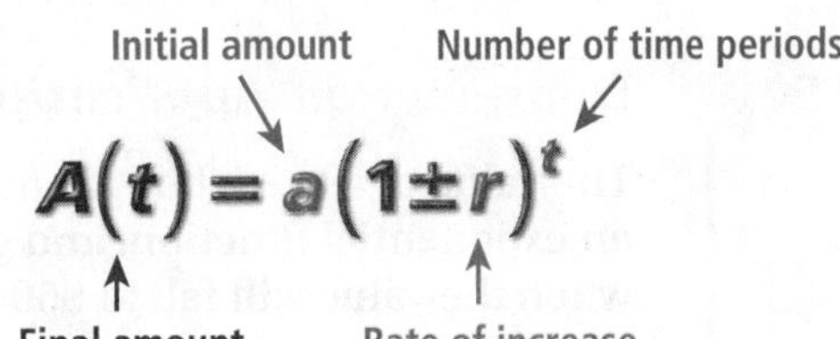

In the formula, the base of the exponential expression, $1 + r$, is called the *growth factor*. Similarly, $1 - r$ is the *decay factor*.

Student to Student

Growth and Decay

Angela Jones, Independence High School

*When a function **increases** by a constant rate, such as 7%, this is the same as multiplying by 100% + 7%, or 107% .*

In decimal form, I would multiply by 1 + 0.07, or 1.07.

*When a function **decreases** by a constant rate, such as 12%, this is the same as multiplying by 100% − 12%, or 88% .*

In decimal form, it's (1 − 0.12), or 0.88.

EXAMPLE 2 Economics Application

Tony purchased a rare 1959 Gibson Les Paul guitar in 2000 for $12,000. Experts estimate that its value will increase by 14% per year. Use a graph to find when the value of the guitar will be $60,000.

Step 1 Write a function to model the growth in value for this guitar.

$f(t) = a(1 + r)^t$ — *Exponential growth function*

$= 12{,}000(1 + 0.14)^t$ — *Substitute 12,000 for a and 0.14 for r.*

$= 12{,}000(1.14)^t$

Helpful Hint

X is used on the graphing calculator for the variable t: **Y1=12000*1.14^X**

Step 2 Graph the function.

When graphing exponential functions in an appropriate domain, you may need to adjust the range a few times to show the key points.

Step 3 Use the graph to predict when the value of the guitar will reach $60,000.

Use the TRACE feature to find the t-value where $f(t) \approx 60{,}000$.

The function value is approximately 60,000 when $t \approx 12.29$. The guitar will be worth $60,000 about 12.29 years after it is purchased, or sometime in 2012.

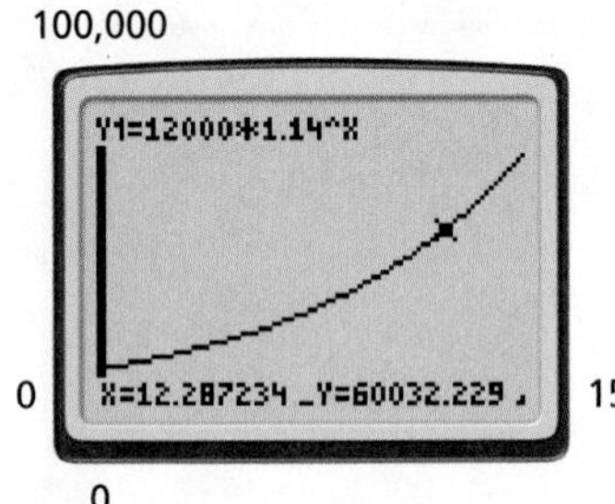

2. In 1981, the Australian humpback whale population was 350 and has increased at a rate of about 14% each year since then. Write a function to model population growth. Use a graph to predict when the population will reach 20,000.

EXAMPLE 3 Depreciation Application

The value of a truck bought new for $28,000 decreases 9.5% each year. Write an exponential function, and graph the function. Use the graph to predict when the value will fall to $5000.

Write a function to model the growth in value for this truck.

$f(x) = a(1 - r)^t$ — *Exponential decay function*

$= 28{,}000(1 - 0.095)^t$ — *Substitute 28,000 for a and 0.095 for r.*

$= 28{,}000(0.905)^t$ — *Simplify.*

Graph the function. Use TRACE to find when the value of the truck will fall below $5000.

It will take about 17.3 years for the value to drop to $5000.

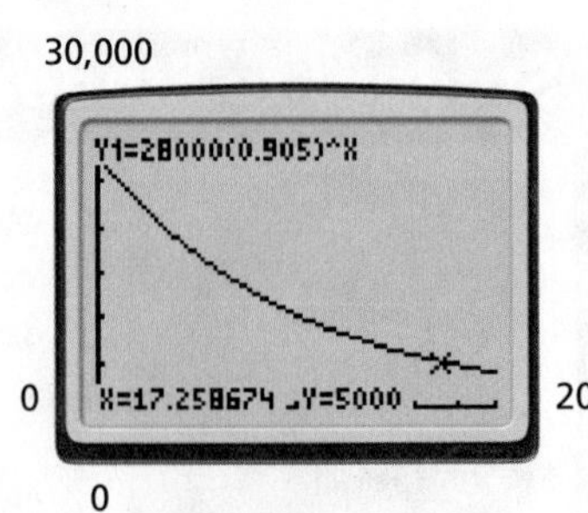

3. A motor scooter purchased for $1000 depreciates at an annual rate of 15%. Write an exponential function, and graph the function. Use the graph to predict when the value will fall below $100.

THINK AND DISCUSS

1. Tell how you can determine, without graphing the function or performing any calculations, whether $f(x) = \left(\frac{2}{3}\right)^x$ increases or decreases over the interval $-16 \le x \le -4$.
2. Discuss the differences between the graph of $f(x) = 1.1^x$ and the graph of $g(x) = 0.9^x$. What happens in each when $x = 0$?
3. Describe the function $f(t) = a(1 - r)^t$ when $0 < r < 1$ and $t > 0$. Describe the function when $-1 < r < 0$ and $t > 0$.

4. **GET ORGANIZED** Copy and complete the graphic organizer. Compare exponential growth and decay.

$f(x) = ab^x$, where $a > 0$	Growth	Decay
Value of b		
General shape of the graph		
What happens to $f(x)$ as x increases?		
What happens to $f(x)$ as x decreases?		

7-1 Exercises

GUIDED PRACTICE

1. **Vocabulary** When the base in an exponential function is between 0 and 1, the function shows __?__. (*exponential growth* or *exponential decay*)

SEE EXAMPLE 1 p. 491

Tell whether the function shows growth or decay. Then graph.

2. $f(x) = 32(0.5^x)$
3. $f(x) = 0.5(1.2^x)$
4. $f(x) = 0.4\left(\frac{3}{4}\right)^x$

SEE EXAMPLE 2 p. 492

5. **Biology** An acidophilus culture containing 150 bacteria doubles in population every hour. Predict the number of bacteria after 12 hours.
   a. Write a function representing the bacteria population for every hour that passes.
   b. Graph the function.
   c. Use the graph to predict the number of bacteria after 12 hours.

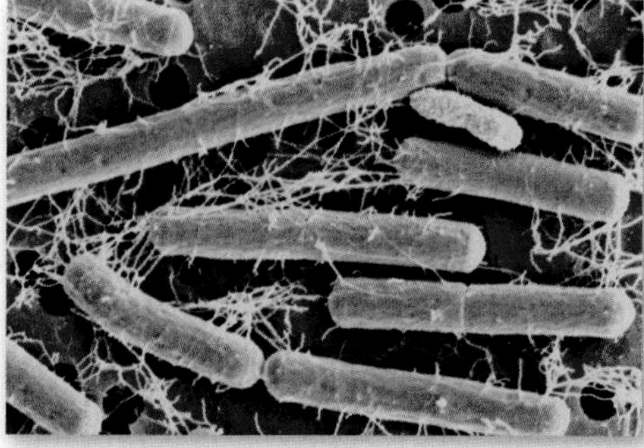

SEE EXAMPLE 3 p. 492

6. **Physics** A new softball dropped onto a hard surface from a height of 25 inches rebounds to about $\frac{2}{5}$ the height on each successive bounce.
   a. Write a function representing the rebound height for each bounce.
   b. Graph the function.
   c. After how many bounces would a new softball rebound less than 1 inch?

PRACTICE AND PROBLEM SOLVING

Independent Practice

For Exercises	See Example
7–9	1
10	2
11	3

Extra Practice

Skills Practice p. S16

Application Practice p. S38

Tell whether the function shows growth or decay. Then graph.

7. $f(x) = \left(\frac{1}{3}\right)^x$ **8.** $f(x) = \left(\frac{1}{3}\right)(1.3)^x$ **9.** $f(x) = 10(2.7)^x$

10. Railroads The amount of freight transported by rail in the United States was about 580 billion *ton-miles* in 1960 and has been increasing at a rate of 2.32% per year since then.

a. Write a function representing the amount of freight, in billions of ton-miles, transported annually (1960 = year 0).

b. Graph the function.

c. In what year would you predict that the number of ton-miles would have exceeded or would exceed 1 trillion (1000 billion)?

11. Medicine A quantity of insulin used to regulate sugar in the bloodstream breaks down by about 5% each minute. A body-weight adjusted dose is generally 10 units.

a. Write a function representing the amount of the dose that remains.

b. Use a calculator to graph the function.

c. About how much insulin remains after 10 minutes?

d. About how long does it take for half of the dose to remain?

LINK

History

The name *Manhattan* is probably a combination of two Native American words, the Delaware word *mannah*, "island," and the Algonquian word *hatin*, "hills." So the name *Manhattan* means "hilly island."

Explain whether each function is exponential.

12. $f(x) = 2x^{10}$ **13.** $f(x) = 0^x$ **14.** $f(x) = 1 \cdot 0.5^x$

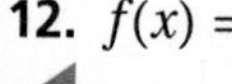

15. History In 1626, the Dutch bought Manhattan Island, now part of New York City, for $24 worth of merchandise. Suppose that, instead, $24 had been invested in an account that paid 3.5% interest each year. Find the balance in 2008.

16. Technology The quantity of new information stored electronically in 2002 was about 5 *exabytes*, or 5×10^{18} bytes. Researchers estimate that this is double what was stored in 1999. Suppose this trend continues. Write and graph a function to predict the pattern of growth beginning in 1999.

17. Business On federal income tax returns, self-employed people can depreciate the value of business equipment. Suppose a computer valued at $2765 depreciates at a rate of 30% per year. Estimate the number of years it will take for the computer's value to be less than $350.

Complete the table for each function. Round each value to the nearest hundredth.

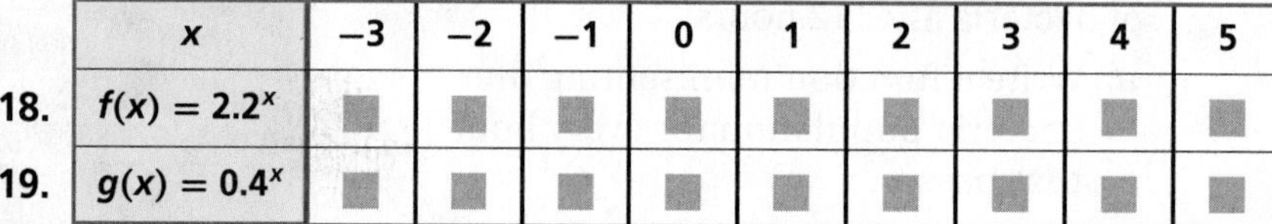

	x	−3	−2	−1	0	1	2	3	4	5
18.	$f(x) = 2.2^x$	■	■	■	■	■	■	■	■	■
19.	$g(x) = 0.4^x$	■	■	■	■	■	■	■	■	■

MULTI-STEP TEST PREP

20. This problem will prepare you for the Multi-Step Test Prep on page 520.

For a certain credit card, the total amount A that you owe after n months is given by $A = P(1.015)^n$, where P is the starting balance.

a. Suppose that you begin with a debt of $1000. Graph the function for the amount that you owe.

b. How much will you owe after one year?

c. How long will it take for the total amount that you owe to reach $1300?

21. **Collectibles** At the peak of a beanbag animal fad, one sales representative sold 12,000 of the animals in one month. Each month after that, the rep sold about 20% fewer animals.

a. About how many beanbag animals did the rep sell in the 6th month after the peak?

b. In which month did the rep first sell fewer than 1000 animals?

22. **Banking** The compound interest formula is $A = P\left(1 + \frac{r}{n}\right)^{nt}$, where A is the amount earned, P is the principal, r is the annual interest rate, t is the time in years, and n is the number of compounding periods per year. Harry invested \$5000 at 5% interest compounded quarterly (4 times per year).

a. How much will the investment be worth after 5 years?

b. When will the investment be worth more than \$10,000?

c. **What if...?** Harry could have invested the same amount in an account that paid 5% interest compounded monthly (12 times per year). How much more would his investment have been worth after 5 years?

23. **Critical Thinking** What are the coordinates of the point that is common to the graph of $f(x) = \left(\frac{2}{3}\right)^x$ and the graph of $f(x) = \left(\frac{3}{2}\right)^x$?

Find the range of each function for the domain $(0, 10]$.

24. $f(x) = 3^x - 2^x$

25. $f(x) = 100(0.9)^x$

26. $f(x) = \frac{3}{4}(2)^x$

27. **Geology** Radon-222 is a gas that escapes from rocks and soil. It can accumulate in buildings and can be dangerous for people who breathe it. Radon-222 decays to polonium and eventually to lead.

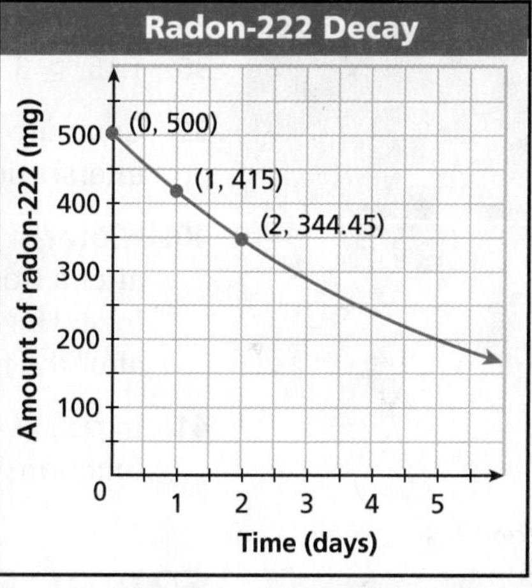

a. Find the percent decrease in the amount of radon-222 each day.

b. Write an exponential decay function for the amount of a 500 mg sample of radon-222 remaining after t days.

c. How much of the radon-222 sample would remain after 14 days?

28. **Estimation** According to the Population Reference Bureau, the world population in 2000 was 6.1 billion and increasing at an annual rate of 1.4%. Estimate the world population in 2020. Then write and evaluate an exponential function to predict the actual population, and compare it to your estimate.

29. **Critical Thinking** Which grows faster as x increases, x^3 or 3^x? Explain.

30. **Write About It** Describe a situation that could be modeled by an exponential function. Give the function and describe the meanings of several function values.

TEST PREP

31. Which function represents exponential decay?

Ⓐ $f(x) = 0.9(1.001^x)$

Ⓑ $f(x) = 1.5\left(\frac{10}{11}\right)^x$

Ⓒ $f(x) = 0.5(2^x)$

Ⓓ $f(x) = \left(\frac{1}{0.5}\right)^x$

32. Which number line represents the values of b in $y = ab^x$ for an exponential decay function?

Ⓕ Ⓗ

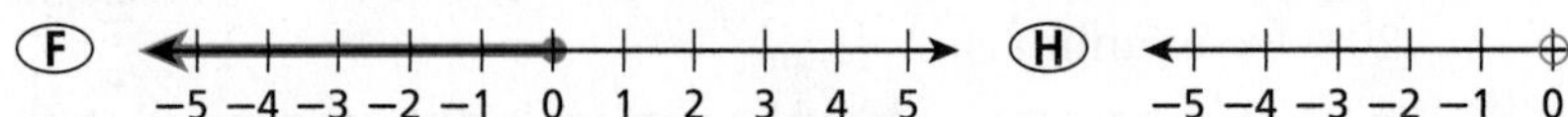

Ⓖ Ⓙ

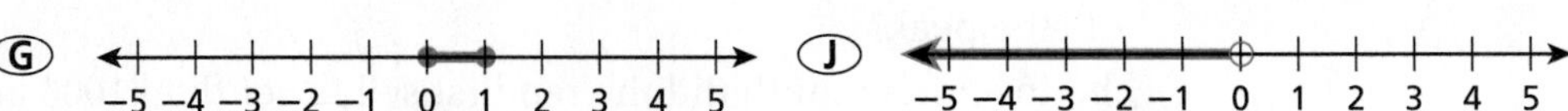

33. **Short Response** What are the values of a and b in $f(x) = ab^x$ for the graph shown?

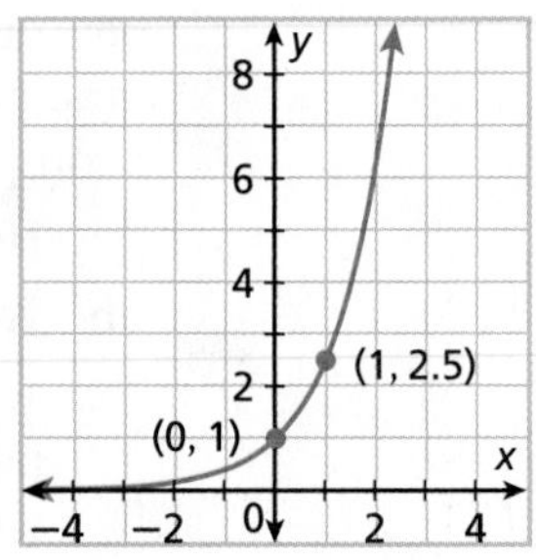

34. The population of a town was 89,443 in 1990 and has increased at a rate of 0.6% per year since then. Which function represents the town's population t years after 1990?

Ⓐ $89{,}443(1.6)^t$ Ⓒ $89{,}443(1.06)^t$

Ⓑ $89{,}443(1.006)^t$ Ⓓ $89{,}443(1.0006)^t$

CHALLENGE AND EXTEND

35. **Critical Thinking** Recall that polynomials are classified by degree. Why doesn't an exponential function have a degree?

Solve by graphing. Write the answer to the nearest hundredth.

36. $1.15^x \geq 3$ 37. $0.97^x < 0.5$ 38. $5 < 1.5^x < 6$

39. Compare the graphs of $y = 2^x$ and $y = x^2$, where $-10 < x < 10$. How many points of intersection are there? Give the coordinates of these points.

40. **Biology** Researchers found that the number of mosquitoes per acre of wetland after a frost is about 10 to the power $\frac{1}{2}d + 2$, where d is the number of days since the frost. How many mosquitoes per acre are there at the time of the frost? How long after the frost does it take for the population to quadruple?

41. In $f(x) = b^x$, why is the domain of b restricted $(b > 0, b \neq 1)$ for exponential functions?

SPIRAL REVIEW

Graph each function with a graphing calculator. Identify the domain and range of the function, and describe the transformation from its parent function. *(Lesson 1-9)*

42. $f(x) = \sqrt{x - 3}$ 43. $f(x) = -x^2 + 1$ 44. $f(x) = 2x^3$ 45. $f(x) = x - 4$

46. **Entertainment** Fred and Katrina are buying video games. Fred bought 3 new video games and 2 old video games for \$235. Katrina bought 1 new video game and 4 old video games for \$195. Find the cost of each type of video game. *(Lesson 3-2)*

Identify whether the function graphed has an odd or even degree and a positive or negative leading coefficient. *(Lesson 6-7)*

47.

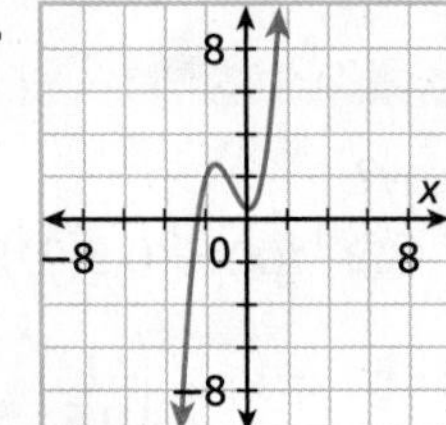

48.

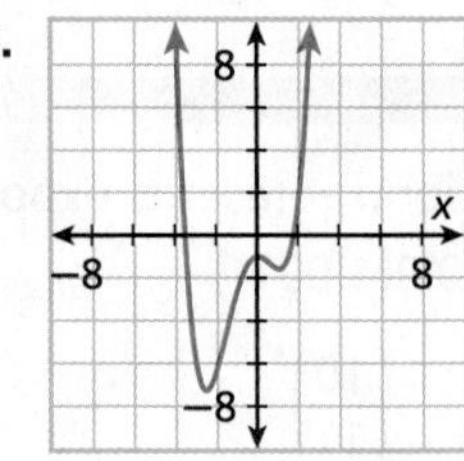

49.

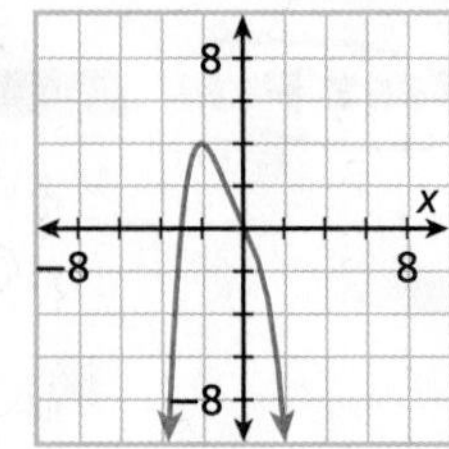

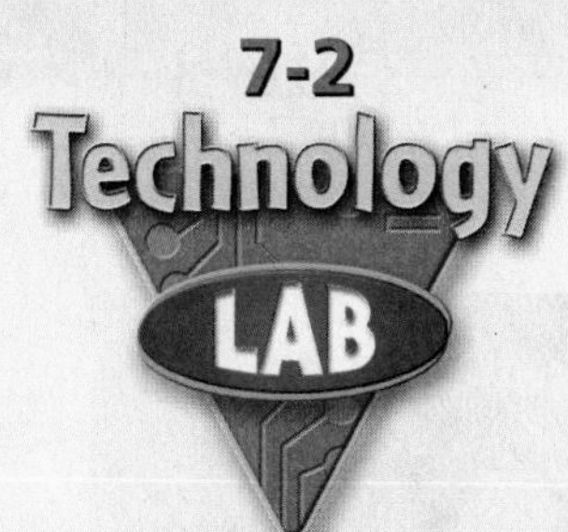

Explore Inverses of Functions

You can use a graphing calculator to explore inverse functions and their relationship to the linear parent function $f(x) = x$.

Activity

Graph the function $f(x) = 2^x$ and its inverse.

1. Graph the function $f(x) = 2^x$ and the linear parent $f(x) = x$ in the decimal window. Enter the functions, and then press ZOOM and select **4:ZDecimal**.

2. Use the **DrawInv** feature to graph the inverse of **Y1**. Enter the DRAW menu by pressing 2nd DRAW PRGM. Then select **8:DrawInv**.

   To select **Y1**, press VARS. Use the arrow keys to move to the **Y-VARS** submenu. Select **1:Function**, and then select **1:Y1** and press ENTER.

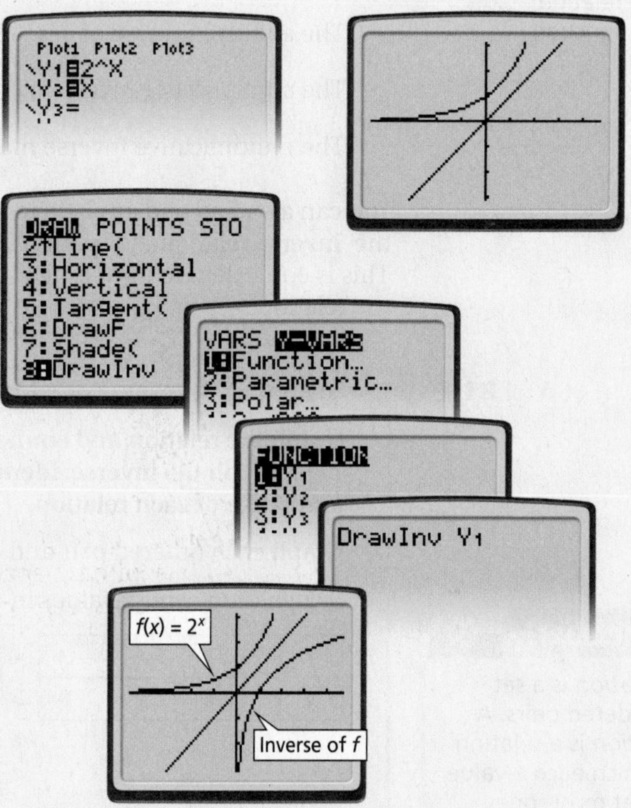

The graph shows the original function $f(x) = 2^x$, its inverse, and the linear parent $f(x) = x$. Notice that the inverse appears to be a function. Its domain is $\{x|x > 0\}$, and its range is $\mathbb{R}$.

Try This

Graph $f(x) = x^2$, its inverse, and $f(x) = x$.

1. Compare the domain and range of $f(x) = x^2$ with the domain and range of its inverse. Is the inverse of $f(x) = x^2$ a function? Explain why or why not.

Graph $f(x) = x^3$, its inverse, and $f(x) = x$.

2. Compare the domain and range of $f(x) = x^3$ with the domain and range of its inverse. Is the inverse of $f(x) = x^3$ a function? Explain why or why not.

3. **Make a Conjecture** Make a conjecture about the relationship between the domain and range of a function and its inverse.

4. **Make a Conjecture** Make a conjecture about the relationship of a function and its inverse to the line $f(x) = x$.

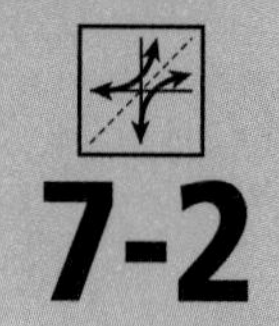

7-2 Inverses of Relations and Functions

Objectives
Graph and recognize inverses of relations and functions.

Find inverses of functions.

Vocabulary
inverse relation
inverse function

Who uses this?

Scuba divers can use an inverse function to determine their depth based on the water pressure. (See Exercise 47.)

You have seen the word *inverse* used in various ways.

The additive inverse of 3 is -3.

The multiplicative inverse of 5 is $\frac{1}{5}$.

The multiplicative inverse matrix of $A = \begin{bmatrix} 3 & 1 \\ 4 & 2 \end{bmatrix}$ is $A^{-1} = \begin{bmatrix} 1 & -0.5 \\ -2 & 1.5 \end{bmatrix}$.

You can also find and apply inverses to relations and functions. To graph the **inverse relation**, you can reflect each point across the line $y = x$. This is equivalent to switching the x- and y-values in each ordered pair of the relation.

EXAMPLE 1 Graphing Inverse Relations

Graph the relation and connect the points. Then graph the inverse. Identify the domain and range of each relation.

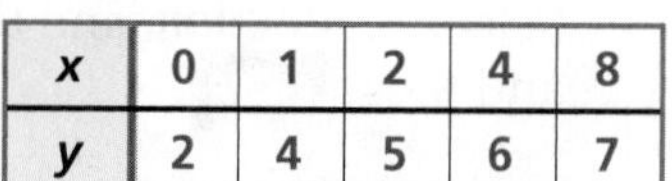

x	0	1	2	4	8
y	2	4	5	6	7

Graph each ordered pair and connect them.

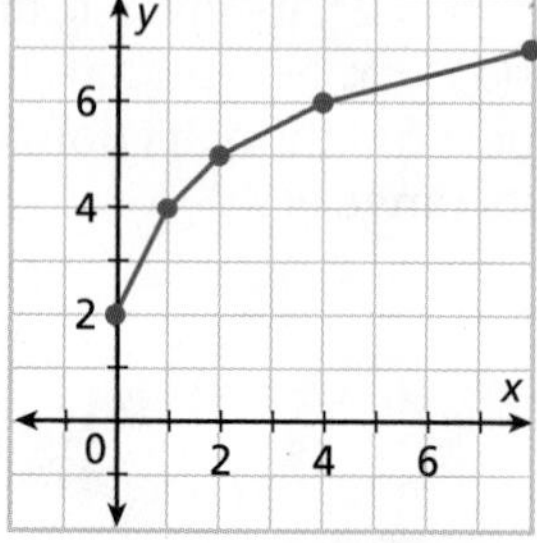

Switch the x- and y-values in each ordered pair.

x	2	4	5	6	7
y	0	1	2	4	8

Remember!

A *relation* is a set of ordered pairs. A *function* is a relation in which each x-value has, at most, one y-value paired with it.

Reflect each point across $y = x$, and connect them. Make sure the points match those in the table.

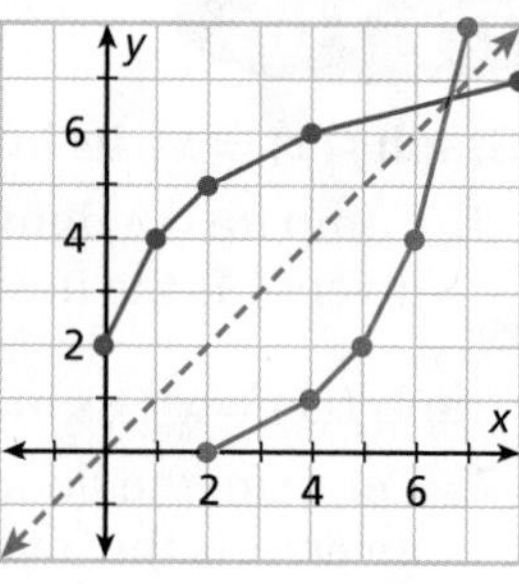

Domain: $\{x \mid 0 \le x \le 8\}$ Range: $\{y \mid 2 \le y \le 7\}$

Domain: $\{x \mid 2 \le x \le 7\}$ Range: $\{y \mid 0 \le y \le 8\}$

1. Graph the relation and connect the points. Then graph the inverse. Identify the domain and range of each relation.

x	1	3	4	5	6
y	0	1	2	3	5

When the relation is also a function, you can write the inverse of the function $f(x)$ as $f^{-1}(x)$. This notation does *not* indicate a reciprocal.

Functions that undo each other are **inverse functions**.

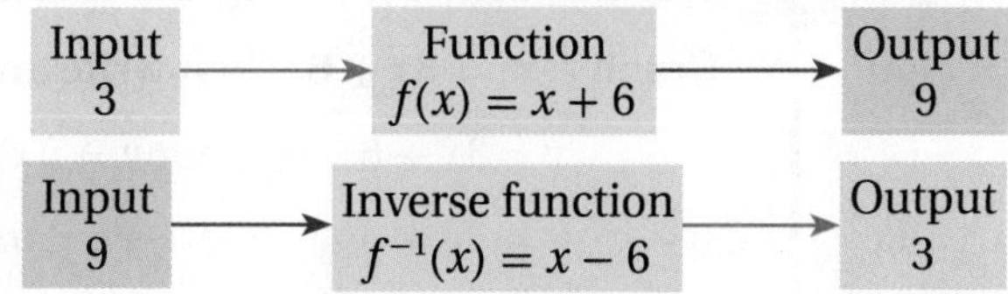

To find the inverse function, use the inverse operation. In the example above, 6 is added to x in $f(x)$, so 6 is subtracted to find $f^{-1}(x)$.

EXAMPLE 2 Writing Inverse Functions by Using Inverse Operations

Use inverse operations to write the inverse of $f(x) = 2x$.

$f(x) = 2x$ *The variable, x, is multiplied by 2.*

$f^{-1}(x) = \frac{x}{2}$ *Divide x by 2 to write the inverse.*

Check Use the input $x = 7$ in $f(x)$.

$f(x) = 2x$

$f(7) = 2(7)$ *Substitute 7 for x.*

$= 14$

Substitute the result into $f^{-1}(x)$.

$f^{-1}(x) = \frac{x}{2}$

$f^{-1}(14) = \frac{14}{2}$ *Substitute 14 for x.*

$= 7$

The inverse function *does* undo the original function. ✔

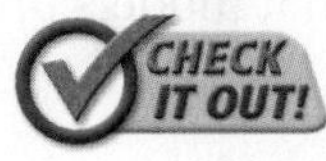

Use inverse operations to write the inverse of each function.

2a. $f(x) = \frac{x}{3}$ **2b.** $f(x) = x + \frac{2}{3}$

Undo operations in the opposite order of the order of operations.

EXAMPLE 3 Writing Inverses of Multi-Step Functions

Use inverse operations to write the inverse of $f(x) = \frac{x}{4} - 5$.

$f(x) = \frac{x}{4} - 5$ *The variable x is divided by 4, then 5 is subtracted.*

$f^{-1}(x) = 4(x + 5)$ *First, undo the subtraction by adding 5 to x. Then, undo the division by multiplying by 4.*

Check Use a sample input.

$f(40) = \frac{40}{4} - 5 = 10 - 5 = 5$ $f^{-1}(5) = 4(5 + 5) = 4(10) = 40$ ✔

Helpful Hint

The *reverse* order of operations:
Addition or Subtraction
Multiplication or Division
Exponents
Parentheses

3. Use inverse operations to write the inverse of $f(x) = 5x - 7$.

You can also find the inverse function by writing the original function with x and y switched and then solving for y.

EXAMPLE 4 Writing and Graphing Inverse Functions

Graph $f(x) = 3x + 6$. Then write and graph the inverse.

$y = 3x + 6$ *Set $y = f(x)$ and graph f.*

$x = 3y + 6$ *Switch x and y.*

$x - 6 = 3y$ *Solve for y.*

$\frac{x-6}{3} = y$

$y = \frac{x-6}{3}$ *Write in y = format.*

$f^{-1}(x) = \frac{x-6}{3}$ *Set $y = f(x)$.*

$= \frac{1}{3}x - 2$ *Simplify. Then graph f^{-1}.*

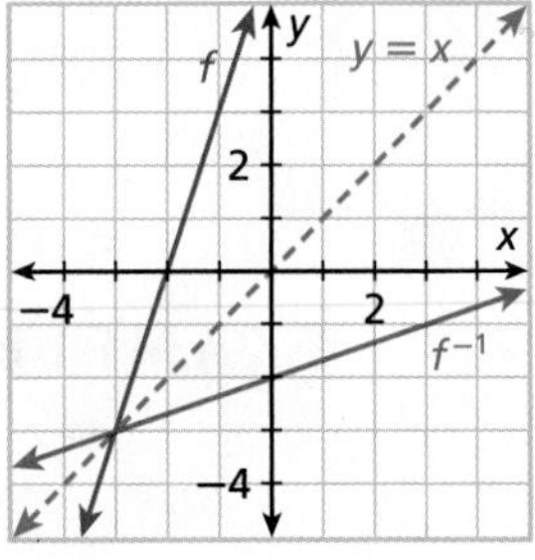

4. Graph $f(x) = \frac{2}{3}x + 2$. Then write the inverse and graph.

Any time you need to undo an operation or work backward from a result to the original input, you can apply inverse functions.

EXAMPLE 5 Retailing Application

A clerk needs to price a digital camera returned by a customer. The customer paid a total of $103.14, which included a gift-wrapping charge of $3 and 8% sales tax. What price should the clerk mark on the tag?

Step 1 Write an equation for the total cost as a function of price.

$c = 1.08(p + 3)$ *Cost c is a function of price p.*

Step 2 Find the inverse function that models price as a function of cost.

$c = 1.08(p + 3)$

$c = 1.08p + 3.24$ *Distribute.*

$c - 3.24 = 1.08p$ *Subtract 3.24 from both sides.*

$\frac{c - 3.24}{1.08} = p$ *Divide to isolate p.*

Step 3 Evaluate the inverse function for $c = \$103.14$.

$p = \frac{103.14 - 3.24}{1.08} = 92.50$

The clerk should mark the tag as $92.50.

Check $c = 1.08(92.50 + 3)$ *Substitute.*

$= 1.08(95.50)$

$= 103.14$ ✓

Remember!

In a real-world situation, don't switch the variables, because they are named for specific quantities.

5. To make tea, use $\frac{1}{6}$ teaspoon of tea per ounce of water plus a teaspoon for the pot. Use the inverse to find the number of ounces of water needed if 7 teaspoons of tea are used.

THINK AND DISCUSS

1. Explain the result of interchanging x and y to find the inverse function of $f(x) = x$. How could you have predicted this from the graph of $f(x)$?
2. Give an example of a function whose inverse is a function. Give an example of a function whose inverse is not a function.
3. Tell what happens when you take the inverse of the inverse of a function. Is the result necessarily a function? Explain.

4. **GET ORGANIZED** Copy and complete the graphic organizer. Show a possible input value, inverse function, and output value for a function $f(x)$.

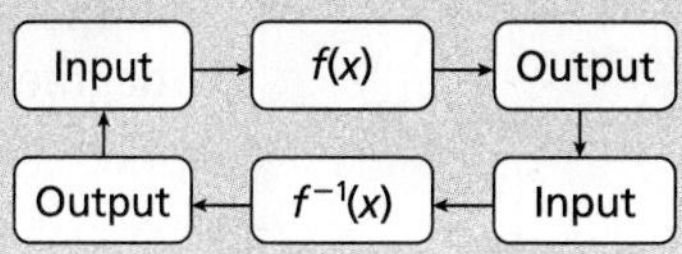

7-2 Exercises

GUIDED PRACTICE

1. **Vocabulary** When switching x and y, the result is always an *inverse* __?__. (*relation* or *function*)

SEE EXAMPLE 1 p. 498

Graph the relation and connect the points. Then graph the inverse. Identify the domain and range of each relation.

2.

x	1	2	3	4
y	1	2	4	8

3.

x	3	4	1	−1
y	−1	−2	−4	−4

SEE EXAMPLE 2 p. 499

Use inverse operations to write the inverse of each function.

4. $f(x) = x + 3$
5. $f(x) = 4x$
6. $f(x) = \frac{x}{2}$
7. $f(x) = x - 2\frac{1}{2}$

SEE EXAMPLE 3 p. 499

8. $f(x) = 5x - 1$
9. $f(x) = \frac{x}{2} + 3$
10. $f(x) = 3 - \frac{1}{2}x$
11. $f(x) = \frac{1}{2}(3 - 3x)$
12. $f(x) = 4(x + 1)$
13. $f(x) = \frac{3x - 5}{2}$

SEE EXAMPLE 4 p. 500

Graph each function. Then write and graph its inverse.

14. $f(x) = 5 - 2x$
15. $f(x) = \frac{x}{4} + 2$
16. $f(x) = 10 + 0.6x$

SEE EXAMPLE 5 p. 500

17. **Meteorology** The formula $C = \frac{5}{9}(F - 32)$ gives degrees Celsius as a function of degrees Fahrenheit. Find the inverse of this function to convert degrees Celsius to Fahrenheit and use it to find 16°C in degrees Fahrenheit.

PRACTICE AND PROBLEM SOLVING

Graph the relation and connect the points. Then graph the inverse. Identify the domain and range of each relation.

18.

x	−1	2	3	5
y	1	3	5	5

19.

x	−4	−2	0	2	4
y	−2	−1	0	1	2

Independent Practice	
For Exercises	See Example
18–19	1
20–22	2
23–25	3
26–28	4
29	5

Extra Practice

Skills Practice p. S16

Application Practice p. S38

Use inverse operations to write the inverse of each function.

20. $f(x) = 0.825x$

21. $f(x) = x - 1\frac{3}{4}$

22. $f(x) = \frac{x}{0.25}$

23. $f(x) = 21 - 32x$

24. $f(x) = 145 + 12.5x$

25. $f(x) = \frac{1}{5}x + 12$

Graph each function. Then write and graph its inverse.

26. $f(x) = \frac{4}{5}(x - 15)$

27. $f(x) = 2 - \frac{x}{3}$

28. $f(x) = 1.21x$

29. **Education** A linear model projects that the number of bachelor's degrees awarded in the United States will increase by 19,500 each year. In 2001, 1.28 million bachelor's degrees were awarded. Use the inverse function to predict the number of years after 2001 that 1.7 million bachelor's degrees will be awarded. *Source: nces.ed.gov*

30. **Critical Thinking** Graph the line that passes through (2, 9) and (3, 4).
    a. What is the slope of this line?
    b. What is the slope of the line that is the inverse of the original line?

LINK

Physics

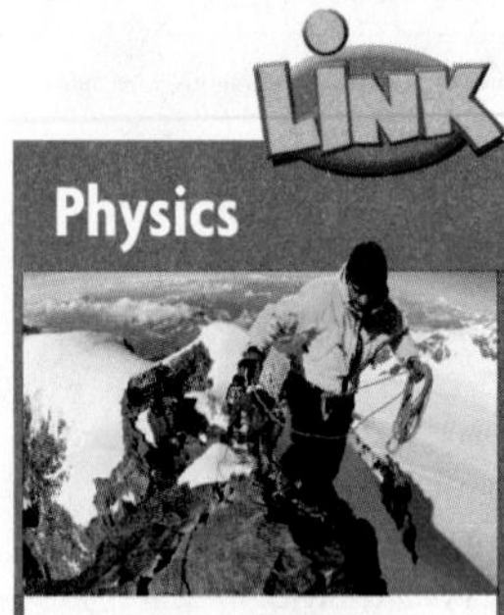

Mountain climbers at very high altitudes can drink tea while it's boiling with bubbles because it's cool enough not to burn them.

31. **Physics** At sea level, the boiling point of water is 212°F. At x thousand feet, the boiling point of water is given by the function $f(x) = 212 - 1.85x$.
    a. Write the inverse function.
    b. Above what altitude, to the nearest 500 feet, does the boiling point of water fall below 200°F?
    c. At the summit of Nepal's Lhotse Mountain, water boils at 160.3°F. What is the mountain peak's altitude?

Geometry **Find the coordinates of the vertices of the inverse for each figure.**

32.

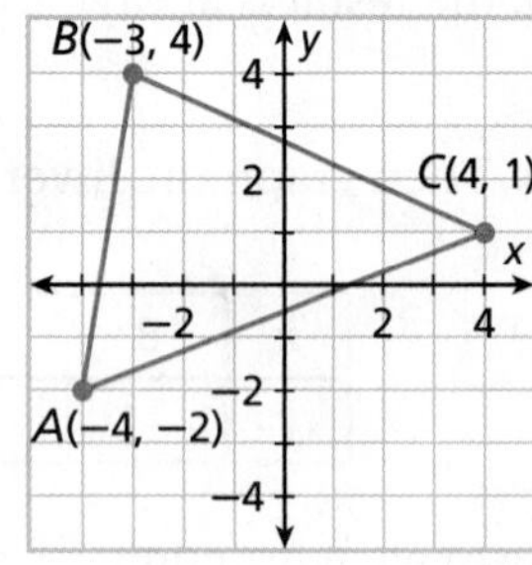

33.

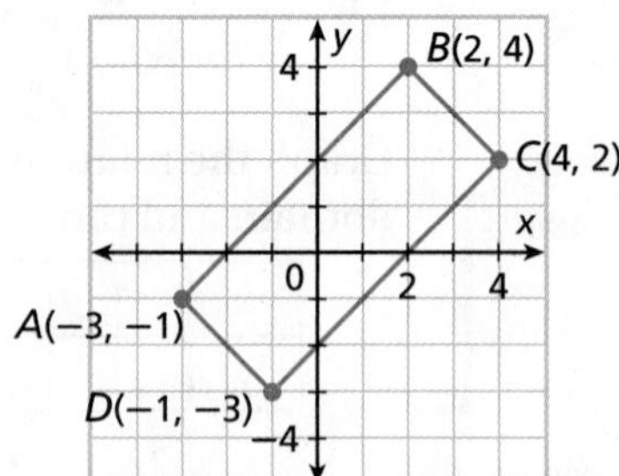

34. **Critical Thinking** What is the inverse of $f(x) = 3$? (Hint: Write this function as $y = 0x + 3$.) Is the inverse a function? Explain.

35. **Animals** In 1999, Warhol the albino ferret ran a 10 m tube race in 12.59 s. Assume that he ran at a constant rate. Write a function that gives distance as a function of time. Write and use the inverse function to find the time it would take Warhol to complete a 25 m race at the same speed.

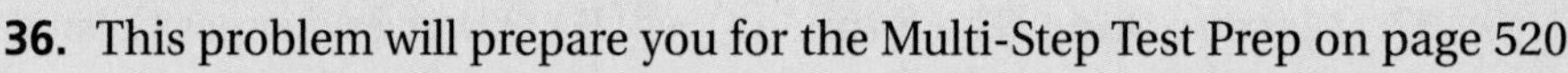

MULTI-STEP TEST PREP

36. This problem will prepare you for the Multi-Step Test Prep on page 520.
    A theater sells tickets for $22. If you pay by credit card, the theater adds a service charge of $3.50 to the entire order.
    a. Write a function that gives the amount billed to the credit card as a function of the number of tickets purchased.
    b. Write the inverse function, and use it to find the number of tickets purchased when the credit card bill is $157.50.
    c. Is it possible to have a total of $332.50 billed to your credit card for these tickets? Why or why not?

37. **ERROR ANALYSIS** Two students found the inverse of $f(x) = \frac{1}{2}x + 1$. Which is incorrect? Explain the error.

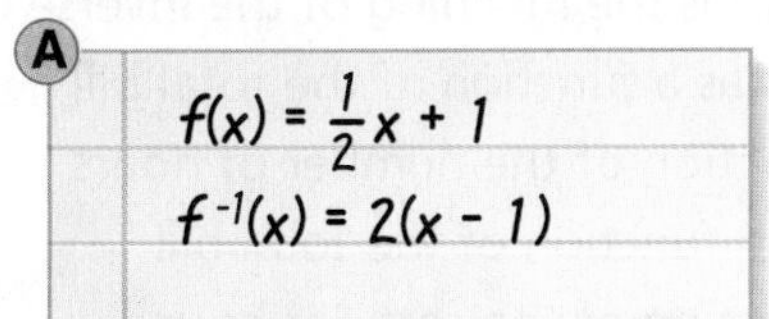

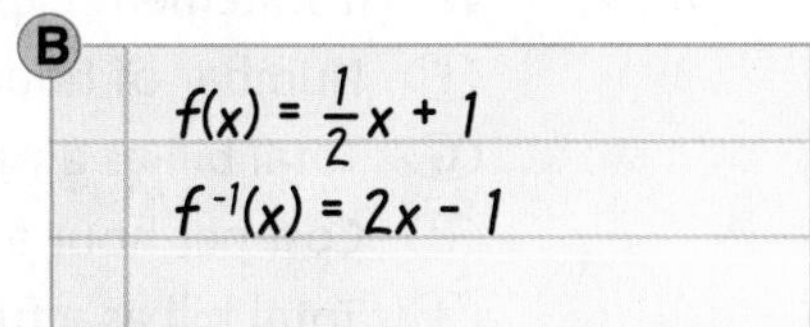

38. **Write About It** Explain the effect on a function and its graph when you switch the coordinates of the ordered pairs.

39. **Critical Thinking** Can the inverse of a relation that is not a function be a function itself? Explain your answer by using an example.

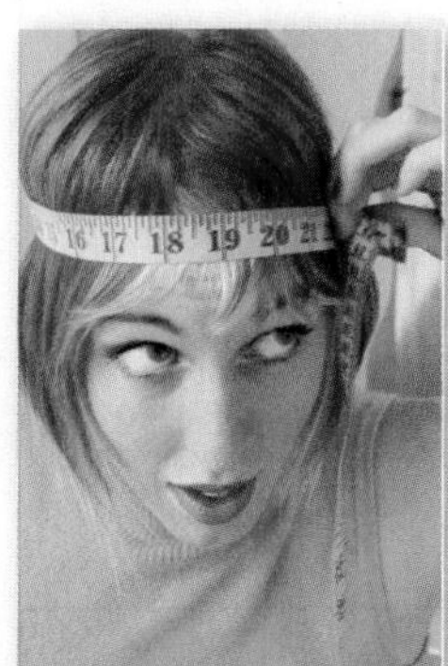

40. **Clothing** Hat size is a linear function of head circumference. A person with a head circumference of $21\frac{1}{2}$ in. has a hat size of $6\frac{7}{8}$, while a person with a head circumference of $21\frac{7}{8}$ in. has a hat size of 7.
   a. Find hat size as a function of head circumference.
   b. Find the inverse. Is it a function? What does the inverse represent?
   c. A hat was found with a size of $7\frac{3}{8}$. What is the head circumference of the owner?

Tell whether each statement is sometimes, always, or never true.

41. The inverse of an ordered pair on a graph is its reflection across the line $y = x$.
42. The inverse of a linear function is a linear function.
43. The inverse of a line with positive slope is a line with negative slope.
44. The inverse of a line with a slope greater than 1 is a line with slope less than 1.
45. The inverse of the inverse of a point (x, y) is the original point.
46. The line $y = k$, where k is a constant, has an inverse.
47. **Diving** Scuba divers must know that the deeper the dive, the greater the water pressure in pounds per square inch (psi) for fresh water diving, as shown in the diagram.
   a. Write the pressure as a function of depth.
   b. Identify a reasonable domain and range of the pressure function.
   c. Find the inverse of the function from part **a.** What does the inverse function represent?
   d. The point (25.9, 25.9) is an approximate solution to both the function from part **a** and its inverse. What does this point mean in the context of the problem?

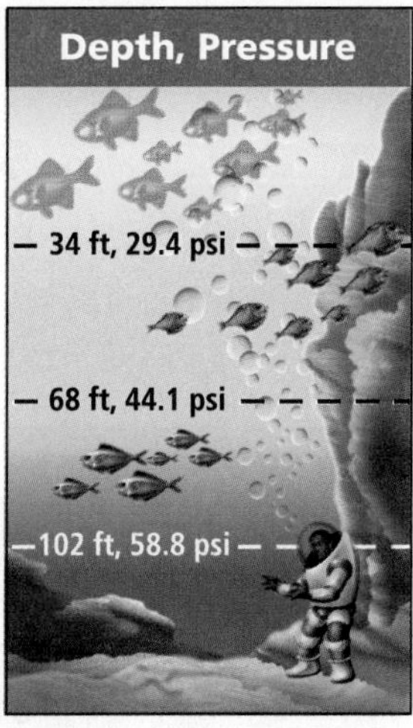

48. Which function is the inverse of $f(x) = 4x - \frac{3}{4}$?

Ⓐ $f^{-1}(x) = \frac{1}{4}x + \frac{3}{16}$

Ⓑ $f^{-1}(x) = -\frac{1}{4}x + 3$

Ⓒ $f^{-1}(x) = \frac{1}{4}x + 3$

Ⓓ $f^{-1}(x) = -\frac{1}{4}x + \frac{3}{16}$

49. Eliza's auto repair bill includes \$175 for parts and \$35 per hour for labor. The bill can be expressed as a function of hours x with the function $f(x) = 175 + 35x$. Which statement explains the meaning of the inverse of the function?

(F) Number of hours as a function of the total bill

(G) Total bill as a function of the number of hours

(H) Cost per hour as a function of the total bill

(J) Total bill as a function of the cost per hour

50. The inverse of a point is $(5, -2)$. What point is this the inverse of?

(A) $(-5, 2)$ (B) $(5, 2)$ (C) $(-2, 5)$ (D) $(2, -5)$

51. **Short Response** Make a table to show the inverse of the relation shown in the graph.

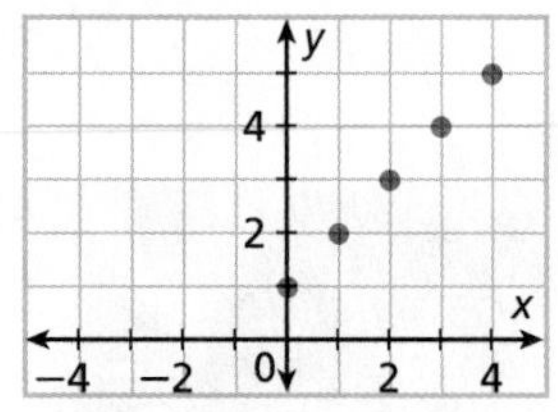

CHALLENGE AND EXTEND

Give the inverse of each linear function, where $y = f(x)$.

52. $y = mx + b$ 53. $ax + by = c$ 54. $y - y_1 = m(x - x_1)$

55. Graph the relation given by the points in the table. Then reflect each point across the line $y = x$ to see the graph of the inverse relation. If the equation of the relation is $f(x) = x^2$, verify algebraically that the equation of the inverse relation is $x = y^2$.

x	y
−3	9
−2	4
−1	1
0	0
1	1
2	4
3	9

56. **Critical Thinking** A linear function and its inverse have the same slope. What must be true of these functions?

Graph each function and its inverse.

57. $y = 3$ 58. $y = x^3$ 59. $y = 2^x$

SPIRAL REVIEW

60. **Business** A stock was purchased for \$45.18 per share. The change in value is shown in the table. *(Lesson 1-1)*

a. Order the stock values from least to greatest. Include the purchase day as day 0.

b. Use set-builder notation to represent the range of the stock value.

Stock Market Value

Day	Change in Value (\$)
1	−0.23
2	+2.58
3	−0.64
4	+1.27
5	−2.12

Write the polynomial equation of least degree with the given roots and leading coefficient of 2. *(Lesson 6-6)*

61. $-3, 2, 1$ 62. $\sqrt{5}, -\sqrt{5}$

63. $1 - i, 2$ 64. $-3, 8, 9$

Tell whether the function shows growth or decay. Then graph. *(Lesson 7-1)*

65. $f(x) = 15\left(\frac{89}{100}\right)^x$ 66. $f(x) = \frac{1}{25}(0.5^x)$

67. $f(x) = 2(1.1^x)$ 68. $f(x) = 0.01(1.9^x)$

7-3 Logarithmic Functions

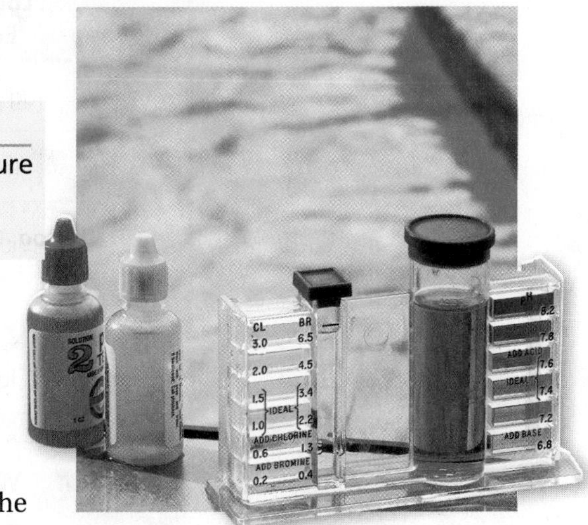

Objectives

Write equivalent forms for exponential and logarithmic functions.

Write, evaluate, and graph logarithmic functions.

Vocabulary

logarithm
common logarithm
logarithmic function

Why learn this?

A logarithmic scale is used to measure the acidity, or pH, of water. (See Example 5.)

How many times would you have to double \$1 before you had \$8? You could use an exponential equation to model this situation. $1(2^x) = 8$. You may be able to solve this equation by using mental math if you know that $2^3 = 8$. So you would have to double the dollar 3 times to have \$8.

How many times would you have to double \$1 to have \$512? You could solve this problem if you could solve $2^x = 8$ by using an inverse operation that undoes raising a base to an exponent. This operation is called finding the logarithm. A **logarithm** is the exponent to which a specified base is raised to obtain a given value.

Reading Math

Read $\log_b a = x$, as "the log base b of a is x." Notice that the log is the exponent.

You can write an exponential equation as a logarithmic equation and vice versa.

Exponential Equation **Logarithmic Equation**

$$b^x = a \qquad \log_b a = x$$

$b > 0, b \neq 1$

EXAMPLE 1 **Converting from Exponential to Logarithmic Form**

Write each exponential equation in logarithmic form.

	Exponential Equation	Logarithmic Form	
a.	$2^6 = 64$	$\log_2 64 = 6$	*The base of the exponent becomes the base of the logarithm.*
b.	$4^1 = 4$	$\log_4 4 = 1$	*The exponent is the logarithm.*
c.	$5^0 = 1$	$\log_5 1 = 0$	*Any nonzero base to the 0 power is 1.*
d.	$5^{-2} = 0.04$	$\log_5 0.04 = -2$	*An exponent (or log) can be negative.*
e.	$3^x = 81$	$\log_3 81 = x$	*The log (and the exponent) can be a variable.*

Write each exponential equation in logarithmic form.

1a. $9^2 = 81$ **1b.** $3^3 = 27$ **1c.** $x^0 = 1(x \neq 0)$

EXAMPLE 2 Converting from Logarithmic to Exponential Form

Write each logarithmic equation in exponential form.

	Logarithmic Equation	Exponential Form	
a.	$\log_{10} 100 = 2$	$10^2 = 100$	*The base of the logarithm becomes the base of the power.*
b.	$\log_7 49 = 2$	$7^2 = 49$	*The logarithm is the exponent.*
c.	$\log_8 0.125 = -1$	$8^{-1} = 0.125$	*A logarithm can be a negative number.*
d.	$\log_5 5 = 1$	$5^1 = 5$	
e.	$\log_{12} 1 = 0$	$12^0 = 1$	

Write each logarithmic equation in exponential form.

2a. $\log_{10} 10 = 1$ **2b.** $\log_{12} 144 = 2$ **2c.** $\log_{\frac{1}{2}} 8 = -3$

A logarithm is an exponent, so the rules for exponents also apply to logarithms. You may have noticed the following properties in the last example.

Special Properties of Logarithms

For any base b such that $b > 0$ and $b \neq 1$,

LOGARITHMIC FORM	EXPONENTIAL FORM	EXAMPLE
Logarithm of Base b		
$\log_b b = 1$	$b^1 = b$	$\log_{10} 10 = 1$ $10^1 = 10$
Logarithm of 1		
$\log_b 1 = 0$	$b^0 = 1$	$\log_{10} 1 = 0$ $10^0 = 1$

A logarithm with base 10 is called a **common logarithm**. If no base is written for a logarithm, the base is assumed to be 10. For example, $\log 5 = \log_{10} 5$.

You can use mental math to evaluate some logarithms.

EXAMPLE 3 Evaluating Logarithms by Using Mental Math

Evaluate by using mental math.

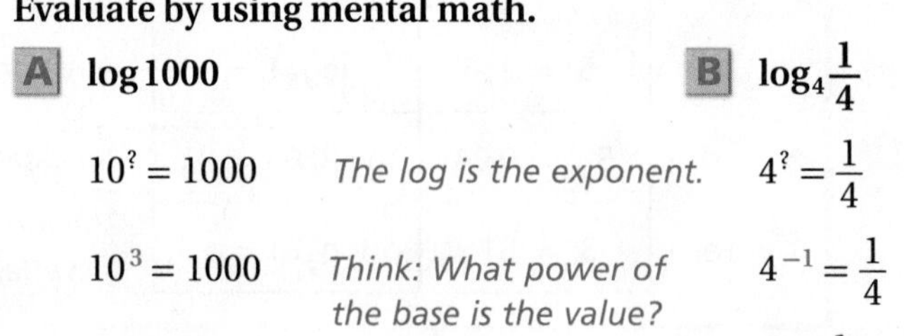

A $\log 1000$

$10^? = 1000$ *The log is the exponent.*

$10^3 = 1000$ *Think: What power of the base is the value?*

$\log 1000 = 3$

B $\log_4 \frac{1}{4}$

$4^? = \frac{1}{4}$

$4^{-1} = \frac{1}{4}$

$\log_4 \frac{1}{4} = -1$

CHECK IT OUT! **Evaluate by using mental math.**

3a. $\log 0.00001$ **3b.** $\log_{25} 0.04$

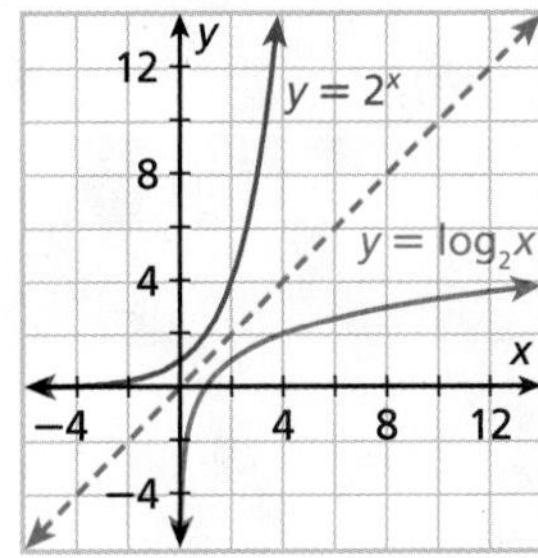

Because logarithms are the inverses of exponents, the inverse of an exponential function, such as $y = 2^x$, is a **logarithmic function**, such as $y = \log_2 x$.

You may notice that the domain and range of each function are switched.

The domain of $y = 2^x$ is all real numbers ($\mathbb{R}$), and the range is $\{y \mid y > 0\}$. The domain of $y = \log_2 x$ is $\{x \mid x > 0\}$, and the range is all real numbers ($\mathbb{R}$).

EXAMPLE 4 Graphing Logarithmic Functions

Use the given x-values to graph each function. Then graph its inverse. Describe the domain and range of the inverse function.

A $f(x) = 3^x$; $x = -2, -1, 0, 1$, and 2

Graph $f(x) = 3^x$ by using a table of values.

x	−2	−1	0	1	2
$f(x) = 3^x$	$\frac{1}{9}$	$\frac{1}{3}$	1	3	9

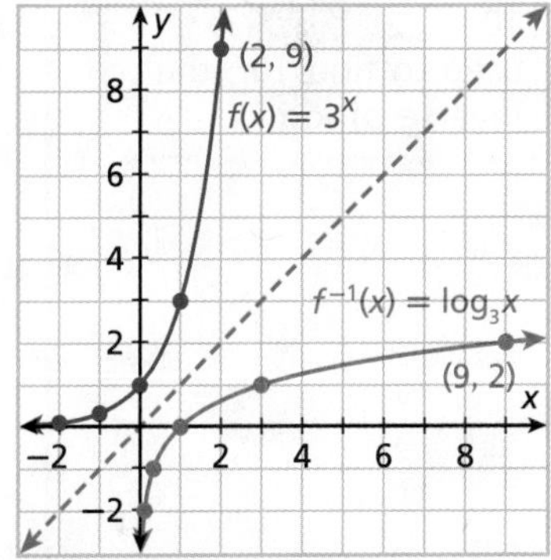

To graph the inverse, $f^{-1}(x) = \log_3 x$, reverse each ordered pair.

x	$\frac{1}{9}$	$\frac{1}{3}$	1	3	9
$f^{-1}(x) = \log_3 x$	−2	−1	0	1	2

The domain of $f^{-1}(x)$ is $\{x \mid x > 0\}$, and the range is $\mathbb{R}$.

B $f(x) = 0.8^x$; $x = -3, 0, 1, 4$, and 7

Graph $f(x) = 0.8^x$ by using a table of values. Round the output values to the nearest tenth, if necessary.

x	−3	0	1	4	7
$f(x) = 0.8^x$	2	1	0.8	0.4	0.2

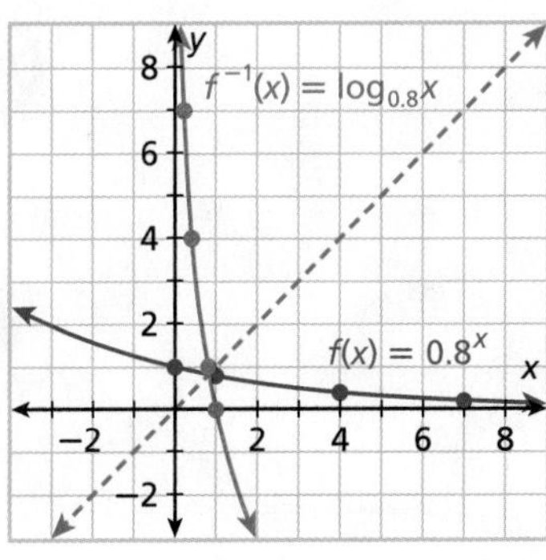

To graph $f^{-1}(x) = \log_{0.8} x$, reverse each ordered pair.

x	2	1	0.8	0.4	0.2
$f^{-1}(x) = \log_{0.8} x$	−3	0	1	4	7

The domain of $f^{-1}(x)$ is $\{x \mid x > 0\}$, and the range is $\mathbb{R}$.

4. Use $x = -2, -1, 1, 2$, and 3 to graph $f(x) = \left(\frac{3}{4}\right)^x$. Then graph its inverse. Describe the domain and range of the inverse function.

EXAMPLE 5 Environmental Application

Chemists regularly test rain samples to determine the rain's acidity, or concentration of hydrogen ions (H^+). Acidity is measured in pH, as given by the function $pH = -\log[H^+]$, where $[H^+]$ represents the hydrogen ion concentration in moles per liter.

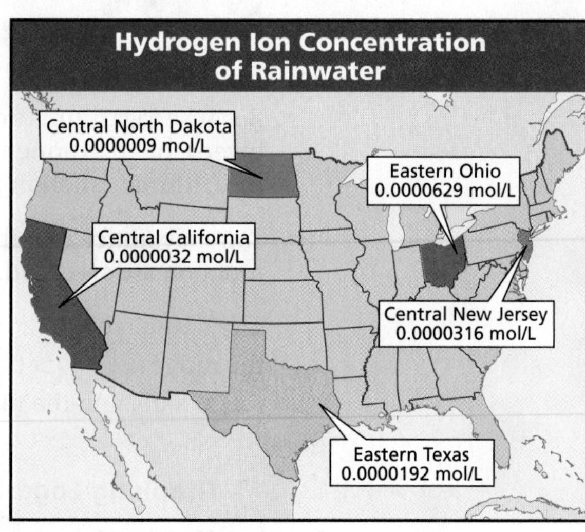

Find the pH of rainwater from each location.

Helpful Hint

The LOG key is used to evaluate logarithms in base 10. 2nd LOG (10^x) is used to find 10^x, the inverse of log.

A Central New Jersey

The hydrogen ion concentration is 0.0000316 moles per liter.

$pH = -\log[H^+]$

$pH = -\log(0.0000316)$ *Substitute the known values in the function.*

Use a calculator to find the value of the logarithm in base 10. Press the LOG key.

The rainwater has a pH of about 4.5.

B Central North Dakota

The hydrogen ion concentration is 0.0000009 moles per liter.

$pH = -\log[H^+]$

$pH = -\log(0.0000009)$ *Substitute the known values in the function.*

Use a calculator to find the value of the logarithm in base 10. Press the LOG key.

The rainwater has a pH of about 6.0.

5. What is the pH of iced tea with a hydrogen ion concentration of 0.000158 moles per liter?

THINK AND DISCUSS

1. Contrast exponential functions with logarithmic functions.
2. Explain whether $\log_b a$ is the same as $\log_a b$. Support your answer.

3. **GET ORGANIZED** Copy and complete the graphic organizer. Use your own words to explain a logarithmic function.

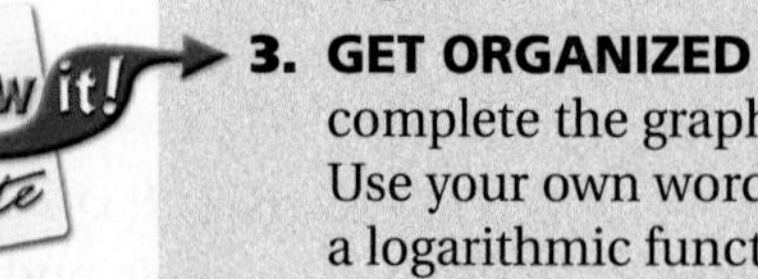

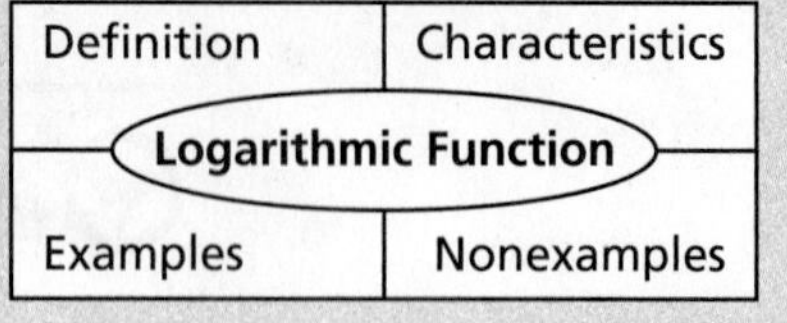

7-3 Exercises

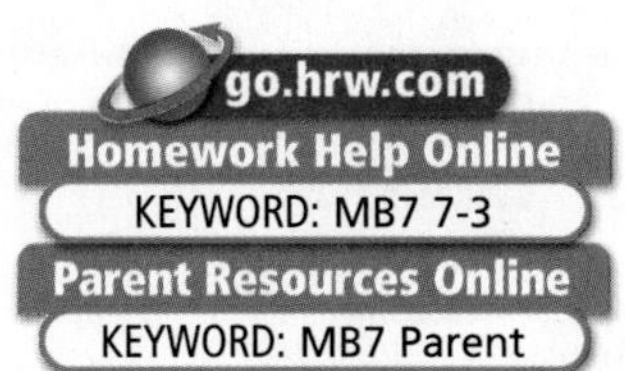

GUIDED PRACTICE

1. **Vocabulary** In the exponential equation $a^x = b$, the logarithm is ___?___. (a, x, or b)

SEE EXAMPLE 1 p. 505

Write each exponential equation in logarithmic form.

2. $2.4^0 = 1$ 3. $4^{1.5} = 8$ 4. $10^{-2} = 0.01$ 5. $3^x = 243$

SEE EXAMPLE 2 p. 506

Write each logarithmic equation in exponential form.

6. $\log_4 0.0625 = -2$ 7. $\log_x(-16) = 3$ 8. $\log_{0.9} 0.81 = 2$ 9. $\log_6 x = 3$

SEE EXAMPLE 3 p. 506

Evaluate by using mental math.

10. $\log_7 343$ 11. $\log_3\left(\frac{1}{9}\right)$ 12. $\log_{0.5} 0.25$ 13. $\log_{1.2} 1.44$

SEE EXAMPLE 4 p. 507

Use the given x-values to graph each function. Then graph its inverse. Describe the domain and range of each function.

14. $f(x) = 5^x$; $x = -2, -1, 0, 1, 1.5$ 15. $f(x) = 0.5^x$; $x = -2, -1, 0, 1, 2$

SEE EXAMPLE 5 p. 508

16. **Chemistry** The acid potential of a solution is given by pOH, where $\text{pOH} = -\log[\text{OH}^-]$, and OH^- represents the concentration of hydroxide ions in moles per liter. The water in one sample contains a hydroxide ion concentration of 0.000000004. What is the pOH of the water?

PRACTICE AND PROBLEM SOLVING

Independent Practice

For Exercises	See Example
17–20	1
21–24	2
25–28	3
29–30	4
31	5

Extra Practice

Skills Practice p. S16
Application Practice p. S38

Write each exponential equation in logarithmic form.

17. $x^{2.5} = 32$ 18. $6^x = 216$ 19. $1.2^0 = 1$ 20. $4^{-1} = 0.25$

Write each logarithmic equation in exponential form.

21. $\log_5 625 = 4$ 22. $\log_2 x = 6$ 23. $\log_{4.5} 1 = 0$ 24. $\log_\pi \pi = 1$

Evaluate by using mental math.

25. $\log_2 1$ 26. $\log 0.001$ 27. $\log_4 64$ 28. $\log_{0.1} 100$

Use the given x-values to graph each function. Then graph its inverse. Describe the domain and range of each function.

29. $f(x) = \left(\frac{4}{5}\right)^x$; $x = -2, -1, 0, 1, 2, 3$ 30. $f(x) = \left(\frac{4}{3}\right)^x$; $x = -2, -1, 0, 1, 2, 3$

31. **Gardening** The flower color of bigleaf hydrangeas is determined by the soil pH. A gardener growing blue hydrangeas believes that lime may be leaching out of a nearby sidewalk and increasing the pH of the soil. The gardener measures the hydrogen ion concentration and finds it to be 0.0000006 moles per liter. Is the soil still good for growing blue flowers? Explain.

$5 < \text{pH} < 5.5$

$5.5 < \text{pH} < 6$

$6 < \text{pH} < 6.5$

32. This problem will prepare you for the Multi-Step Test Prep on page 520.

For a certain credit card, given a starting balance of P and an ending balance of A, the function $n = \frac{\log A - \log P}{\log(1.0175)}$ gives the number of months that have passed, assuming that there were no payments or additional purchases during that time.

a. You started with a debt of \$1000 and now owe \$1210.26. For how many months has the debt been building? Use a calculator.

b. How many additional months will it take until the debt exceeds \$1420?

c. What do you notice from the results of parts **a** and **b**?

33. **Critical Thinking** If $\log_a b = 0$, what is the value of b? Explain.

34. **Sound** The loudness of sound is measured on a logarithmic scale according to the formula $L = 10\log\left(\frac{I}{I_0}\right)$, where L is the loudness of sound in decibels (dB), I is the intensity of sound, and I_0 is the intensity of the softest audible sound.

a. Find the loudness in decibels of each sound listed in the table.

b. The sound at a rock concert is found to have a loudness of 110 decibels. Where should this sound be placed in the table in order to keep the sound intensities in order from least to greatest?

c. **What if...?** A decibel is $\frac{1}{10}$ of a *bel*. Is a jet plane louder than a sound that measures 20 *bels*? Explain.

Sound	Intensity
Jet takeoff	$10^{15}I_0$
Jackhammer	$10^{12}I_0$
Hair dryer	$10^{7}I_0$
Whisper	$10^{3}I_0$
Leaves rustling	$10^{2}I_0$
Softest audible sound	I_0

35. **Critical Thinking** If n is an integer, and 10^n is written in expanded form, can you find $\log 10^n$ by counting the number of zeros in 10^n? Support your answer with an example or counterexample.

36. **Estimation** Given that $\log 100 = 2$ and $\log 1000 = 3$, estimate the values of $\log 200$ and $\log 500$.

37. **Food** The hydrogen ion concentrations of three juice samples are given. Identify the type of juice in each sample.

a. 0.00014 moles per liter

b. 0.0081 moles per liter

c. 0.00074 moles per liter

Juice	pH Range
Lemon	2.0–2.6
Grapefruit	2.9–3.2
Orange	3.3–4.1
Tomato	4.1–4.6

38. **Write About It** Explain why $\log_0 3$ and $\log_1 3$ do not exist.

39. The graph of which function is shown?

(A) $f(x) = \log x$

(B) $f(x) = \log_2 x$

(C) $f(x) = \log_4 x$

(D) $f(x) = 2^x$

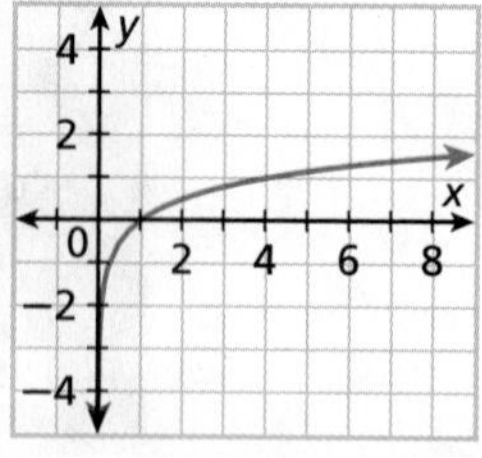

40. Which logarithmic equation is equivalent to $2^7 = 128$?

Ⓕ $\log_7 2 = 128$ Ⓗ $\log_2 7 = 128$

Ⓖ $\log_2 128 = 7$ Ⓙ $\log_7 128 = 2$

41. Which is the best estimate of $\log 50$?

Ⓐ 1.7 Ⓑ 2.5 Ⓒ 5 Ⓓ 10

42. Which graph is the best representation of $f(x) = \log_{0.5} x$?

Ⓕ 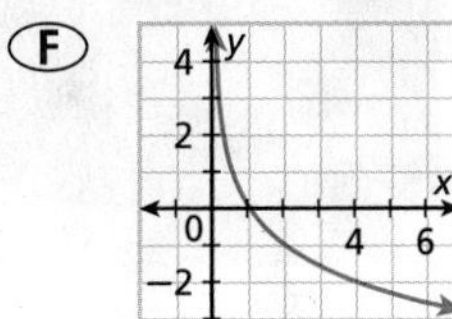

Ⓖ 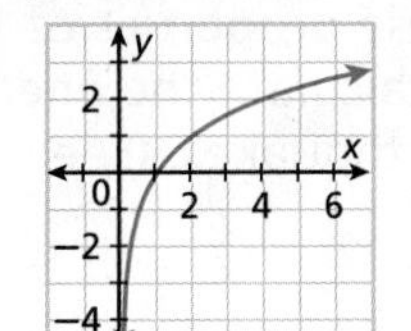

Ⓗ 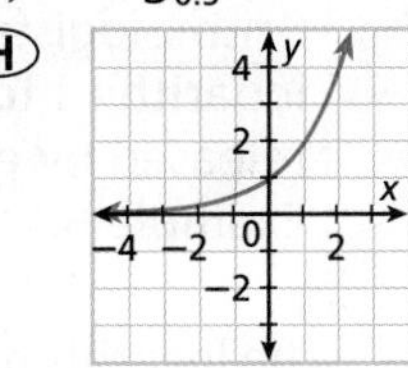

Ⓙ 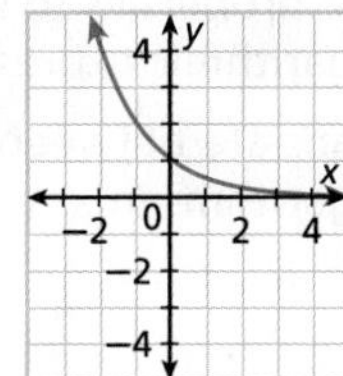

43. **Gridded Response** Evaluate $\log_2 64$.

CHALLENGE AND EXTEND

44. Graph $\log_7 x$ and $\log_{0.7} x$. Describe the difference between the two functions in terms of their graphs.

45. Evaluate $\log_3 9$, $\log_3 27$, and $\log_3 243$. Make a statement about the relationship between the three logarithms. Generalize the result by using variables.

46. Prove that $\log_7 7^{2x+1} = 2x + 1$, giving a reason for each step.

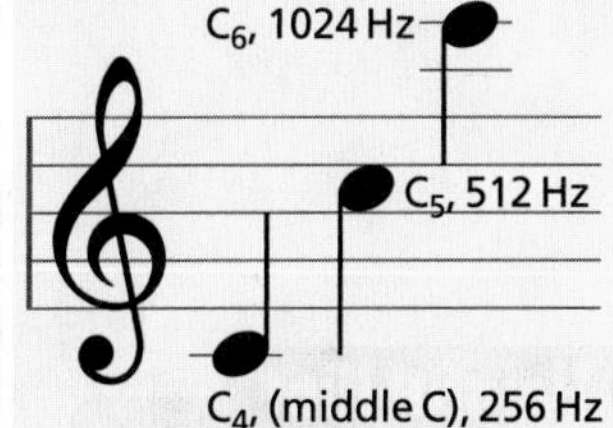

47. **Music** Musical scales are logarithmic. One scale uses a pitch standard called "scientific pitch." In this scale, the frequency of each C note, in vibrations per second, or Hz, can be expressed as a power of 2, as shown.

  a. Express the frequency of the note C_7 in exponential form and in logarithmic form.

  b. If the frequency of one note C is 32 vibrations per second, how many octaves higher or lower than middle C is this note? Explain by using logarithms.

SPIRAL REVIEW

Simplify each expression. Assume that all variables are nonzero. *(Lesson 1-5)*

48. $\left[(2a^4)(5b^2)\right]^2$

49. $\dfrac{8s^2t^6}{4st^8}$

50. $-2t^2(5st^{-1})$

51. $7a^{-2}b^3(3ab + 4a^{-1}b^2)$

52. **Construction** A brick fell at a construction site from a height of 25 feet. Use $h(t) = h_0 - 16t^2$, where h is the height in feet and t is the time in seconds, to determine the time that it took for the brick to hit the ground. *(Lesson 5-3)*

Complete the table of values for each function. Round to the nearest hundredth. *(Lesson 7-1)*

	x	−2	−1	0	1	2
53.	$f(x) = 1.7^x$	■	■	■	■	■
54.	$f(x) = 0.6^x$	■	■	■	■	■
55.	$f(x) = 0.3^x$	■	■	■	■	■

7-4 Properties of Logarithms

Objectives

Use properties to simplify logarithmic expressions.

Translate between logarithms in any base.

Who uses this?

Seismologists use properties of logarithms to calculate the energy released by earthquakes. (See Example 6.)

The logarithmic function for pH that you saw in the previous lesson, $\text{pH} = -\log[\text{H}^+]$, can also be expressed in exponential form, as $10^{-\text{pH}} = [\text{H}^+]$. Because logarithms are exponents, you can derive the properties of logarithms from the properties of exponents.

Remember that to *multiply* powers with the same base, you *add* exponents.

$$b^m b^n = b^{m+n}$$

Product Property of Logarithms

For any positive numbers m, n, and $b\ (b \neq 1)$,

WORDS	NUMBERS	ALGEBRA
The logarithm of a product is equal to the sum of the logarithms of its factors.	$\log_3 1000 = \log_3(10 \cdot 100)$ $= \log_3 10 + \log_3 100$	$\log_b mn = \log_b m + \log_b n$

Helpful Hint

Think:
$\log j + \log a + \log m = \log jam$

The property above can be used in reverse to write a sum of logarithms (exponents) as a single logarithm, which can often be simplified.

EXAMPLE 1 Adding Logarithms

Express as a single logarithm. Simplify, if possible.

A $\log_4 2 + \log_4 32$

$\log_4(2 \cdot 32)$ — *To add the logarithms, multiply the numbers.*

$\log_4 64$ — *Simplify.*

3 — *Think: $4^? = 64$*

Express as a single logarithm. Simplify, if possible.

1a. $\log_5 625 + \log_5 25$ **1b.** $\log_{\frac{1}{3}} 27 + \log_{\frac{1}{3}} \frac{1}{9}$

Remember that to *divide* powers with the same base, you *subtract* exponents.

$$\frac{b^m}{b^n} = b^{m-n}$$

Because logarithms are exponents, subtracting logarithms with the same base is the same as finding the logarithm of the quotient with that base.

Quotient Property of Logarithms

For any positive numbers m, n, and $b\ (b \neq 1)$,

WORDS	NUMBERS	ALGEBRA
The logarithm of a quotient is the logarithm of the dividend minus the logarithm of the divisor.	$\log_5\left(\frac{16}{2}\right) = \log_5 16 - \log_5 2$	$\log_b \frac{m}{n} = \log_b m - \log_b n$

Caution!

Just as a^5b^3 cannot be simplified, logarithms must have the *same* base to be simplified.

The property above can also be used in reverse.

EXAMPLE 2 Subtracting Logarithms

Express $\log_2 32 - \log_2 4$ as a single logarithm. Simplify, if possible.

$\log_2 32 - \log_2 4$	
$\log_2(32 \div 4)$	*To subtract the logarithms, divide the numbers.*
$\log_2 8$	*Simplify.*
3	*Think: $2^? = 8$*

2. Express $\log_7 49 - \log_7 7$ as a single logarithm. Simplify, if possible.

Because you can multiply logarithms, you can also take powers of logarithms.

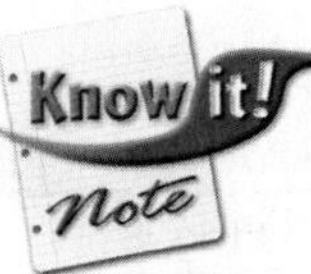

Power Property of Logarithms

For any real number p and positive numbers a and $b\ (b \neq 1)$,

WORDS	NUMBERS	ALGEBRA
The logarithm of a power is the product of the exponent and the logarithm of the base.	$\log 10^3$ $\log(10 \cdot 10 \cdot 10)$ $\log 10 + \log 10 + \log 10$ $3 \log 10$	$\log_b a^p = p \log_b a$

EXAMPLE 3 Simplifying Logarithms with Exponents

Express as a product. Simplify, if possible.

 $\log_3 81^2$

$2 \log_3 81$

$2(4) = 8$ — *Because $3^4 = 81$, $\log_3 81 = 4$.*

 $\log_5\left(\frac{1}{5}\right)^3$

$3 \log_5 \frac{1}{5}$

$3(-1) = -3$ — *$5^{-1} = \frac{1}{5}$*

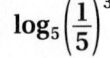

Express as a product. Simplify, if possible.

3a. $\log 10^4$ **3b.** $\log_5 25^2$ **3c.** $\log_2\left(\frac{1}{2}\right)^5$

Exponential and logarithmic operations undo each other since they are inverse operations.

Inverse Properties of Logarithms and Exponents

For any base b such that $b > 0$ and $b \neq 1$,

ALGEBRA	EXAMPLE
$\log_b b^x = x$	$\log_{10} 10^7 = 7$
$b^{\log_b x} = x$	$10^{\log_{10} 2} = 2$

EXAMPLE 4 **Recognizing Inverses**

Simplify each expression.

A $\log_8 8^{3x+1}$

$\log_8 8^{3x+1}$

$3x + 1$

B $\log_5 125$

$\log_5 (5 \cdot 5 \cdot 5)$

$\log_5 5^3$

3

C $2^{\log_2 27}$

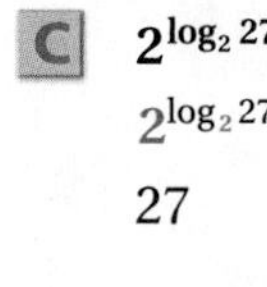

$2^{\log_2 27}$

27

CHECK IT OUT! **4a.** Simplify $\log 10^{0.9}$. **4b.** Simplify $2^{\log_2 (8x)}$.

Most calculators calculate logarithms only in base 10 or base e (see Lesson 7-6). You can change a logarithm in one base to a logarithm in another base with the following formula.

Change of Base Formula

For $a > 0$ and $a \neq 1$ and any base b such that $b > 0$ and $b \neq 1$,

ALGEBRA	EXAMPLE
$\log_b x = \dfrac{\log_a x}{\log_a b}$	$\log_4 8 = \dfrac{\log_2 8}{\log_2 4}$

EXAMPLE 5 **Changing the Base of a Logarithm**

Evaluate $\log_4 8$.

Method 1 Change to base 10.

$$\log_4 8 = \frac{\log 8}{\log 4}$$

$$\approx \frac{0.0903}{0.602} \quad \textit{Use a calculator.}$$

$$= 1.5 \quad \textit{Divide.}$$

Method 2 Change to base 2, because both 4 and 8 are powers of 2.

$$\log_4 8 = \frac{\log_2 8}{\log_2 4} = \frac{3}{2}$$

$$= 1.5$$

CHECK IT OUT! **5a.** Evaluate $\log_9 27$. **5b.** Evaluate $\log_8 16$.

Logarithmic scales are useful for measuring quantities that have a very wide range of values, such as the intensity (loudness) of a sound or the energy released by an earthquake.

EXAMPLE 6 Geology Application

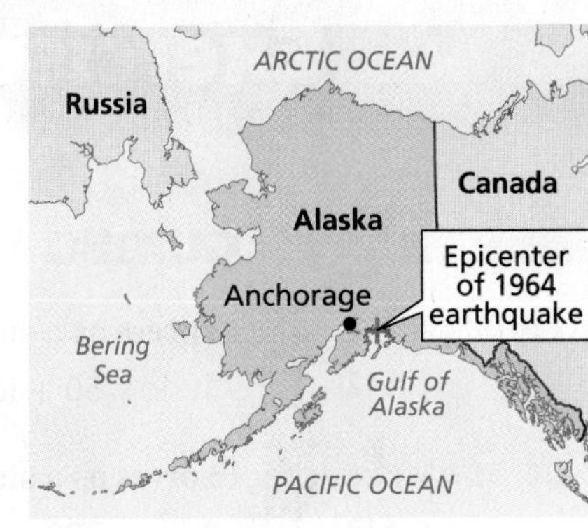

Seismologists use the Richter scale to express the energy, or magnitude, of an earthquake. The Richter magnitude of an earthquake, M, is related to the energy released in ergs E shown by the formula $M = \frac{2}{3}\log\left(\frac{E}{10^{11.8}}\right)$.

In 1964, an earthquake centered at Prince William Sound, Alaska, registered a magnitude of 9.2 on the Richter scale. Find the energy released by the earthquake.

> **Helpful Hint**
>
> The Richter scale is logarithmic, so an increase of 1 corresponds to a release of 10 times as much energy.

$9.2 = \frac{2}{3}\log\left(\frac{E}{10^{11.8}}\right)$	*Substitute 9.2 for M.*
$\left(\frac{3}{2}\right)9.2 = \log\left(\frac{E}{10^{11.8}}\right)$	*Multiply both sides by $\frac{3}{2}$.*
$13.8 = \log\left(\frac{E}{10^{11.8}}\right)$	*Simplify.*
$13.8 = \log E - \log 10^{11.8}$	*Apply the Quotient Property of Logarithms.*
$13.8 = \log E - 11.8$	*Apply the Inverse Properties of Logarithms and Exponents.*
$25.6 = \log E$	
$10^{25.6} = E$	*Given the definition of a logarithm, the logarithm is the exponent.*
$3.98 \times 10^{25} = E$	*Use a calculator to evaluate.*

The energy released by an earthquake with a magnitude of 9.2 is 3.98×10^{25} ergs.

6. How many times as much energy is released by an earthquake with a magnitude of 9.2 than by an earthquake with a magnitude of 8?

THINK AND DISCUSS

1. Explain how to graph $y = \log_5 x$ on a calculator.

2. Tell how you could find $10^{25.6}$ in Example 6 by applying a law of exponents.

3. Describe what happens when you use the change-of-base formula, $\log_b x = \frac{\log_a x}{\log_a b}$, when $x = a$.

4. GET ORGANIZED Copy and complete the graphic organizer. Use your own words to show related properties of exponents and logarithms.

Property of Exponents	Property of Logarithms

7-4 Exercises

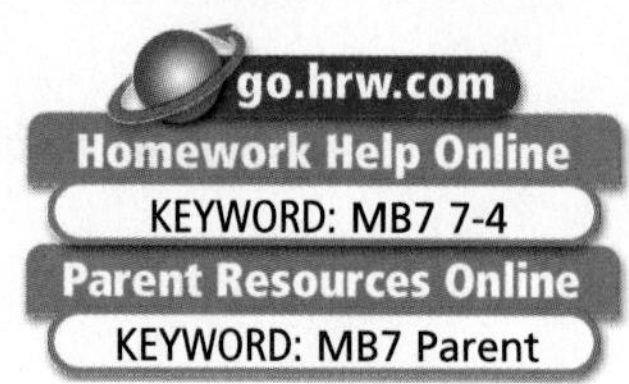

GUIDED PRACTICE

SEE EXAMPLE 1 p. 512

Express as a single logarithm. Simplify, if possible.

1. $\log_5 50 + \log_5 62.5$
2. $\log 100 + \log 1000$
3. $\log_3 3 + \log_3 27$

SEE EXAMPLE 2 p. 513

Express as a single logarithm. Simplify, if possible.

4. $\log_4 320 - \log_4 5$
5. $\log 5.4 - \log 0.054$
6. $\log_6 496.8 - \log_6 2.3$

SEE EXAMPLE 3 p. 513

Simplify, if possible.

7. $\log_8 8^2$
8. $\log_3 3^5$
9. $\log_7 49^3$
10. $\log_{\frac{1}{2}}(0.25)^4$

SEE EXAMPLE 4 p. 514

11. $\log_2 2^{\frac{x}{2}+5}$
12. $2.5^{\log_{2.5} 19}$
13. $\log_4 1024$
14. $\log_2(0.5)^4$

SEE EXAMPLE 5 p. 514

Evaluate.

15. $\log_9\left(\frac{1}{27}\right)$
16. $\log_8 32$
17. $\log_5 10$
18. $\log_2 27$

SEE EXAMPLE 6 p. 515

19. **Geology** The Richter magnitude M of an earthquake is related to the energy released in ergs E shown by the formula $M = \frac{2}{3}\log\left(\frac{E}{10^{11.8}}\right)$. How many times as much energy was released by the 1811 New Madrid, Missouri, earthquake than by the Fort Tejon, California, earthquake?

Largest Earthquakes in Continental U.S.

Location	Year	M
New Madrid, MO	1811	8.1
New Madrid, MO	1812	8.0
Fort Tejon, CA	1957	7.9
San Francisco, CA	1906	7.8
Imperial Valley, CA	1892	7.8

PRACTICE AND PROBLEM SOLVING

Independent Practice

For Exercises	See Example
20–22	1
23–25	2
26–28	3
29–31	4
32–34	5
35	6

Extra Practice

Skills Practice p. S16
Application Practice p. S38

Express as a single logarithm. Simplify, if possible.

20. $\log_8 4 + \log_8 16$
21. $\log 2 + \log 5$
22. $\log_{2.5} 3.125 + \log_{2.5} 5$
23. $\log 1000 - \log 100$
24. $\log_2 16 - \log_2 2$
25. $\log_{1.5} 6.75 - \log_{1.5} 2$

Simplify, if possible.

26. $\log_2 16^3$
27. $\log(100)^{0.1}$
28. $\log_5 125^{\frac{1}{3}}$
29. $\log_3 3^{7+x}$
30. $3^{\log_3 4.52}$
31. $\log_9 6561$

Evaluate.

32. $\log_{\frac{1}{2}} 16$
33. $\log_{25} 125$
34. $\log_4 9$

35. **Sound** After some complaints, it was found that the music from an outdoor concert was 5 decibels louder than the city's allowable level of 100 decibels. The loudness L of sound in decibels is given by $L = 10\log\left(\frac{I}{I_0}\right)$, where I is the intensity of sound and I_0 is the intensity of the softest audible sound. How many times more intense is the concert sound than the allowable level?

36. **Astronomy** The difference between the apparent magnitude (brightness) m of a star, and its absolute magnitude M is given by the formula $m - M = 5 \log \frac{d}{10}$, where d is the distance of the star from Earth, measured in parsecs.

   a. Find the distance d of Antares from Earth.

   b. Sigma Sco is 225 parsecs from Earth. Find its absolute magnitude.

   c. How many times as great is the distance to Antares as the distance to Rho Oph?

Write the equivalent logarithmic form for each equation.

37. $b^{m+n} = b^m b^n$

38. $b^{m-n} = \dfrac{b^m}{b^n}$

39. $(b^m)^n = b^{mn}$

Simplify, if possible.

40. $\log_2 32 - \log_2 128$

41. $\log 0.1 + \log 1 + \log 10$

42. $2 - \log_{11} 121$

43. $\log_{\frac{1}{2}} 2 + \log_{\frac{1}{2}} 2^{\frac{1}{2}}$

44. $7^{\log_7 7} - \log_7 7^7$

45. $\dfrac{10^{\log 10}}{\log 10^{10}}$

46. **Critical Thinking** Use the properties of logarithms with the fact that $\log 2 \approx 0.301$ to evaluate.

   a. $\log 20$

   b. $\log 200$

   c. $\log 2000$

LINK

Math History

Scottish mathematician John Napier (1550–1617) invented logarithms and named them by joining the Greek words *logos* (ratio) and *arithmos* (number).

47. **Chemistry** Most swimming pool experts recommend a pH of between 7.0 and 7.6 for water in a swimming pool. Use $\text{pH} = -\log[\text{H}^+]$, and write an expression for the difference in hydrogen ion concentration over this pH range.

48. **Multi-Step** Suppose that the population of one endangered species decreases at a rate of 4% per year. In one habitat, the current population of the species is 143.

   a. Write an exponential function for the population by year.

   b. Write a logarithmic function for the time based upon population.

   c. Write the keystrokes necessary to enter the logarithmic function on a calculator.

   d. After how long will the population drop below 30, to the nearest year?

49. **Finance** A stock priced at \$40 increases at a rate of 8% per year. Write and evaluate a logarithmic expression for the number of years that it will take for the value of the stock to reach \$50. (*Hint:* Write the expression in exponential form first.)

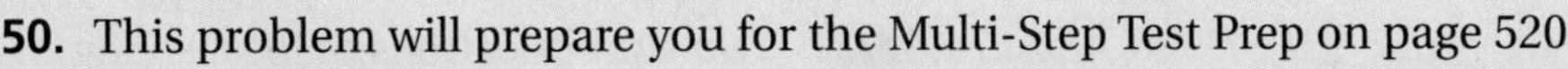

MULTI-STEP TEST PREP

50. This problem will prepare you for the Multi-Step Test Prep on page 520.

For a certain credit card with 19.2% annual interest compounded monthly, the total amount A that you owe after n months is given by $A = P(1.016)^n$, where P is the starting balance.

   a. You start with a balance of \$500. Write and solve a logarithmic expression for the number of months it will take for the debt to double.

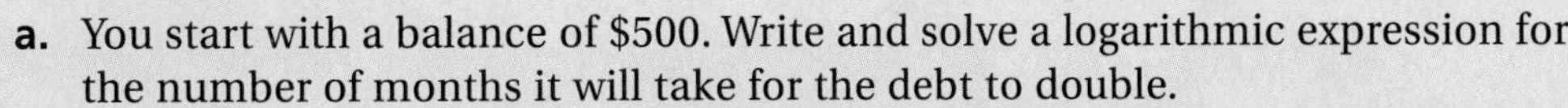

   b. How many additional months will it take for the debt to double again?

   c. Does the amount of time that it takes the debt to double depend on the starting balance?

Graphing Calculator Use the change of base formula and a graphing calculator to graph.

51. $y = \log_3 x$ **52.** $y = 2\log_5 x$ **53.** $y = \frac{\log_{12} x}{3}$

54. Write About It Explain how to graph a logarithm in a base other than 10 on a calculator.

55. Critical Thinking Given $\log_{12} 20 \approx 1.2$ and $\log_{12} 33 \approx 1.4$, find each approximate value.

a. $\log_{12} 1.65$ **b.** $\log_{12} 660$ **c.** $\log_{12} 400$

56. Critical Thinking There is an interesting relationship between logarithms and scientific notation.

a. Find the logarithm of 2.5.

b. Find the logarithm of the mass of the *Titanic*. Compare it to your answer from part **a.**

c. Make a Conjecture A lion has a mass of 2.5×10^2 kg. Find the logarithm of this number. Use your answers and the answers to parts **a** and **b,** to explain how to find the base 10 logarithm of a number written in scientific notation.

d. Use your conjecture to find the logarithm of the mass of a dime. Does your conjecture hold for scientific notation with negative exponents?

mass: $\approx 2.5 \times 10^7$ kg

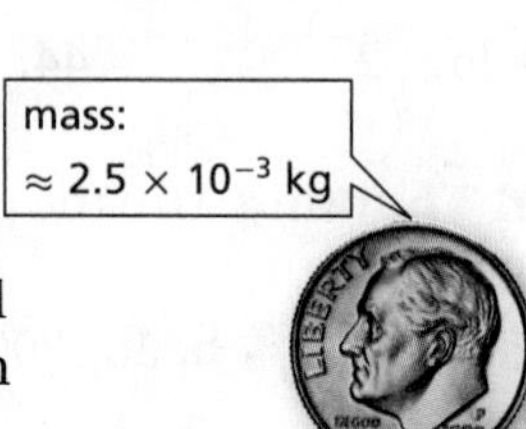

mass: $\approx 2.5 \times 10^{-3}$ kg

Assume $b > 0$ and $b \neq 1$. Tell whether each statement is sometimes, always, or never true.

57. A logarithm with base b can be changed to another rational-number base.

58. The logarithm with base 6 of 6 raised to an expression is equal to the expression.

59. Subtracting log base b of 1 from a number is just the number itself.

60. The base of a logarithm can be a negative number.

61. The logarithm of the square of a number is equal to twice the logarithm of the number.

62. Logarithms with different bases can be added without changing a base.

63. $\frac{\log_b 16}{\log_b 8}$ can be simplified.

64. A logarithm of a logarithm of a number is the number.

65. ///ERROR ANALYSIS/// Two simplifications of $\log 80 + \log 20$ are shown. Which of these is incorrect? Explain.

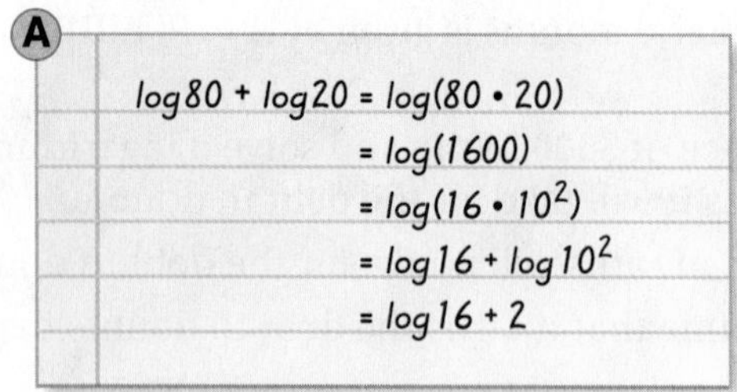

A

$\log 80 + \log 20 = \log(80 \cdot 20)$
$= \log(1600)$
$= \log(16 \cdot 10^2)$
$= \log 16 + \log 10^2$
$= \log 16 + 2$

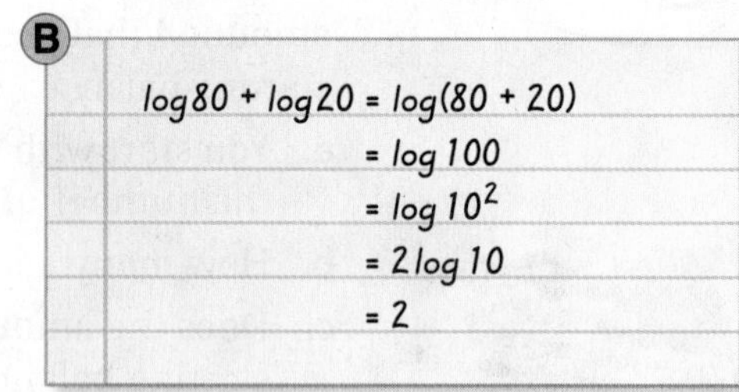

B

$\log 80 + \log 20 = \log(80 + 20)$
$= \log 100$
$= \log 10^2$
$= 2\log 10$
$= 2$

66. Which statement is NOT true?

Ⓐ $\log 140 - \log 35 = \log 4$

Ⓑ $\dfrac{\log 140}{\log 35} = \log 4$

Ⓒ $\log 35 + \log 4 = \log 140$

Ⓓ $\log \dfrac{140}{35} = \log 4$

67. Simplify $\log_9 x^2 + \log_9 x$.

Ⓕ $\log_9 (x^2 + x)$ Ⓖ $\log_9 3x$ Ⓗ $3\log_9 x$ Ⓙ $3(x^2 + x)$

68. Which logarithmic expression is equal to $\log 6$?

Ⓐ $\log 3 + \log 2$ Ⓑ $\log 3 + \log 3$ Ⓒ $(\log 3)(\log 2)$ Ⓓ $(\log 3)(\log 3)$

CHALLENGE AND EXTEND

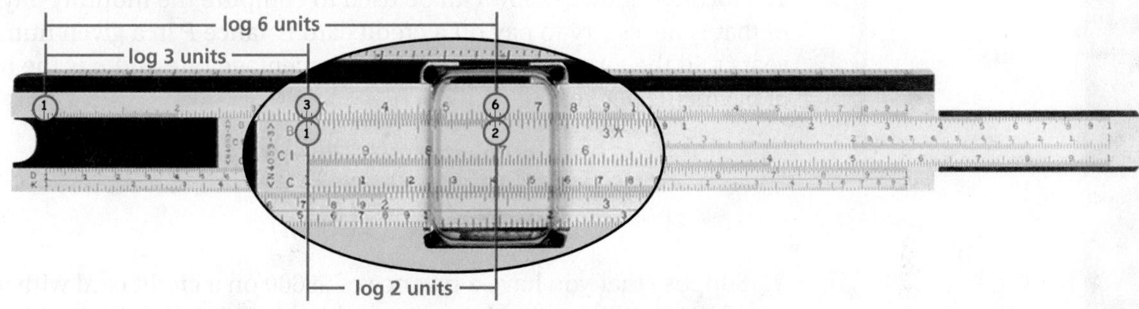

69. **Math History** The slide rule used two number lines that slid against each other. The scale on each was logarithmic, so the properties of logarithms could be applied to multiply and divide numbers.
   a. Explain how the product of 2 and 3 is shown on the slide rule.
   b. How does this show the product property of logarithms?

Find the domain of each function.

70. $f(x) = \log(x^2 - 4)$ 71. $f(x) = \log x - \log(x - 1)$ 72. $f(x) = \log\left(\dfrac{x}{x^2 - 1}\right)$

73. $f(x) = \log\left(\dfrac{1}{x}\right)^2$ 74. $f(x) = -\sqrt{\log(x + 1)}$ 75. $f(x) = \sqrt{-2\log(-x)}$

76. Prove: $\log_b a^p = p\log_b a$. 77. Simplify $\log_9 3^{2x}$.

Solve.

78. $\log_x 25 = 2$ 79. $\log_x(-8) = 3$ 80. $0 = \log_x 1$

SPIRAL REVIEW

Solve. *(Lesson 2-1)*

81. $9 = 3(x - 14)$ 82. $4(x + 1) = 3(2x - 6)$

83. $-20 + 8n = n + 29$ 84. $8\left(n + \dfrac{3}{4}\right) = 10n - 4$

Express each number in terms of *i*. *(Lesson 5-5)*

85. $3\sqrt{-16}$ 86. $-\frac{1}{2}\sqrt{-40}$ 87. $4\sqrt{-8}$ 88. $\sqrt{-125}$

Write each exponential equation in logarithmic form. *(Lesson 7-3)*

89. $5^3 = 125$ 90. $10^{-1} = 0.1$ 91. $36^{0.5} = 6$ 92. $4^x = 256$

Evaluate. *(Lesson 7-3)*

93. $\log_{12} 1$ 94. $\log_5 25$ 95. $\log_{16} 4$ 96. $\log_{625} 0.04$

CHAPTER 7

SECTION 7A

Exponential Functions and Logarithms

Charged Up There are more than 1 billion credit cards in circulation in the United States, and the average American carries a credit card debt of approximately \$8600. Given that many credit cards charge an annual percentage rate (APR) of 18.3%, it can be difficult to escape the "credit hole."

The formula shown below can be used to compute the monthly payment M that is necessary to pay off a credit card balance P in a given number of years t. In the formula, r is the annual percentage rate and n is the number of payments per year.

$$M = \frac{P\left(\frac{r}{n}\right)}{1 - \left(1 + \frac{r}{n}\right)^{-nt}}$$

1. Suppose that you have a balance of \$8600 on a credit card with an APR of 18.3%. What monthly payment should you make in order to pay off the debt in exactly five years?

2. How much money do you end up paying altogether over the five years?

In order to calculate the number of years necessary for a given payment schedule, the formula can be written as shown.

$$t = \frac{\log\left(1 - \frac{Pr}{Mn}\right)}{-n \log\left(1 + \frac{r}{n}\right)}$$

3. If you can afford only a monthly payment of \$160, how long will it take to pay off the credit card debt?

4. Suppose you can afford a monthly payment of \$130. Will you be able to pay off the debt? If so, how long will it take? If not, why not?

5. What is the minimum monthly payment that will work toward paying off the debt?

"I didn't have time to mow the lawn, so I used your credit card to have it carpeted."

CHAPTER 7

SECTION 7A

Quiz for Lesson 7-1 Through 7-4

7-1 Exponential Functions, Growth, and Decay

Tell whether the function shows growth or decay. Then graph.

1. $f(x) = \left(\frac{1}{4}\right)^x$ **2.** $f(x) = \frac{1}{5}(0.2)^x$ **3.** $f(x) = 14(1.4^x)$ **4.** $f(x) = 6.4\left(1\frac{3}{8}\right)^x$

5. Suppose that the number of bacteria in a culture was 1000 on Monday and the number has been increasing at a rate of 50% per day since then.

a. Write a function representing the growth of the culture per day.

b. Graph the function, and use the graph to predict the number of bacteria in the culture the following Monday.

7-2 Inverses of Relations and Functions

Graph each relation. Then graph its inverse.

6.

x	−1	0	1	2	3
y	0	4	8	12	16

7.

x	0	1	2	3	4
y	−1	$-\frac{1}{3}$	$\frac{1}{3}$	1	$1\frac{2}{3}$

Graph each function. Then write and graph the inverse.

8. $f(x) = x + 2.1$ **9.** $f(x) = \frac{3}{4} - x$ **10.** $f(x) = 5x + 4$ **11.** $f(x) = 0.4\left(\frac{x}{2} + 1.5\right)$

12. Rebekah's computer repair bill includes \$210 for parts and \$55 per hour for labor. Her bill can be expressed as a function of hours x by $f(x) = 210 + 55x$. Find the inverse function. Use it to find the number of hours of labor if her bill was \$402.50.

7-3 Logarithmic Functions

Write the exponential equation in logarithmic form.

13. $3^2 = 9$ **14.** $17.6^0 = 1$ **15.** $2^{-2} = 0.25$ **16.** $0.5^x = 0.0625$

Write the logarithmic equation in exponential form.

17. $\log_4 64 = 3$ **18.** $\log_{\frac{1}{5}} 25 = -2$ **19.** $\log_{0.99} 1 = 0$ **20.** $\log_e x = 5$

21. Use the given x-values to graph $f(x) = \left(\frac{5}{6}\right)^x$; $x = -1, 0, 1, 2, 3$. Then graph the inverse function.

7-4 Properties of Logarithms

Express as a single logarithm. Simplify, if possible.

22. $\log_3 81 + \log_3 9$ **23.** $\log_{\frac{1}{5}} 25 + \log_{\frac{1}{5}} 5$ **24.** $\log_{1.2} 2.16 - \log_{1.2} 1.5$

Simplify each expression.

25. $\log_4 256^2$ **26.** $\log_7 343$ **27.** $17^{\log_{17} 0.73}$

Evaluate.

28. $\log_{27} 243$ **29.** $\log_{10} 0.01$ **30.** $\log_5 625$

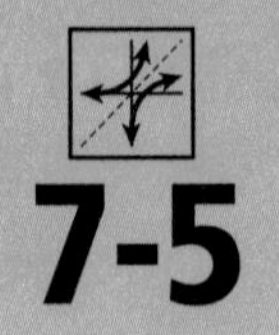

7-5 Exponential and Logarithmic Equations and Inequalities

Objectives
Solve exponential and logarithmic equations and inequalities.

Solve problems involving exponential and logarithmic equations.

Vocabulary
exponential equation
logarithmic equation

Who uses this?
Exponential scales are used to measure light in photography. (See Exercise 40.)

An **exponential equation** is an equation containing one or more expressions that have a variable as an exponent. To solve exponential equations:

- Try writing them so that the bases are all the same. If $b^x = b^y$, then $x = y$ $(b \neq 0, b \neq 1)$.
- Take the logarithm of both sides. If $a = b$, then $\log a = \log b$ $(a > 0, b > 0)$.

EXAMPLE 1 Solving Exponential Equations

Solve and check.

A $8^x = 2^{x+6}$

$(2^3)^x = 2^{x+6}$ *Rewrite each side with the same base; 8 is a power of 2.*

$2^{3x} = 2^{x+6}$ *To raise a power to a power, multiply exponents.*

$3x = x + 6$ *Bases are the same, so the exponents must be equal.*

$x = 3$ *Solve for x.*

Check

8^x	2^{x+6}
8^3	2^{3+6}
8^3	2^9
512	512 ✓

The solution is $x = 3$.

B $5^{x-2} = 200$

$\log 5^{x-2} = \log 200$ *200 is not a power of 5, so take the log of both sides.*

$(x-2)\log 5 = \log 200$ *Apply the Power Property of Logarithms.*

$x - 2 = \dfrac{\log 200}{\log 5}$ *Divide both sides by log 5.*

$x = 2 + \dfrac{\log 200}{\log 5} \approx 5.292$

Check Use a calculator.

```
5^(5.292-2)
            199.9904485
```

The solution is $x \approx 5.292$.

Helpful Hint

When you use a rounded number in a check, the result will not be exact, but it should be reasonable.

Solve and check.

1a. $3^{2x} = 27$ **1b.** $7^{-x} = 21$ **1c.** $2^{3x} = 15$

EXAMPLE 2 Money Application

You can choose a prize of either a \$20,000 car or one penny on the first day, double that (2 cents) on the second day, and so on for a month. On what day would you receive more than the value of the car?

\$20,000 is 2,000,000 cents. On day 1, you would receive 1 cent, or 2^0 cents. On day 2, you would receive 2 cents, or 2^1 cents, and so on. So, on day n you would receive 2^{n-1} cents.

Solve $2^{n-1} > 2 \times 10^6$. *Write 2,000,000 in scientific notation.*

$\log 2^{n-1} > \log(2 \times 10^6)$ *Take the log of both sides.*

$(n-1)\log 2 > \log 2 + \log 10^6$ *Use the Power Property and Product Property.*

$(n-1)\log 2 > \log 2 + 6$ *$\log 10^6$ is 6.*

$n - 1 > \dfrac{\log 2 + 6}{\log 2}$ *Divide both sides by $\log 2$.*

$n > \approx \dfrac{0.301 + 6}{0.301} + 1$ *Evaluate by using a calculator.*

$n > \approx 21.93$ *Round this up to the next whole number.*

Beginning on day 22, you would receive more than the value of the car.

Check On day 22, you would receive 2^{22-1} cents.

$2^{22-1} = 2^{21} = 2{,}097{,}152$ cents, or \$20,971.52.

2. In Example 2, suppose that you receive triple the amount each day. On what day would you receive at least a million dollars?

A **logarithmic equation** is an equation with a logarithmic expression that contains a variable. You can solve logarithmic equations by using the properties of logarithms.

$$\text{If } \log_b x = \log_b y \text{ then } x = y$$

EXAMPLE 3 Solving Logarithmic Equations

Solve.

A $\log_3(x - 5) = 2$

$3^{\log_3(x-5)} = 3^2$ *Use 3 as the base for both sides.*

$x - 5 = 9$ *Use inverse properties to remove 3 to the log base 3.*

$x = 14$ *Simplify.*

Remember!

Review the properties of logarithms from Lesson 7-4.

B $\log 45x - \log 3 = 1$

$\log\left(\dfrac{45x}{3}\right) = 1$ *Write as a quotient.*

$\log(15x) = 1$ *Divide.*

$10^{\log 15x} = 10^1$ *Use 10 as a base for both sides.*

$15x = 10$ *Use inverse properties on the left side.*

$x = \dfrac{2}{3}$

Solve.

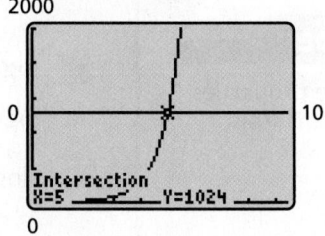 $\log_4 x^2 = 7$

$2\log_4 x = 7$	*Power Property of Logarithms*
$\log_4 x = \frac{7}{2}$	*Divide both sides by 2 to isolate $\log_4 x$.*
$x = 4^{\frac{7}{2}}$	*Definition of a logarithm*
$x = (2^2)^{\frac{7}{2}}$	*4 is a power of 2.*
$x = 2^7$, or 128	

 $\log x + \log(x+9) = 1$

$\log x(x+9) = 1$	*Product Property of Logarithms.*
$10^{\log x(x+9)} = 10^1$	*Exponential form*
$x(x+9) = 10$	*Use the inverse properties.*
$x^2 + 9x - 10 = 0$	*Multiply and collect terms.*
$(x-1)(x+10) = 0$	*Factor.*
$x - 1 = 0$ or $x + 10 = 0$	*Set each of the factors equal to zero.*
$x = 1$ or $x = -10$	*Solve.*

Caution!

Watch out for calculated solutions that are not solutions of the original equation.

Check Check both solutions in the original equation.

$\log x + \log(x+9)$	1
$\log 1 + \log(1+9)$	1
$\log 1 + \log 10$	1
$0 + 1$	1
1	1 ✔

$\log x + \log(x+9)$	1
$\log(-10) + \log(-10+9)$	1 ✘

log(−10) is undefined.

The solution is $x = 1$.

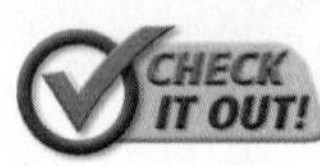

3a. Solve $3 = \log 8 + 3\log x$. **3b.** Solve $2\log x - \log 4 = 0$.

EXAMPLE 4 Using Tables and Graphs to Solve Exponential and Logarithmic Equations and Inequalities

Use a table and graph to solve.

 $2^{2x} = 1024$

Use a graphing calculator. Enter **2^(2X)** as **Y1** and **1024** as **Y2**.

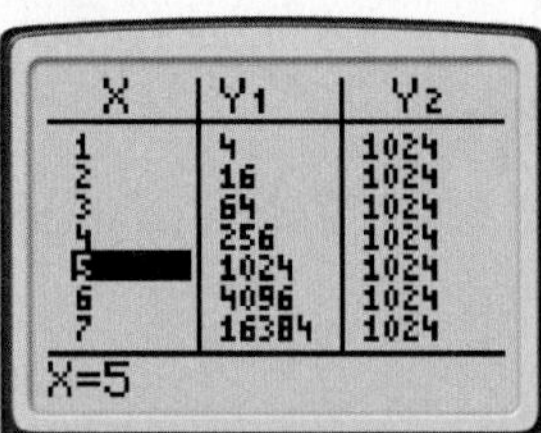

X	Y1	Y2
1	4	1024
2	16	1024
3	64	1024
4	256	1024
5	1024	1024
6	4096	1024
7	16384	1024

X=5

In the table, find the x-value where Y1 and Y2 are equal.

2000

0 10

Intersection X=5 Y=1024

0

In the graph, find the x-value at the point of intersection.

The solution is $x = 5$.

Use a table and graph to solve.

B $\log x - \log 2 \leq \log 75$

Use a graphing calculator. Enter $\log x - \log 2$ as **Y1** and $\log 75$ as **Y2**.

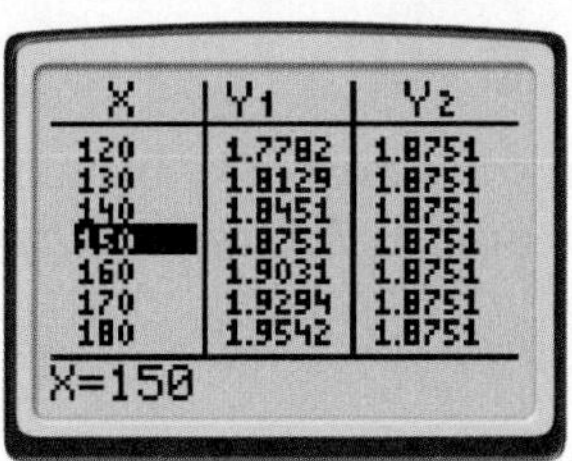

In the table, find the x-values where Y1 is less than or equal to Y2.

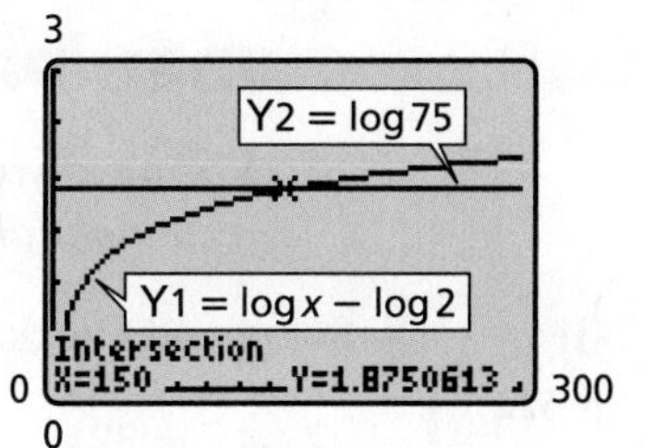

In the graph, find the x-value at the point of intersection.

The solution set is $\{x \mid 0 < x \leq 150\}$.

Check Use algebra.

$$\log x - \log 2 \leq \log 75$$

$$\log\left(\frac{x}{2}\right) \leq \log 75 \quad \textit{Quotient Property of Logarithms}$$

$$10^{\log\left(\frac{x}{2}\right)} \leq 10^{\log 75} \quad \textit{Use 10 as a base for both sides.}$$

$$\frac{x}{2} \leq 75 \quad \textit{Inverse Property}$$

$$x \leq 150 \checkmark \quad \textit{log x is only defined for } x > 0.$$

Use a table and graph to solve.

4a. $2^x = 4^{x-1}$ **4b.** $2^x > 4^{x-1}$ **4c.** $\log x^2 = 6$

THINK AND DISCUSS

1. Explain why a and b must be equal if $\log a = \log b$ $(a > 0, b > 0)$.
2. Give only the first step you would use to solve each equation.
   - **a.** $\log x^5 = 10$
   - **b.** $\log 2x + \log 2 = 1$
   - **c.** $x^4 = 100$
   - **d.** $\log(x + 1000) = 2$
   - **e.** $\log(x + 4) + \log x = 2$
   - **f.** $\log_6(x + 6) = 3$
3. Explain whether a logarithmic equation can have a negative number as a solution. Justify your answer. Give an example, if possible.

4. **GET ORGANIZED** Copy and complete the graphic organizer. Write the strategies and points to remember in your own words for both exponential and logarithmic equations.

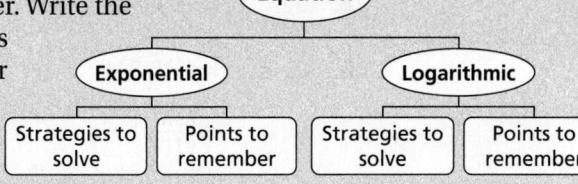

Equation
- Exponential
  - Strategies to solve
  - Points to remember
- Logarithmic
  - Strategies to solve
  - Points to remember

7-5 Exercises

go.hrw.com
Homework Help Online
KEYWORD: MB7 7-5
Parent Resources Online
KEYWORD: MB7 Parent

GUIDED PRACTICE

1. **Vocabulary** You can solve a(n) __?__ by taking the logarithm of both sides. (*exponential equation* or *logarithmic equation*)

SEE EXAMPLE 1 p. 522

Solve and check.

2. $4^{2x} = 32^{\frac{1}{2}}$
3. $9^x = 3^{x-2}$
4. $2^x = 4^{x+1}$
5. $4^x = 10$
6. $\left(\frac{1}{4}\right)^{2x} = \left(\frac{1}{2}\right)^x$
7. $2.4^{3x+1} = 9$

SEE EXAMPLE 2 p. 523

8. **Population** The population of a small coastal resort town, currently 3400, grows at a rate of 3% per year. This growth can be expressed by the exponential equation $P = 3400(1 + 0.03)^t$, where P is the population after t years. Find the number of years it will take for the population to exceed 10,000.

SEE EXAMPLE 3 p. 523

Solve.

9. $\log_2(7x + 1) = \log_2(2 - x)$
10. $\log_6(2x + 3) = 3$
11. $\log 72 - \log\left(\frac{2x}{3}\right) = 0$
12. $\log_3 x^9 = 12$
13. $\log_7(3 - 4x) = \log_7\left(\frac{x}{3}\right)$
14. $\log 50 + \log\left(\frac{x}{2}\right) = 2$
15. $\log x + \log(x + 48) = 2$
16. $\log\left(x + \frac{3}{10}\right) + \log x + 1 = 0$

SEE EXAMPLE 4 p. 524

Use a table and graph to solve.

17. $2^{2x+1} = 256$
18. $2^x 3^x \le 7776$
19. $2\log x^4 = 16$
20. $x > 10\log x$

PRACTICE AND PROBLEM SOLVING

Independent Practice

For Exercises	See Example
21–26	1
27	2
28–33	3
34–36	4

Extra Practice

Skills Practice p. S17
Application Practice p. S38

Solve and check.

21. $2^{x-1} = \frac{1}{64}$
22. $\left(\frac{1}{4}\right)^x = 8^{x-1}$
23. $\left(\frac{1}{5}\right)^{x-2} = 125^{\frac{x}{2}}$
24. $\left(\frac{1}{2}\right)^{-x} = 1.6$
25. $(1.5)^{x-1} = 14.5$
26. $3^{\frac{x}{2}+1} = 12.2$
27. **Pets** A veterinarian has instructed Harrison to give his 75 lb dog one 325 mg aspirin tablet for arthritis. The amount of aspirin A remaining in the dog's body after t minutes can be expressed by $A = 325\left(\frac{1}{2}\right)^{\frac{t}{15}}$. Write and solve a logarithmic inequality to find the time it takes for the amount of aspirin to drop below 50 mg.

Solve.

28. $\log_3(7x) = \log_3(2x + 0.5)$
29. $\log_2\left(1 + \frac{x}{2}\right) = 4$
30. $\log 5x - \log(15.5) = 2$
31. $\log_5 x^4 = 2.5$
32. $\log x - \log\left(\frac{x}{100}\right) = x$
33. $2 - \log 3x = \log\left(\frac{x}{12}\right)$

Use a table and graph to solve.

34. $2 \cdot 3^{x-1} = 162$
35. $4x < 2^{x+1}$
36. $\log(2x - 17) + \log x \ge 2$

37. Solve $\log x = \log(x^2 - 12)$. Explain your answer.

38. Solve $5^{2x} = 100$ to the nearest hundredth.

39. Solve $2^{x+2} = 64$ using more than one method.

40. **Photography** On many cameras, the amount of light admitted through the lens can be controlled by changing the size of the opening, or *aperture*. The size of the aperture is measured as an f-stop setting. The relationship between the f-stop and the amount of light admitted can be represented by the equation $n = \log_2 \frac{1}{\ell}$, where n is the change in f-stop setting from the starting value, f/5.6.

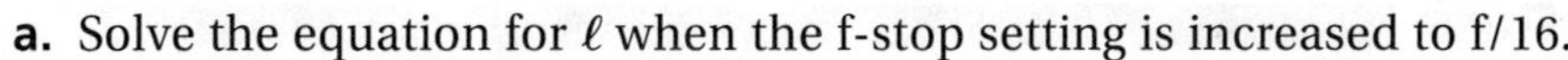

F-stop Setting	f/2	f/2.8	f/4	f/5.6	f/8	f/11	f/16
Change in F-stop Setting	−3	−2	−1	0	1	2	3

a. Solve the equation for ℓ when the f-stop setting is increased to f/16.

b. Solve the equation for n when the light admitted through the lens is twice the amount at f/5.6. What is the f-stop setting? Use a calculator to verify the solution.

LINK

Music

Pianos could be considered both percussion and stringed instruments, with hammers that hit each string. Pianos are usually located near the drums in an orchestra.

41. **Music** The frequency of a note on the piano, in Hz, is related to its position on the keyboard by the function $f(n) = 440 \cdot 2^{\frac{n}{12}}$, where n is the number of keys above or below the note concert A. (A negative value for n means that the key is to the left of, or lower on the keyboard than, concert A.) Find the position n of the key that has a frequency of 110 Hz.

42. **Finance** Suppose that \$250 is deposited into an account that pays 4.5% compounded quarterly. The equation $A = P\left(1 + \frac{r}{4}\right)^n$ gives the amount A in the account after n quarters for an initial investment P that earns interest at a rate r. Solve for n to find how long it will take for the account to contain at least \$500. (*Hint:* Divide both sides by P first.)

43. **Critical Thinking** How many real-number solutions are there for $\log x^2 < 2\log x$? Use a calculator to graph and verify the answer. Explain what the graph indicates about the answer.

44. **///ERROR ANALYSIS///** When a student solved $\log x + 4 = 8$, he arrived at 99,999,996. Give a possible reason for the error.

45. **Write About It** Describe two methods you can use to solve an exponential equation. Give an example of when you would use each method.

MULTI-STEP TEST PREP

46. This problem will prepare you for the Multi-Step Test Prep on page 552.

The number of farms in Iowa (in thousands) can be modeled by $N(t) = 119(0.987)^t$, where t is the number of years since 1980.

a. Has the number of farms in Iowa been increasing or decreasing since 1980? How can you tell?

b. Find the number of farms in Iowa in 1980 and 2000.

c. According to the model, when will be the number of farms in Iowa be about 80,000?

47. **Meteorology** In one part of the atmosphere where the temperature is a constant –70°F, pressure can be expressed as a function of altitude by the equation $P(h) = 128(10)^{-0.0682h}$, where P is the atmospheric pressure in kilopascals (kPa) and h is the altitude in kilometers above sea level. The pressure ranges from 2.55 kPa to 22.9 kPa in this region.

a. What are the lowest and highest altitudes where this model is appropriate? In what part of the atmosphere is the model useful?

b. **What if...?** A kilopascal is 0.145 psi. Would the model predict a sea-level pressure less than or greater than the actual sea-level pressure, 14.7 psi? Explain.

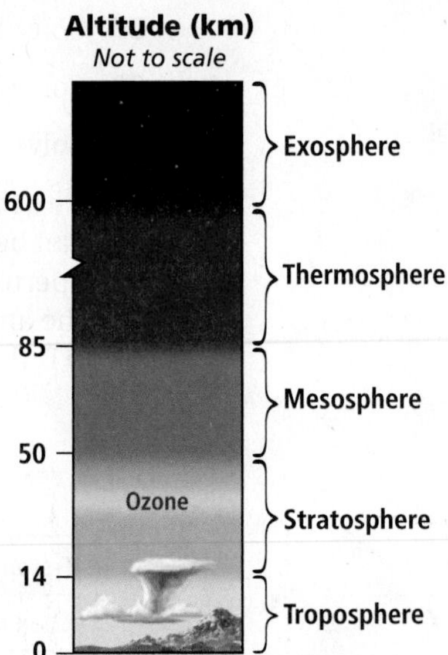

48. What is the solution of the equation $b^x = c$?

Ⓐ $x = \frac{\log b}{\log c}$ Ⓑ $x = \frac{\log c}{\log b}$ Ⓒ $x = \frac{\log b}{c}$ Ⓓ $x = \frac{\log c}{b}$

49. What is the solution of $\log(x - 21) = 2 - \log x$?

Ⓕ $x = 4$ Ⓖ $x = \frac{25}{4}$ Ⓗ $x = \frac{21}{2}$ Ⓙ $x = 25$

50. Which expression has the greatest value when $p = 5$ and $q = 2$?

Ⓐ $\log 2p - \log 3q$ Ⓒ $2\log q - 3\log p$

Ⓑ $\log p^2 - \log q^3$ Ⓓ $\log p - \log q$

CHALLENGE AND EXTEND

51. If $\log_x x = x$, can the equation be solved for x? Explain.

52. Solve $x = 0.125^{\log_2 5}$ algebraically.

53. For what domain is $\log_3 36 - \log_3 x > 1$? Use a calculator to graph and support your solution.

SPIRAL REVIEW

54. **Photography** It costs \$0.75 to develop an 8-by-10-inch photograph and \$0.35 to develop a 4-by-6-inch photograph. Eli has \$5.25. Use x as the number of 8-by-10-inch photographs and y as the number of 4-by-6-inch photographs. *(Lesson 2-5)*

a. Write an inequality for the number of each type of photograph Eli can buy.

b. Graph the inequality. How many 4-by-6-inch photographs can Eli buy if he buys four 8-by-10-inch photographs?

Find the determinant of each matrix. *(Lesson 4-4)*

55. $\begin{bmatrix} 4 & 2 \\ 1 & 7 \end{bmatrix}$ 56. $\begin{bmatrix} -1 & -5 \\ 9 & 10 \end{bmatrix}$ 57. $\begin{bmatrix} \frac{1}{2} & -1 \\ 0 & 6 \end{bmatrix}$ 58. $\begin{bmatrix} \frac{2}{3} & \frac{1}{3} \\ 6 & 9 \end{bmatrix}$

Use inverse operations to find $f^{-1}(x)$. *(Lesson 7-2)*

59. $f(x) = 4x + 3$ 60. $f(x) = 6(x - 2)$ 61. $f(x) = \frac{x}{3} + 9$ 62. $f(x) = \frac{7x - 1}{5}$

Exponents in Probability

You can use exponents to determine a probability when a certain experiment is repeated.

Recall that the probability P of an event is $P(\text{Event } E) = \dfrac{\textbf{number of favorable outcomes}}{\textbf{total number of outcomes}}$.

For example, when rolling a number cube with six possible outcomes, the probability of rolling an odd prime number, 3 or 5, is $\frac{2}{6}$, or $\frac{1}{3}$. The probability of rolling an odd prime number two rolls in a row is $\frac{1}{3} \cdot \frac{1}{3}$. If the probability of an event is r and the events are independent, then the probability of getting the same result when the event is repeated n times is **P(Event E occurring n times in succession)** $= r^n$

Examples

A machine on an assembly line makes an acceptable product 90% of the time. The machine makes 10 samples of the product.

1 What is the probability that all 10 samples are acceptable, to the nearest percent?

$P(\text{All 10 samples are acceptable}) = 0.9^{10}$ *Substitute 0.9 for r and 10 for n in r^n.*

≈ 0.35 *Use a calculator.*

The probability that all 10 samples are acceptable is about 35%.

2 At what number of samples does the probability fall below 10%?

You can solve an inequality.

$0.9^n < 0.1$

$\log 0.9^n < \log 0.1$ *Take the log of both sides.*

$n \log 0.9 < \log 0.1$ *Use the Power Property of Logarithms.*

$n > \dfrac{\log 0.1}{\log 0.9}$ *← = −1* *← ≈ −0.0458*

$n > \approx 21.85$

For 22 or more samples, the probability that all are acceptable drops below 10%.

Try This

1. You toss a coin 6 times. Find the probability of getting heads every time.
2. You toss a number cube 10 times. Find the probability that no roll is a six.
3. A basketball player has a 70% chance of making each free throw. For what number of free throws does the probability of making them all drop below 10%?
4. A test contains multiple-choice questions with 4 choices for each question. For what number of questions does the probability of guessing all of them correctly drop below 0.01%?

Explore the Rule of 72

You can use a spreadsheet to discover a rule to estimate the time needed to double an investment at different interest rates.

Use with Lesson 7-6

Activity

Use a spreadsheet to find the number of years it will take for an investment to double at 3% annual interest. Find the product of the interest rate and the doubling time.

Find a formula for doubling time as a function of interest rate. Use the compound interest formula.

$A = P\left(1 + \frac{r}{n}\right)^{nt}$ — *A is the total amount, P is the principal, r is the interest rate, n is the number of compounding periods, and t is the time in years.*

$2 = 1(1 + r)^t$ — *Substitute 2 for A, 1 for P, and 1 for n. Then solve for t.*

$\log 2 = \log(1 + r)^t$ — *Take the log of both sides.*

$\log 2 = t \log(1 + r)$ — *Power Property of Logarithms*

$t = \frac{\log 2}{\log(1 + r)}$ — *Divide both sides by log(1 + r) to solve for t.*

1. In cells A1 through C1, enter column headings for rate, doubling time, and their product. Enter **3%** in cell A2.

2. In cell B2, enter the formula derived above as shown in the screenshot.

	A	B	C
1	Rate	Doubling Time	Product
2	3%	=LOG(2)/LOG(1+A2)	

3. In cell C2, enter the formula for the product as shown.

	A	B	C
1	Rate	Doubling Time	Product
2	3%	23.44977225	=A2*B2

The spreadsheet shows that at 3% annual interest, an investment will double in about 23.4 years. The product of the interest rate and the doubling time is about 70.

	A	B	C
1	Rate	Doubling Time	Product
2	3%	23.44977225	0.703493168

Try This

1. Complete cells A3 through A20 with interest rates from 3.5% to 12%.
2. Copy and paste the formula from cell B2 into cells B3 through B20.
3. Copy and paste the formula from cell C2 into cells C3 through C20.
4. What is the lowest interest rate that gives you a doubling time less than 9 years?
5. **Make a Conjecture** The rule of 72 is a rule used by investors to estimate the time it will take for an investment to double at a certain rate. Explain why.
6. **Critical Thinking** Write an equation for the rule of 72.

7-6 The Natural Base, e

Objectives
Use the number e to write and graph exponential functions representing real-world situations.

Solve equations and problems involving e or natural logarithms.

Vocabulary
natural logarithm
natural logarithmic function

Why learn this?
Scientists use natural logarithms and carbon dating to determine the ages of ancient bones and fossils. (See Example 4.)

Recall the *compound interest formula* $A = P\left(1 + \frac{r}{n}\right)^{nt}$, where A is the total amount, P is the principal, r is the annual interest rate, n is the number of times the interest is compounded per year, and t is the time in years.

Suppose that \$1 is invested at 100% interest $(r = 1)$ compounded n times for one year as represented by the function $f(n) = \left(1 + \frac{1}{n}\right)^n$.

As n gets very large, interest is *continuously compounded.* Examine the graph of $f(n) = \left(1 + \frac{1}{n}\right)^n$. The function has a horizontal asymptote. As n becomes infinitely large, the value of the function approaches approximately 2.7182818.... This number is called e. Like π, the constant e is an irrational number.

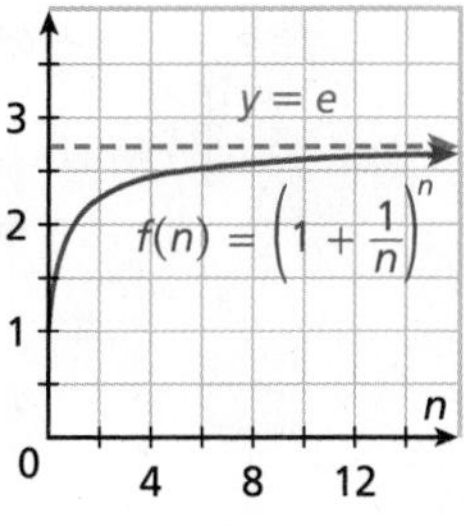

Caution!
The decimal value of e looks like it repeats: 2.718281828.... The value is actually 2.7182818284590.... There is no repeating portion.

Exponential functions with e as a base have the same properties as the functions you have studied. The graph of $f(x) = e^x$ is like other graphs of exponential functions, such as $f(x) = 3^x$.

The domain of $f(x) = e^x$ is all real numbers. The range is $\{y \mid y > 0\}$.

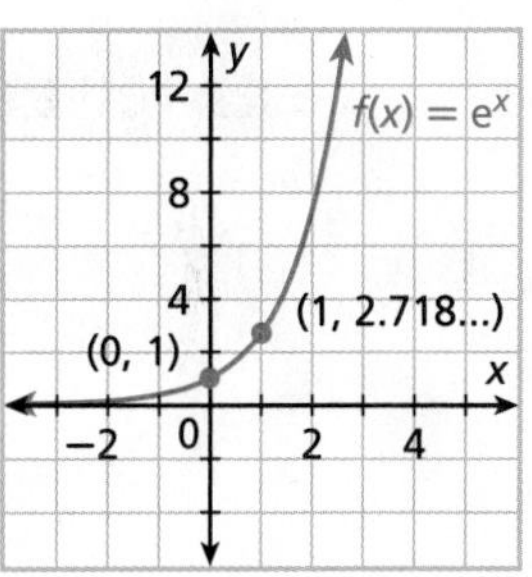

EXAMPLE 1 Graphing Exponential Functions

Graph $f(x) = e^x + 2$.

Make a table. Because e is irrational, the table values are rounded to the nearest tenth.

x	−3	−2	−1	0	1	2	3
$f(x) = e^x + 2$	2.0	2.1	2.4	3	4.7	9.4	22.1

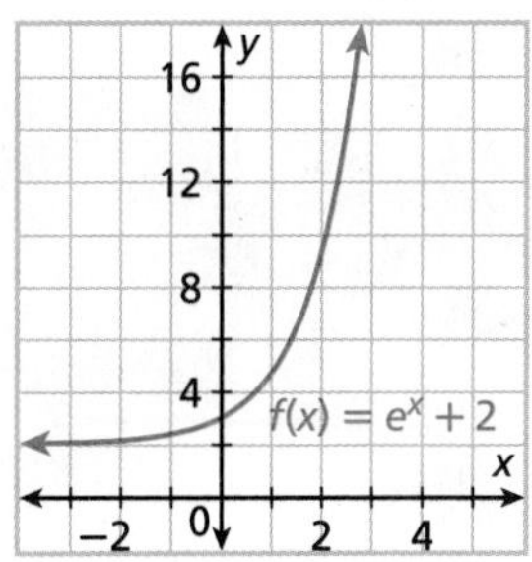

1. Graph $f(x) = e^x - 3$.

A logarithm with a base of e is called a **natural logarithm** and is abbreviated as "ln" (rather than as $\log_e$). Natural logarithms have the same properties as log base 10 and logarithms with other bases.

The **natural logarithmic function** $f(x) = \ln x$ is the inverse of the natural exponential function $f(x) = e^x$.

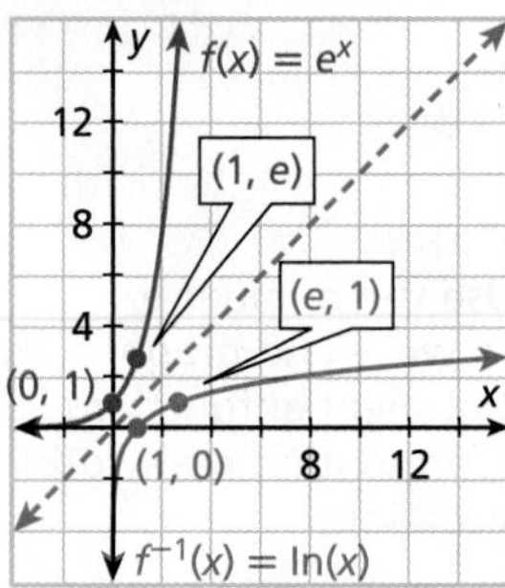

The domain of $f(x) = \ln x$ is $\{x \mid x > 0\}$.
The range of $f(x) = \ln x$ is all real numbers.

All of the properties of logarithms from Lesson 7-4 also apply to natural logarithms.

EXAMPLE 2 Simplifying Expressions with e or ln

Simplify.

A $\ln e^{-2t}$

$\ln e^{-2t} = -2t$

B $e^{\ln(t-1)}$

$e^{\ln(t-1)} = t - 1$

C $e^{5\ln x}$

$e^{5\ln x} = e^{\ln x^5} = x^5$

Simplify.

2a. $\ln e^{3.2}$ **2b.** $e^{2\ln x}$ **2c.** $\ln e^{x+4y}$

The formula for continuously compounded interest is $A = Pe^{rt}$, where A is the total amount, P is the principal, r is the annual interest rate, and t is the time in years.

EXAMPLE 3 *Economics Application*

What is the total amount for an investment of $1000 invested at 5% for 10 years compounded continuously?

$A = Pe^{rt}$

$A = 1000e^{0.05(10)}$ *Substitute 1000 for P, 0.05 for r, and 10 for t.*

$A \approx 1648.72$ *Use the e^x key on a calculator.*

```
1000e^(0.05*10)
        1648.721271
```

The total amount is $1648.72.

3. What is the total amount for an investment of $100 invested at 3.5% for 8 years and compounded continuously?

The *half-life* of a substance is the time it takes for half of the substance to breakdown or convert to another substance during the process of decay. Natural decay is modeled by the function below.

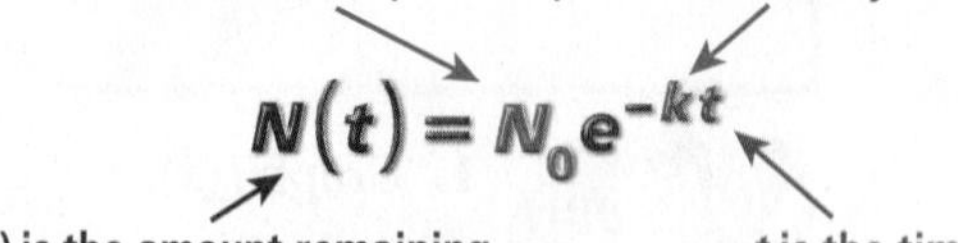

N_0 is the initial amount (at $t = 0$). k is the decay constant.

$N(t)$ is the amount remaining. t is the time.

EXAMPLE 4 Paleontology Application

A paleontologist uncovers a fossil of a saber-toothed cat in California. He analyzes the fossil and concludes that the specimen contains 15% of its original carbon-14. Carbon-14 has a half-life of 5730 years. Use carbon-14 dating to determine the age of the fossil.

Step 1 Find the decay constant for carbon-14.

$N(t) = N_0 e^{-kt}$ — *Use the natural decay function.*

$\frac{1}{2} = 1e^{-k(5730)}$ — *Substitute 1 for N_0, 5730 for t, and $\frac{1}{2}$ for N(t), because half of the initial quantity will remain.*

$\ln \frac{1}{2} = \ln e^{-5730k}$ — *Simplify and take the ln of both sides.*

$\ln 2^{-1} = -5730k$ — *Write $\frac{1}{2}$ as 2^{-1}, and simplify the right side.*

$-\ln 2 = -5730k$ — *$\ln 2^{-1} = -1 \ln 2 = -\ln 2$*

$k = \frac{\ln 2}{5730} \approx 0.00012$

Step 2 Write the decay function and solve for *t*.

$N(t) = N_0 e^{-0.00012t}$ — *Substitute 0.00012 for k.*

$15 = 100e^{-0.00012t}$ — *Substitute 100 for N_0 and 15 for N(t), since N(t) is 15% of N_0.*

$0.15 = e^{-0.00012t}$ — *Divide both sides by 100.*

$\ln 0.15 = \ln e^{-0.00012t}$ — *Take the ln of both sides.*

$\ln 0.15 = -0.00012t$ — *Simplify.*

$t = -\frac{\ln 0.15}{0.00012} \approx 15{,}809$

The fossil is approximately 15,800 years old.

4. Determine how long it will take for 650 mg of a sample of chromium-51, which has a half-life of about 28 days, to decay to 200 mg.

THINK AND DISCUSS

1. Tell how e and π are alike. Tell how they are different.
2. Explain how e and ln are related.

3. **GET ORGANIZED** Copy and complete the graphic organizer. Fill in each box to compare and contrast the two kinds of logarithms. Give general forms and examples. Simplify, if appropriate.

	Common Logarithms	Natural Logarithms
Base		
Logarithmic Form		
Exponential Form		
$\log_b 1$		
$\log_b b$		
$\log_b b^x$		
$b^{\log_b x}$		

7-6 Exercises

go.hrw.com
Homework Help Online
KEYWORD: MB7 7-6
Parent Resources Online
KEYWORD: MB7 Parent

GUIDED PRACTICE

1. **Vocabulary** Write the logarithm of a number x to the natural base e as a function of x. This function is called the __?__.

SEE EXAMPLE 1 p. 531

Graph.

2. $f(x) = e^x - 4$
3. $f(x) = -e^x$
4. $f(x) = 4 - e^x$
5. $f(x) = e^{1-x}$

SEE EXAMPLE 2 p. 532

Simplify.

6. $\ln e^1$
7. $\ln e^{x-y}$
8. $\ln e^{\left(-\frac{x}{3}\right)}$
9. $e^{\ln 2x}$
10. $e^{3\ln x}$

SEE EXAMPLE 3 p. 532

11. **Economics** Emma receives \$7750 and invests it in an account that earns 4% interest compounded continuously. What is the total amount of her investment after 5 years?

SEE EXAMPLE 4 p. 533

12. **Physics** Technetium-99m, a radioisotope used to image the skeleton and the heart muscle, has a half-life of about 6 hours. Find the decay constant. Use the decay function $N(t) = N_0 e^{-kt}$ to determine the amount of a 250 mg dose that remains after 24 hours.

PRACTICE AND PROBLEM SOLVING

Independent Practice

For Exercises	See Example
13–16	1
17–20	2
21	3
22	4

Extra Practice
Skills Practice p. S17
Application Practice p. S38

Graph.

13. $f(x) = e^x + 1$
14. $f(x) = e^x - 1$
15. $f(x) = 1 - e^x$
16. $f(x) = 10 - e^x$

Simplify.

17. $\ln e^0$
18. $\ln e^{2a}$
19. $e^{\ln(c+2)}$
20. $e^{4\ln x}$

21. **Economics** Aidan has \$7565 in his checking account. He invests \$5000 of it in an account that earns 3.5% interest compounded continuously. What is the total amount of his investment after 3 years?

22. **Environment** An accident in 1986 at the Chernobyl nuclear plant in the Ukraine released a large amount of plutonium (Pu-239) into the atmosphere. The half-life of Pu-239 is about 24,110 years. Find the decay constant. Use the function $N(t) = N_0 e^{-kt}$ to find what remains of an initial 20 grams of Pu-239 after 5000 years. How long will it take for these 20 grams to decay to 1 gram?

23. **Calculator** Find the approximate values of $\ln 10$ and $\log e$.
    a. How are these numbers related?
    b. How can you use the change of base formula to support your answer?

24. Show that $\ln x = \ln 10 \times \log x$.

25. **Multi-Step** Newton's law of cooling states that the temperature of an object decreases exponentially as a function of time, according to $T = T_s + (T_0 - T_s)e^{-kt}$, where T_0 is the initial temperature of the liquid, T_s is the surrounding temperature, and k is a constant. For a time in minutes, the constant for coffee is approximately 0.283. The corner coffee shop has an air temperature of 70°F and serves coffee at 206°F. Coffee experts say coffee tastes best at 140°F.
    a. How long does it take for the coffee to reach its best temperature?
    b. The air temperature on the patio is 86°F. How long does it take for coffee to reach its best temperature there?
    c. Graph the cooling functions from parts **a** and **b.** Use the graph to find the time it takes for the coffee to cool to 71°F.

26. Graph the functions $y = \frac{\ln x}{\ln 6}$ and $y = \frac{\log x}{\log 6}$. Explain how the graphs compare with each other and with the graph of $y = \log_6 x$.

Match each transformation of $f(x) = \ln x$ with one of the following graphs.

A.

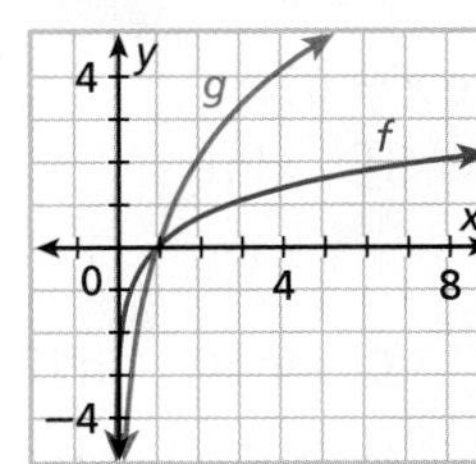

B.

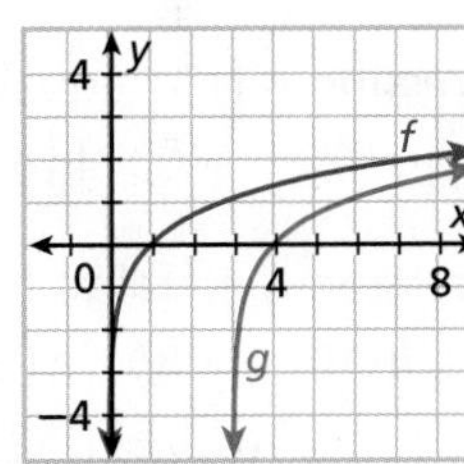

C.

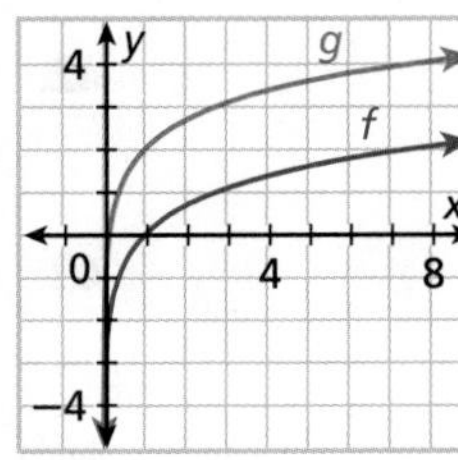

LINK

Ecology

The George River herd, the largest caribou herd in the world, reached its peak population in 1993 at about 776,000.

27. $g(x) = \ln(x - 3)$

28. $g(x) = 3\ln x$

29. $g(x) = \ln x + 3$

30. **Ecology** The George River herd of caribou in Canada was estimated to be about 4700 in 1954 and grew at an exponential rate to about 472,000 in 1984.
   a. Use the exponential growth function $P(t) = P_0 e^{kt}$, where P_0 is the initial population and $P(t)$ is the population at time t, to determine the growth factor k.
   b. **What if...?** If the herd had continued to grow at the same rate, what would its population be in 2010?

Solve.

31. $\ln 5 + \ln x = 1$

32. $\ln 5 - \ln x = 3$

33. $\ln 10 + \ln x^2 = 10$

34. $2\ln x - 2 = 0$

35. $4\ln x - \ln x^4 = 0$

36. $e^{\ln x^3} = 8$

37. **Logistics** A *logistic function*, such as $f(x) = \frac{1}{(1 + e^{-x})}$, can be used to describe the spread of an epidemic in a population.
   a. Graph the function.
   b. How many asymptotes does the function have?
   c. Describe the function in the context of the real-world situation of an epidemic.

38. **Critical Thinking** The graphs of $f(x) = 2^x$, $f(x) = 10^x$, and $f(x) = e^x$ are shown.
   a. Identify the graph of each function.
   b. Name the coordinates of the point that all three functions have in common.
   c. Explain why this point is common to all three functions.

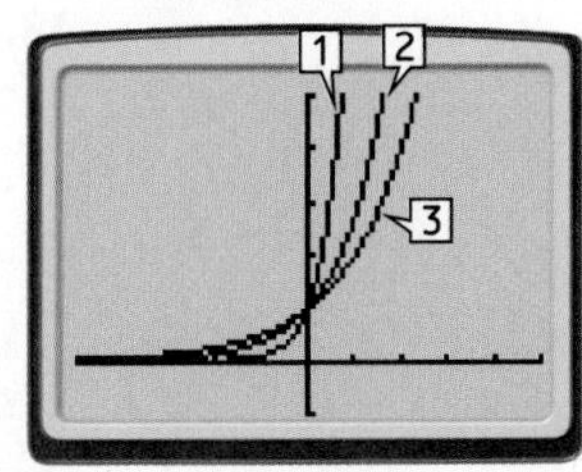

39. **Write About It** Compare compounding interest continuously with compounding daily. How much more is an investment worth when compounding interest continuously? Include an example.

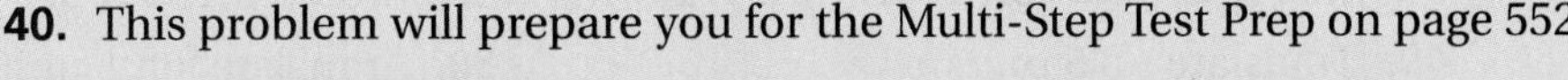

MULTI-STEP TEST PREP

40. This problem will prepare you for the Multi-Step Test Prep on page 552.

In 1990, there were 33,500 farms in North Dakota. In 2000, there were 30,800.
   a. Find the value of k for the exponential function $N(t) = N_0 e^{kt}$ to model the number of farms.
   b. Use your model to predict the number of farms in North Dakota in 2010.
   c. From 1990 to 2000, the average farm increased from 1209 acres to 1279 acres. Use an exponential model to predict the average farm size in 2010.

41. Which group shows values in the order from least to greatest?

   Ⓐ $\log e, \ln 10, \log 10, \ln 1$ Ⓒ $\ln 1, \log e, \log 10, \ln 10$

   Ⓑ $\ln 1, \log e, \ln 10, \log 10$ Ⓓ $\ln 1, \log 10, \ln 10, \log e$

42. Which expression is NOT equal to x where $x \neq 0$?

   Ⓕ $e^{\ln x}$ Ⓖ $\ln e^x$ Ⓗ $x \ln e$ Ⓙ $x + \ln e$

43. Which expression is equal to $\log 50$?

   Ⓐ $\ln 50 \div \ln 10$ Ⓑ $\ln(50 \div 10)$ Ⓒ $\ln 50 + \ln 10$ Ⓓ $\ln 50(\ln 10)$

44. **Short Response** Write an expression that is equivalent to $-\ln x$ without using a negative sign.

CHALLENGE AND EXTEND

45. **Finance** For how many compounding periods in a year would the yield of an investment after 1 year at 8% interest be at least 99.9% of the yield if interest were compounded continuously? Does changing the interest rate change the answer? Explain.

46. Graph the function $f(x) = \frac{1}{\sqrt{2\pi}} e^{-\left(\frac{x^2}{2}\right)}$. Describe the graph, the domain, and the range.

47. Consider the graph of $f(x) = \ln x$.
   a. What function represents the reflection of f across the y-axis?
   b. What function represents the reflection of f across the x-axis?
   c. What function represents the reflection of f across both axes?
   d. Graph the function and the three reflections. Name any asymptotes that the four graphs have in common.

SPIRAL REVIEW

48. **Entertainment** The graph shows the price of a movie ticket by age of the viewer. Sketch a graph to represent each situation below, and identify the transformation of the original graph that it represents. *(Lesson 1-8)*
   a. Before 5:00 P.M., tickets are half price.
   b. The maximum age of viewer for each ticket price is decreased by 3 years.
   c. The price for each ticket doubles for a newly released movie.

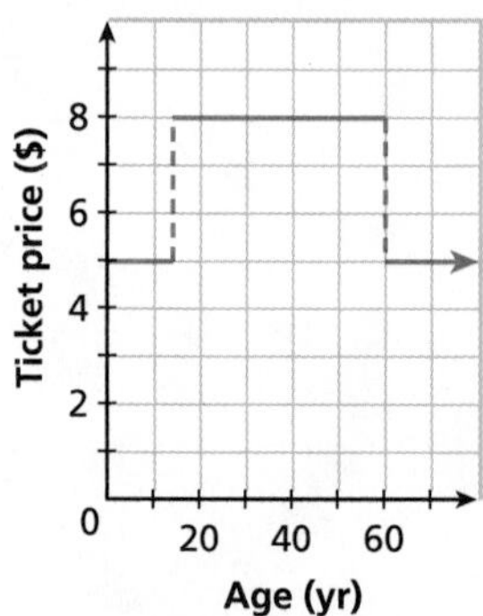

Write a function that transforms $f(x) = -2x^2 + 3x - 4$ in each of the following ways. Support your solution by using a graphing calculator. *(Lesson 6-8)*

49. Translate up 5 units
50. Translate left 2 units
51. Reflect across the x-axis
52. Stretch horizontally by a factor of 2

Express as a single logarithm. Simplify, if possible. *(Lesson 7-4)*

53. $\log_2 8 + \log_2 \frac{1}{2}$
54. $\log_4 64 - \log_4 1$
55. $\log_3 243 - \log_3 2187$
56. $\log_5 25 + \log_5 125$
57. $\log_8 8 + \log_8 \frac{1}{8}$
58. $\log x^2 - \log x$

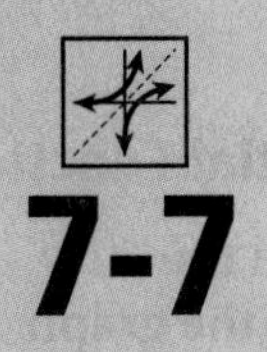

7-7 Transforming Exponential and Logarithmic Functions

Objectives

Transform exponential and logarithmic functions by changing parameters.

Describe the effects of changes in the coefficients of exponential and logarithmic functions.

Who uses this?

Psychologists can use transformations of exponential functions to describe knowledge retention rates over time. (See Example 5.)

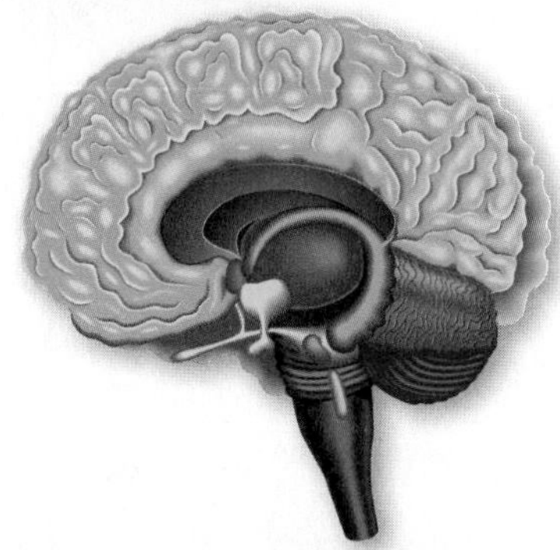

The hippocampus, in orange, directs the storage of memory in the brain.

You can perform the same transformations on exponential functions that you performed on polynomial, quadratic, and linear functions.

Transformations of Exponential Functions

Transformation	$f(x)$ Notation	Examples	
Vertical translation	$f(x) + k$	$y = 2^x + 3$	3 units up
		$y = 2^x - 6$	6 units down
Horizontal translation	$f(x - h)$	$y = 2^{x-2}$	2 units right
		$y = 2^{x+1}$	1 unit left
Vertical stretch or compression	$af(x)$	$y = 6(2^x)$	stretch by 6
		$y = \frac{1}{2}(2^x)$	compression by $\frac{1}{2}$
Horizontal stretch or compression	$f\left(\frac{1}{b}x\right)$	$y = 2^{\left(\frac{1}{5}x\right)}$	stretch by 5
		$y = 2^{3x}$	compression by $\frac{1}{3}$
Reflection	$-f(x)$	$y = -2^x$	across x-axis
	$f(-x)$	$y = 2^{-x}$	across y-axis

Helpful Hint

It may help you remember the direction of the shift if you think of "*h* is for **h**orizontal."

EXAMPLE 1  **Translating Exponential Functions**

Make a table of values, and graph the function $g(x) = 2^x - 4$. Describe the asymptote. Tell how the graph is transformed from the graph of $f(x) = 2^x$.

x	−2	−1	0	1	2	3
$g(x)$	−3.75	−3.5	−3	−2	0	4

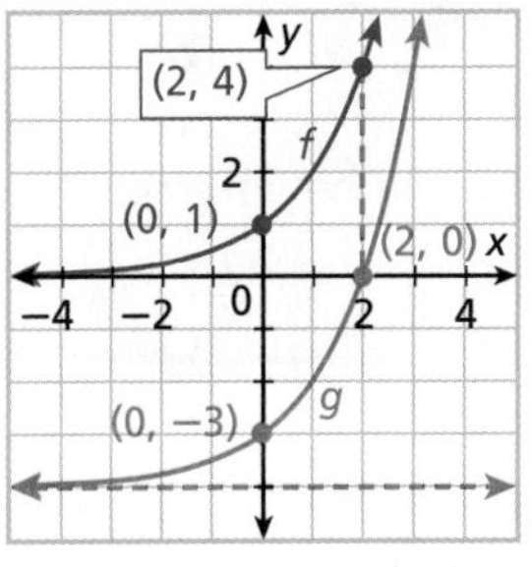

The asymptote is $y = -4$, and the graph approaches this line as the value of x decreases. The transformation moves the graph of $f(x) = 2^x$ down 4 units. The range changes to $\{y \mid y > -4\}$.

1. Make a table of values, and graph $j(x) = 2^{x-2}$. Describe the asymptote. Tell how the graph is transformed from the graph of $f(x) = 2^x$.

EXAMPLE 2 Stretching, Compressing, and Reflecting Exponential Functions

Graph the exponential function. Find the *y*-intercept and the asymptote. Describe how the graph is transformed from the graph of its parent function.

A $g(x) = 2(3^x)$

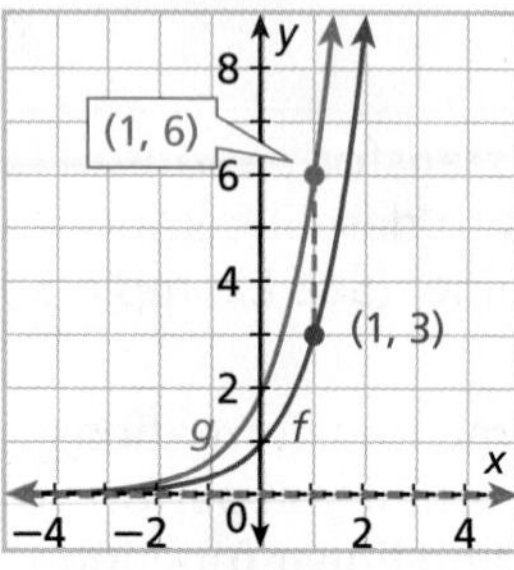

parent function: $f(x) = 3^x$

y-intercept: 2, asymptote: $y = 0$

The graph of $g(x)$ is a vertical stretch of the parent function $f(x) = 3^x$ by a factor of 2.

B $h(x) = -\frac{1}{4}(2^x)$

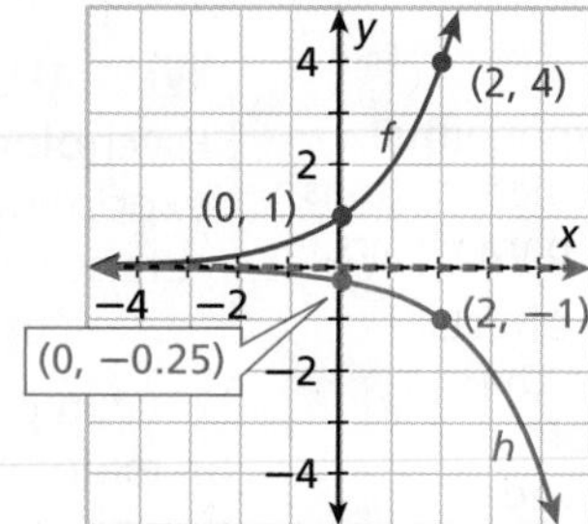

parent function: $f(x) = 2^x$

y-intercept: $-\frac{1}{4}$, asymptote: $y = 0$

The graph of $h(x)$ is a reflection of the parent function $f(x) = 2^x$ across the *x*-axis and a vertical compression by a factor of $\frac{1}{4}$. The range is $\{y \mid y < 0\}$.

Graph the exponential function. Find the *y*-intercept and the asymptote. Describe how the graph is transformed from the graph of its parent function.

2a. $h(x) = \frac{1}{3}(5^x)$ **2b.** $g(x) = 2(2^{-x})$

Remember!

Transformations of $\ln x$ work the same way because $\ln x$ means $\log_e x$.

Because a log is an exponent, transformations of logarithmic functions are similar to transformations of exponential functions. You can stretch, reflect, and translate the graph of the parent logarithmic function $f(x) = \log_b x$.

Examples are given in the table below for $f(x) = \log x$.

Transformations of Logarithmic Functions

Transformation	f(x) Notation	Examples	
Vertical translation	$f(x) + k$	$y = \log x + 3$	3 units up
		$y = \log x - 4$	4 units down
Horizontal translation	$f(x - h)$	$y = \log(x - 2)$	2 units right
		$y = \log(x + 1)$	1 unit left
Vertical stretch or compression	$af(x)$	$y = 6\log x$	stretch by 6
		$y = \frac{1}{2}\log x$	compression by $\frac{1}{2}$
Horizontal stretch or compression	$f\left(\frac{1}{b}x\right)$	$y = \log\left(\frac{1}{5}x\right)$	stretch by 5
		$y = \log(3x)$	compression by $\frac{1}{3}$
Reflection	$-f(x)$	$y = -\log x$	across *x*-axis
	$f(-x)$	$y = \log(-x)$	across *y*-axis

EXAMPLE 3 Transforming Logarithmic Functions

Graph each logarithmic function. Find the asymptote. Then describe how the graph is transformed from the graph of its parent function.

A $q(x) = -\ln(x - 4)$

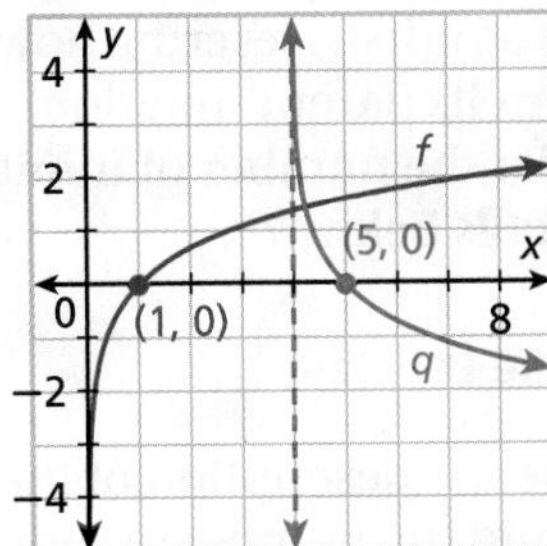

asymptote: $x = 4$

The graph of $q(x)$ is a translation of the parent function $f(x) = \ln x$ 4 units right and a reflection across the x-axis. The domain is $\{x \mid x > 4\}$.

$p(x) = 3\log x + 5$

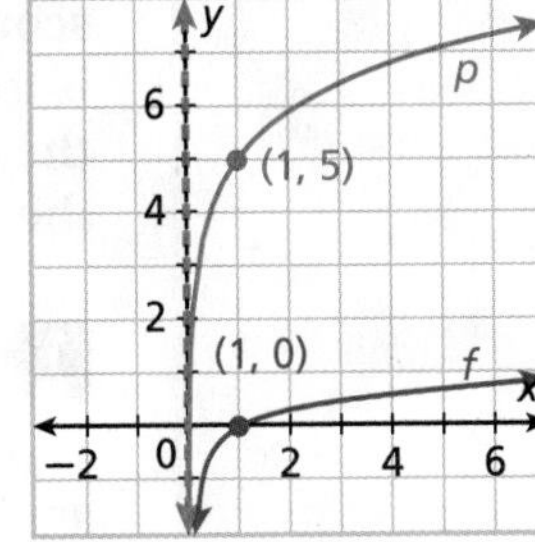

asymptote: $x = 0$

The graph of $p(x)$ is a vertical stretch of the parent function $f(x) = \log x$ by a factor of 3 and a translation 5 units up.

3. Graph the logarithmic function $p(x) = -\ln(x + 1) - 2$. Find the asymptote. Then describe how the graph is transformed from the graph of its parent function.

EXAMPLE 4 Writing Transformed Functions

Write each transformed function.

A $f(x) = 0.2^x$ is translated 2 units right, compressed vertically by a factor of $\frac{1}{3}$, and reflected across the x-axis.

0.2^x	*Begin with the rule for the parent function.*
0.2^{x-2}	*To translate 2 units right, replace x with x − 2.*
$g(x) = \left(-\frac{1}{3}\right)0.2^{x-2}$	*Compress vertically by $\frac{1}{3}$ and reflect across the x-axis.*

B $f(x) = \ln x$ is translated 1 unit left and 3 units up and horizontally stretched by a factor of 5.

$$g(x) = \ln\left(\frac{x}{5} + 1\right) + 3$$

When you write a transformed function, you many want to graph it as a check.

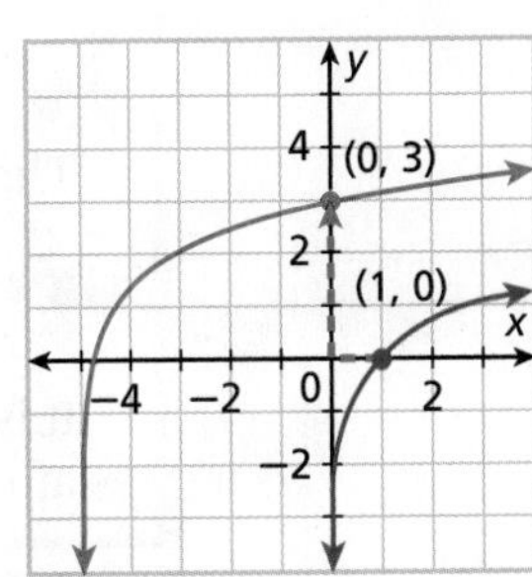

4. Write the transformed function when $f(x) = \log x$ is translated 3 units left and stretched vertically by a factor of 2.

EXAMPLE 5 Problem-Solving Application

A group of students retake the written portion of a driver's test after several months without reviewing the material. A model used by psychologists describes retention of the material by the function $a(t) = 85 - 15\log(t + 1)$, where a is the average score at time t (in months). Describe how the model is transformed from its parent function. Then use the model to predict the number of months when the average score falls below 70.

1 Understand the Problem

The **answers** will be the description of the transformations in $a(t) = 85 - 15\log(t + 1)$ and the number of months when the score falls below 70.

List the important information:

- The model is the function $a(t) = 85 - 15\log(t + 1)$.
- The function is a transformation of $f(t) = \log(t)$.
- The problem asks for t when $a < 70$.

2 Make a Plan

Rewrite the function in a more familiar form, and then use what you know about the effect of changing the parent function to describe the transformations. Substitute known values into $a(t) = 85 - 15\log(t + 1)$, and solve for the unknown.

3 Solve

Rewrite the function, and describe the transformations.

$a(t) = 85 - 15\log(t + 1)$

$a(t) = -15\log(t + 1) + 85$ *Commutative Property*

The graph of $f(t) = \log(t)$ is reflected across the x-axis, vertically stretched by a factor of 15, and translated 85 units up and 1 unit left. The domain $\{t \mid t \geq 0\}$ makes sense in the problem.

Find the time when the average score drops below 70.

$70 > -15\log(t + 1) + 85$ *Substitute 70 for $a(t)$ and replace = with >.*

$-15 > -15\log(t + 1)$ *Subtract 85 from both sides.*

$1 < \log(t + 1)$ *Divide by −15, and reverse the inequality symbol.*

$10^1 < t + 1$ *Change to exponential form.*

$9 < t$

The model predicts a score below 70 after 9 months.

4 Look Back

It is reasonable that scores would drop from 85 to below 70 nine months after the students take the test without reviewing the material.

5. **What if...?** When would the average score drop to 0? Is your answer reasonable?

THINK AND DISCUSS

1. Describe the domain of $f(x) = \log_b(-x)$.
2. Explain how the process of transforming exponential and logarithmic functions is similar to transforming quadratic functions.
3. Tell which transformations of $f(x) = a^x$ change the domain or range. Tell which transformations of $f(x) = \log_b x$ change the domain or range. Are these transformations the same?

4. **GET ORGANIZED** Copy and complete the graphic organizer. Give an example of an indicated transformation for both types of exponential and logarithmic functions. Remember, e is a constant.

Transformation	$f(x) = 5^x$ $f(x) = e^x$	$f(x) = \log_b x$ $f(x) = \ln x$
Vertical translation		
Horizontal translation		
Reflection		
Vertical stretch		
Vertical compression		

7-7 Exercises

GUIDED PRACTICE

SEE EXAMPLE 1 p. 537

Make a table of values, and graph each function. Describe the asymptote. Tell how the graph is transformed from the graph of $f(x) = 3^x$.

1. $g(x) = 3^x + 2$
2. $h(x) = 3^x - 2$
3. $j(x) = 3^{x+1}$

SEE EXAMPLE 2 p. 538

Graph each exponential function. Find the y-intercept and the asymptote. Describe how the graph is transformed from the graph of its parent function.

4. $g(x) = 3(4^x)$
5. $h(x) = \frac{1}{3}(4^x)$
6. $j(x) = -\frac{1}{3}(4^x)$
7. $k(x) = -2(4^x)$
8. $m(x) = -(4^{-x})$
9. $n(x) = e^{2x}$

SEE EXAMPLE 3 p. 539

Graph each logarithmic function. Find the asymptote. Then describe how the graph is transformed from the graph of its parent function.

10. $g(x) = 2.5\log x$
11. $h(x) = 2.5\log(x + 3)$
12. $j(x) = -\frac{1}{3}\ln x + 1.5$

SEE EXAMPLE 4 p. 539

Write each transformed function by using the given parent function and the indicated transformations.

13. The parent exponential function $f(x) = 0.7^x$ is horizontally stretched by a factor of 3, reflected across the x-axis, and translated 2 units left.
14. The parent logarithmic function $f(x) = \log x$ is translated 12 units right, vertically compressed by a factor of $\frac{1}{2}$, and translated 25 units up.

SEE EXAMPLE 5 p. 540

15. **Forestry** The height of a poplar tree in feet, at age t years can be modeled by the function $h(t) = 6 + 3\ln(t + 1)$. Describe how the model is transformed from its parent function. Then use the model to predict the number of years when the height will exceed 17 feet.

PRACTICE AND PROBLEM SOLVING

Independent Practice	
For Exercises	See Example
16–18	1
19–24	2
25–27	3
28–30	4
31	5

Extra Practice

Skills Practice p. S17
Application Practice p. S38

Make a table of values, and graph each function. Describe the asymptote. Tell how the graph is transformed from the graph of $f(x) = 5^x$.

16. $g(x) = 5^x - 1$ **17.** $h(x) = 5^{x+2}$ **18.** $j(x) = 5^{x-1} - 1$

Graph each exponential function. Find the y-intercept and the asymptote. Describe how the graph is transformed from the graph of its parent function.

19. $g(x) = 4\left(\frac{1}{2}\right)^x$ **20.** $h(x) = 0.25\left(\frac{1}{2}\right)^x$ **21.** $j(x) = -0.25\left(\frac{1}{2}\right)^x$

22. $k(x) = -\left(\frac{1}{2}\right)^{\frac{x}{2}}$ **23.** $m(x) = 4\left(\frac{1}{2}\right)^{-x}$ **24.** $n(x) = -4\left(\frac{1}{2}\right)^{-x}$

Graph each logarithmic function. Find the asymptote. Describe how the graph is transformed from the graph of its parent function.

25. $g(x) = \ln(x - 5)$ **26.** $h(x) = \frac{4}{5}\log(x + 3) - 2$ **27.** $m(x) = -4\log x$

Write each transformed function.

28. The function $f(x) = \left(\frac{1}{2}\right)^x$ is translated 4 units right, reflected across the x-axis, and vertically stretched by a factor of 1.5.

29. The function $f(x) = \ln x$ is translated 3 units left, horizontally compressed by a factor of $\frac{1}{4}$ and translated 0.5 units down.

30. The function $f(x) = e^x$ is horizontally stretched by a factor of 3, reflected across the y-axis, and translated 1 unit right.

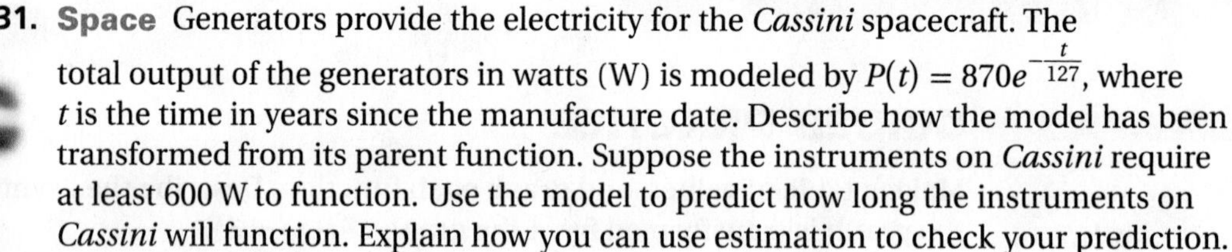

31. Space Generators provide the electricity for the *Cassini* spacecraft. The total output of the generators in watts (W) is modeled by $P(t) = 870e^{-\frac{t}{127}}$, where t is the time in years since the manufacture date. Describe how the model has been transformed from its parent function. Suppose the instruments on *Cassini* require at least 600 W to function. Use the model to predict how long the instruments on *Cassini* will function. Explain how you can use estimation to check your prediction.

32. Critical Thinking What vertical transformation of $f(x) = e^x$ is equivalent to the horizontal translation $g(x) = e^{x+2}$? Write the transformed function.

For Exercises 33–37, match each order of transformation of $f(x) = e^x$ with its transformed function.

33. stretch by a factor of 2, reflect across the x-axis, and translate 5 units down.

34. stretch by a factor of 2, translate 5 units down, and reflect across the x-axis

35. reflect across the x-axis, stretch by a factor of 2, and translate 5 units down.

36. reflect across the x-axis, translate 5 units down, and stretch by a factor of 2.

37. translate 5 units down, stretch by a factor of 2, and reflect across the x-axis.

A. $g(x) = -2e^x - 5$

B. $g(x) = 2[-(e^x - 5)]$

C. $g(x) = 2(-e^x - 5)$

D. $g(x) = 2(-e^x) - 5$

E. $g(x) = -(2e^x - 5)$

F. $g(x) = -2(e^x - 5)$

State the domain and range of each function. Then find the intercepts. If necessary, round to the nearest hundredth.

38. $f(x) = 2^{x-2} + 4$ **39.** $g(x) = 5\log(x + 3)$

Tell whether each statement is sometimes, always, or never true.

40. A vertical translation of $f(x) = \log x$ changes its asymptote.

41. A vertical translation of $f(x) = e^x$ changes its asymptote.

42. A horizontal translation of $f(x) = \log x$ has a range of $\mathbb{R}$.

43. The graph of a transformation of $f(x) = \ln x$ intersects the graph of $f(x)$.

44. Banking The function $A(t) = 1000\left(1 + \frac{r}{n}\right)^{nt}$ can be used to calculate the growth of an investment of \$1000 in an account where the interest is compounded n times per year at an annual rate r. Suppose that you invest \$1000 in such an account compounded quarterly (4 times per year).

a. What annual rate would double your investment in 5 years?

b. At an annual rate of 3.5%, how long (to the nearest year) would it take for your investment to double?

c. What does the model predict for the amount in the account after 10 years if the investment continues to grow at an annual rate of 3.5%?

Match each equation with one of the following graphs.

A.

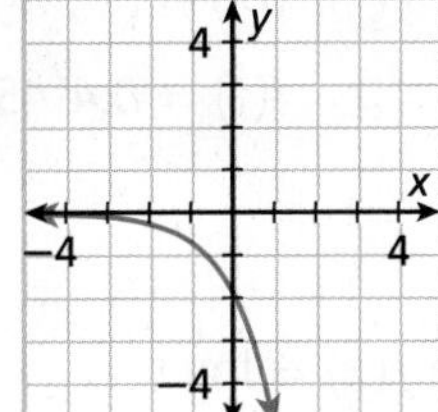

B.

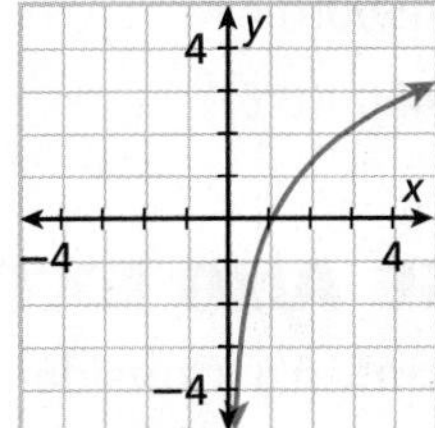

C.

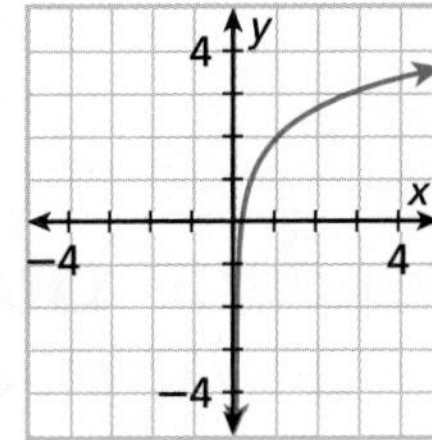

LINK

Medicine

Insulin is a hormone that allows the body's cells, including red blood cells, to absorb glucose. Synthetic insulin can help diabetics maintain a healthy level of blood sugar.

45. $f(x) = \ln x + 2$ **46.** $f(x) = -2e^x$ **47.** $f(x) = 2\ln x$

48. Medicine A dose of synthetic insulin breaks down in the bloodstream over time. The amount of insulin in the blood with an initial dose of A_0 mg, under some conditions, is given by $A = A_0 0.97^t$, where t is the time in minutes. The standard dose is 10 mg. Describe each transformation.

a. The initial dose is changed from 10 mg to 20 mg.

b. The breakdown of the medicine does not begin for 5 minutes.

c. The breakdown time period is increased from one-minute intervals to two-minute intervals.

d. **What if...?** The breakdown rate of 0.97 is reduced to 0.95. Is this a transformation of A?

49. Critical Thinking Describe how changing the value of h and changing the value of k differ in the effect on the graph of $f(x) = a\left(b^{x-h}\right) + k$.

50. Write About It Explain how to translate, reflect, stretch, and compress the graph of $f(x) = b^x$.

MULTI-STEP TEST PREP

51. This problem will prepare you for the Multi-Step Test Prep on page 552.

The number of farms in a county is modeled by $N(t) = 1257(0.99)^t$, where t is the number of years since 1990.

a. One-third of the farms in the county always produce soybeans. Write a new function that models the number of soybean farms.

b. Write a new function that gives the number of soybean farms m months after January 1, 1990.

c. How many soybean farms were there at the end of May 1991?

52. Which function is vertically stretched by a factor of 3 and translated 2 units left from its parent function?

Ⓐ $f(x) = 3(2^{x+2})$

Ⓑ $f(x) = 2^{3x} - 2$

Ⓒ $f(x) = 3\log(x - 2)$

Ⓓ $f(x) = \log(3x + 2)$

53. Which list shows the functions in order from the most compressed horizontally from $f(x) = \log x$ to the most stretched?

Ⓕ $f(x) = \log(x - 10)$, $f(x) = \log(10x)$, $f(x) = \log\left(\frac{x}{10}\right)$

Ⓖ $f(x) = \log\left(\frac{x}{10}\right)$, $f(x) = \log(x - 10)$, $f(x) = \log(10x)$

Ⓗ $f(x) = \log(10x)$, $f(x) = \log(x - 10)$, $f(x) = \log\left(\frac{x}{10}\right)$

Ⓙ $f(x) = \log\left(\frac{x}{10}\right)$, $f(x) = \log(10x)$, $f(x) = \log(x - 10)$

54. The trade-in value of Cindy's car is \$4500 and decreases by about 40% per year. Which choice represents the trade-in value as a function of time?

Ⓐ $f(t) = 4500(0.4)^t$

Ⓑ $f(t) = 4500(0.6)^t$

Ⓒ $f(t) = 0.6(4500)^t$

Ⓓ $f(t) = 0.4(4500)^t$

CHALLENGE AND EXTEND

55. Critical Thinking Consider the function $f(x) = \log x$.

a. Identify the transformation applied to $f(x)$ to create $g(x) = \log x + 1$.

b. Identify the transformation applied to $f(x)$ to create $h(x) = \log(10x)$.

c. Use a graphing calculator to compare the graphs and tables of both functions. What do you notice?

d. Use the properties of logarithms to explain your answer to part **c.**

56. Graphing Calculator Graph the function $y = -\ln(x + 2)$ in the standard window. Make a conjecture explaining why the calculator screen appears to show that the graph stops abruptly and does not extend infinitely in two directions.

57. What can you say about the value of $f(x)$ as the value of x gets closer and closer to h in the standard equation for a logarithmic function, $f(x) = a\log(x - h) + k$, given that a, h, and $k \geq 0$?

SPIRAL REVIEW

Find the minimum or maximum value. Then state the domain and range of the function. *(Lesson 5-2)*

58. $f(x) = x^2 - 2x + 5$

59. $f(x) = 4x^2 + x - 5$

60. $f(x) = -x^2 - x + 1$

61. The table shows the volumes of containers of varying heights. Write a cubic function to model the volume. *(Lesson 6-9)*

Height (in.)	5	7	10	12	15
Volume (qt)	5.5	12.5	33.5	56.8	109.5

Simplify each expression. *(Lesson 7-6)*

62. $\ln e^{x+2}$

63. $\ln e^{-5x}$

64. $e^{\ln(x-1)}$

65. $e^{\ln\left(\frac{x}{4}\right)}$

7-8 Curve Fitting with Exponential and Logarithmic Models

Objectives
Model data by using exponential and logarithmic functions.

Use exponential and logarithmic models to analyze and predict.

Vocabulary
exponential regression
logarithmic regression

Who uses this?

Gem cutters know that values of precious stones of similar quality are exponentially related to the gems' weights. (See Example 2.)

Analyzing data values can identify a pattern, or repeated relationship, between two quantities.

Look at this table of values for the exponential function $f(x) = 2(3^x)$.

x	−1	0	1	2	3
$f(x)$	$\frac{2}{3}$	2	6	18	54

$\times 3 \quad \times 3 \quad \times 3 \quad \times 3$

Remember!

For linear functions (first degree), first differences are constant. For quadratic functions, second differences are constant, and so on.

Notice that the *ratio* of each y-value and the previous one is constant. Each value is three times the one before it, so the ratio of function values is constant for equally spaced x-values. This data can be fit by an exponential function of the form $f(x) = ab^x$.

EXAMPLE 1 **Identifying Exponential Data**

Determine whether f is an exponential function of x of the form $f(x) = ab^x$. If so, find the constant ratio.

A

x	−1	0	1	2	3
$f(x)$	−3	−1	1	3	5

$+2 \quad +2 \quad +2 \quad +2$ *First differences*

y is a linear function of x.

B

x	−1	0	1	2	3
$f(x)$	$\frac{1}{2}$	1	2	4	8

$+\frac{1}{2} \quad +1 \quad +2 \quad +4$

Ratios $\frac{1}{\frac{1}{2}} = \frac{2}{1} = \frac{4}{2} = \frac{8}{4} = 2$

This data set is exponential, with a constant ratio of 2.

Determine whether y is an exponential function of x of the form $f(x) = ab^x$. If so, find the constant ratio.

1a.

x	−1	0	1	2	3
$f(x)$	$2.\overline{6}$	4	6	9	13.5

1b.

x	−1	0	1	2	3
$f(x)$	−3	2	7	12	17

In Chapters 2 and 5, you used a graphing calculator to perform *linear regressions* and *quadratic regressions* to make predictions. You can also use an *exponential model,* which is an exponential function that represents a real data set.

Once you know that data are exponential, you can use **ExpReg** (exponential regression) on your calculator to find a function that fits. This method of using data to find an exponential model is called an **exponential regression**. The calculator fits exponential functions to ab^x, so translations cannot be modeled.

EXAMPLE 2 *Gemology Application*

The table gives the approximate values of diamonds of the same quality. Find an exponential model for the data. Use the model to estimate the weight of a diamond worth \$2325.

Diamond Values	
Weight (carats)	Value (\$)
0.5	920
1.0	1160
2.0	1580
3.0	2150
4.0	2900

Step 1 Enter the data into two lists in a graphing calculator. Use the exponential regression feature.

An exponential model is $V(w) \approx 814.96(1.38)^w$, where V is the diamond value and w is the weight in carats.

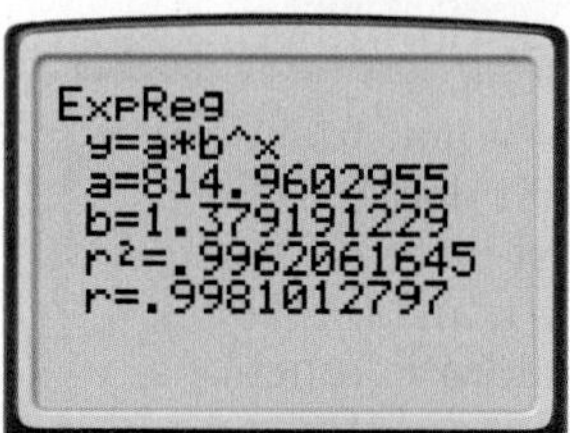

Remember!

If you do not see r^2 and **r** when you calculate regression, use 2nd 0 (CATALOG) and turn these features on by selecting **DiagnosticOn**.

Step 2 Graph the data and the function model to verify that it fits the data.

To enter the regression equation as **Y1** from the Y= screen, press VARS, choose **5:Statistics**, press ENTER, scroll to the **EQ** menu and select **1:RegEQ.**

VARS Y-VARS
1:Window...
2:Zoom...
3:GDB...
4:Picture...
5:Statistics...
6:Table...
7:String...

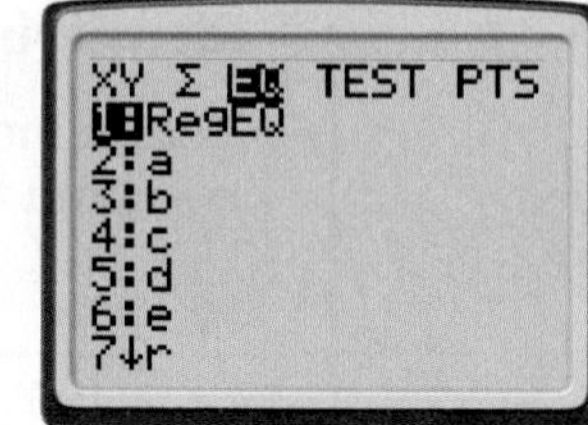

Enter 2325 as **Y2**. Use the intersection feature. You may need to adjust the window dimensions to find the intersection.

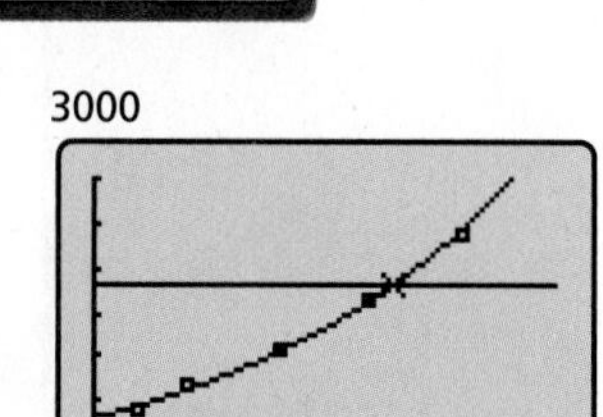

A diamond weighing about 3.26 carats will have a value of \$2325.

2. Use exponential regression to find a function that models this data. When will the number of bacteria reach 2000?

Time (min)	0	1	2	3	4	5
Bacteria	200	248	312	390	489	610

Many natural phenomena can be modeled by natural log functions. You can use a **logarithmic regression** to find a function.

EXAMPLE 3 *Physics Application*

The table gives the Richter scale equivalent for an explosion involving a quantity of TNT. Find a natural log model for the data. Use the model to estimate the number of tons of TNT that would be the equivalent of an earthquake measuring 6.5 on the Richter scale.

Richter Scale TNT Equivalence

TNT (tons)	Magnitude
1 TON	2.0
10 TONS	3.0
1000 TONS	4.0
10,000 TONS	5.0

Enter the data into two lists in a graphing calculator. Then use the logarithmic regression feature. Press STAT **CALC 9:LnReg.** A logarithmic model is $R(t) \approx 2 + 0.29 \ln t$, where R is the Richter scale reading and t is the equivalent number of tons of TNT.

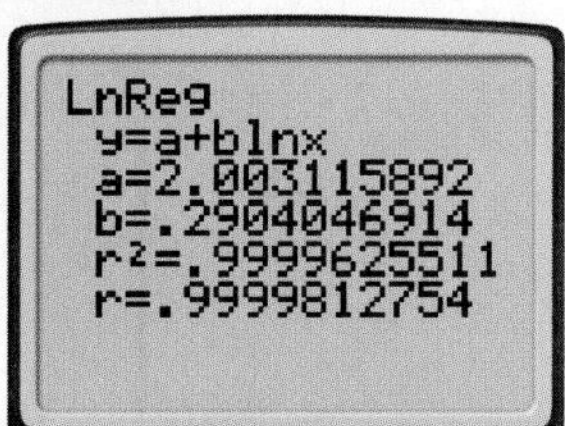

The calculated value of r^2 shows that the function fits the data.

Graph the data and function model to verify that it fits the data.

Use the intersection feature to find x when y is 6.5. The TNT equivalent of an earthquake measuring 6.5 on the Richter scale is about 5.3 million tons.

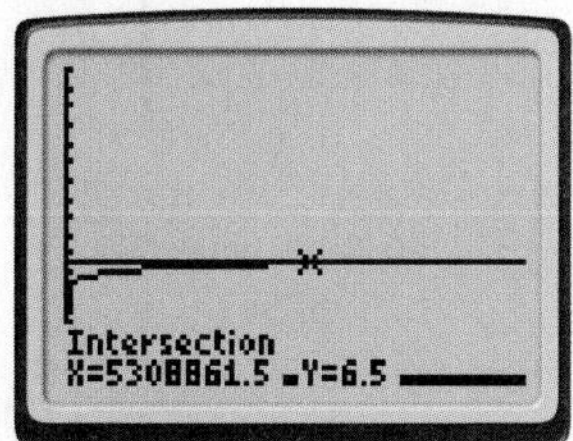

Helpful Hint

Most calculators that perform logarithmic regression use ln rather than log.

3. Use logarithmic regression to find a function that models this data. When will the speed reach 8.0 m/s?

Time (min)	1	2	3	4	5	6	7
Speed (m/s)	0.5	2.5	3.5	4.3	4.9	5.3	5.6

THINK AND DISCUSS

1. Explain how you can determine whether or not a data set can be fit by an exponential function of the form $f(x) = ab^x$.

2. Explain why having only two data points is not enough to tell you whether the data set is exponential or logarithmic.

3. GET ORGANIZED Copy and complete the graphic organizer. Show the procedures and tools for finding an exponential or logarithmic model.

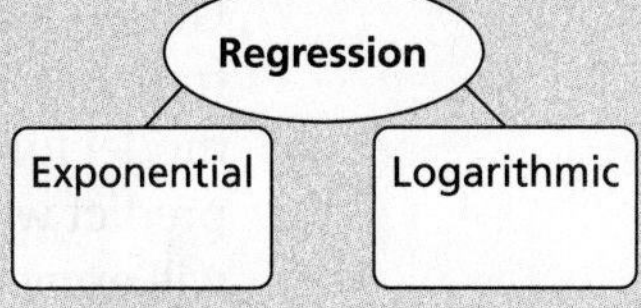

7-8 Exercises

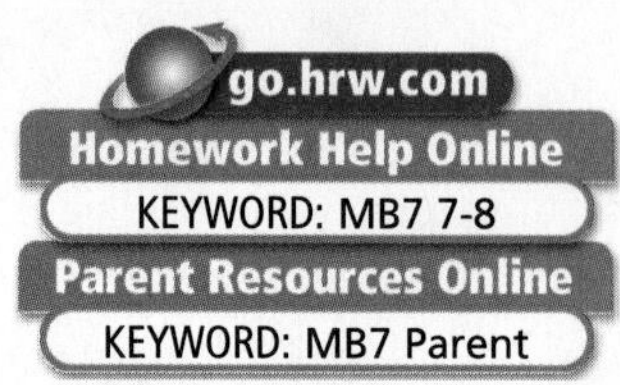

GUIDED PRACTICE

1. **Vocabulary** __?__ is useful when data can be modeled by a function of the form $f(x) = ab^x$. (*Exponential regression* or *Logarithmic regression*)

SEE EXAMPLE 1 p. 545

Determine whether f is an exponential function of x of the form $f(x) = ab^x$. If so, find the constant ratio.

2.

x	-1	0	1	2	3
$f(x)$	$-2\frac{5}{7}$	-1	11	95	683

3.

x	-1	0	1	2	3
$f(x)$	27	18	12	8	$5\frac{1}{3}$

4.

x	-1	0	1	2	3
$f(x)$	5	1	-3	-7	-11

5.

x	-1	0	1	2	3
$f(x)$	$2\frac{1}{4}$	3	4	$5\frac{1}{3}$	$7\frac{1}{9}$

SEE EXAMPLE 2 p. 546

6. **Physics** The table gives the approximate number of degrees Fahrenheit above room temperature of a cup of tea as it cools. Find an exponential model for the data. Use the model to estimate how long it will take the tea to reach a temperature that is less than 40 degrees above room temperature.

Cooling Tea					
Time (min)	0	1	2	3	4
Degrees above room temperature (°F)	132	120	110	101	93

SEE EXAMPLE 3 p. 547

7. **Community** The table shows the population milestones for a small town following its incorporation. Find a natural log model for the data. Use the model to predict how long it will take for the population to reach 8000.

Town Population Milestones					
Time (mo)	6	18	42	90	150
Population	3000	4000	5000	6000	7000

PRACTICE AND PROBLEM SOLVING

Independent Practice

For Exercises	See Example
8–11	1
12	2
13	3

Extra Practice
Skills Practice p. S17
Application Practice p. S38

Determine whether f is an exponential function of x of the form $f(x) = ab^x$. If so, find the constant ratio.

8.

x	-1	0	1	2	3
$f(x)$	1.25	1	0.75	0.5	0.25

9.

x	-5	-3	1	3	5
$f(x)$	20	6	2	12	30

10.

x	-1	0	1	2	3
$f(x)$	0.667	1	1.5	2.25	3.375

11.

x	-1	0	1	2	3
$f(x)$	-16	-8	-4	-2	-1

12. **Social Studies** The table gives the United States Hispanic population from 1980 to 2000. Find an exponential model for the data. Use the model to predict when the Hispanic population will exceed 120 million.

United States Hispanic Population			
Years After 1970	10	20	30
Population (millions)	14.6	22.5	35.3

Source: Census 2000

13. **Telecommunication** The table gives the number of telecommuters in the United States from 1990 to 2000. Find an exponential model for the data. Use the model to estimate when the number of telecommuters will exceed 100 million.

U.S. Telecommuters											
Years After 1990	0	1	2	3	4	5	6	7	8	9	10
Telecommuters (millions)	4.4	5.5	6.6	7.3	9.1	8.5	8.7	11.1	15.7	19.6	23.6

Source: Federal Highway Administration

14. **Ecology** Data on an endangered crane species indicate that their numbers are increasing. The table shows the population size over the last 55 years. Find a logarithmic model for the data. Predict the year when the population will reach 500.

Crane Population					
Population Size	18	40	85	120	185
Years Since 1940	5	22	40	47	57

Decide whether the data set is exponential, and if it is, use exponential regression to find a function that models the data.

15.

x	1	2	3	4
$f(x)$	11	95	683	4799

16.

x	−1	0	2	3
$f(x)$	4	2	0.5	0.25

American alligator, Everglades National Park

17. **Critical Thinking** According to one source, the population of nesting wading birds in the wetlands of the Florida Everglades Park System has decreased from more than a half-million in the 1930s to less than 15,000 today. What do you need to know to determine whether this decrease in numbers is exponential? Explain.

18. **Ecology** One research study showed that the rate of calf survival in Yellowstone elk herds depends on spring snow depths. At snow depths of about 5000 mm, the rate of survival is about 0.9 per hundred cows; at 6700 mm it is about 0.3; and at 8250 mm, it is about 0.17. Find an exponential function to model the data. Use the model to predict the calf survival rate per hundred cows at snow depths of 4000 mm.

19. **Technology** Holiday season sales of a portable digital music player are shown in the graph. Assume that growth rate continues in the same way. Write an exponential function to model the data. Use the model to predict sales in three years.

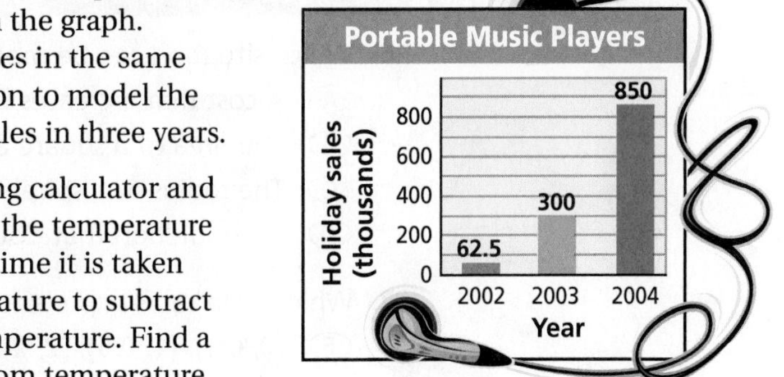

20. **Data Collection** Use a graphing calculator and a temperature probe to measure the temperature of a refrigerated liquid from the time it is taken from refrigeration. Use the list feature to subtract the temperatures from room temperature. Find a model for the difference from room temperature over time. Describe the model and explain why you chose it.

21. **Make a Conjecture** Make a table of values for an exponential function with $x = 1, 2, 3, \ldots 8$. Find the first differences, second differences, and third differences. Make a conjecture about the nth differences, assuming that the domain of the function is all natural numbers.

22. This problem will prepare you for the Multi-Step Test Prep on page 552.

The table shows the total amount of farmland in Vermont since 1970.

a. Use exponential regression to find a function that models the data.

b. According to the model, by what percent does the amount of farmland decrease each year?

c. Predict the amount of farmland in 2010.

Farmland in Vermont

Year	Farmland (thousands of acres)
1970	2010
1980	1740
1990	1440
2000	1270

23. Recreation At the Autosport Show in Birmingham, England, in January 2001, karting champion Stuart Ziemelis demonstrated an electric race kart with a top speed of over 100 mi/h and acceleration from 0-to-60 mi/h in less than 4 s. The *difference* between the race kart's speed S and its top speed can be modeled by $(100 - S) = 100(0.795)^t$, where t is the time in seconds after the start.

a. Predict the electric race kart's speed at 1, 2, and 8 s.

b. Use your answers to part **a** to verify that the speed is an exponential function of time. Use exponential regression to find the function that models the speed.

24. Write About It Describe how to tell whether data is exponential rather than linear, quadratic, or cubic.

25. Biology The number of fronds of duckweed present during an experiment are given in the table.

Day	0	2	3	4	5	6
Fronds	18	32	43	57	76	101

a. Which fits the data better, an exponential function or a linear function?

b. Enter the day numbers in L1 and the logarithm of each number of fronds in L2 (use either log or ln). Which fits this data better, an exponential function or a linear function? Why?

26. Which situation can be modeled by an exponential function?

Ⓐ A cost that increases by $100 each month

Ⓑ The area of a square as the length increases by increments of 10 cm

Ⓒ The radius of a spiral that gets 10% larger with each rotation

Ⓓ A population that doubles as the time doubles

27. Which data set is exponential?

Ⓕ (0, 0.1), (1, 0.5), (2, 2.5), (3, 12.5)

Ⓖ (0, −1), (1, 0), (2, 7), (3, 20)

Ⓗ (0, −1), (1, 0.5), (2, 2), (3, 3.5)

Ⓙ (0, −1), (1, 2), (2, 11), (3, 26)

28. Gridded Response Find the missing value if f is an exponential function.

x	0	1	2	3
y	2	3.5	■	10.71875

CHALLENGE AND EXTEND

29. Find an exponential function that goes through the points $(2, 48)$ and $(4, 300)$. Show your work.

30. **Environment** Helena works in a chemistry laboratory. Due to equipment failure, she may have inhaled toxic fumes. Five hours after the incident, a blood sample shows a toxin concentration of 0.01006 mg/cm^3. Two hours later, another sample detects a concentration of 0.00881 mg/cm^3. Assume that concentration varies exponentially with time.
    a. Write an exponential function to model the data.
    b. There is a health risk if the toxin concentration was as high as 0.015 mg/cm^3. Was the initial concentration above this level?
    c. Helena can return to work when the concentration drops below 0.00010 mg/cm^3. How many hours (to the nearest hour) after the incident will this be?

31. The calculator uses logarithms to fit data to exponential and logarithmic functions. Determine what domains or ranges of data cause the calculator to get an error when using the exponential regression and logarithmic regression functions.

SPIRAL REVIEW

Solve. *(Lesson 5-3)*

32. $|-5x| = 45$
33. $|x + 4| = 0$
34. $|2x - 4| = 3$
35. $2|2x| + 1 = 10$

Find the zeros of each function by factoring. *(Lesson 5-3)*

36. $f(x) = x^2 + 2x - 3$
37. $f(x) = 3x^2 + 24x$
38. $f(x) = 2x^2 + 10x + 12$
39. $f(x) = x^2 + 9x - 36$

Solve and check. *(Lesson 7-5)*

40. $\frac{1}{64} = 4^{x+5}$
41. $81^x = 3^{x+4}$
42. $8^{\frac{x}{3}} = \left(\frac{1}{2}\right)^{x+2}$
43. $216^x = 6^{2x}$

Career Path

go.hrw.com
Career Resources Online
KEYWORD: MB7 Career

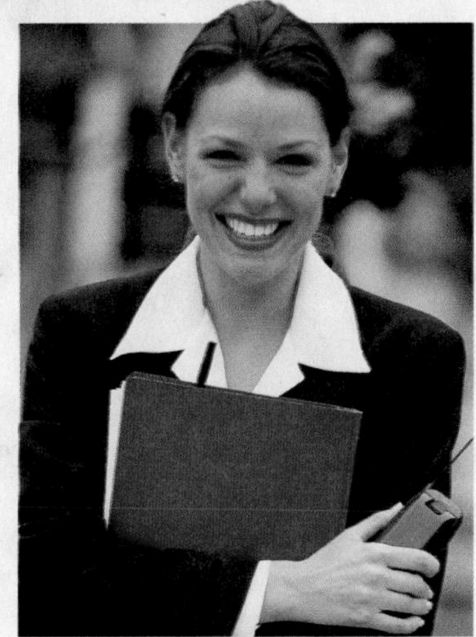

Colleen Murray
Real estate agent

Q: What high school math classes did you take?
A: Algebra 1, Geometry, Business Math, and Algebra 2.

Q: How did you become a real estate agent?
A: After high school, I took an online training course in real estate. Then I had to pass a state license exam.

Q: How is math used in real estate?
A: We calculate house prices, interest rates, payments, taxes, closing costs, commissions, and other fees. I use geometry to calculate areas and formulas to convert between units of measurement, such as square feet to acres.

Q: What are your future plans?
A: I may look into becoming a broker. Then I can supervise other agents and manage my own office.

CHAPTER 7

SECTION 7B

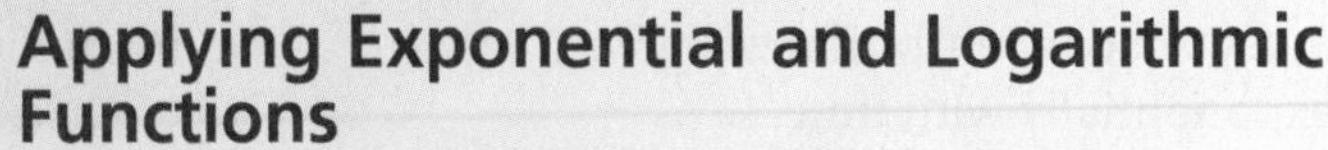

Applying Exponential and Logarithmic Functions

Down on the Farm According to data from the U.S. Department of Agriculture, the number of farms in the United States has been decreasing over the past several decades. During this time, however, the average size of each farm has increased.

1. From 1940 to 1980, the average size A of a U.S. farm can be modeled by the function $A(t) = 174e^{0.022t}$, where t is the number of years since 1940. What was the average farm size in 1940? in 1980?
2. In what year did the average farm size reach 250 acres?
3. During the period from 1940 to 1980, how many years did it take for the average farm size to double?
4. The table shows the number of farms in the United States since 1940. Find an exponential model for the data.

Farms in the United States

Year	Number of Farms (millions)
1940	6.35
1950	5.65
1960	3.96
1970	2.95
1980	2.44
1990	2.15
2000	2.17

5. Predict the number of farms in the United States in 2010.
6. According to your model, how many years does it take for the number of farms to decrease by 50%?
7. According to your model, when will the number of farms in the United States fall below 1 million?

CHAPTER 7

SECTION 7B

Quiz for Lessons 7-5 Through 7-8

7-5 Exponential and Logarithmic Equations and Inequalities

Solve.

1. $3^x = \frac{1}{27}$
2. $49^{x+4} < 7^{\frac{x}{2}}$
3. $13^{3x-1} = 91$
4. $2^{x+4} = 20$
5. $\log_4(x - 1) \geq 3$
6. $\log_2 x^{\frac{1}{3}} = 5$
7. $\log 16x - \log 4 = 2$
8. $\log x + \log(x + 3) = 1$
9. Suppose that you deposit \$500 into an account that pays 3.5% compounded quarterly. The equation $A = P\left(1 + \frac{r}{4}\right)^n$ gives the amount A in the account after n quarters for an initial investment of P that earns interest at a rate of r. Use logarithms to solve for n to find how long it will take for the account to contain at least \$2000.

7-6 The Natural Base, *e*

Graph.

10. $f(x) = e^x + 3$
11. $f(x) = 3 - e^x$
12. $f(x) = \frac{e^x}{3}$
13. $f(x) = 3(e^x - 1)$

Simplify.

14. $\ln e^2$
15. $\ln e^{\frac{x}{2}}$
16. $e^{\ln(1-3a)}$
17. $\ln e^{b+5}$
18. Carbon-14 is a useful dating tool for specimens between 500 and 25,000 years old, such as ancient manuscripts and artifacts. Carbon-14's half-life is 5730 years.
    - **a.** Use the formula $\frac{1}{2} = e^{-kt}$ to find the value of the decay constant for carbon-14.
    - **b.** Use the decay function $N_t = N_0 e^{-kt}$ to determine how much of 10 grams of carbon-14 will remain after 1000 years.

7-7 Transforming Exponential and Logarithmic Functions

Graph the function. Find the *y*-intercept and asymptote. Describe how the graph is transformed from the graph of the parent function.

19. $g(x) = 1.5(3^x)$
20. $k(x) = e^{\frac{x}{2}}$

Graph the function. Find the *x*-intercept and asymptote. Describe how the graph is transformed from the graph of the parent function.

21. $n(x) = 3.5 \log(x + 1)$
22. $p(x) = -\ln(x + 2)$

Write the transformed function.

23. $f(x) = 0.5^x$ is horizontally compressed by a factor of $\frac{1}{2}$ and reflected across the x-axis.

7-8 Curve Fitting with Exponential and Logarithmic Models

Determine whether *y* is an exponential function of *x*. If so, find the constant ratio. Then use exponential regression to find a function that models the data.

24.

x	0	1	2	3	4	5
y	1.5	3	6	12	24	48

25.

x	0	1	2	3	4	5
y	1.5	2.4	3.3	4.2	5.1	6.0

CHAPTER 7

Study Guide: Review

Vocabulary

Complete the sentences below with vocabulary words from the list above.

1. A(n) ___?___ has a base of e.
2. A(n) ___?___ is a line that a graphed function approaches but does not touch.
3. To graph a(n) ___?___, reflect each point in the relation across the line $y = x$.

7-1 Exponential Functions, Growth, and Decay *(pp. 490–496)*

EXAMPLE

A quantity of a certain vitamin is eliminated from the bloodstream at about 15% per hour.

- Will the function that represents this situation show growth or decay?

  It will show decay because the quantity decreases.

- Write a function to show the amount of the vitamin that remains t hours after the peak level of 400 mg.

  $f(x) = 400(0.85)^t$

- Graph the function. Use the graph to predict the amount remaining after 7 hours.

  After 7 hours, about 130 mg are left.

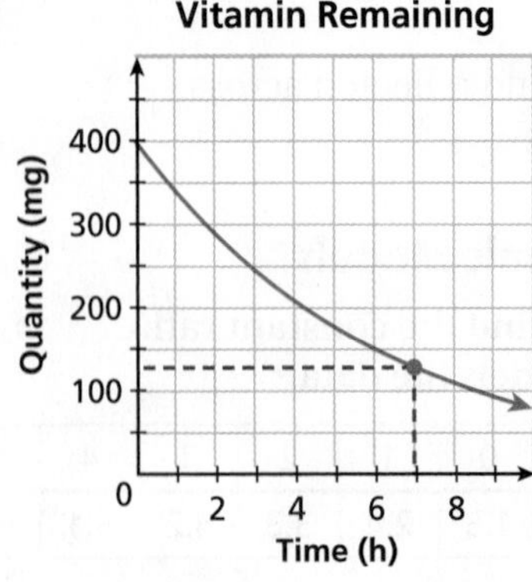

EXERCISES

Tell whether the function shows growth or decay. Then graph.

4. $f(x) = 0.5(1.25)^x$
5. $f(x) = 0.5\left(\frac{3}{2}\right)^x$
6. $f(x) = 2.5(0.25)^x$
7. $f(x) = 2(1 + 0.25)^x$

Use the following data to answer the questions.

The student population in a small resort town has increased by 2% per year for the last 5 years. This year's population is 765 students.

8. Will the function that represents this situation show growth or decay?
9. Suppose that the student population continues to follow the same trend. Write a function to show the number of students as a function of the year, starting with the current year.
10. Graph the function.
11. Use the graph to predict the number of students in 5 years.
12. When will the population exceed 1000 students?

7-2 Inverses of Relations and Functions *(pp. 498–504)*

EXAMPLE

- **Graph the function $f(x) = \frac{4}{5} - 3x$. Then write its inverse and graph.**

$y = -3x + \frac{4}{5}$ *Set y = f(x) and graph*

$x = -3y + \frac{4}{5}$ *Interchange x and y.*

$3y = -x + \frac{4}{5}$ *Solve for y.*

$y = -\frac{1}{3}x + \frac{4}{15}$

Write the inverse and graph.

$f^{-1}(x) = -\frac{1}{3}x + \frac{4}{15}$

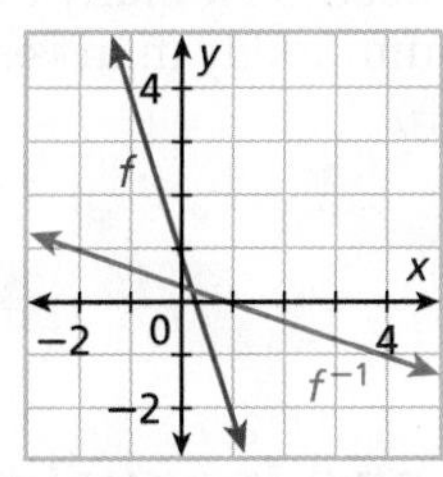

EXERCISES

13. Graph the relation and connect the points. Then graph and write the inverse.

x	−1	0	1	2	3
y	1	0.2	0.04	0.008	0.001

This year the population of a species decreased by 3% from last year.

14. Write an expression for the size of the population this year P_T as a function of last year's population P_L.

15. Write an expression for the year as a function of the size of the population.

16. The formula $M = \frac{5}{8}K$ gives the approximate distance in miles as a function of kilometers. Write and use the inverse of this function to express 25 miles in kilometers.

7-3 Logarithmic Functions *(pp. 505–511)*

EXAMPLES

- **Write the exponential equation $9^{1.5} = 27$ in logarithmic form.**

$9^{1.5} = 27$

$\log_9 27 = 1.5$ *A logarithm is an exponent.*

- **Evaluate $\log_4 64$.**

Because $4^3 = 64$, $\log_4 64 = 3$.

- **Graph $f(x) = 0.6^x$. Then graph its inverse. Describe the domain and range of the inverse function.**

x	−2	−1	0	1	2
f(x)	2.8	1.7	1	0.6	0.4

To graph the inverse, reverse each ordered pair.

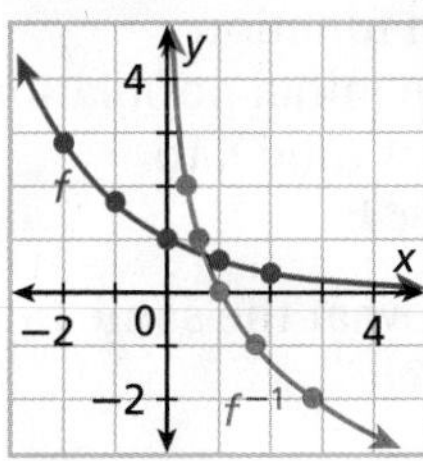

For the inverse function, the domain is $\{x \mid x > 0\}$, and the range is $\mathbb{R}$.

EXERCISES

Write each exponential equation in logarithmic form.

17. $3^5 = 243$ **18.** $1 = 9^0$ **19.** $\left(\frac{1}{3}\right)^{-3} = 27$

Write each logarithmic equation in exponential form.

20. $\log_2 16 = 4$ **21.** $\log 10 = 1$ **22.** $2 = \log_{0.6} 0.36$

Evaluate by using mental math.

23. $\log_7 49$ **24.** $\log_{0.5} 0.25$

25. $\log_{12}\left(\frac{1}{12}\right)$ **26.** $\log 0.01$ **27.** $\log_2 1$

28. Make a table of ordered pairs for $f(x) = \left(\frac{1}{2}\right)^x$. Graph the function and its inverse. Describe the domain and range of the inverse function.

7-4 Properties of Logarithms *(pp. 512–519)*

EXAMPLES

Express as a single logarithm and simplify.

- $\log 25 + \log 40$
  $= \log(25 \cdot 40) = \log 1000 = 3$
- $\log_5 125 - \log_5 25$
  $= \log_5\left(\frac{125}{25}\right) = \log_5 5 = 1$
- $\log_3 8^2$
  $= 2\log_3 8 = 2 \cdot 2 = 4$
- **Evaluate $\log_5 16$.**
  $= \frac{\log 16}{\log 5}$ *Use the change of base formula.*
  $\approx \frac{1.2}{0.7} \approx 1.72$ *Use a calculator to evaluate.*

EXERCISES

Express as a single logarithm and simplify.

29. $\log_2 8 + \log_2 16$

30. $\log 100 + \log 10{,}000$

31. $\log_2 128 - \log_2 2$

32. $\log 10 - \log 0.1$

33. $\log_5 25^2$

34. $\log 10^5 + \log 10^4$

35. The apparent loudness of the music today at Sam's Café was 10 decibels greater than the loudness yesterday. Apparent loudness L is given by $L = 10\log\frac{I}{I_0}$, where I is the intensity of sound, in W/m^2 and I_0 is the lowest intensity that the ear can detect. How many times more intense was the sound today than yesterday?

7-5 Exponential and Logarithmic Equations and Inequalities *(pp. 522–528)*

EXAMPLES

Solve.

- $5^x = 50$
  $\log 5^x = \log 50$
  $x\log 5 = \log 50$
  $x = \frac{\log 50}{\log 5} \approx 2.43$
- $\log_9 x^2 = 5$
  $2\log_9 x = 5$
  $\log_9 x = \frac{5}{2}$
  $x = 9^{\frac{5}{2}}$
  $x = (3^2)^{\frac{5}{2}} = 3^5 = 243$

EXERCISES

Solve and check.

36. $3^{x-1} = \frac{1}{9}$

37. $\left(\frac{1}{2}\right)^x \le 64$

38. $\log x^{\frac{5}{2}} > 2.5$

39. $A = P(1 + r)^n$ gives amount A in an account after n years for an initial investment P that earns interest at an annual rate r. How long will it take for \$250 to increase to \$500 at 4% annual interest?

7-6 The Natural Base, *e* *(pp. 531–536)*

EXAMPLE

- **Simplify $e^{\ln(2s+1)}$.**
  $e^{\ln(2s+1)} = 2s + 1$ *e to the ln of a number is just the number.*
- **What is the total value of an investment of \$5000 that earned 6% interest compounded continuously for 5 years?**
  $A = 5000e^{0.06(5)}$ *Substitute in $A = Pe^{rt}$.*
  $A \approx 6749.29$ *Use a calculator.*
  The value is \$6749.29.

EXERCISES

40. The population of whooping cranes was about 22 in 1940 and grew at an exponential rate to about 194 in 2003.

a. Use the exponential growth function $P(t) = P_0e^{kt}$, where P_0 is the initial population and $P(t)$ is the population at time t, to determine the growth factor k.

b. If the flock continues to grow at the same rate, how large will it be in 2020?

7-7 Transforming Exponential and Logarithmic Functions *(pp. 537–544)*

EXAMPLES

Write each transformed function.

- $f(x) = \left(\frac{1}{3}\right)^x$ is shifted 1 unit left, stretched vertically by a factor of 2, and reflected across the y-axis.

$\left(\frac{1}{3}\right)^x$ *Begin with the rule for the parent function.*

$\left(\frac{1}{3}\right)^{x+1}$ *To shift 1 unit left, replace x with x + 1.*

$2\left(\frac{1}{3}\right)^{x+1}$ *Stretch vertically by 2.*

$g(x) = 2\left(\frac{1}{3}\right)^{-x+1}$ *Reflect across the y-axis.*

- $f(x) = \log x$ is shifted 2 units right and 1 unit down and is compressed vertically by a factor of 0.3.

$$g(x) = \log\left(\frac{x}{0.3} - 2\right) - 1$$

EXERCISES

Write the transformed function.

41. $f(x) = e^x$ is reflected across the x-axis, stretched vertically by a factor of 3, and shifted 2 units down.

Graph each function. Find the intercept and asymptote. Describe how the graph is transformed from the graph of the parent function.

42. $k(x) = \frac{3}{5}(1.5)^{6x}$

43. $m(x) = 2\log\left(x + \frac{1}{2}\right)$

The trade-in value of Marc's truck is $5300. A truck dealer tells him that the trade-in value of a truck decreases by about 35% each year.

44. Write an equation for the trade-in value as a function of time.

45. Describe how the graph of this function is transformed from the graph of the parent function.

7-8 Curve Fitting with Exponential and Logarithmic Models *(pp. 545–551)*

EXAMPLES

- **Use logarithmic regression to find a function that models the increase in the number of pepper trees in a wilderness preserve over six years. Predict the year when the number of trees will reach 70.**

Year	1	2	3	4	5	6
Trees	14	30	40	46	53	55

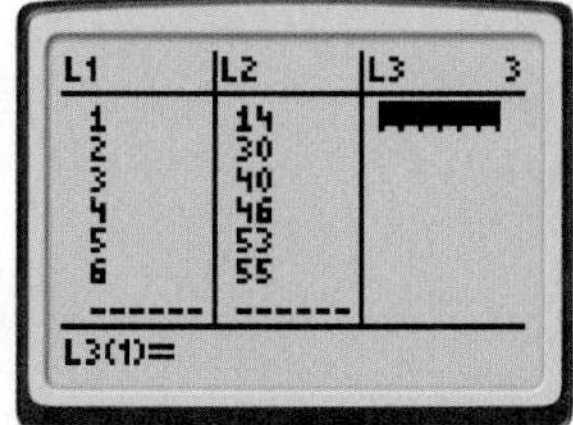

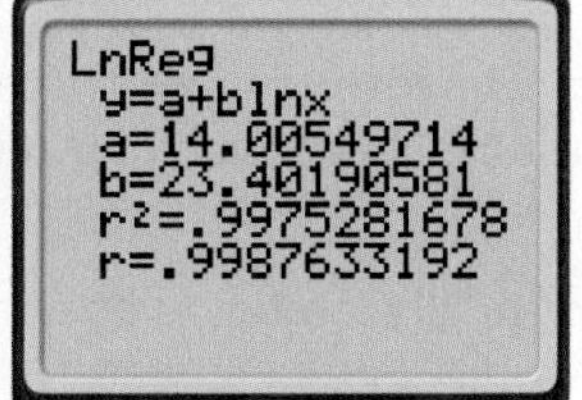

$y \approx 14 + 23.4 \ln x$ *Write the model.*

$\ln x \approx \frac{70 - 14}{23.4} \approx 2.39$ *Substitute 70 for y. Then solve for ln x.*

$x \approx e^{2.39} \approx 10.9$ *Solve for x.*

There will be 70 trees in about 11 years.

EXERCISES

The table gives the population size of a flock of birds in one habitat over the last 57 years.

Years Since Data Was First Collected	Population Size
5	18
22	22
40	85
57	185

46. Use exponential regression, **ExpReg**, to find an exponential function that models the data.

47. Use logarithmic regression, **LnReg**, to find a logarithmic function that models the data.

48. Compare r^2-values of the two functions. Tell which function best models the data and why.

CHAPTER 7

Chapter Test

Tell whether the function shows growth or decay. Then graph.

1. $f(x) = 0.4^x$
2. $f(x) = 1.3\left(\frac{2}{5}\right)^x$
3. $f(x) = \frac{7}{8}(1.1)^x$
4. $f(x) = 50(1 + 0.04)^x$
5. Gina buys a car for $13,500. Assume that its value will decrease by about 15% per year. Write an exponential function to model the value of the car. Graph the function. When will the value fall below $3000?

Graph each function. Then write its inverse and graph.

6. $f(x) = x - 1.06$
7. $f(x) = \frac{5}{6}x - 1.06$
8. $f(x) = 1.06 - \frac{5}{6}x$
9. $f(x) = \frac{1}{4}\left(1.06 - \frac{5}{6}x\right)$

Write in the alternative form (exponential or logarithmic).

10. $16^{\frac{1}{4}} = 2$
11. $16^{-0.5} = \frac{1}{4}$
12. $\log_{\frac{1}{4}} 64 = -3$
13. $\log_{81} \frac{1}{3} = -\frac{1}{4}$

Use the given *x*-values to graph each function. Then write and graph its inverse. Describe the domain and range of the inverse function.

14. $f(x) = \left(\frac{1}{4}\right)^x$; $x = -1, 0, 2, 4$
15. $f(x) = 2.5^x$; $x = -1, 0, 1, 2, 3$
16. $f(x) = 5^{-x}$; $x = -1, 0, 1, 2, 3$

Simplify.

17. $\log_4 128 - \log_4 8$
18. $\log_2 12.8 + \log_2 5$
19. $\log_3 243^2$
20. $5^{\log_5 x}$

Solve.

21. $3^{x-1} = 729^{\frac{x}{2}}$
22. $5^{1.5-x} \le 25$
23. $\log_4(x + 48) = 3$
24. $\log(6x^2) - \log 2x = 1$
25. The rate at which a liquid vitamin breaks down in the average human body can be modeled by $y = D(0.95)^x$, where *y* ml of the original dose *D* remains after *x* minutes. How long will it take for an original dose of 15 ml to be reduced to less than 5 ml?
26. Plutonium Pu-239 has a half-life of about 24,000 years. The formula $\frac{1}{2} = e^{-kt}$ relates the half-life *t* to the decay constant *k* for a given substance. How much of a 100-gram quantity of plutonium will remain after 5 years?
27. $f(x) = \ln x$ is shifted 2 units left and 1 unit up and is vertically stretched by a factor of 3. Write the transformed function.
28. Use logarithmic regression to find the function that models the population data in the table. In what year will the population exceed 100?

Population	50	62	78
Year	1	2	3

FOCUS ON SAT SUBJECT TESTS

The SAT Mathematics Subject Test Level 2 test is meant to be taken by students who have completed two years of algebra and one year of geometry and have studied elementary functions, trigonometry, and some precalculus topics, such as limits.

The questions are placed in an order of increasing difficulty. Because each question is worth the same amount of points, answer as many of the less difficult questions as you can before tackling the more difficult ones.

You may want to time yourself as you take this practice test. It should take you about 6 minutes to complete.

1. If $f^{-1}(x) = \frac{4}{3}x + 8$, what is $f(x)$?

(A) $f(x) = \frac{3}{4}(x - 8)$

(B) $f(x) = \frac{3}{4}x - 8$

(C) $f(x) = \frac{3}{4}(x + 6)$

(D) $f(x) = \frac{4}{3}(x - 8)$

(E) $f(x) = \frac{4}{3}x - 6$

2. If $f(x) = e^x$, then which of the following is $f^{-1}(7)$?

(A) e^7

(B) 7

(C) $\log 7$

(D) $\ln 7$

(E) $\ln\left(e^7\right)$

3. If $e^x e^{2.5} = e^{2.5x}$, what is the vaue of x?

(A) 0

(B) 1

(C) $\frac{5}{3}$

(D) $\mathbb{R}$

(E) $\varnothing$

4. What is $\log_{27} 9$?

(A) $\frac{1}{2}$

(B) $\frac{2}{3}$

(C) $\frac{3}{2}$

(D) 2

(E) 3

5. What is the y-coordinate of the point where the graphs of $y = \log_2\left(\frac{3}{4}x - \frac{23}{4}\right)$ and $y = \log_2\left(-2x + \frac{65}{4}\right)$ intersect?

(A) -2

(B) $\frac{1}{4}$

(C) $\frac{1}{2}$

(D) 2

(E) 8

6. If $\log_9\left\{\log_2[\log_4(x)]\right\} = \frac{1}{2}$, then what is x?

(A) 1.73

(B) 8

(C) 81

(D) 6561

(E) 65,536

CHAPTER 7

TEST TACKLER

Standardized Test Strategies

Any Question Type: Read a Test Item for Understanding

Test items given on a standardized test may vary in type from multiple choice to gridded response to short and extended response. All test items should be read thoroughly so that you recognize important information and have a complete understanding of what is being asked.

EXAMPLE 1

Extended Response The value of a computer purchased new for $2300 goes down by 15.5% each year. Write and graph an exponential function to estimate the value of the computer after 3 years. When will the value of the computer fall below $500?

READ the problem again.

RESTATE the important parts of the test item by using your own words:

What information are you given? The cost of the computer: $2300
The annual percent decrease: 15.5%

What are you asked to do?
1. Write an exponential function.
2. Graph the exponential function.
3. Estimate the computer's value after 3 years.
4. Find when the value will fall below $500.

What should your response include?
1. An exponential function
2. A graph
3. An estimated value, in dollars
4. The time in years

NOTE: Your response should include four parts.

EXAMPLE 2

Short Response Two samples of water taken Monday from a wastewater treatment holding tank have a pH of 4.2 and 4.9. To record the pH for the day, a technician finds the average pH for the two samples. What is the difference in the average pH for Monday and the sample that is most acidic?

READ the problem again.

RESTATE the important parts of the test item by using your own words:

What information are you given? The pH of two samples: 4.2, 4.9

What are you asked to do? Subtract: $\text{pH}_{\text{average}} - \text{pH}_{\text{most acidic sample}}$

Make a plan for your response. Calculate the average pH.
Identify the most acidic sample.
Find the difference.

NOTE: The question requires an intermediate step.

Break a test item into parts to help you organize your approach to the problem.

Read each test item, and answer the questions that follow.

Item A

Gridded Response What is the total amount, to the nearest whole dollar, for an investment of $800 invested at 3.5% for 15 years and compounded continuously?

1. What information are you given?
2. What are you asked to find?
3. Antonio solved this problem and got an incorrect answer of $1220 after using the formula $I = Prt$. What important word(s) did Antonio overlook that may have led him to the correct formula? Explain.
4. Cleo solved this problem by using the formula $800(1 + 0.035)^{15}$ and got an answer of $1340. Did Cleo solve the problem correctly? Explain.

Item B

Gridded Response A doctor prescribed a daily 15-milligram dose of vitamin D to a 55-year-old man. The man weighs 225 pounds. The half-life of vitamin D is about 25 days. The amount A of vitamin D left after t days can be expressed by the exponential function $A = 15\left(\frac{1}{2}\right)^{\frac{t}{25}}$. Find the number of days (to the nearest day) that it takes for the initial dose of vitamin D to drop below 9 milligrams.

5. What information are you given?
6. Identify any information not necessary for your calculations. Explain.
7. Describe a plan that you can use to solve this problem.
8. A student gridded a decimal answer for his response. What part of the problem statement did he overlook?

Item C

Short Response Martha has $6435 in her home safe. She decides to take two-thirds of this amount and invest it in an account that earns 4.25% interest, compounded continuously. What is the total amount of money that Martha has in 3 years?

9. List the information given and what you are being asked to find.
10. Are there intermediate steps that you need to perform to solve the problem? If so, describe the steps.

Item D

Extended Response A runner ran a 3000 m race in 12 minutes and 48 seconds. Write a function that gives distance as a function of time. Write and use the inverse function to find the time it would take the runner to complete a 10,000 m race at the same speed.

11. How many parts are there to this question? Make a list of what needs to be included in your response.
12. What question are you to answer? What units would be acceptable for your answer?

Item E

Short Response Which data set is best represented by using a logarithmic model? Explain your reasoning, and give the function of the logarithmic model.

A)

x	1	20	40	60	80
y	88	218	341	647	980

B)

x	5	15	25	35	45
y	26	43	52	59	61

13. To determine which data set *best* represents a logarithmic model, what intermediate step must you perform to make a comparison?
14. Make a plan for your response.

CHAPTER 7

STANDARDIZED TEST PREP

go.hrw.com
State Test Practice Online
KEYWORD: MB7 TestPrep

CUMULATIVE ASSESSMENT, CHAPTERS 1–7

Multiple Choice

1. Which graph is the inverse of $f(x) = -3x + 6$?

Ⓐ
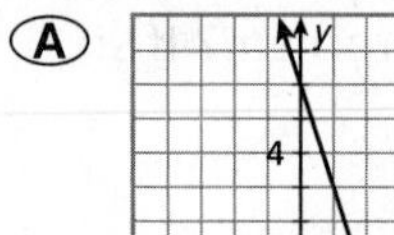

Ⓒ
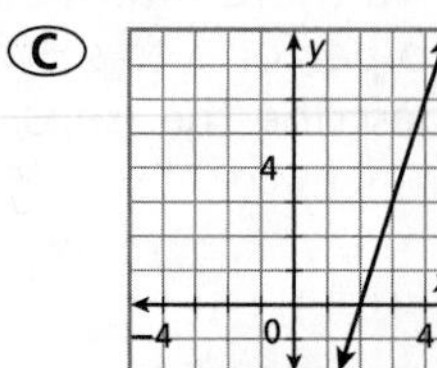

Ⓑ
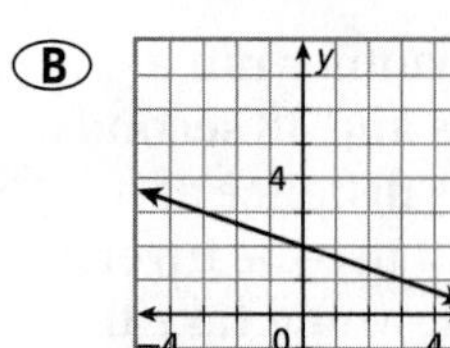

Ⓓ
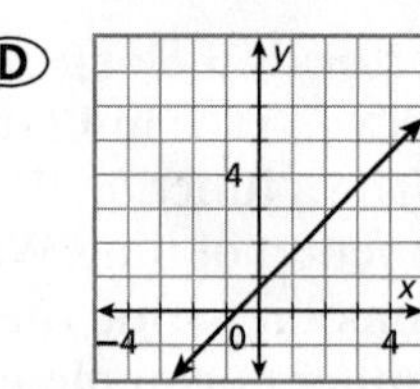

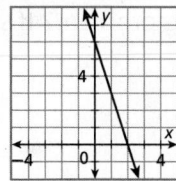

2. Which is equivalent to $\log_5 12 - \log_5 4$?

Ⓕ $\log_5 48$

Ⓖ $\log_5 8$

Ⓗ $\log_5 16$

Ⓙ $\log_5 3$

3. What is the value of x in the equation $\log_4(x-1)^3 = 9$?

Ⓐ $x = 27$

Ⓑ $x = 64$

Ⓒ $x = 65$

Ⓓ $x = 81$

4. The parent logarithmic function $f(x) = \ln x$ is shifted 2 units to the right and 7 units down and is horizontally stretched by a factor of 6. Which is the transformed function?

Ⓕ $f(x) = 6\ln(x-2) - 7$

Ⓖ $f(x) = \ln\left(\frac{x}{6} - 2\right) - 7$

Ⓗ $f(x) = 6\ln(x+2) + 7$

Ⓙ $f(x) = 6\ln\left(\frac{x}{6} + 2\right) + 7$

5. Which equation best fits the data in the scatter plot?

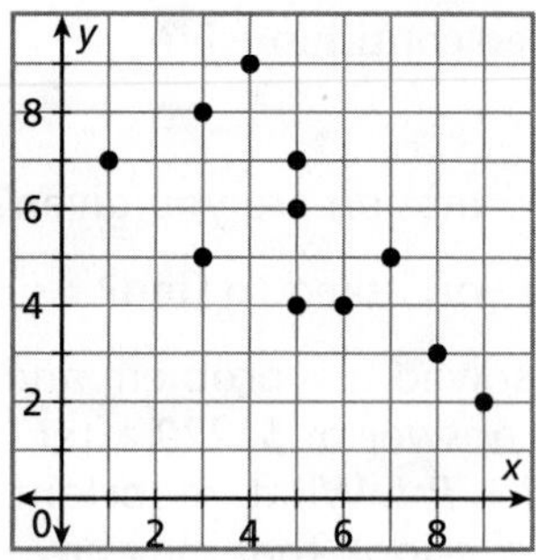

Ⓐ $y = -\frac{10}{11}x + 10$

Ⓑ $y = \frac{10}{11}x + 10$

Ⓒ $y = -\frac{11}{10}x + 1$

Ⓓ $y = \frac{11}{10}x + 1$

6. Which is a factor of $P(x) = 8x^3 - 26x^2 + 17x + 6$?

Ⓕ $4x - 1$

Ⓖ $x + 2$

Ⓗ $2x + 3$

Ⓙ $2x - 3$

7. Which function has a zero of 1?

Ⓐ $f(x) = 2^x - 2$

Ⓑ $f(x) = 2^x + 2$

Ⓒ $f(x) = 2^{x-2}$

Ⓓ $f(x) = 2^{x+2}$

8. The linear correlation coefficient r relating two sets of data is found to be -0.24, and the line of best fit has a y-intercept of 10. Which of the following is NOT necessarily true?

Ⓕ As the values of one set of data increase, the values of the other set decrease.

Ⓖ For positive values of x, the y-value of the line of best fit is less than 10.

Ⓗ The line of best fit is a good model for the data.

Ⓙ The line of best fit has a negative slope.

9. Which has a vertex at (–2, –3)?

Ⓐ $y = x^2 + 4x + 1$

Ⓑ $y = x^2 + 4x - 1$

Ⓒ $y = x^2 - 4x + 1$

Ⓓ $y = x^2 - 4x - 1$

10. What is the product $3(x + y)^4$?

Ⓕ $x^4 + 4x^3y + 6x^2y^2 + 4xy^3 + y^4$

Ⓖ $3x^4 + 12x^3y + 18x^2y^2 + 12xy^3 + 3y^4$

Ⓗ $81x^4 + y^4$

Ⓙ $3x^4 + 3y^4$

11. A line in $y = mx + b$ form has a positive slope and a y-intercept of 5. The slope of the line is decreased. Which of the following must be true?

Ⓐ The x-intercept of the new line is less than the x-intercept of the original line.

Ⓑ The original line and the new line intersect only at (0, 5).

Ⓒ The slope of the new line is greater than 0.

Ⓓ The new line is parallel to the original line.

In Item 12, you can replace a missing number with a variable, such as *x*. Choose a different variable if there is already an *x* in the problem.

Gridded Response

12. What number is missing in the matrix?

$$\begin{bmatrix} 5 & 8 \\ 4 & 3 \end{bmatrix} \times \begin{bmatrix} & 2 \\ -6 & 0 \end{bmatrix} = \begin{bmatrix} -28 & 10 \\ -2 & 8 \end{bmatrix}$$

13. Evaluate $\log_{6.25} 2.5$.

14. Find the positive zero of the equation $f(x) = x^2 + 2.6x - 7.31$ by using the Quadratic Formula.

15. What is the multiplicity of the root 2 in the equation $x^3 - 8x^2 + 20x - 16 = 0$?

16. Use the parent function $f(x) = x^2$. What is the horizontal compression factor of the function $g(x) = \frac{1}{2}(5x)^2 - 4$?

17. What power of 2 has a value of 268,435,456?

Short Response

18. A school is selling used computers and printers. The school sells the computers for \$500 each and the printers for \$50 each. The goal is for the school to make at least \$5200. The school expects to sell at least five computers for every two printers.

a. Write a system of inequalities that models this situation, where x is the number of computers sold, and y is the number of printers sold.

b. Graph the system of inequalities.

19. Radium-226, which has a half-life of 1620 years, is used in medicine for treatment of disease.

a. Find the value of k for radium-226.

b. How much of a 100-gram dose of radium-226 will remain after 3240 years? Round to the nearest gram.

20. Twenty equally spaced points along a 6-foot board are marked for drilling. The distance from the first and last point to the ends is equal to the space between points. What is the distance between consecutive points, to the nearest hundredth of an inch?

Extended Response

21. The chart below shows how many hours students in different grades study each night.

Grade (x)	4	6	8	10	12
Hours (y)	$\frac{1}{4}$	$\frac{1}{2}$	1	2	4

a. Determine if the data set is exponential or logarithmic.

b. Graph the points.

c. Find a function to model the data. Round to the nearest ten thousandth.

d. In which grade do students study 45 minutes each night? Round to the nearest grade.

e. How long do third graders study each night? Round to the nearest half minute.

CHAPTER

8 Rational and Radical Functions

Chapter Focus

- Apply algebraic reasoning to solve problems with rational and radical expressions.
- Make connections among multiple representations of rational and radical functions.

Race to the Finish

You can use rational expressions and functions to determine a bicyclist's average speed in a race with multiple stages.

Chapter Project Online
KEYWORD: MB7 ChProj

ARE YOU READY?

Vocabulary

Match each term on the left with a definition on the right.

1. asymptote
2. rational number
3. reflection
4. translation
5. zero of a function

A. any number that can be expressed as a quotient of two integers, where the denominator is not zero

B. a transformation that flips a figure across a line

C. any number x such that $f(x) = 0$

D. a line that a curve approaches as the value of x or y becomes very large or very small

E. a whole number or its opposite

F. a transformation that moves each point in a figure the same distance in the same direction

Properties of Exponents

Simplify each expression. Assume that all variables are nonzero.

6. $\dfrac{x^{11}y^5}{x^4y^7}$
7. $\left(\dfrac{3x^2y}{z}\right)^4$
8. $(x^3)^{-2}$
9. $(3x^3y)(6xy^5)$
10. $(2x^{-4})^3$
11. $12x^0$

Combine Like Terms

Simplify each expression.

12. $5x^2 + 10x - 4x + 6$
13. $3x + 12 - 10x$
14. $x^2 + x + 3x^2 - 4x$

Greatest Common Factor

Find the greatest common factor of each pair of expressions.

15. $3a^2$ and $12a$
16. c^2d and cd^2
17. $16x^4$ and $40x^3$

Factor Trinomials

Factor each trinomial.

18. $x^2 - 4x - 5$
19. $x^2 + 2x - 24$
20. $x^2 + 12x + 32$
21. $x^2 + 9x + 18$
22. $x^2 - 6x + 9$
23. $x^2 - 8x - 20$

Solve Quadratic Equations

Solve.

24. $5x^2 = 45$
25. $4x^2 - 7 = 93$
26. $2(x - 2)^2 = 32$

CHAPTER 8

Study Guide: Preview

Where You've Been

Previously, you

- solved problems with linear functions.
- simplified polynomial expressions.
- graphed functions with asymptotes.
- solved quadratic equations and inequalities.

In This Chapter

You will study

- solving problems with variation functions.
- simplifying rational and radical expressions.
- graphing rational and radical functions.
- solving rational and radical equations and inequalities.

Where You're Going

You can use the skills in this chapter

- in future math classes, including Precalculus.
- to solve problems in other classes, such as Chemistry, Physics, and Biology.
- outside of school to make predictions involving time, money, or speed.

Key Vocabulary/Vocabulario

complex fraction	fracción compleja
constant of variation	constante de variación
continuous function	función continua
direct variation	variación directa
discontinuous function	función discontinua
extraneous solutions	soluciones extrañas
hole (in a graph)	hoyo (en una gráfica)
inverse variation	variación inversa
radical equation	ecuación radical
radical function	función radical
rational equation	ecuación racional
rational exponent	exponente racional
rational function	función racional

Vocabulary Connections

To become familiar with some of the vocabulary terms in the chapter, consider the following. You may refer to the chapter, the glossary, or a dictionary if you like.

1. The word *extraneous* contains the word *extra*. What does *extra* mean? What do you think an **extraneous solution** is?
2. The graph of a **continuous function** has no gaps or breaks. How do you think a **discontinuous function** differs from a continuous function?
3. Do you think a **hole** could occur in the graph of a *continuous function* or a *discontinuous function*? Why?
4. A rational number can be written as a ratio of two integers. What do you think a **rational exponent** is?

Study Strategy: Make Flash Cards

You can use flash cards to help you remember a sequence of steps, the definitions of vocabulary words, or important formulas and properties.

Use these hints to make useful flash cards:

- Write a vocabulary word or the name of a formula or property on one side of a card and the meaning on the other.
- When memorizing a sequence of steps, make a flash card for each step.
- Use examples or diagrams if needed.
- Label each card with a lesson number in case you need to look back at your textbook for more information.

From Lesson 7-4

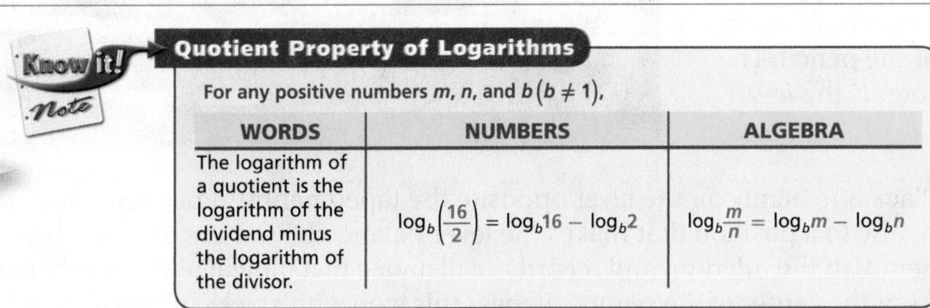

Know it! Note

Quotient Property of Logarithms

For any positive numbers m, n, and $b\ (b \neq 1)$,

WORDS	NUMBERS	ALGEBRA
The logarithm of a quotient is the logarithm of the dividend minus the logarithm of the divisor.	$\log_b\left(\frac{16}{2}\right) = \log_b 16 - \log_b 2$	$\log_b \frac{m}{n} = \log_b m - \log_b n$

Sample Flash Card

Lesson 7-4

Quotient Property of Logarithms

$\log_b \frac{m}{n} = ?$

Front

$\log_b \frac{m}{n} = \log_b m - \log_b n$

example:

$\log_2\left(\frac{16}{2}\right) = \log_2 16 - \log_2 2$

Back

Try This

Make flash cards that can help you remember each piece of information.

1. The Product of Powers Property states that to multiply powers with the same base, add the exponents. (See Lesson 1-5.)
2. The quadratic formula, $x = \frac{-b \pm \sqrt{b^2 - 4ac}}{2a}$, can be used to find the roots of an equation with the form $ax^2 + bx + c = 0\ (a \neq 0)$. (See Lesson 5-6.)

Model Inverse Variation

In this activity, you will explore the relationship between the mass of an object and the object's distance from the pivot point, or fulcrum, of a balanced lever.

Use with Lesson 8-1

Activity

1. Secure a pencil to a tabletop with tape. The pencil will be the *fulcrum*.

2. Draw an arrow on a piece of tape, and use the arrow to mark the midpoint of a ruler. Then tape a penny to the end of the ruler.

3. Place the midpoint of the ruler on top of the pencil. The ruler is the *lever*.

4. Place one penny on the lever opposite the taped penny. If needed, move the untaped penny to a position that makes the lever balanced. Find the distance from the untaped penny to the fulcrum, and record the distance in a table like the one below. (Measure from the center of the penny.) Repeat this step with stacks of two to seven pennies.

Let x be the number of pennies and y be the distance from the fulcrum. Plot the points from your table on a graph. Then draw a smooth curve through the points.

Number of Pennies	1	2	3	4	5	6	7
Distance from Fulcrum (cm)	■	■	■	■	■	■	■

Try This

1. Multiply the corresponding x- and y-values together. What do you notice?
2. Use your answer to Problem 1 to write an equation relating distance from the fulcrum to the number of pennies.
3. Would it be possible to balance a stack of 20 pennies on the lever? Use your equation from Problem 2 to justify your answer.
4. **Make a Conjecture** The relationship between the mass of an object on a balanced lever and the object's distance from the fulcrum can be modeled by an *inverse variation* function. Based on your data and graph, how are the variables in an inverse variation related?

8-1 Variation Functions

Objective
Solve problems involving direct, inverse, joint, and combined variation.

Vocabulary
direct variation
constant of variation
joint variation
inverse variation
combined variation

Why learn this?
You can use variation functions to determine how many people are needed to complete a task, such as building a home, in a given time. (See Example 5.)

In Chapter 2, you studied many types of linear functions. One special type of linear function is called *direct variation*. A **direct variation** is a relationship between two variables x and y that can be written in the form $y = kx$, where $k \neq 0$. In this relationship, k is the **constant of variation**. For the equation $y = kx$, y varies directly as x.

A direct variation equation is a linear equation in the form $y = mx + b$, where $b = 0$ and the constant of variation k is the slope. Because $b = 0$, the graph of a direct variation always passes through the origin.

EXAMPLE 1 Writing and Graphing Direct Variation

Given: y varies directly as x, and $y = 14$ when $x = 3.5$. Write and graph the direct variation function.

$y = kx$	*y varies directly as x.*
$14 = k(3.5)$	*Substitute 14 for y and 3.5 for x.*
$4 = k$	*Solve for the constant of variation k.*
$y = 4x$	*Write the variation function by using the value of k.*

Graph the direct variation function.

The y-intercept is 0, and the slope is 4.

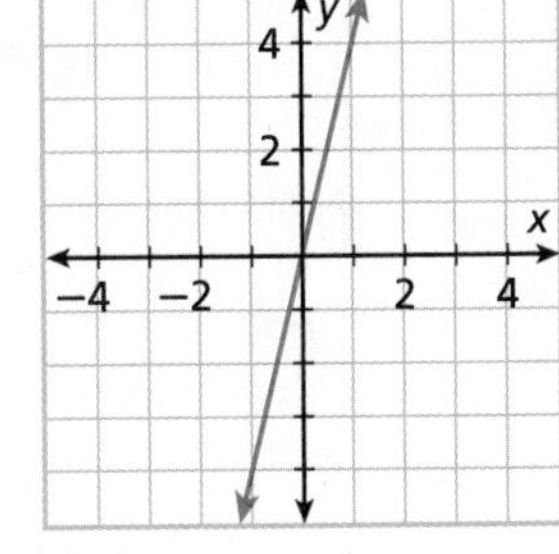

Check Substitute the original values of x and y into the equation.

$y = 4x$	
14	4(3.5)
14	14 ✓

Helpful Hint

If k is positive in a direct variation, the value of y increases as the value of x increases.

1. Given: y varies directly as x, and $y = 6.5$ when $x = 13$. Write and graph the direct variation function.

When you want to find specific values in a direct variation problem, you can solve for k and then use substitution or you can use the proportion derived below.

$$y_1 = kx_1 \rightarrow \frac{y_1}{x_1} = k \quad \text{and} \quad y_2 = kx_2 \rightarrow \frac{y_2}{x_2} = k \quad \text{so,} \quad \frac{y_1}{x_1} = \frac{y_2}{x_2}.$$

EXAMPLE 2 Solving Direct Variation Problems

The circumference of a circle C varies directly as the radius r, and $C = 7\pi$ ft when $r = 3.5$ ft. Find r when $C = 4.5\pi$ ft.

Reading Math

The phrases "y varies directly as x" and "y is directly proportional to x" have the same meaning.

Method 1 Find k.

$C = kr$

$7\pi = k(3.5)$ *Substitute.*

$2\pi = k$ *Solve for k.*

Write the variation function.

$C = (2\pi)r$ *Use 2π for k.*

$4.5\pi = (2\pi)r$ *Substitute 4.5π for C.*

$2.25 = r$ *Solve for r.*

Method 2 Use a proportion.

$\frac{C_1}{r_1} = \frac{C_2}{r_2}$

$\frac{7\pi}{3.5} = \frac{4.5\pi}{r}$ *Substitute.*

$7\pi r = 15.75\pi$ *Find the cross products.*

$r = 2.25$ *Solve for r.*

The radius r is 2.25 ft.

2. The perimeter P of a regular dodecagon varies directly as the side length s, and $P = 18$ in. when $s = 1.5$ in. Find s when $P = 75$ in.

A **joint variation** is a relationship among three variables that can be written in the form $y = kxz$, where k is the constant of variation. For the equation $y = kxz$, y varies jointly as x and z.

EXAMPLE  3 Solving Joint Variation Problems

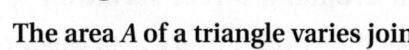

The area A of a triangle varies jointly as the base b and the height h, and $A = 12\text{ m}^2$ when $b = 6$ m and $h = 4$ m. Find b when $A = 36\text{ m}^2$ and $h = 8$ m.

Step 1 Find k.

$A = kbh$ *Joint variation*

$12 = k(6)(4)$ *Substitute.*

$\frac{1}{2} = k$ *Solve for k.*

Step 2 Use the variation function.

$A = \frac{1}{2}bh$ *Use $\frac{1}{2}$ for k.*

$36 = \frac{1}{2}b(8)$ *Substitute.*

$9 = b$ *Solve for b.*

The base b is 9 m.

3. The lateral surface area L of a cone varies jointly as the base radius r and the slant height ℓ, and $L = 63\pi\text{ m}^2$ when $r = 3.5$ m and $\ell = 18$ m. Find r to the nearest tenth when $L = 8\pi\text{ m}^2$ and $\ell = 5$ m.

A third type of variation describes a situation in which one quantity increases and the other decreases. For example, the table shows that the time needed to drive 600 miles decreases as speed increases.

Speed (mi/h)	Time (h)	Distance (mi)
30	20	600
40	15	600
50	12	600

This type of variation is an inverse variation. An **inverse variation** is a relationship between two variables x and y that can be written in the form $y = \frac{k}{x}$, where $k \neq 0$. For the equation $y = \frac{k}{x}$, y varies inversely as x.

EXAMPLE 4 Writing and Graphing Inverse Variation

Given: y varies inversely as x, and $y = 3$ when $x = 8$. Write and graph the inverse variation function.

$y = \frac{k}{x}$ *y varies inversely as x.*

$3 = \frac{k}{8}$ *Substitute 3 for y and 8 for x.*

$k = 24$ *Solve for k.*

$y = \frac{24}{x}$ *Write the variation function.*

Helpful Hint

When graphing an inverse variation function, use values of x that are factors of k so that the y-values will be integers.

To graph, make a table of values for both positive and negative values of x. Plot the points, and connect them with two smooth curves. Because division by 0 is undefined, the function is undefined when $x = 0$.

x	y
−3	−8
−4	−6
−8	−3
−12	−2

x	y
3	8
4	6
8	3
12	2

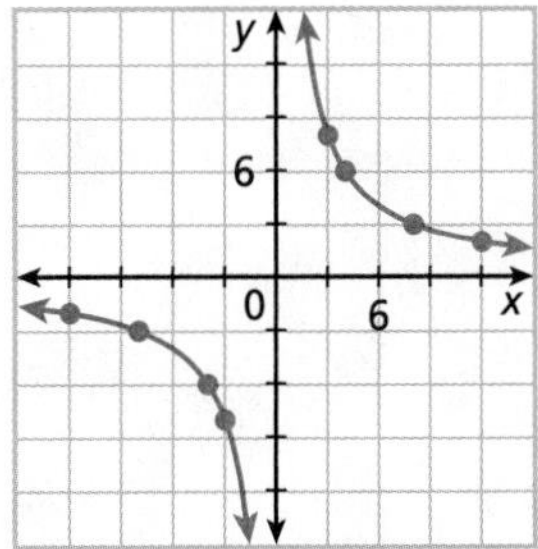

4. Given: y varies inversely as x, and $y = 4$ when $x = 10$. Write and graph the inverse variation function.

When you want to find specific values in an inverse variation problem, you can solve for k and then use substitution or you can use the equation derived below.

$$y_1 = \frac{k}{x_1} \rightarrow y_1x_1 = k \quad \text{and} \quad y_2 = \frac{k}{x_2} \rightarrow y_2x_2 = k \quad \text{so,} \quad y_1x_1 = y_2x_2.$$

EXAMPLE 5 *Community Service Application*

The time t that it takes for a group of volunteers to construct a house varies inversely as the number of volunteers v. If 20 volunteers can build a house in 62.5 working hours, how many volunteers would be needed to build a house in 50 working hours?

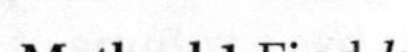

Method 1 Find k.

$t = \frac{k}{v}$

$62.5 = \frac{k}{20}$ *Substitute.*

$1250 = k$ *Solve for k.*

$t = \frac{1250}{v}$ *Use 1250 for k.*

$50 = \frac{1250}{v}$ *Substitute 50 for t.*

$v = 25$ *Solve for v.*

Method 2 Use $t_1v_1 = t_2v_2$.

$t_1v_1 = t_2v_2$

$62.5(20) = 50v$ *Substitute.*

$1250 = 50v$ *Simplify.*

$25 = v$ *Solve for v.*

So 25 volunteers would be needed to build a home in 50 working hours.

5. What if...? How many working hours would it take 15 volunteers to build a house?

You can use algebra to rewrite variation functions in terms of k.

Direct Variation	**Inverse Variation**
$y = kx \rightarrow k = \frac{y}{x}$	$y = \frac{k}{x} \rightarrow k = xy$
Constant ratio	Constant product

Notice that in direct variation, the *ratio* of the two quantities is constant. In inverse variation, the *product* of the two quantities is constant.

EXAMPLE  6 Identifying Direct and Inverse Variation

Determine whether each data set represents a direct variation, an inverse variation, or neither.

 **A**

x	3	8	10
y	9	24	30

In each case, $\frac{y}{x} = 3$. The ratio is constant, so this represents a direct variation.

 **B**

x	4.5	12	2
y	8	3	18

In each case, $xy = 36$. The product is constant, so this represents an inverse variation.

CHECK IT OUT! **Determine whether each data set represents a direct variation, an inverse variation, or neither.**

6a.

x	3.75	15	5
y	12	3	9

6b.

x	1	40	26
y	0.2	8	5.2

A **combined variation** is a relationship that contains both direct and inverse variation. Quantities that vary directly appear in the numerator, and quantities that vary inversely appear in the denominator.

EXAMPLE 7 *Chemistry Application*

Helpful Hint

A kelvin (K) is a unit of temperature that is often used by chemists.

0°C = 273.15 K
100°C = 373.15 K

The volume V of a gas varies inversely as the pressure P and directly as the temperature T. A certain gas has a volume of 10 liters (L), a temperature of 300 kelvins (K), and a pressure of 1.5 atmospheres (atm). If the gas is compressed to a volume of 7.5 L and is heated to 350 K, what will the new pressure be?

Step 1 Find k.

$V = \frac{kT}{P}$ *Combined variation*

$10 = \frac{k(300)}{1.5}$ *Substitute.*

$0.05 = k$ *Solve for k.*

Step 2 Use the variation function.

$V = \frac{0.05T}{P}$ *Use 0.05 for k.*

$7.5 = \frac{0.05(350)}{P}$ *Substitute.*

$P = 2.\overline{3}$ *Solve for P.*

The new pressure will be $2.\overline{3}$, or $2\frac{1}{3}$, atm.

CHECK IT OUT! **7.** If the gas is heated to 400 K and has a pressure of 1 atm, what is its volume?

THINK AND DISCUSS

1. Explain why the graph of a direct variation is a line.
2. Describe the type of variation between the length and the width of a rectangular room with an area of 400 ft^2.

3. **GET ORGANIZED** Copy and complete the graphic organizer. In each box, write the general variation equation, draw a graph, or give an example.

Type of Variation	Equation	Graph	Example
Direct			
Joint			
Inverse			

8-1 Exercises

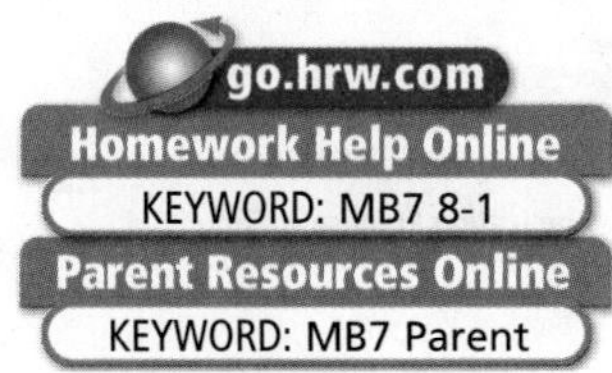

GUIDED PRACTICE

1. **Vocabulary** A variation function in which k is positive and one quantity decreases when the other increases is a(n) __?__. (*direct variation* or *indirect variation*)

SEE EXAMPLE 1 p. 569

Given: y varies directly as x. Write and graph each direct variation function.

2. $y = 6$ when $x = 3$
3. $y = 45$ when $x = -5$
4. $y = 54$ when $x = 4.5$

SEE EXAMPLE 2 p. 570

5. **Physics** The wavelength λ of a wave of a certain frequency varies directly as the velocity v of the wave, and $\lambda = 60$ ft when $v = 15$ ft/s. Find λ when $v = 3$ ft/s.
6. **Work** The dollar amount d that Julia earns varies directly as the number of hours t that she works, and $d = \$116.25$ when $t = 15$ h. Find t when $d = \$178.25$.

SEE EXAMPLE 3 p. 570

7. **Geometry** The volume V of a rectangular prism of a particular height varies jointly as the length ℓ and the width w, and $V = 224$ ft^3 when $\ell = 8$ ft and $w = 4$ ft. Find ℓ when $V = 210$ ft^3 and $w = 5$ ft.
8. **Economics** The total cost C of electricity for a particular light bulb varies jointly as the time t that the light bulb is used and the cost k per kilowatt-hour, and $C = 12$¢ when $t = 50$ h and $k = 6$¢ per kilowatt-hour. Find C to the nearest cent when $t = 30$ h and $k = 8$¢ per kilowatt-hour.

SEE EXAMPLE 4 p. 571

Given: y varies inversely as x. Write and graph each inverse variation function.

9. $y = 2$ when $x = 7$
10. $y = 8$ when $x = 4$
11. $y = \frac{1}{2}$ when $x = -10$

SEE EXAMPLE 5 p. 571

12. **Travel** The time t that it takes for a salesman to drive a certain distance d varies inversely as the average speed r. It takes the salesman 4.75 h to travel between two cities at 60 mi/h. How long would the drive take at 50 mi/h?

SEE EXAMPLE 6 p. 572

Determine whether each data set represents a direct variation, an inverse variation, or neither.

13.

x	2	5	9
y	3	6	4

14.

x	6	4	1
y	2	3	12

15.

x	24	4	12
y	30	5	15

SEE EXAMPLE 7
p. 572

16. **Cars** The power P that must be delivered by a car engine varies directly as the distance d that the car moves and inversely as the time t required to move that distance. To move the car 500 m in 50 s, the engine must deliver 147 kilowatts (kW) of power. How many kilowatts must the engine deliver to move the car 700 m in 30 s?

PRACTICE AND PROBLEM SOLVING

Independent Practice

For Exercises	See Example
17–19	1
20–21	2
22–23	3
24–26	4
27	5
28–30	6
31	7

Extra Practice

Skills Practice p. S18
Application Practice p. S39

Given: y varies directly as x. Write and graph each direct variation function.

17. $y = 4$ when $x = 8$
18. $y = 12$ when $x = 2$
19. $y = -15$ when $x = 5$

20. **Medicine** The dosage d of a drug that a physician prescribes varies directly as the patient's mass m, and $d = 100$ mg when $m = 55$ kg. Find d to the nearest milligram when $m = 70$ kg.

21. **Nutrition** The number of Calories C in a horned melon varies directly as its weight w, and $C = 25$ Cal when $w = 3.5$ oz. How many Calories are in the horned melon shown on the scale? Round to the nearest Calorie.

12.35 oz

22. **Agriculture** The number of bags of soybean seeds N that a farmer needs varies jointly as the number of acres a to be planted and the pounds of seed needed per acre p, and $N = 980$ when $a = 700$ acres and $p = 70$ lb/acre. Find N when $a = 1000$ acres and $p = 75$ lb/acre.

23. **Physics** The heat Q required to raise the temperature of water varies jointly as the mass m of the water and the amount of temperature change T, and $Q = 20{,}930$ joules (J) when $m = 1$ kg and $T = 5°C$. Find m when $Q = 8372$ J and $T = 10°C$.

LINK

Entertainment

Broadway shows are plays or musicals presented in larger theaters near New York City's Times Square. In 2004, 11.3 million tickets were sold to Broadway shows for a total of almost $750 million.

Given: y varies inversely as x. Write and graph the inverse variation function.

24. $y = 1$ when $x = 0.8$
25. $y = 1.75$ when $x = 6$
26. $y = -2$ when $x = 3$

27. **Entertainment** The number of days it takes a theater crew to set up a stage for a musical varies inversely as the number of workers. If the stage can be set up in 3 days by 20 workers, how many days would it take if only 12 workers were available?

Determine whether each data set represents a direct variation, an inverse variation, or neither.

28.

x	5	6.25	10
y	5	4	2.5

29.

x	5	7	9
y	3	5	7

30.

x	8	14	24
y	12	21	36

31. **Chemistry** The volume V of a gas varies inversely as the pressure P and directly as the temperature T. A certain gas has a volume of 20 L, a temperature of 320 K, and a pressure of 1 atm. If the gas is compressed to a volume of 15 L and is heated to 330 K, what will the new pressure be?

Tell whether each statement is sometimes, always, or never true.

32. Direct variation is a linear function.
33. A linear function is a direct variation.
34. An inverse variation is a linear function.
35. In a direct variation, $x = 0$ when $y = 0$.
36. The graph of an inverse variation passes through the origin.

37. This problem will prepare you for the Multi-Step Test Prep on page 608.

In an auto race, a car with an average speed of 200 mi/h takes an average of 31.5 s to complete one lap of the track.

a. Write an inverse variation function that gives the average speed s of a car in miles per hour as a function of the time t in seconds needed to complete one lap.

b. How many seconds does it take the car to complete one lap at an average speed of 210 mi/h?

38. **Data Collection** Use a graphing calculator, a motion detector, and a light detector to measure the intensity of light as distance from the light source increases. Position the detectors next to each other. Place a flashlight in front of the detectors, and then pull the flashlight away from them. Find an appropriate model for the intensity of the light as a function of the square of the distance from the light source.

39. **Multi-Step** Interest earned on a certificate of deposit (CD) at a certain rate varies jointly as the principal in dollars and the time in years.

a. Diane purchased a CD for \$2500 that earned \$12.50 simple interest in 3 months. Write a variation function for this data.

b. At which bank did Diane buy her CD?

c. How much interest would Diane earn in 6 months on a \$3000 CD bought from the same bank?

Complete each table.

40. y varies jointly as x and z.

x	y	z
2	■	4
5	52.5	7
1.5	−36	■
■	1.38	23

41. y varies directly as x and inversely as z.

x	y	z
25	13.75	4
■	1	11
17	18.7	■
10	■	5

42. **Estimation** Shane swims 42 laps in 26 min 19 s. Without using a calculator, estimate how many minutes it would take Shane to swim 15 laps at the same average speed.

43. **Critical Thinking** Explain why only one point (x, y) is needed to write a direct variation function whose graph passes through this point.

44. **Write About It** Explain how to identify the type of variation from a list of ordered pairs.

45. Which of the following would best be represented by an inverse variation function?

Ⓐ The distance traveled as a function of speed

Ⓑ The total cost as a function of the number of items purchased

Ⓒ The area of a circular swimming pool as a function of its radius

Ⓓ The number of posts in a 20-ft fence as a function of distance between posts

46. Which statement is best represented by the graph?

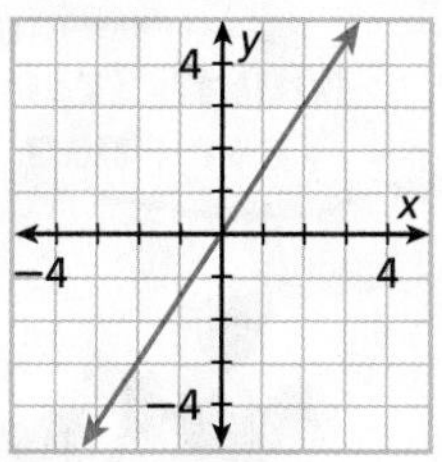

Ⓕ y varies directly as x^2.

Ⓖ y varies inversely as x.

Ⓗ y varies directly as x.

Ⓙ x varies inversely as y.

47. Which equation is best represented by the following statement: y varies directly as the square root of x?

Ⓐ $y = \frac{k}{\sqrt{x}}$ Ⓑ $y = \frac{k}{x^2}$ Ⓒ $k = \sqrt{xy}$ Ⓓ $y = k\sqrt{x}$

48. **Gridded Response** The cost per student of a ski trip varies inversely as the number of students who attend. It will cost each student \$250 if 24 students attend. How many students would have to attend to get the cost down to \$200?

CHALLENGE AND EXTEND

49. Given: y varies jointly as x and the square of z, and $y = 189$ when $x = 7$ and $z = 9$. Find y when $x = 2$ and $z = 6$.

50. **Government** The number of U.S. Representatives that each state receives can be approximated with a direct variation function where the number of representatives (rounded to the nearest whole number) varies directly with the state's population.

a. Given that Pennsylvania has 19 representatives, find k to eight decimal places and write the direct variation function.

b. Find the number of representatives for each state shown.

c. Given that Texas had 32 U.S. representatives in the year 2000, estimate the state's population in that year.

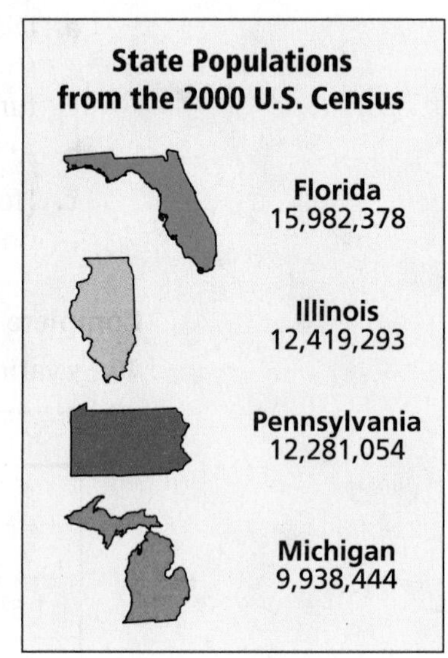

State Populations from the 2000 U.S. Census
Florida
15,982,378
Illinois
12,419,293
Pennsylvania
12,281,054
Michigan
9,938,444

51. **Estimation** Given: y is inversely proportional to x, directly proportional to z^2, and the constant of variation is 7π. Estimate the value of y when $x = 12$ and $z = 2$.

SPIRAL REVIEW

52. **Architecture** Brad stands next to the Eiffel Tower. He is 6 ft 8 in. tall and casts a shadow of 9 ft 4 in. The Eiffel Tower is 985 ft tall. How long is the Eiffel Tower's shadow, in feet? *(Lesson 2-2)*

Write an equation of the line that includes the points in the table. *(Lesson 2-4)*

53.

x	1	3	5	7	9
y	1.5	4	6.5	9	11.5

54.

x	−4	−2	0	2	4
y	10	9	8	7	6

Make a table of values, and graph the exponential function. Describe the asymptote. Tell how the graph is transformed from the graph of $f(x) = 4^x$. *(Lesson 7-7)*

55. $g(x) = \frac{1}{2}(4^x) - 2$

56. $h(x) = (4^{x-1}) + 1$

8-2 Multiplying and Dividing Rational Expressions

Objectives
Simplify rational expressions.
Multiply and divide rational expressions.

Vocabulary
rational expression

Why learn this?
You can simplify rational expressions to determine the probability of hitting an archery target. (See Exercise 35.)

In Lesson 8-1, you worked with inverse variation functions such as $y = \frac{5}{x}$. The expression on the right side of this equation is a *rational expression.* A **rational expression** is a quotient of two polynomials. Other examples of rational expressions include the following:

$$\frac{x^2 - 4}{x + 2} \qquad \frac{10}{x^2 - 6} \qquad \frac{x + 3}{x - 7}$$

Because rational expressions are ratios of polynomials, you can simplify them the same way as you simplify fractions. Recall that to write a fraction in simplest form, you can divide out common factors in the numerator and denominator.

$$\frac{9}{24} = \frac{3 \cdot \cancel{3}}{8 \cdot \cancel{3}} = \frac{3}{8}$$

EXAMPLE 1 Simplifying Rational Expressions

Simplify. Identify any x-values for which the expression is undefined.

A $\frac{3x^7}{2x^4}$

$\frac{3}{2}x^{7-4} = \frac{3}{2}x^3$ *Quotient of Powers Property*

The expression is undefined at $x = 0$ because this value of x makes $2x^4$ equal 0.

B $\frac{x^2 - 2x - 3}{x^2 + 5x + 4}$

$\frac{(x-3)\cancel{(x+1)}}{\cancel{(x+1)}(x+4)} = \frac{(x-3)}{(x+4)}$ *Factor; then divide out common factors.*

The expression is undefined at $x = -1$ and $x = -4$ because these values of x make the factors $(x + 1)$ and $(x + 4)$ equal 0.

Check Substitute $x = -1$ and $x = -4$ into the original expression.

$$\frac{(-1)^2 - 2(-1) - 3}{(-1)^2 + 5(-1) + 4} = \frac{0}{0} \qquad \frac{(-4)^2 - 2(-4) - 3}{(-4)^2 + 5(-4) + 4} = \frac{21}{0}$$

Both values of x result in division by 0, which is undefined.

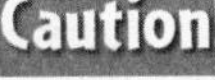

Caution!
When identifying values for which a rational expression is undefined, identify the values of the variable that make the original denominator equal to 0.

Simplify. Identify any x-values for which the expression is undefined.

1a. $\frac{16x^{11}}{8x^2}$ **1b.** $\frac{3x + 4}{3x^2 + x - 4}$ **1c.** $\frac{6x^2 + 7x + 2}{6x^2 - 5x - 6}$

EXAMPLE 2 Simplifying by Factoring −1

Simplify $\frac{2x - x^2}{x^2 - x - 2}$. Identify any x-values for which the expression is undefined.

$$\frac{-1(x^2 - 2x)}{x^2 - x - 2}$$ *Factor out −1 in the numerator so that x^2 is positive, and reorder the terms.*

$$\frac{-1(x)\cancel{(x-2)}}{\cancel{(x-2)}(x+1)}$$ *Factor the numerator and denominator. Divide out common factors.*

$$\frac{-x}{x+1}$$ *Simplify.*

The expression is undefined at $x = 2$ and $x = -1$.

Check The calculator screens suggest that $\frac{2x - x^2}{x^2 - x - 2} = \frac{-x}{x+1}$ except when $x = 2$ or $x = -1$.

X	Y1	Y2
-3	-1.5	-1.5
-2	-2	-2
-1	ERROR	ERROR
0	0	0
1	-.5	-.5
2	ERROR	-.6667
3	-.75	-.75

X=-3

Simplify. Identify any x-values for which the expression is undefined.

2a. $\frac{10 - 2x}{x - 5}$ **2b.** $\frac{-x^2 + 3x}{2x^2 - 7x + 3}$

You can multiply rational expressions the same way that you multiply fractions.

Multiplying Rational Expressions
1. Factor all numerators and denominators completely.
2. Divide out common factors of the numerators and denominators.
3. Multiply numerators. Then multiply denominators.
4. Be sure the numerator and denominator have no common factors other than 1.

EXAMPLE 3 Multiplying Rational Expressions

Multiply. Assume that all expressions are defined.

A 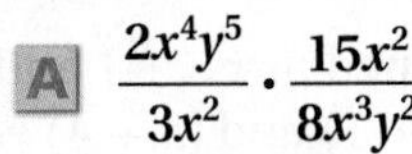

$$\frac{2x^4y^5}{3x^2} \cdot \frac{15x^2}{8x^3y^2}$$

$$\frac{\cancel{2}x^{\cancel{4}1}y^{\cancel{5}3}}{\cancel{3}\cancel{x^2}} \cdot \frac{{}^5\cancel{15}\cancel{x^2}}{{}_4\cancel{8}\cancel{x^3}\cancel{y^2}}$$

$$\frac{5xy^3}{4}$$

B 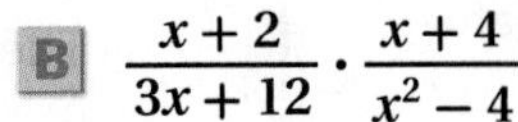

$$\frac{x+2}{3x+12} \cdot \frac{x+4}{x^2-4}$$

$$\frac{\cancel{x+2}}{3\cancel{(x+4)}} \cdot \frac{\cancel{x+4}}{\cancel{(x+2)}(x-2)}$$

$$\frac{1}{3(x-2)} \text{ or } \frac{1}{3x-6}$$

Multiply. Assume that all expressions are defined.

3a. $\frac{x}{15} \cdot \frac{x^7}{2x} \cdot \frac{20}{x^4}$ **3b.** $\frac{10x - 40}{x^2 - 6x + 8} \cdot \frac{x+3}{5x+15}$

You can also divide rational expressions. Recall that to divide by a fraction, you multiply by its reciprocal. $\frac{1}{2} \div \frac{3}{4} = \frac{1}{2} \cdot \frac{4^2}{3} = \frac{2}{3}$

EXAMPLE 4 Dividing Rational Expressions

Divide. Assume that all expressions are defined.

A $\frac{4x^3}{9x^2y} \div \frac{16}{9y^5}$

$\frac{4x^3}{9x^2y} \cdot \frac{9y^5}{16}$ *Rewrite as multiplication by the reciprocal.*

$\frac{4x^{3\,1}}{9x^2y} \cdot \frac{9y^{5\,4}}{16_4}$

$\frac{xy^4}{4}$

B $\frac{x^5 - 4x^3}{x^2 - x - 2} \div \frac{x^5 - x^4 - 2x^3}{x^2 - 1}$

$\frac{x^5 - 4x^3}{x^2 - x - 2} \cdot \frac{x^2 - 1}{x^5 - x^4 - 2x^3}$

$\frac{x^3(x^2 - 4)}{x^2 - x - 2} \cdot \frac{x^2 - 1}{x^3(x^2 - x - 2)}$

$\frac{x^3(x-2)(x+2)}{(x-2)(x+1)} \cdot \frac{(x-1)(x+1)}{x^3(x-2)(x+1)}$

$\frac{(x+2)(x-1)}{(x+1)(x-2)}$ or $\frac{x^2 + x - 2}{x^2 - x - 2}$

Divide. Assume that all expressions are defined.

4a. $\frac{x^2}{4} \div \frac{x^4y}{12y^2}$

4b. $\frac{2x^2 - 7x - 4}{x^2 - 9} \div \frac{4x^2 - 1}{8x^2 - 28x + 12}$

EXAMPLE 5 Solving Simple Rational Equations

Solve. Check your solution.

A $\frac{x^2 - 9}{x + 3} = 7$

$\frac{(x-3)(x+3)}{x+3} = 7$ *Note that $x \neq -3$.*

$x - 3 = 7$

$x = 10$

Check $\frac{x^2 - 9}{x + 3} = 7$

$\frac{(10)^2 - 9}{10 + 3}$	7
$\frac{91}{13}$	7
7	7 ✔

B $\frac{x^2 + 3x - 4}{x - 1} = 5$

$\frac{(x-1)(x+4)}{x-1} = 5$ *Note that $x \neq 1$.*

$x + 4 = 5$

$x = 1$

Because the left side of the original equation is undefined when $x = 1$, there is no solution.

Check A graphing calculator shows that 1 is not a solution.

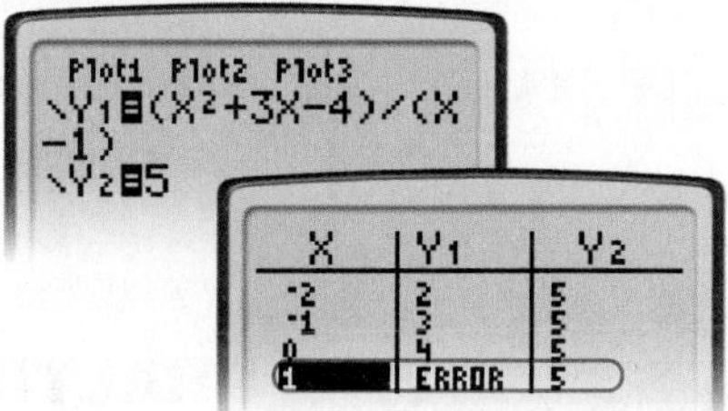

Caution!

As you simplify a rational expression, take note of values that must be excluded. The excluded values are those that make the rational expression undefined.

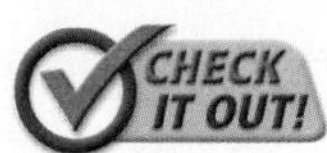

Solve. Check your solution.

5a. $\frac{x^2 + x - 12}{x + 4} = -7$

5b. $\frac{4x^2 - 9}{(2x + 3)} = 5$

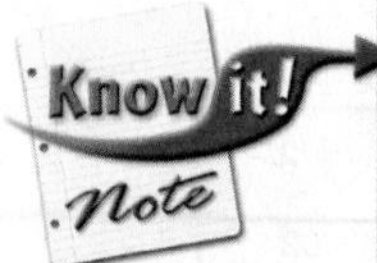

THINK AND DISCUSS

1. Explain how you find undefined values for a rational expression.
2. Explain why it is important to check solutions to rational equations.
3. **GET ORGANIZED** Copy and complete the graphic organizer. In each box, write a worked-out example.

	Numerical Fractions	Rational Expressions
Simplifying		
Multiplying		
Dividing		

8-2 Exercises

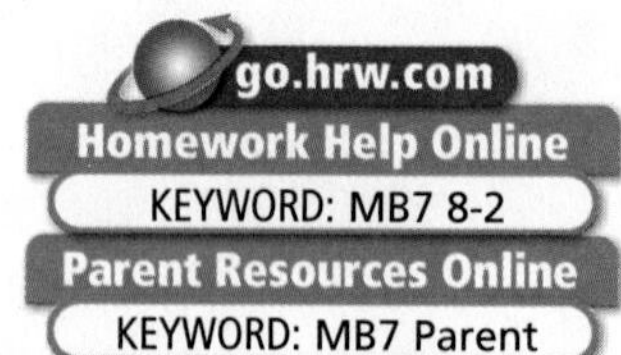

go.hrw.com
Homework Help Online
KEYWORD: MB7 8-2
Parent Resources Online
KEYWORD: MB7 Parent

GUIDED PRACTICE

1. **Vocabulary** How can you tell if an algebraic expression is a *rational expression*?

SEE EXAMPLE 1 p. 577

Simplify. Identify any x-values for which the expression is undefined.

2. $\dfrac{4x^6}{2x-6}$
3. $\dfrac{6x^2+13x-5}{6x^2-23x+7}$
4. $\dfrac{x+4}{3x^2+11x-4}$

SEE EXAMPLE 2 p. 578

5. $\dfrac{-x-4}{x^2-x-20}$
6. $\dfrac{6x^2+7x-3}{-3x^2+x}$
7. $\dfrac{6x^3+6x}{x^2+1}$

SEE EXAMPLE 3 p. 578

Multiply. Assume that all expressions are defined.

8. $\dfrac{x-2}{2x-3} \cdot \dfrac{4x-6}{x^2-4}$
9. $\dfrac{x-2}{x-3} \cdot \dfrac{2x-6}{x+5}$
10. $\dfrac{x^2-16}{x^2-4x+4} \cdot \dfrac{x-2}{x^2+6x+8}$

SEE EXAMPLE 4 p. 579

Divide. Assume that all expressions are defined.

11. $\dfrac{x^5y^4}{3xy} \div \dfrac{1}{x^3y}$
12. $\dfrac{x+3}{x^2-2x+1} \div \dfrac{x+3}{x-1}$
13. $\dfrac{x^2-25}{2x^2+5x-12} \div \dfrac{x^2-3x-10}{x^2+9x+20}$
14. $\dfrac{x^2+2x+1}{x^2-3x-18} \div \dfrac{x^2-1}{x^2-7x+6}$

SEE EXAMPLE 5 p. 579

Solve. Check your solution.

15. $\dfrac{16x^2-9}{4x+3} = -6$
16. $\dfrac{2x^2+7x-15}{2x-3} = 10$
17. $\dfrac{x^2-4}{x-2} = 1$

PRACTICE AND PROBLEM SOLVING

Simplify. Identify any x-values for which the expression is undefined.

18. $\dfrac{4x-8}{x^2-2x}$
19. $\dfrac{8x-4}{2x^2+9x-5}$
20. $\dfrac{x^2-36}{x^2-12x+36}$
21. $\dfrac{3x+18}{24-2x-x^2}$
22. $\dfrac{-2x^2-9x}{4x^2-81}$
23. $\dfrac{4x+20}{-5-x}$

Independent Practice

For Exercises	See Example
18–20	1
21–23	2
24–27	3
28–31	4
32–34	5

Extra Practice

Skills Practice p. S18

Application Practice p. S39

Multiply. Assume that all expressions are defined.

24. $\dfrac{x^2y}{4xy} \cdot \dfrac{x}{6} \cdot \dfrac{3y^5}{x^4}$

25. $\dfrac{x-4}{x-3} \cdot \dfrac{2x-1}{x+4}$

26. $\dfrac{x^2-2x-8}{9x^2-16} \cdot \dfrac{3x^2+10x+8}{x^2-16}$

27. $\dfrac{4x^2-20x+25}{x^2-4x} \cdot \dfrac{3x-12}{2x-5}$

Divide. Assume that all expressions are defined.

28. $\dfrac{4x^2+15x+9}{8x^2+10x+3} \div \dfrac{x^2+4x}{2x+1}$

29. $\dfrac{x^2-4x-5}{x^2-3x+2} \div \dfrac{x^2-3x-10}{x^2-4}$

30. $\dfrac{x+2}{x-4} \div \dfrac{1}{3x-12}$

31. $\dfrac{x^2-2x-3}{x^2-x-2} \div \dfrac{x^2+2x-15}{x^2+x-6}$

Solve. Check your solution.

32. $\dfrac{3x^2+10x+8}{-x-2} = -2$

33. $\dfrac{x^2-9}{x-3} = 5$

34. $\dfrac{x^2+3x-28}{(x+7)(x-4)} = -11$

LINK

Archery

Archery was practiced in ancient times on every inhabited continent except Australia. The painting in the photo above dates from about 1400 B.C.E. and shows archers from ancient Egypt.

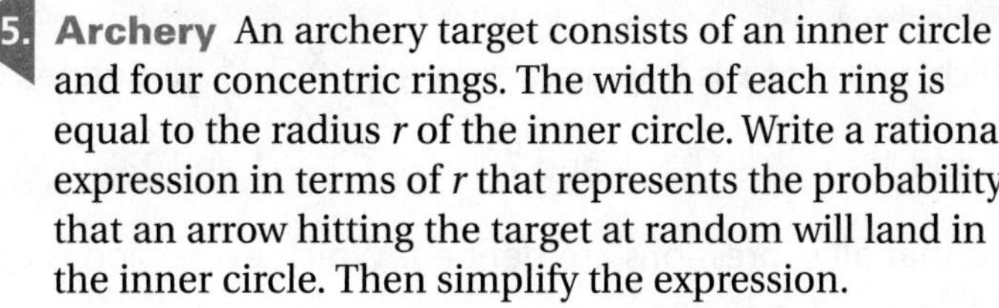

35. **Archery** An archery target consists of an inner circle and four concentric rings. The width of each ring is equal to the radius r of the inner circle. Write a rational expression in terms of r that represents the probability that an arrow hitting the target at random will land in the inner circle. Then simplify the expression.

Multiply or divide. Assume that all expressions are defined.

36. $\dfrac{2x}{3} \cdot \dfrac{x^3}{6x-8}$

37. $\dfrac{4x^2-3x}{4x^2-1} \cdot \dfrac{2x+1}{x}$

38. $\dfrac{1}{25x^2-49} \div \dfrac{x}{10x-14}$

39. $2xy \cdot \dfrac{2x^2}{y} \cdot \dfrac{y^2}{2x}$

40. $\dfrac{14x^4}{xy} \cdot \dfrac{x^3}{6y^3} \div \dfrac{5x^2}{12y^5}$

41. $(y+4) \div \dfrac{4x+4+xy+y}{3}$

42. **Critical Thinking** What polynomial completes the equation $\dfrac{x-5}{x-2} \cdot \dfrac{■}{x-5} = x+1$?

43. **Geometry** Use the table to determine the following.

	Square Prism	Cylinder
Area of Base	s^2	πr^2
Volume	s^2h	$\pi r^2 h$
Surface Area	$2s^2 + 4sh$	$2\pi r^2 + 2\pi rh$

a. For each figure, find the ratio of the volume to the area of the base.

b. For each figure, find the ratio of the surface area to the volume.

c. **What if...?** If the radius and the height of a cylinder were doubled, what effect would this have on the ratio of the cylinder's surface area to its volume?

44. This problem will prepare you for the Multi-Step Test Prep on page 608.

For a car moving with initial speed v_0 and acceleration a, the distance d that the car travels in time t is given by $d = v_0t + \frac{1}{2}at^2$.

a. Write a rational expression in terms of t for the average speed of the car during a period of acceleration. Simplify the expression.

b. During a race, a driver accelerates for 3 s at a rate of 10 ft/s^2 in order to pass another car. The driver's initial speed was 264 ft/s. What was the driver's average speed during the acceleration?

45. **ERROR ANALYSIS** Two students simplified the same expression. Which is incorrect? Explain the error.

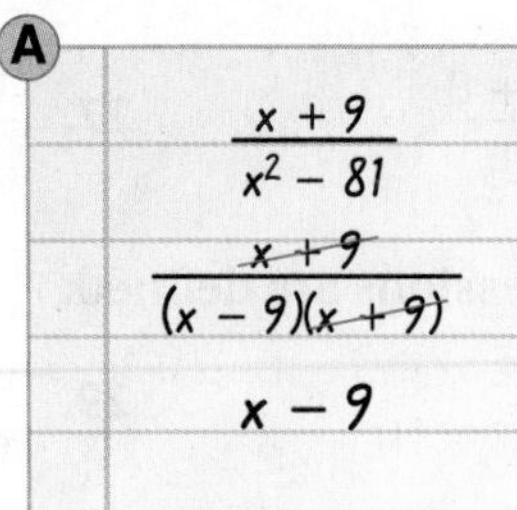

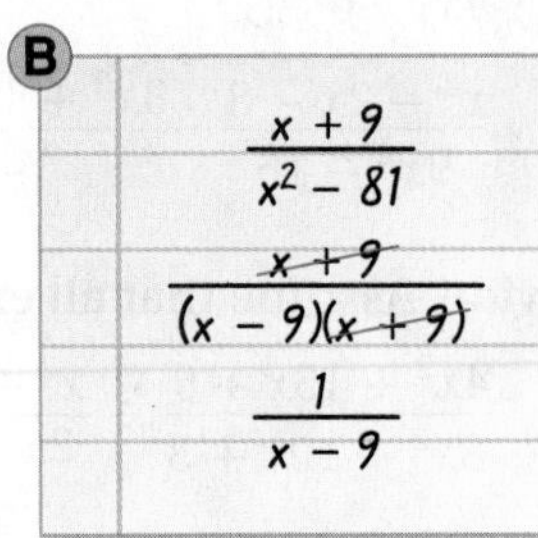

46. **Write About It** You can use polynomial division to find that $\frac{x^3-7x+6}{x-2} = x^2+2x-3$. Is this equation true for all values of x? Explain.

TEST PREP

47. For which values of x is the expression $\frac{x^2-x-12}{x^2+x-2}$ undefined?

Ⓐ 0 and 1 Ⓑ 1 and 2 Ⓒ −1 and 2 Ⓓ −2 and 1

48. Assume that all expressions are defined. Which expression is equivalent to $\frac{x^2+7x+10}{x^2-6x} \div \frac{x^3-4x}{x^2-8x+12}$?

Ⓕ $\frac{x+5}{x^2}$ Ⓖ $\frac{x^2}{x+5}$ Ⓗ $\frac{(x+5)(x+2)^2}{(x-6)^2}$ Ⓙ $\frac{(x-6)^2}{(x+5)(x+2)^2}$

49. The area of a rectangle is equal to $x^2+13x+36$ square units. If the length of the rectangle is equal to $x+9$ units, which expression represents its width?

Ⓐ $x+4$ Ⓑ $x+27$ Ⓒ x^2+4 Ⓓ x^2+27

CHALLENGE AND EXTEND

Multiply or divide. Assume that all expressions are defined.

50. $\frac{8x^3-1}{x+2} \cdot \frac{x^2-4}{2x^2-5x+2}$

51. $\frac{2x^2-50}{x^3+125} \cdot \frac{x^3-125}{x^2-10x+25}$

52. $\frac{x^2-16}{x-3} \div \left(\frac{x^2-9}{x+4}\right)^{-1}$

53. $\frac{x^5-4x^3-x^2+4}{x^3-2x^2+x-2} \div \frac{3x^3+3x^2+3x}{x^2-1} \cdot \frac{6x}{x^2-2x+1}$

SPIRAL REVIEW

Find each product. *(Lesson 6-2)*

54. $6x^2(x^4-2)$

55. $(x+5)(3x^2-7x-1)$

56. $8x^2y^3(xy^2-4x+7y)$

57. **Biology** The table shows the number of births in a population of mice over a 5-year period. Find an exponential model for the data. Use the model to estimate the number of births in the 8th year. *(Lesson 7-8)*

Years	1	2	3	4	5
Births	70,000	120,000	170,000	220,400	271,100

Given: y varies directly as x. Write and graph each direct variation function. *(Lesson 8-1)*

58. $y = 7$ when $x = 14$

59. $y = 8$ when $x = -2$

8-3 Adding and Subtracting Rational Expressions

Objectives
Add and subtract rational expressions.

Simplify complex fractions.

Vocabulary
complex fraction

Why learn this?
You can add and subtract rational expressions to estimate a train's average speed. (See Example 6.)

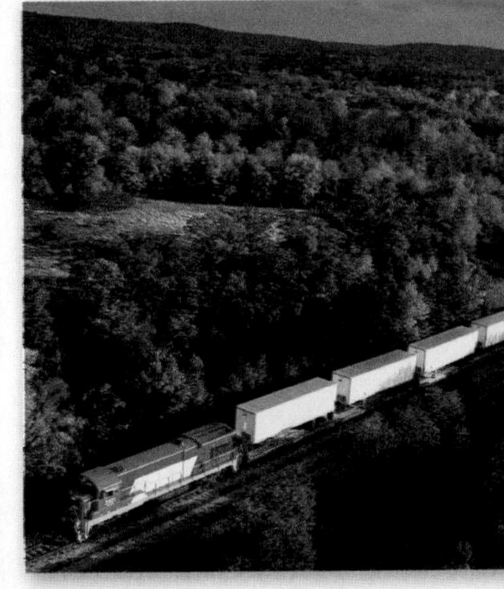

Adding and subtracting rational expressions is similar to adding and subtracting fractions. To add or subtract rational expressions with like denominators, add or subtract the numerators and use the same denominator.

$$\frac{1}{5} + \frac{3}{5} = \frac{4}{5} \qquad \frac{6}{7} - \frac{4}{7} = \frac{2}{7}$$

EXAMPLE 1 Adding and Subtracting Rational Expressions with Like Denominators

Add or subtract. Identify any x-values for which the expression is undefined.

A $\frac{3x-4}{x+3} + \frac{2x+5}{x+3}$

$\frac{3x-4+2x+5}{x+3}$ *Add the numerators.*

$\frac{5x+1}{x+3}$ *Combine like terms.*

The expression is undefined at $x = -3$ because this value makes $x + 3$ equal 0.

B $\frac{2x-1}{x^2+2} - \frac{4x+4}{x^2+2}$

$\frac{2x-1-(4x+4)}{x^2+2}$ *Subtract the numerators.*

$\frac{2x-1-4x-4}{x^2+2}$ *Distribute the negative sign.*

$\frac{-2x-5}{x^2+2}$ *Combine like terms.*

There is no real value of x for which $x^2 + 2 = 0$; the expression is always defined.

Add or subtract. Identify any x-values for which the expression is undefined.

1a. $\frac{6x+5}{x^2-3} + \frac{3x-1}{x^2-3}$ **1b.** $\frac{3x^2-5}{3x-1} - \frac{2x^2-3x-2}{3x-1}$

To add or subtract rational expressions with unlike denominators, first find the least common denominator (LCD). The LCD is the least common multiple of the polynomials in the denominators.

Know it! Note

Least Common Multiple (LCM) of Polynomials
To find the LCM of polynomials:
1. Factor each polynomial completely. Write any repeated factors as powers. For example, $x^3 + 6x^2 + 9x = x(x + 3)^2$.
2. List the different factors. If the polynomials have common factors, use the highest power of each common factor.

EXAMPLE 2 Finding the Least Common Multiple of Polynomials

Find the least common multiple for each pair.

A $2x^3y^4$ **and** $3x^5y^3$

$$2x^3y^4 = 2 \cdot x^3 \cdot y^4$$

$$3x^5y^3 = 3 \cdot x^5 \cdot y^3$$

The LCM is $2 \cdot 3 \cdot x^5 \cdot y^4$, or $6x^5y^4$.

B $x^2 + 3x - 4$ **and** $x^2 - 3x + 2$

$$x^2 + 3x - 4 = (x + 4)(x - 1)$$

$$x^2 - 3x + 2 = (x - 2)(x - 1)$$

The LCM is $(x + 4)(x - 1)(x - 2)$.

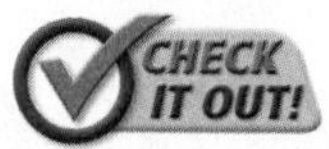

Find the least common multiple for each pair.

2a. $4x^3y^7$ and $3x^5y^4$ **2b.** $x^2 - 4$ and $x^2 + 5x + 6$

To add rational expressions with unlike denominators, rewrite both expressions with the LCD. This process is similar to adding fractions.

$$\frac{2}{6} + \frac{3}{10} = \frac{2}{2 \cdot 3}\left(\frac{5}{5}\right) + \frac{3}{2 \cdot 5}\left(\frac{3}{3}\right)$$

$$= \frac{10}{30} + \frac{9}{30} = \frac{19}{30}$$

EXAMPLE 3 Adding Rational Expressions

Add. Identify any x-values for which the expression is undefined.

A $\dfrac{x-1}{x^2+3x+2} + \dfrac{x}{x+1}$

$$\frac{x-1}{(x+2)(x+1)} + \frac{x}{x+1}$$ *Factor the denominators.*

$$\frac{x-1}{(x+2)(x+1)} + \frac{x}{x+1}\left(\frac{x+2}{x+2}\right)$$ *The LCD is $(x + 2)(x + 1)$, so multiply $\frac{x}{x+1}$ by $\frac{x+2}{x+2}$.*

$$\frac{x-1+x(x+2)}{(x+2)(x+1)}$$ *Add the numerators.*

$$\frac{x^2+3x-1}{(x+2)(x+1)}$$ *Simplify the numerator.*

$$\frac{x^2+3x-1}{(x+2)(x+1)} \text{ or } \frac{x^2+3x-1}{x^2+3x+2}$$ *Write the sum in factored or expanded form.*

The expression is undefined at $x = -2$ and $x = -1$ because these values of x make the factors $(x + 2)$ and $(x + 1)$ equal 0.

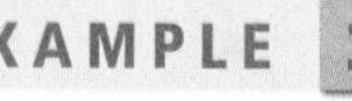

Multiplying by 1 or a form of 1, such as $\frac{x+2}{x+2}$, does not change the value of an expression.

Add. Identify any x-values for which the expression is undefined.

B $\dfrac{x}{x+3} + \dfrac{-18}{x^2 - 9}$

$\dfrac{x}{x+3} + \dfrac{-18}{(x+3)(x-3)}$ — *Factor the denominators.*

$\dfrac{x}{x+3}\left(\dfrac{x-3}{x-3}\right) + \dfrac{-18}{(x+3)(x-3)}$ — *The LCD is $(x + 3)(x - 3)$, so multiply $\frac{x}{x+3}$ by $\frac{x-3}{x-3}$.*

$\dfrac{x(x-3) + (-18)}{(x+3)(x-3)}$ — *Add the numerators.*

$\dfrac{x^2 - 3x - 18}{(x+3)(x-3)}$ — *Write the numerator in standard form.*

$\dfrac{\cancel{(x+3)}(x-6)}{\cancel{(x+3)}(x-3)}$ — *Factor the numerator.*

$\dfrac{x-6}{x-3}$ — *Divide out common factors.*

The expression is undefined at $x = -3$ and $x = 3$ because these values of x make the factors $(x + 3)$ and $(x - 3)$ equal 0.

Helpful Hint

Always simplify the sum or difference of rational expressions. A rational expression can be simplified if its numerator and denominator contain the same factor.

Add. Identify any x-values for which the expression is undefined.

3a. $\dfrac{3x}{2x-2} + \dfrac{3x-2}{3x-3}$ **3b.** $\dfrac{x}{x+3} + \dfrac{2x+6}{x^2+6x+9}$

EXAMPLE 4 Subtracting Rational Expressions

Subtract $\dfrac{2x^2 - 16}{x^2 - 4} - \dfrac{x+4}{x+2}$. Identify any x-values for which the expression is undefined.

$\dfrac{2x^2 - 16}{(x-2)(x+2)} - \dfrac{x+4}{x+2}$ — *Factor the denominators.*

$\dfrac{2x^2 - 16}{(x-2)(x+2)} - \dfrac{x+4}{x+2}\left(\dfrac{x-2}{x-2}\right)$ — *The LCD is $(x - 2)(x + 2)$, so multiply $\frac{x+4}{x+2}$ by $\frac{x-2}{x-2}$.*

$\dfrac{2x^2 - 16 - (x+4)(x-2)}{(x-2)(x+2)}$ — *Subtract the numerators.*

$\dfrac{2x^2 - 16 - (x^2 + 2x - 8)}{(x-2)(x+2)}$ — *Multiply the binomials in the numerator.*

$\dfrac{2x^2 - 16 - x^2 - 2x + 8}{(x-2)(x+2)}$ — *Distribute the negative sign.*

$\dfrac{x^2 - 2x - 8}{(x-2)(x+2)}$ — *Write the numerator in standard form.*

$\dfrac{(x-4)\cancel{(x+2)}}{(x-2)\cancel{(x+2)}}$ — *Factor the numerator.*

$\dfrac{x-4}{x-2}$ — *Divide out common factors.*

The expression is undefined at $x = 2$ and $x = -2$ because these values of x make the factors $(x - 2)$ and $(x + 2)$ equal 0.

Subtract. Identify any x-values for which the expression is undefined.

4a. $\frac{3x-2}{2x+5} - \frac{2}{5x-2}$ **4b.** $\frac{2x^2+64}{x^2-64} - \frac{x-4}{x+8}$

Some rational expressions are *complex fractions*. A **complex fraction** contains one or more fractions in its numerator, its denominator, or both. Examples of complex fractions are shown below.

$$\frac{x+2}{\frac{3}{x}} \qquad \frac{1+\frac{1}{x}}{4x+5} \qquad \frac{\frac{x+3}{x}}{\frac{x+4}{7x}}$$

Recall that the bar in a fraction represents division. Therefore, you can rewrite a complex fraction as a division problem and then simplify. You can also simplify complex fractions by using the LCD of the fractions in the numerator and denominator.

EXAMPLE 5 Simplifying Complex Fractions

Simplify $\frac{\frac{2}{x}+\frac{x}{4}}{\frac{x+1}{x}}$. Assume that all expressions are defined.

Method 1 Write the complex fraction as division.

$\left(\frac{2}{x}+\frac{x}{4}\right) \div \frac{x+1}{x}$ *Write as division.*

$\left(\frac{2}{x}+\frac{x}{4}\right) \cdot \frac{x}{x+1}$ *Multiply by the reciprocal.*

$\left[\frac{2}{x}\left(\frac{4}{4}\right)+\frac{x}{4}\left(\frac{x}{x}\right)\right] \cdot \frac{x}{x+1}$ *The LCD is 4x.*

$\left[\frac{2(4)+x(x)}{4x}\right] \cdot \frac{x}{x+1}$ *Add the numerators.*

$\frac{8+x^2}{4\cancel{x}} \cdot \frac{\cancel{x}}{x+1}$ *Simplify and divide out common factors.*

$\frac{8+x^2}{4(x+1)}$ or $\frac{x^2+8}{4x+4}$ *Multiply.*

Method 2 Multiply the numerator and denominator of the complex fraction by the LCD of the fractions in the numerator and denominator.

$\frac{\frac{2}{\cancel{x}}(4\cancel{x})+\frac{x}{\cancel{4}}(\cancel{4}x)}{\frac{x+1}{\cancel{x}}(4\cancel{x})}$ *The LCD is 4x.*

$\frac{(2)(4)+(x)(x)}{(x+1)(4)}$ *Divide out common factors.*

$\frac{8+x^2}{(x+1)(4)}$ or $\frac{x^2+8}{4x+4}$ *Simplify.*

Simplify. Assume that all expressions are defined.

5a. $\frac{\frac{x+1}{x^2-1}}{\frac{x}{x-1}}$ **5b.** $\frac{\frac{20}{x-1}}{\frac{6}{3x-3}}$ **5c.** $\frac{\frac{1}{x}+\frac{1}{2x}}{\frac{x+4}{x-2}}$

Student to Student

Simplifying Complex Fractions

Brian Carr
Riverside High School

When I simplify complex fractions, I draw arrows connecting the outermost and innermost numbers.

$$\frac{\frac{3}{5}}{\frac{1}{2}} = \frac{6}{5} = 1\frac{1}{5}$$

Then I make a new fraction by writing the product of the outermost numbers as the numerator and the product of the innermost numbers as the denominator.

It also works for rational expressions.

$$\frac{\frac{x^2}{x+1}}{\frac{x}{2}} = \frac{2x^2}{x(x+1)} = \frac{2x}{x+1}$$

EXAMPLE 6 ***Transportation Application***

A freight train averages 30 mi/h traveling to its destination with full cars and 40 mi/h on the return trip with empty cars. What is the train's average speed for the entire trip? Round to the nearest tenth.

Total distance: $2d$ — *Let d represent the one-way distance.*

Total time: $\frac{d}{30} + \frac{d}{40}$ — *Use the formula $t = \frac{d}{r}$.*

Average speed: $\frac{2d}{\frac{d}{30} + \frac{d}{40}}$ — *The average speed is $\frac{\text{total distance}}{\text{total time}}$.*

$\frac{2d(120)}{\frac{d}{30}(120) + \frac{d}{40}(120)}$ — *The LCD of the fractions in the denominator is 120.*

$\frac{240d}{4d + 3d}$ — *Simplify.*

$\frac{240\cancel{d}}{7\cancel{d}} \approx 34.3$ — *Combine like terms and divide out common factors.*

The train's average speed is 34.3 mi/h.

6. Justin's average speed on his way to school is 40 mi/h, and his average speed on the way home is 45 mi/h. What is Justin's average speed for the entire trip? Round to the nearest tenth.

THINK AND DISCUSS

1. Explain how to find the LCD of two rational expressions.

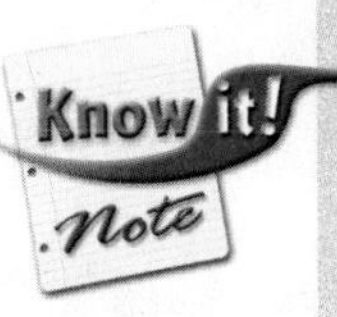

2. GET ORGANIZED Copy and complete the graphic organizer. In each box, write an example and show how to simplify it.

Rational Expressions
- Adding (like denominators)
- Subtracting (unlike denominators)
- Simplifying a complex fraction

8-3 Exercises

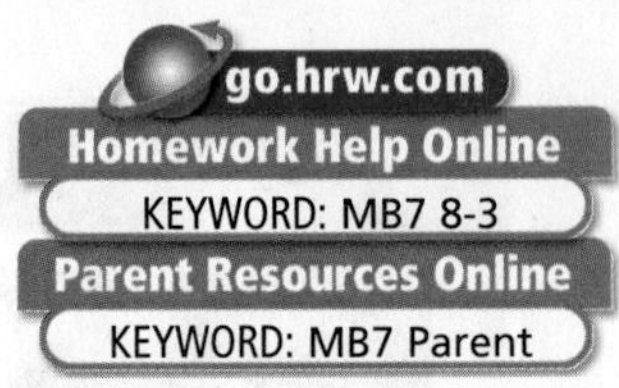

GUIDED PRACTICE

1. **Vocabulary** How does a *complex fraction* differ from other types of fractions?

SEE EXAMPLE 1 p. 583

Add or subtract. Identify any x-values for which the expression is undefined.

2. $\frac{2x-3}{4x-1}+\frac{3x+4}{4x-1}$
3. $\frac{3x-4}{4x+5}-\frac{5x+3}{4x+5}$
4. $\frac{4x-3}{2x-5}-\frac{4x+3}{2x-5}$

SEE EXAMPLE 2 p. 584

Find the least common multiple for each pair.

5. $4x^2y^3$ and $16x^4y$
6. x^2-25 and $x^2+10x+25$

SEE EXAMPLE 3 p. 584

Add or subtract. Identify any x-values for which the expression is undefined.

7. $\frac{3x-2}{x+6}+\frac{2x-3}{2x-1}$
8. $\frac{4x-5}{12x+4}+\frac{3x-1}{3x+1}$
9. $\frac{3x-4}{x^2-9}+\frac{2x-1}{x+3}$

SEE EXAMPLE 4 p. 585

10. $\frac{3x-5}{2x-5}-\frac{2x-5}{3x+1}$
11. $\frac{2x+8}{x^2-16}-\frac{3}{x-4}$
12. $\frac{x+2}{x^2+4x+3}-\frac{x+1}{x+3}$

SEE EXAMPLE 5 p. 586

Simplify. Assume that all expressions are defined.

13. $\dfrac{\frac{2x-3}{x-2}}{\frac{4x-3}{x^2-4}}$
14. $\dfrac{\frac{3x-7}{4x+5}}{\frac{6x-1}{5x-6}}$
15. $\dfrac{\frac{2}{x}+\frac{1}{x}}{\frac{2x}{x+2}}$

SEE EXAMPLE 6 p. 587

16. **Track** Yvette ran at an average speed of 6.20 ft/s during the first two laps of a race and an average speed of 7.75 ft/s during the second two laps of a race. What was Yvette's average speed for the entire race? Round to the nearest tenth.

PRACTICE AND PROBLEM SOLVING

Independent Practice

For Exercises	See Example
17–19	1
20–21	2
22–24	3
25–27	4
28–30	5
31	6

Extra Practice

Skills Practice p. S18
Application Practice p. S39

Add or subtract. Identify any x-values for which the expression is undefined.

17. $\frac{2x-3}{4x-7}+\frac{2x-3}{4x-7}$
18. $\frac{x-5}{3x+4}-\frac{3x-5}{3x+4}$
19. $\frac{x^2-3}{2x+7}-\frac{2x-5}{2x+7}$

Find the least common multiple for each pair.

20. $12x^2y^3$ and $14x^3y^2$
21. $16x^2-25$ and $4x^2-x-5$

Add or subtract. Identify any x-values for which the expression is undefined.

22. $\frac{3x-2}{x+2}+\frac{2x}{4x-1}$
23. $\frac{2x-7}{x-2}+\frac{8x}{3x-6}$
24. $\frac{5x}{4x^2}+\frac{7}{x+1}$
25. $\frac{4x-3}{x^2-9}-\frac{2x-3}{x-3}$
26. $\frac{x}{2x+3}-\frac{2x+1}{2x-3}$
27. $\frac{1}{x-4}-\frac{2}{x^2-6x+8}$

Simplify. Assume that all expressions are defined.

28. $\dfrac{\frac{2x-5}{x^2-9}}{\frac{3x-1}{x+3}}$
29. $\dfrac{\frac{3x-2}{x^2-4}}{\frac{5x+1}{x^2+x-6}}$
30. $\dfrac{\frac{x}{x+1}}{x+\frac{x}{3}}$

31. **Chemistry** A solution is heated from 0°C to 100°C. Between 0°C and 50°C, the rate of temperature increase is 1.5°C/min. Between 50°C and 100°C, the rate of temperature increase is 0.4°C/min. What is the average rate of temperature increase during the entire heating process? Round to the nearest tenth.

32. This problem will prepare you for the Multi-Step Test Prep on page 608.

An auto race consists of 8 laps. A driver completes the first 3 laps at an average speed of 185 mi/h and the remaining laps at an average speed of 200 mi/h.

a. Let d represent the length of one lap. Write an expression in terms of d that represents the time in hours that it takes the driver to complete the race.

b. What is the driver's average speed during the race to the nearest mile per hour?

Add or subtract. Identify any x-values for which the expression is undefined.

33. $\frac{2}{x+4} + \frac{x}{x-3}$ **34.** $\frac{2x}{x^2-36} + \frac{x+4}{x+6}$ **35.** $\frac{2}{x^2-x-20} + \frac{3}{x^2+7x+12}$

36. $\frac{7x}{x^2-5x} + \frac{x^2}{x-5}$ **37.** $\frac{2x}{x-1} - \frac{9}{x-2}$ **38.** $\frac{2x+3}{3x+4} - \frac{x}{9x+12}$

39. $\frac{4x^2}{3x+4} - \frac{2}{2x-3}$ **40.** $\frac{6}{x^2+4x-32} - \frac{x-5}{x-4}$ **41.** $\frac{x+7}{x^2+13x+42} - \frac{10x}{x^2+8x+7}$

42. Environment The junior and senior classes of a high school are cleaning up a beach. Each class has pledged to clean 1600 m of shoreline. The junior class has 12 more students than the senior class.

a. Let s represent the number of students in the senior class. Write and simplify an expression in terms of s that represents the difference between the number of meters of shoreline each senior must clean and the number each junior must clean.

b. If there are 48 seniors, how many more meters of shoreline must each senior clean than the number each junior must clean? Round to the nearest tenth of a meter.

c. Multi-Step If it takes each student about 10 min to clean 15 m of shoreline, approximately how much sooner will the junior class finish than the senior class?

Simplify. Assume that all expressions are defined.

43. $\frac{\frac{4}{x+2}}{\frac{x+2}{6}}$ **44.** $\frac{\frac{2}{3x-4}}{5x+3}$ **45.** $\frac{\frac{1}{2x}+\frac{2}{3x}}{\frac{x-1}{x-3}}$

LINK Architecture

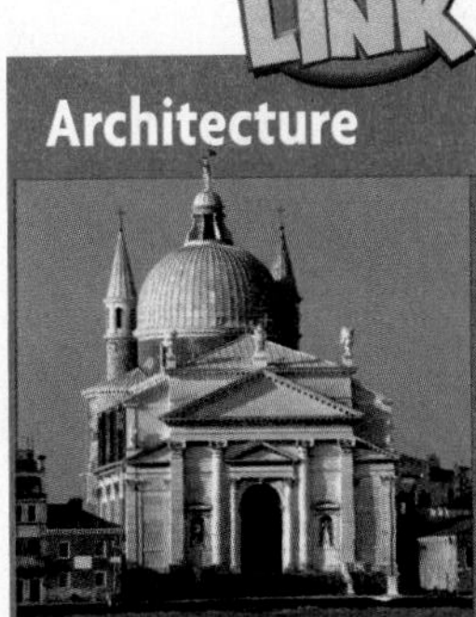

Andrea Palladio stated that his preferred room shapes were squares, circles, and rectangles with precise length-to-width ratios. Some of these shapes can be seen above in Il Redentore church that Palladio designed.

46. Architecture The Renaissance architect Andrea Palladio preferred that the length and width of rectangular rooms be limited to certain ratios. These ratios are listed in the table. Palladio also believed that the height of a room with vaulted ceilings should be the harmonic mean of the length and width.

a. The harmonic mean of two positive numbers a and b is equal to $\frac{2}{\frac{1}{a}+\frac{1}{b}}$. Simplify this expression.

b. Complete the table for a rectangular room with a width of 30 feet that meets Palladio's requirements for its length and height. If necessary, round to the nearest tenth.

c. What if...? A Palladian room has a length-to-width ratio of 4:3. If the length of this room is doubled, what effect should this change have on the room's width and height, according to Palladio's principles?

Rooms with a Width of 30 ft

Length-to-Width Ratio	Length (ft)	Height (ft)
2:1	■	■
3:2	■	■
4:3	■	■
5:3	■	■
$\sqrt{2}$:1	■	■

47. Critical Thinking Write two expressions whose sum is $\frac{x-3}{x+2}$.

48. **Write About It** The first step in adding rational expressions is to write them with a common denominator. This denominator does not necessarily need to be the least common denominator (LCD). Why is it often easier to use the LCD than it is to use other common denominators?

49. Which best represents $\frac{3}{3x} + \frac{5}{9x}$?

(A) $\frac{2}{3x}$ (B) $\frac{7}{2x}$ (C) $\frac{8}{9x}$ (D) $\frac{14}{9x}$

50. Which of the following is equivalent to $\frac{5}{x+2} - \frac{8}{x+4}$?

(F) $\frac{-3x+4}{x^2+8}$ (G) $\frac{-5}{x+4}$ (H) $\frac{-3x+4}{x^2+6x+8}$ (J) $\frac{-3x+36}{x^2+6x+8}$

51. Which of the following is equivalent to $\frac{\frac{8}{7x}}{\frac{-4}{x+1}}$?

(A) $-\frac{2x+2}{7x}$ (B) $-\frac{32}{7x^2+7}$ (C) $-\frac{2}{7x^2+7}$ (D) $-\frac{7x}{2x+2}$

52. A three-day bicycle race has 3 stages of equal length. The table shows a rider's average speed in each of the stages. What is the rider's average speed for the entire race, rounded to the nearest tenth of a kilometer per hour?

(F) 29.5 km/h (H) 30.2 km/h

(G) 29.7 km/h (J) 30.7 km/h

Race Results	
Stage	**Speed (km/h)**
1	35.5
2	31.1
3	25.6

CHALLENGE AND EXTEND

Simplify. Assume that all expressions are defined.

53. $\frac{x-1}{x+2} + \frac{4}{x^2-4} - \frac{6x}{x-2}$

54. $\frac{x^{-1}+y^{-1}}{x^{-1}-y^{-1}}$

55. $(x+2)^{-2} - (x^2-4)^{-1}$

56. $(x-y)^{-1} - (x+y)^{-1}$

57. What polynomial completes the equation $\frac{\blacksquare}{x^3+4x^2-5x} - \frac{x+4}{x^2-x} = \frac{5}{x+5}$?

SPIRAL REVIEW

Evaluate each expression for the given values of the variables. *(Lesson 1-4)*

58. $\frac{-x^2}{y^2-x^2}$ for $x = -2$ and $y = 3$

59. $\frac{m^2-mn}{n^2+10}$ for $m = -4$ and $n = 0$

Graph each logarithmic function. Find the asymptote. Then describe how the graph is transformed from the graph of its parent function. *(Lesson 7-7)*

60. $g(x) = 2\log(x-1)$

61. $h(x) = \log(x+4)$

Simplify. Identify any x-values for which the expression is undefined. *(Lesson 8-2)*

62. $\frac{2x^2+5x^3}{x}$

63. $\frac{x^2-2x-48}{x^2+10x+24}$

64. $\frac{x-2}{x^2-3x+2}$

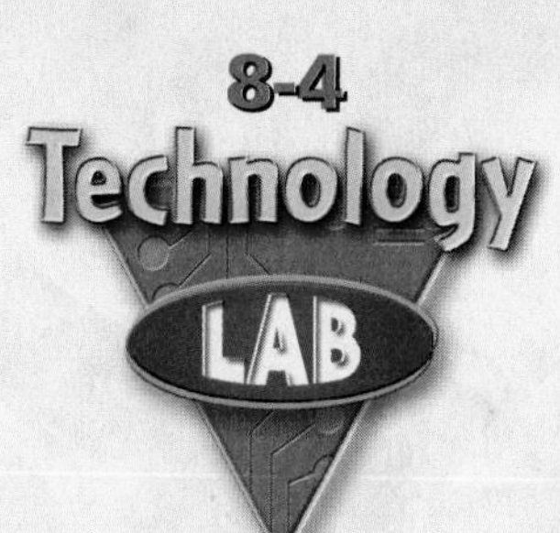

Explore Holes in Graphs

You can use a graphing calculator to explore the relationship between the graphs of rational functions and their simplified forms.

Activity

Use a graph and a table to identify holes in the graph of $f(x) = \dfrac{(x+1)(x-1)}{(x-1)}$.

1 Graph the function $f(x) = \frac{(x+1)(x-1)}{(x-1)}$ in the square window.

The graph appears to be identical to the graph of the function in simplified form, $f(x) = x + 1$.

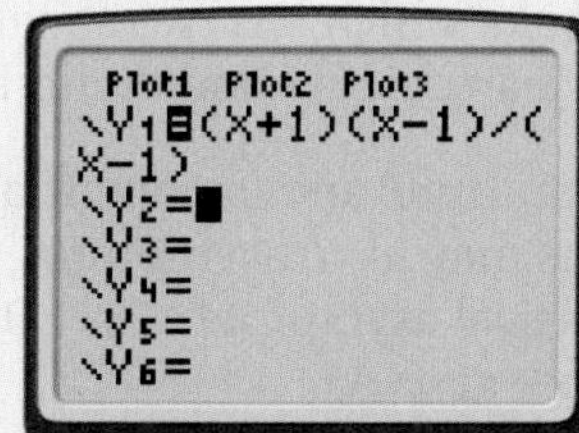

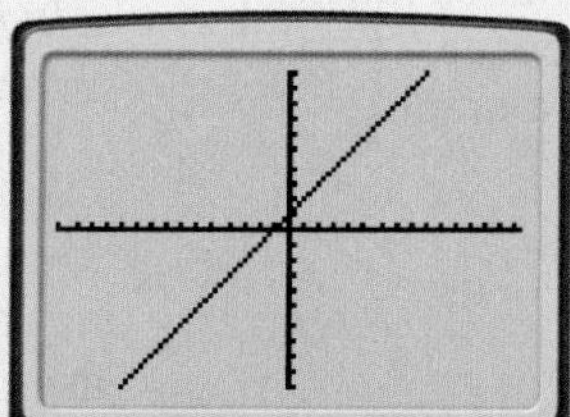

2 Change the window on your graph to the decimal window by pressing ZOOM and selecting **4:ZDecimal**.

Notice that there is a break, or *hole,* in the graph when $x = 1$ because the function is undefined at that x-value.

The hole appears only if you are in a friendly window that allows the calculator to evaluate the function exactly at that point.

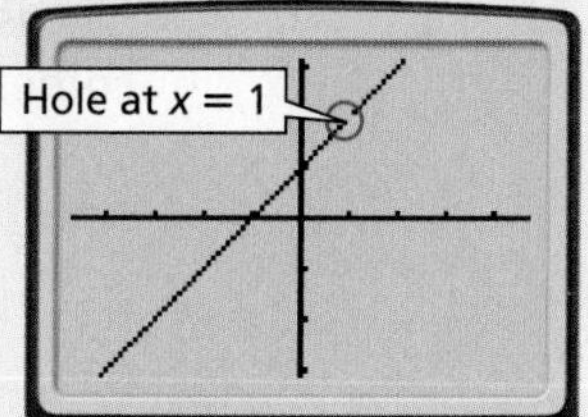

3 Use a table to compare the function $f(x) = \frac{(x+1)(x-1)}{(x-1)}$ to the linear function $f(x) = x + 1$. The table suggests that the graphs are identical except when $x = 1$.

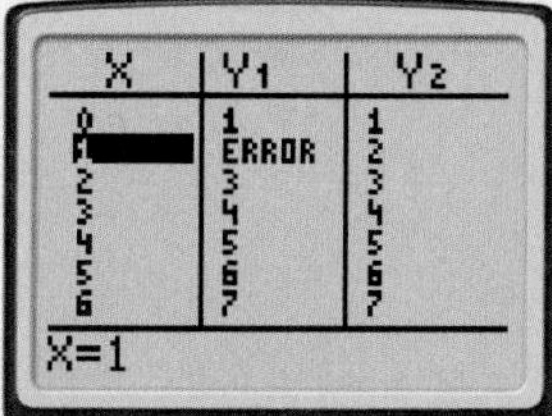

X	Y1	Y2
0	1	1
1	ERROR	2
2	3	3
3	4	4
4	5	5
5	6	6
6	7	7

X=1

Try This

Use a graph and a table to identify the hole in the graph of each function.

1. $f(x) = \dfrac{(x-2)(x+3)}{x+3}$ **2.** $g(x) = \dfrac{(x+1)(x+3)}{x+1}$ **3.** $h(x) = \dfrac{x(x+2)}{x+2}$

4. Make a Conjecture Make a conjecture about where the holes in the graph of a rational function appear, based on the factors of the numerator and the denominator.

Use a graph and a table to identify the hole(s) in the graph of each function. Confirm your answer by factoring.

5. $f(x) = \dfrac{x^2 - 4x + 3}{x - 3}$ **6.** $g(x) = \dfrac{x^2 + x - 2}{x - 1}$ **7.** $h(x) = \dfrac{x^3 - x}{x^2 - 1}$

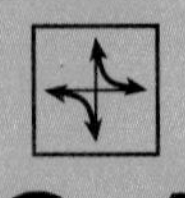

8-4 Rational Functions

Objectives
Graph rational functions.

Transform rational functions by changing parameters.

Vocabulary
rational function
discontinuous function
continuous function
hole (in a graph)

Why learn this?

Rational functions can be used to model the cost per person for group events, such as a band trip to a bowl game. (See Exercise 32.)

A **rational function** is a function whose rule can be written as a ratio of two polynomials. The parent rational function is $f(x) = \frac{1}{x}$. Its graph is a *hyperbola*, which has two separate branches. You will learn more about hyperbolas in Chapter 10.

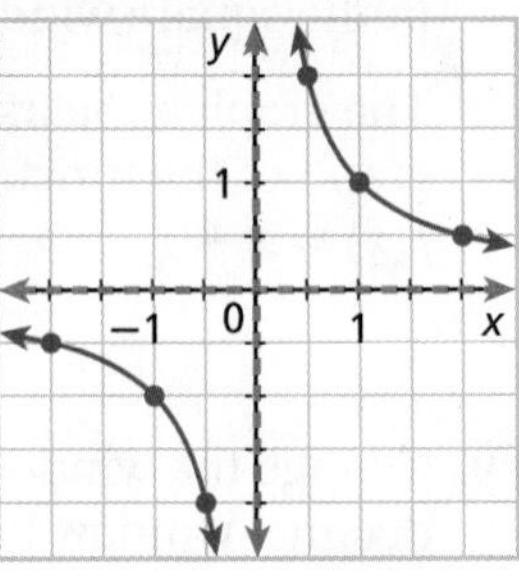

Like logarithmic and exponential functions, rational functions may have asymptotes. The function $f(x) = \frac{1}{x}$ has a vertical asymptote at $x = 0$ and a horizontal asymptote at $y = 0$.

The rational function $f(x) = \frac{1}{x}$ can be transformed by using methods similar to those used to transform other types of functions.

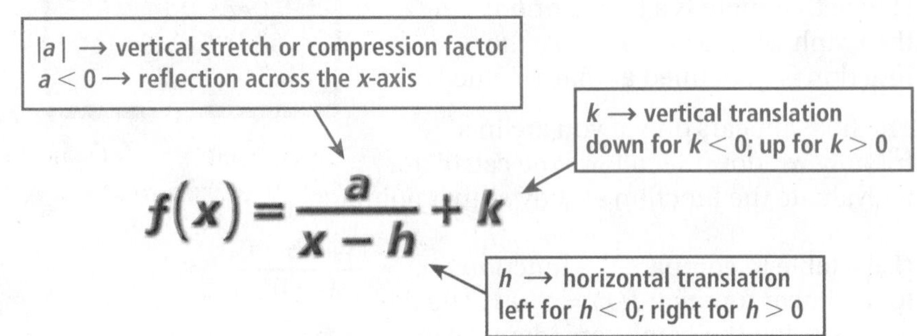

EXAMPLE 1 Transforming Rational Functions

Using the graph of $f(x) = \frac{1}{x}$ as a guide, describe the transformation and graph each function.

A $g(x) = \frac{1}{x - 3}$

Because $h = 3$, translate f 3 units right.

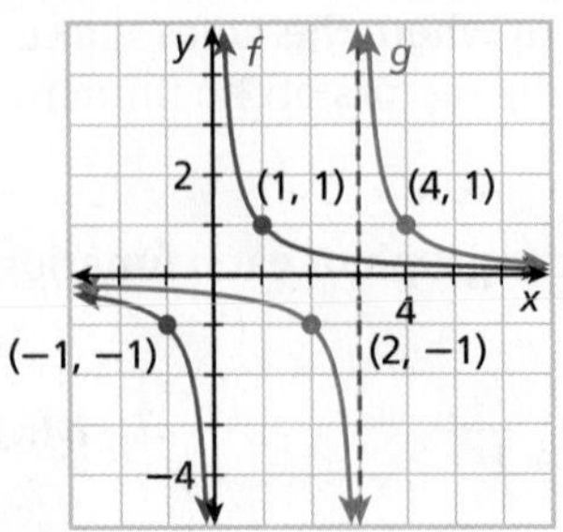

B $g(x) = \frac{1}{x} - 2$

Because $k = -2$, translate f 2 units down.

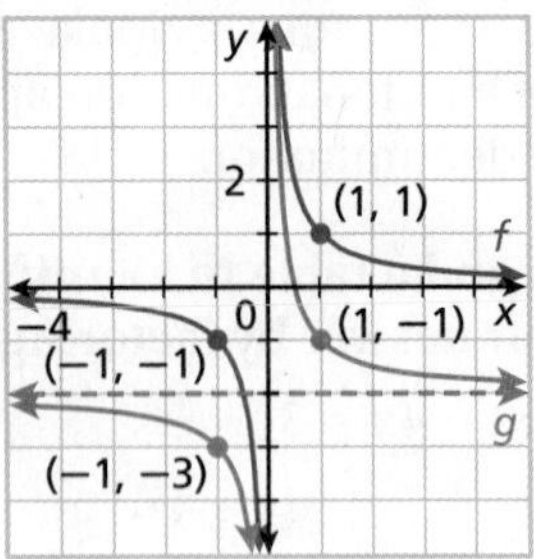

Using the graph of $f(x) = \frac{1}{x}$ as a guide, describe the transformation and graph each function.

1a. $g(x) = \dfrac{1}{x+4}$ **1b.** $g(x) = \dfrac{1}{x} + 1$

The values of h and k affect the locations of the asymptotes, the domain, and the range of rational functions whose graphs are hyperbolas.

Rational Functions

For a rational function of the form $f(x) = \dfrac{a}{x-h} + k$,

- the graph is a hyperbola.
- there is a vertical asymptote at the line $x = h$, and the domain is $\{x \mid x \neq h\}$.
- there is a horizontal asymptote at the line $y = k$, and the range is $\{y \mid y \neq k\}$.

EXAMPLE 2 Determining Properties of Hyperbolas

Identify the asymptotes, domain, and range of the function $g(x) = \dfrac{1}{x+2} + 4$.

$g(x) = \dfrac{1}{x-(-2)} + 4$ *$h = -2$, $k = 4$*

Vertical asymptote: $x = -2$ *The value of h is −2.*

Domain: $\{x \mid x \neq -2\}$

Horizontal asymptote: $y = 4$ *The value of k is 4.*

Range: $\{y \mid y \neq 4\}$

Check Graph the function on a graphing calculator. The graph suggests that the function has asymptotes at $x = -2$ and $y = 4$.

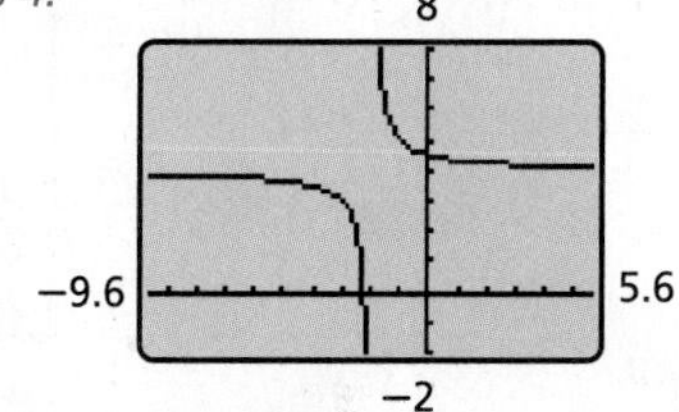

Caution!

Graphing calculators may incorrectly connect two branches of the graph of a rational function with a nearly vertical segment that looks like an asymptote.

2. Identify the asymptotes, domain, and range of the function $g(x) = \frac{1}{x-3} - 5$.

A **discontinuous function** is a function whose graph has one or more gaps or breaks. The hyperbola graphed above and many other rational functions are discontinuous functions.

A **continuous function** is a function whose graph has no gaps or breaks. The functions you have studied before this, including linear, quadratic, polynomial, exponential, and logarithmic functions, are continuous functions.

The graphs of some rational functions are not hyperbolas. Consider the rational function $f(x) = \frac{(x-3)(x+2)}{x+1}$ and its graph. The numerator of this function is 0 when $x = 3$ or $x = -2$. Therefore, the function has x-intercepts at −2 and 3. The denominator of this function is 0 when $x = -1$. As a result, the graph of the function has a vertical asymptote at the line $x = -1$.

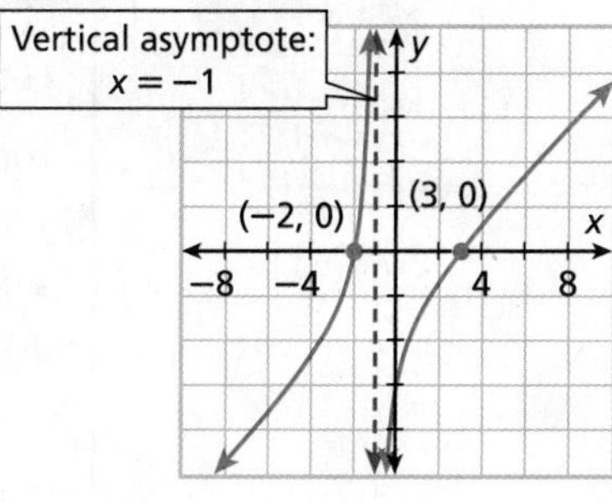

Zeros and Vertical Asymptotes — Rational Functions

If $f(x) = \frac{p(x)}{q(x)}$, where p and q are polynomial functions in standard form with no common factors other than 1, then the function f has

- zeros at each real value of x for which $p(x) = 0$.
- a vertical asymptote at each real value of x for which $q(x) = 0$.

EXAMPLE 3 Graphing Rational Functions with Vertical Asymptotes

Identify the zeros and vertical asymptotes of $f(x) = \frac{x^2 - 2x - 3}{x - 2}$. Then graph.

Remember!

For a review of factoring and finding zeros of polynomial functions, see Lessons 6-4 and 6-5.

Step 1 Find the zeros and vertical asymptotes.

$f(x) = \frac{(x+1)(x-3)}{x-2}$ *Factor the numerator.*

Zeros: -1 and 3 *The numerator is 0 when $x = -1$ or $x = 3$.*

Vertical asymptote: $x = 2$ *The denominator is 0 when $x = 2$.*

Step 2 Graph the function.

Plot the zeros and draw the asymptote. Then make a table of values to fill in missing points.

x	−4	−1	0	1.5	2.5	3	5
y	−3.5	0	1.5	7.5	−3.5	0	4

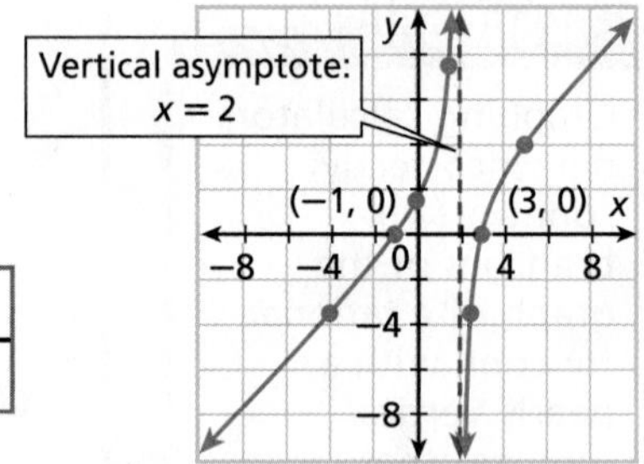

3. Identify the zeros and vertical asymptotes of $f(x) = \frac{x^2 + 7x + 6}{x + 3}$. Then graph.

Some rational functions, including those whose graphs are hyperbolas, have a horizontal asymptote. The existence and location of a horizontal asymptote depends on the degrees of the polynomials that make up the rational function.

Note that the graph of a rational function can sometimes cross a horizontal asymptote. However, the graph will approach the asymptote when $|x|$ is large.

Horizontal Asymptotes — Rational Functions

Let $f(x) = \frac{p(x)}{q(x)}$, where p and q are polynomial functions in standard form with no common factors other than 1. The graph of f has at most one horizontal asymptote.

- If degree of p > degree of q, there is no horizontal asymptote.
- If degree of p < degree of q, the horizontal asymptote is the line $y = 0$.
- If degree of p = degree of q, the horizontal asymptote is the line $y = \frac{\text{leading coefficient of } p}{\text{leading coefficient of } q}$.

EXAMPLE 4 Graphing Rational Functions with Vertical and Horizontal Asymptotes

Identify the zeros and asymptotes of each function. Then graph.

A $f(x) = \dfrac{x^2 + x - 6}{x}$

$f(x) = \dfrac{(x + 3)(x - 2)}{x}$ — *Factor the numerator.*

Zeros: -3 and 2 — *The numerator is 0 when $x = -3$ or $x = 2$.*

Vertical asymptote: $x = 0$ — *The denominator is 0 when $x = 0$.*

Horizontal asymptote: none — *Degree of p > degree of q*

Graph with a graphing calculator or by using a table of values.

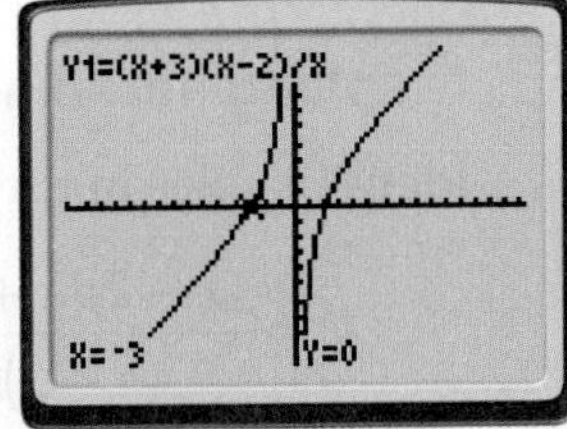

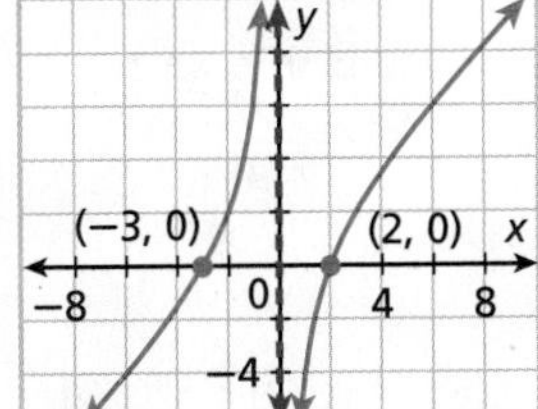

B $f(x) = \dfrac{x - 1}{x^2}$

Zero: 1 — *The numerator is 0 when $x = 1$.*

Vertical asymptote: $x = 0$ — *The denominator is 0 when $x = 0$.*

Horizontal asymptote: $y = 0$ — *Degree of p < degree of q*

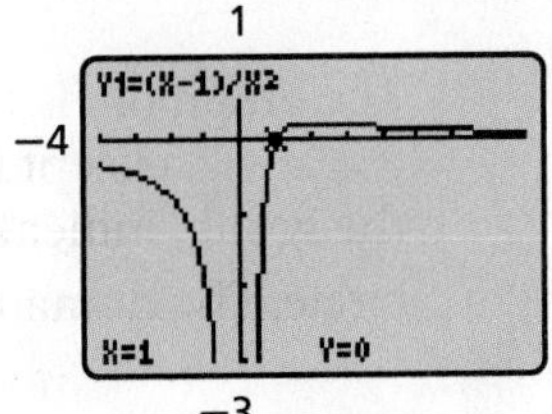

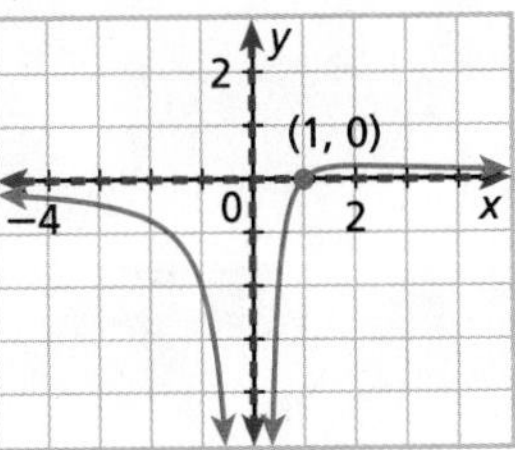

Remember!

Recall from Lesson 6-1 that the leading coefficient of a polynomial is the coefficient of the first term when the polynomial is written in standard form.

C $f(x) = \dfrac{2x^2 - 2}{x^2 - 4}$

$f(x) = \dfrac{2(x + 1)(x - 1)}{(x + 2)(x - 2)}$ — *Factor the numerator and denominator.*

Zeros: -1 and 1 — *The numerator is 0 when $x = -1$ or $x = 1$.*

Vertical asymptotes: $x = -2$, $x = 2$ — *The denominator is 0 when $x = \pm 2$.*

Horizontal asymptote: $y = 2$ — *The horizontal asymptote is* $y = \dfrac{\text{leading coefficient of } p}{\text{leading coefficient of } q} = \dfrac{2}{1} = 2.$

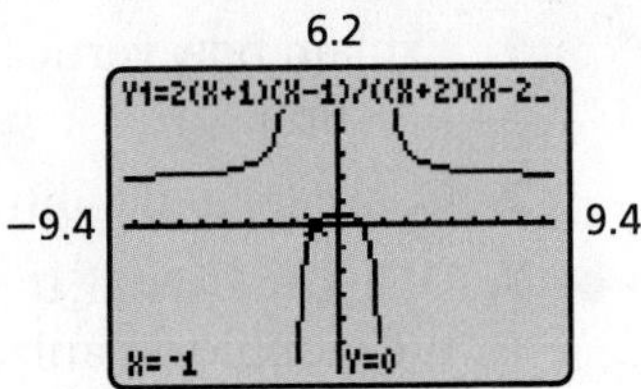

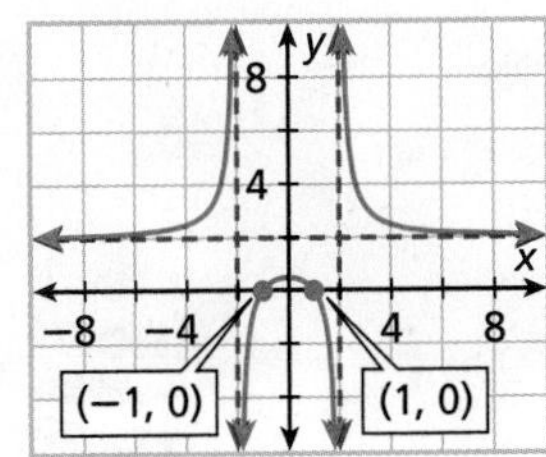

Identify the zeros and asymptotes of each function. Then graph.

4a. $f(x) = \dfrac{x^2 + 2x - 15}{x - 1}$ **4b.** $f(x) = \dfrac{x - 2}{x^2 + x}$ **4c.** $f(x) = \dfrac{3x^2 + x}{x^2 - 9}$

In some cases, both the numerator and the denominator of a rational function will equal 0 for a particular value of x. As a result, the function will be undefined at this x-value. If this is the case, the graph of the function may have a *hole*. A **hole** is an omitted point in a graph.

Holes in Graphs | **Rational Functions**

If a rational function has the same factor $x - b$ in both the numerator and the denominator, then there is a hole in the graph at the point where $x = b$, unless the line $x = b$ is a vertical asymptote.

EXAMPLE 5 Graphing Rational Functions with Holes

Identify holes in the graph of $f(x) = \frac{x^2 - 4}{x + 2}$. Then graph.

$$f(x) = \frac{(x-2)(x+2)}{(x+2)}$$ *Factor the numerator.*

There is a hole in the graph at $x = -2$. *The expression $x + 2$ is a factor of both the numerator and the denominator.*

For $x \neq -2$, $f(x) = \frac{(x-2)\cancel{(x+2)}}{\cancel{(x+2)}} = x - 2$ *Divide out common factors.*

The graph of f is the same as the graph of $y = x - 2$, except for the hole at $x = -2$. On the graph, indicate the hole with an open circle. The domain of f is $\{x \mid x \neq -2\}$.

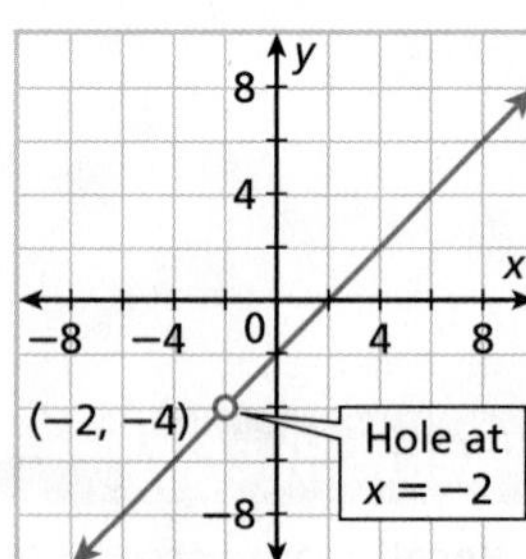

5. Identify holes in the graph of $f(x) = \frac{x^2 + x - 6}{x - 2}$. Then graph.

THINK AND DISCUSS

1. Explain how vertical asymptotes relate to the domain of a rational function.
2. Compare and contrast rational functions and polynomial functions.

3. **GET ORGANIZED** Copy and complete the graphic organizer. In each box, write the formula or method for identifying the characteristic of graphs of rational functions.

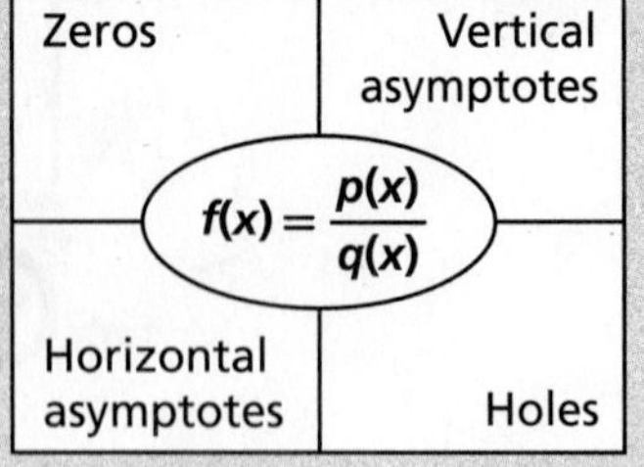

8-4 Exercises

go.hrw.com
Homework Help Online
KEYWORD: MB7 8-4
Parent Resources Online
KEYWORD: MB7 Parent

GUIDED PRACTICE

1. **Vocabulary** A function with a hole in its graph is __?__. (*continuous* or *discontinuous*)

SEE EXAMPLE 1 p. 592

Using the graph of $f(x) = \frac{1}{x}$ as a guide, describe the transformation and graph each function.

2. $g(x) = \frac{1}{x} - 2$
3. $g(x) = \frac{1}{x + 5}$
4. $g(x) = \frac{1}{x - 1} + 4$

SEE EXAMPLE 2 p. 593

Identify the asymptotes, domain, and range of each function.

5. $f(x) = \frac{1}{x} - 1$
6. $f(x) = \frac{1}{x + 4} + 3$
7. $f(x) = \frac{2}{x - 2} - 8$

SEE EXAMPLE 3 p. 594

Identify the zeros and vertical asymptotes of each function. Then graph.

8. $f(x) = \frac{x^2 - x - 12}{x}$
9. $f(x) = \frac{x^2 - 5x}{x - 2}$
10. $f(x) = \frac{x^2}{x - 1}$

SEE EXAMPLE 4 p. 595

Identify the zeros and asymptotes of each function. Then graph.

11. $f(x) = \frac{x^2 + 3x + 2}{3 - x}$
12. $f(x) = \frac{x - 2}{x^2 + 6x}$
13. $f(x) = \frac{5x + 2}{x + 1}$

SEE EXAMPLE 5 p. 596

Identify holes in the graph of each function. Then graph.

14. $f(x) = \frac{x^2 - 5x + 6}{x^2 - 4x + 3}$
15. $f(x) = \frac{x^2 - 4x + 4}{x - 2}$
16. $f(x) = \frac{4x + 20}{2x + 10}$

PRACTICE AND PROBLEM SOLVING

Independent Practice

For Exercises	See Example
17–19	1
20–22	2
23–25	3
26–28	4
29–31	5

Extra Practice
Skills Practice p. S18
Application Practice p. S39

Using the graph of $f(x) = \frac{1}{x}$ as a guide, describe the transformation and graph each function.

17. $g(x) = \frac{1}{x} - 5$
18. $g(x) = \frac{1}{x + 3}$
19. $g(x) = \frac{2}{x}$

Identify the asymptotes, domain, and range of each function.

20. $f(x) = \frac{1}{x + 6}$
21. $f(x) = \frac{4}{x} + 5$
22. $f(x) = \frac{3}{x - 4} - 1$

Identify the zeros and vertical asymptotes of each function. Then graph.

23. $f(x) = \frac{(x + 2)(x - 5)}{(x - 2)}$
24. $f(x) = \frac{(2 - x)(4 + x)}{(x - 1)}$
25. $h(x) = \frac{x^2 - 4}{x + 3}$

Identify the zeros and asymptotes of each function. Then graph.

26. $f(x) = \frac{x^2 - x - 2}{1 - x}$
27. $f(x) = \frac{x - 3}{x^2 - 4}$
28. $f(x) = \frac{2x^2 + x}{1 - x^2}$

Identify holes in the graph of each function. Then graph.

29. $f(x) = \frac{x^4}{x}$
30. $f(x) = \frac{-x^2 + x}{x - 1}$
31. $f(x) = \frac{x^2 - 14x + 49}{x - 7}$

32. **Band** Members of a high school band plan to play at a college bowl game. The trip will cost \$350 per band member plus a \$2000 deposit.
    a. Write a function to represent the total average cost of the trip per band member.
    b. Graph the function.
    c. **What if...?** Find the total average cost per person if 40 band members attend the bowl game.

Identify all zeros, asymptotes, and holes in the graph of each function.

33. $f(x) = \dfrac{x^2 - 2x - 3}{x^2 - 3x}$
34. $f(x) = \dfrac{x^3 - 1}{x - 1}$
35. $f(x) = \dfrac{6x - 5}{2 - 3x}$
36. $f(x) = \dfrac{x^2 + 6x + 8}{x^2}$
37. $f(x) = \dfrac{x}{x^2 - 9}$
38. $f(x) = \dfrac{x^2 - 9}{x^2 - 4}$

Write a rational function with the given characteristics.

39. zeros at -1 and 3 and vertical asymptote at $x = 0$
40. zero at 2, vertical asymptotes at $x = -2$ and $x = 0$, and horizontal asymptote at $y = 0$
41. zero at 2, vertical asymptote at $x = -1$, horizontal asymptote at $y = 1$, and hole at $x = -3$

LINK

Math History

The Granger Collection, New York

The Agnesi curve is named for Maria Agnesi (1718–1799), a mathematician from Milan who wrote one of the earliest surviving mathematical works composed by a woman.

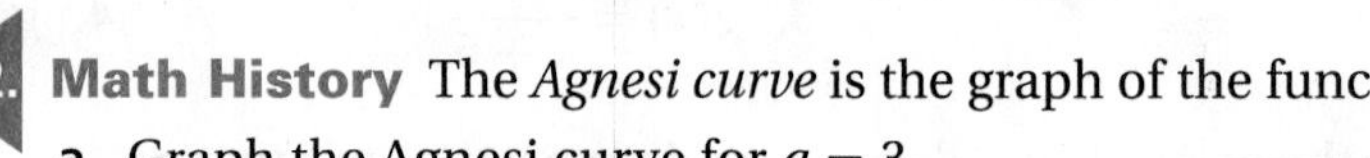

42. **Math History** The *Agnesi curve* is the graph of the function $y = \dfrac{a^3}{x^2 + a^2}$.
   a. Graph the Agnesi curve for $a = 3$.
   b. What are the domain and the range of the function?
   c. Identify all asymptotes of the function.

43. **Chemistry** A chemist has 100 g of a 12% saline solution that she wants to strengthen to 25%. The percentage P of salt in the solution by mass can be modeled by $P(x) = \dfrac{100(12 + x)}{100 + x}$, where x is the number of grams of salt added.
   a. Graph the function for $0 \le x \le 100$.
   b. Use your graph to estimate how much salt the chemist must add to create a 25% solution.

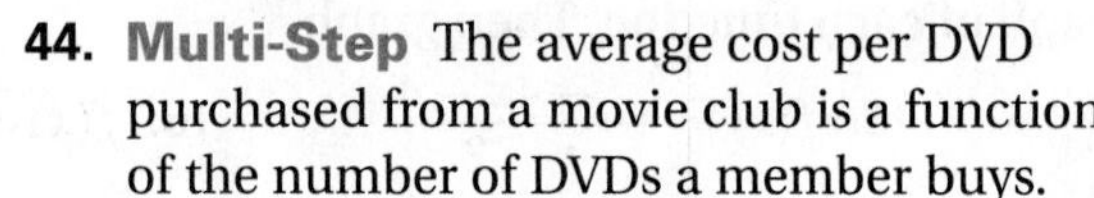

44. **Multi-Step** The average cost per DVD purchased from a movie club is a function of the number of DVDs a member buys.
   a. Graph the data in the table.
   b. The function that describes the data in the table has the form $f(x) = \frac{40}{x} + k$, where k is a constant. What is the value of k?
   c. What is the total cost of buying 15 DVDs from the club?

Number of DVDs	Average Cost ($)
1	55
2	35
4	25
5	23
10	19
20	17

45. **/// ERROR ANALYSIS ///** A student wrote the following description for the graph of $f(x) = \dfrac{(x - 1)(2x - 3)}{(x + 1)(x - 1)}$. Explain the error. Write a correct description.
   The graph has vertical asymptotes at $x = 1$ and $x = -1$ and a horizontal asymptote at $y = 2$.

46. **Critical Thinking** Is it possible to have a rational function with no vertical asymptotes? Explain.

MULTI-STEP TEST PREP

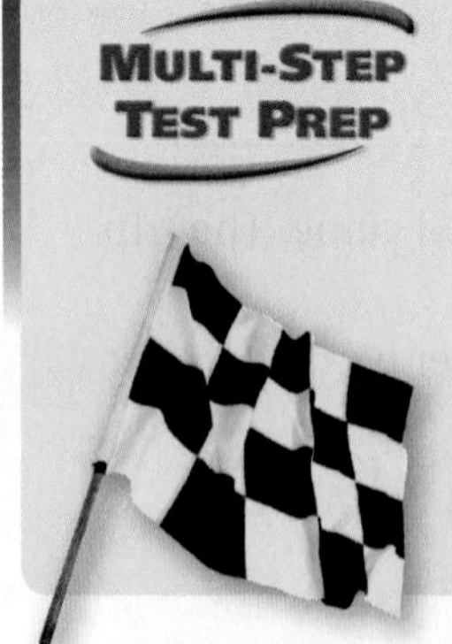

47. This problem will prepare you for the Multi-Step Test Prep on page 608.
   A race car driver makes a pit stop at the beginning of a lap. The time t in seconds that it takes the driver to complete the lap, including the pit stop, can be modeled by $t(r) = \dfrac{12r + 9000}{r}$, where r is the driver's average speed in miles per hour after the pit stop.
   a. Graph the function.
   b. What is the horizontal asymptote of the function, and what does it represent?
   c. The driver's average speed after the pit stop is 200 mi/h. How long does it take the driver to complete the lap, including the pit stop?

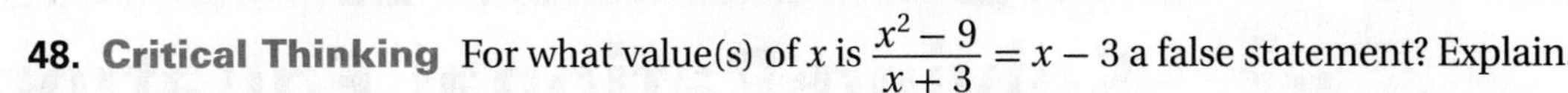

48. **Critical Thinking** For what value(s) of x is $\frac{x^2-9}{x+3} = x - 3$ a false statement? Explain.

49. **Write About It** Explain how to identify the domain of a rational function.

TEST PREP

50. The graph of which of the following rational functions has a hole?

Ⓐ $f(x) = \frac{x^2+5x+4}{x^2+x-12}$

Ⓑ $f(x) = \frac{x^2-2x+1}{x^2+7x-15}$

Ⓒ $f(x) = \frac{x^2-9}{x^2-2x-7}$

Ⓓ $f(x) = \frac{x^2+x-30}{x^2+5x-14}$

51. Which function is shown in the graph?

Ⓕ $f(x) = \frac{x^2+x-2}{x^2-3x+2}$

Ⓖ $f(x) = \frac{x^2+3x+2}{x^2-x-2}$

Ⓗ $f(x) = \frac{x^2+x-2}{x^2+3x+2}$

Ⓙ $f(x) = \frac{x^2-3x+2}{x^2+x-2}$

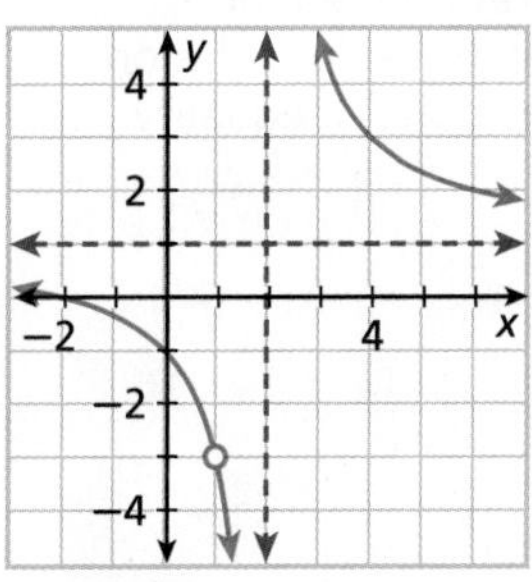

52. What is the horizontal asymptote of $f(x) = \frac{(2x+4)(3x+6)}{(x-1)(x+6)}$?

Ⓐ $y = -6$

Ⓑ $y = -2$

Ⓒ $y = 2$

Ⓓ $y = 6$

CHALLENGE AND EXTEND

Identify all zeros, asymptotes, and holes in the graph of each function. Then graph.

53. $f(x) = \frac{(x^2-3x+2)(x-3)}{(x-1)(x^2-5x+6)}$

54. $f(x) = \frac{(x^2-9)(3x+2)}{(x^2-4)(x-3)}$

55. Let $f(x) = \frac{1}{x^2-2x+c}$. Find c such that the graph of f has the given number of vertical asymptotes.

a. none b. one c. two

Write a rational function with the given characteristics.

56. no zeros, no vertical asymptotes, and a horizontal asymptote at $y = 1$

57. zero at 0, vertical asymptotes at $x = -3$ and $x = 3$, and holes at $x = -1$ and $x = 1$

SPIRAL REVIEW

58. **Sports** In the 1972–1973 school year, 817,073 females participated in high school sports in the United States. By the 2002–2003 school year, this number had increased to 2,856,358. To the nearest percent, what was the percent increase in the number of females participating in high school sports? *(Lesson 2-2)*

Solve. *(Lesson 7-5)*

59. $\log_3(5x-2) = \log_3(2x+8)$

60. $\log_2 x^2 = 4$

61. $\log_x \frac{1}{27} = 3$

62. $\log_4 48 - \log_4 4x = 4$

Add or subtract. Identify any x-values for which the expression is undefined. *(Lesson 8-3)*

63. $\frac{5x-7}{2x+1} + \frac{3x-6}{2x+1}$

64. $\frac{x-1}{x+2} - \frac{x+1}{x-3}$

8-5 Solving Rational Equations and Inequalities

Objective
Solve rational equations and inequalities.

Vocabulary
rational equation
extraneous solution
rational inequality

Who uses this?
Kayakers can use rational equations to determine how fast a river is moving. (See Example 3.)

A **rational equation** is an equation that contains one or more rational expressions. The time t in hours that it takes to travel d miles can be determined by using the equation $t = \frac{d}{r}$, where r is the average rate of speed. This equation is a rational equation.

To solve a rational equation, start by multiplying each term of the equation by the least common denominator (LCD) of all of the expressions in the equation. This step eliminates the denominators of the rational expressions and results in an equation you can solve by using algebra.

EXAMPLE 1 Solving Rational Equations

Solve the equation $x + \frac{8}{x} = 6$.

$x(x) + \frac{8}{x}(x) = 6(x)$ — *Multiply each term by the LCD, x.*

$x^2 + 8 = 6x$ — *Simplify. Note that $x \neq 0$.*

$x^2 - 6x + 8 = 0$ — *Write in standard form.*

$(x - 2)(x - 4) = 0$ — *Factor.*

$x - 2 = 0$ or $x - 4 = 0$ — *Apply the Zero Product Property.*

$x = 2$ or $x = 4$ — *Solve for x.*

Check

$x + \frac{8}{x} = 6$	
$2 + \frac{8}{2}$	6
6	6 ✓

$x + \frac{8}{x} = 6$	
$4 + \frac{8}{4}$	6
6	6 ✓

Remember!
Factoring is not the only method of solving the quadratic equation that results in Example 1. You could also complete the square or use the Quadratic Formula.

Solve each equation.

1a. $\frac{10}{3} = \frac{4}{x} + 2$ **1b.** $\frac{6}{x} + \frac{5}{4} = -\frac{7}{4}$ **1c.** $x = \frac{6}{x} - 1$

An **extraneous solution** is a solution of an equation derived from an original equation that is not a solution of the original equation. When you solve a rational equation, it is possible to get extraneous solutions. These values should be eliminated from the solution set. Always check your solutions by substituting them into the original equation.

EXAMPLE 2 Extraneous Solutions

Solve each equation.

A $\frac{3x}{x-3} = \frac{2x+3}{x-3}$

$\frac{3x}{x-3}(x-3) = \frac{2x+3}{x-3}(x-3)$ *Multiply each term by the LCD, x − 3.*

$\frac{3x}{\cancel{x-3}}\cancel{(x-3)} = \frac{2x+3}{\cancel{x-3}}\cancel{(x-3)}$ *Divide out common factors.*

$3x = 2x + 3$ *Simplify. Note that x ≠ 3.*

$x = 3$ *Solve for x.*

The solution $x = 3$ is extraneous because it makes the denominators of the original equation equal to 0. Therefore, the equation has no solution.

> **Remember!**
> A rational expression is undefined for any value of a variable that makes a denominator in the expression equal to 0.

Check Substitute 3 for x in the original equation.

$$\frac{3(3)}{3-3} = \frac{2(3)+3}{3-3}$$

$$\frac{9}{0} \mid \frac{9}{0} \; ✗$$ *Division by 0 is undefined.*

B $\frac{2x-9}{x-7} + \frac{x}{2} = \frac{5}{x-7}$

$\frac{2x-9}{x-7} \cdot 2(x-7) + \frac{x}{2} \cdot 2(x-7) = \frac{5}{x-7} \cdot 2(x-7)$ *Multiply each term by the LCD, 2(x − 7).*

$\frac{2x-9}{\cancel{x-7}} \cdot 2\cancel{(x-7)} + \frac{x}{\cancel{2}} \cdot \cancel{2}(x-7) = \frac{5}{\cancel{x-7}} \cdot 2\cancel{(x-7)}$ *Divide out common factors.*

$2(2x-9) + x(x-7) = 5(2)$ *Simplify. Note that x ≠ 7.*

$4x - 18 + x^2 - 7x = 10$ *Use the Distributive Property.*

$x^2 - 3x - 28 = 0$ *Write in standard form.*

$(x-7)(x+4) = 0$ *Factor.*

$x - 7 = 0$ or $x + 4 = 0$ *Use the Zero Product Property.*

$x = 7$ or $x = -4$ *Solve for x.*

The solution $x = 7$ is extraneous because it makes the denominators of the original equation equal to 0. The only solution is $x = -4$.

Check Write $\frac{2x-9}{x-7} + \frac{x}{2} = \frac{5}{x-7}$ as $\frac{2x-9}{x-7} + \frac{x}{2} - \frac{5}{x-7} = 0$. Graph the left side of the equation as **Y1** and identify the values of x for which **Y1** $= 0$.

The graph intersects the x-axis only when $x = -4$. Therefore, $x = -4$ is the only solution.

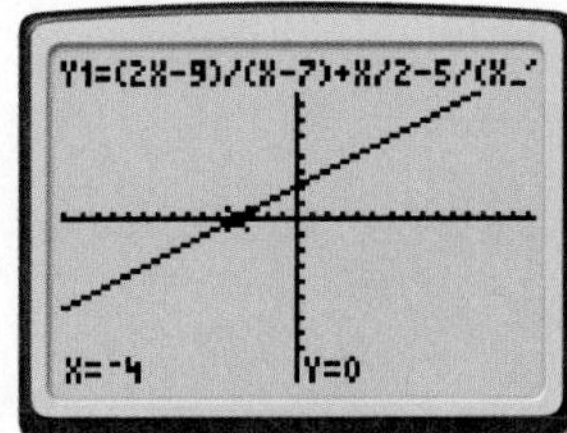

Solve each equation.

2a. $\frac{16}{x^2-16} = \frac{2}{x-4}$ **2b.** $\frac{1}{x-1} = \frac{x}{x-1} + \frac{x}{6}$

EXAMPLE 3 Problem-Solving Application

A kayaker spends an afternoon paddling on a river. She travels 3 mi upstream and 3 mi downstream in a total of 4 h. In still water, the kayaker can travel at an average speed of 2 mi/h. Based on this information, what is the average speed of the river's current? Is your answer reasonable?

1 Understand the Problem

The **answer** will be the average speed of the current.

List the **important information:**

- The kayaker spent 4 hours kayaking.
- She went 3 mi upstream and 3 mi downstream.
- Her average speed in still water is 2 mi/h.

2 Make a Plan

Let c represent the speed of the current. When the kayaker is going upstream, her speed is equal to her speed in still water minus c. When the kayaker is going downstream, her speed is equal to her speed in still water plus c.

	Distance (mi)	Average Speed (mi/h)	Time (h)
Up	3	$2 - c$	$\frac{3}{2-c}$
Down	3	$2 + c$	$\frac{3}{2+c}$

Helpful Hint

distance = rate × time
Therefore,
time = $\frac{\text{distance}}{\text{rate}}$.

total time = time upstream + time downstream

$$4 = \frac{3}{2-c} + \frac{3}{2+c}$$

3 Solve

$$4(2-c)(2+c) = \frac{3}{2-c}(2-c)(2+c) + \frac{3}{2+c}(2-c)(2+c)$$ *The LCD is $(2-c)(2+c)$.*

$$4(2-c)(2+c) = 3(2+c) + 3(2-c)$$ *Simplify. Note that $c \neq \pm 2$.*

$$16 - 4c^2 = 6 + 3c + 6 - 3c$$ *Use the Distributive Property.*

$$16 - 4c^2 = 12$$ *Combine like terms.*

$$-4c^2 = -4$$ *Solve for c.*

$$c = \pm 1$$

The speed of the current cannot be negative. Therefore, the average speed of the current is 1 mi/h.

4 Look Back

If the speed of the current is 1 mi/h, the kayaker's speed when going upstream is $2 - 1 = 1$ mi/h. It will take her 3 h to travel 3 mi upstream. Her speed when going downstream is $2 + 1 = 3$ mi/h. It will take her 1 hour to travel 3 mi downstream. The total trip will take 4 h, which is the given time.

Use the information given above to answer the following.

3. On a different river, the kayaker travels 2 mi upstream and 2 mi downstream in a total of 5 h. What is the average speed of the current of this river? Round to the nearest tenth.

EXAMPLE 4 Work Application

Jason can clean a large tank at an aquarium in about 6 hours. When Jason and Lacy work together, they can clean the tank in about 3.5 hours. About how long would it take Lacy to clean the tank if she works by herself?

Jason's rate: $\frac{1}{6}$ of the tank per hour

Lacy's rate: $\frac{1}{h}$ of the tank per hour, where h is the number of hours needed to clean the tank by herself

Jason's rate × hours worked	+	Lacy's rate × hours worked	=	1 complete job
$\frac{1}{6}(3.5)$	+	$\frac{1}{h}(3.5)$	=	1

$\frac{1}{6}(3.5)(6h) + \frac{1}{h}(3.5)(6h) = 1(6h)$ *Multiply by the LCD, 6h.*

$3.5h + 21 = 6h$ *Simplify.*

$21 = 2.5h$ *Solve for h.*

$8.4 = h$

It will take Lacy about 8.4 hours, or 8 hours 24 minutes, to clean the tank when working by herself.

4. Julien can mulch a garden in 20 minutes. Together, Julien and Remy can mulch the same garden in 11 minutes. How long will it take Remy to mulch the garden when working alone?

A **rational inequality** is an inequality that contains one or more rational expressions. One way to solve rational inequalities is by using graphs and tables.

EXAMPLE 5 Using Graphs and Tables to Solve Rational Equations and Inequalities

Solve $\frac{x}{x-4} \leq 2$ by using a graph and a table.

Use a graph. On a graphing calculator, let **Y1** $= \frac{x}{x-4}$ and **Y2** $= 2$.

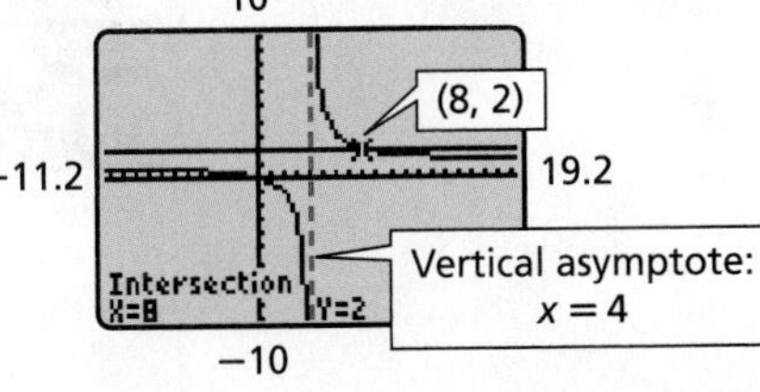

The graph of **Y1** is at or below the graph of **Y2** when $x < 4$ or when $x \geq 8$.

Use a table. The table shows that **Y1** is undefined when $x = 4$ and that **Y1** ≤ **Y2** when $x < 4$ or when $x \geq 8$.

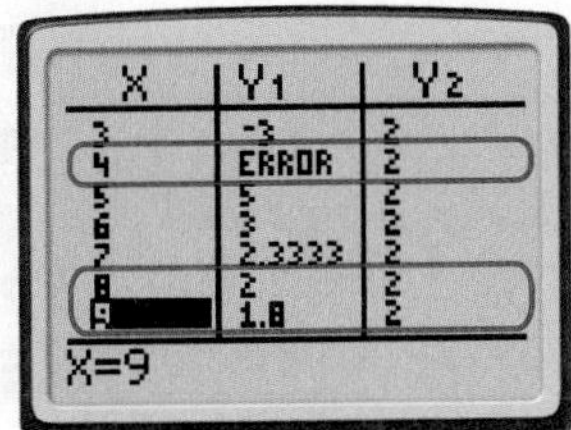

The solution of the inequality is $x < 4$ or $x \geq 8$.

Remember!

The solution $x < 4$ or $x \geq 8$ can be written in set-builder notation as $\{x \mid x < 4 \cup x \geq 8\}$

Solve by using a graph and a table.

5a. $\frac{x}{x-3} \geq 4$

5b. $\frac{8}{x+1} = -2$

You can also solve rational inequalities algebraically. You start by multiplying each term by the least common denominator (LCD) of all the expressions in the inequality. However, you must consider two cases: the LCD is positive or the LCD is negative.

Remember!

If you multiply or divide both sides of an inequality by a negative value, you must reverse the inequality symbol.

EXAMPLE 6 Solving Rational Inequalities Algebraically

Solve the inequality $\frac{8}{x+5} \le 4$ algebraically. Check your answer for reasonableness.

Case 1 LCD is positive.

Step 1 Solve for x.

$\frac{8}{x+5}(x+5) \le 4(x+5)$ *Multiply by the LCD.*

$8 \le 4x + 20$ *Simplify. Note that $x \neq -5$.*

$-12 \le 4x$ *Solve for x.*

$-3 \le x$

Step 2 Consider the sign of the LCD.

$x + 5 > 0$ *LCD is positive.*

$x > -5$ *Solve for x.*

For Case 1, the solution must satisfy $x \ge -3$ *and* $x > -5$, which simplifies to $x \ge -3$.

Case 2 LCD is negative.

Step 1 Solve for x.

$\frac{8}{x+5}(x+5) \ge 4(x+5)$ *Multiply by the LCD. Reverse the inequality.*

$8 \ge 4x + 20$ *Simplify. Note that $x \neq -5$.*

$-12 \ge 4x$ *Solve for x.*

$-3 \ge x$

Step 2 Consider the sign of the LCD.

$x + 5 < 0$ *LCD is negative.*

$x < -5$ *Solve for x.*

For Case 2, the solution must satisfy $x \le -3$ *and* $x < -5$, which simplifies to $x < -5$.

The solution set of the original inequality is the union of the solutions to both Case 1 and Case 2. The solution to the inequality $\frac{8}{x+5} \le 4$ is $x < -5$ or $x \ge -3$, or $\{x \mid x < -5 \cup x \ge -3\}$. The expression will be less than 4 when the denominator is negative or is very large, so the answer is reasonable.

Solve each inequality algebraically.

6a. $\frac{6}{x-2} \ge -4$ **6b.** $\frac{9}{x+3} < 6$

THINK AND DISCUSS

1. Explain why multiplying both sides of a rational equation by the LCD eliminates all of the denominators.
2. Explain why rational equations may have extraneous solutions.
3. Describe two methods for solving the inequality $\frac{12}{x} > 3$.

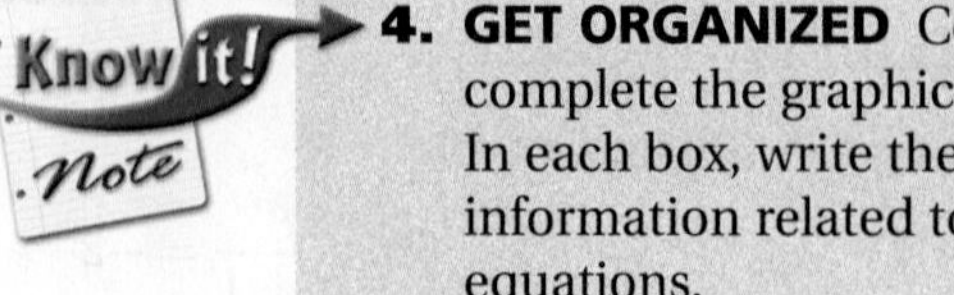

4. **GET ORGANIZED** Copy and complete the graphic organizer. In each box, write the appropriate information related to rational equations.

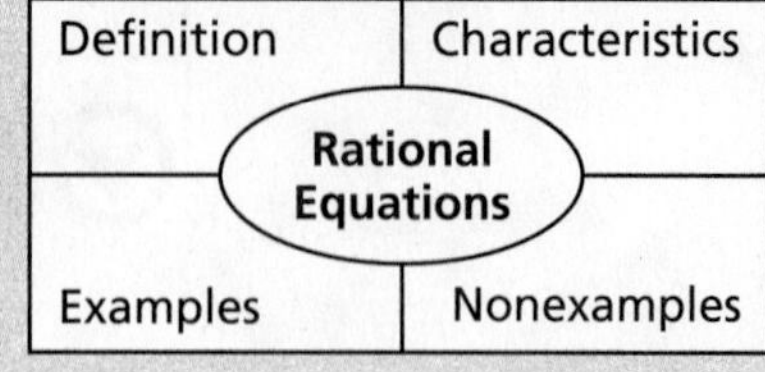

8-5 Exercises

go.hrw.com
Homework Help Online
KEYWORD: MB7 8-5
Parent Resources Online
KEYWORD: MB7 Parent

GUIDED PRACTICE

1. **Vocabulary** How does a *rational expression* differ from a *rational equation*?

SEE EXAMPLE 1 p. 600

Solve each equation.

2. $\frac{1}{8} + \frac{2}{t} = \frac{17}{8t}$
3. $7 = \frac{1}{w} - 4$
4. $\frac{1}{r-5} = \frac{7}{2r}$
5. $\frac{1}{x} = \frac{x}{6} - \frac{5}{6}$
6. $m + \frac{12}{m} = 7$
7. $k + \frac{1}{k} = 2$

SEE EXAMPLE 2 p. 601

8. $\frac{-2x}{x+2} + \frac{x}{3} = \frac{4}{x+2}$
9. $\frac{x}{x-3} + \frac{x}{2} = \frac{6x}{2x-6}$
10. $\frac{3}{x(x+1)} - 1 = \frac{3}{x^2+x}$

SEE EXAMPLE 3 p. 602

11. **Transportation** A river barge travels at an average of 8 mi/h in still water. The barge travels 60 mi up the Mississippi River and 60 mi down the river in a total of 16.5 h. What is the average speed of the current in this section of the Mississippi River? Round to the nearest tenth. Is your answer reasonable?

SEE EXAMPLE 4 p. 603

12. **Work** Each month Leo must make copies of a budget report. When he uses both the large and the small copier, the job takes 30 min. If the small copier is broken, the job takes him 50 min. How long will the job take if the large copier is broken?

SEE EXAMPLE 5 p. 603

Solve by using a graph and a table.

13. $\frac{x-5}{x} > 2$
14. $\frac{3}{x+6} = 3$
15. $\frac{x+3}{2x} < 2$

SEE EXAMPLE 6 p. 604

Solve each inequality algebraically.

16. $\frac{4}{x+1} < 4$
17. $\frac{12}{x-4} \le 3$
18. $\frac{10}{x+8} > 2$

PRACTICE AND PROBLEM SOLVING

Independent Practice	
For Exercises	See Example
19–24	1
25–27	2
28	3
29	4
30–32	5
33–35	6

Extra
Skills Practice p. S19
Application Practice p. S39

Solve each equation.

19. $4 + \frac{1}{x} = \frac{10}{2x}$
20. $\frac{5}{4} = \frac{n-3}{n-4}$
21. $\frac{1}{a-7} = 3$
22. $\frac{1}{x} - \frac{3}{4} = \frac{x}{4}$
23. $\frac{14}{z} = 9 - z$
24. $x + \frac{4}{x} = 4$
25. $\frac{4x}{x-3} + \frac{x}{2} = \frac{12}{x-3}$
26. $\frac{3x}{x+1} = \frac{2x-1}{x+1}$
27. $\frac{2}{x(x-1)} = 1 + \frac{2}{x-1}$
28. **Multi-Step** A passenger jet travels from Los Angeles to Mumbai, India, in 22 h. The return flight takes 17 h. The difference in flight times is caused by winds over the Pacific Ocean that blow primarily from west to east. If the jet's average speed in still air is 550 mi/h, what is the average speed of the wind during the round-trip flight? Round to the nearest mile per hour. Is your answer reasonable?
29. **Art** A glassblower can produce a set of simple glasses in about 2 h. When the glassblower works with an apprentice, the job takes about 1.5 h. How long would it take the apprentice to make a set of glasses when working alone?

Solve by using a graph and a table.

30. $\frac{1}{x} > 1$
31. $\frac{x+1}{x+2} = 2$
32. $\frac{x}{x-5} \le 0$

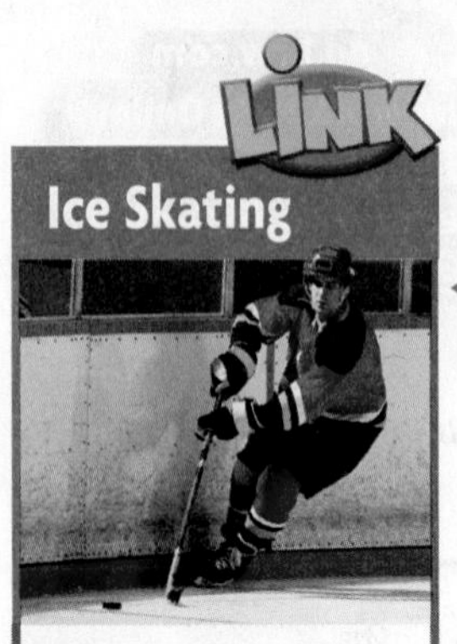

The temperature of the ice in many indoor skating rinks is kept between 24°F and 28°F. Ice that is colder than these temperatures may chip too easily, and ice that is warmer may result in too much friction as skate blades pass over it.

Solve each inequality algebraically.

33. $\frac{1}{3x} < 2$ **34.** $\frac{9}{x-4} \geq -6$ **35.** $\frac{9}{x+10} > 3$

36. Ice Skating A new skating rink will be approximately rectangular in shape and will have an area of no more than 17,000 square feet.

a. Write an inequality expressing the possible perimeter P of the skating rink in feet in terms of its width w.

b. Is 400 feet a reasonable value for the perimeter? Explain.

37. Baseball The baseball card shows statistics for a professional player during four seasons.

a. A player's batting average is equal to his number of hits divided by his number of at bats. For which year listed on the card did Derek Jeter have the greatest batting average?

b. Write and solve an equation to find how many additional consecutive hits h Jeter would have needed to raise his batting average in 2004 to that of his average in 2001.

c. What if...? How many additional hits in a row would Jeter have needed to raise his batting average in 2003 to .500? Check your answer for reasonableness.

YEAR	HITS	AT BATS
2001	191	614
2002	191	644
2003	156	482
2004	188	643

Solve each equation or inequality.

38. $\frac{15n}{n-3} = \frac{5}{n-3} - 8$ **39.** $\frac{z}{z+1} = \frac{z}{z-4}$ **40.** $\frac{4}{x} + 6 = \frac{1}{x^2}$

41. $\frac{8}{x} - \frac{3}{x} = \frac{6}{x-1}$ **42.** $\frac{2(x+4)}{x-4} = \frac{3x}{x-4}$ **43.** $\frac{1}{a-1} + \frac{4}{a+1} = \frac{7}{a^2-1}$

44. $\frac{6}{r} \geq \frac{5}{2}$ **45.** $\frac{8}{x+1} > 4$ **46.** $x \geq \frac{4}{x}$

Use a graphing calculator to solve each rational equation. Round your answers to the nearest hundredth.

47. $\frac{1}{x^2} = 5$ **48.** $\frac{1}{x^2} = x^2 - 1$ **49.** $\frac{1}{x-1} = x - 1$

50. Critical Thinking The reciprocal of a number plus $\frac{7}{2}$ equals 2. Find the number.

51. This problem will prepare you for the Multi-Step Test Prep on page 608.

The average speed for the winner of the 2002 Indy 500 was 25 mi/h greater than the average speed for the 2001 winner. In addition, the 2002 winner completed the 500 mi race 32 min faster than the 2001 winner.

a. Let s represent the average speed of the 2001 winner in miles per hour. Write expressions in terms of s for the time in hours that it took the 2001 and 2002 winners to complete the race.

b. Write a rational equation that can be used to determine s. Solve your equation to find the average speed of the 2001 winner to the nearest mile per hour.

52. **Critical Thinking** An equation has the form $\frac{a}{x} + \frac{x}{b} = c$, where a, b, and c are constants and $b \neq 0$. How many values of x could make this equation true?

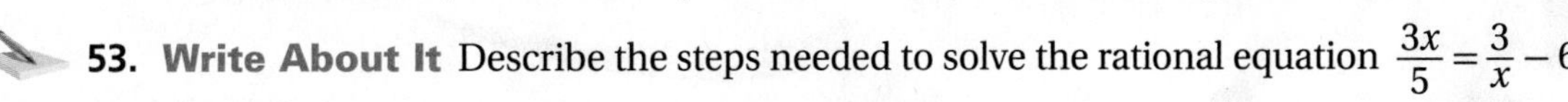

53. **Write About It** Describe the steps needed to solve the rational equation $\frac{3x}{5} = \frac{3}{x} - 6$.

TEST PREP

54. What value of x makes the equation $\frac{1}{x} + \frac{3}{x+3} = \frac{6}{x}$ true?

Ⓐ $-\frac{15}{2}$ Ⓑ $-\frac{12}{5}$ Ⓒ $-\frac{3}{2}$ Ⓓ $-\frac{6}{7}$

55. How many solutions does the equation $\frac{x+2}{x-4} - \frac{1}{x} = \frac{4}{x^2 - 4x}$ have?

Ⓕ 0 Ⓖ 1 Ⓗ 2 Ⓙ 3

56. If $x \neq -2$, which is equivalent to $\frac{4x}{x-2} = 6 + \frac{10}{x-2}$?

Ⓐ $\frac{4x}{x-2} = \frac{16}{x-2}$

Ⓑ $4x = 6(x-2) + 10$

Ⓒ $4x = 6 + 10$

Ⓓ $\frac{4}{-2} = 6 + \frac{5}{x-1}$

57. **Short Response** Water flowing through both a small pipe and a large pipe can fill a water tank in 7 h. Water flowing through the small pipe alone can fill the tank in 15 h.

a. Write an equation that can be used to find the number of hours it would take to fill the tank using only the large pipe.

b. How many hours would it take to fill the tank using only the large pipe? Show your work, or explain how you determined your answer.

CHALLENGE AND EXTEND

Solve each equation or inequality.

58. $\frac{4x}{x^2 + x - 6} = \frac{7x}{x^2 - 5x - 24}$

59. $\frac{1 - 4x^{-1} + 3x^{-2}}{1 - 9x^{-2}} = \frac{x-1}{x+3}$

60. $\frac{3x}{x+2} - \frac{2}{x+4} \geq 7$

61. $\frac{6}{x-3} > \frac{x}{4} + 5$

62. Marcus and Will are painting a barn. Marcus paints about twice as fast as Will. On the first day, they have worked for 6 h and completed about $\frac{1}{3}$ of the job when Will gets injured. If Marcus has to complete the rest of the job by himself, about how many additional hours will it take him?

SPIRAL REVIEW

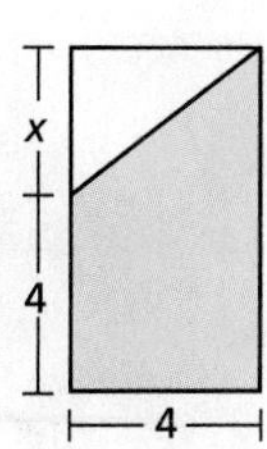

63. Write and simplify an expression in terms of x that represents the area of the shaded portion of the rectangle. *(Previous course)*

Simplify by rationalizing each denominator. *(Lesson 1-3)*

64. $\frac{-3\sqrt{3}}{\sqrt{8}}$

65. $\frac{5}{4\sqrt{7}}$

Given: y varies inversely as x. Write and graph each inverse variation function. *(Lesson 8-1)*

66. $y = -2$ when $x = 5$

67. $y = 2$ when $x = \frac{3}{2}$

CHAPTER 8

MULTI-STEP TEST PREP

SECTION 8A

Rational Functions

Math in the Fast Lane The Indianapolis 500 is one of the most exciting events in sports. Each spring, 33 drivers compete in the 500 mi race, sometimes hitting speeds of more than 220 mi/h.

Winners of the Indianapolis 500		
Year	**Winner**	**Winning Time**
1911	Roy Harroun	6 h 42 min
1990	Arie Luyendyk	2 h 41 min 18 s
2004	Buddy Rice	3 h 15 s

1. Write a rational function that can be used to model the race, where the independent variable represents the average speed in miles per hour and the dependent variable represents the time in hours it takes to complete the race. What type of variation function is it?
2. To the nearest mile per hour, how much faster was the average winning speed in 2004 than in 1911?
3. In 1990, Arie Luyendyk set the record for the fastest Indy 500 average speed, about 186 mi/h. The time in hours to finish the race based on Arie Luyendyk's record can be modeled by the function $t = \frac{500}{186 + s}$, where s is the speed above 186 in miles per hour. Graph the function, and evaluate it for $s = 10$. What does this value of the function represent?
4. During the race, a driver completes one lap with an average speed of 200 mi/h and then completes the following lap at an average speed of 210 mi/h. What is the driver's average speed for the two laps, to the nearest tenth of a mile per hour?
5. Each lap in the Indy 500 is 2.5 mi. A driver completes two laps in 1.5 min. The average speed during the second lap is 8 mi/h faster than the average speed during the first lap. Find the driver's average speed for each of the two laps, to the nearest mile per hour.

Quiz for Lessons 8-1 Through 8-5

8-1 Variation Functions

1. The mass m in kilograms of a bronze statue varies directly as its volume V in cubic centimeters. If a statue made from 1000 cm^3 of bronze has a mass of 8.7 kg, what is the mass of a statue made from 4500 cm^3 of bronze?
2. The time t in hours needed to clean the rides at an amusement park varies inversely with the number of workers n. If 6 workers can clean the rides in 6 hours, how many hours will it take 10 workers to clean the rides?

8-2 Multiplying and Dividing Rational Expressions

Simplify. Identify any x-values for which the expression is undefined.

3. $\frac{5x^3}{10x^2 + 5x}$
4. $\frac{x^2 - 2x - 3}{x^2 + 5x + 4}$
5. $\frac{-x + 6}{x^2 - 3x - 18}$

Multiply or divide. Assume that all expressions are defined.

6. $\frac{x + 3}{x + 2} \cdot \frac{2x - 4}{x^2 - 9}$
7. $\frac{9x^6 y}{27x^2 y^5} \div \frac{x}{6y^2}$
8. $\frac{2x^3 - 18x}{x^2 - 2x - 8} \div \frac{x^2 + x - 12}{x^2 - 16}$

8-3 Adding and Subtracting Rational Expressions

Add or subtract. Identify any x-values for which the expression is undefined.

9. $\frac{3x + 2}{x - 2} - \frac{x + 5}{x - 2}$
10. $\frac{x^2 - x}{x^2 - 25} + \frac{3}{x + 5}$
11. $\frac{x}{x - 3} - \frac{1}{x + 3}$
12. A plane's average speed when flying from one city to another is 550 mi/h and is 430 mi/h on the return flight. To the nearest mile per hour, what is the plane's average speed for the entire trip?

8-4 Rational Functions

Using the graph of $f(x) = \frac{1}{x}$ as a guide, describe the transformations and graph each function.

13. $g(x) = \frac{1}{x - 4}$
14. $g(x) = \frac{1}{x + 1} + 2$

Identify the zeros and asymptotes of each function. Then graph.

15. $f(x) = \frac{x^2 - 16}{x - 3}$
16. $f(x) = \frac{2x}{x^2 - 4}$

8-5 Solving Rational Equations and Inequalities

Solve each equation.

17. $y - \frac{10}{y} = 3$
18. $\frac{x}{x - 8} = \frac{24 - 2x}{x - 8}$
19. $\frac{-3x}{3} - \frac{x + 15}{x + 9} = 1$
20. A restaurant has two pastry ovens. When both ovens are used, it takes about 3 hours to bake the bread needed for one day. When only the large oven is used, it takes about 4 hours to bake the bread for one day. Approximately how long would it take to bake the bread for one day if only the small oven were used?

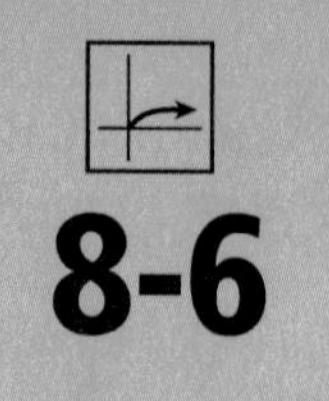

8-6 Radical Expressions and Rational Exponents

Objectives
Rewrite radical expressions by using rational exponents.
Simplify and evaluate radical expressions and expressions containing rational exponents.

Vocabulary
index
rational exponent

Who uses this?
Guitar makers use radical expressions to ensure that the strings produce the correct notes. (See Example 6.)

You are probably familiar with finding the square and square root of a number. These two operations are inverses of each other. Similarly, there are roots that correspond to larger powers.

5 and −5 are **square** roots of 25 because $5^2 = 25$ and $(-5)^2 = 25$.
2 is the **cube** root of 8 because $2^3 = 8$.
2 and −2 are **fourth** roots of 16 because $2^4 = 16$ and $(-2)^4 = 16$.
a is the nth root of b if $a^n = b$.

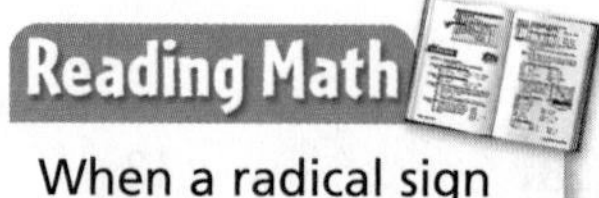

Reading Math
When a radical sign shows no index, it represents a square root.

The nth root of a real number a can be written as the radical expression $\sqrt[n]{a}$, where n is the **index** (plural: *indices*) of the radical and a is the radicand. When a number has more than one real root, the radical sign indicates only the principal, or positive, root.

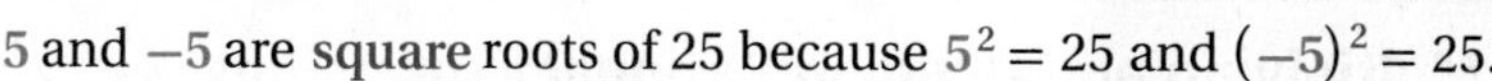

Numbers and Types of Real Roots

Case	Roots	Example
Odd index	1 real root	The real 3rd root of 8 is 2.
Even index; positive radicand	2 real roots	The real 4th roots of 16 are ±2.
Even index; negative radicand	0 real roots	−16 has no real 4th roots.
Radicand of 0	1 root of 0	The 3rd root of 0 is 0.

EXAMPLE 1 Finding Real Roots

Find all real roots.

A **fourth roots of 81**
A positive number has two real fourth roots. Because $3^4 = 81$ and $(-3)^4 = 81$, the roots are 3 and −3.

B **cube roots of −125**
A negative number has one real cube root. Because $(-5)^3 = -125$, the root is −5.

C **sixth roots of −729**
A negative number has no real sixth roots.

Find all real roots.
1a. fourth roots of −256 **1b.** sixth roots of 1 **1c.** cube roots of 125

The properties of square roots in Lesson 1-3 also apply to nth roots.

Properties of nth Roots

For $a > 0$ and $b > 0$,

WORDS	NUMBERS	ALGEBRA
Product Property of Roots The nth root of a product is equal to the product of the nth roots.	$\sqrt[3]{16} = \sqrt[3]{8} \cdot \sqrt[3]{2} = 2\sqrt[3]{2}$	$\sqrt[n]{ab} = \sqrt[n]{a} \cdot \sqrt[n]{b}$
Quotient Property of Roots The nth root of a quotient is equal to the quotient of the nth roots.	$\sqrt{\frac{25}{16}} = \frac{\sqrt{25}}{\sqrt{16}} = \frac{5}{4}$	$\sqrt[n]{\frac{a}{b}} = \frac{\sqrt[n]{a}}{\sqrt[n]{b}}$

EXAMPLE 2 Simplifying Radical Expressions

Simplify each expression. Assume that all variables are positive.

Remember!

When an expression contains a radical in the denominator, you must rationalize the denominator. To do so, rewrite the expression so that the denominator contains no radicals.

A $\sqrt[3]{27x^6}$

$\sqrt[3]{3^3 \cdot x^3 \cdot x^3}$ *Factor into perfect cubes.*

$\sqrt[3]{3^3} \cdot \sqrt[3]{x^3} \cdot \sqrt[3]{x^3}$ *Product Property*

$3 \cdot x \cdot x$ *Simplify.*

$3x^2$

B $\sqrt[3]{\frac{x^3}{7}}$

$\frac{\sqrt[3]{x^3}}{\sqrt[3]{7}}$ *Quotient Property*

$\frac{x}{\sqrt[3]{7}}$ *Simplify the numerator.*

$\frac{x}{\sqrt[3]{7}} \cdot \frac{\sqrt[3]{7}}{\sqrt[3]{7}} \cdot \frac{\sqrt[3]{7}}{\sqrt[3]{7}}$ *Rationalize the denominator.*

$\frac{x\sqrt[3]{7^2}}{\sqrt[3]{7^3}}$ *Product Property*

$\frac{x\sqrt[3]{49}}{7}$ *Simplify.*

Simplify each expression. Assume that all variables are positive.

2a. $\sqrt[4]{16x^4}$ **2b.** $\sqrt[4]{\frac{x^8}{3}}$ **2c.** $\sqrt[3]{x^7} \cdot \sqrt[3]{x^2}$

A **rational exponent** is an exponent that can be expressed as $\frac{m}{n}$, where m and n are integers and $n \neq 0$. Radical expressions can be written by using rational exponents.

Rational Exponents

For any natural number n and integer m,

WORDS	NUMBERS	ALGEBRA
The exponent $\frac{1}{n}$ indicates the nth root.	$16^{\frac{1}{4}} = \sqrt[4]{16} = 2$	$a^{\frac{1}{n}} = \sqrt[n]{a}$
The exponent $\frac{m}{n}$ indicates the nth root raised to the mth power.	$8^{\frac{2}{3}} = (\sqrt[3]{8})^2 = 2^2 = 4$	$a^{\frac{m}{n}} = (\sqrt[n]{a})^m = \sqrt[n]{a^m}$

EXAMPLE 3 Writing Expressions in Radical Form

Write the expression $(-125)^{\frac{2}{3}}$ in radical form, and simplify.

> **Writing Math**
>
> The denominator of a rational exponent becomes the index of the radical.

Method 1 Evaluate the root first.		**Method 2** Evaluate the power first.	
$\left(\sqrt[3]{-125}\right)^2$	*Write with a radical.*	$\sqrt[3]{(-125)^2}$	*Write with a radical.*
$(-5)^2$	*Evaluate the root.*	$\sqrt[3]{15,625}$	*Evaluate the power.*
25	*Evaluate the power.*	25	*Evaluate the root.*

CHECK IT OUT! **Write each expression in radical form, and simplify.**

3a. $64^{\frac{1}{3}}$ **3b.** $4^{\frac{5}{2}}$ **3c.** $625^{\frac{3}{4}}$

EXAMPLE  4 Writing Expressions by Using Rational Exponents

Write each expression by using rational exponents.

A $\sqrt[4]{7^3}$

$7^{\frac{3}{4}}$ $\quad \sqrt[n]{a^m} = a^{\frac{m}{n}}$

B $\sqrt[3]{11^6}$

$11^{\frac{6}{3}}$ $\quad \sqrt[n]{a^m} = a^{\frac{m}{n}}$

$11^2 = 121$ *Simplify.*

CHECK IT OUT! **Write each expression by using rational exponents.**

4a. $\left(\sqrt[4]{81}\right)^3$ **4b.** $\sqrt[3]{10^9}$ **4c.** $\sqrt[4]{5^2}$

Rational exponents have the same properties as integer exponents. (See Lesson 1-5.)

Know it! Note

Properties of Rational Exponents

For all nonzero real numbers *a* and *b* and rational numbers *m* and *n*,

WORDS	NUMBERS	ALGEBRA
Product of Powers Property To multiply powers with the same base, add the exponents.	$12^{\frac{1}{2}} \cdot 12^{\frac{3}{2}} = 12^{\frac{1}{2}+\frac{3}{2}} = 12^2 = 144$	$a^m \cdot a^n = a^{m+n}$
Quotient of Powers Property To divide powers with the same base, subtract the exponents.	$\dfrac{125^{\frac{2}{3}}}{125^{\frac{1}{3}}} = 125^{\frac{2}{3}-\frac{1}{3}} = 125^{\frac{1}{3}} = 5$	$\dfrac{a^m}{a^n} = a^{m-n}$
Power of a Power Property To raise one power to another, multiply the exponents.	$\left(8^{\frac{2}{3}}\right)^3 = 8^{\frac{2}{3}\cdot 3} = 8^2 = 64$	$(a^m)^n = a^{m \cdot n}$
Power of a Product Property To find the power of a product, distribute the exponent.	$(16 \cdot 25)^{\frac{1}{2}} = 16^{\frac{1}{2}} \cdot 25^{\frac{1}{2}} = 4 \cdot 5 = 20$	$(ab)^m = a^m b^m$
Power of a Quotient Property To find the power of a quotient, distribute the exponent.	$\left(\dfrac{16}{81}\right)^{\frac{1}{4}} = \dfrac{16^{\frac{1}{4}}}{81^{\frac{1}{4}}} = \dfrac{2}{3}$	$\left(\dfrac{a}{b}\right)^m = \dfrac{a^m}{b^m}$

EXAMPLE 5 Simplifying Expressions with Rational Exponents

Simplify each expression.

A 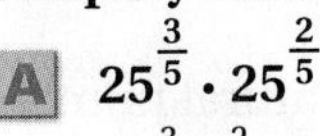
$25^{\frac{3}{5}} \cdot 25^{\frac{2}{5}}$

$25^{\frac{3}{5}+\frac{2}{5}}$ *Product of Powers*

25^{1} *Simplify.*

25 *Evaluate the power.*

Check Enter the expression in a graphing calculator.

25^(3/5)*25^(2/5)
25

B 
$\dfrac{8^{\frac{1}{3}}}{8^{\frac{2}{3}}}$

$8^{\frac{1}{3}-\frac{2}{3}}$ *Quotient of Powers*

$8^{-\frac{1}{3}}$ *Simplify.*

$\dfrac{1}{8^{\frac{1}{3}}}$ *Negative Exponent Property*

$\dfrac{1}{2}$ *Evaluate the power.*

Check Enter the expression in a graphing calculator.

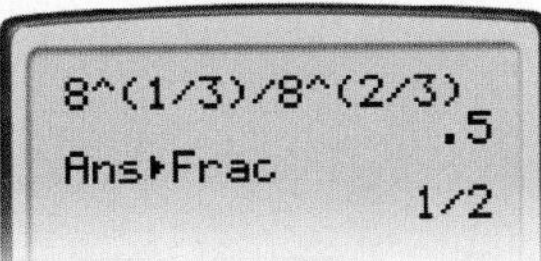

Simplify each expression.

5a. $36^{\frac{3}{8}} \cdot 36^{\frac{1}{8}}$ **5b.** $(-8)^{-\frac{1}{3}}$ **5c.** $\dfrac{5^{\frac{9}{4}}}{5^{\frac{1}{4}}}$

EXAMPLE 6 *Music Application*

Frets are small metal bars positioned across the neck of a guitar so that the guitar can produce the notes of a specific scale.

To find the distance a fret should be placed from the bridge, multiply the length of the string by $2^{-\frac{n}{12}}$, where n is the number of notes higher than the string's root note. Where should a fret be placed to produce a G note on the E string (3 notes higher)?

E string
Frets
64 cm
Bridge

$64\left(2^{-\frac{n}{12}}\right) = 64\left(2^{-\frac{3}{12}}\right)$ *Use 64 cm for the length of the string, and substitute 3 for n.*

$= 64\left(2^{-\frac{1}{4}}\right)$ *Simplify.*

$= 64\left(\dfrac{1}{2^{\frac{1}{4}}}\right)$ *Negative Exponent Property*

$= \dfrac{64}{2^{\frac{1}{4}}}$ *Simplify.*

≈ 53.82 *Use a calculator.*

64/(2^(1/4))
53.81737058

The fret should be placed about 53.82 cm from the bridge.

6. Where should a fret be placed to produce the E note that is one octave higher on the E string (12 notes higher)?

THINK AND DISCUSS

1. Explain why $\sqrt[n]{a^n}$ is equal to a for all natural numbers a and n.

2. **GET ORGANIZED** Copy and complete the graphic organizer. In each box, give a numeric and an algebraic example of the given property of rational exponents.

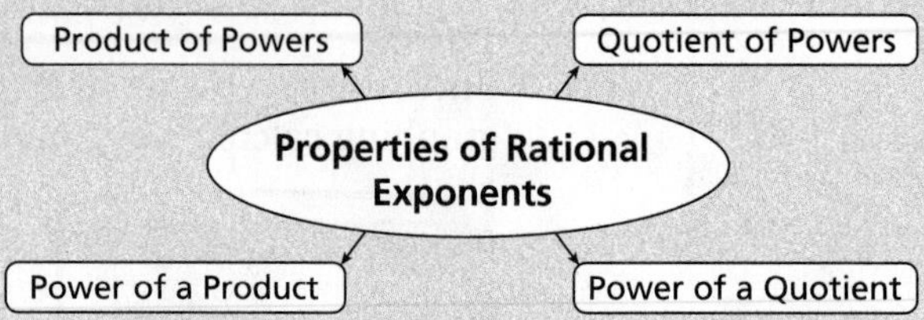

8-6 Exercises

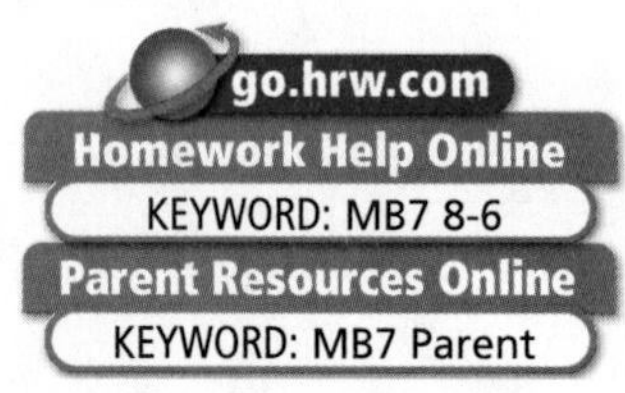

GUIDED PRACTICE

1. **Vocabulary** The *index* of the expression $\sqrt[3]{4^2}$ is __?__. (2, 3, or 4)

SEE EXAMPLE 1 p. 610

Find all real roots.

2. cube roots of 27
3. fourth roots of 625
4. cube roots of 0

SEE EXAMPLE 2 p. 611

Simplify each expression. Assume that all variables are positive.

5. $\sqrt[3]{8x^3}$
6. $\sqrt[4]{\dfrac{32}{x^4}}$
7. $\sqrt[3]{\dfrac{125x^6}{6}}$
8. $\sqrt{50x^3}$
9. $\sqrt[4]{x^8} \cdot \sqrt[3]{x^4}$
10. $\sqrt[3]{\dfrac{x^5}{4}}$
11. $\dfrac{\sqrt{40x^4}}{\sqrt[3]{-x^3}}$
12. $\sqrt[4]{\dfrac{x^{12}y^4}{3}}$

SEE EXAMPLE 3 p. 612

Write each expression in radical form, and simplify.

13. $36^{\frac{3}{2}}$
14. $32^{\frac{3}{5}}$
15. $(-27)^{\frac{1}{3}}$
16. $8^{\frac{2}{3}}$

SEE EXAMPLE 4 p. 612

Write each expression by using rational exponents.

17. $\sqrt[5]{9^{10}}$
18. $\sqrt{8^3}$
19. $\left(\sqrt[6]{5}\right)^3$
20. $\left(\sqrt[3]{27}\right)^2$

SEE EXAMPLE 5 p. 613

Simplify each expression.

21. $13^{\frac{1}{2}} \cdot 13^{\frac{3}{2}}$
22. $\dfrac{9^{\frac{4}{3}}}{9^{\frac{2}{3}}}$
23. $\left(64^{\frac{1}{2}}\right)^{\frac{1}{3}}$
24. $\left(\dfrac{8}{27}\right)^{\frac{1}{3}}$
25. $25^{-\frac{1}{2}}$
26. $7^{\frac{1}{4}} \cdot 7^{-\frac{3}{4}}$
27. $(-125)^{-\frac{1}{3}}$
28. $\left(6^{\frac{1}{2}}\right)^6$

SEE EXAMPLE 6 p. 613

29. **Geometry** The side length of a cube can be determined by finding the cube root of the volume. What is the side length to the nearest *inch* of the cube shown?

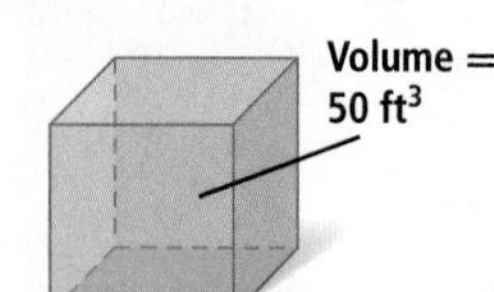

PRACTICE AND PROBLEM SOLVING

Independent Practice

For Exercises	See Example
30–32	1
33–40	2
41–44	3
45–48	4
49–56	5
57	6

Extra Practice

Skills Practice p. S19

Application Practice p. S39

Find all real roots.

30. cube roots of -64 **31.** fifth roots of 32 **32.** fourth roots of -16

Simplify each expression. Assume that all variables are positive.

33. $\sqrt[3]{9x} \cdot \sqrt[3]{3x^2}$ **34.** $\sqrt[4]{324x^8}$ **35.** $\sqrt[3]{\dfrac{x^6}{250}}$ **36.** $\sqrt{\dfrac{x^5}{45}}$

37. $\sqrt[3]{56x^9}$ **38.** $\dfrac{\sqrt[4]{x^{10}}}{\sqrt[4]{x^4}}$ **39.** $\sqrt[5]{x^7} \cdot \sqrt[5]{x^6}$ **40.** $\sqrt[3]{-54x^9y^3}$

Write each expression in radical form, and simplify.

41. $64^{\frac{1}{2}}$ **42.** $216^{\frac{2}{3}}$ **43.** $(-1000)^{\frac{4}{3}}$ **44.** $6^{\frac{3}{2}}$

Write each expression by using rational exponents.

45. $\sqrt[3]{14^3}$ **46.** $\left(\sqrt[5]{-8}\right)^4$ **47.** $\left(\sqrt[4]{144}\right)^2$ **48.** $\sqrt{48^3}$

Simplify each expression.

49. $(8 \cdot 64)^{\frac{2}{3}}$ **50.** $144^{-\frac{1}{2}}$ **51.** $\left(\dfrac{2^3}{27}\right)^{\frac{1}{3}}$ **52.** $2^{\frac{1}{2}} \cdot 2^{\frac{1}{4}}$

53. $\left(\dfrac{49}{81}\right)^{-\frac{1}{2}}$ **54.** $\dfrac{12^{\frac{1}{4}}}{12^{\frac{3}{4}}}$ **55.** $\left(5^{\frac{1}{3}}\right)^{\frac{1}{3}}$ **56.** $\left(\dfrac{27}{27^{\frac{1}{3}}}\right)^{\frac{1}{2}}$

57. Banking The initial amount deposited in a savings account is \$1000. The amount a in dollars in the account after t years can be represented by the function $a(t) = 1000\left(2^{\frac{t}{24}}\right)$. To the nearest dollar, what will the amount in the account be after 6 years?

Biology

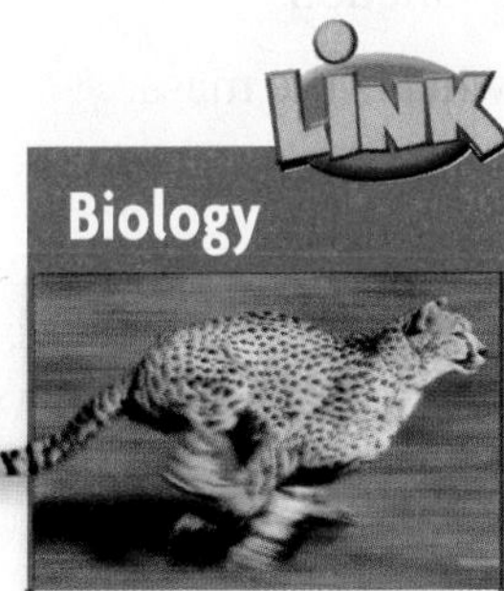

Suppose that a cheetah, a lion, a house cat, and the fastest human runner competed in a 100 m race. At top speed, the cheetah would finish in 3.20 s, the lion in 4.47 s, the house cat in 7.46 s, and the human in 9.77 s.

58. Biology The formula $P = 73.3\sqrt[4]{m^3}$, known as Kleiber's law, relates the metabolism rate P of an organism in Calories per day and the body mass m of the organism in kilograms. The table shows the typical body mass of several members of the cat family.

Typical Body Mass

Animal	Mass (kg)
House cat	4.5
Cheetah	55.0
Lion	170.0

a. What is the metabolism rate of a cheetah to the nearest Calorie per day?

b. Multi-Step Approximately how many more Calories of food does a lion need to consume each day than a house cat does?

59. Medicine Iodine-131 is a radioactive material used to treat certain types of cancer. Iodine-131 has a half-life of 8 days, which means that it takes 8 days for half of an initial sample to decay. The percent of radioactive material that remains after t days can be determined from the expression $100\left(\frac{1}{2}\right)^{\frac{t}{h}}$, where h is the half-life in days.

a. What percent of a sample of iodine-131 will remain after 20 days?

b. What if...? Another form of radioactive iodine used in cancer treatment is iodine-125. Iodine-125 has a half-life of 59 days. A hospital has 20 g of iodine-125 and 20 g of iodine-131 left over from treating patients. How much more iodine-125 than iodine-131 will remain after a period of 30 days?

60. Meteorology The formula $W = 35.74 + 0.6215T - 35.75V^{\frac{4}{25}} + 0.4275TV^{\frac{4}{25}}$ relates the wind chill temperature W to the air temperature T in degrees Fahrenheit and the wind speed V in miles per hour. Use a calculator to find the wind chill to the nearest degree when the air temperature is 40°F and the wind speed is 35 mi/h.

MULTI-STEP TEST PREP

61. This problem will prepare you for the Multi-Step Test Prep on page 636.

For a pendulum with a length L in meters, the expression $2\pi\sqrt{\frac{L}{g}}$ models the time in seconds for the pendulum to complete one back-and-forth swing. In this expression, g is the acceleration due to gravity, 9.8 m/s^2.

a. Simplify the expression by rationalizing the denominator.

b. To the nearest tenth of a second, how long does it take a pendulum with a length of 0.35 m to complete one back-and-forth swing?

Write each expression by using rational exponents. Assume that all variables are positive.

62. $\sqrt[4]{20x^3}$ **63.** $\sqrt{(5x)^7}$ **64.** $\left(\sqrt[5]{-9}\sqrt[3]{x}\right)^4$ **65.** $\left(\sqrt[4]{11x^8}\right)^6$

Simplify each expression, and write it by using a radical. Assume that all variables are positive.

66. $(-8x^{12})^{\frac{2}{3}}$ **67.** $5^{\frac{7}{4}}x^{\frac{3}{4}}$ **68.** $(-12x^{15})^{\frac{3}{5}}$

69. $(a^2b^4)^{\frac{1}{3}}$ **70.** $\left(\frac{a^4}{b}\right)^{\frac{1}{4}}$ **71.** $a^{\frac{3}{4}}(4b^6)^{\frac{1}{4}}$

72. Botany Duckweed is a quickly growing plant that floats on the surface of lakes and ponds. The initial mass of a population of duckweed plants is 100 kg. The mass of the population doubles every 60 h and can be represented by the function $m(t) = 100 \cdot 2^{\frac{t}{60}}$, where t is time in hours. To the nearest kilogram, what is the mass of the plants after 24 h?

Explain whether each statement is sometimes, always, or never true for nonzero values of the variable.

73. $\sqrt[3]{x^6} = x^2$ **74.** $(x)^{\frac{1}{3}} = (-x)^{\frac{1}{3}}$ **75.** $-\sqrt[4]{x^8} = x^{-2}$ **76.** $-\sqrt[3]{x} < 0$

Estimation Identify the pair of consecutive integers that each value is between. Then use a calculator to check your answer.

77. $\sqrt[3]{18}$ **78.** $\sqrt[4]{200}$ **79.** $\sqrt[3]{-80}$

80. Physics Air pressure decreases with altitude according to the formula $P = 14.7(10)^{-0.000014a}$, where P is the air pressure in pounds per square inch and a is the altitude in feet above sea level.

a. Use the formula to estimate the air pressure in Denver, Colorado, which is 5280 ft above sea level.

b. Use the formula to estimate the air pressure at the top of Mount Everest, which is 29,028 ft above sea level.

81. ///ERROR ANALYSIS/// Below are two methods of simplifying an expression. Which is incorrect? Explain the error.

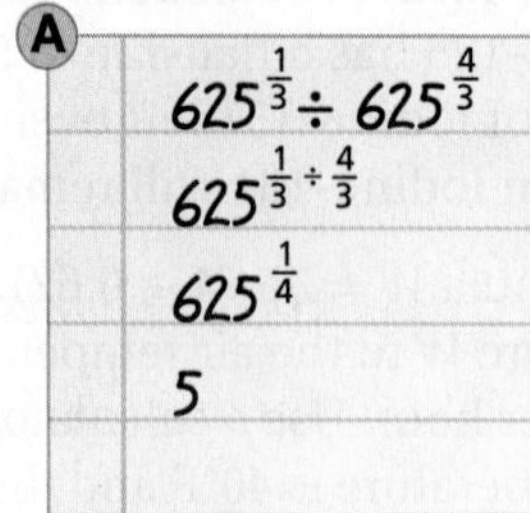

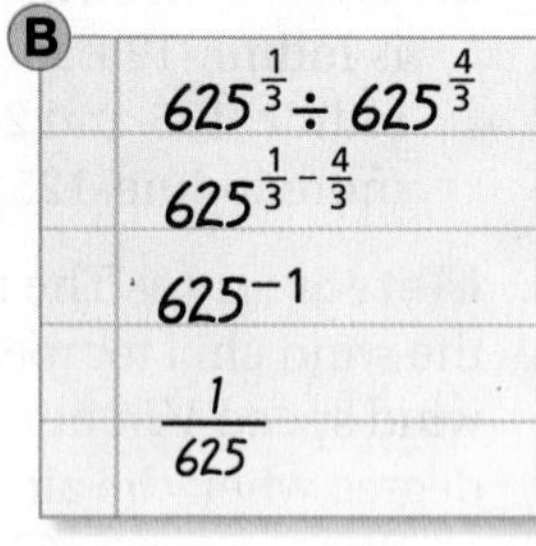

82. How many different positive integer values of n result in a whole number nth root of 64? What are these values?

83. **Critical Thinking** Describe two ways to find the sixth root of 10 on a calculator.

84. **Write About It** Explain whether the expression $x^{2.4}$ contains a rational exponent.

TEST PREP

85. Which of the following represents a real number?

(A) $6^{-\frac{4}{3}}$ (B) $(-9)^{\frac{3}{2}}$ (C) $\sqrt[4]{-11}$ (D) $\left(\sqrt[4]{-14}\right)^3$

86. The surface area S of a sphere with volume V is $S = (4\pi)^{\frac{1}{3}}(3V)^{\frac{2}{3}}$. What effect does increasing the volume of a sphere by a factor of 8 have on its surface area?

(F) The surface area doubles.
(G) The surface area triples.
(H) The surface area increases by a factor of 4.
(J) The surface area increases by a factor of 8.

87. If $a = x^6$, what is $\sqrt[4]{a}$?

(A) $\left(\sqrt{x}\right)^3$ (B) x^2 (C) $x^2\sqrt{x}$ (D) $x^{\frac{2}{3}}$

88. Which expression is equivalent to $\sqrt[3]{\frac{56a^6}{7}}$?

(F) $2a^2$ (G) $8a^2$ (H) $2a^3$ (J) $8a^3$

CHALLENGE AND EXTEND

89. Write an expression by using rational exponents for the square root of the square root of the square root of 20.

90. Simplify the expression $2^{\frac{1}{3}} \cdot 4^{\frac{1}{6}} \cdot 8^{\frac{1}{9}}$.

91. **Critical Thinking** For what real values of a is $\sqrt[3]{a}$ greater than a?

92. Any nonzero real number has three cube roots, only one of which is real. Show that the cube roots of 1 are 1, $\frac{-1 + i\sqrt{3}}{2}$, and $\frac{-1 - i\sqrt{3}}{2}$.

SPIRAL REVIEW

Add or subtract, if possible. *(Lesson 4-1)*

$A = \begin{bmatrix} -2 & -1 & 0 \\ 3 & 2 & 6 \end{bmatrix}$ $B = \begin{bmatrix} 1 & -1 \\ 0 & -2 \end{bmatrix}$ $C = \begin{bmatrix} 5 & 7 \\ 0 & -4 \end{bmatrix}$ $D = \begin{bmatrix} 9 & 8 & -2 \\ 6 & 3 & -1 \end{bmatrix}$

93. $A + D$ 94. $B - C$ 95. $B + C$

Use the description to write each quadratic function in vertex form. *(Lesson 5-1)*

96. The parent function $f(x) = x^2$ is vertically compressed by a factor of 3 and then translated 1 unit right to create g.

97. The parent function $f(x) = x^2$ is reflected across the x-axis and translated 3 units up to create h.

Identify the zeros and the asymptotes of each function. Then graph. *(Lesson 8-4)*

98. $f(x) = \frac{x^2 - 4}{x + 5}$ 99. $f(x) = \frac{x + 3}{x^2 + 6x + 5}$ 100. $f(x) = \frac{4x - 3}{x + 6}$

Area and Volume Relationships

When you change the linear dimensions of a solid figure, its surface area and volume may change in different ways.

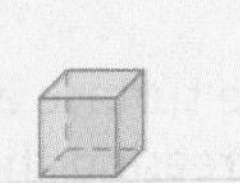

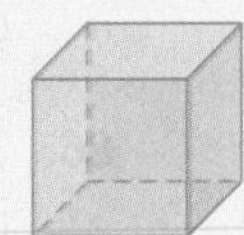

Recall that when you multiply the side length of a cube by a constant a, the surface area increases by a factor of a^2 and the volume increases by a factor of a^3, as shown.

Side Length	$s = 1$ cm	$s = 2(1) = 2$ cm
Surface Area	$A = 6$ cm^2	$A = 2^2(6) = 24$ cm^2
Volume	$V = 1$ cm^3	$V = 2^3(1) = 8$ cm^3

When you want to change the surface area or volume of a figure but maintain the same linear proportions, you can use the reverse process. If the surface area increases by a factor of a, the linear dimensions increase by a factor of $\sqrt{a}$. If the volume increases by a factor of a, the linear dimensions increase by a factor of $\sqrt[3]{a}$.

Example

A cylindrical water storage tank has a radius of 5 ft and a height of 10 ft. A new tank similar to the first is constructed with 20% more capacity. What are the radius and height of the new tank?

The capacity of the larger tank is 120% of the smaller tank. So, the volume is increased by a factor of 1.2.

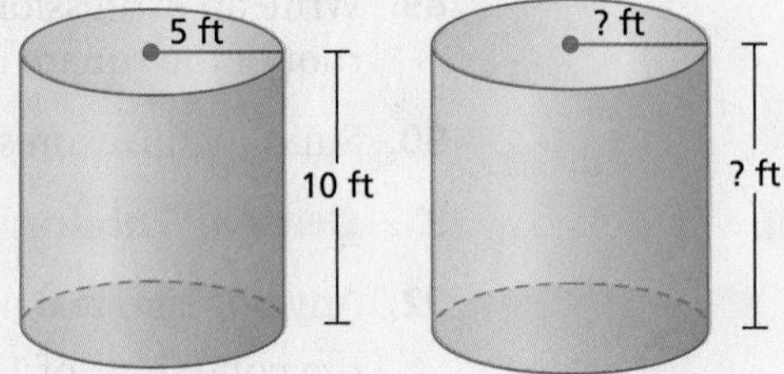

Step 1 Find the scale factor for the linear dimensions.

$\sqrt[3]{1.2} \approx 1.0627$ *Take the cube root.*

Step 2 Find the new dimensions.

$1.0627(5) \approx 5.31$

$1.0627(10) \approx 10.63$

Multiply the original dimensions by the scale factor.

The radius is about 5.31 ft, and the height is about 10.63 ft.

Try This

Solve each problem. If necessary, round your answers to the nearest thousandth.

1. Marsha wants to double the surface area of a circular pond. How should she change the radius? the diameter?
2. The volume of a sphere is increased by a factor of 100. The new radius is 30 cm. What was the radius of the original sphere?
3. The surface area of a cube is decreased from 150 cm^2 to 96 cm^2. By what factor has the volume changed?
4. A store owner wants to create giant ice-cream cones that contain 3 times the volume of a traditional cone. How should he change the radius and height of the traditional cone?

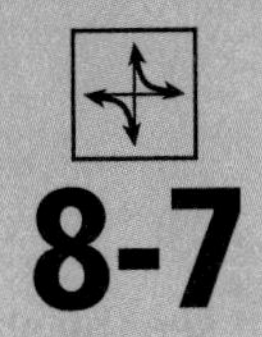

8-7 Radical Functions

Objectives
Graph radical functions and inequalities.
Transform radical functions by changing parameters.

Vocabulary
radical function
square-root function

Who uses this?
Aerospace engineers use transformations of radical functions to adjust for gravitational changes on other planets. (See Example 5.)

Recall that exponential and logarithmic functions are inverse functions. Quadratic and cubic functions have inverses as well. The graphs below show the inverses of the quadratic parent function and the cubic parent function.

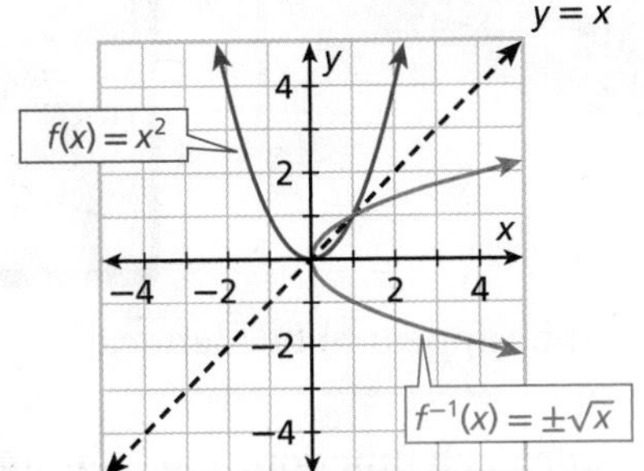

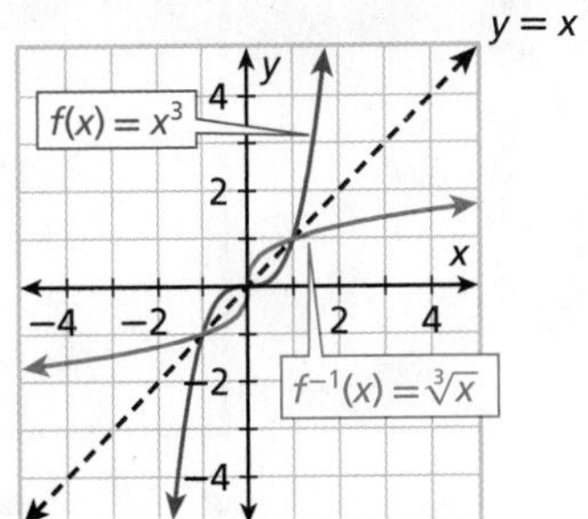

Notice that the inverse of $f(x) = x^2$ is not a function because it fails the vertical line test. However, if we limit the domain of $f(x) = x^2$ to $x \geq 0$, its inverse is the function $f^{-1}(x) = \sqrt{x}$.

A **radical function** is a function whose rule is a radical expression. A **square-root function** is a radical function involving $\sqrt{x}$. The square-root parent function is $f(x) = \sqrt{x}$. The cube-root parent function is $f(x) = \sqrt[3]{x}$.

EXAMPLE 1 Graphing Radical Functions

Graph the function, and identify its domain and range.

A $f(x) = \sqrt{x}$

Make a table of values. Plot enough ordered pairs to see the shape of the curve. Because the square root of a negative number is imaginary, choose only nonnegative values for x.

Helpful Hint
When using a table to graph square-root functions, choose x-values that make the radicands perfect squares.

x	$f(x) = \sqrt{x}$	$(x, f(x))$
0	$f(0) = \sqrt{0} = 0$	(0, 0)
1	$f(1) = \sqrt{1} = 1$	(1, 1)
4	$f(4) = \sqrt{4} = 2$	(4, 2)
9	$f(9) = \sqrt{9} = 3$	(9, 3)

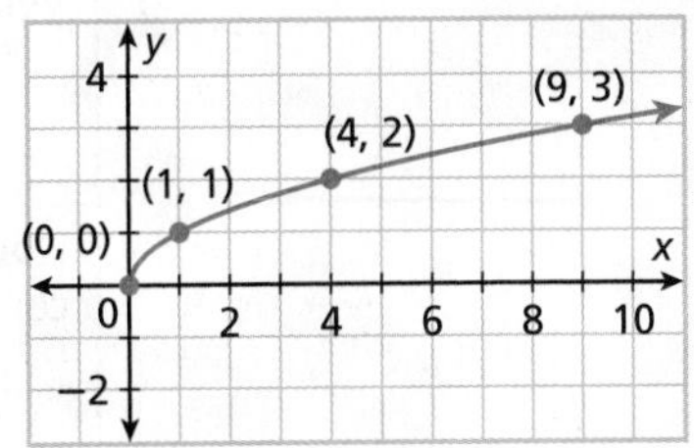

The domain is $\{x \mid x \geq 0\}$, and the range is $\{y \mid y \geq 0\}$.

Graph the function, and identify its domain and range.

B $f(x) = 4\sqrt[3]{x+4}$

Make a table of values. Plot enough ordered pairs to see the shape of the curve. Choose both negative and positive values for x.

Helpful Hint

When using a table to graph cube-root functions, choose x-values that make the radicands perfect cubes.

x	$4\sqrt[3]{x+4}$	$(x, f(x))$
−12	$4\sqrt[3]{-12+4} = 4\sqrt[3]{-8} = -8$	(−12, −8)
−5	$4\sqrt[3]{-5+4} = 4\sqrt[3]{-1} = -4$	(−5, −4)
−4	$4\sqrt[3]{-4+4} = 4\sqrt[3]{0} = 0$	(−4, 0)
−3	$4\sqrt[3]{-3+4} = 4\sqrt[3]{1} = 4$	(−3, 4)
4	$4\sqrt[3]{4+4} = 4\sqrt[3]{8} = 8$	(4, 8)

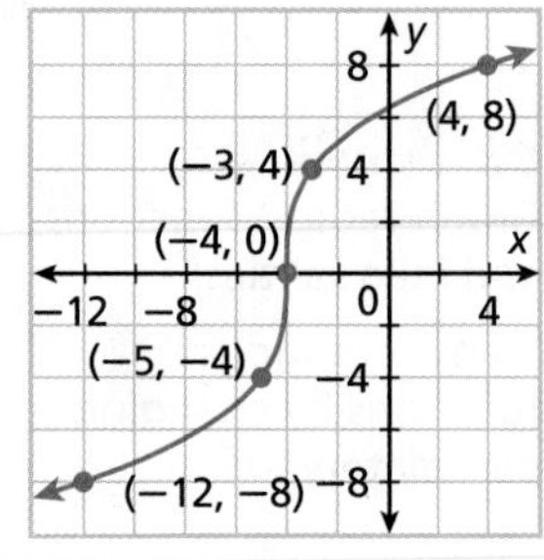

The domain is the set of all real numbers. The range is also the set of all real numbers.

Check Graph the function on a graphing calculator.

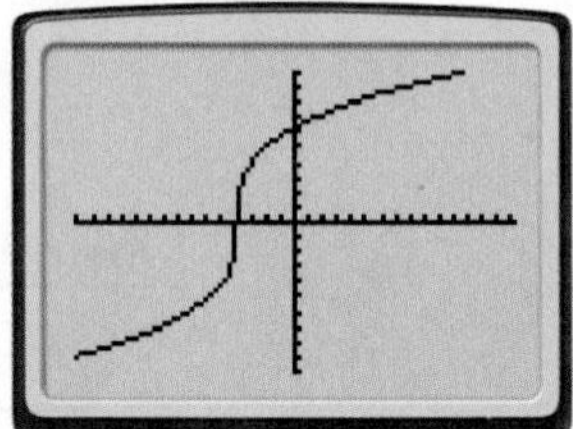

The graphs appear to be identical.

Graph each function, and identify its domain and range.

1a. $f(x) = \sqrt[3]{x}$ **1b.** $f(x) = \sqrt{x+1}$

The graphs of radical functions can be transformed by using methods similar to those used to transform linear, quadratic, polynomial, and exponential functions. This lesson will focus on transformations of square-root functions.

Transformations of the Square-Root Parent Function $f(x) = \sqrt{x}$

Transformation	$f(x)$ Notation	Examples
Vertical translation	$f(x) + k$	$y = \sqrt{x} + 3$ 3 units up $y = \sqrt{x} - 4$ 4 units down
Horizontal translation	$f(x - h)$	$y = \sqrt{x-2}$ 2 units right $y = \sqrt{x+1}$ 1 unit left
Vertical stretch/compression	$af(x)$	$y = 6\sqrt{x}$ vertical stretch by 6 $y = \frac{1}{2}\sqrt{x}$ vertical compression by $\frac{1}{2}$
Horizontal stretch/compression	$f\left(\frac{1}{b}x\right)$	$y = \sqrt{\frac{1}{5}x}$ horizontal stretch by 5 $y = \sqrt{3x}$ horizontal compression by $\frac{1}{3}$
Reflection	$-f(x)$ $f(-x)$	$y = -\sqrt{x}$ across x-axis $y = \sqrt{-x}$ across y-axis

EXAMPLE 2 Transforming Square-Root Functions

Using the graph of $f(x) = \sqrt{x}$ as a guide, describe the transformation and graph each function.

A $g(x) = \sqrt{x} - 2$

$g(x) = f(x) - 2$

Translate f 2 units down.

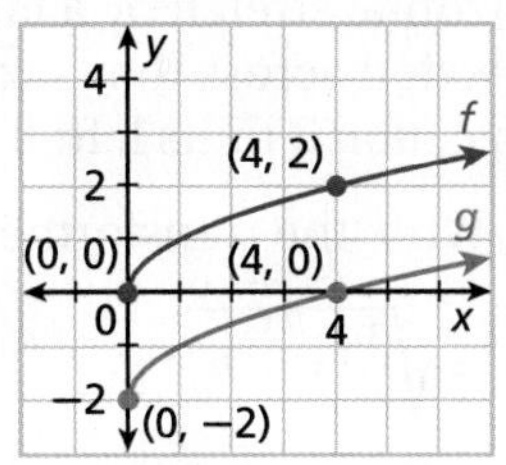

B $g(x) = 3\sqrt{x}$

$g(x) = 3 \cdot f(x)$

Stretch f vertically by a factor of 3.

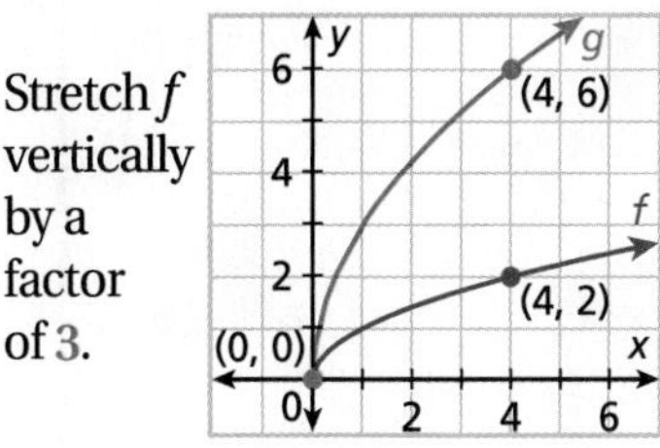

Using the graph of $f(x) = \sqrt{x}$ as a guide, describe the transformation and graph each function.

2a. $g(x) = \sqrt{x} + 1$

2b. $g(x) = \frac{1}{2}\sqrt{x}$

Transformations of square-root functions are summarized below.

$|a| \rightarrow$ vertical stretch or compression factor
$a < 0 \rightarrow$ reflection across the x-axis

$h \rightarrow$ horizontal translation

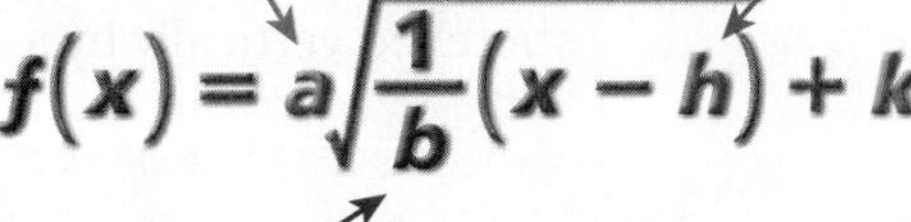

$$f(x) = a\sqrt{\frac{1}{b}(x - h)} + k$$

$|b| \rightarrow$ horizontal stretch or compression factor
$b < 0 \rightarrow$ reflection across the y-axis

$k \rightarrow$ vertical translation

EXAMPLE 3 Applying Multiple Transformations

Using the graph of $f(x) = \sqrt{x}$ as a guide, describe the transformation and graph each function.

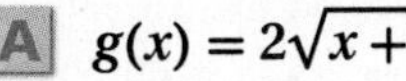

A $g(x) = 2\sqrt{x+3}$

Stretch f vertically by a factor of 2, and translate it 3 units left.

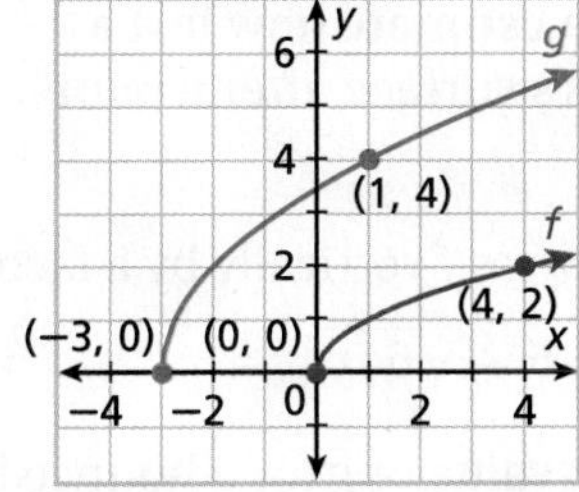

B $g(x) = \sqrt{-x} - 2$

Reflect f across the y-axis, and translate it 2 units down.

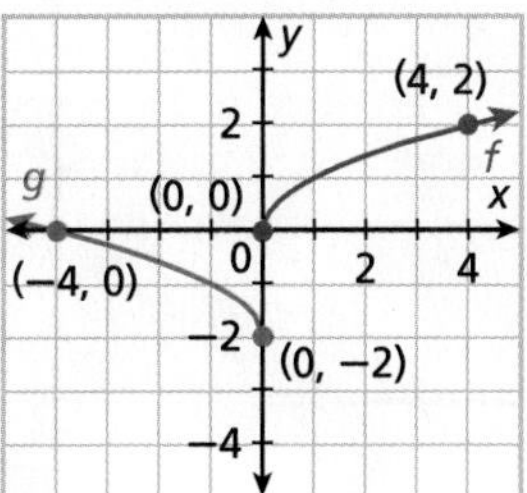

Using the graph of $f(x) = \sqrt{x}$ as a guide, describe the transformation and graph each function.

3a. $g(x) = \sqrt{-x} + 3$

3b. $g(x) = -3\sqrt{x} - 1$

EXAMPLE 4 Writing Transformed Square-Root Functions

Use the description to write the square-root function g.

The parent function $f(x) = \sqrt{x}$ is stretched horizontally by a factor of 2, reflected across the y-axis, and translated 3 units left.

Step 1 Identify how each transformation affects the function.

Horizontal stretch by a factor of 2: $|b| = 2$
Reflection across the y-axis: b is negative
$\Big\}\ b = -2$

Translation 3 units left: $h = -3$

Step 2 Write the transformed function.

$$g(x) = \sqrt{\frac{1}{b}(x - h)}$$

$$g(x) = \sqrt{\frac{1}{-2}\left[x-(-3)\right]} \qquad \textit{Substitute } -2 \textit{ for } b \textit{ and } -3 \textit{ for } h.$$

$$g(x) = \sqrt{-\frac{1}{2}(x + 3)} \qquad \textit{Simplify.}$$

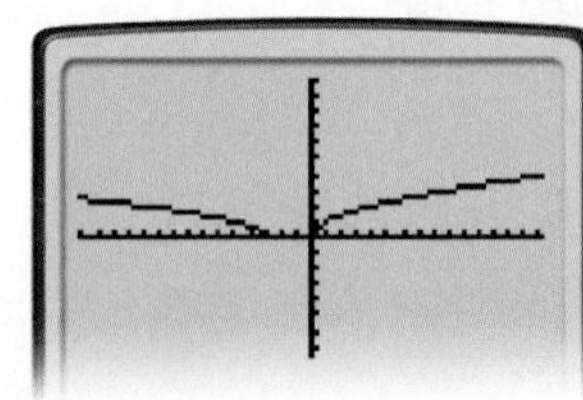

Check Graph both functions on a graphing calculator. The graph of g indicates the given transformations of f.

Use the description to write the square-root function g.

4. The parent function $f(x) = \sqrt{x}$ is reflected across the x-axis, stretched vertically by a factor of 2, and translated 1 unit up.

EXAMPLE 5 *Space Exploration Application*

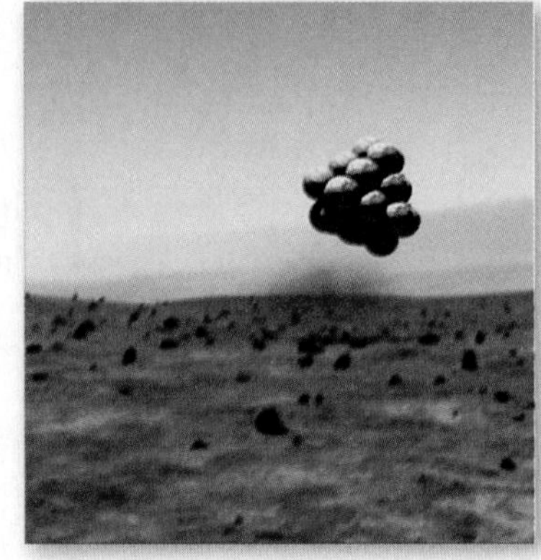

Special airbags are used to protect scientific equipment when a rover lands on the surface of Mars. On Earth, the function $f(x) = \sqrt{64x}$ approximates an object's downward velocity in feet per second as the object hits the ground after bouncing x ft in height.

The corresponding function for Mars is compressed vertically by a factor of about $\frac{3}{5}$. Write the corresponding function g for Mars, and use it to estimate how fast a rover will hit Mars's surface after a bounce of 45 ft in height.

Step 1 To compress f vertically by a factor of $\frac{3}{5}$, multiply f by $\frac{3}{5}$.

$$g(x) = \frac{3}{5}f(x) = \frac{3}{5}\sqrt{64x}$$

Step 2 Find the value of g for a bounce height of 45 ft.

$$g(45) = \frac{3}{5}\sqrt{64(45)} \approx 32 \qquad \textit{Substitute 45 for x and simplify.}$$

The rover will hit Mars's surface with a downward velocity of about 32 ft/s at the end of the bounce.

Use the information on the previous page to answer the following.

5. The downward velocity function for the Moon is a horizontal stretch of f by a factor of about $\frac{25}{4}$. Write the velocity function h for the Moon, and use it to estimate the downward velocity of a landing craft at the end of a bounce 50 ft in height.

In addition to graphing radical functions, you can also graph radical inequalities. Use the same procedure you used for graphing linear and quadratic inequalities.

EXAMPLE 6 Graphing Radical Inequalities

Graph the inequality $y < \sqrt{x} + 2$.

Step 1 Use the related equation $y = \sqrt{x} + 2$ to make a table of values.

x	0	1	4	9
y	2	3	4	5

Step 2 Use the table to graph the boundary curve. The inequality sign is <, so use a dashed curve and shade the area below it.

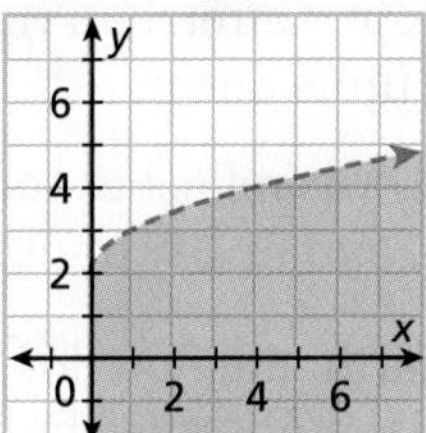

Because the value of x cannot be negative, do not shade left of the y-axis.

Check Choose a point in the solution region, such as $(1, 0)$, and test it in the inequality.

$$y < \sqrt{x} + 2$$

$$0 \overset{?}{<} \sqrt{1} + 2$$

$$0 < 3 \checkmark$$

Graph each inequality.

6a. $y > \sqrt{x + 4}$

6b. $y \geq \sqrt[3]{x - 3}$

THINK AND DISCUSS

1. Explain whether radical functions have asymptotes.

2. Explain how to determine the domain of the function $f(x) = \sqrt{2x + 2}$.

3. GET ORGANIZED Copy and complete the graphic organizer. In each box, give an example of the transformation of the square-root function $f(x) = \sqrt{x}$.

Transformation	Equation	Graph
Vertical translation		
Horizontal translation		
Reflection		
Vertical stretch		

8-7 Exercises

go.hrw.com
Homework Help Online
KEYWORD: MB7 8-7
Parent Resources Online
KEYWORD: MB7 Parent

GUIDED PRACTICE

1. **Vocabulary** Explain why $f(x) = \sqrt{3x} + 4$ is a radical function.

SEE EXAMPLE 1 p. 619

Graph each function, and identify its domain and range.

2. $f(x) = \sqrt{x + 6}$
3. $f(x) = \sqrt{x} - 1$
4. $f(x) = 2\sqrt{x - 3}$
5. $f(x) = 3\sqrt[3]{x}$
6. $f(x) = \sqrt[3]{x} + 2$
7. $f(x) = \sqrt[3]{x - 2}$

SEE EXAMPLE 2 p. 621

Using the graph of $f(x) = \sqrt{x}$ as a guide, describe the transformation and graph each function.

8. $g(x) = \sqrt{x} - 7$
9. $h(x) = 3\sqrt{x}$
10. $j(x) = \sqrt{x - 5}$

SEE EXAMPLE 3 p. 621

11. $g(x) = \frac{1}{2}\sqrt{x} - 1$
12. $h(x) = \sqrt{\frac{1}{3}(x + 4)}$
13. $j(x) = \sqrt{-(x - 3)}$
14. $g(x) = -2\sqrt{x} - 4$
15. $h(x) = \sqrt{-2(x + 2)}$
16. $j(x) = 3\sqrt{x + 3} + 3$

SEE EXAMPLE 4 p. 622

Use the description to write the square-root function g.

17. The parent function $f(x) = \sqrt{x}$ is stretched vertically by a factor of 4 and then translated 5 units left and 2 units down.
18. The parent function $f(x) = \sqrt{x}$ is reflected across the y-axis, then compressed horizontally by a factor of $\frac{1}{2}$, and finally translated 7 units right.

SEE EXAMPLE 5 p. 622

19. **Space Exploration** On Earth, the function $f(x) = \frac{6}{5}\sqrt{x}$ approximates the distance in miles to the horizon observed by a person whose eye level is x feet above the ground. The graph of the corresponding function for Mars is a horizontal stretch of f by a factor of about $\frac{9}{5}$. Write the corresponding function g for Mars, and use it to estimate the distance to the horizon for an astronaut whose eyes are 6 ft above Mars's surface.

SEE EXAMPLE 6 p. 623

Graph each inequality.

20. $y \geq \sqrt{x}$
21. $y \leq \sqrt{x - 4}$
22. $y < \sqrt{x} - 3$
23. $y > \sqrt[3]{x}$

PRACTICE AND PROBLEM SOLVING

Independent Practice

For Exercises	See Example
24–29	1
30–32	2
33–38	3
39–41	4
42	5
43–46	6

Extra Practice

Skills Practice p. S19
Application Practice p. S39

Graph each function, and identify its domain and range.

24. $f(x) = \sqrt{x - 2}$
25. $f(x) = -3\sqrt{x}$
26. $f(x) = 2\sqrt{x + 1} - 3$
27. $f(x) = \sqrt[3]{x + 1}$
28. $f(x) = \sqrt[3]{x} - 4$
29. $f(x) = -2\sqrt[3]{x - 3}$

Using the graph of $f(x) = \sqrt{x}$ as a guide, describe the transformation and graph each function.

30. $g(x) = \sqrt{x} + 2$
31. $h(x) = \sqrt{x - 4}$
32. $j(x) = 0.5\sqrt{x}$
33. $g(x) = \sqrt{3(x + 5)}$
34. $h(x) = \frac{1}{4}\sqrt{-x}$
35. $j(x) = \sqrt{x + 4} - 1$
36. $g(x) = -4\sqrt{x} + 1$
37. $h(x) = 3\sqrt{-x} + 2$
38. $j(x) = \frac{1}{3}\sqrt{-(x + 2)}$

Use the description to write the square-root function g.

39. The parent function $f(x) = \sqrt{x}$ is compressed vertically by a factor of $\frac{1}{3}$ and then translated 3 units left.
40. The parent function $f(x) = \sqrt{x}$ is reflected across the y-axis, stretched horizontally by a factor of 6, and then translated 2 units right.

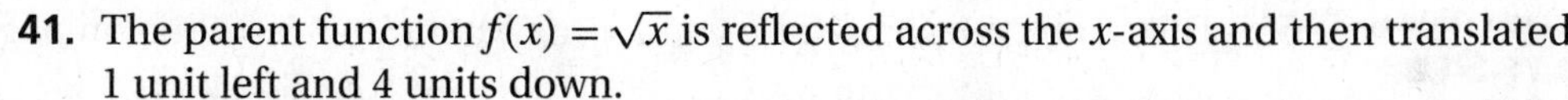

41. The parent function $f(x) = \sqrt{x}$ is reflected across the x-axis and then translated 1 unit left and 4 units down.

42. **Manufacturing** A company manufactures cans for pet food. The function $f(x) = \sqrt{\frac{x}{40}}$ models the radius in centimeters of a can holding x cm^3 of dog food. The graph of the corresponding function for cans of cat food is a horizontal compression of f by a factor of about $\frac{3}{5}$. Write the corresponding function g for cans of cat food, and use it to estimate the radius of a can holding 216 cm^3 of cat food.

Okapi

Graph each inequality.

43. $y < \sqrt{x+5}$
44. $y \geq \sqrt{x-1}$
45. $y > \sqrt[3]{x} + 2$
46. $y \leq \sqrt[3]{x+3}$

47. **Biology** The function $h(m) = 241m^{-\frac{1}{4}}$ can be used to approximate an animal's resting heart rate h in beats per minute, given its mass m in kilograms.
   a. A common shrew is one of the world's smallest mammals. What is the resting heart rate of a common shrew with a mass of 0.01 kg?
   b. An okapi is an African animal related to the giraffe. What is the resting heart rate of an okapi with a mass of 300 kg?

Describe how $f(x) = \sqrt{x}$ was transformed to produce each function.

48. $g(x) = 6\sqrt{x+1}$
49. $h(x) = 3\sqrt{x-1} - 9$
50. $j(x) = -\sqrt{x-3} - 7$

Match each function to its graph.

51. $f(x) = \sqrt{x+2} - 2$
52. $g(x) = \sqrt{x-2} + 2$
53. $h(x) = \sqrt{-(x+2)} + 2$
54. $j(x) = -\sqrt{x-2} - 2$

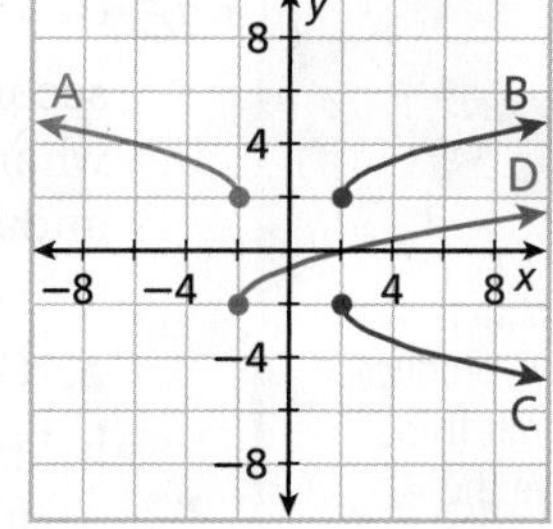

55. **Aviation** Pilots use the function $D(A) = 3.56\sqrt{A}$ to approximate the distance D in kilometers to the horizon from an altitude A in meters.
   a. What is the approximate distance to the horizon observed by a pilot flying at an altitude of 11,000 m?

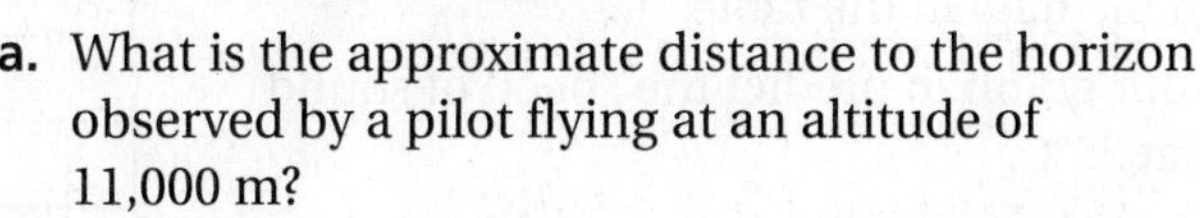

   b. **What if...?** How will the approximate distance to the horizon appear to change if the pilot descends by 4000 m?

56. **Earth Science** The speed in miles per hour of a tsunami can be modeled by the function $s(d) = 3.86\sqrt{d}$, where d is the average depth in feet of the water over which the tsunami travels. Graph this function. Use the graph to predict the speed of a tsunami over water with a depth of 1500 feet.

57. **Astrophysics** New stars can form inside an interstellar cloud of gas when a cloud fragment, called a clump, has a mass M that is greater than what is known as the Jean's mass. The Jean's mass M_J is given by $M_J = 100\sqrt{\frac{(T+273)^3}{n}}$, where T is the temperature of the gas in degrees Celsius and n is the density of the gas in molecules per cubic centimeter. An astronomer discovers a gas clump with $M = 137$, $T = -263$, and $n = 1000$. Will the clump form a star? Justify your answer.

58. **Multi-Step** The formula $v = \sqrt{4909gR}$ approximates the velocity in miles per hour necessary to escape the gravity of a planet with acceleration due to gravity g in ft/s^2 and radius R in miles. On Earth, which has a radius of 3960 mi, the acceleration due to gravity is 32 ft/s^2. On the Moon, which has a radius of 1080 mi, the acceleration due to gravity is about $\frac{1}{6}$ that on Earth. How much faster would a vehicle need to be traveling to escape Earth's gravity than to escape the Moon's gravity?

MULTI-STEP TEST PREP

59. This problem will prepare you for the Multi-Step Test Prep on page 636.

For a pendulum with length x in meters, the function $T(x) = 2\pi\sqrt{\frac{x}{9.8}}$ gives the period of the pendulum in seconds. The period of a pendulum is the time it takes the pendulum to complete one back-and-forth swing.

a. Graph the function.

b. Describe the graph of T as a transformation of $f(x) = \sqrt{x}$.

c. By what factor must the length of a pendulum be increased to double its period?

Tell whether each statement is sometimes, always, or never true.

60. For $n > 0$, the value of $\sqrt{n}$ is greater than the value of $\sqrt[3]{n}$.

61. The domain of a radical function is all real numbers.

62. The range of $f(x) = a\sqrt[3]{x-h}$, where a and h are nonzero real numbers, is all real numbers.

63. The range of $f(x) = a\sqrt{x} + k$, where a and k are nonzero real numbers, is all real numbers.

Graph each inequality, and tell whether the point $(1, 2)$ is a solution.

64. $f(x) \geq \sqrt{x-3}$ **65.** $f(x) \leq \sqrt{x+5}$ **66.** $f(x) > \sqrt[3]{x} - 3$

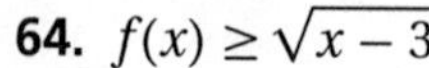

LINK

Physics

A sonic boom is a shock wave produced by an aircraft flying at or above the speed of sound in air. Occasionally, an unusual cone-shaped cloud forms around a plane when the plane's speed is near that of sound, as shown above.

67. Physics The speed s of sound in air in meters per second is given by the function $s = \sqrt{k(T + 273.15)}$, where T is the air temperature in degrees Celsius and k is a positive constant. The table shows the speed of sound in air at a pressure of 1 atmosphere.

Temperature (°C)	Speed of Sound in Air (m/s)
0	331
10	337
20	343
30	348
40	354

a. Graph the data in the table.

b. Use your graph to predict the speed of sound in air at 25°C.

c. Based on the function above, at what temperature would the speed of sound in air be 0 m/s? Explain.

68. Medicine A pharmaceutical company samples the raw materials it receives before they are used in the manufacture of drugs. For inactive ingredients, the company uses the function $s(x) = \sqrt{x} + 1$ to determine the number of samples s that should be taken from a shipment of x containers.

a. Describe the graph of s as a transformation of $f(x) = \sqrt{x}$. Then graph the function.

b. How many samples should be taken from a shipment of 45 containers of an inactive ingredient?

69. Multi-Step The time t in seconds required for an object to fall from a certain height can be modeled by the function $t = \frac{\sqrt{h}}{4}$, where h is the initial height of the object in feet. To the nearest tenth of a second, how much longer will it take for a piece of an iceberg to fall to the ocean from a height of 240 ft than from a height of 100 ft?

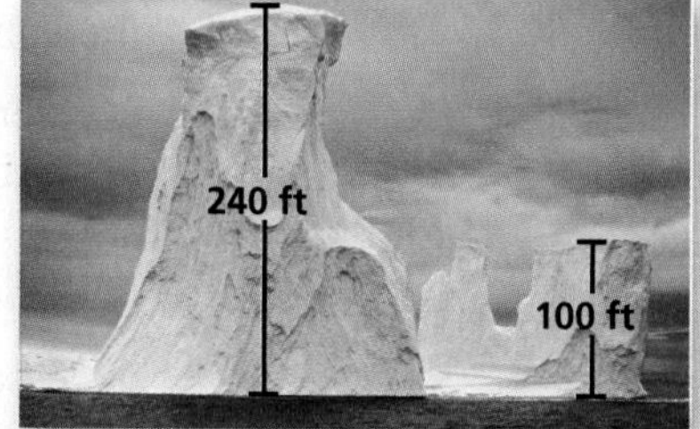

70. Critical Thinking Explain why a vertical compression of a square-root function by a factor of $\frac{1}{2}$ is equivalent to a horizontal stretch of a square-root function by a factor of 4.

71. **Critical Thinking** Why does the square-root function have a limited domain but the cube-root function does not?

72. **Write About It** Describe how a horizontal translation and a vertical translation of the function $f(x) = \sqrt{x}$ each affects the function's domain and range.

TEST PREP

73. What is the domain of the function $f(x) = \sqrt{x - 9}$?
    - Ⓐ All real numbers
    - Ⓑ $x \geq -9$
    - Ⓒ $x \geq 0$
    - Ⓓ $x \geq 9$

74. Which situation could best be modeled by a cube-root function?
    - Ⓕ The volume of a cube as a function of its edge length
    - Ⓖ The diameter of a circle as a function of its area
    - Ⓗ The edge length of a cube as a function of its surface area
    - Ⓙ The radius of a sphere as a function of its volume

75. The function g is a translation 2 units left and 5 units up of $f(x) = \sqrt{x}$. Which of the following represents g?
    - Ⓐ $g(x) = \sqrt{x + 2} + 5$
    - Ⓑ $g(x) = 2\sqrt{x} + 5$
    - Ⓒ $g(x) = \sqrt{x + 5} + 2$
    - Ⓓ $g(x) = 5\sqrt{x - 2}$

76. Which function has a range of $\{y \mid y \leq -2\}$?
    - Ⓕ $f(x) = \sqrt{x} - 2$
    - Ⓖ $f(x) = \sqrt{x - 2}$
    - Ⓗ $f(x) = \sqrt{-x} - 2$
    - Ⓙ $f(x) = -\sqrt{x} - 2$

77. **Short Response** Describe how the graph of $f(x) = \sqrt{x}$ was transformed to produce the graph shown. Then write the equation of the graphed function.

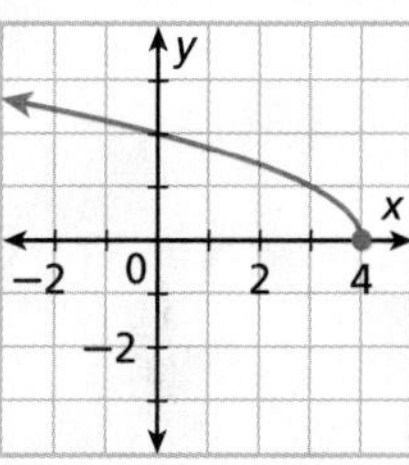

CHALLENGE AND EXTEND

78. The function $f(x) = \sqrt{x}$ is transformed solely by using translations and reflections to produce g. The domain of g is all real numbers greater than or equal to 3, and the range is all real numbers less than or equal to 2. What is the equation that represents g?

79. Write the equation of a square-root function whose graph has its endpoint at $(-3, 4)$ and passes through the point $(2, 2)$.

SPIRAL REVIEW

Solve and graph. *(Lesson 2-1)*

80. $-4x + 5 < -7$
81. $12 \geq 4(x - 5)$
82. $2(x + 1) \geq x - 2$

Use substitution to solve each system of equations. *(Lesson 3-2)*

83. $\begin{cases} y = 2x - 10 \\ 2x + y = 14 \end{cases}$
84. $\begin{cases} y = 3x - 2 \\ 3x = 2y \end{cases}$
85. $\begin{cases} -8x + y = 36 \\ y = x - 4 \end{cases}$

Solve each equation. *(Lesson 8-5)*

86. $\frac{7}{x} + x = \frac{16}{3}$
87. $4 + \frac{2}{x} = \frac{9}{2}$
88. $\frac{-5x^2}{x + 5} = \frac{3x - 2}{x + 5}$

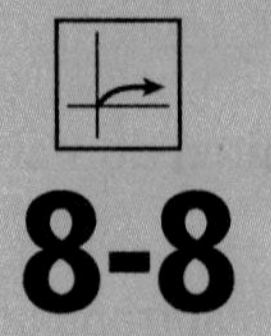

8-8 Solving Radical Equations and Inequalities

IT'S AMAZING HOW PEOPLE SLOW DOWN WHEN YOU POINT A HAIR DRYER AT THEM.

Objective
Solve radical equations and inequalities.

Vocabulary
radical equation
radical inequality

Who uses this?

Police officers can use radical equations to determine whether a car is speeding. (See Example 6.)

A **radical equation** contains a variable within a radical. Recall that you can solve quadratic equations by taking the square root of both sides. Similarly, radical equations can be solved by raising both sides to a power.

Solving Radical Equations	
Steps	**Example**
1. Isolate the radical.	$\sqrt[3]{x} - 2 = 0$ $\sqrt[3]{x} = 2$
2. Raise both sides of the equation to the power equal to the index of the radical.	$(\sqrt[3]{x})^3 = (2)^3$
3. Simplify and solve.	$x = 8$

EXAMPLE  1 Solving Equations Containing One Radical

Solve each equation.

A $2\sqrt{x+1} = 14$

$\frac{2\sqrt{x+1}}{2} = \frac{14}{2}$ *Divide by 2.*

$\sqrt{x+1} = 7$ *Simplify.*

$\left(\sqrt{x+1}\right)^2 = 7^2$ *Square both sides.*

$x + 1 = 49$ *Simplify.*

$x = 48$ *Solve for x.*

Check $2\sqrt{x+1} = 14$

$2\sqrt{48+1}$	14
$2\sqrt{49}$	14
$2(7)$	14 ✓

B $5\sqrt[3]{4x+3} = 15$

$\frac{5\sqrt[3]{4x+3}}{5} = \frac{15}{5}$ *Divide by 5.*

$\sqrt[3]{4x+3} = 3$ *Simplify.*

$\left(\sqrt[3]{4x+3}\right)^3 = 3^3$ *Cube both sides.*

$4x + 3 = 27$ *Simplify.*

$4x = 24$ *Solve for x.*

$x = 6$

Check $5\sqrt[3]{4x+3} = 15$

$5\sqrt[3]{4(6)+3}$	15
$5\sqrt[3]{27}$	15
$5(3)$	15 ✓

Remember!

For a square root, the index of the radical is 2.
$\sqrt{x+1} = \sqrt[2]{x+1}$

Solve each equation.

1a. $4 + \sqrt{x-1} = 5$ **1b.** $\sqrt[3]{3x-4} = 2$ **1c.** $6\sqrt{x+10} = 42$

EXAMPLE 2 Solving Equations Containing Two Radicals

Solve $\sqrt{35x} = 5\sqrt{x+2}$.

$\left(\sqrt{35x}\right)^2 = \left(5\sqrt{x+2}\right)^2$	*Square both sides.*
$35x = 25(x+2)$	*Simplify.*
$35x = 25x + 50$	*Distribute 25.*
$10x = 50$	*Solve for x.*
$x = 5$	

Check

$$\begin{array}{c|l} \sqrt{35x} & = 5\sqrt{x+2} \\ \hline \sqrt{35 \cdot 5} & 5\sqrt{5+2} \\ 5\sqrt{7} & 5\sqrt{7}\ \checkmark \end{array}$$

Solve each equation.

2a. $\sqrt{8x+6} = 3\sqrt{x}$

2b. $\sqrt[3]{x+6} = 2\sqrt[3]{x-1}$

Raising each side of an equation to an even power may introduce extraneous solutions.

EXAMPLE 3 Solving Equations with Extraneous Solutions

Solve $\sqrt{x+18} = x - 2$.

Helpful Hint

You can also use the intersect feature on a graphing calculator to find the point where the two curves intersect.

Method 1 Use a graphing calculator. Let **Y1** $= \sqrt{x+18}$ and **Y2** $= x - 2$.

The graphs intersect in only one point, so there is exactly one solution.

The solution is $x = 7$.

Intersection X=7 Y=5

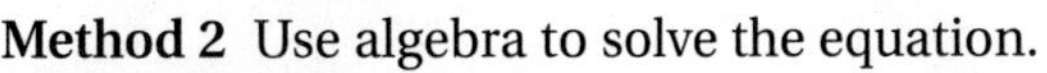

Method 2 Use algebra to solve the equation.

Step 1 Solve for x.

$\sqrt{x+18} = x - 2$	
$\left(\sqrt{x+18}\right)^2 = (x-2)^2$	*Square both sides.*
$x + 18 = x^2 - 4x + 4$	*Simplify.*
$0 = x^2 - 5x - 14$	*Write in standard form.*
$0 = (x+2)(x-7)$	*Factor.*
$x + 2 = 0$ or $x - 7 = 0$	*Solve for x.*
$x = -2$ or $x = 7$	

Step 2 Use substitution to check for extraneous solutions.

$$\begin{array}{c|l} \sqrt{x+18} & = x - 2 \\ \hline \sqrt{-2+18} & -2-2 \\ \sqrt{16} & -4 \\ 4 & -4\ \times \end{array} \qquad \begin{array}{c|l} \sqrt{x+18} & = x - 2 \\ \hline \sqrt{7+18} & 7-2 \\ \sqrt{25} & 5 \\ 5 & 5\ \checkmark \end{array}$$

Because $x = -2$ is extraneous, the only solution is $x = 7$.

Solve each equation.

3a. $\sqrt{2x+14} = x + 3$

3b. $\sqrt{-9x+28} = -x + 4$

You can use similar methods to solve equations containing rational exponents. You raise both sides of the equation to the reciprocal of the exponent. You can also rewrite any expressions with rational exponents in radical form and solve as you would other radical equations.

EXAMPLE  Solving Equations with Rational Exponents

Solve each equation.

A $(3x - 1)^{\frac{1}{5}} = 2$

$\sqrt[5]{3x-1} = 2$	*Write in radical form.*
$\left(\sqrt[5]{3x-1}\right)^5 = 2^5$	*Raise both sides to the fifth power.*
$3x - 1 = 32$	*Simplify.*
$3x = 33$	*Solve for x.*
$x = 11$	

Remember!

To find a power of a power, multiply the exponents.

$\left[(x + 12)^{\frac{1}{2}}\right]^2$

$(x + 12)^{\frac{1}{2} \cdot 2}$

$x + 12$

B $x = (x + 12)^{\frac{1}{2}}$

Step 1 Solve for x.

$x^2 = \left[(x + 12)^{\frac{1}{2}}\right]^2$	*Raise both sides to the reciprocal power.*
$x^2 = x + 12$	*Simplify.*
$x^2 - x - 12 = 0$	*Write in standard form.*
$(x + 3)(x - 4) = 0$	*Factor.*
$x + 3 = 0$ or $x - 4 = 0$	*Solve for x.*
$x = -3$ or $x = 4$	

Step 2 Use substitution to check for extraneous solutions.

x	$(x + 12)^{\frac{1}{2}}$
-3	$(-3 + 12)^{\frac{1}{2}}$
-3	$9^{\frac{1}{2}}$
-3	3 ✗

x	$(x + 12)^{\frac{1}{2}}$
4	$(4 + 12)^{\frac{1}{2}}$
4	$16^{\frac{1}{2}}$
4	4 ✓

The only solution is $x = 4$.

Solve each equation.

4a. $(x + 5)^{\frac{1}{3}} = 3$ **4b.** $(2x + 15)^{\frac{1}{2}} = x$ **4c.** $3(x + 6)^{\frac{1}{2}} = 9$

A **radical inequality** is an inequality that contains a variable within a radical. You can solve radical inequalities by graphing or by using algebra.

EXAMPLE  Solving Radical Inequalities

Solve $\sqrt{2x + 4} \le 4$.

Method 1 Use a graph and a table.

On a graphing calculator, let **Y1** $= \sqrt{2x + 4}$ and **Y2** $= 4$. The graph of **Y1** is at or below the graph of **Y2** for values of x between -2 and 6. Notice that **Y1** is undefined when $x < -2$.

The solution is $-2 \le x \le 6$.

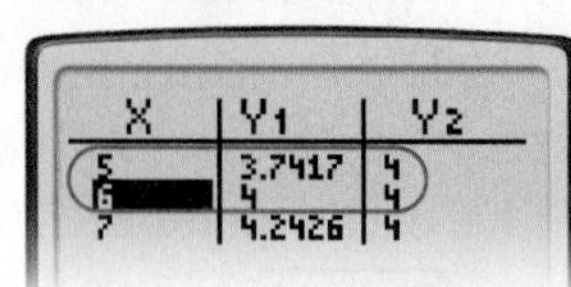

Method 2 Use algebra to solve the inequality.

Step 1 Solve for x.

$\sqrt{2x+4} \leq 4$

$\left(\sqrt{2x+4}\right)^2 \leq (4)^2$ *Square both sides.*

$2x + 4 \leq 16$ *Simplify.*

$2x \leq 12$ *Solve for x.*

$x \leq 6$

Remember!

A radical expression with an even index and a negative radicand has no real roots.

Step 2 Consider the radicand.

$2x + 4 \geq 0$ *The radicand cannot be negative.*

$2x \geq -4$ *Solve for x.*

$x \geq -2$

The solution of $\sqrt{2x+4} \leq 4$ is $x \geq -2$ and $x \leq 6$, or $-2 \leq x \leq 6$.

Solve each inequality.

5a. $\sqrt{x-3} + 2 \leq 5$

5b. $\sqrt[3]{x+2} \geq 1$

EXAMPLE 6 *Automobile Application*

The speed s in miles per hour that a car is traveling when it goes into a skid can be estimated by using the formula $s = \sqrt{30fd}$, where f is the coefficient of friction and d is the length of the skid marks in feet.

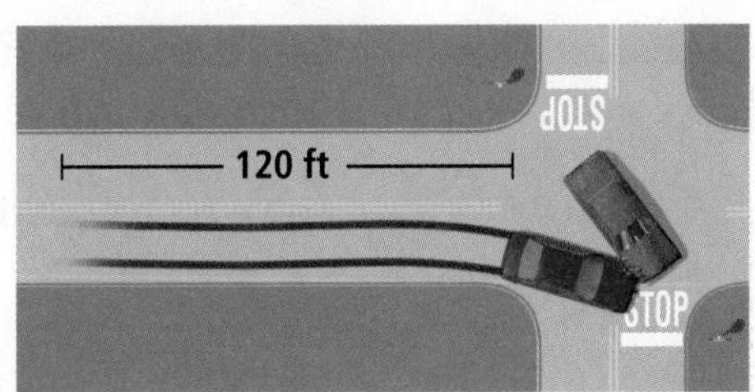

After an accident, a driver claims to have been traveling the speed limit of 45 mi/h. The coefficient of friction under accident conditions was 0.7. Is the driver telling the truth about his speed? Explain.

Use the formula to determine the greatest possible length of the driver's skid marks if he were traveling 45 mi/h.

$s = \sqrt{30fd}$

$45 = \sqrt{30(0.7)d}$ *Substitute 45 for s and 0.7 for f.*

$45 = \sqrt{21d}$ *Simplify.*

$(45)^2 = \left(\sqrt{21d}\right)^2$ *Square both sides.*

$2025 = 21d$ *Simplify.*

$96 \approx d$ *Solve for d.*

If the driver were traveling 45 mi/h, the skid marks would measure about 96 ft. Because the skid marks actually measure 120 ft, the driver must have been driving faster than 45 mi/h.

6. A car skids to a stop on a street with a speed limit of 30 mi/h. The skid marks measure 35 ft, and the coefficient of friction was 0.7. Was the car speeding? Explain.

THINK AND DISCUSS

1. Describe two methods that can be used to solve $\sqrt{x+2} = 6$.
2. Explain the relationship between solving a quadratic equation of the form $x^2 = a$ and a square-root equation of the form $\sqrt{x} = b$, where a and b are real numbers.
3. **GET ORGANIZED** Copy and complete the graphic organizer. In each box, write a step needed to solve a radical equation with extraneous solutions.

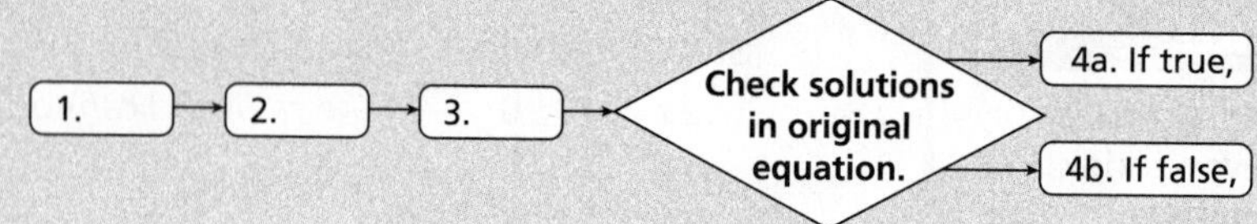

8-8 Exercises

GUIDED PRACTICE

1. **Vocabulary** Is $4x + \sqrt{9} = 5$ a *radical equation*? Explain.

SEE EXAMPLE 1 p. 628

Solve each equation.

2. $\sqrt{x-9} = 5$
3. $\sqrt{3x} = 6$
4. $\sqrt[3]{x-2} = 2$

SEE EXAMPLE 2 p. 629

5. $\sqrt{3x-1} = \sqrt{2x+4}$
6. $2\sqrt{x} = \sqrt{x+9}$
7. $\sqrt[5]{x+4} = \sqrt[5]{3x-2}$
8. $2\sqrt[3]{x} = \sqrt[3]{x+7}$
9. $\sqrt{x+6} - \sqrt{2x-4} = 0$
10. $4\sqrt{x+1} = 3\sqrt{x+2}$

SEE EXAMPLE 3 p. 629

11. $\sqrt{x+56} = x$
12. $\sqrt{x+18} = x-2$
13. $\sqrt{3x-11} = x-3$
14. $\sqrt{x+6} - x = 4$
15. $\sqrt{-x-1} = x+1$
16. $\sqrt{15x+10} = 2x+3$

SEE EXAMPLE 4 p. 630

17. $(x-5)^{\frac{1}{2}} = 3$
18. $(2x+1)^{\frac{1}{3}} = 2$
19. $(4x+5)^{\frac{1}{2}} = x$
20. $2(x-50)^{\frac{1}{3}} = -10$
21. $2(x+1)^{\frac{1}{2}} = 1$
22. $(45-9x)^{\frac{1}{2}} = x-5$

SEE EXAMPLE 5 p. 630

Solve each inequality.

23. $\sqrt{x+5} - 1 \le 4$
24. $\sqrt{2x} + 6 \le 10$
25. $\sqrt{2x+5} < 5$

SEE EXAMPLE 6 p. 631

26. **Stunts** The formula $s = \sqrt{21d}$ relates a stunt car's speed s in miles per hour at the beginning of a skid to the length d of the skid in feet. A stunt driver must skid her car to a stop just in front of a wall. When the driver starts her skid, she is traveling at 64 mi/h. When the driver comes to a stop, how many feet will be between her car and the wall? Round to the nearest foot.

PRACTICE AND PROBLEM SOLVING

Independent Practice

For Exercises	See Example
27–32	1
33–35	2
36–38	3
39–41	4
42–44	5
45	6

Extra Practice

Skills Practice p. S19

Application Practice p. S39

Solve each equation.

27. $\sqrt{x-12}=9$
28. $\sqrt[3]{2x+1}-3=0$
29. $5\sqrt{x+7}=25$
30. $\sqrt[4]{2x+6}=2$
31. $3=\frac{1}{4}\sqrt{3x+30}$
32. $-3=2\sqrt{x-7}-7$
33. $\sqrt{4x+12}=\sqrt{6x}$
34. $5\sqrt{x-1}=\sqrt{x+1}$
35. $\sqrt[3]{4x}=\sqrt[3]{x+7}$
36. $x+3=\sqrt{x+5}$
37. $\sqrt{3x+13}+3=2x$
38. $\sqrt{x+8}-x=-4$
39. $(x-9)^{\frac{1}{2}}=4$
40. $(5x+1)^{\frac{1}{4}}=4$
41. $(3x+28)^{\frac{1}{2}}=x$

Solve each inequality.

42. $\sqrt{3x+3}\le 6$
43. $\sqrt{x-3}\le 4$
44. $\sqrt{8x+1}\ge 7$

45. **Construction** The diameter d in inches of a rope needed to lift a weight of w tons is given by the formula $d=\frac{\sqrt{15w}}{\pi}$. How much weight can be lifted with a rope with a diameter of 1.5 in.?

46. **Geometry** The length of a diagonal d of a rectangular prism is given by $d=\sqrt{\ell^2+w^2+h^2}$, where ℓ is the length, w is the width, and h is the height.

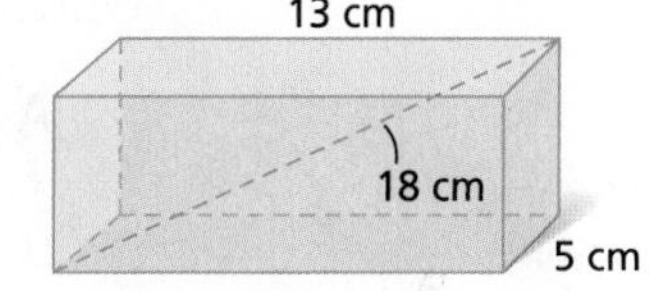

a. What is the height of the prism shown? Round to the nearest tenth.

b. **What if...?** Suppose that the length, width, and height of the prism are doubled. What effect will this change have on the length of the diagonal?

LINK

Tornadoes

The Fujita Tornado Scale goes up to category F12, even though scientists expect that Earth's most powerful tornadoes will reach wind speeds of no higher than those of category F5.

Solve each equation for the indicated variable.

47. $r=\sqrt{\frac{A}{\pi}}$ for A
48. $r=\sqrt[3]{\frac{3V}{4\pi}}$ for V
49. $v=\sqrt{\frac{2E}{m}}$ for E

50. **Tornadoes** The Fujita Tornado Scale is used to estimate the wind velocity of a tornado based on the damage that the tornado causes. The equation $V=k(F+2)^{\frac{3}{2}}$ can be used to determine a tornado's minimum wind velocity V in miles per hour, where k is a constant and F is the tornado's category number on the Fujita Scale.

Fujita Tornado Scale

Damage Level	Category	Minimum Wind Velocity (mi/h)
Moderate	F1	73
Significant	F2	113
Severe	F3	158
Devastating	F4	207
Incredible	F5	261

a. Based on the information in the table, what is the value of the constant k?

b. What would be the minimum wind velocity of an F6 tornado?

c. Winds on Neptune can reach velocities of more than 600 mi/h. Use the equation given above to determine the Fujita category of this wind velocity.

51. **Amusement Parks** For a spinning amusement park ride, the velocity v in meters per second of a car moving around a curve with a radius r meters is given by $v=\sqrt{ar}$, where a is the car's acceleration in m/s^2.

a. For safety reasons, a ride has a maximum acceleration of 39.2 m/s^2. If the cars on the ride have a velocity of 14 m/s, what is the smallest radius that any curve on the ride may have?

b. What is the acceleration of a car moving at 8 m/s around a curve with a radius of 2.5 m?

52. This problem will prepare you for the Multi-Step Test Prep on page 636.

The time T in seconds for a pendulum to complete one back-and-forth swing is given by $T = 2\pi\sqrt{\frac{L}{9.8}}$, where L is the length of the pendulum in meters.

a. Find the length of a pendulum that completes one back-and-forth swing in 2.2 s. Round to the nearest hundredth of a meter.

b. A clockmaker needs a pendulum that will complete 120 back-and-forth swings in one minute. To the nearest hundredth of a meter, how long should the pendulum be?

53. Art Gabriel plans to cover a circular area on a mural with yellow paint.

a. Write a radical inequality that can be used to determine the possible radius r of the circle given that Gabriel has enough paint to cover at most A ft^2.

b. If Gabriel can cover up to 80 ft^2, is 20 a reasonable value of r? Explain.

54. ERROR ANALYSIS Below are two solutions to the equation $2\sqrt{3x+3} = 12$. Which is incorrect? Explain the error.

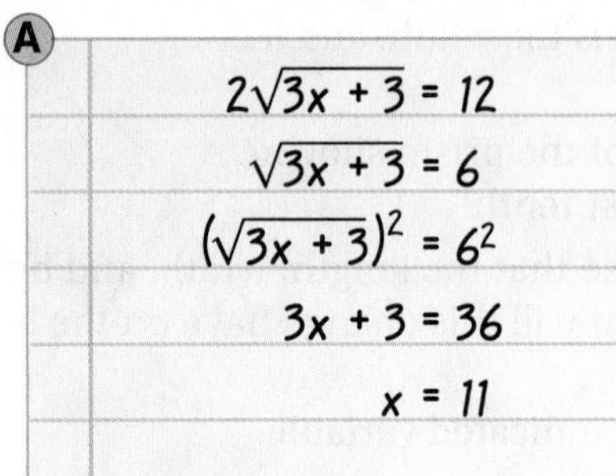

A

$2\sqrt{3x+3} = 12$

$\sqrt{3x+3} = 6$

$(\sqrt{3x+3})^2 = 6^2$

$3x + 3 = 36$

$x = 11$

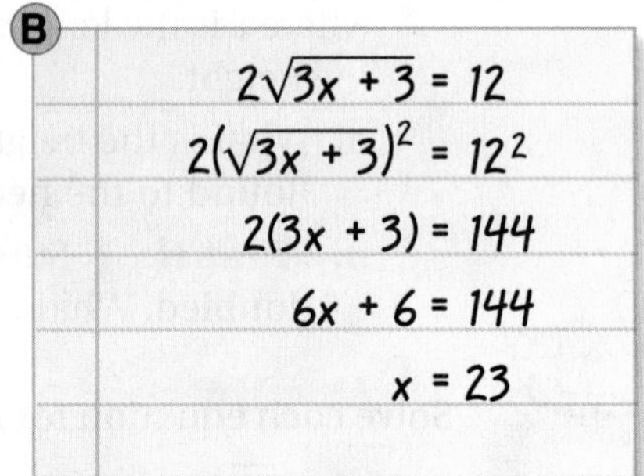

B

$2\sqrt{3x+3} = 12$

$2(\sqrt{3x+3})^2 = 12^2$

$2(3x+3) = 144$

$6x + 6 = 144$

$x = 23$

Graphing Calculator **Use a graphing calculator to solve each equation. Graph each side of the equation on the same screen, and find the point(s) of intersection.**

55. $1.6x - 4 = 1.4\sqrt{x + 8.7}$ **56.** $3(x + 7.4)^{\frac{2}{3}} = 8.8$ **57.** $\sqrt[3]{x^2 + 4.2} = 2.7x - 4.2$

58. Multi-Step On a clear day, the approximate distance d in miles that a person can see is given by $d = 1.2116\sqrt{h}$, where h is the person's height in feet above the ocean.

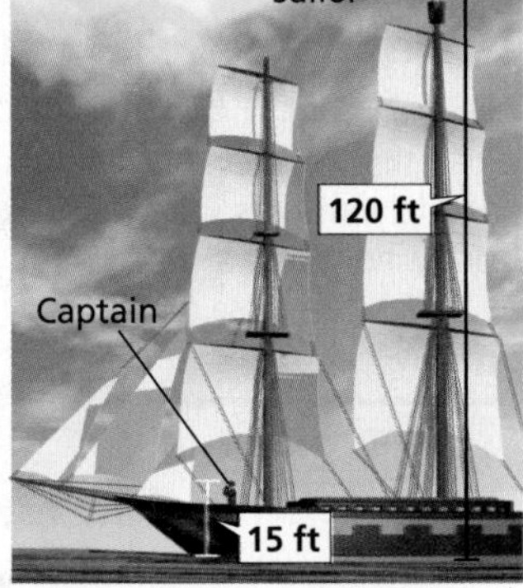

a. To the nearest tenth of a mile, how far can the captain on the clipper ship see?

b. How much farther, to the nearest tenth of a mile, will the sailor be able to see than will the captain?

c. A pirate ship is approaching the clipper ship at a relative speed of 10 mi/h. Approximately how many minutes sooner will the sailor be able to see the pirate ship than will the captain?

59. Chemistry The formula $s = \sqrt[3]{\frac{m}{\rho}}$ relates the side length s of a metal cube to its mass m and its density ρ. The density of gold is 19.30 g/cm^3, and the density of lead is 11.34 g/cm^3. How much greater is the mass of a cube of gold than the mass of a cube of lead if both cubes have a side length of 5 cm?

60. Critical Thinking Without solving the equation, how can you tell that $\sqrt{5x + 17} + 5 = 2$ has no real solutions?

61. Write About It Describe how solving a radical equation is similar to solving a rational equation.

TEST PREP

62. Solve $\sqrt[3]{2x+4} = 3$.

Ⓐ −0.5 Ⓑ −1.5 Ⓒ 2.5 Ⓓ 11.5

63. How many solutions does $x - 1 = \sqrt{5x - 9}$ have?

Ⓕ 0 Ⓖ 1 Ⓗ 2 Ⓙ 3

64. The surface area S of a cone is given by the formula $S = \pi\sqrt{r^2 + h^2}$, where r is the radius of the base and h is the height. What is the approximate height of a cone with a surface area of 40 square inches and a base radius of 8 inches?

Ⓐ 5 inches Ⓒ 15 inches

Ⓑ 10 inches Ⓓ 20 inches

65. The equation $V = \left(\frac{A}{6}\right)^{\frac{3}{2}}$ relates the volume V of a cube to its surface area A. Which of the following is equivalent to this equation?

Ⓕ $A = 6V^{\frac{2}{3}}$ Ⓖ $A = (6V)^{\frac{2}{3}}$ Ⓗ $A = 36V^{\frac{1}{3}}$ Ⓙ $A = (216V)^{\frac{1}{2}}$

66. **Gridded Response** What value of x makes $(2x - 3)^{\frac{1}{4}} = 3$ a true statement?

CHALLENGE AND EXTEND

Indicate whether each of the following statements is sometimes, always, or never true. Equations of the form $\sqrt{x+a} = b$ have at least one real solution when

67. Both a and b are positive.

68. Both a and b are negative.

69. a is negative and b is positive.

70. a is positive and b is negative.

Solve each equation.

71. $\sqrt{x} = \frac{9}{\sqrt{x}}$

72. $\sqrt{\sqrt{x+2}} = 4$

73. $\sqrt{x^2 - 64} = x - 4$

74. **Biology** The surface area S of a human body in square meters can be approximated by $S = \sqrt{\frac{hm}{36}}$, where h is height in meters and m is mass in kilograms. Between the ages of 4 and 17, an athlete's height increased by 75% and mass increased by 350%. By approximately what percent did the surface area of the athlete's skin increase?

SPIRAL REVIEW

75. **Entertainment** The cost of driving through a safari park is \$2.00 per person and \$10.00 per car. For each car, the total cost C can be modeled by the function $C(n) = 2.00n + 10.00$, where n is the number of people. *(Lesson 2-6)*

   a. The manager of the park announces a half-price discount on the charge per car. Write the new cost function $D(n)$. Assume that the charge per person does not change.

   b. Graph $C(n)$ and $D(n)$ in the same coordinate plane.

   c. Describe the transformation that has been applied.

Use inverse operations to write the inverse of each function. *(Lesson 7-2)*

76. $f(x) = \frac{x}{2} + 4$

77. $f(x) = -3x - 1$

78. $f(x) = \frac{x-2}{7}$

Simplify each expression. Assume that all variables are positive. *(Lesson 8-6)*

79. $\sqrt[3]{64x^9}$

80. $\sqrt[4]{\frac{x^8}{81}}$

81. $\sqrt[3]{\frac{18x^{-2}}{x^4}}$

CHAPTER 8

SECTION 8B

MULTI-STEP TEST PREP

Radical Functions

Tick Tock A pendulum clock keeps time by using weights, gears, and a pendulum. The length of the pendulum determines how fast it swings, and the speed of the pendulum determines how fast the hands of the clock advance.

A clockmaker is building a replica of an antique pendulum clock for a museum display and finds that it is running too slowly. As he attempts to fix the clock, he tries pendulums of different lengths. He records the pendulum length and period data shown in the table. The period of a pendulum is the time it takes for the pendulum to complete one back-and-forth swing.

Pendulum Swings	
Length (cm)	Period (s)
10	0.6
20	0.9
30	1.1
40	1.3
50	1.4
60	1.6

1. Create a scatter plot of the data, using pendulum length as the independent variable and period as the dependent variable.
2. Experiment with a graphing calculator to find a function rule that models the data in the scatter plot. Describe your model as a transformation of $f(x) = \sqrt{x}$.
3. What is a reasonable domain for this situation? Explain.
4. Use your model to determine the period of a pendulum that has a length of 16 cm. Round to the nearest tenth of a second.
5. From his observations, the clockmaker concludes that the pendulum needs to have a period of 1 s. To the nearest centimeter, how long should the pendulum be?
6. The function $y = 2\pi\sqrt{\frac{x}{9.8}}$ gives the period y of a pendulum in seconds in terms of the pendulum's length x in meters. Graph this function with the data from the table and explain whether the function is a reasonable model for the data.

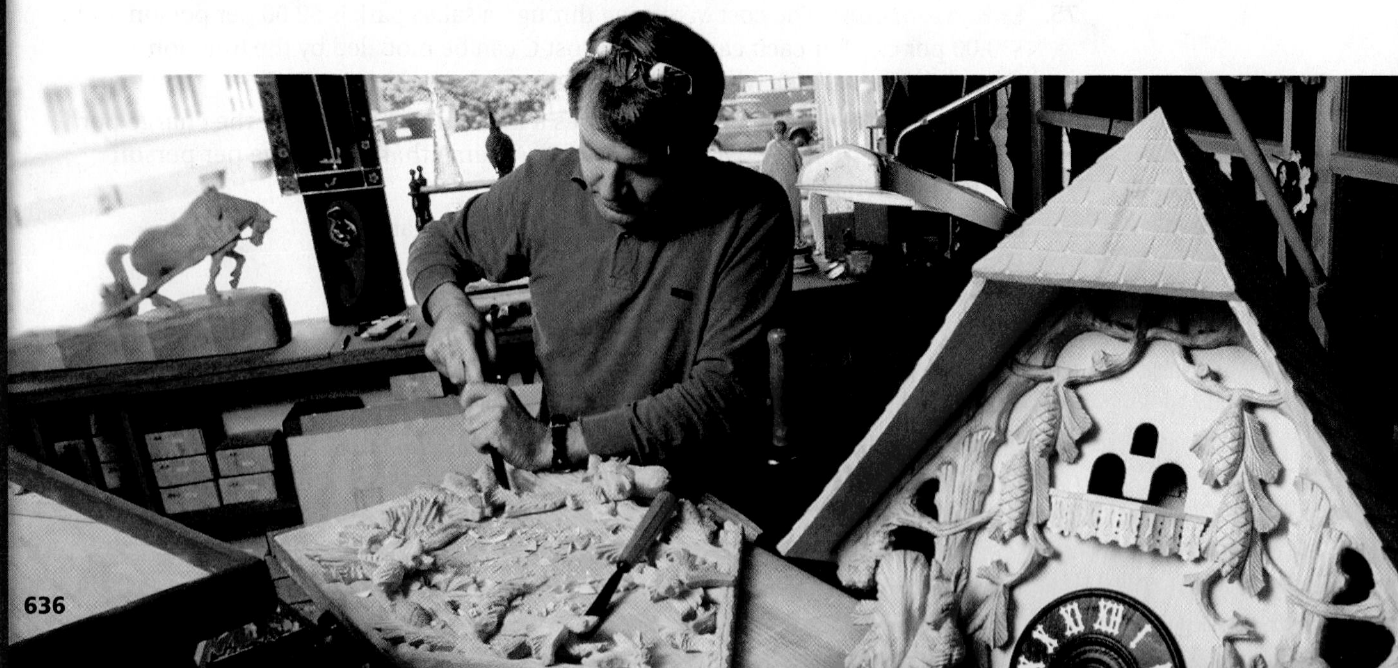

Quiz for Lessons 8-6 Through 8-8

8-6 Radical Expressions and Rational Exponents

Simplify each expression. Assume that all variables are positive.

1. $\sqrt{32x^3}$
2. $\sqrt[3]{8y^{12}z^6}$
3. $\sqrt[4]{\frac{a^4}{9}}$

Write each expression in radical form, and simplify.

4. $4^{\frac{3}{2}}$
5. $16^{\frac{5}{4}}$
6. $(-27)^{\frac{2}{3}}$

Write each expression by using rational exponents.

7. $\sqrt[4]{8^3}$
8. $(\sqrt[5]{243})^2$
9. $(\sqrt[3]{-1000})^2$

10. In an experiment involving fruit flies, the initial population is 112. The growth of the population can be modeled by the function $n(t) = 112 \cdot 2^{\frac{t}{50}}$, where n is the number of fruit flies and t is the time in hours. Based on this model, what is the population of fruit flies after 1 week?

8-7 Radical Functions

Graph each function, and identify its domain and range.

11. $f(x) = -\sqrt{x} + 4$
12. $f(x) = \sqrt[3]{x+1}$

13. Water is draining from a tank connected to two pipes. The speed f in feet per second at which water drains through the first pipe can be modeled by $f(x) = \sqrt{64(x-2)}$, where x is the depth of the water in the tank in feet. The graph of the corresponding function for the second pipe is a translation of f 4 units right. Write the corresponding function g, and use it to estimate the speed at which water drains through the second pipe when the depth of the water is 10 ft.

14. Use the description to write the square-root function g. The parent function $f(x) = \sqrt{x}$ is reflected across the x-axis and then translated 2 units right and 3 units down.

Graph each inequality.

15. $y > \sqrt{x} + 4$
16. $y \leq \sqrt{x-2}$

8-8 Solving Radical Equations and Inequalities

Solve each equation.

17. $-2\sqrt[3]{5x-5} = -10$
18. $\sqrt{x+4} = x - 8$
19. $3\sqrt[3]{x-2} = \sqrt[3]{6x}$

20. The formula $d = \sqrt[3]{\frac{4w}{0.02847}}$ relates the average diameter d of a cultured pearl in millimeters to its weight w in carats. To the nearest tenth of a carat, what is the weight of a cultured pearl with an average diameter of 7 mm?

Solve each inequality.

21. $\sqrt{x+5} < 4$
22. $\sqrt[3]{2x} \geq -2$
23. $\sqrt{x-6} - 10 \leq 4$

CHAPTER 8

Study Guide: Review

Vocabulary

Complete the sentences below with vocabulary words from the list above.

1. A(n) ___?___ is a function whose rule is a ratio of two polynomials.

2. A(n) ___?___ is a relationship that can be written in the form $y = kx$, where k is the ___?___.

8-1 Variation Functions *(pp. 569–576)*

EXAMPLES

■ **The cost in dollars of apples a varies directly as the number of pounds p, and $a = 3.12$ when $p = 2.4$. Find p when $a = 1.04$.**

$\frac{a_1}{p_1} = \frac{a_2}{p_2}$ *Use a proportion.*

$\frac{3.12}{2.4} = \frac{1.04}{p_2}$ *Substitute.*

$3.12p = 2.4(1.04)$ *Find the cross products.*

$p = 0.8$ *Solve for p.*

Apples that cost \$1.04 have a weight of 0.8 lb.

■ **The base b of a parallelogram with fixed area varies inversely as the height h, and $b = 12$ cm when $h = 8$ cm. Find b when $h = 3$ cm.**

$b = \frac{k}{h}$ *b varies inversely with h.*

$12 = \frac{k}{8}$ *Substitute.*

$k = 96$ *Solve for k.*

$b = \frac{96}{h}$ *Substitute 96 for k.*

$b = \frac{96}{3}$ *Substitute 3 for h.*

$b = 32$ *Solve for b.*

The base is 32 cm when the height is 3 cm.

EXERCISES

Given: y varies directly as x. Write and graph each direct variation function.

3. $y = 2$ when $x = 6$

4. $y = 4$ when $x = 1$

5. The number of tiles n needed to cover a floor varies directly as the area a of the floor, and $n = 180$ when $a = 20\text{ ft}^2$. Find n when $a = 34\text{ ft}^2$.

6. The simple interest I earned over a particular period of time varies jointly as the principal P and rate r, and $I = \$264$ when $P = \$1100$ and $r = 0.12$. Find P when $I = \$360$ and $r = 0.09$.

Given: y varies inversely as x. Write and graph each inverse variation function.

7. $y = 3$ when $x = 2$

8. $y = 4$ when $x = 1$

9. For a fixed voltage, the current I flowing in a wire varies inversely as the resistance R of the wire. If the current is 8 amperes when the resistance is 15 ohms, what will the resistance be when the current is 5 amperes?

10. Determine whether the data set represents a direct variation, an inverse variation, or neither.

x	2	5	10
y	25	10	5

8-2 Multiplying and Dividing Rational Expressions *(pp. 577–582)*

EXAMPLES

- **Simplify $\frac{4-x}{x^2-x-20}$. Identify any x-values for which the expression is undefined.**

$$\frac{-1(x+4)}{(x-5)(x+4)} = \frac{-1}{x-5}$$ *Factor. Then divide out common factors.*

Undefined at $x = 5$ and $x = -4$

- **Divide. Assume that all expressions are defined.**

$$\frac{x^2-9}{x+2} \div \frac{x+3}{x^2+7x+10}$$

$$\frac{x^2-9}{x+2} \cdot \frac{x^2+7x+10}{x+3}$$ *Rewrite as multiplication.*

$$\frac{(x-3)(x+3)}{x+2} \cdot \frac{(x+2)(x+5)}{x+3} = (x-3)(x+5)$$

EXERCISES

Simplify. Identify any x-values for which the expression is undefined.

11. $\frac{24x^{14}}{9x^{16}}$ **12.** $\frac{6x^3}{3x+12}$ **13.** $\frac{x^2+x-12}{x^2+5x+4}$

Multiply. Assume that all expressions are defined.

14. $\frac{x+5}{3x+1} \cdot \frac{9x+3}{x^2-25}$ **15.** $\frac{x}{x-4} \cdot \frac{-x+2}{x^2+x-6}$

16. $\frac{x^2+2x-3}{x^2-x-2} \cdot \frac{x-2}{x+3}$ **17.** $\frac{9x^2-1}{x^2-9} \cdot \frac{x+3}{3x+1}$

Divide. Assume that all expressions are defined.

18. $\frac{x^3y}{4xy^4} \div \frac{x}{8y^2}$ **19.** $\frac{x^2+2x-15}{x-2} \div \frac{x^2-9}{2x-4}$

20. $\frac{3x-21}{3x} \div \frac{x^2-49}{x^2+7x}$ **21.** $\frac{x^2+4x+3}{x^2+2x-8} \div \frac{3x+3}{x-2}$

8-3 Adding and Subtracting Rational Expressions *(pp. 583–590)*

EXAMPLES

- **Add. Identify any x-values for which the expression is undefined.**

$$\frac{6x-3}{x^2-x-12} + \frac{x}{x+3}$$

$$\frac{6x-3}{(x-4)(x+3)} + \frac{x}{x+3}\left(\frac{x-4}{x-4}\right)$$

$$\frac{6x-3+x(x-4)}{(x-4)(x+3)}$$ *Add the numerators.*

$$\frac{x^2+2x-3}{(x-4)(x+3)}$$ *Simplify the numerator.*

$$\frac{(x+3)(x-1)}{(x-4)(x+3)} = \frac{x-1}{x-4}$$ *Factor the numerator.*

Undefined at $x = 4$ and $x = -3$

- **Simplify. Assume that all expressions are defined.**

$$\frac{\frac{x+2}{6x}}{\frac{x}{x-4}} = \frac{\frac{x+2}{6x}(6x)(x-4)}{\frac{x}{x-4}(6x)(x-4)}$$ *The LCD is $(6x)(x-4)$.*

$$\frac{(x+2)(x-4)}{x(6x)} = \frac{(x+2)(x-4)}{6x^2}$$

EXERCISES

Add. Identify any x-values for which the expression is undefined.

22. $\frac{4}{x^2+4} + \frac{x^2+8}{x^2+4}$ **23.** $\frac{1}{x+3} + \frac{1}{x-3}$

24. $\frac{x}{x^2-4} + \frac{1}{x-2}$ **25.** $\frac{2x-3}{3x+7} + \frac{6}{4x-1}$

Find the least common multiple for each pair.

26. $x^2 - 9$ and $x^2 - 6x + 9$

27. $x^2 + 2x - 35$ and $x^2 + 9x + 14$

Subtract. Identify any x-values for which the expression is undefined.

28. $\frac{2x}{x+4} - \frac{3}{x+4}$ **29.** $\frac{x}{x+5} - \frac{5}{x-5}$

30. $\frac{1}{x^2-x-6} - \frac{x}{x+2}$ **31.** $\frac{2x}{2x+1} - \frac{7}{3x-1}$

Simplify. Assume that all expressions are defined.

32. $\frac{\frac{x-6}{5}}{\frac{x+2}{8}}$ **33.** $\frac{\frac{x+3}{3x}}{\frac{x^2-9}{6x-9}}$ **34.** $\frac{\frac{x}{4}-\frac{1}{x}}{\frac{x+2}{x-2}}$

35. A jet's average speed is 520 mi/h when flying from Dallas to Chicago and 580 mi/h on the return trip. What is the jet's average speed for the entire trip?

8-4 Rational Functions *(pp. 592–599)*

EXAMPLES

■ **Using the graph of $f(x) = \frac{1}{x}$ as a guide, describe the transformation and graph $g(x) = \frac{1}{x} - 3$.**

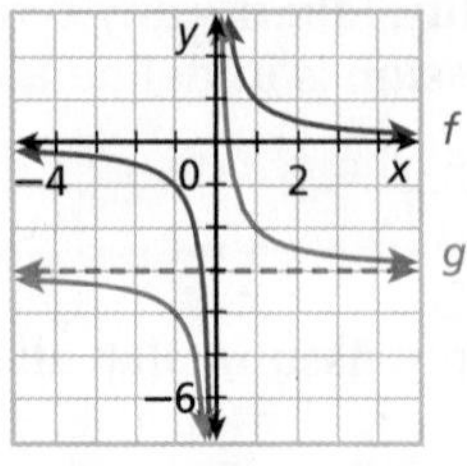

Because $k = -3$, translate f down 3 units.

■ **Identify the zeros and asymptotes of $f(x) = \frac{2x-4}{x+3}$. Then graph.**

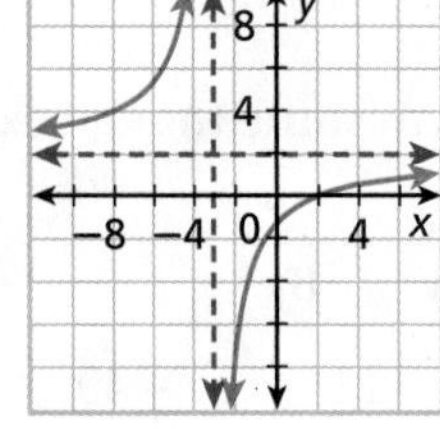

Zero: 2

Vertical asymptote: $x = -3$

Horizontal asymptote: $y = 2$

EXERCISES

Using the graph of $f(x) = \frac{1}{x}$ as a guide, describe the transformation and graph each function.

36. $g(x) = \dfrac{1}{x-4}$

37. $g(x) = \dfrac{1}{x-2} + 3$

Identify the asymptotes, domain, and range of each function.

38. $f(x) = \dfrac{2}{x-1} - 3$

39. $f(x) = \dfrac{3}{x+2} + 1$

Identify the zeros and asymptotes of each function. Then graph.

40. $f(x) = \dfrac{x^2 - 3x}{x+4}$

41. $f(x) = \dfrac{x-3}{x^2 + 6x + 5}$

42. $f(x) = \dfrac{2x-4}{x+3}$

43. $f(x) = \dfrac{x^2 - 9}{x-2}$

44. Identify holes in the graph of $f(x) = \frac{x^2 - 3x - 18}{x+3}$. Then graph.

8-5 Solving Rational Equations and Inequalities *(pp. 600–607)*

EXAMPLE

■ **Solve the equation $\frac{30}{x+1} + x = 10$.**

$$\frac{30}{x+1}(x+1) + x(x+1) = 10(x+1)$$

$30 + x^2 + x = 10x + 10$ *Simplify. $x \neq -1$*

$x^2 - 9x + 20 = 0$ *Write in standard form.*

$(x-4)(x-5) = 0$ *Factor.*

$x = 4$ or $x = 5$ *Solve for x.*

EXERCISES

Solve each equation.

45. $x - \dfrac{6}{x} = 1$

46. $\dfrac{4x}{x-5} = \dfrac{3x+5}{x-5}$

47. $\dfrac{3x}{x+2} = \dfrac{2x+2}{x+2}$

48. $\dfrac{x}{x+4} + \dfrac{x}{2} = \dfrac{2x}{2x+8}$

Solve each inequality.

49. $\dfrac{x+4}{x} > -2$

50. $\dfrac{2}{x-3} < 4$

8-6 Radical Expressions and Rational Exponents *(pp. 610–617)*

EXAMPLES

Simplify each expression. Assume that all variables are positive.

■ $\sqrt[3]{-8x^9} = \sqrt[3]{(-2^3)} \cdot \sqrt[3]{x^3} \cdot \sqrt[3]{x^3} \cdot \sqrt[3]{x^3} = -2x^3$

■ $\sqrt[4]{8x^6} \cdot \sqrt[4]{2x^2} = \sqrt[4]{16x^8} = \sqrt[4]{2^4} \cdot \sqrt[4]{x^4} \cdot \sqrt[4]{x^4} = 2x^2$

■ **Write the expression $\left(\sqrt{16}\right)^3$ by using rational exponents.**

$16^{\frac{3}{2}}$ $\qquad \left(\sqrt[n]{a}\right)^m = a^{\frac{m}{n}}$

EXERCISES

Simplify each expression. Assume that all variables are positive.

51. $\sqrt[3]{27x^6}$

52. $\sqrt[4]{81x^{12}}$

53. $\sqrt[3]{\dfrac{8x^3}{3}}$

Write each expression by using rational exponents.

54. $\left(\sqrt[3]{-27}\right)^2$

55. $\sqrt[4]{16^3}$

56. $\left(\sqrt{9}\right)^3$

Simplify each expression.

57. $17^{\frac{1}{3}} \cdot 17^{\frac{2}{3}}$

58. $(9^4)^{\frac{1}{2}}$

59. $\left(\dfrac{1}{16}\right)^{\frac{1}{4}}$

8-7 Radical Functions (pp. 619–627)

EXAMPLE

■ **Graph $f(x) = \frac{\sqrt{x+8}}{2}$, and identify its domain and range.**

Make a table of values. Then graph.

x	y
−8	0
−7	0.5
−4	1
1	1.5
8	2

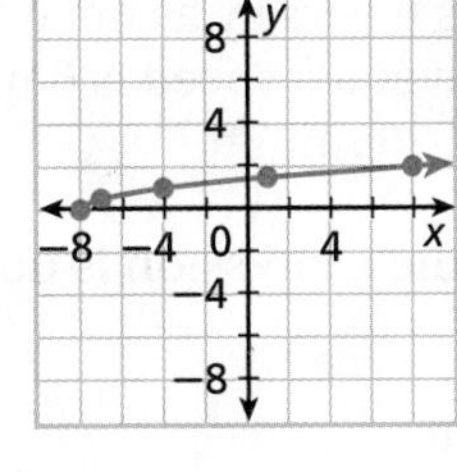

D: $\{x \mid x \geq -8\}$; R: $\{y \mid y \geq 0\}$

EXERCISES

Graph each function, and identify its domain and range.

60. $f(x) = \sqrt{x} + 5$ **61.** $f(x) = -4\sqrt[3]{x}$

Using the graph of $f(x) = \sqrt{x}$ as a guide, describe the transformation and graph each function.

62. $g(x) = -\sqrt{x} + 1$ **63.** $h(x) = \sqrt{4x}$

64. $j(x) = \sqrt{-(x-8)}$ **65.** $k(x) = -\frac{1}{2}\sqrt{x} + 1$

66. Use the description to write the square-root function g. The parent function $f(x) = \sqrt{x}$ is stretched vertically by a factor of 3 and translated 4 units left.

Graph each inequality.

67. $y < \sqrt{x}$ **68.** $y < \sqrt[3]{x+4}$

8-8 Solving Radical Equations and Inequalities (pp. 628–635)

EXAMPLES

Solve each equation.

■ $4\sqrt[3]{x-4} = 12$

$\sqrt[3]{x-4} = 3$ *Divide by 4.*

$\left(\sqrt[3]{x-4}\right)^3 = 3^3$ *Cube both sides.*

$x - 4 = 27$ *Simplify.*

$x = 31$ *Solve for x.*

■ $\sqrt{x+15} = x - 5$

$\left(\sqrt{x+15}\right)^2 = (x-5)^2$ *Square both sides.*

$x + 15 = x^2 - 10x + 25$

$x^2 - 11x + 10 = 0$ *Write in standard form.*

$(x-10)(x-1) = 0$ *Factor.*

$x = 10$ or $x = 1$ *Solve for x.*

Use substitution to check for extraneous solutions.

$\sqrt{x+15}$	$= x - 5$
$\sqrt{10+15}$	$10 - 5$
5	5 ✔

$\sqrt{x+15}$	$= x - 5$
$\sqrt{1+15}$	$1 - 5$
4	−4 ✘

The solution $x = 1$ is extraneous. The only solution is $x = 10$.

EXERCISES

Solve each equation.

69. $\sqrt{x+6} - 7 = -2$ **70.** $\frac{\sqrt[3]{2x-2}}{6} = 1$

71. $\sqrt{10x} = 3\sqrt{x+1}$ **72.** $2\sqrt[5]{x} = \sqrt[5]{64}$

73. $\sqrt{6x-12} = x - 2$ **74.** $\sqrt{x+1} = x - 5$

75. $(4x+7)^{\frac{1}{2}} = 3$ **76.** $(x-4)^{\frac{1}{4}} = 3$

77. $x = (2x+35)^{\frac{1}{2}}$ **78.** $(x+3)^{\frac{1}{3}} = -6$

Solve each inequality.

79. $\sqrt{x-4} \leq 3$ **80.** $\sqrt{2x+7} - 6 > -1$

81. $\sqrt{3x} - 4 < 2$ **82.** $\sqrt[3]{x-1} > -2$

83. The time T in seconds required for a pendulum to complete one back-and-forth swing can be determined from the formula $T = 2\pi\sqrt{\frac{L}{9.8}}$, where L is the length of the pendulum in meters. Estimate the length of a pendulum that completes one back-and-forth swing in 2.5 s.

84. A tetrahedron is a triangular pyramid with four congruent faces. The side length s in meters of a tetrahedron is given by the formula $s = \left(6V\sqrt{2}\right)^{\frac{1}{3}}$, where V is the volume of the tetrahedron in cubic meters. What is the volume of a tetrahedron with a side length of 8 m? Round to the nearest tenth.

CHAPTER 8

CHAPTER TEST

1. The monthly minimum payment p due on a certain credit card with a fixed rate varies directly as the balance b, and $p = \$19.80$ when $b = \$1100$. Find p when $b = \$3000$.

2. The time t that it takes Hannah to bike to school varies inversely as her average speed s. If she can bike to school in 25 min when her average speed is 6 mi/h, what would her average speed need to be to get to school in 20 min?

3. Simplify $\frac{x^2 - x - 6}{x^2 - 4x + 3}$. Identify any x-values for which the expression is undefined.

Multiply or divide. Assume that all expressions are defined.

4. $\frac{x - 9}{2x - 10} \cdot \frac{x - 5}{x^2 - 81}$

5. $\frac{3x^3 - 9x^2}{x^2 - 16} \div \frac{2x - 6}{x^2 - 8x + 16}$

Add or subtract. Identify any x-values for which the expression is undefined.

6. $\frac{5}{x - 5} + \frac{x}{2x - 10}$

7. $\frac{5x}{x - 7} - \frac{9x - 6}{x + 3}$

8. Lorraine averaged 62 words per minute when typing the first 3 pages of a 6-page report. Her average typing speed for the last 3 pages was 45 words per minute. To the nearest word per minute, what was Lorraine's average typing speed for the entire report?

9. Identify the zeros and asymptotes of $f(x) = \frac{3x + 3}{x + 2}$. Then graph.

Solve each equation.

10. $2 + \frac{3}{x - 1} = 10$

11. $\frac{x}{x - 1} + \frac{x}{3} = \frac{5}{x - 1}$

12. Beth can tile a floor in about 6 h. When Beth and Mike work together, they can tile a floor in about 2.4 h. About how long would it take Mike to tile a floor if he works by himself?

Simplify each expression. Assume that all variables are positive.

13. $\sqrt[3]{-32x^6}$

14. $8^{-\frac{2}{3}}$

15. $\frac{27^{\frac{2}{3}}}{27^{\frac{1}{3}}}$

16. Write the expression $\sqrt[5]{x^2}$ by using a rational exponent.

17. Graph the function $f(x) = \sqrt{x + 2} - 4$ and identify its domain and range.

18. Graph the inequality $y \le \sqrt{x} - 2$.

Solve each equation.

19. $\sqrt{x + 7} = 5$

20. $\sqrt{2x + 1} = \sqrt{x + 9}$

21. $(3x + 1)^{\frac{1}{3}} = -2$

22. The formula $s = \sqrt{\frac{A}{4.828}}$ can be used to approximate the side length s of a regular octagon with area A. A stop sign is shaped like a regular octagon with a side length of 12.4 in. To the nearest square inch, what is the area of the stop sign?

23. Solve the inequality $\sqrt{2x + 1} > 3$.

COLLEGE ENTRANCE EXAM PRACTICE

FOCUS ON SAT

There is a set of criteria that your calculator must meet in order for it to be allowed in the testing facility when you take the SAT. For example, calculators that make noise or have QWERTY keypads are not allowed. For complete guidelines, check www.collegeboard.com.

If you do not already have a graphing calculator, consider purchasing or borrowing one because it may give you an advantage when solving some problems on the SAT. Be sure to spend time getting used to any new calculator before test day.

You may want to time yourself as you take this practice test. It should take you about 6 minutes to complete.

1. Which of the following functions is graphed below?

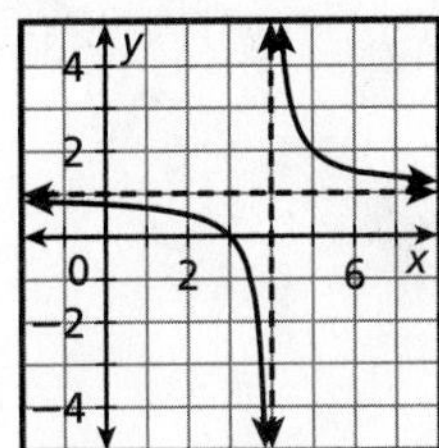

(A) $f(x) = (x + 3)(x - 4)$

(B) $f(x) = (x - 3)(x + 4)$

(C) $f(x) = \frac{x - 3}{x - 4}$

(D) $f(x) = \frac{x - 3}{x + 4}$

(E) $f(x) = \frac{x + 3}{x + 4}$

2. If each of the following expressions is defined, which is equivalent to $x - 1$?

(A) $\frac{(x + 1)(x - 1)}{x - 1}$

(B) $\frac{(x - 1)(x + 2)}{x + 1} \cdot \frac{x + 1}{x + 2}$

(C) $\frac{(x + 1)(x + 2)}{x - 2} \div \frac{x + 2}{x - 2}$

(D) $\frac{x + 1}{x + 2} + \frac{x - 1}{x + 2}$

(E) $\frac{2x - 2}{x - 2} - \frac{x - 1}{x - 2}$

3. The cube root of the square of a real number n is 16. What is the value of n?

(A) $\frac{4}{3}$

(B) $\frac{8}{3}$

(C) 4

(D) 12

(E) 64

4. If y varies inversely as the square of x and $y = 1$ when $x = 2$, what is the value of y when $x = -4$?

(A) -2

(B) $-\frac{1}{2}$

(C) $\frac{1}{4}$

(D) 4

(E) 16

5. If $\sqrt[3]{12x + 28} = 4$, what is the value of x^3?

(A) -8

(B) 3

(C) 12

(D) 27

(E) 64

CHAPTER 8

TEST TACKLER

Standardized Test Strategies

Any Question Type: Use a Diagram

Diagrams are often useful when you are solving problems. For some problems, a diagram is provided for you and you must correctly interpret it. In other situations, you can sketch your own diagram to help you visualize a problem.

EXAMPLE 1

Short Response The height h of a square pyramid can be determined from the equation $h = \sqrt{\ell^2 - \left(\frac{s}{2}\right)^2}$, where ℓ is the slant height of the pyramid and s is the side length of the square base. What is the slant height ℓ of the square pyramid shown? Show your work.

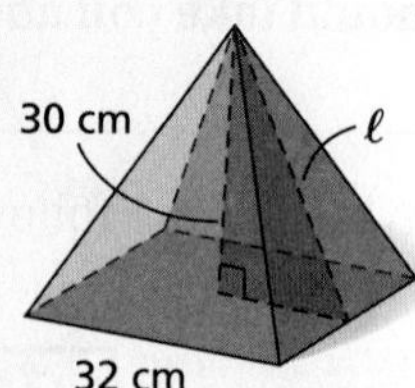

To solve this problem, you must use information from the diagram.

$30 = \sqrt{\ell^2 - \left(\frac{32}{2}\right)^2}$	*Substitute 30 for h and 32 for s.*
$30 = \sqrt{\ell^2 - 16^2}$	*Simplify.*
$900 = \ell^2 - 256$	*Square both sides.*
$1156 = \ell^2$	*Add 256 to both sides.*
$\pm 34 = \ell$	*Solve for ℓ.*

The slant height of the pyramid is 34 centimeters.

EXAMPLE 2

Multiple Choice A circular fountain with radius r feet is built into a square base with a side length of $3r$ feet. What is the probability that a penny hitting the square base at random will land in the circular fountain?

Ⓐ $\frac{\pi}{9}$ Ⓑ $\frac{\pi}{3}$ Ⓒ $\frac{1}{3}$ Ⓓ $\frac{1}{9}$

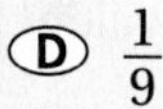

A diagram would be helpful with this problem. Sketch a square with side length 3r to represent the square base. Then sketch a circle inside it with radius r to represent the circular fountain.

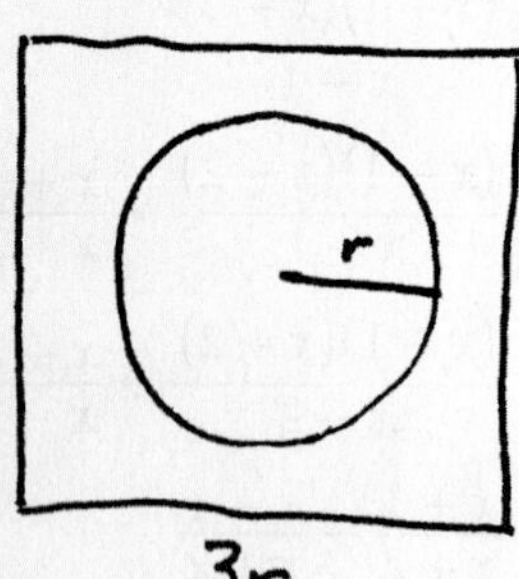

$\frac{\pi r^2}{(3r)^2}$	*The probability that the penny will land in the fountain is the ratio of the area of the fountain to the area of the base.*
$\frac{\pi r^2}{9r^2} = \frac{\pi}{9}$	*Simplify.*

The correct answer is A.

If you sketch your own diagram to help you solve a problem, be sure to label it with any measurements you are given.

Read each test item and answer the questions that follow.

Item A
Multiple Choice What is the area of this composite figure?

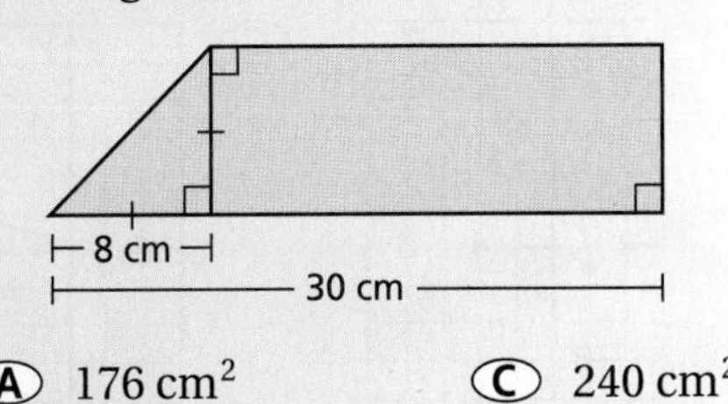

Ⓐ 176 cm^2 Ⓒ 240 cm^2

Ⓑ 208 cm^2 Ⓓ 272 cm^2

1. How can you use the information given in the diagram to determine the length of the rectangle?
2. Explain how you can use the diagram to determine the rectangle's width.
3. What is the area of the triangle? What is the area of the rectangle?

Item B
Multiple Choice A square courtyard has a perimeter of 200 meters. What is the approximate length of a sidewalk that lies along one of the courtyard's diagonals?

Ⓕ 50 meters Ⓗ 71 meters

Ⓖ 57 meters Ⓙ 87 meters

4. Sketch a diagram that can help you visualize the situation.
5. How can you use the information given in the problem to label each side of the courtyard in your diagram with its length?
6. Into what shapes does the diagonal sidewalk divide the courtyard?
7. What equation can you use to determine the length of the sidewalk?

Item C
Short Response What are the measures of the three numbered angles of this triangle? Explain how you determined your answer.

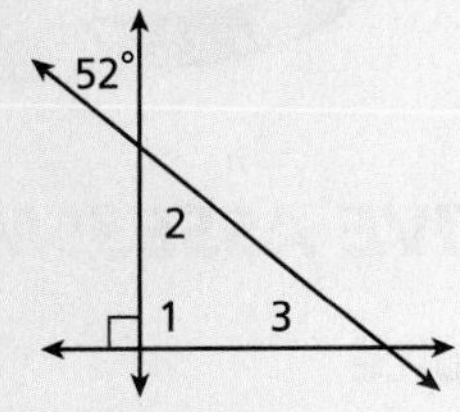

8. Based on the information in the diagram, what type of angle is $\angle 1$? What is its measure?
9. What is the relationship between the $52°$ angle and $\angle 2$? What is the measure of $\angle 2$?
10. How can you use the measures of $\angle 1$ and $\angle 2$ to determine the measure of $\angle 3$?

Item D
Extended Response A rectangular pool is surrounded on all four sides by a tiled lounging area. The length of the pool is 5 feet greater than the width. The width of the lounging area is 10 feet greater than twice the width of the pool. The length of the lounging area is 5 times the width of the pool.

a. Write a rational expression that represents the ratio of the area of the pool to the entire area of the pool and lounging area.

b. Determine the value of the ratio if the width of the pool is 30 feet.

11. Sketch a diagram that can help you visualize the situation.
12. Explain how you determined the labels for the dimensions of your diagram.
13. Is it necessary to draw your diagram to scale? Why or why not?
14. What expression represents the area of the pool? What expression represents the entire area of the pool and lounging area?

CHAPTER 8

STANDARDIZED TEST PREP

go.hrw.com
State Test Practice Online
KEYWORD: MB7 TestPrep

CUMULATIVE ASSESSMENT, CHAPTERS 1–8

Multiple Choice

1. Given: y varies jointly as x and z, and $y = 16$ when $x = \frac{1}{2}$ and $z = 8$. What equation represents the joint variation function?

   Ⓐ $y = \frac{4x}{z}$

   Ⓑ $y = 4x$

   Ⓒ $y = \frac{1}{4}xz$

   Ⓓ $y = 4xz$

2. What is the solution of the equation $\sqrt{3x + 2} = 3\sqrt{2x - 2}$?

   Ⓕ $x = \frac{4}{15}$

   Ⓖ $x = \frac{8}{15}$

   Ⓗ $x = \frac{4}{3}$

   Ⓙ $x = \frac{8}{3}$

3. Which is equivalent to $(3 - 5i)(2 + i)$?

   Ⓐ 11

   Ⓑ $11 - 7i$

   Ⓒ $11 + 7i$

   Ⓓ $1 - 7i$

4. Which is equivalent to $\frac{4x^2y^3}{5xy^2} \div \frac{2y}{10xy}$?

   Ⓕ $\frac{4y}{25}$

   Ⓖ $\frac{4x^2}{y}$

   Ⓗ $4x^2y$

   Ⓙ $4x^2y^5$

5. What is the slope of the line $3y = 2x + 9$?

   Ⓐ $\frac{2}{3}$

   Ⓑ $\frac{3}{2}$

   Ⓒ 3

   Ⓓ 9

6. Which expression can be simplified to a rational number?

   Ⓕ $\sqrt{1} + \sqrt{8}$

   Ⓖ $\sqrt{10} \cdot \sqrt{25}$

   Ⓗ $\left(\sqrt{15}\right)^2$

   Ⓙ $\sqrt{\frac{20}{4}}$

7. Which is the graph of the function $f(x) = 4\sqrt{x + 2} - 3$?

   Ⓐ 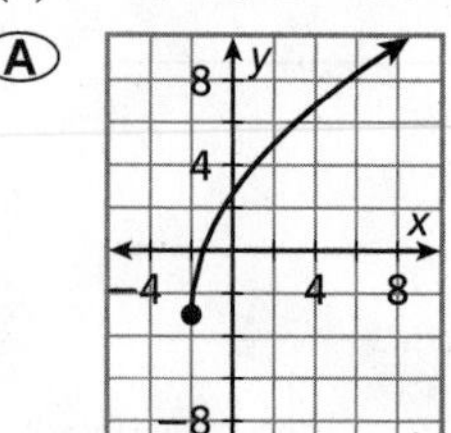

   Ⓒ 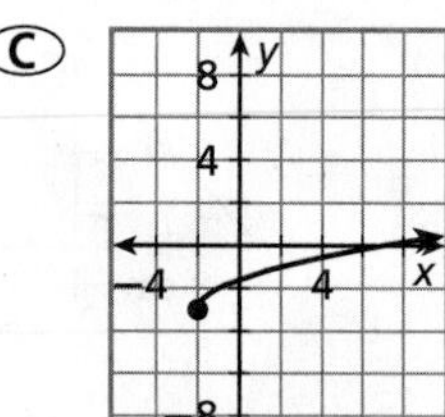

   Ⓑ 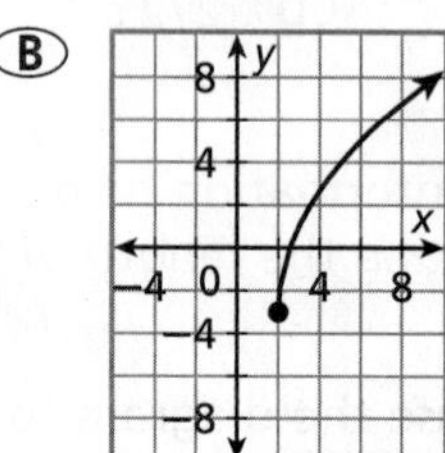

   Ⓓ 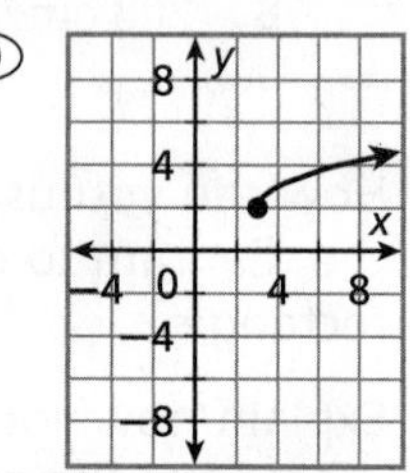

8. At track practice, Jamie ran 0.5 mile farther than twice the distance Rochelle ran. If x represents the distance in miles that Rochelle ran, which expression represents the distance that Jamie ran?

   Ⓕ $0.5(2x)$

   Ⓖ $0.5x + 2$

   Ⓗ $2(x + 0.5)$

   Ⓙ $2x + 0.5$

9. Which equation best describes the relationship between x and y shown in the table?

x	1	3	6	10	15
y	−1	5	14	26	41

   Ⓐ $y = -3x + 2$

   Ⓑ $y = -2x + 1$

   Ⓒ $y = 2x - 3$

   Ⓓ $y = 3x - 4$

10. A triangle with vertices at $(1, 4)$, $(-2, 3)$, and $(5, 0)$ is translated 2 units right and 3 units down. Which are the coordinates of a vertex of the image?

   Ⓕ $(-5, 5)$

   Ⓖ $(-1, 1)$

   Ⓗ $(0, 0)$

   Ⓙ $(3, 3)$

If you have extra time at the end of a test, go back and check your answers. Remember that you can always check the solution to an equation by substituting your answer to see if it makes the equation true.

11. What is the standard form of the expression $(2x^2 - x + 4) - (3x^3 + x^2 - 2x)$?

Ⓐ $-3x^3 - x^2 - 3x + 4$

Ⓑ $-3x^3 + x^2 + x + 4$

Ⓒ $x^2 + x + 4 - 3x^3$

Ⓓ $3x^3 + 3x^2 + 3x + 4$

12. At what point does the graph of $f(x) = \frac{2x^2 - x - 3}{x + 1}$ have a hole?

Ⓕ $(-1, -5)$ Ⓗ $(1.5, 0)$

Ⓖ $(-1, 0)$ Ⓙ $(1.5, 2.5)$

13. What function is graphed below?

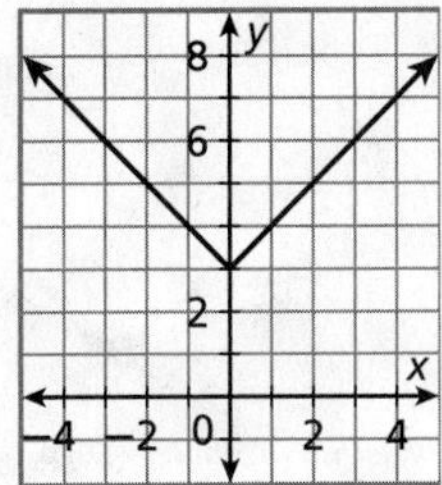

Ⓐ $f(x) = |3x|$ Ⓒ $f(x) = 3|x|$

Ⓑ $f(x) = |x + 3|$ Ⓓ $f(x) = |x| + 3$

Gridded Response

14. What value of x makes the equation true?

$\frac{7}{4} = \frac{3}{x} + 1$

15. What value completes the square for the expression below?

$x^2 - 3x + \blacksquare$

16. Simplify the expression.

$(\sqrt[3]{-8})^2$

17. What value of x makes the equation true?

$\log_5(x + 8) = 2$

18. Simplify the expression.

$\frac{5x}{x + \frac{1}{4}} - \frac{20x}{4x + 1}$

Short Response

19. The function $K = \frac{5}{9}(F - 32) + 273$ expresses temperature in kelvins K as a function of temperature in degrees Fahrenheit F.

a. Find the inverse of the function.

b. What does the inverse represent?

c. Use the inverse to find the temperature in degrees Fahrenheit that is equivalent to 300 kelvins.

20. The WNBA Most Valuable Player award is given to the player with the greatest number of total points, which are tallied based on the number of first-, second-, and third-place votes that the player receives. The table shows the number of votes for the top three nominees in 2004. Find the number of points awarded for each vote.

Player	First-Place Votes	Second-Place Votes	Third-Place Votes	Total Points
L. Leslie	33	0	19	425
L. Jackson	15	18	15	351
D. Taurasi	0	13	7	126

21. The graph of $f(x) = \frac{1}{2}x^2 + c$ is a parabola with its vertex at $(0, 3)$.

a. What is the value of c? Explain how you determined this value.

b. Graph the function f.

Extended Response

22. The information in the table describes a polynomial function.

Leading Coefficient	1
Degree	3
Zeros	−1, 2, 4
Local Minimum	≈ −4.1
Local Maximum	≈ 8.2
***y*-intercept**	8

a. Describe the end behavior of the graph of the function. Justify your answer.

b. How many turning points does the graph of the function have? Justify your answer.

c. Sketch a graph of the function.

Real-World CONNECTIONS

The Return of the Trumpeter Swan

The majestic trumpeter swan was once abundant throughout Michigan, but by 1900, the species had been hunted almost to extinction. Since 1985, the Detroit Zoo has been working with Michigan State University to reintroduce the species to Michigan's wetlands. The program has been a great success—the population of trumpeter swans continues to grow every year.

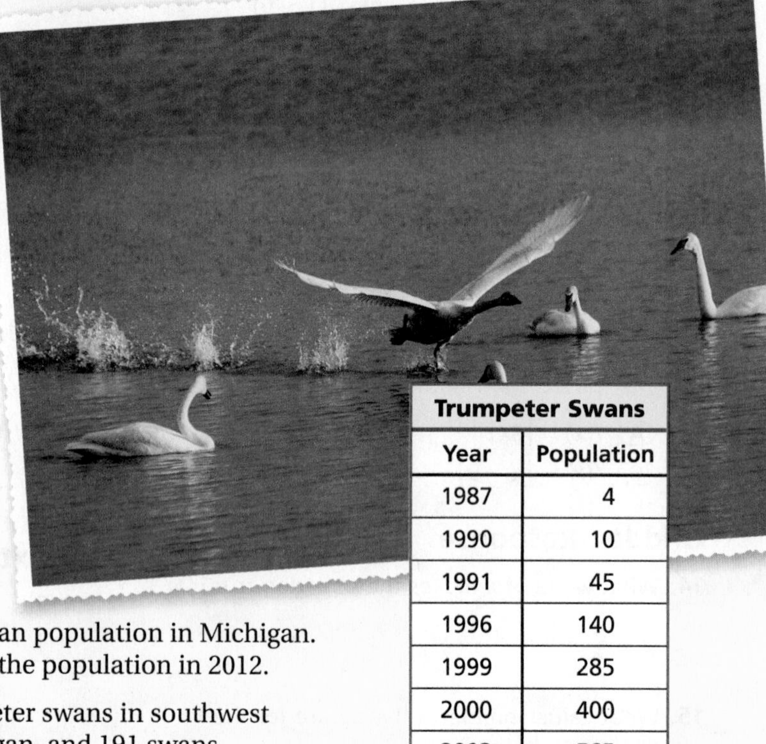

Trumpeter Swans	
Year	**Population**
1987	4
1990	10
1991	45
1996	140
1999	285
2000	400
2003	565

Choose one or more strategies to solve each problem. For 1–3, use the table.

1. The table shows the growth of the swan population in Michigan. Use an exponential model to predict the population in 2012.
2. In 2000, there were about 100 trumpeter swans in southwest Michigan, 50 swans in eastern Michigan, and 191 swans in Seney National Wildlife Refuge. If this population distribution continues, about how many swans will be in each region in 2012?
3. In what year do you predict that the total population of trumpeter swans in Michigan will exceed 6000? Justify your answer.
4. A cygnet is a young swan. In 1997, there were 60 trumpeter swan cygnets in Michigan. In each of the next 2 years, their population increased by 30% compared with the year before. If this rate of increase continues, in what year will the population of cygnets exceed 1500?

The Motor City

In 1903, Henry Ford opened a small car company in Detroit that employed 10 people. Within a decade, Detroit had become the heart of America's automotive industry, earning it the nickname the "Motor City." Today, Detroit remains an important center for automotive research.

Choose one or more strategies to solve each problem. For 1–3, use the table.

Stopping Distances on Dry Pavement	
Speed (mi/h)	**Distance (ft)**
10	4.2
20	16.8
30	37.8
40	67.2

1. Automotive engineers use the equation $s = \sqrt{30fd}$ to study the relationship between a vehicle's speed s in miles per hour and its stopping distance d in feet once the brakes have been applied. In this equation, f is the coefficient of friction, which depends in part on the condition of the road.
   a. Determine the coefficient of friction to the nearest tenth for dry pavement.
   b. Predict the stopping distance to the nearest foot for a vehicle moving at 65 mi/h.
2. For a vehicle on wet pavement, the coefficient of friction is 0.4. How does driving on wet pavement affect the stopping distance for a given speed?
3. Engineers want to design brakes that will reduce stopping distances by 10%. How would this change the equation relating speed and stopping distance?
4. The equation $v_{\text{max}} = \sqrt{14.88fr}$ gives the maximum velocity in miles per hour that a vehicle can safely travel around a curve that has a radius of r feet. If the velocity is greater than v_{max}, the tires will slip. Engineers find that under snowy conditions, $v_{\text{max}} = 15$ mi/h for a freeway off-ramp that has a radius of 50 ft. To the nearest tenth, what is the coefficient of friction for the off-ramp in these conditions?

CHAPTER

9 Properties and Attributes of Functions

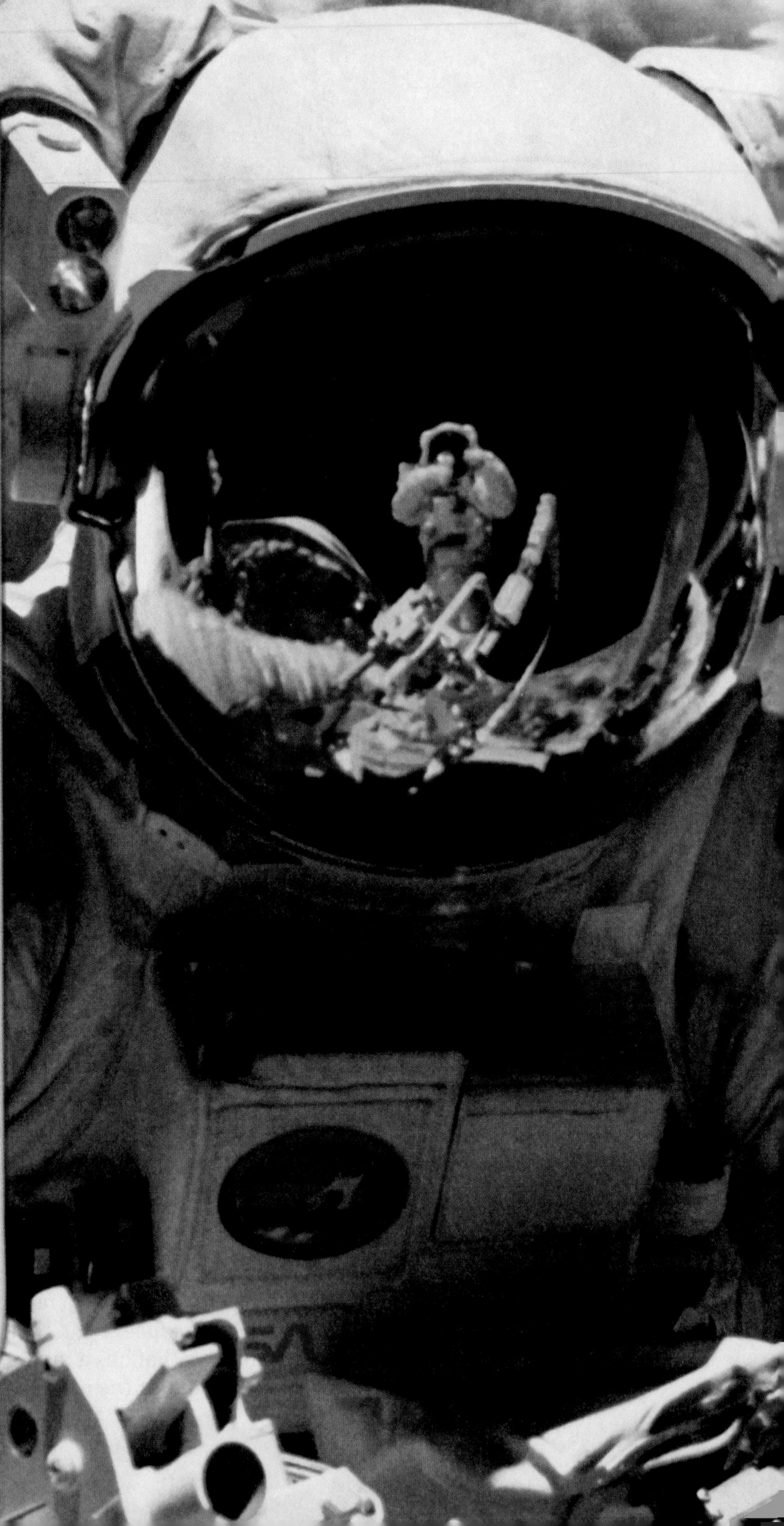

Chapter Focus

- Make connections among representations of various function families.
- Operate and solve problems with functions and their inverses.

COSMIC DEBRIS

Space missions have left more than 28,000 pieces of debris floating in space. You can analyze the debris trends by using functions and graphs.

go.hrw.com
Chapter Project Online
KEYWORD: MB7 ChProj

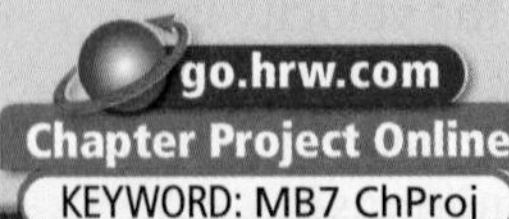

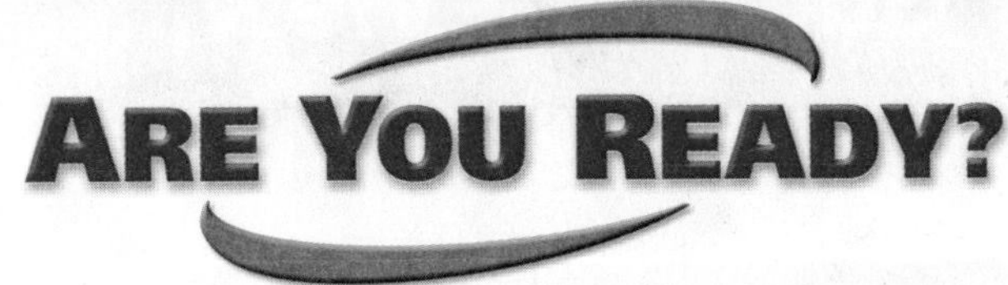

ARE YOU READY?

Vocabulary

Match each term on the left with a definition on the right.

1. translation
2. slope
3. regression
4. correlation

A. the statistical study of the relationship between variables

B. the constant rate of change of a linear function

C. the ratio between two sets of measurements

D. a transformation that moves each point in a figure or graph the same distance in the same direction

E. a measure of the strength and direction of the linear relationship between two variables

Connect Words and Algebra

Write an equation to represent each situation.

5. The cost of renting a recording studio is \$30 for the first hour and \$20 for each additional hour.
6. The volume of water in a tank is equal to 30 gallons plus 8 gallons for every minute the pump is on.

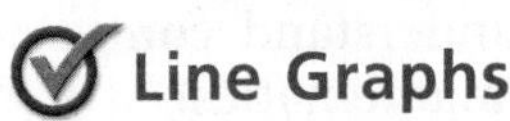

Line Graphs

Find each value for the graph of $f(x)$ shown.

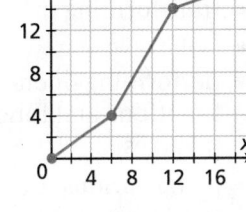

7. $f(6)$
8. $f(15)$
9. x such that $f(x) = 2$
10. x such that $f(x) = 9$
11. Find the slope of the line segment between $x = 6$ and $x = 12$.
12. Find the slope of the line segment between $x = 12$ and $x = 18$.

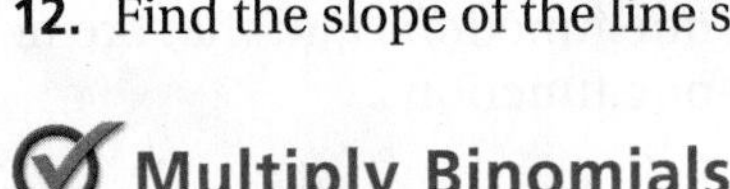

Multiply Binomials

Multiply. Then simplify.

13. $(x - 6)(x + 4)$
14. $(6 - x)(4 - x)$
15. $(5x + 8)(2x - 7)$
16. $(x^2 - 7)(4x + 5)$
17. $(3x^2 + 8)(7x^2 + 8)$
18. $(x - 8)(x + 8)$

Simplify Polynomial Expressions

Simplify.

19. $8(3x^5) - (2x)^3(5x^2)$
20. $5(x + 3)^2 - 6(x + 3)$
21. $3x(4 - x^3) - 6x^2(x + 4)$
22. $3x^3(x^2 + 4) - x(x^4 - 5)$

CHAPTER 9 Study Guide: Preview

Where You've Been

Previously, you

- studied different functions, graphs, and equations.
- transformed linear, quadratic, exponential, and radical functions.
- performed operations on many types of expressions.
- used linear, quadratic, and exponential functions to model real-world data.

In This Chapter

You will study

- multiple representations of functions.
- transforming piecewise functions.
- performing operations on functions and function inverses.
- using various functions to model real-world data.

Where You're Going

You can use the skills in this chapter

- in all of your future math classes, including Calculus and Statistics.
- in other classes, such as Health, Chemistry, Physics, and Economics.
- outside of school to model data and make predictions in sports, travel, and finance.

Key Vocabulary/Vocabulario

composition of functions	composición de funciones
one-to-one function	función uno a uno
piecewise function	función a trozos
step function	función escalón

Vocabulary Connections

To become familiar with some of the vocabulary terms in the chapter, consider the following. You may refer to the chapter, the glossary, or a dictionary if you like.

1. One definition of the word *composition* is "the act or process of putting together." How can you use this definition of *composition* to understand **composition of functions** in mathematics?
2. Imagine looking at a set of stairs from the side. Would a graph that looked like stairs represent a function? What might a **step function** look like?
3. Recall the definition of a function. What do you think a **one-to-one function** is? Give examples of functions from mathematics and from real life that are one-to-one functions and that are not one-to-one functions.

CHAPTER 9

Reading Strategy: Read Problems for Understanding

Read a problem once to become aware of the concept being reviewed. Then read it again slowly and carefully to identify what the problem is asking. As you read, highlight key information given in the problem statement. When dealing with a multi-step problem, break the problem into parts and then make a plan to solve it.

19. Space Exploration On Earth, the function $f(x) = \frac{6}{5}\sqrt{x}$ approximates the distance in miles to the horizon observed by a person whose eye level is x feet above the ground. The graph of the corresponding function for Mars is a horizontal stretch of f by a factor of about $\frac{9}{5}$. Write the corresponding function g for Mars, and use it to estimate the distance to the horizon for an astronaut whose eyes are 6 ft above Mars's surface.

Step	Question	Answer
Step 1	What concept is being reviewed?	• transforming a rational function by changing its parameters
Step 2	What are you being asked to do?	• Rewrite the function to include the new parameter. • Evaluate the revised function for a given value.
Step 3	What is the key information needed to solve the problem?	• The function $f(x) = \frac{6}{5}\sqrt{x}$ represents the distance on Earth • The function for Mars is a horizontal stretch by a factor of $\frac{9}{5}$ • The astronaut's eye level on Mars is 6 ft.
Step 4	What is my plan to solve this multi-part problem?	• Revise the given function to account for horizontal stretch on Mars. • Evaluate the revised function for $x = 6$.

Try This

For each problem, complete each step in the four-step method described above.

1. A rectangle has a length of $(x + 5)$ units and a width of $(x + 4)$ units. Write and graph a rational function R to represent the ratio of the area to the perimeter. Identify a reasonable domain and range of the function.

2. The diameter d (in inches) of a rope needed to lift w tons is given by $d = \frac{\sqrt{15w}}{\pi}$. How much more can be lifted with a rope 1.25 inches in diameter than with a rope 0.75 inch in diameter?

9-1 Multiple Representations of Functions

Objectives

Translate between the various representations of functions.

Solve problems by using the various representations of functions.

Who uses this?

An amusement park manager can use representations of functions, such as graphs and tables, to analyze ticket sales. (See Example 1.)

An amusement park manager estimates daily profits by multiplying the number of tickets sold by 20. This verbal description is useful, but other representations of the function may be more useful.

Equation

$p = 20n$

or

$p(n) = 20n$

Table

n	p
50	1000
100	2000
150	3000
200	4000

Graph

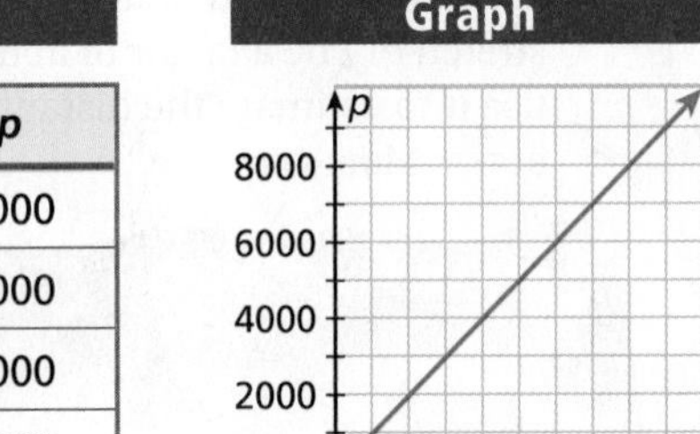

These different representations can help the manager set, compare, and predict prices.

EXAMPLE 1 ***Business Application***

A manager at an amusement park monitors the ticket sales at the park over a four-day weekend. Match each situation to one of the following graphs. Sketch a possible graph of the situation if the situation does not match any of the given graphs.

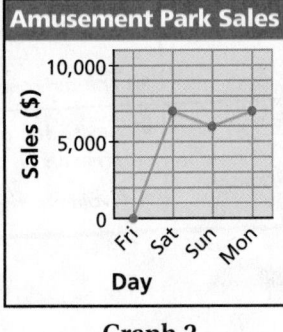

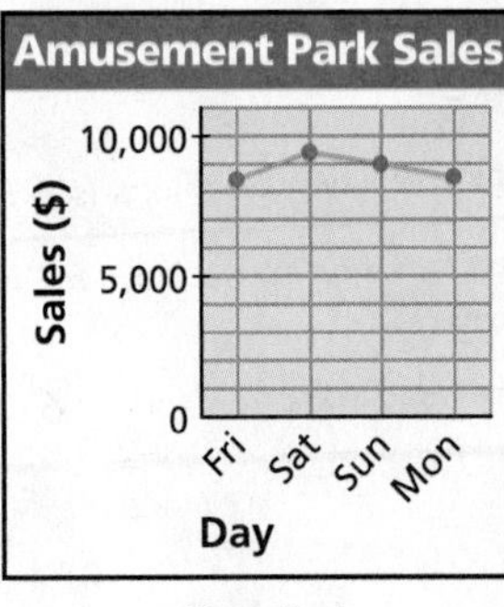

Graph 1

Amusement Park Sales

Sales ($): 10,000; 5,000; 0

Day: Fri, Sat, Sun, Mon

Graph 2

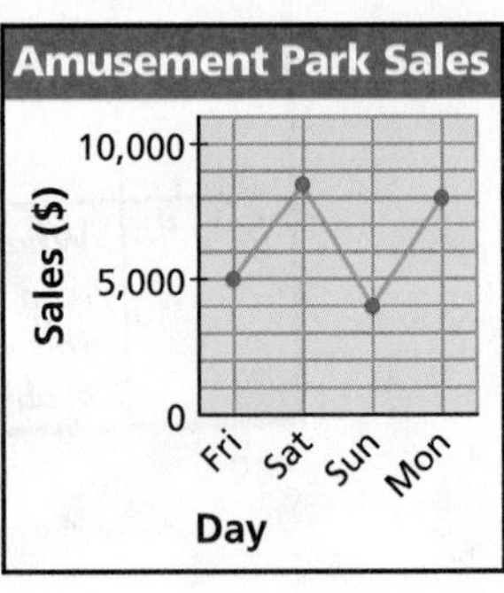

Graph 3

A **The park was closed on Friday for repairs.**

graph 2 *The graph shows no ticket sales on Friday.*

B **The park hosted a big concert on Saturday and a parade on Monday.**

graph 3 *The graph shows increased ticket sales on Saturday and Monday.*

C **The park was very busy during the holiday weekend.**

graph 1 *The graph shows high ticket sales every day.*

What if...? Sketch a possible graph to represent the following.

1a. The weather was beautiful on Friday and Saturday, but it rained all day on Sunday and Monday.

1b. Only $\frac{1}{2}$ of the rides were running on Friday and Sunday.

Because each representation of a function (words, equation, table, or graph) describes the same relationship, you can often use any representation to generate the others.

EXAMPLE 2 Recreation Application

Kurt is rappelling down a 500-foot cliff at a rate of 6 feet per second. Create a table, equation, and graph to represent Kurt's height from the ground with relation to time. When will Kurt reach the ground?

Step 1 Create a table.

Let t be the time in seconds and h be Kurt's height, in feet, from the ground.

Kurt begins at a height of 500 feet, and the height decreases by 6 feet each second.

t	h	
0	500	
1	494	$500 - 6$
2	488	$500 - 6(2)$
3	482	$500 - 6(3)$
4	476	$500 - 6(4)$
5	470	$500 - 6(5)$

Step 2 Write an equation.

Height	is equal to	500	minus	6 feet per second.
h	$=$	500	$-$	$6t$

Step 3 Find the intercepts and graph the equation.

h-intercept: 500

Solve for t when $h = 0$.

$$h = 500 - 6t$$
$$0 = 500 - 6t$$
$$-500 = -6t$$
$$t = \frac{-500}{-6} = 83\frac{1}{3}$$

t-intercept: $83\frac{1}{3}$

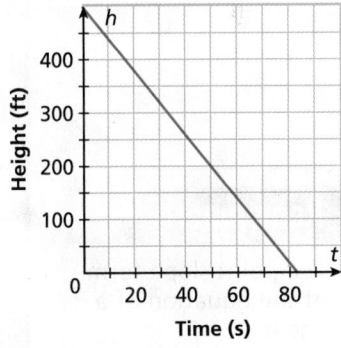

Kurt will reach the ground after $83\frac{1}{3}$ seconds.

2. The table shows the height, in feet, of an arrow in relation to its horizontal distance from the archer. Create a graph, an equation, and a verbal description to represent the height of the arrow with relation to its horizontal distance from the archer.

Arrow Distance and Height

Distance from Archer (ft)	0	75	150	225	300	375
Height (ft)	6.55	59.80	90.55	98.80	84.50	47.50

Translating Between Multiple Representations	
When given a(n)...	**Try to...**
Table	• Find finite differences or ratios to determine which parent function best describes the data. • Graph points as ordered pairs and look for a pattern. • Match the data to the related parent function, if applicable, and perform a regression.
Graph	• Identify which parent function the graph most resembles, and then use key points (intercepts, maxima, minima, and so on) from the graph to help write an equation. • Locate several points on the graph and write them in a table. • Use slope; increasing, decreasing, or constant intervals; and intercepts to write a verbal description.
Equation	• Make a table of values. You may use a graphing calculator. • Make a graph by using transformations of parent functions or a graphing calculator.
Verbal Description	• Identify dependent and independent variables, and write an algebraic equation. • Generate a table of values by using the pattern described. • Sketch a graph of the situation by using hints from the description about increasing, decreasing, or constant intervals, as well as intercepts.

EXAMPLE 3 Using Multiple Representations to Solve Problems

A **Stacy runs three days a week at a track. Stacy starts keeping time when she starts warming up and notes after every 2 laps how long she has been at the track. The table shows the times for several laps. Use a graph and an equation to find the time it will take Stacy to run 20 laps.**

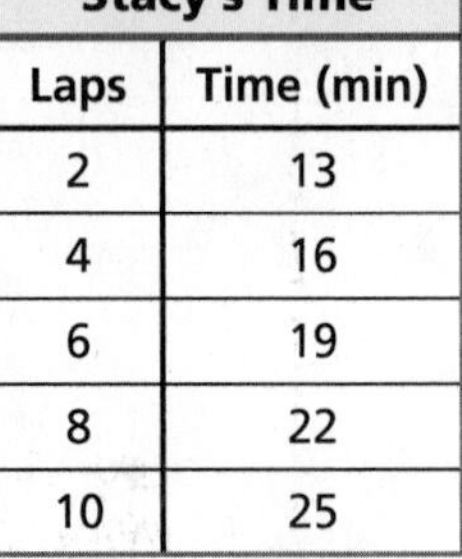

Stacy's Time	
Laps	**Time (min)**
2	13
4	16
6	19
8	22
10	25

Step 1 Graph the data.

The data appear to be linear.

Step 2 Write a linear equation.

Let x = the number of laps and y = the time in minutes.

$m = \frac{y_2 - y_1}{x_2 - x_1} = \frac{16 - 13}{4 - 2} = \frac{3}{2}$ *Find the slope. Use any two points.*

$y - y_1 = m(x - x_1)$ *Point-slope form*

$y - 13 = \frac{3}{2}(x - 2)$ *Use (2, 13) and slope $\frac{3}{2}$.*

$y = \frac{3}{2}x + 10$ *Simplify.*

Step 3 Evaluate the function for 20 laps.

$y = \frac{3}{2}(20) + 10 = 40.$

It will take Stacy 40 minutes to complete 20 laps.

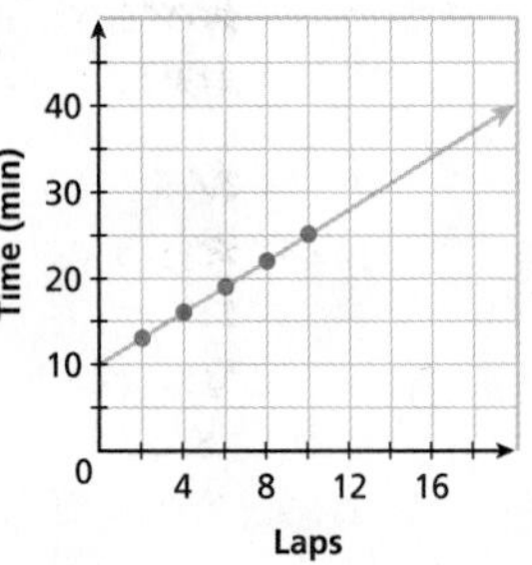

Remember!

The point-slope form of the equation of a line is $y - y_1 = m(x - x_1)$, where m is the slope and (x_1, y_1) is a point on the line. (Lesson 2-4)

B **The owner of an orange grove finds that if 26 trees are planted per acre, each mature tree yields about 576 oranges per year. For each additional tree planted per acre, the number of oranges produced annually by each tree decreases by 12. Use a table, a graph, and an equation to find how many trees per acre should be planted to maximize the yield per acre.**

Make a table for an acre of orange trees. Because the orchard owner is interested in the total number of oranges, make a graph by using trees t as the independent variable and total oranges as the dependent variable.

Orange Tree Yield

Trees	Oranges per Tree	Total Oranges
26	576	14,976
27	564	15,228
28	552	15,456
29	540	15,660
30	528	15,840
31	516	15,996
32	504	16,128

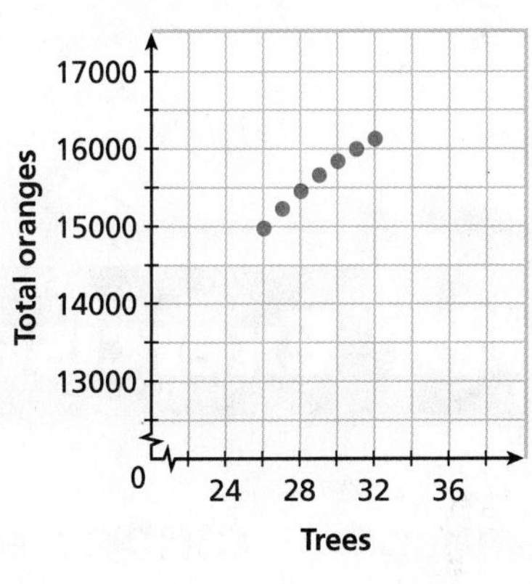

The data do not appear to be linear, so check finite differences.

Total oranges	14,976	15,228	15,456	15,660	15,840	15,996	16,128
First differences	252	228	204	180	156	132	
Second differences	−24	−24	−24	−24	−24		

Remember!

First differences are constant in linear functions. Second differences are constant in quadratic functions. (Lesson 5-9)

Because the second differences are constant, a quadratic model is appropriate. Use a graphing calculator to perform a quadratic regression on the data.

The equation $y = -12x^2 + 888x$ models the data, and the graph appears to fit. Use the **TRACE** or **MAXIMUM** feature to identify the maximum orange yield.

The maximum occurs when 37 trees are planted on each acre.

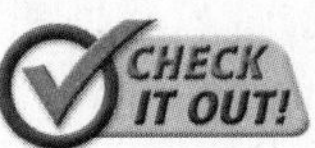

3. Bartolo opened a new sporting goods business and has recorded his sales each week. To break even, Bartolo needs to sell $48,000 worth of merchandise in a week. Assuming the sales trend continues, use a graph and an equation to find the number of weeks before Bartolo breaks even.

Bartolo's Sales

Week	Sales ($)
1	25,000
2	27,500
3	30,250
4	33,275
5	36,603

THINK AND DISCUSS

1. Explain how to use a table to help create an equation for a set of data.
2. Give an example of a real-world situation where a graph might be the most useful representation of a set of data.
3. **GET ORGANIZED** Copy and complete the graphic organizer. In each box give an example.

Know it! Note

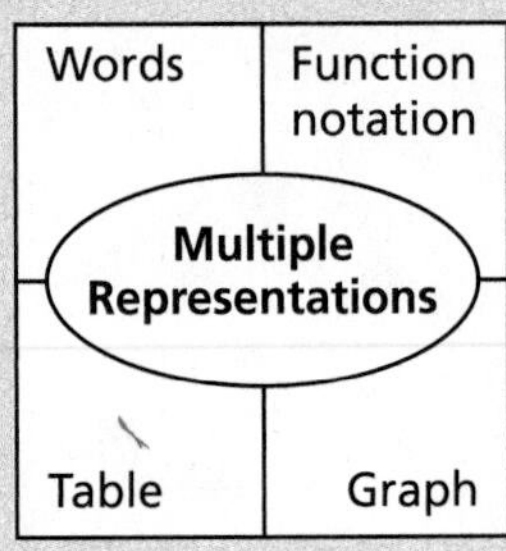

9-1 Exercises

go.hrw.com
Homework Help Online
KEYWORD: MB7 9-1
Parent Resources Online
KEYWORD: MB7 Parent

GUIDED PRACTICE

SEE EXAMPLE 1 p. 654

Match each situation to its corresponding graph. Sketch a possible graph of the situation if the situation does not match any of the given graphs.

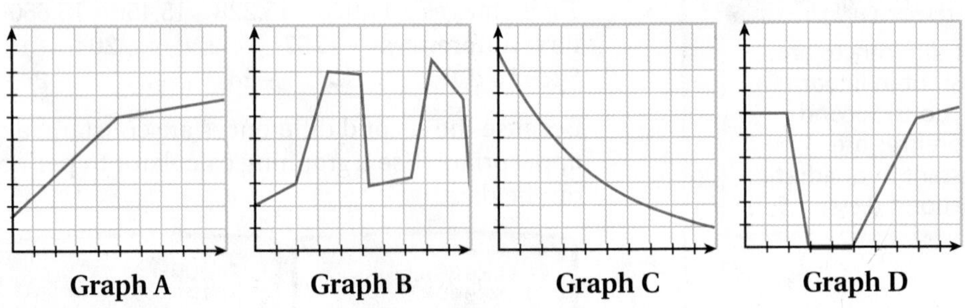

1. Due to a product recall, a company's profits drop sharply into a loss but rebound a few weeks later.
2. The value of a car declines as the car gets older.
3. A souvenir shop's sales are seasonal, with high sales in summer and winter and low sales in spring and fall.
4. An airplane ascends to a peak height of 30,000 feet and then descends to a cruising altitude of 24,000 feet.

SEE EXAMPLE 2 p. 655

5. **Education** Part-time students at a university must pay an enrollment fee of \$179.35, plus \$218.40 per credit hour. Create a table, an equation, and a graph that give the total cost of enrollment as a function of credit hours.

SEE EXAMPLE 3 p. 656

6. **Recreation** Claire is hiking up the South Kaibab Trail at the Grand Canyon. The table shows Claire's altitude above sea level every 15 minutes after she starts to hike. Use a graph and an equation to find how long it will take Claire to reach the rim of the canyon at 7260 feet.

Claire's Altitude

Time (min)	Altitude (ft)
15	2940
30	3240
45	3540
60	3840
75	4140

PRACTICE AND PROBLEM SOLVING

Independent Practice	
For Exercises	See Example
7–10	1
11–12	2
13–14	3

Extra Practice

Skills Practice p. S20

Application Practice p. S40

Match each situation to its corresponding graph. Sketch a possible graph of the situation if the situation does not match any of the given graphs.

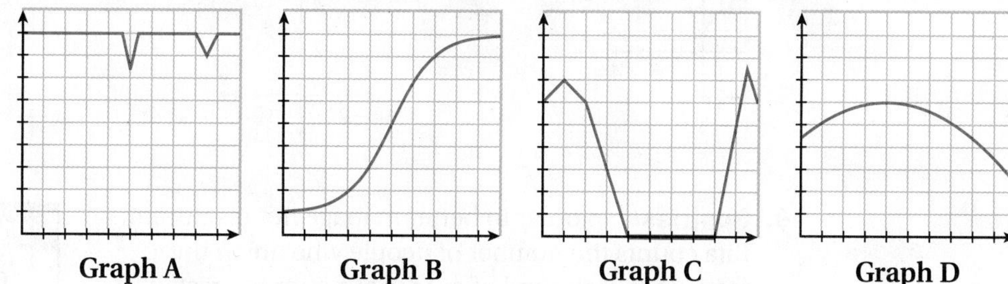

7. The sales of lift tickets at a ski resort are highest at the beginning and end of the year.

8. The attendance at a pop singer's concerts is steadily high except on two nights.

9. The population of a city peaked in the 1980s and has been decreasing slowly but steadily in the years since.

10. Sales of a new type of cell phone increase rapidly and then level off.

11. Health Carl has a severe fever, so his doctor advises him to take his temperature every 4 hours until it falls below 100°F. The table shows Carl's temperature with relation to time. Create a graph, an equation, and a verbal description to represent Carl's temperature with relation to time. When will Carl's temperature drop below 100°F?

Carl's Temperature

Time (h)	Temperature (°F)
0	101.10
4	102.82
8	103.78
12	103.98
16	103.42
20	102.10

12. Transportation A truck begins a trip of 1675 miles. The truck averages 55 miles per hour, including stops. Create a table, a graph, and an equation to represent the distance that the truck has left to travel with relation to time.

LINK

Whales

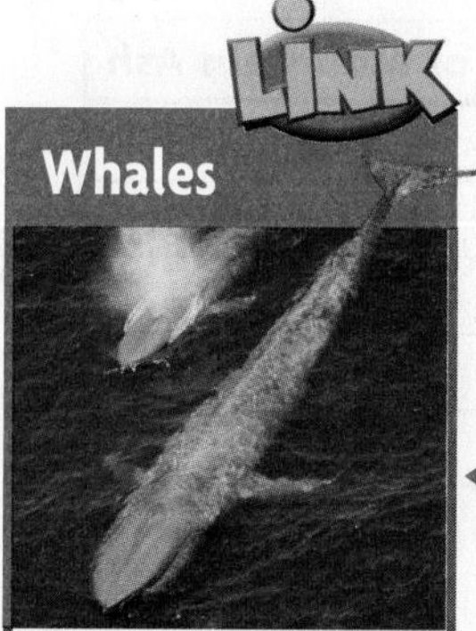

Blue whales are the largest and loudest animals on Earth. Their calls can reach intensity levels of 180 decibels, louder than a jet airplane.

13. Whales Researchers are studying the growth of a young blue whale. The graph shows the approximate weight of the whale from birth to 8 months.

a. Find an equation for the weight of the whale as a function of time, and describe the relationship in words.

b. Will the weight of the whale continue to increase by the same amount each month? Explain your answer.

Weight of a Blue Whale from Birth

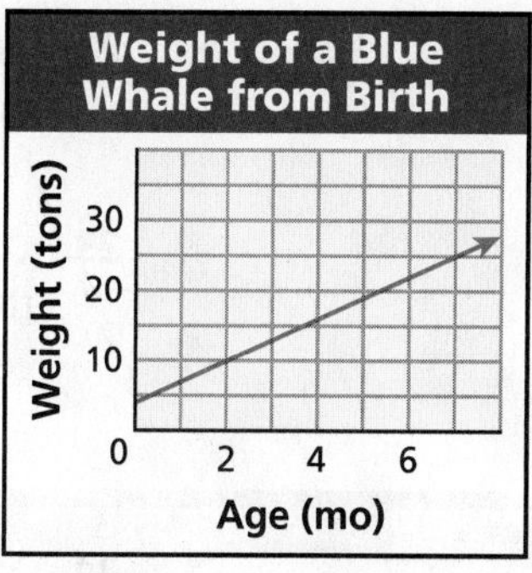

14. Business Alex is painting a house. When Alex starts work on Monday morning, there are 2452 square feet of surface area that remain to be painted. Alex can paint 64 square feet of surface area in an hour.

a. Write an equation for the amount of surface area that Alex has left to paint after t hours.

b. If Alex works for 40 hours a week, will he be able to finish painting the house in a week?

15. Sports The owners of a minor league hockey team have found that when they charge \$12 for a lower-level seat, they average 800 fans per game. For every \$1 increase in ticket price, the attendance decreases by an average of 50 people. Find the ticket price that will maximize revenue for the team's owners.

Classify each function as linear, absolute-value, quadratic, exponential, or rational, and justify your choice.

16.

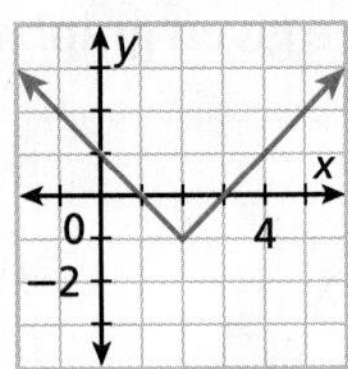

17.

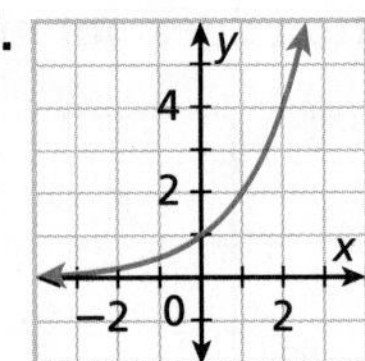

18.

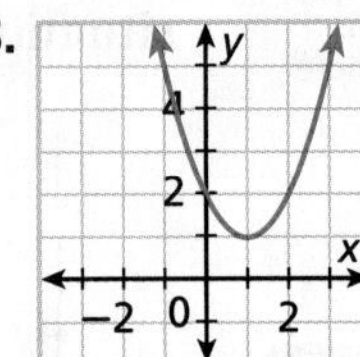

19. Business In order to better manage her restaurant, Rita counts the number of people who are in the restaurant at the end of every hour after the restaurant is opened. The results are shown in the graph.

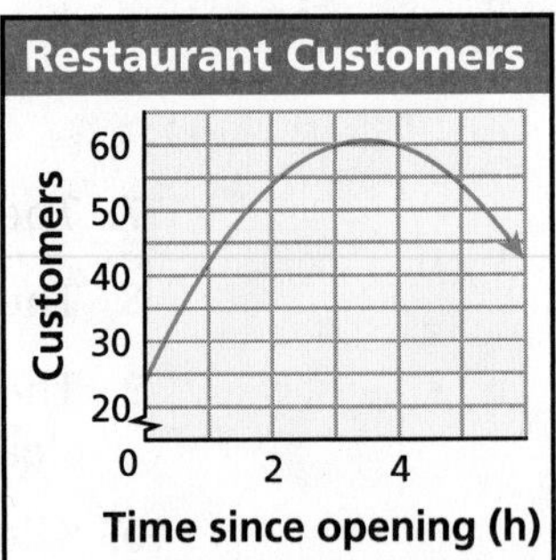

a. Write a function for the graph.

b. According to your function, what was the maximum number of customers in Rita's restaurant on this evening?

c. Based on the function, when will there be no customers in Rita's restaurant?

20. Hobbies Susan collects antique dolls. In 2005, her collection contained 6 dolls. She plans to double the number of dolls in her collection every year. Use a table, a graph, and an equation to determine when Susan will have more than 100 dolls in her collection.

21. Forestry The *Sorbus aucuparia*, or mountain ash tree, typically grows to the heights shown in the table.

a. Create a graph of height versus time.

b. Write a function that models the height.

c. During which year would you expect the height to reach 18 ft?

Growth of Mountain Ash

Year	Height (ft)
1	4
3	7
6	10
10	13

22. Write About It Describe a different situation in which you would find each representation of a function, including a table, a graph, and an equation, useful.

23. Critical Thinking When would a graph give you more evidence about a relationship than a table would? When would a table give more evidence than a graph would?

MULTI-STEP TEST PREP

24. This problem will prepare you for the Multi-Step Test Prep on page 680.

A group of people stand in a circle and hold hands. One person squeezes the hand of the person on her left, who then squeezes the hand of the next person, and so on. The table shows the time that it takes the signal to go all the way around the circle.

a. Create a graph of time versus the number of participants.

b. Write a function that models the situation.

c. Suppose the signal takes about a minute to go around the circle. How many participants are there?

Time for Hand Squeeze to Complete a Cycle

People	Time (s)
5	2.10
8	3.36
14	5.88
23	9.66

TEST PREP

25. Business This graph shows data on the number of olive slices on pizzas of different radii. Let r represent the radius of the pizza and n represent the number of olive slices. Identify the equation that best represents the relationship between the radius and the number of olive slices.

Number of Olive Slices on Pizzas

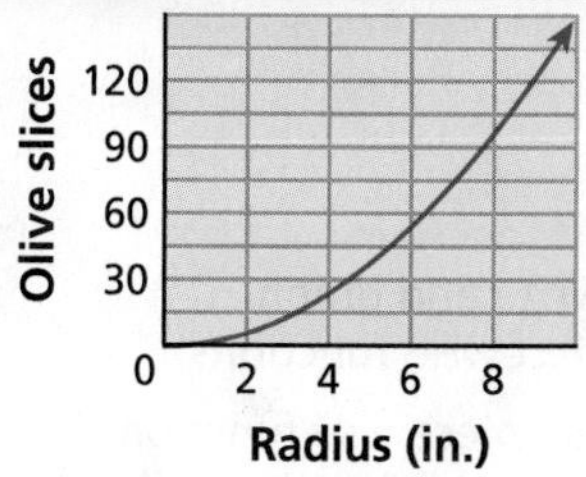

Ⓐ $n = -\frac{3}{2}r^2$ Ⓒ $n = \frac{3}{2}r^2$

Ⓑ $n = -6r$ Ⓓ $n = 6r$

26. A charity is selling American flags to celebrate Independence Day. The charity's profit in dollars is modeled by $p = \frac{1}{2}n$, where n is the number of flags sold. Which of the following choices identifies the same function?

Ⓐ The profit is $2 per flag.

Ⓑ

n	1	2	3
p	2	4	6

Ⓒ For every 2 flags sold, the profit is $1.

Ⓓ

n	1	2	3	4
p	0.5	1.5	2.5	3.5

27. Short Response Which type of function would best model the cost for carpeting a square room as a function of the room's width? Explain your answer.

CHALLENGE AND EXTEND

Write an equation and create a graph for each situation described.

28. The volume of a box for a glass decoration is found by doubling the radius of the decoration, raising it to the third power, and then adding 10.

29. The total cost of an item at a sale is found by taking off a 20% discount, subtracting a $10-off coupon, and adding 6.5% sales tax.

30. Finance Sharmila was able to save $500 from her summer job. She put the money into a mutual fund. This table shows how the value of Sharmila's money has grown.

a. Write an appropriate model for the amount that Sharmila will have in this mutual fund after t years.

b. Use your model to predict when Sharmila will have $2000 in the mutual fund.

Sharmila's Mutual Fund

Year	Value ($)
1	545.00
2	594.00
3	647.51
4	705.79
5	769.31

SPIRAL REVIEW

Find the vertex of each function. *(Lesson 2-9)*

31. $f(x) = |x + 3| - 4$

32. $f(x) = -|x - 1| - 2$

33. Tim paid $200 to have his lawn fertilized. The lawn-care company charged $0.25 per square foot. If Tim's lawn is a rectangle with a length that is twice its width, find the dimensions of the lawn. *(Lesson 5-4)*

Graph each function, and identify its domain and range. *(Lesson 8-7)*

34. $f(x) = \sqrt{x + 3}$

35. $f(x) = 3\sqrt{x - 1}$

9-2 Piecewise Functions

Objectives
Write and graph piecewise functions.

Use piecewise functions to describe real-world situations.

Vocabulary
piecewise function
step function

Why learn this?

You can use piecewise functions to model an athlete's performance in a triathlon. (See Example 4.)

A **piecewise function** is a function that is a combination of one or more functions. The rule for a piecewise function is different for different parts, or pieces, of the domain. For instance, movie ticket prices are often different for different age groups. So the function for movie ticket prices would assign a different value (ticket price) for each domain interval (age group).

EXAMPLE 1 ***Entertainment Application***

Create a table and a verbal description to represent the graph.

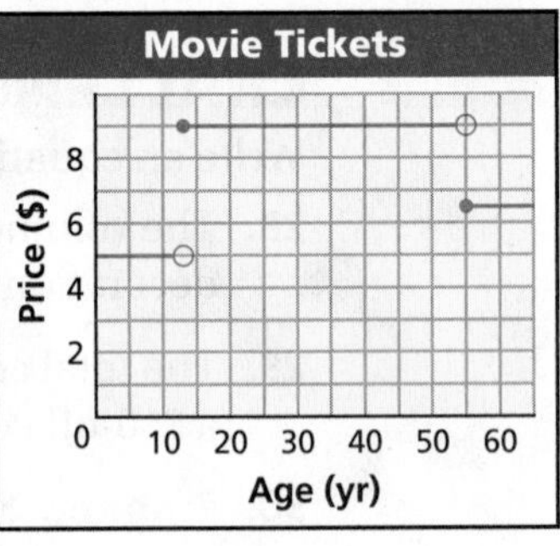

Step 1 Create a table.

Because the endpoints of each segment of the graph identify the intervals of the domain, use the endpoints and points close to them as the domain values in the table.

Remember!

When using interval notation, square brackets [ ] indicate an included endpoint, and parentheses ( ) indicate an excluded endpoint. (Lesson 1-1)

Movie Tickets

Age	Price ($)
0–12	5.00
13–54	9.00
55+	6.50

The domain of the function is divided into three intervals:

Ages 12 and under ⟶ $[0, 13)$
Ages 13 and under 55 ⟶ $[13, 55)$
Ages 55 and over ⟶ $[55, \infty)$

Step 2 Write a verbal description.

Use the domain intervals and the prices from the table.

Movie tickets are \$5.00 for children ages 12 and under, \$9.00 for people ages 13 through 54, and \$6.50 for seniors ages 55 years and older.

1. Create a table and a verbal description to represent the graph.

A piecewise function that is constant for each interval of its domain, such as the ticket price function, is called a **step function**. You can describe piecewise functions with a function rule. The rule for the movie ticket prices from Example 1 is shown.

$$f(x) = \begin{cases} 5 & \text{if } 0 < x < 13 \\ 9 & \text{if } 13 \le x < 55 \\ 6.5 & \text{if } x \ge 55 \end{cases}$$

Read this as "f of x is 5 if x is greater than 0 and less than 13, 9 if x is greater than or equal to 13 and less than 55, and 6.5 if x is greater than or equal to 55."

To evaluate any piecewise function for a specific input, find the interval of the domain that contains that input and then use the rule for that interval.

EXAMPLE 2 Evaluating a Piecewise Function

Evaluate each piecewise function for $x = -2$ and $x = 5$.

A $f(x) = \begin{cases} -5 & \text{if } x \le 0 \\ 4 & \text{if } 0 < x \le 3 \\ 12 & \text{if } x > 3 \end{cases}$

$f(-2) = -5$ *Because $-2 \le 0$, use the rule for $x \le 0$.*

$f(5) = 12$ *Because $5 > 3$, use the rule for $x > 3$.*

B $g(x) = \begin{cases} 3x + 4 & \text{if } x < 5 \\ x^2 - 3 & \text{if } x \ge 5 \end{cases}$

$g(-2) = 3(-2) + 4 = -2$ *Because $-2 < 5$, use the rule for $x < 5$.*

$g(5) = 5^2 - 3 = 22$ *Because $5 \ge 5$, use the rule for $x \ge 5$.*

Evaluate each piecewise function for $x = -1$ and $x = 3$.

2a. $f(x) = \begin{cases} 12 & \text{if } x < -3 \\ 15 & \text{if } -3 \le x < 6 \\ 20 & \text{if } x \ge 6 \end{cases}$ **2b.** $g(x) = \begin{cases} 3x^2 + 1 & \text{if } x < 0 \\ 5x - 2 & \text{if } x \ge 0 \end{cases}$

You can graph a piecewise function by graphing each piece of the function.

EXAMPLE 3 Graphing Piecewise Functions

Graph each function.

A $f(x) = \begin{cases} -4 & \text{if } x < 2 \\ 4 & \text{if } x \ge 2 \end{cases}$

The function is composed of two constant pieces that will be represented by horizontal rays. Because the domain is divided at $x = 2$, evaluate both branches of the function at $x = 2$. The function is -4 when $x < 2$, so plot the point $(2, -4)$ with an open circle and draw a horizontal ray to the left. The function is 4 when $x \ge 2$, so plot the point $(2, 4)$ with a solid dot and draw a horizontal ray to the right.

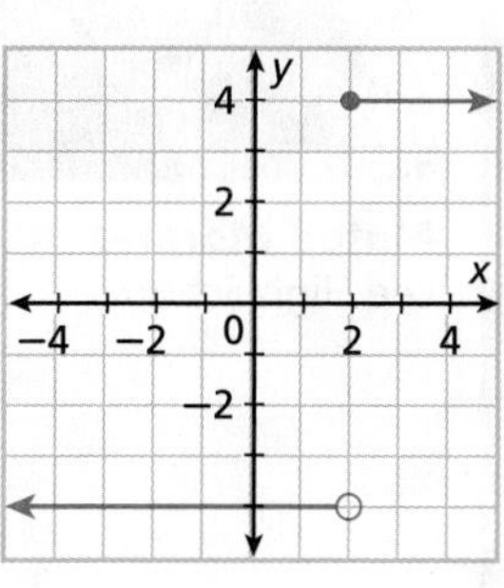

Graph each function.

B $g(x) = \begin{cases} 3x + 8 & \text{if } x \leq -3 \\ -2x & \text{if } -3 < x < 1 \\ x^2 - 3 & \text{if } x \geq 1 \end{cases}$

The function is composed of two linear pieces and a quadratic piece. The domain is divided at $x = -3$ and $x = 1$.

Use a table of values to graph each piece.

x	$g(x) = 3x + 8$	$g(x) = -2x$	$g(x) = x^2 - 3$
−4	−4		
−3	−1	6	
−2		4	
−1		2	
0		0	
1		−2	−2
2			1
3			6

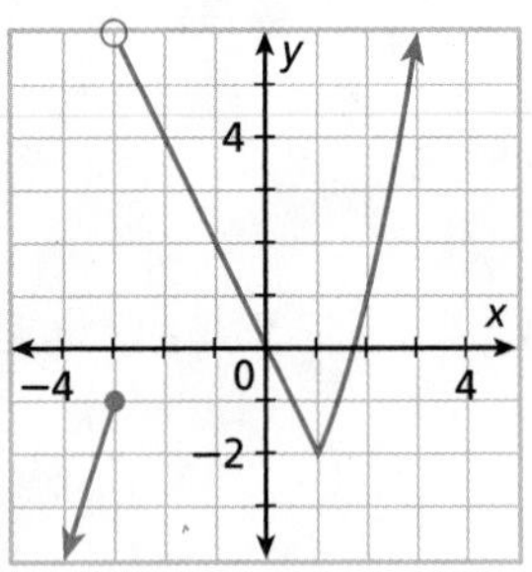

Add a closed circle at $(-3, -1)$ and an open circle at $(-3, 6)$ so that the graph clearly shows the function value when $x = -3$.

No circle is required at $(1, -2)$ because the function is connected at that point.

Graph each function.

3a. $f(x) = \begin{cases} 4 & \text{if } x \leq -1 \\ -2 & \text{if } x > -1 \end{cases}$

3b. $g(x) = \begin{cases} -3x & \text{if } x < 2 \\ x + 3 & \text{if } x \geq 2 \end{cases}$

Notice that piecewise functions are not necessarily *continuous*, meaning that the graph of the function may have breaks or gaps.

To write the rule for a piecewise function, determine where the domain is divided and write a separate rule for each piece. Combine the pieces by using the correct notation.

Student to Student

Graphing Piecewise Functions

Mateo Morales
Lee High School

When I graph a piecewise function, I like to graph each piece like it's a separate function. Then I go back and erase the parts that are outside of the restricted domain.

Example: $f(x) = \begin{cases} x + 4 & \text{if } x < -2 \\ -2x & \text{if } x \geq -2 \end{cases}$

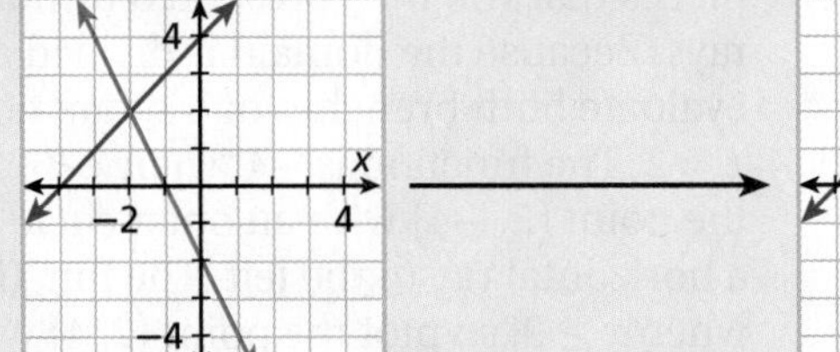

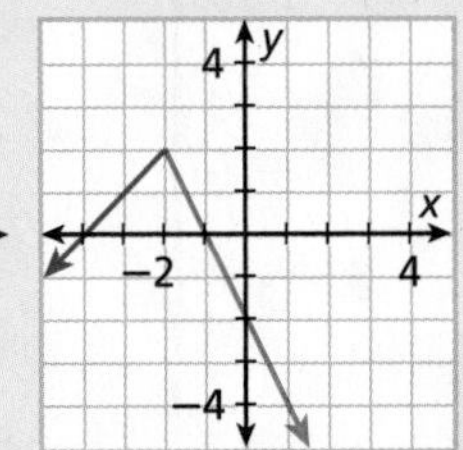

EXAMPLE 4 Sports Application

David is completing a 100-mile triathlon. He swims 2 miles in 1 hour, then bikes 80 miles in 4 hours, and finally he runs 18 miles in 3 hours. Sketch a graph of David's distance versus time. Then write a piecewise function for the graph.

> **Remember!**
> The distance formula $d = rt$ can be rearranged to find rates: $r = \frac{d}{t}$.

Step 1 Make a table to organize the data. Use the distance formula to find David's rate for each leg of the race.

David's Race

Activity	Time (h)	Distance (mi)	Rate (mi/h)
Swimming	1	2	2
Biking	4	80	20
Running	3	18	6

Step 2 Because time is the independent variable, determine the intervals for the function.

Swimming: $0 \le t \le 1$ *He swims for 1 hour.*

Biking: $1 < t \le 5$ *He bikes for the next 4 hours.*

Running: $5 < t \le 8$ *He runs the final 3 hours.*

Step 3 Graph the function.

After 1 hour, David has covered 2 miles. On the next leg, he reaches a distance of 82 total miles after 5 total hours. Finally, he completes the 100 miles after 8 hours.

Triathlon Distance Covered

Distance (mi): 0, 20, 40, 60, 80, 100
Time (h): 2, 4, 6, 8

Step 4 Write a linear function for each leg.

Use point-slope form: $y - y_1 = m(x - x_1)$.

Swimming: $d = 2t$ *Use $m = 2$ and $(0, 0)$.*

Biking: $d = 20t - 18$ *Use $m = 20$ and $(5, 82)$.*

Running: $d = 6t + 52$ *Use $m = 6$ and $(8, 100)$.*

The function rule is $d(t) = \begin{cases} 2t & \text{if } 0 \le t \le 1 \\ 20t - 18 & \text{if } 1 < t \le 5 \\ 6t + 52 & \text{if } 5 < t \le 8 \end{cases}$.

4. Shelly earns \$8 an hour. She earns \$12 an hour for each hour over 40 that she works. Sketch a graph of Shelly's earnings versus the number of hours that she works up to 60 hours. Then write a piecewise function for the graph.

THINK AND DISCUSS

1. Tell whether it is possible to have a continuous step function.

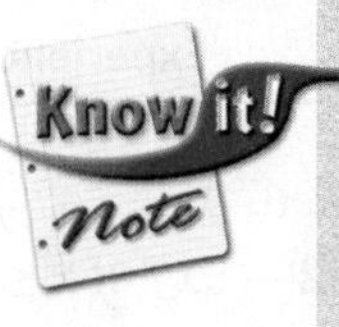

2. GET ORGANIZED Copy and complete the graphic organizer. Describe the domain and range for each function. Then include an example.

Function	Domain	Range	Example
Piecewise			
Step			

9-2 Exercises

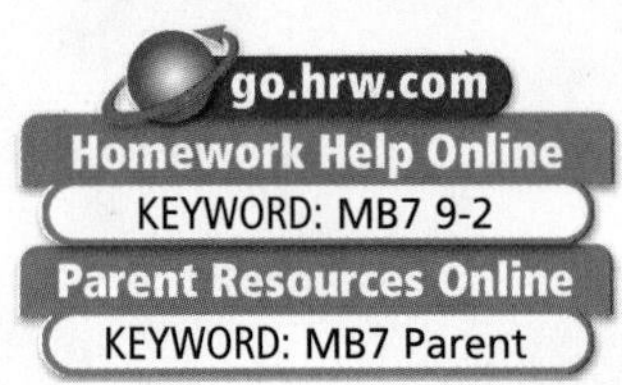

GUIDED PRACTICE

1. **Vocabulary** How are step functions related to piecewise functions?

SEE EXAMPLE 1 p. 662

Create a table and a verbal description to represent each graph.

2. 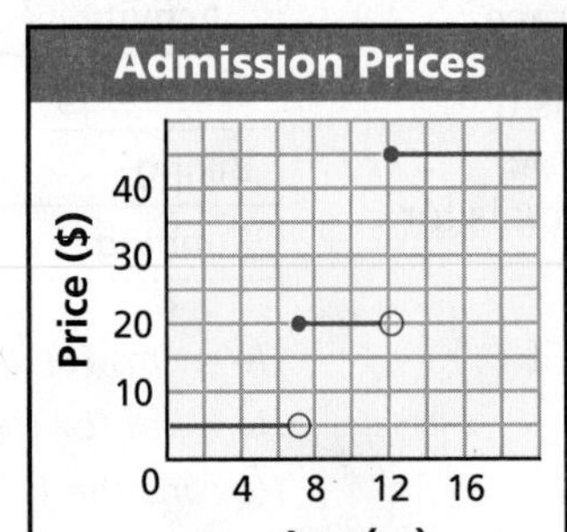

3. 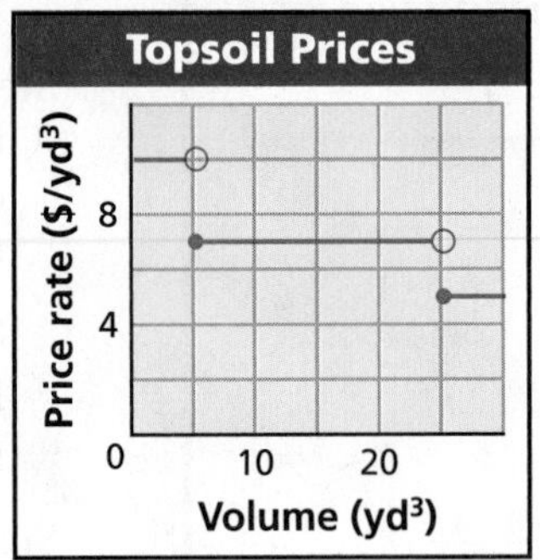

SEE EXAMPLE 2 p. 663

Evaluate each piecewise function for $x = -6$ and $x = 3$.

4. $f(x) = \begin{cases} -8 & \text{if } x \leq -5 \\ 0 & \text{if } -5 < x < 5 \\ 5 & \text{if } x \geq 5 \end{cases}$

5. $g(x) = \begin{cases} 5x - 9 & \text{if } x < 2 \\ 4 - x^2 & \text{if } x \geq 2 \end{cases}$

SEE EXAMPLE 3 p. 663

Graph each function.

6. $f(x) = \begin{cases} 7 & \text{if } x < -2 \\ -2 & \text{if } x \geq -2 \end{cases}$

7. $g(x) = \begin{cases} -2x + 8 & \text{if } x \leq 4 \\ \frac{1}{2}x & \text{if } x > 4 \end{cases}$

SEE EXAMPLE 4 p. 665

8. The cost of renting a canoe is $20 for the first 4 hours and $3 per hour for additional hours. Sketch a graph of the cost of renting a canoe from 0 to 8 hours. Then write a piecewise function for the graph.

PRACTICE AND PROBLEM SOLVING

Independent Practice

For Exercises	See Example
9–10	1
11–12	2
13–14	3
15	4

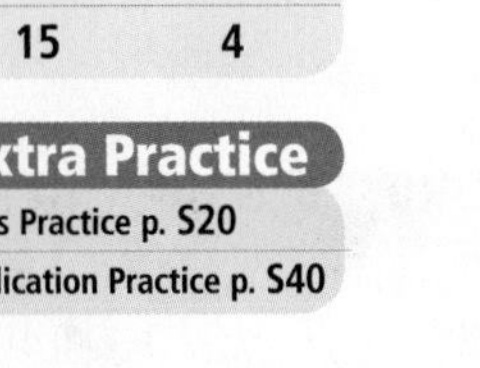

Create a table and a verbal description to represent each graph.

9. 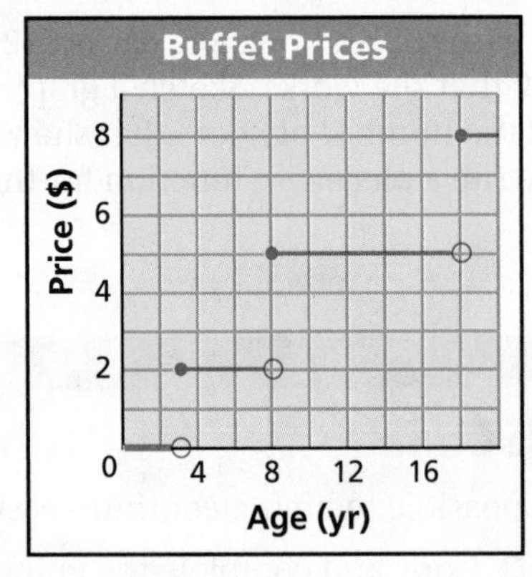

10. 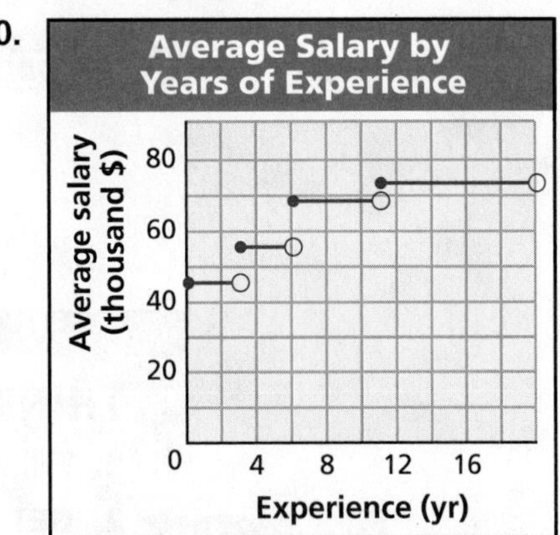

Evaluate each piecewise function for $x = -2$, $x = 2$, and $x = 6$.

11. $g(x) = \begin{cases} 9x - 2 & \text{if } x < -3 \\ x^2 - 3 & \text{if } -3 \leq x < 1 \\ 5 & \text{if } x \geq 1 \end{cases}$

12. $f(x) = \begin{cases} 12 - 9x & \text{if } x \leq 0 \\ x^2 + 3x & \text{if } 0 < x < 3 \\ 4^x & \text{if } x \geq 3 \end{cases}$

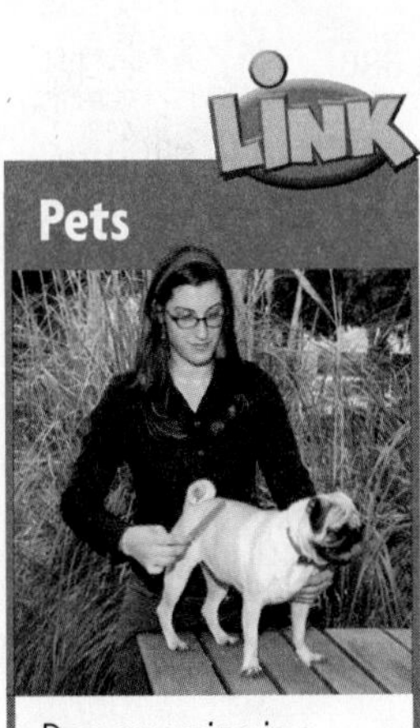

Dog grooming is a $2 billion industry in the United States. There is evidence that there were dog-grooming parlors in France as early as the 1700s.

Graph each function.

13. $f(x) = \begin{cases} \frac{3}{4}x + 1 & \text{if } x < 4 \\ \frac{3}{4}x - 2 & \text{if } x \geq 4 \end{cases}$

14. $g(x) = \begin{cases} -2x - 5 & \text{if } x < -2 \\ x^2 - 3 & \text{if } x \geq -2 \end{cases}$

15. Pets A dog groomer charges different prices based on the weight of the dog. Sketch a graph of the cost of grooming a dog from 0 to 100 pounds. Then write a piecewise function for the graph.

Grooming Prices	
Weight (lb)	**Price ($)**
15 and under	30
Over 15 and up to 50	50
Over 50	75

Write a piecewise function for each graph.

16.

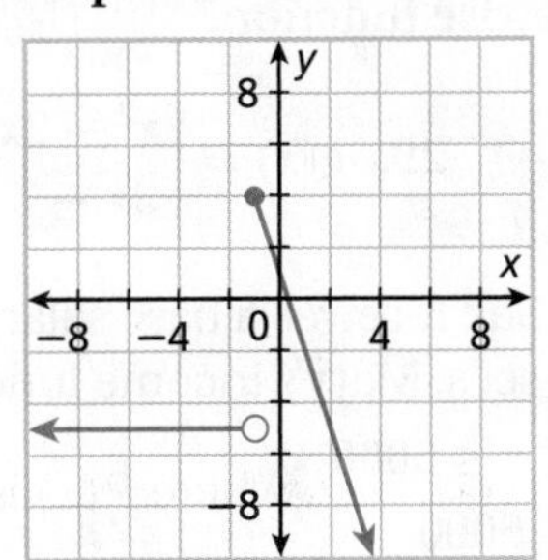

17.

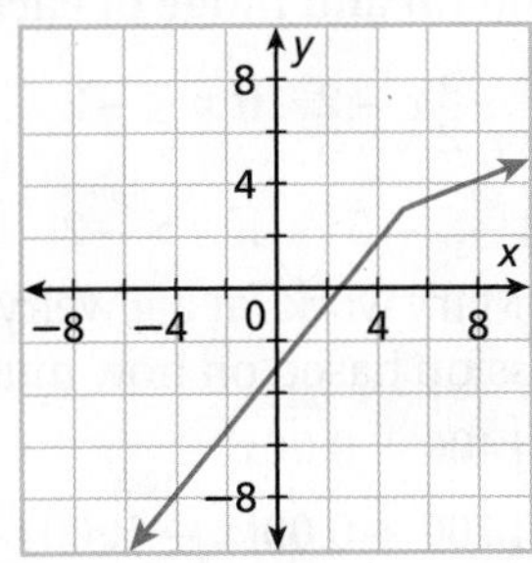

18.

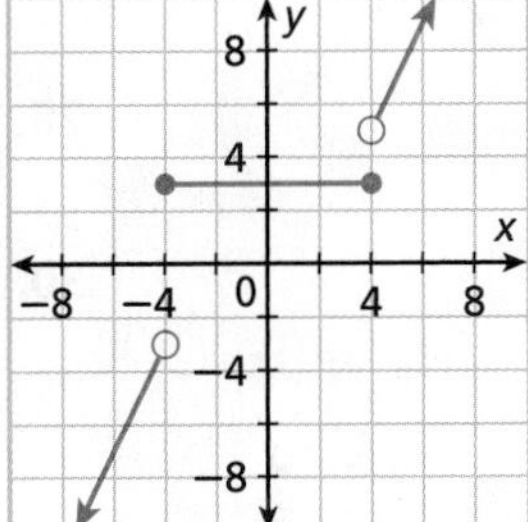

19. Parking A parking garage charges $6 for the first 4 hours that a car is parked in the lot. After that, the garage charges an additional $3 an hour. Write a piecewise function for the cost of parking a car in this garage for x hours.

20. Travel Derek and his friends drove from San Francisco to Lake Tahoe to go skiing. The average speed that they traveled during each leg of the trip is shown on the map. They drove 30 min in the city, 3 h on the highway, and 30 min up the mountain.

a. Write a piecewise function to represent the distance that Derek traveled during his 4 h trip.

b. Graph the function.

c. What if...? How much longer would the trip have taken if Derek had averaged 50 mi/h on the highway?

Average Speed

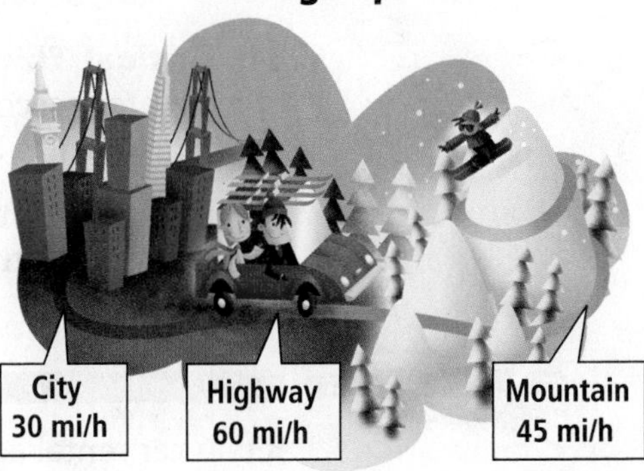

Write each absolute-value function as a piecewise function.

21. $f(x) = |x|$

22. $g(x) = |x - 4|$

23. $h(x) = 2|x| - 4$

24. Shipping An overnight delivery service charges $11 for a package that weighs 2 pounds or less. The delivery service charges $3 for each additional pound. Sketch a graph of the cost of shipping a package from 0 to 8 pounds. Then write a piecewise function for the graph.

Graph each function.

25. $h(x) = \begin{cases} \frac{1}{2}x^2 & \text{if } x \leq 0 \\ 2^x - 4 & \text{if } 0 < x \leq 3 \\ 2x - 2 & \text{if } x > 3 \end{cases}$

26. $h(x) = \begin{cases} -3 & \text{if } x \leq 0 \\ 3^x - 4 & \text{if } x > 0 \end{cases}$

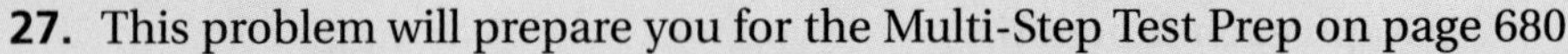

MULTI-STEP TEST PREP

27. This problem will prepare you for the Multi-Step Test Prep on page 680.

A human chain is formed by 60 people standing with their arms outstretched, each holding the hand of the person on either side. The first 30 people in the chain have arm spans of 6 feet. The next 30 people have arm spans of 5.5 feet. At the word "go," the first person squeezes the hand of the second person, then the second person squeezes the hand of the third, and so on. Assume that each person takes $\frac{1}{3}$ second to pass along the signal.

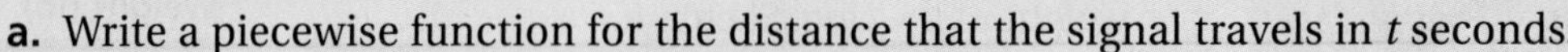

a. Write a piecewise function for the distance that the signal travels in t seconds.

b. Does the signal travel faster in the first half of the chain or the second half? How is this shown in the function?

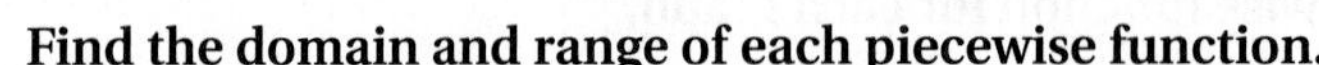

Find the domain and range of each piecewise function.

28. $f(x) = \begin{cases} -\frac{5}{2}x - 2 & \text{if } x \le -2 \\ -x - 5 & \text{if } x > -2 \end{cases}$

29. $g(x) = \begin{cases} x^2 - 2x - 3 & \text{if } x < 4 \\ 3x - 7 & \text{if } x \ge 4 \end{cases}$

30. **Sales** Mary works at a jewelry store. She receives a base salary every week plus a commission based on how much she sells. Mary's income function can be modeled by $P(x) = \begin{cases} 400 + 0.06x & \text{if } 0 \le x \le 5000 \\ 700 + 0.09(x - 5000) & \text{if } x > 5000 \end{cases}$, where $P(x)$ is her income and x is the amount of her sales in dollars.
   a. Write a description of Mary's income function.
   b. How much will Mary earn in a week in which she sells \$4000 worth of jewelry?
   c. Find the value of the jewelry that Mary must sell in a week if she wants to earn \$900 for that week.

31. **Critical Thinking** Why would a piecewise function best describe the height of an elevator t seconds after it leaves the bottom floor of a building? Would the piecewise function also be a step function?

32. **Write About It** Explain why piecewise functions are often good for representing real-world situations. Include at least two examples.

TEST PREP

33. A car rental agency charges \$15 a day for driving a car 200 miles or less. If a car is driven over 200 miles, the renter must pay \$0.05 for each mile over 200 driven. Which of the following functions represents the cost to drive a car from this agency x miles in a day?

Ⓐ $C(x) = \begin{cases} 15 & \text{if } 0 \le x \le 200 \\ 0.05x & \text{if } x > 200 \end{cases}$

Ⓒ $C(x) = \begin{cases} 15 & \text{if } 0 \le x \le 200 \\ 15 + 0.05(x - 200) & \text{if } x > 200 \end{cases}$

Ⓑ $C(x) = \begin{cases} 0.05 & \text{if } 0 \le x \le 200 \\ 15x & \text{if } x > 200 \end{cases}$

Ⓓ $C(x) = \begin{cases} 15 & \text{if } 0 \le x \le 200 \\ 15 + 0.05x & \text{if } x > 200 \end{cases}$

34. Which of the following is a continuous function?

Ⓕ $f(x) = \begin{cases} 3x - 4 & \text{if } x < 0 \\ -1 & \text{if } x \ge 0 \end{cases}$

Ⓗ $h(x) = \begin{cases} x^2 & \text{if } x < -2 \\ 2x & \text{if } x \ge -2 \end{cases}$

Ⓖ $g(x) = \begin{cases} 5x - 4 & \text{if } x < 3 \\ 2x + 5 & \text{if } x \ge 3 \end{cases}$

Ⓙ $j(x) = \begin{cases} 3x + 4 & \text{if } x \le -1 \\ 3^x + 4 & \text{if } x > -1 \end{cases}$

35. Let $f(x) = \begin{cases} 1 - 5x & \text{if } x < -5 \\ 3 - x^3 & \text{if } -5 \le x < -2 \\ 5 - x^2 & \text{if } x \ge -2 \end{cases}$. Find $f(-2)$.

Ⓐ -5 Ⓑ 1 Ⓒ 9 Ⓓ 11

CHALLENGE AND EXTEND

The *greatest integer function* returns the greatest integer less than or equal to a given number. The greatest integer function is written $f(x) = \lfloor x \rfloor$ and is often written as int(x) on graphing calculators. For example, if hamburgers cost \$1.79 each, the function $f(x) = \left\lfloor \frac{x}{1.79} \right\rfloor$ would return the number of hamburgers you could buy for x dollars.

36. Write a function for the number of orders of fries that can be bought with x dollars if an order of fries costs \$1.29. Then use your function to find the number of orders of fries that you can buy with \$10.

The *least integer function* returns the least integer greater than or equal to a given number. The least integer function is written $f(x) = \lceil x \rceil$. For example, $f(2.9) = \lceil 2.9 \rceil = 3$.

37. At a parking garage, parking costs \$4 for up to 1 hour. After that, it costs \$1.50 for each additional hour or fraction thereof. Write a function to represent the cost of parking for x hours. Then use the function to find the cost of parking for 5 hours and 23 minutes.

SPIRAL REVIEW

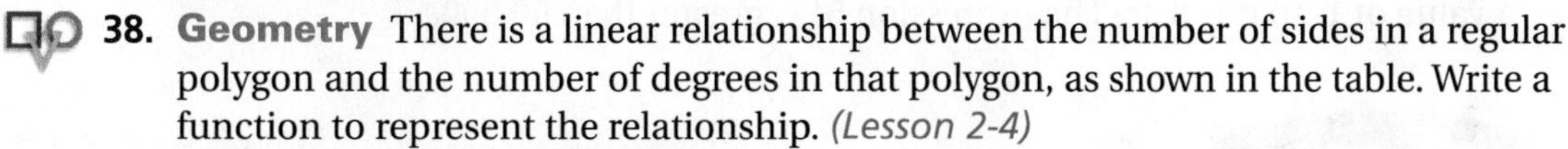

38. **Geometry** There is a linear relationship between the number of sides in a regular polygon and the number of degrees in that polygon, as shown in the table. Write a function to represent the relationship. *(Lesson 2-4)*

Sides	3	4	5	6	8
Sum of Interior Angles (°)	180	360	540	720	1080

Identify the asymptotes, domain, and range of each function. *(Lesson 8-4)*

39. $f(x) = \dfrac{4}{x-1} - 3$

40. $f(x) = \dfrac{3}{x+2} + 1$

41. $f(x) = \dfrac{5}{x-3} + 1$

Match each situation with one of the following graphs. *(Lesson 9-1)*

A.

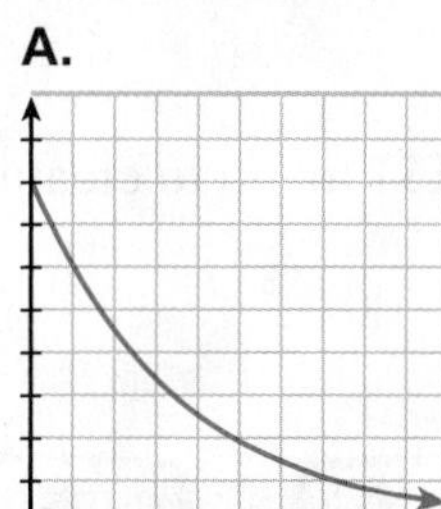

B.

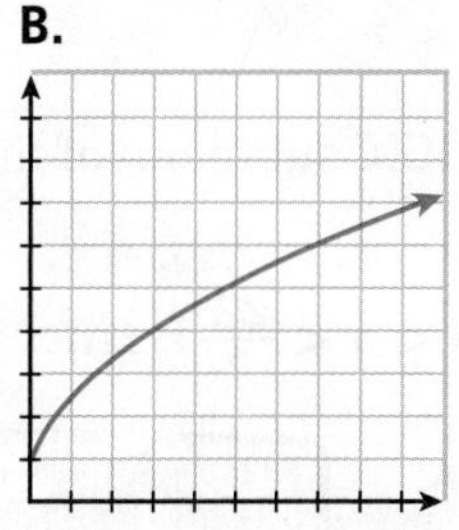

C.

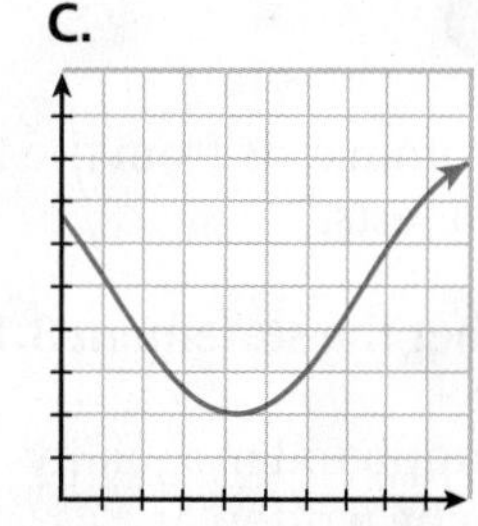

D.

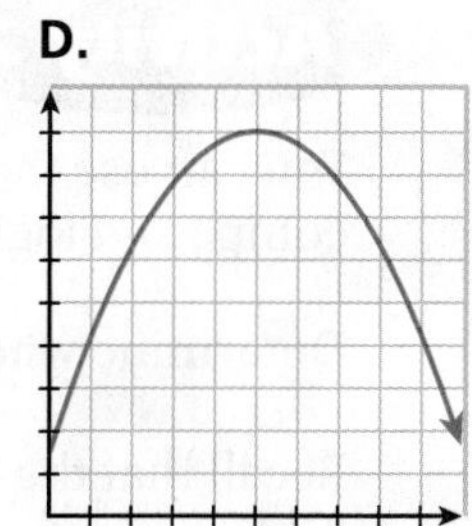

42. A company releases a product without advertisement, and the profit drops. Then the company advertises, and the profit increases.

43. The value of a computer declines over time.

44. The sales for an ice cream store are low in winter, high in spring and fall, and extremely high in summer.

45. The temperature rises steadily from 12:00 P.M. to 5:00 P.M.

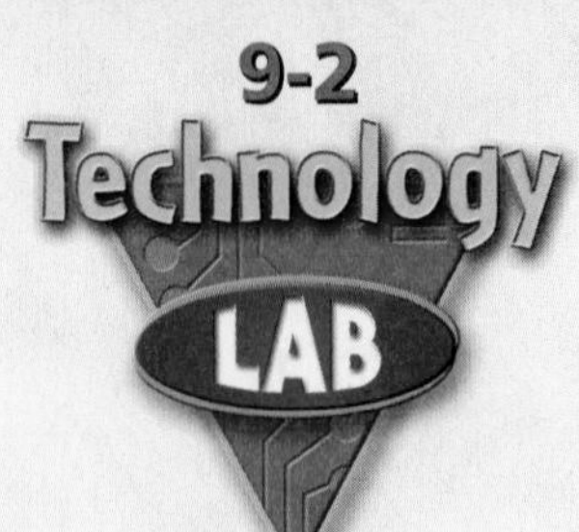

Graph Piecewise Functions

You can graph piecewise functions on a graphing calculator by using logical tests to restrict the domain for each piece of the function.

Activity 1

A graphing calculator can determine whether mathematical statements, such as $5 > 3$, are true. You can enter these statements by using the **TEST** menu. The calculator returns a value of 1 if the statement is true and a value of 0 if the statement is false.

Determine whether the statement 5^7 is greater than or less than 50,000.

Enter the first expression. Access the **TEST** menu (as shown) by pressing 2nd MATH. Choose the less-than symbol (**5:<**), and then enter the second expression. Enter the second inequality using the greater-than symbol (**3:>**).

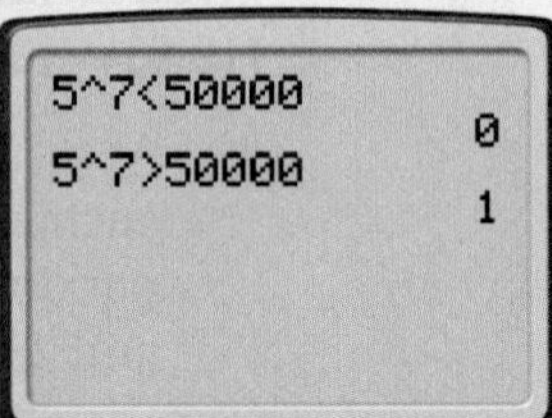

The first inequality returns a value of 0, so it is false. The second inequality returns a value of 1, so it is true. The expression 5^7 is greater than 50,000.

Try This

Use logical tests to determine whether each statement is true or false.

1. $4 - 3 \stackrel{?}{=} 3 - 4$
2. $(-6)^4 \stackrel{?}{\geq} 1000$
3. $\frac{3}{16} \stackrel{?}{<} 0.1875$
4. $\frac{3}{16} \stackrel{?}{>} 0.1875$
5. **Draw a Conclusion** What conclusion can you make about $\frac{3}{16}$ and 0.1875 based on the answers to Problems 3 and 4?

Activity 2

You can use the commands from the **LOGIC** submenu of the **TEST** menu to create compound logical tests.

Determine whether the statement $3.14 < \pi < \frac{22}{7}$ is true.

Recall that the compound inequality $3.14 < \pi < \frac{22}{7}$ can be written as $3.14 < \pi$ and $\pi < \frac{22}{7}$. Enter the first inequality, and then access the **LOGIC** submenu by pressing 2nd MATH ▶. Choose **1: and,** and then enter the second inequality.

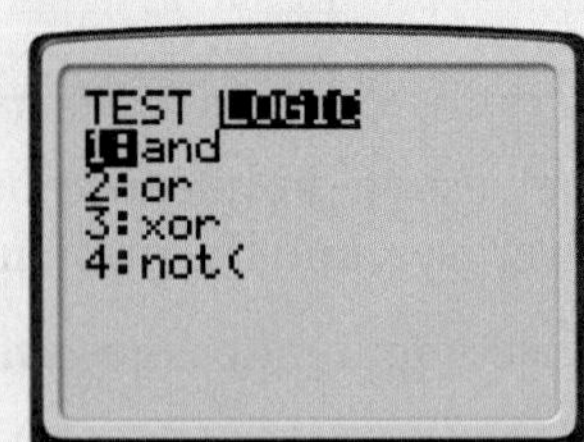

Because the statement returns a value of 1, the statement is true: $3.14 < \pi < \frac{22}{7}$. ✔

Try This

Use logical tests to determine whether each statement is true or false.

6. $-2^2 < -2 < (-2)^2$

7. $(-2)^1 < (-2)^2 < (-2)^3$

8. $\sqrt{2} < 2 < 2^2$

9. $\sqrt{\frac{1}{2}} < \frac{1}{2} < \left(\frac{1}{2}\right)^2$

10. Make a Conjecture What conjecture can you make about the relationship between a number, its square, and its square root if the number is greater than 1? What if the number is between 0 and 1?

Activity 3

Graph the piecewise function $f(x) = \begin{cases} 2x + 7 & \text{if } x \le -2 \\ 3 & \text{if } -2 < x \le 2 \\ x + 1 & \text{if } x > 2 \end{cases}$.

1 Enter the first part of the function rule as **Y1**. Then divide by the domain interval of the first part of the rule. Be sure to enclose both the first part of the rule and the domain interval in parentheses as shown.

The domain interval is a logical test. When the logical test is true, the calculator returns a value of 1, so **Y1** is equal to $2x + 7$. When the logical test is false, the calculator returns a value of 0, so **Y1** is undefined.

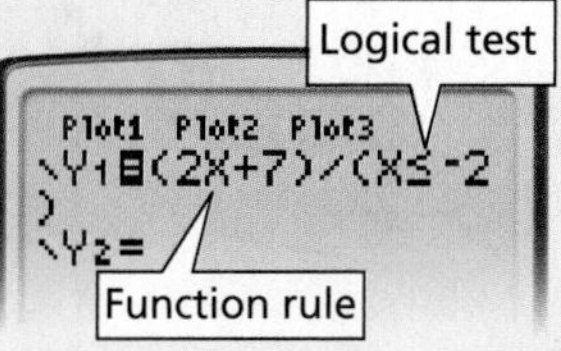

2 Use similar methods to enter the second part of the rule, divided by its domain interval, as **Y2**. Because the domain interval is a compound inequality, use the **and** command from the **LOGIC** menu.

```
Plot1 Plot2 Plot3
\Y1=(2X+7)/(X≤-2
)
\Y2=(3)/(X>-2 an
d X≤2)
\Y3=(X+1)/(X>2)
\Y4=
\Y5=
```

3 Finally, enter the third part of the rule, divided by its domain interval, as **Y3**, and graph in the standard square window.

4 The table shows values for each part of the rule. Notice that for each part, the value of y is undefined outside of the domain interval. (To see values of **Y3**, use the ▶ key to scroll to the right.)

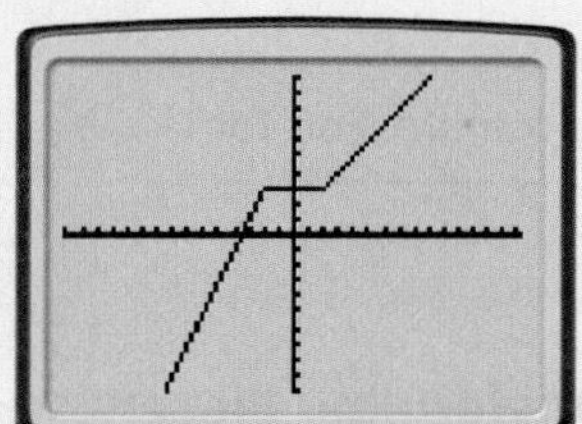

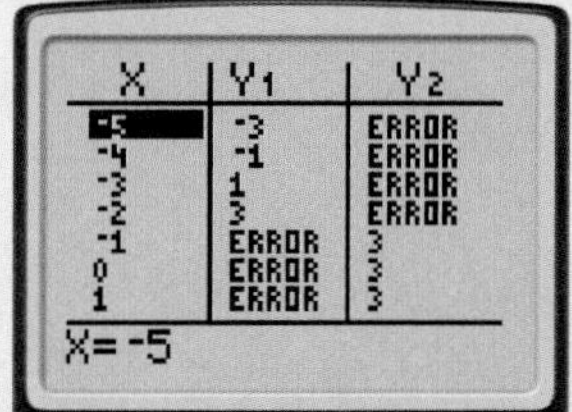

Try This

Graph each piecewise function.

11. $g(x) = \begin{cases} x & \text{if } x < 0 \\ -x & \text{if } x \ge 0 \end{cases}$

12. $h(x) = \begin{cases} 2x + 8 & \text{if } x \le -2 \\ x^2 & \text{if } x > -2 \end{cases}$

13. $f(x) = \begin{cases} -3x & \text{if } x < 1 \\ x - 4 & \text{if } 1 \le x < 5 \\ -\frac{1}{2}x + \frac{7}{2} & \text{if } x \ge 5 \end{cases}$

14. Critical Thinking Explain how dividing the function by a logical test value visually restricts the domain of the function on your graph.

15. Critical Thinking Explain how you can use the table feature of a graphing calculator to evaluate a piecewise function.

9-3 Transforming Functions

"If you miss a payment, we show up and embarrass you in front of your friends."

Objectives

Transform functions.

Recognize transformations of functions.

Why learn this?

Transformations can be used to describe changes in college tuition fees. (See Example 4.)

In previous lessons, you learned how to transform several types of functions. You can transform piecewise functions by applying transformations to each piece independently. Recall the rules for transforming functions given in the table.

Transformations of $f(x)$	
Horizontal Translation	**Vertical Translation**
$f(x) \rightarrow f(x - h)$ left for $h < 0$ right for $h > 0$	$f(x) \rightarrow f(x) + k$ down for $k < 0$ up for $k > 0$
Reflection Across y-axis	**Reflection Across x-axis**
$f(x) \rightarrow f(-x)$ The graph is reflected across the y-axis.	$f(x) \rightarrow -f(x)$ The graph is reflected across the x-axis.
Horizontal Stretch/Compression	**Vertical Stretch/Compression**
$f(x) \rightarrow f\left(\frac{1}{b}x\right)$ stretch for $b > 1$ compression for $0 < b < 1$	$f(x) \rightarrow af(x)$ stretch for $a > 1$ compression for $0 < a < 1$

Caution!

Horizontal translations change both the rules and the intervals of piecewise functions. Vertical translations change only the rules.

EXAMPLE 1 Transforming Piecewise Functions

Given $f(x) = \begin{cases} x + 3 & \text{if } x > 0 \\ 2x + 3 & \text{if } x \le 0 \end{cases}$, write the rule for $g(x)$, a horizontal translation of $f(x)$ 4 units right.

Each piece of $f(x)$ must be shifted 4 units right. Replace every x in the function with $(x - 4)$, and simplify.

$$g(x) = f(x - 4) = \begin{cases} (x - 4) + 3 & \text{if } (x - 4) > 0 \\ 2(x - 4) + 3 & \text{if } (x - 4) \le 0 \end{cases}$$

$$= \begin{cases} x - 1 & \text{if } x > 4 \\ 2x - 5 & \text{if } x \le 4 \end{cases}$$

Check Graph both functions to support your answer.

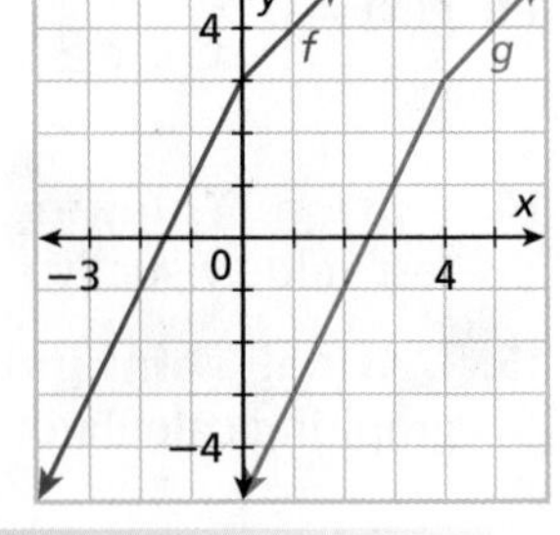

1. Given $f(x) = \begin{cases} x^2 & \text{if } x \le 0 \\ x - 3 & \text{if } x > 0 \end{cases}$, write the rule for $g(x)$, a horizontal stretch of $f(x)$ by a factor of 2.

When functions are transformed, the intercepts may or may not change. By identifying the transformations, you can determine the intercepts, which can help you graph a transformed function.

Effects of Transformations on Intercepts of $f(x)$	
Horizontal Stretch or Compression by a Factor of b	**Vertical Stretch or Compression by a Factor of a**
x-intercepts are multiplied by b. y-intercept stays the same.	x-intercepts stay the same. y-intercept is multiplied by a.
Reflection Across y-axis	**Reflection Across x-axis**
x-intercepts are negated. y-intercept stays the same.	x-intercepts stay the same. y-intercept is negated.

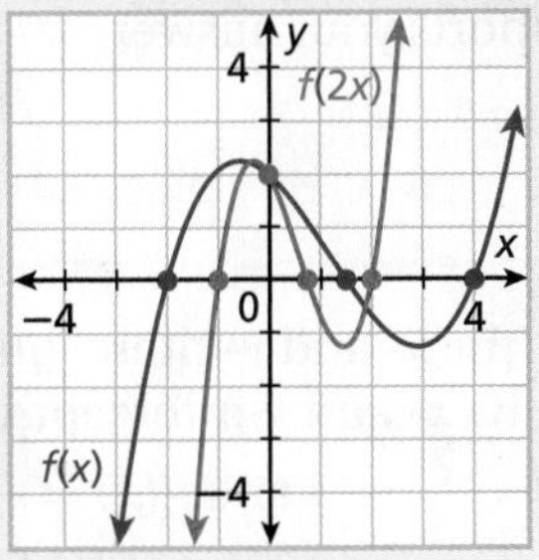

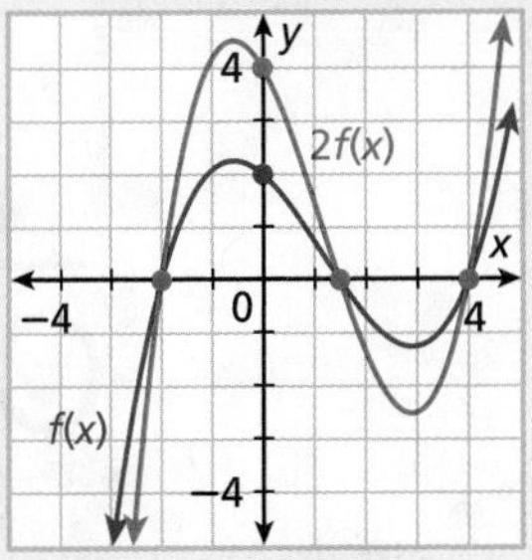

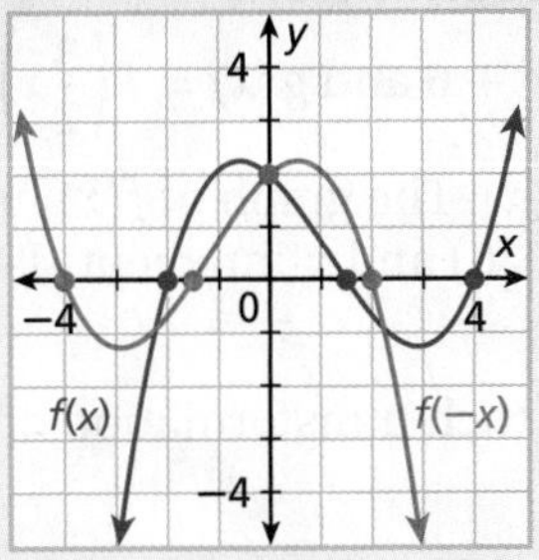

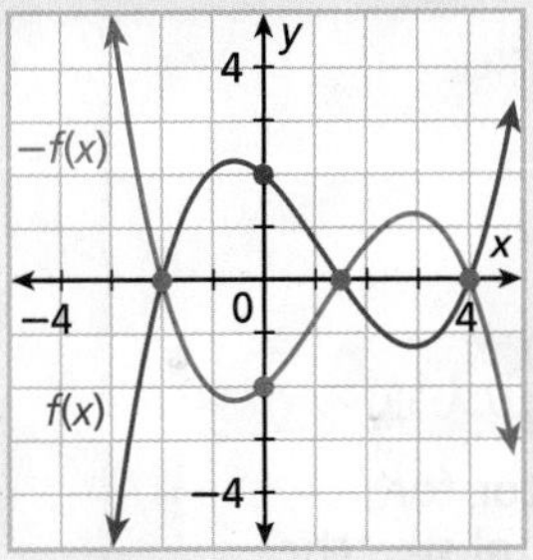

EXAMPLE 2 Identifying Intercepts

Identify the x- and y-intercepts of $f(x)$. Without graphing $g(x)$, identify its x- and y-intercepts.

A $f(x) = \frac{1}{2}x - 3$ and $g(x) = 3f(x)$

Find the intercepts of the original function.

$f(0) = \frac{1}{2}(0) - 3 = -3$ $\qquad 0 = \frac{1}{2}x - 3$

$f(0) = -3$ $\qquad 6 = x$

The y-intercept is -3, and the x-intercept is 6. Note that $g(x)$ is a vertical stretch of $f(x)$ by a factor of 3. So the x-intercept of $g(x)$ is also 6. The y-intercept is $3(-3)$, or -9.

Check A graph supports your answer.

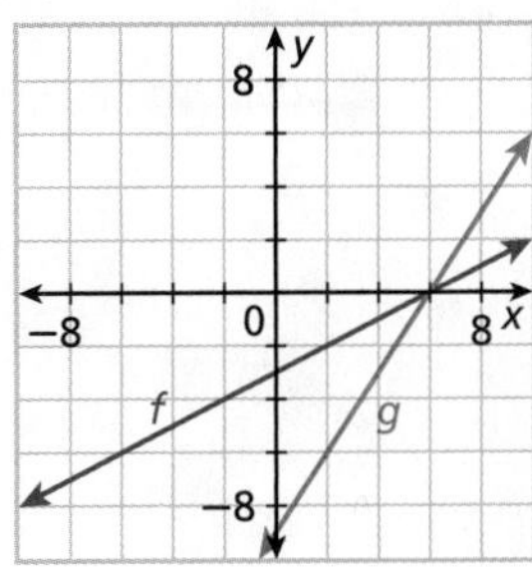

Identify the x- and y-intercepts of $f(x)$. Without graphing $g(x)$, identify its x- and y-intercepts.

B $f(x) = x^2 - 4$ **and** $g(x) = f(2x)$

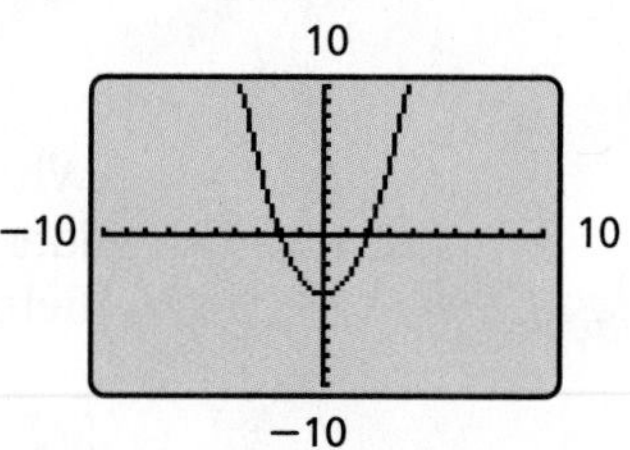

From the graph of $f(x)$, the y-intercept is -4 and the x-intercepts are -2 and 2.

Note that $g(x)$ is a horizontal compression by a factor of $\frac{1}{2}$. So the x-intercepts of $g(x)$ will be $\frac{1}{2}(-2)$ and $\frac{1}{2}(2)$, or -1 and 1. The y-intercept is unchanged at -4.

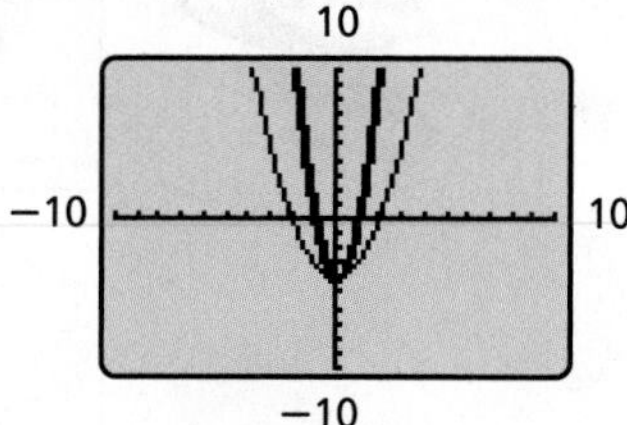

Check A graph supports your answer.

Identify the x- and y-intercepts of $f(x)$. Without graphing $g(x)$, identify its x- and y-intercepts.

2a. $f(x) = \frac{2}{3}x + 4$ and $g(x) = -f(x)$

2b. $f(x) = x^2 - 9$ and $g(x) = \frac{1}{3}f(x)$

EXAMPLE 3 Combining Transformations

Given $f(x) = -\frac{2}{3}x^2 + 6$ **and** $g(x) = f\left(\frac{3}{2}x\right) + 4$**, graph** $g(x)$**.**

Remember!

The factor for horizontal stretches and compressions is the reciprocal of the coefficient in the equation.

$$\frac{1}{\frac{3}{2}} = \frac{2}{3}$$

Step 1 Graph $f(x)$. The graph of $f(x)$ has y-intercept $(0, 6)$ and x-intercepts $(-3, 0)$ and $(3, 0)$.

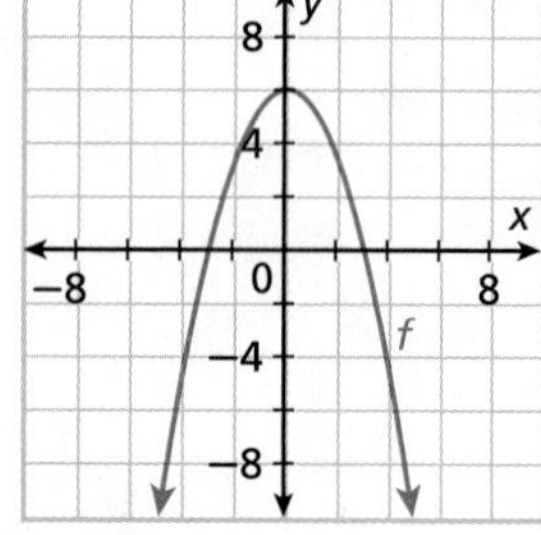

Step 2 Analyze each transformation one at a time.

The first transformation is a horizontal compression by a factor of $\frac{2}{3}$. After the horizontal compression, the x-intercepts will be -2 and 2, but the y-intercept will remain 6.

The second transformation is a vertical translation of 4 units up. Use a table to shift each identified point up 4 units.

Intercept Points	(−2, 0)	(2, 0)	(0, 6)
Shifted	(−2, 4)	(2, 4)	(0, 10)

Step 3 Graph the final result.

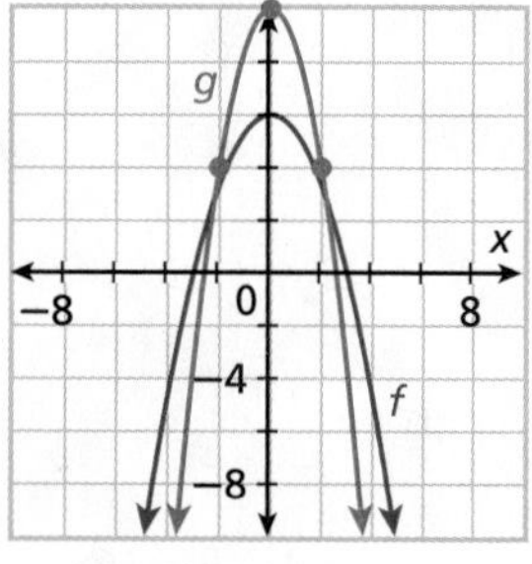

3. Given $f(x) = 2^x - 4$ and $g(x) = -\frac{1}{2}f(x)$, graph $g(x)$.

EXAMPLE 4 Problem-Solving Application

PROBLEM SOLVING

A college charges different fees according to the number of credit hours in which students have enrolled. The fee scale is modeled by the piecewise function below, where x is the number of credit hours.

$$f(x) = \begin{cases} 110x & \text{if } 0 < x < 12 \\ 1320 & \text{if } 12 \le x \le 18 \\ 150(x-18) + 1320 & \text{if } x > 18 \end{cases}$$

The college plans to increase all fees by 10% for the fall semester. In the spring semester, the college plans to add an administrative fee of $75 to each enrollment. Write the rule for the fee function for the spring semester.

1 Understand the Problem

The new fee function will include two changes, a 10% increase and an additional fee of $75. The 10% increase is equivalent to multiplying all of the parts of the function by 110%, or 1.1. This will be a vertical stretch by a factor of 1.1. The administrative fee will be a vertical translation of 75 units up.

2 Make a Plan

Perform each transformation, one at a time, and then write the new rule.

3 Solve

First find the fees for the fall semester.

$$f_{\text{fall}}(x) = (1.1)f(x) = \begin{cases} (1.1)110x & \text{if } 0 < x < 12 \\ (1.1)1320 & \text{if } 12 \le x \le 18 \\ (1.1)[150(x-18) + 1320] & \text{if } x > 18 \end{cases}$$

Multiply all parts by 1.1.

$$= \begin{cases} 121x & \text{if } 0 < x < 12 \\ 1452 & \text{if } 12 \le x \le 18 \\ 165(x-18) + 1452 & \text{if } x > 18 \end{cases}$$

Then find the fees for the spring semester.

$$f_{\text{spring}}(x) = f_{\text{fall}}(x) + 75 = \begin{cases} 121x + 75 & \text{if } 0 < x < 12 \\ 1452 + 75 & \text{if } 12 \le x \le 18 \\ 165(x-18) + 1452 + 75 & \text{if } x > 18 \end{cases}$$

$$= \begin{cases} 121x + 75 & \text{if } 0 < x < 12 \\ 1527 & \text{if } 12 \le x \le 18 \\ 165(x-18) + 1527 & \text{if } x > 18 \end{cases}$$

4 Look Back

Check your answer by trying a few values. For 20 hours, the original fee would have been $1620. A 10% increase plus a $75 fee would amount to $1857. Evaluate the function for $x = 20$ to check.

$$f_{\text{spring}}(20) = \{165(20-18) + 1527 = 1857 \checkmark$$

Continue by checking each piece of the function.

4. A movie theater charges $5 for children under 12 and $7.50 for anyone 12 and over. The theater decides to increase its prices by 20%. It charges an additional $0.50 fee for online ticket purchases. Write a function for the online ticket prices.

THINK AND DISCUSS

1. Identify the transformations that leave the y-intercept unchanged.
2. Explain why the point (0, 0) is unchanged under any stretch or compression.

3. **GET ORGANIZED** Copy and complete the graphic organizer. Identify the effects of each transformation on the intercepts.

Transformation	*x*-intercepts	*y*-intercept
Horizontal stretch or compression by a factor of *b*		
Vertical stretch or compression by a factor of *a*		
Reflection across *y*-axis		
Reflection across *x*-axis		

9-3 Exercises

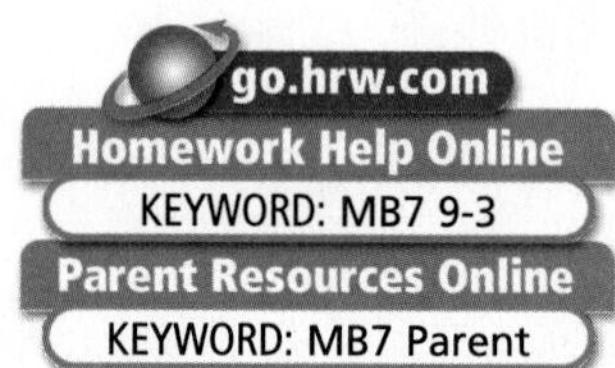

GUIDED PRACTICE

SEE EXAMPLE 1 p. 672

Given $f(x) = \begin{cases} x - 3 & \text{if } x \le 0 \\ 4x & \text{if } x > 0 \end{cases}$, write the rule for each function.

1. $g(x)$, a horizontal translation of $f(x)$ 6 units left
2. $h(x)$, a horizontal compression by a factor of $\frac{1}{4}$

SEE EXAMPLE 2 p. 673

Identify the x- and y-intercepts of $f(x)$. Without graphing $g(x)$, identify its x- and y-intercepts.

3. $f(x) = 4x + 12$ and $g(x) = \frac{1}{6}f(x)$
4. $f(x) = -x^2 + 16$ and $g(x) = f(4x)$

SEE EXAMPLE 3 p. 674

Given $f(x)$, graph $g(x)$.

5. $f(x) = -x^2 + 1$ and $g(x) = f(2x) - 1$
6. $f(x) = |x - 1| - 2$ and $g(x) = -2f(x)$

SEE EXAMPLE 4 p. 675

7. **Taxes** The state income tax in Connecticut is modeled by the function $T(x) = \begin{cases} 0.02x & \text{if } 0 < x \le 10{,}000 \\ 0.05x & \text{if } x > 10{,}000 \end{cases}$, where x is income in dollars. Suppose that Connecticut decided to increase its tax rates by 20% and add a filing fee of \$100 dollars. Write a function for the new state income tax.

PRACTICE AND PROBLEM SOLVING

Given $f(x) = \begin{cases} x^2 & \text{if } x < 1 \\ 4x & \text{if } x \ge 1 \end{cases}$, write the rule for each function.

8. $g(x)$, a vertical compression of $f(x)$ by a factor of $\frac{1}{4}$
9. $h(x)$, a horizontal stretch by a factor of 2
10. $p(x)$, a vertical translation 3 units down

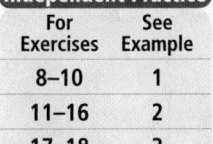

Independent Practice

For Exercises	See Example
8–10	1
11–16	2
17–18	3
19	4

Extra Practice

Skills Practice p. S20

Application Practice p. S40

Identify the x- and y-intercepts of $f(x)$. Without graphing $g(x)$, identify its x- and y-intercepts.

11. $f(x) = -\frac{3}{2}x + 9$ and $g(x) = \frac{2}{3}f(x)$

12. $f(x) = x^2 - 25$ and $g(x) = f\left(\frac{5}{3}x\right)$

13. $f(x) = -\frac{2}{5}x + 2$ and $g(x) = f(2x)$

14. $f(x) = x^2 - 3x - 4$ and $g(x) = -f\left(\frac{1}{3}x\right)$

15. $f(x) = 3^x - 1$ and $g(x) = 2f(x) - 4$

16. $f(x) = x^3 + 8$ and $g(x) = f\left(-\frac{1}{2}x\right)$

Given $f(x)$, graph $g(x)$.

17. $f(x) = \frac{1}{2}x + 4$ and $g(x) = 3f(-x)$

18. $f(x) = \left(\frac{1}{2}\right)^x - 2$ and $g(x) = -f(2x)$

19. Business The amount that a caterer charges to cater a party for n people is given by the function $C(n) = \begin{cases} 18n & \text{if } n \le 50 \\ 400 + 10n & \text{if } n > 50 \end{cases}$.

a. During a sale, the caterer reduces the amount charged by 10%. Find the function for how much the caterer will charge during the sale.

b. If the caterer then decides to take an additional \$2 off per person, find the function for how much the caterer will charge.

LINK

Safety

In some cities, automatic cameras are used to identify and photograph vehicles that are speeding. The first stationary speed camera in Washington, D.C., detected more than 10,000 speeding drivers in its first 15 days of operation.

20. Safety Speeding fines in Washington, D.C., are shown in the table.

a. Write a function to represent speeding fines.

b. If the speeding offense occurs in a school zone, the city adds a fine of \$50. Write a function for the increased fines in a school zone.

c. **What if...?** The city is considering increasing speeding fines by 15%. Write a new function for the increased speeding fines.

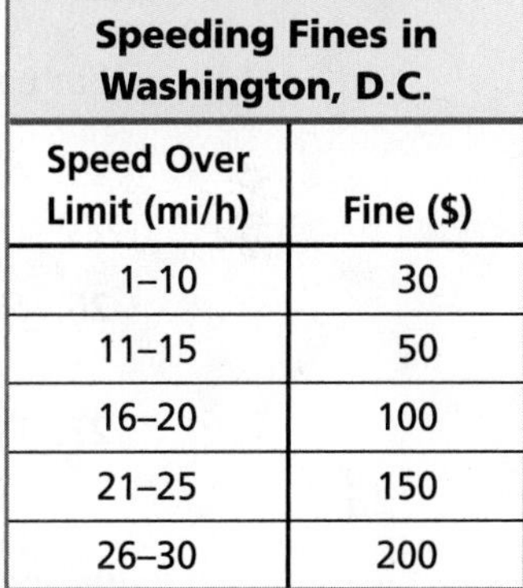

Speeding Fines in Washington, D.C.

Speed Over Limit (mi/h)	Fine (\$)
1–10	30
11–15	50
16–20	100
21–25	150
26–30	200

21. Critical Thinking Suppose that the graph of $f(x)$ has n x-intercepts.

a. How many x-intercepts does the graph of $bf(ax)$ have? Explain.

b. Explain why you cannot tell how many x-intercepts the graph of $f(x - h) + k$ has.

22. Money A credit card company charges a person taking a cash advance on its credit card at an ATM a \$6 transaction fee if \$200 or less is withdrawn. For amounts over \$200, the transaction fee is 3% of the amount withdrawn.

a. Write a function for the transaction fee to withdraw x dollars.

b. Suppose that the company wants to increase fees by 15% in order to reflect increased costs. Adjust your function to include the increase.

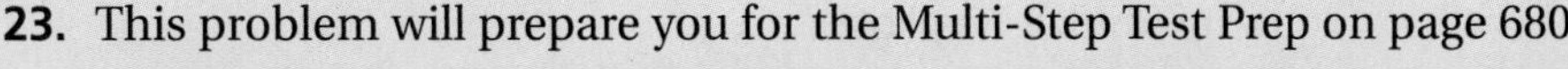

23. This problem will prepare you for the Multi-Step Test Prep on page 680.

At a party, the host whispers a phrase into the ear of a guest who then whispers the phrase into the ear of the person standing next to him. The process is repeated down the line until the last person says the phrase out loud. The time in seconds for the phrase to move through the line is modeled by $T(n) = \begin{cases} 3.5n & \text{if } n \le 8 \\ 4.5n - 8 & \text{if } n > 8 \end{cases}$, where n is the number of guests in the line.

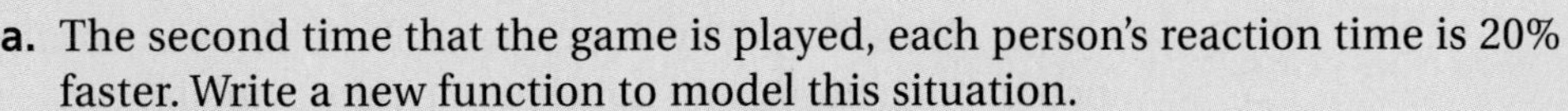

a. The second time that the game is played, each person's reaction time is 20% faster. Write a new function to model this situation.

b. Describe the effect of this improvement on the graph of $T(n)$.

24. **Technology** Morphing is a computerized technique for making one picture turn into another picture. Morphing is created by transforming specific points from one location to another.

    a. Graph the functions $f(x) = \left\{\frac{1}{2}x + 4 \text{ for } 1 \le x \le 2\right.$, $g(x) = \left\{-x^2 + 6x - 7 \text{ for } 2 \le x \le 4\right.$, and $h(x) = \left\{-\frac{1}{2}x + 7 \text{ for } 4 \le x \le 5\right.$ on the same coordinate grid.

    b. Graph the transformed functions $f_{new}(x) = -f(x) + 8$, $g_{new}(x) = -g(x) + 3$, and $h_{new}(x) = -h(x) + 8$.

    c. Describe the morph that you created.

For each function, give the new function rule after the given transformation.

25. $f(x) = \begin{cases} 2^x - 1 & \text{if } x \le -3 \\ -5x + 3 & \text{if } x > -3 \end{cases}$ after a translation of 7 units down

26. $f(x) = \begin{cases} 3x^2 & \text{if } x < 1 \\ -2x + 4 & \text{if } x \ge 1 \end{cases}$ after a vertical stretch by a factor of 5

27. **Food** A farmers' market sells fruits and vegetables at a flat rate with discounts for larger purchases.

    a. Sketch a graph of the cost of 0 to 10 pounds of produce.

    b. Write a piecewise function for the cost of x pounds of produce.

    c. **What if...?** During a sale, the market offers a buy-one-get-one-free sale. Graph the new cost function and describe the transformation from the original function.

28. **Business** A company's profit model is given by $P(n) = -0.002n^2 + 19n - 9000$, where $P(n)$ is the profit in dollars and n is the number of items produced. Based on some new data, the profit model for next year is predicted to be $R(n) = P(0.8n)$.

    a. How will the change affect the number of items the company should produce to maximize its profit?

    b. Find the number of items the company should produce to maximize profit under the new model.

29. **Critical Thinking** A linear function has an x-intercept equal to 2 and a y-intercept equal to 3. The function is stretched vertically by a factor of 2, then translated 3 units down, and then stretched horizontally by a factor of 2. What are the new intercepts?

30. **Critical Thinking** Why does a vertical translation not affect the domain of a function but a horizontal translation might? Explain.

31. **Write About It** Can a graph that is not continuous be transformed into a continuous graph by using stretches and compressions only? Explain.

TEST PREP

32. For the graphs shown, which of the following is $g(x)$?

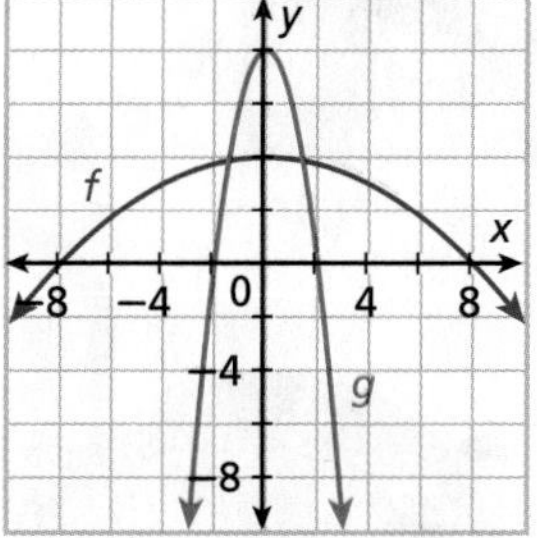

Ⓐ $g(x) = 2f\left(\frac{1}{4}x\right)$ Ⓒ $g(x) = 2f(4x)$

Ⓑ $g(x) = \frac{1}{2}f\left(\frac{1}{4}x\right)$ Ⓓ $g(x) = \frac{1}{2}f(4x)$

33. Suppose that $f(x) = \begin{cases} 2x & x > 8 \\ x^2 & x \leq 8 \end{cases}$.
Which of the following is $g(x) = f(4x)$?

Ⓕ $g(x) = \begin{cases} \frac{x}{2} & \text{if } x > 2 \\ \frac{x^2}{16} & \text{if } x \leq 2 \end{cases}$ Ⓗ $g(x) = \begin{cases} 8x & \text{if } x > 32 \\ 4x^2 & \text{if } x \leq 32 \end{cases}$

Ⓖ $g(x) = \begin{cases} \frac{x}{2} & \text{if } x > 8 \\ \frac{x^2}{16} & \text{if } x \leq 8 \end{cases}$ Ⓙ $g(x) = \begin{cases} 8x & \text{if } x > 2 \\ 16x^2 & \text{if } x \leq 2 \end{cases}$

34. The y-intercept of $g(x) = \frac{3}{5}f(5x)$ is 15. Which of the following is the y-intercept of $f(x)$?

Ⓐ 3 Ⓑ 9 Ⓒ 25 Ⓓ 75

CHALLENGE AND EXTEND

35. **Geometry** Consider the function $f(x) = \begin{cases} \frac{2}{3}x + 4 & \text{if } x < 0 \\ -\frac{1}{2}x + 4 & \text{if } x \geq 0 \end{cases}$.

a. Graph the function, and find its intercepts. Then find the area bounded by the function and the x-axis.

b. Graph the transformation $g(x) = 4f(2x)$. Find the area bounded by $g(x)$ and the x-axis.

c. Write a function $h(x)$ that creates an area of 7 square units.

36. Consider the functions $f(x) = 2x^3 - 3x^2 - 11x + 6$, $g(x) = 3f\left(\frac{1}{2}x\right)$, and $h(x) = -g\left(\frac{1}{2}x\right)$.

a. Find the x- and y-intercepts of $g(x)$.

b. Find the x- and y-intercepts of $h(x)$.

SPIRAL REVIEW

37. **Geology** An earthquake map claims that about 43% of the earthquakes in the United States between 1999 and 2002 occurred in California. There were 973 earthquakes between 1999 and 2002 in the United States. About how many earthquakes occurred in California? *(Lesson 2-2)*

Find the maximum or minimum value of each function. Then state the domain and range of the function. *(Lesson 5-2)*

38. $f(x) = 4x^2 - 2x + 8$

39. $g(x) = -3x^2 + 6x - 9$

Evaluate each piecewise function for $x = -4$, $x = 0$, and $x = 5$. *(Lesson 9-2)*

40. $f(x) = \begin{cases} 3 & \text{if } x < 1 \\ x^2 - 4 & \text{if } x \geq 1 \end{cases}$

41. $f(x) = \begin{cases} 5 - 2x & \text{if } x < -3 \\ 4 + x & \text{if } x \geq -3 \end{cases}$

CHAPTER 9

MULTI-STEP TEST PREP

SECTION 9A

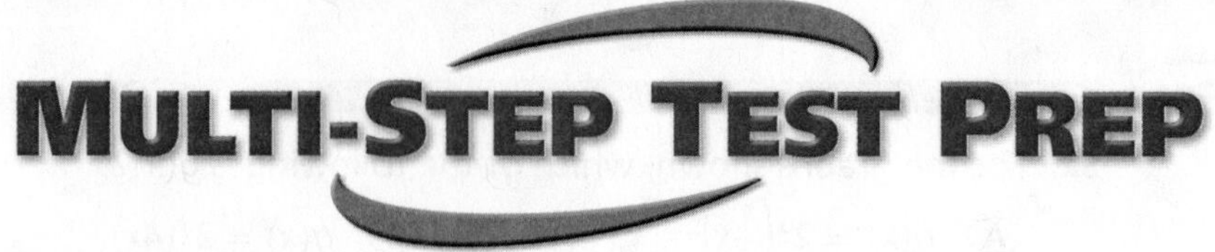

Functions and Their Graphs

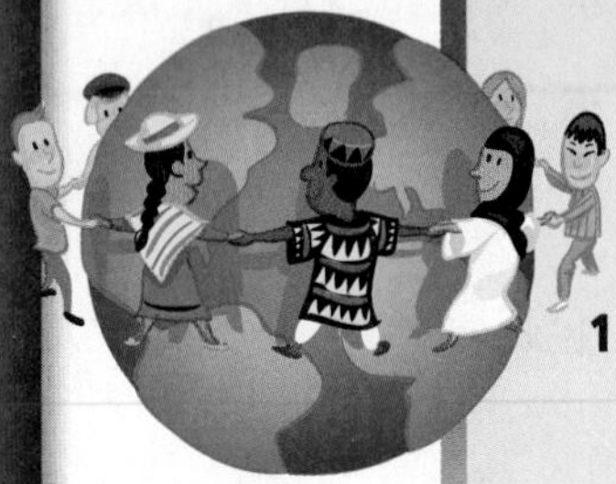

Hands Around the World Imagine a human chain of people holding hands. Assume that each person stands with his or her arms fully outstretched.

1. Suppose that the chain could go all the way around the planet. Then the chain's length would be equal to the circumference of the earth at the equator (about 24,000 miles). Assuming that the average adult arm span is 6 feet, how many people would it take to make this human chain?
2. At the word "go!" the first person in the chain squeezes the hand of the second person, who in turn immediately squeezes the hand of the third person, and so on. Given that it takes 20 seconds for the 60th person to react to having his or her hand squeezed, how many hours would it take the signal to travel all the way around the world?
3. Sketch a graph of the distance in feet that the signal travels in the span of 0 to 1000 seconds. Identify the slope of the line.
4. Researchers at the University of British Columbia have measured muscle reaction times of 0.1 second for Olympic sprinters. If the human chain consisted entirely of Olympic sprinters, how long would it take for the signal to travel all the way around the world?
5. Create a graph of the distance the signal travels in the chain of Olympic sprinters. How does the slope compare to the graph in Problem 3?
6. Suppose that the first half of a human chain is formed by 500 Olympic sprinters and the second half is formed by 500 people whose reaction time is 0.9 second. Write and graph a piecewise function that describes the distance traveled by the signal as a function of time.

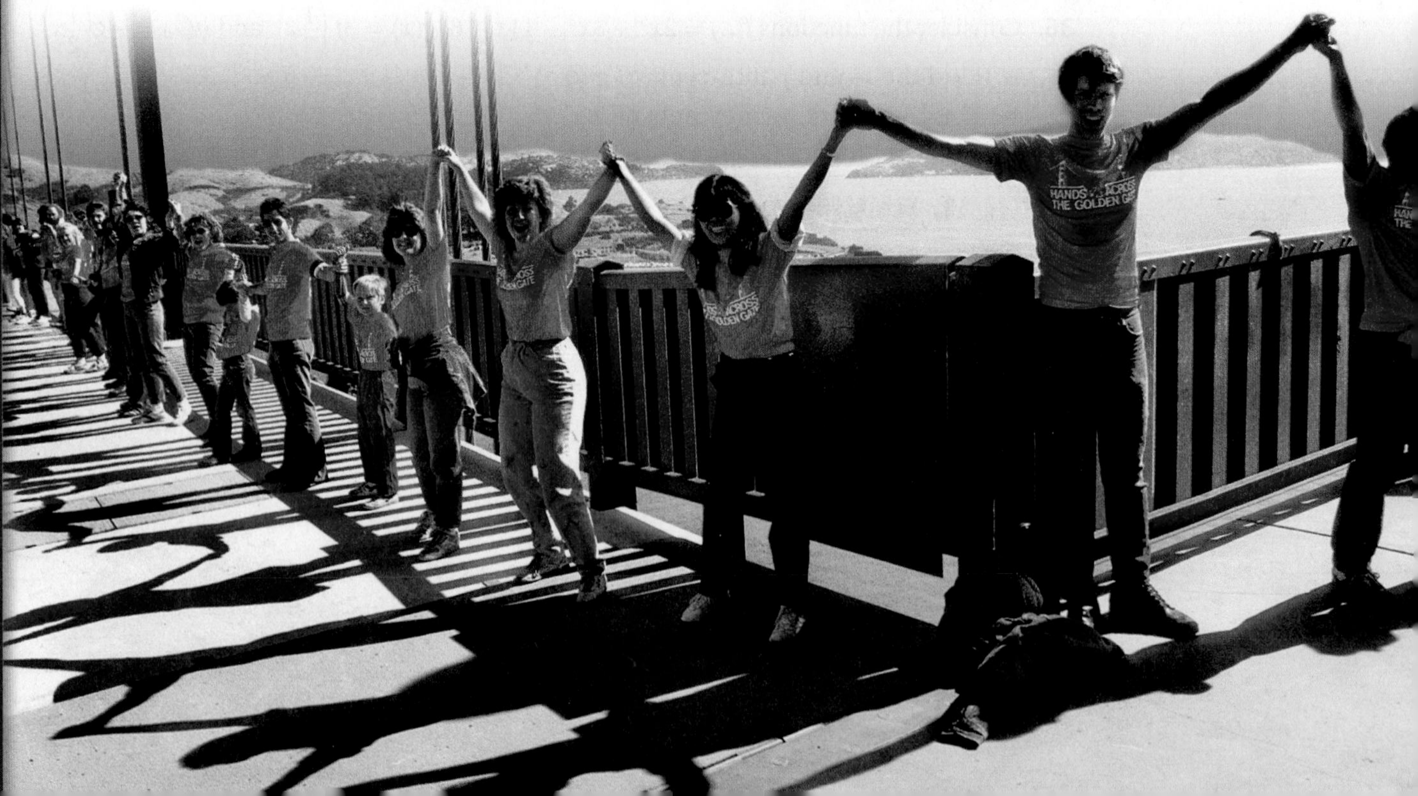

READY TO GO ON?

Quiz for Lessons 9-1 Through 9-3

9-1 Multiple Representations of Functions

1. Amanda must read a 294-page book for her history class over the next week. Amanda has found that she can read 42 pages in an hour. Create a table, a graph, and an equation to represent the number of pages that Amanda has left to read with relation to time.

2. The height of a rocket at different times after it was fired is shown in the table.

Time (s)	0	1	2	3	4	5
Height (m)	50.0	65.1	70.4	65.9	51.5	27.5

a. Find an appropriate model for the height of the rocket.
b. Find the maximum height of the rocket.
c. How long will the rocket stay in the air?

9-2 Piecewise Functions

Graph each function.

3. $f(x) = \begin{cases} 3 & \text{if } x < 0 \\ 2x + 3 & \text{if } x \geq 0 \end{cases}$

4. $h(x) = \begin{cases} -x + 1 & \text{if } x < -3 \\ -x & \text{if } -3 \leq x < 1 \\ -x - 1 & \text{if } x \geq 1 \end{cases}$

5. The cost of renting a mountain bike is $25 for the first 3 hours and $5 for each additional hour. Sketch a graph of the cost of renting a mountain bike for 0 to 8 hours. Then write a piecewise function for the graph.

Write a piecewise function for each graph.

6. 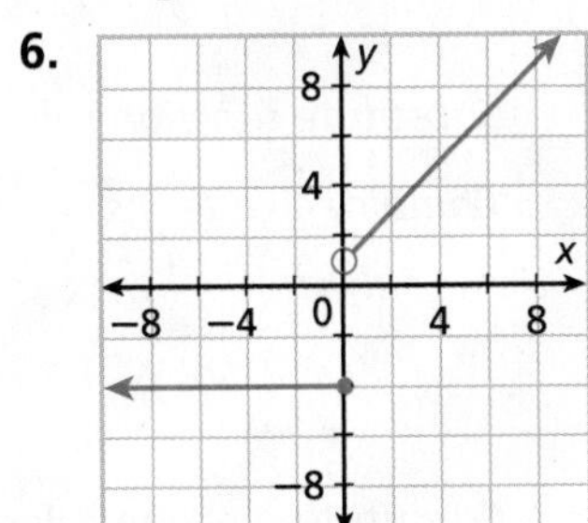

7. 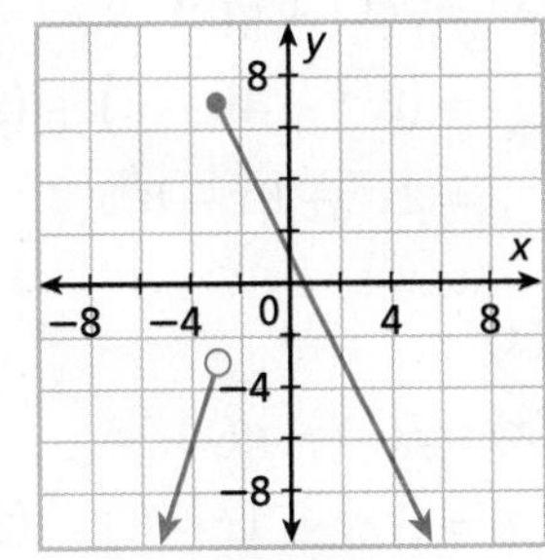

8. 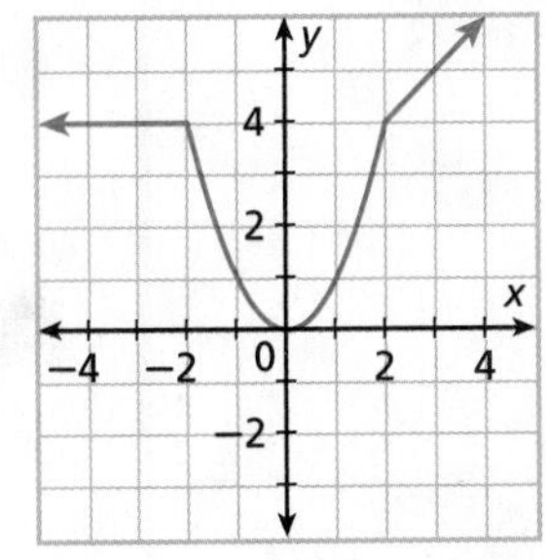

9-3 Transforming Functions

Identify the x- and y-intercepts of $f(x)$. Without graphing $g(x)$, identify its x- and y-intercepts.

9. $f(x) = 2x - 2$ and $g(x) = -f\left(\frac{1}{2}x\right)$

10. $f(x) = x^2 - 4$ and $g(x) = 2f(x)$

Given $f(x)$, graph $g(x)$.

11. $f(x) = |x| - 3$ and $g(x) = 2f(x) + 3$

12. $f(x) = x^2 + 1$ and $g(x) = -3f(x)$

fog

9-4 Operations with Functions

Objectives
Add, subtract, multiply, and divide functions.

Write and evaluate composite functions.

Vocabulary
composition of functions

Who uses this?
Importers can use function operations to determine the costs of items that are purchased in foreign currencies. (See Example 5.)

You can perform operations on functions in much the same way that you perform operations on numbers or expressions. You can add, subtract, multiply, or divide functions by operating on their rules.

Notation for Function Operations	
Operation	**Notation**
Addition	$(f+g)(x) = f(x) + g(x)$
Subtraction	$(f-g)(x) = f(x) - g(x)$
Multiplication	$(fg)(x) = f(x) \cdot g(x)$
Division	$\left(\frac{f}{g}\right)(x) = \frac{f(x)}{g(x)}$, where $g(x) \neq 0$

EXAMPLE 1 **Adding and Subtracting Functions**

Given $f(x) = 2x^2 + 4x - 6$ and $g(x) = 2x - 2$, find each function.

A $(f+g)(x)$

$(f+g)(x) = f(x) + g(x)$

$= (2x^2 + 4x - 6) + (2x - 2)$ *Substitute function rules.*

$= 2x^2 + 6x - 8$ *Combine like terms.*

B $(f-g)(x)$

$(f-g)(x) = f(x) - g(x)$

$= (2x^2 + 4x - 6) - (2x - 2)$ *Substitute function rules.*

$= 2x^2 + 4x - 6 - 2x + 2$ *Distributive Property*

$= 2x^2 + 2x - 4$ *Combine like terms.*

Given $f(x) = 5x - 6$ and $g(x) = x^2 - 5x + 6$, find each function.

1a. $(f+g)(x)$ **1b.** $(f-g)(x)$

When you divide functions, be sure to note any domain restrictions that may arise.

EXAMPLE 2 Multiplying and Dividing Functions

Given $f(x) = 2x^2 + 4x - 6$ and $g(x) = 2x - 2$, find each function.

A $(gf)(x)$

$$\begin{aligned}(gf)(x) &= g(x) \cdot f(x) \\ &= (2x-2)(2x^2+4x-6) && \textit{Substitute function rules.} \\ &= 2x(2x^2+4x-6) - 2(2x^2+4x-6) && \textit{Distributive Property} \\ &= 4x^3 + 8x^2 - 12x - 4x^2 - 8x + 12 && \textit{Multiply.} \\ &= 4x^3 + 4x^2 - 20x + 12 && \textit{Combine like terms.}\end{aligned}$$

B $\left(\frac{f}{g}\right)(x)$

$$\begin{aligned}\left(\frac{f}{g}\right)(x) &= \frac{f(x)}{g(x)} \\ &= \frac{2x^2+4x-6}{2x-2} && \textit{Set up the division as a rational expression.} \\ &= \frac{2(x-1)(x+3)}{2(x-1)} && \textit{Factor completely. Note that } x \neq 1. \\ &= \frac{\cancel{2(x-1)}(x+3)}{\cancel{2(x-1)}} && \textit{Divide out common factors.} \\ &= x + 3, \text{ where } x \neq 1 && \textit{Simplify.}\end{aligned}$$

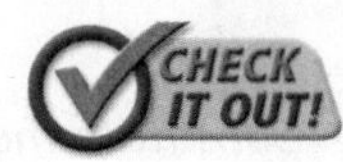

Given $f(x) = x + 2$ and $g(x) = x^2 - 4$, find each function.

2a. $(fg)(x)$

2b. $\left(\frac{g}{f}\right)(x)$

Another function operation uses the output from one function as the input for a second function. This operation is called the **composition of functions**.

Composition of Functions

The composition of functions f and g is notated

$$(f \circ g)(x) = f(g(x)).$$

The domain of $(f \circ g)(x)$ is all values of x in the domain of g such that $g(x)$ is in the domain of f.

Reading Math

The composition $(f \circ g)(x)$ or $f(g(x))$ is read "f of g of x."

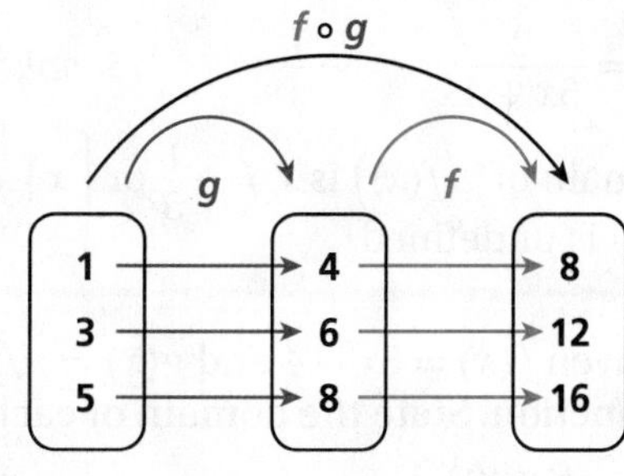

To find $(f \circ g)(1)$, first find $g(1)$.

$g(1) = 4$

Then use 4 as the input into f:

$f(4) = 8$

So $(f \circ g)(1) = f(g(1)) = 8$.

The order of function operations is the same as the order of operations for numbers and expressions. To find $f(g(3))$, evaluate $g(3)$ first and then substitute the result into f.

EXAMPLE 3 Evaluating Composite Functions

Given $f(x) = 3x + 1$ and $g(x) = x^3$, find each value.

> **Caution!**
>
> Be careful not to confuse the notation for multiplication of functions with composition.
> $fg(x) \neq f(g(x))$

A $f(g(2))$

Step 1 Find $g(2)$.

$g(2) = 2^3$ *$g(x) = x^3$*

$= 8$

Step 2 Find $f(8)$.

$f(8) = 3(8) + 1$ *$f(x) = 3x + 1$*

$= 25$

So $f(g(2)) = 25$.

B $g(f(2))$

Step 1 Find $f(2)$.

$f(2) = 3(2) + 1$ *$f(x) = 3(x) + 1$*

$= 7$

Step 2 Find $g(7)$.

$g(7) = 7^3$ *$g(x) = x^3$*

$= 343$

So $g(f(2)) = 343$.

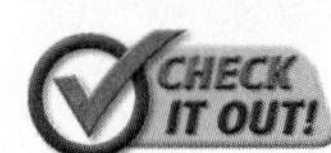

Given $f(x) = 2x - 3$ and $g(x) = x^2$, find each value.

3a. $f(g(3))$ **3b.** $g(f(3))$

You can use algebraic expressions as well as numbers as inputs into functions. To find a rule for $f(g(x))$, substitute the rule for g into f.

EXAMPLE 4 Writing Composite Functions

Given $f(x) = 5x + 2$ and $g(x) = \frac{2}{x - 1}$, write each composite function. State the domain of each.

A $f(g(x))$

$f(g(x)) = f\left(\frac{2}{x - 1}\right)$ *Substitute the rule for g into f.*

$= 5\left(\frac{2}{x - 1}\right) + 2$ *Use the rule for f. Note that $x \neq 1$.*

$= \frac{10}{x - 1} + 2, x \neq 1$ *Simplify.*

The domain of $f(g(x))$ is $x \neq 1$ or $\{x \mid x \neq 1\}$ because $g(1)$ is undefined.

B $g(f(x))$

$g(f(x)) = g(5x + 2)$ *Substitute the rule for f into g.*

$= \frac{2}{(5x + 2) - 1}$ *Use the rule for g.*

$= \frac{2}{5x + 1}, x \neq -\frac{1}{5}$ *Simplify. Note that $x \neq -\frac{1}{5}$.*

The domain of $g(f(x))$ is $x \neq -\frac{1}{5}$ or $\left\{x \mid x \neq -\frac{1}{5}\right\}$ because $f\left(-\frac{1}{5}\right) = 1$ and $g(1)$ is undefined.

Given $f(x) = 3x - 4$ and $g(x) = \sqrt{x} + 2$, write each composite function. State the domain of each.

4a. $f(g(x))$ **4b.** $g(f(x))$

Composite functions can be used to simplify a series of functions.

EXAMPLE 5 Business Application

Lisa imports scooters from Italy. The cost of the scooters is given in euros. The total cost of each scooter includes a 10% service charge and 75 euros for shipping.

EXCHANGE RATES	
CURRENCY	UNITS PER U.S. DOLLAR
BRITISH POUND	0.53
EUROPEAN EURO	0.77
JAPANESE YEN	103.60
MEXICAN PESO	11.30

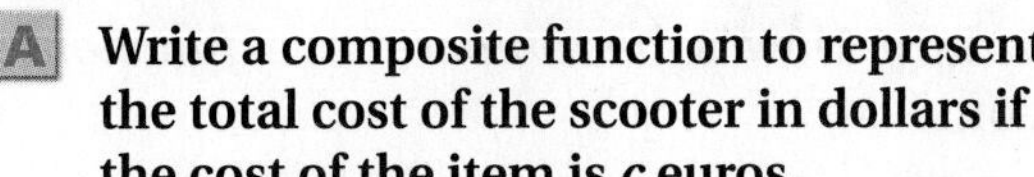

A **Write a composite function to represent the total cost of the scooter in dollars if the cost of the item is c euros.**

Step 1 Write a function for the total cost in euros.

$E(c) = c + 0.1c + 75$

$= 1.1c + 75$

Step 2 Write a function for the cost in dollars based on the cost in euros.

$D(c) = \frac{c}{0.77}$ *Use the exchange rate table.*

Step 3 Find the composition $D(E(c))$.

$D(E(c)) = \frac{E(c)}{0.77}$ *Substitute E(c) for c.*

$= \frac{1.1c + 75}{0.77}$ *Replace E(c) with its rule.*

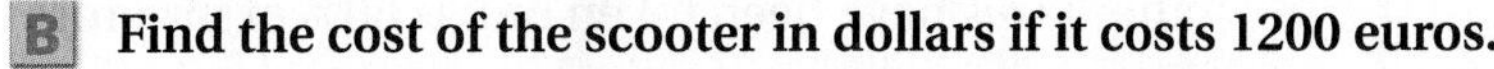

B **Find the cost of the scooter in dollars if it costs 1200 euros.**

Evaluate the composite function for $c = 1200$.

$D(E(1200)) = \frac{1.1(1200) + 75}{0.77}$

≈ 1811.69

The scooter would cost $1811.69, including all charges.

During a sale, a music store is selling all drum kits for 20% off. Preferred customers also receive an additional 15% off.

5a. Write a composite function to represent the final cost of a kit that originally cost c dollars.

5b. Find the cost of a drum kit priced at $248 that a preferred customer wants to buy.

THINK AND DISCUSS

1. Explain why $(f + g)x = (g + f)x$ for any functions f and g.

2. Find two functions such that $f(g(x)) = g(f(x))$.

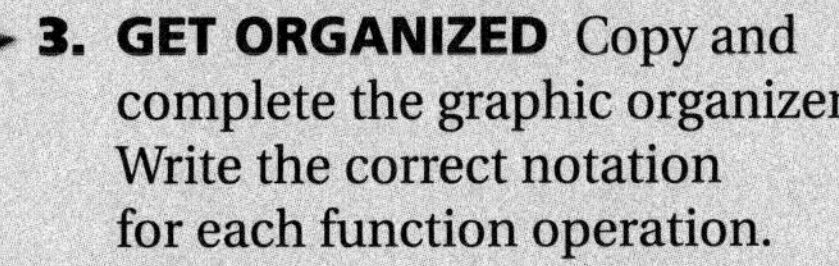

3. GET ORGANIZED Copy and complete the graphic organizer. Write the correct notation for each function operation.

Operation	Notation
Addition	
Subtraction	
Multiplication	
Division	
Composition	

9-4 Exercises

go.hrw.com
Homework Help Online
KEYWORD: MB7 9-4
Parent Resources Online
KEYWORD: MB7 Parent

GUIDED PRACTICE

1. **Vocabulary** How is the *composition of functions* different from the other function operations?

SEE EXAMPLE 1 p. 682

Given $f(x) = 8x + 13$ and $g(x) = x^2 - 5x$, find each function.

2. $(f + g)(x)$
3. $(f - g)(x)$
4. $(g - f)(x)$

SEE EXAMPLE 2 p. 683

Given $f(x) = 2x^2 + 2x$ and $g(x) = x + 1$, find each function.

5. $(fg)(x)$
6. $\left(\frac{f}{g}\right)(x)$
7. $\left(\frac{g}{f}\right)(x)$

SEE EXAMPLE 3 p. 684

Given $f(x) = 3x^2$ and $g(x) = 7 - x$, find each value.

8. $f(g(5))$
9. $g(f(5))$
10. $f(g(-2))$

SEE EXAMPLE 4 p. 684

Given $f(x) = x^2$, $g(x) = 2x - 3$, and $h(x) = \sqrt{x + 1}$, write each composite function. State the domain of each.

11. $f(g(x))$
12. $g(f(x))$
13. $f(h(x))$

SEE EXAMPLE 5 p. 685

14. **Consumer Economics** Ron is saving money for college. Each month he deposits 10% of his net income plus an additional $50 into a savings account. His net income, after taxes have been taken out, is 80% of his gross income.
    a. Write a composite function for the amount that Ron saves each month if his gross income is g.
    b. Find the amount that Ron saves in a month when his gross income is $2400.

PRACTICE AND PROBLEM SOLVING

Independent Practice

For Exercises	See Example
15–18	1
19–23	2
24–29	3
30–32	4
33	5

Extra Practice
Skills Practice p. S21
Application Practice p. S40

Given $f(x) = 2x^2 - 8$, $g(x) = x^2 + 5x + 6$, and $h(x) = 2x + 4$, find each function.

15. $(f + g)(x)$
16. $(f - g)(x)$
17. $(f + h)(x)$
18. $(g - h)(x)$
19. $(fg)(x)$
20. $\left(\frac{f}{g}\right)(x)$
21. $\left(\frac{h}{f}\right)(x)$
22. $(gh)(x)$
23. $\left(\frac{g}{h}\right)(x)$

Given $f(x) = 2\sqrt{x + 3}$ and $g(x) = -3x + 1$, find each value.

24. $f(g(1))$
25. $g(f(1))$
26. $f(g(4))$
27. $g(f(6))$
28. $f\left(g\left(\frac{4}{3}\right)\right)$
29. $g(f(97))$

Given $f(x) = 4x + 3$, $g(x) = \frac{x}{x+3}$, and $h(x) = -x^2 - 2$, write each composite function. State the domain of each.

30. $f(g(x))$
31. $g(f(x))$
32. $f(h(x))$
33. **Business** The cost of carpeting a room is $4 per square yard plus $100. Each square yard is equal to 9 square feet.
    a. Write a composite function for the cost of carpeting a room that covers x square feet.
    b. Find the square footage of a room that costs $380 to carpet.

34. This problem will prepare you for the Multi-Step Test Prep on page 706.

When the air in a hot-air balloon is heated to 100°F, each cubic foot of air can lift about 7 g.

a. Write a function $f(x)$ for the number of grams that can be lifted by a balloon containing x ft^3 of air.

b. The equation $g(x) = \frac{x}{453.6}$ converts x grams to pounds. Write a composite function for the number of pounds that can be lifted by a balloon containing x ft^3 of air.

c. Approximately how many cubic feet of air are needed to lift 1000 lb?

35. Consumer Economics Lanie has two coupons for a shoe store. One is for $10 off, and the other is for 15% off.

a. Write a function $f(p)$ for the final cost of an item of original price p if Lanie uses only the $10-off coupon.

b. Write a function $g(p)$ for the final cost of an item of original price p if Lanie uses only the 15%-off coupon.

c. Find $f(g(p))$ and $g(f(p))$.

d. Which coupon should Lanie apply first? Explain.

e. Find the lowest price that Lanie could pay for a pair of shoes priced at $49.

Earthquakes

Earthquakes are generally caused by movement along faults. Faults are cracks in Earth's crust, the largest of which occur at tectonic plate boundaries.

36. Earthquakes The shock waves created from an earthquake travel away from the epicenter at a rate of 9 km/s. As the radius of the circular waves increases, more and more area is affected by the earthquake.

a. Find a function for the total area in square kilometers affected by the earthquake after t s.

b. Geologists predict that the earthquake will be felt over an area of approximately 35,000 km^2. How long after the earthquake begins will this area be affected?

37. Population The population of Las Vegas, Nevada, can be approximated by the function $p(t) = 160{,}000 \cdot 1.05^t$, where t is the number of years since 1980. The number of doctors in Las Vegas can be approximated by the function $d(p) = 0.0044p$, where p is the population.

a. Find a function for the number of doctors in Las Vegas as a function of the number of years t since 1980.

b. Estimation Estimate the number of doctors in Las Vegas in 2010.

c. Approximately when will the number of doctors in Las Vegas exceed 5000?

38. Critical Thinking Given $f(x) = x$ and given any function $g(x)$, is $f(g(x))$ always equal to $g(f(x))$? Explain.

Use the tables to find each value.

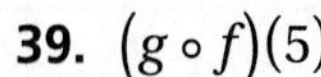

39. $(g \circ f)(5)$ **40.** $(f \circ g)(3)$

41. $g(f(4))$ **42.** $f(g(2))$

x	2	3	4	5
f(x)	0	1	2	3

x	1	2	3	4
g(x)	1	2	4	8

43. Critical Thinking Can you use the tables to find $f(g(4))$? Explain your answer.

44. Write About It Is the sum of two linear functions also a linear function? Is the product of two linear functions also a linear function? Explain.

45. If $(f \circ g)(x) = (3x + 4)^2$, which of the following could be true?

Ⓐ $f(x) = 3x + 4$ and $g(x) = x^2$

Ⓑ $f(x) = x^2$ and $g(x) = 3x + 4$

Ⓒ $f(x) = (3x)^2$ and $g(x) = 4^2$

Ⓓ $f(x) = 3x + 4$ and $g(x) = \sqrt{x}$

46. If $f(x) = 2x + 1$ and $g(x) = 5x - 2$, then which of the following is $(fg)(5)$?

Ⓕ 253

Ⓖ 53

Ⓗ 47

Ⓙ 13

47. Given $f(x) = 4 - x^2$ and $g(x) = \frac{1}{2}x - 2$, which of the following is $(f \circ g)(x)$?

Ⓐ $(f \circ g)(x) = -\frac{1}{2}x^2$

Ⓑ $(f \circ g)(x) = -\frac{1}{4}x^2 + 2x$

Ⓒ $(f \circ g)(x) = -\frac{1}{2}x^3 + 2x^2 + 2x - 8$

Ⓓ $(f \circ g)(x) = -x^2 + \frac{1}{2}x + 2$

48. **Gridded Response** Given that $f(x) = (x + 1)^2$ and $g(x) = 3x$, find $(f + g)(2)$.

CHALLENGE AND EXTEND

49. Given $f(x) = 2x - 6$ and $f(g(x)) = 3x^2 + 4$, find $g(x)$.

50. Given $f(x) = 3x + 8$ and $g(x) = \begin{cases} x^2 & \text{if } x < 0 \\ 5x + 2 & \text{if } x \geq 0 \end{cases}$, find $g(f(x))$.

51. **Physics** When a ball is thrown up a hill, the height y of the ball is given by the function $y = -0.12x^2 + 2.8x$, where x is the horizontal distance from the thrower. The hill is represented by the linear function $y = \frac{2}{5}x$.

a. Find the maximum height of the ball above the ground.

b. Find the height of the ball when it hits the ground.

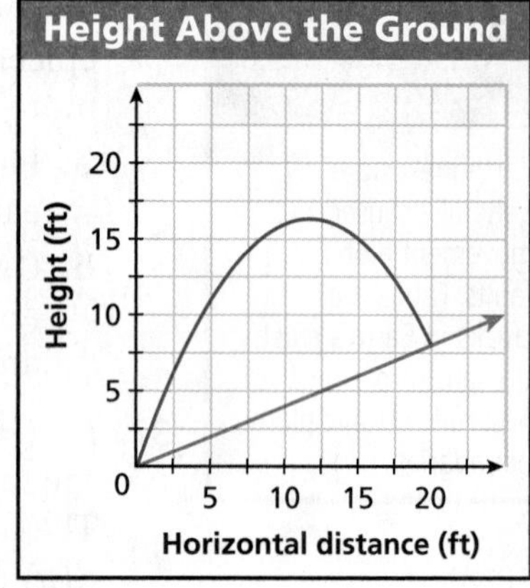

SPIRAL REVIEW

52. **Business** The value of a computer purchased for \$800 depreciates by 20% each year. *(Lesson 7-1)*

a. Write a function to model the value of the computer after t years.

b. How much will the computer be worth in 10 years?

Decide whether the data set is exponential, and if it is, use exponential regression to find a function that models the data. *(Lesson 7-8)*

53.

x	2	3	4	5	6
y	5	10	20	40	80

54.

x	1	2	3	4	5
y	5	10	15	20	25

Given $f(x) = \begin{cases} 8x & x \geq 0 \\ x - 9 & x < 0 \end{cases}$, **write the rule for each function.** *(Lesson 9-3)*

55. $g(x)$, a horizontal translation of $f(x)$ 5 units to the left

56. $h(x)$, a vertical stretch by a factor of 3

Using Geometric Formulas

Geometric formulas can be used to find lengths of sides or edges. Solve the formula for the variable that you need. In these formulas, *s* is the length of a side or an edge and *r* is the radius.

Regular Hexagon

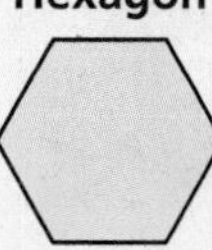

$A = \frac{3s^2}{2}\sqrt{3}$

Regular Octagon

$A = 2s^2(\sqrt{2} + 1)$

Regular Tetrahedron

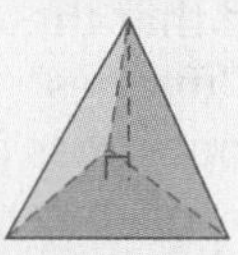

$V = \frac{s^3}{12}\sqrt{2}$

Regular Octahedron

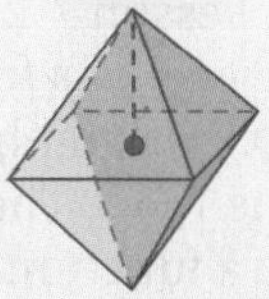

$V = \frac{s^3}{3}\sqrt{2}$

Sphere

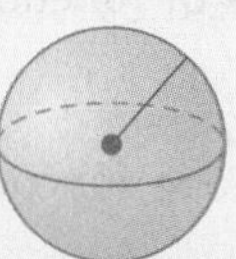

$A = 4\pi r^2$

$V = \frac{4\pi r^3}{3}$

Example

A rectangle is 30 cm long and 10 cm wide. Find the length of the sides of a regular octagon that has the same area as this rectangle.

1 Find the area of the rectangle.

$30 \cdot 10 = 300$ *The area is 300 cm².*

2 Use the octagon formula. Solve for *s*, the length of one side.

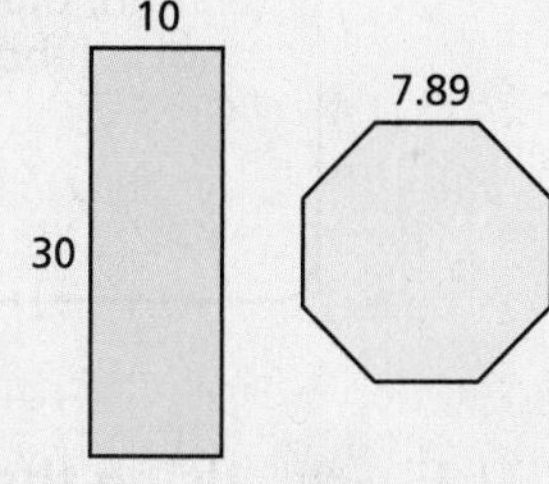

$$A = 2s^2(\sqrt{2} + 1)$$

$$\frac{A}{2(\sqrt{2} + 1)} = s^2$$ *Divide both sides by $2(\sqrt{2} + 1)$.*

$$s = \sqrt{\frac{A}{2(\sqrt{2} + 1)}}$$ *Take the square root of both sides.*

3 Substitute 300 for the area *A*, and solve for the side length.

$$s \approx \sqrt{\frac{300}{2(1.41 + 1)}} \approx \sqrt{\frac{300}{4.82}} \approx \sqrt{62.24} \approx 7.89$$ *Use 1.41 as an approximation for $\sqrt{2}$.*

Try This

Solve each problem. Start by solving the appropriate formula for *s* or *r*.

1. What is the radius of a sphere made with 1000 cubic feet of clay?
2. Jake used 540 square inches of mosaic tile to build a tabletop in the shape of a regular hexagon. How long is one edge of this tabletop?
3. A tent shaped like a tetrahedron has 30 cubic feet of air space. Describe the base of this tent.
4. Cyndi wants to construct an octahedron that has the same volume as a sphere with a radius of 9 cm. What length should she make each edge of the octahedron?

9-5 Functions and Their Inverses

Objectives
Determine whether the inverse of a function is a function.

Write rules for the inverses of functions.

Vocabulary
one-to-one function

Who uses this?

Nurses can use inverse functions to approximate the ages of infants. (See Exercise 37.)

In Lesson 7-2, you learned that the inverse of a function $f(x)$ "undoes" $f(x)$. Its graph is a reflection across the line $y = x$. The inverse may or may not be a function.

Recall that the vertical-line test (Lesson 1-6) can help you determine whether a relation is a function. Similarly, the *horizontal-line test* can help you determine whether the inverse of a function is a function.

Horizontal-line Test

WORDS	EXAMPLES	
If any horizontal line passes through more than one point on the graph of a relation, the inverse relation is not a function.	Inverse is a function.	Inverse is not a function.

EXAMPLE 1 Using the Horizontal-Line Test

Use the horizontal-line test to determine whether the inverse of each relation is a function.

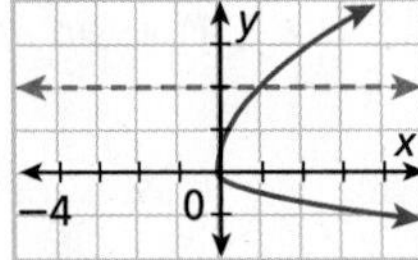

The inverse is a function because no horizontal line passes through two points on the graph.

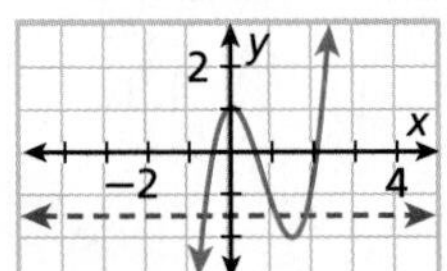

The inverse is not a function because a horizontal line passes through more than one point on the graph.

1. Use the horizontal-line test to determine whether the inverse of the relation is a function.

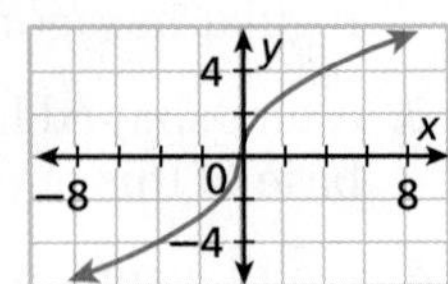

Recall from Lesson 7-2 that to write the rule for the inverse of a function, you can exchange x and y and solve the equation for y. Because the values of x and y are switched, the domain of the function will be the range of its inverse and vice versa.

EXAMPLE 2 Writing Rules for Inverses

Find the inverse of $f(x) = \left(\frac{1}{2}x + 2\right)^2$. Determine whether it is a function, and state its domain and range.

Step 1 Graph the function.

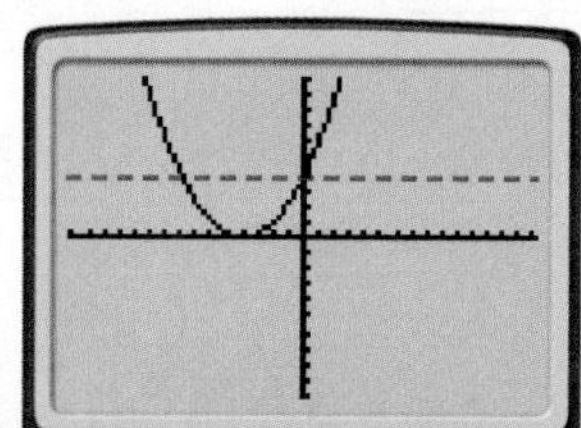

The horizontal-line test shows that the inverse is not a function. Note that the domain of f is all real numbers and the range is $\{y \mid y \geq 0\}$.

Step 2 Find the inverse.

$$y = \left(\frac{1}{2}x + 2\right)^2$$ *Rewrite the function using y instead of f(x).*

$$x = \left(\frac{1}{2}y + 2\right)^2$$ *Switch x and y in the equation.*

$$\sqrt{x} = \sqrt{\left(\frac{1}{2}y + 2\right)^2}$$ *Take the square root of both sides.*

$$\pm\sqrt{x} = \frac{1}{2}y + 2$$ *Note the domain restriction $x \geq 0$.*

$$\pm\sqrt{x} - 2 = \frac{1}{2}y$$ *Subtract 2 from each side.*

$$y = 2\left(\pm\sqrt{x} - 2\right)$$ *Isolate y.*

$$y = \pm 2\sqrt{x} - 4$$ *Simplify.*

Because of the $\pm$ symbol, there may be two y-values for an x-value. This confirms that the inverse is not a function. Because the inverse is not a function, you cannot use the notation $f^{-1}(x)$.

The domain of the inverse is the range of $f(x)$: $\{x \mid x \geq 0\}$. The range is the domain of $f(x)$: all real numbers.

Check Graph both relations to see that they are symmetric about $y = x$. To graph the inverse, you will have to graph the positive and negative cases separately.

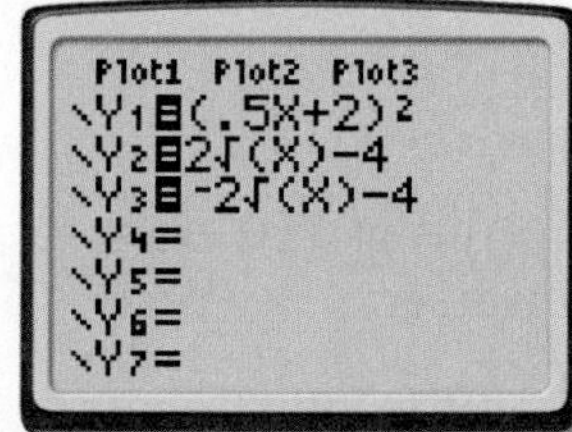

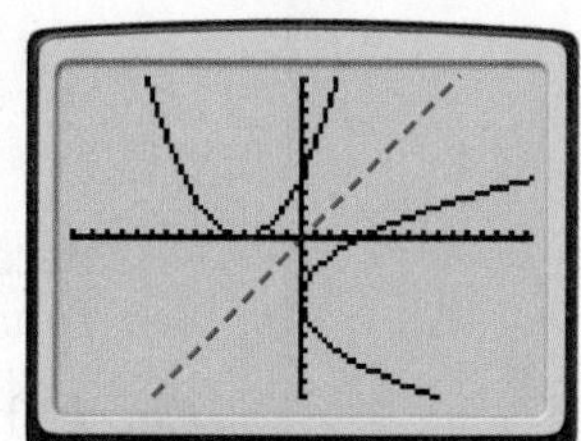

Caution!

When you take the square root of both sides of a quadratic equation be sure to add the $\pm$ symbol. (Lesson 5-4)

2. Find the inverse of $f(x) = x^3 - 2$. Determine whether it is a function, and state its domain and range.

You have seen that the inverses of functions are not necessarily functions. When both a relation and its inverse are functions, the relation is called a *one-to-one function*. In a **one-to-one function**, each y-value is paired with exactly one x-value.

You can use composition of functions to verify that two functions are inverses. Because inverse functions "undo" each other, when you compose two inverses the result is the input value x.

Identifying Inverse Functions

WORDS	ALGEBRA	EXAMPLE
If the compositions of two functions equal the input value, the functions are inverses.	If $f(g(x)) = g(f(x)) = x$, then $f(x)$ and $g(x)$ are inverse functions.	$f(x) = 3x$ and $g(x) = \frac{1}{3}x$ $f(g(x)) = 3\left(\frac{1}{3}x\right) = x$ $g(f(x)) = \frac{1}{3}(3x) = x$

EXAMPLE 3 Determining Whether Functions Are Inverses

Determine by composition whether each pair of functions are inverses.

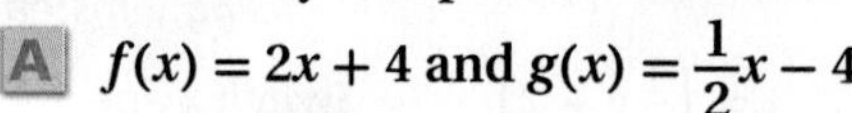

A $f(x) = 2x + 4$ and $g(x) = \frac{1}{2}x - 4$

Find the composition $f(g(x))$.

$f(g(x)) = 2\left(\frac{1}{2}x - 4\right) + 4$ *Substitute $\frac{1}{2}x - 4$ for x in f.*

$= (x - 8) + 4$ *Use the Distributive Property.*

$= x - 4$ *Simplify.*

Because $f(g(x)) \neq x$, f and g are not inverses. There is no need to check $g(f(x))$.

Check The graphs are not symmetric about the line $y = x$.

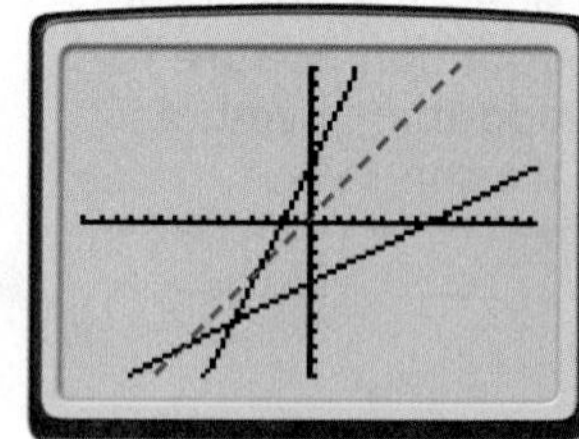

B For $x \geq 0$, $f(x) = \frac{1}{4}x^2$ and $g(x) = 2\sqrt{x}$.

Find the compositions $f(g(x))$ and $g(f(x))$.

$f(g(x)) = \frac{1}{4}(2\sqrt{x})^2$ $\quad g(f(x)) = 2\sqrt{\frac{1}{4}x^2}$

$= \frac{1}{4}(4x)$ $\quad = 2\left(\frac{1}{2}x\right)$

$= x, x \geq 0$ $\quad = x$

Because $f(g(x)) = g(f(x)) = x$ for $x \geq 0$, f and g are inverses.

Check The graphs are symmetric about the line $y = x$ when $x \geq 0$.

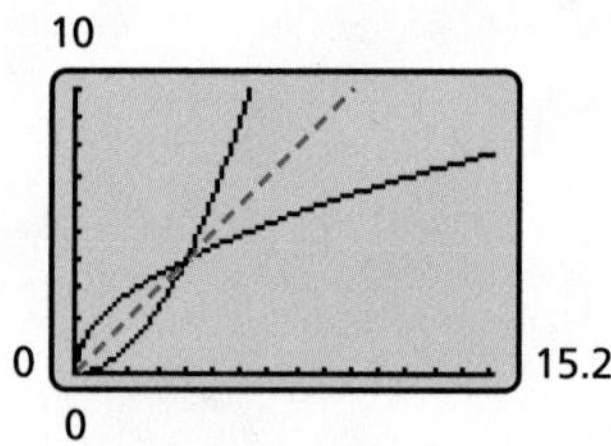

Determine by composition whether each pair of functions are inverses.

3a. $f(x) = \frac{2}{3}x + 6$ and $g(x) = \frac{3}{2}x - 9$

3b. $f(x) = x^2 + 5$ and $g(x) = \sqrt{x} - 5$ for $x \geq 0$

THINK AND DISCUSS

1. Explain why the horizontal-line test works.
2. Explain the relationship between the domain and range of a function and the domain and range of its inverse.

3. **GET ORGANIZED** Copy and complete the graphic organizer. Describe how each method or characteristic is used to find or verify inverses.

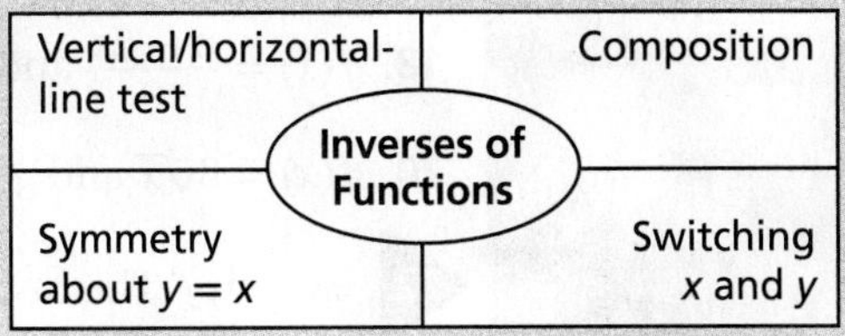

Vertical/horizontal-line test	Composition
Symmetry about $y = x$	Switching x and y

(Center: Inverses of Functions)

9-5 Exercises

GUIDED PRACTICE

SEE EXAMPLE 1 p. 690

Use the horizontal-line test to determine whether the inverse of each relation is a function.

1. 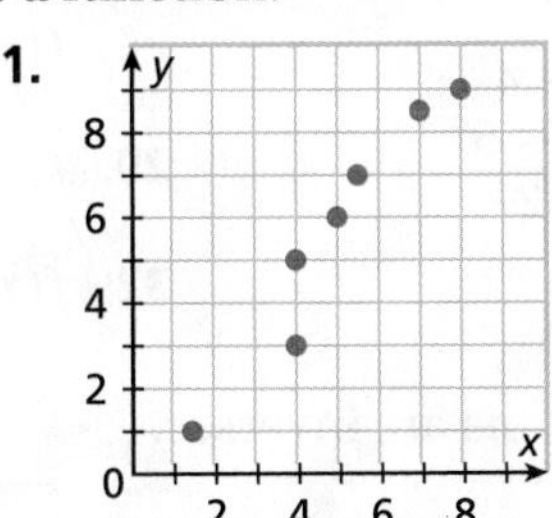
2. 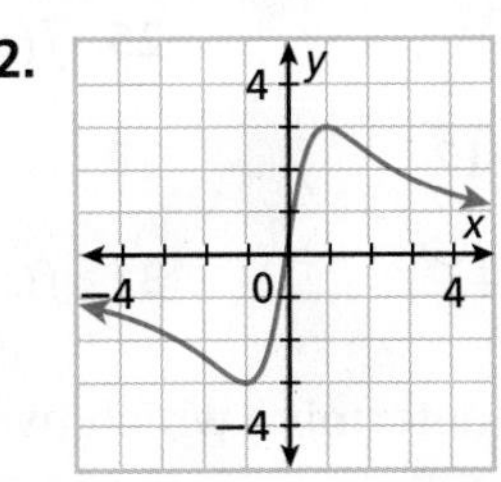
3. 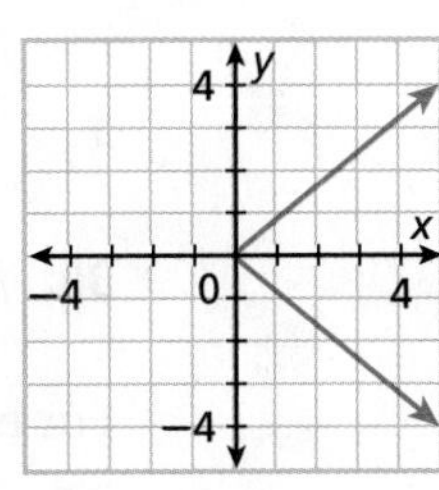

SEE EXAMPLE 2 p. 691

Find the inverse of each function. Determine whether the inverse is a function, and state its domain and range.

4. $f(x) = -3x + 21$
5. $g(x) = x^2 - 9$
6. $h(x) = \frac{x + 5}{8}$

SEE EXAMPLE 3 p. 692

Determine by composition whether each pair of functions are inverses.

7. $f(x) = 4x - 12$ and $g(x) = -4x + 8$
8. $f(x) = \sqrt{3x}$ and $g(x) = \frac{x^2}{3}$ for $x \geq 0$

PRACTICE AND PROBLEM SOLVING

Independent Practice

For Exercises	See Example
9–11	1
12–17	2
18–21	3

Extra Practice

Skills Practice p. S21

Application Practice p. S40

Use the horizontal-line test to determine whether the inverse of each relation is a function.

9. 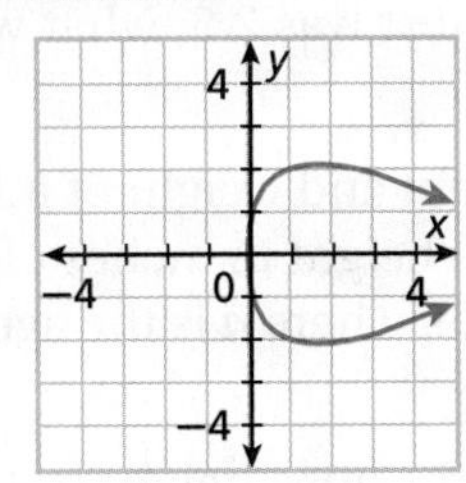
10. 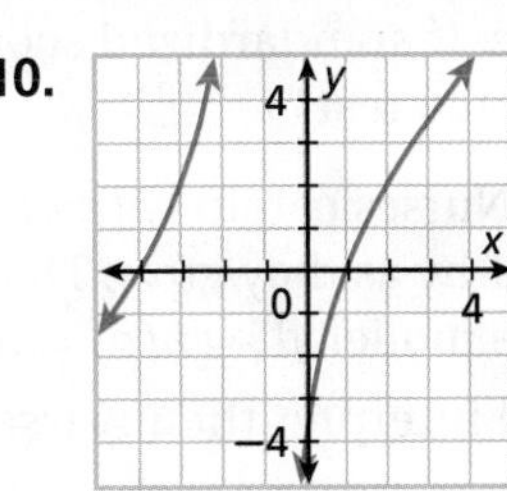
11. 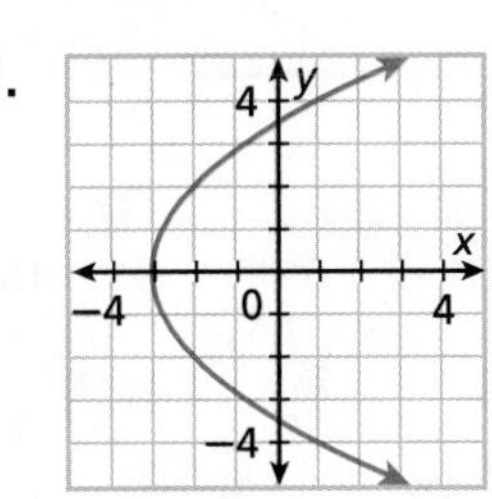

Find the inverse of each function. Determine whether the inverse is a function, and state its domain and range.

12. $f(x) = \frac{3}{5}x$ **13.** $f(x) = 8x^3$ **14.** $f(x) = \frac{x}{x+1}$

15. $f(x) = \frac{5x+9}{6}$ **16.** $f(x) = (x-4)^2$ **17.** $f(x) = 5 + \sqrt{x+8}$

Determine by composition whether each pair of functions are inverses.

18. $f(x) = \frac{5-2x}{9}$ and $g(x) = -\frac{9}{2}x + \frac{5}{2}$ **19.** $f(x) = \frac{5}{x+1}$ and $g(x) = \frac{x-1}{5}$ for $x \neq -1$

20. $f(x) = 3\sqrt{x}$ and $g(x) = \frac{1}{3}x^2$ for $x \geq 0$ **21.** $f(x) = \log\frac{x}{2}$ and $g(x) = 2(10^x)$ for $x > 0$

LINK

Biology

There are about 900 species of crickets worldwide. Many male crickets make chirping noises either by rubbing their wings together or by rubbing their wing cases against their hind legs.

22. Biology The number of times that a cricket chirps per minute can be found by using the function $N(F) = 4F - 160$, where F is the temperature in degrees Fahrenheit.

a. Find and interpret the inverse of $N(F)$.

b. What is the temperature when the cricket is chirping 60 times a minute?

c. How many times will the cricket chirp in 1 minute at a temperature of 80°F?

23. Business The managers of a pizza restaurant have found that the function $t(d) = 20 + 2.5d$ models the length of time in minutes, after it is ordered, for a pizza to be delivered a distance of d miles.

a. Write the inverse of $t(d)$, and explain what it represents.

b. How far away can a customer live and still get a pizza within 30 minutes of placing an order?

Write the rule for the inverse of each function. Then state its domain and range.

24. $f(x) = \frac{7-8x}{3}$ **25.** $f(x) = \frac{5}{x+4}$ **26.** $f(x) = 5(x+6)^2$

27. $f(x) = \sqrt[3]{x-12}$ **28.** $f(x) = \frac{x^3-5}{12}$ **29.** $f(x) = 7^x$

30. $f(x) = \ln(x+2)$ **31.** $f(x) = 3e^{x+5}$ **32.** $f(x) = \frac{\log(x+8)}{4}$

For each graph, determine which two functions are inverses.

33.

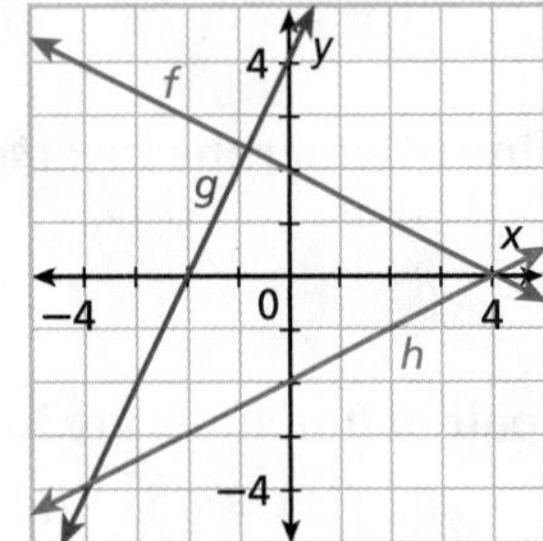

34.

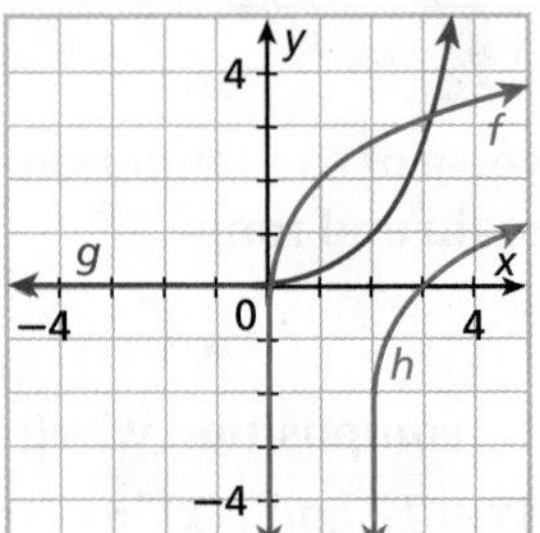

35.

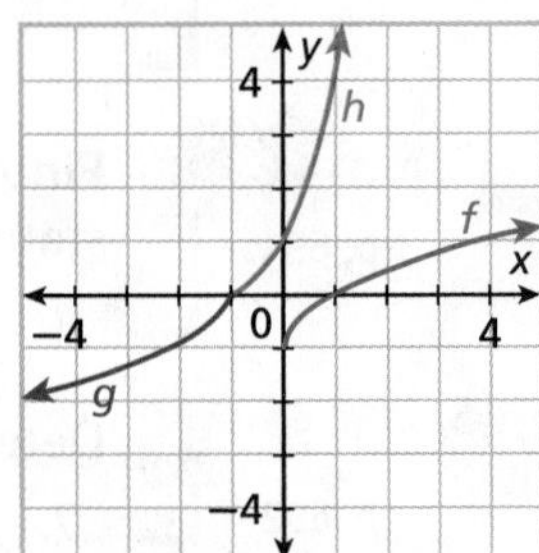

36. Statistics A person's standardized score on a test is given by the function $z(x) = \frac{x-250}{40}$, where x is the actual score on the test.

a. Find and interpret the inverse of $z(x)$.

b. If a person's standardized score on a test was 2.5, what was the person's actual score on the test?

37. Medicine Nurses carefully track the height and weight of infants to ensure that they are healthy as they grow. The average height in inches of a girl in the first 3 years of life can be modeled by $h(a) = 3\sqrt{a} + 19$, where a is the age of the girl in months.

a. Find and interpret the inverse of $h(a)$.

b. Estimation Estimate the age of a girl whose height is $32\frac{1}{2}$ inches.

38. This problem will prepare you for the Multi-Step Test Prep on page 706.

If an object is dropped from a hot-air balloon at an altitude of 500 ft, the object's height after t seconds can be modeled by $h(t) = -16t^2 + 500$.

a. Find and interpret the inverse of $h(t)$.

b. How long does it take the object to hit the ground?

c. How long does it take the object to fall if it lands on the roof of a building that is 128 ft tall?

39. **Conservation** As a brown bear with a radio collar walks along a river, the distance from the bear to an observation post after t seconds is given by the function $d(t) = \sqrt{1600 + 9t^2}$.

a. Find and interpret the inverse of $d(t)$.

b. If the tracking equipment has a range of 5500 feet, how long will a person in the observation post be able to track the bear before having to move?

40. **Photography** The cost in dollars of enlarging a photo is given by the function $c = 0.1\ell^2$, where ℓ is the length of the enlargement in inches.

a. Write the inverse of the function, and explain what it represents.

b. Determine the length of an enlargement that costs \$25.60.

41. **Manufacturing** The surface area of an aluminum can is given by the function $S(h) = 18\pi + 6\pi h$.

a. Find and interpret the inverse of $S(h)$.

b. Find the height to the nearest hundredth of a centimeter of a can with a surface area of 500 cm^2.

42. **Critical Thinking** Identify two functions that are their own inverses.

43. **Geometry** The area of a square is $A = s^2$, where s is the length of a side.

a. Find and interpret the inverse of the function.

b. Explain how an architect or city planner might use the inverse.

c. **Estimation** Estimate the side length of a square park that covers an area of 800,000 square feet.

44. **Critical Thinking** If a relation is not a function, can its inverse be a function? Use an example to illustrate your answer.

45. **Write About It** Describe two ways to determine whether two functions are inverses of each other. How would your methods apply to determining whether a function is its own inverse?

46. The formula for converting from degrees Celsius to degrees Fahrenheit is $F = \frac{9}{5}C + 32$. Which of the following formulas converts degrees Fahrenheit to degrees Celsius?

Ⓐ $C = \frac{9}{5}F - 32$

Ⓑ $C = \frac{9}{5}(F - 32)$

Ⓒ $C = \frac{5}{9}F + 32$

Ⓓ $C = \frac{5}{9}(F - 32)$

47. Which of the following is true about the relation graphed?

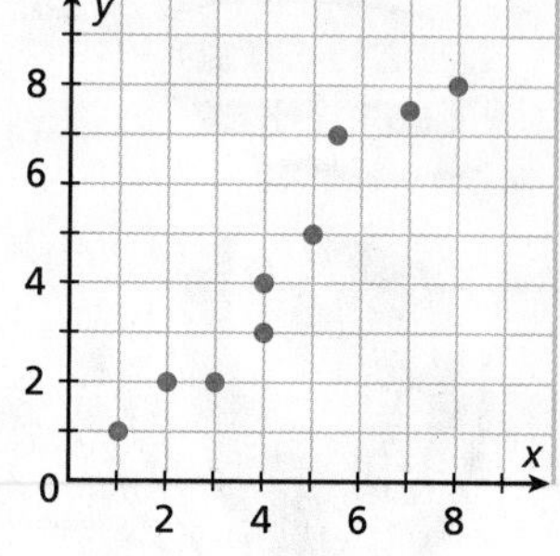

Ⓕ Both the relation and its inverse are functions.
Ⓖ The relation is a function, but its inverse is not a function.
Ⓗ The relation is not a function, but its inverse is a function.
Ⓙ Neither the relation nor its inverse is a function.

48. Which of the following is the inverse of $f(x) = \sqrt{x} + 1$?
Ⓐ $f^{-1}(x) = x^2 - 1, x \geq 0$
Ⓑ $f^{-1}(x) = (x - 1)^2, x \geq 0$
Ⓒ $f^{-1}(x) = x^2 + 1, x \geq 0$
Ⓓ $f^{-1}(x) = (x + 1)^2, x \geq 0$

49. For a certain function, $f(0) = 2$ and $f^{-1}(4) = 1$. Which of the following is also true?
Ⓕ $f^{-1}(0) = 2$
Ⓖ $f^{-1}(2) = 0$
Ⓗ $f(4) = 1$
Ⓙ $f(2) = 0$

50. Which function has an inverse that is NOT a function?
Ⓐ $f(x) = 2x^3 + 3$
Ⓑ $f(x) = \sqrt{2x} + 5$
Ⓒ $f(x) = x^2 - 1$
Ⓓ $f(x) = 3^x + 1$

51. **Short Response** Given that $f(x)$ is a quadratic function, is its inverse a function? Explain.

CHALLENGE AND EXTEND

52. Use the Quadratic Formula to find a rule for the inverse of $f(x) = 3x^2 - 6x - 9$.

Find a rule for the inverse of each function.

53. $f(x) = \dfrac{3 + \ln x}{3 - \ln x}$

54. $f(x) = \dfrac{5\log(x^3) - 3\log(x^2)}{3}$

55. Is $f^{-1}\left(g^{-1}(x)\right) = \left(f\left(g(x)\right)\right)^{-1}$ correct? Support your answer.

56. **Personal Finance** A financial manager predicts that if a person leaves \$1000 in his mutual fund, the value of the money after t years will be $V(t) = 1000\left(1.08^t\right)$.
a. Find and interpret the inverse of $V(t)$.
b. If a person puts \$1000 into this mutual fund, predict how much money the person will have in the fund in 10 years.
c. If a person puts \$1000 into this mutual fund, after how many years will the person have \$4000 in the fund?

SPIRAL REVIEW

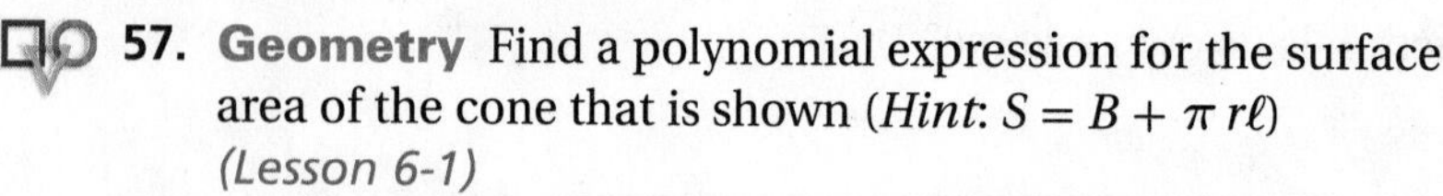

57. **Geometry** Find a polynomial expression for the surface area of the cone that is shown (*Hint:* $S = B + \pi r\ell$) (Lesson 6-1)

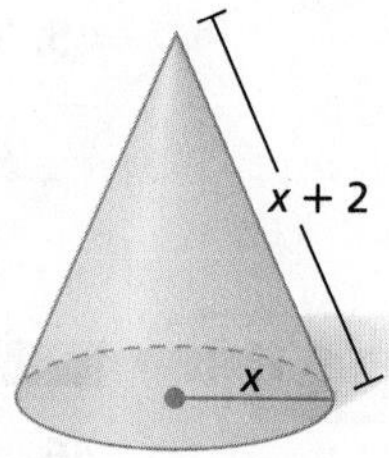

Find each product. (Lesson 6-2)

58. $(x + 2)(x^4 + x^2 + 1)$
59. $(x + 3)(x^2 - 3x + 9)$
60. $(x^3 - x^2)(x^2 + 2x)$

Given $f(x) = 9x - 5$ and $g(x) = x^2 - x - 1$, find each function. (Lesson 9-4)

61. $(f + g)(x)$
62. $(f - g)(x)$
63. $(g - f)(x)$

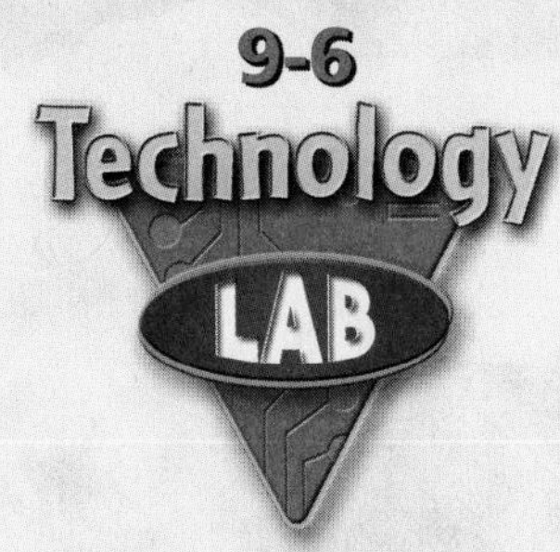

Explore Symmetry

A graph is *symmetric with respect to the y-axis* if a reflection of the graph across the y-axis produces an identical graph. A graph is *symmetric with respect to the origin* if a 180° rotation of the graph about the origin produces an identical graph.

Use with Lesson 9-6

y-Axis Symmetry	Origin Symmetry
(−2, 4); (2, 4); Line of reflection; *y*; *x*	*y*; (2, 4); *x*; 180° rotation about the origin; (−2, −4)

Activity

Graph and classify the function $f(x) = \frac{1}{2}x^4 - 4x^2$. Then describe the symmetry of the graph.

1 Enter the function rule for **Y1**, and view the graph in a friendly window.

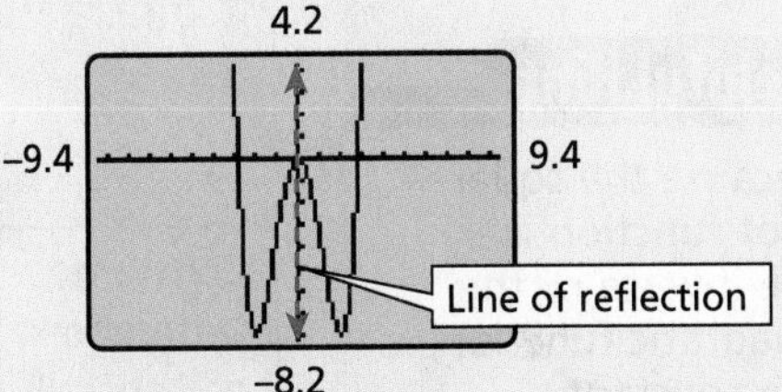

2 Classify the function. The expression $\frac{1}{2}x^4 - 4x^2$ is a polynomial, so $f(x) = \frac{1}{2}x^4 - 4x^2$ is a polynomial function.

3 Examine the symmetry of the graph. The *y*-axis divides the graph into two parts that appear to be reflections of each other, so the graph appears to have *y*-axis symmetry. The graph does not appear to have origin symmetry.

Confirm the symmetry of the graph by viewing a table of values. Except for the origin, the table includes only pairs of points that are reflections of each other across the *y*-axis.

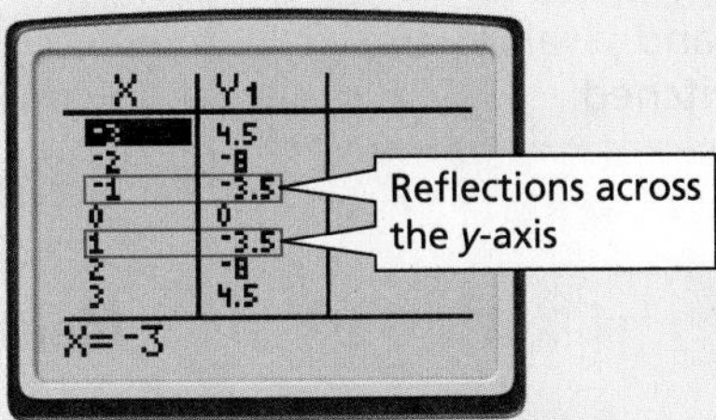

Try This

Graph and classify each function. Then describe the symmetry of the graph.

1. $f(x) = |x|$

2. $f(x) = -2x$

3. $f(x) = 3^x$

4. $f(x) = \frac{3}{x}$

5. $f(x) = x^3 - 5x$

6. $f(x) = x^2 + 4$

7. A power function can be written in the form $f(x) = ax^n$, where a and n are real numbers and $a \neq 0$. Graph several power functions with positive integer values of n.

a. Make a Conjecture Describe the symmetry of the graphs of power functions for which n is a positive odd integer.

b. Make a Conjecture Describe the symmetry of the graphs of power functions for which n is a positive even integer.

9-6 Modeling Real-World Data

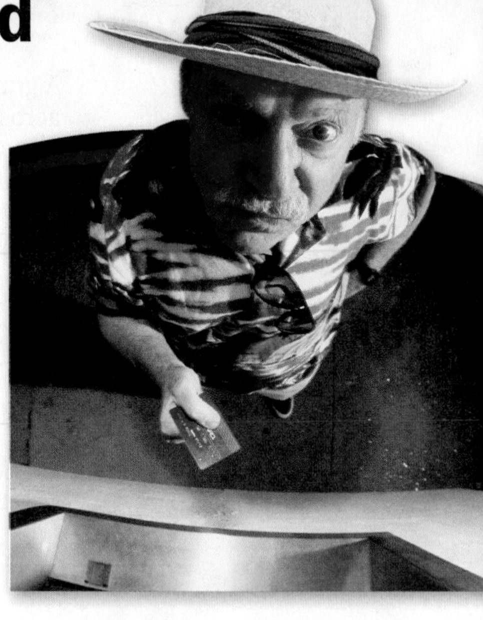

Objectives

Apply functions to problem situations.

Use mathematical models to make predictions.

Who uses this?

You can use mathematical models to analyze and predict the number of automated teller machines (ATMs) in use. (See Example 3.)

Much of the data that you encounter in the real world may form a pattern. Many times the pattern of the data can be modeled by one of the functions you have studied. You can then use the functions to analyze trends and make predictions. Recall some of the parent functions that you have studied so far.

Families of Functions

Family	Linear	Quadratic	Exponential	Square Root
Rule	$f(x) = x$	$f(x) = x^2$	$f(x) = b^x, b > 0$	$f(x) = \sqrt{x}$
Graph				
Constant Differences or Ratios	Constant first differences between y-values for evenly spaced x-values	Constant second differences between y-values for evenly spaced x-values	Constant ratios between y-values for evenly spaced x-values	Constant second differences between x-values for evenly spaced y-values

Helpful Hint

Because the square-root function is the inverse of the quadratic function, the constant differences for x- and y-values are switched.

EXAMPLE 1 Identifying Models by Using Constant Differences or Ratios

Use constant differences or ratios to determine which parent function would best model the given data set.

A The length of a spring depends on the mass attached.

Mass (kg)	4	5	6	7	8	9	10
Length (cm)	30.6	32	33.4	34.8	36.2	37.6	39

Notice that the mass data are evenly spaced. Check the first differences between the lengths to see if the data set is linear.

Length (cm)	30.6	32	33.4	34.8	36.2	37.6	39

First differences 1.4 1.4 1.4 1.4 1.4 1.4

Because the first differences are a constant 1.4, a linear model will best model the data.

Use constant differences or ratios to determine which parent function would best model the given data set.

B **The age of a tree can be determined from its diameter.**

Diameter (cm)	1.6	3.6	6.4	10.0	14.4	19.6	25.6
Age (yr)	2	3	4	5	6	7	8

Notice that the age data are evenly spaced. Check the first differences between diameters.

Diameter (cm)	1.6	3.6	6.4	10.0	14.4	19.6	25.6

First differences 2 2.8 3.6 4.4 5.2 6

Second differences 0.8 0.8 0.8 0.8 0.8

Because the second differences of the independent variable are constant when the dependent variables are evenly spaced, a square-root function will best model the data.

Check A scatter plot reveals a shape similar to the square-root parent function $f(x) = \sqrt{x}$.

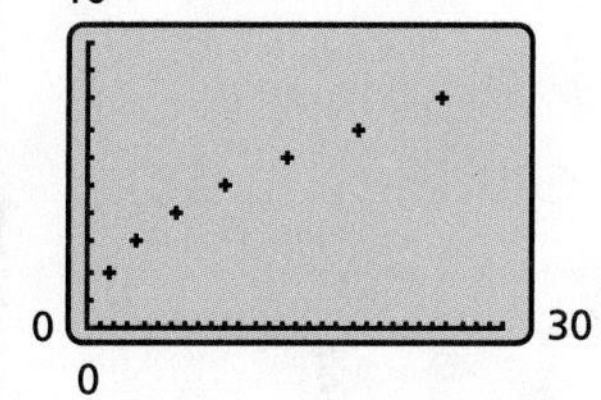

C **The volume of a liquid remaining after evaporation depends on the time elapsed.**

Time (h)	1	2	3	4	5	6
Volume (mL)	512	384	288	216	162	121.5

Because the time data are evenly spaced, check the differences between the volumes.

Volume (mL)	512	384	288	216	162	121.5

First differences −128 −96 −72 −54 −40.5

Second differences 32 24 18 13.5

Neither the first nor second differences are constant. Check ratios between the volumes.

$$\frac{384}{512} = 0.75, \frac{288}{384} = 0.75, \frac{216}{288} = 0.75, \frac{162}{216} = 0.75, \text{ and } \frac{121.5}{162} = 0.75.$$

Because the ratios between the values of the dependent variable are constant, an exponential function would best model the data.

Check A scatter plot reveals a shape similar to an exponential decay function.

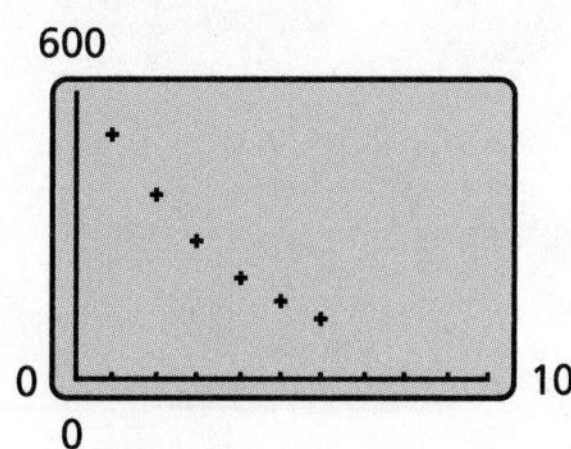

Use constant differences or ratios to determine which parent function would best model the given data set.

1a.

x	12	48	108	192	300
y	10	20	30	40	50

1b.

x	21	22	23	24
y	243	324	432	576

Real-world data rarely have differences or ratios that are mathematically constant, but you can analyze them to see if they are close to constant. You can also use a scatter plot to visually determine which model best suits a data set. Then you can perform a regression to find a function to model the data. Recall that the correlation coefficient r helps you see how well the model fits the data (Lesson 2-7).

EXAMPLE 2 Conservation Application

A zoologist is monitoring the size of a herd of buffalo in the years since the herd was released into a wilderness area. Write a function that models the given data.

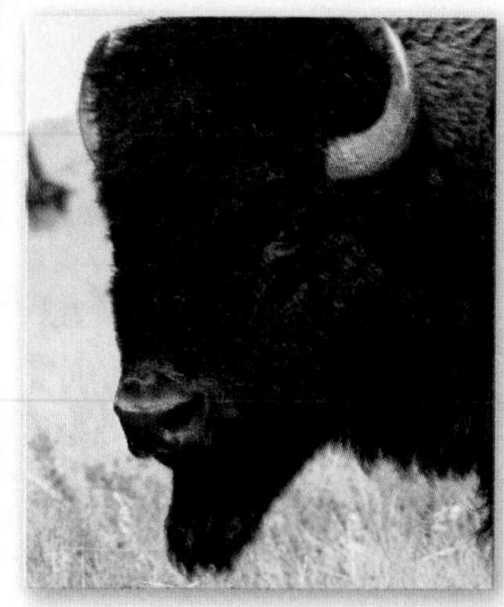

Time (yr)	5	6	7	8	9	10
Buffalo	124	150	185	213	261	322

Step 1 Make a scatter plot of the data.

The data appear to form a quadratic or an exponential pattern.

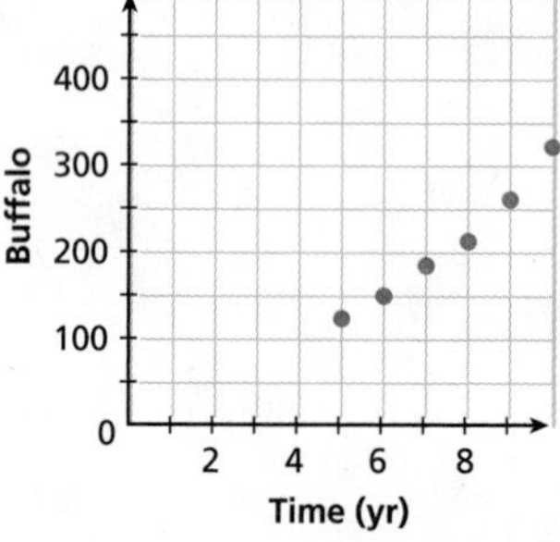

Step 2 Analyze differences.

Buffalo	124	150	185	213	261	322

First differences 26 35 28 48 61

Second differences 9 −7 20 13

Helpful Hint

To display the correlation coefficient r on some calculators, you must turn on the diagnostic mode.

Press 2nd 0 (CATALOG), and choose **DiagnosticOn**.

Step 3 Neither the first nor the second differences are close to constant, so analyze the ratios.

$$\frac{150}{124} = 1.210, \frac{185}{150} = 1.233, \frac{213}{185} = 1.151, \frac{261}{213} = 1.225, \text{ and } \frac{322}{261} = 1.234$$

The ratios are all close to 1.2, indicating that an exponential model would be appropriate.

Step 4 Use your graphing calculator to perform an exponential regression.

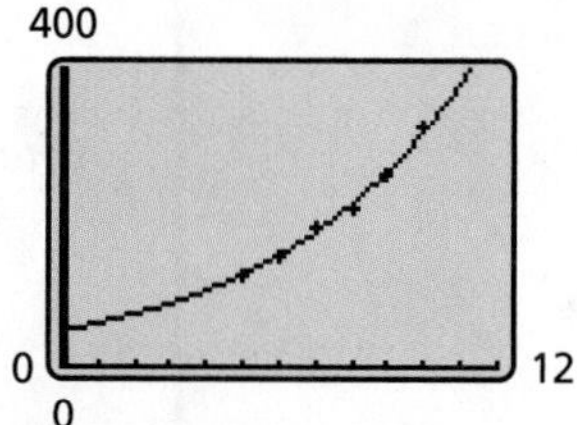

An exponential function that models the data is $f(x) = 48.581(1.207^x)$. The correlation coefficient r is very close to 1, which indicates a good fit.

2. Write a function that models the given data.

x	12	14	16	18	20	22	24
y	110	141	176	215	258	305	356

When data are not ordered or evenly spaced, you may have to try several models to determine which best approximates the data. Graphing calculators often indicate the value of the *coefficient of determination,* indicated by r^2 or R^2. The closer the coefficient is to 1, the better the model approximates the data.

EXAMPLE 3 *Banking Application*

The data set shows the approximate number of automated teller machines (ATMs) in operation in the United States. Using 1990 as a reference year, write a function that models the data.

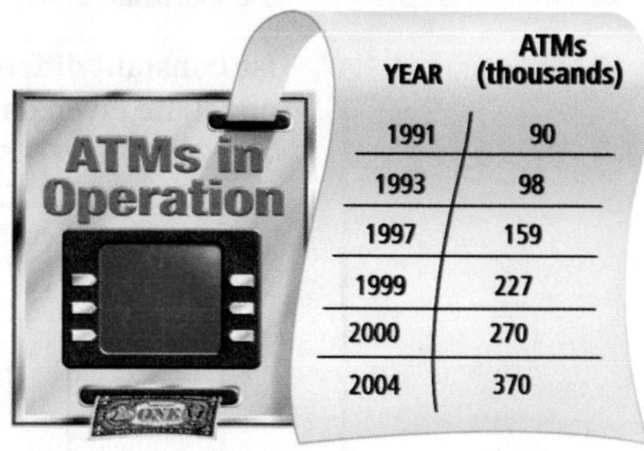

YEAR	ATMs (thousands)
1991	90
1993	98
1997	159
1999	227
2000	270
2004	370

The data are not evenly spaced, so you cannot analyze differences or ratios.

Create a scatter plot of the data. Use 1990 as year 0. The data appears to be quadratic, cubic, or exponential.

Use the calculator to perform each type of regression.

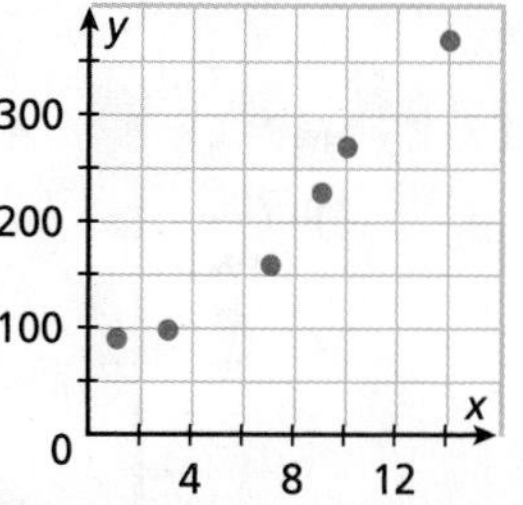

Compare the values of r^2. The cubic model seems to be the best fit. The function $f(x) \approx 0.2x^3 + 5.44x^2 - 22.13x + 110.07$ models the data.

3. Write a function that models the data.

Fertilizer/Acre (lb)	11	14	25	31	40	50
Yield/Acre (bushels)	245	302	480	557	645	705

THINK AND DISCUSS

1. Explain the limitations of finding constant differences or ratios when working with real-world data.

2. GET ORGANIZED Copy and complete the graphic organizer. Explain how each method can help you determine which model best fits a data set.

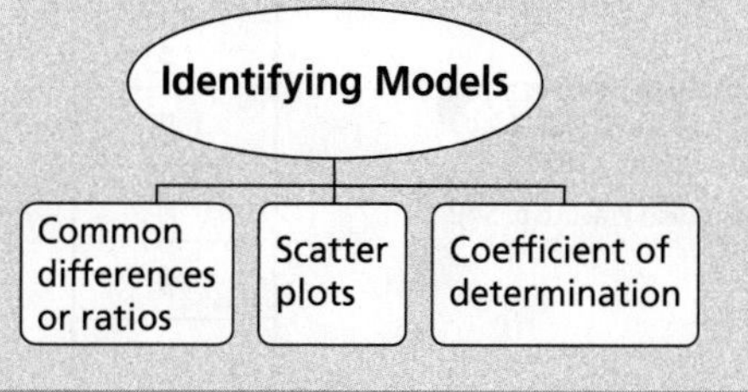

9-6 Exercises

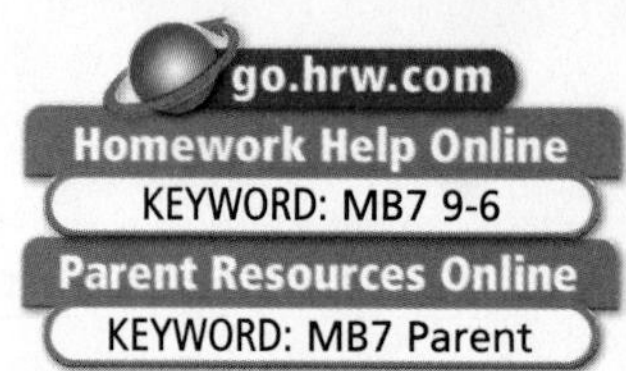

GUIDED PRACTICE

SEE EXAMPLE 1 p. 698

Use constant differences or ratios to determine which parent function would best model the given data set.

1.

x	y
6	69.6
13	51.4
20	33.2
27	15
34	−3.2
41	−21.4

2.

x	y
11	2
47	6
99	10
167	14
251	18
351	22

3.

x	y
0	125
1	150
2	180
3	216
4	259.2
5	311.04

SEE EXAMPLE 2 p. 700

4. This table shows the mass in grams m of the radioactive substance iodine-131 remaining in a container t days after the beginning of an experiment.

Time t (days)	0	1	2	3	4	5	6
Mass m (g)	1000	917.40	841.62	772.10	708.33	649.82	596.14

a. Write a function that models the data.

b. Use your model to predict the number of grams of iodine-131 that will be left after 20 days.

c. Use your model to predict when there will be less than 50 grams remaining.

SEE EXAMPLE 3 p. 701

5. The table shows the value of a stock at various points in the past 24 months since Carla bought the stock.

Time t (months)	0	4	9	12	15	20	24
Stock Value v ($)	62	54	45	48	55	53	60

a. Write a function that models the data.

b. Use your model to predict the stock price 6 months after Carla bought it.

c. Would you recommend that Carla use your model to predict the value of her stock a year from now? Why or why not?

PRACTICE AND PROBLEM SOLVING

Independent Practice

For Exercises	See Example
6–8	1
9	2
10	3

Extra Practice

Skills Practice p. S21
Application Practice p. S40

Use constant differences or ratios to determine which parent function would best model the given data set.

6.

x	y
1	380
3	343
5	310
7	279
9	252
11	228

7.

x	y
2	97
8	202
14	253
20	250
26	193
32	82

8.

x	y
4	4
9	6
16	8
25	10
36	12

9. **Agriculture** A farmer is experimenting with the amount of fertilizer to put on his corn fields. Different amounts of fertilizer are applied to each field, and the resulting yields are measured. Write a function that models the given data.

Fertilizer/Acre (lb)	45	70	90	115	125	135	150
Yield/Acre (bushels)	29	60	70	88	84	86	76

10. **Biology** The table shows the estimated number of *E. coli* bacteria in a lab dish *t* minutes after the start of an experiment.

Time (min)	0	10	20	30	40	50	60
Bacteria	300	423	596	842	1188	1686	2354

LINK
Math History

In 1806, French mathematician Adrien-Marie Legendre (1752–1833) modeled the orbit of a comet by fitting a quadratic curve to location data.

a. Using *t* as the independent variable, find the model that best fits the data.
b. Use your model to predict the number of bacteria after 3 hours.
c. How long does it take the population of *E. coli* to triple?

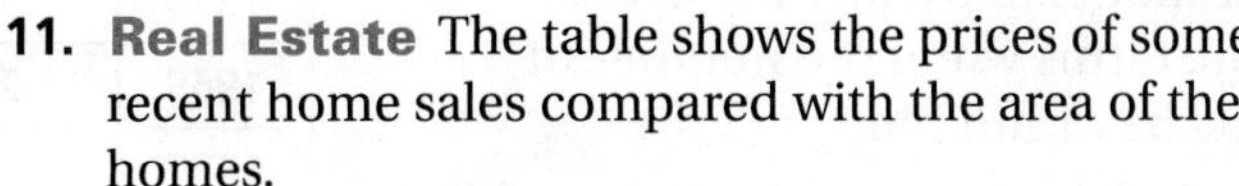

11. **Real Estate** The table shows the prices of some recent home sales compared with the area of the homes.

a. Using area as the independent variable, find a model for the data.
b. Use your model to predict the number of square feet in a house that is priced at $175,000.
c. How accurate do you think your answer to part **b** is?

Area of Homes Sold

Area (ft^2)	Price ($)
2675	179,000
1170	125,900
1486	136,750
2510	172,500
2444	169,900
2980	187,000

12. **Economics** An economist is studying the median yearly income of workers by their ages.

Age (yr)	18	28	38	48	58	68
Median Income ($)	17,480	30,650	37,440	41,230	37,570	21,390

a. Find an appropriate model for the data.
b. Use your model to predict the median income for a worker who is 43 years old.

13. **Data Collection** Use a graphing calculator and a motion detector to measure the distance of a ball or a toy car as it travels down a ramp. Set the motion detector at the top of the ramp and release the object to collect the data.
a. Find an appropriate model for distance versus time.
b. Use your model to predict the distance the object would travel in 1 minute if the ramp continued indefinitely.

14. **Health** The table shows the mean age of mothers in the United States when they had their first child.

Year	1980	1985	1990	1995	2000
Mean Age of Mother at First Birth	22.7	23.7	24.2	24.5	24.9

a. Using 1980 as a reference year, find both a quadratic and cubic model for the data.
b. Use both models to predict the mean age of a mother at first birth in 2010.
c. Explain which prediction you think is more accurate.

15. This problem will prepare you for the Multi-Step Test Prep on page 706.

The table shows how the volume v of air in a hot-air balloon relates to the temperature t of the air.

Temperature (°F)	Volume (ft²)
100	30,000
106	33,000
112	36,300
118	39,930

a. Find an exponential model for the data.

b. Use your model to predict the volume of the air when its temperature is 109°F.

c. Would your model be accurate for any air temperature greater than 118°F? Why or why not?

16. **Agriculture** The table shows the number and the average area of farms in the United States in the last century.

a. Using the number of farms as the independent variable, find a model for the average size of farms.

b. Use your model to predict the average size of the farms when the number of farms reaches 1 million.

c. Use your model to estimate the average size of the farms when there were 4.5 million farms.

Number and Size of U.S. Farms

Year	Farms (millions)	Average Area (acres)
1910	6.4	139
1930	6.3	157
1950	5.4	216
1969	2.7	390
1987	2.1	462
1997	1.9	487

17. **Baseball** The Fan Cost Index tracks the cost for a family of four to attend a Major League Baseball game.

Year	1991	1994	1997	2000	2003
FCI	\$79.41	\$96.41	\$107.26	\$132.44	\$151.19

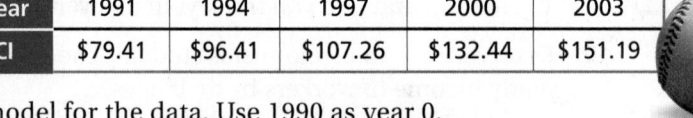

a. Find a model for the data. Use 1990 as year 0.

b. How fast has the FCI been increasing according to your model?

c. The FCI in 2004 was \$155.52. How close is the actual value to the value predicted by your model?

d. Use your model to predict when the FCI will reach \$200.

e. Because of inflation, something that cost \$1.00 in 1991 cost \$1.34 in 2003. How does the change in the FCI compare with inflation?

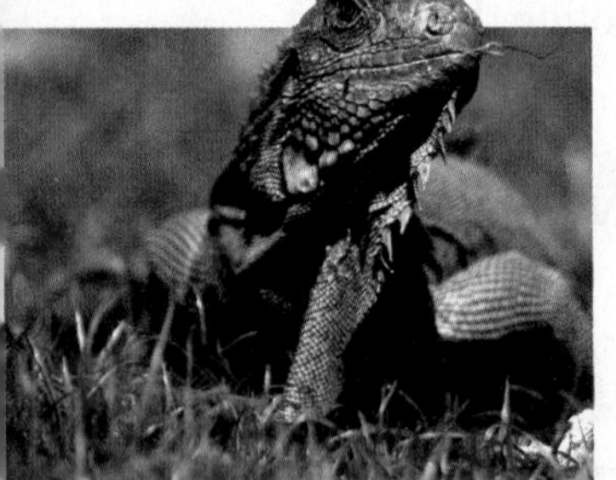

Green iguana

18. **Biology** The table shows the number of species of reptiles and amphibians and the area in square miles for some islands in the Caribbean.

a. Using number of species as the independent variable, find an appropriate model for the data.

b. Use your model to predict the area of an island with 75 species of reptiles and amphibians.

c. How accurate do you think your prediction in part **b** is? Explain.

Species	Area (mi²)
11	5
16	32
53	3,435
45	4,244
108	29,371
100	44,218

19. **Critical Thinking** Sometimes data that appear linear are better modeled by a quadratic function. What can you conclude about the value of a in the quadratic model of such a data set?

20. **Write About It** Suppose that a model can be found that provides a good fit for data on two variables. What evidence does the model give of a cause-and-effect relationship between the two variables? Use examples in your explanation.

TEST PREP

21. Which of the following is true for the data in the table?

x	y
3	2
4	23
5	50
6	83
7	122
8	167

Ⓐ The first differences of values of the dependent variable are constant.
Ⓑ The second differences of values of the dependent variable are constant.
Ⓒ The ratios of values of the dependent variable are constant.
Ⓓ The ratios of values of the independent variable are constant.

22. Find n so that an exponential model will fit the data exactly.

Ⓕ $n = 40$ Ⓗ $n = 45$
Ⓖ $n = 49$ Ⓙ $n = 52$

x	5	6	7
y	16	28	n

23. Find n so that a quadratic model will fit the data exactly.

Ⓐ $n = 60$ Ⓒ $n = 80$
Ⓑ $n = 70$ Ⓓ $n = 90$

x	5	6	7	8
y	12	32	58	n

CHALLENGE AND EXTEND

24. The function $P(t) = \frac{a}{1 + be^{-kt}}$, called a *logistic function*, is often used when there are factors such as food or space that limit a population's growth. The number of fish in a stocked pond can be modeled by the function $F(t) = \frac{4000}{1 + 5.7e^{-0.2t}}$, where t is the number of months after the pond is stocked.
    a. Predict the number of fish in the lake after 10 months.
    b. When will the population of fish reach 3000?
    c. Find the maximum number of fish that the pond can hold if the function is correct.

25. **Graphing Calculator** Another type of regression you can perform is a power regression. Use the **PwrReg** feature to find a model for the given data. Which parent function best fits the data?

x	1	24	41	74
y	1	4.9	6.4	8.6

SPIRAL REVIEW

Graph each system of inequalities. *(Lesson 3-3)*

26. $\begin{cases} y \geq 3x + 1 \\ y \leq x - 3 \end{cases}$

27. $\begin{cases} y \geq x - 8 \\ y \leq -\frac{4}{3}x + \frac{1}{3} \end{cases}$

28. $\begin{cases} y \leq 5x \\ y \geq x + 2 \end{cases}$

29. **Business** The profit for a company in thousands of dollars is modeled by the function $p(x) = -x^3 + 12x^2 - 12x - 80$, where x is the number of items produced in thousands. *(Lesson 5-5)*
    a. Find the zeros of the function.
    b. Which zero represents the number of items that the company must produce to break even?

Determine by composition whether each pair of functions are inverses. *(Lesson 9-5)*

30. $f(x) = x^2 + 1$ and $g(x) = \sqrt{x} + 1$

31. $f(x) = -4 + 5x$ and $g(x) = \frac{1}{5}x + \frac{4}{5}$

CHAPTER 9

MULTI-STEP TEST PREP

SECTION 9B

Functional Relationships

Full of Hot Air When you ride in a hot-air balloon that is rising vertically, the distance to the farthest object that you can see increases as the balloon's height increases. The table shows data that were collected on a hot-air balloon.

Balloon's Height (m)	7.8	31.3	70.5	125.4	196.0
Distance That You Can See (km)	10	20	30	40	50

1. Which is the independent variable? Why?
2. Which parent function best models the data set? Why?
3. Write a function $f(x)$ that models the data.
4. If you are in a hot-air balloon at a height of 100 m, how far would you expect to be able to see?
5. Write the inverse function of $f(x)$, and explain what it represents.
6. Find the approximate minimum height for a hot-air balloon if you want to be able to see objects that are 25 km away.
7. The function $g(x) = 0.3x$ converts distances in feet to approximate distances in meters. Write a composite function for the distance that you can see in kilometers from a height of x feet.

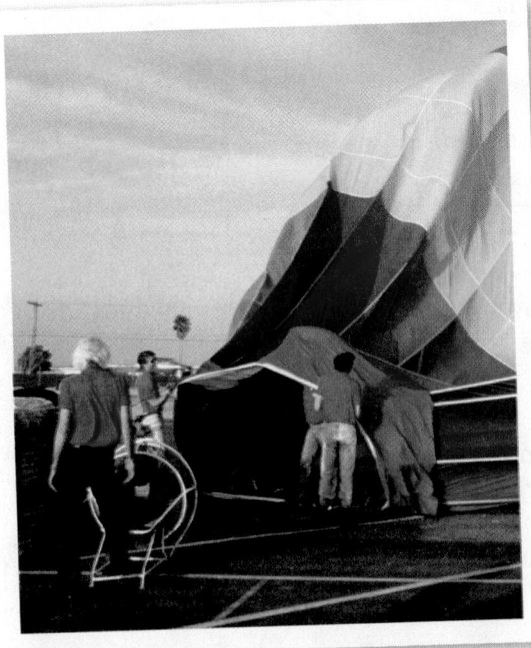

READY TO GO ON?

Quiz for Lessons 9-4 Through 9-6

9-4 Operations with Functions

Given $f(x) = \dfrac{5}{x+3}$, $g(x) = x - 6$, and $h(x) = x^2 - 4x - 12$, find each function or value.

1. $(f - g)(2)$
2. $(g + h)(x)$
3. $\left(\dfrac{g}{h}\right)(8)$
4. $\left(\dfrac{h}{g}\right)(x)$
5. $(gh)(5)$
6. $(gf)(x)$
7. $g(f(-2))$
8. $h(g(x))$
9. Find $(f \circ g)(x)$. State the domain of the composite function.
10. Erin receives a 30% employee discount at the camera store where she works. During a sale, she receives an additional 20% off the discounted price. Write a composite function for the price Erin pays for an item with an original price of p dollars.

9-5 Functions and Their Inverses

State whether the inverse of each relation is a function.

11.
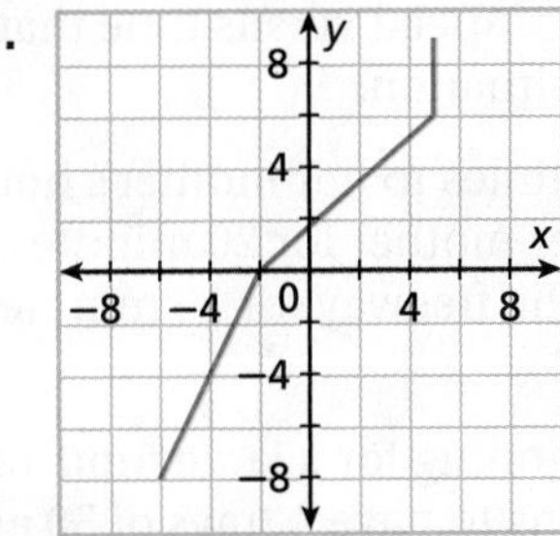

12.
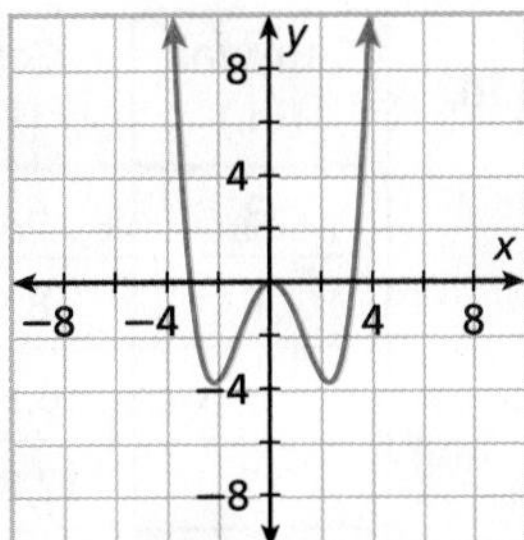

Write the rule for the inverse of each function. Then state the domain and range of the inverse.

13. $f(x) = \dfrac{2}{3}x - 12$
14. $g(x) = \dfrac{12}{x-5}$
15. $h(x) = x^2 - 4$
16. $n(x) = 3^x$

9-6 Modeling Real-World Data

17. Use finite differences or ratios to determine which parent function would best model this set of data.

x	0	1	2	3	4
y	625	375	225	135	81

18. The table shows the average temperature in degrees Fahrenheit and the average utility bill for the households in a town in recent months. Using average temperature as the independent variable, find a model for the average bill.

Average Monthly Temperature (°F)	Average Monthly Utility Bill ($)
61	108
80	103
46	148
72	89
50	125
88	132

CHAPTER 9

Study Guide: Review

Vocabulary

composition of functions 683

one-to-one function 691

piecewise function 662

step function 663

Complete the sentences below with vocabulary words from the list above.

1. In a(n) ___?___, each y-value is paired with exactly one x-value.
2. A(n) ___?___ is a piecewise function that is constant for each interval of its domain.
3. The function operation that uses the output from one function as the input for a second function is the ___?___.

9-1 Multiple Representations of Functions *(pp. 654–661)*

EXAMPLE

■ **The managers of a town are interested in the cost of snow removal over the winter. The table shows the cost of removing various amounts of snow. Use a graph and an equation to find the cost to remove 24 inches of snow.**

Snowfall (in.)	Cost ($)
3	6,950
6	8,900
9	10,850
12	12,800

A scatter plot shows that the data is linear.

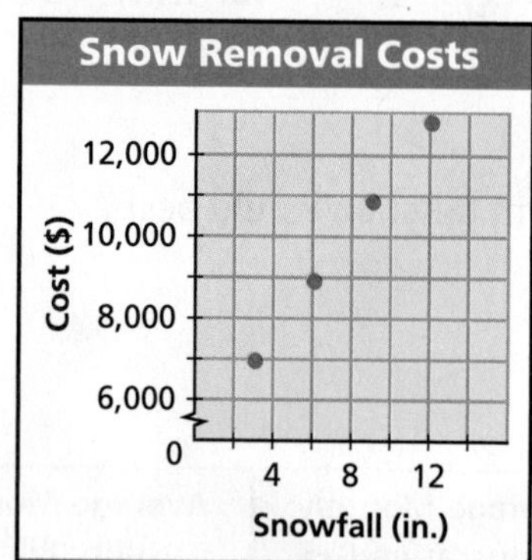

Find the slope of the line by using two points.

$$m = \frac{8900 - 6950}{6 - 3} = \frac{1950}{3} = 650$$

Write an equation by using one of the points.

$$y - 6950 = 650(x - 3)$$
$$y = 650x + 5000$$

The cost for removing 24 inches of snow is
$y = 5000 + 650(24) = \$20{,}600$.

EXERCISES

4. Draw a graph of speed versus time that represents the following situation.

   Avery drove 5 miles to her mother's house and visited with her mother for 20 minutes. Then she drove on the freeway for 15 minutes before arriving home.

5. A caterer is planning for a large fund-raising dinner. He plans to have 4 trays of 30 appetizers each on the buffet. In addition, he will prepare an additional 4 appetizers per guest. Create a table, a graph, and an equation to represent the number of appetizers with relation to the number of guests.

6. The scatter plot shows how long it takes to fill various cylindrical containers of different radii.

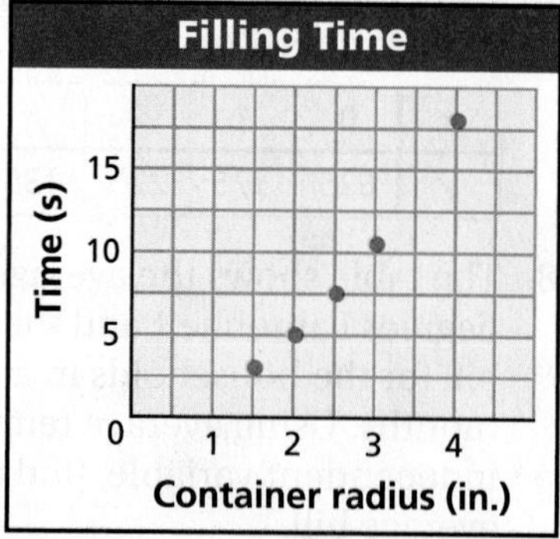

   a. Create a table and an equation for the data.

   b. Use your equation to predict the time that it would take to fill a cylindrical container with a radius of 7 inches.

9-2 Piecewise Functions *(pp. 662–669)*

EXAMPLES

■ Evaluate $f(x) = \begin{cases} 5x + 2 & \text{if } x \le 1 \\ x^2 - 6 & \text{if } x > 1 \end{cases}$ for $x = -2$ and $x = 5$.

$f(-2) = 5(-2) + 2 = -8$ *Use the rule for $x \le 1$.*

$f(5) = 5^2 - 6 = 19$ *Use the rule for $x > 1$.*

■ Graph $g(x) = \begin{cases} 2x + 4 & \text{if } x < -2 \\ -3x + 2 & \text{if } x \ge -2 \end{cases}$.

The domain of the function is split at $x = -2$. Use a table of values to graph both pieces.

x	g(x) = 2x + 4	g(x) = −3x + 2
−4	−4	■
−3	−2	■
−2	0	8
−1	■	5
0	■	2

Use an open circle at $(-2, 0)$ and a closed circle at $(-2, 8)$.

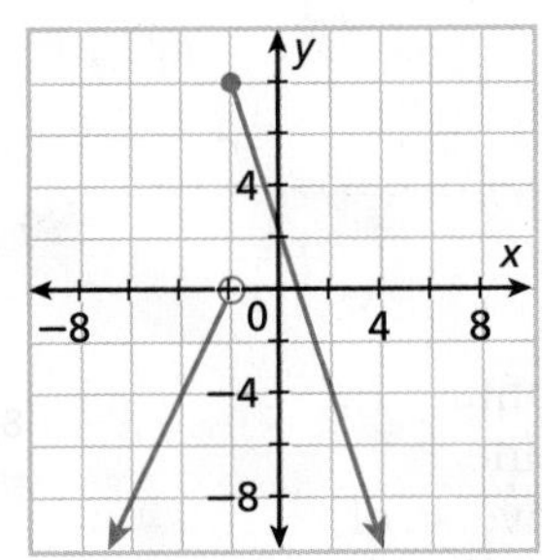

EXERCISES

7. Evaluate $f(x) = \begin{cases} \sqrt{5x + 9} & \text{if } x \ge 4 \\ 9 - 7x & \text{if } x < 4 \end{cases}$ for $x = -6$ and $x = 8$.

Graph each function.

8. $f(x) = \begin{cases} 2x - 4 & \text{if } x < 0 \\ 5 & \text{if } x \ge 0 \end{cases}$

9. $g(x) = \begin{cases} \frac{3}{2}x - 1 & \text{if } x \le 2 \\ \sqrt{x + 2} & \text{if } x > 2 \end{cases}$

10. Write a piecewise function for this graph.

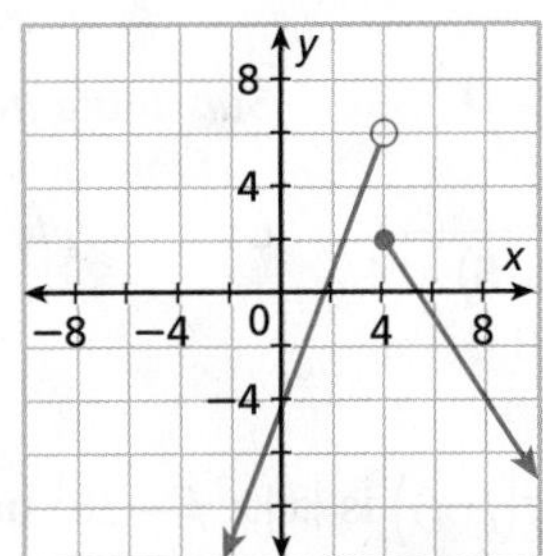

11. A bicycle delivery service charges \$6 to deliver a package that weighs 8 ounces or less. For each additional ounce, the service charges \$1.50 per ounce. Write a piecewise function for the amounts that this company charges to deliver packages that weigh 3 pounds or less.

9-3 Transforming Functions *(pp. 672–679)*

EXAMPLE

■ **Given $f(x) = \begin{cases} 2x - 2 & \text{if } x \le 3 \\ -4x + 16 & \text{if } x > 3 \end{cases}$, write the rule for $g(x)$, a horizontal translation of $f(x)$ 5 units left.**

Each piece of $f(x)$ must be shifted 5 units left. Replace every x with $(x + 5)$, and simplify.

$$g(x) = f(x + 5) = \begin{cases} 2(x + 5) - 2 & \text{if } (x + 5) \le 3 \\ -4(x + 5) + 16 & \text{if } (x + 5) > 3 \end{cases}$$

$$= \begin{cases} 2x + 8 & \text{if } x \le -2 \\ -4x - 4 & \text{if } x > -2 \end{cases}$$

EXERCISES

12. Given $f(x) = \begin{cases} 2x - 2 & \text{if } x \le 3 \\ -4x + 16 & \text{if } x > 3 \end{cases}$, write the rule for $h(x)$, a vertical translation of $f(x)$ 2 units up.

13. Given $f(x) = \begin{cases} 3x + 2 & \text{if } x \le 0 \\ x^2 & \text{if } x > 0 \end{cases}$, write the rule for $g(x)$, a horizontal translation of $f(x)$ 7 units right.

14. Given $f(x) = 2x^2 + 1$ and $g(x) = f\left(\frac{1}{2}x\right) + 1$, graph $g(x)$.

9-4 Operations with Functions *(pp. 682–688)*

EXAMPLES

Given $f(x) = x + 3$ and $g(x) = x^2 - 9$, find each function.

- $\left(\frac{g}{f}\right)(x)$

$$\left(\frac{g}{f}\right)(x) = \frac{g(x)}{f(x)} = \frac{x^2 - 9}{x + 3}$$
$$= \frac{(x+3)(x-3)}{x+3} = x - 3, x \neq -3$$

- **Given $f(x) = x + 6$ and $g(x) = \frac{18}{x+4}$, find $g(f(x))$. State its domain.**

$g(f(x)) = g(x + 6)$ *Substitute the rule for f into g.*

$= \frac{18}{(x+6)+4}$ *Use the rule for g.*

$= \frac{18}{x+10}$

The domain of $g(f(x))$ is $\{x | x \neq -10\}$ because the function is undefined at $x = -10$.

EXERCISES

Given $f(x) = x^2 - 5x - 14$ and $g(x) = x - 7$, find each function.

15. $(f + g)(x)$
16. $(f - g)(x)$
17. $(g - f)(x)$
18. $(fg)(x)$
19. $\left(\frac{f}{g}\right)(x)$
20. $\left(\frac{g}{f}\right)(x)$

Let $f(x) = x - 2$ and $g(x) = \frac{8}{x+1}$.

21. Find $f(g(-2))$ and $g(f(-2))$.
22. Find $f(g(1))$, and $g(f(1))$.
23. Find $g(f(x))$, and state its domain.
24. Find $f(g(x))$ and state its domain.
25. Because of high fuel costs, an airline begins adding a fuel surcharge of \$30 to the price of each airline ticket the airline sells. Also, the airline must add 9% to the price for airport and sales taxes. Write a composite function for how much a person would pay for a ticket with this airline that is x dollars before surcharges and taxes.

9-5 Functions and Their Inverses *(pp. 690–696)*

EXAMPLES

- **Find the inverse of $f(x) = -3(x - 6)^2$. Determine whether it is a function, and state its domain and range.**

$y = -3(x - 6)^2$ *Rewrite the function by using y.*

$x = -3(y - 6)^2$ *Switch x and y in the equation.*

$-\frac{x}{3} = (y - 6)^2$ *Divide both sides by −3.*

$\pm\sqrt{-\frac{x}{3}} = y - 6$ *Take the square root of both sides.*

$y = \pm\sqrt{-\frac{x}{3}} + 6$ *Simplify.*

$f^{-1}(x) = \pm\sqrt{-\frac{x}{3}} + 6$ *Rewrite as $f^{-1}(x)$.*

Because there is a positive y-value and a negative y-value for any $x < 0$, the inverse is not a function. Because the radicand must be greater than or equal to 0, the domain is $\{x | x \leq 0\}$. The range is $\mathbb{R}$.

EXERCISES

26. Use the horizontal-line test to determine whether the inverse of the relation graphed is a function.

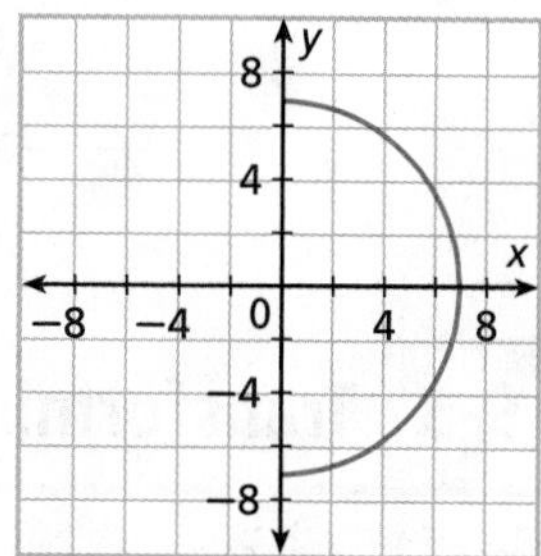

Find the inverse of each function. Determine whether the inverse is a function, and state its domain and range.

27. $f(x) = 5 - 8x$
28. $f(x) = \left(\frac{1}{3}x + 2\right)^2$
29. $f(x) = \frac{5}{2x+8}$
30. $f(x) = 3 + \sqrt{x - 5}$

EXAMPLES

- **Determine by composition whether $f(x) = \frac{1}{3}x - 4$ and $g(x) = 12 + 3x$ are inverses.**

Find both compositions.

$$f(g(x)) = \frac{1}{3}(12 + 3x) - 4 = 4 + x - 4 = x$$

$$g(f(x)) = 12 + 3\left(\frac{1}{3}x - 4\right) = 12 + x - 12 = x$$

Because $f(g(x)) = g(f(x)) = x$, f and g are inverses.

EXERCISES

Determine by composition whether each pair of functions are inverses.

31. $f(x) = 3x - 5$ and $g(x) = \frac{x-3}{5}$

32. $f(x) = \sqrt[3]{x-5}$ and $g(x) = x^3 + 5$

33. The formula for the surface area of a sphere with radius r is $A(r) = 4\pi r^2$. Find and interpret the inverse of $A(r)$.

9-6 Modeling Real-World Data *(pp. 698–705)*

EXAMPLE

- **The table shows the ticket prices to a minor league baseball game in relation to the number of years since the team began playing.**

Baseball Ticket Prices	
Year	Price ($)
1	9.50
2	10.25
3	11.10
4	12.00
5	12.92

Step 1 Check the first differences of the prices.

0.75 0.85 0.90 0.92

Because the first differences are not constant, a linear model is not a good fit.

Step 2 Check the second differences.

0.10 0.05 0.02

Because the second differences are not constant, a quadratic model is not a good fit.

Step 3 Check the ratios.

$\frac{10.25}{9.5} \approx 1.08$, $\frac{11.10}{10.25} \approx 1.08$, $\frac{12}{11.10} \approx 1.08$, $\frac{12.92}{12} \approx 1.08$

The ratios are close to 1.08. An exponential model is a good fit.

Step 4 Perform an exponential regression.

An appropriate model is $f(x) = 8.79(1.08)^x$.

EXERCISES

34. The table shows the city of Culver's water use in relation to daily high temperature.

Water Use in Culver	
Daily High Temperature (°F)	Water Use (million gal)
55	71.3
60	78.7
65	86.9
70	96
75	106
80	117

a. Find an appropriate model for this data. Use temperature t as the independent variable.

b. Use your model to predict the number of gallons that Culver will use when the high temperature is 85°F.

c. Use your model to predict the high temperature when the water use is 50 million gallons.

CHAPTER 9

Chapter Test

1. James receives a salary of $300 per week plus a commission of 3% of the amount he sells. Create a table, a graph, and an equation to represent his weekly earnings on sales of 0 to 10,000 dollars.

2. While standing at the top of a cliff, Kurt accidentally knocks a stone loose. The table shows the height of the stone in meters after t seconds.

   a. Create a graph and an equation for the data by using time t as the independent variable.

   b. How high is the cliff?

   c. Find the height of the stone after 10 seconds.

   d. When will the stone hit the ground?

Height of Falling Stone	
Time (s)	**Height (m)**
1	615.1
2	600.4
3	575.9
4	541.6
5	497.5
6	443.6

Graph each function.

3. $f(x) = \begin{cases} -x - 3 & \text{if } x < 1 \\ 2x - 6 & \text{if } x \geq 1 \end{cases}$

4. $g(x) = \begin{cases} 5 & \text{if } x \leq -2 \\ -x^2 - 4x & \text{if } x > -2 \end{cases}$

Given $f(x)$, graph $g(x)$.

5. $f(x) = 2x - 4$ and $g(x) = -\frac{1}{2}f(x) - 1$

6. $f(x) = x^2 - 2$ and $g(x) = -f(x + 2)$

Given $f(x) = 4x^2 - 9$ and $g(x) = 2x + 3$, find each function or value.

7. $(f - g)(4)$

8. $g(f(3))$

9. $(fg)(5)$

10. $\left(\frac{g}{f}\right)(x)$

11. Ramon pays a 10% insurance fee for each piece of jewelry in his store. He then prices the item for sale at 150% of his total cost. Write a composite function for the price of an item with an original cost of c dollars.

Write the rule for the inverse of each function. Determine whether the inverse is a function, and state its domain and range.

12. $f(x) = 12 - 5x$

13. $g(x) = \frac{10}{x + 4}$

14. $h(x) = \frac{(x + 5)^2}{2}$

15. The table shows the average sales prices of houses and the houses' distances from downtown.

   a. Find an appropriate model for the data by using distance d as the independent variable.

   b. Use your model to predict the average sales prices of houses that are 20 miles from downtown.

Sales Prices of Houses	
Distance from Downtown (mi)	**Average Sales Price ($)**
2	118,496
4	109,016
6	100,295
8	92,271
10	84,890
12	78,098

FOCUS ON SAT STUDENT-PRODUCED RESPONSES

Some questions on the SAT require you to enter your answer in a special grid. Your answers must be positive integers, fractions, or decimals. You cannot enter negative numbers or mixed numbers in the grid.

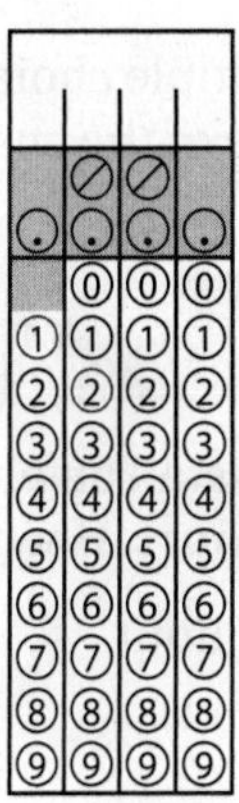

Some questions may have multiple answers; in these cases you may enter any one correct answer. If the solution is an inequality, be sure that you choose a number from the solution region.

You may want to time yourself as you take this practice test. It should take you about 9 minutes to complete.

---

1. If 5 less than 3 times a number is equal to 2 more than twice the number, what is the number?

2. The graph of $f(x)$ is shown.

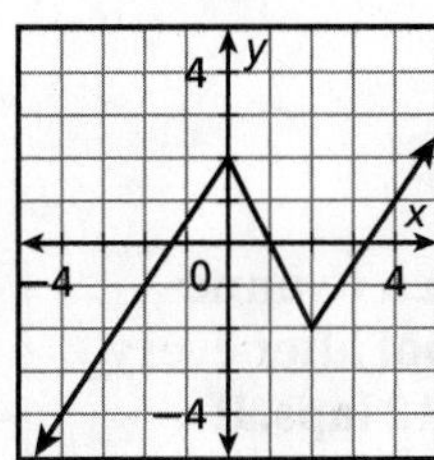

If $g(x) = -f(x) + 1$, what is $g(2)$?

3. Give a possible value for x in the inequality $-4(2x - 3) > 4x - 24$.

4. Let the operations ♦ and ♥ be defined for real numbers a and b as shown.

$a \blacklozenge b = 2a - b$

$a \heartsuit b = \frac{a + b}{2}$

What is the value of $(4 \heartsuit 9) \blacklozenge 3$?

5. Maria drove to her grandmother's house at an average speed of 60 miles per hour. On the way home, she averaged only 45 miles per hour due to traffic. If she spent a total of $3\frac{1}{2}$ hours driving, how many miles is the trip to her grandmother's house?

6. The table shows some values for the function f.

x	−2	0	2	4
$f(x)$	7	4	1	−2

What is the value of $f^{-1}(-2)$?

Standardized Test Strategies

Multiple Choice: Eliminate Answer Choices

With some multiple choice test items, you can use mental math or logic to quickly eliminate some of the answer choices before you begin solving the problem.

EXAMPLE 1

Tyler can install an air conditioning unit in 3 hours. If Laura helps him, the job is done in 2 hours. How many hours would it take Laura working alone?

Ⓐ 1 hour Ⓒ 6 hours

Ⓑ 2 hours Ⓓ 8 hours

READ *the question. Then try to* ***eliminate*** *some of the answer choices.*

Use logic:
When Tyler works alone, the job gets done in 3 hours. When working with Laura, the job takes only 2 hours. So, it is reasonable to assume that Laura working alone takes MORE THAN 2 hours to complete the job.

Based on this logic, **eliminate** choices A and B.
Set up and solve a rational equation to find the correct answer, C.

EXAMPLE 2

Ryanne swims six days a week. Her coach starts keeping time when Ryanne starts warming up and notes how long Ryanne has been at the pool after every 2 laps. The table shows the time that it takes for Ryanne to swim 12 laps. If Ryanne wants to swim 24 laps, how long will it take?

Laps	Time (min)
2	6
4	10
6	14
8	18
10	22
12	26

Ⓕ 28 minutes Ⓗ 48 minutes

Ⓖ 38 minutes Ⓙ 50 minutes

LOOK *at the data, and* ***eliminate*** *some answer choices.*

Use mental math and logic:
From the data in the table, you can tell that Ryanne swims 2 laps every 4 minutes. So it takes her 2 minutes to swim 1 lap.

So 24 laps would take $24(2) = 48$ minutes. You can eliminate any answer choice that is LESS THAN 48 minutes: choices F and G.

Before you select choice H as your answer, be careful. Look at the data in the table again. The first 2 laps that Ryanne swims take her **6** minutes, not 4 minutes, so your estimate of 48 laps is a bit low. Therefore, **eliminate** choice H. Choice J is the correct answer.

Try to eliminate unreasonable answer choices. Some choices may be too great or too small or may have incorrect units.

Read each test item and answer the questions that follow.

Item A

The width of a rectangle is 6 feet less than its length. Which of the following systems of equations can be used to find the dimensions of the rectangle if the perimeter of the rectangle is 56 feet?

Ⓐ $\ell = w - 6$; $2\ell + 2w = 56$

Ⓑ $w = \ell - 6$; $2(\ell + w) = 56$

Ⓒ $\ell = w - 6$; $\ell w = 56$

Ⓓ $w = \ell - 6$; $\ell w = \ell 6$

1. What is the perimeter formula for the area of a rectangle? Based on this formula, are there any choices that you can eliminate immediately? If so, which choices and why?
2. Read the first sentence of the test item again and write an expression. Are there any more answer choices that you can eliminate? Explain.

Item B

The volume V of a gas varies inversely with the pressure P and directly with the temperature T. A certain gas has a volume of 30 liters, a temperature of 345 kelvins, and a pressure of 1 atmosphere. If the gas is compressed to a volume of 20 liters and heated to 375 kelvins, what will the new pressure be?

Ⓕ 0.72 atmosphere

Ⓖ 0.72 liter

Ⓗ 1.5 atmospheres

Ⓙ 1.63 atmospheres

3. Are there any answer choices that logically do not make sense and can be eliminated? If so, which choices and why?
4. Because the volume of a gas varies inversely with the pressure, if the volume decreases, should the pressure increase or decrease? Can you eliminate any of the answer choices by using this information?

Item C

A moving truck company charges $125 a day for driving its truck 50 miles or less. The company charges an additional $0.05 per mile for all miles driven over 50 miles. Which of the following functions represents the fee for this moving truck for x miles in a day?

Ⓐ $C(x) = \begin{cases} 125 & \text{if } 0 \le x \le 50 \\ 2.5 & \text{if } x > 50 \end{cases}$

Ⓑ $C(x) = \begin{cases} 125 & \text{if } 0 \le x \le 50 \\ 125 + 0.05(x - 50) & \text{if } x > 50 \end{cases}$

Ⓒ $C(x) = \begin{cases} 50 & \text{if } 0 \le x \le 50 \\ 50 + 0.05x & \text{if } x > 50 \end{cases}$

Ⓓ $C(x) = \begin{cases} 0.05 & \text{if } 0 \le x \le 50 \\ 125x & \text{if } x > 50 \end{cases}$

5. Look at answer choice A. Why can it be eliminated immediately?
6. Sarah wants to eliminate choice C. Do you agree? Explain.

Item D

Which function corresponds to the graph?

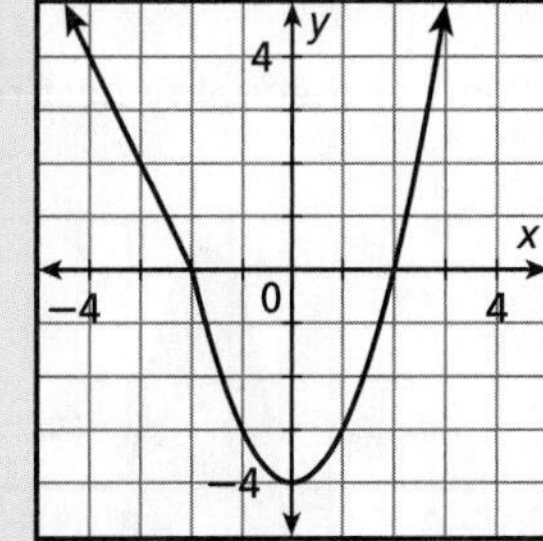

Ⓕ $g(x) = \begin{cases} x^2 - 4 & \text{if } x \ge 0 \\ -2x - 4 & \text{if } x < 0 \end{cases}$

Ⓖ $g(x) = \begin{cases} x - 4 & \text{if } x \ge -2 \\ -2x & \text{if } x < -2 \end{cases}$

Ⓗ $g(x) = \begin{cases} x^2 - 4 & \text{if } x \ge -2 \\ -2x - 4 & \text{if } x < -2 \end{cases}$

Ⓙ $g(x) = \begin{cases} x^2 & \text{if } x \ge -2 \\ -2x + 4 & \text{if } x < -2 \end{cases}$

7. Describe the functions on the graph. Which answer choice can be eliminated based on the shape of the function?
8. Kaye looked at the domain of the function and decided to eliminate choice F. Do you agree with Kaye's decision? Explain.

CHAPTER 9

STANDARDIZED TEST PREP

CUMULATIVE ASSESSMENT, CHAPTERS 1–9

Multiple Choice

1. Which is the graph of $f(x) = |x + 1| - 2$?

Ⓐ 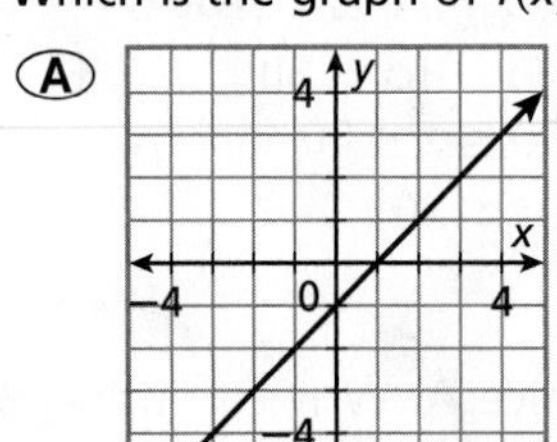

Ⓒ 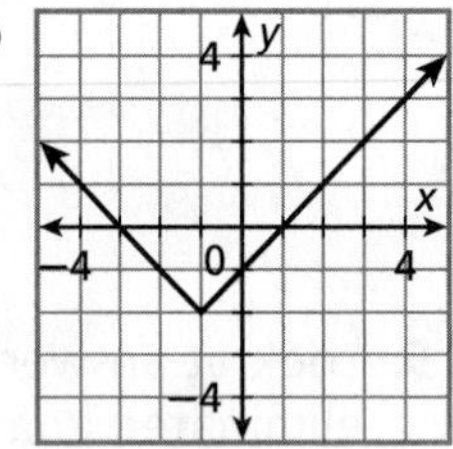

Ⓑ 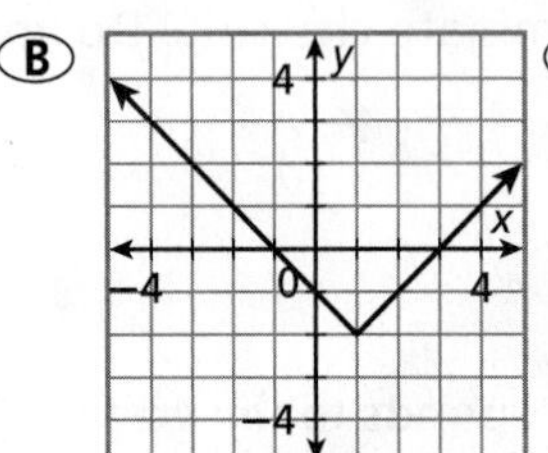

Ⓓ 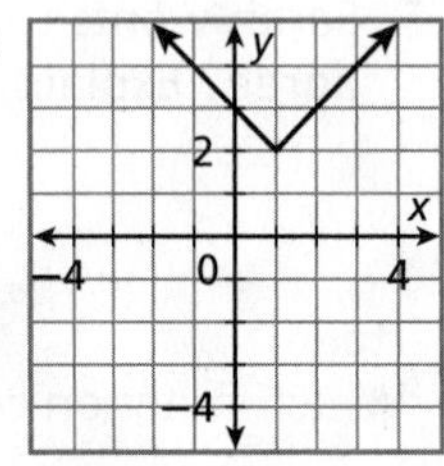

2. Which equation or inequality best represents the graph?

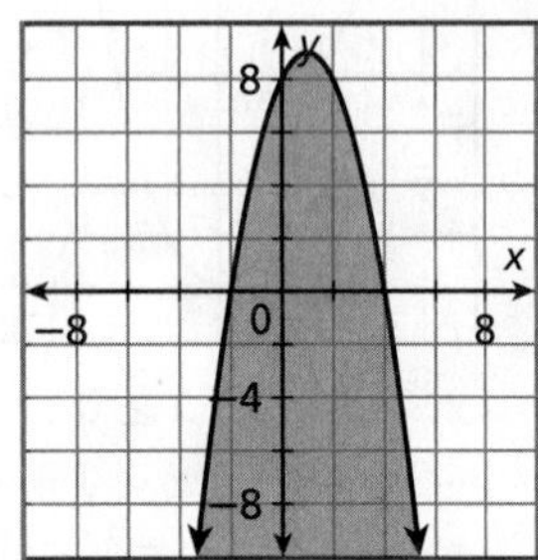

Ⓕ $y = x^2 + 2x + 8$

Ⓖ $y = -x^2 + 2x + 8$

Ⓗ $y \leq x^2 + 2x + 8$

Ⓙ $y \leq -x^2 + 2x + 8$

3. Which is the augmented matrix for this system of equations?

$$\begin{cases} -5y = 8 - x \\ y + 3x = 10 \end{cases}$$

Ⓐ $\left[\begin{array}{cc|c} -5 & 8 & -1 \\ 1 & 3 & 10 \end{array}\right]$

Ⓒ $\left[\begin{array}{cc|c} 1 & -5 & 8 \\ 1 & 3 & 10 \end{array}\right]$

Ⓑ $\left[\begin{array}{cc|c} 1 & -5 & 8 \\ 3 & 1 & 10 \end{array}\right]$

Ⓓ $\left[\begin{array}{cc|c} -5 & 8 & -1 \\ 3 & 1 & 10 \end{array}\right]$

4. Which description best reflects the graph shown?

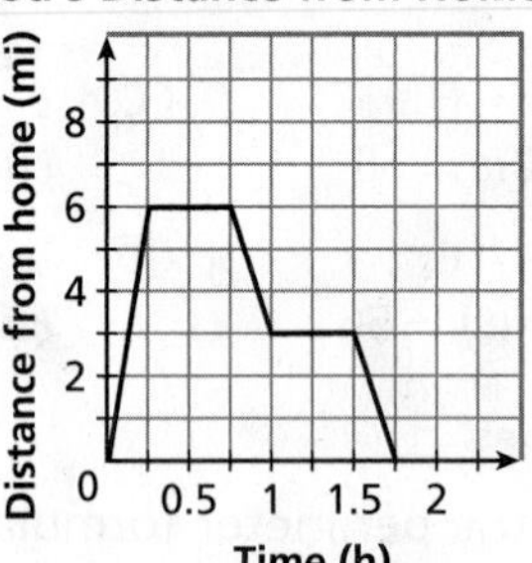

Ⓕ Lou drove 6 miles to the library, spent an hour there, and then drove straight home.

Ⓖ Lou drove 6 miles to the library, spent half an hour there, stopped by the video store for half an hour, and then drove home.

Ⓗ Lou drove 3 miles to the library, spent half an hour there, drove another 3 miles to the movie store, and then drove home.

Ⓙ Lou drove 6 miles to the library, spent half an hour there, drove another 3 miles to the video store, and spent an hour there.

5. Evaluate the piecewise function for $x = -1$.

$$f(x) = \begin{cases} x^2 + 4x - 8 & x < -1 \\ x^3 - x^2 + 5 & x \geq -1 \end{cases}$$

Ⓐ −13　　Ⓒ 3

Ⓑ −11　　Ⓓ 5

6. Solve for x.

$\sqrt{2x - 4} = x - 6$

Ⓕ $x = 10$　　Ⓗ $x = 2$ and $x = 20$

Ⓖ $x = 4$ and $x = 10$　　Ⓙ $x = 2$ and $x = 12$

7. Given $f(x) = 2x^2 - 7x - 30$ and $g(x) = x - 6$, find $\left(\frac{f}{g}\right)(x)$.

Ⓐ $2x - 5$　　Ⓒ $\frac{(2x - 5)(x + 6)}{x - 6}$

Ⓑ $2x + 5$　　Ⓓ $\frac{(2x - 10)(9x + 3)}{x - 6}$

8. Which transformation of triangle ABC creates an image with a vertex at $(-2, 1)$?

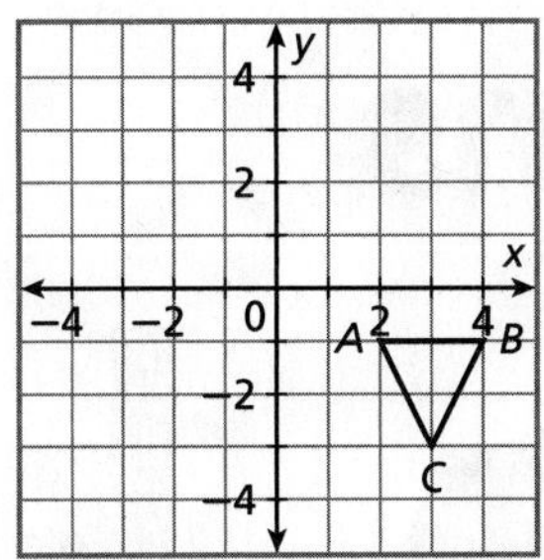

Ⓕ Reflect ΔABC across the x-axis.

Ⓖ Reflect ΔABC across the y-axis.

Ⓗ Translate ΔABC 3 units left and 3 units up.

Ⓙ Rotate ΔABC 180° about the origin.

In Item 9, examine one part of the function at a time, eliminating answer choices until you find a graph that matches all parts of the function.

9. Which is the graph of $f(x) = -\frac{1}{2}x^2 + 6$?

Ⓐ
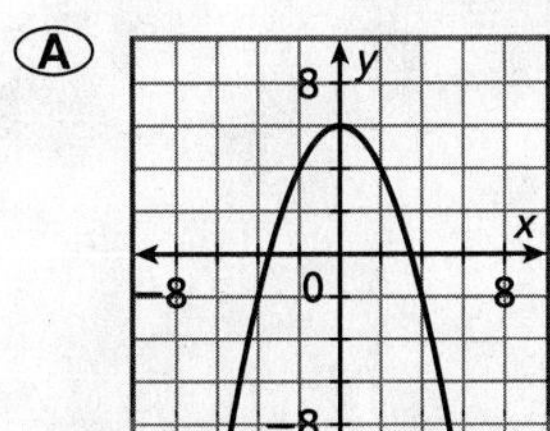

Ⓒ
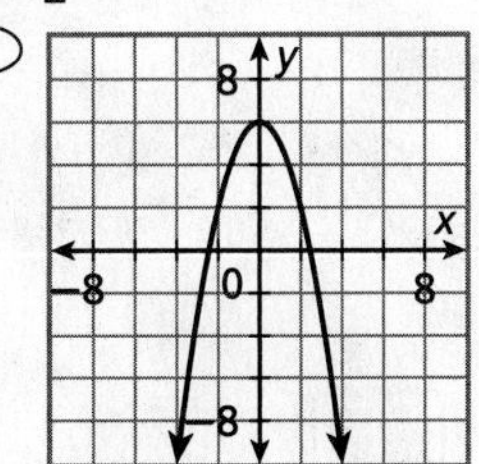

Ⓑ
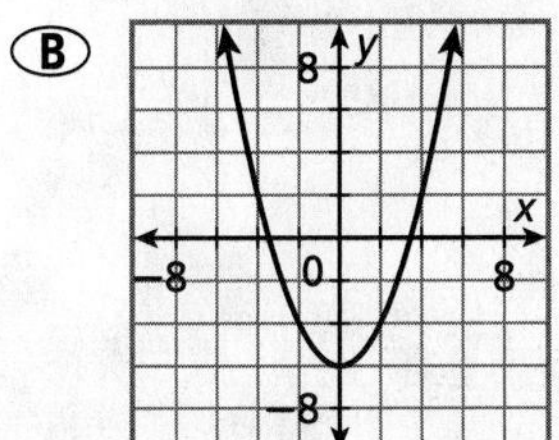

Ⓓ
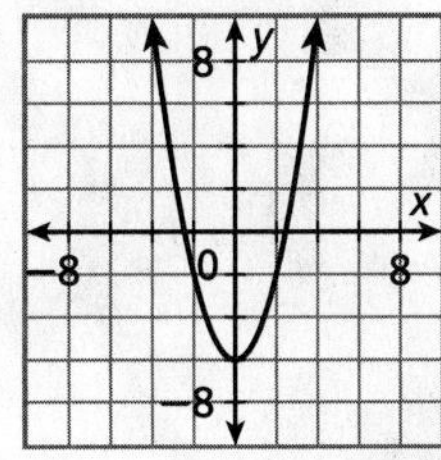

Gridded Response

10. Find the value of $\log_4 256^3$.

11. What is the value of c in the given equation?

$4(5i - 2) + 3 = 2(10i + c) - 7$

12. Find the value of the given expression when $x = 5$.

$$\left(\frac{x^2 + 5x - 36}{2x^2 - 10x + 8}\right)\left(\frac{x^2 + x - 2}{x^2 + 11x + 18}\right)$$

Short Response

13. The equation $f(x) = x^2 + 1$ is a function.

a. Find the inverse of the function.

b. Graph $f(x) = x^2 + 1$ and its inverse.

c. Explain whether the inverse is a function.

14. Use the points below.

$(0, 6)$, $(2, 2)$, and $(5, 11)$

a. Write a quadratic function that fits the points.

b. Check the quadratic function that you wrote by substituting the ordered pairs. Verify that each is a solution.

c. Graph the equation.

d. Find $f(7)$ and $f(-7)$.

15. Consider the function $f(x) = x^2 - 4$.

a. Identify two different transformations of f so that the vertex would be $(1, 4)$.

b. Identify two different transformations of f so that its graph would pass through $(0, 2)$ and $(-4, 2)$.

Extended Response

16. The volume of gas in a car depends on the number of miles that have been driven since the tank was last filled.

Distance driven (mi)	0	50	100	150	200
Gas (gal)	10	8	6	4	2

a. Use constant differences or ratios to determine which parent function would best model the given data.

b. Write the equation for the data.

c. How many gallons are left after 75 miles?

d. Can the car be driven for 300 miles? Why or why not?

e. Find and interpret the inverse of the equation.

CHAPTER

10 Conic Sections

- Develop conceptual understanding of conic sections.
- Applying algebraic representations of conic sections to solve problems.

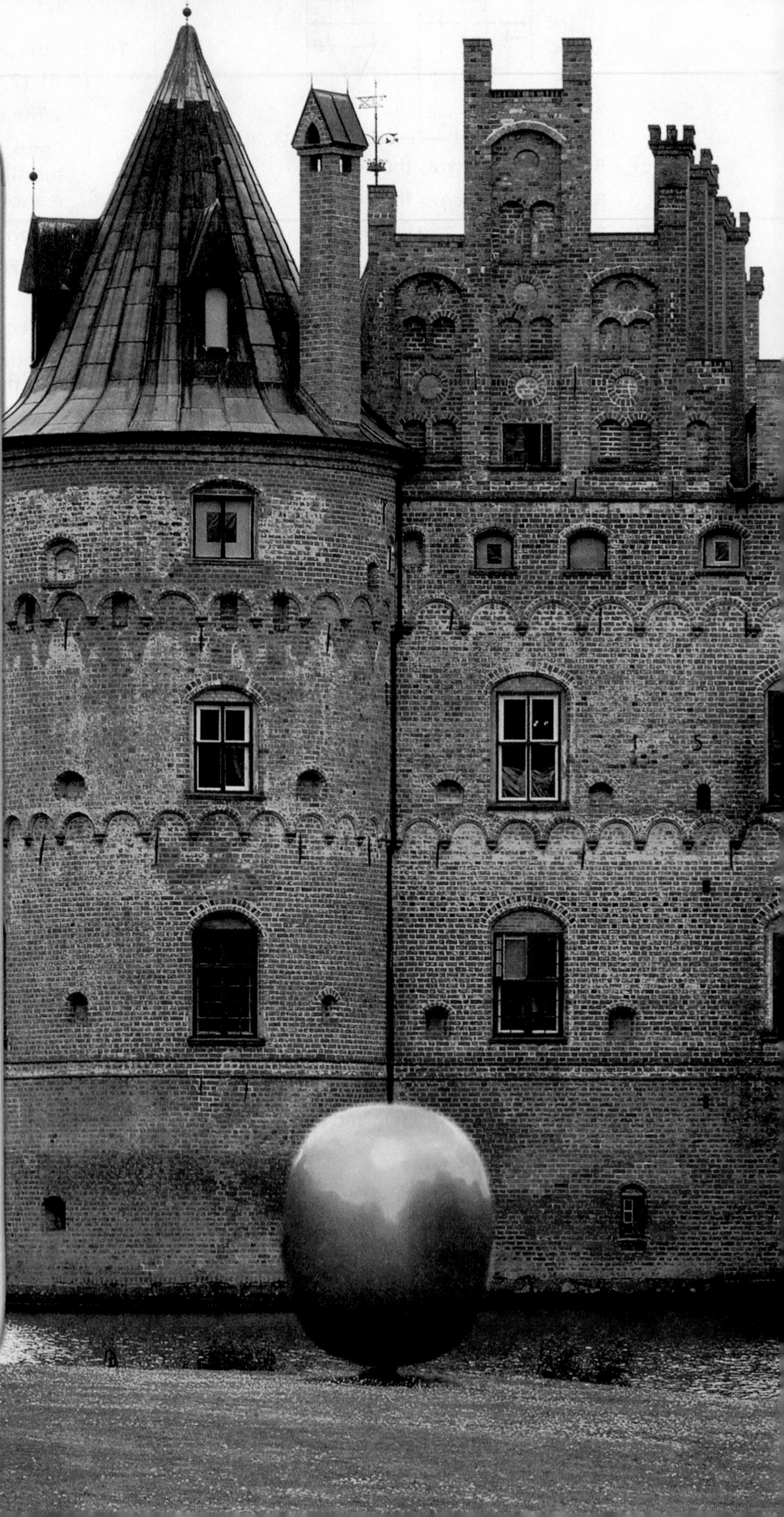

CRACKING THE SUPER EGG

You can use conic sections to create your own super egg and discover the many different uses of super ellipses.

Chapter Project Online
KEYWORD: MB7 ChProj

Vocabulary

Match each term on the left with a definition on the right.

1. vertex of a parabola
2. axis of symmetry
3. solution set of a system of equations
4. asymptote

A. a line that divides a plane figure or a graph into two congruent reflected halves
B. a line approached by the graph of a function
C. a line that is neither horizontal nor vertical
D. the turning point of a parabola
E. the set of points that make all equations in a system true

Circumference and Area of Circles

Find the circumference and area of each circle.

5. 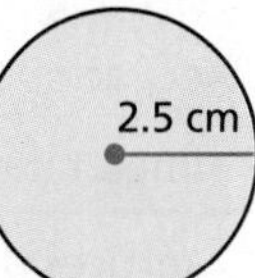

6. 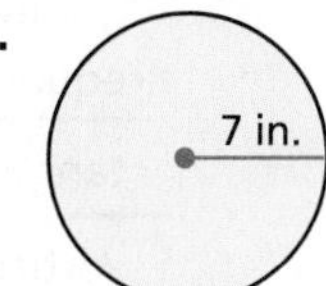

Area of Polygons

Find the area of each figure.

7. 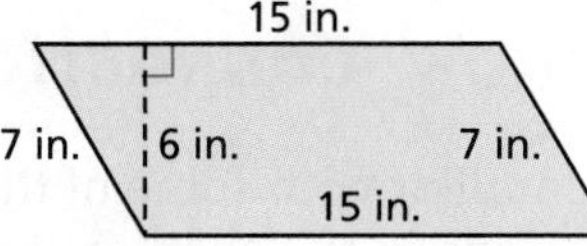

8. 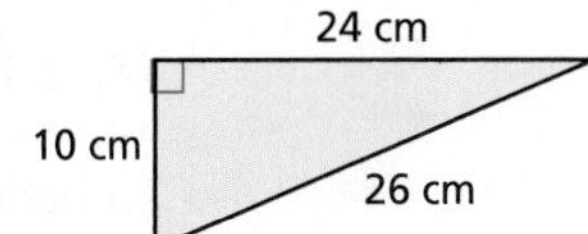

9. 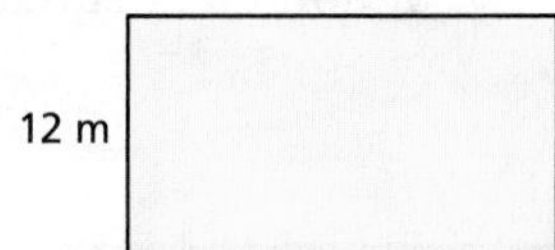

Find Areas in the Coordinate Plane

Find the area of each figure.

10. 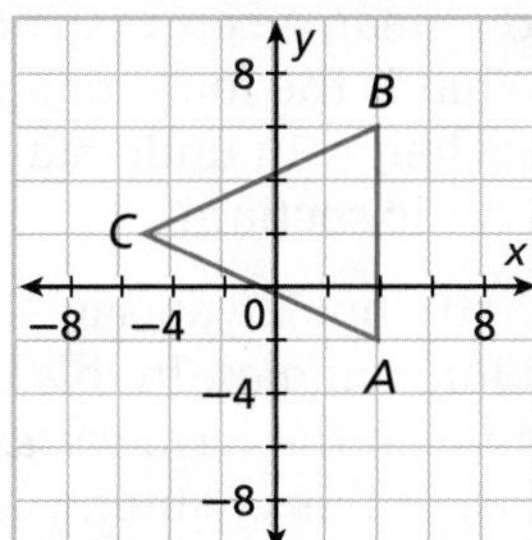

11. 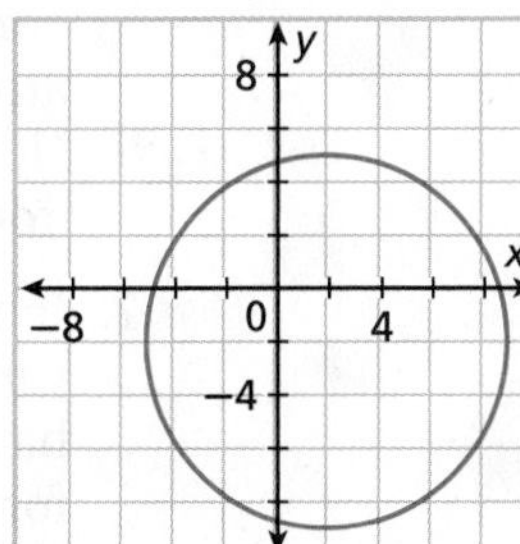

12. 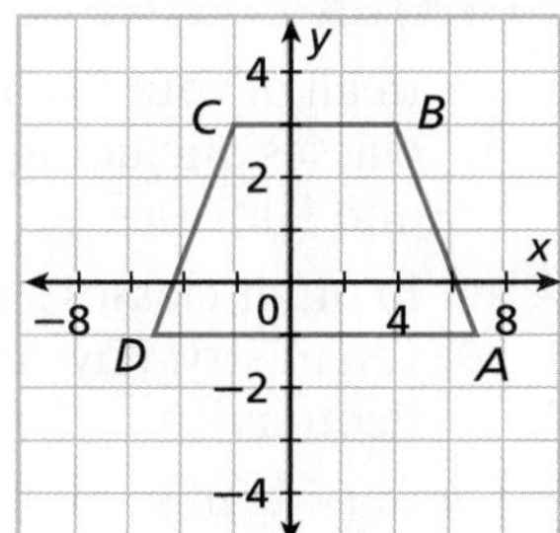

Complete the Square

Complete the square for each expression. Write the resulting expression as a binomial squared.

13. $x^2 - 4x + \blacksquare$

14. $x^2 - x + \blacksquare$

15. $x^2 + 6x + \blacksquare$

CHAPTER 10

Study Guide: Preview

Where You've Been

Previously, you

- graphed parabolas defined by quadratic functions.
- studied graphs of piecewise functions.
- solved systems of linear equations.

In This Chapter

You will study

- graphs of parabolas and other conic sections that are not functions.
- graphs of conic sections represented by two functions together.
- methods for solving systems of nonlinear equations.

Where You're Going

You can use the skills in this chapter

- in all of your future math classes, including Calculus and Statistics.
- in other classes such as Chemistry, Physics, and Economics.
- outside of school in engineering, architecture, astronomy, photography, and communications.

Key Vocabulary/Vocabulario

circle	círculo
conic section	sección cónica
directrix	directriz
ellipse	elipse
foci of an ellipse	focos de una elipse
foci of a hyperbola	focos de una hipérbola
focus of a parabola	foco de una parábola
hyperbola	hipérbola
nonlinear system of equations	sistema no lineal de ecuaciones
tangent line	línea tangente
vertices of an ellipse	vértices de una elipse
vertices of a hyperbola	vértices de una hipérbola

Vocabulary Connections

To become familiar with some of the vocabulary terms in the chapter, consider the following. You may refer to the chapter, the glossary, or a dictionary if you like.

1. When you use the word *focus* in most contexts, you mean a center of activity or attention. What is the focus of a painting? How can this help you understand a **focus** of a conic section?
2. In the geometry book, you saw the term *vertex* used for triangles. In this book you have already seen the term *vertex* used for parabolas. In this chapter, you will see the term **vertex** used for ellipses and hyperbolas. Why is the same term used in all of these different situations?
3. How often does a *tangent* touch a circle? Can curves other than circles also have **tangents**? What do you mean when you say that someone went "off on a tangent" during a discussion?

Study Strategy: Learn Vocabulary

Understanding math terminology and vocabulary is important to learning and using new math concepts. You have already learned many new terms and as you progress in your studies of math, you will need to learn many more.

To learn new vocabulary:

- Look for the meaning of a new word through the context in which it is introduced.
- Use the prefix or suffix to determine the meaning of the root word.
- Relate the new term to familiar, everyday words.

Once you know what a word means, write its definition in your own words.

Vocabulary Word	Study Tips	Definition
Polynomial	Prefix *poly-*, meaning "many"	A monomial or a sum or difference of monomials
Conjunction	Prefix *con-*, meaning "connect" or "together"	A compound statement that uses the word *and*
Extraneous Solution	Relate to the word *extra*, meaning "not needed."	Extra roots that are not solutions to the original equation
Slope	Think of a *ski slope*.	The measure of the steepness of a line

polynomial = many
conjunction = connect or together
extraneous solution = not needed
slope = ski slope

Fill in the chart with information that can help you learn the vocabulary words.

	Vocabulary Word	Study Tips	Definition
1.	Trinomial	■	■
2.	Disjunction	■	■
3.	Variable	■	■
4.	Multiplicity	■	■

Use the given prefix's meaning to write the definition of the corresponding vocabulary words.

5. *dia-* through, across, between: diameter; diagonal

6. *trans-* across, beyond, through: transformation; translation

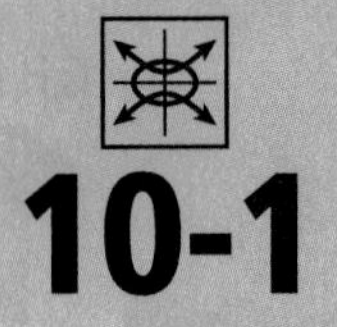

10-1 Introduction to Conic Sections

Objectives
Recognize conic sections as intersections of planes and cones.

Use the distance and midpoint formulas to solve problems.

Vocabulary
conic section

Who uses this?
Archaeologists use distance and midpoint to organize excavation sites. (See Exercise 43.)

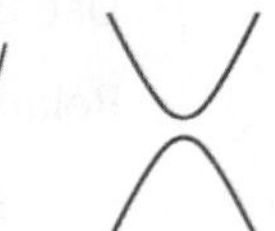

In Chapter 5, you studied the parabola. The parabola is one of a family of curves called *conic sections*. **Conic sections** are formed by the intersection of a double right cone and a plane. There are four types of conic sections: circles, ellipses, hyperbolas, and parabolas.

Although the parabolas you studied in Chapter 5 are functions, most conic sections are not. This means that you often must use two functions to graph a conic section on a calculator.

A circle is defined by its center and its radius. An ellipse, an elongated shape similar to a circle, has two perpendicular axes of different lengths.

EXAMPLE 1 Graphing Circles and Ellipses on a Calculator

Graph each equation on a graphing calculator. Identify each conic section. Then describe the center and intercepts.

A $x^2 + y^2 = 25$

Step 1 Solve for y so that the expression can be used in a graphing calculator.

$y^2 = 25 - x^2$ *Subtract x^2 from both sides.*

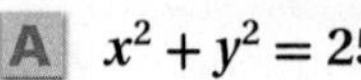

$y = \pm\sqrt{25 - x^2}$ *Take the square root of both sides.*

Step 2 Use two equations to see the complete graph.

$y_1 = \sqrt{25 - x^2}$

$y_2 = -\sqrt{25 - x^2}$

Use a square window on your graphing calculator for an accurate graph. The graphs meet and form a complete circle, even though it may not appear that way on your calculator.

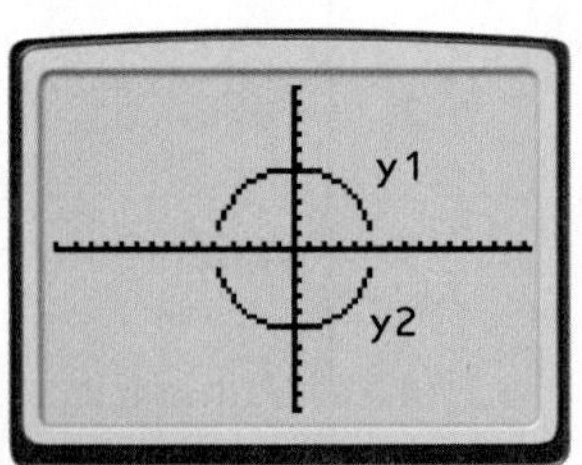

The graph is a circle with center $(0, 0)$ and intercepts $(5, 0)$, $(-5, 0)$, $(0, 5)$, and $(0, -5)$.

Check Use a table to confirm the intercepts.

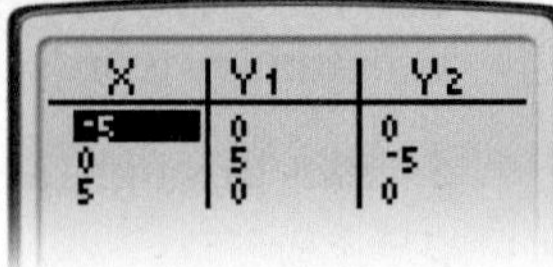

Remember!
When you take the square root of both sides of an equation, remember that you must include the positive and negative roots.

Graph each equation on a graphing calculator. Identify each conic section. Then describe the center and intercepts.

B $16x^2 + 9y^2 = 144$

Step 1 Solve for y so that the expression can be used in a graphing calculator.

$9y^2 = 144 - 16x^2$ *Subtract $16x^2$ from both sides.*

$y^2 = \frac{144 - 16x^2}{9}$ *Divide both sides by 9.*

$y = \pm\sqrt{\frac{144 - 16x^2}{9}}$ *Take the square root of both sides.*

Step 2 Use two equations to see the complete graph.

$$y_1 = \sqrt{\frac{144 - 16x^2}{9}}$$

$$y_2 = -\sqrt{\frac{144 - 16x^2}{9}}$$

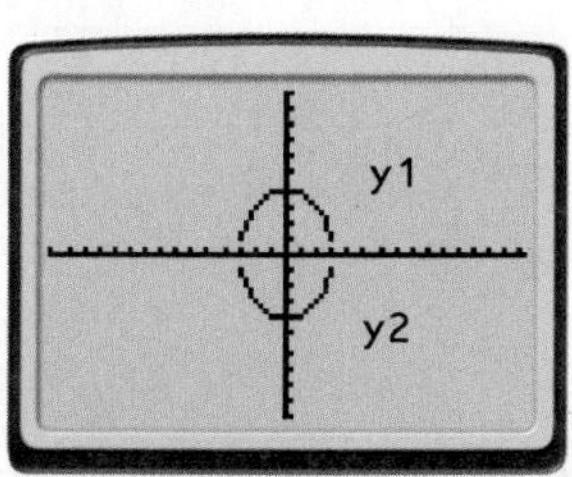

Use a square window on your graphing calculator. The graphs meet and form a complete ellipse, even though it may not appear that way on your calculator.

The graph is an ellipse with center (0, 0) and intercepts (3, 0), (−3, 0), (0, 4), and (0, −4).

Check Use a table to confirm the intercepts.

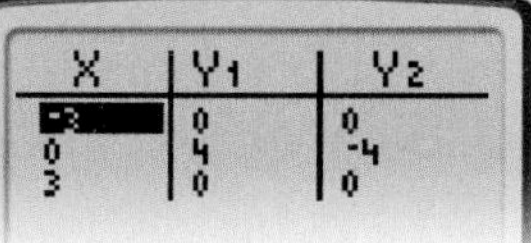

Graph each equation on a graphing calculator. Identify each conic section. Then describe the center and intercepts.

1a. $x^2 + y^2 = 49$ **1b.** $9x^2 + 25y^2 = 225$

A parabola is a single curve, whereas a hyperbola has two congruent branches. The equation of a parabola usually contains either an x^2 term or a y^2 term, but not both. The equations of the other conics will usually contain both x^2 and y^2 terms.

EXAMPLE 2 Graphing Parabolas and Hyperbolas on a Calculator

Graph each equation on a graphing calculator. Identify each conic section. Then describe the vertices and the direction that the graph opens.

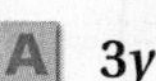

A $3y^2 = x$

Step 1 Solve for y so that the expression can be used in a graphing calculator.

$y^2 = \frac{x}{3}$ *Divide both sides by 3.*

$y = \pm\sqrt{\frac{x}{3}}$ *Take the square root of both sides.*

Step 2 Use two equations to see the complete graph.

$$y_1 = \sqrt{\frac{x}{3}} \text{ and } y_2 = -\sqrt{\frac{x}{3}}$$

The graph is a parabola with vertex (0, 0) that opens to the right.

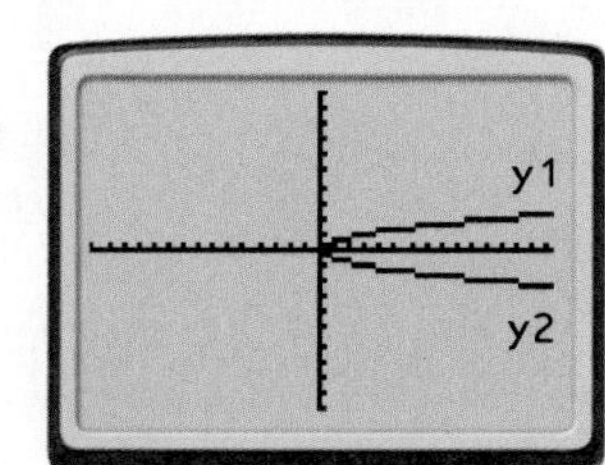

Graph each equation on a graphing calculator. Identify each conic section. Then describe the vertices and the direction that the graph opens.

B $x^2 - y^2 = 4$

Step 1 Solve for y so that the expression can be used in a graphing calculator.

$-y^2 = 4 - x^2$	*Subtract x^2 from both sides.*
$y^2 = -(4 - x^2)$	*Multiply both sides by −1.*
$y^2 = -4 + x^2$	*Distribute.*
$y^2 = x^2 - 4$	*Rearrange.*
$y = \pm\sqrt{x^2 - 4}$	*Take the square root of both sides.*

Helpful Hint

Because hyperbolas contain two curves that open in opposite directions, classify them as opening horizontally, vertically, or neither.

Step 2 Use two equations to see the complete graph.

$y_1 = \sqrt{x^2 - 4}$

$y_2 = -\sqrt{x^2 - 4}$

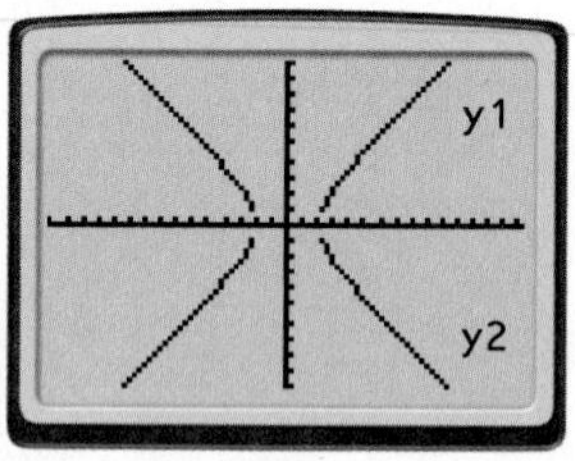

The graph is a hyperbola that opens horizontally with vertices at (2, 0) and (−2, 0).

CHECK IT OUT! **Graph each equation on a graphing calculator. Identify each conic section. Then describe the vertices and the direction that the graph opens.**

2a. $2y^2 = x$ **2b.** $x^2 - y^2 = 16$

Every conic section can be defined in terms of distances. You can use the Midpoint and Distance Formulas to find the center and radius of a circle.

Know it! Note

Midpoint and Distance Formulas

FORMULA	EXAMPLE	GRAPH
The **midpoint** (x_M, y_M) of the segment with endpoints (x_1, y_1) and (x_2, y_2) is $(x_M, y_M) = \left(\frac{x_1 + x_2}{2}, \frac{y_1 + y_2}{2}\right)$.	The midpoint of the segment with endpoints (1, 2) and (5, 8) is $\left(\frac{1+5}{2}, \frac{2+8}{2}\right) = (3, 5)$.	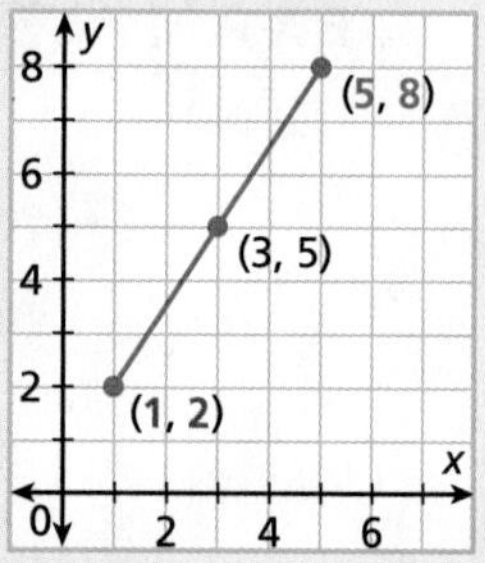
The **distance** d between the points with coordinates (x_1, y_1) and (x_2, y_2) is $d = \sqrt{(x_2 - x_1)^2 + (y_2 - y_1)^2}$.	The distance between the points (2, 1) and (6, 4) is $\sqrt{(6-2)^2 + (4-1)^2} = 5$.	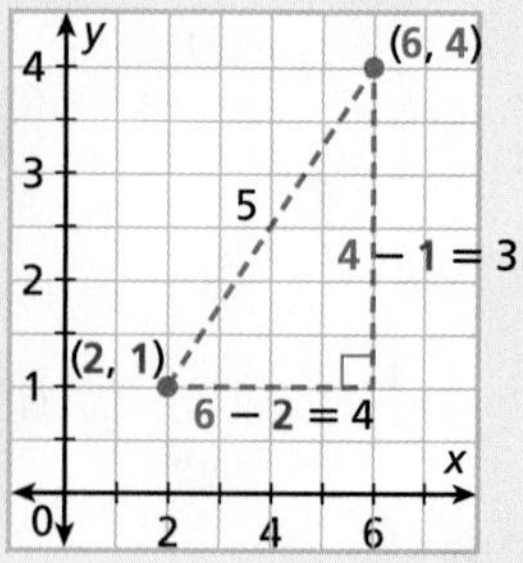

Because a diameter must pass through the center of a circle, the midpoint of a diameter is the center of the circle. The radius of a circle is the distance from the center to any point on the circle and equal to half the diameter.

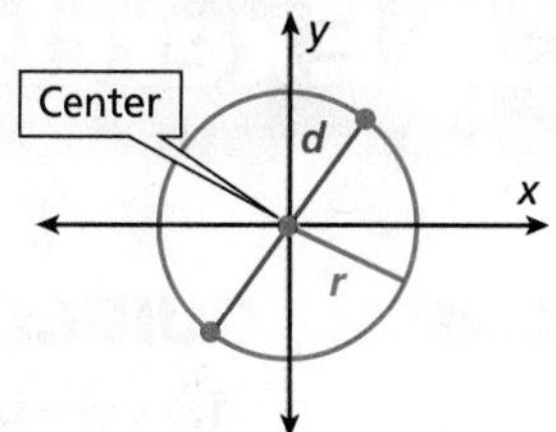

EXAMPLE 3 Finding the Center and Radius of a Circle

Find the center and radius of a circle that has a diameter with endpoints (3, 12) and (9, 4).

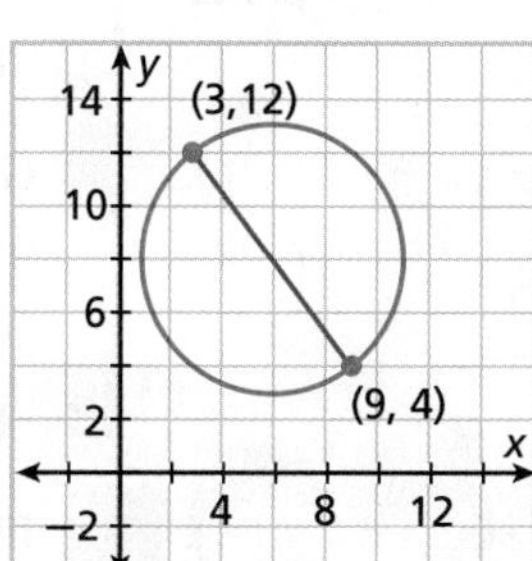

Step 1 Find the center of the circle.

Use the Midpoint Formula with the endpoints, (3, 12) and (9, 4).

$$\left(\frac{3+9}{2}, \frac{12+4}{2}\right) = (6, 8)$$

The center of the circle is (6, 8).

Helpful Hint

The midpoint formula uses averages. You can think of x_M as the average of the x-values and y_M as the average of the y-values.

Step 2 Find the radius.

Use the Distance Formula with (6, 8) and (3, 12).

$$r = \sqrt{(6-3)^2 + (8-12)^2}$$
$$= \sqrt{3^2 + (-4)^2}$$
$$= \sqrt{9+16}$$
$$= 5$$

The radius of the circle is 5.

Check Use the other endpoint (9, 4) and the center (6, 8). The radius should equal 5 for any point on the circle.

$$r = \sqrt{(9-6)^2 + (4-8)^2} = 5 \checkmark$$

The radius is the same using (9, 4).

3. Find the center and radius of a circle that has a diameter with endpoints (2, 6) and (14, 22).

THINK AND DISCUSS

1. If you know one endpoint and the midpoint of a line segment, how could you find the other endpoint of the segment?
2. Find the domain and range of each of the graphs in Examples 1 and 2.

3. **GET ORGANIZED** Copy and complete the graphic organizer. List the types of conic sections, and sketch an example of each.

Conic Sections

10-1 Exercises

go.hrw.com
Homework Help Online
KEYWORD: MB7 10-1
Parent Resources Online
KEYWORD: MB7 Parent

GUIDED PRACTICE

1. **Vocabulary** What are the four different types of *conic sections*?

SEE EXAMPLE 1 p. 722

Graph each equation on a graphing calculator. Identify each conic section. Then describe the center and intercepts.

2. $3x^2 + 3y^2 = 48$
3. $9x^2 + 16y^2 = 144$
4. $x^2 + y^2 = 36$

SEE EXAMPLE 2 p. 723

Graph each equation on a graphing calculator. Identify each conic section. Then describe the vertices and the direction that the graph opens.

5. $5y^2 = x$
6. $x^2 = y^2 + 9$
7. $y^2 - x^2 = 25$
8. $12y = 6x^2$
9. $2x^2 - y^2 = 4$
10. $-y^2 = 4 + x$

SEE EXAMPLE 3 p. 725

Find the center and radius of a circle that has a diameter with the given endpoints.

11. $(3, 6)$ and $(13, 30)$
12. $(-4, 1)$ and $(-16, -8)$
13. $(6, -9)$ and $(-8, 39)$

PRACTICE AND PROBLEM SOLVING

Independent Practice

For Exercises	See Example
14–22	1
23–31	2
32–34	3

Extra Practice

Skills Practice p. S22
Application Practice p. S41

Graph each equation on a graphing calculator. Identify each conic section. Then describe the center and intercepts.

14. $49x^2 + 36y^2 = 1764$
15. $\frac{x^2}{9} + \frac{y^2}{9} = 1$
16. $243 - 3x^2 - 3y^2 = 0$
17. $\frac{x^2}{4} = 1 - \frac{y^2}{25}$
18. $4x^2 + 81y^2 = 324$
19. $\frac{4x^2}{25} + \frac{4y^2}{225} = 1$
20. $\frac{3}{4}x^2 + \frac{3}{4}y^2 = 75$
21. $4x^2 + 4y^2 = 81$
22. $x^2 + y^2 = \frac{4}{9}$

Graph each equation on a graphing calculator. Identify each conic section. Then describe the vertices and the direction that the graph opens.

23. $y = 2x^2$
24. $x^2 = y^2 + 64$
25. $x + 2y^2 = 0$
26. $x = \frac{2}{3}y^2$
27. $0 = 1 + \frac{x^2}{64} - \frac{y^2}{36}$
28. $5y^2 - 5x^2 = 180$
29. $x = 4y^2 - 3$
30. $y = 4 - \frac{x^2}{5}$
31. $9x^2 - 16y^2 = 144$

Find the center and radius of a circle that has a diameter with the given endpoints.

32. $(20, 21)$ and $(12, 6)$
33. $\left(\frac{9}{2}, \frac{5}{2}\right)$ and $\left(\frac{5}{2}, \frac{17}{2}\right)$
34. $(7, -5)$ and $(-1, 10)$

35. **Geometry** A circle has center $(-7, 10)$ and contains the point $(23, -6)$.
    a. Find the circumference and area of the circle.
    b. Find the other endpoint of the diameter with one endpoint $(23, -6)$.

MULTI-STEP TEST PREP

36. This problem will prepare you for the Multi-Step Test Prep on page 758.
    The orbit of an asteroid can be modeled by the equation $16x^2 + 25y^2 = 400$.
    a. Graph the equation on a graphing calculator, and identify the conic section.
    b. Identify the *x*- and *y*-intercepts of the orbit.
    c. Suppose that each unit of the coordinate plane represents 50 million miles. What is the maximum width of the asteroid's orbit?

Use your graphing calculator to match each equation to one of the following graphs.

A.

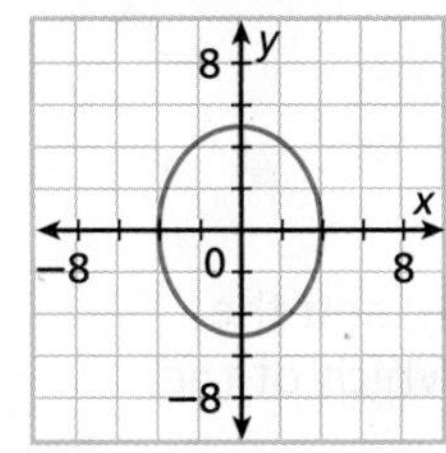

B.

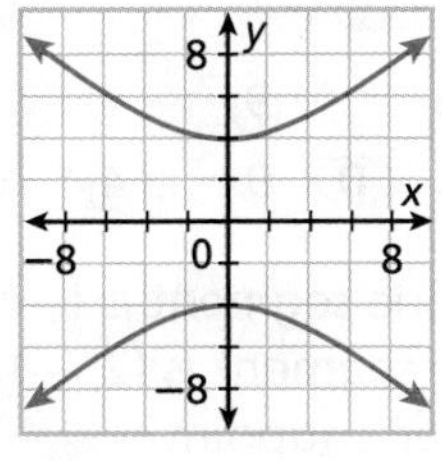

C.

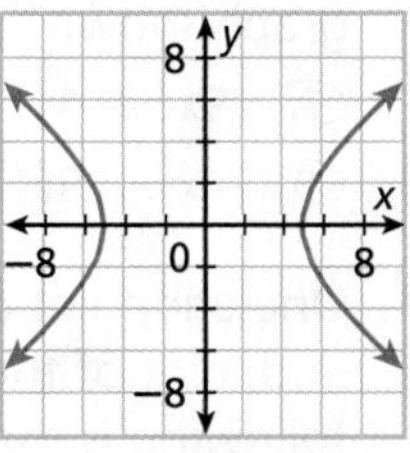

D.

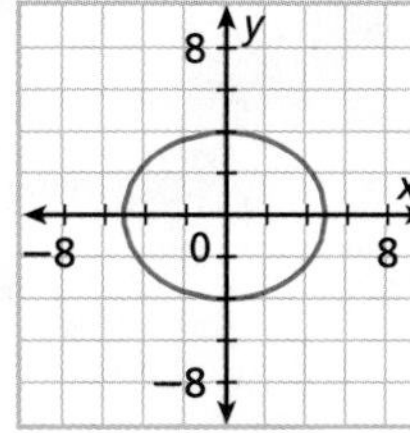

37. $16x^2 + 25y^2 = 400$

38. $16x^2 - 25y^2 = 400$

39. $25x^2 + 16y^2 = 400$

40. $25y^2 - 16x^2 = 400$

41. Geometry A quadrilateral has vertices $A(2, 3)$, $B(12, 3)$, $C(18, 11)$, and $D(8, 11)$.

a. Find the length of each side.

b. Classify the figure *ABCD*.

c. Find the area of *ABCD*.

LINK

Archaeology

Chichén Itzá, in Yucatán, Mexico, was a major city of the Maya civilization. Its city center covers about 2 square miles and was used primarily for religious ceremonies. Today the ruins are the most visited archaeological site in Mexico.

42. Critical Thinking How can you tell if the graph of an equation in the form $ax^2 + by^2 = c$ is a circle or an ellipse?

43. Archaeology Archaeologists exploring an underwater site have set up a grid so that they can precisely label where any artifacts they discover were found. The archaeologists have found two treasure chests at points *B* and *C* and a ship's wheel at point *A*. Which treasure is the wheel closer to? Explain.

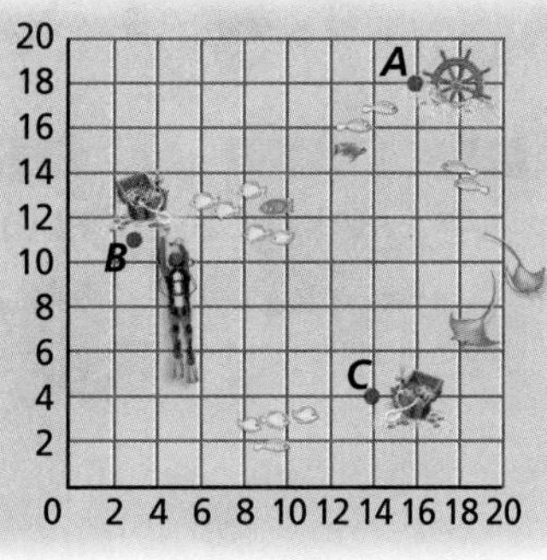

44. ///ERROR ANALYSIS/// Which solution is incorrect? Explain the error. Find the distance between $(0, 0)$ and $(2, 3)$.

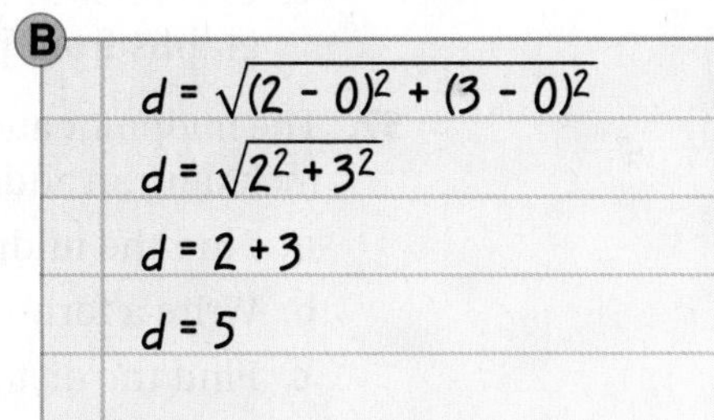

45. Geometry A triangle has vertices $A(8, 2)$, $B(13, 14)$, and $C(-4, 6)$.

a. Find the length of $\overline{AB}$.

b. Find the length of the segment joining the midpoints of $\overline{BC}$ and $\overline{AC}$.

c. Find the slopes of $\overline{AB}$ and the segment joining the midpoints of the other two sides. What do the slopes tell you about the two segments?

Tell whether each statement is sometimes, always, or never true. If it is sometimes true, give examples to support your answer.

46. A circle is a function.

47. The domain of a parabola is all real numbers.

48. The distance between two points is positive.

49. Write About It If a right triangle has a hypotenuse with length *c* and legs with lengths *a* and *b*, the Pythagorean Theorem states that $a^2 + b^2 = c^2$. Explain how the Distance Formula is related to the Pythagorean Theorem.

50. Which of the following could be the equation of the graph shown?

Ⓐ $9x^2 - 4y^2 = 36$ Ⓒ $9y^2 - 4x^2 = 36$

Ⓑ $4x^2 + 9y^2 = 36$ Ⓓ $9x^2 + 4y^2 = 36$

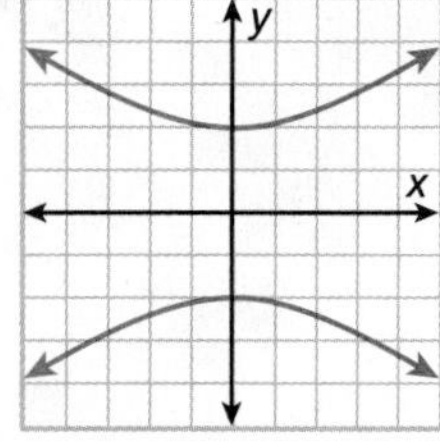

51. One endpoint of a line segment is $(-4, -8)$, and the midpoint of the line segment is $(2, -12)$. Which of the following is the other endpoint?

Ⓕ $(-1, -10)$ Ⓖ $(3, -2)$ Ⓗ $(-8, 16)$ Ⓙ $(8, -16)$

52. Which of the following are the x-intercepts of the graph of $4x^2 + 25y^2 = 100$?

Ⓐ $(2, 0)$ and $(-2, 0)$ Ⓒ $(5, 0)$ and $(-5, 0)$

Ⓑ $(4, 0)$ and $(-4, 0)$ Ⓓ $(10, 0)$ and $(-10, 0)$

53. What is the distance between the points $(-2, 6)$ and $(5, 30)$?

Ⓕ $3\sqrt{145}$ Ⓖ 31 Ⓗ $3\sqrt{65}$ Ⓙ 25

CHALLENGE AND EXTEND

Find a so that the two points are the given distance apart.

54. $(-5, 8)$ and $(3, a)$; 17

55. $(4, -10)$ and $(a, 5)$; 39

56. Multi-Step A degenerate conic is formed when a plane passes through the vertex of a hollow double cone. A point, a line, and a pair of intersecting lines are all degenerate conics.

a. The graph of $y^2 - x^2 = 0$ is a degenerate hyperbola. Graph $y^2 - x^2 = 0$.

b. What is the graph of $x^2 + y^2 = 0$?

c. Explain how a plane could intersect a hollow double cone to result in the graphs from parts **a** and **b.**

57. The midpoint and distance formulas can be extended to three dimensions by including an additional term in each formula for the variable z.

a. Find the midpoint of the segment with endpoints $(6, -3, -9)$ and $(12, 7, -13)$.

b. Write a formula to find the midpoint of a segment in three dimensions.

c. Find the distance between the points $(1, 2, 3)$ and $(5, 8, 10)$.

d. Write a formula to find the distance between two points in three dimensions.

SPIRAL REVIEW

58. Construction A construction crew is repainting the center line on a 12 mi road. If the crew has completed 2.5 mi after 45 min, about how much more time should the painting take? *(Lesson 2-2)*

Find the zeros of each function by factoring. *(Lesson 5-3)*

59. $f(x) = x^2 - 2x - 48$

60. $f(x) = x^2 + 12x + 27$

61. $f(x) = x^2 - 11x + 28$

62. $f(x) = x^2 + 10x - 24$

63. $f(x) = 2x^2 - 25x + 33$

64. $f(x) = 3x^2 + 22x + 24$

Graph each exponential function. Find the y-intercept and the asymptote. Then describe how the graph transformed from the graph of its parent function $f(x) = 5^x$. *(Lesson 7-7)*

65. $f(x) = -\frac{1}{2}(5^x) + 3$

66. $f(x) = 4(5^x)$

67. $f(x) = 6(5^x) - 1$

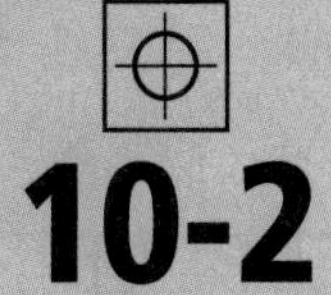

10-2 Circles

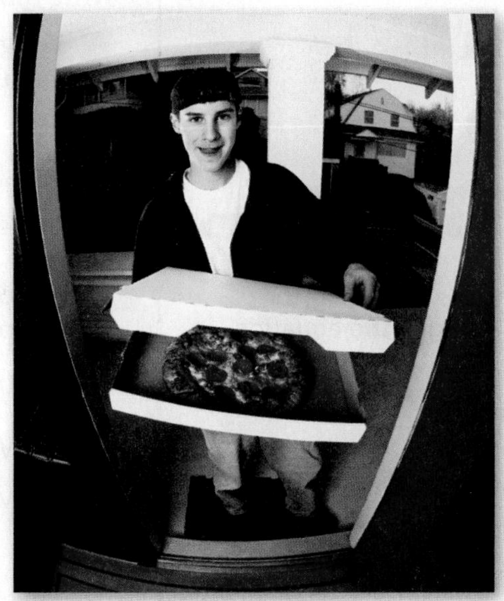

Objectives
Write an equation for a circle.

Graph a circle, and identify its center and radius.

Vocabulary
circle
tangent

Why learn this?
You can use circles to find locations within a given radius of an address. (See Example 3.)

A **circle** is the set of points in a plane that are a fixed distance, called the radius, from a fixed point, called the center. Because all of the points on a circle are the same distance from the center of the circle, you can use the Distance Formula to find the equation of a circle.

EXAMPLE 1 Using the Distance Formula to Write the Equation of a Circle

Write the equation of a circle with center $(2, 1)$ and radius $r = 5$.

Use the Distance Formula with $(x_2, y_2) = (x, y)$, $(x_1, y_1) = (2, 1)$, and distance equal to the radius, 5.

$$d = \sqrt{(x_2 - x_1)^2 + (y_2 - y_1)^2} \quad \textit{Use the Distance Formula.}$$

$$5 = \sqrt{(x - 2)^2 + (y - 1)^2} \quad \textit{Substitute.}$$

$$5^2 = (x - 2)^2 + (y - 1)^2 \quad \textit{Square both sides.}$$

$$25 = (x - 2)^2 + (y - 1)^2$$

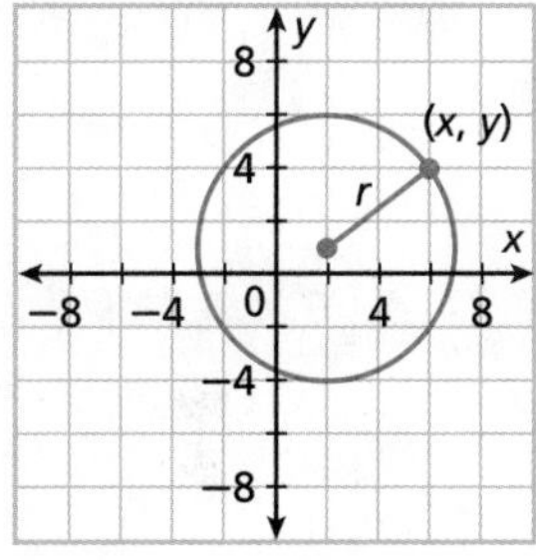

1. Write the equation of a circle with center $(4, 2)$ and radius $r = 7$.

Notice that r^2 and the center are visible in the equation of a circle. This leads to a general formula for a circle with center (h, k) and radius r.

Equation of a Circle

EQUATION	EXAMPLE	GRAPH
The equation of a circle with center (h, k) and radius r is $(x - h)^2 + (y - k)^2 = r^2$.	The equation of the circle with center $(5, -2)$ and radius $r = 8$ is $(x - 5)^2 + (y - (-2))^2 = 8^2$ or $(x - 5)^2 + (y + 2)^2 = 64$.	y, x, r, (h, k), 4, −4, 0, 4, 8, 12, −4, −8

EXAMPLE 2 Writing the Equation of a Circle

Write the equation of each circle.

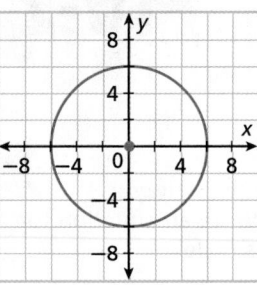

A **the graphed circle with center $(0, 0)$ and radius $r = 6$**

$(x - h)^2 + (y - k)^2 = r^2$ *Equation of a circle*

$(x - 0)^2 + (y - 0)^2 = 6^2$ *Substitute.*

$x^2 + y^2 = 36$

Helpful Hint

If the center of the circle is at the origin, the equation simplifies to $x^2 + y^2 = r^2$.

B **the circle with center $(2, 4)$ and containing the point $(8, 12)$**

$r = \sqrt{(8-2)^2 + (12-4)^2}$ *Use the Distance Formula to find the radius.*

$= \sqrt{6^2 + 8^2}$

$= \sqrt{100} = 10$

$(x - 2)^2 + (y - 4)^2 = 10^2$ *Substitute the values into the equation of a circle.*

$(x - 2)^2 + (y - 4)^2 = 100$

2. Find the equation of the circle with center $(-3, 5)$ and containing the point $(9, 10)$.

The location of points in relation to a circle can be described by inequalities. The points inside the circle satisfy the inequality $(x - h)^2 + (y - k)^2 < r^2$. The points outside the circle satisfy the inequality $(x - h)^2 + (y - k)^2 > r^2$.

EXAMPLE 3 *Consumer Application*

Raul and his friends are deciding where to have a pizza party based on the delivery area of the pizza restaurant. The restaurant is located at the point $(-1, 2)$, and the letters represent the homes of Raul and his friends. Which houses are within a 3-mile radius of the restaurant and will get free delivery?

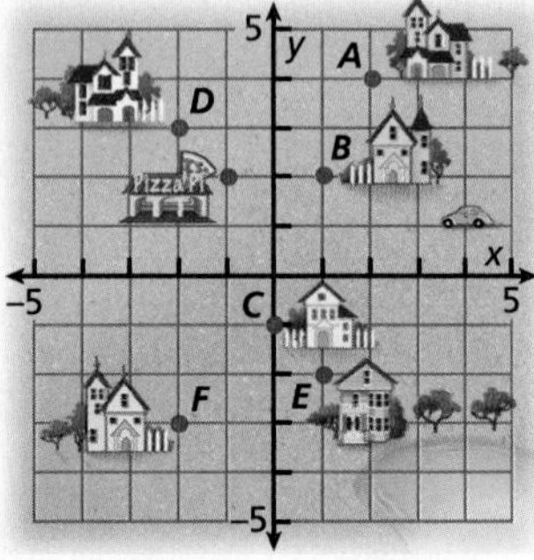

Graph the circle with center $(-1, 2)$ and radius 3. The points inside the circle will satisfy the inequality $(x + 1)^2 + (y - 2)^2 < 3^2$.

Points D and B are within a 3-mile radius.

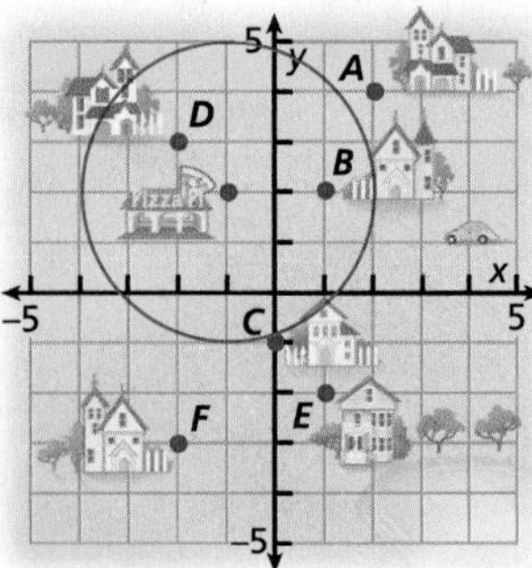

Check Point $C(0, -1)$ is near the boundary.

$(0 + 1)^2 + (-1 - 2)^2 < 3^2$

$(1)^2 + (-3)^2 < 3^2$

$1 + 9 < 9$ ✗ *Point $C(0, -1)$ is not inside the circle.*

3. What if...? Which homes are within a 3-mile radius of a restaurant located at $(2, -1)$?

A **tangent** is a line in the same plane as the circle that intersects the circle at exactly one point. Recall from geometry that a tangent to a circle is perpendicular to the radius at the point of tangency.

EXAMPLE 4 Writing the Equation of a Tangent

Write the equation of the line that is tangent to the circle $25 = x^2 + y^2$ at the point $(3, 4)$.

Step 1 Identify the center and radius of the circle.

From the equation $25 = x^2 + y^2$, the circle has center $(0, 0)$ and radius $r = 5$.

Step 2 Find the slope of the radius at the point of tangency and the slope of the tangent.

$m = \frac{y_2 - y_1}{x_2 - x_1}$ *Use the slope formula.*

$m = \frac{4 - 0}{3 - 0}$ *Substitute $(3, 4)$ for (x_2, y_2) and $(0, 0)$ for (x_1, y_1).*

$m = \frac{4}{3}$ *The slope of the radius is $\frac{4}{3}$.*

Because the slopes of perpendicular lines are negative reciprocals, the slope of the tangent is $-\frac{3}{4}$.

Step 3 Find the slope-intercept equation of the tangent by using the point $(3, 4)$ and the slope $m = -\frac{3}{4}$.

$y - y_1 = m(x - x_1)$ *Use the point-slope formula.*

$y - 4 = -\frac{3}{4}(x - 3)$ *Substitute $(3, 4)$ for (x_1, y_1) and $-\frac{3}{4}$ for m.*

$y = -\frac{3}{4}x + \frac{25}{4}$ *Rewrite in slope-intercept form.*

The equation of the line that is tangent to $25 = x^2 + y^2$ at $(3, 4)$ is $y = -\frac{3}{4}x + \frac{25}{4}$.

Check Graph the circle and the line.

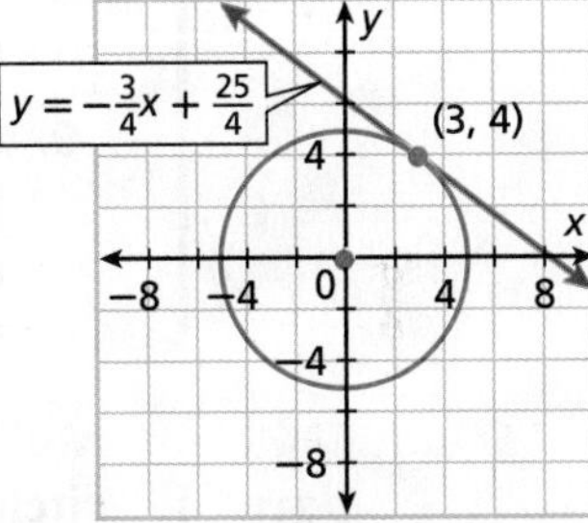

Remember!

To review linear functions, see Lesson 2-4.

4. Write the equation of the line that is tangent to the circle $25 = (x - 1)^2 + (y + 2)^2$ at the point $(5, -5)$.

THINK AND DISCUSS

1. Explain the transformation of $x^2 + y^2 = 1$ that is necessary to get the equation $(x - h)^2 + (y - k)^2 = 1$.

2. Explain what happens to the radius if the equation of a circle changes from $x^2 + y^2 = 4$ to $x^2 + y^2 = 16$.

Know it! Note

3. GET ORGANIZED Copy and complete the graphic organizer. Sketch each circle, and give its equation.

	$r = 1$	$r = 3$
Center (0, 0)		
Center (1, 2)		

10-2 Exercises

go.hrw.com
Homework Help Online
KEYWORD: MB7 10-2
Parent Resources Online
KEYWORD: MB7 Parent

GUIDED PRACTICE

1. **Vocabulary** How can you recognize a *tangent* of a circle?

SEE EXAMPLE 1 p. 729

Write the equation of each circle.

2. center $(6, -5)$ and radius $r = 4$
3. center $(-11, 3)$ and radius $r = 9$

SEE EXAMPLE 2 p. 730

4. 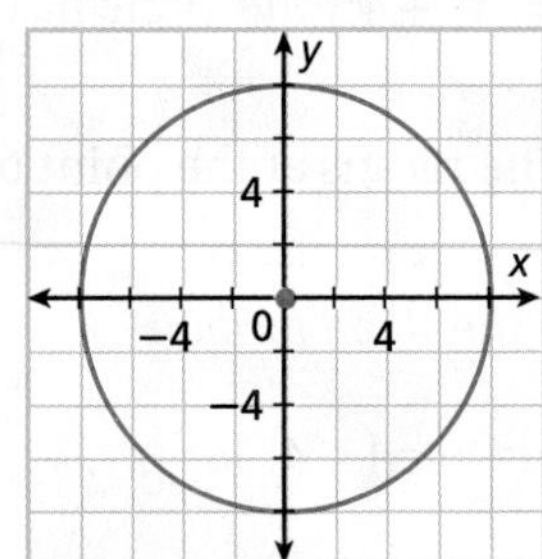

5.

6. center $(-1, 9)$ and containing the point $(2, 5)$
7. center $(-2, -5)$ and containing the point $(-10, -20)$

SEE EXAMPLE 3 p. 730

Depending on its strength, an earthquake can be felt in locations miles away from the epicenter.

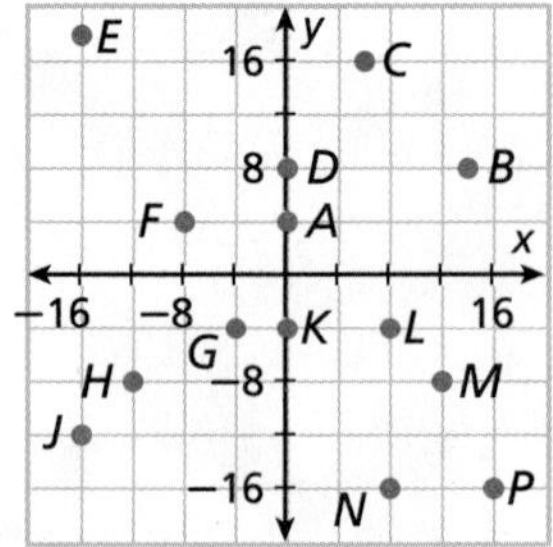

8. **Multi-Step** Suppose that the epicenter of the earthquake is located at the point $(5, -2)$ and the earthquake is felt up to 10 mi away. Which labeled points represent locations that are affected by the earthquake?
9. **Multi-Step** Suppose that the epicenter of the earthquake is located at the point $(-5, -7)$ and the earthquake is felt up to 8 mi away. Which labeled points represent locations that are affected by the earthquake?

SEE EXAMPLE 4 p. 731

Multi-Step Write the equation of the line that is tangent to each circle at the given point.

10. $x^2 + y^2 = 100$; $(8, 6)$
11. $(x + 6)^2 + (y + 4)^2 = 25$; $(-9, -8)$

PRACTICE AND PROBLEM SOLVING

Independent Practice

For Exercises	See Example
12–13	1
14–17	2
18–19	3
20–21	4

Extra Practice
Skills Practice p. S22
Application Practice p. S41

Write the equation of each circle.

12. center $(3, 2)$ and radius $r = 7$
13. center $(5, 1)$ and radius $r = 10$

14. 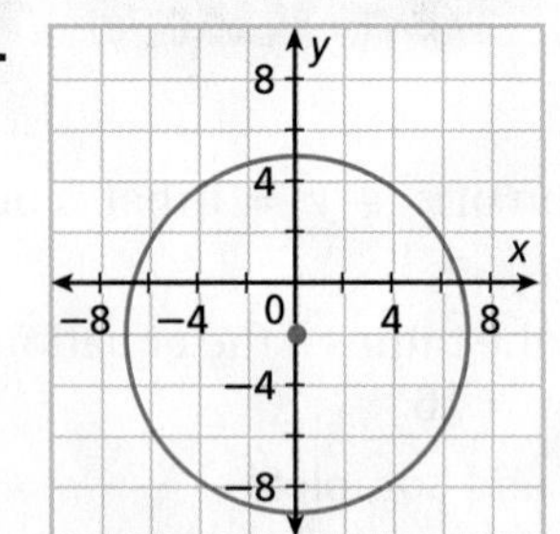

15. 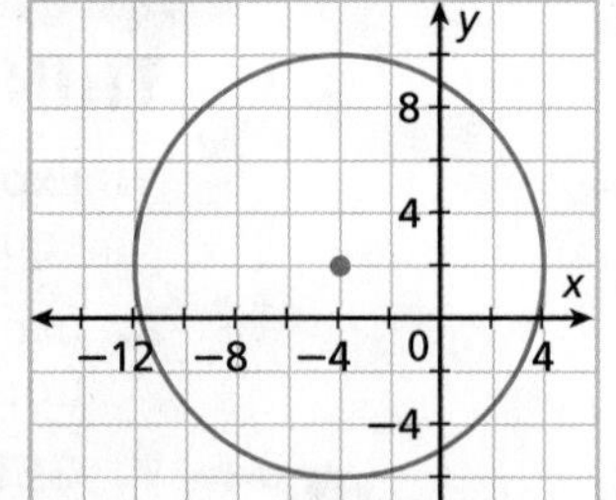

16. center $(12, -3)$ and containing the point $(-12, 7)$
17. center $(-6, -4)$ and containing the point $(-2, -1)$

Aida's puppy escaped from the backyard and is lost. Aida has created a map of places that the puppy may have gone.

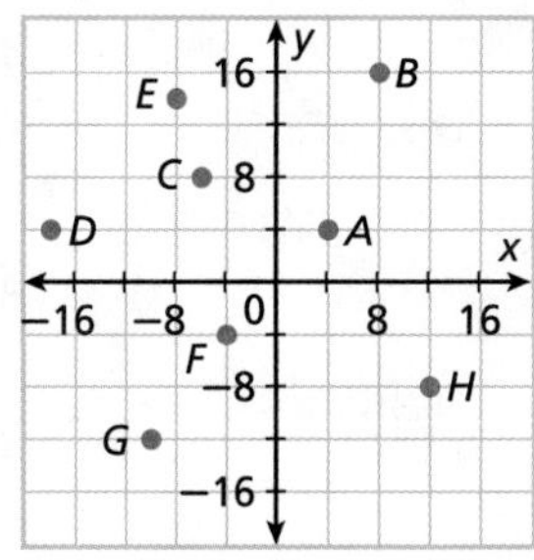

18. **Multi-Step** Suppose that Aida's house is located at the point $(3, 8)$. The puppy has been gone for 4 hours, and Aida estimates that the puppy cannot have traveled more than 12 miles. Which labeled points represent possible locations of the puppy?

19. **Multi-Step** Suppose that Aida's house is located at the point $(-6, 15)$. The puppy has been gone for 1 hour, and Aida estimates that the puppy cannot have traveled more than 3 miles. Which labeled points represent possible locations of the puppy?

History

Stonehenge, in southern England, is thought to have been built in three stages, from 2950-1600 B.C.E. It is not a single structure but consists of many stone, earth, and wood constructions.

Multi-Step Write the equation of the line that is tangent to each circle at the given point.

20. $x^2 + y^2 = 169, (-5, 12)$

21. $(x - 2)^2 + (y - 4)^2 = 289, (-15, 4)$

22. **History** The outermost ring of the ancient monument Stonehenge can be modeled by the equation $x^2 + y^2 = 27{,}225$. The Sarsen Circle, the center ring of stones usually associated with the monument, can be modeled by the equation $x^2 + y^2 = 2916$.
    a. The Heel Stone is located outside of the circles, approximately at the point $(0, 300)$. Find the maximum and minimum distances, in feet, to the Heel Stone from both the outer and inner circles.
    b. Graph the outer circle and the Sarsen Circle.
    c. Two Station Stones surrounded by circular ditches are located within the outer circle. One stone is located at approximately $(-100, 100)$ and is surrounded by a ditch of radius 12 ft. Write an equation to model the ditch around this Station Stone.

Find the domain and range of each relation.

23. $x^2 + y^2 = 36$

24. $(x - 2)^2 + (y + 7)^2 = 81$

25. $(x + 2)^2 + (y)^2 = 9$

26. **Geometry** The circle with center $(2, 3)$ and the circle with center $(-1, -1)$ are tangent at the point $(5, 7)$.
    a. Find an equation for the small circle.
    b. Find an equation for the large circle.
    c. Find the equation of the line that is tangent to both circles.

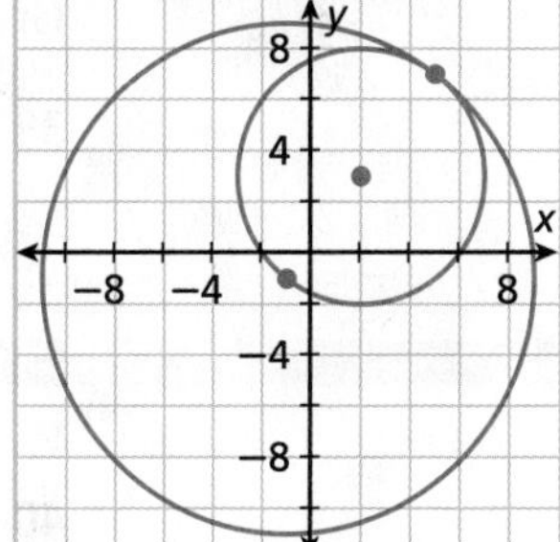

Geometry Find the center and radius of each circle.

27. $(x + 4)^2 + y^2 = 64$

28. $\left(x - \frac{2}{3}\right)^2 + \left(y - \frac{5}{8}\right)^2 = 49$

MULTI-STEP TEST PREP

29. This problem will prepare you for the Multi-Step Test Prep on page 758.

    The orbit of Venus is nearly circular. An astronomer develops a model for the orbit in which the Sun has coordinates $(-5, 20)$, the circular orbit of Venus passes through $(62, 20)$, and each unit of the coordinate plane represents 1 million miles.
    a. Write an equation for the orbit of Venus.
    b. How far is Venus from the Sun?
    c. How far does Venus travel as it makes one complete orbit of the Sun?

30. **Entertainment** A radio station emits a signal that can be received by anyone within 120 miles of the station's transmitter. Write and graph an inequality for the region covered by the radio station with the transmitter located at $(0, 0)$.

31. **Critical Thinking** Is it possible to have two different lines that are tangent to the same circle at the same point? Explain.

32. **Write About It** How could you show that the line with equation $y = -\frac{5}{12}x + \frac{28}{3}$ is tangent to the circle with equation $169 = (x-3)^2 + (y+6)^2$ at the point $(8, 6)$?

TEST PREP

33. Which of the following lines is tangent at $(13, 9)$ to the circle with center $(5, 3)$?

Ⓐ $y = \frac{3}{4}x - \frac{3}{4}$ Ⓑ $y = -\frac{3}{4}x + \frac{75}{4}$ Ⓒ $y = -\frac{4}{3}x + \frac{79}{3}$ Ⓓ $y = \frac{4}{3}x - \frac{25}{3}$

34. Which of the following points is inside the circle with the equation $121 = (x-5)^2 + (y+9)^2$?

Ⓕ $(12, 2)$ Ⓖ $(-8, 6)$ Ⓗ $(2, -6)$ Ⓙ $(-9, -3)$

35. **Short Response** Give the equation of a circle with center $(-4, 8)$ and radius $r = 9$.

CHALLENGE AND EXTEND

36. A *sphere* is the set of all points in three-dimensional space that are a fixed distance from a fixed point, called the center. The equation of a sphere with center (a, b, c) and radius r is $(x-a)^2 + (y-b)^2 + (z-c)^2 = r^2$. Write the equation of a sphere with center $(1, -3, 4)$ and radius 5.

37. The lines $y = -3x + 1$ and $y = 2x - 9$ each contain diameters of a particular circle. The point $(9, 19)$ is on the circle.
    a. Find the center of the circle.
    b. Write the equation of the circle.

Graph each system of inequalities.

38. $\begin{cases} x - 3y > -12 \\ (x-2)^2 + (y-1)^2 \le 49 \end{cases}$

39. $\begin{cases} (x-3)^2 + (y-2)^2 \le 36 \\ (x-4)^2 + (y+4)^2 \le 25 \end{cases}$

SPIRAL REVIEW

Write the equation of each line. *(Lesson 2-4)*

40. slope 2 through $(1, 4)$

41. slope $\frac{1}{2}$ through $(-2, 1)$

42. slope $\frac{4}{3}$ and y-intercept 1

43. **Travel** Patrick drives a bus. When he picks up 20 passengers or fewer, his route takes him 15 minutes plus half a minute for each passenger. When Patrick picks up more than 20 passengers, his route takes him 20 minutes plus 1 minute for every passenger. *(Lesson 9-2)*
    a. Write a piecewise function for the amount of time that Patrick's route requires.
    b. Graph the function.
    c. How long does it take Patrick to pick up 20 passengers?

Graph each equation on a graphing calculator. Identify each conic section. Then describe the vertices and the direction that the graph opens. *(Lesson 10-1)*

44. $\frac{y^2}{3} = x$

45. $16y^2 = -x$

46. $4x^2 - 9y^2 = 36$

Surface Area and Volume

You can use formulas to find the surface area and volume of three-dimensional figures such as cylinders, cones, and spheres.

	Cylinder with radius r and height h	Cone with radius r and height h	Sphere with radius r
Solid			
Volume	$V = \pi r^2 h$	$V = \frac{1}{3}\pi r^2 h$	$V = \frac{4}{3}\pi r^3$
Surface Area	$S = 2\pi r(r + h)$	$S = \pi r\sqrt{r^2 + h^2} + \pi r^2$	$S = 4\pi r^2$

Example

Find the surface area and volume of the cone shown.

In order to use the formulas, identify the radius and height of the cone. $r = 5$ and $h = 12$. Find the surface area. Use the formula.

$S = \pi r\sqrt{r^2 + h^2} + \pi r^2$ *Formula for surface area of a cone.*

$S = \pi \cdot 5\sqrt{(5)^2 + (12)^2} + \pi(5)^2$ *Substitute 5 for r and 12 for h.*

$S = 90\pi$ *Simplify.*

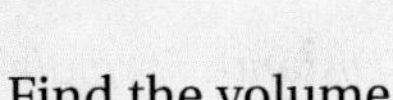

Find the volume.

$V = \frac{1}{3}\pi r^2 h$ *Formula for the volume of a cone.*

$V = \frac{1}{3}\pi(5)^2(12)$ *Substitute 5 for r and 12 for h.*

$V = 100\pi$ *Simplify.*

Try This

Find the surface area and volume of each figure.

1.

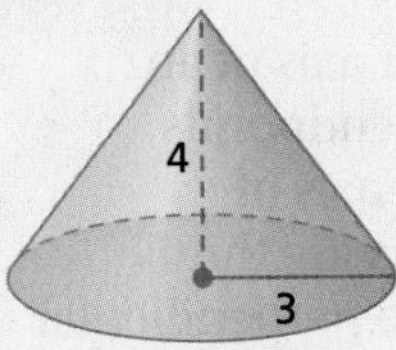

2.

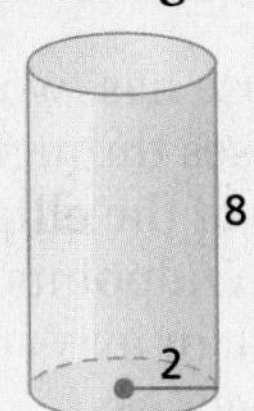

3.

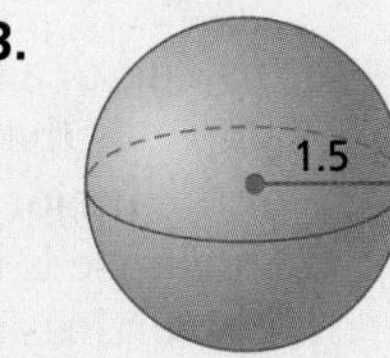

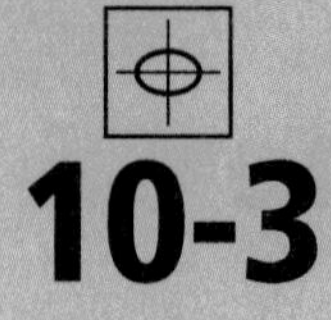

10-3 Ellipses

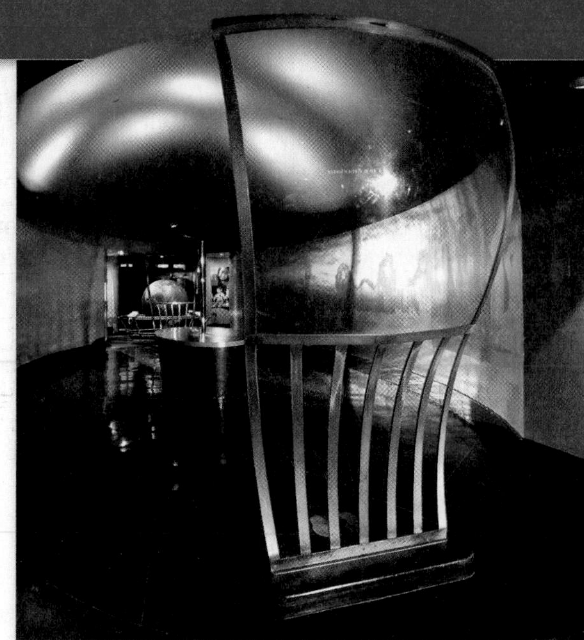

Objectives
Write the standard equation for an ellipse.

Graph an ellipse, and identify its center, vertices, co-vertices, and foci.

Vocabulary
ellipse
focus of an ellipse
major axis
vertices of an ellipse
minor axis
co-vertices of an ellipse

Who uses this?

The whispering gallery at the Chicago Museum of Science and Industry was designed by using an ellipse. (See Exercise 31.)

If you pulled the center of a circle apart into two points, it would stretch the circle into an ellipse.

An **ellipse** is the set of points $P(x, y)$ in a plane such that the sum of the distances from any point P on the ellipse to two fixed points F_1 and F_2, called the **foci** (singular: focus), is the constant sum $d = PF_1 + PF_2$. This distance d can be represented by the length of a piece of string connecting two pushpins located at the foci.

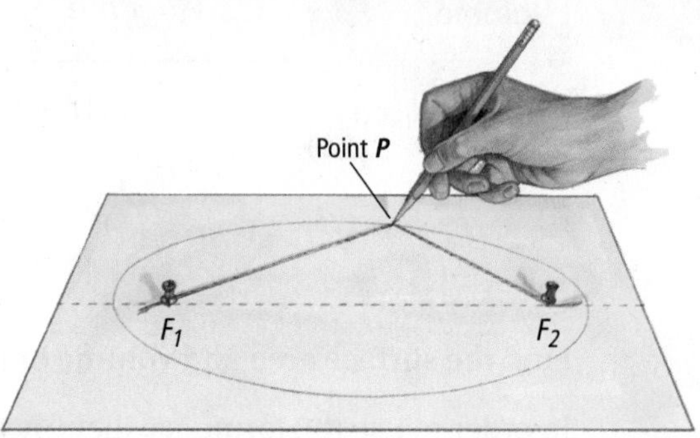

You can use the distance formula to find the constant sum of an ellipse.

EXAMPLE 1 Using the Distance Formula to Find the Constant Sum of an Ellipse

Find the constant sum for an ellipse with foci $F_1\ (-3, 0)$ and $F_2\ (3, 0)$ and the point on the ellipse $(0, 4)$.

$d = PF_1 + PF_2$ *Definition of the constant sum of an ellipse*

$d = \sqrt{(x_1 - x_3)^2 + (y_1 - y_3)^2} + \sqrt{(x_2 - x_3)^2 + (y_2 - y_3)^2}$ *Distance Formula*

$d = \sqrt{(-3 - 0)^2 + (0 - 4)^2} + \sqrt{(3 - 0)^2 + (0 - 4)^2}$ *Substitute.*

$d = \sqrt{25} + \sqrt{25}$ *Simplify.*

$d = 10$

The constant sum is 10.

1. Find the constant sum for an ellipse with foci $F_1\ (0, -8)$ and $F_2\ (0, 8)$ and the point on the ellipse $(0, 10)$.

Instead of a single radius, an ellipse has two axes. The longer axis of an ellipse is the **major axis** and passes through both foci. The endpoints of the major axis are the **vertices of the ellipse**. The shorter axis of an ellipse is the **minor axis**. The endpoints of the minor axis are the **co-vertices of the ellipse**. The major axis and minor axis are perpendicular and intersect at the center of the ellipse.

The standard form of an ellipse centered at (0, 0) depends on whether the major axis is horizontal or vertical.

Horizontal

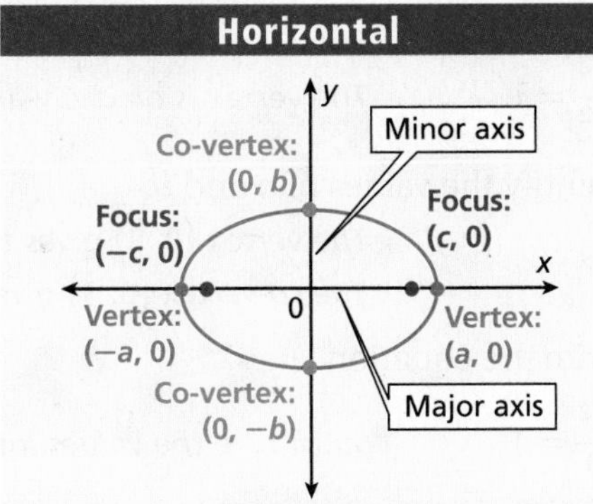

Vertical

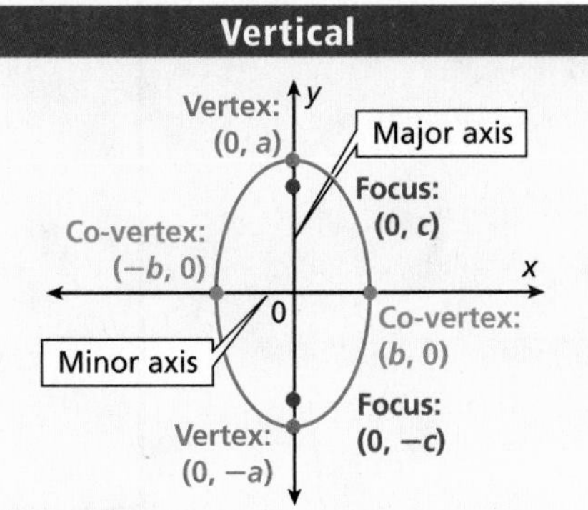

The values a, b, and c are related by the equation $c^2 = a^2 - b^2$. Also note that the length of the major axis is $2a$, the length of the minor axis is $2b$, and $a > b$.

Standard Form for the Equation of an Ellipse Center at (0, 0)

MAJOR AXIS	HORIZONTAL	VERTICAL
Equation	$\frac{x^2}{a^2} + \frac{y^2}{b^2} = 1$	$\frac{y^2}{a^2} + \frac{x^2}{b^2} = 1$
Vertices	$(a, 0), (-a, 0)$	$(0, a), (0, -a)$
Foci	$(c, 0), (-c, 0)$	$(0, c), (0, -c)$
Co-vertices	$(0, b), (0, -b)$	$(b, 0), (-b, 0)$

EXAMPLE 2 Using Standard Form to Write an Equation for an Ellipse

Write an equation in standard form for each ellipse with center (0, 0).

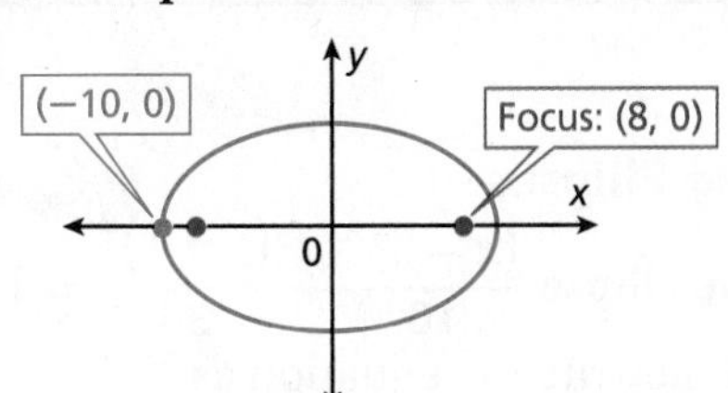

Step 1 Choose the appropriate form of equation.

$\frac{x^2}{a^2} + \frac{y^2}{b^2} = 1.$ *The horizontal axis is longer.*

Step 2 Identify the values of a and c.

$a = 10$ *The vertex (−10, 0) gives the value of a.*

$c = 8$ *The focus (8, 0) gives the value of c.*

Step 3 Use the relationship $c^2 = a^2 - b^2$ to find b^2.

$8^2 = 10^2 - b^2$ *Substitute 10 for a and 8 for c.*

$b^2 = 36$

Step 4 Write the equation.

$\frac{x^2}{100} + \frac{y^2}{36} = 1$ *Substitute the values into the equation of an ellipse.*

Write an equation in standard form for each ellipse with center (0, 0).

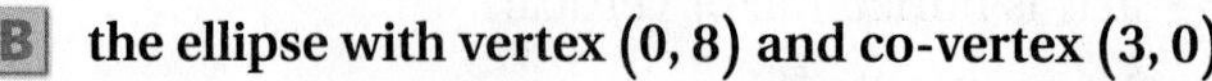

B **the ellipse with vertex $(0, 8)$ and co-vertex $(3, 0)$**

Step 1 Choose the appropriate form of equation.

$$\frac{y^2}{a^2} + \frac{x^2}{b^2} = 1$$ *The vertex is on the y-axis.*

Step 2 Identify the values of a and b.

$a = 8$ *The vertex $(0, 8)$ gives the value of a.*

$b = 3$ *The co-vertex $(0, 3)$ gives the value of b.*

Step 3 Write the equation.

$$\frac{y^2}{64} + \frac{x^2}{9} = 1$$ *Substitute the values into the equation of an ellipse.*

CHECK IT OUT!

Write an equation in standard form for each ellipse with center $(0, 0)$.

2a. Vertex $(9, 0)$ and co-vertex $(0, 5)$

2b. Co-vertex $(4, 0)$ focus $(0, 3)$

Ellipses may also be translated so that the center is not the origin.

Standard Form for the Equation of an Ellipse Center at (h, k)

MAJOR AXIS	HORIZONTAL	VERTICAL
Equation	$\frac{(x-h)^2}{a^2} + \frac{(y-k)^2}{b^2} = 1$	$\frac{(y-k)^2}{a^2} + \frac{(x-h)^2}{b^2} = 1$
Vertices	$(h+a, k), (h-a, k)$	$(h, k+a), (h, k-a)$
Foci	$(h+c, k), (h-c, k)$	$(h, k+c), (h, k-c)$
Co-vertices	$(h, k+b), (h, k-b)$	$(h+b, k), (h-b, k)$

EXAMPLE 3 Graphing Ellipses

Graph the ellipse $\frac{(x-3)^2}{16} + \frac{(y-1)^2}{36} = 1$.

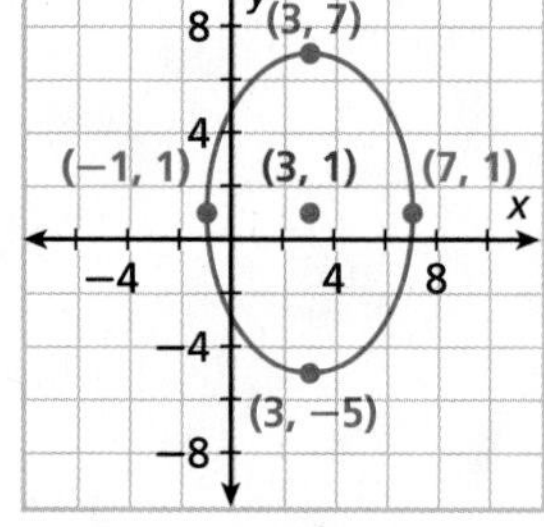

Step 1 Rewrite the equation as

$$\frac{(x-3)^2}{4^2} + \frac{(y-1)^2}{6^2} = 1.$$

Step 2 Identify the values of h, k, a, and b.

$h = 3$ and $k = 1$, so the center is $(3, 1)$.

$a = 6$ and $b = 4$; Because $6 > 4$, the major axis is vertical.

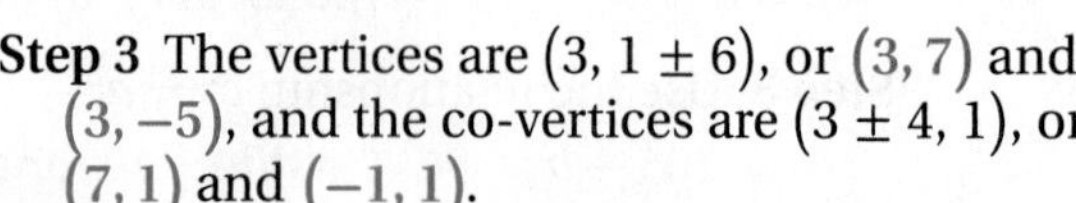

Step 3 The vertices are $(3, 1 \pm 6)$, or $(3, 7)$ and $(3, -5)$, and the co-vertices are $(3 \pm 4, 1)$, or $(7, 1)$ and $(-1, 1)$.

CHECK IT OUT!

Graph each ellipse.

3a. $\frac{x^2}{64} + \frac{y^2}{25} = 1$

3b. $\frac{(x-2)^2}{25} + \frac{(y-4)^2}{9} = 1$

EXAMPLE 4 Engineering Application

A road passes through a tunnel in the form of a semi-ellipse. In order to widen the road to accommodate more traffic, engineers must design a larger tunnel that is twice as wide and 1.5 times as tall as the original tunnel. The design for the original tunnel can be modeled by the equation $\frac{x^2}{100} + \frac{y^2}{64} = 1$, measured in feet.

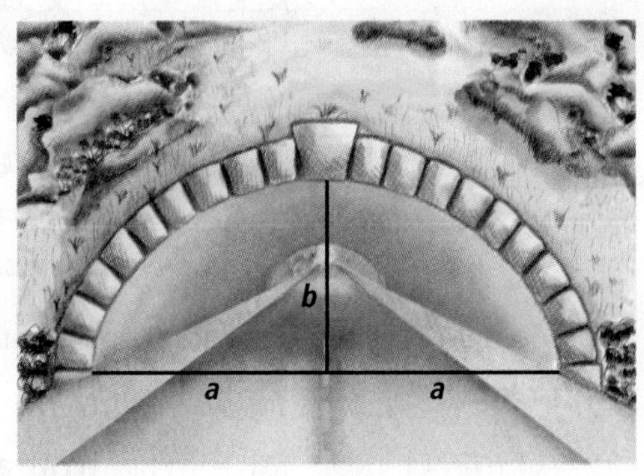

a. Find the dimensions of the larger tunnel.

Step 1 Find the dimensions of the original tunnel.

Because $100 > 64$, the major axis of the tunnel is horizontal.

$a^2 = 100$, so $a = 10$ and the width of the tunnel is $2a = 20$ ft.

$b^2 = 64$, so $b = 8$ and the height of the tunnel is 8 ft.

Step 2 Find the dimensions of the larger tunnel.

The width of the larger tunnel is $2(20) = 40$ ft.

The height is $1.5(8) = 12$ ft.

b. Write an equation for the design of the larger tunnel.

Step 1 Use the dimensions of the larger tunnel to find the values of a and b.

For the larger tunnel, $a = 20$ and $b = 12$.

Step 2 Write the equation.

The equation in standard form for the larger tunnel is $\frac{x^2}{20^2} + \frac{y^2}{12^2} = 1$, or $\frac{x^2}{400} + \frac{y^2}{144} = 1$.

Engineers have designed a tunnel with the equation $\frac{x^2}{64} + \frac{y^2}{36} = 1$, measured in feet. A design for a larger tunnel needs to be twice as wide and 3 times as tall.

4a. Find the dimensions for the larger tunnel.

4b. Write an equation for the design of the larger tunnel.

THINK AND DISCUSS

1. Explain where the foci are located in relation to the vertices.

2. Compare circles and ellipses by using lines of symmetry.

3. GET ORGANIZED Copy and complete the graphic organizer. Give an equation for each type of ellipse.

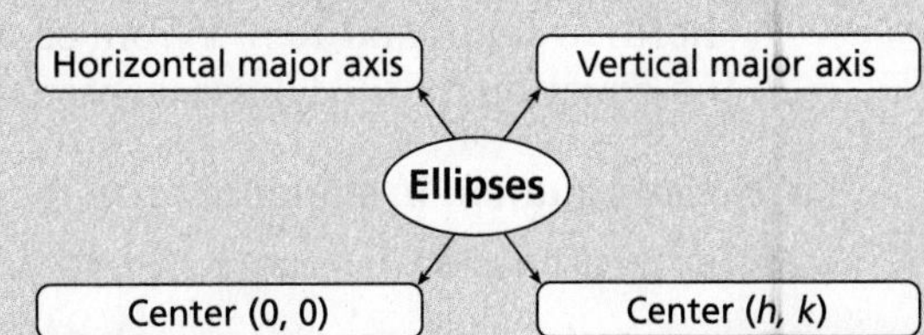

10-3 Exercises

go.hrw.com
Homework Help Online
KEYWORD: MB7 10-3
Parent Resources Online
KEYWORD: MB7 Parent

GUIDED PRACTICE

1. **Vocabulary** How can you tell the difference between the *major axis* and the *minor axis* of an ellipse?

SEE EXAMPLE 1 p. 736

Find the constant sum of an ellipse with the given foci and point on the ellipse.

2. $F_1(-5, 0), F_2(5, 0), P(0, -12)$
3. $F_1(0, -12), F_2(0, 12), P(9, 0)$

SEE EXAMPLE 2 p. 737

Multi-Step Write an equation in standard form for each ellipse with center (0, 0).

4. vertex $(-9, 0)$, co-vertex $(0, 7)$
5. vertex $(0, 25)$, focus $(0, -20)$
6. co-vertex $(10, 0)$, focus $(0, 24)$
7. vertex $(-7, 0)$, focus $(\sqrt{13}, 0)$

SEE EXAMPLE 3 p. 738

Graph each ellipse.

8. $\frac{x^2}{36} + \frac{y^2}{81} = 1$
9. $\frac{x^2}{121} + \frac{y^2}{49} = 1$
10. $\frac{(x-5)^2}{16} + \frac{(y+2)^2}{36} = 1$
11. $\frac{(x+1)^2}{64} + \frac{(y-6)^2}{9} = 1$

SEE EXAMPLE 4 p. 739

12. **Engineering** Engineers are building semi-elliptical bridges across two rivers. The larger river is 4 times as wide as the smaller river and must accommodate boats that are 3 times as tall. The equation for the bridge over the smaller river is $\frac{x^2}{225} + \frac{y^2}{144} = 1$, measured in feet.
    a. Find the dimensions of the larger bridge.
    b. Write an equation for the design of the larger bridge.

PRACTICE AND PROBLEM SOLVING

Independent Practice

For Exercises	See Example
13–14	1
15–18	2
19–22	3
23	4

Extra Practice
Skills Practice p. S22
Application Practice p. S41

Find the constant sum of an ellipse with the given foci and point on the ellipse.

13. $F_1(-20, 0), F_2(20, 0), P(-21, 0)$
14. $F_1(0, -8), F_2(0, 8), P(9, 13.6)$

Multi-Step Write an equation in standard form for each ellipse with center (0, 0).

15. vertex $(5, 0)$, co-vertex $(0, -2)$
16. co-vertex $(0, -8)$, focus $(6, 0)$
17. co-vertex $(4, 0)$, focus $(0, -3)$
18. vertex $(0, -9)$, focus $(0, 3\sqrt{5})$

Graph each ellipse.

19. $\frac{(x+2)^2}{169} + \frac{(y-7)^2}{25} = 1$
20. $\frac{(x-6)^2}{36} + \frac{(y-4)^2}{100} = 1$
21. $\frac{x^2}{256} + \frac{y^2}{196} = 1$
22. $\frac{x^2}{225} + \frac{y^2}{289} = 1$

23. **National Parks** South of the White House in Washington, D.C., is the President's Park South, or the Ellipse, which hosts events such as the White House Garden Tours. The Ellipse is 880 ft from north to south and 1057 ft from east to west. Write an equation for the Ellipse, centered at the origin.

Write an equation in standard form for each ellipse.

24. tangent to the x-axis at $(9, 0)$ and tangent to the y-axis at $(0, -6)$
25. center $(-4, 7)$, vertex $(-4, -3)$, focus $(-4, 0)$

26. **Estimation** An ellipse has a vertex at the point $(2.4, -6.1)$, focus $(0.35, -6.1)$, and center $(-4.5, -6.1)$. Estimate the coordinates of the co-vertices.

Write an equation for each graph, and give the domain and range. (*Hint:* The domain and range depend on the center and the lengths of the major and minor axes.)

27.

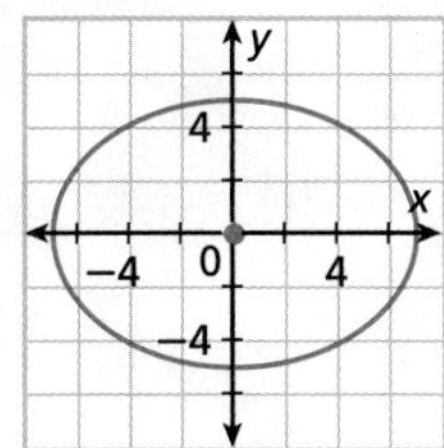

28.

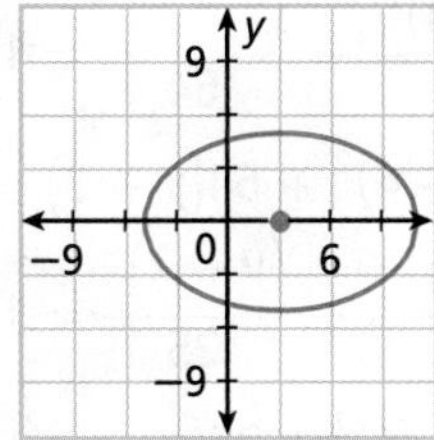

29.

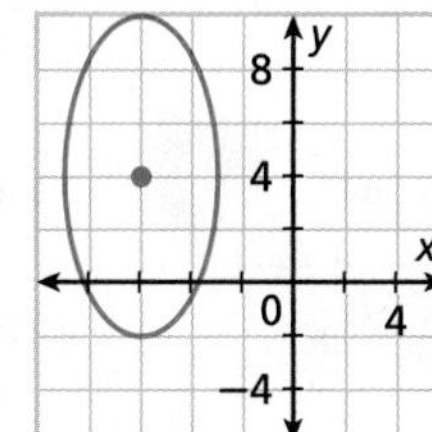

LINK

History

Located in Rome, Italy, the Colosseum was designed to hold as many as 50,000 spectators, who would arrive and leave through 80 entrances.

30. **History** The Roman Colosseum is shaped like a large ellipse, with an external width of 188 m and a length of 156 m. Write an equation that can be used to model the shape of the Colosseum.

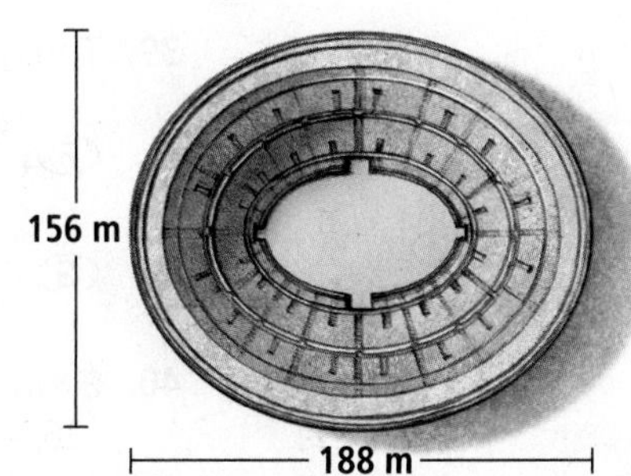

31. **Architecture** As a result of their unique elliptical shapes, whispering galleries enable the smallest sound generated at one focus to be carried across the room to the other focus. The whispering gallery at the Chicago Museum of Science and Industry is 47 ft 4 in. long and 13 ft 6 in. wide.

   a. Supposing that the center of the floor of the whispering gallery is located at the origin, write an equation for the gallery floor.

   b. Find the coordinates of the foci. How far apart are they?

Find the center, vertices, co-vertices, foci, domain, and range of each ellipse.

32. $\dfrac{(x-1)^2}{225} + \dfrac{(y+5)^2}{324} = 1$

33. $9(x+9)^2 + 81(y+4)^2 = 729$

34. **Critical Thinking** An ellipse is defined by the distance $PF_1 + PF_2 = d$. Could the distance between the foci be less than $PF_1 + PF_2$? Explain.

35. **Geometry** The area of an ellipse in standard form is given by $A = \pi ab$.

   a. **Critical Thinking** How is the formula for the area of an ellipse related to the formula for the area of a circle?

   b. Find the area of $\dfrac{(x+2)^2}{169} + \dfrac{(y-7)^2}{25} = 1$.

MULTI-STEP TEST PREP

36. This problem will prepare you for the Multi-Step Test Prep on page 758.

The figure shows the elliptical orbit of Mars, where each unit of the coordinate plane represents 1 million kilometers. As shown, the planet's maximum distance from the Sun is 249 million kilometers and its minimum distance from the Sun is 207 million kilometers.

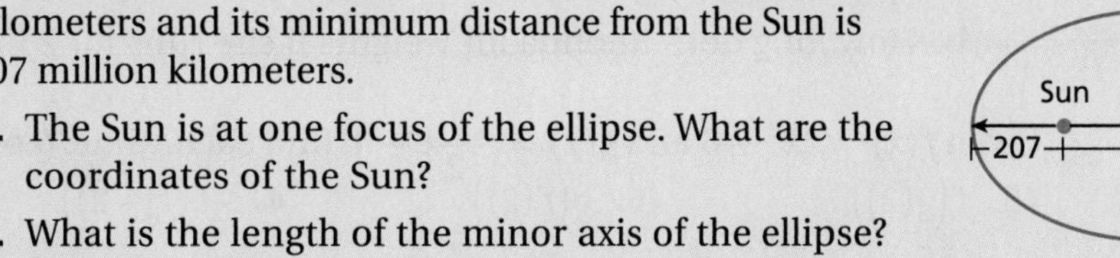

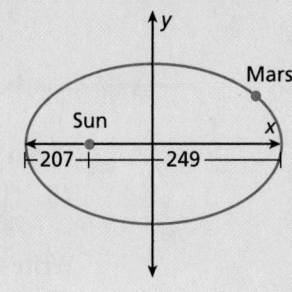

   a. The Sun is at one focus of the ellipse. What are the coordinates of the Sun?

   b. What is the length of the minor axis of the ellipse?

   c. Write an equation that models the orbit of Mars.

37. **Write About It** How is the distance $PF_1 + PF_2$ related to the length of the ellipse's major axis?

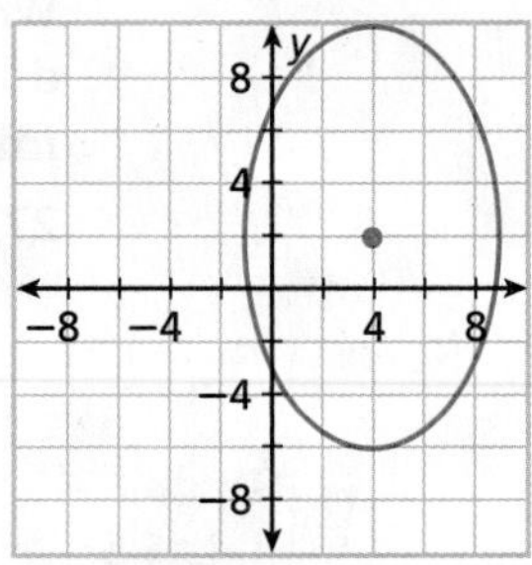

38. Which of the following is the equation for the graph?

Ⓐ $\dfrac{(x-4)^2}{25} - \dfrac{(y-2)^2}{64} = 1$

Ⓑ $25(x-4)^2 + 64(y-2)^2 = 1600$

Ⓒ $\dfrac{(x-4)^2}{64} + \dfrac{(y-2)^2}{25} = 1$

Ⓓ $64(x-4)^2 + 25(y-2)^2 = 1600$

39. The graph of which equation has the greatest distance between foci?

Ⓕ $\dfrac{(x-12)^2}{49} + \dfrac{(y+23)^2}{25} = 1$

Ⓗ $\dfrac{(x-1)^2}{20} + \dfrac{(y-1)^2}{150} = 1$

Ⓖ $\dfrac{x^2}{625} + \dfrac{y^2}{576} = 1$

Ⓙ $\dfrac{x^2}{175} + \dfrac{y^2}{225} = 1$

40. **Short Response** Give an equation for the ellipse with center $(2, -3)$, focus $(26, -3)$, and major axis length 50.

CHALLENGE AND EXTEND

41. The eccentricity of an ellipse is defined as $e = \frac{c}{a}$. Recall that $c^2 = a^2 - b^2$ for an ellipse in standard form.
    - **a.** Find the eccentricity of the ellipse with equation $\frac{x^2}{841} + \frac{y^2}{400} = 1$.
    - **b.** Find the equation of the ellipse with vertices $(13, 0)$ and $(-13, 0)$ and $e = \frac{5}{13}$.
    - **c.** What are the possible values for the eccentricity of an ellipse?
    - **d.** Describe the relationship between eccentricity and the shape of an ellipse.

42. **Astronomy** The path that the Moon travels around Earth is an ellipse with Earth at one focus. The length of the major axis is about 477,700 mi, and the length of the minor axis is about 476,980 mi.
    - **a.** Write an equation for the Moon's orbit.
    - **b.** Find the minimum and maximum distances from Earth to the Moon.

43. Write an equation for an ellipse with foci $F_1\,(-3, 0)$ and $F_2\,(3, 0)$ and a constant sum of 10. (*Hint:* Use $d = PF_1 + PF_2$ and the point (x, y).)

SPIRAL REVIEW

44. **Recreation** Rhonda exercises no more than 60 minutes a day. She runs and lifts weights. *(Lesson 2-5)*
    - **a.** Write and graph an inequality for the number of minutes that Rhonda can run and lift weights each day.
    - **b.** How long does Rhonda lift weights if she runs for 25 minutes?

Given $f(x) = 2x^2 + 6$ and $g(x) = -\frac{1}{2}x + 4$, find each value. *(Lesson 9-4)*

45. $f(g(2))$
46. $g(f(2))$
47. $f(g(-2))$
48. $g(f(-2))$

Write the equation of each circle. *(Lesson 10-2)*

49. center $(0, -1)$, containing the point $(6, 7)$
50. center $(-5, 9)$, radius $r = 6$

Locate the Foci of an Ellipse

You have seen how an ellipse is defined by its foci and how to draw an ellipse given the foci. You can find the foci of a given ellipse by using a compass.

Use with Lesson 10-3

Activity

Find the foci of the ellipse with major axis length 20 and minor axis length 12.

1. Graph the ellipse so that the center is at $(0, 0)$. Mark the endpoints of the major axis: $(-10, 0)$ and $(10, 0)$. Mark the endpoints of the minor axis at $(0, -6)$ and $(0, 6)$. Draw the ellipse.

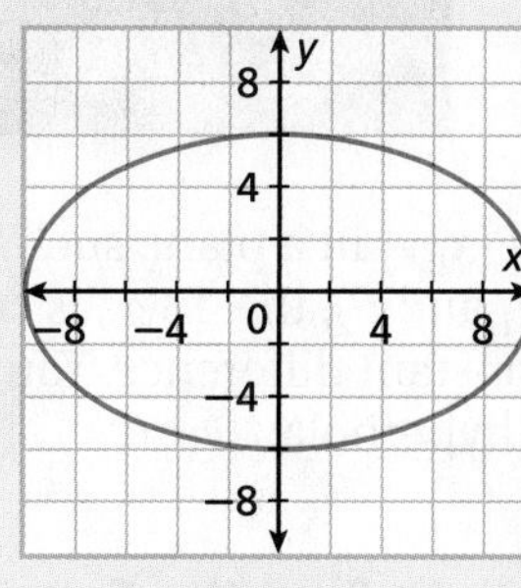

2. Use a compass to draw a circle with radius 10 units centered at $(0, 0)$.

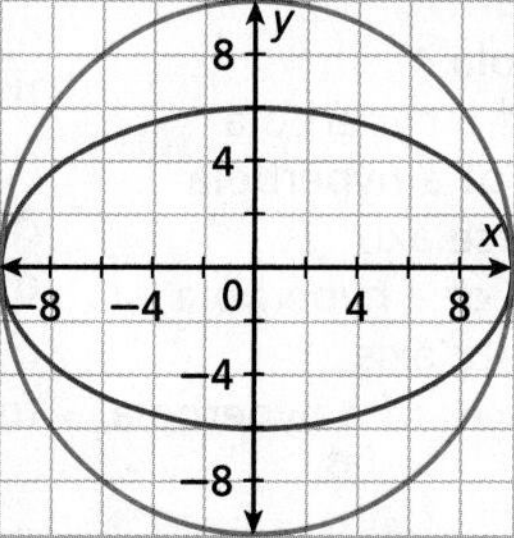

3. Draw the line with equation $y = 6$ on the graph. Mark the points where the line intersects the circle.

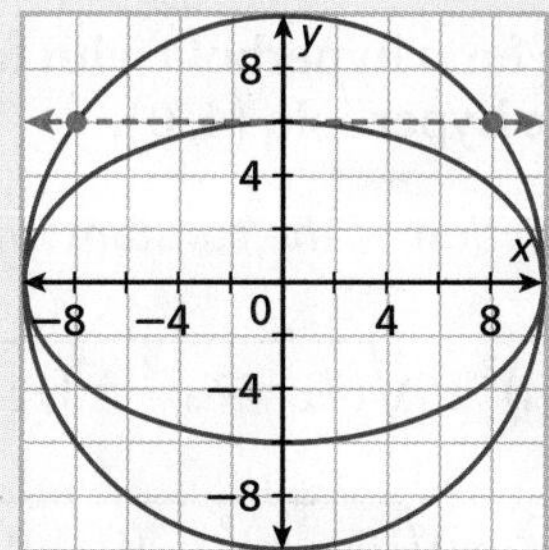

4. Draw lines from the points where $y = 6$ intersects the circle perpendicular to the x-axis. The foci of the ellipse are the points where the perpendicular lines intersect the x-axis. Where are the foci of your ellipse? Check by using the formula $c^2 = a^2 - b^2$.

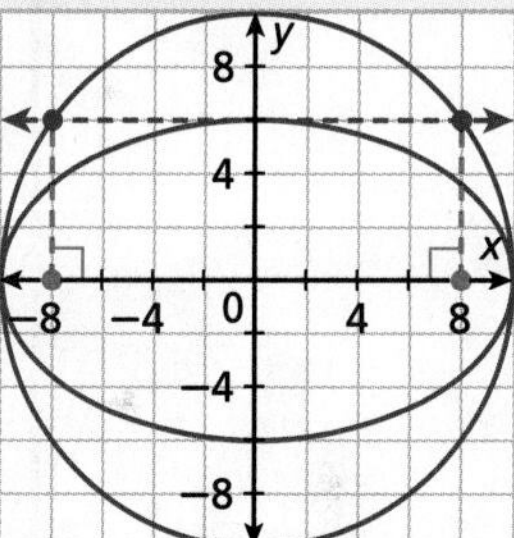

Try This

Use a compass to find the foci of each ellipse with a horizontal major axis.

1. major axis length 26, minor axis length 10
2. major axis length 34, minor axis length 16

Use a compass to find the foci of each ellipse with a vertical major axis.

3. major axis length 25, minor axis length 24
4. major axis length 20, minor axis length 12
5. **Critical Thinking** In Step 3 above, what other line could you have drawn to get the same foci?
6. **Critical Thinking** Why does this method of locating the foci of an ellipse work?

10-4 Hyperbolas

Objectives

Write the standard equation for a hyperbola.

Graph a hyperbola, and identify its vertices, co-vertices, center, foci, and asymptotes.

Vocabulary

hyperbola
focus of a hyperbola
branch of a hyperbola
transverse axis
vertices of a hyperbola
conjugate axis
co-vertices of a hyperbola

Who uses this?

Biologists use hyperbolas to locate and track whales based on the sounds that the whales make. (See Exercise 33.)

What would happen if you pulled the two foci of an ellipse so far apart that they moved outside the ellipse? The result would be a *hyperbola*, another conic section.

A **hyperbola** is the set of points $P(x, y)$ in a plane such that the difference of the distances from P to fixed points F_1 and F_2, the **foci**, is constant. For a hyperbola, $d = |PF_1 - PF_2|$, where d is the constant difference. You can use the distance formula to find the equation of a hyperbola.

EXAMPLE 1 Using the Distance Formula to Find the Constant Difference of a Hyperbola

Find the constant difference for a hyperbola with foci $F_1(-5, 0)$ and $F_2(5, 0)$ and the point on the hyperbola $(4, 0)$.

$d = |PF_1 - PF_2|$ *Definition of the constant difference of a hyperbola*

$= \left|\sqrt{(x_1 - x_3)^2 + (y_1 - y_3)^2} - \sqrt{(x_2 - x_3)^2 + (y_2 - y_3)^2}\right|$ *Distance Formula*

$= \left|\sqrt{(-5 - 4)^2 + (0 - 0)^2} - \sqrt{(5 - 4)^2 + (0 - 0)^2}\right|$ *Substitute.*

$= \left|\sqrt{81} - \sqrt{1}\right|$ *Simplify.*

$= 8$

The constant difference is 8.

1. Find the constant difference for a hyperbola with foci at $F_1(0, -10)$ and $F_2(0, 10)$ and the point on the hyperbola $(6, 7.5)$.

As the graphs in the following table show, a hyperbola contains two symmetrical parts called **branches**.

A hyperbola also has two axes of symmetry. The **transverse axis** of symmetry contains the vertices and, if it were extended, the foci of the hyperbola. The **vertices of a hyperbola** are the endpoints of the transverse axis.

The **conjugate axis** of symmetry separates the two branches of the hyperbola. The **co-vertices of a hyperbola** are the endpoints of the conjugate axis. The transverse axis is not always longer than the conjugate axis.

The standard form of the equation of a hyperbola depends on whether the hyperbola's transverse axis is horizontal or vertical.

Horizontal

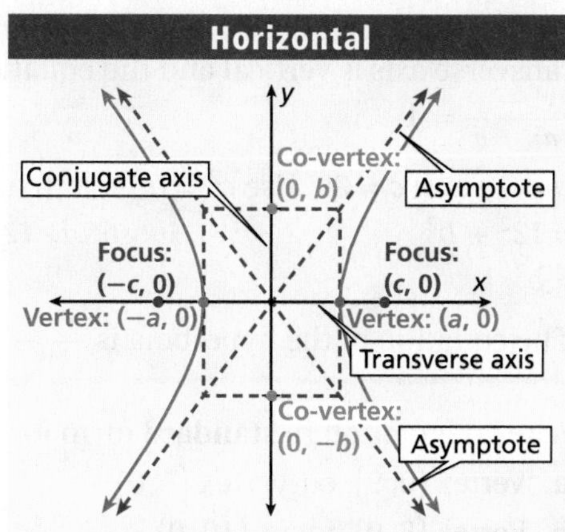

Vertical

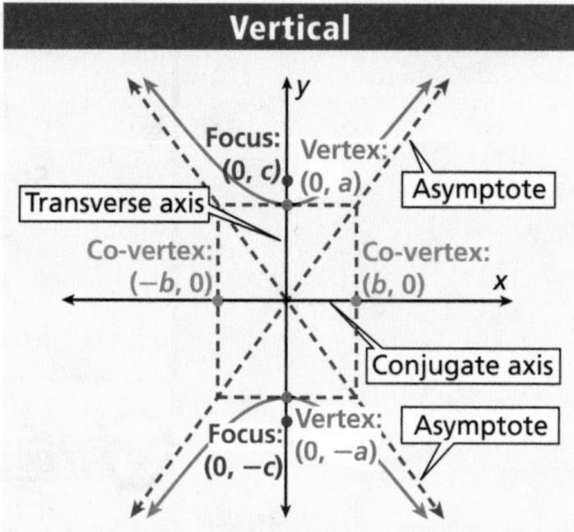

The values a, b, and c are related by the equation $c^2 = a^2 + b^2$. Also note that the length of the transverse axis is $2a$ and the length of the conjugate axis is $2b$.

Standard Form for the Equation of a Hyperbola Center at (0, 0)

TRANSVERSE AXIS	HORIZONTAL	VERTICAL
Equation	$\frac{x^2}{a^2} - \frac{y^2}{b^2} = 1$	$\frac{y^2}{a^2} - \frac{x^2}{b^2} = 1$
Vertices	$(a, 0), (-a, 0)$	$(0, a), (0, -a)$
Foci	$(c, 0), (-c, 0)$	$(0, c), (0, -c)$
Co-vertices	$(0, b), (0, -b)$	$(b, 0), (-b, 0)$
Asymptotes	$y = \pm\frac{b}{a}x$	$y = \pm\frac{a}{b}x$

EXAMPLE 2 Writing Equations of Hyperbolas

Write an equation in standard form for each hyperbola.

A

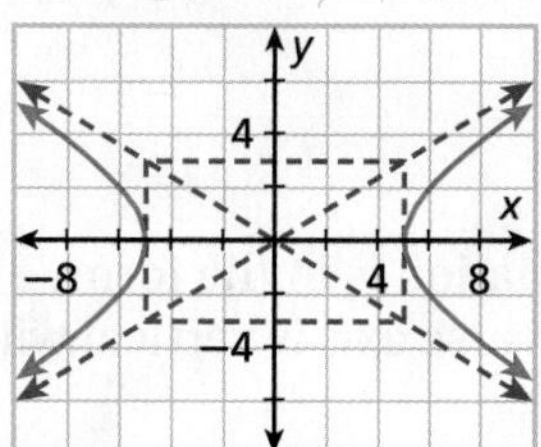

Step 1 Identify the form of the equation.

The graph opens horizontally, so the equation will be in the form $\frac{x^2}{a^2} - \frac{y^2}{b^2} = 1$.

Step 2 Identify the center and vertices.

The center of the graph is $(0, 0)$, the vertices are $(-5, 0)$ and $(5, 0)$, and the co-vertices are $(0, -3)$ and $(0, 3)$. So $a = 5$ and $b = 3$.

Step 3 Write the equation.

Because $a = 5$ and $b = 3$, the equation of the graph is $\frac{x^2}{5^2} - \frac{y^2}{3^2} = 1$, or $\frac{x^2}{25} - \frac{y^2}{9} = 1$.

Write an equation in standard form for each hyperbola.

B **the hyperbola with center (0, 0), vertex (0, 12), and focus (0, 20)**

Step 1 Because the vertex and the focus are on the vertical axis, the transverse axis is vertical and the equation is in the form $\frac{y^2}{a^2} - \frac{x^2}{b^2} = 1$.

Step 2 $a = 12$ and $c = 20$; Use $c^2 = a^2 + b^2$ to solve for b^2.

$20^2 = 12^2 + b^2$ *Substitute 12 for a and 20 for c.*

$256 = b^2$

Step 3 The equation of the hyperbola is $\frac{y^2}{144} - \frac{x^2}{256} = 1$

Write an equation in standard form for each hyperbola.

2a. Vertex (0, 9), co-vertex (7, 0)

2b. Vertex (8, 0), focus (10, 0)

As with circles and ellipses, hyperbolas do not have to be centered at the origin.

Standard Form for the Equation of a Hyperbola Center at (h, k)

TRANSVERSE AXIS	HORIZONTAL	VERTICAL
Equation	$\frac{(x-h)^2}{a^2} - \frac{(y-k)^2}{b^2} = 1$	$\frac{(y-k)^2}{a^2} - \frac{(x-h)^2}{b^2} = 1$
Vertices	$(h+a, k), (h-a, k)$	$(h, k+a), (h, k-a)$
Foci	$(h+c, k), (h-c, k)$	$(h, k+c), (h, k-c)$
Co-vertices	$(h, k+b), (h, k-b)$	$(h+b, k), (h-b, k)$
Asymptotes	$y - k = \pm\frac{b}{a}(x-h)$	$y - k = \pm\frac{a}{b}(x-h)$

EXAMPLE 3 Graphing a Hyperbola

Find the vertices, co-vertices, and asymptotes of each hyperbola, and then graph.

A $\frac{y^2}{25} - \frac{x^2}{36} = 1$

Step 1 The equation is in the form $\frac{y^2}{a^2} - \frac{x^2}{b^2} = 1$, so the transverse axis is vertical with center (0, 0).

Step 2 Because $a = 5$ and $b = 6$, the vertices are (0, 5) and (0, −5) and the co-vertices are (6, 0) and (−6, 0).

Step 3 The equations of the asymptotes are $y = \frac{5}{6}x$ and $y = -\frac{5}{6}x$.

Step 4 Draw a box by using the vertices and co-vertices. Draw the asymptotes through the corners of the box.

Step 5 Draw the hyperbola by using the vertices and the asymptotes.

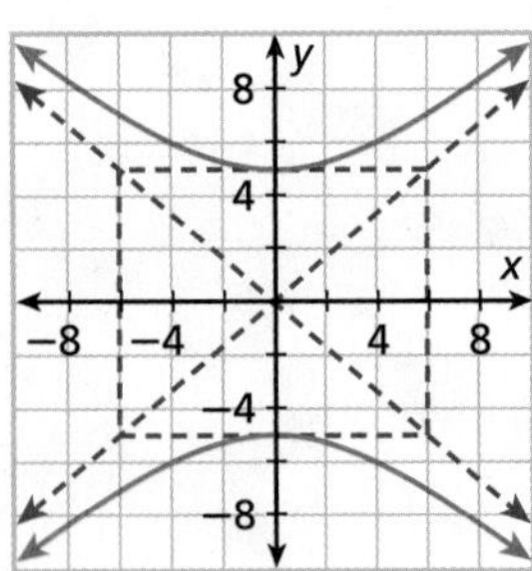

Find the vertices, co-vertices, and asymptotes of each hyperbola, and then graph.

B $\dfrac{(x-2)^2}{16} - \dfrac{(y+3)^2}{49} = 1$

Step 1 The equation is in the form $\dfrac{(x-h)^2}{a^2} - \dfrac{(y-k)^2}{b^2} = 1$ so the transverse axis is horizontal with center $(2, -3)$.

Step 2 Because $a = 4$ and $b = 7$, the vertices are $(6, -3)$ and $(-2, -3)$ and the co-vertices are $(2, 4)$ and $(2, -10)$.

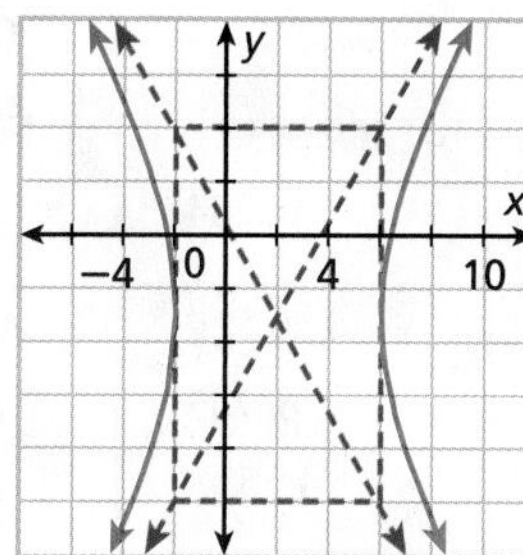

Step 3 The equations of the asymptotes are $y + 3 = \frac{7}{4}(x-2)$ and $y + 3 = -\frac{7}{4}(x-2)$.

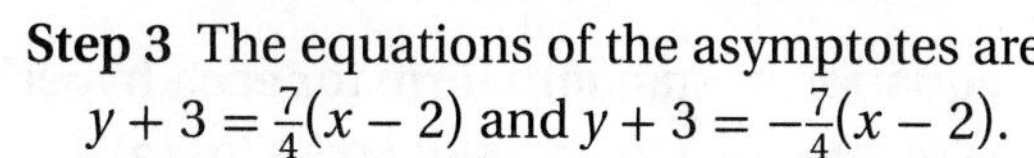

Step 4 Draw a box by using the vertices and co-vertices. Draw the asymptotes through the corners of the box.

Step 5 Draw the hyperbola by using the vertices and the asymptotes.

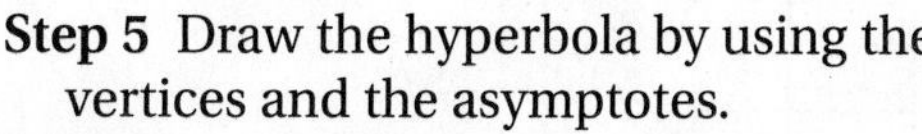

Caution!

The graph of the hyperbola must pass through the vertices and approach both of the asymptotes.

Find the vertices, co-vertices, and asymptotes of each hyperbola, and then graph.

3a. $\dfrac{x^2}{16} - \dfrac{y^2}{36} = 1$ **3b.** $\dfrac{(y+5)^2}{9} - \dfrac{(x-1)^2}{1} = 1$

Notice that as the parameters change, the graph of the hyperbola is transformed.

Parameter	Transformation
h	Translates the graph left for $h > 0$ and right for $h < 0$
k	Translates the graph up for $k > 0$ and down for $k < 0$
a	Stretches the graph in the direction of the transverse axis; as a increases, the vertices move farther apart.
b	Stretches the graph in the direction of the conjugate axis; as b increases, the co-vertices move farther apart.

THINK AND DISCUSS

1. When is the transverse axis of a hyperbola shorter than its conjugate axis?
2. How do you tell when a hyperbola has a horizontal transverse axis?

3. **GET ORGANIZED** Copy and complete the graphic organizer. Label all of the parts of the hyperbola.

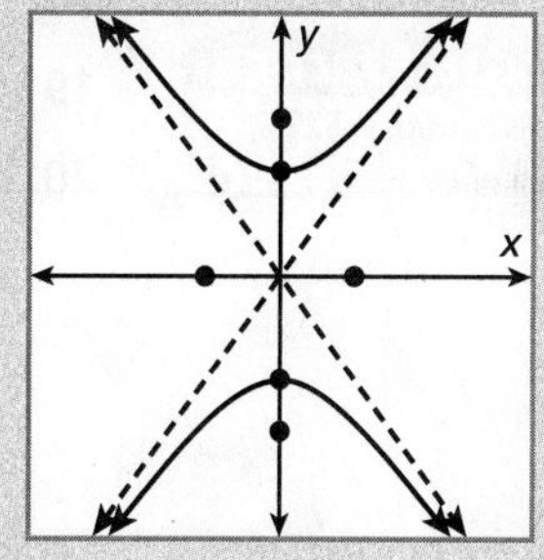

10-4 Exercises

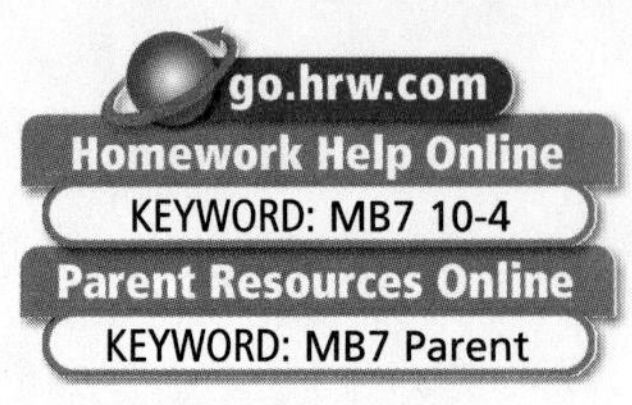

GUIDED PRACTICE

1. **Vocabulary** The vertices of a hyperbola lie on the __?__ (*transverse axis* or *conjugate axis*).

SEE EXAMPLE 1 p. 744

Find the constant difference for a hyperbola with the given foci and point on the hyperbola.

2. $F_1(-13, 0), F_2(13, 0), P(5, 0)$
3. $F_1(0, -17), F_2(0, 17), P(0, -15)$

SEE EXAMPLE 2 p. 745

Write an equation in standard form for each hyperbola.

4. center $(0, 0)$, vertex $(0, 5)$, and focus $(0, 13)$
5. center $(0, 0)$, vertex $(9, 0)$, and co-vertex $(0, 7)$
6. 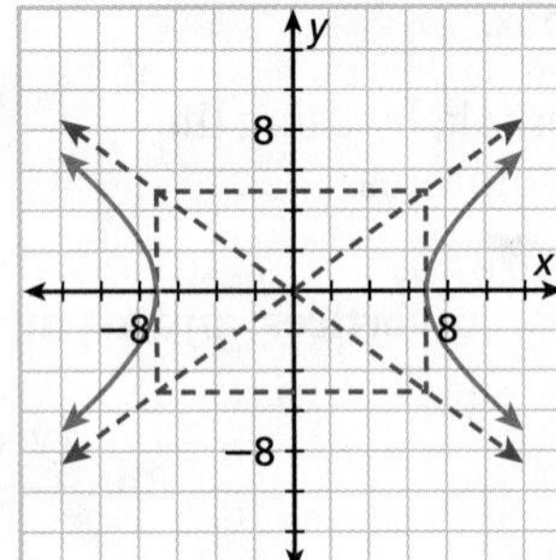

7. 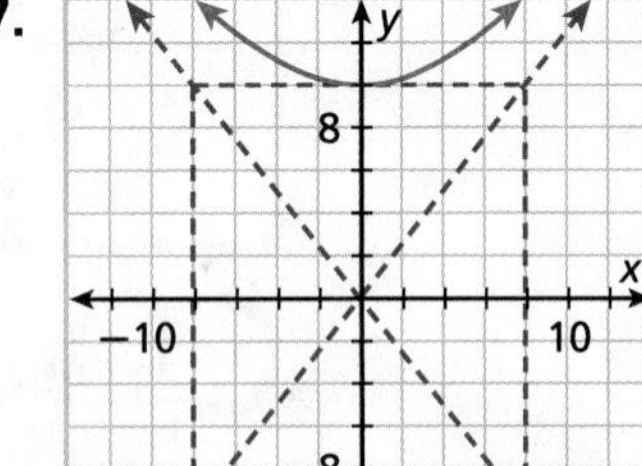

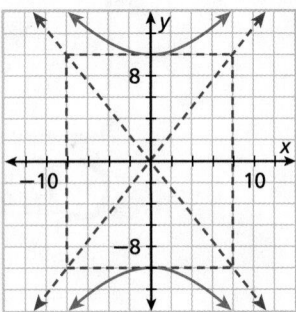

SEE EXAMPLE 3 p. 746

Find the vertices, co-vertices, and asymptotes of each hyperbola, and then graph.

8. $\frac{x^2}{49} - \frac{y^2}{36} = 1$
9. $\frac{x^2}{25} - \frac{y^2}{64} = 1$
10. $\frac{y^2}{25} - \frac{x^2}{36} = 1$
11. $\frac{y^2}{100} - \frac{x^2}{81} = 1$
12. $\frac{(x-4)^2}{9} - \frac{(y-3)^2}{64} = 1$
13. $\frac{(x-4)^2}{16} - \frac{(y+6)^2}{49} = 1$
14. $\frac{(y+8)^2}{36} - \frac{(x+3)^2}{25} = 1$
15. $\frac{(y+7)^2}{4} - \frac{x^2}{25} = 1$

PRACTICE AND PROBLEM SOLVING

Independent Practice

For Exercises	See Example
16–17	1
18–21	2
22–29	3

Extra Practice

Skills Practice p. S22

Application Practice p. S41

Find the constant difference for a hyperbola with the given foci and point on the hyperbola.

16. $F_1(0, -10), F_2(0, 10), P(0, 6)$
17. $F_1(-29, 0), F_2(29, 0), P(21, 0)$

Write an equation in standard form for each hyperbola.

18. center $(0, 0)$, vertex $(15, 0)$, co-vertex $(0, -13)$
19. center $(0, 0)$, vertex $(-8, 0)$, focus $(17, 0)$
20. 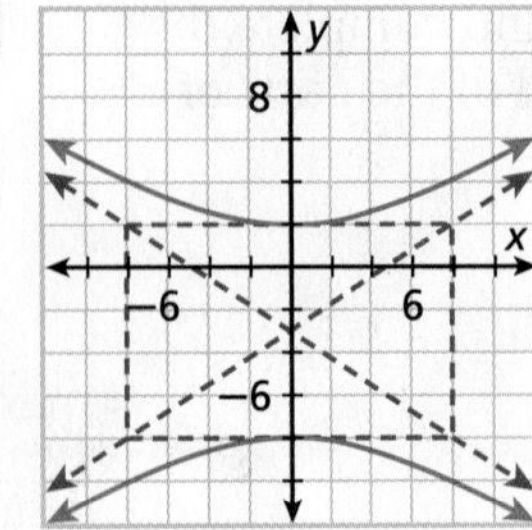

21. 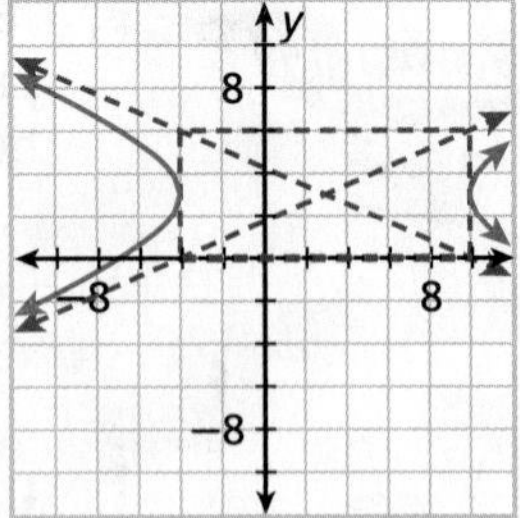

Find the vertices, co-vertices, and asymptotes of each hyperbola, and then graph.

22. $\frac{x^2}{64} - \frac{y^2}{36} = 1$ **23.** $\frac{y^2}{25} - \frac{x^2}{81} = 1$ **24.** $\frac{y^2}{81} - \frac{x^2}{16} = 1$ **25.** $\frac{x^2}{4} - \frac{y^2}{121} = 1$

26. $\frac{(y-1)^2}{64} - \frac{(x+2)^2}{36} = 1$ **27.** $\frac{(x+5)^2}{25} - \frac{(y-3)^2}{16} = 1$

28. $\frac{(y-8)^2}{25} - \frac{(x+6)^2}{36} = 1$ **29.** $\frac{(x-6)^2}{9} - \frac{(y-2)^2}{16} = 1$

30. Architecture If the x-axis is placed at a height of 100 meters, the outer edge of a cooling tower can be modeled by the hyperbola $\frac{x^2}{900} - \frac{y^2}{1600} = 1$, measured in meters. If the tower is 150 meters tall, find the width of the cooling tower at the top.

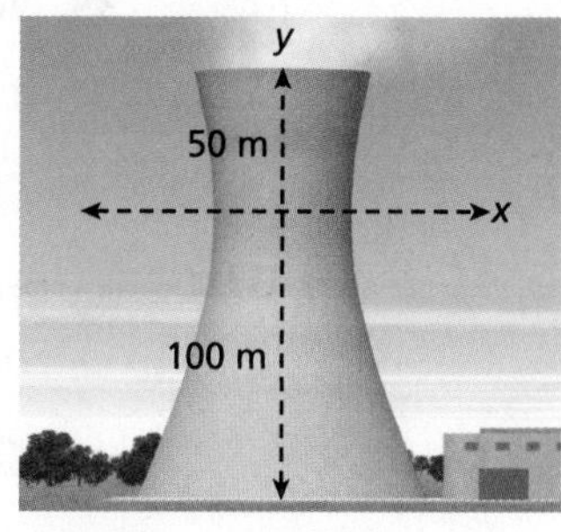

LINK

Physics

The saying "lightning never strikes twice in the same place" is often disproven. The Empire State Building is struck by lightning about 100 times each year and serves as a lightning rod for the surrounding area.

31. Critical Thinking What happens to the graph of $\frac{x^2}{a^2} - \frac{y^2}{16} = 1$ as the values of a increase? What happens to the graph of $\frac{x^2}{16} - \frac{y^2}{b^2} = 1$ as the values of b increase?

32. Physics Two people standing 10,000 feet apart see lightning strike. One person hears the thunder 5 seconds after the other person. Because sound travels at 1100 feet per second, one person is 5500 feet farther from the lightning strike than the other. The possible locations of the strike then form a hyperbola with the two people at the foci. Place the origin midway between the two people, and write an equation that could be used to represent the possible locations of the lightning strike.

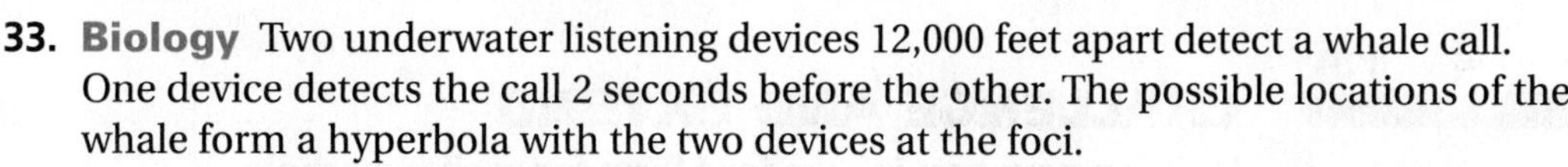

33. Biology Two underwater listening devices 12,000 feet apart detect a whale call. One device detects the call 2 seconds before the other. The possible locations of the whale form a hyperbola with the two devices at the foci.

a. If the speed of sound in water is 5000 feet per second, write an equation for the possible locations of the whale. (*Hint:* Place the origin midway between the devices.)

b. What if...? Could the location of the whale be more precisely located if there were a third listening device? Explain.

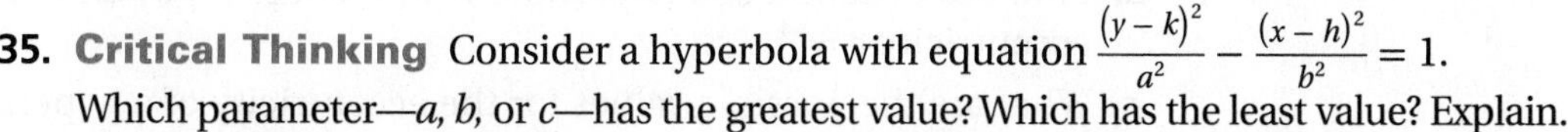

34. Critical Thinking How could you identify the domain and range of a hyperbola? Explain.

35. Critical Thinking Consider a hyperbola with equation $\frac{(y-k)^2}{a^2} - \frac{(x-h)^2}{b^2} = 1$. Which parameter—$a$, b, or c—has the greatest value? Which has the least value? Explain.

36. Write About It Suppose you have two hyperbolas that are the same except that the transverse axis and conjugate axis are switched. How does switching the axes affect the equations of the asymptotes for the two hyperbolas? Why?

37. This problem will prepare you for the Multi-Step Test Prep on page 758.

A comet's path as it approaches the Sun is modeled by one branch of the hyperbola $\frac{y^2}{900} - \frac{x^2}{44{,}896} = 1$, where the Sun is at the corresponding focus. Each unit of the coordinate plane represents 1 million miles.

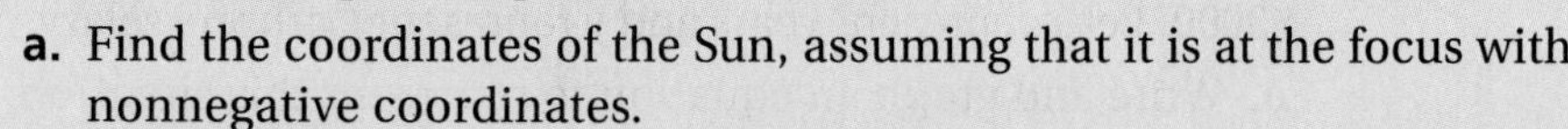

a. Find the coordinates of the Sun, assuming that it is at the focus with nonnegative coordinates.

b. How close does the comet come to the Sun?

c. When the comet is far from the Sun, the comet's path can be modeled by the hyperbola's asymptotes. Write the equations of the asymptotes.

38. Which of the following is the equation of the graph shown?

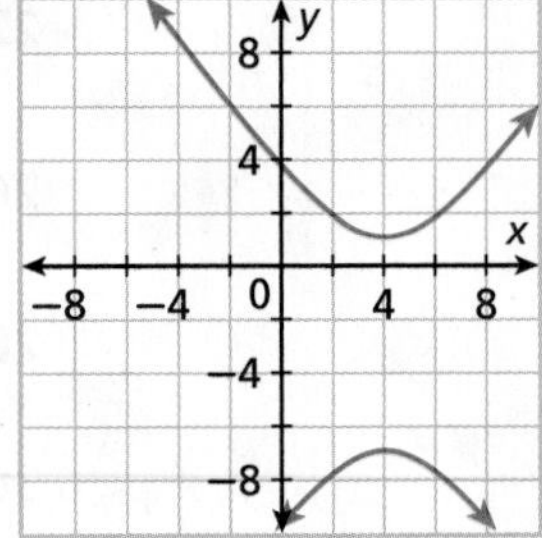

Ⓐ $\frac{(x-3)^2}{16} - \frac{(y+4)^2}{9} = 1$ Ⓒ $\frac{(y-3)^2}{16} - \frac{(x+4)^2}{9} = 1$

Ⓑ $\frac{(x+3)^2}{16} - \frac{(y-4)^2}{9} = 1$ Ⓓ $\frac{(y+3)^2}{16} - \frac{(x-4)^2}{9} = 1$

39. Which of the following is an asymptote of the graph of $1 = \frac{x^2}{4} - \frac{y^2}{9}$?

Ⓕ $y = -\frac{2}{3}x$ Ⓖ $y = \frac{3}{2}x$ Ⓗ $y = -\frac{9}{4}x$ Ⓙ $y = \frac{4}{9}x$

40. The graph of which of the following equations will have the greatest distance between foci?

Ⓐ $\frac{(x-6)^2}{36} - \frac{(y+2)^2}{81} = 1$ Ⓒ $\frac{(y+115)^2}{49} - \frac{(x-225)^2}{100} = 1$

Ⓑ $\frac{(x+22)^2}{45} - \frac{(y-36)^2}{125} = 1$ Ⓓ $\frac{(y-59)^2}{90} - \frac{(x+76)^2}{95} = 1$

41. What is the length of the conjugate axis of the hyperbola with equation $\frac{x^2}{49} - \frac{y^2}{121} = 1$?

Ⓕ 7 Ⓖ 11 Ⓗ 14 Ⓙ 22

CHALLENGE AND EXTEND

Write an equation in standard form for each hyperbola.

42. co-vertex $(-12, 0)$, asymptote $y = -\frac{4}{3}x$

43. vertex $(27, -9)$, asymptote $y + 9 = -\frac{3}{5}(x - 7)$

44. The eccentricity of a hyperbola is defined as $e = \frac{c}{a}$. Recall that $c^2 = a^2 + b^2$ for a hyperbola in standard form.

a. Find the eccentricity of $\frac{(x-4)^2}{144} - \frac{(y+2)^2}{1225} = 1$.

b. Find the equation of a hyperbola with vertices $(0, 6)$ and $(0, -6)$, and eccentricity $e = \frac{4}{3}$.

c. What are the possible values for the eccentricity of a hyperbola?

d. Describe the relationship between eccentricity and the shape of a hyperbola.

45. Use the distance formula to write the equation of a hyperbola with foci at $F_1(-5, 0)$ and $F_2(5, 0)$ and $d = 8$. (*Hint:* Use $d = PF_1 - PF_2$ and the point (x, y).)

SPIRAL REVIEW

Graph each function by using a table. *(Lesson 5-1)*

46. $f(x) = 2x^2 + 3x - 6$ 47. $f(x) = -x^2 + 2x + 5$ 48. $f(x) = x^2 - 5x + 4$

49. **Finance** Carlton's starting salary was \$30,000. Every year, he received a raise of \$3000. Let x represent years and y represent Carlton's salary. *(Lesson 9-1)*

a. Write and graph an equation to represent this situation.

b. After how many years will Carlton earn \$60,000?

Write an equation in standard form for each ellipse with center (0, 0). *(Lesson 10-3)*

50. vertex $(5, 0)$, co-vertex $(0, 4)$ 51. vertex $(0, -2)$, focus $(0, \sqrt{2})$

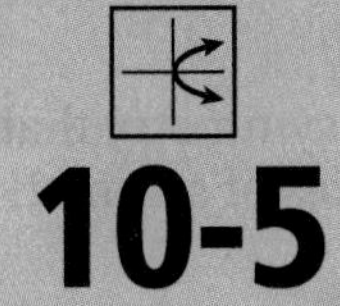

10-5 Parabolas

Objectives
Write the standard equation of a parabola and its axis of symmetry.
Graph a parabola, and identify its focus, directrix, and axis of symmetry.

Vocabulary
focus of a parabola
directrix

Why learn this?
Parabolas are used with microphones to pick up sounds from sports events. (See Example 4.)

In Chapter 5, you learned that the graph of a quadratic function is a parabola. Because a parabola is a conic section, it can also be defined in terms of distance.

A parabola is the set of all points $P(x, y)$ in a plane that are an equal distance from both a fixed point, the **focus**, and a fixed line, the **directrix**. A parabola has an axis of symmetry perpendicular to its directrix and that passes through its vertex. The vertex of a parabola is the midpoint of the segment connecting the focus and the directrix.

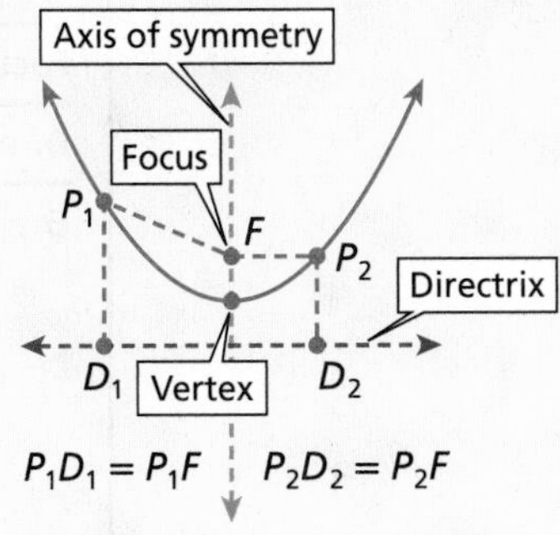

EXAMPLE 1 Using the Distance Formula to Write the Equation of a Parabola

Use the Distance Formula to find the equation of a parabola with focus $F(0, 3)$ and directrix $y = -3$.

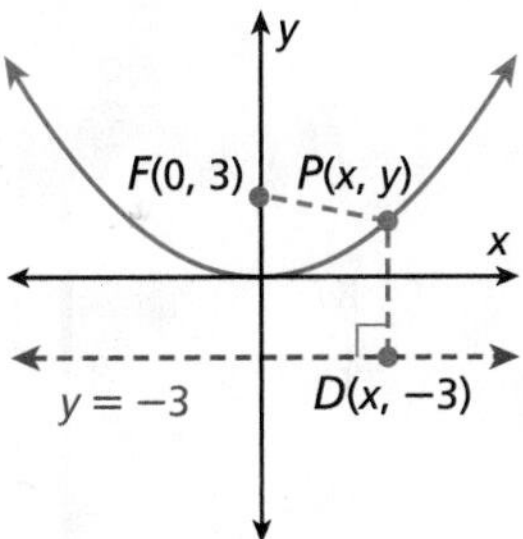

$PF = PD$ *Definition of a parabola*

$\sqrt{(x - x_1)^2 + (y - y_1)^2} = \sqrt{(x - x_2)^2 + (y - y_2)^2}$ *Distance Formula*

$\sqrt{(x - 0)^2 + (y - 3)^2} = \sqrt{(x - x)^2 + (y + 3)^2}$ *Substitute (0, 3) for (x_1, y_1) and (x, −3) for (x_2, y_2).*

$\sqrt{x^2 + (y - 3)^2} = \sqrt{(y + 3)^2}$ *Simplify.*

$x^2 + (y - 3)^2 = (y + 3)^2$ *Square both sides.*

$x^2 + y^2 - 6y + 9 = y^2 + 6y + 9$ *Expand.*

$x^2 - 6y = 6y$ *Subtract y^2 and 9 from both sides.*

$x^2 = 12y$ *Add 6y to both sides.*

$y = \frac{1}{12}x^2$ *Solve for y.*

Remember!
The distance from a point to a line is defined as the length of the line segment from the point perpendicular to the line.

1. Use the Distance Formula to find the equation of a parabola with focus $F(0, 4)$ and directrix $y = -4$.

Previously, you have graphed parabolas with vertical axes of symmetry that open upward or downward. Parabolas may also have horizontal axes of symmetry and may open to the left or right.

The equations of parabolas use the parameter p. The $|p|$ gives the distance from the vertex to both the focus and the directrix.

Standard Form for the Equation of a Parabola Vertex at $(0, 0)$

AXIS OF SYMMETRY	HORIZONTAL $y = 0$	VERTICAL $x = 0$
Equation	$x = \frac{1}{4p}y^2$	$y = \frac{1}{4p}x^2$
Direction	Opens right if $p > 0$ Opens left if $p < 0$	Opens upward if $p > 0$ Opens downward if $p < 0$
Focus	$(p, 0)$	$(0, p)$
Directrix	$x = -p$	$y = -p$
Graph	$D(-p, y)$, $P(x, y)$, $F(p, 0)$, $x = -p$, x, y	$F(0, p)$, $P(x, y)$, $D(x, -p)$, $y = -p$, x, y

EXAMPLE 2 **Writing Equations of Parabolas**

Write the equation in standard form for each parabola.

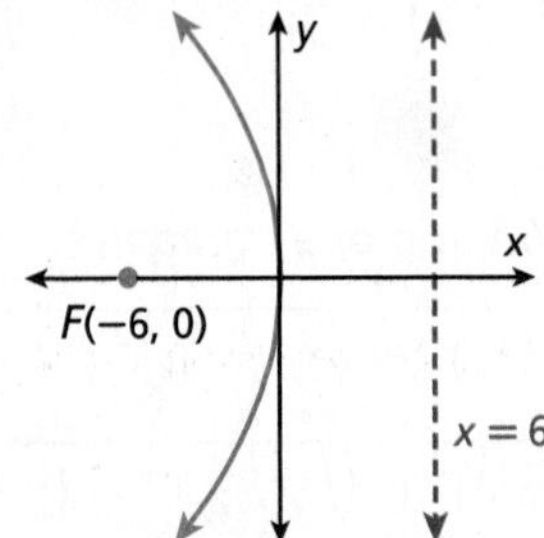

Step 1 Because the axis of symmetry is horizontal and the parabola opens to the left, the equation is in the form $x = \frac{1}{4p}y^2$ with $p < 0$.

Step 2 The distance from the focus $(-6, 0)$ to the vertex $(0, 0)$ is 6, so $p = -6$ and $4p = -24$.

Step 3 The equation of the parabola is $x = -\frac{1}{24}y^2$.

Check Use your graphing calculator. The graph of the equation appears to match.

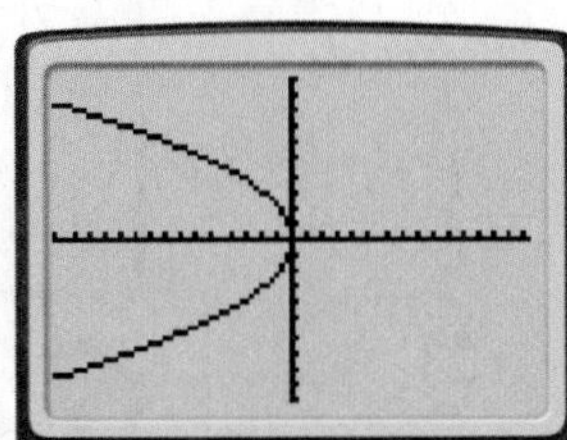

Write the equation in standard form for each parabola.

B the parabola with vertex $(0, 0)$ and directrix $y = -2.5$.

Step 1 Because the directrix is a horizontal line, the equation is in the form $y = \frac{1}{4p}x^2$. The vertex is above the directrix, so the graph will open upward.

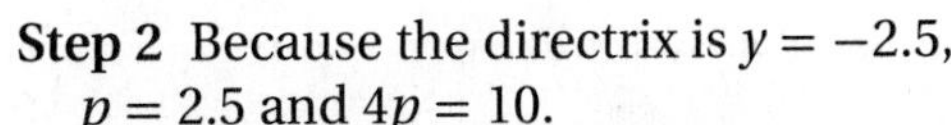

Step 2 Because the directrix is $y = -2.5$, $p = 2.5$ and $4p = 10$.

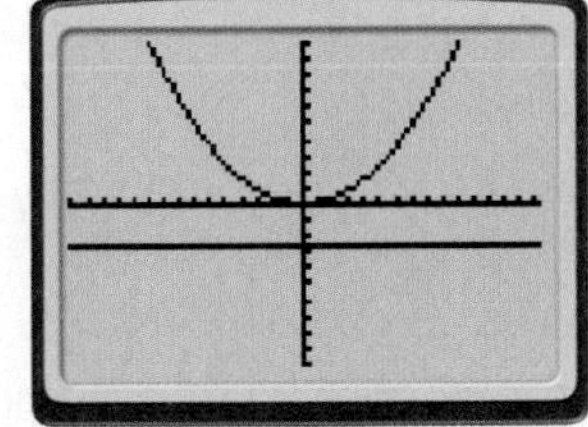

Step 3 The equation of the parabola is $y = \frac{1}{10}x^2$.

Check Use your graphing calculator.

Write the equation in standard form for each parabola.

2a. vertex $(0, 0)$, directrix $x = 1.25$

2b. vertex $(0, 0)$, focus $(0, -7)$

The vertex of a parabola may not always be the origin. Adding or subtracting a value from x or y translates the graph of a parabola. Also notice that the values of p stretch or compress the graph.

Standard Form for the Equation of a Parabola Vertex at (h, k)

AXIS OF SYMMETRY	HORIZONTAL $y = k$	VERTICAL $x = h$
Equation	$x - h = \frac{1}{4p}(y - k)^2$	$y - k = \frac{1}{4p}(x - h)^2$
Direction	Opens right if $p > 0$ Opens left if $p < 0$	Opens upward if $p > 0$ Opens downward if $p < 0$
Focus	$(h + p, k)$	$(h, k + p)$
Directrix	$x = h - p$	$y = k - p$
Graph	y, x, $y = k$, $F(h + p, k)$, (h, k), $x = h - p$	$x = h$, y, x, $F(h, k + p)$, (h, k), $y = k - p$

EXAMPLE 3 Graphing Parabolas

Find the vertex, value of p, axis of symmetry, focus, and directrix of the parabola $x - 2 = -\frac{1}{16}(y + 5)^2$. Then graph.

Step 1 The vertex is $(2, -5)$.

Step 2 $\frac{1}{4p} = -\frac{1}{16}$, so $4p = -16$ and $p = -4$.

Step 3 The graph has a horizontal axis of symmetry, with equation $y = -5$, and opens left.

Step 4 The focus is $(2 + (-4), -5)$, or $(-2, -5)$.

Step 5 The directrix is a vertical line $x = 2 - (-4)$, or $x = 6$.

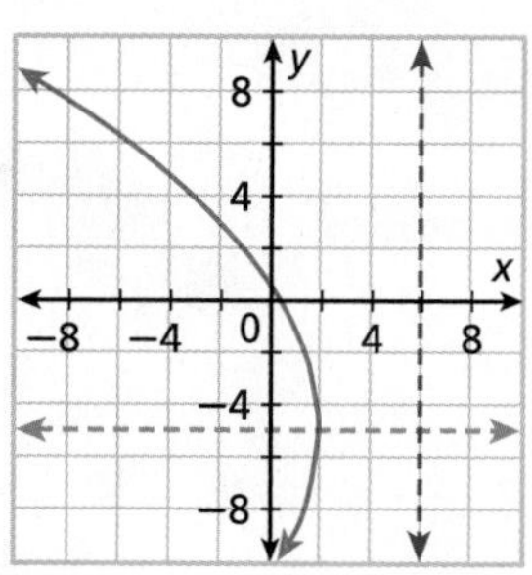

Find the vertex, value of *p*, axis of symmetry, focus, and directrix of each parabola. Then graph.

3a. $x - 1 = \frac{1}{12}(y - 3)^2$ **3b.** $y - 4 = -\frac{1}{2}(x - 8)^2$

Light or sound waves collected by a parabola will be reflected by the curve through the focus of the parabola, as shown in the figure. Waves emitted from the focus will be reflected out parallel to the axis of symmetry of a parabola. This property is used in communications technology.

EXAMPLE  4 Using the Equation of a Parabola

Engineers are constructing a parabolic microphone for use at sporting events. The surface of the parabolic microphone will reflect sounds to the focus of the microphone at the end of a part called a feedhorn. The equation for the cross section of the parabolic microphone dish is $x = \frac{1}{32}y^2$, measured in inches. How long should the engineers make the feedhorn?

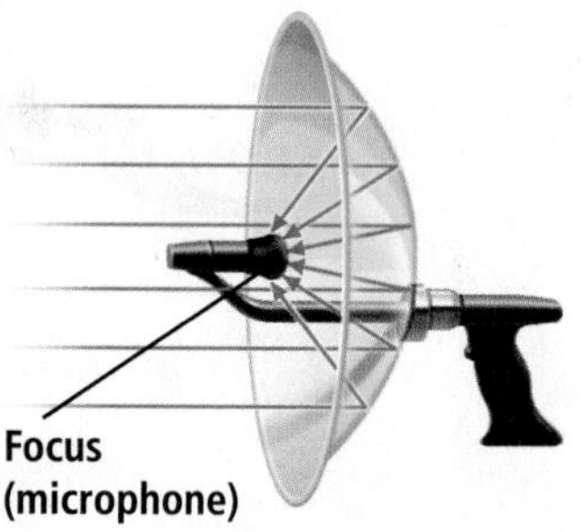

The equation for the cross section is in the form $x = \frac{1}{4p}y^2$, so $4p = 32$ and $p = 8$. The focus should be 8 inches from the vertex of the cross section. Therefore, the feedhorn should be 8 inches long.

4. Find the length of the feedhorn for a microphone with a cross section equation $x = \frac{1}{44}y^2$.

THINK AND DISCUSS

1. By using the standard form of a parabola's equation, how can you tell which direction a parabola opens?

2. How does knowing the value of *p* help you in finding the focus and the directrix of a parabola?

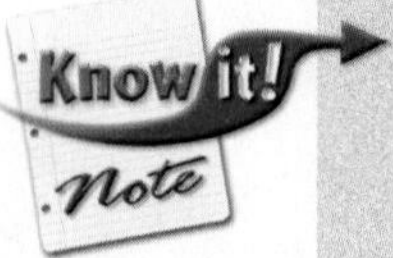

3. GET ORGANIZED Copy and complete the graphic organizer. Sketch an example and give an equation for each type of parabola.

Opens upward	Opens right
Parabola	
Opens downward	Opens left

10-5 Exercises

go.hrw.com
Homework Help Online
KEYWORD: MB7 10-5
Parent Resources Online
KEYWORD: MB7 Parent

GUIDED PRACTICE

1. **Vocabulary** Describe the relationship between a parabola and its *directrix*.

SEE EXAMPLE 1 p. 751

Use the distance formula to find the equation of a parabola with the given focus and directrix.

2. $F(0, -5)$, $y = 5$
3. $F(7, 0)$, $x = -7$
4. $F(-3, 0)$, $x = 6$

SEE EXAMPLE 2 p. 752

Write the equation in standard form for each parabola.

5. 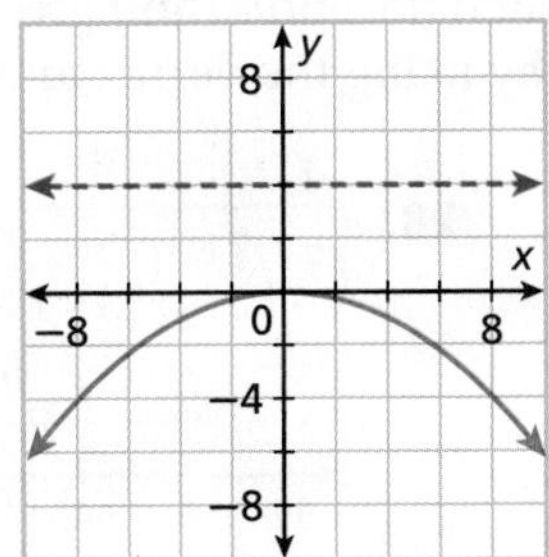

6. 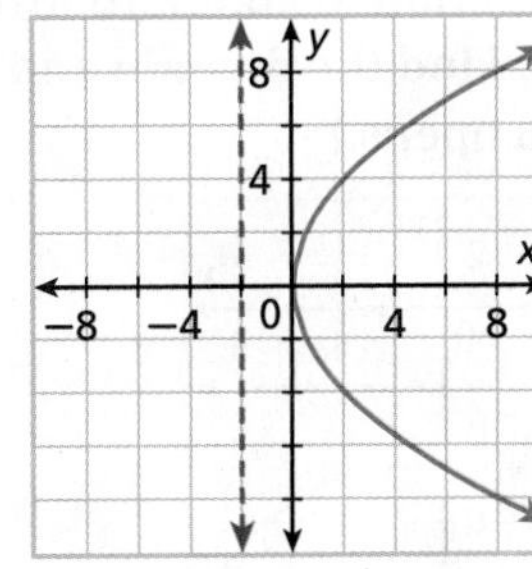

7. 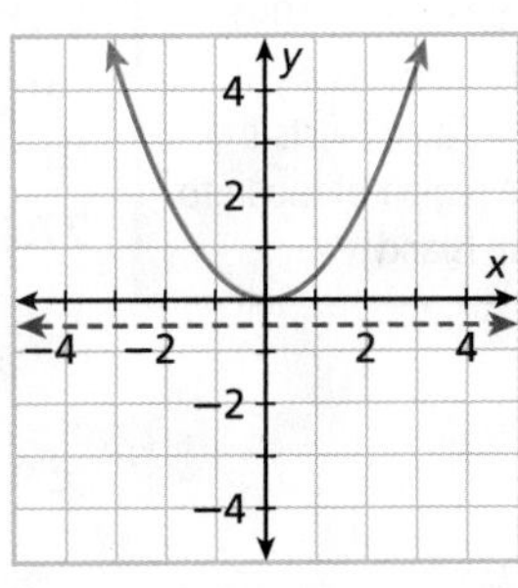

8. vertex $(0, 0)$, focus $(0, 1)$
9. vertex $(0, 0)$, focus $(-8, 0)$

SEE EXAMPLE 3 p. 753

Find the vertex, value of *p*, axis of symmetry, focus, and directrix of each parabola, and then graph.

10. $y = \frac{1}{32}(x + 2)^2$
11. $x = \frac{1}{24}(y - 4)^2$
12. $y + 1 = \frac{1}{16}(x - 2)^2$

SEE EXAMPLE 4 p. 754

13. **Communications** The equation for the cross section of a parabolic satellite TV dish is $y = \frac{1}{38}x^2$, measured in inches. How far is the focus from the vertex of the cross section?

PRACTICE AND PROBLEM SOLVING

Independent Practice

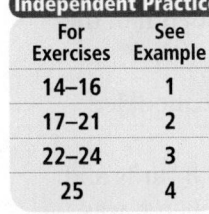

For Exercises	See Example
14–16	1
17–21	2
22–24	3
25	4

Extra Practice

Skills Practice p. S23
Application Practice p. S41

Use the distance formula to find the equation of a parabola with the given focus and directrix.

14. $F(0, 3)$, $y = -5$
15. $F(-2, 0)$, $x = 8$
16. $F(7, 0)$, $x = -1$

Write the equation in standard form for each parabola.

17. 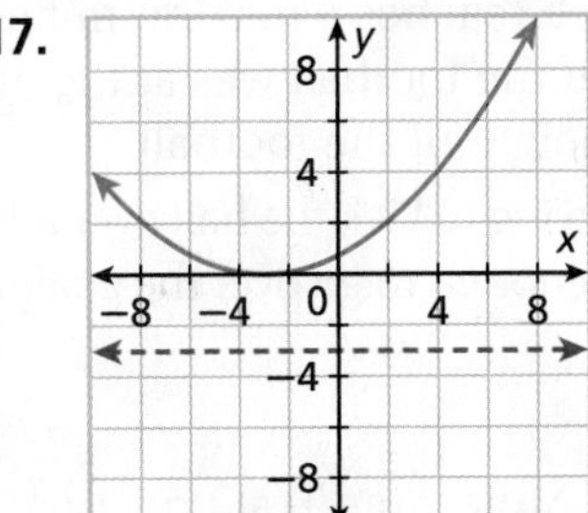

18. 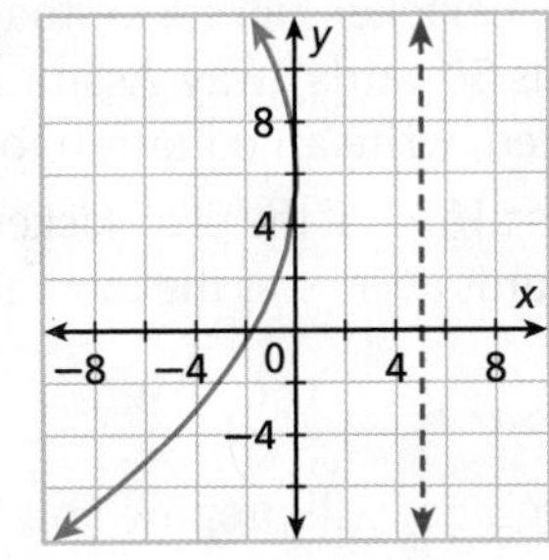

19. 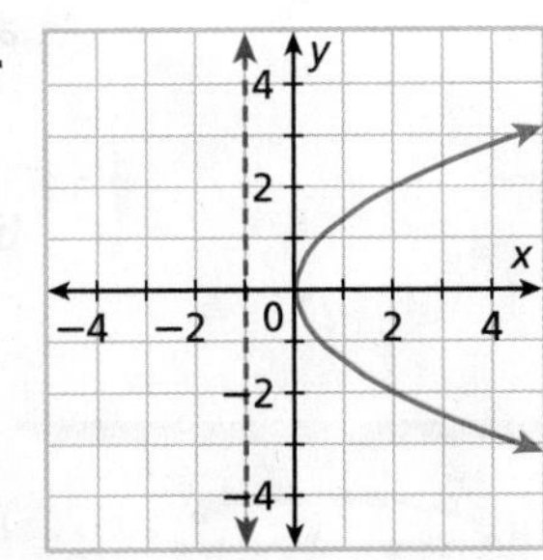

20. vertex $(0, 0)$, focus $\left(\frac{1}{2}, 0\right)$
21. vertex $(0, 0)$, focus $(0, -6)$

Find the vertex, value of *p*, axis of symmetry, focus, and directrix of each parabola, and then graph.

22. $y = \frac{1}{8}(x - 1)^2$
23. $x = 2y^2 + 1$
24. $x - 2 = \frac{1}{2}(y + 1)^2$

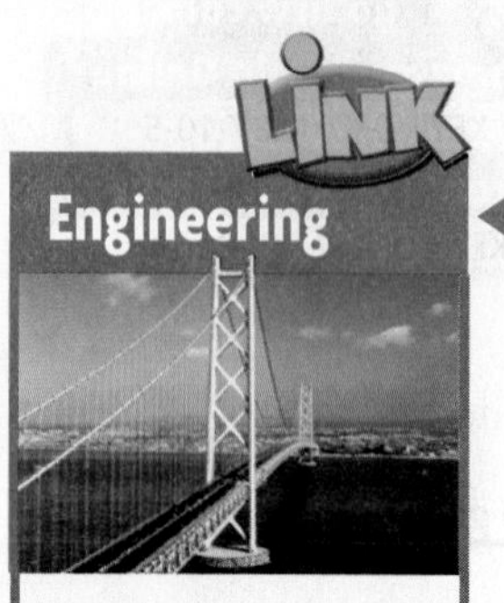

Engineering

The Akashi-Kaikyo Bridge is the longest suspension bridge in the world with a main span of 1991 m. Also known as the Pearl Bridge, it connects the Kobe region of Japan to Awaji Island.

25. **Communications** Find an equation for a cross section of a parabolic microphone whose feedhorn is 9 inches long if the end of the feedhorn is placed at the origin.

26. **Engineering** The main cables of a suspension bridge are ideally parabolic. The cables over a bridge that is 400 feet long are attached to towers that are 100 feet tall. The lowest point of the cable is 40 feet above the bridge.

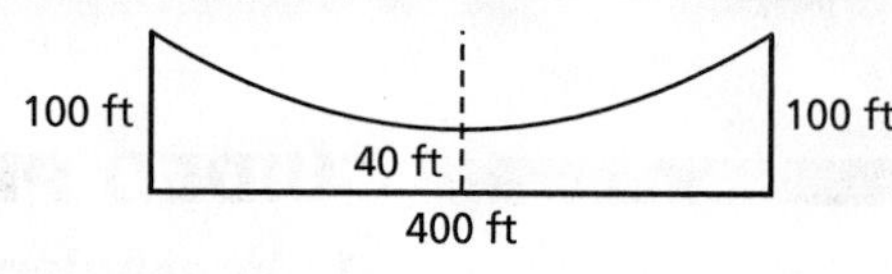

   a. Find the coordinates of the vertex and the tops of the towers if the bridge represents the x-axis and the axis of symmetry is the y-axis.
   b. Find an equation that can be used to model the cables.

Write the equation in standard form for each parabola, and give the domain and range. (*Hint:* Find the domain and range by using the vertex and the direction that the parabola opens.)

27.

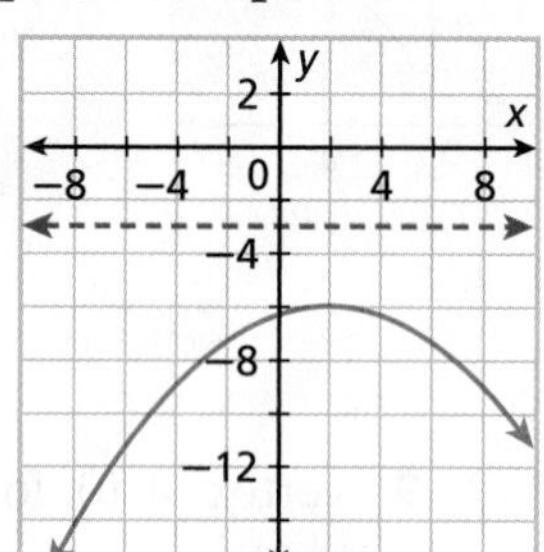

28.

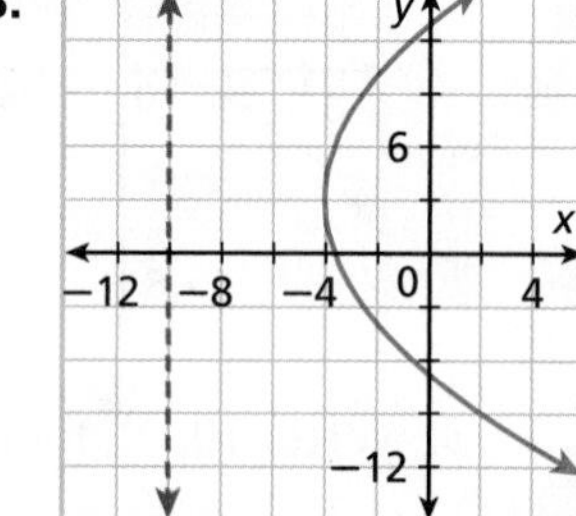

29. vertex $(-7, -3)$, focus $(2, -3)$
30. vertex $(5, -2)$, focus $(5, -8)$
31. focus $(0, 0)$, directrix $y = 10$
32. focus $(2, 6)$, directrix $y = -8$
33. focus $(4, -5)$, directrix $x = 12$
34. focus $(-3, 1)$, directrix $x = -15$

35. **Engineering** A spotlight has parabolic cross sections.
   a. Write an equation for a cross section of the spotlight if the bulb is 5 inches from the vertex and the vertex is placed at the origin.
   b. Write an equation for a cross section of the spotlight if the bulb is 4 inches from the vertex and the bulb is placed at the origin.
   c. If the spotlight has a diameter of 24 inches at its opening, find the depth of the spotlight if the bulb is 5 inches from the vertex.

36. **Sports** When a football is kicked, the path that the ball travels can be modeled by a parabola.
   a. A placekicker kicks a football, which reaches a maximum height of 8 yards and lands 50 yards away. Assuming that the football was at the origin when it was kicked, write an equation for the height of the football.
   b. **What if...?** If the placekicker was trying to kick the ball over a 10-foot-high goalpost 40 yards away, was the football high enough to go over the goalpost? Explain.

MULTI-STEP TEST PREP

37. This problem will prepare you for the Multi-Step Test Prep on page 758.

The path of a comet is modeled by the parabola $y = -\frac{1}{532}(x + 96)^2 + 174$, where each unit of the coordinate plane represents 1 million kilometers.
   a. The Sun is at the focus of the parabolic path. Find the coordinates of the Sun.
   b. How close does the comet come to the Sun?
   c. What are the coordinates of the comet when it is at its closest point to the Sun?

Graph each equation. Identify the vertex, value of p, axis of symmetry, focus, and directrix for each equation.

38. $20(y-2) = (x+6)^2$

39. $y = -2(x+4)^2 + 5$

40. $(y+7)^2 = \frac{x}{16}$

41. $x + 3 = \frac{1}{8}(y-2)^2$

42. Critical Thinking Find the distance d from the focus to the points on the parabola that are on the line perpendicular to the axis of symmetry and through the focus. Explain your answer.

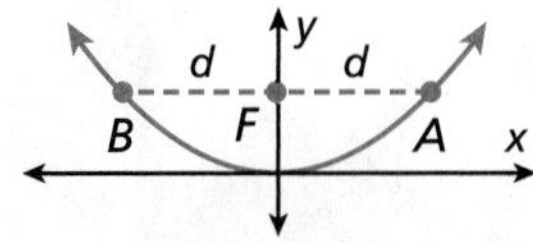

43. Write About It Explain how changing the value of p will affect the vertex, focus, and directrix of the parabola $y - k = \frac{1}{4p}(x-h)^2$.

44. The graph of which of the following parabolas opens to the left?

Ⓐ $16y - 4x^2 = 12$ Ⓑ $16y + 4x^2 = 12$ Ⓒ $16x - 4y^2 = 12$ Ⓓ $16x + 4y^2 = 12$

45. Which of the following is the axis of symmetry for the graph of $x - 4 = \frac{1}{8}(y+2)^2$?

Ⓕ $x = 0$ Ⓖ $y = -2$ Ⓗ $x = 4$ Ⓙ $y = 8$

46. Which of the following graphs has the directrix $y = 4$?

Ⓐ $y + 3 = \frac{1}{4}(x-1)^2$

Ⓑ $y - 5 = \frac{1}{4}(x+2)^2$

Ⓒ $x - 5 = \frac{1}{4}(y+4)^2$

Ⓓ $x + 3 = \frac{1}{4}(y-2)^2$

47. Short Response What are the coordinates of the focus for the graph of $x - 3 = \frac{1}{16}y^2$?

CHALLENGE AND EXTEND

Write the equation in standard form for each parabola.

48. vertex $(6, 8)$, contains the point $(4, -2)$, axis of symmetry $x = 6$

49. focus $(6, 5)$, axis of symmetry $x = 6$, contains the point $(10, 5)$

Multi-Step The latus rectum of a parabola is the line segment perpendicular to the axis of symmetry through the focus, with endpoints on the parabola. Find the length of the latus rectum of each parabola.

50. $y = \frac{1}{8}x^2$

51. $y - k = \frac{1}{4p}(x-h)^2$

SPIRAL REVIEW

52. Write and graph a system of linear inequalities whose solution region is the triangle given by the vertices $(0, 2)$, $(1, 4)$, and $(2, 1)$. *(Lesson 3-3)*

Find the inverse of each function. Tell whether the inverse is a function, and state its domain and range. *(Lesson 9-5)*

53. $f(x) = 4x + 22$ **54.** $f(x) = 3x^2 + 1$ **55.** $f(x) = \frac{x-2}{3}$ **56.** $f(x) = \frac{1}{x-1}$

Find the vertices, co-vertices, and asymptotes of each hyperbola, and then graph. *(Lesson 10-4)*

57. $\frac{x^2}{81} - \frac{y^2}{25} = 1$ **58.** $\frac{y^2}{9} - \frac{x^2}{16} = 1$ **59.** $\frac{y^2}{64} - \frac{x^2}{4} = 1$ **60.** $\frac{x^2}{49} - \frac{y^2}{36} = 1$

CHAPTER 10

SECTION 10A

Understanding Conic Sections

The Solar System Johannes Kepler (1571–1630) is generally credited as the first astronomer to recognize the role of the conic sections in describing our solar system. Kepler's first law of planetary motion states that the path of every planet is an ellipse with the Sun at one focus.

1. Although the orbit of Earth around the Sun is elliptical, it very closely resembles a circle. The orbit can be modeled by $x^2 + y^2 = 8649$, where the Sun is at the origin and each unit of the coordinate plane represents 1 million miles. How far does Earth travel in 1 year as it makes one complete orbit?

2. The figure shows the elliptical orbit of Mercury, whose minimum distance to the Sun is 29 million miles and whose maximum distance to the Sun is 43 million miles. According to Kepler's laws, the average distance of a planet to the Sun is equal to half the length of the orbit's major axis. What is the average distance of Mercury to the Sun?

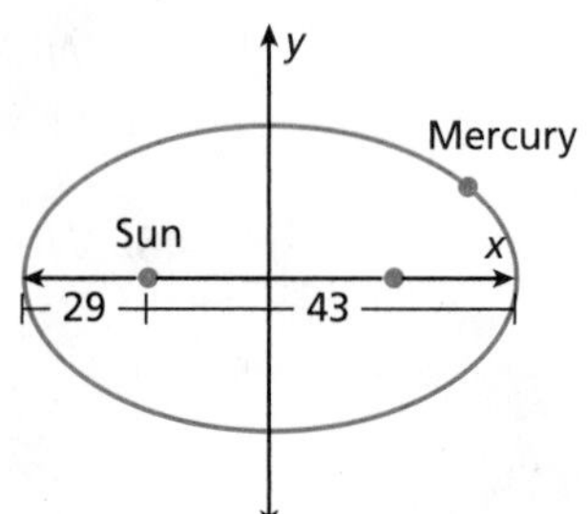

3. Write an equation that models the orbit of Mercury.

4. A comet that passes through the solar system just once has a path that is modeled by a hyperbola or a parabola. Astronomers discover a comet whose path is modeled by $\frac{x^2}{2500} - \frac{y^2}{37{,}500} = 1$, with the Sun at one focus. How close will the comet come to the Sun?

5. The path of another comet is modeled by $336(x - 89) = (y - 62)^2$, with the Sun at the focus. In this model, what are the coordinates of the Sun? How close will this comet come to the Sun?

READY TO GO ON?

Quiz for Lessons 10-1 Through 10-5

10-1 Introduction to Conic Sections

1. The delivery area of a furniture store extends to the locations $(-7, 12)$ and $(5, -4)$. Write an equation for the delivery area of the store if a line between the locations represents a diameter of the delivery area.

Identify and describe each conic section.

2. $\frac{(x+2)^2}{64} + \frac{(y-8)^2}{64} = 1$
3. $25x^2 + 36y^2 = 900$
4. $x = \frac{y^2}{3} + 2$
5. $\frac{y^2}{25} - \frac{x^2}{25} = 1$

10-2 Circles

Write the equation of each circle.

6. center $(-3, 7)$ and radius $r = 12$
7. center $(4, -2)$ and containing the point $(-4, 13)$
8. Write the equation of the line that is tangent to $x^2 + y^2 = 225$ at $(9, -12)$.

10-3 Ellipses

Find the center, vertices, co-vertices, and foci of each ellipse. Then graph.

9. $\frac{x^2}{81} + \frac{y^2}{100} = 1$
10. $4(x-2)^2 + 16(y+3)^2 = 64$
11. Write the equation of the ellipse with center $(3, 5)$, vertex $(-10, 5)$, and focus $(8, 5)$.
12. A semi-elliptical bridge over a stream that is 30 feet wide must be 12 feet high at its highest point to accommodate boat traffic. Write an equation for a cross section of the bridge.

10-4 Hyperbolas

Find the center, vertices, co-vertices, foci, and asymptotes for each hyperbola. Then graph.

13. $\frac{y^2}{49} - \frac{x^2}{25} = 1$
14. $\frac{(x-5)^2}{36} - \frac{(y+3)^2}{9} = 1$
15. Write the equation of the hyperbola with vertices $(2, 3)$ and $(2, 9)$ and co-vertex $(7, 6)$.

10-5 Parabolas

Find the vertex, value of *p*, axis of symmetry, focus, and directrix for each parabola. Then graph.

16. $x = -\frac{1}{12}y^2$
17. $y = 2(x+3)^2 + 4$
18. Write the equation of the parabola with focus $(5, 2)$ and directrix $x = 1$.
19. A cross section of a parabolic microphone has the equation $35x = y^2$, where x and y are measured in inches. How far from the vertex of the microphone should the feedhorn be placed?

10-6 Identifying Conic Sections

Objectives
Identify and transform conic sections.

Use the method of completing the square to identify and graph conic sections.

Why learn this?

The path of an airplane in a dive can be modeled by a branch of a hyperbola or a parabola. (See Example 4.)

In Lessons 10-2 through 10-5, you learned about the four conic sections. Recall the equations of conic sections in standard form. In these forms, the characteristics of the conic sections can be identified.

Know it! Note

Standard Forms for the Conic Sections with Center (h, k)

Circle	$(x-h)^2+(y-k)^2=r^2$	
	HORIZONTAL AXIS	**VERTICAL AXIS**
Ellipse	$\frac{(x-h)^2}{a^2}+\frac{(y-k)^2}{b^2}=1$	$\frac{(x-h)^2}{b^2}+\frac{(y-k)^2}{a^2}=1$
Hyperbola	$\frac{(x-h)^2}{a^2}-\frac{(y-k)^2}{b^2}=1$	$\frac{(y-k)^2}{a^2}-\frac{(x-h)^2}{b^2}=1$
Parabola	$x-h=\frac{1}{4p}(y-k)^2$	$y-k=\frac{1}{4p}(x-h)^2$

EXAMPLE 1 Identifying Conic Sections in Standard Form

Identify the conic section that each equation represents.

A $\frac{(x-7)^2}{5^2}-\frac{(y+2)^2}{2^2}=1$

This equation is of the same form as a hyperbola with a horizontal transverse axis.

B $y-3=\frac{1}{12}(x-4)^2$

This equation is of the same form as a parabola with a vertical axis of symmetry.

C $\frac{(x-1)^2}{8^2}+\frac{(y-1)^2}{10^2}=1$

This equation is of the same form as an ellipse with a vertical major axis.

Identify the conic section that each equation represents.

1a. $x^2+(y+14)^2=11^2$ **1b.** $\frac{(y-6)^2}{2^2}-\frac{(x-1)^2}{21^2}=1$

Student to Student

Classifying Conic Sections

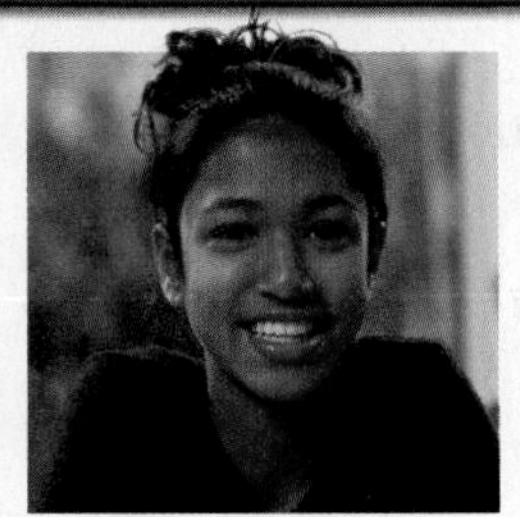

Mercedes Raya
Central High School

I can classify an equation in standard form just by looking. This is a good way for me to check my work.

Only one squared term → it's a parabola.

A squared term minus a squared term → it's a hyperbola.

A squared term plus a squared term → it's a circle or an ellipse.

All conic sections can be written in the general form $Ax^2 + Bxy + Cy^2 + Dx + Ey + F = 0$. The conic section represented by an equation in general form can be determined by the coefficients.

Classifying Conic Sections

For an equation of the form $Ax^2 + Bxy + Cy^2 + Dx + Ey + F = 0$ (A, B, and C do not all equal 0.)

CONIC SECTION	COEFFICIENTS
Circle	$B^2 - 4AC < 0$, $B = 0$, and $A = C$
Ellipse	$B^2 - 4AC < 0$ and either $B \neq 0$ or $A \neq C$
Hyperbola	$B^2 - 4AC > 0$
Parabola	$B^2 - 4AC = 0$

EXAMPLE 2 **Identifying Conic Sections in General Form**

Identify the conic section that each equation represents.

A $6x^2 + 9y^2 + 12x - 15y - 25 = 0$

$A = 6, B = 0, C = 9$ — *Identify the values for A, B, and C.*

$B^2 - 4AC$

$0^2 - 4(6)(9)$ — *Substitute into $B^2 - 4AC$.*

-216 — *Simplify. The conic is either a circle or an ellipse.*

$A \neq C$ — *The conic is not a circle.*

Because $B^2 - 4AC < 0$ and $A \neq C$, the equation represents an ellipse.

B $4x^2 + 4xy + y^2 - 12x + 8y + 36 = 0$

$A = 4, B = 4, C = 1$ — *Identify the values for A, B, and C.*

$B^2 - 4AC$

$4^2 - 4(4)(1)$ — *Substitute into $B^2 - 4AC$.*

0 — *Simplify.*

Because $B^2 - 4AC = 0$, the equation represents a parabola.

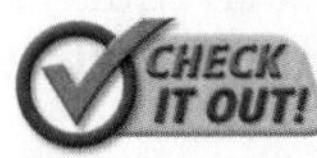

Identify the conic section that each equation represents.

2a. $9x^2 + 9y^2 - 18x - 12y - 50 = 0$

2b. $12x^2 + 24xy + 12y^2 + 25y = 0$

If you are given the equation of a conic in standard form, you can write the equation in general form by expanding the binomials.

If you are given the general form of a conic section, you can use the method of completing the square from Lesson 5-4 to write the equation in standard form.

EXAMPLE 3 Finding the Standard Form of the Equation for a Conic Section

Find the standard form of each equation by completing the square. Then identify and graph each conic.

A $x^2 - 12x - 16y + 36 = 0$

$x^2 - 12x + \blacksquare = 16y - 36 + \blacksquare$ *Prepare to complete the square in x.*

$x^2 - 12x + \left(\frac{-12}{2}\right)^2 = 16y - 36 + \left(\frac{-12}{2}\right)^2$ *Add $\left(-\frac{12}{2}\right)^2$, or 36, to both sides to complete the square.*

$(x-6)^2 = 16y$ *Factor and simplify.*

$\frac{1}{16}(x-6)^2 = y$ *Divide both sides by 16.*

$y = \frac{1}{16}(x-6)^2$ *Rewrite in standard form.*

Because the conic is of the form $y - k = \frac{1}{4p}(x-h)^2$, it is a parabola with vertex $(6, 0)$ and $p = 4$, and it opens upward. The focus is $(6, 4)$ and the directrix is $y = -4$.

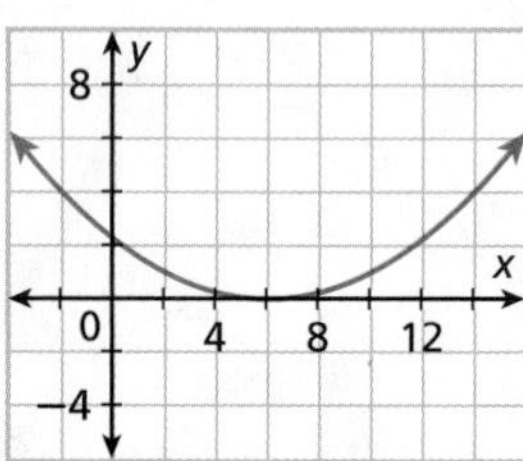

Remember!

You must factor out the leading coefficient of x^2 and y^2 before completing the square.

B $x^2 + 4y^2 + 4x - 24y + 36 = 0$

$x^2 + 4x + \blacksquare + 4y^2 - 24y + \blacksquare = -36 + \blacksquare + \blacksquare$ *Rearrange to prepare for completing the square in x and y.*

$x^2 + 4x + \blacksquare + 4(y^2 - 6y + \blacksquare) = -36 + \blacksquare + \blacksquare$ *Factor 4 from the y terms.*

$x^2 + 4x + \left(\frac{4}{2}\right)^2 + 4\left[y^2 - 6y + \left(-\frac{6}{2}\right)^2\right] = -36 + \left(\frac{4}{2}\right)^2 + 4\left(-\frac{6}{2}\right)^2$ *Complete both squares.*

$(x+2)^2 + 4(y-3)^2 = 4$ *Factor and simplify.*

$\frac{(x+2)^2}{4} + \frac{(y-3)^2}{1} = 1$ *Divide both sides by 4.*

Because the conic is of the form $\frac{(x-h)^2}{a^2} + \frac{(y-k)^2}{b^2} = 1$, it is an ellipse with center $(-2, 3)$, horizontal major axis length 4, and minor axis length 2. The co-vertices are $(-2, 4)$ and $(-2, 2)$, and the vertices are $(-4, 3)$ and $(0, 3)$.

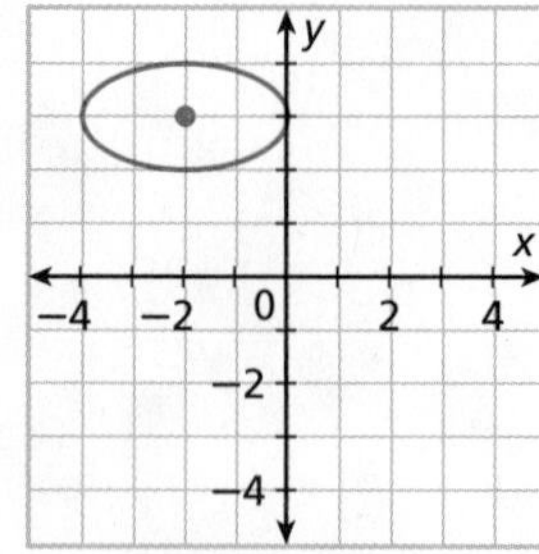

Find the standard form of each equation by completing the square. Then identify and graph each conic.

3a. $y^2 - 9x + 16y + 64 = 0$

3b. $16x^2 + 9y^2 - 128x + 108y + 436 = 0$

EXAMPLE 4 Aviation Application

At an air show, an airplane makes a dive that can be modeled by the equation $-4x^2 + 16y^2 - 16x + 32y - 64 = 0$, measured in hundreds of feet, with the ground represented by the x-axis. How close to the ground does the airplane pass?

The graph of $-4x^2 + 16y^2 - 16x + 32y - 64 = 0$ is a conic section. Write the equation in standard form.

$$-4x^2 - 16x + \blacksquare + 16y^2 + 32y + \blacksquare = 64 + \blacksquare + \blacksquare$$

Rearrange to prepare for completing the square in x and y.

$$-4(x^2 + 4x + \blacksquare) + 16(y^2 + 2y + \blacksquare) = 64 + \blacksquare + \blacksquare$$

Factor −4 from the x terms and 16 from the y terms.

$$-4\left[x^2 + 4x + \left(\frac{4}{2}\right)^2\right] + 16\left[y^2 + 2y + \left(\frac{2}{2}\right)^2\right] = 64 - 4\left(\frac{4}{2}\right)^2 + 16\left(\frac{2}{2}\right)^2$$

Complete both squares.

$$16(y+1)^2 - 4(x+2)^2 = 64 \qquad \textit{Simplify.}$$

$$\frac{(y+1)^2}{4} - \frac{(x+2)^2}{16} = 1 \qquad \textit{Divide both sides by 64.}$$

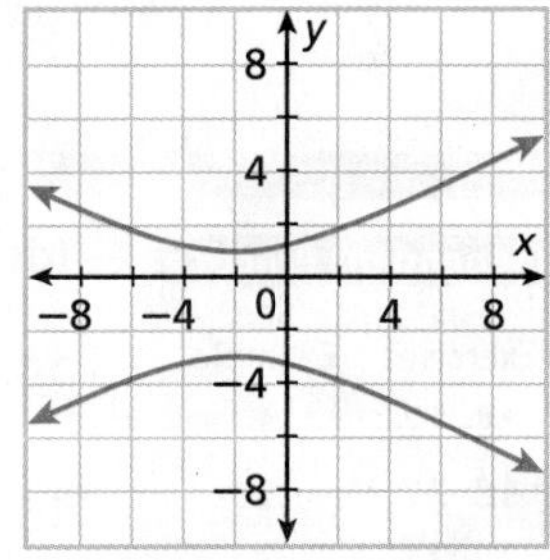

Because the conic is of the form $\frac{(y-k)^2}{a^2} - \frac{(x-h)^2}{b^2} = 1$, it is a hyperbola with vertical transverse axis length 4 and center $(-2, -1)$. The vertices are then $(-2, 1)$ and $(-2, -3)$. Because distance above ground is always positive, the airplane will be on the upper branch of the hyperbola. The relevant vertex is $(-2, 1)$ with y-coordinate 1.

The minimum height of the plane is 100 feet.

4. An airplane makes a dive that can be modeled by the equation $-16x^2 + 9y^2 + 96x + 36y - 252 = 0$, measured in hundreds of feet. How close to the ground does the airplane pass?

THINK AND DISCUSS

1. In the equation $Ax^2 + Bxy + Cy^2 + Dx + Ey + F = 0$, if $B = 0$, what must be true about either A or C for the equation to represent a parabola?

2. When solving by completing the square, what must be added to both sides of the equation if one side has $5x^2 - 30x$? Explain.

3. GET ORGANIZED Copy and complete the graphic organizer. Give an example of coefficients for each conic section in general form.

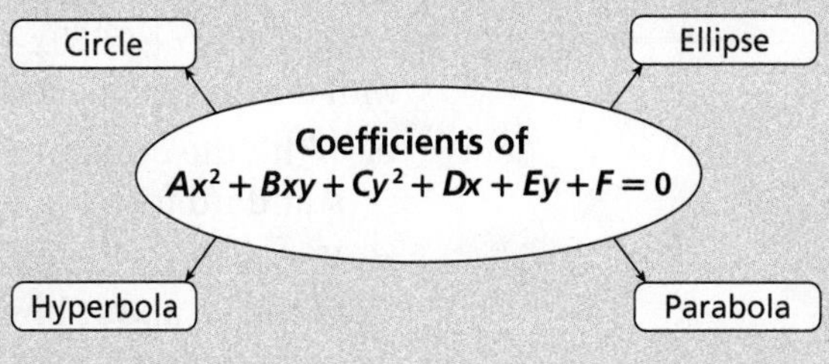

10-6 Exercises

go.hrw.com
Homework Help Online
KEYWORD: MB7 10-6
Parent Resources Online
KEYWORD: MB7 Parent

GUIDED PRACTICE

Identify the conic section that each equation represents.

SEE EXAMPLE 1 p. 760

1. $\dfrac{(x+4)^2}{2^2} + \dfrac{(y-3)^2}{3^2} = 1$
2. $\dfrac{(x-8)^2}{5^2} - \dfrac{y^2}{5^2} = 1$
3. $y + 9 = 4(x-1)^2$
4. $(x-2)^2 + (y-6)^2 = 13^2$

SEE EXAMPLE 2 p. 761

5. $12x^2 + 18y^2 - 8x + 9y - 10 = 0$
6. $-4y^2 + 15x + 12y - 8 = 0$
7. $10x^2 + 15xy + 10y^2 + 15x + 25y + 9 = 0$
8. $6x^2 = 14x + 12y^2 - 16y + 20$

SEE EXAMPLE 3 p. 762

Find the standard form of each equation by completing the square. Then identify and graph each conic.

9. $x^2 + y^2 - 16x + 10y + 53 = 0$
10. $x^2 + 14x - 12y + 97 = 0$
11. $25x^2 + 9y^2 + 72y - 81 = 0$
12. $16x^2 + 36y^2 + 160x - 432y + 1120 = 0$

SEE EXAMPLE 4 p. 763

13. **Multi-Step** A moth is circling an outdoor light in a path that can be modeled by the equation $4x^2 + 9y^2 - 108y = -288$, measured in inches. How close does the moth pass to a lizard located at the origin?

PRACTICE AND PROBLEM SOLVING

Independent Practice

For Exercises	See Example
14–17	1
18–21	2
22–31	3
32	4

Extra Practice
Skills Practice p. S23
Application Practice p. S41

Identify the conic section that each equation represents.

14. $\dfrac{(y-11)^2}{2^2} - \dfrac{(x+15)^2}{9^2} = 1$
15. $x - 4 = \dfrac{1}{16}(y-3)^2$
16. $(x+2)^2 + (y-4)^2 = 3^2$
17. $\dfrac{(x+2)^2}{6^2} + \dfrac{(y-7)^2}{8^2} = 1$
18. $12x^2 - 18y^2 - 18x - 12y + 12 = 0$
19. $7x^2 + 28x - 29y - 16 = 0$
20. $-12x^2 - 3y^2 + 7x + 9y - 5 = 0$
21. $12x^2 + 9y^2 - 2xy + 9 = 8y - 3y^2$

Find the standard form of each equation by completing the square. Then identify and graph each conic.

22. $x^2 + 20x - 4y + 100 = 0$
23. $x^2 + y^2 - 8y - 33 = 0$
24. $9x^2 + 36y^2 - 72x - 180 = 0$
25. $25x^2 - 4y^2 - 72y - 424 = 0$
26. $x^2 - 2x - 20y - 79 = 0$
27. $x^2 + y^2 + 10x + 4y + 9 = 0$
28. $64x^2 + 49y^2 + 256x - 196y - 2684 = 0$
29. $9x^2 - 4y^2 + 18x + 56y - 223 = 0$
30. $y^2 + 6x + 12y - 6 = 0$
31. $x^2 + y^2 - 5x + 9y + 10.5 = 0$

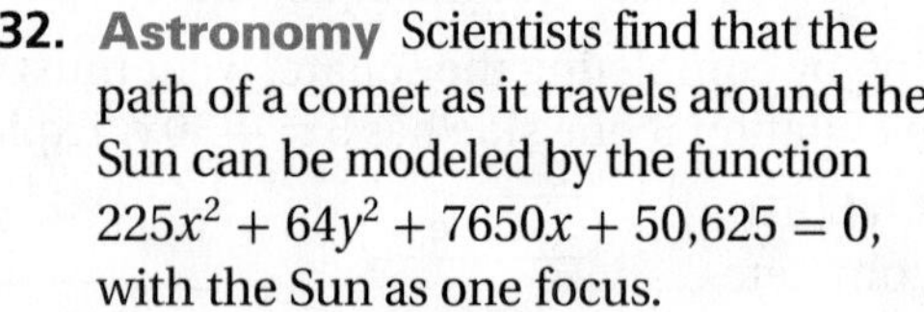

32. **Astronomy** Scientists find that the path of a comet as it travels around the Sun can be modeled by the function $225x^2 + 64y^2 + 7650x + 50{,}625 = 0$, with the Sun as one focus.
    a. Write the equation in standard form.
    b. If measurements are in millions of miles, about how close will the comet come to the sun?

Comet C/2001 Q4

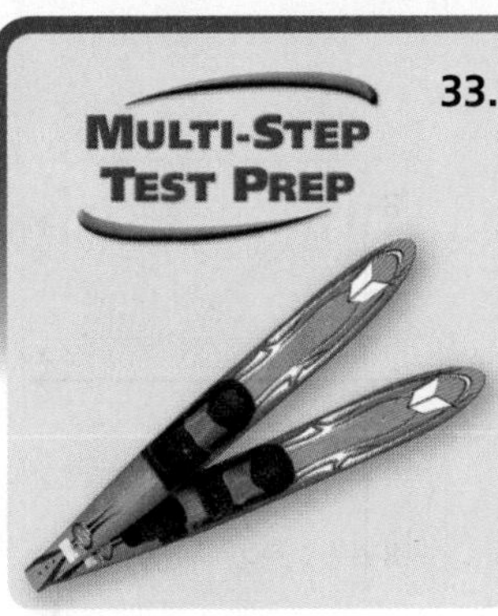

33. This problem will prepare you for the Multi-Step Test Prep on page 776.

A water-skier is towed along a path that can be modeled by $25x^2 + 4y^2 + 300x - 24y + 836 = 0$. Each unit of the coordinate plane represents 10 m.

a. What is the shape of the water-skier's path?

b. The edge of a dock is represented by the y-axis. How close does the water-skier come to the dock?

c. A second water-skier is towed along the same path. What is the maximum possible distance between the two water-skiers?

Write each equation in the form $Ax^2 + Bxy + Cy^2 + Dx + Ey + F = 0$.

34. $(x-7)^2 + (y+12)^2 = 81$ **35.** $\frac{(x-5)^2}{25} + \frac{(y+8)^2}{36} = 1$ **36.** $\frac{(x+10)^2}{49} - \frac{(y-6)^2}{81} = 1$

Determine whether the origin lies inside, outside, or on the graph of each equation.

37. $36x^2 + 4y^2 - 432x + 1152 = 0$ **38.** $4x^2 + 36y^2 - 48x = 0$

39. $16x^2 + 64y^2 - 192x + 16y - 447 = 0$ **40.** $3x^2 + 3y^2 = 147$

LINK Math History

In 1604, German astronomer Johannes Kepler introduced a new way of thinking about the conic sections—as a family of related curves. For example, the parabola could be considered simply a hyperbola with one focus at infinity.

41. Multi-Step A model of the solar system includes a satellite orbiting the Moon on a path that can be modeled by the equation $6x^2 + 6y^2 = 24$, measured in centimeters (1 cm:10,000 km). If the Moon is located at the point $(0, 38.4)$, how close will the satellite pass to the Moon in the model?

42. Critical Thinking What does the graph of $x^2 - xy = 0$ look like? Explain.

43. Agriculture A farmer is planning to fence in part of the farm. Placing the farmhouse at the origin, the farmer finds that the path for the fence can be modeled by the equation $x^2 + y^2 - 80x - 60y - 37{,}500 = 0$, measured in feet.

a. Write the equation in standard form.

b. Find the area enclosed by the fence.

c. Is the farmhouse inside or outside of the fence?

44. ///ERROR ANALYSIS/// In which case below was the conic section $4y^2 + 3x - 12y = 2x^2 + 18$ identified incorrectly? Explain the error.

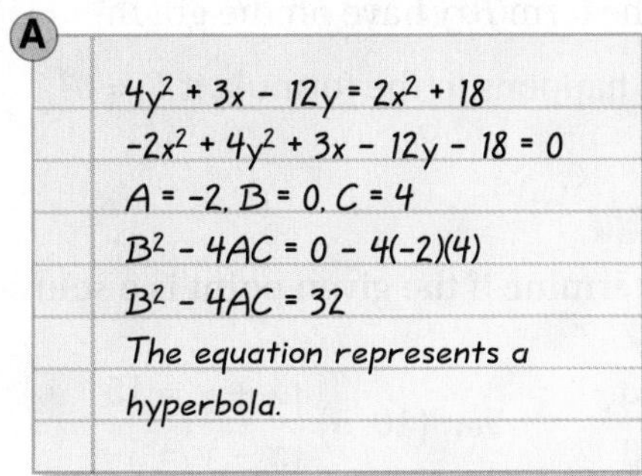
A

$4y^2 + 3x - 12y = 2x^2 + 18$
$-2x^2 + 4y^2 + 3x - 12y - 18 = 0$
$A = -2, B = 0, C = 4$
$B^2 - 4AC = 0 - 4(-2)(4)$
$B^2 - 4AC = 32$
The equation represents a hyperbola.

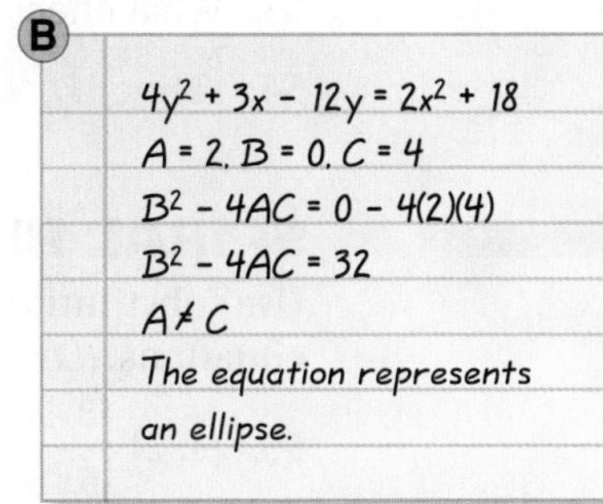
B

$4y^2 + 3x - 12y = 2x^2 + 18$
$A = 2, B = 0, C = 4$
$B^2 - 4AC = 0 - 4(2)(4)$
$B^2 - 4AC = 32$
$A \neq C$
The equation represents an ellipse.

45. Sports The path followed by a baseball after it is hit can be modeled by the equation $2x^2 - 800x + 1000y - 4000 = 0$, measured in feet.

a. Write the equation in standard form.

b. What is the maximum height of the ball?

c. What was the height of the ball when it was hit?

d. What if...? How would changing the 4000 in the equation to 5000 change your answers to parts **b** and **c?**

46. Write About It Compare the equations and graphs of parabolas and hyperbolas.

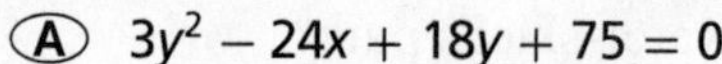

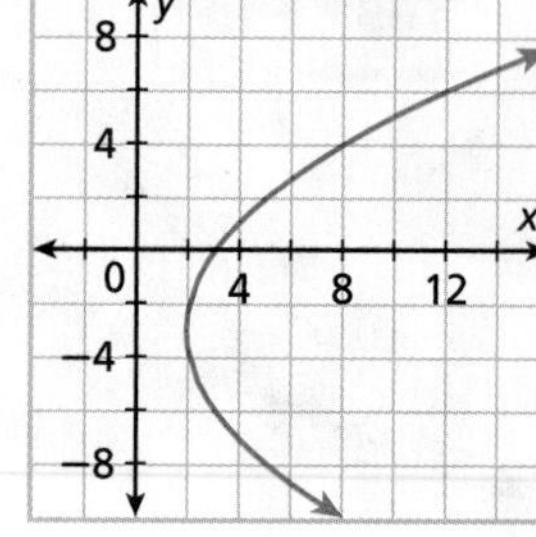

47. Which of the following is the equation for the graph shown?

Ⓐ $3y^2 - 24x + 18y + 75 = 0$

Ⓑ $5x^2 + 30x - 40y + 125 = 0$

Ⓒ $2x^2 - 3y^2 + 18x - 24y + 75 = 0$

Ⓓ $3x^2 + 2y^2 - 24x + 18y + 125 = 0$

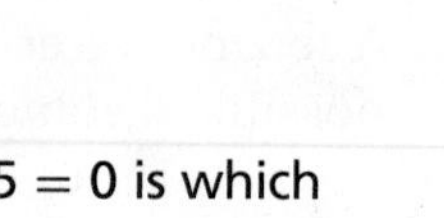

48. The graph of $9x^2 + 15x - 9y^2 - 15y + 25 = 0$ is which of the following?

Ⓕ Circle　　Ⓖ Ellipse

Ⓗ Hyperbola　　Ⓙ Parabola

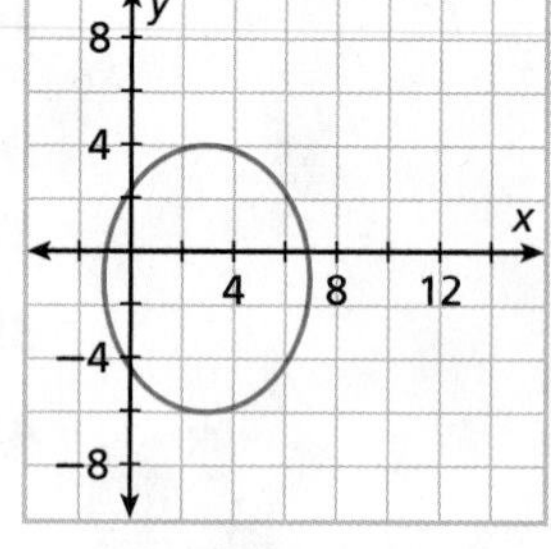

49. Which of the following is the equation for the graph shown?

Ⓐ $25x^2 + 25y^2 - 150x + 32y - 159 = 0$

Ⓑ $25x^2 - 150x + 32y = 159$

Ⓒ $25x^2 - 150x = 16y^2 - 32y + 159$

Ⓓ $16y^2 + 32y - 159 = 150x - 25x^2$

50. **Short Response** Write the equation $x^2 + y^2 + 8x - 6y + 16 = 0$ in standard form, and identify the conic section that it represents. What are the coordinates of the center?

CHALLENGE AND EXTEND

In order to graph the general form of conic sections, $Ax^2 + Bxy + Cy^2 + Dx + Ey + F = 0$, use the quadratic formula,

$$y = \frac{-(Bx+E) \pm \sqrt{(Bx+E)^2 - 4C(Ax^2 + Dx + F)}}{2C}$$ **, and a graphing calculator.**

51. Graph $4x^2 + 8xy - 9y^2 - 36 = 0$.

52. Graph $9x^2 - 12xy + 16y^2 - 144 = 0$.

53. What effect does the term Bxy have on the graph?

54. **What if...?** What happens to the formula if $C = 0$?

SPIRAL REVIEW

Use substitution to determine if the given point is a solution to the system of equations. *(Lesson 3-1)*

55. $(1, 2)\begin{cases} 8y - 3x = 13 \\ 5x + 6y = 18 \end{cases}$

56. $(10, 5)\begin{cases} x + y = 15 \\ x - y = 5 \end{cases}$

57. $(-2, 4)\begin{cases} x = 8 - y \\ 2x - 7y = -32 \end{cases}$

Use elimination to solve each system of equations. *(Lesson 3-2)*

58. $\begin{cases} 7x - 2y = 20 \\ -7x + 10y = 12 \end{cases}$

59. $\begin{cases} 3x + 4y = 16 \\ 2x - 4y = 4 \end{cases}$

60. $\begin{cases} x + 5y = -13 \\ -2x - 7y = 14 \end{cases}$

61. **Business** In 1980, a baseball card was valued at \$1.65. The value of the baseball card increased at a rate of 5% per year. *(Lesson 7-1)*

a. Write an equation to model the value of the baseball card where t is the number of years since 1980.

b. What was the value of the baseball card in 2004?

10-6 Technology LAB

Conic-Section Art

You can use graphs of conic sections to design and create pictures on the coordinate grid.

Use with Lesson 10-6

go.hrw.com
Lab Resources Online
KEYWORD: MB7 LAB10

Activity

Create a picture of a dragonfly by using one circle and six ellipses.

1 Graph the head by using $x^2 + (y - 5)^2 = 1$.

Solve for y, $y = \pm\sqrt{1 - x^2} + 5$, and graph. There are two ways to enter the two halves of the circle into the calculator.

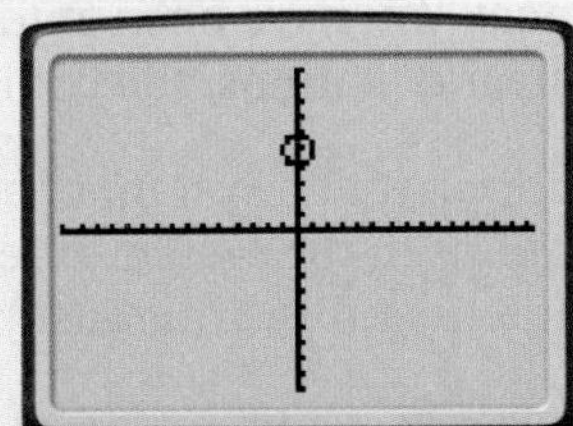

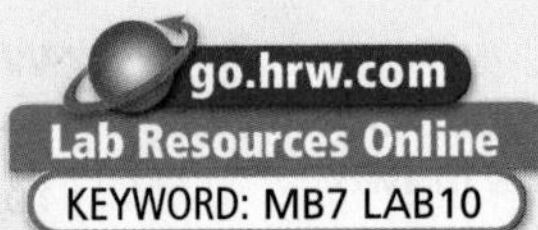

2 The part of the equation $\{-1, 1\}$ represents $\pm$ and can be used to graph both halves of a conic section at one time.

```
Plot1 Plot2 Plot3
\Y1={-1,1}√(1-X²
)+5
```

3 Graph the body parts and one right wing by using $x^2 + \frac{(y-2)^2}{4} = 1$, $x^2 + \frac{(y+4)^2}{16} = 1$, *and* $\frac{(x-6)^2}{25} + (y - 1)^2 = 1$.

```
Plot1 Plot2 Plot3
\Y2={-1,1}√(4-4X
²)+2
\Y3={-1,1}√(16-1
6X²)-4
\Y4={-1,1}√(1-((
X-6)²)/25)+1
```

4 Graph the other right wing and left wings by using $\frac{(x-5)^2}{16} + (y - 3)^2 = 1$, $\frac{(x+6)^2}{25} + (y - 1)^2 = 1$, *and* $\frac{(x+5)^2}{16} + (y - 3)^2 = 1$.

```
Plot1 Plot2 Plot3
\Y5={-1,1}√(1-((
X-5)²)/16)+3
\Y6={-1,1}√(1-((
X+6)²)/25)+1
\Y7={-1,1}√(1-((
X+5)²)/16)+3
```

5 The dragonfly is now complete.

Turn off the axes by using the **Format** function and setting **AxesOff**.

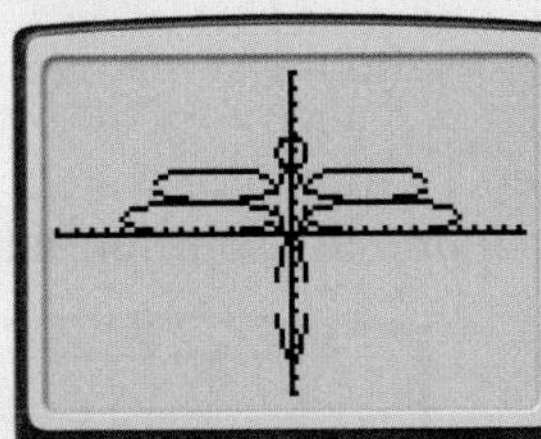

Try This

1. Create your own picture by using the graphs of conic sections. Use at least four conic sections. You may also use lines if necessary.
2. Trade equations with a classmate, and attempt to re-create his or her picture by using only the equations.

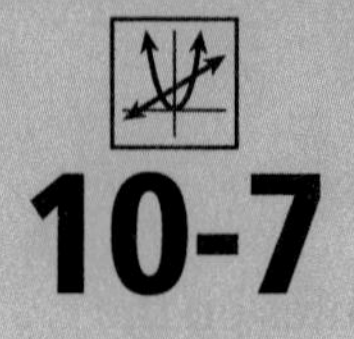

10-7 Solving Nonlinear Systems

Objective
Solve systems of equations in two variables that contain at least one second-degree equation.

Vocabulary
nonlinear system of equations

Who uses this?
Harbormasters can solve nonlinear systems to ensure that ships traveling in a variety of patterns do not collide. (See Example 4.)

A **nonlinear system of equations** is a system in which at least one of the equations is not linear. You have been studying one class of nonlinear equations, the conic sections.

The solution set of a system of equations is the set of points that make all of the equations in the system true, or where the graphs intersect. For systems of nonlinear equations, you must be aware of the number of possible solutions.

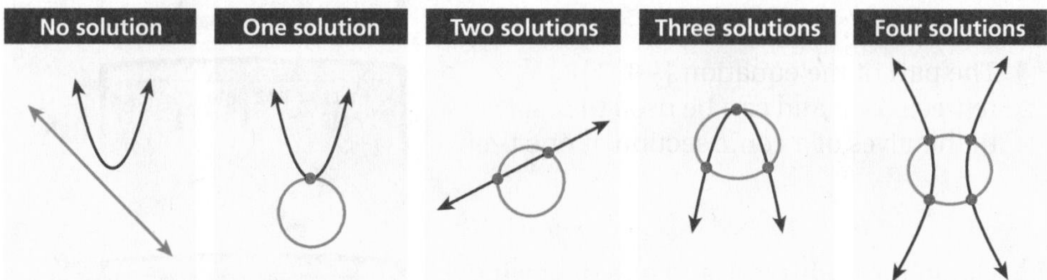

You can use your graphing calculator to find solutions to systems of nonlinear equations and to check algebraic solutions.

EXAMPLE 1 **Solving a Nonlinear System by Graphing**

Solve $\begin{cases} 2x - y = 1 \\ y + 7 = 2(x+1)^2 \end{cases}$ by graphing.

The graph of the first equation is a line, and the graph of the second equation is a parabola, so there may be as many as two points of intersection.

Step 1 Solve each equation for y.

$y = 2x - 1$ *Solve the first equation for y.*

$y = 2(x+1)^2 - 7$ *Solve the second equation for y.*

Step 2 Graph the system on your calculator, and use the intersect feature to find the solution set.

The points of intersection are $(-2, -5)$ and $(1, 1)$.

Check Substitute the points into each equation.

Check $(-2, -5)$.

y	$2x - 1$
-5	$2(-2) - 1$
-5	-5 ✓

y	$2(x+1)^2 - 7$
-5	$2(-2+1)^2 - 7$
-5	-5 ✓

Check $(1, 1)$.

y	$2x - 1$
1	$2(1) - 1$
1	1 ✓

y	$2(x+1)^2 - 7$
1	$2(1+1)^2 - 7$
1	1 ✓

The solution set of the system is $\{(-2, -5), (1, 1)\}$.

1. Solve $\begin{cases} 3x + y = 4.5 \\ y = \frac{1}{2}(x-3)^2 \end{cases}$ by graphing.

The substitution method for solving linear systems can also be used to solve nonlinear systems algebraically.

EXAMPLE 2 Solving a Nonlinear System by Substitution

Solve $\begin{cases} x^2 + y^2 = 25 \\ y + 5 = \frac{1}{2}x^2 \end{cases}$ **by using the substitution method.**

The graph of the first equation is a circle, and the graph of the second equation is a parabola. There may be as many as four points of intersection.

Step 1 It is simplest to solve for x^2 because both equations have x^2 terms.

$x^2 = 2y + 10$ *Solve for x^2 in the second equation.*

Step 2 Use substitution.

$(2y + 10) + y^2 = 25$ *Substitute this value into the first equation.*

$y^2 + 2y - 15 = 0$ *Simplify, and set equal to 0.*

$(y - 3)(y + 5) = 0$ *Factor.*

$y = 3$ or $y = -5$

Step 3 Substitute 3 and -5 into $x^2 = 2y + 10$ to find values for x.

$x^2 = 2(3) + 10$
$x^2 = 16$
$x = \pm 4$
$(4, 3)$ and $(-4, 3)$ are solutions.

$x^2 = 2(-5) + 10$
$x^2 = 0$
$x = 0$
$(0, -5)$ is a solution.

The solution set of the system is $\{(4, 3), (-4, 3), (0, -5)\}$.

Check Use a graphing calculator. The graph supports that there are three points of intersection.

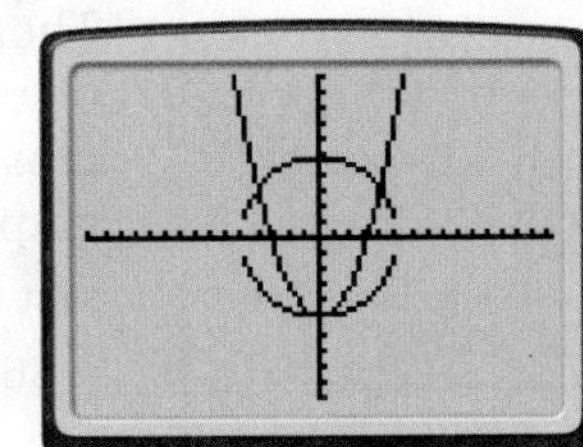

Solve each system of equations by using the substitution method.

2a. $\begin{cases} x + y = -1 \\ x^2 + y^2 = 25 \end{cases}$

2b. $\begin{cases} x^2 + y^2 = 25 \\ y - 5 = -x^2 \end{cases}$

The elimination method can also be used to solve systems of nonlinear equations.

EXAMPLE 3 Solving a Nonlinear System by Elimination

Solve $\begin{cases} 25x^2 + 9y^2 = 225 \\ 16x^2 - 9y^2 = 144 \end{cases}$ **by using the elimination method.**

The graph of the first equation is an ellipse, and the graph of the second equation is a hyperbola. There may be as many as four points of intersection.

Remember!

In Example 3, you can check your work on a graphing calculator.

Step 1 Eliminate y.

$$\begin{array}{rl} 25x^2 + 9y^2 = 225 & \\ + \; 16x^2 - 9y^2 = 144 & \textit{Add the equations.} \\ \hline 41x^2 \qquad = 369 & \\ x^2 = 9, \text{ so } x = \pm 3 & \textit{Solve for x.} \end{array}$$

Step 2 Find the values for y.

$$\begin{array}{rl} 25(9) + 9y^2 = 225 & \textit{Substitute 9 for } x^2. \\ 225 + 9y^2 = 225 & \textit{Simplify.} \\ y = 0 & \end{array}$$

The solution set of the system is $\{(3, 0), (-3, 0)\}$.

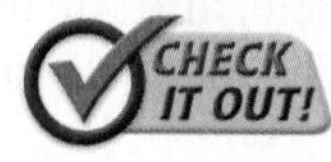

3. Solve $\begin{cases} 25x^2 + 9y^2 = 225 \\ 25x^2 - 16y^2 = 400 \end{cases}$ by using the elimination method.

EXAMPLE 4 *Problem-Solving Application*

A tour boat travels around a small island in a pattern that can be modeled by the equation $36x^2 + 25y^2 = 900$, with the island at the origin. Suppose that a fishing boat approaches the island on a path that can be modeled by the equation $y - 3 = \frac{1}{5}x^2$. Is there any danger of collision?

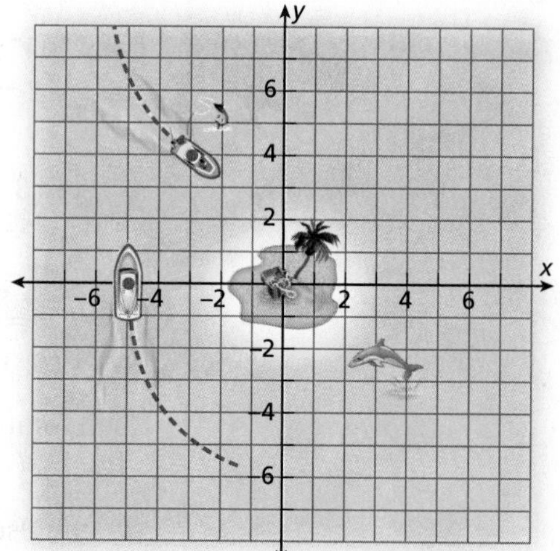

1 Understand the Problem

There is a potential danger of a collision if the two paths cross. The paths will cross if the graphs of the equations intersect.

List the important information:

- $36x^2 + 25y^2 = 900$ represents the path of the tour boat.
- $y - 3 = \frac{1}{5}x^2$ represents the path of the fishing boat.

2 Make a Plan

To see if the graphs intersect, solve the system $\begin{cases} 36x^2 + 25y^2 = 900 \\ y - 3 = \frac{1}{5}x^2 \end{cases}$

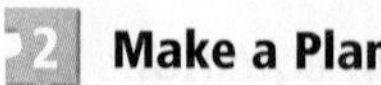

3 Solve

The graph of the first equation is an ellipse, and the graph of the second equation is a parabola. There may be as many as four points of intersection.

$x^2 = 5y - 15$ *Solve the second equation for x^2.*

$36(5y - 15) + 25y^2 = 900$ *Substitute this value into the first equation.*

$25y^2 + 180y - 1440 = 0$ *Simplify, and set equal to 0.*

$$y = \frac{-180 \pm \sqrt{180^2 - 4(25)(-1440)}}{2(25)}$$ *Use the quadratic formula.*

$y = \frac{-180 \pm 420}{50}$, or $y = 4.8$ and $y = -12$

Substitute $y = 4.8$ and $y = -12$ into $x^2 = 5y - 15$ to find the values for x.

$x^2 = 5(4.8) - 15$ $\quad$ $x^2 = 5(-12) - 15$

$x^2 = 9$, or $x = \pm 3$ $\quad$ $x^2 = -75$ *There are no real values of $\sqrt{-75}$.*

The real solutions to the system are $(3, 4.8)$ and $(-3, 4.8)$.

4 Look Back

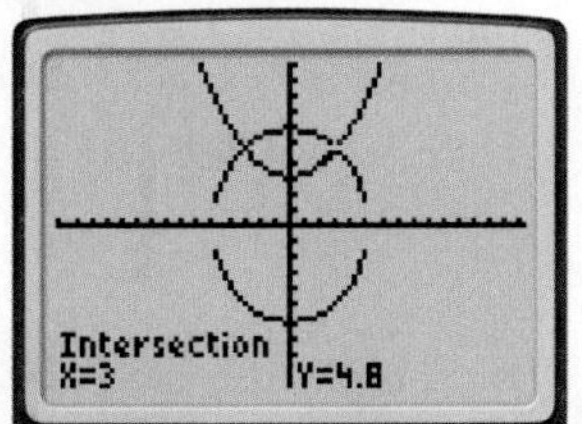

The graph supports that there are two points of intersection. Because the paths intersect, the boats are in danger of colliding if they arrive at the intersections $(3, 4.8)$ or $(-3, 4.8)$ at the same time.

4. What if...? Suppose the paths of the boats can be modeled by the system $\begin{cases} 36x^2 + 25y^2 = 900 \\ y + 2 = -\frac{1}{10}x^2 \end{cases}$.

Is there any danger of collision?

THINK AND DISCUSS

1. What can you tell about the graphs if the system has no solution?

2. Describe the steps for solving a nonlinear system of equations by graphing.

3. GET ORGANIZED Copy and complete the graphic organizer. Use the table to record information on the intersection of a hyperbola and a circle.

	Graph	Example
No Solution		
One Solution		
Two Solutions		
Three Solutions		
Four Solutions		

10-7 Exercises

go.hrw.com
Homework Help Online
KEYWORD: MB7 10-7
Parent Resources Online
KEYWORD: MB7 Parent

GUIDED PRACTICE

1. **Vocabulary** How is a *nonlinear system of equations* different from a linear system of equations?

SEE EXAMPLE 1 p. 768

Solve each system of equations by graphing.

2. $\begin{cases} y + 3x = 0 \\ y - 6 = -3x^2 \end{cases}$
3. $\begin{cases} y + 2 = \frac{1}{4}(x - 4)^2 \\ x - y = 6 \end{cases}$
4. $\begin{cases} y + 2x = 10 \\ x = \frac{1}{8}(y - 2)^2 \end{cases}$

SEE EXAMPLE 2 p. 769

Solve each system of equations by using the substitution method.

5. $\begin{cases} y + x = 17 \\ x^2 + y^2 = 169 \end{cases}$
6. $\begin{cases} x^2 + y^2 = 25 \\ y - x = 7 \end{cases}$
7. $\begin{cases} x^2 + y^2 = 36 \\ x + 2y = 16 \end{cases}$
8. $\begin{cases} x^2 + y^2 = 100 \\ x + 2 = \frac{1}{8}y^2 \end{cases}$
9. $\begin{cases} x^2 + y^2 = 36 \\ y + 6 = \frac{1}{3}x^2 \end{cases}$
10. $\begin{cases} x^2 + y^2 = 25 \\ y - 6.25 = -\frac{1}{4}x^2 \end{cases}$

SEE EXAMPLE 3 p. 770

Solve each system of equations by using the elimination method.

11. $\begin{cases} x^2 + y^2 = 20 \\ 4x^2 + y^2 = 68 \end{cases}$
12. $\begin{cases} 9x^2 + 5y^2 = 45 \\ 6y^2 - 27x^2 = 54 \end{cases}$
13. $\begin{cases} 4x^2 + 3y^2 = 12 \\ 5x^2 + 6y^2 = 30 \end{cases}$

SEE EXAMPLE 4 p. 770

14. **Radio** The range of a radio station is bounded by the circle with equation $x^2 + y^2 = 2025$. A stretch of highway near the station is modeled by the equation $y - 15 = \frac{1}{20}x^2$. At what points does a car on the highway enter or exit the broadcast range of the station?

PRACTICE AND PROBLEM SOLVING

Independent Practice

For Exercises	See Example
15–17	1
18–23	2
24–29	3
30	4

Extra Practice
Skills Practice p. S23
Application Practice p. S41

Solve each system of equations by graphing.

15. $\begin{cases} 2y - x = 10 \\ y - 3 = \frac{1}{8}(x + 4)^2 \end{cases}$
16. $\begin{cases} x - 6 = -\frac{1}{6}y^2 \\ 2x + y = 6 \end{cases}$
17. $\begin{cases} y^2 - x^2 = 36 \\ 2x + y = -\frac{3}{2} \end{cases}$

Solve each system of equations by using the substitution method.

18. $\begin{cases} x^2 + y^2 = 13 \\ x - y = 1 \end{cases}$
19. $\begin{cases} y^2 - 4x^2 = 16 \\ y - x = 4 \end{cases}$
20. $\begin{cases} x^2 - y^2 = 16 \\ x + y^2 = 4 \end{cases}$
21. $\begin{cases} y = \frac{1}{4}(x - 3)^2 \\ 3x - 2y = 13 \end{cases}$
22. $\begin{cases} -3 = 2x^2 - y \\ x^2 - 36 = 9y^2 \end{cases}$
23. $\begin{cases} x^2 + y^2 = 8 \\ x^2 - y = 6 \end{cases}$

Solve each system of equations by using the elimination method.

24. $\begin{cases} 2x^2 + 3y^2 = 83 \\ 4x^2 - 2y^2 = -34 \end{cases}$
25. $\begin{cases} \frac{x^2}{5} + \frac{y^2}{3} = 15 \\ x^2 + y^2 = 20 \end{cases}$
26. $\begin{cases} x^2 + y^2 = 16 \\ y^2 - 2x^2 = 16 \end{cases}$
27. $\begin{cases} x - y = 7 \\ x^2 - y = 7 \end{cases}$
28. $\begin{cases} 4x^2 + y^2 = 1 \\ -x^2 + y^2 = 1 \end{cases}$
29. $\begin{cases} x^2 + y^2 = 9 \\ x^2 - 4y^2 = 4 \end{cases}$

10-2 Circles *(pp. 729–734)*

EXAMPLES

- **Write the equation of the circle with center $(-5, 9)$ and radius $r = 16$.**

Substitute into the general equation of a circle, $(x - h)^2 + (y - k)^2 = r^2$.

$$(x - (-5))^2 + (y - 9)^2 = 16^2$$

$$(x + 5)^2 + (y - 9)^2 = 256 \qquad \textit{Simplify.}$$

- **Write an equation of the line that is tangent at (12, 9) to the circle with equation $x^2 + y^2 = 225$.**

The circle has center $(0, 0)$. The tangent is perpendicular to the radius at the point of tangency.

Find the slope of the radius and the slope of the tangent.

$$m_r = \frac{9 - 0}{12 - 0} = \frac{9}{12} = \frac{3}{4} \qquad \textit{The slope of the radius is } \tfrac{3}{4}.$$

$$m_t = -\frac{4}{3} \qquad \textit{Use the negative reciprocal.}$$

$$y - 9 = -\frac{4}{3}(x - 12) \qquad \textit{Use point-slope form.}$$

EXERCISES

Find the center and the radius of each circle.

12. $(x - 6)^2 + y^2 = 361$
13. $(x + 12)^2 + (y - 4)^2 = 15$

Write the equation of each circle.

14. center $(8, -7)$ and radius $r = 14$
15. center $(3, 6)$ and containing the point $(7, -2)$
16. diameter with endpoints $(2, 5)$ and $(-8, 11)$

Write an equation of the line that is tangent to the given circle at the given point.

17. $x^2 + y^2 = 34$ at $(3, 5)$
18. $(x + 3)^2 + y^2 = 16$ at $(-3, 4)$
19. $(x - 2)^2 + (y + 7)^2 = 44$ at $(6, -2)$
20. $(x + 4)^2 + (y - 1)^2 = 89$ at $(1, -7)$

10-3 Ellipses *(pp. 736–742)*

EXAMPLE

- **Graph $\frac{(x + 1)^2}{25} + \frac{(y - 4)^2}{9} = 1$. Then find the foci of the ellipse.**

Rewrite the equation as $\frac{(x + 1)^2}{5^2} + \frac{(y - 4)^2}{3^2} = 1$.

The center is $(-1, 4)$. Because $5 > 3$, the major axis is horizontal, $a = 5$ and $b = 3$. The vertices are $(-1 \pm 5, 4)$, or $(-6, 4)$ and $(4, 4)$. The co-vertices are $(-1, 4 \pm 3)$ or $(-1, 7)$ and $(-1, 1)$.

In an ellipse, $c^2 = a^2 - b^2$. In this ellipse, $c^2 = 5^2 - 3^2 = 16$, so $c = 4$.

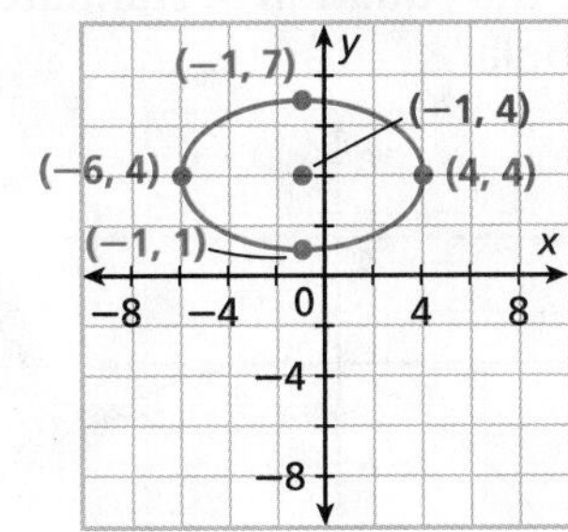

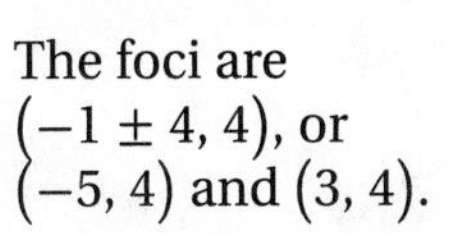

The foci are $(-1 \pm 4, 4)$, or $(-5, 4)$ and $(3, 4)$.

EXERCISES

Find the center, vertices, co-vertices, and foci of each ellipse. Then graph.

21. $\frac{x^2}{9} + \frac{y^2}{36} = 1$
22. $25x^2 + 64y^2 = 1600$
23. $\frac{(x - 3)^2}{49} + \frac{(y + 2)^2}{64} = 1$

Find the equation of each ellipse.

24.

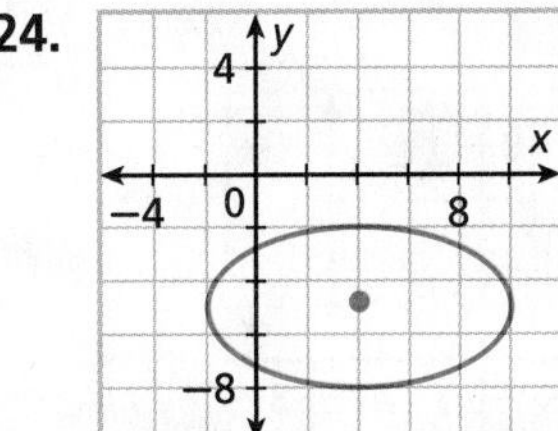

25. co-vertices at $(12, 0)$ and $(-12, 0)$ and major axis length 30
26. vertices at $(-8, 3)$ and $(4, 3)$ and foci at $(-5, 3)$ and $(1, 3)$

10-4 Hyperbolas *(pp. 744–750)*

EXAMPLE

■ **Find the center, vertices, co-vertices, foci, and asymptotes of $\frac{y^2}{16} - \frac{x^2}{9} = 1$. Then graph.**

The equation is in the form $\frac{y^2}{a^2} - \frac{x^2}{b^2}$, so the transverse axis is vertical. The center is $(0, 0)$.

Because $a = 4$ and $b = 3$, the vertices are $(0, 4)$ and $(0, -4)$ and the co-vertices are $(3, 0)$ and $(-3, 0)$. The equations of the asymptotes are $y = \frac{4}{3}x$ and $y = -\frac{4}{3}x$.

In a hyperbola, $c^2 = a^2 + b^2$. In this hyperbola, $c^2 = 4^2 + 3^2 = 25$, so $c = 5$ and the foci are $(0, 5)$ and $(0, -5)$.

Draw a box by using the vertices and co-vertices. Draw the asymptotes through the corners of the box. Draw the hyperbola by using the vertices and the asymptotes.

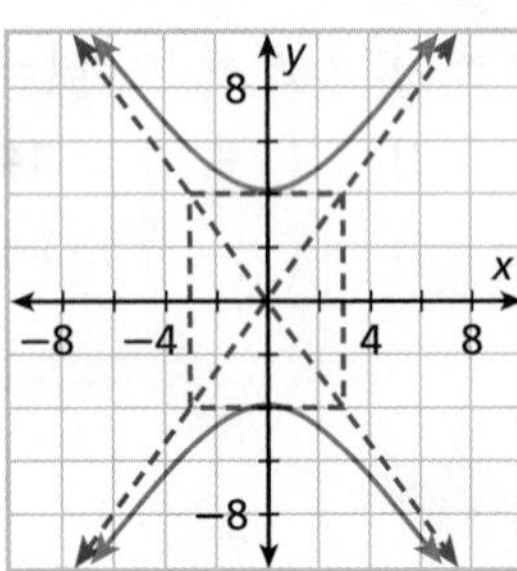

EXERCISES

Find the center, vertices, co-vertices, foci, and asymptotes of each hyperbola, and then graph.

27. $\frac{x^2}{25} - \frac{y^2}{49} = 1$

28. $64y^2 - 36x^2 = 2304$

29. $\frac{(x-3)^2}{4} - \frac{(y+6)^2}{49} = 1$

Write an equation in standard form for each hyperbola.

30.

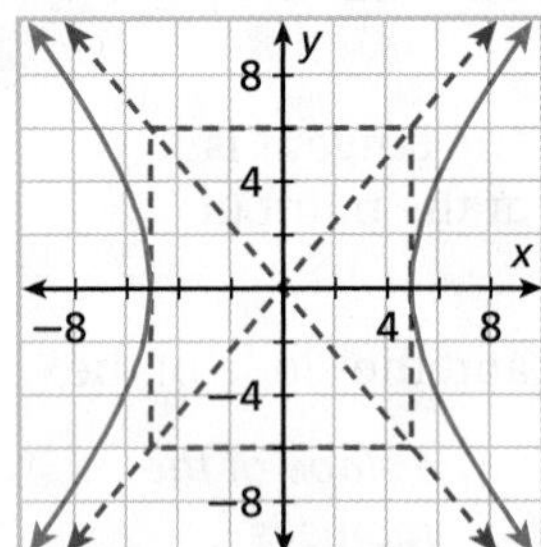

31. vertices $(11, 0)$ and $(-11, 0)$ and conjugate axis length 8

32. co-vertices $(6, 0)$ and $(-6, 0)$ and asymptotes $y = \frac{5}{6}x$ and $y = -\frac{5}{6}x$

33. length of transverse axis 10 and foci at $(-7, 18)$ and $(-7, -8)$

10-5 Parabolas *(pp. 751–757)*

EXAMPLE

■ **Find the vertex, value of *p*, axis of symmetry, focus, and directrix of $x - 2 = -\frac{1}{16}(y+3)^2$. Then graph.**

The equation is in the form $x - h = \frac{1}{4p}(y-k)^2$ with $p < 0$, so the graph opens to the left.

The vertex is $(2, -3)$, and the axis of symmetry is $y = -3$.

Because $\frac{1}{4p} = -\frac{1}{16}$, $p = -4$. The focus is $(2 - 4, -3)$, or $(-2, -3)$.

The directrix is $x = 2 + 4$, or $x = 6$.

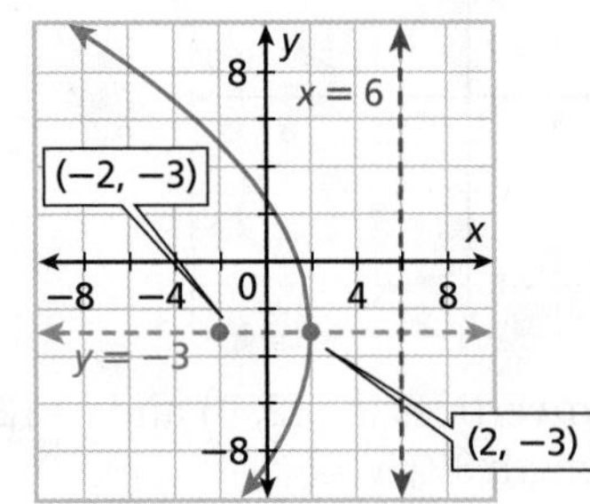

EXERCISES

Find the vertex, value of *p*, axis of symmetry, focus, and directrix for each parabola. Then graph.

34. $y = -\frac{1}{12}x^2$

35. $x = 2y^2$

36. $y - 5 = (x + 4)^2$

37. $x - 4 = -\frac{1}{6}(y + 2)^2$

Write the equation in standard form for each parabola.

38.

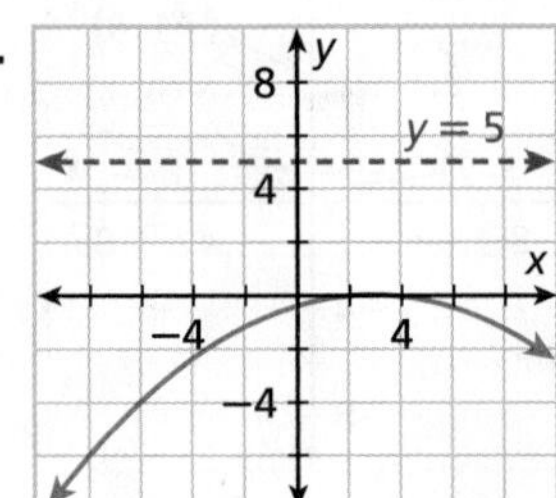

39. vertex $(4, 6)$, axis of symmetry $y = 6$, $p = -2.5$

40. focus $(12, -4)$ and directrix $x = 6$

10-6 Identifying Conic Sections *(pp. 760–766)*

EXAMPLES

- **Identify the conic section represented by $3x^2 + 5xy - 8y^2 + 3x - 5y = 2$.**

$A = 3, B = 5, C = -8$ *Identify values of A, B, and C.*

$B^2 - 4AC = 5^2 - 4(3)(-8) = 121$ *Substitute.*

Because $B^2 - 4AC > 0$, the equation represents a hyperbola.

- **Find the standard form of the equation by completing the square. Then identify the conic.**

$y^2 - 4x - 10y = -13$

$y^2 - 10y + \blacksquare = 4x - 13 + \blacksquare$ *Rearrange.*

$y^2 - 10y + \left(\frac{10}{2}\right)^2 = 4x - 13 + \left(\frac{10}{2}\right)^2$ *Add $\left(\frac{10}{2}\right)^2$ to both sides.*

$(y - 5)^2 = 4x + 12$ *Factor, and simplify.*

$x + 3 = \frac{1}{4}(y - 5)^2$ *Rewrite in standard form.*

The equation represents a parabola.

EXERCISES

Identify the conic section that each equation represents.

41. $\frac{x^2}{12} = 1 - \frac{y^2}{9}$
42. $(x - 5)^2 = \frac{2}{3}(y + 4)^2 + 1$
43. $(x - 8)^2 = \frac{1}{12}(y + 5)$
44. $7x^2 + 7y^2 - 15x = 25$
45. $15x^2 - 6xy + 9y^2 - 12x - 12y + 15 = 0$

Find the standard form of each equation by completing the square. Then identify and graph each conic.

46. $y^2 - 4x + 12y = -24$
47. $2x^2 + 6y^2 + 16x = -20$
48. $x^2 + y^2 + 10x - 8y + 5 = 0$
49. $4x^2 - 8y^2 + 8x - 48y - 100 = 0$

10-7 Solving Nonlinear Systems *(pp. 768–775)*

EXAMPLE

- **Solve $\begin{cases} x^2 - y^2 = 16 \\ y^2 - x = 4 \end{cases}$ by using the substitution method.**

The graph of the first equation is a hyperbola. The graph of the second equation is a parabola. There may be as many as four points of intersection.

It is simplest to solve for y^2 because both equations have y^2 terms.

$y^2 = x + 4$ *Solve the second equation for y^2.*

$x^2 - (x + 4) = 16$ *Substitute this value into the first equation.*

$(x - 5)(x + 4) = 0$ *Simplify, and factor.*

$x = 5$ or $x = -4$

$y^2 = 5 + 4 = 9$ or $y^2 = -4 + 4 = 0$ *Substitute.*

$y = \pm 3$ when $x = 5$ and $y = 0$ when $x = -4$. The solution set is $\{(5, 3), (5, -3), (-4, 0)\}$.

EXERCISES

Solve each system of equations by graphing.

50. $\begin{cases} y + 6 = \frac{1}{2}(x - 2)^2 \\ y + 2x = -2 \end{cases}$
51. $\begin{cases} 25x^2 + 16y^2 = 400 \\ 16y = -5(x - 4)^2 \end{cases}$

Solve each system by using the substitution method.

52. $\begin{cases} 2x^2 - 2y^2 = 56 \\ x^2 + y^2 = 100 \end{cases}$
53. $\begin{cases} 2x^2 - y^2 = 14 \\ y - 2x = -4 \end{cases}$

Solve each system by using the elimination method.

54. $\begin{cases} 4y^2 - 8x^2 = 16 \\ 4x^2 + 5y^2 = 20 \end{cases}$
55. $\begin{cases} 3x^2 - 2y^2 = 76 \\ 5x^2 + 3y^2 = 228 \end{cases}$

Solve each system by using any method.

56. $\begin{cases} 3x^2 + 5y^2 = 192 \\ 3y - x = 16 \end{cases}$
57. $\begin{cases} \frac{x^2}{25} - \frac{y^2}{16} = 1 \\ 30x^2 + 20y^2 = 600 \end{cases}$

CHAPTER 10

CHAPTER TEST

1. The transmission of a radio signal can be received at the locations $(1, -10)$ and $(-11, 6)$. Write an equation for the range of the signal if a line between the locations represents a diameter of the range.
2. Write the equation of the line that is tangent to $(x + 2)^2 + (y - 8)^2 = 40$ at $(3, -1)$.
3. Find the center, vertices, co-vertices, and foci of the ellipse with equation $49(x + 4)^2 + 16(y - 2)^2 = 784$. Then graph.
4. A shelter for a patch of young strawberry plants is constructed in the form of an ellipse. If the shelter is 4.5 feet high at its highest point and the patch is 19 feet wide, write an equation for the ellipse.
5. Find the center, vertices, co-vertices, foci, and asymptotes of the hyperbola with equation $\frac{x^2}{25} - \frac{y^2}{144} = 1$. Then graph.
6. Write the equation of the hyperbola with vertices $(0, 7)$ and $(0, -7)$ and conjugate axis length 28.
7. Find the vertex, value of p, axis of symmetry, focus, and directrix of the parabola with equation $y + 4 = \frac{1}{24}(x - 2)^2$. Then graph.
8. The filament of a flashlight bulb is located at the focus, which is 0.75 centimeters from the vertex of the flashlight's parabolic reflector. Write an equation for the cross section of the parabolic reflector if the vertex is at the origin and the reflector is pointed to the left.

Identify the conic section that each equation represents.

9. $\frac{x - 2}{4} = \frac{(y + 5)^2}{12}$

10. $1 - \frac{(x + 5)^2}{8} = \frac{(y - 4)^2}{8}$

11. $7x^2 + 5xy - 2y^2 + 8x - 26 = 0$

Find the standard form of each equation by completing the square. Then identify the conic.

12. $x^2 + y^2 - 16x + 20y + 124 = 0$

13. $6x^2 + 4y^2 + 84x - 24y + 306 = 0$

Find the solutions to the system by using the substitution or elimination method.

14. $\begin{cases} 2y - 3x = 1 \\ x + 4 = \frac{1}{4}(y - 2)^2 \end{cases}$

15. $\begin{cases} y + x = 2 \\ x^2 + y^2 = 52 \end{cases}$

16. $\begin{cases} 3x^2 - 4y^2 = 143 \\ 5x^2 - 5y^2 = 280 \end{cases}$

17. Two trapeze artists are swinging through the air along the paths shown in the graph. One performer releases the swing and travels in a path that can be modeled by the equation $y = -\frac{1}{4}x^2 + 16$. The performer's partner moves along a path that can be modeled by the equation $y = \frac{1}{2}x^2 + 16$. At what point will the performer be caught by his partner?

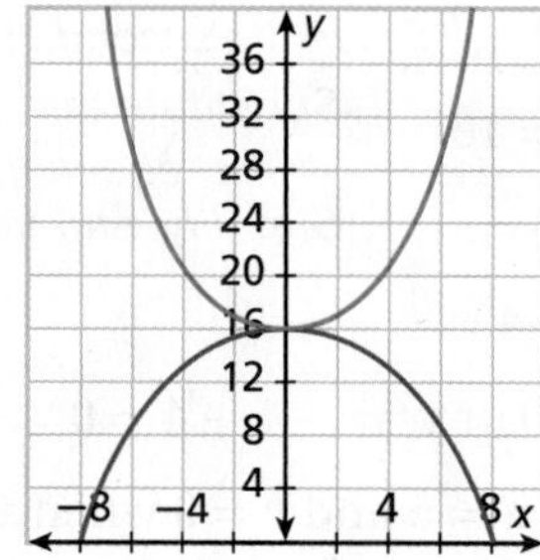

CHAPTER 10

FOCUS ON SAT MATHEMATICS SUBJECT TESTS

The topics covered on each SAT Mathematics Subject Tests vary only slightly each time the test is administered. You can find out the general distribution of questions across topics and then determine which areas need more of your attention when you are studying for the test.

To prepare for the SAT Mathematics Subject Tests, start reviewing course material a couple of months before your test date. Take sample tests to find the areas you might need to focus on more. Remember that you are not expected to have studied all of the topics on the test.

You may want to time yourself as you take this practice test. It should take you about 6 minutes to complete.

1. The graph of the equation $x^2 + y^2 - 2x + 3y + 8 = 0$ is which of the following?

(A) Parabola

(B) Circle

(C) Hyperbola

(D) Ellipse

(E) Point

2. What is the length of the major axis of the ellipse with equation $\frac{(x-1)^2}{4} + (y+3)^2 = 9$?

(A) 2

(B) 3

(C) 4

(D) 6

(E) 12

3. What is the distance from the focus to the vertex of a parabola with equation $x = \frac{1}{12}(y-1)^2$?

(A) 3

(B) 6

(C) 12

(D) 48

(E) 144

4. Which of the following is the equation of an asymptote of the graph of $\frac{(y+2)^2}{9} - \frac{(x-5)^2}{4} = 1$?

(A) $y + 2 = \frac{3}{2}(x-5)$

(B) $y + 2 = \frac{2}{3}(x-5)$

(C) $y + 2 = \frac{9}{4}(x-5)$

(D) $y = \frac{3}{2}x$

(E) $y = \frac{2}{3}x$

5. The circle with equation $x^2 + y^2 + sx + ty + 33 = 0$ has center (4, 5). What is $\frac{s}{t}$?

(A) $-\frac{5}{4}$

(B) $-\frac{4}{5}$

(C) $\frac{4}{5}$

(D) $\frac{5}{4}$

(E) There is not enough information to determine the answer.

CHAPTER 10

TEST TACKLER

Standardized Test Strategies

Multiple Choice: Context-Based Test Items

You will encounter some multiple-choice test items where the problem statement does not give you an actual problem to solve but requires you to use the answer choices provided to determine which choice fits the context of the problem statement. Depending on the problem, you can use a variety of methods, such as substitution, graphing, or elimination, to obtain the correct answer.

EXAMPLE 1

Which of the following equations, when graphed, has x-intercepts at $(5, 0)$ and $(-5, 0)$?

Ⓐ $2x^2 + 25y^2 = 150$

Ⓑ $8x^2 + 50y^2 = 200$

Ⓒ $5x^2 + 5y^2 = 100$

Ⓓ $4x^2 + 5y^2 = 50$

Although there are many equations that have x-intercepts at $(5, 0)$ and $(-5, 0)$, you need to select the equation from the four choices given. For this problem, you can use either of these two methods:

Substitution Method Substitute $x = 5$ and $y = 0$ into the equation, and simplify. Then substitute $x = -5$ and $y = 0$ into the equation, and simplify. Find which equation makes a true statement with the given x-intercepts.

Try choice A: $2x^2 + 25y^2 = 150$; $2(5)^2 + 25(0)^2 = 50$
Because the first equation does not make a true statement, $150 \neq 50$, choice A is incorrect.

Try choice B: $8x^2 + 50y^2 = 200$; $8(5)^2 + 50(0)^2 = 200$; $8(-5)^2 + 50(0)^2 = 200$
Because both equations make a true statement, choice B is correct.

Try choice C and choice D to confirm that you found the correct answer.

Graphing Method Solve each equation in the answer choices for y. Then graph each equation on a graphing calculator. Look for the graph that intersects the x-axis at $(5, 0)$ and $(-5, 0)$.

Try choice A: $2x^2 + 25y^2 = 150$

$$y = \pm\sqrt{\frac{(150 - 2x^2)}{25}}$$

When graphed on a calculator, the graph crosses the x-axis at about (8.5, 0) and (−8.5, 0). Choice A is incorrect.

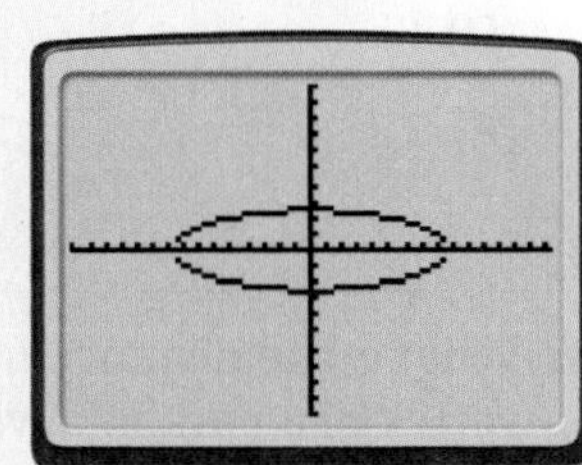

Try choice B: $8x^2 + 50y^2 = 200$

$$y = \pm\sqrt{\frac{(200 - 8x^2)}{50}}$$

When graphed on a calculator, the graph crosses the x-axis at (5, 0) and (−5, 0). Choice B is the correct answer.

Try choice C and choice D to confirm that you found the correct answer.

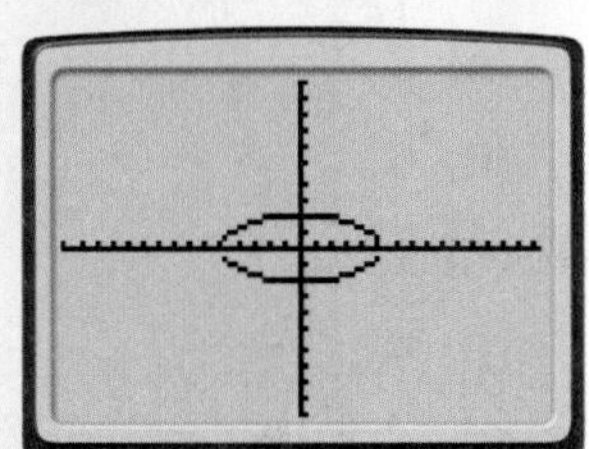

Underline the context of the problem statement to make sure that you are clear about what is being asked.

Read each test item and answer the questions that follow.

Item A

Which equation, when graphed, is a parabola that opens to the right?

Ⓐ $4y - 2x^2 = 6$ Ⓒ $4x - 2y^2 = 6$

Ⓑ $4y + 2x^2 = 6$ Ⓓ $4x + 2y^2 = 6$

1. On a coordinate grid, sketch two or three parabolas that open to the right. Can they all be represented by the same equation? If not, what do these equations have in common?
2. From what you know about parabolas, can any of the answer choices be eliminated? Explain.
3. Describe how to determine which answer choice is correct.

Item B

The graph of which of the following ellipses has the smallest distance between foci?

Ⓕ $\frac{(x+16)^2}{64} + \frac{(y-9)^2}{25} = 1$

Ⓖ $\frac{x^2}{4} + \frac{y^2}{81} = 1$

Ⓗ $\frac{(x-1)^2}{1} + \frac{(y-1)^2}{100} = 1$

Ⓙ $\frac{x^2}{289} + \frac{y^2}{169} = 1$

4. If you read only the problem statement and not the answer choices, can you solve the problem? Explain.
5. How can you find the distance between foci if you know *a* and *b*?

Item C

Which of the following points is inside the circle described by the following equation?

$$(x-2)^2 + (y-6)^2 = 9$$

Ⓐ $(0, 0)$ Ⓒ $(5, 6)$

Ⓑ $(-2, 4)$ Ⓓ $(3, 5)$

6. Describe how you can use your graphing calculator to determine the correct answer.
7. Can you use algebra to determine the correct answer? If so, describe your method.

Item D

A power outage affects areas *L*, *M*, and *N*. Which of the following best describes the power outage?

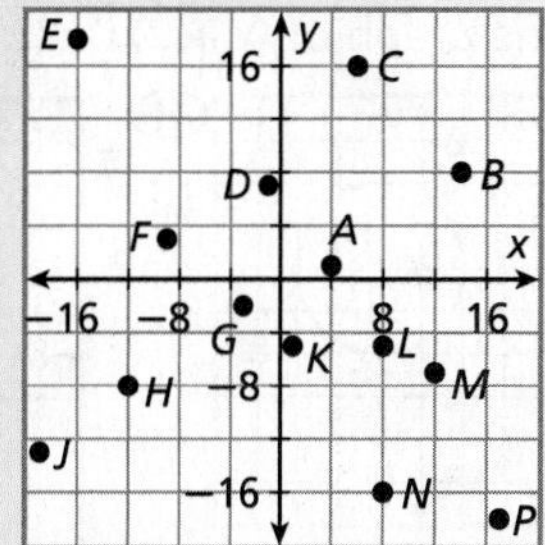

Ⓕ The main generator is located at $(12, -9)$ and shuts down power up to 9 miles away.

Ⓖ The main generator is located at $(4, -6)$ and shuts down power up to 8 miles away.

Ⓗ The main generator is located at $(10, -3)$ and shuts down power up to 5 miles away.

Ⓙ The main generator is located at $(-8, -15)$ and shuts down power up to 15 miles away.

8. What does the problem state about areas *L*, *M*, and *N*? What can you interpret about the areas not mentioned?
9. A student found that areas *L* and *M* are within the circle described by choice H. Can the student stop working and select choice H as the correct response? Explain.
10. Describe a method that you can use to determine the correct answer.

CHAPTER 10

STANDARDIZED TEST PREP

go.hrw.com
State Test Practice Online
KEYWORD: MB7 TestPrep

CUMULATIVE ASSESSMENT, CHAPTERS 1–10

Multiple Choice

1. Which conic section does the equation $\frac{x^2}{20} + \frac{y^2}{52} = 1$ represent?

   (A) Circle

   (B) Parabola

   (C) Hyperbola

   (D) Ellipse

2. Which is the graph of $(x + 2)^2 + (y - 2)^2 = 16$?

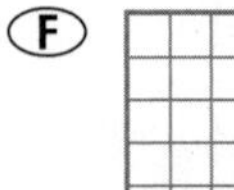

(F)

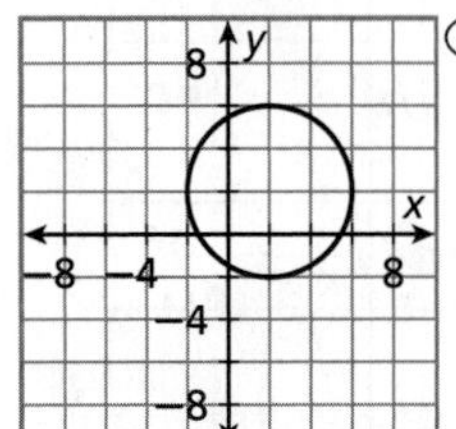

(H)

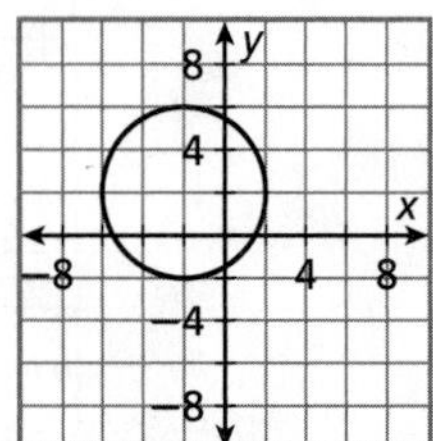

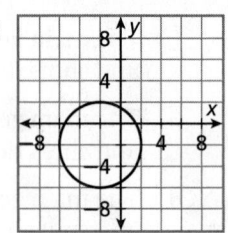

(G)

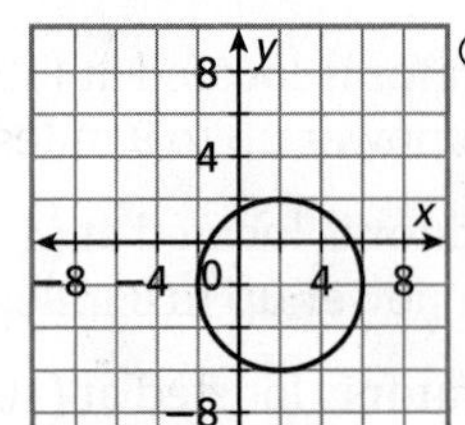

(J)

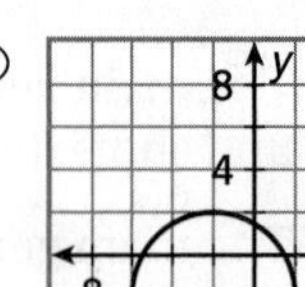

3. What system of linear inequalities can be used to represent the graph?

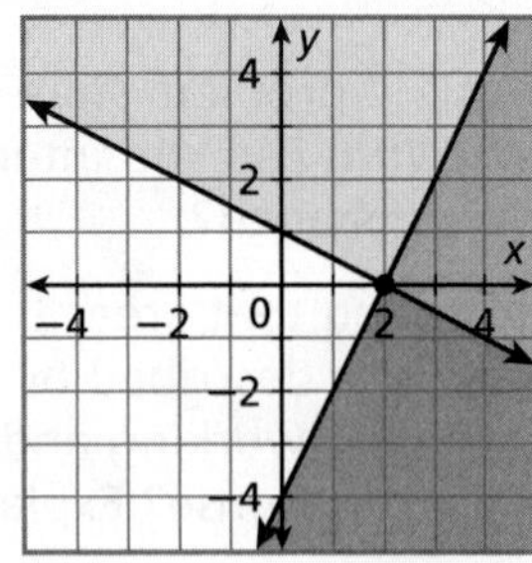

   (A) $\begin{cases} y \le 2x - 4 \\ 2y \ge -x + 2 \end{cases}$

   (B) $\begin{cases} y < 2x - 4 \\ 2y > -x + 2 \end{cases}$

   (C) $\begin{cases} y \le 2x - 4 \\ 2y \le -x + 2 \end{cases}$

   (D) $\begin{cases} y < 2x - 4 \\ 2y < -x + 2 \end{cases}$

4. What equation can be used to represent the graph?

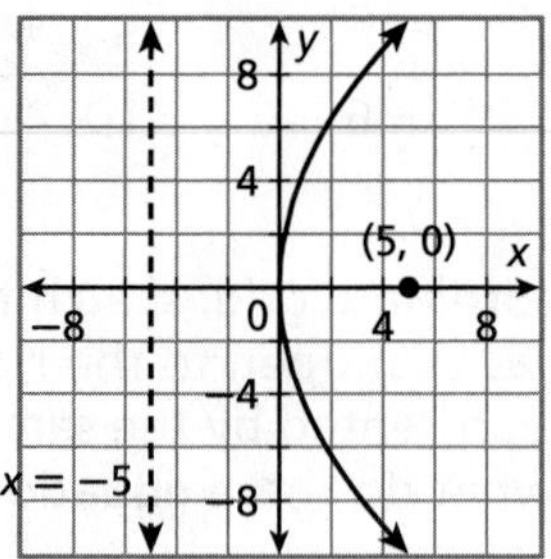

   (F) $x = -\frac{1}{20}y^2$

   (G) $x = \frac{1}{20}y^2$

   (H) $y = \frac{1}{20}x^2$

   (J) $y = -\frac{1}{20}x^2$

5. Solve $\begin{cases} x^2 + 4y^2 = 64 \\ x + 8 = \frac{1}{2}y^2 \end{cases}$ by using the substitution method.

   (A) $\{(-8, 0), (0, 4), (0, -4)\}$

   (B) $\{(0, -8), (4, 0), (-4, 0)\}$

   (C) $\{(-8, 0), (0, 4)\}$

   (D) $\{(0, 4), (0, -4)\}$

6. Find all of the roots of the polynomial equation $x^5 + x^4 - x^3 - x^2 - 20x - 20 = 0$.

   (F) $\sqrt{5}, -\sqrt{5}, -1$

   (G) $i, -i, \sqrt{5}, -\sqrt{5}, -1$

   (H) $2i, -2i, \sqrt{5}, -\sqrt{5}, -1$

   (J) $4i, -4i, \sqrt{5}, -\sqrt{5}, -1$

7. At age 20, Jon invested \$50 at 6.75% compounded continuously. Jon is now 50. What is the present value of Jon's investment?

   (A) \$4,545.67

   (B) \$378.81

   (C) \$17,534.57

   (D) \$2,314.46

In Item 15, recall that the notation $(f \circ g)(x)$ is equivalent to $f(g(x))$. Begin by substituting the value for x into the function $g(x)$.

8. Simplify.

$$\frac{x+1}{3x+4} + \frac{x-1}{4x-7}$$

Ⓕ $\frac{2x}{7x-3}$

Ⓖ $\frac{7x^2-17x-11}{(3x+4)(4x-7)}$

Ⓗ $\frac{7x^2+17x-11}{(3x+4)(4x-7)}$

Ⓙ $\frac{7x^2-2x-11}{(3x+4)(4x-7)}$

9. What is the inverse of the function $f(x) = \frac{7x-4}{3}$?

Ⓐ $f^{-1}(x) = \frac{3}{7x-4}$

Ⓑ $f^{-1}(x) = \frac{3x+4}{7}$

Ⓒ $f^{-1}(x) = \frac{3}{7}x - \frac{3}{4}$

Ⓓ $f^{-1}(x) = \frac{3}{7}x - \frac{4}{7}$

10. Solve for x : $3^{2x-1} = 27^{x+4}$.

Ⓕ 5

Ⓖ $\frac{7}{5}$

Ⓗ −2

Ⓙ −13

Gridded Response

11. What is the x-intercept of the axis of symmetry of the function $f(x) = 5x^2 - \frac{1}{2}x - 4$?

12. Evaluate.

$\log_{256} 16$

13. Solve for x.

$$\frac{8}{x+4} - \frac{2}{x} = \frac{5}{x+4}$$

14. Simplify.

$$\left(\sqrt[3]{2^9}\right)^2$$

15. Given $f(x) = 3x^2 - 1$ and $g(x) = \frac{1}{x+5}$, what is the value of $(f \circ g)(-6)$?

Short Response

16. A hyperbola has center $(3, -5)$, focus $(-10, -5)$, and vertex $(15, -5)$.

a. Write the equation for the hyperbola.

b. What are the equations of the asymptotes of the hyperbola?

17. The approximate heart rate of an adult can be modeled by $f(x) = -(x-5)^2 + 75$, where x is the age (in tens) of the person.

a. Find the inverse for the function, and explain what it represents.

b. Approximate the age of a person whose heart rate is 65.

18. The pentagon below has vertices at $(1, 2)$, $(2, 4)$, $(4, 5)$, $(5, 2)$, and $(4, -1)$.

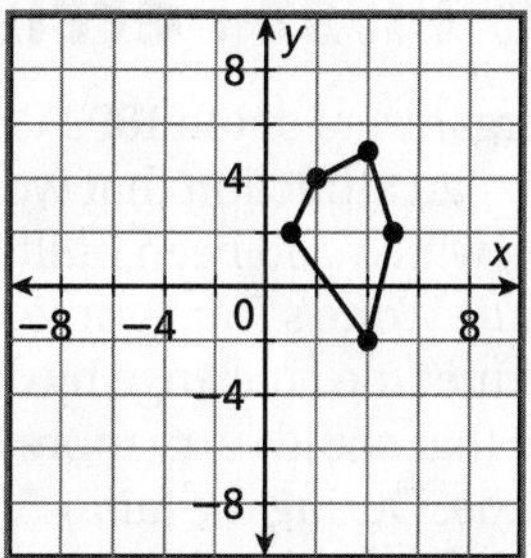

a. Write the matrix used to transform the pentagon 3 units to the left and 5 units down.

b. What are the coordinates of the transformed pentagon?

Extended Response

19. Joan's grandmother gave her a diamond necklace valued at \$4500. The value of the necklace is predicted to appreciate 7.5% per year.

a. Write a function to model the predicted growth in the value of the necklace.

b. Graph the function.

c. What is the predicted value of the necklace in 10 years?

d. Based on the model, what was the value of the necklace 30 years ago?

Real-World CONNECTIONS

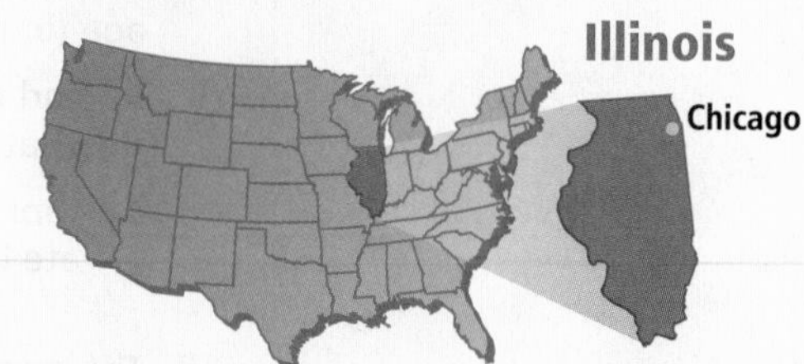

The First Ferris Wheel

The organizers of the 1893 World's Fair in Chicago wanted an attraction that would outdo the Eiffel Tower, which had been built four years earlier for the Paris World's Fair. A bridge builder named George Ferris met the challenge by designing a colossal wheel that could carry more than 2100 passengers at a time. During the fair, 1.5 million visitors paid the 50-cent fee for a 20-minute ride on Ferris's wheel.

Choose one or more strategies to solve each problem. For 1, use the table.

Building Ferris's Wheel	
Date	**Total Number of Cars Attached**
June 10, 1893	1
June 11, 1893	6
June 13, 1893	21

1. Each car of the wheel could carry up to 60 passengers. Because of the cars' enormous size, it took several days to hang all of the cars on the wheel. Develop a model to predict the number of cars that had been attached to the wheel by June 14, 1893.

2. As the wheel revolved, the paths of the cars could be modeled by $x^2 + y^2 - 250y = 0$. Find the diameter of the wheel.

3. Approximately how many feet has a car traveled after one complete revolution of the wheel?

4. A car starts at the bottom of the wheel. After 2 min 15 s, the car's horizontal distance to the central axle is 125 ft. How long does it take the car to make one complete revolution?

Soldier Field

Chicago's Soldier Field was built in 1924 as a multipurpose sports stadium. Since 1970, it has been the home of the National Football League's Chicago Bears. In 2003, a new 61,500-seat stadium was built within the shell of the original structure so that the historic colonnades and exterior walls of the old Soldier Field could be preserved.

Choose one or more strategies to solve each problem.

1. The renovated stadium can be modeled by an ellipse centered at the origin, a vertex at $(425, 0)$, and a focus at $(301, 0)$, measured in feet. Find the length and width of the stadium to the nearest foot.

For 2, use the diagram.

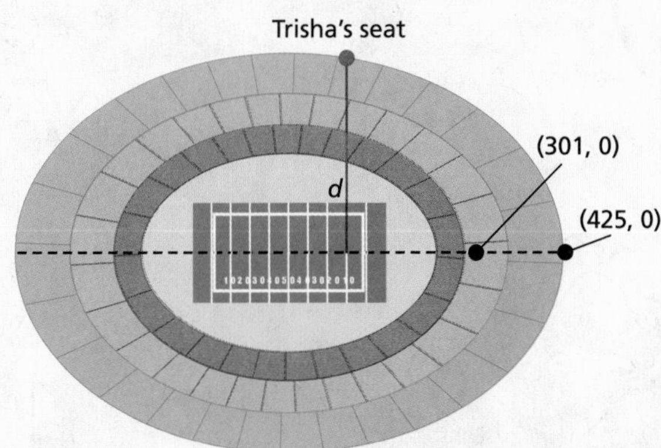

2. Trisha bought tickets to a Bears game. As shown, her seat is on the 20-yard line, in the last row of the stadium. What is the horizontal distance d to the nearest foot from her seat to the middle of the playing field?

3. During the game, a player makes a kick from the 40-yard line. The ball reaches a maximum height of 9 yards and lands 60 yards away. If the path of the ball is modeled by a parabola, does the ball clear the 10-foot-tall goalpost located 50 yards away? If so, by how many feet?

CHAPTER

11 Probability and Statistics

Chapter Focus

- Apply concepts of probability to solve problems.
- Analyze and interpret data sets.

APPROXIMATE WAIT TIME FROM HERE 4872 MINUTES

Wait a Second!

You can use probability and statistics to analyze *queuing*, the study of waiting in line.

go.hrw.com
Chapter Project Online
KEYWORD: MB7 ChProj

ARE YOU READY?

Vocabulary

Match each term on the left with a definition on the right.

1. mean	**A.** a comparison of two quantities by division
2. median	**B.** the sum of the values in a set divided by the number of values
3. ratio	**C.** the value, or values, that occur most often
4. mode	**D.** the result of addition
	E. the middle value, or mean of the two middle values, of a set when the set is ordered numerically

Tree Diagrams

5. Natalie has three colors of wrapping paper (purple, blue, and yellow) and three colors of ribbon (gold, white, and red). Make a tree diagram showing all possible ways that she can wrap a present using one color of paper and one color of ribbon.

Add and Subtract Fractions

Add or subtract.

6. $1 - \frac{14}{20}$ **7.** $\frac{3}{8} + \frac{5}{6}$ **8.** $\frac{8}{15} - \frac{2}{5}$ **9.** $\frac{1}{12} + \frac{1}{10}$

Multiply and Divide Fractions

Multiply or divide.

10. $\frac{1}{2} \cdot \frac{3}{7}$ **11.** $2\frac{1}{3} \cdot \frac{1}{4}$ **12.** $\frac{4}{5} \div \frac{1}{2}$ **13.** $5\frac{1}{3} \div \frac{1}{4}$

Percent Problems

Solve.

14. What number is 7% of 150? **15.** 90% of what number is 45?

16. A $24 item receives a price increase of 12%. How much was the price increased?

17. Twenty percent of the water in a large aquarium should be changed weekly. How much water should be changed each week if an aquarium holds 65 gallons of water?

Find Measures of Central Tendency

Find the mean, median, and mode of each data set.

18. $\{9, 4, 2, 6, 4\}$ **19.** $\{1, 1, 1, 2, 2, 2\}$

20. $\{1, 2, 3, 4, 5, 6\}$ **21.** $\{18, 14, 20, 18, 14, 3, 18\}$

CHAPTER 11

Study Guide: Preview

Where You've Been

Previously, you

- made tree diagrams to find the number of possible combinations of a group of objects.
- made lists to count and arrange objects.
- calculated measures of central tendency.

In This Chapter

You will study

- solving problems involving counting and arranging.
- finding theoretical, experimental, and binomial probabilities.
- analyzing data to include expected value and standard deviation.

Where You're Going

You can use the skills in this chapter

- to find probabilities involved in games and events involving chance.
- to calculate and report appropriate measures when analyzing data.
- to form a solid foundation for studies in advanced statistics.

Key Vocabulary/Vocabulario

binomial experiment	experimento binomial
combination	combinación
conditional probability	probabilidad condicional
dependent events	sucesos dependientes
experimental probability	probabilidad experimental
factorial	factorial
independent events	sucesos independientes
outcome	resultado
permutation	permutación
theoretical probability	probabilidad teórica

Vocabulary Connections

To become familiar with some of the vocabulary terms in the chapter, consider the following. You may refer to the chapter, the glossary, or a dictionary if you like.

1. A number is the product of its *factors*. What operation do you think is involved in finding a **factorial** ?
2. A *theory* can be described as a sound and rational explanation. An *experiment* can be described as a procedure carried out in a controlled environment. Knowing this, how do you think **theoretical probability** differs from **experimental probability** ?
3. A *conditional* is used to describe something that will be done only if another thing is done. Do you think **conditional probability** is used with **independent events** or **dependent events** ? Why?
4. Each possible result of an experiment is an **outcome** . How many possible outcomes do you think a **binomial experiment** has? Why?

Writing Strategy: Translate Between Words and Math

It is important to correctly interpret the type of math being described by a verbal or written description. Listen/look for key words to help you translate between the words and the math.

15. In 1626, the Dutch bought Manhattan Island for \$24 worth of merchandise. Suppose that, instead, \$24 had been invested in an account that paid 3.5% interest compounded annually. Find the balance in 2008.

compounded: *Compounding indicates an exponential function.*

31. Gardeners check the pH level of soil to ensure a pH of 6 or 7. Soil is usually more acidic in areas where rainfall is high, whereas soil in dry areas is usually more alkaline. The pH level of a certain soil sample is 5.5. What is the difference in hydrogen ion concentration, or $[H^+]$, between the sample and an acceptable level?

pH

hydrogen ion concentration: *These terms indicate a logarithmic function.*

parabola: *A parabola indicates a quadratic function.*

27. You are given a parabola with two points that have the same y-value, $(-7, 11)$ and $(3, 11)$. Explain how to find the equation for the axis of symmetry of this parabola.

Try This

Identify the key word and the type of function being described.

1. Kelly invested \$2000 in a savings account at a simple interest rate of 2.5%. How much money will she have in 8 months?
2. The diameter d in inches of a chain needed to move p pounds is given by the square root of $85p$, divided by pi. How much more can be lifted with a chain 2.5 inches in diameter than by a rope 0.5 inch in diameter?
3. A technician took a blood sample from a patient and detected a toxin concentration of 0.01006 mg/cm^3. Two hours later, the technician took another sample and detected a concentration of 0.00881 mg/cm^3. Assume that the concentration varies exponentially with time. Write a function to model the data.
4. Students found that the number of mosquitoes per acre of wetland grows by about 10 to the power $\frac{1}{2}d + 2$, where d is the number of days since the last frost. Write and graph the function representing the number of mosquitoes on each day.

11-1 Permutations and Combinations

Objectives
Solve problems involving the Fundamental Counting Principle.

Solve problems involving permutations and combinations.

Vocabulary
Fundamental Counting Principle
permutation
factorial
combination

Why learn this?
Permutations can be used to determine the number of ways to select and arrange artwork so as to give a new look each day. (See Example 2B.)

You have previously used tree diagrams to find the number of possible combinations of a group of objects. In this lesson, you will learn to use the **Fundamental Counting Principle**.

Fundamental Counting Principle

If there are n items and m_1 ways to choose a first item, m_2 ways to choose a second item after the first item has been chosen, and so on, then there are $m_1 \cdot m_2 \cdot \ldots \cdot m_n$ ways to choose n items.

EXAMPLE 1 Using the Fundamental Counting Principle

A **For the lunch special, you can choose an entrée, a drink, and one side dish. How many meal choices are there?**

number of main dishes	times	number of beverages	times	number of sides	equals	number of choices
3	×	4	×	3	=	36

There are 36 meal choices.

B **In Utah, a license plate consists of 3 digits followed by 3 letters. The letters *I*, *O*, and *Q* are not used, and each digit or letter may be used more than once. How many different license plates are possible?**

digit		*digit*		*digit*		*letter*		*letter*		*letter*	
10	×	10	×	10	×	23	×	23	×	23	= 12,167,000

There are 12,167,000 possible license plates.

Helpful Hint

In Example 1B, there are 10 possible digits and $26 - 3 = 23$ possible letters.

1a. A "make-your-own-adventure" story lets you choose 6 starting points, gives 4 plot choices, and then has 5 possible endings. How many adventures are there?

1b. A password is 4 letters followed by 1 digit. Uppercase letters (A) and lowercase letters (a) may be used and are considered different. How many passwords are possible?

A **permutation** is a selection of a group of objects in which order is important.

There is one way to arrange one item A.

A second item B can be placed first or second.

A third item C can be first, second, or third for each order above.

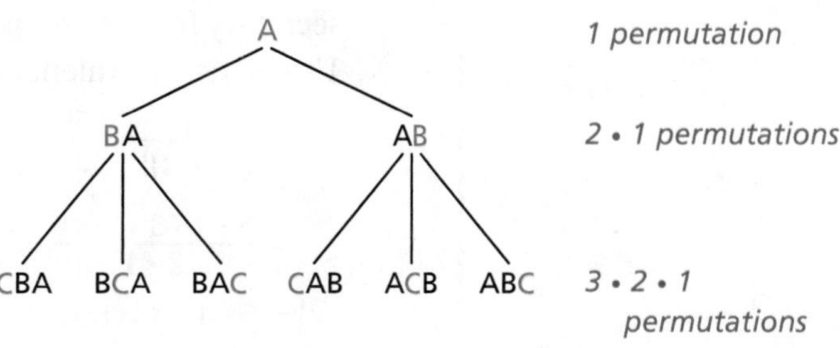

You can see that the number of permutations of 3 items is $3 \cdot 2 \cdot 1$. You can extend this to permutations of n items, which is $n \cdot (n-1) \cdot (n-2) \cdot (n-3) \cdot \ldots \cdot 1$. This expression is called *n factorial,* and is written as $n!$.

n Factorial

For any whole number n,

WORDS	NUMBERS	ALGEBRA
The **factorial** of a number is the product of the natural numbers less than or equal to the number. 0! is defined as 1.	$6! = 6 \cdot 5 \cdot 4 \cdot 3 \cdot 2 \cdot 1 = 720$	$n! = n \cdot (n-1) \cdot (n-2) \cdot (n-3) \cdot \ldots \cdot 1$

Sometimes you may not want to order an entire set of items. Suppose that you want to select and order 3 people from a group of 7. One way to find possible permutations is to use the Fundamental Counting Principle.

First Person		Second Person		Third Person		*There are 7 people. You are choosing 3 of them in order.*
7 choices	•	6 choices	•	5 choices	=	210 permutations

Another way to find the possible permutations is to use factorials. You can divide the total number of arrangements by the number of arrangements that are not used. In the example above, there are 7 total people and 4 whose arrangements do not matter.

$$\frac{\text{arrangements of 7 people}}{\text{arrangements of 4 people}} = \frac{7!}{4!} = \frac{7 \cdot 6 \cdot 5 \cdot \cancel{4} \cdot \cancel{3} \cdot \cancel{2} \cdot \cancel{1}}{\cancel{4} \cdot \cancel{3} \cdot \cancel{2} \cdot \cancel{1}} = 210$$

This can be generalized as a formula, which is useful for large numbers of items.

Permutations

NUMBERS	ALGEBRA
The number of permutations of 7 items taken 3 at a time is $_7P_3 = \frac{7!}{(7-3)!} = \frac{7!}{4!}$.	The number of permutations of n items taken r at a time is $_nP_r = \frac{n!}{(n-r)!}$.

EXAMPLE 2 Finding Permutations

A **How many ways can a club select a president, a vice president, and a secretary from a group of 5 people?**

This is the equivalent of selecting and arranging 3 items from 5.

$$_5P_3 = \frac{5!}{(5-3)!} = \frac{5!}{2!}$$ *Substitute 5 for n and 3 for r in $\frac{n!}{(n-r)!}$.*

$$= \frac{5 \cdot 4 \cdot 3 \cdot \cancel{2 \cdot 1}}{\cancel{2 \cdot 1}}$$ *Divide out common factors.*

$$= 5 \cdot 4 \cdot 3 = 60$$

There are 60 ways to select the 3 people.

B **An art gallery has 9 fine-art photographs from an artist and will display 4 from left to right along a wall. In how many ways can the gallery select and display the 4 photographs?**

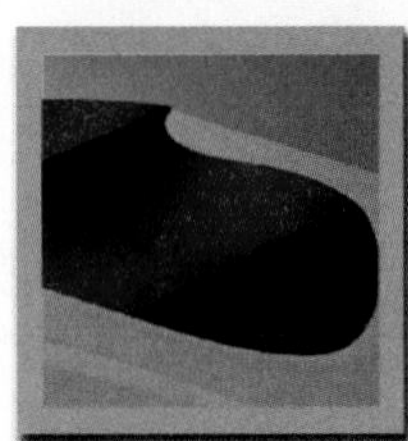

$$_9P_4 = \frac{9!}{(9-4)!} = \frac{9!}{5!} = \frac{9 \cdot 8 \cdot 7 \cdot 6 \cdot \cancel{5 \cdot 4 \cdot 3 \cdot 2 \cdot 1}}{\cancel{5 \cdot 4 \cdot 3 \cdot 2 \cdot 1}}$$ *Divide out common factors.*

$$= 9 \cdot 8 \cdot 7 \cdot 6$$
$$= 3024$$

There are 3024 ways that the gallery can select and display the photographs.

Helpful Hint

The number of factors left after dividing is the number of items selected. In Example 2B, there are 4 photographs and 4 factors in $9 \cdot 8 \cdot 7 \cdot 6$.

2a. Awards are given out at a costume party. How many ways can "most creative," "silliest," and "best" costume be awarded to 8 contestants if no one gets more than one award?

2b. How many ways can a 2-digit number be formed by using only the digits 5–9 and by each digit being used only once?

A **combination** is a grouping of items in which order does not matter. There are generally fewer ways to select items when order does not matter. For example, there are 6 ways to order 3 items, but they are all the same combination:

6 permutations → {ABC, ACB, BAC, BCA, CAB, CBA}

1 combination → {ABC}

To find the number of combinations, the formula for permutations can be modified.

$$\text{number of permutations} = \frac{\text{ways to arrange all items}}{\text{ways to arrange items not selected}}$$

Because order does not matter, divide the number of permutations by the number of ways to arrange the selected items.

$$\text{number of combinations} = \frac{\text{ways to arrange all items}}{(\text{ways to arrange selected items})(\text{ways to arrange items not selected})}$$

Combinations

NUMBERS	ALGEBRA
The number of combinations of 7 items taken 3 at a time is $_7C_3 = \frac{7!}{3!(7-3)!}$.	The number of combinations of n items taken r at a time is $_nC_r = \frac{n!}{r!(n-r)!}$.

When deciding whether to use permutations or combinations, first decide whether order is important. Use a permutation if order matters and a combination if order does not matter.

EXAMPLE 3 *Pet Adoption Application*

Katie is going to adopt kittens from a litter of 11. How many ways can she choose a group of 3 kittens?

Step 1 Determine whether the problem represents a permutation or combination.

The order does not matter. The group Kitty, Smoky, and Tigger is the same as Tigger, Kitty, and Smoky. It is a combination.

Step 2 Use the formula for combinations.

$$_{11}C_3 = \frac{11!}{3!(11-3)!} = \frac{11!}{3!(8!)} \quad n = 11 \text{ and } r = 3$$

$$= \frac{11 \cdot 10 \cdot 9 \cdot \cancel{8 \cdot 7 \cdot 6 \cdot 5 \cdot 4 \cdot 3 \cdot 2 \cdot 1}}{3 \cdot 2 \cdot 1(\cancel{8 \cdot 7 \cdot 6 \cdot 5 \cdot 4 \cdot 3 \cdot 2 \cdot 1})} \quad \textit{Divide out common factors.}$$

$$= \frac{11 \cdot 10 \cdot 9}{3 \cdot 2 \cdot 1} = \frac{11 \cdot \cancel{10}^5 \cdot \cancel{9}^3}{_1\cancel{3} \cdot {}_1\cancel{2} \cdot 1} = 165$$

There are 165 ways to select a group of 3 kittens from 11.

Helpful Hint

You can find permutations and combinations by using **nPr** and **nCr**, respectively, on scientific and graphing calculators.

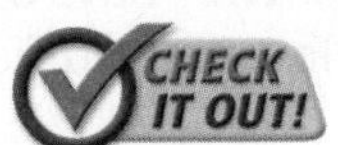

3. The swim team has 8 swimmers. Two swimmers will be selected to swim in the first heat. How many ways can the swimmers be selected?

THINK AND DISCUSS

1. Give a situation in which order matters and one in which order does not matter.
2. Give the value of $_nC_n$, where n is any integer. Explain your answer.
3. Tell what $_3C_4$ would mean in the real world and why it is not possible.
4. **GET ORGANIZED** Copy and complete the graphic organizer.

	Fundamental Counting Principle	Permutation	Combination
Formula			
Examples			

11-1 Exercises

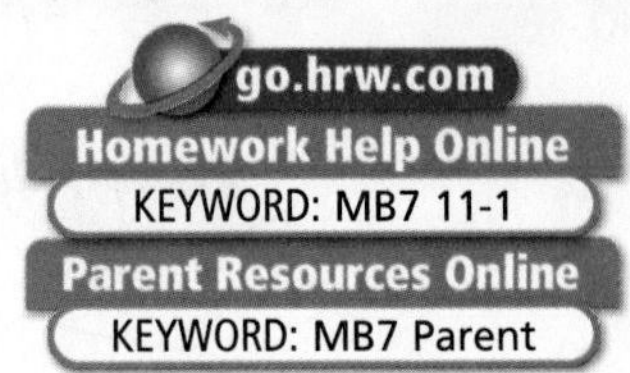

GUIDED PRACTICE

1. **Vocabulary** When you open a rotating combination lock, order is __?__ (*important* or *not important*), so this is a __?__ (*permutation* or *combination*).

SEE EXAMPLE 1 p. 794

2. Jamie purchased 3 blouses, 3 jackets, and 2 skirts. How many different outfits using a blouse, a jacket, and a skirt are possible?
3. An Internet code consists of one digit followed by one letter. The number zero and the letter *O* are excluded. How many codes are possible?

SEE EXAMPLE 2 p. 796

4. Nate is on a 7-day vacation. He plans to spend one day jet skiing and one day golfing. How many ways can Nate schedule the 2 activities?
5. How many ways can you listen to 3 songs from a CD that has 12 selections?
6. Members from 6 different school organizations decorated floats for the homecoming parade. How many different ways can first, second, and third prize be awarded?

SEE EXAMPLE 3 p. 797

7. A teacher wants to send 4 students to the library each day. There are 21 students in the class. How many ways can he choose 4 students to go to the library on the first day?
8. Gregory has a coupon for $1 off the purchase of 3 boxes of Munchie brand cereal. The store has 5 different varieties of Munchie brand cereal. How many ways can Gregory choose 3 boxes of cereal so that each box is a different variety?

PRACTICE AND PROBLEM SOLVING

Independent Practice

For Exercises	See Example
9–10	1
11–13	2
14	3

Extra Practice

Skills Practice p. S24
Application Practice p. S42

9. **Hiking** A hiker can take 4 trails to the lake and then 3 trails from the lake to the cabins. How many routes are there from the lake to the cabins?
10. The cheerleading squad is making posters. They have 3 different colors of poster board and 4 different colors of markers. How many different posters can be made by using one poster board and one marker?
11. How many ways can you choose a manager and assistant from a 9-person task force?
12. How many identification codes are possible by using 3 letters if no letter may be repeated?
13. There are 5 airplanes ready to depart. Runway A and runway D are available. How many ways can 2 planes be assigned to runways without using the same runway?
14. **Food** How many choices of 3 hamburger toppings are possible?

15. **What if...?** In the United Kingdom's National Lottery, you must correctly select a group of 6 numbers from 49. Suppose that the contest were changed to selecting 7 numbers. How many more ways would there be to select the numbers?

Evaluate.

16. ${}_6P_6$
17. ${}_5C_5$
18. ${}_9P_1$
19. ${}_6C_1$
20. $\dfrac{2!}{6!}$
21. $\dfrac{4!3!}{2!}$
22. $\dfrac{9!}{7!}$
23. $\dfrac{8! - 5!}{(8-5)!}$

Geometry **Find the number of ways that each selection can be made.**

24. two marked points to determine slope

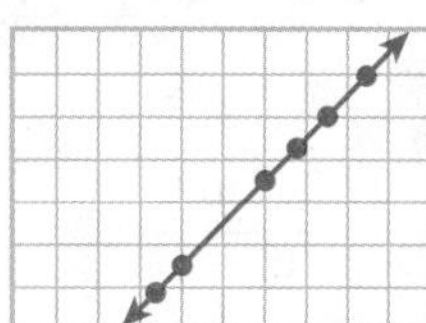

25. four points to form a quadrilateral

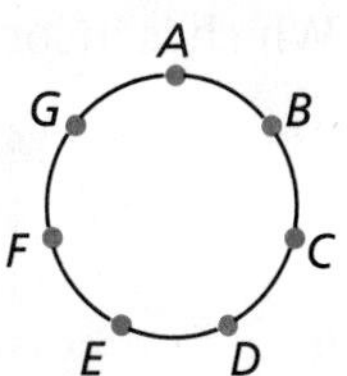

Compare. Write >, <, or =.

26. $_7P_3$ ■ $_7C_4$ **27.** $_7P_4$ ■ $_7P_3$ **28.** $_7C_3$ ■ $_7C_4$ **29.** $_{10}C_{10}$ ■ $_{10}P_{10}$

30. Copy and complete the table. Use the table to explain why 0! is defined as 1.

$n!$	4!	3!	2!	1!
$n(n-1)!$	$4(3!) = 24$	■	■	■

LINK

Music

There are many change-ringing societies and groups, especially in the United Kingdom. Bell ringers work together to follow patterns and called changes to avoid repeating sequences.

31. Critical Thinking Why are there more unique permutations of the letters in YOUNG than in GEESE?

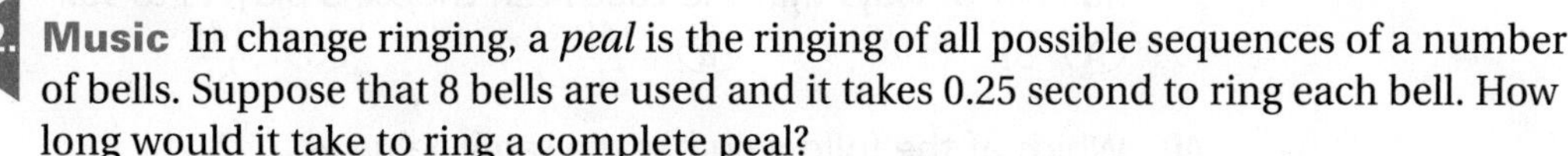

32. Music In change ringing, a *peal* is the ringing of all possible sequences of a number of bells. Suppose that 8 bells are used and it takes 0.25 second to ring each bell. How long would it take to ring a complete peal?

33. Multi-Step Amy, Bob, Charles, Dena, and Esther are club officers.

a. Copy and complete the table to show the ways that a president, a vice president, and a secretary can be chosen if Amy is chosen president. (Use first initials for names.)

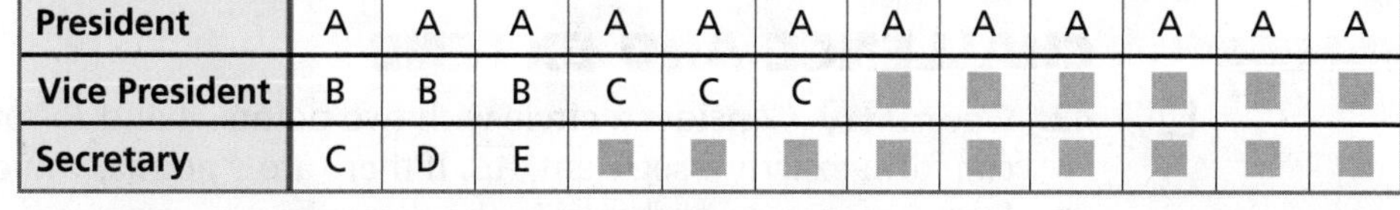

President	A	A	A	A	A	A	A	A	A	A	A	A
Vice President	B	B	B	C	C	C	■	■	■	■	■	■
Secretary	C	D	E	■	■	■	■	■	■	■	■	■

b. Extend the table to show the number of ways that the three officers can be chosen if Bob is chosen president. Make a conjecture as to the number of ways that a president, a vice president, and a secretary can be chosen.

c. Use a formula to find the number of different ways that a president, a vice president, and a secretary can be chosen. Compare your result with part **b.**

d. How many different ways can 3 club officers be chosen to form a committee? Compare this with the answer to part **c.** Which answer is a number of permutations? Which answer is a number of combinations?

34. Critical Thinking Use the formulas to divide $_nP_r$ by $_nC_r$. Predict the result of dividing $_6P_3$ by $_6C_3$. Check your prediction. What meaning does the result have?

35. Write About It Find $_9C_2$ and $_9C_7$. Find $_{10}C_6$ and $_{10}C_4$. Explain the results.

36. This problem will prepare you for the Multi-Step Test Prep on page 826.

While playing the game of Yahtzee, Jen rolls 5 dice and gets the result shown at right.

a. How many different ways can she arrange the dice from left to right?

b. How many different ways can she choose 3 of the dice to reroll?

37. **ERROR ANALYSIS** Below are two solutions for “How many Internet codes can be made by using 3 digits if 0 is excluded and digits may not be repeated?” Which is incorrect? Explain the error.

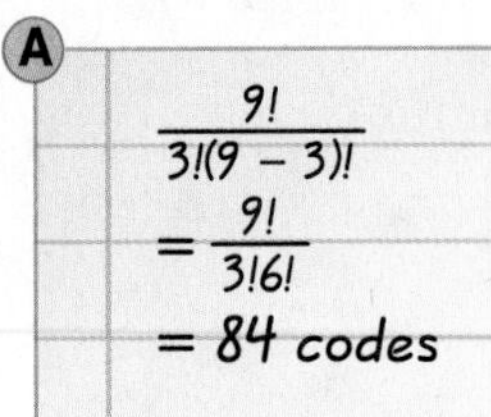

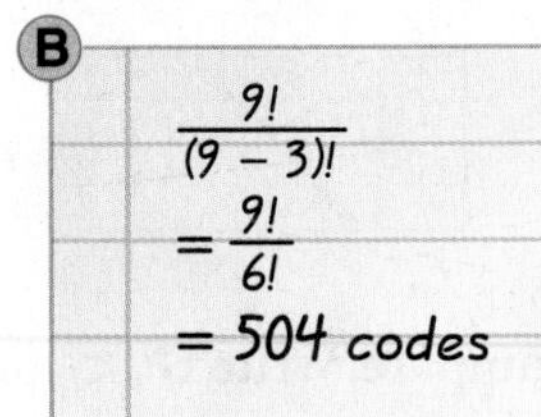

38. **Critical Thinking** Explain how to use the Fundamental Counting Principle to answer the question in Exercise 37.

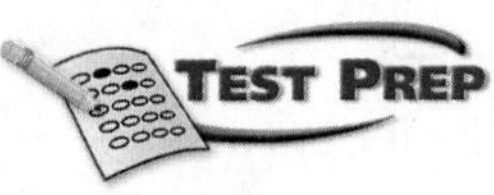

39. There are 14 players on the team. Which of the following expressions models the number of ways that the coach can choose 5 players to start the game?

Ⓐ $5!$ Ⓑ $\dfrac{14!}{5!}$ Ⓒ $\dfrac{14!}{9!}$ Ⓓ $\dfrac{14!}{5!9!}$

40. Which of the following has the same value as ${}_9C_4$?

Ⓕ ${}_9P_4$ Ⓖ ${}_4C_9$ Ⓗ ${}_9P_5$ Ⓙ ${}_9C_5$

41. **Short Response** Rene can choose 1 elective each of the 4 years that she is in high school. There are 15 electives. How many ways can Rene choose her electives?

CHALLENGE AND EXTEND

42. **Geometry** Consider a circle with two points, A and B. You can form exactly 1 segment, $\overline{AB}$. If there are 3 points, you can form 3 segments as shown in the diagram.

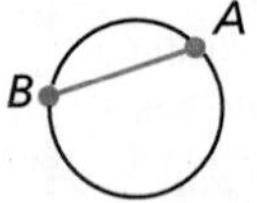

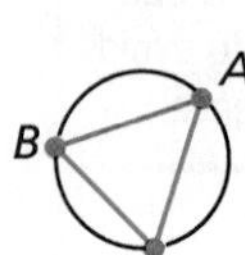

a. How many segments can be formed from 4 points, 5 points, 6 points, and n points? Write your answer for n points as a permutation or combination.

b. How many segments can be formed from 20 points?

43. **Government** How many ways can a jury of 12 and 2 alternate jurors be selected from a pool of 30 potential jurors? (*Hint:* Consider how order is both important and unimportant in selection.) Leave your answer in unexpanded notation.

SPIRAL REVIEW

44. **Money** The cost to rent a boat increased from \$0.15 per mile to \$0.45 per mile. Write a function $p(x)$ for the initial cost and a function $P(x)$ for the cost after the price increase. Graph both functions on the same coordinate plane. Describe the transformation. *(Lesson 1-8)*

Solve each proportion. *(Lesson 2-2)*

45. $\dfrac{17}{n} = \dfrac{11}{77}$ 46. $\dfrac{2.9}{3.7} = \dfrac{x}{23.31}$ 47. $\dfrac{2.2}{n} = \dfrac{1.6}{9.5}$ 48. $\dfrac{x}{36} = \dfrac{98}{18}$

Identify the conic section that each equation represents. *(Lesson 10-6)*

49. $6x^2 + 3xy - 9y^2 + 5x - 2y - 16 = 0$ 50. $8x^2 + 8y^2 - 6x + 7y - 9 = 0$

Relative Area

In *geometric probability,* the probability of an event corresponds to ratios of the areas (or lengths or volumes) or parts of one or more figures.

In the spinners shown, the probability of landing on a color is based on relative area.

$\frac{1}{2}$ shaded $\quad$ $\frac{3}{8}$ shaded $\quad$ $\frac{1}{4}$ shaded

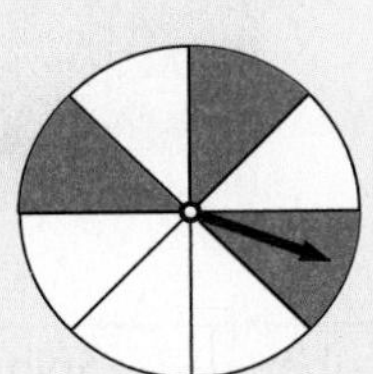

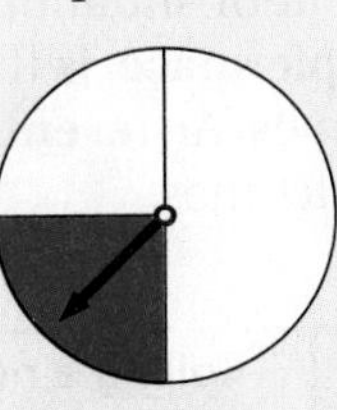

Area Formulas	
Figure	**Formula**
Rectangle	$A = bh$
Square	$A = s^2$
Triangle	$A = \frac{1}{2}bh$
Trapezoid	$A = \frac{1}{2}h(b_1 + b_2)$
Circle	$A = \pi r^2$

Use the area formulas at right to help you determine relative area.

Example

What portion of the rectangle is shaded? Write the relative area as a fraction, a decimal, and a percent.

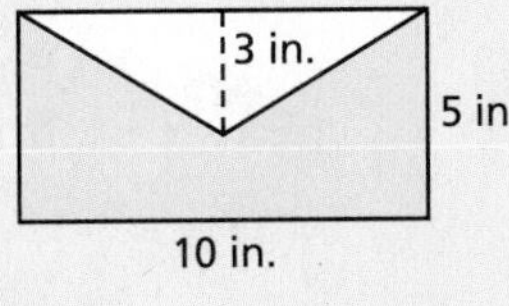

Find the ratio of the area of the shaded region to the area of the rectangle.

$A = 10(5) = 50 \text{ in}^2$ *Area of the rectangle:* $A = bh$

$A = \frac{1}{2}(3)(10) = 15 \text{ in}^2$ *Area of the unshaded triangle:* $A = \frac{1}{2}bh$

$$\frac{\text{area of shaded region}}{\text{area of the rectangle}} = \frac{50 - 15}{50} = \frac{35}{50} = \frac{7}{10} = 0.7\text{, or } 70\%$$

Try This

What portion of each figure is shaded? Write the relative area as a fraction, a decimal, and a percent.

1. 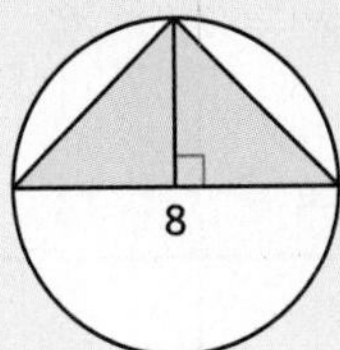

2. 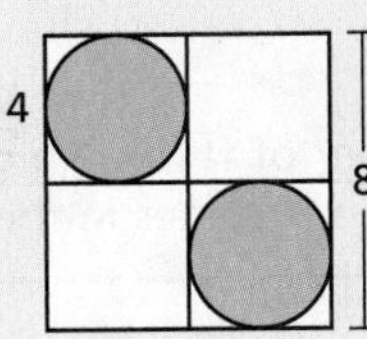

3. 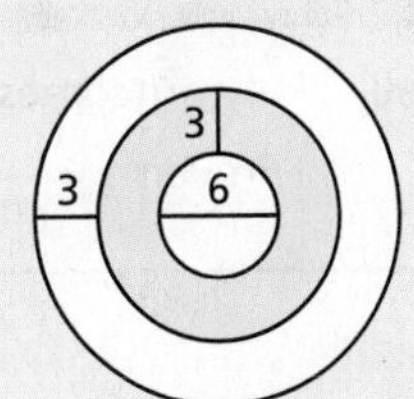

4. 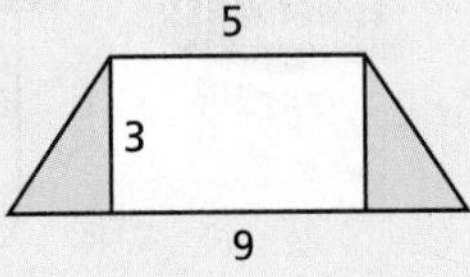

5. Write the relative area of each sector of the spinner as a fraction, decimal, and percent.

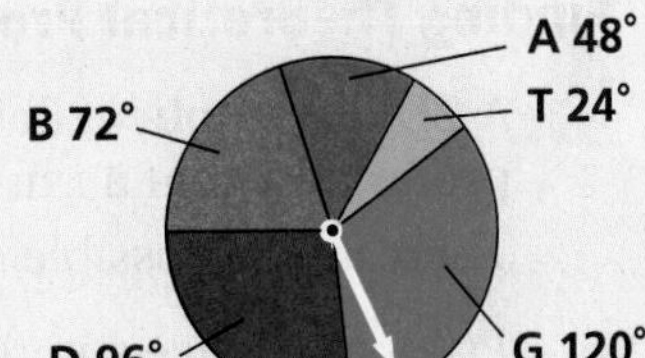

11-2 Theoretical and Experimental Probability

Objectives

Find the theoretical probability of an event.

Find the experimental probability of an event.

Vocabulary

probability
outcome
sample space
event
equally likely outcomes
favorable outcomes
theoretical probability
complement
geometric probability
experiment
trial
experimental probability

Why learn this?

You can use probability to find the chances of hitting or missing a target in the game Battleship. (See Example 2.)

Probability is the measure of how likely an event is to occur. Each possible result of a probability experiment or situation is an **outcome**. The **sample space** is the set of all possible outcomes. An **event** is an outcome or set of outcomes.

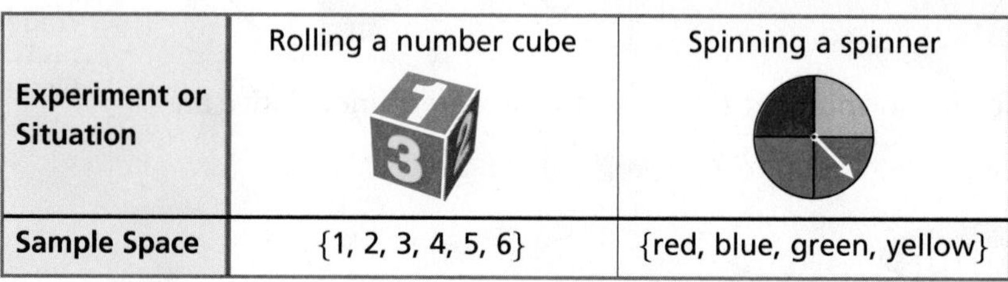

Experiment or Situation	Rolling a number cube	Spinning a spinner
Sample Space	{1, 2, 3, 4, 5, 6}	{red, blue, green, yellow}

Probabilities are written as fractions or decimals from 0 to 1, or as percents from 0% to 100%.

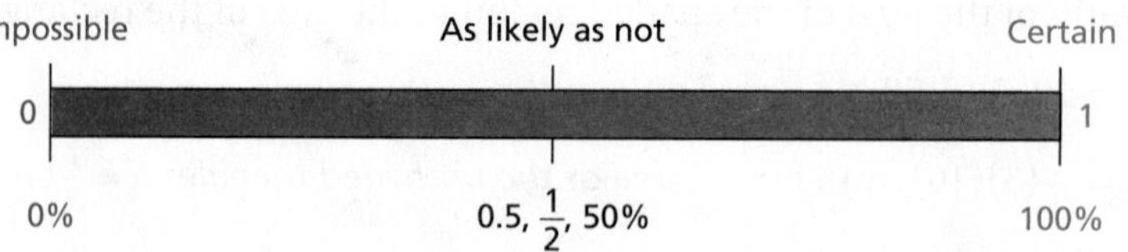

Equally likely outcomes have the same chance of occurring. When you toss a fair coin, heads and tails are equally likely outcomes. **Favorable outcomes** are outcomes in a specified event. For equally likely outcomes, the **theoretical probability** of an event is the ratio of the number of favorable outcomes to the total number of outcomes.

Theoretical Probability

For equally likely outcomes,

$$P(\text{event}) = \frac{\text{number of favorable outcomes}}{\text{number of outcomes in the sample space}}.$$

EXAMPLE 1 Finding Theoretical Probability

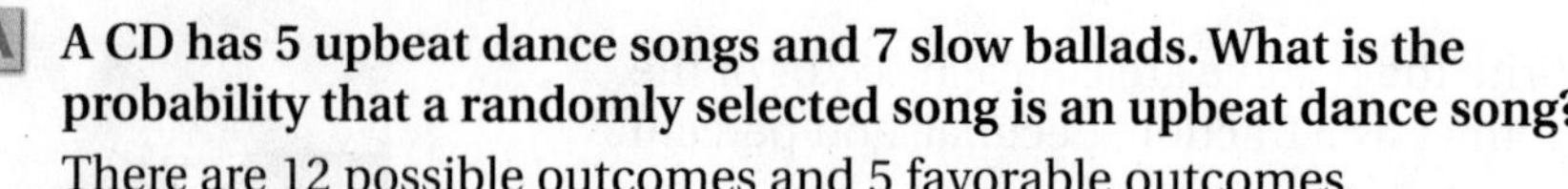

A **A CD has 5 upbeat dance songs and 7 slow ballads. What is the probability that a randomly selected song is an upbeat dance song?**

There are 12 possible outcomes and 5 favorable outcomes.

$P(\text{upbeat dance song}) = \frac{5}{12} \approx 41.7\%$

B **A red number cube and a blue number cube are rolled. If all numbers are equally likely, what is the probability that the sum is 10?**

There are 36 possible outcomes.

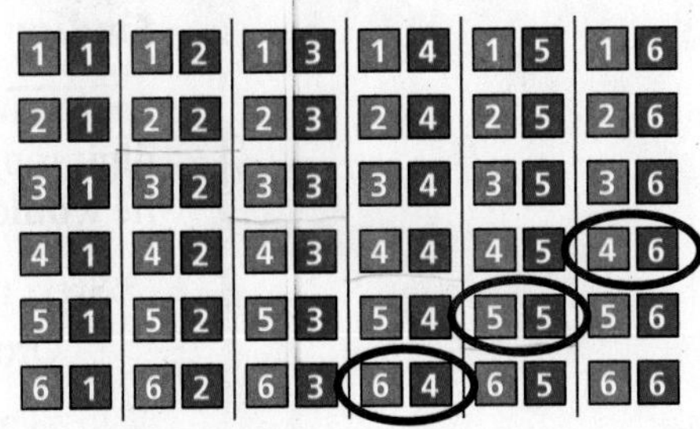

$$P(\text{sum is } 10) = \frac{\text{number of outcomes with sum of 10}}{36}$$

$$P(\text{sum is } 10) = \frac{3}{36} = \frac{1}{12}$$ *3 outcomes with a sum of 10: (4, 6) (5, 5), and (6, 4)*

A red number cube and a blue number cube are rolled. If all numbers are equally likely, what is the probability of each event?

1a. The sum is 6.

1b. The difference is 6.

1c. The red cube is greater.

The sum of all probabilities in the sample space is 1. The **complement** of an event E is the set of all outcomes in the sample space that are not in E.

Complement

The probability of the complement of event E is

$$P(\text{not } E) = 1 - P(E).$$

EXAMPLE 2 *Entertainment Application*

The game Battleship is played with 5 ships on a 100-hole grid. Players try to guess the locations of their opponent's ships and sink them. At the start of the game, what is the probability that the first shot misses all targets?

$P(\text{miss}) = 1 - P(\text{hit})$ *Use the complement.*

$P(\text{miss}) = 1 - \frac{17}{100}$ *There are 17 total holes covered by game pieces.*

$= \frac{83}{100}$, or 83%

There is an 83% chance of the first shot missing all targets.

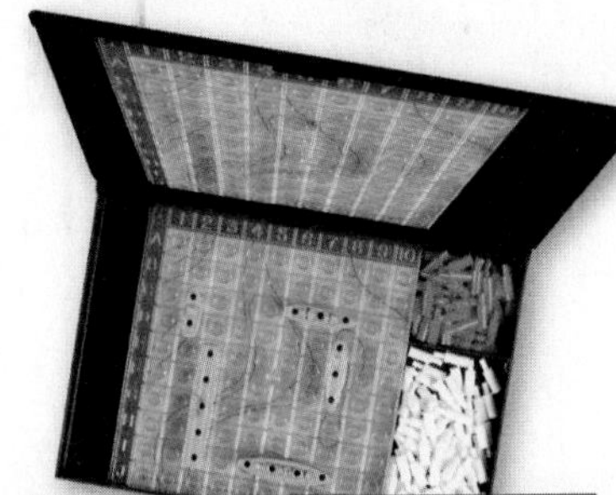

Battleship Pieces

Game Piece	Number of Holes Covered
Destroyer	2
Cruiser	3
Submarine	3
Battleship	4
Carrier	5

2. Two integers from 1 to 10 are randomly selected. The same number may be chosen twice. What is the probability that both numbers are less than 9?

EXAMPLE 3 Finding Probability with Permutations or Combinations

Each student received a 4-digit code to use the library computers, with no digit repeated. Manu received the code 7654. What was the probability that he would receive a code of consecutive numbers?

Step 1 Determine whether the code is a permutation or a combination.
Order is important, so it is a permutation.

Step 2 Find the number of outcomes in the sample space.
The sample space is the number of permutations of 4 of 10 digits.

$$_{10}P_4 = \frac{10!}{6!} = \frac{10 \cdot 9 \cdot 8 \cdot 7 \cdot \cancel{6 \cdot 5 \cdot 4 \cdot 3 \cdot 2 \cdot 1}}{\cancel{6 \cdot 5 \cdot 4 \cdot 3 \cdot 2 \cdot 1}} = 5040$$

Step 3 Find the favorable outcomes.
The favorable outcomes are the codes 0123, 1234, 2345, 3456, 4567, 5678, 6789, and the reverse of each of these numbers. There are 14 favorable outcomes.

Step 4 Find the probability.

$$P(\text{consecutive numbers}) = \frac{14}{5040} = \frac{1}{360}$$

The probability that Manu would receive a code of consecutive numbers was $\frac{1}{360}$.

3. A DJ randomly selects 2 of 8 ads to play before her show. Two of the ads are by a local retailer. What is the probability that she will play both of the retailer's ads before her show?

Geometric probability is a form of theoretical probability determined by a ratio of lengths, areas, or volumes.

EXAMPLE 4 Finding Geometric Probability

Three semicircles with diameters 2, 4, and 6 cm are arranged as shown in the figure. If a point inside the figure is chosen at random, what is the probability that the point is inside the shaded region?

4 cm
2 cm
6 cm

Find the ratio of the area of the shaded region to the area of the entire semicircle. The area of a semicircle is $\frac{1}{2}\pi r^2$.

First, find the area of the entire semicircle.

$A_t = \frac{1}{2}\pi(3^2) = 4.5\pi$ *Total area of largest semicircle*

Next, find the unshaded area.

$A_u = \left[\frac{1}{2}\pi(2^2)\right] + \left[\frac{1}{2}\pi(1^2)\right] = 2\pi + 0.5\pi = 2.5\pi$ *Sum of areas of the unshaded semicircles*

Subtract to find the shaded area.

$A_s = 4.5\pi - 2.5\pi = 2\pi$ *Area of shaded region*

$\frac{A_s}{A_t} = \frac{2\pi}{4.5\pi} = \frac{2}{4.5} = \frac{4}{9}$ *Ratio of shaded region to total area*

The probability that the point is in the shaded region is $\frac{4}{9}$.

4. Find the probability that a point chosen at random inside the large triangle is in the small triangle.

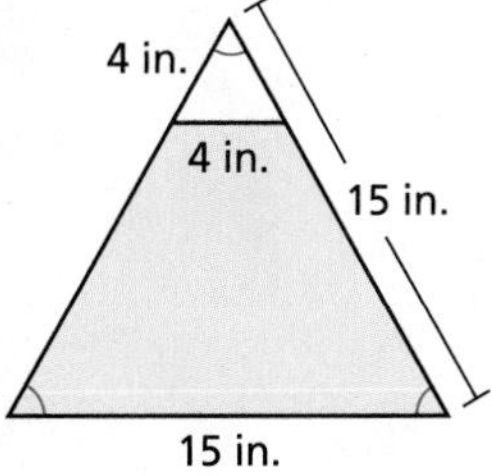

You can estimate the probability of an event by using data, or by **experiment**. For example, if a doctor states that an operation "has an 80% probability of success," 80% is an estimate of probability based on similar case histories.

Each repetition of an experiment is a **trial**. The sample space of an experiment is the set of all possible outcomes. The **experimental probability** of an event is the ratio of the number of times that the event occurs, the *frequency*, to the number of trials.

Experimental Probability

$$\text{experimental probability} = \frac{\text{number of times the event occurs}}{\text{number of trials}}$$

Experimental probability is often used to estimate theoretical probability and to make predictions.

EXAMPLE 5 Finding Experimental Probability

The bar graph shows the results of 100 tosses of an oddly shaped number cube. Find each experimental probability.

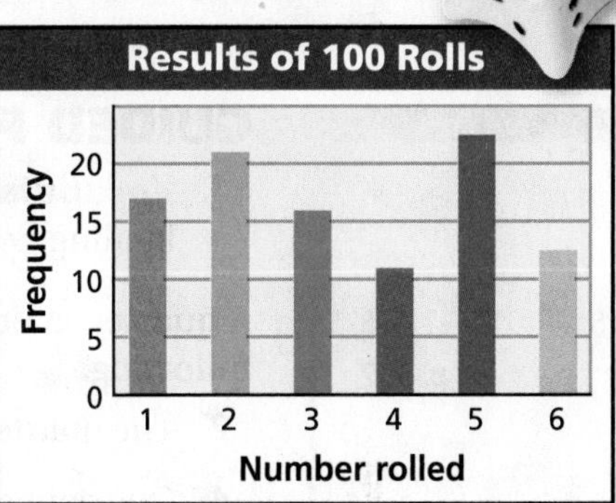

A rolling a 3

The outcome 3 occurred 16 times out of 100 trials.

$P(3) = \frac{16}{100} = \frac{4}{25} = 0.16$

Helpful Hint

Frequencies must be whole numbers, so they can be easily read from the graph in Example 5.

B rolling a perfect square

$$P(\text{perfect square}) = \frac{17 + 11}{100}$$

$$= \frac{28}{100} = \frac{7}{25} = 0.28$$

The numbers 1 and 4 are perfect squares. 1 occurred 17 times and 4 occurred 11 times.

C rolling a number other than 5

Use the complement.

$$P(5) = \frac{22}{100}$$

5 occurred 22 times out of 100 trials.

$$1 - P(5) = 1 - \frac{22}{100} = \frac{78}{100} = \frac{39}{50} = 0.78$$

5. The table shows the results of choosing one card from a deck of cards, recording the suit, and then replacing the card.

Card Suit	Hearts	Diamonds	Clubs	Spades
Number	5	9	7	5

5a. Find the experimental probability of choosing a diamond.

5b. Find the experimental probability of choosing a card that is not a club.

THINK AND DISCUSS

1. Explain whether the probability of an event can be 1.5.
2. Tell which events have the same probability when two number cubes are tossed: sum of 7, sum of 5, sum of 9, and sum of 11.
3. Compare the theoretical and experimental probabilities of getting heads when tossing a coin if Joe got heads 8 times in 20 tosses of the coin.

4. **GET ORGANIZED** Copy and complete the graphic organizer. Give an example of each probability concept.

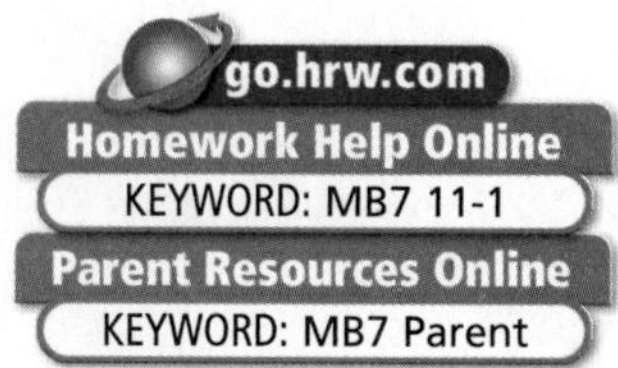

11-2 Exercises

go.hrw.com
Homework Help Online
KEYWORD: MB7 11-1
Parent Resources Online
KEYWORD: MB7 Parent

GUIDED PRACTICE

1. **Vocabulary** A fair coin is tossed 8 times and lands heads up 3 times. The ___?___ of landing heads is $\frac{1}{2}$.(*theoretical probability* or *experimental probability*)

SEE EXAMPLE 1 p. 802

A quarter, a nickel, and a penny are flipped. Find the probability of each of the following.

2. The quarter shows heads.
3. The penny and nickel show heads.
4. One coin shows heads.
5. All three coins land the same way.

SEE EXAMPLE 2 p. 803

6. What is the probability that a random 2-digit number (00-99) does not end in 5?
7. What is the probability that a randomly selected date in one year is not in the month of December or January?

SEE EXAMPLE 3 p. 804

8. A clerk has 4 different letters that need to go in 4 different envelopes. What is the probability that all 4 letters are placed in the correct envelopes?
9. There are 12 balloons in a bag: 3 each of blue, green, red, and yellow. Three balloons are chosen at random. Find the probability that all 3 of the balloons are green.

SEE EXAMPLE 4 p. 804

Use the diagram for Exercises 10 and 11. Find each probability.

10. that a point chosen at random is in the shaded area
11. that a point chosen at random is in the smallest circle

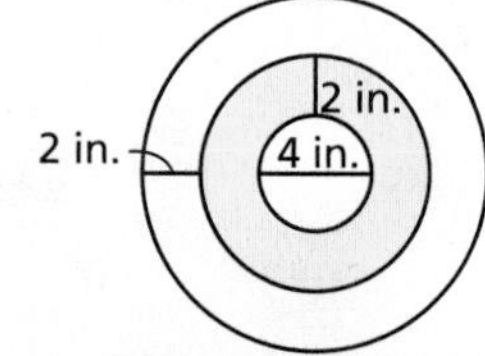

SEE EXAMPLE 5 p. 805

Use the table for Exercises 12 and 13.

12. Find the experimental probability of spinning red.
13. Find the experimental probability of spinning red or blue.

Spinner Experiment

Color	Red	Green	Blue
Spins	5	8	7

PRACTICE AND PROBLEM SOLVING

Independent Practice	
For Exercises	See Example
14–15	1
16	2
17–18	3
19	4
20	5

Extra Practice

Skills Practice p. S24
Application Practice p. S42

There are 3 green marbles, 7 red marbles, and 5 white marbles in a bag. Find the probability of each of the following.

14. The chosen marble is white.

15. The chosen marble is red or white.

16. Two integers from 1 to 8 are randomly selected. The same number can be chosen both times. What is the probability that both numbers are greater than 2?

17. **Swimming** The coach randomly selects 3 swimmers from a team of 8 to swim in a heat. What is the probability that she will choose the three strongest swimmers?

18. **Books** There are 7 books numbered 1–7 on the summer reading list. Peter randomly chooses 2 books. What is the probability that Peter chooses books numbered 1 and 2?

19. **Games** In the game of corntoss, players throw corn-filled bags at a hole in a wooden platform. If a bag that hits the platform can hit any location with an equal likelihood, find the probability that a tossed bag lands in the hole.

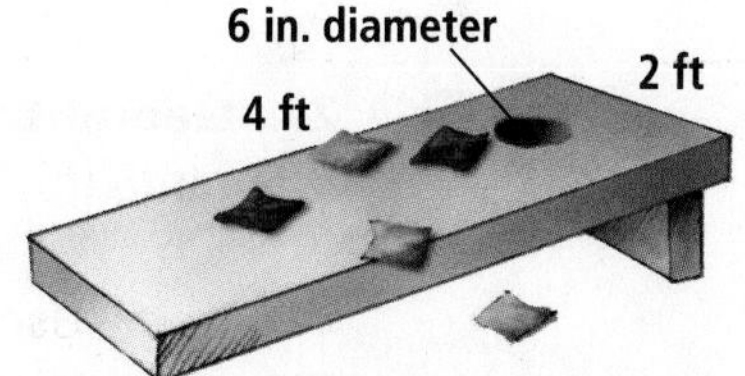

20. **Cards** An experiment consists of choosing one card from a standard deck and then replacing it. The experiment was done several times, and the results are: 8 hearts, 8 diamonds, 6 spades, and 6 clubs. Find the experimental probability that a card is red.

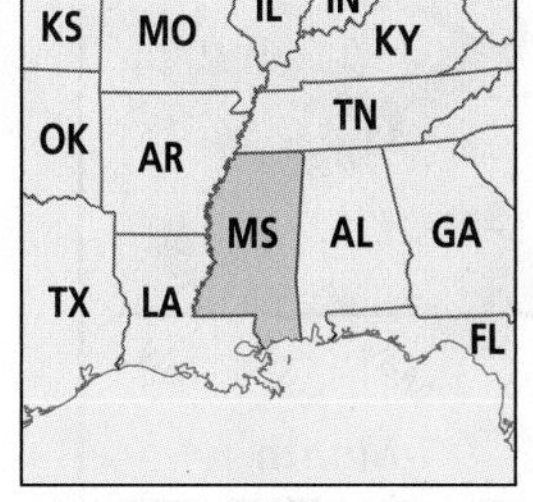

21. **Critical Thinking** Explain whether the experimental probability of tossing tails when a fair coin is tossed 25 times is always, sometimes, or never equal to the theoretical probability.

22. **Games** A radio station in Mississippi is giving away a trip to the Mississippi coast from any other state in the United States. Assuming an equally likely chance for a winner from any other state, what is the probability that the winner will be from a state that does not border Mississippi?

23. **Geometry** **Use the figure.**
    a. A circle with radius r is inscribed in a square with side length $2r$. What is the ratio of the area of the circle to the area of the square?
    b. A square board has an inscribed circle with a 15 in. radius. A small button is dropped 10,000 times on the board, landing inside the circle 7852 times. How can you use this experiment to estimate a value for π?

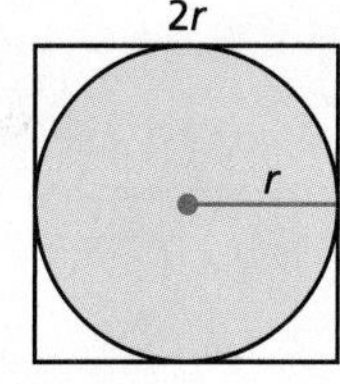

24. **Games** The sides of a backgammon die are marked with the numbers 2, 4, 8, 16, 32, and 64. Describe an outcome that has a probability of $\frac{2}{3}$.

25. **Computer** A player in a computer basketball program has a constant probability of making each free throw. Jack notes the success rate over a period of time.
    a. Find the experimental probability for each set of 25 attempts as a decimal.
    b. Find the experimental probability for the entire experiment.
    c. What is the best estimate of the theoretical probability? Justify your answer.

Free Throw Shooting

Attempts	Free Throws Made
1–25	17
26–50	21
51–75	19
76–100	16

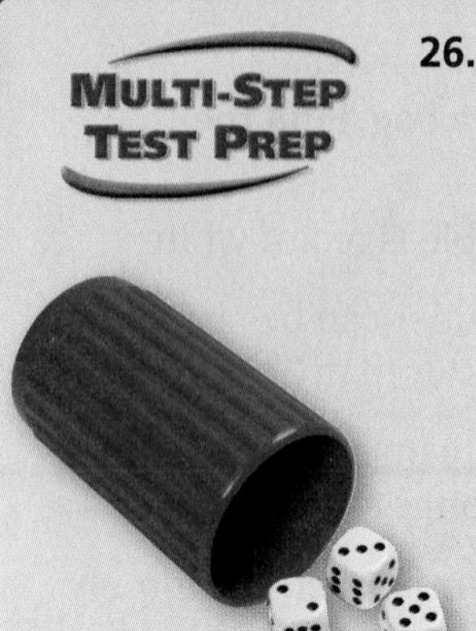

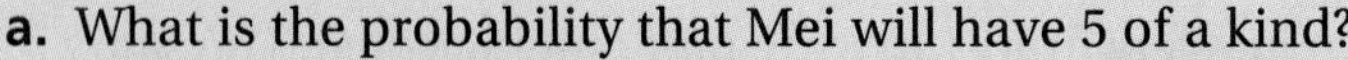

26. This problem will prepare you for the Multi-Step Test Prep on page 826.

While playing Yahtzee and rolling 5 dice, Mei gets the result shown at right. Mei decides to keep the three 4's and reroll the other 2 dice.

a. What is the probability that Mei will have 5 of a kind?

b. What is the probability that she will have 4 of a kind (four 4's plus something else)?

c. What is the probability that she will have exactly three 4's?

d. How are the answers to parts **a, b,** and **c** related?

27. **Geometry** The points along $\overline{AF}$ are evenly spaced. A point is randomly chosen. Find the probability that the point lies on $\overline{BD}$.

1 2 3 4 5 6
A B C D E F

Weather Use the graph and the following information for Exercises 28–30.
The table shows the number of days that the maximum temperature was above 90°F in Death Valley National Park in 2002.

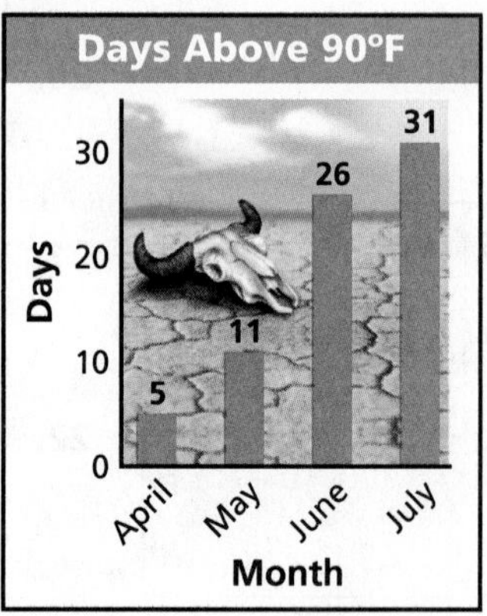

28. What is the experimental probability that the maximum temperature will be greater than 90°F on a given day in April?

29. For what month would you estimate the theoretical probability of a maximum temperature no greater than 90°F to be about 0.13? Explain.

30. May has 31 days. How would the experimental probability be affected if someone mistakenly used 30 days to calculate the experimental probability that the maximum temperature will not be greater than 90°F on a given day in May?

31. **Critical Thinking** Is it possible for the experimental probability of an event to be 0 if the theoretical probability is 1? Is it possible for the experimental probability of an event to be 0 if the theoretical probability is 0.99? Explain.

32 **Geometry** The two circles circumscribe and inscribe the square. Find the probability that a random point in the large circle is within the inner circle. (*Hint:* Use the Pythagorean Theorem.)

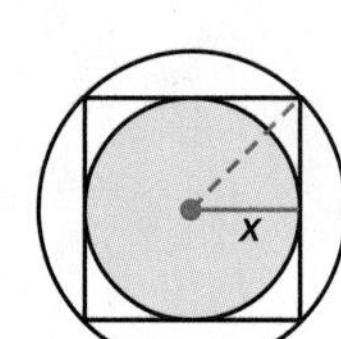

33. **Critical Thinking** Lexi tossed a fair coin 20 times, resulting in 12 heads and 8 tails. What is the theoretical probability that Lexi will get heads on the next toss? Explain.

34. **Athletics** Do male or female high school basketball players have a better chance of playing on college teams? on professional teams? Explain.

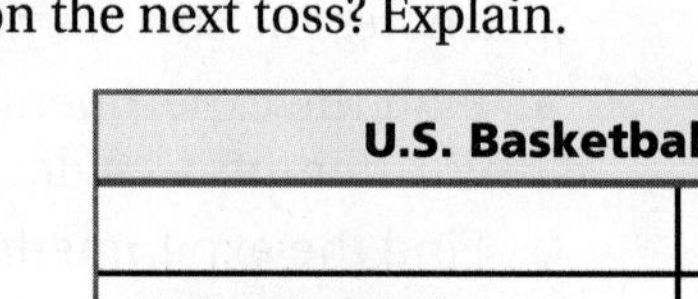

U.S. Basketball Players

	Men	Women
High School Players	549,500	456,900
College Players	4,500	4,100
College Players Drafted by Pro Leagues	44	32

Source: www.ncaa.org

35. **Write About It** Describe the difference between theoretical probability and experimental probability. Give an example in which they may differ.

TEST PREP

36. A fair coin is tossed 25 times, landing tails up 14 times. What is the experimental probability of heads?

(A) 0.44 (B) 0.50 (C) 0.56 (D) 0.79

37. **Geometry** Find the probability that a point chosen at random in the large rectangle at right will lie in the shaded area, to the nearest percent.

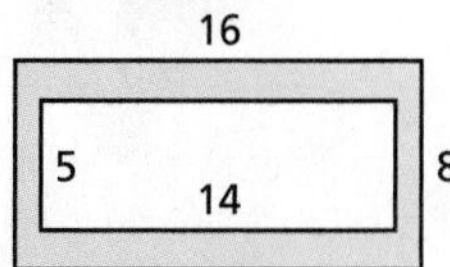

(F) 18% (G) 45% (H) 55% (J) 71%

38. How many outcomes are in the sample space when a quarter, a dime, and a nickel are tossed?

(A) 3 (B) 6 (C) 8 (D) 12

39. Two number cubes are rolled. What is the theoretical probability that the sum is 5?

(F) $\frac{1}{3}$ (G) $\frac{1}{6}$ (H) $\frac{1}{9}$ (J) $\frac{1}{12}$

40. **Short Response** Find the probability that a point chosen at random on the part of the number line shown will lie between points B and C.

4 8 12 24
A B C D

CHALLENGE AND EXTEND

41. The graph illustrates a statistical property known as the *law of large numbers*. Make a conjecture about the effect on probability as the number of trials gets very large. Give an example of how the probability might be affected for a real-world situation.

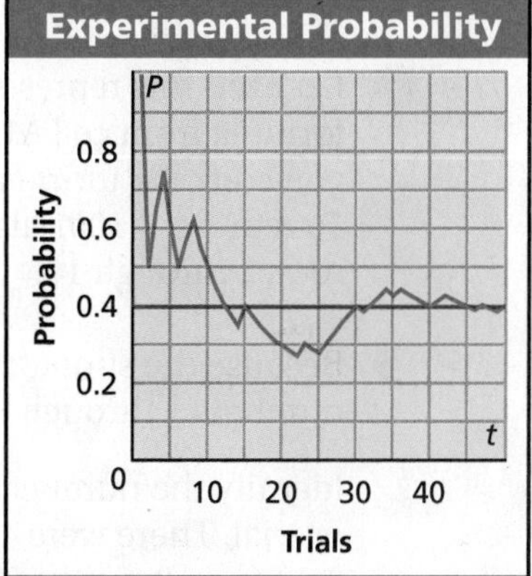

42. Four trumpet players' instruments are mixed up, and the trumpets are given to the players just before a concert. What is the probability that *no one* gets his or her trumpet back?

43. The table shows the data from a spinner experiment. Draw a reasonable spinner with 6 regions that may have been used for this experiment.

Spinner Experiment				
Color	Red	Blue	Green	Yellow
Occurrences	23	44	7	26

SPIRAL REVIEW

Find the minimum or maximum value of each function. *(Lesson 5-2)*

44. $f(x) = 0.25x^2 - 0.85x + 1$

45. $f(x) = -2x^2 + 20x - 34$

Write the equation in standard form for each parabola. *(Lesson 10-5)*

46. vertex $(0, 0)$, directrix $x = -3$

47. vertex $(0, 0)$, directrix $y = 5$

48. A coach chooses 5 players for a basketball team from a group of 11. *(Lesson 11-1)*
   a. How many ways can she choose 5 players?
   b. How many ways can she choose 5 players to play different positions?

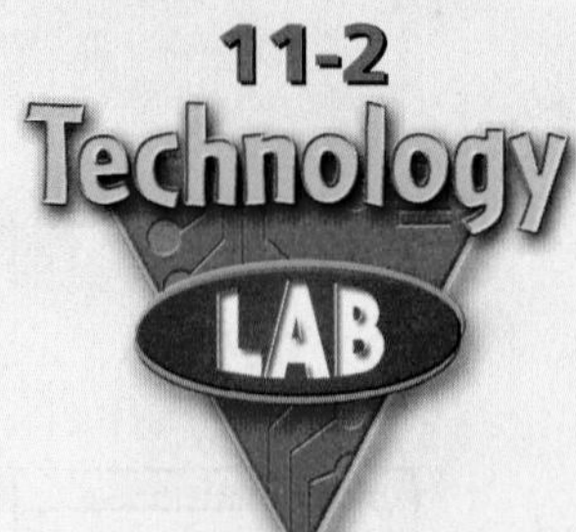

Explore Simulations

A *simulation* is a model that uses random numbers to approximate experimental probability. You can use a spreadsheet to perform simulations. The **RAND( )** function generates random decimal values greater than or equal to 0 and less than 1. The **INT** function gives the greatest integer less than or equal to the input value. The functions can be used together to generate random integers as shown in the table

Random Numbers		
Formula	**Output**	**Example**
=RAND()	Decimal values $0 \le n < 1$	0.279606096
=**100***RAND()	Decimal values $0 \le n < 100$	27.9606096
=**INT**(100*RAND())	Integers $0 \le n \le 99$	27
=INT(100*RAND())**+1**	Integers $1 \le n \le 100$	28

Activity

Use a simulation to find the experimental probability that a 65% free throw shooter will make at least 4 of his next 5 attempts.

1. To represent a percent, enter the formula for random integers from 1 to 100 into cell A1.

A1 | fx =INT(100*RAND())+1

	A	B	C	D	E
1	38				

2. Let each row represent a trial of 5 attempts. Copy the formula from cell A1 into cells B1 through E1. Each time you copy the formula, the random values will change. To represent 10 trials, copy the formulas from row 1 into rows 2 through 10.

A1 | fx =INT(100*RAND())+1

	A	B	C	D	E
1	72	98	34	74	87

3. Because the shooter makes 65% of his attempts, let the numbers 1 through 65 represent a successful attempt.

	A	B	C	D	E
1	✓ 25	✓ 2	✓ 62	✓ 26	✓ 38
2	✓ 30	✓ 32	66	88	✓ 9
3	✓ 27	✓ 18	✓ 9	✓ 9	93
4	98	✓ 34	✓ 10	86	99
5	87	✓ 64	✓ 4	74	✓ 36
6	✓ 5	97	69	83	✓ 51
7	✓ 39	✓ 39	80	95	97
8	✓ 32	✓ 64	✓ 51	✓ 64	✓ 46
9	✓ 52	81	✓ 39	✓ 5	✓ 36
10	✓ 48	✓ 46	✓ 45	69	✓ 21

Identify the number of successful attempts in each row, or trial. There were 4 or more successes in trials 1, 3, 8, 9, and 10. So there is about a $\frac{5}{10}$, or 50%, experimental probability that the shooter will make at least 4 of his next 5 attempts.

Note that each time you run the simulation, you may get a different probability. The more trials you perform, the more reliable your estimate will be.

Try This

Use a simulation to find each experimental probability.

1. An energy drink game advertises a 25% chance of winning with each bottle cap. Find the experimental probability that a 6-pack will contain at least 3 winners.
2. In a game with a 40% chance of winning, your friend challenges you to win 4 times in a row. Find the experimental probability of this happening in the next 4 games.
3. **Critical Thinking** How would you design a simulation to find the probability that a baseball player with a .285 batting average will get a hit in 5 of his next 10 at bats?

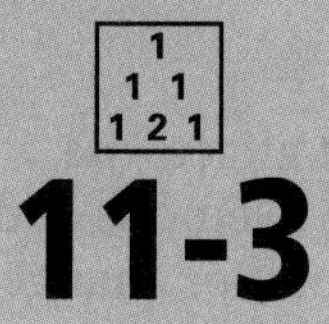

11-3 Independent and Dependent Events

Objectives

Determine whether events are independent or dependent.

Find the probability of independent and dependent events.

Vocabulary

independent events
dependent events
conditional probability

Who uses this?

Political analysts can use demographic information and probabilities to predict the results of elections. (See Example 3.)

Events are **independent events** if the occurrence of one event does not affect the probability of the other.

If a coin is tossed twice, its landing heads up on the first toss and landing heads up on the second toss are independent events. The outcome of one toss does not affect the probability of heads on the other toss. To find the probability of tossing heads twice, multiply the individual probabilities, $\frac{1}{2} \cdot \frac{1}{2}$, or $\frac{1}{4}$.

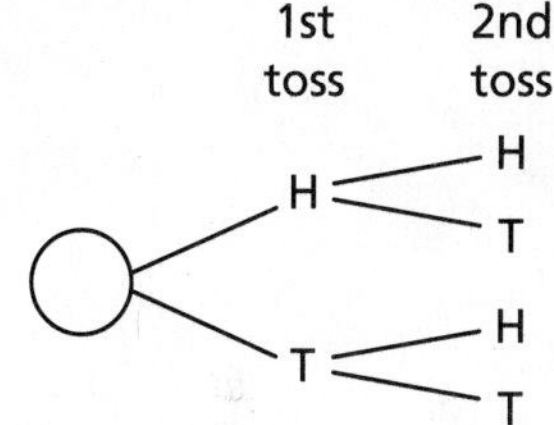

Know it! Note

Probability of Independent Events

If A and B are independent events, then $P(A \text{ and } B) = P(A) \cdot P(B)$.

EXAMPLE 1 Finding the Probability of Independent Events

Find each probability.

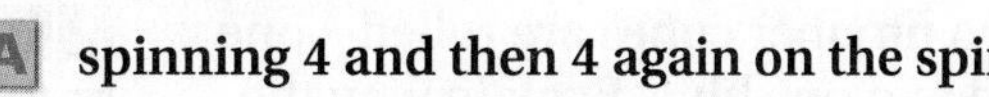

A spinning 4 and then 4 again on the spinner

Spinning a 4 once does not affect the probability of spinning a 4 again, so the events are independent.

$P(4 \text{ and then } 4) = P(4) \cdot P(4)$

$\frac{3}{8} \cdot \frac{3}{8} = \frac{9}{64}$ *3 of the 8 equal sectors are labeled 4.*

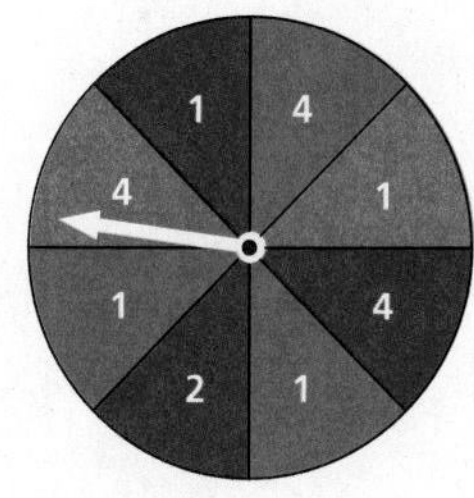

B spinning red, then green, and then red on the spinner

The result of any spin does not affect the probability of any other outcome.

$P(\text{red, then green, and then red}) = P(\text{red}) \cdot P(\text{green}) \cdot P(\text{red})$

$= \frac{1}{4} \cdot \frac{3}{8} \cdot \frac{1}{4} = \frac{3}{128}$ *2 of the 8 equal sectors are red; 3 are green.*

Find each probability.

1a. rolling a 6 on one number cube and a 6 on another number cube

1b. tossing heads, then heads, and then tails when tossing a coin 3 times

Events are **dependent events** if the occurrence of one event affects the probability of the other. For example, suppose that there are 2 lemons and 1 lime in a bag. If you pull out two pieces of fruit, the probabilities change depending on the outcome of the first.

The tree diagram shows the probabilities for choosing two pieces of fruit from a bag containing 2 lemons and 1 lime.

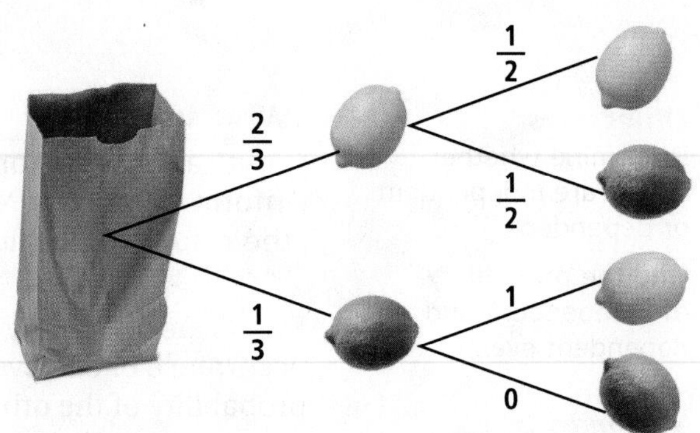

The probability of a specific event can be found by multiplying the probabilities on the branches that make up the event. For example, the probability of drawing two lemons is $\frac{2}{3} \cdot \frac{1}{2} = \frac{1}{3}$.

To find the probability of dependent events, you can use **conditional probability** $P(B \mid A)$, the probability of event B, given that event A has occurred.

Probability of Dependent Events

If A and B are dependent events, then $P(A \text{ and } B) = P(A) \cdot P(B \mid A)$, where $P(B \mid A)$ is the probability of B, given that A has occurred.

EXAMPLE 2 Finding the Probability of Dependent Events

Two number cubes are rolled—one red and one blue. Explain why the events are dependent. Then find the indicated probability.

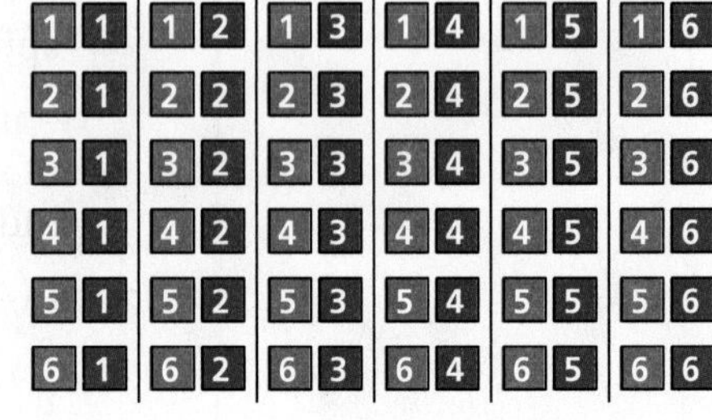

The red cube shows a 1, and the sum is less than 4.

Step 1 Explain why the events are dependent.

$$P(\text{red } 1) = \frac{6}{36} = \frac{1}{6}$$ *Of 36 outcomes, 6 have a red 1.*

$$P(\text{sum} < 4 \mid \text{red } 1) = \frac{2}{6} = \frac{1}{3}$$ *Of 6 outcomes with a red 1, 2 have a sum less than 4.*

The events "the red cube shows a 1" and "the sum is less than 4" are dependent because $P(\text{sum} < 4)$ is different when it is known that a red 1 has occurred.

Step 2 Find the probability.

$$P(A \text{ and } B) = P(A) \cdot P(B \mid A)$$
$$P(\text{red } 1 \text{ and sum} < 4) = P(\text{red } 1) \cdot P(\text{sum} < 4 \mid \text{red } 1)$$
$$= \frac{1}{6} \cdot \frac{2}{3} = \frac{1}{18}$$

Helpful Hint

In Example 2A, you can check to see that 2 of the 36 outcomes, or $\frac{1}{18}$, have a red 1 and a sum less than 4: (1, 1) and (1, 2).

Explain why the events are dependent. Then find the indicated probability.

B **The blue cube shows a multiple of 3, and the sum is 8.**

The events are dependent because $P(\text{sum is } 8)$ is different when the blue cube shows a multiple of 3.

$P(\text{blue multiple of } 3) = \frac{2}{6} = \frac{1}{3}$ *Of 6 outcomes for blue, 2 have a multiple of 3.*

$P(\text{sum is } 8 \mid \text{blue multiple of } 3) = \frac{2}{12} = \frac{1}{6}$ *Of 12 outcomes that have a blue multiple of 3, 2 have a sum 8.*

$P(\text{blue multiple of 3 and sum is } 8) =$

$P(\text{blue multiple of } 3) \cdot P(\text{sum is } 8 \mid \text{blue multiple of } 3) = \left(\frac{1}{3}\right)\left(\frac{1}{6}\right) = \frac{1}{18}$

Two number cubes are rolled—one red and one black. Explain why the events are dependent, and then find the indicated probability.

2. The red cube shows a number greater than 4, and the sum is greater than 9.

Conditional probability often applies when data fall into categories.

EXAMPLE 3 Using a Table to Find Conditional Probability

Largest Texas Counties' Votes for President 2004 (thousands)			
County	Bush	Kerry	Other
Harris	581	472	5
Dallas	345	336	4
Tarrant	349	207	3
Bexar	260	210	3
Travis	148	197	5

The table shows the approximate distribution of votes in Texas' five largest counties in the 2004 presidential election. Find each probability.

A **that a voter from Tarrant County voted for George Bush**

$P(\text{Bush} \mid \text{Tarrant}) = \frac{349}{559} \approx 0.624$ *Use the Tarrant row. Of 559,000 Tarrant voters, 349,000 voted for Bush.*

B **that a voter voted for John Kerry and was from Dallas County**

$P(\text{Dallas} \mid \text{Kerry}) = \frac{336}{1422}$ *Of 1,422,000 who voted for Kerry, 336,000 were from Dallas County.*

$P(\text{Kerry and Dallas} \mid \text{Kerry}) = \frac{1422}{3125} \cdot \frac{336}{1422}$ *There were 3,125,000 total voters.*

≈ 0.108

Find each probability.

3a. that a voter from Travis county voted for someone other than George Bush or John Kerry

3b. that a voter was from Harris county and voted for George Bush

In many cases involving random selection, events are independent when there is replacement and dependent when there is not replacement.

EXAMPLE 4 Determining Whether Events Are Independent or Dependent

Two cards are drawn from a deck of 52. Determine whether the events are independent or dependent. Find the probability.

> **Remember!**
> A standard card deck contains 4 suits of 13 cards each. The face cards are the jacks, queens, and kings.

A selecting two aces when the first card is replaced

Replacing the first card means that the occurrence of the first selection will not affect the probability of the second selection, so the events are independent.

$P(\text{ace} \mid \text{ace on first draw}) = P(\text{ace}) \cdot P(\text{ace})$

$= \frac{4}{52} \cdot \frac{4}{52} = \frac{1}{169}$ *4 of the 52 cards are aces.*

B selecting a face card and then a 7 when the first card is not replaced

Not replacing the first card means that there will be fewer cards to choose from, affecting the probability of the second selection, so the events are dependent.

$P(\text{face card}) \cdot P(7 \mid \text{first card was a face card})$

$= \frac{12}{52} \cdot \frac{4}{51} = \frac{4}{221}$ *There are 12 face cards, four 7's and 51 cards available for the second selection.*

A bag contains 10 beads—2 black, 3 white, and 5 red. A bead is selected at random. Determine whether the events are independent or dependent. Find the indicated probability.

4a. selecting a white bead, replacing it, and then selecting a red bead

4b. selecting a white bead, not replacing it, and then selecting a red bead

4c. selecting 3 nonred beads without replacement

THINK AND DISCUSS

1. Describe some independent events.
2. Extend the rule for the probability of independent events to more than two independent events. When might this be used?
3. **GET ORGANIZED** Copy and complete the graphic organizer. In each box, compare independent and dependent events and their related probabilities.

Probability of Independent Events vs. Probability of Dependent Events

Similarities	Differences

11-3 Exercises

go.hrw.com
Homework Help Online
KEYWORD: MB7 11-3
Parent Resources Online
KEYWORD: MB7 Parent

GUIDED PRACTICE

1. **Vocabulary** Two events are __?__ if the occurrence of one event does not affect the probability of the other event. (*independent* or *dependent*)

SEE EXAMPLE 1 p. 811

Find each probability.

2. rolling a 1 and then another 1 when a number cube is rolled twice
3. a coin landing heads up on every toss when it is tossed 3 times

SEE EXAMPLE 2 p. 812

Two number cubes are rolled—one blue and one yellow. Explain why the events are dependent. Then find the indicated probability.

4. The blue cube shows a 4 and the product is less than 20.
5. The yellow cube shows a multiple of 3, given that the product is 6.

SEE EXAMPLE 3 p. 813

The table shows the results of a quality-control study of a lightbulb factory. A lightbulb from the factory is selected at random. Find each probability.

Lightbulb Quality		
	Shipped	Not Shipped
Defective	10	45
Not Defective	942	3

6. that a shipped bulb is not defective
7. that a bulb is defective and shipped

SEE EXAMPLE 4 p. 814

A bag contains 20 checkers—10 red and 10 black. Determine whether the events are independent or dependent. Find the indicated probability.

8. selecting 2 black checkers when they are chosen at random with replacement
9. selecting 2 black checkers when they are chosen at random without replacement

PRACTICE AND PROBLEM SOLVING

Independent Practice

For Exercises	See Example
10–11	1
12–14	2
15–16	3
17–18	4

Extra Practice

Skills Practice p. S24
Application Practice p. S42

Find each probability.

10. choosing the same activity when two friends each randomly choose 1 of 4 extracurricular activities to participate in
11. rolling an even number and then rolling a 6 when a number cube is rolled twice

Two number cubes are rolled—one blue and one yellow. Explain why the events are dependent. Then find the indicated probability.

12. The yellow cube is greater than 5 and the product is greater than 24.
13. The blue cube is less than 3 and the product is 8.
14. The table shows immigration to the United States from three countries in three different years. A person is randomly selected. Find each probability.
    a. that a selected person is from Cuba, given that the person immigrated in 1990
    b. that a person came from Spain and immigrated in 2000
    c. that a selected person immigrated in 1995, given that the person was from Ghana.

Immigration to the United States			
Country	1990	1995	2000
Cuba	10,645	17,937	20,831
Ghana	4,466	3,152	4,344
Spain	1,886	1,321	1,264

Employment Find each probability.

15. that a person with an advanced degree is employed

16. that a person is not a high school graduate and is not employed

Employment by Education Level, Ages 21–24		
Education Level	Employed (millions)	Not employed (millions)
Not a high school graduate	1.060	0.834
High school graduate	2.793	1.157
Some college	4.172	1.634
Bachelor's degree	1.53	0.372
Advanced degree	0.104	0.041

A bag contains number slips numbered 1 to 9. Determine whether the events are independent or dependent, and find the indicated probability.

17. selecting 2 even numbers when 2 slips are chosen without replacement

18. selecting 2 even numbers when 2 slips are chosen with replacement

Determine whether the events are independent or dependent.

19. A coin comes up heads, and a number cube rolled at the same time comes up 6.

20. A 4 is drawn from a deck of cards, set aside, and then an ace is drawn.

21. A 1 is rolled on a number cube, and then a 4 is rolled on the same number cube.

22. A dart hits the bull's-eye, and a second dart also hits the bull's eye.

LINK

Tennis

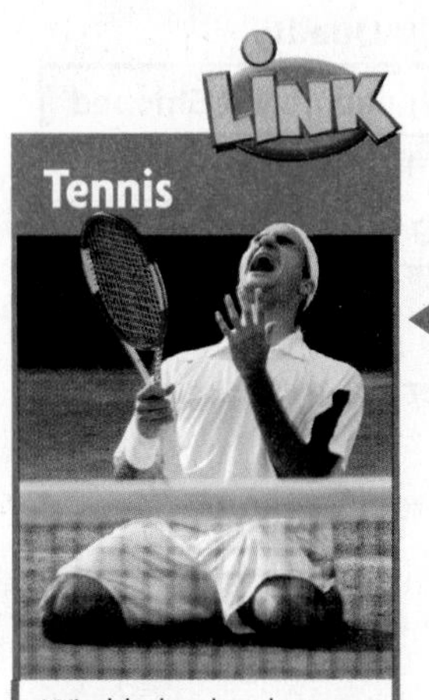

Wimbledon has been played annually since 1877 at the All England Lawn Tennis and Croquet Club.

23. **Tennis** In the 2004 Wimbledon Men's Tennis Championship final, Roger Federer defeated Andy Roddick in three sets.

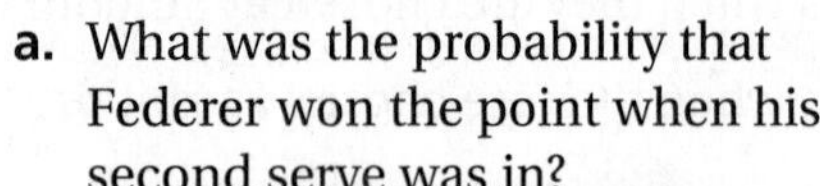

a. What was the probability that Federer won the point when his second serve was in?

b. When Federer lost a point, what was the probability that he *double faulted*?

Roger Federer's Service Points		
	Won	Lost
First Serve In	64	31
Second Serve In	34	22
Second Serve Out (Double Fault)	0	3

24. **Multi-Step** At one high school, the probability that a student is absent today, given that the student was absent yesterday, is 0.12. The probability that a student is absent today, given that the student was present yesterday, is 0.05. The probability that a student was absent yesterday is 0.1. Draw a tree diagram to represent the situation. What is the probability that a randomly selected student was present yesterday and today?

MULTI-STEP TEST PREP

25. This problem will prepare you for the Multi-Step Test Prep on page 826.

While playing Yahtzee, Jake rolls 5 dice and gets the result shown at right. The rules allow him to reroll these dice 2 times. Jake decides to try for all 5's, so he rerolls the 2 and the 3.

a. What is the probability that Jake gets no additional 5's in either of the 2 rolls?

b. What is the probability that he gets all 5's on his first reroll of the 2 and the 3?

c. What is the probability that he gets all 5's on his first reroll, given that at least one of the dice is a 5?

Estimation Use the graph to estimate each probability.

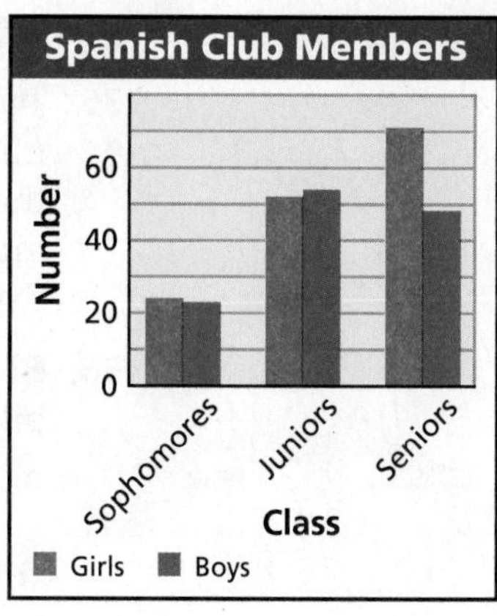

26. that a Spanish club member is a girl
27. that a senior Spanish club member is a girl
28. that a male Spanish club member is a senior
29. **Critical Thinking** A box contains 100 balloons. Eighty are yellow, and 20 are green. Fifty are marked "Happy Birthday!" and 50 are not. A balloon is randomly chosen from the box. How many yellow "Happy Birthday!" balloons must be in the box if the event "a balloon is yellow" and the event "a balloon is marked 'Happy Birthday!'" are independent?
30. **Travel** Airline information for three years is given in the table.
    a. Complete the table.
    b. What was the probability that a scheduled flight in 2004 was canceled?
    c. An on-time flight is selected randomly for study. What is the probability that it was a flight from 2005?

Scheduled Flights (thousands) January to July

	2003	2004	2005	Total
On Time		3197	3237	
Delayed	598		877	2321
Canceled	61	68		
Total	3761		4196	

Source: Bureau of Transportation Statistics

31. **Write About It** The "law of averages" is a nonmathematical term that means that events eventually "average out." So, if a coin comes up heads 10 tosses in a row, there is a greater probability that it will come up tails on the eleventh toss. Explain the error in this thinking.

32. What is the probability that a person's birthday falls on a Saturday next year, given that it falls on a Saturday this year?

    Ⓐ 0 Ⓑ $\frac{1}{7}$ Ⓒ $\frac{1}{2}$ Ⓓ 1

33. Which of the following has the same probability as rolling doubles on 2 number cubes 3 times in a row?

    Ⓕ A single number cube is rolled 3 times. The cube shows 5 each time.

    Ⓖ Two number cubes are rolled 3 times. Each time the sum is 6.

    Ⓗ Two number cubes are rolled 3 times. Each time the sum is greater than 2.

    Ⓙ Three number cubes are rolled twice. Each time all cubes show the same number (triples).

34. **Extended Response** Use the tree diagram.

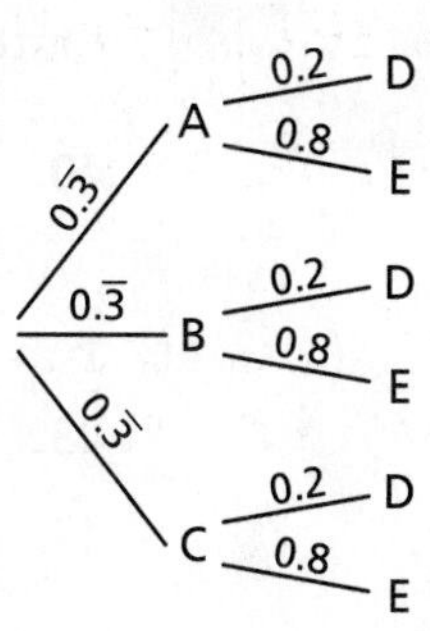

    a. Find $P(D \mid A)$, $P(D \mid B)$, and $P(D \mid C)$.
    b. Does the tree diagram represent independent or dependent events? Explain your answer.
    c. Describe a scenario for which the tree diagram could be used to find probabilities.

CHALLENGE AND EXTEND

35. Two number cubes are rolled in succession and the numbers that they show are added together. What is the only sum for which the probability of the sum is independent of the number shown on the first roll? Explain.

36. Birthdays People born on February 29 have a birthday once every 4 years.

a. What is the smallest group of people in which there is a greater than 50% chance that 2 people share a birthday? (Do not include February 29.)

b. What is the probability that in a group of 150 people, none are born on February 29?

c. What is the least number of people such that there is a greater than 50% chance that one of the people in the group has a birthday on February 29?

37. There are 150 people at a play. Ninety are women, and 60 are men. Half are sitting in the lower level, and half are sitting in the upper level. There are 35 women sitting in the upper level. A person is selected at random for a prize. What is the probability that the person is sitting in the lower level, given that the person is a woman? Is the event "person is sitting in the lower level" independent of the event "person is a woman"? Explain.

38. Medicine Suppose that strep throat affects 2% of the population and a test to detect it produces an accurate result 99% of the time.

a. Complete the table.

b. What is the probability that someone who tests positive actually has strep throat?

Per 10,000 People Tested			
	Have strep	Do not have strep	Total
Test Positive	■	■	■
Test Negative	■	■	■
Total	■	■	10,000

SPIRAL REVIEW

39. Sports A basketball player averaged 18.3 points per game in the month of December. In January, the same basketball player averaged 32.5 points per game. *(Lesson 2-6)*

a. Write the average number of points scored as a function of games played for both months, $p(d)$ and $p(j)$.

b. Graph $p(d)$ and $p(j)$ on the same coordinate plane.

c. Describe the transformation that occurred.

Solve each system of equations by graphing. Round your answer to the nearest tenth. *(Lesson 10-7)*

40. $\begin{cases} 2x^2 - 4y^2 = 12 \\ y = 2 \end{cases}$

41. $\begin{cases} 4x^2 - 2y^2 = 18 \\ -x^2 + 6y^2 = 22 \end{cases}$

42. $\begin{cases} x^2 + y^2 = 16 \\ 2y + 5x^2 = -3 \end{cases}$

Two number cubes are rolled. Find each probability. *(Lesson 11-2)*

43. The sum is 12.

44. The sum is less than 5.

45. At least one number is odd.

46. At least one number is less than 3.

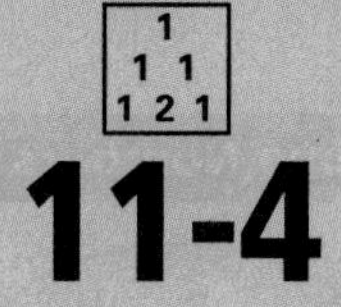

11-4 Compound Events

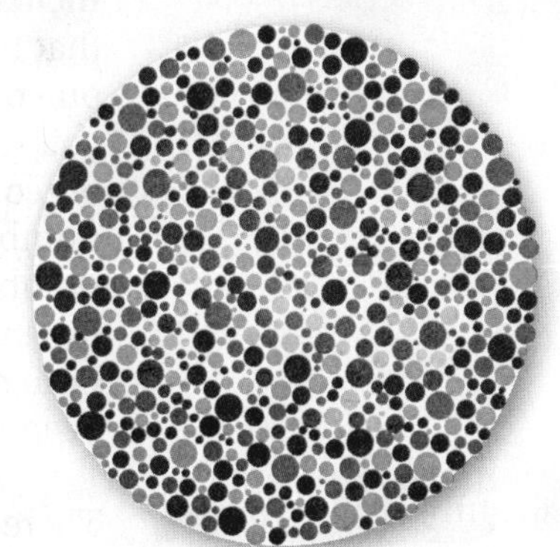

Objectives

Find the probability of mutually exclusive events.

Find the probability of inclusive events.

Vocabulary

simple event
compound event
mutually exclusive events
inclusive events

Why learn this?

You can use the probability of compound events to determine the likelihood that a person of a specific gender is color-blind. (See Example 3.)

A **simple event** is an event that describes a single outcome. A **compound event** is an event made up of two or more simple events. **Mutually exclusive events** are events that cannot both occur in the same trial of an experiment. Rolling a 1 and rolling a 2 on the same roll of a number cube are mutually exclusive events.

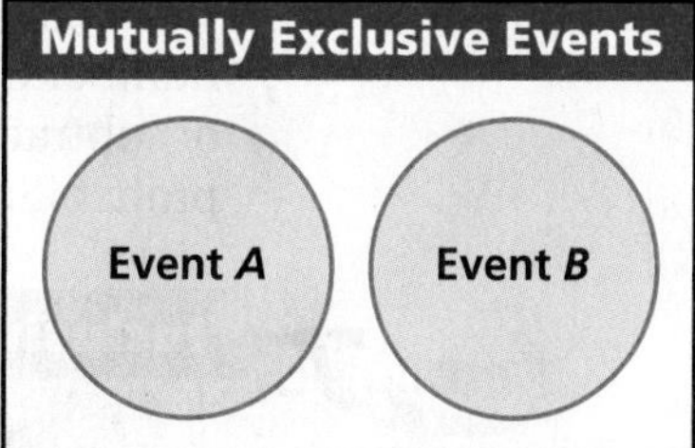

Mutually Exclusive Events

WORDS	ALGEBRA	EXAMPLE
The probability of two mutually exclusive events *A* or *B* occurring is the sum of their individual probabilities.	For two mutually exclusive events *A* and *B*, $P(A \cup B) = P(A) + P(B)$.	When a number cube is rolled, $P(\text{less than } 3) = P(1 \text{ or } 2) = P(1) + P(2) = \frac{1}{6} + \frac{1}{6} = \frac{1}{3}$.

Remember!

Recall that the union symbol ∪ means "or."

EXAMPLE 1 Finding Probabilities of Mutually Exclusive Events

A drink company applies one label to each bottle cap: "free drink," "free meal," or "try again." A bottle cap has a $\frac{1}{10}$ probability of being labeled "free drink" and a $\frac{1}{25}$ probability of being labeled "free meal."

a. Explain why the events "free drink" and "free meal" are mutually exclusive.

Each bottle cap has only one label applied to it.

b. What is the probability that a bottle cap is labeled "free drink" or "free meal"?

$$P(\text{free drink} \cup \text{free meal}) = P(\text{free drink}) + P(\text{free meal})$$
$$= \frac{1}{10} + \frac{1}{25} = \frac{5}{50} + \frac{2}{50} = \frac{7}{50}$$

1. Each student cast one vote for senior class president. Of the students, 25% voted for Hunt, 20% for Kline, and 55% for Vila. A student from the senior class is selected at random.

a. Explain why the events "voted for Hunt," "voted for Kline," and "voted for Vila" are mutually exclusive.

b. What is the probability that a student voted for Kline or Vila?

Inclusive events are events that have one or more outcomes in common. When you roll a number cube, the outcomes "rolling an even number" and "rolling a prime number" are not mutually exclusive. The number 2 is both prime and even, so the events are inclusive.

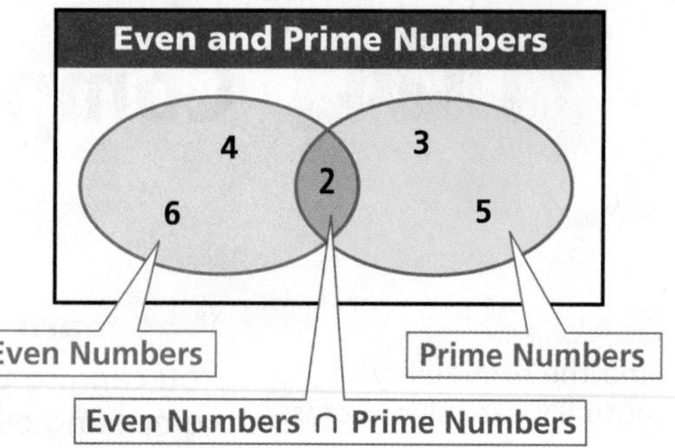

Remember!

Recall that the intersection symbol ∩ means "and."

There are 3 ways to roll an even number, $\{2, 4, 6\}$.

There are 3 ways to roll a prime number, $\{2, 3, 5\}$.

The outcome "2" is counted twice when outcomes are added $(3 + 3)$. The actual number of ways to roll an even number or a prime is $3 + 3 - 1 = 5$. The concept of subtracting the outcomes that are counted twice leads to the following probability formula.

Inclusive Events

WORDS	The probability of two inclusive events *A* or *B* occurring is the sum of their individual probabilities minus the probability of *both* occurring.
ALGEBRA	For two inclusive events *A* and *B*, $P(A \cup B) = P(A) + P(B) - P(A \cap B)$.
EXAMPLE	When you roll a number cube, $P(\text{even number or prime}) =$ $P(\text{even or prime}) = P(\text{even}) + P(\text{prime}) - P(\text{even and prime})$ $= \frac{3}{6} + \frac{3}{6} - \frac{1}{6} = \frac{5}{6}$.

EXAMPLE 2 Finding Probabilities of Inclusive Events

Find each probability on a die.

A rolling a 5 or an odd number

$P(5 \text{ or odd}) = P(5) + P(\text{odd}) - P(5 \text{ and odd})$

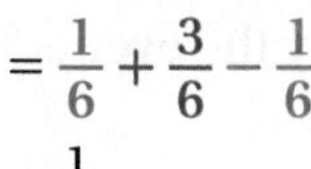

$= \frac{1}{6} + \frac{3}{6} - \frac{1}{6}$ *5 is also an odd number.*

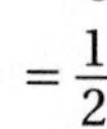

$= \frac{1}{2}$

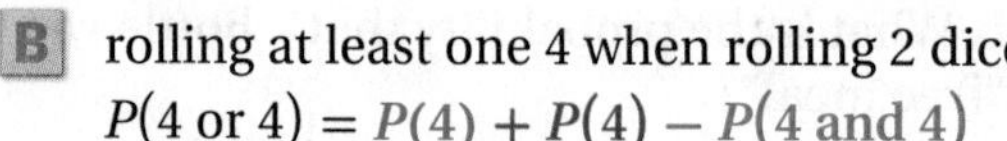

B rolling at least one 4 when rolling 2 dice

$P(4 \text{ or } 4) = P(4) + P(4) - P(4 \text{ and } 4)$

$= \frac{1}{6} + \frac{1}{6} - \frac{1}{36}$ *There is 1 outcome in 36 where both dice show 4.*

$= \frac{11}{36}$

A card is drawn from a deck of 52. Find the probability of each.

2a. drawing a king or a heart

2b. drawing a red card (hearts or diamonds) or a face card (jack, queen, or king)

EXAMPLE 3 ***Health Application***

Of 3510 drivers surveyed, 1950 were male and 103 were color-blind. Only 6 of the color-blind drivers were female. What is the probability that a driver was male or was color-blind?

Helpful Hint

As you work through Example 3, fill in the Venn diagram with information as you find it.

Step 1 Use a Venn diagram.

Label as much information as you know. Being male and being color-blind are inclusive events.

3510 total drivers

male drivers	overlap	color-blind drivers
1853	97	6

Step 2 Find the number in the overlapping region.

Subtract 6 from 103. This is the number of color-blind males, 97.

Step 3 Find the probability.

$= P(\text{male} \cup \text{color-blind}) =$

$= P(\text{male}) + P(\text{color-blind}) - P(\text{male} \cap \text{color-blind})$

$= \frac{1950}{3510} + \frac{103}{3510} - \frac{97}{3510} = \frac{1956}{3510} \approx 0.557$

The probability that a driver was male or was color-blind is about 55.7%.

3. Of 160 beauty spa customers, 96 had a hair styling and 61 had a manicure. There were 28 customers who had only a manicure. What is the probability that a customer had a hair styling or a manicure?

Recall from Lesson 11-2 that the complement of an event with probability p, all outcomes that are not in the event, has a probability of $1 - p$. You can use the complement to find the probability of a compound event.

EXAMPLE 4 ***Book Club Application***

There are 5 students in a book club. Each student randomly chooses a book from a list of 10 titles. What is the probability that at least 2 students in the group choose the same book?

$P(\text{at least 2 students choose same}) = 1 - P(\text{all choose different})$ *Use the complement.*

$$P(\text{all choose different}) = \frac{\text{number of ways 5 students can choose different books}}{\text{total number of ways 5 students can choose books}}$$

$$= \frac{{}_{10}P_5}{10^5}$$

$$= \frac{10 \cdot 9 \cdot 8 \cdot 7 \cdot 6}{10 \cdot 10 \cdot 10 \cdot 10 \cdot 10} = \frac{30{,}240}{100{,}000} = 0.3024$$

$P(\text{at least 2 students choose same}) = 1 - 0.3024 = 0.6976$

The probability that at least 2 students choose the same book is 0.6976, or 69.76%.

4. In one day, 5 different customers bought earrings from the same jewelry store. The store offers 62 different styles. Find the probability that at least 2 customers bought the same style.

THINK AND DISCUSS

1. Explain why the formula for inclusive events, $P(A \cup B) = P(A) + P(B) - P(A \cap B)$, also applies to mutually exclusive events.
2. Tell whether the probability of sharing a birthday with someone else in the room is the same whether your birthday is March 13 or February 29. Explain.

3. **GET ORGANIZED** Copy and complete the graphic organizer. Give at least one example for each.

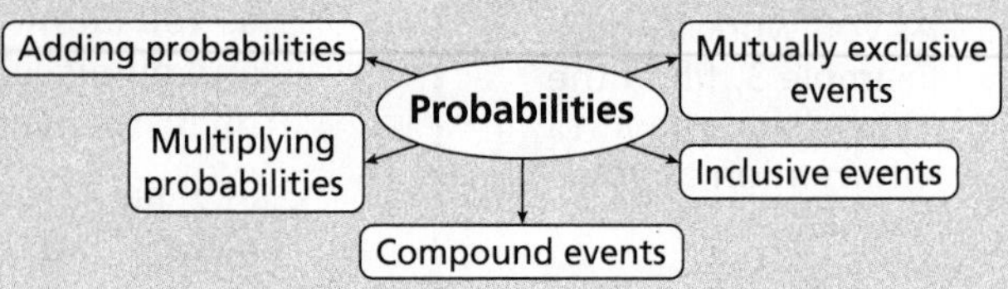

11-4 Exercises

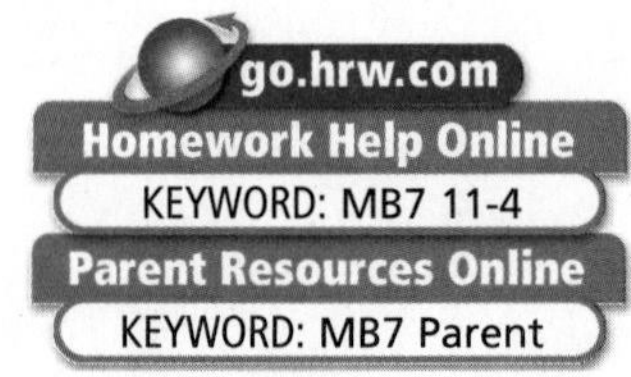

GUIDED PRACTICE

1. **Vocabulary** A compound event where one outcome overlaps with another is made up of two __?__. (*inclusive event* or *mutually exclusive events*)

A bag contains 25 marbles: 10 black, 13 red, and 2 blue. A marble is drawn from the bag at random.

SEE EXAMPLE 1 p. 819

2. Explain why the events "getting a black marble" and "getting a red marble" are mutually exclusive.
3. What is the probability of getting a red or a blue marble?
4. A car approaching an intersection has a 0.1 probability of turning left and a 0.2 probability of turning right. Explain why the events are mutually exclusive. What is the probability that the car will turn?

SEE EXAMPLE 2 p. 820

Numbers 1–10 are written on cards and placed in a bag. Find each probability.

5. choosing a number greater than 5 or choosing an odd number
6. choosing an 8 or choosing a number less than 5
7. choosing at least one even number when selecting 2 cards from the bag

SEE EXAMPLE 3 p. 821

Five years after 650 high school seniors graduated, 400 had a college degree and 310 were married. Half of the students with a college degree were married.

8. What is the probability that a student has a college degree or is married?
9. What is the probability that a student has a college degree or is not married?
10. What is the probability that a student does not have a college degree or is married?

SEE EXAMPLE 4 p. 821

11. A vending machine offers 8 different drinks. One day, 6 employees each purchased a drink from the vending machine. Find the probability that at least 2 employees purchased the same drink.

PRACTICE AND PROBLEM SOLVING

Independent Practice	
For Exercises	See Example
12–13	1
14–15	2
16–18	3
19	4

Extra Practice

Skills Practice p. S24
Application Practice p. S42

Jump ropes are given out during gym class. A student has a $\frac{1}{6}$ chance of getting a red jump rope and a $\frac{1}{3}$ chance of getting a green jump rope. Meg is given a jump rope.

12. Explain why the events "getting a red jump rope" and "getting a green jump rope" are mutually exclusive.

13. What is the probability that Meg gets a red or green jump rope?

The letters *A–P* are written on cards and placed in a bag. Find the probability of each outcome.

14. choosing an *E* or choosing a *G*

15. choosing an *E* or choosing a vowel

Lincoln High School has 98 teachers. Of the 42 female teachers, 8 teach math. One-seventh of all of the teachers teach math.

16. What is the probability that a teacher is a woman or teaches math?

17. What is the probability that a teacher is a man or teaches math?

18. What is the probability that a teacher is a man or does not teach math?

19. A card is drawn from a deck of 52 and recorded. Then the card is replaced, and the deck is shuffled. This process is repeated 13 times. What is the probability that at least one of the cards drawn is a heart?

20. Critical Thinking Events *A* and *B* are mutually exclusive. Must the complements of events *A* and *B* be mutually exclusive? Explain by example.

LINK

Television

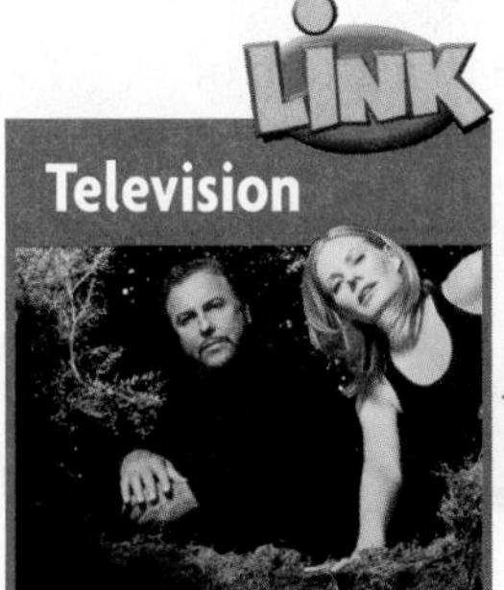

In 2004, about 109.6 million U.S. households had televisions. Nielsen's *rating points*, such as those for *CSI*, represent the percent of these households tuned to a show.

21. Television According to Nielsen Media Research, on June 21, 2005, from 9 to 10 P.M., the NBA Finals Game 7 between San Antonio and Detroit had a 22 *share* (was watched by 22% of television viewers), while *CSI* had a 15 share. What is the probability that someone who was watching television during this time watched the NBA Finals or *CSI*? Do you think that this is theoretical or experimental probability? Explain.

School Arts Use the table for Exercises 22 and 23.

22. What would you need to know to find the probability that a U.S. public school offers music or dance classes?

23. What is the minimum probability that a U.S. public school offers visual arts or drama? What is the maximum probability?

Arts Offered by U.S. Public Schools

Class Type	Music	Visual arts	Dance	Drama and theater
Percent of Schools	94%	87%	20%	19%

24. Geometry A square dartboard contains a red square and a blue square that overlap. A dart hits a random point on the board.

a. Find $P(\text{red} \cap \text{blue})$.
b. Find $P(\text{red})$.
c. Find $P(\text{red} \cup \text{blue})$.
d. Find $P(\text{yellow})$.

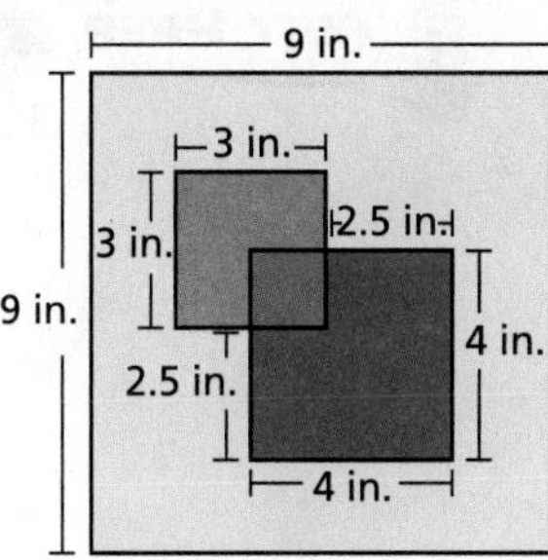

25. Genetics One study found that 8% of men and 0.5% of women are born color-blind. Of the study participants, 52% were men.

a. Which probability would you expect to be greater: that a study participant is male *and* born color-blind or that a participant is male *or* born color-blind? Explain.

b. What is the probability that a study participant is male and born color-blind? What is the probability that a study participant is male or born color-blind?

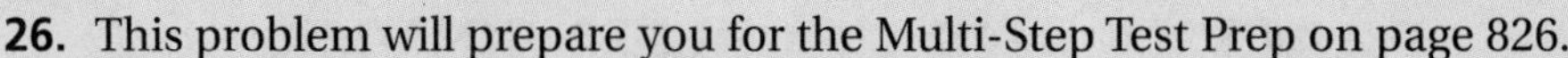

26. This problem will prepare you for the Multi-Step Test Prep on page 826.

While playing Yahtzee, Amanda rolls five dice and gets the result shown. She decides to keep the 1, 2, and 4, and reroll the 5 and 6.

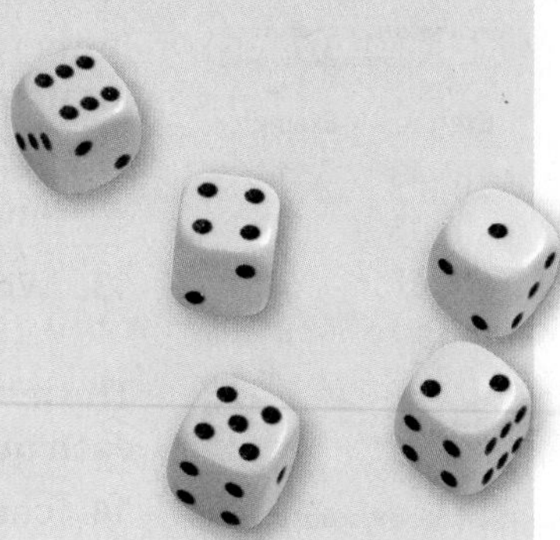

a. After rerolling the 5 and 6, what is the probability that Amanda will have a "large straight" (1-2-3-4-5) or three 4's?

b. After rerolling the 5 and 6, what is the probability that Amanda will have a "small straight" (1-2-3-4 plus anything else) or a pair of 3's?

27. **Public Safety** In a study of canine attacks, the probability that the victim was under 18 years of age was 0.8. The probability that the attack occurred on the dog owner's property was 0.64. The probability that the victim was under 18 years of age or the attack occurred on the owner's property was 0.95. What was the probability that the victim was under 18 years of age and the attack occurred on the owner's property?

28. **Politics** A 4-person leadership committee is randomly chosen from a group of 24 candidates. Ten of the candidates are men, and 14 are women.

a. What is the probability that the committee is all male or all female?

b. What is the probability that the committee has at least 1 man or at least 1 woman?

29. **Multi-Step** The game Scrabble contains letter tiles that occur in different numbers. Suppose that one tile is selected.

a. What is the probability of choosing a vowel if *Y* is not included?

b. What is the probability of choosing a *Y*?

c. What is the probability of choosing a vowel if *Y* is included? How does this relate to the answer to parts **a** and **b**?

Distribution of Scrabble Tiles

Tiles	Frequency
J, K, Q, X, Z	1
B, C, F, H, M, P, V, W, Y, blank	2
G	3
D, L, S, U	4
N, R, T	6
O	8
A, I	9
E	12

30. **Write About It** Demonstrate two ways to find the probability of a coin's landing heads up at least once in 2 tosses of a coin.

TEST PREP

31. For a quilt raffle, 2500 tickets numbered 0001–2500 are sold. Jamie has number 1527. The winning raffle number is read one digit at a time. The first winning number begins "One...". After the first digit is called, Jamie's chances of winning do which of the following?

Ⓐ Go to 0

Ⓑ Stay the same

Ⓒ Increase from $\frac{1}{2500}$ to $\frac{1}{1527}$

Ⓓ Increase from $\frac{1}{2500}$ to $\frac{1}{1000}$

32. A fair coin is tossed 4 times. Given that each of the first 3 tosses land tails up, what is the probability that all 4 tosses land tails up?

Ⓕ 0.5

Ⓖ Greater than 0.5

Ⓗ 0.5^4

Ⓙ Between 0.5^4 and 0.5

33. If Travis rolls a 5 on a number cube, he lands on "roll again." If Travis rolls a number greater than 3, he'll pass "start" and collect \$100. What is the probability that Travis rolls again or collects \$100?

Ⓐ $\frac{1}{6}$ Ⓑ $\frac{1}{5}$ Ⓒ $\frac{1}{4}$ Ⓓ $\frac{1}{2}$

34. **Short Response** What is the probability of an event or its complement? Explain.

CHALLENGE AND EXTEND

35. What is the probability that at least 2 people in a group of 10 people have the same birthday? (Assume no one in the group was born on February 29th.)

Travel For Exercises 36–38, use the Venn diagram, which shows the transportation methods used by 162 travelers. Find each probability if a traveler is selected at random.

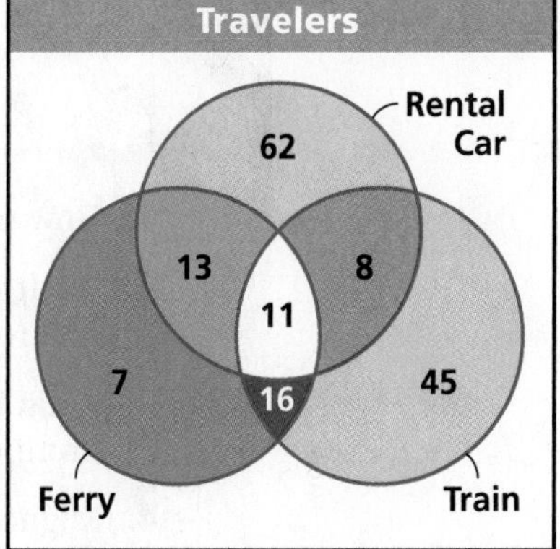

36. $P(\text{ferry or train})$

37. $P(\text{ferry or rental car})$

38. $P(\text{train and ferry, or train and rental car})$

Use the table of probabilities and the following information for Exercises 39–41. Hint: Draw a Venn diagram.

For any three events A, B, and C, $P(A \text{ or } B \text{ or } C) =$
$P(A) + P(B) + P(C) - P(A \cap B) - P(A \cap C) - P(B \cap C) + P(A \cap B \cap C)$

Event	$P(A)$	$P(B)$	$P(C)$	$P(A \cap B)$	$P(A \cap C)$	$P(B \cap C)$	$P(A \cap B \cap C)$
Probability	0.5	0.3	0.7	0.2	0.3	0.1	0.1

39. Find $P(B \cup C)$. 40. Find $P(A \cup B \cup C)$. 41. Find $P(B \cap (A \cup C))$.

SPIRAL REVIEW

Write a cubic function for each graph. *(Lesson 6-9)*

42.

x	y
−4	0
−1	0
0	−4
2	0

43.

x	y
−5	0
−2	0
−1	24
3	0

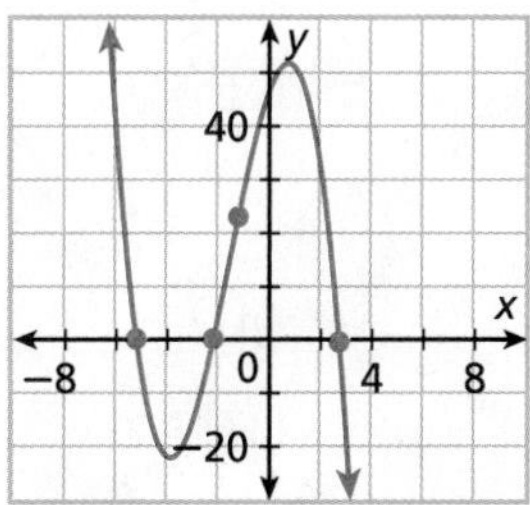

Graph each function. *(Lesson 9-2)*

44. $f(x) = \begin{cases} 2 & \text{if } x < -1 \\ 2x + 4 & \text{if } x \geq -1 \end{cases}$

45. $g(x) = \begin{cases} 1 - x^2 & \text{if } x < 1 \\ x^2 - 1 & \text{if } x \geq 1 \end{cases}$

Find each probability. *(Lesson 11-3)*

46. A coin is tossed twice and it lands heads up both times.

47. A coin is tossed 4 times and it lands heads up, heads up, tails up, and then tails up.

48. Two number cubes are rolled. The sum is greater than 10. The first number cube is 6.

CHAPTER 11

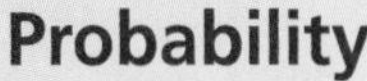

MULTI-STEP TEST PREP

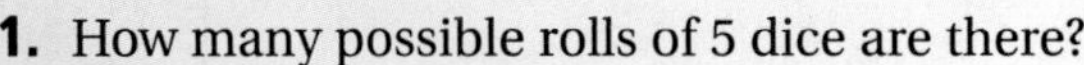

SECTION 11A

Probability

Roll Call Yahtzee is played with 5 dice. A player rolls all 5 dice and may choose to roll any or all of the dice a second time and then a third time. At that point, the player scores points for various combinations of dice, such as 3 of a kind, 4 of a kind, or 5 of a kind.

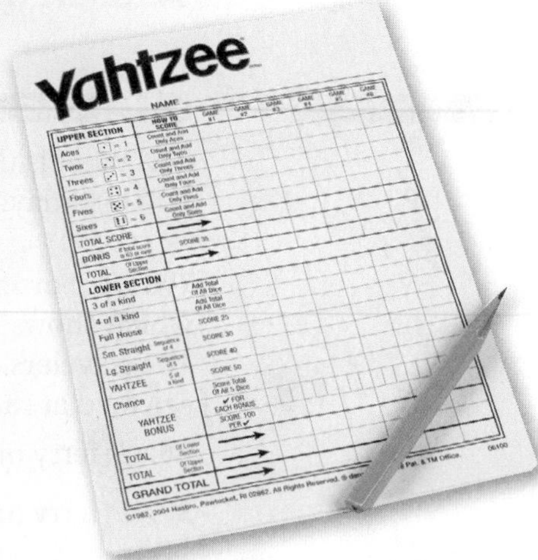

1. How many possible rolls of 5 dice are there?
2. What is the probability of rolling five 6's on the first roll of the dice?
3. What is the probability of rolling 5 of any one number on the first roll?
4. Miguel's first roll is shown at right. He decides to reroll the 6's. What is the probability that he has a 1, 2, 3, 4, and 5 after this roll?

5. What is the probability that Miguel has a 1, 2, 3, 4, and 5 after the roll, given that at least one of the dice comes up a 4?
6. What is the probability that Miguel has a 1, 2, 3, 4, and 5 or a pair of 2's after the roll in Problem 4?
7. What is the probability that Miguel has a 1, 2, 3, 4, and any other number or a pair of 4's after the roll in Problem 4?

Quiz for Lessons 11-1 Through 11-4

11-1 Permutations and Combinations

1. A security code consists of 5 digits (0–9), and a digit may not be used more than once. How many possible security codes are there?
2. Adric owns 8 pairs of shoes. How many ways can he choose 4 pairs of shoes to pack into his luggage?
3. A plumber received calls from 5 customers. There are 6 open slots on today's schedule. How many ways can the plumber schedule the customers?

11-2 Theoretical and Experimental Probability

4. A cooler contains 18 cans: 9 of lemonade, 3 of iced tea, and 6 of cola. Dee selects a can without looking. What is the probability that Dee selects iced tea?
5. Jordan has 9 pens in his desk; 2 are out of ink. If his mom selects 2 pens from his desk, what is the probability that both are out of ink?
6. Find the probability that a point chosen at random inside the figure shown is in the shaded area.
7. A number cube is tossed 50 times, and a 2 is rolled 12 times. Find the experimental probability of not rolling a 2.

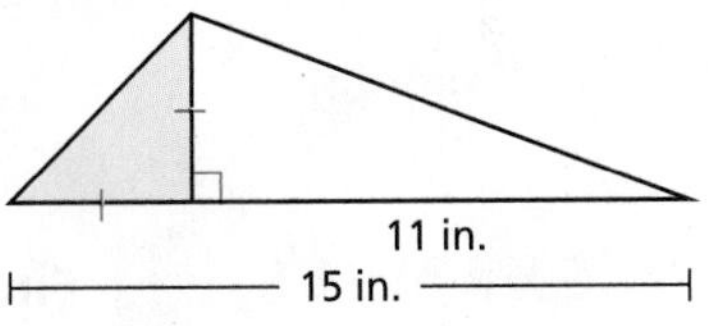

11-3 Independent and Dependent Events

8. Explain why the events "getting tails, then tails, then tails, then tails, then heads when tossing a coin 5 times" are independent, and find the probability.
9. Two number cubes are rolled—one red and one black. Explain why the events "the red cube shows a 6" and "the sum is greater than or equal to 10" are dependent, and find the probability.
10. The table shows the breakdown of math students for one school year. Find the probability that a Geometry student is in the 11th grade.
11. A bag contains 25 checkers—15 red and 10 black. Determine whether the events "a red checker is selected, not replaced, and then a black checker is selected" are independent or dependent, and find the probability.

Math Students by Grade

	Geometry	Algebra 2
9th Grade	26	0
10th Grade	68	24
11th Grade	33	94

11-4 Compound Events

Numbers 1–30 are written on cards and placed in a bag. One card is drawn. Find each probability.

12. drawing an even number or a 1
13. drawing an even number or a multiple of 7
14. Of a company's 85 employees, 60 work full time and 40 are married. Half of the full-time workers are married. What is the probability that an employee works part time or is not married?

11-5 Measures of Central Tendency and Variation

Objectives
Find measures of central tendency and measures of variation for statistical data.

Examine the effects of outliers on statistical data.

Vocabulary
expected value
probability distribution
variance
standard deviation
outlier

Who uses this?
Statisticians can use measures of central tendency and variation to analyze World Series results. (See Example 2.)

Recall that the *mean, median,* and *mode* are measures of central tendency—values that describe the center of a data set.

The *mean* is the sum of the values in the set divided by the number of values. It is often represented as $\bar{x}$. The *median* is the middle value or the mean of the two middle values when the set is ordered numerically. The *mode* is the value or values that occur most often. A data set may have one mode, no mode, or several modes.

EXAMPLE 1 Finding Measures of Central Tendency

Reading Math
A set of *univariate* data involves a single variable. The data set in Example 1 involves only one variable—number of days—so it is univariate.

Find the mean, median, and mode of the data.

Number of days from mailing to delivery: 6, 4, 3, 4, 2, 5, 3, 4, 5, 2, 3, 4

Mean: $\frac{6+4+3+4+2+5+3+4+5+2+3+4}{12} = \frac{45}{12} = 3.75$ days

Median: 2 2 3 3 3 4 ¦ 4 4 4 5 5 6 $\frac{4+4}{2} = 4$ days

Mode: The most common result is 4 days.

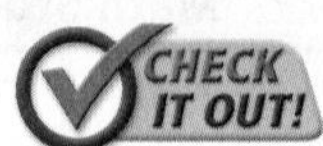

Find the mean, median, and mode of each data set.

1a. $\{6, 9, 3, 8\}$ **1b.** $\{2, 5, 6, 2, 6\}$

A *weighted average* of a data set gives greater importance, or weight, to some values in the set than to others. To find a weighted average, multiply each value by its weight. Then divide the sum of these products by the sum of the weights.

Suppose a teacher grades students' work in a class by using a weighted average in which homework has a weight of 30%, tests have a weight of 40%, and the final exam has a weight of 30%. Mia has a homework score of 84, a test score of 88, and a final exam score of 91.

$$\text{Mia's weighted average} = \frac{84(0.30) + 88(0.40) + 91(0.30)}{0.30 + 0.40 + 0.30} = \frac{87.7}{1.00} = 87.7$$

For an experiment with numerical outcomes, the **expected value** is the weighted average of the possible outcomes. The weight for each outcome is its probability.

EXAMPLE 2 Finding Expected Value

The probability distribution for the number of games played in each World Series for the years 1923–2004 is given below. Find the expected number of games in a World Series.

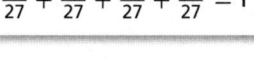

Helpful Hint

The sum of all of the probabilities in a probability distribution is 1. In Example 2,

$\frac{5}{27} + \frac{5}{27} + \frac{6}{27} + \frac{11}{27} = 1$

World Series Games				
Number of Games *n* in World Series	4	5	6	7
Probability of *n* Games	$\frac{5}{27}$	$\frac{5}{27}$	$\frac{6}{27}$	$\frac{11}{27}$

$$\text{expected value} = 4\left(\frac{5}{27}\right) + 5\left(\frac{5}{27}\right) + 6\left(\frac{6}{27}\right) + 7\left(\frac{11}{27}\right)$$ *Use the weighted average.*

$$= \frac{20}{27} + \frac{25}{27} + \frac{36}{27} + \frac{77}{27} = \frac{158}{27} \approx 5.85$$ *Simplify.*

The expected number of games in a World Series is about 5.85.

CHECK IT OUT! **2.** The probability distribution of the number of accidents in a week at an intersection, based on past data, is given below. Find the expected number of accidents for one week.

Number of accidents *n*	0	1	2	3
Probability of *n* accidents	0.75	0.15	0.08	0.02

A *box-and-whisker plot* shows the spread of a data set. It displays 5 key points: the **minimum** and **maximum** values, the **median**, and the **first** and **third quartiles.**

Reading Math

The first quartile is sometimes called the 25th percentile, and the third quartile is sometimes called the 75th percentile.

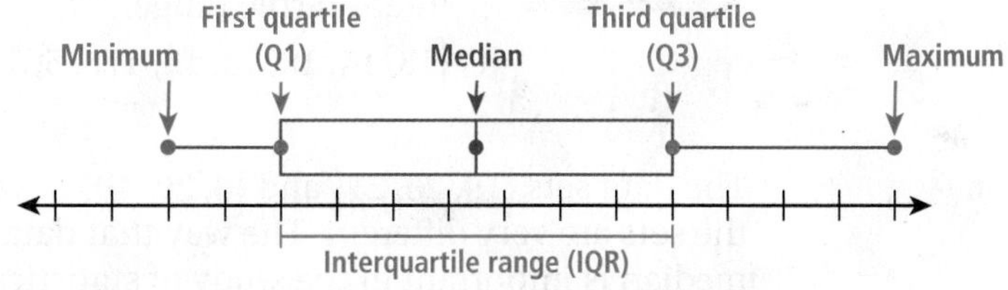

The quartiles are the medians of the lower and upper halves of the data set. If there are an odd number of data values, do not include the median in either half.

The *interquartile range*, or IQR, is the difference between the 1st and 3rd quartiles, or Q3 – Q1. It represents the middle 50% of the data.

Student to Student — Box-and-Whisker Plots

Jenny Rivera
Lincoln High School

I know I have to sort the data before I can make a box-and-whisker plot. I enter the data into my graphing calculator list. Then I use the STAT sort feature to sort the list in ascending order.

Other times, I'll use a spreadsheet and sort the data there.

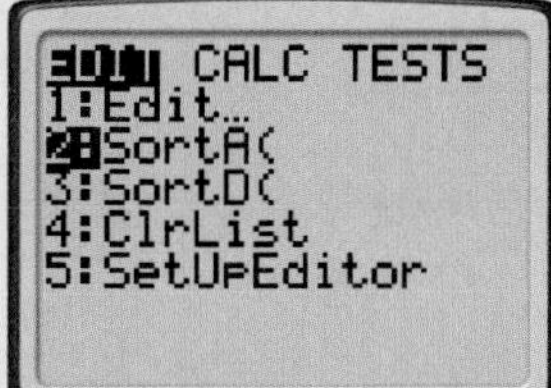

EXAMPLE 3 Making a Box-and-Whisker Plot and Finding the Interquartile Range

Make a box-and-whisker plot of the data. Find the interquartile range.
$\{5, 3, 9, 2, 14, 6, 8, 9, 5, 8, 13, 3, 15, 7, 4, 2, 12, 8\}$

Step 1 Order the data from least to greatest.

2, 2, 3, 3, 4, 5, 5, 6, 7, 8, 8, 8, 9, 9, 12, 13, 14, 15

Step 2 Find the minimum, maximum, median, and quartiles.

(2, 2, 3, 3, 4, 5, 5, 6, 7), (8, 8, 8, 9, 9, 12, 13, 14, 15)

Minimum — First quartile — Median 7.5 — Third quartile — Maximum

Step 3 Draw a box-and-whisker plot.

Draw a number line, and plot a point above each of the five values. Then draw the box from the first quartile to the third quartile with a line segment through the median. Draw whiskers from the box to the minimum and maximum.

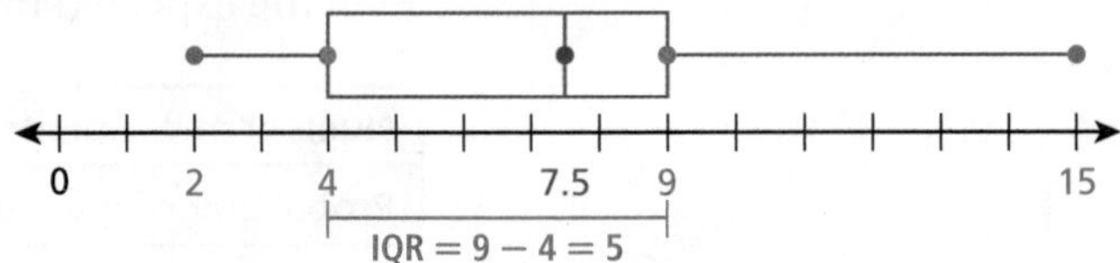

The interquartile range is 5, the length of the box in the diagram.

3. Make a box-and-whisker plot of the data. Find the interquartile range.
$\{13, 14, 18, 13, 12, 17, 15, 12, 13, 19, 11, 14, 14, 18, 22, 23\}$

The data sets $\{19, 20, 21\}$ and $\{0, 20, 40\}$ have the same mean and median, but the sets are very different. The way that data are spread out from the mean or median is important in the study of statistics.

A *measure of variation* is a value that describes the spread of a data set. The most commonly used measures of variation are the *range*, the interquartile range, the *variance*, and the *standard deviation*.

The **variance**, denoted by σ^2, is the average of the squared differences from the mean. **Standard deviation**, denoted by σ, is the square root of the variance and is one of the most common and useful measures of variation.

Low standard deviations indicate data that are clustered near the measures of central tendency, whereas high standard deviations indicate data that are spread out from the center.

Reading Math

The symbol commonly used to represent the mean is $\bar{x}$, or "*x* bar." The symbol for standard deviation is the lowercase Greek letter *sigma*, σ.

Finding Variance and Standard Deviation
Step 1. Find the mean of the data, $\bar{x}$.
Step 2. Find the difference between the mean and each data value, and square it.
Step 3. Find the variance, σ^2, by adding the squares of all of the differences from the mean and dividing by the number of data values.
Step 4. Find the standard deviation, σ, by taking the square root of the variance.

EXAMPLE 4 Finding the Mean and Standard Deviation

The data represent the number of milligrams of a substance in a patient's blood, found on consecutive doctor visits. Find the mean and the standard deviation of the data.

$\{14, 13, 16, 9, 3, 7, 11, 12, 11, 4\}$

Step 1 Find the mean.

$$\bar{x} = \frac{14 + 13 + 16 + 9 + 3 + 7 + 11 + 12 + 11 + 4}{10} = 10$$

Step 2 Find the difference between the mean and each data value, and square it.

Data Value x	14	13	16	9	3	7	11	12	11	4
$x - \bar{x}$	4	3	6	−1	−7	−3	1	2	1	−6
$(x - \bar{x})^2$	16	9	36	1	49	9	1	4	1	36

Step 3 Find the variance.

$$\sigma^2 = \frac{16 + 9 + 36 + 1 + 49 + 9 + 1 + 4 + 1 + 36}{10} = 16.2$$

Find the average of the last row of the table.

Step 4 Find the standard deviation.

$$\sigma = \sqrt{16.2} \approx 4.02$$

The standard deviation is the square root of the variance.

The mean is 10 mg, the standard deviation is about 4.02 mg.

4. Find the mean and standard deviation for the data set of the number of elevator stops for several rides.

$\{0, 3, 1, 1, 0, 5, 1, 0, 3, 0\}$

Remember!

Enter lists in the graphing calculator by pressing STAT and choosing **1:Edit...**

An **outlier** is an extreme value that is much less than or much greater than the other data values. Outliers have a strong effect on the mean and standard deviation. If an outlier is the result of measurement error or represents data from the wrong population, it is usually removed. There are different ways to determine whether a value is an outlier. One is to look for data values that are more than 3 standard deviations from the mean.

EXAMPLE 5 Examining Outliers

The number of electoral votes in 2004 for 11 western states are shown. Find the mean and the standard deviation of the data. Identify any outliers, and describe how they affect the mean and the standard deviation.

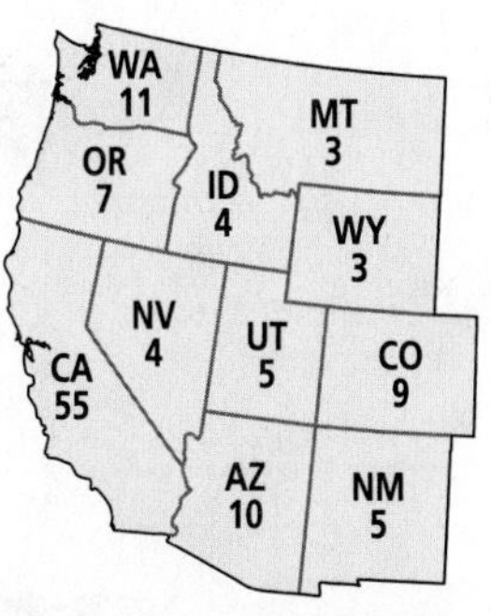

Step 1 Enter the data values into list **L1** on a graphing calculator.

Step 2 Find the mean and standard deviation.

On the graphing calculator, press STAT, scroll to the **CALC** menu, and select **1:1-Var Stats.**

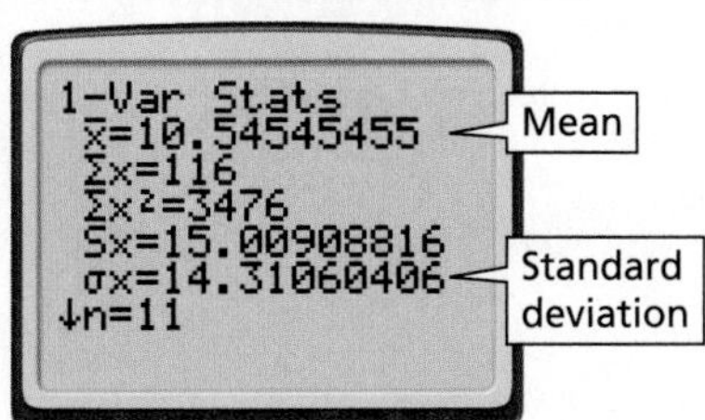

The mean is about 10.5, and the standard deviation is about 14.3.

Step 3 Identify the outliers.

Look for data values that are more than 3 standard deviations away from the mean in either direction.

Three standard deviations is about $3(14.3) = 42.9$.

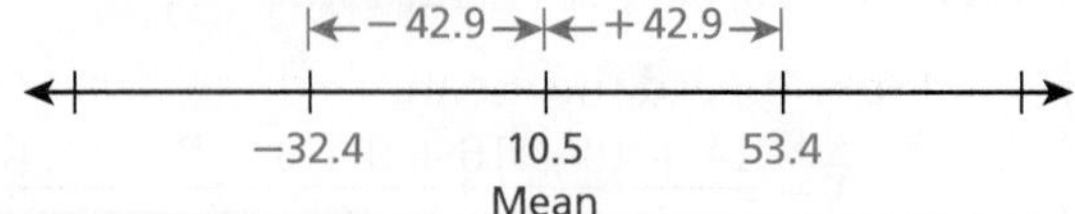

Values 42.9 units below the mean are negative and would not make sense in the problem (a state cannot have a negative number of electoral votes).

Values greater than 53.4 are outliers, so 55, the number of California electoral votes, is an outlier.

Check $\frac{|\text{value} - \text{mean}|}{\text{standard deviation}} = \frac{|55 - 10.5|}{14.3} \approx 3.1$

55 is about 3.1 standard deviations from the mean, so it is an outlier.

Step 4 Remove the outlier to see the effect that it has on the mean and standard deviation.

All data **Without outlier**

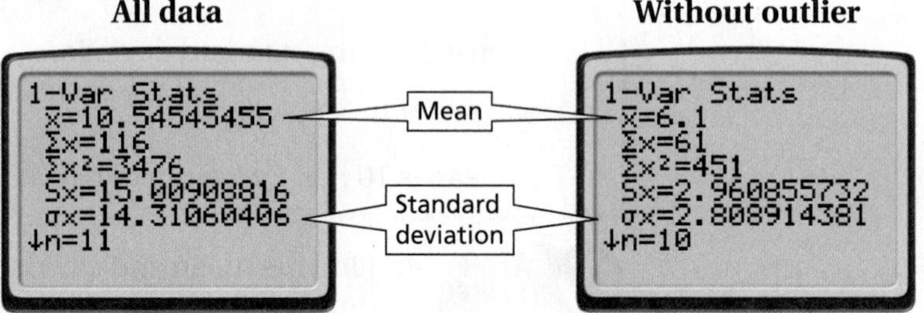

The outlier in the data set causes the mean to increase from 6.1 to ≈ 10.5 and the standard deviation to increase from ≈ 2.8 to ≈ 14.3.

5. In the 2003 and 2004 American League Championship Series, the New York Yankees scored the following numbers of runs against the Boston Red Sox: 2, 6, 4, 2, 4, 6, 6, 10, 3, 19, 4, 4, 2, 3. Identify the outlier, and describe how it affects the mean and standard deviation.

THINK AND DISCUSS

1. Describe the effect of adding a constant to each data value on the mean.

2. Describe the effect of adding a constant to each data value on the standard deviation.

3. What effect does doubling the variance have on the standard deviation?

Know it! Note

4. GET ORGANIZED Copy and complete the graphic organizer. In each box, define and give an example of each measure.

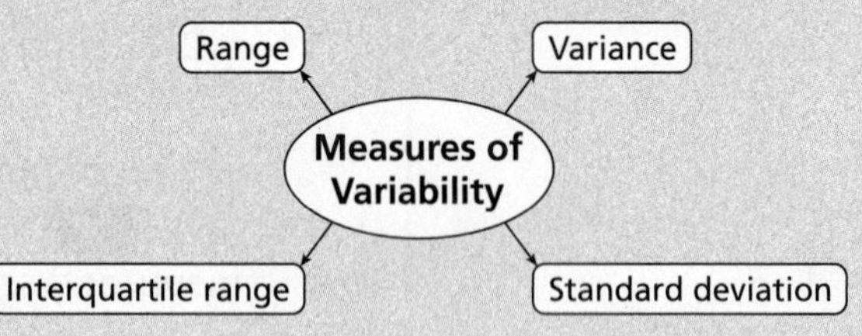

11-5 Exercises

GUIDED PRACTICE

1. **Vocabulary** A measure of variation, or spread of a data set, is the __?__. *(variance* or *expected value)*

SEE EXAMPLE 1 p. 828

Find the mean, median, and mode of each data set.

2. $\{5, 7, 4, 7, 6, 7\}$
3. $\{2, 4, 4, 6, 6, 6, 7, 8\}$
4. $\{10, 14, 18, 22, 26\}$

SEE EXAMPLE 2 p. 829

5. Find the expected value of the prize.

Prize Giveaway						
Value	\$0	\$1	\$5	\$20	\$100	\$1000
Probability	0.9359	0.05	0.01	0.003	0.001	0.0001

SEE EXAMPLE 3 p. 830

Make a box-and-whisker plot of the data. Find the interquartile range.

6. $\{3, 5, 2, 2, 8, 9, 1, 11\}$
7. $\{2, 4, 1, 4, 2, 2, 7, 4\}$
8. $\{33, 34, 31, 27, 22\}$

SEE EXAMPLE 4 p. 831

Find the variance and standard deviation.

9. $\{3, 3, 4, 5, 5\}$
10. $\{10, 12, 14, 15, 18, 20, 23\}$
11. $\{7, 14, 21, 28, 35, 42\}$

SEE EXAMPLE 5 p. 831

12. **Measurement** Students in a fourth-grade class were asked to measure the widths of their desks in centimeters. They recorded the following measures: 49, 50, 49, 48, 49, 19, 50, 49, 48, 50, 49, and 50. Identify the outlier, and describe how it affects the mean and the standard deviation.

PRACTICE AND PROBLEM SOLVING

Independent Practice

For Exercises	See Example
13–15	1
16	2
17–19	3
20–22	4
23	5

Extra Practice

Skills Practice p. S25
Application Practice p. S42

Find the mean, median, and mode of each data set.

13. $\{4, 16, 25, 9, 36, 49\}$
14. $\{1, 7, 7, 2, 3, 14, 127, 8\}$
15. $\{5, 10, 15, 20, 25\}$

16. Find the expected number of heads.

Three Coins Are Tossed				
Number of Heads	0	1	2	3
Probability	$\frac{1}{8}$	$\frac{3}{8}$	$\frac{3}{8}$	$\frac{1}{8}$

Make a box-and-whisker plot of the data. Find the interquartile range.

17. $\{12, 15, 12, 6, 18, 29\}$
18. $\{2, 2, 3, 8, 2, 8, 2, 42\}$
19. $\{3, 4, 3, 1, 2\}$

Find the variance and standard deviation.

20. $\{4, 4, 4, 4, 5\}$
21. $\{8, 12, 30, 35, 48, 50, 62\}$
22. $\{14, 26, 40, 52\}$

23. **Football** The 2004 Cincinnati Bengals scored 24, 16, 9, 17, 17, 23, 20, 26, 17, 14, 58, 27, and 28 points in their first 13 games. Find the mean and the standard deviation of the data. Identify the outlier, and describe how it affects the mean and the standard deviation.

24. **Critical Thinking** Write a set of data in which neither the mean nor the median are data values.

25. **Shopping** You are at a store and want to purchase an accurate room thermometer. One says 73°F, six say 75°F, eight say 76°F, and one says 37°F. Which measure of central tendency would you be least likely to use to pick a thermometer? Explain.

For a data set with a first quartile of Q1 and a third quartile of Q3, a value less than Q1 – 1.5(IQR) or greater than Q3 + 1.5(IQR) may be considered to be an outlier. Use this rule to identify any outliers in each data set. Show your work.

26. {2, 3, 4, 5, 5, 25}   **27.** {91, 90, 79, 15, 82, 90, 88}   **28.** {1, 36, 34, 33, 35, 92}

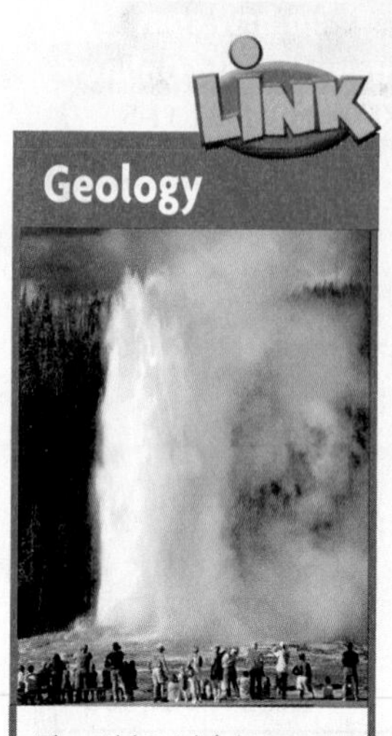

The Old Faithful Geyser at Yellowstone National Park can send 8500 gallons of boiling water to a height of 185 feet.

Geology Use the graph of 222 eruptions of the Old Faithful Geyser for Exercises 29 and 30.

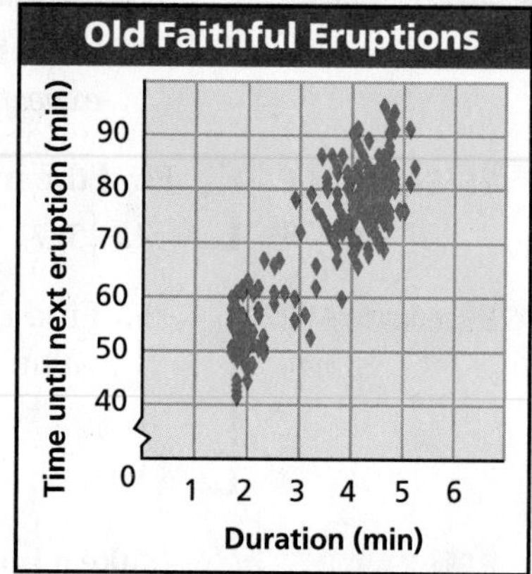

29. The duration has a mean of 3.6 min and a standard deviation of 1.1 min. What duration time intervals would be outliers? Describe any outliers for duration on the graph.

30. The time between eruptions has a mean of 71 min and a standard deviation of 12.8 min. What time intervals would be outliers? Describe any outliers for time intervals on the graph.

Estimation Use the box-and-whisker plots for Exercises 31–34.

Home Runs by Season

Babe Ruth

Hank Aaron

0 10 20 30 40 50 60

31. Which player hit the most home runs in a season? By approximately how many home runs did he do so?

32. Which player had the greater median number of home runs? Estimate how much greater.

33. Estimate the interquartile range for both players.

34. Which data set has the smaller standard deviation? Explain.

35. You have a 0.1% chance of winning \$500 and a 99.9% chance of losing \$1. What is the expected value of your gain? (*Hint*: The two possible outcomes for this "experiment" are + 500 and –1.)

36. Suppose that you have a 10% chance of winning \$100, a 30% chance of losing \$2, and a 60% chance of breaking even. What is the expected value?

37. ///ERROR ANALYSIS/// Two students attempt to find the standard deviation of 4, 6, 8, and 10. Which is incorrect? Explain the error.

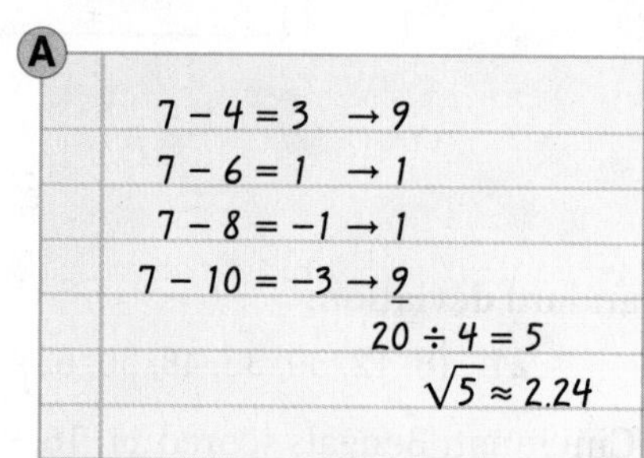

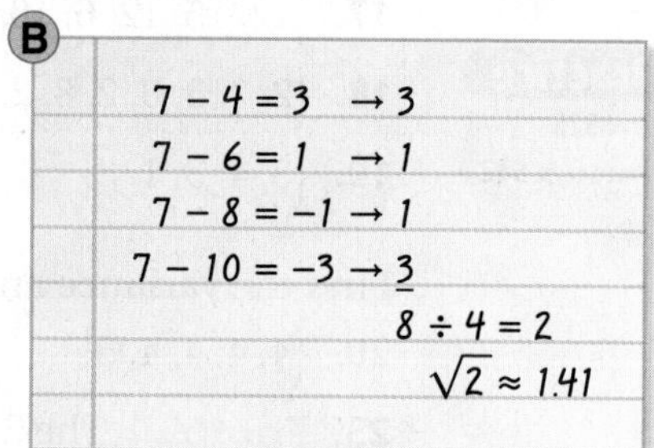

38. Write About It Is an expected value always, sometimes, or never a value in the data set? Give an example to justify your answer.

39. Games In a game, you multiply the values of two number cubes.

a. What is the expected value of this product?

b. What is the probability that a product is greater than the expected value?

c. What is the probability that a product is less than the expected value?

d. Are the answers to parts **b** and **c** equal? Explain.

40. This problem will prepare you for the Multi-Step Test Prep on page 844. The table shows the total annual precipitation for San Diego, California.

Year	1994	1995	1996	1997	1998
Precipitation (in.)	9.4	17.0	7.3	7.0	16.1

Year	1999	2000	2001	2002	2003
Precipitation (in.)	5.4	6.9	8.5	4.2	9.2

a. Find the mean annual precipitation and the standard deviation.

b. In what years was the precipitation more than one standard deviation from the mean?

c. Find the median and interquartile range for the data.

41. Which data set would give the smallest standard deviation?

Ⓐ $\{1, 5, 7, 50\}$

Ⓑ $\{2, 10, 102, 110\}$

Ⓒ $\{100, 200, 300, 400\}$

Ⓓ $\{100, 101, 102, 105\}$

42. Which of the following is NOT true about the data sets $\{0, 48, 49, 50, 51, 52, 100\}$ and $\{0, 1, 2, 50, 98, 99, 100\}$?

Ⓕ The means are equal.

Ⓖ The ranges are equal.

Ⓗ The variances are equal.

Ⓙ The medians are equal.

43. The mean score on a test is 50. Which cannot be true?

Ⓐ Half the scores are 0, and half the scores are 100.

Ⓑ The range is 50.

Ⓒ Half the scores are 25, and half the scores are 50.

Ⓓ Every score is 50.

CHALLENGE AND EXTEND

44. A data set has a mean of 4, a median of 3, and a standard deviation of 1.6.

a. Suppose that every value of the data set is multiplied by 5. What is the mean, median, and standard deviation of the new data set?

b. Suppose that 5 is added to every value of the original data set. What is the mean, median, and standard deviation of the new data set?

45. A deck of cards is shuffled. What is the expected number of cards that will be in the same position that they were in originally? (*Hint:* Look at decks of 1, 2, 3, and 4 cards.)

SPIRAL REVIEW

46. **Business** Li was paid \$725 a month plus \$1.75 for every magazine she sold. Li earned \$1425 one month. How many magazines did Li sell? *(Lesson 2-1)*

Find each product. *(Lesson 6-2)*

47. $(2 - x^2)(2x^2 + 5x - 3)$

48. $4xy^2(x^2y + 3x^2 - 2y)$

A number cube is rolled. Find each probability. *(Lesson 11-4)*

49. an even number or a 1

50. an odd number or a 4

51. a number divisible by 2 or 6

Collect Experimental Data

You can perform an experiment to generate, collect, organize, and analyze data in order to form mathematical conjectures.

Make a table of the sum of two number cubes.

Blue cube (columns); Red cube (rows)

	1	2	3	4	5	6
1	2	3	4	5	6	7
2	3	4	5	6	7	8
3	4	5	6	7	8	9
4	5	6	7	8	9	10
5	6	7	8	9	10	11
6	7	8	9	10	11	12

Try This

1. Describe any symmetry you notice in the table.
2. Make a probability distribution by using theoretical probabilities.

Sums	2	3	4	5	6	7	8	9	10	11	12
Probability	■	■	■	■	■	■	■	■	■	■	■

3. Find the expected value by using the theoretical probability distribution.
4. Which sum is most likely? least likely?
5. Do any two different sums have the same probability? If so, what are those sums?
6. Roll two number cubes 36 times. Record the results in a table.
7. Make a probability distribution of your data.
8. Find the expected value by using your probability distribution.

Answer the following questions based on your experiment.

9. Which sum was most likely? least likely?
10. Did any two different sums have the same probability? If so, what are those sums?
11. Compare your results with the theoretical results.
12. Combine the results of your experiment with those of other students. How do the experimental results of the group compare with your results? with the theoretical results?

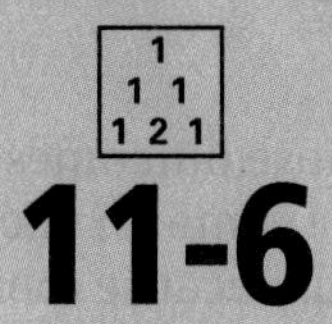

11-6 Binomial Distributions

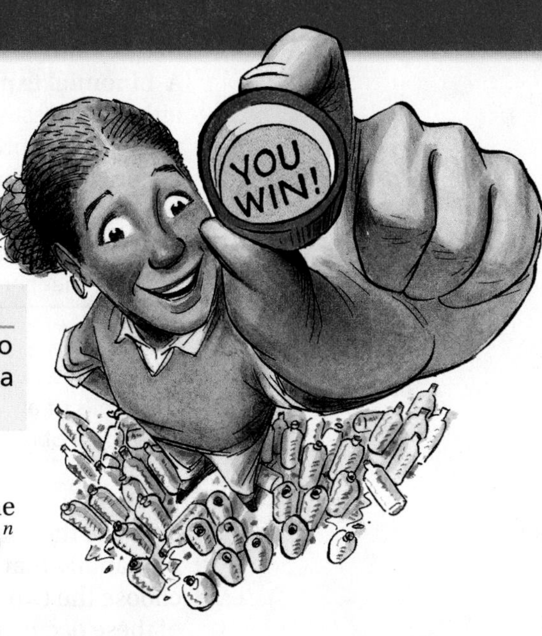

Objectives

Use the Binomial Theorem to expand a binomial raised to a power.

Find binomial probabilities and test hypotheses.

Vocabulary

Binomial Theorem
binomial experiment
binomial probability

Why learn this?

You can use binomial distributions to determine your chances of winning a marketing contest. (See Example 3.)

You used Pascal's triangle to find binomial expansions in Lesson 6-2. The coefficients of the expansion of $(x + y)^n$ are the numbers in Pascal's triangle, which are actually combinations.

Pascal's Triangle	Combinations (Binomial Coefficients)	Binomial Expansion
1	${}_0C_0$	$(x+y)^0 = 1$
1 1	${}_1C_0 \quad {}_1C_1$	$(x+y)^1 = x + y$
1 2 1	${}_2C_0 \quad {}_2C_1 \quad {}_2C_2$	$(x+y)^2 = x^2 + 2xy + y^2$
1 3 3 1	${}_3C_0 \quad {}_3C_1 \quad {}_3C_2 \quad {}_3C_3$	$(x+y)^3 = x^3 + 3x^2y + 3xy^2 + y^3$

The pattern in the table can help you expand any binomial by using the **Binomial Theorem**.

Binomial Theorem

For any whole number n,

$$(x+y)^n = {}_nC_0x^ny^0 + {}_nC_1x^{n-1}y^1 + {}_nC_2x^{n-2}y^2 + \cdots + {}_nC_{n-1}x^1y^{n-1} + {}_nC_nx^0y^n$$

EXAMPLE 1 **Expanding Binomials**

Use the Binomial Theorem to expand each binomial.

A $(x+y)^4$ *The sum of the exponents for each term is 4.*

$$\begin{aligned}(x+y)^4 &= {}_4C_0x^4y^0 + {}_4C_1x^3y^1 + {}_4C_2x^2y^2 + {}_4C_3x^1y^3 + {}_4C_4x^0y^4\\ &= 1x^4y^0 + 4x^3y^1 + 6x^2y^2 + 4x^1y^3 + 1x^0y^4\\ &= x^4 + 4x^3y + 6x^2y^2 + 4xy^3 + y^4\end{aligned}$$

B $(3p+q)^3$

$$\begin{aligned}(3p+q)^3 &= {}_3C_0(3p)^3q^0 + {}_3C_1(3p)^2q^1 + {}_3C_2(3p)^1q^2 + {}_3C_3(3p)^0q^3\\ &= 1\cdot 27p^3\cdot 1 + 3\cdot 9p^2q + 3\cdot 3pq^2 + 1\cdot 1q^3\\ &= 27p^3 + 27p^2q + 9pq^2 + q^3\end{aligned}$$

Remember!

In the expansion of $(x + y)^n$, the powers of x decrease from n to 0 and the powers of y increase from 0 to n. Also, the sum of the exponents is n for each term. (Lesson 6-2)

Use the Binomial Theorem to expand each binomial.

1a. $(x-y)^5$ **1b.** $(a+2b)^3$

A **binomial experiment** consists of n independent trials whose outcomes are either successes or failures; the probability of success p is the same for each trial, and the probability of failure q is the same for each trial. Because there are only two outcomes, $p + q = 1$, or $q = 1 - p$. Below are some examples of binomial experiments:

Experiment	Success	Failure	P(success)	P(failure)
10 flips of a coin	Heads	Tails	$p = 0.5$	$q = 1 - p = 0.5$
100 rolls of a number cube	Roll a 3.	Roll any other number.	$p = \frac{1}{6}$	$q = \frac{5}{6}$

Suppose the probability of being left-handed is 0.1 and you want to find the probability that 2 out of 3 people will be left-handed. There are ${}_3C_2$ ways to choose the two left-handed people: LLR, LRL, and RLL. The probability of each of these occurring is 0.1(0.1)(0.9). This leads to the following formula.

Binomial Probability

If a binomial experiment has n trials in which p is the probability of success and q is the probability of failure in any given trial, then the **binomial probability** that there will be exactly r successes is:

$$P(r) = {}_nC_r\, p^r q^{n-r}$$

EXAMPLE 2 Finding Binomial Probabilities

One in 5 boats going through a *slough* at midday will bypass the harbor and head out to sea. Four boats are going through the slough.

A What is the probability that exactly 2 boats will head out to sea?

The probability that a boat will head out to sea is $\frac{1}{5}$, or 0.2.

$P(r) = {}_nC_r p^r q^{n-r}$

$P(2) = {}_4C_2(0.2)^2(0.8)^{4-2}$ *Substitute 4 for n, 2 for r, 0.2 for p, and 0.8 for q.*

$= 6(0.04)(0.64) = 0.1536$

The probability that exactly 2 of the boats will head out to sea is about 15.4%.

B What is the probability that at least 2 boats will head out to sea?

At least 2 boats is the same as exactly 2, 3, or 4 boats heading out to sea.

$P(2) + P(3) + P(4)$

$0.1536 + {}_4C_3(0.2)^3(0.8)^{4-3} + {}_4C_4(0.2)^4(0.8)^{4-4}$

$0.1536 + 0.0256 + 0.0016 = 0.1808$

The probability that at least 2 boats will head out to sea is about 18.1%.

2a. Students are assigned randomly to 1 of 3 guidance counselors. What is the probability that Counselor Jenkins will get 2 of the next 3 students assigned?

2b. Ellen takes a multiple-choice quiz that has 5 questions, with 4 answer choices for each question. What is the probability that she will get at least 2 answers correct by guessing?

EXAMPLE 3 Problem-Solving Application

Vince buys 10 juice drinks. What is the probability that he will get at least 2 prizes?

Sweepstakes Prizes Chances of Winning	
Free drink	1 in 5
Water bottle	1 in 22
T-shirt	1 in 250
Music player	1 in 100,000
Car	1 in 20,000,000
Any prize	1 in 4

1 Understand the Problem

The **answer** will be the probability that Vince will get at least 2 prizes.

List the important information:

- Vince buys 10 juice drinks.
- The binomial probability that each bottle wins a prize is $\frac{1}{4}$.

2 Make a Plan

The direct way to solve the problem is to calculate $P(2) + P(3) + P(4) + \cdots + P(10)$.

An easier way is to use the complement. "Getting 0 or 1 prize" is the complement of "getting at least 2 prizes." Find this probability, and then subtract the result from 1.

3 Solve

Step 1 Find $P(0 \text{ or } 1 \text{ prize})$.

$$\begin{aligned} &P(0) \qquad + \qquad P(1) \\ &= {}_{10}C_0\,(0.25)^0(0.75)^{10-0} + {}_{10}C_1(0.25)^1(0.75)^{10-1} \\ &= 1(1)(0.75)^{10} + 10(0.25)(0.75)^9 \\ &\approx 0.0563 + 0.1877 \\ &\approx 0.2440 \end{aligned}$$

Step 2 Use the complement to find the probability.

$1 - 0.2440$ *Subtract from 1.*

≈ 0.7560

The probability that Vince will get at least 2 prizes is about 0.76.

4 Look Back

The answer is reasonable, as the expected number of winners is $\frac{1}{4}$ of 10, = 2.5, which is greater than 2. So the probability that Vince will get at least 2 prizes should be greater than 0.5.

3a. Wendy takes a multiple-choice quiz that has 20 questions. There are 4 answer choices for each question. What is the probability that she will get at least 2 answers correct by guessing?

3b. A machine has a 98% probability of producing a part within acceptable tolerance levels. The machine makes 25 parts an hour. What is the probability that there are 23 or fewer acceptable parts?

THINK AND DISCUSS

1. Describe and explain the sum of p and q for a binomial experiment.
2. Tell what three expressions are multiplied to find the probability that there will be r successes in a binomial experiment of n trials.

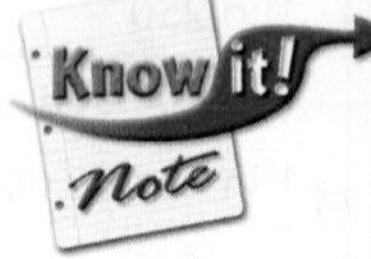

3. **GET ORGANIZED** Copy and complete the graphic organizer. Solve each problem that you include.

Binomial Experiments	
Probability	**Example**
Probability of r successes in n trials	
Probability of at least r successes	
Probability of at most r successes	
Probability using a complement	

11-6 Exercises

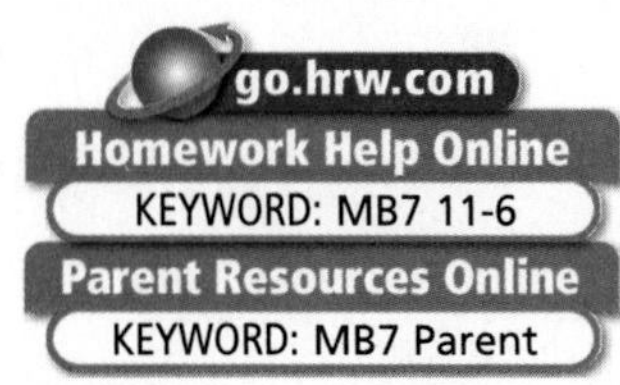

GUIDED PRACTICE

1. **Vocabulary** There are __?__ possible outcomes in each trial of a *binomial experiment.*

SEE EXAMPLE 1 p. 837

Use the Binomial Theorem to expand each binomial.

2. $(x + 3)^4$
3. $(3x + 5)^3$
4. $(p - 2)^6$
5. $(x + y)^6$

SEE EXAMPLE 2 p. 838

6. **School** The principal will randomly choose 6 students from a large school to represent the school in a newspaper photograph. The probability that a chosen student is an athlete is 30% (assume that this doesn't change). What is the probability that 4 athletes are chosen? What is the probability that at least 4 athletes are chosen?
7. **Shopping** Wilma bought 4 boxes of Crunch-A-Lot cereal. One out of every 5 boxes has a coupon for a free box of Crunch-A-Lot. What is the probability that Wilma got 3 coupons? What is the probability that Wilma got at least 2 coupons?

SEE EXAMPLE 3 p. 839

8. **Manufacturing** In a manufacturing plant, there is a 2% chance that a stamp will be placed on a box upside down. The plant shipped 30 boxes today. What is the probability that at least 2 of the boxes have an upside-down stamp?

PRACTICE AND PROBLEM SOLVING

Use the Binomial Theorem to expand each binomial.

9. $(y + 5)^4$
10. $(2m - 1)^3$
11. $(4 + 3x)^5$
12. $(2a + 3c)^3$
13. **Civil Rights** In a survey of more than 100,000 high school students in 2004 by researchers at the University of Connecticut, 83% agreed with the statement "People should be allowed to express unpopular opinions." If 8 students are selected at random, what is the probability that at least 6 agree with the statement?

Independent Practice	
For Exercises	See Example
9–12	1
13–14	2
15–16	3

Extra Practice

Skills Practice p. S25
Application Practice p. S42

14. Five marbles are randomly selected with replacement. The probability that a black marble is chosen is 15%. What is the probability that 2 marbles are black? What is the probability that at least 2 marbles are black?

15. **Genetics** A woman is expecting triplets. What is the probability that there are 2 girls and 1 boy? What is the probability that all 3 babies are girls?

16. **Botany** A tree has a 25% chance of flowering. In a random sample of 15 trees, what is the probability that at least 4 develop flowers?

Use the Binomial Theorem to expand each binomial.

17. $(x-y)^5$ 18. $(c+6)^3$ 19. $(4k-1)^4$ 20. $(p+q)^7$

Evaluate $P(r) = {}_nC_r\, p^r q^{n-r}$, where $q = 1 - p$.

21. $p = 0.8, n = 3, r = 2$ 22. $p = 0.5, n = 5, r = 1$ 23. $p = \frac{1}{3}, n = 4, r = 2$

24. **Travel** A small airline overbooks flights on the assumption that several passengers will not show up. Suppose that the probability that a passenger shows up is 0.91. What is the probability that a 20-seat flight with 22 tickets sold will be able to seat all passengers who arrive?

25. **Genetics** A hedgehog has a litter of 4. What is the probability that all 4 are male? What is the probability that at least 3 are male?

Find each probability when a fair coin is tossed 10 times.

26. more than 7 heads 27. at least 2 heads 28. exactly 5 heads

29. **Quality Control** An auto part has a 95% chance of being made within its tolerance level and a 5% chance of being pulled as defective. What is the probability that in a box of 8 parts, no more than 1 is defective?

30. **Graphing Calculator** The **randBin** function simulates a binomial experiment and reports the number of successes. To simulate a binomial experiment with $n = 6$ and $p = 0.3$ five times, press MATH, move to **PRB**, select **randBin(** and enter 6, 0.3, and 5, separated by commas.
    a. Simulate a binomial experiment with $n = 5$ and $p = 0.8$ five times.
    b. Use the formula to find the probability of at least 4 successes.
    c. How do your simulation results compare?

31. **Multi-Step** For $P = 0.8$ and $n = 10$, use a calculator to find the binomial probabilities for $r = 0$ to $r = 10$. Round to the nearest hundredth. Construct a bar graph of the probabilities. Describe the shape of the graph. How does the graph relate to the expected value?

32. **Critical Thinking** Which is more likely, a family with 4 children of 2 girls and 2 boys or a family of 4 children with 3 of one gender and 1 of the other? Explain.

33. This problem will prepare you for the Multi-Step Test Prep on page 844.

Based on historical data, the expected number of rainy days in San Antonio, Texas, during a calendar year is 82. Assume that rainy days are independent events.
    a. What is the probability that there will be rain on any given day in San Antonio?
    b. What is the probability that there will be exactly 3 rainy days during any given week?
    c. What is the probability that there will be at least 3 rainy days during any given week?

34. There are 10 marbles in a bag. Half are striped, and half are not striped. Explain why choosing 3 marbles without replacement and noting whether they are striped does not fit the definition of a binomial experiment.

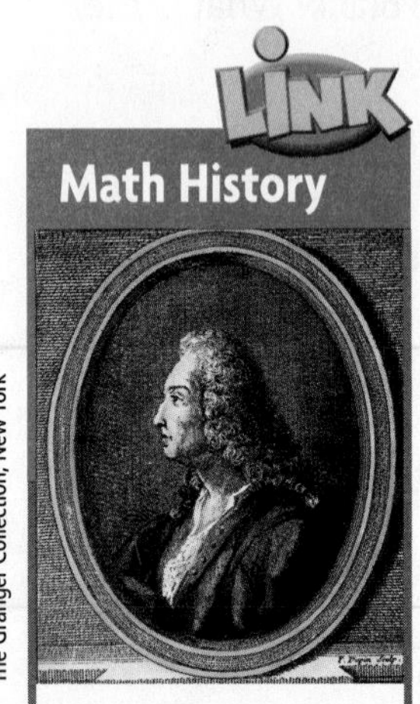

The Granger Collection, New York

The trials in a binomial experiment are often called Bernoulli trials after Italian mathematician Jacob Bernoulli (1654–1705).

35. **Air Travel** In 2003, 20.46% of all direct flights from Dallas/Fort Worth to Los Angeles International Airport were delayed. Kelly flew that route 4 times and was on a delayed flight 3 times. What is the probability that she would have been on a delayed flight at least 3 times?

36. **Games** As the ball drops, it has an equal chance of making a left turn or right turn at each peg.

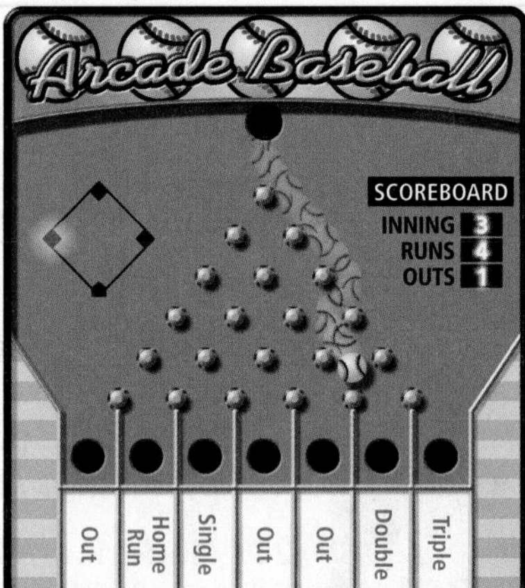

a. What is the probability of a home run?

b. What is the probability of an out?

c. What is the probability of a hit (a single, double, triple, or home run)?

d. How are the answers to parts **b** and **c** related?

37. **Pets** A survey showed that 45% of dog owners take their dog with them on vacation. If 5 dog owners go on vacation, what is the probability that fewer than 3 take their dog?

38. **Write About It** Describe a situation for which it would be beneficial to use the complement to find binomial probabilities.

Estimation Use the graph for Exercises 39 and 40. The graph shows the probability of *r* successes in 10 trials of a binomial experiment.

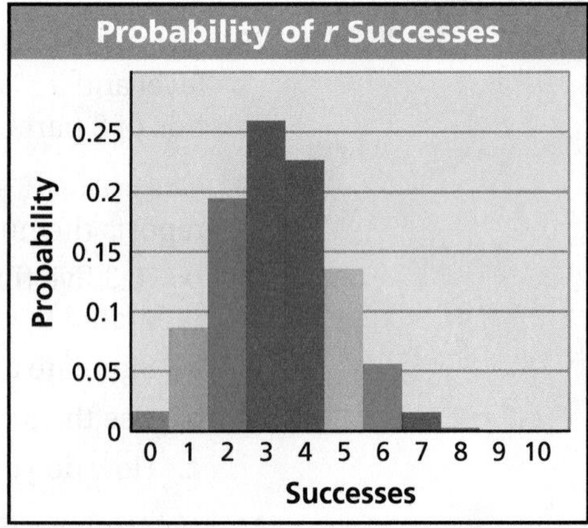

39. Estimate the probability of 2 or fewer successes.

40. Estimate the binomial probability p. Explain how you arrived at your answer.

41. Which of the following is NOT true about a binomial experiment?

Ⓐ The outcomes are either successes or failures.

Ⓑ The trials are dependent.

Ⓒ The probability of success is constant.

Ⓓ The trials are identical.

42. In a binomial experiment with 2 trials and a probability of success on each trial of 40%, what is the probability of exactly 1 success?

Ⓕ 16% Ⓖ 36% Ⓗ 48% Ⓙ 52%

43. In a binomial experiment, the probability of success is 20%. Which gives the probability of 3 successes in 5 trials?

Ⓐ $3(0.2)^3(0.8)^2$ Ⓑ $10(0.2)^3(0.8)^2$ Ⓒ $3(0.2)^2(0.8)^3$ Ⓓ $10(0.2)^2(0.8)^3$

44. **Gridded Response** A part has a 4% chance of being discarded for imperfections. Out of 10 randomly selected parts, what is the probability that no more than 1 has an imperfection? Round to the nearest whole percent.

45. **Short Response** About 18.8% of the people in the United States have one of the 100 most common last names. What is the probability that in a group of 10 randomly-selected people, 3 or more have one of these names?

CHALLENGE AND EXTEND

46. **Genetics** There is about a 0.1 probability that a person is left-handed. There are 650 people in an auditorium.
    a. What is the expected number of left-handed people in the auditorium? Explain.
    b. The standard deviation for a binomial experiment with n trials is given by $\sqrt{npq}$. Describe the number of left-handed people that you would expect in the auditorium as an interval within 1 standard deviation of the expected number.

47. Find each probability. Which is greater?
    a. rolling at least one 1 in 6 rolls of a die
    b. rolling at least two 1's in 12 rolls of a die

48. **Calculator** The **binomcdf** function, found in 2nd 0 (CATALOG), computes the cumulative probability of r successes in a binomial experiment of n trials with a probability of success p. To compute the probability of at most 3 successes in a binomial experiment with $n = 6$ and $p = 0.3$, use **binomcdf**, enter 6, 0.3, and 3, separated by commas, and press ENTER. Use the **binomcdf** function to find the probability of *at least* 4 successes in a binomial experiment of 20 trials with probability of success 0.4.

49. Show why any number ${}_{n+1}C_{r+1}$ in Pascal's triangle is the sum of the two numbers above it, ${}_nC_r$ and ${}_nC_{r+1}$ where r is not equal to 0 or n, and $n > 1$.

50. **Bowling** A bowler has a 0.4 probability of making exactly 1 strike in 2 frames, either in the first frame or the second frame. Assume that the bowler's probability p of getting a strike is the same for any frame.
    a. Write an equation and solve for p.
    b. Find the probability that the bowler makes strikes in both frames.

SPIRAL REVIEW

For each function, evaluate $f(-3)$, $f(0)$, and $f(2)$. *(Lesson 1-7)*

51. $f(x) = -x^2 + 2x - 4$

52. $f(x) = (-x)^2 - 3x + 1$

Determine whether y is an exponential function of x. If so, use exponential regression to find a function that models the data. *(Lesson 7-8)*

53.

x	1	2	3	4	5
y	1.4	2.6	3.8	5.0	6.2

54.

x	1	2	3	4	5
y	10	22	36	52	70

Find the mean, median, and mode of each data set. *(Lesson 11-5)*

55. $\{2, 18, 15, 14, 18\}$

56. $\{6, 13, 9, 7, 6, 4\}$

57. $\{24, 20, 32, 24, 16, 34\}$

58. $\{10, 5, 15, 5, 8\}$

CHAPTER 11

MULTI-STEP TEST PREP

SECTION 11B

Data Analysis and Statistics

Rain Reign Many people think of Seattle, Washington, as one of the rainiest cities in the United States. The table provides precipitation data for Seattle and Atlanta, Georgia, over a 10-year period. By analyzing this data set, you can decide for yourself whether Seattle deserves its soggy reputation.

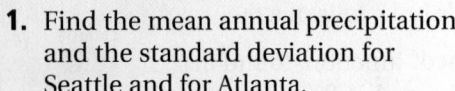

Annual Precipitation (in.)		
Year	**Seattle**	**Atlanta**
1994	34.8	60.0
1995	42.6	52.8
1996	50.7	44.6
1997	43.3	51.7
1998	44.1	46.2
1999	42.1	38.9
2000	28.7	35.6
2001	37.6	38.4
2002	31.4	47.6
2003	41.5	52.9

1. Find the mean annual precipitation and the standard deviation for Seattle and for Atlanta.
2. For which city do the data cluster more closely around the mean?
3. Find the interquartile range for Seattle and for Atlanta.
4. For which city do the data cluster more closely around the median?
5. During a calendar year, the expected number of rainy days in Atlanta is 115. Find the probability that it will rain on any given day. Then find the probability that it will rain there on at least 2 days during any given week.
6. Based on your findings, why do you think Seattle, rather than Atlanta, has a reputation as a rainy city?

CHAPTER 11

SECTION 11B

Quiz for Lessons 11-5 Through 11-6

11-5 Measures of Central Tendency and Variation

1. Mr. Ortega took the following number of sick days per year for the last 5 years: 4, 2, 6, 3, 2. Find the mean, median, and mode of the data set.
2. The probability distribution for the number of defects in a shipment of alarm clocks, based on past data, is given below. Find the expected number of defects in a shipment of alarm clocks.

Number of Defects, n	0	1	2	3	4
Probability of n Defects	0.82	0.11	0.04	0.02	0.01

3. Make a box-and-whisker plot of the data. Find the interquartile range.
   Ages of employees at a movie theater: 17, 23, 18, 22, 45, 28, 21, 25
4. The lengths of fish caught, in inches, during one fishing trip are given. Find the lengths within 1 standard deviation of the mean.

   Lengths of fish caught: 14, 28, 16, 20, 22, 33, 12, 30, 30, 25

The data set shows the amount of money, rounded to the nearest dollar, spent by 20 consecutive shoppers at a home-improvement store.

35, 18, 49, 55, 280, 29, 42, 61, 19, 80, 33, 45, 67, 28, 71, 37, 48, 50, 31, 22

5. Find the mean and standard deviation of the data.
6. Identify the outlier, and describe how it affects the mean and standard deviation.

11-6 Binomial Distributions

7. Use the Binomial Theorem to expand $(m - 2n)^3$.

The spinner shown is spun 10 times.

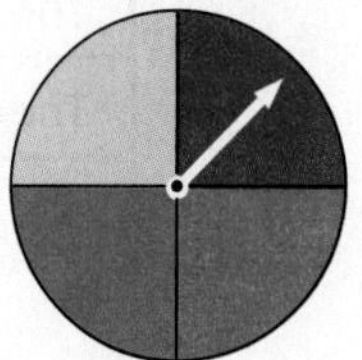

8. What is the probability that the spinner will land in the blue area exactly 5 times?
9. What is the probability that the spinner will land in the blue area at least 3 times?

A multiple-choice quiz has 5 questions. Each question has 3 possible answers. A student guesses the answer to each question. Find each probability.

10. The student answers all 5 questions correctly.
11. The student answers exactly 1 question correctly.
12. The student answers all 5 questions incorrectly.
13. The student answers at least 1 question correctly.

EXTENSION Normal Distributions

Objectives

Recognize normally distributed data.

Use the characteristics of the normal distribution to solve problems.

A *random variable* is associated with the possible outcomes of an experiment. For example, if the random variable X is associated with the possible outcomes of rolling a number cube, the possible values of X are 1, 2, 3, 4, 5, and 6.

A *probability distribution* shows the probabilities that correspond to the possible values of a random variable. Probability distributions can be based on either discrete or continuous data.

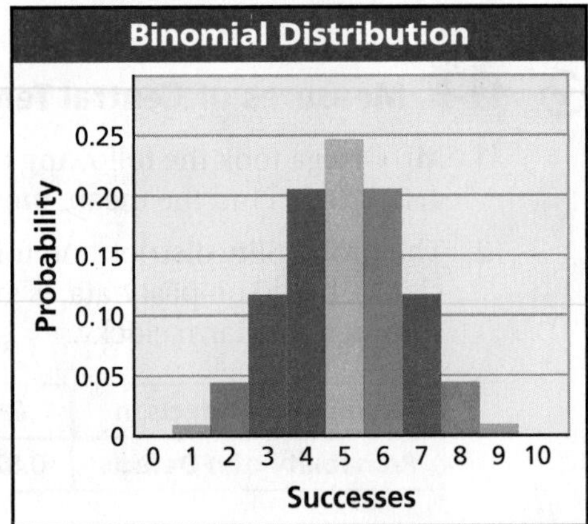

The binomial distributions that you studied in Lesson 11-6 were *discrete probability distributions* because there were a finite number of possible outcomes.

In a *continuous probability distribution,* the outcome can be any real number—for example, the time it takes to complete a task.

You may be familiar with the bell-shaped curve called the *normal curve.* A *normal distribution* is a function of the mean and standard deviation of a data set that assigns probabilities to intervals of real numbers associated with continuous random variables.

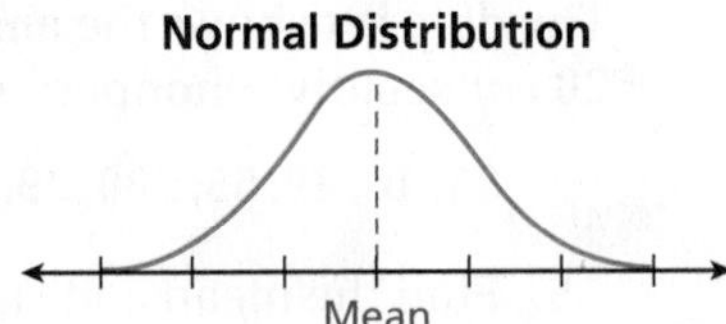

Normal Distributions
The probability assigned to a real-number interval is the area under the normal curve in that interval. Because the area under the curve represents probability, the total area under the curve is 1.
The maximum value of a normal curve occurs at the mean.
The normal curve is symmetric about a vertical line through the mean.
The normal curve has a horizontal asymptote at $y = 0$.

The figure shows the percent of data in a normal distribution that falls within a number of standard deviations from the mean.

The diagram shows the following:

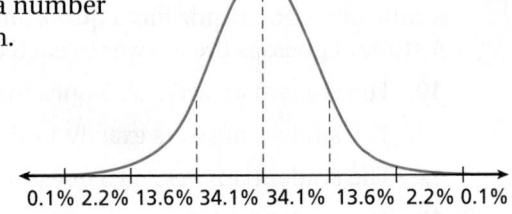

- About 68% lie within 1 standard deviation of the mean.
- About 95% lie within 2 standard deviations of the mean.
- More than 99.7% lie within 3 standard deviations of the mean.

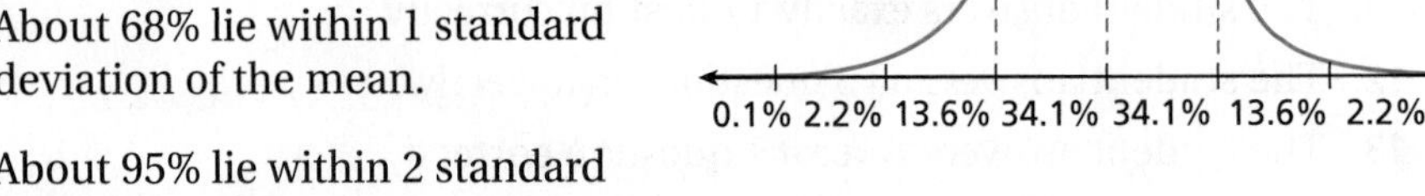

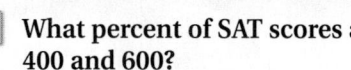

EXAMPLE 1 Finding Normal Probabilities

The SAT is designed so that scores are normally distributed with a mean of 500 and a standard deviation of 100.

A **What percent of SAT scores are between 400 and 600?**

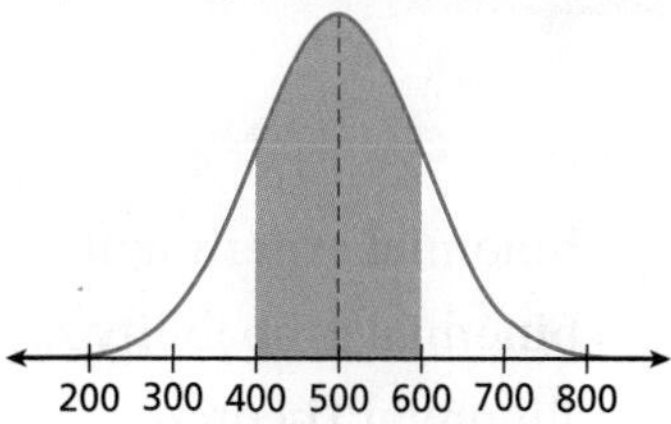

Both 400 and 600 are 1 standard deviation from the mean. Use the percents from the figure on the previous page.

$34.1\% + 34.1\% = 68.2\%$

About 68.2% of the scores are between 400 and 600.

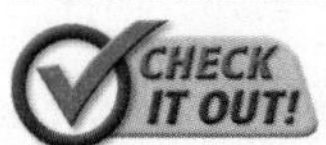

Reading Math

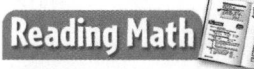

Each end of a normal distribution is called a *tail.*

B **What is the probability that an SAT score is above 600?**

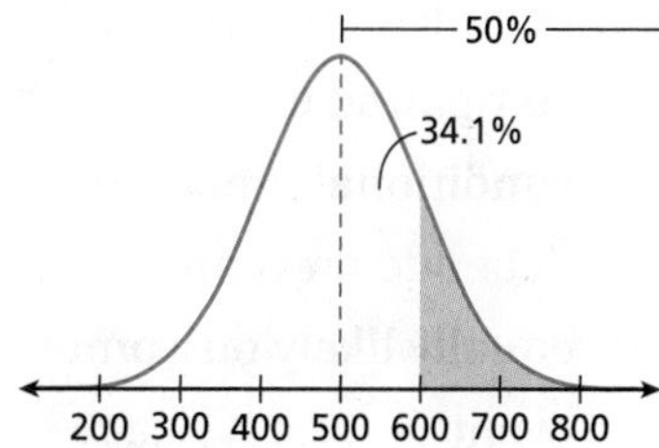

Because the graph is symmetric, the right side of the graph shows 50% of the data.

$50\% - 34.1\% = 15.9\%$

The probability that an SAT score is above 600 is about 0.159, or 15.9%.

C **What is the probability that an SAT score is less than 300 or greater than 700?**

$50\% - (34.1\% + 13.6\%) = 2.3\%$ *Percent of data > 700*

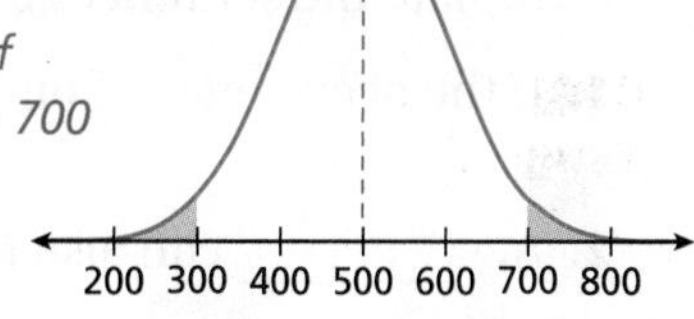

Because the curve is symmetric, the probability that an SAT score is less than 300 or greater than 700 is about $2(2.3\%)$, or 4.6%.

CHECK IT OUT! **Use the information above to answer the following.**

1. What is the probability that an SAT score is above 300?

EXTENSION Exercises

A standardized test has a mean of 50 and a standard deviation of 4. Find the probability of test scores in the following ranges.

1. between 42 and 58
2. below 46
3. between 46 and 54

The amount of coffee in a can has a mean of 350 g and a standard deviation of 4 g.

4. What percent of cans have less than 338 g of coffee?
5. What is the probability that a can has between 342 g and 350 g of coffee?
6. What is the probability that a can has less than 342 g or more than 346 g of coffee?

Flight 202's arrival time is normally distributed with a mean arrival time of 4:30 P.M. and a standard deviation of 15 minutes.

7. Find the probability that an arrival time is after 4:45 P.M.
8. Find the probability that an arrival time is between 4:15 P.M. and 5:00 P.M.

CHAPTER 11

Study Guide: Review

Vocabulary

binomial experiment	838	experiment	805	outlier	831
binomial probability	838	experimental probability	805	permutation	795
Binomial Theorem	837	factorial	795	probability	802
combination	796	favorable outcomes	802	probability distribution	828
complement	803	Fundamental Counting Principle	794	sample space	802
compound event	819	geometric probability	804	simple event	819
conditional probability	812	inclusive events	820	standard deviation	830
dependent events	812	independent events	811	theoretical probability	802
equally likely outcomes	802	mutually exclusive events	819	trial	805
event	802	outcome	802	variance	830
expected value	828				

Complete the sentences below with vocabulary words from the list above.

1. If the occurrence of one event affects the probability of the other, then the events are ___?___.
2. A(n) ___?___ can also be called a weighted average.
3. When arranging items, order is important when using a(n) ___?___.

11-1 Permutations and Combinations *(pp. 794–800)*

EXAMPLES

- **If you have 8 vases to choose from, how many ways can you arrange 5 of them on a shelf?**

The order matters, so it is a permutation.

$$_8P_5 = \frac{8!}{(8-5)!} = \frac{8 \cdot 7 \cdot 6 \cdot 5 \cdot 4 \cdot \cancel{3} \cdot \cancel{2} \cdot \cancel{1}}{\cancel{3} \cdot \cancel{2} \cdot \cancel{1}}$$
$$= 8 \cdot 7 \cdot 6 \cdot 5 = 6720$$

There are 6720 ways to arrange the vases.

- **If 7 pizza toppings are available, how many ways can you choose 2 toppings?**

The order does not matter, so it is a combination.

$$_7C_2 = \frac{7!}{2!(7-2)!} = \frac{7 \cdot 6 \cdot \cancel{5} \cdot \cancel{4} \cdot \cancel{3} \cdot \cancel{2} \cdot \cancel{1}}{2 \cdot 1(\cancel{5} \cdot \cancel{4} \cdot \cancel{3} \cdot \cancel{2} \cdot \cancel{1})}$$
$$= \frac{42}{2} = 21$$

There are 21 ways to choose the toppings.

EXERCISES

4. How many different 7-digit telephone numbers can be made if the first digit cannot be 7, 8, or 9?
5. From a group of 12 volunteers, a surveyor must choose 5 to complete an advanced survey. How many groups of 5 people can be chosen?
6. In one day, a salesman plans to visit 6 out of 14 companies that are in the neighborhood. How many ways can he plan the visits?
7. How many ways can 7 people arrange themselves inside a van that has 10 seats?
8. The caterer told Kathy that she can choose 3 entrées from the 6 listed on the menu. How many groups of 3 entrées can she choose?

11-2 Theoretical and Experimental Probability *(pp. 802–809)*

EXAMPLES

A paper clip holder has 100 paper clips: 30 are red, 20 are yellow, 25 are green, 15 are pink, and 10 are black. A paper clip is randomly chosen. Find each probability.

- The paper clip is green.

$$P(\text{green}) = \frac{\text{number of green paper clips}}{\text{total number of paper clips}}$$

$$= \frac{25}{100} = \frac{1}{4}$$

- The paper clip is not pink.

$$P(\text{not pink}) = 1 - P(\text{pink}) = 1 - \frac{15}{100} = \frac{17}{20}$$

- **Carl and Pedro each put their names in a hat for a door prize. Two names will be selected, and there are a total of 40 names in the hat. What is the probability that Carl wins the first prize and Pedro wins the second?**

The number of outcomes in the sample space is the number of ways that 2 people can be selected from 40 and then ordered.

$$P(\text{Carl, then Pedro}) = \frac{1}{{}_{40}P_2} = \frac{1}{1560}$$

- **A dart is randomly thrown at the dartboard. What is the probability that it lands in the outer ring?**

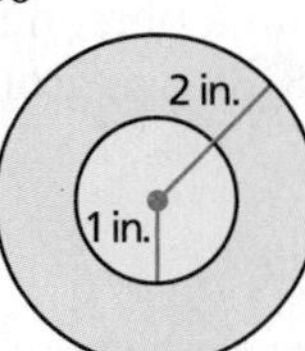

$$P(\text{outer ring}) = \frac{\text{area of outer ring}}{\text{area of dart board}}$$

$$= \frac{\text{area of large circle} - \text{area of inner circle}}{\text{area of large circle}}$$

$$= \frac{\pi(3)^2 - \pi(1)^2}{\pi(3)^2} = \frac{9\pi - 1\pi}{9\pi} = \frac{8\pi}{9\pi} = \frac{8}{9}$$

- **The table shows the results of 75 tosses of a number cube. Find the experimental probability of rolling a 4.**

1	2	3	4	5	6
10	12	16	15	9	13

$$P(4) = \frac{\text{number of times 4 occurred}}{\text{number of trials}} = \frac{15}{75}$$

$$= \frac{1}{5} = 0.2$$

EXERCISES

Two number cubes are rolled. What is the probability of each event?

9. Sum is 8.
10. Difference is 1.
11. Sum is even.
12. Product is less than 30.
13. The 10-member math team randomly selects 4 representatives to send to a meet. What is the probability that the 4 members chosen are the 4 with the lowest math grades?
14. A 5-digit code is given to all cashiers at a store to let them log onto the cash register. What is the probability that an employee receives a code with all 5 numbers the same?
15. Find the probability that a point chosen at random inside the rectangle is in the shaded area.

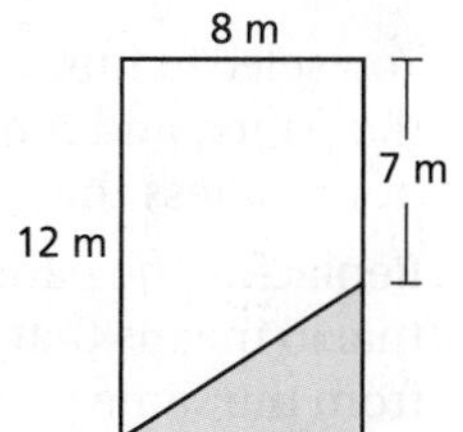

16. Find the probability that a point chosen at random inside the square is not inside the circle.

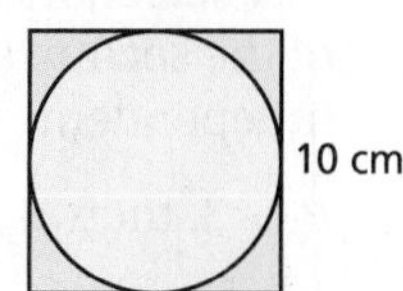

The bar graph shows the results of tossing two pennies 50 times. Find the experimental probability of each of the following.

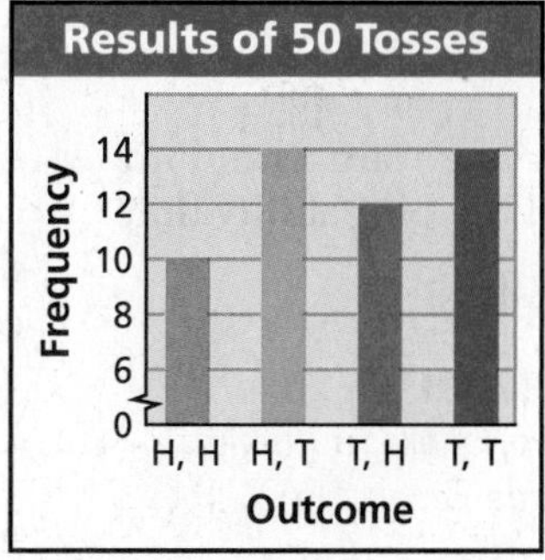

17. tossing 2 heads
18. tossing at least 1 tail
19. not tossing a head
20. tossing exactly 1 tail

Two pennies are tossed. Find the theoretical probability of each of the following.

21. tossing 2 heads
22. tossing at least 1 tail
23. not tossing a head
24. tossing exactly 1 tail

11-3 Independent and Dependent Events *(pp. 811–818)*

EXAMPLES

A bag contains slips of papers with the following numbers: 2, 2, 3, 3, 4, 5, 6. Determine whether the events are independent or dependent, and find the indicated probability.

- You select a 3, keep the paper, and then your friend selects a 3.

  Keeping the paper with the first 3 changes the number of 3's left in the bag for your friend to choose from, so the events are dependent.

  $P(3, \text{then } 3) = P(3) \cdot P(3 \mid 3).$

  $= \frac{2}{7} \cdot \frac{1}{6} = \frac{2}{42} = \frac{1}{21}$

- You select a number greater than 3, replace the paper, and then your friend selects a number less than 3.

  Replacing the paper with the number greater than 3 means that your friend will also select from the same papers, so the occurrence of the first selection does not affect the probability of the second selection. The events are independent.

  $P(> 3, \text{then} < 3) = P(> 3) \cdot P(< 3)$

  $= \frac{3}{7} \cdot \frac{2}{7} = \frac{6}{49}$

EXERCISES

Explain why the events are independent, and find the probability.

25. rolling "doubles" 3 times in a row when rolling 2 number cubes

26. selecting a red pen and then a blue pen, when selecting 2 pens from a bag of 10 red and 15 blue pens with replacement

The table shows the age and marital status of the members of an environmental group. One person from the group is randomly selected. Find each probability.

Marital Status by Age				
	18–34	35–50	51–65	66+
Married	6	20	22	4
Single	14	22	11	0

27. that the selected person is single, given that he or she is in the 35–50 age group

28. that a married person is 66 or older

29. that a person aged 18–50 is married

30. that a person in the group is single and in the 18–34 age group

11-4 Compound Events *(pp. 819–825)*

EXAMPLES

Andy is using his calculator to obtain a random number from 10 to 20. Find the probability that

- Andy gets a 15 or a multiple of 2.

  10 11 12 13 14 15 16 17 18 19 20

  $\frac{1}{11} + \frac{6}{11} = \frac{7}{11}$ *The events are mutually exclusive.*

- Andy gets a multiple of 3 or a multiple of 5.

  10 11 12 13 14 15 16 17 18 19 20

  $\frac{3}{11} + \frac{3}{11} - \frac{1}{11} = \frac{5}{11}$ *The events are inclusive.*

- Andy gets all different numbers if he has the calculator randomly select 5 numbers.

  $\frac{{}_{11}P_5}{11^5} = \frac{11 \cdot 10 \cdot 9 \cdot 8 \cdot 7}{11 \cdot 11 \cdot 11 \cdot 11 \cdot 11} = \frac{55{,}440}{161{,}051} \approx 0.3442$

EXERCISES

A store is handing out coupons. One-third of the coupons offer a 10% discount, half offer a 15% discount, and one-sixth offer a 20% discount. A customer is handed a coupon.

31. Explain why the events "10% discount" and "15% discount" are mutually exclusive.

32. What is the probability that the coupon offers a 10% discount or a 15% discount?

A card is drawn from a deck of 52. Find the probability of each outcome.

33. drawing a red card or drawing a 5

34. drawing a club or drawing a heart

35. Of 120 males and 180 females who took an eye exam, 170 passed. One-third of the males did not pass. What is the probability that a person who took the exam passed or was male?

11-5 Measures of Central Tendency and Variation *(pp. 828–835)*

EXAMPLES

■ **The probability distribution for the number of substitute teachers needed is given. Find the expected number of substitute teachers needed on any given day.**

Number of Substitutes *n*	0	1	2	3	4
Probability of *n* Substitutes	0.05	0.08	0.38	0.41	0.08

$0(0.05)+1(0.08)+2(0.38)+3(0.41)+4(0.08)=2.39$

The expected number of substitutes is 2.39.

■ **The number of books in each box shipped from a warehouse is given. Find the number within 1 standard deviation of the mean.**

12, 10, 4, 8, 24, 16, 14, 10, 10, 8, 16

Step 1 Find the mean.

$$\frac{12+10+4+8+24+16+14+10+10+8+16}{11}=12$$

Step 2 Find the variance. Add the squares of all the differences from the mean, and divide by the number of data values.

$$\frac{0+4+64+16+144+16+4+4+4+16+16}{11}\approx 26.2$$

Step 3 Take the square root: $\sqrt{26.2}\approx 5.1$

The number within 1 standard deviation of the mean is $\approx 12 \pm 5.1$, or $[6.9, 17.1]$.

EXERCISES

Find the mean, median, and mode of each data set.

36. 5, 8, 0, 8, 6

37. 12, 15, 13, 13, 15, 12

38. The probability distribution for the number of arrests made in a small town on one day is given below. Find the expected number of arrests on any one day.

Number of Arrests *n*	0	1	2	3
Probability of *n* Arrests	0.65	0.22	0.1	0.03

39. Make a box-and-whisker plot of the data. Then find the interquartile range.

33, 52, 65, 48, 83, 29, 33, 50, 71

40. The number of races that a runner won every year for 10 years is given. Find the number of wins within 1 standard deviation of the mean. 5, 7, 4, 11, 8, 10, 8, 6, 9, 7

41. The principal reported that the mean of a standardized test score for the school was 81.3 and the standard deviation was 4.4. Sharon scored 96. Is her score an outlier? Explain.

42. On 6 quizzes, Aaron scored 73, 88, 86, 90, 87, and 29. Find the mean and standard deviation of the data. On his seventh quiz, he scored 32. Describe how his seventh score affects the mean and standard deviation.

11-6 Binomial Distributions *(pp. 837–843)*

EXAMPLES

Sheila bought 5 energy bars. Each has a 1 in 10 chance of winning a free energy bar.

■ What is the probability that Sheila will win 3 energy bars?

$P(3)={}_5C_3(0.1)^3(0.9)^{5-3}$ $\quad P(r)={}_nC_r p^r q^{n-r}$

$=10(0.001)(0.81)=0.0081$

■ What is the probability that Sheila will win at least 1 energy bar?

$P(\text{at least } 1)=1-P(0)$

$P(0)={}_5C_0(0.1)^0(0.9)^{5-0}\approx 0.5905$

$1-0.5905=0.4095$

EXERCISES

Use the Binomial Theorem to expand each binomial.

43. $(5+2x)^3$

44. $(x-2y)^4$

45. The probability of Ike making a free throw is 0.65. He shoots 75 free throws. Find the expected number of free throws made and the standard deviation.

46. A spinner is divided into 6 equal sections, numbered 1 through 6. It is spun 8 times. What is the probability that the spinner lands on 1 exactly 3 times? What is the probability that the spinner lands on 1 at least 2 times?

CHAPTER 11

1. A mall employee is dressing a mannequin. There are 6 pairs of shoes, 4 types of jeans, and 8 sweaters. Using 1 of each, how many ways can the mannequin be dressed?
2. How many ways can you award first, second, and third place to 8 contestants?
3. How many ways can a group of 3 students be chosen from a class of 30?
4. Four cards are randomly selected from a standard deck of 52 playing cards. What is the probability that the cards are all jacks, all queens, or all kings?
5. The table shows the results of tossing 2 coins. Find the experimental probability of tossing 2 tails.

HH	HT	TH	TT
3	6	5	6

Each letter of the alphabet is written on a card. The cards are placed into a bag. Determine whether the events are independent or dependent, and find the indicated probability.

6. The letter D is drawn, replaced in the bag, and then the letter J is drawn.
7. Three vowels are drawn without replacement.

A card is drawn from a bag containing the 9 cards shown. Find each probability.

8. selecting a C or an even number
9. selecting an odd number or a multiple of 3
10. The probability distribution for the number of absent students on any given day for a certain class is given. Find the expected number of absent students.

Number of Students Absent n	0	1	2	3	4
Probability of n Absent Students	$\frac{7}{20}$	$\frac{5}{20}$	$\frac{4}{20}$	$\frac{3}{20}$	$\frac{1}{20}$

The number of known satellites of the planets in the solar system (as of 2005) is given.

	Mercury	Venus	Earth	Mars	Jupiter	Saturn	Uranus	Neptune	Pluto
Moons	0	0	1	2	63	33	27	13	1

Source: NASA Planetary Data System, 2005

11. Make a box-and-whisker plot of the data. Find the interquartile range.
12. Is 63 an outlier? Explain.
13. Identify the outlier in the following data set: 93, 107, 110, 103, 98, 95, 12, 111, 128, 99, 114, and 90. Describe how the outlier affects the mean and the standard deviation.
14. Use the Binomial Theorem to expand $(3x + y)^4$.

The probability of winning a carnival game is 15%. Elaine plays 10 times.

15. Find the probability that Elaine will win 2 times.
16. Find the probability that Elaine will win at least 2 times.

FOCUS ON SAT MATHEMATICS SUBJECT TESTS

The reference information at the beginning of a test is usually the same each time the test is given. Memorize this information so that you won't have to refer back to it during the test. When you take the test, note whether any information is different from what you expected.

If you do not know how to solve a general problem, try working out a simple example or two to see if a general solution method becomes apparent. But do not spend too much time on examples. If you are still stuck after a while, move on to the next problem.

You may want to time yourself as you take this practice test. It should take you about 6 minutes to complete.

---

1. Two cards are drawn from a standard deck of 52 cards. What is the probability that a king and a queen are drawn?

(A) $\frac{1}{169}$

(B) $\frac{2}{169}$

(C) $\frac{8}{663}$

(D) $\frac{14}{663}$

(E) $\frac{4}{169}$

---

2. A number cube is rolled twice. What is the probability of getting a 6 at least once?

(A) $\frac{1}{36}$

(B) $\frac{1}{6}$

(C) $\frac{11}{36}$

(D) $\frac{1}{3}$

(E) $\frac{5}{6}$

---

3. Your CD player can hold 6 CDs. You have 10 CDs to choose from, one of which is your favorite and is always in your player. How many ways can the player be filled if order does not matter?

(A) 126

(B) 210

(C) 720

(D) 15,120

(E) 151,200

---

4. Of 100 students, 37 play an instrument, 45 play sports, and 11 do both. What is the probability that a student neither plays an instrument nor plays sports?

(A) 0.145

(B) 0.18

(C) 0.29

(D) 0.40

(E) 0.82

---

5. A student's mean score after 4 quizzes was 72. After the fifth quiz, the mean increased to 75. What was the student's score on the fifth quiz?

(A) 60

(B) 72

(C) 84

(D) 87

(E) 100

CHAPTER 11

TEST TACKLER

Standardized Test Strategies

Multiple Choice: None of the Above or All of the Above

Given a multiple-choice test item where one of the answer choices is *none of the above* or *all of the above,* the correct response is the best, most-complete answer choice available.

To answer these types of test items, compare each answer choice with the question and determine if the answer is true or false. If you determine that more than one of the choices is true, then the correct choice is likely to be *all of the above.*

If you do not know how to solve the problem and have to guess at the answer, more often than not, *all of the above* is correct and *none of the above* is incorrect.

EXAMPLE 1

There are 8 players on the chess team. Which of the following models the number of ways that the coach can choose 2 players to start the game?

Ⓐ $_8C_2$

Ⓑ $\dfrac{8!}{2!(6!)}$

Ⓒ 28

Ⓓ All of the above

LOOK at each choice separately, and determine if it is true or false.

As you consider each choice, mark it "true" or "false."

Consider Choice A: *Because order does not matter, this is a combination problem. The number of combinations of 8 players, taken 2 at a time, is given by $_nC_r$, where $n = 8$ and $r = 2$. So, $_8C_2$ is a correct model of the combination.*

Choice A is *"true."* The answer could be choice A, but you need to check if choices B and C are also correct because the answer could be *all of the above.*

Consider Choice B: *The number of combinations of 8 players, taken two at a time, is given by $_nC_r = \frac{n!}{r!(n-r)!}$, where $n = 8$ and $r = 2$.*

$$_nC_r = \frac{n!}{r!(n-r)!} = \frac{8!}{2!(8-2)!} = \frac{8!}{2!(6)!}$$

Choice B is also a correct model of the combination. Choice B is *"true."* The answer is likely to be choice D, *all of the above,* but you still should check to see if choice C is true.

Consider Choice C: *The number of combinations of 8 players, taken two at a time, is given by $_nC_r = \frac{n!}{r!(n-r)!}$, where $n = 8$ and $r = 2$.*

$$_nC_r = \frac{n!}{r!(n-r)!} = \frac{8!}{2!(8-2)!} = \frac{8!}{2!(6)!} = 28$$

Choice C is also a correct model of the combination. Choice C is *"true."* Because choices A, B, and C are all *"true,"* the correct answer choice is choice D, *all of the above.*

Be careful of problems with double negatives. Read the problem statement and each answer choice twice before selecting an answer.

Read each test item and answer the questions that follow.

Item A

The mean score on a test is 68. Which can NOT be true about the scores?

Ⓐ Every score is 68.

Ⓑ Half are 68, and half are 0.

Ⓒ Half are 94, and half are 38.

Ⓓ None of these

1. What is the definition of *mean*?
2. Read the problem statement again. If an answer choice is true, is that the correct response? Explain.
3. Willie determined that both choices A and C could be true statements, so he chose choice D as his response. Do you agree? If not, what would you have done differently?

Item B

For a number cube, what is the probability of rolling a 2 or a number greater than 4?

Ⓕ 50%

Ⓖ $P(\text{rolling a } 2 \cup \text{rolling 5 or 6}) = P(\text{rolling a } 2) + P(\text{rolling 5 or 6})$

Ⓗ $\frac{1}{6} + \frac{2}{6}$

Ⓙ All of the above

4. Is this event mutually exclusive or inclusive? How do you know? Determine if choice G is a true or false statement.
5. If you roll a number cube, what is the probability of rolling a 2? What is the probability of rolling a 5 or 6?
6. Simplify choice H to find its value. Is this value equivalent to any other answer choices?
7. How many answer choices are correct? What is the correct response?

Item C

Suppose that a dart lands at a random point on the circular dartboard. Find the probability that the dart lands inside only the dark gray or white region. The radius of the dartboard is 3 inches.

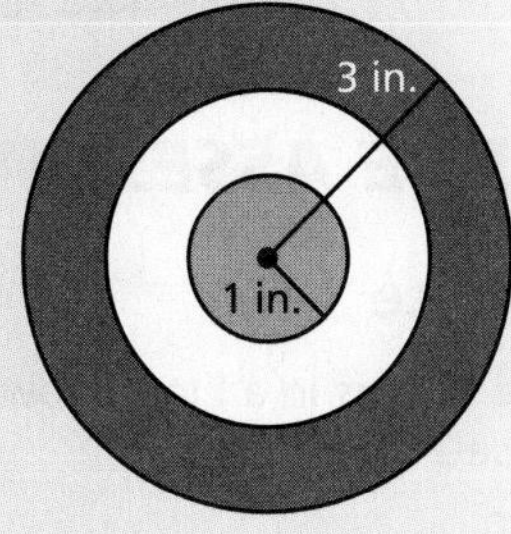

Ⓐ $\frac{1}{9}$

Ⓑ 8π

Ⓒ $\frac{8}{9}$

Ⓓ None of these

8. A student finds that both choice A and choice B are incorrect. To save time, he chooses choice D as his answer because he figures it is likely that choice C will also be incorrect. Do you think that this student made a wise decision? Explain.
9. What is the formula for the area of a circle? What is the area of this dartboard? How can you determine the area of the dark gray and white regions?
10. Find if choice A, B, or C is true, and determine the response to the test item.

Item D

Each gym member receives a 3-digit code to use for a locker combination with no digit repeated. Grace received the code 210. What was the probability that she would receive a code of consecutive numbers?

Ⓕ $1.1\overline{6}\%$

Ⓖ $\frac{1}{45}$

Ⓗ $\frac{1}{{}_{10}P_3}$

Ⓙ All of the above

11. How can you determine if choice J is correct?
12. Are the values given in choices F, G, and H equivalent? What does this tell you about choice J?

CHAPTER 11

STANDARDIZED TEST PREP

go.hrw.com
State Test Practice Online
KEYWORD: MB7 TestPrep

CUMULATIVE ASSESSMENT, CHAPTERS 1–11

Multiple Choice

1. There were 8 dogs in a litter. How many ways can Mike choose 2 dogs?

(A) 20,160

(B) 56

(C) 28

(D) $\frac{1}{28}$

2. What is the median of the test scores given?
$\{97, 78, 61, 90, 95, 96, 80, 67, 86, 88, 90, 92\}$

(F) 85

(G) 88

(H) 89

(J) 90

3. The table shows the number of teachers, coaches, and students at a high school of each gender. What is the probability, to the nearest hundredth, that a coach is male?

School Population and Gender		
	Male	Female
Teachers	12	24
Coaches	17	9
Students	429	453

(A) 0.65

(B) 0.35

(C) 0.04

(D) 0.02

4. For $f(x) = ab^x$, if x increases by 1, the value of $f(x)$ does which of the following?

(F) $f(x)$ increases by b.

(G) $f(x)$ is multiplied by b.

(H) $f(x)$ increases by a.

(J) $f(x)$ is multiplied by a.

5. A slice of an 18-inch diameter pizza that is cut into sixths sells for \$3.25. At this rate, how much should a slice that is one eighth of a 16-inch diameter pizza sell for, to the nearest \$0.05?

(A) \$1.75

(B) \$1.95

(C) \$2.15

(D) \$2.45

6. Which graph shows a line with a slope of $-\frac{4}{3}$ that passes through $(5, 2)$?

(F)

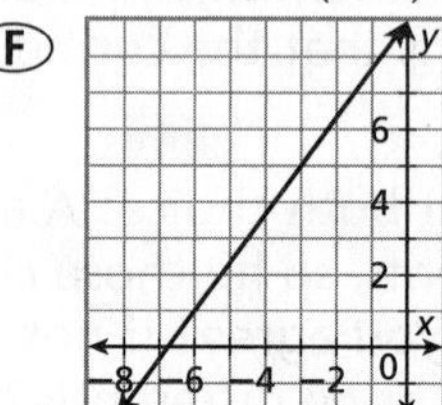

(H)

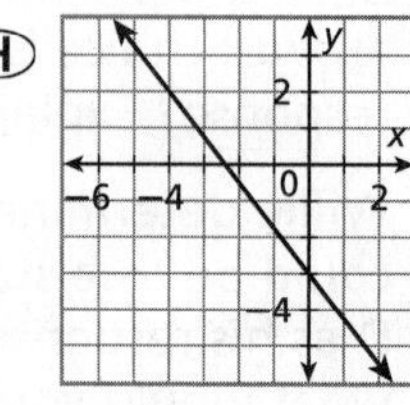

(G)

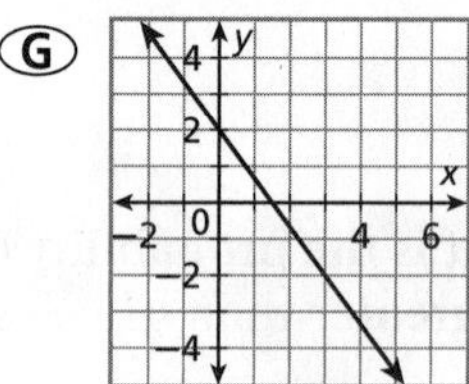

(J)

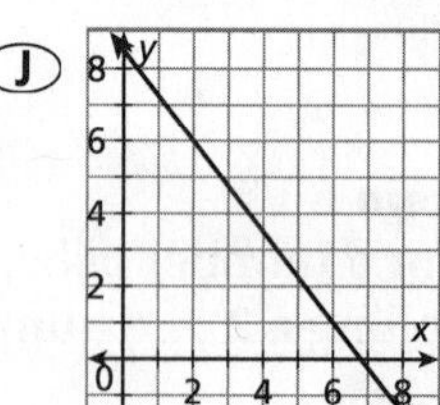

7. Which type of function is shown in the graph?

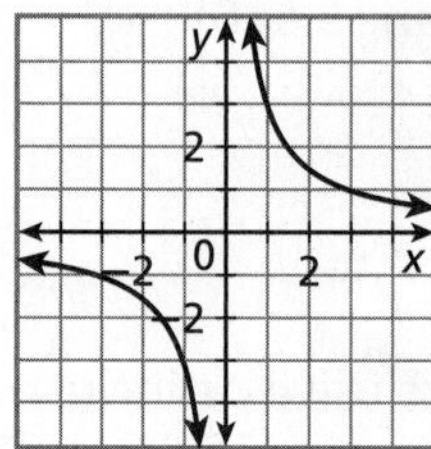

(A) exponential

(B) polynomial

(C) radical

(D) rational

8. Which conic section does the equation represent?
$2x^2 + 9xy + 10y^2 + 4x + 5y + 8 = 0$

(F) Parabola

(G) Hyperbola

(H) Ellipse

(J) Circle

In item 9, remember that a real number with a 0 exponent is 1. You can use mental math to quickly evaluate each function and compare your result to the corresponding value in the graphed function.

9. Which is the equation of the graph below?

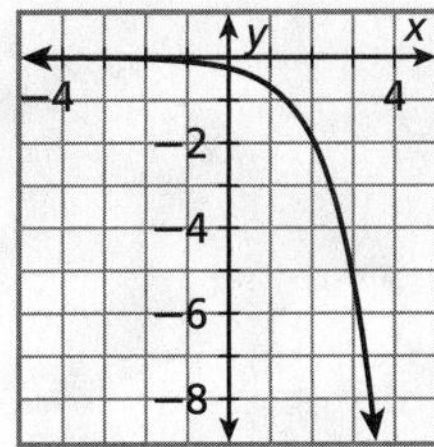

(A) $f(x) = 0.25(2.75^x)$

(B) $f(x) = -2.75(0.25^x)$

(C) $f(x) = 2.75(0.25^x)$

(D) $f(x) = -0.25(2.75^x)$

Gridded Response

10. What value of x makes the equation true?
$6(x - i) - 2i = (4 - i)^2$

11. Use long division to find the coefficient of the x term in the quotient.
$(2x^3 + 5x^2 + 10x + 7) \div (x + 1)$

Use the spinner for Items 12 and 13.

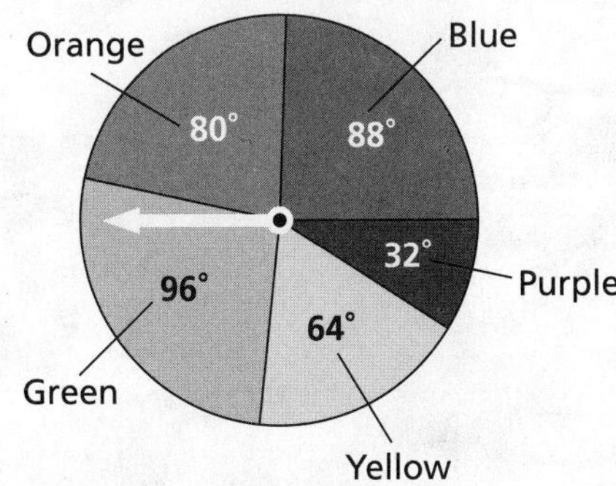

12. What is the probability of the spinner landing on the orange or purple sector, to the nearest hundredth?

13. What is the probability that the spinner will land on green in at least 2 of the next 3 spins? Write the answer to the nearest thousandth.

Short Response

14. Find the center and the radius of a circle that has a diameter with the endpoints $(-2, 8)$ and $(4, 2)$.

   a. What is the length of the diameter?

   b. The endpoints $(4, 8)$ and $(-2, y)$ are located on the circle. Find the missing value of y.

15. The table below shows the number of students that graduated from a high school from 1920 to 2000, measured every 20 years.

x	1920	1940	1960	1980	2000
y	9	59	159	409	909

   a. Write a polynomial function for the data. Let x be the number of years since 1920. Round your answer to the nearest thousandth.

   b. At this rate how many students will graduate in 2020? Round your answer to the nearest student.

   c. About how many students graduated in 1990? Round your answer to the nearest student.

16. The Badgers won 70% of their games this season. They won 5 of the 12 games they played during their last road trip. Before the road trip, the Badgers had won 75% of their games.

   a. How many wins and losses did the Badgers have during the season?

   b. How many wins and losses did the Badgers have before their last road trip?

Extended Response

17. Randy wants to collect 515 baseball cards. Each week Randy buys 15 baseball cards.

   a. Create a table to represent this situation where t is the amount of time in weeks and c is the number of cards that Randy still wants to buy.

   b. Write an equation to model the data in the table.

   c. Graph the equation.

   d. After how many weeks will Randy meet his goal?

CHAPTER 12

Sequences and Series

Chapter Focus

- Represent sequences and series algebraically to solve problems.
- Prove statements by mathematical induction.

GOLDEN RECTANGLES

The Fibonacci sequence has connections to geometry, art, and architecture. Explore them by using golden rectangles.

go.hrw.com
Chapter Project Online
KEYWORD: MB7 ChProj

ARE YOU READY?

Vocabulary

Match each term on the left with a definition on the right.

1. exponential function
2. function
3. linear equation
4. quadratic function

A. a pairing in which there is exactly one output value for each input value
B. an equation whose graph is a straight line
C. a function defined by a quotient of two polynomials
D. a function of the form $f(x) = ax^2 + bx + c$, where $a \neq 0$
E. a function of the form $f(x) = ab^x$, where $a \neq 0$ and $b \neq 1$

Simplify Radical Expressions

Simplify each expression.

5. $\sqrt{25} \cdot \sqrt{36}$
6. $\sqrt{121} - \sqrt{81}$
7. $\sqrt{\frac{1}{49}}$
8. $\frac{\sqrt{16}}{\sqrt{64}}$

Evaluate Powers

Evaluate.

9. $(-3)^3$
10. $(-5)^4$
11. $1 - (-2^3)^3$
12. $\frac{2^2 \cdot 2^7}{(2^2)^5}$

Solve for a Variable

Solve each equation for *x*.

13. $y = 12x - 5$
14. $y = -\frac{x}{3} + 1$
15. $y = -9 + x^2$
16. $y = -4(x^2 - 9)$

Evaluate Expressions

Evaluate each expression for $x = 2, y = 12$, and $z = 24$.

17. $\frac{y(y+1)}{3x}$
18. $z + (y - 1)x$
19. $y\left(\frac{x+z}{2}\right)$
20. $z\left(\frac{1-y}{1-x}\right)$

Counterexamples

Find a counterexample to show that each statement is false.

21. $n^2 = n$, where n is a real number
22. $n^3 \geq n^2 \geq n$, where n is a real number
23. $\frac{1}{n} > \frac{1}{n^2}$, where n is a real number
24. $\frac{2}{n} \neq \frac{n}{2}$, where n is a real number

CHAPTER 12

Study Guide: Preview

Where You've Been

Previously, you

- studied sets of numbers, including natural numbers and perfect squares.
- used patterns of differences or ratios to classify data.
- graphed and evaluated linear and exponential functions.

In This Chapter

You will study

- patterns of numbers, called *sequences,* and their sums, called *series.*
- patterns to determine whether sequences are arithmetic or geometric.
- how to write and evaluate sequences and series.

Where You're Going

You can use the skills learned in this chapter

- in future math classes, especially Precalculus and Calculus.
- in Physics classes to model patterns, such as the heights of bouncing objects.
- outside of school to calculate the growth of financial investments.

Key Vocabulary/Vocabulario

converge	convergir
diverge	divergir
explicit formula	fórmula explícita
finite sequence	sucesión finita
infinite sequence	sucesión infinita
iteration	iteración
limit	límite
recursive formula	fórmula recurrente
sequence	sucesión
series	serie
term of a sequence	término de una sucesión

Vocabulary Connections

To become familiar with some of the vocabulary terms in the chapter, consider the following. You may refer to the chapter, the glossary, or a dictionary if you like.

1. What does the word **sequence** mean in everyday usage? What might a number sequence refer to?
2. The word *finite* means "having definite or definable limits." Give examples of sentences that use the word *finite.* Explain what a **finite sequence** might refer to.
3. Using the previous definition of *finite,* give examples of sentences that use the word *infinite.* Explain what an **infinite sequence** might refer to.
4. What does a television series refer to? What might a mathematical **series** mean?
5. State what a term of a polynomial refers to. Then write a possible description for a **term of a sequence** .

Writing Strategy: Write a Convincing Argument

Being able to write a convincing argument about a math concept shows that you understand the material well. You can use a four-step method to write an effective argument as shown in the response to the exercise below.

From Lesson 11-2

35. Write About It Describe the difference between theoretical probability and experimental probability. Give an example in which they may differ.

Step 1 **Identify the goal.**

The goal is to describe the difference between theoretical and experimental probability.

Step 2 **Provide a statement of response to the goal.**

Theoretical probability is based purely on mathematics, but experimental probability is based on the results of an experiment.

Step 3 **Provide the evidence to support your statement.**

In a coin toss, the theoretical probability of tossing heads is $\frac{\text{number of favorable outcomes}}{\text{number of outcomes in the sample space}} = \frac{1}{2}$.

The experimental probability of tossing heads is $\frac{\text{number of times the event occurs}}{\text{number of trials}}$.

In one trial, the result is either heads or tails, so the experimental probability will be 1 or 0. The theoretical probability is still $\frac{1}{2}$.

Step 4 **Summarize your argument.**

Because theoretical probability is based solely on the mathematical outcomes, it never changes. Experimental probability is based on actual results, so it may change with each trial of an experiment.

Try This

Use the four-step method described above to answer each question.

1. A number cube is rolled 20 times and lands on the number 3 twice. What is the fewest number of rolls needed for the experimental probability of rolling a 3 to equal the theoretical probability of rolling a 3? Explain how you got your answer.

2. Aidan has narrowed his college choices down to 9 schools. He plans to visit 3 or 4 schools before the end of his junior year. How many more ways can he visit a group of 4 schools than a group of 3 schools? Explain.

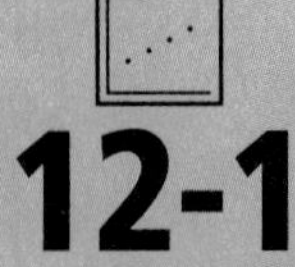

12-1 Introduction to Sequences

Objectives
Find the *n*th term of a sequence.

Write rules for sequences.

Vocabulary
sequence
term of a sequence
infinite sequence
finite sequence
recursive formula
explicit formula
iteration

Who uses this?
Sequences can be used to model many natural phenomena, such as the changes in a rabbit population over time.

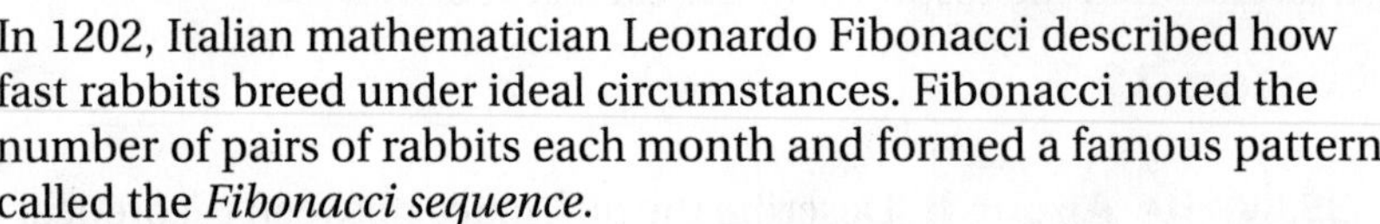

In 1202, Italian mathematician Leonardo Fibonacci described how fast rabbits breed under ideal circumstances. Fibonacci noted the number of pairs of rabbits each month and formed a famous pattern called the *Fibonacci sequence.*

A **sequence** is an ordered set of numbers. Each number in the sequence is a **term of the sequence**. A sequence may be an **infinite sequence** that continues without end, such as the natural numbers, or a **finite sequence** that has a limited number of terms, such as $\{1, 2, 3, 4\}$.

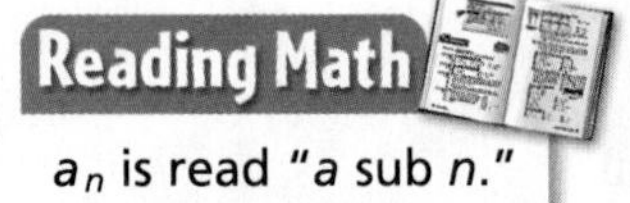

Reading Math
a_n is read "a sub *n*."

You can think of a sequence as a function with sequential natural numbers as the domain and the terms of the sequence as the range. Values in the domain are called *term numbers* and are represented by n. Instead of function notation, such as $a(n)$, sequence values are written by using subscripts. The first term is a_1, the second term is a_2, and the nth term is a_n. Because a sequence is a function, each number n has only one term value associated with it, a_n.

Term number	n	1	2	3	4	5	Domain
Term value	a_n	1	1	2	3	5	Range

In the Fibonacci sequence, the first two terms are 1 and each term after that is the sum of the two terms before it. This can be expressed by using the rule $a_1 = 1$, $a_2 = 1$, and $a_n = a_{n-2} + a_{n-1}$, where $n \geq 3$. This is a *recursive formula.* A **recursive formula** is a rule in which one or more previous terms are used to generate the next term.

EXAMPLE 1 Finding Terms of a Sequence by Using a Recursive Formula

Find the first 5 terms of the sequence with $a_1 = 5$ and $a_n = 2a_{n-1} + 1$ for $n \geq 2$.

The first term is given, $a_1 = 5$.

Substitute a_1 into the rule to find a_2. Continue using each term to find the next term.

n	$2a_{n-1} + 1$	a_n
1	*Given*	5
2	$2(5) + 1$	11
3	$2(11) + 1$	23
4	$2(23) + 1$	47
5	$2(47) + 1$	95

The first 5 terms are 5, 11, 23, 47, and 95.

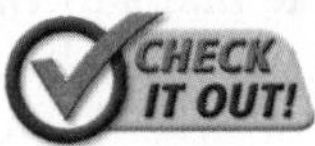

CHECK IT OUT! **Find the first 5 terms of each sequence.**

1a. $a_1 = -5$, $a_n = a_{n-1} - 8$ **1b.** $a_1 = 2$, $a_n = -3a_{n-1}$

In some sequences, you can find the value of a term when you do not know its preceding term. An **explicit formula** defines the nth term of a sequence as a function of n.

EXAMPLE 2 Finding Terms of a Sequence by Using an Explicit Formula

Find the first 5 terms of the sequence $a_n = 2^n - 3$.

Make a table. Evaluate the sequence for $n = 1$ through $n = 5$.

n	$2^n - 3$	a_n
1	$2^1 - 3$	−1
2	$2^2 - 3$	1
3	$2^3 - 3$	5
4	$2^4 - 3$	13
5	$2^5 - 3$	29

The first 5 terms are −1, 1, 5, 13, and 29.

Check Use a graphing calculator. Enter $y = 2^x - 3$ and make a table.

X	Y1
1	-1
2	1
3	5
4	13
5	29

Find the first 5 terms of each sequence.

2a. $a_n = n^2 - 2n$ **2b.** $a_n = 3n - 5$

You can use your knowledge of functions to write rules for sequences.

EXAMPLE 3 Writing Rules for Sequences

Write a possible explicit rule for the nth term of each sequence.

A 3, 6, 12, 24, 48, ...

Examine the differences and ratios.

Ratios 2 2 2 2

Terms	3	6	12	24	48

1st differences 3 6 12 24

2nd differences 3 6 12

The ratio is constant. The sequence is exponential with a base of 2.

Look for a pattern with powers of 2.

$a_1 = 3 = 3(2)^0$, $a_2 = 6 = 3(2)^1$, $a_3 = 12 = 3(2)^2$, ...

A pattern is $3(2)^{n-1}$. One explicit rule is $a_n = 3(2)^{n-1}$.

B 2.5, 4, 5.5, 7, 8.5, ...

Examine the differences.

Terms	2.5	4	5.5	7	8.5

1st differences 1.5 1.5 1.5 1.5

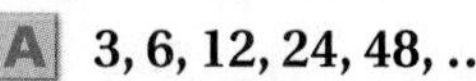

The first differences are constant, so the sequence is linear.

The first term is 2.5, and each term is 1.5 more than the previous.

A pattern is $2.5 + 1.5(n - 1)$, or $1.5n + 1$. One explicit rule is $a_n = 1.5n + 1$.

Remember!

Linear patterns have constant first differences. Quadratic patterns have constant second differences. Exponential patterns have constant ratios. (Lesson 9-6)

Write a possible explicit rule for the nth term of each sequence.

3a. 7, 5, 3, 1, −1, ... **3b.** $1, \frac{1}{2}, \frac{1}{3}, \frac{1}{4}, \frac{1}{5}, \ldots$

EXAMPLE 4 Physics Application

A ball is dropped and bounces to a height of 5 feet. The ball rebounds to 60% of its previous height after each bounce. Graph the sequence and describe its pattern. How high does the ball bounce on its 9th bounce?

Because the ball first bounces to a height of 5 feet and then bounces to 60% of its previous height on each bounce, the recursive rule is $a_1 = 5$ and $a_n = 0.6a_{n-1}$. Use this rule to find some other terms of the sequence and graph them.

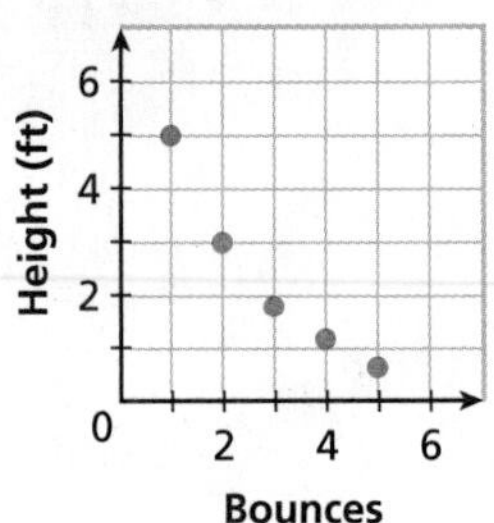

Caution!

Do not connect the points on the graph because the number of bounces is limited to the set of natural numbers.

$a_2 = 0.6(5) = 3$

$a_3 = 0.6(3) = 1.8$

$a_4 = 0.6(1.8) = 1.08$

The graph appears to be exponential. Use the pattern to write an explicit rule.

$a_n = 5(0.6)^{n-1}$, where n is the bounce number

Use this rule to find the bounce height for the 9th bounce.

$a_9 = 5(0.6)^{9-1} \approx 0.084$ foot, or approximately 1 inch.

The ball is about 0.084 feet high on the 9th bounce.

4. An ultra-low-flush toilet uses 1.6 gallons every time it is flushed. Graph the sequence of total water used after n flushes, and describe its pattern. How many gallons have been used after 10 flushes?

Recall that a fractal is an image made by repeating a pattern (Lesson 5-5). Each step in this repeated process is an **iteration**, the repetitive application of the same rule.

EXAMPLE 5 Iteration of Fractals

The Sierpinski triangle is a fractal made by taking an equilateral triangle, removing an equilateral triangle from the center, and repeating for each new triangle. Find the number of triangles in the next 2 iterations.

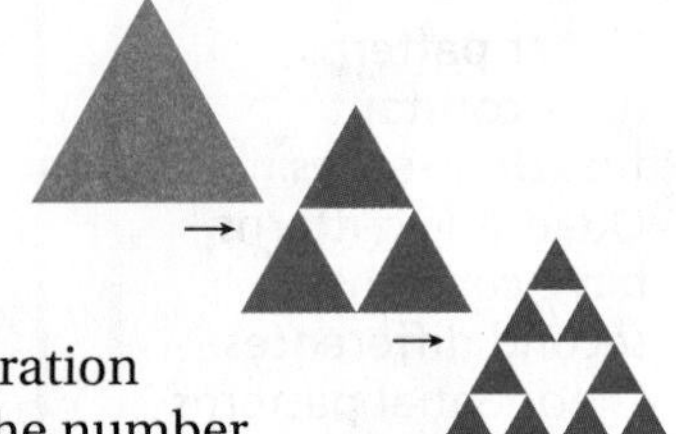

By removing the center of each triangle, each iteration turns every triangle into 3 smaller triangles. So the number of triangles triples with each iteration.

The number of triangles can be represented by the sequence $a_n = 3^{n-1}$.

The 4th and 5th terms are $a_4 = 3^{4-1} = 27$ and $a_5 = 3^{5-1} = 81$.

The next two iterations result in 27 and 81 triangles.

5. The Cantor set is a fractal formed by repeatedly removing the middle third of a line segment as shown. Find the number of segments in the next 2 iterations.

THINK AND DISCUSS

1. Explain the difference between a recursive rule and an explicit rule.
2. Identify three possible next terms for the sequence 1, 2, 4, ...
3. Describe how a sequence is a function. Do all sequences have the same domain? Explain.

4. **GET ORGANIZED** Copy and complete the graphic organizer. Summarize what you have learned about sequences.

Definition	Two types of sequences
Sequences	
Examples	Two possible formulas

12-1 Exercises

GUIDED PRACTICE

1. **Vocabulary** A formula that uses one or more previous terms to find the next term is a(n) __?__ formula. (*explicit* or *recursive*)

SEE EXAMPLE 1 p. 862

Find the first 5 terms of each sequence.

2. $a_1 = 1, a_n = 4a_{n-1} - 1$ 3. $a_1 = 3, a_n = a_{n-1} + 11$ 4. $a_1 = 500, a_n = \frac{a_{n-1}}{5}$

SEE EXAMPLE 2 p. 863

5. $a_n = 12(n - 2)$ 6. $a_n = \left(-\frac{1}{2}\right)^{n-1}$ 7. $a_n = -3n^2$

8. $a_n = n(n - 1)$ 9. $a_n = 4^{n-1}$ 10. $a_n = (n + 1)^2$

SEE EXAMPLE 3 p. 863

Write a possible explicit rule for the *n*th term of each sequence.

11. 6, 9, 12, 15, 18, ... 12. $\frac{1}{2}, \frac{2}{3}, \frac{3}{4}, \frac{4}{5}, \frac{5}{6}, \ldots$ 13. 25, 15, 5, −5, −15, ...

SEE EXAMPLE 4 p. 864

14. **Income** Billy earns $25,000 the first year and gets a 5% raise each year. Graph the sequence, and describe its pattern. How much will he earn per year after 5 years? 10 years?

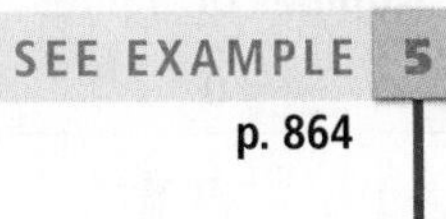
SEE EXAMPLE 5 p. 864

15. **Patterns** Find the number of segments in the next 2 terms of the pattern shown.

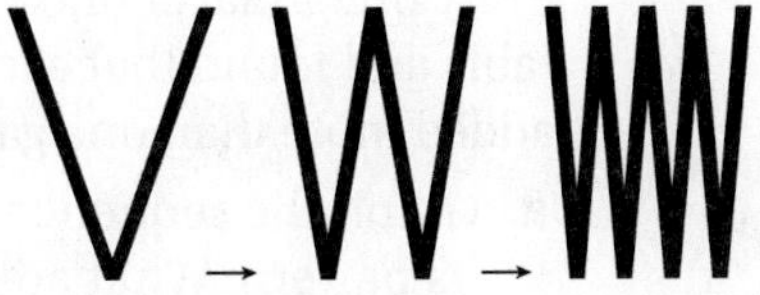

PRACTICE AND PROBLEM SOLVING

Find the first 5 terms of each sequence.

16. $a_1 = 7, a_n = a_{n-1} - 3$ 17. $a_n = \frac{1}{n^2}$ 18. $a_1 = 4, a_n = 1.5a_{n-1} - 2$

19. $a_n = (2)^{n-1} + 8$ 20. $a_n = 2n^2 - 12$ 21. $a_1 = -2, a_n = -3a_{n-1} - 1$

Independent Practice	
For Exercises	See Example
16–18	1
19–21	2
22–24	3
25	4
26	5

Extra Practice

Skills Practice p. S26
Application Practice p. S43

Write a possible explicit rule for the *n*th term of each sequence.

22. 2, 8, 18, 32, 50, … **23.** 9, 5, 1, −3, −7, … **24.** 5, 0.5, 0.05, 0.005, …

25. Architecture Chairs for an orchestra are positioned in a curved form with the conductor at the center. The front row has 16 chairs, and each successive row has 4 more chairs. Graph the sequence and describe its pattern. How many chairs are in the 6th row?

26. Fractals Find the number of squares in the next 2 iterations of Cantor dust as shown.

Find the first 5 terms of each sequence.

27. $a_1 = 12, a_n = \frac{1}{2}a_{n-1} + 2$ **28.** $a_1 = 1, a_n = \frac{2}{a_{n-1}}$ **29.** $a_1 = -10, a_n = -a_{n-1} + 10$

30. $a_n = 2n^2 - 12$ **31.** $a_n = 8 - \frac{1}{10}n$ **32.** $a_n = 5(-1)^{n+1}(3)^{n-1}$

33. ///ERROR ANALYSIS/// Two attempts to find the first 5 terms of the sequence $a_1 = 3$ and $a_n = 2n + 1$ are shown. Which is incorrect? Explain the error.

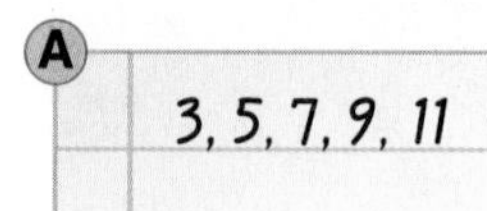

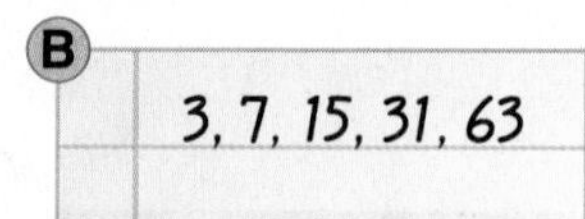

Math History

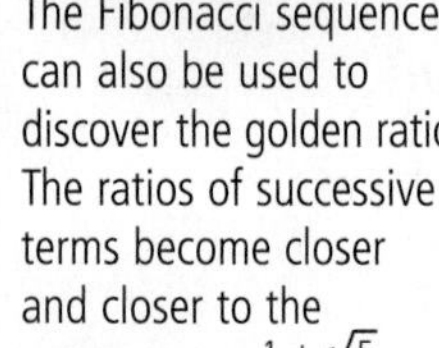

The Fibonacci sequence can also be used to discover the golden ratio. The ratios of successive terms become closer and closer to the golden ratio, $\frac{1 + \sqrt{5}}{2}$.

The Granger Collection, New York

Write a possible explicit rule for each sequence, and find the 10th term.

34. $16, 4, 1, \frac{1}{4}, \frac{1}{16}, \ldots$ **35.** $\frac{15}{9}, \frac{14}{9}, \frac{13}{9}, \frac{12}{9}, \frac{11}{9}, \ldots$ **36.** −5.0, −2.5, 0, 2.5, 5.0, …

37. $1, -\frac{1}{2}, \frac{1}{3}, -\frac{1}{4}, \frac{1}{5}, \ldots$ **38.** 0.04, 0.4, 4, 40, 400, … **39.** 24, 21, 16, 9, 0, …

40. Fibonacci Recall from the lesson that the Fibonacci sequence models the number of pairs of rabbits after a certain number of months. The sequence begins 1, 1, …, and each term after that is the sum of the two terms before it.

a. Find the first 12 terms of the Fibonacci sequence.

b. How many pairs of rabbits are produced under ideal circumstances at the end of one year?

Find the number of dots in the next 2 figures for each dot pattern.

41.

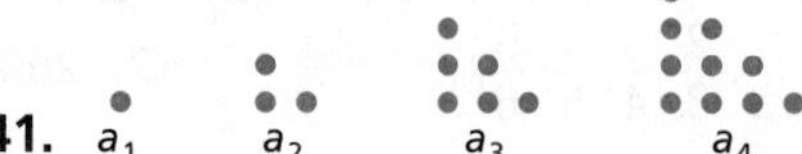

42. a_1 a_2 a_3 a_4

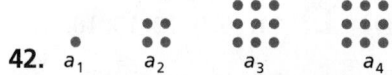

43. Chess Ronnie is scheduling a chess tournament in which each player plays every other player once. He created a table and found that each new player added more than one game.

a. Graph the sequence and describe its pattern. What are the next 2 terms in the sequence?

b. Use a regression to find an explicit rule for the sequence.

c. What if…? How would the schedule change if each player played every other player *twice*? Make a table, and describe how the sequence is transformed.

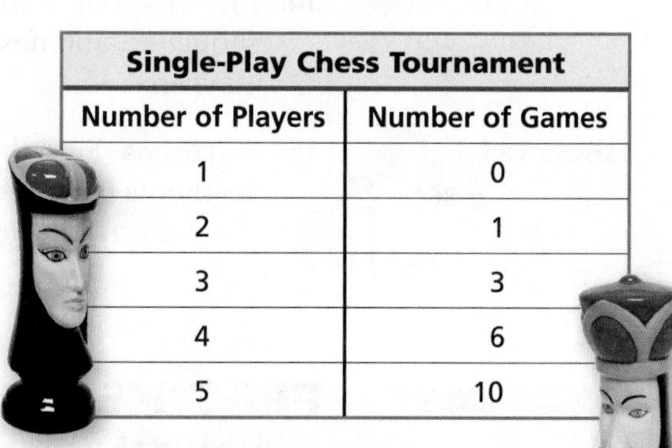

Single-Play Chess Tournament

Number of Players	Number of Games
1	0
2	1
3	3
4	6
5	10

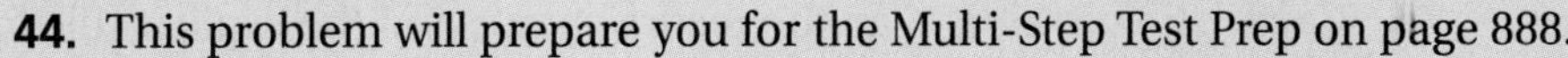

44. This problem will prepare you for the Multi-Step Test Prep on page 888.

A kite is made with 1 tetrahedron in the first (top) layer, 3 tetrahedrons in the second layer, 6 tetrahedrons in the third layer, and so on. Each tetrahedron is made by joining six sticks of equal length.

a. The rule $a_n = a_{n-1} + 6n$ gives the number of sticks needed to make the nth layer of the kite, where $a_1 = 6$. Find the first five terms of the sequence.

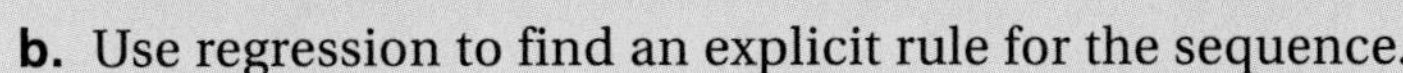

b. Use regression to find an explicit rule for the sequence.

c. How many sticks are needed to build the 10th layer of the kite?

45. Geometry The sum of the interior angle measures for the first 5 regular polygons is shown.

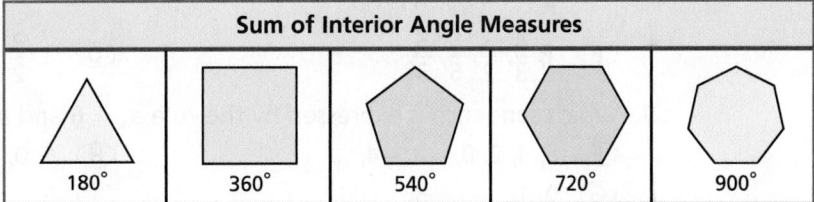

Sum of Interior Angle Measures				
180°	360°	540°	720°	900°

a. Write an explicit rule for the nth term of the sequence of the sum of the angle measures. What is the sum of the measures of the interior angles of a 12-sided regular polygon?

b. Recall that all angles are congruent in a regular polygon. Make a table for the measure of an interior angle for each regular polygon. Graph the data, and describe the pattern.

c. Write an explicit rule for the nth term of the sequence described in part **b.**

d. Find the measure of an interior angle of a 10-sided regular polygon.

46. Estimation Estimate the 20th term of the sequence 7.94, 8.935, 9.93, 10.925, 11.92, ... Explain how you reached your estimate.

47. Music Music involves arranging different pitches through time. The musical notation below indicates the duration of various notes (and rests).

Symbols for Musical Notes and Rests

a. Write a numerical sequence that shows the progression of notes (and rests). Write a recursive formula and an explicit formula to generate this sequence.

b. In 4/4 time, a whole note represents 4 beats, a half note represents 2 beats, a quarter note represents 1 beat, and so on. Write a sequence for the number of beats that each note in the progression represents. Then write a recursive formula and an explicit formula to generate this sequence. How is this sequence related to the sequence in part **a**?

48. **Critical Thinking** Can the recursive rule and the explicit rule for a formula ever be the same?

49. **Write About It** Explain how an infinite sequence is different from a finite sequence.

TEST PREP

50. Which is the next term in the sequence −9, −6, −3 , 0, ...?

   Ⓐ −3 Ⓑ 0 Ⓒ 3 Ⓓ 6

51. Which rule describes the given sequence 4, 12, 36, 108, ...?

   Ⓕ $a_n = 4 + 3n$
   Ⓖ $a_n = 3 + 4n$
   Ⓗ $a_1 = 4,\ a_n = 3a_{n-1},\ n \geq 2$
   Ⓙ $a_1 = 3,\ a_n = 4a_{n-1},\ n \geq 2$

52. Which sequence is expressed by the rule $a_n = \frac{2n}{n+1}$?

   Ⓐ $\frac{2}{3}, \frac{4}{5}, \frac{6}{7}, \frac{8}{9}, \frac{10}{11}, \ldots$
   Ⓑ $1, \frac{4}{3}, \frac{3}{2}, \frac{8}{5}, \frac{5}{3}, \ldots$
   Ⓒ $0, 1, 2, \frac{3}{2}, \frac{8}{5}, \ldots$
   Ⓓ $2, \frac{3}{2}, \frac{8}{5}, \frac{5}{3}, \frac{12}{7}, \ldots$

53. Which sequence is expressed by the rule $a_1 = 6$ and $a_n = 12 - 2a_{n-1},\ n \geq 2$?

   Ⓕ 6, 4, 2, 0, −2, −4, ...
   Ⓖ 0, 12, −12, 36, −60, ...
   Ⓗ 6, 0, 12, −12, 36, ...
   Ⓙ 6, 0, −6, −12, −18, ...

54. **Gridded Response** Find the next term in the sequence −32, 16, −8, 4, −2, ...

CHALLENGE AND EXTEND

Write an explicit rule for each sequence and find the 10th term.

55. $-\frac{2}{3}, \frac{5}{3}, 8, \frac{61}{3}, \frac{122}{3}, \ldots$

56. −2, 6, −12, 20, −30, ...

57. 0.9, 0.8, 0.6, 0.3, −0.1, ...

58. **Geometry** Draw 5 circles. Place 1 point on the first circle, 2 points on the second, 3 points on the third, and so forth. Then connect every point with every other point in each circle, and count the maximum number of nonoverlapping regions that are formed inside each circle.

   a. Write the resulting sequence.

   b. Although the sequence appears to double, the sixth circle has less than 32 possible regions. Try to find them all by carefully drawing this figure. How many did you get?

SPIRAL REVIEW

Simplify. Assume that all expressions are defined. *(Lesson 8-2)*

59. $\frac{x^2 - 9}{x^2 + 5x + 6}$

60. $\frac{4x^2 - 5x}{8x^2 + 18x - 35}$

61. $\frac{4x - 12}{x^2 - 25} \div \frac{8x - 24}{2x - 10}$

62. $\frac{x^2 - 5x - 6}{x^2 - 3x - 18} \cdot \frac{x^2 + x - 6}{x^2 - x - 2}$

Add or subtract. *(Lesson 8-4)*

63. $\frac{2x - 3}{x + 1} + \frac{4x - 9}{x - 1}$

64. $\frac{9x}{8x - 4} - \frac{10x + 3}{12x - 6}$

65. $\frac{x^2}{2x + 7} - \frac{x}{x + 2}$

66. **Literature** Christopher is reading a book containing 854 pages at a rate of 1.5 pages per minute. Create a table, equation, and graph to represent the number of pages remaining to be read P in relation to time t. *(Lesson 9-1)*

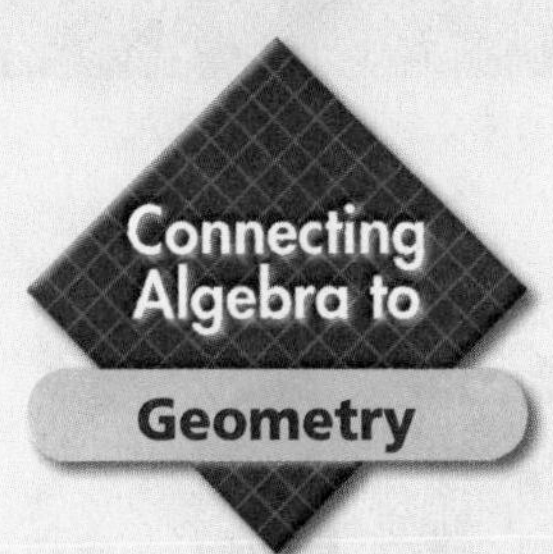

Geometric Patterns and Tessellations

Sequences of figures can often be described with number patterns.

Polygonal numbers can be represented by dots arranged in the form of polygons. The first four hexagonal numbers are illustrated. The sums show a pattern. The sequence for the total number of dots is 1, 6, 15, 28, ...

$n = 1$ 1

$n = 2$ $1 + 5 = 6$

$n = 3$ $1 + 5 + 9 = 15$

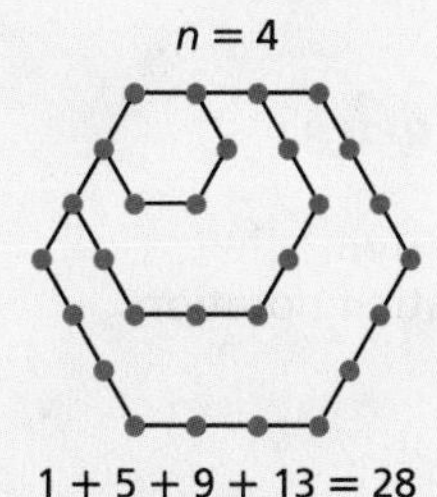

$n = 4$ $1 + 5 + 9 + 13 = 28$

Example

The figure shows how regular hexagons can be used to tessellate, or cover, the plane. Write a sequence for the number of hexagons added at each stage. Describe the pattern in the sequence, and find the next term.

Show the number of hexagons added at each stage.

Level	1	2	3	4
Number of Hexagons	1	6	12	18

From the second term on, the number added appears to increase by 6 each time. The next level probably would have 24 hexagons. You can check your conjecture by constructing the next stage of the tessellation and counting the hexagons.

Try This

Write a sequence for the number of polygons added at each stage of the figure. Describe the pattern in the sequence, and find the next term.

1.

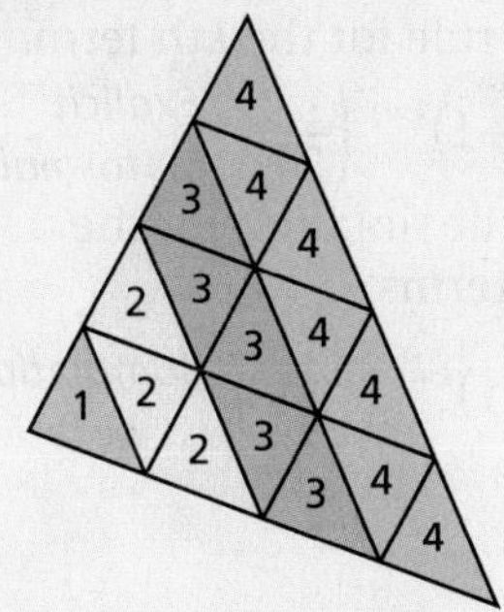

2.

4	4	4	4	4	4	4
4	3	3	3	3	3	4
4	3	2	2	2	3	4
4	3	2	1	2	3	4
4	3	2	2	2	3	4
4	3	3	3	3	3	4
4	4	4	4	4	4	4

3.

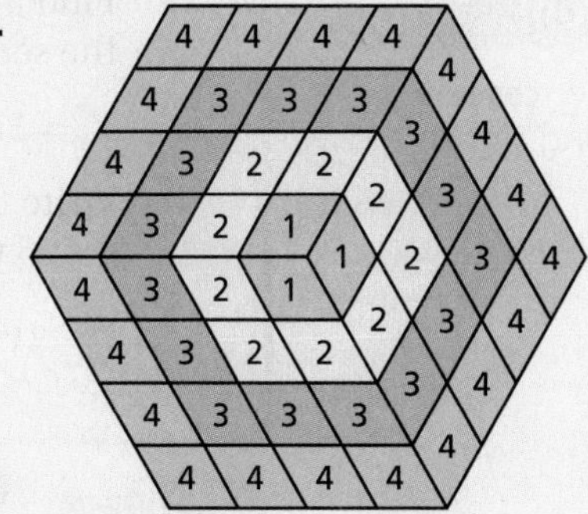

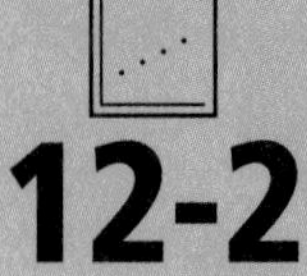

12-2 Series and Summation Notation

Objective
Evaluate the sum of a series expressed in sigma notation.

Vocabulary
series
partial sum
summation notation

Why learn this?
You can use sums of sequences to find the size of a house of cards. (See Example 4.)

In Lesson 12-1, you learned how to find the *n*th term of a sequence. Often we are also interested in the sum of a certain number of terms of a sequence. A **series** is the indicated sum of the terms of a sequence. Some examples are shown in the table.

Sequence	1, 2, 3, 4	2, 4, 6, 8, ...	$\frac{1}{2}, \frac{1}{3}, \frac{1}{4}, \frac{1}{5}, \frac{1}{6}$
Series	$1 + 2 + 3 + 4$	$2 + 4 + 6 + 8 + \cdots$	$\frac{1}{2} + \frac{1}{3} + \frac{1}{4} + \frac{1}{5} + \frac{1}{6}$

Because many sequences are infinite and do not have defined sums, we often find partial sums. A **partial sum**, indicated by S_n, is the sum of a specified number of terms of a sequence.

For the even numbers:

$S_1 = 2$ *Sum of first term*

$S_2 = 2 + 4 = 6$ *Sum of first 2 terms*

$S_3 = 2 + 4 + 6 = 12$ *Sum of first 3 terms*

$S_4 = 2 + 4 + 6 + 8 = 20$ *Sum of first 4 terms*

A series can also be represented by using **summation notation**, which uses the Greek letter $\sum$ (capital *sigma*) to denote the sum of a sequence defined by a rule, as shown.

$$\sum_{k=1}^{5} 2k$$

5 ← Last value of *k*
2k ← Explicit formula for sequence
k=1 ← First value of *k*

EXAMPLE 1 Using Summation Notation

Write each series in summation notation.

A $3 + 6 + 9 + 12 + 15$

Find a rule for *k*th term of the sequence.

$a_k = 3k$ *Explicit formula*

Write the notation for the first 5 terms.

$\sum_{k=1}^{5} 3k$ *Summation notation*

B $\frac{1}{2} - \frac{1}{4} + \frac{1}{8} - \frac{1}{16} + \frac{1}{32} - \frac{1}{64}$

Find a rule for the *k*th term.

$a_k = (-1)^{k+1}\left(\frac{1}{2}\right)^k$ *Explicit formula*

Write the notation for the first 6 terms.

$\sum_{k=1}^{6} (-1)^{k+1}\left(\frac{1}{2}\right)^k$ *Summation notation*

Caution!
For sequences with alternating signs:
Use $(-1)^{k+1}$ if $a_1 = +$.
Use $(-1)^k$ if $a_1 = -$.

CHECK IT OUT! **Write each series in summation notation.**

1a. $\frac{2}{4} + \frac{2}{9} + \frac{2}{16} + \frac{2}{25} + \frac{2}{36}$ **1b.** $-2 + 4 - 6 + 8 - 10 + 12$

EXAMPLE 2 Evaluating a Series

Expand each series and evaluate.

A $\sum_{k=3}^{6} \frac{1}{2^k}$

$$\sum_{k=3}^{6} \frac{1}{2^k} = \frac{1}{2^3} + \frac{1}{2^4} + \frac{1}{2^5} + \frac{1}{2^6}$$ *Expand the series by replacing k.*

$$= \frac{1}{8} + \frac{1}{16} + \frac{1}{32} + \frac{1}{64}$$ *Evaluate powers.*

$$= \frac{8}{64} + \frac{4}{64} + \frac{2}{64} + \frac{1}{64} = \frac{15}{64}$$ *Simplify.*

B $\sum_{k=1}^{4} (10 - k^2)$

$$\sum_{k=1}^{4} (10 - k^2) = (10 - 1^2) + (10 - 2^2) + (10 - 3^2) + (10 - 4^2)$$ *Expand.*

$$= 9 + 6 + 1 + (-6)$$ *Simplify.*

$$= 10$$

Caution!

Watch out! A series can have a first value other than $k = 1$, such as in Example 2A, where k begins at 3.

CHECK IT OUT! Expand each series and evaluate.

2a. $\sum_{k=1}^{4} (2k - 1)$

2b. $\sum_{k=1}^{5} -5(2)^{k-1}$

Finding the sum of a series with many terms can be tedious. You can derive formulas for the sums of some common series.

In a *constant series,* such as $3 + 3 + 3 + 3 + 3$, each term has the same value.

$$\sum_{k=1}^{5} 3 = \underbrace{3 + 3 + 3 + 3 + 3}_{5 \text{ terms}} = 5 \cdot 3 = 15$$

The formula for the sum of a constant series is $\sum_{k=1}^{n} c = nc$, as shown.

$$\sum_{k=1}^{n} c = \underbrace{c + c + c + \cdots + c}_{n \text{ terms}} = nc$$

A *linear series* is a counting series, such as the sum of the first 10 natural numbers. Examine when the terms are rearranged.

$$\sum_{1}^{10} k = 1 + 2 + 3 + 4 + 5 + 6 + 7 + 8 + 9 + 10$$
$$= (1 + 10) + (2 + 9) + (3 + 8) + (4 + 7) + (5 + 6)$$
$$= \underbrace{11 + 11 + 11 + 11 + 11}_{5 \text{ terms}} = 5(11) = 55$$

Notice that 5 is half of the number of terms and 11 represents the sum of the first and the last term, 1 + 10. This suggests that the sum of a linear series is $\sum_{k=1}^{n} k = \frac{n}{2}(1 + n)$, which can be written as $\sum_{k=1}^{n} k = \frac{n(n+1)}{2}$.

Similar methods will help you find the sum of a *quadratic series.*

Summation Formulas

CONSTANT SERIES	LINEAR SERIES	QUADRATIC SERIES
$\sum_{k=1}^{n} c = nc$	$\sum_{k=1}^{n} k = \frac{n(n+1)}{2}$	$\sum_{k=1}^{n} k^2 = \frac{n(n+1)(2n+1)}{6}$

EXAMPLE 3 Using Summation Formulas

Evaluate each series.

A $\sum_{k=5}^{10} 8$ *Constant series*

Method 1 Use the summation formula.

There are 6 terms.

$$\sum_{k=5}^{10} 8 = nc = 6(8) = 48$$

Method 2 Expand and evaluate.

$$\sum_{k=5}^{10} 8 = \underbrace{8 + 8 + 8 + 8 + 8 + 8}_{6 \text{ terms}} = 48$$

> **Caution!**
>
> When counting the number of terms, you must include both the first and the last. For example, $\sum_{k=5}^{10} 8$ has six terms, not five.
> $k = 5, 6, 7, 8, 9, 10$

B $\sum_{k=1}^{5} k$ *Linear series*

Method 1 Use the summation formula.

$$\sum_{k=1}^{5} k = \frac{n(n+1)}{2} = \frac{5(6)}{2} = 15$$

Method 2 Expand and evaluate.

$$\sum_{k=1}^{5} k = 1 + 2 + 3 + 4 + 5 = 15$$

C $\sum_{k=1}^{7} k^2$ *Quadratic series*

Method 1 Use the summation formula.

$$\sum_{k=1}^{7} k^2 = \frac{n(n+1)(2n+1)}{6}$$
$$= \frac{7(7+1)(2 \cdot 7 + 1)}{6}$$
$$= \frac{56(15)}{6}$$
$$= 140$$

Method 2 Use a graphing calculator.

```
1²+2²+3²+4²+5²+6
²+7²
                140
```

Evaluate each series.

3a. $\sum_{k=1}^{60} 4$ **3b.** $\sum_{k=1}^{15} k$ **3c.** $\sum_{k=1}^{10} k^2$

EXAMPLE 4 *Problem-Solving Application*

Ricky is building a card house similar to the one shown. He wants the house to have as many stories as possible with a deck of 52 playing cards. How many stories will Ricky's house have?

1 Understand the Problem

The **answer** will be the number of stories, or rows, in the card house.

List the important information:

- He has 52 playing cards.
- The house should have as many stories as possible.

2 Make a Plan

Make a diagram of the house to better understand the problem. Find a pattern for the number of cards in each story. Write and evaluate the series.

3 Solve

Make a table and a diagram.

Row	1	2	3	4
Diagram	/\	/\/\	/\/\/\	/\/\/\/\
Cards	2	5	8	11

The number of cards increases by 3 in each row. Write a series to represent the total number of cards in n rows.

$\sum_{k=1}^{n}(3k-1)$, where k is the row number and n is the total number of rows

Evaluate the series for several n-values.

$$\sum_{k=1}^{4}(3k-1) = [3(1)-1] + [3(2)-1] + [3(3)-1] + [3(4)-1]$$
$$= 26$$

$$\sum_{k=1}^{5}(3k-1) = [3(1)-1] + [3(2)-1] + [3(3)-1] + [3(4)-1] + [3(5)-1]$$
$$= 40$$

$$\sum_{k=1}^{6}(3k-1) = [3(1)-1] + [3(2)-1] + [3(3)-1] + [3(4)-1] + [3(5)-1] + [3(6)-1]$$
$$= 57$$

Because Ricky has only 52 cards, the house can have at most 5 stories.

Look Back

Use the table to continue the pattern. The 5th row would have 14 cards. $S_5 = 2 + 5 + 8 + 11 + 14 = 40$. The next row would have more than 12 cards, so the total would be more than 52.

4. A flexible garden hose is coiled for storage. Each subsequent loop is 6 inches longer than the preceding loop, and the innermost loop is 34 inches long. If there are 6 loops, how long is the hose?

THINK AND DISCUSS

1. Explain the difference between a sequence and a series.

2. Explain what each of the variables represents in the notation $\sum_{k=m}^{n} k$.

3. GET ORGANIZED Copy and complete the graphic organizer. Write the general notation and an example for each term.

	Sequence	Series
Notation		
Example		

12-2 Exercises

go.hrw.com
Homework Help Online
KEYWORD: MB7 12-2
Parent Resources Online
KEYWORD: MB7 Parent

GUIDED PRACTICE

1. **Vocabulary** Give an example of *summation notation.*

SEE EXAMPLE 1 p. 870

Write each series in summation notation.

2. $1 + \frac{1}{4} + \frac{1}{9} + \frac{1}{16} + \frac{1}{25}$
3. $-3 + 6 - 9 + 12 - 15$
4. $1 + 10 + 100 + 1000 + 10{,}000$
5. $100 + 95 + 90 + 85 + 80$

SEE EXAMPLE 2 p. 871

Expand each series and evaluate.

6. $\sum_{k=1}^{5} k^3$
7. $\sum_{k=1}^{4} (-1)^{k+1} \frac{12}{k^2}$
8. $\sum_{k=5}^{10} -5k$

SEE EXAMPLE 3 p. 872

Evaluate each series.

9. $\sum_{k=1}^{21} k$
10. $\sum_{k=1}^{20} k^2$
11. $\sum_{k=15}^{35} 6$

SEE EXAMPLE 4 p. 872

12. **Finance** Melinda makes monthly car payments of \$285 each month. How much will she have paid after 2 years? 5 years?

PRACTICE AND PROBLEM SOLVING

Independent Practice

For Exercises	See Example
13–16	1
17–19	2
20–22	3
23	4

Extra Practice

Skills Practice p. S26
Application Practice p. S43

Write each series in summation notation.

13. $1.1 + 2.2 + 3.3 + 4.4 + 5.5$
14. $\frac{1}{2} + \frac{2}{3} + \frac{3}{4} + \frac{4}{5} + \frac{5}{6}$
15. $11 - 12 + 13 - 14 + 15 - 16$
16. $1 + 2 + 4 + 8 + 16 + 32$

Expand each series and evaluate.

17. $\sum_{k=1}^{5} [8(k+1)]$
18. $\sum_{k=2}^{7} (-2)^k$
19. $\sum_{k=1}^{4} \frac{k-1}{k+1}$

Evaluate each series.

20. $\sum_{k=1}^{99} k$
21. $\sum_{k=11}^{88} 2.5$
22. $\sum_{k=1}^{25} k^2$

23. **Retail** A display of soup cans is arranged with 1 can on top and each row having an additional can. How many cans are in a display of 20 rows?

Write each series in summation notation.

24. $-1 + 4 - 9 + 16 - 25 + 36$
25. $25 + 24 + 23 + \cdots + 1$
26. $\frac{1}{3} + \frac{1}{9} + \frac{1}{27} + \frac{1}{81} + \frac{1}{243}$
27. $-800 - 80 - 8 - 0.8 - 0.08$
28. $10.8 + 10.5 + 10.2 + 9.9$
29. $9 - 16 + 25 - 36 + 49 - 64$
30. $-3.9 + 4.4 - 4.9 + 5.4 - 5.9$
31. $0 + 3.4 + 6.8 + 10.2 + 13.6$
32. $3 + \frac{3}{2} + 1 + \frac{3}{4} + \frac{3}{5}$
33. $1000 + 100 + 10 + 1 + \frac{1}{10}$

34. **Travel** The distance from St. Louis, Missouri, to Los Angeles, California, is 1596 miles. Michael plans to travel half the distance on the first day and half the remaining distance each day after that. Write a series in summation notation for the total distance he will travel in 5 days. How far will Michael travel in the 5 days?

35. **Safety** An employer uses a telephone tree to notify employees in the case of an emergency closing. When the office manager makes the decision to close, she calls 3 people. Each of these people calls 3 other people, and so on.

a. Make a tree diagram with 3 levels to represent the problem situation.

b. Write and evaluate a series to find the total number of people notified after 5 levels of calls.

c. **What if...?** Suppose that the phone tree involves calling 5 people at each level. How many more people would be notified after 5 levels of calls?

LINK

Math History

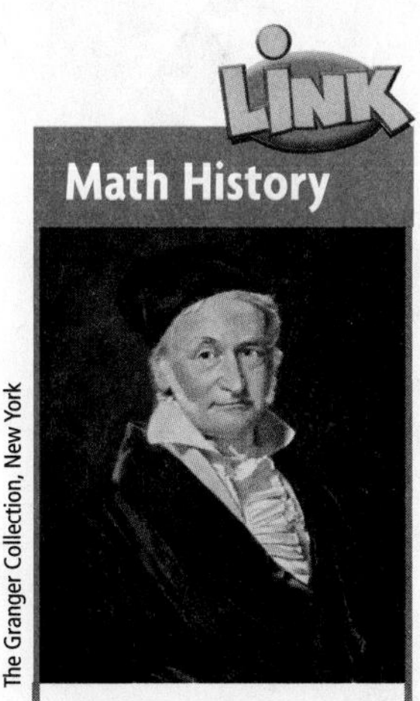

The Granger Collection, New York

At the age of 10, German mathematician Carl Friedrich Gauss discovered a quick method for adding the first 100 natural numbers. His method gave us the summation formula for a linear series.

Expand each series and evaluate.

36. $\sum_{k=1}^{6}(k^2+1)$ 37. $\sum_{k=1}^{6}(-1)^k 5k$ 38. $\sum_{k=3}^{6}\frac{1}{2k}$

39. $\sum_{k=1}^{6}(3k-2)$ 40. $\sum_{k=6}^{11}12(k-2)$ 41. $\sum_{k=1}^{5}\frac{k^2}{5k}$

42. **Architecture** A hotel is being built in the shape of a pyramid, as shown in the diagram. Each square floor is 10 feet longer and 10 feet wider than the floor above it.

a. Write a series that represents the total area of n floors of the hotel.

b. How many stories must the hotel be to have at least 50,000 square feet of floor area?

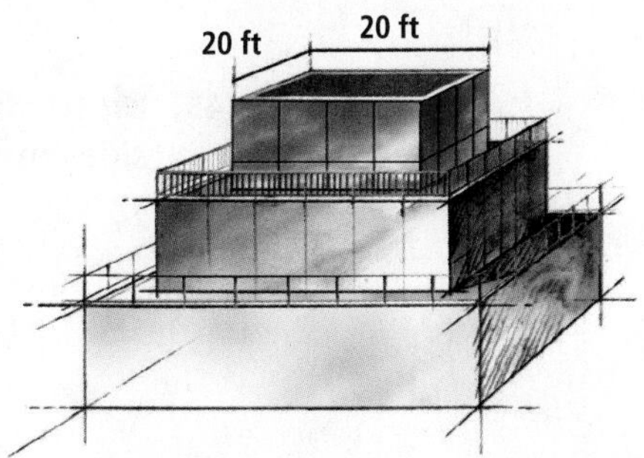

Estimation **Use mental math to estimate each sum. Then compare your answer to the sum obtained by using a calculator.**

43. $10 + 11 + 12 + \cdots + 29 + 30$

44. $1 + 3 + 5 + \cdots + 97 + 99$

45. $-2 + (-4) + (-6) + \cdots + (-98) + (-100)$

46. **Physics** The distance that an object falls in equal time intervals is represented in the table. Rules created by Leonardo da Vinci and Galileo are shown. (In this general case, specific units do not apply to time or distance.)

Distance Fallen in Each Time Interval		
Time Interval	**Leonardo's Rule**	**Galileo's Rule**
1	1	1
2	2	3
3	3	5
4	4	7
5	5	9

a. Write the series for each rule for 5 intervals, and find the respective sums. What does the sum of the series for 5 intervals represent?

b. Write each series in summation notation. Then evaluate each series for $n = 10$.

c. By the current rule, the distance fallen in each interval is 1, 4, 9, 16, 25.... How do Leonardo's rule and Galileo's rule compare to the current rule?

47. **Critical Thinking** Some mathematical properties may be applied to series.

a. Evaluate $\sum_{k=1}^{10}3n$ and $3\sum_{k=1}^{10}n$. Make a conjecture based on your answer.

b. Evaluate $\sum_{k=1}^{10}n + \sum_{k=1}^{10}2$ and $\sum_{k=1}^{10}(n+2)$. Make a conjecture based on your answer.

48. This problem will prepare you for the Multi-Step Test Prep on page 888. The series $\sum_{k=1}^{n}(3k^2 + 3k)$ gives the total number of sticks needed to make a tetrahedral kite with n layers.

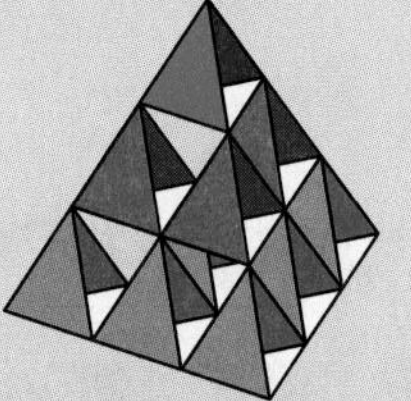

a. Expand and evaluate the series to find out how many sticks are needed to make a kite with 5 layers.

b. Use the properties
$$\sum_{k=1}^{n}(a_k + b_k) = \sum_{k=1}^{n} a_k + \sum_{k=1}^{n} b_k \text{ and } \sum_{k=1}^{n} ca_k = c\sum_{k=1}^{n} a_k$$
to rewrite the series as a multiple of a quadratic series plus a multiple of a linear series.

c. Use summation formulas to determine how many sticks are needed to make a kite with 17 layers.

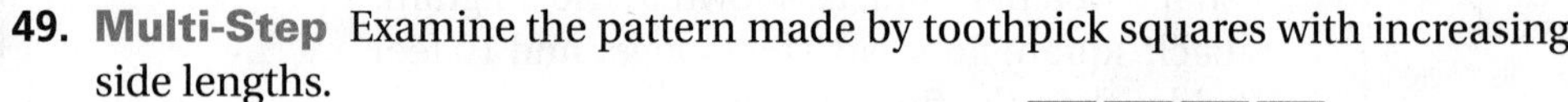

49. **Multi-Step** Examine the pattern made by toothpick squares with increasing side lengths.

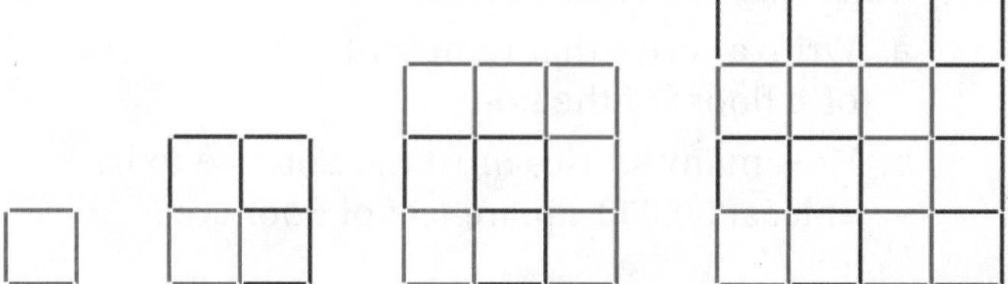

a. Write a sequence for the number of toothpicks added to form each new square.

b. Write and evaluate a series in summation notation to represent the total number of toothpicks in a square with a side length of 6 toothpicks.

50. **Critical Thinking** Are the sums of 1 + 3 + 5 + 7 + 9 and 9 + 7 + 5 + 3 + 1 the same? Do these series have the same summation notation? Explain.

51. **Write About It** Explain why S_n represents a partial sum and not a complete sum of the terms of a sequence.

52. Which notation accurately reflects the series $\sum_{k=1}^{7}(-1)^k(3k)$?

Ⓐ 3 + 6 + 9 + 12 + 15 + 18 + 21
Ⓑ 3 − 6 + 9 − 12 + 15 − 18 + 21
Ⓒ −3 + 6 − 9 + 12 − 15 + 18 − 21
Ⓓ −3 − 6 − 9 − 12 − 15 − 18 − 21

53. Which notation accurately reflects the series $\frac{1}{2} + \frac{1}{4} + \frac{1}{6} + \frac{1}{8}$?

Ⓕ $\sum_{k=1}^{4}\frac{k}{2}$ Ⓖ $\sum_{k=1}^{4}\frac{1}{2^k}$ Ⓗ $\sum_{k=1}^{4}\frac{1}{2k}$ Ⓙ $\sum_{k=1}^{4}\frac{1}{k+2}$

54. What is the value of $\sum_{k=1}^{6} k^2$?

Ⓐ 36 Ⓑ 55 Ⓒ 91 Ⓓ 273

55. Find the sum of the series $\frac{1}{3} + \frac{1}{6} + \frac{1}{12} + \frac{1}{24}$?

Ⓕ $\frac{1}{45}$ Ⓖ $\frac{4}{45}$ Ⓗ $\frac{7}{12}$ Ⓙ $\frac{5}{8}$

56. **Short Response** The number of cans in each row of a pyramidal stack is 1, 4, 9, 16, ... Would a sequence or series be used to find the number of cans in the 20th row? Explain.

CHALLENGE AND EXTEND

The product of a sequence of terms can be represented by using *pi notation,* which uses the Greek letter Π (capital *pi*). Expand each product and evaluate.

57. $\prod_{k=1}^{5} k$

58. $\prod_{k=1}^{4} (-1)^k$

Prove each summation property for the sequences a_k and b_k.

59. $\sum_{k=1}^{n} ca_k = c\sum_{k=1}^{n} a_k$

60. $\sum_{k=1}^{n} (a_k + b_k) = \sum_{k=1}^{n} a_k + \sum_{k=1}^{n} b_k$

61. **Critical Thinking** What might the sum of the sequence $1 - 1 + 1 - 1 + 1 - 1 + \cdots$ be if it continues forever? Explain.

SPIRAL REVIEW

Find the intercepts of each line, and graph the lines. *(Lesson 2-3)*

62. $3x - 4y = 12$

63. $-6x + 3y = -18$

64. $10x + 15y = -5$

65. **Architecture** The height in feet of an elevator above ground is modeled by $h(t) = 8|t - 6| + 10$, where t is the time in seconds. What is the minimum height of the elevator? *(Lesson 2-9)*

Find the first 5 terms of each sequence. *(Lesson 12-1)*

66. $a_n = \left(\frac{1}{2}n + 2\right)^2$

67. $a_1 = 2, a_n = (a_{n-1})^2 - 1$

68. $a_n = \frac{4^n}{2}$

Career Path

go.hrw.com
Career Resources Online
KEYWORD: MB7 Career

Steven Howe
Nursing student

Q: What high school math classes did you take?

A: Algebra 1, Geometry, Business Math, and Algebra 2

Q: Why did you decide to pursue a career in nursing?

A: I've always liked science, especially biology and anatomy. I also wanted a career where I can help people, so a job in medicine seemed perfect.

Q: How is math used in nursing?

A: Nurses have to make a lot of calculations to ensure that patients receive the correct dosages of medicine. They also use complicated instruments to measure and monitor different body functions.

Q: What are your future plans?

A: I'll finish my associate's degree in nursing at the end of the semester. I hope to get a job at one of the local hospitals.

Evaluate Sequences and Series

Graphing calculators have built-in features that help you generate the terms of a sequence and find the sums of series.

Use with Lesson 12-2

Activity

Use a graphing calculator to find the first 7 terms of the sequence $a_n = 1.5n + 4$. Then find the sum of those terms.

NAMES OPS MATH
1:SortA(
2:SortD(
3:dim(
4:Fill(
5:seq(
6:cumSum(
7↓ΔList(

1 Find the first 7 terms of the sequence.

Enter the **LIST** operations menu by pressing 2nd STAT (LIST) and scrolling right to the **OPS** menu. Then select the sequence command **5:seq(**.

The sequence command takes the following four expressions separated by commas.

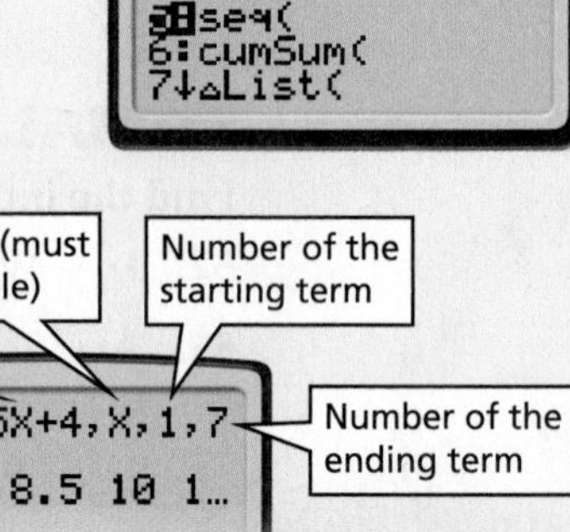

Enter the rule, using x as the variable. Enter 1 for the starting term and 7 for the ending term. Close the parentheses, and then press ENTER.

seq(1.5X+4,X,1,7
)
…0 11.5 13 14.5}

The terms of the sequence will be displayed in brackets. Use the arrow keys to scroll to see the rest of the terms.

The first 7 terms are 5.5, 7, 8.5, 10, 11.5, 13, and 14.5.

2 Find the sum of the terms.

Enter the **LIST** math menu by pressing 2nd STAT (LIST), and scrolling right to the **MATH** menu. Then select the sum command **5:sum(**.

Follow the steps for entering a sequence as shown in Step 1.

The sum of the first 7 terms is 70.

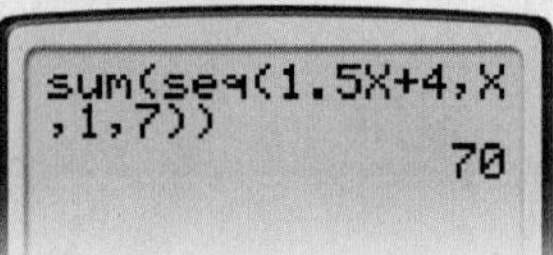

Try This

Find the first 8 terms of each sequence. Then find the sum of those 8 terms.

1. $a_n = 2n^2 - 5$

2. $a_n = \frac{1}{4}(2)^{n-1}$

3. $a_n = 0.3n + 1.6$

4. $a_n = 20n$

5. $a_n = n^3 - 2n$

6. $a_n = 0.1(5)^n$

7. Critical Thinking Find the next 5 terms of the sequence 200, 182, 164, 146, 128, ... Then find the sum of those 5 terms.

12-3 Arithmetic Sequences and Series

Objectives
Find the indicated terms of an arithmetic sequence.

Find the sums of arithmetic series.

Vocabulary
arithmetic sequence
arithmetic series

Who uses this?
You can use arithmetic sequences to predict the cost of mailing letters.

The cost of mailing a letter in 2005 based on its weight in ounces gives the sequence 0.37, 0.60, 0.83, 1.06, ... This sequence is called an **arithmetic sequence** because its successive terms differ by the same number d $(d \neq 0)$, called the *common difference.* For the mail costs, d is 0.23, as shown.

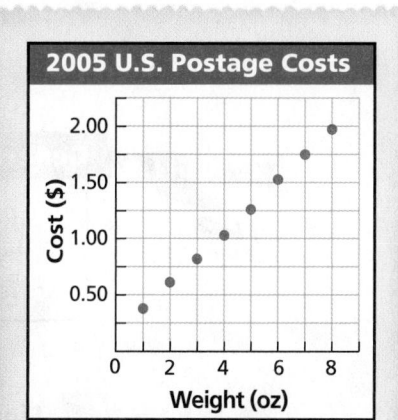

Term	a_1	a_2	a_3	a_4
Value	0.37	0.60	0.83	1.06

Differences 0.23 0.23 0.23

Recall that linear functions have a constant first difference. Notice also that when you graph the ordered pairs (n, a_n) of an arithmetic sequence, the points lie on a straight line. Thus, you can think of an arithmetic sequence as a linear function with sequential natural numbers as the domain.

EXAMPLE 1 **Identifying Arithmetic Sequences**

Determine whether each sequence could be arithmetic. If so, find the common first difference and the next term.

A $-3, 2, 7, 12, 17, \ldots$

$-3, \quad 2, \quad 7, \quad 12, \quad 17$

Differences 5 5 5 5

The sequence could be arithmetic with a common difference of 5.
The next term is $17 + 5 = 22$.

B $-4, -12, -24, -40, -60, \ldots$

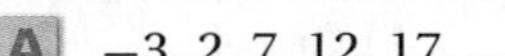

$-4, \quad -12, \quad -24, \quad -40, \quad -60$

Differences $-8 \quad -12 \quad -16 \quad -20$

The sequence is not arithmetic because the first differences are not common.

Determine whether each sequence could be arithmetic. If so, find the common difference and the next term.

1a. $1.9, 1.2, 0.5, -0.2, -0.9, \ldots$ **1b.** $\frac{11}{2}, \frac{11}{3}, \frac{11}{4}, \frac{11}{5}, \frac{11}{6}, \ldots$

Each term in an arithmetic sequence is the sum of the previous term and the common difference. This gives the recursive rule $a_n = a_{n-1} + d$. You also can develop an explicit rule for an arithmetic sequence.

Notice the pattern in the table. Each term is the sum of the first term and a multiple of the common difference.

This pattern can be generalized into a rule for all arithmetic sequences.

Postage Costs per Ounce	
n	a_n
1	$a_1 = 0.37 + 0(0.23)$
2	$a_2 = 0.37 + 1(0.23)$
3	$a_3 = 0.37 + 2(0.23)$
4	$a_4 = 0.37 + 3(0.23)$
n	$a_n = 0.37 + (n - 1)(0.23)$

General Rule for Arithmetic Sequences

The nth term a_n of an arithmetic sequence is given by

$$a_n = a_1 + (n - 1)d$$

where a_1 is the first term and d is the common difference.

EXAMPLE 2 **Finding the nth Term Given an Arithmetic Sequence**

Find the 10th term of the arithmetic sequence 32, 25, 18, 11, 4, ...

Step 1 Find the common difference: $d = 25 - 32 = -7$.

Step 2 Evaluate by using the formula.

$a_n = a_1 + (n - 1)d$ — *General rule*

$a_{10} = 32 + (10 - 1)(-7)$ — *Substitute 32 for a_1, 10 for n, and −7 for d.*

$= -31$ — *Simplify.*

The 10th term is −31.

Check Continue the sequence.

n	1	2	3	4	5	6	7	8	9	10
a_n	32	25	18	11	4	−3	−10	−17	−24	−31 ✓

Find the 11th term of each arithmetic sequence.

2a. −3, −5, −7, −9, ...

2b. 9.2, 9.15, 9.1, 9.05, ...

Student to Student *Finding the nth Term*

Diana Watson
Bowie High School

I like to check the value of a term by using a graphing calculator.

I enter the function for the nth, or general, term. For Example 2A, enter $y = 32 + (x - 1)(-7)$.

I then use the table feature. Start at 1 (for n = 1), and use a step of 1. Then find the desired term (y-value) as shown for n = 10.

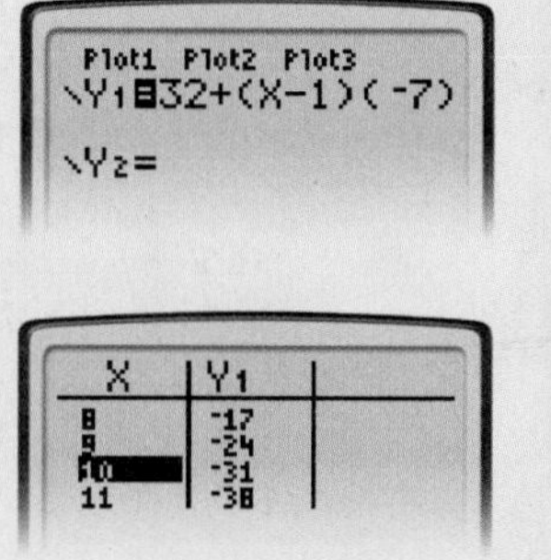

EXAMPLE 3 **Finding Missing Terms**

Find the missing terms in the arithmetic sequence 11, ▇, ▇, ▇, −17.

Step 1 Find the common difference.

$a_n = a_1 + (n - 1)d$	*General rule*
$-17 = 11 + (5 - 1)d$	*Substitute −17 for a_n, 11 for a_1, and 5 for n.*
$-7 = d$	*Solve for d.*

Step 2 Find the missing terms using $d = -7$ and $a_1 = 11$.

$a_2 = 11 + (2 - 1)(-7)$	$a_3 = 11 + (3 - 1)(-7)$	$a_4 = 11 + (4 - 1)(-7)$
$= 4$	$= -3$	$= -10$

The missing terms are 4, −3, and −10.

3. Find the missing terms in the arithmetic sequence 2, ▇, ▇, ▇, 0.

Because arithmetic sequences have a common difference, you can use any two terms to find the difference.

EXAMPLE 4 **Finding the *n*th Term Given Two Terms**

Find the 6th term of the arithmetic sequence with $a_9 = 120$ and $a_{14} = 195$.

Step 1 Find the common difference.

$a_n = a_1 + (n - 1)d$	
$a_{14} = a_9 + (14 - 9)d$	*Let $a_n = a_{14}$ and $a_1 = a_9$. Replace 1 with 9.*
$a_{14} = a_9 + 5d$	*Simplify.*
$195 = 120 + 5d$	*Substitute 195 for a_{14} and 120 for a_9.*
$75 = 5d$	
$15 = d$	

Step 2 Find a_1.

$a_n = a_1 + (n - 1)d$	*General rule*
$120 = a_1 + (9 - 1)(15)$	*Substitute 120 for a_9, 9 for n, and 15 for d.*
$120 = a_1 + 120$	*Simplify.*
$0 = a_1$	

Step 3 Write a rule for the sequence, and evaluate to find a_6.

$a_n = a_1 + (n - 1)d$	*General rule*
$a_n = 0 + (n - 1)(15)$	*Substitute 0 for a_1 and 15 for d.*
$a_6 = 0 + (6 - 1)15$	*Evaluate for n = 6.*
$= 75$	

The 6th term is 75.

Find the 11th term of each arithmetic sequence.

4a. $a_2 = -133$ and $a_3 = -121$ **4b.** $a_3 = 20.5$ and $a_8 = 13$

In Lesson 12-2 you wrote and evaluated series. An **arithmetic series** is the indicated sum of the terms of an arithmetic sequence. You can derive a general formula for the sum of an arithmetic series by writing the series in forward and reverse order and adding the results.

$$\begin{aligned} S_n &= a_1 + (a_1 + d) + (a_1 + 2d) + \ldots + a_n \\ S_n &= a_n + (a_n - d) + (a_n - 2d) + \ldots + a_1 \\ \hline 2S_n &= \underbrace{(a_1 + a_n) + (a_1 + a_n) + (a_1 + a_n) \ldots + (a_1 + a_n)}_{(a_1 + a_n) \text{ is added } n \text{ times}} \end{aligned}$$

$$2S_n = n(a_1 + a_n)$$

$$S_n = \frac{n(a_1 + a_n)}{2}, \text{ or } S_n = n\left(\frac{a_1 + a_n}{2}\right)$$

Sum of the First n Terms of an Arithmetic Series

WORDS	NUMBERS	ALGEBRA
The sum of the first n terms of an arithmetic series is the product of the number of terms and the average of the first and last terms.	The sum of $2 + 4 + 6 + 8 + 10$ is $5\left(\frac{2 + 10}{2}\right) = 5(6) = 30.$	$S_n = n\left(\frac{a_1 + a_n}{2}\right)$, where n is the number of terms, a_1 is the first term, and a_n is the nth term.

EXAMPLE 5 Finding the Sum of an Arithmetic Series

Find the indicated sum for each arithmetic series.

A S_{15} for $25 + 12 + (-1) + (-14) + \cdots$

Find the common difference.

$d = 12 - 25 = -13$

Find the 15th term.

$a_{15} = 25 + (15 - 1)(-13)$

$= -157$

Find S_{15}.

$S_n = n\left(\frac{a_1 + a_n}{2}\right)$ *Sum formula*

$S_{15} = 15\left(\frac{25 + (-157)}{2}\right)$ *Substitute.*

$= 15(-66) = -990$

Check Use a graphing calculator.

B $\sum_{k=1}^{12} (3 + 4k)$

Find the 1st and 12th terms.

$a_1 = 3 + 4(1) = 7$

$a_{12} = 3 + 4(12) = 51$

Find S_{12}.

$S_n = n\left(\frac{a_1 + a_n}{2}\right)$

$S_{12} = 12\left(\frac{7 + 51}{2}\right)$

$= 348$

Check Use a graphing calculator.

Remember!

These sums are actually *partial sums.* You cannot find the complete sum of an infinite arithmetic series because the term values increase or decrease indefinitely.

Find the indicated sum for each arithmetic series.

5a. S_{16} for $12 + 7 + 2 + (-3) + \cdots$ **5b.** $\sum_{k=1}^{15} (50 - 20k)$

EXAMPLE 6 Theater Application

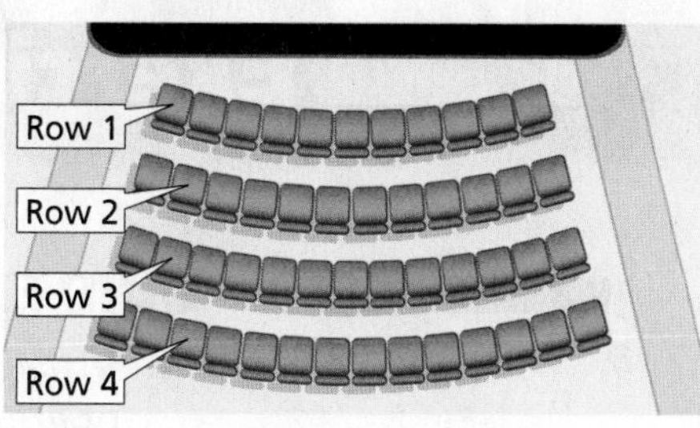

The number of seats in the first 14 rows of the center orchestra aisle of the Marquis Theater on Broadway in New York City form an arithmetic sequence as shown.

A How many seats are in the 14th row?

Write a general rule using $a_1 = 11$ and $d = 1$.

$$a_n = a_1 + (n - 1)d \quad \textit{Explicit rule for nth term}$$

$$a_{14} = 11 + (14 - 1)1 \quad \textit{Substitute.}$$

$$= 11 + 13$$

$$= 24 \quad \textit{Simplify.}$$

There are 24 seats in the 14th row.

B How many seats in total are in the first 14 rows?

Find S_{14} using the formula for finding the sum of the first n terms.

$$S_n = n\left(\frac{a_1 + a_n}{2}\right) \quad \textit{Formula for first n terms}$$

$$S_{14} = 14\left(\frac{11 + 24}{2}\right) \quad \textit{Substitute.}$$

$$= 14\left(\frac{35}{2}\right)$$

$$= 245 \quad \textit{Simplify.}$$

There are 245 seats in rows 1 through 14.

6. **What if...?** Suppose that each row after the first had 2 additional seats.
   a. How many seats would be in the 14th row?
   b. How many total seats would there be in the first 14 rows?

THINK AND DISCUSS

1. Compare an arithmetic sequence with a linear function.
2. Describe the effect that a negative common difference has on an arithmetic sequence.
3. Explain how to find the 6th term in a sequence when you know the 3rd and 4th terms.
4. Explain how to find the common difference when you know the 7th and 12th terms of an arithmetic sequence.

5. **GET ORGANIZED** Copy and complete the graphic organizer. Write in each rectangle to summarize your understanding of arithmetic sequences.

Definition	Characteristics
Arithmetic Sequences	
Examples	Formulas

12-3 Exercises

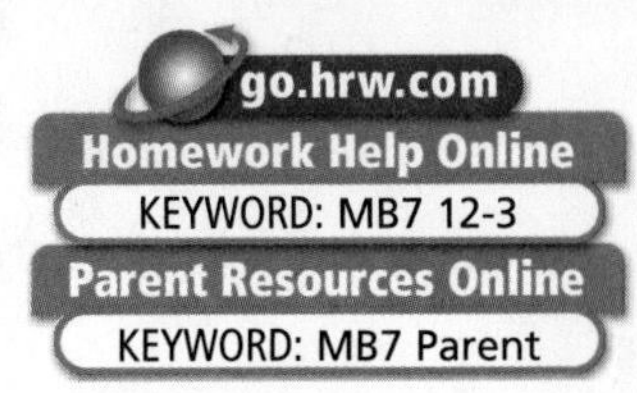

GUIDED PRACTICE

1. **Vocabulary** The expression $10 + 20 + 30 + 40 + 50$ is an __?__. (*arithmetic sequence* or *arithmetic series*)

SEE EXAMPLE 1 p. 879

Determine whether each sequence could be arithmetic. If so, find the common difference and the next term.

2. 46, 39, 32, 25, 18, ...
3. 28, 21, 15, 10, 6, ...
4. $\frac{12}{3}, \frac{10}{3}, \frac{8}{3}, \frac{6}{3}, \frac{4}{3}, \ldots$

SEE EXAMPLE 2 p. 880

Find the 8th term of each arithmetic sequence.

5. 3, 8, 13, 18, ...
6. $10, 9\frac{3}{4}, 9\frac{1}{2}, 9\frac{1}{4}, \ldots$
7. −3.2, −3.4, −3.6, −3.8, ...

SEE EXAMPLE 3 p. 881

Find the missing terms in each arithmetic sequence.

8. 13, ■, ■, 25
9. 9, ■, ■, ■, 37
10. 1.4, ■, ■, ■, −1

SEE EXAMPLE 4 p. 881

Find the 9th term of each arithmetic sequence.

11. $a_4 = 27$ and $a_5 = 19$
12. $a_3 = 12.2$ and $a_4 = 12.6$
13. $a_3 = -5$ and $a_6 = -11$
14. $a_{10} = 100$ and $a_{20} = 50$
15. $a_7 = -42$ and $a_{11} = -28$
16. $a_4 = \frac{3}{4}$ and $a_8 = \frac{1}{2}$

SEE EXAMPLE 5 p. 882

Find the indicated sum for each arithmetic series.

17. S_{15} for $5 + 9 + 13 + 17 + \cdots$
18. $\sum_{k=1}^{12}(-2 + 6k)$
19. S_{18} for $3.2 + 2.9 + 2.6 + 2.3 + \cdots$

SEE EXAMPLE 6 p. 883

20. **Salary** Juan has taken a job with an initial salary of $26,000 and annual raises of $1250.
    a. What will his salary be in his 6th year?
    b. How much money in total will Juan have earned after six years?

PRACTICE AND PROBLEM SOLVING

Independent Practice

For Exercises	See Example
21–23	1
24–26	2
27–29	3
30–32	4
33–35	5
36	6

Extra Practice
Skills Practice p. S26
Application Practice p. S43

Determine whether each sequence could be arithmetic. If so, find the common difference and the next term.

21. 288, 144, 72, 36, 18, ...
22. −2, −12, −22, −32, −42, ...
23. 0.99, 0.9, 0.81, 0.72, ...

Find the 11th term of each arithmetic sequence.

24. 12, 11.9, 11.8, 11.7, ...
25. $\frac{2}{5}, \frac{3}{5}, \frac{4}{5}, 1, \ldots$
26. −3.0, −2.5, −2.0, −1.5, ...

Find the missing terms in each arithmetic sequence.

27. 77, ■, ■, ■, 33
28. −29, ■, ■, −2
29. 2.3, ■, ■, ■, 1.5

Find the 12th term of each arithmetic sequence.

30. $a_4 = 18.4$ and $a_5 = 16.2$
31. $a_4 = -2$ and $a_8 = 46$
32. $a_{22} = -49$ and $a_{25} = -58$

Find the indicated sum for each arithmetic series.

33. S_{15} for $-18 + (-16) + (-14) + \cdots$
34. $\sum_{k=1}^{20}(88 - 3k)$
35. $\sum_{k=1}^{14}\left(14 - \frac{1}{2}k\right)$

One of London's most recognizable landmarks, Big Ben sits atop the Palace of Westminister, where the British Parliament meets. The name Big Ben actually refers to the 13.8-ton bell that chimes the hours.

36. **Consumer Economics** Clarissa is buying a prom dress on layaway. She agrees to make a \$15 payment and increase the payment by \$5 each week.
   a. What will her payment be in the 9th week?
   b. How much money in total will Clarissa have paid after 9 weeks?

37. **Clocks** A clock chimes every hour. The clock chimes once at 1 o'clock, twice at 2 o'clock, and so on.
   a. How many times will the clock chime from 1 P.M. through midnight? in exactly one 24-hour period?
   b. **What if...?** Another clock also chimes once on every half hour. How does this affect the sequence and the total number of chimes per day?

Find the indicated sum for each arithmetic series.

38. $\sum_{k=1}^{16}(555 - 11k)$

39. $\sum_{k=1}^{15}(4 - 0.5k)$

40. $\sum_{k=1}^{18}\left(-33 + \frac{5}{2}k\right)$

41. S_{16} for $7.5 + 7 + 6.5 + 6.0 + \cdots$

42. S_{18} for $2 + 9 + 16 + 23 + \cdots$

43. **Architecture** The Louvre pyramid in Paris, France, is built of glass panes. There are 4 panes in the top row, and each additional row has 4 more panes than the previous row.

   a. Write a series in summation notation to describe the total number of glass panes in n rows of the pyramid.
   b. If the pyramid were made of 18 complete rows, how many panes would it have?
   c. The actual pyramid has 11 panes less than a complete 18-row pyramid because of the space for the entrance. Find the total number of panes in the Louvre pyramid.

44. **Physics** Water towers are tall to provide enough water pressure to supply all of the houses and businesses in the area of the tower. Each foot of height provides 0.43 psi (pounds per square inch) of pressure.
   a. Write a sequence for the pressure in psi for each foot of height.
   b. What is the minimum height that supplies 50 psi, a typical minimum supply pressure?
   c. What is the minimum height that supplies 100 psi, which is a typical maximum pressure?
   d. Graph the sequence, and discuss the relationship between the height found for a pressure of 50 psi and the height found at 100 psi.

45. **Exercise** Sheila begins an exercise routine for 20 minutes each day. Each week she plans to add 5 minutes per day to the length of her routine.
   a. For how many minutes will she exercise each day of the 6th week?
   b. What happens to the length of Sheila's exercise routine if she continues this increasing pattern for 2 years?

46. **Geology** Every year the continent of North America moves farther away from Europe.
   a. How much farther from Europe will North America be in 50 years?
   b. How many years until an extra mile is added? (*Hint:* 1 mi ≈ 1609 m)

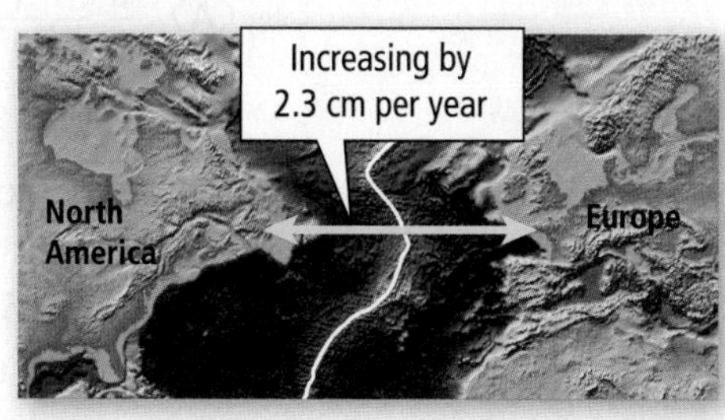

47. This problem will prepare you for the Multi-Step Test Prep on page 888.

You can make a simple tetrahedral kite with one peak by using 4 tetrahedrons. You can also make long kites with multiple peaks by successively adding 3 tetrahedrons as shown.

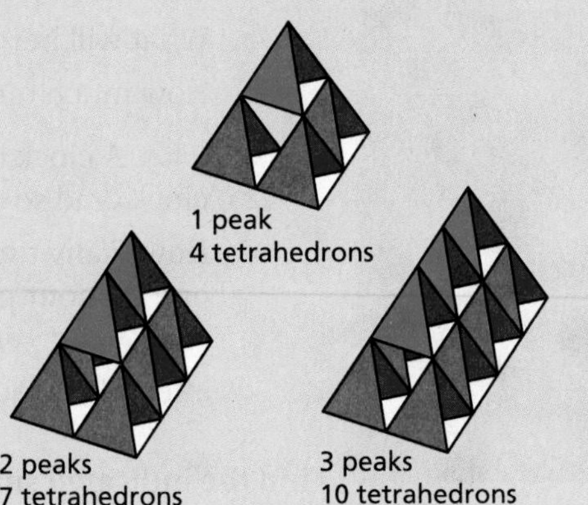

a. How many tetrahedrons are needed to make a kite with 20 peaks?

b. A kite maker wants to build one example of every kite with 1 to 20 peaks. How many tetrahedrons will be needed?

48. **Finance** The starting salary for a summer camp counselor is \$395 per week. In each of the subsequent weeks, the salary increases by \$45 to encourage experienced counselors to work for the entire summer. If the salary is \$710 in the last week of the camp, for how many weeks does the camp run?

49. **Sports** A town is planning a 5K race. The race route will begin at 1st street, travel 30 blocks down Main Street, and finish on 31st Street. The race planners want to have water stations at each turn. In addition, they want to place 5 more water stations evenly distributed between 1st Street and 31st Street on Main Street.

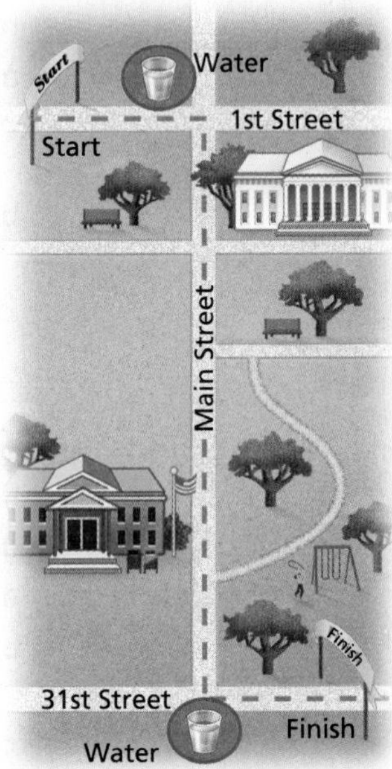

a. At what street intersections should the water stations be placed?

b. If each block is 0.1 mile, what is the maximum distance a runner will be from a water station while on Main Street?

50. **Critical Thinking** What is the least number of terms you need to write the general rule for an arithmetic sequence? How many points do you need to write an equation of a line? Are these answers related? Explain.

51. **Write About It** An arithmetic sequence has a positive common difference. What happens to the nth term as n becomes greater and greater? What happens if the sequence has a negative common difference?

52. Which sequence could be an arithmetic sequence?

Ⓐ $\frac{1}{2}, \frac{1}{3}, \frac{1}{4}, \frac{1}{5}, \ldots$

Ⓑ 2.2, 4.4, 6.6, 8.8, ...

Ⓒ 2, 4, 8, 16, ...

Ⓓ 2, 4, 7, 11, ...

53. A catering company charges a setup fee of \$45 plus \$12 per person. Which of the following sequences accurately reflects this situation?

Ⓕ $a_n = 45 + 12(n - 1)$

Ⓖ 45, 57, 69, 81, 93, ...

Ⓗ $a_n = 57 + 12n$

Ⓙ 57, 69, 81, 93, 105, ...

54. Which graph might represent the terms of an arithmetic sequence?

Ⓐ 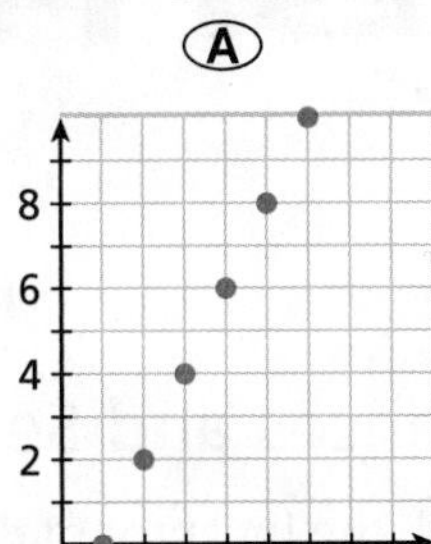

Ⓑ 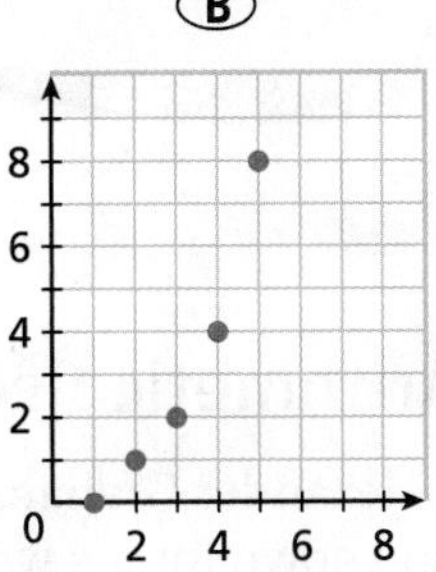

Ⓒ 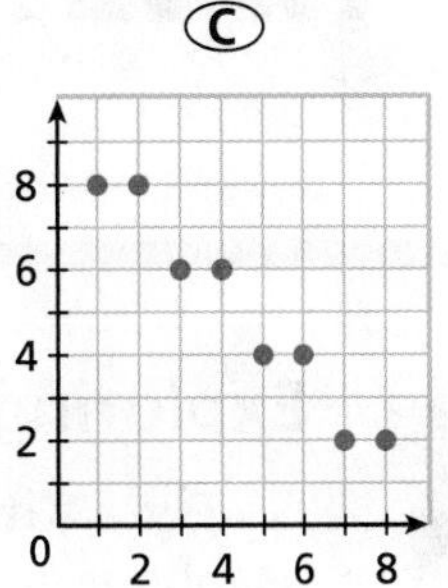

Ⓓ 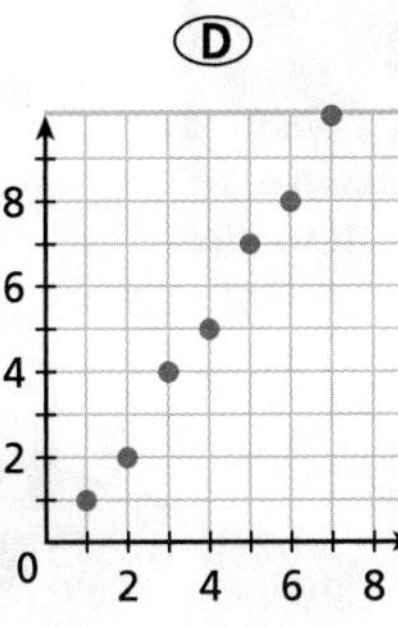

55. Given the arithmetic sequence 4, ■, ■, ■, 40, what are the three missing terms?

Ⓕ 11, 22, 33 Ⓗ 14, 24, 34

Ⓖ 13, 22, 31 Ⓙ 16, 24, 36

56. Which represents the sum of the arithmetic series 19 + 16 + 13 + 10 + 7 + 4?

Ⓐ $\sum_{k=1}^{6} 19 - 3k$ Ⓒ $\sum_{k=1}^{6} (22 - 3k)$

Ⓑ $\sum_{k=1}^{6} 19 - 4k$ Ⓓ $\sum_{k=1}^{6} [22 - 3(k - 1)]$

57. **Gridded Response** What is the 13th term of the arithmetic sequence 54, 50, 46, 42, ...

CHALLENGE AND EXTEND

58. Consider the two terms of an arithmetic series a_n and a_m.
   a. Show that the common difference is $d = \frac{a_n - a_m}{n - m}$.
   b. Use the new formula to find the common difference for the arithmetic sequence with $a_{12} = 88$ and $a_{36} = 304$.

59. Find a formula for the sum of an arithmetic sequence that does NOT include the last term. When might this formula be useful?

60. The sum of three consecutive terms of an arithmetic sequence is 60. If the product of these terms is 7500, what are the terms?

61. **Critical Thinking** What does $a_{2n} = 2a_n$ mean and for what arithmetic sequences is it true?

SPIRAL REVIEW

Tell whether the function shows growth or decay. Then graph. *(Lesson 7-1)*

62. $f(x) = 1.25(0.75)^x$ 63. $f(x) = 1.43(5.32)^x$ 64. $f(x) = 0.92(0.64)^x$

65. **Sound** The loudness of sound is given by $L = 10\log\left(\frac{I}{I_0}\right)$, where L is the loudness of sound in decibels, I is the intensity of sound, and I_0 is the intensity of the softest audible sound. A sound meter at an auto race had a relative intensity of $10^{9.2}\, I_0$. Find the loudness of the sound in decibels. *(Lesson 7-3)*

Write each series in summation notation. *(Lesson 12-2)*

66. $1 + \frac{1}{2} + \frac{1}{3} + \frac{1}{4} + \frac{1}{5}$ 67. $\frac{4}{5} + \frac{8}{5} + \frac{12}{5} + \frac{16}{5} + 4$

68. $-1 + 2 + 7 + 14 + 23$ 69. $-\frac{1}{3} - \frac{2}{3} - 1 - \frac{4}{3} - \frac{5}{3}$

CHAPTER 12

Multi-Step Test Prep

SECTION 12A

Exploring Arithmetic Sequences and Series

Go Fly a Kite! Alexander Graham Bell, the inventor of the telephone, is also known for his work with tetrahedral kites. In 1902, Bell used the kites to prove that it is possible to build an arbitrarily large structure that will fly. The kites are made up of tetrahedrons (four-sided triangular figures) with two sides covered with fabric. As shown in the figure, the size of a tetrahedral kite is determined by how many layers it has.

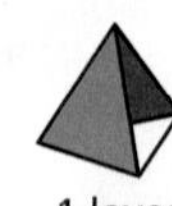

1 layer

2 layers

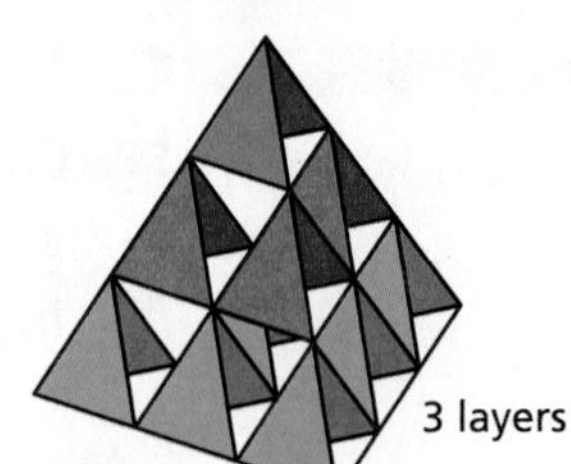

3 layers

1. The first layer of a tetrahedral kite has 1 tetrahedron, the second layer has 3 tetrahedrons, and the third layer has 6 tetrahedrons. Write a sequence that shows how many tetrahedrons are in each of the first 10 layers.
2. Write a recursive formula for the sequence.
3. Write an explicit rule for the nth term of the sequence.
4. How many tetrahedrons are there in the 25th layer?
5. Write a series in summation notation that gives the total number of tetrahedrons in a kite with 25 layers.
6. Evaluate the series in problem 5 to find the total number of tetrahedrons in a kite with 25 layers. (*Hint:* Use the properties

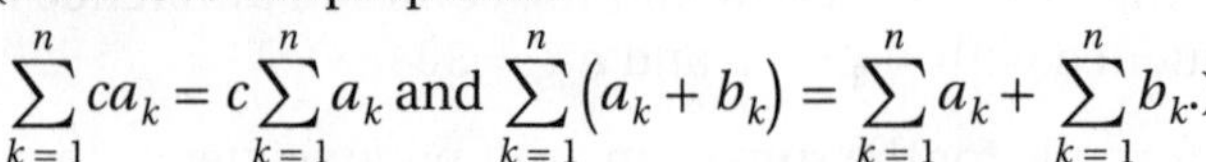

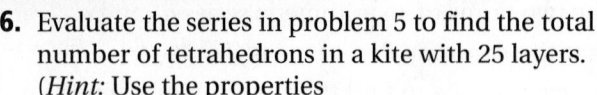

$$\sum_{k=1}^{n} ca_k = c\sum_{k=1}^{n} a_k \text{ and } \sum_{k=1}^{n}\left(a_k + b_k\right) = \sum_{k=1}^{n} a_k + \sum_{k=1}^{n} b_k.)$$

7. You see someone flying a large tetrahedral kite at a kite festival. You look up and estimate that the bottom layer of the kite contains between 100 and 110 tetrahedrons. How many layers does the kite have? How many tetrahedrons did it take to build the kite?

READY TO GO ON?

Quiz for Lessons 12-1 Through 12-3

12-1 Introduction to Sequences

Find the first 5 terms of each sequence.

1. $a_n = \frac{2}{3}n$
2. $a_n = 4^{n-1}$
3. $a_1 = -1$ and $a_n = 2a_{n-1} - 12$
4. $a_n = n^2 - 2n$

Write a possible explicit rule for the *n*th term of each sequence.

5. 8, 11, 14, 17, 20, ...
6. −2, −8, −18, −32, −50, ...
7. 1000, 200, 40, 8, $\frac{8}{5}$, ...
8. 437, 393, 349, 305, 261, ...
9. A car traveling at 55 mi/h passes a mile marker that reads mile 18. If the car maintains this speed for 4 hours, what mile marker should the car pass? Graph the sequence for *n* hours, and describe its pattern.

12-2 Series and Summation Notation

Expand each series and evaluate.

10. $\sum_{k=1}^{4}(-14 - 2k)$
11. $\sum_{k=1}^{4}\left(\frac{k}{k+2}\right)$
12. $\sum_{k=1}^{5}(-1)^k(k^2 - 2)$

Evaluate each series.

13. $\sum_{k=1}^{5}\frac{1}{2}$
14. $\sum_{k=1}^{40}k^2$
15. $\sum_{k=1}^{15}k$
16. The first row of a theater has 20 seats, and each of the following rows has 3 more seats than the preceding row. How many seats are in the first 12 rows?

12-3 Arithmetic Sequences and Series

Find the 8th term of each arithmetic sequence.

17. 10.00, 10.11, 10.22, 10.33, ...
18. −5, −13, −21, −29, ...
19. $a_2 = 57.5$ and $a_5 = 80$
20. $a_{10} = 141$ and $a_{13} = 186$

Find the missing terms in each arithmetic sequence.

21. −23, ■, ■, −89
22. 31, ■, ■, ■, 79

Find the indicated sum for each arithmetic series

23. S_{10} for 40 + 30 + 20 + 10 + ⋯
24. $\sum_{k=5}^{8}4k$
25. $\sum_{k=1}^{11}(0.5k + 5.5)$
26. S_{14} for −6 −1 + 4 + 9 + ⋯
27. Suppose that you make a bank deposit of $1 the first week, $1.50 the second week, $2 the third week, and so on. How much will you contribute to the account on the last week of the year (52nd week)? What is the total amount that you have deposited in the bank after one year?

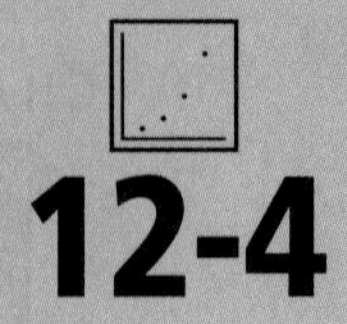

12-4 Geometric Sequences and Series

Objectives

Find terms of a geometric sequence, including geometric means.

Find the sums of geometric series.

Vocabulary

geometric sequence
geometric mean
geometric series

Who uses this?

Sporting-event planners can use geometric sequences and series to determine the number of matches that must be played in a tournament. (See Example 6.)

Serena Williams was the winner out of 128 players who began the 2003 Wimbledon Ladies' Singles Championship. After each match, the winner continues to the next round and the loser is eliminated from the tournament. This means that after each round only half of the players remain.

The number of players remaining after each round can be modeled by a *geometric sequence.* In a **geometric sequence**, the ratio of successive terms is a constant called the *common ratio r* $(r \neq 1)$. For the players remaining, r is $\frac{1}{2}$.

Term	a_1	a_2	a_3	a_4
Value	128	64	32	16

Ratios $\frac{64}{128} = \frac{1}{2}$ $\frac{32}{64} = \frac{1}{2}$ $\frac{16}{32} = \frac{1}{2}$

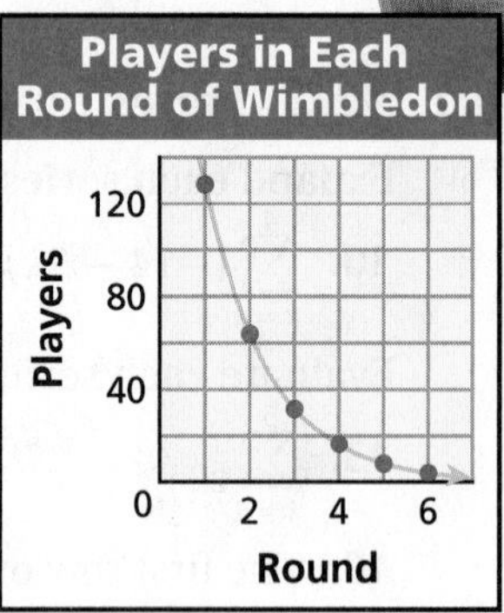

Recall that exponential functions have a common ratio. When you graph the ordered pairs (n, a_n) of a geometric sequence, the points lie on an exponential curve as shown. Thus, you can think of a geometric sequence as an exponential function with sequential natural numbers as the domain.

EXAMPLE 1 Identifying Geometric Sequences

Determine whether each sequence could be geometric or arithmetic. If possible, find the common ratio or difference.

A 8, 12, 18, 27, ...

8, 12, 18, 27

Diff. 4 6 9

Ratio $\frac{3}{2}$ $\frac{3}{2}$ $\frac{3}{2}$

It could be geometric, with $r = \frac{3}{2}$.

B 8, 16, 24, 32, ...

8, 16 24, 32

Diff. 8 8 8

Ratio 2 $\frac{3}{2}$ $\frac{4}{3}$

It could be arithmetic, with $d = 8$.

C 6, 10, 15, 21, ...

6, 10, 15, 21

Diff. 4 5 6

Ratio $\frac{5}{3}$ $\frac{3}{2}$ $\frac{7}{5}$

It is neither.

Determine whether each sequence could be geometric or arithmetic. If possible, find the common ratio or difference.

1a. $\frac{1}{4}, \frac{1}{12}, \frac{1}{36}, \frac{1}{108}, \ldots$

1b. 1.7, 1.3, 0.9, 0.5, ...

1c. −50, −32, −18, −8, ...

Each term in a geometric sequence is the product of the previous term and the common ratio, giving the recursive rule for a geometric sequence.

$$a_n = a_{n-1} r$$

nth term → a_n; First term → a_{n-1}; Common ratio → r

You can also use an explicit rule to find the *n*th term of a geometric sequence. Each term is the product of the first term and a power of the common ratio as shown in the table.

Tennis Players in Each Round of Wimbledon

Round	1	2	3	4	n
Players	128	64	32	16	a_n
Formula	$a_1 = 128\left(\frac{1}{2}\right)^0$	$a_2 = 128\left(\frac{1}{2}\right)^1$	$a_3 = 128\left(\frac{1}{2}\right)^2$	$a_4 = 128\left(\frac{1}{2}\right)^3$	$a_n = 128\left(\frac{1}{2}\right)^{n-1}$

This pattern can be generalized into a rule for all geometric sequences.

General Rule for Geometric Sequences

The *n*th term a_n of a geometric sequence is

$$a_n = a_1 r^{n-1},$$

where a_1 is the first term and r is the common ratio.

EXAMPLE 2 Finding the *n*th Term Given a Geometric Sequence

Find the 9th term of the geometric sequence −5, 10, −20, 40, −80, ...

Step 1 Find the common ratio.

$$r = \frac{a_2}{a_1} = \frac{10}{-5} = -2$$

Step 2 Write a rule, and evaluate for $n = 9$.

$a_n = a_1 r^{n-1}$ *General rule*

$a_9 = -5(-2)^{9-1}$ *Substitute −5 for a_1, 9 for n, and −2 for r.*

$= -5(256) = -1280$

The 9th term is −1280.

Check Extend the sequence.

$a_5 = -80$ *Given*

$a_6 = -80(-2) = 160$

$a_7 = 160(-2) = -320$

$a_8 = -320(-2) = 640$

$a_9 = 640(-2) = -1280$ ✓

Find the 9th term of each geometric sequence.

2a. $\frac{3}{4}, -\frac{3}{8}, \frac{3}{16}, -\frac{3}{32}, \frac{3}{64}, \ldots$

2b. 0.001, 0.01, 0.1, 1, 10, ...

EXAMPLE 3 Finding the *n*th Term Given Two Terms

Find the 10th term of the geometric sequence with $a_5 = 96$ and $a_7 = 384$.

Step 1 Find the common ratio.

$a_7 = a_5 r^{(7-5)}$	*Use the given terms.*
$a_7 = a_5 r^2$	*Simplify.*
$384 = 96r^2$	*Substitute 384 for a_7 and 96 for a_5.*
$4 = r^2$	*Divide both sides by 96.*
$\pm 2 = r$	*Take the square root of both sides.*

Caution!

When given two terms of a sequence, be sure to consider positive and negative values for *r* when necessary.

Step 2 Find a_1.

Consider both the positive and negative values for *r*.

$a_n = a_1 r^{n-1}$		$a_n = a_1 r^{n-1}$	*General rule*
$96 = a_1(2)^{5-1}$	or	$96 = a_1(-2)^{5-1}$	*Use $a_5 = 96$ and $r = \pm 2$.*
$6 = a_1$		$6 = a_1$	

Step 3 Write the rule and evaluate for a_{10}.

Consider both the positive and negative values for *r*.

$a_n = a_1 r^{n-1}$		$a_n = a_1 r^{n-1}$	*General rule*
$a_n = 6(2)^{n-1}$	or	$a_n = 6(-2)^{n-1}$	*Substitute for a_1 and r.*
$a_{10} = 6(2)^{10-1}$		$a_{10} = 6(-2)^{10-1}$	*Evaluate for $n = 6$.*
$a_{10} = 3072$		$a_{10} = -3072$	

The 10th term is 3072 or −3072.

Find the 7th term of the geometric sequence with the given terms.

3a. $a_4 = -8$ and $a_5 = -40$ **3b.** $a_2 = 768$ and $a_4 = 48$

Geometric means are the terms between any two nonconsecutive terms of a geometric sequence.

Geometric Mean

If *a* and *b* are positive terms of a geometric sequence with exactly one term between them, the geometric mean is given by the following expression.

$$\sqrt{ab}$$

EXAMPLE 4 Finding Geometric Means

Find the geometric mean of $\frac{1}{2}$ and $\frac{1}{32}$.

$$\sqrt{ab} = \sqrt{\left(\frac{1}{2}\right)\left(\frac{1}{32}\right)}$$

$$= \sqrt{\frac{1}{64}} = \frac{1}{8} \quad \textit{Use the formula.}$$

4. Find the geometric mean of 16 and 25.

The indicated sum of the terms of a geometric sequence is called a **geometric series**. You can derive a formula for the partial sum of a geometric series by subtracting the product of S_n and r from S_n as shown.

$$\begin{aligned} S_n &= a_1 + a_1 r + a_1 r^2 + \cdots + a_1 r^{n-1} \\ -rS_n &= \quad - a_1 r - a_1 r^2 - \cdots - a_1 r^{n-1} - a_1 r^n \\ \hline S_n - rS_n &= a_1 \qquad\qquad\qquad\qquad\qquad - a_1 r^n \\ S_n(1-r) &= a_1(1-r^n) \\ S_n &= a_1\left(\frac{1-r^n}{1-r}\right) \end{aligned}$$

Sum of the First *n* Terms of a Geometric Series

The partial sum S_n of the first n terms of a geometric series $a_1 + a_2 + \cdots + a_n$ is given by

$$S_n = a_1\left(\frac{1-r^n}{1-r}\right),\ r \neq 1$$

where a_1 is the first term and r is the common ratio.

Remember!

These sums are partial sums because you are finding the sum of a finite number of terms. In Lesson 12-5, you will find the sums of infinite geometric series.

EXAMPLE 5 Finding the Sum of a Geometric Series

Find the indicated sum for each geometric series.

A S_7 for $3 - 6 + 12 - 24 + \cdots$

Step 1 Find the common ratio.

$$r = \frac{a_2}{a_1} = \frac{-6}{3} = -2$$

Step 2 Find S_7 with $a_1 = 3$, $r = -2$, and $n = 7$.

$$S_n = a_1\left(\frac{1-r^n}{1-r}\right) \quad \textit{Sum formula}$$

$$S_7 = 3\left(\frac{1-(-2)^7}{1-(-2)}\right) \quad \textit{Substitute.}$$

$$= 3\left(\frac{1-(-128)}{3}\right)$$

$$= 129$$

Check Use a graphing calculator.

```
sum(seq(3(-2)^(X
-1),X,1,7,1))
                129
```

✔

B $\displaystyle\sum_{k=1}^{5}\left(\frac{1}{3}\right)^{k-1}$

Step 1 Find the first term.

$$a_1 = \left(\frac{1}{3}\right)^{1-1} = \left(\frac{1}{3}\right)^0 = 1$$

Step 2 Find S_5.

$$S_n = a_1\left(\frac{1-r^n}{1-r}\right) \quad \textit{Sum formula}$$

$$S_5 = 1\left(\frac{1-\left(\frac{1}{3}\right)^5}{1-\left(\frac{1}{3}\right)}\right) \quad \textit{Substitute.}$$

$$= \left(\frac{1-\left(\frac{1}{243}\right)}{\frac{2}{3}}\right)$$

$$= \frac{242}{243}\cdot\frac{3}{2} = \frac{121}{81} \approx 1.49$$

Check Use a graphing calculator.

```
sum(seq((1/3)^(X
-1),X,1,5,1))
         1.49382716
```

✔

Find the indicated sum for each geometric series.

5a. S_6 for $2 + 1 + \frac{1}{2} + \frac{1}{4} + \cdots$ **5b.** $\displaystyle\sum_{k=1}^{6} -3(2)^{k-1}$

EXAMPLE 6 Sports Application

The Wimbledon Ladies' Singles Championship begins with 128 players. The players compete until there is 1 winner. How many matches must be scheduled in order to complete the tournament?

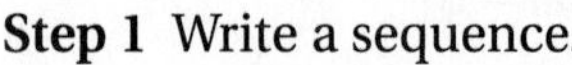

Step 1 Write a sequence.

Let n = the number of rounds,

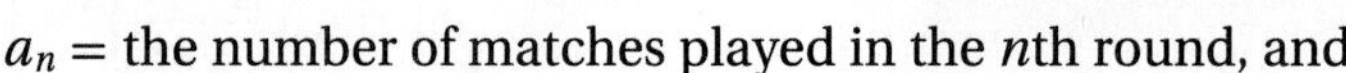

a_n = the number of matches played in the nth round, and

S_n = the total number of matches played through n rounds.

$$a_n = 64\left(\frac{1}{2}\right)^{n-1}$$ *The first round requires 64 matches, so $a_1 = 64$. Each successive match requires $\frac{1}{2}$ as many, so $r = \frac{1}{2}$.*

Remember!

For a review of solving exponential equations, see Lesson 7-5.

Step 2 Find the number of rounds required.

$$1 = 64\left(\frac{1}{2}\right)^{n-1}$$ *The final round will have 1 match, so substitute 1 for a_n.*

$$\frac{1}{64} = \left(\frac{1}{2}\right)^{n-1}$$ *Isolate the exponential expression by dividing by 64.*

$$\left(\frac{1}{2}\right)^{6} = \left(\frac{1}{2}\right)^{n-1}$$ *Express $\frac{1}{64}$ as a power of $\frac{1}{2}$: $\frac{1}{64} = \left(\frac{1}{2}\right)^6$.*

$$6 = n - 1$$ *Equate the exponents.*

$$7 = n$$ *Solve for n.*

Step 3 Find the total number of matches after 7 rounds.

$$S_7 = 64\left(\frac{1-\left(\frac{1}{2}\right)^7}{1-\left(\frac{1}{2}\right)}\right) = 127$$ *Sum function for geometric series.*

127 matches must be scheduled to complete the tournament.

CHECK IT OUT!

6. **Real Estate** A 6-year lease states that the annual rent for an office space is \$84,000 the first year and will increase by 8% each additional year of the lease. What will the total rent expense be for the 6-year lease?

THINK AND DISCUSS

1. Find the next three terms of the geometric sequence that begins 3, 6, ... Then find the next three terms of the arithmetic sequence that begins 3, 6, ...
2. Compare the geometric mean of 4 and 16 with the mean, or average.

3. **GET ORGANIZED** Copy and complete the graphic organizer. In each box, summarize your understanding of geometric sequences.

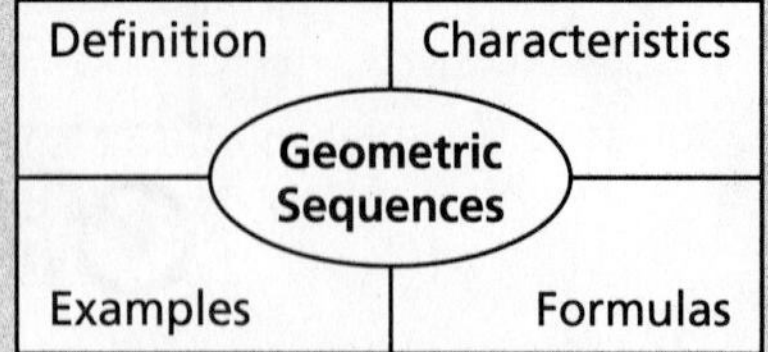

12-4 Exercises

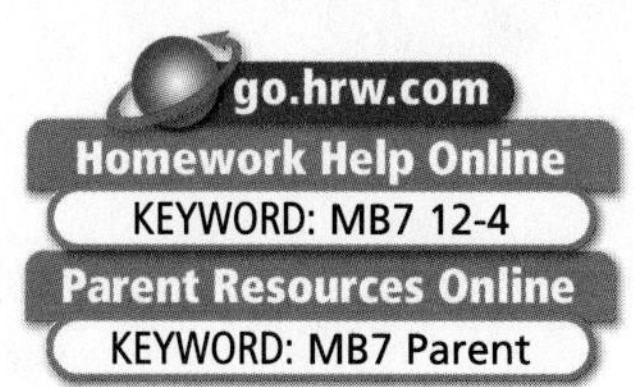

GUIDED PRACTICE

1. **Vocabulary** The term between two given terms in a geometric sequence is the __?__. (*geometric mean* or *geometric series*)

SEE EXAMPLE 1 p. 890

Determine whether each sequence could be geometric or arithmetic. If possible, find the common ratio or difference.

2. −10, −12, −14, −16, ...
3. $\frac{1}{2}$, 1, 2, 3, ...
4. −320, −80, −20, −5, ...

SEE EXAMPLE 2 p. 891

Find the 10th term of each geometric sequence.

5. 2, 6, 18, 54, 162, ...
6. 5000, 500, 50, 5, 0.5, ...
7. −0.125, 0.25, −0.5, 1, −2,...

SEE EXAMPLE 3 p. 892

Find the 6th term of the geometric sequence with the given terms.

8. $a_4 = -12, a_5 = -4$
9. $a_2 = 4, a_5 = 108$
10. $a_3 = 3, a_5 = 12$

SEE EXAMPLE 4 p. 892

Find the geometric mean of each pair of numbers.

11. 6 and $\frac{3}{8}$
12. 2 and 32
13. 12 and 192

SEE EXAMPLE 5 p. 893

Find the indicated sum for each geometric series.

14. S_6 for $2 + 0.2 + 0.02 + \cdots$
15. $\sum_{k=1}^{5} (-3)^{k-1}$
16. S_5 for $12 - 24 + 48 - 96 + \cdots$
17. $\sum_{k=1}^{9} 256\left(\frac{1}{2}\right)^{k-1}$

SEE EXAMPLE 6 p. 894

18. **Salary** In his first year, a math teacher earned $32,000. Each successive year, he earned a 5% raise. How much did he earn in his 20th year? What were his total earnings over the 20-year period?

PRACTICE AND PROBLEM SOLVING

Independent Practice

For Exercises	See Example
19–21	1
22–25	2
26–28	3
29–31	4
32–35	5
36	6

Extra Practice
Skills Practice p. S27
Application Practice p. S43

Determine whether each sequence could be geometric or arithmetic. If possible, find the common ratio or difference.

19. −36, −49, −64, −81, ...
20. −2, −6, −18, −54, ...
21. 2, 7, 12, 17, ...

Find the 9th term of each geometric sequence.

22. $\frac{1}{2}, \frac{1}{10}, \frac{1}{50}, \frac{1}{250}, \frac{1}{1250}, \ldots$
23. 3, −6, 12, −24, 48, ...
24. 3200, 1600, 800, 400, 200, ...
25. 8, 24, 72, 216, 648, ...

Find the 7th term of the geometric sequence with the given terms.

26. $a_4 = 54, a_5 = 162$
27. $a_5 = 13.5, a_6 = 20.25$
28. $a_4 = -4, a_6 = -100$

Find the geometric mean of each pair of numbers.

29. 9 and $\frac{1}{9}$
30. 18 and 2
31. $\frac{1}{5}$ and 45

Find the indicated sum for each geometric series.

32. S_6 for $1 + 5 + 25 + 125 + \cdots$
33. S_8 for $10 + 1 + \frac{1}{10} + \frac{1}{100} + \cdots$
34. $\sum_{k=1}^{6} -1\left(\frac{1}{3}\right)^{k-1}$
35. $\sum_{k=1}^{7} 8(10)^{k-1}$

36. **Genealogy** You have 2 biological parents, 4 biological grandparents, and 8 biological great grandparents.

a. How many direct ancestors do you have in the 6 generations before you? 12 generations?

b. **What if...?** How does the explicit rule change if you are considered the first generation?

LINK

Collectibles

The most expensive rock'n'roll memorabilia ever purchased was John Lennon's Rolls Royce, with a price tag of $2.2 million.

Given each geometric sequence, (a) write an explicit rule for the sequence, (b) find the 10th term, and (c) find the sum of the first 10 terms.

37. $\frac{1}{16}, \frac{1}{8}, \frac{1}{4}, \frac{1}{2}, \ldots$

38. 4, 0.4, 0.04, 0.004, ...

39. 8, 16, 32, 64, ...

40. $-22, -11, -\frac{11}{2}, -\frac{11}{4}, \ldots$

41. 162, −54, 18, −6, ...

42. 12.5, 62.5, 312.5, 1562.5, ...

43. **Collectibles** Louis bought a vintage Rolling Stones concert shirt for $20. He estimates that the shirt will increase in value by 15% per year.

a. How much is the shirt worth after 4 years? after 8 years?

b. Does the shirt increase more in value during the first 4 years or the second 4 years? Explain.

44. **College Tuition** New grandparents decide to pay for their granddaughter's college education. They give the girl a penny on her first birthday and double the gift on each subsequent birthday. How much money will the girl receive when she is 18? 21? Will the money pay for her college education? Explain.

45. **Technology** You receive an e-mail asking you to forward it to 5 other people to ensure good luck. Assume that no one breaks the chain and that there are no duplications among the recipients. How many e-mails will have been sent after 10 generations, including yours, have received and sent the e-mail?

46. **Fractals** The Sierpinski carpet is a fractal based on a square. In each iteration, the center of each shaded square is removed.

a. Given that the area of the original square is 1 square unit, write a sequence for the area of the *n*th iteration of the Sierpinski carpet.

b. In which iteration will the area be less than $\frac{1}{2}$ of the original area?

47. **Paper** A piece of paper is 0.1 mm thick. When folded, the paper is twice as thick.

a. Studies have shown that you can fold a piece of paper a maximim of 7 times. How thick will the paper be if it is folded on top of itself 7 times?

b. Assume that you could fold the paper as many times as you want. How many folds would be required for the paper to be taller than Mount Everest (8850 m)?

48. **Measurement** Several common U.S. paper sizes are shown in the table.

a. Examine the length and width measures for the different paper sizes. What interrelationships do you observe?

b. How are the areas for each paper size (from A to E) mathematically related and what name is this relationship given?

Common U.S. Paper Sizes

U.S. Paper Size	Dimensions (in.)
A (letter)	$8\frac{1}{2} \times 11$
B (ledger)	11×17
C	17×22
D	22×34
E	34×44

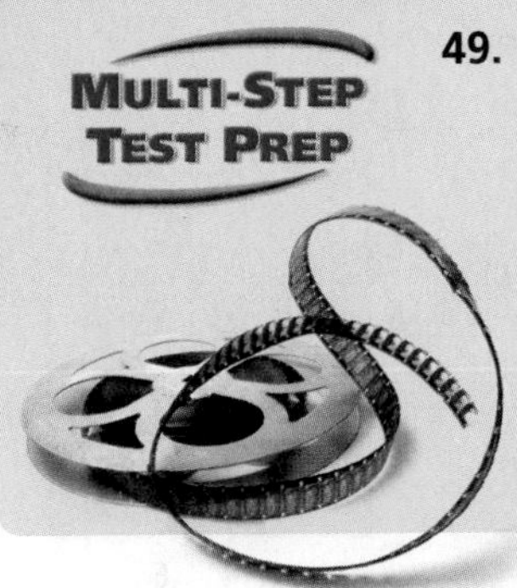

49. This problem will prepare you for the Multi-Step Test Prep on page 908.

A movie earned \$60 million in its first week of release and \$9.6 million in the third week of release. The sales each week can be modeled by a geometric sequence.

a. Estimate the movie's sales in its second week of release.

b. By what percent did the sales decrease each week?

c. In what week would you expect sales to be less than \$1 million?

d. Estimate the movie's total sales during its 8-week release period.

50. **Biology** The population growth of bacteria in a petri dish each hour creates a geometric sequence. After 1 hour there were 4 bacteria cells, and after 5 hours there were 324 cells. How many cells were found at hours 2, 3, and 4?

51. **Critical Thinking** Find an arithmetic sequence, a geometric sequence, and a sequence that is neither arithmetic nor geometric that begins 1, 4, ...

52. **Finance** Suppose that you pay \$750 in rent each month. Suppose also that your rent is increased by 10% each year thereafter.

a. Write a series that describes the total rent paid each year over the first 5 years, and find its sum.

b. Use sigma notation to represent the series for the total rent paid each year over the first 10 years, and evaluate it.

53. **Music** The frequencies produced by playing C notes in ascending octaves make up a geometric sequence. C0 is the lowest C note audible to the human ear.

a. The note commonly called middle C is C4. Find the frequency of middle C.

b. Write a geometric sequence for the frequency of C notes in hertz where $n = 1$ represents C1.

c. Humans cannot hear sounds with frequencies greater than 20,000 Hz. What is the first C note that humans cannot hear?

Scale of C's

Note	Frequency (Hz)
C0	16.24
C1	32.7
C2	65.4
C3	130.8
C4	■

54. **Medicine** During a flu outbreak, a hospital recorded 16 cases the first week, 56 cases the second week, and 196 cases the third week.

a. Write a geometric sequence to model the flu outbreak.

b. If the hospital did nothing to stop the outbreak, in which week would the total number infected exceed 10,000?

55. **Graphing Calculator** Use the **SEQ** and **SUM** features to find each indicated sum of the geometric series $8 + 6 + 4.5 + \cdots$ to the nearest thousandth.

a. S_{10} b. S_{20} c. S_{30} d. S_{40}

e. Does the series appear to be approaching any particular value? Explain.

56. **Critical Thinking** If a geometric sequence has $r > 1$, what happens to the terms as n increases? What happens if $0 < r < 1$?

57. **Write About It** What happens to the terms of a geometric sequence when the first term is tripled? What happens to the sum of this geometric sequence?

58. Find the sum of the first 6 terms for the geometric series $4.5 + 9 + 18 + 36 + \cdots$.

Ⓐ 67.5 Ⓑ 144 Ⓒ 283.5 Ⓓ 445.5

59. Which graph might represent the terms of a geometric sequence?

Ⓕ

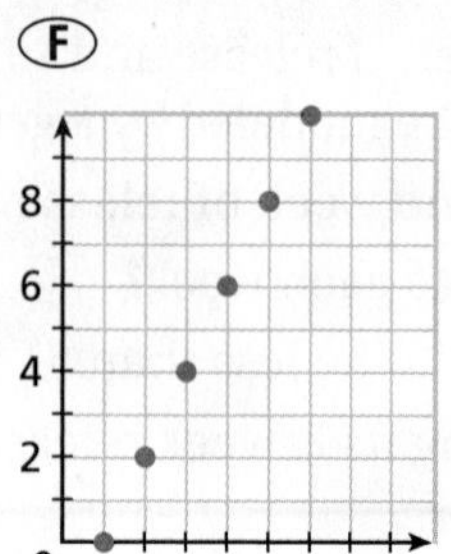

Ⓖ

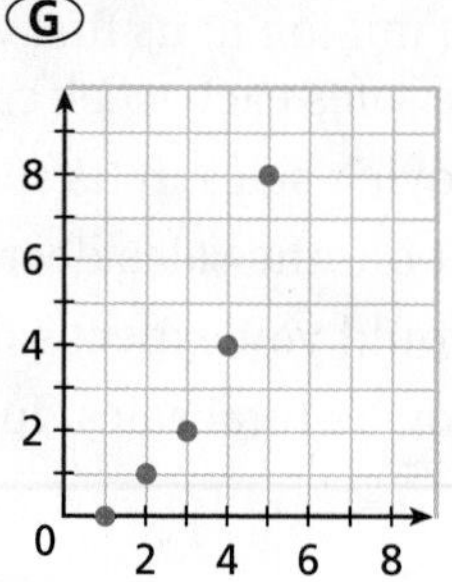

Ⓗ

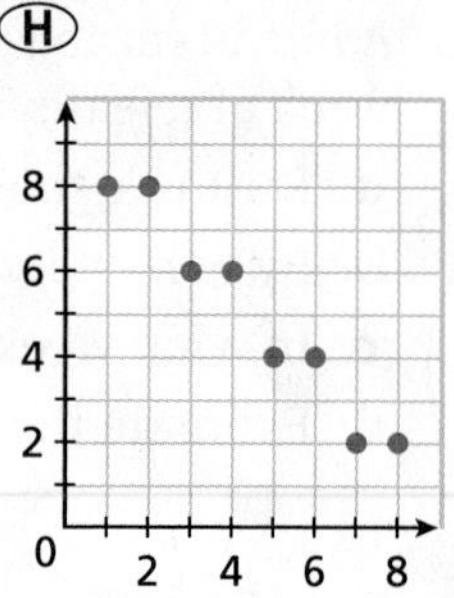

Ⓙ

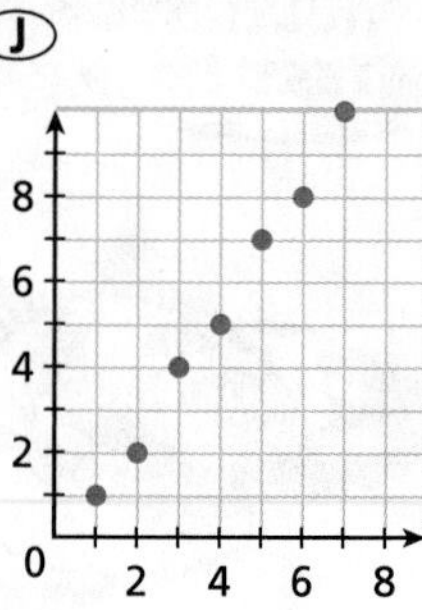

60. Find the first 3 terms of the geometric sequence with $a_7 = -192$ and $a_9 = -768$.

Ⓐ 3, −6, 12

Ⓑ −3, 12, −48

Ⓒ −3, 6, −12 or −3, −6, −12

Ⓓ 3, −12, 48 or −3, −12, −48

61. Which represents the sum of the series 10 − 15 + 22.5 − 33.75 + 50.625?

Ⓕ $\sum_{k=1}^{5} 10\left(\frac{3}{2}\right)^{k-1}$

Ⓗ $\sum_{k=1}^{5} -10\left(\frac{3}{2}\right)^{k-1}$

Ⓖ $\sum_{k=1}^{5} 10\left(-\frac{3}{2}\right)^{k-1}$

Ⓙ $\sum_{k=1}^{5} 10\left(-\frac{3}{2}\right)^{k}$

62. **Short Response** Why does the general rule for a geometric sequence use $n - 1$ instead of n? Explain.

CHALLENGE AND EXTEND

Graphing Calculator **For each geometric sequence, find the first term with a value greater than 1,000,000.**

63. $a_1 = 10$ and $r = 2$

64. $a_1 = \frac{1}{4}$ and $r = 4$

65. $a_1 = 0.01$ and $r = 3.2$

66. The sum of three consecutive terms of a geometric sequence is 73.5. If the product of these terms is 2744, what are the terms?

67. Consider the geometric sequence whose first term is 55 with the common ratio $\frac{1+\sqrt{5}}{2}$.

a. Find the next 5 terms rounded to the nearest integer.

b. Add each pair of successive terms together. What do you notice?

c. Make a conjecture about this sequence.

SPIRAL REVIEW

Identify the zeros and asymptotes of each function. *(Lesson 8-2)*

68. $f(x) = \frac{x^2 + 2x - 3}{x + 1}$

69. $f(x) = \frac{x + 5}{x^2 - x - 6}$

70. $f(x) = \frac{x^2 - 16}{4x}$

71. **Shopping** During a summer sale, a store gives a 20% discount on all merchandise. On Mondays, the store takes another 10% off of the sale price. *(Lesson 9-4)*

a. Write a composite function to represent the cost on Monday of an item with an original price of x dollars.

b. Find the cost on Monday of an item originally priced at $275.

Find the 10th term of each arithmetic sequence. *(Lesson 12-3)*

72. 78, 65, 52, 39, 26, ...

73. 1.7, 7.3, 12.9, 18.5, 24.1, ...

74. 9.42, 9.23, 9.04, 8.85, 8.66, ...

75. 16.4, 26.2, 36, 45.8, 55.6, ...

Explore Infinite Geometric Series

You can explore infinite geometric series by using a sequence of squares.

Use with Lesson 12-5

Activity

1. On a piece of graph paper, draw a 16×16 unit square. Note that its perimeter is 64 units.
2. Starting at one corner of the original square, draw a new square with side lengths half as long, or in this case, 8×8 units. Note that its perimeter is 32 units.
3. Create a table as shown at right. Fill in the perimeters and the cumulative sum of the perimeters that you have found so far.

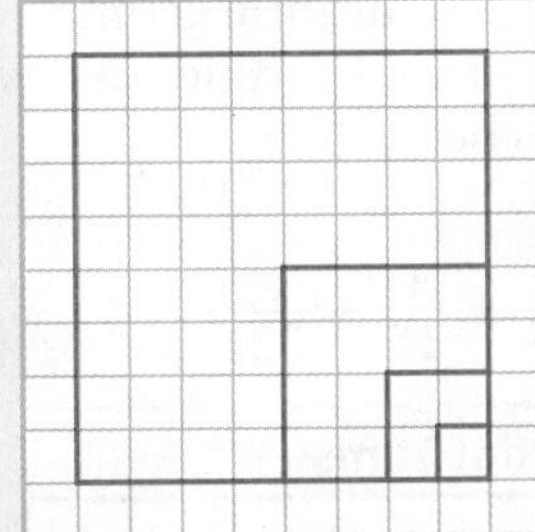

Square	Perimeter	Sum
16×16	64	64
8×8	32	96
4×4	■	■
2×2	■	■
1×1	■	■
$\frac{1}{2} \times \frac{1}{2}$	■	■

Try This

1. Copy the table, and complete the first 6 rows.
2. Use summation notation to write a geometric series for the perimeters.
3. Use a graphing calculator to find the sum of the first 20 terms of the series.
4. **Make a Conjecture** Make a conjecture about the sum of the perimeter series if it were to continue indefinitely.
5. Evaluate $\frac{64}{1 - \frac{1}{2}}$. How does this relate to your answer to Problem 4?
6. Copy and complete the table by finding the area of each square and the cumulative sums.
7. Use summation notation to write a geometric series for the areas.
8. Use a graphing calculator to find the sum of the first 10 terms of the series.
9. **Make a Conjecture** Make a conjecture about the sum of the area series if it were to continue indefinitely.
10. Evaluate $\frac{256}{1 - \frac{1}{4}}$. How does this relate to your answer to Problem 9?
11. **Draw a Conclusion** Write a formula for the sum of an infinite geometric sequence.

Square	Area	Sum
16×16	■	■
8×8	■	■
4×4	■	■
2×2	■	■
1×1	■	■
$\frac{1}{2} \times \frac{1}{2}$	■	■

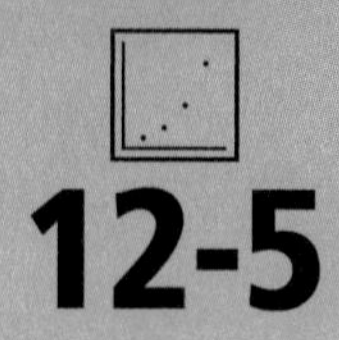

12-5 Mathematical Induction and Infinite Geometric Series

Objectives
Find sums of infinite geometric series.
Use mathematical induction to prove statements.

Vocabulary
infinite geometric series
converge
limit
diverge
mathematical induction

Why learn this?
You can use infinite geometric series to explore repeating patterns. (See Exercise 58.)

In Lesson 12-4, you found partial sums of geometric series. You can also find the sums of some infinite geometric series. An **infinite geometric series** has infinitely many terms. Consider the two infinite geometric series below.

$$S_n = \frac{1}{2} + \frac{1}{4} + \frac{1}{8} + \frac{1}{16} + \frac{1}{32} + \cdots$$

Partial Sums						
n	1	2	3	4	5	6
S_n	$\frac{1}{2}$	$\frac{3}{4}$	$\frac{7}{8}$	$\frac{15}{16}$	$\frac{31}{32}$	$\frac{63}{64}$

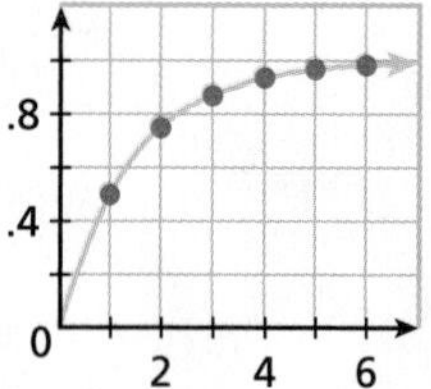

$$R_n = \frac{1}{32} + \frac{1}{16} + \frac{1}{8} + \frac{1}{4} + \frac{1}{2} + \cdots$$

Partial Sums						
n	1	2	3	4	5	6
R_n	$\frac{1}{32}$	$\frac{3}{32}$	$\frac{7}{32}$	$\frac{15}{32}$	$\frac{31}{32}$	$\frac{63}{32}$

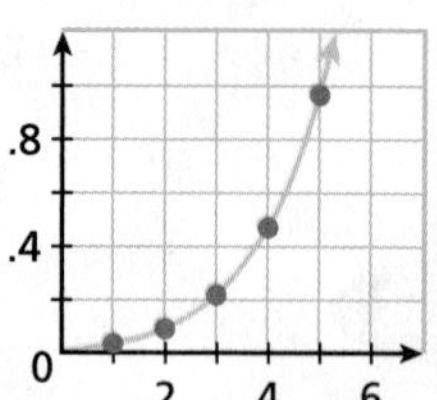

Notice that the series S_n has a common ratio of $\frac{1}{2}$ and the partial sums get closer and closer to 1 as n increases. When $|r| < 1$ and the partial sum approaches a fixed number, the series is said to **converge**. The number that the partial sums approach, as n increases, is called a **limit**.

For the series R_n, the opposite applies. Its common ratio is 2, and its partial sums increase toward infinity. When $|r| \geq 1$ and the partial sum does not approach a fixed number, the series is said to **diverge**.

EXAMPLE 1 Finding Convergent or Divergent Series

Determine whether each geometric series converges or diverges.

A $20 + 24 + 28.8 + 34.56 + \cdots$

$$r = \frac{24}{20} = 1.2, |r| \geq 1$$

The series diverges and does not have a sum.

B $1 + \frac{1}{3} + \frac{1}{9} + \frac{1}{27} + \frac{1}{81} + \cdots$

$$r = \frac{\frac{1}{3}}{1} = \frac{1}{3}, |r| < 1$$

The series converges and has a sum.

Determine whether each geometric series converges or diverges.

1a. $\frac{2}{3} + 1 + \frac{3}{2} + \frac{9}{4} + \frac{27}{8} + \cdots$ **1b.** $32 + 16 + 8 + 4 + 2 + \cdots$

If an infinite series converges, we can find the sum. Consider the series $S_n = \frac{1}{2} + \frac{1}{4} + \frac{1}{8} + \frac{1}{16} + \frac{1}{32} + \cdots$ from the previous page. Use the formula for the partial sum of a geometric series with $a_1 = \frac{1}{2}$ and $r = \frac{1}{2}$.

$$S_n = a_1\left(\frac{1-r^n}{1-r}\right) = \frac{1}{2}\left(\frac{1-\left(\frac{1}{2}\right)^n}{1-\frac{1}{2}}\right) = \frac{1\left(1-\left(\frac{1}{2}\right)^n\right)}{2\left(\frac{1}{2}\right)} = \frac{1-\left(\frac{1}{2}\right)^n}{1} = 1-\left(\frac{1}{2}\right)^n$$

Graph the simplified equation on a graphing calculator. Notice that the sum levels out and converges to 1.

As n approaches infinity, the term $\left(\frac{1}{2}\right)^n$ approaches zero. Therefore, the sum of the series is 1. This concept can be generalized for all convergent geometric series and proved by using calculus.

Sum of an Infinite Geometric Series

The sum of an infinite geometric series S with common ratio r and $|r| < 1$ is

$$S = \frac{a_1}{1-r},$$

where a_1 is the first term.

EXAMPLE 2 Finding the Sums of Infinite Geometric Series

Find the sum of each infinite geometric series, if it exists.

A $5 + 4 + 3.2 + 2.56 + \cdots$

$r = 0.8$ *Converges: $|r| < 1$*

$S = \frac{a_1}{1-r}$ *Sum formula*

$= \frac{5}{1-0.8} = \frac{5}{0.2} = 25$

Check Graph $y = 5\left(\frac{1-(0.8)^x}{1-0.8}\right)$ on a graphing calculator. The graph approaches $y = 25$. ✔

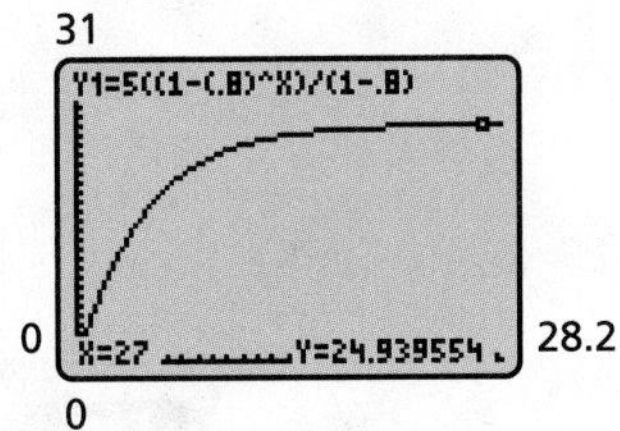

Helpful Hint

You can graph a geometric series by using the sum formula from Lesson 12-4: $S_n = a_1\left(\frac{1-r^n}{1-r}\right)$ with S_n as y and n as x and with values substituted for r and a_1.

B $\sum_{k=1}^{\infty} \frac{2}{3^{k-1}}$

$\sum_{k=1}^{\infty} \frac{2}{3^{k-1}} = \frac{2}{1} + \frac{2}{3} + \frac{2}{9} + \cdots$ *Evaluate.*

$r = \frac{\frac{2}{3}}{2} = \frac{2}{6} = \frac{1}{3}$ *Converges: $|r| < 1$*

$S = \frac{a_1}{1-r} = \frac{2}{1-\frac{1}{3}} = \frac{2}{\frac{2}{3}} = \frac{6}{2} = 3$

Check Graph $y = 2\left(\frac{1-\left(\frac{1}{3}\right)^x}{1-\frac{1}{3}}\right)$ on a graphing calculator. The graph approaches $y = 3$. ✔

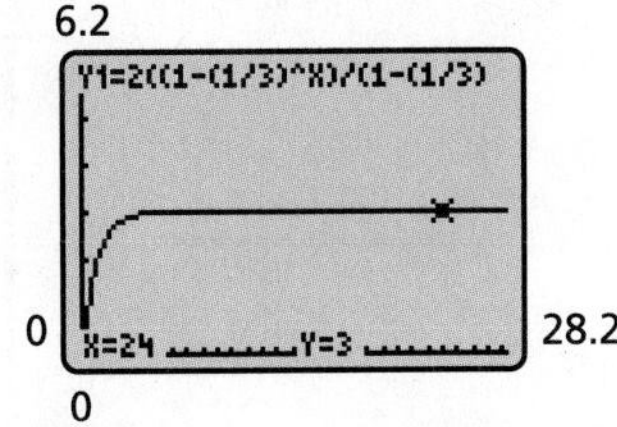

Find the sum of each infinite geometric series, if it exists.

2a. $25 - 5 + 1 - \frac{1}{5} + \frac{1}{25} - \cdots$ **2b.** $\sum_{k=1}^{\infty} \left(\frac{2}{5}\right)^k$

You can use infinite series to write a repeating decimal as a fraction.

EXAMPLE 3 Writing Repeating Decimals as Fractions

Write 0.232323... as a fraction in simplest form.

Step 1 Write the repeating decimal as an infinite geometric series.

$0.232323... = 0.23 + 0.0023 + 0.000023 + \cdots$ *Use the pattern for the series.*

Step 2 Find the common ratio.

$$r = \frac{0.0023}{0.23}$$

$$= \frac{1}{100}, \text{ or } 0.01$$

$|r| < 1$; the series converges to a sum.

Step 3 Find the sum.

$$S = \frac{a_1}{1 - r}$$ *Apply the sum formula.*

$$= \frac{0.23}{1 - 0.01} = \frac{0.23}{0.99} = \frac{23}{99}$$

Check Use a calculator to divide the fraction $\frac{23}{99}$. ✔

Remember!

Recall that every repeating decimal, such as 0.232323..., or $0.\overline{23}$, is a rational number and can be written as a fraction.

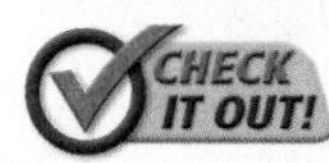

3. Write 0.111... as a fraction in simplest form.

You have used series to find the sums of many sets of numbers, such as the first 100 natural numbers. The formulas that you used for such sums can be proved by using a type of mathematical proof called **mathematical induction**.

Proof by Mathematical Induction

To prove that a statement is true for all natural numbers *n*,

Step 1 The base case: Show that the statement is true for $n = 1$.

Step 2 Assume that the statement is true for a natural number *k*.

Step 3 Prove that the statement is true for the natural number $k + 1$.

EXAMPLE 4 Proving with Mathematical Induction

Use mathematical induction to prove that the sum of the first n natural numbers is $1 + 2 + 3 + \cdots + n = \frac{n(n+1)}{2}$.

Step 1 Base case: Show that the statement is true for $n = 1$.

$$1 = \frac{n(n+1)}{2} = \frac{1(1+1)}{2} = \frac{2}{2} = 1$$ *The base case is true.*

Step 2 Assume that the statement is true for a natural number *k*.

$$1 + 2 + 3 + \cdots + k = \frac{k(k+1)}{2}$$ *Replace n with k.*

Step 3 Prove that it is true for the natural number $k + 1$.

$$1 + 2 + \cdots + k = \frac{k(k+1)}{2}$$

$$1 + 2 + \cdots + k + (k+1) = \frac{k(k+1)}{2} + (k+1)$$ *Add the next term $(k + 1)$ to each side.*

$$= \frac{k(k+1)}{2} + \frac{2(k+1)}{2}$$ *Find the common denominator.*

$$= \frac{k(k+1) + 2(k+1)}{2}$$ *Add numerators.*

$$= \frac{(k+1)(k+2)}{2}$$ *Factor out $k + 1$.*

$$= \frac{(k+1)[(k+1)+1]}{2}$$ *Write with $k + 1$.*

Therefore, $1 + 2 + 3 + \cdots + n = \frac{n(n+1)}{2}$.

4. Use mathematical induction to prove that the sum of the first n odd numbers is $1 + 3 + 5 + \cdots + (2n - 1) = n^2$.

Mathematical statements that seem to be true may in fact be false. By finding a counterexample, you can disprove a statement.

EXAMPLE 5 Using Counterexamples

Helpful Hint

Often counter-examples can be found using special numbers like 1, 0, negative numbers, or fractions.

Identify a counterexample to disprove $2^n \geq n^2$, where n is a real number.

$2^0 \geq (0)^2$	$2^1 \geq (1)^2$	$2^4 \geq (4)^2$	$2^{-1} \geq (-1)^2$
$1 \geq 0$ ✔	$2 \geq 1$ ✔	$24 \geq 16$ ✔	$\frac{1}{2} \geq 1$ ✘

$2^n \geq n^2$ is not true for $n = -1$, so it is not true for all real numbers.

5. Identify a counterexample to disprove $\frac{a^2}{2} \leq 2a + 1$, where a is a real number.

THINK AND DISCUSS

1. Explain how to determine whether a geometric series converges or diverges.

2. Explain how to represent the repeating decimal $0.8\overline{3}$ as an infinite geometric series.

3. GET ORGANIZED Copy and complete the graphic organizer. Summarize the different infinite geometric series.

	Example	Common Ratio	Sum
Convergent Series			
Divergent Series			

12-5 Exercises

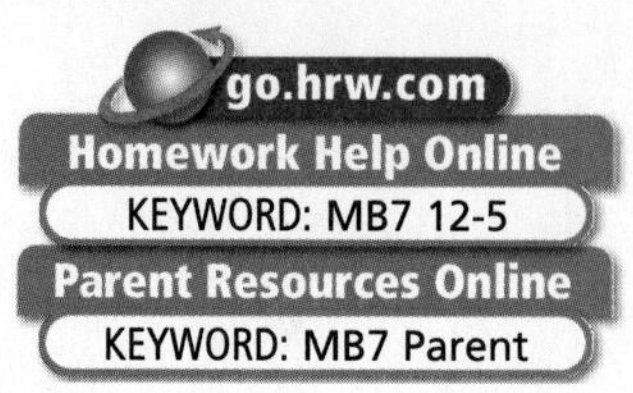

GUIDED PRACTICE

1. **Vocabulary** An infinite geometric series whose sum approaches a fixed number is said to __?__. (*converge* or *diverge*)

SEE EXAMPLE 1 p. 900

Determine whether each geometric series converges or diverges.

2. $1 - \frac{1}{3} + \frac{1}{9} - \frac{1}{27} + \frac{1}{81} + \cdots$
3. $1 - 5 + 25 - 125 + 625 + \cdots$
4. $27 + 18 + 12 + 8 + \cdots$

SEE EXAMPLE 2 p. 901

Find the sum of each infinite geometric series, if it exists.

5. $\frac{3}{4} + \frac{1}{2} + \frac{1}{3} + \frac{2}{9} + \cdots$
6. $\sum_{k=1}^{\infty} 4(0.25)^k$
7. $800 + 200 + 50 + \cdots$

SEE EXAMPLE 3 p. 902

Write each repeating decimal as a fraction in simplest form.

8. $0.888\ldots$
9. $0.\overline{56}$
10. $0.131313\ldots$

SEE EXAMPLE 4 p. 902

11. Use mathematical induction to prove that the sum of the first n even numbers is $2 + 4 + 6 + \cdots + 2n = n(n + 1)$.

SEE EXAMPLE 5 p. 903

Identify a counterexample to disprove each statement, where n is a real number.

12. $n^4 \geq 1$
13. $\log n > 0$
14. $n^3 \leq 3n^2$

PRACTICE AND PROBLEM SOLVING

Independent Practice

For Exercises	See Example
15–17	1
18–20	2
21–23	3
24	4
25–27	5

Extra Practice

Skills Practice p. S27
Application Practice p. S43

Determine whether each geometric series converges or diverges.

15. $3 + \frac{3}{5} + \frac{3}{25} + \frac{3}{125} + \frac{3}{625} + \cdots$
16. $5 + 10 + 20 + 40 + \cdots$
17. $2 - 4 + 8 - 16 + 32 + \cdots$

Find the sum of each infinite geometric series, if it exists.

18. $\sum_{k=1}^{\infty} 60\left(\frac{1}{10}\right)^k$
19. $\frac{8}{5} - \frac{4}{5} + \frac{2}{5} - \frac{1}{5} + \cdots$
20. $\sum_{k=1}^{\infty} 3.5^k$

Write each repeating decimal as a fraction in simplest form.

21. $0.\overline{6}$
22. $0.90909\ldots$
23. $0.541541541\ldots$
24. Use mathematical induction to prove
$$\frac{1}{1(2)} + \frac{1}{2(3)} + \frac{1}{3(4)} + \cdots + \frac{1}{n(n+1)} = \frac{n}{n+1}.$$

Identify a counterexample to disprove each statement, where a is a real number.

25. $a^3 \neq -a^2$
26. $a^4 > 0$
27. $5a^2 > 2^a$
28. **ERROR ANALYSIS** Two possible sums for the series $\frac{1}{5} + \frac{2}{5} + \frac{4}{5} + \cdots$ are shown. Which is incorrect? Explain the error.

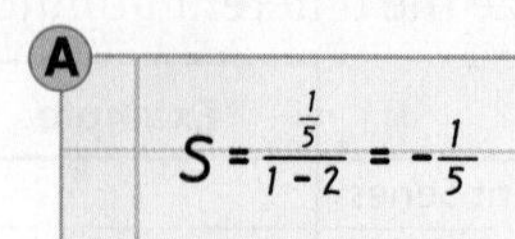

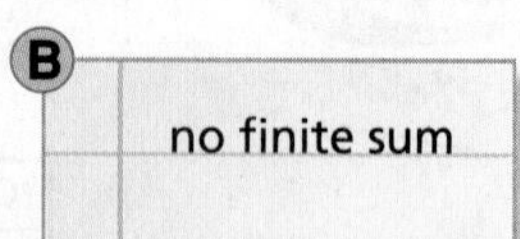

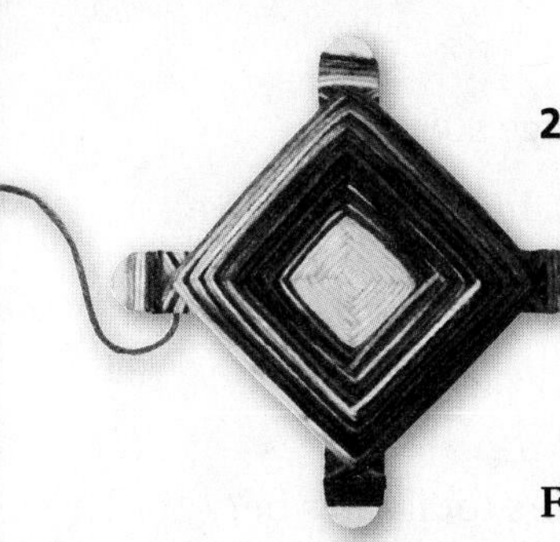

29. **Art** Ojos de Dios are Mexican holiday decorations. They are made of yarn, which is wrapped around sticks in a repeated square pattern. Suppose that the side length of the outer square is 8 inches. The side length of each inner square is 90% of the previous square's length. How much yarn will be required to complete the decoration? (Assume that the pattern is represented by an infinite geometric series.)

Find the sum of each infinite geometric series, if it exists.

30. $215 - 86 + 34.4 - 13.76 + \cdots$

31. $500 + 400 + 320 + \cdots$

32. $8 - 10 + 12.5 - 15.625 + \cdots$

33. $\sum_{k=1}^{\infty} -5\left(\frac{1}{8}\right)^{k-1}$

34. $\sum_{k=1}^{\infty} 2\left(\frac{1}{4}\right)^{k-1}$

35. $\sum_{k=1}^{\infty} \left(\frac{5}{3}\right)^{k-1}$

36. $-25 - 30 - 36 - 43.2 + \cdots$

37. $\sum_{k=1}^{n} 200(0.6)^{k-1}$

38. **Geometry** A circle of radius r has smaller circles drawn inside it as shown. Each smaller circle has half the radius of the previous circle.
    a. Write an infinite geometric series in terms of r that expresses the circumferences of the circles, and find its sum.
    b. Find the sum of the circumferences for the infinite set of circles if the first circle has a radius of 3 cm.

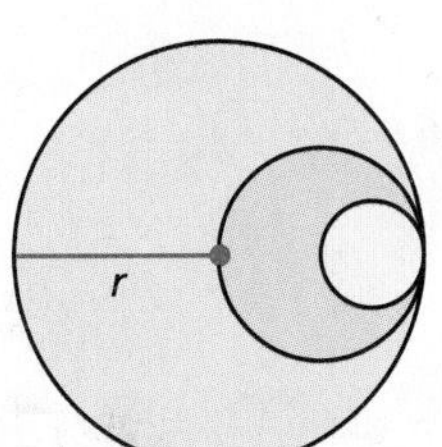

Write each repeating decimal as a fraction in simplest form.

39. $0.\overline{4}$

40. $0.\overline{9}$

41. $0.\overline{123}$

42. $0.\overline{18}$

43. $0.\overline{5}$

44. $0.\overline{054}$

45. **Music** Due to increasing online downloads, CD sales have declined in recent years. Starting in 2001, the number of CDs shipped each year can be modeled by a geometric sequence.
    a. Estimate the number of CDs that will be shipped in 2010.
    b. Estimate the total number of CDs shipped from 2001 through 2010.
    c. Suppose that the geometric series continued indefinitely. Find the total number of CDs shipped from 2001.

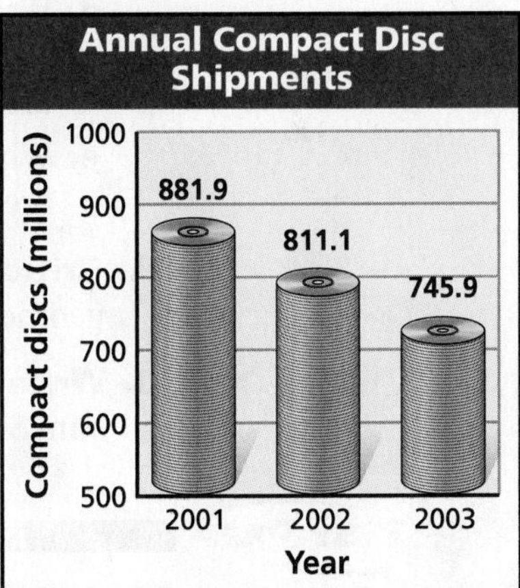

Use mathematical induction to prove each statement.

46. $1 + 2 + 4 + \cdots + 2^{n-1} = 2^n - 1$

47. $1 + 4 + \cdots + n^2 = \frac{n(n+1)(2n+1)}{6}$

48. $1(2) + 2(3) + 2(4) + \cdots + n(n+1) = \frac{n(n+1)(n+2)}{3}$

49. $\frac{1}{2} + \frac{1}{4} + \frac{1}{8} + \cdots + \left(\frac{1}{2}\right)^n = 1 - \left(\frac{1}{2}\right)^n$

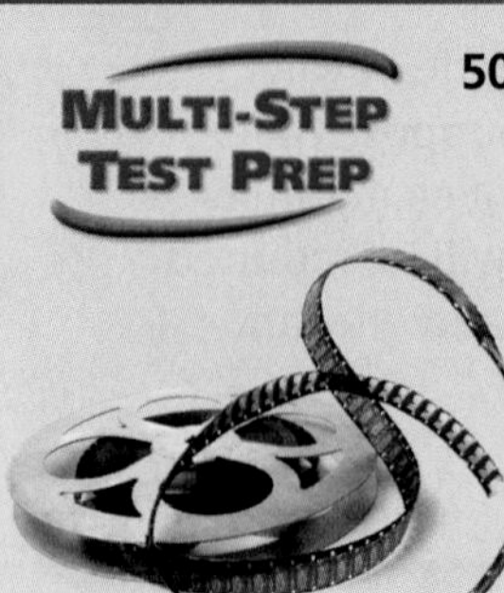

MULTI-STEP TEST PREP

50. This problem will prepare you for the Multi-Step Test Prep on page 908.

A movie earned \$80 million in the first week that it was released. In each successive week, sales declined by about 40%.

a. Write a general rule for a geometric sequence that models the movie's sales each week.

b. Estimate the movie's total sales in the first 6 weeks.

c. If this pattern continued indefinitely, what would the movie's total sales be?

51. Game Shows Imagine that you have just won the grand prize on a game show. You can choose between two payment options as shown. Which would you choose, and why?

PRIZE PAYMENT OPTIONS	
A.	**B.**
\$1 million the first year and half of the previous year's amount for eternity	**\$100,000 a year for 20 years**

Identify a counterexample to disprove each statement, where x is a real number.

52. $\dfrac{x^4}{x^3} \le 2x$ **53.** $x^4 - 1 \ge 0$ **54.** $\ln x^5 > \ln x$

55. $2x^2 \le 3x^3$ **56.** $2x^2 - x \ge 0$ **57.** $12x - x^2 > 25$

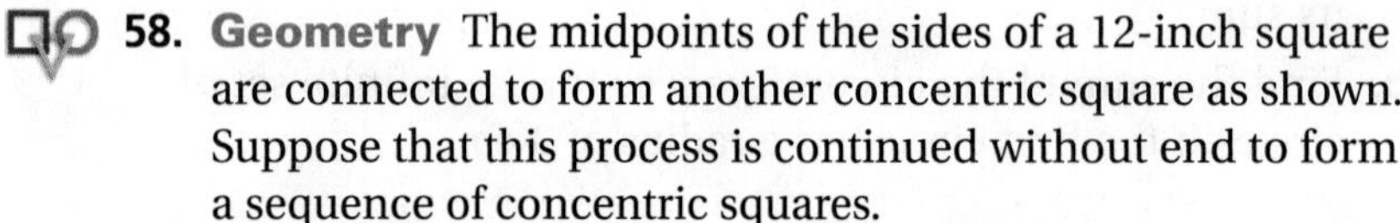

58. Geometry The midpoints of the sides of a 12-inch square are connected to form another concentric square as shown. Suppose that this process is continued without end to form a sequence of concentric squares.

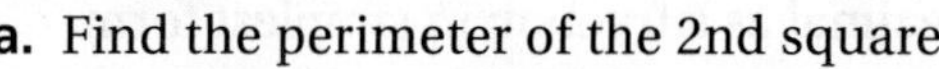

a. Find the perimeter of the 2nd square.

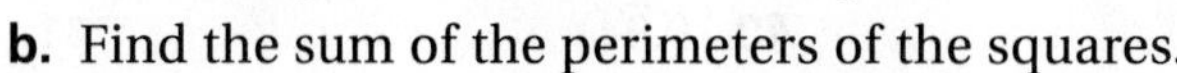

b. Find the sum of the perimeters of the squares.

c. Find the sum of the areas of the squares.

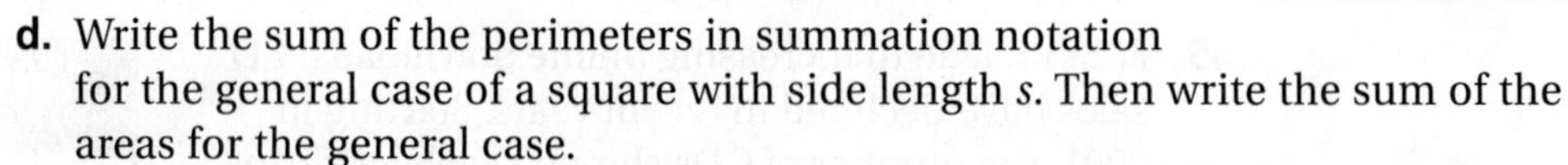

d. Write the sum of the perimeters in summation notation for the general case of a square with side length s. Then write the sum of the areas for the general case.

e. Which series decreases faster, the sum of the perimeters or the sum of the areas? How do you know?

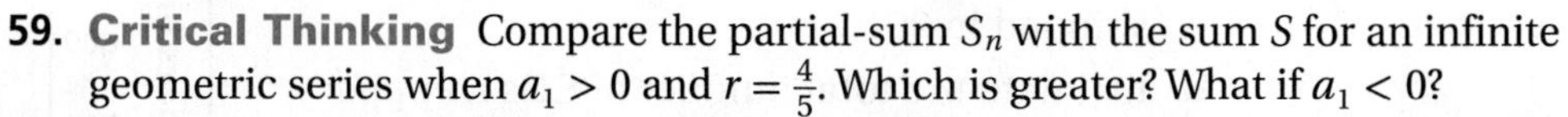

59. Critical Thinking Compare the partial-sum S_n with the sum S for an infinite geometric series when $a_1 > 0$ and $r = \frac{4}{5}$. Which is greater? What if $a_1 < 0$?

60. Write About It Why might the notation for a partial sum S_n change for the sum S for an infinite geometric series?

TEST PREP

61. Which infinite geometric series converges?

Ⓐ $\sum_{k=1}^{\infty}\left(\frac{5}{4}\right)^k$ Ⓑ $\sum_{k=1}^{\infty}5\left(\frac{1}{4}\right)^k$ Ⓒ $\sum_{k=1}^{\infty}\frac{1}{4}(5)^k$ Ⓓ $\sum_{k=1}^{\infty}\left(\frac{1}{4}\right)^k 5^k$

62. What is the sum of the infinite geometric series $1 - \frac{1}{2} + \frac{1}{4} - \frac{1}{8} + \frac{1}{16} + \cdots$?

Ⓕ 2   Ⓖ $\frac{2}{3}$ Ⓗ $\frac{1}{2}$ Ⓙ $\frac{1}{3}$

63. An infinite geometric series has a sum of 180 and a common ratio of $\frac{2}{3}$. What is the first term of the series?

Ⓐ 60   Ⓑ 120   Ⓒ 270   Ⓓ 540

64. Which graph represents a converging infinite geometric series?

Ⓕ 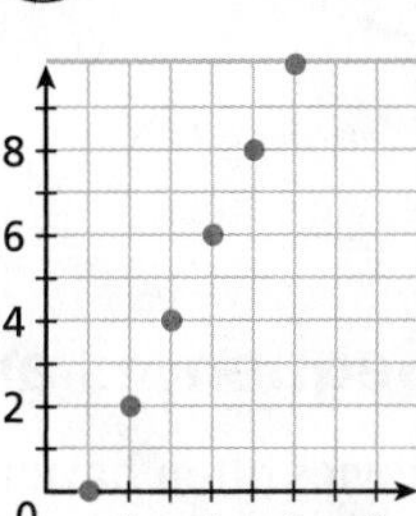

Ⓖ 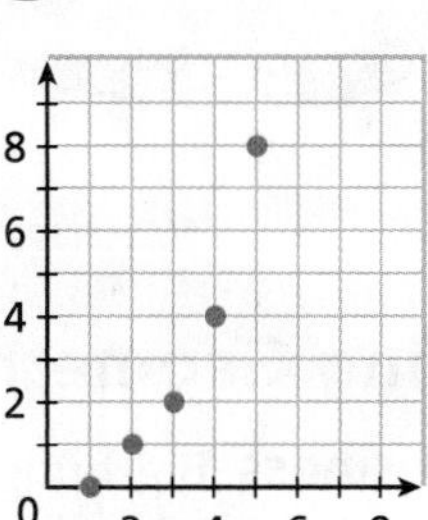

Ⓗ 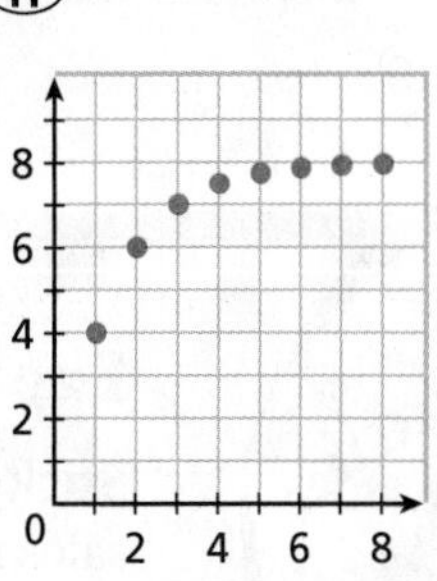

Ⓙ 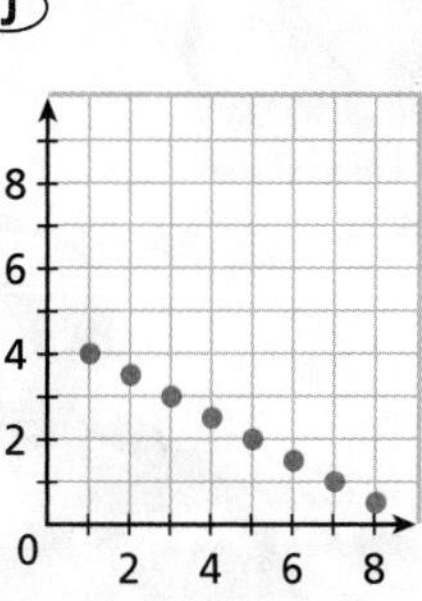

65. **Extended Response** Use mathematical induction to prove $3 + 5 + \cdots + (2n + 1) = n(n + 2)$. Show all of your work.

CHALLENGE AND EXTEND

Write each repeating decimal as a fraction in simplest form.

66. $0.1\overline{6}$ **67.** $0.41\overline{6}$ **68.** $0.5\overline{286}$

69. Critical Thinking Can an infinite arithmetic series approach a limit like an infinite geometric series? Explain why or why not.

70. Geometry Consider the construction that starts with a 12-inch square and contains concentric squares as indicated. Notice that a spiral is formed by the sequence of segments starting at a corner and moving inward as each midpoint is reached. A second similar spiral determines the area shown in blue.

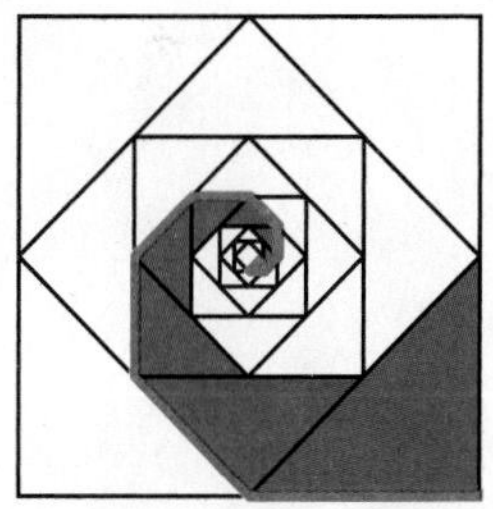

a. Use the sum of a series to find the length of the spiral indicated in red.

b. Use the sum of a series to find the polygonal area indicated in blue.

c. Is your answer to the sum of the polygonal area in part **b** reasonable? Explain.

SPIRAL REVIEW

71. Football A kickoff specialist kicks 80% of his kickoffs into the end zone. What is the probability that he kicks at least 4 out of 5 of his next kickoffs into the end zone? *(Lesson 11-6)*

72. Geometry Consider the pattern of figures shown. *(Lesson 12-3)*

a. Find the number of dots in each of the next 3 figures in the pattern.

b. Write a general rule for the sequence of the number of dots in the nth figure.

c. How many dots will be in the 22nd figure in the pattern?

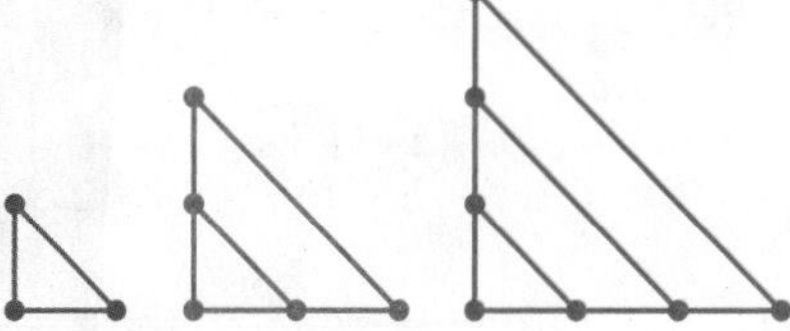

Determine whether each sequence could be geometric or arithmetic. If possible, find the common ratio or difference. *(Lesson 12-4)*

73. 297, 99, 33, 11, … **74.** $\frac{4}{3}, \frac{8}{3}, 4, \frac{16}{3}, \ldots$

75. 25, 100, 250, 1000, … **76.** 4, 4.8, 5.76, 6.912, …

CHAPTER 12

MULTI-STEP TEST PREP

SECTION 12B

Exploring Geometric Sequences and Series

Sticky Business Big-budget movies often have their greatest sales in the first weekend, and then weekend sales decrease with each passing week. After a movie has been released for a few weeks, movie studios may try to predict the total sales that the movie will generate.

Weekend Box Office Sales (million $)		
Weekend	***Spider-Man***	***Spider-Man 2***
1	114.9	115.8
2	71.4	45.2
3	45.0	24.8

1. Find the ratios of the sequences of weekend sales for *Spider-Man* and *Spider-Man 2*.
2. Write the rule for a geometric sequence that could be used to estimate the sales for *Spider-Man* in a given weekend.
3. Use the sequence from Problem 2 to predict *Spider-Man's* weekend sales for weeks 4 and 5.
4. Write and evaluate a series in summation notation to find *Spider-Man's* total weekend sales for the first 5 weekends of its release.
5. Suppose that the series from Problem 4 continued infinitely. Estimate the total weekend sales for *Spider-Man*. The actual total weekend sales for *Spider-Man* were about $311.1 million. How does this compare with your estimate?
6. Would a geometric sequence be a good model for the weekend sales of *Spider-Man 2*? Justify your answer.

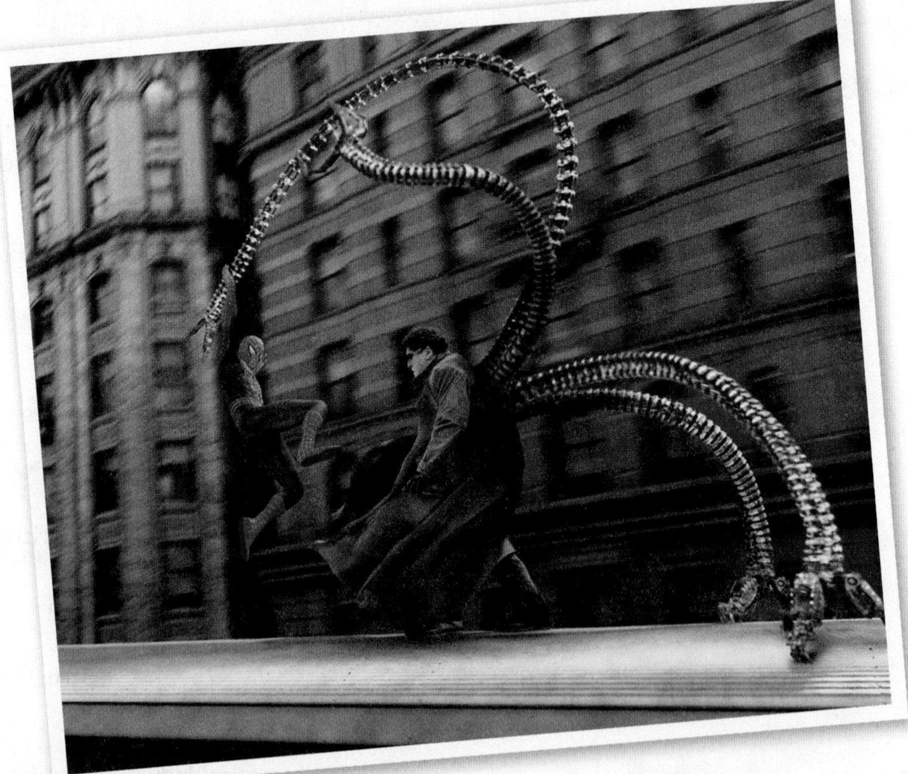

READY TO GO ON?

Quiz for Lessons 12-4 Through 12-5

12-4 Geometric Sequences and Series

Find the 8th term of each geometric sequence.

1. $\frac{2}{5}, \frac{6}{5}, \frac{18}{5}, \frac{54}{5}, \ldots$
2. $-16, -40, -100, -250, \ldots$
3. $-1, 11, -121, 1331, \ldots$
4. $2, 20, 200, 2000, \ldots$

Find the 10th term of each geometric sequence with the given terms.

5. $a_1 = 3.3$ and $a_2 = 33$
6. $a_4 = -1$ and $a_6 = -4$
7. $a_6 = 20.25$ and $a_8 = 9$
8. $a_3 = 57$ and $a_5 = 513$

Find the geometric mean of each pair of numbers.

9. $\frac{1}{3}$ and $\frac{1}{27}$
10. 4.5 and 450
11. 32 and $\frac{1}{8}$

Find the indicated sum for each geometric series.

12. S_6 for $8 - 16 + 32 - 64 + \cdots$
13. S_5 for $1 + \frac{2}{3} + \frac{4}{9} + \frac{8}{27} + \cdots$
14. $\sum_{k=1}^{7} (8)^k$
15. $\sum_{k=1}^{5} 18\left(\frac{1}{6}\right)^{k-1}$
16. The cost for electricity is expected to rise at an annual rate of 8%. In its first year, a business spends \$3000 for electricity.
    a. How much will the business pay for electricity in the 6th year?
    b. How much in total will be paid for electricity over the first 6 years?

12-5 Mathematical Induction and Infinite Geometric Series

Find the sum of each infinite series, if it exists.

17. $25 + 20 + 16 + 12.8 + \cdots$
18. $15 - 18 + 21.6 - 25.92 + \cdots$
19. $\sum_{k=1}^{\infty} (-1)^k \left(\frac{2}{3}\right)^k$
20. $\sum_{k=1}^{\infty} 4(0.22)^k$

Use mathematical induction to prove $4 + 8 + 12 + \cdots + 4n = 2n(n + 1)$.

21. Step 1
22. Step 2
23. Step 3
24. A table-tennis ball is dropped from a height of 5 ft. The ball rebounds to 60% of its previous height after each bounce.
    a. Write an infinite geometric series to represent the distance that the ball travels after it initially hits the ground. (*Hint:* The ball travels up and down on each bounce.)
    b. What is the total distance that the ball travels after it initially hits the ground?

EXTENSION Area Under a Curve

Objective
Approximate area under a curve by using rectangles.

Finding the area under a curve is an important topic in higher mathematics, such as calculus. You can approximate the area under a curve by using a series of rectangles as shown in Example 1.

EXAMPLE 1 Finding Area Under a Curve

Estimate the area under the curve $f(x) = -\frac{1}{2}x^2 + 2x + 3\frac{1}{8}$ over $0 \le x \le 5$.

Graph the function. Divide the area into 5 rectangles, each with a width of 1 unit.

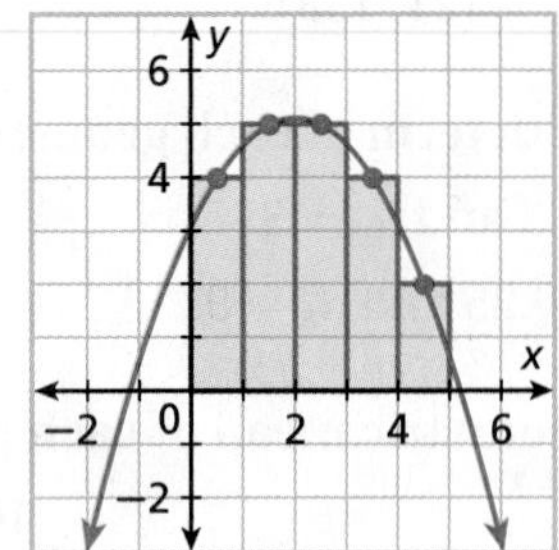

x	$f(x)$
0.5	4
1.5	5
2.5	5
3.5	4
4.5	2

Remember!
Area is measured in square units.

Find the height of each rectangle by evaluating the function at the center of each rectangle, as shown in the table.

Approximate the area by finding the sum of the areas of the rectangles.

$A \approx 1(4) + 1(5) + 1(5) + 1(4) + 1(2) = 20$

The estimate of 20 square units is very close to the actual area of $19\frac{19}{24}$ square units, which can be found by using calculus.

1. Estimate the area under the curve $f(x) = -x^2 + 5x + 5.75$ over $0 \le x \le 6$. Use 6 intervals.

You can formalize the procedure for finding the area under the curve of a function by using the sum of a series.

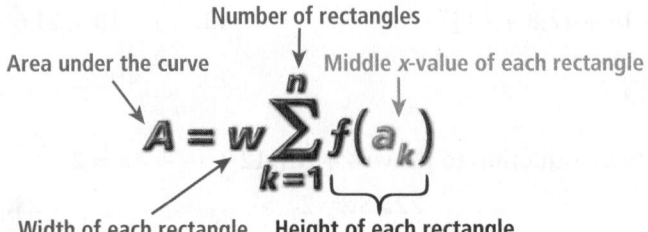

Number of rectangles

Area under the curve

Middle x-value of each rectangle

$$A = w\sum_{k=1}^{n} f(a_k)$$

Width of each rectangle

Height of each rectangle

EXAMPLE 2 Finding Area Under a Curve by Using a Series

Use the sum of a series to estimate the area under the curve $f(x) = -x^2 + 50x$ over $0 \le x \le 50$.

Step 1 Graph the function.

Step 2 Divide the area into 5 rectangles, each with a width of 10 units.

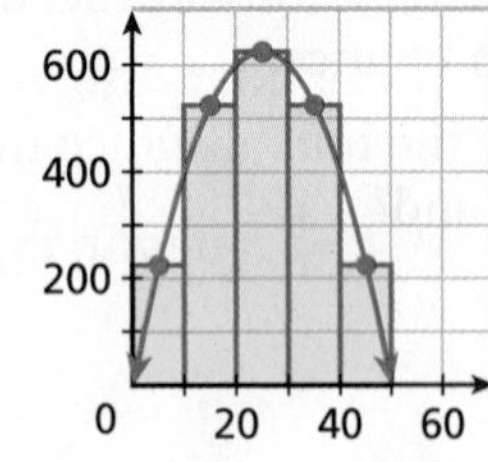

a_k	$f(a_k)$
$a_1 = 5$	225
$a_2 = 15$	525
$a_3 = 25$	625
$a_4 = 35$	525
$a_5 = 45$	225

Step 3 Find the value of the function at the center of each rectangle, as shown in the table.

Step 4 Write the sum that approximates the area.

$$A \approx 10\sum_{k=1}^{5} f(a_k) = 10\left[f(a_1) + f(a_2) + f(a_3) + f(a_4) + f(a_5)\right]$$
$$= 10\left[(225) + (525) + (625) + (525) + (225)\right]$$
$$= 10(2125) = 21{,}250$$

The estimated area is 21,250 square units.

2. Use the sum of a series to estimate the area under the curve $f(x) = -x^2 + 9x + 3$ over $0 \le x \le 9$. Use 3 intervals.

EXTENSION Exercises

Estimate the area under each curve. Use 4 intervals.

1. $f(x) = -\frac{1}{2}x^2 + 12x + 2$ over $0 \le x \le 24$

2. $f(x) = -x^2 + 8x + 4$ over $0 \le x \le 8$

3. $f(x) = -\frac{1}{4}x^2 + 5x$ over $0 \le x \le 16$

4. $f(x) = -0.1x^2 + 20x$ over $0 \le x \le 200$

Use the sum of a series to estimate the area under each curve. Use 5 intervals.

5. $f(x) = -x^2 + 10x + 5$ over $0 \le x \le 10$

6. $f(x) = -x^2 + 30x$ over $0 \le x \le 20$

7. $f(x) = -\frac{1}{10}x^2 + 400$ over $0 \le x \le 50$

8. $f(x) = -0.2x^2 + 28x + 300$ over $0 \le x \le 150$

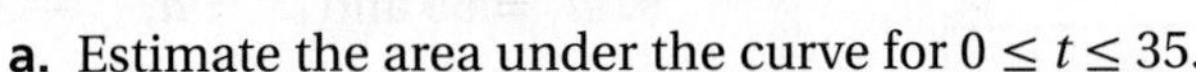

9. Physics The graph shows a car's speed versus time as the car accelerates. This realistic curve can be approximated by $v(t) = -0.1t^2 + 7.3t$, where v is the velocity in feet per second and t is the time in seconds.

a. Estimate the area under the curve for $0 \le t \le 35$.

b. What does the area under the curve represent? Explain. (*Hint:* Consider the units of your answer to part **a.**)

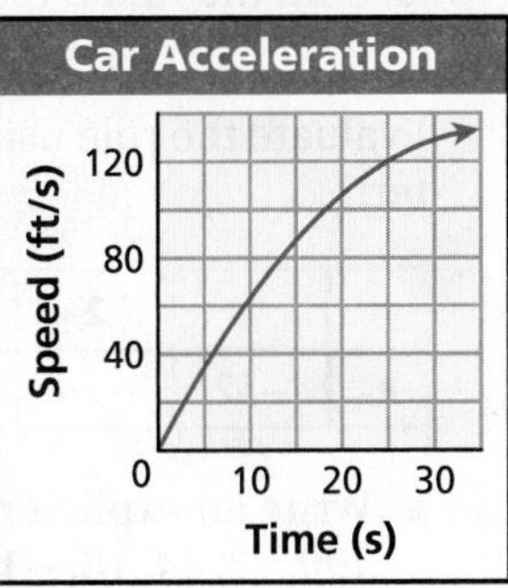

10. Energy Conservation Daily electricity use peaks in the early afternoon and can be approximated by a parabola. Suppose that the rate of electricity use in kilowatts (kW) is modeled by the function $f(x) = -1.25x^2 + 30x + 700$, where x represents the time in hours.

a. Write a sum to represent the area under the curve for a domain of $0 \le x \le 24$.

b. Estimate the area under the curve.

11. Write About It Explain how the units of the values on the x-axis and the units of the values on the y-axis can be used to find the units that apply to the area under a curve.

12. Critical Thinking For a given function and domain, how would increasing the number of rectangles affect the approximation of the area under the curve?

CHAPTER 12

Study Guide: Review

Vocabulary

Complete the sentences below with vocabulary words from the list above.

1. A(n) ___?___ has a common difference, and a(n) ___?___ has a common ratio.
2. A series that has no limit ___?___, whereas a series that approaches a limit ___?___.
3. A(n) ___?___ defines the nth term. A(n) ___?___ defines the next term by using one or more of the previous terms.
4. A(n) ___?___ continues without end, and a(n) ___?___ has a last term.
5. Each step in a repeated process is called a(n) ___?___.

12-1 Introduction to Sequences *(pp. 862–868)*

EXAMPLES

■ **Find the first 5 terms of the sequence with $a_1 = -52$; $a_n = 0.5a_{n-1} + 2$.**

Evaluate the rule using each term to find the next term.

n	1	2	3	4	5
a_n	−52	−24	−10	−3	0.5

■ **Write an explicit rule for the nth term of 100, 72, 44, 16, −12, ...**

Examine the differences or ratios.

Terms	100	72	44	16	−12
1st differences		28	28	28	28

The first differences are constant, so the sequence is linear.

The first term is 100, and each term is 28 less than the previous term.

The explicit rule is $a_n = 100 - 28(n - 1)$.

EXERCISES

Find the first 5 terms of each sequence.

6. $a_n = n - 9$
7. $a_n = \frac{1}{2}n^2$
8. $a_n = \left(-\frac{3}{2}\right)^{n-1}$
9. $a_1 = 55$ and $a_n = a_{n-1} - 2$
10. $a_1 = 200$ and $a_n = \frac{1}{5}a_{n-1}$
11. $a_1 = -3$ and $a_n = -3a_{n-1} + 1$

Write a possible explicit rule for the nth term of each sequence.

12. −4, −8, −12, −16, −20, ...
13. 5, 20, 80, 320, 1280, ...
14. −24, −19, −14, −9, −4, ...
15. 27, 18, 12, 8, $\frac{16}{3}$, ...
16. **Sports** Suppose that a basketball is dropped from a height of 3 ft. If the ball rebounds to 70% of its height after each bounce, how high will the ball reach after the 4th bounce? the 9th bounce?

12-2 Series and Summation Notation (pp. 870–877)

EXAMPLES

- **Expand $\sum_{k=1}^{5}(-1)^{n+1}(11-2n)$, and evaluate.**

$$\sum_{k=1}^{5}(-1)^{n+1}(11-2n) = (-1)^2(11-2) + (-1)^3(11-4) + (-1)^4(11-6) + (-1)^5(11-8) + (-1)^6(11-10)$$

$$= 9 - 7 + 5 - 3 + 1$$

$$= 5 \quad \textit{Simplify.}$$

- **Evaluate $\sum_{k=1}^{8} k^2$.**

Use summation formula for a quadratic series.

$$\sum_{k=1}^{8} k^2 = \frac{n(n+1)(2n+1)}{6}$$

$$= \frac{8(8+1)(2\cdot 8+1)}{6} = \frac{72(17)}{6} = 204$$

EXERCISES

Expand each series and evaluate.

17. $\sum_{k=1}^{4} k^2(-1)^k$

18. $\sum_{k=1}^{5}(0.5k+4)$

19. $\sum_{k=1}^{5}(-1)^{k+1}(2k-1)$

20. $\sum_{k=1}^{4}\frac{5k}{k^2}$

Evaluate each series.

21. $\sum_{k=1}^{8} -5$

22. $\sum_{k=1}^{10} k^2$

23. $\sum_{k=1}^{12} k$

24. **Finance** A household has a monthly mortgage payment of \$1150. How much is paid by the household after 2 years? 15 years?

12-3 Arithmetic Sequences and Series (pp. 879–887)

EXAMPLES

- **Find the 12th term for the arithmetic sequence 85, 70, 55, 40, 25, ….**

Find the common difference:
$d = 70 - 85 = -15.$

$a_n = a_1 + (n-1)d$ *General rule*

$a_{12} = 85 + (12-1)(-15)$ *Substitute.*

$= -80$ *Simplify.*

- **Find $\sum_{k=1}^{11}(-2-33k)$.**

Find the 1st and 11th terms.

$a_1 = -2 - 33(1) = -35$

$a_{11} = -2 - 33(11) = -365$

Find S_{11}.

$S_n = n\left(\frac{a_1 + a_n}{2}\right)$ *Sum formula*

$S_{11} = 11\left(\frac{-35-365}{2}\right)$ *Substitute.*

$= -2200$

EXERCISES

Find the 11th term of each arithmetic sequence.

25. 23, 19, 15, 11, …

26. $\frac{1}{5}, \frac{3}{5}, 1, \frac{7}{5}, \frac{9}{5}, \ldots$

27. −9.2, −8.4, −7.6, −6.8, …

28. $a_3 = 1.5$ and $a_4 = 5$

29. $a_6 = 47$ and $a_8 = 21$

30. $a_5 = -7$ and $a_9 = 13$

Find the indicated sum for each arithmetic series.

31. S_{18} for $-1 - 5 - 9 - 13 + \cdots$

32. S_{12} for $\frac{1}{3} + \frac{1}{6} + 0 - \frac{1}{6} + \cdots$

33. $\sum_{k=1}^{15}(-14+3k)$

34. $\sum_{k=1}^{15}\left(\frac{3}{2}k + 10\right)$

35. **Savings** Kelly has \$50 and receives \$8 a week for allowance. He wants to save all of his money to buy a new mountain bicycle that costs \$499. Write an arithmetic sequence to represent the situation. Then find whether Kelly will be able to buy the new bicycle after one year (52 weeks).

12-4 Geometric Sequences and Series *(pp. 890–898)*

EXAMPLES

- **Find the 8th term of the geometric sequence 6, 24, 96, 384, ….**

Find the common ratio. $r = \frac{24}{6} = 4$

Write a rule, and evaluate for $n = 8$.

$a_n = a_1 r^{n-1}$ *General rule*

$a_8 = 6(4)^{8-1} = 98{,}304$

- **Find the 8th term of the geometric sequence with $a_4 = -1000$ and $a_6 = -40$.**

Step 1 Find the common ratio.

$a_6 = a_4 r^{(6-4)}$ *Use the given terms.*

$-40 = -1000r^2$ *Substitute.*

$\frac{1}{25} = r^2$ *Simplify.*

$\pm\frac{1}{5} = r$

Step 2 Find a_1 using both possible values for r.

$-1000 = a_1\left(\frac{1}{5}\right)^{4-1}$ or $-1000 = a_1\left(-\frac{1}{5}\right)^{4-1}$

$a_1 = -125{,}000$ or $a_1 = 125{,}000$

Step 3 Write the rule and evaluate for a_8 by using both possible values for r.

$a_n = a_1 r^{n-1}$ $\qquad a_n = a_1 r^{n-1}$

$a_n = -125{,}000\left(\frac{1}{5}\right)^{n-1}$ or $a_n = 125{,}000\left(-\frac{1}{5}\right)^{n-1}$

$a_8 = -125{,}000\left(\frac{1}{5}\right)^{8-1}$ $\qquad a_8 = 125{,}000\left(-\frac{1}{5}\right)^{8-1}$

$a_8 = -1.6$ $\qquad a_8 = -1.6$

- **Find $\sum_{k=1}^{7} -2(5)^{k-1}$.**

Find the common ratio. $r = \frac{a_2}{a_1} = \frac{-6}{3} = -2$

Find S_7

$S_n = a_1\left(\frac{1-r^n}{1-r}\right)$ *Sum formula*

$S_7 = 3\left(\frac{1-(-2)^7}{1-(-2)}\right)$ *Substitute.*

$= 3\left(\frac{1-(-128)}{3}\right) = 129$

EXERCISES

Find the 8th term of each geometric sequence.

36. 40, 4, 0.4, 0.04, 0.004, …
37. $\frac{1}{18}, \frac{1}{6}, \frac{1}{2}, \frac{3}{2}, \ldots$
38. −16, −8, −4, −2, …
39. −6, 12, −24, 48, …

Find the 9th term of the geometric sequence with the given terms.

40. $a_3 = 24$ and $a_4 = 96$
41. $a_1 = \frac{2}{3}$ and $a_2 = -\frac{4}{3}$
42. $a_4 = -1$ and $a_6 = -4$
43. $a_3 = 4$ and $a_6 = 500$

Find the geometric mean of each pair of numbers.

44. 10 and 2.5
45. $\frac{1}{2}$ and 8
46. $\frac{\sqrt{3}}{96}$ and $\frac{\sqrt{3}}{6}$
47. $\frac{5}{12}$ and $\frac{125}{108}$

Find the indicated sum for each geometric series.

48. S_5 for $1 + \frac{1}{3} + \frac{1}{9} + \frac{1}{27} + \cdots$
49. S_6 for $-\frac{4}{5} + 8 - 80 + 800 + \cdots$
50. $\sum_{k=1}^{8} (4)^{k-1}$
51. $\sum_{k=1}^{7} -2(5)^{k-1}$
52. $\sum_{k=1}^{6} 60\left(-\frac{1}{2}\right)^{k-1}$
53. $\sum_{k=1}^{5} 18\left(\frac{1}{2}\right)^{k-1}$
54. **Depreciation** A new photocopier costs $9000 and depreciates each year such that it retains only 65% of its preceding year's value. What is the value of the photocopier after 5 years?
55. **Rent** A one-bedroom apartment rents for $650 a month. The rent is expected to increase by 6% per year.
    a. What will be the annual rent expense on the apartment after 5 years?
    b. What will be the total amount spent on rent if a person rents the apartment for the entire 5-year period?

12-5 Mathematical Induction and Infinite Geometric Series (pp. 900–907)

EXAMPLES

Find the sum of each infinite series, if it exists.

■ $-9261 + 441 - 21 + 1 + \cdots$

$r = \frac{441}{-9261} = -\frac{1}{21}$ *Converges: $|r| < 1$*

$S = \frac{a_1}{1 - r}$ *Sum formula*

$= \frac{-9261}{1 - \left(-\frac{1}{21}\right)} = \frac{-9261}{\frac{22}{21}}$

$= -\frac{194{,}481}{22}$, or $-8840.0\overline{45}$

■ $\sum_{k=1}^{\infty} -5\left(\frac{7}{10}\right)^{k-1}$

$= -5 - \frac{35}{10} - \frac{245}{100} + \cdots$ *Evaluate.*

$r = \frac{-\frac{35}{10}}{-5} = \frac{7}{10}$ *Converges: $|r| < 1$*

$S = \frac{a_1}{1 - r} = \frac{-5}{1 - \frac{7}{10}} = \frac{-5}{\frac{3}{10}} = -\frac{50}{3}$, or $-16.\overline{6}$

■ **Use mathematical induction to prove $2 + 5 + \cdots + (3n - 1) = \frac{n}{2}(3n + 1)$.**

Step 1 Base case: Show that the statement is true for $n = 1$.

$2 = \frac{n}{2}(3n + 1) = \frac{1}{2}(3 \cdot 1 + 1) = 2$ *True*

Step 2 Assume that the statement is true for a natural number k.

$2 + 5 + \cdots + (3k - 1) = \frac{k}{2}(3k + 1)$ *Replace n with k.*

Step 3 Prove that it is true for the natural number $k + 1$.

$2 + 5 + \ldots + (3k - 1) + 3(k + 1) - 1$ *Add to both sides.*

$= \frac{k}{2}(3k + 1) + 3(k + 1) - 1$

$= \frac{k(3k + 1)}{2} + (3k + 3 - 1)$ *Multiply.*

$= \frac{3k^2 + k}{2} + \frac{2(3k + 2)}{2}$ *Simplify and rewrite with like denominators.*

$= \frac{3k^2 + 7k + 4}{2}$ *Add.*

$= \frac{(k + 1)(3k + 4)}{2}$ *Factor.*

$= \frac{(k + 1)}{2}\left(3(k + 1) + 1\right)$ *Write with k + 1.*

EXERCISES

Find the sum of each infinite series, if it exists.

56. $-2700 + 900 - 300 + 100 + \cdots$

57. $-1.2 - 0.12 - 0.012 - 0.0012 + \cdots$

58. $-49 - 42 - 36 - \frac{216}{7} + \cdots$

59. $4 + \frac{4}{5} + \frac{4}{25} + \frac{4}{125} + \cdots$

60. $\sum_{k=1}^{\infty} \frac{9}{3^k}$

61. $\sum_{k=1}^{\infty} -7\left(\frac{3}{5}\right)^k$

62. $\sum_{k=1}^{\infty} (-1)^{k+1}\left(\frac{1}{8^k}\right)$

63. $\sum_{k=1}^{\infty} \left(\frac{4}{3}\right)^k$

Use mathematical induction to prove each statement.

64. $2 + 4 + 8 + \cdots + 2^n = 2^{n+1} - 2$

65. $1 + 5 + 25 + \cdots + 5^{n-1} = \frac{5^n - 1}{4}$

66. $\frac{1}{3} + \frac{1}{15} + \cdots + \frac{1}{4n^2 - 1} = \frac{n}{2n + 1}$

67. Recreation A child on a swing is let go from a vertical height so that the distance that he travels in the first back-and-forth swing is exactly 9 feet.

a. If each swing decreases the distance by 85%, write an infinite geometric series that expresses the distance that the child travels in feet.

b. What is the total distance that the child in the swing travels before the swing stops?

CHAPTER 12

CHAPTER TEST

Find the first 5 terms of each sequence.

1. $a_n = n^2 - 4$
2. $a_1 = 48$ and $a_n = \frac{1}{2}a_{n-1} - 8$

Write a possible explicit rule for the *n*th term of each sequence.

3. $-4, -2, 0, 2, 4, \ldots$
4. $54, 18, 6, 2, \frac{2}{3}, \ldots$

Expand each series and evaluate.

5. $\sum_{k=1}^{4} 5k^3$
6. $\sum_{k=1}^{7} (-1)^{k+1}(k)$

Find the 9th term of each arithmetic sequence.

7. $-19, -13, -7, -1, \ldots$
8. $a_2 = 11.6$ and $a_5 = 5$
9. Find 2 missing terms in the arithmetic sequence 125, ■, ■, 65.

Find the indicated sum for each arithmetic series.

10. S_{20} for $4 + 7 + 10 + 13 + \ldots$
11. $\sum_{k=1}^{12} (-9k + 8)$
12. The front row of a theater has 16 seats and each subsequent row has 2 more seats than the row that precedes it. How many seats are in the 12th row? How many seats in total are in the first 12 rows?

Find the 10th term of each geometric sequence.

13. $\frac{3}{256}, \frac{3}{64}, \frac{3}{16}, \frac{3}{4}, \ldots$
14. $a_4 = 2$ and $a_5 = 8$
15. Find the geometric mean of 4 and 25.

Find the indicated sum for each geometric series.

16. S_6 for $2 + 1 + \frac{1}{2} + \frac{1}{4} + \ldots$
17. $\sum_{k=1}^{6} 250\left(-\frac{1}{5}\right)^{k-1}$
18. You invest \$1000 each year in an account that pays 5% annual interest. How much is the first \$1000 you invested worth after 10 full years of interest payments? How much in total do you have in your account after 10 full years?

Find the sum of each infinite geometric series, if it exists.

19. $200 - 100 + 50 - 25 + \ldots$
20. $\sum_{k=1}^{\infty} 2\left(\frac{7}{8}\right)^k$

Use mathematical induction to prove $\frac{1}{2} + \frac{3}{2} + \frac{5}{2} + \cdots + \frac{2n-1}{2} = \frac{n^2}{2}$.

21. Step 1
22. Step 2
23. Step 3

10. What transformation has been applied to f to get g?

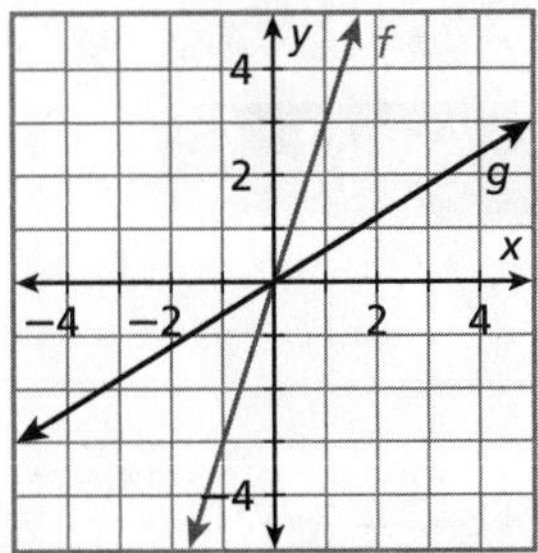

Ⓕ Horizontal compression by $\frac{1}{5}$

Ⓖ Horizontal stretch by 5

Ⓗ Vertical compression by $\frac{1}{3}$

Ⓙ Vertical stretch by 5

In Item 11, you may choose to graph, factor, complete the square, or use the Quadratic Formula to find the zeros.

11. Find the zeros of $f(x) = 2x^2 + 5x - 12$.

Ⓐ $-4, \frac{3}{2}$

Ⓑ $-2, 3$

Ⓒ $-\frac{3}{2}, 4$

Ⓓ $\frac{3}{2}, 2$

Gridded Response

12. Find the common ratio of the geometric sequence.

125, 50, 20, 8, ...

13. A card is drawn from a deck of 52. What is the probability of drawing a 10 or a diamond, to the nearest hundredth?

14. What is the sum of the arithmetic series?

$\sum_{k=1}^{8} (7k - 3)$

15. What is the y-value of the point that represents the solution to the given system of equations, to the nearest hundredth?

$\begin{cases} 2y - 2 = 4x \\ 6 - x = 8y \end{cases}$

Short Response

16. Use the function $f(x) = \sqrt[3]{5x}$ to answer the following questions.
    a. What is the domain and range?
    b. What is the inverse of $f(x)$?
    c. What is the domain and range of the inverse function?
    d. Graph $f(x)$ and $f^{-1}(x)$ on the same coordinate plane.

17. Use the infinite geometric series $\sum_{n=1}^{\infty} \frac{5}{4^{n-1}}$ to answer the following questions.
    a. Determine if the series converges or diverges.
    b. Find the sum of the infinite series, if it exists.

18. A grocery store display contains 3 cans on the top row and an additional can in each row forming a triangular shape.
    a. Would you use a sequence or a series to represent the number of cans in the nth row? Explain.
    b. How many cans are in the 12th row?
    c. What does the series $\sum_{k=1}^{n} (k + 2)$ represent? Explain.

Extended Response

19. A test to be on a trivia show has two parts. 60% of contestants pass the first part, and 20% pass the second part.
    a. Draw a tree diagram that gives the probabilities for a contestant's possible outcomes on the test.
    b. If a contestant must pass both parts of the test to be on the show, how many contestants out of a group of 50 would likely make the show? Show your work.
    c. Is it more likely that a contestant would pass both parts or fail both parts of the test? Explain.

Real-World CONNECTIONS

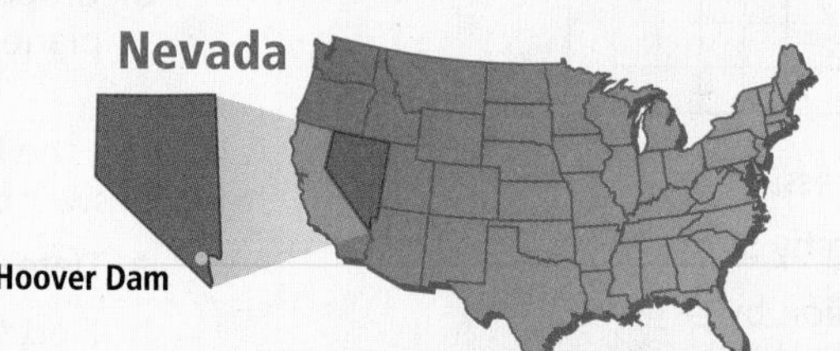

The Hoover Dam

Since its completion in 1935, the Hoover Dam has often been cited as one of the seven engineering wonders of the world. Its 6.6 million tons of concrete tame the waters of the Colorado River and form Lake Mead, the largest man-made reservoir in the United States.

Choose one or more strategies to solve each problem. For 1 and 2, use the table.

Traffic Forecasts for the Hoover Dam			
Year	2007	2008	2009
Number of Cars per Day	16,300	16,780	17,260

1. The Hoover Dam serves as a bridge between the Nevada and Arizona sides of the Colorado River. Traffic analysts project that the traffic on the dam will increase according to an arithmetic sequence. How many cars, on average, would you predict to cross the dam each day in 2017?
2. Approximately how many vehicles will cross the dam in the years 2007 through 2017, inclusive? (*Hint:* Assume 365 days per year.)
3. Small trucks make up 18% of the traffic on the dam, and RVs account for another 4%. All trucks and RVs are inspected before they are allowed to cross.
   a. Assuming that other types of vehicles are not inspected, what is the probability that three consecutive vehicles arriving at a checkpoint will be inspected?
   b. What is the probability that 3 out of 5 vehicles arriving at a checkpoint will need to be inspected?

 Silver and Gold Mining

Nevada's nickname is the Silver State, which is not surprising considering that more than 10 million ounces of the metal are mined in Nevada each year. Gold mining is also an essential part of Nevada's economy. In fact, if Nevada were a nation, it would rank third in the world in gold production behind South Africa and Australia.

Choose one or more strategies to solve each problem.

1. Nevada experienced a gold-mining boom from 1981 to 1990. During this period, the number of thousands of ounces of gold mined each year can be modeled by a geometric sequence in which $a_1 = 375$ (that is, 375,000 ounces were mined in 1981) and the common ratio is 1.35. Approximately how many ounces of gold were mined in 1990?
2. What was the total gold production in the years 1981 through 1990, inclusive?
3. In a particular mine, the probability of discovering a profitable quantity of gold in a sector is approximately 40%. What is the probability that the miners will discover a profitable quantity of gold in 3 of the next 4 sectors?

For 4, use the table.

4. Nevada experienced a silver boom during the 1990s. An industry analyst is collecting detailed data for all of the years from 1991 to 2000 in which silver production was outside of 1 standard deviation of the mean. For which years should she collect this data?

Nevada Silver Production

Year	Production (million oz)
1991	18.6
1992	19.7
1993	23.2
1994	22.8
1995	24.6
1996	20.7
1997	24.7
1998	21.5
1999	19.5
2000	23.2

CHAPTER

13 Trigonometric Functions

Chapter Focus

- Develop conceptual understanding of trigonometric functions.
- Solve problems with trigonometric functions and their inverses.

GEARING UP!

The shape and size of gear teeth determine whether gears fit together. You can use trigonometry to make a working model of a set of gears.

go.hrw.com
Chapter Project Online
KEYWORD: MB7 ChProj

Vocabulary

Match each term on the left with a definition on the right.

1. acute angle
2. function
3. domain
4. reciprocal

A. the set of all possible input values of a relation or function
B. an angle whose measure is greater than 90°
C. a relation with at most one y-value for each x-value
D. an angle whose measure is greater than 0° and less than 90°
E. the multiplicative inverse of a number

Ratios

Use $\triangle ABC$ to write each ratio.

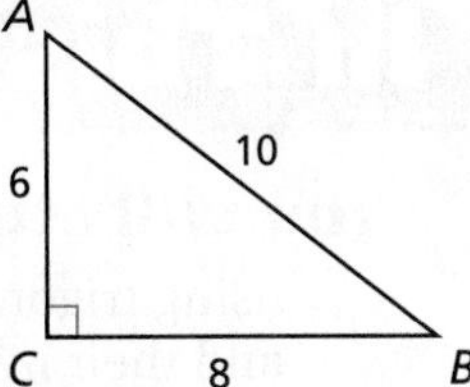

5. BC to AB
6. AC to BC
7. the length of the longest side to the length of the shortest side
8. the length of the shorter leg to the length of the hypotenuse

Classify Triangles

Classify each triangle as acute, right, or obtuse.

9. 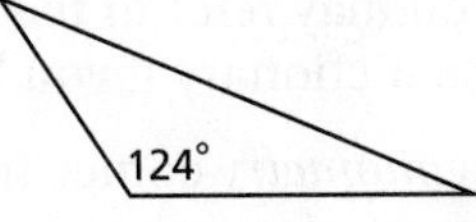

10. 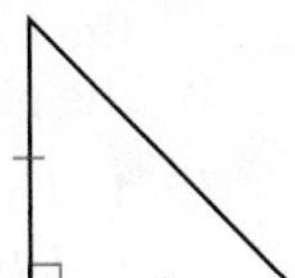

11. 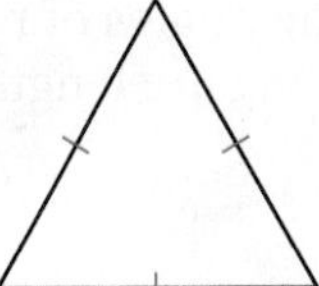

Triangle Sum Theorem

Find the value of x in each triangle.

12. 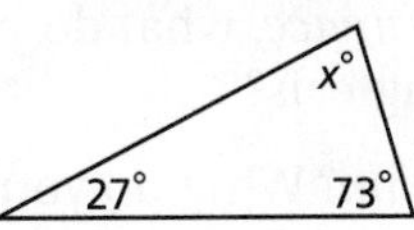

13. 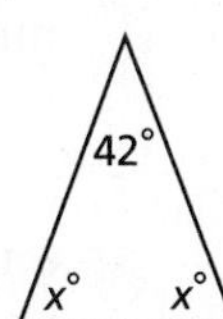

14. 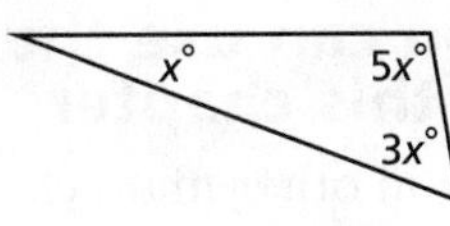

Pythagorean Theorem

Find the missing length for each right triangle with legs a and b and hypotenuse c. Round to the nearest tenth.

15. $a = 16$, $b = $ ■, $c = 20$
16. $a = 3$, $b = 5$, $c = $ ■
17. $a = 9$, $b = $ ■, $c = 18$
18. $a = 7$, $b = 14$, $c = $ ■

CHAPTER 13

Study Guide: Preview

Where You've Been

Previously, you

- used inverses of functions.
- measured indirectly using ratios and proportional reasoning.
- found equations of circles on the coordinate plane.

In This Chapter

You will study

- using trigonometric functions and their inverses.
- measuring indirectly using side lengths and angles of triangles.
- using angles of rotation and finding arc lengths of circles.

Where You're Going

You can use the skills in this chapter

- in other math classes, such as Precalculus.
- in scientific fields such as astronomy, forensics, geology, and engineering.
- outside of school in navigation, surveying, drafting, architecture, landscaping, and aviation.

Key Vocabulary/Vocabulario

angle of rotation	ángulo de rotación
coterminal angle	ángulo coterminal
initial side	lado inicial
radian	radián
reference angle	ángulo de referencia
standard position	posición estándar
terminal side	lado terminal
trigonometric function	función trigonométrica
unit circle	círculo unitario

Vocabulary Connections

To become familiar with some of the vocabulary terms in the chapter, consider the following. You may refer to the chapter, the glossary, or a dictionary if you like.

1. The word *trigonometry* comes from Greek words meaning "triangle measurement." What types of problems might you be able to solve by using **trigonometric functions**?
2. What is a reference book? Based on this meaning of *reference*, what do you think a **reference angle** is?
3. What is a *rotation*? What do you think an **angle of rotation** is?
4. The origin of the word *unit* is a Latin word meaning "one." What do you think the radius of a **unit circle** is?

Reading Strategy: Interpret and Read Diagrams

Diagrams are informational tools. Be sure to read and understand the information provided in these visual aids before you attempt to work a problem.

From Lesson 10-3

MULTI-STEP TEST PREP

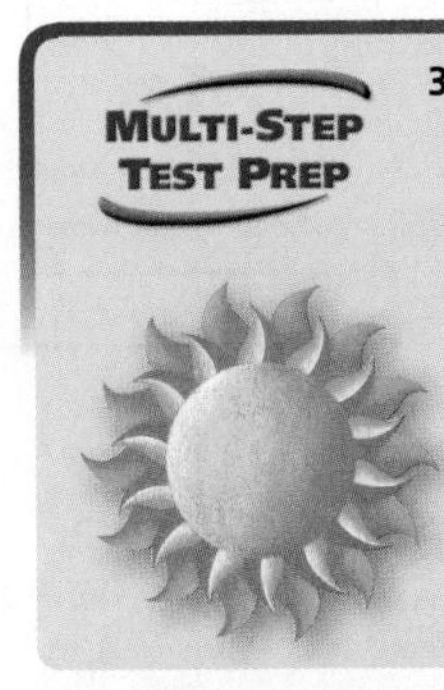

36. This problem will prepare you for the Multi-Step Test Prep on page 758.

The figure shows the elliptical orbit of Mars, where each unit of the coordinate plane represents 1 million kilometers. As shown, the planet's maximum distance from the Sun is 249 million kilometers and its minimum distance from the Sun is 207 million kilometers.

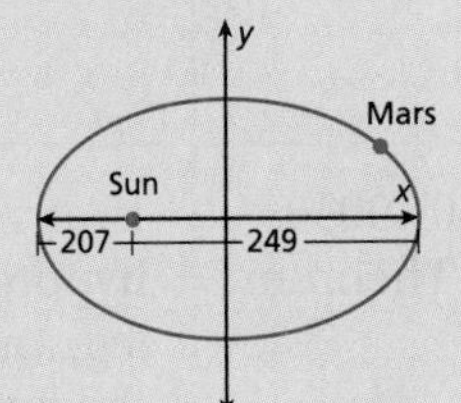

a. The Sun is at one focus of the ellipse. What are the coordinates of the Sun?

b. What is the length of the minor axis of the ellipse?

c. Write an equation that models the orbit of Mars.

1. **Examine the diagram.** A point labeled *Sun* lies on the major axis of what appears to be an ellipse. The distances from this point to the vertices are labeled 207 and 249.
2. **Reread the problem, and identify key information about the diagram.** Each unit represents 1 million kilometers. The Sun is at one focus of the ellipse.
3. **Interpret this information.** The labels 207 and 249 represent 207 million kilometers and 249 million kilometers. The length of the major axis can be found by adding these two measurements.
4. **Now you are ready to solve the problem.**

Try This

Read the problem from Chapter 10, and examine the diagram. Then answer the questions below.

26. Engineering The main cables of a suspension bridge are ideally parabolic. The cables over a bridge that is 400 feet long are attached to towers that are 100 feet tall. The lowest point of the cable is 40 feet above the bridge.

100 ft | 40 ft | 100 ft | 400 ft

a. Find the coordinates of the vertex and the tops of the towers if the bridge represents the x-axis and the axis of symmetry is the y-axis.

1. What information is provided in the diagram?
2. What information regarding the diagram is provided in the problem?
3. What conclusions can you draw from the information related to the diagram?

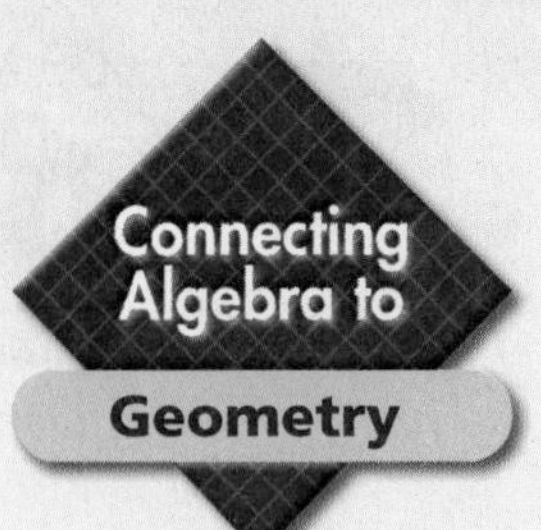

Special Right Triangles

Review the relationships of the side lengths of special right triangles below. You can use these relationships to find side lengths of special right triangles.

Special Right Triangles	
45°-45°-90° Triangle Theorem	In any 45°-45°-90° triangle, the length of the hypotenuse is $\sqrt{2}$ times the length of a leg.
30°-60°-90° Triangle Theorem	In any 30°-60°-90° triangle, the length of the hypotenuse is 2 times the length of the shorter leg, and the length of the longer leg is $\sqrt{3}$ times the length of the shorter leg.

Example

Find the unknown side lengths for the triangle shown.

The triangle is a 30°-60°-90° triangle, and the length of the hypotenuse is 8.

Step 1 Find the length of the shorter leg.

$8 = 2y$ *hypotenuse = 2 · shorter leg*

$4 = y$ *Solve for y, the length of the shorter leg.*

Step 2 Find the length of the longer leg.

$4\sqrt{3}$ *longer leg = $\sqrt{3}$ · shorter leg*

The length of the shorter leg is 4, and the length of the longer leg is $4\sqrt{3}$.

Check Use the Pythagorean Theorem.

$$4^2 + \left(4\sqrt{3}\right)^2 = 8^2$$

$16 + 48$	64
64	64 ✓

Find the unknown side lengths for each triangle.

1.

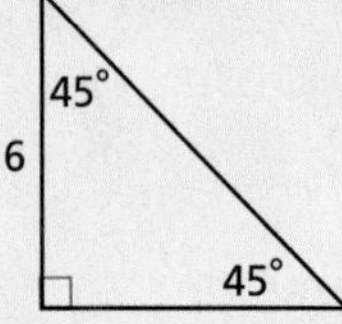

2.

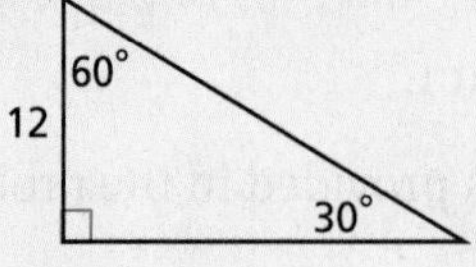

3.

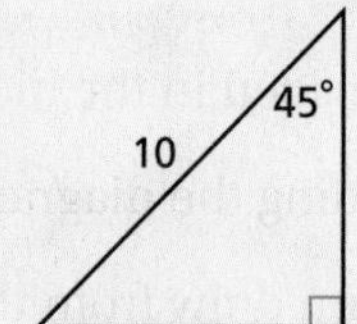

4.

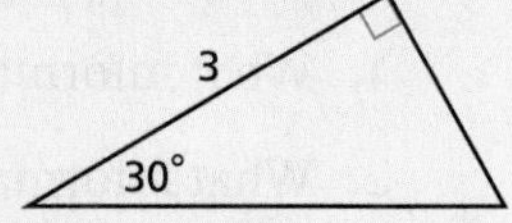

13-1 Right-Angle Trigonometry

Objectives
Understand and use trigonometric relationships of acute angles in triangles.

Determine side lengths of right triangles by using trigonometric functions.

Vocabulary
trigonometric function
sine
cosine
tangent
cosecant
secant
cotangent

Who uses this?
Trigonometry can be used to measure the heights of objects, such as an eruption of a geyser, that cannot be measured directly. (See Example 4.)

Trigonometry comes from Greek words meaning "triangle measurement." Trigonometry can be used to solve problems involving triangles.

A **trigonometric function** is a function whose rule is given by a trigonometric ratio. A *trigonometric ratio* compares the lengths of two sides of a right triangle. The Greek letter theta θ is traditionally used to represent the measure of an acute angle in a right triangle. The values of trigonometric ratios depend upon θ.

Know it! Note

Trigonometric Functions

WORDS	NUMBERS	SYMBOLS
The **sine** (sin) of angle θ is the ratio of the length of the **opposite** leg to the length of the **hypotenuse**.	$\sin\theta = \frac{4}{5}$	$\sin\theta = \frac{\text{opp.}}{\text{hyp.}}$
The **cosine** (cos) of angle θ is the ratio of the length of the **adjacent** leg to the length of the **hypotenuse**.	$\cos\theta = \frac{3}{5}$	$\cos\theta = \frac{\text{adj.}}{\text{hyp.}}$
The **tangent** (tan) of angle θ is the ratio of the length of the **opposite** leg to the length of the **adjacent** leg.	$\tan\theta = \frac{4}{3}$	$\tan\theta = \frac{\text{opp.}}{\text{adj.}}$

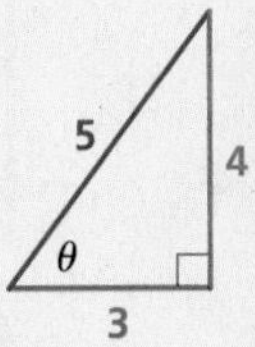

The triangle shown at right is similar to the one in the table because their corresponding angles are congruent. No matter which triangle is used, the value of $\sin\theta$ is the same. The values of the sine and other trigonometric functions depend only on angle θ and not on the size of the triangle.

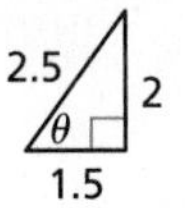

$$\sin\theta = \frac{2}{2.5} = \frac{4}{5}$$

EXAMPLE 1 Finding Trigonometric Ratios

Find the value of the sine, cosine, and tangent functions for θ.

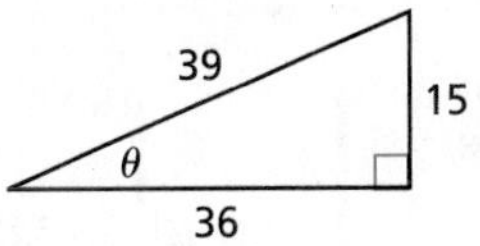

$$\sin\theta = \frac{\text{opp.}}{\text{hyp.}} = \frac{15}{39} = \frac{5}{13} \qquad \cos\theta = \frac{\text{adj.}}{\text{hyp.}} = \frac{36}{39} = \frac{12}{13} \qquad \tan\theta = \frac{\text{opp.}}{\text{adj.}} = \frac{15}{36} = \frac{5}{12}$$

CHECK IT OUT!

1. Find the value of the sine, cosine, and tangent functions for θ.

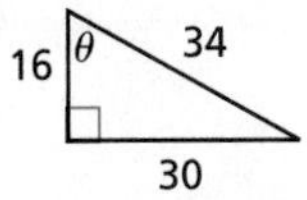

You will frequently need to determine the value of trigonometric ratios for 30°, 60°, and 45° angles as you solve trigonometry problems. Recall from geometry that in a 30°-60°-90° triangle, the ratio of the side lengths is $1:\sqrt{3}:2$, and that in a 45°-45°-90° triangle, the ratio of the side lengths is $1:1:\sqrt{2}$.

Know it! Note

Trigonometric Ratios of Special Right Triangles

Diagram	Sine	Cosine	Tangent
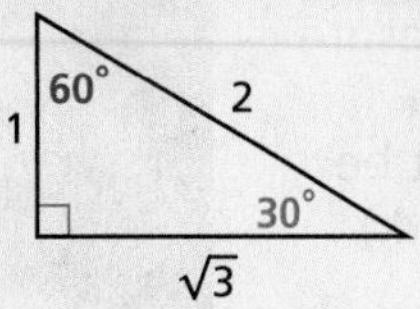	$\sin 30° = \frac{1}{2}$ $\sin 60° = \frac{\sqrt{3}}{2}$	$\cos 30° = \frac{\sqrt{3}}{2}$ $\cos 60° = \frac{1}{2}$	$\tan 30° = \frac{1}{\sqrt{3}} = \frac{\sqrt{3}}{3}$ $\tan 60° = \frac{\sqrt{3}}{1} = \sqrt{3}$
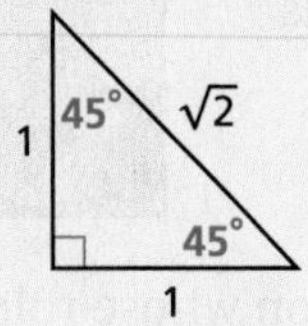	$\sin 45° = \frac{1}{\sqrt{2}} = \frac{\sqrt{2}}{2}$	$\cos 45° = \frac{1}{\sqrt{2}} = \frac{\sqrt{2}}{2}$	$\tan 45° = \frac{1}{1} = 1$

EXAMPLE 2 Finding Side Lengths of Special Right Triangles

Use a trigonometric function to find the value of x.

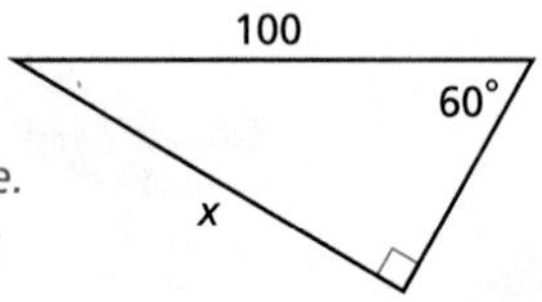

$\sin\theta = \frac{\text{opp.}}{\text{hyp.}}$ — *The sine function relates the opposite leg and the hypotenuse.*

$\sin 60° = \frac{x}{100}$ — *Substitute 60° for θ, x for opp., and 100 for hyp.*

$\frac{\sqrt{3}}{2} = \frac{x}{100}$ — *Substitute $\frac{\sqrt{3}}{2}$ for sin 60°.*

$50\sqrt{3} = x$ — *Multiply both sides by 100 to solve for x.*

CHECK IT OUT! **2.** Use a trigonometric function to find the value of x.

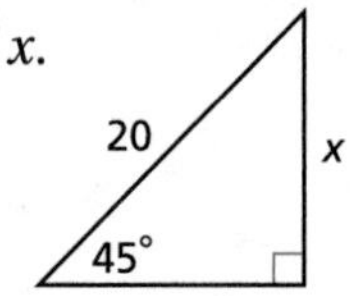

EXAMPLE 3 *Construction Application*

A builder is constructing a wheelchair ramp from the ground to a deck with a height of 18 in. The angle between the ground and the ramp must be 4.8°. To the nearest inch, what should be the distance d between the end of the ramp and the deck?

$\tan\theta = \frac{\text{opp.}}{\text{adj.}}$

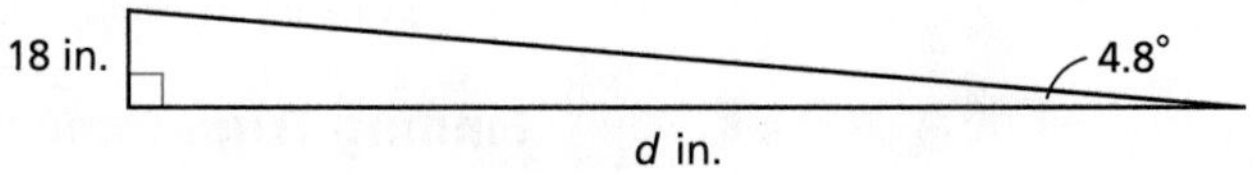

$\tan 4.8° = \frac{18}{d}$ — *Substitute 4.8° for θ, 18 for opp., and d for adj.*

$d(\tan 4.8°) = 18$ — *Multiply both sides by d.*

$d = \frac{18}{\tan 4.8°}$ — *Divide both sides by tan 4.8°.*

$d \approx 214$ — *Use a calculator to simplify.*

The distance should be about 214 in., or 17 ft 10 in.

Caution!

Make sure that your graphing calculator is set to interpret angle values as degrees. Press MODE. Check that **Degree** and not **Radian** is highlighted in the third row.

3. A skateboard ramp will have a height of 12 in., and the angle between the ramp and the ground will be 17°. To the nearest inch, what will be the length ℓ of the ramp?

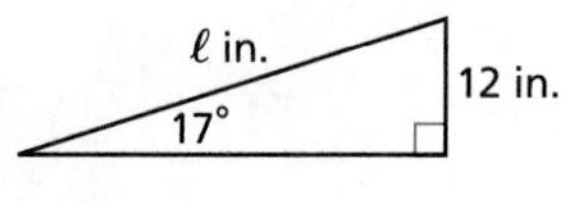

When an object is above or below another object, you can find distances indirectly by using the *angle of elevation* or the *angle of depression* between the objects.

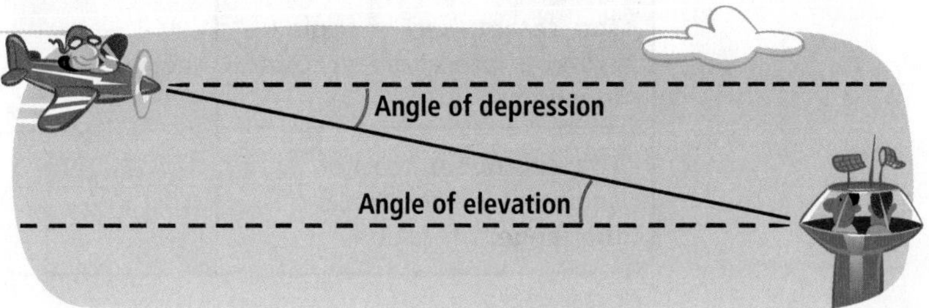

EXAMPLE 4 Geology Application

A park ranger whose eye level is 5 ft above the ground measures the angle of elevation to the top of an eruption of Old Faithful geyser to be 34.6°. If the ranger is standing 200 ft from the geyser's base, what is the height of the eruption to the nearest foot?

Step 1 Draw and label a diagram to represent the information given in the problem.

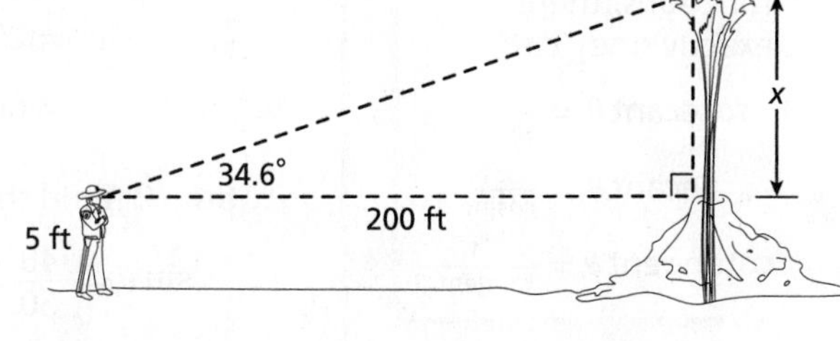

Step 2 Let x represent the height of the eruption compared with the ranger's eye level. Determine the value of x.

$\tan\theta = \frac{\text{opp.}}{\text{adj.}}$ *Use the tangent function.*

$\tan 34.6° = \frac{x}{200}$ *Substitute 34.6° for θ, x for opp., and 200 for adj.*

$200(\tan 34.6°) = x$ *Multiply both sides by 200.*

$138 \approx x$ *Use a calculator to solve for x.*

Step 3 Determine the overall height of the eruption.

$x + 5 = 138 + 5$ *The ranger's eye level is 5 ft above the ground, so add 5 ft to x to find the overall height of the eruption.*

$= 143$

The height of the eruption is about 143 ft.

4. A surveyor whose eye level is 6 ft above the ground measures the angle of elevation to the top of the highest hill on a roller coaster to be 60.7°. If the surveyor is standing 120 ft from the hill's base, what is the height of the hill to the nearest foot?

The reciprocals of the sine, cosine, and tangent ratios are also trigonometric ratios. They are the trigonometric functions *cosecant, secant,* and *cotangent.*

Reciprocal Trigonometric Functions

WORDS	NUMBERS	SYMBOLS
The **cosecant** (csc) of angle θ is the reciprocal of the sine function.	$\csc\theta = \frac{5}{4}$	$\csc\theta = \frac{1}{\sin\theta} = \frac{\text{hyp.}}{\text{opp.}}$
The **secant** (sec) of angle θ is the reciprocal of the cosine function.	$\sec\theta = \frac{5}{3}$	$\sec\theta = \frac{1}{\cos\theta} = \frac{\text{hyp.}}{\text{adj.}}$
The **cotangent** (cot) of angle θ is the reciprocal of the tangent function.	$\cot\theta = \frac{3}{4}$	$\cot\theta = \frac{1}{\tan\theta} = \frac{\text{adj.}}{\text{opp.}}$

EXAMPLE  5

Finding All Trigonometric Ratios

Find the values of the six trigonometric functions for θ.

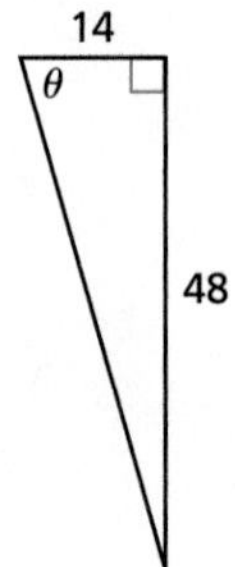

Step 1 Find the length of the hypotenuse.

$a^2 + b^2 = c^2$ *Pythagorean Theorem*

$c^2 = 14^2 + 48^2$ *Substitute 14 for a and 48 for b.*

$c^2 = 2500$ *Simplify.*

$c = 50$ *Solve for c. Eliminate the negative solution.*

Step 2 Find the function values.

$$\sin\theta = \frac{48}{50} = \frac{24}{25} \qquad \cos\theta = \frac{14}{50} = \frac{7}{25} \qquad \tan\theta = \frac{48}{14} = \frac{24}{7}$$

$$\csc\theta = \frac{1}{\sin\theta} = \frac{25}{24} \qquad \sec\theta = \frac{1}{\cos\theta} = \frac{25}{7} \qquad \cot\theta = \frac{1}{\tan\theta} = \frac{7}{24}$$

Helpful Hint

In each reciprocal pair of trigonometric functions, there is exactly one "*co*."

cosecant $\theta = \frac{1}{\text{sine }\theta}$

secant $\theta = \frac{1}{\text{cosine }\theta}$

cotangent $\theta = \frac{1}{\text{tangent }\theta}$

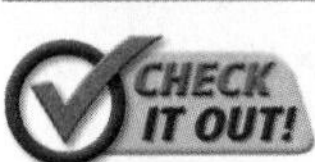

5. Find the values of the six trigonometric functions for θ.

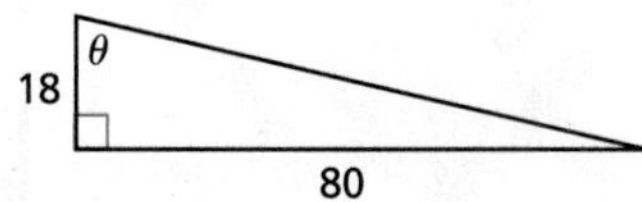

THINK AND DISCUSS

1. The sine of an acute angle in a right triangle is 0.6. Explain why the cosine of the other acute angle in the triangle must be 0.6.

2. If the secant of an acute angle in a right triangle is 2, which trigonometric ratio for that angle has a value of 0.5? Explain.

3. GET ORGANIZED Copy and complete the graphic organizer. For each trigonometric function, give the name, the side length ratio, and the reciprocal function.

	Sin	Cos	Tan
Function Name			
Side Length Ratio			
Reciprocal Function			

13-1 Exercises

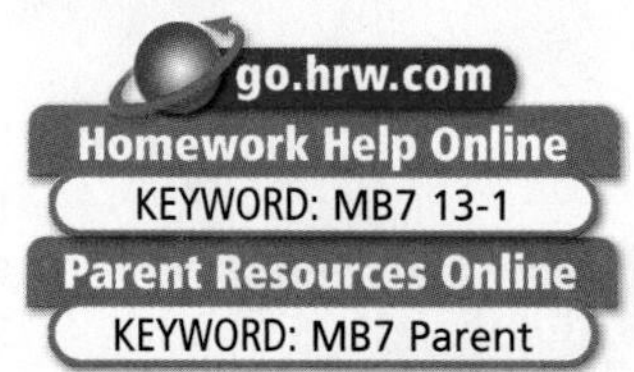

GUIDED PRACTICE

1. **Vocabulary** The ratio of the length of the opposite leg to the length of the adjacent leg of an acute angle of a right triangle is the __?__ of the angle. (*tangent* or *cotangent*)

SEE EXAMPLE 1 p. 929

Find the value of the sine, cosine, and tangent functions for θ.

2. 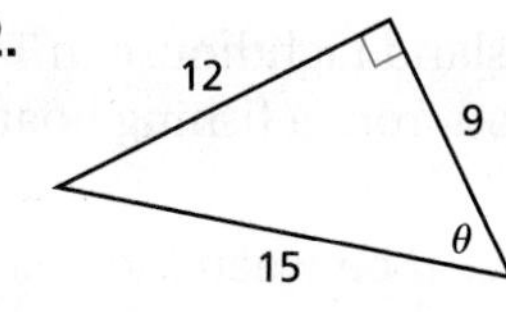

3. 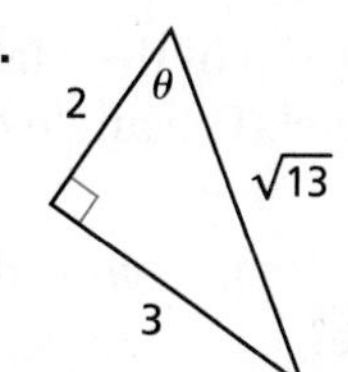

4.

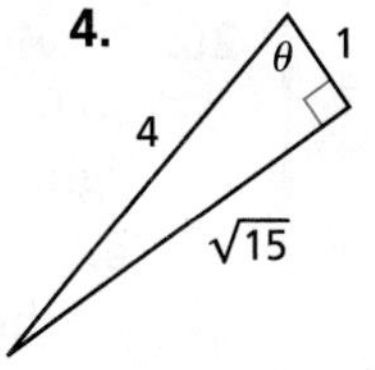

SEE EXAMPLE 2 p. 930

Use a trigonometric function to find the value of x.

5. 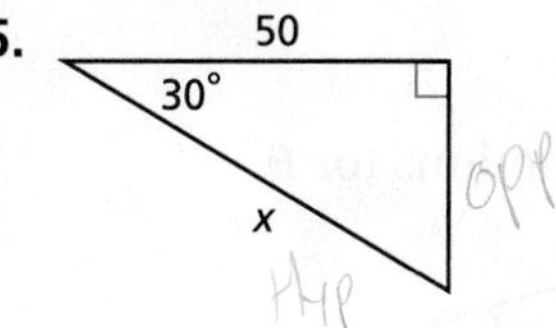

6. 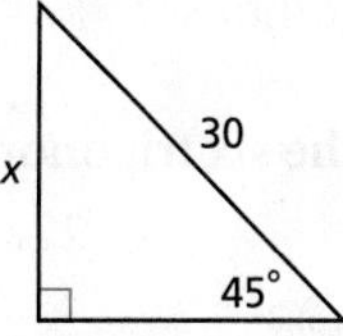

7.

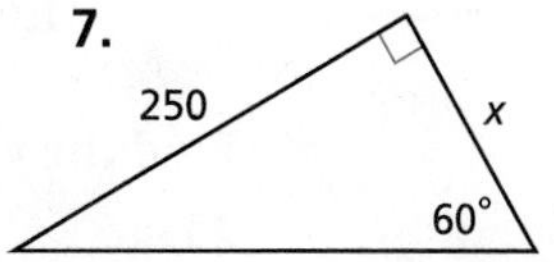

SEE EXAMPLE 3 p. 930

8. **Engineering** An escalator in a mall must lift customers to a height of 22 ft. If the angle between the escalator stairs and the ground floor will be 30°, what will be the length ℓ of the escalator?

SEE EXAMPLE 4 p. 931

9. **Recreation** The pilot of a hot-air balloon measures the angle of depression to a landing spot to be 20.5°. If the pilot's altitude is 90 m, what is the horizontal distance between the balloon and the landing spot? Round to the nearest meter.

SEE EXAMPLE 5 p. 932

Find the values of the six trigonometric functions for θ.

10. 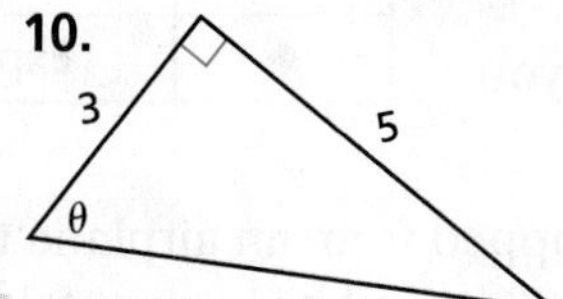

11. 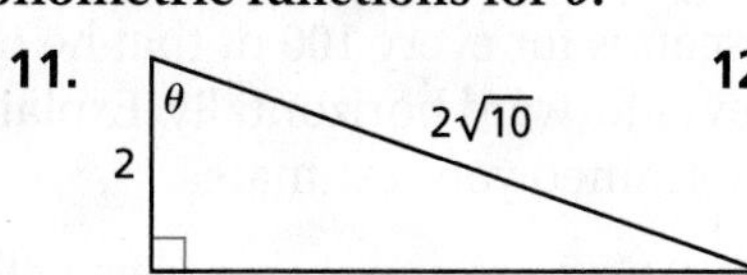

12. 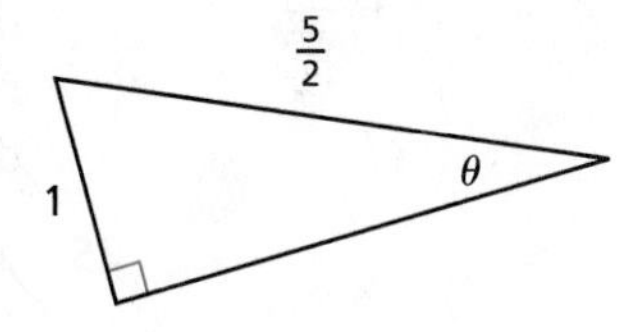

PRACTICE AND PROBLEM SOLVING

Independent Practice

For Exercises	See Example
13–15	1
16–18	2
19	3
20	4
21–23	5

Extra Practice

Skills Practice p. S28

Application Practice p. S44

Find the value of the sine, cosine, and tangent functions for θ.

13. 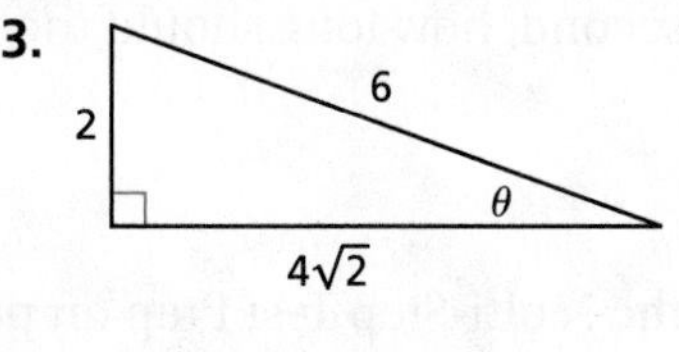

14.

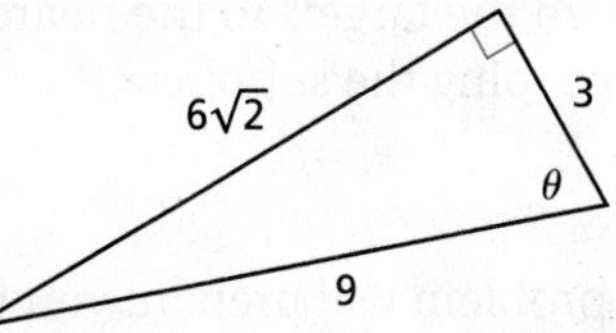

15. 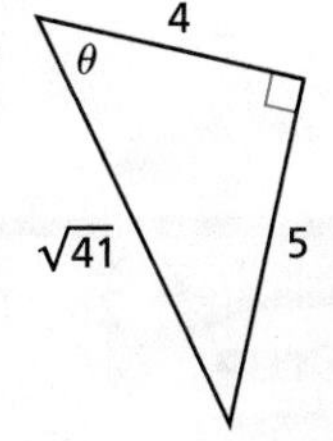

Use a trigonometric function to find the value of x.

16.

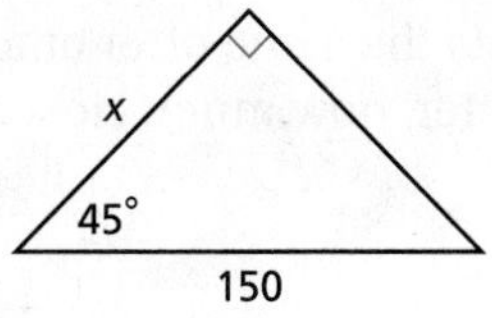

17. 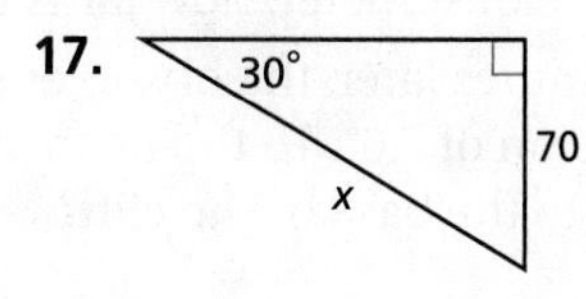

18.

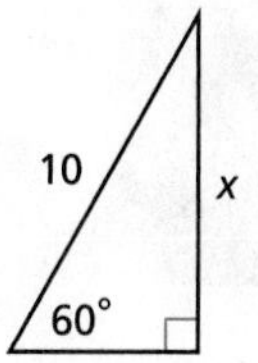

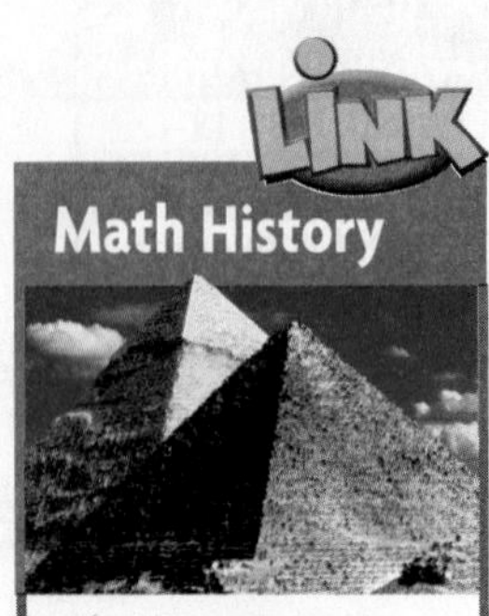

Thales of Miletus (624–547 B.C.E.) was a Greek mathematician reputed to have measured the height of the Egyptian pyramids by using the lengths of shadows and indirect measurement.

19. **History** Today, the Great Pyramid in Egypt is not as tall as when it was originally built. The square base of the pyramid has a side length of 230 m, and the sides of the pyramid meet the base at an angle of 52°.

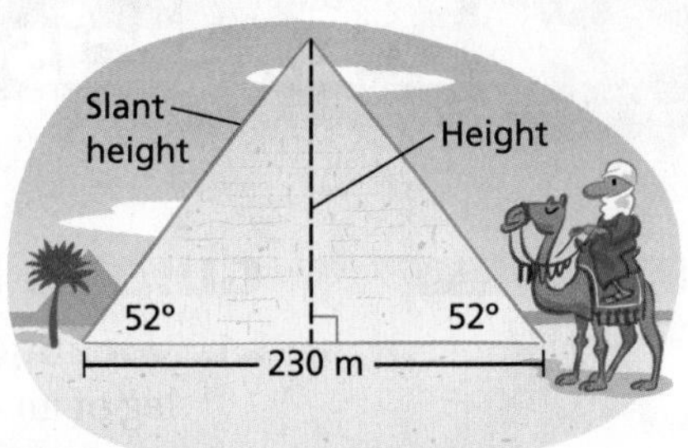

a. What was the original height of the pyramid to the nearest meter?

b. What was the original slant height of the pyramid to the nearest meter?

20. **Navigation** The top of the Matagorda Island Lighthouse in Texas is about 90 ft above sea level. The angle of elevation from a fishing boat to the top of the lighthouse is 10°.

a. To the nearest foot, what is the distance d between the boat and the base of the lighthouse?

b. **What if...?** After the boat drifts for half an hour, the angle of elevation has decreased to 4.5°. To the nearest foot, how much farther has the boat moved from the lighthouse?

Find the values of the six trigonometric functions for θ.

21. 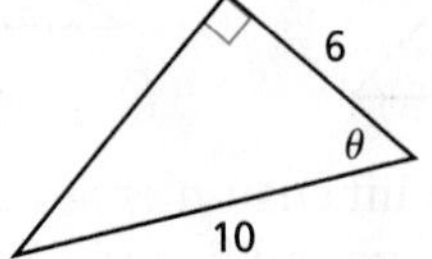

22. 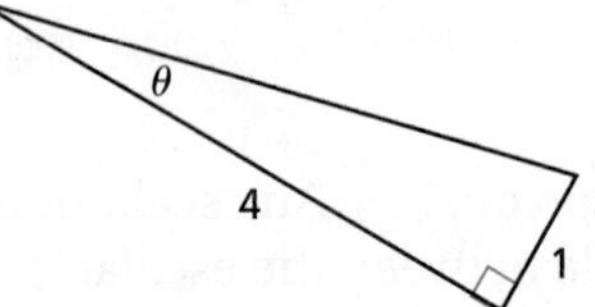

23. 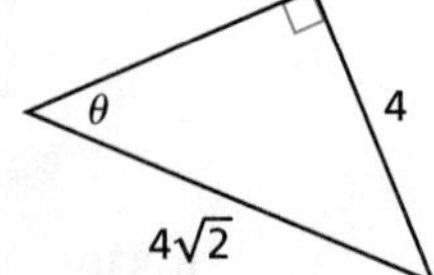

24. **Estimation** One factor that determines a ski slope's difficulty is the slope angle. The table shows the typical slope angles for the most common difficulty categories. For each category, estimate how many meters a skier descends for every 100 m that he or she moves forward horizontally. Explain how you determined your estimates.

Slope Ratings

Symbol	Difficulty	Slope Angle
●	Beginner	5° to 10°
■	Intermediate	10° to 20°
◆	Expert	20° to 35°

25. **Multi-Step** A supply package will be dropped from an airplane to an Arctic research station. The plane's altitude is 2000 ft, and its horizontal speed is 235 ft/s. The angle of depression to the target is 14°.

a. To the nearest foot, what is the plane's horizontal distance from the target?

b. The plane needs to drop the supplies when it is a horizontal distance of 500 ft from the target. To the nearest second, how long should the pilot wait before dropping the supplies?

MULTI-STEP TEST PREP

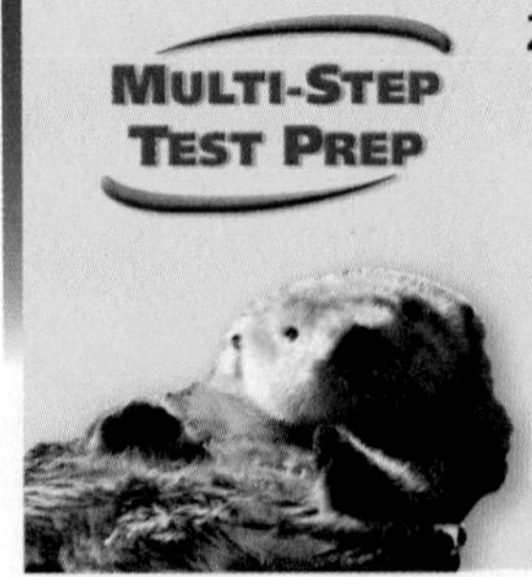

26. This problem will prepare you for the Multi-Step Test Prep on page 956.

An observer on a sea cliff with a height of 12 m spots an otter through a pair of binoculars at an angle of depression of 5.7°.

a. To the nearest meter, how far is the otter from the base of the cliff?

b. Five minutes later, the observer sights the same otter at an angle of depression of 7.6°. To the nearest meter, how much closer has the otter moved to the base of the cliff?

27. **Surveying** Based on the measurements shown in the diagram, what is the width w of the river to the nearest foot?

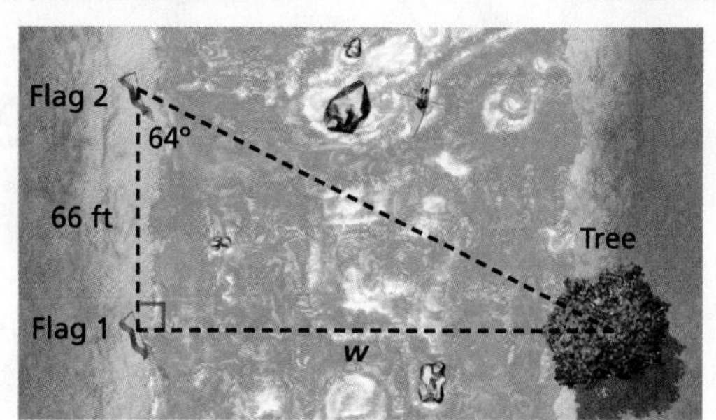

28. **Critical Thinking** Show that $\frac{\sin\theta}{\cos\theta} = \tan\theta$.

29. **Write About It** Suppose that you are given the measure of an acute angle in a right triangle and the length of the leg adjacent to this angle. Describe two different methods that you could use to find the length of the hypotenuse.

Use the diagram for Exercises 30 and 31.

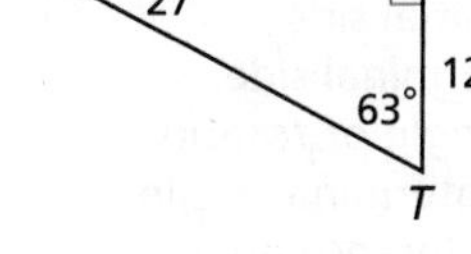

30. Which of the following is equal to cos 27°?

Ⓐ csc 63° Ⓑ sec 63° Ⓒ tan 63° Ⓓ sin 63°

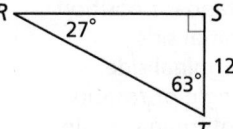

31. Which expression represents the length of $\overline{RS}$?

Ⓕ 12 cot 27° Ⓖ 12 csc 27° Ⓗ 12 sin 27° Ⓙ 12 tan 27°

32. If $\tan\theta = \frac{3}{4}$, what is $\cos\theta$?

Ⓐ $\frac{3}{5}$ Ⓑ $\frac{4}{5}$ Ⓒ $\frac{5}{4}$ Ⓓ $\frac{4}{3}$

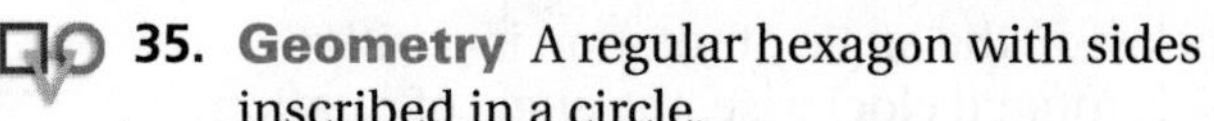

CHALLENGE AND EXTEND

33. **Geometry** Two right triangles each have an acute angle with a sine ratio of 0.6. Prove that the triangles are similar.

34. For an acute angle of a right triangle, which trigonometric ratios are always greater than 1? Which are always less than 1? Explain.

35. **Geometry** A regular hexagon with sides of length 3 ft is inscribed in a circle.

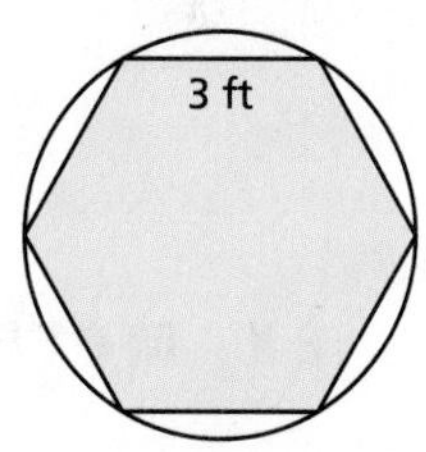

a. Use a trigonometric ratio to find the radius of the circle.

b. Determine the area of the hexagon.

36. Explain why the sine of an acute angle is equal to the cosine of its complement.

SPIRAL REVIEW

Solve each proportion. *(Lesson 2-2)*

37. $\frac{4}{17} = \frac{x}{136}$ 38. $\frac{60.3}{x} = \frac{6.7}{3}$ 39. $\frac{196}{x} = \frac{0.05}{9.8}$

40. The students at a high school are randomly assigned a computer password. Each password consists of 4 characters, each of which can be a letter from A to Z or a digit from 0 to 9. What is the probability that a randomly chosen password will consist only of digits? *(Lesson 11-2)*

Find the sum of each infinite series, if it exists. *(Lesson 12-5)*

41. $\sum_{n=1}^{\infty}\left(\frac{1}{3}\right)^n$ 42. $\sum_{n=1}^{\infty} 3n - 5$ 43. $10 + 4 + 1.6 + 0.64 + \cdots$

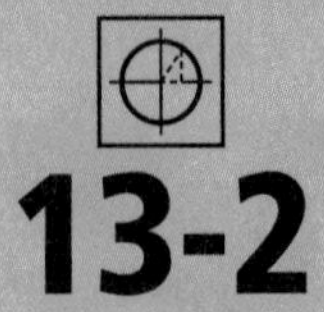

13-2 Angles of Rotation

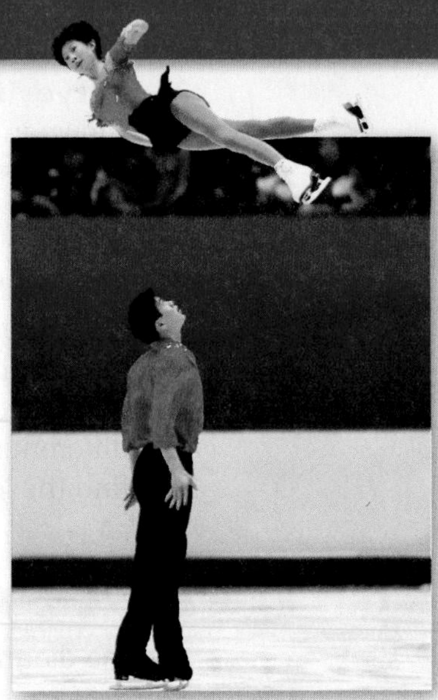

Objectives

Draw angles in standard position.

Determine the values of the trigonometric functions for an angle in standard position.

Vocabulary

standard position
initial side
terminal side
angle of rotation
coterminal angle
reference angle

Why learn this?

You can use angles of rotation to determine the rate at which a skater must spin to complete a jump. (See Exercise 51.)

In Lesson 13-1, you investigated trigonometric functions by using acute angles in right triangles. The trigonometric functions can also be evaluated for other types of angles.

An angle is in **standard position** when its vertex is at the origin and one ray is on the positive x-axis. The **initial side** of the angle is the ray on the x-axis. The other ray is called the **terminal side** of the angle.

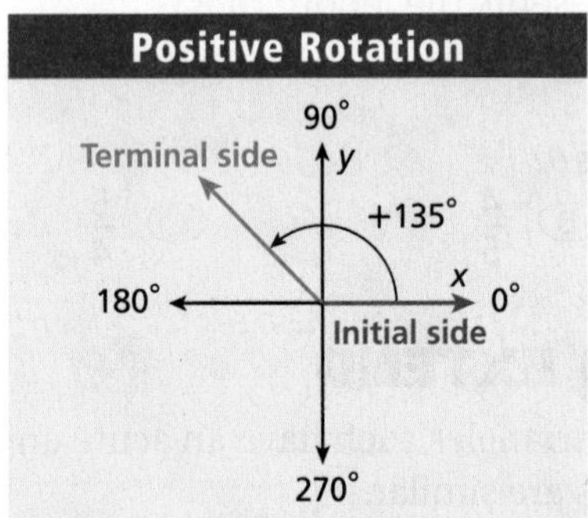

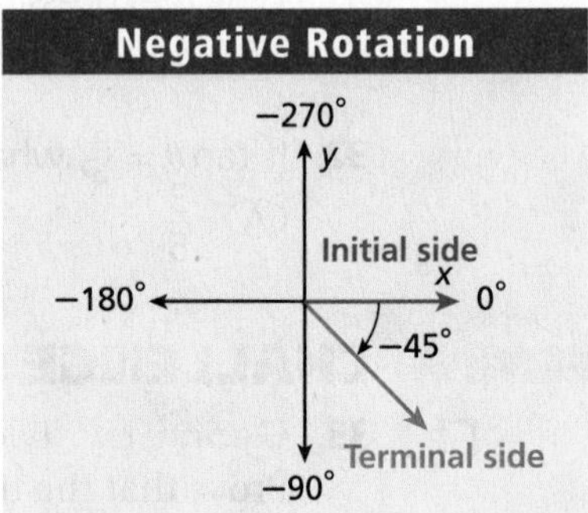

An **angle of rotation** is formed by rotating the terminal side and keeping the initial side in place. If the terminal side is rotated counterclockwise, the angle of rotation is positive. If the terminal side is rotated clockwise, the angle of rotation is negative. The terminal side can be rotated more than 360°.

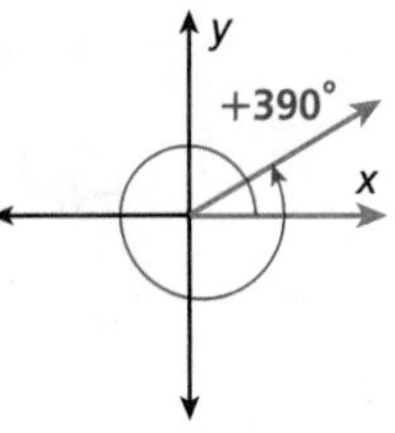

EXAMPLE 1 Drawing Angles in Standard Position

Remember!

A 360° rotation is a complete rotation. A 180° rotation is one-half of a complete rotation.

Draw an angle with the given measure in standard position.

A 300°

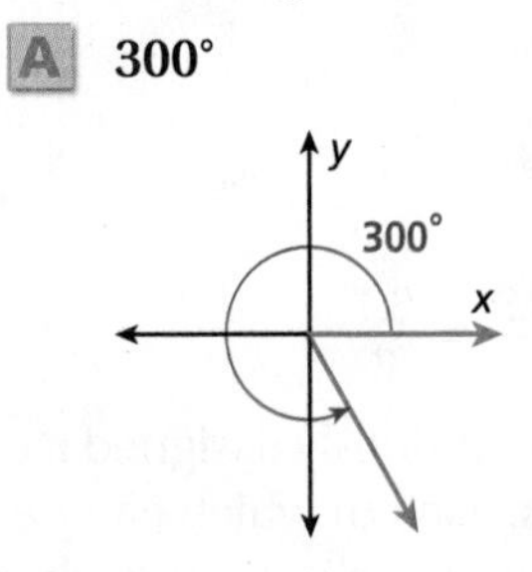

Rotate the terminal side 300° counterclockwise.

B −150°

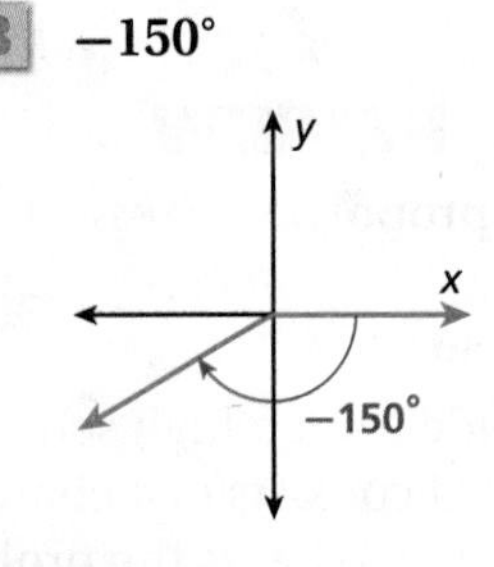

Rotate the terminal side 150° clockwise.

C 900°

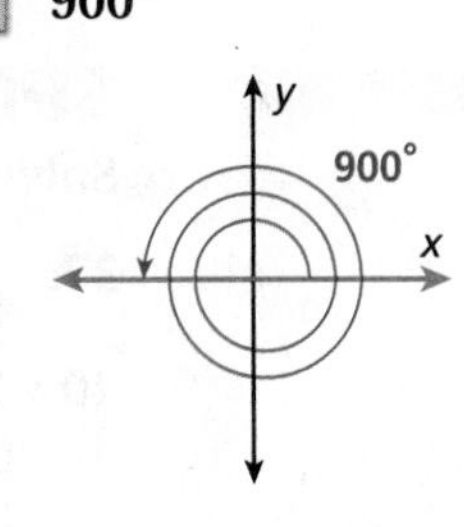

Rotate the terminal side 900° counterclockwise.
900° = 360° + 360° + 180°

Draw an angle with the given measure in standard position.

1a. 210° **1b.** 1020° **1c.** −300°

Coterminal angles are angles in standard position with the same terminal side. For example, angles measuring 120° and −240° are coterminal.

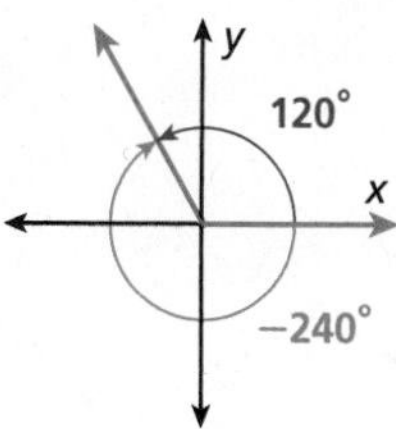

There are infinitely many coterminal angles. One way to find the measure of an angle that is coterminal with an angle θ is to add or subtract integer multiples of 360°.

EXAMPLE 2 Finding Coterminal Angles

Find the measures of a positive angle and a negative angle that are coterminal with each given angle.

A $\theta = 40°$

$40° + 360° = 400°$ *Add 360° to find a positive coterminal angle.*

$40° - 360° = -320°$ *Subtract 360° to find a negative coterminal angle.*

Angles that measure 400° and −320° are coterminal with a 40° angle.

B $\theta = 380°$

$380° - 360° = 20°$ *Subtract 360° to find a positive coterminal angle.*

$380° - 2(360°) = -340°$ *Subtract a multiple of 360° to find a negative coterminal angle.*

Angles that measure 20° and −340° are coterminal with a 380° angle.

Find the measures of a positive angle and a negative angle that are coterminal with each given angle.

2a. $\theta = 88°$ **2b.** $\theta = 500°$ **2c.** $\theta = -120°$

For an angle θ in standard position, the **reference angle** is the positive acute angle formed by the terminal side of θ and the x-axis. In Lesson 13-3, you will learn how to use reference angles to find trigonometric values of angles measuring greater than 90° or less than 0°.

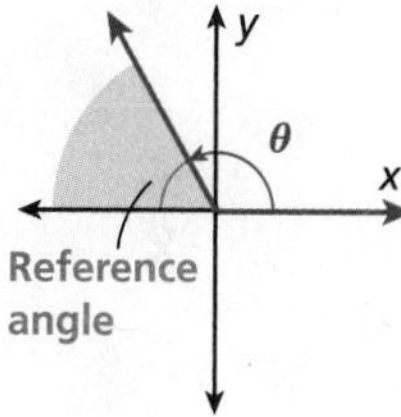

EXAMPLE 3 Finding Reference Angles

Find the measure of the reference angle for each given angle.

A $\theta = 150°$

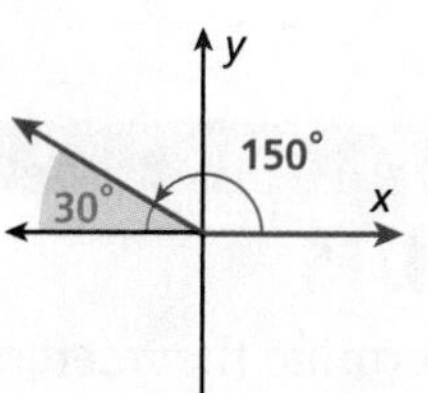

The measure of the reference angle is 30°.

B $\theta = -130°$

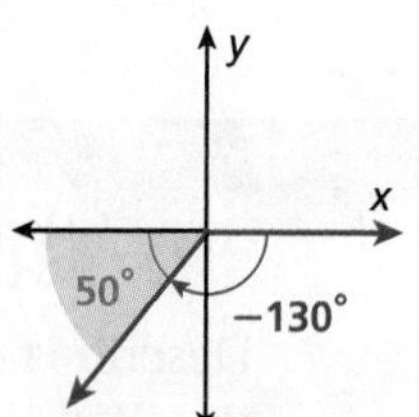

The measure of the reference angle is 50°.

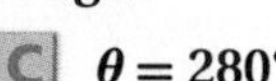
C $\theta = 280°$

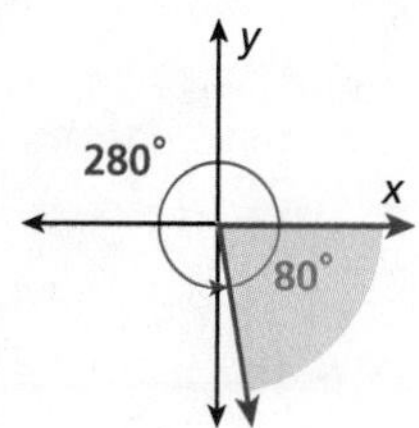

The measure of the reference angle is 80°.

Find the measure of the reference angle for each given angle.

3a. $\theta = 105°$ **3b.** $\theta = -115°$ **3c.** $\theta = 310°$

To determine the value of the trigonometric functions for an angle θ in standard position, begin by selecting a point P with coordinates (x, y) on the terminal side of the angle. The distance r from point P to the origin is given by $\sqrt{x^2 + y^2}$.

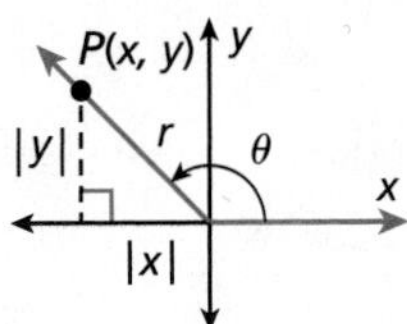

Trigonometric Functions

For a point $P(x, y)$ on the terminal side of θ in standard position and $r = \sqrt{x^2 + y^2}$,

SINE	COSINE	TANGENT
$\sin\theta = \frac{y}{r}$	$\cos\theta = \frac{x}{r}$	$\tan\theta = \frac{y}{x}, x \neq 0$

EXAMPLE 4 Finding Values of Trigonometric Functions

$P(4, -5)$ is a point on the terminal side of θ in standard position. Find the exact value of the six trigonometric functions for θ.

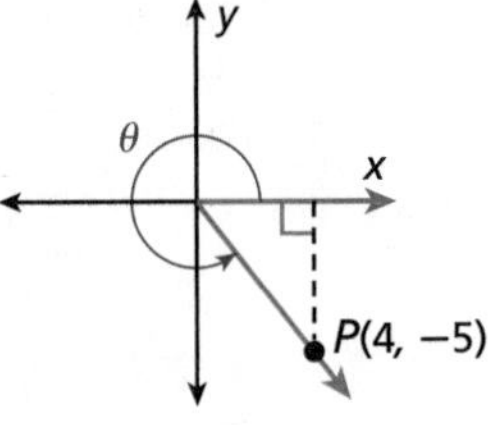

Step 1 Plot point P, and use it to sketch a right triangle and angle θ in standard position. Find r.

$$r = \sqrt{4^2 + (-5)^2} = \sqrt{16 + 25} = \sqrt{41}$$

Helpful Hint

Because r is a distance, its value is always positive, regardless of the sign of x and y.

Step 2 Find $\sin\theta$, $\cos\theta$, and $\tan\theta$.

$$\sin\theta = \frac{y}{r} = \frac{-5}{\sqrt{41}} = -\frac{5\sqrt{41}}{41}$$

$$\cos\theta = \frac{x}{r} = \frac{4}{\sqrt{41}} = \frac{4\sqrt{41}}{41}$$

$$\tan\theta = \frac{y}{x} = \frac{-5}{4} = -\frac{5}{4}$$

Step 3 Use reciprocals to find $\csc\theta$, $\sec\theta$, and $\cot\theta$.

$$\csc\theta = \frac{1}{\sin\theta} = -\frac{\sqrt{41}}{5} \qquad \sec\theta = \frac{1}{\cos\theta} = \frac{\sqrt{41}}{4} \qquad \cot\theta = \frac{1}{\tan\theta} = -\frac{4}{5}$$

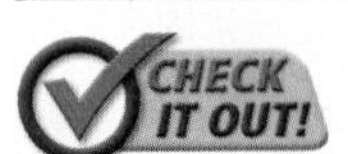

4. $P(-3, 6)$ is a point on the terminal side of θ in standard position. Find the exact value of the six trigonometric functions for θ.

THINK AND DISCUSS

1. Describe how to determine the reference angle of an angle whose terminal side is in Quadrant III.

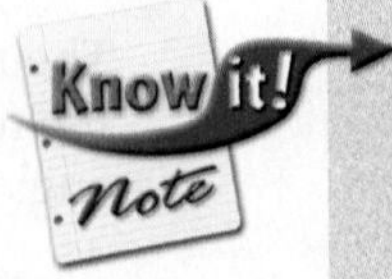

2. **GET ORGANIZED** Copy and complete the graphic organizer. In each box, describe how to determine the given angle or position for an angle θ.

Standard position	Reference angle
Angle θ	
Positive coterminal angle	Negative coterminal angle

13-2 Exercises

go.hrw.com
Homework Help Online
KEYWORD: MB7 13-2
Parent Resources Online
KEYWORD: MB7 Parent

GUIDED PRACTICE

1. **Vocabulary** If a 45° angle is in standard position, its __?__ side lies above the x-axis. (*initial* or *terminal*)

SEE EXAMPLE 1 p. 936

Draw an angle with the given measure in standard position.

2. 60° 3. −135° 4. 450° 5. −1125°

SEE EXAMPLE 2 p. 937

Find the measures of a positive angle and a negative angle that are coterminal with each given angle.

6. $\theta = 75°$ 7. $\theta = 720°$ 8. $\theta = -25°$ 9. $\theta = -390°$

SEE EXAMPLE 3 p. 937

Find the measure of the reference angle for each given angle.

10. $\theta = 95°$ 11. $\theta = -250°$ 12. $\theta = 230°$ 13. $\theta = -160°$
14. $\theta = 345°$ 15. $\theta = -130°$ 16. $\theta = -15°$ 17. $\theta = 220°$

SEE EXAMPLE 4 p. 938

***P* is a point on the terminal side of θ in standard position. Find the exact value of the six trigonometric functions for θ.**

18. $P(-3, 2)$ 19. $P(4, -2)$ 20. $P(0, -6)$ 21. $P(-3, -4)$
22. $P(5, -3)$ 23. $P(1, 6)$ 24. $P(-6, -5)$ 25. $P(-3, 6)$

PRACTICE AND PROBLEM SOLVING

Independent Practice

For Exercises	See Example
26–29	1
30–33	2
34–41	3
42–49	4

Extra Practice
Skills Practice p. S28
Application Practice p. S44

Draw an angle with the given measure in standard position.

26. −120° 27. 225° 28. −570° 29. 750°

Find the measures of a positive angle and a negative angle that are coterminal with each given angle.

30. $\theta = 254°$ 31. $\theta = 1020°$ 32. $\theta = -165°$ 33. $\theta = -610°$

Find the measure of the reference angle for each given angle.

34. $\theta = -25°$ 35. $\theta = 50°$ 36. $\theta = -185°$ 37. $\theta = 200°$
38. $\theta = 390°$ 39. $\theta = -95°$ 40. $\theta = 160°$ 41. $\theta = 325°$

***P* is a point on the terminal side of θ in standard position. Find the exact value of the six trigonometric functions for θ.**

42. $P(2, -5)$ 43. $P(5, -2)$ 44. $P(-4, 5)$ 45. $P(4, 3)$
46. $P(-6, 2)$ 47. $P(3, -6)$ 48. $P(2, -4)$ 49. $P(5, 4)$

50. **Recreation** A carousel has eight evenly spaced seats shaped like animals. During each ride, the carousel makes between 8 and 9 clockwise revolutions. At the end of one ride, the carousel stops so that the lion is in the position where the zebra was when the ride started. Through how many degrees did the carousel rotate on this ride?

51. **Multi-Step** A double axel is a figure-skating jump in which the skater makes 2.5 revolutions in the air. If a skater is in the air for 0.66 s during a double axel, what is her average angular speed to the nearest degree per second?

Determine the exact coordinates of point *P*.

52.
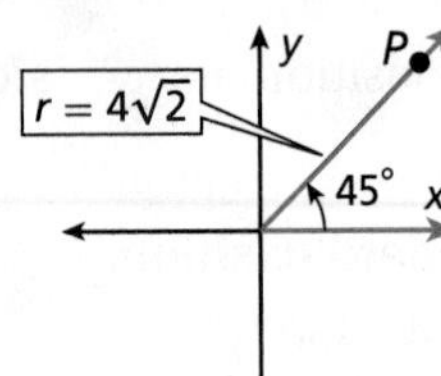

53.
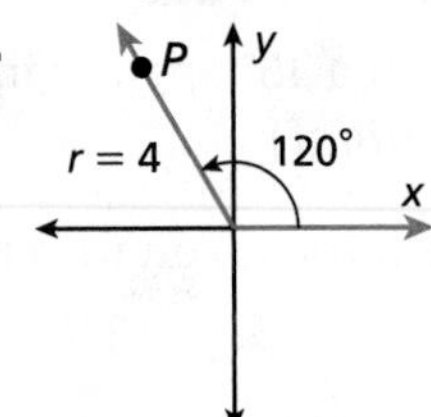

54.
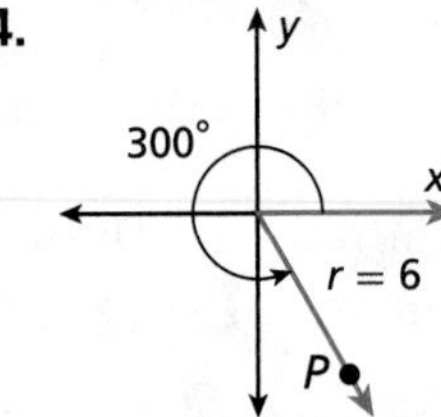

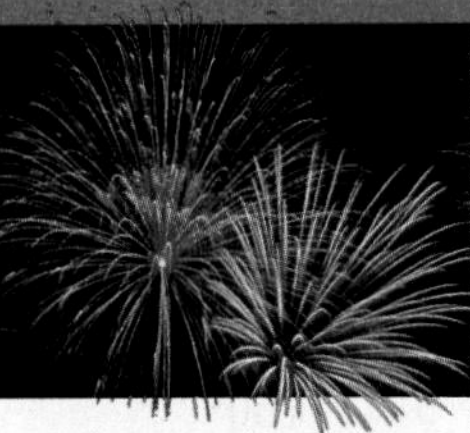

LINK

Fireworks

In professional fireworks displays, the chemicals that produce colored bursts of light are encased in spherical shells. In general, a firework rises about 100 ft for each inch of shell diameter.

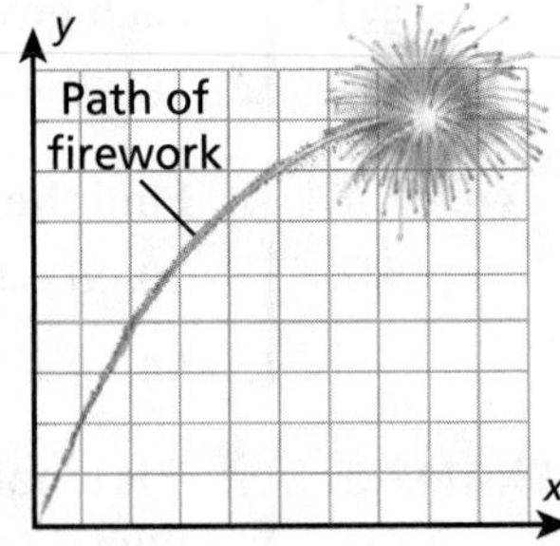

55. **Fireworks** The horizontal distance x and vertical distance y in feet traveled by a firework can be modeled by the functions $x(t) = v(\cos\theta)t$ and $y(t) = -16t^2 + v(\sin\theta)t$. In these functions, v is the initial velocity of the firework, θ is the angle at which the firework is launched, and t is the time in seconds. A firework is launched with an initial velocity of 166 ft/s at an angle of 75°.

a. To the nearest foot, what is the maximum height that the firework will reach?

b. To achieve the greatest effect, the firework should explode when it reaches its maximum height. To the nearest second, how long after the launch should the firework explode?

c. To the nearest foot, what is the horizontal distance that the firework will have traveled when the maximum height is reached?

d. **What if...?** To the nearest foot, how much higher would the firework travel if it were fired at an angle of 90°?

56. **///ERROR ANALYSIS///** $P(2, -2)$ is a point on the terminal side of an angle θ in standard position. Two attempts at finding $\csc\theta$ are shown below. Which is incorrect? Explain the error.

A

$r = \sqrt{2^2 + (-2)^2} = \sqrt{8}$

$\csc\theta = \frac{\sqrt{8}}{2}$

$\csc\theta = \frac{2\sqrt{2}}{2} = \sqrt{2}$

B

$r = \sqrt{2^2 + (-2)^2} = \sqrt{8}$

$\csc\theta = \frac{\sqrt{8}}{-2}$

$\csc\theta = -\frac{2\sqrt{2}}{2} = -\sqrt{2}$

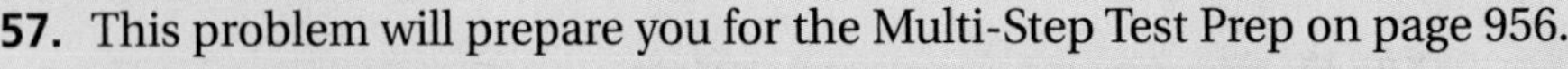

MULTI-STEP TEST PREP

57. This problem will prepare you for the Multi-Step Test Prep on page 956.

An aquarium has a cylindrical tank that rotates at a constant speed about an axis through the center of the cylinder's bases. In 1 minute, the tank rotates through an angle of 48°.

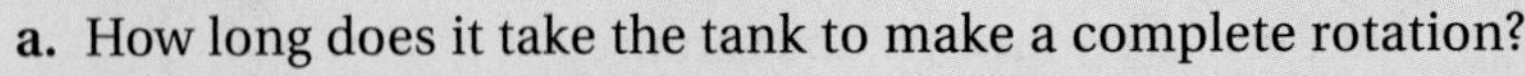

a. How long does it take the tank to make a complete rotation?

b. The tank rotates only during the aquarium's operating hours. If the aquarium is open from 9:30 A.M. to 6:00 P.M., how many rotations does the tank make in one day?

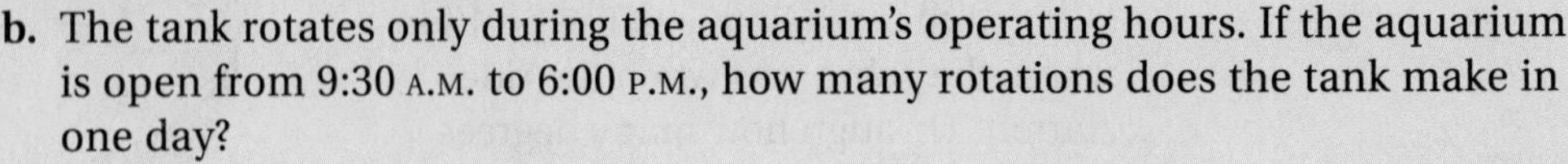

Use your calculator to find the value of each trigonometric function. Round to the nearest thousandth.

58. $\sin 260°$ **59.** $\cos(-130°)$ **60.** $\csc 200°$

Find all values of θ that have a reference angle with the given measure for $0° \le \theta < 360°$.

61. 30° **62.** 55° **63.** 82°

64. Critical Thinking Explain how the tangent of an angle in standard position is related to the slope of the terminal side of the angle.

65. Write About It Explain how to determine whether sin 225° is positive or negative without using a calculator.

66. Which of the following angles have a reference angle with a measure of 30°?

I. $\theta = 120°$ II. $\theta = -150°$ III. $\theta = 330°$

Ⓐ III only Ⓑ I and II only Ⓒ II and III only Ⓓ I, II, and III

67. In standard position, the terminal side of $\angle P$ passes through point $(-3, 4)$, and the terminal side of $\angle Q$ passes through point $(3, 4)$. Which trigonometric function has the same value for both angles?

Ⓕ sine Ⓖ cosine Ⓗ tangent Ⓙ secant

68. Which angle in standard position is coterminal with an angle that measures $-120°$?

Ⓐ $\theta = 60°$ Ⓑ $\theta = 120°$ Ⓒ $\theta = 240°$ Ⓓ $\theta = 300°$

CHALLENGE AND EXTEND

P is a point on the terminal side of θ in standard position. Find the value of the sine, cosine, and tangent of θ in terms of a and b. Assume that a and b are positive.

69. $P(a, b)$ **70.** $P\left(\frac{1}{a}, a\right)$ **71.** $P(a^2, ab)$

72. Write an expression that can be used to determine all of the coterminal angles of an angle that measures 50°.

73. For what values of θ, if any, are the six trigonometric functions undefined?

SPIRAL REVIEW

Use finite differences to determine the degree of the polynomial that best describes the data. *(Lesson 6-9)*

74.

x	0	1	2	3	4	5
y	−3	−1	3	9	17	27

75.

x	0	1	2	3	4	5
y	2	−2	0	14	46	102

Given $f(x) = 2x - 2$ and $g(x) = x^2 + 1$, find each value. *(Lesson 9-4)*

76. $f(g(3))$ **77.** $g(f(4))$ **78.** $f(g(-1))$

Find the value of the sine, cosine, and tangent functions for θ. *(Lesson 13-1)*

79.

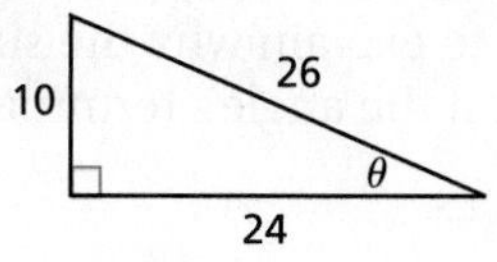

80.

θ
9
6

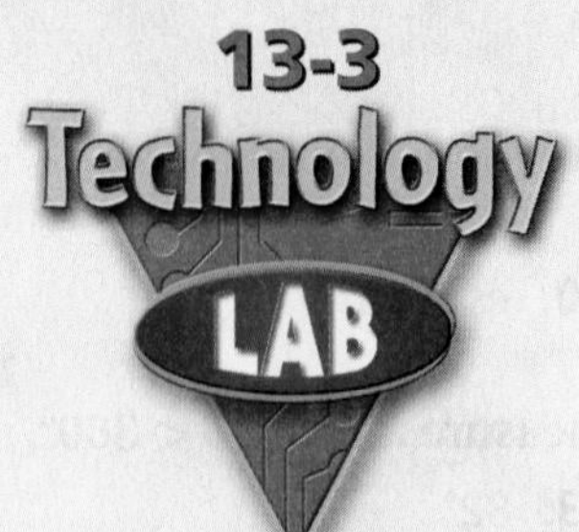

Explore the Unit Circle

A *unit circle* is a circle with a radius of 1 unit centered at the origin on the coordinate plane. You can use a graphing calculator to plot a unit circle based on the cosine and sine functions. You can then use the unit circle to explore the values of these functions for various angle measures.

Use with Lesson 13-3

go.hrw.com
Lab Resources Online
KEYWORD: MB7 Lab13

Activity

Use the sine and cosine functions to graph a unit circle, and use it to determine sin 30° and cos 30°.

1. Press MODE and make sure that the angle mode is set to **Degree**. Set the graphing mode to **Par** (Parametric).

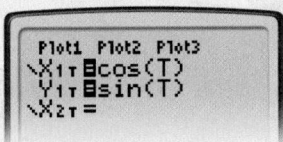

2. Press Y=, and enter **cos(T)** for $\mathbf{X_{1T}}$ and **sin(T)** for $\mathbf{Y_{1T}}$.

3. Press WINDOW and set **Tmin** to 0, **Tmax** to 360, and **Tstep** to 2. Set **Xmin** and **Ymin** to −1, **Xmax** and **Ymax** to 1, and **Xscl** and **Yscl** to 0.1.

4. Press ZOOM and select **5:Zsquare**. A circle with a radius of 1 unit is displayed.

5. Press TRACE. Use the arrow keys to move the cursor to the point where **T=30**.

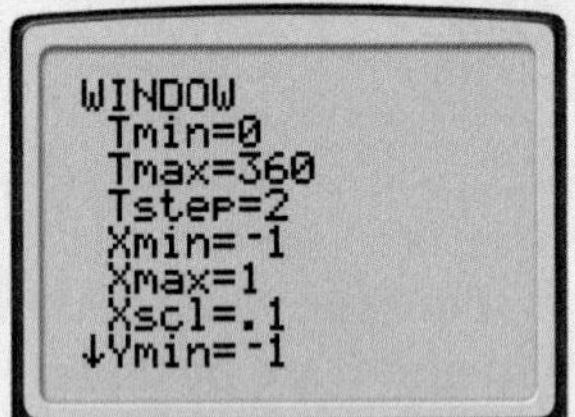

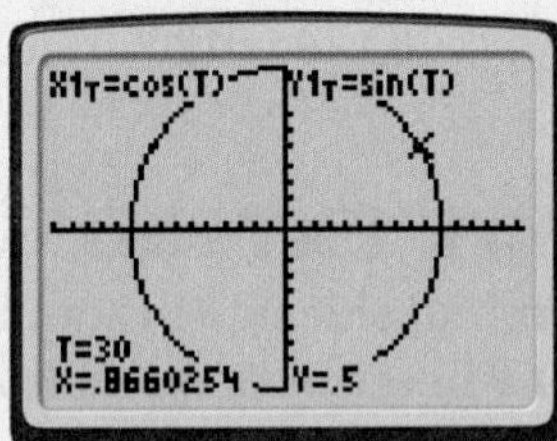

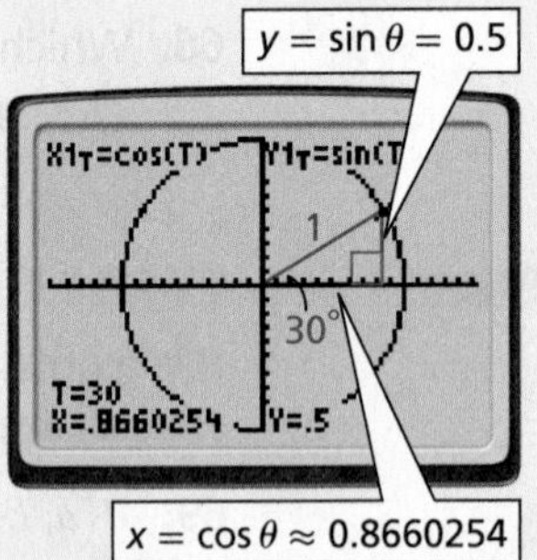

From Lesson 13-1, you know that $\sin 30° = \frac{1}{2} = 0.5$ and that $\cos 30° = \frac{\sqrt{3}}{2} \approx 0.8660254$. These values agree with those shown on the graph.

Notice that the unit circle can be used to define the cosine and sine functions. For an angle θ in standard position whose terminal side passes through point $P(x, y)$ on the unit circle, $\sin \theta = y$ and $\cos \theta = x$.

Try This

Use the unit circle on your graphing calculator to determine the values of the sine and cosine functions of each angle.

1. $\theta = 150°$
2. $\theta = 244°$
3. $\theta = 90°$
4. **Make a Conjecture** How can you verify that the unit circle displayed on your graphing calculator has a radius of 1 unit?
5. **Make a Conjecture** Use the graph of the unit circle to explain why the sine function is negative for an angle θ in standard position if the angle's terminal side lies in Quadrants III or IV.

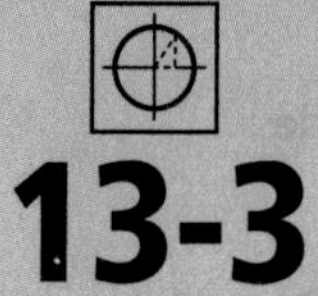

13-3 The Unit Circle

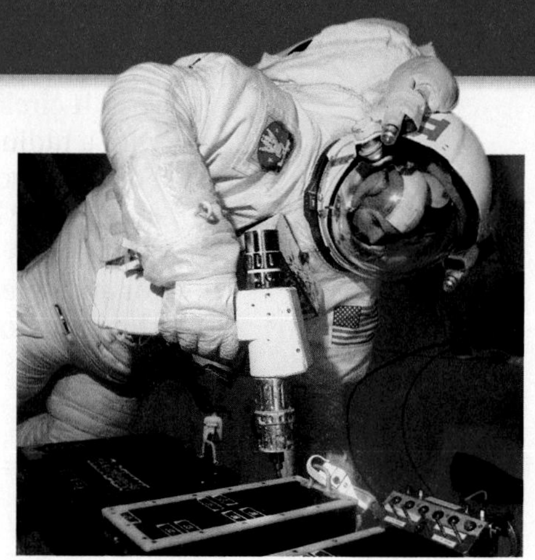

Objectives

Convert angle measures between degrees and radians.

Find the values of trigonometric functions on the unit circle.

Vocabulary

radian

unit circle

Who uses this?

Engineers can use angles measured in radians when designing machinery used to train astronauts. (See Example 4.)

So far, you have measured angles in degrees. You can also measure angles in *radians*.

A **radian** is a unit of angle measure based on arc length. Recall from geometry that an *arc* is an unbroken part of a circle. If a central angle θ in a circle of radius r intercepts an arc of length r, then the measure of θ is defined as 1 radian.

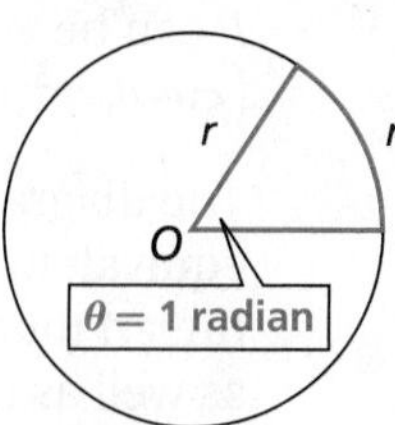

The circumference of a circle of radius r is $2\pi r$. Therefore, an angle representing one complete clockwise rotation measures 2π radians. You can use the fact that 2π radians is equivalent to 360° to convert between radians and degrees.

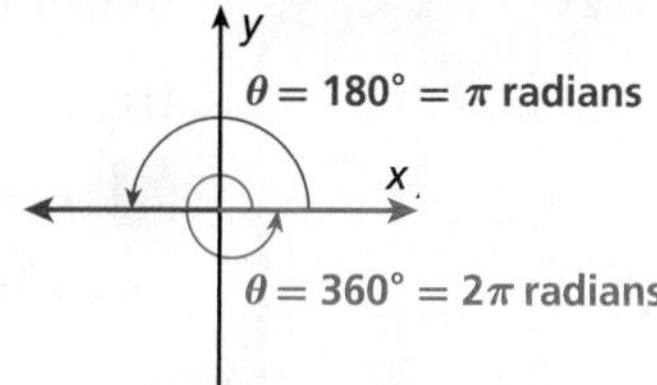

Converting Angle Measures

DEGREES TO RADIANS	RADIANS TO DEGREES
Multiply the number of degrees by $\left(\frac{\pi \text{ radians}}{180°}\right)$.	Multiply the number of radians by $\left(\frac{180°}{\pi \text{ radians}}\right)$.

EXAMPLE 1 **Converting Between Degrees and Radians**

Reading Math

Angles measured in radians are often not labeled with the unit. If an angle measure does not have a degree symbol, you can usually assume that the angle is measured in radians.

Convert each measure from degrees to radians or from radians to degrees.

A −45°

$$-45\cancel{°}\left(\frac{\pi \text{ radians}}{180\cancel{°}}\right) = -\frac{\pi}{4} \text{ radians}$$ *Multiply by* $\left(\frac{\pi \text{ radians}}{180°}\right)$.

B $\frac{5\pi}{6}$ radians

$$\left(\frac{5\cancel{\pi}}{6} \cancel{\text{radians}}\right)\left(\frac{180°}{\cancel{\pi} \cancel{\text{radians}}}\right) = 150°$$ *Multiply by* $\left(\frac{180°}{\pi \text{ radians}}\right)$.

Convert each measure from degrees to radians or from radians to degrees.

1a. 80° **1b.** $\frac{2\pi}{9}$ radians **1c.** −36° **1d.** 4π radians

A **unit circle** is a circle with a radius of 1 unit. For every point $P(x, y)$ on the unit circle, the value of r is 1. Therefore, for an angle θ in standard position:

$$\sin\theta = \frac{y}{r} = \frac{y}{1} = y$$

$$\cos\theta = \frac{x}{r} = \frac{x}{1} = x$$

$$\tan\theta = \frac{y}{x}$$

So the coordinates of P can be written as $(\cos\theta, \sin\theta)$.

The diagram shows the equivalent degree and radian measures of special angles, as well as the corresponding x- and y-coordinates of points on the unit circle.

The Unit Circle

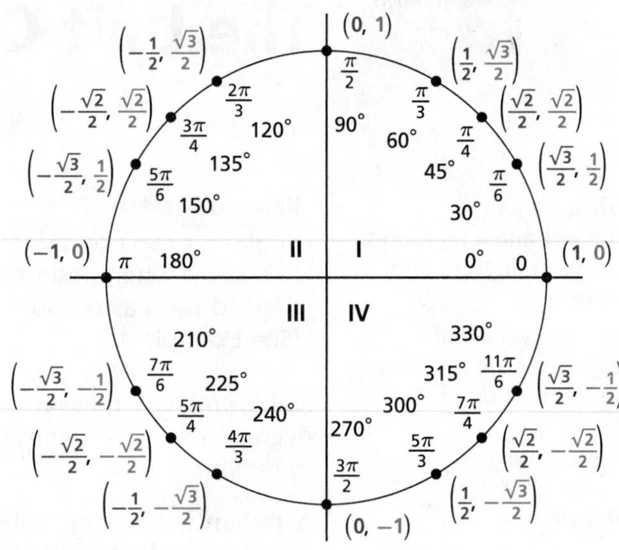

EXAMPLE 2 Using the Unit Circle to Evaluate Trigonometric Functions

Use the unit circle to find the exact value of each trigonometric function.

 **A** $\cos 210°$

The angle passes through the point $\left(-\frac{\sqrt{3}}{2}, -\frac{1}{2}\right)$ on the unit circle.

$\cos 210° = x$ *Use* $\cos\theta = x$.

$= -\frac{\sqrt{3}}{2}$

 **B** $\tan\frac{5\pi}{3}$

The angle passes through the point $\left(\frac{1}{2}, -\frac{\sqrt{3}}{2}\right)$ on the unit circle.

$\tan\frac{5\pi}{3} = \frac{y}{x}$ *Use* $\tan\theta = \frac{y}{x}$.

$= \frac{-\frac{\sqrt{3}}{2}}{\frac{1}{2}} = -\frac{\sqrt{3}}{2} \cdot \frac{2}{1} = -\sqrt{3}$

Use the unit circle to find the exact value of each trigonometric function.

2a. $\sin 315°$ **2b.** $\tan 180°$ **2c.** $\cos\frac{4\pi}{3}$

You can use reference angles and Quadrant I of the unit circle to determine the values of trigonometric functions.

Trigonometric Functions and Reference Angles
To find the sine, cosine, or tangent of θ:
Step 1 Determine the measure of the reference angle of θ.
Step 2 Use Quadrant I of the unit circle to find the sine, cosine, or tangent of the reference angle.
Step 3 Determine the quadrant of the terminal side of θ in standard position. Adjust the sign of the sine, cosine, or tangent based upon the quadrant of the terminal side.

The diagram shows how the signs of the trigonometric functions depend on the quadrant containing the terminal side of θ in standard position.

	QII	QI
	$\sin\theta: +$ $\cos\theta: -$ $\tan\theta: -$	$\sin\theta: +$ $\cos\theta: +$ $\tan\theta: +$
	QIII	**QIV**
	$\sin\theta: -$ $\cos\theta: -$ $\tan\theta: +$	$\sin\theta: -$ $\cos\theta: +$ $\tan\theta: -$

EXAMPLE 3 Using Reference Angles to Evaluate Trigonometric Functions

Use a reference angle to find the exact value of the sine, cosine, and tangent of 225°.

Step 1 Find the measure of the reference angle.

The reference angle measures 45°.

Step 2 Find the sine, cosine, and tangent of the reference angle.

$\sin 45° = \frac{\sqrt{2}}{2}$ — *Use* $\sin\theta = y$.

$\cos 45° = \frac{\sqrt{2}}{2}$ — *Use* $\cos\theta = x$.

$\tan 45° = 1$ — *Use* $\tan\theta = \frac{y}{x}$.

Step 3 Adjust the signs, if needed.

$\sin 225° = -\frac{\sqrt{2}}{2}$ — *In Quadrant III,* $\sin\theta$ *is negative.*

$\cos 225° = -\frac{\sqrt{2}}{2}$ — *In Quadrant III,* $\cos\theta$ *is negative.*

$\tan 225° = 1$ — *In Quadrant III,* $\tan\theta$ *is positive.*

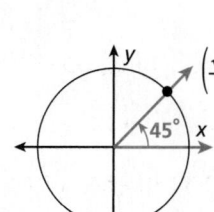

Use a reference angle to find the exact value of the sine, cosine, and tangent of each angle.

3a. 270° **3b.** $\frac{11\pi}{6}$ **3c.** $-30°$

If you know the measure of a central angle of a circle, you can determine the length s of the arc intercepted by the angle.

$$\frac{\text{radian measure of } \theta}{\text{radian measure of circle}} \rightarrow \frac{\theta}{2\pi} = \frac{s}{2\pi r} \leftarrow \frac{\text{arc length intercepted by } \theta}{\text{arc length intercepted by circle}}$$

$$\theta = \frac{s}{r} \quad \text{Multiply each side by } 2\pi.$$

$$s = r\theta \quad \text{Solve for } s.$$

Arc Length Formula

For a circle of radius r, the arc length s intercepted by a central angle θ (measured in radians) is given by the following formula.

$$s = r\theta$$

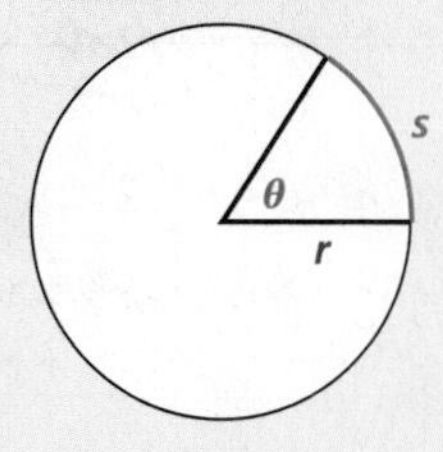

EXAMPLE 4 Engineering Application

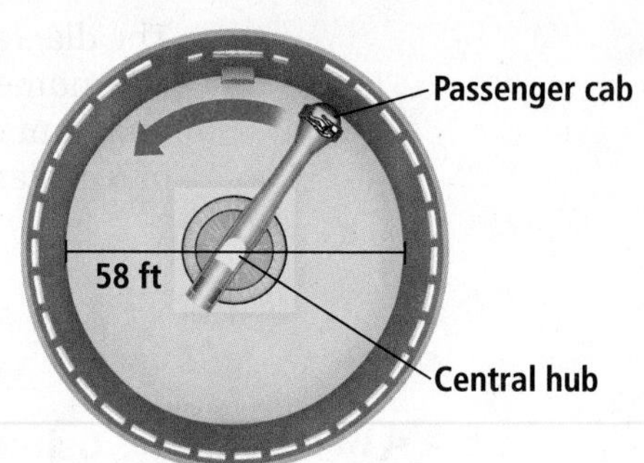

A human centrifuge is a device used in training astronauts. The passenger cab of the centrifuge shown makes 32 complete revolutions about the central hub in 1 minute. To the nearest foot, how far does an astronaut in the cab travel in 1 second?

Step 1 Find the radius of the centrifuge.

$r = \frac{58}{2} = 29$ ft *The radius is $\frac{1}{2}$ of the diameter.*

Step 2 Find the angle θ through which the cab rotates in 1 second.

$\frac{\text{radians rotated in 1 s}}{\text{1 s}} = \frac{\text{radians rotated in 60 s}}{\text{60 s}}$ *Write a proportion.*

$\frac{\theta \text{ radians}}{\text{1 s}} = \frac{32(2\pi) \text{ radians}}{\text{60 s}}$ *The cab rotates θ radians in 1 s and $32(2\pi)$ radians in 60 s.*

$60 \cdot \theta = 32(2\pi)$ *Cross multiply.*

$\theta = \frac{32(2\pi)}{60}$ *Divide both sides by 60.*

$\theta = \frac{16\pi}{15}$ *Simplify.*

Step 3 Find the length of the arc intercepted by $\frac{16\pi}{15}$ radians.

$s = r\theta$ *Use the arc length formula.*

$s = 29\left(\frac{16\pi}{15}\right)$ *Substitute 29 for r and $\frac{16\pi}{15}$ for θ.*

$s \approx 97$ *Simplify by using a calculator.*

The astronaut travels about 97 feet in 1 second.

4. An hour hand on Big Ben's Clock Tower in London is 14 ft long. To the nearest tenth of a foot, how far does the tip of the hour hand travel in 1 minute?

THINK AND DISCUSS

1. Explain why the tangent of a 90° angle is undefined.
2. Describe how to use a reference angle to determine the sine of an angle whose terminal side in standard position is in Quadrant IV.

3. **GET ORGANIZED** Copy and complete the graphic organizer. In each box, give an expression that can be used to determine the value of the trigonometric function.

	Acute Angle of Right Triangle	Angle of Rotation with $P(x, y)$	Angle with $P(x, y)$ on Unit Circle
$\sin\theta$			
$\cos\theta$			
$\tan\theta$			

13-3 Exercises

go.hrw.com
Homework Help Online
KEYWORD: MB7 13-3
Parent Resources Online
KEYWORD: MB7 Parent

GUIDED PRACTICE

1. **Vocabulary** What is the radius of a *unit circle*? the circumference?

SEE EXAMPLE 1 p. 943

Convert each measure from degrees to radians or from radians to degrees.

2. $30°$ 3. $-75°$ 4. $-150°$ 5. $135°$

6. $\frac{3\pi}{5}$ 7. $-\frac{5\pi}{8}$ 8. $-\frac{\pi}{3}$ 9. $\frac{4\pi}{9}$

SEE EXAMPLE 2 p. 944

Use the unit circle to find the exact value of each trigonometric function.

10. $\sin 150°$ 11. $\tan 315°$ 12. $\cot \frac{11\pi}{6}$ 13. $\cos \frac{2\pi}{3}$

SEE EXAMPLE 3 p. 945

Use a reference angle to find the exact value of the sine, cosine, and tangent of each angle.

14. $240°$ 15. $120°$ 16. $\frac{7\pi}{4}$ 17. $\frac{\pi}{3}$

SEE EXAMPLE 4 p. 946

18. **Engineering** An engineer is designing a curve on a highway. The curve will be an arc of a circle with a radius of 1260 ft. The central angle that intercepts the curve will measure $\frac{\pi}{6}$ radians. To the nearest foot, what will be the length of the curve?

PRACTICE AND PROBLEM SOLVING

Independent Practice

For Exercises	See Example
19–26	1
27–30	2
31–34	3
35	4

Extra Practice

Skills Practice p. S28
Application Practice p. S44

Convert each measure from degrees to radians or from radians to degrees.

19. $240°$ 20. $115°$ 21. $-25°$ 22. $-315°$

23. $-\frac{\pi}{9}$ 24. $\frac{2\pi}{5}$ 25. $\frac{7\pi}{2}$ 26. $-\frac{4\pi}{3}$

Use the unit circle to find the exact value of each trigonometric function.

27. $\tan 300°$ 28. $\sin 120°$ 29. $\cos \frac{5\pi}{6}$ 30. $\sec \frac{\pi}{3}$

Use a reference angle to find the exact value of the sine, cosine, and tangent of each angle.

31. $225°$ 32. $135°$ 33. $\frac{11\pi}{6}$ 34. $-\frac{5\pi}{6}$

35. **Geography** New York City is located about 40° north of the equator. If Earth's radius is about 4000 miles, approximately how many miles south would a plane need to fly from New York City to reach the equator?

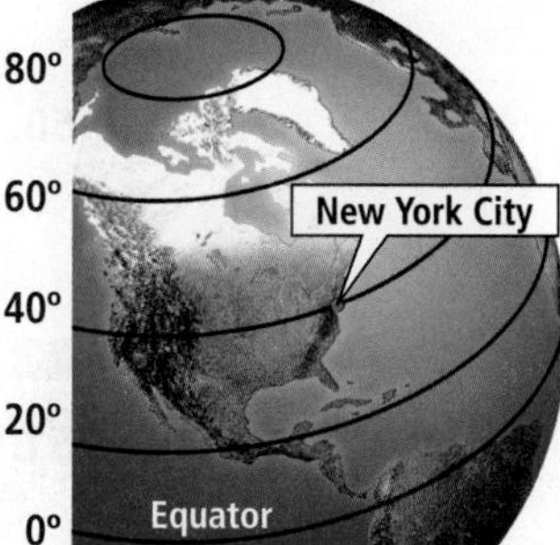

Draw an angle with the given measure in standard position. Then determine the measure of its reference angle.

36. $\frac{\pi}{3}$ 37. $\frac{7\pi}{4}$ 38. $\frac{5\pi}{6}$

39. **Electronics** A DVD rotates through an angle of 20π radians in 1 second. At this speed, how many revolutions does the DVD make in 1 minute?

40. **Work** A cashier is unsure whether a group of customers ordered and ate a large or a medium pizza. All that remains is one crust, which has an arc length of about $4\frac{1}{4}$ in. All pizzas are divided into 12 equal pieces. If medium pizzas have a diameter of 12 in. and large pizzas have a diameter of 16 in., what size did the customers order? Explain how you determined your answer.

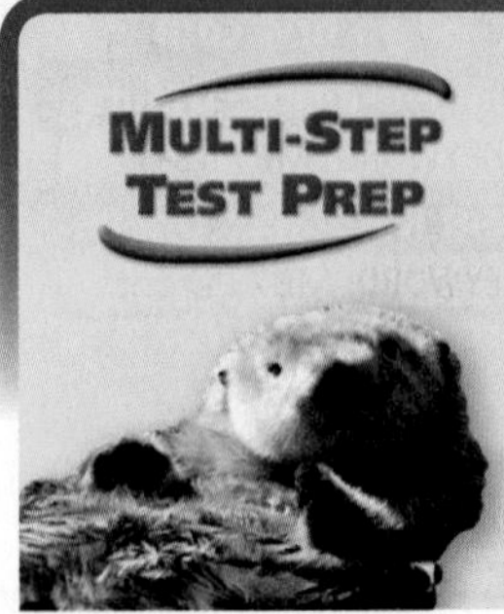

41. This problem will prepare you for the Multi-Step Test Prep on page 956.
A railing along an observation deck at an aquarium has a length of 22 ft. The railing is shaped like an arc that represents $\frac{1}{8}$ of a circle.
   a. What is the measure, to the nearest degree, of the central angle that intercepts the railing?
   b. To the nearest foot, what is the radius of the circle on which the railing is based?

Find the measure of an angle that is coterminal with each given angle.

42. $\theta = \frac{\pi}{8}$ **43.** $\theta = \pi$ **44.** $\theta = \frac{3\pi}{4}$ **45.** $\theta = -\frac{4\pi}{3}$

46. Astronomy The table shows the radius of Earth and Pluto and the number of hours that each takes to rotate on its axis.

	Radius at Equator (km)	Rotational Period (h)
Earth	6378	24
Pluto	1195	153

   a. How many days does it take Earth to rotate through an angle of 2π radians?
   b. Through what angle, in radians, do Earth and Pluto rotate in 1 hour?
   c. **What if...?** Suppose that a scientific expedition is sent to Pluto. In 1 hour, how much farther would a person at Earth's equator move than an astronaut at Pluto's equator, as a result of the bodies' rotations? Round to the nearest kilometer.

47. Quadrantal angles are angles whose terminal sides lie on the x- or y-axis in standard position. Explain how to use the unit circle to determine the sine of the quadrantal angles 0, $\frac{\pi}{2}$, π, and $\frac{3\pi}{2}$ radians.

48. Multi-Step A rear windshield wiper moves through an angle of 135° on each swipe. To the nearest inch, how much greater is the length of the arc traced by the top end of the wiper blade than the length of the arc traced by the bottom end of the wiper blade?

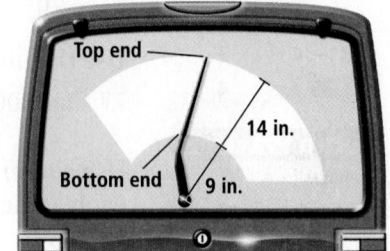

Top end
14 in.
Bottom end
9 in.

49. Critical Thinking If P is a point on the terminal side of θ in standard position, under what conditions are the coordinates of P equal to $(\cos\theta, \sin\theta)$?

50. Write About It Explain how to determine the value of $\sin(-\theta)$ if you know the value of $\sin\theta$.

51. Which angle measure is closest to 2.5 radians?

Ⓐ 90° Ⓑ 120° Ⓒ 150° Ⓓ 225°

52. What is the value of $\cot\left(\frac{5\pi}{6}\right)$?

Ⓕ $-\sqrt{3}$ Ⓖ $-\frac{\sqrt{3}}{3}$ Ⓗ $\frac{\sqrt{3}}{3}$ Ⓙ $\sqrt{3}$

53. Short Response If the tangent of an angle θ is $-\sqrt{3}$ and the cosine of θ is $\frac{1}{2}$, what is the value of the other four trigonometric functions of θ? Explain how you determined your answer.

CHALLENGE AND EXTEND

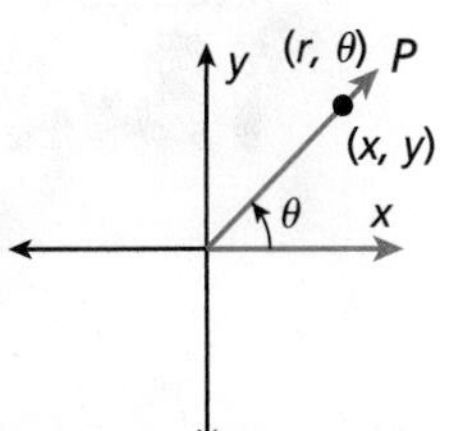

Polar Coordinates **In the rectangular coordinate system, the coordinates of point P are (x, y). In the polar coordinate system, the coordinates of point P are (r, θ). Convert each point from polar coordinates to rectangular coordinates.**

54. $\left(6\sqrt{2}, \frac{\pi}{4}\right)$ **55.** $\left(10, \frac{7\pi}{6}\right)$ **56.** $\left(5, \frac{5\pi}{3}\right)$

57. **Photography** A photographer taking nighttime photos of wildlife is using a searchlight attached to the roof of a truck. The light has a range of 250 m and can be rotated horizontally through an angle of 150°. Estimate the area of ground that can be lit by the searchlight without moving the truck. Explain how you determined your estimate.

58. What is the range of each of the six trigonometric functions for the domain $\{\theta \mid -90° < \theta < 90°\}$?

SPIRAL REVIEW

Graph each function, and identify its domain and range. *(Lesson 8-7)*

59. $f(x) = \sqrt{x+4}$ **60.** $f(x) = \sqrt[3]{x} - 3$ **61.** $f(x) = -3\sqrt{x}$

Find the 12th term of each geometric sequence. *(Lesson 12-4)*

62. 900, 180, 36, 7.2, ... **63.** −6, 24, −96, 384, ... **64.** $\frac{1}{8}, \frac{3}{8}, 1\frac{1}{8}, 3\frac{3}{8}, \ldots$

Find the measure of the reference angle for each given angle. *(Lesson 13-2)*

65. $\theta = 135°$ **66.** $\theta = -295°$ **67.** $\theta = 175°$ **68.** $\theta = -155°$

Career Path

go.hrw.com
Career Resources Online
KEYWORD: MB7 Career

Darryl Wright
Surveying Assistant

Q: What high school math classes did you take?

A: Algebra 1, Geometry, Algebra 2, and Trigonometry

Q: What do you like about surveying?

A: I like being outside and being in the construction industry. It's cool to see a bridge or building built where there wasn't anything before. I also like the high-tech instruments we get to use.

Q: How is math used in surveying?

A: Surveying is basically measuring a lot of distances and angles, so we use trigonometry and geometry all the time. I also do unit conversions to make sure the measurements are in the correct form.

Q: What are your future plans?

A: I'm taking classes at a community college and working toward an associate's degree in surveying. At the same time, I'm gaining work experience that will eventually help me become a licensed surveyor.

13-4 Inverses of Trigonometric Functions

Objectives
Evaluate inverse trigonometric functions.

Use trigonometric equations and inverse trigonometric functions to solve problems.

Vocabulary
inverse sine function
inverse cosine function
inverse tangent function

Who uses this?
Hikers can use inverse trigonometric functions to navigate in the wilderness. (See Example 3.)

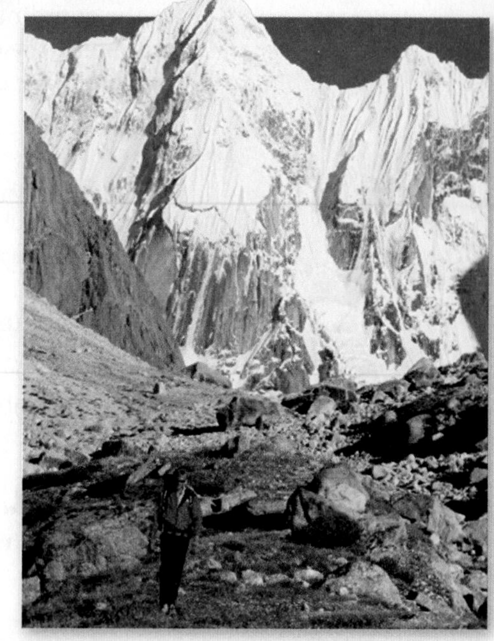

You have evaluated trigonometric functions for a given angle. You can also find the measure of angles given the value of a trigonometric function by using an *inverse trigonometric* relation.

Function	Inverse Relation
$\sin\theta = a$	$\sin^{-1} a = \theta$
$\cos\theta = a$	$\cos^{-1} a = \theta$
$\tan\theta = a$	$\tan^{-1} a = \theta$

Reading Math

The expression $\sin^{-1}$ is read as "the inverse sine." In this notation, $^{-1}$ indicates the *inverse* of the sine function, NOT the *reciprocal* of the sine function.

The inverses of the trigonometric functions are not functions themselves because there are many values of θ for a particular value of a. For example, suppose that you want to find $\cos^{-1}\frac{1}{2}$. Based on the unit circle, angles that measure $\frac{\pi}{3}$ and $\frac{5\pi}{3}$ radians have a cosine of $\frac{1}{2}$. So do all angles that are coterminal with these angles.

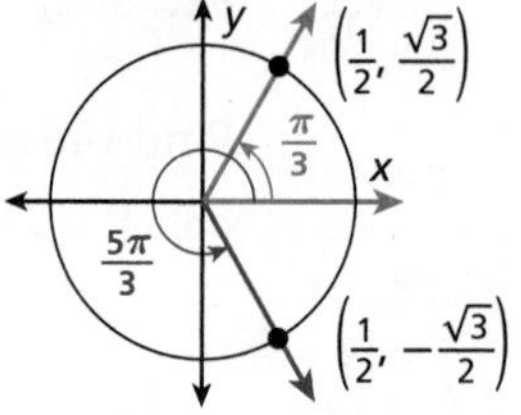

EXAMPLE 1 Finding Trigonometric Inverses

Find all possible values of $\sin^{-1}\frac{\sqrt{2}}{2}$.

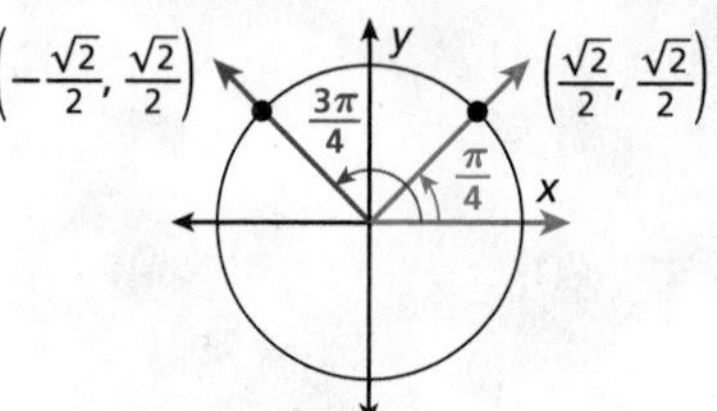

Step 1 Find the values between 0 and 2π radians for which $\sin\theta$ is equal to $\frac{\sqrt{2}}{2}$.

$$\frac{\sqrt{2}}{2} = \sin\frac{\pi}{4}, \qquad \frac{\sqrt{2}}{2} = \sin\frac{3\pi}{4}$$

Use y-coordinates of points on the unit circle.

Step 2 Find the angles that are coterminal with angles measuring $\frac{\pi}{4}$ and $\frac{3\pi}{4}$ radians.

$$\frac{\pi}{4} + (2\pi)n, \qquad \frac{3\pi}{4} + (2\pi)n$$

Add integer multiples of 2π radians, where n is an integer.

1. Find all possible values of $\tan^{-1}1$.

Because more than one value of θ produces the same output value for a given trigonometric function, it is necessary to restrict the domain of each trigonometric function in order to define the inverse trigonometric functions.

Trigonometric functions with restricted domains are indicated with a capital letter. The domains of the Sine, Cosine, and Tangent functions are restricted as follows.

$\text{Sin}\,\theta = \sin\theta$ for $\left\{\theta \mid -\frac{\pi}{2} \le \theta \le \frac{\pi}{2}\right\}$ *θ is restricted to Quadrants I and IV.*

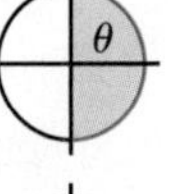

$\text{Cos}\,\theta = \cos\theta$ for $\left\{\theta \mid 0 \le \theta \le \pi\right\}$ *θ is restricted to Quadrants I and II.*

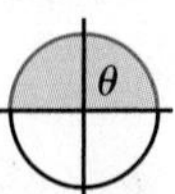

$\text{Tan}\,\theta = \tan\theta$ for $\left\{\theta \mid -\frac{\pi}{2} < \theta < \frac{\pi}{2}\right\}$ *θ is restricted to Quadrants I and IV.*

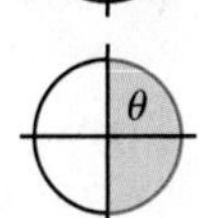

These functions can be used to define the inverse trigonometric functions. For each value of a in the domain of the inverse trigonometric functions, there is only one value of θ. Therefore, even though $\tan^{-1}1$ has many values, $\text{Tan}^{-1}1$ has only one value.

Inverse Trigonometric Functions

WORDS	SYMBOL	DOMAIN	RANGE
The **inverse sine function** is $\text{Sin}^{-1}a = \theta$, where $\text{Sin}\,\theta = a$.	$\text{Sin}^{-1}a$	$\left\{a \mid -1 \le a \le 1\right\}$	$\left\{\theta \mid -\frac{\pi}{2} \le \theta \le \frac{\pi}{2}\right\}$ $\left\{\theta \mid -90^\circ \le \theta \le 90^\circ\right\}$
The **inverse cosine function** is $\text{Cos}^{-1}a = \theta$, where $\text{Cos}\,\theta = a$.	$\text{Cos}^{-1}a$	$\left\{a \mid -1 \le a \le 1\right\}$	$\left\{\theta \mid 0 \le \theta \le \pi\right\}$ $\left\{\theta \mid 0^\circ \le \theta \le 180^\circ\right\}$
The **inverse tangent function** is $\text{Tan}^{-1}a = \theta$, where $\text{Tan}\,\theta = a$.	$\text{Tan}^{-1}a$	$\left\{a \mid -\infty < a < \infty\right\}$	$\left\{\theta \mid -\frac{\pi}{2} < \theta < \frac{\pi}{2}\right\}$ $\left\{\theta \mid -90^\circ < \theta < 90^\circ\right\}$

Reading Math

The inverse trigonometric functions are also called the arcsine, arccosine, and arctangent functions.

EXAMPLE 2 Evaluating Inverse Trigonometric Functions

Evaluate each inverse trigonometric function. Give your answer in both radians and degrees.

A $\text{Cos}^{-1}\frac{1}{2}$

$\frac{1}{2} = \text{Cos}\,\theta$ *Find the value of θ for $0 \le \theta \le \pi$ whose Cosine is $\frac{1}{2}$.*

$\frac{1}{2} = \text{Cos}\frac{\pi}{3}$ *Use x-coordinates of points on the unit circle.*

$\text{Cos}^{-1}\frac{1}{2} = \frac{\pi}{3}$, or $\text{Cos}^{-1}\frac{1}{2} = 60^\circ$

$\left(\frac{1}{2}, \frac{\sqrt{3}}{2}\right)$; $\frac{\pi}{3}$, or 60°; x; y

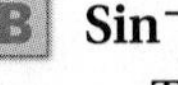
B $\text{Sin}^{-1}2$

The domain of the inverse sine function is $\left\{a \mid -1 \le a \le 1\right\}$. Because 2 is outside this domain, $\text{Sin}^{-1}2$ is undefined.

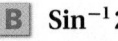

Evaluate each inverse trigonometric function. Give your answer in both radians and degrees.

2a. $\text{Sin}^{-1}\left(-\frac{\sqrt{2}}{2}\right)$ **2b.** $\text{Cos}^{-1}0$

You can solve trigonometric equations by using trigonometric inverses.

EXAMPLE 3 Navigation Application

A group of hikers plans to walk from a campground to a lake. The lake is 2 miles east and 0.5 mile north of the campground. To the nearest degree, in what direction should the hikers head?

Step 1 Draw a diagram.

The hikers' direction should be based on θ, the measure of an acute angle of a right triangle.

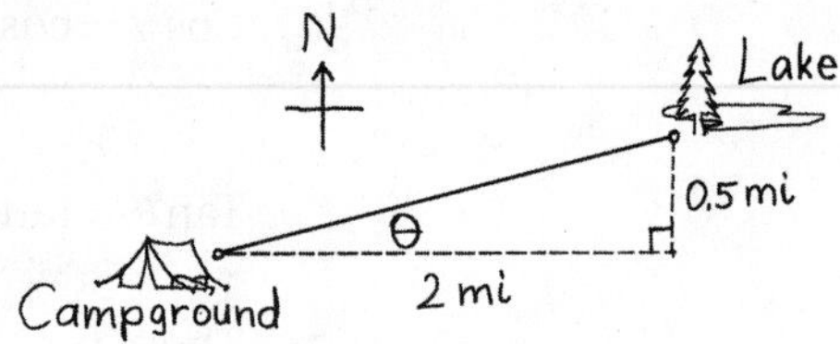

> **Caution!**
>
> If the answer on your calculator screen is 0.2449786631 when you enter $\tan^{-1}(0.25)$, your calculator is set to radian mode instead of degree mode.

Step 2 Find the value of θ.

$\tan\theta = \dfrac{\text{opp.}}{\text{adj.}}$ *Use the tangent ratio.*

$\tan\theta = \dfrac{0.5}{2} = 0.25$ *Substitute 0.5 for opp. and 2 for adj. Then simplify.*

$\theta = \text{Tan}^{-1}0.25$

$\theta \approx 14°$

The hikers should head 14° north of east.

Use the information given above to answer the following.

3. An unusual rock formation is 1 mile east and 0.75 mile north of the lake. To the nearest degree, in what direction should the hikers head from the lake to reach the rock formation?

EXAMPLE  Solving Trigonometric Equations

Solve each equation to the nearest tenth. Use the given restrictions.

 **$\cos\theta = 0.6$, for $0° \le \theta \le 180°$**

The restrictions on θ are the same as those for the inverse cosine function.

$\theta = \text{Cos}^{-1}(0.6) \approx 53.1°$ *Use the inverse cosine function on your calculator.*

 **$\cos\theta = 0.6$, for $270° < \theta < 360°$**

The terminal side of θ is restricted to Quadrant IV. Find the angle in Quadrant IV that has the same cosine value as 53.1°.

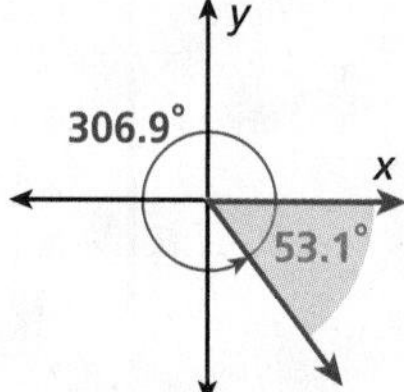

$\theta \approx 360° - 53.1° \approx 306.9°$ *θ has a reference angle of 53.1°, and $270° < \theta < 360°$.*

Solve each equation to the nearest tenth. Use the given restrictions.

4a. $\tan\theta = -2$, for $-90° < \theta < 90°$

4b. $\tan\theta = -2$, for $90° < \theta < 180°$

THINK AND DISCUSS

1. Given that θ is an acute angle in a right triangle, describe the measurements that you need to know to find the value of θ by using the inverse cosine function.
2. Explain the difference between $\tan^{-1}a$ and $\text{Tan}^{-1}a$.

3. **GET ORGANIZED** Copy and complete the graphic organizer. In each box, give the indicated property of the inverse trigonometric functions.

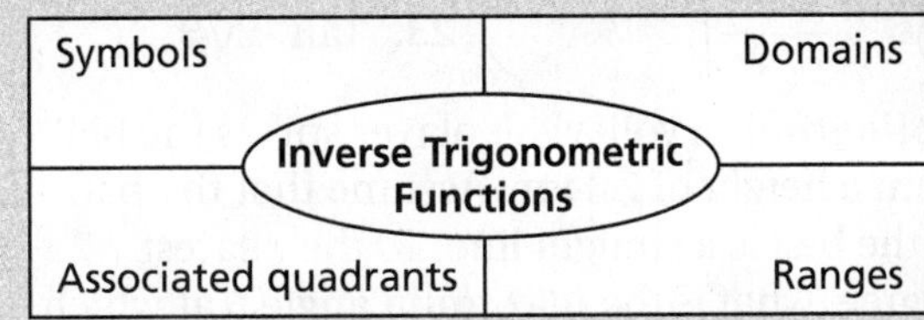

13-4 Exercises

GUIDED PRACTICE

1. **Vocabulary** Explain how the inverse tangent function differs from the reciprocal of the tangent function.

SEE EXAMPLE 1 p. 950

Find all possible values of each expression.

2. $\sin^{-1}\left(-\frac{1}{2}\right)$
3. $\tan^{-1}\frac{\sqrt{3}}{3}$
4. $\cos^{-1}\left(-\frac{\sqrt{2}}{2}\right)$

SEE EXAMPLE 2 p. 951

Evaluate each inverse trigonometric function. Give your answer in both radians and degrees.

5. $\text{Cos}^{-1}\frac{\sqrt{3}}{2}$
6. $\text{Tan}^{-1}1$
7. $\text{Cos}^{-1}2$
8. $\text{Tan}^{-1}\left(-\sqrt{3}\right)$
9. $\text{Sin}^{-1}\frac{\sqrt{2}}{2}$
10. $\text{Sin}^{-1}0$

SEE EXAMPLE 3 p. 952

11. **Architecture** A point on the top of the Leaning Tower of Pisa is shifted about 13.5 ft horizontally compared with the tower's base. To the nearest degree, how many degrees does the tower tilt from vertical?

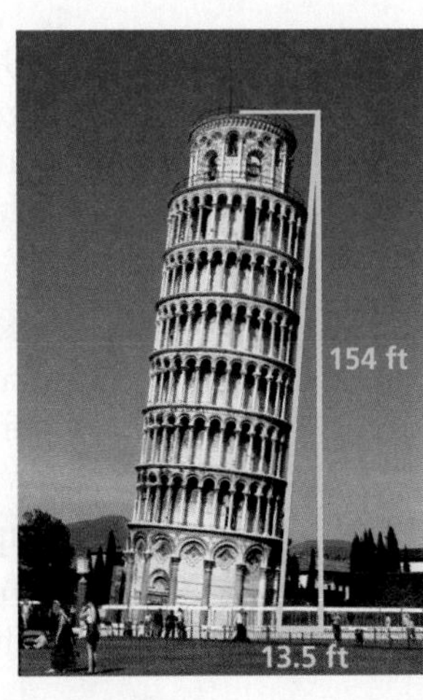

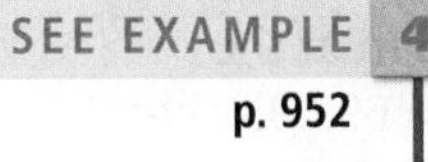
SEE EXAMPLE 4 p. 952

Solve each equation to the nearest tenth. Use the given restrictions.

12. $\tan\theta = 1.4$, for $-90° < \theta < 90°$
13. $\tan\theta = 1.4$, for $180° < \theta < 270°$
14. $\cos\theta = -0.25$, for $0 \le \theta \le 180°$
15. $\cos\theta = -0.25$, for $180° < \theta < 270°$

PRACTICE AND PROBLEM SOLVING

Independent Practice

For Exercises	See Example
16–18	1
19–24	2
25	3
26–29	4

Extra Practice

Skills Practice p. S29
Application Practice p. S44

Find all possible values of each expression.

16. $\cos^{-1} 1$ **17.** $\sin^{-1} \frac{\sqrt{3}}{2}$ **18.** $\tan^{-1}(-1)$

Evaluate each inverse trigonometric function. Give your answer in both radians and degrees.

19. $\text{Sin}^{-1} \frac{\sqrt{3}}{2}$ **20.** $\text{Cos}^{-1}(-1)$ **21.** $\text{Tan}^{-1}\left(-\frac{\sqrt{3}}{3}\right)$

22. $\text{Cos}^{-1}\left(-\frac{\sqrt{3}}{2}\right)$ **23.** $\text{Tan}^{-1} \sqrt{3}$ **24.** $\text{Sin}^{-1} \sqrt{3}$

25. Volleyball A volleyball player spikes the ball from a height of 2.44 m. Assume that the path of the ball is a straight line. To the nearest degree, what is the maximum angle θ at which the ball can be hit and land within the court?

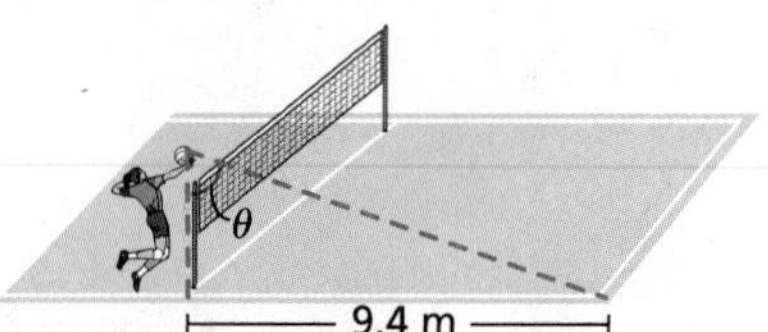

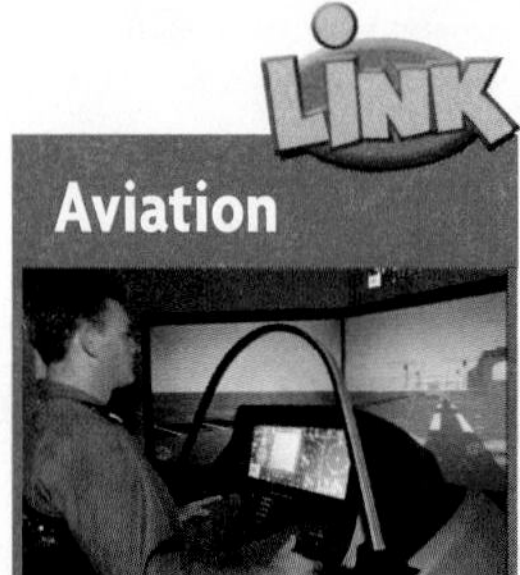

Aviation

A flight simulator is a device used in training pilots that mimics flight conditions as realistically as possible. Some flight simulators involve full-size cockpits equipped with sound, visual, and motion systems.

Solve each equation to the nearest tenth. Use the given restrictions.

26. $\sin \theta = -0.75$, for $-90° \le \theta \le 90°$ **27.** $\sin \theta = -0.75$, for $180° < \theta < 270°$

28. $\cos \theta = 0.1$, for $0° \le \theta \le 180°$ **29.** $\cos \theta = 0.1$, for $270° < \theta < 360°$

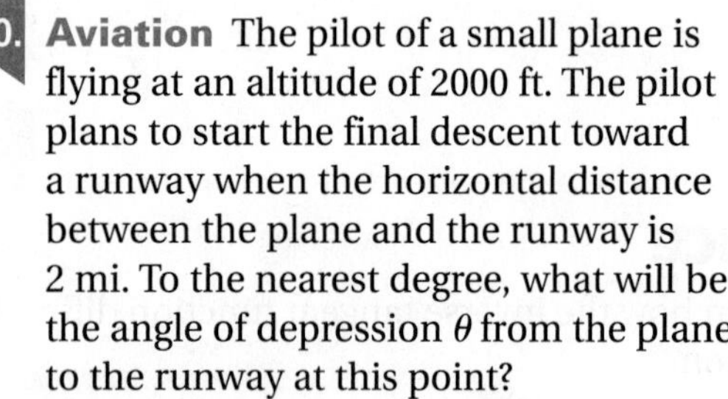

30. Aviation The pilot of a small plane is flying at an altitude of 2000 ft. The pilot plans to start the final descent toward a runway when the horizontal distance between the plane and the runway is 2 mi. To the nearest degree, what will be the angle of depression θ from the plane to the runway at this point?

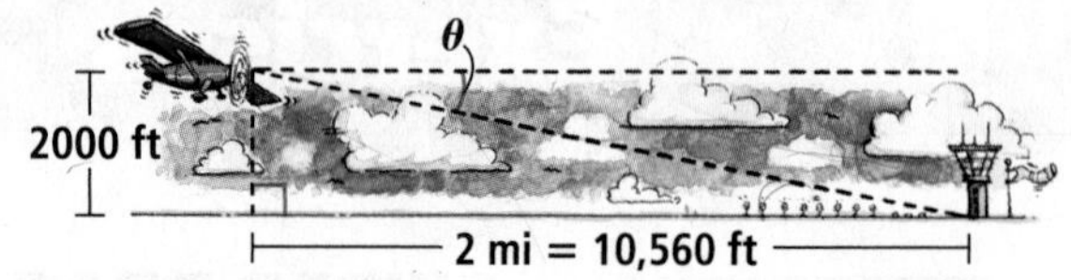

31. Multi-Step The table shows the dimensions of three pool styles offered by a construction company.

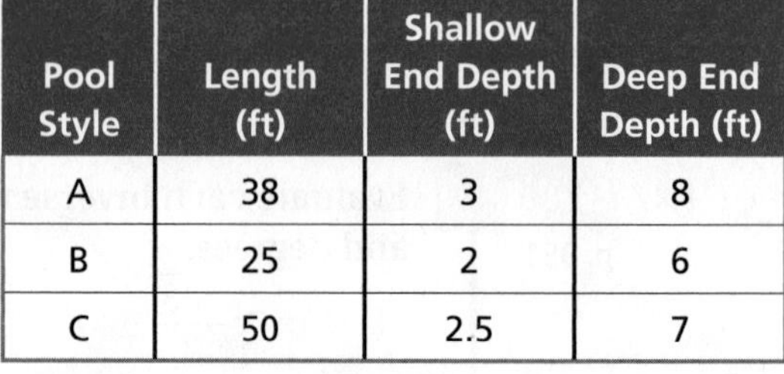

Pool Style	Length (ft)	Shallow End Depth (ft)	Deep End Depth (ft)
A	38	3	8
B	25	2	6
C	50	2.5	7

a. To the nearest tenth of a degree, what angle θ does the bottom of each pool make with the horizontal?

b. Which pool style's bottom has the steepest slope? Explain.

c. What if...? If the slope of the bottom of a pool can be no greater than $\frac{1}{6}$, what is the greatest angle θ that the bottom of the pool can make with the horizontal? Round to the nearest tenth of a degree.

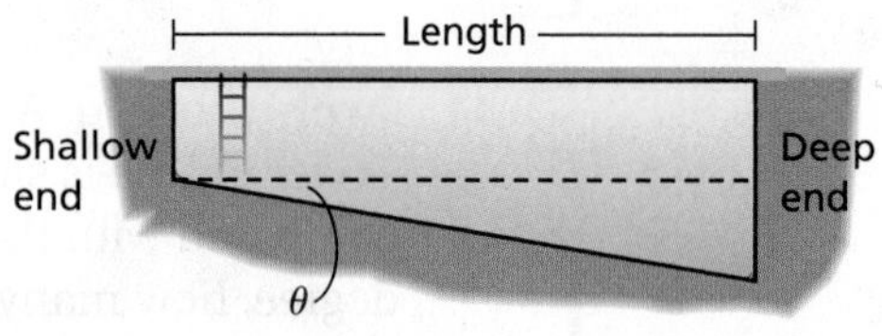

32. Navigation Lines of longitude are closer together near the poles than at the equator. The formula for the length ℓ of 1° of longitude in miles is $\ell = 69.0933 \cos \theta$, where θ is the latitude in degrees.

a. At what latitude, to the nearest degree, is the length of a degree of longitude approximately 59.8 miles?

b. To the nearest mile, how much longer is the length of a degree of longitude at the equator, which has a latitude of 0°, than at the Arctic Circle, which has a latitude of about 66°N?

MULTI-STEP TEST PREP

33. This problem will prepare you for the Multi-Step Test Prep on page 956.

Giant kelp is a seaweed that typically grows about 100 ft in height, but may reach as high as 175 ft.

a. A diver positions herself 10 ft from the base of a giant kelp so that her eye level is 5 ft above the ocean floor. If the kelp is 100 ft in height, what would be the angle of elevation from the diver to the top of the kelp? Round to the nearest tenth of a degree.

b. The angle of elevation from the diver's eye level to the top of a giant kelp whose base is 30 ft away is 75.5°. To the nearest foot, what is the height of the kelp?

Find each value.

34. $\text{Cos}^{-1}(\cos 0.4)$ **35.** $\tan(\text{Tan}^{-1} 0.7)$ **36.** $\sin(\text{Cos}^{-1} 0)$

37. Critical Thinking Explain why the domain of the Cosine function is different from the domain of the Sine function.

38. Write About It Is the statement $\text{Sin}^{-1}(\sin\theta) = \theta$ true for all values of θ? Explain.

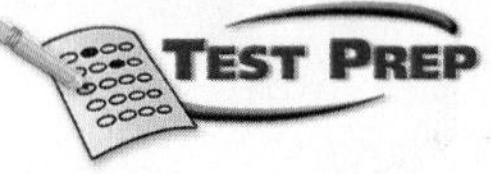

TEST PREP

39. For which equation is the value of θ in radians a positive value?

Ⓐ $\text{Cos}\,\theta = -\frac{1}{2}$ Ⓑ $\text{Tan}\,\theta = -\frac{\sqrt{3}}{3}$ Ⓒ $\text{Sin}\,\theta = -\frac{\sqrt{3}}{2}$ Ⓓ $\text{Sin}\,\theta = -1$

40. A caution sign next to a roadway states that an upcoming hill has an 8% slope. An 8% slope means that there is an 8 ft rise for 100 ft of horizontal distance. At approximately what angle does the roadway rise from the horizontal?

Ⓕ 2.2° Ⓖ 4.6° Ⓗ 8.5° Ⓙ 12.5°

41. What value of θ makes the equation $2\sqrt{2}(\text{Cos}\,\theta) = -2$ true?

Ⓐ 45° Ⓑ 60° Ⓒ 135° Ⓓ 150°

CHALLENGE AND EXTEND

42. If $\text{Sin}^{-1}\left(-\frac{\sqrt{2}}{2}\right) = -\frac{\pi}{4}$, what is the value of $\text{Csc}^{-1}\left(-\sqrt{2}\right)$?

Solve each inequality for $\{\theta \mid 0 \le \theta \le 2\pi\}$.

43. $\cos\theta \le \frac{1}{2}$ **44.** $2\sin\theta - \sqrt{3} > 0$ **45.** $\tan 2\theta \ge 1$

SPIRAL REVIEW

Graph each function. Identify the parent function that best describes the set of points, and describe the transformation from the parent function. *(Lesson 1-9)*

46. $\{(-2, -4), (-1, -0.5), (0, 0), (1, 0.5), (2, 4)\}$ **47.** $\{(-4, 1), (-2, 3), (0, 5), (2, 7), (4, 9)\}$

Find the inverse of each function. Determine whether the inverse is a function, and state its domain and range. *(Lesson 9-5)*

48. $f(x) = 3(x + 2)^2$ **49.** $f(x) = \frac{x}{4} + 1$ **50.** $f(x) = -2x^2 + 5$

Convert each measure from degrees to radians or from radians to degrees. *(Lesson 13-3)*

51. 240° **52.** $-\frac{5\pi}{4}$ **53.** 420°

CHAPTER 13

MULTI-STEP TEST PREP

SECTION 13A

Trigonometry and Angles

By the Sea The Monterey Bay Aquarium in California is visited by almost 2 million people each year. The aquarium is home to more than 550 species of plants and animals.

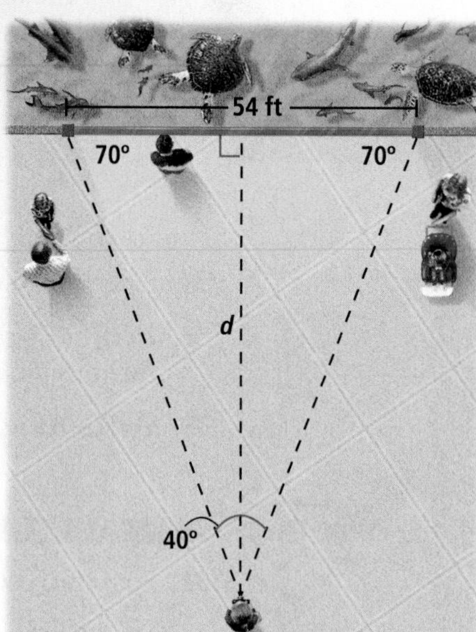

1. The window in front of the aquarium's Outer Bay exhibit is 54 ft long. Maria's camera has a viewing angle of 40°, as shown. To the nearest foot, how far would Maria need to stand from the window in order to include the entire window in a photo? This distance is labeled *d*.

2. Warty sea cucumbers may be found in Monterey Bay to a depth of about 64 m. A research vessel is anchored to the seafloor by a 70 m chain that makes an angle of 56° with the ocean's surface. Is the research vessel located over water that is too deep for warty sea cucumbers? Justify your answer.

3. A crystal jellyfish in a cylindrical aquarium tank is carried by a current in a circular path with a diameter of 2.5 m. In 1 min, the jellyfish is carried 26 cm by the current. At this rate, how long will it take the current to move the jellyfish in a complete circle? Round to the nearest minute.

4. A sea otter is released from the aquarium's rehabilitation program with a radio transmitter implanted in its abdomen. The transmitter indicates that the otter is 400 m west and 80 m south of an observation deck. How many degrees south of west should an aquarium worker standing on the deck aim his binoculars in order to see the otter? Round to the nearest degree.

READY TO GO ON?

CHAPTER 13

SECTION 13A

Quiz for Lessons 13-1 Through 13-4

13-1 Right-Angle Trigonometry

Find the values of the six trigonometric functions for θ.

1. 9, 41, θ, 40

2. 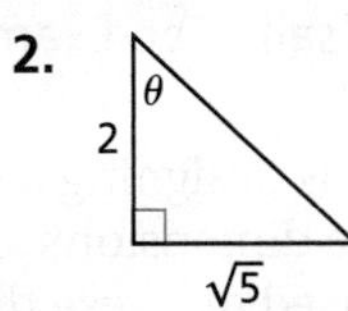

Use a trigonometric function to find the value of x.

3. 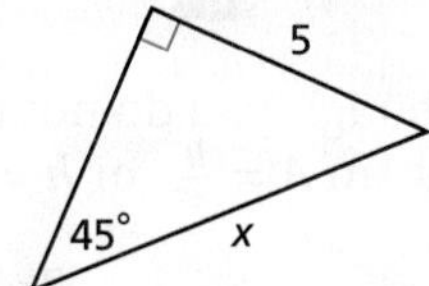

4. 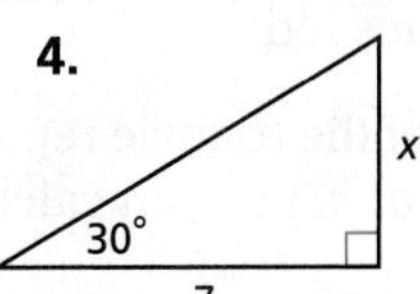

5. A biologist's eye level is 5.5 ft above the ground. She measures the angle of elevation to an eagle's nest on a cliff to be 66° when she stands 50 ft from the cliff's base. To the nearest foot, what is the height of the eagle's nest?

13-2 Angles of Rotation

Draw an angle with the given measure in standard position.

6. $-270°$

7. $405°$

Point P is a point on the terminal side of θ in standard position. Find the exact value of the six trigonometric functions for θ.

8. $P(12, -5)$

9. $P(-2, 7)$

13-3 The Unit Circle

Convert each measure from degrees to radians or from radians to degrees.

10. $-120°$

11. $63°$

12. $\frac{3\pi}{8}$

13. $-\frac{10\pi}{3}$

Use the unit circle to find the exact value of each trigonometric function.

14. $\cos 210°$

15. $\tan 120°$

16. $\cos \frac{\pi}{2}$

17. $\tan \frac{5\pi}{4}$

18. A bicycle tire rotates through an angle of 3.4π radians in 1 second. If the radius of the tire is 0.34 m, what is the bicycle's speed in meters per second? Round to the nearest tenth.

13-4 Inverses of Trigonometric Functions

Evaluate each inverse trigonometric function. Give your answer in both radians and degrees.

19. $\text{Sin}^{-1} \frac{\sqrt{3}}{2}$

20. $\text{Tan}^{-1}\left(-\frac{\sqrt{3}}{3}\right)$

21. A driver uses a ramp when unloading supplies from his delivery truck. The ramp is 10 feet long, and the bed of the truck is 4 feet off the ground. To the nearest degree, what angle does the ramp make with the ground?

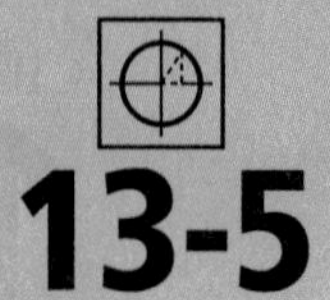

13-5 The Law of Sines

Objectives

Determine the area of a triangle given side-angle-side information.

Use the Law of Sines to find the side lengths and angle measures of a triangle.

Who uses this?

Sailmakers can use sine ratios to determine the amount of fabric needed to make a sail. (See Example 1.)

A sailmaker is designing a sail that will have the dimensions shown in the diagram. Based on these dimensions, the sailmaker can determine the amount of fabric needed.

The area of the triangle representing the sail is $\frac{1}{2}bh$. Although you do not know the value of h, you can calculate it by using the fact that $\sin A = \frac{h}{c}$, or $h = c \sin A$.

Helpful Hint

An angle and the side opposite that angle are labeled with the same letter. Capital letters are used for angles, and lowercase letters are used for sides.

$\text{Area} = \frac{1}{2}bh$ *Write the area formula.*

$\text{Area} = \frac{1}{2}bc\sin A$ *Substitute c sin A for h.*

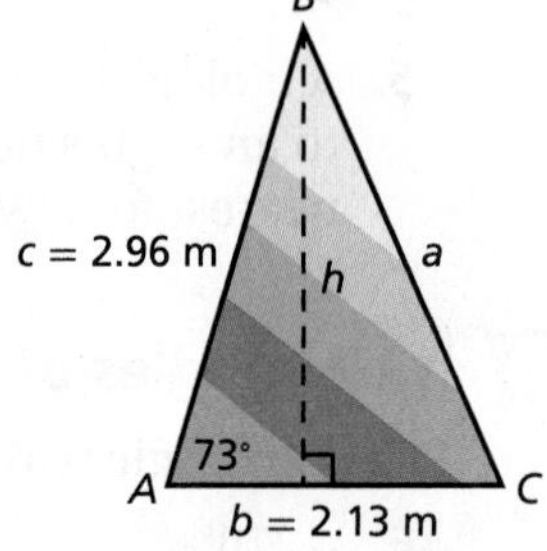

This formula allows you to determine the area of a triangle if you know the lengths of two of its sides and the measure of the angle between them.

Area of a Triangle

For $\triangle ABC$,

$\text{Area} = \frac{1}{2}bc \sin A$

$\text{Area} = \frac{1}{2}ac \sin B$

$\text{Area} = \frac{1}{2}ab \sin C$

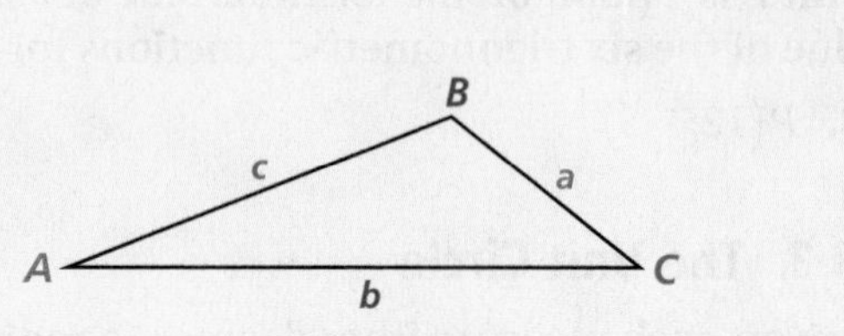

EXAMPLE 1 **Determining the Area of a Triangle**

Find the area of the sail shown at the top of the page. Round to the nearest tenth.

$\text{area} = \frac{1}{2}bc \sin A$ *Write the area formula.*

$= \frac{1}{2}(2.13)(2.96) \sin 73°$ *Substitute 2.13 for b, 2.96 for c, and 73° for A.*

≈ 3.014655113 *Use a calculator to evaluate the expression.*

The area of the sail is about 3.0 m^2.

1. Find the area of the triangle. Round to the nearest tenth.

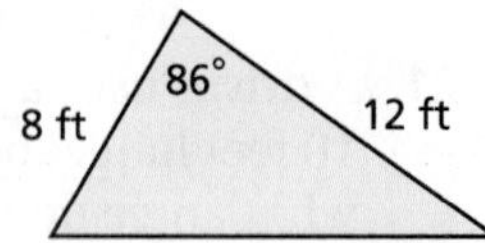

The area of $\triangle ABC$ is equal to $\frac{1}{2}bc\sin A$ or $\frac{1}{2}ac\sin B$ or $\frac{1}{2}ab\sin C$. By setting these expressions equal to each other, you can derive the Law of Sines.

$$\frac{1}{2}bc\sin A = \frac{1}{2}ac\sin B = \frac{1}{2}ab\sin C$$

$$bc\sin A = ac\sin B = ab\sin C \qquad \textit{Multiply each expression by 2.}$$

$$\frac{\cancel{b}\cancel{c}\sin A}{a\cancel{b}\cancel{c}} = \frac{\cancel{a}\cancel{c}\sin B}{\cancel{a}b\cancel{c}} = \frac{\cancel{a}\cancel{b}\sin C}{\cancel{a}\cancel{b}c} \qquad \textit{Divide each expression by abc.}$$

$$\frac{\sin A}{a} = \frac{\sin B}{b} = \frac{\sin C}{c} \qquad \textit{Divide out common factors.}$$

Law of Sines

For $\triangle ABC$, the Law of Sines states that

$$\frac{\sin A}{a} = \frac{\sin B}{b} = \frac{\sin C}{c}.$$

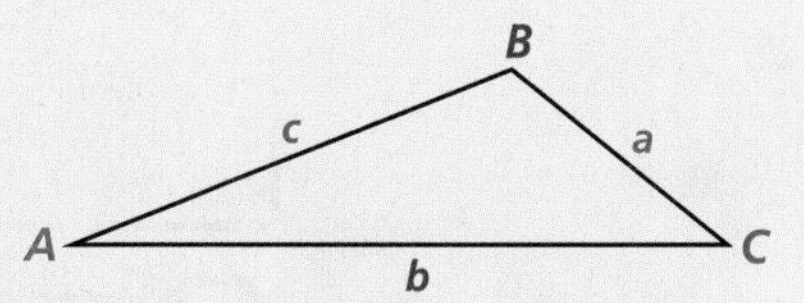

The Law of Sines allows you to solve a triangle as long as you know either of the following:

1. Two angle measures and any side length—angle-angle-side (AAS) or angle-side-angle (ASA) information
2. Two side lengths and the measure of an angle that is not between them—side-side-angle (SSA) information

EXAMPLE 2 Using the Law of Sines for AAS and ASA

Solve the triangle. Round to the nearest tenth.

A

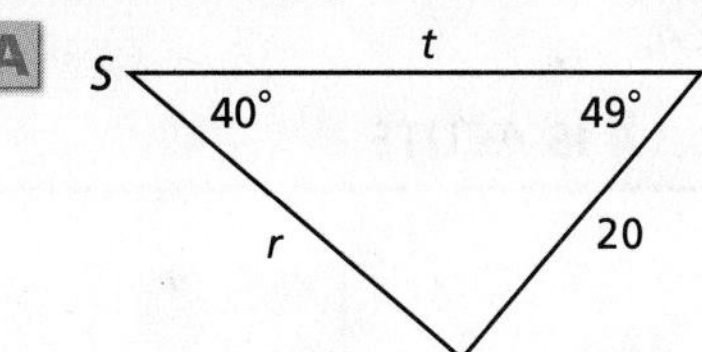

Reading Math

The expression "solve a triangle" means to find the measures of all unknown angles and sides.

Step 1 Find the third angle measure.

$m\angle R + m\angle S + m\angle T = 180°$	*Triangle Sum Theorem*
$49° + 40° + m\angle T = 180°$	*Substitute 49° for m∠R and 40° for m∠S.*
$m\angle T = 91°$	*Solve for m∠T.*

Step 2 Find the unknown side lengths.

$\frac{\sin R}{r} = \frac{\sin S}{s}$	*Law of Sines*	$\frac{\sin S}{s} = \frac{\sin T}{t}$
$\frac{\sin 49°}{r} = \frac{\sin 40°}{20}$	*Substitute.*	$\frac{\sin 40°}{20} = \frac{\sin 91°}{t}$
$r\sin 40° = 20\sin 49°$	*Cross multiply.*	$t\sin 40° = 20\sin 91°$
$r = \frac{20\sin 49°}{\sin 40°}$	*Solve for the unknown side.*	$t = \frac{20\sin 91°}{\sin 40°}$
$r \approx 23.5$		$t \approx 31.1$

Solve the triangle. Round to the nearest tenth.

B

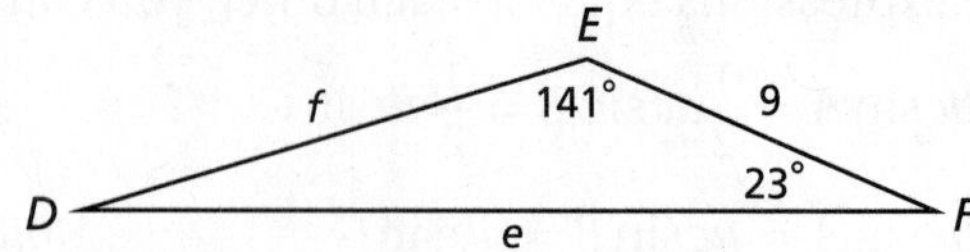

Step 1 Find the third angle measure.

$m\angle D = 180° - 141° - 23° = 16°$ *Triangle Sum Theorem*

Step 2 Find the unknown side lengths.

$\dfrac{\sin D}{d} = \dfrac{\sin E}{e}$	*Law of Sines*	$\dfrac{\sin D}{d} = \dfrac{\sin F}{f}$
$\dfrac{\sin 16°}{9} = \dfrac{\sin 141°}{e}$	*Substitute.*	$\dfrac{\sin 16°}{9} = \dfrac{\sin 23°}{f}$
$e = \dfrac{9 \sin 141°}{\sin 16°} \approx 20.5$		$f = \dfrac{9 \sin 23°}{\sin 16°} \approx 12.8$

Solve each triangle. Round to the nearest tenth.

2a.

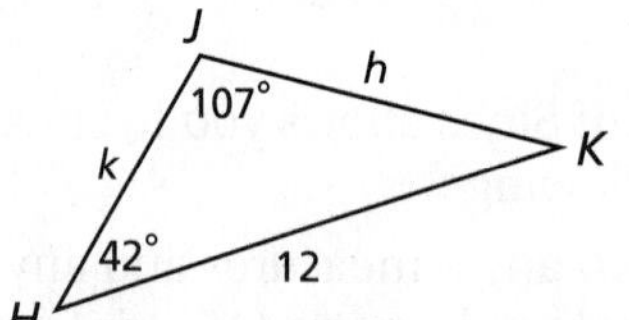

2b.

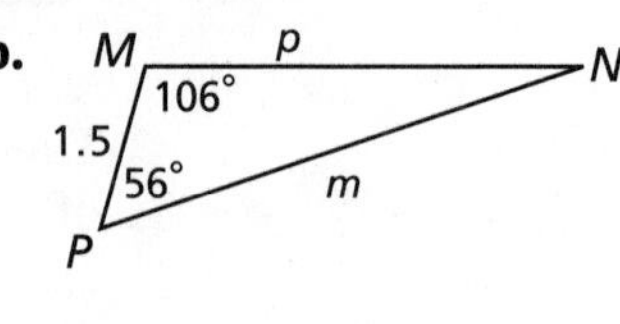

When you use the Law of Sines to solve a triangle for which you know side-side-angle (SSA) information, zero, one, or two triangles may be possible. For this reason, SSA is called the *ambiguous case*.

Ambiguous Case **Possible Triangles**

Given *a*, *b*, and m∠*A*,

∠A IS ACUTE.		∠A IS RIGHT OR OBTUSE.
$a < h$ No triangle	$a = h$ One triangle	$a \le b$ No triangle
$h < a < b$ Two triangles	$a \ge b$ One triangle	$a > b$ One triangle

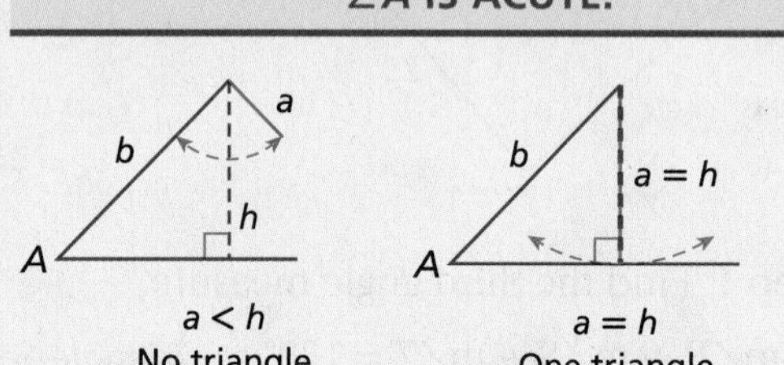

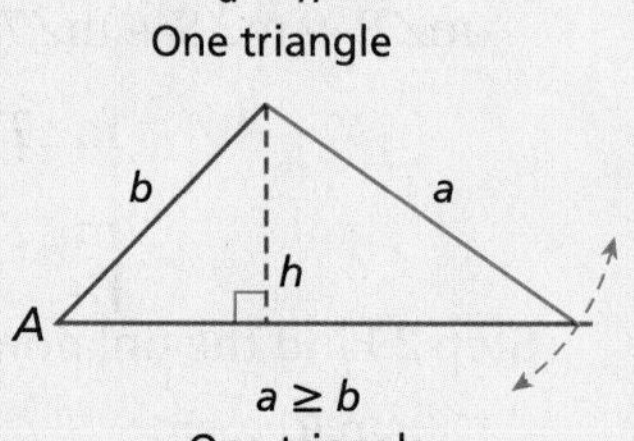

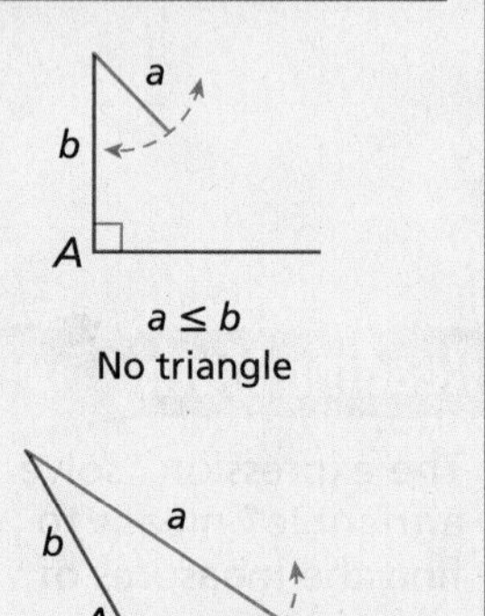

Remember!

When one angle in a triangle is obtuse, the measures of the other two angles must be acute.

Solving a Triangle Given *a*, *b*, and m∠*A*
1. Use the values of *a*, *b*, and m∠*A* to determine the number of possible triangles.
2. If there is one triangle, use the Law of Sines to solve for the unknowns.
3. If there are two triangles, use the Law of Sines to find $m\angle B_1$ and $m\angle B_2$. Then use these values to find the other measurements of the two triangles.

EXAMPLE 3 Art Application

Maggie is designing a mosaic by using triangular tiles of different shapes. Determine the number of triangles that Maggie can form using the measurements $a = 11$ cm, $b = 17$ cm, and $m\angle A = 30°$. Then solve the triangles. Round to the nearest tenth.

Step 1 Determine the number of possible triangles. In this case, $\angle A$ is acute. Find h.

$$\sin 30° = \frac{h}{17} \qquad \textit{sin } \theta = \frac{\textit{opp.}}{\textit{hyp.}}$$

$$h = 17 \sin 30° \approx 8.5 \text{ cm} \qquad \textit{Solve for h.}$$

Because $h < a < b$, two triangles are possible.

Triangle 1

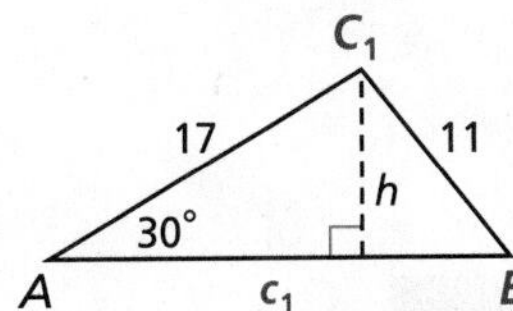

Triangle 2

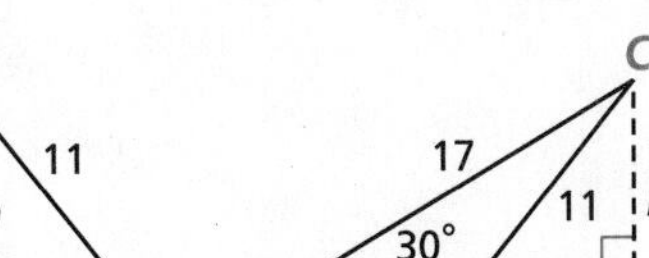

Step 2 Determine $m\angle B_1$ and $m\angle B_2$.

$$\frac{\sin A}{a} = \frac{\sin B}{b} \qquad \textit{Law of Sines}$$

$$\frac{\sin 30°}{11} = \frac{\sin B}{17} \qquad \textit{Substitute.}$$

$$\sin B = \frac{17 \sin 30°}{11} \qquad \textit{Solve for sin B.}$$

$$\sin B \approx 0.773$$

Let $\angle B_1$ represent the acute angle with a sine of 0.773. Use the inverse sine function on your calculator to determine $m\angle B_1$.

$$m\angle B_1 = \text{Sin}^{-1}\left(\frac{17 \sin 30°}{11}\right) \approx 50.6°$$

Let $\angle B_2$ represent the obtuse angle with a sine of 0.773.

$$m\angle B_2 = 180° - 50.6° = 129.4° \qquad \textit{The reference angle of } \angle B_2 \textit{ is 50.6°.}$$

Helpful Hint

Because $\angle B_1$ and $\angle B_2$ have the same sine value, they also have the same reference angle.

Step 3 Find the other unknown measures of the two triangles.

Solve for $m\angle C_1$.

$$30° + 50.6° + m\angle C_1 = 180°$$

$$m\angle C_1 = 99.4°$$

Solve for $m\angle C_2$.

$$30° + 129.4° + m\angle C_2 = 180°$$

$$m\angle C_2 = 20.6°$$

Solve for c_1.

$$\frac{\sin A}{a} = \frac{\sin C_1}{c_1} \qquad \textit{Law of Sines}$$

$$\frac{\sin 30°}{11} = \frac{\sin 99.4°}{c_1} \qquad \textit{Substitute.}$$

$$c_1 = \frac{11 \sin 99.4°}{\sin 30°} \qquad \textit{Solve for the unknown side.}$$

$$c_1 \approx 21.7 \text{ cm}$$

Solve for c_2.

$$\frac{\sin A}{a} = \frac{\sin C_2}{c_2}$$

$$\frac{\sin 30°}{11} = \frac{\sin 20.6°}{c_2}$$

$$c_2 = \frac{11 \sin 20.6°}{\sin 30°}$$

$$c_2 \approx 7.7 \text{ cm}$$

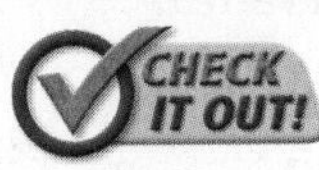

3. Determine the number of triangles Maggie can form using the measurements $a = 10$ cm, $b = 6$ cm, and $m\angle A = 105°$. Then solve the triangles. Round to the nearest tenth.

THINK AND DISCUSS

1. Explain how right triangle trigonometry can be used to determine the area of an obtuse triangle.

2. Explain why using the Law of Sines when given AAS or ASA is different than when given SSA.

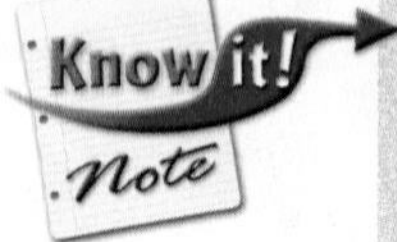

3. GET ORGANIZED Copy and complete the graphic organizer. In each box, give the conditions for which the ambiguous case results in zero, one, or two triangles.

SSA: Given a, b, and $m\angle A$			
Angle A	**0 triangles**	**1 triangle**	**2 triangles**
Obtuse			
Acute			

13-5 Exercises

go.hrw.com
Homework Help Online
KEYWORD: MB7 13-5
Parent Resources Online
KEYWORD: MB7 Parent

GUIDED PRACTICE

SEE EXAMPLE 1 p. 958

Find the area of each triangle. Round to the nearest tenth.

1.

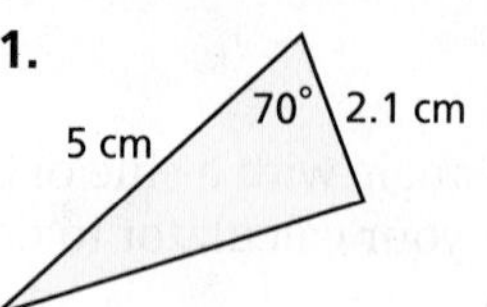

2.

12.7 ft, 110°, 9.9 ft, 18.6 ft

3.

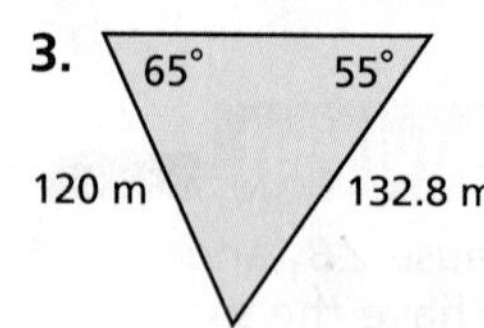

SEE EXAMPLE 2 p. 959

Solve each triangle. Round to the nearest tenth.

4.

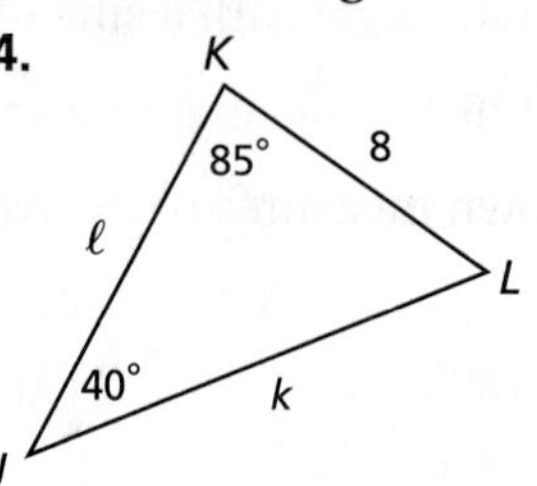

5.

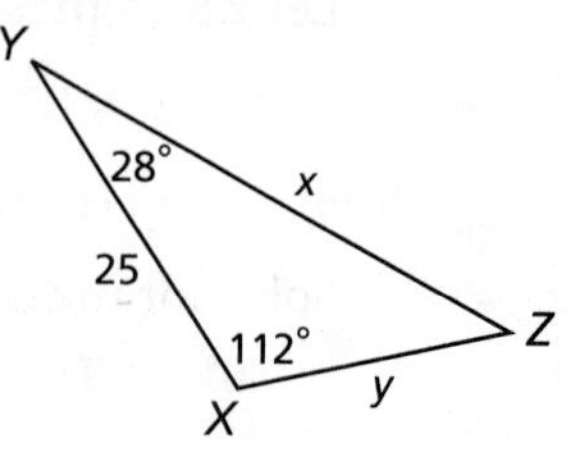

6.

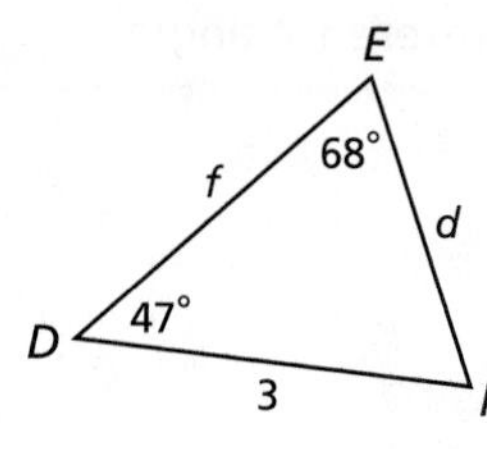

7.

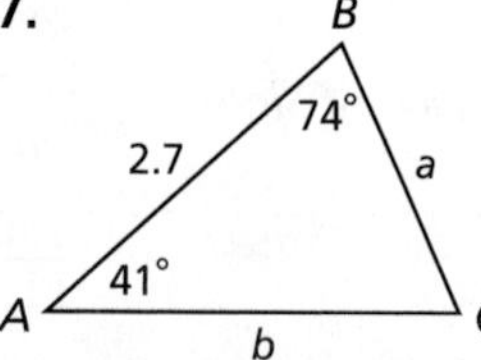

8.

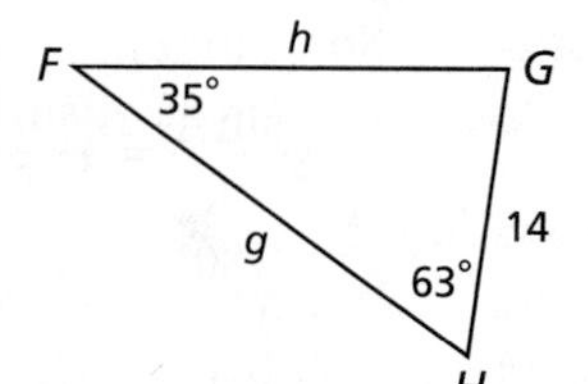

9.

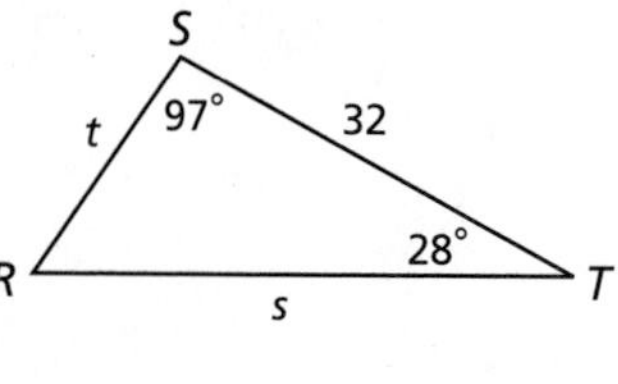

SEE EXAMPLE 3 p. 961

Gardening **A landscape architect is designing triangular flower beds. Determine the number of different triangles that he can form using the given measurements. Then solve the triangles. Round to the nearest tenth.**

10. $a = 6$ m, $b = 9$ m, $m\angle A = 55°$

11. $a = 10$ m, $b = 4$ m, $m\angle A = 120°$

12. $a = 8$ m, $b = 9$ m, $m\angle A = 35°$

13. $a = 7$ m, $b = 6$ m, $m\angle A = 45°$

Independent Practice	
For Exercises	See Example
14–16	1
17–19	2
20–23	3

Extra Practice

Skills Practice p. S29

Application Practice p. S44

PRACTICE AND PROBLEM SOLVING

Find the area of each triangle. Round to the nearest tenth.

14.

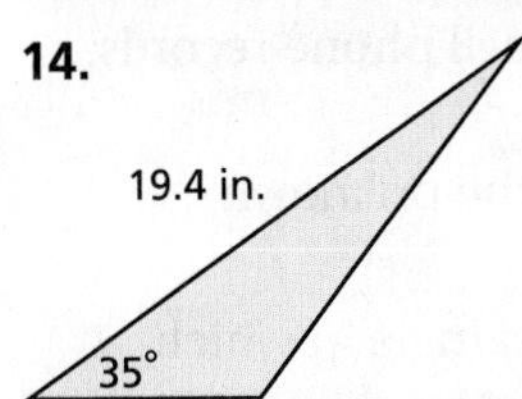

15.

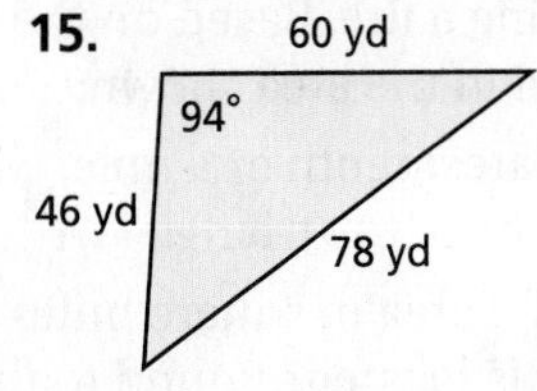

16.

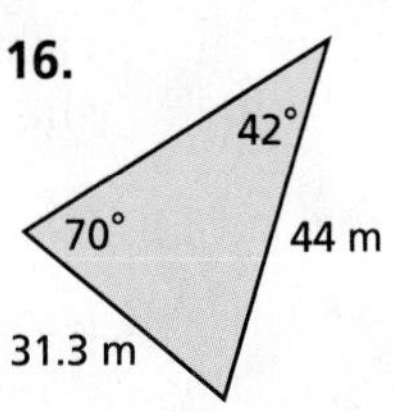

Solve each triangle. Round to the nearest tenth.

17.

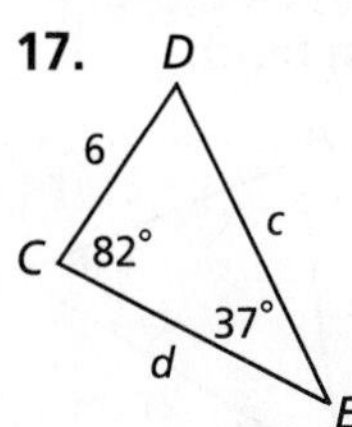

18.

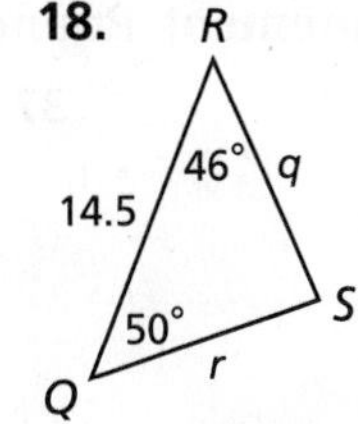

19.

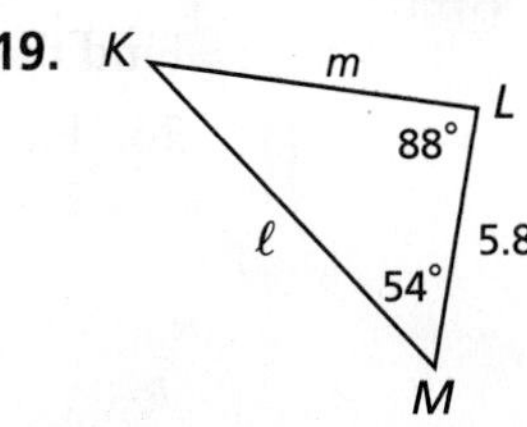

Art **An artist is designing triangular mirrors. Determine the number of different triangles that she can form using the given measurements. Then solve the triangles. Round to the nearest tenth.**

20. $a = 6$ cm, $b = 4$ cm, $m\angle A = 72°$

21. $a = 3.0$ in., $b = 3.5$ in., $m\angle A = 118°$

22. $a = 4.2$ cm, $b = 5.7$ cm, $m\angle A = 39°$

23. $a = 7$ in., $b = 3.5$ in., $m\angle A = 130°$

24. **Astronomy** The diagram shows the relative positions of Earth, Mars, and the Sun on a particular date. What is the distance between Mars and the Sun on this date? Round to the nearest million miles.

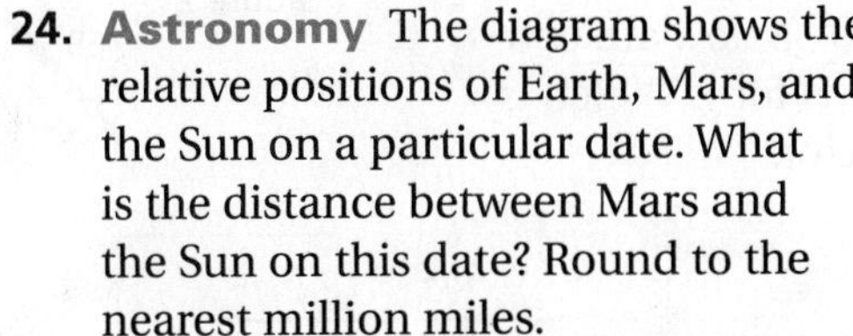

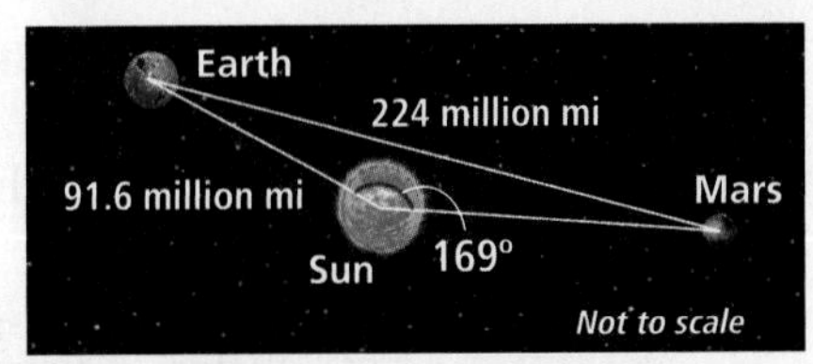

Use the given measurements to solve △ABC. Round to the nearest tenth.

25. $m\angle A = 54°$, $m\angle B = 62°$, $a = 14$

26. $m\angle A = 126°$, $m\angle C = 18°$, $c = 3$

27. $m\angle B = 80°$, $m\angle C = 41°$, $b = 25$

28. $m\angle A = 24°$, $m\angle B = 104°$, $c = 10$

29. **Rock Climbing** A group of climbers needs to determine the distance from one side of a ravine to another. They make the measurements shown. To the nearest foot, what is the distance d across the ravine?

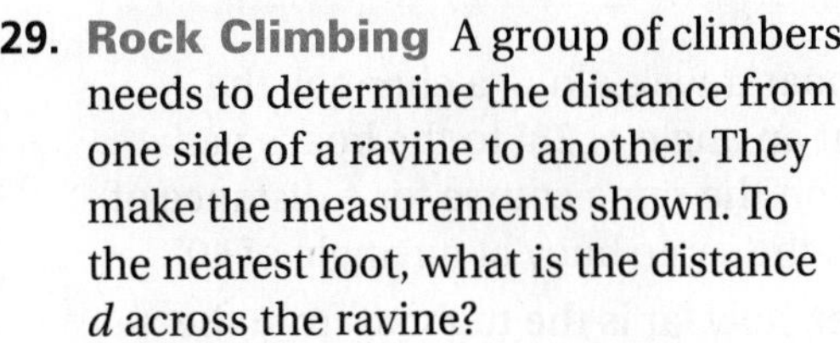

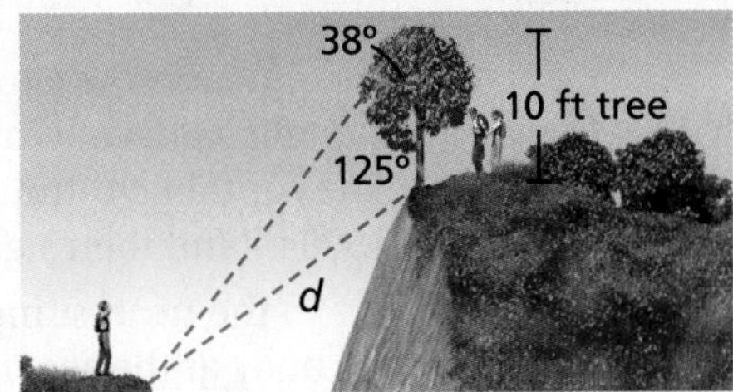

Determine the number of different triangles that can be formed using the given measurements. Then solve the triangles. Round to the nearest tenth.

30. $m\angle C = 45°$, $b = 10$, $c = 5$

31. $m\angle B = 135°$, $b = 12$, $c = 8$

32. $m\angle A = 60°$, $a = 9$, $b = 10$

33. $m\angle B = 30°$, $a = 6$, $b = 3$

34. **Painting** Trey needs to paint a side of a house that has the measurements shown. What is the area of this side of the house to the nearest square foot?

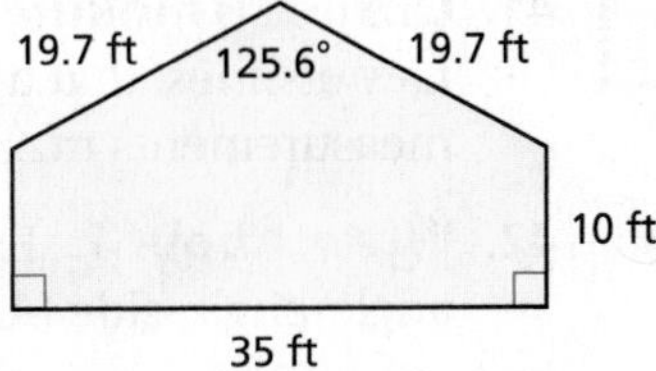

35. This problem will prepare you for the Multi-Step Test Prep on page 974.

An emergency dispatcher must determine the position of a caller reporting a fire. Based on the caller's cell phone records, she is located in the area shown.

a. To the nearest tenth of a mile, what are the unknown side lengths of the triangle?

b. What is the area in square miles of the triangle in which the caller is located? Round to the nearest tenth.

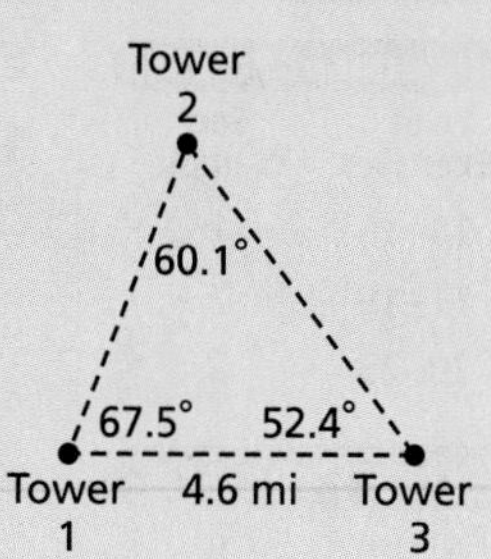

Find the indicated measurement. Round to the nearest tenth.

36. Find $m\angle B$.

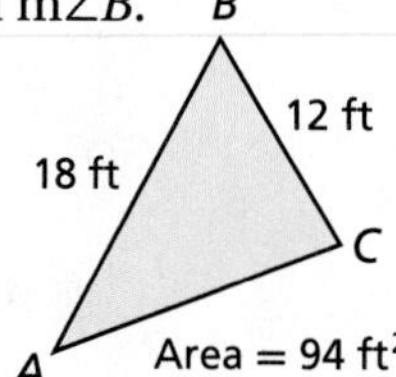

37. Find c.

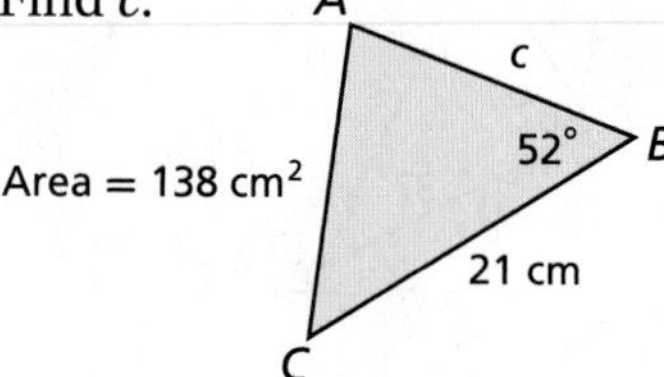

38. Multi-Step A new road will be built from a town to a nearby highway. So far, two routes have been proposed. To the nearest tenth of a mile, how much shorter is route 2 than route 1?

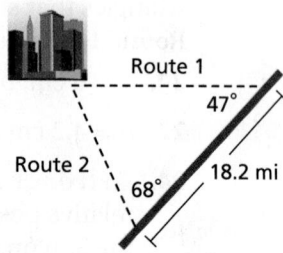

Route 1
47°
Route 2
68°
18.2 mi

39. ///ERROR ANALYSIS/// Below are two attempts at solving $\triangle FGH$ for g. Which is incorrect? Explain the error.

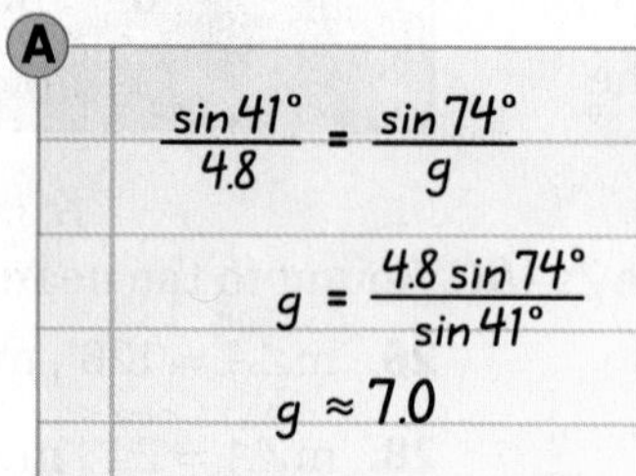

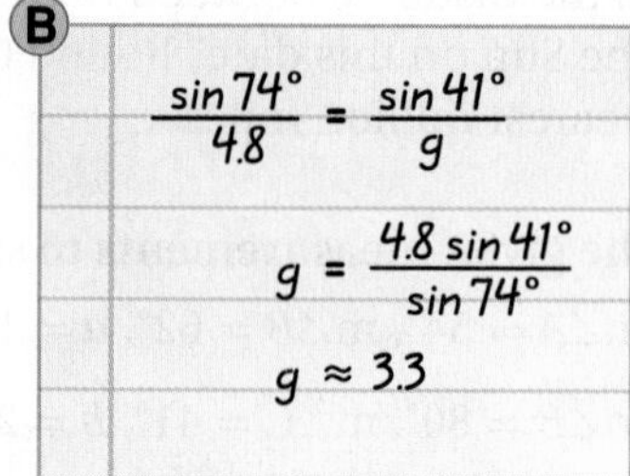

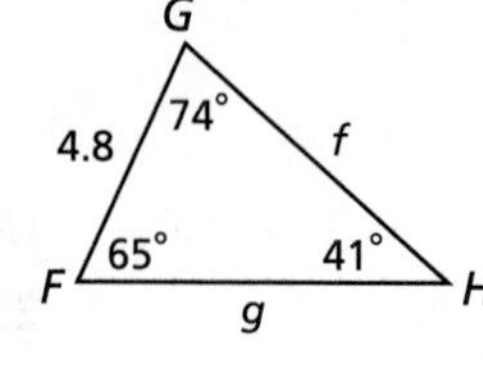

LINK

Navigation

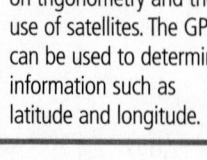

Ship captains rely heavily on GPS technology. GPS stands for "Global Positioning System," a navigation system based on trigonometry and the use of satellites. The GPS can be used to determine information such as latitude and longitude.

40. Navigation As a tugboat travels along a channel, the captain sights a buoy at an angle of 28° to the boat's path. The captain continues on the same course for a distance of 1500 m and then sights the same buoy at an angle of 40°.

a. To the nearest meter, how far is the tugboat from the buoy at the second sighting?

b. To the nearest meter, how far was the tugboat from the buoy when the captain first sighted the bouy?

c. What if...? If the tugboat continues on the same course, what is the closest that it will come to the buoy? Round to the nearest meter.

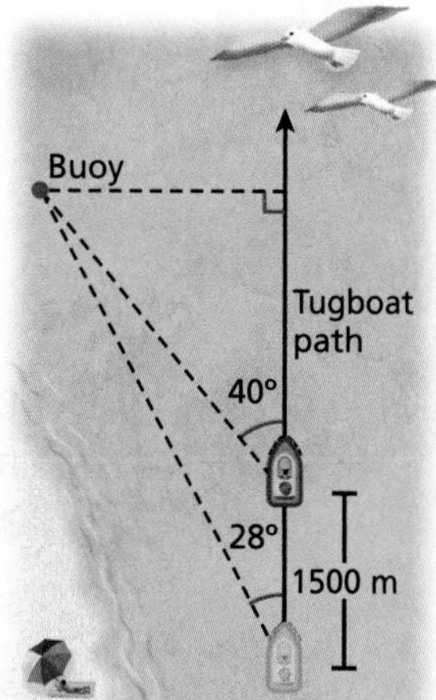

41. Critical Thinking How can you tell, without using the Law of Sines, that a triangle cannot be formed by using the measurements $m\angle A = 92°$, $m\angle B = 104°$, and $a = 18$?

42. Write About It Explain how to solve a triangle when angle-angle-side (AAS) information is known.

TEST PREP

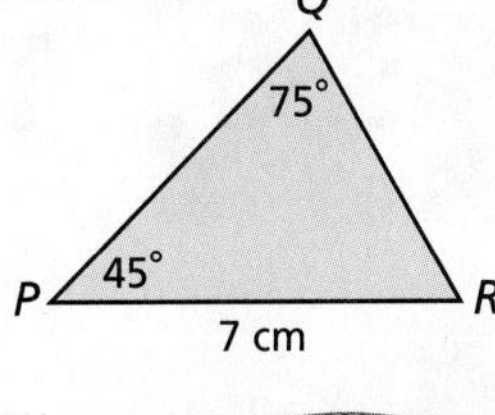

43. What is the area of $\triangle PQR$ to the nearest tenth of a square centimeter?

Ⓐ 2.4 cm^2 Ⓒ 23.5 cm^2

Ⓑ 15.5 cm^2 Ⓓ 40.1 cm^2

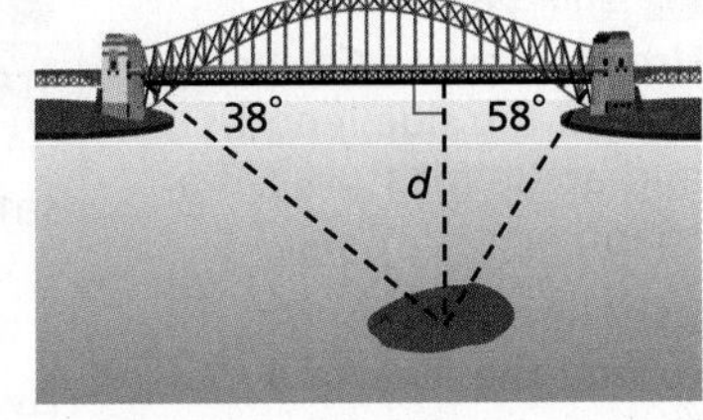

44. A bridge is 325 m long. From the west end, a surveyor measures the angle between the bridge and an island to be 38°. From the east end, the surveyor measures the angle between the bridge and the island to be 58°. To the nearest meter, what is the distance *d* between the bridge and the island?

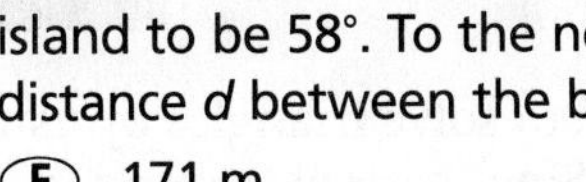

Ⓕ 171 m Ⓗ 217 m

Ⓖ 201 m Ⓙ 277 m

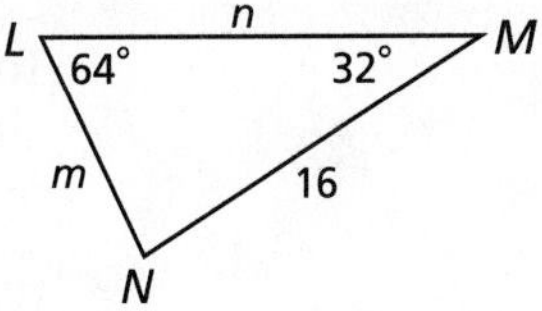

45. **Short Response** Examine $\triangle LMN$ at right.

a. Write an expression that can be used to determine the value of *m*.

b. Is there more than one possible triangle that can be constructed from the given measurements? Explain your answer.

CHALLENGE AND EXTEND

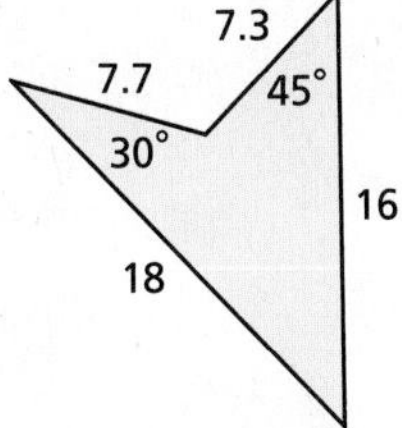

46. What is the area of the quadrilateral at right to the nearest square unit?

47. **Critical Thinking** The lengths of two sides of a triangle are $a = 3$ and $b = 2\sqrt{3}$. For what values of $m\angle A$ do two solutions exist when you solve the triangle by using the Law of Sines?

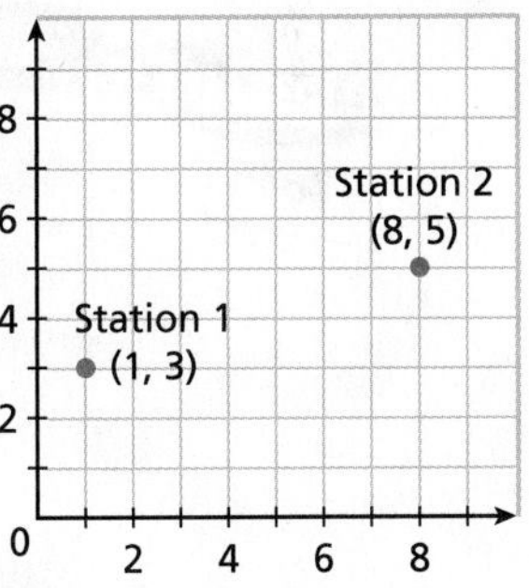

48. **Multi-Step** The map shows the location of two ranger stations. Each unit on the map represents 1 mile. A ranger at station 1 saw a meteor that appeared to land about 72° north of east. A ranger at station 2 saw the meteor appear to land about 45° north of west. Based on this information, about how many miles from station 1 did the meteor land? Explain how you determined your answer.

SPIRAL REVIEW

Find the intercepts of each line, and graph the line. *(Lesson 2-3)*

49. $x + y = 5$ **50.** $3x - y = 9$ **51.** $2x + 6y = 12$

Solve each equation. *(Lesson 8-5)*

52. $\frac{4x}{x-1} = \frac{2x+9}{x-1}$ **53.** $\frac{7x-9}{x^2-4} = \frac{4}{x+2}$ **54.** $\frac{x}{3} - \frac{4x}{7} = \frac{x-2}{3}$

Evaluate each inverse trigonometric function. Give your answer in both radians and degrees. *(Lesson 13-4)*

55. $\text{Cos}^{-1}\left(-\frac{\sqrt{2}}{2}\right)$ **56.** $\text{Tan}^{-1}\sqrt{3}$ **57.** $\text{Sin}^{-1}\frac{1}{2}$

13-6 The Law of Cosines

Objectives

Use the Law of Cosines to find the side lengths and angle measures of a triangle.

Use Heron's Formula to find the area of a triangle.

Who uses this?

Trapeze artists can use the Law of Cosines to determine whether they can perform stunts safely. (See Exercise 27.)

In the previous lesson, you learned to solve triangles by using the Law of Sines. However, the Law of Sines cannot be used to solve triangles for which side-angle-side (SAS) or side-side-side (SSS) information is given. Instead, you must use the Law of Cosines.

To derive the Law of Cosines, draw $\triangle ABC$ with altitude $\overline{BD}$. If x represents the length of $\overline{AD}$, the length of $\overline{DC}$ is $b - x$.

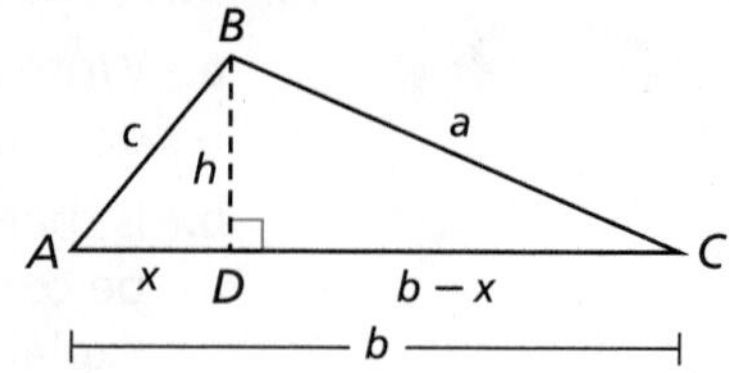

Write an equation that relates the side lengths of $\triangle DBC$.

$a^2 = (b - x)^2 + h^2$	*Pythagorean Theorem*
$a^2 = b^2 - 2bx + x^2 + h^2$	*Expand $(b - x)^2$.*
$a^2 = b^2 - 2bx + c^2$	*In $\triangle ABD$, $c^2 = x^2 + h^2$. Substitute c^2 for $x^2 + h^2$.*
$a^2 = b^2 - 2b(c\cos A) + c^2$	*In $\triangle ABD$, $\cos A = \frac{x}{c}$, or $x = c\cos A$. Substitute $c\cos A$ for x.*
$a^2 = b^2 + c^2 - 2bc\cos A$	

The previous equation is one of the formulas for the Law of Cosines.

Law of Cosines

For $\triangle ABC$, the Law of Cosines states that

$$a^2 = b^2 + c^2 - 2bc\cos A.$$
$$b^2 = a^2 + c^2 - 2ac\cos B.$$
$$c^2 = a^2 + b^2 - 2ab\cos C.$$

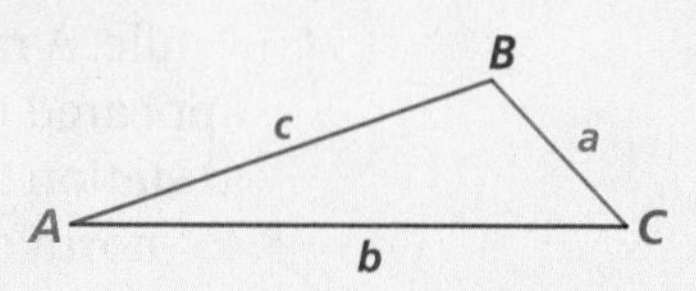

EXAMPLE 1 Using the Law of Cosines

Use the given measurements to solve $\triangle ABC$. Round to the nearest tenth.

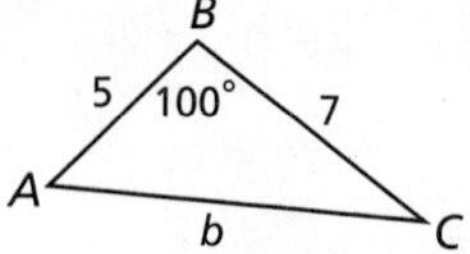

Step 1 Find the length of the third side.

$b^2 = a^2 + c^2 - 2ac\cos B$	*Law of Cosines*
$b^2 = 7^2 + 5^2 - 2(7)(5)\cos 100°$	*Substitute.*
$b^2 \approx 86.2$	*Use a calculator to simplify.*
$b \approx 9.3$	*Solve for the positive value of b.*

Step 2 Find an angle measure.

$$\frac{\sin A}{a} = \frac{\sin B}{b} \qquad \textit{Law of Sines}$$

$$\frac{\sin A}{7} = \frac{\sin 100°}{9.3} \qquad \textit{Substitute.}$$

$$\sin A = \frac{7\sin 100°}{9.3} \qquad \textit{Solve for } \sin A.$$

$$m\angle A = \text{Sin}^{-1}\left(\frac{7\sin 100°}{9.3}\right) \approx 47.8° \qquad \textit{Solve for } m\angle A.$$

Step 3 Find the third angle measure.

$$47.8° + 100° + m\angle C \approx 180° \qquad \textit{Triangle Sum Theorem}$$

$$m\angle C \approx 32.2° \qquad \textit{Solve for } m\angle C.$$

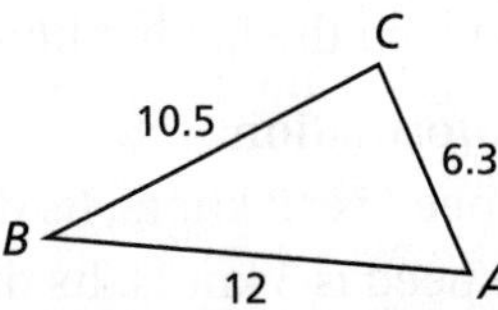

Remember!

The largest angle of a triangle is the angle opposite the longest side.

Step 1 Find the measure of the largest angle, $\angle C$.

$$c^2 = a^2 + b^2 - 2ab\cos C \qquad \textit{Law of Cosines}$$

$$12^2 = 10.5^2 + 6.3^2 - 2(10.5)(6.3)\cos C \qquad \textit{Substitute.}$$

$$\cos C \approx 0.0449 \qquad \textit{Solve for } \cos C.$$

$$m\angle C \approx \text{Cos}^{-1}(0.0449) \approx 87.4° \qquad \textit{Solve for } m\angle C.$$

Step 2 Find another angle measure.

$$b^2 = a^2 + c^2 - 2ac\cos B \qquad \textit{Law of Cosines}$$

$$6.3^2 = 10.5^2 + 12^2 - 2(10.5)(12)\cos B \qquad \textit{Substitute.}$$

$$\cos B \approx 0.8514 \qquad \textit{Solve for } \cos B.$$

$$m\angle B \approx \text{Cos}^{-1}(0.8514) \approx 31.6° \qquad \textit{Solve for } m\angle B.$$

Step 3 Find the third angle measure.

$$m\angle A + 31.6° + 87.4° \approx 180° \qquad \textit{Triangle Sum Theorem}$$

$$m\angle A \approx 61.0° \qquad \textit{Solve for } m\angle A.$$

Use the given measurements to solve $\triangle ABC$. Round to the nearest tenth.

1a. $b = 23$, $c = 18$, $m\angle A = 173°$ **1b.** $a = 35$, $b = 42$, $c = 50.3$

Student to Student

Solving Triangles

Stefan Maric
Wylie High School

If I solve a triangle using the Law of Sines, I like to use the Law of Cosines to check my work. I used the Law of Sines to solve the triangle below.

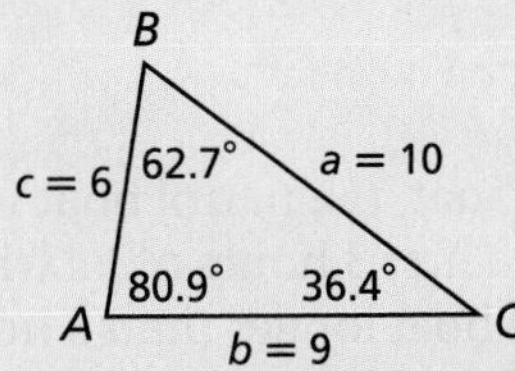

I can check that the length of side b really is 9 by using the Law of Cosines.

$b^2 = a^2 + c^2 - 2ac\cos B$

9^2	$10^2 + 6^2 - 2(10)(6)\cos 62.7°$
81	81.0 ✔

The Law of Cosines shows that I was right.

EXAMPLE 2 *Problem-Solving Application*

A coast guard patrol boat and a fishing boat leave a dock at the same time on the courses shown. The patrol boat travels at a speed of 12 nautical miles per hour (12 knots), and the fishing boat travels at a speed of 5 knots. After 3 hours, the fishing boat sends a distress signal picked up by the patrol boat. If the fishing boat does not drift, how long will it take the patrol boat to reach it at a speed of 12 knots?

1 Understand the Problem

The **answer** will be the number of hours that the patrol boat needs to reach the fishing boat.

List the important information:

- The patrol boat's speed is 12 knots. Its direction is 15° east of north.
- The fishing boat's speed is 5 knots. Its direction is 130° east of north.
- The boats travel 3 hours before the distress call is given.

2 Make a Plan

Determine the angle between the boats' courses and the distance that each boat travels in 3 hours. Use this information to draw and label a diagram. Then use the Law of Cosines to find the distance d between the boats at the time of the distress call. Finally, determine how long it will take the patrol boat to travel this distance.

3 Solve

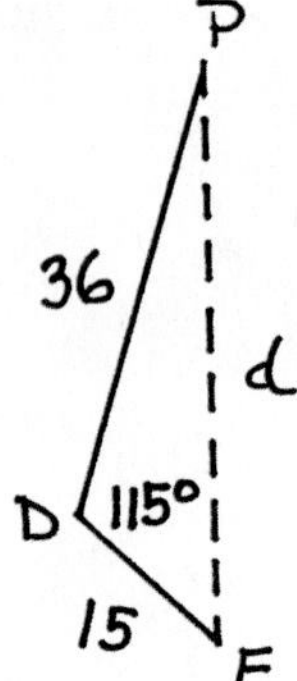

Step 1 Draw and label a diagram.

The angle between the boats' courses is 130° − 15° = 115°. In 3 hours, the patrol boat travels 3(12) = 36 nautical miles and the fishing boat travels 3(5) = 15 nautical miles.

Step 2 Find the distance d between the boats.

$d^2 = p^2 + f^2 - 2pf\cos D$ — *Law of Cosines*

$d^2 = 15^2 + 36^2 - 2(15)(36)\cos 115°$ — *Substitute 15 for p, 36 for f, and 115° for D.*

$d^2 \approx 1977.4$ — *Use a calculator to simplify.*

$d \approx 44.5$ — *Solve for the positive value of d.*

Step 3 Determine the number of hours.

The patrol boat must travel about 44.5 nautical miles to reach the fishing boat. At a speed of 12 nautical miles per hour, it will take the patrol boat $\frac{44.5}{12} \approx 3.7$ hours to reach the fishing boat.

Helpful Hint

There are two solutions to $d^2 = 1977.4$. One is positive, and one is negative. Because d represents a distance, the negative solution can be disregarded.

4 Look Back

To reach the fishing boat, the patrol boat will have to travel a greater distance than it did during the first 3 hours of its trip. Therefore, it makes sense that it will take the patrol boat longer than 3 hours to reach the fishing boat. An answer of 3.7 hours seems reasonable.

2. A pilot is flying from Houston to Oklahoma City. To avoid a thunderstorm, the pilot flies 28° off of the direct route for a distance of 175 miles. He then makes a turn and flies straight on to Oklahoma City. To the nearest mile, how much farther than the direct route was the route taken by the pilot?

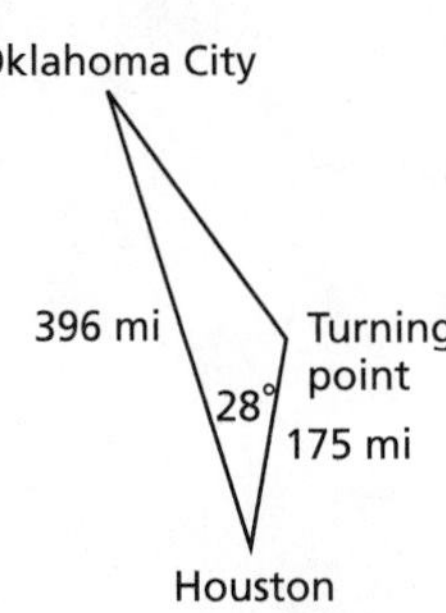

The Law of Cosines can be used to derive a formula for the area of a triangle based on its side lengths. This formula is called Heron's Formula.

Heron's Formula

For $\triangle ABC$, where s is half of the perimeter of the triangle, or $\frac{1}{2}(a + b + c)$,

Area $= \sqrt{s(s-a)(s-b)(s-c)}$

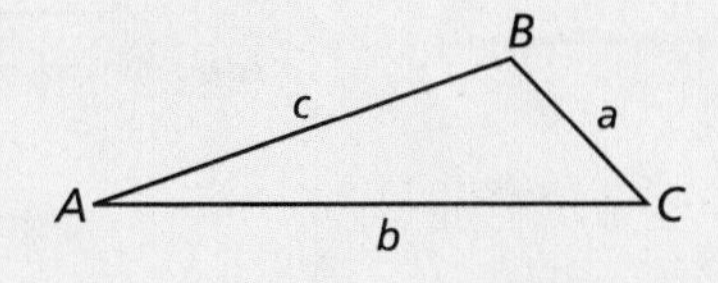

EXAMPLE 3 Architecture Application

A blueprint shows a reception area that has a triangular floor with sides measuring 22 ft, 30 ft, and 34 ft. What is the area of the floor to the nearest square foot?

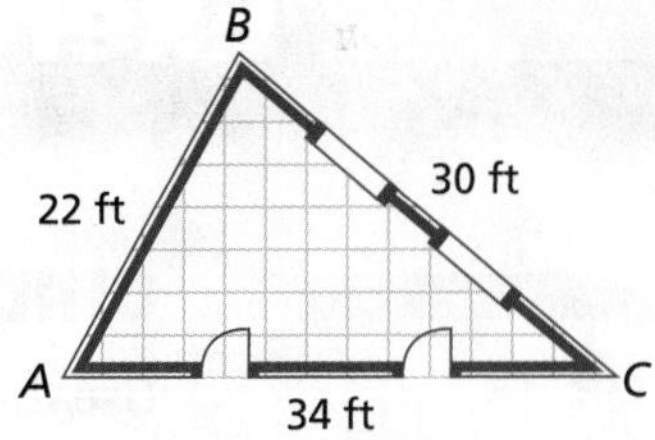

Step 1 Find the value of s.

$s = \frac{1}{2}(a + b + c)$ *Use the formula for half of the perimeter.*

$s = \frac{1}{2}(30 + 34 + 22) = 43$ *Substitute 30 for a, 34 for b, and 22 for c.*

Step 2 Find the area of the triangle.

$A = \sqrt{s(s-a)(s-b)(s-c)}$ *Heron's Formula*

$A = \sqrt{43(43-30)(43-34)(43-22)}$ *Substitute 43 for s.*

$A \approx 325$ *Use a calculator to simplify.*

The area of the floor is 325 ft^2.

Check Find the measure of the largest angle, $\angle B$.

$b^2 = a^2 + c^2 - 2ac\cos B$ *Law of Cosines*

$34^2 = 30^2 + 22^2 - 2(30)(22)\cos B$ *Substitute.*

$\cos B \approx 0.1727$ *Solve for cos B.*

$m\angle B \approx 80.1°$ *Solve for m∠B.*

Find the area of the triangle by using the formula area $= \frac{1}{2}ac\sin B$.

area $= \frac{1}{2}(30)(22)\sin 80.1° \approx 325$ ft^2 ✔

3. The surface of a hotel swimming pool is shaped like a triangle with sides measuring 50 m, 28 m, and 30 m. What is the area of the pool's surface to the nearest square meter?

THINK AND DISCUSS

1. Explain why you cannot solve a triangle if you are given only angle-angle-angle (AAA) information.
2. Describe the steps that you could use to find the area of a triangle by using Heron's Formula when you are given side-angle-side (SAS) information.

3. **GET ORGANIZED** Copy and complete the graphic organizer. List the types of triangles that can be solved by using each law. Consider the following types of triangles: ASA, AAS, SAS, SSA, and SSS.

13-6 Exercises

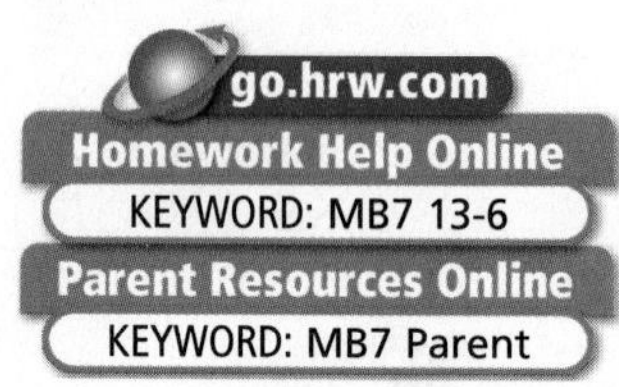

GUIDED PRACTICE

SEE EXAMPLE 1 p. 966

Use the given measurements to solve each triangle. Round to the nearest tenth.

1.
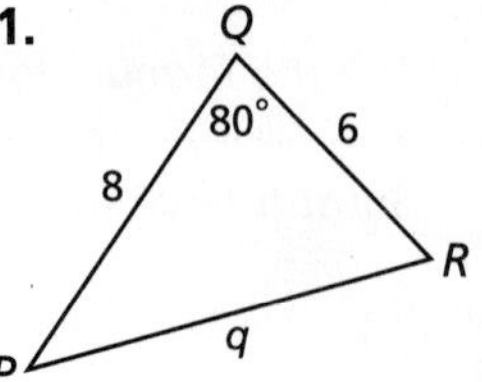

2.
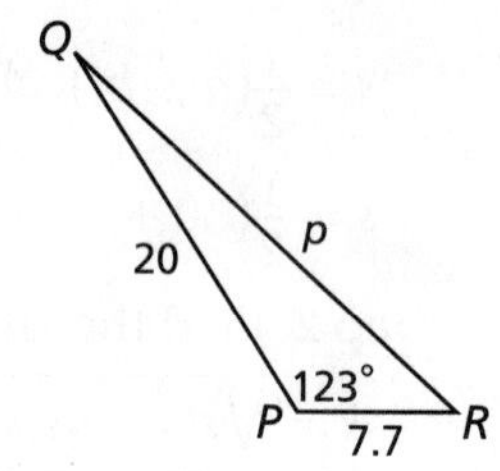

3.
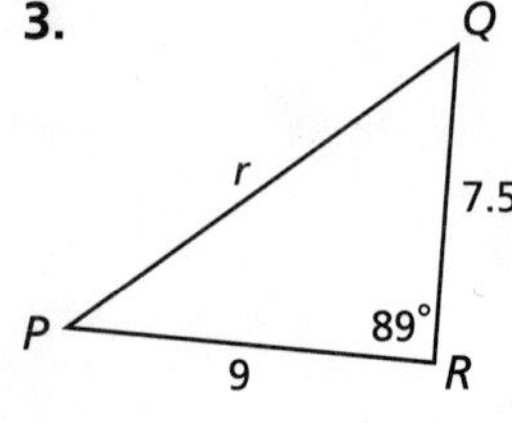

4.
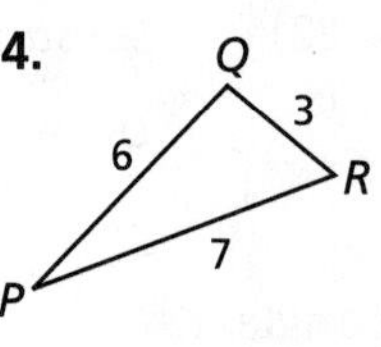

5.
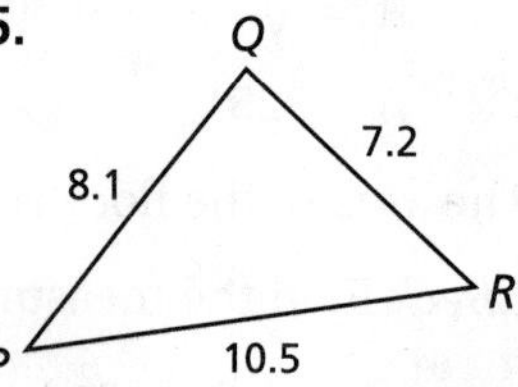

6.
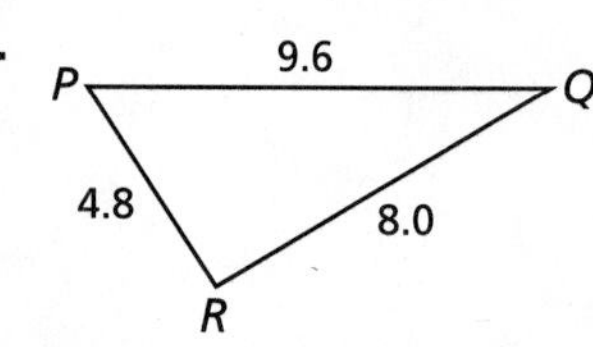

SEE EXAMPLE 2 p. 968

7. **Recreation** A triangular hiking trail is being built in the area shown. At an average walking speed of 2 m/s, how many minutes will it take a hiker to make a complete circuit around the triangular trail? Round to the nearest minute.

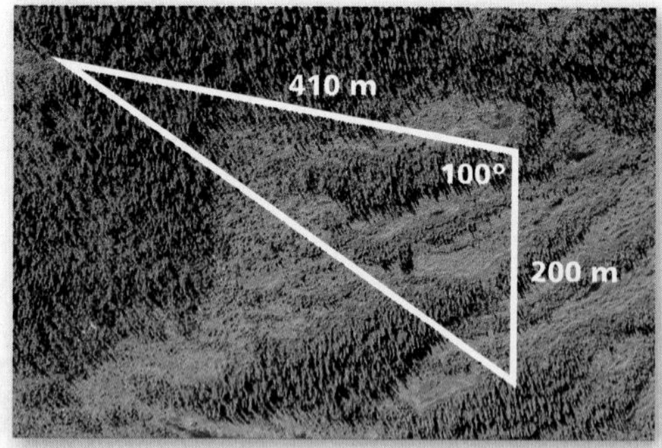

SEE EXAMPLE 3 p. 969

8. **Agriculture** A triangular wheat field has side lengths that measure 410 ft, 500 ft, and 420 ft. What is the area of the field to the nearest square foot?

PRACTICE AND PROBLEM SOLVING

Independent Practice

For Exercises	See Example
9–14	1
15	2
16	3

Extra Practice

Skills Practice p. S29
Application Practice p. S44

Use the given measurements to solve each triangle. Round to the nearest tenth.

9.
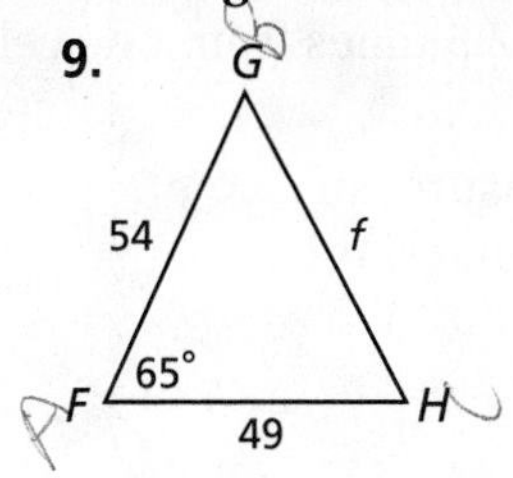

10.
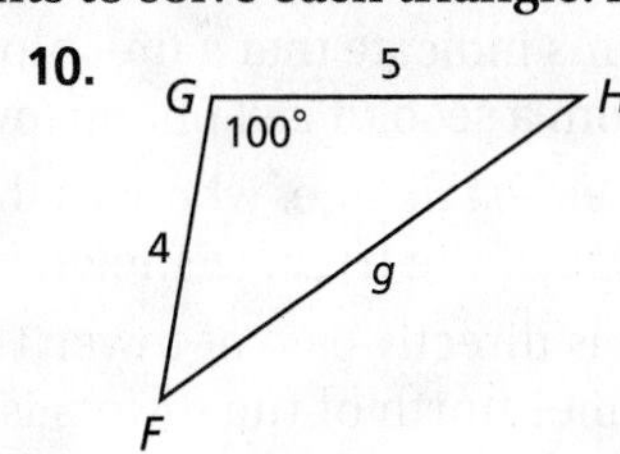

11.
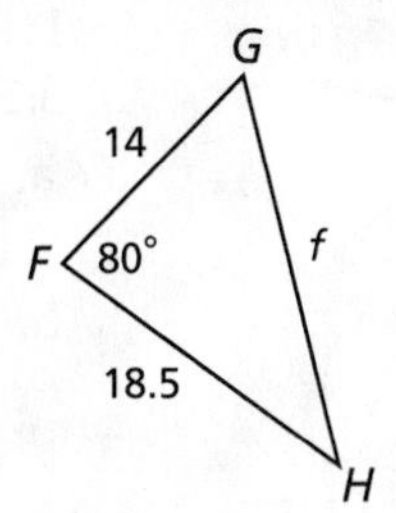

12.
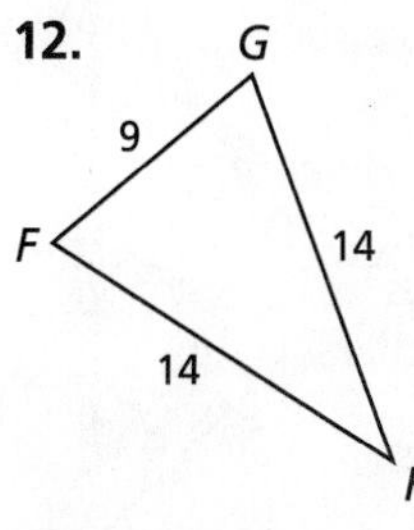

13.
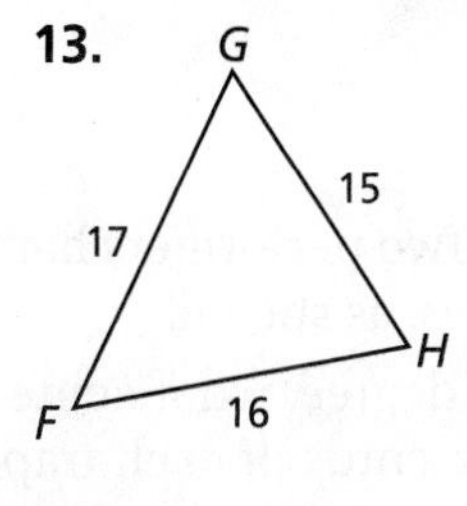

14.
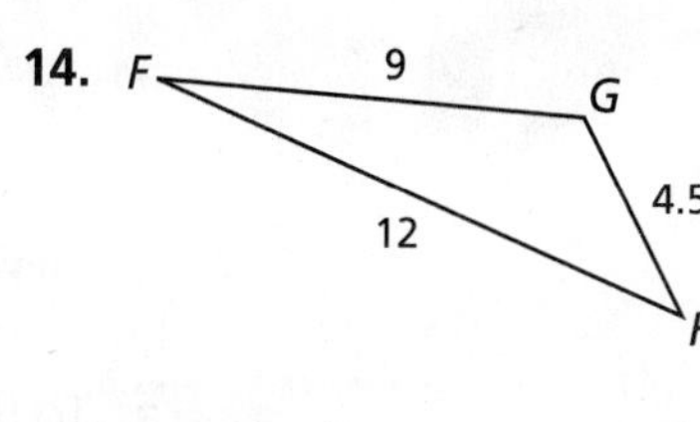

15. Ecology An ecologist is studying a pair of zebras fitted with radio-transmitter collars. One zebra is 1.4 mi from the ecologist, and the other is 3.5 mi from the ecologist. To the nearest tenth of a mile, how far apart are the two zebras?

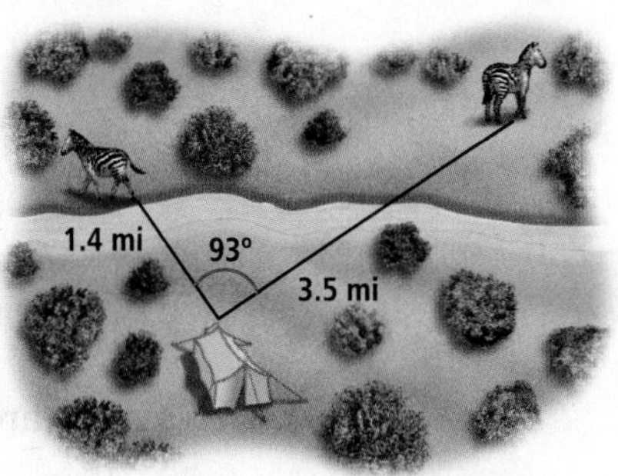

16. Art How many square meters of fabric are needed to make a triangular banner with side lengths of 2.1 m, 1.5 m, and 1.4 m? Round to the nearest tenth.

Use the given measurements to solve $\triangle ABC$. Round to the nearest tenth.

17. $m\angle A = 120°, b = 16, c = 20$

18. $m\angle B = 78°, a = 6, c = 4$

19. $m\angle C = 96°, a = 13, b = 9$

20. $a = 14, b = 9, c = 10$

21. $a = 5, b = 8, c = 6$

22. $a = 30, b = 26, c = 35$

23. Commercial Art A graphic artist is asked to draw a triangular logo with sides measuring 15 cm, 18 cm, and 20 cm. If she draws the triangle correctly, what will be the measures of its angles to the nearest degree?

24. Aviation The course of a hot-air balloon takes the balloon directly over points A and B, which are 500 m apart. Several minutes later, the angle of elevation from an observer at point A to the balloon is 43.3°, and the angle of elevation from an observer at point B to the balloon is 58.2°. To the nearest meter, what is the balloon's altitude?

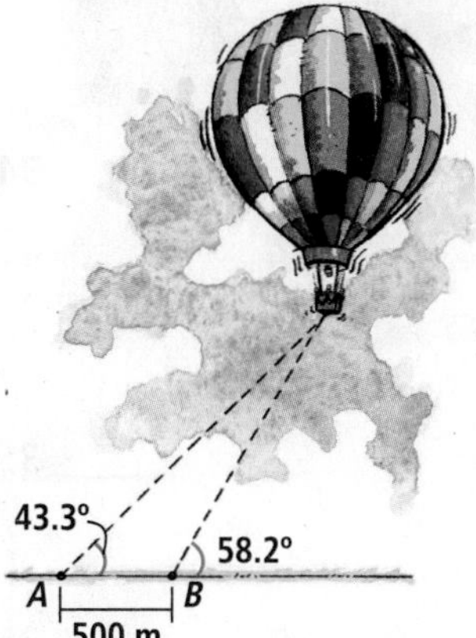

25. Multi-Step A student pilot takes off from a local airstrip and flies 70° south of east for 160 miles. The pilot then changes course and flies due north for another 80 miles before turning and flying directly back to the airstrip.

a. How many miles is the third stage of the pilot's flight? Round to the nearest mile.

b. To the nearest degree, what angle does the pilot turn the plane through in order to fly the third stage?

26. This problem will help prepare you for the Multi-Step Test Prep on page 974.

Phone records indicate that a fire is located 2.5 miles from one cell phone tower and 3.2 miles from a second cell phone tower.

a. To the nearest degree, what are the measures of the angles of the triangle shown in the diagram?

b. Tower 2 is directly east of tower 1. How many miles north of the towers is the fire? This distance is represented by n in the diagram.

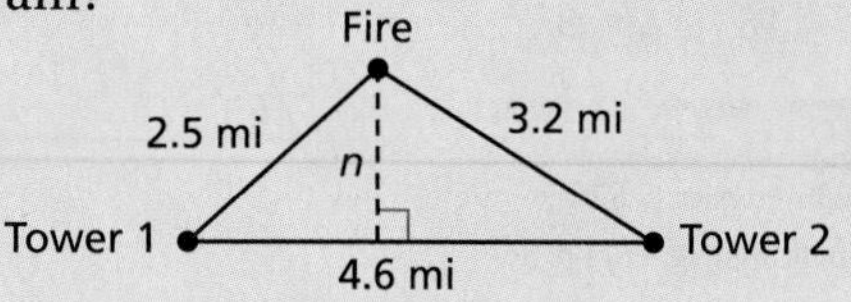

27. Entertainment Two performers hang by their knees from trapezes, as shown.

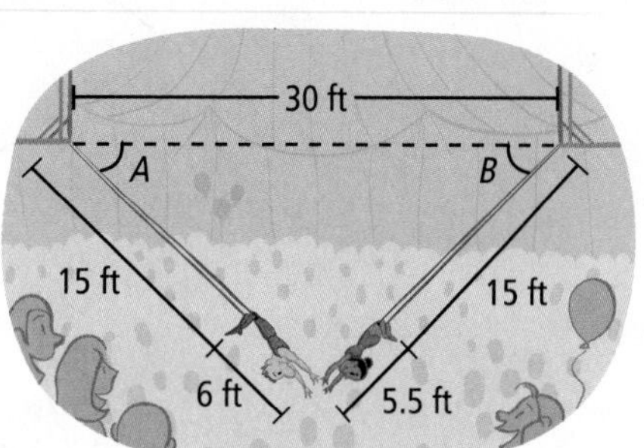

a. To the nearest degree, what acute angles A and B must the cords of each trapeze make with the horizontal if the performer on the left is to grab the wrists of the performer on the right and pull her away from her trapeze?

b. **What if...?** Later, the performer on the left grabs the trapeze of the performer on the right and lets go of his trapeze. To the nearest degree, what angles A and B must the cords of each trapeze make with the horizontal for this trick to work?

Find the area of the triangle with the given side lengths. Round to the nearest tenth.

28. 15 in., 18 in., 24 in.

29. 30 cm, 35 cm, 47 cm

30. 28 m, 37 m, 33 m

31. 3.5 ft, 5 ft, 7.5 ft

32. Estimation The adjacent sides of a parallelogram measure 3.1 cm and 3.9 cm. The measures of the acute interior angles of the parallelogram are 58°. Estimate the lengths of the diagonals of the parallelogram without using a calculator, and explain how you determined your estimates.

33. Surveying Barrington Crater in Arizona was produced by the impact of a meteorite. Based on the measurements shown, what is the diameter d of Barrington Crater to the nearest tenth of a kilometer?

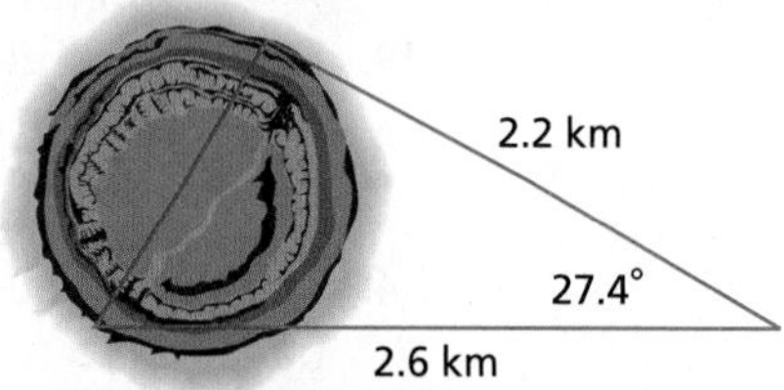

34. Travel The table shows the distances between three islands in Hawaii. To the nearest degree, what is the angle between each pair of islands in relation to the third island?

Distances Between Islands (mi)

	Kauai	Molokai	Lanai
Kauai	0	155.7	174.8
Molokai	155.7	0	26.1
Lanai	174.8	26.1	0

35. Critical Thinking Use the Law of Cosines to explain why $c^2 = a^2 + b^2$ for $\triangle ABC$, where $\angle C$ is a right angle.

36. Critical Thinking Can the value of s in Heron's Formula ever be less than the length of the longest side of a triangle? Explain.

37. Write About It Describe two different methods that could be used to solve a triangle when given side-side-side (SSS) information.

38. What is the approximate measure of $\angle K$ in the triangle shown?

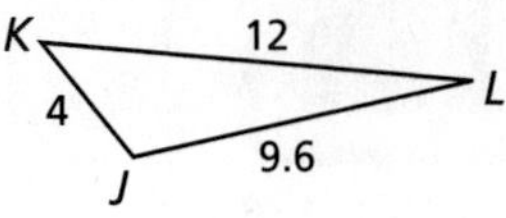

Ⓐ 30° Ⓒ 54°

Ⓑ 45° Ⓓ 60°

39. For $\triangle RST$ with side lengths r, s, and t, which equation can be used to determine r?

Ⓕ $r = \sqrt{s^2 + t^2 - 2st \sin R}$ Ⓗ $r = \sqrt{s^2 + t^2 - 2st \cos R}$

Ⓖ $r = \sqrt{s^2 - t^2 - 2st \sin R}$ Ⓙ $r = \sqrt{s^2 - t^2 - 2st \cos R}$

40. A team of archaeologists wants to dig for fossils in a triangular area marked by three stakes. The distances between the stakes are shown in the diagram. Which expression represents the dig area in square feet?

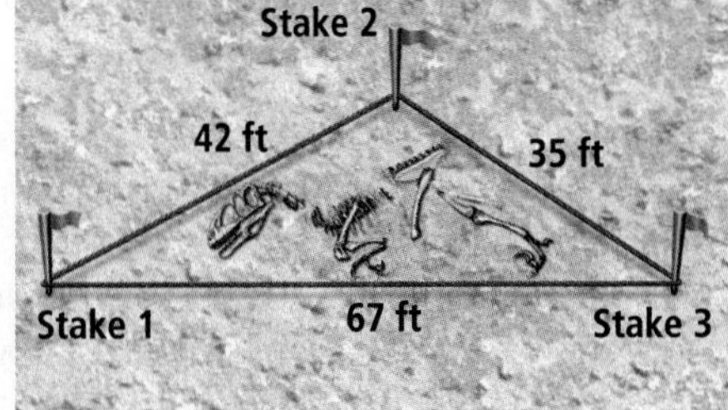

Ⓐ $\sqrt{72(30)(37)(5)}$

Ⓑ $\sqrt{48(6)(13)(19)}$

Ⓒ $\sqrt{144(42)(35)(67)}$

Ⓓ $\sqrt{144(102)(109)(77)}$

CHALLENGE AND EXTEND

41. Abby uses the Law of Cosines to find $m\angle A$ when $a = 2$, $b = 3$, and $c = 5$. The answer she gets is 0°. Did she make an error? Explain.

42. Geometry What are the angle measures of an isosceles triangle whose base is half as long as its congruent legs? Round to the nearest tenth.

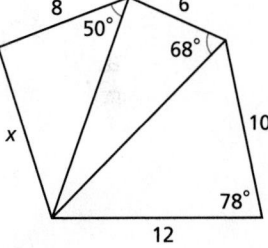

43. Use the figure shown to solve for x. Round to the nearest tenth.

SPIRAL REVIEW

Solve each equation. *(Lesson 5-5)*

44. $x^2 + 25 = 0$ **45.** $3x^2 = -48$ **46.** $\frac{1}{2}x^2 + 18 = 0$

Identify the x- and y-intercepts of $f(x)$. Without graphing $g(x)$, identify its x- and y-intercepts. *(Lesson 9-3)*

47. $f(x) = 2x - 8$ and $g(x) = \frac{1}{2}f(x)$ **48.** $f(x) = x^2 - 4$ and $g(x) = -f(x)$

49. $f(x) = \frac{1}{2}x + 6$ and $g(x) = f(3x)$ **50.** $f(x) = x^3 + 1$ and $g(x) = -4f(x)$

Solve each triangle. Round to the nearest tenth. *(Lesson 13-5)*

51.

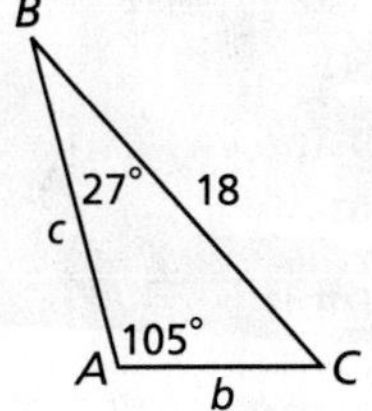

52.

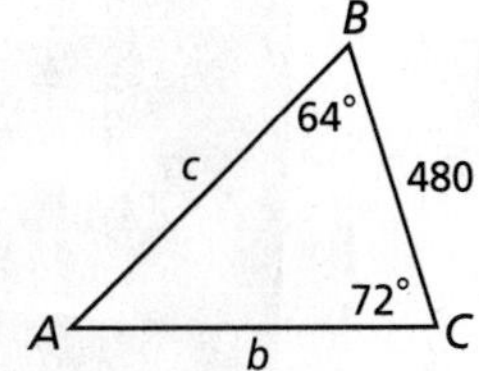

CHAPTER 13 MULTI-STEP TEST PREP

SECTION 13B

Applying Trigonometric Functions

Where's the Fire? A driver dials 9-1-1 on a cell phone to report smoke coming from a building. Before the driver can give the building's address, the call is cut short. The 9-1-1 dispatcher is still able to determine the driver's location based on the driver's position in relation to nearby cell phone towers.

1. When the driver makes the call, he is located in the triangular area between the three cell phone towers shown. To the nearest tenth of a mile, what is the distance between tower 3 and each of the other towers?

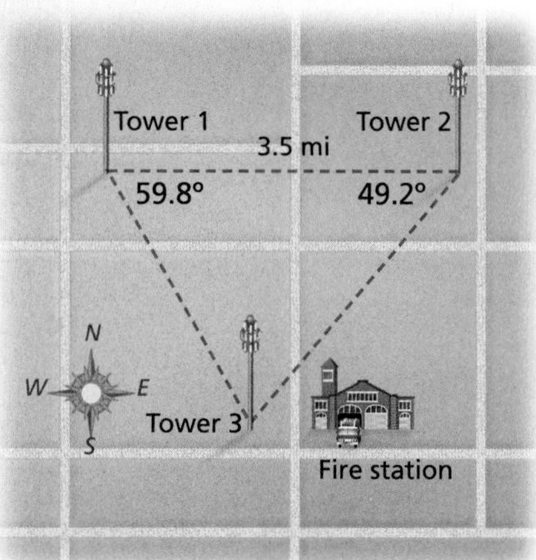

2. What is the area in square miles of the triangle with the three cell phone towers at its vertices? Round to the nearest tenth.
3. The driver is 1.7 miles from tower 1 and 2.4 miles from tower 2 when the call is made. Make a sketch of the triangle with tower 1, tower 2, and the driver at its vertices. To the nearest tenth of a degree, what are the measures of the angles of this triangle?
4. Tower 2 is directly east of tower 1. How many miles east of tower 1 is the driver? How many miles south of tower 1 is the driver? Round to the nearest tenth.
5. A fire station is located 1 block from tower 3. Estimate the distance between the fire station and the fire. Explain how you determined your estimate.

READY TO GO ON?

CHAPTER 13

SECTION 13B

Quiz for Lessons 13-5 Through 13-6

13-5 The Law of Sines

Find the area of each triangle. Round to the nearest tenth.

1. 4 ft, 55°, 2.4 ft

2. 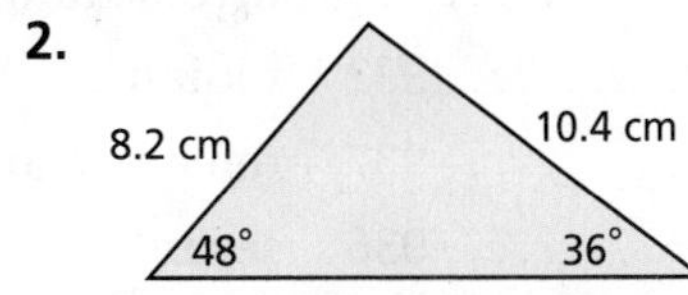

Solve each triangle. Round to the nearest tenth.

3. 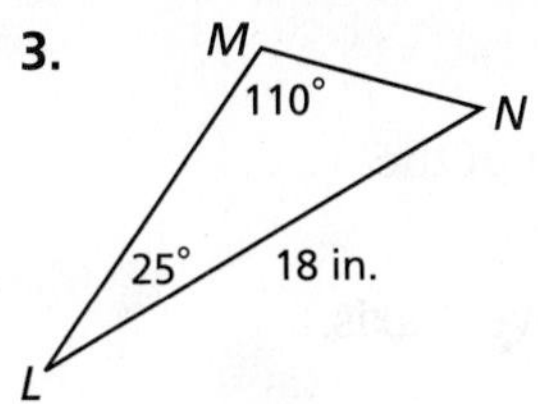

4. 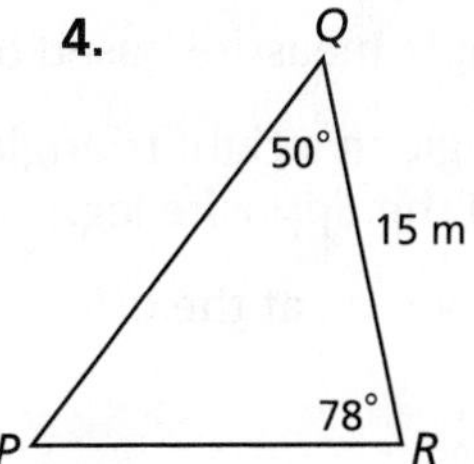

Derrick is designing triangular panes for a stained glass window. Determine the number of different triangles that he can form using the given measurements. Then solve the triangles. Round to the nearest tenth.

5. $a = 2.1$ cm, $b = 1.8$ cm, $m\angle A = 42°$

6. $a = 3$ cm, $b = 4.6$ cm, $m\angle A = 95°$

7. The rangers at two park stations spot a signal flare at the same time. Based on the measurements shown in the diagram, what is the distance between each park station and the point where the flare was set off? Round to the nearest tenth.

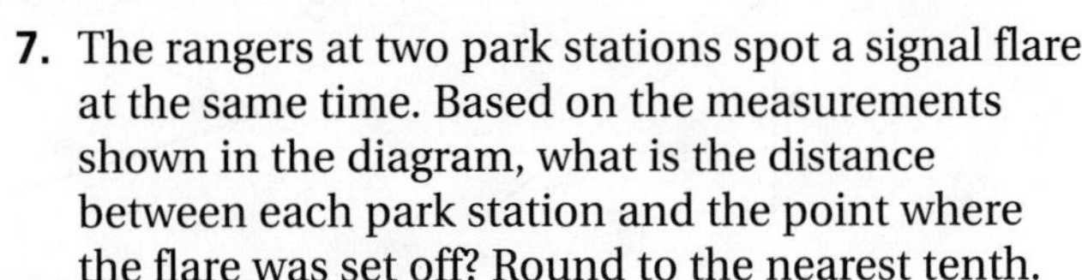

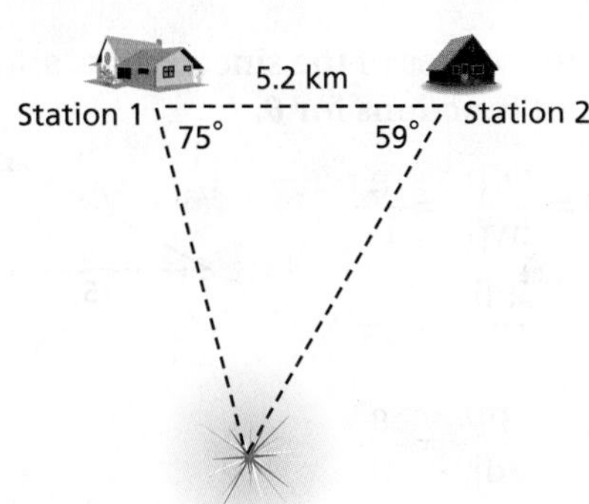

13-6 The Law of Cosines

Use the given measurements to solve each triangle. Round to the nearest tenth.

8. 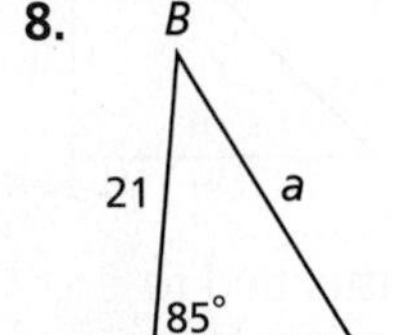

9. 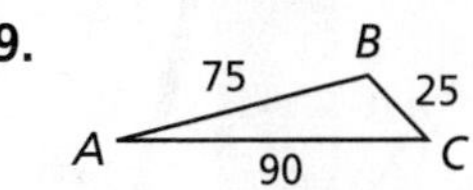

10. A civil engineer is working on plans for a new road called Pine Avenue. This road will intersect Market Boulevard and 3rd Street as shown. To the nearest degree, what is the measure of the angle that Pine Avenue will make with Market Boulevard?

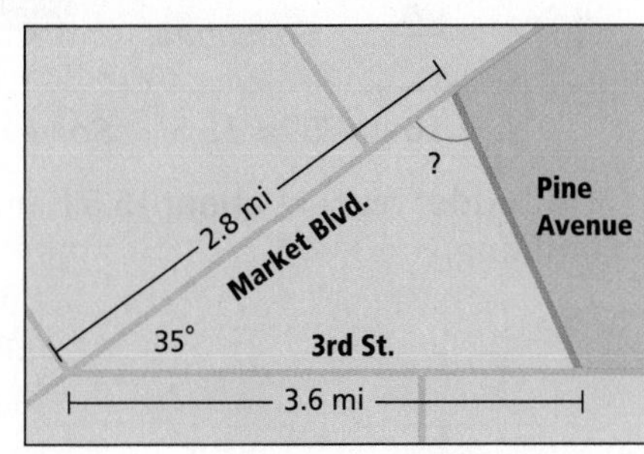

11. A school courtyard is shaped like a triangle. Its sides measure 25 yards, 27.5 yards, and 32 yards. What is the area of the courtyard to the nearest square yard?

CHAPTER 13

Study Guide: Review

Vocabulary

Complete the sentences below with vocabulary words from the list above.

1. A(n) ___?___ is a unit of angle measure based on arc length.
2. The ___?___ of an acute angle in a right triangle is the ratio of the length of the hypotenuse to the length of the opposite leg.
3. An angle in ___?___ has its vertex at the origin and one ray on the positive x-axis.

13-1 Right-Angle Trigonometry *(pp. 929–935)*

EXAMPLES

■ **Find the values of the sine, cosine, and tangent functions for θ.**

$$\sin\theta = \frac{\text{opp.}}{\text{hyp.}} = \frac{8}{17}$$

17 8 θ 15

$$\cos\theta = \frac{\text{adj.}}{\text{hyp.}} = \frac{15}{17}$$

$$\tan\theta = \frac{\text{opp.}}{\text{adj.}} = \frac{8}{15}$$

■ **A 16 ft ladder is leaned against a building as shown. How high up the building does the ladder reach?**

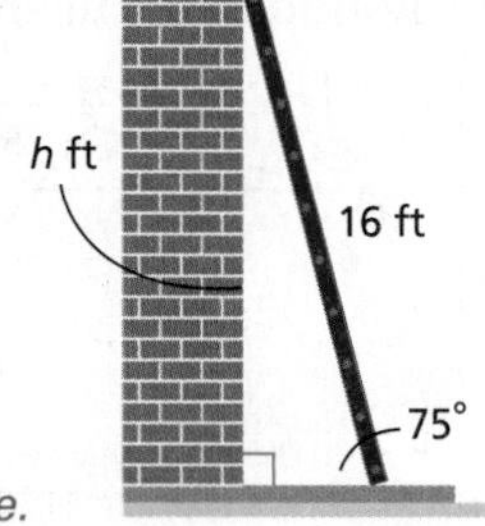

$$\sin\theta = \frac{\text{opp.}}{\text{hyp.}}$$

$\sin 75^\circ = \frac{h}{16}$ *Substitute.*

$h = 16\sin 75^\circ \approx 15.5$ *Solve for h.*

The ladder reaches about 15.5 ft up the building.

EXERCISES

Find the values of the six trigonometric functions for θ.

4.

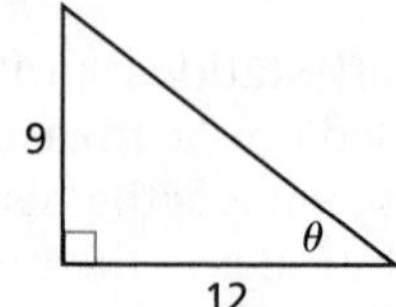

5.

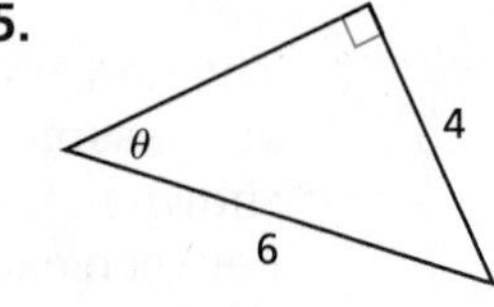

Use a trigonometric function to find the value of x.

6.

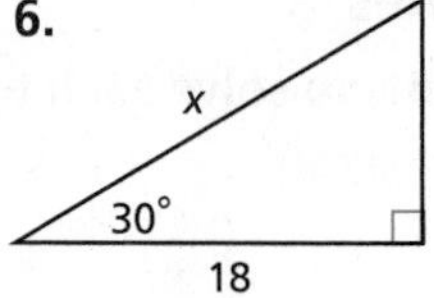

7.

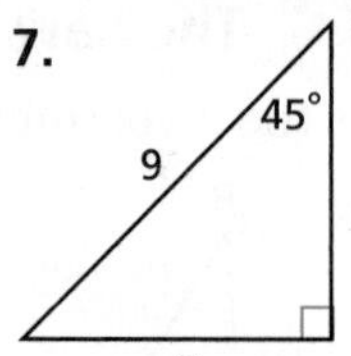

8. A support wire is being attached to a telephone pole as shown in the diagram. To the nearest foot, how long does the wire need to be?

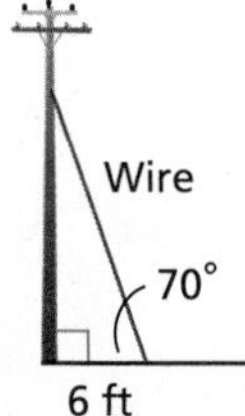

9. The angle of depression from a watchtower to a forest fire is 8°. If the watchtower is 25 m high, what is the distance between the base of the tower and the fire to the nearest meter?

13-2 Angles of Rotation *(pp. 936–941)*

EXAMPLES

■ **Draw a −290° angle in standard position.**

Rotate the terminal side 290° clockwise.

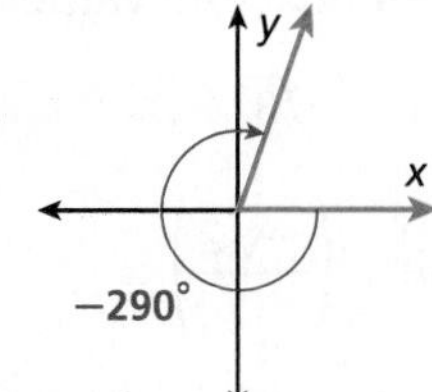

■ **$P(-5, 12)$ is a point on the terminal side of θ in standard position. Find the exact value of the six trigonometric functions of θ.**

$r = \sqrt{(-5)^2 + (12)^2} = 13$ *Find r.*

$\sin\theta = \frac{y}{r} = \frac{12}{13}$ $\cos\theta = \frac{x}{r} = \frac{-5}{13} = -\frac{5}{13}$

$\tan\theta = \frac{y}{x} = \frac{12}{-5} = -\frac{12}{5}$ $\csc\theta = \frac{1}{\sin\theta} = \frac{13}{12}$

$\sec\theta = \frac{1}{\cos\theta} = -\frac{13}{5}$ $\cot\theta = \frac{1}{\tan\theta} = -\frac{5}{12}$

EXERCISES

Draw an angle with the given measure in standard position.

10. 195° **11.** −220° **12.** −450°

Find the measures of a positive angle and a negative angle that are coterminal with each given angle.

13. $\theta = 115°$ **14.** $\theta = 382°$ **15.** $\theta = -135°$

Find the measure of the reference angle for each given angle.

16. $\theta = 84°$ **17.** $\theta = 127°$ **18.** $\theta = -105°$

***P* is a point on the terminal side of θ in standard position. Find the exact value of the six trigonometric functions for θ.**

19. $P(-4, 3)$ **20.** $P(5, 12)$ **21.** $P(-15, -8)$

22. $P(8, -3)$ **23.** $P(-9, -1)$ **24.** $P(-5, 10)$

13-3 The Unit Circle *(pp. 943–949)*

EXAMPLES

Convert each measure from degrees to radians or from radians to degrees.

■ −60°

$-60°\left(\frac{\pi \text{ radians}}{180°}\right) = -\frac{\pi}{3}$ radians

■ $\frac{5\pi}{3}$ radians

$\left(\frac{5\pi}{3} \text{ radians}\right)\left(\frac{180°}{\pi \text{ radians}}\right) = 300°$

■ **Use a reference angle to find the exact value of tan 150°.**

Step 1 The reference angle measures 30°.

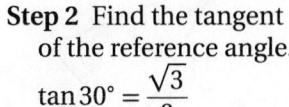

Step 2 Find the tangent of the reference angle.

$\tan 30° = \frac{\sqrt{3}}{3}$

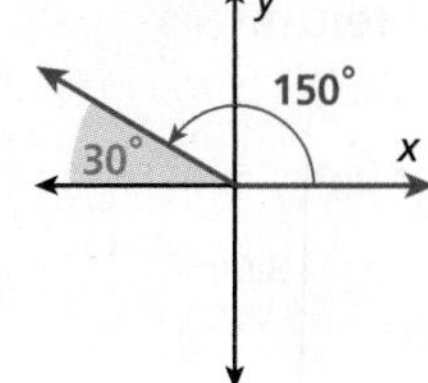

Step 3 Adjust the sign, if needed.

The tangent ratio is negative if the terminal side of the angle is in Quadrant II.

$\tan 150° = -\frac{\sqrt{3}}{3}$

EXERCISES

Convert each measure from degrees to radians or from radians to degrees.

25. 270° **26.** −120° **27.** 400°

28. $\frac{\pi}{6}$ **29.** $-\frac{\pi}{9}$ **30.** $\frac{9\pi}{4}$

Use the unit circle to find the exact value of each trigonometric function.

31. $\cos 240°$ **32.** $\tan\frac{3\pi}{4}$ **33.** $\sec 300°$

Use a reference angle to find the exact value of the sine, cosine, and tangent of each angle measure.

34. $\frac{7\pi}{6}$ **35.** 300° **36.** $-\frac{\pi}{3}$

37. A circle has a radius of 16 in. To the nearest inch, what is the length of an arc of the circle that is intercepted by a central angle of 80°?

38. The minute hand on a clock on a town hall tower is 1.5 meters in length.

a. Find the angle in radians through which the minute hand rotates in 10 minutes.

b. To the nearest tenth of a meter, how far does the tip of the minute hand travel in 10 minutes?

13-4 Inverses of Trigonometric Functions *(pp. 950–955)*

EXAMPLES

■ **Evaluate $\text{Sin}^{-1}\left(-\frac{\sqrt{3}}{2}\right)$. Give your answer in both radians and degrees.**

$-\frac{\sqrt{3}}{2} = \text{Sin}\,\theta$ *Find the value of θ for $-\frac{\pi}{2} \le \theta \le \frac{\pi}{2}$.*

$-\frac{\sqrt{3}}{2} = \text{Sin}\left(-\frac{\pi}{3}\right)$ *Use y-coordinates of points on the unit circle.*

$\text{Sin}^{-1}\left(-\frac{\sqrt{3}}{2}\right) = -\frac{\pi}{3}$, or $\text{Sin}^{-1}\left(-\frac{\sqrt{3}}{2}\right) = -60°$

■ **A boat is 2.8 miles east and 1.3 miles north of a dock. To the nearest degree, in what direction should the boat head to reach the dock?**

Step 1 Draw a diagram.

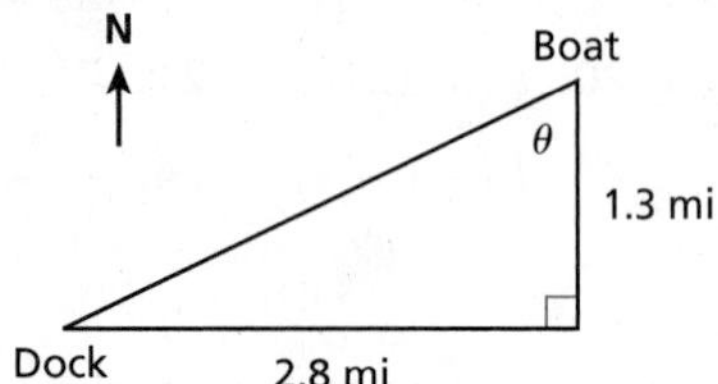

Step 2 Find the value of θ.

$\tan\theta = \frac{\text{opp.}}{\text{adj.}}$ *Use the tangent ratio.*

$\tan\theta = \frac{2.8}{1.3}$ *Substitute.*

$\theta = \text{Tan}^{-1}\left(\frac{2.8}{1.3}\right) \approx 65°$ *Solve for θ.*

The boat should head 65° west of south.

EXERCISES

Find all possible values of each expression.

39. $\tan^{-1}\sqrt{3}$

40. $\cos^{-1}\left(-\frac{\sqrt{3}}{2}\right)$

41. $\sin^{-1}\left(-\frac{\sqrt{2}}{2}\right)$

42. $\tan^{-1}\left(-\frac{\sqrt{3}}{3}\right)$

Evaluate each inverse trigonometric function. Give your answer in both radians and degrees.

43. $\text{Sin}^{-1}\left(-\frac{1}{2}\right)$

44. $\text{Tan}^{-1}\frac{\sqrt{3}}{3}$

45. $\text{Cos}^{-1}(-1)$

46. $\text{Sin}^{-1}\frac{\sqrt{2}}{2}$

47. A skateboard ramp is 39 inches long and rises to a height of 22 inches. To the nearest degree, what angle does the ramp make with the ground?

48. A parasail is a parachute that lifts a person into the air when he or she is towed by a boat. Shelley is parasailing at a height of 100 feet. If 152 feet of towline attaches her to the boat, what is the angle of depression from Shelley to the boat? Round to the nearest degree.

Solve each equation to the nearest tenth. Use the given restrictions.

49. $\sin\theta = 0.3$, for $-90° \le \theta \le 90°$

50. $\sin\theta = 0.3$, for $90° \le \theta \le 180°$

51. $\tan\theta = 2.2$, for $-90° < \theta < 90°$

52. $\tan\theta = 2.2$, for $180° \le \theta \le 270°$

13-5 The Law of Sines *(pp. 958–965)*

EXAMPLES

■ **Find the area of the triangle. Round to the nearest tenth.**

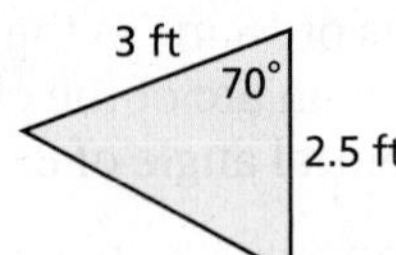

$\text{Area} = \frac{1}{2}ab\sin C$ *Use the area formula*

$= \frac{1}{2}(3)(2.5)\sin 70°$ *Substitute.*

$\approx 3.5\text{ ft}^2$ *Evaluate.*

EXERCISES

Find the area of each triangle. Round to the nearest tenth.

53.

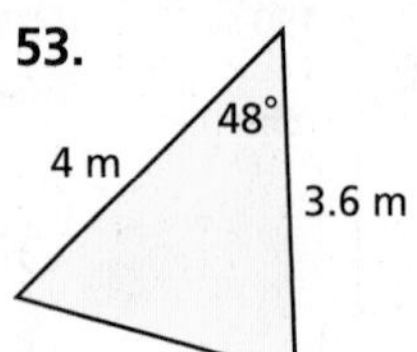

54.

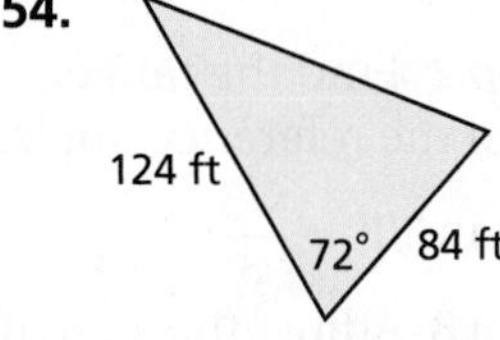

55.

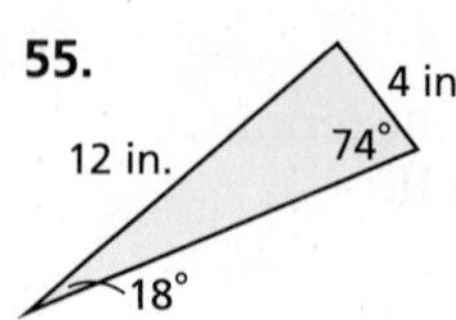

56.

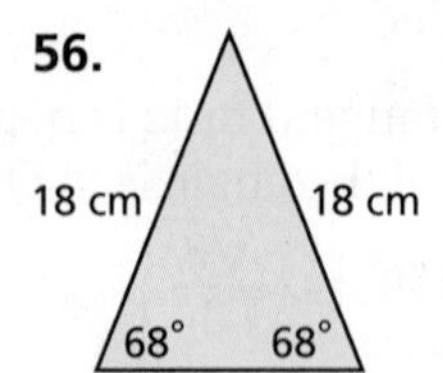

■ **Solve the triangle. Round to the nearest tenth.**

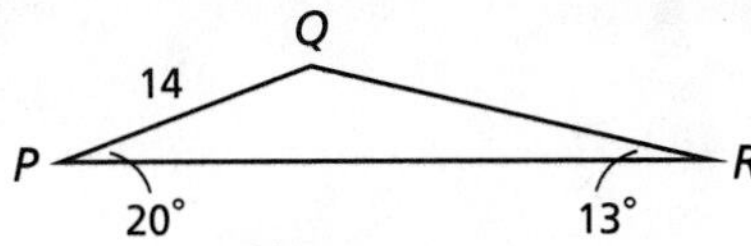

Step 1 Find the third angle measure.

$m\angle Q° = 180° - 20° - 13° = 147°$

Step 2 Use the Law of Sines to find the unknown side lengths.

$$\frac{\sin P}{p} = \frac{\sin R}{r} \qquad \frac{\sin Q}{q} = \frac{\sin R}{r}$$

$$\frac{\sin 20°}{p} = \frac{\sin 13°}{14} \qquad \frac{\sin 147°}{q} = \frac{\sin 13°}{14}$$

$$p = \frac{14 \sin 20°}{\sin 13°} \qquad q = \frac{14 \sin 147°}{\sin 13°}$$

$$p \approx 21.3 \qquad q \approx 33.9$$

Solve each triangle. Round to the nearest tenth.

57. **58.**

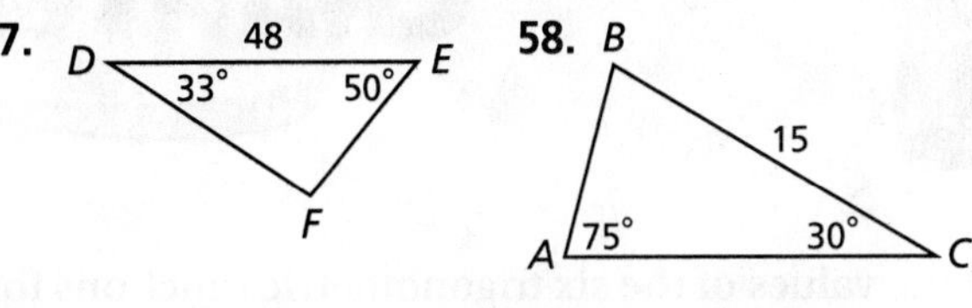

59. **60.**

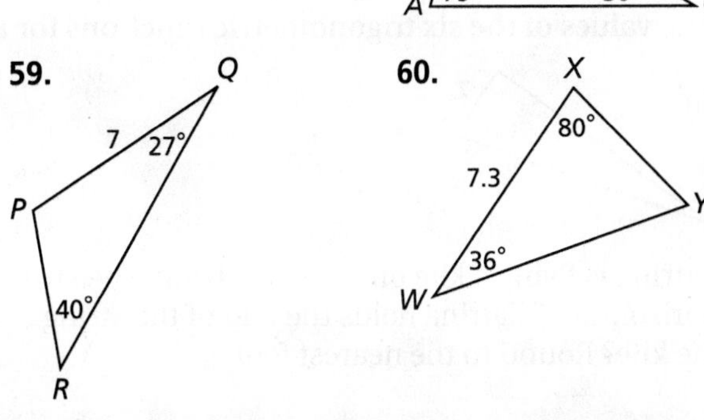

61. A graphic artist is designing a triangular logo. Determine the number of different triangles that he can form using the measurements $a = 14$ cm, $b = 16$ cm, and $m\angle A = 55°$. Then solve the triangles. Round to the nearest tenth.

13-6 The Law of Cosines *(pp. 966–973)*

EXAMPLES

■ **Use the given measurements to solve $\triangle ABC$. Round to the nearest tenth.**

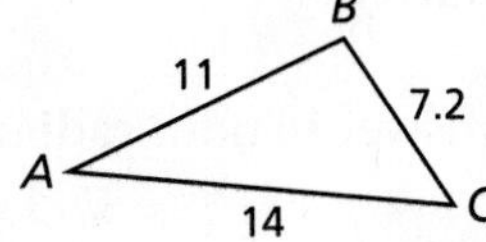

Step 1 Find the measure of the largest angle, $\angle B$.

$$b^2 = a^2 + c^2 - 2ac \cos B$$

$$14^2 = 7.2^2 + 11^2 - 2(7.2)(11) \cos B$$

$$m\angle B \approx 98.4°$$

Step 2 Find another angle measure.

$$a^2 = b^2 + c^2 - 2bc \cos A$$

$$7.2^2 = 14^2 + 11^2 - 2(14)(11) \cos A$$

$$m\angle A \approx 30.6°$$

Step 3 Find the third angle measure.

$$m\angle C \approx 180° - 30.6° - 98.4° \approx 51.0°$$

■ **A triangular tile has sides measuring 4 in., 5 in., and 8 in. What is the area of the tile to the nearest square inch?**

$s = \frac{1}{2}(4 + 5 + 8) = 8.5$ *Find the value of s.*

$A = \sqrt{s(s - a)(s - b)(s - c)}$ *Heron's Formula*

$A = \sqrt{8.5(8.5 - 4)(8.5 - 5)(8.5 - 8)} \approx 8.2 \text{ in}^2$

EXERCISES

Use the given measurements to solve $\triangle ABC$. Round to the nearest tenth.

62. $m\angle C = 29°$, $a = 14$, $b = 30$

63. $m\angle A = 110°$, $b = 18$, $c = 12$

64. $a = 12$, $b = 3$, $c = 10$

65. $a = 7$, $b = 9$, $c = 11$

66. A bicycle race has a triangular course with the dimensions shown.

a. To the nearest tenth of a kilometer, how long is the race?

b. At an average speed of 28 km/h, how many hours will it take a rider to complete the race? Round to the nearest tenth.

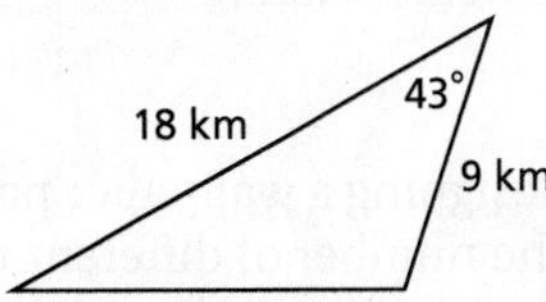

67. A triangular wading pool has side lengths that measure 10 ft, 12 ft, and 16 ft. What is the area of the pool's surface to the nearest square foot?

68. A triangular pennant has side lengths that measure 24 in., 24 in., and 8 in. What is the area of the pennant to the nearest square inch?

Find the values of the six trigonometric functions for θ.

1. 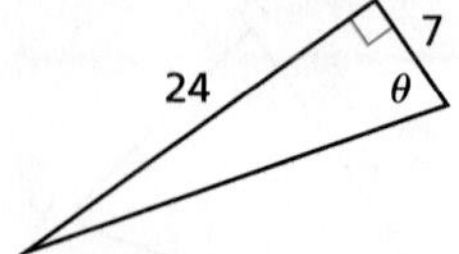

2. 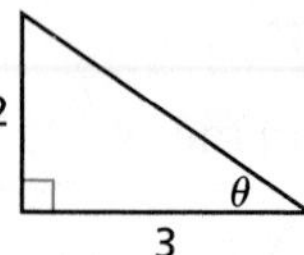

3. Katrina is flying a kite on 150 ft of string. The string makes an angle of 62° with the horizontal. If Katrina holds the end of the string 5 ft above the ground, how high is the kite? Round to the nearest foot.

Draw an angle with the given measure in standard position.

4. 100° **5.** −210°

***P* is a point on the terminal side of θ in standard position. Find the exact value of the six trigonometric functions of θ.**

6. $P(-32, 24)$ **7.** $P(-3, -7)$

Convert each measure from degrees to radians or from radians to degrees.

8. 310° **9.** −36° **10.** $\frac{2\pi}{9}$ **11.** $-\frac{5\pi}{6}$

Use the unit circle to find the exact value of each trigonometric function.

12. $\cos 210°$ **13.** $\tan\frac{11\pi}{6}$

Evaluate each inverse trigonometric function. Give your answer in both radians and degrees.

14. $\text{Cos}^{-1}\frac{\sqrt{2}}{2}$ **15.** $\text{Sin}^{-1}\left(-\frac{\sqrt{3}}{2}\right)$

16. A limestone cave is 6.2 mi south and 1.4 mi east of the entrance of a national park. To the nearest degree, in what direction should a group at the entrance head in order to reach the cave?

17. Find the area of $\triangle DEF$. Round to the nearest tenth.

18. Use the given measurements to solve $\triangle DEF$. Round to the nearest tenth.

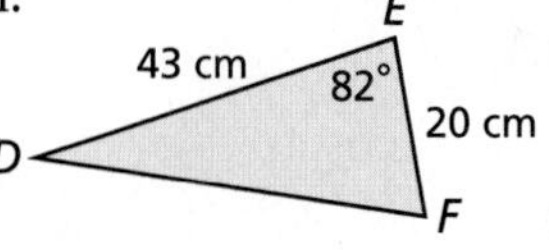

19. An artist is designing a wallpaper pattern based on triangles. Determine the number of different triangles she can form using the measurements $a = 28$, $b = 13$, and $m\angle A = 102°$. Then solve the triangles. Round to the nearest tenth.

20. Solve $\triangle LMN$. Round to the nearest tenth.

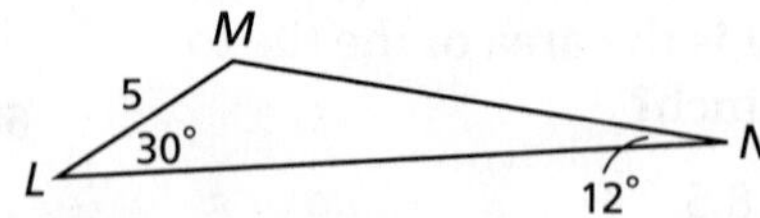

21. A lawn next to an office building is shaped like a triangle with sides measuring 16 ft, 24 ft, and 30 ft. What is the area of the lawn to the nearest square foot?

FOCUS ON SAT MATHEMATICS SUBJECT TESTS

Though both the SAT Mathematics Subject Tests Level 1 and Level 2 may include questions involving basic trigonometric functions, only the Level 2 test may include questions involving the Law of Sines, the Law of Cosines, and radian measure.

You may want to time yourself as you take this practice test. It should take you about 6 minutes to complete.

If you take the Level 1 test, make sure that your calculator is set to degree mode, because no questions will require you to use radians. If you take the Level 2 test, you will need to determine whether to use degree or radian mode as appropriate.

1. A right triangle has an angle measuring 22°. The shorter leg of the triangle has a length of 3 inches. What is the area of the triangle?

(A) 1.8 in^2

(B) 4.2 in^2

(C) 7.4 in^2

(D) 11.1 in^2

(E) 12.0 in^2

2. If $0 \le \theta \le \frac{\pi}{2}$ and $\cos^{-1}(\sin\theta) = \frac{\pi}{3}$, then what is the value of θ?

(A) $\frac{\pi}{6}$

(B) $\frac{\pi}{2}$

(C) $\frac{5\pi}{6}$

(D) $\frac{4\pi}{3}$

(E) $\frac{3\pi}{2}$

3. A triangle has side lengths of 7, 26, and 31. What is the measure of the smallest angle of the triangle?

(A) 8°

(B) 10°

(C) 26°

(D) 30°

(E) 40°

4. A manufacturer must produce a metal bar with a triangular cross section that meets the specifications shown. What is the length of side a?

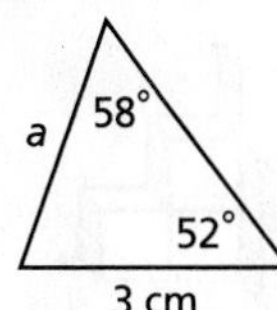

Note: Figure not drawn to scale

(A) 2.4 cm

(B) 2.6 cm

(C) 2.8 cm

(D) 3.2 cm

(E) 3.6 cm

5. If $\sin B = \frac{5}{9}$ in the figure below, what is $\tan A$?

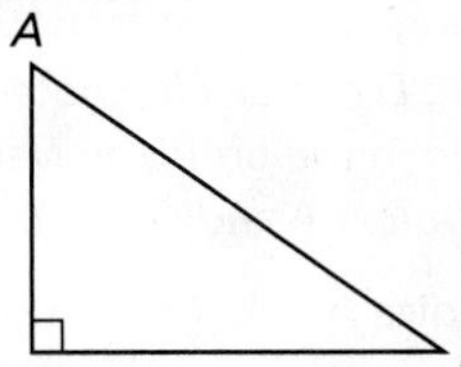

Note: Figure not drawn to scale

(A) 0.45

(B) 0.67

(C) 0.83

(D) 1.50

(E) 1.80

CHAPTER 13 TEST TACKLER

Standardized Test Strategies

Multiple Choice: Spatial-Reasoning Problems

Some problems test your ability to use spatial reasoning. To solve these problems, you must be able to recognize different views of geometric figures. Orthographic drawings and nets are two common ways of representing three-dimensional objects. An *orthographic drawing* usually presents three views of a three-dimensional object: top, front, and side. A *net* is a diagram that can be folded to form a three-dimensional figure.

EXAMPLE 1

The drawing shows the top view of a structure made from cubes as well as the number of cubes in each column of the structure. Which three-dimensional view represents the same structure?

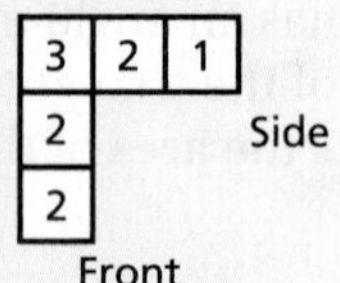

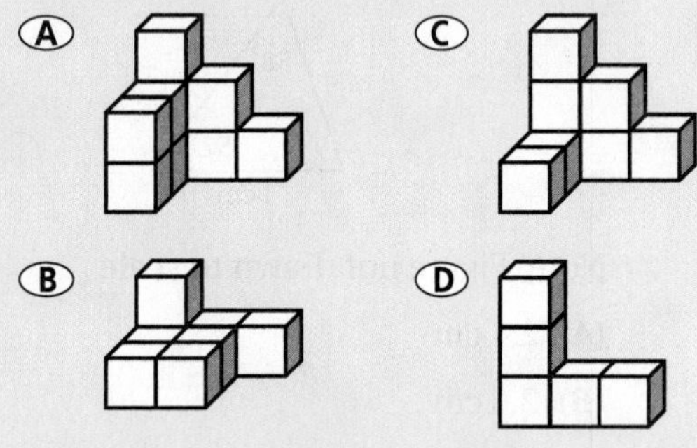

Start by sketching the top view of each answer choice.

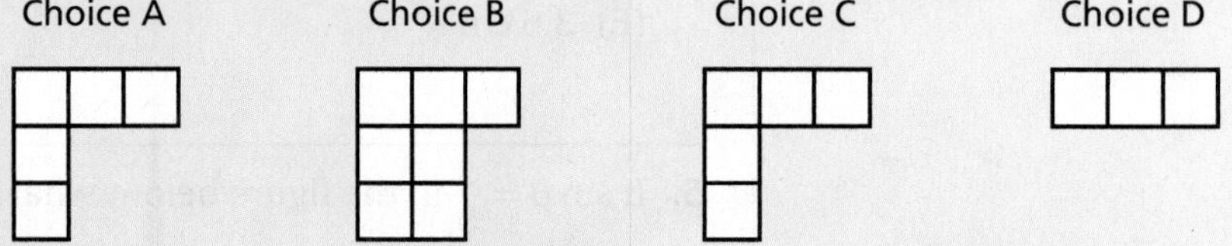

Choices B and D can be eliminated because their top views do not match the one given in the problem. Next, count the number of cubes in each column of choices A and C.

Choice A

3	2	1
2		
2		

Choice C

3	2	1
1		
1		

The two front columns of choice C have only 1 cube each instead of 2. Therefore, choice C can be eliminated. Each column of choice A, however, has the correct number of cubes.

The correct answer is choice A.

If you have trouble visualizing the geometric figures, make a quick sketch. Your sketch does not need to be exact, but it should show the sides or faces of the figures in the correct relationships to each other.

Read each test item and answer the questions that follow.

Item A

The front, top, and side views of a solid are shown below. What is the volume of the solid?

1.7 m, 2 m, Front; 4 m, 2 m, Top; 1.7 m, 4 m, Side

Ⓐ 6.8 m^3

Ⓑ 9.1 m^3

Ⓒ 13.6 m^3

Ⓓ 16.5 m^3

1. Make a sketch of the figure. What type of figure do the three views show?
2. How can you determine the volume of this figure?

Item B

What three-dimensional figure does this net represent?

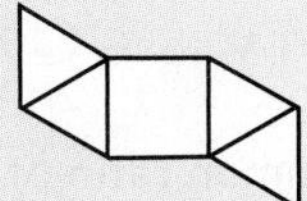

Ⓕ Square pyramid

Ⓖ Triangular pyramid

Ⓗ Rectangular prism

Ⓙ Triangular prism

3. What type and number of faces does the figure have?
4. What type and number of faces does each of the answer choices have?

Item C

Which of the following is the front view of the figure shown?

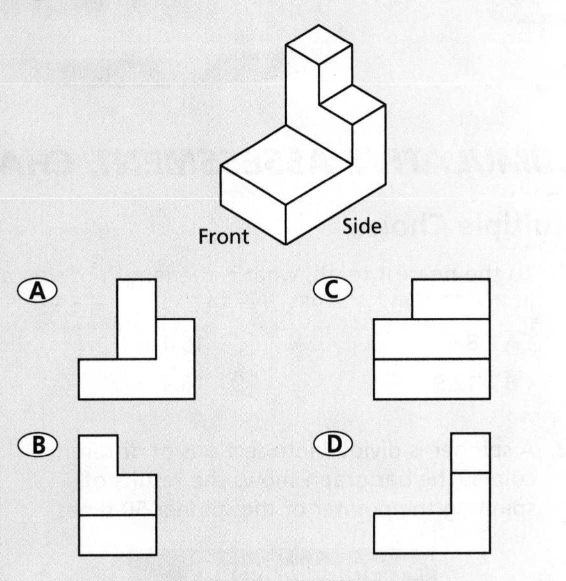

5. Make a sketch of the figure. Shade the faces on the front of the figure.
6. Describe the shapes of these faces.

Item D

Which is a true statement about the net of the cube shown?

Ⓕ The face with the star and the face with the circle are parallel.

Ⓖ The face with the heart and the face with the circle are perpendicular.

Ⓗ The faces with the triangles are parallel.

Ⓙ The face with the number 5 and the face with the star are perpendicular.

7. Which faces of the cube are opposite each other? Are opposite faces parallel or perpendicular to each other?
8. Can faces that share an edge be parallel to each other? Explain.

CHAPTER 13

STANDARDIZED TEST PREP

go.hrw.com
State Test Practice Online
KEYWORD: MB7 TestPrep

CUMULATIVE ASSESSMENT, CHAPTERS 1–13

Multiple Choice

1. To the nearest tenth, what is the length of side a in $\triangle ABC$ if $m\angle A = 98°$, $b = 14.2$, and $c = 5.9$?

Ⓐ 8.4
Ⓑ 12.9
Ⓒ 15.4
Ⓓ 16.1

2. A spinner is divided into sections of different colors. The bar graph shows the results of spinning the pointer of the spinner 50 times.

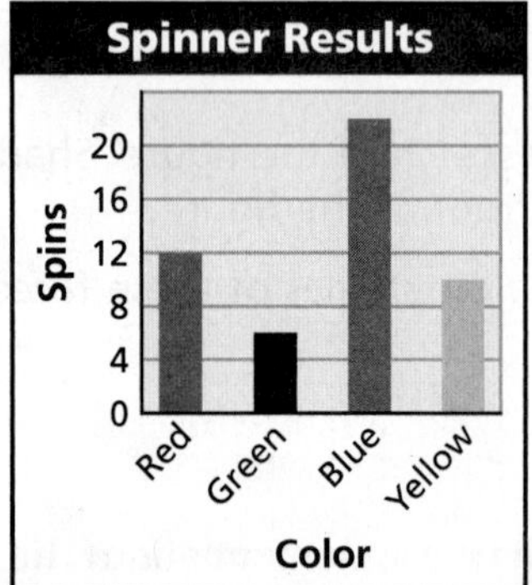

What is the experimental probability that the pointer of the spinner will land on a blue section?

Ⓕ 0.05
Ⓖ 0.22
Ⓗ 0.25
Ⓙ 0.44

3. If $-\frac{\pi}{2} \le \theta \le \frac{\pi}{2}$, what value of θ makes the equation $\sin^{-1}\left(\frac{1}{2}\right) = \theta$ true?

Ⓐ $\frac{\pi}{6}$
Ⓑ $\frac{\pi}{4}$
Ⓒ $\frac{\pi}{3}$
Ⓓ $\frac{5\pi}{6}$

4. What is the inverse of the matrix $\begin{bmatrix} -3 & 4 \\ 0 & -1 \end{bmatrix}$?

Ⓕ $\begin{bmatrix} -\frac{1}{3} & -\frac{4}{3} \\ 0 & -1 \end{bmatrix}$
Ⓖ $\begin{bmatrix} 1 & 0 \\ -4 & 3 \end{bmatrix}$
Ⓗ $\begin{bmatrix} -\frac{1}{3} & \frac{1}{4} \\ 0 & -1 \end{bmatrix}$
Ⓙ $\begin{bmatrix} -1 & -4 \\ 0 & -3 \end{bmatrix}$

5. What is the equation of a hyperbola with center $(0, 0)$, a vertex at $(0, 6)$, and a focus at $(0, 10)$?

Ⓐ $\frac{x^2}{36} - \frac{y^2}{64} = 1$
Ⓑ $\frac{y^2}{36} - \frac{x^2}{64} = 1$
Ⓒ $\frac{y^2}{36} + \frac{x^2}{64} = 1$
Ⓓ $\frac{y^2}{64} - \frac{x^2}{36} = 1$

6. What is the 7th term of the following geometric sequence?

125, 25, 5, 1, ...

Ⓕ 0.2
Ⓖ 0.04
Ⓗ 0.008
Ⓙ 0.0016

7. What type of function best models the data in the table?

x	−2	−1	0	1	2
y	6.35	11.6	29.35	59.6	102.35

Ⓐ linear
Ⓑ quadratic
Ⓒ cubic
Ⓓ square root

8. If $f(x) = \frac{3}{2}x - 4$ and $g(x) = \frac{1}{2}f(x)$, what is the y-intercept of $g(x)$?

Ⓕ −4
Ⓖ −2
Ⓗ $\frac{1}{2}$
Ⓙ $\frac{8}{3}$

9. What is the common ratio of the exponential function represented by the table?

x	−2	−1	0	1	2
y	2.56	3.2	4	5	6.25

Ⓐ 0.16
Ⓑ 0.25
Ⓒ 0.64
Ⓓ 1.25

10. What effect does a translation 3 units right have on the graph of $f(x) = 2x - 5$?

Ⓕ The slope increases.
Ⓖ The slope decreases.
Ⓗ The value of the y-intercept increases.
Ⓙ The value of the y-intercept decreases.

One way to check whether two expressions are equivalent is to substitute the same value for the variable in each expression. If the expressions simplify to different values, then they are *not* equivalent.

11. Which of the following is equivalent to $(x + 4)^3$?

Ⓐ $x^3 + 64$

Ⓑ $x^3 + 8x + 16$

Ⓒ $4x^3 + 32x^2 + 64x$

Ⓓ $x^3 + 12x^2 + 48x + 64$

12. What is $\cos\theta$?

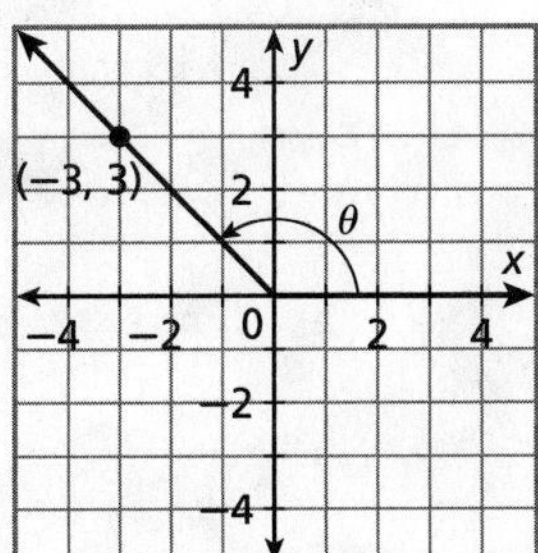

Ⓕ -1

Ⓖ $-\frac{\sqrt{2}}{2}$

Ⓗ $\frac{\sqrt{2}}{2}$

Ⓙ 1

13. What is the measure in degrees of an angle that measures $\frac{3\pi}{4}$ radians?

Ⓐ 45°

Ⓑ 90°

Ⓒ 135°

Ⓓ 180°

Gridded Response

14. To the nearest hundredth, what is the value of x in the triangle below?

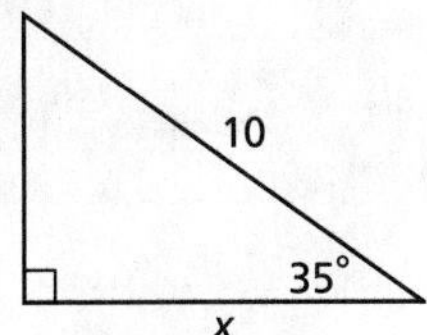

15. What is the 15th term of an arithmetic sequence with $a_{11} = 425$ and $a_{17} = 515$?

16. How many different triangles can be formed with the following measurements?

$a = 6.38$, $b = 4.72$, $m\angle A = 132°$

17. The function $h(t) = -4.9t^2 + 4.9t + 1.75$ models the height in meters of a lacrosse ball, where t is the time in seconds since the ball was thrown. Based on the model, what is the maximum height in meters that the ball will reach?

Short Response

18. Tickets for the water park cost \$12 for children under 13, \$20 for people ages 13 to 60, and \$15 for people over 60 years of age.

a. Write a function to represent the cost y in dollars of a ticket to the water park given a person's age x in years.

b. Graph the function.

19. What are the constraints on the region bounded by the quadrilateral below?

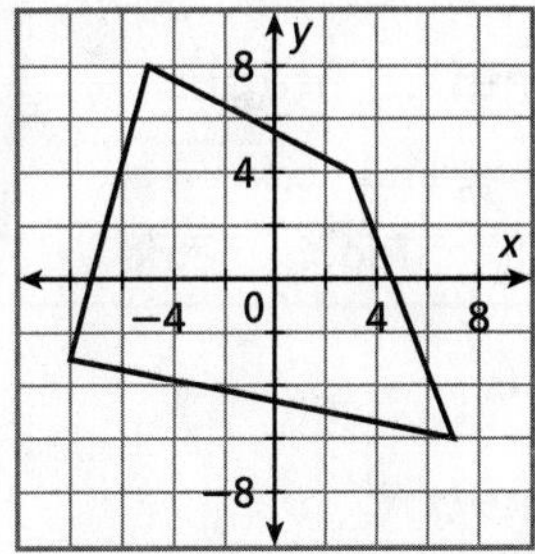

20. The table shows the number of Atlantic hurricanes for the years 1997–2004.

Atlantic Hurricanes			
Year	**Number**	**Year**	**Number**
1997	3	2001	9
1998	10	2002	4
1999	8	2003	7
2000	8	2004	9

a. Make a box-and-whisker plot of the hurricane data.

b. What is the mean number of hurricanes per year for the time period shown in the table?

Extended Response

21. The choir director at a high school wants to rent an auditorium for an upcoming performance. To pay for the auditorium, \$550 must be raised in ticket sales. The cost of the tickets will depend on the number of people who are expected to attend the performance.

a. Write a function to represent the number of dollars y a ticket should cost when x is the number of people who are expected to attend the performance.

b. What are the asymptotes of the function?

c. Graph the function.

d. What is a reasonable domain and range for the function? Explain.

e. How much should tickets cost if 250 people are expected to attend the performance?

CHAPTER 14

Trigonometric Graphs and Identities

Chapter Focus

- Make connections among representations of trigonometric functions.
- Use reasoning to solve problems involving trigonometric ratios.

Spinning Wheels

You can use graphs of trigonometric functions and trigonometric identities to model the motion of a circle or a wheel in a variety of situations.

go.hrw.com
Chapter Project Online
KEYWORD: MB7 ChProj

Vocabulary

Match each term on the left with a definition on the right.

1. cosecant
2. cosine
3. hypotenuse
4. tangent of an angle

A. the ratio of the length of the leg adjacent the angle to the length of the opposite leg

B. the ratio of the length of the leg adjacent the angle to the length of the hypotenuse

C. the ratio of the length of the leg opposite the angle to the length of the adjacent leg

D. the ratio of the length of the hypotenuse to the length of the leg opposite the angle

E. the side opposite the right angle

Divide Fractions

Divide.

5. $\dfrac{\frac{3}{5}}{\frac{5}{2}}$ **6.** $\dfrac{\frac{3}{4}}{\frac{1}{2}}$ **7.** $\dfrac{-\frac{3}{8}}{\frac{1}{8}}$ **8.** $\dfrac{\frac{2}{3}}{-\frac{7}{4}}$

Simplify Radical Expressions

Simplify each expression.

9. $\sqrt{6} \cdot \sqrt{2}$ **10.** $\sqrt{100 - 64}$ **11.** $\dfrac{\sqrt{9}}{\sqrt{36}}$ **12.** $\sqrt{\dfrac{4}{25}}$

Multiply Binomials

Multiply.

13. $(x + 11)(x + 7)$ **14.** $(y - 4)(y - 9)$

15. $(2x - 3)(x + 5)$ **16.** $(k + 3)(3k - 3)$

17. $(4z - 4)(z + 1)$ **18.** $(y + 0.5)(y - 1)$

Special Products of Binomials

Multiply.

19. $(2x + 5)^2$ **20.** $(3y - 2)^2$

21. $(4x - 6)(4x + 6)$ **22.** $(2m + 1)(2m - 1)$

23. $(s + 7)^2$ **24.** $(-p + 4)(-p - 4)$

CHAPTER 14

Study Guide: Preview

Where You've Been

In previous chapters, you

- solved problems involving triangles and trigonometric ratios.
- factored to solve quadratic equations.
- applied function models to solve real-world problems.
- solved equations by using algebra and graphs.

In This Chapter

You will study

- problems involving trigonometric functions.
- factoring to solve trigonometric equations.
- trigonometric function models of real-world problems.
- solving trigonometric equations by using algebra and graphs.

Where You're Going

You can use the skills in this chapter

- in your future math classes, particularly Calculus.
- in other classes, such as Physics, Biology, and Economics.
- outside of school to observe cyclical patterns and make conjectures.

Key Vocabulary/Vocabulario

amplitude	amplitud
cycle	ciclo
frequency	frecuencia
period	periodo
periodic function	función periódica
phase shift	cambio de fase
rotation matrix	matriz de rotación

Vocabulary Connections

To become familiar with some of the vocabulary terms in the chapter, consider the following. You may refer to the chapter, the glossary, or a dictionary if you like.

1. What does the word *amplify* mean? What might the **amplitude** of a pendulum swing refer to?
2. What does a **cycle** refer to in everyday language? Give examples of cyclical phenomena.
3. Give an example of something that occurs *frequently*. To describe how often something occurs, like brushing our teeth, we can say "we brush twice a day." Describe the **frequency** of your example.
4. What does **period** mean in everyday language? What might a **periodic function** refer to?
5. What result might you expect from using a **rotation matrix**?

Study Strategy: Prepare for Your Final Exam

Math is a cumulative subject, so your final exam will probably cover all of the material that you have learned from the beginning of the course. Preparation is essential for you to be successful on your final exam. It may help you to make a study timeline like the one below.

2 weeks before the final:

- Look at previous exams and homework to determine areas I need to focus on; rework problems that were incorrect or incomplete.
- Make a list of all formulas and theorems that I need to know for the final.
- Create a practice exam using problems from the book that are similar to problems from each exam.

1 week before the final:

- Take the practice exam and check it. For each problem I miss, find two or three similar ones and work those.
- Work with a friend in the class to quiz each other on formulas, postulates, and theorems from my list.

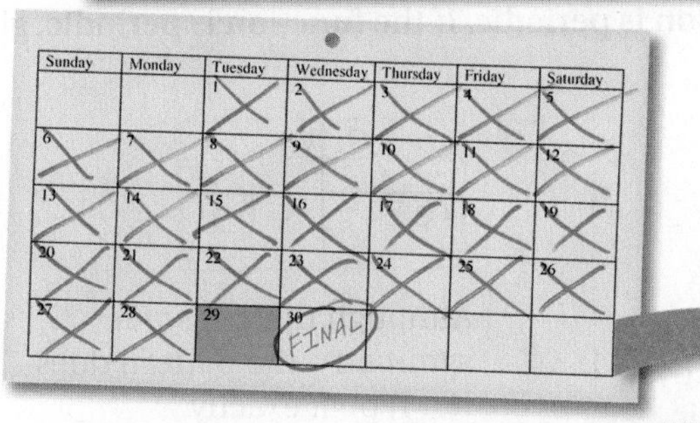

1 day before the final:

- Make sure I have pencils and a calculator (check batteries!).

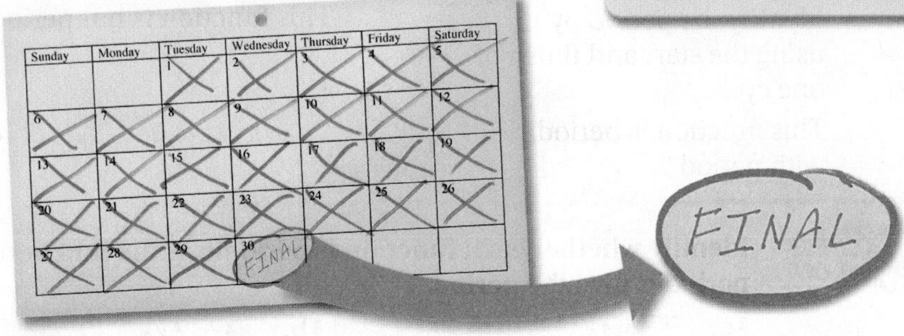

FINAL

Try This

1. Create a timeline that you will use to study for your final exam.

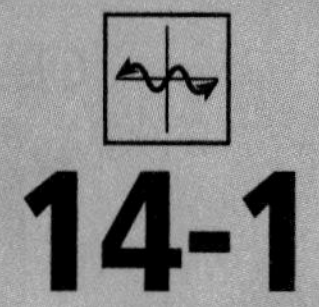

14-1 Graphs of Sine and Cosine

Objective
Recognize and graph periodic and trigonometric functions.

Vocabulary
periodic function
cycle
period
amplitude
frequency
phase shift

Why learn this?
Periodic phenomena such as sound waves can be modeled with trigonometric functions. (See Example 3.)

Periodic functions are functions that repeat exactly in regular intervals called **cycles**. The length of the cycle is called its **period**. Examine the graphs of the periodic function and nonperiodic function below. Notice that a cycle may begin at any point on the graph of a function.

Periodic	Not Periodic
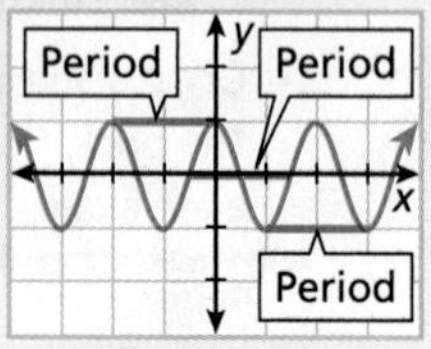 Period, Period, Period (x, y axes)	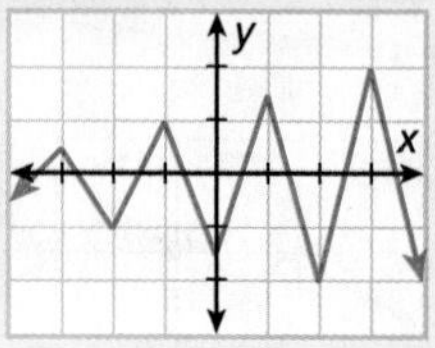 (x, y axes)

EXAMPLE 1 Identifying Periodic Functions

Identify whether each function is periodic. If the function is periodic, give the period.

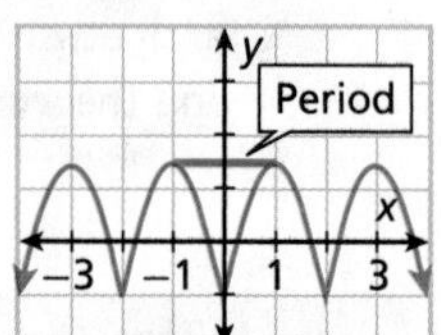

The pattern repeats exactly, so the function is periodic. Identify the period by using the start and finish of one cycle.

This function is periodic with period 2.

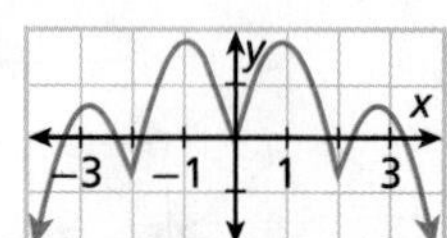

Although there is some symmetry, the pattern does not repeat exactly.

This function is not periodic.

Identify whether each function is periodic. If the function is periodic, give the period.

1a.

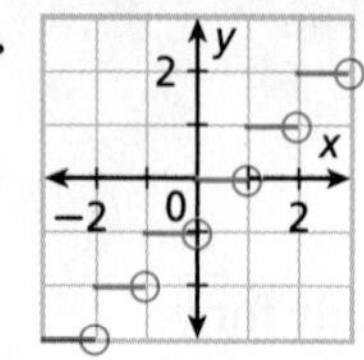

1b.

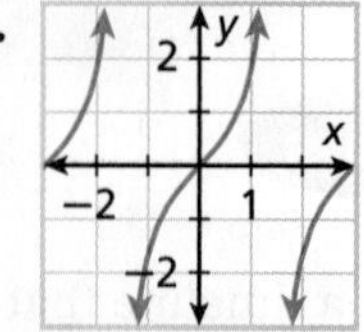

The trigonometric functions that you studied in Chapter 13 are periodic. You can graph the function $f(x) = \sin x$ on the coordinate plane by using y-values from points on the unit circle where the independent variable x represents the angle θ in standard position.

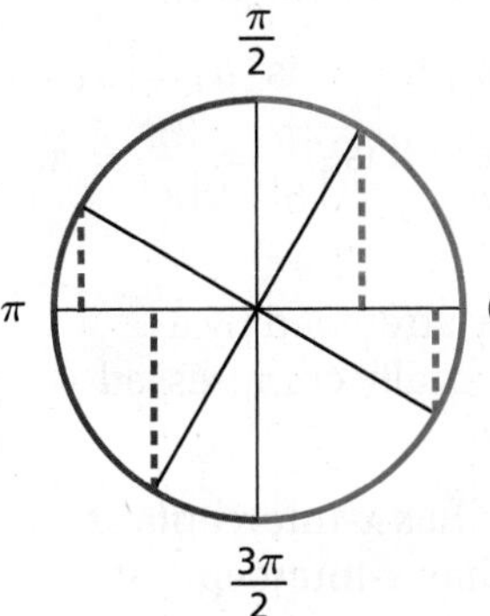

$x(=\theta)$	y
$\frac{\pi}{3}$	$\frac{\sqrt{3}}{2}$
$\frac{5\pi}{6}$	$\frac{1}{2}$
$\frac{4\pi}{3}$	$-\frac{\sqrt{3}}{2}$
$\frac{11\pi}{6}$	$-\frac{1}{2}$

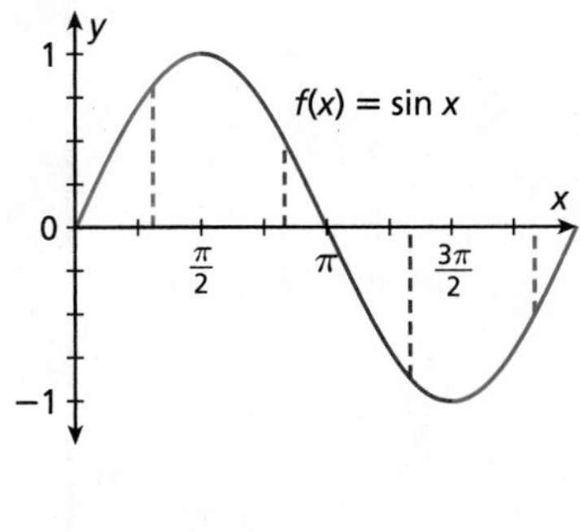

Similarly, the function $f(x) = \cos x$ can be graphed on the coordinate plane by using x-values from points on the unit circle.

The **amplitude** of sine and cosine functions is half of the difference between the maximum and minimum values of the function. The amplitude is always positive.

Characteristics of the Graphs of Sine and Cosine

FUNCTION	$y = \sin x$	$y = \cos x$
GRAPH		
DOMAIN	$\{x \mid x \in \mathbb{R}\}$	$\{x \mid x \in \mathbb{R}\}$
RANGE	$\{y \mid -1 \le y \le 1\}$	$\{y \mid -1 \le y \le 1\}$
PERIOD	2π	2π
AMPLITUDE	1	1

Helpful Hint

The graph of the sine function passes through the origin. The graph of the cosine function has y-intercept 1.

You can use the parent functions to graph transformations $y = a \sin bx$ and $y = a \cos bx$. Recall that a indicates a vertical stretch $(|a| > 1)$ or compression $(0 < |a| < 1)$, which changes the amplitude. If a is less than 0, the graph is reflected across the x-axis. The value of b indicates a horizontal stretch or compression, which changes the period.

Transformations of Sine and Cosine Graphs

For the graphs of $y = a \sin bx$ or $y = a \cos bx$ where $a \neq 0$ and x is in radians,

- the amplitude is $|a|$.
- the period is $\frac{2\pi}{|b|}$.

EXAMPLE 2 Stretching or Compressing Sine and Cosine Functions

Using $f(x) = \sin x$ as a guide, graph the function $g(x) = 3\sin 2x$. Identify the amplitude and period.

Step 1 Identify the amplitude and period.

Because $a = 3$, the amplitude is $|a| = |3| = 3$.

Because $b = 2$, the period is $\frac{2\pi}{|b|} = \frac{2\pi}{|2|} = \pi$.

Step 2 Graph.

The curve is vertically stretched by a factor of 3 and horizontally compressed by a factor of $\frac{1}{2}$.

The parent function f has x-intercepts at multiples of π and g has x-intercepts at multiples of $\frac{\pi}{2}$.

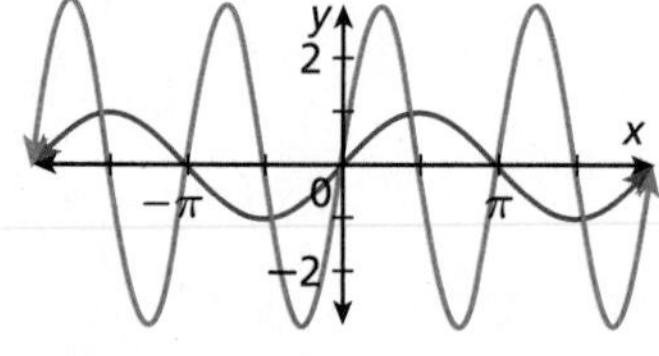

The maximum value of g is 3, and the minimum value is -3.

2. Using $f(x) = \cos x$ as a guide, graph the function $h(x) = \frac{1}{3}\cos 2x$. Identify the amplitude and period.

Sine and cosine functions can be used to model real-world phenomena, such as sound waves. Different sounds create different waves. One way to distinguish sounds is to measure *frequency*. **Frequency** is the number of cycles in a given unit of time, so it is the reciprocal of the period of a function.

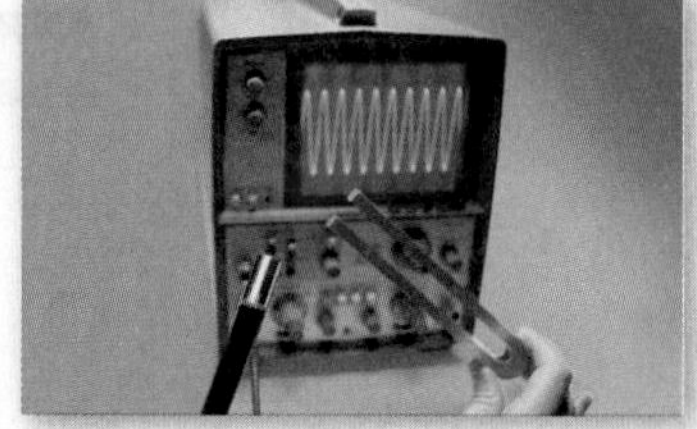

Hertz (Hz) is the standard measure of frequency and represents one cycle per second. For example, the sound wave made by a tuning fork for middle A has a frequency of 440 Hz. This means that the wave repeats 440 times in 1 second.

EXAMPLE 3 *Sound Application*

Use a sine function to graph a sound wave with a period of 0.005 second and an amplitude of 4 cm. Find the frequency in hertz for this sound wave.

Use a horizontal scale where one unit represents 0.001 second. The period tells you that it takes 0.005 seconds to complete one full cycle. The maximum and minimum values are given by the amplitude.

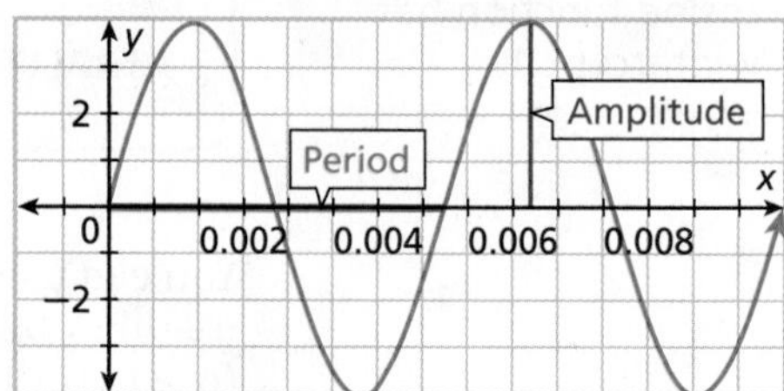

$$\text{frequency} = \frac{1}{\text{period}}$$

$$= \frac{1}{0.005} = 200 \text{ Hz}$$

The frequency of the sound wave is 200 Hz.

3. Use a sine function to graph a sound wave with a period of 0.004 second and an amplitude of 3 cm. Find the frequency in hertz for this sound wave.

Sine and cosine can also be translated as $y = \sin(x - h) + k$ and $y = \cos(x - h) + k$. Recall that a vertical translation by k units moves the graph up $(k > 0)$ or down $(k < 0)$.

A **phase shift** is a horizontal translation of a periodic function. A phase shift of h units moves the graph left $(h < 0)$ or right $(h > 0)$.

EXAMPLE 4 Identifying Phase Shifts for Sine and Cosine Functions

Using $f(x) = \sin x$ as a guide, graph $g(x) = \sin\left(x + \frac{\pi}{2}\right)$. Identify the x-intercepts and phase shift.

Step 1 Identify the amplitude and period.

Amplitude is $|a| = |1| = 1$.

The period is $\frac{2\pi}{|b|} = \frac{2\pi}{|1|} = 2\pi$.

Step 2 Identify the phase shift.

$x + \frac{\pi}{2} = x - \left(-\frac{\pi}{2}\right)$ *Identify h.*

Because $h = -\frac{\pi}{2}$, the phase shift is $\frac{\pi}{2}$ radians to the left.

All x-intercepts, maxima, and minima of $f(x)$ are shifted $\frac{\pi}{2}$ units to the left.

Step 3 Identify the x-intercepts.

The first x-intercept occurs at $-\frac{\pi}{2}$. Because $\sin x$ has two x-intercepts in each period of 2π, the x-intercepts occur at $-\frac{\pi}{2} + n\pi$, where n is an integer.

Step 4 Identify the maximum and minimum values.

The maximum and minimum values occur between the x-intercepts. The maxima occur at $2\pi n$ and have a value of 1. The minima occur at $\pi + 2\pi n$ and have a value of -1.

Step 5 Graph using all of the information about the function.

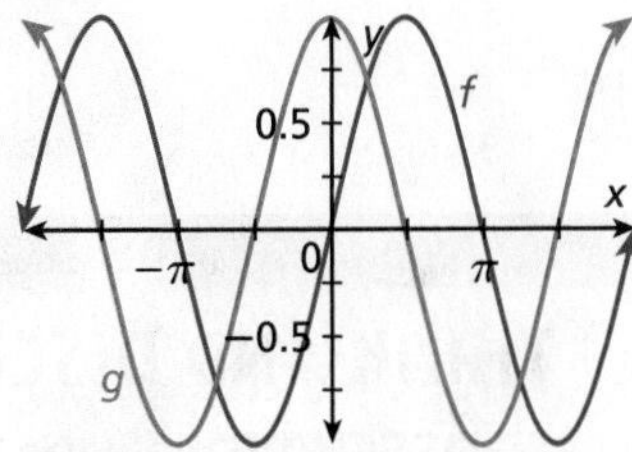

Helpful Hint

The repeating pattern is maximum, intercept, minimum, intercept,.... So intercepts occur twice as often as maximum or minimum values.

4. Using $f(x) = \cos x$ as a guide, graph $g(x) = \cos(x - \pi)$. Identify the x-intercepts and phase shift.

You can combine the transformations of trigonometric functions. Use the values of a, b, h, and k to identify the important features of a sine or cosine function.

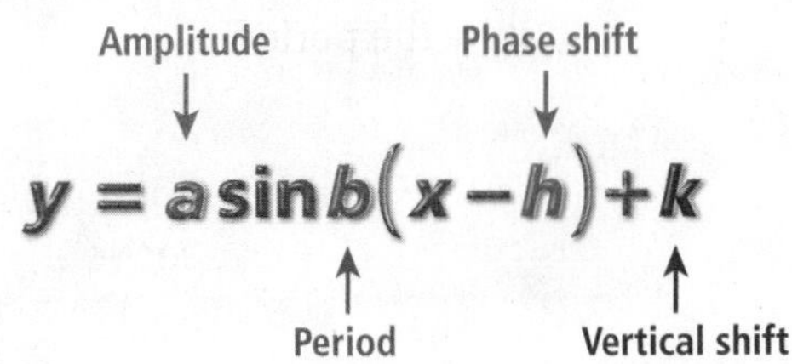

EXAMPLE 5 *Entertainment Application*

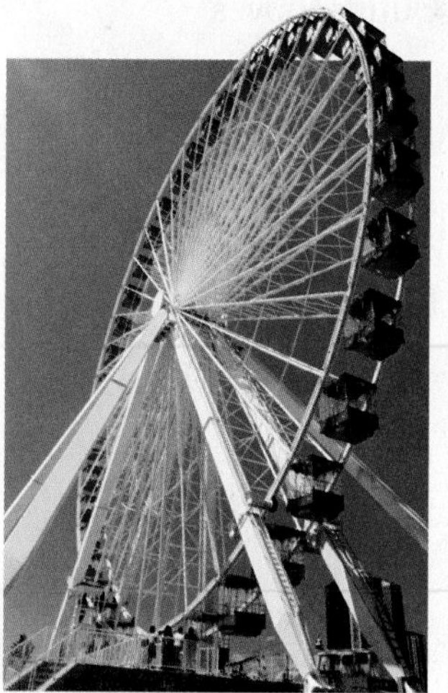

The Ferris wheel at the landmark Navy Pier in Chicago takes 7 minutes to make one full rotation. The height H in feet above the ground of one of the six-person gondolas can be modeled by $H(t) = 70\sin\frac{2\pi}{7}(t - 1.75) + 80$, where t is time in minutes.

a. Graph the height of a cabin for two complete periods.

$H(t) = 70\sin\frac{2\pi}{7}(t - 1.75) + 80$ *$a = 70$, $b = \frac{2\pi}{7}$, $h = 1.75$, $k = 80$*

Step 1 Identify the important features of the graph.

Amplitude: 70

Period: $\frac{2\pi}{|b|} = \frac{2\pi}{\left|\frac{2\pi}{7}\right|} = 7$

The period is equal to the time required for one full rotation.

Phase shift: 1.75 minutes right

Vertical shift: 80

There are no x-intercepts.

Maxima: $80 + 70 = 150$ at 3.5 and 10.5

Minima: $80 - 70 = 10$ at 0, 7, and 14

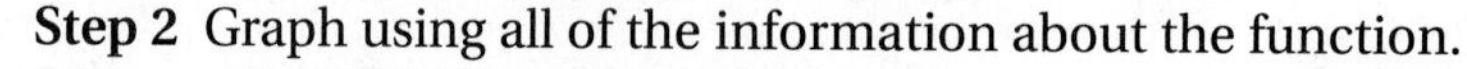

Step 2 Graph using all of the information about the function.

b. What is the maximum height of a cabin?

The maximum height is $80 + 70 = 150$ feet above the ground.

5. What if...? Suppose that the height H of a Ferris wheel can be modeled by $H(t) = -16\cos\frac{\pi}{45}t + 24$, where t is the time in seconds.

a. Graph the height of a cabin for two complete periods.

b. What is the maximum height of a cabin?

THINK AND DISCUSS

1. **DESCRIBE** how the frequency and period of a periodic function are related. How does this apply to the graph of $f(x) = \cos x$?

2. **EXPLAIN** how the maxima and minima are related to the amplitude and period of sine and cosine functions.

3. **GET ORGANIZED** Copy and complete the graphic organizer. For each type of transformation, give an example and state the period.

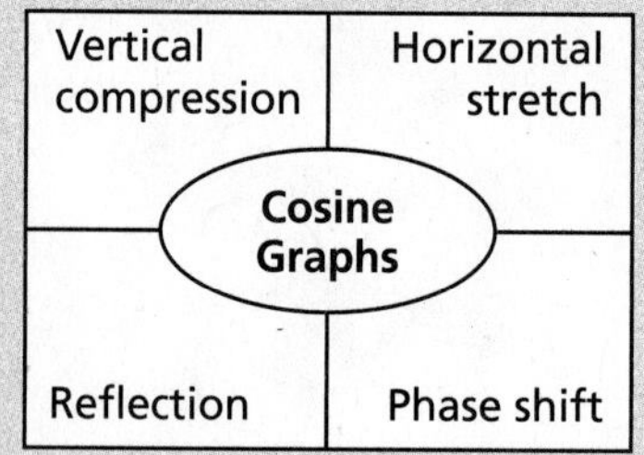

14-1 Exercises

go.hrw.com
Homework Help Online
KEYWORD: MB7 14-1
Parent Resources Online
KEYWORD: MB7 Parent

GUIDED PRACTICE

1. **Vocabulary** Periodic functions repeat in regular intervals called __?__. *(cycles* or *periods)*

SEE EXAMPLE 1 p. 990

Identify whether each function is periodic. If the function is periodic, give the period.

2. 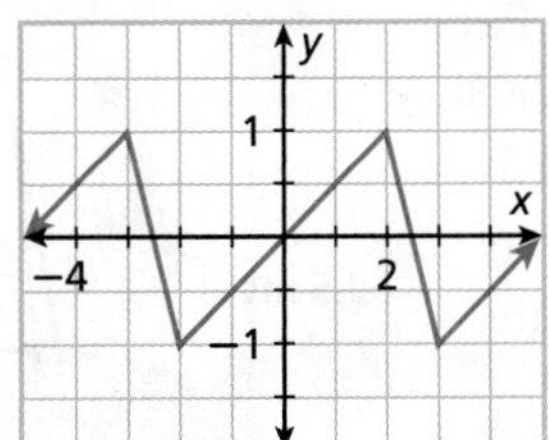

3. 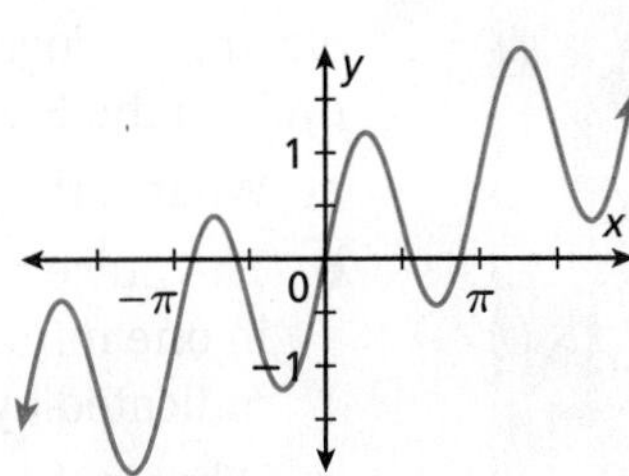

SEE EXAMPLE 2 p. 992

Using $f(x) = \sin x$ or $f(x) = \cos x$ as a guide, graph each function. Identify the amplitude and the period.

4. $f(x) = 2\sin\frac{1}{2}x$
5. $h(x) = \frac{1}{4}\cos x$
6. $k(x) = \sin \pi x$

SEE EXAMPLE 3 p. 992

7. **Sound** Use a sine function to graph a sound wave with a period of 0.01 second and an amplitude of 6 in. Find the frequency in hertz for this sound wave.

SEE EXAMPLE 4 p. 993

Using $f(x) = \sin x$ or $f(x) = \cos x$ as a guide, graph each function. Identify the x-intercepts and the phase shift.

8. $f(x) = \sin\left(x + \frac{3\pi}{2}\right)$
9. $g(x) = \cos\left(x - \frac{\pi}{2}\right)$
10. $h(x) = \sin\left(x - \frac{\pi}{4}\right)$

SEE EXAMPLE 5 p. 994

11. **Recreation** The height H in feet above the ground of the seat of a playground swing can be modeled by $H(\theta) = -4\cos\theta + 6$, where θ is the angle that the swing makes with a vertical extended to the ground. Graph the height of a swing's seat for $0° \le \theta \le 90°$. How high is the swing when $\theta = 60°$?

PRACTICE AND PROBLEM SOLVING

Independent Practice

For Exercises	See Example
12–13	1
14–17	2
18	3
19–22	4
23	5

Extra Practice

Skills Practice p. S30
Application Practice p. S45

Identify whether each function is periodic. If the function is periodic, give the period.

12. 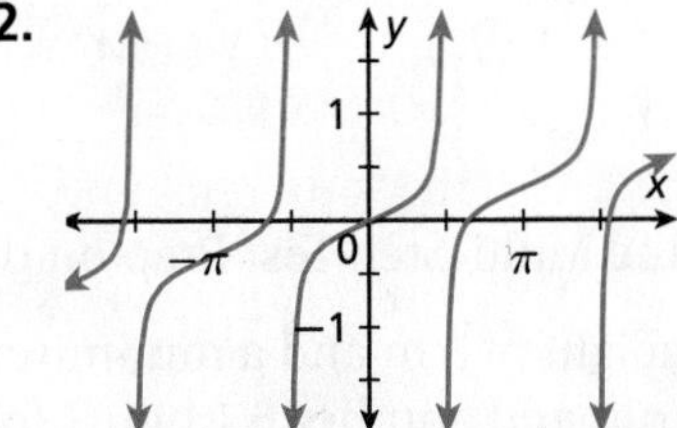

13. 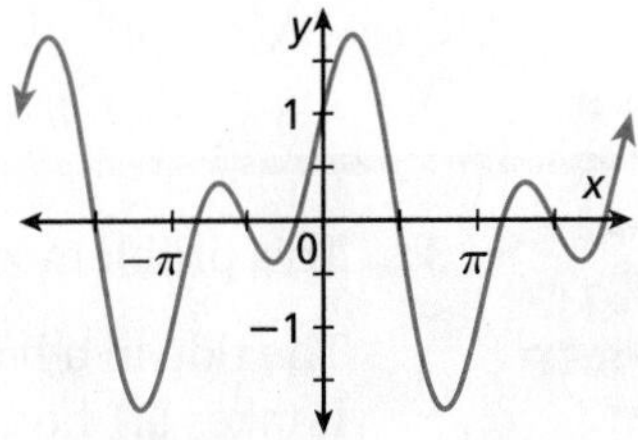

Using $f(x) = \sin x$ or $f(x) = \cos x$ as a guide, graph each function. Identify the amplitude and period.

14. $f(x) = 4\cos x$
15. $g(x) = \frac{3}{2}\sin x$
16. $g(x) = -\cos 4x$
17. $j(x) = 6\sin\frac{1}{3}x$

18. **Sound** Use a sine function to graph a sound wave with a period of 0.025 seconds and an amplitude of 5 in. Find the frequency in hertz for this sound wave.

Using $f(x) = \sin x$ or $f(x) = \cos x$ as a guide, graph each function. Identify the x-intercepts and phase shift.

19. $f(x) = \sin(x + \pi)$

20. $h(x) = \cos(x - 3\pi)$

21. $g(x) = \sin\left(x + \frac{3\pi}{4}\right)$

22. $j(x) = \cos\left(x + \frac{\pi}{4}\right)$

23. Oceanography The depth d in feet of the water in a bay at any time is given by $d(t) = \frac{3}{2}\sin\left(\frac{5\pi}{31}t\right) + 23$, where t is the time in hours. Graph the depth of the water. What are the maximum and minimum depths of the water?

LINK

Medicine

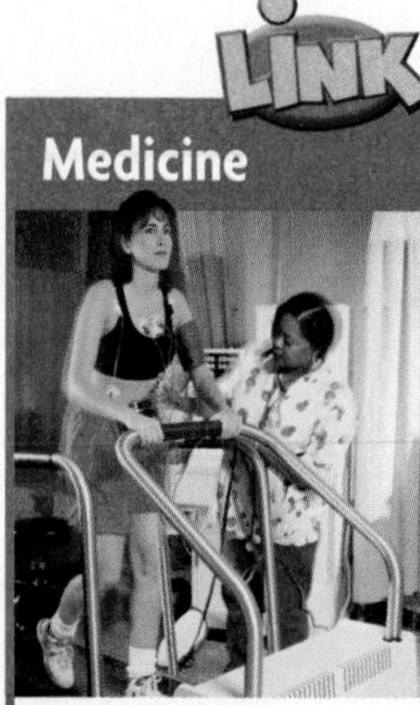

An EKG measures the electrical signals that control the rhythm of a beating heart. EKGs are used to diagnose and monitor heart disease.

24. Medicine The figure shows a normal adult electrocardiogram, known as an EKG. Each cycle in the EKG represents one heartbeat.

a. What is the period of one heartbeat?

b. The pulse rate is the number of beats in one minute. What is the pulse rate indicated by the EKG?

c. What is the frequency of the EKG?

d. How does the pulse rate relate to the frequency in hertz?

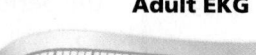

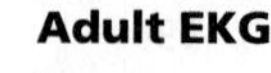

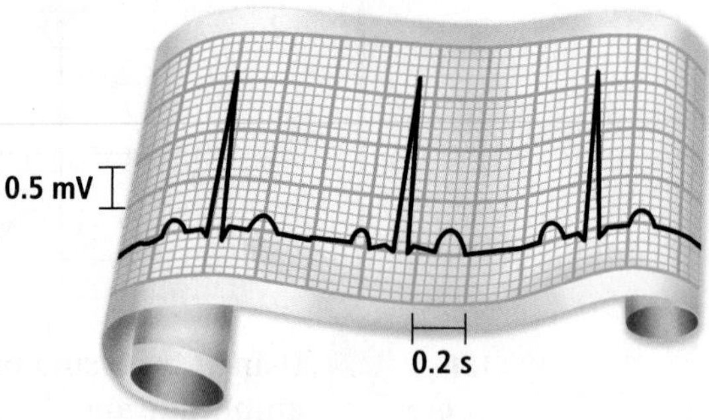

Determine the amplitude and period for each function. Then describe the transformation from its parent function.

25. $f(x) = \sin\left(x + \frac{\pi}{4}\right) - 1$

26. $h(x) = \frac{3}{4}\cos\frac{\pi}{4}x$

27. $h(x) = \cos(2\pi x) - 2$

28. $j(x) = -3\sin 3x$

Estimation Use a graph of sine or cosine to estimate each value.

29. $\sin 160°$

30. $\cos 50°$

31. $\sin 15°$

32. $\cos 95°$

Write both a sine and a cosine function for each set of conditions.

33. amplitude of 6, period of π

34. amplitude of $\frac{1}{4}$, phase shift of $\frac{2}{3}\pi$ left

Write both a sine and a cosine function that could be used to represent each graph.

35.

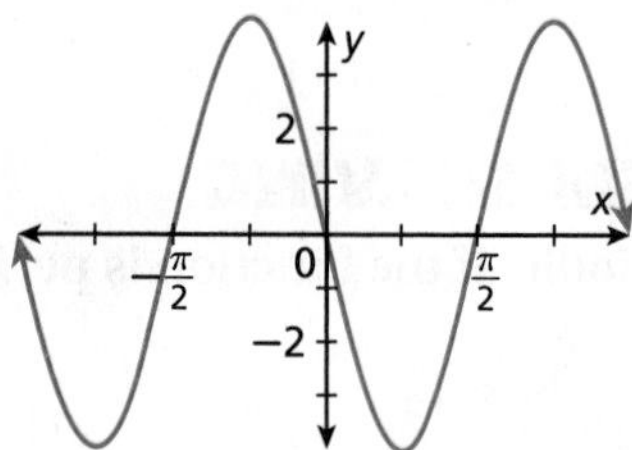

36.

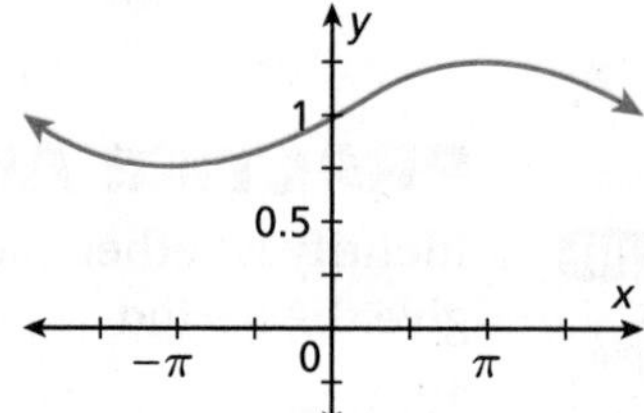

37. This problem will prepare you for the Multi-Step Test Prep on page 1004.

The tide in a bay has a maximum height of 3 m and a minimum height of 0 m. It takes 6.1 hours for the tide to go out and another 6.1 hours for it to come back in. The height of the tide h is modeled as a function of time t.

a. What are the period and amplitude of h? What are the maximum and minimum values?

b. Assume that high tide occurs at $t = 0$. What are $h(0)$ and $h(6.1)$?

c. Write h in the form $h(t) = a\cos bt + k$.

38. **Critical Thinking** Given the amplitude and period of a sine function, can you find its maximum and minimum values and their corresponding x-values? If not, what information do you need and how would you use it?

39. **Write About It** What happens to the period of $f(x) = \sin b\theta$ when $b > 1$? $b < 1$? Explain.

TEST PREP

40. Which trigonometric function best matches the graph?

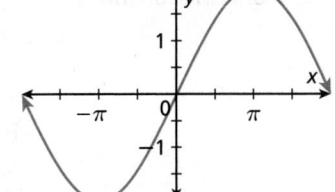

Ⓐ $y = \frac{1}{2}\sin x$ Ⓒ $y = \frac{1}{2}\sin 2x$

Ⓑ $y = 2\sin x$ Ⓓ $y = 2\sin\frac{1}{2}x$

41. What is the amplitude for $y = -4\cos 3\pi x$?

Ⓕ -4 Ⓗ 4

Ⓖ 3 Ⓙ 3π

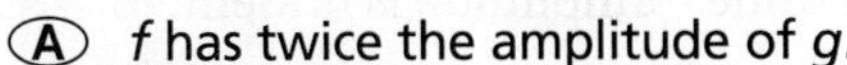

42. Based on the graphs, what is the relationship between f and g?

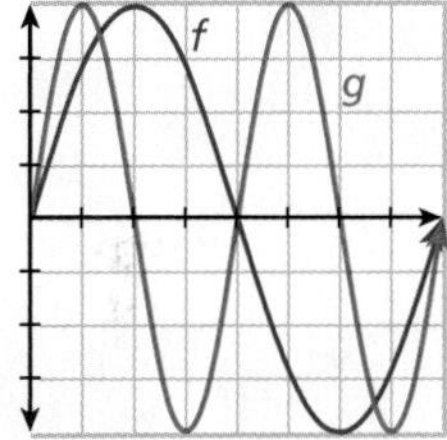

Ⓐ f has twice the amplitude of g.

Ⓑ f has twice the period of g.

Ⓒ f has twice the frequency of g.

Ⓓ f has twice the cycle of g.

43. **Short Response** Using $y = \sin x$ as a guide, graph $y = -4\sin 2(x - \pi)$ on the interval $[0, 2\pi]$ and describe the transformations.

CHALLENGE AND EXTEND

44. Graph $f(x) = \text{Sin}^{-1}x$ and $g(x) = \text{Cos}^{-1}x$. (*Hint:* Use what you learned about graphs of inverse functions in Lesson 9-5 and inverse trigonometric functions in Lesson 13-4.)

Consider the functions $f(\theta) = \frac{1}{2}\sin\theta$ and $g(\theta) = 2\cos\theta$ for $0° \le \theta \le 360°$.

45. On the same set of coordinate axes, graph $f(\theta)$ and $g(\theta)$.

46. What are the approximate coordinates of the points of intersection of $f(\theta)$ and $g(\theta)$?

47. When is $f(\theta) > g(\theta)$?

SPIRAL REVIEW

Use interval notation to represent each set of numbers. *(Lesson 1-1)*

48. $-7 < x \le 5$ 49. $x \le -2$ or $1 \le x < 13$ 50. $0 \le x \le 9$

51. **Flowers** Adam has \$100 to purchase a combination of roses, lilies, and carnations. Roses cost \$6 each, lilies cost \$2 each, and carnations cost \$4 each. *(Lesson 3-5)*

Roses	6	■	3	7
Lilies	■	8	5	■
Carnations	11	15	■	13

a. Write a linear equation in three variables to represent this situation.

b. Complete the table.

Use the given measurements to solve $\triangle ABC$. Round to the nearest tenth. *(Lesson 13-6)*

52. $b = 20$, $c = 11$, $A = 165°$ 53. $a = 11.9$, $b = 14.7$, $c = 26.1$

14-2 Graphs of Other Trigonometric Functions

Objective
Recognize and graph trigonometric functions.

Why learn this?
You can use the graphs of reciprocal trigonometric functions to model rotating objects such as lights. (See Exercise 25.)

The tangent and cotangent functions can be graphed on the coordinate plane. The tangent function is undefined when $\theta = \frac{\pi}{2} + \pi n$, where n is an integer. The cotangent function is undefined when $\theta = \pi n$. These values are excluded from the domain and are represented by vertical asymptotes on the graph. Because tangent and cotangent have no maximum or minimum values, amplitude is undefined.

To graph tangent and cotangent, let the variable x represent the angle θ in standard position.

Characteristics of the Graphs of Tangent and Cotangent

FUNCTION	$y = \tan x$	$y = \cot x$
GRAPH		
DOMAIN	$\left\{x \mid x \neq \frac{\pi}{2} + \pi n,\right.$ where n is an integer$\left.\right\}$	$\left\{x \mid x \neq \pi n,\right.$ where n is an integer$\left.\right\}$
RANGE	$\{y \mid -\infty < y < \infty\}$	$\{y \mid -\infty < y < \infty\}$
PERIOD	π	π
AMPLITUDE	undefined	undefined

Like sine and cosine, you can transform the tangent function.

Transformations of Tangent Graphs

For the graph of $y = a \tan bx$, where $a \neq 0$ and x is in radians,

- the period is $\frac{\pi}{|b|}$.
- the asymptotes are located at $x = \frac{\pi}{2|b|} + \frac{\pi n}{|b|}$, where n is an integer.

EXAMPLE 1 Transforming Tangent Functions

Using $f(x) = \tan x$ as a guide, graph $g(x) = \tan 2x$. Identify the period, x-intercepts, and asymptotes.

Step 1 Identify the period.

Because $b = 2$, the period is $\frac{\pi}{|b|} = \frac{\pi}{|2|} = \frac{\pi}{2}$.

Step 2 Identify the x-intercepts.

An x-intercept occurs at $x = 0$. Because the period is $\frac{\pi}{2}$, the x-intercepts occur at $\frac{\pi}{2}n$, where n is an integer.

Step 3 Identify the asymptotes.

Because $b = 2$, the asymptotes occur at $x = \frac{\pi}{2|2|} + \frac{\pi n}{|2|}$, or $x = \frac{\pi}{4} + \frac{\pi n}{2}$.

Step 4 Graph using all of the information about the function.

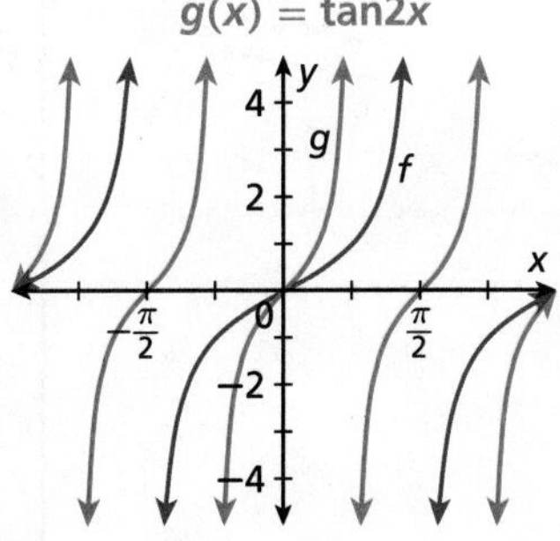

1. Using $f(x) = \tan x$ as a guide, graph $g(x) = 3\tan\frac{1}{2}x$. Identify the period, x-intercepts, and asymptotes.

Know it! Note — **Transformations of Cotangent Graphs**

For the graph of $y = a\cot bx$, where $a \neq 0$ and x is in radians,

- the period is $\frac{\pi}{|b|}$.
- the asymptotes are located at $x = \frac{\pi n}{|b|}$, where n is an integer.

EXAMPLE 2 Graphing the Cotangent Function

Using $f(x) = \cot x$ as a guide, graph $g(x) = \cot 0.5x$. Identify the period, x-intercepts, and asymptotes.

Step 1 Identify the period.

Because $b = 0.5$, the period is $\frac{\pi}{|b|} = \frac{\pi}{|0.5|} = 2\pi$.

Step 2 Identify the x-intercepts.

An x-intercept occurs at $x = \pi$. Because the period is 2π, the x-intercepts occur at $x = \pi + 2\pi n$, where n is an integer.

Step 3 Identify the asymptotes.

Because $b = 0.5$, the asymptotes occur at

$$x = \frac{\pi n}{|0.5|} = 2\pi n.$$

Step 4 Graph using all of the information about the function.

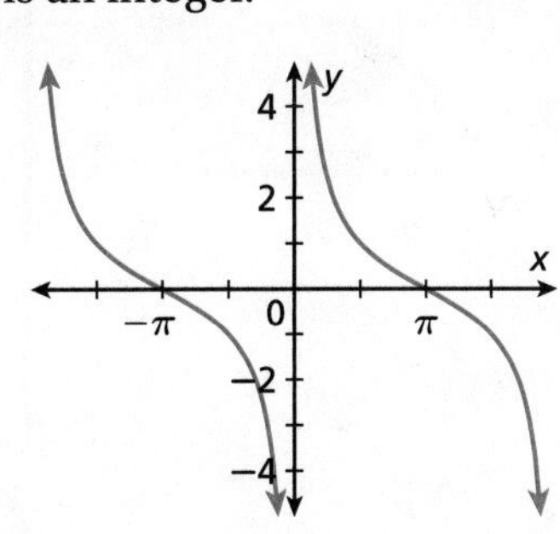

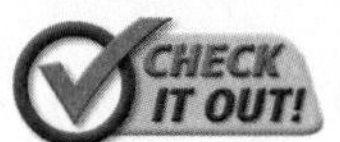

2. Using $f(x) = \cot x$ as a guide, graph $g(x) = -\cot 2x$. Identify the period, x-intercepts, and asymptotes.

Recall that $\sec\theta = \frac{1}{\cos\theta}$. So, secant is undefined where cosine equals zero and the graph will have vertical asymptotes at those locations. Secant will also have the same period as cosine. Sine and cosecant have a similar relationship. Because secant and cosecant have no absolute maxima or minima, amplitude is undefined.

Characteristics of the Graphs of Secant and Cosecant

FUNCTION	$y = \sec x$	$y = \csc x$
GRAPH		
DOMAIN	$\left\{x \mid x \neq \frac{\pi}{2} + \pi n,\right.$ where n is an integer$\left.\right\}$	$\left\{x \mid x \neq \pi n,\right.$ where n is an integer$\left.\right\}$
RANGE	$\{y \mid y \leq -1, \text{ or } y \geq 1\}$	$\{y \mid y \leq -1, \text{ or } y \geq 1\}$
PERIOD	2π	2π
AMPLITUDE	undefined	undefined

You can graph transformations of secant and cosecant by using what you learned in Lesson 14-1 about transformations of graphs of cosine and sine.

EXAMPLE 3 Graphing Secant and Cosecant Functions

Using $f(x) = \cos x$ as a guide, graph $g(x) = \sec 2x$. Identify the period and asymptotes.

Step 1 Identify the period.

Because $\sec 2x$ is the reciprocal of $\cos 2x$, the graphs will have the same period.

Because $b = 2$ for $\cos 2x$, the period is $\frac{2\pi}{|b|} = \frac{2\pi}{|2|} = \pi$.

Step 2 Identify the asymptotes.

Because the period is π, the asymptotes occur at $x = \frac{\pi}{2|2|} + \frac{\pi}{|2|}n = \frac{\pi}{4} + \frac{\pi}{2}n$, where n is an integer.

Step 3 Graph using all of the information about the function.

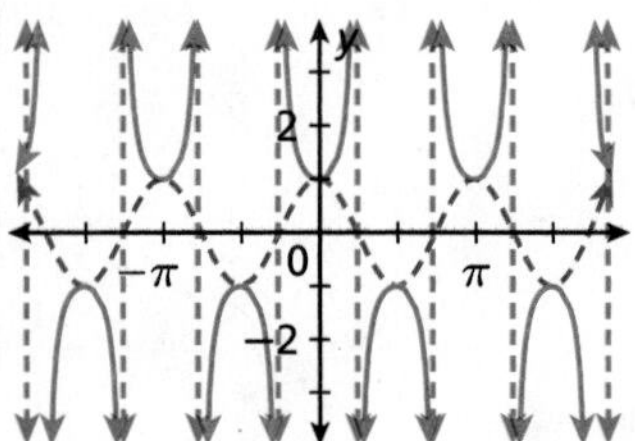

3. Using $f(x) = \sin x$ as a guide, graph $g(x) = 2\csc x$. Identify the period and asymptotes.

THINK AND DISCUSS

1. **EXPLAIN** why $f(x) = \sin x$ can be used to graph $g(x) = \csc x$.
2. **EXPLAIN** how the zeros of the cosine function relate to the vertical asymptotes of the graph of the tangent function.

3. **GET ORGANIZED** Copy and complete the graphic organizer.

Function	Zeros	Asymptotes	Period
$y = \sec x$			
$y = \csc x$			
$y = \cot x$			
$y = \tan x$			

14-2 Exercises

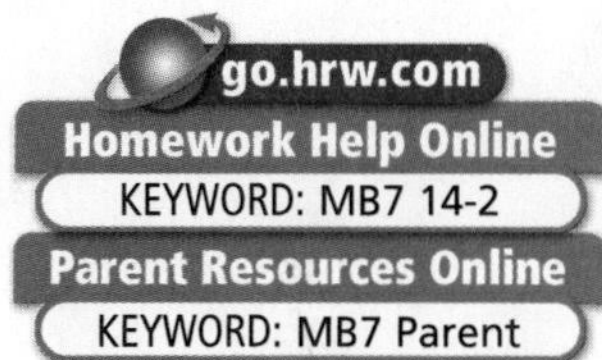

GUIDED PRACTICE

SEE EXAMPLE 1 p. 999

Using $f(x) = \tan x$ as a guide, graph each function. Identify the period, x-intercepts, and asymptotes.

1. $k(x) = 2\tan(3x)$
2. $g(x) = \tan\frac{1}{4}x$
3. $h(x) = \tan 2\pi x$

SEE EXAMPLE 2 p. 999

Using $f(x) = \cot x$ as a guide, graph each function. Identify the period, x-intercepts, and asymptotes.

4. $j(x) = 0.25\cot x$
5. $p(x) = \cot 2x$
6. $g(x) = \frac{3}{2}\cot x$

SEE EXAMPLE 3 p. 1000

Using $f(x) = \cos x$ or $f(x) = \sin x$ as a guide, graph each function. Identify the period and asymptotes.

7. $g(x) = \frac{1}{2}\sec x$
8. $q(x) = \sec 4x$
9. $h(x) = 3\csc x$

PRACTICE AND PROBLEM SOLVING

Independent Practice

For Exercises	See Example
10–13	1
14–16	2
17–19	3

Extra Practice

Skills Practice p. S30

Application Practice p. S45

Using $f(x) = \tan x$ as a guide, graph each function. Identify the period, x-intercepts, and asymptotes.

10. $p(x) = \tan\frac{3}{2}x$
11. $g(x) = \tan\left(x + \frac{\pi}{4}\right)$
12. $h(x) = \frac{1}{2}\tan 4x$
13. $j(x) = -2\tan\frac{\pi}{2}x$

Using $f(x) = \cot x$ as a guide, graph each function. Identify the period, x-intercepts, and asymptotes.

14. $h(x) = 4\cot x$
15. $g(x) = \cot\frac{1}{4}x$
16. $j(x) = 0.1\cot x$

Using $f(x) = \cos x$ or $f(x) = \sin x$ as a guide, graph each function. Identify the period and asymptotes.

17. $g(x) = -\sec x$
18. $k(x) = \frac{1}{2}\csc x$
19. $h(x) = \csc(-x)$

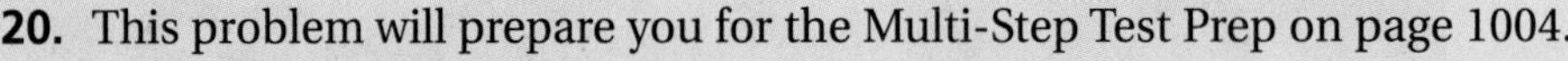

20. This problem will prepare you for the Multi-Step Test Prep on page 1004.

Between 1:00 P.M. ($t = 1$) and 6:00 P.M. ($t = 6$), the height (in meters) of the tide in a bay is modeled by $h(t) = 0.4 \csc \frac{5\pi}{31}t$.

a. Graph the function for the range $1 \le t \le 6$.

b. At what time does low tide occur?

c. What is the height of the tide at low tide?

d. What is the maximum height of the tide during this time span? When does this occur?

Find four values for which each function is undefined.

21. $f(\theta) = \tan\theta$ 22. $g(\theta) = \cot\theta$ 23. $h(\theta) = \sec\theta$ 24. $j(\theta) = \csc\theta$

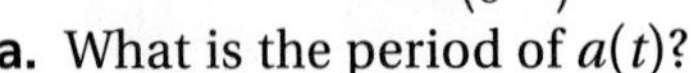

25. **Law Enforcement** A police car is parked on the side of the road next to a building. The flashing light on the car is 6 feet from the wall and completes one full rotation every 3 seconds. As the light rotates, it shines on the wall. The equation representing the distance a in feet is $a(t) = 6\sec\left(\frac{2}{3}\pi t\right)$.

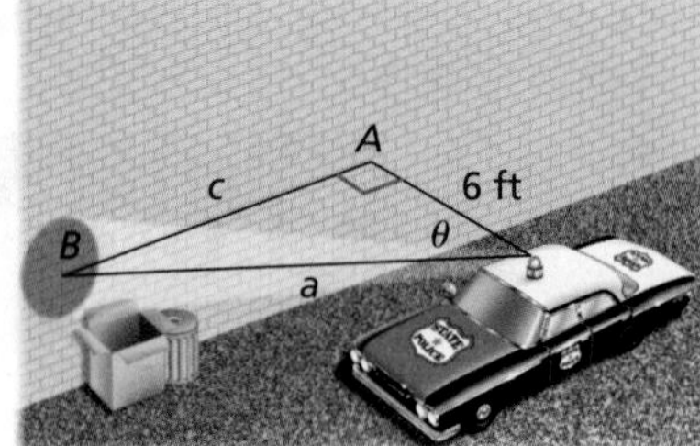

a. What is the period of $a(t)$?

b. Graph the function for $0 \le t \le 3$.

c. **Critical Thinking** Identify the location of any asymptotes. What do the asymptotes represent?

Math History

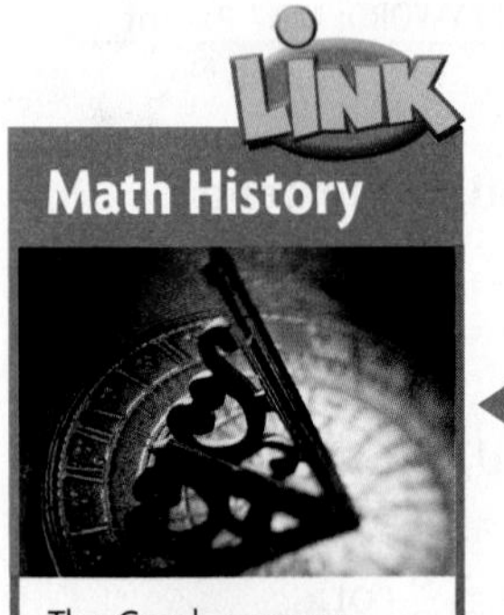

The Greek gnomon was a tall staff, but gnomon is also the part of a sundial that casts a shadow. Based on the variation of shadows at high noon, a gnomon can be used to determine the day of the year, in addition to the time of day.

26. **Math History** The ancient Greeks used a *gnomon,* a type of tall staff, to tell the time of day based on the lengths of shadows and the altitude θ of the sun above the horizon.

a. Use the figure to write a cotangent function that can be used to find the length of the shadow s in terms of the height of the gnomon h and the angle θ.

b. Graph your answer to part **a** for a gnomon of height 6 ft.

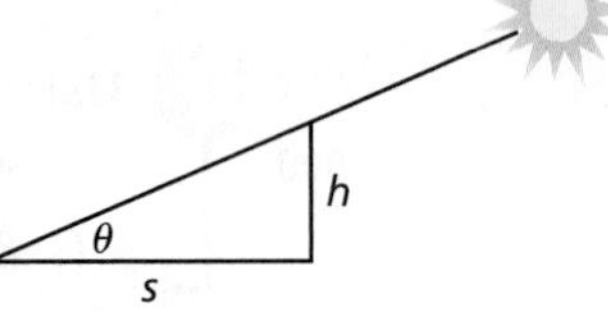

Complete the table by labeling each function as increasing or decreasing.

		$0 < x < \frac{\pi}{2}$	$\frac{\pi}{2} < x < \pi$	$\pi < x < \frac{3\pi}{2}$	$\frac{3\pi}{2} < x < 2\pi$
27.	$\sin x$	■	■	■	■
28.	$\csc x$	■	■	■	■
29.	$\cos x$	■	■	■	■
30.	$\sec x$	■	■	■	■
31.	$\tan x$	■	■	■	■
32.	$\cot x$	■	■	■	■

33. **Critical Thinking** Based on the table above, what do you observe about the increasing/decreasing relationship between reciprocal pairs of trigonometric functions?

34. **Critical Thinking** How do the signs (whether a function is positive or negative) of reciprocal pairs of trigonometric functions relate?

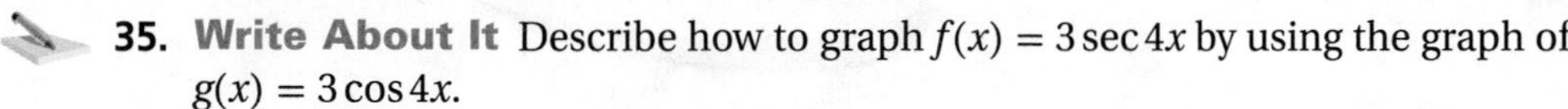

35. **Write About It** Describe how to graph $f(x) = 3\sec 4x$ by using the graph of $g(x) = 3\cos 4x$.

TEST PREP

36. Which is NOT in the domain of $y = \cot x$?

Ⓐ $-\frac{\pi}{2}$ Ⓑ 0 Ⓒ $\frac{\pi}{2}$ Ⓓ $\frac{3\pi}{2}$

37. What is the range of $f(x) = 3\csc 2\theta$?

Ⓕ $\{y \mid y \leq -1 \text{ or } y \geq 1\}$

Ⓖ $\{y \mid y \leq -3 \text{ or } y \geq 3\}$

Ⓗ $\{y \mid y \leq -2 \text{ or } y \geq 2\}$

Ⓙ $\{y \mid y \leq -\frac{1}{2} \text{ or } y \geq \frac{1}{2}\}$

38. Which could be the equation of the graph?

Ⓐ $y = \tan 2x$ Ⓒ $y = 2\tan x$

Ⓑ $y = \cot 2x$ Ⓓ $y = 2\cot x$

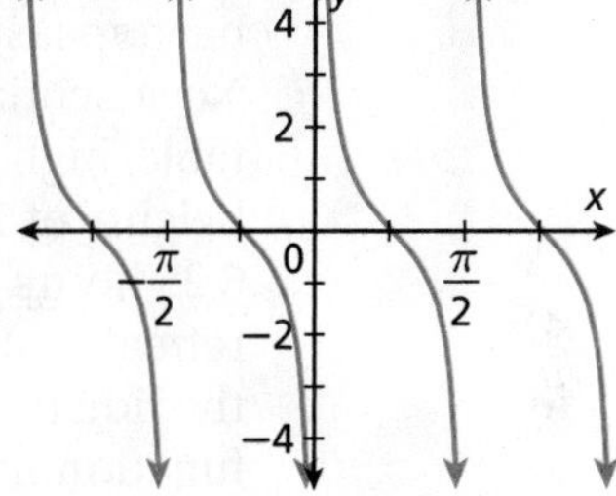

39. What is the period of $y = \tan\frac{1}{2}x$?

Ⓕ $\frac{\pi}{2}$ Ⓗ 2π

Ⓖ π Ⓙ 4π

40. The graph of which function has a period of $\frac{2\pi}{3}$ and an asymptote at $x = \frac{\pi}{2}$?

Ⓐ $y = \sec\frac{3}{2}x$ Ⓒ $y = \csc\frac{3}{2}x$

Ⓑ $y = \sec 3x$ Ⓓ $y = \csc 3x$

CHALLENGE AND EXTEND

Describe the period, local maximum and minimum values, and phase shift.

41. $f(x) = 4 - 3\csc \pi(x - 1)$

42. $g(x) = 4\cot\frac{1}{2}\left(x - \frac{\pi}{2}\right)$

43. $h(x) = 0.5\sec 2\left(x + \frac{\pi}{4}\right)$

44. $f(x) = 9 + 2\tan 3(x + \pi)$

45. $g(x) = 0.62 + 0.76\sec x$

46. $h(x) = \csc\frac{\pi}{2}\left(x + \frac{5}{7}\right)$

Graph each trigonometric function and its inverse. Identify the domain and range of the corresponding inverse function.

47. $f(x) = \text{Sec}\,x$ for $0 \leq x \leq \pi$ and $x \neq \frac{\pi}{2}$

48. $f(x) = \text{Tan}\,x$ for $-\frac{\pi}{2} < x < \frac{\pi}{2}$

49. $g(x) = \text{Csc}\,x$ for $-\frac{\pi}{2} \leq x \leq \frac{\pi}{2}$ and $x \neq 0$

50. $g(x) = \text{Cot}\,x$ for $0 < x < \pi$

SPIRAL REVIEW

Find the additive and multiplicative inverse for each number. *(Lesson 1-2)*

51. $-\frac{1}{10}$

52. 0.2

53. $-3\sqrt{5}$

54. $\frac{4}{9}$

55. **Technology** Marjorie's printer prints 30 pages per minute. How many pages does Marjorie's printer print in 22 seconds? *(Lesson 2-2)*

Convert each measure from degrees to radians or from radians to degrees. *(Lesson 13-3)*

56. $45°$

57. $\frac{3\pi}{4}$ radians

58. $225°$

59. $-\frac{\pi}{3}$ radians

CHAPTER 14

MULTI-STEP TEST PREP

SECTION 14A

Trigonometric Graphs

The Tide Is Turning Tides are caused by several factors, but the main factor is the gravitational pull of the Moon. As the Moon revolves around Earth, the Moon causes large bodies of water to swell toward it resulting in rising and falling tides. You can use trigonometric functions to develop a model of a simplified tide.

Tides at the Bay of Fundy

	Time (h)	Height (m)
High Tide	$t = 0$	16.3
Low Tide	$t = 6.25$	0

1. The highest tides in the world have been measured at the Bay of Fundy, in Nova Scotia, Canada. As shown in the table, high tides in the bay can reach heights of 16.3 m. Assume that it takes 6.25 hours for the tide to completely retreat and then another 6.25 hours for the tide to come back in. Write a periodic function based on the cosine function that models the height of the tide over time.
2. What are the amplitude, period, maximum and minimum values, and phase shift of the function?
3. Graph the function.
4. At time $t = 0$, the tide is at 16.3 m. What is the tide's height after 3 hours? after 9 hours?
5. Will a high tide occur at the same time each day at the Bay of Fundy? Why or why not?
6. It is possible to write a function that models the height of the tide based on the sine function. What is the function? What is the phase shift?

READY TO GO ON?

Quiz for Lessons 14-1 Through 14-2

14-1 Graphs of Sine and Cosine

Identify whether each function is periodic. If the function is periodic, give the period.

1. 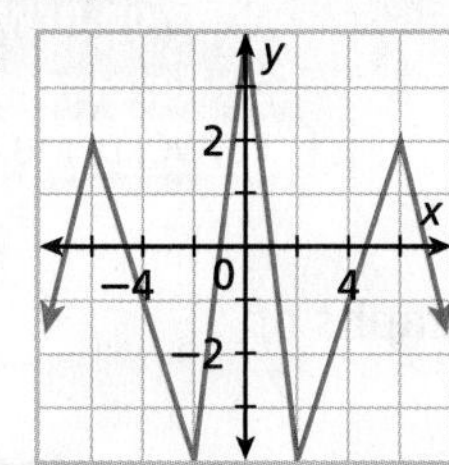

2. 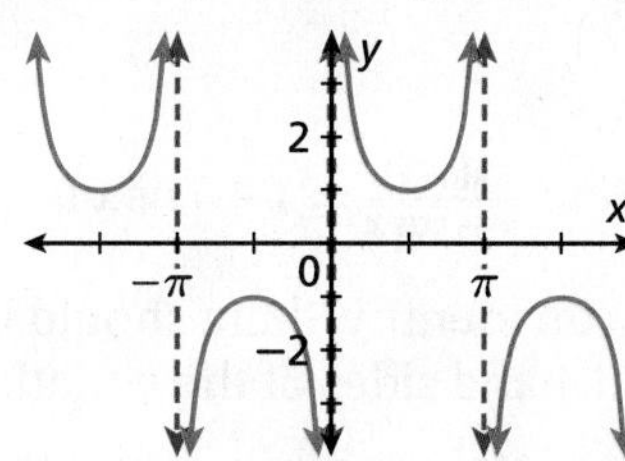

3. 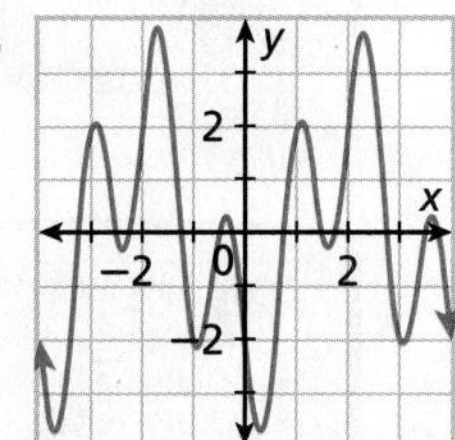

4. 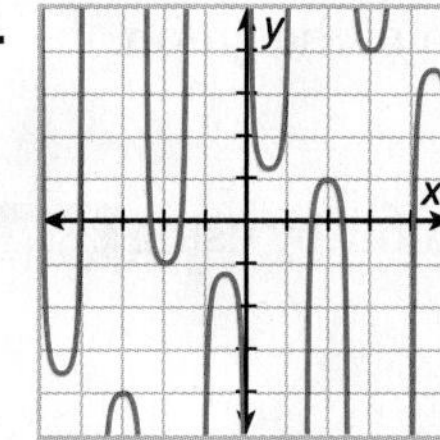

Using $f(x) = \sin x$ or $f(x) = \cos x$ as a guide, graph each function. Identify the amplitude and period.

5. $f(x) = \sin 4x$
6. $g(x) = -3\sin x$
7. $h(x) = 0.25\cos \pi x$

Using $f(x) = \sin x$ or $f(x) = \cos x$ as a guide, graph each function. Identify the x-intercepts and phase shift.

8. $f(x) = \cos\left(x - \frac{3\pi}{2}\right)$
9. $g(x) = \sin\left(x - \frac{3\pi}{4}\right)$
10. $h(x) = \cos\left(x + \frac{5\pi}{4}\right)$

11. The torque τ applied to a bolt is given by $\tau(x) = Fr\sin x$, where r is the length of the wrench in meters, F is the applied force in newtons, and x is the angle between F and r in radians. Graph the torque for a 0.5 meter wrench and a force of 500 newtons for $0 \le x \le \frac{\pi}{2}$. What is the torque for an angle of $\frac{\pi}{3}$?

14-2 Graphs of Other Trigonometric Functions

Using $f(x) = \tan x$ as a guide, graph each function. Identify the period, x-intercepts, and asymptotes.

12. $f(x) = \frac{1}{2}\tan 4x$
13. $g(x) = -2\tan \frac{1}{2}x$
14. $h(x) = \tan \frac{1}{2}\pi x$

Using $f(x) = \cot x$ as a guide, graph each function. Identify the period, x-intercepts, and asymptotes.

15. $g(x) = -2\cot x$
16. $h(x) = \cot 0.5x$
17. $j(x) = \cot 4x$

Using $f(x) = \cos x$ or $f(x) = \sin x$ as a guide, graph each function. Identify the period and asymptotes.

18. $f(x) = -2\sec x$
19. $g(x) = \frac{1}{4}\csc x$
20. $h(x) = \sec \pi x$

Graph Trigonometric Identities

You can use a graphing calculator to compare graphs and make conjectures about trigonometric identities.

Use with Lesson 14-3

go.hrw.com
Lab Resources Online
KEYWORD: MB7 Lab14

Activity

Determine whether $\frac{\sin^2 x}{1 - \cos x} = 1 + \cos x$ is a possible identity.

If the equation is an identity, there should be no visible difference in the graphs of the left- and right-hand sides of the equation.

1. Enter $\frac{\sin^2 x}{1 - \cos x}$ as **Y1** and $1 + \cos x$ as **Y2**. For **Y2**, select the mode represented by the 0 with a line through it. This will help you see the path of the graph.

2. Set the graphing window by using ZOOM and **7:ZTrig.**

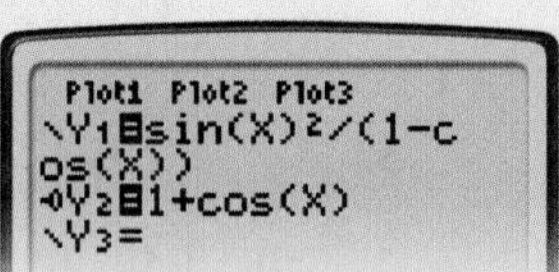

3. Watch the calculator as the graphs are generated. As **Y2** is being graphed, a circle will move along the path of the graph.

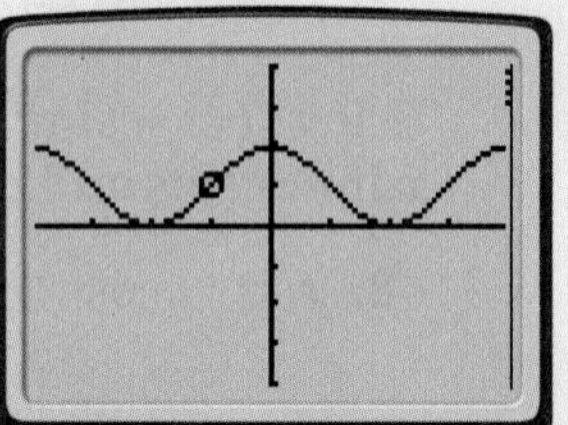

4. The path of the circle, **Y2**, traced the graph of **Y1**. The graphs appear to be the same.

   Because the graphs appear to be identical, $\frac{\sin^2 x}{1 - \cos x} = 1 + \cos x$ is most likely an identity. Use algebra to confirm.

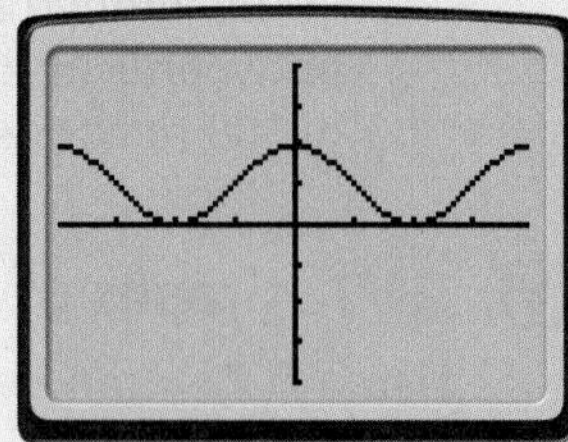

Try This

1. **Make a Conjecture** Determine whether $\sec x - \tan x \sin x = \cos x$ is a possible identity.
2. Prove or disprove your answer to Problem 1 by using algebra.
3. **Make a Conjecture** Determine whether $\frac{1 + \tan x}{1 + \cot x} = \tan x$ is a possible identity.
4. Prove or disprove your answer to Problem 3 by using algebra.

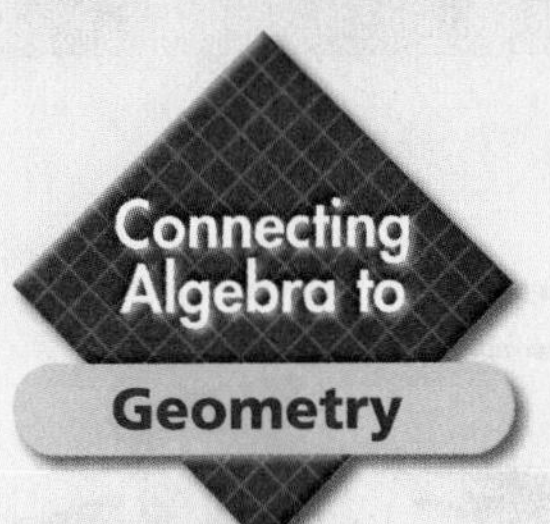

Angle Relationships

Angle relationships in circles and polygons can be used to solve problems.

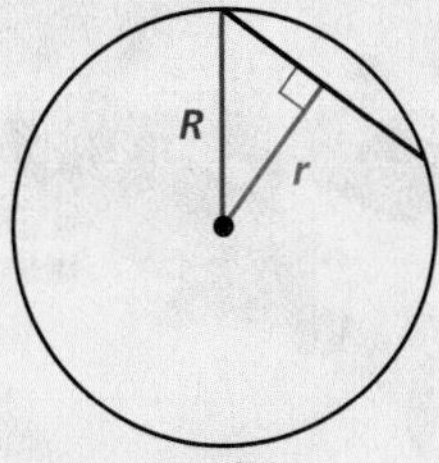

R radius

R
r
θ
s

r	**apothem**
s	**length of side**
θ	**interior angle**
n	**number of sides**

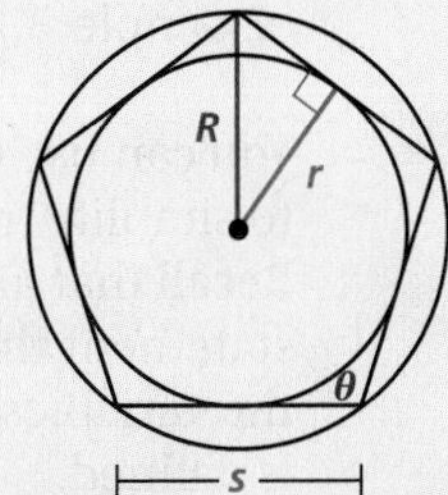

R	**radius of circumscribed circle**
r	**radius of inscribed circle**

The figures show regular polygons. A **regular polygon** has sides of equal length and equal interior angles. Here are some useful relationships for regular polygons.

R bisects θ. $\qquad \theta = \left(\frac{n-2}{n}\right)180^\circ \qquad r = R\cos\left(\frac{180^\circ}{n}\right) \qquad s = 2r\tan\left(\frac{180^\circ}{n}\right) = 2R\sin\left(\frac{180^\circ}{n}\right)$

Example

A regular octagon is inscribed in a circle with a radius of 5 cm. What is the length of each side of the octagon?

Make a sketch of the problem.

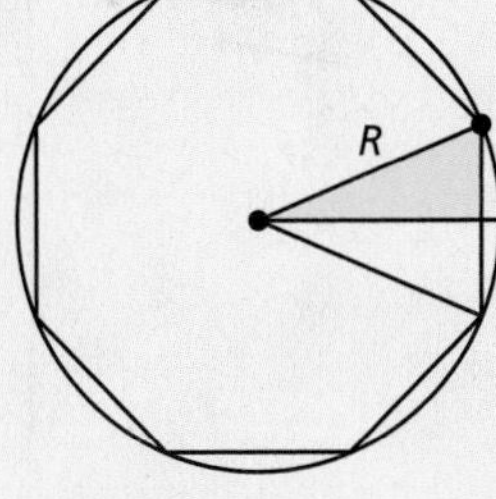

$s = 2R\sin\left(\frac{180^\circ}{n}\right)$ *Choose a formula relating the radius of the circumscribed circle to the side length of the polygon.*

$s = 2(5)\sin\left(\frac{180^\circ}{8}\right)$ *Substitute 5 for R and 8 for n.*

$s = 10\sin 22.5^\circ \approx 3.83 \text{ cm}$

Try This

Solve each problem. Round each answer to the nearest hundredth.

1. A circle is inscribed in an equilateral triangle with 8 in. sides. What is the diameter of the circle? What is the altitude of the triangle?
2. An isosceles right triangle is inscribed in a semicircle with a radius of 20 cm. What are the lengths of the three sides of the triangle?
3. The interior angles of a regular polygon each measure 150°. If this polygon is inscribed in a circle with a 10 in. diameter, how long is each side of the polygon?
4. Use the figure to find the side lengths of all three shaded triangles if the diameter of the circle is 10 cm. Round to the nearest hundredth if necessary.

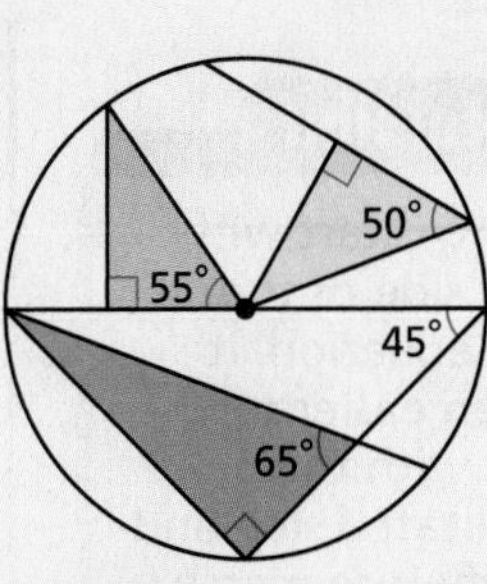

14-3 Fundamental Trigonometric Identities

Objective
Use fundamental trigonometric identities to simplify and rewrite expressions and to verify other identities.

Who uses this?
Ski supply manufacturers can use trigonometric identities to determine the type of wax to use on skis. (See Example 3.)

You can use trigonometric identities to simplify trigonometric expressions. Recall that an identity is a mathematical statement that is true for all values of the variables for which the statement is defined.

A derivation for a Pythagorean identity is shown below.

$$x^2 + y^2 = r^2 \qquad \textit{Pythagorean Theorem}$$

$$\frac{x^2}{r^2} + \frac{y^2}{r^2} = 1 \qquad \textit{Divide both sides by } r^2.$$

$$\cos^2\theta + \sin^2\theta = 1 \qquad \textit{Substitute } \cos\theta \textit{ for } \frac{x}{r} \textit{ and } \sin\theta \textit{ for } \frac{y}{r}.$$

Fundamental Trigonometric Identities

Reciprocal Identities	Tangent and Cotangent Ratio Identities	Pythagorean Identities	Negative-Angle Identities
$\csc\theta = \frac{1}{\sin\theta}$	$\tan\theta = \frac{\sin\theta}{\cos\theta}$	$\cos^2\theta + \sin^2\theta = 1$	$\sin(-\theta) = -\sin\theta$
$\sec\theta = \frac{1}{\cos\theta}$	$\cot\theta = \frac{\cos\theta}{\sin\theta}$	$1 + \tan^2\theta = \sec^2\theta$	$\cos(-\theta) = \cos\theta$
$\cot\theta = \frac{1}{\tan\theta}$		$\cot^2\theta + 1 = \csc^2\theta$	$\tan(-\theta) = -\tan\theta$

To prove that an equation is an identity, alter one side of the equation until it is the same as the other side. Justify your steps by using the fundamental identities.

EXAMPLE 1 **Proving Trigonometric Identities**

Helpful Hint
You may start with either side of the given equation. It is often easier to begin with the more complicated side and simplify it to match the simpler side.

Prove each trigonometric identity.

 **A** $\boldsymbol{\sec\theta = \csc\theta\tan\theta}$

$\sec\theta = \csc\theta\tan\theta$ *Choose the right-hand side to modify.*

$= \left(\frac{1}{\sin\theta}\right)\left(\frac{\sin\theta}{\cos\theta}\right)$ *Reciprocal and ratio identities*

$= \frac{1}{\cos\theta}$ *Simplify.*

$= \sec\theta$ *Reciprocal identity*

Prove each trigonometric identity.

B $\csc(-\theta) = -\csc\theta$

$\csc(-\theta) = -\csc\theta$	*Choose the left-hand side to modify.*
$\dfrac{1}{\sin(-\theta)} =$	*Reciprocal identity*
$\dfrac{1}{-\sin\theta} =$	*Negative-angle identity*
$-\left(\dfrac{1}{\sin\theta}\right) = -\csc\theta$	
$-\csc\theta = -\csc\theta$	*Reciprocal identity*

CHECK IT OUT! **Prove each trigonometric identity.**

1a. $\sin\theta\cot\theta = \cos\theta$

1b. $1 - \sec(-\theta) = 1 - \sec\theta$

You can use the fundamental trigonometric identities to simplify expressions.

EXAMPLE 2 Using Trigonometric Identities to Rewrite Trigonometric Expressions

Rewrite each expression in terms of cos θ, and simplify.

A $\dfrac{\sin^2\theta}{1 - \cos\theta}$

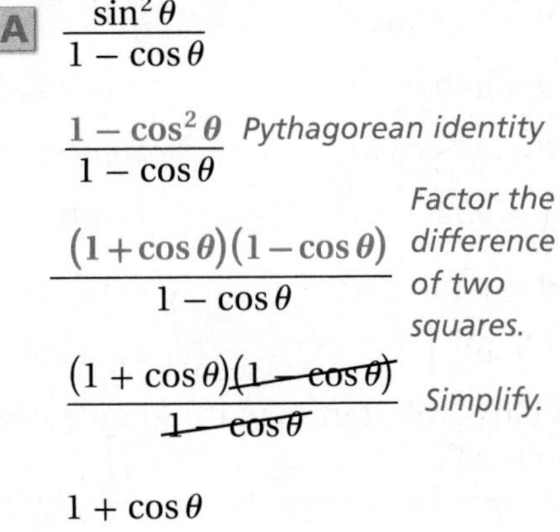

$\dfrac{1 - \cos^2\theta}{1 - \cos\theta}$	*Pythagorean identity*
$\dfrac{(1+\cos\theta)(1-\cos\theta)}{1 - \cos\theta}$	*Factor the difference of two squares.*
$\dfrac{(1 + \cos\theta)\cancel{(1 - \cos\theta)}}{\cancel{1 - \cos\theta}}$	*Simplify.*
$1 + \cos\theta$	

B $\sec\theta - \tan\theta\sin\theta$

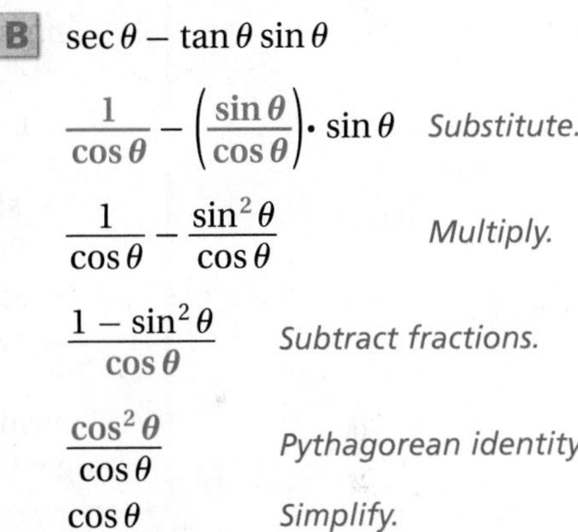

$\dfrac{1}{\cos\theta} - \left(\dfrac{\sin\theta}{\cos\theta}\right)\cdot\sin\theta$	*Substitute.*
$\dfrac{1}{\cos\theta} - \dfrac{\sin^2\theta}{\cos\theta}$	*Multiply.*
$\dfrac{1 - \sin^2\theta}{\cos\theta}$	*Subtract fractions.*
$\dfrac{\cos^2\theta}{\cos\theta}$	*Pythagorean identity*
$\cos\theta$	*Simplify.*

Helpful Hint

If you get stuck, try converting all of the trigonometric functions into sine and cosine functions.

CHECK IT OUT! **Rewrite each expression in terms of sin θ, and simplify.**

2a. $\dfrac{\cos^2\theta}{1 - \sin\theta}$

2b. $\cot^2\theta$

Student to Student *Graphing to Check for Equivalent Expressions*

Julia Zaragoza
Oak Ridge
High School

I like to use a graphing calculator to check for equivalent expressions.

For Example 2A, enter $y = \dfrac{\sin^2\theta}{(1 - \cos\theta)}$ *and* $y = 1 + \cos\theta$. *Graph both functions in the same viewing window.*

The graphs appear to coincide, so the expressions are most likely equivalent.

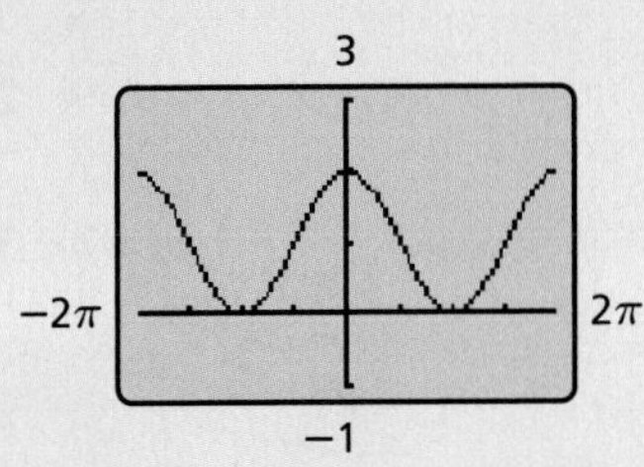

EXAMPLE 3 Sports Application

A ski supply company is testing the friction of a new ski wax by placing a waxed wood block on an inclined plane of wet snow. The incline plane is slowly raised until the wood block begins to slide.

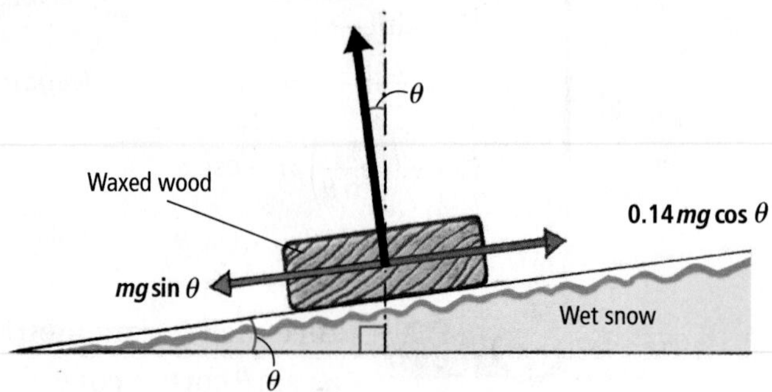

The symbol μ is read as "mu."

At the instant the block starts to slide, the component of the weight of the block parallel to the incline, $mg\sin\theta$, and the resistive force of friction, $\mu mg\cos\theta$, are equal. μ is the coefficient of friction. At what angle will the block start to move if $\mu = 0.14$?

Set the expression for the weight component equal to the expression for the force of friction.

$mg\sin\theta = \mu mg\cos\theta$

$\sin\theta = \mu\cos\theta$	*Divide both sides by mg.*
$\sin\theta = 0.14\cos\theta$	*Substitute 0.14 for μ.*
$\frac{\sin\theta}{\cos\theta} = 0.14$	*Divide both sides by $\cos\theta$.*
$\tan\theta = 0.14$	*Ratio identity*
$\theta \approx 8°$	*Evaluate inverse tangent.*

The wood block will start to move when the wet snow incline is raised to an angle of about 8°.

3. Use the equation $mg\sin\theta = \mu mg\cos\theta$ to determine the angle at which a waxed wood block on a wood incline with $\mu = 0.4$ begins to slide.

THINK AND DISCUSS

1. **DESCRIBE** how you prove that an equation is an identity.
2. **EXPLAIN** which identity can be used to prove that $(1 - \cos\theta)(1 + \cos\theta) = \sin^2\theta$.

3. **GET ORGANIZED** Copy and complete the graphic organizer by writing the three Pythagorean identities.

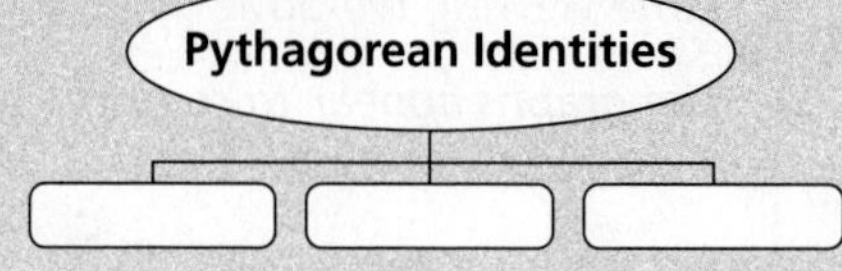

14-3 Exercises

go.hrw.com
Homework Help Online
KEYWORD: MB7 14-3
Parent Resources Online
KEYWORD: MB7 Parent

GUIDED PRACTICE

SEE EXAMPLE 1 p. 1008

Prove each trigonometric identity.

1. $\sin\theta\sec\theta = \tan\theta$
2. $\cot(-\theta) = -\cot\theta$
3. $\cos^2\theta\left(\sec^2\theta - 1\right) = \sin^2\theta$

SEE EXAMPLE 2 p. 1009

Rewrite each expression in terms of cos *θ*, and simplify.

4. $\csc\theta\tan\theta$
5. $\left(1 + \sec^2\theta\right)\left(1 - \sin^2\theta\right)$
6. $\sin^2\theta + \cos^2\theta + \tan^2\theta$

SEE EXAMPLE 3 p. 1010

7. **Physics** Use the equation $mg\sin\theta = \mu mg\cos\theta$ to determine the angle at which a glass-top table can be tilted before a glass plate on the table begins to slide. Assume $\mu = 0.94$.

PRACTICE AND PROBLEM SOLVING

Independent Practice	
For Exercises	See Example
8–11	1
12–15	2
16	3

Extra Practice
Skills Practice p. S31
Application Practice p. S45

Prove each trigonometric identity.

8. $\sec\theta\cot\theta = \csc\theta$
9. $\dfrac{\sin\theta - \cos\theta}{\sin\theta} = 1 - \cot\theta$
10. $\tan\theta\sin\theta = \sec\theta - \cos\theta$
11. $\sec^2\theta\left(1 - \cos^2\theta\right) = \tan^2\theta$

Rewrite each expression in terms of sin *θ*, and simplify.

12. $\dfrac{\cos^2\theta}{1 + \sin\theta}$
13. $\dfrac{\tan\theta}{\cot\theta}$
14. $\cos\theta\cot\theta + \sin\theta$
15. $\dfrac{\sec^2\theta - 1}{1 + \tan^2\theta}$

16. **Physics** Use the equation $mg\sin\theta = \mu mg\cos\theta$ to determine the steepest slope of the street shown on which a car with rubber tires can park without sliding.

Multi-Step Rewrite each expression in terms of a single trigonometric function.

17. $\tan\theta\cot\theta$
18. $\sin\theta\cot\theta\tan\theta$
19. $\cos\theta + \sin\theta\tan\theta$
20. $\sin\theta\csc\theta - \cos^2\theta$
21. $\cos^2\theta\sec\theta\csc\theta$
22. $\cos\theta\left(\tan^2\theta + 1\right)$
23. $\csc\theta\left(1 - \cos^2\theta\right)$
24. $\csc\theta\cos\theta\tan\theta$
25. $\dfrac{\sin\theta}{1 - \cos^2\theta}$
26. $\dfrac{\sin^2\theta}{1 - \cos^2\theta}$
27. $\dfrac{\tan\theta}{\sin\theta\sec\theta}$
28. $\dfrac{\cos\theta}{\sin\theta\cot\theta}$
29. $\tan\theta\left(\tan\theta + \cot\theta\right)$
30. $\sin^2\theta + \cos^2\theta + \cot^2\theta$
31. $\sin^2\theta\sec\theta\csc\theta$

Verify each identity.

32. $\dfrac{\cos\theta - 1}{\cos^2\theta} = \sec\theta - \sec^2\theta$
33. $\sin^2\theta\left(\csc^2\theta - 1\right) = \cos^2\theta$
34. $\tan\theta + \cot\theta = \sec\theta\csc\theta$
35. $\dfrac{\cos\theta}{1 - \sin^2\theta} = \sec\theta$
36. $\dfrac{1 - \cos^2\theta}{\tan\theta} = \sin\theta\cos\theta$
37. $\dfrac{\csc^2\theta}{1 + \tan^2\theta} = \cot^2\theta$

Prove each fundamental identity without using any of the other fundamental identities. (*Hint:* Use the trigonometric ratios with *x*, *y*, and *r*.)

38. $\tan\theta = \dfrac{\sin\theta}{\cos\theta}$
39. $\cot\theta = \dfrac{\cos\theta}{\sin\theta}$
40. $1 + \cot^2\theta = \csc^2\theta$
41. $\csc\theta = \dfrac{1}{\sin\theta}$
42. $\sec\theta = \dfrac{1}{\cos\theta}$
43. $1 + \tan^2\theta = \sec^2\theta$

MULTI-STEP TEST PREP

44. This problem will prepare you for the Multi-Step Test Prep on page 1034.

The displacement y of a mass attached to a spring is modeled by $y(t) = 5 \sin t$, where t is the time in seconds. The displacement z of another mass attached to a spring is modeled by $z(t) = 2.6 \cos t$.

a. The two masses are set in motion at $t = 0$. When do the masses have the same displacement for the first time?

b. What is the displacement at this time?

c. At what other times will the masses have the same displacement?

Graphing Calculator **Use a graphing calculator to determine whether each of the following equations represents an identity. (*Hint:* You may need to rewrite the equations in terms of sine, cosine, and tangent.)**

45. $(\csc\theta - 1)(\csc\theta + 1) = \tan^2\theta$

46. $\sec\theta - \cos\theta = \sin\theta$

47. $\cos\theta(\sec\theta + \cos\theta\csc^2\theta) = \csc^2\theta$

48. $\cot\theta(\cos\theta + \sin\theta\tan\theta) = \csc\theta$

49. $\cos\theta = 0.99\cos\theta$

50. $\sin\theta\cos\theta = \tan\theta - \tan\theta\sin^2\theta$

51. **Physics** A conical pendulum is created by a pendulum that travels in a circle rather than side to side and traces out the shape of a cone. The radius r of the base of the cone is given by the formula $r = \frac{g\tan\theta}{\omega^2}$, where g represents the force of gravity and ω represents the angular velocity of the pendulum.

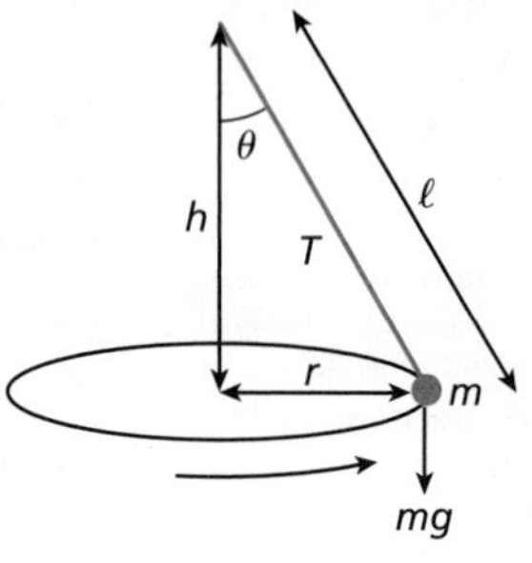

a. Use $\omega = \sqrt{\frac{g}{\ell\cos\theta}}$ and fundamental trigonometric identities to rewrite the formula for the radius.

b. Find a formula for ℓ in terms of g, ω, and a single trigonometric function.

Critical Thinking **A function is called odd if $f(-x) = -f(x)$ and even if $f(-x) = f(x)$.**

52. Which of the six trigonometric functions are odd? Which are even?

53. What distinguishes the graph of an odd function from an even function or a function that is neither odd nor even?

54. Determine whether the following functions are odd, even, or neither.

a.

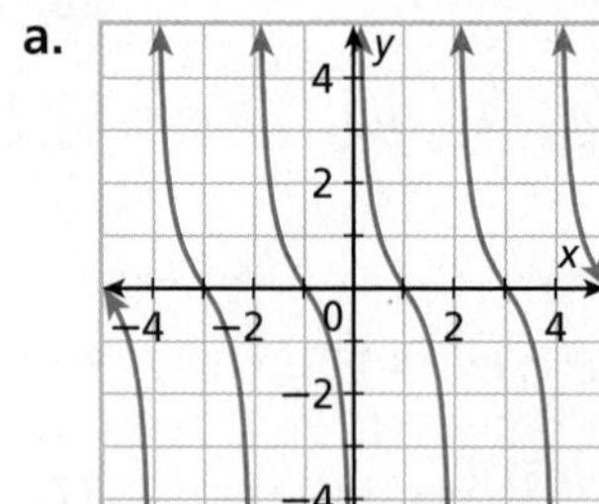

b.

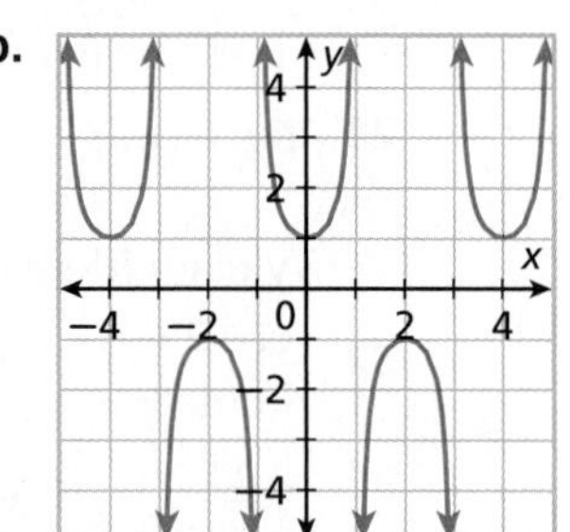

55. **Critical Thinking** In how many equivalent forms can $\tan\theta = \frac{\sin\theta}{\cos\theta}$ be expressed? Write at least three of its forms.

56. **Write About It** Use the fact that $\sin(-\theta) = -\sin\theta$ and $\cos(-\theta) = \cos\theta$ to explain why $\tan(-\theta) = -\tan\theta$.

TEST PREP

57. Which expression is equivalent to $\sec\theta \sin\theta$?

Ⓐ $\sin\theta$ Ⓑ $\cos\theta$ Ⓒ $\csc\theta$ Ⓓ $\tan\theta$

58. Which expression is NOT equivalent to the other expressions?

Ⓕ $\sec\theta \csc\theta$ Ⓖ $\dfrac{1}{\sin\theta\cos\theta}$ Ⓗ $\dfrac{\tan\theta}{\sin^2\theta}$ Ⓙ $\dfrac{\cos^2\theta}{\cot\theta}$

59. Which trigonometric statement is NOT an identity?

Ⓐ $1 + \cos^2\theta = \sin^2\theta$ Ⓒ $1 + \tan^2\theta = \sec^2\theta$

Ⓑ $\csc^2\theta - 1 = \cot^2\theta$ Ⓓ $1 - \sin^2\theta = \cos^2\theta$

60. Which is equivalent to $1 - \sec^2\theta$?

Ⓕ $\tan^2\theta$ Ⓖ $-\tan^2\theta$ Ⓗ $\cot^2\theta$ Ⓙ $-\cot^2\theta$

61. **Short Response** Verify that $\sin\theta + \cot\theta\cos\theta = \csc\theta$ is an identity. Write the justification for each step.

CHALLENGE AND EXTEND

Write each expression as a single fraction.

62. $\dfrac{1}{\cos\theta} + \dfrac{1}{\cos^2\theta}$

63. $\dfrac{\cos\theta}{\sin\theta} + \dfrac{\sin\theta}{\cos\theta}$

64. $1 - \dfrac{\cos\theta}{\sin\theta}$

65. $\dfrac{1}{1-\cos\theta} - \dfrac{\cos\theta}{1-\cos^2\theta}$

Simplify.

66. $\dfrac{\frac{1}{\sin^2\theta} - 1}{\frac{\cos^2\theta}{\sin^2\theta}}$

67. $\dfrac{\frac{1}{\sin\theta} + \frac{1}{\cos\theta}}{\frac{1}{\sin\theta\cos\theta}}$

68. $\dfrac{\frac{1}{\sin\theta} - \frac{1}{\cos\theta}}{\frac{\sin\theta}{\cos\theta} - \frac{\cos\theta}{\sin\theta}}$

69. $\dfrac{1 - \frac{1}{\sin\theta}}{1 - \frac{1}{\sin^2\theta}}$

SPIRAL REVIEW

70. **Travel** A statistician kept a record of the number of tourists in Hawaii for six months. Match each situation to its corresponding graph. *(Lesson 9-1)*

A

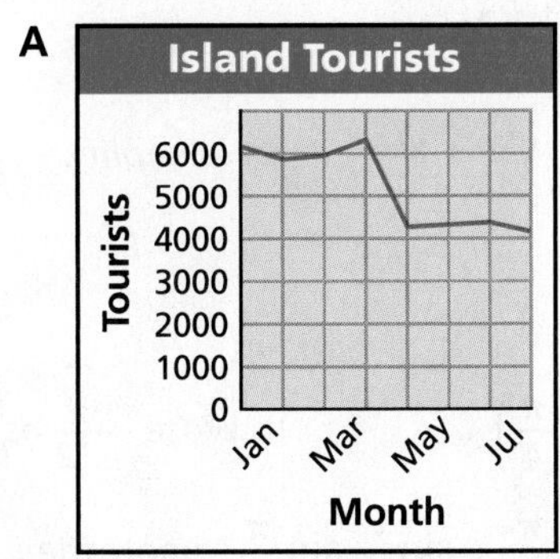

B

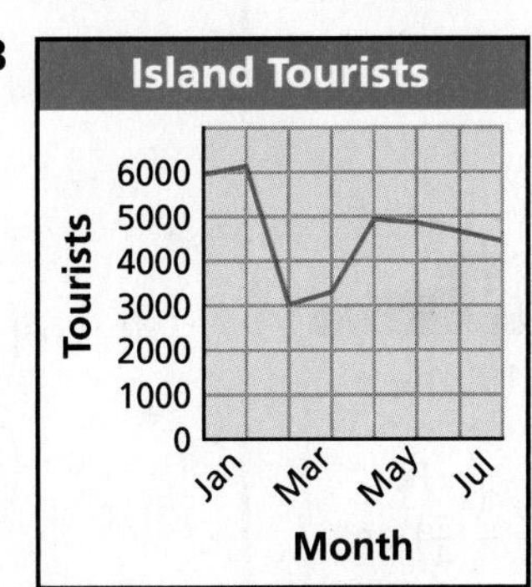

a. There were predictions of hurricanes in March and April.

b. High airfares and high temperatures cause tourism to drop off in the summer.

Find each probability. *(Lesson 11-3)*

71. rolling a 4 on a number cube and a 4 on another number cube

72. getting heads on both tosses when a coin is tossed 2 times

Find four values for which each function is undefined. *(Lesson 14-2)*

73. $y = -\tan\theta$

74. $y = \sec(0.5\theta)$

75. $y = -\csc\theta$

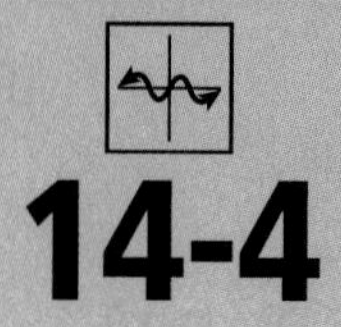

14-4 Sum and Difference Identities

Objectives
Evaluate trigonometric expressions by using sum and difference identities.

Use matrix multiplication with sum and difference identities to perform rotations.

Vocabulary
rotation matrix

Why learn this?

You can use sum and difference identities and matrices to form images made from rotations. (See Example 4.)

Matrix multiplication and sum and difference identities are tools to find the coordinates of points rotated about the origin on a plane.

Sum and Difference Identities	
Sum Identities	**Difference Identities**
$\sin(A+B) = \sin A\cos B + \cos A\sin B$	$\sin(A-B) = \sin A\cos B - \cos A\sin B$
$\cos(A+B) = \cos A\cos B - \sin A\sin B$	$\cos(A-B) = \cos A\cos B + \sin A\sin B$
$\tan(A+B) = \dfrac{\tan A + \tan B}{1 - \tan A\tan B}$	$\tan(A-B) = \dfrac{\tan A - \tan B}{1 + \tan A\tan B}$

EXAMPLE 1 Evaluating Expressions with Sum and Difference Identities

Find the exact value of each expression.

A $\sin 75°$

$\sin 75° = \sin(30° + 45°)$ *Write 75° as the sum 30° + 45° because trigonometric values of 30° and 45° are known.*

$= \sin 30° \cos 45° + \cos 30° \sin 45°$ *Apply identity for sin(A + B).*

$= \frac{1}{2} \cdot \frac{\sqrt{2}}{2} + \frac{\sqrt{3}}{2} \cdot \frac{\sqrt{2}}{2}$ *Evaluate.*

$= \frac{\sqrt{2}}{4} + \frac{\sqrt{6}}{4} = \frac{\sqrt{2}+\sqrt{6}}{4}$ *Simplify.*

B $\cos\left(-\frac{\pi}{12}\right)$

$\cos\left(-\frac{\pi}{12}\right) = \cos\left(\frac{\pi}{6} - \frac{\pi}{4}\right)$ *Write $-\frac{\pi}{12}$ as the difference $\frac{\pi}{6} - \frac{\pi}{4}$.*

$= \cos\frac{\pi}{6}\cos\frac{\pi}{4} + \sin\frac{\pi}{6}\sin\frac{\pi}{4}$ *Apply the identity for cos(A − B).*

$= \frac{\sqrt{3}}{2} \cdot \frac{\sqrt{2}}{2} + \frac{1}{2} \cdot \frac{\sqrt{2}}{2}$ *Evaluate.*

$= \frac{\sqrt{6}}{4} + \frac{\sqrt{2}}{4} = \frac{\sqrt{2}+\sqrt{6}}{4}$ *Simplify.*

Helpful Hint

In Example 1B, there is more than one way to get $-\frac{\pi}{12}$. For example, $\left(\frac{\pi}{6} - \frac{\pi}{4}\right)$ or $\left(\frac{\pi}{4} - \frac{\pi}{3}\right)$.

Find the exact value of each expression.

1a. $\tan 105°$ **1b.** $\sin\left(-\frac{11\pi}{12}\right)$

Shifting the cosine function right π radians is equivalent to reflecting it across the x-axis. A proof of this is shown in Example 2 by using a difference identity.

Phase Shift Right π Radians

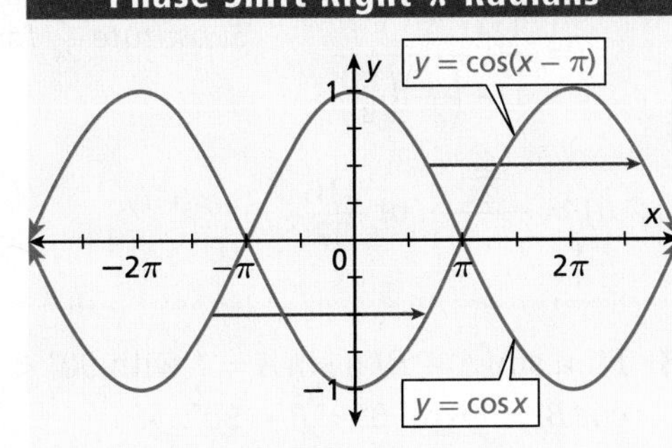

Reflection Across x-axis

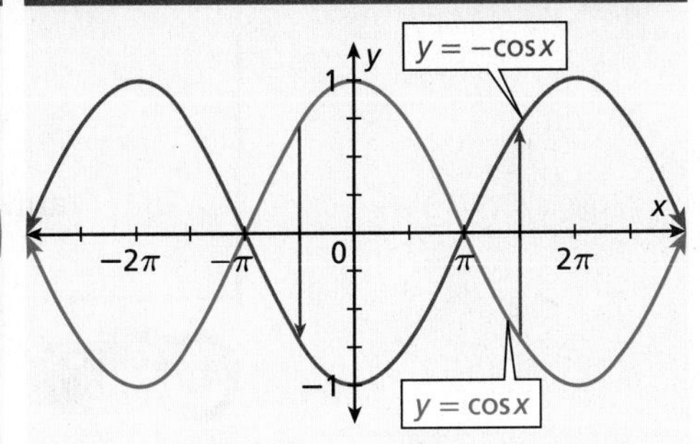

EXAMPLE 2 Proving Identities with Sum and Difference Identities

Prove the identity $\cos(x - \pi) = -\cos x$.

$\cos(x - \pi) = -\cos x$	*Choose the left-hand side to modify.*
$\cos x \cos \pi + \sin x \sin \pi =$	*Apply the identity for cos(A − B).*
$-1 \cdot \cos x + 0 \cdot \sin x =$	*Evaluate.*
$-\cos x = -\cos x$	*Simplify.*

2. Prove the identity $\cos\left(x + \frac{\pi}{2}\right) = -\sin x$.

EXAMPLE 3 Using the Pythagorean Theorem with Sum and Difference Identities

Remember!

Refer to Lessons 13-2 and 13-3 to review reference angles.

Find $\tan(A + B)$ if $\sin A = -\frac{7}{25}$ with $180° < A < 270°$ and if $\cos B = \frac{8}{17}$ with $0° < B < 180°$.

Step 1 Find $\tan A$ and $\tan B$.

Use reference angles and the ratio definitions $\sin A = \frac{y}{r}$ and $\cos B = \frac{x}{r}$. Draw a triangle in the appropriate quadrant and label x, y, and r for each angle.

In Quadrant III (QIII), $180° < A < 270°$ and $\sin A = -\frac{7}{25}$.

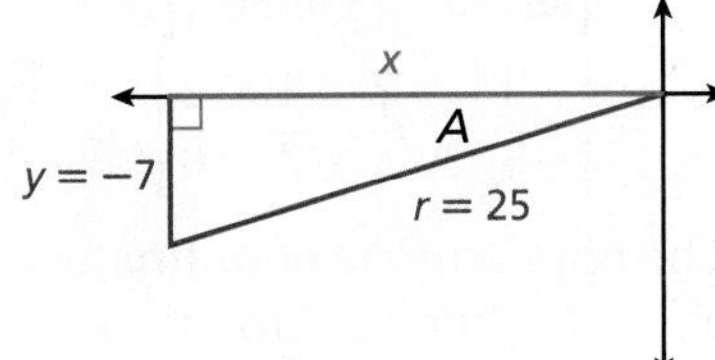

$x^2 + (-7)^2 = 25^2$

$x = -\sqrt{625 - 49} = -24$

Thus, $\tan A = \frac{y}{x} = \frac{7}{24}$.

In Quadrant I (QI), $0° < B < 180°$ and $\cos B = \frac{8}{17}$.

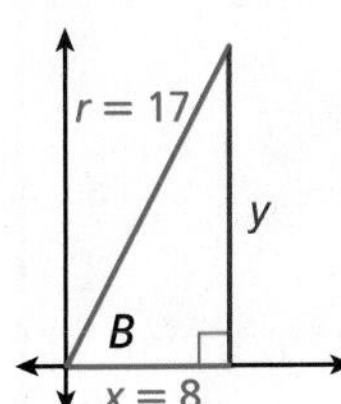

$8^2 + y^2 = 17^2$

$y = \sqrt{289 - 64} = 15$

Thus, $\tan B = \frac{y}{x} = \frac{15}{8}$.

Step 2 Use the angle-sum identity to find $\tan(A + B)$.

$$\tan(A+B) = \frac{\tan A + \tan B}{1 - \tan A \tan B}$$ *Apply identity for $\tan(A + B)$.*

$$= \frac{\left(\frac{7}{24}\right) + \left(\frac{15}{8}\right)}{1 - \left(\frac{7}{24}\right)\left(\frac{15}{8}\right)}$$ *Substitute $\frac{7}{24}$ for $\tan A$ and $\frac{15}{8}$ for $\tan B$.*

$$\tan(A+B) = \frac{\frac{52}{24}}{1 - \frac{35}{64}}, \text{ or } \frac{416}{87}$$ *Simplify.*

3. Find $\sin(A - B)$ if $\sin A = \frac{4}{5}$ with $90° < A < 180°$ and if $\cos B = \frac{3}{5}$ with $0° < B < 90°$.

To rotate a point $P(x,y)$ through an angle θ, use a **rotation matrix**.

The sum identities for sine and cosine are used to derive the system of equations that yields the rotation matrix.

Using a Rotation Matrix

If $P(x, y)$ is any point in a plane, then the coordinates $P'(x', y')$ of the image after a rotation of θ degrees counterclockwise about the origin can be found by using the rotation matrix:

$$\begin{bmatrix} \cos\theta & -\sin\theta \\ \sin\theta & \cos\theta \end{bmatrix}\begin{bmatrix} x \\ y \end{bmatrix} = \begin{bmatrix} x' \\ y' \end{bmatrix}$$

EXAMPLE 4 Using a Rotation Matrix

Find the coordinates, to the nearest hundredth, of the points in the figure shown after a 30° rotation about the origin.

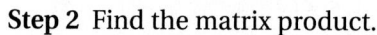

Step 1 Write matrices for a 30° rotation and for the points in the figure.

$$R_{30°} = \begin{bmatrix} \cos 30° & -\sin 30° \\ \sin 30° & \cos 30° \end{bmatrix}$$ *Rotation matrix*

$$S = \begin{bmatrix} 0 & 0 & \sqrt{3} & -\sqrt{3} \\ 2 & 4 & 1 & 1 \end{bmatrix}$$ *Matrix of point coordinates*

Step 2 Find the matrix product.

$$R_{30°} \times S = \begin{bmatrix} \cos 30° & -\sin 30° \\ \sin 30° & \cos 30° \end{bmatrix}\begin{bmatrix} 0 & 0 & \sqrt{3} & -\sqrt{3} \\ 2 & 4 & 1 & 1 \end{bmatrix}$$

$$= \begin{bmatrix} -1 & -2 & 1 & -2 \\ \sqrt{3} & 2\sqrt{3} & \sqrt{3} & 0 \end{bmatrix}$$

Step 3 The approximate coordinates of the points after a 30° rotation are $A'\left(-1, \sqrt{3}\right)$, $B'\left(-2, 2\sqrt{3}\right)$, $C'\left(1, \sqrt{3}\right)$, and $D'(-2, 0)$.

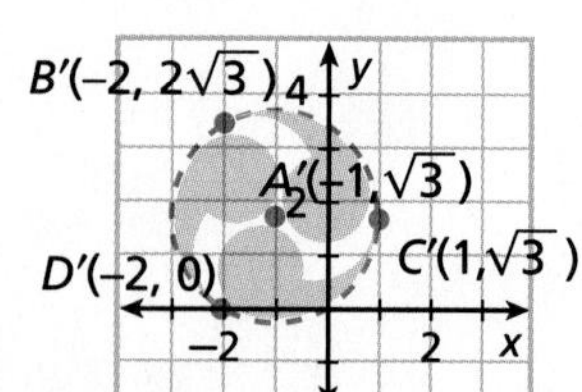

4. Find the coordinates, to the nearest hundredth, of the points in the original figure after a 60° rotation about the origin.

THINK AND DISCUSS

1. **DESCRIBE** three different ways that you can use the difference identity to find the exact value of $\sin 15°$.
2. **EXPLAIN** the similarities and differences between the identity formulas for sine and cosine. How do the signs of the terms relate to whether the identity is a sum or a difference?
3. **GET ORGANIZED** Copy and complete the graphic organizer. For each type of function, give the sum and difference identity and an example.

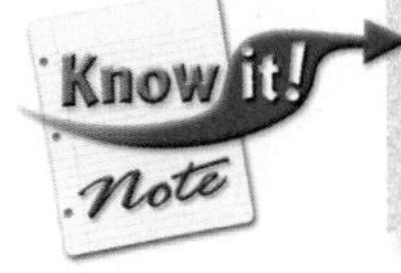

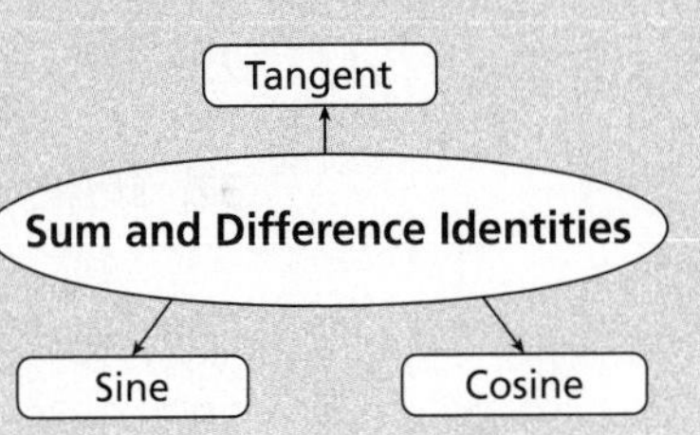

14-4 Exercises

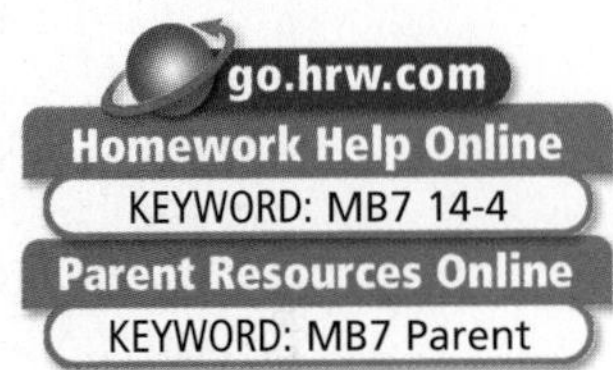

GUIDED PRACTICE

1. **Vocabulary** A geometric rotation requires that a center point of rotation be defined. Which point and which direction does a rotation matrix such as R_θ assume?

SEE EXAMPLE 1 p. 1014

Find the exact value of each expression.

2. $\cos 105°$
3. $\sin \frac{11\pi}{12}$
4. $\tan \frac{\pi}{12}$
5. $\cos(-75°)$

SEE EXAMPLE 2 p. 1015

Prove each identity.

6. $\sin\left(\frac{\pi}{2} + x\right) = \cos x$
7. $\tan(\pi + x) = \tan x$
8. $\cos\left(\frac{3\pi}{2} - x\right) = -\sin x$

SEE EXAMPLE 3 p. 1015

Find each value if $\sin A = -\frac{12}{13}$ with $180° < A < 270°$ and if $\sin B = \frac{4}{5}$ with $90° < B < 180°$.

9. $\sin(A + B)$
10. $\cos(A - B)$
11. $\tan(A + B)$
12. $\tan(A - B)$

SEE EXAMPLE 4 p. 1016

13. Find the coordinates, to the nearest hundredth, of the vertices of triangle ABC with $A(0, 2)$, $B(0, -1)$, and $C(3, 0)$ after a 120° rotation about the origin.

PRACTICE AND PROBLEM SOLVING

Independent Practice

For Exercises	See Example
14–17	1
18–20	2
21–24	3
25	4

Extra Practice

Skills Practice p. S31
Application Practice p. S45

Find the exact value of each expression.

14. $\sin \frac{7\pi}{12}$
15. $\tan 165°$
16. $\sin 195°$
17. $\cos \frac{11\pi}{12}$

Prove each identity.

18. $\cos\left(\frac{3\pi}{2} + x\right) = \sin x$
19. $\sin\left(\frac{3\pi}{2} + x\right) = -\cos x$
20. $\tan(x - 2\pi) = \tan x$

Find each value if $\cos A = -\frac{12}{13}$ with $90° < A < 180°$ and if $\sin B = -\frac{4}{5}$ with $270° < B < 360°$.

21. $\sin(A + B)$
22. $\tan(A - B)$
23. $\cos(A + B)$
24. $\cos(A - B)$

25. Find the coordinates, to the nearest hundredth, of the vertices of figure ABC with $A(0, 2)$, $B(1, 2)$, and $C(0, 1)$ after a 45° rotation about the origin.

Find the exact value of each expression.

26. $\sin 165°$

27. $\tan(-105°)$

28. $\cos 195°$

29. $\sin(-15°)$

30. $\cos\frac{19\pi}{12}$

31. $\tan\frac{5\pi}{12}$

32. $\sin 255°$

33. $\tan 195°$

34. $\cos\frac{\pi}{12}$

Find the value for each unknown angle given that $0° \le \theta \le 180°$.

35. $\cos(\theta - 30°) = \frac{1}{2}$

36. $\cos(20° + \theta) = \frac{\sqrt{2}}{2}$

37. $\sin(180° - \theta) = \frac{1}{2}$

38. **Physics** Light enters glass of thickness t at an angle θ_i and leaves the glass at the same angle θ_i. However, the exiting ray of light is offset from the initial ray by a distance $\Delta = \left(\frac{\sin(\theta_i - \theta_r)}{\sin\theta_i \cos\theta_r}\right)t$, indicated in the figure shown.

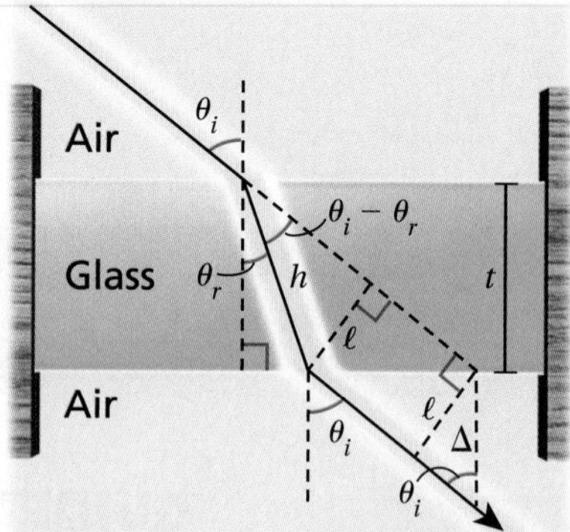

a. Write the formula for Δ in terms of tangent and cotangent by using the difference identities and other trigonometric identities.

b. Use the figure to write a ratio for $\sin(\theta_i - \theta_r)$.

Multi-Step **Find $\tan(A + B)$, $\cos(A + B)$, and $\sin(A - B)$ for each situation.**

39. $\sin A = -\frac{7}{25}$ with $180° < A < 270°$ and $\cos B = \frac{12}{13}$ with $0° < B < 90°$

40. $\sin A = -\frac{1}{3}$ with $270° < A < 360°$ and $\sin B = \frac{4}{5}$ with $0° < B < 90°$

41. The figure $PQRS$ will be rotated about the origin repeatedly to create the logo for a new product.

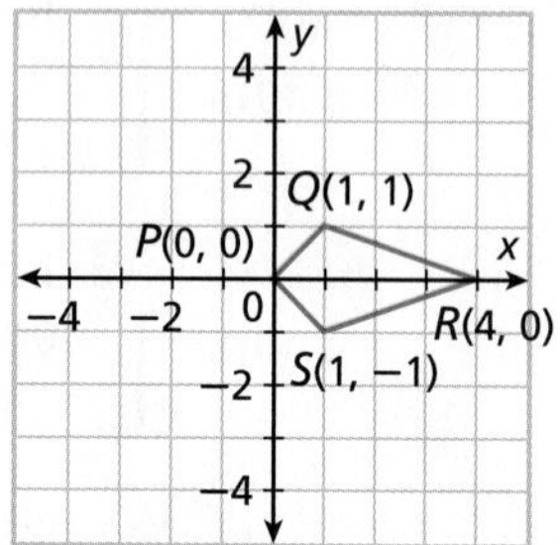

a. Write the rotation matrices for 90°, 180°, and 270° rotations.

b. Use your answers to part **a** to find the coordinates of the vertices of the figure after each of the three rotations.

c. Graph the three rotations on the same graph as $PQRS$ to create the logo.

42. **Critical Thinking** Is it possible to find the exact value of $\sin\left(\frac{11\pi}{24}\right)$ by using sum or difference identities? Explain.

MULTI-STEP TEST PREP

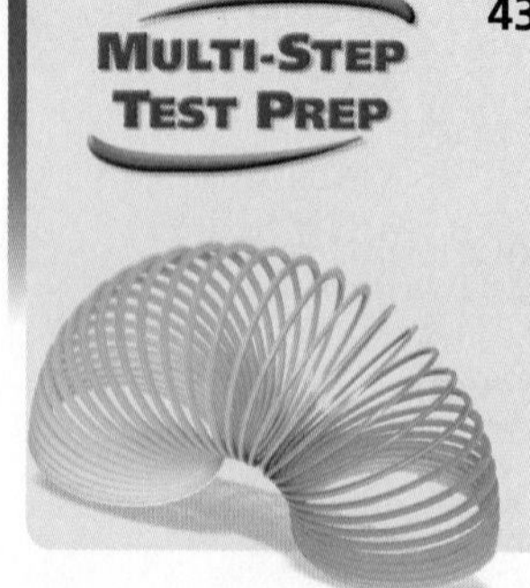

43. This problem will prepare you for the Multi-Step Test Prep on page 1034.

The displacement y of a mass attached to a spring is modeled by $y(t) = 4.2\sin\left(\frac{2\pi}{3}t - \frac{\pi}{2}\right)$, where t is the time in seconds.

a. What are the amplitude and period of the function?

b. Use a trigonometric identity to write the displacement, using only the cosine function.

c. What is the displacement of the mass when $t = 8$ s?

 **Geometry** Find the coordinates, to the nearest hundredth, of the vertices of figure $ABCD$ with $A(0, 3)$, $B(1, 4)$, $C(2, 3)$, and $D(2, 0)$ after each rotation about the origin.

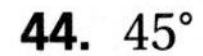

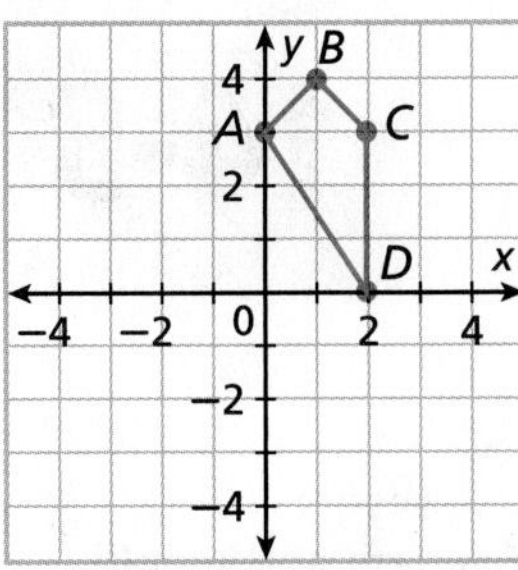

44. 45°
45. 60°
46. 120°
47. −30°

48. **Write About It** In general, does $\sin(A + B) = \sin A + \sin B$? Give an example to support your response.

TEST PREP

49. Which is the value of $\cos 15° \cos 45° - \sin 15° \sin 45°$?

Ⓐ $\frac{1}{2}$ Ⓑ $\frac{\sqrt{2}}{2}$ Ⓒ $-\frac{\sqrt{2}}{2}$ Ⓓ $\frac{2+\sqrt{2}}{2}$

50. Which gives the value for x if $\sin\left(\frac{\pi}{2} + x\right) = \frac{1}{2}$?

Ⓕ $\frac{\pi}{6}$ Ⓖ $\frac{\pi}{4}$ Ⓗ $\frac{\pi}{3}$ Ⓙ $\frac{\pi}{2}$

51. Given $\sin A = \frac{1}{2}$ with $0° < A < 90°$ and $\cos B = \frac{3}{5}$ with $0° < B < 90°$, which expression gives the value of $\cos(A - B)$?

Ⓐ $\frac{3\sqrt{3}+4}{10}$ Ⓑ $\frac{3\sqrt{3}-4}{10}$ Ⓒ $\frac{3+4\sqrt{3}}{10}$ Ⓓ $\frac{3-4\sqrt{3}}{10}$

52. **Short Response** Find the exact value for $\sin(-15°)$. Show your work.

CHALLENGE AND EXTEND

53. Verify that the rotation matrix for θ is the inverse of the rotation matrix for $-\theta$.

54. Derive the identity for $\tan(A + B)$.

55. Derive the rotation matrix by using the sum identities for sine and cosine and recalling from Lesson 13-2 that any point $P(x, y)$ can be represented as $(r\cos\alpha, r\sin\alpha)$ by using a reference angle.

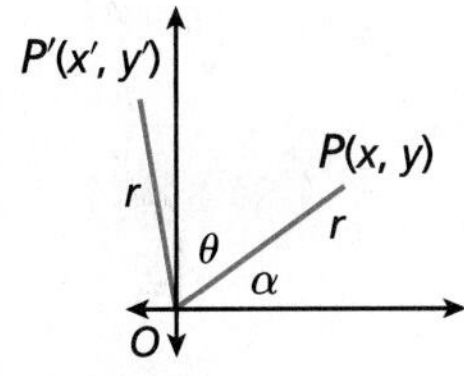

Find the angle by which a figure ABC with vertices $A(1, 0)$, $B(0, 2)$, and $C(-1, 0)$ was rotated to get $A'B'C'$.

56. $A'(0, 1)$, $B'(-2, 0)$, $C'(0, -1)$
57. $A'\left(\frac{\sqrt{2}}{2}, \frac{\sqrt{2}}{2}\right)$, $B'(-\sqrt{2}, \sqrt{2})$, $C'\left(-\frac{\sqrt{2}}{2}, -\frac{\sqrt{2}}{2}\right)$
58. $A'(-1, 0)$, $B'(0, -2)$, $C'(1, 0)$
59. $A'\left(\frac{\sqrt{3}}{2}, \frac{1}{2}\right)$, $B'(-1, \sqrt{3})$, $C'\left(-\frac{\sqrt{3}}{2}, -\frac{1}{2}\right)$

SPIRAL REVIEW

Divide. Assume that all expressions are defined. *(Lesson 8-2)*

60. $\frac{3x^2}{7y^3} \div \frac{6x}{21y}$
61. $\frac{x^2 + x - 2}{x^2 - 2x - 8} \div \frac{x^2 + 3x + 2}{x^2 - 3x - 4}$
62. $\frac{9x^3y^2}{15xy^4} \div \frac{6x^4y}{3x^2y^5}$

Identify the conic section that each equation represents. *(Lesson 10-6)*

63. $x^2 + 2xy + y^2 + 12x - 25 = 0$
64. $5x^2 + 5y^2 + 20x - 15y = 0$

Rewrite each expression in terms of a single trigonometric function. *(Lesson 14-3)*

65. $\frac{\cot\theta \sec\theta}{\sin\theta \cos\theta}$
66. $\cot\theta \tan\theta \csc\theta$
67. $\frac{\tan\theta}{\sec\theta} \sin\theta$

14-5 Double-Angle and Half-Angle Identities

Objective
Evaluate and simplify expressions by using double-angle and half-angle identities.

Who uses this?
Double-angle formulas can be used to find the horizontal distance for a projectile such as a golf ball. (See Exercise 49.)

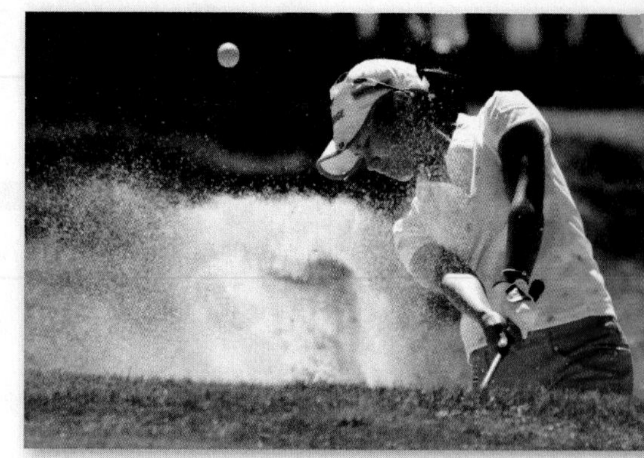

You can use sum identities to derive the *double-angle identities.*

$$\sin 2\theta = \sin(\theta + \theta)$$
$$= \sin\theta\cos\theta + \cos\theta\sin\theta$$
$$= 2\sin\theta\cos\theta$$

You can derive the double-angle identities for cosine and tangent in the same way. There are three forms of the identity for $\cos 2\theta$, which are derived by using $\sin^2\theta + \cos^2\theta = 1$. It is common to rewrite expressions as functions of θ only.

Know it! Note

Double-Angle Identities		
$\sin 2\theta = 2\sin\theta\cos\theta$	$\cos 2\theta = \cos^2\theta - \sin^2\theta$ $\cos 2\theta = 2\cos^2\theta - 1$ $\cos 2\theta = 1 - 2\sin^2\theta$	$\tan 2\theta = \dfrac{2\tan\theta}{1 - \tan^2\theta}$

EXAMPLE 1 Evaluating Expressions with Double-Angle Identities

Find $\sin 2\theta$ and $\cos 2\theta$ if $\cos\theta = -\frac{3}{4}$ and $90° < \theta < 180°$.

Step 1 Find $\sin\theta$ to evaluate $\sin 2\theta = 2\sin\theta\cos\theta$.

Method 1 Use the reference angle.

In QII, $90° < \theta < 180°$, and $\cos\theta = -\frac{3}{4}$.

$(-3)^2 + y^2 = 4^2$ *Use the Pythagorean Theorem.*

$y = \sqrt{16 - 9} = \sqrt{7}$ *Solve for y.*

$\sin\theta = \dfrac{\sqrt{7}}{4}$

$r = 4$
y
θ
$x = -3$

Method 2 Solve $\sin^2\theta = 1 - \cos^2\theta$.

$\sin^2\theta = 1 - \cos^2\theta$

$\sin\theta = \sqrt{1 - \left(-\frac{3}{4}\right)^2}$ *Substitute $-\frac{3}{4}$ for cosθ.*

$= \sqrt{1 - \frac{9}{16}} = \frac{\sqrt{7}}{4}$ *Simplify.*

$\sin\theta = \dfrac{\sqrt{7}}{4}$

Caution!
The signs of x and y depend on the quadrant for angle θ.

	sin	cos
QI	+	+
QII	+	−
QIII	−	−
QIV	−	+

Step 2 Find $\sin 2\theta$.

$\sin 2\theta = 2\sin\theta\cos\theta$	*Apply the identity for* $\sin 2\theta$.
$= 2\left(\frac{\sqrt{7}}{4}\right)\left(-\frac{3}{4}\right)$	*Substitute* $\frac{\sqrt{7}}{2}$ *for* $\sin\theta$ *and* $-\frac{3}{4}$ *for* $\cos\theta$.
$= -\frac{3\sqrt{7}}{8}$	*Simplify.*

Step 3 Find $\cos 2\theta$.

$\cos 2\theta = 2\cos^2\theta - 1$	*Select a double-angle identity.*
$= 2\left(-\frac{3}{4}\right)^2 - 1$	*Substitute* $-\frac{3}{4}$ *for* $\cos\theta$.
$= 2\left(\frac{9}{16}\right) - 1$	*Simplify.*
$= \frac{1}{8}$	

1. Find $\tan 2\theta$ and $\cos 2\theta$ if $\cos\theta = \frac{1}{3}$ and $270° < \theta < 360°$.

You can use double-angle identities to prove trigonometric identities.

EXAMPLE 2 Proving Identities with Double-Angle Identities

Prove each identity.

A $\sin^2\theta = \frac{1}{2}(1 - \cos 2\theta)$

$\sin^2\theta = \frac{1}{2}(1 - \cos 2\theta)$	*Choose the right-hand side to modify.*
$= \frac{1}{2}\left(1 - \left(1 - 2\sin^2\theta\right)\right)$	*Apply the identity for* $\cos 2\theta$.
$= \frac{1}{2}\left(2\sin^2\theta\right)$	*Simplify.*
$\sin^2\theta = \sin^2\theta$	

Helpful Hint

Choose to modify either the left side or the right side of an identity. Do not work on both sides at once.

B $(\cos\theta + \sin\theta)^2 = 1 + \sin 2\theta$

$(\cos\theta + \sin\theta)^2 = 1 + \sin 2\theta$	*Choose the left-hand side to modify.*
$\cos^2\theta + 2\cos\theta\sin\theta + \sin^2\theta =$	*Expand the square.*
$\left(\cos^2\theta + \sin^2\theta\right) + \left(2\cos\theta\sin\theta\right) =$	*Regroup.*
$1 + \sin 2\theta =$	*Rewrite using* $1 = \cos^2\theta + \sin^2\theta$ *and* $\sin 2\theta = 2\sin\theta\cos\theta$.
$1 + \sin 2\theta = 1 + \sin 2\theta$	

Prove each identity.

2a. $\cos^4\theta - \sin^4\theta = \cos 2\theta$ **2b.** $\sin 2\theta = \frac{2\tan\theta}{1 + \tan^2\theta}$

You can use double-angle identities for cosine to derive the *half-angle identities* by substituting $\frac{\theta}{2}$ for θ. For example, $\cos 2\theta = 2\cos^2\theta - 1$ can be rewritten as $\cos\theta = 2\cos^2\frac{\theta}{2} - 1$. Then solve for $\cos\frac{\theta}{2}$.

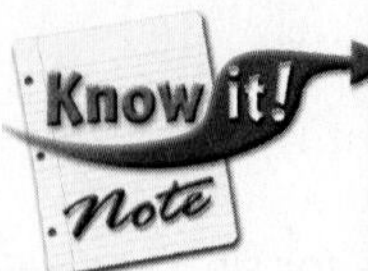

Half-Angle Identities

$$\sin\frac{\theta}{2} = \pm\sqrt{\frac{1-\cos\theta}{2}} \qquad \cos\frac{\theta}{2} = \pm\sqrt{\frac{1+\cos\theta}{2}} \qquad \tan\frac{\theta}{2} = \pm\sqrt{\frac{1-\cos\theta}{1+\cos\theta}}$$

Choose + or − depending on the location of $\frac{\theta}{2}$.

Half-angle identities are useful in calculating exact values for trigonometric expressions.

In Example 3, the expressions $-\frac{\sqrt{2+\sqrt{3}}}{2}$ and $\frac{\sqrt{2-\sqrt{2}}}{2}$ are in reduced form and cannot be simplified further.

EXAMPLE 3 Evaluating Expressions with Half-Angle Identities

Use half-angle identities to find the exact value of each trigonometric expression.

A $\cos 165°$

$\cos\frac{330°}{2}$

$-\sqrt{\frac{1+\cos 330°}{2}}$ *Negative in QII*

$-\sqrt{\frac{1+\left(\frac{\sqrt{3}}{2}\right)}{2}}$ $\cos 330° = \frac{\sqrt{3}}{2}$

$-\sqrt{\left(\frac{2+\sqrt{3}}{2}\right)\left(\frac{1}{2}\right)}$ *Simplify.*

$-\frac{\sqrt{2+\sqrt{3}}}{2}$

Check Use your calculator.

B $\sin\frac{\pi}{8}$

$\sin\frac{1}{2}\left(\frac{\pi}{4}\right)$

$+\sqrt{\frac{1-\cos\left(\frac{\pi}{4}\right)}{2}}$ *Positive in QI*

$\sqrt{\frac{1-\frac{\sqrt{2}}{2}}{2}}$ $\cos\frac{\pi}{4} = \frac{\sqrt{2}}{2}$

$\sqrt{\left(\frac{2-\sqrt{2}}{2}\right)\left(\frac{1}{2}\right)}$ *Simplify.*

$\frac{\sqrt{2-\sqrt{2}}}{2}$

Check Use your calculator.

Use half-angle identities to find the exact value of each trigonometric expression.

3a. $\tan 75°$ **3b.** $\cos\frac{5\pi}{8}$

EXAMPLE 4 Using the Pythagorean Theorem with Half-Angle Identities

Find $\sin\frac{\theta}{2}$ and $\tan\frac{\theta}{2}$ if $\sin\theta = -\frac{5}{13}$ and $180° < \theta < 270°$.

Step 1 Find $\cos\theta$ to evaluate the half-angle identities.

Use the reference angle.

In QIII, $180° < \theta < 270°$, and $\sin\theta = -\frac{5}{13}$.

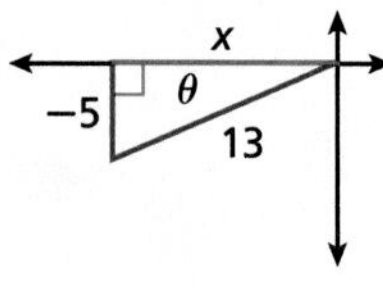

$x^2 + (-5)^2 = 13^2$ *Pythagorean Theorem*

$x = -\sqrt{169-25} = -12$ *Solve for the missing side x.*

Thus, $\cos\theta = -\frac{12}{13}$.

Step 2 Evaluate $\sin\frac{\theta}{2}$.

$\sin\frac{\theta}{2}$

$+\sqrt{\frac{1-\cos\theta}{2}}$ *Choose + for $\sin\frac{\theta}{2}$ where $90° < \frac{\theta}{2} < 135°$.*

$\sqrt{\frac{1-\left(-\frac{12}{13}\right)}{2}}$ *Evaluate.*

$\sqrt{\left(\frac{25}{13}\right)\left(\frac{1}{2}\right)}$ *Simplify.*

$\sqrt{\frac{25}{26}}$

$\frac{5\sqrt{26}}{26}$

Step 3 Evaluate $\tan\frac{\theta}{2}$.

$\tan\frac{\theta}{2}$

$-\sqrt{\frac{1-\cos\theta}{1+\cos\theta}}$ *Choose − for $\tan\frac{\theta}{2}$ where $90° < \frac{\theta}{2} < 135°$.*

$-\sqrt{\frac{1-\left(-\frac{12}{13}\right)}{1+\left(-\frac{12}{13}\right)}}$ *Evaluate.*

$-\sqrt{\left(\frac{25}{13}\right)\left(\frac{13}{1}\right)}$ *Simplify.*

$-\sqrt{25}$

-5

Caution!

Be careful to choose the correct sign for $\sin\frac{\theta}{2}$ and $\cos\frac{\theta}{2}$. If $180° < \theta < 270°$, then $90° < \frac{\theta}{2} < 135°$.

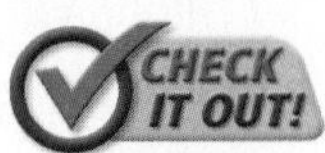

4. Find $\sin\frac{\theta}{2}$ and $\cos\frac{\theta}{2}$ if $\tan\theta = \frac{4}{3}$ and $0° < \theta < 90°$.

THINK AND DISCUSS

1. **EXPLAIN** which double-angle identity you would use to simplify $\frac{\cos 2\theta}{\sin\theta + \cos\theta}$.
2. **DESCRIBE** how to determine the sign of the value for $\sin\frac{\theta}{2}$ and for $\cos\frac{\theta}{2}$.

3. **GET ORGANIZED** Copy and complete the graphic organizer. In each box, write one of the identities.

Double-Angle Identity for Cosine

14-5 Exercises

go.hrw.com
Homework Help Online
KEYWORD: MB7 14-5
Parent Resources Online
KEYWORD: MB7 Parent

GUIDED PRACTICE

SEE EXAMPLE 1 p. 1020

Find $\sin 2\theta$, $\cos 2\theta$, and $\tan 2\theta$ for each set of conditions.

1. $\cos\theta = -\frac{5}{13}$ and $\frac{\pi}{2} < \theta < \pi$

2. $\sin\theta = \frac{4}{5}$ and $0° < \theta < 90°$

SEE EXAMPLE 2 p. 1021

Prove each identity.

3. $2\cos 2\theta = 4\cos^2\theta - 2$

4. $\sin^2\theta = 1 - \frac{\cos 2\theta + 1}{2}$

5. $\frac{1 + \cos 2\theta}{\sin 2\theta} = \cot\theta$

6. $\sin 2\theta = \frac{2\tan\theta}{1 + \tan^2\theta}$

SEE EXAMPLE 3 p. 1022

Use half-angle identities to find the exact value of each trigonometric expression.

7. $\cos 67.5°$

8. $\cos\frac{\pi}{12}$

9. $\tan\frac{3\pi}{8}$

10. $\sin 112.5°$

SEE EXAMPLE 4 p. 1022

Find $\sin\frac{\theta}{2}$, $\cos\frac{\theta}{2}$, and $\tan\frac{\theta}{2}$ for each set of conditions.

11. $\sin\theta = -\frac{24}{25}$ and $180° < \theta < 270°$

12. $\cos\theta = \frac{1}{4}$ and $270° < \theta < 360°$

PRACTICE AND PROBLEM SOLVING

Independent Practice

For Exercises	See Example
13–14	1
15–18	2
19–22	3
23–24	4

Extra Practice

Skills Practice p. S31
Application Practice p. S45

Find $\sin 2\theta$, $\cos 2\theta$, and $\tan 2\theta$ for each set of conditions.

13. $\cos\theta = -\frac{7}{25}$ and $90° < \theta < 180°$

14. $\tan\theta = \frac{20}{21}$ and $0 \le \theta \le \frac{\pi}{2}$

Prove each identity.

15. $\frac{\sin 2\theta}{\sin\theta} = 2\cos\theta$

16. $\cos^2\theta = \frac{1}{2}(1 + \cos 2\theta)$

17. $\tan\theta = \frac{1 - \cos 2\theta}{\sin 2\theta}$

18. $\tan\theta = \frac{\sin 2\theta}{1 + \cos 2\theta}$

Use half-angle identities to find the exact value of each trigonometric expression.

19. $\sin\frac{7\pi}{12}$

20. $\cos\frac{5\pi}{12}$

21. $\sin 22.5°$

22. $\tan 15°$

Find $\sin\frac{\theta}{2}$, $\cos\frac{\theta}{2}$, and $\tan\frac{\theta}{2}$ for each set of conditions.

23. $\tan\theta = -\frac{12}{35}$ and $\frac{3\pi}{2} < \theta < 2\pi$

24. $\sin\theta = -\frac{3}{5}$ and $180° < \theta < 270°$

Multi-Step **Rewrite each expression in terms of trigonometric functions of θ rather than multiples of θ. Then simplify.**

25. $\sin 3\theta$

26. $\sin 4\theta$

27. $\cos 3\theta$

28. $\cos 4\theta$

29. $\cos 2\theta + 2\sin^2\theta$

30. $\cos 2\theta + 1$

31. $\tan 2\theta(2 - \sec^2\theta)$

32. $\frac{\cos 2\theta}{\cos\theta + \sin\theta}$

33. $\frac{\cos\theta\sin 2\theta}{1 + \cos 2\theta}$

34. $\frac{\cos 2\theta - 1}{\sin^2\theta}$

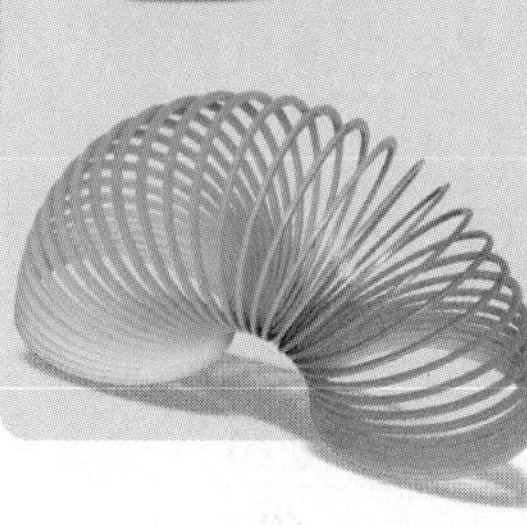

35. This problem will prepare you for the Multi-Step Test Prep on page 1034.

The displacement y of a mass attached to a spring is modeled by $y(t) = 3.1 \sin 2t$, where t is the time in seconds.

a. Rewrite the function by using a double-angle identity.

b. The displacement w of another mass attached to a spring is given by $w(t) = 3.8 \cos t$. The two masses are set in motion at $t = 0$. When do the masses have the same displacement for the first time?

c. What is the displacement at this time?

Multi-Step **Find $\sin 2\theta$, $\cos 2\theta$, $\tan 2\theta$, $\sin\frac{\theta}{2}$, $\cos\frac{\theta}{2}$, and $\tan\frac{\theta}{2}$ for each set of conditions.**

36. $\cos\theta = \frac{3}{8}$ and $\frac{\pi}{2} < \theta < \pi$

37. $\cos\theta = -\frac{\sqrt{5}}{3}$ and $180° < \theta < 270°$

38. $\sin\theta = \frac{2}{5}$ and $0° < \theta < 90°$

39. $\tan\theta = -\frac{1}{2}$ and $\frac{3\pi}{2} < \theta < 2\pi$

Use half-angle identities to find the exact value of each trigonometric expression.

40. $\cos\frac{7\pi}{8}$

41. $\sin\frac{11\pi}{12}$

42. $\cos 105°$

43. $\sin(-15°)$

LINK

Physics

The Tevatron at Fermi National Accelerator Lab in Batavia, Illinois, uses superconducting magnets to study subatomic particles by colliding matter and antimatter inside of a ring with a diameter of 6.3 km.

44. **Physics** The change in momentum of a scattered nuclear particle is given by $\Delta P = P_f - P_i$, where P_f is the final momentum, and P_i is the initial momentum.

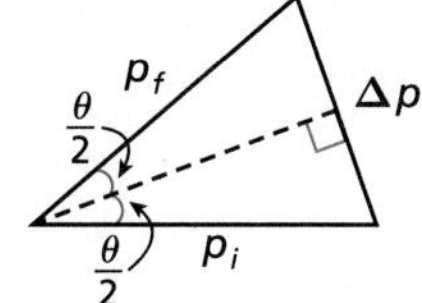

a. Use the diagram and the Pythagorean Theorem to write a formula for ΔP in terms of P_i. Then write a formula for ΔP in terms of P_f.

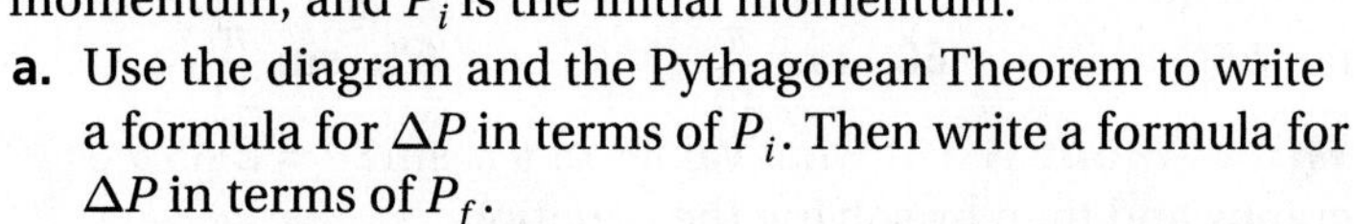

b. Compare your two answers to part **a.** What does this tell you about the magnitude, or size, of the momentum before and after the "collision"?

c. Write the formula for ΔP in terms of $\cos\theta$.

Prove each identity.

45. $\cos^2\frac{\theta}{2} = \frac{\sin^2\theta}{2(1-\cos\theta)}$

46. $\cos 2\theta = \frac{1-\tan^2\theta}{1+\tan^2\theta}$

47. $\frac{\tan\theta + \sin\theta}{2\tan\theta} = \cos^2\frac{\theta}{2}$

48. **Graphing Calculator** Graph $y = \frac{(\cos x)(1-\cos 2x)}{\sin 2x}$ to discover an identity. Then prove the identity.

49. **Multi-Step** A golf ball is hit with an initial velocity of v_0 in feet per second at an angle of elevation θ. The function $d(\theta) = \frac{{v_0}^2 \sin\theta\cos\theta}{16}$ gives the horizontal distance d in feet that the ball travels.

a. Rewrite the function in terms of the double angle 2θ.

b. Calculate the horizontal distance for an initial velocity of 80 ft/s for angles of 15°, 30°, 45°, 60°, and 75°.

c. For a given velocity, what angle gives the maximum horizontal distance?

d. **What if...?** If the initial velocity is 80 ft/s, through what approximate range of angles will the ball travel horizontally at least 175 ft?

50. **Critical Thinking** Explain how to find the exact value for $\sin 7.5°$.

51. **Write About It** How do you know when to use a double-angle or a half-angle identity?

TEST PREP

52. What is the value of $\sin 2\theta$ if $\cos\theta = -\frac{\sqrt{2}}{2}$ and $90° < \theta < 180°$?

Ⓐ $\frac{1}{2}$ Ⓑ $\frac{\sqrt{2}}{2}$ Ⓒ 1 Ⓓ −1

53. What is the value for $\cos 2\theta$ if $\sin\theta = \cos\theta$?

Ⓕ 0 Ⓖ 1 Ⓗ $2\sin^2\theta$ Ⓙ $2\cos^2\theta$

54. What is the value for $\sin\frac{\theta}{2}$ if $\cos\theta = -\frac{12}{13}$ and $90° < \theta < 180°$?

Ⓐ $\frac{\sqrt{26}}{26}$ Ⓑ $-\frac{\sqrt{26}}{26}$ Ⓒ $\frac{5\sqrt{26}}{26}$ Ⓓ $-\frac{5\sqrt{26}}{26}$

55. What is the exact value for $\sin 157.5°$?

Ⓕ $-\frac{\sqrt{2-\sqrt{2}}}{2}$ Ⓖ $\frac{\sqrt{2-\sqrt{2}}}{2}$ Ⓗ $-\frac{\sqrt{2+\sqrt{2}}}{2}$ Ⓙ $\frac{\sqrt{2+\sqrt{2}}}{2}$

56. **Short Response** Verify that $\frac{\cos 2\theta}{\sin\theta + \cos\theta} = \cos\theta - \sin\theta$ for $0 \le \theta \le \frac{\pi}{2}$. Show each step in your justification process.

CHALLENGE AND EXTEND

57. Derive the double-angle formula for $\tan 2\theta$ by using the ratio identity for tangent and the double-angle identities for sine and cosine.

58. Derive the half-angle formula for $\tan\frac{\theta}{2}$ by using the ratio identity for tangent.

Use half-angle identities to find the exact value of each expression.

59. $\tan 7.5°$ 60. $\tan\frac{\pi}{16}$ 61. $\sin\frac{\pi}{24}$ 62. $\cos 11.25°$

63. **Write About It** For what values of θ is $\sin 2\theta = 2\sin\theta$ true? Explain first by using graphs and then by solving the equation.

64. Derive the product-to-sum formulas $\sin A \sin B = \frac{1}{2}\left[\cos(A-B) - \cos(A+B)\right]$ and $\cos A \cos B = \frac{1}{2}\left[\cos(A+B) + \cos(A-B)\right]$ by using the angle sum and difference formulas.

SPIRAL REVIEW

Use the vertical-line test to determine whether each relation is a function. *(Lesson 1-6)*

65. 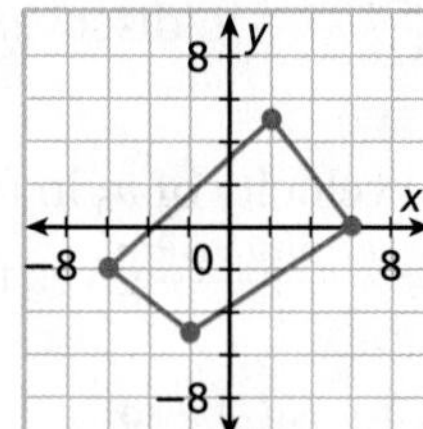

66. 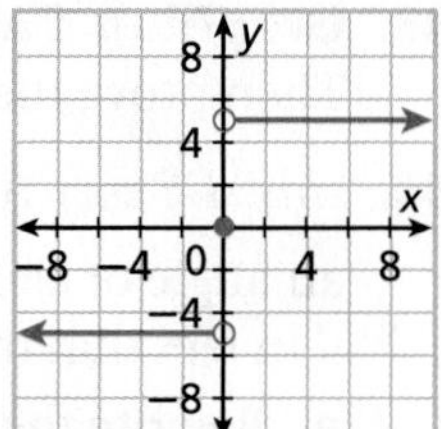

Add or subtract. Identify any x-values for which the expression is undefined. *(Lesson 8-3)*

67. $\frac{3x-2}{x+7} + \frac{2x+14}{x+7}$ 68. $\frac{4x-1}{x} + \frac{6x-2}{2x}$

69. $\frac{7x+4}{x+1} - \frac{5x+8}{x-3}$ 70. $\frac{x+9}{x^2} - \frac{x}{x+2}$

Find the exact value of each expression. *(Lesson 14-4)*

71. $\sin\left(-\frac{\pi}{12}\right)$ 72. $\sin 105°$ 73. $\cos\frac{7\pi}{12}$ 74. $\cos 255°$

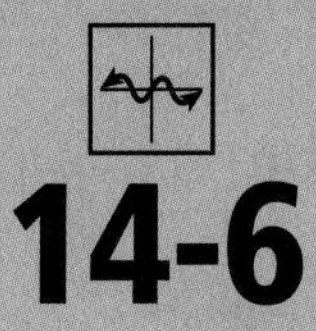

14-6 Solving Trigonometric Equations

Objectives
Solve equations involving trigonometric functions.

Why learn this?
You can use trigonometric equations to determine the day of the year that the sun will rise at a given time. (See Example 4.)

Unlike trigonometric identities, most trigonometric equations are true only for certain values of the variable, called *solutions*. To solve trigonometric equations, apply the same methods used for solving algebraic equations.

EXAMPLE 1 **Solving Trigonometric Equations with Infinitely Many Solutions**

Find all of the solutions of $3\tan\theta = \tan\theta + 2$.

Method 1 Use algebra.

Solve for θ over one cycle of the tangent, $-90° < \theta < 90°$.

$3\tan\theta = \tan\theta + 2$

$3\tan\theta - \tan\theta = 2$ — *Subtract $\tan\theta$ from both sides.*

$2\tan\theta = 2$ — *Combine like terms.*

$\tan\theta = 1$ — *Divide by 2.*

$\theta = \tan^{-1} 1$ — *Apply the inverse tangent.*

$\theta = 45°$ — *Find θ when $\tan\theta = 1$.*

Find all real number values of θ, where n is an integer.

$\theta = 45° + 180°n$ — *Use the period of the tangent function.*

Helpful Hint

Compare Example 1 with this solution:

$3x = x + 2$
$3x - x = 2$
$2x = 2$
$x = 1$

Method 2 Use a graph.

Graph $y = 3\tan\theta$ and $y = \tan\theta + 2$ in the same viewing window for $-90° \le \theta \le 90°$.

Use the intersect feature of your graphing calculator to find the points of intersection.

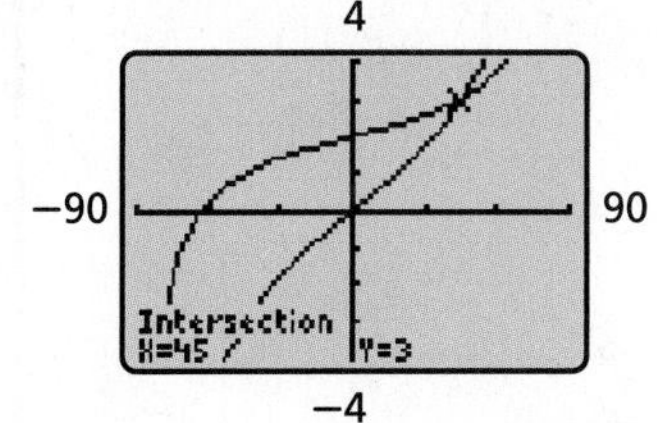

The graphs intersect at $\theta = 45°$. Thus, $\theta = 45° + 180°n$, where n is an integer.

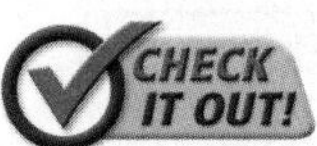

1. Find all of the solutions of $2\cos\theta + \sqrt{3} = 0$.

Some trigonometric equations can be solved by applying the same methods used for quadratic equations.

EXAMPLE 2 Solving Trigonometric Equations in Quadratic Form

Solve each equation for the given domain.

A $\sin^2\theta - 2\sin\theta = 3$ **for** $0 \le \theta < 2\pi$

$\sin^2\theta - 2\sin\theta - 3 = 0$ *Subtract 3 from both sides.*

$(\sin\theta + 1)(\sin\theta - 3) = 0$ *Factor the quadratic expression by comparing it with $x^2 - 2x - 3 = 0$.*

$\sin\theta = -1$ or $\sin\theta = 3$ *Apply the Zero Product Property.*

$\sin\theta = 3$ has no solution because $-1 \le \sin\theta \le 1$.

$\theta = \frac{3\pi}{2}$ *The only solution will come from $\sin\theta = -1$.*

B $\cos^2\theta + 2\cos\theta - 1 = 0$ **for** $0° \le \theta < 360°$

The equation is in quadratic form but cannot easily be factored. Use the Quadratic Formula.

$\cos\theta = \frac{-(2) \pm \sqrt{(2)^2 - 4(1)(-1)}}{2(1)}$ *Substitute 1 for a, 2 for b, and −1 for c.*

$\cos\theta = -1 \pm \sqrt{2}$ *Simplify.*

$-1 - \sqrt{2} < -1$ so $\cos\theta = -1 - \sqrt{2}$ has no solution.

$\theta = \cos^{-1}(-1 + \sqrt{2})$ *Apply the inverse cosine.*

$\approx 65.5°$ or $294.5°$ *Use a calculator. Find both angles for $0° \le \theta < 360°$.*

Caution!

A trigonometric equation may have zero, one, two, or an infinite number of solutions, depending on the equation and domain of θ.

Solve each equation for $0 \le \theta < 2\pi$.

2a. $\cos^2\theta + 2\cos\theta = 3$ **2b.** $\sin^2\theta + 5\sin\theta - 2 = 0$

You can often write trigonometric equations involving more than one function as equations of only one function by using trigonometric identities.

EXAMPLE 3 Solving Trigonometric Equations with Trigonometric Identities

Use trigonometric identities to solve each equation for $0 \le \theta < 2\pi$.

A $2\cos^2\theta = \sin\theta + 1$

$2(1 - \sin^2\theta) - \sin\theta - 1 = 0$ *Substitute $1 - \sin^2\theta$ for $\cos^2\theta$ by the Pythagorean identity.*

$-2\sin^2\theta - \sin\theta + 2 - 1 = 0$ *Simplify.*

$2\sin^2\theta + \sin\theta - 1 = 0$ *Multiply by −1.*

$(2\sin\theta - 1)(\sin\theta + 1) = 0$ *Factor.*

$\sin\theta = \frac{1}{2}$ or $\sin\theta = -1$ *Apply the Zero Product Property.*

$\theta = \frac{\pi}{6}$ or $\frac{5\pi}{6}$ or $\theta = \frac{3\pi}{2}$

Check Use the intersect feature of your graphing calculator. A graph supports your answer.

2

0 2π

0 $\frac{\pi}{6}$ $\frac{5\pi}{6}$ $\frac{3\pi}{2}$

Use trigonometric identities to solve each equation for $0° \le \theta < 360°$.

B $\cos 2\theta + 3\cos\theta + 2 = 0$

$2\cos^2\theta - 1 + 3\cos\theta + 2 = 0$ — *Substitute $2\cos^2\theta - 1$ for $\cos 2\theta$ by the double-angle identity.*

$2\cos^2\theta + 3\cos\theta + 1 = 0$ — *Combine like terms.*

$(2\cos\theta + 1)(\cos\theta + 1) = 0$ — *Factor.*

$\cos\theta = -\frac{1}{2}$ — *Apply the Zero Product Property.*

or

$\cos\theta = -1$

$\theta = 120°$ or $240°$ or $\theta = 180°$

Check Use the intersect feature of your graphing calculator. A graph supports your answer.

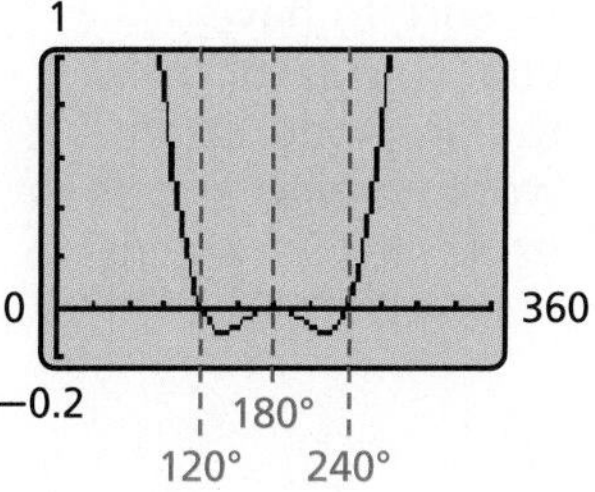

Use trigonometric identities to solve each equation for the given domain.

3a. $4\sin^2\theta + 4\cos\theta = 5$ for $0° \le \theta < 360°$

3b. $\sin 2\theta = -\cos\theta$ for $0 \le \theta < 2\pi$

EXAMPLE  4

Problem-Solving Application

The first sunrise in the United States each day is observed from Cadillac Mountain on Mount Desert Island in Maine. The time of the sunrise can be modeled by $t(m) = 1.665\sin\frac{\pi}{6}(m + 3) + 5.485$, where t is hours after midnight and m is the number of months after January 1. When does the sun rise at 7 A.M.?

1 Understand the Problem

The **answer** will be months of the year.

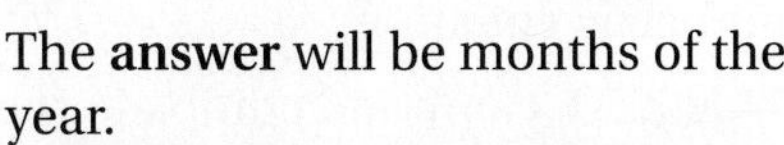

List the important information:

- The function model is $t(m) = 1.665\sin\frac{\pi}{6}(m + 3) + 5.485$.
- Sunrise is at 7 A.M., which is represented by $t = 7$.
- m represents the number of months after January 1.

2 Make a Plan

Substitute 7 for t in the model. Then solve the equation for m by using algebra.

Solve

$$7 = 1.665\sin\frac{\pi}{6}(m+3) + 5.485 \qquad \textit{Substitute 7 for t.}$$

$$\frac{7-5.485}{1.665} = \sin\frac{\pi}{6}(m+3) \qquad \textit{Isolate the sine term.}$$

$$\sin^{-1}(0.9\overline{099}) = \frac{\pi}{6}(m+3) \qquad \textit{Apply the inverse sine.}$$

Sine is positive in Quadrants I and II. Compute both values.

QI: $\sin^{-1}(0.9\overline{099}) = \frac{\pi}{6}(m+3)$

$$1.143 \approx \frac{\pi}{6}(m+3)$$

$$\left(\frac{6}{\pi}\right)1.143 \approx m+3$$

$$-0.817 \approx m$$

QII: $\pi - \sin^{-1}(0.9\overline{099}) = \frac{\pi}{6}(m+3)$

$$\pi - 1.143 \approx \frac{\pi}{6}(m+3)$$

$$\left(\frac{6}{\pi}\right)(\pi - 1.143) \approx m+3$$

$$0.817 \approx m$$

The value $m = 0.817$ corresponds to late January and the value $m = -0.817$ corresponds to early December.

Caution!

Be sure to have your calculator in radian mode when working with angles expressed in radians.

4 Look Back

Check your answer by using a graphing calculator. Enter $y = 1.665\sin\frac{\pi}{6}(x+3) + 5.485$ and $y = 7$. Graph the functions on the same viewing window, and find the points of intersection.

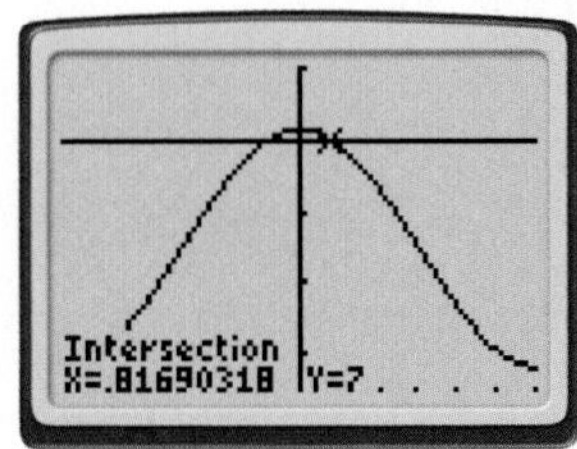

The graphs intersect at about 0.817 and −0.817.

4. The number of hours h of sunlight in a day at Cadillac Mountain can be modeled by $h(d) = 3.31\sin\frac{\pi}{182.5}(d - 85.25) + 12.22$, where d is the number of days after January 1. When are there 12 hours of sunlight?

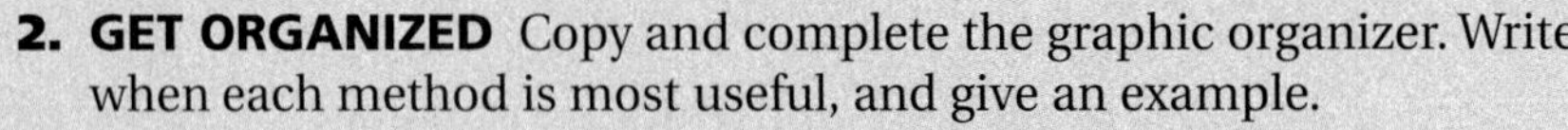

THINK AND DISCUSS

1. **DESCRIBE** the general procedure for finding all real-number solutions of a trigonometric equation.

2. **GET ORGANIZED** Copy and complete the graphic organizer. Write when each method is most useful, and give an example.

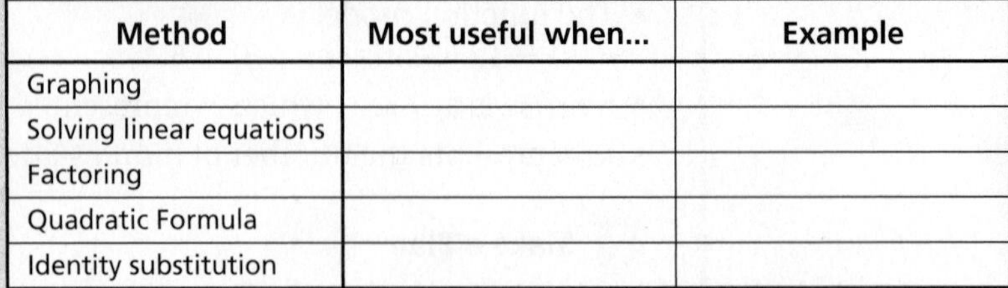

Method	Most useful when...	Example
Graphing		
Solving linear equations		
Factoring		
Quadratic Formula		
Identity substitution		

14-6 Exercises

go.hrw.com
Homework Help Online
KEYWORD: MB7 14-6
Parent Resources Online
KEYWORD: MB7 Parent

GUIDED PRACTICE

SEE EXAMPLE 1 p. 1027

Find all of the solutions of each equation.

1. $6\cos\theta - 1 = 2$
2. $2\sin\theta - \sqrt{3} = 0$
3. $\cos\theta = \sqrt{3} - \cos\theta$

SEE EXAMPLE 2 p. 1028

Solve each equation for the given domain.

4. $2\sin^2\theta + 3\sin\theta = -1$ for $0 \le \theta < 2\pi$
5. $\cos^2\theta - 4\cos\theta + 1 = 0$ for $0° \le \theta < 360°$

SEE EXAMPLE 3 p. 1028

Multi-Step **Use trigonometric identities to solve each equation for the given domain.**

6. $2\sin^2\theta - \cos 2\theta = 0$ for $0° \le \theta < 360°$
7. $\sin^2\theta + \cos\theta = -1$ for $0 \le \theta < 2\pi$

SEE EXAMPLE 4 p. 1029

8. **Heating** The amount of energy from natural gas used for heating a manufacturing plant is modeled by $E(m) = 350\sin\frac{\pi}{6}(m + 1.5) + 650$, where E is the energy used in dekatherms, and m is the month where $m = 0$ represents January 1. When is the gas usage 825 dekatherms? Assume an average of 30 days per month.

PRACTICE AND PROBLEM SOLVING

Independent Practice

For Exercises	See Example
9–12	1
13–14	2
15–16	3
17	4

Extra Practice

Skills Practice p. S31
Application Practice p. S45

Find all of the solutions of each equation.

9. $1 - 2\cos\theta = 0$
10. $\sqrt{3}\tan\theta - 3 = 0$
11. $2\cos\theta + \sqrt{3} = 0$
12. $2\sin\theta + 1 = 2 + \sin\theta$

Solve each equation for the given domain.

13. $2\cos^2\theta + \cos\theta - 1 = 0$ for $0 \le \theta < 2\pi$
14. $\sin^2\theta + 2\sin\theta - 2 = 0$ for $0° \le \theta < 360°$

Multi-Step **Use trigonometric identities to solve each equation for the given domain.**

15. $\cos 2\theta + \cos\theta + 1 = 0$ for $0° \le \theta < 360°$
16. $\cos 2\theta = \sin\theta$ for $0 \le \theta < 2\pi$
17. **Multi-Step** The amount of energy used by a large office building is modeled by $E(t) = 100\sin\frac{\pi}{12}(t - 8) + 800$, where E is the energy in kilowatt-hours, and t is the time in hours after midnight.
    a. During what time in the day is the electricity use 850 kilowatt-hours?
    b. When are the least and greatest amounts of electricity used? Are your answers reasonable? Explain.

Solve each equation algebraically for $0° \le \theta < 360°$.

18. $2\sin^2\theta = \sin\theta$
19. $2\cos^2\theta = \sin\theta + 1$
20. $\cos 2\theta - 2\sin\theta + 2 = 0$
21. $2\cos^2\theta + 3\sin\theta = 3$
22. $\cos^2\theta + \sin\theta - 1 = 0$
23. $2\sin^2\theta + \sin\theta = 0$

Solve each equation algebraically for $0 \le \theta < 2\pi$.

24. $\sin^2\theta - \sin\theta = 0$
25. $\cos^2\theta - 3\cos\theta = 4$
26. $\cos\theta(0.5 + \cos\theta) = 0$
27. $2\sin^2\theta - 3\sin\theta = 2$
28. $\cos^2\theta + \frac{1}{2}\cos\theta = 5$
29. $\sin^2\theta + 3\sin\theta + 3 = 0$
30. $\cos^2\theta + 4\cos\theta - 3 = 0$
31. $\tan^2\theta = \sqrt{3}\tan\theta$

32. **Sports** A baseball is thrown with an initial velocity of 96 feet per second at an angle θ degrees with a horizontal.

a. The horizontal range R in feet that the ball travels can be modeled by $R(\theta) = \frac{v^2 \sin 2\theta}{32}$. At what angle(s) with the horizontal will the ball travel 250 feet?

b. The maximum vertical height H_{max} in feet that the ball travels upward can be modeled by $H_{max}(\theta) = \frac{v^2 \sin^2 \theta}{64}$. At what angle(s) with the horizontal will the ball travel 50 feet?

Performing Arts

Traditional Japanese kabuki theaters were round and were able to be rotated to change scenes. The stages were also equipped with trapdoors and bridges that led through the audience.

33. **Performing Arts** A theater has a rotating stage that can be turned for different scenes. The stage has a radius of 18 feet, and the area in square feet of the segment of the circle formed by connecting two radii as shown is $A = \frac{r^2}{2}(\theta - \sin \theta)$, with θ in radians.

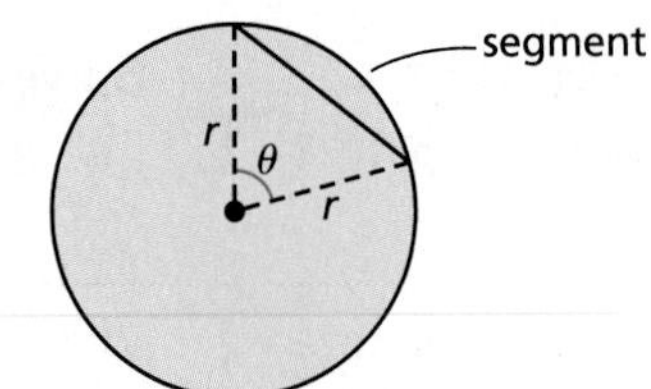

a. What angle gives a segment area of 92 square feet? How many such sets can simultaneously fit on the full rotating stage?

b. What angle gives a segment area of 50 square feet? About how many such sets can simultaneously fit on the full rotating stage?

34. **Oceanography** The height of the water on a certain day at a pier in Cape Cod, Massachusetts, can be modeled by $h(t) = 4.5 \sin \frac{\pi}{6.25}(t + 4) + 7.5$, where h is the height in feet and t is the time in hours after midnight.

a. On this particular day, when is the height of the water 5 feet?

b. How much time is there between high and low tides?

c. What is the period for the tide?

d. Does the cycle of tides fit evenly in a 24-hour day? Explain.

35. **/// ERROR ANALYSIS ///** Below are two solution procedures for solving $\sin^2 \theta - \frac{1}{2} \sin \theta = 0$ for $0° \le \theta < 360°$. Which is incorrect? Explain the error.

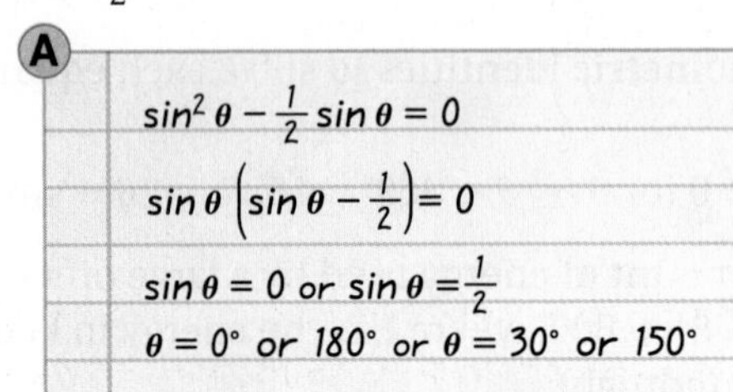
A

$\sin^2 \theta - \frac{1}{2} \sin \theta = 0$

$\sin \theta \left(\sin \theta - \frac{1}{2}\right) = 0$

$\sin \theta = 0$ or $\sin \theta = \frac{1}{2}$

$\theta = 0°$ or $180°$ or $\theta = 30°$ or $150°$

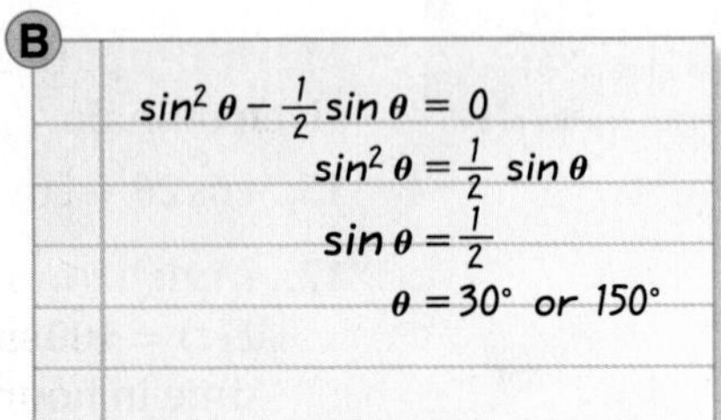
B

$\sin^2 \theta - \frac{1}{2} \sin \theta = 0$

$\sin^2 \theta = \frac{1}{2} \sin \theta$

$\sin \theta = \frac{1}{2}$

$\theta = 30°$ or $150°$

36. **Critical Thinking** What is the difference between a trigonometric equation and a trigonometric identity? Explain by using examples.

37. **Graphing Calculator** Use your graphing calculator to find all solutions of the equation $2 \cos x = 0.25x$.

MULTI-STEP TEST PREP

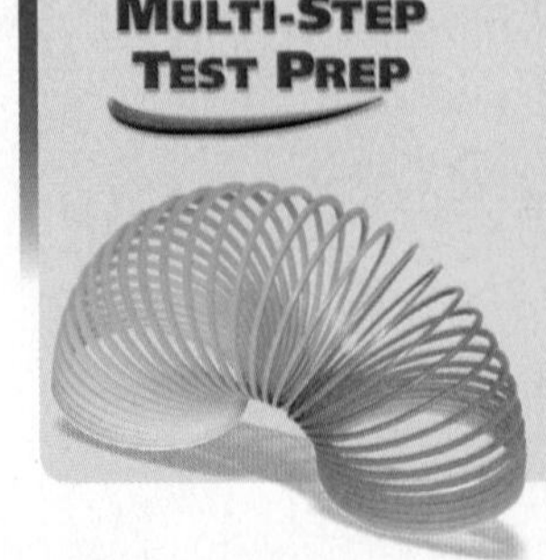

38. This problem will prepare you for the Multi-Step Test Prep on page 1034.

The displacement in centimeters of a mass attached to a spring is modeled by $y(t) = 2.9 \cos\left(\frac{2\pi}{3}t + \frac{\pi}{4}\right) + 3$, where t is the time in seconds.

a. What are the maximum and minimum displacements of the mass?

b. The mass is set in motion at $t = 0$. When is the displacement of the mass equal to 1 cm for the first time?

c. At what other times will the displacement be 1 cm?

Estimation Use a graphing calculator to approximate the solution to each equation to the nearest tenth of a degree for $0° \leq \theta < 360°$.

39. $\tan\theta - 12 = -1$

40. $\sin\theta + \cos\theta + 1.25 = 0$

41. $4\sin^2(2\theta - 30) = 4$

42. $\tan^2\theta + \tan\theta = 3$

43. $\sin^2\theta + 5\sin\theta = 3.5$

44. $\cos^2\theta - \cos 2\theta + 1 = 0$

45. Write About It How many solutions can a trigonometric equation have? Explain by using examples.

TEST PREP

46. Which values are solutions of $2\cos\theta + \sqrt{3} = 2\sqrt{3}$ for $0° \leq \theta < 360°$?

Ⓐ 30° or 150°

Ⓑ 30° or 330°

Ⓒ 60° or 120°

Ⓓ 60° or 320°

47. Which gives an approximate solution to $5\tan\theta - \sqrt{3} = \tan\theta$ for $-90° \leq \theta \leq 90°$?

Ⓕ −23.4°   Ⓖ −19.1°   Ⓗ 19.1°   Ⓙ 23.4°

48. Which value for θ is NOT a solution to $\sin^2\theta = \sin\theta$?

Ⓐ 0°   Ⓑ 90°   Ⓒ 180°   Ⓓ 270°

49. Which gives all of the solutions of $\cos\theta - 1 = -\frac{1}{2}$ for $0 \leq \theta < 2\pi$?

Ⓕ $\frac{2\pi}{3}$ or $\frac{5\pi}{3}$

Ⓖ $\frac{\pi}{3}$ or $\frac{2\pi}{3}$

Ⓗ $\frac{2\pi}{3}$ or $\frac{4\pi}{3}$

Ⓙ $\frac{\pi}{3}$ or $\frac{5\pi}{3}$

50. Which gives the solution to $\sin^2\theta - \sin\theta - 2 = 0$ for $0° \leq \theta < 360°$?

Ⓐ 90°

Ⓑ 270°

Ⓒ 90° or 270°

Ⓓ No solution

51. Short Response Solve $2\cos^2\theta + \cos\theta - 2 = 0$ algebraically. Show the steps in the solution process.

CHALLENGE AND EXTEND

Solve each equation algebraically for $0° \leq \theta < 360°$.

52. $9\cos^3\theta - \cos\theta = 0$

53. $4\cos^3\theta - \cos\theta = 0$

54. $16\sin^4\theta - 16\sin^2\theta + 3 = 0$

55. $\sin^2\theta - 4.5\sin\theta = 2.5$

56. $|\sin\theta| = \frac{1}{2}$

57. $|\cos\theta| = \frac{\sqrt{3}}{2}$

SPIRAL REVIEW

Order the given numbers from least to greatest. *(Lesson 1-1)*

58. $\frac{\sqrt{3}}{2}, -1, 0.8\overline{6}, 1, \frac{5}{6}$

59. $2\sqrt{5}, \frac{19}{4}, 4.\overline{47}, \sqrt{21}, \frac{\pi}{0.65}$

60. Technology An e-commerce company constructed a Web site for a local business. Each time a customer purchases a product on the Web site, the e-commerce company receives 5% of the sale. Write a function to represent the e-commerce company's revenue based on total website sales per day. What is the value of the function for an input of 259, and what does it represent? *(Lesson 1-7)*

Simplify each expression by writing it only in terms of θ. *(Lesson 14-5)*

61. $\cos 2\theta - 2\cos^2\theta$

62. $\frac{\sin 2\theta}{2\sin\theta}$

63. $\cos 2\theta + \sin^2\theta$

64. $\frac{\cos 2\theta + 1}{2}$

CHAPTER 14

MULTI-STEP TEST PREP

SECTION 14B

Trigonometric Identities

Spring into Action Simple harmonic motion refers to motion that repeats in a regular pattern. The bouncing motion of a mass attached to a spring is a good example of simple harmonic motion. As shown in the figure, the displacement y of the mass as a function of time t in seconds is a sine or cosine function. The amplitude is the distance from the center of the motion to either extreme. The period is the time that it takes to complete one full cycle of the motion.

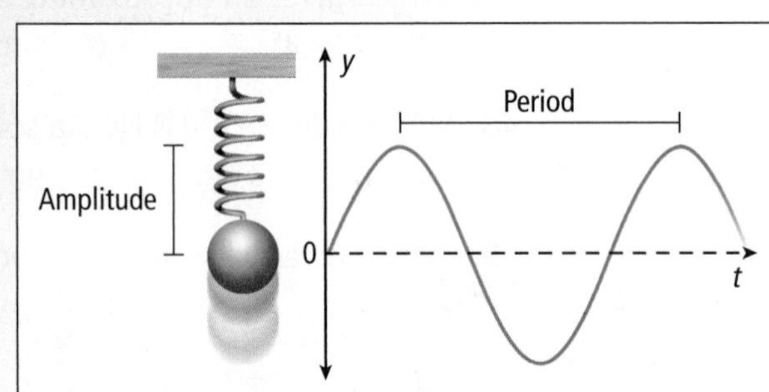

1. The displacement in inches of a mass attached to a spring is modeled by $y_1(t) = 3\sin\left(\frac{2\pi}{5}t + \frac{\pi}{2}\right)$, where t is the time in seconds. What is the amplitude of the motion? What is the period?
2. What is the initial displacement when $t = 0$ s? How long does it take until the displacement is 1.8 in.?
3. At what other times will the displacement be 1.8 in.?
4. Use trigonometric identities to write the displacement by using only the cosine function.
5. The displacement of a second mass attached to a spring is modeled by $y_2(t) = \sin\frac{2\pi}{5}t$. Both masses are set in motion at $t = 0$ s. How long does it take until both masses have the same displacement?
6. The displacement of a third mass attached to a spring is modeled by $y_3(t) = \cos\frac{\pi}{5}t$. The second and third masses are set in motion at $t = 0$ s. How long does it take until both masses have the same displacement?

READY TO GO ON?

CHAPTER 14

SECTION 14B

Quiz for Lessons 14-3 Through 14-6

14-3 Fundamental Trigonometric Identities

Prove each trigonometric identity.

1. $\sin^2\theta \sec\theta \csc\theta = \tan\theta$
2. $\sin(-\theta)\sec\theta\cot\theta = -1$
3. $\dfrac{\cot^2\theta - 1}{\cot^2\theta + 1} = 1 - 2\sin^2\theta$

Rewrite each expression in terms of a single trigonometric function.

4. $\cot\theta\sec\theta$
5. $\dfrac{1}{\cos(-\theta)}$
6. $\dfrac{\csc^2\theta}{\tan\theta + \cot\theta}$

14-4 Sum and Difference Identities

Find the exact value of each expression.

7. $\cos\dfrac{5\pi}{12}$
8. $\sin(-75°)$
9. $\tan 75°$

Find each value if $\sin A = \frac{1}{4}$ with $90° < A < 180°$ and if $\cos B = \frac{12}{13}$ with $270° < B < 360°$.

10. $\sin(A + B)$
11. $\cos(A + B)$
12. $\cos(A - B)$
13. Find the coordinates, to the nearest hundredth, of the vertices of figure $ABCD$ with $A(0, 0)$, $B(4, 1)$, $C(0, 2)$, and $D(-1, 1)$ after a 120° rotation about the origin.

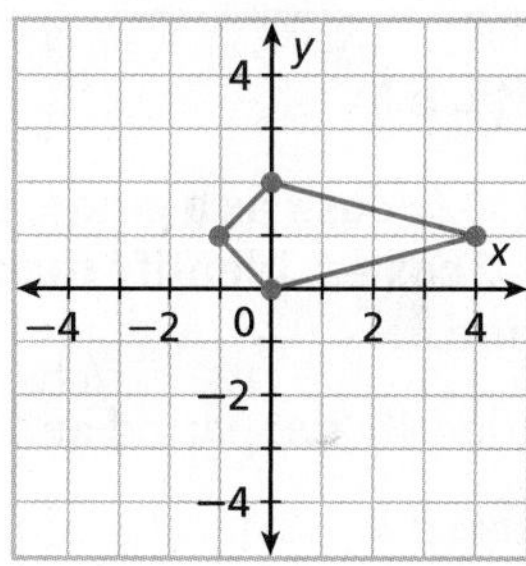

14-5 Double-Angle and Half-Angle Identities

Find each expression if $\cos\theta = -\frac{4}{5}$ and $180° < \theta < 270°$.

14. $\sin 2\theta$
15. $\cos 2\theta$
16. $\tan 2\theta$
17. $\sin\dfrac{\theta}{2}$
18. $\cos\dfrac{\theta}{2}$
19. $\tan\dfrac{\theta}{2}$
20. Use half-angle identities to find the exact value of cos 22.5°.

14-6 Solving Trigonometric Equations

21. Find all solutions of $1 + 2\sin\theta = 0$ where θ is in radians.

Solve each equation for $0° \le \theta < 360°$.

22. $\cos 2\theta + 2\cos\theta = 3$
23. $8\sin^2\theta - 2\sin\theta = 1$

Use trigonometric identities to solve each equation for $0 \le \theta < 2\pi$.

24. $\cos 2\theta = 3\cos\theta + 1$
25. $\sin^2\theta + \cos\theta + 1 = 0$
26. The average daily *minimum* temperature for Houston, Texas, can be modeled by $T(x) = -15.85\cos\frac{\pi}{6}(x - 1) + 76.85$, where T is the temperature in degrees Fahrenheit, x is the time in months, and $x = 0$ is January 1. When is the temperature 65°F? 85°F?

CHAPTER 14

Study Guide: Review

Vocabulary

Complete the sentences below with vocabulary words from the list above.

1. The shortest repeating portion of a periodic function is known as a(n) ___?___.
2. The number of cycles in a given unit of time is called ___?___.
3. The ___?___ gives the length of a complete cycle for a periodic function.
4. A horizontal translation of a periodic function is known as a(n) ___?___.

14-1 Graphs of Sine and Cosine *(pp. 990–997)*

EXAMPLES

■ **Using $f(x) = \cos x$ as a guide, graph $g(x) = -2\cos\frac{\pi}{2}x$. Identify the amplitude and period.**

Step 1 Identify the period and amplitude.

Because $a = -2$, amplitude is $|a| = |-2| = 2$.

Because $b = \frac{\pi}{2}$, the period is $\frac{2\pi}{|b|} = \frac{2\pi}{\left|\frac{\pi}{2}\right|} = 4$.

Step 2 Graph.

The curve is reflected over the x-axis.

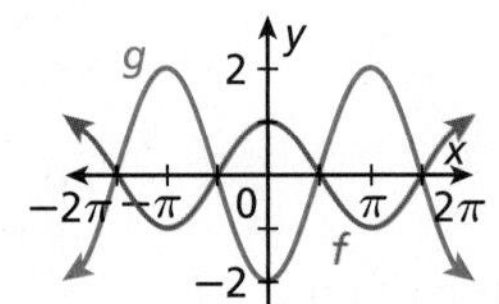

■ **Using $f(x) = \sin x$ as a guide, graph $g(x) = \sin\left(x - \frac{5\pi}{4}\right)$. Identify the x-intercepts and phase shift.**

The amplitude is 1. The period is 2π.

$-\frac{5\pi}{4}$ indicates a shift $\frac{5\pi}{4}$ units right.

The first x-intercept occurs at $\frac{\pi}{4}$. Thus, the intercepts occur at $\frac{\pi}{4} + n\pi$, where n is an integer.

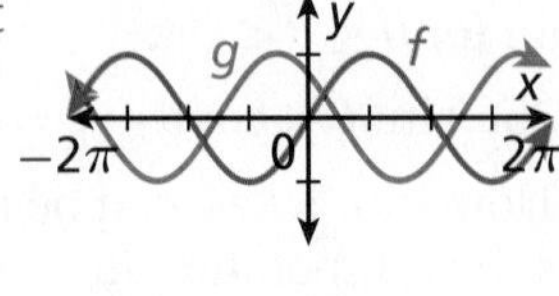

EXERCISES

Using $f(x) = \sin x$ or $f(x) = \cos x$ as a guide, graph each function. Identify the amplitude and period.

5. $f(x) = \cos 3x$
6. $g(x) = \cos\frac{1}{2}x$
7. $h(x) = -\frac{1}{3}\sin x$
8. $j(x) = 2\sin \pi x$
9. $f(x) = \frac{1}{2}\cos 2x$
10. $g(x) = \frac{\pi}{2}\sin \pi x$

Using $f(x) = \sin x$ or $f(x) = \cos x$ as a guide, graph each function. Identify the x-intercepts and phase shift.

11. $f(x) = \cos(x + \pi)$
12. $g(x) = \sin\left(x + \frac{\pi}{4}\right)$
13. $h(x) = \sin\left(x - \frac{3\pi}{2}\right)$
14. $j(x) = \cos\left(x + \frac{3\pi}{2}\right)$

Biology In photosynthesis, a plant converts carbon dioxide and water to sugar and oxygen. This process is studied by measuring a plant's carbon assimilation C (in micromoles of CO_2 per square meter per second). For a bean plant, $C(t) = 1.2\sin\frac{\pi}{12}(t - 6) + 7$, where t is time in hours starting at midnight.

15. Graph the function for two complete cycles.
16. What is the period of the function?
17. What is the maximum and at what time does it occur?

14-2 Graphs of Other Trigonometric Functions *(pp. 998–1003)*

EXAMPLE

- **Using $f(x) = \cot x$ as a guide, graph $g(x) = \cot\frac{\pi}{2}x$. Identify the period, x-intercepts, and asymptotes.**

Step 1 Identify the period.

Because $b = \frac{\pi}{2}$, the period is $\frac{\pi}{|b|} = \frac{\pi}{\left|\frac{\pi}{2}\right|} = 2$.

Step 2 Identify the x-intercepts.

The first x-intercept occurs at 1. Thus, the x-intercepts occur at $1 + 2n$, where n is an integer.

Step 3 Identify the asymptotes.

The asymptotes occur at $x = \frac{\pi n}{|b|} = \frac{\pi n}{\left|\frac{\pi}{2}\right|} = 2n$.

Step 4 Graph.

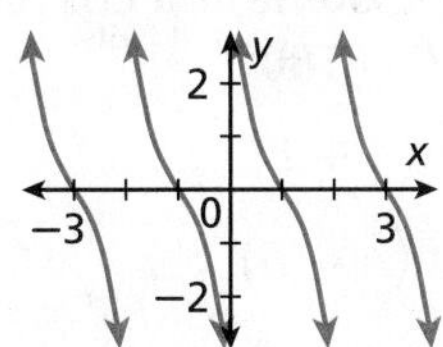

EXERCISES

Using $f(x) = \tan x$ or $f(x) = \cot x$ as a guide, graph each function. Identify the period, x-intercepts, and asymptotes.

18. $f(x) = \frac{1}{4}\tan x$
19. $g(x) = \tan \pi x$
20. $h(x) = \tan\frac{1}{2}\pi x$
21. $g(x) = 5\cot x$
22. $j(x) = -0.5\cot x$
23. $j(x) = \cot \pi x$

Using $f(x) = \cos x$ or $f(x) = \sin x$ as a guide, graph each function. Identify the period and asymptotes.

24. $f(x) = 2\sec x$
25. $g(x) = \csc 2x$
26. $h(x) = 4\csc x$
27. $j(x) = 0.2\sec x$
28. $h(x) = \sec(-x)$
29. $j(x) = -2\csc x$

14-3 Fundamental Trigonometric Identities *(pp. 1008–1013)*

EXAMPLES

- **Prove $\frac{\tan\theta}{1-\cos^2\theta} = \sec\theta\csc\theta$.**

$\frac{\left(\frac{\sin\theta}{\cos\theta}\right)}{(\sin^2\theta)} =$ *Modify the left side. Apply the ratio and Pythagorean identities.*

$\left(\frac{\sin\theta}{\cos\theta}\right)\left(\frac{1}{\sin^2\theta}\right) =$ *Multiply by the reciprocal.*

$\left(\frac{1}{\cos\theta}\right)\left(\frac{1}{\sin\theta}\right) =$ *Simplify.*

$\sec\theta\csc\theta$ *Reciprocal identities*

- **Rewrite $\frac{\cot\theta + \tan\theta}{\csc\theta}$ in terms of a single trigonometric function, and simplify.**

$(\cot\theta + \tan\theta)\sin\theta$ *Given.*

$\left(\frac{\cos\theta}{\sin\theta} + \frac{\sin\theta}{\cos\theta}\right)\sin\theta$ *Ratio identities*

$\frac{\cos^2\theta + \sin^2\theta}{\cos\theta}$ *Add fractions and simplify.*

$\frac{1}{\cos\theta} = \sec\theta$ *Pythagorean and reciprocal identities*

EXERCISES

Prove each trigonometric identity.

30. $\sec\theta\sin\theta\cot\theta = 1$
31. $\frac{\sin^2(-\theta)}{\tan\theta} = \sin\theta\cos\theta$
32. $(\sec\theta + 1)(\sec\theta - 1) = \tan^2\theta$
33. $\cos\theta\sec\theta + \cos^2\theta\csc^2\theta = \csc^2\theta$
34. $(\tan\theta + \cot\theta)^2 = \sec^2\theta + \csc^2\theta$
35. $\tan\theta + \cot\theta = \sec\theta\csc\theta$
36. $\sin^2\theta\tan\theta = \tan\theta - \sin\theta\cos\theta$
37. $\frac{\tan\theta}{1-\cos^2\theta} = \sec\theta\csc\theta$

Rewrite each expression in terms of a single trigonometric function, and simplify.

38. $\cot\theta\sec\theta$
39. $\frac{\sec\theta\sin\theta}{\cot\theta}$
40. $\frac{\tan(-\theta)}{\cot\theta}$
41. $\frac{\cos\theta\cot\theta}{\csc^2\theta - 1}$

14-4 Sum and Difference Identities (pp. 1014–1019)

EXAMPLES

■ **Find $\sin(A+B)$ if $\cos A = -\frac{1}{3}$ with $180° < A < 270°$ and if $\sin B = \frac{4}{5}$ with $90° < B < 180°$.**

Step 1 Find $\sin A$ and $\cos B$ by using the Pythagorean Theorem with reference triangles.

$180° < A < 270°$ $90° < B < 180°$

$\cos A = -\frac{1}{3}$ $\sin B = \frac{4}{5}$

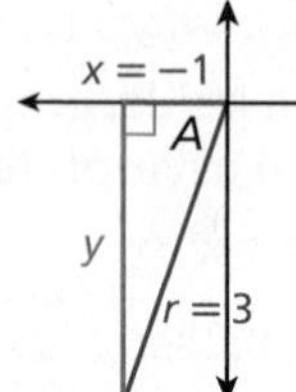

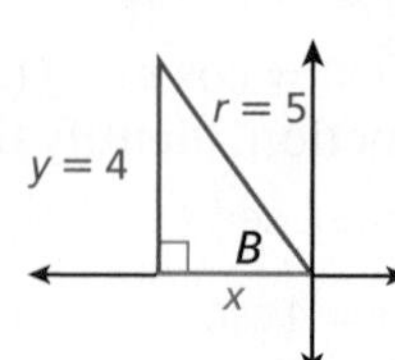

$y = -\sqrt{8}$, $\sin A = \frac{-\sqrt{8}}{3}$ $x = -3$, $\cos B = \frac{-3}{5}$

Step 2 Use the angle-sum identity.

$$\begin{aligned}\sin(A+B) &= \sin A\cos B + \cos A \sin B\\ &= \left(\frac{-\sqrt{8}}{3}\right)\left(\frac{-3}{5}\right) + \left(-\frac{1}{3}\right)\left(\frac{4}{5}\right)\\ &= \frac{3\sqrt{8}-4}{15}\end{aligned}$$

■ **Find the coordinates to the nearest hundredth of the vertices of figure ABC with $A(0, 2)$, $B(1, 2)$, and $C(0, 1)$ after a 60° rotation about the origin.**

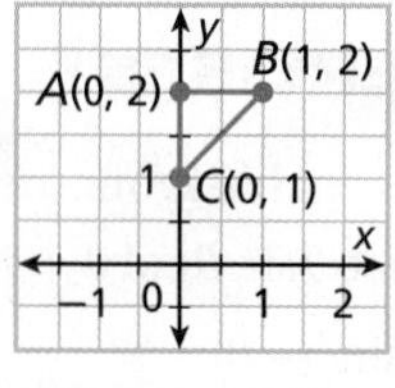

Step 1 Write matrices for a 60° rotation and for the points in the figure.

$$R_{60°} = \begin{bmatrix}\cos 60° & -\sin 60°\\ \sin 60° & \cos 60°\end{bmatrix}$$ *Rotation matrix*

$$S = \begin{bmatrix}0 & 1 & 0\\ 2 & 2 & 1\end{bmatrix}$$ *Matrix of points*

Step 2 Find the matrix product.

$$R_{60°} \times S = \begin{bmatrix}\cos 60° & -\sin 60°\\ \sin 60° & \cos 60°\end{bmatrix}\begin{bmatrix}0 & 1 & 0\\ 2 & 2 & 1\end{bmatrix}$$

$$\approx \begin{bmatrix}-1.73 & -1.23 & -0.87\\ 1 & 1.87 & 0.5\end{bmatrix}$$

Step 3 The approximate coordinates of the points after a 60° rotation are $A'(-1.73, 1)$, $B'(-1.23, 1.87)$, and $C'(-0.87, 0.5)$.

EXERCISES

Find the exact value of each expression.

42. $\sin\frac{19\pi}{12}$ **43.** $\cos 165°$

44. $\cos 15°$ **45.** $\tan\frac{\pi}{12}$

Find each value if $\tan A = \frac{3}{4}$ with $0° < A < 90°$ and if $\tan B = -\frac{5}{12}$ with $90° < B < 180°$.

46. $\sin(A+B)$ **47.** $\cos(A+B)$

48. $\tan(A-B)$ **49.** $\tan(A+B)$

50. $\sin(A-B)$ **51.** $\cos(A-B)$

Find each value if $\sin A = \frac{\sqrt{7}}{4}$ with $0° < A < 90°$ and if $\cos B = -\frac{5}{13}$ with $90° < B < 180°$.

52. $\sin(A+B)$ **53.** $\cos(A+B)$

54. $\tan(A-B)$ **55.** $\tan(A+B)$

56. $\sin(A-B)$ **57.** $\cos(A-B)$

Find the coordinates, to the nearest hundredth, of the vertices of figure $ABCD$ with $A(0, 0)$, $B(3, 0)$, $C(4, 2)$, and $D(1, 2)$ after each rotation about the origin.

58. 30° rotation   **59.** 45° rotation

60. 60° rotation   **61.** 90° rotation

Find the coordinates, to the nearest hundredth, of the vertices of figure $ABCD$ with $A(0, 0)$, $B(5, 2)$, $C(0, 4)$, and $D(-5, 2)$ after each rotation about the origin.

62. 120° rotation   **63.** 180° rotation

64. 240° rotation   **65.** 270° rotation

14-5 Double-Angle and Half-Angle Identities *(pp. 1020–1026)*

EXAMPLES

Find each expression if $\sin\theta = \frac{1}{4}$ and $270° < \theta < 360°$.

- $\sin 2\theta$

For $\sin\theta = \frac{1}{4}$ in QIV, $\cos\theta = -\frac{\sqrt{15}}{4}$.

$\sin 2\theta = 2\sin\theta\cos\theta$ *Identity for $\sin 2\theta$*

$= 2\left(\frac{1}{4}\right)\left(-\frac{\sqrt{15}}{4}\right) = -\frac{\sqrt{15}}{8}$ *Substitute.*

- $\cos\frac{\theta}{2}$

$\cos\frac{\theta}{2} = \pm\sqrt{\frac{1+\cos\theta}{2}}$ *Identity for $\cos\frac{\theta}{2}$*

$= -\sqrt{\frac{1+\left(-\frac{\sqrt{15}}{4}\right)}{2}}$ *Negative for $\cos\frac{\theta}{2}$ in QII*

$= -\sqrt{\left(\frac{4-\sqrt{15}}{4}\right)\left(\frac{1}{2}\right)} = -\frac{\sqrt{4-\sqrt{15}}}{\sqrt{8}}$

EXERCISES

Find each expression if $\tan\theta = \frac{4}{3}$ and $0° < \theta < 90°$.

66. $\sin 2\theta$
67. $\cos 2\theta$
68. $\tan\frac{\theta}{2}$
69. $\sin\frac{\theta}{2}$

Find each expression if $\cos\theta = \frac{3}{4}$ and $\frac{3\pi}{2} < \theta < 2\pi$.

70. $\tan 2\theta$
71. $\cos 2\theta$
72. $\cos\frac{\theta}{2}$
73. $\sin\frac{\theta}{2}$

Use half-angle identities to find the exact value of each trigonometric expression.

74. $\sin\frac{\pi}{12}$
75. $\cos 75°$

14-6 Solving Trigonometric Equations *(pp. 1027–1033)*

EXAMPLES

- **Find all of the solutions of $3\cos\theta - \sqrt{3} = \cos\theta$.**

$3\cos\theta - \sqrt{3} = \cos\theta$

$3\cos\theta - \cos\theta = \sqrt{3}$ *Subtract $\tan\theta$.*

$2\cos\theta = \sqrt{3}$ *Combine like terms.*

$\cos\theta = \frac{\sqrt{3}}{2}$ *Divide by 2.*

$\theta = \cos^{-1}\left(\frac{\sqrt{3}}{2}\right)$ *Apply the inverse cosine.*

$\theta = 30°$ or $330°$ *Find θ for $0° \le \theta < 360°$.*

$\theta = 30° + 360°n$

or $330° + 360°n$

- **Solve $6\sin^2\theta + 5\sin\theta = -1$ for $0° \le \theta < 360°$.**

$6\sin^2\theta + 5\sin\theta + 1 = 0$ *Set equal to 0.*

$(2\sin\theta + 1)(3\sin\theta + 1) = 0$ *Factor.*

$\sin\theta = -1$ or $\sin\theta = 3$ *Zero Product Property*

$\theta = 210°, 330°$

or $\approx 199.5°, 340.5°$ *$\sin\theta = 3$ has no solution since $-1 \le \sin\theta \le 1$.*

EXERCISES

Find all of the solutions of each equation.

76. $\sqrt{2}\cos\theta + 1 = 0$
77. $\cos\theta = 2 + 3\cos\theta$
78. $\tan^2\theta + \tan\theta = 0$
79. $\sin^2\theta - \cos^2\theta = \frac{1}{2}$

Solve each equation for $0 \le \theta < 2\pi$.

80. $2\cos^2\theta - 3\cos\theta = 2$
81. $\cos^2\theta + 5\cos\theta - 6 = 0$
82. $\sin^2\theta - 1 = 0$
83. $2\sin^2\theta - \sin\theta = 3$

Use trigonometric identities to solve each equation for $0 \le \theta < 2\pi$.

84. $\cos 2\theta = \cos\theta$
85. $\sin 2\theta + \cos\theta = 0$

86. Earth Science The number of minutes of daylight for each day of the year can be modeled with a trigonometric function. For Washington, D.C., S is the number of minutes of daylight in the model $S(d) = 180\sin(0.0172d - 1.376) + 720$, where d is the number of days since January 1.

a. What is the maximum number of daylight minutes, and when does it occur?

b. What is the minimum number of daylight minutes, and when does it occur?

CHAPTER 14

Chapter Test

1. Using $f(x) = \cos x$ as a guide, graph $g(x) = \frac{1}{2}\cos 2x$. Identify the amplitude and period.
2. Using $f(x) = \sin x$ as a guide, graph $g(x) = \sin\left(x + \frac{\pi}{3}\right)$. Identify the x-intercepts and phase shift.
3. A torque τ in newton meters (N•m) applied to an object is given by $\tau(\theta) = Fr\sin\theta$, where r is the length of the lever arm in meters, F is the applied force in newtons, and θ is the angle between F and r in degrees. Find the amount and angle for the maximum torque and the minimum torque for a lever arm of 0.5 m and a force of 500 newtons, where $0° \le \theta \le 90°$.
4. Using $f(x) = \tan x$ as a guide, graph $g(x) = 2\tan \pi x$. Identify the period, x-intercepts, and asymptotes.
5. Using $f(x) = \cot x$ as a guide, graph $g(x) = \cot 4x$. Identify the period, x-intercepts, and asymptotes.
6. Using $f(x) = \sin x$ as a guide, graph $g(x) = \frac{1}{4}\csc x$. Identify the period and asymptotes.
7. Prove the trigonometric identity $\cot\theta = \cos^2\theta\sec\theta\csc\theta$.

Rewrite each expression in terms of a single trigonometric function.

8. $(\sec\theta + 1)(\sec\theta - 1)$
9. $\dfrac{\sin(-\theta)}{\cos(-\theta)}$

Find each value if $\tan A = \frac{3}{4}$ with $0° < A < 90°$ and if $\sin B = -\frac{12}{13}$ with $180° < B < 270°$.

10. $\sin(A + B)$
11. $\cos(A - B)$
12. Find the coordinates, to the nearest hundredth, of the vertices of figure $ABCD$ with $A(0, 1)$, $B(2, 1)$, $C(3, 3)$, and $D(-1, 3)$ after a 30° rotation about the origin.

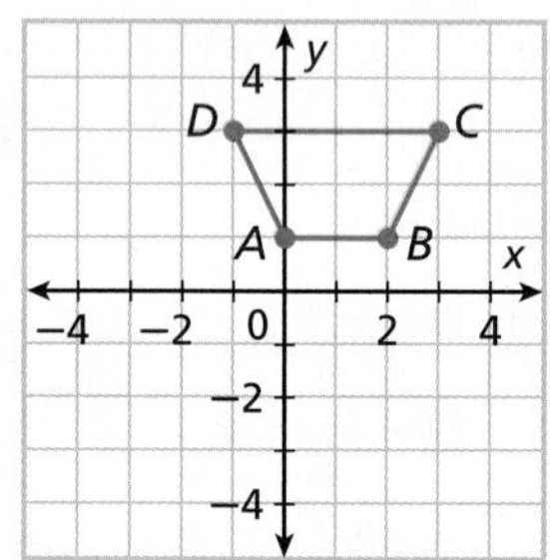

Find each expression if $\tan\theta = -\frac{12}{5}$ and $90° < \theta < 180°$.

13. $\sin 2\theta$
14. $\cos 2\theta$
15. $\cos\dfrac{\theta}{2}$
16. Use half-angle identities to find the exact value of $\sin\dfrac{3\pi}{8}$.
17. Find all of the solutions of $\tan\theta + \sqrt{3} = 0$.
18. Solve $2\sin^2\theta = \sin\theta$ for $0° \le \theta < 360°$.
19. Use trigonometric identities to solve $2\cos^2\theta + 3\sin\theta = 0$ for $0 \le \theta < 2\pi$.
20. The voltage at a wall plug in a home can be modeled by $V(t) = 156\sin 2\pi(60t)$, where V is the voltage in volts and t is time in seconds. At what times is the voltage equal to 110 volts?

College Entrance Exam Practice

CHAPTER 14

FOCUS ON SAT MATHEMATICS SUBJECT TESTS

To help decide which standardized tests you should take, make a list of colleges that you might like to attend. Find out the admission requirements for each school. Make sure that you register for and take the appropriate tests early enough for colleges to receive your scores.

If your calculator malfunctions while you are taking an SAT Mathematics Subject Test, you may be able to have your score for that test canceled. To do so, you must inform a supervisor at the test center immediately when the malfunction occurs.

You may want to time yourself as you take this practice test. It should take you about 6 minutes to complete.

1. Identify the range of $f(x) = 3\sin x$.

(A) $-1 \leq f(x) \leq 1$

(B) $-3 < f(x) < 3$

(C) $0 \leq f(x) \leq 3$

(D) $-3 \leq f(x) \leq 3$

(E) $-\infty < f(x) < \infty$

2. If $2\sin^2\theta + 5\sin\theta = 3$, what could the value of θ be?

(A) $\frac{\pi}{6}$

(B) $\frac{\pi}{3}$

(C) $\frac{2\pi}{3}$

(D) $\frac{7\pi}{6}$

(E) $\frac{11\pi}{6}$

3. If $\sec\theta = 4$, what is $\tan^2\theta$?

(A) $\frac{1}{16}$

(B) 3

(C) 5

(D) 15

(E) 17

4. Given the figure, what is the value of $\cos(A - B)$?

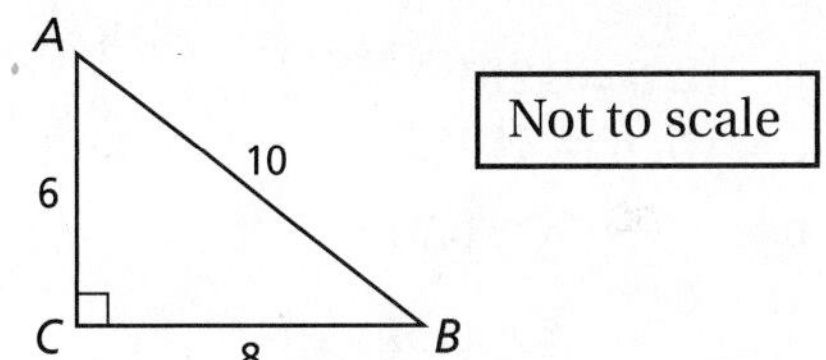

(A) 0

(B) $\frac{7}{25}$

(C) $\frac{24}{25}$

(D) 1

(E) $\frac{28}{25}$

5. If $\sin\theta = \frac{7}{9}$, what is $\cos 2\theta$?

(A) $-\frac{8\sqrt{2}}{9}$

(B) $-\frac{17}{81}$

(C) $\frac{17}{81}$

(D) $\frac{56\sqrt{2}}{81}$

(E) $\frac{8\sqrt{2}}{9}$

CHAPTER 14

TEST TACKLER

Standardized Test Strategies

Multiple Choice: Choose Answer Combinations

You may be given a test item in which you are asked to choose from a combination of statements. To answer these types of test items, try comparing each given statement with the question and determining whether the statement is true or false. If you determine that more than one of the statements is correct, choose the combination that contains each correct statement.

EXAMPLE 1

Which exact solution makes the equation $2\cos^2\theta - 3\cos\theta = 2$ true?

I. $\theta = 2°$
II. $\theta = 120°$
III. $\theta = 240°$

Look at each statement separately, and determine if it is true or false.

Ⓐ I only
Ⓑ II and III
Ⓒ II only
Ⓓ I, II, and III

As you consider each statement, mark it true or false.

Consider statement I: Substitute 2° for θ in the equation.

$$2\cos^2(2°) - 3\cos(2°) \approx -1.0006$$
$$\neq 2$$

Statement I is false.
So, the answer is ***not*** choice A or D.

Consider statement II: Substitute 120° for θ in the equation.

$$2\cos^2(120°) - 3\cos(120°) = 2$$

Statement II is true.
The answer *could be* choice B or C.

Consider statement III: Substitute 240° for θ in the equation.

$$2\cos^2(240°) - 3\cos(240°) = 2$$

Statement III is true.

Because both statements II and III are true, choice B is the correct response.

You can also use a table to keep track of whether the statements are true or false.

Statement	True/False
I	False
II	True
III	True

As you eliminate a statement, cross out the corresponding answer choice(s).

Read each test item and answer the questions that follow.

Item A

Which expression is equivalent to $\tan^2\theta$?

I. $\sec^2\theta - 1$

II. $\sec^2\theta + 1$

III. $\dfrac{1}{\csc^2\theta - 1}$

IV. $\dfrac{1-\cos^2\theta}{1-\sin^2\theta}$

(A) I and II

(B) II and III

(C) I and III

(D) I, III, and IV

1. What are some of the identities that involve the tangent function?
2. Determine whether statements I, II, III, and IV are true or false. Explain your reasoning.
3. Sally realized that statement III was true and selected choice B as her response. Do you agree? If not, what would you have done differently?

Item B

For the graph of $f(x) = 3\sin x + 2$, which of the statements are true?

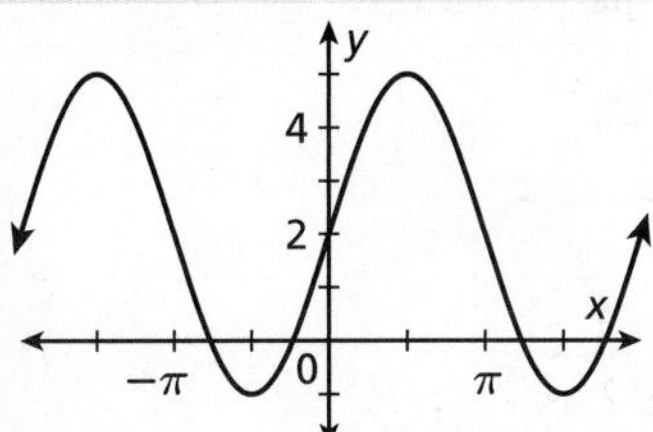

I. The function has a period of $\frac{2\pi}{3}$.

II. The function has an amplitude of 3.

III. The function has a period of 2π.

(F) I only

(G) III only

(H) II only

(J) II and III

4. How do you determine the period of a trigonometric function?
5. How do you determine the amplitude of a trigonometric function?
6. Using your response to Problems 4 and 5, which of the three statements are true? Explain.

Item C

Which identities do you need to use to prove that $\tan\theta\csc\theta = \sec\theta$?

I. $\tan\theta = \dfrac{\sin\theta}{\cos\theta}$

II. $\sec^2\theta = \tan^2\theta + 1$

III. $\csc\theta = \dfrac{1}{\sin\theta}$

(A) I only

(B) II only

(C) I and II

(D) I and III

7. Is statement I true or false? Can any answer choice be eliminated? Explain.
8. Is statement II true or false? Should you select the answer choice yet? Explain.
9. Is statement III true or false? Explain.
10. Which combination of statements is correct? How do you know?

Item D

For the graph of the function $f(x) = \sec 4x$, which are equations of some of the asymptotes?

I. $x = \dfrac{\pi}{8}$

II. $x = \dfrac{\pi}{2}$

III. $x = -\dfrac{3\pi}{4}$

(F) I only

(G) II and III

(H) I, II, and III

(J) I and III

11. Create a table, and determine whether each statement is true or false.
12. Using your table, which choice is the most accurate?

CHAPTER 14

STANDARDIZED TEST PREP

go.hrw.com
State Test Practice Online
KEYWORD: MB7 TestPrep

CUMULATIVE ASSESSMENT, CHAPTERS 1–14

Multiple Choice

1. What is the exact value of tan 15°?

Ⓐ $\frac{\sqrt{6}-\sqrt{2}}{4}$

Ⓑ $\frac{\sqrt{6}+\sqrt{2}}{4}$

Ⓒ $2+\sqrt{3}$

Ⓓ $2-\sqrt{3}$

2. Where do the asymptotes occur in the given equation?

$y = \frac{1}{3}\cot 2x$

Ⓕ $2\pi n$

Ⓖ $\frac{\pi n}{2}$

Ⓗ $3\pi n$

Ⓙ $\frac{\pi n}{3}$

3. What is the period of the given equation?

$y = 5\cos\frac{1}{3}x$

Ⓐ $\frac{2\pi}{5}$

Ⓑ $\frac{5}{3}$

Ⓒ $\frac{2\pi}{3}$

Ⓓ 6π

4. A movie has 14 dialogue scenes and 10 action scenes. If these are the only two types of scenes, what is the probability that a randomly selected scene will be an action scene?

Ⓕ $\frac{5}{12}$

Ⓖ $\frac{7}{12}$

Ⓗ $\frac{5}{7}$

Ⓙ $\frac{7}{5}$

5. What is the value of $f(x) = 3x^3 + 4x^2 + 7x + 10$ for $x = -2$?

Ⓐ −44

Ⓑ −12

Ⓒ 0

Ⓓ 36

6. Which graph shows an inverse variation function for which $y = 2$ when $x = -1$?

Ⓕ
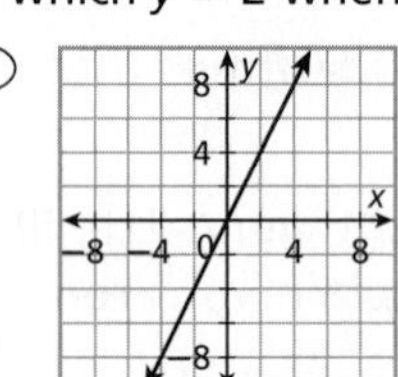

Ⓗ
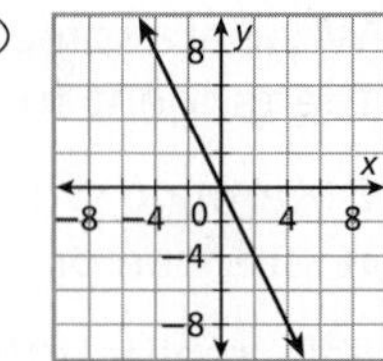

Ⓖ
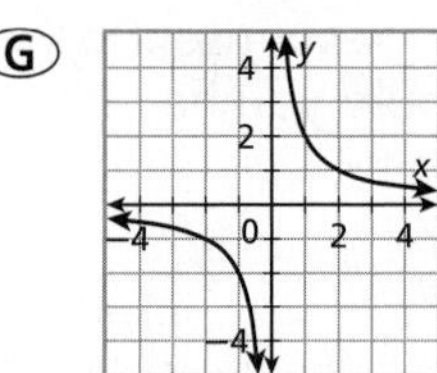

Ⓙ
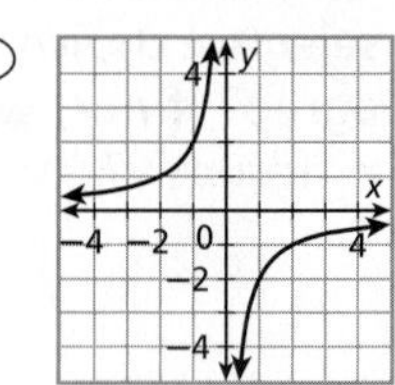

7. What is the exact value of cos157.5° using half-angle identities?

Ⓐ $-\frac{\sqrt{2-\sqrt{2}}}{2}$

Ⓑ $\frac{\sqrt{2-\sqrt{2}}}{2}$

Ⓒ $-\frac{\sqrt{2+\sqrt{2}}}{2}$

Ⓓ $\frac{\sqrt{2+\sqrt{2}}}{2}$

8. What type of function is $f(x) = -2x^3 - x + 10$?

Ⓕ cubic

Ⓖ exponential

Ⓗ quadratic

Ⓙ rational

9. Which is a solution of $2\cos\theta = 2\sin\theta$ for $\pi \le \theta \le 3\pi$?

Ⓕ $\frac{\pi}{4}$

Ⓖ π

Ⓗ $\frac{5\pi}{4}$

Ⓙ 3π

10. Which is the equation of a circle with center $(3, 2)$ and radius 5?

Ⓐ $25 = (x - 3)^2 + (y - 2)^2$

Ⓑ $5 = (x - 3)^2 + (y - 2)^2$

Ⓒ $25 = (x + 3)^2 + (y + 2)^2$

Ⓓ $5 = (x + 3)^2 + (y + 2)^2$

Gridded Response

11. What is the value of x?

$5\sqrt{2x - 7} + 4 = 9$

12. What is the value of $\cos\theta$? Round to the nearest thousandth.

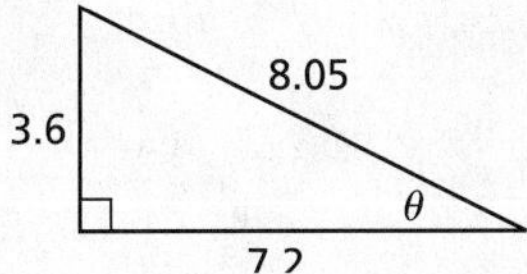

In Item 13, the answer will be a *y*-value only. It will be quickest and most efficient to isolate *x* in one equation and substitute for *x* in the second equation because then the first variable for which you obtain a value will be *y*.

13. What is the y-value of the solution of the following system of nonlinear equations?

$$\begin{cases} x - 4 = \frac{1}{4}y^2 \\ \frac{(x + 1)^2}{25} + \frac{y^2}{36} = 1 \end{cases}$$

14. Find the sum of the arithmetic series $\sum_{k=1}^{14}(3k - 5)$.

Short Response

15. The chart below shows the names of the students on the academic bowl team.

Robin	Drew	Jim
Greg	Sarah	Mindy
Ashley	Tina	Justin
David	Amy	Kevin

a. Only 2 students can be chosen for the final academic bowl. How many different ways can the students be selected?

b. Explain why you solved the problem the way that you did.

16. Given the sequence:

4, 12, 36, 108, 324, ...

a. Write the explicit rule for the nth term.

b. Find the 10th term.

Extended Response

17. The chart below shows the grades in Mr. Bradshaw's class.

90	85	72	86	94	96
85	95	94	68	71	85
93	98	84	83	80	89

Round each answer to the nearest tenth.

a. Find the mean.

b. Find the median.

c. Find the mode.

d. Find the variance.

e. Find the standard deviation.

f. Find the range.

The Rock and Roll Hall of Fame

The Rock and Roll Hall of Fame in downtown Cleveland traces the history of rock music through live performances and interactive exhibits. Designed by renowned architect I. M. Pei, the 50,000-square-foot exhibition space houses everything from vintage posters to handwritten lyrics to John Lennon's report card.

Choose one or more strategies to solve each problem.
For 1 and 2, use the diagram.

1. Visitors enter the museum through an enormous glass entryway in the shape of a tetrahedron. The figure shows the dimensions of the tetrahedron. What is the pitch of the tetrahedron's slanted facade? (*Hint:* The pitch is shown in the figure by angle θ.)

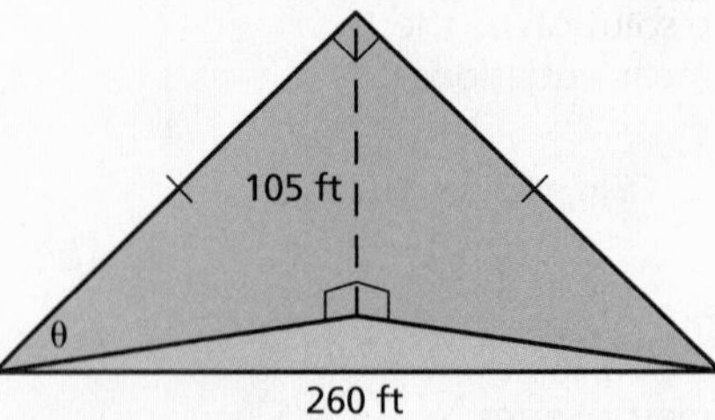

2. What is the area of the triangular floor space enclosed by the glass tetrahedron?
3. The Hall of Fame exhibits are displayed in an eight-story, 162-foot tower. Pei originally designed a 200-foot tower but had to reduce its height in order to meet the requirements of a nearby airport. From the top of the existing tower, an observer sights the entrance to the museum's plaza with an angle of depression of 18°. What would be the angle of depression to the entrance of the plaza from Pei's original tower?

Marblehead Lighthouse

Since its construction in 1821, Marblehead Lighthouse has stood at the entrance to Sandusky Bay, guiding sailors along Lake Erie's rocky shores. The 65-foot tower is one of Ohio's best-known landmarks and the oldest continuously operating lighthouse on the Great Lakes.

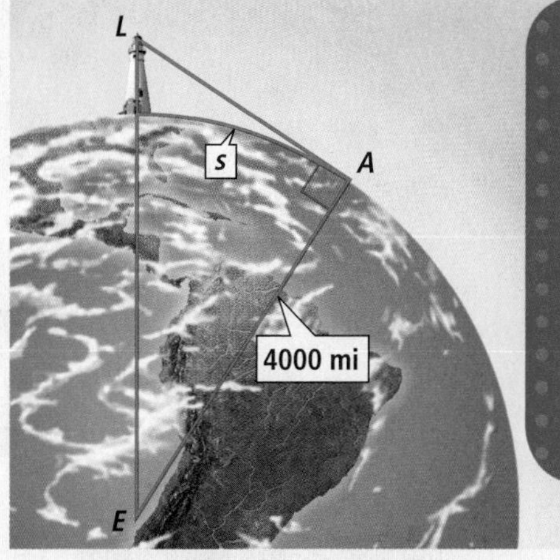

Choose one or more strategies to solve each problem.

1. The range of a lighthouse is the maximum distance at which its light is visible. In the figure, point A is the farthest point from which it is possible to see the light at the top of the lighthouse L. The distance along Earth s is the range. Assuming that the radius of Earth is 4000 miles, find the range of Marblehead Lighthouse.

2. In 1897, a new lighting system was installed in the lighthouse. A set of descending weights rotated the tower's lantern to produce a flashing light. The rotation could be modeled by the function $f(x) = \sin \frac{\pi}{5}x$, where x is the time in seconds since the weights were released. The light briefly flashed on whenever $f(x) = 1$. How many times per minute did the light flash?

3. Today the flashing light of Marblehead Lighthouse can be modeled by $g(x) = \sin \frac{\pi}{3}x$. How many seconds are there between each flash? Does the light flash more or less frequently than in 1897?

Real-World Connections

Additional Topics

ADDITIONAL TOPIC

A-1 Theoretical and Reasonable Domain and Range

Objectives

Identify the theoretical domain and range of functions.

Identify the reasonable domain and range of functions.

The *theoretical domain* of a function $y = f(x)$ is the set of all possible values of the independent variable x. The *theoretical range* of a function $y = f(x)$ is the set of all possible values of the dependent variable y. The table describes the domain and range of different types of functions.

Theoretical Domain and Range

Function	Domain	Range
Absolute value	All real numbers	Determined by the minimum or maximum
Polynomial	All real numbers	• Odd degree: All real numbers • Even degree: Determined by the minimum or maximum
Exponential	All real numbers	Determined by the horizontal asymptote
Logarithmic	Determined by the vertical asymptote	All real numbers
Rational (hyperbola as graph)	Determined by the vertical asymptote	Determined by the horizontal asymptote
Radical	• Square root: Determined by the expression under the radical sign • Cube root: All real numbers	• Square root: Determined by the minimum or maximum • Cube root: All real numbers
Periodic (sine or cosine)	All real numbers	Determined by the minimum and maximum values

EXAMPLE 1

Determining Theoretical Domain and Range

State the domain and range of each function.

A $y = 3x^5 - 7x^2 + 1$

The function is a polynomial function of degree 5.

The domain of a polynomial function is all real numbers.

Because the degree is odd, the range is all real numbers.

B $y = \sqrt{x - 2} - 1$

The function is a square-root function.

The expression under the radical symbol must be nonnegative, so the domain is $\{x \mid x \geq 2\}$.

Graph the function to find its minimum value. The minimum value is -1, so the range is $\{y \mid y \geq -1\}$.

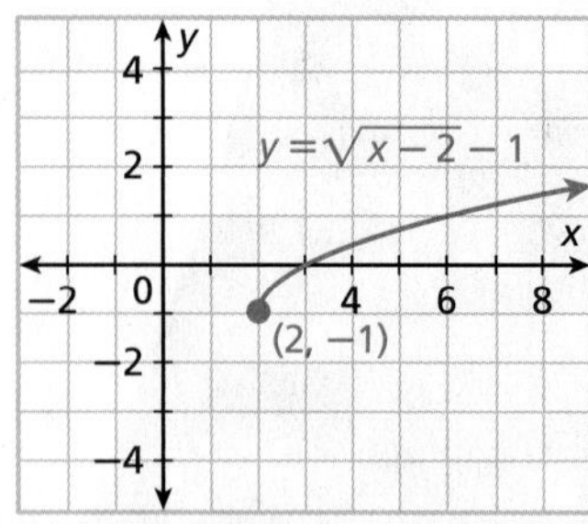

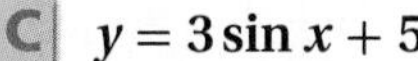

C $y = 3\sin x + 5$

The function is a sine function.

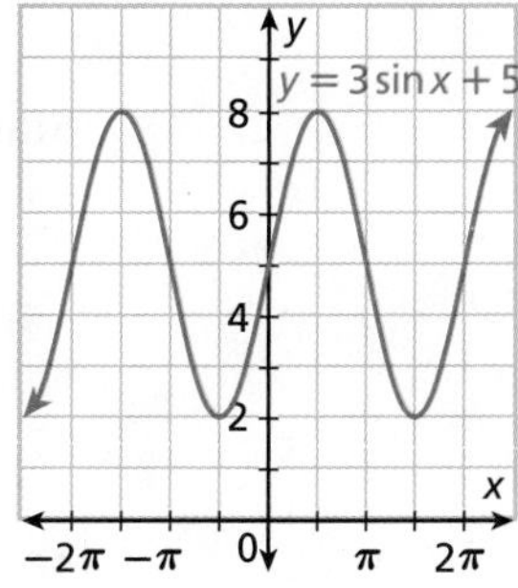

The domain of a sine function is all real numbers.

Remember!

Recall from Lesson 14-1 that for a function of the form $y = a\sin x + k$, the amplitude is $|a|$ and the vertical shift is k.

The amplitude of the function is 3, and the vertical shift is 5.

Minima: $5 - 3 = 2$

Maxima: $5 + 3 = 8$

The range is $\{y \mid 2 \le y \le 8\}$.

CHECK IT OUT! **State the domain and range of each function.**

1a. $y = x^4 + x^2 - 5$ **1b.** $y = -2^x$ **1c.** $y = \dfrac{1}{x - 6}$

In some situations, the theoretical domain and theoretical range must be restricted to values that make sense in a real-world context. These restrictions result in the *reasonable domain* and *reasonable range.*

EXAMPLE 2 Determining Reasonable Domain and Range

Nicole drives 300 miles and goes no faster than the speed limit of 60 miles per hour. The time y it takes Nicole to drive 300 miles varies inversely as her speed x. Write a function to describe the situation, and state the reasonable domain and range.

Remember!

Recall from Chapter 8 that an inverse variation is a type of rational function. The graph of an inverse variation is a hyperbola.

Step 1 Write the function and identify the theoretical domain and range.

$y = \dfrac{300}{x}$ *An inverse variation has the form $y = \frac{k}{x}$.*

Theoretical domain: $\{x \mid x \neq 0\}$ *Vertical asymptote: $x = 0$*

Theoretical range: $\{y \mid y \neq 0\}$ *Horizontal asymptote: $y = 0$*

Step 2 Identify the reasonable domain and range.

Reasonable domain: $\{x \mid 0 < x \le 60\}$ *Nicole's speed is greater than 0 and no greater than 60 miles per hour.*

The minimum time for the trip occurs when Nicole drives at the maximum speed of 60 miles per hour.

$y = \dfrac{300}{60} = 5$ *Substitute 60 for x in the function.*

Reasonable range: $\{y \mid y \ge 5\}$ *It takes Nicole at least 5 hours to drive 300 miles.*

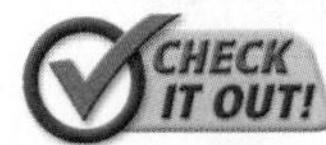

CHECK IT OUT! **2.** Trevyn buys a new car for \$17,000. The value v of the car in dollars is a function of the time t in years since the car was purchased. The value of the car decreases 10% each year. Write a function to describe the situation, and state the reasonable domain and range.

A-1 Exercises

State the domain and range of each function.

1. $y = 5^x$
2. $y = -3x^3 + 4x^2 - x$
3. $y = \sqrt{x+3} + 4$
4. $y = \dfrac{2}{x+7}$
5. $y = x^2 + 4x - 5$
6. $y = -2x - 6$
7. $y = \dfrac{1}{2}\cos x + 4$
8. $y = \log_3 x + 7$
9. $y = \sqrt[3]{x} + 5$
10. $y = -\dfrac{1}{10}x^7$
11. $y = -\sin 2x + 1$
12. $y = |x| - 3$

Write a function for each situation, and state the reasonable domain and range.

13. A cylinder with volume V in cubic centimeters has a height of 26 centimeters and a radius of r centimeters.

14. Anne buys a rare baseball card for \$320. The value v of the card in dollars is a function of the time t in years since the card was purchased. The value increases 4% per year.

15. **Design** Marcus is making a box with an open top. He starts with a square piece of metal with a side length of 30 centimeters. He cuts identical squares from each corner and folds up the sides.

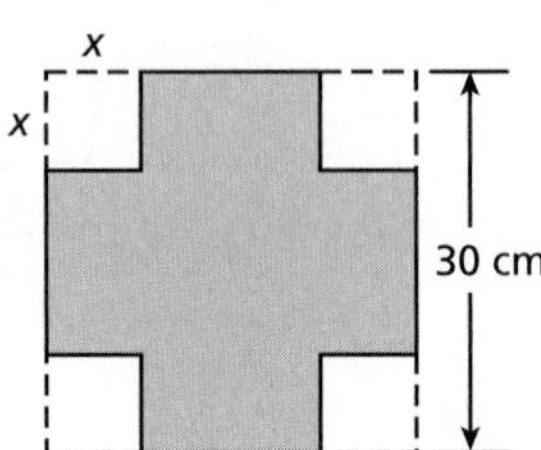

   a. Write a function V that gives the volume of the box when squares of side length x are cut from the corners.
   b. State the reasonable domain and range of the function. (*Hint*: Use a graphing calculator.)

16. **Physics** A model rocket is launched from the ground with an initial vertical velocity of 80 feet per second.
   a. Write a function h that gives the height of the rocket in feet at time t in seconds. (*Hint*: See the general projectile motion function in Lesson 5-3.)
   b. State the reasonable domain and range of the function.
   c. How long does the rocket remain in the air? Is your answer related to the reasonable domain or the reasonable range? Explain.

17. **Travel** A group visits a museum and hires a guide who charges \$60 for a tour. The cost for each person is \$12 for the museum entry fee, plus his or her share of the \$60 fee for the guide.
   a. Write a function f that gives the cost in dollars for each person if there are x people in the tour group.
   b. Describe the reasonable domain and range of the function.

Determine the theoretical domain and range of each function.

18.

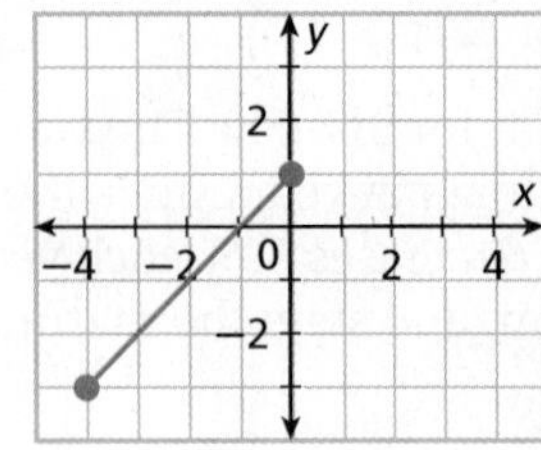

19.

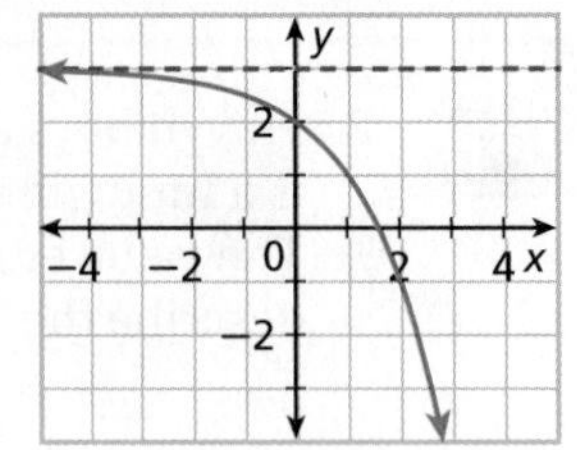

20.

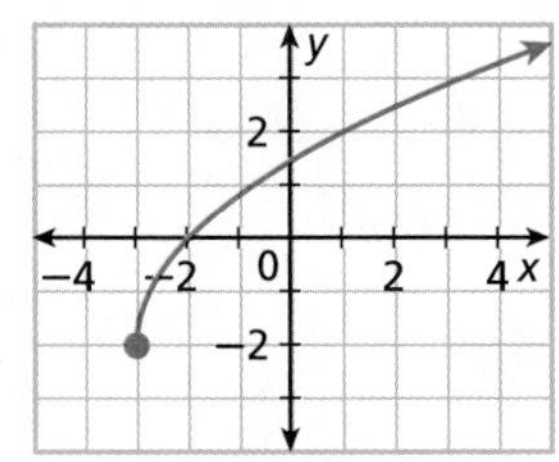

ADDITIONAL TOPIC

A-2

Comparing and Contrasting Functions

Objective
Compare and contrast functions.

Different types of functions have different characteristics. The table below shows some of the key characteristics that can be used to compare and contrast functions.

Key Characteristics of Functions	
Characteristic	**Example:** $f(x) = x^2 + 4x + 3$
Function type	Quadratic
Type and number of zeros	2 real zeros (–3 and –1)
Maximum or minimum value (if any)	Minimum: –1
Continuity	Continuous function
End behavior	As $x \to +\infty$, $f(x) \to +\infty$. As $x \to -\infty$, $f(x) \to +\infty$.
Domain and range	D: $\mathbb{R}$; R: $\{y \mid y \geq -1\}$

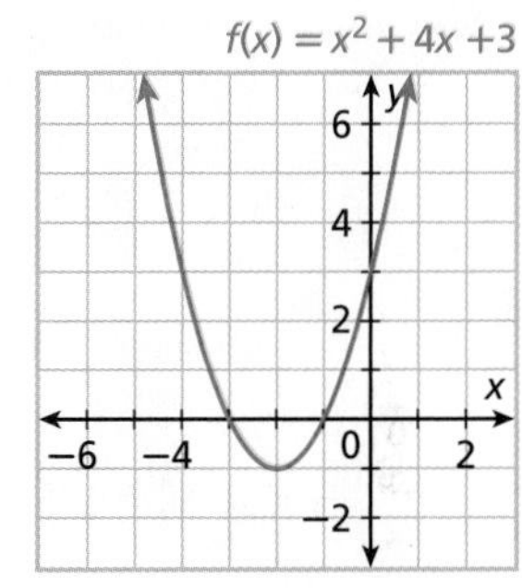

When comparing and contrasting two functions, it is often helpful to start by graphing both functions on the same coordinate plane. Then use the graphs and the function rules to help you identify characteristics of the functions.

EXAMPLE 1 **Comparing and Contrasting Functions**

Describe how the functions are alike and how they are different.

A $f(x) = \frac{1}{2}x^3$ **and** $g(x) = x^3 - 4x$

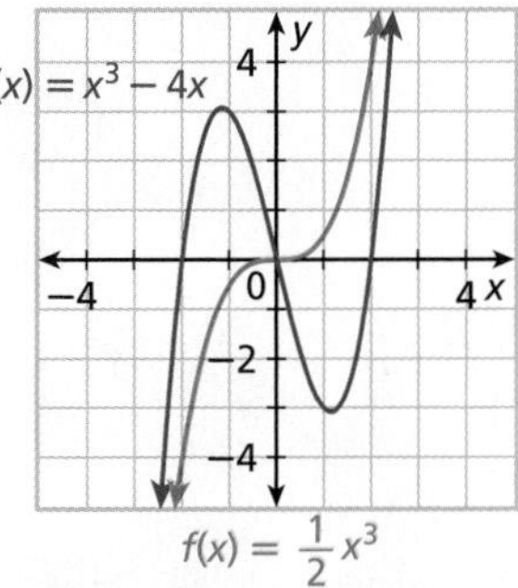

Graph both functions and then compare them.

Remember!
Recall that a power function can be written in the form $f(x) = ax^n$, where a and n are real numbers and $a \neq 0$.

Function type: Both functions are cubic polynomials, but f is also a power function.

Type and number of zeros: Both functions have a real zero at 0, but g also has real zeros at –2 and 2.

Maximum or minimum: Neither has a maximum or minimum, but g has a local maximum of about 3.08 and a local minimum of about –3.08.

Continuity: Both functions are continuous.

End behavior: Both have the same type of end behavior. As $x \to +\infty$, $f(x) \to +\infty$ and $g(x) \to +\infty$. As $x \to -\infty$, $f(x) \to -\infty$ and $g(x) \to -\infty$.

Domain and range: Both functions have a domain and range of all real numbers.

B $f(x) = \frac{2}{x}$ and $g(x) = \left(\frac{1}{2}\right)^{x-2}$

Graph both functions and then compare them.

Function type: f is a rational function, and g is an exponential function.

Type and number of zeros: Neither function has real zeros.

Maximum or minimum: Neither function has a maximum or minimum value.

Continuity: g is continuous, but f is discontinuous. The graph of f has a gap when $x = 0$.

End behavior: As $x \to +\infty$, $f(x) \to 0$ and $g(x) \to 0$. As $x \to -\infty$, $f(x) \to 0$ but $g(x) \to +\infty$.

Domain and range: The domain of f is $\{x | x \neq 0\}$, and the domain of g is all real numbers. The range of f is $\{y | y \neq 0\}$, and the range of g is $\{y | y > 0\}$.

1. Describe how the functions $f(x) = |x| - 3$ and $g(x) = x^2 - 3$ are alike and how they are different.

EXAMPLE 2 *Biology Application*

Wildlife biologists have developed two models for predicting the population of white-tailed deer in a state park over the next 10 years.

Model 1: $f(x) = 25(1.02)^x$ **Model 2: $g(x) = 0.1x^2 + 25$**

Both models give the deer population in thousands, where x is the time in years. Compare the two functions. Which model predicts a greater population at the end of the 10-year period?

- Model 1 is an exponential function, and model 2 is a quadratic function.
- Because the models are valid for the next 10 years, the reasonable domain of both functions is $\{x | 0 \leq x \leq 10\}$.
- Model 1 predicts that the population will increase from 25,000 to about 30,475. Model 2 predicts that the population will increase from 25,000 to 35,000.

Model 2 predicts a greater population of deer at the end of the 10-year period.

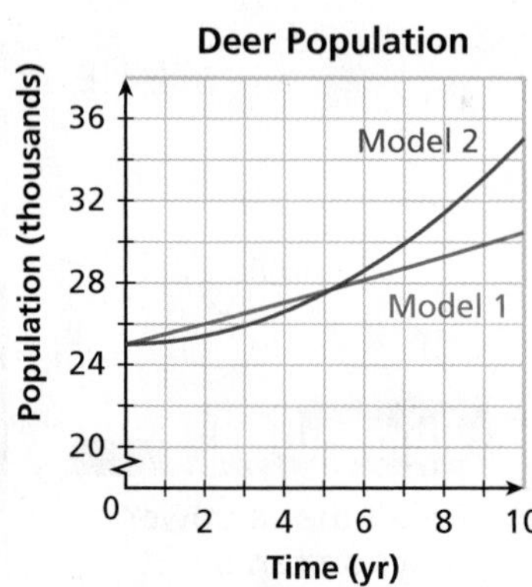

2. The following functions model the prices of stock in two companies over a 5-day trading period.

Stock 1: $f(x) = 3 \sin x + 18$ Stock 2: $g(x) = 0.3x^3 - 3x^2 + 6x + 20$

Both models give the price of the stock in dollars, where x is the time in days. Compare the two functions. Which stock price was higher at the end of day 3?

A-2 Exercises

Describe how the functions are alike and how they are different.

1. $f(x) = 2\cos x$ and $g(x) = 2\sin x$
2. $f(x) = \left(\frac{1}{3}\right)^x$ and $g(x) = \frac{3}{x}$
3. $f(x) = 3x^2 - 2$ and $g(x) = \frac{1}{3}x^4 - 2$
4. $f(x) = \sqrt{x} + 4$ and $g(x) = \log x + 4$
5. **Aviation** The following functions model the altitude of two planes over a period of 20 minutes.

   Plane 1: $f(x) = 2\sqrt{x} + 25$ Plane 2: $g(x) = 6\sqrt[3]{x+5} + 20$

   Both models give the altitude in thousands of feet, where x is the time in minutes. Compare the two functions. Are the planes ever at the same height during the 20-minute period?

Classify each function as a power, polynomial, rational, exponential, radical, or periodic function.

6. $f(x) = 2x^4 + 3x$
7. $f(x) = 3^x - 3$
8. $f(x) = \frac{x+1}{x^2 - 1}$
9. $f(x) = \frac{1}{5}x^5$
10. $f(x) = \cos(x - 2)$
11. $f(x) = \sqrt[3]{x} + 4$

Describe how the functions shown in each graph are alike and how they are different.

12. 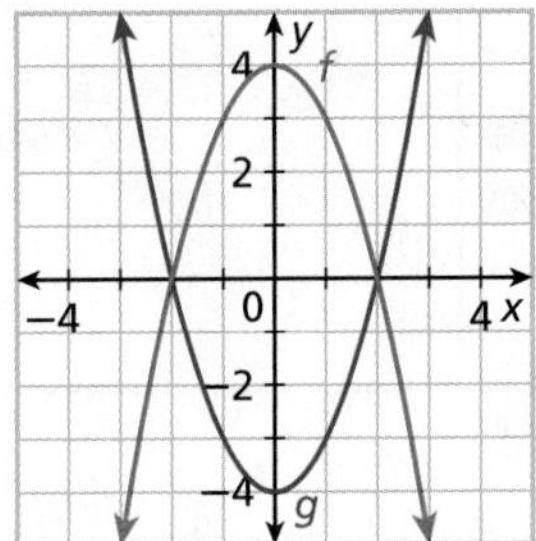

13. 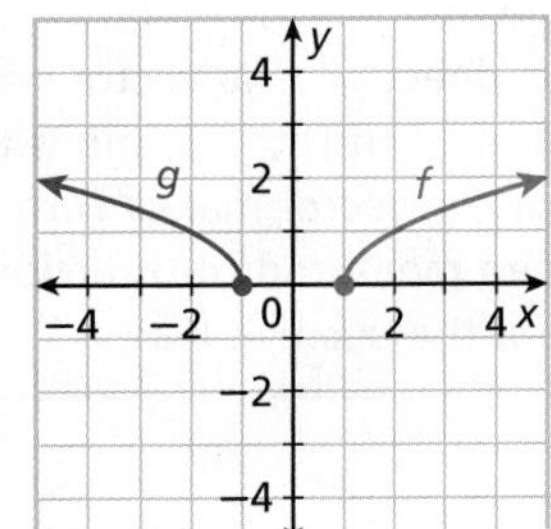

14. 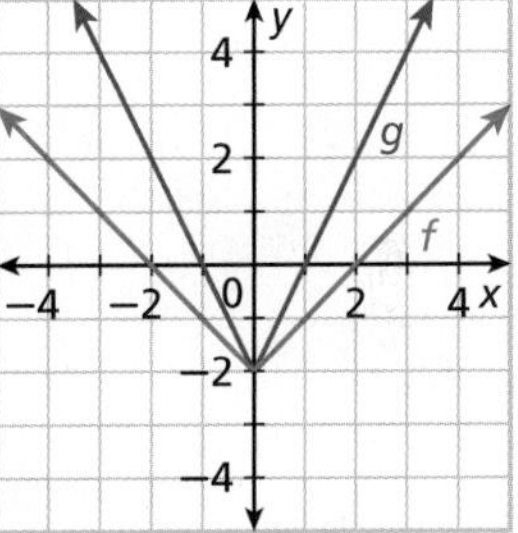

Give an example of a function with the given characteristics.

15. A function with no real zeros and a domain of all real numbers
16. A discontinuous function with exactly one real zero
17. A function with real zeros at –2 and 2 and a minimum of -4
18. **Consumer Economics** The value in dollars of a particular car over time can be modeled by the function $f(x) = 25{,}000(0.85)^x$, where x is the age of the car in years. The value of a particular truck over time can be modeled by the function $g(x) = \frac{10{,}000}{x+1} + 10{,}000$, where x is the age of the truck in years.
    - a. Compare the two functions.
    - b. Justin is planning to buy one of the two vehicles and keep it for 5 years. Would it make more economic sense for Justin to buy the car or the truck? Use mathematics to justify your answer.
19. **Critical Thinking** How are quadratic functions similar to absolute-value functions? How are they different?

ADDITIONAL TOPIC

A-3 Vectors

Objectives
Find the magnitude and direction of vectors.

Solve problems with vectors.

Vocabulary
vector
component form
magnitude
direction
resultant vector

A **vector** is a quantity that has both length and direction. You can use an arrow to represent a vector. The vector shown below can be named $\overrightarrow{PQ}$ or $\vec{v}$. Always list the initial point first when using two points to name a vector.

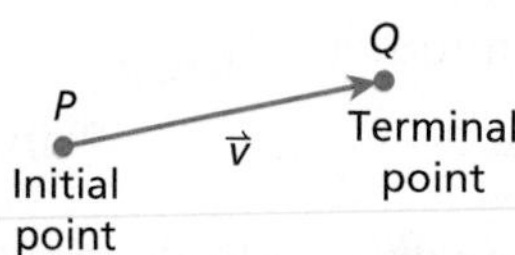

You can also name a vector by using *component form*. The **component form** $\langle x, y\rangle$ of a vector lists the horizontal and vertical change in units from the initial point to the terminal point. The component form of $\overrightarrow{AB}$ is $\langle 2, 3\rangle$.

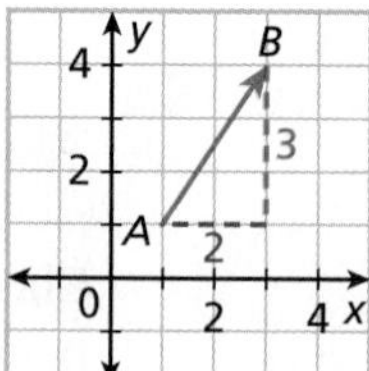

Properties of Vectors

WORDS	EXAMPLE
Magnitude The **magnitude** of a vector is its length. The magnitude of vector $\overrightarrow{AB}$ is written $\lvert\overrightarrow{AB}\rvert$.	The magnitude of $\overrightarrow{AB}$ is 5.
Direction The **direction** of a vector whose initial point is the origin is the angle that the vector makes with the *x*-axis when measured counterclockwise from the positive *x*-axis.	The direction of $\overrightarrow{AB}$ is 60°.

EXAMPLE 1 **Finding the Magnitude and Direction of a Vector**

Find the magnitude and direction of the vector $\langle 2, 3\rangle$ to the nearest tenth.

Step 1 Draw the vector on a coordinate plane.

If you use the origin as the initial point, the terminal point will be (2, 3).

Step 2 Find the magnitude of the vector by finding the distance from the initial point to the terminal point.

$$\lvert\langle 2, 3\rangle\rvert = \sqrt{(2-0)^2 + (3-0)^2}$$
$$= \sqrt{2^2 + 3^2} \quad \textit{Follow the order of operations.}$$
$$= \sqrt{4+9}$$
$$= \sqrt{13}$$
$$\approx 3.6 \quad \textit{Estimate the square root.}$$

Helpful Hint

If the initial point of a vector $\langle x, y\rangle$ is the origin, then the magnitude of the vector is $\sqrt{x^2 + y^2}$.

Step 3 Find the direction of the vector by using the tangent function.

$$\tan\theta = \frac{\text{opp.}}{\text{adj.}} = \frac{3}{2}$$

$$\theta = \text{Tan}^{-1}\left(\frac{3}{2}\right)$$

$$\theta \approx 56.3°$$ *Use a calculator.*

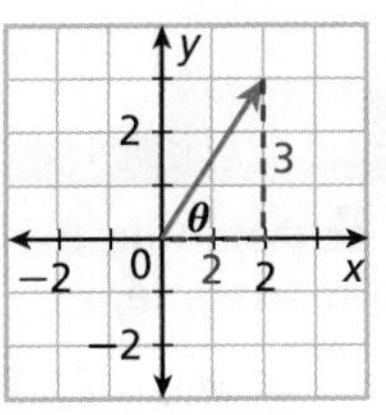

The magnitude of the vector is 3.6, and its direction is 56.3°.

1. Find the magnitude and direction of the vector $\langle 5, 8\rangle$ to the nearest tenth.

A **resultant vector** is a vector that represents the sum of two or more vectors. To add vectors numerically, add their components. If $\vec{u} = \langle x_1, y_1\rangle$ and $\vec{v} = \langle x_2, y_2\rangle$, then $\vec{u} + \vec{v} = \langle x_1 + x_2, y_1 + y_2\rangle$.

EXAMPLE 2 *Recreation Application*

Adriana is paddling a canoe across a river. She paddles due east at an average speed of 2 mi/h. The current moves the canoe due north at an average speed of 4.5 mi/h. To the nearest tenth, what are the canoe's actual speed and direction?

Step 1 Draw vectors to represent the situation.

Let $\vec{p}$ represent Adriana's paddling, and let $\vec{c}$ represent the current.

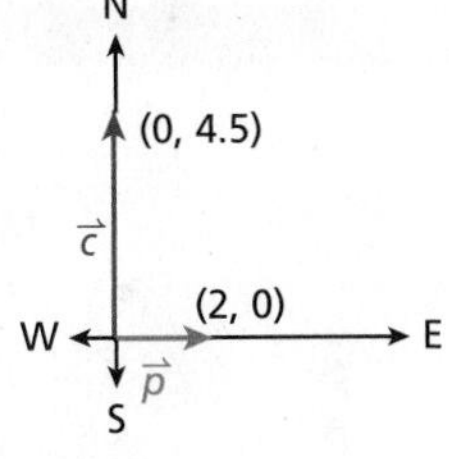

Step 2 Add the vectors.

$$\langle 2, 0\rangle + \langle 0, 4.5\rangle = \langle 2 + 0, 0 + 4.5\rangle$$

$$= \langle 2, 4.5\rangle$$

Step 3 Find the magnitude of the resultant vector to determine the canoe's speed.

$$|\langle 2, 4.5\rangle| = \sqrt{(2-0)^2 + (4.5-0)^2}$$

$$\approx 4.9$$

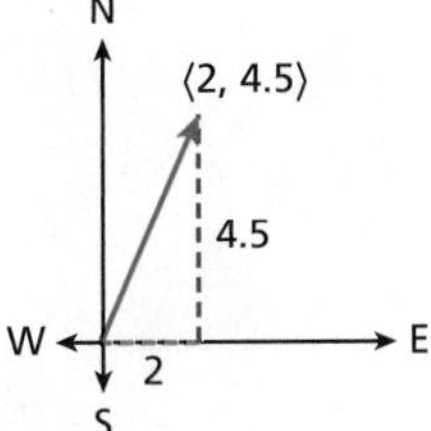

Step 4 Find the direction of the resultant vector to determine the canoe's direction.

$$\tan\theta = \frac{4.5}{2}$$

$$\theta = \text{Tan}^{-1}\left(\frac{4.5}{2}\right)$$

$$\approx 66.0°$$

The canoe's actual speed is 4.9 mi/h, and its direction is 66.0° north of east.

Writing Math

Since Adriana paddles 2 mi/h in the direction of the *x*-axis, $\vec{p}$ has a horizontal component of 2 and a vertical component of 0. So the component form of $\vec{p}$ is $\langle 2, 0\rangle$.

2. A small plane heads due south at an average speed of 140 mi/h. The wind blows the plane due east at an average speed of 40 mi/h. To the nearest whole number, what are the plane's actual speed and direction?

EXAMPLE 3 Finding the Components of a Vector

A golf ball is hit with an initial velocity of 46 m/s at an angle of 18° from the horizontal. Write the velocity vector in component form, and explain what the components mean. Round your answers to the nearest whole number.

> **Remember!**
>
> For an acute angle θ in a right triangle, $\cos\theta = \frac{\text{adj.}}{\text{hyp.}}$ and $\sin\theta = \frac{\text{opp.}}{\text{hyp.}}$.

Use trigonometric functions to find the components of the velocity vector.

$\cos 18° = \frac{x}{46}$ → $x = 46\cos 18° \approx 44$

$\sin 18° = \frac{y}{46}$ → $y = 46\sin 18° \approx 14$

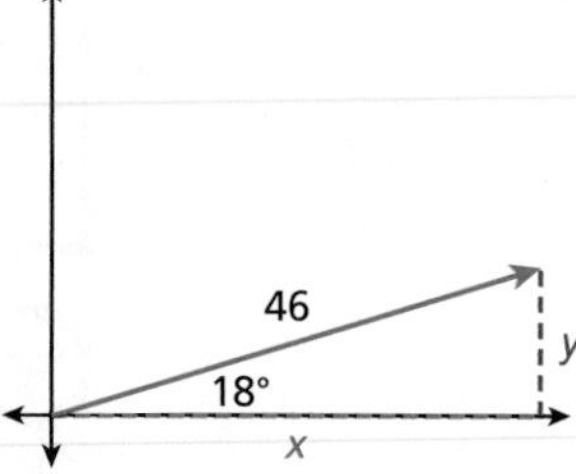

The component form of the velocity vector is $\langle 44, 14\rangle$. The ball's initial horizontal speed is 44 mi/h, and its initial vertical speed is 14 mi/h.

3. A firework leaves the ground with an initial velocity of 180 ft/s at an angle of 82° from the horizontal. Write the velocity vector in component form, and explain what the components mean. Round your answers to the nearest whole number.

A-3 Exercises

Find the magnitude and direction of each vector to the nearest tenth.

1. $\langle 10, 4\rangle$
2. $\langle 6, 6\rangle$
3. $\langle 7, 2\rangle$
4. $\langle 0, 5\rangle$

5. **Fitness** A swimmer heads due south across a lake at an average speed of 90 yd/min. Surface waves push the swimmer due east at an average speed of 13 yd/min. To the nearest whole number, what are the swimmer's actual speed and direction?

6. **Transportation** A helicopter heads due west at an average speed of 85 mi/h. The wind blows the helicopter due north at an average speed of 15 mi/h. To the nearest tenth, what are the helicopter's actual speed and direction?

For Exercises 7 and 8, write the velocity vector in component form, and explain what the components mean. Round your answers to the nearest tenth.

7. **Sports** Aaron shoots an arrow with an initial velocity of 58 m/s at an angle of 3° from the horizontal.

8. **Recreation** A roller coaster is moving uphill at a velocity of 11 mi/h at an angle of 22° from the horizontal.

Draw each vector on a coordinate plane. Find its magnitude to the nearest tenth.

9. $\langle -3, 5\rangle$
10. $\langle -6, -2\rangle$
11. $\langle 4, -7\rangle$
12. $\langle -8, 0\rangle$

Find each vector sum. Then find the magnitude and direction of the resultant vector. Round the magnitude and direction to the nearest tenth.

13. $\langle 4, 9\rangle + \langle 10, 2\rangle$ **14.** $\langle 6, 5\rangle + \langle 1, 7\rangle$ **15.** $\langle 3, 11\rangle + \langle 8, 2\rangle$

Write each vector in component form. Round values to the nearest tenth.

16. magnitude 18, direction 82° **17.** magnitude 75, direction 30°

18. magnitude 5.9, direction 46° **19.** magnitude 110, direction 6°

20. Recreation Marianne hiked 3 miles in a direction 31° north of east. To the nearest tenth of a mile, how far east is she from her starting point? How far north is she from her starting point?

21. Multi-Step A player kicks a football with an initial velocity of 78 ft/s at an angle of 42° from the horizontal.

a. Write the velocity vector in component form, and explain what the components mean. Round your answers to the nearest whole number.

b. The function $h(t) = -16t^2 + v_0t$ represents the height h in feet that the football will reach after t seconds, where v_0 is the initial vertical velocity of the ball. What is the value of v_0?

c. The crossbar between the goal posts is 10 feet high. Will the football go high enough to pass over the crossbar? Explain how you determined your answer.

22. Multi-Step Burton is crossing a river in a kayak. He paddles due east at an average speed of 180 ft/min. The current moves the kayak due south at an average speed of 115 ft/min.

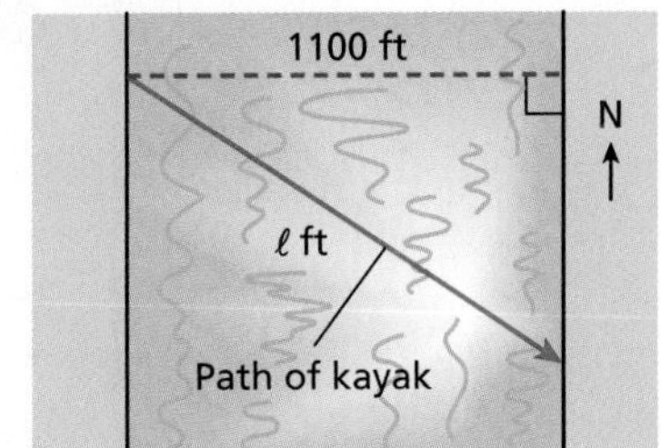

a. To the nearest whole number, find the kayak's actual speed and direction.

b. The distance from one bank of the river to the other is 1100 feet. To the nearest foot, what is the length ℓ of the path that the kayak will take across the river?

c. To the nearest minute, how long will it take Burton to cross the river?

The vector $\langle x, y\rangle$ can describe a translation of a figure x units horizontally and y units vertically. For example, a translation 2 units right and 1 unit down can be described by the vector $\langle 2, -1\rangle$. Write a vector in component form to describe each translation of $\triangle ABC$ to $\triangle A'B'C'$.

23.

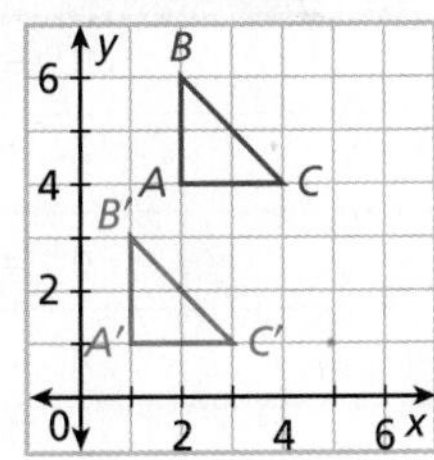

24.

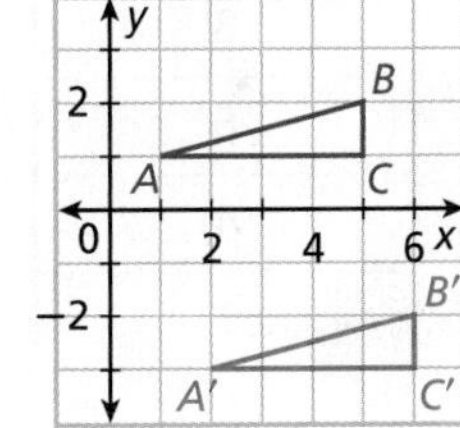

25.

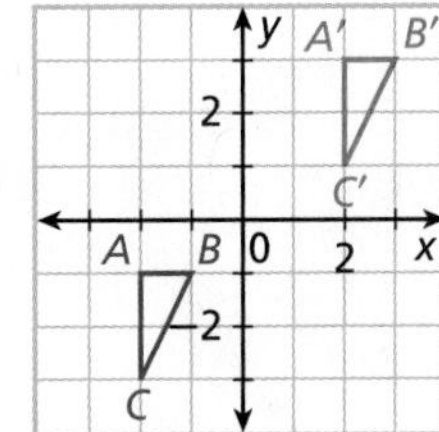

One way to graph complex numbers is by using vectors. For example, you can graph $4 + 2i$ by graphing the vector whose initial point is the origin and whose terminal point is (4, 2) in the complex plane. Use a vector to graph each complex number.

26. $5 + 3i$ **27.** $-1 + 6i$ **28.** $8 - 8i$

ADDITIONAL TOPIC

A-4 Reasoning and Proof

Objectives
Use inductive and deductive reasoning to make and verify conjectures.

Vocabulary
inductive reasoning
conjecture
deductive reasoning
proof

You use *inductive reasoning* when you draw a conclusion from a pattern. **Inductive reasoning** is the process of reasoning that a rule or statement is true because specific cases are true. A **conjecture** is a statement that is believed to be true because it is based on inductive reasoning.

EXAMPLE 1 Using Inductive Reasoning to Make Conjectures

Write a conjecture to answer each question.

A **What is the next term in the sequence 2.4, 3.7, 5, 6.3, 7.6,...?**

Look for a pattern in the terms.

2.4, 3.7, 5, 6.3, 7.6, ... *You can add 1.3 to each term to find the next term.*

+1.3 +1.3 +1.3 +1.3

$7.6 + 1.3 = 8.9$ *Add 1.3 to 7.6 to find the next term.*

Conjecture: The next term in the sequence is 8.9.

B **How does the graph of $g(x) = -(x + b)$ differ from the graph of $f(x) = -x$ when b is a positive integer?**

Graph *f*. Then graph *g* for several positive integer values of *b*, and look for a pattern.

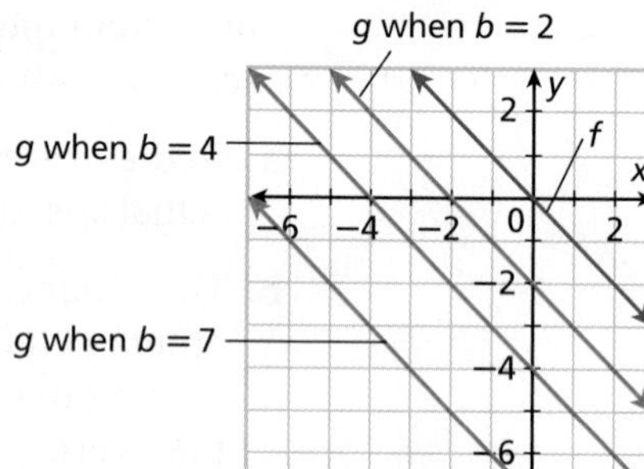

Conjecture: When *b* is a positive integer, the graph of *g* is the graph of *f* translated down *b* units.

C **Given that *a* is even and *n* is a positive integer, is a^n always, sometimes, or never even?**

List some examples, and look for a pattern.

a (even)	*n* (positive integer)	a^n
8	1	$8^1 = 8 \longrightarrow$ even
6	2	$6^2 = 36 \longrightarrow$ even
4	3	$4^3 = 64 \longrightarrow$ even
2	4	$2^4 = 16 \longrightarrow$ even

Conjecture: The value of a^n is always even when *a* is even and *n* is a positive integer.

Write a conjecture to answer each question.

1a. What is the next term in the sequence 96, 48, 24, 12, 6,...?

1b. How does the graph of $g(x) = (x + n)^2$ differ from the graph of $f(x) = x^2$ when n is a positive integer?

1c. Given that a and b are real numbers and $a < b$, is $b - a$ always, sometimes, or never negative?

To show that a conjecture is always true, you must prove it by using *deductive reasoning*. **Deductive reasoning** is the process of using logic to draw conclusions from given facts, definitions, and properties.

A **proof** is an argument that uses logic, definitions, properties, and previously proven statements to show that a conclusion is true. An *algebraic proof* uses algebraic properties such as the properties of equality.

EXAMPLE 2 Writing an Algebraic Proof

Write an algebraic proof for each statement.

A **The expression $2(6 + x) + 3x$ is equivalent to $5x + 12$.**

List a justification for each step.

$2(6 + x) + 3x$	Given expression
$2(6) + 2(x) + 3x$	Distributive Property
$12 + 2x + 3x$	Multiply.
$12 + (2x + 3x)$	Associative Property of Addition
$12 + 5x$	Combine like terms.
$5x + 12$	Commutative Property of Addition

B **The solution of $2x - 12 = 6$ is $x = 9$.**

List a justification for each step.

$2x - 12 = 6$	Given equation
$+12 \quad +12$	Addition Property of Equality
$2x + 0 = 18$	Add.
$2x = 18$	Additive Identity Property
$\frac{2x}{2} = \frac{18}{2}$	Division Property of Equality
$x = 9$	Divide.

Remember!

The Additive Identity Property states that for any real number a, $a + 0 = a$.

C **The expression $\frac{x^7}{x^3} \cdot 2x^{-1}$ is equivalent to $2x^3$. Assume all variables are positive.**

List a justification for each step.

$\frac{x^7}{x^3} \cdot 2x^{-1}$	Given expression
$x^4 \cdot 2x^{-1}$	Quotient of Powers Property
$2 \cdot x^4 \cdot x^{-1}$	Commutative Property of Multiplication
$2(x^4 \cdot x^{-1})$	Associative Property of Multiplication
$2x^3$	Product of Powers Property

Write an algebraic proof for each statement.

2a. The expression $(3x^2y^{-1})^2$ is equivalent to $\frac{9x^4}{y^2}$. Assume all variables are positive.

2b. The solution set of $5x < 2x + 12$ is $x < 4$.

A *coordinate proof* uses both coordinate geometry and algebra to prove conjectures about figures in the coordinate plane. You can use slope, the Distance Formula, the Midpoint Formula, and the coordinates of vertices to prove statements about geometric figures.

EXAMPLE 3 Writing a Coordinate Proof

$\triangle ABC$ has vertices $A(2, 4)$, $B(4, 8)$ and $C(6, 2)$. Write a coordinate proof to show that $\triangle ABC$ is a right triangle.

Find the slope of $\overline{AB}$ and $\overline{AC}$.

slope of $\overline{AB} = \frac{8-4}{4-2} = \frac{4}{2} = 2$

slope of $\overline{AC} = \frac{2-4}{6-2} = \frac{-2}{4} = -\frac{1}{2}$

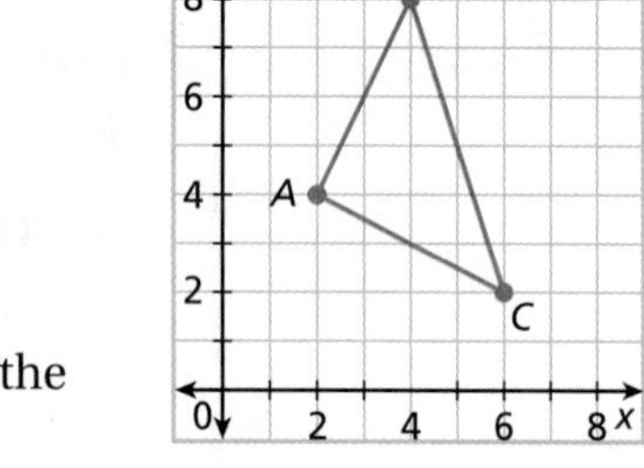

The product of the slopes is $2\left(-\frac{1}{2}\right) = -1$, so the segments are perpendicular.

Because $\overline{AB}$ and $\overline{AC}$ are perpendicular, $\angle A$ is a right angle and $\triangle ABC$ is a right triangle.

Remember!

Two different nonvertical lines are parallel if they have the same slope. Two nonvertical lines are perpendicular if the product of their slopes is −1.

3. Quadrilateral *ABCD* has vertices $A(2, 0)$, $B(2, 6)$, $C(5, 6)$, and $D(4, 0)$. Write a coordinate proof to show that *ABCD* is a trapezoid.

A-4 Exercises

Write a conjecture to answer each question.

1. What is the next term in the sequence 6, −12, 24, −48, 96,...?

2. What is the next term in the sequence $\frac{1}{2}, \frac{5}{6}, 1\frac{1}{6}, 1\frac{1}{2}, 1\frac{5}{6}, ...$?

3. How does the graph of $g(x) = |x - n|$ differ from the graph of $f(x) = |x|$ when n is a positive integer?

4. Is the product of three odd numbers always, sometimes, or never odd?

Write an algebraic proof to prove each statement.

5. The expression $(x-3)(x+1)$ is equivalent to $x^2 - 2x - 3$.

6. The expression $(3x)(4x)(x^3)$ is equivalent to $12x^5$.

7. The solutions of $2x^2 - 72 = 0$ are $x = -6$ and $x = 6$.

8. The solution set of $6(x-5) \geq -24$ is $x \geq 1$.

9. $\triangle ABC$ has vertices $A(2, 4)$, $B(7, 7)$, and $C(4, 2)$. Write a coordinate proof to show that $\triangle ABC$ is an isosceles triangle.

10. Quadrilateral $ABCD$ has vertices $A(1, 5)$, $B(3, 7)$, $C(4, 3)$, and $D(2, 1)$. Write a coordinate proof to show that $ABCD$ is a parallelogram.

For Exercises 11 and 12, state whether each conclusion involves the use of inductive or deductive reasoning.

11. If you add the same quantity to both sides of an equation, the equation will still be true. A problem states that $2x - 5 = -20$. Using this information, Arianna concludes that $2x - 5 + 5 = -20 + 5$.

12. The first 9 terms of the Fibonacci sequence are 1, 1, 2, 3, 5, 8, 13, 21, and 34. Of these terms, the third, sixth, and ninth are even. Based on this information, Ty concludes that every third term of the Fibonacci sequence is even.

State the property that justifies each equation. Assume all variables are positive.

13. $(4n)^3 = 4^3 \cdot n^3$

14. $4a^2(a + 3) = 4a^2 \cdot a + 4a^2 \cdot 3$

15. $\sqrt[3]{8x^6} = \sqrt[3]{8} \cdot \sqrt[3]{x^6}$

16. $5t + (-5t) = 0$

17. $\frac{c}{c - 6} \cdot 1 = \frac{c}{c - 6}$

18. $\frac{z^6}{2z^3} = \frac{z^3}{2}$

19. **Math History** The twin prime conjecture (which has not yet been proven) states that there are an infinite number of twin prime. A twin prime is a pair of consecutive odd numbers that are both prime. For example, 5 and 7 are a twin prime. Give four other examples that support the twin prime conjecture.

20. **Surveying** A surveyor graphs the coordinates of a plot of land on the map shown. Each unit on the map represents 100 feet. Write a coordinate proof to show that the plot of land is rectangular.

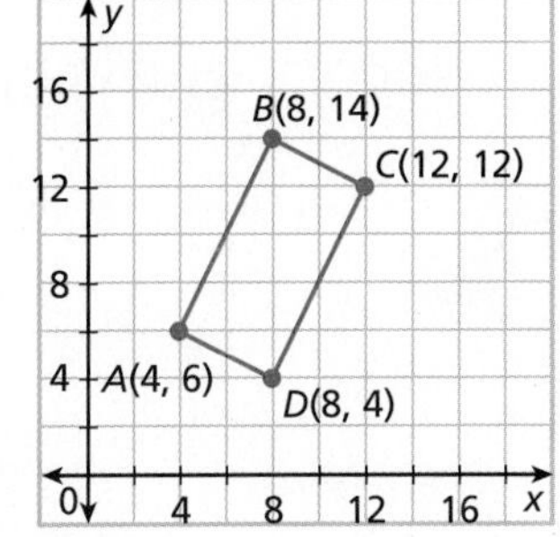

21. **Music** An online music store sells songs for \$0.88 each. Another online music store sells songs for \$0.63 each plus a one-time membership fee of \$4.00.

    a. Write an inequality that can be used to find the number of songs s for which the total cost is less at the first store than at the second store.

    b. Solve the inequality, and support your solution with an algebraic proof.

    c. Explain what the solution means in the context of the problem.

Determine whether each triangle is scalene, isosceles, or equilateral. Use a coordinate proof to support your answer.

22.

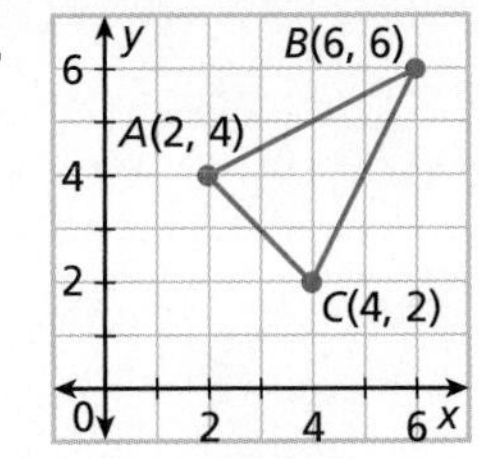

23.
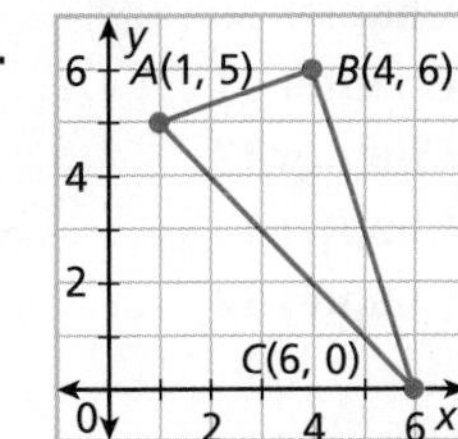

24.
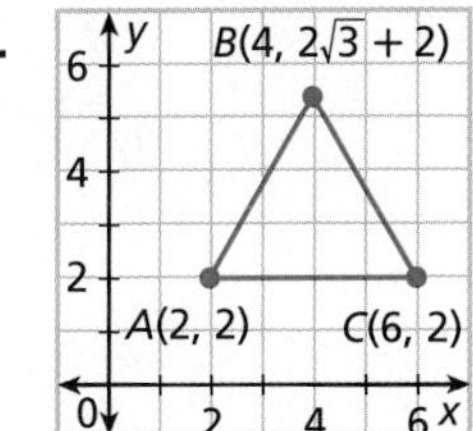

Student Handbook

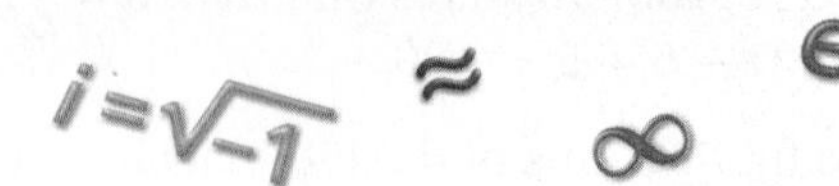

Extra Practice

Student Handbook

Extra Practice

Chapter 1 ■ Skills Practice

Lesson 1-1

Order the given numbers from least to greatest. Then classify each number by the subsets of the real numbers to which it belongs.

1. $2.3, \frac{5}{2}, \sqrt{10}, 2.\overline{4}, 2\sqrt{3}$ **2.** $-3, -\sqrt{12}, \frac{2}{5}, -2\pi, -\pi$ **3.** $\sqrt{9}, 3.0\overline{2}, 3\frac{1}{16}, 3\frac{2}{30}, \pi$

Use interval notation to represent each set of numbers.

4. $-40 \le x < -12$ **5.** $-1 < x < 5$ or $x \ge 13$ **6.**

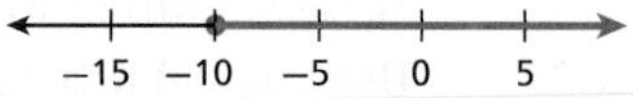

Rewrite each set in the indicated notation.

7. $x \le 0$ or $4 < x < 8$; set-builder notation **8.** all odd natural numbers; roster notation

Lesson 1-2

Identify the property demonstrated by each equation.

9. $12 + a = a + 12$ **10.** $3 \cdot (9 \cdot 2) = (3 \cdot 9) \cdot 2$ **11.** $2(\sqrt{10} + 4) = 2(\sqrt{10}) + 2(4)$

Use mental math to find each value.

12. a 15% tip on a bill of \$34.60 **13.** a 30% discount on a \$67.80 item

Classify each statement as sometimes, always, or never true. Give examples or properties to support your answer.

14. $a + 4 = b + 4$ **15.** $12b = 6b + 6b$ **16.** $ab = ac$

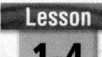

Lesson 1-3

Estimate to the nearest tenth.

17. $\sqrt{90}$ **18.** $\sqrt{62}$ **19.** $-\sqrt{48}$ **20.** $\sqrt{23}$

Simplify each expression.

21. $\frac{\sqrt{242}}{\sqrt{2}}$ **22.** $\frac{\sqrt{20}}{\sqrt{120}}$ **23.** $2\sqrt{5} + 4\sqrt{20}$ **24.** $2\sqrt{72} - \sqrt{18}$

Lesson 1-4

Write an algebraic expression to represent each situation.

25. the area in square inches of a triangle with base b inches and height 12 inches

26. the amount in dollars remaining from \$55 after spending d dollars

Evaluate each expression for the given values of the variables.

27. $2a^2 + 5a - 3b$ for $a = 4$ and $b = -3$ **28.** $\frac{x + y}{2xy + 2}$ for $x = 3$ and $y = 5$

Simplify each expression.

29. $3n + 5n - 2(n + 2)$ **30.** $3(x - 7) + 4x^2$ **31.** $-4a + 2(12 - 4a)$

Lesson 1-5

Simplify each expression. Assume all variables are nonzero.

32. 4^0 **33.** $3^2 \cdot 3^{-5}$ **34.** $(3x^2y)^4$ **35.** $\frac{(5x)^2}{5y^{-4}}$

Simplify each expression. Write the answer in scientific notation.

36. $(1.4 \times 10^{12})(2.2 \times 10^3)$ **37.** $\frac{(9.9 \times 10^6)}{(2.2 \times 10^3)}$ **38.** $\frac{24 \times 10^{-5}}{6 \times 10^4}$

Chapter 1 ■ Skills Practice

Lesson 1-6 **Give the domain and range for each relation.**

39. 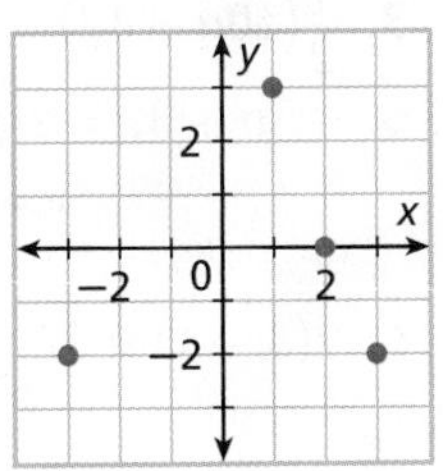

40.

x	y
−5	−10
−2	−2
0	5
4	19

41. 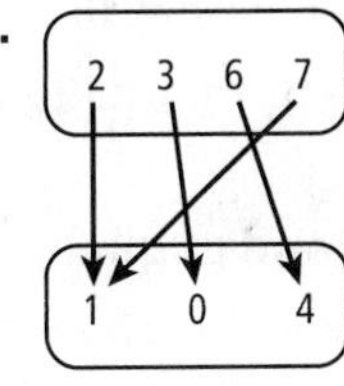

Determine whether each relation is a function.

42.

Average Regular Gasoline Prices August 2005				
Date	8/8	8/15	8/22	8/29
Cost ($/gal)	2.37	2.55	2.61	2.61

43. from a person's age to his or her height

Lesson 1-7 **For each function, evaluate $f(0), f(3)$, and $f(-2)$.**

44. $f(x) = -4x + 10$

45. $f(x) = \frac{1}{2}x^2$

46. $f(x) = x^2 - 2x + 5$

Graph each function.

47. $g(x) = \frac{1}{2}x - 4$

48.

x	1	2	3	4
y	1	3	5	7

49. $h(x) = -2x + 5$

Lesson 1-8 **Perform the given translation on the point $(-3, 4)$. Give the coordinates of the translated point.**

50. 3 units right

51. 5 units up

52. 2 units left, 2 units down

Use a table to perform each transformation of $y = f(x)$. Use the same coordinate plane as the original function.

53. reflection across the y-axis

54. translation 2 units up

55. vertical compression by a factor of $\frac{1}{2}$

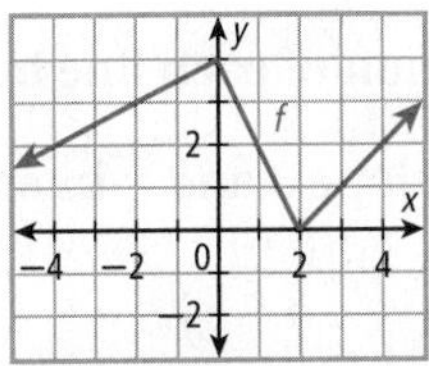

Lesson 1-9 **Identify the parent function for g from its function rule. Then graph g on your calculator and describe what transformation of the parent function it represents.**

56. $g(x) = (x + 3)^3$

57. $g(x) = \sqrt{x - 4}$

58. $g(x) = x^2 + 3$

Graph the data from the table. Describe the parent function and the transformation that best approximates the data set.

59.

x	−2	−1	0	1	2
y	−4	−0.5	0	0.5	4

60.

x	1	3	5	7	9
y	16	4	0	4	16

Chapter 2 ▪ Skills Practice

Lesson 2-1

Solve.

1. $4(x - 3) = 48$
2. $6x + 10 = -2x + 26$
3. $\frac{1}{2}(10a + 12) = a - 6$
4. $3z + 12 = \frac{1}{2}(4z + 4)$
5. $11w + 4 = 58 - 7w$
6. $-5p + 32 = 2(p - 2)$

Solve and graph.

7. $3x + 7 < 28$
8. $12y - 3 \leq 57$
9. $2(4 - x) < 10$

Lesson 2-2

Solve each proportion.

10. $\frac{3x}{15} = \frac{3}{5}$
11. $\frac{8}{5x} = \frac{2}{11}$
12. $\frac{-4}{5} = \frac{14}{y}$
13. $\frac{2.2}{3} = \frac{n}{5}$
14. $\frac{9.5}{3} = \frac{6 + m}{6}$
15. $\frac{-1}{9} = \frac{1.5}{3 - x}$

Lesson 2-3

Determine whether each data set could represent a linear function.

16.

x	−2	1	4	7
$f(x)$	−14	−5	4	13

17.

x	−2	−1	0	1
$f(x)$	6	0	−2	0

Graph each line.

18. slope $\frac{2}{3}$; passes through $(3, 4)$
19. slope $-\frac{5}{3}$; passes through $(6, -1)$

Find the intercepts of each line, and graph the lines.

20. $-2y + x = 8$
21. $3x + y = 6$

Write each function in slope-intercept form. Then graph the function.

22. $3y - 2x = 3$
23. $4y + 3x = 20$

Lesson 2-4

Find the slope of each line.

24.

x	−2	1	4	7
$f(x)$	−14	−5	4	13

25. a line through $(-1, 20)$ and $(3, -4)$

Write the equation of each line in slope-intercept form.

26. a line with slope 3 and x-intercept $\frac{4}{3}$
27. a line with slope $-\frac{3}{2}$ passing through $(4, 1)$

28.

x	−2	0	5	6
$f(x)$	14	15	17.5	18

29.

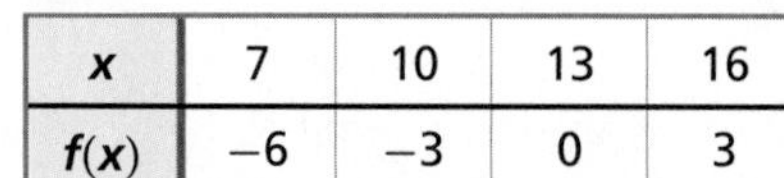

x	7	10	13	16
$f(x)$	−6	−3	0	3

30.

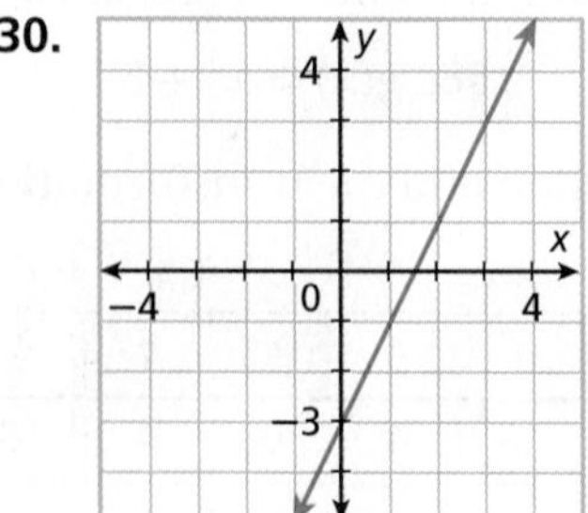

31.

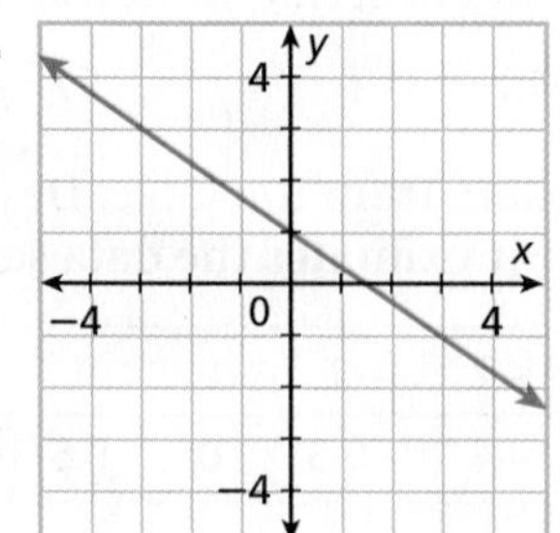

Extra Practice

Chapter 2 ■ Skills Practice

Lesson 2-5

Graph each inequality using intercepts.

32. $y - x > 4$ **33.** $2y - 8x \leq -4$ **34.** $4y + 3x \geq 12$

Solve each inequality for y. Graph the solution.

35. $6x + 6y < 18$ **36.** $12 > 2(x - 3y)$ **37.** $6y \leq 9x - 36$

Lesson 2-6

Let $g(x)$ be the indicated transformation of $f(x)$. Write the rule for $g(x)$.

38. $f(x) = \frac{4}{7}x + 1$; vertical translation 3 units down

39. $f(x) = -4x + 9$; horizontal stretch by a factor of 4

40. linear function defined in the table; reflection across the y-axis

x	−1	0	2	5
y	−17	−11	1	19

Let $g(x)$ be the indicated transformation of $f(x) = x$. Write the rule for $g(x)$.

41. vertical stretch by a factor of 2 followed by a horizontal shift 2 units right

42. horizontal shift 5 units left followed by a reflection across the x-axis

43. vertical stretch by a factor of $\frac{3}{2}$ followed by a vertical shift 8 units down

Lesson 2-7

44. If the points in a scatter plot have a positive correlation, then the r-value is ___?___. If the points have no correlation, then the r-value is ___?___.

45. Make a scatter plot of the data shown in the table.

x	0	2	3	4	6	9
y	18	15	14	10	5	1

46. Find the correlation coefficient and the equation of the line of best fit. Draw the line of best fit on your scatter plot.

Lesson 2-8

Solve each compound inequality. Then graph the solution set.

47. $3 - x > 4$ or $2x + 7 \geq 17$ **48.** $8x \leq 0$ and $4x + 6 \geq -10$

Solve each equation.

49. $|x - 9| = 1$ **50.** $|5x + 5| = 20$ **51.** $4|-2x| = 48$

Solve each inequality. Then graph the solution set.

52. $|x + 7| > 4$ **53.** $|2x - 5| < 21$ **54.** $3\left|\frac{1}{2}x + 1\right| \geq 12$

Lesson 2-9

Let $g(x)$ be the indicated transformation of $f(x) = |x|$. Write the rule for $g(x)$.

55. 7 units up **56.** 3 units right

Translate $f(x) = |x|$ so that the vertex is at the given point. Then graph.

57. $(1, 4)$ **58.** $(-3, 2)$ **59.** $(1.5, -2.5)$

Perform each transformation. Then graph.

60. Stretch $f(x) = |x - 1|$ vertically by a factor of 2.

61. Reflect $f(x) = |x + 4| - 1$ across the y-axis.

Extra Practice

Chapter 3 ■ Skills Practice

Lesson 3-1

Use substitution to determine if the given ordered pair is an element of the solution set for the system of equations.

1. $(2, 8)$ $\begin{cases} y - 2x = 4 \\ 2y + x = -8 \end{cases}$

2. $(4, 13)$ $\begin{cases} y - 3x = 1 \\ 4x - y = 3 \end{cases}$

3. $(3, 2.5)$ $\begin{cases} 2y - x = 2 \\ 3x - 2y = 4 \end{cases}$

4. $(5, 4)$ $\begin{cases} x - y = 1 \\ x - 2y = 8 \end{cases}$

Use a graph and a table to solve each system. Check your answer.

5. $\begin{cases} 4y - x = 12 \\ 3x - 4y = -16 \end{cases}$

6. $\begin{cases} 3x + 3y = 6 \\ 2x - y = 4 \end{cases}$

7. $\begin{cases} 2y - x = 12 \\ 5x - 2y = -4 \end{cases}$

8. $\begin{cases} y - x = 4 \\ 2y + x = -4 \end{cases}$

Classify each system and determine the number of solutions.

9. $\begin{cases} y - 3x = 2 \\ 2y - 6x = 10 \end{cases}$

10. $\begin{cases} y - x = 3 \\ 3x - 4y = 10 \end{cases}$

11. $\begin{cases} 2y + 3x = 8 \\ 3x + 2y = 8 \end{cases}$

12. $\begin{cases} 4y - x = 6 \\ 2x - 8y = -12 \end{cases}$

Lesson 3-2

Use substitution to solve each system of equations.

13. $\begin{cases} x + y = 22 \\ y = x - 4 \end{cases}$

14. $\begin{cases} y = 2x + 2 \\ 3x + 2y = 18 \end{cases}$

15. $\begin{cases} 4x - y = 3 \\ 3y + 3x = 36 \end{cases}$

16. $\begin{cases} 9x - 3y = 3 \\ 2y - 4x = 16 \end{cases}$

Use elimination to solve each system of equations.

17. $\begin{cases} 3x + y = 5 \\ -2x - y = 1 \end{cases}$

18. $\begin{cases} 3x + y = 11 \\ 3y - 3x = -3 \end{cases}$

19. $\begin{cases} 2y + 5x = 7 \\ 2x - 4y = 10 \end{cases}$

20. $\begin{cases} \frac{1}{3}y + 2x = 11 \\ y - 3x = -12 \end{cases}$

Classify each system and determine the number of solutions.

21. $\begin{cases} 2y + x = 10 \\ -y + 4x = 4 \end{cases}$

22. $\begin{cases} 2y - x = 2 \\ 2x - 4y = 12 \end{cases}$

23. $\begin{cases} 4x - 8y = 16 \\ 12y - 6x = -24 \end{cases}$

24. $\begin{cases} y - \frac{2}{3}x = 3 \\ 2x - 3y = 15 \end{cases}$

Lesson 3-3

Graph each system of inequalities.

25. $\begin{cases} y \le 2x + 3 \\ y \ge x + 4 \end{cases}$

26. $\begin{cases} x + 2y \le 10 \\ -x + 2y > 12 \end{cases}$

27. $\begin{cases} y > 3x + 3 \\ 2y - 3x > 12 \end{cases}$

28. $\begin{cases} 3x + y < 4 \\ 2y - \frac{1}{2}x \ge 8 \end{cases}$

Graph each system of inequalities and classify the figure created by the solution region.

29. $\begin{cases} y \le 2x + 4 \\ y \ge 2x - 1 \\ y \le 4 \\ y \ge -1 \end{cases}$

30. $\begin{cases} y \le 3x \\ y \le -3x + 13 \\ y \ge 0 \end{cases}$

31. $\begin{cases} x \ge -1 \\ x \le 3 \\ y \ge 1 \\ y \le 8 \end{cases}$

32. $\begin{cases} y + x \le 8 \\ y - x \le 1 \\ y \le 3 \\ y \ge -1 \end{cases}$

33. Write a system of inequalities to describe the graph.

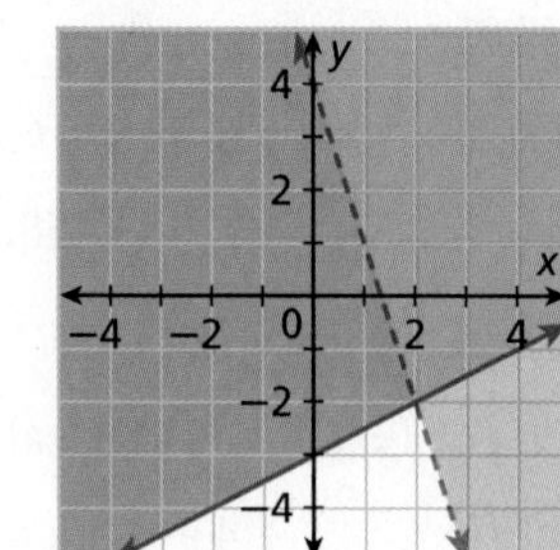

Chapter 3 ■ Skills Practice

Lesson 3-4

Graph each feasible region.

34. $\begin{cases} y \geq 0 \\ x \geq 1 \\ y \leq -x + 8 \\ y \leq 3x \end{cases}$ **35.** $\begin{cases} y \geq -1 \\ x \geq -2 \\ y \leq -2x + 10 \\ y \leq \frac{1}{2}x + 5 \end{cases}$ **36.** $\begin{cases} y \geq -8 \\ x \geq -4 \\ y \leq -2x + 1 \\ y \leq -\frac{1}{4}x - 6 \end{cases}$ **37.** $\begin{cases} y \geq -3 \\ x \leq 1 \\ y \leq x + 8 \\ y \geq -x - 6 \end{cases}$

Maximize or minimize each objective function.

38. Maximize $P = 5x + 3y$ for the constraints from Exercise 34.

39. Maximize $P = 1.2x + 9.5y$ for the constraints from Exercise 35.

40. Minimize $P = 11x - 2.5y$ for the constraints from Exercise 36.

41. Minimize $P = 8x + 24y$ for the constraints from Exercise 37.

42. Maximize $P = 5.5x + 9y$ for the constraints shown on the coordinate grid below.

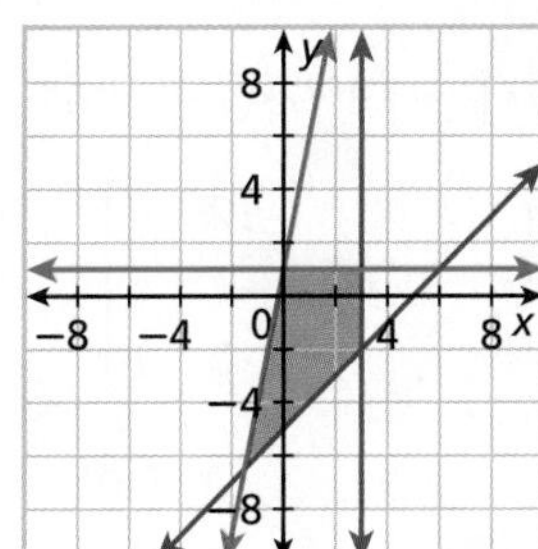

Lesson 3-5

Graph each point in three-dimensional space.

43. $(0, 4, -2)$ **44.** $(1, 3, 3)$ **45.** $(2, -3, -5)$ **46.** $(-3, -1, 4)$

Graph each linear equation in three-dimensional space.

47. $2x + 2y + z = 10$ **48.** $3x - 2y + 2z = 6$

49. $6x + 4y + 3z = 12$ **50.** $\frac{1}{2}x + 4y - z = 4$

Lesson 3-6

Use substitution or elimination to solve each system of equations.

51. $\begin{cases} 3x + y - z = 2 \\ 5x + 3y + 4z = -5 \\ -2x + y + 8z = -12 \end{cases}$ **52.** $\begin{cases} 2x + 2y - z = 16 \\ 4x - 2y + 2z = 0 \\ -3x - y + 3z = -19 \end{cases}$

53. $\begin{cases} 3x + 4y + 2z = 1 \\ -x + y - 4z = -17 \\ 2x + 8y + 4z = 14 \end{cases}$ **54.** $\begin{cases} -x + 3y + 3z = 11 \\ -3x + 5y - 7z = 1 \\ 4x - 2y + 3z = 11 \end{cases}$

Classify each system as consistent or inconsistent, and determine the number of solutions.

55. $\begin{cases} 3x + 3y - z = -3 \\ 5x + y + 2z = 14 \\ -4x + 2y + z = -9 \end{cases}$ **56.** $\begin{cases} 2x + 3y + z = 12 \\ 2x + 3y + z = -8 \\ 4x - y - 4z = 15 \end{cases}$ **57.** $\begin{cases} 8x - 4y - 16z = 12 \\ -2x + y + 4z = -3 \\ 3x - 2z + 9z = 18 \end{cases}$

Extra Practice

Chapter 4 ■ Skills Practice

Lesson 4-1

Use the following matrices for Exercises 1–4. Add or subtract, if possible.

$$A=\begin{bmatrix}1 & 3 & 6\\ 2 & -5 & 0\end{bmatrix} \qquad B=\begin{bmatrix}1.2 & 3.5 & 4\\ 2.2 & 2.7 & -0.5\end{bmatrix} \qquad C=\begin{bmatrix}-1 & 3 & 9\\ 4 & -5 & -2.2\\ 2 & 1 & 12\end{bmatrix}$$

1. $A+B$ **2.** $A+C$ **3.** $B-A$ **4.** $C-B$

Use the following matrices for Exercises 5–8. Evaluate, if possible.

$$A=\begin{bmatrix}4 & 7 & 3\\ 2 & 12 & -4\end{bmatrix} \qquad B=\begin{bmatrix}-3 & 10 & -9\\ 2 & 0 & -6\end{bmatrix} \qquad C=\begin{bmatrix}16 & 8\\ -3 & 2\\ 21 & 0\end{bmatrix}$$

5. $4A$ **6.** $-2C$ **7.** $\frac{1}{2}A+B$ **8.** $2C-A$

Lesson 4-2

Tell whether each product is defined. If so, give its dimensions.

9. $A_{2\times 4}$ and $B_{4\times 5}$; AB **10.** $C_{3\times 3}$ and $D_{2\times 3}$; CD **11.** $E_{4\times 7}$ and $F_{7\times 6}$; EF

Use the following matrices for Exercises 12–15. Find each product, if possible.

$$A=\begin{bmatrix}-1 & 2 & 5\\ 2 & -4 & 0\end{bmatrix} \quad B=\begin{bmatrix}2 & 5\\ 3 & 9\end{bmatrix} \quad C=\begin{bmatrix}3 & 7 & 1\\ 10 & 4 & -2\end{bmatrix} \quad D=\begin{bmatrix}12 & 0\\ -4 & 4\\ 5 & 1\end{bmatrix} \quad E=\begin{bmatrix}5 & 1 & -3\end{bmatrix}$$

12. AD **13.** BC **14.** ED **15.** CB

Use the following matrices for Exercises 16–19. Evaluate, if possible.

$$A=\begin{bmatrix}9 & 6\\ 0 & -2\end{bmatrix} \qquad B=\begin{bmatrix}3 & 5 & 10\\ -3 & -1 & 6\\ 2 & 3 & 6\end{bmatrix} \qquad C=\begin{bmatrix}12 & 0 & 5\\ -5 & 7 & 8\end{bmatrix}$$

16. A^2 **17.** A^3 **18.** B^2 **19.** C^2

Lesson 4-3

Translate the polygon with coordinates $M(3, 0)$, $N(2, 4)$, $O(-1, 3)$, and $P(-2, -1)$ as indicated. Find the coordinates of the vertices of the image, and graph.

20. 3 units right and 2 units down **21.** 1 unit left and 4 units up

Use a matrix to reduce or enlarge the polygon with coordinates $M(3, 0)$, $N(2, 4)$, $O(-1, 3)$, and $P(-2, -1)$ by the given factor. Find the coordinates of the vertices of the image, and graph.

22. Reduce polygon *MNOP* by a factor of 0.25.

23. Enlarge polygon *MNOP* by a factor of 3.

Reflect the figure with coordinates $A(-1, 1)$, $B(1, -3)$, $C(5, -1)$, and $D(2, 4)$ across the given line. Find the coordinates of the vertices of the image, and graph.

24. Reflect *ABCD* across the *x*-axis. **25.** Reflect *ABCD* across the *y*-axis.

Use each matrix to rotate the figure with coordinates $E(2, 2)$, $F(4, 0)$, $G(-3, -3)$, and $H(-2, 3)$ about the origin. Graph and describe the image.

26. $\begin{bmatrix}0 & -1\\ 1 & 0\end{bmatrix}$ **27.** $\begin{bmatrix}-1 & 0\\ 0 & -1\end{bmatrix}$

Extra Practice

Chapter 4 ■ Skills Practice

Lesson 4-4

Find the determinant of each matrix.

28. $\begin{bmatrix} -3 & 4 \\ 5 & -2 \end{bmatrix}$ 29. $\begin{bmatrix} 0.75 & 3 \\ 1.5 & 4 \end{bmatrix}$ 30. $\begin{bmatrix} \frac{1}{4} & \frac{1}{2} \\ \frac{2}{3} & 8 \end{bmatrix}$ 31. $\begin{bmatrix} 10 & -5 \\ 12 & \frac{1}{2} \end{bmatrix}$

Use Cramer's rule to solve each system of equations.

32. $\begin{cases} 3x + 2y = 1 \\ -4x + 5y = -32 \end{cases}$

33. $\begin{cases} x + 4y = 15 \\ 3x - 10 = 2y \end{cases}$

34. $\begin{cases} 10x + 23 = 7y \\ 2y - 10 = 4x \end{cases}$

35. $\begin{cases} \frac{1}{2}x + \frac{3}{2}y = -1 \\ \frac{1}{4}x + 1 + y = 0 \end{cases}$

Find the determinant of each matrix.

36. $\begin{bmatrix} 2 & 3 & 5 \\ -1 & 4 & 4 \\ 5 & 0 & 9 \end{bmatrix}$ 37. $\begin{bmatrix} 3 & -6 & -1 \\ 2 & 2 & 2 \\ 7 & 1 & -3 \end{bmatrix}$ 38. $\begin{bmatrix} 9 & 3 & 0 \\ 5 & -5 & 1 \\ 2 & 3 & -2 \end{bmatrix}$

Lesson 4-5

Determine whether the given matrices are inverses.

39. $\begin{bmatrix} 1 & -8 \\ 2 & 4 \end{bmatrix} \begin{bmatrix} 0.2 & 0.4 \\ -0.1 & 0.05 \end{bmatrix}$

40. $\begin{bmatrix} 9 & 3 \\ -6 & -6 \end{bmatrix} \begin{bmatrix} \frac{1}{6} & \frac{1}{12} \\ -\frac{1}{6} & -\frac{1}{4} \end{bmatrix}$

41. $\begin{bmatrix} 1 & 2 \\ 2 & 1 \end{bmatrix} \begin{bmatrix} 1 & -\frac{1}{2} \\ -\frac{1}{2} & 1 \end{bmatrix}$

42. $\begin{bmatrix} 14 & 7 \\ 20 & 1 \end{bmatrix} \begin{bmatrix} 1 & 0 \\ 0 & 1 \end{bmatrix}$

Find the inverse of the matrix, if it is defined.

43. $\begin{bmatrix} -\frac{1}{3} & \frac{2}{3} \\ \frac{2}{3} & -\frac{1}{3} \end{bmatrix}$ 44. $\begin{bmatrix} 3 & 6 \\ -9 & -6 \end{bmatrix}$ 45. $\begin{bmatrix} 3 & 3 \\ -2 & -2 \end{bmatrix}$ 46. $\begin{bmatrix} 1 & -4 \\ -\frac{1}{2} & 3 \end{bmatrix}$

Write the matrix equation for the system and solve.

47. $\begin{cases} 4x + 2y = 12 \\ 6x - y = -2 \end{cases}$

48. $\begin{cases} \frac{1}{3}x + 2y = -3 \\ y - 4 = -2x \end{cases}$

49. $\begin{cases} 3x + 3y = 12 \\ 2x + 9.5 = 5y \end{cases}$

Lesson 4-6

Write the augmented matrix for each system of equations.

50. $\begin{cases} 2x + 8 = 5y \\ 3y - 7 = 12x \end{cases}$

51. $\begin{cases} 9 - y = 2x \\ 3y = 18 \end{cases}$

52. $\begin{cases} 2x + 9y = 10 \\ 3x - z = 8 \\ 5z + 5 = 13y \end{cases}$

53. $\begin{cases} 4 - 5y = 8x \\ 13x + 12 = z \\ 4z - 2y = 0 \end{cases}$

Write the augmented matrix and use row reduction to solve.

54. $\begin{cases} 4x - 2y = 26 \\ x + 6y = -13 \end{cases}$

55. $\begin{cases} 8x - \frac{1}{2} = -3y \\ 4y - 8 = 4x \end{cases}$

56. $\begin{cases} 6x + \frac{1}{2}y = 6 \\ y + 14x = 12 \end{cases}$

57. $\begin{cases} 12x + y = -6 \\ 2y - 2x = 14 \end{cases}$

Extra Practice

Chapter 5 ■ Skills Practice

Lesson 5-1

Graph each function by using a table.

1. $f(x) = \frac{1}{2}x^2 - 4$
2. $f(x) = 2x^2 - x + 3$
3. $f(x) = -x^2 - 3x$

Using the graph of $f(x) = x^2$ as a guide, describe the transformations, and then graph each function.

4. $g(x) = (x + 2)^2 + 1$
5. $g(x) = -2x^2$
6. $g(x) = \frac{1}{4}x^2$

Use the description to write each quadratic function in vertex form.

7. The parent function $f(x) = x^2$ is vertically stretched by a factor of 3 and translated 6 units right to create g.
8. The parent function $f(x) = x^2$ is reflected across the x-axis and translated 12 units down to create g.

Lesson 5-2

Identify the axis of symmetry for the graph of each function.

9. $f(x) = 2x^2 + 1$
10. $f(x) = (x + 3)^2 - 5$
11. $f(x) = 3(x - 2)^2$

For each function, (a) determine whether the graph opens upward or downward, (b) find the axis of symmetry, (c) find the vertex, (d) find the y-intercept, and (e) graph the function.

12. $f(x) = 2x^2 - 4x + 5$
13. $f(x) = -\frac{1}{2}x^2 - 2x + 3$
14. $f(x) = -x^2 - 8x - 6$

Find the minimum or maximum value of each function. Then state the domain and range of the function.

15. $f(x) = 3x^2 + 60x + 294$
16. $f(x) = -2x^2 + 28x - 95$
17. $f(x) = 2x^2 + 14x + 30$

Lesson 5-3

Find the zeros of each function by using a graph and a table.

18. $f(x) = x^2 + 5x + 6$
19. $f(x) = x^2 - 3x - 28$
20. $f(x) = -x^2 + 12x - 20$

Find the zeros of each function by factoring.

21. $f(x) = x^2 + 2x - 35$
22. $f(x) = x^2 - 8x - 9$
23. $f(x) = 2x^2 - 9x$
24. $f(x) = x^2 + 10x + 25$
25. $f(x) = x^2 - 49$
26. $f(x) = x^2 - 12x + 36$

Write a quadratic function in standard form for each given set of zeros.

27. 5 and 8
28. −3 and 1
29. 6 and 6
30. 12 and 0

Lesson 5-4

Solve each equation.

31. $4x^2 - 10 = 90$
32. $x^2 + 8x + 16 = 10$
33. $x^2 + 4x + 4 = 8$

Complete the square for each expression. Write the resulting expression as a binomial squared.

34. $x^2 - 16x + \blacksquare$
35. $x^2 + 22x + \blacksquare$
36. $x^2 + 7x + \blacksquare$

Solve each equation by completing the square.

37. $x^2 + 8x = -10$
38. $x^2 - 12x = 13$
39. $x^2 + 20 = 10x$
40. $2x^2 + 12x = 14$
41. $3x^2 - 18 = 48x$
42. $x^2 - 5 = 2x$

Write each function in vertex form, and identify its vertex.

43. $f(x) = x^2 - 2x + 17$
44. $f(x) = x^2 + 4x - 8$
45. $f(x) = 4x^2 - 24x + 31$

Chapter 5 ■ Skills Practice

Lesson 5-5

Express each number in terms of *i*.

46. $2\sqrt{-81}$ **47.** $-\sqrt{-144}$ **48.** $\sqrt{-128}$ **49.** $5\sqrt{-48}$

Solve each equation.

50. $169 + x^2 = 0$ **51.** $2x^2 = -200$ **52.** $x^2 = -90$

Find the zeros of each function.

53. $f(x) = x^2 + 8x + 20$ **54.** $f(x) = x^2 - 14x + 65$ **55.** $f(x) = x^2 - 2x + 46$

Find each complex conjugate.

56. $12i$ **57.** $3 - 6i$ **58.** $10i - 3$ **59.** $2\sqrt{7} - 10i$

Lesson 5-6

Find the zeros of each function by using the Quadratic Formula.

60. $f(x) = x^2 - 10x + 3$ **61.** $f(x) = 2x^2 + 5x + 1$ **62.** $f(x) = -x^2 + 8x - 3$

63. $f(x) = x^2 - 6x + 40$ **64.** $f(x) = x^2 + 7x + 13$ **65.** $f(x) = 2x^2 - 9x + 25$

Find the type and number of solutions for each equation.

66. $x^2 + 8x = -16$ **67.** $x^2 + 3 = 10x$ **68.** $5 + 2x^2 = 12x$ **69.** $4x^2 + 2x = -9$

Lesson 5-7

Graph each inequality.

70. $y \geq (x + 3)^2 + 2$ **71.** $y < 2x^2 - 4x - 1$ **72.** $y < -x^2 + 11x - 24$

Solve each inequality.

73. $x^2 + 13x + 20 < -2$ **74.** $x^2 - 11x \geq -10$ **75.** $x^2 + 6x + 3 > 10$

76. $x^2 - 2x - 20 > 28$ **77.** $2x^2 - 9x \leq 5$ **78.** $3x^2 + 1 \geq 4x$

Lesson 5-8

Determine whether each data set could represent a quadratic function. Explain.

79.

x	3	4	5	6	7
y	−2	−5	−6	−5	−2

80.

x	−2	−1	0	1	2
y	−5	2	3	4	11

81.

x	−6	−5	−4	−3	−2
y	19	10	7	10	19

Write a quadratic function that fits each set of points.

82. $(-2, 0)$, $(1, 6)$, and $(3, -10)$ **83.** $(-4, -25)$, $(0, -9)$, and $(2, 5)$

Lesson 5-9

Graph each complex number.

84. -3 **85.** $2i$ **86.** $2 + 4i$ **87.** $-3 - 3i$

Find each absolute value.

88. $|6 + 9i|$ **89.** $|-3 + 4i|$ **90.** $|-7i|$

Simplify. Write the result in the form $a + bi$.

91. $(3 + 7i) + (-2 + 3i)$ **92.** $(-9 - 4i) + (5 + i)$ **93.** $(10 + 6i) - (3i - 12)$

94. $-3i(9 - 2i)$ **95.** $(2 - i)(4 + 3i)$ **96.** $(6 + 4i)(4 - 5i)$

97. $\frac{11 + 3i}{2 + i}$ **98.** $\frac{-44 - 40i}{-8 + 2i}$ **99.** $\frac{5 + 12i}{3 + 2i}$

Extra Practice

Chapter 6 ■ Skills Practice

Lesson 6-1

Identify the degree of each monomial.

1. $7x^2$
2. $-12x$
3. $2x^3y^3$
4. 8

Rewrite each polynomial in standard form. Then identify the leading coefficient, degree, and number of terms. Name the polynomial.

5. $5x^2 + 6 + 9x - 10x^3$
6. $3 - 12x^4 - 6x^2$
7. $14x + 15x^5$

Add or subtract. Write your answer in standard form.

8. $(12x^2 + 4x - 9) + (3x^3 - 7x^2 - 1)$
9. $(34 + 8x^3 - 9x^2) - (3x^3 + 10x^2 - 4x - 4)$

Graph each polynomial function on a calculator. Describe the graph, and identify the number of real zeros.

10. $f(x) = 5x^3 + 4x - 6$
11. $g(x) = 2x^4 - 12x + 3$
12. $h(x) = 3x^3 - 4x + 1$

Lesson 6-2

Find each product.

13. $3ab(2a^2 - 5ab + 9b)$
14. $-5cd^3(8d + 3c - c^2d)$
15. $(x + 3)(2x^2 - x + 6)$
16. $(2x - 1)(-x^2 + 5x + 5)$
17. $(2x + 6)^3$
18. $(y - 2)^4$

Expand each expression.

19. $(x - y)^5$
20. $(y + 4)^4$
21. $(2x + y)^5$
22. $(x - 2y)^4$

Lesson 6-3

Divide by using long division.

23. $(6x^2 + 7x - 2) \div (x + 4)$
24. $(2x^2 - 9x + 10) \div (2x - 1)$

Divide by using synthetic division.

25. $(3x^3 + 4x^2 - 8) \div (x - 2)$
26. $(2x^3 + 3x^2 - 6x - 4) \div (x - 1)$

Use synthetic division to evaluate the polynomial for the given value.

27. $P(x) = -2x^3 + 7x^2 - 3x - 9$ for $x = -2$
28. $P(x) = 6x^3 - 7x^2 + 10$ for $x = 0.5$

Lesson 6-4

Determine whether the given binomial is a factor of the polynomial $P(x)$.

29. $(x + 2)$; $P(x) = 3x^3 + 11x^2 + 2x - 16$
30. $(x - 4)$; $P(x) = 12x^3 + 9x^2 - 2x + 8$
31. $(x + 1)$; $P(x) = x^4 - 3x^3 + 10x + 4$
32. $(x - 3)$; $P(x) = x^3 - 3x^2 - 4x + 12$

Factor each expression.

33. $2x^3 + 12x^2 - 4x - 24$
34. $2x^3 + 5x^2 - 18x - 45$
35. $4x^3 + 12x^2 + 12x + 36$
36. $a^3 + 27$
37. $128b - 2b^4$
38. $4c^5 + 32c^2$

Lesson 6-5

Solve each polynomial equation by factoring.

39. $2x^3 + 3x^2 - 8x - 12 = 0$
40. $-3x^3 + 30x^2 + 5x - 50 = 0$

Identify the roots of each equation. State the multiplicity of each root.

41. $x^3 + 15x^2 + 75x + 125 = 0$
42. $x^3 - 2x^2 - 32x + 96 = 0$
43. $8x^3 - 12x^2 + 6x - 1 = 0$
44. $4x^3 + 16x^2 - 25x - 100 = 0$

Identify all of the real roots of each equation.

45. $2x^4 - x^3 - 14x^2 - 5x + 6 = 0$
46. $6x^3 - 11x^2 - 19x - 6 = 0$

Extra Practice

Chapter 6 ■ Skills Practice

Lesson 6-6 **Write the simplest polynomial function with the given zeros.**

47. $-1, 1, 4$ **48.** $-3, \frac{1}{2}, \frac{1}{3}$ **49.** $-3, 1, \frac{2}{3}$ **50.** $-5, 1, 2$

Solve each equation by finding all roots.

51. $x^4 - 5x^3 + 15x^2 - 45x + 54 = 0$ **52.** $2x^4 + 5x^3 - 10x^2 + 10x + 8 = 0$

Write the simplest polynomial function with the given zeros.

53. $3, \sqrt{5}$ **54.** $1 + i, 2$ **55.** $-2, 2i$ **56.** $1, \sqrt{2}, i$

Lesson 6-7 **Identify the leading coefficient, degree, and end behavior.**

57. $P(x) = 7x^3 - 12x^2 + 9x - 10$ **58.** $Q(x) = -3x^5 + 8x^4 - 16x + 1$

Identify whether the function graphed has an odd or even degree and a positive or negative leading coefficient.

59.

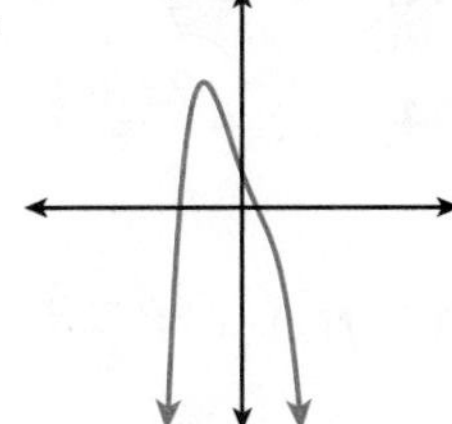

60.

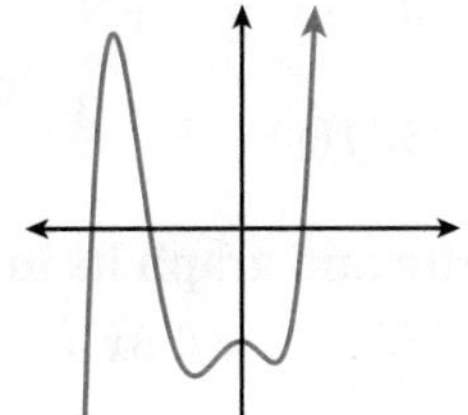

61.

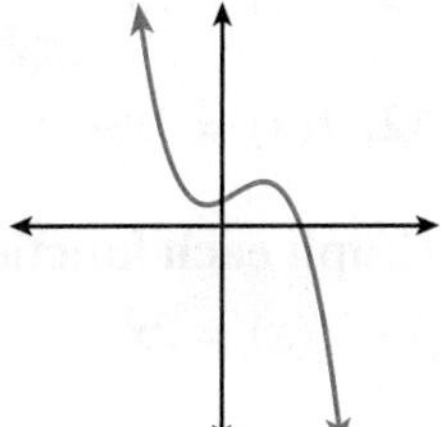

Graph each function.

62. $Q(x) = -4x^3 - 12x^2 + x + 3$ **63.** $R(x) = 2x^4 + x^3 - 19x^2 - 9x + 9$

Graph each function on a calculator, and estimate the local maxima and minima.

64. $S(x) = -2x^4 + x^3 + 5x^2 + 6$ **65.** $T(x) = x^3 + 5x^2 + 3x + 1$

Lesson 6-8 **For $f(x) = 2x^3 - 3$, write the rule for each function and sketch the graph.**

66. $g(x) = f(x) + 6$ **67.** $h(x) = f(x - 2)$ **68.** $j(x) = f(-x)$ **69.** $k(x) = \frac{1}{2}f(x)$

Let $f(x) = -3x^4 + 2x^2 - 7x + 10$. Write a function g that performs each transformation.

70. Reflect $f(x)$ across the y-axis. **71.** Reflect $f(x)$ across the x-axis.

Let $f(x) = x^3 - 7x^2 + 5$. Graph f and g on the same coordinate plane. Describe g as a transformation of f.

72. $g(x) = f(x + 4)$ **73.** $g(x) = -2f(x)$ **74.** $g(x) = f(-x) - 3$

Write a function that transforms $f(x) = 3x^3 - 5x^2 + x + 1$ in each of the following ways. Support your solution by using a graphing calculator.

75. Stretch vertically by a factor of 3 and move 1 unit to the right.

76. Reflect across the y-axis and move 1 unit down.

Lesson 6-9 **Use finite differences to determine the degree of the polynomial that best describes the data.**

77.

x	−2	−1	0	1	2	3
y	−24	−4	6	12	20	36

78.

x	−2	−1	0	1	2	3
y	−27	0	9	12	69	288

Extra Practice

Chapter 7 ■ Skills Practice

Lesson 7-1

Tell whether the function shows growth or decay. Then graph.

1. $f(x) = 12(2.4)^x$
2. $f(x) = 20\left(\frac{4}{5}\right)^x$
3. $f(x) = 0.25(5)^x$

Explain whether each function is exponential.

4. $f(x) = 4x^9$
5. $f(x) = 0.6^x$
6. $f(x) = 10(0)^x$

Lesson 7-2

Graph the relation and connect the points. Then graph the inverse. Identify the domain and range of each relation.

7.

x	1	2	3	4
y	−1	0	2	4

8.

x	−3	−1	2	4
y	−3	−1	−1	−3

Use inverse operations to write the inverse of each function.

9. $f(x) = 15x$
10. $f(x) = x + 9$
11. $f(x) = \frac{x}{7}$
12. $f(x) = 3x + 2$
13. $f(x) = 5 - \frac{3}{4}x$
14. $f(x) = \frac{2x+1}{5}$

Graph each function. Then write and graph its inverse.

15. $f(x) = 2x + 4$
16. $f(x) = 0.8x + 1$
17. $f(x) = \frac{4x-5}{3}$

Lesson 7-3

Write each exponential equation in logarithmic form.

18. $3^5 = 243$
19. $51^0 = 1$
20. $16^{1.5} = 64$
21. $7^x = 343$

Write each logarithmic equation in exponential form.

22. $\log_{64}512 = 1.5$
23. $\log_2 0.125 = -3$
24. $\log_4 x = 70$
25. $\log_x 12 = 3$

Evaluate by using mental math.

26. $\log_{10}1000$
27. $\log_5 0.2$
28. $\log_{0.5}0.125$
29. $\log_{1.1}1.21$

Use the given *x*-values to graph each function. Then graph its inverse. Describe the domain and range of the inverse function.

30. $f(x) = 4^x$; $x = -2, -1, 0, 1, 2$
31. $f(x) = 0.2^x$; $x = -2, -1, 0, 1, 2$

Lesson 7-4

Express as a single logarithm. Simplify, if possible.

32. $\log_2 10 + \log_2 12.8$
33. $\log_4 8 + \log_4 2$
34. $\log_5 1.25 + \log_5 4$
35. $\log_6 144 - \log_6 4$
36. $\log 10{,}000 - \log 100$
37. $\log_8 8 - \log_8 1$

Simplify, if possible.

38. $\log_8 64^4$
39. $\log_7 49^5$
40. $\log_9 1^4$
41. $\log_3 3^{5x+8}$
42. $4^{\log_4 12}$
43. $\log_{1.4}1.4^5$

Evaluate.

44. $\log_4 256$
45. $\log_4\left(\frac{1}{64}\right)$
46. $\log_3 7$
47. $\log_4 13$

Chapter 7 ■ Skills Practice

Lesson 7-5

Solve and check.

48. $3^{x+1} = 9^4$ **49.** $32^{x-2} = 8^x$ **50.** $9^x = 12$ **51.** $3.5^{2x-1} = 15$

Solve.

52. $\log_6(4x - 9) = \log_6(x)$ **53.** $\log_7(10x + 13) = 3$ **54.** $\log(20x) - \log 4 = 2$

55. $\log_9 x^3 = 8$ **56.** $\log x + \log(2x - 1) = 1$ **57.** $\log_3\left(\frac{2}{x}\right) + 2 = 0$

Use a table and a graph to solve.

58. $3^{4x-3} = 243$ **59.** $3^x 4^x \geq 1728$ **60.** $\log x^3 = x - 94$ **61.** $3\log x^2 < 6$

Lesson 7-6

Graph.

62. $f(x) = e^x - 1$ **63.** $f(x) = -2e^x + 3$ **64.** $f(x) = 2 - e^{-x}$ **65.** $f(x) = 1.5e^{x+1}$

Simplify.

66. $\ln e^{20}$ **67.** $\ln e^{2x+10}$ **68.** $e^{\ln 5x^2}$ **69.** $e^{2\ln 2x}$

Lesson 7-7

Make a table of values and graph each function. Describe the asymptote, the domain, and the range. Tell how the graph is transformed from the graph of $f(x) = 4^x$.

70. $g(x) = 4^x - 2$ **71.** $h(x) = 4^{x+2}$ **72.** $j(x) = 4^{x-1} - 4$

Graph each exponential function. Find the y-intercept, the asymptote, the domain, and the range. Describe how the graph is transformed from the graph of its parent function.

73. $g(x) = -\frac{1}{2}(3^x)$ **74.** $h(x) = 3(2^{-x})$ **75.** $j(x) = 5e^{x+1}$

Graph each logarithmic function. Find the asymptote. Then describe how the graph is transformed from the graph of its parent function.

76. $g(x) = -4\log x$ **77.** $h(x) = 3\ln(3 - x)$ **78.** $j(x) = \ln(0.5x) - 3$

Write each transformed function by using the given parent function and the indicated transformations.

79. The parent function $f(x) = 6^x$ is horizontally stretched by a factor of 3 and translated 4 units to the left.

80. The parent function $f(x) = \log x$ is vertically compressed by a factor of $\frac{1}{5}$, reflected across the y-axis, and translated 10 units down.

Lesson 7-8

Determine whether f is an exponential function of x. If so, find the constant ratio.

81.

x	−2	−1	1	2	3
y	0.4	2	10	50	250

82.

x	−2	−1	0	1	2
y	−17	−2	13	28	43

83.

x	−2	−1	0	1	2
y	4	2	1	0.5	0.25

84.

x	−2	−1	0	1	2
y	−6	1	12	37	54

Extra Practice

Chapter 8 ■ Skills Practice

Lesson 8-1

Given: y varies directly as x. Write and graph each direct variation function.

1. $y = 8$ when $x = 2$
2. $y = 21$ when $x = 3$
3. $y = 4$ when $x = 2.5$

Given: y varies inversely as x. Write and graph each inverse variation function.

4. $y = 4$ when $x = 2$
5. $y = 4$ when $x = \frac{1}{2}$
6. $y = \frac{3}{5}$ when $x = 10$

Determine whether each data set represents a direct variation, an inverse variation, or neither.

7.

x	1	3	6
y	2.5	7.5	15

8.

x	2	4	8
y	6	10	18

9.

x	2	8	20
y	5	1.25	0.5

Lesson 8-2

Simplify. Identify any x-values for which the expression is undefined.

10. $\dfrac{6x^3}{27x^2 + 12x}$
11. $\dfrac{x^2 - x - 2}{3x - 6}$
12. $\dfrac{-x^2 + 16}{-x^2 - 9x - 20}$

Multiply or divide. Assume that all expressions are defined.

13. $\dfrac{4xy^3}{5x^2} \cdot \dfrac{20x^3y^2}{-16xy^7}$
14. $\dfrac{x^2 - 9}{2x + 10} \cdot \dfrac{x + 5}{x - 3}$
15. $\dfrac{x - 4}{2x^2} \cdot \dfrac{x}{x^2 - x - 12}$
16. $\dfrac{3x^3}{4x + 4} \div \dfrac{9x}{x + 1}$
17. $\dfrac{12x^3y^6}{9xy} \div \dfrac{6y^2}{3x}$
18. $\dfrac{x^2 - 16}{x^2 + 4x + 3} \div \dfrac{x - 4}{x + 1}$

Lesson 8-3

Find the least common multiple for each pair.

19. $6x^3y$ and $2xy^2$
20. $x^2 + 5x$ and $x^2 - 25$
21. $x^2 - 3x - 18$ and $x^2 - 5x - 6$

Add or subtract. Identify any x-values for which the expression is undefined.

22. $\dfrac{x + 9}{2x + 1} + \dfrac{3x + 6}{2x + 1}$
23. $\dfrac{2}{x + 3} + \dfrac{4x}{x^2 - 9}$
24. $\dfrac{1}{x^2 + 6x + 8} + \dfrac{1}{x^2 - 6x - 16}$
25. $\dfrac{x - 6}{x + 5} - \dfrac{8x + 7}{x + 5}$
26. $\dfrac{x}{x + 1} - \dfrac{3}{x + 4}$
27. $\dfrac{7}{x - 9} - \dfrac{2x - 6}{x^2 - 13x + 36}$

Simplify. Assume that all expressions are defined.

28. $\dfrac{\frac{3x}{3x + 21}}{\frac{9x^2}{x + 7}}$
29. $\dfrac{\frac{x}{x - 1}}{\frac{10x^2}{-4x + 4}}$
30. $\dfrac{\frac{1}{x - 2}}{\frac{x + 3}{x^2 - 4}}$

Lesson 8-4

Using the graph of $f(x) = \frac{1}{x}$ as a guide, describe the transformation and graph each function.

31. $g(x) = \dfrac{1}{x - 4}$
32. $g(x) = \dfrac{1}{x} + 6$
33. $g(x) = \dfrac{1}{x + 2} - 5$

Identify the zeros and asymptotes of each function. Then graph.

34. $f(x) = \dfrac{x^2 - 5x - 24}{2x + 1}$
35. $f(x) = \dfrac{2x^2 - 3x - 2}{x - 4}$
36. $f(x) = \dfrac{-3x^2 + 8x - 4}{x^2 - 25}$

Identify holes in the graph of each function. Then graph.

37. $f(x) = \dfrac{x^2 - 4x - 21}{x + 3}$
38. $f(x) = \dfrac{x^2 - 4x - 5}{x^2 - 25}$
39. $f(x) = \dfrac{x^2 - 3x}{4x - 12}$

Extra Practice

Chapter 8 ■ Skills Practice

Lesson 8-5

Solve each equation.

40. $12 + \frac{2}{3x} = 6$ **41.** $x - \frac{1}{x} = \frac{35}{x}$ **42.** $\frac{x}{x+1} + \frac{x}{4} = \frac{3x}{4x+4}$

43. $\frac{x-1}{x-4} = \frac{x+6}{x}$ **44.** $\frac{6x}{x+5} = \frac{2x-20}{x+5}$ **45.** $\frac{4}{x-4} = \frac{-x}{x-4} + \frac{x}{2}$

Solve each inequality by using a graph and a table.

46. $\frac{2x+1}{x} \geq 3$ **47.** $\frac{4}{x+3} < 2$ **48.** $\frac{x-4}{2x} \geq 2$

Solve each inequality algebraically.

49. $\frac{3}{x+2} \leq 1$ **50.** $\frac{10}{x-2} < 2$ **51.** $\frac{15}{x+3} \leq 1$

Lesson 8-6

Simplify each expression. Assume all variables are positive.

52. $\sqrt[3]{343x^9}$ **53.** $\sqrt[5]{\frac{x^5}{32}}$ **54.** $\sqrt[4]{\frac{x^8y^4}{10}}$

Write each expression in radical form, and simplify.

55. $81^{\frac{3}{2}}$ **56.** $243^{\frac{2}{5}}$ **57.** $(-8)^{\frac{4}{3}}$

Write each expression using rational exponents.

58. $\sqrt[5]{10^2}$ **59.** $\sqrt[4]{17^3}$ **60.** $\left(\sqrt[5]{8}\right)^3$

Simplify each expression.

61. $8^{\frac{1}{2}} \cdot 8^{\frac{5}{2}}$ **62.** $\frac{4^{\frac{7}{2}}}{4^{\frac{1}{2}}}$ **63.** $\left(100^{\frac{1}{2}}\right)^3$

Lesson 8-7

Graph each function, and identify its domain and range.

64. $f(x) = \sqrt{x-4} + 1$ **65.** $f(x) = -\frac{1}{2}\sqrt{x}$ **66.** $f(x) = 2\sqrt[3]{x+2}$

Using the graph of $f(x) = \sqrt{x}$ as a guide, describe the transformation and graph each function.

67. $g(x) = \sqrt{x-8}$ **68.** $g(x) = -6\sqrt{x}$ **69.** $g(x) = \frac{1}{3}\sqrt{x} + 2$

Graph each inequality.

70. $y \geq \sqrt{x+2} - 3$ **71.** $y < 2\sqrt{-x}$ **72.** $y > -4\sqrt[3]{x} + 4$

Lesson 8-8

Solve each equation.

73. $\sqrt{2x+10} = 10$ **74.** $\sqrt{4x+4} = 2\sqrt{4x-9}$ **75.** $3\sqrt[3]{x} = \sqrt[3]{7x+40}$

76. $\sqrt{2x+48} = x$ **77.** $2x + 5 = \sqrt{4x+10}$ **78.** $x + 6 = \sqrt{4x+21}$

79. $(3x-5)^{\frac{1}{2}} = 4$ **80.** $(x-4)^{\frac{1}{3}} = -2$ **81.** $(8x-7)^{\frac{1}{2}} = x$

Solve each inequality.

82. $\sqrt{x-7} < 3$ **83.** $\sqrt{3x+1} + 2 \leq 6$ **84.** $\sqrt{2x-3} > 5$

Chapter 9 ■ Skills Practice

Lesson 9-1

Match each situation to its corresponding graph. Sketch a possible graph of the situation if the situation does not match any of the given graphs.

Graph A

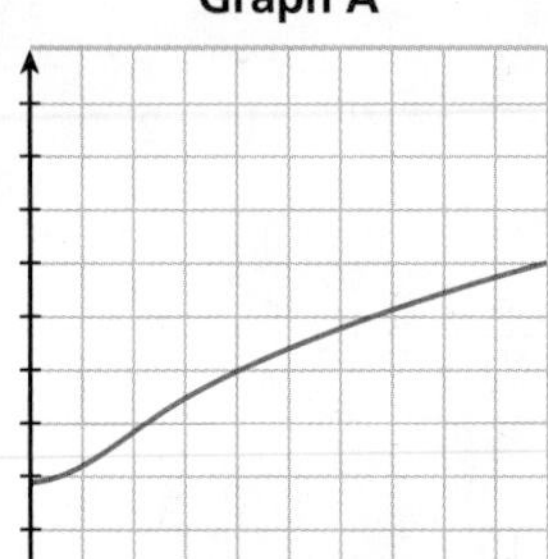

Graph B

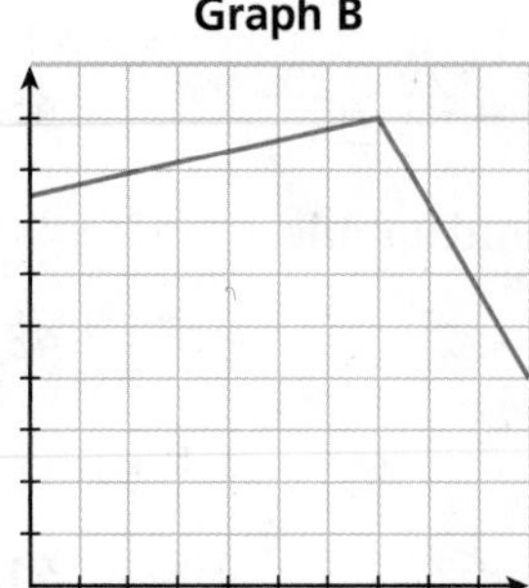

Graph C

Graph D

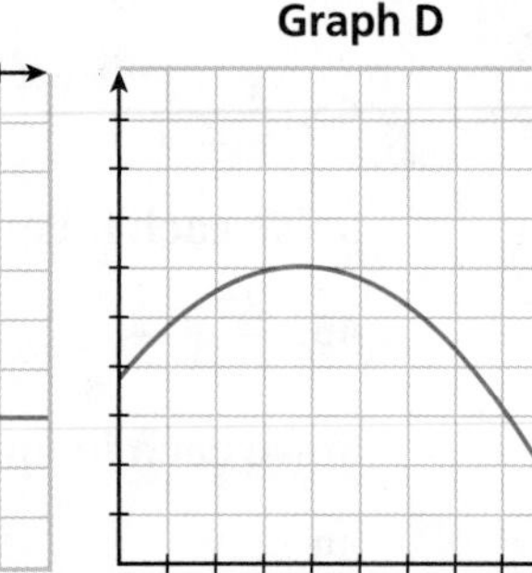

1. A state senator's high approval rating is rising steadily but then drops sharply after a scandal.
2. The value of an antique chair increases steadily.
3. Sales of a valuable stock dip and then recover.
4. A scuba diver descends to 60 ft below sea level and swims around at that depth.

Lesson 9-2

Create a table and a verbal description to represent each graph.

5.

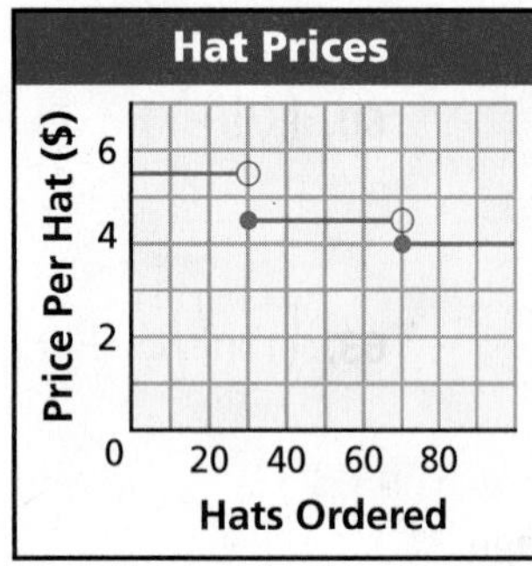

6.

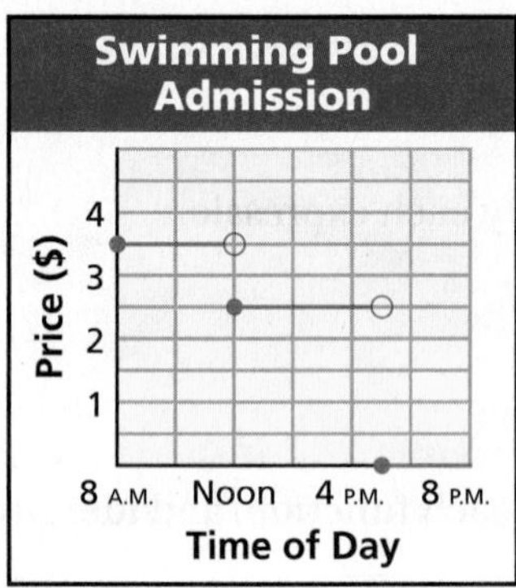

Evaluate each piecewise function for $x = -2$ and $x = 5$.

7. $f(x) = \begin{cases} 10 & \text{if } x \le -4 \\ 7 & \text{if } -4 < x \le 2 \\ 3 & \text{if } x > 2 \end{cases}$

8. $g(x) = \begin{cases} x + 2 & \text{if } x < 0 \\ 4 - x & \text{if } x \ge 0 \end{cases}$

9. $h(x) = \begin{cases} x^2 - 3 & \text{if } x \le 2 \\ x + 1 & \text{if } x > 2 \end{cases}$

Graph each function.

10. $f(x) = \begin{cases} 4 & \text{if } x < -1 \\ -1 & \text{if } x \ge -1 \end{cases}$

11. $g(x) = \begin{cases} 2x - 4 & \text{if } x \le 2 \\ -2x + 2 & \text{if } x > 2 \end{cases}$

12. $h(x) = \begin{cases} 2 & \text{if } x < 3 \\ x^2 - 7 & \text{if } x \ge 3 \end{cases}$

Lesson 9-3

Given $f(x) = \begin{cases} 2x - 2 & \text{if } x < 1 \\ -3x & \text{if } x \ge 1 \end{cases}$, write the rule for each function.

13. $g(x)$, a vertical stretch by a factor of 3

14. $h(x)$, a reflection across the y-axis

Identify the x- and y-intercepts of $f(x)$. Without graphing $g(x)$, identify its x- and y-intercepts.

15. $f(x) = -3x + 6$ and $g(x) = f(-2x)$

16. $f(x) = (x - 3)^2$ and $g(x) = -2f(x)$

Chapter 9 ■ Skills Practice

Lesson 9-4

Given $f(x)$, graph $g(x)$.

17. $f(x) = \frac{1}{2}x - 4$ and $g(x) = f(-x) + 2$ **18.** $f(x) = |x + 2|$ and $g(x) = \frac{1}{2}f(x - 1) - 4$

Given $f(x) = -2x + 5$ and $g(x) = 4x^2 - 11$, find each function.

19. $(f + g)(x)$ **20.** $(f - g)(x)$ **21.** $(g - f)(x)$

Given $f(x) = x - 3$ and $g(x) = x^2 + 3x - 18$, find each function.

22. $(fg)(x)$ **23.** $\left(\frac{f}{g}\right)(x)$ **24.** $\left(\frac{g}{f}\right)(x)$

Given $f(x) = \frac{1}{2}x + 5$ and $g(x) = -2x^2$, find each value.

25. $f(g(2))$ **26.** $g(f(2))$ **27.** $g(f(-6))$

Given $f(x) = \sqrt{x}$, $g(x) = 2x + 3$, and $h(x) = x^2 + 20$, write each composite function. State the domain of each.

28. $f(g(x))$ **29.** $g(f(x))$ **30.** $g(h(x))$

Lesson 9-5

Use the horizontal-line test to determine whether the inverse of each relation is a function.

31.

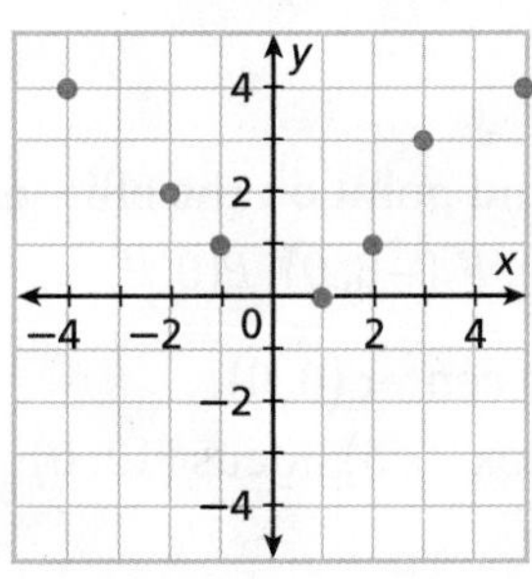

32.

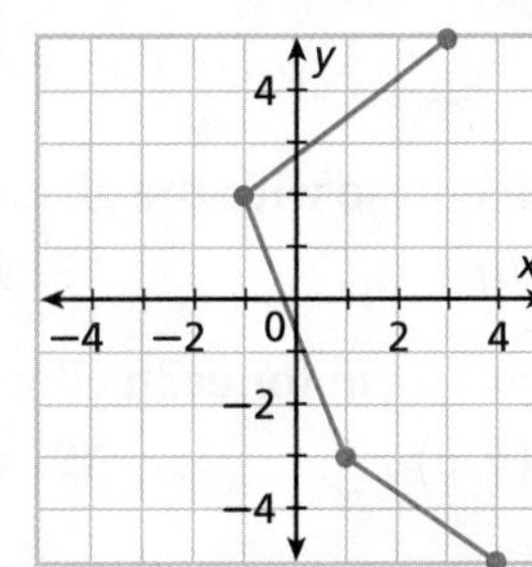

33.

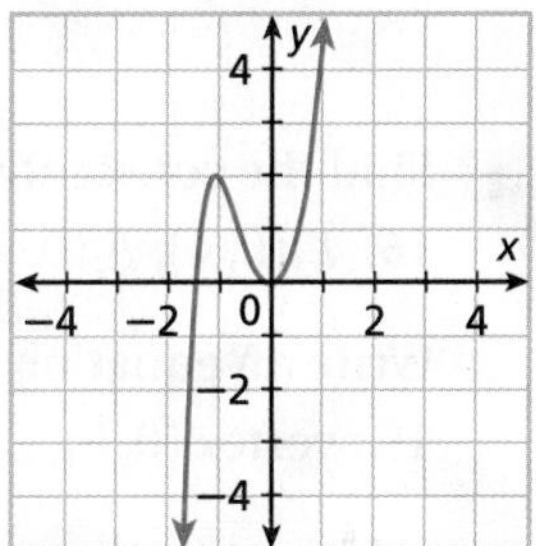

Find the inverse of each function. Determine whether the inverse is a function, and state its domain and range.

34. $f(x) = \frac{1}{2}x - 7$ **35.** $g(x) = 10 - x^2$ **36.** $h(x) = \frac{3}{4 + x}$

Determine by composition whether each pair of functions are inverses.

37. $f(x) = \frac{3}{4}x^2$ and $g(x) = \sqrt{\frac{4}{3}x}$ for $x \geq 0$ **38.** $f(x) = \frac{12x + 1}{5}$ and $g(x) = \frac{5}{12x - 1}$

Lesson 9-6

Use constant differences or ratios to determine which parent function would best model the given data set.

39.

x	y
1	6
3	−12
5	−30
7	−48
9	−66

40.

x	y
2	−3
4	6
6	21
8	42
10	69

41.

x	y
0	0.5
1	2
2	8
3	32
4	128

Extra Practice

Lesson 10-1

Graph each equation on a graphing calculator. Identify each conic section. Then describe the center and intercepts.

1. $4x^2 + 16y^2 = 64$
2. $x^2 + y^2 = 4$
3. $4x^2 + 4y^2 = 100$

Graph each equation on a graphing calculator. Identify each conic section. Then describe the vertices and the direction that the graph opens.

4. $x^2 = y^2 + 16$
5. $-10y^2 = x$
6. $2y^2 - x^2 = 5$

Find the center and radius of a circle that has a diameter with the given endpoints.

7. $(-2, -1)$ and $(6, 3)$
8. $(-4, 0)$ and $(2, 8)$
9. $(2, 1)$ and $(8, -1)$

Lesson 10-2

Write the equation of each circle.

10. center $(-4, 3)$ and radius $r = 3$
11. center $(4, 6)$ and radius $r = 9$
12. center $(-3, 3)$ and containing the point $(-3, 0)$
13. center $(2, -5)$ and containing the point $(4, -3)$

Write the equation of the line that is tangent to each circle at the given point.

14. $(x + 2)^2 + (y + 4)^2 = 25$; $(-5, 0)$
15. $(x - 4)^2 + y^2 = 100$; $(10, 8)$

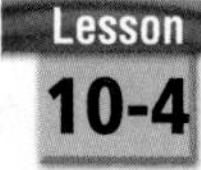

Lesson 10-3

Find the constant sum of an ellipse with the given foci and point on the ellipse.

16. $F_1(0, 4)$, $F_2(0, -4)$, $P(3, 0)$
17. $F_1(6, 0)$, $F_2(-6, 0)$, $P(0, 8)$

Write an equation in standard form for each ellipse with center $(0, 0)$.

18. vertex $(0, 6)$, co-vertex $(5, 0)$
19. co-vertex $(0, 5)$, focus $(12, 0)$

Graph each ellipse.

20. $\frac{x^2}{16} + \frac{y^2}{49} = 1$
21. $\frac{x^2}{100} + \frac{y^2}{36} = 1$
22. $\frac{(x-3)^2}{25} + \frac{(y+2)^2}{64} = 1$

Lesson 10-4

Find the constant difference for a hyperbola with the given foci and point on the hyperbola.

23. $F_1(-15, 0)$, $F_2(15, 0)$, $P(12, 0)$
24. $F_1(0, 16)$, $F_2(0, -16)$, $P(0, 10)$

Write an equation in standard form for each hyperbola.

25.

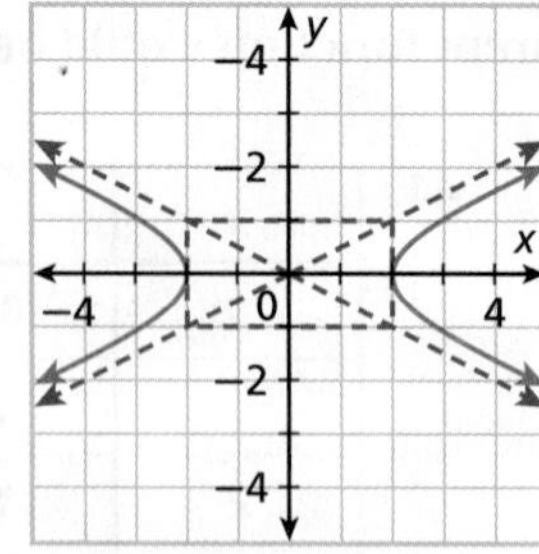

26.

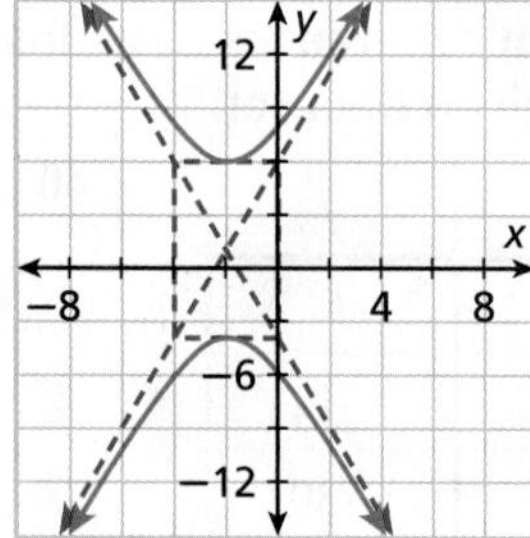

Find the vertices, co-vertices, and asymptotes of each hyperbola, and then graph.

27. $\frac{x^2}{25} - \frac{y^2}{9} = 1$
28. $\frac{(x-4)^2}{16} - \frac{(y+2)^2}{4} = 1$
29. $\frac{(y-2)^2}{9} - (x-2)^2 = 1$

Chapter 14 ■ Skills Practice

Lesson 14-3

Prove each trigonometric identity.

22. $\sec(-\theta) = \sec\theta$
23. $\dfrac{1 - \cos\theta}{\sin\theta} = \dfrac{\sin\theta}{1 + \cos\theta}$
24. $\tan^2\theta\left(1 - \sin^2\theta\right) = \sin^2\theta$

Rewrite each expression in terms of cos θ and simplify.

25. $\sec\theta\left(1 - \sin^2\theta\right)$
26. $\dfrac{\sin^2\theta}{1 + \cos\theta}$
27. $\dfrac{\csc\theta - \sin\theta}{\cot\theta}$

Rewrite each expression in terms of sin θ and simplify.

28. $\dfrac{\tan\theta + 1}{\sec\theta + \csc\theta}$
29. $\dfrac{\cot\theta}{\csc\theta}$
30. $1 - \cot\theta\cos\theta\sin\theta$

Lesson 14-4

Find each value if $\sin A = \frac{12}{13}$ with $0° < A < 90°$ and if $\cos B = -\frac{3}{5}$ with $90° < B < 180°$.

31. $\sin(A + B)$
32. $\cos(A - B)$
33. $\tan(A + B)$

Find the coordinates, to the nearest hundredth, of the vertices of figure *ABCD* with $A(-2, -2)$, $B(-2, 3)$, $C(1, 3)$, and $D(1, -2)$ after each rotation about the origin.

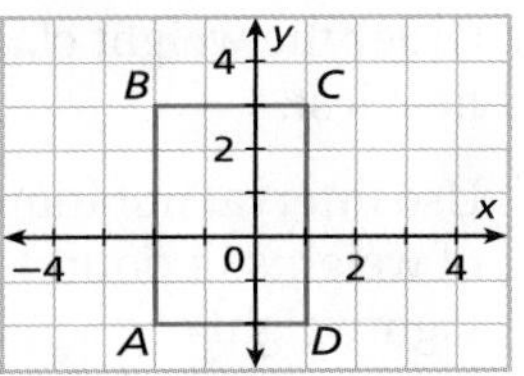

34. 135°
35. 270°

Lesson 14-5

Find sin 2θ, cos 2θ, and tan 2θ for each set of conditions.

36. $\sin\theta = \frac{12}{13}$ and $0° < \theta < 90°$
37. $\cos\theta = -\frac{3}{5}$ and $180° < \theta < 270°$
38. $\tan\theta = -\frac{3}{2}$ and $\frac{3\pi}{2} < \theta < 2\pi$
39. $\sin\theta = \frac{1}{3}$ and $\frac{\pi}{2} < \theta < \pi$

Prove each identity.

40. $\dfrac{\cos 2\theta}{\cos\theta + \sin\theta} = \cos\theta - \sin\theta$
41. $\dfrac{\cos\theta\sin 2\theta}{1 + \cos 2\theta} = \sin\theta$
42. $\cos 2\theta + 2\sin^2\theta = 1$
43. $(\sin\theta - \cos\theta)^2 = 1 - \sin 2\theta$

Find $\sin\frac{\theta}{2}$, $\cos\frac{\theta}{2}$, and $\tan\frac{\theta}{2}$ for each set of conditions.

44. $\sin\theta = \frac{3}{5}$ and $90° < \theta < 180°$
45. $\tan\theta = -\frac{7}{24}$ and $270° < \theta < 360°$
46. $\tan\theta = -\frac{\sqrt{5}}{2}$ and $\frac{\pi}{2} < \theta < \pi$
47. $\cos\theta = \frac{1}{5}$ and $0 < \theta < \frac{\pi}{2}$

Lesson 14-6

Find all of the solutions of each equation.

48. $2\cos\theta = \sqrt{2}$
49. $2\sin\theta + 5 = 6$
50. $3\tan\theta = 2\tan\theta - 1$
51. $\tan\theta = 2\tan\theta - \sqrt{3}$

Solve each equation for the given domain.

52. $\cos^2\theta - 3\cos\theta - 4 = 0$ for $0 \le \theta < 2\pi$
53. $2\sin^2\theta - 5\sin\theta + 2 = 0$ for $0 \le \theta < 2\pi$
54. $\sin^2\theta + 3\sin\theta + 1 = 0$ for $0° \le \theta < 360°$
55. $\cos^2\theta + 4\cos\theta - 2 = 0$ for $0° \le \theta < 360°$

Use trigonometric identities to solve each equation for the given domain.

56. $\cos 2\theta + 3\cos\theta = 1$ for $0 \le \theta < 2\pi$
57. $\cos 2\theta + 5\sin\theta = -2$ for $0 \le \theta < 2\pi$
58. $2\sin^2\theta = 3 - 3\cos\theta$ for $0° \le \theta < 360°$
59. $\sin 2\theta = \cos\theta$ for $0° \le \theta < 360°$

Extra Practice

Extra Practice

Chapter 1 ▪ Applications Practice

Sports Use the following information for Exercises 1–3.

In women's boxing, some of the official weight classes in pounds are defined in the table below. Each class includes the lightest weight in the range but not the heaviest weight. *(Lesson 1-1)*

Middleweight 154–160	Featherweight 122–126
Jr. Middleweight 147–154	Bantamweight 115–118
Super Lightweight 135–140	Welterweight 140–147

1. Order the weight classes from lightest to heaviest.
2. Use interval notation to represent the set of weights in pounds that define the Super Lightweight class.
3. Use set-builder notation to represent the set of weights in pounds that define the Welterweight class.
4. **Commerce** A sweater is on sale for 20% off. The regular price of the sweater is \$60. Use mental math to determine the sale price of the sweater. Explain how you determined your answer. *(Lesson 1-2)*
5. **Construction** A builder is covering a rectangular floor with square tiles. A row of 46 tiles fits along the length of the room, and a row of 26 tiles fits along the width of the room. If each tile covers 20.25 in^2, what are the dimensions of the room in feet? *(Lesson 1-3)*

Money Use the following information for Exercises 6 and 7.

Charles pays \$1.25 for a newspaper using only quarters and dimes. Let q represent the number of quarters he uses. *(Lesson 1-4)*

6. Write an expression in terms of q for the number of dimes Charles uses.
7. If Charles uses 3 quarters, how many dimes does he use?
8. **Astronomy** The diameter of the Sun is 1.392×10^6 km. What is the radius of the Sun in kilometers? Express your answer in scientific notation. *(Lesson 1-5)*
9. **Shipping** The table shows the cost of shipping packages that weigh up to 3 lb. Is the relation from weight to cost a function? Is the relation from cost to weight a function? Explain. *(Lesson 1-6)*

Weight (lb)	Cost (\$)
Up to 1 lb	3.69
More than 1 lb and up to 2 lb	3.85
More than 2 lb and up to 3 lb	4.65

Communication Use the following information for Exercises 10 and 11.

A cell phone plan charges \$2.99 per month for 300 text messages plus \$0.05 for each additional text message. *(Lesson 1-7)*

10. Write a function to represent the monthly charge in dollars for x text messages.
11. What is the value of the function for an input of 450, and what does it represent?
12. **Recreation** A bowling alley charges \$4.00 to rent shoes and \$2.75 per game. As part of a promotion, the alley lowers the price of shoes to \$3.00. What kind of transformation describes the change in the total cost of bowling x games per person? *(Lesson 1-8)*
13. **Sports** Each team in a soccer league plays each of the other teams one time during a season. Graph the relationship between the number of teams and the total number of games and identify which parent function best describes the data. Then use the graph to estimate the total number of games per season when there are 8 teams in the league. *(Lesson 1-9)*

Total Number of Games per Season					
Teams	4	6	10	12	14
Games	6	15	45	66	91

Chapter 2 ■ Applications Practice

1. **Poetry** An English sonnet is made up of 14 lines of text. Rebecca is working on a poetry project for her English class that must be at least 100 lines long. Rebecca has already written 61 lines of haiku, free-verse poems, and limericks, and she plans to write the rest in sonnet form. How many sonnets must she write to complete the project? *(Lesson 2-1)*

2. **Nutrition** Tom follows a strict diet in which he gets 22% of his daily Calories from fat. His diet contains 363 Calories of fat each day. What is his total daily caloric intake? *(Lesson 2-2)*

Home Economics Use the following information for Exercises 3 and 4.

Jonathan owes his parents $150 for car repairs. For each hour of chores he does, Jonathan's parents credit him $8 toward his debt. *(Lesson 2-3)*

3. Make a graph showing the amount that Jonathan owes his parents versus the number of hours he does chores.

4. What are the intercepts of the graph? What do they mean?

Consumer Economics Use the following information for Exercises 5 and 6.

The table below shows the cost of several long-distance calls made using the same calling plan. *(Lesson 2-4)*

Time (min)	7	12	15	24
Cost ($)	$1.80	$2.55	$3.00	$4.35

5. Find the function that represents the data and write it in slope-intercept form. What do the slope and y-intercept represent?

6. Make a graph to show the cost of all phone calls up to 20 minutes.

7. **Sports** The basketball team is losing by 8 points. They score either 2 points or 3 points for each basket they make. Write and graph an inequality for the number of 2-point and 3-point baskets the team needs to make in order to win the game if the other team scores 16 more points. *(Lesson 2-5)*

Careers Use the following information for Exercises 8 and 9.

At a spa each masseur earns $80 per day plus $15 per massage. Starting next month, the per-massage fee will be raised to $30. *(Lesson 2-6)*

8. Write $f(x)$ to represent the original earnings and $g(x)$ to represent the new earnings.

9. Graph $f(x)$ and $g(x)$ on the same coordinate plane. Describe the transformation.

10. **Astronomy** The table below shows the distances from four planets to the Sun and the time it takes in Earth days for each planet to complete its revolution around the Sun.

Planet	Mercury	Venus	Earth	Mars
Distance (million km)	58	108	150	228
Revolution (Earth days)	88	225	365	687

Make a scatter plot using distance as the independent variable. Find the line of best fit and correlation coefficient. *(Lesson 2-7)*

11. **Meteorology** A meteorologist predicts that Sunday's high temperature will be 76°F. Her predictions are generally accurate to within 4°F. Write and solve an absolute-value inequality to find the possible high temperatures. *(Lesson 2-8)*

12. **Architecture** The TransAmerica Pyramid in San Francisco is 324 meters high and 81 meters wide at its base. The diagram shows a side view of the building. The vertex is at $(40.5, 324)$. Write an absolute-value equation to describe the graph. *(Lesson 2-9)*

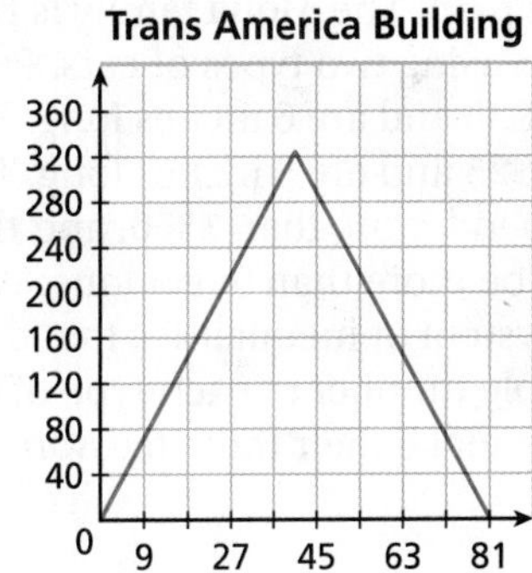

Extra Practice

Chapter 3 ■ Applications Practice

Oceanography **Use the following information for Exercises 1–3.**

A dolphin and a shark are swimming toward the same fish. The dolphin is 88 meters away and is swimming at a rate of 10.7 meters per second. The shark is 100 meters away and is swimming at a rate of 12.2 meters per second. *(Lesson 3-1)*

1. Write and graph a system of equations that could be used to model the distance of both the dolphin and the shark from the fish.
2. In how many seconds will the dolphin and the shark be the same distance from the fish?
3. What will that distance be?
4. **Chemistry** A chemist needs 16 ounces of a 10% potassium chloride solution. Solution A contains 12% potassium chloride, and solution B contains 8% potassium chloride. How much of each solution must the chemist combine? *(Lesson 3-2)*
5. **Consumer Economics** At the hardware store, Leslie bought 2 boxes of nails and 3 boxes of screws and paid $13.95 before tax. Michael bought 4 boxes of nails and 1 box of screws and paid $12.15 before tax. Find the cost of a box of nails and the cost of a box of screws. *(Lesson 3-2)*
6. **Entertainment** Hillary and Rob are at a multimedia store buying CDs and DVDs. The CDs cost $14 each, and the DVDs cost $12 each. Their total budget is $150, and Hillary wants to make sure that they buy at least as many DVDs as they buy CDs. Write and graph a system of inequalities that describes the possible number of CDs and DVDs they can buy. *(Lesson 3-3)*
7. **Construction** The Moua family is building a toy train using two types of cars. Passenger cars cost $30 and are 6 inches long. Freight cars cost $25 and are 9 inches long. They cannot spend more than $350, and the train must not be more than 9 feet long. Write and graph a system of inequalities that describes the possible number of each type of car they can use to make their train. *(Lesson 3-3)*

Business **Use the following information for Exercises 8 and 9.**

Leona owns a small business selling earrings and necklaces. Each pair of earrings takes 30 minutes to make and yields $3 of profit. Each necklace takes 1 hour to make and yields $7 of profit. Leona works no more than 7 hours per day, and she always makes at least 4 pairs of earrings each day. *(Lesson 3-4)*

8. Write a system of inequalities and graph the feasible region for how many earrings and necklaces Leona can make in a day.
9. Write an equation describing Leona's profit P. How many of each product should she make each day to maximize her profits?

Interior Design **Use the following information for Exercises 10 and 11.**

Mrs. Walsh has $150 to spend on decorations for her living room. She plans to buy candles, picture frames, and decorative pillows. The candles are 3 for $20, the picture frames cost $15 each, and the pillows cost $25 each. *(Lesson 3-5)*

10. Write a linear equation in three variables to represent this situation.
11. If Mrs. Walsh buys 6 candles and 4 frames, how many pillows can she buy?

Fitness **Use the following information for Exercises 12 and 13.**

Each day at the gym, Jaya cycles on the stationary bicycle, lifts weights, and swims laps. The table shows the number of minutes she spent doing each activity and the number of Calories she burned on 3 different days. *(Lesson 3-6)*

Day	Cycling	Weight Lifting	Swimmimg	Total Calories
1	30	30	20	455
2	25	45	15	432.5
3	25	20	30	495

12. How many Calories per minute does each activity burn?
13. How many Calories would Jaya burn if she spent 40 minutes cycling, 20 minutes lifting weights, and 20 minutes swimming?

Extra Practice

Chapter 4 ■ Applications Practice

Transportation **Use the following information for Exercises 1 and 2.**

The table shows the costs for different bus tickets from San Antonio to Dallas. *(Lesson 4-1)*

Category	Child	Student	Adult	Senior
One-Way	\$18.00	\$23.50	\$41.00	\$34.50
Round-Trip	\$34.00	\$45.00	\$79.00	\$66.00

1. Next year, the bus company will raise the price of each ticket by 3%. Use a scalar product to find the new ticket prices.
2. Due to a rise in gas prices this month, the bus company is temporarily charging passengers an extra \$2.50 per one-way ticket and \$4.50 per round-trip ticket. Use matrix addition to find the new ticket prices.
3. **Taxes** Different portions of Mr. Waller's income are taxed at different rates. Use matrix multiplication to find the total amount of taxes he paid each year. *(Lesson 4-2)*

Tax Rates			Mr. Waller's Income		
Year	Job	Home Business	Source	2004	2005
2004	23%	31%	Job	\$23,550	\$25,750
2005	24%	31%	Home Business	\$5,600	\$5,200

4. **Design** The Fishing Club's new logo is shaped like a fish on a fishing line. On a coordinate plane, the vertices of the image are $(-1, 1)$, $(2, -3)$, $(0, -5)$, $(4, -5)$, $(5, 1)$, $(2, 5)$ and $(2, 10)$. Find the vertices of the figure after it is enlarged by a factor of 2 and reflected across the x-axis. *(Lesson 4-3)*

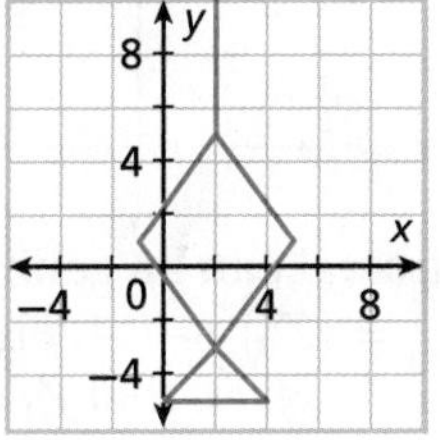

Gardening **Use the following information for Exercises 5 and 6.**

Mrs. Alarcón bought 3 geraniums, 2 ferns, and 2 petunias for \$67.00. Mrs. Muñiz bought 4 geraniums, 4 petunias, and 1 fern for \$89.50. The geraniums cost \$3.50 more than the ferns. *(Lesson 4-4)*

5. Write the coefficient matrix for the problem.
6. Use Cramer's rule to find the cost of each type of plant.

Sports **Use the following information for Exercises 7–9.**

The gymnastics coach kept track of how many of each type of deduction some of his gymnasts received during the balance beam exercise at their last meet. *(Lesson 4-5)*

	Stepping Out of Bounds	Heavy Brush of Hands/ Feet	Out of Sync with Music	Total Points Lost
Amber	2	1	1	0.55
Marcia	1	2	1	0.75
Jenna	3	1	2	0.70

7. Write the appropriate matrix equation.
8. Find the inverse of the coefficient matrix.
9. Solve the matrix equation to find the amount of each deduction.

Manufacturing **Use the following information for Exercises 10 and 11.**

A manufacturing company makes wooden boxes in small, medium, and large sizes out of the same wood. The table shows how many of each box were made and how much wood was used on 3 different days. *(Lesson 4-6)*

	Small	Medium	Large	Wood Used
Mon	10	12	8	4468 in^2
Tue	7	15	10	5068 in^2
Wed	20	9	5	4298 in^2

10. Write an augmented matrix to describe the situation.
11. Use row operations to find the amount of wood used to make each size of box.

Extra Practice

Chapter 5 ■ Applications Practice

Construction **Use the following information for Exercises 1 and 2.**

A landscape designer is using square stepping stones in a backyard. The function $f(x) = 8x^2$ represents the area in square inches that will be covered by 8 stepping stones with side length x inches. *(Lesson 5-1)*

1. Write a function g for the area that will be covered by 16 stepping stones with side length x inches. Describe g as a transformation of f.

2. The landscape designer decides to use smaller stones with a side length of $(x - 2)$ inches. Write a function h for the area that will be covered by 8 of the smaller stones. Describe h as a transformation of f.

Entertainment **Use the following information for Exercises 3 and 4.**

Part of a roller coaster's path can be modeled by the function $f(x) = -\frac{4}{49}x^2 + \frac{40}{7}x$, where x is the horizontal distance in feet the roller coaster has traveled and f is its height in feet above the ground. *(Lesson 5-2)*

3. What is the roller coaster's maximum height above the ground on this part of the path?

4. How far has the roller coaster traveled horizontally when it reaches its maximum height?

Sports **Use the following information for Exercises 5–7.**

A kickball player kicks a ball from ground level with an initial vertical velocity of 24 ft/s.

5. Write a function in standard form for the ball's height h in feet, where t is the time in seconds after the ball is thrown. *(Lesson 5-3)*

6. How long is the ball in the air? *(Lesson 5-3)*

7. Complete the square to rewrite h in vertex form. What is the ball's maximum height? *(Lesson 5-4)*

8. **School** In a student's science fair project, he claims that the height h in feet above the ground of an object shot from a catapult can be modeled by $h(t) = 16t^2 - 32t + 32$, where t is the time in seconds after the object is shot. What are the zeros of this function? Explain why the values of the zeros indicate that the student's model is incorrect. *(Lesson 5-5)*

9. **Forestry** A wind gust blows a cone from a branch on a redwood tree. The cone's height h in meters above the ground can be modeled by $h(t) = -4.9t^2 - t + 75$, where t is the time in seconds since the cone broke from the branch. To the nearest tenth of a second, how long does the cone fall before hitting the ground? *(Lesson 5-6)*

10. **Business** The weekly profit p in dollars generated by a smoothie stand can be modeled by the function $p(c) = -302c^2 + 1635c - 1712$, where c is the cost in dollars per smoothie. For what range of smoothie costs will the stand generate at least $450 per week? *(Lesson 5-7)*

11. **Law Enforcement** The table shows the cost of speeding tickets in a certain town, based on how many miles per hour over the speed limit the driver was traveling. Find a quadratic model for the fine given the number of miles per hour over the speed limit. Estimate the fine for a driver traveling 8 mi/h over the speed limit. *(Lesson 5-8)*

Miles per Hour over the Speed Limit	Fine ($)
5	55
10	70
15	95
20	130

12. **Fractals** A fractal can be generated from the formula $Z_{n+1} = (Z_n)^2 + 0.4$. Find the value of Z_2 for this fractal given that $Z_1 = 0.5 - 0.5i$ and $Z_2 = (Z_1)^2 + 0.4$.

Chapter 6 ■ Applications Practice

Manufacturing **Use the following information for Exercises 1 and 2.**

A company produces globes in two different sizes. The large globes have a radius of x inches, and the small globes have a radius of $x - 2$ inches. *(Lesson 6-1)*

1. Write functions to find the volume of each globe size.

2. Evaluate each function for $x = 8$.

Business **Use the following information for Exercises 3 and 4.**

Mr. Schwartz models the number of items his business sold during its first 10 years as $N(x) = 0.07x^3 + 9x^2 - 16x + 80$. His average profit per item (in dollars) can be modeled as $P(x) = 0.5x + 10$. *(Lesson 6-2)*

3. Write a polynomial $T(x)$ that can be used to model the total profit for his company during these years.

4. Evaluate $T(4)$ and explain its significance.

5. **Entertainment** The concert attendance for a music group can be described by the function $F(x) = \frac{1}{4}x^3 + 2x^2 + 50$, where x is the number of concerts since its debut. Use synthetic division to find the number of people who attended the fourth concert. *(Lesson 6-3)*

Sports **Use the following information for Exercises 6 and 7.**

The manager of a basketball team charted the team's progress for the season. For each game, she took the team's points and subtracted the points that the other team scored. The team's performance can be modeled by the function $P(x) = x^3 - 9x^2 + 18x$, where x represents the number of games since the start of the season. *(Lesson 6-4)*

6. Find the zeros of the function. What do they represent?

7. Write the function in factored form.

8. **Packaging** A company packages its ink pens in a box whose length is 3 inches longer than its width and whose height is 2 inches shorter than its width. The volume of the box is 18 in^3. What are the dimensions of the box? *(Lesson 6-5)*

9. **Medicine** A medicine capsule is shaped like a cylinder with a hemisphere at each end. The cylindrical portion of the capsule is 3 cm long, and the volume is $\frac{9}{4}\pi$ cm^3. Find the radius of the capsule. *(Lesson 6-6)*

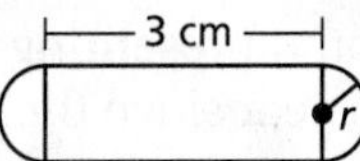

Investing **Use the following information for Exercises 10–12.**

Sharon tracked the closing value of a stock that she owns each day over a 25-day period. On average, the stock followed the curve $F(x) = -0.005x^3 + 0.05x^2 + x + 31.25$. *(Lesson 6-7)*

10. Graph the function on a graphing calculator.

11. What is the maximum value that the stock hit, and on approximately what day did it occur?

12. What is the y-intercept of the graph, and what does it signify?

School **Use the following information for Exercises 13 and 14.**

The enrollment of students at a school each year since 2000 can be modeled by the function $S(x) = -0.005x^5 + 0.07x^4 - 0.5x^2 + 278$. *(Lesson 6-8)*

13. Write the function $T(x) = S(x) - 50$.

14. Graph S and T on the same coordinate plane. Describe T as a transformation of S.

15. **Government** The table below shows the number of city employees during a 6-year period. Use a polynomial model to estimate the number of city employees in 2007. *(Lesson 6-9)*

Year	City Employees
2000	165
2001	168
2002	181
2003	210
2004	261
2005	340

Extra Practice

Chapter 7 ■ Applications Practice

School **Use the following information for Exercises 1–3.**

A school's honor society was founded in 1970 with 120 members. Since then, the society membership has increased by about 10% each year. *(Lesson 7-1)*

1. Write a function representing the number of members each year since the club's founding (1970 = year 0).
2. Graph the function through the year 2005.
3. In which year did the number of members exceed 1000?

Chemistry **Use the following information for Exercises 4–6.**

A glass was filled with 6 inches of water and left out on the counter. The amount of water in inches left in the glass after d days is $f(d) = 6 - 0.2d$. *(Lesson 7-2)*

4. Write the inverse function $f^{-1}(d)$.
5. After how many days was there 3.4 inches of water left in the glass?
6. After how many days was the glass empty?

Biology **Use the following information for Exercises 7 and 8.**

The number of bacteria in a culture after t hours is $f(t) = 3^{\frac{t}{2}}$. *(Lesson 7-3)*

7. How many bacteria are in the culture after 10 hours?
8. Replace $f(t)$ with y and write the function in logarithmic form.

Sound **Use the following information for Exercises 9 and 10.**

The loudness L of sound in decibels is given by $L = 10 \log\left(\frac{I}{I_0}\right)$, where I is the intensity of sound and I_0 is the intensity of the softest audible sound. *(Lesson 7-4)*

9. Rewrite this equation as the difference of two logarithms.
10. When is the equation undefined?

11. **Investing** A stock is losing value at a rate of 5% per month. An investor made an initial purchase of \$1500 worth of stock. The value of her shares of stock after m months is $A = 1500(0.95)^m$. Solve for m to find how many months it will take for the stockholder's shares to be worth less than \$1000. *(Lesson 7-5)*
12. **Economics** Ivy's parents invested \$2700 for college in an account that receives 3.5% interest compounded continuously. What will the total amount of their investment be when Ivy starts college in 8 years? *(Lesson 7-6)*
13. **Physics** Americium-241, a radioactive element used in smoke detectors, has a half-life of 7370 years. Find the decay constant, then use the decay function $N(t) = N_0 e^{-kt}$ to determine the amount of atoms that remain from a sample of 1000 atoms after 20,000 years. *(Lesson 7-6)*

Art **Use the following information for Exercises 14–16.**

A small painting by Mondrian was valued at \$10,500 in the year 2000. Since then its value has been increasing by 3% each year. The value of the painting x years after the year 2000 is $V = 10{,}500(1.03)^x$. Write a function for each transformation described below and explain the effect on the graph of the parent function. *(Lesson 7-7)*

14. The initial value in 2000 is adjusted to \$9500.
15. The value is \$1500 more each year.
16. The value of the painting increases by 3% every 2 years.
17. **Business** The table gives the number of employees at a company in the years since it was founded. Find a logarithmic model for the data. Predict when the company will have 60 employees. *(Lesson 7-8)*

Company Employees

Years since Founding	1	2	3	4	5	6
Employees	12	26	34	40	44	48

Chapter 8 ■ Applications Practice

1. **Physics** The amount of force F exerted by an object varies directly as the object's acceleration a. An object accelerating at 5 m/s^2 exerts a force of 10 Newtons. How much force would the same object exert at an acceleration of 7 m/s^2? *(Lesson 8-1)*

2. **Transportation** The time t required for a bus to travel a certain distance varies inversely as its average speed r. It takes the bus 2.2 h to travel between two cities at 50 mi/h. How long would the same drive take at 40 mi/h? *(Lesson 8-1)*

Recreation **Use the following information for Exercises 3 and 4.**

At a carnival booth, contestants can win a prize by throwing a dart at a square board. The total area of the board in square feet can be represented by the expression $4x^2 + 24x + 36$. *(Lesson 8-2)*

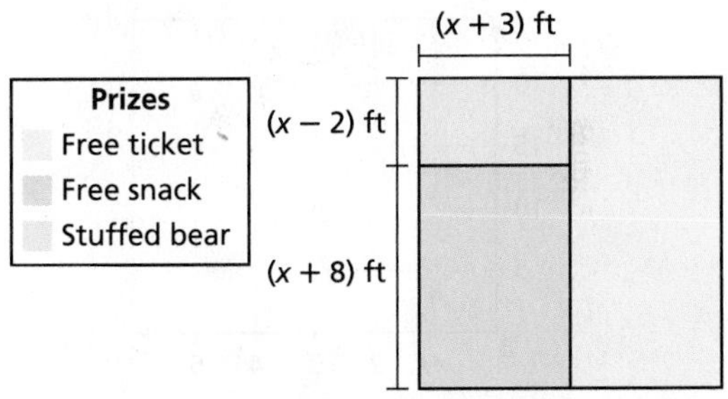

3. If a dart hits the board at random, what is the probability in terms of x of winning a bear?

4. If a dart hits the board at random, what is the probability in terms of x of winning a snack?

5. **Fitness** Geoff ran a 6 mi race for charity. During the first 4 mi of the race, he averaged 6 mi/h. During the last 2 mi, he averaged 5.5 mi/h. What was Geoff's average speed in miles per hour for the entire race? Round to the nearest hundredth. *(Lesson 8-3)*

School **Use the following information for Exercises 6 and 7.**

A science class is taking a field trip to a planetarium. Admission costs \$8 per student, plus there is a tour charge of \$80 per class. *(Lesson 8-4)*

6. Write and graph a function to represent the total average cost of the field trip per student.

7. Find the total average cost per student if 25 students go on the field trip.

8. **Travel** A tour boat travels 12 mi up a river and 12 mi down the river in a total of 5.5 h. In still water, the boat travels at an average speed of 5.5 mi/h. Based on this information, what is the speed of the river's current? *(Lesson 8-5)*

9. **Carpentry** A carpenter can build a cabinet in 4 h. When his son assists him, they can build the same type of cabinet in 2.5 h. About how long would it take the carpenter's son to build a cabinet by himself? *(Lesson 8-5)*

10. **Measurement** A large cubic storage box has a volume of $166\frac{3}{8}$ ft^3. The box is labeled with a strip of tape that wraps once around the entire box. What is the length of the tape that labels the box? *(Lesson 8-6)*

Physics **Use the following information for Exercises 11 and 12.**

The period of a pendulum is the time it takes for the pendulum to complete one back-and-forth swing. The function $f(x) = 2\pi\sqrt{\frac{x}{32}}$ gives the period f of a pendulum in seconds where x is the length of the pendulum in feet. *(Lesson 8-7)*

11. Write a function g for the period of a pendulum of length $(x + 2)$ ft.

12. Describe the function g as a transformation of f.

13. **Geometry** The length of a diagonal d of a rectangular prism is given by $d = \sqrt{\ell^2 + w^2 + h^2}$, where ℓ is the length, w is the width, and h is the height. What is the minimum height in inches of a box with a length of 15 in. and a width of 12 in. that will hold a 20 in. baton? Round your answer to the nearest tenth. *(Lesson 8-8)*

Chapter 9 ■ Applications Practice

1. **Ecology** The table shows the population of a colony of penguins over a 6-year period. Use a graph and an equation to predict the number of penguins in the colony in 2010. *(Lesson 9-1)*

Penguin Colony Population	
Year	Population
2000	112
2001	123
2002	135
2003	149
2004	164
2005	180

Shipping Use the following information for Exercises 2 and 3.

A shipping company charges different rates depending on the weight of the package to be shipped. *(Lesson 9-2)*

Shipping Costs	
Weight (lb)	Cost ($)
Under 2	$3.50
2 to 7	$6.00
More than 7	$9.00

2. Write a piecewise function to represent shipping costs for packages up to 10 lb.
3. Graph the function.

Recreation Use the following information for Exercises 4 and 5.

The zoo charges $7.00 per person for admittance. For groups of 20 people or more, the zoo charges $6.00 per person plus a one-time administrative fee of $10. *(Lesson 9-3)*

4. Write a function to represent the cost of admittance to the zoo for x people.
5. The zoo decides to raise the group administrative fee by $5. Write the resulting function. How does this affect the graph of the function?

Politics Use the following information for Exercises 6 and 7.

Approximately 2 in 3 people surveyed support a bill to raise the salaries of local police officers. Of those who support the bill, 60% also support a raise in taxes to pay for the bill. *(Lesson 9-4)*

6. Write a composite function for the number of people who support the bill and think that taxes should be raised.
7. The total number of people who support both the bill and the tax is 90. How many people were surveyed?

Scouting Use the following information for Exercises 8–10.

The graph shows the number of merit badges that scouts from the same troop have earned, based on the number of years they have been in the troop. *(Lesson 9-5)*

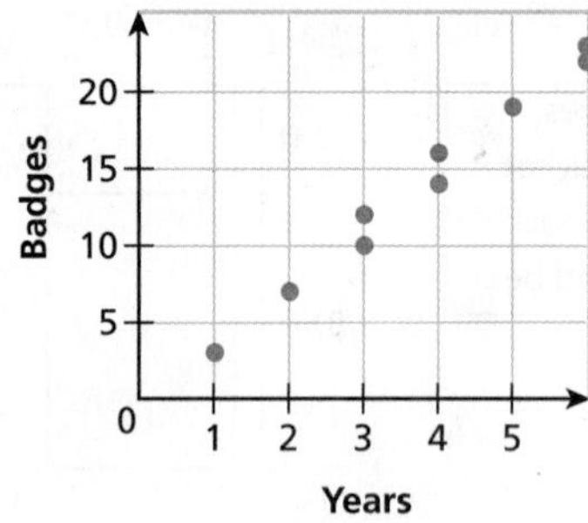

8. Graph the inverse of $f(x)$.
9. Is $f(x)$ a function? Is its inverse a function?
10. Use your graph to predict how long a scout has been in the troop if he has earned 36 badges.

Nutrition Use the following information for Exercises 11 and 12.

The table shows the number of Calories and grams of fat in selected sandwiches. *(Lesson 9-6)*

Sandwich Nutrition Information					
Fat (g)	6	8	12	15	20
Calories	372	396	442	477	535

11. Write a function that models the data.
12. Use your model to predict the number of Calories in a sandwich containing 25 grams of fat.

Chapter 10 ■ Applications Practice

Geometry **Use the following information for Exercises 1–3.**

A circle has center $(7, 8)$ and contains the point $(11, 11)$. *(Lesson 10-1)*

1. Find the circumference of the circle.
2. Find the area of the circle.
3. Find the other endpoint of the diameter with one endpoint $(11, 5)$.

Design **Use the following information for Exercises 4–6.**

Grace is designing a courtyard for a client. The courtyard will include a small circular fountain inside a large circular patio, which will be surrounded by a square fence. The plans have been overlaid on a coordinate plane, as shown below. *(Lesson 10-2)*

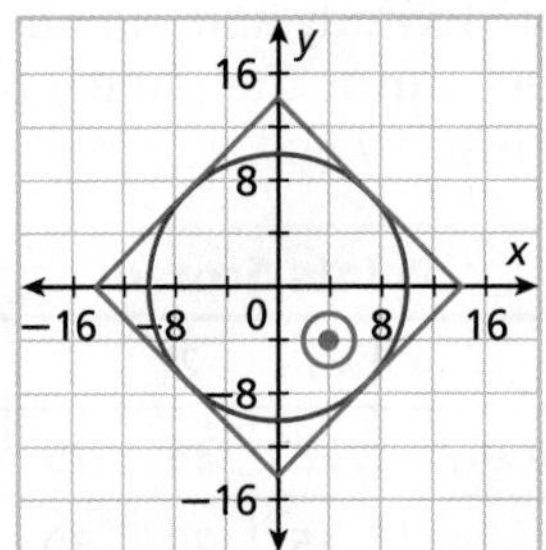

4. Find an equation for the fountain.
5. Find an equation for the circular patio.
6. Each side of the fence is tangent to the patio. Find the equation for the part of the fence that passes through the point $\left(-5\sqrt{2}, 5\sqrt{2}\right)$.

Architecture **Use the following information for Exercises 7 and 8.**

The Oval Office in the White House has a major axis 35 ft 10 in. long and a minor axis 29 ft long. *(Lesson 10-3)*

7. Suppose that the center of the floor of the Oval Office is located at the origin. Write an equation that can be used to model the office floor.
8. Find the coordinates of the foci.

9. **Sports** Two people watching a baseball game are seated 2000 feet apart. One person hears the crack of the bat 1 second before the other person. Because sound travels at 1100 feet per second, one person must be 1100 feet closer to the bat than the other. The possible locations of the batter form a hyperbola with the two people as foci. Write an equation that could be used to represent the possible locations of the batter. (*Hint:* Place the origin midway between the two people.) *(Lesson 10-4)*

10. **Recreation** A half-pipe, similar to those used by skateboarders, is parabolic in shape. Use the intersection of the ground and the center of the half-pipe as the origin and write an equation to model the shape of the curved interior of the structure. *(Lesson 10-5)*

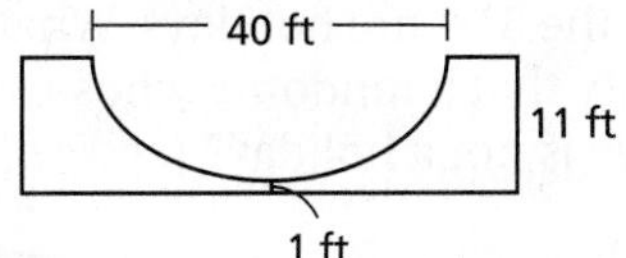

Fitness **Use the following information for Exercises 11 and 12.**

A runner is running on a track. His path in yards can be modeled by the equation $x^2 - 160x + 4y^2 - 160y + 7840 = 0$. *(Lesson 10-6)*

11. Write the equation in standard form by completing the square.
12. There is a drinking fountain in the center of the track. What are the coordinates of the fountain? What is the farthest distance that a runner would have to travel from the track to the fountain?

13. **Ecology** A water tank has spilled, and the flooded area in square feet can be modeled by the equation $x^2 + y^2 = 225$. Near the spilled tank, there is a garden whose shape can be modeled by the equation $\frac{(x-9)^2}{25} + \frac{(y-6)^2}{36} = 1$. At what points do the boundaries of the spill and the garden intersect? *(Lesson 10-7)*

Chapter 11 ■ Applications Practice

Music **Use the following information for Exercises 1 and 2.**

Serialism is a form of music in which the composer arranges each of the 12 tones in an octave to form a musical phrase. *(Lesson 11-1)*

1. How many ways can the 12 tones of an octave be arranged?
2. How many different musical phrases could a composer create by arranging only 5 of the 12 tones of an octave?
3. **Drama** A drama class is performing the Greek tragedy *Antigone,* by Sophocles. Of the 15 students in the class, 6 will make up the chorus. How many different ways can the chorus be selected? *(Lesson 11-1)*
4. **Holidays** Of December's 31 days, the 25th and the 31st are holidays. What is the probability that a randomly chosen day in December is not a holiday? *(Lesson 11-2)*
5. **Games** If Sara's dart lands in a red equilateral triangle, she wins a prize. Each triangle has a base of 2 in. If all locations on the 12 in. diameter target are equally likely, what is the probability that Sara wins a prize? *(Lesson 11-2)*

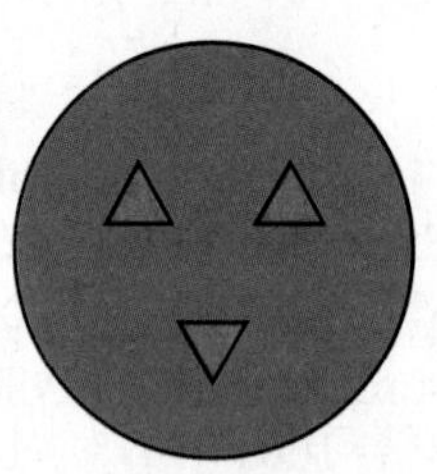

Literature **Use the following information for Exercises 6 and 7.**

The works of Chilean poet Pablo Neruda have been published in many languages. The school library has copies of two of his books in both English and Spanish. The table shows how many times each book has been checked out. *(Lesson 11-3)*

Books Checked Out		
	Canto General	*Extravagario*
English	23	27
Spanish	17	14

6. What is the probability that *Canto General* was checked out in Spanish?
7. What is the probability that a student who checked out a Pablo Neruda book selected *Extravagario* in English?

Immigration **Use the following information for Exercises 8 and 9.**

A group of 100 immigrants was studied over a one-year period. During the study, 63 of the immigrants found jobs, and 14 returned to their country of origin. Of the immigrants who found jobs, 6 of them returned to their countries before the end of the study. *(Lesson 11-4)*

8. What is the probability that an immigrant found a job or returned to his or her country of origin?
9. What is the probability that an immigrant did not find a job or returned to his country of origin?

Basketball **Use the following information for Exercises 10–12.**

The table below shows the number of points scored by Tracy McGrady and Yao Ming of the Houston Rockets during the same 5 games of the 2005 season. *(Lesson 11-5)*

Points Scored					
Game	1	2	3	4	5
Tracy McGrady	28	36	25	37	27
Yao Ming	15	20	30	8	33

10. Find the mean of both sets of data.
11. Find the standard deviation of both sets of data.
12. Determine whether there is an outlier. If so, describe how it affects the mean and standard deviation.

Nutrition **Use the following information for Exercises 13 and 14.**

At a frozen yogurt store, 75% of customers ask for a cup, while the others ask for a cone. At closing time, the store has 7 people waiting and only 2 cones left. *(Lesson 11-6)*

13. What is the probability that exactly 2 people will want cones?
14. What is the probability that no more than 2 people will want cones?

Chapter 12 ■ Applications Practice

Housing Use the following information for Exercises 1 and 2.

Lily moved into her apartment in 2001, when the rent was \$650. Every year since then, the landlord has raised the rent by 5%. *(Lesson 12-1)*

1. Graph the sequence and describe its pattern.
2. How much will Lily's rent be in 2010?
3. **Fractals** Find the number of red circles in the next 2 terms of the fractal. *(Lesson 12-1)*

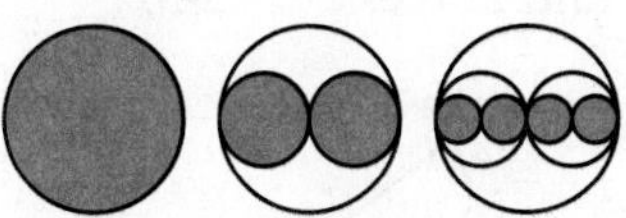

4. **Awards** A local charity started its Volunteer Hall of Fame by inducting the first honoree in 1997. The next year it inducted 2 new members, and in 1999 it inducted 3 new members. Each year since then, it has added one more member than it did the previous year. How many members will the Volunteer Hall of Fame have in 2009? *(Lesson 12-2)*

Fractals Use the following information for Exercises 5 and 6.

The number of circles in the first iteration of the fractal is $3^0 = 1$. The number of circles in the second iteration of the fractal is $3^0 + 3^1 = 4$. The number of circles in the third iteration of the fractal is $3^0 + 3^1 + 3^2 = 13$. *(Lesson 12-2)*

5. Use summation notation to write an expression for the number of circles in the nth iteration of the fractal.
6. Find the number of circles in the 5th iteration of the fractal.

Fitness Use the following information for Exercises 7–9.

When a member first joins a health club, he or she pays \$240 for the first year. Each year after that, the yearly fee is reduced by \$10. *(Lesson 12-3)*

7. What is the yearly fee for the 7th year?
8. How much will a member have paid after belonging to the health club for 10 years?
9. If a member has paid a total of \$2450 in fees, how long has she been a member of the health club?

Communication Use the following information for Exercises 10–12.

The Parent Teacher Association spreads news using a phone tree. The president and vice president start the phone tree by calling 3 people each. Each of the 6 people called then have 3 new people to call, and so on, until every member of the PTA has been called. *(Lesson 12-4)*

10. Write a sequence to describe the phone tree.
11. How many people are on the 5th row of the phone tree?
12. It takes a total of 6 rows to finish the phone tree. Write an expression in summation notation to express the number of people called in the entire phone tree. How many members does the Parent Teacher Association have?

Business Use the following information for Exercises 13 and 14.

The table shows the annual revenue generated by a new product in its first 4 years. *(Lesson 12-5)*

Annual Revenue				
Year	**2001**	**2002**	**2003**	**2004**
Sales (thousand \$)	375	225	135	81

13. Assume that the trend continues. Estimate the revenue generated in 2008.
14. Assume that the sales trend continues indefinitely. Estimate the total revenue the product will generate.

Extra Practice

Chapter 13 ■ Applications Practice

1. **Aviation** A plane is flying at an altitude of 6500 ft. The pilot sights the runway of an airport at an angle of depression of 6°. To the nearest tenth of a mile, what is the horizontal distance from the plane to the runway? *(Lesson 13-1)*

2. **Architecture** Thomas stands 250 m from the base of the Sears Tower in Chicago. His eye level is 1.75 m above the ground, and he measures the angle of elevation to the top of the tower to be 60.4°. Based on this information, what is the height of the Sears Tower to the nearest meter? *(Lesson 13-1)*

Recreation Use the following information for Exercises 3 and 4.

A Ferris wheel makes one complete revolution in 40 s. *(Lesson 13-2)*

3. Through what angle, in degrees, does a car of the Ferris wheel rotate in 70 s?

4. How long does it take a car of the Ferris wheel to rotate through an angle of 792° ?

5. **Landscape Design** A path through a park is shaped like an arc of a circle with a radius of 25 ft. The central angle that intercepts the path measures $\frac{\pi}{2}$ radians. To the nearest foot, how long is the path? *(Lesson 13-3)*

6. **Entertainment** A standard circus ring is 42 ft in diameter. A clown on a bicycle rides once around the circumference of the ring in 10 s. To the nearest tenth of a foot, how far does the clown travel in 1 second? *(Lesson 13-3)*

7. **Astronomy** Venus is approximately 108 million km from the Sun and takes 225 days to complete an orbit. Based on this information, how far does Venus travel in its nearly circular orbit around the Sun in 1 day? Round to the nearest million kilometers. *(Lesson 13-3)*

8. **Construction** The entrance to a store is 6 in. above the level of the sidewalk. A contractor is building an access ramp to the entrance that will cover a horizontal distance of 6 ft. To the nearest degree, what angle will the ramp make with the sidewalk? *(Lesson 13-4)*

9. **Safety** The "1-to-4" rule states that when a ladder is leaning against a wall, the bottom of the ladder should be 1 ft away from the wall for every 4 ft that the top of the ladder rises on the wall. To the nearest degree, what angle should the ladder make with the ground? *(Lesson 13-4)*

10. **Surveying** A surveyor is measuring a triangular plot of land, as shown. To the nearest foot, what is the distance between stakes 1 and 2? *(Lesson 13-5)*

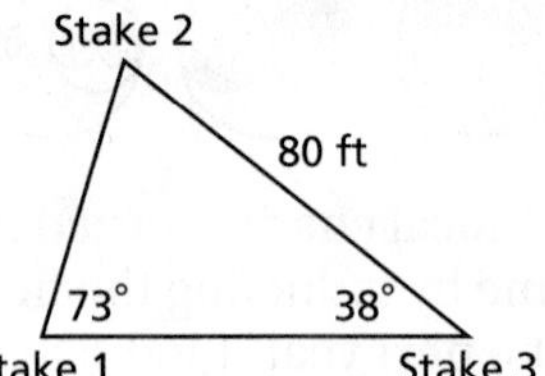

Hobbies Use the following information for Exercises 11 and 12.

Andrew uses pieces of wood to build triangular picture frames. Determine the number of triangles he can form using the given side and angle measurements. Then solve the triangles. Round to the nearest tenth. *(Lesson 13-5)*

11. $a = 10.5$ cm, $b = 12$ cm, $m\angle A = 60°$

12. $a = 8$ cm, $b = 15$ cm, $m\angle A = 44°$

13. **Hiking** Anne and Keisha leave their campsite at the same time. Anne hikes due east at 2 mi/h. Keisha heads 65° east of north at 3 mi/h. To the nearest tenth of a mile, what is the distance d between the hikers after 3 hours? *(Lesson 13-6)*

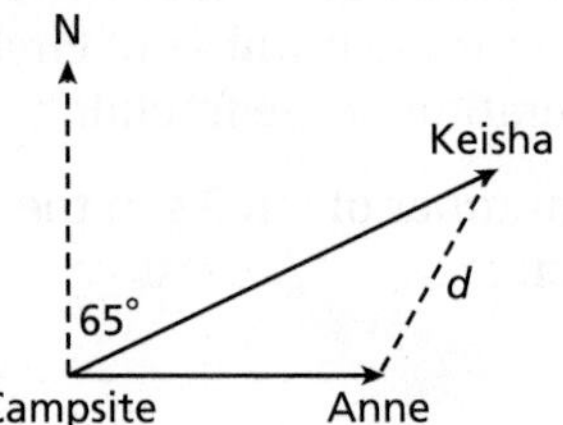

14. A museum has a triangular window with sides measuring 9 ft, 11 ft, and 14 ft. What is the area of the window to the nearest square foot? *(Lesson 13-6)*

Chapter 14 ■ Applications Practice

1. **Sound** Use a sine function to graph a sound wave with a period of 0.006 second and an amplitude of 5 cm. Find the frequency in hertz for this sound wave. *(Lesson 14-1)*

Recreation **Use the following information for Exercises 2–4.**

As a cyclist rides her bike, the height in inches above the ground of one of the pedals is modeled by $H(t) = 6\cos 2\pi t + 12$, where t is the time in seconds. *(Lesson 14-1)*

2. Graph the height of the pedal for two complete periods.
3. What is the maximum and minimum height of the pedal?
4. How many complete revolutions does the pedal make in one minute?

Use the following information for Exercises 5 and 6.

As a swimming pool is drained, the depth of the water in feet is modeled by $D(t) = 1.05 \cot \frac{\pi}{8}\left(t + \frac{1}{2}\right)$, where t is the time in hours. *(Lesson 14-2)*

5. Graph the depth of the water in the swimming pool for $0 \le t \le 3$.
6. What is the starting depth of the water? Round to the nearest inch.

Use the following information for Exercises 7 and 8.

The minute hand of a clock begins on the 12 and moves around the dial. The slope of the line represented by the minute hand is given by the function $S(t) = -\tan 2\pi(t - 0.25)$, where t is the time in hours. *(Lesson 14-2)*

7. Graph the slope of the minute hand for six complete periods.
8. What is the period of the function?
9. **Physics** Use the equation $mg \sin\theta = \mu mg \cos\theta$ to determine the angle at which a steel table can be tilted before a copper pan on the table begins to slide. Assume $\mu = 0.53$ and round your answer to the nearest degree. *(Lesson 14-3)*

Geometry **Use the following information for Exercises 10 and 11.**

Find the coordinates, to the nearest hundredth, of the vertices of $\triangle ABC$ after the given rotation. *(Lesson 14-4)*

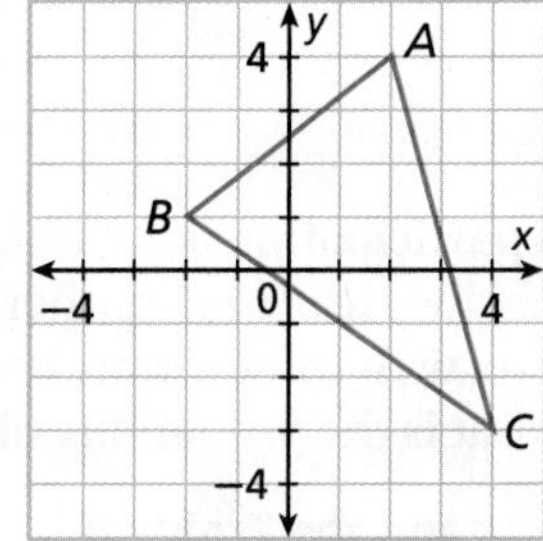

10. A 60° rotation about the origin
11. A 135° rotation about the origin

Physics **Use the following information for Exercises 12 and 13.**

The horizontal component of the acceleration of an object sliding down a frictionless inclined plane is $a(\theta) = 9.8 \sin\theta \cos\theta$, where θ is the angle of the inclined plane and where acceleration is measured in meters per second per second $\left(\frac{m}{s^2}\right)$. *(Lesson 14-5)*

12. Rewrite the function in terms of the double angle 2θ.
13. Graph the function for $0 \le \theta \le \frac{\pi}{2}$. For what angle does the object have the greatest acceleration in the horizontal direction?
14. The population in thousands of a seaside town is modeled by $P(t) = 10\sin\frac{\pi}{180}(t - 160) + 15$, where t is the day of the year and $t = 0$ represents January 1. How many days after January 1 is the population equal to 22,000? *(Lesson 14-6)*
15. The temperature in New York City during one day in the summer is modeled by $F(t) = 16\sin\frac{\pi}{12}(t - 8) + 68$, where F is the temperature in degrees Fahrenheit and t is the time in hours after midnight. At what times during the day is the temperature 80°F? *(Lesson 14-6)*

Extra Practice

Problem Solving Handbook

Draw a Diagram

You can draw a diagram that represents the information in a problem to help you understand and solve the problem.

Problem Solving Strategies

Draw a Diagram	Make a Table
Make a Model	Solve a Simpler Problem
Guess and Test	Use Logical Reasoning
Work Backward	Use a Venn Diagram
Find a Pattern	Make an Organized List

EXAMPLE

Carmen is participating in an online contest to win a car. She is given a choice of three doors. Each door leads to another level with three doors, and each of those leads to another level with three doors. Behind one of those final doors is the grand prize of a new car. What is the probability of winning the car if she chooses doors at random?

1 Understand the Problem

List the important information.

- She begins with three doors.
- Each of those doors leads to three other doors, and each of those doors leads to another three doors.
- One of the final doors leads to the car.
- The probability of winning is the number of cars divided by the total number of final door choices.

The answer will be the probability of finding the car.

2 Make a Plan

Use a tree diagram to show the possible door choices. This will show the number of possible paths Carmen could choose.

3 Solve

Draw the tree diagram. Draw three doors to represent the original three doors. Draw three more doors for each door and connect them with lines. Repeat to have three rows of doors.

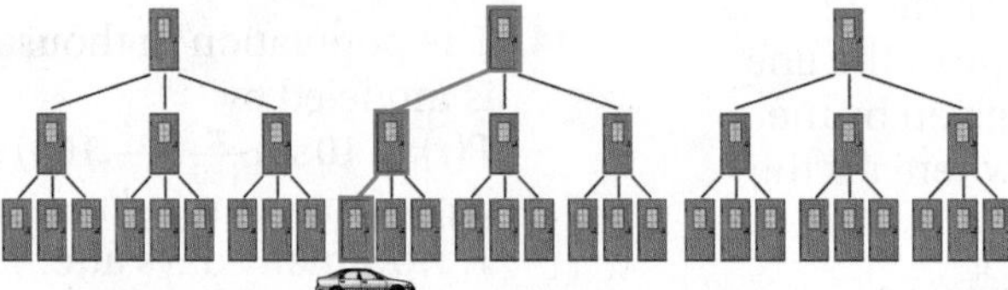

The highlighted path shows that there is exactly one way to win the car.

The total number of paths is 27.

The probability of winning the car is $\frac{1}{27} \approx 3.7\%$.

4 Look Back

Check that you drew your diagram correctly. Does the diagram accurately represent the information given in the question?

PRACTICE

1. Bob has a green, a blue, a red, and a yellow marble in a bag. He randomly selects one marble at a time from the bag until the bag is empty. What is the probability that the blue marble is chosen immediately before the red one?

Problem-Solving Handbook

Make a Model

For problems that involve objects, it is sometimes useful to make a model to help you solve the problem.

Problem Solving Strategies

Draw a Diagram	Make a Table
Make a Model	Solve a Simpler Problem
Guess and Test	Use Logical Reasoning
Work Backward	Use a Venn Diagram
Find a Pattern	Make an Organized List

EXAMPLE

Ryan created a pyramid with a square base out of cans of soup for a store display. When he had finished, he needed to know the number of cans that he had used. The pyramid has four levels. The top level has one can, and each row beneath it has one additional can added to each side length. How many cans are in the pyramid?

Understand the Problem

List the important information.

- There are four levels.
- The top level has one can.
- The side length increases by one as you go down each level.

The answer will be the number of cans in the pyramid.

Make a Plan

You can use blocks to make a model of the problem. Use the blocks to create the pyramid in the problem. Remember to count the number of blocks as you go.

Solve

Since each level has one can added to the side length, the side length of the bottom level is 4. Make a 4-by-4 square of blocks for the base. Count the number of blocks used. The level above has side lengths of 3, so make a 3-by-3 square on top of the base. Count the number of blocks used in this level. Continue to the top of the pyramid. The total number of blocks is the sum of the blocks at each level: $16 + 9 + 4 + 1 = 30$.

Look Back

Make sure the pyramid matches the given information. There should be four levels increasing by one in side length as you go down the pyramid.

PRACTICE

1. Paul wants to make a pyramid with an equilateral triangle base out of cans. Paul has 25 cans. He wants the pyramid to have one can on the top, and he wants the number of cans on each side of the following triangle layers to increase by one. How tall can Paul make the pyramid? How many cans will he have left over?
2. A display of cereal boxes is arranged with 1 box on top and each row having an additional box. How many boxes are in a display of 9 rows?

Guess and Test

One way to solve a problem is to guess the answer and test to see whether it is correct. You can continue to guess and test until you find the correct answer.

Problem Solving Strategies

Draw a Diagram	Make a Table
Make a Model	Solve a Simpler Problem
Guess and Test	Use Logical Reasoning
Work Backward	Use a Venn Diagram
Find a Pattern	Make an Organized List

EXAMPLE

Tom is playing a game where he draws marbles out of a bag. Red marbles are worth 3 points, and blue ones are worth 2 points. Tom drew 8 marbles and won 20 points. How many marbles of each color does Tom have?

1 Understand the Problem

List the important information.

- Red marbles are worth 3 points.
- Blue marbles are worth 2 points.
- The total number of points is 20.
- The total number of marbles is 8.

2 Make a Plan

Start with a guess in which the total number of marbles is 8. Test to see whether the total number of points is 20.

3 Solve

Make a first guess of 3 red and 5 blue, and find the total number of points.

Guess: 3 red and 5 blue

Test: $(3 \times 3) + (5 \times 2) = 19$

The number of points is too small. Increase the number of red marbles and decrease the number of blue marbles.

Guess: 5 red and 3 blue

Test: $(5 \times 3) + (3 \times 2) = 21$

The number of points is too high. Decrease the number of red marbles and increase the number of blue marbles.

Guess: 4 red and 4 blue

Test: $(4 \times 3) + (4 \times 2) = 20$

Tom should have drawn 4 red marbles and 4 blue marbles.

4 Look Back

Test the answer to see whether the number of marbles satisfies the question.

4 red marbles and 4 blue marbles are 8 marbles and are worth 20 points.

PRACTICE

1. Fred has 7 coins. All the coins are nickels or dimes. The total value of the coins is \$0.55. How many of each type of coin does he have?
2. The sum of Beth's age and Brian's age is 20. Three times Beth's age plus 2 times Brian's age is 55. How old are Beth and Brian?

Work Backward

Sometimes in a problem you are given an end result and asked to find a fact that leads to the result. In these cases, you can work backward to solve the problem.

Problem Solving Strategies

Draw a Diagram	Make a Table
Make a Model	Solve a Simpler Problem
Guess and Test	Use Logical Reasoning
Work Backward	Use a Venn Diagram
Find a Pattern	Make an Organized List

EXAMPLE

Laura is delivering meals to retirement communities. She dropped off 2 less than $\frac{1}{2}$ of the meals at the first community. Then she dropped off $\frac{1}{3}$ of the remaining meals plus 2 at the second community. She has 8 meals left. How many meals did she have to start?

1 Understand the Problem

List the important information.

- Laura delivered $\frac{1}{2}$ of the meals minus 2 at the first community.
- Laura delivered $\frac{1}{3}$ of the meals plus 2 at the second community.
- She has 8 meals left.

The answer will be the number of meals that she had at the start.

2 Make a Plan

Start with the 8 meals and work backward through the given information to determine the beginning number of meals.

3 Solve

She has 8 meals at the end, so start with 8 meals.

She delivered $\frac{1}{3}$ of the meals plus 2 at the second community, so add 2 to the number of meals and multiply by $\frac{3}{2}$ to undo giving $\frac{1}{3}$ away. $\quad \frac{3}{2}(8 + 2) = 15$

She had 15 meals before she visited the second community.

She delivered $\frac{1}{2}$ of the meals minus 2 at the first community, so subtract 2 and multiply by 2 to undo giving $\frac{1}{2}$ away. $\quad 2(15 - 2) = 26$

Laura started with 26 meals.

4 Look Back

Use the starting amount of 26 meals and work from the beginning of the problem following the steps.

Start: 26

Subtract $\frac{1}{2}$ of the meals plus 2 more: 15

Subtract $\frac{2}{3}$ of the meals minus 2 more: 8

PRACTICE

1. A tree is growing in Danny's yard. When Danny first observed the tree, he noticed that the number of branches on the tree had doubled that year. The year after, the number of branches tripled minus 3. The year after that, the tree doubled its number of branches, plus 6. How many branches did the tree originally have if it currently has 120 branches?

Find a Pattern

When the pieces of information in a problem have a relationship, you can find a pattern to help solve the problem.

Problem Solving Strategies

Draw a Diagram	Make a Table
Make a Model	Solve a Simpler Problem
Guess and Test	Use Logical Reasoning
Work Backward	Use a Venn Diagram
Find a Pattern	Make an Organized List

EXAMPLE

Fred has 3 homework problems the first day of school. The second day he has 5. The third day he has 7. The fourth day he has 9. If this pattern continues, how many homework problems will Fred have on the tenth day of school?

Understand the Problem

List the important information.

- On day 1 he has 3 homework problems, on day 2 he has 5 homework problems, on day 3 he has 7 homework problems, and on day 4 he has 9 homework problems.

The answer will be the number of homework problems Fred will have on day 10.

Make a Plan

Find a pattern by comparing the number of homework problems Fred has each day. Then use this pattern to determine the number of homework problems he will have on day 10.

Solve

Organize the data and find the pattern.

Day	Number of Homework Problems	Pattern
1	3	$3 + 2(1 - 1)$
2	5	$3 + 2(2 - 1)$
3	7	$3 + 2(3 - 1)$
4	9	$3 + 2(4 - 1)$

The pattern is that he gains 2 homework problems each day. Since he has 3 problems the first day and the number of days that have passed is the day number minus 1, the number of homework problems Fred has on the day n is $3 + 2(n - 1)$. The number of homework problems Fred will have on day 10 is $3 + 2(10 - 1) = 21$.

Look Back

Since the pattern is that he gains 2 homework problems each day, continue the data in a table to make sure that he will have 21 homework problems on the tenth day. Check that the formula you developed satisfies the information given in the question.

PRACTICE

1. Joseph is making signs for his student council election campaign. He made 1 sign the first day, 4 signs the second day, 7 signs the third day, and 10 signs the fourth day. How many signs will he make on the tenth day?
2. A flower is growing in a field. In year 1 there are two flowers in the field, in year 2 there are 3, in year 3 there are 5, in year 4 there are 9, in year 5 there are 17, and in year 6 there are 33. How many flowers will there be in year 11?

Make a Table

When you are solving problems that involve a large amount of data, it is often useful to make a table to organize and analyze the data.

Problem Solving Strategies

Draw a Diagram	**Make a Table**
Make a Model	Solve a Simpler Problem
Guess and Test	Use Logical Reasoning
Work Backward	Use a Venn Diagram
Find a Pattern	Make an Organized List

EXAMPLE

Peter, Michael, and Lisa work at the same shop. Peter works every 2 days, Michael works every 4 days, and Lisa works every 5 days. They all worked today. In how many days will they all work together again? How many days will each person work between now and when they all work together next?

1 Understand the Problem

List the important information.

- Peter works every 2 days, Michael every 4 and Lisa every 5.
- They all worked together today.

The answers will be:

- the number of days until they work together again and
- the number of days each person will work between now and then.

2 Make a Plan

Make a table, using ✔'s to show the days each person works.

3 Solve

Start with a ✔ in each person's row on day 0. For Peter, place a ✔ every 2 days. For Michael, place a ✔ every 4 days. For Lisa, place a ✔ every 5 days.

Day	0	1	2	3	4	5	6	7	8	9	10	11	12	13	14	15	16	17	18	19	20
Peter	✔		✔		✔		✔		✔		✔		✔		✔		✔		✔		✔
Michael	✔				✔				✔				✔				✔				✔
Lisa	✔					✔					✔					✔					✔

They will all work together again in 20 days. Peter will work nine, Michael will work 4, and Lisa will work 3 days between now and then.

4 Look Back

Check the information in the table. Make sure that no mistakes have been made in counting and that the data matches the information given in the question.

PRACTICE

1. If Peter works every 3 days, Michael works every 5 days, and Lisa works every 6 days, when will the next day be that they all work together if they all worked together today? How many days will each person work between now and when they all work together next?
2. A restaurant receives a shipment of produce every 2 days, a shipment of meat every 9 days, and a shipment of frozen food every 12 days. When will be the next day that all three shipments arrive if all three shipments arrived today? How many of each type of shipment will the restaurant receive between now and then.

Solve a Simpler Problem

When solving a complex problem, it is sometimes helpful to write a simpler problem, solve it, and then use a similar method to solve the complex problem.

Problem Solving Strategies

Draw a Diagram	Make a Table
Make a Model	**Solve a Simpler Problem**
Guess and Test	Use Logical Reasoning
Work Backward	Use a Venn Diagram
Find a Pattern	Make an Organized List

EXAMPLE

In a garden, there are 2 flowers, 1 red and 1 blue. Each year, the number of red flowers increases by 1 and the number of blue flowers increases by 2. What percent of the flowers will be red 10 years from now?

1 Understand the Problem

List the important information.

- The field begins with 1 red and 1 blue flower.
- Each year, the number of red flowers increases by 1.
- Each year, the number of blue flowers increases by 2.

The answer will be the percent of red flowers after 10 years have passed.

2 Make a Plan

Solve a simpler problem: Find the pattern in the number of red flowers and the total number of flowers in ten years.

3 Solve

Make a table. Separate the two patterns. Identify each pattern and develop a formula.

Year	Red Flowers	Pattern	Blue Flowers	Total Flowers	Pattern
0	1	1 + (0)	1	2	2 + 3(0)
1	2	1 + (1)	3	5	2 + 3(1)
2	3	1 + (2)	5	8	2 + 3(2)
3	4	1 + (3)	7	11	2 + 3(3)

If n is the nth year, then the number of red flowers is $1 + n$ and the total number of flowers is $2 + 3n$. The percent of flowers that are red is the ratio of the number of red flowers to the total number of flowers.

So the percent of red flowers in the nth year is $\frac{1+n}{2+3n}$, and in 10 years the percent of flowers that are red is $\frac{1+10}{2+3(10)} = \frac{11}{32} = 34.375\%$.

4 Look Back

Check that the answer is reasonable. Since the blue flowers grow faster than the red flowers and the garden starts with an equal number of each, there should be more blue flowers than red flowers. Therefore, the percent of red flowers should be less than 50%.

PRACTICE

1. In a field of flowers, there are 2 flowers; 1 yellow and 1 orange. Each year, the number of yellow flowers increases by 3, and the number of orange flowers increases by 4. What percent of the flowers will be yellow in 20 years?

Problem-Solving Handbook

Use Logical Reasoning

Use logical reasoning to help you solve problems by identifying the facts and using them to draw conclusions.

Problem Solving Strategies

Draw a Diagram	Make a Table
Make a Model	Solve a Simpler Problem
Guess and Test	**Use Logical Reasoning**
Work Backward	Use a Venn Diagram
Find a Pattern	Make an Organized List

EXAMPLE

Friends Jeff, Luca, Linda, and Blair are each a different age between 11 and 14. Each person has a different favorite color and sport. The sports are baseball, football, tennis and hockey. The colors are red, blue, green, and yellow. Jeff is 11 and likes to play baseball. The football player is the oldest and dislikes red. The hockey player's favorite color is blue. Linda does not play football. Blair likes the color green, plays tennis, and is a year younger than Linda. Find each person's age, favorite color, and sport.

1 Understand the Problem

List the important information.

- Jeff is 11 and likes to play baseball.
- The football player is the oldest and dislikes red.
- The hockey player's favorite color is blue.
- Linda does not play football.
- Blair likes the color green, plays tennis, and is a year younger than Linda.

The answer will be each person's age, favorite color, and sport.

2 Make a Plan

Start with the given clues. Use logical reasoning to make a table of the facts.

3 Solve

Make a table. Work with the clues one at a time. Place a ✓ in a box if the clue matches the person and an *X* if it does not.

	R	Bl	G	Y	Ba	F	T	H	11	12	13	14
Jeff	✓	X	X	X	✓	X	X	X	✓	X	X	X
Luca	X	X	X	✓	X	✓	X	X	X	X	X	✓
Linda	X	✓	X	X	X	X	X	✓	X	X	✓	X
Blair	X	X	✓	X	X	X	✓	X	X	✓	X	X

Jeff is 11, plays baseball, and likes red. Luca is 14, plays football, and likes yellow. Linda is 13, plays hockey, and likes blue. Blair is 12, plays tennis, and likes green.

4 Look Back

Compare your answer to the clues in the problem. Make sure none of the conclusions conflict with the clues.

PRACTICE

1. Friends Bob, Gary, Roxanne, and Robin have last names that begin with the letters *B, S, T,* and *H.* Their ages are 10, 12, 14, and 16, and their hair colors are blond, black, brown, and red. Bob's last initial is *B.* Robin is a teenager. Roxanne does not have red hair. Bob is 2 years older than Roxanne. The oldest has the last initial *S* and brown hair. Gary's last initial comes before Roxanne's in the alphabet. Gary is 10 and has black hair. Find each person's last initial, age, and hair color.

Use a Venn Diagram

Venn diagrams can be useful in solving problems with sets that overlap each other.

Problem Solving Strategies

Draw a Diagram	Make a Table
Make a Model	Solve a Simpler Problem
Guess and Test	Use Logical Reasoning
Work Backward	**Use a Venn Diagram**
Find a Pattern	Make an Organized List

EXAMPLE

There were three science lectures that students could attend, one on physics, one on chemistry, and one on biology. Four students attended all lectures, 6 students went to both the biology and physics lectures, 10 students went to both the chemistry and physics lectures, and 16 students went to both the chemistry and biology lectures. If a total of 30 students attended the physics lecture, 50 students attended the chemistry lecture, and 60 students attended the biology lecture, how many students went to at least one lecture?

1 Understand the Problem

List the important information.

- all lectures: 4
- biology and physics: 6
- chemistry and physics: 10
- chemistry and biology: 16
- physics: total of 30
- chemistry: total of 50
- biology: total of 50

The answer will be the number of students that went to at least one lecture.

2 Make a Plan

Use a Venn diagram to show the number of students that attended each lecture.

3 Solve

Draw and label three overlapping circles. In the section where all the circles overlap, place a 4 because 4 students attended all the lectures. In each section where only two circles overlap, place the number of students that went to both those two lectures. Calculate the number of students that went to only one lecture by taking the number of students that attended each lecture and subtracting the number that also attended other lectures. The sum of the numbers in each circle should be the total number of students that attended that lecture.

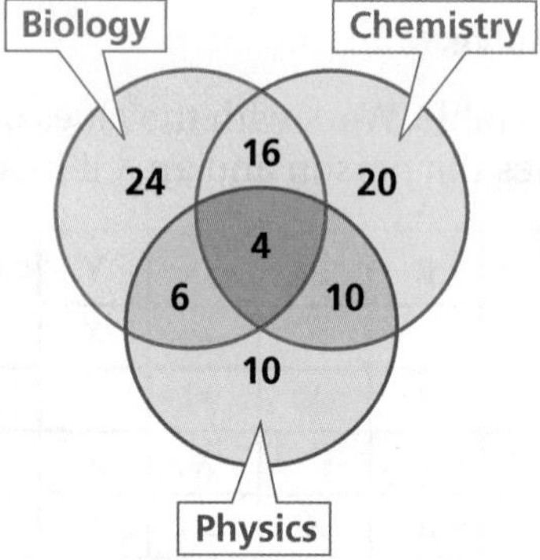

The total number of students is the sum of the numbers in all the circles. Therefore, the number of students is $24 + 6 + 10 + 16 + 4 + 10 + 20 = 90$.

4 Look Back

Check your Venn diagram against the initial data to make certain that the diagram agrees with the question asked.

PRACTICE

1. In summer school the math courses offered were Algebra, Geometry, and Calculus. Three students took all three courses, 5 students took only Algebra and Geometry, 1 student took only Calculus and Geometry, and 10 students took only Algebra and Calculus. If there were 28 students in Algebra, 24 students in Geometry, and 30 students in Calculus, how many students took at least one math course?

Problem-Solving Handbook

Make an Organized List

When you are solving a problem that contains a lot of information, it may be helpful to make an organized list to record the possible outcomes.

Problem Solving Strategies

Draw a Diagram	Make a Table
Make a Model	Solve a Simpler Problem
Guess and Test	Use Logical Reasoning
Work Backward	Use a Venn Diagram
Find a Pattern	**Make an Organized List**

EXAMPLE

Pete's Pizza has four toppings to choose from: pepperoni, ham, extra cheese, and mushrooms. How many possible pizzas are there if you can have 0, 1, 2, 3, or 4 toppings and cannot get the same topping twice?

1 Understand the Problem

List the important information.

- There are 4 possible toppings.
- A pizza can have 0 to 4 toppings.
- You cannot have the same topping twice.

The answer will be the number of pizzas that are possible.

Make a Plan

Make an organized list of the possible combinations of toppings. List all the possible combinations.

3 Solve

Make a column for each number of toppings on the pizza. Let P = pepperoni, H = ham, C = extra cheese, and M = mushrooms.

0 Toppings	1 Topping	2 Toppings	3 Toppings	4 Toppings
Plain Cheese	P	PH	PHC	PHCM
	H	PC	PHM	
	C	PM	PCM	
	M	HC	HCM	
		HM		
		CM		

Adding the number of choices yields 16 possible pizzas.

Look Back

Make sure all the possible choices are shown in the table and that none repeat.

PRACTICE

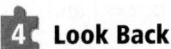

1. Pete's Pizza has decided that customers may repeat toppings but choose no more than a total of two toppings per pizza. How many pizzas are now possible?
2. Calvin has a bag with 5 balls inside. The balls are all distinct and labeled A through E. How many three-letter "words" can he create by randomly removing a ball and not replacing it? (Consider a word to be any permutation of three letters.)
3. Matty is going to run some errands. She may stop by the cleaners, the video store, and the grocery store. If she plans to make at least 1 stop, how many possible routes can she take?

Selected Answers

Chapter 1

1-1

Check It Out! **1a.** $-2, -\sqrt{3}, -0.321, \frac{3}{2}, \pi$ **b.** -2: $\mathbb{R}, \mathbb{Q}, \mathbb{Z}$; $-\sqrt{3}$: $\mathbb{R}$, irrational; -0.321: $\mathbb{R}, \mathbb{Q}$; $\frac{3}{2}$: $\mathbb{R}, \mathbb{Q}$; π: $\mathbb{R}$, irrational **2a.** $(-\infty, -1]$ **b.** $(-\infty, 2]$ or $(3, 11]$ **3a.** even numbers between 1 and 9 **b.** $\{3, 4, 5, 6, 7\}$ **c.** $\{x \mid x \geq 99\}$

Exercises **1.** roster notation **3.** $-\frac{100}{4}, -6.897, \frac{1}{8}, \sqrt{4}, \sqrt{6}$; $-\frac{100}{4}$: $\mathbb{R}, \mathbb{Q}, \mathbb{Z}$; -6.897: $\mathbb{R}, \mathbb{Q}$; $\frac{1}{8}$: $\mathbb{R}, \mathbb{Q}$; $\sqrt{4}$: $\mathbb{R}, \mathbb{Q}, \mathbb{Z}, \mathbb{W}, \mathbb{N}$; $\sqrt{6}$: $\mathbb{R}$, irrational **5.** $(-10, 10]$ **7.** $[1, 20)$ or $(30, \infty)$ **9.** $\{x \mid -5 \leq x < 3\}$ **11.** $\{-5, -4, -3, -2, -1, 0, 1, 2, 3, 4, 5\}$ **13.** $-2, -\sqrt{2}, -1.\overline{25}, \frac{\sqrt{2}}{3}, \frac{1}{2}$; -2: $\mathbb{R}, \mathbb{Q}, \mathbb{Z}$; $-\sqrt{2}$: $\mathbb{R}$, irrational; $-1.\overline{25}$: $\mathbb{R}, \mathbb{Q}$; $\frac{\sqrt{2}}{3}$: $\mathbb{R}$, irrational; $\frac{1}{2}$: $\mathbb{R}, \mathbb{Q}$ **15.** $(-\infty, 5)$ or $(5, \infty)$ **17.** $[-3, 3]$ **19.** $\{11, 22, 33, 44, 55, 66, 77, \ldots\}$ **21.** $\{x \mid -9 \leq x \leq -1$ and x is odd$\}$ **23.** $\mathbb{Q}$ **27.** numbers greater than or equal to -4 and less than 8; cannot be expressed in roster notation; $\{x \mid -4 \leq x < 8\}$ **29.** numbers greater than 0 and less than 1; cannot be expressed in roster notation; $(0, 1)$ **31.** $(-\infty, 2)$ or $(2, \infty)$; $\{x \mid x \neq 2\}$ **33.** $(1, 10)$; $\{x \mid 1 < x < 10\}$ **35.** $(-\infty, 5)$ or $(5, 10]$; $\{x \mid x < 5$ or $5 < x \leq 10\}$ **37.** false **39.** true **41.** $\{x \mid 11 \leq x \leq 12\}$; $\{x \mid 12 \leq x \leq 13\}$; $\{x \mid 14 \leq x \leq 16\}$ **45.** $(-\infty, -1]$ or $(3, 6)$ or $[9, \infty)$

47. −2 0 2 4 6 8 10 12

49. −2 −1 0 1 2 3 4 5

51. −3 −2 −1 0 1 2 3 4

53. $\mathbb{N}$ **55.** $\mathbb{W}$ **57a.** interior designer, police officer, pediatric nurse, marine biologist, astronaut **b.** The order would not change. **c.** The order would not change. **d.** {46,000, 52,900, 59,800, 79,350, 106,950} **63.** D **65.** B **67.** finite; $\mathbb{Q}$ **69.** finite; $\mathbb{Q}, \mathbb{Z}, \mathbb{W}, \mathbb{N}$ **75.** \$20, \$20, and \$10

1-2

Check It Out! **1a.** -500; $\frac{1}{500}$ **b.** 0.01; -100 **2a.** Commutative Property of Multiplication **b.** Associative Property of Multiplication **3.** \$3.12 **4a.** always true by the Additive Inverse Property **b.** sometimes true; possible answer: true when $a = 0$, $b = 1$, and $c = 2$; false when $a = 1$, $b = 2$, and $c = 3$

Exercises **1.** 36; $-\frac{1}{36}$ **3.** $-2\sqrt{2}$; $\frac{1}{2\sqrt{2}}$ **5.** $\frac{1}{500}$; -500 **7.** Associative Property of Multiplication **9.** Commutative Property of Multiplication **11.** \$7.33 **13.** sometimes true **15.** 2.5; $-\frac{2}{5}$ **17.** -2π; $\frac{1}{2\pi}$ **19.** $-\frac{1}{20}$; 20 **21.** Distributive Property **23.** Additive Identity Property **25.** \$9.80 **27.** never true by the Multiplicative Inverse Property **29.** $4(11.99) - 2(8.88) =$ \$30.20 **31.** $3(0.9)(9.96) + 5(0.75)(11.99) = 71.8545 \approx$ \$71.85 **33.** $\approx$ 2 loops **35.** 5; Associative Property of Addition **37.** 0; Additive Identity Property **39.** $\frac{5}{4}$; Multiplicative Inverse Property **41.** yes **45.** Multiplicative Identity Property **47.** Distributive Property; Associative Property of Addition **49.** Distributive Property **53.** D **55.** C **57.** $n = 2$ **59.** 66.7% **61.** $-4\sqrt{2}$ **63.** $(-10, 0]$ **65.** cannot be notated

1-3

Check It Out! **1.** -7.4 **2a.** $4\sqrt{3}$ **b.** $\frac{3}{2}$ **c.** 10 **d.** 7 **3a.** $\frac{3\sqrt{35}}{7}$ **b.** $\frac{\sqrt{10}}{2}$ **4a.** $13\sqrt{5}$ **b.** $-\sqrt{5}$

Exercises **1.** radicand **3.** 4.5 **5.** 3.6 **7.** 12 **9.** $4\sqrt{5}$ **11.** $-5\sqrt{2}$ **13.** $-\frac{\sqrt{7}}{7}$ **15.** $5\sqrt{2}$ **17.** $\sqrt{2}$ **19.** -3.9 **21.** 9.9 **23.** $-\frac{1}{11}$ **25.** $-8\sqrt{5}$ **27.** $5\sqrt{17}$ **29.** $-3\sqrt{21}$ **31.** $\frac{9\sqrt{2}}{4}$ **33.** $\frac{\sqrt{3}}{30}$ **35.** $7\sqrt{7}$ **37.** $23\sqrt{3}$ **39.** $8\sqrt{7}$ **41.** $-3\sqrt{6}$ **43.** 33.9 cm **45.** 99.0 in. **47.** about 50 in. by 50 in. **49.** 180 **51.** $2\sqrt{5} - 5\sqrt{2}$ **53.** $\frac{3\sqrt{35} + \sqrt{5}}{5}$ **55.** $\frac{16\sqrt{10}}{5}$ **57.** 600 ft by 600 ft **59.** 7467.3 ft **61.** 8167.7 ft **63.** always true **65.** no **67a.** ≈ 7.81 s **67b.** ≈ 3.20 s **69.** H **71.** 8.9 **73a.** 6 in.; $6\sqrt{5}$ in. **b.** 54 in^2 **c.** $18 + 6\sqrt{2} + 6\sqrt{5}$ in. **75.** tetrahedron or triangular pyramid **77.** triangular prism **79.** $1.5 < x < 8$ **81.** $\frac{3}{4} < x < \frac{5}{2}$ **83.** Commutative Property of Addition **85.** Distributive Property

1-4

Check It Out! **1a.** $18 + y$ **b.** $3600h$ **2.** -15 **3.** $-6x - 8xy - 9y$ **4a.** $8000 - 30h$ **b.** \$7160

Exercises **1.** $0.79c$ **3.** 9 **5.** $-12a + 9$ **7.** $1 + 5ab - 25a - b^2$ **9.** $(180 - x)°$ **11.** -18 **13.** 115 **15.** $3x - 12y + 2$ **17.** $5 - 3m - 2n$ **19a.** $500 - 20m$ **b.** 460 min or 7 h 40 min **21.** $5g^2 - 6g + 1$; 28 **23.** $\frac{a^2 - 2b^2 + 2a}{2 + a}$; -7

25.

x	$(x-4)^2$	x^2+16	$x^2-8x+16$
1	9	17	9
0	4	20	4
2	1	25	1
4	0	32	0

$(x - 4)^2 = x^2 - 8x + 16$ **27.** $7a + 4b$ **29a.** $4125 - 175d$ **b.** \$3250 **c.** They save \$175 per day. **31.** $y = -40$; $y = -25$; $y = -7$; $y = -5$; $y = -10$ **33.** $y = 7$; $y = 15$; $y = 1$; $y = -13$; $y = -5$ **37.** G **39.** $a = 8$ **41.** $a = 22$ **43a.** 4; undefined; -48; undefined; 36; $\frac{147}{8}$ **b.** $x = 1$ and $x = 3$ **c.** $\{x \mid x \neq 1$ and $x \neq 3\}$ **45.** square pyramid **47.** $\mathbb{Q}$ **49.** irrational **51.** $3\sqrt{6}$ **53.** 14

1-5

Check It Out! **1a.** $(2a)(2a)(2a)(2a)(2a)$ **b.** $3 \cdot b \cdot b \cdot b \cdot b$ **c.** $-(2x - 1)(2x - 1)(2x - 1) \cdot y \cdot y$ **2a.** 9 **b.** $-\frac{1}{3125}$ **3a.** $125x^{18}$ **b.** $-\frac{1}{8a^9b^3}$ **4a.** 2.5×10^{-4} **b.** 1.24×10^{-9} **5.** ≈ 8.33 min

Exercises 3. $(12xy)(12xy)(12xy)(12xy)$ **5.** $\left(-\frac{1}{2}d\right)\left(-\frac{1}{2}d\right)\left(-\frac{1}{2}d\right)$ **7.** 1 **9.** $\frac{1}{10}$ **11.** cd^6 **13.** $\frac{10y^{10}}{x^4}$ **15.** $-4m^4n^6$ **17.** $\frac{y^3}{x^4}$ **19.** 3×10^{11} **21.** 400 **23.** $5 \cdot x \cdot x \cdot x$ **25.** $2a(-b^2 - a)(-b^2 - a)$ **27.** $-\frac{4}{3}$ **29.** -1 **31.** $-x^{20}y^{10}$ **33.** $-16a^5b^7$ **35.** 1.5×10^9 **37.** 1.55 min **39.** $2^6, 2^2, 2^5, 2^{-8}; 16^{-2}, 4^1, 2^5, 8^2$ **41.** $-2^6, 2^0, 2^4, 2^{-2}; -8^2, 2^{-2}, 4^0, 16^1$ **43.** $3m^5n^4$ **45.** $\frac{3x}{2y^3}$ **47.** $-24a^3b^7$ **49.** $\frac{9m^2}{25n^2}$ **51.** 1296 **53.** 1728 **55a.** 3742 km/h **b.** ≈ 288,609 times as fast **c.** ≈ 1.28 s **57.** $-\frac{7x^3}{4y^2}$ **59.** $\frac{100}{x^4z^6}$ **61.** $\frac{8m^4}{n^2}$ **63.** Laos; 25.6 **65.** Vietnam; 615.6 **67.** $\approx 2.84 \times 10^9$ beats **69.** $\approx 1.27 \times 10^5$ hairs **71.** Power of a Product Property or Power of a Power Property **73.** Power of a Quotient Property or Power of a Power Property **77.** 6.5×10^{-15} **79.** 3.5×10^{14} **81.** 1.1346×10^{24} **83.** C **85.** C **87.** $\approx 2.0363 \times 10^{-4}$ **91.** $\frac{1}{3}$ **93.** 8 **95.** $-\frac{1}{3}$

1-6

Check It Out! 1. D: $\{-2, -1, 0, 1, 2, 3\}$; R: $\{-3, -2, -1, 0, 1, 2\}$ **2a.** function **b.** not a function **3a.** function **b.** not a function; (1, 2) and (1, −2)

Exercises 1. range **3.** D: {2000, 2001, 2002, 2003}; R: {5.39, 5.65, 5.80, 6.03} **5.** not a function **7.** function **9.** D: {Irene, Anna, Lea, Kate}; R: {12, 16, 22} **11.** function **13.** not a function **15.** function **17.** D: $\{-2, -1, 0, 1, 2\}$; R: $\{-2, 0, 2\}$ **19.** D: {jumbo, extra large, large, medium}; R: {1.75, 2, 2.25, 2.5} **21a.** function **b.** function **c.** not a function **d.** function **e.** not a function **23.** D: {a, b, c, d}; R: {1, 2, 4}; function **25.** D: {1, 3, 5, 7, 9}; R: {3}; function **27.** D: {3, 4, 5, 6, 7}; R: $\{-1, 2, 3\}$; function **29.** D: {Monday, Tuesday, Wednesday, Thursday, Friday, Saturday, Sunday}; R: {24}; function **31.** B to A **33.** A to B **35.** B to A **37.** both **39.** No; the relation is not a function. **41a.** Yes, the relation is a function. **b.** It is a function. **c.** 2d: ≈ 0.0183 oz; 3d: ≈ 0.0282 oz; 4d: ≈ 0.0506 oz; 5d: ≈ 0.0590 oz; 6d: ≈ 0.0884 oz **45.** F **47.** $b \in \mathbb{R}$ and $a \neq \{-1, 0, 1, 2\}$ **49.** One to one; each length in feet corresponds to only one length in inches. **51.** 288 ft **53.** $36\pi \approx 113.1$ ft^2 **55.** 4.7 **57.** 9.5 **59.** $\frac{20}{w}$ **61.** $\frac{x^{21}}{z^7}$

1-7

Check It Out! 1a. $f(0) = 0; f\left(\frac{1}{2}\right) = -\frac{7}{4}; f(-2) = 12$ **b.** $f(0) = 1; f\left(\frac{1}{2}\right) = 0; f(-2) = 5$

2a.

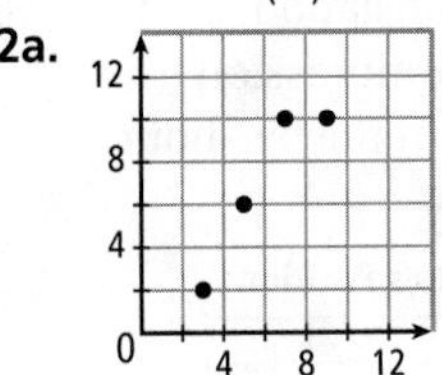

b.

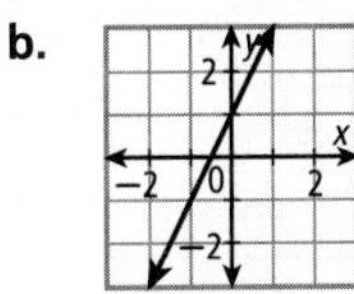

3a. $f(x) = 0.27x$ **b.** 6.48; the price to develop 24 prints, in dollars

Exercises 1. independent **3.** $f(0) = 9; f(1.5) = 11.25; f(-4) = 25$ **5.** $f(0) = 3; f(1.5) = 4; f(-4) = 4$ **7.** $f(0) = -5; f(1.5) = 1; f(-4) = 1$

9.

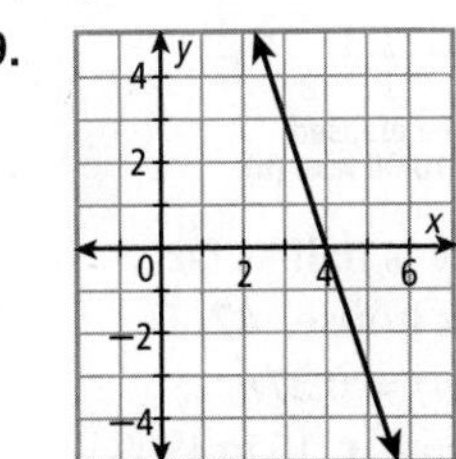

11. $f(x) = 125x$; 6250; the loss if 50 customers purchase the living room set, in dollars **13.** $f(0) = 0; f\left(\frac{3}{2}\right) = -\frac{3}{4}; f(-1) = -2$ **15.** $f(0) = 2; f\left(\frac{3}{2}\right) = 5; f(-1) = 0$ **17.** $f(0) = 0; f\left(\frac{3}{2}\right) = 3; f(-1) = \frac{1}{2}$

19.

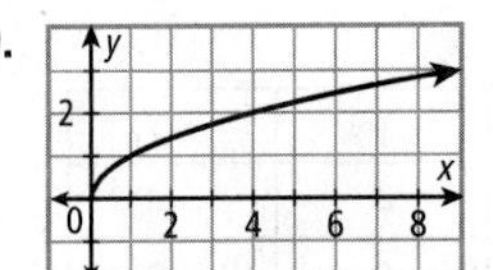

21. $f(m) = 160 + 4m$; 192; a fine of \$192 for driving 8 mi/h over the speed limit **23.** $f(-3.5) = -16.5; f(-1) = -9; f\left(\frac{1}{4}\right) = -5.25; f(2) = 0; f(11) = 27$ **25.** $f(-4) = -3; f(0) = -\frac{1}{3}; f\left(\frac{1}{2}\right) = 0; f(5) = 3$ **27.** $f(-2)\,0 = -1; f(-1) = 2; f(1) = 2; f(2) = -1$ **29.** D: $\{A \mid A \geq 0\}$; R: $\{y \mid y \in W\}$ **31.** D: $\{t \mid t \geq 0\}$; R: $\{y \mid -16 < y \leq 32.8\}$ **33.** $t = 35$; the number of years it takes for plan h to reach a value of \$7500 **35.** $t = 40$; the time when plan g is worth $\frac{1}{2}$ the value of plan h **37.** $h(40) - g(40) = 5000$; the difference in the value of the plans after 40 years **39.** When $x = 3$, $f(x) = \frac{1}{x-3} = \frac{1}{0}$, but division by 0 is undefined. **41.** For $-5 < x < 0$, x represents negative hours, and distance traveled would be negative. **43.** independent: number of shirts; dependent: total cost; domain: $x \geq 15$ **45.** $f(x) = 2.37x$ **47.** $f(x) = 0.8x$ **51.** H **53.** 31 **55.** $g\left(-\frac{h}{4}\right) = 1$ **57.** $r(t^4) = \frac{\sqrt{t^{16}+4}}{t^4}$ **59.** $12x - xy + 8$ **61.** $\frac{c-2}{c}$ **63.** b is any value. **65.** yes

1-8

Check It Out! 1a. (3, 3) **b.** (−2, 1)

2a.

$x+3$	x	y
1	−2	4
2	−1	0
3	0	2
5	2	2

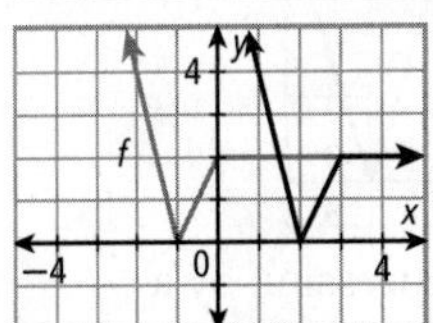

Selected Answers

b.

x	y	$-y$
−2	4	−4
−1	0	0
0	2	−2
2	2	−2

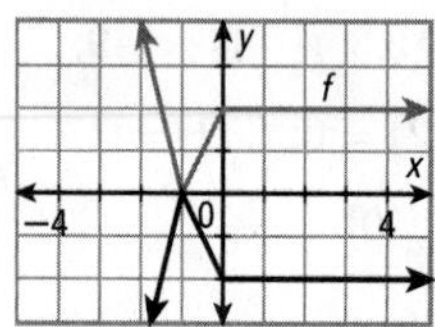

3.

x	y	$2y$
−1	3	6
0	0	0
2	2	4
4	2	4

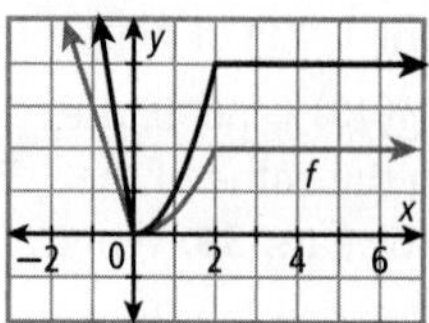

4. vertical compression by a factor of $\frac{3}{4}$

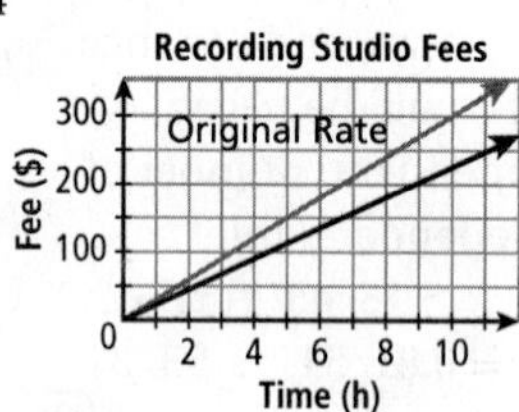

Exercises **1.** compression **3.** $(4, -1)$

5.

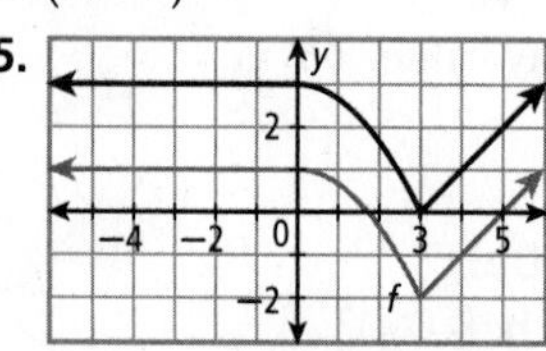

7.

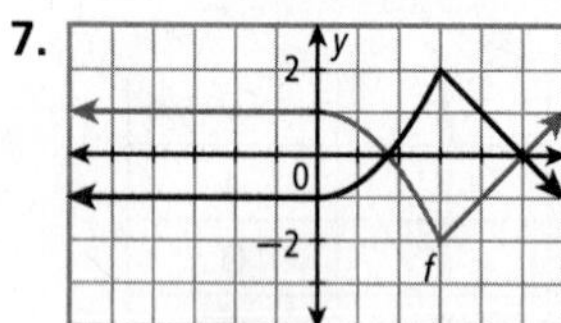

9.

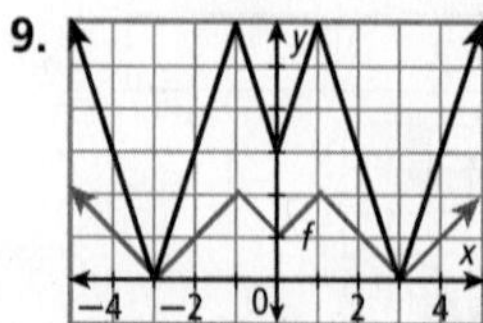

11. vertical compression by a factor of $\frac{1}{2}$ **13.** horizontal shift right 5 units **15.** $(3, 5)$

17.

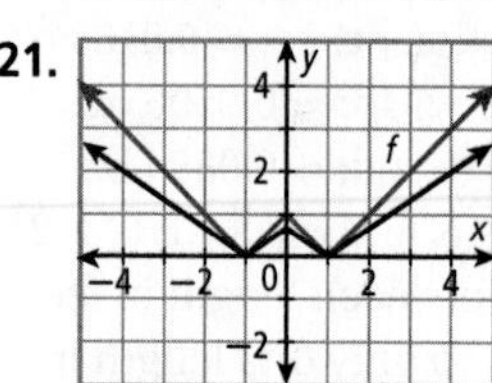

21.

25. vertical shift down 5 units **27.** horizontal stretch by a factor of 2 **29.** 10 square units; the same as the original **31.** 7 square units; smaller than the original **33.** 10 square units; the same as the original **35.** 30 square units; larger than the original **37a.** vertical translation **b.** horizontal compression **c.** the increase in the per-hour labor rate

39.

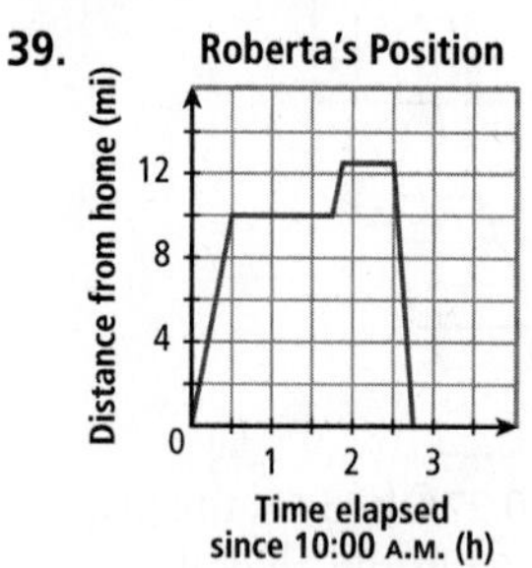

41.

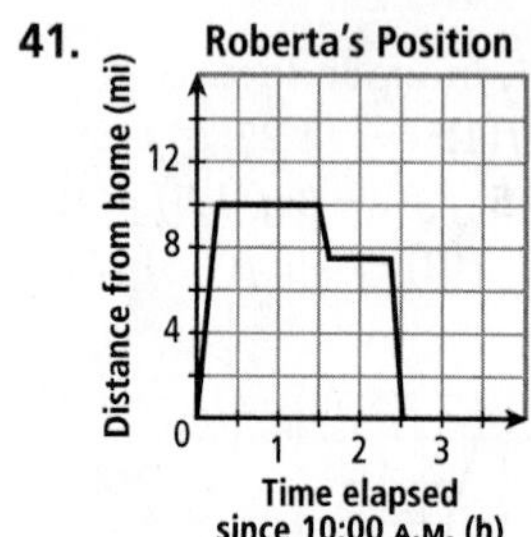

43. The library is half as far from Roberta's house. **47.** H **49.** H **53a.** $c(n) = 0.37n$ **b.** vertical stretch **c.** 15 in 1999 and 13 in 2002 **d.** The number of letters that can be mailed for $5.00 must be rounded down to the nearest whole number. **55.** 110 **57.** yes **59.** $f(1) = -\frac{1}{2}$; $f(-3) = -\frac{17}{2}$; $f\left(\frac{1}{4}\right) = -2$ **61.** $f(1) = 0$; $f(-3) = 64$; $f\left(\frac{1}{4}\right) = \frac{225}{256}$

1-9

Check It Out! **1a.** cubic; translation 2 units up **b.** quadratic; reflection across the y-axis **2.** linear; vertical stretch by a factor of 3

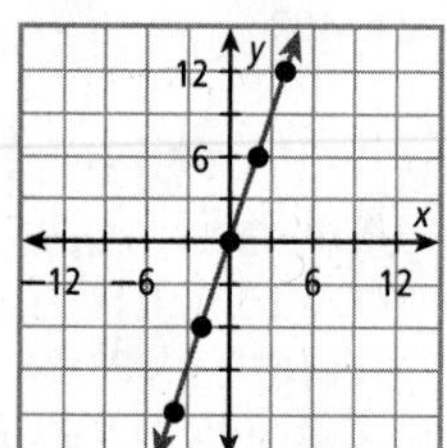

3. linear; about $72

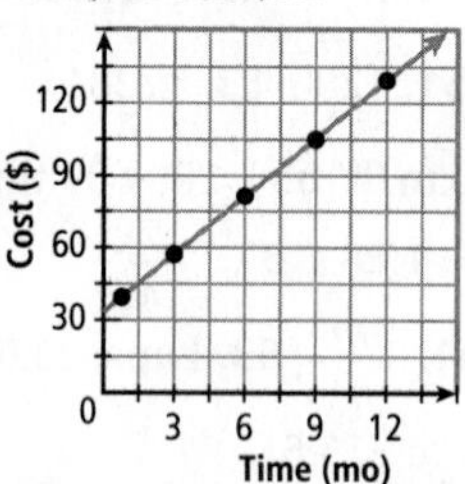

Exercises **3.** quadratic; translation 1 unit left **5.** square root; translation 3 units left **7.** linear; translation $\sqrt{2}$ units down **9.** cubic; vertical compression or horizontal stretch **11.** quadratic; translation 1 unit down **13.** cubic; translation 3 units up **15.** square root; vertical stretch or horizontal compression **17.** D: $\{x \mid x \geq 0\}$; R: $\{y \mid y \geq 0\}$; vertical stretch by a factor of 3 **19.** D: $\{x \mid x \geq 0\}$; R: $\{y \mid y \leq 0\}$; reflection across the x-axis **21.** D: $\{x \mid x \in \mathbb{R}\}$; R: $\{y \mid y \leq 1\}$; reflection across the x-axis and then a vertical shift up 1 unit **23.** $195 **25.** quadratic; horizontal shift right 7 units **27.** linear; reflection across the y-axis and a vertical shift down 1 unit **29.** linear; $\approx$ 1500 pixels **31.** quadratic; $\approx$ 1417 pixels **33.** Cubic; D: $\{\ell \mid \ell \geq 0\}$; R: $\{y \mid y \geq 0\}$; the domain and range are restricted. **35.** Linear; D: $\{n \mid n \in \mathbb{N}\}$; R: $\{y \mid y \in \mathbb{N}\}$; the domain and range are restricted. **37.** Square root; D: $\{a \mid a \geq 0\}$; R: $\{y \mid y \geq 0\}$; the domain and range are the same. **39a.** linear **b.** cubic **c.** quadratic **d.** square root

e. linear; horizontal stretch by a factor of 2 and a vertical shift up 3 units **43.** H **45.** G **47.** quadratic **49.** linear **51.** 7.5×10^9 **53.** 2.0×10^{-25} **55.** $f(-5) = 15; f\left(-\frac{2}{3}\right) = -\frac{8}{9};$ $f(1.6) = 5.76; f(4) = 24$ **57.** $(4, -10)$

Study Guide: Review

1. domain; range **2.** $\{x \mid x \geq -5\}$ **3.** $(-1, 5]$ **4.** $\{4, 5, 6, 7, \ldots\}$ **5.** $\{x \mid x < -2 \text{ or } x > 5\}$ **6.** integers greater than −4 and less than or equal to 5 **7.** $[5.5, 5.6]$ **8.** Commutative Property of Multiplication **9.** Distributive Property **10.** $-0.55; \frac{1}{0.55}$ **11.** $\frac{7}{8}; -\frac{8}{7}$ **12.** $-1.\overline{2}; \frac{1}{1.\overline{2}}$ or $\frac{9}{11}$ **13.** 3.5 **14.** 7.4 **15.** 8.6 **16.** 5.4 **17.** $4\sqrt{2}$ **18.** 4 **19.** $-4\sqrt{2}$ **20.** $3\sqrt{7}$ **21.** $\frac{7\sqrt{2}}{2}$ **22.** $\frac{\sqrt{10}}{5}$ **23.** −96 **24.** 14 **25.** $\frac{1}{8}$ **26.** $11x - 3y$ **27.** $18 - 5a + b$ **28.** $-3x - 12y$ **29.** $a^2c + 2bc$ **30.** $\frac{-8x^{15}}{y^9}$ **31.** $\frac{-12x^7}{7y^9}$ **32.** $\frac{r^4}{s^4}$ **33.** $\frac{4m^6}{n^4}$ **34.** 7×10^7 **35.** 5.4×10^1 **36.** D: $\{3, 5, 7\}$; R: $\{-1, 0, 9\}$; not a function **37.** D: $[-2, \infty)$; R: $[-4, \infty)$; not a function **38.** D: $\{-2, 0, 3, 4\}$; R: $\{3, 4\}$; function **39.** D: $\{5, 10, 15, 20, 25\}$; R: $\{-5, -4, -3, -2, -1\}$; function **40.** D: {a, b, c}; R: {Alabama, Alaska, Arizona, Arkansas, California, Colorado, Connecticut}; not a function **41.** $f(2) = -2; f\left(\frac{1}{2}\right) = \frac{7}{4}; f(-2) = -2$ **42.** $f(2) = -16; f\left(\frac{1}{2}\right) = -\frac{17}{2}; f(-2) = 4$ **43.** $f(2) = -1; f\left(\frac{1}{2}\right) = 1; f(-2) = 2$ **44.** $f(2) = \frac{1}{2}; f\left(\frac{1}{2}\right) = 2; f(-2) = -\frac{1}{2}$

45.

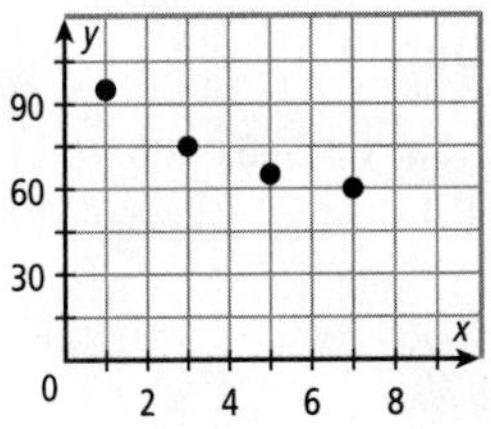

46.

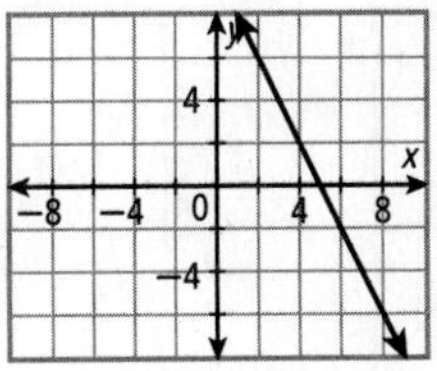

47. $A(s) = 6s^2$, where A is the surface area in square units and s is the side length in linear units; $A(10) = 600$; the surface area for a cube of side length 10 cm is 600 cm². **48.** $(0, -5)$ **49.** $(5, 1)$ **50.** vertical compression by a factor of $\frac{1}{2}$ **51.** vertical stretch by a factor of 1.1 **52.** translation 1 unit up **53.** quadratic function; translation 1 unit down **54.** square-root function; reflection across the x-axis **55.** linear function; about 90 psi

Chapter 2

2-1

Check It Out! 1. 44 **2a.** $p = -4$ **b.** $r = \frac{1}{2}$ **3.** $w = 3$ **4a.** ∅ **b.** ℝ

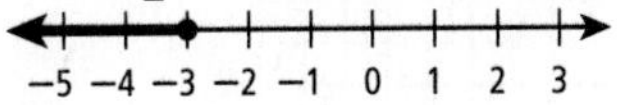

5. $x \leq -3$

Exercises 1. identity **3.** $x = 14$ **5.** $x = -6$ **7.** $x = -3$ **9.** $x = 2$ **11.** $r = -6$ **13.** ∅ **15.** ℝ **17.** ∅ **19.** $x > \frac{7}{3}$ **21.** 28 s **23.** $x = 16$ **25.** $x = \frac{19}{2}$ **27.** $n = 6$ **29.** $x = 2$ **31.** $t = -8$ **33.** ∅ **35.** ∅ **37.** $x \geq -2$

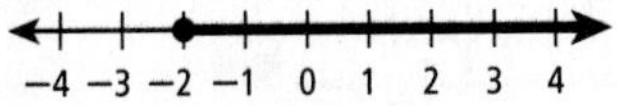

39. $x \leq -12$ **41.** \$0.04 **43a.** no more than 10 **b.** no more than 21 **c.** no more than 13 **45.** $m\angle D = 70°$; $m\angle E = 20°$ **47.** 10 tragedies; 17 comedies; 10 histories. **49.** $k = -10$ **53.** C **55.** D **57.** 12 **59.** $x < -\frac{8}{5}$ **61a.** ≈ 111 min **b.** ≈ 75 min **63.** $8\sqrt{10}$ **65.** $2\sqrt{15}$ **67.** function **69.** Yes

2-2

Check It Out! 1a. $y = 11$ **b.** $x = 42$ **2.** 1240 students **3.** ≈ 53 in.

4.

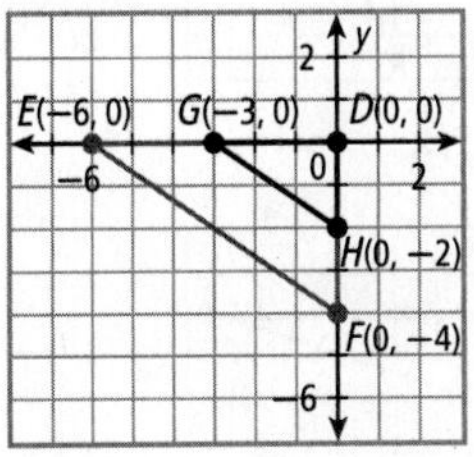

5. 27 ft

Exercises 1. rate **3.** $n = 8$ **5.** $t = 54$ **7.** $x = 20$ **9.** $x = -21$ **11.** 24 mi/gal **13.** 52.5 ft **15.** $y = 6.2$ **17.** $x = 10$ **19.** \$1.22 **21.** 36 ft **23.** $t = 0.168$ **25.** $u = 8$ **27.** $h = -30$ **29.** $x = 0$ **33.** The person would be 22 ft tall. **35a.** ≈ 128.57 **35b.** ≈ 128.59 times as long **37.** ≈ 0.0018% **39.** 5.4 in. **41.** $AB = 16\frac{2}{3}$; $EF = 22\frac{1}{2}$ **43.** HO **45.** 145 ft **49.** G **51.** G **53.** $h = 8.6$ **55.** $z = 8$ or $z = -8$ **57.** no **59.** 3 **61.** 350 **63.** 0.025 **65.** cone **67.** hexagonal prism or cylinder **69.** $f(x) = x$; vertical translation, up 4, then stretch by a scale factor of 3 **71.** $f(x) = \sqrt{x}$; horizontal translation, left 1, then reflection.

2-3

Check It Out! 1a. yes **b.** no

2.

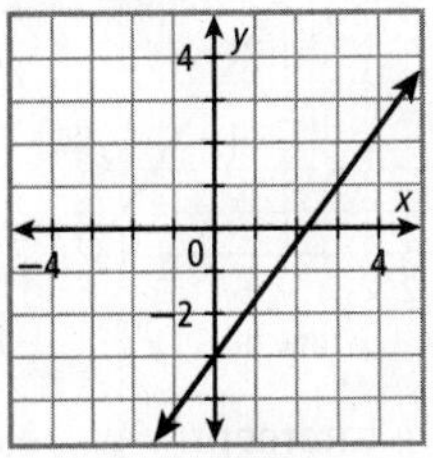

3. $x = -4$; $y = 12$

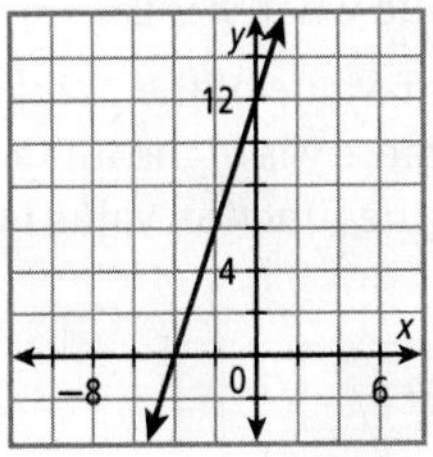

Selected Answers

4a. $y = 2x - 9$

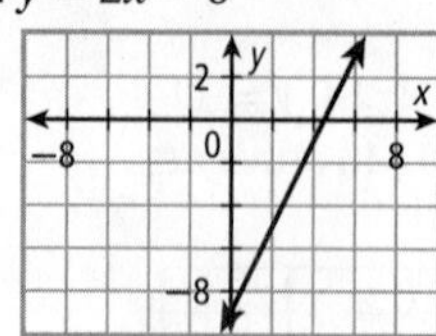

b. $y = \frac{1}{3}x - 2$

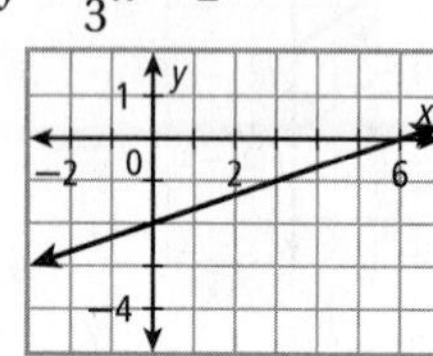

5a. horizontal;

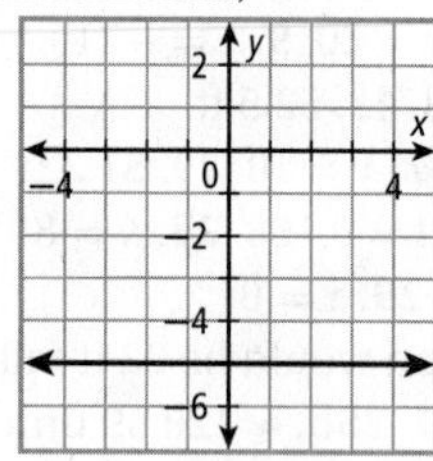

b.

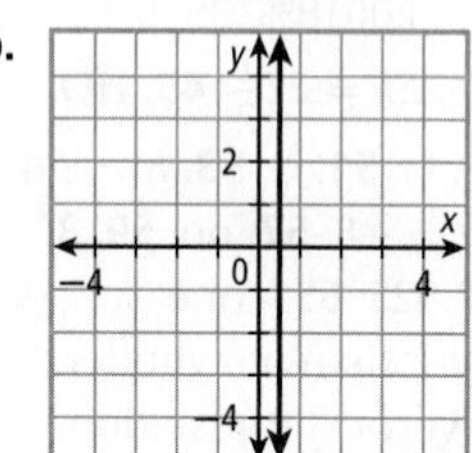

6. 64 mi/h

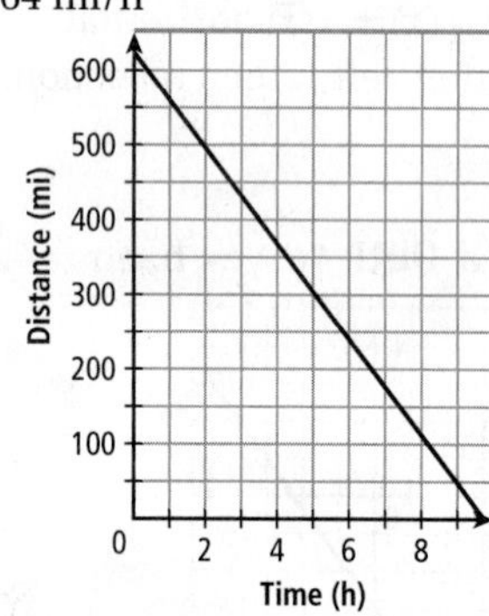

Exercises 1. y-intercept: y-value of the point on the y-axis where x is 0; function value when x is 0

x-intercept: x-value of the point on the x-axis where y is 0; the input value when the function value is 0

3. yes

5.

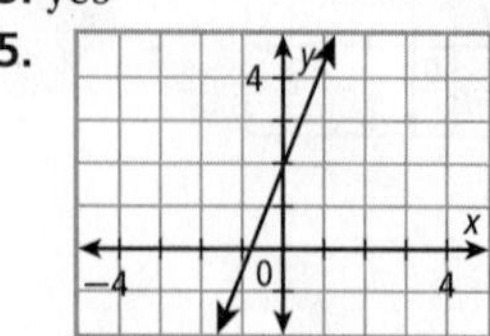

7.

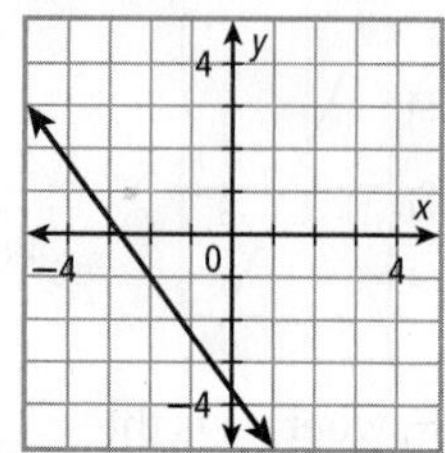

9. $x = 6$; $y = 5$

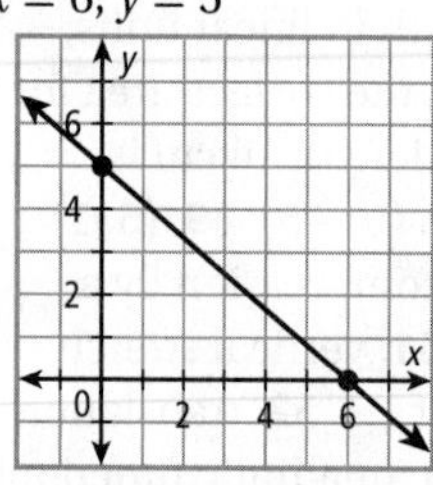

11. $x = -6$; $y = 15$

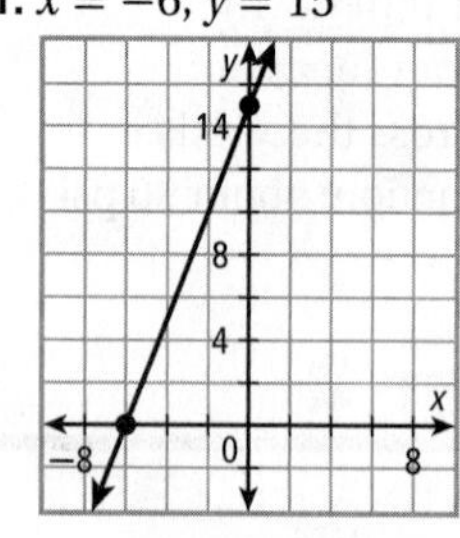

13. $y = -5x + 4$

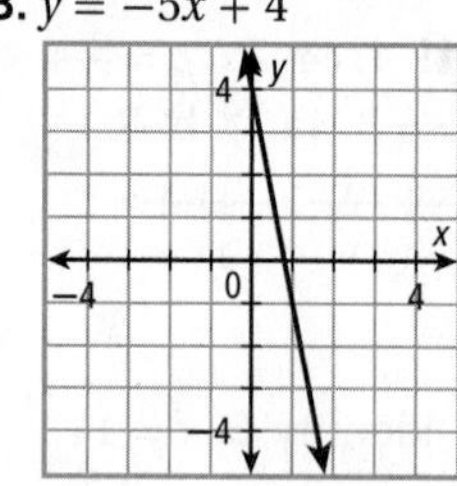

15. $y = -2x + 5$

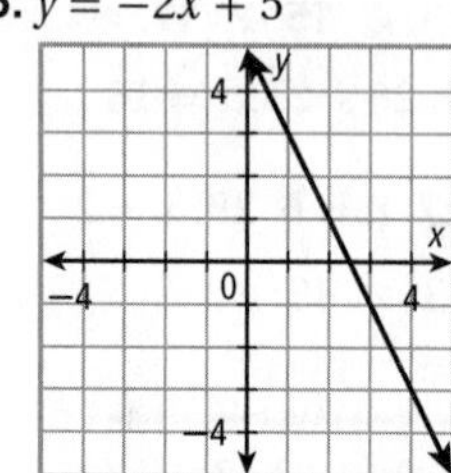

17. vertical

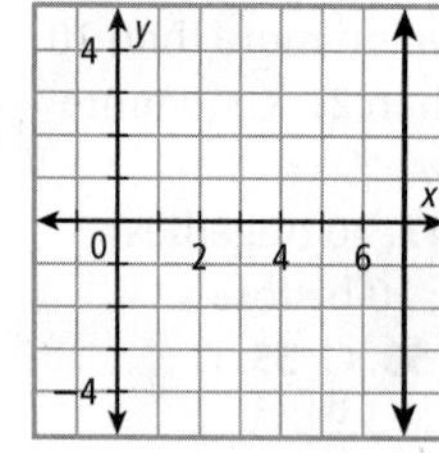

19. vertical

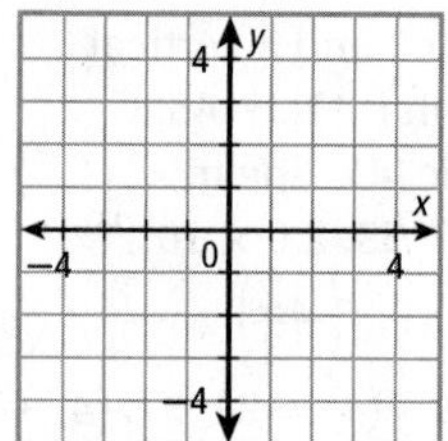

21. \$73.50/h

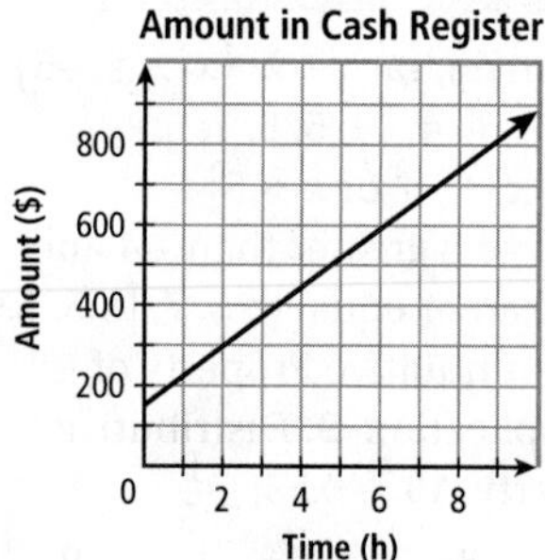

23. yes

25.

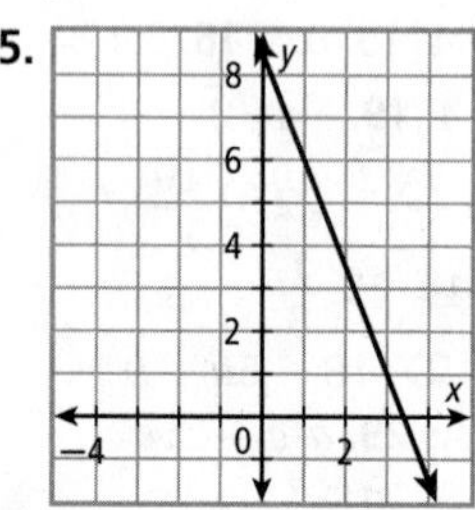

29. $x = 4$; $y = -8$
31. $x = -2$; $y = 3$
33. $y = 3x - 2$
35. $y = \frac{4}{3}x + 2$ **37.** horizontal
39. horizontal
47a. yes **b.** \$1.99 **c.** 1.19
49. sometimes **51a.** ≈ 1.97
51c. the number of leagues per foot
51d. $\approx$ 364.6 million ft; 10,172
53a. $-\frac{A}{B}; \frac{C}{B}$ **b.** 3; $-\frac{9}{2}$ **55a.** adult \$5, student \$2 **b.** y-intercept: 110; x-intercept: 44 **59.** D **61.** B
63. 0.125 **65a.** $\frac{9}{4}$; -9; 4
b. y-intercept: b; x-intercept: a
c. $\frac{x}{6} + \frac{y}{15} = 1$ **67.** $\frac{1}{2}$ **69.** $-\frac{27}{32}$
71. 81.9 **73.** $f(0) = 7; f(-3) = 6$
75. $f(0) = 0; f(-3) = -9$
77. $x = -24$ **79.** $t = 6$

2-4

Check It Out! 1. $y = \frac{3}{4}x + 3$

2a. 1 b. 0 **3a.** $y = -5x + 8$
b. $y = 2x + 1$

4a. $c = 2.5n + 4$; \$49

b.

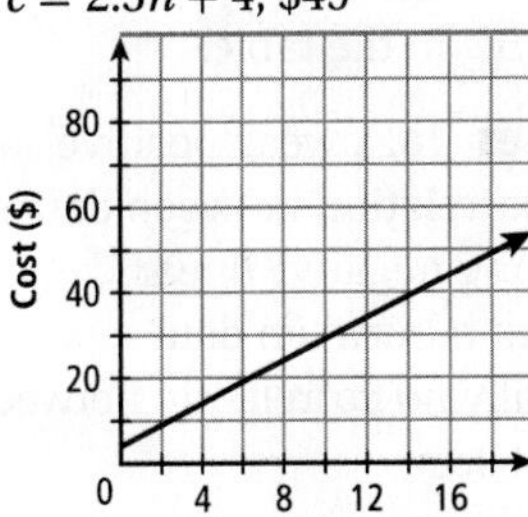

5a. $y = 5x - 1$ **b.** $y = -\frac{6}{5}x - 2$

Exercises **1.** $y = 2x + 1$

3. $y = \frac{1}{4}x + 3$ **5.** $\frac{7}{5}$ **7.** $y = -\frac{4}{3}x - \frac{8}{3}$

9a. $t = -\frac{1}{550}x + 212$

b.

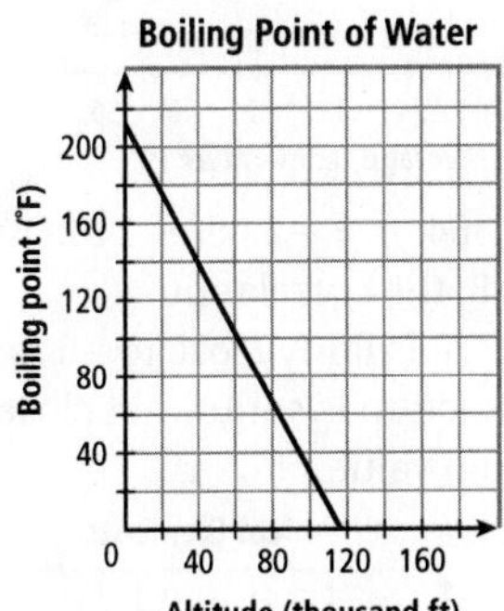

c. 192° **11.** $y = -\frac{9}{5}x - 4$

13. $y = \frac{5}{3}x - 2$ **15.** $\frac{2}{3}$

17. $y = \frac{7}{3}x + 4$

19a. $f = \frac{4}{9}T - \frac{64}{3}$

19.

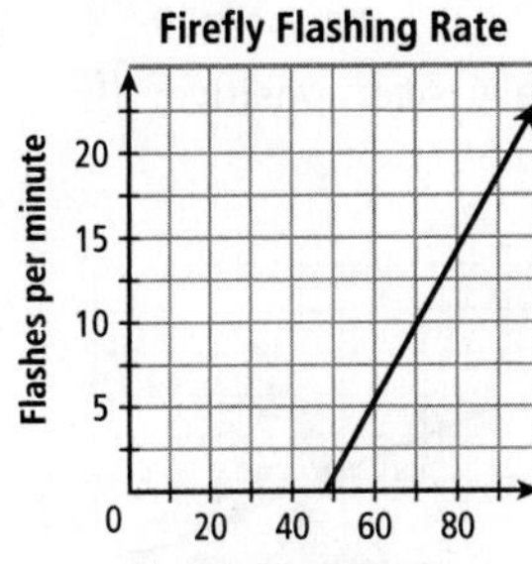

c. 104.25°F **d.** ≈ -5.8 times; no

21. $y = -\frac{1}{3}x + 3$ **23.** neither

25. parallel **27.** $f(x) = 2x - 1$

29. $y = 4x + 3$

31. $y = -\frac{11}{8}x + \frac{1}{8}$ **33.** $y = 21x - 40$

35. $y = \frac{1}{6}x + \frac{4}{3}$ **37.** $y = -3x - 8$

39. slope $\overline{AB}$ = slope $\overline{DC} = -\frac{1}{3}$; slope $\overline{AD}$ = slope $\overline{BC} = 3$; rectangle

41. trapezoid **45.** G **49.** no

53. $(-\infty, -4)$ **55.** no **57.** yes

2-5

Check It Out!

1a.

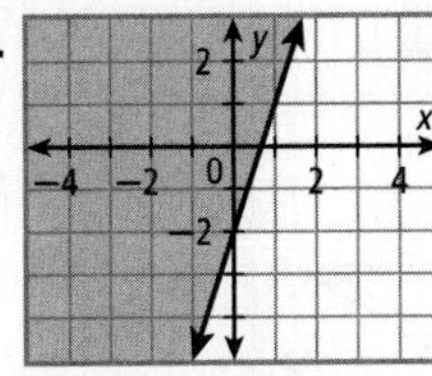

b.

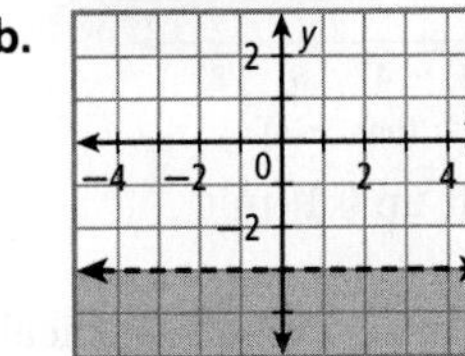

2.

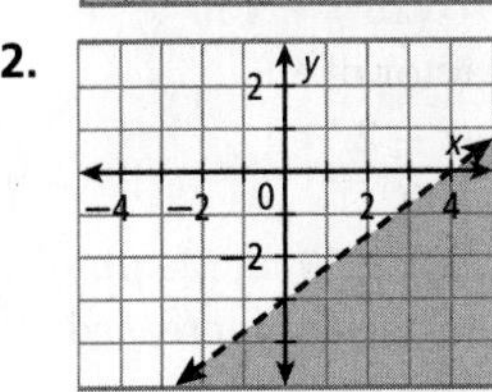

3. $40x + 125y \le 1500$

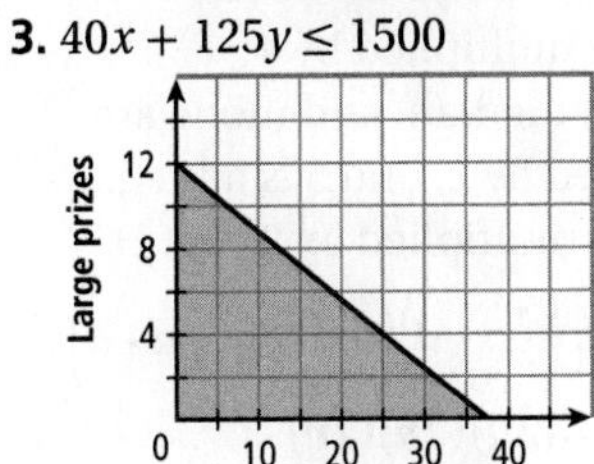

no more than 25

4.

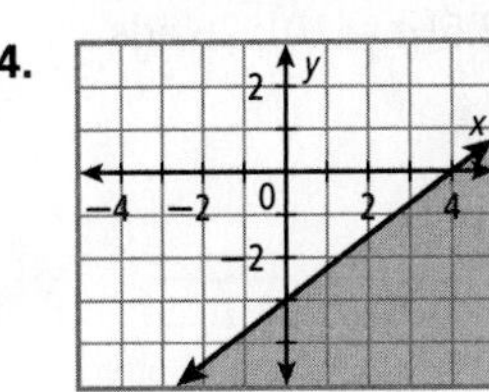

Exercises

3.

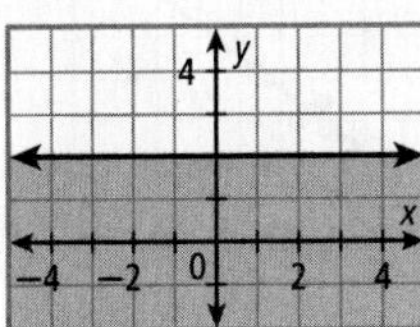

5.

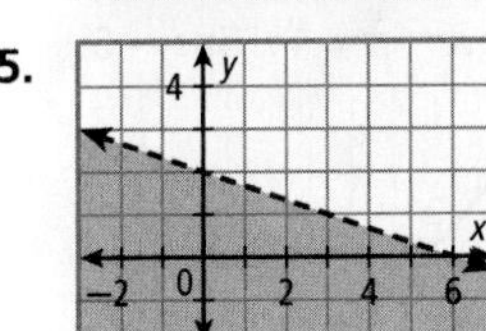

7.

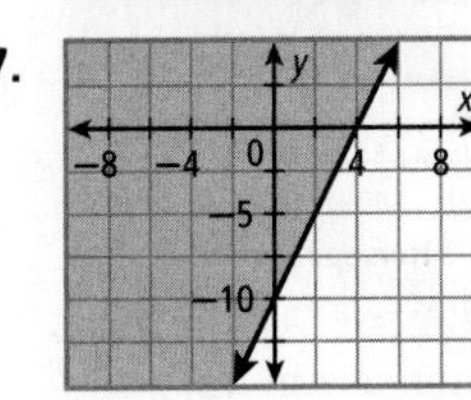

9a. $2.29x + 3.75y \le 7.00$

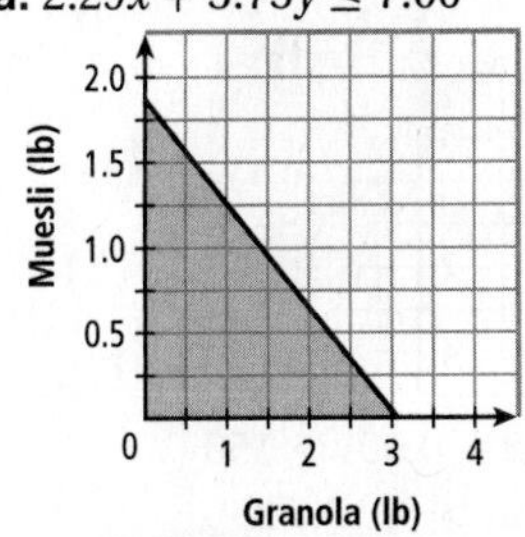

b. no more than 0.6 lb

11. $y \le +3x - 4$

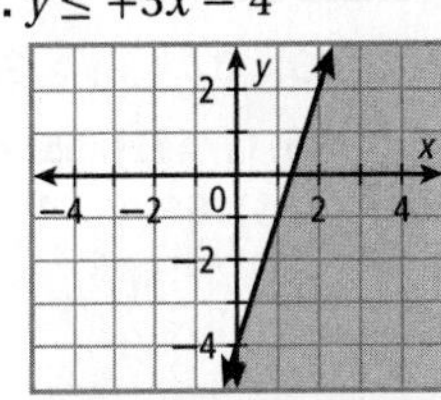

13. $y < 3x + 4$

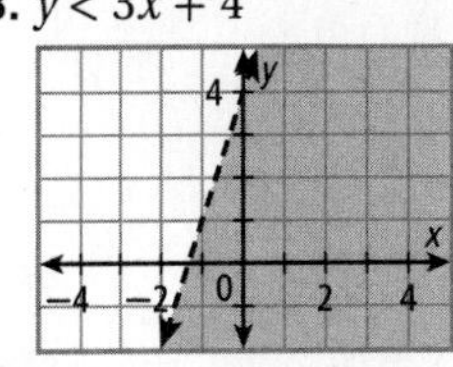

15.

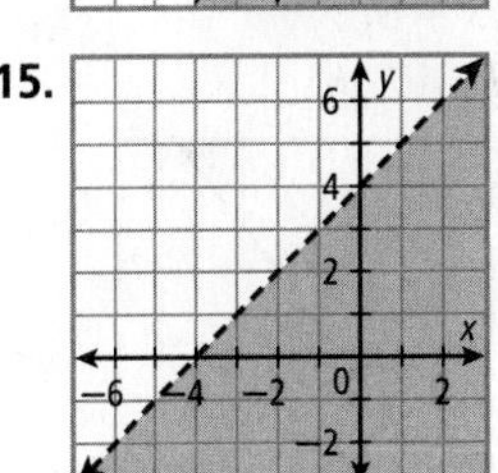

17.

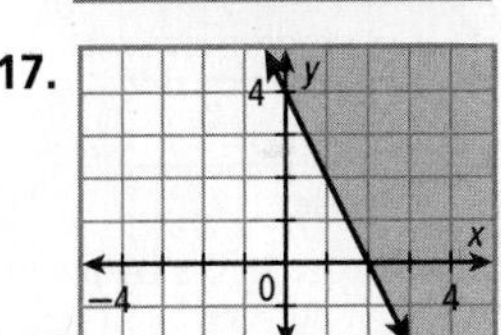

19. $200x + 500y \le 10{,}000$

21a. $8x + 12y \le 200$;

b. no more than 10 h

23. $y \le 5x - 4$

25.

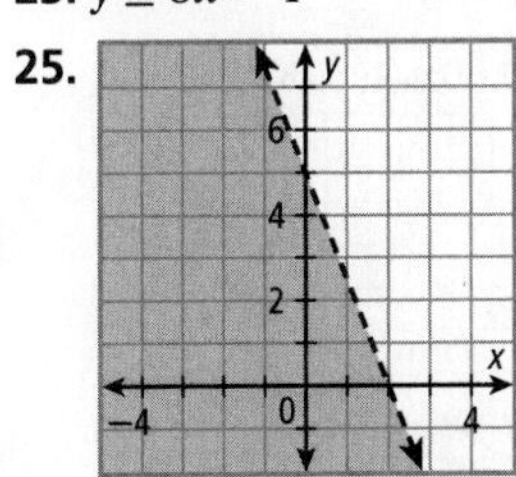

29.

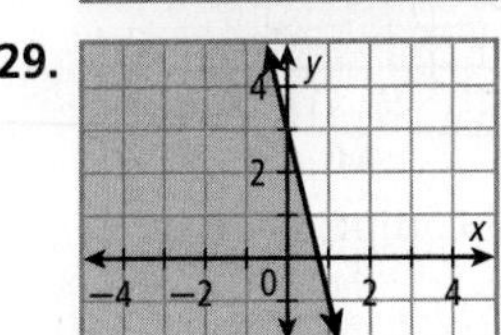

31. 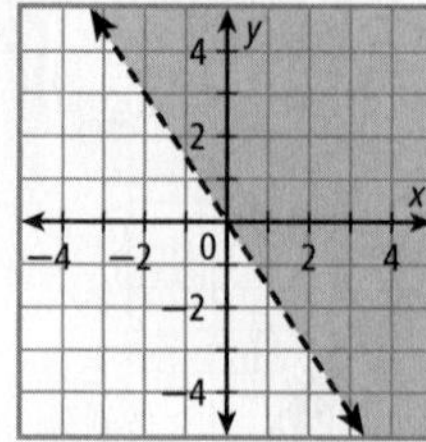

35a. $1.25x + 0.50y \geq 150$
b. yes 37a. $> \approx 18.5$ h
b. possible distances from port
c. between 176 and 380 mi
39. $y > -\frac{4}{3}x + 2$ 43a. $8x + 6y \geq 220$
b. $8x + 6y \leq 300$ 45. G 47. J 55. no
57. $(-5, 3)$ 59. $(-4, 6)$ 61. $x = 1$
63. $y = 0.25x - 7.25$

2-6

Check It Out!

1a. $g(x) = 3(x - 2) + 1$
b. $g(x) = -(x + 2)$
2. $g(x) = \frac{1}{4}(3x + 2)$
3. $g(x) = \frac{1}{2}(x + 8)$
4a. $S(n) = 25n - 75$
b. 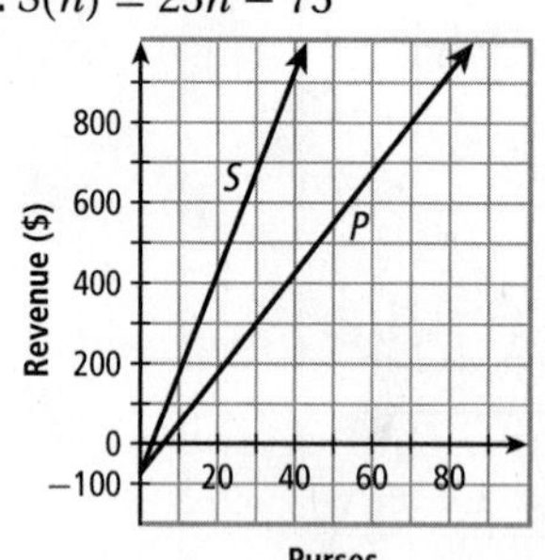

4c. horizontal compression by a factor of $\frac{1}{2}$

Exercises 1. $g(x) = -\frac{3}{2}x + 2$
3. $g(x) = x - 6$
5. $g(x) = \frac{2}{3}x - 6$
7a. $D(n) = 0.60n + 5.00$
b. 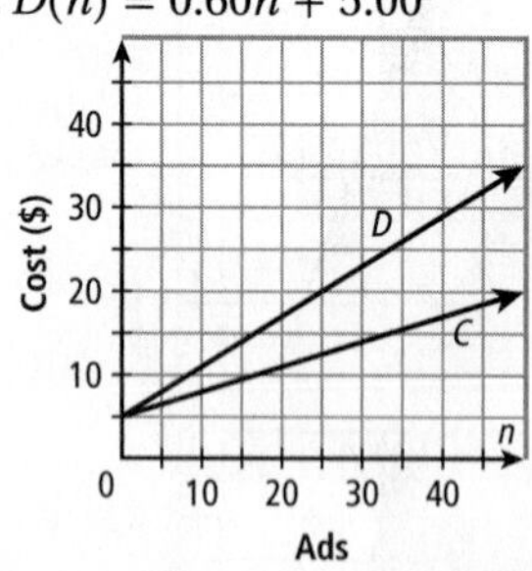

c. horizontal compression by a factor of $\frac{1}{2}$
9. $g(x) = \frac{1}{2}x - 4$
11. $g(x) = 1.2(-0.5x + 0.5)$
13. $g(x) = \frac{1}{2.75}(x + 1)$
15a. $g(x) = 0.15x + 0.35$
b. 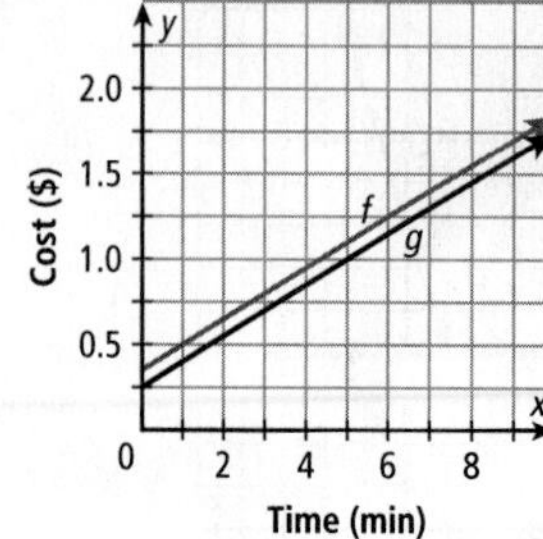

c. vertical shift up 0.1 unit
17. $g(x) = 2x$
19. $T(n) = 0.10\left(\frac{n}{15}\right) = \frac{n}{150}$; vertical stretch by a factor of 1.6
21a. $g(x) = -x - 2$
b. $h(x) = -x + 2$
23a. 22.125; 20; 23; 59 b. Mean, median, and mode are increased by 7. Range stays the same.
c. All are multiplied by 4.
d. Mean, median, and mode are multiplied by 2, and 5 is added. Range is multiplied by 2. 25. H
27. F 31. $\left(\frac{3}{5}d \cdot d\right)\left(\frac{3}{5}d \cdot d\right)\left(\frac{3}{5}d \cdot d\right)$
33. $-(2n)(2n)(2n)(2n)$
35. horizontal
37. neither
39. $B(a) = 32.5(a - 10)$; 26 ads

2-7

Check It Out!

1. 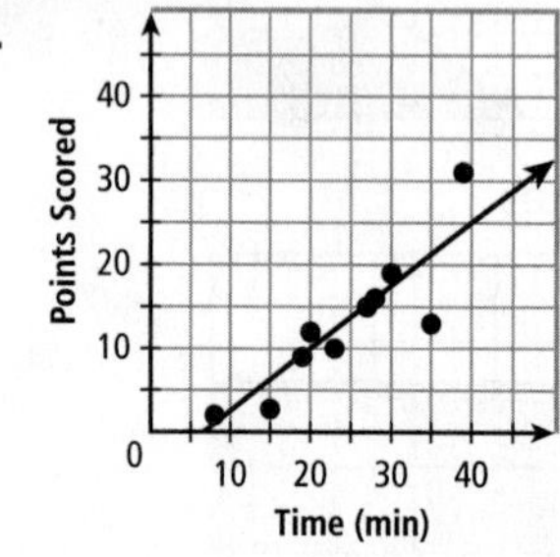

Possible answer: $p = 0.75m - 5$
2a. 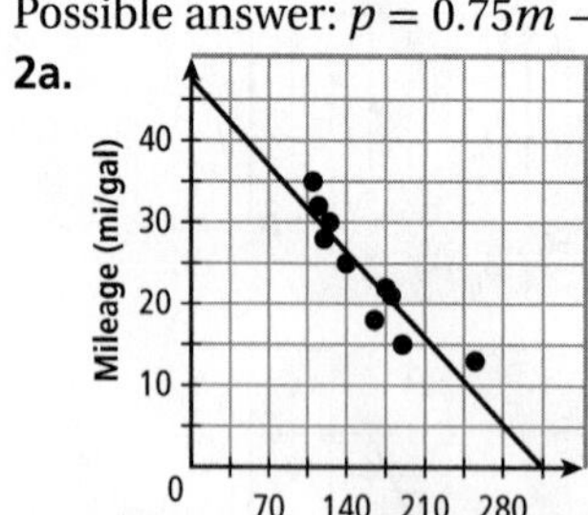

b. $r \approx -0.916$; $y \approx -0.15x + 47.5$; for a 1-unit increase in hp, gas mileage drops ≈ 0.15 mi/gal
c. ≈ 16.0 mi/gal 3. ≈ 10 g; not close to the 15 g in the table.

Exercises 1a. a weak positive linear correlation between data sets
b. a strong negative linear correlation between data sets
c. virtually no correlation between the data sets
3a–b. 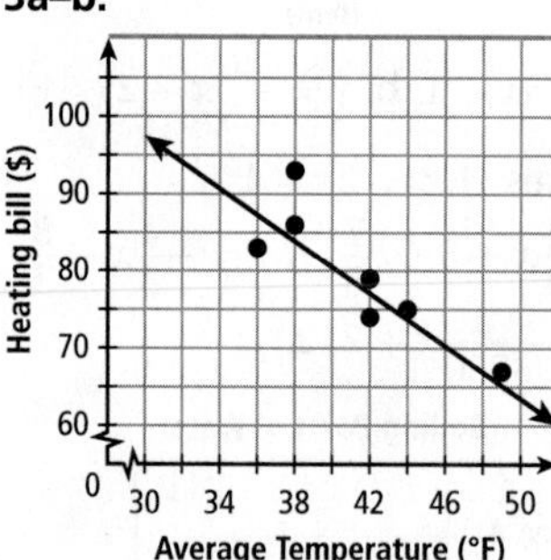

$r \approx -0.864$; $h \approx -1.68t + 148.88$
c. \$81.68; the correlation coefficient is fairly close to -1, so the prediction is somewhat close to the actual value.
5. 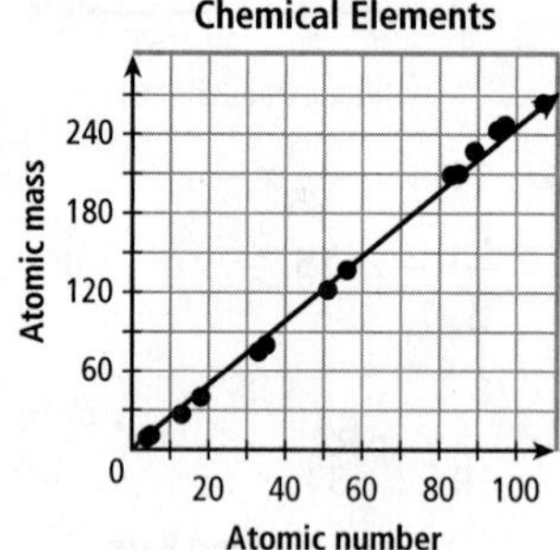

Possible answer: positive; $w = 2.5n - 5.5$
7a–b. 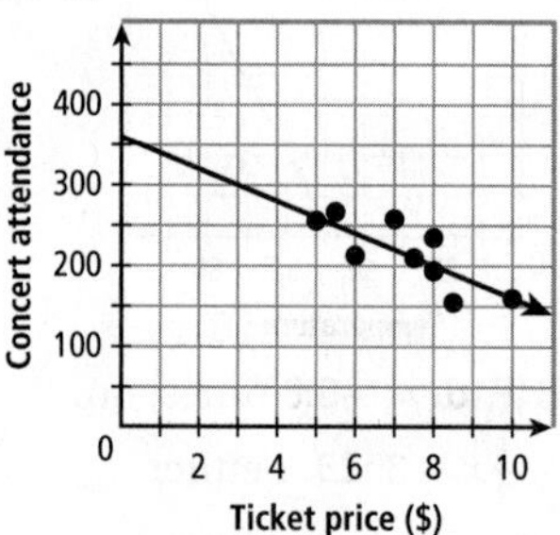

$r \approx -0.801$ $a \approx -20.95p + 368.89$
c. 180 people; fairly accurate.
9. $r \approx 0$ 11. $r \approx 0.9$
13. Possible answers:
13a. $s = 95.5 - p$

b. $s = 100.5 - p$;

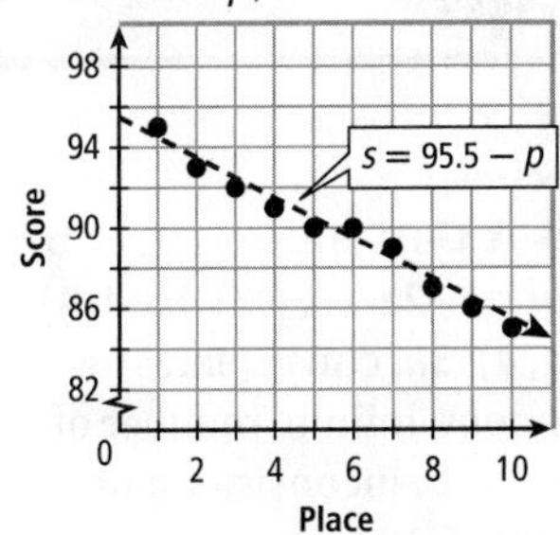

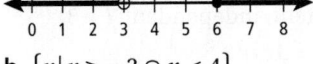

15a. $r = 0.994$; $y \approx 1.20x - 3.66$
b. A 1 cm increase in femur length corresponds to a 1.2 cm increase in humerus length. **c.** 44.7 cm; the data is nearly linear, so the prediction is probably accurate.
19. C **21.** B **23a.** $r = 0$
b. The data appear related but not linear. **25.** $8x^2 - 10x^2y + 4xy - 6$
27. $-g^2 + g - 12$
29. $x < -6$
31. $\varnothing$ **33.** $f(x) = x + 6$; $g(x) = -x - 6$; $g(x) = -f(x)$; reflection across the x-axis

2-8

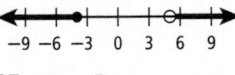

Check It Out! 1a. $\{x \mid x < 3 \cup x \geq 6\}$
b. $\{x \mid x \geq -3 \cap x < 4\}$
c. $\{x \mid x < 17\}$
d. $\{x \mid 4 < x \leq 8\}$
2a. $-22, 4$ **b.** $-5, 5$
3a. $\{x \mid x < -1 \cup x > 5\}$
b. $\varnothing$
4a. $\{x \mid -3 \leq x \leq 13\}$
b. $\varnothing$

Exercises 1. disjunction
3. $-2 < x \leq 6$
5. $-3, -7$ **7.** $3, -3$
9. $x < -1$ or $x > 7$
11. $-8 < x < 4$

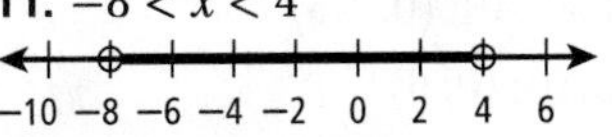

13. $\varnothing$ **15.** $-1 \leq x \leq 5$
17. $-5, -9$ **19.** $3, -3$
21. $x \leq -7$ or $x \geq -3$
23. $x \leq -7$ or $x \geq 3$
25. $x < -8$ or $x > 3$
27. $-8 < x < 7$
29. $x < -6$ or $x \geq -1$
31. $-4 \leq x < 3$
33. $x \leq -4$ or $x > 5$
35. $x > -5$
37. $7, -\frac{19}{5}$
39. $x \leq 2$ or $x \geq 3$

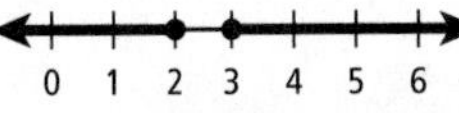

41. $x < -\frac{23}{4}$ or $x > \frac{13}{4}$
45. $|20x - 3400| \leq 100$; $165 \leq x \leq 175$
47. sometimes **55.** B **57.** D
58. F **59.** $x = 1$ or -4 **61.** B
63a. Associative Property
b. no **65.** ≈ 27 mi/gal
67. $n = 6$; Distributive Property
69. 60°; 80°; 100°; 120° **71.** 95°; 110°; 75°; 80°

2-9

Check It Out!
1a. $g(x) = |x| - 4$

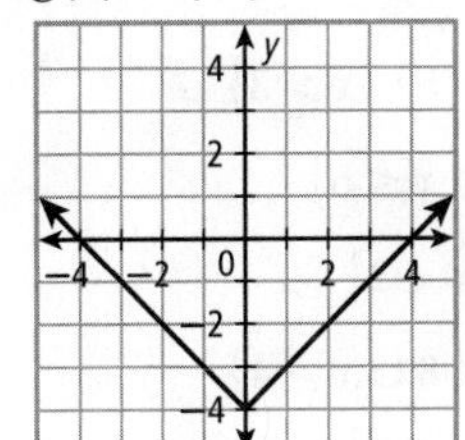

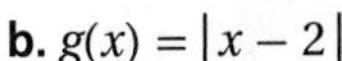

b. $g(x) = |x - 2|$

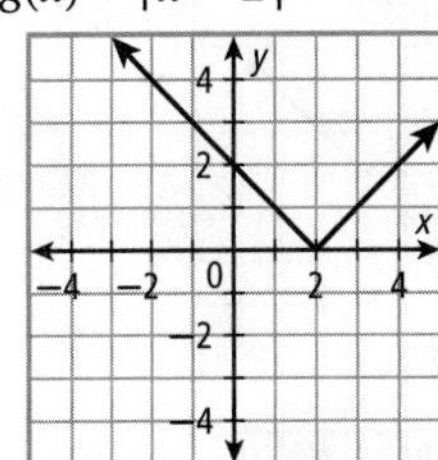

2. $g(x) = |x - 4| - 2$

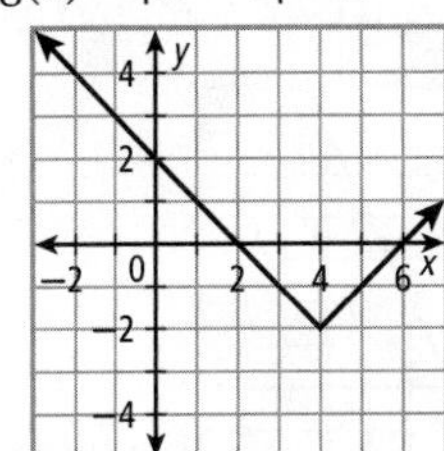

3a. $g(x) = -|-x - 4| + 3$

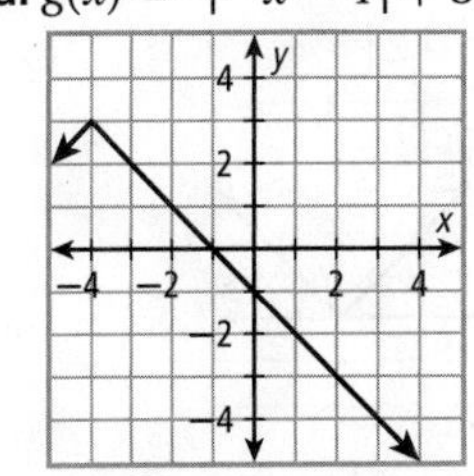

b. $g(x) = \frac{1}{2}(|x| + 1)$

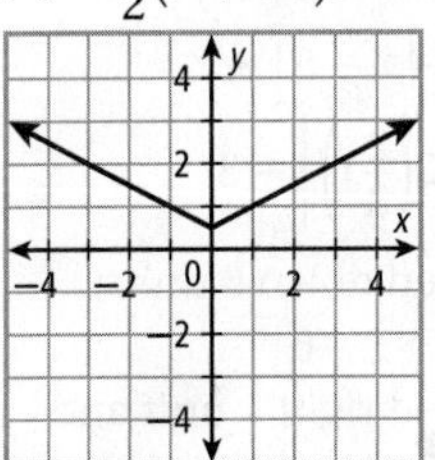

c. $g(x) = |2x| - 3$

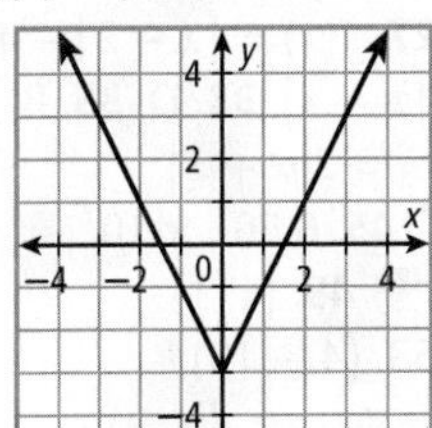

Exercises 1. The graph is the line $y = x$ where negative x-values are reflected over the x-axis, creating a **V**.
3. $g(x) = |x + 4|$

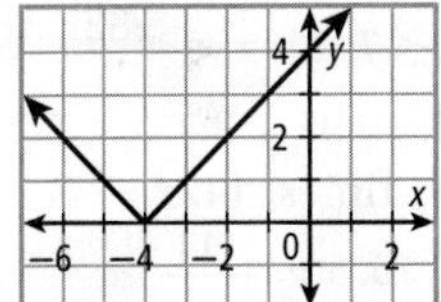

Selected Answers

5. $g(x) = |x - 1| + 6$

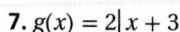

7. $g(x) = 2|x + 3|$

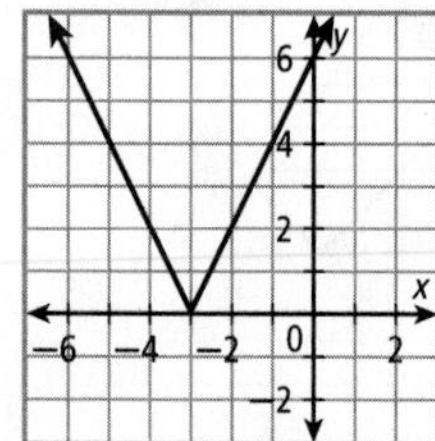

9. $g(x) = |x - 2|$

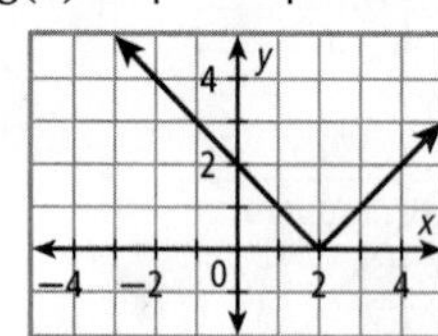

11. $g(x) = |x + 4|$
13. $g(x) = |x - 1.5| + 4.5$
15. $g(x) = -|x - 5| - 2$
17. $f(x) = \left|2\left(\frac{2}{3}x\right)\right| - 3$
19. translated down 6 units; D: $\mathbb{R}$; R: $\{y \mid y \geq -6\}$
21. translated right 1 unit and vertically stretched by a factor of 2; D: $\mathbb{R}$; R: $\{y \mid y \geq 0\}$
23. $(-5, 9)$ **27.** $f(x) = |x - 2| - 4$
29. $f(x) = -|x - 4|$ **33.** D **35.** B
37. B **41.** $f(x) = 2|x + 3|$
43. 7.5×10^9 **45.** 6.561×10^7
47. 2.0×10^{-25} **49.** $(1, 1)$
51. $(6, -5)$ **53.** $(4, -10)$
55. $\varnothing$

Study Guide: Review

1. contradiction **2.** point-slope form **3.** correlation **4.** $x = \frac{13}{2}$
5. $\mathbb{R}$ **6.** $x = -\frac{4}{7}$ **7.** $x = \frac{31}{2}$ **8.** $x = \frac{51}{41}$
9. 140 **10.** $x \leq 7$ **11.** $x < -\frac{32}{3}$
12. $x \leq 9$ **13.** $19.95 + 2.75x < 50$; fewer than 11 times **14.** $x = 33$
15. $x = -15$ **16.** $x = -\frac{11}{3}$
17. $x = \frac{19}{18}$ **18.** 4.5 ft **19.** yes
20. $(5, 0)$; $(0, 2)$
21. $(3, 0)$; $(0, -2)$
22. $(-2.25, 0)$; $(0, 1.5)$
23. $(1.5, 0)$; $(0, 6)$
24. $y = -2x + 5$
25. $y = \frac{5}{3}x + 3$
26. $y = -\frac{3}{2}x + 2$
27. $y = -\frac{2}{3}x + 9$
28. vertical **29.** horizontal
30. $-27.5t + 500$
31. $y = \frac{1}{2}x + 4$
32. $y = 3x$
33. $y = \frac{3}{2}x - 8$
34. $y = -\frac{2}{3}x + 2$
35. $y > -3$
36. $y \leq x + 3$
37. $y > -\frac{1}{2}x - 3$
38. $y < 3x - 4$
39. $y < -2x + 3$
40. $12x + 21y \leq 2520$
41. $g(x) = x - 8$
42. $g(x) = 3x + 15$
43. $g(x) = x - 4$
44. $g(x) = -x - 5$
45. $g(x) = -x - 12$
46a.

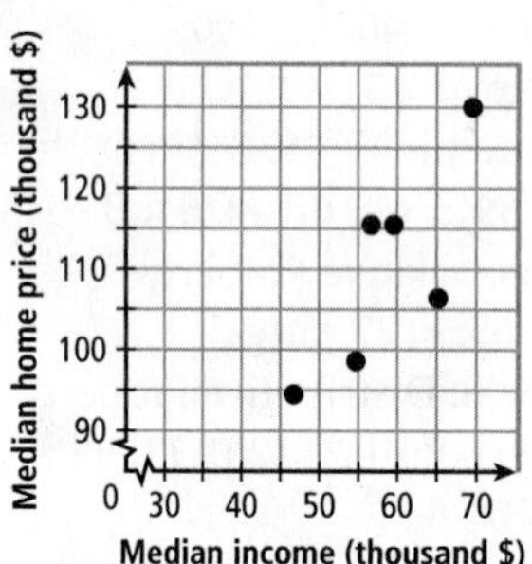

b. $r = 0.800$; $P = 1.279I + 35.074$
47. $x = 28$ or $x = -12$
48. $x = 66$ or $x = -54$
49. $\varnothing$
50. $\{x \mid x < -5 \cup x > 3\}$
51. $\{x \mid -2 \leq x \leq 5\}$
52. $\{x \mid 1 < x < 3\}$
53. $\{x \mid x \leq -8 \cup x \geq 4\}$
54. $g(x) = |x + 5| + 7$
55. $g(x) = |x - 6| - 9$
56. $g(x) = |-x - 4| + 1$
57. $g(x) = \frac{|3x + 1|}{3}$
58. $g(x) = -|x - 3| - 5$

Chapter 3

3-1

Check It Out! **1a.** solution. **b.** not a solution. **2a.** $(0, -3)$ **b.** $(4, 4)$ **c.** $(-1, 4)$ **3a.** consistent, dependent; infinite number of solutions **b.** inconsistent; no solution **4.** 10 min

Exercises **1.** inconsistent **3.** not a solution **5.** solution **7.** $(-2, 5)$ **9.** $(2, 3)$ **11.** consistent, dependent; infinite number of solutions **13.** inconsistent; no solution **15.** solution **17.** not a solution **19.** $(3, 1)$ **21.** $(1, -4)$ **23.** consistent, dependent; infinite number of solutions **25.** consistent, independent; one solution **27.** 10 system sales **29.** solution **31.** not a solution; $(-3, 0)$

33a. $\begin{matrix} \ell = 10{,}000 - 200x \\ m = 5{,}000 + 50x \end{matrix}$

b. 20 min **c.** 6000 ft

35. $\begin{cases} y = 2x - 3 \\ y = -x + 6 \end{cases}$ consistent, independent; $(3, 3)$

37. $\begin{cases} y = 3x - 3 \\ y = 3x + 1 \end{cases}$ inconsistent; no solution

39. $(-0.25, 4)$ **41.** $(2.831, -30.403)$ **45.** Consistent, independent **47.** D **49.** B **51.** $\left(\frac{100}{7}, \frac{6200}{7}\right)$ **53.** infinite number of solutions **55.** The solution has no meaning in the real world. **57.** $\frac{2\sqrt{3}}{3}$ **59.** $\frac{\sqrt{2}}{2}$ **61.** -3 **63.** 40h

3-2

Check It Out! **1a.** $(4, 7)$ **b.** $(3, -4)$ **2a.** $\left(\frac{3}{4}, -4\right)$ **b.** $(6, -4)$ **3a.** consistent, dependent; infinite number of solutions **b.** inconsistent; no solution **4.** 18.75 lb of Sumatra beans and 31.25 lb of Kona beans

Exercises **1.** elimination **3.** $(8, -11)$ **5.** $(-2, -1)$ **7.** $(-55, -21)$ **9.** $(-2, 5)$

11. inconsistent; no solution **13.** consistent, dependent; infinite number of solutions **15.** $\left(-6, \frac{3}{2}\right)$ **17.** $\left(\frac{1}{4}, 1\right)$ **19.** $(-7, -6)$ **21.** $(-2.45, -4.8)$ **23.** consistent, dependent; infinite number of solutions **25.** consistent, dependent; infinite number of solutions **27.** $x + y = 1200$; $x = \frac{1}{2}y$; $(400{,}800)$ **29.** $(6, 2)$ **31.** $(20, -3)$ **33a.** 22 **b.** The total number of coins increases. **c.** 12 dimes and 18 nickels **35a.** 266.5 mi **b.** $y = 128.43x$ **c.** ≈ 7.12 mi **37.** student = \$5.50 and adult = \$7.50 **41.** G **43.** $(2, -1)$; independent, consistent **47a.** $p = 22\frac{7}{9}$; $q = 8\frac{8}{9}$ **b.** $p = 17\frac{2}{3}$; $q = 29\frac{1}{3}$ **49.** $28c^2 + 1$; 253 **51.** $\frac{2}{9y^2}$; $\frac{2}{81}$ **53.** $f(x) = -1.5x - 0.5$

55. 

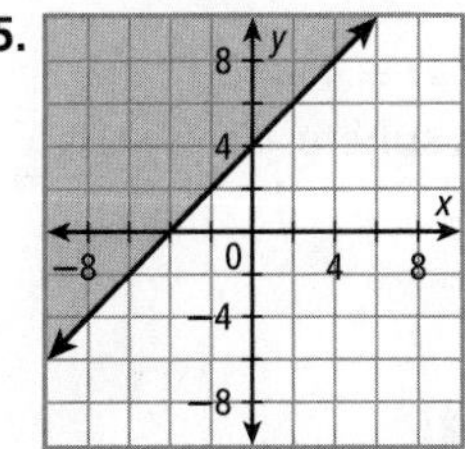

3-3

Check It Out!

1a.

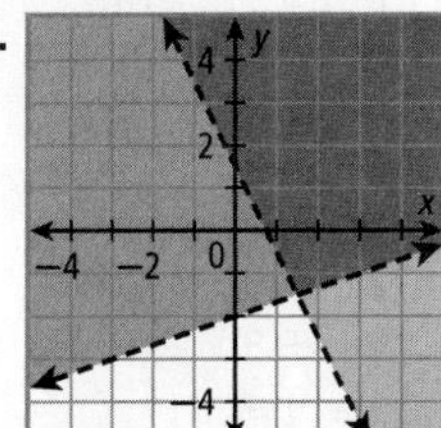

b.

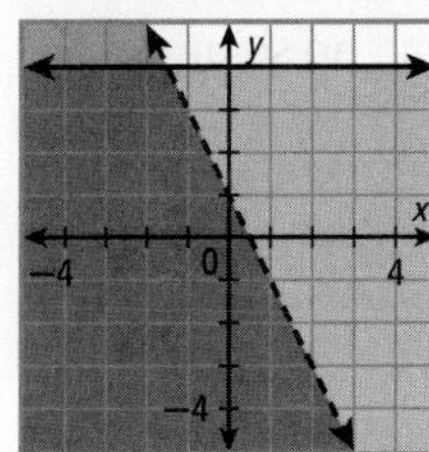

2. $\begin{cases} d + s \leq 40 \\ 2d + 2.5s \geq 90 \end{cases}$

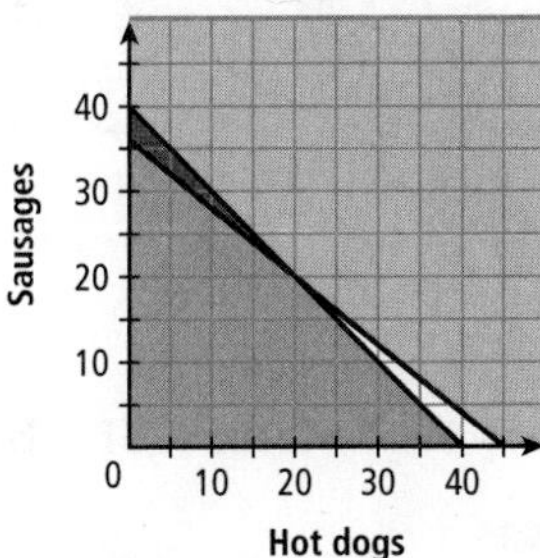

3a. triangle

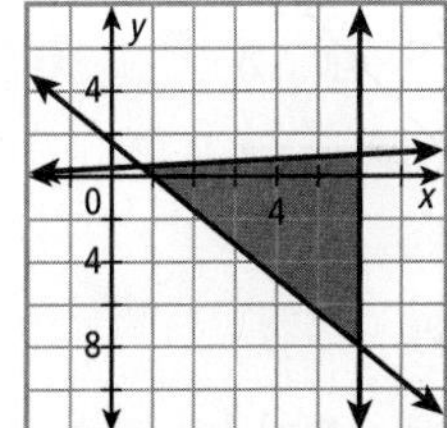

b. trapezoid

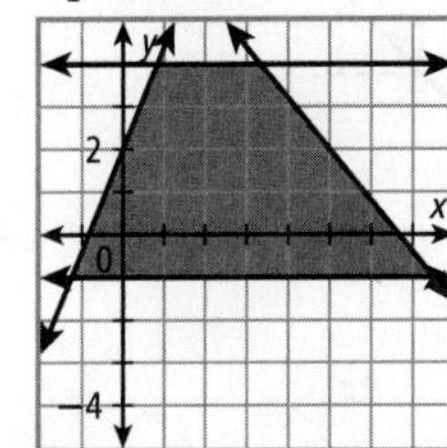

Exercises

3.

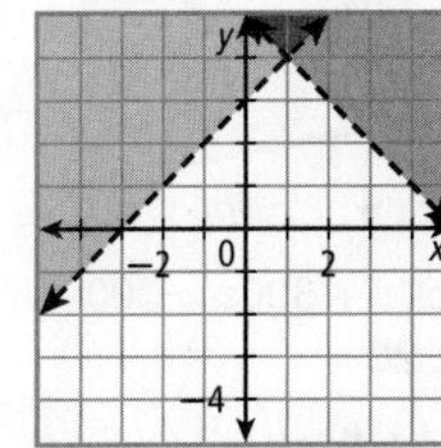

5.

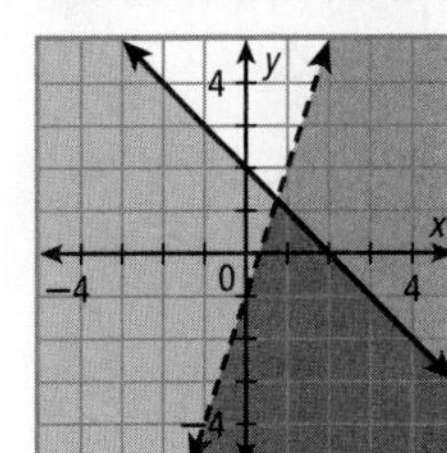

7. rectangle **9.** isosceles triangle

11.

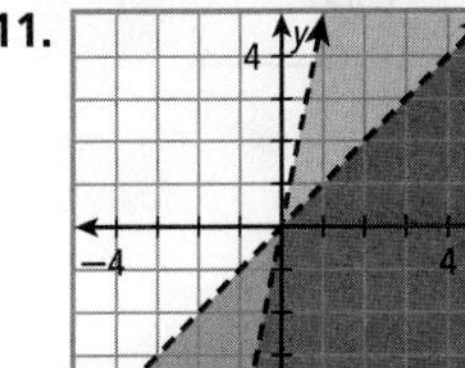

13.

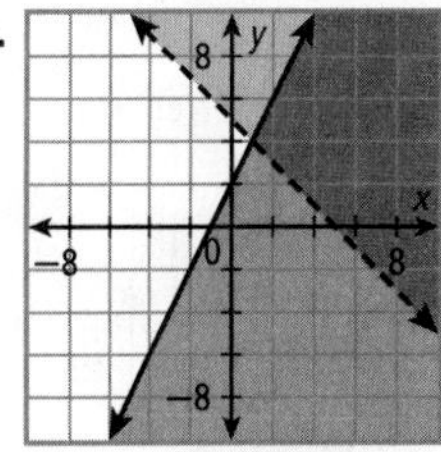

15. $\begin{cases} x + y \leq 10{,}000 \\ y \leq 0.2x \\ x \geq 0 \\ y \geq 0 \end{cases}$

17. trapezoid

19. isosceles right triangle

27. $\begin{cases} x \geq 0 \\ y \geq 0 \\ x + y \leq 114{,}650 \\ x + y \geq 56{,}801 \\ y \geq x + 2000 \end{cases}$

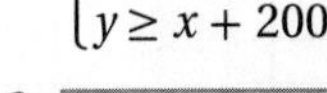

29.

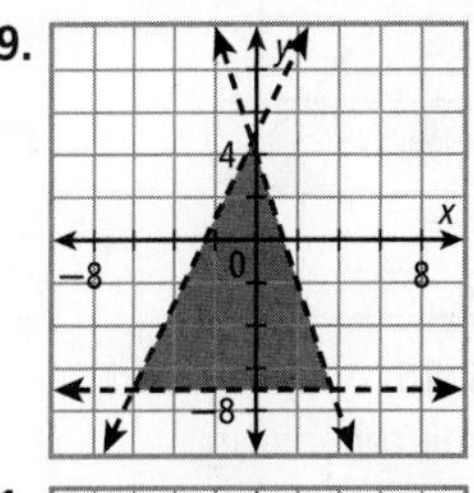

31.

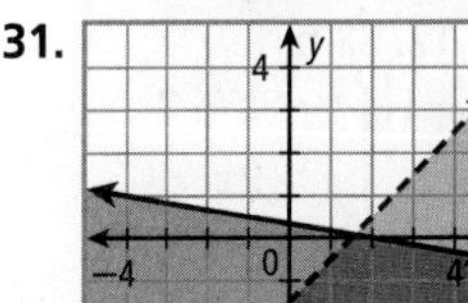

35. G **39.** \$20,000 **41.** $\frac{3}{4}$; $-\frac{4}{3}$ **43.** 1; -1 **45.** $y = -3$ **47.** $y = -\frac{1}{3}x + 9$ **49.** $y = -x + 5$

3-4

Check It Out!

1.

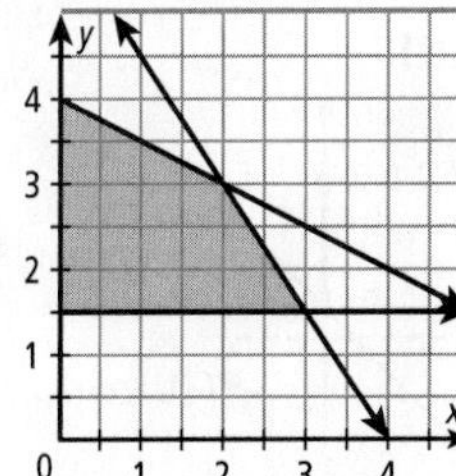

2. $P = 140$ **3.** 8 of bookcase A and 4 of bookcase B

Exercises

1. Constraints

3.

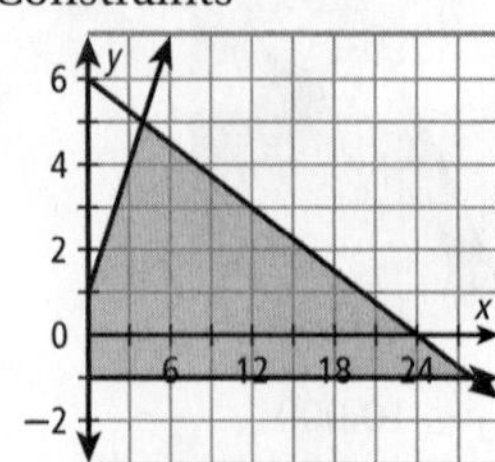

5. $P = 106$ **7.** $P = 3.9$

9.

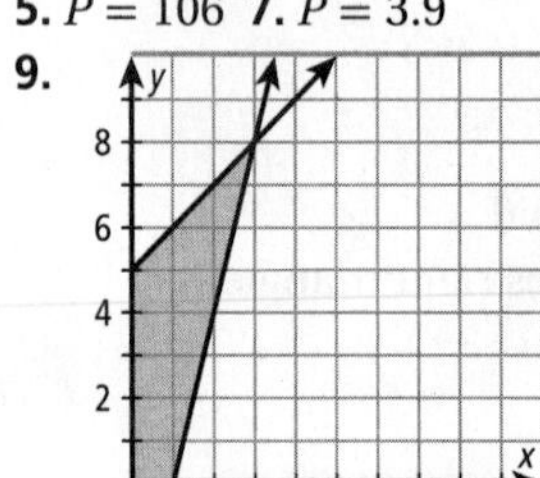

11.

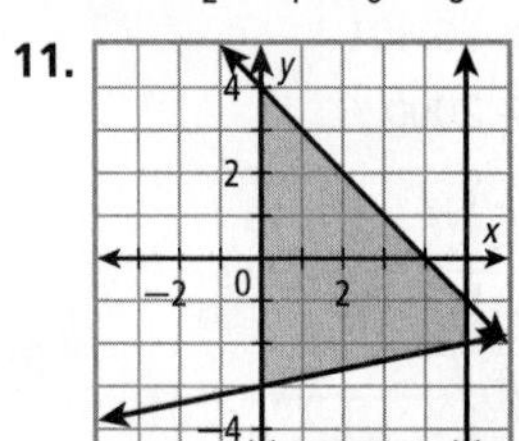

13. $P = -36$ **15.** 60 radio and 24 prime-time television commercials **17.** 32 h

19. right triangle; $\begin{cases} y \le x + 2 \\ y \ge 2x \\ y \ge -\frac{1}{2}x \end{cases}$

21. 20 stops **23.** 40 Soy Joy and 20 Vitamin Boost **27.** D **29.** G

31. $f(7) = \frac{1}{11}; f\left(-\frac{1}{2}\right) = -\frac{1}{4}$

33. $f(7) = 8; f\left(-\frac{1}{2}\right) = \frac{1}{2}$

37. right triangle

3-5

Check It Out!

1.

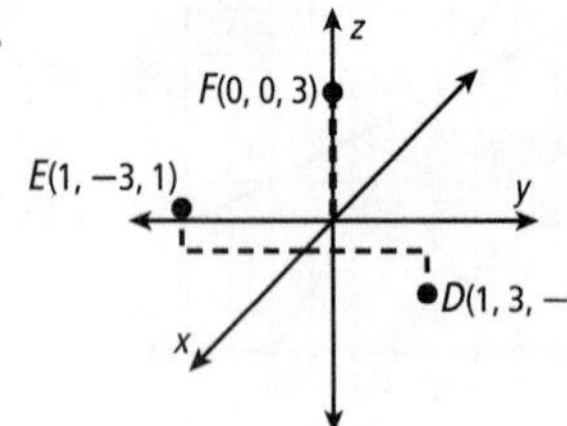

2.

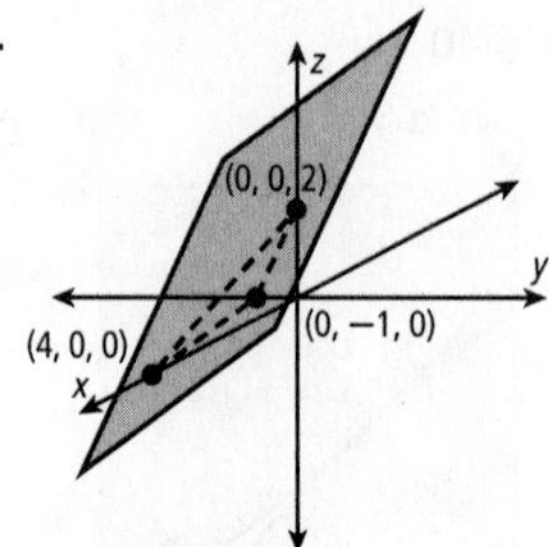

3a. $3.5x + 1.5y + 0.75z = 61.5$ **b.** 15

Exercises

3.

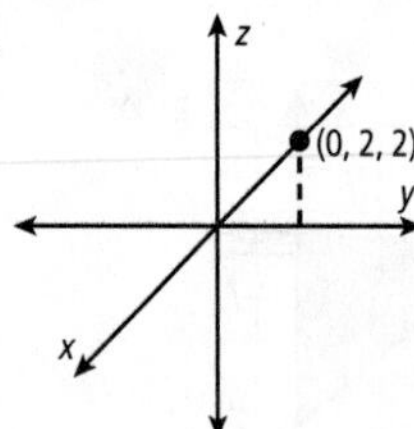

5.

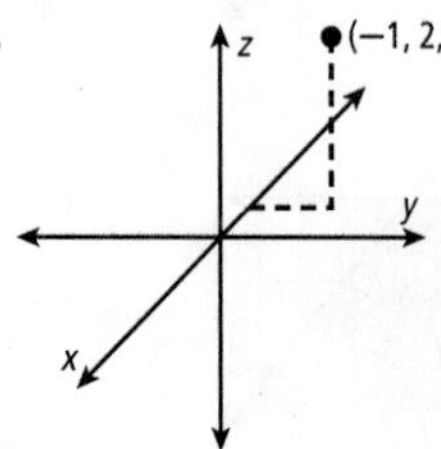

7.

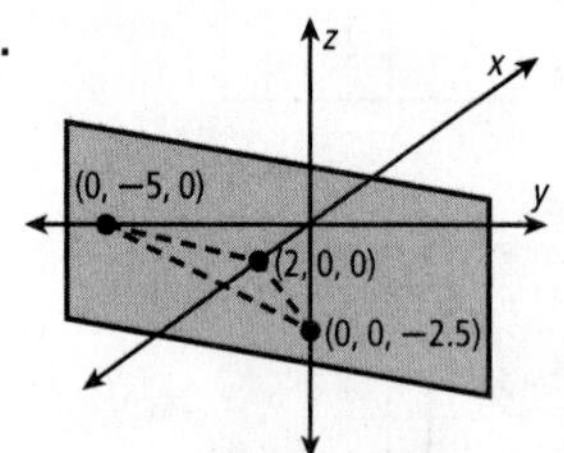

9a. $225x + 150y + 300z = 3000$ **b.** 1; 6; 6; 0 **c.** 20

11.

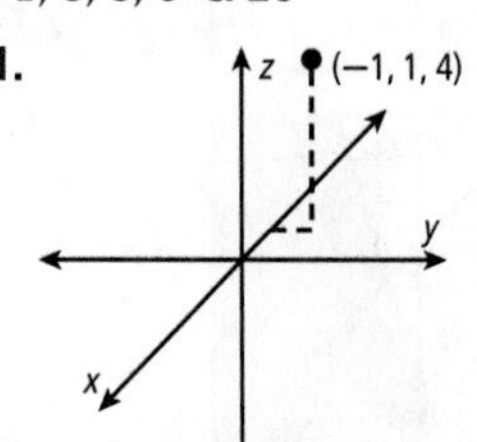

15.

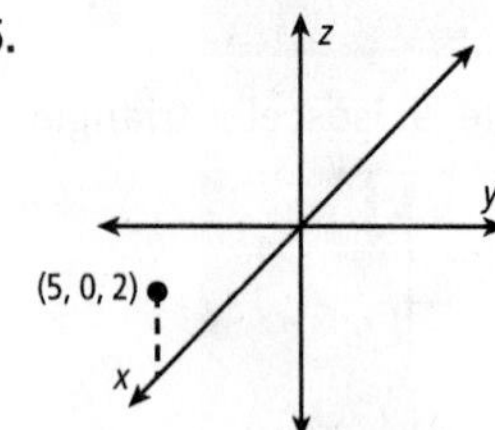

19.

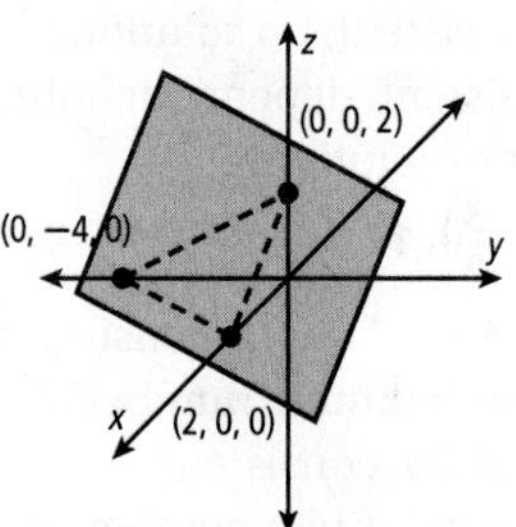

23.

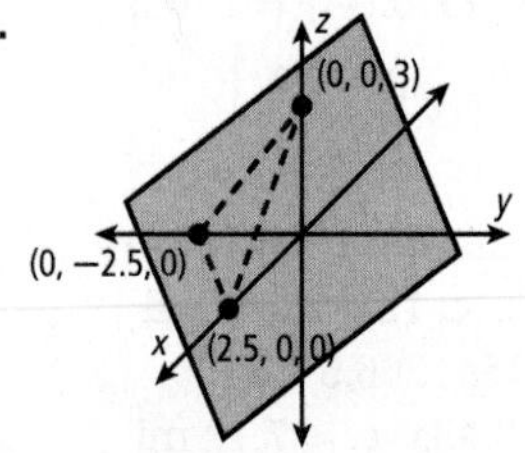

29. No. **31b.** $(7, 12, 8.5)$ **c.** $(7, 12, 12.5)$ **33.** A **35.** H

37.

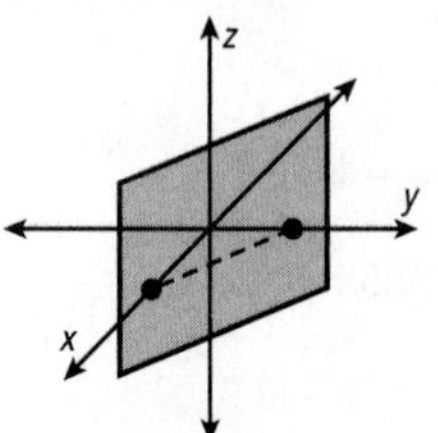

41. $x + 2y - 4z = 4$ **43.** square pyramid **45.** sphere **47.** $x = 10$; $y = 2$ **49.** $x = 5$; $y = \frac{1}{3}$

3-6

Check It Out!

1. $x = -2, y = 1, z = 2$

2. first place—3 points; second place—2 points; third place—1 point

3a. consistent; infinite number of solutions **b.** inconsistent; no solution

Exercises

1. $x = -4, y = 3, z = 3$

3. $x = 1, y = 3, z = 1$

5. inconsistent; no solution

7. inconsistent; no solution

9. $x = 3, y = 1, z = 6$

11. Talent—30%; Presentation—20%; Star Quality—50%

13. inconsistent; no solution

15. $m\angle A = 120°$; $m\angle B = 45°$; $m\angle A = 15°$ **19a.** (5, −2, 50) **b.** 50 ft **c.** (5, −2, 0) **21.** J

23. $w = 1, x = -2, y = -1, z = 3$

25. $(3, 3)$ **27.** 7.15 m by 5.2 m

29. $y = \frac{2}{3}x - 4$

Extension

Check It Out!

1a. $\begin{cases} x = 5t \\ y = 20t \end{cases}$

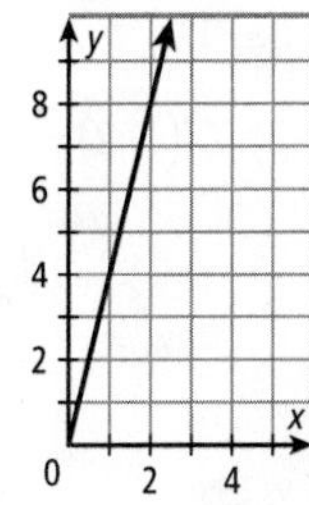

b. At $t = 10$, the helicopter has a ground distance of 50 ft from its takeoff point and an altitude of 200 ft. **2.** $y = 4x$

Exercises

1.

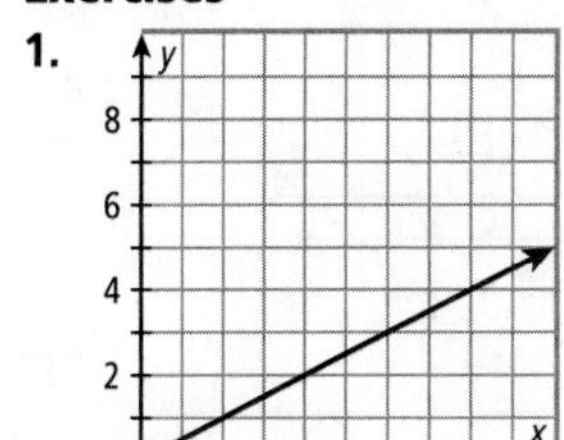

3.

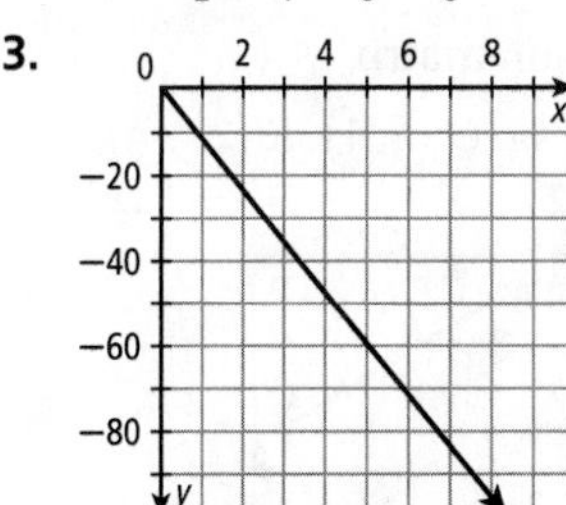

5. $y = \frac{2}{3}x$ **7.** $y = 10x$

9a. $\begin{cases} x = 1.8t \\ y = -0.9t \end{cases}$

b. -45 m **c.** $-77{,}760$ m

Study Guide: Review

1. dependent **2.** elimination **3.** system of linear inequalities; feasible region **4.** three-dimensional coordinate system; ordered triple **5.** consistent **6.** $(5, 10)$ **7.** $(4, 2)$ **8.** $(-4, -1)$ **9.** $(0, -2)$ **10.** independent; one solution **11.** dependent; infinitely many solutions **12.** inconsistent; no solution **13.** independent; 1 solution **14.** 3 locks **15.** $(1, 3)$ **16.** $(6, 5)$ **17.** $(-2, -8)$ **18.** $(4, -2)$ **19.** $(4, 5)$ **20.** $(3, 4)$ **21.** $(5, 2)$ **22.** $(2, 1)$ **23.** 48 oz pine; 32 oz lavender

24.

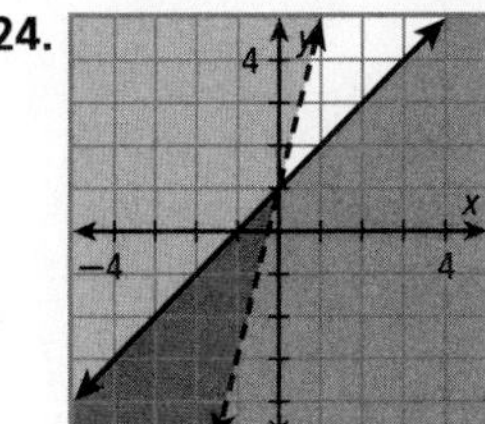

25.

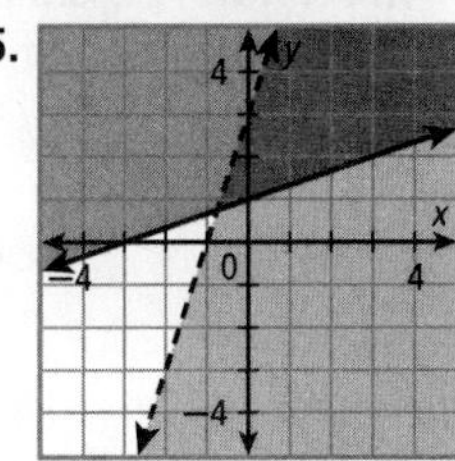

26. right triangle **27.** trapezoid

28. $\begin{cases} x + y \le 120 \\ 8x + 11.5y < 1200 \end{cases}$

29.

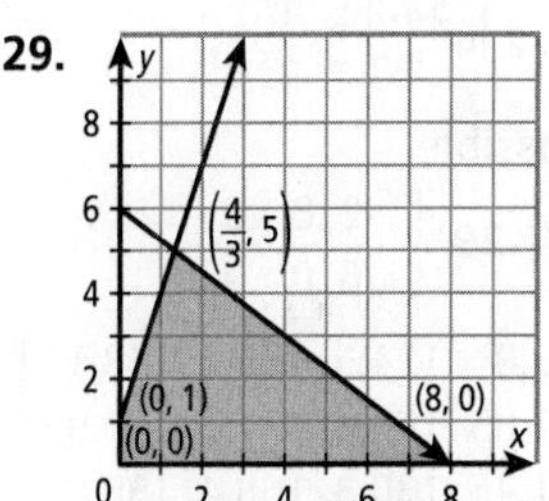

30.

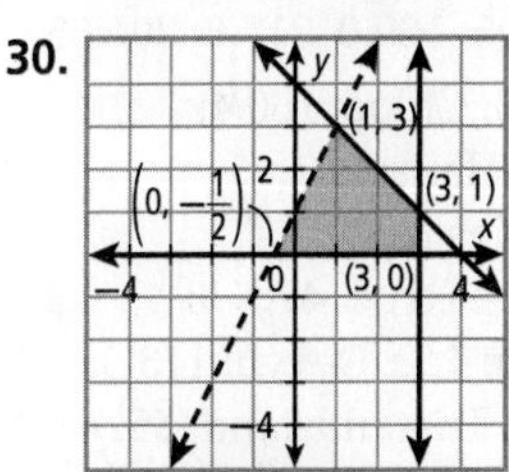

31.

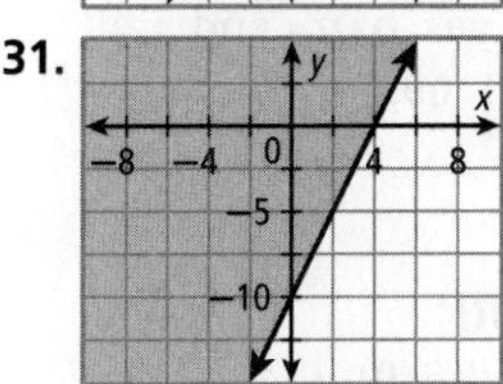

32.

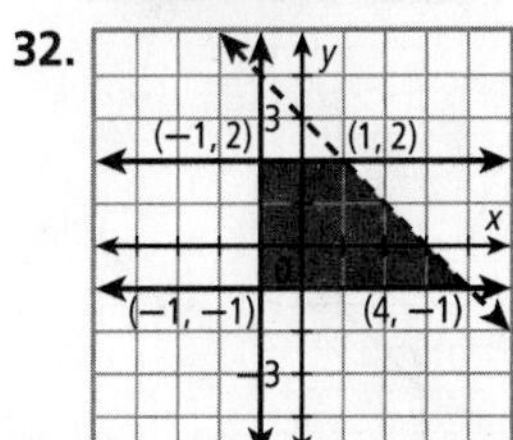

33. 58 **34.** -4.5

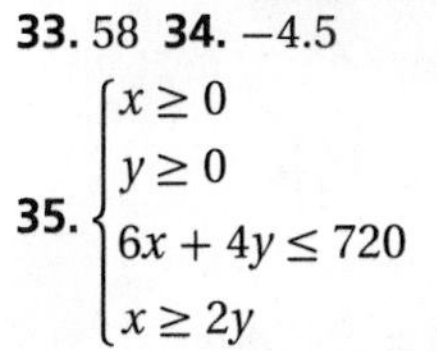

35. $\begin{cases} x \ge 0 \\ y \ge 0 \\ 6x + 4y \le 720 \\ x \ge 2y \end{cases}$

36. $P = 8x + 9y$ **37.** \$1125 **38.** 25 phones with contracts and 5 without contracts

39–42.

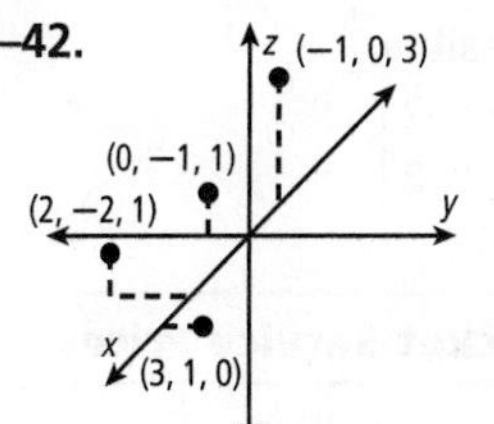

43.

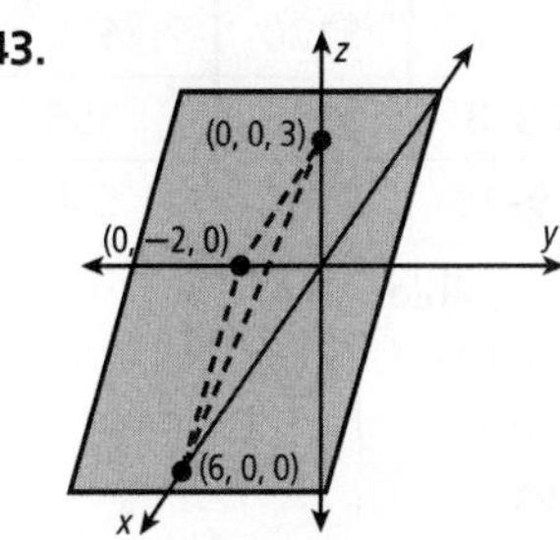

44.

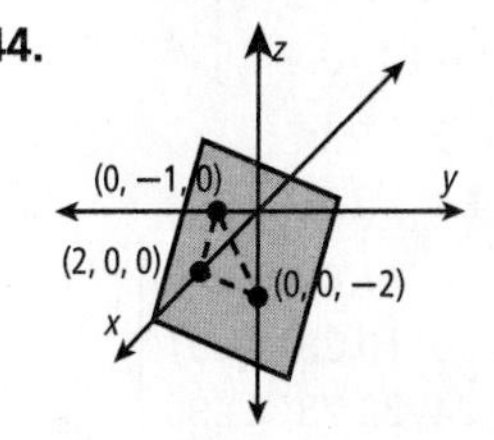

45.

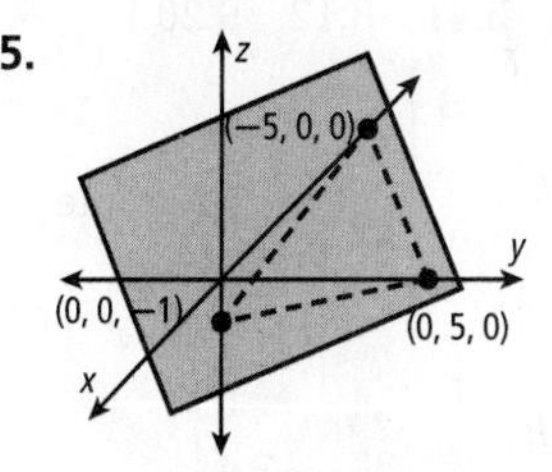

46.

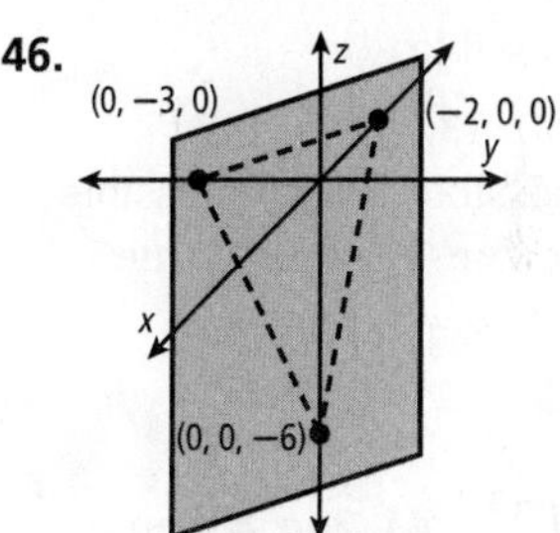

47. $2d + 9p + 4c = 35$, where d = drinks, p = pizza, c = ice cream **48.** $(1, 2, 3)$ **49.** $(1, -1, 2)$ **50.** inconsistent, no solution **51.** dependent, infinitely many solutions

Chapter 4

4-1

Check It Out!

1a. 3×4 **b.** 11 **c.** m_{14} and m_{23}

2a. $\begin{bmatrix} 4 & 0 & -8 \\ 6 & 2 & 18 \end{bmatrix}$

b. not possible

c. $\begin{bmatrix} -4 & 2 & 2 \\ 0 & -2 & 2 \end{bmatrix}$

3.

Ticket Service Prices		
Day	Plaza	Balcony
Days 1–2	$120	$70
Days 3–8	$100	$56
Days 9–10	$160	$90

4a. not possible

b. $\begin{bmatrix} -1 & -10 \\ -6 & 47 \end{bmatrix}$ **c.** $\begin{bmatrix} -9 & 4.5 & 12 \end{bmatrix}$

Exercises

1. entry **3.** $\begin{bmatrix} 1.5 & 7.8 & 4 \\ -1.2 & 0.4 & 1 \end{bmatrix}$

5. $\begin{bmatrix} -1.5 & 0.2 & -2 \\ 1.2 & -4.4 & 1 \end{bmatrix}$

7. $P_T = \begin{bmatrix} 9.74 & 14.07 & 15.16 \\ 6.50 & 10.28 & 11.91 \\ 16.24 & 22.73 & 24.90 \\ 5.41 & 8.12 & 9.20 \end{bmatrix}$

9. $\begin{bmatrix} -\frac{1}{2} & \frac{1}{2} & 3 \\ 2 & 0 & \frac{1}{2} \\ \frac{1}{2} & 1 & \frac{1}{2} \end{bmatrix}$ **11.** not possible

13. $F - E = \begin{bmatrix} -7.4 & 0 \\ 37 & -2.4 \end{bmatrix}$

15. not possible

17. $\begin{bmatrix} 29{,}061 & 13{,}483 & 20{,}147 \end{bmatrix}$

19. not possible **21.** not possible

23. never true **27.** always true

29. $a = -6$; $b = 11$; $c = 4$

31. no **33.** F **35.** $\frac{1}{2}$

39. $\begin{bmatrix} 2.5 & -4 \\ 1 & -7 \end{bmatrix}$ **41.** $20n$ **43.** no

4-2

Check It Out!

1a. no **b.** no **c.** 4 × 3

2a. $\begin{bmatrix} 67 & 5 \\ 62 & 72 \\ 66 & -6 \end{bmatrix}$ **2b.** $\begin{bmatrix} 3 & 41 & 97 \\ -30 & 78 & 128 \end{bmatrix}$

3. $\begin{bmatrix} 2436 & 1196 & 1240 \\ 1605 & 786 & 819 \end{bmatrix}$; 819

4a. not possible

b. $A^3 = \begin{bmatrix} 259 & 129 \\ -86 & -42 \end{bmatrix}$

c. $B^3 = \begin{bmatrix} 82 & 103 & 2 \\ 125 & 33 & -39 \\ 17 & -12 & 34 \end{bmatrix}$

d. $I^4 = \begin{bmatrix} 1 & 0 \\ 0 & 1 \end{bmatrix}$

Exercises

1. multiplicative identity matrix

3. no **5.** yes; 5 × 5 **7.** yes; 2 × 2

9. $\begin{bmatrix} -2 & -18 & -9 \\ 4 & 29 & 15 \\ -2 & 3 & 0 \end{bmatrix}$ **11.** not possible

13. $\begin{bmatrix} 4 & 2 \\ 1 & -3 \end{bmatrix}$ **15.** $\begin{bmatrix} -1 & 2 \\ -1 & -2 \end{bmatrix}$

17. not possible **19.** no

21. yes; 3 × 1 **23.** no

25. not possible

27. $\begin{bmatrix} 27 & -10 \\ -10 & 3 \\ -5 & 1 \end{bmatrix}$ **29.** $\begin{bmatrix} -2 & 3 & -4 \\ 1 & -1 & 1 \\ 4 & 1 & 3 \end{bmatrix}$

31. $\begin{bmatrix} -1 & 2 \\ -1 & -2 \end{bmatrix}$ **33.** $\begin{bmatrix} 6 & 2 & 1 \\ 5 & 4 & 1 \\ 7 & 3 & 3 \end{bmatrix}$

35. not possible

37. $\begin{bmatrix} 5 & 11 \\ 7 & 27 \end{bmatrix}$ **39.** $\begin{bmatrix} -2 & 8 & 12 \\ 6 & 0 & 4 \end{bmatrix}$

41a. $SD = \begin{bmatrix} 122.8 & 124.5 & 160.2 & 148.1 \\ 161.85 & 160.4 & 207.8 & 191.95 \\ 131.45 & 130.3 & 168.4 & 155.85 \\ 168.95 & 169.0 & 217.8 & 201.65 \end{bmatrix}$

b. Ted: 122.8; Chloe: 160.4; Biko: 168.4; Hana: 201.65

43. sometimes true

45. sometimes true **47.** −8

49. Madison: 122; Devyn: 113.5; Ali: 69.5 **51.** Tristan Island **55.** *G*

57. *BA* **59a.** yes **b.** p_{12} and p_{21}

61. 10 **63.** 11 **69.** not possible

4-3

Check It Out!

1. $G'(5, 3)$, $H'(6, 0)$, $J'(4, -2)$

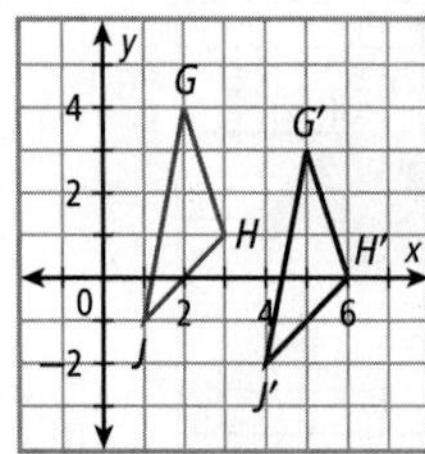

2. $D'\left(2\frac{2}{3}, 4\right)$, $E'\left(6\frac{2}{3}, 1\frac{1}{3}\right)$, $F'\left(-2\frac{2}{3}, -9\frac{1}{3}\right)$

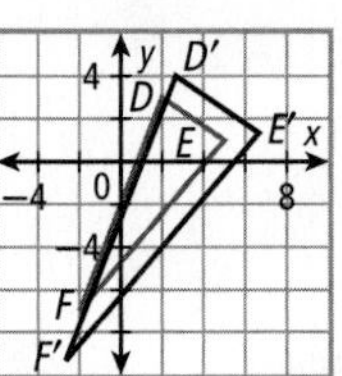

3. $J'(3, -4)$, $K'(4, -2)$, $L'(1, 2)$

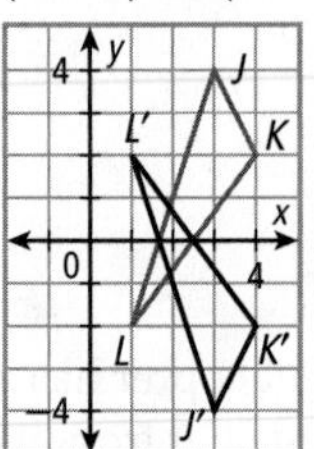

4. $A'(0, 0)$, $B'(-4, 0)$, $C'(0, 3)$; the image is rotated 180°.

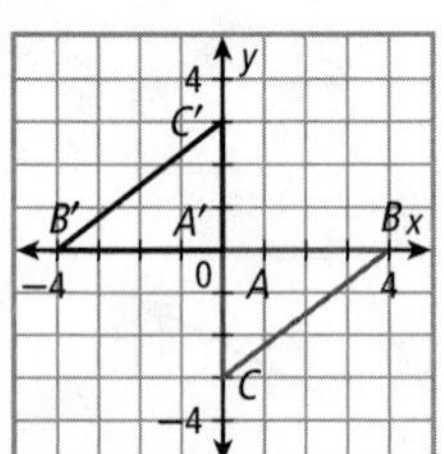

Exercises

1. reflection matrix

3. $P'(-1, 4)$, $Q'(4, 1)$, $R'(2, -4)$, $S'(-1, -2)$

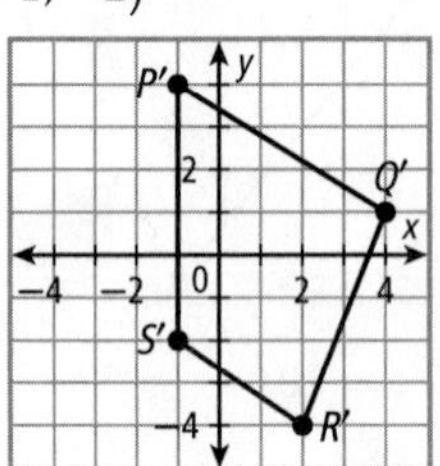

5. $P'(-4, 8)$, $Q'(6, 2)$, $R'(2, -8)$, $S'(-4, -4)$

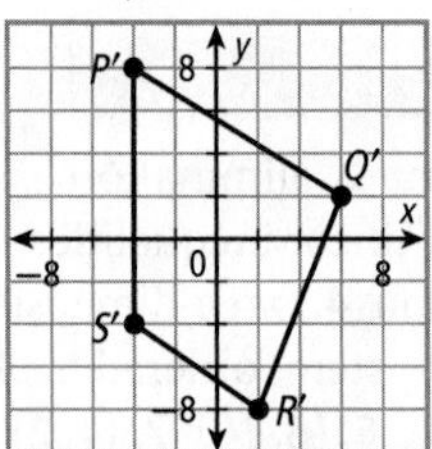

7. $A'(3, -2)$, $B'(4, 0)$, $C'(3, 2)$, $D'(1, 2)$, $E'(-1, -1)$

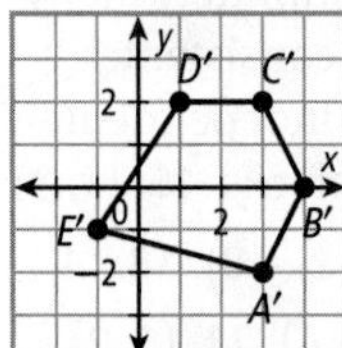

9. 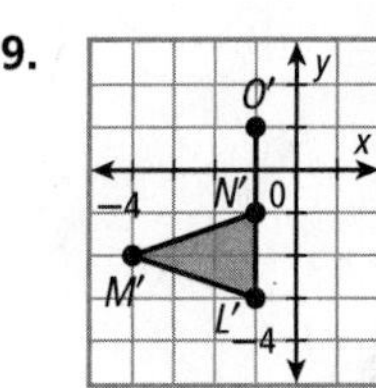

The image is rotated 180°.

11. $W'\left(\frac{3}{2}, 3\right)$, $X'\left(-3, \frac{9}{2}\right)$, $Y'\left(-\frac{9}{2}, 6\right)$, $Z'\left(-6, \frac{3}{2}\right)$

13. 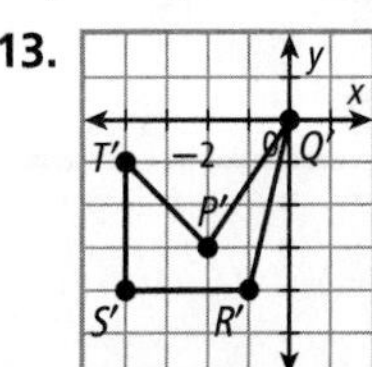

The image is rotated 90° counterclockwise.

15a. $\begin{bmatrix} -2.5 & 2.5 & 4.5 & 0.5 & -4 \\ 3 & 3 & -2 & -4.5 & -1.5 \end{bmatrix}$

15b. counterclockwise

19. $(-8, 3)$, $(-6, 3.5)$, $(-4, 3)$, $(-2, 2.5)$, $(2, 3)$, $(1.5, 0)$, $(-1, 0)$

21. $(-5, -4)$, $(-3, -4.5)$, $(-1, -4)$, $(1, -3.5)$, $(5, -4)$, $(4.5, -1)$, $(2, -1)$

23. $(-4, -5)$, $(-4.5, -3)$, $(-4, -1)$, $(-3.5, 1)$, $(-4, 5)$, $(-1, 4.5)$, $(-1, 2)$

25. $\begin{bmatrix} 1 & 0 \\ 0 & -1 \end{bmatrix}$; $\begin{bmatrix} -1 & 0 \\ 0 & 1 \end{bmatrix}$

27. B **29.** C **33.** yes **35.** yes **37.** not possible

4-4

Check It Out!

1a. 10 **b.** $-2\frac{1}{4}$ **c.** $\pi - \frac{1}{2}$

2. $D = \begin{vmatrix} 6 & -2 \\ 3 & -1 \end{vmatrix} = 0$

$\begin{vmatrix} c_1 & b_1 \\ c_2 & b_2 \end{vmatrix} = \begin{vmatrix} 14 & -2 \\ 7 & -1 \end{vmatrix} = 0$

dependent; infinitely many solutions.

3. 75 **4.** 240 g protein, 380 g carbohydrates, and 80 g fat

Exercises

1. A 0 entry in a coefficient matrix corresponds to a coefficient of 0 for one variable in one equation. **3.** 2.25 **5.** 0 **7.** no solution **9.** $\left(2\frac{1}{2}, -\frac{1}{4}\right)$ **11.** 0

13. trail mix \$2.99; mixed nuts \$6.98; dried fruit \$3.99 **15.** −1

17. $\pi r^2 - 2r^2$ **19.** $(\approx 1.27, \approx 1.11)$

21. $\left(-4\frac{2}{3}, \frac{7}{9}\right)$ **23.** 1.2

25. bicycling: 420 Cal/h; racquetball: 540 Cal/h; swimming: 600 Cal/h **27.** 17 square units

29. 1 point: 9 voters; 2 points: 11 voters; 3 points: 18 voters **31.** −16

33. a. 235 dimes, 190 nickels

b. \$33 **37.** D **39.** 2.5, or $\frac{5}{2}$ **43.** 254

45. $\left(-\frac{4}{3}, -4\right)$ **47.** $\left(-\frac{1}{3}, -\frac{2}{3}\right)$

49. $D'(1, -1)$, $E'(4, 2)$, $F'(-2, 3)$, $G'(-1, 1)$

51. $D'(3, 3)$, $E'(12, -6)$, $F'(-6, -9)$, $G'(-3, -3)$

4-5

Check It Out!

1. yes

2. $\begin{bmatrix} \frac{1}{6} & \frac{1}{6} \\ \frac{1}{4} & -\frac{1}{4} \end{bmatrix}$ **3.** $\begin{bmatrix} 1 & 1 \\ 2 & 3 \end{bmatrix}\begin{bmatrix} x \\ y \end{bmatrix} = \begin{bmatrix} 4 \\ 9 \end{bmatrix}$; $(3, 1)$

4. smarty pants

Exercises

1. Set the product of the coefficient matrix and the variable matrix equal to the constant matrix. **3.** no

5. $\begin{bmatrix} 2 & 0 \\ 1 & 3 \end{bmatrix}$ **7.** no inverse **9.** $\begin{bmatrix} 8 & -7 \\ -9 & 8 \end{bmatrix}$

11. $\begin{bmatrix} 5 & 9 \\ -4 & -7 \end{bmatrix}\begin{bmatrix} x \\ y \end{bmatrix} = \begin{bmatrix} 1 \\ 2 \end{bmatrix}$; $(-25, 14)$

13. $\begin{bmatrix} 7 & -4 \\ -5 & 3 \end{bmatrix}$; in New Delhi

15. yes **17.** $\begin{bmatrix} 8 & -2 \\ -6 & 1 \end{bmatrix}$

19. $\begin{bmatrix} 8 & -3 \\ -5 & 2 \end{bmatrix}$ **21.** $\begin{bmatrix} -11 & -3 \\ 7 & 2 \end{bmatrix}$

23. $\begin{bmatrix} 1 & 2 \\ 2 & 1 \end{bmatrix}\begin{bmatrix} x \\ y \end{bmatrix} = \begin{bmatrix} 6 \\ 9 \end{bmatrix}$; $(4, 1)$

25. $\begin{bmatrix} 4 & -3 \\ -9 & 7 \end{bmatrix}$; Monday early

27a. $\begin{bmatrix} 6 & 2 \\ 1 & 1 \end{bmatrix}$ **b.** $\begin{bmatrix} 6 & 2 \\ 1 & 1 \end{bmatrix}\begin{bmatrix} x \\ y \end{bmatrix} = \begin{bmatrix} 34 \\ 7 \end{bmatrix}$

c. $\begin{bmatrix} \frac{1}{4} & -\frac{1}{2} \\ -\frac{1}{4} & \frac{3}{2} \end{bmatrix}$

d. 5 six-person boats and 2 two-person boats

31. 46 \$50 bills and 27 \$100 bills

33a. They are halved. **37.** $\begin{bmatrix} \frac{1}{a} \end{bmatrix}$

39. The two matrices are inverses of each other. **41.** H **43.** F

45. points/game: 2; assists/game: 5; turnovers/game: −4; steals/game: 3

47a. play to win

b. $\begin{bmatrix} 1 & -1 & 0 \\ 0 & 1 & -1 \\ 0 & 0 & 1 \end{bmatrix}$

c. $\begin{bmatrix} -3 & -12 & 23 & -11 \\ -6 & -13 & 0 & 20 \\ 18 & 25 & 0 & 0 \end{bmatrix}$

49. 0.175 **51.** $(1, 1, 0)$

53. 8.5 **55.** −43

4-6

Check It Out!

1a. $\left[\begin{array}{cc|c} -1 & -1 & 0 \\ -1 & -1 & -2 \end{array}\right]$

b. $\left[\begin{array}{ccc|c} -5 & -4 & 0 & 12 \\ 1 & 0 & 1 & 3 \\ 0 & 4 & 3 & 10 \end{array}\right]$

2a. $\left[\begin{array}{cc|c} 4 & 4 & 32 \\ 1 & 3 & 16 \end{array}\right]$; $(4, 4)$

b. $\left[\begin{array}{cc|c} 9 & 3 & 15 \\ -6 & -2 & 10 \end{array}\right]$; no solution

3a. $\left[\begin{array}{ccc|c} 3 & -1 & 5 & -1 \\ 1 & 0 & 2 & 1 \\ 1 & 3 & -1 & 25 \end{array}\right]$; $(5, 6, -2)$

b. $t = 820$; $d = 1600$; 1600 days.

Exercises

1. The coefficients are in columns to the left of the vertical bar that separates them from the constant terms.

3. $\left[\begin{array}{ccc|c} 1 & 1 & 1 & 10 \\ 2 & 0 & 1 & 12 \\ 0 & -1 & 1 & 3 \end{array}\right]$

5. $\left[\begin{array}{ccc|c} -3 & 1 & 0 & -2 \\ 0 & \frac{1}{4} & -1 & -1 \\ -\frac{1}{2} & 0 & 1 & 8 \end{array}\right]$

7. $\left[\begin{array}{cc|c} -1 & 8 & 7 \\ \frac{1}{2} & 3 & 0 \end{array}\right]$; $\left(-3, \frac{1}{2}\right)$

Selected Answers

9. $\left[\begin{array}{cc|c} 1 & -1 & -4 \\ 4 & -4 & -3 \end{array}\right]$; the system is inconsistent.

11. $\left[\begin{array}{ccc|c} \frac{1}{2} & \frac{3}{2} & -1 & 0 \\ -2 & 1 & 0 & 4 \\ 1 & 1 & 1 & 3 \end{array}\right]$

13. $\left[\begin{array}{ccc|c} 0.1 & 0.2 & 0.15 & 1.0 \\ 1 & 1 & -1 & 0 \\ 1.3 & -2 & 0 & 0 \end{array}\right]$

15. $\left[\begin{array}{cc|c} 5 & -1 & 2 \\ 1 & -1 & -4 \end{array}\right]$; (1.5, 5.5)

17. 12 roosters, 4 hens, and 84 chicks.

23. $\left[\begin{array}{cc|c} 3 & -1 & -9 \\ -4 & 7 & 12 \end{array}\right]$; (−3, 0)

25. $\left[\begin{array}{ccc|c} 2 & 5 & -1 & 0 \\ -1 & 3 & 0 & -7 \\ 1 & 0 & 7 & 25 \end{array}\right]$; (4, −1, 3)

27b. first-place: 3 points, second-place: 2 points, third-place: 1 point.

29. (−1, 4, 2) 31. $\left(\frac{5}{6}, \frac{5}{6}, -\frac{5}{2}\right)$

33a. $\begin{cases} 2x + 7y = 24 \\ 4x + 13y = 46 \end{cases}$

33b. $\left[\begin{array}{cc|c} 2 & 7 & 24 \\ 4 & 13 & 46 \end{array}\right]$ 33c. (5, 2)

33d. meal: 5 tickets, ride: 2 tickets 35. A 37. C 41. a reduction by a factor of $\frac{3}{8}$ 43. $P = 6$ at (0, 3)

45. $\begin{bmatrix} 3 & -1 \\ 1 & 2 \end{bmatrix}\begin{bmatrix} x \\ y \end{bmatrix} = \begin{bmatrix} 0 \\ 7 \end{bmatrix}$; (1, 3)

Extension

Check it Out!

1. $A^3 = \begin{bmatrix} 6 & 1 & 0 & 0 & 5 \\ 3 & 4 & 1 & 3 & 5 \\ 3 & 1 & 1 & 1 & 3 \\ 4 & 1 & 2 & 6 & 2 \\ 2 & 2 & 1 & 4 & 2 \end{bmatrix}$;

5 3-step paths from *B* to *F* and from *F* to itself

Exercises

1. $\begin{bmatrix} 1 & 0 & 1 & 0 & 0 & 1 \\ 0 & 0 & 1 & 1 & 0 & 0 \\ 1 & 0 & 0 & 1 & 0 & 0 \\ 0 & 0 & 1 & 0 & 0 & 0 \\ 0 & 0 & 0 & 0 & 0 & 1 \\ 0 & 1 & 0 & 0 & 2 & 0 \end{bmatrix}$

3. *A* to *D*, *A* to *E*, *B* to *A*, *B* to *C*, *C* to *D*, *C* to *E*, *D* to *C*, *E* to *F*, *F* to *B*

5. For vertex *A*, one 1-step roundtrip is possible. For *A*, *C*, *D*, *E*, and *F*, at least one 2-step roundtrip is possible. For *A* and *C*, at least one 3-step roundtrip is possible.

Study Guide: Review

1. scalar 2. constant matrix 3. square matrix 4. not possible

5. $\begin{bmatrix} 0.4 & 0.6 \\ 0.8 & 1 \end{bmatrix}$ 6. $\begin{bmatrix} 2 & -\frac{7}{3} & \frac{4}{3} \\ -\frac{11}{3} & \frac{2}{3} & 1 \end{bmatrix}$

7. $\begin{bmatrix} 6 & -9 & 4 \\ -9 & 2 & 5 \end{bmatrix}$ 11. $\begin{bmatrix} -4 & -3 & 5 \\ 4 & 2 & -8 \\ -2 & -4 & -5 \end{bmatrix}$

12. $\begin{bmatrix} -7 & 9 \\ -3 & -3 \\ -8 & -1 \end{bmatrix}$ 13. not defined

14. $\begin{bmatrix} -3 & 5 & 10 \\ -12 & 2 & 9 \end{bmatrix}$ 15. not possible

16. $\begin{bmatrix} 15 & 1 & 7 \\ -1 & 5 & 5 \\ -7 & 5 & 9 \end{bmatrix}$ 17. $\begin{bmatrix} 71 & -7 \\ 70 & -6 \end{bmatrix}$

18a. $A = \begin{bmatrix} 5 & 2.5 \\ 7.5 & 4.25 \\ 9 & 5.75 \end{bmatrix}$; $B = \begin{bmatrix} 67 & 196 & 245 \\ 104 & 75 & 154 \end{bmatrix}$

18b. Thursday: \$595; Friday: \$1788.75; Saturday: \$3090.50 18c. adults: \$4010; students: \$1464.25 19. (0, 0), (1, 4), (4, 5), and (2, 1) 20. (−3, −1.5), (−1.5, 4.5), (3, 6), and (0, 0)

21. (−2, 1), (−1, −3); (2, −4), (0, 0); reflected across the *x*-axis.

22. (−1, 2), (3, 1), (4, −2), and (0, 0); rotated 90°clockwise.

23. 2 24. 0 25. $\frac{1}{2}$ 26. 22 27. −31

28. 0 29. (5, 4) 30. (2, −5)

31. infinitely many solutions

32. (2, 4, −3) 33. no solution

34. (0.5, 2, 1.5) 35a. $\begin{vmatrix} 2 & 3 \\ -1 & 1 \end{vmatrix} = 5$

35b. (1, 2) 36b. 72 small, 18 medium, and 12 large

37. $\begin{bmatrix} 0.15 & -0.1 \\ 0.05 & 0.3 \end{bmatrix}$ 38. $\begin{bmatrix} \frac{4}{3} & \frac{8}{3} \\ 0 & 5 \end{bmatrix}$

39. no inverse

40. $\begin{bmatrix} -0.25 & -0.25 & 0.5 \\ 1.5 & 0.5 & -1 \\ -2.25 & -0.25 & 1.5 \end{bmatrix}$

41. $\begin{bmatrix} -2 & 0 & 2 \\ -5 & -1 & 7 \\ 6 & 2 & -8 \end{bmatrix}$

42. does not exist 43. (20, 10) 44. (5, 4) 45. (4, 3, 2) 46. (−1, −2.5, 3.5) 47. (0.25, −0.5) 48. (−2, −6) 49. (0.1, −0.05, 0.2) 50. (1, 1, 2) 51. 12 first-place, 4 second-place, 11 third-place

Chapter 5

5-1

Check It Out!

1.

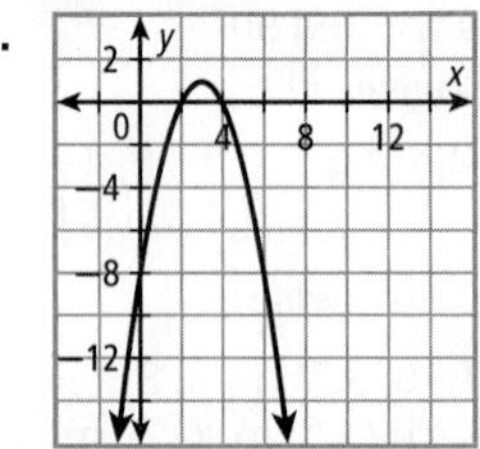

x	−1	1	3	5	7
g(*x*)	−15	−3	1	−3	−15

2a.

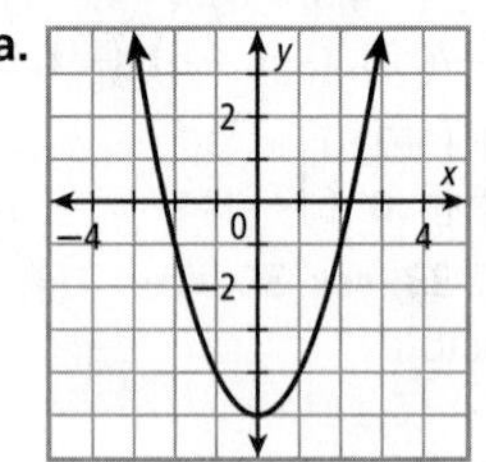

g is *f* translated 5 units down.

b.

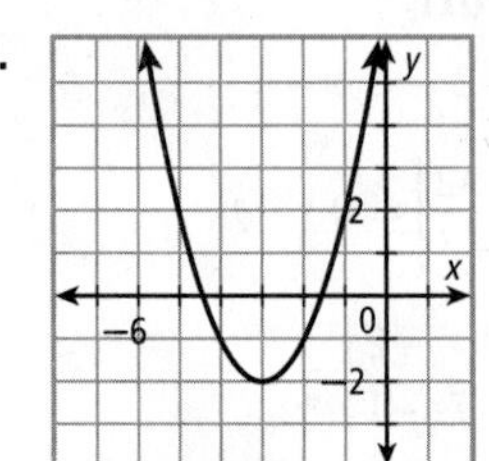

h is *f* translated 3 units left and 2 units down.

3a.

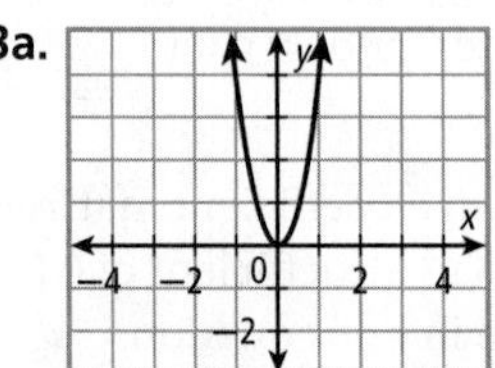

g is a horizontal compression of *f* by a factor of $\frac{1}{2}$.

b. 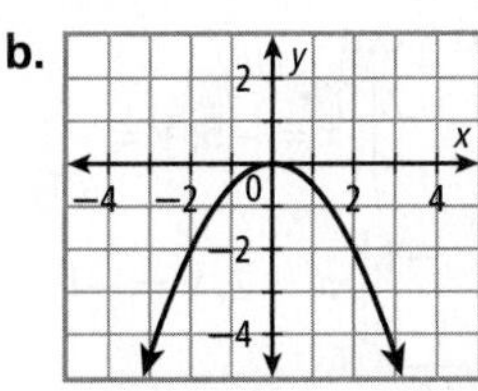

h is *f* reflected across the *x*-axis and vertically compressed by a factor of $\frac{1}{2}$. **4a.** $g(x) = \frac{1}{3}(x-2)^2 - 4$ **b.** $g(x) = -(x+5)^2 + 1$ **5.** Vertical compression by a factor of $\frac{13}{15}$; the braking distance will be less with optimally inflated new tires than with tires having more wear.

Exercises 1. vertex

3. 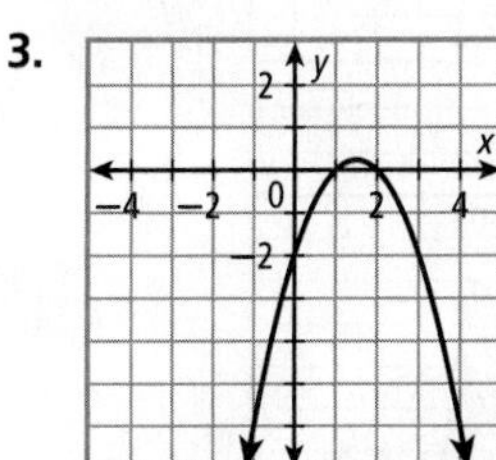

5. *d* is *f* translated 4 units right. **7.** *h* is *f* translated 1 unit left and 3 units down. **9.** *h* is a horizontal stretch of *f* by a factor of 8. **11.** *h* is *f* reflected across the *x*-axis and horizontally compressed by a factor of $\frac{1}{5}$. **13.** *d* is *f* reflected across the *x*-axis and vertically compressed by a factor of $\frac{2}{3}$. **15.** $h(x) = -x^2 - 6$

17. 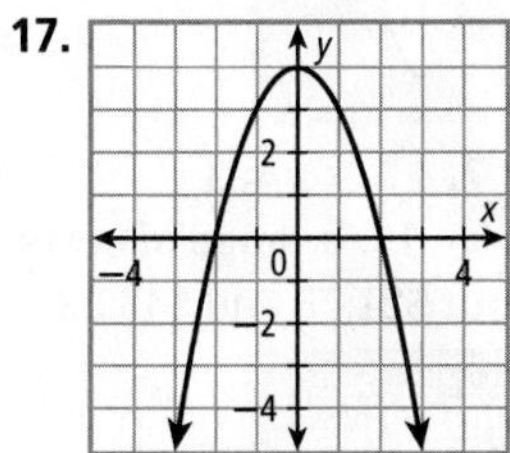

19. 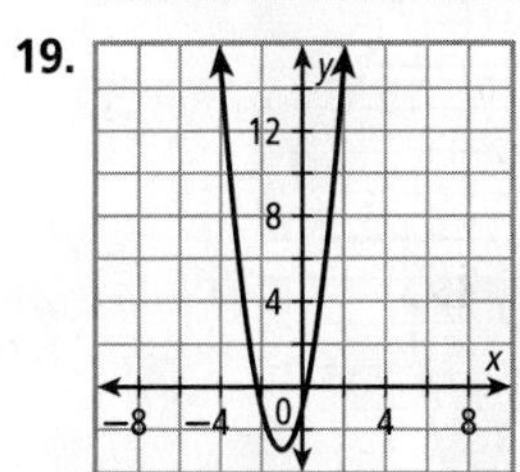

21. *h* is *f* translated 5 units left. **23.** *g* is *f* translated 4 units left and 3 units down. **25.** *j* is *f* translated 4 units right and 9 units down. **27.** *h* is *f* reflected across the *x*-axis and vertically stretched by a factor of 20. **29.** $g(x) = -\frac{1}{2}(x-1)^2$

31. Vertical translation; at any given speed, the gas mileage for an SUV is 18 mi/gal less than for a compact car. **33.** *p* is *f* reflected across the *x*-axis and translated 4 units right. **35.** *h* is *f* vertically stretched by a factor of 4 and translated 2 units down. **37.** *g* is *f* horizontally compressed by a factor of $\frac{1}{3}$ and translated 1 unit up. **39.** C **41.** A **43.** horizontal line; linear or constant function **45a.** vertical compression by a factor of 0.38 and translation 3.5 units right and 59 units up **b.** $y = -6.08(t-4)^2 + 95$ **47.** J **49.** G **51.** translation 6 units right and 6 units up: $y = -3(x-3)^2 + 3$ **55.** $f(x) = \sqrt{x}$ **57.** $y = 2x + 10$

5-2

Check It Out! 1. $x = 3$

2a. 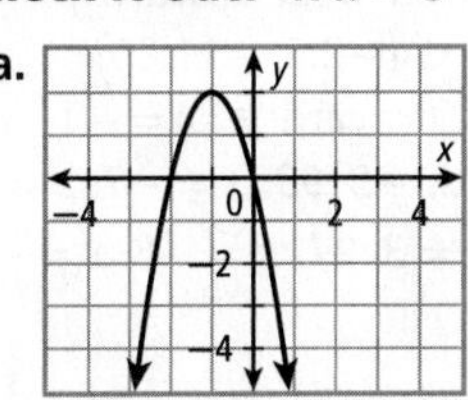

downward; $x = -1$; $(-1, 2)$; 0

b. 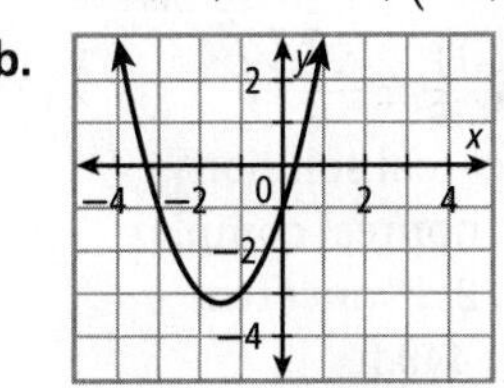

upward; $x = -\frac{3}{2}$; $\left(-\frac{3}{2}, -\frac{13}{4}\right)$; −1

3a. minimum: −6; D: ℝ; R: $\{y \mid y \geq -6\}$ **b.** maximum: −4; D: ℝ; R: $\{y \mid y \leq -4\}$ **4.** 30.0 mi/gal at 49 mi/h

Exercises 1. minimum **3.** $x = 0$ **5.** downward; $x = -1$; $(-1,-7)$; −8 **7.** downward; $x = 2$; $(2, 3)$; −1 **9.** maximum: $\frac{1}{4}$; D: ℝ; R: $\left\{y \mid y \leq \frac{1}{4}\right\}$ **11.** 3.125 m **13.** $x = 1$ **15.** upward; $x = -\frac{1}{2}$; $\left(-\frac{1}{2}, -\frac{9}{4}\right)$; −2 **17.** upward; $x = 2$; $(2, -6)$; −4 **19.** upward; $x = -\frac{1}{3}$; $\left(-\frac{1}{3}, -\frac{25}{3}\right)$; −8 **21.** downward; $x = 0$; $(0,-2)$; −2 **23.** upward; $x = -2$; $(-2,1)$; 2 **25.** maximum: 9; D: ℝ; R: $\{y \mid y \leq 9\}$ **27.** maximum: −4; D: ℝ; R: $\{y \mid y \leq -4\}$ **29.** minimum: 0; D: ℝ; R: $\{y \mid y \geq 0\}$

31. 64 ft **33a.** 562.5 mm **b.** 93.75 to 1 **c.** 168.75 m **35.** minimum: ≈ −3.029771 **37.** minimum: ≈ −1.253333 **41a.** about 1.6 s **b.** about 45 ft **43.** G **45.** G **51.** $60\sqrt{2}$ **53.** $\frac{3\sqrt{5}}{5}$ **55.** $f(0) = 10$; $f\left(\frac{1}{2}\right) = \frac{29}{4}$; $f(-2) = 26$ **57.** $f(0) = -20$; $f\left(\frac{1}{2}\right) = -22$; $f(-2) = -12$ **59.** $y + 4 = 3(x-1)$ **61.** $y - 5 = -2(x-3)$

5-3

Check It Out! 1. −3,1 **2a.** −1, 6 **b.** 0, 8 **3.** 3 s **4a.** $x = 2$ **b.** $x = -\frac{3}{5}$, $x = \frac{3}{5}$ **5.** Possible answer: $f(x) = x^2 - 25$

Exercises 1. roots **3.** 2, 4 **5.** 1, 6 **7.** −4, 0 **9.** −2, 8 **11.** 4 s **13.** $x = 2$ **19.** −3, 2 **21.** −8, −3 **23.** 0, 9 **25.** −8, 1 **27.** 4 s **29.** $x = -\frac{9}{2}$, $x = \frac{9}{2}$ **31.** $x = -\frac{1}{2}$, $x = \frac{1}{2}$ **33.** $x = \frac{2}{7}$ **37.** 0, 6 **39.** 6 **41.** 11 **43.** 5, 6 **45.** −7, −2 **47a.** $h(t) = -16t^2 + 16t + 5$ **b.** 1.25 s **49.** $x = -5$, $x = -1$ **51.** $x = -\frac{1}{3}$ **53.** $x = -2$, $x = 3$ **55a.** $(0, -16)$ **b.** −16 **c.** −4, 4 **57a.** $(1, 2)$ **b.** 0 **c.** 0, 2 **59a.** $\left(-\frac{1}{6}, -4\frac{1}{12}\right)$ **b.** −4 **c.** $-1\frac{1}{3}$, 1 **61.** 20 ft by 4 ft **63.** 10 m by 5 m **67.** B **69.** C **71.** $x = 0$, $x = \frac{3}{2}$ **73.** $x = \frac{1}{4}$, $x = \frac{1}{2}$ **75a.** $(a+b)(a^2 - ab + b^2) = a^3 - a^2b + ab^2 + a^2b - ab^2 + b^3 = a^3 + b^3$ **b.** $(2x+3)(4x^2 - 6x + 9)$ **c.** $a^3 - b^3 = (a-b)(a^2 + ab + b^2)$ **d.** $(x-1)(x^2 + x + 1)$ **77.** 8.64×10^{12} **79.** 6.5×10^{-10} **81.** $w = 2.2$ **83.** *h* is a vertical compression of *f* by a factor of 0.5. **85.** *g* is *f* translated 1 unit left.

5-4

Check It Out! 1a. $x = \pm\frac{5}{2}$ **b.** $x = -11$, $x = 3$ **2a.** $x^2 + 4x + 4 = (x+2)^2$ **b.** $x^2 - 4x + 4 = (x-2)^2$ **c.** $x^2 + 3x + \frac{9}{4} = \left(x + \frac{3}{2}\right)^2$ **3a.** $x = \frac{9 \pm \sqrt{89}}{2}$ **b.** $x = -1$, $x = 9$

Selected Answers

4a. $f(x) = (x + 12)^2 + 1$; $(-12, 1)$ **b.** $g(x) = 5(x - 5)^2 + 3$; $(5, 3)$

Exercises **1.** $\left(\frac{b}{2}\right)^2$ **3.** $x = 1, x = 9$ **5.** $x^2 + 14x + 49 = (x + 7)^2$ **7.** $x^2 - 9x + \frac{81}{4} = \left(x - \frac{9}{2}\right)^2$ **9.** $x = 2, x = 4$ **11.** $x = -2 \pm 2\sqrt{7}$ **13.** $x = -2 \pm \frac{\sqrt{46}}{2}$ **15.** $g(x) = (x - 5)^2 - 14$; $(5, -14)$ **17.** $f(x) = (x + 4)^2 - 26$; $(-4, -26)$ **19.** $h(x) = 3(x - 2)^2 - 16$; $(2, -16)$ **21.** $x = -7, x = 13$ **23.** $x^2 - 18x + 81 = (x - 9)^2$ **25.** $x^2 - \frac{1}{2}x + \frac{1}{16} = \left(x - \frac{1}{4}\right)^2$ **27.** $x = 2 \pm \sqrt{3}$ **29.** $x = 2, x = 6$ **31.** $x = -1 \pm \frac{2\sqrt{3}}{3}$ **33.** $g(x) = (x + 7)^2 + 22$; $(-7, 22)$ **35.** $f(x) = (x + 2)^2 - 11$; $(-2, -11)$ **37.** $h(x) = 2(x + 1.5)^2 + 20.5$; $(-1.5, 20.5)$ **39a.** about 12.3 s **b.** about 2.3 s **41.** $x = \pm\sqrt{3}$ **43.** $x = \pm 5$ **45.** $x = -13 \pm \sqrt{7}$ **47.** $x = \frac{-3 \pm 5\sqrt{2}}{2}$ **49.** $x = \frac{-3 \pm \sqrt{5}}{3}$ **51.** $x = -5, x = -3$ **53.** $x = \frac{-2 \pm \sqrt{7}}{3}$ **55.** $x = \frac{7 \pm \sqrt{57}}{2}$ **57.** $x = -3 \pm \sqrt{5}$ **59.** $x = 4 \pm 2\sqrt{10}$ **61a.** 1.7 s **b.** 71 ft/s **65.** $x = \pm 7.416$ **67.** $x = \pm 4.192$ **69.** $x = \pm 1.528$ **73.** B **75.** A **77.** 2.5 **79.** $b = \pm 24$ **81.** $b = \pm 18$ **83.** $2\sqrt{5} \pm 1$ **85a.** 135,000 ft^2 **b.** 450 ft by 300 ft **c.** 129,600 ft^2 **87.** $\{x \mid -6 \le x \le 14\}$ **89.** $\{x \mid -1 \le x \le 5\}$ **91.** 3×3 **93.** 1368; the amount in dollars the Hernandez family budgeted for housing **95.** $x = 0$; $(0, -1)$

5-5

Check It Out! **1a.** $2i\sqrt{3}$ **b.** $12i$ **c.** $-i\sqrt{7}$ **2a.** $x = \pm 6i$ **b.** $x = \pm 4i\sqrt{3}$ **c.** $x = \pm\frac{5}{3}i$ **3a.** $x = -4$; $y = -\frac{3}{10}$ **b.** $x = -\frac{8}{5}$; $y = -\frac{\sqrt{6}}{6}$ **4a.** $-2 \pm 3i$ **b.** $4 \pm i\sqrt{2}$ **5a.** $9 + i$ **b.** $\sqrt{3} - i$ **c.** $8i$

Exercises **1.** imaginary **3.** $2i$ **5.** $12i$ **7.** $x = \pm 6i$ **9.** $x = \pm 11i$ **11.** $x = 1$; $y = -1$ **13.** $-3 \pm 5i$ **15.** $\sqrt{5} - 5i$ **17.** $6 - i\sqrt{2}$ **19.** $-i\sqrt{10}$ **21.** $5i\sqrt{2}$ **23.** $x = \pm 4i$ **25.** $x = \pm 8i$ **27.** $x = -3$; $y = -5$ **29.** $\frac{3 \pm i\sqrt{7}}{8}$ **31.** $\frac{3 \pm i\sqrt{21}}{3}$ **33.** $-\frac{\sqrt{3}}{2} + 2i$ **35.** $-1 - \frac{i}{10}$ **37.** $1 - 14i$ **39.** $-2\sqrt{5} - 4i$ **41.** $9 + i\sqrt{2}$ **43.** $c = 0, d = 5$ **45.** $c = \pm 2, d = 4$ **47.** $x = \pm 9i$ **49.** $x = \pm 12i$ **51.** $x = \pm 2i\sqrt{2}$ **53.** $x = -5 \pm 2i$ **55.** $x = -1 \pm 2i$ **57.** $x = 12 \pm i\sqrt{5}$ **59.** always true **61.** sometimes true **63.** sometimes true **65.** sometimes true **67.** $-1 \pm 4i$ **69.** $-8 \pm 3i$ **71.** $8 \pm 2i$ **73.** The complex conjugate of a real number a is the number a. **75a.** $t = \frac{7}{2} \pm \frac{\sqrt{3}}{2}i$ **b.** no **c.** 196 ft **77.** F **79.** G **81.** When $a < 0$, the 2 solutions are imaginary and complex. When $a > 0$, the 2 solutions are real and complex. **85.** $T^2 = \begin{bmatrix} 12 & -3 & 5 \\ 2 & 7 & -1 \\ -4 & 4 & -2 \end{bmatrix}$ **87.** not defined **89a.** upward **b.** $x = -2.5$ **c.** $(-2.5, -11.25)$ **d.** -10 **91a.** upward **b.** $x = -1$ **c.** $(-1, -5)$ **d.** -3 **93.** $x = -7, x = 2$ **95.** $x = \frac{3}{4}, x = 3$ **97.** $x = -8, x = -3$

5-6

Check It Out! **1a.** $\frac{-3 \pm \sqrt{37}}{2}$ **b.** $4 \pm \sqrt{6}$ **2.** $\frac{1}{6} \pm \frac{\sqrt{95}}{6}i$ **3a.** 1 distinct real solution **b.** 2 distinct nonreal complex solutions **c.** 2 distinct real solutions **4.** 449 ft

Exercises **3.** $\frac{2 \pm \sqrt{7}}{3}$ **5.** $-6, 1$ **7.** $\pm\frac{\sqrt{38}}{2}$ **9.** $-3 \pm i\sqrt{3}$ **11.** $-2 \pm i\sqrt{6}$ **13.** $\frac{-7 \pm i\sqrt{111}}{20}$ **15.** 2 distinct real solutions **17.** 14 in. and 20 in. **19.** $-6, 0$ **21.** $-1 \pm \sqrt{10}$ **23.** $\pm\frac{\sqrt{21}}{7}$ **25.** $\frac{-1 \pm i\sqrt{3}}{2}$ **27.** $\frac{-7 \pm 3\sqrt{17}}{4}$ **29.** $\frac{2 \pm 2i\sqrt{2}}{3}$ **31.** 2 distinct real solutions **33.** 1 distinct real solution **35.** 2 distinct real solutions **37a.** 9 s **b.** 6 s **39.** $\frac{1 \pm \sqrt{3}}{2}$ **41.** $\frac{-3 \pm \sqrt{17}}{4}$ **43.** $\frac{1 \pm i\sqrt{87}}{2}$ **45.** $x = -2, x = 5$ **47.** $x = -2.5, x = 1.5$ **49.** $x = -3, x = 7$ **51.** $x = \pm 5$ **53.** $x = 8$ **55.** 3 in. **57.** $c = -36$ **61.** B **63.** C **65.** 15 cm and 8 cm **73.** $\left[\begin{array}{cc|c} 2 & -3 & -7 \\ 1 & -6 & 1 \end{array}\right]$; $x = -5$; $y = -1$ **75.** $\left[\begin{array}{cc|c} 4 & 5 & -1 \\ 2 & -7 & 9 \end{array}\right]$; $x = 1$; $y = -1$ **77.** $x = 4 \pm \sqrt{14}$

5-7

Check It Out! **1a.**

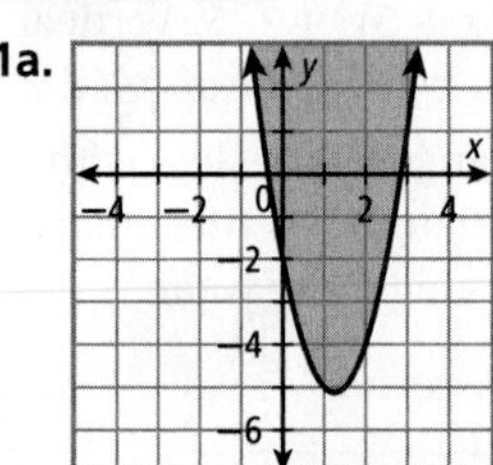

b.

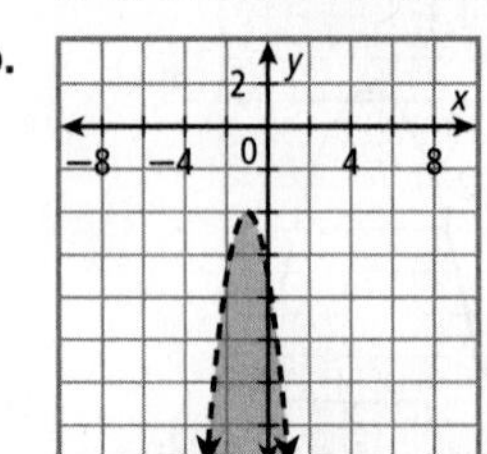

2a. $-1 < x < 2$ **b.** $x \le 0$ or $x \ge 2.5$ **3a.** $x \le 2$ *or* $x \ge 4$ **b.** $x < -1$ or $x > 2.5$ **4.** fewer than 14 or more than 36 people

Exercises **3.**

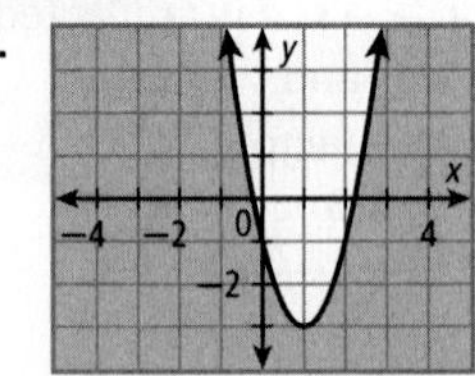

5. $0 \le x \le 5$ **7.** $1.5 \le x \le 3$ **9.** $-8 < x < -5$ **11.** a range of costs between about \$21.78 and \$48.22 **13.**

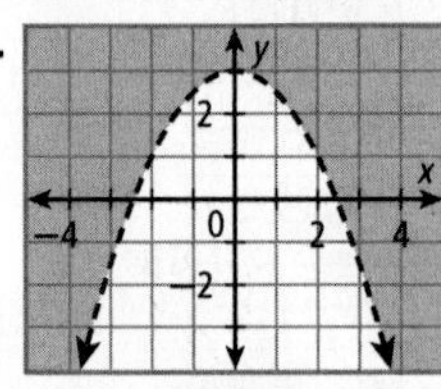

15.

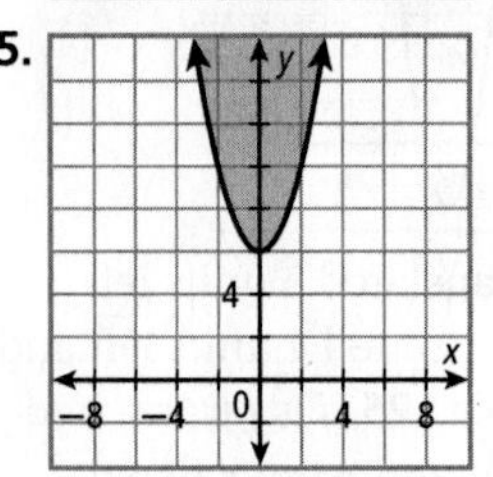

17.

19. $x \le -1$ or $x \ge -0.5$
21. $x < -2$ or $x > 4$ **23.** $2 < x < 10$
25. $-1 \le x \le 2.5$ **27.** at distances less than about 3 ft and at distances greater than about 102 ft

29. 

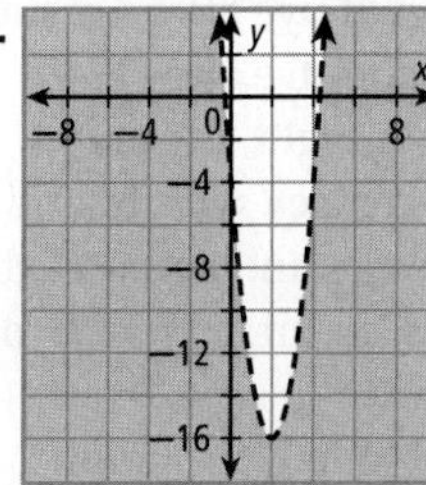

33.

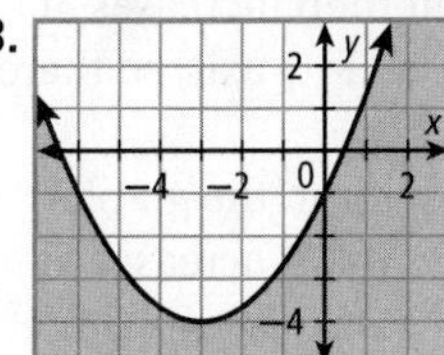

35. $-3 \le x \le 8$

37. $\dfrac{-1-\sqrt{17}}{4} < x < \dfrac{-1+\sqrt{17}}{4}$

39. $-1 - \dfrac{\sqrt{6}}{3} < x < -1 + \dfrac{\sqrt{6}}{3}$

41. $\dfrac{-5-\sqrt{61}}{6} \le x \le \dfrac{-5+\sqrt{61}}{6}$

43. $x \le \dfrac{1-\sqrt{6}}{5}$ or $x \ge \dfrac{1+\sqrt{6}}{5}$

45. $x < 3$ or $x > 9$ **47.** a distance between 0 ft and about 31 ft
49. A **51a.** $A(x) = -\frac{1}{2}x^2 + 10x$
b. $3.7 \le x \le 16.3$ **c.** $0 < x \le 5.5$ or $14.5 \le x \le 20$ **53b.** a width between 5 ft and 15 ft **c.** a width of 10 ft **55.** $0.9 \le x \le 14.1$
57. $x \le -2.2$ or $x \ge 0.7$ **59.** It is not **63.** J **65.** $x < -3$ or $x > -1$
69. 121.5 square units
75. $c = 9$

5-8

Check It Out! 1a. Quadratic; second differences are constant for equally spaced x-values.
b. Not quadratic; first differences are constant so the function is linear. **2.** $f(x) = -x^2 + 4x - 3$
3. $L(d) \approx 14.3d^2 - 112.4d + 430.1$; about 446 ft

Exercises 3. Not quadratic; second differences are not constant for equally spaced x-values.
5. $y = x^2 - 2x - 3$ **7.** $y = x^2 - 3x + 4$
9. $y = -\frac{1}{2}x^2 + 4x - 3$ **11.** $C(x) \approx 0.0098x^2 + 0.62x + 3.8$; about \$31.20
13. Quadratic; second differences are constant for equally spaced x-values. **15.** $y = \frac{4}{3}x^2 - x - \frac{7}{3}$
17. $y = 0.5x^2 - 3x - 8$
19. $y \approx -3.7x^2 + 216x + 781$; about \$3290 million, or \$3.29 billion

21. The function is $A(b) = \left(\frac{1}{2}h\right)b$, which is linear. **23.** The function is $A(s) = s^2$, which is quadratic.
25. -3 **27.** -1
29a. $p(s) = -0.125s^2 + 5.25s - 35.05$ **b.** \$18.95 **c.** a maximum point; the price and size of the most expensive pizza
d. \$9.95; $-\$1.05$ **31.** not quadratic
33. quadratic; $y = 5x^2 + 2x$
35. not quadratic **39a.** $y \approx -10.7x + 208.1$ **b.** no **c.** linear; $y = 4x + 8$
41. $t(n) = \frac{1}{2}n^2 + \frac{1}{2}n$
43b. $y \approx 0.5x + 3$
c. $y \approx -0.13x^2 + 2.8x - 6$
45. B **47.** D
49. $y = 2x^2 - 5$ **53.** yes
55. The matrix is undefined.

57. $\begin{bmatrix} \frac{1}{3} & -\frac{8}{3} \\ 0 & -2 \end{bmatrix}$ **59.** $\pm 3i$

5-9

Check It Out!
1.

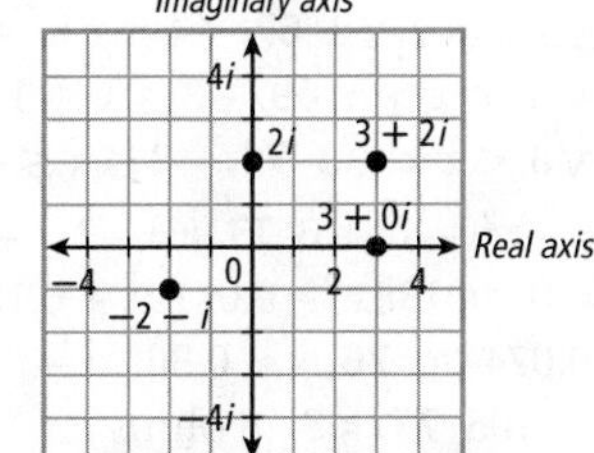

2a. $\sqrt{5}$ **b.** $\frac{1}{2}$ **c.** 23 **3a.** $-3 - i$
b. $-3 - 3i$ **c.** 8

4a.

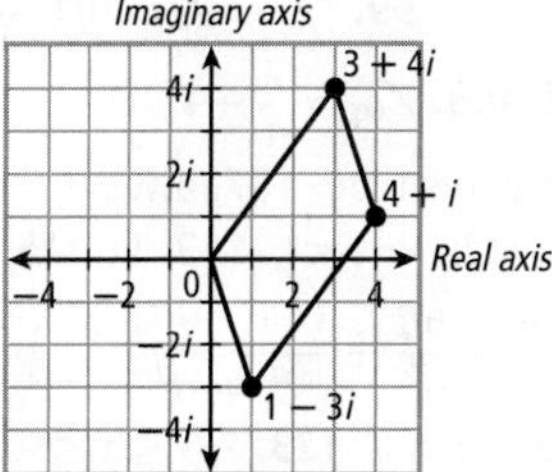

$4 + i$

b.

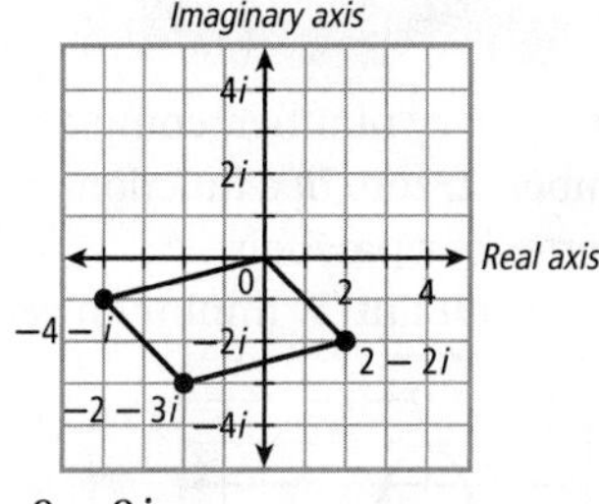

$-2 - 3i$

5a. $10 + 6i$ **b.** $20 - 28i$
c. 13 **6a.** $-\frac{1}{2}i$ **b.** -1
7a. $-8 + 3i$ **b.** $\frac{7}{5} + \frac{1}{5}i$
Exercises 1. real; imaginary
3, 5.

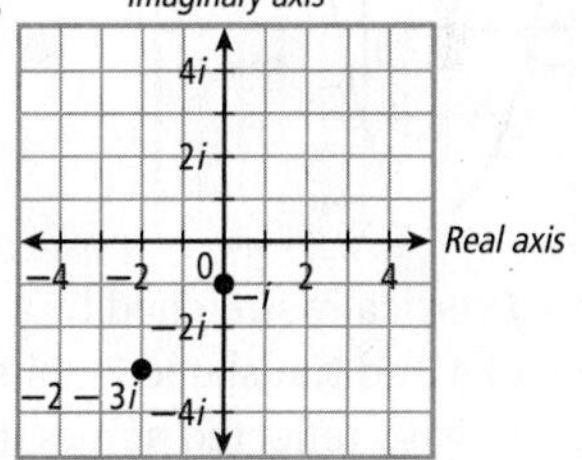

7. 33.3 **9.** 13 **11.** 15 **13.** $3 - 5i$
15. $-9 + 15i$ **17.** $-28 - 19i$
19. $-3 - i$ **21.** 5 **23.** $37 - 5i$
25. $8 + 6i$ **27.** $-i$ **29.** -1 **31.** $\frac{21}{10} + \frac{17}{10}i$
33. $4 - i$ **35.** $-2 + \frac{1}{2}i$
37, 39.

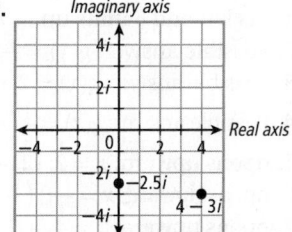

41. 18 **43.** 10 **45.** $2\sqrt{29}$ **47.** $-11 + 7i$
49. $28 + 41i$ **51.** $-4 + 9i$ **53.** $4 + 6i$
55. $48 + 12i$ **57.** 53 **59.** $24 + 78i$
61. $-i$ **63.** -5 **65.** $\frac{13}{10} - \frac{11}{10}i$
67. $4 + i$ **69.** $\frac{3}{4} + \frac{9}{4}i$ **71.** $3i$
73. $-2 - i$ **75.** $\sqrt{10}$ **77.** $2\sqrt{10}$
79. 0 **81.** $\frac{\sqrt{10}}{2}$ **83.** $\sqrt{11}$ **85.** $9.5 + 2.9i$
87. $-9.7 + 1.3i$ **89.** $-1 + 4i$
91. $-5 + 12i$ **93.** $10 - 5i$ **95.** 0

97. $1 - 12i$ **99.** $\frac{26}{37} + \frac{8}{37}i$ **101.** $\frac{8}{13} + \frac{12}{13}i$ **103.** $Z_{eq} = \frac{7}{4} - i$
105. always true **107.** always true
109. A is incorrect. **113.** D **115.** C
119. $\frac{ac + bd}{c^2 + d^2} + \frac{(bc - ad)}{c^2 + d^2}i$
121. $0 \le x \le 2$ **123.** $-5 \le x \le \frac{3}{2}$
125. Yes

Study Guide: Review

1. imaginary number; complex number **2.** zero of a function
3. vertex of a parabola
4. discriminant **5.** minimum value
6.

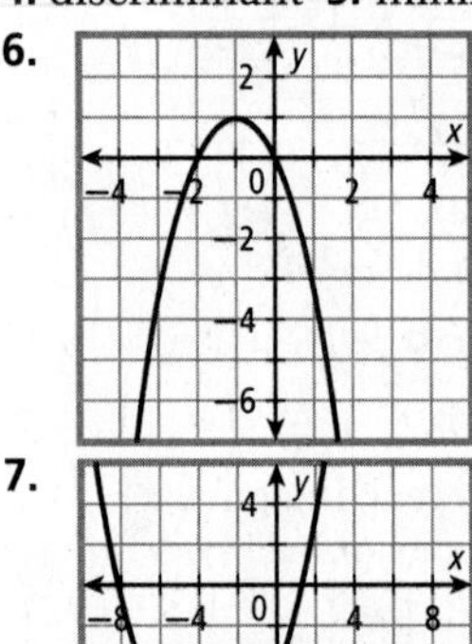

7.

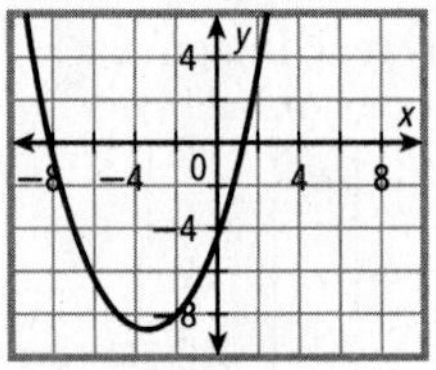

8. g is f vertically stretched by a factor of 4 and translated 2 units right. **9.** g is f reflected across the x-axis, vertically stretched by a factor of 2, and translated 1 unit left. **10.** g is f vertically compressed by a factor of $\frac{1}{3}$ and translated 3 units down. **11.** g is f reflected across the x-axis and translated 2 units left and 6 units up.
12. Possible answer: $g(x) = -x^2 - 3$
13. Possible answer: $g(x) = 2(x - 4)^2$
14. Possible answer: $g(x) = \frac{1}{4}(x + 1)^2$
15. opens upward; $x = 2$; $(2, -1)$; 3
16. opens upward; $x = -1$; $(-1, 2)$; 3
17. opens upward; $x = 1.5$; $(1.5, -2.25)$; 0 **18.** opens upward; $x = 2$; $(2, 2)$; 4 **19.** minimum: 5
20. maximum: 4.5 **21.** minimum: -5.25 **22.** maximum: 18
23. maximum: 12 **24.** minimum: 7
25. $x = -1$ or $x = 8$ **26.** $x = 2$ or $x = 3$ **27.** $x = -12$ or $x = 12$
28. $x = 0$ or $x = 21$ **29.** $x = 2$
30. $x = -1$ or $x = -3$ **31.** $x = 2$ or $x = -16$ **32.** $x = -\frac{1}{3}$ **33.** Possible answer: $f(x) = x^2 + x - 6$
34. Possible answer: $f(x) = x^2 - 1$
35. Possible answer: $f(x) = x^2 - 9x + 20$ **36.** Possible answer: $f(x) = x^2 + 5x + 6$ **37.** Possible answer: $f(x) = x^2 + 10x + 25$
38. Possible answer: $f(x) = x^2 - 9x$
39. $x = 4$ or $x = 12$ **40.** $x = -14$ or $x = -6$ **41.** $x = -2$ or $x = 8$
42. $x = 7 \pm \sqrt{62}$ **43.** $f(x) = (x - 2)^2 + 5$; $(2, 5)$ **44.** $g(x) = (x + 1)^2 - 8$; $(-1, -8)$ **45.** $x = \pm 9i$ **46.** $x = \pm 5i$
47. $x = -3 \pm i$ **48.** $x = -6 \pm 3i$
49. $x = 7 \pm i\sqrt{26}$ **50.** $x = 11 \pm 2i\sqrt{3}$
51. $-5i - 4$ **52.** $3 - i\sqrt{5}$
53. $\frac{3 \pm \sqrt{41}}{2}$ **54.** $5 \pm 2i\sqrt{3}$
55. $\frac{5}{2} \pm \frac{i\sqrt{11}}{2}$ **56.** $-\frac{3}{2} \pm i\frac{\sqrt{3}}{2}$
57. $\frac{5}{2} \pm i\frac{\sqrt{15}}{2}$ **58.** 1 distinct real solution **59.** 2 real solutions
60. 2 nonreal complex solutions
61. 2 real solutions **62.** 2 nonreal complex solutions **63.** 2 nonreal complex solutions
64.

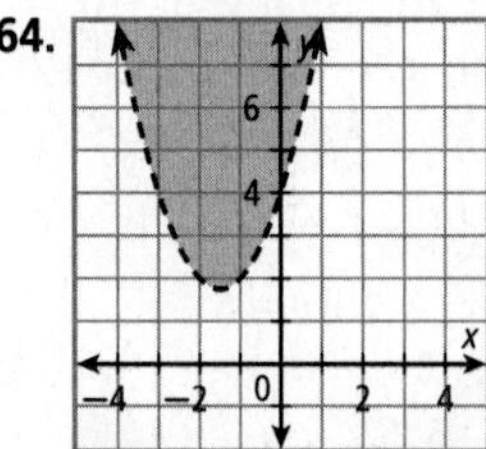

65.

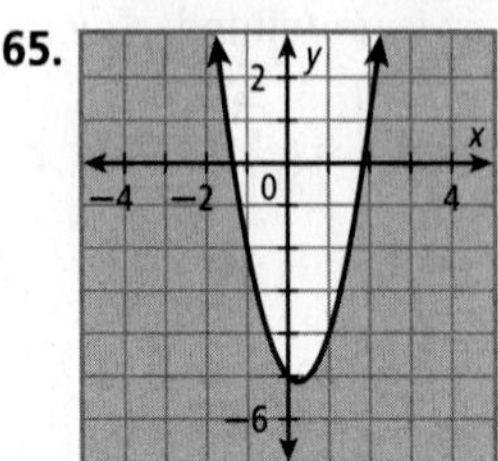

66. $x \le -3$ or $x \ge 1$ **67.** $-4 < x < -1$
68. $x < 1$ or $x > 5$ **69.** $-3 \le x \le 3$
70. $-\sqrt{3} < x < \sqrt{3}$ **71.** $-2 \le x \le \frac{2}{3}$
72. $y = -x^2 - 3x + 6$ **73.** $y = -2x^2 + x$
74. $y \approx 0.000188x^2 - 0.0112x + 0.182$
75. ≈ 0.074 in. **76.** $y \approx 0.360x^2 - 11.9x + 105$ **77.** ≈ 37.8 ohms
78. 3 **79.** $2\sqrt{5}$ **80.** 20 **81.** 7
82. $7 + 4i$ **83.** $6 + 2i$ **84.** -6
85. $-20 - 15i$ **86.** $46 + 28i$
87. 13 **88.** $9 - 19i$
89. $-57 - 51i$ **90.** 1 **91.** $-5i$
92. $-\frac{9}{2} + i$ **93.** $\frac{7}{25} + \frac{26}{25}i$
94. $2 - 6i$ **95.** $4 + 5i$

Chapter 6

6-1

Check It Out! 1a. 3 **b.** 0 **c.** 5 **d.** 9 **2a.** $-2x^2 + 4x + 2$; -2; 2; 3; quadratic trinomial
b. $x^3 - 18x^2 + 2x - 5$; 1; 3; 4; cubic polynomial with 4 terms
3a. $16x^3 - 30x^2 + 6x - 16$
b. $5x^3 - 9x^2 - 3x + 14$
4. $f(4) = 3.8398$; $f(17) = 1.6368$; the concentration of dye after 4 s; the concentration of dye after 17 s
5a. From left to right, the graph increases, decreases slightly, and then increases again. It crosses the x-axis 3 times, so there appear to be 3 real zeros.
b. From right to left, the graph decreases and then increases. It does not cross the x-axis, so there are no real zeros.
c. From left to right, the graph decreases and then increases. It crosses the x-axis twice, so there appear to be 2 real zeros.
d. From left to right, the graph alternately decreases and increases, changing direction 3 times. It crosses the x-axis 4 times, so there appear to be 4 real zeros.

Exercises 1. The leading coefficient of a polynomial is the number being multiplied by the variable with the greatest degree. **3.** 5 **5.** 6 **7.** $3x^2 + 5x - 4$; 3; 2; 3; quadratic trinomial
9. $4x^4 + 8x^2 - 3x + 1$; 4; 4; 4; quartic with 4 terms
11. $3x^2 + 12x + 3$
13. $-5x^2 - 7x - 5$ **15.** From left to right, the graph increases. It crosses the x-axis once, so there appears to be 1 real zero. **17.** From left to right, the graph decreases. It crosses the x-axis once, so there appears to be 1 real zero. **19.** 8
21. 0 **23.** $2x^4 + 3x^3 + x^2 - 7x$; 2; 4; 4; quartic with 4 terms
25. $2x^3 + 10x - 9$; 2; 3; 3; cubic trinomial **27.** $x^3 + x^2$
29. $5y^3 - 3y^2 + 2y + 2$
31a. $d(1) = -3$; $d(2) = -28$
33. From left to right, the graph increases. There is 1 real zero.

35. The graph decreases, increases, and then decreases. There is 1 real zero. **41.** $S(x) = 4\pi x^2 + 8\pi x$ **43.** $S(x) = 5\pi x^2 + \frac{31}{2}\pi x + 12\pi$ **45a.** \$12.04 **b.** \$27.52 **47.** sometimes true **49.** sometimes true **51a.** The x-intercepts are -3, 1, and 4. **b.** The x-intercepts are -1, -2, 3, and 1. **c.** The x-intercepts are 0, -1, and 2. **d.** The x-intercepts are -2 and 3. **e.** The x-intercepts are $-\frac{1}{2}$, 0, and $\frac{1}{2}$. **53.** Yes **55.** J **57.** J **67.** vertical **69.** horizontal **71.** shift left 3 units and up 2 units

6-2

Check It Out!

1a. $12c^3d^3 - 18c^2d^3 + 42c^2d^4$ **b.** $6x^2y^4 + x^2y^3 - 28x^2y^2 + 30x^2y$ **2a.** $9b^3 - 9b^2c - 4bc^2 + 4c^3$ **b.** $x^4 + x^3 - 21x^2 + 13x - 2$ **3.** $T(x) = -0.00008x^4 - 0.0028x^3 + 0.028x^2 + 0.3x + 9$ **4a.** $x^4 + 16x^3 + 96x^2 + 256x + 256$ **b.** $8x^3 - 12x^2 + 6x - 1$ **5a.** $x^3 + 6x^2 + 12x + 8$ **b.** $x^5 - 20x^4 + 160x^3 - 640x^2 + 1280x - 1024$ **c.** $81x^4 + 108x^3 + 54x^2 + 12x + 1$

Exercises

1. $-20c^3d^5 - 12c^4d^4$ **3.** $5x^3y + 8x^2y - 7xy$ **5.** $x^3 + x^2y - 3xy^2 + y^3$ **7.** $3x^5 + 15x^4 + 16x^3 - 3x^2 + 6x - 2$ **9.** $-0.02x^4 - 0.3x^3 + 4.4x^2 - 14.2x + 20$ **11.** $x^4 + 4x^3y + 6x^2y^2 + 4xy^3 + y^4$ **13.** $x^3 - 9x^2y + 27xy^2 - 27y^3$ **15.** $16x^4 + 32x^3y + 24x^2y^2 + 8xy^3 + y^4$ **17.** $32x^5 - 80x^4y + 80x^3y^2 - 40x^2y^3 + 10xy^4 - y^5$ **19.** $6x^4 + 27x^3 - 18x^2$ **21.** $12r^5 + 28r^4 - 60r^3 + 28r^2$ **23.** $6x^3 + 7x^2y - 16xy^2 + 10y^3$ **25.** $12x^4 + 17x^3 + 8x^2 + x - 2$ **27.** $8x^3 - 24x^2 + 24x - 8$ **29.** $x^4 - 4x^3y + 6x^2y^2 - 4xy^3 + y^4$ **31.** $x^4 - 12x^3y + 54x^2y^2 - 108xy^3 + 81y^4$ **33.** $x^5 + 5x^4y + 10x^3y^2 + 10x^2y^3 + 5xy^4 + y^5$ **35.** equivalent **37.** not equivalent **39.** $T(x) = -0.0003x^4 - 0.0164x^3 + 2.572x^2 - 14.12x + 116.2$ **41.** $p^3 - 6p^2q + 12pq^2 - 8q^3$ **43.** $x^6 + x^4y^3 + x^3y^3 + xy^6$ **45.** $5x^3y + x^2y - 9xy + 10x^3 + 2x^2 - 18x$ **47.** $3x^4 - 24x^3 + 72x^2 - 96x + 48$ **49.** $-x^5 - 14x^3 - 45x^2 + 30x - 450$ **51.** $2x^6 - 3x^5 - 8x^4 + 12x^3 + 14x - 21$ **53.** No **55a.** $f(n) = \frac{1}{4}n^4 + n^3 + \frac{5}{4}n^2 + \frac{1}{2}n$ **b.** 7098 **59.** J **61.** H **63.** $x^{10} - 10x^9 + 45x^8 - 120x^7 + 210x^6 - 252x^5 + 210x^4 - 120x^3 + 45x^2 - 10x + 1$ **65.** $m^6 - 3m^4n^2 + 3m^2n^4 - n^6$ **67.** $B(x) = x - 3$ **69.** $B(x) = x^3 + 1$ **71.** $\begin{bmatrix} 8 & 1 \\ 4 & 13 \end{bmatrix}$ **73.** $\begin{bmatrix} 4 & -2 & 10 \\ -4 & 10 & 6 \\ -4 & -6 & 6 \end{bmatrix}$ **75.** $4x^4 - 6x^3 + 5x^2 + 3x$; 4; 4; 4; quartic with 4 terms **77.** $3x^5 - 4x^2 - 2x + 9$; 3; 5; 4; quintic with 4 terms

6-3

Check It Out!

1a. $5x + 1 - \frac{13}{3x + 1}$ **b.** $x + 8 - \frac{4}{x - 3}$ **2a.** $6x - 23 + \frac{63}{x + 3}$ **b.** $x + 3$ **3a.** $P(-3) = 4$ **b.** $P\left(\frac{1}{5}\right) = 5$ **4.** $y - 5$

Exercises **3.** $x + 2 + \frac{1}{x - 1}$ **5.** $7x - 2$ **7.** $x - 6$ **9.** $P(-8) = 42$ **11.** $P(-1) = 6$ **13.** $x + 4$ **15.** $x^2 - 1$ **17.** $\frac{1}{2}x^3 - 2x^2 - \frac{7}{2}$ **19.** $x + 4 + \frac{2}{x + 1}$ **21.** $x + 1 - \frac{2}{x + 8}$ **23.** $2x + 14 - \frac{1}{x - \frac{1}{2}}$ **25.** $P(4) = 9$ **27.** $P\left(-\frac{1}{3}\right) = \frac{5}{3}$ **29.** $I(t) = 0.5t^2 + 4t$ **31.** $a = 2$; $b = 8$; $c = 29$ **33.** $a = 3$; $b = 9$; $c = -4$ **35.** $x - 2$ **37.** $D(h) = \frac{1}{\pi} - \frac{4}{\pi h} + \frac{20}{\pi h^2}$ **39.** $y^2 + 5$ **41.** $x^2 - 5x - 12$ **43.** $t - 4$ **45.** $x^3 + 3x^2 - 10x - 1$ **47.** $x^3 - x^2 + 3x - 4 + \frac{1}{x - 6}$ **49.** Solution B is correct. **53.** B **55.** D **57.** $P(-4) = -1{,}189{,}150$ **59.** $P(1) = 0$ **61.** $k = 18$ **65.** max = 1.25; D: $\mathbb{R}$; R: $\{y \mid y \le 1.25\}$ **67.** min = -2; D: $\mathbb{R}$; R: $\{y \mid y \ge -2\}$ **69.** $12x^3y^3 + 24x^3y + 20x^2y^4$ **71.** $4x^3 - 8x^2y + 8xy^2 - 4y^3$

6-4

Check It Out!

1a. no **b.** yes **2a.** $(x + 3)(x - 3)(x - 2)$ **b.** $(x^2 + 4)(2x + 1)$ **3a.** $(2 + z^2)(4 - 2z^2 + z^4)$ **b.** $2x^2(x - 2)(x^2 + 2x + 4)$ **4.** $x = 1, 3, 4$; $V(x) = (x - 1)(x - 3)(x - 4)$

Exercises

1. yes **3.** yes **5.** $(x + 2)(x - 2)(x + 5)$ **7.** $2(x + 2)(x - 2)(x - 1)$ **9.** $3(x - 2)(4x + 1)$ **11.** $2t^4(t + 3)(t^2 - 3t + 9)$ **13.** $(3 + x)(9 - 3x + x^2)$ **15.** $(y - 5)(y^2 + 5y + 25)$ **17.** no **19.** yes **21.** $(b + 2)(b - 2)(4b + 3)$ **23.** $(x + 3)(x - 3)(3x + 1)$ **25.** $(x + 2)(x - 2)(5x - 1)$ **27.** $(s - 1)(s + 1)(s^2 + s + 1)(s^2 - s + 1)$ **29.** $6x(x - 3)(x^2 + 3x + 9)$ **31.** $y^2(y + 3)(y^2 - 3y + 9)$ **33.** $x^2(x^2 - 7)(x^2 - 7)$ **35.** $(x - 2)(x + 2)(4x + 1)$ **37.** $x(2x^2 - 1)(2x^2 - 3)(2x^2 + 3)$ **39.** $a = 3$; $d = 72$ **41.** $P(x) = (x - 2)(x^3 + 5x + 1)$ **43.** $P(x) = (x + 2)(2x^4 - 6x + 3)$ **45a.** $f(t) = -t(t - 8)(t - 18)(t - 18)$ **b.** \$2,535,000 **c.** $f(15) = -945$ **47.** $B(x) = x^3 - 2x^2 + 4x - 8$ **51.** J **53.** $[(x - 3) + 2][(x - 3)^2 - 2(x - 3) + 4]$; $(x - 1)(x^2 - 8x + 19)$

Selected Answers

57. $(3x - 5)(3x - 5)$

59. $\left(x - \frac{22}{3}\right)\left(x + \frac{35}{6}\right)$ **61.** 20

63. $\frac{19}{26} + \frac{17}{26}i$ **65.** $P(5) = 64$

67. $P(-1) = 20$

6-5

Check It Out!

1a. $x = 0, -1, 6$ **b.** $x = -5, 2, 5$
2a. $x = 2$ with multiplicity 4
b. $x = 0$ with multiplicity 3; $x = -1$ with multiplicity 1; $x = 6$ with multiplicity 2 **3.** 2 ft
4. $x = -\frac{1}{2}, 1 \pm \sqrt{5}$

Exercises

3. $x = 6, -6, 1, -1$
5. $x = 0, \frac{1}{3}, -4$
7. $x = -5, -2, 2, 5$
9. $x = -2$, 2 with multiplicity 3
11. $x = -6, \pm\sqrt{5}$ **13.** $x = -5, 1, 4$
15. $x = -3, 3$ **17.** $x = -8, 0, 8$
19. $x = \frac{5}{2}, \pm\sqrt{2}$ **21.** $x = 0$ with multiplicity 2; $x = 8$ with multiplicity 3 **23.** 3 in. by 3 in.
25. $x = -\frac{4}{3}, \pm\sqrt{2}$ **27a.** $\pm1, \pm2, \pm4$
b. $x = -2, 2$ **c.** 2 **d.** $x = -2.62, -0.38$ **29.** $x = 3, 2 \pm \sqrt{2}$
31. $x = -5, -2, 3, 5$
33. $x = -1, 0, 1, 2 \pm \sqrt{5}$ **35a.** 126 ft
b. The coaster passes through 2 tunnels within the first 100 s.
c. Possible answer: $h(t) = 3(t - 3)(t - 5)$ **41.** F **43.** H
45. $k = -18$ **47.** $k = 6$
49. $x < -3$ or $x > 2$ **51.** $-1 < x < 1$
53. $4(2x + 1)(x + 1)(x - 1)$

6-6

Check It Out!

1a. $P(x) = x^3 - 4x^2 - 4x + 16$
1b. $x^3 - \frac{11}{3}x^2 + 2x$
2. $x = -5, 1, 2i, -2i$
3. $P(x) = x^5 - 5x^4 + 9x^3 - 17x^2 + 20x + 12$ **4.** $r = 9$ ft

Exercises

1. $P(x) = x^3 - \frac{10}{3}x^2 + 3x - \frac{2}{3}$
3. $P(x) = x^3 - \frac{1}{2}x^2 - 4x + 2$
5. $x = 2, \frac{2 \pm \sqrt{2}i}{3}$
7. $P(x) = x^3 - 4x^2 + 6x - 4$
9. $P(x) = x^5 - 2x^4 + 2x^3 - 4x^2 - 8x + 16$
11. $P(x) = x^3 - 3x - 2$
13. $P(x) = x^3 + 3x^2 - 6x - 8$
15. $x = 1, 3$ **17.** $x = \frac{3}{2}, 2i, -2i$
19. $x = 1, -1, \pm\sqrt{3}$
21. $P(x) = x^5 + 3x^4 - 13x^3 - 39x^2 + 40x + 120$ **23.** $r = 9$ ft
25. $x = 2, -4, -1$
27. $x = -1$ **29.** $x = 3, \frac{-1 \pm i\sqrt{3}}{2}$
31. $x = 0, 7, 3 \pm 2i$
33. $x = \pm3i, \pm i\sqrt{5}$ **35.** $x = -1, 2, 3$
37a. $x^3 - 6x^2 - 243 = 0$ **b.** 9 m
c. They are complex.
39. $P(x) = x^4 + 12x^2 - 64$
41. $P(x) = x^3 - 4x^2 + 5x - 2$
43. $P(x) = x^4 - 6x^3 + 18x^2 - 54x + 81$
45. never true **47.** Sometimes true
49. $x = 0$ or $x \approx \pm0.537$
51. $x \approx -0.782, 0.975, 3.965$
53. $r = 6$ **57.** B **59.** D **61.** D
63. $f(3i) = 0; f(-\sqrt{3}) = -36 - 12\sqrt{3}$ **65.** $x = \pm3i$
67. $(a + bi)(a - bi)$
69. $(a + bi)(a - bi)(a^4 - 2a^2b^2 + b^4)$
71. $x^4 + 2x^2 + 1 = 0; \pm i$
73. shift right 2 units, reflection across x-axis, and shift up 3 units
75. $(9, -3)$ **77.** $x = 0, 42, 1$
79. $x = 0, -8, 2$

6-7

Check It Out!

1a. 2; 5; as $x \to -\infty$, $P(x) \to -\infty$, as $x \to +\infty$, $P(x) \to \infty$ **b.** -3; 2; as $x \to -\infty$, $P(x) \to -\infty$ as $x \to +\infty$, $P(x) \to -\infty$
2a. odd; negative **b.** even; positive
3a.

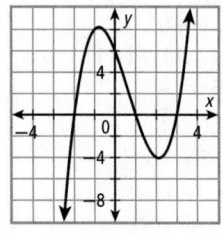

b.

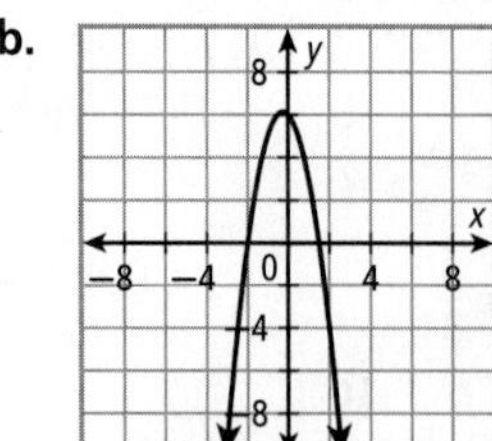

4a.

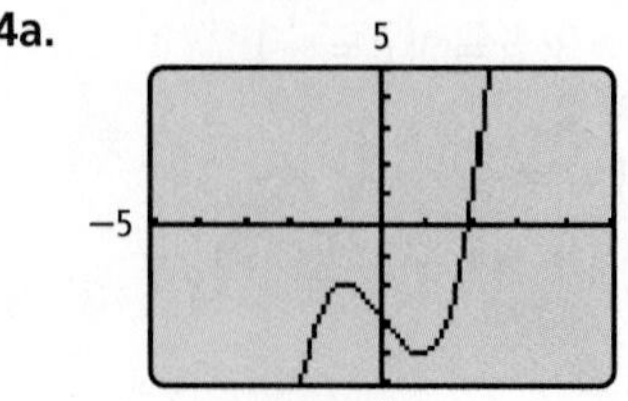

min $= -4.0887$; max $= -1.9113$
b.

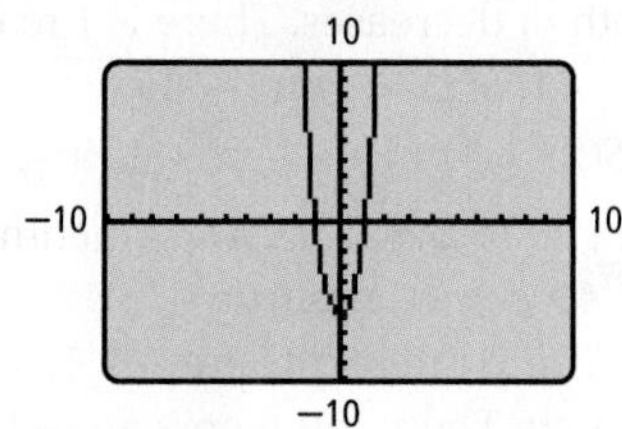

min $= 6$
5. 420.1 ft^3

Exercises

1. A graph "turns around" at a turning point.
3. -2; 7; $x \to -\infty$ $Q \to +\infty$, $x \to +\infty$ $Q \to -\infty$ **5.** 3; 2; $x \to \infty$ $S \to +\infty$, $x \to +\infty$ $S \to +\infty$ **7.** even; positive
9. even; negative
11.

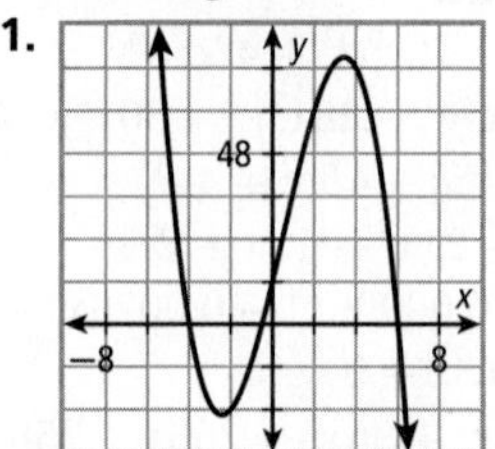

13. max $= -2.9098$; min $= -14.0902$
15. 2; 3; $x \to -\infty$ $P \to -\infty$, $x \to +\infty$ $P \to +\infty$
17. -1; 5; $x \to -\infty$ $R \to \infty$ $x \to +\infty$ $R \to +\infty$
19. even; negative **21.** odd; negative
23.

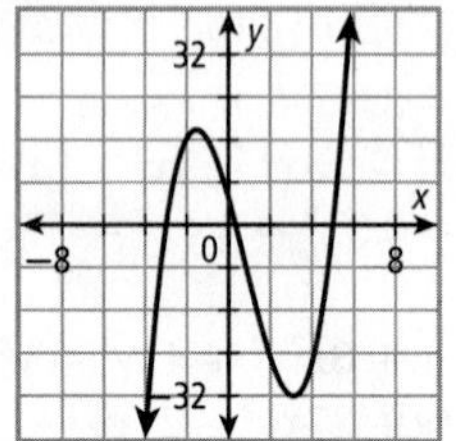

25.

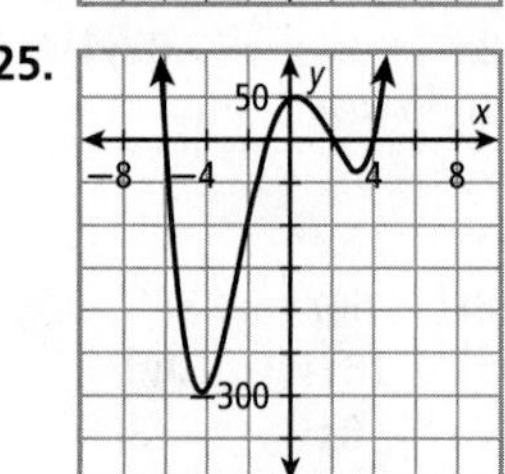

27. min $= 20$ **29.** max $= -1$
31. 3.425 L; 0.5 s **33.** B **35.** A
37. $+\infty$; $+\infty$ **39.** $+\infty$; $+\infty$
41. $-\infty$; $-\infty$
45a. $V(x) = -\frac{1}{3}x^3 + \frac{10}{3}x^2$
b. ≈ 49.4 in^3 **c.** approximately 6.7 in. × 3.3 in. × 6.7 in.
49. H
57. no **59.** $h(t) = -16(t - 2)^2 + 70$; vertex $(2, 70)$ **61.** $10x - 2 + \frac{8}{x + 1}$

6-8

Check It Out!

1a. $g(x) = x^3 - 1$

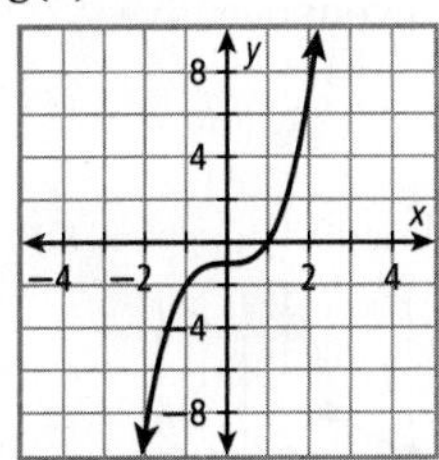

b. $g(x) = x^3 + 6x^2 + 12x + 12$

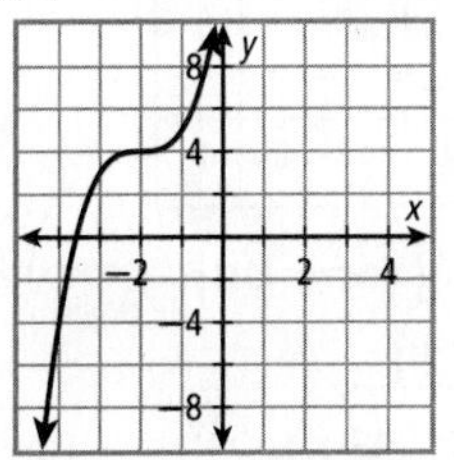

2a. $g(x) = -x^3 + 2x^2 + x - 2$ **b.** $g(x) = -x^3 - 2x^2 + x + 2$ **3a.** vertical compression

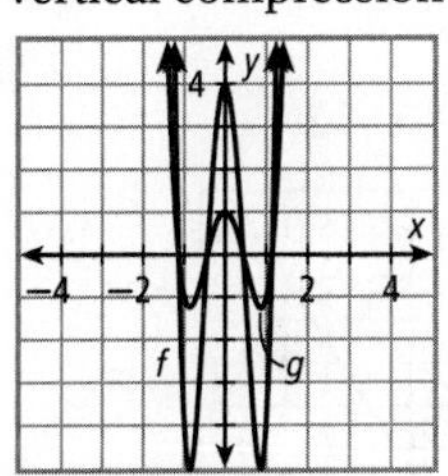

b. horizontal stretch

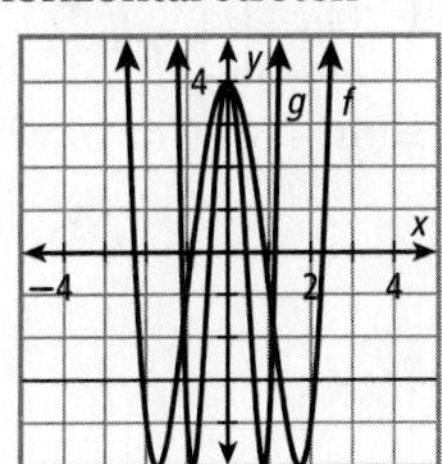

4a. $g(x) = 4(x - 3)^3 - 1 = 4x^3 - 3x^2 + 108x - 109$

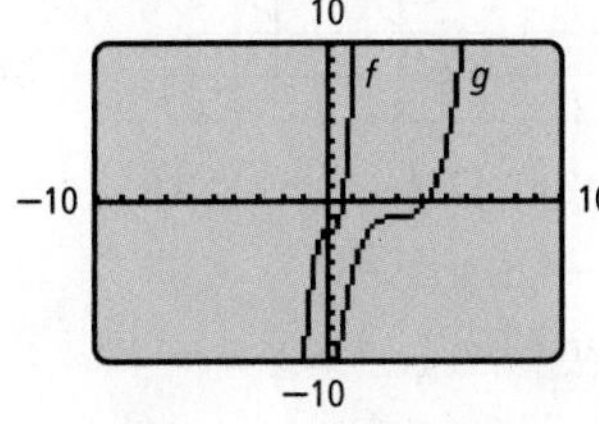

b. $g(x) = -8(x + 3)^3 + 2 = -8x^3 - 96x^2 - 384x - 510$

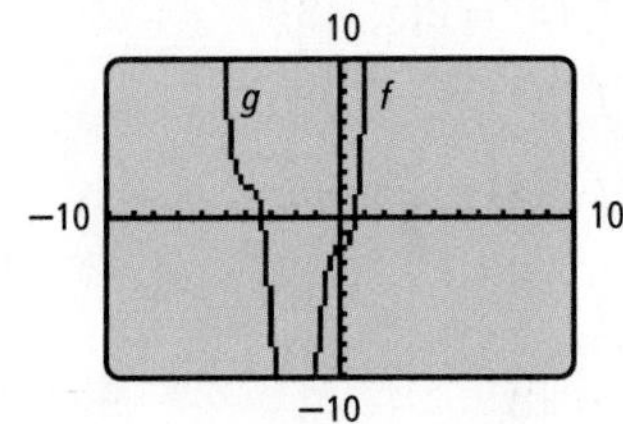

5. $g(x) = 0.01x^3 + 0.55x^2 - 5.85x + 134.25$
Possible answer: The model represents the number of sales since March.

Exercises

1. $g(x) = x^4 - 4$ **3.** $j(x) = 81x^4 - 8$ **5.** $g(x) = x^3 + 3x^2 + 2x + 1$ **7.** horizontal stretch **9.** horizontal compression and vertical shift **11.** $g(x) = -32x^3 + 2$ **13.** $c(x) = 4x^3 - 6x + 60$; the cost has doubled. **15.** $h(x) = x^3 - 9x^2 + 27x - 31$ **17.** $g(x) = -x^3 + 2x^2 - 5x + 3$ **19.** vertical stretch **21.** horizontal stretch **23.** $g(x) = \frac{1}{3}x^4 - 1$ **25.** $V\left(\frac{2}{3}x\right) = \frac{8}{27}x^3 + \frac{4}{3}x^2 + \frac{2}{3}x + 8$ **27a.** $v > 2.04$ **b.** $G(v) = 0.24v^2 + 2.4v + 6$; a shift 5 units left **c.** $v \geq 0$ **d.** a vertical stretch **31.** B **33.** B **35.** shift right 2 units **37.** shift right 3 units and up 8 units **39.** $w(t) = 60t$; yes **41.** $3x^5 - 3x^4 + 5x^2 - 4x$ **43.** $x = -2, 1, \pm i\sqrt{5}$ **45.** $x = -4, -1, 2, \pm 2i\sqrt{2}$

6-9

Check It Out!

1. cubic **2.** $f(x) = 0.001x^3 - 0.113x^2 + 4.134x - 24.867$ **3.** $\approx \$11,482.84$

Exercises **1.** linear **3.** quartic **5.** 831 patients **7.** quartic **9.** $f(x) = 0.821x^2 - 1.821x + 23.357$ **13a.** $f(x) = 0.019x^3 - 0.185x^2 + 0.95x + 12.056$; $R^2 = 0.9944$ **b.** $f(x) = 0.0075x^4 - 0.071x^3 + 0.143x^2 + 0.604x + 12.083$; $R^2 = 0.9967$ **c.** no **15.** yes **17.** C **19.** $f(x) = x^3 - 5x + 4$ **25.** $4a - 25a^3$ **27.** cubic parent function; shift right 1 unit and up 2 units. **29.** 4; 5; $x \to -\infty$, $f(x) \to -\infty$; $x \to +\infty$, $f(x) \to +\infty$

Study Guide: Review

1. monomial **2.** synthetic division **3.** multiplicity **4.** end behavior **5.** $-3x^3 + 4x^2 + 6x + 7$; -3; 3; 4: cubic polynomial with 4 terms **6.** $-x^5 + 2x^4 + 5x^3 + 8x$; -1; 5; 4: quintic polynomial with 4 terms **7.** $9x^2 - 11x + 1$; 9; 2; 3: quadratic trinomial **8.** $x^4 - 6x^2$; 1; 4; 2: quartic binomial **9.** $8x^3 + x^2 - 4x$ **10.** $-5x^3 + 6x^2 + 10x - 1$ **11.** $-6x^2 - x + 9$ **12.** $-4x^4 - x^3 - 3$ **13.** From left to right, it alternately increases and decreases, changing direction 3 times and crossing the x-axis 2 times. There appear to be 2 real zeros. **14.** From left to right, it increases, decreases slightly, and then increases again. It crosses the x-axis 1 time. There appears to be 1 real zero. **15.** From left to right, it alternately decreases and increases, changing direction 3 times. It crosses the x-axis 4 times. There appear to be 4 real zeros. **16.** From left to right, it increases, decreases, and then increases again. It crosses the x-axis 3 times. There appear to be 3 real zeros. **17.** $15x^3 - 10x^2$ **18.** $-6t^3 + 18t^2 - 3t$ **19.** $a^3b^2 - a^2b^2 + a^2b^3$ **20.** $x^3 - 4x^2 + x + 6$ **21.** $2x^4 + 3x^3 - 5x^2 + 2x + 5$ **22.** $x^3 - 9x^2 + 27x - 27$ **23.** $x^5 + 4x^4 - 3x^3 - 11x^2 + 4x$ **24.** $16x^4 + 32x^3 + 24x^2 + 8x + 1$ **25.** $4\pi x^4 - 4\pi x^3 - 12\pi x^2$ **26.** $x^2 - 7x + 16 - \frac{39}{x + 2}$ **27.** $4x^3 + 2x^2 + 4x + 1 + \frac{5}{2x - 1}$ **28.** $x^2 - x + \frac{2}{x - 3}$ **29.** $x^2 + 2x + 6 + \frac{11}{x - 2}$ **30.** $x^2 + 2x + 2$ in.; remainder 2 in. **31.** no **32.** yes **33.** yes **34.** $(x - 1)(x - 4)(x + 4)$ **35.** $(x - 2)(2x - 1)(2x + 1)$ **36.** $3(x + 3)(x^2 - 3x + 9)$ **37.** $2(2x - 1)(4x^2 + 2x + 1)$ **38.** 1, 2 **39.** $-2, -2 \pm \sqrt{3}$ **40.** -1 **41.** $-3, 3, \pm\sqrt{3}$ **42.** $-1, \pm\sqrt{2}$ **43.** $1, 2 \pm 2\sqrt{2}$ **44.** 2 m **45.** $P(x) = x^3 - 3x^2 - 10x + 24$ **46.** $P(x) = x^3 - \frac{1}{2}x^2 - \frac{13}{2}x - 3$ **47.** $P(x) = x^3 + x^2 - 2x - 2$ **48.** $P(x) = x^3 + 3x^2 + x + 3$ **49.** $P(x) = x^4 - 5x^2 + 6$ **50.** $P(x) = x^4 - 2x^3 + 2x^2 - 8x - 8$ **51.** $1, -2i, 2i$ **52.** $-i, i, -\sqrt{2}, \sqrt{2}$ **53.** $\pm 4, \pm\frac{1}{2}i$ **54.** $\pm\sqrt{5}, -3$ **55.** -2; 3; as $x \to -\infty$, $f(x) \to +\infty$; as $x \to +\infty$, $f(x) \to -\infty$

Selected Answers

56. 1; 4; as $x \to \pm\infty, f(x) \to +\infty$
57. -3; 6; as $x \to \pm\infty, f(x) \to -\infty$
58. 7; 5; as $x \to -\infty, f(x) \to -\infty$, as $x \to +\infty, f(x) \to +\infty$

59.

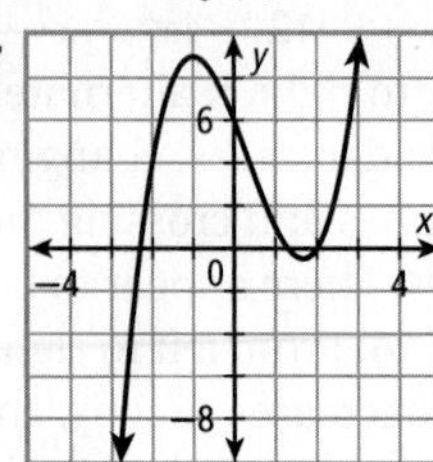

60.

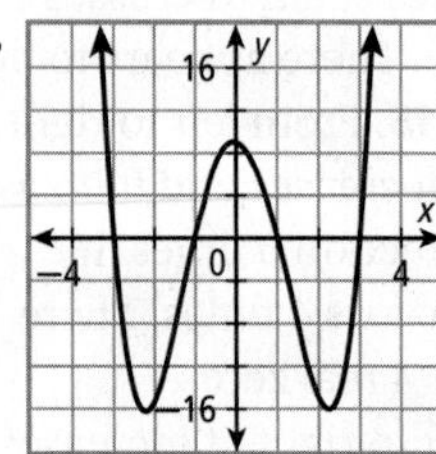

61.

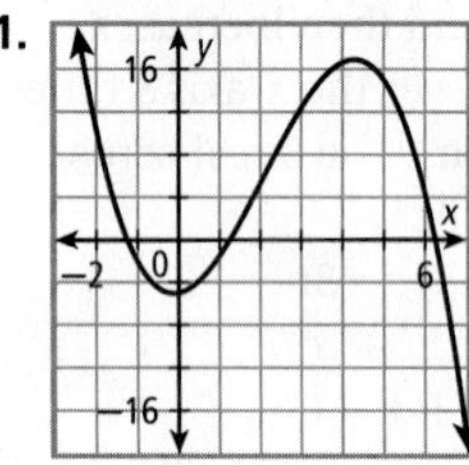

62. $g(x) = 2x^4 - 12x^2 + 1$
63. $g(x) = -x^4 + 6x^2 + 6$
64. $g(x) = (-x - 3)^4 + 6(-x - 3)^2 - 4$
65. $f(x) \approx -6\frac{2}{3}x^4 + 80x^3 - 328\frac{1}{3}x^2 + 575x - 72$
66. $f(x) \approx 80.5x^3 - 523.5x^2 + 1790x + 544$

Chapter 7

7-1

Check It Out!

1. growth

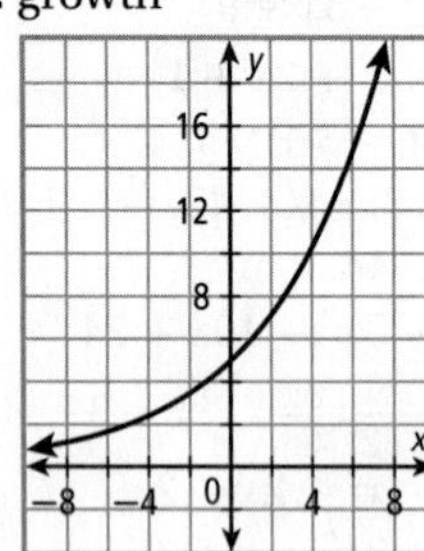

2. $P(t) = 350(1.14)^t$

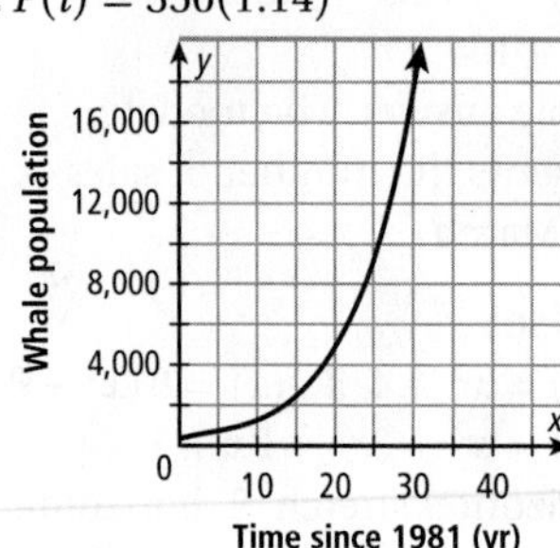

30.9 yr

3. $v(t) = 1000(0.85)^t$

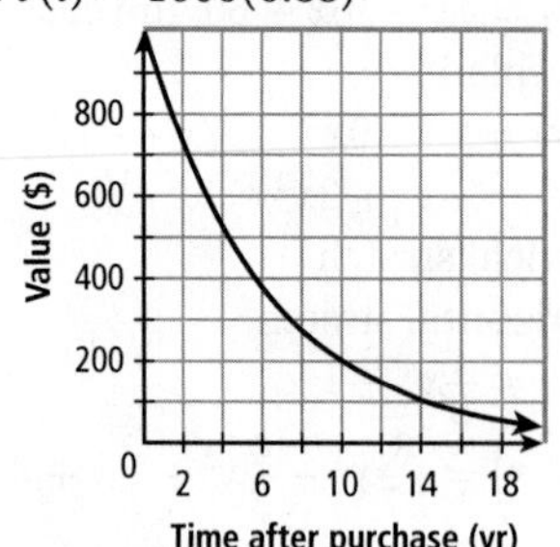

14.2 yr

Exercises **1.** exponential decay. **3.** growth

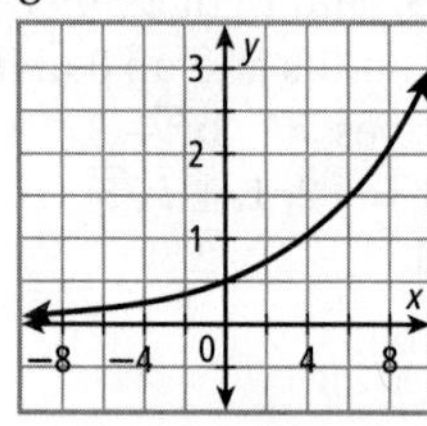

5a. $f(x) = 150(2^x)$
b.

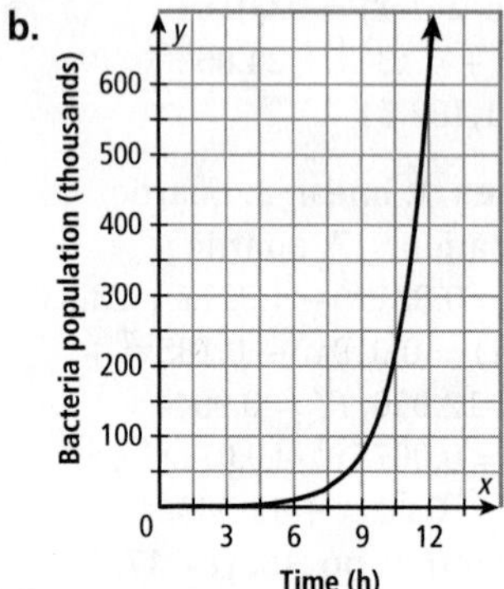

c. $\approx 600{,}000$
7. decay **9.** growth
11a. $f(x) = 10(0.95)^x$ **c.** ≈ 6 units
d. 13.6 min. **13.** no
15. $\approx \$12{,}000{,}000$ **17.** ≈ 5.8 yr
19. 15.63; 6.25; ...; 0.03; 0.01
21a. ≈ 3146 **b.** 12th month
25. (34.868, 100] **27a.** 17%
b. $A(t) = 500(0.83)^t$ **c.** ≈ 36.8 mg
29. 3^x **31.** B **37.** $x > 22.76$
39. 2; (2, 4), $(\approx -0.767, \approx 0.588)$

43. D: $\mathbb{R}$; R: $\{y \mid y \le 1\}$; $f(x) = x^2$ reflected across x-axis and shifted 1 unit up **47.** odd; positive **49.** even; negative

7-2

Check It Out!

1.

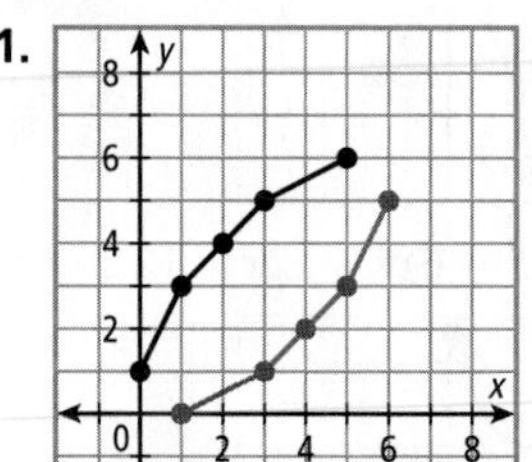

relation: D: $\{1 \le x \le 6\}$; R: $\{0 \le y \le 5\}$
inverse: D: $\{0 \le y \le 5\}$; R: $\{1 \le x \le 6\}$
2a. $f^{-1}(x) = 3x$ **b.** $f^{-1}(x) = x - \frac{2}{3}$
3. $f^{-1}(x) = \frac{x + 7}{5}$
4. $f^{-1}(x) = \frac{3}{2}x - 3$

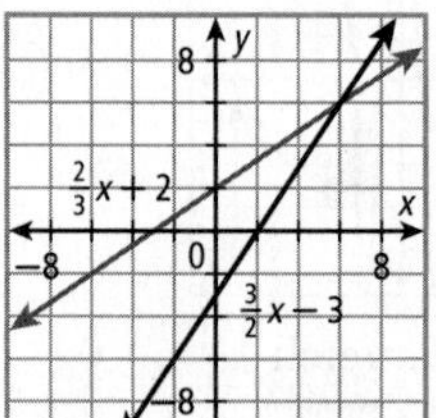

5. inverse: $z = 6t - 6$; 36 oz of water

Exercises

1. relation
3.

relation: D: $\{-1 \le x \le 4\}$; R: $\{-4 \le y \le -1\}$
inverse: D: $\{-4 \le y \le -1\}$; R: $\{-1 \le x \le 4\}$
5. $f^{-1}(x) = \frac{1}{4}x$ **7.** $f^{-1}(x) = x + 2\frac{1}{2}$
9. $f^{-1}(x) = 2(x - 3)$
11. $f^{-1}(x) = -\frac{2}{3}x + 1$
13. $f^{-1}(x) = \frac{2}{3}x + \frac{5}{3}$

15. 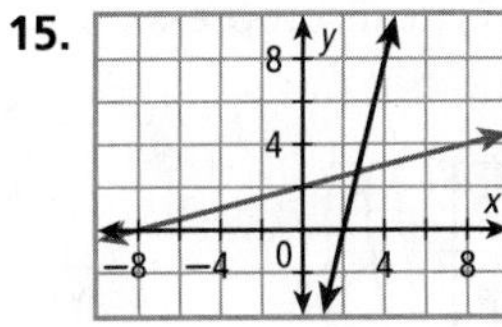

$f^{-1}(x) = 4(x - 2)$

17. $F = \frac{9}{5}C + 32$; 61° F

19.  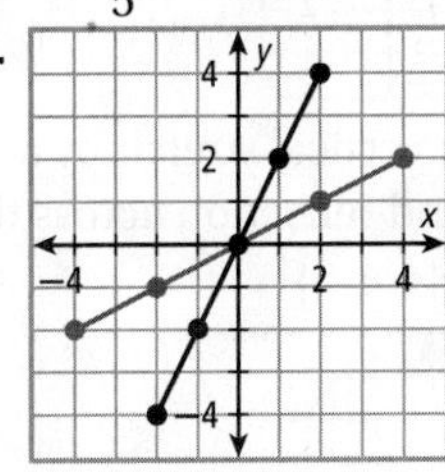

relation: D: $\{-4 \le x \le 4\}$;
R: $\{-2 \le y \le 2\}$
inverse: D: $\{-2 \le y \le 2\}$;
R: $\{-4 \le x \le 4\}$

21. $f^{-1}(x) = x + 1\frac{3}{4}$

23. $f^{-1}(x) = -\frac{1}{32}x + \frac{21}{32}$

25. $f^{-1}(x) = 5x - 60$

27. $f^{-1}(x) = -3x + 6$

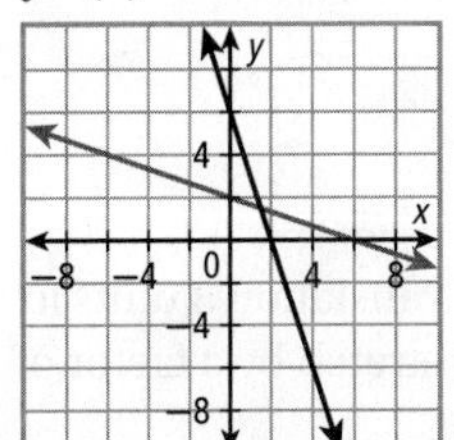

29. 22 **31a.** $f^{-1}(x) = \frac{212 - x}{1.85}$
b. 6500 ft **c.** 27,946 ft

33. $(4, 2), (2, 4), (-3, -1), (-1, -3)$

35. $f(x) = \frac{10}{12.59}x$; $f^{-1}(x) = 1.259x$; 31.48 s **37.** B **39.** yes **41.** always **43.** never **45.** always

47a. $P = \frac{147}{340}d + 14.7$
b. D: $\{d \mid d \ge 0\}$; R: $\{P \mid P \ge 14.7\}$
c. $d = \frac{340}{147}P - 34$; depth as a function of pressure **49.** F

51.

x	1	2	3	4	5
y	0	1	2	3	4

53. $y = -\frac{b}{a}x + \frac{c}{a}$

61. $2x^3 - 14x + 12 = 0$

63. $2x^3 - 8x^2 + 12x - 8 = 0$

65. decay **67.** growth

7-3

Check It Out! 1a. $\log_9 81 = 2$
b. $\log_3 27 = 3$ **c.** $\log_x 1 = 0$
2a. $10^1 = 10$ **b.** $12^2 = 144$
c. $\left(\frac{1}{2}\right)^{-3} = 8$ **3a.** -5 **b.** -1

4. 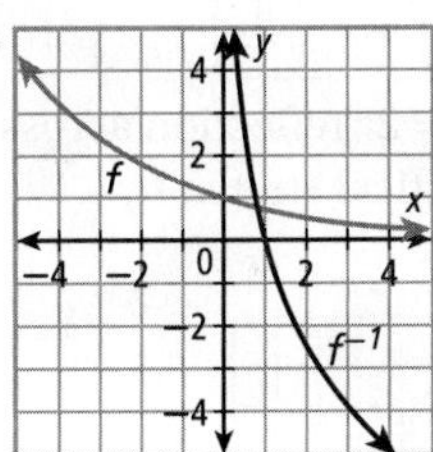

$f(x)$: D: $\mathbb{R}$; R: $\{y \mid y > 0\}$; $f^{-1}(x)$: D: $\{x \mid x > 0\}$; R: $\mathbb{R}$ **5.** about 3.8

Exercises

1. x **3.** $\log_4 8 = 1.5$ **5.** $\log_3 243 = x$
7. $x^3 = -16$ **9.** $6^3 = x$ **11.** -2 **13.** 2
15. $f(x)$: D: $\mathbb{R}$, R: $\{y \mid y > 0\}$; $f^{-1}(x)$: D: $\{x \mid x > 0\}$; R: $\mathbb{R}$
17. $\log_x 32 = 2.5$ **19.** $\log_{1.2} 1 = 0$
21. $5^4 = 625$ **23.** $4.5^0 = 1$ **25.** 0 **27.** 3
29. $f(x)$: D: $\mathbb{R}$, R: $\{y \mid y > 0\}$; $f^{-1}(x)$: D: $\{x \mid x > 0\}$; R: $\mathbb{R}$ **31.** no **33.** 1
35. yes **37a.** orange **b.** lemon
c. grapefruit **39.** C **41.** A **43.** 6
47a. $2^{11} = 2048$ Hz, $\log_2 2048 = 11$
b. 3 octaves lower **49.** $\frac{2s}{t^2}$
51. $21a^{-1}b^4 + 28a^{-3}b^5$
53. 0.35; 0.59; 1; 1.7; 2.89
55. 11.11; 3.33; 1; 0.3; 0.09

7-4

Check It Out!
1a. $\log_5 (625 \bullet 25) = 6$
b. $\log_{\frac{1}{3}} 3 = -1$ **2.** $\log_7 7 = 1$
3a. $4 \log 10 = 4$ **b.** $4 \log_5 5 = 4$
c. $-5 \log_2 2 = -5$ **4a.** 0.9 **b.** $8x$
5a. 1.5 **b.** $1.\overline{3}$ **6.** ≈ 63

Exercises

1. $\log_5 3125 = 5$ **3.** $\log_3 81 = 4$
5. $\log 100 = 2$ **7.** 2 **9.** 6 **11.** $\frac{x}{2} + 5$
13. 5 **15.** -1.5 **17.** ≈ 1.43
19. 2 times as large **21.** $\log 10 = 1$
23. $\log 10 = 1$ **25.** $\log_{1.5} 3.375 = 3$
27. 0.2 **29.** $7 + x$ **31.** 4 **33.** 1.5
35. ≈ 3.16 times as intense
37. $\log_b m + \log_b n = \log_b mn$
39. $n\log_b b^m = mn$
41. 0 **43.** $-\frac{3}{2}$ **45.** 1
47. $10^{-7} - 10^{-7.6}$
49. $t = \log_{1.08}\left(\frac{50}{40}\right)$; 2.9
55a. ≈ 0.2 **b.** ≈ 2.6 **c.** ≈ 2.4
57. sometimes **59.** always
61. always **63.** sometimes **65.** B
67. H **71.** $\{x \mid x > 1\}$ **73.** $\{x \mid x > 0\}$
75. $\{x \mid -1 \le x < 0\}$ **77.** x **79.** $\varnothing$
81. 17 **83.** 7 **85.** $12i$ **87.** $8i\sqrt{2}$
89. $\log_5 125 = 3$ **91.** $\log_{36} 6 = 0.5$
93. 0 **95.** 0.5

7-5

Check It Out!
1a. 1.5 **b.** ≈ -1.565 **c.** ≈ 1.302
2. day 18 **3a.** 5 **b.** 2 **4a.** $x = 2$
b. $x < 2$ **c.** $x = 1000$

Exercises

1. exponential equation **3.** $x = -2$
5. $x \approx 1.661$ **7.** $x \approx 0.503$ **9.** $x = \frac{1}{8}$
11. $x = 108$ **13.** $x = \frac{9}{13}$ **15.** $x = 2$
17. $x = 3.5$ **19.** $x = 100$ **21.** $x = -5$
23. $x = 0.8$ **25.** ≈ 7.595
27. ≈ 41 min **29.** $x = 30$ **31.** ≈ 2.73
33. $x = 20$ **35.** $x < 1$ **37.** $x = 4$
39. $x = 4$ **41.** 24 keys below concert A **43.** 0 **47a.** 11 km; 25 km **b.** greater **49.** J **51.** no
53. $\{x \mid 0 < x < 12\}$ **55.** 26 **57.** 3
59. $f^{-1}(x) = \frac{1}{4}x - \frac{3}{4}$
61. $f^{-1}(x) = 3x - 27$

7-6

Check It Out!
1. 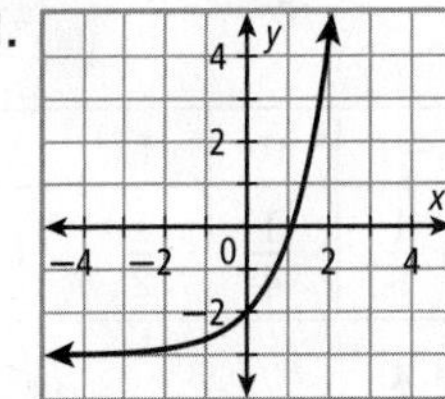

2a. 3.2 **b.** x^2 **c.** $x + 4y$
3. \$132.31 **4.** ≈ 47.6 days

Exercises

1. $f(x) = \ln x$; natural logarithm

3. 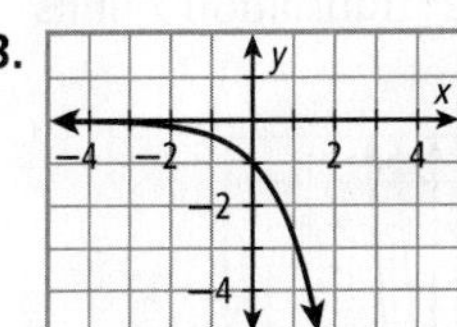

5. 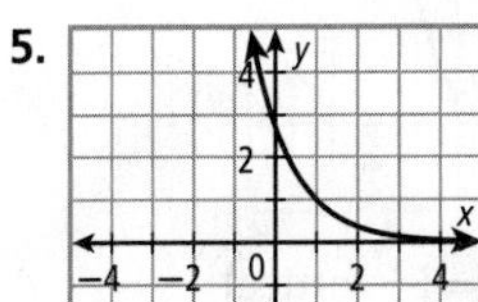

Selected Answers

7. $x - y$ **9.** $2x$ **11.** \$9465.87

13.

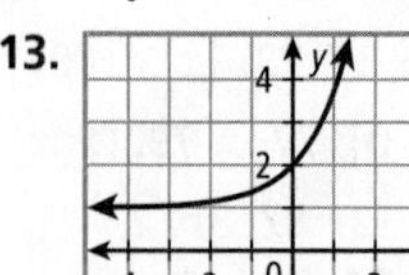

15.

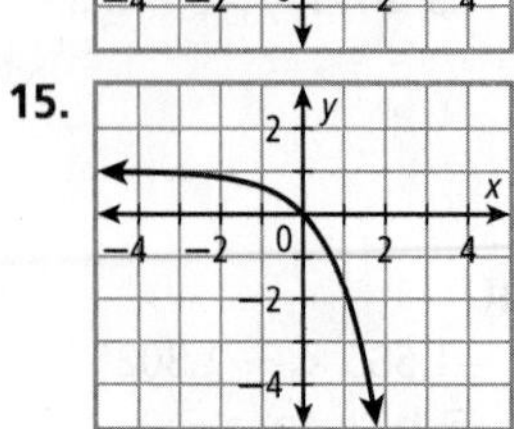

17. 0 **19.** $c + 2$ **21.** \$5553.55

23a. They are reciprocals.

25a. ≈ 2.4 min **b.** ≈ 2.8 min

c. room: ≈ 17.4 min

27. B **29.** C **31.** $x = \frac{e}{5} \approx 0.54$

33. $x = \frac{e^5}{\sqrt{10}} \approx 47$

35. $\{x \mid x > 0\}$ **37b.** 2

41. C **43.** A **45.** 4; yes

47a. $f(x) = \ln(-x)$ **b.** $f(x) = -\ln x$

c. $f(x) = -\ln(-x)$

d. one asymptote: $x = 0$

49. $g(x) = f(x) + 5 = -2x^2 + 3x + 1$

51. $g(x) = -f(x) = 2x^2 - 3x + 4$

53. $\log_2 4 = 2$

55. $\log_3\left(\frac{243}{2187}\right) = -2$

57. $\log_8 1 = 0$

7-7

Check It Out!

1.

x	−2	−1	0	1	2
$j(x)$	$\frac{1}{16}$	$\frac{1}{8}$	$\frac{1}{4}$	$\frac{1}{2}$	1

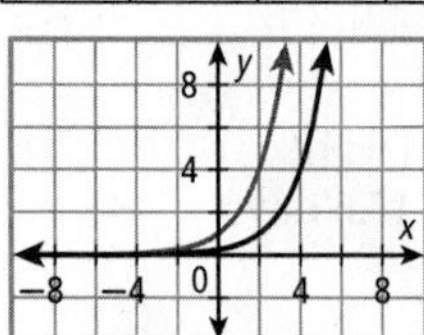

$y = 0$; $j(x) = 2^x$ translation 2 units right

2a.

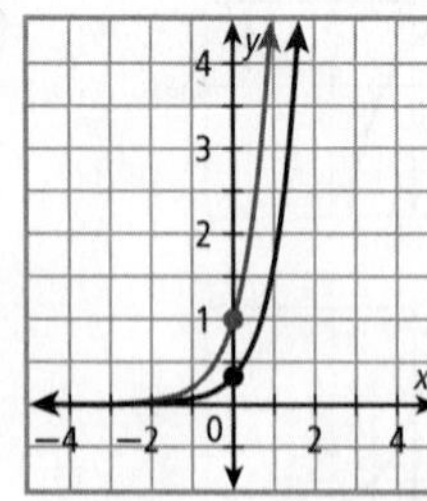

$\frac{1}{3}$; $y = 0$; $f(x) = 5^x$ vertical compression by a factor of 3

b.

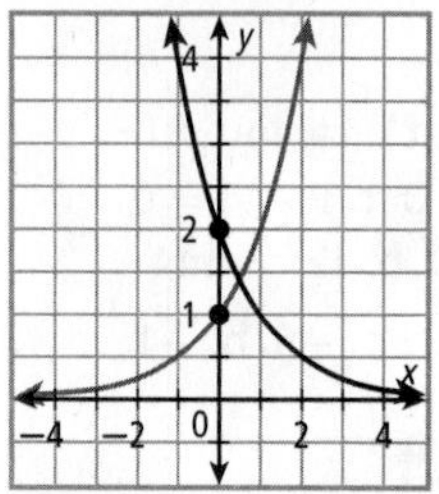

2; $y = 0$; $j(x) = 2^x$ reflection across y-axis and vertical stretch by a factor of 2

3.

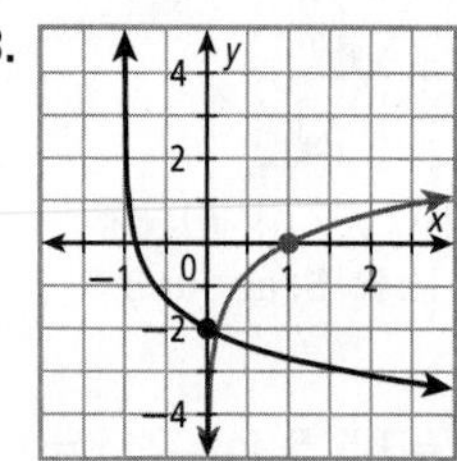

$x = -1$; translation of $f(x) = \ln x$ 1 unit left, reflection across the x-axis, and translation 2 units down; D: $\{x \mid x > -1\}$

4. $g(x) = 2\log(x + 3)$

5. $t = 38{,}679$ yr; no

Exercises

1.

x	−2	−1	0	1	2
$g(x)$	2.1	2.3	3	5	11

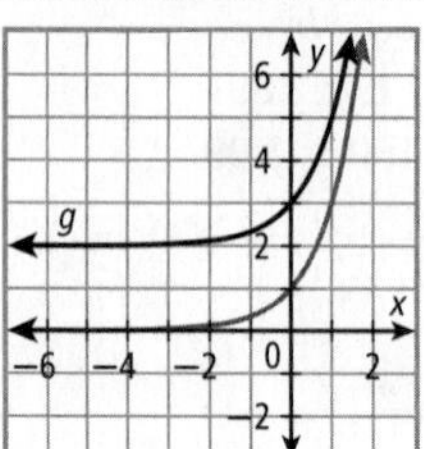

$y = 2$; translation 2 units up; R: $\{y \mid y > 2\}$

3.

x	−3	−2	−1	0	1
$j(x)$	0.11	0.33	1	3	9

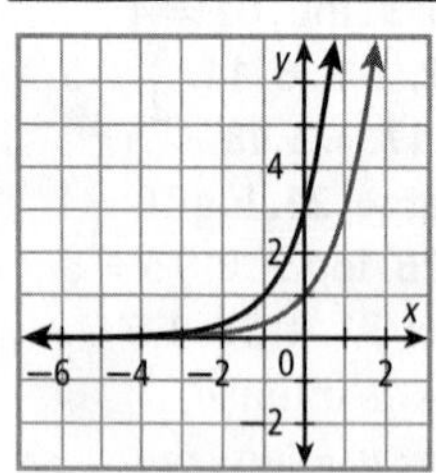

$y = 0$; translation 1 unit left

5. $\frac{1}{3}$; $y = 0$; vertical compression by a factor of $\frac{1}{3}$

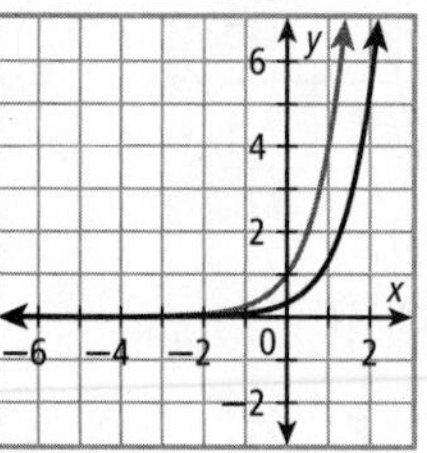

7. −2; $y = 0$; vertical stretch by a factor of 2 and reflection across the x-axis; R: $\{y \mid y < 0\}$

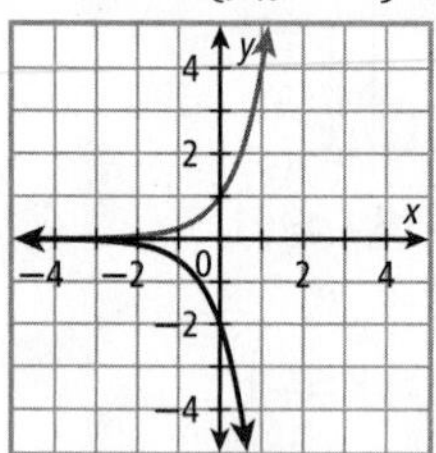

9. 1; $y = 0$; horizontal compression by a factor of $\frac{1}{2}$

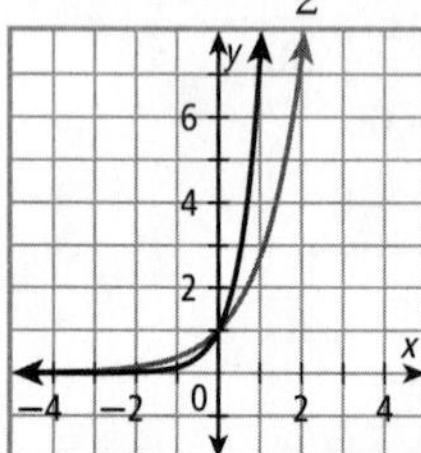

11. $x = -3$; translation 3 units left and vertical stretch by a factor of 2.5; D: $\{x \mid x > -3\}$

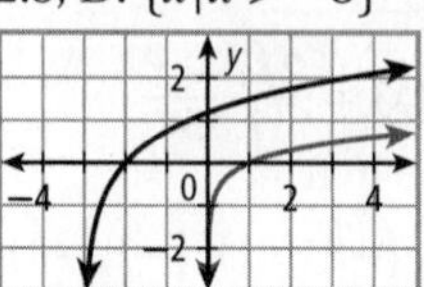

13. $g(x) = -0.7^{\left(\frac{x}{3} + 2\right)}$

15. translated 1 unit left, stretched vertically by a factor of 3, and translated 6 units up; D: $\{t \mid t \geq 0\}$; after about 39 years

17.

x	−2	−1	0	1	2
$h(x)$	1	5	25	125	625

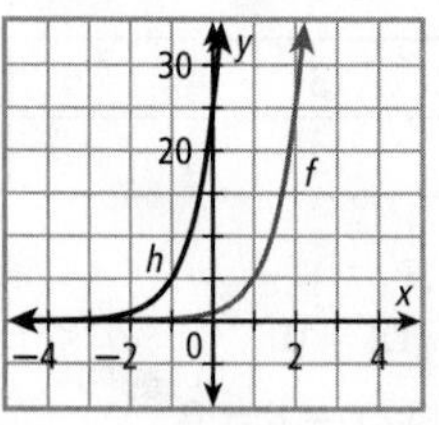

$y = 0$; translation 2 units left

19. 4; $y = 0$; vertical stretch by a factor of 4 **21.** −0.25; $y = 0$; vertical compression by a factor of 0.25 and reflection across the x-axis; R: $\{y|y < 0\}$ **23.** 4; $y = 0$; vertical stretch by a factor of 4 and reflection across the y-axis
25. $x = 5$; translation 5 units right; D: $\{x|x > 5\}$ **27.** $x = 0$; vertical stretch by a factor of 4 and reflection across the x-axis
29. $f(x) = \ln(4x + 3) - 0.5$
31. ≈ 47 yr **33.** A **35.** D **37.** F
39. D: $\{x \mid x \geq -3\}$; R: $\mathbb{R}$; x-intercept: −2; y-intercept: 2.39 **41.** always
43. sometimes **45.** C **47.** B
51a. $N(t) = 419(0.99)^t$
b. $N(t) = 419(0.99)^{\frac{m}{12}}$
c. 413 **53.** H **59.** min: $\left(-\frac{1}{8}, -\frac{81}{16}\right)$; D: $\mathbb{R}$; R: $\left\{y|y \geq -\frac{81}{16}\right\}$
61. $f(x) \approx 0.032x^3 - 0.0076x^2 + 0.073x + 1.30$ **63.** $-5x$ **63.** $\frac{x}{4}$

7-8

Check It Out!

1a. yes; 1.5 **b.** no
2. $B(t) \approx 199(1.25)^t$; ≈10.3 min
3. $S(t) \approx 0.59 + 2.64 \ln t$; ≈16.6 min

Exercises

1. exponential regression **3.** yes; $\frac{2}{3}$
5. yes; $\frac{4}{3}$ **7.** $P(t) \approx 621.6 + 1221 \ln t$; ≈ 421 mo **9.** no **11.** yes; $\frac{1}{2}$
13. $T(t) \approx 4.45(1.165)^t$; ≈ 2011
15. yes; $f(x) = 1.55(7.54)^x$
19. $s(t) = 68.24(3.69)^t$; ≈ 46.5 million **23a.** 20.5 mi/h; 36.8 mi/h; 84.0 mi/h **b.** $s = 100(0.8^t)$
25a. exponential **b.** linear **27.** F
29. $f(x) = 7.68(2.5)^x$ **33.** $x = -4$
35. $x = \pm\frac{9}{4}$ **37.** $x = -8, 0$
39. $x = -12, 3$ **41.** $x = \frac{4}{3}$ **43.** $x = 0$

Study Guide: Review

1. natural logarithmic function
2. asymptote
3. inverse relation
4. growth **5.** growth
6. decay **7.** growth
8. growth
9. $P(t) = 765(1.02)^t$

10.

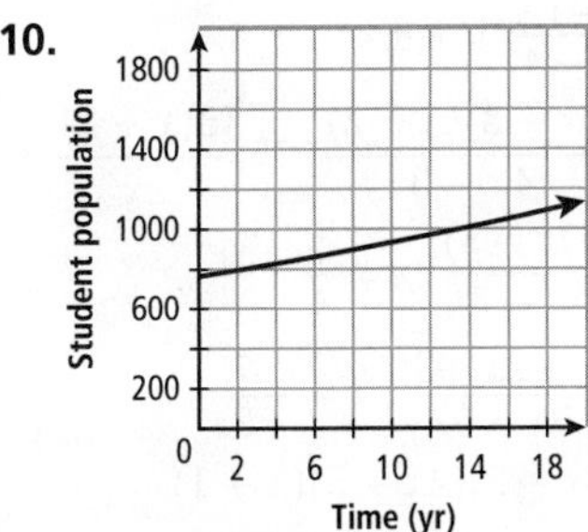

11. ≈ 845 **12.** ≈ 13.5 yr

13.

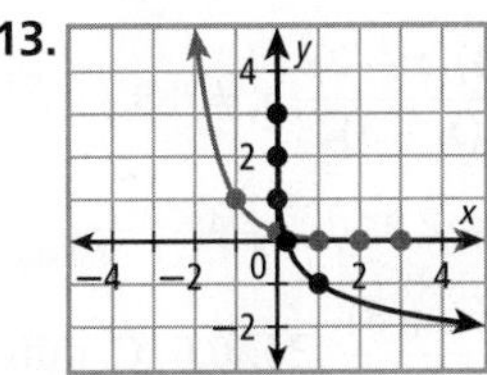

14. $P_T = P_L(1 - 0.03)$
15. $P_L = \frac{P_T}{0.97}$ **16.** $K = \frac{8}{5}M$; 40 km
17. $\log_3 243 = 5$ **18.** $\log_9 1 = 0$
19. $\log_{\frac{1}{3}} 27 = -3$ **20.** $2^4 = 16$
21. $10^1 = 10$ **22.** $0.6^2 = 0.36$
23. 2 **24.** 2 **25.** −1 **26.** −2 **27.** 0
28.

x	−2	−1	0	1	2
y	4	2	1	0.5	0.25

D: $\{x|x > 0\}$; R: $\mathbb{R}$
29. $\log_2 128 = 7$
30. $\log 1{,}000{,}000 = 6$
31. $\log_2 64 = 6$ **32.** $\log 100 = 2$
33. $\log_5 5^4 = 4$ **34.** $9 \log 10 = 9$
35. 10 times **36.** −1 **37.** $x \geq -6$
38. $x > 10$ **39.** 17.67 quarters, or 4.4 yr **40.** $k = 0.0346$
41. $g(x) = -3e^x - 2$ **42.** 0.6; $y = 0$; vertically compressed by a factor of $\frac{3}{5}$ and horizontally compressed by a factor of $\frac{1}{6}$ **43.** 0.5; $x = -0.5$; translated $\frac{1}{2}$ unit left and vertically stretched by a factor of 2
44. $V(t) = 5300(1 - 0.35)^t$
45. vertically stretched by a factor of 3500 **46.** $f(x) \approx 11.26(1.05)^x$
47. $f(x) \approx -97.8 + 56.4 \ln x$
48. The exponential function; $r^2 \approx 0.94$ versus $r^2 \approx 0.60$ for the logarithmic function

Chapter 8

8-1

Check It Out!

1. $y = 0.5x$

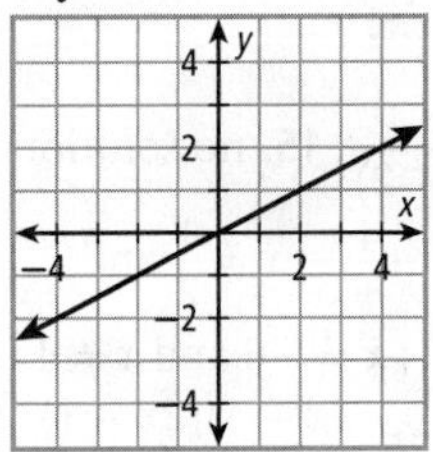

2. 6.25 in. **3.** 1.6 m
4. $y = \frac{40}{x}$

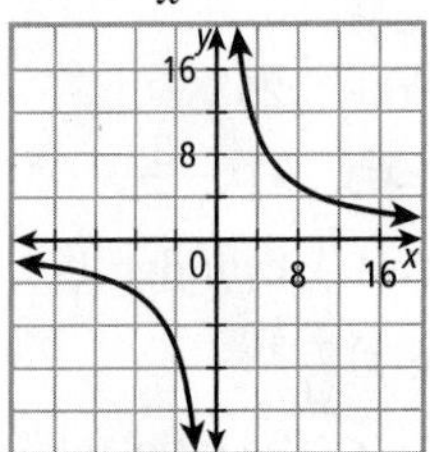

5. $83\frac{1}{3}$ working hours
6a. inverse **b.** direct **7.** 20 L

Exercises **1.** indirect variation
3. $y = -9x$ **5.** 12 ft **7.** 6 ft
9. $y = \frac{14}{x}$ **11.** $y = -\frac{5}{x}$ **13.** neither
15. direct **17.** $y = \frac{1}{2}x$ **19.** $y = -3x$
21. 88 Cal **23.** 0.2 kg **25.** $y = \frac{10.5}{x}$
27. 5 days **29.** neither
31. 1.375 atm **33.** sometimes
35. always **37a.** $s = \frac{6300}{t}$ **b.** 30 s
39a. $I = 0.02Pt$ **b.** True Federal Bank **c.** \$30 **41.** $x = 5$; $y = 4.4$; $z = 2$ **45.** D **47.** D **49.** 24 **51.** $y \approx 7$
53. $y = \frac{5}{4}x + \frac{1}{4}$ **55.** asymptote: $y = -2$; vertically compressed by a factor of $\frac{1}{2}$ and translated 2 units down

8-2

Check It Out!

1a. $2x^9$; $x \neq 0$ **b.** $\frac{1}{x-1}$; $x \neq -\frac{4}{3}$ and $x \neq 1$ **c.** $\frac{(2x+1)}{(2x-3)}$; $x \neq -\frac{2}{3}$ and $x \neq \frac{3}{2}$ **2a.** −2; $x \neq 5$ **b.** $\frac{-x}{2x-1}$; $x \neq 3$ and $x \neq \frac{1}{2}$ **3a.** $\frac{2x^3}{3}$ **b.** $\frac{2}{x-2}$
4a. $\frac{3y}{x^2}$ **b.** $\frac{4(x-4)}{x+3}$
5a. no solution **b.** $x = 4$

Exercises

3. $\frac{(2x+5)}{(2x-7)}$; $x \neq \frac{1}{3}$ and $x \neq \frac{7}{2}$
5. $\frac{-1}{x-5}$; $x \neq -4$ and $x \neq 5$
7. $6x$; defined for all real values of x
9. $\frac{2(x-2)}{(x+5)}$ **11.** $\frac{x^7y^4}{3}$
13. $\frac{(x+5)^2}{(2x-3)(x+2)}$ **15.** no solution
17. $x = -1$ **19.** $\frac{4}{x+5}$; $x \neq \frac{1}{2}$ and $x \neq -5$ **21.** $\frac{-3}{x-4}$; $x \neq -6$ and $x \neq 4$
23. -4; $x \neq -5$ **25.** $\frac{(x-4)(2x-1)}{(x-3)(x+4)}$
27. $\frac{3(2x-5)}{x}$ **29.** $\frac{x+1}{x-1}$ **31.** $\frac{x+3}{x+5}$
33. $x = 2$ **35.** $\frac{\pi r^2}{\pi (5r)^2}$; $\frac{1}{25}$
37. $\frac{4x-3}{2x-1}$ **39.** $2x^2y^2$ **41.** $\frac{3}{x+1}$
43a. square prism: $\frac{h}{1}$; cylinder: $\frac{h}{1}$
b. square prism: $\frac{2s+4h}{sh}$; cylinder: $\frac{2r+2h}{rh}$ **c.** The ratio would be reduced by a factor of $\frac{1}{2}$.
45. Student A **47.** D **49.** A
51. $\frac{2(x^2+5x+25)}{x^2-5x+25}$
53. $\frac{2(x+1)(x+2)}{x^2+1}$
55. $3x^3 + 8x^2 - 36x - 5$
57. $y \approx 56{,}800(1.39)^x$; about 800,000 births **59.** $y = -4x$

8-3

Check It Out!

1a. $\frac{9x+4}{x^2-3}$; $x \neq \pm\sqrt{3}$
b. $\frac{x^2+3x-3}{3x-1}$; $x \neq \frac{1}{3}$ **2a.** $12x^5y^7$
b. $(x+2)(x-2)(x+3)$
3a. $\frac{15x-4}{6(x-1)}$; $x \neq 1$ **b.** $\frac{x+2}{x+3}$; $x \neq -3$ **4a.** $\frac{15x^2-20x-6}{(2x+5)(5x-2)}$; $x \neq -\frac{5}{2}$ and $x \neq \frac{2}{5}$ **b.** $\frac{x+4}{x-8}$; $x \neq \pm 8$ **5a.** $\frac{1}{x}$ **b.** 10 **c.** $\frac{3(x-2)}{2x(x+4)}$
6. 42.4 mi/h

Exercises **3.** $\frac{-2x-7}{4x+5}$; $x \neq -\frac{5}{4}$
5. $16x^4y^3$ **7.** $\frac{2(4x^2+x-8)}{(x+6)(2x-1)}$; $x \neq -6$ and $x \neq \frac{1}{2}$
9. $\frac{2x^2-4x-1}{(x+3)(x-3)}$; $x \neq \pm 3$
11. $\frac{-1}{x-4}$; $x \neq \pm 4$
13. $\frac{(2x-3)(x+2)}{4x-3}$ **15.** $\frac{3(x+2)}{2x^2}$
17. $\frac{2(2x-3)}{4x-7}$; $x \neq \frac{7}{4}$
19. $\frac{x^2-2x+2}{2x+7}$; $x \neq -\frac{7}{2}$
21. $(4x-5)(4x+5)(x+1)$
23. $\frac{7(2x-3)}{3(x-2)}$; $x \neq 2$
25. $\frac{-(2x+3)(x-2)}{(x-3)(x+3)}$; $x \neq \pm 3$
27. $\frac{1}{x-2}$; $x \neq 2$ and $x \neq 4$
29. $\frac{(3x-2)(x+3)}{(5x+1)(x+2)}$ **31.** 0.6 °C/min
33. $\frac{x^2+6x-6}{(x+4)(x-3)}$; $x \neq -4$ and $x \neq 3$
35. $\frac{5x-9}{(x-5)(x+4)(x+3)}$; $x \neq -4$, $x \neq -3$, and $x \neq 5$
37. $\frac{2x^2-13x+9}{(x-1)(x-2)}$; $x \neq 1$ and $x \neq 2$
39. $\frac{2(4x^3-6x^2-3x-4)}{(3x+4)(2x-3)}$; $x \neq -\frac{4}{3}$ and $x \neq \frac{3}{2}$
41. $\frac{-9x^2-52x+7}{(x+7)(x+6)(x+1)}$; $x \neq -7$, $x \neq -6$, and $x \neq -1$ **43.** $\frac{24}{(x+2)^2}$
45. $\frac{7(x-3)}{6x(x-1)}$ **49.** D **51.** A
53. $\frac{-5x^2-15x+6}{(x+2)(x-2)}$
55. $\frac{-4}{(x+2)^2(x-2)}$
57. $6x^2 + 4x + 20$ **59.** $\frac{8}{5}$
61. The asymptote is $x = -4$. The transformation is a translation 4 units left.

8-4

Check It Out!

1a. g is f translated 4 units left.

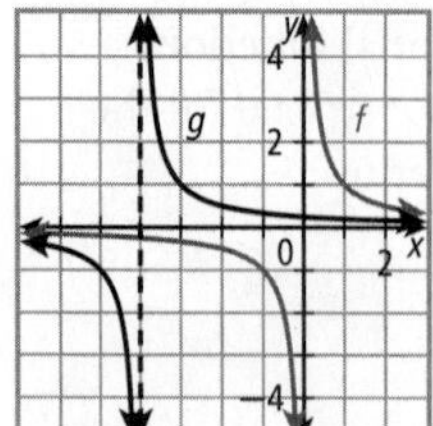

b. g is f translated 1 unit up.

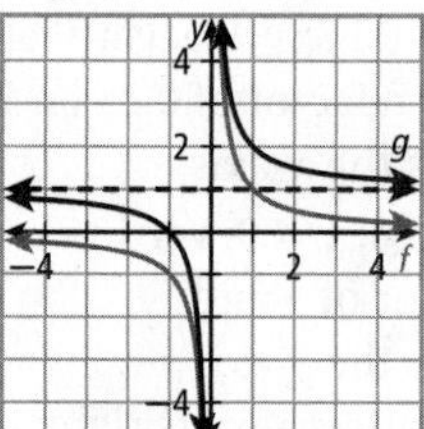

2. asymptotes: $x = 3$, $y = -5$; D: $\{x \mid x \neq 3\}$; R: $\{y \mid y \neq -5\}$
3. zeros: $-6, -1$; asymptote: $x = -3$

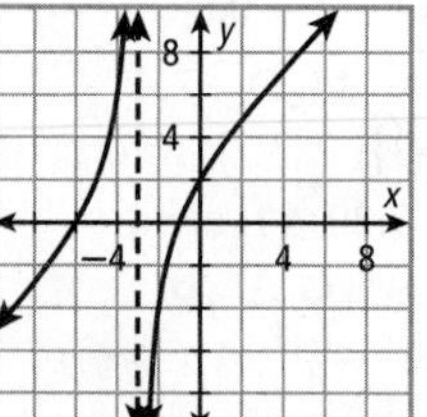

4a. zeros: $-5, 3$; asymptote: $x = 1$

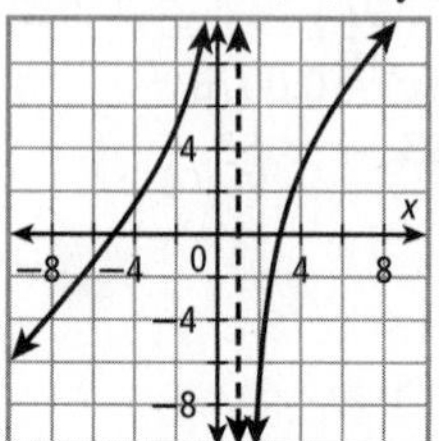

b. zero: 2; asymptotes: $x = -1$, $x = 0$, $y = 0$

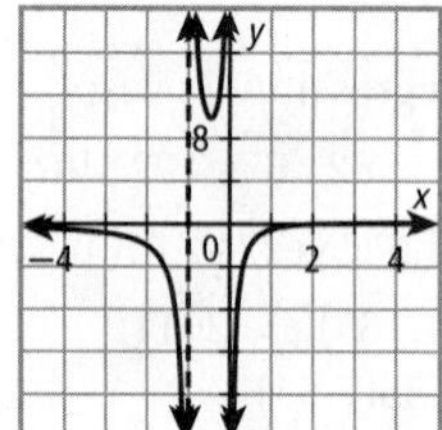

c. zeros: $-\frac{1}{3}, 0$; asymptotes: $x = -3$, $x = 3$, $y = 3$

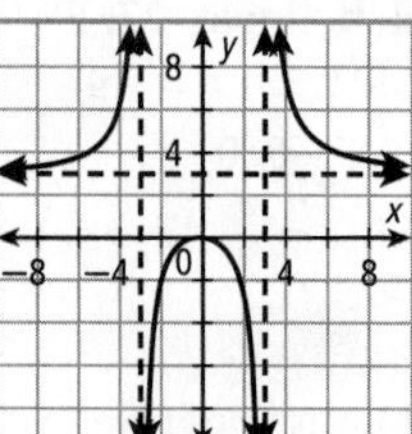

5. hole at $x = 2$

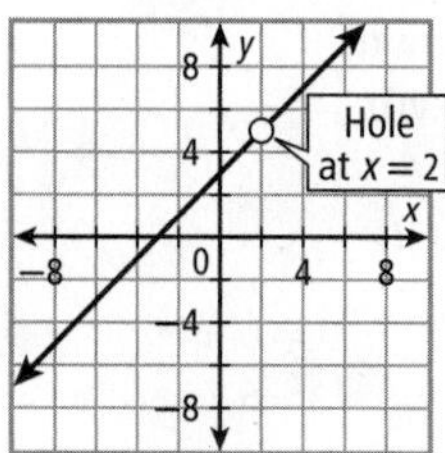

Exercises **1.** discontinuous **3.** g is f translated 5 units left. **5.** asymptotes: $x = 0$, $y = -1$; D: $\{x \mid x \neq 0\}$; R: $\{y \mid y \neq -1\}$ **7.** asymptotes: $x = 2$, $y = -8$; D: $\{x \mid x \neq 2\}$; R: $\{y \mid y \neq -8\}$ **9.** zeros: 0, 5; vertical asymptote: $x = 2$ **11.** zeros: $-2, -1$; asymptote: $x = 3$ **13.** zero: $-\frac{2}{5}$; asymptotes: $x = -1$, $y = 5$ **15.** hole at $x = 2$ **17.** g is f translated 5 units down. **19.** g is f vertically stretched by a factor of 2. **21.** asymptotes: $x = 0$, $y = 5$; D: $\{x \mid x \neq 0\}$; R: $\{y \mid y \neq 5\}$ **23.** zeros: -2, 5; vertical asymptote: $x = 2$ **25.** zeros: -2, 2; vertical asymptote: $x = -3$ **27.** zero: 3; asymptotes: $x = -2$, $x = 2$, $y = 0$ **29.** hole at $x = 0$ **31.** hole at $x = 7$ **33.** zero: -1; asymptotes: $x = 0$, $y = 1$; hole at $x = 3$ **35.** zero: $\frac{5}{6}$; asymptotes: $x = \frac{2}{3}$, $y = -2$ **37.** zero: 0; asymptotes: $x = 3$, $x = -3$, $y = 0$ **43b.** ≈ 17 g

47b. $t = 12$; the number of seconds the driver spent at the pit stop **c.** 57 s **51.** F **53.** holes at $x = 1$, $x = 2$, $x = 3$ **59.** $x = \frac{10}{3}$ **61.** $x = \frac{1}{3}$ **63.** $\frac{8x - 13}{2x + 1}$; $x \neq -\frac{1}{2}$

8-5

Check It Out! **1a.** $x = 3$ **b.** $x = -2$ **c.** $x = -3$, $x = 2$ **2a.** no solution **b.** $x = -6$ **3.** 1.5 mi/h **4.** about 24 min **5a.** $3 < x \leq 4$ **b.** $x = -5$

6a. $x \leq \frac{1}{2}$ or $x > 2$ **b.** $x < -3$ or $x > -\frac{3}{2}$

Exercises **3.** $w = \frac{1}{11}$ **5.** $x = -1$, $x = 6$ **7.** $k = 1$ **9.** $x = 0$, $x = 7$ **11.** 2.4 mi/h **13.** $-5 < x < 0$ **15.** $x < 0$ or $x > 1$ **17.** $x < 4$ or $x \geq 8$ **19.** $x = 1$ **21.** $a = \frac{22}{3}$ **23.** $z = 2$, $z = 7$ **25.** $x = -8$ **27.** $x = -2$ **29.** about 6 h **31.** $x = -3$ **33.** $x < 0$ or $x > \frac{1}{6}$ **35.** $-10 < x < -7$ **37a.** 2003 **b.** 18 hits **c.** 170 hits **39.** $z = 0$ **41.** $x = -5$ **43.** $a = 2$ **45.** $-1 < x < 1$

47. $x = \pm 0.45$ **49.** $x = 0$, $x = 2$ **51a.** 2001 winner: $\frac{500}{s}$; 2002 winner: $\frac{500}{s + 25}$ **b.** 141 mi/h **55.** G **57b.** about 13 h **59.** all real numbers except -3, 0, and 3 **61.** $x < -21$ or $3 < x < 4$

63. $4(x + 4) - \frac{1}{2}(4x) = 2x + 16$ **65.** $\frac{5\sqrt{7}}{28}$ **67.** $y = \frac{3}{x}$

8-6

Check It Out! **1a.** no real roots **b.** ± 1 **c.** 5 **2a.** $2x$ **b.** $\frac{\sqrt[4]{27}}{3}x^2$ **c.** x^3 **3a.** 4 **b.** 32 **c.** 125 **4a.** $81^{\frac{3}{4}}$ **b.** 1000 **c.** $5^{\frac{1}{2}}$ **5a.** 6 **b.** $-\frac{1}{2}$ **c.** 25 **6.** 32 cm from the bridge

Exercises **1.** 3 **3.** ± 5 **5.** $2x$ **7.** $\frac{5x^2\sqrt[3]{36}}{6}$ **9.** $x^3\sqrt[3]{x}$ **11.** $-2x\sqrt{10}$ **13.** 216 **15.** -3 **17.** $9^{\frac{10}{5}} = 9^2 = 81$ **19.** $5^{\frac{1}{2}}$ **21.** 169 **23.** 2 **25.** $\frac{1}{5}$ **27.** $-\frac{1}{5}$ **29.** 44 in. **31.** 2 **33.** $3x$ **35.** $\frac{x^2\sqrt[3]{4}}{10}$ **37.** $2x^3\sqrt[3]{7}$ **39.** $x^2\sqrt[5]{x^3}$ **41.** 8 **43.** 10,000 **45.** $14^{\frac{3}{3}} = 14^1 = 14$ **47.** $144^{\frac{1}{2}} = 12$ **49.** 64 **51.** $\frac{2}{3}$ **53.** $\frac{9}{7}$ **55.** $5^{\frac{1}{9}}$, or $\sqrt[9]{5}$ **57.** \$1189 **59a.** about 18% **b.** about 12.6 g **61a.** $\frac{2\pi\sqrt{Lg}}{g}$ **b.** 1.2 s **63.** $(5x)^{\frac{7}{2}}$ **65.** $11^{\frac{3}{2}}x^{12}$ **67.** $5\sqrt[4]{125x^3}$ **69.** $b\sqrt[3]{a^2b}$ **71.** $b\sqrt[4]{4a^3b^2}$ **73.** always **75.** never **77.** 2 and 3; about 2.62 **79.** -5 and -4; about -4.31 **81.** A is incorrect. **85.** A **87.** A **89.** $20^{\frac{1}{8}}$ **91.** $a < -1$ or $0 < a < 1$

93. $A + D = \begin{bmatrix} 7 & 7 & -2 \\ 9 & 5 & 5 \end{bmatrix}$

95. $B + C = \begin{bmatrix} 6 & 6 \\ 0 & -6 \end{bmatrix}$

97. $h(x) = -x^2 + 3$ **99.** zero: -3; asymptotes: $x = -5$, $x = -1$, $y = 0$

8-7

Check It Out! **1a.** D: $\{x \mid x \in \mathbb{R}\}$; R: $\{y \mid y \in \mathbb{R}\}$

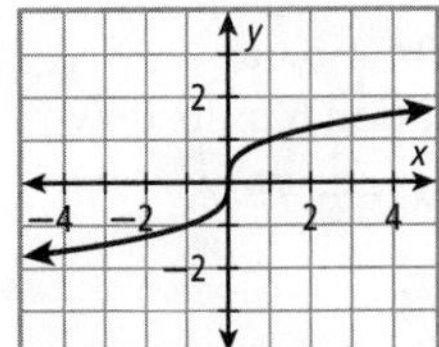

b. D: $\{x \mid x \geq -1\}$; R: $\{y \mid y \geq 0\}$

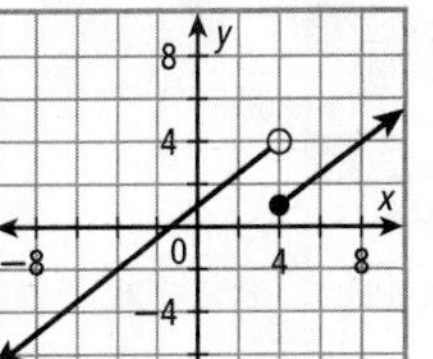

2a. g is f translated 1 unit up.

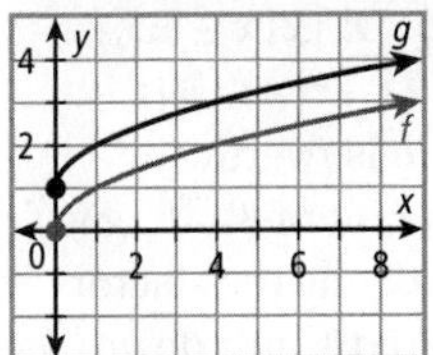

b. g is f vertically compressed by a factor of $\frac{1}{2}$.

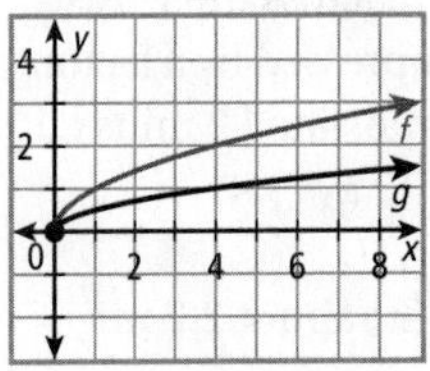

3a. g is f reflected across the y-axis and translated 3 units up.

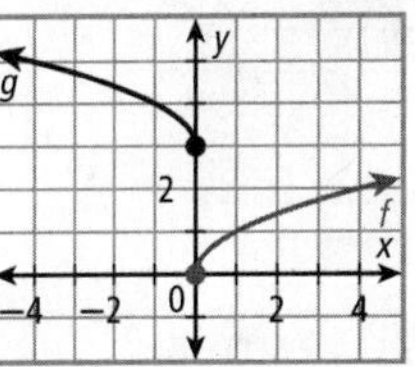

b. g is f vertically stretched by a factor of 3, reflected across the x-axis, and translated 1 unit down.

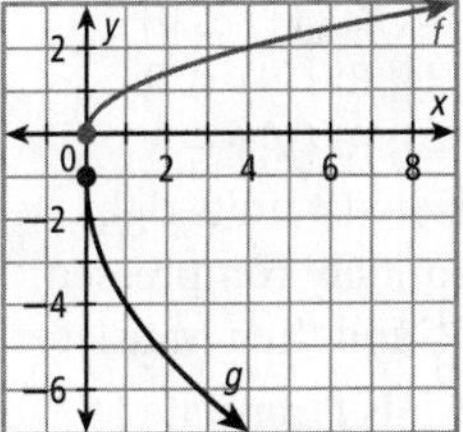

4. $g(x) = -2\sqrt{x} + 1$

5. $h(x) = \sqrt{\frac{256}{25}x}$; about 23 ft/s

6a.

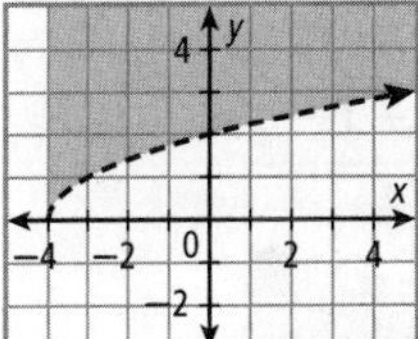

b.

Exercises **3.** D: $\{x \mid x \geq 0\}$; R: $\{y \mid y \geq -1\}$ **5.** D: $\{x \mid x \in \mathbb{R}\}$; R: $\{y \mid y \in \mathbb{R}\}$ **7.** D: $\{x \mid x \in \mathbb{R}\}$; R: $\{y \mid y \in \mathbb{R}\}$ **9.** h is f vertically stretched by a factor of 3. **11.** g is f compressed vertically by a factor of $\frac{1}{2}$ and translated 1 unit down. **13.** j is f reflected across the y-axis and then translated 3 units right. **15.** h is f reflected across the y-axis, horizontally compressed by a factor of $\frac{1}{2}$, and then translated 2 units left. **17.** $g(x) = 4\sqrt{(x+5)} - 2$

19. $g(x) = \frac{6}{5}\sqrt{\frac{5}{9}x}$; about 2.2 mi

21.

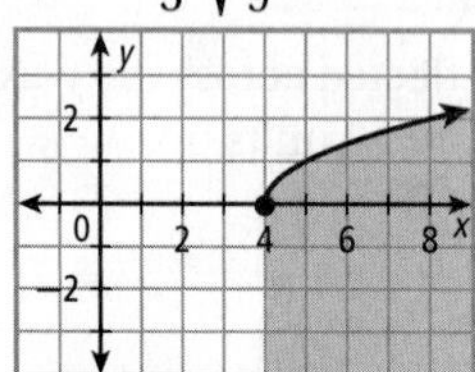

23.

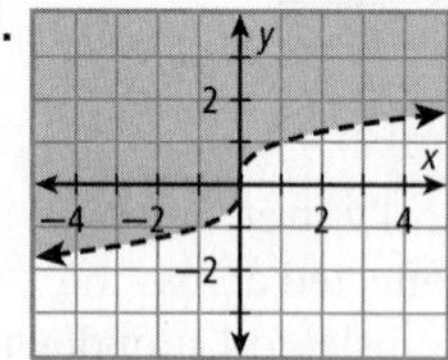

25. D: $\{x \mid x \geq 0\}$; R: $\{y \mid y \leq 0\}$ **27.** D: $\{x \mid x \in \mathbb{R}\}$; R: $\{y \mid y \in \mathbb{R}\}$ **29.** D: $\{x \mid x \in \mathbb{R}\}$; R: $\{y \mid y \in \mathbb{R}\}$ **31.** h is f translated 4 units right. **33.** g is f horizontally compressed by a factor of $\frac{1}{3}$ and then translated 5 units left. **35.** j is f translated 4 units left and 1 unit down. **37.** h is f reflected across the y-axis, vertically stretched by a factor of 3, and then translated 2 units up.

39. $g(x) = \frac{1}{3}\sqrt{x+3}$

41. $g(x) = -\sqrt{x+1} - 4$

43.

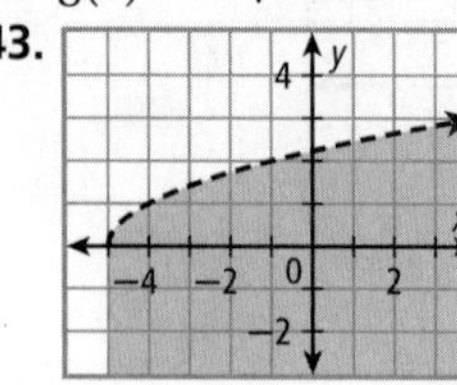

45.

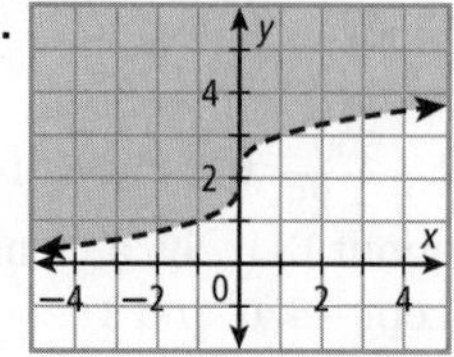

47a. ≈ 762 beats/min **b.** ≈ 58 beats/min **49.** a vertical stretch by a factor of 3 followed by a translation 1 unit right and 9 units down **51.** D **53.** A **55a.** about 373 km **b.** It will appear to decrease by about 76 km. **57.** yes **59c.** by a factor of 4 **61.** sometimes **63.** never **65.** yes **67b.** about 346 m/s **c.** -273.15°C **69.** 1.4 s **73.** D **75.** A **79.** $f(x) = -2\sqrt{\frac{1}{5}(x+3)} + 4$ **81.** $x \leq 8$ **83.** $x = 6, y = 2$ **85.** $x = -\frac{40}{7}, y = -\frac{68}{7}$ **87.** $x = 4$

8-8

Check It Out! **1a.** $x = 2$ **b.** $x = 4$ **c.** $x = 39$ **2a.** $x = 6$ **b.** $x = 2$ **3a.** $x = 1$ **b.** $x = -4, x = 3$ **4a.** $x = 22$ **b.** $x = 5$ **c.** $x = 3$ **5a.** $3 \leq x \leq 12$ **b.** $x \geq -1$ **6.** If the car were traveling 30 mi/h, its skid marks would have measured about 43 ft. Because the actual skid marks measure less than 43 ft, the car was not speeding.

Exercises **1.** No; the expression under the radical does not contain a variable. **3.** $x = 12$ **5.** $x = 5$ **7.** $x = 3$ **9.** $x = 10$ **11.** $x = 8$ **13.** $x = 4, x = 5$ **15.** $x = -1$ **17.** $x = 14$ **19.** $x = 5$ **21.** $x = -\frac{3}{4}$ **23.** $-5 \leq x \leq 20$ **25.** $\frac{-5}{2} \leq x < 10$ **27.** $x = 93$ **29.** $x = 18$ **31.** $x = 38$ **33.** $x = 6$ **35.** $x = \frac{7}{3}$ **37.** $x = 4$ **39.** $x = 25$ **41.** $x = 7$ **43.** $3 \leq x \leq 19$ **45.** about 1.5 tons **47.** $A = \pi r^2$ **49.** $E = \frac{1}{2}mv^2$ **51a.** 5 m **b.** 25.6 m/s^2 **53a.** $r \leq \sqrt{\frac{A}{\pi}}$ **b.** no **55.** $x \approx 5.84$ **57.** $x \approx 2.35$ **59.** 995 g **63.** H **65.** F **67.** always true **69.** always true **71.** $x = 9$ **73.** $x = 10$ **75a.** $D(n) = 2.00n + 5.00$ **c.** vertical translation 5 units down **77.** $f^{-1}(x) = -\frac{1}{3}x - \frac{1}{3}$ **79.** $4x^3$ **81.** $\frac{\sqrt[3]{18x}}{x}$

Study Guide: Review

1. rational function **2.** direct variation; constant of variation **3.** $y = \frac{1}{3}x$ **4.** $y = 4x$ **5.** 306 tiles **6.** \$2000 **7.** $y = \frac{6}{x}$ **8.** $y = \frac{4}{x}$ **9.** 24 ohms **10.** inverse variation **11.** $\frac{8}{3x^2}$; $x \neq 0$ **12.** $\frac{2x^3}{x+4}$; $x \neq -4$ **13.** $\frac{x-3}{x+1}$; $x \neq -4, x \neq -1$ **14.** $\frac{3}{x-5}$ **15.** $\frac{-x}{(x-4)(x+3)}$ **16.** $\frac{x-1}{x+1}$ **17.** $\frac{3x-1}{x-3}$ **18.** $\frac{2x}{y}$ **19.** $\frac{2(x+5)}{x+3}$ **20.** 1 **21.** $\frac{x+3}{3(x+4)}$ **22.** $\frac{x^2+12}{x^2+4}$ **23.** $\frac{2x}{(x+3)(x-3)}$; $x \neq \pm 3$ **24.** $\frac{2(x+1)}{(x+2)(x-2)}$; $x \neq \pm 2$ **25.** $\frac{8x^2+4x+45}{(3x+7)(4x-1)}$; $x \neq -\frac{7}{3}$, $x \neq \frac{1}{4}$ **26.** $(x-3)^2(x+3)$ **27.** $(x-5)(x+2)(x+7)$ **28.** $\frac{2x-3}{x+4}$; $x \neq -4$ **29.** $\frac{x^2-10x-25}{(x+5)(x-5)}$; $x \neq \pm 5$ **30.** $\frac{-(x^2-3x-1)}{(x-3)(x+2)}$; $x \neq -2, x \neq 3$ **31.** $\frac{6x^2-16x-7}{(2x+1)(3x-1)}$; $x \neq -\frac{1}{2}$, $x \neq \frac{1}{3}$ **32.** $\frac{8(x-6)}{5(x+2)}$ **33.** $\frac{2x-3}{x(x-3)}$ **34.** $\frac{(x-2)^2}{4x}$ **35.** ≈ 548 mi/h **36.** g is f translated 4 units right. **37.** g is f translated 2 units right and 3 units up. **38.** asymptotes: $x = 1, y = -3$; D: $\{x \mid x \neq 1\}$; R: $\{y \mid y \neq -3\}$ **39.** asymptotes: $x = -2, y = 1$; D: $\{x \mid x \neq -2\}$; R: $\{y \mid y \neq 1\}$ **40.** zeros: 0, 3; asymptote: $x = -4$ **41.** zero: 3; asymptotes: $x = -5, x = -1, y = 0$ **42.** zero: 2; asymptotes: $x = -3$, $y = 2$ **43.** zeros: -3, 3; asymptote: $x = 2$ **44.** hole at $x = -3$ **45.** $x = -2$ or $x = 3$ **46.** no solution **47.** $x = 2$ **48.** $x = 0$ **49.** $x < -\frac{4}{3}$ or $x > 0$ **50.** $x < 3$ or $x > \frac{7}{2}$ **51.** $3x^2$ **52.** $3x^3$ **53.** $2x\frac{\sqrt[3]{9}}{3}$ **54.** $(-27)^{\frac{2}{3}}$ **55.** $16^{\frac{3}{4}}$

56. $9^{\frac{3}{2}}$ **57.** 17 **58.** 81 **59.** $\frac{1}{2}$
60. D: $\{x \mid x \geq 0\}$; R: $\{y \mid y \geq 5\}$
61. D: $\mathbb{R}$; R: $\mathbb{R}$ **62.** g is f reflected across the x-axis and translated 1 unit up. **63.** h is f compressed horizontally by a factor of $\frac{1}{4}$.
64. j is f reflected across the y-axis and translated 8 units right.
65. k is f reflected across the x-axis, compressed vertically by a factor of $\frac{1}{2}$, and translated 1 unit up.
66. $g(x) = 3\sqrt{x+4}$

67.

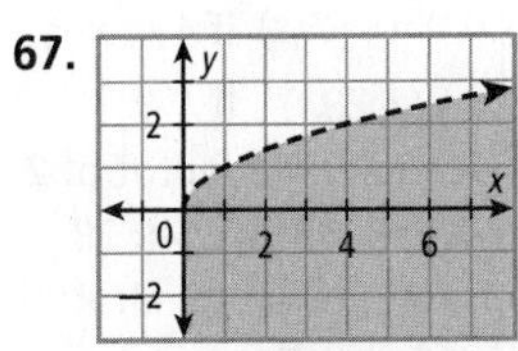

68.

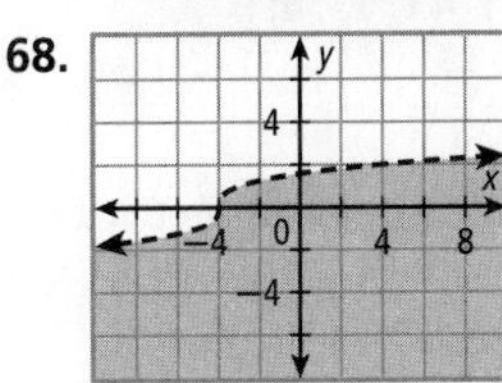

69. $x = 19$ **70.** $x = 109$ **71.** $x = 9$
72. $x = 2$ **73.** $x = 2$ or $x = 8$
74. $x = 8$ **75.** $x = 0.5$ **76.** $x = 85$
77. $x = 7$ **78.** $x = -219$
79. $4 \leq x \leq 13$ **80.** $x > 9$
81. $0 \leq x < 12$ **82.** $x > -7$
83. ≈ 1.6 m **84.** 60.3 m^3

Chapter 9

9-1

Check It Out!

1.

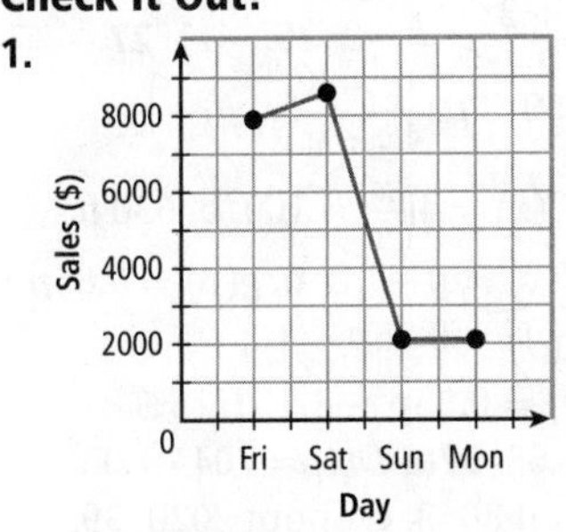

b.

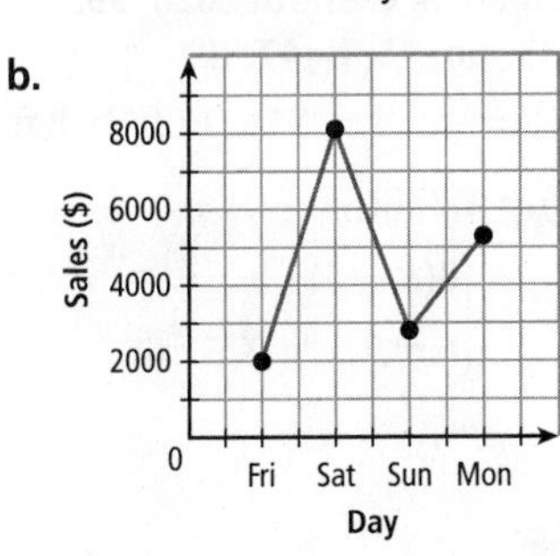

2.

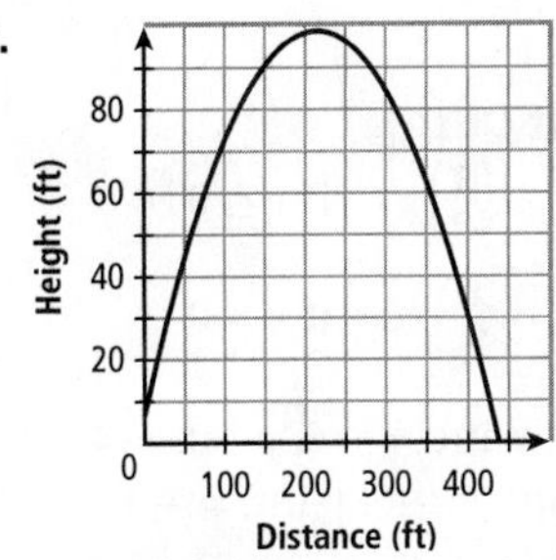

$h(x) = -0.002x^2 + 0.86x + 6.55$

3.

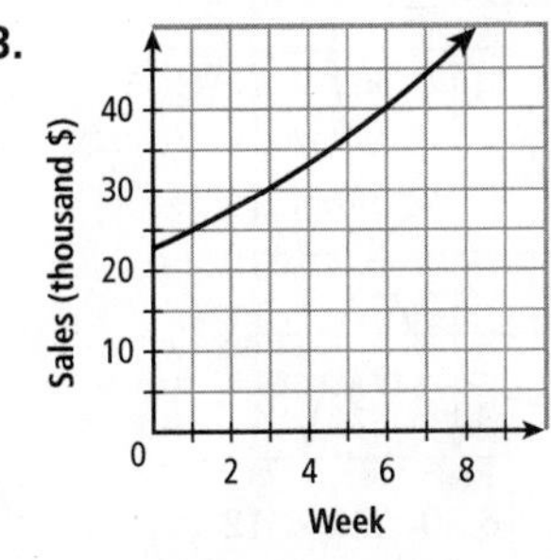

$f(x) \approx 22{,}727.15(1.1)^x$; 8 weeks

Exercises **1.** graph D **3.** graph B

5.

Enrollment Costs	
Credit Hours	**Cost ($)**
1	397.75
2	616.15
3	834.55
4	1053.00
5	1271.40

$C = 179.35 + 218.4x$

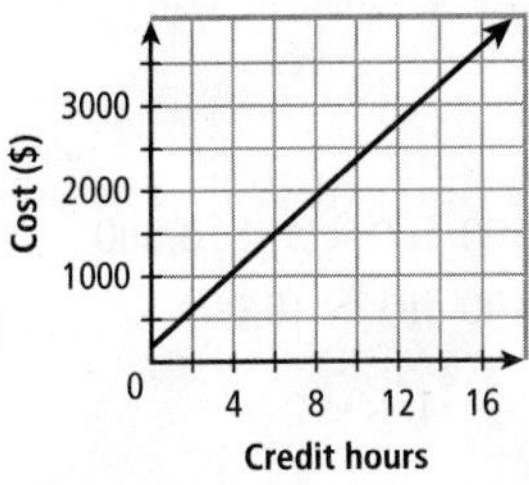

7. graph C **9.** graph D **11.** $T(t) = -0.02375t^2 + 0.525t + 101.1$
13a. $W(t) = 3t + 4$; The whale weighs 4 tons at birth and gains 3 tons per month. **15.** $14
17. exponential function
19a. $C(t) = -3t^2 + 21t + 24$
b. ≈ 61 **c.** 8 h after opening
21b. $h(t) \approx 0.0071t^3 - 0.1714t^2 + 2.1t + 2.071$ **c.** during year 15
25. C **29.** $C(p) = 1.065(0.8p - 10)$
31. $(-3, -4)$ **33.** 40×20 ft
35. D: $\{x \mid x \geq 1\}$; R: $\{y \mid y \geq 0\}$

9-2

Check It Out!

1.

Time Range (h)	Green Fee ($)
[8 A.M. – noon)	28
[noon – 4 P.M.)	24
[4 P.M. – 9 P.M.)	12

The green fee is $28 from 8 A.M. up to noon, $24 from noon up to 4 P.M., and $12 from 4 P.M. up to 9 P.M.
2a. 15; 15 **b.** 4; 13
3a.

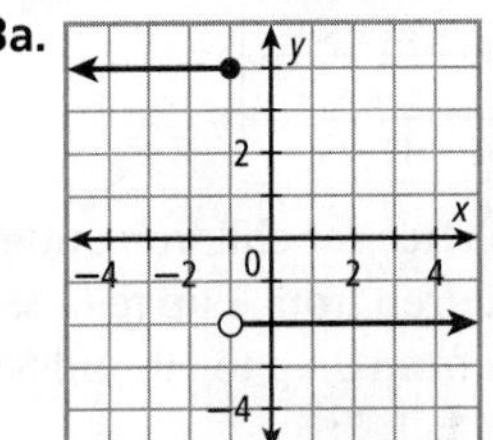

b.

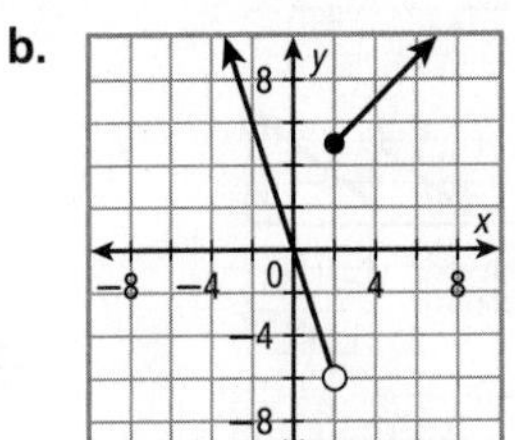

4.

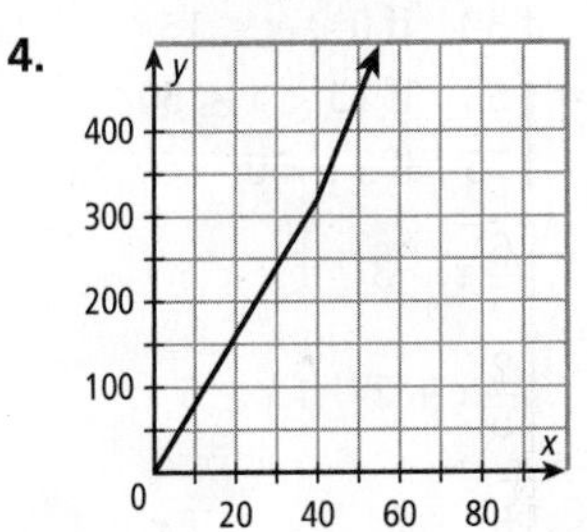

$$f(h) = \begin{cases} 8h & \text{if } 0 \leq h \leq 40 \\ 12(h-40) + 320 & \text{if } h > 40 \end{cases}$$

Exercises **1.** Step functions are a subset of piecewise functions. A step function is a piecewise function that is constant over each interval in its domain. **3.** The price per yard is $10 for less than 5 yd^3, $7 for 5 yd^3 up to 25 yd^3, and $4 for 25 yd^3 or more.

Topsoil Prices	
Price per Cubic Yard ($)	**Volume (yd^3)**
10	$0 \leq x < 5$
7	$5 \leq x < 25$
4	$x \geq 25$

5. −39; −5

7.

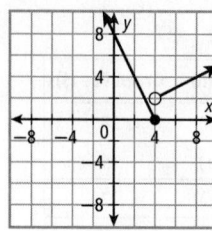

9.

Buffet Prices	
Price ($)	**Age (yr)**
0	$0 < x < 3$
2	$3 \le x < 8$
5	$8 \le x < 18$
8	$18 \le x$

The buffet is free for children under 3, \$2 for children from 3 up to 8, \$5 for children from 8 up to 18, and \$8 for adults. **11.** 1; 5; 5

13.

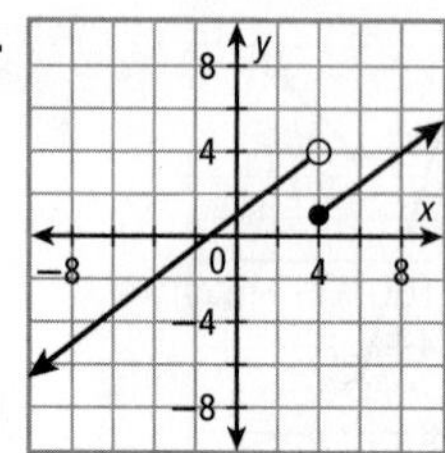

15. $f(x) = \begin{cases} 30 & \text{if } 0 < x \le 15 \\ 50 & \text{if } 15 < x \le 50 \\ 75 & \text{if } x > 50 \end{cases}$

17. $f(x) = \begin{cases} \frac{6}{5}x - 3 & \text{if } x < 5 \\ \frac{2}{5}x + 2 & \text{if } x \ge 5 \end{cases}$

19. $f(x) = \begin{cases} 6 & \text{if } x \le 4 \\ 6 + 3(x - 4) & \text{if } x > +4 \end{cases}$

21. $f(x) = \begin{cases} +x & \text{if } x \ge 0 \\ -x & \text{if } x < 0 \end{cases}$

23. $h(x) = \begin{cases} 2x - 4 & \text{if } x \ge 0 \\ -2x - 4 & \text{if } x < 0 \end{cases}$

27a. $d(t) = \begin{cases} 18t & \text{if } 0 \le t \le 10 \\ 16.5(t - 10) + 180 & \text{if } 10 < t \le 20 \end{cases}$

b. First half; the slope is steeper. **29.** D: ℝ; R: $\{y \mid y \ge -4\}$ **33.** C **35.** B **37.** $f(x) = 4 + 1.5(\lceil x \rceil - 1)$; \$11.50 **39.** vertical: $x = 1$; horizontal: $y = -3$; D: $\{x \mid x \ne 1\}$; R: $\{y \mid y \ne -3\}$ **41.** vertical: $x = 3$; horizontal: $y = 1$; D: $\{x \mid x \ne 3\}$; R: $\{y \mid y \ne 1\}$ **43.** A **45.** B

9-3

Check It Out!

1. $g(x) = \begin{cases} \left(\frac{x}{2}\right)^2 & \text{if } x \le 0 \\ \frac{x}{2} - 3 & \text{if } x > 0 \end{cases}$

2a. $f(x)$: x-int. = −6, y-int. = 4; $g(x)$: x-int. = −6, y-int. = −4

b. $f(x)$: x-int. = ±3, y-int. = −9; $g(x)$: x-int. = ±3, y-int. = −3

3.

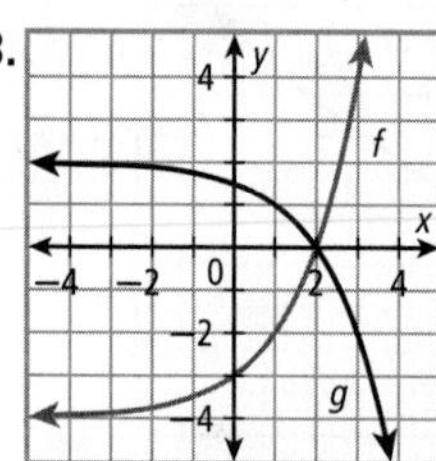

4. $f(x) = \begin{cases} 6.50 & \text{if } x < 12 \\ 9.50 & \text{if } x \ge 12 \end{cases}$

Exercises

1. $g(x) = \begin{cases} x + 3 & \text{if } x \le -6 \\ 4(x + 6) & \text{if } x > -6 \end{cases}$

3. $f(x)$: x-int. = −3, y-int. = 12; $g(x)$: x-int. = −3, y-int. = 2

5.

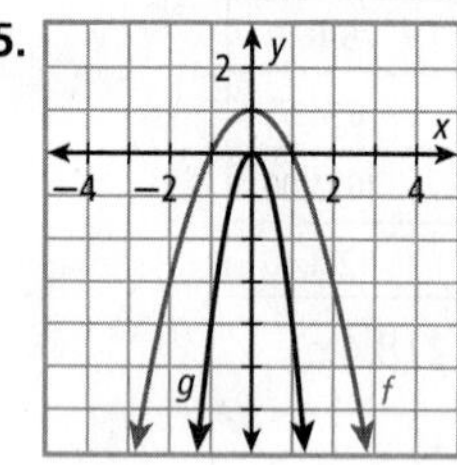

7. $T(x) = \begin{cases} 0.024x + 100 & \text{if } 0 < x \le 10{,}000 \\ 0.060x + 100 & \text{if } x > 10{,}000 \end{cases}$

9. $h(x) = \begin{cases} \left(\frac{x}{2}\right)^2 & \text{if } x < 2 \\ 2x & \text{if } x \ge 2 \end{cases}$

11. $f(x)$: x-int. = 6, y-int. = 9; $g(x)$: x-int. = 6, y-int. = 6

13. $f(x)$: x-int. = 5, y-int. = 2; $g(x)$: x-int. = 2.5, y-int. = 2

15. $f(x)$: x-int. = 0, y-int. = 0; $g(x)$: x-int. = 1, y-int. = −4

17.

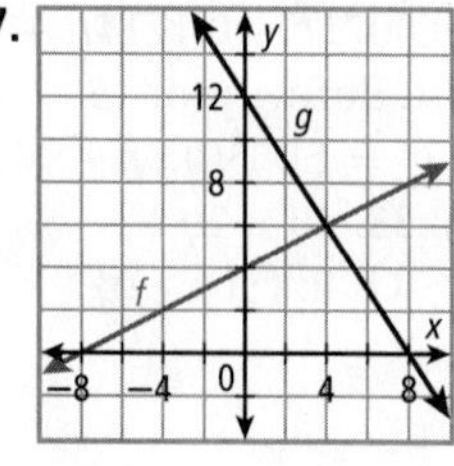

19a. $f(n) = \begin{cases} 16.2n & \text{if } n \le 50 \\ 360 + 9n & \text{if } n > 50 \end{cases}$

b. $f(n) = \begin{cases} 14.2n & \text{if } n \le 50 \\ 360 + 7n & \text{if } n > 50 \end{cases}$

21a. n x-intercepts

23a. $T(n) = \begin{cases} 2.8n & \text{if } n \le 8 \\ 3.6n - 6.4 & \text{if } n > 8 \end{cases}$

25. $f(x) - 7 = \begin{cases} 2^x - 8 & \text{if } x \le -3 \\ -5x - 4 & \text{if } x > -3 \end{cases}$

27b. $C(x) = \begin{cases} 1.29x & \text{if } 0 < x < 4 \\ 0.85(1.29x) & \text{if } 4 \le x < 7 \\ 0.7(1.29x) & \text{if } x \ge 7 \end{cases}$

c. horizontal stretch by a factor of 2 **29.** x-int: 2; y-int: 3 **33.** J **35a.** 28 **b.** 56 **37.** about 418 **39.** −6; D: ℝ; R: $\{y \mid y \le -6\}$ **41.** 13; 4; 9

9-4

Check It Out! **1a.** $(f + g)(x) = x^2$ **b.** $(f - g)(x) = -x^2 + 10x - 12$ **2a.** $(fg)(x) = x^3 + 2x^2 - 4x - 8$ **b.** $\left(\frac{g}{f}\right)(x) = x - 2, x \ne -2$ **3a.** 15 **b.** 9 **4a.** $f(g(x)) = 3\sqrt{x} + 2, x \ge 0$ **b.** $g(f(x)) = \sqrt{3x - 4} + 2, x \ge \frac{4}{3}$ **5a.** $f(c) = 0.68c$ **b.** \$168.64

Exercises **3.** $-x^2 + 13x + 13$ **5.** $2x^3 + 4x^2 + 2x$ **7.** $\frac{1}{2x}, x \ne 0$ or -1 **9.** −68 **11.** $4x^2 - 12x + 9$; ℝ **13.** $x + 1; x \ge -1$ **15.** $3x^2 + 5x - 2$ **17.** $2x^2 + 2x - 4$ **19.** $2x^4 + 10x^3 + 4x^2 - 40x - 48$ **21.** $\frac{1}{x - 2}, x \ne -2$ or 2 **23.** $\frac{x + 3}{2}, x \ne -2$ **25.** −11 **27.** −17 **29.** −59 **31.** $\frac{4x + 3}{4x + 6}; x \ne -\frac{3}{2}$ **33a.** $C(x) = 4\left(\frac{x}{9}\right) + 100$ **b.** 630 ft² **35a.** $f(p) = p - 10$ **b.** $g(p) = 0.85p$ **c.** $f(g(p)) = 0.85p - 10$; $g(f(p)) = 0.85p - 8.5$ **d.** 15% **e.** \$31.65 **37a.** $D(t) = 704 \cdot 1.05^t$ **b.** about 3043 **c.** about 2020 **39.** 4 **41.** 2 **43.** no **45.** B **47.** B **49.** $g(x) = \frac{3}{2}x^2 + 5$ **51a.** 12 ft **b.** 8 ft **53.** $f(x) = 1.25(2^t)$

55. $g(x) = \begin{cases} 8(x + 5) & x \ge -5 \\ x - 4 & x < -5 \end{cases}$

9-5

Check It Out! 1. function **2.** $f^{-1}(x) = \sqrt[3]{x+2}$; function; D: $\mathbb{R}$; R: $\mathbb{R}$ **3a.** yes **b.** no

Exercises 1. function **3.** function **5.** $y = \pm\sqrt{x+9}$; not a function; D: $\{x \mid x \geq -9\}$; R: $\mathbb{R}$ **7.** no **9.** not a function **11.** function

13. $f^{-1}(x) = \frac{\sqrt[3]{x}}{2}$; function; D: $\mathbb{R}$; R: $\mathbb{R}$ **15.** $f^{-1}(x) = \frac{6}{5}x - \frac{9}{5}$; function; D: $\mathbb{R}$; R: $\mathbb{R}$

17. $f^{-1}(x) = (x-5)^2 - 8$; function; D: $\{x \mid x \geq 5\}$; R: $\{y \mid y \geq -8\}$ **19.** no

21. yes **23a.** $d(t) = \frac{t-20}{2.5}$

b. within 4 mi **25.** $y = \frac{5}{x} - 4$; D: $\{x \mid x \neq 0\}$; R: $\{y \mid y \neq -4\}$

27. $y = x^3 + 12$; D: $\mathbb{R}$; R: $\mathbb{R}$

29. $y = \log_7 x$; D: $\{x \mid x > 0\}$; R: $\mathbb{R}$

31. $y = \ln\left(\frac{x}{3}\right) - 5$; D: $\{x \mid x > 0\}$; R: $\mathbb{R}$

33. g and h **35.** f and h

37a. $a(h) = \left(\frac{h-19}{3}\right)^2$

b. about 20.25 mo

39a. $t(d) = \frac{\sqrt{d^2 - 1600}}{3}$

b. $\approx$ 1833.28 s (about 31 min)

41a. $h(s) = \frac{s - 18\pi}{6\pi}$ **b.** 23.53 cm

43a. $s = \sqrt{A}$ **c.** $\approx$ 894 ft **47.** J

49. G **53.** $y = e^{\frac{3x-3}{x+1}}$

55. $f^{-1}(g^{-1}(x)) \neq (f(g(x)))^{-1}$

57. $2\pi x^2 + 2\pi x$ **59.** $x^3 + 27$

61. $x^2 + 8x - 6$ **63.** $x^2 - 10x + 4$

9-6

Check It Out! 1a. square root **b.** exponential

2. $f(x) = \frac{1}{2}x^2 + \frac{5}{2}x + 8$

3. $f(x) \approx -0.2x^2 + 23.99x + 5.28$

Exercises 1. linear **3.** exponential **5a.** $V(t) \approx 0.08t^2 - 2.04t + 60.86$ **b.** about \$51.68 **7.** quadratic **9.** $f(x) \approx -0.009x^2 + 2.28x - 55.31$ **11a.** $y \approx 34.37x + 85{,}851.76$ **b.** about 2594 ft^2 **15a.** $V(t) \approx 6126.9(1.016)^t$ **b.** about 34,611 ft^3 **17a.** $f(x) \approx 75.95(1.055^x)$ **b.** about 5.5%/yr **c.** The model predicts \$160.65, which is about \$5 more than the actual FCI. **d.** about 2008 **21.** B **23.** D

25. $f(x) \approx x^{0.5}$; $f(x) = \sqrt{x}$ **29.** a. -2, 4, and 10 **31.** yes

Study Guide: Review

1. one-to-one function
2. step function
3. composition of functions

4.

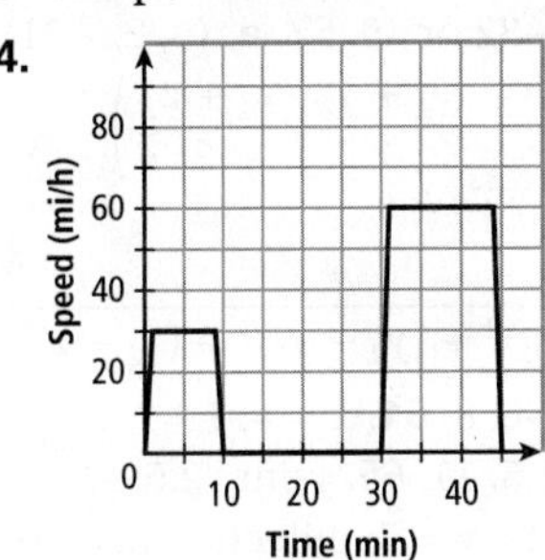

5.

Guests	10	20	30	40	50
Appetizers	160	200	240	280	320

$y = 4x + 120$

6a.

Radius (in.)	1.5	2	2.5	3	4
Time (s)	3	5	7.5	10.5	18

$y = x^2 + \frac{1}{2}x$ **b.** 52.5 s **7.** 51; 7

8.

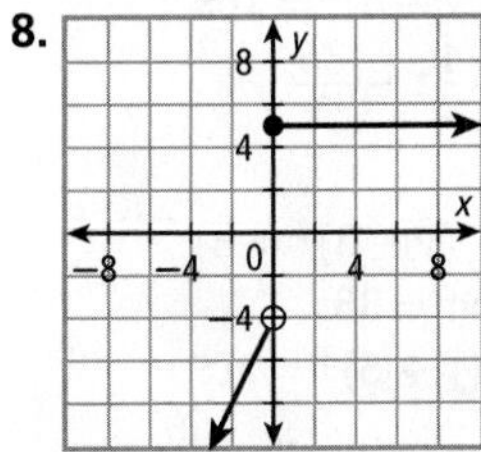

9.

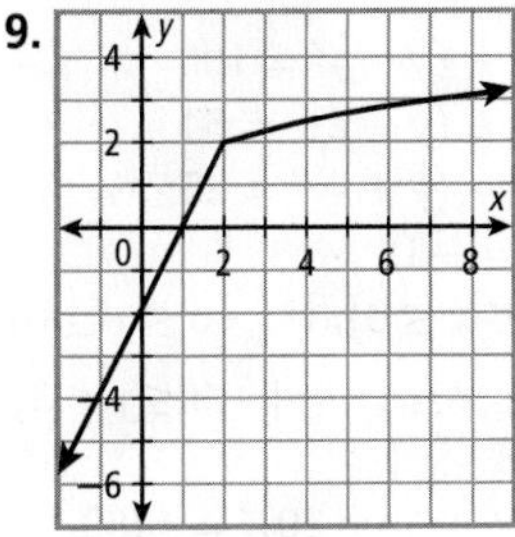

10. $f(x) = \begin{cases} \frac{5}{2}x - 4 & \text{if } x < 4 \\ -\frac{3}{2}x + 8 & \text{if } x \geq 4 \end{cases}$

11. $f(x) = \begin{cases} 6 & 0 < x \leq 8 \\ 6 + 1.5(x-8) & 8 < x \leq 48 \end{cases}$

12. $h(x) = \begin{cases} 2x & \text{if } x \leq 3 \\ -4x + 18 & \text{if } x > 3 \end{cases}$

13. $g(x) = \begin{cases} 3(x-7) + 2 & \text{if } x \leq 7 \\ (x-7)^2 & \text{if } x > 7 \end{cases}$

14.

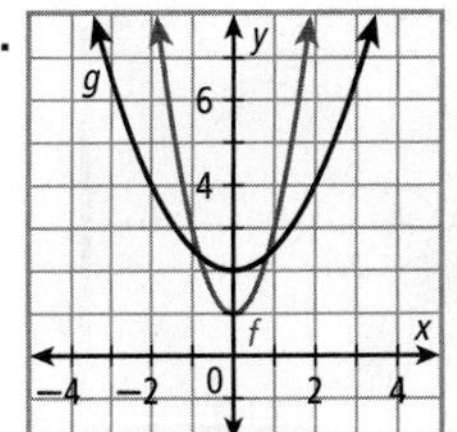

15. $x^2 - 4x - 21$ **16.** $x^2 - 6x - 7$
17. $-x^2 + 6x + 7$
18. $x^3 - 12x^2 + 21x + 98$
19. $x + 2, x \neq 7$ **20.** $\frac{1}{x+2}, x \neq 7$ or -2 **21.** -10; $-\frac{8}{3}$ **22.** 2; undefined

23. $g(f(x)) = \frac{8}{x-1}$; D: $\{x \mid x \neq 1\}$

24. $f(g(x)) = \frac{8}{x+1} - 2$; D: $\{x \mid x \neq -1\}$

25. $P(x) = 1.09(x + 30)$ **26.** function

27. $f^{-1}(x) = \frac{-x+5}{8}$; function; D: $\mathbb{R}$; R: $\mathbb{R}$ **28.** $y = \pm 3\sqrt{x} - 6$; not a function; D: $\{x \mid x \geq 0\}$; R: $\mathbb{R}$

29. $f^{-1}(x) = \frac{5}{2x} - 4$; function; D: $\{x \mid x \neq 0\}$; R: $\{y \mid y \neq -4\}$

30. $f^{-1}(x) = (x-3)^2 + 5$; function; D: $\{x \mid x \geq 3\}$; R: $\{y \mid y \geq 5\}$ **31.** no

32. yes **33.** $r = \sqrt{\frac{A}{4\pi}}$; r is the radius for a sphere with a given surface area.

34a. $f(x) = 23.96(1.02)^x$

b. $\approx$ 129.0 million gal **c.** $\approx$ 37°F

Chapter 10

10-1

Check It Out!

1a.

circle; center: (0, 0); intercepts: (0, ±7), (±7, 0)

b.

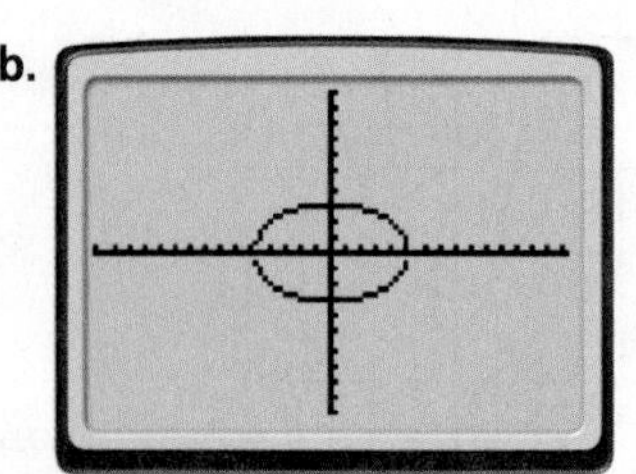

ellipse; center: (0, 0); intercepts: (±5, 0), (0, ±3)

2a.

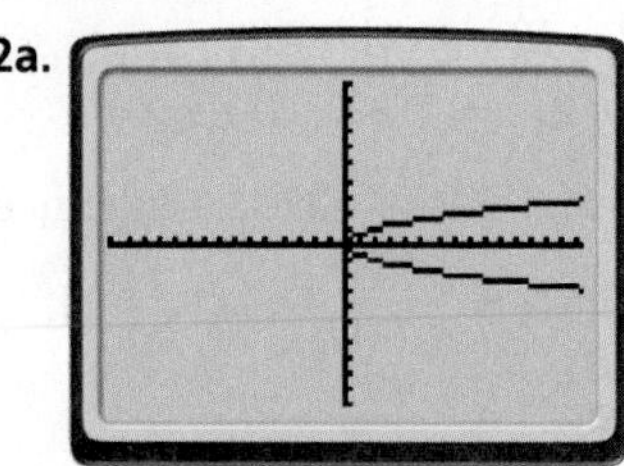

parabola; vertex: (0, 0); opens right

b.

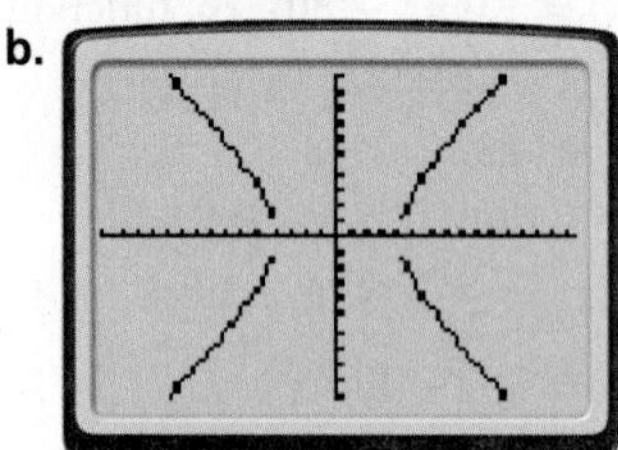

hyperbola; vertices: (±4, 0); opens horizontally **3.** Center: (8, 14); $r = 10$

Exercises **1.** circles, ellipses, hyperbolas, and parabolas **3.** ellipse; center: (0, 0); intercepts: (0, ±3), (±4, 0) **5.** parabola; vertex: (0, 0); opens right **7.** hyperbola; vertices: (0, ±5); opens vertically **9.** hyperbola; vertices: $(\pm\sqrt{2}, 0)$; opens horizontally **11.** center: (8, 18); $r = 13$ **13.** center: (−1, 15); $r = 25$ **15.** circle; center: (0, 0); intercepts: (0, ±3), (±3, 0) **17.** ellipse; center: (0, 0); intercepts: (0, ±5), (±2, 0) **19.** ellipse; center: (0, 0); intercepts: $\left(0, \pm\frac{15}{2}\right), \left(\pm\frac{5}{2}, 0\right)$ **21.** circle; center: (0, 0); intercepts: $\left(0, \pm\frac{9}{2}\right), \left(\pm\frac{9}{2}, 0\right)$ **23.** parabola; vertex: (0, 0); opens upward **25.** parabola; vertex: (0, 0); opens left **27.** hyperbola; vertices: (0, ±6); opens vertically **29.** parabola; vertex: (−3, 0); opens right **31.** hyperbola; vertices: (±4, 0); opens horizontally **33.** center: $\left(\frac{7}{2}, \frac{11}{2}\right)$; $r = \sqrt{10}$ **35a.** $C = 68\pi$; $A = 1156\pi$ **b.** (−37, 26) **37.** D **39.** A **41a.** $AB = 10$; $AD = 10$; $BC = 10$; $CD = 10$ **b.** rhombus **c.** 80 square units **43.** C **45a.** 13 units **b.** 6.5 units **c.** $\frac{12}{5}; \frac{12}{5}$ **47.** Sometimes true **51.** J **53.** J **55.** $a = -32$ or 40 **57. a.** (9, 2, −11) **b.** $\left(\frac{x_1 + x_2}{2}, \frac{y_1 + y_2}{2}, \frac{z_1 + z_2}{2}\right)$ **c.** $d = \sqrt{101}$ **d.** $d = \sqrt{(x_2 - x_1)^2 + (y_2 - y_1)^2 + (z_2 - z_1)^2}$ **59.** $x = -6, 8$ **61.** $x = 4, 7$ **63.** $x = 1.5, 11$ **65.** y-int.: 2.5; asymptote: $y = 3$; reflection across the x-axis, vertical compression by a factor of $\frac{1}{2}$, shift 3 units up **67.** y-int.: 5; asymptote: $y = -1$; vertical stretch by a factor of 6, shift 1 unit down

10-2

Check It Out!
1. $(x - 4)^2 + (y - 2)^2 = 49$
2. $(x + 3)^2 + (y - 5)^2 = 169$
3. C, E **4.** $y = \frac{4}{3}x - \frac{35}{3}$

Exercises
3. $(x + 11)^2 + (y - 3)^2 = 81$
5. $(x - 3)^2 + y^2 = 36$
7. $(x + 2)^2 + (y + 5)^2 = 289$
9. K, H, G **11.** $y = -\frac{3}{4}x - \frac{59}{4}$
13. $(x - 5)^2 + (y - 1)^2 = 100$
15. $(x + 4)^2 + (y - 2)^2 = 64$
17. $(x + 6)^2 + (y + 4)^2 = 25$
19. E **21.** $x = -15$
23. $\{x \mid -6 \le x \le 6\}$; $\{y \mid -6 \le y \le 6\}$
25. $\{x \mid -5 \le x \le 1\}$; $\{y \mid -3 \le y \le 3\}$
27. (−4, 0); 8
29a. $(x + 5)^2 + (y - 20)^2 = 4489$
b. 67 million mi **c.** 134π million mi
31. No **33.** C **35.** $(x + 4)^2 + (y - 8)^2 = 81$ **37a.** (2, −5)
b. $(x - 2)^2 + (y + 5)^2 = 625$
41. $y = \frac{1}{2}x + 2$

43a. $f(x) = \begin{cases} \frac{1}{2}x + 15 & 0 \le x \le 20 \\ x + 20 & x > 20 \end{cases}$

c. 25 min **45.** parabola; vertex: (0, 0); opens left

10-3

Check It Out! **1.** 20
2a. $\frac{x^2}{81} + \frac{y^2}{25} = 1$ **b.** $\frac{y^2}{25} + \frac{x^2}{16} = 1$

3a.

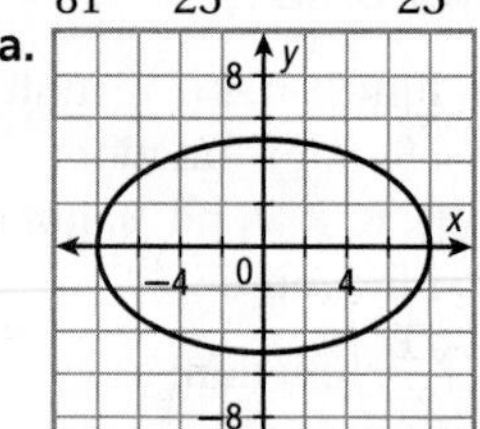

b.

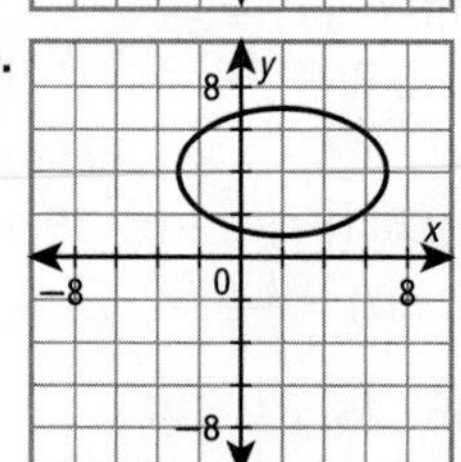

4a. width: 32 ft; height: 18 ft
b. $\frac{x^2}{256} + \frac{y^2}{324} = 1$

Exercises **1.** The major axis of an ellipse is always longer than the minor axis of an ellipse. **3.** 30
5. $\frac{y^2}{625} + \frac{x^2}{225} = 1$ **7.** $\frac{x^2}{49} + \frac{y^2}{36} = 1$

9.

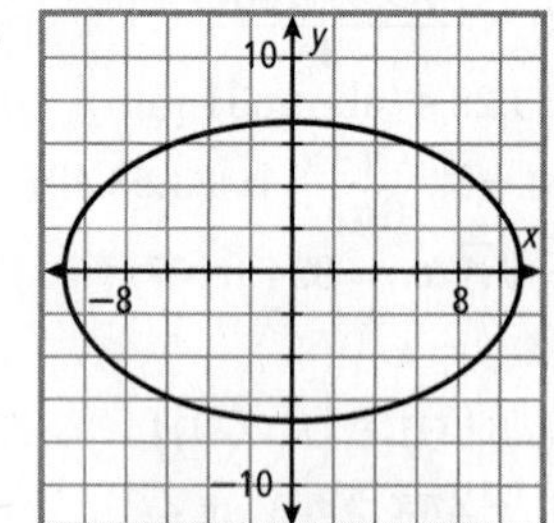

11.

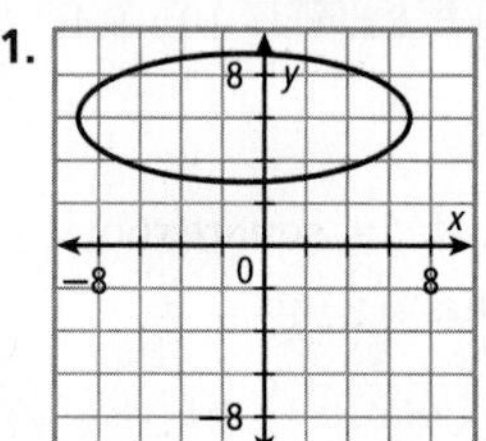

13. 42 **15.** $\frac{x^2}{25} + \frac{y^2}{4} = 1$
17. $\frac{y^2}{25} + \frac{x^2}{16} = 1$

19.

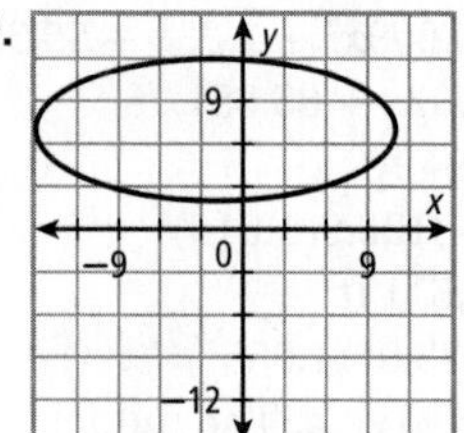

21.

23. $\frac{x^2}{279{,}312.25} + \frac{y^2}{193{,}600} = 1$
25. $\frac{(y-7)^2}{100} + \frac{(x+4)^2}{51} = 1$
27. $\frac{x^2}{49} + \frac{y^2}{25} = 1$; D: $\{x \mid -7 \le x \le 7\}$; R: $\{y \mid -5 \le y \le 5\}$
29. $\frac{(y-4)^2}{36} + \frac{(x+6)^2}{9} = 1$; $\{x \mid -9 \le x \le -3\}$, $\{y \mid -2 \le y \le 10\}$
31a. $\frac{9x^2}{5041} + \frac{16y^2}{729} = 1$
b. $(\pm 22.68, 0)$; ~45.36 ft **33.** center: $(-9, -4)$; vertices: $(0, -4)$, $(-18, -4)$; co-vertices: $(-9, -7)$, $(-9, -1)$; foci: $(-9 \pm 6\sqrt{2}, -4)$; D: $\{x \mid -18 \le x \le 0\}$; R: $\{y \mid -7 \le y \le -1\}$ **35a.** Instead of r^2, the formula for the area of an ellipse uses the values of *a* and *b* because an ellipse can be defined by *a* and *b* rather than a radius.
b. 65π **37.** The length of an ellipse's major axis is equal to the distance $PF_1 + PF_2$. **39.** H
41a. $\frac{21}{29}$ **b.** $\frac{x^2}{169} + \frac{y^2}{144} = 1$
c. $0 < e < 1$ **43.** $\frac{x^2}{25} + \frac{y^2}{16} = 1$
45. 24 **47.** 56
49. $x^2 + (y+1)^2 = 100$

10-4

Check It Out! 1. 12
2a. $\frac{y^2}{81} - \frac{x^2}{49} = 1$ **b.** $\frac{x^2}{64} - \frac{y^2}{36} = 1$
3a. vertices: $(\pm 4, 0)$; co-vertices: $(0, \pm 6)$; asymptotes: $y = \pm\frac{3}{2}x$

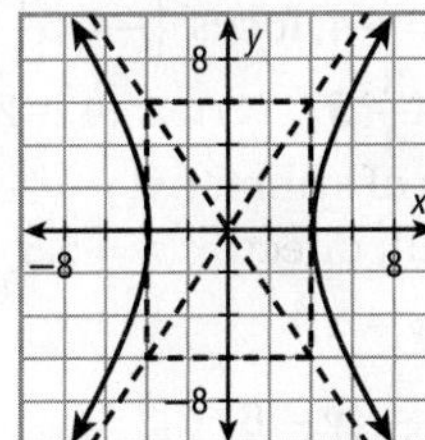

b. vertices: $(1, -4)$, $(1, -6)$; co-vertices: $(4, -5)$, $(-2, -5)$; asymptotes: $y = \pm\frac{1}{3}(x-1) - 5$

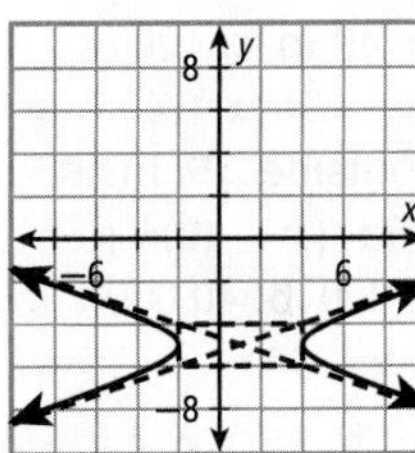

Exercises 1. transverse axis
3. 30 **5.** $\frac{x^2}{81} - \frac{y^2}{49} = 1$
7. $\frac{y^2}{100} - \frac{x^2}{64} = 1$
9. vertices: $(\pm 5, 0)$; co-vertices: $(0, \pm 8)$; asymptotes: $y = \pm\frac{8}{5}x$
11. vertices: $(0, \pm 10)$; co-vertices: $(\pm 9, 0)$; asymptotes: $y = \pm\frac{10}{9}x$
13. vertices: $(8, -6)$, $(0, -6)$; co-vertices: $(4, 1)$, $(4, -13)$; asymptotes: $y = \pm\frac{7}{4}(x-4) - 6$
15. vertices: $(0, -5)$, $(0, -9)$; co-vertices: $(\pm 5, -7)$; asymptotes: $y = \pm\frac{2}{5}x - 7$ **17.** 42
19. $\frac{x^2}{64} - \frac{y^2}{225} = 1$
21. $\frac{(x-3)^2}{49} - \frac{(y-3)^2}{9} = 1$
23. vertices: $(0, \pm 5)$; co-vertices: $(\pm 9, 0)$; asymptotes: $y = \pm\frac{5}{9}x$
25. vertices: $(\pm 2, 0)$; co-vertices: $(0, \pm 11)$; asymptotes: $y = \pm\frac{11}{2}x$
27. vertices: $(0, 3)$, $(-10, 3)$; co-vertices: $(-5, 7)$, $(-5, -1)$; asymptotes: $y = \pm\frac{4}{5}(x+5) + 3$
29. vertices: $(9, 2)$, $(3, 2)$; co-vertices: $(6, 6)$, $(6, -2)$; asymptotes: $y = \pm\frac{4}{3}(x-6) + 2$
33b. Yes **35.** $c^2 = a^2 + b^2$, so *c* always has the greatest value. There is not enough information given to determine whether *a* or *b* has the least value. **37a.** $(0, 214)$
b. 184 million mi **c.** $y \approx \pm 0.142x$
39. G **41.** J
43. $\frac{(x-7)^2}{400} - \frac{(y+9)^2}{144} = 1$
45. $\frac{x^2}{16} - \frac{y^2}{9} = 1$
47.

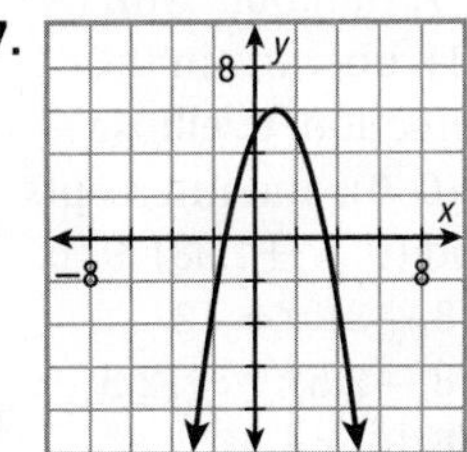

49a. $y = 30{,}000 + 3{,}000x$ **b.** 10 yr
51. $\frac{y^2}{4} + \frac{x^2}{2} = 1$

10-5

Check It Out! 1. $y = \frac{1}{16}x^2$
2. a. $x = -\frac{1}{5}y^2$ **b.** $y = -\frac{1}{28}x^2$
3a. vertex: $(1, 3)$; $p = 3$; axis of symmetry: $y = 3$; focus: $(4, 3)$; directrix: $x = -2$

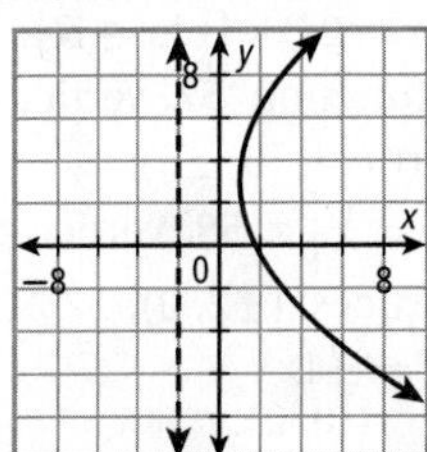

b. vertex: $(8, 4)$; $p = -\frac{1}{2}$; axis of symmetry: $x = 8$; focus: $(8, 3.5)$; directrix: $y = 4.5$

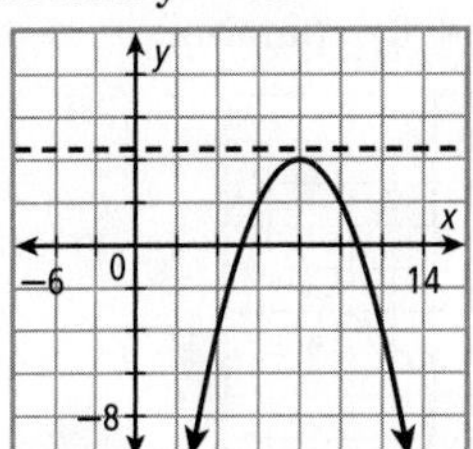

4. 11 in.

Exercises 3. $x = \frac{1}{28}y^2$
5. $y = -\frac{1}{16}x^2$ **7.** $y = \frac{1}{2}x^2$
9. $x = -\frac{1}{32}y^2$ **11.** vertex: $(0, 4)$; $p = 6$; axis of symmetry: $y = 4$; focus: $(6, 4)$; directrix: $x = -6$
13. 9.5 in **15.** $x - 3 = -\frac{1}{20}y^2$
17. $y = \frac{1}{12}(x+3)^2$ **19.** $x = \frac{1}{4}y^2$
21. $y = -\frac{1}{24}x^2$ **23.** vertex: $(1, 0)$; $p = \frac{1}{8}$; axis of symmetry: $y = 0$; focus: $\left(\frac{9}{8}, 0\right)$; directrix: $x = \frac{7}{8}$
27. $y + 6 = -\frac{1}{12}(x-2)^2$; D: $\{x \mid x \in \mathbb{R}\}$; R: $\{y \mid y \le -6\}$
29. $x + 7 = \frac{1}{36}(y+3)^2$; D: $\{x \mid x \ge -7\}$; R: $\{y \mid y \in \mathbb{R}\}$
31. $y - 5 = -\frac{1}{20}x^2$; D: $\{x \mid x \in \mathbb{R}\}$; R: $\{y \mid y \le 5\}$ **33.** $x - 8 = -\frac{1}{16}(y+5)^2$; D: $\{x \mid x \le 8\}$; R: $\{y \mid y \in \mathbb{R}\}$ **35a.** $y = \frac{1}{20}x^2$
b. $y + 4 = \frac{1}{16}x^2$ **c.** 7.2 in
37a. $(-96, 41)$ **b.** 133 million km
c. $(-96, 174)$ **39.** vertex: $(-4, 5)$;

$p = -\frac{1}{8}$; axis of symmetry: $x = -4$; focus: $\left(-4, 4\frac{7}{8}\right)$; directrix: $y = 5\frac{1}{8}$ **41.** vertex: $(-3, 2)$; $p = 2$; axis of symmetry: $y = 2$; focus: $(-1, 2)$; directrix: $x = -5$ **45.** G **47.** $(7, 0)$ **49.** $y - 7 = -\frac{1}{8}(x-6)^2$ or $y - 3 = \frac{1}{8}(x - 6)^2$ **51.** $4p$ **53.** $f^{-1}(x) = \frac{x - 22}{4}$; D: $\{x \mid x \in \mathbb{R}\}$; R: $\{y \mid y \in \mathbb{R}\}$; function **55.** $f^{-1}(x) = 3x + 2$; D: $\{x \mid x \in \mathbb{R}\}$; R: $\{y \mid y \in \mathbb{R}\}$; function **57.** vertices: $(\pm 9, 0)$; co-vertices: $(0, \pm 5)$; asymptotes: $y = \pm\frac{5}{9}x$ **59.** vertices: $(0, \pm 8)$; co-vertices: $(\pm 2, 0)$; asymptotes: $y = \pm 4x$

10-6

Check It Out! 1a. circle **b.** hyperbola **2a.** circle **b.** parabola **3a.** $x = \frac{1}{9}(y + 8)^2$; parabola

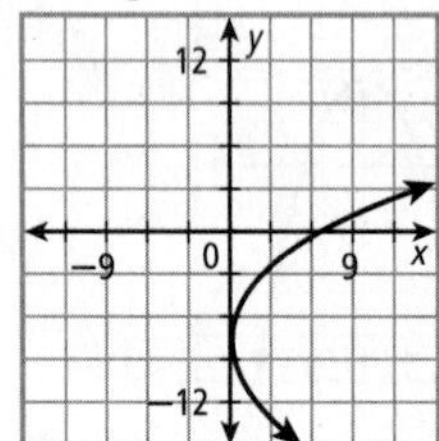

b. $\frac{(x - 4)^2}{9} + \frac{(y + 6)^2}{16} = 1$; ellipse

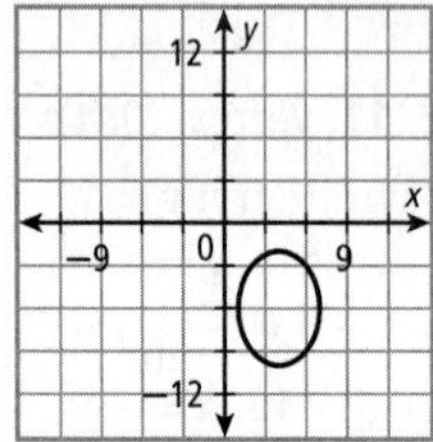

4. 200 ft

Exercises 1. ellipse **3.** parabola **5.** ellipse **7.** ellipse **9.** $(x - 8)^2 + (y + 5)^2 = 36$; circle **11.** $\frac{x^2}{9} + \frac{(y + 4)^2}{25} = 1$; ellipse **13.** 4 in **15.** parabola **17.** ellipse **19.** parabola **21.** ellipse **23.** $x^2 + (y - 4)^2 = 49$; circle **25.** $\frac{x^2}{4} - \frac{(y + 9)^2}{25} = 1$; hyperbola **27.** $(x + 5)^2 + (y + 2)^2 = 20$; circle **29.** $\frac{(x + 1)^2}{4} - \frac{(y - 7)^2}{9} = 1$; hyperbola **31.** $(x - 2.5)^2 + (y + 4.5)^2 = 16$; circle **33a.** ellipse **b.** 40 m **c.** 100 m **35.** $36x^2 + 25y^2 - 360x + 400y + 1600 = 0$ **37.** outside **39.** inside **41.** 36.4 cm **43a.** $(x - 40)^2 + (y - 30)^2 = 40{,}000$ **b.** $40{,}000\pi$ **c.** inside **45a.** $y - 84 = -\frac{1}{500}(x-200)^2$ **b.** 84 ft **c.** 4 ft **47.** A **49.** D **53.** It rotates the graph. **55.** no **57.** no **59.** $(4, 1)$ **61a.** $f(x) = 1.65(1 + 0.05)^t$ **b.** $5.32

10-7

Check It Out! 1. $(0, 4.5)$ **2a.** $(-4, 3), (3, -4)$ **b.** $(0, 5), (\pm 3, -4)$ **3.** no solution **4.** yes, at $(\pm 4, -3.6)$

Exercises 3. $(4, -2), (8, 2)$ **5.** $(12, 5), (5, 12)$ **7.** no solution **9.** $(0, -6), \left(\pm 3\sqrt{3}, 3\right)$ **11.** $(\pm 4, 2), (\pm 4, -2)$ **13.** no solution **15.** $(0, 5), (-4, 3)$ **17.** $(2.5, -6.5), (-4.5, 7.5)$ **19.** $(0, 4), \left(\frac{8}{3}, \frac{20}{3}\right)$ **21.** $(5, 1), (7, 4)$ **23.** $(\pm 2, -2), \left(\pm\sqrt{7}, 1\right)$ **25.** no solution **27.** $(0, -7), (1, -6)$ **29.** $\left(2\sqrt{2}, \pm 1\right), \left(-2\sqrt{2}, \pm 1\right)$ **31.** $(0, 0), (1, 1)$ **33.** $(6, 1), (-26, -3)$ **35.** $(0, \pm 3)$ **37.** $(2, \pm 4)$ **39.** no solution **41.** $(10, \pm 4), (-10, \pm 4)$ **43.** 25 s **45.** $(2.8, -2.6), (3.3, 2.9), (-7.9, -1.3), (-8.1, 1.5)$ **47a.** hyperbola **b.** yes; approximately $(6.69, 2.68)$, $(1.31, 2.68)$ **49.** $(-2, 0)$ **53.** G **55.** $(4, \pm 3)$ **57.** $(3, 4), (4, 3)$ **61.** about $100 **63.** cylinder **65.** 4 **67.** $-\frac{2}{5}$ **69.** $f(x) = 5x - 2$

Study Guide: Review

1. transverse axis **2.** tangent line **3.** focus; directrix **4.** conic section **5.** circle with center $(0, 0)$ and radius $r = 9$ **6.** hyperbola with center $(0, 0)$ and intercepts $(5, 0)$ and $(-5, 0)$ **7.** parabola with vertex $(0, -1)$, opening in the positive x-direction **8.** ellipse with center $(0, 0)$, and intercepts $(\pm 3.5, 0)$, and $(0, \approx \pm 1.98)$ **9.** B **10.** center: $(3, -3)$; $r = 12$ **11.** center: $(8, -2.5)$; $r = 12.5$ **12.** center: $(6, 0)$; $r = 19$ **13.** center: $(-12, 4)$; $r = \sqrt{15}$ **14.** $(x - 8)^2 + (y + 7)^2 = 196$ **15.** $(x - 3)^2 + (y - 6)^2 = 80$ **16.** $(x + 3)^2 + (y - 8)^2 = 34$ **17.** $y - 5 = -\frac{3}{5}(x - 3)$ **18.** $y = 4$ **19.** $y + 2 = -\frac{4}{5}(x - 6)$ **20.** $y + 7 = \frac{5}{8}(x - 1)$ **21.** center: $(0, 0)$; vertices: $(0, \pm 6)$; co-vertices: $(\pm 3, 0)$; foci: $\left(0, \pm 3\sqrt{3}\right)$ **22.** center: $(0, 0)$; vertices: $(\pm 8, 0)$; co-vertices: $(0, \pm 5)$; foci: $\left(\pm\sqrt{39}, 0\right)$ **23.** center: $(3, -2)$; vertices: $(3, 6)$, $(3, -10)$; co-vertices: $(10, -2)$, $(-4, -2)$; foci: $\left(3, -2 \pm \sqrt{15}\right)$ **24.** $\frac{(x - 4)^2}{36} + \frac{(y + 5)^2}{9} = 1$ **25.** $\frac{x^2}{144} + \frac{y^2}{225} = 1$ **26.** $\frac{(x + 2)^2}{36} + \frac{(y - 3)^2}{27} = 1$ **27.** center: $(0, 0)$; vertices: $(\pm 5, 0)$; co-vertices: $(0, \pm 7)$; foci: $\left(\pm\sqrt{74}, 0\right)$; asymptotes: $y = \pm\frac{7}{5}x$ **28.** center: $(0, 0)$; vertices: $(0, \pm 6)$; co-vertices: $(\pm 8, 0)$; foci: $(0, \pm 10)$; asymptotes: $y = \pm\frac{3}{4}x$ **29.** center: $(3, -6)$; vertices: $(5, -6)$, $(1, -6)$; co-vertices: $(3, 1)$, $(3, -13)$; foci: $\left(3 \pm \sqrt{53}, -6\right)$; asymptotes: $y + 6 = \pm\frac{7}{2}(x - 3)$ **30.** $\frac{x^2}{25} - \frac{y^2}{36} = 1$ **31.** $\frac{x^2}{121} - \frac{y^2}{16} = 1$ **32.** $\frac{y^2}{25} - \frac{x^2}{36} = 1$ **33.** $\frac{(y - 5)^2}{25} - \frac{(x + 7)^2}{144} = 1$ **34.** vertex: $(0, 0)$; $p = -3$; axis of symmetry: $x = 0$; focus: $(0, -3)$; directrix: $y = 3$ **35.** vertex: $(0, 0)$; $p = \frac{1}{8}$; axis of symmetry: $y = 0$; focus: $\left(\frac{1}{8}, 0\right)$; directrix: $x = -\frac{1}{8}$ **36.** vertex: $(-4, 5)$; $p = \frac{1}{4}$; axis of symmetry: $x = -4$; focus: $\left(-4, 5\frac{1}{4}\right)$; directrix: $y = 4\frac{3}{4}$ **37.** vertex: $(4, -2)$; $p = -1.5$; axis of symmetry: $y = -2$; focus: $(2.5, -2)$; directrix: $x = 5.5$ **38.** $y = -\frac{1}{20}(x - 3)^2$ **39.** $x - 4 = -\frac{1}{10}(y - 6)^2$ **40.** $x - 9 = \frac{1}{12}(y + 4)^2$ **41.** ellipse **42.** hyperbola **43.** parabola **44.** circle **45.** ellipse **46.** $x + 3 = \frac{1}{4}(y + 6)^2$; parabola

47. $\frac{(x+4)^2}{6} + \frac{y^2}{2} = 1$; ellipse
48. $(x+5)^2 + (y-4)^2 = 36$; circle
49. $\frac{(x+1)^2}{8} - \frac{(y+3)^2}{4} = 1$; hyperbola **50.** $(2, -6)$, $(-2, 2)$
51. $(4, 0)$, $(0, -5)$
52. $(8, \pm 6)$, $(-8, \pm 6)$
53. $(3, 2)$, $(5, 6)$ **54.** $(0, 2)$, $(0, -2)$
55. $(6, 4)$, $(6, -4)$, $(-6, 4)$, $(-6, -4)$
56. $(2, 6)$, $(-7, 3)$ **57.** no solution

Chapter 11

11-1

Check It Out! 1a. 120 **b.** 73,116,160 **2a.** 336 **b.** 20 **3.** 28

Exercises 1. important; permutation **3.** 225 **5.** 1320 **7.** 5985 **9.** 12 **11.** 72 **13.** 20 **15.** 71,916,768 **17.** 1 **19.** 6 **21.** 72 **23.** 6700 **25.** 35 **27.** > **29.** <
33a.

President	A	A	A	A	A	A	A	A	A	A	A	A
Vice President	B	B	B	C	C	C	D	D	D	E	E	E
Secretary	C	D	E	B	D	E	B	C	E	B	C	D

b.

President	B	B	B	B	B	B	B	B	B	B	B	B
Vice President	A	A	A	C	C	C	D	D	D	E	E	E
Secretary	C	D	E	A	D	E	A	C	E	A	C	D

60 ways
c. 60 **d.** 10; 60; 10 **37.** A **39.** D **41.** 1365 **43.** $({}_{30}C_{12})({}_{18}C_2)$ **45.** $n = 119$ **47.** $n = 13.0625$ **49.** hyperbola

11-2

Check It Out! 1a. $\frac{5}{36}$ **b.** 0 **c.** $\frac{5}{12}$ **2.** $\frac{16}{25}$ **3.** $\frac{1}{28}$ **4.** $\frac{16}{225}$ **5a.** $\frac{9}{26}$ **b.** $\frac{19}{26}$

Exercises 1. theoretical probability **3.** $\frac{1}{4}$ **5.** $\frac{1}{4}$ **7.** $\frac{303}{365}$ **9.** $\frac{1}{220}$ **11.** $\frac{1}{9}$ **13.** $\frac{3}{5}$ **15.** $\frac{4}{5}$ **17.** $\frac{1}{56}$ **19.** $\approx \frac{1}{42}$ **21.** never **23a.** $\frac{\pi}{4}$ **25a.** 0.68; 0.84; 0.76; 0.64 **b.** 0.73 **27.** $\frac{2}{5}$ **29.** June; ≈ 0.13 **31.** no; yes **33.** $\frac{1}{2}$ **37.** G **39.** H **45.** max.: 16 **47.** $y = -\frac{1}{20}x^2$

11-3

Check It Out! 1a. $\frac{1}{36}$ **b.** $\frac{1}{8}$ **2.** $\frac{5}{36}$ **3a.** ≈ 0.014 **b.** ≈ 0.186 **4a.** independent; $\frac{3}{20}$ **b.** dependent; $\frac{1}{6}$ **c.** dependent; $\frac{1}{12}$

Exercises 1. independent **3.** $\frac{1}{8}$ **5.** The probability that the yellow cube shows a multiple of 3 increases from $\frac{1}{3}$ if the product is 6; $\frac{1}{2}$ **7.** $\frac{1}{100}$ **9.** dependent; $\frac{9}{38}$ **11.** $\frac{1}{12}$ **13.** The probability that the product is 8 increases from $\frac{1}{18}$ if the blue cube is less than 3; $\frac{1}{36}$ **15.** ≈ 0.72 **17.** dependent; $\frac{1}{6}$ **19.** independent **21.** independent **23a.** ≈ 0.61 **b.** ≈ 0.05 **25a.** $\frac{625}{1296}$ **b.** $\frac{1}{36}$ **c.** $\frac{1}{6}$ **27.** ≈ 0.6 **29.** 40 **33.** F **35.** 7 **37.** $\frac{11}{18}$; no **39a.** $P(d) = 18.3$g; $P(j) = 32.5$g **c.** vertical stretch by a factor of ≈ 1.78 **41.** $x \approx \pm 2.6$; $y \approx \pm 2.2$ **43.** $\frac{1}{36}$ **45.** $\frac{3}{4}$

11-4

Check It Out! 1a. Each student can vote only once. **b.** 75% **2a.** $\frac{4}{13}$ **b.** $\frac{8}{13}$ **3.** $\frac{31}{40}$ **4.** ≈ 0.1524

Exercises 1. inclusive events **3.** $\frac{3}{5}$ **5.** $\frac{4}{5}$ **7.** $\frac{7}{9}$ **9.** $\frac{54}{65}$ **11.** ≈ 0.92 **13.** $\frac{1}{2}$ **15.** $\frac{1}{4}$ **17.** $\frac{32}{49}$ **19.** $1 - 0.75^{13} \approx 0.976$ **21.** 0.37; experimental **23.** 87%; 100% **25b.** 4.16%; 52.24% **27.** 0.49 **29a.** 0.42 **b.** 0.02 **c.** 0.44; it is the sum of the probabilities. **31.** D **33.** D **35.** ≈ 0.12 **37.** $\frac{13}{18}$ **39.** 0.9 **41.** 0.2 **43.** $y = -1.5x^3 - 6x^2 + 16.5x + 45$ **47.** $\frac{1}{16}$

11-5

Check It Out! 1a. 6.5; 7; no mode **b.** 4.2; 5; 2 and 6 **2.** 0.37
3.
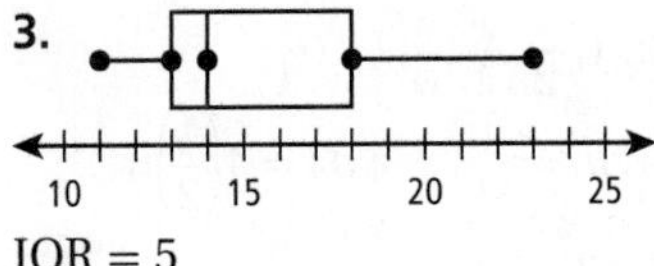

IQR = 5

4. 1.4; ≈ 1.6 **5.** 19; the mean increases from ≈ 4.3 to ≈ 5.4, and the standard deviation increases from ≈ 2.2 to ≈ 4.3.

Exercises 1. variance **3.** 5.375; 6; 6 **5.** \$0.36
7.
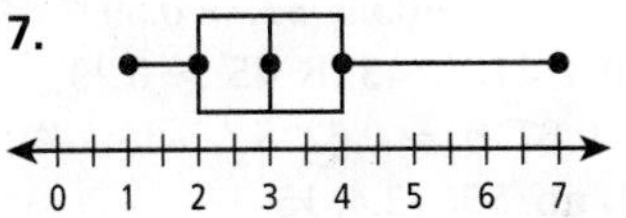

IQR = 2
9. 0.8; 0.89 **11.** 142.92; 11.95 **13.** $23.1\overline{6}$; 20.5; no mode **15.** 15; 15; no mode
17.
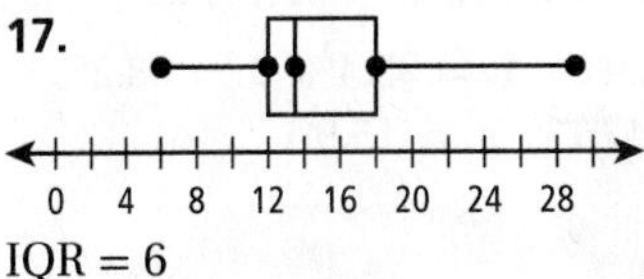

IQR = 6
19.
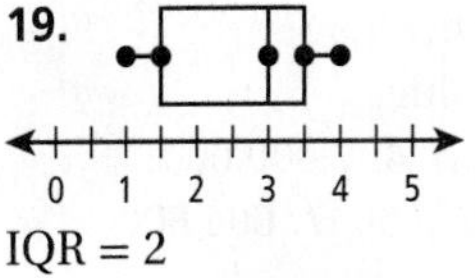

IQR = 2
21. 343.71; 18.54 **23.** 58; the mean increases from ≈ 19.8 to ≈ 22.8, and the standard deviation increases from ≈ 5.6 to ≈ 11.5. **25.** the mean; 37° is an outlier and affects the mean greatly. **27.** 15; $Q_1 - 1.5(IQR) = 79 - 1.5(90-79) = 62.5$; $15 < 62.5$ **29.** < 0.3 min or > 6.9 min; none **31.** Ruth **35.** – \$0.499 **37.** B **39a.** 12.25 **b.** $\frac{13}{36}$ **c.** $\frac{23}{36}$ **d.** no **41.** D **43.** C **45.** 1 **47.** $-2x^4 - 5x^3 + 7x^2 + 10x - 6$ **49.** $\frac{2}{3}$ **51.** $\frac{1}{2}$

11-6

Check It Out! 1a. $x^5 - 5x^4y + 10x^3y^2 - 10x^2y^3 + 5xy^4 - y^5$ **b.** $a^3 + 6a^2b + 12ab^2 + 8b^3$ **2a.** $\frac{2}{9} \approx 0.22$ **b.** $\frac{47}{128} \approx 0.37$ **3a.** ≈ 0.98 **b.** ≈ 0.09

Exercises 1. 2 **3.** $27x^3 + 135x^2 + 225x + 125$ **5.** $x^6 + 6x^5y + 15x^4y^2 + 20x^3y^3 + 15x^2y^4 + 6xy^5 + y^6$ **7.** ≈ 0.026 ≈ 0.181 **9.** $y^4 + 20y^3 + 150y^2 + 500y + 625$ **11.** $1024 + 3840x + 5760x^2 + 4320x^3 + 1620x^4 + 243x^5$ **13.** ≈ 0.86 **15.** $\frac{3}{8}$; $\frac{1}{8}$

17. $x^5 - 5x^4y + 10x^3y^2 - 10x^2y^3 + 5xy^4 - y^5$ **19.** $256k^4 - 256k^3 + 96k^2 - 16k + 1$ **21.** 0.384 **23.** $\frac{8}{27}$
25. $\frac{1}{16}; \frac{5}{16}$ **27.** ≈ 0.989
29. ≈ 0.94 **33a.** $\frac{82}{365}$ **b.** ≈ 0.14
c. ≈ 0.19 **35.** ≈ 0.03 **37.** ≈ 0.59
39. ≈ 0.3 **41.** B **43.** B **45.** ≈ 0.29
47a. ≈ 0.67 **b.** ≈ 0.62 **51.** −19; −4; −4 **53.** no **55.** 13.4; 15; 18
57. 25; 24; 24

Extension

Check it Out! 1. $\approx 97.7\%$

Exercises 1. $\approx 95.4\%$ **3.** $\approx 68.2\%$ **5.** $\approx 47.7\%$ **7.** $\approx 15.9\%$

Study Guide: Review

1. dependent events
2. expected value
3. permutation **4.** 7,000,000
5. 792 **6.** 2,162,160 **7.** 604,800
8. 20 **9.** $\frac{5}{36}$ **10.** $\frac{5}{18}$ **11.** $\frac{1}{2}$
12. $\frac{11}{12}$ **13.** $\frac{1}{210}$ **14.** $\frac{1}{10{,}000}$
15. $\frac{5}{24}$ **16.** ≈ 0.21 **17.** $\frac{1}{5}$
18. $\frac{4}{5}$ **19.** $\frac{7}{25}$ **20.** $\frac{13}{25}$ **21.** $\frac{1}{4}$
22. $\frac{3}{4}$ **23.** $\frac{1}{4}$ **24.** $\frac{1}{2}$ **25.** $\frac{1}{216}$
26. $\frac{6}{25}$ **27.** $\frac{11}{21}$ **28.** $\frac{1}{13}$
29. $\frac{13}{31}$ **30.** $\frac{14}{99}$ **31.** Each coupon offers only 1 discount. **32.** $\frac{5}{6}$
33. $\frac{7}{13}$ **34.** $\frac{1}{2}$ **35.** $\frac{7}{10}$
36. mean: 5.4; median: 6; mode: 8 **37.** mean: $13.\overline{3}$; median: 13; modes: 12, 13, and 15
38. 0.51
39.

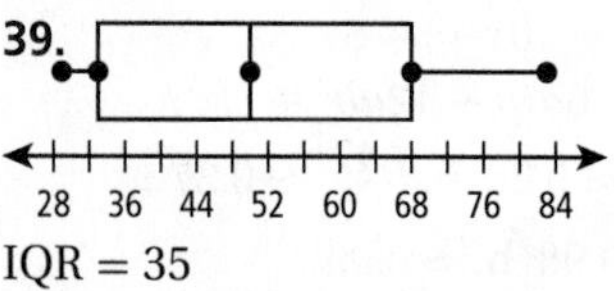

IQR = 35

40. [5.4, 9.6] **41.** yes **42.** The mean decreases from 75.5 to 69.3, and the standard deviation increases from ≈ 21.5 to ≈ 25.1.
43. $125 + 150x + 60x^2 + 8x^3$
44. $x^4 - 8x^3y + 24x^2y^2 - 32xy^3 + 16y^4$ **45.** 48.75; ≈ 4.13
46. ≈ 0.10; ≈ 0.40

Chapter 12

12-1

Check It Out! 1a. −5, −13, −21, −29, −37 **b.** 2, −6, 18, −54, 162
2a. −1, 0, 3, 8, 15 **b.** −2, 1, 4, 7, 10
3a. $a_n = 9 - 2n$ **b.** $a_n = \frac{1}{n}$
4.

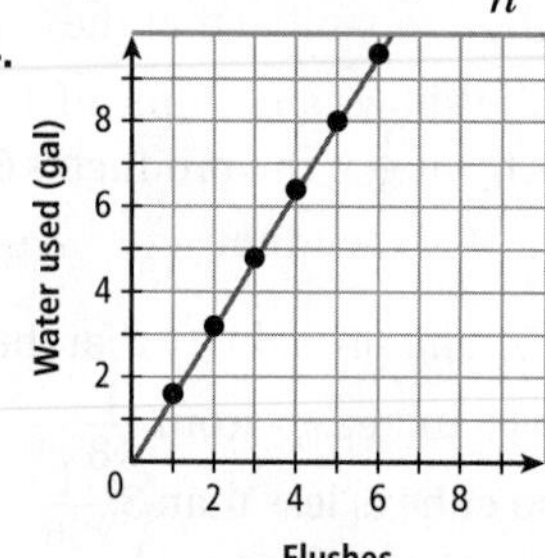

The graph shows the points lie on a line with positive slope; 16 gal. **5.** 8, 16

Exercises 1. recursive **3.** 3, 14, 25, 36, 47 **5.** −12, 0, 12, 24, 36
7. −3, −12, −27, −48, −75 **9.** 1, 4, 16, 64, 256 **11.** $a_n = 3 + 3n$
13. $a_n = 35 - 10n$ **15.** 16, 32
17. −2, 5, −16, 47, −142 **19.** 9, 10, 12, 16, 24 **21.** $1, \frac{1}{4}, \frac{1}{9}, \frac{1}{16}, \frac{1}{25}$
23. $a_n = 13 - 4n$ **25.** linear with a slope of 4; 36 **27.** 12, 8, 6, 5, $4\frac{1}{2}$ **29.** 10, 20, −10, 20, −10
31. 7.9, 7.8, 7.7, 7.6, 7.5 **33.** B is incorrect. The formula is explicit, not recursive. **35.** $a_n = \frac{16}{9} - \frac{1}{9}n$; $\frac{2}{3}$ **37.** $a_n = \frac{(-1)^{n+1}}{n}$; $-\frac{1}{10}$
39. $a_n = 25 - n^2$; −75 **41.** 15, 21
43a. 15, 21 **b.** $a_n = \frac{1}{2}n^2 - \frac{1}{2}n$
c.

Players	1	2	3	4	5
Games	0	2	6	12	20

The sequence is twice the previous sequence. The function is a vertical stretch by a factor of 2.
45a. $a_n = 180(n - 2)$ for $n \geq 3$; 1800°
c. $a_n = \frac{180(n-2)}{n}$ for $n \geq 3$
47a. $1, \frac{1}{2}, \frac{1}{4}, \frac{1}{8}, \frac{1}{16}, \frac{1}{32}$;
$a_1 = 1, a_n = \frac{1}{2}a_{n-1}$; $a_n = \left(\frac{1}{2}\right)^{n-1}$
b. $4, 2, 1, \frac{1}{2}, \frac{1}{4}, \frac{1}{8}$;
$a_1 = 4, a_n = \frac{1}{2}a_{n-1}$; $a_n = 4\left(\frac{1}{2}\right)^{n-1}$
51. H **53.** H **55.** $a_n = \frac{n^3}{3} - 1$; $\frac{997}{3}$
57. $a_n = -0.05n^2 + 0.05n + 0.9$; −3.6 **59.** $\frac{x-3}{x+2}$ **61.** $\frac{1}{x+5}$
63. $\frac{2(3x^2 - 5x - 3)}{(x+1)(x-1)}$
65. $\frac{x(x^2 - 7)}{(2x+7)(x+2)}$

12-2

Check It Out! 1a. $\sum_{k=1}^{5} \frac{2}{(k+1)^2}$
b. $\sum_{k=1}^{6} (-1)^k(2k)$
2a. $1 + 3 + 5 + 7 = 16$
b. $-5 - 10 - 20 - 40 - 80 = -155$
3a. 240 **b.** 120 **c.** 385 **4.** 294 in., or $24\frac{1}{2}$ ft

Exercises 1. $\sum_{k=1}^{n} k$
3. $\sum_{k=1}^{5} (-1)^k(3k)$
5. $\sum_{k=1}^{5} [100 - 5(k - 1)]$
7. $12 - 3 + \frac{4}{3} - \frac{3}{4} = 9\frac{7}{12}$
9. 231 **11.** 126 **13.** $\sum_{k=1}^{5} 1.1k$
15. $\sum_{k=1}^{6} (-1)^{k+1}(k + 10)$
17. $16 + 24 + 32 + 40 + 48 = 160$
19. $0 + \frac{1}{3} + \frac{2}{4} + \frac{3}{5} = \frac{43}{30}$ **21.** 195
23. 210 cans **25.** $\sum_{k=1}^{25} (26 - k)$
27. $\sum_{k=1}^{5} -800\left(\frac{1}{10}\right)^{k-1}$
29. $\sum_{k=1}^{6} (-1)^{k+1}(k + 2)^2$
31. $\sum_{k=1}^{5} 3.4k - 3.4$, or $\sum_{k=1}^{5} 3.4(k - 1)$
33. $\sum_{k=1}^{5} \frac{1000}{10^{k-1}}$ **35b.** $\sum_{k=1}^{5} 3^k = 3 + 9 + 27 + 81 + 243 = 363$
c. 3542
37. $-5 + 10 - 15 + 20 - 25 + 30 = 15$
39. $1 + 4 + 7 + 10 + 13 + 16 = 51$
41. $\frac{1}{5} + \frac{2}{5} + \frac{3}{5} + \frac{4}{5} + 1 = 3$
43. 420 **45.** −2550
47a. Both equal 165; $\sum_{k=1}^{n} ca_k = c\sum_{k=1}^{n} a_k$.
b. Both equal 75; $\sum_{k=1}^{n} (a_k + b_k) = \sum_{k=1}^{n} a_k + \sum_{k=1}^{n} b_k$. **49. a.** $a_n = 4n$
b. $\sum_{k=1}^{6} 4k$; 84 toothpicks **53.** H

55. J **57.** 1 · 2 · 3 · 4 · 5 = 120

59. $\sum_{k=1}^{n} ca_k = ca_1 + ca_2 + \cdots + ca_n$

$= c(a_1 + a_2 + \cdots + a_n)$

$= c\sum_{k=1}^{n} a_k$

63. x-int.: 3; y-int.: −6 **65.** 10 ft **67.** 2, 3, 8, 63, 3968

12-3

Check It Out! 1a. arithmetic; $d = -0.7$; −1.6 **b.** not arithmetic **2a.** −23 **b.** 8.7 **3.** $\frac{3}{2}, 1, \frac{1}{2}$ **4a.** −25 **b.** 8.5 **5a.** −408 **b.** −1650 **6a.** 37 seats **b.** 336 total seats

Exercises 1. arithmetic series **3.** not arithmetic **5.** 38 **7.** −4.6 **9.** 16, 23, 30 **11.** −13 **13.** −17 **15.** −35 **17.** 495 **19.** 11.7 **21.** not arithmetic **23.** arithmetic; −0.09; 0.63 **25.** $\frac{12}{5}$ **27.** 66, 55, 44 **29.** 2.1, 1.9, 1.7 **31.** 94 **33.** −60 **35.** 143.5 **37a.** 78; 156 **b.** adds 1 to each term of the sequence; adds 24 to the total number per day **39.** 0 **41.** 60 **43a.** $\sum_{k=1}^{n} 4k$ **b.** 684 **c.** 673 **45.** 45 minutes; after 2 years, her exercise routine would be over 8 h long, which is not realistic. **47a.** 61 **b.** 650 **49a.** 6th, 11th, 16th, 21st, and 26th Streets **b.** 0.25 mi **53.** J **55.** G **57.** 6 **63.** growth **65.** 92 dB **67.** $\sum_{k=1}^{5} \frac{4k}{5}$ **69.** $\sum_{k=1}^{5} -\frac{k}{3}$

12-4

Check It Out! 1a. geometric; $r = \frac{1}{3}$ **b.** arithmetic; $d = -0.4$ **c.** neither **2a.** $\frac{3}{1024}$ **b.** 100,000 **3a.** −1000 **b.** $\frac{3}{4}$ or $-\frac{3}{4}$ **4.** 20 **5a.** $\frac{63}{16}$ **b.** −189 **6.** $616,218.04

Exercises 1. geometric mean **3.** neither **5.** 39,366 **7.** 64 **9.** 324 **11.** $\frac{3}{2}$ **13.** 48 **15.** 61 **17.** 511 **19.** neither **21.** arithmetic; $d = 5$ **23.** 768 **25.** 52,488 **27.** 30.375 **29.** 1 **31.** 3 **33.** 11.111111 **35.** 8,888,888 **37.** $a_n = \frac{1}{16}(2)^{n-1}$; $a_{10} = 32$; $S_{10} = \frac{1023}{16} \approx 63.94$

39. $a_n = 8(2)^{n-1}$; $a_{10} = 4096$; $S_{10} = 8184$ **41.** $a_n = 162\left(-\frac{1}{3}\right)^{n-1}$; $a_{10} = -\frac{2}{243}$; $S_{10} = 121\frac{121}{243} \approx 121.5$

43a. $34.98; $61.18 **45.** 2,441,406 **47a.** 12.8 mm **b.** 27 folds **49a.** $24 million **b.** 60% **c.** week 6 **d.** about $99.93 million

53a. about 261.6 Hz **b.** $a_n \approx 16.3(2)^n$ **c.** C11 **55a.** 30.198 **b.** 31.899 **c.** 31.994 **d.** 32.000 **e.** Yes, the series appears to be approaching 32. **59.** G **61.** G **63.** $a_{18} = 1,310,720$ **65.** $a_{17} \approx 1,208,925.82$ **67a.** 89, 144, 233, 377, 610 **b.** Their sum is the next term. **69.** zero: −5; vertical asymptotes: $x = -2$ and $x = 3$; horizontal asymptote: $y = 0$ **71a.** $f(x) = 0.9(0.8x) = 0.72x$

b. $198 **73.** 52.1 **75.** 104.6

12-5

Check It Out! 1a. diverges **b.** converges **2a.** $\frac{125}{6}$ **b.** $\frac{2}{3}$ **3.** $\frac{1}{9}$

4. Step 1: $\sum_{k=1}^{1}(2k-1) = 1;\ 1^2 = 1$

Step 2: $1 + 3 + \cdots + (2k-1) = k^2$

Step 3: $1 + 3 + \cdots + (2k-1) + [2(k+1)-1]$
$= k^2 + [2(k+1)-1]$
$= k^2 + 2k + 1$
$= (k+1)^2$

5. $a = 5$: $\frac{5^2}{2} \overset{?}{\leq} 2(5) + 1$

$12.5 \nleq 11$

Exercises 1. converge **3.** diverges **5.** $\frac{9}{4}$ **7.** $1066\frac{2}{3}$ **9.** $\frac{56}{99}$

11. Step 1: $2 \cdot 1 = n(n+1)$
$= 1(1+1) = 2$

Step 2: $2 + 4 + \cdots + 2(k)$
$= (k)(k+1)$

Step 3: $2 + 4 + \cdots + 2k + 2(k+1) = k(k+1) + 2(k+1)$
$= k^2 + k + 2k + 2$
$= k^2 + 3k + 2$
$= (k+1)(k+2)$

13. Possible answer: $n = 1$ **15.** converges **17.** diverges **19.** $\frac{16}{15}$ **21.** $\frac{2}{3}$ **23.** $\frac{541}{999}$ **25.** $a = 0$ **27.** $a = 0$ **29.** 320 in., or $26\frac{2}{3}$ ft **31.** 2500 **33.** $-\frac{40}{7}$ **35.** No sum exists. **37.** 500 **39.** $\frac{4}{9}$ **41.** $\frac{41}{333}$ **43.** $\frac{5}{9}$ **45a.** about 415.0 million

b. about 6.2 billion **c.** about 11 billion **53.** $x = \frac{1}{2}$ **55.** $x = -2$ **57.** $x = 0$ **59.** For $a_1 > 0$, $S > S_n$, and both sums are positive. For $a_1 < 0$, $S_n > S$, and both sums are negative. **61.** B **63.** A **67.** $\frac{5}{12}$ **69.** No; the partial sums will approach infinity if $d > 0$ and negative infinity if $d < 0$. **71.** 73.728 % **73.** geometric; $r = \frac{1}{3}$ **75.** geometric; $r = 0.25$

Extension

Check It Out! 1. 53 square units **2.** 155.25 square units

Exercises 1. 1236 square units **3.** 304 square units **5.** 220 square units **7.** 15,875 square units **9a.** about 3056 square units

Study Guide: Review

1. arithmetic; geometric **2.** diverges; converges **3.** explicit formula; recursive formula **4.** infinite sequence; finite sequence **5.** iteration **6.** −8, −7, −6, −5, −4 **7.** $\frac{1}{2}, 2, \frac{9}{2}, 8, \frac{25}{2}$ **8.** $1, -\frac{3}{2}, \frac{9}{4}, -\frac{27}{8}, \frac{81}{16}$ **9.** 55, 53, 51, 49, 47 **10.** $200, 40, 8, \frac{8}{5}, \frac{8}{25}$ **11.** −3, 10, −29, 88, −263 **12.** $a_n = -4n$ **13.** $a_n = 5(4)^{n-1}$ **14.** $a_n = 5n - 29$ **15.** $a_n = 27\left(\frac{2}{3}\right)^{n-1}$ **16.** 0.72 ft, or 8.6 in.; 0.12 ft, or 1.5 in. **17.** $-1 + 4 - 9 + 16 = 10$ **18.** $4.5 + 5.0 + 5.5 + 6.0 + 6.5 = 27.5$ **19.** $1 - 3 + 5 - 7 + 9 = 5$ **20.** $5 + \frac{5}{2} + \frac{5}{3} + \frac{5}{4} = \frac{125}{12}$ **21.** −40 **22.** 385 **23.** 78

24. $27,600; $207,000 **25.** 17 **26.** $\frac{21}{5}$ **27.** −1.2 **28.** 29.5 **29.** −18 **30.** 23 **31.** −630 **32.** −7 **33.** 150 **34.** 330

35. 50, 58, 66, 74,...; no, because he will have a total savings of only $458

36. 0.000004 **37.** $\frac{243}{2}$ **38.** $-\frac{1}{8}$ **39.** 768 **40.** 98,304 **41.** $\frac{512}{3}$ **42.** ±32 **43.** 62,500 **44.** 5 **45.** 2 **46.** $\frac{\sqrt{3}}{24}$ **47.** $\frac{25}{36}$ **48.** $\frac{121}{81}$ **49.** 72,727.2 **50.** 21,845 **51.** −39,062 **52.** $\frac{315}{8} = 39.375$ **53.** $\frac{279}{8} = 34.875$

54. $1044.26 **55.** $9847.32; $43,969.32

56. −2025 **57.** $-\frac{4}{3}$ or $-1.\overline{3}$

58. −343 **59.** 5 **60.** 4.5 **61.** $-\frac{21}{2}$

62. $\frac{1}{9}$ **63.** No sum exists.

64. Step 1: $2^1 = 2^{1+1} - 2 = 2$

Step 2: $2 + \cdots + 2^k = 2^{k+1} - 2$

Step 3: $2 + \cdots + 2^k + 2^{k+1}$

$= 2^{k+1} - 2 + 2^{k+1}$

$= 2(2^{k+1}) - 2$

$= 2^{k+2} - 2 = 2^{k+1+1} - 2$

65. Step 1: $5^{1-1} = \frac{5^1 - 1}{4} = 1$

Step 2: $1 + \cdots + 5^{k-1} = \frac{5^k - 1}{4}$

Step 3: $1 + \cdots + 5^{k-1} + 5^k$

$= \frac{5^k - 1}{4} + 5^k$

$= \frac{5^k - 1}{4} + \frac{4(5^k)}{4}$

$= \frac{5^k + 4(5^k) - 1}{4}$

$= \frac{5(5^k) - 1}{4} = \frac{5^{k+1} - 1}{4}$

66. Step 1: $\frac{1}{4(1^2) - 1}$

$= \frac{1}{2(1) + 1}$

$= \frac{1}{3}$

Step 2: $\frac{1}{3} + \cdots + \frac{1}{4k^2 - 1}$

$= \frac{k}{2k + 1}$

Step 3: $\frac{1}{3} + \cdots + \frac{1}{4k^2 - 1} +$

$\frac{1}{4(k + 1)^2 - 1}$

$= \frac{k}{2k + 1} + \frac{1}{4(k + 1)^2 - 1}$

$= \frac{k}{2k + 1} + \frac{1}{4k^2 + 8k + 3}$

$= \frac{k}{2k + 1} +$

$\frac{1}{(2k + 1)(2k + 3)}$

$= \frac{k(2k + 3)}{(2k + 1)(2k + 3)} +$

$\frac{1}{(2k + 1)(2k + 3)}$

$= \frac{k(2k + 3) + 1}{(2k + 1)(2k + 3)}$

$= \frac{2k^2 + 3k + 1}{(2k + 1)(2k + 3)}$

$= \frac{\cancel{(2k + 1)}(k + 1)}{\cancel{(2k + 1)}(2k + 3)}$

$= \frac{k + 1}{2k + 2 + 1}$

$= \frac{k + 1}{2(k + 1) + 1}$

67a. $\sum_{k=1}^{\infty} 9(0.85)^{k-1}$ **b.** 60 ft

Chapter 13

13-1

Check It Out! 1. $\sin\theta = \frac{15}{17}$; $\cos\theta = \frac{8}{17}$; $\tan\theta = \frac{15}{8}$ **2.** $x = 10\sqrt{2}$ **3.** 41 in. **4.** 220 ft **5.** $\sin\theta = \frac{40}{41}$; $\cos\theta = \frac{9}{41}$; $\tan\theta = \frac{40}{9}$; $\csc\theta = \frac{41}{40}$; $\sec\theta = \frac{41}{9}$; $\cot\theta = \frac{9}{40}$

Exercises 1. tangent **3.** $\sin\theta = \frac{3\sqrt{13}}{13}$; $\cos\theta = \frac{2\sqrt{13}}{13}$; $\tan\theta = \frac{3}{2}$ **5.** $x = \frac{100\sqrt{3}}{3}$ **7.** $x = \frac{250\sqrt{3}}{3}$ **9.** 241 m **11.** $\sin\theta = \frac{3\sqrt{10}}{10}$; $\cos\theta = \frac{\sqrt{10}}{10}$; $\tan\theta = 3$; $\csc\theta = \frac{\sqrt{10}}{3}$; $\sec\theta = \sqrt{10}$; $\cot\theta = \frac{1}{3}$ **13.** $\sin\theta = \frac{1}{3}$; $\cos\theta = \frac{2\sqrt{2}}{3}$; $\tan\theta = \frac{\sqrt{2}}{4}$ **15.** $\sin\theta = \frac{5\sqrt{41}}{41}$; $\cos\theta = \frac{4\sqrt{41}}{41}$; $\tan\theta = \frac{5}{4}$ **17.** $x = 140$ **19a.** 147 m **b.** 187 m **21.** $\sin\theta = \frac{4}{5}$; $\cos\theta = \frac{3}{5}$; $\tan\theta = \frac{4}{3}$; $\csc\theta = \frac{5}{4}$; $\sec\theta = \frac{5}{3}$; $\cot\theta = \frac{3}{4}$ **23.** $\sin\theta = \frac{\sqrt{2}}{2}$; $\cos\theta = \frac{\sqrt{2}}{2}$; $\tan\theta = 1$; $\csc\theta = \sqrt{2}$; $\sec\theta = \sqrt{2}$; $\cot\theta = 1$ **25a.** 8022 ft **b.** 32 s **27.** 135 ft **31.** F **35a.** 3 ft **b.** $13.5\sqrt{3}$ ft² **37.** $x = 32$ **39.** $x = 38{,}416$ **41.** $\frac{1}{2}$ **43.** $16\frac{2}{3}$

13-2

Check It Out!

1a.

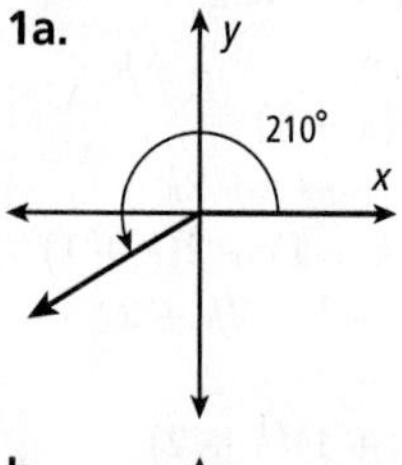

y, 210°, x

b.

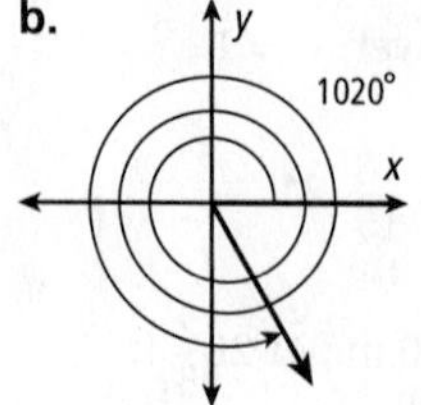

c.

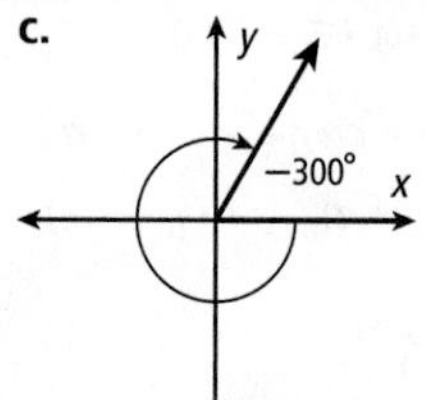

2a. Possible answer: 448°; −272° **b.** Possible answer: 860°; −220° **c.** Possible answer: 240°; −480°

3a. 75° **b.** 65° **c.** 50°

4. $\sin\theta = \frac{2\sqrt{5}}{5}$; $\cos\theta = -\frac{\sqrt{5}}{5}$; $\tan\theta = -2$; $\csc\theta = \frac{\sqrt{5}}{2}$; $\sec\theta = -\sqrt{5}$; $\cot\theta = -\frac{1}{2}$

Exercises 1. terminal

3.

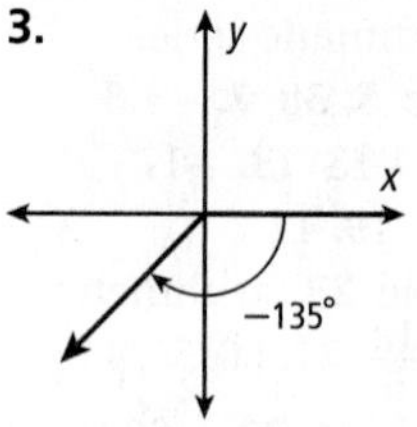

y, x, −135°

5.

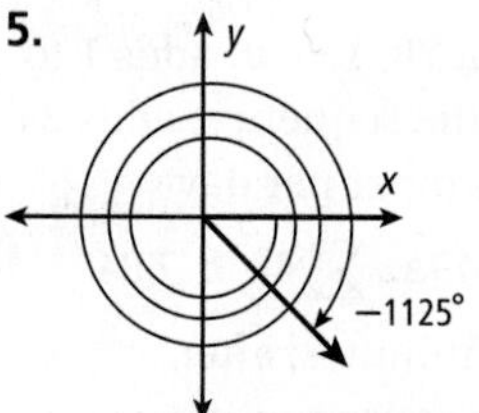

11. 70° **13.** 20° **15.** 50° **17.** 40° **19.** $\sin\theta = -\frac{\sqrt{5}}{5}$; $\cos\theta = \frac{2\sqrt{5}}{5}$; $\tan\theta = -\frac{1}{2}$; $\csc\theta = -\sqrt{5}$; $\sec\theta = \frac{\sqrt{5}}{2}$; $\cot\theta = -2$ **21.** $\sin\theta = -\frac{4}{5}$; $\cos\theta = -\frac{3}{5}$; $\tan\theta = \frac{4}{3}$; $\csc\theta = -\frac{5}{4}$; $\sec\theta = -\frac{5}{3}$; $\cot\theta = \frac{3}{4}$ **23.** $\sin\theta = \frac{6\sqrt{37}}{37}$; $\cos\theta = \frac{\sqrt{37}}{37}$; $\tan\theta = 6$; $\csc\theta = \frac{\sqrt{37}}{6}$; $\sec\theta = \sqrt{37}$; $\cot\theta = \frac{1}{6}$ **25.** $\sin\theta = \frac{2\sqrt{5}}{5}$; $\cos\theta = -\frac{\sqrt{5}}{5}$; $\tan\theta = -2$; $\csc\theta = \frac{\sqrt{5}}{2}$; $\sec\theta = -\sqrt{5}$; $\cot\theta = -\frac{1}{2}$

27.

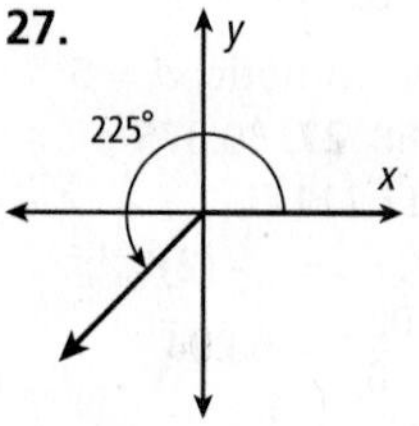

y, 225°, x

Selected Answers

29. 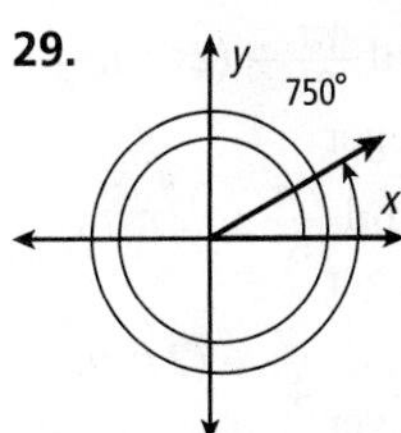

35. 50° **37.** 20° **39.** 85° **41.** 35°
43. $\sin\theta = -\frac{2\sqrt{29}}{29}$; $\cos\theta = \frac{5\sqrt{29}}{29}$; $\tan\theta = -\frac{2}{5}$; $\csc\theta = -\frac{\sqrt{29}}{2}$; $\sec\theta = \frac{\sqrt{29}}{5}$; $\cot\theta = -\frac{5}{2}$
45. $\sin\theta = \frac{3}{5}$; $\cos\theta = \frac{4}{5}$; $\tan\theta = \frac{3}{4}$; $\csc\theta = \frac{5}{3}$; $\sec\theta = \frac{5}{4}$; $\cot\theta = \frac{4}{3}$
47. $\sin\theta = -\frac{2\sqrt{5}}{5}$; $\cos\theta = \frac{\sqrt{5}}{5}$; $\tan\theta = -2$; $\csc\theta = -\frac{\sqrt{5}}{2}$; $\sec\theta = \sqrt{5}$; $\cot\theta = -\frac{1}{2}$
49. $\sin\theta = \frac{4\sqrt{41}}{41}$; $\cos\theta = \frac{5\sqrt{41}}{41}$; $\tan\theta = \frac{4}{5}$; $\csc\theta = \frac{\sqrt{41}}{4}$; $\sec\theta = \frac{\sqrt{41}}{5}$; $\cot\theta = \frac{5}{4}$ **51.** 1364°/s **53.** $(-2, 2\sqrt{3})$
55a. 402 ft **b.** 5 s **c.** 215 ft **d.** 29 ft
57a. 7.5 min **b.** 68 rotations
59. −0.643 **61.** 30°, 150°, 210°, 330°
63. 82°, 98°, 262°, 278° **67.** F
69. $\sin\theta = \frac{b\sqrt{a^2+b^2}}{a^2+b^2}$; $\cos\theta = \frac{a\sqrt{a^2+b^2}}{a^2+b^2}$; $\tan\theta = \frac{b}{a}$
71. $\sin\theta = \frac{b\sqrt{a^2+b^2}}{a^2+b^2}$; $\cos\theta = \frac{a\sqrt{a^2+b^2}}{a^2+b^2}$; $\tan\theta = \frac{b}{a}$
73. sine and cosine: none; tangent and secant: for $\theta = 90°$ for $\theta = 270°$ and all angles coterminal with these angles; cosecant and cotangent: for $\theta = 0°$ for $\theta = 180°$ and all angles coterminal with these angles **75.** 3 **77.** $g(f(4)) = 37$
79. $\sin\theta = \frac{5}{13}$; $\cos\theta = \frac{12}{13}$; $\tan\theta = \frac{5}{12}$

13-3

Check It Out! 1a. $\frac{4\pi}{9}$ radians **b.** 40° **c.** $-\frac{\pi}{5}$ radians **d.** 720°
2a. $-\frac{\sqrt{2}}{2}$ **b.** 0 **c.** $-\frac{1}{2}$
3a. $\sin 270° = -1$; $\cos 270° = 0$; $\tan 270°$: undefined
b. $\sin\frac{11\pi}{6} = -\frac{1}{2}$; $\cos\frac{11\pi}{6} = \frac{\sqrt{3}}{2}$; $\tan\frac{11\pi}{6} = -\frac{\sqrt{3}}{3}$
c. $\sin(-30°) = -\frac{1}{2}$; $\cos(-30°) = \frac{\sqrt{3}}{2}$; $\tan(-30°) = -\frac{\sqrt{3}}{3}$ **4.** 1.5 ft
Exercises 1. 1 unit; 2π units
3. $-\frac{5\pi}{12}$ radians **5.** $\frac{3\pi}{4}$ radians
7. −112.5° **9.** 80° **11.** −1 **13.** $-\frac{1}{2}$
15. $\sin 120° = \frac{\sqrt{3}}{2}$; $\cos 120° = -\frac{1}{2}$; $\tan 120° = -\sqrt{3}$
17. $\sin\frac{\pi}{3} = \frac{\sqrt{3}}{2}$; $\cos\frac{\pi}{3} = \frac{1}{2}$; $\tan\frac{\pi}{3} = \sqrt{3}$ **19.** $\frac{4\pi}{3}$ radians
21. $-\frac{5\pi}{36}$ radians **23.** −20°
25. 630° **27.** $-\sqrt{3}$ **29.** $-\frac{\sqrt{3}}{2}$
31. $\sin 225° = -\frac{\sqrt{2}}{2}$; $\cos 225° = -\frac{\sqrt{2}}{2}$; $\tan 225° = 1$
33. $\sin\frac{11\pi}{6} = -\frac{1}{2}$; $\cos\frac{11\pi}{6} = \frac{\sqrt{3}}{2}$; $\tan\frac{11\pi}{6} = -\frac{\sqrt{3}}{3}$ **35.** about 2793 mi
37. reference angle: $\frac{\pi}{4}$
39. 600 revolutions/min
41a. 45° **b.** 28 ft **51.** C
53. $\sin\theta = -\frac{\sqrt{3}}{2}$; $\csc\theta = -\frac{2\sqrt{3}}{3}$; $\sec\theta = 2$; $\cot\theta = -\frac{\sqrt{3}}{3}$
55. $(-5\sqrt{3}, -5)$ **59.** D: $\{x \mid x \geq -4\}$; R: $\{y \mid y \geq 0\}$ **61.** D: $\{x \mid x \geq 0\}$; R: $\{y \mid y \leq 0\}$ **63.** 25,165,824
65. 45° **67.** 5°

13-4

Check It Out! 1. $\frac{\pi}{4} + (2\pi)n$ or $\frac{5\pi}{4} + (2\pi)n$, where n is an integer
2a. $-\frac{\pi}{4}$ or −45° **b.** $\frac{\pi}{2}$ or 90°
3. 37° north of east **4a.** $\theta = -63.4°$
b. $\theta = 116.6°$
Exercises 3. $\frac{\pi}{6} + (2\pi)n$ and $\frac{7\pi}{6} + (2\pi)n$, where n is an integer
5. $\frac{\pi}{6}$; 30° **7.** undefined **9.** $\frac{\pi}{4}$; 45°
11. 5° **13.** $\theta = 234.5°$ **15.** $\theta = 255.5°$
17. $\frac{\pi}{3} + (2\pi)n$ and $\frac{2\pi}{3} + (2\pi)n$, where n is an integer **19.** $\frac{\pi}{3}$; 60°
21. $-\frac{\pi}{6}$; −30° **23.** $\frac{\pi}{3}$; 60° **25.** 75°
27. $\theta = 228.6°$ **29.** $\theta = 275.7°$
31a. style A: 7.5°; style B: 9.1°; style C: 5.1° **b.** style B **c.** 9.5°
33a. 84.0° **b.** 121 ft **35.** 0.7
39. A **41.** C **43.** $\frac{\pi}{3} \leq \theta \leq \frac{5\pi}{3}$
45. $\frac{\pi}{8} \leq \theta < \frac{\pi}{4}$ or $\frac{5\pi}{8} \leq \theta < \frac{3\pi}{4}$ or $\frac{9\pi}{8} \leq \theta < \frac{5\pi}{4}$ or $\frac{13\pi}{8} \leq \theta < \frac{7\pi}{4}$
47. linear; translation 5 units up (or 5 units left) **49.** $f^{-1}(x) = 4x - 4$; function; D: ℝ; R: ℝ **51.** $\frac{4\pi}{3}$ radians
53. $\frac{7\pi}{3}$ radians

13-5

Check It Out! 1. 47.9 ft^2
2a. $m\angle K = 31°$; $k \approx 6.5$; $h \approx 8.4$
b. $m\angle N = 18°$; $m \approx 4.7$; $p \approx 4.0$
3. 1 triangle; $m\angle B \approx 35.4°$; $m\angle C \approx 39.6°$; $c \approx 6.6$ cm
Exercises 1. 4.9 cm^2 **3.** 6900.5 m^2
5. $m\angle Z = 40°$; $x \approx 36.1$; $y \approx 18.3$
7. $m\angle C = 65°$; $a \approx 2.0$; $b \approx 2.9$
9. $m\angle R = 55°$; $s \approx 38.8$; $t \approx 18.3$
11. 1 triangle; $m\angle B \approx 20.3°$; $m\angle C \approx 39.7°$; $c \approx 7.4$ m
13. 1 triangle; $m\angle B \approx 37.3°$; $m\angle C \approx 97.7°$; $c \approx 9.8$ m
15. 1376.6 yd^2 **17.** $m\angle D = 61°$; $c \approx 9.9$; $d \approx 8.7$ **19.** $m\angle K = 38°$; $\ell \approx 9.4$; $m \approx 7.6$ **21.** 0 triangles
23. 1 triangle; $m\angle B \approx 22.5°$; $m\angle C \approx 27.5°$; $c \approx 4.2$ in.
25. $m\angle C = 64°$; $b \approx 15.3$; $c \approx 15.6$
27. $m\angle A = 59°$; $a \approx 21.8$; $c \approx 16.7$
29. 21 ft **31.** 1 triangle; $m\angle A \approx 16.9°$; $m\angle C \approx 28.1°$; $a \approx 4.9$ **33.** 1 triangle; $m\angle A = 90°$; $m\angle C = 60°$; $c \approx 5.2$
35a. distance from tower 1 to tower 2: 4.2 mi; distance from tower 2 to tower 3: 4.9 mi **b.** 8.9 mi^2
37. 16.7 cm **39.** B is incorrect.
43. B **45b.** no **47.** $0° < m\angle A < 60°$
49. y-intercept: 5; x-intercept: 5
51. y-intercept: 2; x-intercept: 6
53. $x = \frac{1}{3}$ **55.** 135°; $\frac{3\pi}{4}$ radians
57. 30°; $\frac{\pi}{6}$ radians

13-6

Check It Out! 1a. $a \approx 40.9$; $m\angle B \approx 3.9°$; $m\angle C \approx 3.1°$
b. $m\angle A \approx 43.4°$; $m\angle B \approx 55.6°$; $m\angle C \approx 81.0°$ **2.** 34 mi **3.** 367 m^2

Exercises **1.** $q \approx 9.1$; m$\angle P \approx 40.5°$; m$\angle R \approx 59.5°$ **3.** $r \approx 11.6$; m$\angle P \approx 40.3°$; m$\angle R \approx 50.7°$ **5.** m$\angle P \approx 43.2°$; m$\angle Q \approx 86.5°$; m$\angle R \approx 50.3°$ **7.** 9 min **9.** $f \approx 55.5$; m$\angle G \approx 53.1°$; m$\angle H \approx 61.9°$ **11.** $f \approx 21.2$; m$\angle G \approx 59.2°$; m$\angle H \approx 40.8°$ **13.** m$\angle F \approx 54°$; m$\angle G \approx 59.6°$; m$\angle H \approx 66.4°$ **15.** 3.8 mi **17.** m$\angle B \approx 26.3°$; m$\angle C \approx 33.7°$; $a \approx 31.2$ **19.** m$\angle A \approx 51.3°$; m$\angle B \approx 32.7°$; $c \approx 16.6$ **21.** m$\angle A \approx 38.6°$; m$\angle B \approx 92.9°$; m$\angle C \approx 48.5°$ **23.** 74°, 46°, and 60° **25a.** 89 mi **b.** 38° **27a.** m$\angle A = 43°$; m$\angle B = 44°$ **b.** m$\angle A = 28°$; m$\angle B = 41°$ **29.** 524.6 cm^2 **31.** 7.3 ft^2 **33.** 1.2 km **39.** H **41.** No, Abby did not make an error. A triangle cannot be formed from sides that measure 2 units, 3 units, and 5 units. **43.** $x = 9.9$ **45.** $x = \pm 4i$ **47.** x-intercept of f: 4; y-intercept of f: −8; x-intercept of g: 4; y-intercept of g: −4 **49.** x-intercept of f: −12; y-intercept of f: 6; x-intercept of g: −4; y-intercept of g: 6 **51.** m$\angle C = 48°$; $b \approx 8.5$; $c \approx 13.8$

Study Guide: Review

1. radian **2.** cosecant **3.** standard position

4. $\sin\theta = \frac{3}{5}$; $\cos\theta = \frac{4}{5}$; $\tan\theta = \frac{3}{4}$; $\csc\theta = \frac{5}{3}$; $\sec\theta = \frac{5}{4}$; $\cot\theta = \frac{4}{3}$

5. $\sin\theta = \frac{2}{3}$; $\cos\theta = \frac{\sqrt{5}}{3}$; $\tan\theta = \frac{2\sqrt{5}}{5}$; $\csc\theta = \frac{3}{2}$; $\sec\theta = \frac{3\sqrt{5}}{5}$; $\cot\theta = \frac{\sqrt{5}}{2}$

6. $x = 12\sqrt{3}$ **7.** $x = \frac{9\sqrt{2}}{2}$

8. 18 ft **9.** 178 m

10.

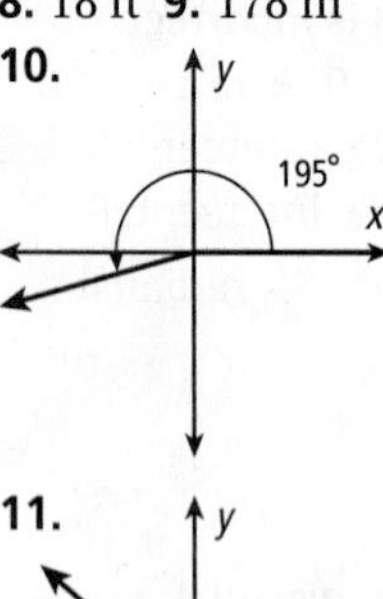

11.

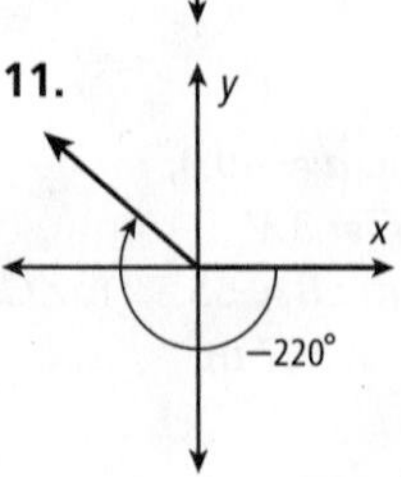

12.

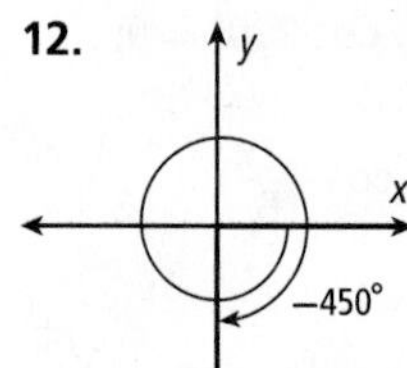

13. Possible answer: 475°; −245°
14. Possible answer: 22°; −338°
15. Possible answer: 225°; −495°
16. 84° **17.** 53° **18.** 75°

19. $\sin\theta = \frac{3}{5}$; $\cos\theta = -\frac{4}{5}$; $\tan\theta = -\frac{3}{4}$; $\csc\theta = \frac{5}{3}$; $\sec\theta = -\frac{5}{4}$; $\cot\theta = -\frac{4}{3}$

20. $\sin\theta = \frac{12}{13}$; $\cos\theta = \frac{5}{13}$; $\tan\theta = \frac{12}{5}$; $\csc\theta = \frac{13}{12}$; $\sec\theta = \frac{13}{5}$; $\cot\theta = \frac{5}{12}$

21. $\sin\theta = -\frac{8}{17}$; $\cos\theta = -\frac{15}{17}$; $\tan\theta = \frac{8}{15}$; $\csc\theta = -\frac{17}{8}$; $\sec\theta = -\frac{17}{15}$; $\cot\theta = \frac{15}{8}$

22. $\sin\theta = -\frac{3\sqrt{73}}{73}$; $\cos\theta = \frac{8\sqrt{73}}{73}$; $\tan\theta = -\frac{3}{8}$; $\csc\theta = -\frac{\sqrt{73}}{3}$; $\sec\theta = \frac{\sqrt{73}}{8}$; $\cot\theta = -\frac{8}{3}$

23. $\sin\theta = -\frac{\sqrt{82}}{82}$; $\cos\theta = -\frac{9\sqrt{82}}{82}$; $\tan\theta = \frac{1}{9}$; $\csc\theta = -\sqrt{82}$; $\sec\theta = -\frac{\sqrt{82}}{9}$; $\cot\theta = 9$

24. $\sin\theta = \frac{2\sqrt{5}}{5}$; $\cos\theta = -\frac{\sqrt{5}}{5}$; $\tan\theta = -2$; $\csc\theta = \frac{\sqrt{5}}{2}$; $\sec\theta = -\sqrt{5}$; $\cot\theta = -\frac{1}{2}$

25. $\frac{3\pi}{2}$ radians **26.** $-\frac{2\pi}{3}$ radians **27.** $\frac{20\pi}{9}$ radians **28.** 30° **29.** −20° **30.** 405° **31.** $-\frac{1}{2}$ **32.** −1 **33.** 2

34. $\sin\frac{7\pi}{6} = -\frac{1}{2}$; $\cos\frac{7\pi}{6} = -\frac{\sqrt{3}}{2}$; $\tan\frac{7\pi}{6} = \frac{\sqrt{3}}{3}$ **35.** $\sin 300° = -\frac{\sqrt{3}}{2}$; $\cos 300° = \frac{1}{2}$; $\tan 300° = -\sqrt{3}$

36. $\sin\left(-\frac{\pi}{3}\right) = -\frac{\sqrt{3}}{2}$; $\cos\left(-\frac{\pi}{3}\right) = \frac{1}{2}$; $\tan\left(-\frac{\pi}{3}\right) = -\sqrt{3}$

37. 22 in. **38a.** $\frac{\pi}{3}$ radians **b.** 1.6 m

39. $\frac{\pi}{3} + (2\pi)n$ and $\frac{4\pi}{3} + (2\pi)n$, where n is an integer
40. $\frac{5\pi}{6} + (2\pi)n$ and $\frac{7\pi}{6} + (2\pi)n$, where n is an integer
41. $\frac{5\pi}{4} + (2\pi)n$ and $\frac{7\pi}{4} + (2\pi)n$, where n is an integer
42. $\frac{5\pi}{6} + (2\pi)n$ and $\frac{11\pi}{6} + (2\pi)n$, where n is an integer
43. −30°; $-\frac{\pi}{6}$ radians **44.** 30°; $\frac{\pi}{6}$ radians **45.** 180°; π radians **46.** 45°; $\frac{\pi}{4}$ radians **47.** 34° **48.** 41° **49.** 17.5° **50.** 162.5° **51.** 65.6° **52.** 245.6° **53.** 5.4 m^2 **54.** 4953.1 ft^2 **55.** 24.0 in.^{2} **56.** 112.5 cm^2 **57.** m$\angle F = 97°$; $d \approx 26.3$; $e \approx 37.0$ **58.** m$\angle B = 75°$; $b = 15$; $c \approx 7.8$ **59.** m$\angle P = 113°$; $p \approx 10.0$; $q \approx 4.9$ **60.** m$\angle Y = 64°$; $w = 4.8$; $x = 8.0$ **61.** 2 triangles; m$\angle B_1 \approx 69.4°$; m$\angle C_1 \approx 55.6°$; $c_1 \approx 14.1$ cm; m$\angle B_2 \approx 110.6°$; m$\angle C_2 \approx 14.4°$; $c_2 \approx 4.3$ cm **62.** m$\angle A \approx 20.9°$; m$\angle B \approx 130.1°$; $c \approx 19.0°$ **63.** m$\angle B \approx 43.0°$; m$\angle C \approx 27.0°$; $a \approx 24.8$ **64.** m$\angle A \approx 125.7°$; m$\angle B \approx 11.7°$; m$\angle C \approx 42.6°$ **65.** m$\angle A \approx 39.4°$; m$\angle B \approx 54.7°$; m$\angle C \approx 85.9°$ **66a.** 40.0 km **b.** 1.4 h **67.** 60 ft^2 **68.** 95 in.^{2}

Chapter 14

14-1

Check It Out! **1a.** not periodic **b.** periodic; 3

2.

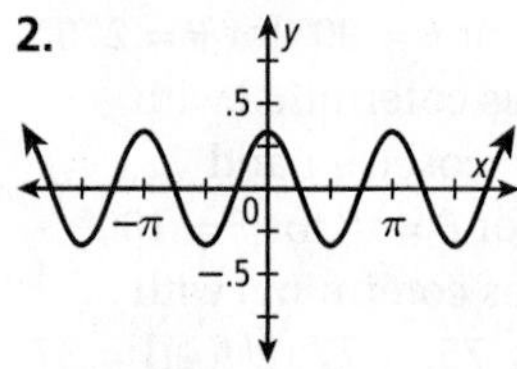

amplitude: $\frac{1}{3}$; period: π

3.

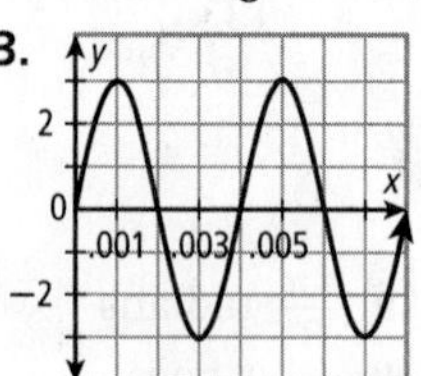

frequency: 250 Hz

Selected Answers

4. 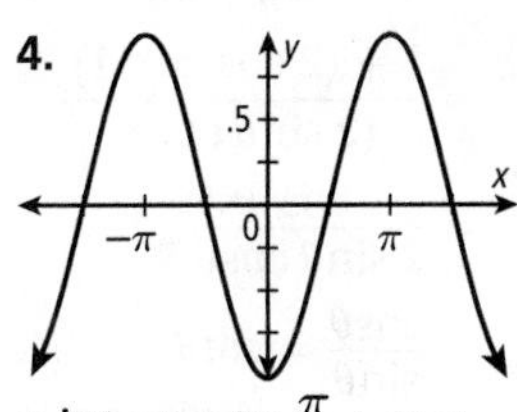

x-intercepts: $\frac{\pi}{2} + n\pi$;
phase shift: π right

5a. 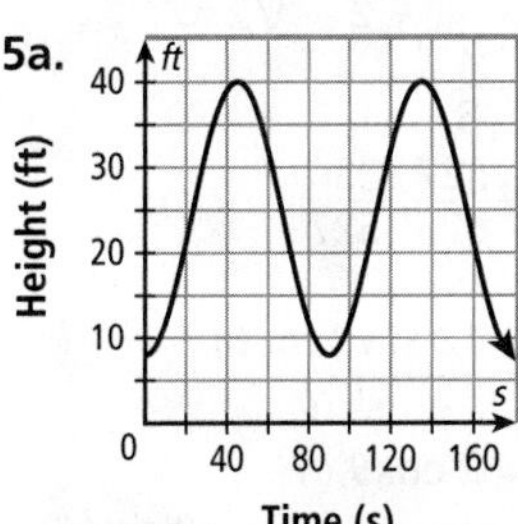

b. 40 ft

Exercises **1.** periods **3.** not periodic **5.** amplitude: $\frac{1}{4}$; period: 2π **7.** frequency: 100 Hz **9.** x-intercepts: πn; phase shift: $\frac{\pi}{2}$right **11.** 4 ft **13.** periodic; 2π **15.** amplitude: $\frac{3}{2}$; period: 2π **17.** amplitude: 6; period: 6π **19.** x-intercepts: πn; phase shift: π left **21.** x-intercepts: $\frac{\pi}{4} + \pi n$; phase shift: $\frac{3\pi}{4}$ left **23.** max.: 24.5 ft; min.: 21.5 ft **25.** amplitude: 1; period: 2π; phase shift $\frac{\pi}{4}$ left and vertical shift 1 down **27.** amplitude: 1; period: 1; horizontal compression and vertical shift 2 down **29.** ≈ 0.3 **31.** ≈ 0.25 **33.** $f(x) = 6 \sin 2x$; $f(x) = 6 \cos 2x$ **35.** $f(x) = -4 \sin 2x$; $g(x) = 4 \cos 2\left(x + \frac{\pi}{4}\right)$ **37a.** period: 12.2; amplitude: 1.5; max.: 3; min.: 0 **b.** $h(0) = 3$; $h(6.1) = 0$ **c.** $h(t) = 1.5 \cos \frac{2\pi}{12.2}t + 1.5$ **39.** The period decreases for $b > 1$ and increases for $b < 1$ because the period is given by $\frac{2\pi}{b}$. **41.** H **43.** phase shift π right, horizontal compression, vertical stretch, and reflection across the x-axis amplitude: 4; period: π; x-intercepts $0, \frac{\pi}{2}, \pi, \frac{3\pi}{2}$, and 2π; max.: 4, min.: -4

45. 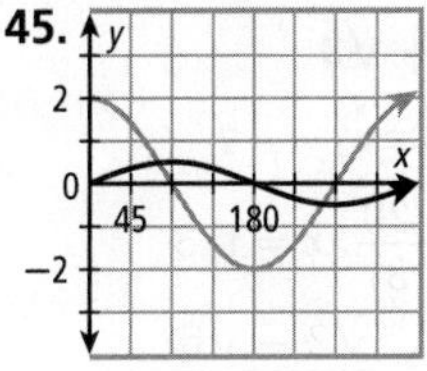

47. $76° < \theta < 256°$ **49.** $(-\infty, -2]$ or $[1, 13)$ **51a.** $6r + 2l + 4c = 100$
b.

Roses	6	4	3	7
Lilies	10	8	5	3
Carnations	11	15	18	13

53. $m\angle A = 10°$; $m\angle B = 12.4°$; $m\angle C = 157.6°$

14-2

Check It Out!

1. 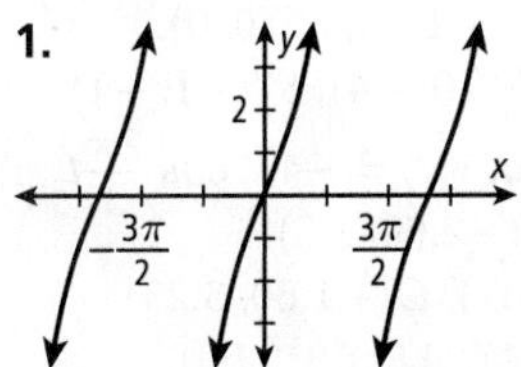

period: 2π; x-intercepts: $2\pi n$; asymptotes: $\pi + 2\pi n$

2. 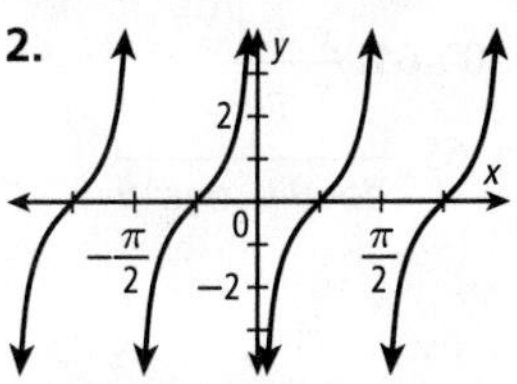

period: $\frac{\pi}{2}$; x-intercepts: $\frac{\pi}{4} + \frac{\pi}{2}n$; asymptotes: $\frac{\pi}{2}n$

3. 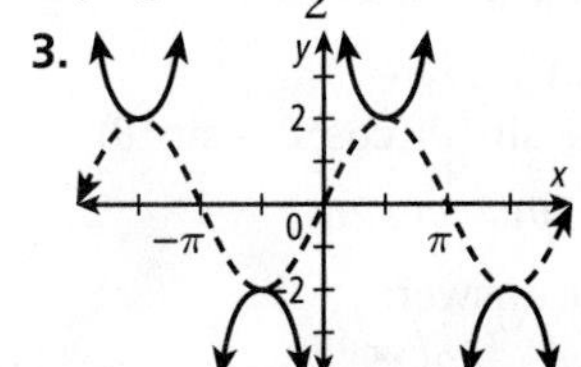

period: 2π; asymptotes: πn

Exercises **1.** period: $\frac{\pi}{3}$; x-intercepts: $\frac{\pi}{3}n$; asymptotes: $\frac{\pi}{6} + \frac{\pi}{3}n$ **3.** period: $\frac{1}{2}$; x-intercepts: $\frac{1}{2}n$; asymptotes: $\frac{1}{4} + \frac{1}{2}n$ **5.** period: $\frac{\pi}{2}$; x-intercepts: $\frac{\pi}{4} + \frac{\pi}{2}n$; asymptotes: $\frac{\pi}{2}n$ **7.** period: 2π; asymptotes: $\frac{\pi}{2} + \pi n$ **9.** period: 2π; asymptotes: πn **11.** period: π; x-intercepts: $\frac{3\pi}{4} + \pi n$; asymptotes: $\frac{\pi}{4} + \pi n$ **13.** period: 2; x-intercepts: $2n$; asymptotes: $1 + 2n$ **15.** period: 4π; x-intercepts: $2\pi + 4\pi n$; asymptotes: $4\pi n$ **17.** period: 2π; asymptotes: $\frac{\pi}{2} + \pi n$ **19.** period: 2π; asymptotes: πn **21.** $\frac{\pi}{2}; \frac{3\pi}{2}; -\frac{\pi}{2}; \frac{5\pi}{2}$ **23.** $\frac{\pi}{2}; \frac{3\pi}{2}; -\frac{\pi}{2}; \frac{5\pi}{2}$

25a. 3 s **c.** $t = \frac{3}{4}$ and $t = \frac{9}{4}$ **27.** increasing; decreasing; decreasing; increasing **29.** decreasing; decreasing; increasing; increasing **31.** increasing; increasing; increasing; increasing **37.** G **39.** H **41.** period: 2; local maximum: 1; local minimum: 7; phase shift: 1 right **47.** D: $\{x \mid x \le -1 \text{ or } x \ge 1\}$; R: $\left\{y \mid 0 \le y \le \pi \text{ and } y \ne \frac{\pi}{2}\right\}$ **49.** D: $\{x \mid x \le -1 \text{ or } x \ge 1\}$; R: $\{y \mid -\frac{\pi}{2} \le y \le \frac{\pi}{2} \text{ and } y \ne 0\}$ **51.** $\frac{1}{10}$; -10 **53.** $3\sqrt{5}$; $-\frac{\sqrt{5}}{15}$ **55.** 11 pages **57.** 135° **59.** $-60°$

14-3

Check It Out!

1a. $\sin\theta \cot\theta = \sin\theta\left(\frac{\cos\theta}{\sin\theta}\right) = \cos\theta$

b. $1 - \sec(-\theta) = 1 - \frac{1}{\cos(-\theta)} = 1 - \frac{1}{\cos\theta} = 1 - \sec\theta$

2a. $1 + \sin\theta$ **b.** $\frac{1}{\sin^2\theta} - 1$ **3.** $\theta \approx 22°$

Exercises

1. $\sin\theta \sec\theta = \sin\theta\left(\frac{1}{\cos\theta}\right) = \frac{\sin\theta}{\cos\theta} = \tan\theta$

3. $\cos^2\theta(\sec^2\theta - 1) = \cos^2\theta(\tan^2\theta) = \cos^2\theta\left(\frac{\sin\theta}{\cos\theta}\right)^2 = \cos^2\theta\left(\frac{\sin^2\theta}{\cos^2\theta}\right) = \sin^2\theta$

5. $1 + \cos^2\theta$ **7.** $\theta \approx 43°$

9. $\frac{\sin\theta - \cos\theta}{\sin\theta} = \frac{\sin\theta}{\sin\theta} - \frac{\cos\theta}{\sin\theta} = 1 - \cot\theta$

11. $\sec^2\theta(1 - \cos^2\theta) = \left(\frac{1}{\cos^2\theta}\right)(\sin^2\theta) = \frac{\sin^2\theta}{\cos^2\theta} = \tan^2\theta$

13. $\frac{\sin^2\theta}{1 - \sin^2\theta}$ **15.** $\sin^2\theta$ **17.** 1 **19.** $\sec\theta$ **21.** $\cot\theta$ **23.** $\sin\theta$ **25.** $\csc\theta$ **27.** 1 **29.** $\sec^2\theta$ **31.** $\tan\theta$

33. $\sin^2\theta(\csc^2\theta - 1) = \sin^2\theta \cot^2\theta = \sin^2\theta\left(\frac{\cos^2\theta}{\sin^2\theta}\right) = \cos^2\theta$

Selected Answers

35. $\frac{\cos\theta}{1-\sin^2\theta} = \frac{\cos\theta}{\cos^2\theta} =$
$\frac{1}{\cos\theta} = \sec\theta$
39. $\cot\theta = \frac{x}{y} = \frac{r\cos\theta}{r\sin\theta}$
$= \frac{\cos\theta}{\sin\theta}$
43. $x^2 + y^2 = r^2$
$\frac{x^2}{x^2} + \frac{y^2}{x^2} = \frac{r^2}{x^2}$
$1 + \left(\frac{y}{x}\right)^2 = \left(\frac{r}{x}\right)^2$
$1 + \tan^2\theta = \sec^2\theta$
45. no **47.** yes **49.** no
51a. $r = \ell\sin\theta$ **b.** $\ell = \frac{g}{\omega^2}\sec\theta$
55. an infinite number of equivalent forms **57.** D **59.** A
63. $\frac{1}{\sin\theta\cos\theta}$ **65.** $\frac{1}{1-\cos^2\theta}$
67. $\sin\theta + \cos\theta$ **69.** $\frac{\sin\theta}{\sin\theta + 1}$
71. $\frac{1}{36}$ **73.** $\frac{\pi}{2}, \frac{3\pi}{2}, -\frac{\pi}{2}, -\frac{3\pi}{2}$
75. $0, \pi, -\pi, 2\pi$

14-4

Check It Out! 1a. $-2-\sqrt{3}$
b. $\frac{\sqrt{2}-\sqrt{6}}{4}$
2. $\cos\left(\frac{\pi}{2}+x\right) = \cos\left(\frac{\pi}{2}\right)\cos x - \sin\left(\frac{\pi}{2}\right)\sin x$
$= (0)\cos x - (1)\sin x$
$= -\sin x$
3. $\frac{24}{25}$ **4.** $A'(-\sqrt{3}, 1), B'(-2\sqrt{3}, 2), C'(0, 2), D'(-\sqrt{3}, -1)$

Exercises 1. A rotation matrix assumes a counterclockwise rotation about the origin.
3. $\frac{\sqrt{6}-\sqrt{2}}{4}$ **5.** $\frac{\sqrt{6}-\sqrt{2}}{4}$
7. $\tan(\pi + x) = \frac{\tan\pi + \tan x}{1 - \tan\pi\tan x}$
$= \frac{0 + \tan x}{1 - 0}$
$= \tan x$
9. $\frac{16}{65}$ **11.** $\frac{16}{63}$ **13.** $A'(-1.73, -1), B'(-0.87, 0.5), C'(-1.5, 2.60)$
15. $\sqrt{3}-2$ **17.** $\frac{-\sqrt{2}-\sqrt{6}}{4}$
19. $\sin\left(\frac{3\pi}{2}+x\right) = \sin\frac{3\pi}{2}\cos x + \cos\frac{3\pi}{2}\sin x$
$= (-1)\cos x + (0)\sin x$
$= -\cos x$

21. $\frac{63}{65}$ **23.** $-\frac{16}{65}$ **25.** $A'(-1.41, 1.41), B'(-0.71, 2.12), C'(-0.71, 0.71)$
27. $2+\sqrt{3}$ **29.** $\frac{\sqrt{2}-\sqrt{6}}{4}$
31. $2+\sqrt{3}$ **33.** $2-\sqrt{3}$ **35.** $\theta = 90°$
37. $\theta = 30°$ or $150°$
39. $\frac{204}{253}; -\frac{253}{325}; \frac{36}{325}$
41a. $\begin{bmatrix} 0 & -1 \\ 1 & 0 \end{bmatrix}; \begin{bmatrix} -1 & 0 \\ 0 & -1 \end{bmatrix}; \begin{bmatrix} 0 & 1 \\ -1 & 0 \end{bmatrix};$
b. $P'(0, 0), Q'(-1, 1), R'(0, 4), S'(1, 1); P''(0, 0), Q''(-1, -1), R''(-4, 0), S''(-1, 1); P'''(0, 0), Q'''(1, -1), R'''(0, -4), S'''(-1, -1)$
43a. 4.2; 3 **b.** $y(t) = -4.2\cos\frac{2\pi}{3}t$
c. 2.1 **45.** $A'(-2.60, 1.5), B'(-2.96, 2.87), C'(-1.60, 3.23), D'(1, 1.73)$ **47.** $A'(1.50, 2.60), B'(2.87, 2.96), C'(3.23, 1.60), D'(1.73, -1)$ **49.** A **51.** A
57. 45° **59.** 30° **61.** $\frac{x-1}{x+2}$
63. parabola **65.** $\frac{1}{\cos\theta - \cos^3\theta}$
67. $\sin^2\theta$

14-5

Check It Out! 1. $\frac{4\sqrt{2}}{7}; -\frac{7}{9}$
2a. Possible answer:
$\cos^4\theta - \sin^4\theta$
$= (\cos^2\theta + \sin^2\theta)(\cos^2\theta - \sin^2\theta)$
$= (1)(\cos 2\theta) = \cos 2\theta$
b. Possible answer:
$\frac{2\tan\theta}{1+\tan^2\theta} = \frac{2\left(\frac{\sin\theta}{\cos\theta}\right)}{\sec^2\theta}$
$= \frac{2\left(\frac{\sin\theta}{\cos\theta}\right)}{\frac{1}{\cos^2\theta}} \cdot \frac{\left(\frac{\cos^2\theta}{1}\right)}{\left(\frac{\cos^2\theta}{1}\right)}$
$= 2\left(\frac{\sin\theta}{\cos\theta}\right)\left(\frac{\cos^2\theta}{1}\right)$
$= 2\sin\theta\cos\theta = \sin 2\theta$
3a. $\sqrt{7+4\sqrt{3}}$ **b.** $-\frac{\sqrt{2-\sqrt{2}}}{2}$
4. $\frac{\sqrt{5}}{5}; \frac{2\sqrt{5}}{5}$

Exercises 1. $-\frac{120}{169}; -\frac{119}{169}; \frac{120}{119}$
3. $2\cos 2\theta = 2(2\cos^2\theta - 1)$
$= 4\cos^2\theta - 2$

5. $\frac{1+\cos 2\theta}{\sin 2\theta} = \frac{1 + (2\cos^2\theta - 1)}{(2\sin\theta\cos\theta)}$
$= \frac{2\cos^2\theta}{2\sin\theta\cos\theta}$
$= \frac{\cos\theta}{\sin\theta} = \cot\theta$
7. $\frac{\sqrt{2-\sqrt{2}}}{2}$ **9.** $\sqrt{\frac{2+\sqrt{2}}{2-\sqrt{2}}}$
11. $\frac{4}{5}; -\frac{3}{5}; -\frac{4}{3}$
13. $-\frac{336}{625}; -\frac{527}{625}; \frac{336}{527}$
15. $\frac{\sin 2\theta}{\sin\theta} = \frac{(2\sin\theta\cos\theta)}{\sin\theta}$
$= 2\cos\theta$
17. $\frac{1-\cos 2\theta}{\sin 2\theta} = \frac{1-(1-2\sin^2\theta)}{2\sin\theta\cos\theta}$
$= \frac{2\sin^2\theta}{2\sin\theta\cos\theta}$
$= \frac{\sin\theta}{\cos\theta} = \tan\theta$
19. $\frac{\sqrt{2+\sqrt{3}}}{2}$ **21.** $\frac{\sqrt{2-\sqrt{2}}}{2}$
23. $\frac{\sqrt{37}}{37}; -\frac{6\sqrt{37}}{37}; -\frac{1}{6}$
25. $3\sin\theta\cos^2\theta - \sin^3\theta$
27. $\cos\theta\left(1 - 4\sin^2\theta\right)$ **29.** 1
31. $2\tan\theta$ **33.** $\sin\theta$
35a. $y(t) = 6.2\sin t\cos t$
b. about 0.66 s **c.** about 3.00 m
37. $\frac{4\sqrt{5}}{9}; \frac{1}{9}; 4\sqrt{5}; \frac{\sqrt{18+6\sqrt{5}}}{6}; -\frac{\sqrt{18-6\sqrt{5}}}{6}; -\frac{\sqrt{3+\sqrt{5}}}{\sqrt{3-\sqrt{5}}}$
39. $-\frac{4}{5}; \frac{3}{5}; -\frac{4}{3}; \sqrt{\frac{5-2\sqrt{5}}{10}}; -\sqrt{\frac{5+2\sqrt{5}}{10}}; -\sqrt{\frac{5-2\sqrt{5}}{5+2\sqrt{5}}}$
41. $\frac{\sqrt{2-\sqrt{3}}}{2}$ **43.** $-\frac{\sqrt{2-\sqrt{3}}}{2}$
49a. $d(\theta) = \frac{v_0^2\sin 2\theta}{32}$
b. 100 ft; ≈ 173 ft; 200 ft; ≈ 173 ft; 100 ft **c.** 45° **d.** $30.52° < \theta < 59.48°$
53. F **55.** G
59. $\sqrt{\frac{2-\sqrt{2+\sqrt{3}}}{2+\sqrt{2+\sqrt{3}}}}$
61. $\frac{1}{2}\sqrt{2-\sqrt{2+\sqrt{3}}}$
65. no **67.** $\frac{5x+12}{x+7}; x \neq 7$
69. $\frac{2x^2-30x-20}{(x+1)(x-3)}; x \neq 1, 3$
71. $\frac{\sqrt{2}-\sqrt{6}}{4}$ **73.** $\frac{\sqrt{2}-\sqrt{6}}{4}$

14-6

Check It Out! 1. $150° + 360n°$, $210° + 360n°$ **2a.** 0 **b.** $\approx 21.9°$, $\approx 158.1°$ **3a.** 60°, 300° **b.** 90°, 210°, 270°, 330° **4.** late March and late September

Exercises 1. $60° + 360n°$, $300° + 360n°$ **3.** $30° + 360n°$, $330° + 360n°$ **5.** $\approx 74.5°$ or 285.5° **7.** π **9.** $60° + 360n°$, $300° + 360n°$ **11.** $150° + 360n°$, $210° + 360n°$ **13.** $\frac{\pi}{3}$, π, or $\frac{5\pi}{3}$ **15.** 90°, 120°, 240°, 270° **17a.** 10:00 A.M. and 6:00 P.M. **19.** 30°, 150°, 270° **21.** 30°, 90°, 150° **23.** 0°, 180°, 210°, 330° **25.** π **27.** $\frac{7\pi}{6}$, $\frac{11\pi}{6}$ **29.** no solution **31.** 0, $\frac{\pi}{3}$, π, $\frac{4\pi}{3}$ **33a.** $\approx\frac{\pi}{2}$; 4 sets **b.** $\approx\frac{2\pi}{5}$; 5 sets **35.** B is incorrect **37.** $x \approx -4.165, -1.797, 1.395, 5.464, 6.831$ **39.** $\approx 84.8°$, $\approx 264.8°$ **41.** 60°, 150°, 240°, 330° **43.** 38.5°, 141.5° **47.** J **49.** J

51. $\theta \approx 38.7°$ or 321.3°. **53.** 90°, 270°, 120°, 240°, 60°, 300° **55.** 210°, 330° **57.** 30°, 150°, 210°, 330° **59.** $2\sqrt{5}$, $4.\overline{47}$, $\sqrt{21}$, $\frac{19}{4}$, $\frac{\pi}{0.65}$ **61.** -1 **63.** $\cos^2\theta$

Study Guide: Review

1. cycle **2.** frequency **3.** period **4.** phase shift **5.** amplitude: 1; period: $\frac{2\pi}{3}$ **6.** amplitude: 1; period: 4π **7.** amplitude: $\frac{1}{3}$; period: 2π **8.** amplitude: 2; period: 2 **9.** amplitude: $\frac{1}{2}$; period: π **10.** amplitude: $\frac{\pi}{2}$; period: 2 **11.** x-intercepts: $\frac{\pi}{2} + \pi n$; phase shift: π left **12.** x-intercepts: $\frac{3\pi}{4} + \pi n$; phase shift: $\frac{\pi}{4}$ left **13.** x-intercepts: $\frac{\pi}{2} + \pi n$; phase shift: $\frac{3\pi}{2}$ right **14.** x-intercepts: πn; phase shift: $\frac{3\pi}{2}$ left

15.

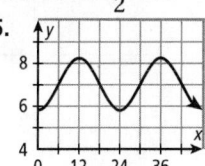

16. 24 h **17.** 8.2; noon **18.** period: π; x-intercepts: πn; asymptotes: $\frac{\pi}{2} + \pi n$ **19.** period: 1; x-intercepts: n; asymptotes: $\frac{1}{2} + n$ **20.** period: 2; x-intercepts: $2n$; asymptotes: $1 + 2n$ **21.** period: π; x-intercepts: $\frac{\pi}{2} + \pi n$; asymptotes: πn **22.** period: π; x-intercepts: $\frac{\pi}{2} + \pi n$; asymptotes: πn **23.** period: 1; x-intercepts: $\frac{1}{2} + n$; asymptotes: n **24.** period: 2π; asymptotes: $\frac{\pi}{2} + \pi n$ **25.** period: π; asymptotes: $\frac{\pi}{2}n$ **26.** period: 2π; asymptotes: πn **27.** period: 2π; asymptotes: $\frac{\pi}{2} + \pi n$ **28.** period: 2π; asymptotes: $\frac{\pi}{2} + \pi n$ **29.** period: 2π; asymptotes: $\pi + \pi n$

30. $\sec\theta\sin\theta\cot\theta$
$$= \left(\frac{1}{\cos\theta}\right)\sin\theta\left(\frac{\cos\theta}{\sin\theta}\right)$$
$$= \left(\frac{\cos\theta}{\cos\theta}\right)\left(\frac{\sin\theta}{\sin\theta}\right) = 1$$

31. $\frac{\sin^2(-\theta)}{\tan\theta} = \frac{(-\sin\theta)(-\sin\theta)}{\frac{\sin\theta}{\cos\theta}}$
$$= (\sin\theta)(\sin\theta)\left(\frac{\cos\theta}{\sin\theta}\right)$$
$$= \sin\theta\cos\theta$$

32. $(\sec\theta + 1)(\sec\theta - 1) = \sec^2\theta - 1$
$$= \tan^2\theta$$

33. $\cos\theta\sec\theta + \cos^2\theta\csc^2\theta =$
$$1 + \cos^2\theta\frac{1}{\sin^2\theta}$$
$$= 1 + \cot^2\theta$$
$$= \csc^2\theta$$

34. $(\tan\theta + \cot\theta)^2 =$
$$\tan^2\theta + 2\tan\theta\cot\theta + \cot^2\theta$$
$$= \tan^2\theta + 2 + \cot^2\theta$$
$$= (\tan^2\theta + 1) + (1 + \cot^2\theta)$$
$$= \sec^2\theta + \csc^2\theta$$

35. $\tan\theta + \cot\theta = \frac{\sin\theta}{\cos\theta} + \frac{\cos\theta}{\sin\theta}$
$$= \frac{\sin^2\theta + \cos^2\theta}{\sin\theta\cos\theta}$$
$$= \frac{1}{\sin\theta\cos\theta}$$
$$= \sec\theta\csc\theta$$

36. $\sin^2\theta\tan\theta = (1 - \cos^2\theta)\tan\theta$
$$= \tan\theta - \cos^2\tan\theta$$
$$= \tan\theta - \cos^2\theta\left(\frac{\sin\theta}{\cos\theta}\right)$$
$$= \tan\theta - \sin\theta\cos\theta$$

37. $\frac{\tan\theta}{1 - \cos^2\theta} = \frac{\left(\frac{\sin\theta}{\cos\theta}\right)}{(\sin^2\theta)}$
$$= \left(\frac{\sin\theta}{\cos\theta}\right)\left(\frac{1}{\sin^2\theta}\right)$$
$$= \left(\frac{1}{\cos\theta}\right)\left(\frac{1}{\sin\theta}\right)$$
$$= \sec\theta\csc\theta$$

38. $\csc\theta$ **39.** $\tan^2\theta$ **40.** $-\tan^2\theta$ **41.** $\sin\theta$ **42.** $\frac{-\sqrt{2} - \sqrt{6}}{4}$ **43.** $\frac{-\sqrt{2} - \sqrt{6}}{4}$ **44.** $\frac{\sqrt{6} + \sqrt{2}}{4}$ **45.** $2 - \sqrt{3}$ **46.** $-\frac{16}{65}$ **47.** $-\frac{63}{65}$ **48.** $\frac{56}{33}$ **49.** $\frac{16}{63}$ **50.** $-\frac{56}{65}$ **51.** $-\frac{33}{65}$ **52.** $\frac{36 - 5\sqrt{7}}{52}$ **53.** $\frac{-15 - 12\sqrt{7}}{52}$ **54.** $\frac{5\sqrt{7} + 36}{15 - 12\sqrt{7}}$ **55.** $\frac{5\sqrt{7} - 36}{15 + 12\sqrt{7}}$ **56.** $\frac{-36 - 5\sqrt{7}}{52}$ **57.** $\frac{-15 + 12\sqrt{7}}{52}$

58. $\approx \begin{bmatrix} 0 & 2.60 & 2.46 & -0.13 \\ 0 & 1.50 & 3.73 & 2.23 \end{bmatrix}$

59. $\approx \begin{bmatrix} 0 & 2.12 & 1.41 & -0.71 \\ 0 & 2.12 & 4.24 & 2.12 \end{bmatrix}$

60. $\approx \begin{bmatrix} 0 & 1.5 & 0.27 & -1.23 \\ 0 & 2.60 & 4.46 & 1.87 \end{bmatrix}$

61. $\begin{bmatrix} 0 & 0 & -2 & -2 \\ 0 & 3 & 4 & 1 \end{bmatrix}$

62. $\approx \begin{bmatrix} 0 & -4.23 & -3.46 & 0.77 \\ 0 & 3.33 & -2 & -5.33 \end{bmatrix}$

63. $\begin{bmatrix} 0 & -5 & 0 & 5 \\ 0 & -2 & -4 & -2 \end{bmatrix}$

64. $\approx \begin{bmatrix} 0 & -0.77 & 3.46 & 4.23 \\ 0 & -5.33 & -2 & 3.33 \end{bmatrix}$

65. $\begin{bmatrix} 0 & 2 & 4 & 2 \\ 0 & -5 & 0 & 5 \end{bmatrix}$ **66.** $\frac{24}{25}$

67. $-\frac{7}{25}$ **68.** $\frac{1}{2}$ **69.** $\frac{\sqrt{5}}{5}$ **70.** $-3\sqrt{7}$ **71.** $\frac{1}{8}$ **72.** $-\frac{\sqrt{14}}{4}$ **73.** $\frac{\sqrt{2}}{4}$ **74.** $\frac{\sqrt{2 - \sqrt{3}}}{2}$ **75.** $\frac{\sqrt{2 - \sqrt{3}}}{2}$ **76.** $135° + 360n°$, $225° + 360n°$ **77.** $180° + 360n°$ **78.** $0° + 180n°$, $135° + 180n°$ **79.** $60° + 180n°$, $120° + 180n°$ **80.** $\frac{2\pi}{3}$, $\frac{4\pi}{3}$ **81.** 0 **82.** $\frac{\pi}{2}$, $\frac{3\pi}{2}$ **83.** $\frac{3\pi}{2}$ **84.** 0, $\frac{2\pi}{3}$, $\frac{4\pi}{3}$ **85.** $\frac{\pi}{2}$, $\frac{7\pi}{6}$, $\frac{3\pi}{2}$, $\frac{11\pi}{6}$ **86a.** 900 min; late June **b.** 540 min; late December

Selected Answers

Glossary/Glosario

go.hrw.com
Multilingual Glossary Online
KEYWORD: MB7 Glossary

A

ENGLISH	SPANISH	EXAMPLES
absolute value of a complex number (p. 382) The absolute value of $a + bi$ is the distance from the origin to the point (a, b) in the complex plane and is denoted $\lvert a + bi \rvert = \sqrt{a^2 + b^2}$.	**valor absoluto de un número complejo** El valor absoluto de $a + bi$ es la distancia desde el origen hasta el punto (a, b) en el plano complejo y se expresa $\lvert a + bi \rvert = \sqrt{a^2 + b^2}$.	$\lvert 2 + 3i \rvert = \sqrt{2^2 + 3^2} = \sqrt{13}$
absolute value of a real number (p. 151) The absolute value of x is the distance from zero to x on a number line, denoted $\lvert x \rvert$. $\lvert x \rvert = \begin{cases} x & \text{if } x \ge 0 \\ -x & \text{if } x < 0 \end{cases}$	**valor absoluto de un número real** El valor absoluto de x es la distancia desde cero hasta x en una recta numérica y se expresa $\lvert x \rvert$. $\lvert x \rvert = \begin{cases} x & \text{si } x \ge 0 \\ -x & \text{si } x < 0 \end{cases}$	$\lvert 3 \rvert = 3$ $\lvert -3 \rvert = 3$
absolute-value function (p. 158) A function whose rule contains absolute-value expressions.	**función de valor absoluto** Función cuya regla contiene expresiones de valor absoluto.	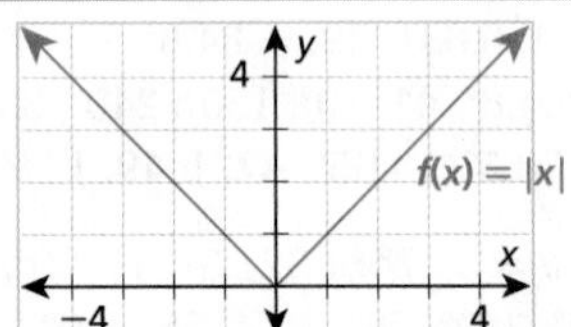
acute angle (p. 960) An angle that measures greater than 0° and less than 90°.	**ángulo agudo** Ángulo que mide más de 0° y menos de 90°.	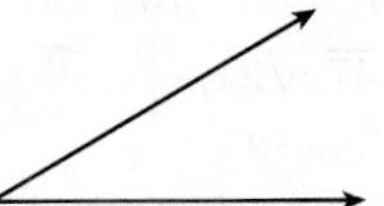
additive inverse of a matrix (p. 249) A matrix where each entry is the opposite of each entry in another matrix. Two matrices are additive inverses if their sum is the zero matrix.	**inverso aditivo de una matriz** Matriz en la cual cada entrada es el opuesto de cada entrada en otra matriz. Dos matrices son inversos aditivos si su suma es la matriz cero.	$\begin{bmatrix} 1 & -2 \\ 0 & 4 \end{bmatrix}$ and $\begin{bmatrix} -1 & 2 \\ 0 & -4 \end{bmatrix}$ are additive inverses.
address (p. 246) The location of an entry in a matrix, given by the row and column in which the entry appears. In matrix A, the address of the entry in row i and column j is a_{ij}.	**dirección** Ubicación de una entrada en una matriz, indicada por la fila y la columna en las que aparece la entrada. En la matriz A, la dirección de la entrada de la fila i y la columna j es a_{ij}.	In the matrix $A = \begin{bmatrix} 2 & 3 \\ 4 & 1 \end{bmatrix}$, the address of the entry 2 is a_{11}, the address of the entry 3 is a_{12}.
algebraic expression (p. 27) An expression that contains at least one variable.	**expresión algebraica** Expresión que contiene por lo menos una variable.	$2x + 3y$
amplitude (p. 991) The amplitude of a periodic function is half the difference of the maximum and minimum values (always positive).	**amplitud** La amplitud de una función periódica es la mitad de la diferencia entre los valores máximo y mínimo (siempre positivos).	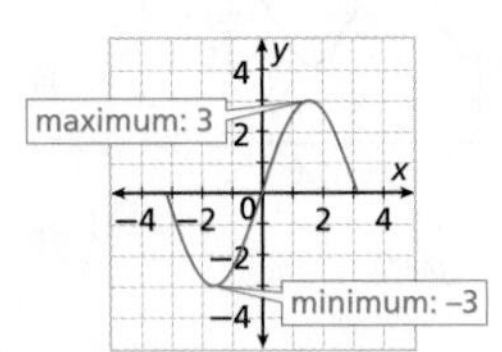 amplitude $= \frac{1}{2}\left[3 - (-3)\right] = 3$

ENGLISH / SPANISH / EXAMPLES

angle of depression (p. 931) The angle formed by a horizontal line and a line of sight to a point below.

ángulo de depresión Ángulo formado por una recta horizontal y una línea visual a un punto inferior.

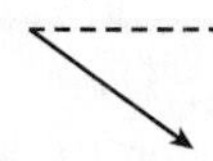

---

angle of elevation (p. 931) The angle formed by a horizontal line and a line of sight to a point above.

ángulo de elevación Ángulo formado por una recta horizontal y una línea visual a un punto superior.

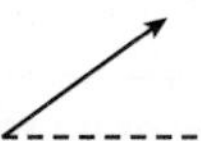

---

angle of rotation (p. 936) An angle formed by a rotating ray, called the terminal side, and a stationary reference ray, called the initial side.

ángulo de rotación Ángulo formado por un rayo en rotación, denominado lado terminal, y un rayo de referencia estático, denominado lado inicial.

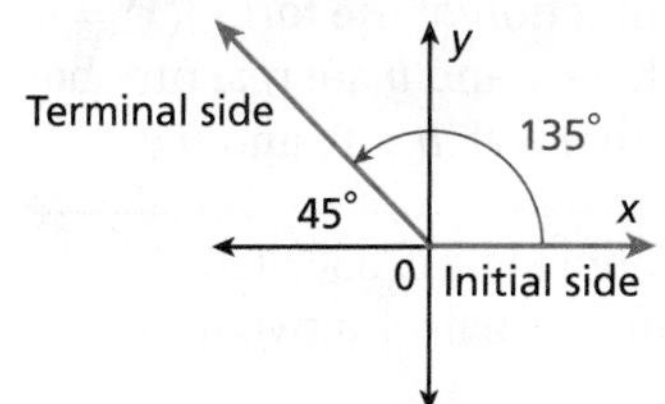

---

arc (p. 943) An unbroken part of a circle consisting of two points on the circle, called the endpoints, and all the points on the circle between them.

arco Parte continua de un círculo formada por dos puntos del círculo denominados extremos y todos los puntos del círculo comprendidos entre éstos.

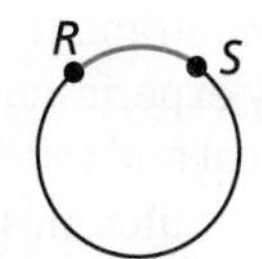

---

arc length (p. 943) The distance along an arc measured in linear units.

longitud de arco Distancia a lo largo de un arco medida en unidades lineales.

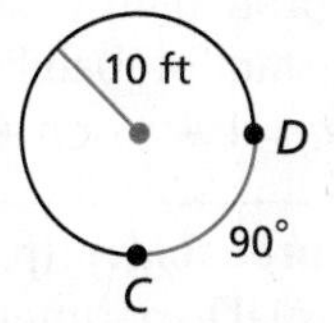

$m\widehat{CD} = 5\pi$ ft

---

arithmetic sequence (p. 879) A sequence whose successive terms differ by the same nonzero number d, called the *common difference*.

sucesión aritmética Sucesión cuyos términos sucesivos difieren en el mismo número distinto de cero d, denominado *diferencia común*.

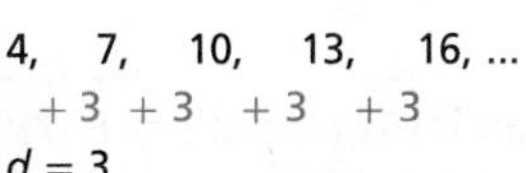

$d = 3$

---

arithmetic series (p. 882) The indicated sum of the terms of an arithmetic sequence.

serie aritmética Suma indicada de los términos de una sucesión aritmética.

$4 + 7 + 10 + 13 + 16 + \ldots$

---

asymptote (p. 490) A line that a graph approaches as the value of a variable becomes extremely large or small.

asíntota Línea recta a la cual se aproxima una gráfica a medida que el valor de una variable se hace sumamente grande o pequeño.

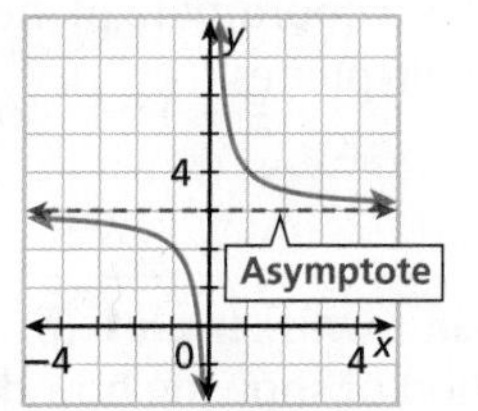

---

augmented matrix (p. 287) A matrix that consists of the coefficients and the constant terms in a system of linear equations.

matriz aumentada Matriz formada por los coeficientes y los términos constantes de un sistema de ecuaciones lineales.

System of equations: $3x + 2y = 5$, $2x - 3y = 1$

Augmented matrix: $\left[\begin{array}{cc|c} 3 & 2 & 5 \\ 2 & -3 & 1 \end{array}\right]$

---

axis of symmetry (p. 323) A line that divides a plane figure or a graph into two congruent reflected halves.

eje de simetría Línea que divide una figura plana o una gráfica en dos mitades reflejadas congruentes.

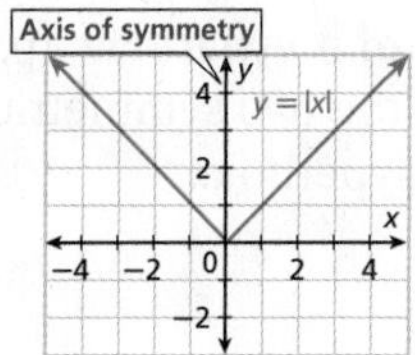

ENGLISH	SPANISH	EXAMPLES
B		
base of a power (p. 34) The number in a power that is used as a factor.	**base de una potencia** Número de una potencia que se utiliza como factor.	$3^4 = 3 \cdot 3 \cdot 3 \cdot 3 = 81$ (base: 3)
base of an exponential function (p. 490) The value of b in a function of the form $f(x) = ab^x$, where a and b are real numbers with $a \neq 0$, $b > 0$, and $b \neq 1$.	**base de una función exponencial** Valor de b en una función del tipo $f(x) = ab^x$, donde a y b son números reales con $a \neq 0$, $b > 0$, y $b \neq 1$.	$f(x) = 5(2)^x$ (base: 2)
binomial (pp. 336, 406) A polynomial with two terms.	**binomio** Polinomio con dos términos.	$x + y$ $2a^2 + 3$ $4m^3n^2 + 6mn^4$
binomial experiment (p. 837) A probability experiment consists of n identical and independent trials whose outcomes are either successes or failures, with a constant probability of success p and a constant probability of failure q, where $q = 1 - p$ or $p + q = 1$.	**experimento binomial** Experimento de probabilidades que comprende n pruebas idénticas e independientes cuyos resultados son éxitos o fracasos, con una probabilidad constante de éxito p y una probabilidad constante de fracaso q, donde $q = 1 - p$ o $p + q = 1$.	A multiple-choice quiz has 10 questions with 4 answer choices. The number of trials is 10. If each question is answered randomly, the probability of success for each trial is $\frac{1}{4} = 0.25$ and the probability of failure is $\frac{3}{4} = 0.75$.
binomial probability (p. 838) In a binomial experiment, the probability of r successes $(0 \leq r \leq n)$ is $P(r) = {}_nC_r \cdot p^r q^{n-r}$.	**probabilidad binomial** En un experimento binomial, la probabilidad de r éxitos $(0 \leq r \leq n)$ es $P(r) = {}_nC_r \cdot p^r q^{n-r}$.	In the binomial experiment above, the probability of randomly guessing 6 problems correctly is $P = {}_{10}C_6\,(0.25)^6\,(0.75)^4 \approx 0.016$.
Binomial Theorem (p. 837) For any positive integer n, $(x+y)^n = {}_nC_0\, x^n y^0 + {}_nC_1\, x^{n-1} y^1 + {}_nC_2\, x^{n-2} y^2 + \cdots + {}_nC_{n-1}\, x^1 y^{n-1} + {}_nC_n\, x^0 y^n$	**Teorema de los binomios** Dado un entero positivo n, $(x+y)^n = {}_nC_0\, x^n y^0 + {}_nC_1\, x^{n-1} y^1 + {}_nC_2\, x^{n-2} y^2 + \cdots + {}_nC_{n-1}\, x^1 y^{n-1} + {}_nC_n\, x^0 y^n$	$(x+2)^4 = {}_4C_0\, x^4 2^0 + {}_4C_1\, x^3 2^1 + {}_4C_2\, x^2 2^2 + {}_4C_1\, x^1 2^3 + {}_4C_4\, x^0 2^4 = x^4 + 8x^3 + 24x^2 + 32x + 16$
boundary line (p. 124) A line that divides a coordinate plane into two half-planes.	**línea de límite** Línea que divide un plano cartesiano en dos semiplanos.	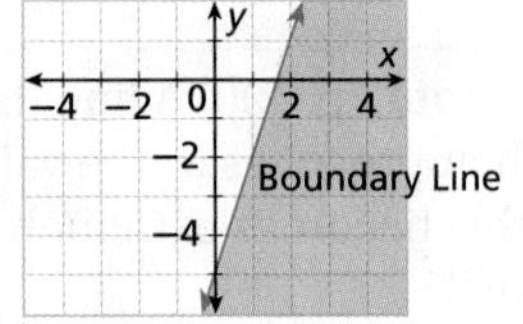
box-and-whisker plot (p. 829) A method of showing how data is distributed by using the median, quartiles, and minimum and maximum values; also called a *box plot*.	**gráfica de mediana y rango** Método para demostrar la distribución de datos utilizando la mediana, los cuartiles y los valores mínimos y máximos; también llamado *gráfica de caja*.	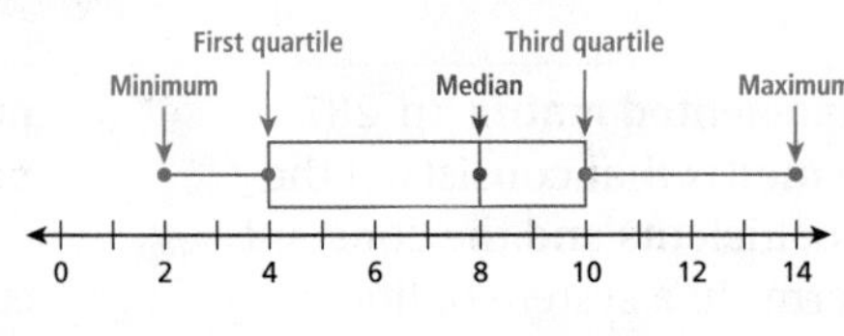
branch of a hyperbola (p. 744) One of the two symmetrical parts of the hyperbola.	**rama de una hipérbola** Una de las dos partes simétricas de la hipérbola.	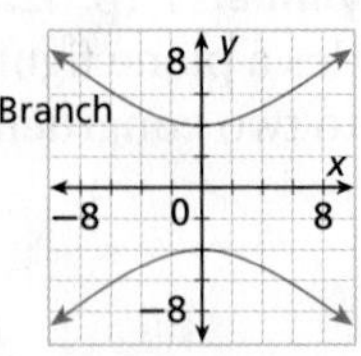

ENGLISH	SPANISH	EXAMPLES

circle (p. 729) The set of points in a plane that are a fixed distance from a given point called the center of the circle.	**círculo** Conjunto de puntos en un plano que se encuentran a una distancia fija de un punto determinado denominado centro del círculo.	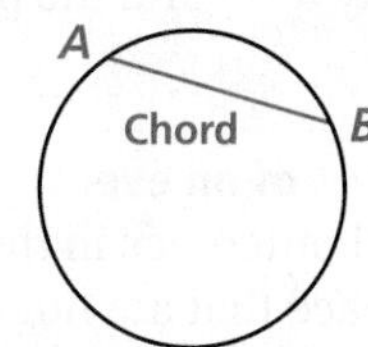
circumference (p. 943) The distance around a circle.	**circunferencia** Distancia alrededor del círculo.	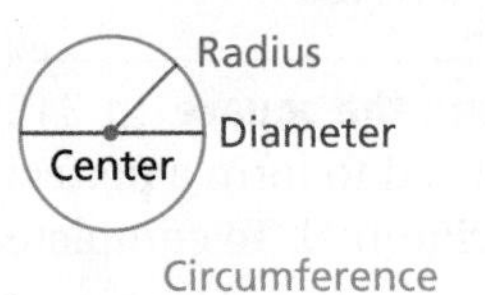
closure (p. 15) A set of numbers is said to be closed, or to have closure, under a given operation if the result of the operation on any two numbers in the set is also in the set.	**cerradura** Se dice que un conjunto de números es cerrado, o tiene cerradura, respecto de una operación determinada, si el resultado de la operación entre dos números cualesquiera del conjunto también está en el conjunto.	The natural numbers are closed under addition because the sum of two natural numbers is always a natural number.
coefficient (p. 47) A number multiplied by a variable.	**coeficiente** Número multiplicado por una variable.	In the expression $2x + 3y$, 2 is the coefficient of x and 3 is the coefficient of y.
coefficient matrix (p. 271) The matrix of the coefficients of the variables in a linear system of equations.	**matriz de coeficientes** Matriz de los coeficientes de las variables en un sistema lineal de ecuaciones.	System of equations: $2x + 3y = 11$, $5x - 4y = 16$; Coefficient matrix: $\begin{bmatrix} 2 & 3 \\ 5 & -4 \end{bmatrix}$
coefficient of determination (p. 376) The number R^2, with $0 \le R^2 \le 1$, that shows the fraction of the data that are close to the curve of best fit and, thus, how well the curve fits the data.	**coeficiente de determinación** El número R^2, con $0 \le R^2 \le 1$, que muestra la fracción de los datos cercanos a la línea de mejor ajuste y, por lo tanto, cuánto se ajusta la línea de mejor ajuste a los datos.	
combination (p. 796) A selection of a group of objects in which order is *not* important. The number of combinations of r objects chosen from a group of n objects is denoted ${}_nC_r$.	**combinación** Selección de un grupo de objetos en la cual el orden *no* es importante. El número de combinaciones de r objetos elegidos de un grupo de n objetos se expresa así: ${}_nC_r$.	For 4 objects *A, B, C,* and *D*, there are ${}_4C_2 = 6$ different combinations of 2 objects: *AB, AC, AD, BC, BD, CD*.
combined variation (p. 572) A relationship containing both direct and inverse variation.	**variación combinada** Relación que contiene variaciones directas e inversas.	$y = \frac{kx}{z}$, where k is the constant of variation
common difference (p. 879) In an arithmetic sequence, the nonzero constant difference of any term and the previous term.	**diferencia común** En una sucesión aritmética, diferencia constante distinta de cero entre cualquier término y el término anterior.	In the arithmetic sequence 3, 5, 7, 9, 11, ..., the common difference is 2.
common logarithm (p. 506) A logarithm whose base is 10, denoted $\log_{10}$ or just log.	**logaritmo común** Logaritmo de base 10, que se expresa $\log_{10}$ o simplemente log.	$\log 100 = \log_{10} 100 = 2$, since $10^2 = 100$.

ENGLISH	SPANISH	EXAMPLES
common ratio (p. 879) In a geometric sequence, the constant ratio of any term and the previous term.	**razón común** En una sucesión geométrica, la razón constante r entre cualquier término y el término anterior.	In the geometric sequence 32, 16, 18, 4, 2 ..., the common ratio is $\frac{1}{2}$.
complement of an event (p. 803) All outcomes in the sample space that are not in an event E, denoted $\overline{E}$.	**complemento de un suceso** Todos los resultados en el espacio muestral que no están en el suceso E y se expresan $\overline{E}$.	In the experiment of rolling a number cube, the complement of rolling a 3 is rolling a 1, 2, 4, 5, or 6.
completing the square (p. 342) A process used to form a perfect-square trinomial. To complete the square of $x^2 + bx$, add $\left(\frac{b}{2}\right)^2$.	**completar el cuadrado** Proceso utilizado para formar un trinomio cuadrado perfecto. Para completar el cuadrado de $x^2 + bx$, hay que sumar $\left(\frac{b}{2}\right)^2$.	$x^2 + 6x + \blacksquare$ Add $\left(\frac{6}{2}\right)^2 = 9$. $x^2 + 6x + 9$ $(x + 3)^2$ *is a perfect square.*
complex conjugate (p. 352) The complex conjugate of any complex number $a + bi$, denoted $\overline{a + bi}$, is $a - bi$.	**conjugado complejo** El conjugado complejo de cualquier número complejo $a + bi$, expresado como $\overline{a + bi}$, es $a - bi$.	$\overline{4 + 3i} = 4 - 3i$ $\overline{4 - 3i} = 4 + 3i$
complex fraction (p. 586) A fraction that contains one or more fractions in the numerator, the denominator, or both.	**fracción compleja** Fracción que contiene una o más fracciones en el numerador, en el denominador, o en ambos.	$\dfrac{\frac{1}{2}}{1 + \frac{2}{3}}$
complex number (p. 351) Any number that can be written as $a + bi$, where a and b are real numbers and $i = \sqrt{-1}$.	**número complejo** Todo número que se puede expresar como $a + bi$, donde a y b son números reales e $i = \sqrt{-1}$.	$4 + 2i$ $5 + 0i = 5$ $0 - 7i = -7i$
complex plane (p. 382) A set of coordinate axes in which the horizontal axis is the real axis and the vertical axis is the imaginary axis; used to graph complex numbers.	**plano complejo** Conjunto de ejes cartesianos en el cual el eje horizontal es el eje real y el eje vertical es el eje imaginario; se utiliza para representar gráficamente números complejos.	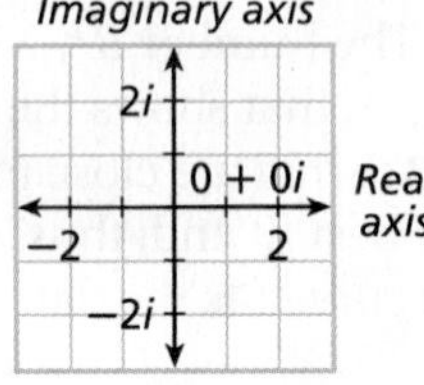
composite figure (p. 349) A plane figure made up of triangles, rectangles, trapezoids, circles, and other simple shapes, or a three-dimensional figure made up of prisms, cones, pyramids, cylinders, and other simple three-dimensional figures.	**figura compuesta** Figura plana compuesta por triángulos, rectángulos, trapecios, círculos y otras formas simples, o figura tridimensional compuesta por prismas, conos, pirámides, cilindros y otras figuras tridimensionales simples.	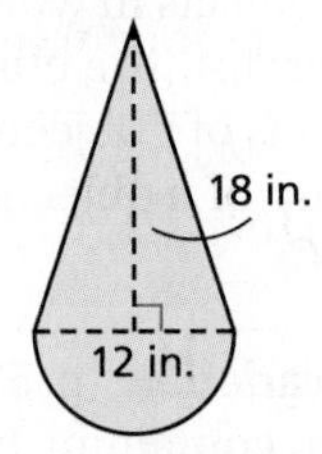
composition of functions (p. 683) The composition of functions f and g, written as $(f \circ g)(x)$ and defined as $f(g(x))$ uses the output of $g(x)$ as the input for $f(x)$.	**composición de funciones** La composición de las funciones f y g, expresada como $(f \circ g)(x)$ y definida como $f(g(x))$ utiliza la salida de $g(x)$ como la entrada para $f(x)$.	If $f(x) = x^2$ and $g(x) = x + 1$, the composite function $(f \circ g)(x) = (x + 1)^2$.
compound event (p. 819) An event made up of two or more simple events.	**suceso compuesto** Suceso formado por dos o más sucesos simples.	In the experiment of tossing a coin and rolling a number cube, the event of the coin landing heads and the number cube landing on 3.

ENGLISH	SPANISH	EXAMPLES
compression (p. 61) A transformation that pushes the points of a graph horizontally toward the *y*-axis or vertically toward the *x*-axis.	**compresión** Transformación que desplaza los puntos de una gráfica horizontalmente hacia el eje *y* o verticalmente hacia el eje *x*.	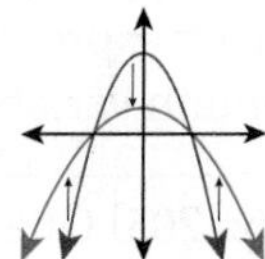
conditional probability (p. 812) The probability of event *B*, given that event *A* has already occurred or is certain to occur, denoted $P(B \mid A)$; used to find probability of dependent events.	**probabilidad condicional** Probabilidad del suceso *B*, dado que el suceso *A* ya ha ocurrido o es seguro que ocurrirá, expresada como $P(B \mid A)$; se utiliza para calcular la probabilidad de sucesos dependientes.	
congruent (p. 60) Having the same size and shape, denoted by ≅.	**congruente** Que tiene el mismo tamaño y forma, expresado por ≅. 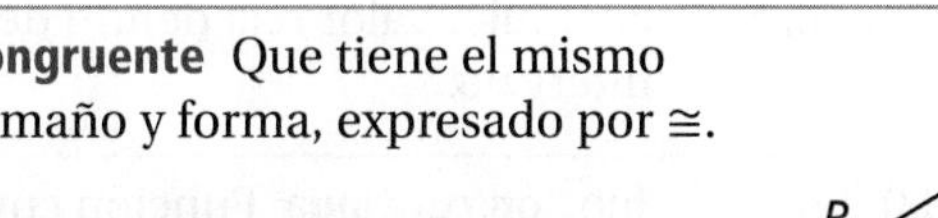	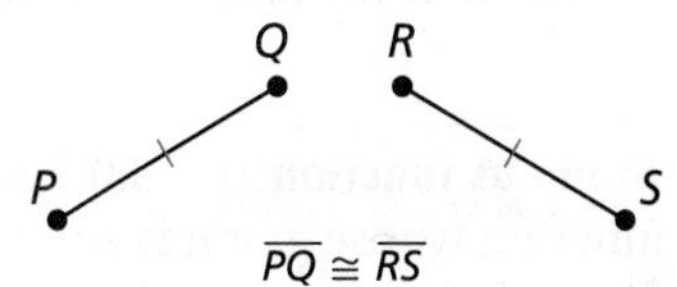
conic section (p. 722) A plane figure formed by the intersection of a double right cone and a plane. Examples include circles, ellipses, hyperbolas, and parabolas.	**sección cónica** Figura plana formada por la intersección de un cono regular doble y un plano. Algunos ejemplos son círculos, elipses, hipérbolas y parábolas.	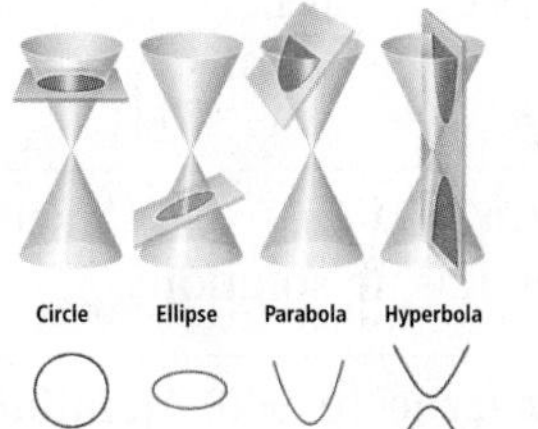
conjugate axis (p. 744) The axis of symmetry of a hyperbola that separates the two branches of the hyperbola.	**eje conjugado** Eje de simetría de una hipérbola que separa las dos ramas de la hipérbola.	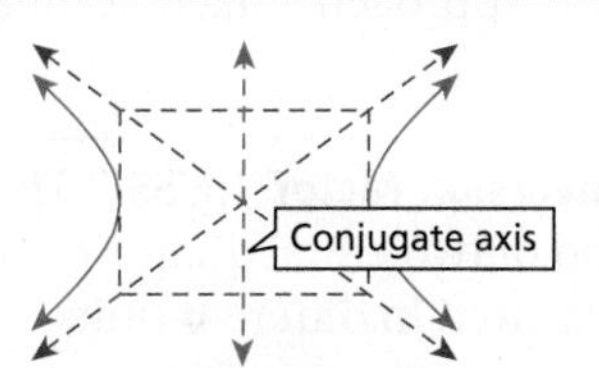
conjunction (p. 150) A compound statement that uses the word *and*.	**conjunción** Enunciado compuesto que contiene la palabra *y*.	3 is less than 5 AND greater than 0.
consistent system (p. 183) A system of equations or inequalities that has at least one solution.	**sistema consistente** Sistema de ecuaciones o desigualdades que tiene por lo menos una solución.	$\begin{cases} x + y = 6 \\ x - y = 4 \end{cases}$ solution: (5, 1)
constant function (p. 67) A function of the form $f(x) = c$, where *c* is a constant.	**función constante** Función del tipo $f(x) = c$, donde *c* es una constante.	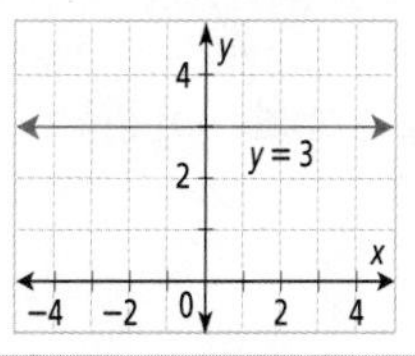
constant matrix (p. 279) The matrix of the constants in a linear system of equations.	**matriz de constantes** Matriz de las constantes de un sistema lineal de ecuaciones.	System of equations $\begin{cases} 2x + 3y = 11 \\ 5x - 4y = 16 \end{cases}$ Constant matrix $\begin{bmatrix} 11 \\ 16 \end{bmatrix}$
constant of variation (p. 569) The constant *k* in direct, inverse, joint, and combined variation equations.	**constante de variación** La constante *k* en ecuaciones de variación directa, inversa, conjunta y combinada.	$y = 5x$ (5: constant of variation)

ENGLISH	SPANISH	EXAMPLES
constant term (pp. 28, 569) A term in a function or expression that does not contain variables.	**término constante** Término de una función o expresión que no contiene variables.	$f(x) = 3x + 5$ ← Constant term (5)
constraint (p. 205) One of the inequalities that define the feasible region in a linear-programming problem.	**restricción** Una de las desigualdades que definen la región factible en un problema de programación lineal.	Constraints: $x > 0$, $y > 0$, $x + y \leq 8$, $3x + 5y \leq 30$ Feasible region 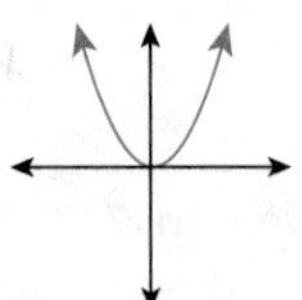
continuous data (p. 846) Data that can take on any real-value measurement within an interval.	**datos continuos** Datos obtenidos por medición que pueden asumir cualquier valor real dentro de un intervalo.	The quantity of water in a glass as the water evaporates is continuous data.
continuous function (p. 593) A function whose graph is an unbroken line or curve with no gaps or breaks.	**función continua** Función cuya gráfica es una línea recta o curva continua, sin espacios ni interrupciones.	
contradiction (p. 92) An equation that has no solutions.	**contradicción** Ecuación que no tiene soluciones.	$x + 1 = x$ $1 = 0$ ✗
converge (p. 900) An infinite series converges when the partial sums approach a fixed number.	**convergir** Una sucesión o serie infinita converge cuando las sumas parciales se aproximan a un número fijo.	$\frac{1}{2} + \frac{1}{4} + \frac{1}{8} + \frac{1}{16} + \ldots$ converges to 1.
conversion factor (p. S57) The ratio of two equal quantities, each measured in different units.	**factor de conversión** Razón entre dos cantidades iguales, cada una medida en unidades diferentes.	$\frac{12 \text{ inches}}{1 \text{ foot}}$
correlation (p. 142) A measure of the strength and direction of the relationship between two variables or data sets.	**correlación** Medida de la fuerza y dirección de la relación entre dos variables o conjuntos de datos.	Positive correlation 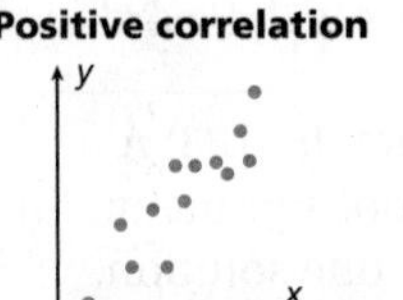 No correlation; Negative correlation

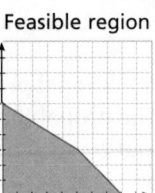

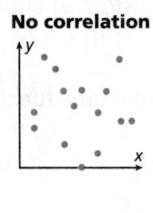

ENGLISH	SPANISH	EXAMPLES
correlation coefficient (p. 143) A number r, where $-1 \leq r \leq 1$, that describes how closely the points in a scatter plot cluster around the least-squares line.	**coeficiente de correlación** Número r, donde $-1 \leq r \leq 1$, que describe a qué distancia de la recta de mínimos cuadrados se agrupan los puntos de un diagrama de dispersión.	An r-value close to 1 describes a strong positive correlation. An r-value close to 0 describes a weak correlation or no correlation. An r-value close to -1 describes a strong negative correlation.
cosecant (p. 932) In a right triangle, the cosecant of angle A is the ratio of the length of the hypotenuse to the length of the side opposite A. It is the reciprocal of the sine function.	**cosecante** En un triángulo rectángulo, la cosecante del ángulo A es la razón entre la longitud de la hipotenusa y la longitud del cateto opuesto a A. Es la inversa de la función seno.	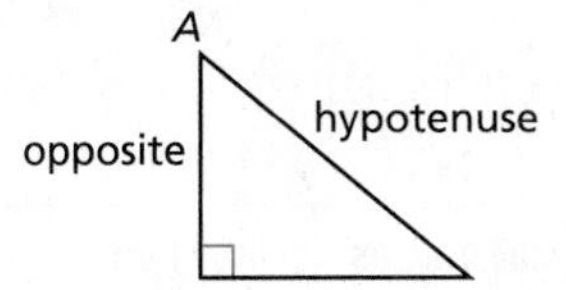 $\csc A = \frac{\text{hypotenuse}}{\text{opposite}} = \frac{1}{\sin A}$
cosine (p. 929) In a right triangle, the cosine of angle A is the ratio of the length of the side adjacent to angle A to the length of the hypotenuse. It is the reciprocal of the secant function.	**coseno** En un triángulo rectángulo, el coseno del ángulo A es la razón entre la longitud del cateto adyacente al ángulo A y la longitud de la hipotenusa. Es la inversa de la función secante.	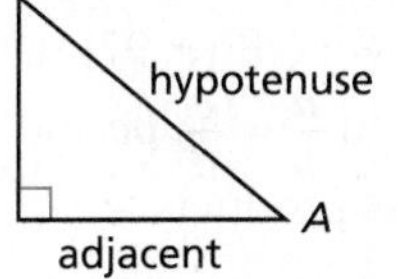 $\cos A = \frac{\text{adjacent}}{\text{hypotenuse}} = \frac{1}{\sec A}$
cotangent (p. 932) In a right triangle, the cotangent of angle A is the ratio of the length of the side adjacent to A to the length of the side opposite A. It is the reciprocal of the tangent function.	**cotangente** En un triángulo rectángulo, la cotangente del ángulo A es la razón entre la longitud del cateto adyacente a A y la longitud del cateto opuesto a A. Es la inversa de la función tangente.	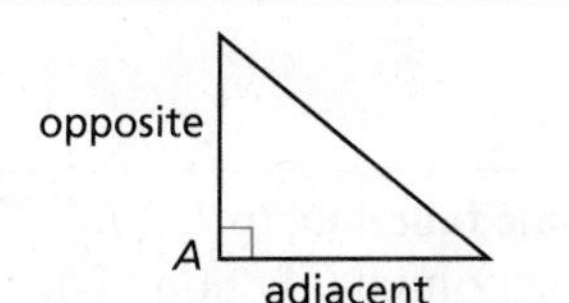 $\cot A = \frac{\text{adjacent}}{\text{opposite}} = \frac{1}{\tan A}$
coterminal angles (p. 937) Two angles in standard position with the same terminal side.	**ángulos coterminales** Dos ángulos en posición estándar con el mismo lado terminal.	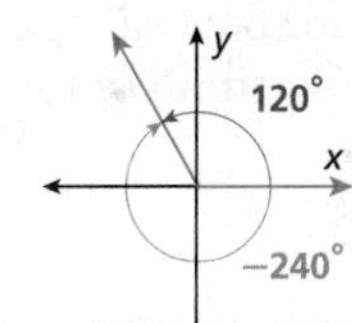
counterexample (p. 903) An example that proves that a conjecture or statement is false.	**contraejemplo** Ejemplo que demuestra que una conjetura o enunciado es falso.	
co-vertices of a hyperbola (p. 744) The endpoints of the conjugate axis.	**co-vértices de una hipérbola** Extremos de un eje conjugado.	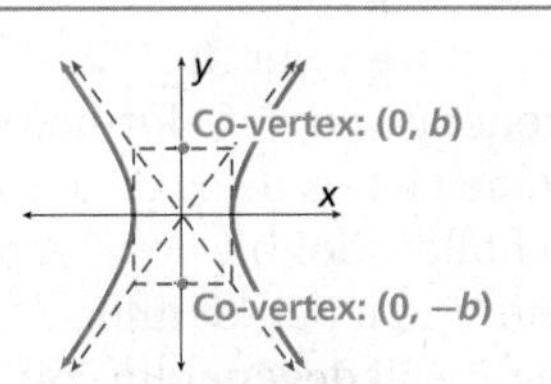
co-vertices of an ellipse (p. 736) The endpoints of the minor axis.	**co-vértices de una elipse** Extremos del eje menor.	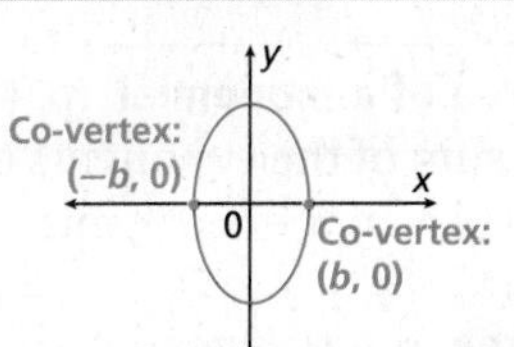

Glossary/Glosario

ENGLISH	SPANISH	EXAMPLES
Cramer's rule (p. 271) A method of solving systems of linear equations by using determinants.	**regla de Cramer** Método para resolver sistemas de ecuaciones lineales utilizando determinantes.	For the system $\begin{cases} x - y = 3 \\ 2x - y = -1 \end{cases}$, $D = \begin{vmatrix} 1 & -1 \\ 2 & -1 \end{vmatrix} = 1(-1) - 2(-1) = 1$ $x = \dfrac{\begin{vmatrix} c_1 & b_1 \\ c_2 & b_2 \end{vmatrix}}{D} = \dfrac{\begin{vmatrix} 3 & -1 \\ -1 & -1 \end{vmatrix}}{1} = \dfrac{-3 - 1}{1} = -4$ $y = \dfrac{\begin{vmatrix} a_1 & c_1 \\ a_2 & c_2 \end{vmatrix}}{D} = \dfrac{\begin{vmatrix} 1 & 3 \\ 2 & -1 \end{vmatrix}}{1} = \dfrac{-1 - 6}{1} = -7$
critical values (p. 367) Values that separate the number line into intervals that either contain solutions or do not contain solutions.	**valores críticos** Valores que separan la recta numérica en intervalos que contienen o no contienen soluciones.	
cross products (p. 97) In the statement $\frac{a}{b} = \frac{c}{d}$, bc and ad are the cross products.	**productos cruzados** En el enunciado $\frac{a}{b} = \frac{c}{d}$, bc y ad son los productos cruzados.	$\frac{1}{2} = \frac{3}{6}$ Cross products: $2 \bullet 3 = 6$ and $1 \bullet 6 = 6$
cube-root function (p. 619) The function $f(x) = \sqrt[3]{x}$.	**función de raíz cúbica** La función $f(x) = \sqrt[3]{x}$.	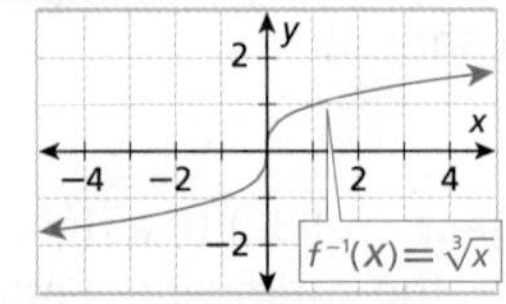
cubic function (p. 67) A polynomial function of degree 3.	**función cúbica** Función polinomial de grado 3.	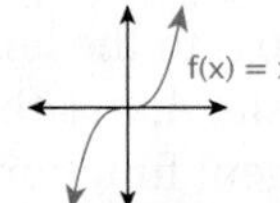
cycle of a periodic function (p. 990) The shortest repeating part of a periodic graph or function.	**ciclo de una función periódica** La parte repetida más corta de una gráfica o función periódica.	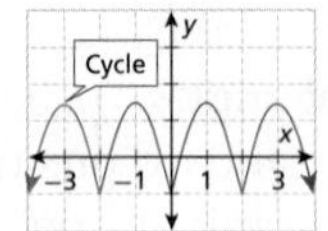

D

ENGLISH	SPANISH	EXAMPLES
decay factor (p. 481) The base $1 - r$ in an exponential expression.	**factor decremental** Base $1 - r$ en una expresión exponencial.	$2(0.93)^t$ ↑ decay factor (representing $1 - 0.07$)
degenerate conic (p. 728) A degenerate conic is formed when a plane passes through the vertex of a hollow double cone. A point, a line, and a pair of intersecting lines are all degenerate conics.	**cónica degenerada** Una cónica degenerada se forma cuando un plano atraviesa el vértice de un cono doble hueco. Un punto, una línea y un par de líneas secantes son cónicas degeneradas.	A point is a circle with no radius.
degree of a monomial (p. 406) The sum of the exponents of the variables in the monomial.	**grado de un monomio** Suma de los exponentes de las variables del monomio.	$4x^2y^5z^3$ Degree: $2 + 5 + 3 = 10$ 5 Degree: 0 $(5 = 5x^0)$
degree of a polynomial (p. 406) The degree of the term of the polynomial with the greatest degree.	**grado de un polinomio** Grado del término del polinomio con el grado máximo.	$3x^2y^2 + 4xy^5 - 12x^3y^2$ Degree 6 $3x^2y^2$: Degree 4; $4xy^5$: Degree 6; $12x^3y^2$: Degree 5

ENGLISH	SPANISH	EXAMPLES
dependent events (p. 812) Events for which the occurrence or nonoccurrence of one event affects the probability of the other event.	**sucesos dependientes** Dos sucesos son dependientes si el hecho de que uno de ellos se cumpla o no afecta la probabilidad del otro.	From a bag containing 3 red marbles and 2 blue marbles, drawing a red marble, and then drawing a blue marble without replacing the first marble.
dependent system (p. 184) A system of equations that has infinitely many solutions.	**sistema dependiente** Sistema de ecuaciones que tiene infinitamente muchas soluciones.	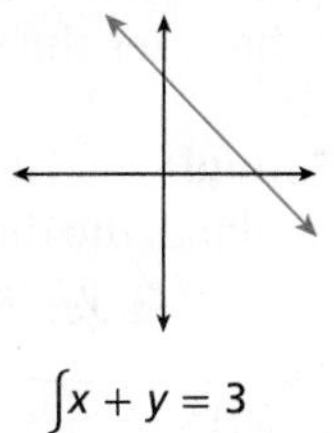 $\begin{cases} x + y = 3 \\ 2x + 2y = 6 \end{cases}$
dependent variable (p. 52) The output of a function; a variable whose value depends on the value of the input, or independent variable.	**variable dependiente** Salida de una función; variable cuyo valor depende del valor de la entrada, o variable independiente.	$y = 2x + 1$ (arrow to y: dependent variable)
determinant (p. 270) A real number associated with a square matrix. The determinant of $A = \begin{bmatrix} a & b \\ c & d \end{bmatrix}$ is $\lvert A \rvert = ad - bc$.	**determinante** Número real asociado con una matriz cuadrada. El determinante de $A = \begin{bmatrix} a & b \\ c & d \end{bmatrix}$ es $\lvert A \rvert = ad - bc$.	$\begin{vmatrix} 2 & -1 \\ 3 & 4 \end{vmatrix} = 2(4) - (-1)(3) = 11$
difference of two squares (p. 336) A polynomial of the form $a^2 - b^2$, which may be written as the product $(a + b)(a - b)$.	**diferencia de dos cuadrados** Polinomio del tipo $a^2 - b^2$, que se puede expresar como el producto $(a + b)(a - b)$.	$x^2 - 4 = (x + 2)(x - 2)$
dimensions of a matrix (p. 246) A matrix with m rows and n columns has dimensions $m \times n$, read "m by n."	**dimensiones de una matriz** Una matriz con m filas y n columnas tiene dimensiones $m \times n$, expresadas "m por n".	$\begin{bmatrix} -3 & 2 & 1 & -1 \\ 4 & 0 & -5 & 2 \end{bmatrix}$ Dimensions 2×4
direct variation (p. 569) A linear relationship between two variables, x and y, that can be written in the form $y = kx$, where k is a nonzero constant.	**variación directa** Relación lineal entre dos variables, x e y, que puede expresarse en la forma $y = kx$, donde k es una constante distinta de cero.	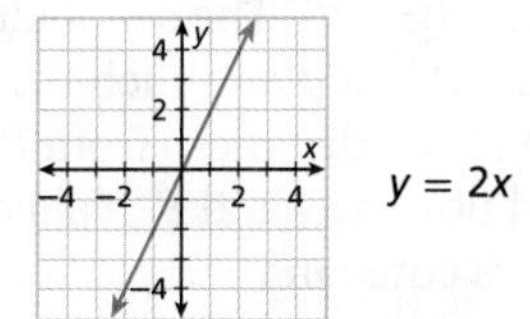 $y = 2x$
directrix (p. 751) A fixed line used to define a *parabola*. Every point on the parabola is equidistant from the directrix and a fixed point called the *focus*.	**directriz** Línea fija utilizada para definir una *parábola*. Cada punto de la parábola es equidistante de la directriz y de un punto fijo denominado *foco*.	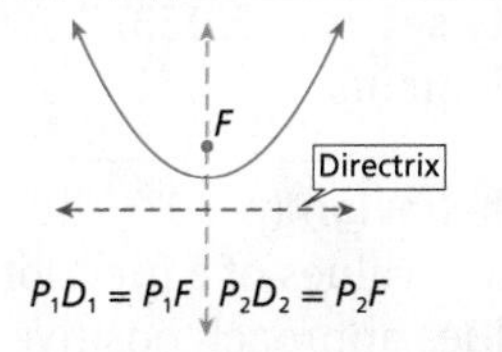 $P_1D_1 = P_1F$ $P_2D_2 = P_2F$
discontinuous function (p. 593) A function whose graph has one or more jumps, breaks, or holes.	**función discontinua** Función cuya gráfica tiene uno o más saltos, interrupciones u hoyos.	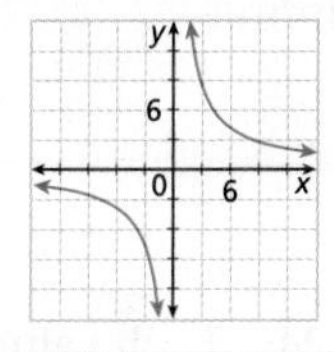
discrete data (p. 846) Data that cannot take on any real-value measurement within an interval.	**datos discretos** Datos que no admiten cualquier medida de valores reales dentro de un intervalo.	the number of pennies in a jar over time

ENGLISH	SPANISH	EXAMPLES
discriminant (p. 357) The discriminant of the quadratic equation $ax^2 + bx + c = 0$ is $b^2 - 4ac$.	**discriminante** El discriminante de la ecuación cuadrática $ax^2 + bx + c = 0$ es $b^2 - 4ac$.	The discriminant of $2x^2 - 5x - 3$ is $(-5)^2 - 4(2)(-3) = 25 + 24 = 49$.
disjunction (p. 150) A compound statement that uses the word *or*.	**disyunción** Enunciado compuesto que contiene la palabra *o*.	John will walk to work OR he will stay home.
Distance Formula (p. 724) In a coordinate plane, the distance from (x_1, y_1) to (x_2, y_2) is $d = \sqrt{(x_2 - x_1)^2 + (y_2 - y_1)^2}$.	**Fórmula de distancia** En un plano cartesiano, la distancia desde (x_1, y_1) hasta (x_2, y_2) es $d = \sqrt{(x_2 - x_1)^2 + (y_2 - y_1)^2}$.	The distance from (2, 1) to (6, 4) is $d = \sqrt{(6-2)^2 + (4-1)^2}$ $= \sqrt{4^2 + 3^2} = \sqrt{9 + 16} = 5$.
diverge (p. 900) An infinite series diverges when the partial sums do not approach a fixed number.	**divergir** Una serie infinita diverge cuando las sumas parciales no se aproximan a un número fijo.	$1 + 2 + 4 + 8 + 16 + \dots$ diverges.
domain (p. 44) The set of all possible input values of a relation or function.	**dominio** Conjunto de todos los posibles valores de entrada de una función o relación.	The domain of the function $f(x) = \sqrt{x}$ is $\{x \mid x \geq 0\}$.

ENGLISH	SPANISH	EXAMPLES
element of a set (p. 6) An item in a set.	**elemento de un conjunto** Componente de un conjunto.	4 is an element of the set of even numbers. $4 \in \{\text{even numbers}\}$
elimination (p. 191) A method used to solve systems of equations in which one variable is eliminated by adding or subtracting two equations of the system.	**eliminación** Método utilizado para resolver sistemas de ecuaciones por el cual se elimina una variable sumando o restando dos ecuaciones del sistema.	
ellipse (p. 736) The set of all points *P* in a plane such that the sum of the distances from *P* to two fixed points F_1 and F_2, called the foci, is constant.	**elipse** Conjunto de todos los puntos *P* de un plano tal que la suma de las distancias desde *P* hasta los dos puntos fijos F_1 y F_2, denominados focos, es constante.	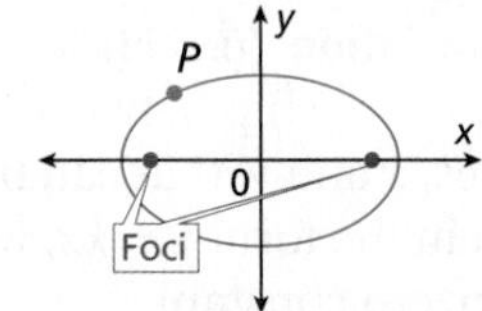
empty set (pp. 6, 153) A set with no elements.	**conjunto vacío** Conjunto sin elementos.	The solution set of $\lvert x \rvert < 0$ is the empty set, $\{\ \}$, or $\varnothing$.
end behavior (p. 453) The trends in the *y*-values of a function as the *x*-values approach positive and negative infinity.	**comportamiento extremo** Tendencia de los valores de *y* de una función a medida que los valores de *x* se aproximan al infinito positivo y negativo.	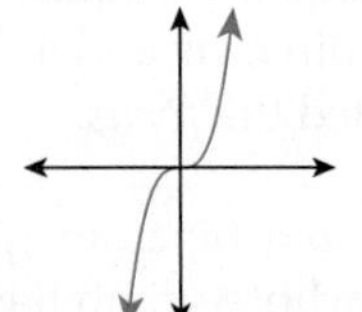 End behavior: $f(x) \to \infty$ as $x \to \infty$; $f(x) \to -\infty$ as $x \to -\infty$
entry (p. 246) Each value in a matrix; also called an element.	**entrada** Cada valor de una matriz; también denominado elemento.	3 is the entry in the first row and second column of $A = \begin{bmatrix} 2 & 3 \\ 0 & 1 \end{bmatrix}$, denoted a_{12}.

ENGLISH	SPANISH	EXAMPLES
equally likely outcomes (p. 802) Outcomes are equally likely if they have the same probability of occurring. If an experiment has n equally likely outcomes, then the probability of each outcome is $\frac{1}{n}$.	**resultados igualmente probables** Los resultados son igualmente probables si tienen la misma probabilidad de ocurrir. Si un experimento tiene n resultados igualmente probables, entonces la probabilidad de cada resultado es $\frac{1}{n}$.	If a coin is tossed, and heads and tails are equally likely, then $P(\text{heads}) = P(\text{tails}) = \frac{1}{2}$.
equation (p. 90) A mathematical statement that two expressions are equivalent.	**ecuación** Enunciado matemático que indica que dos expresiones son equivalentes.	$x + 4 = 7$ $2 + 3 = 6 - 1$ $(x - 1)^2 + (y + 2)^2 = 4$
evaluate (p. 28) To find the value of an algebraic expression by substituting a number for each variable and simplifying by using the order of operations.	**evaluar** Calcular el valor de una expresión algebraica sustituyendo cada variable por un número y simplificando mediante el orden de las operaciones.	Evaluate $2x + 7$ for $x = 3$. $2x + 7$ $2(3) + 7$ $6 + 7$ 13
event (p. 802) An outcome or set of outcomes in a probability experiment.	**suceso** Resultado o conjunto de resultados en un experimento de probabilidad.	In the experiment of rolling a number cube, the event "an odd number" consists of the outcomes 1, 3, and 5.
expected value (p. 828) The weighted average of the numerical outcomes of a probability experiment.	**valor esperado** Promedio ponderado de los resultados numéricos de un experimento de probabilidad.	The table shows the probability of getting a given score by guessing on a three-question quiz. (see table below) The expected value is a score of $0(0.42) + 1(0.42) + 2(0.14) + 3(0.02) = 0.76$.

Score	0	1	2	3
Probability	0.42	0.42	0.14	0.02

ENGLISH	SPANISH	EXAMPLES
experiment (p. 805) An operation, process, or activity in which outcomes can be used to estimate probability.	**experimento** Una operación, proceso o actividad cuyo resultado se puede usar para estimar la probabilidad.	Tossing a coin 10 times and noting the number of heads.
experimental probability (p. 805) The ratio of the number of times an event occurs to the number of trials, or times, that an activity is performed.	**probabilidad experimental** Razón entre la cantidad de veces que ocurre un suceso y la cantidad de pruebas, o veces, que se realiza una actividad.	Kendra made 6 of 10 free throws. The experimental probability that she will make her next free throw is $P(\text{free throw}) = \frac{\text{number made}}{\text{number attempted}} = \frac{6}{10}$.
explicit formula (p. 863) A formula that defines the nth term a_n, or general term, of a sequence as a function of n.	**fórmula explícita** Fórmula que define el enésimo término a_n, o término general, de una sucesión como una función de n.	Sequence: 4, 7, 10, 13, 16, 19, ... Explicit formula: $a_n = 1 + 3n$
exponent (p. 34) The number that indicates how many times the base in a power is used as a factor.	**exponente** Número que indica la cantidad de veces que la base de una potencia se utiliza como factor.	$3^4 = 3 \cdot 3 \cdot 3 \cdot 3 = 81$ (the 4 is labeled "exponent")
exponential decay (p. 490) An exponential function of the form $f(x) = ab^x$ in which $0 < b < 1$. If r is the rate of decay, then the function can be written $y = a(1 - r)^t$, where a is the initial amount and t is the time.	**decremento exponencial** Función exponencial del tipo $f(x) = ab^x$ en la cual $0 < b < 1$. Si r es la tasa decremental, entonces la función se puede expresar como $y = a(1 - r)^t$, donde a es la cantidad inicial y t es el tiempo.	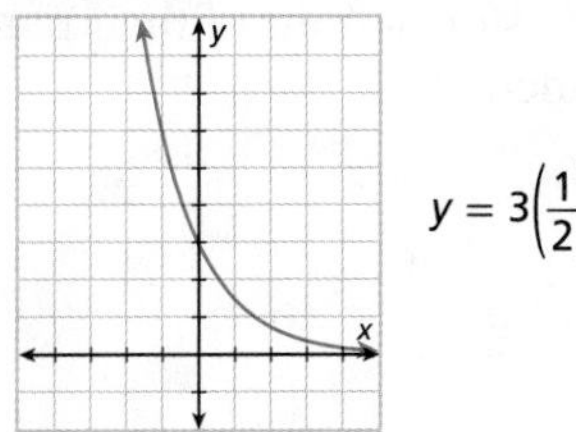 $y = 3\left(\frac{1}{2}\right)^x$

ENGLISH	SPANISH	EXAMPLES
exponential equation (p. 522) An equation that contains one or more exponential expressions.	**ecuación exponencial** Ecuación que contiene una o más expresiones exponenciales.	$2^{x+1} = 8$
exponential function (p. 490) A function of the form $f(x) = ab^x$, where a and b are real numbers with $a \neq 0$, $b > 0$, and $b \neq 1$.	**función exponencial** Función del tipo $f(x) = ab^x$, donde a y b son números reales con $a \neq 0$, $b > 0$ y $b \neq 1$.	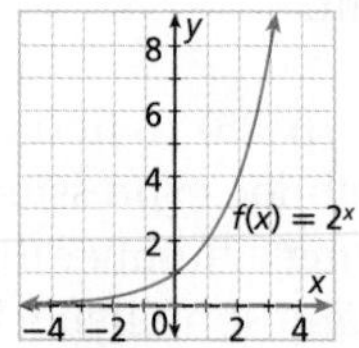
exponential growth (p. 490) An exponential function of the form $f(x) = ab^x$ in which $b > 1$. If r is the rate of growth, then the function can be written $y = a(1 + r)^t$, where a is the initial amount and t is the time.	**crecimiento exponencial** Función exponencial del tipo $f(x) = ab^x$ en la que $b > 1$. Si r es la tasa de crecimiento, entonces la función se puede expresar como $y = a(1 + r)^t$, donde a es la cantidad inicial y t es el tiempo.	
exponential regression (p. 546) A statistical method used to fit an exponential model to a given data set.	**regresión exponencial** Método estadístico utilizado para ajustar un modelo exponencial a un conjunto de datos determinado.	ExpReg y=a*b^x a=814.9602955 b=1.379191229 r²=.9962061645 r=.9981012797
extraneous solution (pp. 524, 600) A solution of a derived equation that is not a solution of the original equation.	**solución extraña** Solución de una ecuación derivada que no es una solución de la ecuación original.	To solve $\sqrt{x} = -2$, square both sides; $x = 4$. ***Check*** $\sqrt{4} = -2$ is false; so 4 is an extraneous solution.

F

ENGLISH	SPANISH	EXAMPLES
Factor Theorem (p. 430) For any polynomial $P(x)$, $(x - a)$ is a factor of $P(x)$ if and only if $P(a) = 0$.	**Teorema del factor** Dado el polinomio $P(x)$, $(x - a)$ es un factor de $P(x)$ si y sólo si $P(a) = 0$.	$(x - 1)$ is a factor of $P(x) = x^2 - 1$ because $P(1) = 1^2 - 1 = 0$.
factorial (p. 795) If n is a positive integer, then n factorial, written $n!$, is $n \cdot (n - 1) \cdot (n - 2) \cdot \ldots \cdot 2 \cdot 1$. The factorial of 0 is defined to be 1.	**factorial** Si n es un entero positivo, entonces el factorial de n, expresado como $n!$, es $n \cdot (n - 1) \cdot (n - 2) \cdot \ldots \cdot 2 \cdot 1$. Por definición, el factorial de 0 será 1.	$7! = 7 \cdot 6 \cdot 5 \cdot 4 \cdot 3 \cdot 2 \cdot 1 = 5040$ $0! = 1$
factoring (p. 334) The process of writing a number or algebraic expression as a product.	**factorización** Proceso por el que se expresa un número o expresión algebraica como un producto.	$x^2 - 4x - 21 = (x - 7)(x + 3)$
family of functions (p. 67) A set of functions whose graphs have basic characteristics in common. Functions in the same family are transformations of their parent function.	**familia de funciones** Conjunto de funciones cuyas gráficas tienen características básicas en común. Las funciones de la misma familia son transformaciones de su función madre.	Some members of the family of quadratic functions with the parent function $f(x) = x^2$ are: $f(x) = 3x^2$ $f(x) = x^2 + 1$ $f(x) = (x - 2)^2$ 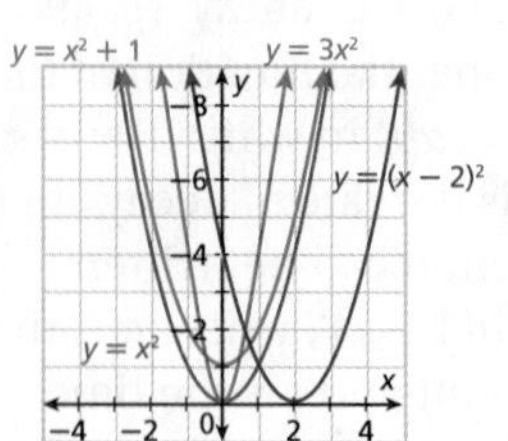

ENGLISH	SPANISH	EXAMPLES
favorable outcome (p. 802) The occurrence of one of several possible outcomes of a specified event or probability experiment.	**resultado favorable** Cuando se produce uno de varios resultados posibles de un suceso específico o experimento de probabilidad.	In the experiment of rolling an odd number on a number cube, the favorable outcomes are 1, 3, and 5.
feasible region (p. 205) The set of points that satisfy the constraints in a linear-programming problem.	**región factible** Conjunto de puntos que cumplen con las restricciones de un problema de programación lineal.	Constraints: $x > 0$ $y > 0$ $x + y \leq 8$ $3x + 5y \leq 30$ 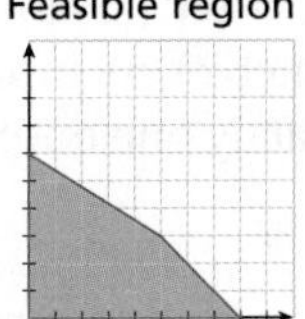
Fibonacci sequence (p. 862) The infinite sequence of numbers beginning with 1, 1 such that each term is the sum of the two previous terms.	**sucesión de Fibonacci** Sucesión infinita de números que comienza con 1, 1 de forma tal que cada término es la suma de los dos términos anteriores.	1, 1, 2, 3, 5, 8, 13, 21, ...
finite sequence (p. 862) A sequence with a finite number of terms.	**sucesión finita** Sucesión con un número finito de términos.	1, 2, 3, 4, 5
finite set (p. 7) A set with a definite, or finite, number of elements.	**conjunto finito** Conjunto con un número de elementos definido o finito.	$\{2, 4, 6, 8, 10\}$
first differences (p. 105) The differences between y-values of a function for evenly spaced x-values.	**primeras diferencias** Diferencias entre los valores de y de una función para valores de x espaciados uniformemente.	x: 0, 1, 2, 3; y: 3, 7, 11, 15; first differences +4 +4 +4
first quartile (p. 829) The median of the lower half of a data set, denoted Q_1. Also called *lower quartile.*	**primer cuartil** Mediana de la mitad inferior de un conjunto de datos, expresada como Q_1. También se llama *cuartil inferior.*	Lower half: 18, (23), 28, Upper half: 36, 42, 49; First quartile
focus (pl. foci) of a hyperbola (p. 744) One of two fixed points F_1 and F_2 that are used to define a hyperbola. For every point P on the hyperbola, $PF_1 - PF_2$ is constant.	**foco de una hipérbola** Uno de los dos puntos fijos F_1 y F_2 utilizados para definir una hipérbola, Para cada punto P de la hipérbola, $PF_1 - PF_2$ es constante.	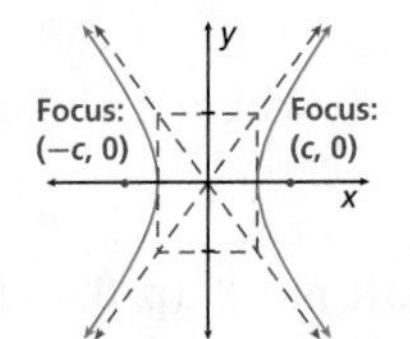
focus (pl. foci) of an ellipse (p. 736) One of two fixed points F_1 and F_2 that are used to define an ellipse. For every point P on the ellipse, $PF_1 + PF_2$ is constant.	**foco de una elipse** Uno de los dos puntos fijos F_1 y F_2 utilizados para definir una elipse. Para cada punto P de la elipse, $PF_1 + PF_2$ es constante.	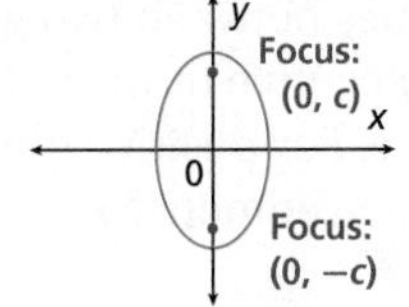
focus (pl. foci) of a parabola (p. 751) A fixed point F used with a *directrix* to define a *parabola.*	**foco de una parábola** Punto fijo F utilizado con una *directriz* para definir una *parábola.*	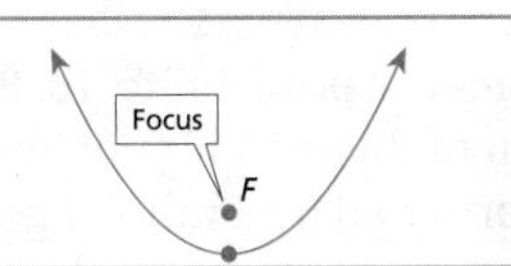
frequency of a data value (p. 828) The number of times the value appears in the data set.	**frecuencia de un valor de datos** Cantidad de veces que aparece el valor en un conjunto de datos.	In the data set 5, 6, 6, 6, 8, 9, the data value 6 has a frequency of 3.

Glossary/Glosario

ENGLISH	SPANISH	EXAMPLES
frequency of a periodic function (p. 992) The number of cycles per unit of time. Also the reciprocal of the period.	**frecuencia de una función periódica** Cantidad de ciclos por unidad de tiempo. También es la inversa del periodo.	The function $y = \sin(2x)$ has a period of π and a frequency of $\frac{1}{\pi}$.
function (p. 45) A relation in which every input is paired with exactly one output.	**función** Una relación en la que cada entrada corresponde exactamente a una salida.	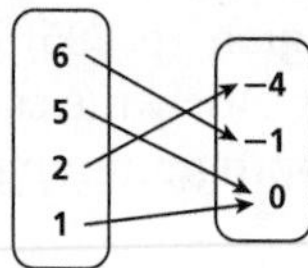
function notation (p. 51) If x is the independent variable and y is the dependent variable, then the function notation for y is $f(x)$, read "f of x," where f names the function.	**notación de función** Si x es la variable independiente e y es la variable dependiente, entonces la notación de función para y es $f(x)$, que se lee "f de x", donde f nombra la función.	equation: $y = 2x$ function notation: $f(x) = 2x$
function rule (p. 53) An algebraic expression that defines a function.	**regla de función** Expresión algebraica que define una función.	$f(x) = 2x^2 + 3x - 7$ ↑ function rule
Fundamental Counting Principle (p. 794) For n items, if there are m_1 ways to choose a first item, m_2 ways to choose a second item after the first item has been chosen, and so on, then there are $m_1 \cdot m_2 \cdot \ldots \cdot m_n$ ways to choose n items.	**Principio fundamental de conteo** Dados n elementos, si existen m_1 formas de elegir un primer elemento, m_2 formas de elegir un segundo elemento después de haber elegido el primero, y así sucesivamente, entonces existen $m_1 \cdot m_2 \cdot \ldots \cdot m_n$ formas de elegir n elementos.	If there are 4 colors of shirts, 3 colors of pants, and 2 colors of shoes, then there are $4 \cdot 3 \cdot 2 = 24$ possible outfits.

G

ENGLISH	SPANISH	EXAMPLES
general form of a conic section (p. 761) $Ax^2 + Bxy + Cy^2 + Dx + Ey + F = 0$, where A and B are not both 0.	**forma general de una sección cónica** $Ax^2 + Bxy + Cy^2 + Dx + Ey + F = 0$, donde A y B no son los dos 0.	A circle with a vertex at $(1, 2)$ and radius 3 has the general form $x^2 + y^2 - 2x - 4y - 4 = 0$.
geometric mean (p. 892) In a geometric sequence, a term that comes between two given nonconsecutive terms of the sequence. For positive numbers a and b, the geometric mean is $\sqrt{ab}$.	**media geométrica** En una sucesión geométrica, un término que se encuentra entre dos términos no consecutivos dados de la sucesión. Dados los números positivos a y b, la media geométrica es $\sqrt{ab}$.	The geometric mean of 4 and 9 is $\sqrt{4(9)} = \sqrt{36} = 6$.
geometric probability (p. 804) A form of theoretical probability determined by a ratio of geometric measures such as lengths, areas, or volumes.	**probabilidad geométrica** Una forma de la probabilidad teórica determinada por una razón de medidas geométricas, como longitud, área o volumen.	 The probability of the pointer landing on red is $\frac{2}{9}$.

ENGLISH	SPANISH	EXAMPLES
geometric sequence (p. 890) A sequence in which the ratio of successive terms is a constant r, called the common ratio, where $r \neq 0$ and $r \neq 1$.	**sucesión geométrica** Sucesión en la que la razón de los términos sucesivos es una constante r, denominada razón común, donde $r \neq 0$ y $r \neq 1$.	1, 2, 4, 8, 16, ... $\cdot 2$ $\cdot 2$ $\cdot 2$ $\cdot 2$ $r = 2$
geometric series (p. 893) The indicated sum of the terms of a geometric sequence.	**serie geométrica** Suma indicada de los términos de una sucesión geométrica.	$1 + 2 + 4 + 8 + 16 + \ldots$
glide reflection (p. 261) A composition of a translation and a reflection across a line parallel to the translation vector.	**deslizamiento con inversión** Composición de una traslación y una reflexión sobre una línea paralela al vector de traslación.	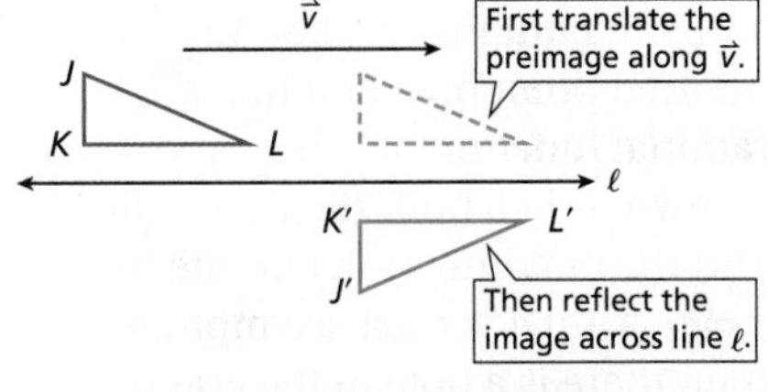
grade (p. 102) A measure of the steepness of surfaces, expressed as a percent.	**grado** Medida de la inclinación de las superficies, expresada como un porcentaje.	A ramp that rises 1 foot for every 5 feet of the horizontal distance has a grade of 20%.
greatest common factor (GCF) (p. 331) The product of the greatest integer and the greatest power of each variable that divides evenly into each term.	**máximo común divisor (MCD)** Producto del entero mayor y la potencia mayor de cada variable que divide exactamente cada término.	The GCF of $4x^3y$ and $6x^2y$ is $2x^2y$. The GCF of 27 and 45 is 9.
greatest-integer function (p. 669) A function denoted by $f(x) = [x]$ or $f(x) = \lfloor x \rfloor$ in which the number x is rounded down to the greatest integer that is less than or equal to x.	**función de entero mayor** Función expresada como $f(x) = [x]$ o $f(x) = \lfloor x \rfloor$ en la cual el número x se redondea hacia abajo hasta el entero mayor que sea menor que o igual a x.	$\lfloor 4.98 \rfloor = 4$ $\lfloor -2.1 \rfloor = -3$
growth factor (p. 491) The base $1 + r$ in an exponential expression.	**factor de crecimiento** La base $1 + r$ en una expresión exponencial.	$12{,}000(1 + 0.14)^t$ growth factor

H

ENGLISH	SPANISH	EXAMPLES
half-life (p. 532) The half-life of a substance is the time it takes for one-half of the substance to decay into another substance.	**vida media** La vida media de una sustancia es el tiempo que tarda la mitad de la sustancia en desintegrarse y transformarse en otra sustancia.	Carbon-14 has a half-life of 5730 years, so 5 g of an initial amount of 10 g will remain after 5730 years.
half-plane (p. 124) The part of the coordinate plane on one side of a line, which may include the line.	**semiplano** Parte del plano cartesiano de un lado de una línea, que puede incluir la línea.	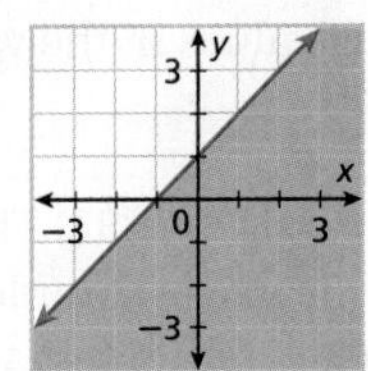

ENGLISH	SPANISH	EXAMPLES
Heron's Formula (p. 969) A triangle with side lengths *a*, *b*, and *c* has area $A = \sqrt{s(s-a)(s-b)(s-c)}$, where *s* is one-half the perimeter, or $s = \frac{1}{2}(a+b+c)$.	**fórmula de Herón** Un triángulo con longitudes de lado *a*, *b* y *c* tiene un área $A = \sqrt{s(s-a)(s-b)(s-c)}$, donde *s* es la mitad del perímetro ó $s = \frac{1}{2}(a+b+c)$.	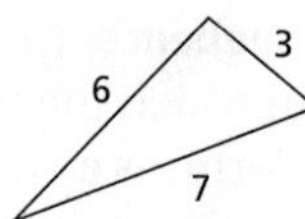 $s = \frac{1}{2}(3+6+7) = 8$ $A = \sqrt{8(8-3)(8-6)(8-7)}$ $= \sqrt{80} = 4\sqrt{5}$ square units
hole (in a graph) (p. 596) An omitted point on a graph. If a rational function has the same factor $x - b$ in both the numerator and the denominator, and the line $x = b$ is not a vertical asymptote, then there is a hole in the graph at the point where $x = b$.	**hoyo (en una gráfica)** Punto omitido en una gráfica. Si una función racional tiene el mismo factor $x - b$ tanto en el numerador como en el denominador, y la línea $x = b$ no es una asíntota vertical, entonces hay un hoyo en la gráfica en el punto donde $x = b$.	$f(x) = \frac{(x-2)(x+2)}{(x+2)}$ has a hole at $x = -2$. 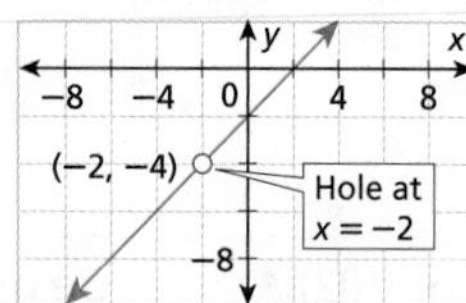
horizontal line (p. 108) A line described by the equation $y = b$, where *b* is the *y*-intercept.	**línea horizontal** Línea descrita por la ecuación $y = b$, donde *b* es la intersección con el eje *y*.	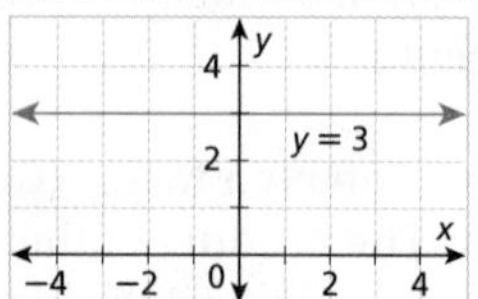
horizontal line test (p. 690) If a horizontal line crosses the graph of a function *f* at more than one point, then the inverse is not a function.	**prueba de la línea horizontal** Si una línea horizontal cruza la gráfica de una función *f* en más de un punto, entonces la inversa no es una función.	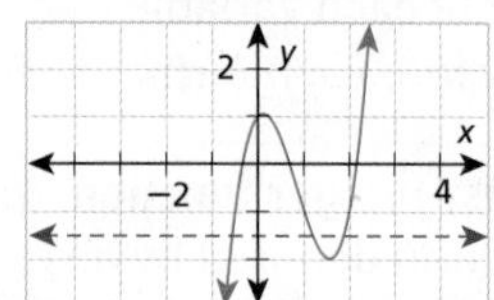 The inverse is not a function.
hyperbola (p. 744) The set of all points *P* in a plane such that the difference of the distances from *P* to two fixed points F_1 and F_2, called the foci, is a constant $d = \lvert PF_1 - PF_2 \rvert$.	**hipérbola** Conjunto de todos los puntos *P* en un plano tal que la diferencia de las distancias de *P* a dos puntos fijos F_1 y F_2, llamados focos, es una constante $d = \lvert PF_1 - PF_2 \rvert$.	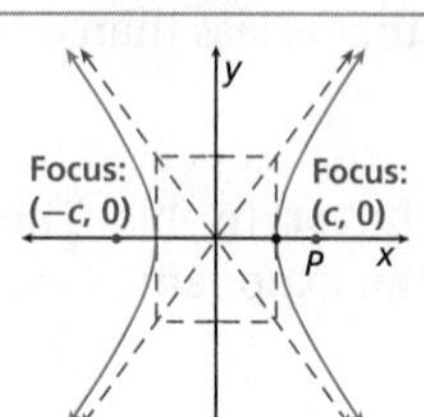
hypotenuse (p. 20) The side opposite the right angle in a right triangle.	**hipotenusa** Lado opuesto al ángulo recto de un triángulo rectángulo.	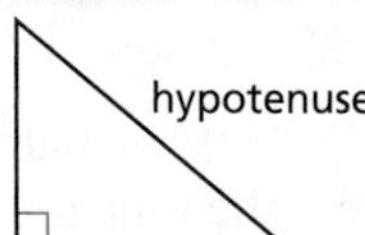

I

ENGLISH	SPANISH	EXAMPLES
identity (p. 92) An equation that is true for all values of the variables.	**identidad** Ecuación verdadera para todos los valores de las variables.	$3 = 3$ $2(x-1) = 2x - 2$
imaginary axis (p. 382) The vertical axis in the complex plane, it graphically represents the purely imaginary part of complex numbers.	**eje imaginario** Eje vertical de un plano complejo. Representa gráficamente la parte puramente imaginaria de los números complejos.	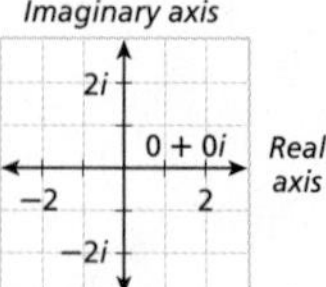

ENGLISH	SPANISH	EXAMPLES

inverse function (p. 499) The function that results from exchanging the input and output values of a one-to-one function. The inverse of $f(x)$ is denoted $f^{-1}(x)$.

función inversa Función que resulta de intercambiar los valores de entrada y salida de una función uno a uno. La función inversa de $f(x)$ se expresa $f^{-1}(x)$.

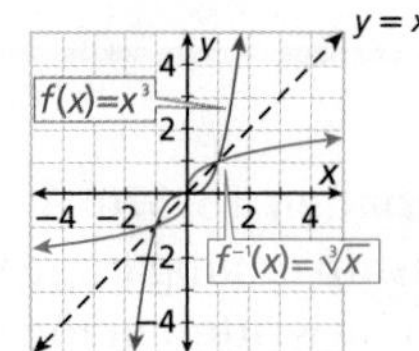

inverse relation (p. 498) The inverse of the relation consisting of all ordered pairs (x, y) is the set of all ordered pairs (y, x). The graph of an inverse relation is the reflection of the graph of the relation across the line $y = x$.

relación inversa La inversa de la relación que consta de todos los pares ordenados (x, y) es el conjunto de todos los pares ordenados (y, x). La gráfica de una relación inversa es el reflejo de la gráfica de la relación sobre la línea $y = x$.

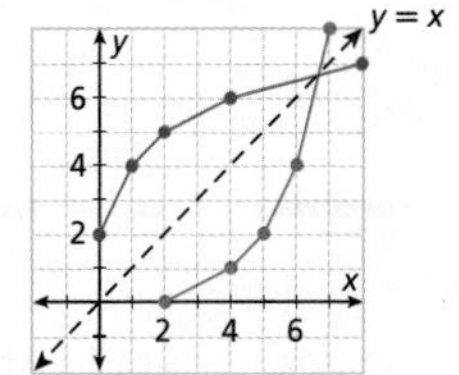

inverse sine function (p. 951) If the domain of the sine function is restricted to $\left[-\frac{\pi}{2}, \frac{\pi}{2}\right]$, then the function $\text{Sin}\,\theta = a$ has an inverse function, $\text{Sin}^{-1} a = \theta$, also called *arcsine*.

función seno inverso Si el dominio de la función seno se restringe a $\left[-\frac{\pi}{2}, \frac{\pi}{2}\right]$, entonces la función $\text{Sen}\,\theta = a$ tiene una función inversa, $\text{Sen}^{-1} a = \theta$, también llamada *arco seno*.

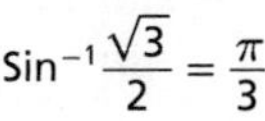

inverse tangent function (p. 951) If the domain of the tangent function is restricted to $\left(-\frac{\pi}{2}, \frac{\pi}{2}\right)$, then the function $\text{Tan}\theta = a$ has an inverse function, $\text{Tan}^{-1} a = \theta$, also called *arctangent*.

función tangente inversa Si el dominio de la función tangente se restringe a $\left(-\frac{\pi}{2}, \frac{\pi}{2}\right)$, entonces la función $\text{Tan}\theta = a$ tiene una función inversa, $\text{Tan}^{-1} a = \theta$, también llamada *arco tangente*.

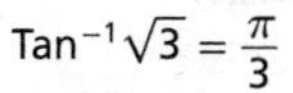

inverse variation (p. 570) A relationship between two variables, x and y, that can be written in the form $y = \frac{k}{x}$, where k is a nonzero constant and $x \neq 0$.

variación inversa Relación entre dos variables, x e y, que puede expresarse en la forma $y = \frac{k}{x}$, donde k es una constante distinta de cero y $x \neq 0$.

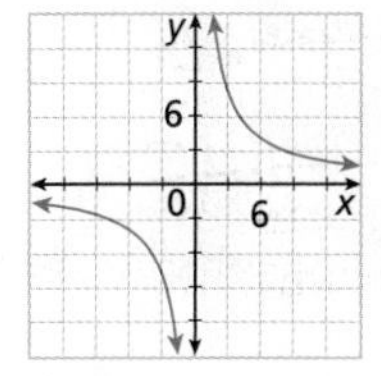

$y = \frac{24}{x}$

irrational number (p. 6) A real number that cannot be expressed as the ratio of two integers.

número irracional Número real que no se puede expresar como una razón de enteros.

$\sqrt{2}, \pi, e$

iteration (p. 864) The repetitive application of the same rule.

iteración Aplicación repetitiva de la misma regla.

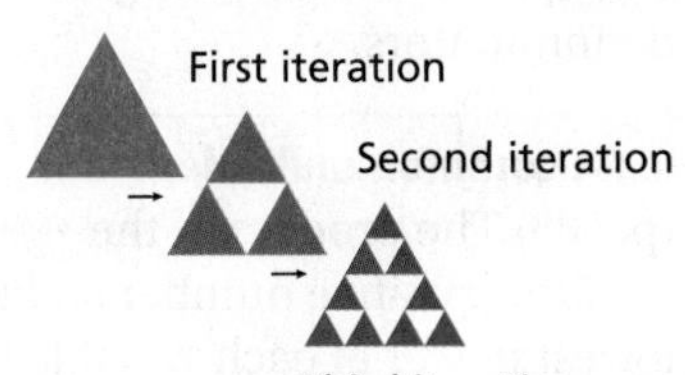

ENGLISH	SPANISH	EXAMPLES

J

joint variation (p. 570) A relationship among three variables that can be written in the form $y = kxz$, where k is a nonzero constant.	**variación conjunta** Relación entre tres variables que se puede expresar de la forma $y = kxz$, donde k es una constante distinta de cero.	$y = 3xz$

L

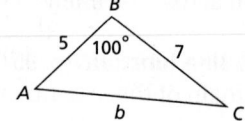

Law of Cosines (p. 966) For $\triangle ABC$ with side lengths a, b, and c, $a^2 = b^2 + c^2 - 2bc \cos A$ $b^2 = a^2 + c^2 - 2ac \cos B$ $c^2 = a^2 + b^2 - 2ab \cos C$.	**Ley de cosenos** Dado $\triangle ABC$ con longitudes de lado a, b y c, $a^2 = b^2 + c^2 - 2bc \cos A$ $b^2 = a^2 + c^2 - 2ac \cos B$ $c^2 = a^2 + b^2 - 2ab \cos C$.	B; 5; 100°; 7; A; b; C $b^2 = 7^2 + 5^2 - 2(7)(5) \cos 100°$ $b^2 \approx 86.2$ $b \approx 9.3$
law of large numbers (p. 809) The tendency of experimental probability to approach theoretical probability as the number of trials gets very large.	**Ley de los números grandes** Tendencia de la probabilidad experimental a acercarse a la probabilidad teórica cuando el número de pruebas es muy grande.	The more times you toss a coin, the closer the experimental probability will be to $\frac{1}{2}$.
Law of Sines (p. 959) For $\triangle ABC$ with side lengths a, b, and c, $\frac{\sin A}{a} = \frac{\sin B}{b} = \frac{\sin C}{c}$.	**Ley de senos** Dado $\triangle ABC$ con longitudes de lado a, b y c, $\frac{\text{sen } A}{a} = \frac{\text{sen } B}{b} = \frac{\text{sen } C}{c}$.	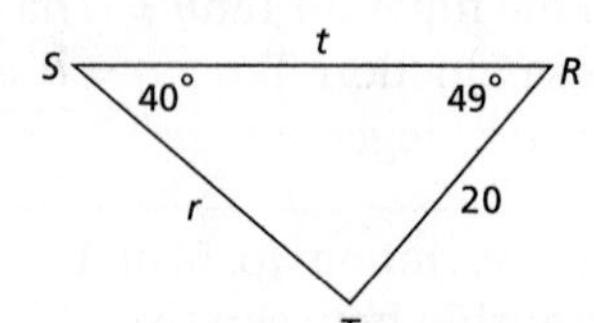 $\frac{\sin 49°}{r} = \frac{\sin 40°}{20}$ $r = \frac{20 \sin 49°}{\sin 40°} \approx 23.5$
leading coefficient (p. 406) The coefficient of the first term of a polynomial in standard form.	**coeficiente principal** Coeficiente del primer término de un polinomio en forma estándar.	$3x^2 + 7x - 2$ Leading coefficient
least common denominator (LCD) (p. 583) The least common multiple of two or more given denominators.	**mínimo común denominador (mcd)** Mínimo común múltiplo de dos o más denominadores dados.	The LCD of $\frac{3}{4}$ and $\frac{5}{6}$ is 12.
least common multiple (LCM) (p. 583) The product of the smallest positive number and the lowest power of each variable that divides evenly into each term.	**mínimo común múltiplo (mcm)** El producto del número positivo más pequeño y la potencia más baja de cada variable que divide exactamente cada término.	The LCM of 10 and 18 is 90. The LCM of $2x^2$ *and* $5x^3$ *is* $10x^3$.
leg of a right triangle (p. 20) One of the two sides of the right triangle that form the right angle.	**cateto de un triángulo rectángulo** Uno de los dos lados de un triángulo rectángulo que forman el ángulo recto.	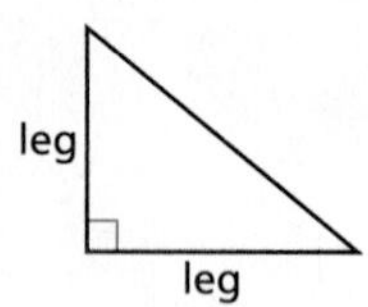

ENGLISH	SPANISH	EXAMPLES

like radical terms (p. 23) Radical terms having the same radicand and index.

radicales semejantes Términos radicales que tienen el mismo radicando e índice.

$3\sqrt{2x}$ and $\sqrt{2x}$ Like radicals
$\sqrt{3x}$ and $\sqrt{2x}$ Unlike radicals

---

like terms (p. 28) Terms with the same variables raised to the same exponents.

términos semejantes Términos con las mismas variables elevadas a los mismos exponentes.

$3a^3b^2$ and $7a^3b^2$ Like terms
$4xy^2$ and $6x^2y$ Unlike terms

---

limit (p. 900) A number (or infinity) that the terms of an infinite sequence or series approach as the term number increases.

límite Número (o infinito) al que se aproximan los términos de una sucesión o serie infinita a medida que aumenta el número de términos.

The series $\frac{1}{2} + \frac{1}{4} + \frac{1}{8} + \frac{1}{16} + \ldots$ has a limit of 1.

---

line of best fit (p. 142) The line that comes closest to all of the points in a data set.

línea de mejor ajuste Línea que más se acerca a todos los puntos de un conjunto de datos.

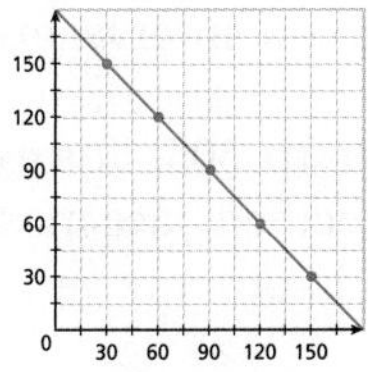

---

linear equation in one variable (p. 90) An equation that can be written in the form $ax = b$, where a and b are constants and $a \neq 0$.

ecuación lineal en una variable Ecuación que puede expresarse en la forma $ax = b$, donde a y b son constantes y $a \neq 0$.

$x + 1 = 7$

---

linear function (p. 105) A function that can be written in the form $f(x) = mx + b$, where x is the independent variable and m and b are real numbers. Its graph is a line.

función lineal Función que puede expresarse en la forma $f(x) = mx + b$, donde x es la variable independiente y m y b son números reales. Su gráfica es una línea.

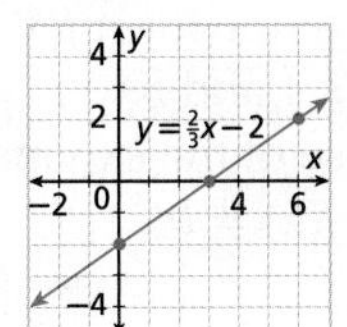

---

linear inequality in two variables (p. 124) An inequality that can be written in one of the following forms: $y < mx + b$, $y > mx + b$, $y \leq mx + b$, $y \geq mx + b$, or $y \neq mx + b$, where m and b are real numbers.

desigualdad lineal en dos variables Desiqualdad que puede expresarse de una de las siguientes formas: $y < mx + b$, $y > mx + b$, $y \leq mx + b$, $y \geq mx + b$, o $y \neq mx + b$, donde m y b son números reales.

$2x + 3y \leq 6$
$y > \frac{1}{2}x - 7$

---

linear programming (p. 205) A method of finding a maximum or minimum value of a linear function, called the *objective function*, that satisfies a given set of conditions, called *constraints*.

programación lineal Método para calcular un valor máximo o mínimo de una función lineal, denominada *función objetiva*, que cumple con una serie dada de condiciones, denominadas *restricciones*.

Constraints

$$\begin{cases} x \geq 0 \\ 40x + 60y \leq 1440 \\ y \geq \frac{1}{3}x \\ y \leq 16 \end{cases}$$

Feasible Region

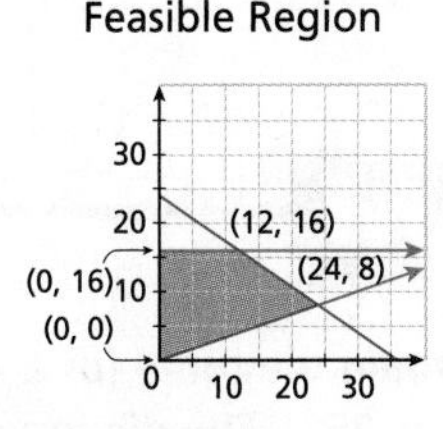

For the given constraints, the objective function $P = 18x + 25y$ is maximized at (24, 8).

---

linear regression (p. 143) A statistical method used to fit a linear model to a given data set.

regresión lineal Método estadístico utilizado para ajustar un modelo lineal a un conjunto de datos determinado.

ENGLISH	SPANISH	EXAMPLES

linear system (p. 182) A system of equations containing only linear equations.

sistema lineal Sistema de ecuaciones que contiene sólo ecuaciones lineales.

$$\begin{cases} y = 2x + 1 \\ x + y = 8 \end{cases}$$

---

local maximum (p. 455) For a function f, $f(a)$ is a local maximum if there is an interval around a such that $f(x) < f(a)$ for every x-value in the interval except a.

máximo local Dada una función f, $f(a)$ es el máximo local si hay un intervalo en a tal que $f(x) < f(a)$ para cada valor de x en el intervalo excepto a.

Local maximum

---

local minimum (p. 455) For a function f, $f(a)$ is a local minimum if there is an interval around a such that $f(x) > f(a)$ for every x-value in the interval except a.

mínimo local Dada una función f, $f(a)$ es el mínimo local si hay un intervalo en a tal que $f(x) > f(a)$ para cada valor de x en el intervalo excepto a.

Local minimum

---

logarithm (p. 505) The exponent that a specified base must be raised to in order to get a certain value.

logaritmo Exponente al cual debe elevarse una base determinada a fin de obtener cierto valor.

$\log_2 8 = 3$, because 3 is the power that 2 is raised to in order to get 8; or $2^3 = 8$.

---

logarithmic equation (p. 523) An equation that contains a logarithm of a variable.

ecuación logarítmica Ecuación que contiene un logaritmo de una variable.

$\log x + 3 = 7$

---

logarithmic function (p. 507) A function of the form $f(x) = \log_b x$, where $b \neq 1$ and $b > 0$, which is the inverse of the exponential function $f(x) = b^x$.

función logarítmica Función del tipo $f(x) = \log_b x$, donde $b \neq 1$ y $b > 0$, que es la inversa de la función exponencial $f(x) = b^x$.

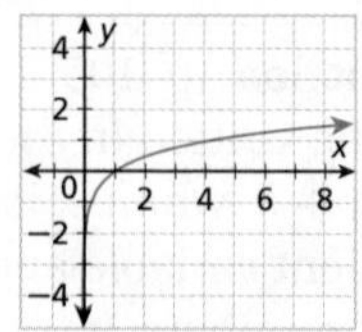

$f(x) = \log_4 x$

---

logarithmic regression (p. 546) A statistical method used to fit a logarithmic model to a given data set.

regresión logarítmica Método estadístico utilizado para ajustar un modelo logarítmico a un conjunto de datos determinado.

---

logistic function (p. 535) An exponential growth function that tapers off at an asymptote.

función logística Función de crecimiento exponencial que disminuye en una asíntota.

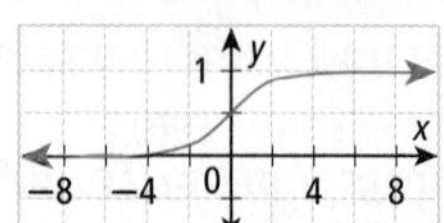

M

main diagonal (of a matrix) (p. 255) The diagonal from the upper left corner to the lower right corner of a matrix.

diagonal principal (de una matriz) Diagonal que se extiende desde la esquina superior izquierda hasta la esquina inferior derecha de una matriz.

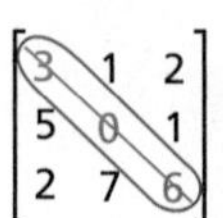

---

major axis (p. 736) The longer axis of an ellipse. The foci of the ellipse are located on the major axis, and its endpoints are the *vertices of the ellipse.*

eje mayor El eje más largo de una elipse. Los focos de la elipse se encuentran sobre el eje mayor y sus extremos son los *vértices de la elipse.*

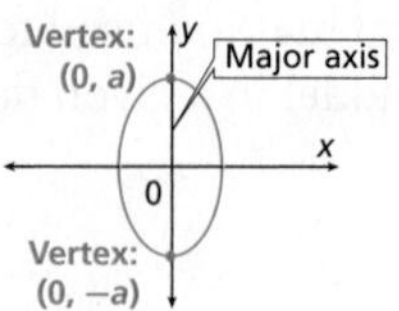

ENGLISH	SPANISH	EXAMPLES
mapping diagram (p. 44) A diagram that shows the relationship of elements in the domain to elements in the range of a relation or function.	**diagrama de correspondencia** Diagrama que muestra la relación entre los elementos del dominio y los elementos del rango de una función.	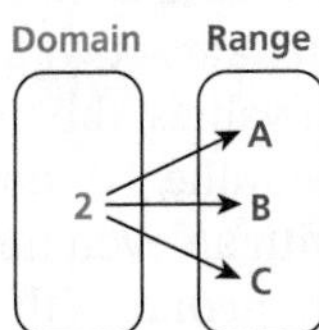
mathematical induction (p. 902) A type of mathematical proof. To prove that a statement is true for all natural numbers n, first show that the statement is true for $n = 1$; then assume it is true for some number k and prove that it is true for $k + 1$. It follows that the statement is true for all values of n.	**inducción matemática** Tipo de demostración matemática. Para demostrar que un enunciado se cumple para todos los números naturales n, primero se demuestra que el enunciado se cumple para $n = 1$; luego se supone que se cumple para un número k y se demuestra que se cumple para $k + 1$. Por lo tanto, el enunciado se cumplirá para todos los valores de n.	
matrix (p. 246) A rectangular array of numbers.	**matriz** Arreglo rectangular de números.	$\begin{bmatrix} 1 & 0 & 3 \\ -2 & 2 & -5 \\ 7 & -6 & 3 \end{bmatrix}$
matrix equation (p. 279) An equation of the form $AX = B$, where A is the coefficient matrix, X is the variable matrix, and B is the constant matrix of a system of equations.	**ecuación matricial** Ecuación del tipo $AX = B$, donde A es la matriz de coeficientes, X es la matriz de variables y B es la matriz de constantes de un sistema de ecuaciones.	System of equations: $\begin{matrix} 2x + 3y = 7 \\ 4x - 6y = 5 \end{matrix}$ Matrix equation: $\begin{bmatrix} 2 & 3 \\ 4 & -6 \end{bmatrix} \begin{bmatrix} x \\ y \end{bmatrix} = \begin{bmatrix} 7 \\ 5 \end{bmatrix}$
matrix product (p. 253) The product of two matrices, where each entry in P_{ij} is the sum of the products of consecutive entries in row i in matrix A and column j in matrix B.	**producto matricial** Producto de dos matrices, donde cada entrada de P_{ij} es la suma de los productos de las entradas consecutivas de la fila i de la matriz A y de la columna j de la matriz B.	$\begin{bmatrix} 1 & 2 \\ 3 & 4 \end{bmatrix} \begin{bmatrix} 5 & 6 \\ 7 & 8 \end{bmatrix} = \begin{bmatrix} 1(5) + 2(7) & 1(6) + 2(8) \\ 3(5) + 4(7) & 3(6) + 4(8) \end{bmatrix}$ $= \begin{bmatrix} 19 & 22 \\ 43 & 50 \end{bmatrix}$
maximum value of a function (p. 326) The y-value of the highest point on the graph of the function.	**máximo de una función** Valor de y del punto más alto en la gráfica de la función.	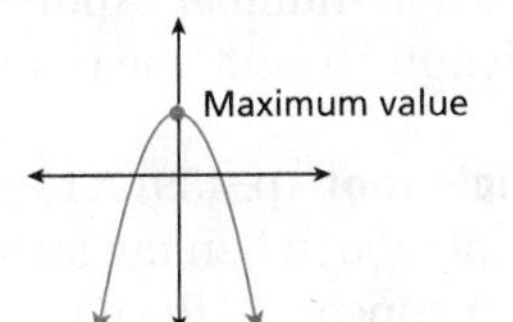
mean (p. 828) The sum of all the values in a data set divided by the number of data values. Also called the *average*.	**media** Suma de todos los valores de un conjunto de datos dividida entre el número de valores de datos. También llamada *promedio*.	Data set: 4, 6, 7, 8, 10 Mean: $\frac{4 + 6 + 7 + 8 + 10}{5} = \frac{35}{5} = 7$
measure of central tendency (p. 828) A measure that describes the center of a data set.	**medida de tendencia dominante** Medida que describe el centro de un conjunto de datos.	the mean, median, or mode
measure of variation (p. 830) A measure that describes the spread of a data set.	**medida de variación** Medida que describe la amplitud de un conjunto de datos.	the range, variance, standard deviation, or interquartile range

ENGLISH	SPANISH	EXAMPLES
median of a data set (p. 828) For an ordered data set with an odd number of values, the median is the middle value. For an ordered data set with an even number of values, the median is the average of the two middle values.	**mediana de un conjunto de datos** Dado un conjunto de datos ordenados con un número impar de valores, la mediana es el valor del medio. Dado un conjunto de datos ordenados con un número par de valores, la mediana es el promedio de los dos valores del medio.	8, 9, (9), 12, 15 Median: 9 4, 6, (7, 10), 10, 12 Median: $\frac{7+10}{2} = 8.5$
midpoint (p. 724) The point that divides a segment into two congruent segments.	**punto medio** Punto que divide un segmento en dos segmentos congruentes.	A B C Point B is the midpoint of $\overline{AC}$.
minimum value of a function (p. 326) The y-value of the lowest point on the graph of the function.	**mínimo de una función** Valor de y del punto más bajo en la gráfica de la función.	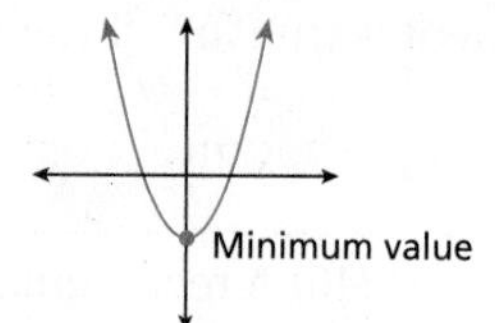
minor axis (p. 736) The shorter axis of an ellipse. Its endpoints are the *co-vertices of the ellipse.*	**eje menor** El eje más corto de una elipse. Sus extremos son los *co-vértices de la elipse.*	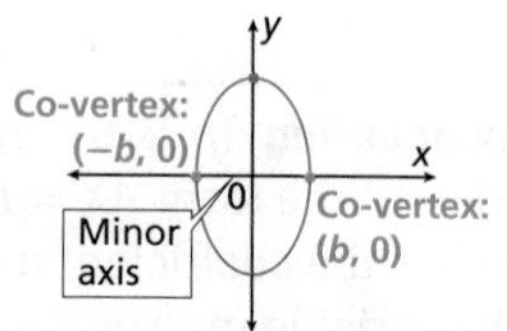
mode (p. 828) The value or values that occur most frequently in a data set; if all values occur only once, the data set is said to have no mode.	**moda** El valor o los valores que se presentan con mayor frecuencia en un conjunto de datos. Si todos los valores se presentan con la misma frecuencia, se dice que el conjunto de datos no tiene moda.	Data set: 3, 6, (8, 8), 10 Mode: 8 Data set: 2, (5, 5), (7, 7) Modes: 5 and 7 Data set: 2, 3, 6, 9, 11 No mode
monomial (p. 406) A number or a product of numbers and variables with whole-number exponents, or a polynomial with one term.	**monomio** Número o producto de números y variables con exponentes de números cabales, o polinomio con un término.	$8x$, 9, $3x^2y^4$
multiple root (p. 439) A root r is a multiple root when the factor $(x - r)$ appears in the equation more than once.	**raíz múltiple** Una raíz r es una raíz múltiple cuando el factor $(x - r)$ aparece en la ecuación más de una vez.	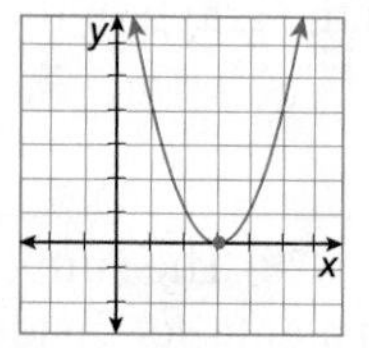 3 is a multiple root of $P(x) = (x - 3)^2$.
multiplicative identity matrix (p. 255) A square matrix with 1 in every entry of the main diagonal and 0 in every other entry.	**matriz de identidad multiplicativa** Una matriz cuadrada que contiene 1 en cada entrada de la diagonal principal y 0 en las demás entradas.	$\begin{bmatrix} 1 & 0 \\ 0 & 1 \end{bmatrix}, \begin{bmatrix} 1 & 0 & 0 \\ 0 & 1 & 0 \\ 0 & 0 & 1 \end{bmatrix}$

ENGLISH	SPANISH	EXAMPLES
multiplicative inverse of a square matrix (p. 278) The multiplicative inverse of square matrix A, if it exists, is notated A^{-1}, where the product of A and A^{-1} is the identity matrix.	**inverso multiplicativo de una matriz cuadrada** El inverso multiplicativo de una matriz cuadrada A, si existe, se escribe A^{-1}, donde el producto de A y A^{-1} es la matriz de identidad.	The multiplicative inverse of $A = \begin{bmatrix} -2 & 5 \\ 1 & -3 \end{bmatrix}$ is $A^{-1} = \begin{bmatrix} -3 & -5 \\ -1 & -2 \end{bmatrix}$, because $AA^{-1} = A^{-1}A = \begin{bmatrix} 1 & 0 \\ 0 & 1 \end{bmatrix}$.
multiplicity (p. 439) If a polynomial $P(x)$ has a multiple root at r, the multiplicity of r is the number of times $(x - r)$ appears as a factor in $P(x)$.	**multiplicidad** Si un polinomio $P(x)$ tiene una raíz múltiple en r, la multiplicidad de r es la cantidad de veces que $(x - r)$ aparece como factor en $P(x)$.	For $P(x) = (x - 3)^2$, the root 3 has a multiplicity of 2.
mutually exclusive events (p. 819) Two events are mutually exclusive if they cannot both occur in the same trial of an experiment.	**sucesos mutuamente excluyentes** Dos sucesos son mutuamente excluyentes si ambos no pueden ocurrir en la misma prueba de un experimento.	In the experiment of rolling a number cube, rolling a 3 and rolling an even number are mutually exclusive events.

N

ENGLISH	SPANISH	EXAMPLES
natural logarithm (p. 532) A logarithm with base e, written as ln.	**logaritmo natural** Logaritmo con base e, que se escribe ln.	$\ln 5 = \log_e 5 \approx 1.6$
natural logarithmic function (p. 532) The function $f(x) = \ln x$, which is the inverse of the natural exponential function $f(x) = e^x$. Domain is $\{x \mid x > 0\}$; range is all real numbers.	**función logarítmica natural** Función $f(x) = \ln x$, que es la inversa de la función exponencial natural $f(x) = e^x$. El dominio es $\{x \mid x > 0\}$; el rango es todos los números reales.	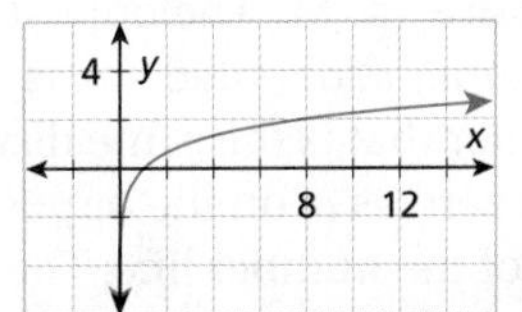
natural number (p. 6) A counting number.	**número natural** Número que sirve para contar.	1, 2, 3, 4, 5, 6, ...
negative exponent (p. 35) A base raised to a negative exponent is equal to the reciprocal of that base raised to the opposite exponent: $b^{-n} = \frac{1}{b^n}$.	**exponente negativo** Una base elevada a un exponente negativo es igual al recíproco de dicha base elevado al exponente opuesto: $b^{-n} = \frac{1}{b^n}$.	$5^{-3} = \frac{1}{5^3} = \frac{1}{125}$
net (p. 421) A diagram of the faces of a three-dimensional figure arranged in such a way that the diagram can be folded to form the three-dimensional figure.	**plantilla** Diagrama de las caras de una figura tridimensional que se puede plegar para formar la figura tridimensional.	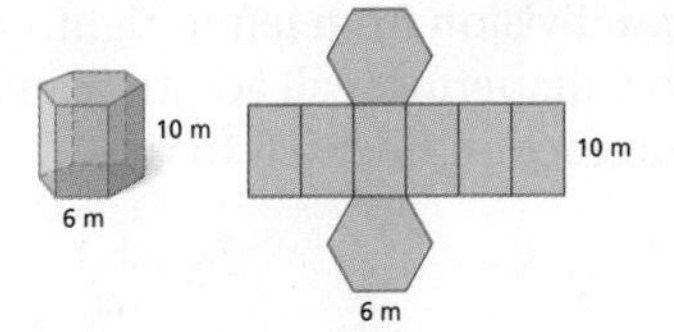
nonlinear system of equations (p. 768) A system in which at least one of the equations is not linear.	**sistema no lineal de ecuaciones** Sistema en el cual por lo menos una de las ecuaciones no es lineal.	$\begin{cases} y = 2x^2 \\ y = -3x^2 + 5 \end{cases}$

ENGLISH	SPANISH	EXAMPLES
***n*th root** (p. 610) The *n*th root of a number *a*, written as $\sqrt[n]{a}$ or $a^{\frac{1}{n}}$, is a number that is equal to *a* when it is raised to the *n*th power.	**enésima raíz** La enésima raíz de un número *a*, que se escribe como $\sqrt[n]{a}$ o $a^{\frac{1}{n}}$, es un número igual a *a* cuando se eleva a la enésima potencia.	$\sqrt[5]{32} = 2$, because $2^5 = 32$.

ENGLISH	SPANISH	EXAMPLES
objective function (p. 206) The function to be maximized or minimized in a linear programming problem.	**función objetiva** Función que se debe maximizar o minimizar en un problema de programación lineal.	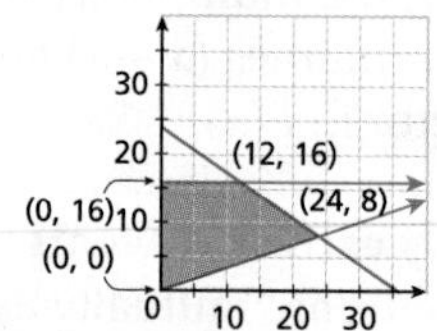 The objective function $P = 18x + 25y$ is maximized at $(24, 8)$.
obtuse angle (p. 198) An angle that measures greater than 90° and less than 180°.	**ángulo obtuso** Ángulo que mide más de 90° y menos de 180°.	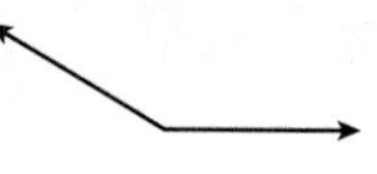
one-to-one function (p. 691) A function in which each *y*-value corresponds to only one *x*-value. The inverse of a one-to-one function is also a function.	**función uno a uno** Función en la que cada valor de *y* corresponde a sólo un valor de *x*. La inversa de una función uno a uno es también una función.	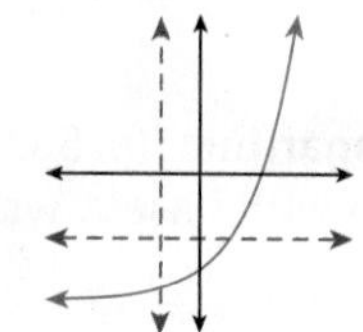
opposite (p. 14) The opposite of a number *a*, denoted $-a$, is the number that is the same distance from zero as *a*, on the opposite side of the number line. The sum of opposites is 0.	**opuesto** El opuesto de un número *a*, expresado $-a$, es el número que se encuentra a la misma distancia de cero que *a*, del lado opuesto de la recta numérica. La suma de los opuestos es 0.	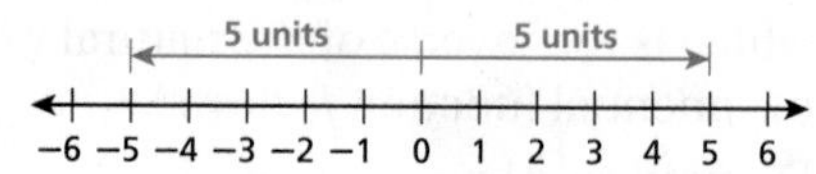 5 and −5 are opposites.
order of operations (p. 28) A process for evaluating expressions: First, perform operations in parentheses or other grouping symbols. Second, evaluate powers and roots. Third, perform all multiplication and division from left to right. Fourth, perform all addition and subtraction from left to right.	**orden de las operaciones** Proceso para evaluar las expresiones: Primero, realizar las operaciones entre paréntesis u otros símbolos de agrupación. Segundo, evaluar las potencias y las raíces. Tercero, realizar todas las multiplicaciones y divisiones de izquierda a derecha. Cuarto, realizar todas las sumas y restas de izquierda a derecha.	$2 + 3^2 - (7 + 5) \div 4 \cdot 3$ $2 + 3^2 - 12 \div 4 \cdot 3$ Add inside parentheses. $2 + 9 - 12 \div 4 \cdot 3$ Evaluate the power. $2 + 9 - 3 \cdot 3$ Divide. $2 + 9 - 9$ Multiply. $11 - 9$ Add. 2 Subtract.
ordered triple (p. 214) A set of three numbers that can be used to locate a point (x, y, z) in a three-dimensional coordinate system.	**tripleta ordenada** Conjunto de tres números que se pueden utilizar para ubicar un punto (x, y, z) en un sistema de coordenadas tridimensional.	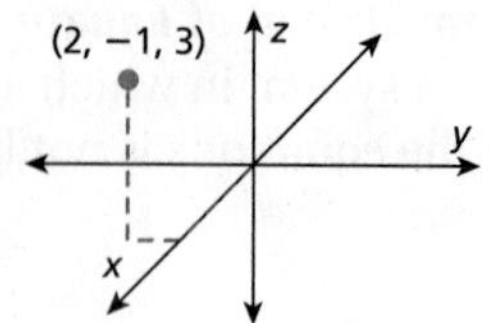

ENGLISH	SPANISH	EXAMPLES

origin (p. 3) The intersection of the x- and y-axes in a coordinate plane. The coordinates of the origin are $(0, 0)$.

origen Intersección de los ejes x e y en un plano cartesiano. Las coordenadas de origen son $(0, 0)$.

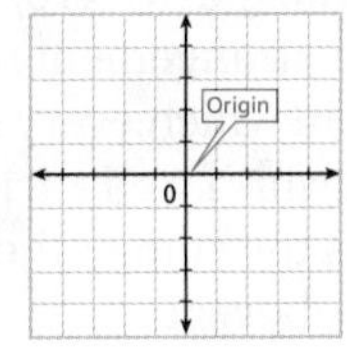

outcome (p. 802) A possible result of a probability experiment.

resultado Resultado posible en un experimento de probabilidad.

In the experiment of rolling a number cube, the possible outcomes are 1, 2, 3, 4, 5, and 6.

outlier (p. 831) A data value that is far removed from the rest of the data. A value less than $Q_1 - 1.5(\text{IQR})$ or greater than $Q_3 + 1.5(\text{IQR})$ is considered to be an outlier.

valor extremo Valor de datos que está muy alejado del resto de los datos. Un valor menor que $Q_1 - 1.5(\text{IQR})$ o mayor que $Q_3 + 1.5(\text{IQR})$ se considera un valor extremo.

parabola (p. 315) The shape of the graph of a quadratic function. Also, the set of points equidistant from a point F, called the *focus*, and a line d, called the *directrix*.

parábola Forma de la gráfica de una función cuadrática. También, conjunto de puntos equidistantes de un punto F, denominado *foco*, y una línea d, denominada *directriz*.

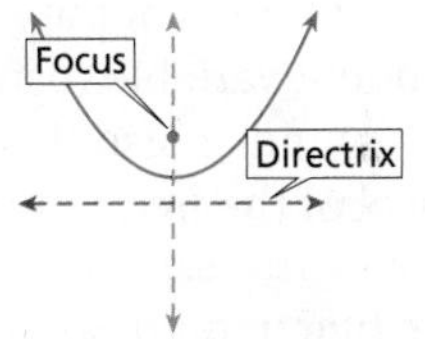

parameter (p. 230) One of the constants in a function or equation that may be changed. Also the third variable in a set of parametric equations.

parámetro Una de las constantes en una función o ecuación que se puede cambiar. También es la tercera variable en un conjunto de ecuaciones paramétricas.

$y = (x - h)^2 + k$

parameters

parametric equations (p. 230) A pair of equations that define the x- and y-coordinates of a point in terms of a third variable called a parameter.

ecuaciones paramétricas Par de ecuaciones que definen las coordenadas x e y de un punto en función de una tercera variable denominada parámetro.

$x(t) = t + 1$

$y(t) = -2t$

parent function (p. 67) The simplest function with the defining characteristics of the family. Functions in the same family are transformations of their parent function.

función madre La función más básica con las características de la familia. Las funciones de la misma familia son transformaciones de su función madre.

$f(x) = x^2$ is the parent function for $g(x) = x^2 + 4$ and $h(x) = 5(x + 2)^2 - 3$.

partial sum (p. 870) Indicated by $S_n = \sum_{i=1}^{n} a_i$, the sum of a specified number of terms n of a sequence whose total number of terms is greater than n.

suma parcial Expresada por $S_n = \sum_{i=1}^{n} a_i$, la suma de un número específico n de términos de una sucesión cuyo número total de términos es mayor que n.

For the sequence $a_n = n^2$, the fourth partial sum of the infinite series $\sum_{k=1}^{\infty} k^2$ is

$\sum_{k=1}^{4} k^2 = 1^2 + 2^2 + 3^2 + 4^2 = 30$.

ENGLISH | **SPANISH** | **EXAMPLES**

Pascal's triangle (p. 416) A triangular arrangement of numbers in which every row starts and ends with 1 and each other number is the sum of the two numbers above it.

triángulo de Pascal Arreglo triangular de números en el cual cada fila comienza y termina con 1 y cada uno de los demás números es la suma de los dos números que están encima de él.

```
        1
      1   1
    1   2   1
  1   3   3   1
1   4   6   4   1
```

---

perfect square (p. 21) A number whose positive square root is a whole number.

cuadrado perfecto Número cuya raíz cuadrada positiva es un número cabal.

36 is a perfect square because $\sqrt{36} = 6$.

---

perfect-square trinomial (p. 336) A trinomial whose factored form is the square of a binomial. A perfect-square trinomial has the form $a^2 - 2ab + b^2 = (a - b)^2$ or $a^2 + 2ab + b^2 = (a + b)^2$.

trinomio cuadrado perfecto Trinomio cuya forma factorizada es el cuadrado de un binomio. Un trinomio cuadrado perfecto tiene la forma $a^2 - 2ab + b^2 = (a - b)^2$ o $a^2 + 2ab + b^2 = (a + b)^2$.

$x^2 + 6x + 9$ is a perfect-square trinomial, because $x^2 + 6x + 9 = (x + 3)^2$.

---

period of a periodic function (p. 990) The length of a cycle measured in units of the independent variable (usually time in seconds). Also the reciprocal of the frequency.

periodo de una función periódica Longitud de un ciclo medido en unidades de la variable independiente (generalmente el tiempo en segundos). También es la inversa de la frecuencia.

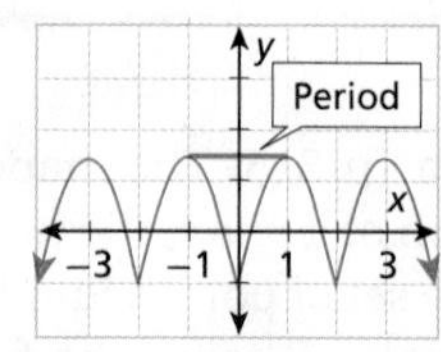

---

periodic function (p. 990) A function that repeats exactly in regular intervals, called *periods.*

función periódica Función que se repite exactamente a intervalos regulares denominados *periodos.*

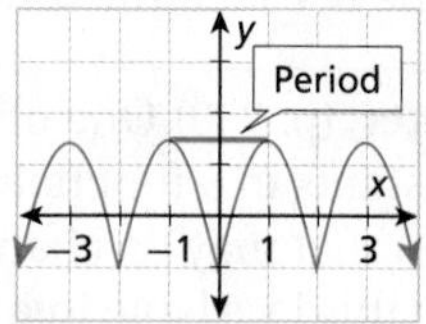

---

permutation (p. 795) An arrangement of a group of objects in which order is important. The number of permutations of r objects from a group of n objects is denoted ${}_nP_r$.

permutación Arreglo de un grupo de objetos en el cual el orden es importante. El número de permutaciones de r objetos de un grupo de n objetos se expresa ${}_nP_r$.

For 4 objects *A, B, C,* and *D,* there are ${}_4P_2 = 12$ different permutations of 2 objects: *AB, AC, AD, BC, BD, CD, BA, CA, DA, CB, DB,* and *DC.*

---

phase shift (p. 993) A horizontal translation of a periodic function.

cambio de fase Traslación horizontal de una función periódica.

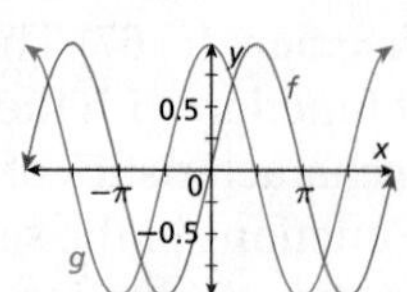

g is a phase shift of f $\frac{\pi}{2}$ units left.

---

piecewise function (p. 662) A function that is a combination of one or more functions.

función a trozos Función que es una combinación de una o más funciones.

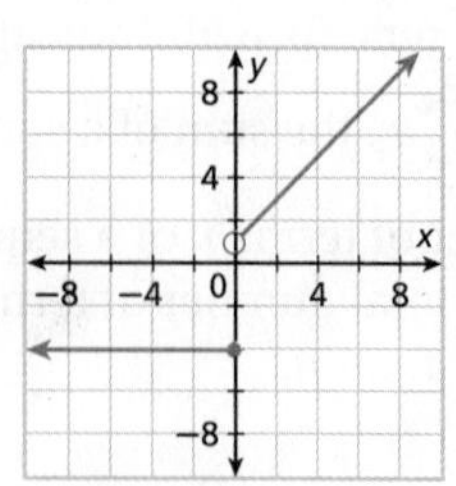

$$f(x) = \begin{cases} -4 & \text{if } x \leq 0 \\ x + 1 & \text{if } x > 0 \end{cases}$$

ENGLISH	SPANISH	EXAMPLES
point-slope form (p. 116) The point-slope form of a linear equation is $y - y_1 = m(x - x_1)$, where m is the slope and (x_1, y_1) is a point on the line.	**forma de punto y pendiente** La forma de punto y pendiente de una ecuación lineal es $y - y_1 = m(x - x_1)$, donde m es la pendiente y (x_1, y_1) es un punto en la línea.	The equation of the line through (2, 1) with slope 3 is $y - 1 = 3(x - 2)$.
polynomial (p. 406) A monomial or a sum or difference of monomials.	**polinomio** Monomio o suma o diferencia de monomios.	$2x^2 + 3x - 7$
polynomial function (p. 408) A function whose rule is a polynomial.	**función polinomial** Función cuya regla es un polinomio.	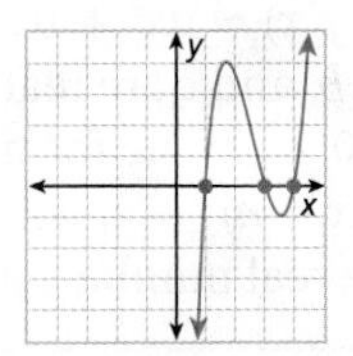 $f(x) = x^3 - 8x^2 + 19x - 12$
power (p. 34) An expression written with a base and an exponent or the value of such an expression.	**potencia** Expresión escrita con una base y un exponente o el valor de dicha expresión.	$2^3 = 8$, so 8 is the third power of 2.
principal root (p. 21) The positive root of a number, indicated by the radical sign.	**raíz principal** Raíz cuadrada positiva de un número, expresada por el signo de radical.	$\sqrt{36} = 6$
probability (p. 802) A number from 0 to 1 (or 0% to 100%) that is the measure of how likely an event is to occur.	**probabilidad** Número entre 0 y 1 (o entre 0% y 100%) que describe cuán probable es que ocurra un suceso.	A bag contains 3 red marbles and 4 blue marbles. The probability of choosing a red marble is $\frac{3}{7}$.
probability distribution for an experiment (p. 828) The function that pairs each outcome with its probability.	**distribución de probabilidad para un experimento** Función que asigna a cada resultado su probabilidad.	A number cube is rolled 10 times. The results are shown in the table. (see table below)
proportion (p. 97) A statement that two ratios are equal; $\frac{a}{b} = \frac{c}{d}$.	**proporción** Enunciado que establece que dos razones son iguales; $\frac{a}{b} = \frac{c}{d}$.	$\frac{2}{3} = \frac{4}{6}$
pure imaginary number (p. 351) *See* imaginary number.	**número imaginario puro** *Ver* número imaginario.	$3i$

Outcome	1	2	3	4	5	6
Probability	$\frac{1}{10}$	$\frac{1}{5}$	$\frac{1}{5}$	0	$\frac{3}{10}$	$\frac{1}{5}$

Q

ENGLISH	SPANISH	EXAMPLES
quadratic equation (p. 334) An equation that can be written in the form $ax^2 + bx + c = 0$, where a, b, and c are real numbers and $a \neq 0$.	**ecuación cuadrática** Ecuación que se puede expresar como $ax^2 + bx + c = 0$, donde a, b y c son números reales y $a \neq 0$.	$x^2 + 3x - 4 = 0$ $x^2 - 9 = 0$

ENGLISH	SPANISH	EXAMPLES

Quadratic Formula (p. 356) The formula $x = \frac{-b \pm \sqrt{b^2 - 4ac}}{2a}$, which gives solutions, or roots, of equations in the form $ax^2 + bx + c = 0$, where $a \neq 0$.

fórmula cuadrática La fórmula $x = \frac{-b \pm \sqrt{b^2 - 4ac}}{2a}$, que da soluciones, o raíces, para las ecuaciones del tipo $ax^2 + bx + c = 0$, donde $a \neq 0$.

The solutions of $2x^2 - 5x - 3 = 0$ are given by

$$x = \frac{-(-5) \pm \sqrt{(-5)^2 - 4(2)(-3)}}{2(2)}$$

$$= \frac{5 \pm \sqrt{25 + 24}}{4} = \frac{5 \pm 7}{4};$$

$x = 3$ or $x = -\frac{1}{2}$.

---

quadratic function (p. 315) A function that can be written in the form $f(x) = ax^2 + bx + c$, where a, b, and c are real numbers and $a \neq 0$, or in the form $f(x) = a(x - h)^2 + k$, where a, h, and k are real numbers and $a \neq 0$.

función cuadrática Función que se puede expresar como $f(x) = ax^2 + bx + c$, donde a, b y c son números reales y $a \neq 0$, o como $f(x) = a(x - h)^2 + k$, donde a, h y k son números reales y $a \neq 0$.

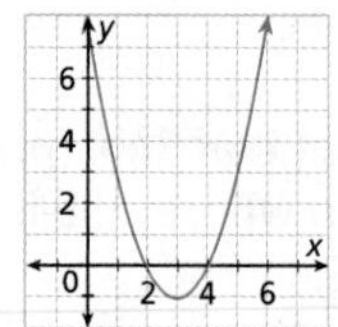

$f(x) = x^2 - 6x + 8$

---

quadratic inequality in two variables (p. 366) An inequality that can be written in one of the following forms:
$y < ax^2 + bx + c$,
$y > ax^2 + bx + c$,
$y \leq ax^2 + bx + c$,
$y \geq ax^2 + bx + c$,
or $y \neq ax^2 + bx + c$,
where a, b, and c are real numbers and $a \neq 0$.

desigualdad cuadrática en dos variables Desigualdad que puede expresarse de una de las siguientes formas:
$y < ax^2 + bx + c$,
$y > ax^2 + bx + c$,
$y \leq ax^2 + bx + c$,
$y \geq ax^2 + bx + c$,
o $y \neq ax^2 + bx + c$,
donde a, b y c son números reales y $a \neq 0$.

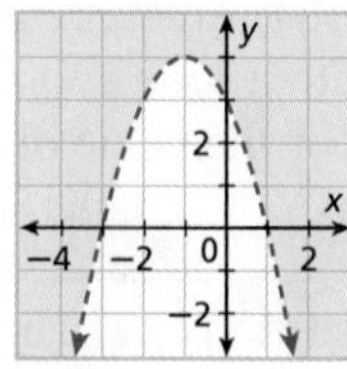

$y > -x^2 - 2x + 3$

---

quadratic model (p. 376) A quadratic function used to represent a set of data.

modelo cuadrático Función cuadrática que se utiliza para representar un conjunto de datos.

x	4	6	8	10
$f(x)$	27	52	89	130

A quadratic model for the data is $f(x) = x^2 + 3.3x - 2.6$.

---

quadratic regression (p. 376) A statistical method used to fit a quadratic model to a given data set.

regresión cuadrática Método estadístico utilizado para ajustar un modelo cuadrático a un conjunto de datos determinado.

radian (p. 943) A unit of angle measure based on arc length. In a circle of radius r, if a central angle has a measure of 1 radian, then the length of the intercepted arc is r units.

2π radians $= 360°$
1 radian $\approx 57°$

radián Unidad de medida de un ángulo basada en la longitud del arco. En un círculo de radio r, si un ángulo central mide 1 radián, entonces la longitud del arco abarcado es r unidades.

2π radianes $= 360°$
1 radián $\approx 57°$

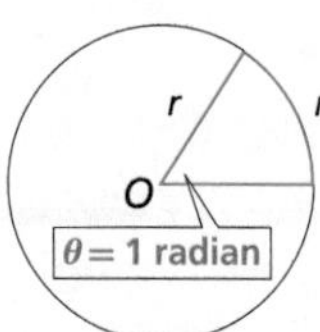

---

radical (p. 21) An indicated root of a quantity.

radical Raíz indicada de una cantidad.

$\sqrt{36} = 6$, $\sqrt[3]{27} = 3$

ENGLISH	SPANISH	EXAMPLES
radical equation (p. 628) An equation that contains a variable within a radical.	**ecuación radical** Ecuación que contiene una variable dentro de un radical.	$\sqrt{x+3}+4=7$
radical function (p. 619) A function whose rule contains a variable within a radical.	**función radical** Función cuya regla contiene una variable dentro de un radical.	Graph with points (0, 0), (1, 1), (4, 2), (9, 3); $f(x)=\sqrt{x}$
radical inequality (p. 630) An inequality that contains a variable within a radical.	**desigualdad radical** Desigualdad que contiene una variable dentro de un radical.	$\sqrt{x+3}\le 7$
radical symbol (p. 21) The symbol $\sqrt{\ }$ used to denote a root. The symbol is used alone to indicate a square root or with an index, $\sqrt[n]{\ }$, to indicate the *n*th root.	**símbolo de radical** Símbolo $\sqrt{\ }$ que se utiliza para expresar una raíz. Puede utilizarse solo para indicar una raíz cuadrada, o con un índice, $\sqrt[n]{\ }$, para indicar la enésima raíz.	$\sqrt{36}=6$, $\sqrt[3]{27}=3$
radicand (p. 21) The expression under a radical sign.	**radicando** Número o expresión debajo del signo de radical.	$\sqrt{x+3}-2$ (Radicand: $x+3$)
random sample A sample selected from a population so that each member of the population has an equal chance of being selected.	**muestra aleatoria** Muestra seleccionada de una población tal que cada miembro de ésta tenga igual probabilidad de ser seleccionado.	Mr. Hansen chose a random sample of the class by writing each student's name on a slip of paper, mixing up the slips, and drawing five slips without looking.
range of a data set (p. 830) The difference of the greatest and least values in the data set.	**rango de un conjunto de datos** La diferencia del mayor y menor valor en un conjunto de datos.	The data set $\{3, 3, 5, 7, 8, 10, 11, 11, 12\}$ has a range of $12-3=9$.
range of a function or relation (p. 44) The set of output values of a function or relation.	**rango de una función o relación** Conjunto de los valores de salida de una función o relación.	The range of $y=x^2$ is $\{y \mid y\ge 0\}$.
rate (p. 98) A ratio that compares two quantities measured in different units.	**tasa** Razón que compara dos cantidades medidas en diferentes unidades.	$\frac{55 \text{ miles}}{1 \text{ hour}}=55$ mi/h
ratio (p. 97) A comparison of two quantities by division.	**razón** Comparación de dos cantidades mediante una división.	$\frac{1}{2}$ or 1:2
rational equation (p. 600) An equation that contains one or more rational expressions.	**ecuación racional** Ecuación que contiene una o más expresiones racionales.	$\frac{x+2}{x^2+3x-1}=6$
rational exponent (p. 611) An exponent that can be expressed as $\frac{m}{n}$ such that if *m* and *n* are integers, then $b^{\frac{m}{n}}=\sqrt[n]{b^m}=\left(\sqrt[n]{b}\right)^m$.	**exponente racional** Exponente que se puede expresar como $\frac{m}{n}$ tal que, si *m* y *n* son números enteros, entonces $b^{\frac{m}{n}}=\sqrt[n]{b^m}=\left(\sqrt[n]{b}\right)^m$.	$4^{\frac{3}{2}}=\sqrt{4^3}=\sqrt{64}=8$ $4^{\frac{3}{2}}=\left(\sqrt{4}\right)^3=2^3=8$

ENGLISH	SPANISH	EXAMPLES
rational expression (p. 577) An algebraic expression whose numerator and denominator are polynomials and whose denominator has a degree ≥ 1.	**expresión racional** Expresión algebraica cuyo numerador y denominador son polinomios y cuyo denominador tiene un grado ≥ 1.	$\frac{x + 2}{x^2 + 3x - 1}$
rational function (p. 592) A function whose rule can be written as a rational expression.	**función racional** Función cuya regla se puede expresar como una expresión racional.	$f(x) = \frac{x + 2}{x^2 + 3x - 1}$
rational inequality (p. 603) An inequality that contains one or more rational expressions.	**desigualdad racional** Desigualdad que contiene una o más expresiones racionales.	$\frac{x + 2}{x^2 + 3x - 1} \geq 6$
rational number (p. 6) A number that can be written in the form $\frac{a}{b}$, where a and b are integers and $b \neq 0$.	**número racional** Número que se puede expresar como $\frac{a}{b}$, donde a y b son números enteros y $b \neq 0$.	$3, 1.75, 0.\overline{3}, -\frac{2}{3}, 0$
rationalizing the denominator (p. 22) A method of rewriting a fraction by multiplying by another fraction that is equivalent to 1 in order to remove radical terms from the denominator.	**racionalizar el denominador** Método que consiste en escribir nuevamente una fracción multiplicándola por otra fracción equivalente a 1 a fin de eliminar los términos radicales del denominador.	$\frac{1}{\sqrt{2}}\left(\frac{\sqrt{2}}{\sqrt{2}}\right) = \frac{\sqrt{2}}{2}$
real axis (p. 382) The horizontal axis in the complex plane; it graphically represents the real part of complex numbers.	**eje real** Eje horizontal de un plano complejo. Representa gráficamente la parte real de los números complejos.	Imaginary axis; $2i$; $0 + 0i$; Real axis; -2; 2; $-2i$
real number (p. 6) A rational or irrational number. Every point on the number line represents a real number.	**número real** Número racional o irracional. Cada punto de la recta numérica representa un número real.	$-5, 0, \frac{2}{3}, \sqrt{2}, 3.1, \pi$
real part of a complex number (p. 351) For a complex number of the form $a + bi$, a is the real part.	**parte real de un número complejo** Dado un número complejo del tipo $a + bi$, a es la parte real.	$5 + 6i$ (Real part: 5; Imaginary part: $6i$)
reciprocal (p. 14) For a real number $a \neq 0$, the reciprocal of a is $\frac{1}{a}$. The product of reciprocals is 1.	**recíproco** Dado el número real $a \neq 0$, el recíproco de a es $\frac{1}{a}$. El producto de los recíprocos es 1.	$\frac{1}{2}$ is the reciprocal of 2. $\frac{5}{3}$ is the reciprocal of $\frac{3}{5}$.
recursive formula (p. 862) A formula for a sequence in which one or more previous terms are used to generate the next term.	**fórmula recurrente** Fórmula para una sucesión en la cual uno o más términos anteriores se utilizan para generar el término siguiente.	For the sequence 5, 7, 9, 11, ..., a recursive formula is $a_1 = 5$ and $a_n = a_{n-1} + 2$.
reduced row-echelon form (p. 288) A form of an augmented matrix in which the coefficient columns form an identity matrix.	**forma escalonada reducida por filas** Forma de matriz aumentada en la que las columnas de coeficientes forman una matriz de identidad.	$\left[\begin{array}{cc\|c} 1 & 0 & -1 \\ 0 & 1 & 3 \end{array}\right]$

ENGLISH	SPANISH	EXAMPLES
reference angle (p. 937) For an angle in standard position, the reference angle is the positive acute angle formed by the terminal side of the angle and the *x*-axis.	**ángulo de referencia** Dado un ángulo en posición estándar, el ángulo de referencia es el ángulo agudo positivo formado por el lado terminal del ángulo y el eje *x*.	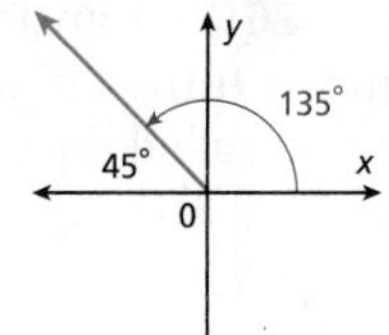
reflection (p. 60) A transformation that reflects, or "flips," a graph or figure across a line, called the line of reflection, such that each reflected point is the same distance from the line of reflection but is on the opposite side of the line.	**reflexión** Transformación que refleja, o invierte, una gráfica o figura sobre una línea, llamada la línea de reflexión, de manera tal que cada punto reflejado esté a la misma distancia de la línea de reflexión pero que se encuentre en el lado opuesto de la línea.	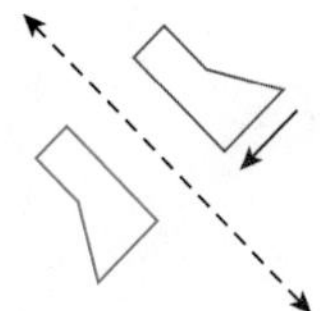
reflection matrix (p. 263) A matrix used to reflect a figure across a specified *line of symmetry.*	**matriz de reflexión** Matriz utilizada para reflejar una figura sobre un *eje de simetría* específico.	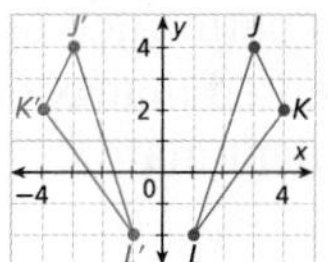 Matrix $\begin{bmatrix} -1 & 0 \\ 0 & 1 \end{bmatrix}$ was used to reflect the figure across the *y*-axis.
regression (p. 142) The statistical study of the relationship between variables.	**regresión** Estudio estadístico de la relación entre variables.	
relation (p. 44) A set of ordered pairs.	**relación** Conjunto de pares ordenados.	$\{(0, 5), (0, 4), (2, 3), (4, 0)\}$
replacement set (p. 55) A set of numbers that can be substituted for a variable.	**conjunto de reemplazo** Conjunto de números que pueden sustituir una variable.	The solution set of $y = x + 3$ for the replacement set $\{1, 2, 3\}$ is $\{4, 5, 6\}$.
right angle (p. 960) An angle that measures 90°.	**ángulo recto** Ángulo que mide 90°.	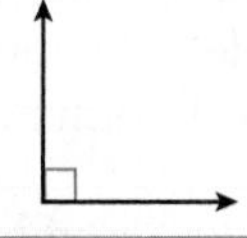
right triangle (p. 20) A triangle with one right angle.	**triángulo rectángulo** Triángulo con un ángulo recto.	
rigid transformation (p. 261) A transformation that does not change the size or shape of a figure.	**transformación rígida** Transformación que no cambia el tamaño o la forma de una figura.	Reflections, rotations, and translations are rigid transformations.
root of an equation (p. 334) Any value of the variable that makes the equation true.	**raíz de una ecuación** Cualquier valor de la variable que transforme la ecuación en verdadera.	The roots of $(x - 2)(x + 1) = 0$ are 2 and -1.
roster notation (p. 7) A way of representing a set by listing the elements between braces, { }.	**notación de lista** Forma de representar un conjunto enumerando los elementos entre llaves, { }.	The first 5 positive odd numbers are $\{1, 3, 5, 7, 9\}$.

ENGLISH	SPANISH	EXAMPLES
rotation (p. 261) A transformation that rotates or turns a figure about a point called the center of rotation.	**rotación** Transformación que hace rotar o girar una figura sobre un punto llamado centro de rotación.	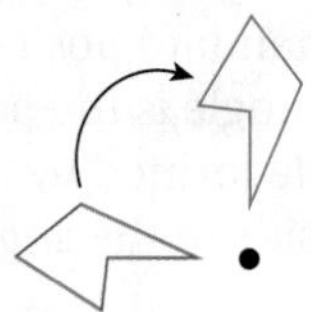
rotation matrix (p. 264) A matrix used to rotate a figure about the origin.	**matriz de rotación** Matriz utilizada para rotar una figura sobre el origen.	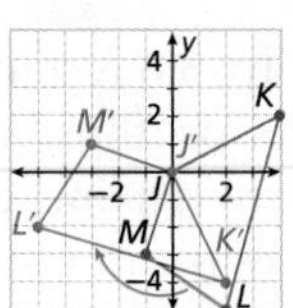 Matrix $\begin{bmatrix} 0 & 1 \\ -1 & 0 \end{bmatrix}$ was used to rotate the figure 90° clockwise.
row operation (p. 288) An operation performed on a row of an augmented matrix that creates an equivalent matrix.	**operación por filas** Operación realizada en una fila de una matriz aumentada que crea una matriz equivalente.	$\left[\begin{array}{cc\|c} 2 & 0 & -2 \\ 0 & 1 & 3 \end{array}\right] = \left[\begin{array}{cc\|c} \frac{1}{2}(2) & \frac{1}{2}(0) & \frac{1}{2}(-1) \\ 0 & 1 & 3 \end{array}\right] = \left[\begin{array}{cc\|c} 1 & 0 & -1 \\ 0 & 1 & 3 \end{array}\right]$
row-reduction method (p. 288) The process of performing elementary row operations on an augmented matrix to transform the matrix to reduced row echelon form.	**método de reducción por filas** Proceso por el cual se realizan operaciones elementales de filas en una matriz aumentada para transformar la matriz en una forma reducida de filas escalonadas.	$\left[\begin{array}{cc\|c} 2 & 0 & -2 \\ 0 & 1 & 3 \end{array}\right] = \left[\begin{array}{cc\|c} \frac{1}{2}(2) & \frac{1}{2}(0) & \frac{1}{2}(-1) \\ 0 & 1 & 3 \end{array}\right] = \left[\begin{array}{cc\|c} 1 & 0 & -1 \\ 0 & 1 & 3 \end{array}\right]$

ENGLISH	SPANISH	EXAMPLES
sample space (p. 802) The set of all possible outcomes of a probability experiment.	**espacio muestral** Conjunto de todos los resultados posibles en un experimento de probabilidades.	In the experiment of rolling a number cube, the sample space is $\{1, 2, 3, 4, 5, 6\}$.
scalar (p. 248) A number that is multiplied by a matrix.	**escalar** Número que se multiplica por una matriz.	$3\begin{bmatrix} 1 & -2 \\ 2 & 3 \end{bmatrix} = \begin{bmatrix} 3 & -6 \\ 6 & 9 \end{bmatrix}$ (3 = scalar)
scale factor (p. 99) The multiplier used on each dimension to change one figure into a similar figure.	**factor de escala** El multiplicador utilizado en cada dimensión para transformar una figura en una figura semejante.	y, 5, A′(4, 6), A(2, 3), B′(0, 2), B(0, 1), x, 0, C(3, 0), C′(6, 0)
scatter plot (p. 142) A graph with points plotted to show a possible relationship between two sets of data.	**diagrama de dispersión** Gráfica con puntos que se usa para demostrar una relación posible entre dos conjuntos de datos.	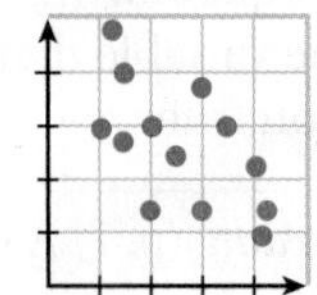

ENGLISH	SPANISH	EXAMPLES
scientific notation (p. 36) A method of writing very large or very small numbers, by using powers of 10, in the form $m \times 10^n$, where $1 \le m < 10$ and n is an integer.	**notación científica** Método que consiste en escribir números muy grandes o muy pequeños utilizando potencias de 10 del tipo $m \times 10^n$, donde $1 \le m < 10$ y n es un número entero.	$1.256\ 10^{13} = 12{,}560{,}000{,}000{,}000$ $7.5 \times 10^{-6} = 0.0000075$
secant of an angle (p. 932) In a right triangle, the ratio of the length of the hypotenuse to the length of the side adjacent to angle A. It is the reciprocal of the cosine function.	**secante de un ángulo** En un triángulo rectángulo, la razón entre la longitud de la hipotenusa y la longitud del cateto adyacente al ángulo A. Es la inversa de la función coseno.	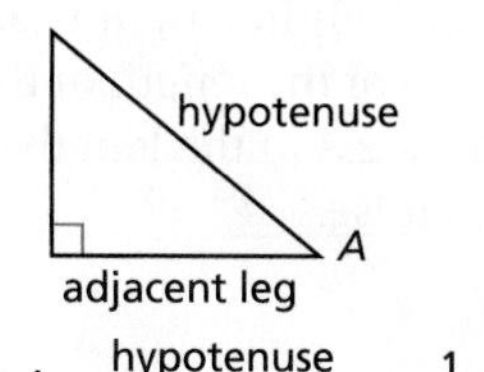 $\sec A = \frac{\text{hypotenuse}}{\text{adjacent}} = \frac{1}{\cos A}$
second differences (p. 374) Differences between first differences of a function.	**segundas diferencias** Diferencias entre las primeras diferencias de una función.	x: 0, 1, 2, 3 y: 1, 4, 9, 16 first differences +3 +5 +7 second differences +2 +2
sequence (p. 862) A list of numbers that often form a pattern.	**sucesión** Lista de números que generalmente forman un patrón.	1, 2, 4, 8, 16, ...
series (p. 870) The indicated sum of the terms of a sequence.	**serie** Suma indicada de los términos de una sucesión.	1 + 2 + 4 + 8 + 16 + ...
set (p. 6) A collection of items called elements.	**conjunto** Grupo de componentes denominados elementos.	$\{1, 2, 3\}$
set-builder notation (p. 8) A notation for a set that uses a rule to describe the properties of the elements of the set.	**notación de conjuntos** Notación para un conjunto que se vale de una regla para describir las propiedades de los elementos del conjunto.	$\{x \mid x > 3\}$ is read, "The set of all x such that x is greater than 3."
Sierpinski triangle (p. 864) A fractal formed from a triangle by removing triangles with vertices at the midpoints of the sides of each remaining triangle.	**triángulo de Sierpinski** Fractal formado a partir de un triángulo al cual se le recortan triángulos cuyos vértices se encuentran en los puntos medios de los lados de cada triángulo restante.	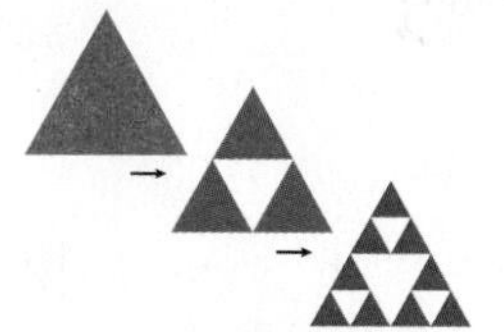
similar (p. 99) Two figures are similar if they have the same shape but not necessarily the same size.	**semejantes** Dos figuras son semejantes si tienen la misma forma pero no necesariamente el mismo tamaño.	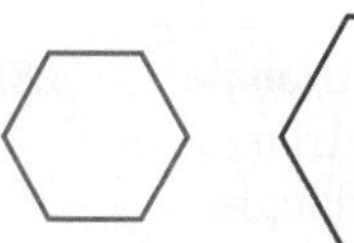
simple event (p. 819) An event consisting of only one outcome.	**suceso simple** Suceso que contiene sólo un resultado.	In the experiment of rolling a number cube, the event consisting of the outcome 3 is a simple event.
simplify (p. 28) To perform all indicated operations.	**simplificar** Realizar todas las operaciones indicadas.	3(4) + 7 12 + 7 19

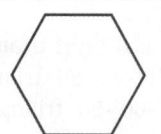

Glossary/Glosario

ENGLISH	SPANISH	EXAMPLES

simulation (p. 810) A model of an experiment, often one that would be too difficult or time-consuming to actually perform.

simulación Modelo de un experimento; generalmente se recurre a la simulación cuando realizar dicho experimento sería demasiado difícil o llevaría mucho tiempo.

A random number generator is used to simulate the roll of a number cube.

---

sine (p. 929) In a right triangle, the ratio of the length of the side opposite $\angle A$ to the length of the hypotenuse.

seno En un triángulo rectángulo, razón entre la longitud del cateto opuesto a $\angle A$ y la longitud de la hipotenusa.

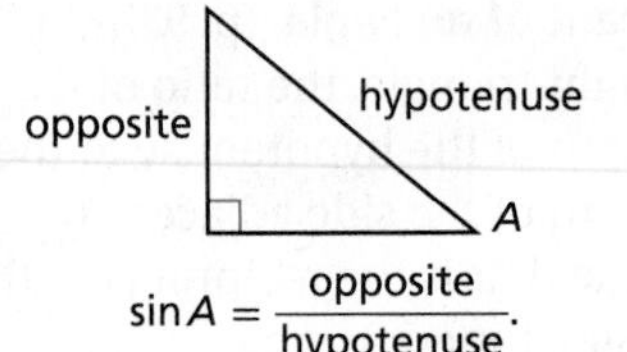

$\sin A = \frac{\text{opposite}}{\text{hypotenuse}}$.

---

slope (p. 106) A measure of the steepness of a line. If (x_1, y_1) and (x_2, y_2) are any two points on the line, the slope of the line, known as m, is represented by the equation $m = \frac{y_2 - y_1}{x_2 - x_1}$.

pendiente Medida de la inclinación de una línea. Dados dos puntos (x_1, y_1) y (x_2, y_2) en una línea, la pendiente de la línea, denominada m, se representa con la ecuación $m = \frac{y_2 - y_1}{x_2 - x_1}$.

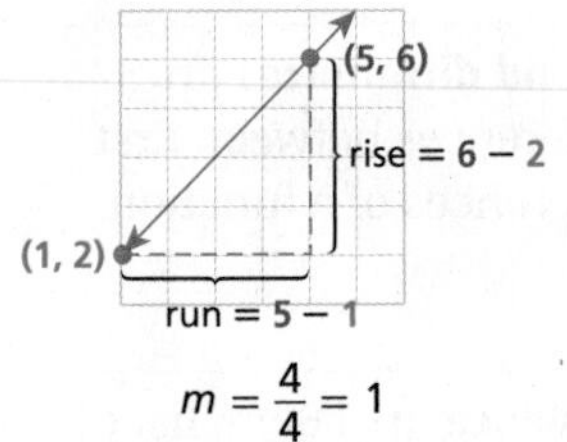

---

slope-intercept form (p. 107) The slope-intercept form of a linear equation is $y = mx + b$, where m is the slope and b is the y-intercept.

forma de pendiente-intersección La forma de pendiente-intersección de una ecuación lineal es $y = mx + b$, donde m es la pendiente y b es la intersección y.

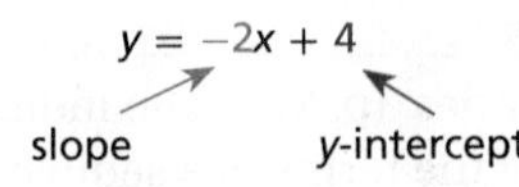

---

solution set of an equation (p. 90) The set of values that make an equation true.

conjunto solución de una ecuación Conjunto de valores que hacen verdadero un enunciado.

The solution set of $x^2 = 9$ is $\{-3, 3\}$.

---

solving a triangle (p. 959) Using given measures to find unknown angle measures or side lengths of a triangle.

resolución de un triángulo Utilizar medidas dadas para hallar las medidas desconocidas de los ángulos o las longitudes de los lados de un triángulo.

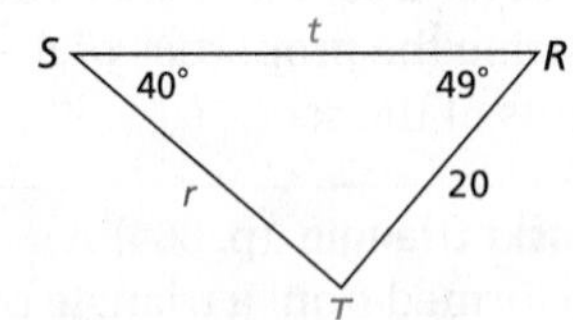

$49° + 40° + m\angle T = 180°$

$m\angle T = 91°$

$\frac{\sin 49°}{r} = \frac{\sin 40°}{20}$ $\quad$ $\frac{\sin 91°}{t} = \frac{\sin 40°}{20}$

$r \approx 23.5$ $\quad$ $t \approx 31.1$

---

special right triangle (p. 928) A 45°-45°-90° triangle or a 30°-60°-90° triangle.

triángulo rectángulo especial Triángulo de 45°-45°-90° o triángulo de 30°-60°-90°.

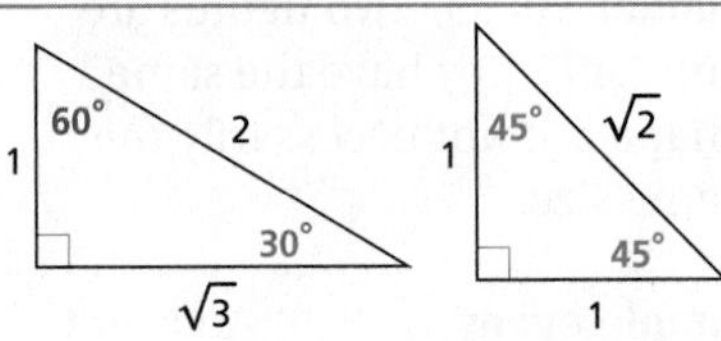

---

square matrix (p. 255) A matrix with the same number of rows as columns.

matriz cuadrada Matriz con el mismo número de filas y columnas.

$\begin{bmatrix} 1 & 2 \\ 0 & -3 \end{bmatrix}, \begin{bmatrix} 1 & -3 & 1 \\ 2 & 0 & -2 \\ 0 & 1 & 3 \end{bmatrix}$

---

square root (p. 21) A number that is multiplied to itself to form a product is called a square root of that product.

raíz cuadrada El número que se multiplica por sí mismo para formar un producto se denomina la raíz cuadrada de ese producto.

-4 and 4 are square roots of 16 because $(-4)^2 = 16$ and $4^2 = 16$.

ENGLISH	SPANISH	EXAMPLES
square-root function (p. 619) A function whose rule contains a variable under a square-root sign.	**función de raíz cuadrada** Función cuya regla contiene una variable bajo un signo de raíz cuadrada.	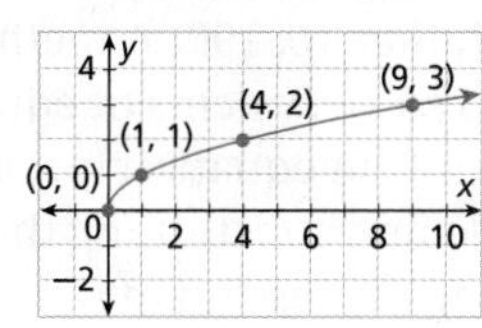 $f(x) = \sqrt{x}$
standard deviation (p. 830) A measure of dispersion of a data set. The standard deviation σ is the square root of the variance.	**desviación estándar** Medida de dispersión de un conjunto de datos. La desviación estándar σ es la raíz cuadrada de la varianza.	Data set: $\{6, 7, 7, 9, 11\}$ Mean: $\frac{6+7+7+9+11}{5} = 8$ Variance: $\frac{1}{5}(4+1+1+1+9) = 3.2$ Standard deviation: $\sigma = \sqrt{3.2} \approx 1.8$
standard form of a linear equation (p. 111) $Ax + By = C$, where A, B, and C are real numbers.	**forma estándar de una ecuación lineal** $Ax + By = C$, donde A, B y C son números reales.	$2x + 3y = 6$
standard form of a polynomial (p. 406) A polynomial in one variable is written in standard form when the terms are in order from greatest degree to least degree.	**forma estándar de un polinomio** Un polinomio de una variable se expresa en forma estándar cuando los términos se ordenan de mayor a menor grado.	$3x^3 - 5x^2 + 6x - 7$
standard form of a quadratic equation (p. 324) $ax^2 + bx + c = 0$, where a, b, and c are real numbers and $a \neq 0$.	**forma estándar de una ecuación cuadrática** $ax^2 + bx + c = 0$, donde a, b y c son números reales y $a \neq 0$.	$2x^2 + 3x - 1 = 0$
standard position (p. 936) An angle in standard position has its vertex at the origin and its initial side on the positive x-axis.	**posición estándar** Ángulo cuyo vértice se encuentra en el origen y cuyo lado inicial se encuentra sobre el eje x.	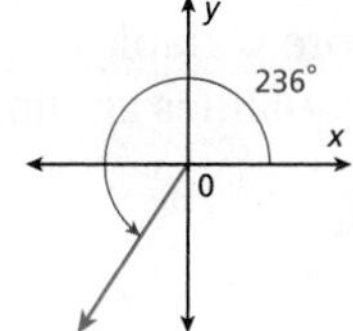
step function (p. 663) A piecewise function that is constant over each interval in its domain.	**función escalón** Función a trozos que es constante en cada intervalo en su dominio.	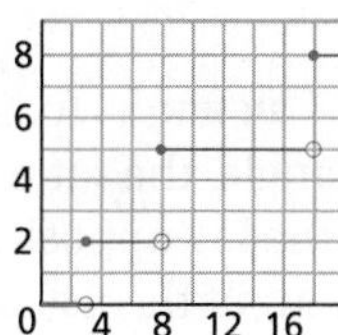
stretch (p. 61) A transformation that pulls the points of a graph horizontally away from the y-axis or vertically away from the x-axis.	**estiramiento** Transformación que desplaza los puntos de una gráfica en forma horizontal alejándolos del eje y o en forma vertical alejándolos del eje x.	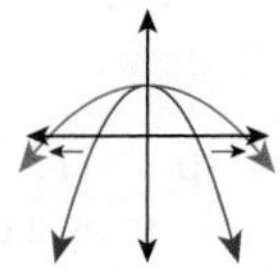
subset (p. 6) A set that is contained entirely within another set. Set B is a subset of set A if every element of B is contained in A, denoted $B \subset A$.	**subconjunto** Conjunto que se encuentra dentro de otro conjunto. El conjunto B es un subconjunto del conjunto A si todos los elementos de B son elementos de A; se expresa $B \subset A$.	The set of integers is a subset of the set of rational numbers, denoted $\mathbb{Z} \subset \mathbb{Q}$.

Glossary/Glosario

ENGLISH	SPANISH	EXAMPLES
substitution (p. 190) A method used to solve systems of equations by solving an equation for one variable and substituting the resulting expression into the other equation(s).	**sustitución** Método utilizado para resolver sistemas de ecuaciones resolviendo una ecuación para una variable y sustituyendo la expresión resultante en las demás ecuaciones.	$\begin{cases} 2x + 3y = -1 \\ x - 3y = 4 \end{cases}$ Solve for x. $x = 4 + 3y$ Substitute into the first equation and solve. $2(4 + 3y) + 3y = -1$ $y = -1$ Then solve for x. $x = 4 + 3(-1) = 1$
summation notation (p. 870) A method of notating the sum of a series using the Greek letter $\sum$ (capital *sigma*).	**notación de sumatoria** Método de notación de la suma de una serie que utiliza la letra griega $\sum$ (SIGMA mayúscula).	$\sum_{k=1}^{5} 3k = 3 + 6 + 9 + 12 + 15 = 45$
synthetic division (p. 423) A shorthand method of dividing by a linear binomial of the form $(x - a)$ by writing only the coefficients of the polynomials.	**división sintética** Método abreviado de división que consiste en dividir por un binomio lineal del tipo $(x - a)$ escribiendo sólo los coeficientes de los polinomios.	$(x^3 - 7x + 6) \div (x - 2)$ $\begin{array}{r\|rrrr} 2 & 1 & 0 & -7 & 6 \\ & & 2 & 4 & 6 \\ \hline & 1 & 2 & -3 & 0 \end{array}$ $(x^3 - 7x + 6) \div (x - 2) = x^2 + 2x - 3$
system of equations (p. 182) A set of two or more equations that have two or more variables.	**sistema de ecuaciones** Conjunto de dos o más ecuaciones que contienen dos o más variables.	$\begin{cases} 2x + 3y = -1 \\ x^2 = 4 \end{cases}$
system of linear equations (p. 182) *See* linear system.	**sistema de ecuaciones lineales** *Ver* sistema lineal.	
system of linear inequalities (p. 199) A system of inequalities in two or more variables in which all of the inequalities are linear.	**sistema de desigualdades lineales** Sistema de desigualdades en dos o más variables en el que todas las desigualdades son lineales.	$\begin{cases} 2x + 3y \geq -1 \\ x - 3y < 4 \end{cases}$

ENGLISH	SPANISH	EXAMPLES
tangent of an angle (p. 929) In a right triangle, the ratio of the length of the leg opposite $\angle A$ to the length of the leg adjacent to $\angle A$.	**tangente de un ángulo** En un triángulo rectángulo, razón entre la longitud del cateto opuesto a $\angle A$ y la longitud del cateto adyacente a $\angle A$.	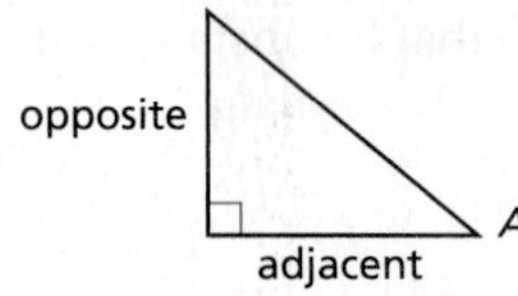 $\tan A = \frac{\text{opposite}}{\text{adjacent}}$
tangent line (p. 731) A line that is in the same plane as a circle and intersects the circle at exactly one point.	**línea tangente** Línea que está en el mismo plano que un círculo y corta al círculo en exactamente un punto.	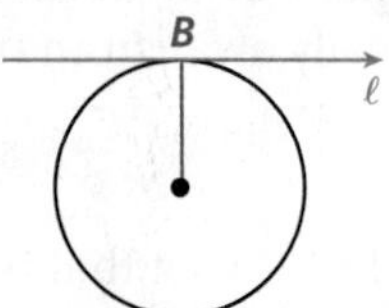
term of an expression (p. 28) The parts of the expression that are added or subtracted.	**término de una expresión** Partes de la expresión que se suman o se restan.	$3x^2 + 6x - 8$ Term Term Term

ENGLISH	SPANISH	EXAMPLES
term of a sequence (p. 862) An element or number in the sequence.	**término de una sucesión** Elemento o número de una sucesión.	5 is the third term in the sequence 1, 3, 5, 7, ...
terminal side (p. 936) For an angle in standard position, the ray that is rotated relative to the positive *x*-axis.	**lado terminal** Dado un ángulo en una posición estándar, el rayo que rota en relación con el eje positivo *x*.	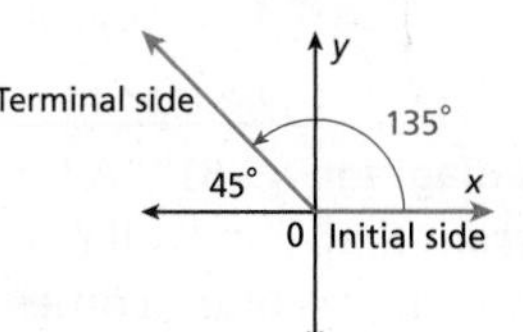
theoretical probability (p. 802) The ratio of the number of equally likely outcomes in an event to the total number of possible outcomes.	**probabilidad teórica** Razón entre el número de resultados igualmente probables de un suceso y el número total de resultados posibles.	The theoretical probability of rolling an odd number on a number cube is $\frac{3}{6} = \frac{1}{2}$.
third quartile (p. 829) The median of the upper half of a data set. Also called *upper quartile.*	**tercer cuartil** La mediana de la mitad superior de un conjunto de datos. También se llama *cuartil superior.*	Lower half Upper half (18, 23, 28,)(29, (36), 42) Third quartile
three-dimensional coordinate system (p. 214) A space that is divided into eight regions by an *x*-axis, a *y*-axis, and a *z*-axis. The locations, or coordinates, of points are given by ordered triples.	**sistema de coordenadas tridimensional** Espacio dividido en ocho regiones por un eje *x*, un eje *y* y un eje *z*. Las ubicaciones, o coordenadas, de los puntos son dadas por tripletas ordenadas.	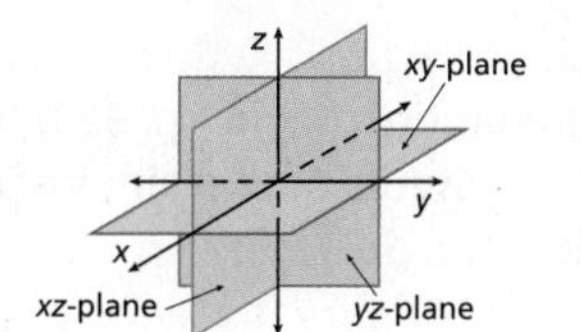
transformation (p. 59) A change in the position, size, or shape of a figure or graph.	**transformación** Cambio en la posición, tamaño o forma de una figura o gráfica.	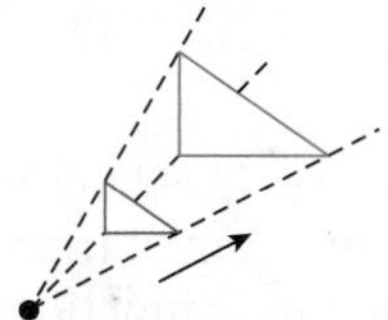
translation (p. 59) A transformation that shifts or slides every point of a figure or graph the same distance in the same direction.	**traslación** Transformación en la que todos los puntos de una figura se mueven la misma distancia en la misma dirección.	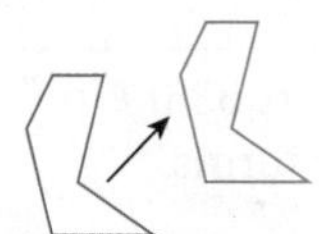
translation matrix (p. 262) A matrix used to translate points on the coordinate plane.	**matriz de traslación** Matriz utilizada para trasladar puntos en el plano cartesiano.	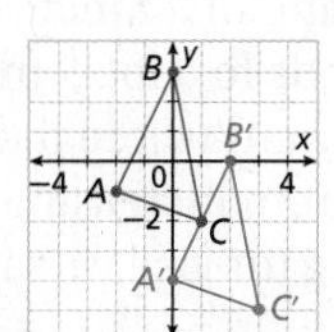 Matrix $\begin{bmatrix} -2 & -2 & -2 \\ 3 & 3 & 3 \end{bmatrix}$ is used to translate the figure 2 units left and 3 units up.
transpose (p. 260) A matrix that reverses the rows and columns of a matrix.	**transposición** Matriz que invierte las filas y columnas de una matriz.	$\begin{bmatrix} 1 & 2 \\ 3 & 4 \\ 5 & 6 \end{bmatrix}$ is the transpose of $\begin{bmatrix} 1 & 3 & 5 \\ 2 & 4 & 6 \end{bmatrix}$.

Glossary/Glosario

ENGLISH	SPANISH	EXAMPLES
transverse axis (p. 744) The axis of symmetry of a hyperbola that contains the vertices and foci.	**eje transversal** Eje de simetría de una hipérbola que contiene los vértices y focos.	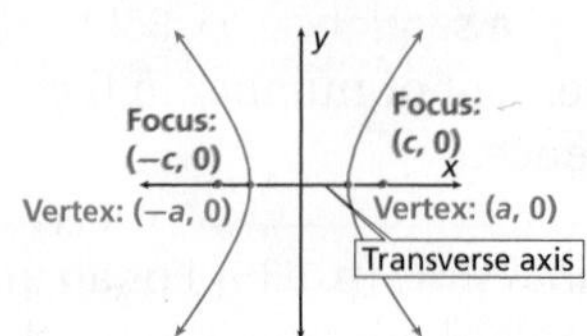
tree diagram (p. 812) A branching diagram that shows all possible combinations or outcomes of an experiment.	**diagrama de árbol** Diagrama con ramificaciones que muestra todas las combinaciones o resultados posibles de un experimento.	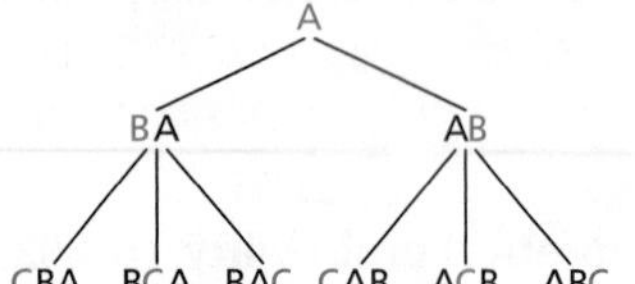
trial (p. 805) In probability, a single repetition or observation of an experiment.	**prueba** En probabilidad, una sola repetición u observación de un experimento.	In the experiment of rolling a number cube, each roll is one trial.
trigonometric function (p. 929) A function whose rule is given by a trigonometric ratio.	**función trigonométrica** Función cuya regla es dada por una razón trigonométrica.	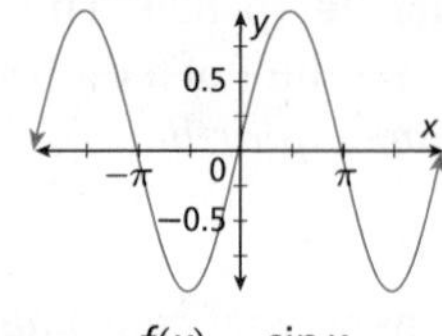 $f(x) = \sin x$
trigonometric ratio (p. 929) Ratio of the lengths of two sides of a right triangle.	**razón trigonométrica** Razón entre dos lados de un triángulo rectángulo.	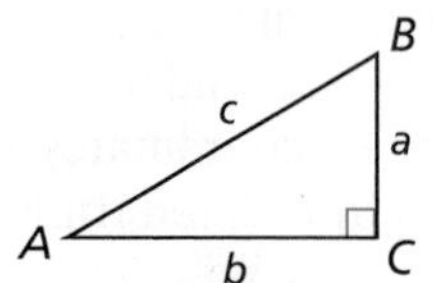 $\sin A = \frac{a}{c}, \cos A = \frac{b}{c}, \tan A = \frac{a}{b}$
trigonometry (p. 929) The study of the measurement of triangles and of trigonometric functions and their applications.	**trigonometría** Estudio de la medición de los triángulos y de las funciones trigonométricas y sus aplicaciones.	
trinomial (p. 336) A polynomial with three terms.	**trinomio** Polinomio con tres términos.	$4x^2 + 3xy - 5y^2$
turning point (p. 455) A point on the graph of a function that corresponds to a local maximum (or minimum) where the graph changes from increasing to decreasing (or vice versa).	**punto de inflexión** Punto de la gráfica de una función que corresponde a un máximo (o mínimo) local donde la gráfica pasa de ser creciente a decreciente (o viceversa).	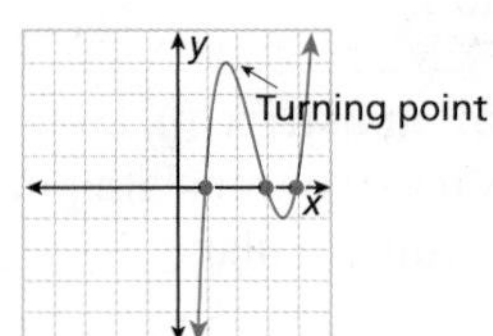

U

ENGLISH	SPANISH	EXAMPLES
unit circle (p. 944) A circle with a radius of 1, centered at the origin.	**círculo unitario** Círculo con un radio de 1, centrado en el origen.	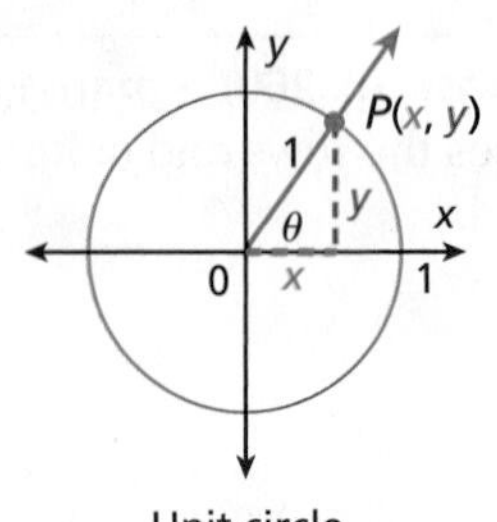 Unit circle

ENGLISH	SPANISH	EXAMPLES

variable (p. 3) A symbol used to represent a quantity that can change.

variable Símbolo utilizado para representar una cantidad que puede cambiar.

$2x + 3$ (arrow to x: variable)

---

variable matrix (p. 279) The matrix of the variables in a linear system of equations.

matriz de variables Matriz de las variables de un sistema lineal de ecuaciones.

System of equations $\begin{cases} 2x + 3y = -1 \\ x - 3y = 4 \end{cases}$ Variable matrix $\begin{bmatrix} x \\ y \end{bmatrix}$

---

variance (p. 830) The average of squared differences from the mean. The square root of the variance is called the *standard deviation.*

varianza Promedio de las diferencias cuadráticas en relación con la media. La raíz cuadrada de la varianza se denomina *desviación estándar.*

Data set: is $\{6, 7, 7, 9, 11\}$

Mean: $\frac{6 + 7 + 7 + 9 + 11}{5} = 8$

Variance: $\frac{1}{5}(4 + 1 + 1 + 1 + 9) = 3.2$

Venn diagram (p. 821) A diagram used to show relationships between sets.

diagrama de Venn Diagrama utilizado para mostrar la relación entre conjuntos.

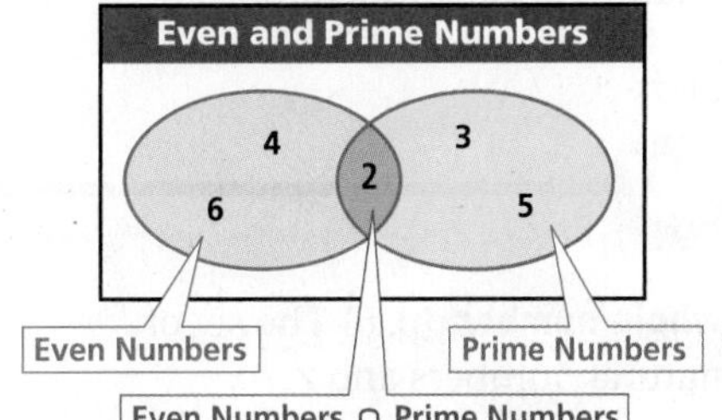

---

vertex form of a quadratic function (p. 318) A quadratic function written in the form $f(x) = a(x - h)^2 + k$, where *a, h,* and *k* are constants and (h, k) is the vertex.

forma en vértice de una función cuadrática Una función cuadrática expresada en la forma $f(x) = a(x - h)^2 + k$, donde *a, h* y *k* son constantes y (h, k) es el vértice.

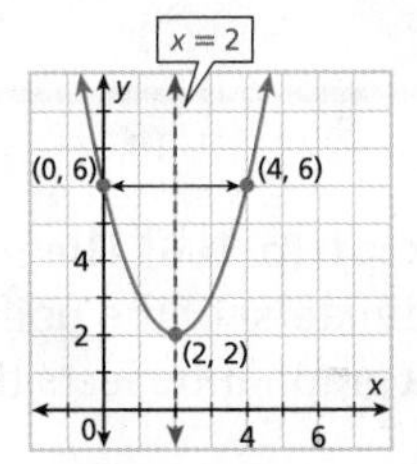

$f(x) = (x - 2)^2 + 2$

---

vertex of a hyperbola (vertices) (p. 744) The endpoints of the transverse axis of the hyperbola.

vértice de una hipérbola Extremos del eje transversal de la hipérbola.

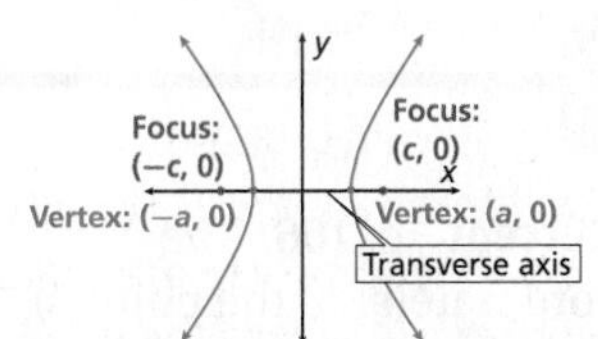

---

vertex of an absolute-value graph (p. 158) The point where the axis of symmetry intersects the graph.

vértice de una gráfica de valor absoluto Punto donde en el eje de simetría interseca la gráfica.

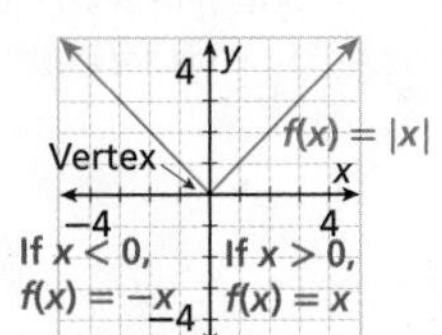

---

vertex of an ellipse (vertices) (p. 736) The endpoints of the major axis of the ellipse.

vértice de una elipse Extremos del eje mayor de la elipse.

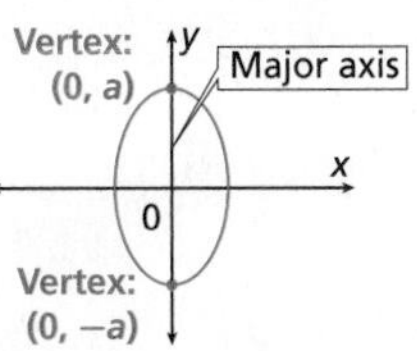

ENGLISH	SPANISH	EXAMPLES
vertex of a parabola (p. 318) The highest or lowest point on the parabola.	**vértice de una parábola** Punto más alto o más bajo de una parábola.	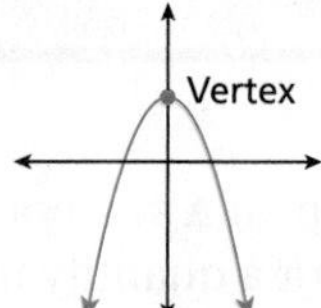
vertical line (p. 108) A line whose equation is $x = a$, where a is the x-intercept. The slope of a vertical line is undefined.	**línea vertical** Línea cuya ecuación es $x = a$, donde a es la intersección con el eje x. La pendiente de una línea vertical es indefinida.	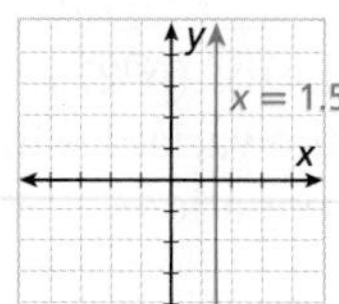
vertical-line test (p. 46) A test used to determine whether a relation is a function. If any vertical line crosses the graph of a relation more than once, the relation is not a function.	**prueba de la línea vertical** Prueba utilizada para determinar si una relación es una función. Si una línea vertical corta la gráfica de una relación más de una vez, la relación no es una función.	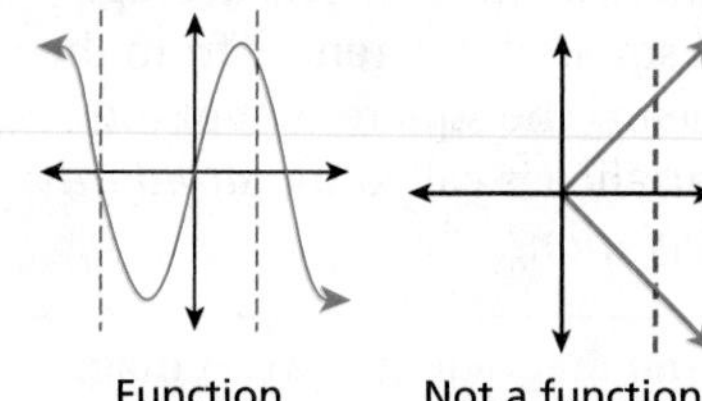

W

whole number (p. 6) The set of natural numbers and zero.	**número cabal** Conjunto de los números naturales y cero.	0, 1, 2, 3, 4, 5, …

X

x-intercept (p. 106) The x-coordinate(s) of the point(s) where a graph intersects the x-axis.	**intersección con el eje x** Coordenada(s) x de uno o más puntos donde una gráfica corta el eje x.	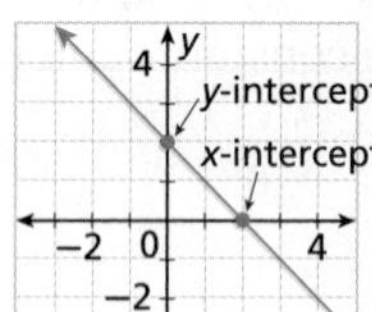

Y

y-intercept (p. 106) The y-coordinate(s) of the point(s) where a graph intersects the y-axis.	**intersección con el eje y** Coordenada(s) y de uno o más puntos donde una gráfica corta el eje y.	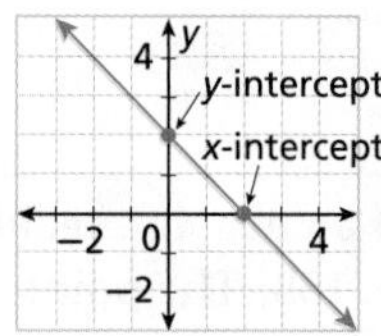

ENGLISH	SPANISH	EXAMPLES

Z

z-axis (p. 214) The third axis in a three-dimensional coordinate system.

eje z Tercer eje en un sistema de coordenadas tridimensional.

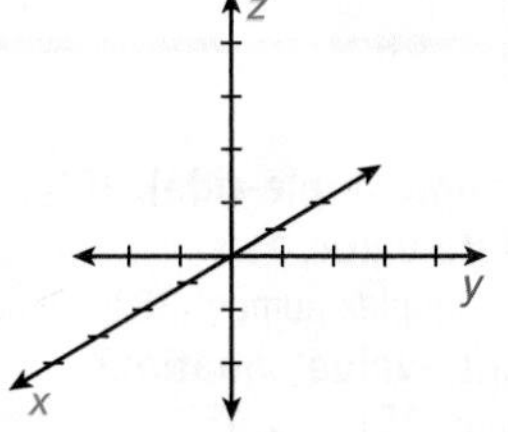

zero exponent (p. 35) For any nonzero real number x, $x^0 = 1$.

exponente cero Dado un número real distinto de cero x, $x^0 = 1$.

$5^0 = 1$

zero of a function (p. 333) For the function f, any number x such that $f(x) = 0$.

cero de una función Dada la función f, todo número x tal que $f(x) = 0$.

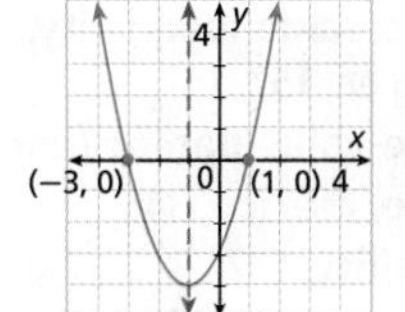

The zeros of $f(x) = x^2 + 2x - 3$ are -3 and 1.

Glossary/Glosario

Index

C

Index

D

E

Index

F

Index

H

Index

M

N

Index

Q

Index

Credits

Abbreviations used: (t) top, (c) center, (b) bottom, (l) left, (r) right, (bkgd) background

Photo Credits

All images by HRW Photo unless otherwise noted.

Master Icons: teens, authors, (all), Sam Dudgeon/HRW Photo

Front Matter: vi (l), © Masa Ushioda/SeaPics.com; vii (r), Cai Yuhao/Imaginechina/ZUMA Press; viii (l), Tom & Pat Leeson; ix (r), Reuters/CORBIS; ix (bkgd), Martin Sasse/laif/Aurora; x (l), Ezra O. Shaw/Allsport/Getty Images; xi (r), Glasswork by Dave Davidson/Image by Jeff Clarke Photography; xii (l), Robert Glusic/Photodisc Green/gettyimages; xiii (r), Lester Lefkowitz/CORBIS; xiv (l), CORBIS; xv (r), Bert Wiklund; xvii (r), SIME s.a.s/eStock Photo; xviii (l), © The Studio Dog/PhotoDisc Green/gettyimages; xix (r), Martin Rogers/Getty Images; xx (t), © PunchStock; xx (b), Stewart Cohen/Photodisc Red/gettyimages; xx (c) LWA-Dann Tardif/CORBIS; xxi (l), NASA; xxi (t), L. Hammel/A. van der Voort/Bildarchiv Monheim GmbH/Alamy Photos; xxi (c), James L. Amos/CORBIS; xxi (r), © Kevin Lamarque/Reuters/CORBIS; xxii (b), Victoria Smith/HRW.

Chapter One: 2–3 (all), © Masa Ushioda/SeaPics.com; 6 (tr), Gary Rhijnsburger/Masterfile; 6 (bl), NASA Kennedy Space Center; 11 (t, inset), Victoria Smith/HRW; 12 (l), Mark A. Schneider/Photo Researchers, Inc.; 14 (tr), on-page credit; 17 (br, inset), Sam Dudgeon/HRW; 18 (cl), Dinodia Picture Agency; 18 (bl), NASA Kennedy Space Center; 21 (tr), © Royalty Free/CORBIS; 25 (tr), Chase Swift/CORBIS; 25 (bl), NASA Kennedy Space Center; 25 (cl), Jason Hawkes Photo Library; 27 (tr), Don Emmert/AFP/Getty Images; 27 (tr), Cartoon copyrighted by Mark Parisi, printed with permission.; 29 (tr), Orlin Wagner/AP/Wide World Photos; 31 (cl), Mike Elicson/AP/Wide World Photos; 31 (bl), NASA Kennedy Space Center; 34 (tr), NASA; 37 (l), NASA/JPL/University of Arizona; 39 (l), James Martin/Getty Images; 40 (tl), NASA Kennedy Space Center; 42 (tl), NASA Kennedy Space Center; 42 (tr), NASA; 44 (tr), Bananastock; 45 (t, tc, bc, b), Victoria Smith/HRW; 48 (tr), United States Mint Image; 49 (tl), Victoria Smith/HRW; 49 (br), Sam Dudgeon/HRW; 51 (tr), Adastra/Getty Images; 53 (tr), Dallas and John Heaton/PictureQuest; 55 (tl), © Royalty Free/CORBIS; 56 (tl), Victoria Smith/HRW; 57 (cl), Len Rubenstein/Index Stock Imagery, Inc.; 60 (t), © PunchStock; 64 (bl), Victoria Smith/HRW; 64 (cl), Terry I. Husebye/workbookstock.com; 67 (t), Alex Rosenfield/Science Photo Library; 71 (bl), Victoria Smith/HRW; 72 (l), NASA; 72 (c), Copyright © Image Source Limited ; 72 (cr), Photodisc/Getty Images; 74 (tl), Victoria Smith/HRW; 74 (br), George H. H. Huey/CORBIS.

Chapter Two: 86–87 (all), Cai Yuhao/Imaginechina/ZUMA Press; 90 (tr), Corel Royalty Free; 91 Reuters/Corbis; 95 (cl), © CORBIS SYGMA; 95 (bl), AbleStock.com; 97 (tr), Brad Wrobleski/Masterfile; 98 (br), Mike Dobel/Alamy Photos; 102 (tl), AbleStock.com; 102 (inset), PictureNet/CORBIS; 102 (bl), D. Hurst/Alamy Photos; 102 (cr), Andrew Brown; Ecoscene/CORBIS; 105 (tr), NASA/Science Photo Library; 110 (cr), Patrick Beckers; 111 (tl), AbleStock.com; 111 (cl), © Image State/Alamy; 115 (tr), Ray Stubblebine/Reuters/CORBIS; 117 (bl), Digital Vision; 118 (inset), Sam Dudgeon/HRW; 118 (inset), Sam Dudgeon/HRW; 118 (inset), Sam Dudgeon/HRW; 121 (cl), Erich Lessing/Art Resource, NY; 121 (tl), AbleStock.com; 124 (tr), Photo by 20th Century Fox/ZUMA Press; 128 (bl), Detlev Van Ravenswaay/Science Photo Library; 129 (tr), ©Alamy Photos; 129 (bl), AbleStock.com; 130 (tr), Andy Christiansen/HRW; 132 (tl), AbleStock.com; 132 (br), ©Onne van der Wal/CORBIS; 134 (tr), © CORBIS; 137 (tr), Sam Dudgeon/HRW; 139 (bl), Steve Vidler/SuperStock; 142 (tr), Annie Griffiths Belt/CORBIS; 144 (tl) Carlos Lopez-Barillas; 147 (tl), Tim Zurowski/CORBIS; 148 (br), James L. Amos/CORBIS; 148 (tl), Steve Vidler/SuperStock; 150 (tr), Courtesy of the Louisville Slugger Museum; 155 (cl), Patrick Hertzog/AFP/Getty Images; 155 (bl), Steve Vidler/SuperStock; 158 (tr), Morton Beebe & Associates; 161 (br), Photodisc/gettyimages; 162 (bl), Steve Vidler/SuperStock; 162 (cr), © PunchStock; 164 (br), Kim Christensen; 164 (tl), Steve Vidler/SuperStock; 174 (br), Bob Krist/CORBIS; 176 (cr), Bob Krist/CORBIS; 177 (b), Jim Wark/Airphoto; 177 (cr), Michael Townsend/Getty Images.

Chapter Three: 178–179 (all), Tom & Pat Leeson; 182 (tr), Richard Price/Getty Images; 186 (tl), © Royalty Free/CORBIS; 187 (tl), Michael Melford/Getty Images; 190 (tr), Eric Vandeville/Gamma; 193 (tl), Krys Bailey/Alamy; 193 (bl), Comstock Royalty Free; 195 (br), Frank Herholdt/Alamy Photos; 195 (tl), Phil Kember/Index Stock Imagery, Inc.; 195 (tr), Javier Pierini/gettyimages; 195 (bl), Jules Frazier/Photodisc Green/gettyimages; 196 (tl), © Royalty Free/CORBIS; 199 (tl), VAN HASSELT JOHN/CORBIS SYGMA; 203 (tl), © Royalty Free/CORBIS; 210 (tl), © Royalty Free/CORBIS; 210 (cl), CORBIS; 212 (tl), © Royalty Free/CORBIS; 212 (br), Paltera Stefano/Gamma; 214 (tr, inset), Gilles Mingasson/Getty Images; 217 (tr), Frank & Joyce Burek/Photodisc/Getty Images; 220 (tr), Al Tielemans/SI/Newsport/CORBIS; 222 (tl), Ralph Freso/East Valley Tribune/AP/Wide World Photos; 225 (bl), ACE STOCK LIMITED/Alamy; 227 (bl), ACE STOCK LIMITED/Alamy; 227 (br), Dean/Alamy; 228 © Mark Peterson/CORBIS; 228 (tl), ACE STOCK LIMITED/Alamy.

Chapter Four: 242–243 (all), Reuters/CORBIS; 242–243 (bkgd), Martin Sasse/laif/Aurora; 244 (tr), United Press International/NewsCom; 248 (cr), © Paul A. Souders/CORBIS; 251 (bl), Photodisc/gettyimages; 253 (tr), ZUMA Press; 255 (tr), Victoria Smith/HRW; 258 (cl), Itar-Tass Photos/NewsCom; 258 (bl), Photodisc/gettyimages; 259 (tl), Jeff Cooper/Salina Journal/AP/Wide World Photos; 262 (tr), The Granger Collection, New York; 266 (tl) © 2005 The M.C. Escher Company-Holland. All rights reserved. www.mcescher.com; 266 (bl), Photodisc/gettyimages; 268 (b), Brian Summers/Veer Images; 268 (tl), Photodisc/gettyimages; 270 (tr), Rosemary Weller/Getty Images; 273 (cr), Sam Dudgeon/HRW; 275 (cl), James L. Amos/CORBIS; 276 (tl), Purestock/SuperStock; 277 (bl), LWA-Dann Tardif/CORBIS; 278 (tr) Philip Kaake/Alamy; 284 (tl), Purestock/SuperStock; 285 (tr), Artville/gettyimages; 287 (tr), © Royalty Free/CORBIS; 289 (bl), © Royalty Free/CORBIS; 292 (tl), Victoria Smith/HRW; 292 (cr), ADAM NADEL/AFP/Getty Images; 292 (bl), Purestock/SuperStock; 293 (t), Victoria Smith/HRW; 294 (br), Stone/Getty Images; 294 Purestock/SuperStock; 307 Copyright © Image Source Limited ; 308 (bl), Courtesy James Island County Park; 308 (cr), Copyright © Image Source Limited ; 309 (tr), Paul Franklin.

Chapter Five: 310–311 (all), Ezra O. Shaw/Allsport/Getty Images; 315 (tr), Bill Brooks/Masterfile; 321 (tl), © Royalty Free/CORBIS; 321 (bl), Andy Christiansen/HRW; 323 (tr), Robert Holland/Image Bank/Getty Images; 329 (cl), James H. Robinson/Photo Researchers, Inc.; 329 (bl), Andy Christiansen/HRW; 333 (tr), Aflo Foto; 339 (bl), Andy Christiansen/HRW; 339 (tl), David Mendelsohn/Masterfile; 341 (tr), David Welling/Nature Picture Library; 346 (br), Peter Guttman/CORBIS; 347 (tl), Andy Christiansen/HRW; 350 (tr), on-page credit; 354 (cl), The Granger Collection, New York; 356 (tr), Reuters/CORBIS; 358 (bl), © BananaStock Ltd.; 362 (tl), Scaled Composites/SPL/Photo Researchers, Inc.; 362 (bl), Andy Christiansen/HRW; 362 (inset), Steve Bloom Images; 364 (tl), Andy Christiansen/HRW; 364 (br), Ray Stubblebine/Reuters/CORBIS; 366 (tr), Paul Kingsley/Alamy; 372 (tl), Andy Christiansen/HRW; 374 (tr), The Granger Collection, New York; 378 (bl), Andy Christiansen/HRW; 380 (l), Science Photo Library/Photo Researchers, Inc.; 382 (tr), Gregory Sams/SPL/Photo Researchers, Inc.; 387 (r), Mehau Kulyk/Photo Researchers, Inc.; 387 (l), A. Pasieka/Photo Researchers, Inc.; 388 (bl), Andy Christiansen/HRW; 390 (tl), Andy Christiansen/HRW; 390 (b), Jennifer Shephard, The Truth/AP/Wide World Photos; 390 (r), Andy Christiansen/HRW.

Chapter Six: 402–403 (all), Glasswork by Dave Davidson/Image by Jeff Clarke Photography; 406 (tr), Dan Lim/Masterfile; 411 (bl), © Hans Neleman/The Image Bank/Getty Images; 414 (tr), Digital Vision/eStock Photo; 417 (tl), © LWA-Dann Tardif/CORBIS; 419 (bl), © Hans Neleman/The Image Bank/Getty Images; 419 (tl), © Bettman/CORBIS; 422 (tr), © Cartoon Stock; 425 (cl), Luscious Frames/Alamy; 427 (bl), © Hans Neleman/The Image Bank/Getty Images; 427 (tl), © Bettman/CORBIS; 428 (tr), © PhotoDisc/gettyimages; 428 (br), © PhotoDisc/gettyimages; 430 (tr), Ian Lloyd/Masterfile; 434 (tl), © Hans Neleman/The Image Bank/Getty Images; 435 (bl), Zuma Press/NewsCom; 436 (tl), © Hans Neleman/The Image Bank/Getty Images; 436 (br), © Neal Preston/CORBIS; 438 (tr), Sam Dudgeon/HRW; 443 (bl), Neil Beer/CORBIS; 443 (cl), © 2005 Busch Entertainment Corporation. All rights reserved; 445 (tr), © Mark M. Lawrence/CORBIS; 450 (tl), Neil Beer/CORBIS; 450 (cl), © James Randklev/CORBIS; 453 (tr), © Craig Lovell/CORBIS; 458 (bl), Neil Beer/CORBIS; 458 (tl), Janine Wiedel Photolibrary/Alamy; 460 (tr), © Black Star/Alamy Photos; 462 (r), Pixonnet.com/Alamy Photos; 464 (bl), Neil Beer/CORBIS; 464 (cl), Tom Stack/Tom Stack & Associates; 466 (tr) Scott Olson/Getty Images; 469 (bl, bc, br), Victoria Smith/HRW; 470 (r), Worldsat International/SPL/Photo Researchers, Inc.; 472 (b), © Richard T. Nowitz/CORBIS; 484 (b), Grace Davies/Omni-Photo Communications; 484 (cr), Courtesy Adventure Aquarium; 485 (r), © Bettman/CORBIS.

Chapter Seven: 486–487 (all), Robert Glusic/Photodisc Green/gettyimages; 490 (tr), Richard Lewis/AP/Wide World Photos; 491 (b), © PunchStock; 493 SciMAT/Photo Researachers, Inc.; 494 (l), Bettmann/CORBIS; 496 (l), CDC/PHIL/CORBIS; 498 (tr) Wolfgang Polzer/Alamy 502 (cl), Vandystadt-Didier Givois/TIPS Images; 503 (l), © PunchStock; 505 (t), Peter Van Steen/HRW; 509 (br), The Garden Picture Library/Alamy Photos; 509 (bc), Steve Satushek/Getty Images; 509 (bl), jack sparticus/Alamy Photos; 512 (tr), Simon Kwong/CORBIS; 517 (tr), Stocktrek Images/Corbis;

517 (cl), George Bernard/Photo Researchers, Inc.; 518 (l), Randy Allbritton/Photodisc Green/gettyimages; 518 (r), Christie's Images/CORBIS; 519 (c, inset), Sam Dudgeon/HRW; 520 (b), Jerry King/eToon.com; 522 (tr), Philippe Petit-Mars/CORBIS; 527 (bl), age fotostock/ImageState; 527 (inset), Sam Dudgeon/HRW; 527 (cl), © photographer/Alamy Photos; 531 (t), D. Schwimmer/Bruce Coleman, Inc.; 533 (t), R.A. Mittermeir/Bruce Coleman, Inc.; 535 (cl), franc Lukasseck/Picture Press/photolibrary; 535 (bl), age fotostock/Imagestate; 537 (tr), doc-stock/Alamy; 540 (all images), © Royalty Free/CORBIS; 542 (cl), David Ducros/Photo Researchers, Inc.; 543 (bl), age fotostock/ImageState; 543 (cl), Susumu Nishinf/SPL/Photo Researchers, Inc; 545 (t), Steve Taylor/Getty Images; 549 (cl), © PunchStock; 550 (t), age fotostock/Imagestate; 551 (bl), © PunchStock; 552 (b), Jim Wark/Airphotona.

Chapter Eight: 546–547 (all), Letser Lefkowitz/CORBIS; 568 (tl, tr, c, b), Andy Christiansen/HRW; 569 (t), Steve Gates/AP/Wide World Photos; 571 (b), Andy Christiansen/HRW; 574 (cl), Robbie Jack/CORBIS; 574 (tr), Sam Dudgeon/HRW; 575 (t), Stockdisc/gettyimages; 577 (t), Design Pics Inc/Alamy; 581 (cl), Dr. E. Strouhal/Werner Forman/Art Resource, NY; 581 (r), PhotoDisc/gettyimages; 581 (bl), Stockdisc/gettyimages; 583 (t), Digital Vision/gettyimages; 587 (t), BananaStock/age fotostock; 589 (cl), L. Hammel/A. van der Voort/Bildarchiv Monheim GmbH/Alamy Photos; 589 (tl), Stockdisc/gettyimages; 592 (t), Simon Hayter/Toronto Star/NewsCom; 598 (tl), The Granger Collection, New York; 598 (bl), Stockdisc/gettyimages; 600 (tr), © Skip Brown/Getty Images; 602 (tr), Photodisc Blue/Getty Images; 606 (r), Ezra Shaw/Getty Images; 606 (t), Stockdisc/gettyimages; 606 (tl), © William Sallaz/Duomo/CORBIS; 608 (l), Stockdisc/gettyimages; 608 (b), Michael Kim/CORBIS; 608 (r), Bettmann/CORBIS; 610 (t), Paul Sancya/AP/Wide World Photos; 615 (cl), Chris Johnsr/National Geographic Image Collection; 616 (cl), David Davis Photoproductions/Alamy; 616 (tl), Comstock Images/Alamy; 619 (t), NASA; 622 (b), NASA; 625 (l), John Boyd/photolibrary.com; 626 (cl), John Gay/Ensign/AP/Wide World Photos; 626 (tl), Comstock Images/Alamy; 626 (br), © Eastcott Momatiuk/Photographer's Choice/Getty Images; 628 (t), The New Yorker Collection, 2002, Leo Cullum from Cartoonbank.com. All rights reserved.; 633 (l), Don Lloyd/The Reporter/AP/Wide World Photos; 634 (t), Comstock Images/Alamy; 636 (t), Comstock Images/Alamy Photos; 636 (b), Bob Krist/CORBIS; 640 (b), Thomas Mangelsen/Minden Pictures; 648 (cr), dbphots/Alamy; 648 (br), aaronpeterson.net/Alamy; 649 (inset), Bettmann/CORBIS; 649 (t), Bruce Ando/Stone/Getty Images.

Chapter Nine: 650–651 (all), CORBIS; 654 (tr), Alan Schein Photography/CORBIS; 659 (cl), Phillip Colla/Oceanlight; 660 (tl, tc, tr), Sam Dudgeon/HRW; 662 (tr), ©Mike Finn-Kelcey/Reuters/CORBIS; 664 (bl), © PunchStock; 667 (l), Victoria Smith/HRW; 672 (t), Mike Baldwin/www.cartoonstock.com; 677 (cl), eye35.com/Alamy ; 678 (tl, tr), Digital Vision/gettyimages; 680 (b), Wernher Krutein; 682 (t, tl), Sam Dudgeon/HRW; 687 (cl), © PunchStock; 690 (t), Sam Dudgeon/HRW; 694 (l), © PunchStock; 695 (t), CORBIS Royalty free; 698 (t), Bruce Ayres/Getty Images; 700 CORBIS Royalty Fee Photographs; 700 (tr), Blaine Harrington III/Corbis; 703 SPL/Photo Researchers, Inc.; 704 (bl), Thomas Cockrem/Alamy; 704 (tl), CORBIS Royalty Free; 706 (c), PhotoDisc/ gettyimages; 706 (b), Gerard Vandystadt/TIPS Images; 706 (tl), Carl & Ann Purcell/CORBIS.

Chapter Ten: 718–719 (all), Bert Wiklund; 727 (l), Jeremy Woodhouse/Digital Vision/gettyimages; 729 (t), Adam Crowley/Photodisc Green/gettyimages; 733 (cl), Jason Hawkes/CORBIS; 736 (tr), Scott Brownell/Museum of Science and Industry, Chicago; 740 (b), Lani Howe/Photri-Microstock; 741 (cl), Free Agents Limited/CORBIS; 744 (tr), Juniors Bildarchiv/Alamy; 749 (cl), Paul Katz/Index Stock Imagery, Inc.; 751 (t), © David Madison Sports Images, Inc.; 755 (l), Kevin Taylor/Alamy; 756 (t), AFP/Getty Images; 757 (cl), Sheila Terry/Photo Researchers, Inc.; 758 (b), Mehau Kulyk/SPL/Photo Researchers, Inc.; 760 (tr), Chuck Eckert/Alamy; 761 (t), © PunchStock; 764 (b), NOAO/AURA/NSF/PHOTO RESEARCHERS, INC; 765 (tl), Victoria Smith/HRW; 768 (t), Travel Ink/Digital Vision/gettyimages; 773 (cl) AFP/Getty Images; 773 (b), Victoria Smith/HRW; 775 (b), Copyright © Image Source Limited ; 776 (t), Victoria Smith/HRW; 776 (b), Randy Faris/CORBIS; 788 (cl), ©CORBIS; 788 (b), Bettmann/CORBIS; 789 (t), Jim Wark/Airphoto; 789 (b), John Gress/Reuters/CORBIS.

Chapter Eleven: 794 (t), Sam Dudgeon/HRW/Artwork by Teri Jonas, Courtesy Wally Workman Gallery, Austin, TX; 796 (l, cl, r): Royalty-free/Corbis; 796 (cr) Ocean with flowers: VisionsofAmerica/Joe Sohm/Digital Vision/Getty Images; 797 (r), Japack Photo Library/Photolibrary; 799 (bl), Sam Dudgeon/HRW; 799 (cl) Luz Martin/Alamy; 799 (br), Sam Dudgeon/HRW; 802 (t), Sam Dudgeon/HRW; 803 (r), Sam Dudgeon/HRW; 805 (r), Sam Dudgeon/HRW; 808 (tl, tr), Sam Dudgeon/HRW; 811 (t), Adey Bryant/www.CartoonStock.com; 813 (r), Jason Reeves/Reuters; 813 (l), Jim Young/Reuters; 814 (t), Sam Dudgeon/HRW; 816 (l), © Kevin Lamarque/Reuters/CORBIS; 816 (bl, br), Sam Dudgeon/HRW; 818 (t), Sam Dudgeon/HRW; 819 Steve Allen/Brand X/Corbis; 820 (r), Sam Dudgeon/HRW; 821 (t), Sam Dudgeon/HRW/The Isahinkai Foundation; 823 (l), CBS/Landov; 824 (l, tr, all inset), Sam Dudgeon/HRW; 826 (all photos), Sam Dudgeon/HRW; 828 (t), Republished with permission of Globe Newspaper Company, Inc./Stan Grossfeld; 829 (b), © Comstock Images/Alamy Photos; 834 (t), © Lester Lefkowitz/CORBIS; 835 (t), © ThinkStock LLC/Index Stock Imagery, Inc.; 836 (t), © ThinkStock LLC/Index Stock Imagery, Inc.; 836 (b), © Ron Sherman/Getty Images; 841 (cl), blickwinkel/Alamy; 841 (b), © ThinkStock LLC/Index Stock Imagery, Inc.; 842 (l), The Granger Collection, New York; 844 (b), Steven Vidler/Eurasia Press/Corbis.

Chapter Twelve: 858–859 (all); SIME s.a.s/eStock Photo; 862 (t), The Image Bank/Getty Images; 866 (l), The Granger Collection, New York; 866 (bl, br), Sam Dudgeon/HRW; 867 (tl), Anthony Lysson; 870 (t), Jim Barcus/Kansas City Star/KRT Photos/NewsCom; 872 (b), Blow Up/Getty Images; 875 (l), The Granger Collection, New York; 876 (tl), Anthony Lysson; 877 (b), Stewart Cohen/Photodisc Red/gettyimages; 879 (tl, tr), United States Mint Image; 879 (tc), ™ Rachel Robinson by CMG Worldwide/www.JackieRobinson.com; Stamp Designs: © 1982, United States Postal Service. Displayed with permission. All rights reserved. Written authorization from the Postal Service is required to use, reproduce, post, transmit, distribute, or publicly display these images.; 880 (b), Lucca DiCecco/Alamy; 882 (t), Anthony Lysson; 885 (t), Chuck Pefley/Alamy Photos; 885 (cr), David Noton/Getty Images; 886 (tl), Anthony Lysson; 888 (b), STEPHANE/Gamma; 890 (tl), Reuters/CORBIS; 890 (cl), PhotoDisc green/gettyimages; 894 (t), REUTERS/Ian Hodgson/CORBIS; 896 (t), Bettman/CORBIS; 897 (t), Ingram Publishing/Alamy; 900 (t), Vaughan Fleming/David Parkeker/Photo Researchers, Inc.; 905 (t), Victoria Smith/HRW; 906 (t), Ingram Publishing/Alamy; 908 (t), Ingram Publishing/Alamy; 908 (b), Sony Pictures/ZUMA; 922 (b), Lester Lefkowitz/CORBIS; 922 (cr), Lake County Museum/CORBIS; 923 (r), Digital Vision/gettyimages; 923 (b), ImageState/Alamy Photos; 923 (c), Don Farrall/Photodisc Green/getty images.

Chapter Thirteen: 924–925 (all), © The Studio Dog/PhotoDisc Green/gettyimages; 929 (t), © John Elk III/Lonely Planet Images; 934 (tl), © Larry Lee Photography/CORBIS; 934 (b), NORBERT WU/Minden Pictures; 936 (t), Photo by Rick Wilking/Reuters; 940 (t), © Steve Allen/Brand X Pictures/Alamy Photos; 940 (b), NORBERT WU/Minden Pictures; 943 (t), NASA Marshall Space Flight Center (NASA-MSFC); 948 (t), NORBERT WU/Minden Pictures; 949 (b), © Michael Keller/CORBIS; 950 (t), Jimmy Chin/National Geographic Image Collection; 953 (b), © GOODSHOOT/Alamy Photos; 954 (l), © DAVID LOH/Reuters/CORBIS; 955 (t, tl), NORBERT WU/Minden Pictures; 956 (b), © Amos Nachoum/CORBIS; 958 (t), © Ron Watts/CORBIS; 964 (t), © D. Hurst/Alamy Photos; 964 (l), © Jay Ireland & Georgienne E. Bradley; 966 (t), © VALLON FABRICE/CORBIS KIPA; 967 (b), © Michael A. Keller/CORBIS; 970 (b), Jim Wark/Airphoto; 972 (t), © D. Hurst/Alamy Photos; 972 (l), © Charles and Josette Lenars/CORBIS; 974 (t), © D. Hurst/Alamy Photos; 974 (b), George Hall/Check Six.

Chapter Fourteen: 986–987 (all), Martin Rogers/Getty Images; 990 (t), Thinkstock/Alamy Photos; 992 (r), Charles D. Winters; 994 (t), Index Stock Imagery/Photo Library; 996 (t), Brand X Pictures/Alamy Photos; 996 (b), Eckhard Slawik/SPL/Photo Researchers, Inc.; 998 (t), Richard Gaul/Getty Images; 1002 (t), Eckhard Slawik/SPL/Photo Researchers, Inc.; 1002 (cl), Allan H Shoemake/Getty Images; 1004 (t), Eckhard Slawik/SPL/Photo Researchers, Inc.; 1004 (bl), Paul A. Souders/CORBIS; 1004 (br), Buddy Mays/CORBIS; 1008 (t), Duomo/CORBIS; 1009 (b), Ken Weingart/SuperStock/Alamy; 1012 (t), Sam Dudgeon/HRW; 1018 (b), Donald Miralle/Getty Images; 1020 (t), Donald Miralle/Getty Images; 1025 (t), Sam Dudgeon/HRW; 1025 (cl), Kevin Fleming/CORBIS; 1027 (t), Cosmo Condina/TIPS Images; 1032 (tl), Yuriko Nakao/Reuters/CORBIS; 1032 (b), Sam Dudgeon/HRW; 1034 (t, b), Sam Dudgeon/HRW; 1046 (cr), Brooks Kraft/CORBIS; 1046 (b), Brownie Harris/CORBIS; 1047 (t), Tom Till/Alamy Photos; 1047 (b), Jeff Greenberg/Index Stock/Photo Library.

Backmatter: 1060, Bettmann/Corbis, S2 (t), John Langford/HRW; S3 (b), John Langford/HRW.